2022

GAAP GUIDE

Restatement and Analysis of Current FASB Standards, organized in a manner consistent with the FASB's Accounting Standards Codification

---

JAN R. WILLIAMS, Ph.D., CPA

TERRY L. NEAL, Ph.D., CPA

JUDITH WEISS, CPA

Wolters Kluwer

Editorial Staff

Editor . . . . Lawrence C. Koral
Production . . . . Jennifer Schencker, Manjula Mahalingam, Prabhu Meenakshisundaram

This publication is designed to provide accurate and authoritative information in regard to the subject matter covered. It is sold with the understanding that the publisher is not engaged in rendering legal, accounting or other professional service. If legal advice or other expert assistance is required, the services of a competent professional person should be sought. All views expressed in this publication are those of the author and not necessarily those of the publisher or any other person.

ISBN: 978-0-8080-5366-8

2700 Lake Cook Road
Riverwoods, IL 60015
800 344 3734
CCHCPELink.com

Do not send returns to the above address. If for any reason you are not satisfied with your book purchase, it can easily be returned within 30 days of shipment. Please go to *support.cch.com/returns* to initiate your return. If you require further assistance with your return, please call: (800) 344-3734 M-F, 8 a.m. – 6 p.m. CT.

Printed in the United States of America

SUSTAINABLE FORESTRY INITIATIVE Certified Sourcing
www.sfiprogram.org
SFI-01028

Contents

Generally Accepted Accounting Principles

Appendices

Preface

The 2022 *GAAP Guide* summarizes and analyzes accounting standards as reflected in the FASB Accounting Standards Codification® (ASC). Accounting Standards Updates (ASUs) are issued throughout the year and represent changes in the ASC. This edition is current through ASU 2021-04, *Earnings Per Share (Topic 260), Debt—Modifications and Extinguishments (Subtopic 470-50), Compensation—Stock Compensation (Topic 718), and Derivatives and Hedging—Contracts in Entity's Own Equity (Subtopic 815-40): Issuer's Accounting for Certain Modifications or Exchanges of Freestanding Equity-Classified Written Call Options (a consensus of the FASB Emerging Issues Task Force).* This ASU is covered in Chapter 11, *Earnings Per Share*, of this edition of the GAAP Guide. Citations to the ASC are identified throughout the text. Users of the 2022 *GAAP Guide* are encouraged to continuously monitor the FASB web site and other sources for additional ASUs that are issued after the 2022 *GAAP Guide* goes to press.

The *GAAP Guide* is an abbreviated summary of generally accepted accounting principles as defined by the ASC. It is intended to assist users in identifying those areas that require direct sourcing into the ASC that are of particular relevance to the unique situations of financial statement preparers and auditors. Significant underlying detail, including implementation guidance, found in the ASC, is not included in the *GAAP Guide.* The authors strongly encourage users to go to the cited ASC sections for additional guidance beyond the summarized material included in this edition.

FASB EFFECTIVE DATE STRUCTURE FOR MAJOR ASUs

Over the years, the FASB received requests from stakeholders to defer the effective dates of major ASUs not yet effective for all entities. Other feedback has been received regarding the challenges of implementing major ASUs for some types of entities, including private companies, smaller public companies, not-for-profit organizations, and employee benefit plans. Such entities are particularly challenged by the time and resources required to implement new guidance, including the availability of internal and external resources, timing and staff education, staff knowledge and experience, comprehensive transition requirements, and other factors.

To address those concerns, the FASB announced in ASU 2019-10, *Financial Instruments—Credit Losses (Topic 326), Derivatives and Hedging (Topic 815), and Leases (Topic 842): Effective Dates*, that it has developed the following effective date structure for major ASUs. This structure is intended to extend and simplify how the effective dates are staggered between larger public companies and all other entities. It is expected that the FASB will continue to allow early application of most ASUs by all entities. Whether early application is available is identified within each emerging ASU.

The FASB's effective date structure for major ASUs is as follows:

Bucket 1 – First effective for public business entities that file with the Securities and Exchange Commission (SEC), excluding entities eligible to be smaller reporting companies (SRCs), as defined by the SEC.

Bucket 2 – An effective date staggered at least two years after the effective date for entities in Bucket 1, for SRCs, all other public business entities, and nonpublic business entities, such as private companies, not-for-profit organizations, and employee benefit plans.

The above structure applies to major ASUs whose implementation represents particular challenges for some entities. Exceptions can be expected for ASUs with a narrow scope, including some ASUs that are applicable immediately upon issuance for all entities.

New ASUs will be incorporated into the *GAAP Guide* in the next edition after the ASU is issued. Existing guidance is retained as long as it remains applicable to any type of reporting entity.

RECENTLY ISSUED ACCOUNTING STANDARDS UPDATES (ASUs)

Following is a listing of the ASUs that were issued after the 2021 *GAAP Guide* was finalized and that have been incorporated into the 2022 *GAAP Guide.*

The effective dates summarized here are intentionally brief. More detailed explanation of the effective dates related to each ASU is available in the discussion of the ASU and at STANDARDS/ACCOUNTING STANDARDS UPDATES—EFFECTIVE DATES on the FASB website (fasb.org). This source provides additional information regarding transition requirements and options, including the availability of early adoption. In some cases, an ASU's effective date is related to that of another ASU, details of which are also available in the above sources.

- **ASU 2020-06** Debt—Debt with Conversion and Other Options (Subtopic 470-20) and Derivatives and Hedging—Contracts in Entity's Own Equity (Subtopic 815-40): Accounting for Convertible Instruments and Contracts in an Entity's Own Equity

  Effective Date: For public business entities that meet the definition of an SEC filer, excluding entities eligible to be smaller reporting entities, the effective date is for fiscal years beginning after December 15, 2021, including interim periods within those fiscal years. For all other entities, the effective date is for fiscal years beginning after December 15, 2023, including interim periods within those fiscal years.

- **ASU 2020-07** Not-for-Profit Entities (Topic 958): Presentation and Disclosures by Not-for-Profit Entities for Contributed Nonfinancial Assets

  Effective Date: The effective date is for annual periods beginning after June 15, 2021 and interim periods within annual periods beginning after June 15, 2022.

- **ASU 2020-08** Codification Improvements to Subtopic 310-20, Receivables—Nonrefundable Fees and Other Costs

  Effective Date: For public business entities, this ASU is effective for fiscal years, and interim periods within those fiscal years, beginning after December 15, 2020. For all other entities, the effective date is for fiscal years beginning after December 15, 2021, and for interim periods within fiscal years beginning after December 15, 2022.

- **ASU 2020-09** Debt (Topic 470): Amendments to SEC Paragraphs Pursuant to SEC Release No. 33-10762

  Effective Date: The final rules became effective on January 4, 2021.

- **ASU 2020-10** Codification Improvements

  Effective Date: For public business entities, this ASU is effective for annual periods beginning after December 15, 2020. For all other entities, the amendments to the ASC are effective for annual periods beginning after December 15, 2021, and for interim periods within annual periods beginning after December 15, 2022.

- **ASU 2020-11** Financial Services—Insurance (Topic 944): Effective Date and Early Application

  Effective Date: In consideration of the implications of the COVID-19 pandemic on an insurance entity's ability to effectively implement ASU 2018-12, *Financial Services—Insurance (Topic 944): Targeted Improvements to the Accounting for Long-Duration Contracts*, this ASU defers the effective date for long-duration contracts by one year. For public business entities that meet the definition of an SEC filer and are not smaller reporting entities, ASU 2018-12 is effective for fiscal years beginning after December 15, 2022 and for interim periods within those fiscal years. For all other entities, the guidance in ASU 2018-12 is effective for fiscal years beginning after December 15, 2024, and interim periods within fiscal years beginning after December 15, 2025.

- **ASU 2021-01** Reference Rate Reform (Topic 848): Scope

  Effective Date: This ASU was issued in January 2021, and is effective immediately for all entities.

- **ASU 2021-02** Franchisors—Revenue from Contracts with Customers (Subtopic 952-606): Practical Expedient

  Effective Date: If an entity has not yet adopted ASC 606, *Revenue from Contracts with Customers*, the existing transition provisions and effective date of ASC 606 apply. If the entity has already adopted ASC 606, the amendments in this ASU are effective in interim and annual periods beginning after December 15, 2020.

- **ASU 2021-03** Intangibles—Goodwill and Other (Topic 350): Accounting Alternative for Evaluating Triggering Events

Effective Date: The amendments in this ASU are effective on a prospective basis for fiscal years beginning after December 15, 2019.

PRACTICE NOTE: An ASU issued in 2021 with an effective date for 2019 requires additional explanation. The FASB had issued ASU 2017-04, *Intangibles—Goodwill and Other (Topic 350): Simplifying the Test for Goodwill Impairment*, which eliminated step 2 of the goodwill impairment test. However, the effective date of that ASU was delayed by the issuance of ASU 2019-10, *Financial Instruments—Credit Losses (Topic 326), Derivatives and Hedging (Topic 815), and Leases (Topic 842): Effective Dates*, which sets the effective date for the guidance in ASU 2017-14 and ASU 2019-10 in ASC 350-20-65-3 to be after **December 15, 2019** for annual and any interim impairment tests performed.

- **ASU 2021-04** Earnings Per Share (Topic 260), Debt—Modifications and Extinguishments (Subtopic 470-50), Compensation—Stock Compensation (Topic 718), and Derivatives and Hedging—Contracts in Entity's Own Equity (Subtopic 815-40): Issuer's Accounting for Certain Modifications or Exchanges of Freestanding Equity-Classified Written Call Options (a consensus of the FASB Emerging Issues Task Force)

  Effective Date: The effective date for all entities is for fiscal years beginning after December 15, 2021, including interim periods within those fiscal years.

RESPONSE TO COVID-19

The collateral effects of the coronavirus (COVID-19) are expected to have a significant impact on the financial reporting of many companies. The FASB has a QUICKLINK that immediately comes up when you access the FASB web site (fasb.org), "FASB Response to COVID-19." The FASB indicates that it is monitoring and responding to the COVID-19 situation and is expected to continuously update this link for developments related to COVID-19.

In response to COVID-19, in an April 8, 2020 press release, (then) FASB chairman Russel G. Golden announced deferrals of the effective dates of revenue recognition and lease standards. This was later formalized in ASU 2020-05. He also made the following specific statements regarding the FASB's plans going forward:

". . . we will temporarily suspend issuance of other public exposure documents and will defer work that requires public outreach on other technical agenda projects to focus on supporting stakeholders as they navigate the impact of the crisis . . . It is important to note that we recognize that there are other standards with effective dates of 2022 and beyond—and that companies implementing them are also suffering from a dislocation of accounting staff and a reallocation of resources. I want to assure them that the FASB is committed to understanding how the COVID-19 crisis is impacting their transition plans, and we will continue to address issues at a future Board meeting, including addressing the need for more time related to adoption."

As the 2022 *GAAP Guide* goes to press, the "FASB Response to COVID-19" link on the FASB web site has several entries related to the FASB's response to COVID-19. The introduction to this link states: "The FASB shares global concerns about the stakeholder impact of the coronavirus (COVID-19) pandemic in the United States and abroad. The FASB is monitoring and responding to the situation and is committed to supporting and assisting our stakeholders during this difficult time." The Staff Q&A on Hedge Accounting during COVID-19 (issued April 28, 2020) and the Staff Q&A Document on Accounting for Leases during COVID-19 (issued April 10, 2020) appear to the authors of the 2022 *GAAP Guide* to be particularly important in implementing GAAP in 2021 and beyond.

In selected chapters in the 2022 *GAAP Guide*, specific references to FASB decisions related to COVID-19 are identified. Following are several examples where specific references to COVID-19 are found:

- The impact of COVID-19 on the alternative available in accounting for goodwill for certain entities (ASU 2021-03) is covered in Chapter 26, *ASC 350—Intangibles—Goodwill and Other*.
- In Chapter 35, *ASC 470—Debt*, users are directed to a fall, 2020 educational paper issued by the FASB that provides additional guidance for stakeholders in applying accounting for debt restructurings and modifications during the difficult COVID-19 time.

- COVID-19–related deferrals of the effective dates in ASU 2020-05 for certain entities related to revenue recognition are covered in Chapter 38, *ASC 606/605—Revenue Recognition*, and in Chapter 56, *ASC 842—Leases.*
- In Chapter 50, *ASC 815—Derivatives and Hedging*, guidance related to COVID-19 is provided from an FASB Staff Q&A.

While the FASB has issued relatively few changes in the ASC that directly relate to COVID-19, following are the existing areas that the authors believe may be particularly useful to issuers and auditors of financial statements in 2021 and beyond to reflect the impact of COVID-19. Whether these are relevant in any situation depends on the unique circumstances surrounding the reporting entity.

- Chapter 2—*ASC 205—Presentation of Financial Statements*
  –Liquidation Basis of Accounting (ASC 205-30)
  –Going Concern (ASC 205-40)
- Chapter 15—*ASC 275—Risks and Uncertainties*
- Chapter 24—*ASC 330—Inventories* (obsolescence)
- Chapter 26—*ASC 350—Intangibles—Goodwill and Other* (impairment)
- Chapter 27—*ASC 360—Property, Plant, and Equipment* (impairment)
- Chapter 33—*ASC 450—Contingencies*
- Chapter 35—*ASC 470—Debt* (classification)
- Chapter 56—*ASC 842—Leases* (concessions)
- Chapter 60—*ASC 852—Reorganizations*

OUTSTANDING PROPOSED ACCOUNTING STANDARDS UPDATES (PASUs)

Proposed ASUs (PASUs) are identified as Important Notices and are briefly described in both the General Guidance and the Interpretive Guidance sections of the appropriate chapters. This feature of the 2022 *GAAP Guide* is intended to alert users to upcoming developments that may have a significant impact on the preparation and auditing of financial statements in the future. As the 2022 *GAAP Guide* goes to press, these exposure drafts have not been issued as final ASUs and will not be in effect until they are finalized. With limited exceptions, final ASUs that have been issued will be incorporated in the next edition of the *GAAP Guide* in the appropriate chapter(s) and the effective dates will be clearly indicated.

The 10 PASUs that are covered as Important Notices in this edition are listed below, in the order of the chapter(s) they are expected to impact when issued as final ASUs. The Exposure Draft numbers begin with the year in which the draft was issued (e.g., Exposure Draft 2020-700 in Chapter 56 was issued in 2020).

Chapter 8

Notes to Financial Statements (Topic 235): Assessing Whether Disclosures are Material (Exposure Draft 2015-310)

Chapter 24

Inventory (Topic 330): Disclosure Framework—Changes to the Disclosure Requirements for Inventory (Exposure Draft 2017-210)

Chapter 43

Compensation—Stock Compensation (Topic 718): Determining the Current Price of an Underlying Share for Equity-Classified Share-Option Awards (a proposal of the Private Company Council) (Exposure Draft 2020-200)

Chapter 46

Income Taxes (Topic 740): Disclosure Framework—Changes to the Disclosure Requirements for Income Taxes (Exposure Draft 2019-500)

Chapter 47

Business Combinations (Topic 805): Accounting for Contract Assets and Contract Liabilities from Contracts with Customers (Exposure Draft 2020-1000)

Chapter 50

Derivative and Hedging (Topic 815): Codification Improvements to Hedge Accounting (Exposure Draft 2019-790)

Derivatives and Hedging (Topic 815): Fair Value Hedging—Portfolio Layer Method (Exposure Draft 2021-002)

Chapter 54

Government Assistance (Topic 832): Disclosures by Business Entities about Government Assistance (Exposure Draft 2015-340)

Chapter 56

Leases (Topic 842): Targeted Improvements (Exposure Draft 2020-700)

Leases (Topic 842): Discount Rate for Lessees That Are Not Public Business Entities (Exposure Draft 2021-003)

About the Authors

Jan R. Williams, Ph.D., CPA, is Dean and Professor Emeritus of the Haslam College of Business at the University of Tennessee, Knoxville (UTK), where he was on the faculty from 1977 through 2013. Following several years of retirement, he served on a short-term basis as Dean of the Massey College of Business at Belmont University. Prior to UTK, he was on the faculties of the University of Georgia and Texas Tech University. His B.S. degree is from George Peabody College (now a college of Vanderbilt University), MBA from Baylor University, and Ph.D. in Business Administration with majors in both accounting and economics from the University of Arkansas. He is a CPA in Arkansas (inactive) and Tennessee (active license).

Dr. Williams has been actively involved in the American Institute of CPAs, the National Association of State Boards of Accountancy, the Tennessee Society of Certified Public Accountants, and several other professional accounting organizations. Throughout his career, he taught university financial accounting courses, as well as continuing professional education for CPAs. In 1994, Dr. Williams received the Outstanding Accounting Educator Award from both the Tennessee Society of CPAs and the AICPA. He authored or co-authored six books and over 125 articles, monographs, and other publications on issues related to financial reporting and accounting and business education. Dr. Williams served as National President of Beta Alpha Psi, President of the American Accounting Association, and Chair of the Board of Directors of the AACSB (Association to Advance Collegiate Schools of Business) International. He received the American Accounting Association's Outstanding Accounting Educator award.

Terry L. Neal, Ph.D., CPA, is the Richard L. Townsend Chaired Professor of Accounting and Head of the Department of Accounting and Information Management of the Haslam College of Business at the University of Tennessee. He also is a Research Fellow at the University of Tennessee's Corporate Governance Center. Dr. Neal currently teaches a graduate course in advanced financial accounting topics, an undergraduate intermediate accounting course, and has also taught undergraduate auditing. He has also taught continuing professional education courses for one of the Big 4 accounting firms for several years. Dr. Neal served as the director of the Ph.D. program in Accounting for several years and taught a doctoral seminar in empirical/archival research, with an emphasis on auditing and corporate governance issues. Dr. Neal also serves as a research fellow of the ERM Initiative at North Carolina State University.

Dr. Neal received a B.S. in accounting from Tennessee Technological University (1988) and a Ph.D. from the University of Tennessee (1998). Prior to joining the faculty at the University of Tennessee, Dr. Neal was on the faculty of the Douglas J. Von Allmen School of Accountancy at the University of Kentucky.

Judith Weiss, CPA, has an M.S. in Accounting from Long Island University, Greenvale, New York, and an M.S. in Education from Queens College, Flushing, New York. After several years in public accounting and private industry, she worked as a technical manager in the AICPA's Accounting Standards Division, where she helped industry committees to develop Audit and Accounting Guides and Statements of Position. As a senior manager in the national offices of Deloitte & Touche LLP and Grant Thornton LLP, she was involved in projects related to standard-setting by the FASB and the AICPA. Ms. Weiss has followed the work of the EITF since its inception and has attended its meetings in person or through the internet regularly since 1991.

Since 1993, Ms. Weiss has combined her extensive experience in the development and implementation of accounting and auditing standards with her technical writing background in writing projects related to accounting standards. She has contributed to several books in the area of accounting and auditing. She also has coauthored articles on accounting standards for several publications, including the *Journal of Accountancy, The CPA Journal, The Journal of Real Estate Accounting and Taxation,* and the *Journal of Corporate Accounting and Finance.*

Acknowledgments

Judith Weiss gives thanks to the late Thomas W. McRae and to Paul Rosenfield, formerly of the AICPA, who taught her about writing and the accounting standards-setting process; former colleagues and friends who helped to make the Guide a reality; and four very important CPAs: her husband, Carl, sons, Daniel and Jonathan, and daughter-in-law, Robyn, for their interest and tireless encouragement in this project.

The authors and publisher wish to thank Duane Rehyl, an accounting and auditing partner with Andrews Hooper Pavlik PLC (AHP), for his technical review and comments on the 2022 edition of *GAAP Guide*.

Generally Accepted Accounting Principles

CHAPTER 1

ASC 105—GENERALLY ACCEPTED ACCOUNTING PRINCIPLES

CONTENTS

GENERAL GUIDANCE

ASC 105-10: OVERALL

GAAP HIERARCHY AND THE ACCOUNTING STANDARDS CODIFICATION

The meaning of the term *generally accepted accounting principles* (GAAP) has varied over time. Originally, GAAP referred to accounting policies and procedures that were widely used in practice. As several standard-setting bodies and professional organizations became more involved in establishing required or preferred practices, the term evolved to refer to the pronouncements issued by particular accounting bodies. Today, the term U.S. GAAP is defined by the Financial Accounting Standards Board's (FASB's) Accounting Standards Codification® (ASC). The ASC is the single source of authoritative accounting principles recognized by the FASB to be applied by nongovernmental entities in the preparation of financial statements in accordance with U.S. GAAP. Rules and interpretative releases of the Securities and Exchange Commission (SEC) under the authority of federal law are also sources of authoritative U.S. GAAP for SEC registrants (ASC 105-10-5-1).

Prior to the issuance of the ASC, the FASB established what was commonly referred to as the GAAP hierarchy. The purpose of the GAAP hierarchy was to assist financial statement preparers, auditors, and users of financial statements in determining the relative priority of the different sources of GAAP used by accountants in preparing financial statements and by auditors to judge the fairness of presentation in those statements. The ASC superseded the GAAP hierarchy, and today all authoritative sources of U.S. GAAP included in the ASC have the same level of authority.

For transactions where guidance for a transaction or event is not specified in the ASC, the reporting entity is to consider accounting principles for similar transactions or events that are covered in the ASC. Following that, the entity considers nonauthoritative guidance from other sources that are not included in the ASC, including FASB Concepts Statements, AICPA Issue Papers, International Financial Reporting Standards, pronouncements of professional associations or regulatory agencies, Technical Information Services Inquiries and Replies included in AICPA Technical Practice Aids, and accounting textbooks (ASC 105-10-5-2, 3).

The ASC codifies the following standards:

- FASB Standards
  - — Statements
  - — Interpretations
  - — Technical Bulletins
  - — Staff Positions
  - — Staff Implementation Guides
- Emerging Issues Task Force
  - — Abstracts
  - — Appendix D Topics
  - — Staff Implementation Guides

- Derivative Implementation Issues
- Accounting Principles Board Opinions
- Accounting Research Bulletins
- Accounting Interpretations
- AICPA
  - Statements of Position
  - Audit and Accounting Guides
  - Practice Bulletins
  - Technical Inquiry Services

PRACTICE POINTER: The ASC can be accessed through the FASB's web site at www.fasb.org. An opportunity is available for limited use of the ASC for those who are not familiar with it. This provides an opportunity to explore the ASC, try its capabilities and functionality, and make an informed decision regarding the subscription options.

PRACTICE POINTER: From time to time, the FASB issues Accounting Standards Updates (ASUs) that represent multiple ASC improvements rather than focusing on one specific financial reporting issue. For example, ASU 2018-09, *Codification Improvements,* included a number of corrections and clarifications in the ASC since its establishment in September 2009 as the sole source of authoritative generally accepted accounting principles. Rather than focusing on a single financial reporting issue, this ASU specifies 30 different issues that deal with a wide range of financial reporting areas, including but not limited to reporting comprehensive income, debt extinguishment, distinguishing liabilities and equity, stock compensation, business combinations, derivatives and hedging, fair value measurement, financial services, and defined contribution pension plans. More recently, similar codification improvement ASUs have been issued (e.g., ASU 2020-03, ASU 2020-08, ASU 2020-10). The titles of all of these ASUs begin with "Codification Improvements . . . ," which signals that the FASB is constantly looking for ways to improve the ASC. This pattern of continuous improvement in the Accounting Standards Codification can be expected to continue as the FASB identifies various corrections and clarifications that are intended to improve financial reporting.

PRACTICE POINTER: As indicated above, ASU 2020-10, *Codification Improvements*, is a recent codification improvement ASU that affects multiple sections of the Accounting Standards Codification covered elsewhere in the 2022 *GAAP Guide.* The following summarizes the transition and effective date information related to ASU 2020-10. A public business entity, a not-for-profit entity that has issued, or is a conduit bond obligor for, securities that are traded, listed, or quoted on an exchange or an over-the-counter market, and an employee benefit plan that files or furnishes financial statements with or to the Securities and Exchange Commission shall apply ASU 2020-10 for annual periods beginning after December 15, 2020, including interim periods within those annual periods. For all other entities, ASU 2020-10 is effective for annual periods beginning after December 15, 2021 and interim periods within annual periods beginning after December 15, 2022. An entity shall recognize and present separately the cumulative effect of the change in accounting principle as an adjustment to the opening balance as of the beginning of the period in which ASU 2020-10 is first applied. (ASC 105-10-65-6)

CHAPTER 2

ASC 205—PRESENTATION OF FINANCIAL STATEMENTS

CONTENTS

PART I: GENERAL GUIDANCE

ASC 205-10: OVERALL

OVERVIEW

Reporting the results of operations, including determining and presenting net income and comprehensive income, is one of the most important aspects of financial reporting. U.S. GAAP provide specific guidance concerning how certain items are to be presented in the income statement.

BACKGROUND

For many years, there were differences of opinion in the accounting profession as to what should be included in net income. Proponents of the *all-inclusive approach* (sometimes called "clean surplus") took the position that all items affecting net increases in owners' equity, except dividends and capital transactions, should be included in computing net income. Alternatively, proponents of the *current operating performance approach* (sometimes called "dirty surplus") advocated limiting the determination of net income to normal, recurring items of profit and loss that relate only to the current period while recognizing other items by direct charges and credits to retained earnings. Differences between the two concepts are seen most clearly in the treatment of the following items:

- Unusual or infrequently occurring items
- Extraordinary items (eliminated by ASU 2015-01)
- Changes in accounting principles

- Discontinued operations
- Prior period adjustments
- Certain items that are now required by U.S. GAAP to be recognized directly in stockholders' equity rather than in net income

Current U.S. GAAP require the presentation of income in a manner that incorporates elements of both the all-inclusive and the current operating performance approaches. Net income includes all items of revenue, expense, gain, and loss during a reporting period, except prior period adjustments, dividends, and capital transactions, and a limited number of items specifically identified as being recognized directly in equity as other comprehensive income. Examples of items recognized directly in equity are certain foreign currency adjustments and certain changes in the value of debt and equity investments.

COMPARATIVE FINANCIAL STATEMENTS

Comparative financial statements generally provide more information than financial statements for a single period. They provide a context for current-year statements, and they furnish useful data about differences in the results of operations for the periods presented and in the financial position, results of operations, and cash flows at the comparison dates (ASC 205-10-45-1). Notes to financial statements, explanations, and accountants' reports containing qualifications that appeared in the statements for preceding years shall be repeated, or at least referred to, in the comparative statements to the extent they continue to be of significance (ASC 205-10-50-2).

Consistency is a major factor in creating comparability. Prior-year amounts and classifications must be comparable with the current period presented, and exceptions must be disclosed clearly (ASC 205-10-45-2 through 4).

ASC 205-20: DISCONTINUED OPERATIONS

DISCONTINUED OPERATIONS

ASC 205 provides guidance with regard to reporting of discontinued operations for either (1) a component or group of components of an entity that is disposed of or is classified as held for sale, or (2) a business or nonprofit activity that is classified as held for sale when acquired (ASC 205-20-15-2). This guidance does not apply for oil and gas properties accounted for using the full cost method of accounting (ASC 205-20-15-3). For purposes of applying ASC 205, a component of an entity comprises operations and cash flows that can be clearly distinguished, operationally and for financial reporting purposes, from the rest of the entity. A component may be a reportable segment or an operating segment as those terms are defined in ASC 280 (Segment Reporting), a subsidiary, or an asset group (ASC Glossary).

PRACTICE NOTE: When a part of an entity is disposed of or otherwise discontinued, there is an inherent lack of comparability between earlier periods, which include that part of the entity, and later periods that exclude that part of the entity. In addition, there is the income effect of the disposal itself that affects comparability. An important aspect of ASC 205 is to use disclosure to compensate for this lack of comparability. The extent of disclosures that are required about a discontinued operation varies depending on the nature of the discontinued operation. Discontinued operations that include an equity method investment, or a business or nonprofit activity classified as held for sale on acquisition, will generally require less extensive disclosures.

The disposal of a component or a group of components of an entity is reported in discontinued operations if the disposal represents a strategic shift that has (or will have) a significant effect on the entity's operations and financial results when any of the following occur (ASC 205-20-45-1B):

- The component or group of components qualifies to be classified as held for sale.
- The component or group of components is disposed of by sale.
- The component or group of components is disposed of other than by sale.

The results of operations of a business or nonprofit activity that, on acquisition, qualifies to be classified as held to sale are reported in discontinued operations (ASC 205-20-45-1D).

A component or a group of components of an entity, or a business or nonprofit activity, qualifies to be classified as held for sale in the period in which all of the following criteria are met (ASC 205-20-45-1E):

- Management commits to a properly authorized plan to sell the entity to be sold.
- The entity to be sold is available for immediate sale in its present condition.

- Actions required to complete the plan to sell the entity to be sold have been initiated, including a program to locate a buyer or buyers.
- The sale of the entity to be sold is probable and is expected to be completed within one year, with exceptions made for certain events or circumstances beyond an entity's control that may extend the time to completion of the sale beyond one year.
- The entity to be sold is being actively marketed at a reasonable price given its current fair value.
- It is unlikely that the plan to sell the entity to be sold will be significantly changed or withdrawn.

Statement in Which Net Income Is Reported

Discontinued operations are reported as a separate component in the statement in which net income is reported by a business entity (the statement of activities of a not-for-profit entity). The presentation of discontinued operations reports the results of operations of a discontinued operation, including any gain or loss recognized, in the period in which the discontinued operation either has been disposed of or is classified as held for sale. Any gain or loss recognized on the disposal, or any loss recognized on classification as held for sale, must be presented separately on the face of the statement where net income is reported or disclosed in the financial statement footnotes (ASC 205-20-45-3).

Illustration of Presentation of Discontinued Operations in Net Income

Based on assumed numbers, the following illustrates the presentation of discontinued operations in income in accordance with U.S. GAAP:

Income (loss) from continuing operations before provision for income taxes	$400,000	
Provision for income taxes	(136,000)	
Income (loss) from continuing operations		$264,000
Discontinued operations (Note: ________)		
Income (loss) from operations of discontinued component A (less applicable income taxes $34,000)	$(66,000)	
Loss (gain) on disposal of component A (less applicable income taxes of $17,000)	(33,000)	
Net income (loss) from discontinued operations		(99,000)
Net income		$165,000

Adjustments to amounts previously reported in discontinued operations in a prior period must be presented separately in the current period in the discontinued operations sections of the statement where net income is reported. The nature and amount of such adjustment shall be disclosed (ASC 205-20-45-4).

PRACTICE NOTE: A gain or loss recognized on the sale of a long-lived asset that is not a discontinued operation is included in income from continuing operations before income taxes in the income statement of a business enterprise and in income from continuing operations of a not-for-profit organization (ASC 360-10-45-5).

Statement of Financial Position

The assets and liabilities of a discontinued operation must be presented separately in the asset and liability sections, respectively, of the statement of financial position in the period(s) that the discontinued operation is classified as held for sale and for all prior periods. Those assets and liabilities cannot be offset and presented as a single amount. If a discontinued operation is disposed of before it qualifies to be classified as held for sale, the assets and liabilities of the discontinued operation is presented separately for the periods presented in the statement of financial position before the period that includes the disposal (ASC 205-20-45-10).

For any discontinued operation initially classified as held for sale in the current period, the major classes of assets and liabilities of the discontinued operation must be either presented on the face of the statement of financial position or disclosed in the financial statement footnotes for all periods presented in the statement of financial position (ASC 205-20-45-11).

Disclosure

The following information is required to be disclosed in conjunction with discontinued operations (ASC 205-20-50-1):

- A description of the facts and circumstances leading to the disposal or expected disposal and, the expected manner and timing of that disposal.
- The gain or loss recognized, if not separately disclosed on the face of the statement where net income is reported as part of discontinued operations.
- If applicable, the segment(s) in which the discontinued operation is reported under ASC 280 (Segment Reporting).

If an entity changes its plan for disposing of a discontinued operation, the notes to the financial statements for the year in which that decision is made should include a description of the facts and circumstances leading to the decision to change the plan as well as the impact of the change on the results of operations for the period and any prior periods presented (ASC 205-20-50-3).

An entity may retain a significant continuing involvement in a discontinued operation after the disposal date. In such cases, the following disclosures are required (ASC 205-20-50-4A, B):

- A description of the nature of the activities that give rise to the continuing involvement.
- The period of time during which the involvement is expected to continue.
- For all periods presented, the amount of any cash inflows and outflows from or to the discontinued operation after the disposal transaction.
- For all periods presented, revenues or expenses presented, if any, in continuing operations after the disposal transaction that before the disposal transaction were eliminated in consolidated financial statements as intra-entity transactions.
- For a discontinued operation in which an entity retains an equity method investment after the disposal, information that allows financial statement users to compare the entity's financial performance from period to period assuming that the entity held the same equity method investment in all periods presented in the statement where net income is reported.

ASC 205-30: LIQUIDATION BASIS OF ACCOUNTING

Liquidation is defined as the process by which an entity converts its assets to cash or other assets and settles its obligations with creditors in anticipation of the entity ceasing all activities. Upon cessation of the entity's activities, any remaining cash or other assets are distributed to the entity's investors or other claimants. Liquidation may be compulsory or voluntary. Dissolution of an entity as a result of that entity being acquired by another entity or merged into another entity in its entirety and with the expectation of continuing its business does not qualify as liquidation. (ASC Glossary)

An entity is required to prepare financial statements in accordance with the liquidation basis of accounting when liquidation is imminent. Liquidation is considered imminent when either of the following occurs:

- A plan for liquidation has been approved by the person or persons with the authority to make such a plan effective, and the likelihood is remote that any of the following will occur:
  - — Execution of the plan will be blocked by other parties (e.g., shareholders with certain rights).
  - — The entity will return from liquidation.
- A plan for liquidation is imposed by other forces (e.g., involuntary bankruptcy) and the likelihood is remote that the entity will return from liquidation. (ASC 205-30-25-2)

Following are several key principles applicable to the liquidation basis of accounting:

- When applying the liquidation basis of accounting, an entity shall recognize other items that it previously had not recognized (e.g., trademarks) but that it expects to either sell in liquidation or use to settle liabilities.
- The entity shall recognize liabilities in accordance with the recognition provisions that would otherwise apply to those liabilities.

- The entity shall accrue estimated costs to dispose of assets or other items that it expects to sell in liquidation and present those costs in the aggregate separately from those assets or items. Discounting provisions in measuring the accrual for estimated disposal costs shall not be used.
- The entity shall accrue costs and income that it expects to incur or earn through the end of its liquidation and when it has a reasonable basis for estimation.
- The entity shall measure assets to reflect the estimated amount of cash or other consideration that it expects to collect in settling or disposing of those assets in carrying out its liquidation plan.
- The entity shall measure liabilities in accordance with the measurement provisions that would otherwise be applied except as noted above for the accrual of estimated disposal costs and expected income and expenses related to liquidation.
- At each reporting date, the entity shall remeasure its assets and other items it expects to sell that it has not previously recognized, liabilities, and the accruals of disposal or other costs or income to reflect the actual or estimated change in carrying value since the previous reporting date. (ASC 205-30-25-1 through 35-1)

An entity applying the liquidation basis shall prepare a statement of net assets in liquidation and a statement of changes in net assets in liquidation. The liquidation basis shall be applied prospectively from the date that the liquidation becomes imminent.

All of the following are required to be disclosed:

- The fact that the financial statements are prepared by the liquidation basis, including the facts and circumstances surrounding the adoption of the liquidation basis.
- A description of the entity's plan for liquidation, including a description of:
  - — The manner in which the disposal of assets and other items is expected to occur.
  - — The manner in which liabilities are expected to be settled.
  - — The expected date by which liquidation is expected to be complete.
- The methods and significant assumptions used to measure assets and liabilities, including any subsequent changes to those methods and assumptions.
- The type and amount of costs and income accrued in the statement of net assets in liquidation for the period over which those costs are expected to be paid or income earned. (ASC 205-30-50-2)

ASC 205-40: GOING CONCERN

OVERVIEW

Unless and until an entity's liquidation becomes imminent, the entity prepares its financial statements on a going concern basis, which assumes that the entity will continue to function and be able to continue to meet its obligations as they become due (ASC 205-40-05-01). However, even if an entity's liquidation is not imminent, there may be conditions and events that exist which raise substantial doubt about the entity's ability to continue as a going concern. In those situations, although the entity continues to prepare its financial statements on a going concern basis, management must also determine whether to disclose certain information about the relevant conditions and events (ASC 205-40-05-02).

PRACTICE NOTE: Substantial doubt about an entity's ability to continue as a going concern exists when these conditions and events indicate that it is probable that the entity will be unable to meet its obligations as they become due within one year after the date that the financial statements are issued (or within one year after the date that the financial statements are available to be issued when applicable) (ASC Glossary).

DISCLOSURE

Evaluating Conditions and Events That May Raise Substantial Doubt

While preparing financial statements for each annual and interim reporting period, an entity's management must evaluate whether there are conditions and events that raise substantial doubt about the entity's ability to continue as a going concern

(ASC 205-40-50-1). Management makes this evaluation based on relevant conditions and events that are known and reasonably knowable at the date that the financial statements are issued (ASC 205-40-50-3).

When making the evaluation of an entity's ability to meet its obligations, management must consider quantitative and qualitative information about the following conditions and events (ASC 205-40-50-5):

- The entity's current financial condition
- The entity's conditional and unconditional obligations due or anticipated within one year after the date that the financial statements are issued
- The funds necessary to maintain the entity's operations considering its current financial condition, obligations, and other expected cash flows
- Other conditions and events that may adversely affect the entity's ability to meet its obligations within one year after the date that the financial statements are issued

Examples of Plans That Management May Implement to Mitigate Concerns

Following are examples (not a comprehensive list) of plans management might consider to mitigate issues that raise doubt about an entity's ability to continue as a going concern:

- Availability and terms of new debt financing or refinancing of existing debt, including factoring of receivables, sale and leaseback of assets.
- For a plan of a closely-held business, an infusion of additional capital funds from the entity's principal shareholder.
- Existing or committed arrangement to restructure or subordinate debt and to guarantee loans of the entity.
- Possible effects on management's borrowing plans of existing restrictions on additional borrowing or the sufficiency of available collateral. (ASC 205-40-55-3)

Consideration of Management's Plans When Substantial Doubt Is Raised

When an entity determines that conditions and events raise substantial doubt about its ability to continue as a going concern, management must evaluate whether its plans to mitigate those conditions and events, when implemented, will alleviate the substantial doubt (ASC 205-40-50-6). However, these management plans should only be considered in evaluating whether the substantial doubt is alleviated if (ASC 205-40-50-7):

- It is probable that the plans will be effectively implemented within one year after the date that the financial statements are issued; and
- It is probable that the plans, when implemented, will mitigate the relevant conditions or events that raise substantial doubt about the entity's ability to continue as a going concern.

PRACTICE NOTE: Generally, to be considered probable of being effectively implemented, the plans must have been approved by management, or others with appropriate authority, before the date that the financial statements are issued (ASC 205-40-50-8).

Disclosures When Management's Plans Alleviate Substantial Doubt

If management's plans are determined to effectively alleviate the substantial doubt about the entity's ability to continue as a going concern, an entity must disclose in the footnotes information that allows financial statement users to understand the following (ASC 205-40-50-12):

- The principal conditions or events that raised substantial doubt about the entity's ability to continue as a going concern (prior to consideration of management's plans);
- Management's evaluation of the significance of those conditions or events in relation to the entity's ability to meet its obligations; and
- Management's plans that alleviated the substantial doubt about the entity's ability to continue as a going concern.

Disclosures When Management's Plans Do Not Alleviate Substantial Doubt

If management's plans are determined to not alleviate the existing substantial doubt, the entity must include a statement in the notes indicating that there is substantial doubt about the entity's ability to continue as a going concern within one year after the date that the financial statements are issued. In addition, the entity must also disclose information that allows financial statement users to understand the following (ASC 205-40-50-13):

- The principal conditions or events that raised substantial doubt about the entity's ability to continue as a going concern;
- Management's evaluation of the significance of those conditions or events in relation to the entity's ability to meet its obligations; and
- Management's plans that are intended to mitigate the conditions or events that raise substantial doubt about the entity's ability to continue as a going concern.

An entity must continue to provide these required disclosures if conditions or events continue to raise substantial doubt in subsequent annual or interim periods. These disclosures should become more extensive as more is known about the relevant conditions or events and about management's plans to alleviate them. These disclosures must also provide appropriate context regarding how the conditions or events have changed between reporting periods. If it is determined in a later reporting period that substantial doubt no longer exists, an entity must disclose how the relevant conditions or events that raised substantial doubt were resolved (ASC 205-40-50-14).

PART II: INTERPRETIVE GUIDANCE

ASC 205-20: DISCONTINUED OPERATIONS

ASC 205-20-45-6 through 45-9, S50-1, S99-3 Illustration of Allocation of Interest to Discontinued Operations

OVERVIEW

A company selling a business segment (or line of business) reports the sale separately as a discontinued operation. The company has debt on its balance sheet.

ACCOUNTING ISSUES

- Can interest expense be allocated to discontinued operations based on the debt's principal amount that will or could be paid with proceeds from the sale of operations?
- If so, how should such interest be allocated?
- Can general overhead expenses be allocated to discontinued operations?

ACCOUNTING GUIDANCE

1. Allocation of interest to discontinued operations is permitted but not required.
2. The following method should be used if allocation of interest to discontinued operations is elected:
   a. Allocate other consolidated interest not attributable to the entity's other operations based on a ratio of net assets to be sold or discontinued less debt required to be paid due to the disposal transaction to the sum of the consolidated entity's total net assets plus consolidated debt *other than:*
      (1) Debt of the discontinued operation that will be assumed by the buyer,
      (2) Debt required to be paid due to the disposal transaction, and
      (3) Debt that can be directly attributed to the entity's other operations.
   b. A uniform consolidated debt-to-equity ratio for all operations is assumed. If that is not the case because the assets being sold are atypical, as in a finance company, a normal debt-to-equity ratio for that type of business can be used.
   c. Interest is allocated to discontinued operations based on debt that can be identified as specifically related to those operations, if allocation based on net assets would not provide meaningful results.
3. General and corporate overhead should not be allocated to discontinued operations.

SEC STAFF COMMENT

The SEC Observer stated that registrants that elect to allocate interest in accordance with the consensus will be expected to clearly disclose their accounting policy, including the method of allocation, and the amount allocated to and included in discontinued operations for all periods presented.

Illustration of Allocation of Interest to Discontinued Operations

Assets	
Assets of discontinued operations	$ 400,000
Other assets	800,000
Total assets	$1,200,000
Liabilities and Equity	
Trade payables and other noninterest-bearing debt	$ 250,000
Debt related to discontinued operations to be assumed by the buyer	100,000
Debt required to be paid due to disposal	150,000
Debt related to other operations	150,000
Debt unrelated to other operations	250,000
Deferred taxes	50,000
Total liabilities	$ 950,000
Stockholders' equity	250,000
Total liabilities and equity	$1,200,000

The consensus applies to the income statement presentation of both continuing and discontinued operations and including presentation of the gain or loss on disposal of a component of an enterprise. The decision whether to allocate interest should be applied consistently to all discontinued operations.

Total interest expense (10% average interest rate × $650,000 interest-bearing debt) = $65,000

Based on the information presented above, interest on consolidated debt not attributable to other operations is computed as a ratio of (1) the net assets to be discontinued less debt required to be paid due to the disposal and (2) the sum of consolidated net assets plus debt unrelated to other operations:

Net assets to be discontinued less debt required to be paid due to disposal	=	$400,000 - $100,000 - $150,000	= .3 interest on consolidated debt
Sum of consolidated net assets* plus debt unrelated to other operations		$250,000 + $250,000	

* ($1,200,000 – $950,000 = $250,000)

Interest on debt unrelated to other operations	= $250,000 ×.10
	= $25,000 × .3
	= $7,500
Interest on debt assumed by buyer	= $100,000 ×.10
	= $10,000
Interest allocated to discontinued operations	= $7,500 + $10,000
	= $17,500

DISCUSSION

This Issue was raised by the FASB staff, who noted that practice is varied. The allocation approach chosen by the EITF is based on the rationale that interest is a cost that should be associated with the assets financed with the debt. The EITF favored an allocation approach based on the amount of debt that will be repaid with the proceeds of the sale of discontinued operations. However, they decided to limit that amount to debt that will be assumed by the buyer and other debt unrelated to operations, such as general corporate debt.

CHAPTER 3

ASC 210—BALANCE SHEET

CONTENTS

PART I: GENERAL GUIDANCE

ASC 210-10: OVERALL

OVERVIEW

The distinction between current and noncurrent assets and liabilities in a classified balance sheet is an important feature of financial reporting. Defined as working capital, the difference between current assets and current liabilities plays an important role in liquidity analysis which is of particular interest to investors, creditors, and other users of financial statements.

BACKGROUND

In the ordinary course of business, there is a continuing circulation of capital within the current assets. For example, a manufacturer expends cash for materials, labor, and factory overhead that are converted into finished inventory. Inventory is then converted into trade receivables and, on collection of receivables, is converted back to cash. The average time elapsing between expenditure of cash and receiving the cash back from the collection of the trade receivable is referred to as the *operating cycle*. One year is used as a basis for segregating current assets in the usual case where more than one operating cycle occurs within a year. When the operating cycle is longer than one year, as with the lumber, tobacco, and distillery businesses, the operating cycle is used for segregating current assets. *In the event that a business clearly has no operating cycle, the one-year rule is used* (ASC 210-10-45-3).

Frequently, businesses have a *natural business year*, at the end of which the company's activity, inventory, and trade receivables are at their lowest point. This is often the point in time selected as the end of the entity's accounting period for financial reporting purposes.

BASIC DEFINITIONS

Current Assets

Resources that are expected to be realized in cash, sold, or consumed during the next year (or longer operating cycle) are classified as current assets. Current assets are sometimes called circulating or working assets; cash that is restricted as to withdrawal or use for other than current operations is not classified as a current asset (ASC 210-10-45-4).

PRACTICE NOTE: This definition of current assets demonstrates the importance of professional judgment in determining the proper treatment of certain items. The words "expected to be realized" indicate that management intent is important. The same asset could be a current asset for one company and not a current asset for another company due to differences in management intent.

The primary types of current assets are cash, cash equivalents, secondary cash resources, receivables, inventories, and prepaid expenses (ASC 210-10-45-1).

Cash and Cash Equivalents

Includes cash and cash equivalents, such as cash on deposit, cash awaiting deposit, and other cash funds that are available for current operations. *Cash equivalents* consist of short-term, highly liquid investments that are (*a*) readily convertible to known amounts of cash and (*b*) so near their maturities that they present insignificant risk of changes in value because of changes in interest rates.

Secondary Cash Resources

A common type of secondary cash resources is marketable securities that are available for current operations.

Receivables

Include trade accounts, notes, and acceptances receivable, as well as receivables from officers and employees, if collectible in the ordinary course of business within one year.

Inventories

Include merchandise, raw materials, work in process, finished goods, operating supplies, and ordinary maintenance material and parts.

Prepaid Expenses

Include prepaid insurance, interest, taxes, advertising, unused royalties, current paid advertising not received, and operating supplies. Prepaid expenses, unlike other current assets, are not expected to be converted into cash; but, if they had not been paid in advance, they would require the use of current assets during the operating cycle.

Asset valuation allowances for losses, such as those for receivables and investments, are deducted from the assets or groups of assets to which the allowances relate (ASC 210-10-45-13).

Current Liabilities

Current liabilities are obligations for which repayment is expected to require the use of current assets or the creation of other current liabilities.

PRACTICE POINTER: The definition of current liabilities is based on the asset category from which the liability is expected to be retired rather than on a specific period of time. As a practical matter, however, most current liabilities are expected to be retired during the period of time encompassed by the definition of current assets. Care should be taken, however, to identify instances where liabilities that are due in the near future should be classified as noncurrent because they will not require the use of current assets. Examples are short-term obligations expected to be refinanced that meet certain specified criteria and liabilities that are within one year of maturity but that will be paid from noncurrent assets (e.g., bond sinking funds).

There are several common types of current liabilities (ASC 210-10-45-8):

Payables from Operations

Include items that have entered the operating cycle, which include trade payables and accrued liabilities such as wages and taxes.

Debt Maturities

Include amounts expected to be liquidated during the current operating cycle, such as short-term notes and the currently maturing portion of long-term debt.

Revenue Received in Advance

Includes collections received in advance of services, for example, prepaid subscriptions and other deferred revenues. This type of current liability is typically liquidated by means other than the payment of cash (e.g., delivery of products, provision of services).

Other Accruals

Include estimates of accrued amounts that are expected to be required to cover expenditures within the year for known obligations (*a*) when the amount can be determined only approximately (provision for accrued bonuses payable) or (*b*) when the specific person(s) to whom payment will be made is (are) unascertainable (provision for warranty of a product) (ASC 210-10-45-6).

Working Capital and Related Ratios

Working capital is the excess of current assets over current liabilities, and it is often used as a measure of the liquidity of an enterprise (ASC 210-10-05-5).

Changes in Each Element of Working Capital

The changes in each element of working capital are the increases or decreases in each current asset and current liability over the amounts in the preceding year.

Illustration of Determining Working Capital

	20X8	20X9	Working Capital Increase or (Decrease)
Current Assets:			
Cash	$10,000	$ 15,000	$ 5,000
Accounts receivable, net	25,000	35,000	10,000
Inventory	50,000	60,000	10,000
Prepaid expenses	1,000	500	(500)
Total current assets	$86,000	$110,500	$ 24,500
Current Liabilities:			
Accounts payable	$10,000	$ 15,000	$ (5,000)
Notes payable-current	20,000	15,000	5,000
Accrued expenses	1,000	1,500	(500)
Total current liabilities	$31,000	$ 31,500	$ (500)
Net working capital	$55,000	$ 79,000	
Increase in working capital			$24,000

The *current ratio*, or *working capital ratio*, is a measure of current position and is useful in analyzing short-term credit. The current ratio is computed by dividing the total current assets by the total current liabilities.

Illustration of Current Ratio

	20X8	20X9
Current assets	$86,000	$110,500
Current liabilities	(31,000)	(31,500)
Working capital	$55,000	$79,000
Current ratio (86 ÷ 31), (110.5 ÷ 31.5)	2.8:1	3.5:1

The *acid-test* or *quick ratio* is determined by dividing those assets typically closest to cash by total current liabilities. The assets used to calculate this ratio consist of only the most liquid assets, typically cash, receivables, and marketable securities.

PRACTICE POINTER: Only receivables and securities *convertible into cash* are included; restricted cash and securities are excluded.

Illustration of Acid-Test Ratio

	20X8	20X9
Cash	$10,000	$15,000
Receivables, net	25,000	35,000
Total *quick* assets	$35,000	$50,000
Total current liabilities	$31,000	$31,500
Acid-test ratio (35 ÷ 31), (50 ÷ 31.5)	1.1:1	1.6:1

PRACTICE POINTER: As illustrated above, inventory is excluded from the numerator in calculating the quick/acid-test ratio. The reasoning behind this is that inventory is often one of the largest current assets and the furthest away from being converted into cash. In considering whether the current or quick/acid-test ratio is a better measure of liquidity, the accounting method used for inventory may be an important factor. Where the LIFO inventory method is used, the current asset amount of inventory consists of the oldest costs and may not be a fair representation of the current value of the inventory. This would make the acid test/quick ratio the preferred liquidity measure. On the other hand, if the FIFO inventory method is used, the current asset amount of inventory represents an amount closer to the current cost, which may make the current ratio a more logical measure of liquidity.

RECEIVABLES

Accounts receivable are reported in the financial statements at net realizable value. Net realizable value is equal to the gross amount of receivables less an estimated allowance for uncollectible accounts.

Two common procedures of accounting for uncollectible accounts are (1) the direct write-off method and (2) the allowance method.

Direct Write-Off Method

This method delays the recognition of uncollectible accounts until a specific account is determined to be uncollectible. The conceptual weaknesses of the direct write-off method are:

- Bad debt expense may not be recognized in the same reporting period as the related sale.
- Accounts receivable are overstated, because no attempt is made to account for the unknown bad debts included therein.

Ordinarily, the direct write-off method is not considered U.S. GAAP, because it results in a mismatching of revenues and expenses (i.e., expenses are recognized in a later period than the revenue to which they relate), overstating the amount of assets and understating the amount of expense. The method may be acceptable in situations where uncollectible accounts are immaterial in amount.

Allowance Method

The allowance method recognizes an estimate of uncollectible accounts each period, even though the specific individual accounts that will not be collected cannot be specifically identified at that time. Estimates of uncollectible accounts usually are made as a percentage of credit sales or ending receivables. This method is consistent with ASC 450 (Contingencies), as explained below.

Under ASC 450, a contingency exists if, at the date of the financial statements, an enterprise does not expect to collect the full amount of its accounts receivable. Under this circumstance, an accrual for a loss contingency must be recognized, if both of the following conditions exist:

- It is *probable* that as of the date of the financial statements an asset has been impaired or a liability incurred, based on information available before the issuance of the financial statements.
- The amount of the loss can be *estimated reasonably*.

If both of the above conditions are met, an accrual for the estimated amount of uncollectible receivables is made even though the specific uncollectible receivables cannot be identified at the time of the accrual. An enterprise may base its estimate of uncollectible receivables on its prior experience, the experience of other enterprises in the same industry, the debtor's ability to pay, or an appraisal of current economic conditions.

PRACTICE NOTE: Estimates of uncollectible amounts are usually made in the aggregate for all credit sales rather than being based on individual accounts. A predictable percentage of credit sales or outstanding accounts receivable are common approaches used to estimate uncollectibles for a reporting period.

Significant uncertainty may exist in the ultimate collection of receivables if an enterprise is unable to estimate reasonably the amount that is uncollectible. If a significant uncertainty exists in the ultimate collection of the receivables, the installment sales method, cost-recovery method, or some other method of revenue recognition may be used. In the event that both of the above conditions for accrual are not met and a loss contingency is at least *reasonably possible*, certain financial statement disclosures are required by ASC 450.

Illustration of Accounting for Uncollectible Accounts by the Allowance Method

AMB Co. estimates uncollectible accounts at 1% of credit sales. For the current year, credit sales totaled $1,000,000. The year-end balances in accounts receivable and the unadjusted allowance for uncollectible accounts are $250,000 and $15,000, respectively.

The entry to record uncollectible accounts ($1,000,000 × 1% = $10,000) is as follows:

Bad debt expense	10,000	
Allowance for uncollectible accounts		10,000

The balance sheet includes accounts receivable of $250,000, allowance for uncollectible accounts of $25,000 ($15,000 + $10,000), and net accounts receivable of $225,000 ($250,000 – $25,000).

When a specific uncollectible account is written off (e.g., $2,100), the reduction in accounts receivable is charged to the allowance:

Allowance for uncollectible accounts	2,100	
Accounts receivable (specific account)		2,100

This entry has no effect on the amount of net accounts receivable, because both the receivables balance and the allowance balance are reduced by the same amount.

If the estimate of uncollectibles is based on the ending balance of accounts receivable, the same procedure is followed, except that the existing balance in the allowance would require consideration. For example, if uncollectible accounts were estimated at 9% of the ending balance in accounts receivable, the bad debt expense for the year would be $7,500, computed as follows:

Required allowance ($250,000 × 9%)	$22,500
Balance before adjustment	(15,000)
Required adjustment	$ 7,500

The balance sheet includes accounts receivable of $250,000, an allowance of $22,500, and a net receivables amount of $227,500.

A variation on the previous method is to "age" accounts receivable, a procedure that recognizes an increasing percentage as uncollectible as accounts become increasingly delinquent. For example, applying this procedure to the $250,000 receivables balance above might result in the following:

	Within 30 Days	*30 Days Overdue*	*60 Days Overdue*	*Past 60 Days Overdue*
Accounts receivable balance	$120,000	$50,000	$50,000	$30,000
Uncollectible %	2%	7%	12%	25%
Uncollectible balance	$2,400	$3,500	$6,000	$7,500

The total uncollectible balance is $19,400, ($2,400 + $3,500 + $6,000 + $7,500), resulting in the recognition of bad debt expense of $4,400, assuming a previous allowance balance of $15,000 ($19,400 – $15,000 = $4,400).

Discounted Notes Receivable

Discounted notes receivable arise when the holder endorses the note (with or without recourse) to a third party and receives a sum of cash. The difference between the amount of cash received by the holder and the maturity value of the note is called the discount. If the note is discounted with recourse, the assignor remains contingently liable for the ultimate payment of the note when it becomes due. If the note is discounted without recourse, the assignor assumes no further liability.

The account "discounted notes receivable" is a contra account, which is deducted from the related receivables for financial statement purposes. The following is the procedure for computing the proceeds of a discounted note:

1. Compute the total maturity value of the note, including interest due at maturity.
2. Compute the discount amount (the maturity value of the note multiplied by the discount rate for the time involved).
3. The difference between the two amounts (1 less 2) equals the proceeds of the note.

Illustration of Discounted Notes Receivable

A $1,000 90-day 10% note is discounted at a bank at 8% when 60 days are remaining to maturity.

Maturity—$1,000 + ($1,000 × .10 × 90/360)	$1,025.00
Discount—$1,025 × .08 × 60/360	(13.67)
Proceeds of note	$1,011.33

Factoring

Factoring is a process by which a company converts its receivables into immediate cash by assigning them to a factor either with or without recourse. *With recourse* means that the assignee can return the receivable to the company and get back the funds paid if the receivable is uncollectible. *Without recourse* means that the assignee assumes the risk of losses on collections. Under factoring arrangements, the customer may or may not be notified.

Pledging

Pledging is the process whereby the company uses existing accounts receivable as collateral for a loan. The company retains title to the receivables but pledges that it will use the proceeds to pay the loan.

CASH SURRENDER VALUE OF LIFE INSURANCE

The proceeds of a life insurance policy usually provide some degree of financial security to one or more beneficiaries named in the policy. Upon death of the insured, the insurance company pays the beneficiary the face amount of the policy, less any outstanding indebtedness.

Insurable Interest

An owner of an insurance interest in life insurance need only exist at the time the policy is issued, while an insurable interest in property insurance must exist at the time of a loss. An insurable interest is a test of financial relationship. A husband may insure the life of his wife, an employer the life of an employee, a creditor the life of a debtor, and a partner the life of a copartner.

An investment in a life insurance policy is accounted for at the amount that can be realized by the owner of the policy as of the date of its statement of financial position. Generally, the amount that can be realized from a life insurance policy is the amount of its *cash surrender value*. The increase in the cash surrender value of an insurance policy for a particular period is recorded by the owner of the policy and the cash surrender value is included as an asset in its statement of financial position. The insurance expense for the same period is the difference between the total amount of premium paid and the amount of increase in the cash surrender value of the policy.

Illustration of Insurable Interest

An enterprise is the owner and sole beneficiary of a $200,000 life insurance policy on its president. The annual premium is $16,000. The policy is starting its fourth year, and the schedule of cash values indicates that at the end of the fourth year the cash value increases $25 per thousand. The enterprise pays the $16,000 premium, and the journal entry to record the transaction is as follows:

Life insurance expense—officers	11,000	
Cash surrender value—life insurance policy (200 × $25)	5,000	
Cash		16,000

The cash surrender value of a life insurance policy is classified either as a current or noncurrent asset in the policy owner's statement of financial position, depending upon the intentions of the policy owner. If the policy owner intends to surrender the policy to the insurer for its cash value within its normal operating cycle, the cash surrender value is classified as a current asset in the statement of financial position. If there is no intention of collecting the policy's cash value within the normal operating cycle of the policy owner, the cash surrender value is classified as a noncurrent asset in the statement of financial position.

LIABILITY CLASSIFICATION ISSUES

ASC 480 more clearly defines the distinction between liabilities and equity. ASC 480 also establishes standards for issuers of financial instruments with characteristics of both liabilities and equity related to the classification and measurement of those instruments.

Current Obligations Expected to Be Refinanced

ASC 210 establishes U.S. GAAP for classifying a short-term obligation that is expected to be refinanced into a long-term liability or stockholders' equity. ASC 210 applies only to those companies that issue classified balance sheets (ASC 210-10-15-3). ASC 470 provides guidance on when a short-term obligation can be excluded from current liabilities and classified as non-current.

Callable Obligations

ASC 470 establishes U.S. GAAP for the current/noncurrent classification in the debtor's balance sheet of obligations that are payable on demand or callable by the creditor.

Compensated Absences

For guidance regarding the proper accrual of the liability for employees' compensated absences, see ASC 420.

OFFSETTING ASSETS AND LIABILITIES—GENERAL

Offsetting is combining a recognized asset and a recognized liability as one net amount in a financial statement. If the amount of the recognized asset is the same as the amount of the recognized liability, then the net or combined amount of both is zero, and, as a result, no amount would appear in the financial statement. If the two amounts are not the same, the net amount of the two items that have been offset is presented in the financial statement and classified in the manner of the larger item.

PRACTICE POINTER: Offsetting results in the loss of information and may be directly affected by materiality. Two material amounts may result in an immaterial amount when they are offset. Unless the two amounts are individually immaterial, offsetting in financial statements is generally discouraged or not allowed except in specific circumstances.

ASC 210-20 discusses the general principle of offsetting in the balance sheet in the context of income tax amounts and provides the following guidance:

- Offsetting assets and liabilities in the balance sheet is acceptable only where a right of setoff exists.
- This includes offsetting cash or other assets against a tax liability or other amounts owed to governments that are not, by their terms, designated specifically for the payment of taxes.
- The only exception to this general principle occurs when it is clear that a purchase of securities that are acceptable for the payment of taxes is in substance an advance payment of taxes that are payable in the relatively near future.

The general principle of financial reporting, which holds that offsetting assets and liabilities is improper except where a right of setoff exists, usually is considered in the context of unconditional receivables from and payables to another party. ASC 210 extends this general principle to *conditional* amounts recognized for contracts under which the amounts to be received or paid or the items to be exchanged depend on future interest rates, future exchange rates, future commodity prices, or other factors.

Four criteria that must be met for the right of setoff to exist (ASC 210-20-45-1):

1. Each party owes the other party specific amounts.
2. The reporting party has the right to set off the amount payable, by contract or other agreement, with the amount receivable from the other party.
3. The reporting party intends to set off.
4. The right of setoff is enforceable at law.

OBSERVATIONS: The importance of managerial intent is apparent in the third criterion, which states that the reporting party *intends* to set off its payable and receivable. When all of these conditions are met, the reporting entity has a valid right of setoff and may present the net amount of the payable or receivable in the balance sheet.

Generally, debts may be set off if they exist between mutual debtors, each acting in its capacity as both debtor and creditor. State laws and the U.S. Bankruptcy Code may impose restrictions on or prohibitions against the right of set off in bankruptcy under certain circumstances.

Illustration of Offsetting Assets and Liabilities

The offsetting of assets and liabilities is an important issue to consider when determining financial statement presentation of current assets and current liabilities. Any time items are set off, information that would otherwise be available is lost. In addition, important financial statement relationships may be altered when assets and liabilities are set off. Consider the following example:

Current Assets	
Receivable from M Co.	$100
Other assets	400
	$500
Current Liabilities	
Payable to M Co.	$ 75
Other liabilities	175
	$250
Current ratio (500/250)	2:1

Now, consider the same situation, except the $75 payable to M Co. is offset against the $100 receivable from M Co.:

Current Assets	
Net receivable from M Co. ($100 –$75)	$25
Other assets	400
	$425
Current Liabilities	
Other liabilities	$175
Current ratio (425/175)	2.4:1

When offsetting is applied, the individual amounts of the receivable and payable are not presented, and only the net amount of $25 is present in the balance sheet. Further, the current ratio is significantly altered by the offsetting activity. This is a simple example, but it illustrates the impact of offsetting and its importance as a financial statement reporting issue.

An exception to the general offsetting rule exists for derivative contracts executed with the same counterparty under a master netting agreement. A master netting agreement is a contractual agreement entered into by two parties to multiple contracts that provides for the net settlement of all contracts covered by the agreement in the event of default under any one contract. For such derivative contracts, assets and liabilities may be offset and presented as a net amount even if the reporting entity does not meet the requirement in ASC 210 that the reporting entity has the intent to net settle. Offsetting derivative assets and liabilities under this exception is an election and the reporting entity must apply the election consistently.

Many sources of authoritative accounting standards specify accounting treatments that result in offsetting or in a balance sheet presentation that has an effect similar to offsetting. ASC 210 is not intended to modify the accounting treatment in any of those particular circumstances.

OFFSETTING OF DERIVATIVES, PURCHASE AND REPURCHASE AGREEMENTS, AND SECURITIES LENDING TRANSACTIONS

ASC 210 provides specific guidance as to when payables under repurchase agreements can be offset with receivables under reverse repurchase agreements. These criteria are (ASC 210-20-45-11):

1. The agreements are executed with the same counterparty.
2. The agreements have the same settlement date, set forth at inception.
3. The agreements are executed in accordance with a master netting arrangement.
4. The securities under the agreements exist in "book entry" form and can be transferred only by means of entries in the records of the transfer system operator or securities custodian.
5. The agreements will be settled on a securities transfer system that operates in the manner described below, and the enterprise must have associated banking arrangements in place as described below. Cash settlements for securities transferred are made under established banking arrangements that provide that the enterprise will need available cash on deposit only for any net amounts that are due at the end of the business day. It must be *probable* that the associated banking arrangements will provide sufficient *daylight overdraft or other intraday credit* at the settlement date for each of the parties.
6. The enterprise intends to use the same account at the clearing bank (or other financial institution) to settle its receivable (i.e., cash inflow from the reverse purchasing agreement) and its payable (i.e., cash outflow to settle the offsetting repurchase agreement).

If these six criteria are met, the enterprise has the option to offset. That choice must be applied consistently.

The third criterion refers to a "master netting arrangement." A master netting arrangement exists if the reporting entity has multiple contracts, whether for the same type of conditional or exchange contract or for different types of contracts, with a single counterparty that are subject to a contractual agreement that provides for the net settlement of all contracts through a single payment in a single currency in the event of default on or termination of any one contract (ASC 210).

The fourth criterion refers to "book entry" form. ASC 210 considers this a key element because it provides control over the securities. The controlling record for a "book entry" security is maintained by the transfer system operator. A securities custodian that has a security account with the transfer system operation may maintain "subsidiary" records of "book entry" securities and may transfer the securities within its subsidiary records; however, a security cannot be traded from the account of that custodian to a new custodian without a "book entry" transfer of the security over the securities transfer system. This form of accounting record facilitates repurchase and reverse repurchase agreement transactions on securities transfer systems.

For a transfer system for repurchase and reverse repurchase agreements to meet the fifth criterion, cash transfers must be initiated by the owner of record of the securities notifying its securities custodian to transfer those securities to the counterparty to the arrangement. Under associated banking arrangements, each party to a same-day settlement of both a repurchase agreement and a reverse repurchase agreement would be obligated to pay a gross amount of cash for the securities transferred from its counterparty, but the party would be able to reduce that gross obligation by notifying its securities custodian to transfer other securities to that counterparty the same day (ASC 210-20-45-14).

In the fifth criterion, the term *probable* has the same definition as in ASC 450, meaning that a transaction or event is more likely to occur than not. The phrase "daylight overdraft or other intraday credit" refers to the feature of the banking arrangement that permits transactions to be completed during the day when insufficient cash is on deposit, provided there is sufficient cash to cover the net cash requirement at the end of the day.

ASC 210 requirements apply to recognized derivatives accounted for in accordance with Topic 815, including bifurcated embedded derivatives, repurchase agreements and reverse repurchase agreements, and securities borrowing and securities lending transactions that are offset in accordance with either Topic 210 or 815. These requirements are also applicable for recognized derivative instruments accounted for in accordance with Topic 815 that are subject to an enforceable master netting arrangement or similar agreement, irrespective of whether they are offset in accordance with Topic 210 or 815 (ASC 210-250-2).

DISCLOSURE STANDARDS

Current assets and current liabilities must be identified clearly in the financial statements, and the basis for determining the stated amounts must be disclosed fully (ASC 210-10-05-5). The following are the common disclosures that are required for current assets and current liabilities in the financial statements or in notes thereto:

- Classification of inventories and the method used (e.g., FIFO, LIFO, average cost).
- Restrictions on current assets.
- Current portions of long-term obligations.
- Description of accounting policies relating to current assets and current liabilities.
- Accounts receivable and notes receivable from officers, employees, or affiliated companies, if material, must be reported separately in the financial statements. (ASC 310-10-45-13)

The above disclosure requirements apply to both of the following:

a. Recognized financial instruments and derivative instruments that are offset.

b. Recognized financial instruments and derivative instruments that are subject to an enforceable master netting arrangement or similar agreement. (ASC 210-20-50-1)

Disclosure is required of information to enable users of an entity's financial statements to evaluate the effect or potential effect of netting arrangements on its financial position. This includes the effort or potential effect of rights of offset associated with the entity's recognized assets and liabilities. (ASC 210-20-50-2) To meet this objective, the entity must disclose at the end of the reporting period the following quantitative information:

1. The gross amounts of those recognized assets and liabilities.
2. The amounts offset to determine the net amounts presented in the statement of financial position.
3. The net amounts presented in the statement of financial position.
4. The amounts subject to an enforceable master netting arrangement or similar arrangement:
   a. The amounts related to recognized financial instruments and other derivative instruments that either management makes a policy election not to offset or do not meet some of the guidance in ASC 210-20-45 or 815-10-45.
   b. The amounts related to financial collateral, including cash collateral.
5. The net amounts after deducting the amounts in (4) from the amounts in (3). (ASC 210-20-50-3)

The above information is required in a tabular form, separately for assets and liabilities unless another format is more appropriate. (ASC 210-20-50-4) A description of the rights of offset associated with an entity's recognized assets and liabilities subject to an enforceable master netting arrangement or similar agreement is required. (ASC 210-20-50-5) If the information above is presented in more than one note to the financial statements, cross-references between notes is required. (ASC 210-20-50-6)

PART II: INTERPRETIVE GUIDANCE

ASC 210-20: OFFSETTING

ASC 210-20-45-9—Assurance That a Right of Setoff Is Enforceable in a Bankruptcy under FASB Interpretation No. 39

At the November 1994 meeting of the EITF, the FASB staff clarified the meaning of the phrase "the right of setoff is enforceable at law," which is one of the conditions for offsetting in ASC 210-20-45.

Some have questioned whether the right of setoff is effective if a debtor is in bankruptcy. Two opposing views were suggested about the relationship between ASC 210-20-45-8, which states that "legal constraints should be considered to determine whether the right of setoff is enforceable," and paragraph 48 of FASB Interpretation No. 39 (FIN-39) (not in ASC), which stated that "this Interpretation does not include a separate requirement for protection in bankruptcy." Some believed that the effectiveness of the right of setoff in bankruptcy needs to be proved, while others believed that it is unnecessary to consider bankruptcy in financial statements that are prepared under the going-concern concept.

The FASB staff's views about the amount of certainty needed to determine whether the right of setoff should be upheld in bankruptcy straddles those two views. They believe that because the phrase "enforceable at law" includes the concept that the right of setoff should be recognized in bankruptcy, FIN-39 does not include a requirement for protection in bankruptcy. To assert in financial statements that the right of setoff is enforceable at law requires support that depends on cost-benefit constraints, and facts and circumstances. Amounts should be offset only if—based on all available positive and negative information about the ability to legally enforce the setoff—"there is reasonable assurance that the right of setoff would be upheld in bankruptcy."

CHAPTER 4

ASC 215—STATEMENT OF SHAREHOLDER EQUITY

ASC 215 does not provide any unique guidance but rather only provides a link to guidance on shareholders' equity in other ASC subtopics (ASC 215-10-05-1).

CHAPTER 5

ASC 220—COMPREHENSIVE INCOME

CONTENTS

GENERAL GUIDANCE

ASC 220-10: OVERALL

OVERVIEW

Reporting the results of operations, including comprehensive income, is one of the most important aspects of financial reporting. U.S. GAAP provide specific guidance concerning how comprehensive income should be presented. For discussion of the guidance concerning how net income should be determined and presented, see Chapter 2, *ASC 205—Presentation of Financial Statements*, and Chapter 6, *ASC 225—Income Statement*.

BACKGROUND

The FASB first introduced the term "comprehensive income" in its conceptual framework. *Comprehensive income* is the change in equity of a business enterprise from transactions, other events, and circumstances from nonowner sources during a period. It includes all changes in equity during a period except those resulting from investments by owners and distributions to owners. The FASB concluded that comprehensive income and its components should be reported as part of a full set of financial statements for a period. Net income or net earnings is a more narrow measurement of performance and is an element of comprehensive income. ASC 220 requires the presentation of comprehensive income and its components, including net income, in the financial statements. (See the background section of Chapter 2, *ASC 205—Presentation of Financial Statements*, for additional information on the presentation of income, including comprehensive income.)

REPORTING COMPREHENSIVE INCOME

Several accounting standards currently require that certain items that qualify as part of comprehensive income be recognized directly in the equity section of the statement of financial position without having been recognized in the determination of net income.

> ***PRACTICE POINTER:*** Reporting items directly into stockholders' equity does not mean those items are charged or credited directly to retained earnings. As explained and illustrated below, such items are carefully labeled as elements of "other comprehensive income." They are outside the determination of net income, but are clearly distinguished from transactions with owners, such as dividends, which are direct adjustments to retained earnings. Elements of other comprehensive income are not charged or credited directly to retained earnings.

ASC 220 applies to all enterprises that provide a full set of financial statements reporting financial position, results of operations, and cash flows. It does *not* apply to (ASC 220-10-15-2, 3):

- Enterprises that have no items of other comprehensive income in any period presented.
- Not-for-profit organizations that must follow ASC 958 (Not-for-Profit Entities).

ASC 220 deals with the presentation and display of comprehensive income, but it does not specify when to recognize or how to measure the components of comprehensive income. Those subjects are covered in other current standards or will be covered in future standards (ASC 220-10-05-1).

Objectives of Presenting Comprehensive Income

Comprehensive income is a measure of all changes in equity of an entity during a period that result from recognized transactions and other economic events of the period *other than transactions with owners in their capacity as owners.* (ASC 220-10-10-1) When used in conjunction with related disclosures and other information in the financial statements, comprehensive income assists investors, creditors, and others in assessing the entity's activities and future cash flows. (ASC 220-10-10-2)

The term *comprehensive income,* as used in ASC 220, includes net income plus all other components of comprehensive income. The term *other comprehensive income* denotes revenues, expenses, gains, and losses that are included in comprehensive income but not included in the determination of net income in accordance with U.S. GAAP. While the terms *comprehensive income* and *other comprehensive income* are used throughout ASC 220, those precise terms are not required to be used in an enterprise's financial statements (ASC 220-10-15-4; ASC Glossary).

PRACTICE NOTE: Before ASC 220, some elements of comprehensive income were presented in the income statement and others were reported directly in the equity section of the statement of financial position as direct adjustments to retained earnings. However, all elements were *not* required to be brought together in a single amount of comprehensive income.

Information an enterprise provides by reporting comprehensive income—along with related disclosures and other information in the financial statements—is believed to help investors, creditors, and others to assess the enterprise's activities and the timing and magnitude of its future cash flows. Given the diverse nature of the components of other comprehensive income, the FASB indicates that detailed information about each component is important. In fact, the FASB states that information about the components of comprehensive income may be more important than the total of comprehensive income, and the required disclosures are intended to support this position (ASC 220-10-10-2, 3).

If a company has no components of comprehensive income other than net income, it is not required to report comprehensive income.

PRACTICE NOTE: Apparently, the FASB believes that in a situation in which there are no elements of other comprehensive income, to designate a single amount as both net income and comprehensive income is potentially confusing to financial statement users. In this situation, the amount is comparable to net income of an enterprise that presents both net income and comprehensive income, so the FASB determined that no reporting of comprehensive income is appropriate. This limits the applicability of ASC 220 because many enterprises do not have transactions that would create a difference between net income and comprehensive income.

Display Alternatives

The requirement to present comprehensive income applies to (1) entities that provide a full set of financial statements that report financial position, results of operations, and cash flows, and (2) investment companies, defined benefit pension plans, and other employment plans that are exempt from the presentation of a statement of cash flows. (ASC 220-10-15-2)

Entities are required to report comprehensive income either in a single continuous financial statement or in two separate but consecutive financial statements. If presented in a single continuous financial statement, the following information is required:

- A total amount of net income together with the components that make up net income.
- A total amount for other comprehensive income together with the components that make up other comprehensive income.
- Total comprehensive income. (ASC 220-10-45-1A)

When an entity reports comprehensive income in two separate consecutive financial statements, the following information is required:

- Components of and the total of net income in the statement of net income.
- Components and the total for other comprehensive income as well as a total for comprehensive income in the statement of other comprehensive income presented immediately after the statement of net income. (ASC 220-10-45-1B)

PRACTICE NOTE: The earlier practice of presenting the components of other comprehensive income as a part of the statement of changes in stockholders' equity (or other similar title) is no longer acceptable. When this alternative was available, it was the most commonly used method of presenting comprehensive income. There was concern that presenting comprehensive income as part of the statement of stockholders' equity did not adequately emphasize the importance of the elements of comprehensive income (see below) other than net income. This might have contributed to the elimination of this alternative.

Components of Net Income

Components of net income are presented in various components, including income from continuing operations and discontinued operations. (ASC 220-10-45-7)

Components of Other Comprehensive Income

Following are items of other comprehensive income required by various ASC sections:

- Foreign currency translation adjustments.
- Gains and losses on foreign currency transactions that are designated as economic hedges of a net investment in a foreign entity.
- Gains and losses on intra-entity foreign currency transactions that are of a long-term-investment nature when the entities to the transactions are consolidated, combined, or accounting for by the equity method.
- Gains and losses on derivative instruments that are designated and qualify as cash flow hedges.
- Unrealized holding gains and losses on available-for-sale securities.
- Unrealized holding gains and losses that result from a debt security being transferred into the available-for-sale and held-to-maturity category from the held-to-maturity category.
- Gains or losses associated with pension and other postretirement benefits that are not recognized immediately as a component of net periodic income.
- Prior service costs or credits associated with pension or other postretirement benefits.
- Transition assets or obligations associated with pension or other postretirement benefits that are not recognized immediately as a component of net periodic benefit cost.
- Changes in fair value attributable to instrument-specific credit risk of liabilities for which the fair value option is selected. (ASC 220-10-45-10A)

Reclassification Adjustments

Items recognized in other comprehensive income that are later recognized in net income require a reclassification adjustment in order to prevent double counting of transactions in the determination of comprehensive income. An example of these transactions is accumulated gains or losses on debt investment securities that are accumulated in stockholders' equity under ASC 320 until the securities are sold. At the time of the sale, any previously recognized gains or losses that were accumulated in stockholders' equity as an element of other comprehensive income are reversed in other comprehensive income and then recognized as an element of net income. The reversal of the previous recognition in other comprehensive income offsets the recognition from the previous period and effectively moves the recognition from other comprehensive income to net income when the gain or loss is realized in a sale (ASC 220-10-45-15).

PRACTICE POINTER: Reclassification adjustments may be displayed on the face of the financial statement in which comprehensive income is reported, or they may be disclosed in notes to the financial statements. For all reclassification adjustments, an enterprise may use either a gross display on the face of the financial statement or a net display on the face of the financial statement or in notes to the financial statements.

Illustration of One- and Two-Statement Formats for Presenting Comprehensive Income

Warner, Inc. has revenues of $1,559,231, expenses of $790,000, and two components of other comprehensive income, as follows:

- Accumulated gains of $100,000 on available-for-sale investments
- Foreign currency translation adjustments (losses) of $25,000

Net income is $500,000 for 20X5, the current year. Warner's income tax rate is 35%.

[This illustration is intended to show both one- and two-statement formats for presenting other comprehensive income in the one- and two-income statement formats. It does not include all of the required disclosures that may be required for specific elements of other comprehensive income.]

Format 1—One Income-Statement Format

Warner, Inc.
Statement of Income and Comprehensive Income for Year 20X5

Revenues		$1,559,231
Expenses		790,000
Income before income tax		$769,231
Income tax		269,231
Net income		$500,000
Other comprehensive income, net of income tax:		
Unrealized holding gains [$100,000 × (1–.35)]	$65,000	
Foreign currency translation [$25,000 × (1–.35)]	(16,250)	48,750
Comprehensive income		$548,750

Format 2—Two Income-Statement Format

Warner, Inc.
Statement of Comprehensive Income for Year 20X5*

Net income		$500,000
Other comprehensive income, net of income tax:		
Unrealized holding gains	$65,000	
Foreign currency translation	(16,250)	48,750
Comprehensive income		$548,750

* The financial statement ending in "net income" is presented as a separate statement and is unchanged by ASC 220.

Reporting Accumulated Other Comprehensive Income

The amount of total accumulated other comprehensive income shall be presented as a component of equity that is separate from the amount of retained earnings and additional paid-in capital. A descriptive title, such as accumulated other comprehensive income, shall be used for that component of equity. (ASC 220-10-45-14)

Either on the face of the financial statements or in a separate note disclosure, the changes in the accumulated balances for each component of other comprehensive income included in that separate component of equity shall be presented. In addition to the presentation of changes in accumulated balances for each component of other comprehensive income, current period reclassifications out of accumulated other comprehensive income and other amounts of current-period other comprehensive income is required. (ASC 220-10-45-14A)

An entity shall separately provide information about the effects on net income of significant amounts reclassified out of each component of accumulated other comprehensive income if those amounts all are required to be reclassified to income in the same reporting period. This information may be presented either on the face of the statement where net income is presented or in as separate disclosure in notes to the financial statements. (ASC 220-10-45-17)

Equity Section of the Statement of Financial Position

At the end of the reporting period, the total of other comprehensive income is transferred to a separate stockholders' equity account, much like net income is transferred to retained earnings. This separate stockholders' equity account should have an appropriate descriptive title, such as *Accumulated Other Comprehensive Income*. Disclosure of the accumulated balances for each classification of that separate component of equity shall be made on the face of the statement of financial position, in a statement of changes in stockholders' equity, or in notes to the financial statements (ASC 220-10-45-14).

PRACTICE POINTER: The accumulated amount of other comprehensive income may not be charged or credited directly into retained earnings. Separate disclosure is required of *accumulated other comprehensive income* as a discrete component of stockholders' equity.

The classifications used in the disclosure of the balances of individual components of other comprehensive income must correspond to the classifications used elsewhere in the same financial statements (ASC 220-10-45-14).

The presentation of unrealized gains and losses on available-for-sale debt securities is aggregated for simplicity and, therefore, does not necessarily comply with all of the disclosures that may be required in all situations (e.g., available-for-sale investments with an allowance for credit losses). (ASC 220-10-55-15B)

Presentation of Income Tax Effects

An entity shall present the amount of income tax expense or benefit allocated to each component of other comprehensive income, including reclassification adjustments, in the statement in which those components are presented or disclose it in the notes to the financial statements. (ASC 220-10-45-12)

Either on the face of the financial statements or as a separate disclosure in notes, the changes in the accumulated balances of each component of other comprehensive income are required. In addition to the presentation in accumulated balances, an entity shall present separately for each component of other comprehensive income, current-period reclassifications out of other comprehensive income and other amounts of current-period other comprehensive income. Both before-tax and net-of-tax presentations are permitted, provided the entity complies with the requirements of ASC 220-10-45-12. (ASC 220-10-45-14A)

An entity shall disclose a description of the accounting policy for releasing income tax effects from accumulated other comprehensive income. Either on the face of the financial statements or as a separate note disclosure, changes in the accumulated balances for each component of equity are required. The entity shall also present separately for each component of other comprehensive income, current-period classifications out of accumulated other comprehensive income, and other amounts of current-period other comprehensive income. (ASC 220-10-50-5)

An entity shall separately provide information about the effects on net income of significant amounts reclassified out of each component of accumulated other comprehensive income if those amounts are required under other ASC topics to be reclassified to net income in their entirety in the reporting period. This disclosure may be done on the face of the statement in which net income is presented or as a separate note to the financial statements. (ASC 220-10- 45-17) If the choice is made to present information about the effects of significant amounts reclassified out of accumulated other comprehensive income on net income, on the face of the statement where net income is presented, the entity shall present parenthetically by component of other comprehensive income the effect of significant reclassification amounts on the respective line items of net income. In addition, the entity shall present parenthetically the aggregate tax effect of all significant reclassifications on the line item for income tax benefit or expense in the statements where net income is presented. (ASC 220-10-45-17A)

If information about significant amounts reclassified out of other comprehensive income is made in notes, it shall disclose the significant amounts by each component of accumulated other comprehensive income and provide a subtotal of each component of comprehensive income. (ASC 220-10-50-6)

Legislation referred to as the Tax Cuts and Jobs Act reduced the U.S. federal corporate income tax rate and made other changes in the U.S. tax law. An entity may elect to reclassify the income tax effects of the Tax Cuts and Jobs Act on items within accumulated other comprehensive income to retained earnings. If an entity does not elect to reclassify items, it shall provide certain disclosures (see ASC 220-10-50-3). If the entity elects to reclassify the income tax effects of Tax Cuts and Jobs Act, the amount of the reclassification includes the following:

- The effect of the change in the U.S. federal corporate income tax rate on the gross deferred tax amounts and related valuation allowances, if any, at the date of the enactment of the Tax Cuts and Jobs Act related to items remaining in other comprehensive income. The effect of the change in the U.S. federal corporate income tax rate on gross valuation allowances that were originally charged to income from continuing operations shall not be included.
- Other income tax effects of the Tax Cuts and Jobs Act on items remaining in accumulated other comprehensive income that entity elects to reclassify. (ASC 220-10-45-21A)

CHAPTER 6

ASC 225—INCOME STATEMENT

CONTENTS

PART I: GENERAL GUIDANCE

ASC 225-10: OVERALL

OVERVIEW

Reporting the results of operations, including determining and presenting net income and comprehensive income, is one of the most important aspects of financial reporting. U.S. GAAP provide specific guidance concerning how certain items are to be presented in the income statement and the statement of comprehensive income. (See Chapter 2, *ASC 205—Presentation of Financial Statements*, and Chapter 5, *ASC 220—Comprehensive Income*, for related material.)

BACKGROUND

For many years, there were differences of opinion in the accounting profession as to what should be included in net income. Proponents of the *all-inclusive approach* took the position that all items affecting net increases in owners' equity, except dividends and capital transactions, should be included in determining net income. Alternatively, proponents of the *current operating performance approach* advocated limiting the income statement to normal, recurring items of profit and loss that related only to ongoing, routine operations during the current period. Other items of profit and loss would be recognized directly in retained earnings. Differences between the two concepts were seen most clearly in the treatment of the following items:

- Unusual or infrequent items
- Changes in accounting principles
- Discontinued operations
- Prior period adjustments
- Certain items that are required by U.S. GAAP to be recognized directly in stockholders' equity rather than in net income

Current U.S. GAAP require the presentation of income in a manner that is between the extremes of all-inclusive and current operating performance. Net income generally includes all items of revenue, expense, gain, and loss during a reporting period, except prior period adjustments, dividends, and capital transactions, and a limited number of items that are required to be recognized directly in equity. (See Chapter 2, *ASC 205—Presentation of Financial Statements*, and Chapter 5, *ASC 220—Comprehensive Income*, for related material and for a complete list of items recognized directly in equity.)

UNUSUAL AND/OR INFREQUENTLY OCCURRING ITEMS

PRACTICE NOTE: For many years, unusual and infrequent items that met the criteria of extraordinary items were considered to be an integral part of income reporting. Extraordinary items were eliminated by ASU 2015-01, *Income Statement—Extraordinary and Unusual Items (Subtopic 225-20): Simplifying Income Statement Presentation by Eliminating the Concept of Extraordinary Items.* While there may be several reasons for this change, one oft-stated rationale was the difficulty of consistently applying the criteria of items that were both unusual and infrequent (i.e., extraordinary items) versus those that were either infrequent or unusual, but not both. In addition to the elimination of extraordinary items, related headings, such as "Income before extraordinary items" are no longer appropriate. As indicated below, items that are unusual in nature or that occur infrequently continue to require disclosure.

A material transaction that is unusual in nature or occurs infrequently or both is reported as a separate component of income from continuing operations. The nature of the item, as well as the financial effects of the item, is presented as a separate component in the income statement or disclosed in notes to the financial statements. Gains and losses of a similar nature that are not individually material shall be aggregated. Unusual and/or infrequently occurring items are not presented on the face of the income statement net of income taxes. Also, the earnings per share effects of these events and transactions shall not be presented on the face of the income statement.

PART II: INTERPRETIVE GUIDANCE

ASC 225-30: BUSINESS INTERRUPTION INSURANCE

ASC 225-30-05-2, 45-1, 50-1; ASC 450-30-60-2 through 60-3 Income Statement Display of Business Interruption Insurance Recoveries

BACKGROUND

Business interruption (BI) insurance is discussed in: ASC 605-40-05-1 through 05-2; 25-1 through 25-4; 30-1; 45-1; 55-66; 60-1, ASC 450-10-60-4 and in ASC 410-30-05-1 through 05-3, 05-5 through 05-25; 10-1; 15-1 through 15-3; 25-1 through 25-15, 25-17, 25-20 through 25-23; 30-1 through 30-19; 35-1 through 35-5, 35-7 through 35-12, 35-12A; 45-1 through 45-5; 50-1 through 50-17; 55-1 through 55-6, 55-14 through 55-17, 55-27 through 55-51; 60-3, 60-8.

ASC 605-40-05-1 through 05-2; 25-1 through 25-4; 30-1; 45-1; 55-66; and 60-1, and ASC 450-10-60-4 provide broad guidance on the recognition, measurement, and classification of insurance recoveries related to property and equipment. Under the Interpretation, gains or losses on involuntary conversions of property and equipment into insurance proceeds should be measured as the difference between the carrying amount of the property or equipment and the insurance proceeds received. Such recoveries are reported in the financial statements on the same line as a reduction of the related loss.

The guidance in ASC 410-30-05-1 through 05-3, 05-5 through 05-25; 10-1; 15-1 through 15-3; 25-1 through 25-15, 25-17, 25-20 through 25-23; 30-1 through 30-19; 35-1 through 35-5, 35-7 through 35-12, 35-12A; 45-1 through 45-5; 50-1 through 50-17; 55-1 through 55-6, 55-14 through 55-17, 55-27 through 55-51; and 60-3, 60-8, which applies to insurance recoveries for environmental remediation costs, requires that expenses related to environmental remediation be reported in *operating* income in financial statements that classify items as operating or nonoperating. Credits from recoveries of such expenses should be reported on the same income statement line as a reduction of the expense.

BI insurance differs from the types of insurance discussed above, because it protects an insured entity's future earnings or profits if its operations are suspended because of a loss of use of equipment and property as a result of a covered event. Such insurance usually reimburses the insured entity for certain costs and losses incurred during a reasonable period in which the entity rebuilds, repairs, or replaces the damaged property. Covered losses include costs related to gross margin not earned because normal operations have been halted, a portion of fixed charges and expenses related to a loss of gross margin, and other expenses such as the rental of temporary facilities and equipment.

ACCOUNTING ISSUE

How should recoveries of business interruption insurance be displayed in the income statement?

ACCOUNTING GUIDANCE

Entities are permitted to decide how to present recoveries from business interruption insurance in their financial statements as long as the presentation is acceptable under current GAAP. In addition, the following disclosures should be made in the period in which such recoveries are reported:

- The nature of the event that caused losses due to business interruption.
- The total amount of recoveries from business interruption insurance reported during the period and the income statement line items in which recoveries are reported.

CHAPTER 7

ASC 230—STATEMENT OF CASH FLOWS

CONTENTS

PART I: GENERAL GUIDANCE

ASC 230-10: OVERALL

OVERVIEW

The statement of cash flows is an important part of a complete set of financial statements prepared in conformity with U.S. GAAP for all business enterprises. Within that statement, cash receipts and payments are classified as operating, investing, and financing activities, which are presented in a manner that reconciles the change in cash from the beginning to the end of the period.

BACKGROUND

Information in a statement of cash flows, when used in conjunction with information available in other financial statements and related disclosures, assists investors, creditors, and other users in assessing the following:

- The enterprise's ability to generate positive future net cash flows
- The enterprise's ability to meet its obligations, pay dividends, and satisfy its needs for external financing
- Reasons for differences between net income and associated cash receipts and payments
- The effects on an enterprise's financial position of both its cash and noncash investing and financing transactions.

ASC 230 (Statement of Cash Flows) requires that a *statement of cash flows* be included as part of a full set of general financial statements that are externally issued by any business enterprise. All business enterprises are required to comply with the provision of ASC 230.

There are certain exemptions from the general requirements in ASC 230. ASC 230 does not apply to: (*a*) certain employee benefit plans and (*b*) highly liquid investment companies that meet certain conditions (ASC 230-10-15-4). Cash receipts and cash payments resulting from transactions in certain securities, other assets, and loans acquired specifically for resale are classified as *operating cash flows* in a statement of cash flows (ASC 230-10-45-20, 21). Banks, savings institutions, and credit unions can report net cash flows from certain transactions instead of gross cash flows (ASC 230-10-45-8). Finally, an enterprise that meets certain conditions can classify the cash flow of a hedging transaction and the cash flow of its related hedged item in the same category of cash flow (operating activity, investing activity, or financing activity).

STATEMENT OF CASH FLOWS—GENERAL

The statement of cash flows specifies the amount of net cash provided or used by an enterprise during a period from (*a*) operating activities, (*b*) investing activities, and (*c*) financing activities. The statement of cash flows indicates the net effect of these cash flows on the enterprise's cash and cash equivalents, and amounts generally described as restricted cash or restricted cash equivalents. The reconciliation of beginning and ending cash and cash equivalents is an important part of the required information in the statement of cash flows. This reconciliation directly ties the statement of cash flows to the amount of cash in comparative statements of financial position or balance sheets. ASC 230 also requires that the statement of cash flows contain separate disclosures of all investing and financing activities of an enterprise that affect its financial position, but do not directly affect its cash flows during the period (ASC 230-10-45-2). Descriptive terms such as *cash* or *cash and cash equivalents* are required in the statement of cash flows, whereas ambiguous terms such as *funds* are inappropriate (ASC 230-10-45-4). As a general rule, offsetting of similar transactions is not permitted in the statement of cash flows (e.g., addition of new debt and repayment of previous debt, the purchase and resale of plant assets). When cash, cash equivalent, and amounts generally described as restricted cash or restricted cash equivalent are presented in more than one line item within the statement of financial position, an entity shall provide the disclosures required in ASC 230-10-50-8.

Cash Equivalents

Cash equivalents are short-term, highly liquid investments that are (*a*) readily convertible to known amounts of cash and (*b*) so near their maturities that they present insignificant risk of changes in value because of changes in interest rates. As a general rule, only investments with *original maturities* of three months or less qualify as cash equivalents (ASC Glossary). Examples of items commonly considered to be cash equivalents include Treasury bills, commercial paper, money market funds, and federal funds that are sold (ASC Glossary).

PRACTICE POINTER: Investments such as those identified above are considered the equivalent of, or essentially the same as, cash itself. An enterprise must disclose its policy for determining which items are treated as cash equivalents. Any change in that policy is accounted for as a change in accounting principle by restating financial statements of earlier years that are presented for comparative purposes (ASC 230-10-50-1). ASC 230 does not specify the accounting treatment of amounts in bank accounts that are unavailable for immediate withdrawal, such as compensating balances in the bank account of a borrower. Logically, these amounts should be treated as cash, with disclosure of any material restrictions on withdrawal.

Gross and Net Cash Flows

As a general rule, ASC 230 requires an enterprise to report gross amounts of its cash receipts and cash payments in the statement of cash flows. For example, outlays for acquisitions of property, plant, and equipment are reported separately from proceeds from the sale of these assets rather than being netted. Similarly, proceeds from borrowing are reported separately from repayments. The gross amounts of cash receipts and cash payments are presumed to be more relevant than net amounts. It may be sufficient in some circumstances, however, to report the net amounts of certain assets and liabilities instead of their gross amounts (ASC 230-10-45-7).

The net changes during a period may be reported for those assets and liabilities in which turnover is quick, amounts are large, and maturities are short (ASC 230-10-45-8). These include cash receipts and cash payments pertaining to (*a*) investments (other than cash equivalents), (*b*) loans receivable, and (*c*) debt, provided the original maturity of the asset or liability is three months or less (ASC 230-10-45-9).

ASC 230 permits banks, savings institutions, and credit unions to report net amounts for (*a*) deposits placed with other financial institutions and withdrawals of deposits, (*b*) time deposits accepted and repayments of deposits, and (*c*) loans made to customers and principal collections of loans.

Classification of Cash Receipts and Cash Payments

Under ASC 230, an enterprise is required to classify its cash receipts and cash payments into operating activities, investing activities, or financing activities (ASC 230-10-45-10).

Operating Activities include all transactions and other events that are not defined as investing or financing activities. Operating activities generally involve producing and delivering goods and providing services (i.e., transactions that enter into the determination of net income) (ASC Glossary).

Cash inflows:

- Cash receipts from sales of goods or services, including receipts from collection or sale of accounts receivable and short-term and long-term notes arising from such sales
- Cash receipts from returns on loans, other debt instruments of other entities, and equity securities
- All other cash receipts not classified as investing or financing activities, such as amounts received to settle lawsuits and refunds from suppliers.

Cash outflows:

- Cash payments for materials for manufacture or goods for resale, including principal payments on accounts payable and short-term and long-term notes to suppliers
- Cash payments to other suppliers and employers for other goods and services
- Cash payments to governments for taxes, duties, fines, or penalties
- Cash payments to lenders and others for interest, including the portion of the payments made to settle zero-coupon debt instruments that is attributable to accreted interest related to the debt discount or the portion of the payments made to settle other debt instruments with coupon interest rates that are insignificant in relation to the effective interest rate of the borrowing that is attributable to accreted interest related to the debt discount. (For all other debt instruments, an issuer shall not bifurcate cash payments to lenders and other creditors at settlement for amounts attributable to accreted interest related to the debt discount, nor classify such amounts as cash outflows from operating activities.)
- Cash payments made to settle an asset retirement obligation
- Cash payments, or the portion of the payments, not made soon after the acquisition date of a business combination by an acquirer to settle a contingent consideration liability that exceed the amount of the contingent consideration liability recognized at the acquisition date, including measurement-period adjustments, less any amounts paid soon after the acquisition date to settle the contingent consideration liability
- All other cash payments not classified as investing or financing activities, such as payments to settle lawsuits, cash contributions to charities, and cash refunds to customers. (ASC 230-10-45-17)

In reporting cash flows from operating activities, entities are encouraged to report major classes of gross cash receipts and gross cash payments, separately reporting the following classes of operating cash receipts and payments:

- Cash collected from customers, including lessees, licenses, and the like
- Interest and dividends received
- Other operating cash receipts, if any
- Cash paid to employees and other suppliers of goods or services

- Interest paid, including the portion of payments made to settle zero-coupon debt instruments that is attributable to accreted interest related to the debt discount or the portion of the payments made to settle other debt instruments with coupon interest rates that are insignificant in relation to the effective interest rate of the borrowing that is attributable to accreted interest related to the debt discount
- Income taxes paid
- Other operating cash payments, if any. (ASC 230-10-45-25)

Investing Activities include making and collecting loans and acquiring and disposing of debt or equity instruments and property, plant, and equipment and other productive assets; that is, assets held for or used in the production of goods or services by the enterprise (other than materials that are part of the enterprise's inventory) (ASC Glossary). Acquiring and disposing of certain loans or other debt or equity instruments that are acquired specifically for resale are excluded from investing activities (ASC Glossary). Cash flows from purchases, sales, and maturities of available-for-sale debt securities are classified as cash flows from investing activities and reported gross in the statement of cash flows (ASC 230-10-45-11).

Cash inflows:

- Receipts from collections or sales of loans and of others' debt instruments and collections on a transferor's beneficial interests in a securitization of the transferor's trade receivables
- Receipts from sales of equity instruments of other enterprises and from returns of investments in those instruments
- Receipts from sales of property, plant, and equipment and other productive assets
- Receipts from sales of loans that were not specifically acquired for resale. (ASC 230-10-45-12)

Cash outflows:

- Payments for loans made by the enterprise and to acquire debt instruments of other entities
- Payments to acquire equity instruments in other enterprises
- Payments at the time of purchase or soon thereafter to acquire property, plant, and equipment and other productive assets, including interest capitalized as part of the cost of those assets
- Payments made soon after the acquisition date of a business combination by an acquirer to settle a contingent consideration liability. (ASC 230-10-45-13)

PRACTICE POINTER: Receipts from sales of equity instruments of other entities, are generally classified as cash inflows from investing activities. Certain donated equity instruments received by NFP organizations are an exception. Cash receipts resulting from the sale of donated financial assets by NFPs that upon receipt were directed without any NFP-imposed limitations for sale and were converted nearly immediately into cash are classified as operating cash flows. If, however, the donor restricted the use of the contributed resource to a long-term purpose, those cash receipts meeting stated criteria are classified as financing activities.

Financing Activities include obtaining resources from owners and providing them with a return on, and return of, their investment; borrowing money and repaying amounts borrowed, or otherwise settling the obligation; and obtaining and paying for other resources obtained from creditors on long-term credit (ASC Glossary).

Cash inflows:

- Proceeds from issuing equity instruments
- Proceeds from issuing bonds, mortgages, notes, and other short-term or long-term borrowing
- Receipts from contributions and investment income that by donor stipulation are restricted for the purposes of acquiring, constructing, or improving property, plant and equipment, or other long-lived assets or establishing or increasing a permanent endowment or term endowment
- Proceeds received from derivative instruments that include financing elements at inception. (ASC 230-10-45-14)

Cash outflows:

- Payments of dividends or other distributions to owners, including outlays to reacquire the enterprise's equity instruments. (Cash paid to a tax authority by a grantor when withholding shares from a grantee's award for tax-withholding purposes is considered an outlay to acquire the entity's equity investments.)

- Repayments of amounts borrowed, including the portion of the repayments made to settle zero-coupon debt instruments that is attributable to the principal or the portion of the repayments made to settle other debt instruments with coupon interest rates that are insignificant in relation to the effective interest rate of the borrowing that is attributable to the principal
- Other principal payments to creditors that have extended long-term credit
- Distributions to counterparties or derivative instruments that include financing elements at inception, other than a financing element inherently included in an at-the-market derivative instruments with no prepayments
- Payments of debt issue costs
- Payments, or the portion of payments, not made soon after the acquisition date of a business combination by an acquirer to settle a contingent consideration liability up to the amount of the contingent consideration liability recognized at the acquisition date, including measurement-period adjustments, less any amounts paid soon after the acquisition date to settle the contingent consideration liability. (ASC 230-10-45-15)

PRACTICE POINTER: Cash received from sales of inventory to customers is presented as cash from operating activities, whether received at the time of sale or collected at some other time, on open account or on a note (short-term, long-term, or installment). Similarly, cash paid to suppliers for inventory is presented as cash used for operating activities, whether paid at the time of purchase or paid at some other time, on open account or on a note (short-term, long-term, or installment).

Selected Classification Issues

Banks, brokers, and dealers in securities and other entities may carry securities and other assets in a trading account. Characteristics of trading account activity are described in ASC Topics 255 and 940. (ASC 230-10-45-18)

Cash receipts and cash payments resulting from purchases and sales of securities classified as trading debt securities accounted for in accordance with ASC 320 and equity securities accounted for in accordance with ASC 321 shall be classified based on the nature and purpose for which the securities were acquired. (ASC 230-10-45-19)

Cash receipts and cash payments resulting from purchases and sales of other securities and other assets are classified as operating cash flows if those assets are acquired specifically for resale and are carried at fair value in a trading account. (ASC 230-10-45-20)

Some loans are similar to debt securities in a trading account in that they are originated or purchased specifically for resale and are held for short periods of time. Cash flows from acquisitions and sales of loans shall be classified as operating cash flows if those loans are acquired specifically for resale and are carried at fair value or at the lower of amortized cost basis or fair value. For example, mortgage loans held for sale are required to be reported at the lower of amortized cost basis or fair value in accordance with ASC 948. (ASC 230-10-45-21)

Cash receipts resulting from the settlement of insurance claims, excluding proceeds received from corporate-owned life insurance policies and bank-owned life insurance policies, are classified on the basis of the related insurance coverage. For insurance, proceeds received in a lump-sum settlement, the entity shall determine the classification on the basis of the nature of each loss included in the settlement. (ASC 230-10-45-21B) Cash receipts resulting from the settlement of corporate-owned life insurance policies, including bank-owned life insurance policies, are classified as investing activities. Cash payments for premiums on corporate-owned life insurance policies, including bank-owned life insurance policies, may be classified as investing activities, operating activities or a combination of investing and operating activities. (ASC 320-10-45-21C)

A cash receipt or a cash payment that can qualify for more than one cash flow activity is appropriately classified as the activity that is likely to be the predominant source of cash flows for that item. For example, the acquisition and sale of equipment used by an enterprise or rented to others generally are investing activities. If the intention of an enterprise is to use or rent the equipment for a short period of time and then sell it, however, the cash receipts and cash payments associated with the acquisition or production of the equipment and the subsequent sale are considered cash flows from operating activities. (ASC 230-10-45-22)

PRACTICE POINTER: For guidance on classifying and reporting cash flows from available-for-sale, held-to-maturity, and trading debt securities, see ASC 320. For guidance on classifying and reporting cash flows from equity securities, see Topic 321.

PRACTICE POINTER: Care should be taken in classifying certain cash flows. The FASB has indicated how to classify certain items that might logically be included in more than one of the major categories of the statement of cash flows. Following are examples of these items:

Interest paid: Presented as an operating activity, despite its close association with financing activities and the fact that dividends paid are presented as a financing activity.

Interest and dividends received: Presented as operating activities, despite their close association with other activities presented as investing activities.

Gains and losses on asset and liability transactions (e.g., sale of plant assets, extinguishment of debt): Presented as investing and financing activities, although the gain/loss was included in net income.

Income taxes: Presented entirely as an operating activity, despite the fact that some gains and losses that may affect income taxes are presented as investing and financing activities.

As a general rule, each cash receipt or cash payment is required to be classified according to its source (operating, investing, or financing) without regard to whether it arose as a hedge of another item. However, ASC 230 indicates that the cash flows from derivative instruments that are accounted for as fair-value or cash-flow hedges under ASC 815 may be classified in the same category as the cash flow of the related hedged item, provided that the enterprise (*a*) discloses this accounting policy and (*b*) reports the gain or loss on the hedging instrument in the same accounting period as the offsetting gain or loss on the hedged item.

Foreign Currency Cash Flows

An enterprise with foreign currency translations or foreign operations shall report, in its statement of cash flows, the reporting currency equivalent of foreign currency cash flows using the exchange rates in effect at the time of the cash flows. An appropriately weighted average exchange rate for the period may be used in lieu of the actual currency rates at the dates of the cash flows, provided that the results are substantially the same. The effect of exchange rate changes on cash balances held in foreign currencies is reported in the statement of cash flows as a separate part of the reconciliation of the change in cash and cash equivalents during the period. (ASC 830-230-45-1)

Exemption for Certain Investment Companies

Investment-type entities that meet certain conditions are not required to include a statement of cash flows as part of their complete financial presentation in accordance with U.S. GAAP. The entities entitled to this exemption are as follows (ASC 230-10-15-4):

- Investment companies that are subject to the registration and regulatory requirements of the Investment Company Act of 1940 (1940 Act)
- Investment enterprises that have essentially the same characteristics as investment companies subject to the 1940 Act
- Common trust funds, variable annuity accounts, or similar funds maintained by a bank, insurance company, or other enterprise in its capacity as a trustee, administrator, or guardian for the collective investment and reinvestment of moneys.

The investment-type entities specified above are not required to include a statement of cash flows in their financial presentations, provided that they meet all of the following conditions (ASC 230-10-15-4):

- Substantially all investments owned by the enterprise were highly liquid during the period covered by the financial statements (highly liquid investments include, but are not limited to, marketable securities and other assets that can be sold through existing markets).
- Substantially all of the investments owned by the enterprise are carried at market value including securities for which market value is calculated by the use of matrix pricing techniques (described in the AICPA Industry Audit

and Accounting Guide titled Audits of Investment Companies). Securities that do not meet this condition are those for which (*a*) market value is not readily ascertainable and (*b*) fair value must be determined in good faith by the board of directors of the enterprise.

- Based on average debt outstanding during the period, the enterprise had little or no debt in relation to average total assets. For these purposes, average debt outstanding generally may exclude obligations from (*a*) redemption of shares by the enterprise, (*b*) unsettled purchases of securities or similar assets, or (*c*) written covered options.
- The enterprise provides a statement of changes in net assets.

CONTENT AND FORM OF STATEMENT OF CASH FLOWS

A statement of cash flows shall disclose separately the amount of net cash provided or used during a period from an enterprise's (*a*) operating activities, (*b*) investing activities, and (*c*) financing activities. The effect of the total amount of net cash provided or used during a period from all sources (operating, investing, and financing) on an enterprise's cash and cash equivalents shall be clearly disclosed in a manner that reconciles beginning and ending cash and cash equivalents (ASC 230-10-45-24).

In reporting cash flows from *operating activities* in the statement of cash flows, ASC 230 encourages but does not require an enterprise to use the *direct method* (ASC 230-10-45-25). Enterprises that do not use the direct method to report their cash flows from operating activities may use the *indirect method* (also referred to as the reconciliation method). The amount of cash flows from operating activities is the same whether calculated and presented by the direct or indirect method. There is no difference in reporting the cash flows from investing and financing activities, regardless of whether the direct or indirect method is used to report cash flows from operations.

Direct Method

A presentation of a statement of cash flows by the direct method reflects the gross amounts of the principal components of cash receipts and cash payments from operating activities, such as cash received from customers and cash paid to suppliers and employees. Using the direct method, the amount of net cash provided by or used in operating activities during the period is equal to the difference between the total amount of gross cash receipts and the total amount of gross cash payments arising from operating activities.

ASC 230 requires enterprises using the direct method of reporting the amount of net cash flow provided from or used by operating activities to present separately, at a minimum, in their statement of cash flows, the following principal components of operating cash receipts and operating cash payments (ASC 230-10-45-25):

- Cash collected from customers, including lessees, licensees, and other similar receipts
- Interest and dividends received
- Any other operating cash receipts
- Cash paid to employees and other suppliers of goods or services including suppliers of insurance, advertising, and other similar cash payments
- Any other operating cash payments, including interest paid, income taxes paid, and other similar cash payments.

PRACTICE POINTER: An enterprise may use an alternate method of computation to arrive at the amounts shown in a statement of cash flows. For example, when preparing a direct method statement of cash flows, an enterprise may make an alternate computation to determine the amount of cash received from customers; i.e., it may start with total sales for the period and adjust that figure for the difference between beginning and ending accounts receivable.

The provisions of ASC 230 encourage, but do not require, an enterprise to include in its statement of cash flows other meaningful details pertaining to its cash receipts and cash payments from operating activities. For example, a retailer or manufacturer might decide to subdivide cash paid to employees and suppliers into cash payments for costs of inventory and cash payments for selling, general, and administrative expenses (ASC 230-10-45-25).

PRACTICE NOTE: While both the direct and indirect methods of presenting operating cash flows are acceptable, ASC 230 encourages the direct method because it reflects the gross amounts of the principal components of cash receipts and cash payments from operating activities. The indirect method does not do this. Also, the direct method is more consistent with the manner of presenting cash flows from financing and investing activities in which gross positive and net cash flows are presented in each category. Despite the FASB's stated preference for the direct method, the predominant method used in practice is the indirect method. This is likely because the direct method requires disclosure of the reconciliation of net income to cash from operations, and this is essentially the information provided in the body of the statement prepared by the indirect method.

Indirect Method

Enterprises that choose not to provide information about major classes of operating cash receipts and cash payments by the direct method, as encouraged by ASC 230. Alternatively, they can determine and report the same amount of net cash flow from operating activities by reconciling net income to net cash flow from operating activities (the indirect or reconciliation method). The adjustments necessary to reconcile net income to net cash flow are made to net income to remove (*a*) the effects of all deferrals of past operating cash receipts and cash payments, such as changes during the period in inventory and deferred income, (*b*) the effects of all accruals of expected future operating cash receipts and cash payments, such as changes during the period in receivables and payables, and (*c*) the effects of all items classified as investing or financing cash flows, such as gains or losses on sales of property, plant, and equipment and discontinued operations (investing activities), and gains or losses on extinguishment of debt (financing activities) (ASC 230-10-45-28).

Reconciliation of Net Income to Net Cash Flow

Regardless of whether an enterprise uses the direct or indirect method of reporting net cash flow from *operating* activities, a reconciliation of net income to net cash flow must be provided in conjunction with the statement of cash flows. The reconciliation of net income to net cash flow from operating activities provides information about the net effects of operating transactions and other events that affect net income and operating cash flows in different periods. This reconciliation separately reflects all major classes of reconciling items. For example, major classes of deferrals of past operating cash receipts and payments and accruals of expected future operating cash receipts and payments, including at a minimum, changes during the period in receivables and payables pertaining to *operating* activities, are reported separately. Enterprises are encouraged to further break down those categories they consider meaningful. For example, changes in trade receivables for an enterprise's sale of goods or services might be reported separately from changes in other operating receivables (ASC 230-10-45-29).

If an enterprise uses the direct method, the reconciliation referred to above is provided in a separate schedule accompanying the statement of cash flows (ASC 230-10-45-30).

If an enterprise uses the indirect method, the reconciliation referred to above typically becomes the operating activities section of the statement of cash flows and no additional disclosure is required. If the reconciliation is included within and as part of the statement of cash flows, all adjustments to net income to determine net cash flow from operating activities must be clearly identified as reconciling items (ASC 230-10-45-31, 32).

PRACTICE NOTE: The fact that the reconciliation of net income to net cash flows from operating activities is required as a supplemental disclosure if a company uses the direct method may be one reason why the majority of companies use the indirect method. The cost of developing the additional information required to use the direct method may also explain the popularity of the indirect method.

Regardless of whether the direct or the indirect method is used to report net cash flow from operating activities, ASC 230 requires the separate disclosure of the amounts of interest paid (net of amounts capitalized) and income taxes paid during the period (ASC 230-10-45-29). If the indirect method is used, the amount of interest paid (net of amounts capitalized), including the portion of the payments made to settle zero-coupon debt instruments that is attributable to accreted interest related to the debt discount or the portion of the payments made to settle other debt instruments with coupon interest rates that are insignificant in relation to the effective interest rate of the borrowing that is attributable to accreted interest related to the debt discount, is required to be disclosed (ASC 230-10-50-2). These disclosures usually are in the operating activities section of the statement if the direct method is used and in a note if the indirect method is used.

Noncash Investing and Financing Activities

Disclosures in conjunction with the statement of cash flows must contain information about all investing and financing activities of an enterprise during a period that affect recognized assets or liabilities but that do not result in cash receipts or cash payments. These disclosures may be either narrative or summarized in a schedule, and they shall clearly relate the cash and noncash aspects of transactions involving similar items. Examples of noncash investing and financing transactions include:

- Converting debt to equity
- Acquiring assets by assuming directly related liabilities (e.g., capital leases, purchasing a building by incurring a mortgage to the seller)
- Obtaining a right-to-use asset in exchange for a lease liability
- Obtaining a beneficial interest as consideration for transferring financial assets (excluding cash), including the transferor's trade receivables, in a securitization transaction
- Obtaining a building or investment asset by receiving a gift
- Exchanging noncash assets or liabilities for other noncash assets or liabilities. (ASC 230-10-50-4)

Only the cash portion of a part-cash, part-noncash transaction is reported in the body of the statement of cash flows (ASC 230-10-50-4).

PRACTICE NOTE: The justification for requiring disclosure of noncash investing and financing activities is that they (1) affect the entity's financial position, and (2) they typically involve the equivalent of two cash transactions combined into a single noncash transaction. For example, the conversion of debt into equity is the equivalent of paying off debt (a negative cash flow) and the sale of additional equity shares (a positive cash flow). Similarly, the exchange of one noncash asset for another noncash asset is equivalent to two cash transactions in which one asset is sold (positive cash flow) and the other purchased (negative cash flow).

Cash Flow per Share

An enterprise is prohibited from reporting any amount representing cash flow per share in its financial statements (ASC 230-10-45-3).

FINANCIAL INSTITUTIONS

Different requirements apply for the statement of cash flows for financial institutions. Cash receipts and payments associated with securities that are carried in *trading accounts* by banks, brokers, and dealers in securities are classified as cash flows from operating activities. In addition, cash inflows and outflows associated with securities classified as trading securities (see ASC 320 (Investments—Debt Securities) and ASC 321 (Investments—Equity Securities)) must be shown as operating cash flows. On the other hand, if securities are acquired for investment purposes, the related cash receipts and cash payments are classified as cash flows from investing activities. Loans are given similar treatment. The cash receipts and cash payments associated with mortgage loans that are held for resale by a bank or mortgage broker are classified as cash flows from operating activities. If the mortgage loans are held for investment purposes, however, the related cash receipts and cash payments are classified as cash flows from investing activities (ASC 230-10-45-12, 21).

Instead of reporting gross amounts of cash flows in their statements of cash flows, as would be required by ASC 230, banks, savings institutions, and credit unions are permitted to report *net* amounts of cash flows that result from (*a*) deposits and deposit withdrawals with other financial institutions, (*b*) time deposits accepted and repayments of deposits, and (*c*) loans to customers and principal collections of loans. Financial institutions have the following choices in reporting cash flows in its statement of cash flows:

- To report the gross amount of all cash receipts and disbursements
- To report the net cash flows in the limited situations allowed by ASC 230, such as loans with maturities of three months or less, and to report gross amounts for all other transactions
- If the enterprise is a bank, savings institution, or credit union, to report net cash flows in the limited situations allowed by U.S. GAAP, such as time deposits, and to report gross amounts for all other transactions
- If the enterprise is a bank, savings institution, or credit union, to report net cash flows in the situations allowed by ASC 230, and to report gross amounts for all other transactions.

If a consolidated enterprise includes a bank, savings institution, or credit union that uses net cash reporting as allowed by ASC 230, the statement of cash flows of the consolidated enterprise must report separately (*a*) the net cash flows of the financial institution and (*b*) the gross cash receipts and cash payments of other members of the consolidated enterprise, including subsidiaries of a financial institution that are not themselves financial institutions.

Illustration of Procedures for Preparing a Statement of Cash Flows

Following are Holcomb Company's balance sheets for the year ending December 31, 20X8 and the quarter ending March 31, 20X9, as well as the income statement for the three months ending March 31, 20X9.

Balance Sheet

	December 31, 20X8	*March 31, 20X9*
Cash	$ 25,300	$ 87,400
Marketable securities	16,500	7,300
Accounts receivable, net	24,320	49,320
Inventory	31,090	48,590
Total current assets	97,210	192,610
Land	40,000	18,700
Building	250,000	250,000
Equipment	—	81,500
Accumulated depreciation	(15,000)	(16,250)
Investment in 30% owned company	61,220	67,100
Other assets	15,100	15,100
Total	$448,530	$608,760
Accounts payable	$ 21,220	$ 17,330
Dividend payable	—	8,000
Income taxes payable	—	34,616
Total current liabilities	21,220	59,946
Other liabilities	186,000	186,000
Bonds payable	50,000	115,000
Discount on bonds payable	(2,300)	(2,150)
Deferred income taxes	510	846
Preferred stock ($2 par)	30,000	—
Common stock ($1 par)	80,000	110,000
Dividends declared	—	(8,000)
Retained earnings	83,100	147,118
Total	$448,530	$608,760

Income Statement

	For the Three Months Ended March 31, 20X9
Sales	$242,807
Gain on sale of marketable investments	2,400
Equity in earnings of 30% owned company	5,880
Gain on condemnation of land	10,700
Total revenues and gains	261,787
Cost of sales	138,407
General and administrative expenses	22,010
Depreciation	1,250
Interest expense	1,150
Income taxes	34,952
	197,769
Net income	$ 64,018

The following information has been identified:

(1) In January 20X9, the company sold marketable securities for cash of $11,600. These securities had been held for several months.

(2) The preferred stock is convertible into common stock at a rate of one share of preferred for three shares of common.

(3) In February 20X9, land was condemned. An award of $32,000 in cash was received in March.

(4) During February 20X9, the company purchased equipment for cash.

(5) During March 20X9, bonds were issued by the company at par for cash.

(6) The investment in the 30% owned company included $3,220 attributable to goodwill at December 31, 20X8.

Worksheet for Preparing the Statement of Cash Flows for the Quarter Ended March 31, 20X9

Real Accounts	*Balances 12/31/X8*	*Changes Debit*	*Changes Credit*	*Balances 3/31/X9*
Debits:				
Cash	$ 25,300	(n) $62,100		$87,400
Marketable Securities	16,500		(f) 9,200	7,300
Accounts Receivable, Net	24,320	(a) 25,000		49,320
Inventory	31,090	(b) 17,500		48,590
Land	40,000		(g) 21,300	18,700
Building	250,000			250,000

Real Accounts	Balances 12/31/X8	Changes Debit	Changes Credit	Balances 3/31/X9
Equipment	0	(h) 81,500		81,500
Investment in 30% Owned Company	61,220	(j) 5,880		67,100
Other Assets	15,100			15,100
Discount on Bonds Payable	2,300		(e) 150	2,150
Dividends Declared	0	(m) 8,000		8,000
	465,830			635,160
Credits:				
Accumulated Depreciation	15,000		(d) 1,250	16,250
Accounts Payable	21,220	(b) 3,890		17,330
Dividend Payable	0		(m) 8,000	8,000
Income Taxes Payable	0		(i) 34,616	34,616
Other Liabilities	186,000			186,000
Bonds Payable	50,000		(k) 65,000	115,000
Deferred Income Taxes	510		(i) 336	846
Preferred Stock	30,000	(l) 30,000		0
Common Stock	80,000		(l) 30,000	110,000
Retained Earnings	83,100		64,018	147,118
	465,830	233,870	233,870	635,160
Nominal Accounts				
Sales			(a) 242,807	
Gain on Sale of Marketable Securities			(f) 2,400	
Equity in Earnings of 30% Owned Company			(j) 5,880	
Gain on Condemnation of Land			(g) 10,700	
Cost of Sales		(b) 138,407		
General and Administrative Expenses		(c) 22,010		
Depreciation		(d) 1,250		
Interest Expense		(e) 1,150		
Income Taxes		(i) 34,952		
		197,769	261,787	
		64,018		
		261,787	261,787	

	Balances 12/31/X8	Changes Debit	Changes Credit	Balances 3/31/X9
Cash Flow Categories				
Operating Activities:				
Cash Collected from Customers		(a) 217,807		
Cash Paid for Goods to Be Sold			(b) 159,797	
Cash Flow Categories				
Cash Paid for General and Administrative Expenses			(c) 22,010	
Cash Paid for Interest			(e) 1,000	
Investing Activities				
Cash Received from Sale of Marketable Securities		(f) 11,600		
Cash Received from Land Condemnation		(g) 32,000		
Cash Paid for Purchase of Equipment			(h) 81,500	
Financing Activities				
Cash Received from Sale of Bonds Payable		(k) 65,000		
		326,407	264,307	
Increase in Cash			(n) 62,100	
		326,407	326,407	

Explanation of Worksheet Entries

(a)	Sales	$242,807
	Less increase in receivables	(25,000)
	Cash collected from customers	$217,807
(b)	Cost of sales	$138,407
	Plus increase in inventory	17,500
	Plus decrease in accounts payable	3,890
	Cash paid for goods to be sold	$159,797
(c)	G&A expenses	$ 22,010
	No adjustments	—
	Cash paid for G&A expenses	$ 22,010

(d) $1,250 reconciliation of depreciation expense and change in accumulated depreciation. No statement of cash flow effects.

(e)	Interest expense	$ 1,150
	Less decrease in discount on bonds payable	(150)
	Cash paid for interest	$ 1,000
(f)	Decrease in marketable securities	$ 9,200
	Plus gain on sale of marketable securities	2,400
	Cash received from sale of marketable securities	$ 11,600
(g)	Decrease in land	$ 21,300
	Plus gain on condemnation of land	10,700
	Cash received from land condemnation	$ 32,000

(h) Increase in equipment account ($81,500) also cash paid for equipment.

(i) Reconciliation of income tax expense ($34,952) to income tax payable ($34,616) and increase in deferred income tax ($336). No statement of cash flow effect.

(j) Reconciliation of $5,880 equity in earnings of 30% owned company (income statement) to change in inventory in 30% owned company. No statement of cash flow effects.

(k)	Increase in bonds payable account	$ 65,000
	No adjustment	—
	Cash received from sale of bonds payable	$ 65,000

(l) Noncash transaction to record retirement of preferred stock and issuance of common stock at $30,000. No statement of cash flow effects, but disclosure is required.

(m) Reconciliation of $8,000 dividends declared to increase in dividends payable. No statement of cash flow effects but disclosure is required.

(n) Reconciliation of $62,100 increase in cash to net of all sources (increases) and uses (decreases) in cash.

Holcomb Company
Statement of Cash Flows (Direct Method)
for the Three Months Ended March 31, 20X9

Cash Flows from Operating Activities		
Cash Received from Customers		$217,807
Cash Paid for Goods to be Sold	$ 159,797	
Cash Paid for General and Administrative Expenses	22,010	
Cash Paid for Interest	1,000	
Cash Disbursed for Operating Activities		182,807
Net Cash Provided by Operating Activities		$ 35,000

Cash Flows from Investing Activities		
Proceeds from Sale of Marketable Securities	$ 11,600	
Proceeds from Condemnation of Land	32,000	
Purchases of Equipment	(81,500)	
Net Cash Used in Investing Activities		(37,900)
Cash Flows from Financing Activities		
Proceeds of Long-Term Debt		65,000
Net Increase in Cash		$ 62,100
Cash, January 1, 20X9		25,300
Cash, March 31, 20X9		$ 87,400
Reconciliation of Net Income to Net Cash Provided by Operating Activities:		
Net Income		$64,018
Adjustments to Reconcile Net Income to Net Cash Provided by Operating Activities:		
Depreciation Expense		1,250
Bond Discount Amortization		150
Increase in Deferred Income Tax		336
Gain on Sale of Marketable Securities		(2,400)
Equity in Earnings of Investee		(5,880)
Gain on Sale of Land		(10,700)
Accounts Receivable Increase		(25,000)
Inventory Increase		(17,500)
Accounts Payable Decrease		(3,890)
Income Taxes Payable Increase		34,616
Net Cash Provided by Operating Activities		$ 35,000

Schedule of Noncash Financing Activities

Retirement of Preferred Stock by Conversion to Common Stock	$ 30,000
Declaration of Cash Dividends to be Paid	$ 8,000

Holcomb Company
Statement of Cash Flows (Indirect Method)
for the Three Months Ended March 31, 20X9

Cash Flows from Operating Activities		
Net Income		$64,018
Adjustments to Reconcile Net Income to Net Cash Provided by Operating Activities:		
Depreciation Expense		1,250
Bond Discount Amortization		150
Increase in Deferred Income Tax		336
Gain on Sale of Marketable Securities		(2,400)
Equity in Earnings of Investee		(5,880)
Gain on Sale of Land		(10,700)
Accounts Receivable Increase		(25,000)
Inventory Increase		(17,500)
Accounts Payable Decrease		(3,890)
Income Taxes Payable Increase		34,616
Net Cash Provided by Operating Activities		$ 35,000
Cash Flows from Investing Activities		
Proceeds from Sale of Marketable Securities	$ 11,600	
Proceeds from Condemnation of Land	32,000	
Purchases of Equipment	(81,500)	
Net Cash Used in Investing Activities		(37,900)
Cash Flows from Financing Activities		
Proceeds of Long-Term Debt		65,000
Net Increase in Cash		$ 62,100
Cash, January 1, 20X9		25,300
Cash, March 31, 20X9		$ 87,400

Schedule of Noncash Financing Activities

Retirement of Preferred Stock by Conversion to Common Stock	$ 30,000
Declaration of Cash Dividends to be Paid	$ 8,000

PART II: INTERPRETIVE GUIDANCE

ASC 230-10: OVERALL

ASC 230-10-45-4 through 45-5, 45-24, 50-7 through 50-8, 55-12A, 55-18A, 55-20; 230-10-65-3; ASC 830-230-45-1; ASC 958-205-55-3, 55-5, 55-21 Statement of Cash Flows (Topic 230) Restricted Cash

BACKGROUND

The Emerging Issues Task Force (EITF) took on this issue, because generally accepted accounting principles (U.S. GAAP) did not provide guidance for the classification of and presentation of changes in restricted cash or restricted cash equivalents (other than limited guidance for not-for-profit entities) that occur when (*a*) cash is transferred between cash, cash equivalents, and amounts referred to as restricted cash or restricted cash equivalents, and (*b*) there are direct cash receipts into restricted cash, restricted cash equivalents, or direct payments made from restricted cash or restricted cash equivalents. As a result, there was diversity in practice. Some entities were classifying transfers between cash and restricted cash or restricted cash equivalents as operating, investing, or financing activities, or as a combination of those activities, in the cash flows statement. In addition, some entities presented as cash inflows and cash outflows direct cash receipts into, and direct cash receipts from, a bank account in which restricted cash was held. Others disclosed those cash flows as noncash investing or financing activities. Further, some entities presented restricted cash and cash equivalents in various line items on the balance sheet with titles that did not indicate that the amounts are restricted cash or restricted cash equivalents. The objective of this project was to provide guidance for the presentation of restricted cash and restricted cash equivalents in the statement of cash flows and to help users to reconcile the information about restricted cash and restricted cash equivalents presented in the cash flow statement with information about those items presented in the balance sheet.

ACCOUNTING GUIDANCE

The following are the amendments to ASC 230, Statement of Cash Flows:

- ASC 230-10-45-4 has been amended to require that a cash flow statement should explain a change during the period in "the total of cash" "and amounts generally described as restricted cash or restricted cash equivalents." That paragraph has been amended further by deleting the third sentence and adding a requirement that an entity provide the disclosures discussed in ASC 230-10-50-8 below if cash, cash equivalents, and amounts generally described as restricted cash or restricted cash equivalents are presented in more than one line item in the balance sheet.
- ASC 230-10-45-5. This paragraph has been amended to provide that because transfers between cash, cash equivalents, and amounts generally described as restricted cash or restricted cash equivalents are part of an entity's cash management activities but not part of its operating, investing, and financing activities, information about those transfers are not reported as cash flow activities in a statement of cash flows.
- ASC 230-10-45-24. The paragraph is amended to provide that a cash flow statement for a period, which provides information about net cash provided or used in an entity's operating, investing, and financing activities, should report the net effect of those flows on "the total of cash . . . and amounts generally described as restricted cash or restricted cash equivalents during the period." In addition, a requirement has been added that the cash flow statement should present that information in a manner that reconciles the beginning and ending totals of those amounts.
- ASC 230-10-50-7. This paragraph and ASC 230-10-50-8 have been added in the Disclosure section under a new heading, Restrictions on Cash and Cash Equivalents. ASC 230-10-50-7 requires an entity to "disclose information about the nature of restrictions on its cash, cash equivalents, and amounts generally described as restricted cash or restricted cash equivalents." It also requires entities under the scope of Topic 958, Not-for-Profit Entities, to provide the required disclosures in ASC 958-210-50-3, which are discussed below.
- ASC 230-10-50-8 provides that an entity that presents cash, cash equivalents, and amounts generally described as restricted cash or restricted cash equivalents in more than one line item of the balance sheet is required to:
  - — Present on the face of the cash flows statement or disclose in the notes to the financial statements, the line items and amounts of cash, cash equivalents, and amounts generally described as restricted cash or restricted cash equivalents for each period that a balance sheet is presented; and
  - — Present a reconciliation of cash, cash equivalents, and restricted cash reported in several line items on the balance sheet in either narrative or tabular format, by adding the amounts of like line items in the balance sheet, and

presenting the sum of those line items, which should be equal to the total amount of cash, cash equivalents, and amounts generally described as restricted cash or restricted cash equivalents in the cash flows statement at the end of the corresponding period presented.

The following are amendments to Subtopic 830-20, Foreign Currency Matters-Statement of Cash Flows:

- ASC 830-230-45-1. This paragraph has been amended by requiring that an entity's cash flow statement should report the effect of rate changes on cash, cash equivalents, and amounts generally described as restricted cash or restricted cash equivalents held in foreign currencies as a separate part of the reconciliation of the change in total cash, cash equivalents, and amounts generally described as restricted cash or restricted cash equivalents during the period.

The following are amendments to Subtopic 958-230, Not-for-Profit Entities—Presentation of Statement of Cash Flows:

- ASC 958-230-55-3. The first sentence of this paragraph has been amended to require that a not-for-profit entity reporting the receipt of cash with a donor-imposed restriction limiting the use of the funds to long-term purposes should adjust the change in net assets in order to reconcile to net cash flows from operating activities, which is necessary if the indirect method of cash flows reporting is used so that those cash receipts are presented as cash inflows from financing activities as required by the guidance in ASC 230-10-45-14(c). The remainder of the paragraph has been deleted.

TRANSITION AND EFFECTIVE DATE

The following is the transition and effective date guidance in ASC 230-10-65-3:

- The guidance is effective for public business entities in financial statement issue for fiscal years that begin after December 15, 2017, and interim periods within those fiscal years.
- For other entities, the guidance is effective for financial statements issued for fiscal years that begin after December 15, 2018, and interim periods in fiscal years that begin after December 15, 2019.
- The guidance should be applied retrospectively to all periods presented.
- Earlier application of the guidance is permitted, including adoption in an interim period. If so, adjustments, if any, should be presented as of the beginning of the fiscal year that includes the interim period.
- The disclosures in ASC 250-10-50-1(a) and (b)1, and ASC 250-10-50-2, as applicable, are required in the first interim and annual period in which an entity adopts the guidance.

ASC 230-10-45-12, 21A; ASC 958-230-55-3 Not-for-Profit Entities: Classification of the Sale of Donated Financial Assets in the Statement of Cash Flows

BACKGROUND

Not-for-profit entities (NFPs) usually receive donations in the form of cash, but to accommodate donors, some NFPs accept donations in the form of financial instruments, which are most often immediately sold and converted into cash to comply with those entities' operating policies. The EITF discussed this issue because of diversity in the way NFPs classified cash receipts from the sale of donated securities in their statements of cash flows. Cash receipts from the sale of donated securities were being presented in the statement of cash flows as investing, financing, or operating cash flows.

Under the guidance in FASB Accounting Standards Codification® (ASC) 230, *Statement of Cash Flows*, an entity may classify cash receipts as operating, investing, or financing activities. Under the guidance in ASC 230-10-45-11 through 45-12, cash flows from a sale of available-for-sale securities and most receipts from sales of other debt and equity instruments should be classified as investing activities. However, under the guidance in ASC 230-10-45-20, cash receipts from assets that were acquired for resale and held in a trading account for a short time should be classified as operating cash flows. According to the guidance in ASC 230-10-45-22, cash flows with features of more than one classification should be classified based on the primary source of the cash flows.

ACCOUNTING ISSUE

How should NFP entities that account for their transactions under the guidance in ASC 958, *Not-for-Profit Entities*, account for donations received in the form of debt or equity instruments?

ACCOUNTING GUIDANCE

ASC 230-10-45-21A provides the following guidance for the classification of donated debt and equity instruments in the cash flow statements of NFPs accounted for under the guidance in ASC 958, *Not-for-Profit Entities*:

- Classify as "operating" cash flows, cash received from the sale of financial assets (donated debt or equity instruments) that were sold with no limitations imposed by the NFP entity and were converted to cash almost immediately after they were received.
- Classify as a "financing" activity, cash received from the sale of financial assets (donated debt or equity instruments), which meets the conditions in ASC 230-10-45-21A, but the use of which has been restricted by a *donor* to a long-term purpose described in ASC 230-10-45-14(c) as intended for "the purposes of acquiring, constructing, or improving, property, plant, equipment, or other long-lived assets or establishing or increasing a permanent endowment or term endowment."

The guidance in ASC 230-10-45-12(a) and 45-12(b) has been amended to exclude certain donated debt and equity instruments discussed in ASC 230-10-45-21A from classification as "investing" activities.

A reference to the guidance in ASC 230-10-45-21A has been added to the implementation guidance in ASC 958-230-55-3, which is related to the accounting for cash received with a donor restriction that limits the use of that cash to a long-term purpose.

ASC 230-10-45-12 through 45-13, 45-15 through 45-17, 45-21B through 21-D, 45-22, 45-22A, 45-25, 50-2, 50-4, 50-10, 50-13, 55-20, 65-2; ASC 958-805-45-11 through 45-12, Classification of Certain Cash Receipts and Cash Payments

BACKGROUND

The Emerging Issues Task Force (EITF) was asked to address the issues discussed in this ASU because of the existence of diversity in practice in the manner in which the guidance in Topic 230, *Statement of Cash Flows*, and other topics has been applied in the classification and presentation of certain cash receipts and cash payments. In some cases, the diverse accounting practices may have occurred as a result of a lack of guidance in Topic 230 for the classification and presentation of some cash receipts and cash payments, or because the existing guidance is unclear. To reduce that diversity, eight issues related to specific transactions are discussed below.

ACCOUNTING GUIDANCE

The following are the issues discussed and the amended guidance as of the effective date of ASU 2016-15 (see below):

- **Issue 1—Debt Prepayment or Debt Extinguishment Costs.** Topic 230 does not provide guidance for the accounting of costs that a borrower may incur when a debt financing arrangement is settled before its maturity date. A prepayment or debt extinguishment penalty provision is often included in a financing agreement as consideration to the lender for interest that the lender will not earn because of an early debt settlement.

  Amended Guidance. ASC 230-10-45-15(g) has been added to require a borrower to classify as cash outflows for *financing* activities all cash payments related to debt prepayment or costs of debt extinguishment, including third-party costs, premiums paid, and other fees paid to lenders that are directly related to a debt prepayment or extinguishment. However, accrued interest should be excluded from those amounts.

- **Issue 2—Settlement of Zero-Coupon Bonds.** Interest on Zero-coupon bonds, which are debt securities that are usually issued or traded at a discount from their face amounts, is not paid until maturity. There was diversity in practice in accounting for the settlement of such bonds, because Topic 230 did not provide specific guidance for the classification of the accreted interest and principal portions of cash payments for zero-coupon bonds in the statement of cash flows.

  Amended Guidance. Topic 230 has been amended as follows:

  — ASC 230-10-45-15(b) has been amended to provide that the portion of repayments to settle zero-coupon bonds that is related to a bond's principal or the principal of other debt instruments with "coupon interest rates that are insignificant in relation to **the effective interest rate** of the borrowing" should be classified as cash *outflows* for *financing* activities.

  — ASC 230-10-45-17(d) has been amended to provide that the portion of cash payments to lenders and other creditors for interest should be classified as a cash *outflow* for *operating* activities, including the portion for accreted interest related to debt discount in payments to settle zero-coupon bonds or other debt instruments with "coupon interest rates that are insignificant in relation to **the effective interest rate** of the borrowing." However, lenders and other creditors should not bifurcate payments on "all other debt instruments" at settlement for amounts attributable to accreted interest related to debt discount and should *not* classify it as a cash outflow for operating activities.

— ASC 230-10-45-25(e), which refers to interest paid and is one of a list of items that must be separately disclosed by entities that report their net cash flows from operating activities by providing separate information about the totals of major classes of gross cash receipts and gross cash payments and the sum of those amounts (the direct method), has been amended to provide that the information about interest paid should include information about (*a*) the portion of a settlement of zero coupon debt instruments for accreted interest related to the debt discount or (*b*) the portion of payments made to settle other debt instruments with "coupon interest rates that are insignificant in relation to **the effective interest rate** of the borrowing that is attributable to accreted interest related to the debt discount."

— ASC 230-10-50-2 has been amended to require that the portion of payments for accreted interest related to debt discount in cash payments made to settle zero-coupon debt instruments or other debt instruments with "coupon interest rates that are insignificant in relation to **the effective interest rate** of the borrowing" be disclosed in cash flow statements presented using the indirect method.

- **Issue 3—Contingent Consideration Payments Made after a Business Combination.** The *Master Glossary* of the FASB Accounting Standards Codification® defines the term, *contingent consideration,* as "an obligation of the acquirer to transfer additional assets or equity interests to the former owners of an acquiree as part of the exchange for control of the acquiree if future events occur or conditions are met." Because, no specific guidance is provided in Topic 230 or Topic 805, Business Combinations, for the classification of such cash payments in the cash flow statement, entities have classified those cash payments in different ways.

  Amended Guidance. Under the ASU's guidance, an acquirer is required to separate payments made to settle a contingent consideration liability after a business combination and classify them as cash outflows for financing and operating activities or as financing and investing activities as follows, depending on when the payments are made:

  — ASC 230-10-45-13(d) has been added to require that disclosure of payments made to settle a contingent consideration liability "soon" after a business combination be classified in the list of cash outflows for an *investing* activity.

  — ASC 230-45-15(f) has been added to require that disclosure of an acquirer's payments or a portion of payments made to settle all or part of a contingent consideration liability recognized at the acquisition date of a business combination, that are "not made soon" thereafter, including measurement-period adjustments, less amounts paid "soon" after the date of the acquisition to settle the liability be classified in the list of cash outflows for *financing* activities.

  — ASC 230-10-45-17(ee) has been added to require disclosure of an acquirer's cash payments to settle a contingent consideration liability or a portion of those payments "not made soon" after the acquisition date of a business combination that exceed the amount of the contingent consideration liability recognized at the acquisition date, including measurement-period adjustments, less amounts paid "soon" after the acquisition date should be classified in the list of cash outflows for *operating* activities. (Also see ASC 230-10-45-15(f))

  — ASC 958-805-45-11, which applies to not-for-profit (NFP) entities, provides that an NFP acquirer should classify cash flows related to an acquisition as an *investing* activity. However, the paragraph has been amended to provide that the guidance does not apply to an acquirer's cash payments made to settle a contingent consideration liability incurred as a result of an acquisition are not paid "soon" after the business combination, but notes that cash payments made "soon" after a business combination's acquisition date to settle a contingent consideration liability should be classified as investing activities.

  — ASC 958-805-45-12 has been added to provide the same guidance as that in ASC 230-10-45-15(f) and ASC 230-10-45-17(ee) for NFPs.

- **Issue 4—Proceeds from the Settlement of Insurance Claims.** Under the existing guidance in topic 230, cash inflows from the settlement of insurance claims are considered to be cash flows from operating activities, except if they are "directly related to investing or financing activities, such as from destruction of a building." There was diversity in the classification of such proceeds because it was unclear whether the phrase "directly related to investing or financing activities" applies to the insurance coverage or to the planned use of the insurance proceeds.

Amended Guidance. The amended guidance clarifies the cash flow classification of proceeds from the settlement of insurance claims as follows:

— ASC 230-10-45-16(c), which is included in the list of disclosures about cash inflows from operating activities has been amended by deleting "proceeds of insurance settlements except for those that are directly related to investing or financing activities, such as from destruction of a building"; which caused the diversity in practice.

— ASC 230-10-45-21B has been added under a new subheading "Proceeds from the Settlement of Insurance Claims." This paragraph provides that cash proceeds received from the settlement of insurance claims, other than those from corporate-owned life insurance policies and bank-owned life insurance policies, should be classified based on the related insurance coverage (i.e., the nature of the loss). The classification of insurance proceeds that are received in a lump sum should be based on the nature of each loss included in the settlement.

Illustrative cash flow statements on the direct and indirect method classify insurance proceeds as follows:

— Cash flows from operating activities—Insurance proceeds received for business interruption (direct method)

— Cash flows from operating activities—Gain on insurance proceeds received for damage to equipment (indirect method)

— Cash flow from investing activities—Insurance proceeds received for damage to equipment (direct and indirect method).

- **Issue 5—Proceeds from the Settlement of Corporate-Owned Life Insurance Policies, including Bank-Owned Policies.** Entities may purchase such policies to fund the cost of employee benefits and to protect against the loss of key employees. One of the primary benefits of using insurance policies for that purpose is an entity's ability to receive death benefits tax-free. In addition, investment income is accumulated tax-free through the build-up of a policy's cash surrender value. There was diversity in practice in the classification of proceeds received from the settlement of corporate-owned life insurance policies that were classified based on an entity's purpose for acquiring those policies. There also has been diversity in the classification of the cost of premiums paid on such insurance policies.

  Amended Guidance. The amended guidance is as follows:

  — ASC 230-10-45-21C is added to provide that cash received from the settlement of corporate-owned life insurance policies, including bank-owned life insurance policies, should be classified as cash flows from *investing* activities. Entities may elect to classify cash payments for premiums on corporate-owned life insurance policies, including bank-owned life insurance policies, as cash outflows from one of the following (*a*) *investing* activities, (*b*) *operating* activities, or (*c*) a combination of *investing* and *operating* activities.

- **Issue 6—Distributions Received from Equity Method Investees.** Cash receipts from equity method investees are commonly classified as cash inflows from operating activities, conforming to the classification of cash receipts of interest and dividends. Cash receipts from an equity method investee that are deemed to be returns of investment are commonly classified as cash inflows from investing activities to conform with the classification of returns of investment in equity financial instruments of other entities. However, there has been diversity in practice in applying those concepts.

  Amended Guidance. The amended guidance is as follows:

  — ASC 230-10-45-21D provides that a reporting entity that applies the equity method should make an accounting policy election to classify distributions received from investees by using one of the following approaches:

  a. *The cumulative earnings approach.* Under this approach, an investor considers an investee's distribution to be a return *on* investment that should be classified as cash inflows from *operating* activities. However, if the difference between the cumulative amount of distributions that an investor has received from an investee and the amount of distributions received in prior periods that were deemed to be returns *of* investment exceeds the investor's recognized cumulative equity in the investee's earnings (as adjusted for amortization of basis differences), a distribution in the current period up to the excess amount should be considered a return *of* investment and should be classified as cash flows from *investing* activities.

  b. *Nature of the distribution approach.* Under this approach, distributions received from an investee should be classified based on the nature of the investee's activity or activities that resulted in the distribution made as a return *on* investment (i.e., classified as a cash inflow from *operating* activities) or a return *of* investment (which is classified as a cash inflow from *investing* activities) if that information is available.

If an entity that has elected to apply the approach discussed in (b) finds that the information necessary to apply that approach to distributions received from an individual equity method investee is not available, it should report a change in accounting principle *retrospectively* by applying the cumulative earnings approach for that investee. In that case, an entity should disclose that a change in accounting principle occurred with regard to the affected investee because of a lack of available information and should provide the disclosures required in ASC 250-10-50-1(b) and ASC 250-10-50-2, as applicable. Regardless of which approach is applied, an entity also should comply with the applicable accounting policy disclosure requirements in ASC 235-10-50-1 through 50-6.

- **Issue 7—Beneficial Interests in Securitization Transactions.** This issue addresses two kinds of securitization transactions with beneficial interests that are accounted for as a sale under the guidance in ASC 860, *Transfers and Servicing*.

  1. In the first transaction, a transferor sells financial assets to an unconsolidated securitization entity for cash and retains a beneficial interest in the financial assets. The transferor receives cash based on the fair value of the financial assets less the beneficial interest retained by the transferor. ASC 230 provided no guidance on whether the retained beneficial interest should be considered a noncash activity or whether the transaction should be presented gross as a cash inflow for the sale of the financial assets and a cash outflow for the purchase of a beneficial asset.
  2. The second transaction involves a transfer of trade receivables in a securitization transaction under which the transferor retains a beneficial interest and has the right to receive cash from the securitization entity's collections on the trade receivables. Because Topic 230 provided no guidance for the classification of cash receipts related to beneficial interests in securitization transactions, transferors were classifying subsequent cash receipts from payments on beneficial interests in trade receivables retained in such transactions as operating activities or as investing activities in their cash flow statements.

  Amended Guidance. The amended guidance for the classification of cash inflows from both transactions is as follows:

  — ASC 230-10-45-12 provides guidance regarding cash flows that are classified as *investing* activities. Subparagraph (a), which provides guidance for the treatment of the second transaction discussed above, has been amended by the addition of the phrase "and collections on a transferor's beneficial interests in a securitization of the transferor's trade receivables."

  — ASC 230-10-50-4, which provides examples of noncash investing and financing activities (e.g., converting debt to equity), has been amended to include the first transaction discussed above by the addition of "obtaining a beneficial interest as consideration for transferring financial assets (excluding cash), including the transferor's trade receivables, in a securitization transaction."

- **Issue 8—Separately Identifiable Cash Flows and Application of the Predominance Principle.** Topic 230 provides that because some cash receipts and payments may have aspects of more than one class of cash flows, the appropriate classification in those situations depends on the nature of the activity that is the predominant source of an item's cash flows. However, there has been diversity in the interpretation and application of the "predominance" principle.

  Accounting Guidance. The following guidance clarifies when an entity should separate cash receipts and cash payments into more than one class of cash flows and when it should classify them into one class of cash flows based on predominance:

  — ASC 230-10-45-22 has been amended by deleting the paragraph's second through sixth sentences and adding guidance providing that the classification of cash receipts and cash payments should first be determined based on the guidance in ASC 230 and other applicable guidance. If there is no specific guidance, each separately identifiable source or separately identifiable use of the cash receipts or cash payments should be determined based on the nature of the underlying cash flows, "including when judgement is necessary to estimate the amount of each separately identifiable source or use." Each separately identifiable source or use within the cash receipts and cash payments should then be classified as financing, investing, or operating activities based on their nature.

— ASC 230-10-45-22A, which also has been added, provides that if cash receipts or payments have aspects of more than one class of cash flows that cannot be separated by source or use (e.g., if an entity acquires or produces a piece of equipment to be rented to others for a period of time and then sold), the appropriate classification should depend on the activity that is likely to be the predominant source or use of cash flows related to the item.

Effective Date and Transition

The following is the transition and effective date guidance in ASC 230-10-65-2:

- The ASU's guidance is effective as follows:
  — For public business entities, the guidance is effective for financial statements issued for fiscal years that begin after December 15, 2017, and interim periods within those fiscal years.
  — For all other entities, the guidance is effective for financial statements issued for fiscal years that begin after December 15, 2018, and interim periods within fiscal years that begin after December 15, 2019.
- The guidance should be applied retrospectively to all periods presented.
- If applying the guidance retrospectively to any prior period presented is impracticable (see ASC 250-10-45-9 through 45-10), an entity should apply the guidance as if the change was made prospectively as of the earliest date practicable.
- Earlier application of the guidance is permitted, including adoption in an interim period. If an entity does so, adjustments, if any, should be presented as of the beginning of the fiscal year that includes the interim period. An entity that early adopts the guidance must adopt all of the guidance in the same period.
- The disclosures in ASC 250-10-50-1(a) and (b)(1) and 250-10-50-2, as applicable, should be provided in the first interim and annual period in which an entity adopts the guidance. If retrospective application to any prior period is impracticable, the disclosures in ASC 250-10-50-1(b)(4) should be provided.

ASC 230-10-45-15 Classification of Debt Issue Costs in the Statement of Cash Flows

BACKGROUND

Entities incur certain costs in connection with issuing debt securities or other short-term or long-term borrowings. Such costs, which include underwriting, accounting, legal fees, and printing, generally are subtracted by the underwriter or lender from the proceeds of the debt or are paid by the borrower directly to the service providers.

Debt issue costs, which are required to be reported in the balance sheet as deferred charges, in accordance with FASB Accounting Standards Codification® (ASC) 835-30-45-3, generally are reported as assets and amortized over the term of the debt.

There has been diversity in practice in the cash flow statement classification of debt issue costs paid directly by a borrower—some have associated such costs with an entity's financing activities while others have associated them with an entity's operating activities. In an informal survey conducted by the FASB staff, debt issue costs were most often classified as a financing activity.

ACCOUNTING ISSUE

How should a borrower's cash payments for debt issue costs be classified in the statement of cash flows?

ACCOUNTING GUIDANCE

A borrower's cash payments for debt issue costs should be classified as a financing activity in the statement of cash flows.

DISCUSSION

The following arguments support classification of debt issue costs as a financing activity:

- There is a direct relationship between the debt issue and the debt issue costs.
- It is inconsistent to classify such costs as an operating activity, because according to the guidance in ASC 230-10-45-17, cash from operations includes activities that are *other* than financing or investing activities. Also, according to the guidance in ASC 230-10-45-22, classification depends on the "predominant source of cash flows for the item."

- Additions to property, plant, and equipment, which are subsequently depreciated, are not included in operating cash flows. Likewise, even though the asset is subsequently amortized, it is not meaningful to include payments for debt issue costs in the operating activity classification.

ASC 230-10-45-17; ASC 410-20-45-3 Classification in the Statement of Cash Flows of Payments Made to Settle an Asset Retirement Obligation within the Scope of FASB Statement No. 143, *Accounting for Asset Retirement Obligations*

BACKGROUND

The guidance in ASC 410-20 applies to *legal* obligations related to the retirement of tangible long-lived assets that result from the acquisition, construction, or development and the normal operation of those assets. Asset retirement obligations under the scope of ASC 410-20 must be recognized at the fair value of the liability in the period incurred. The associated costs should be capitalized as part of a long-lived asset's carrying amount and amortized to expense using a systematic and rational method over the asset's useful life. A liability must be recognized on the acquisition date for an existing retirement obligation related to acquired tangible long-lived assets as if the obligation had been incurred on that date. The guidance in this Issue does *not* apply to obligations under the scope of ASC 410-20, which are related to the treatment of environmental contamination that occurs after its guidance has been adopted.

Although under the guidance in ASC 230 cash receipts and payments should be classified as operating, investing, or financing activities, neither ASC 230 nor ASC 410-20 provide guidance for the classification of cash paid for obligations associated with the retirement of tangible long-lived assets and associated retirement costs.

ACCOUNTING ISSUE

How should cash paid to settle an asset retirement obligation be classified in the cash flow statement?

ACCOUNTING GUIDANCE

A cash payment made to settle an asset retirement obligation should be classified in the statement of cash flows as an *operating* activity.

CHAPTER 8

ASC 235—ACCOUNTING POLICIES AND STANDARDS

CONTENTS

GENERAL GUIDANCE

ASC 235-10: OVERALL

OVERVIEW

Accounting policies are important in understanding an entity's financial statements. FASB standards require the disclosure of accounting policies as an integral part of financial statements when those statements intend to present financial position, cash flows, and results of operations in conformity with U.S. GAAP.

BACKGROUND

In the United States, GAAP have been codified gradually over many years. During those years, a hierarchy of U.S. GAAP established the relative authority of the various pronouncements that had been issued by different standard-setting bodies (e.g., Committee on Accounting Procedures, Accounting Principles Board, and FASB). That hierarchy was replaced by the FASB Accounting Standards Codification (ASC). ASC 105 in Chapter 1 of this *Guide* contains further discussion of the U.S. GAAP hierarchy and Accounting Standards Codification.

All financial statements that present financial position, cash flows, and results of operations in accordance with U.S. GAAP must include disclosure of significant accounting policies. This includes financial statements of not-for-profit entities. Unaudited interim financial statements that do not include changes in accounting policies since the end of the preceding year are not required to disclose accounting policies in interim statements (ASC 235-10-50-1, 2).

DISCLOSURE OF SIGNIFICANT ACCOUNTING POLICIES

U.S. GAAP require a description of all significant accounting policies of a reporting entity as an integral part of the financial statements. The most common and preferred presentation of disclosing accounting policies is in the first note of the financial statements, under the caption "Summary of Significant Accounting Policies" or similar description. ASC 235 specifically states this preference, but recognizes the need for flexibility in terms of format (ASC 235-10-50-6).

Examples of areas of accounting for which policies are required to be disclosed are (ASC 235-10-50-4):

- Basis of consolidation
- Depreciation methods
- Inventory methods
- Amortization of intangibles
- Recognition of profit on long-term construction contracts

- Recognition of revenue from contracts with customers
- Recognition of revenue from leasing operations

Accounting principles and methods of applying them should be disclosed. Informed professional judgment is necessary to select for disclosure those principles that materially affect financial position, cash flows, and results of operations. Accounting principles and their method of application in the following areas are considered particularly important (ASC 235-10-50-3):

- A selection from existing acceptable alternatives (This could include elections to adopt Accounting Standards Updates (ASUs) related to Private Company Council options.)
- Areas peculiar to a specific industry in which the entity functions
- Unusual and innovative applications of U.S. GAAP

Disclosure of accounting policies is not intended to duplicate information presented elsewhere in the financial statements. In disclosing accounting policies, reference may be required to information presented elsewhere in the report, such as in the case of a change in an accounting principle that requires specific treatment (ASC 235-10-50-5).

PRACTICE POINTER: Many pronouncements, which are now part of the Accounting Standards Codification, require disclosure of information about accounting policies in specific financial reporting situations. For example, ASC 230 (Statement of Cash Flows) requires disclosure of the accounting policy for defining the term *cash equivalents*. Because there are so many requirements of this type embedded in the authoritative accounting literature, a financial statement disclosure checklist is a useful tool to guard against the inadvertent omission of required information. An unresolved issue is determining the materiality threshold of items for purposes of disclosing accounting policies.

Illustration of Disclosure of Significant Accounting Policies

Principles of consolidation The consolidated financial statements include the assets, liabilities, revenues, expenses, and cash flows of all significant subsidiaries. All significant intercompany transactions have been eliminated in consolidation. Investments in significant companies that are 20% to 50% owned are accounted for by the equity method, which requires the corporation's share of earnings to be included in income. All other investments are carried at market value or amortized cost in conformity with ASC 320 (Investments—Debt Securities) and ASC 321 (Investments—Equity Securities).

Cash equivalents Securities with maturities of three months or less when purchased are treated as cash equivalents in presenting the statement of cash flows.

Accounts receivable The company grants trade credit to its customers. Receivables are valued at management's estimate of the amount that will ultimately be collected. The allowance for doubtful accounts is based on specific identification of uncollectible accounts and the company's historical collection experience.

Plant assets and depreciation Plant assets are carried at cost, less accumulated depreciation. Expenditures for replacements are capitalized, and the replaced items are retired. Maintenance and repairs are charged to operations. Gains and losses from the sale of plant assets are included in net income. Depreciation is calculated on a straight-line basis utilizing the assets' estimated useful lives. The corporation and its subsidiaries use accelerated depreciation methods for tax purposes where appropriate.

Inventories Inventories are stated at the lower of cost or market using the last-in, first-out (LIFO) method for substantially all qualifying domestic inventories and the average cost method for other inventories.

Patents, trademarks, and goodwill Amounts paid for purchased patents and trademarks and for securities of newly acquired subsidiaries in excess of the fair value of the net assets of such subsidiaries are charged to patents, trademarks, and goodwill, respectively. Intangible assets with finite useful lives are amortized over those useful lives. Intangible assets with indefinite useful lives are not amortized, but these assets are evaluated, at least annually, for impairment.

Earnings per share Earnings per share figures are based on the weighted-average number of shares of common stock outstanding in each year. There would have been no material dilutive effect on net income per share for 20X2 or 20X3 if convertible securities had been converted and if outstanding stock options had been exercised.

Pension plans The company has pension plans that cover substantially all salaried employees. Benefits are based primarily on each employee's years of service and average compensation during the last five years of employment. Company policy is to fund annual periodic pension cost to the maximum allowable for federal income tax purposes.

Income taxes Income taxes are accounted for by the asset/liability approach in accordance with ASC 740 (Income Taxes). Deferred taxes represent the expected future tax consequences when the reported amounts of assets and liabilities are recovered or paid. They arise from differences between the financial reporting and tax bases of assets and liabilities and are adjusted for changes in tax laws and tax rates when those changes are enacted. The provision for income taxes represents the total of income taxes paid or payable for the current year, plus the change in deferred taxes during the year.

Interest costs Interest related to construction of qualifying assets is capitalized as part of construction costs in accordance with ASC 835 (Capitalization of Interest Cost).

PRACTICE POINTER: ASC 235 states a preference for all accounting policies to be presented together, and for that presentation to be between the financial statements and their notes or as the first note. In meeting this requirement, some companies present information in the policy statement that is not directly related to accounting policy. For example, in addition to stating the accounting policy regarding the inventory cost method used, a company also may indicate the dollar breakdown of raw materials, work-in-process, and finished goods. In the authors' opinion, this tends to obscure the accounting policy information. Similarly, in addition to stating depreciation policy, some companies include information regarding balances (i.e., book values) of plant assets in different categories. The authors encourage limiting disclosure in the policy statement to accounting policy matters and to presenting other information in other notes, possibly with cross-references. For example, in the section of the policy statement that states inventory policy, a cross-reference to another note covering in detail information about the amount of various types of inventory may be appropriate.

ASSESSING MATERIALITY IN NOTES TO FINANCIAL STATEMENTS

IMPORTANT NOTICE FOR 2022

The FASB has outstanding a proposed ASU that may have a significant impact on financial statements in the future. This proposed ASU relates to the FASB's disclosure framework project whose objective is to improve the effectiveness of disclosures in notes to the financial statements by facilitating clear communication of the information required by U.S. GAAP. It represents the FASB's response to requests for guidance on when disclosures are relevant for a particular reporting entity. A 2013 study conducted by the FASB indicated that additional explanation is needed to appropriately consider materiality in deciding which information to provide in notes. The outcome could result in reducing or eliminating irrelevant disclosures.

Achieving the objective of improving disclosures in notes to the financial statements includes developing a framework that promotes consistent decisions by the FASB about disclosure requirement and the appropriate exercise of discretion by reporting entities.

The proposed ASU would clarify the way materiality should be considered when assessing requirements for providing information in notes to financial statements. The proposed ASU would not change any specific disclosure requirements.

The proposed amendments to ASC 235 are the following:

- Materiality would be applied to both quantitative and qualitative disclosures individually and in the aggregate in the context of the financial statements taken as a whole. Some, all, or none of the requirements in a disclosure section may be considered material.
- Materiality would be referred to as a legal concept.
- The omission of the disclosure of immaterial information is not an accounting error.

This proposed ASU has been outstanding since 2015. There are other projects on the FASB's agenda that may change disclosure requirements in several areas. Given the length of time this exposure draft has been outstanding, the future of this project and its impact on future financial statements is uncertain.

Pension plans. The company has pension plans that cover substantially all salaried employees. Benefits are based primarily on each employee's years of service and average compensation during the last five years of employment. Company policy is to fund annual periodic pension cost to the maximum allowable for federal income tax purposes.

Income taxes. Income taxes are accounted for by the asset/liability approach in accordance with ASC 740 (Income Taxes). Deferred taxes represent the expected future tax consequences when the reported amounts of assets and liabilities are recovered or paid. They arise from differences between the financial reporting and tax bases of assets and liabilities and are adjusted for changes in tax laws and tax rates when those changes are enacted. The provision for income taxes represents the total of income taxes paid or payable for the current year, plus the change in deferred taxes during the year.

Interest costs. Interest related to construction of qualifying assets is capitalized as part of construction costs, in accordance with ASC 835 (Capitalization of Interest Cost).

PRACTICE POINTER: ASC 235 states a preference for all accounting policies to be presented together, and for that presentation to be between the financial statements and their notes or as the first note. In meeting this requirement, some companies present information in the policy statement that is not directly related to accounting policy. For example, in addition to stating the accounting policy regarding the inventory cost method used, a company also may indicate the dollar breakdown of raw materials, work-in-process, and finished goods. In the authors' opinion, this tends to obscure the accounting policy information. Similarly, in addition to stating depreciation policy, some companies include information regarding balances (i.e., book values) of plant assets in different categories. The authors encourage limiting disclosure in the policy statement to accounting policy matters and to presenting other information in other notes, possibly with cross-references. For example, in the section of the policy statement that states inventory policy, a cross-reference to another note covering in detail information about the amount of various types of inventory may be appropriate.

ASSESSING MATERIALITY IN NOTES TO FINANCIAL STATEMENTS

IMPORTANT NOTICE FOR 2022

The FASB has outstanding a proposed ASU that may have a significant impact on financial statements in the future. This proposed ASU relates to the FASB's disclosure framework project whose objective is to improve the effectiveness of disclosures in notes to the financial statements by facilitating clear communication of the information required by U.S. GAAP. It represents the FASB's response to requests for guidance on when disclosures are relevant for a particular reporting entity. A 2012 study conducted by the FASB indicated that additional explanation is needed to appropriately consider materiality in deciding which information to provide in notes. The outcome could result in reducing or eliminating irrelevant disclosures.

Achieving the objective of improving disclosures in notes to the financial statements includes developing a framework that promotes consistent decisions by the FASB about disclosure requirement and the appropriate exercise of discretion by reporting entities.

The proposed ASU would clarify the way materiality should be considered when assessing requirements for providing information in notes to financial statements. The proposed ASU would not change any specific disclosure requirements.

The proposed amendments to ASC 235 are the following:

- Materiality would be considered both quantitatively and qualitatively for disclosures individually and in the aggregate in the context of the financial statements taken as a whole. Some, all, or none of the requirements in a disclosure section may be considered material.
- Materiality would be referred to as a legal concept.
- The omission of the disclosure of immaterial information is not an accounting error.

The proposed ASU has been outstanding since 2015. There are other projects on the FASB's agenda that may change disclosure requirements in several areas. Given the length of time the exposure draft has been outstanding, the future of this project and its impact on future financial statements is uncertain.

CHAPTER 9

ASC 250—ACCOUNTING CHANGES AND ERROR CORRECTIONS

CONTENTS

GENERAL GUIDANCE

ASC 250-10: OVERALL

OVERVIEW

Accounting changes are broadly classified as (*a*) changes in an accounting principle, (*b*) changes in an accounting estimate, and (*c*) changes in the reporting entity (ASC Glossary). *Corrections of errors in previously issued financial statements are not accounting changes but are covered in the same accounting literature because of their similarity to accounting changes* (ASC 250-10-05-4).

Two different accounting methods are used within U.S. GAAP to account for accounting changes and corrections of errors: (1) current and prospective method, and (2) retroactive restatement method.

PRACTICE POINTER: These methods are not alternatives for the same type of accounting change or correction of an error. The authoritative literature clearly identifies the situations in which each is to be applied.

BACKGROUND

Changes in accounting principle, estimate, and entity are described in the authoritative literature as follows:

- *Change in accounting principle*—Results from the adoption of a generally accepted accounting principle different from the one used previously for financial reporting purposes. The term *principle* includes not only principles and practices, but also methods of applying them (ASC Glossary).
- *Change in accounting estimate*—Necessary consequence of periodic presentations of financial statements and the many estimates and assumptions that underlie those statements. A change in estimate results in a change in the carrying amount of an existing asset or liability or a change in the future accounting treatment of an existing asset or liability (ASC Glossary).

- *Change in accounting entity*—A special type of change in accounting principle that results when the reporting entity is different from that of previous periods. This type of change is characterized by (*a*) presenting consolidated or combined financial statements in place of individual company statements, (*b*) changing specific subsidiaries that make up the group of companies for which consolidated financial statements are presented, and (*c*) changing the companies included in combined financial statements (ASC Glossary).

Corrections of errors are not accounting changes. However, corrections of errors are similar to accounting changes and are sometimes confused with accounting changes. As a result, the authoritative literature discusses the correction of errors in the same authoritative literature as accounting changes (ASC 250-10-05-4). Errors in financial statements result from mathematical mistakes, mistakes in the application of accounting principles, and the oversight or misuse of facts that existed at the time financial statements were prepared. A change from an unacceptable accounting principle or method to an acceptable one is also considered a correction of an error (ASC Glossary).

Two approaches for dealing with accounting changes and corrections of errors are included in ASC 250: (1) the current and prospective method, and (2) the retroactive restatement method. In the current and prospective method, the impact of the change is reflected in current and future financial statements without adjustment to prior years. In the retroactive restatement method, prior years' financial statements are restated to include the effect of the change.

The following areas are not considered changes in an accounting principle (ASC 250-10-45-1):

- A principle, practice, or method adopted for the first time on new or previously immaterial events or transactions
- A principle, practice, or method adopted or modified because of events or transactions that are clearly different in substance

---

PRACTICE POINTER: A situation that is not mentioned in ASC 250 is changing from an accelerated depreciation method to the straight-line method at a point in the life of the asset, usually when depreciation by the accelerated method falls below the straight-line method. This is not considered a change in accounting principle provided the change is planned at the time the accelerated method is adopted and the policy is applied consistently (ASC 250-10-45-20).

A change in the composition of the elements of cost (material, labor, and overhead) included in inventory is an accounting change that requires justification based on the rule of preferability (ASC 250-10-55-1).

The primary source of U.S. GAAP for accounting changes and error corrections is ASC 250. ASC 250 applies to all voluntary changes in accounting principle and to changes required by an accounting pronouncement in the unusual circumstance that the pronouncement does not indicate a specific transition method (ASC 250-10-05-2). ASC 250 requires the retrospective application of the new accounting principle to prior periods' financial statements. Retrospective application is defined as the application of a different accounting principle to prior accounting periods as if that principle had always been used or as the adjustment of previously issued financial statements to reflect a change in the reporting entity (ASC Glossary). Any voluntary change in accounting principle must be justified on the basis of its preferability (ASC 250-10-45-2). (ASU 2016-03 removes the requirement to assess preferability on the four Private Company Council (PCC) ASUs issued in 2014.)

ASC 250 establishes retrospective application as the required method for reporting a change in accounting principle in the absence of explicit transition requirements specified in a newly adopted accounting standard. The standard provides guidance on when retrospective application is impracticable and for reporting a change in accounting principle in that circumstance. Error corrections are to be reported by restating previously issued financial statements (ASC 250-10-05-4). ASC 250 applies to financial statements of business enterprises and not-for-profit organizations. It also applies to financial summaries of information based on primary financial statements that include an accounting period in which an accounting change or error correction is reflected (ASC 250-10-15-3).

ASC 250 provides standards of accounting and reporting, followed by specific disclosure requirements, for four situations: changes in accounting principle, changes in accounting estimate, changes in reporting entity, and corrections of errors in previously issued financial statements.

CHANGES IN ACCOUNTING PRINCIPLE

The following are examples of common changes in accounting principle:

- A change in the method of pricing inventory, such as LIFO to FIFO or FIFO to LIFO
- A change in the method of depreciation for plant assets
- A change in the method of accounting for software development costs.

Financial reporting standards presume that an accounting principle, once adopted, will not be changed in accounting for events and transactions of the same type. Consistent use of accounting principles from period to period is an important dimension of high-quality financial statements that facilitate analysis and enhance comparability (ASC 250-10-45-1). A reporting entity shall change an accounting principle only if the change is required by a newly issued accounting pronouncement or the entity can justify the use of a different allowable accounting principle on the basis that it is preferable (ASC 250-10-45-2).

PRACTICE NOTE: Justifying a change in accounting principle on the basis of preferability is difficult. One commonly-accepted rationale for changing an accounting principle is to align the company's accounting with widely-used industry practices.

An entity making a change in accounting principle will report that change by retrospective application of the new principle to all periods, unless it is impracticable to do so. Retrospective application requires the following three steps (ASC 250-10-45-5):

Step 1. The cumulative effect of the change to the new principle on periods prior to those presented shall be reflected in the carrying amount of assets and liabilities as of the beginning of the first period presented.

Step 2. An offsetting adjustment, if any, shall be made to the opening balance of retained earnings for that period.

Step 3. Financial statements for each individual prior period presented are adjusted to reflect the period-specific effects of applying the new principle.

Impracticable

The term "impracticable," as used in ASC 250, means that at least one of the following applies (ASC 250-10-45-9):

- After making every reasonable effort to do so, the entity is unable to apply the requirement.
- Retrospective application requires assumptions about management's intent in a prior period that cannot be independently substantiated.
- Retrospective application requires significant estimates, and it is impossible to develop objective information about those estimates that provide evidence of circumstances that existed on the date(s) at which those amounts would be recognized, measured, or disclosed under retrospective application and would have been available when the financial statements for that period were issued.

If the cumulative effect of applying a change in accounting principle to all prior periods can be determined, but it is impracticable to determine the period-specific effects of that change on all prior periods presented, the cumulative effect of the change is applied to the carrying amounts of assets and liabilities as of the beginning of the earliest period to which the new accounting principle can be applied. The offsetting adjustment, if any, is to the opening balance of retained earnings for that period (ASC 250-10-45-6).

If it is impracticable to determine the cumulative effect of applying a change in accounting principle to any prior period, the new principle is applied as if the change was made prospectively as of the earliest date practicable. A change from the first-in, first-out (FIFO) inventory method to the last-in, first-out (LIFO) inventory method when the effects of having been on LIFO in the past cannot be determined is an example of such a situation (ASC 250-10-45-7).

Justification

Changing an accounting principle must be supported by a justification on the basis of preferability. (This does not apply to the adoption of the PCC ASUs.) The issuance of an accounting pronouncement may require the use of a new accounting principle, interpreting an existing principle, expressing a preference for an accounting principle, or rejecting a specific principle. Any of these may require an entity to change an accounting principle. Such a requirement is sufficient justification for making a change in an accounting principle. The burden of justifying other changes in accounting principle rests with the reporting entity making the change (ASC 250-10-45-13).

Retrospective application shall ordinarily include only the direct effects of a change in accounting principle, including the income tax effects. If indirect effects are actually incurred and recognized, they shall be reported in the period in which the accounting change is made (ASC 250-10-45-8).

A change in accounting principle made in an interim period shall be reported by retrospective application. However, the impracticability exception stated above may not be applied to prechange interim periods of the fiscal year in which the change is made. When retrospective application to prechange interim periods is impractical, the desired change may only be made as of the beginning of a subsequent fiscal year (ASC 250-10-45-14).

Publicly traded companies that do not issue separate fourth-quarter reports must disclose in a note to their annual reports any effect of an accounting change made during the fourth quarter (ASC 250-10-45-15).

Illustration of the Application of ASC 250—Change in Accounting Principle

Universal Technologies Inc. changes from the LIFO method of inventory valuation to the FIFO method at January 1, 20X7. Universal Technologies had used the LIFO method since its inception on January 1, 20X4. The change in inventory method is preferable.

Sales are $15,000 for each year from 20X4 through 20X7 and selling, general, and administrative expenses are $5,000 in each year. Universal Technologies' effective income tax rate is 30% in each year and it has no temporary or permanent income tax differences. Income taxes accrued at the end of each year are paid in cash at the beginning of the next year. Universal Technologies' annual report to shareholders includes three years of income statements and statements of cash flows and two years of balance sheets. (Earnings per share computations are ignored.)

Universal Technologies has determined that the effect of changing from LIFO inventory valuation to FIFO inventory valuation has the following effects on inventory and cost of goods sold for each year from 20X4 through 20X7:

	Inventory Determined by		*Cost of Sales Determined by*	
Date	*LIFO Method*	*FIFO Method*	*LIFO Method*	*FIFO Method*
1/1/20X4	0	0	0	0
12/31/20X4	600	400	4,800	5,000
12/31/20X5	1,000	1,440	5,000	4,360
12/31/20X6	1,200	1,100	5,200	5,740
12/31/20X7	1,600	2,340	5,000	4,160

Universal Technologies' originally reported income statements for 20X4 through 20X6 (using the LIFO inventory method) are:

Income Statement (as originally reported)

	20X6	*20X5*	*20X4*
Sales	$15,000	$15,000	$15,000
Cost of goods sold	5,200	5,000	4,800
Selling, general, and administrative expenses	5,000	5,000	5,000
Income before income taxes	4,800	5,000	5,200
Income taxes	1,440	1,500	1,560
Net income	$ 3,360	$ 3,500	$ 3,640

Universal Technologies' income statements showing the retrospective application of the FIFO inventory method (from the LIFO method) are:

Income Statement

	20X7	*20X6*	*20X5*
		As Adjusted (Note A)	As Adjusted (Note A)
Sales	$15,000	$15,000	$15,000
Cost of goods sold	4,160	5,740	4,360
Selling, general, and administrative expenses	5,000	5,000	5,000
Income before income taxes	5,840	4,260	5,640
Income taxes	1,752	1,278	1,692
Net income	$ 4,088	$ 2,982	$ 3,948

NOTE A: Change in Method of Inventory Valuation On January 1, 20X7, Universal Technologies Inc. changed from the LIFO inventory valuation method to the FIFO inventory valuation method. The FIFO inventory valuation method was adopted [provide justification for why the FIFO method is preferable to the LIFO method] and the comparative financial statements for 20X6 and 20X5 have been adjusted to apply the FIFO method on a retrospective basis. The following financial statement line items for fiscal years 20X7, 20X6, and 20X5 were affected by the change in accounting principle.

Income Statement—20X7

	As Computed Under LIFO	*As Reported Under FIFO*	*Effect of Change*
Cost of goods sold	$5,000	$4,160	$(840)
Income before taxes	$5,000	$5,840	$ 840
Income tax expense	$1,500	$1,752	$ 252
Net income	$3,500	$4,088	$ 588

Income Statement—20X6

	As Originally Reported	*As Adjusted*	*Effect of Change*
Cost of goods sold	$5,200	$5,740	$540
Income before taxes	$4,800	$4,260	$(540)
Income tax expense	$1,440	$1,278	$(162)
Net income	$3,360	$2,982	$(378)

Income Statement—20X5

	As Originally Reported	*As Adjusted*	*Effect of Change*
Cost of goods sold	$5,000	$4,360	$(640)
Income before taxes	$5,000	$5,640	$ 640
Income tax expense	$1,500	$1,692	$ 192
Net income	$3,500	$3,948	$ 448

Balance Sheet—12/31/X7

	As Computed Under FIFO	*As Reported Under FIFO*	*Effect of Change*
Cash	$113,900	$113,930	$ 30
Inventory	$ 1,600	$ 2,340	$740
Total assets	$115,500	$116,270	$770
Income tax liability	$ 1,500	$ 1,752	$252
Retained earnings	$ 14,000	$ 14,518	$518

Balance Sheet—12/31/X6

	As Originally Reported	*As Adjusted*	*Effect of Change*
Cash	$ 10,740	$110,608	$(132)
Inventory	$ 1,200	$ 1,100	$(100)
Total assets	$111,940	$111,708	$(232)
Income tax liability	$ 1,440	$ 1,278	$(162)
Retained earnings	$ 10,500	$ 10,430	$ (70)

Balance Sheet—12/31/X5

	As Originally Reported	*As Adjusted*	*Effect of Change*
Cash	$107,640	$107,700	$ 60
Inventory	$ 1,000	$ 1,440	$440
Total assets	$108,640	$109,140	$500
Income tax liability	$ 1,500	$ 1,692	$192
Retained earnings	$ 7,140	$ 7,448	$308

As a result of the accounting change, retained earnings as of January 1, 20X5 decreased from $3,640, as originally reported using the LIFO method, to $3,500 using the FIFO method.

Statement of Cash Flows—20X7

	As Computed Under LIFO	*As Reported Under FIFO*	*Effect of Change*
Net income	$3,500	$ 4,088	$ 588
(Increase) decrease in inventory	$ (400)	$ (1,240)	$ (840)
Increase (decrease) in income tax liability	$ 60	$ 474	$ 414
Net cash provided by operating activities	$3,160	$ 3,322	$ 162
Change in cash	$3,160	$ 3,322	$ 162

Statement of Cash Flows—20X6

	As Originally Reported	*As Adjusted*	*Effect of Change*
Net income	$3,360	$2,982	$(378)
(Increase) decrease in inventory	$ (200)	$ 340	$ 540
Increase (decrease) in income tax liability	$ (60)	$ (414)	$(354)
Net cash provided by operating activities	$3,100	$2,908	$(192)
Change in cash	$3,100	$2,908	$(192)

Statement of Cash Flow—20X5

	As Originally Reported	*As Adjusted*	*Effect of Change*
Net income	$ 3,500	$ 3,948	$ 448
(Increase) decrease in inventory	$ (400)	$ (1,040)	$ (640)
Increase (decrease) in income tax liability	$ (60)	$ 192	$ 252
Net cash provided by operating activities	$ 3,040	$ 3,100	$ 60
Change in cash	$ 3,040	$ 3,100	$ 60

Disclosure

The following items are required disclosures in the period during which the change in accounting principle is made (ASC 250-10-50-1):

- The nature of and reason for the change in principle, including an explanation of why the new principle is preferable.
- The method of applying the change, and:
  - — A description of the prior-period information that has been retrospectively adjusted, if any.
  - — The effect of the change on income from continuing operations, net income, any other affected financial statement item, and any affected per-share amounts for the current period and any prior periods retrospectively adjusted.
  - — The cumulative effect of the change on retained earnings (or other components of equity or net assets in the statement of financial position) as of the beginning of the earliest period presented.
  - — If retrospective application to all periods is impracticable, the reasons therefore and a description of the alternative method used to report the change.
- If indirect effects of a change in accounting principle are recognized:
  - — A description of the indirect effects, including the amounts that have been recognized in the current period and the related per-share amounts, if applicable.
  - — Unless impracticable, the amount of the total recognized indirect effects of the accounting change and the related per-share amounts, if applicable, that are attributable to each prior period presented.

In the fiscal year in which a different accounting principle is adopted, financial information reported for interim periods after the date of adoption will disclose the effect of the change in income from continuing operations, net income, and related per-share amounts, if applicable, for the post-change interim periods (ASC 250-10-50-3).

CHANGES IN ACCOUNTING ESTIMATE

A change in accounting estimate is accounted for in the period of change if the change affects only that period, or is accounted for in the period of change and future periods if the change affects both. A change in accounting estimate is not accounted for by restating or retrospectively adjusting amounts reported in financial statements of prior periods or by reporting pro forma amounts for prior periods (ASC 250-10-45-17).

Distinguishing between a change in accounting principle and a change in accounting estimate may be difficult. In some cases, a change in estimate is effected by a change in accounting principle, such as when a depreciation method is changed to reflect a change in the estimated future benefits of the asset or the pattern of consumption of those benefits. The change in principle cannot be separated from the effect of the change in accounting estimate. Changes of this type are considered changes in estimate (ASC 250-10-45-17). Similar to other changes in accounting principle, a change in accounting estimate that is effected by a change in accounting principle is appropriate only if the new principle is justifiable on the basis that it is preferable (ASC 250-10-45-18).

Illustration of Current and Prospective Method

In 20X6, Martin Co. paid $150,000 for a building that was expected to have a ten-year life with an estimated value at the end of that period of $25,000. Straight-line depreciation was used through 20X9. In 20Y0, management's reassessment of the useful lives of all assets resulted in a decision that the useful life would be 15 years from the time of purchase, at which time the estimated value would be approximately $10,000.

The book value of the asset at the time of the change is computed as follows:

Cost	$150,000
Accumulated depreciation [($150,000 – $25,000)/10] × 4	(50,000)
Book value	$100,000

Depreciation for 20Y0 and each of the next 11 years (15 years total – 4 years depreciated to date) is computed and recorded as follows:

Book value at time of change	$100,000
Estimated residual value	(10,000)
Depreciable cost	$90,000
Depreciation per year ($90,000/11)	$8,182

Entry: Depreciation Expense	8,182	
Accumulated Depreciation		8,182

To summarize, depreciation recognized over the estimated life of the asset is as follows: $12,500 for each of four years (prior to the change in estimated life) and $8,182 for each of 11 years (following the change in estimated life), totaling $140,000 ($150,000 – $10,000).

No cumulative effect is recorded. Disclosure is required of the nature of the change and the impact on income ($12,500 – $8,182 = $4,318) as follows:

During 20Y0, management determined that the useful life of the building was longer than originally expected. A change in accounting estimate was recognized to reflect this decision, resulting in an increase in net income of $4,318.

Disclosure

The effect on income from continuing operations, net income, and any related per-share amounts of the current period must be disclosed for a change in estimate that affects several future periods. Disclosure of those effects is not necessary for estimates made each period in the ordinary course of accounting for items, such as uncollectible accounts or inventory obsolescence. Effects of such a change in estimate must be disclosed, however, if the effect is material (ASC 250-10-50-4).

When an entity effects a change in estimate by changing an accounting principle, the disclosures required for a change in accounting principles (stated above) are required. If a change in estimate does not have a material effect in the period of change, but is expected to have a material effect in later periods, a description of the change is required whenever the financial statements of the period of the change are presented (ASC 250-10-50-4).

CHANGES IN REPORTING ENTITY

ASC 250 specifies that an accounting change that results in financial statements that are, in effect, those of a different reporting entity must be retrospectively applied so that the specific entities that comprise the reporting entity in the current period are comparable to the specific entities that comprised the reporting entity in previous years. Previously issued interim financial information shall be presented on a retrospective basis with the following exception: the amount of interest cost previously capitalized on investments accounted for by the equity method will not be changed when retrospectively applying the accounting change to the financial statements of prior periods (ASC 250-10-45-21).

Disclosure

When there has been a change in reporting entity, the financial statements of the period of change must include a description of the nature of the change and the reason for the change. The effect of the change on net income, other comprehensive income, and any related per-share amounts must be disclosed for all periods presented (ASC 250-10-50-6).

CORRECTIONS OF ERRORS IN PREVIOUSLY ISSUED FINANCIAL STATEMENTS

An error in financial statements of prior periods that is discovered after those statements are issued is reported as a prior-period adjustment by restating the prior period financial statements. This requires the following three steps (ASC 250-10-45-23):

Step 1. The cumulative effect of the error on periods prior to the period in which the error is discovered and corrected is reflected in the carrying amounts of assets and liabilities as of the beginning of that period.

Step 2. An offsetting adjustment, if any, is made to the opening balance of retained earnings (or other component of equity or net assets in the statement of financial position) for that period.

Step 3. Financial statements for each individual prior period presented are adjusted to reflect correction of the period-specific effects of the error.

PRACTICE POINTER: Distinguishing between a *change in accounting estimate* and the *correction of an error* may be difficult and may require professional judgment. In the final analysis, the difference often comes down to the timing of the availability of the information upon which the change or correction is made. If the information is newly available, the adjustment is a change in accounting estimate. If the information was previously available, but was not used or was incorrectly used, the adjustment is a correction of an error. This classification is important because a change in estimate is accounted for prospectively while a correction of an error requires restatement of previously issued financial statements.

Illustration of Correction of Error in Previously Issued Financial Statements

In 20X7 and 20X8, Warren, Inc., inappropriately capitalized $100,000 of period costs as fixed assets in each year. This intentional misstatement was discovered and corrected in 20X9. The period costs inappropriately capitalized as fixed assets were being depreciated on a straight-line basis (with no salvage value) over 10 years. Warren, Inc. accounted for the $100,000 of period costs correctly in 20X9. Warren, Inc.'s effective tax rate is 30%, and all income taxes due are paid in full during the year in which they are incurred. Warren, Inc.'s income statements, balance sheets, and statements of retained earnings as originally filed are as follows:

Income Statements (as originally presented)

	20X8	*20X7*
Revenues	$500,000	$500,000
Cost of goods sold	250,000	250,000
Other expenses (excluding depreciation)	100,000	100,000
Depreciation expense	20,000	10,000
Income before taxes	130,000	140,000
Income tax expense (at 30%)	39,000	42,000
Net income	$ 91,000	$ 98,000

Balance Sheets (as originally presented)

	20X8	*20X7*
Cash	$119,000	$100,000
Receivables	80,000	60,000
Inventories	80,000	108,000
Income tax refund receivable	—	—
Fixed assets (net)	170,000	90,000
Total assets	$449,000	$358,000
Accounts payable	$ 20,000	$ 20,000
Long-term liabilities	40,000	40,000
Total liabilities	60,000	60,000
Paid-in capital	200,000	200,000
Retained earnings	189,000	98,000
Total stockholders' equity	389,000	298,000
Total liabilities and stockholders' equity	$449,000	$358,000

Statements of Retained Earnings (as originally presented)

	20X8	*20X7*
Balance, January 1	$98,000	$—
Net income	91,000	98,000
Balance, December 31	$189,000	$ 98,000

The entry to record the correction of this error in 20X9 is as follows:

Accumulated depreciation	30,000	
Retained earnings [($200,000 – $30,000) × .7]	119,000	
Income tax refund receivable	51,000	
Fixed assets		200,000

In 20X9, Warren, Inc. presents income statements and statements of retained earnings for 20X9 and 20X8 and a balance sheet for 20X9. (Warren, Inc.'s statement of cash flows and required disclosures are not presented.)

Income Statements

	20X9	*20X9 (as restated)*
Revenues	$500,000	$500,000
Cost of goods sold	250,000	250,000
Other expenses (excluding depreciation)	–200,000	–200,000
Depreciation expense	—	—
Income before taxes	50,000	50,000
Income tax expense (at 30%)	15,000	15,000
Net income	$ 35,000	$ 35,000

Statements of Retained Earnings

	20X9	*20X8 (as restated)*
Balance, January 1	$ 70,000	$ 98,000
Adjustment to correct the error of improper capitalization of period expenses (net of tax)		(63,000)*
Adjusted balance, January 1	70,000	35,000
Net income	35,000	35,000
Balance, December 31	$105,000	$70,000

———-

* ($10,000 – $100,000) × (1–.3)

Balance Sheet

	20X9
Cash	$110,000
Receivables	94,000
Inventories	110,000
Income tax refund receivable	51,000
Fixed assets (net)	-0-
Total assets	$365,000
Accounts payable	$20,000
Long-term liabilities	40,000
Total liabilities	60,000

	20X9
Paid-in capital	200,000
Retained earnings	105,000
Total stockholders' equity	305,000
Total liabilities and stockholders' equity	$365,000

Disclosure

When financial statements have been restated for the correction of an error, the entity must disclose the nature of the error and the fact that previously issued financial statements have been restated. Prior period adjustments are excluded from the determination of net income (ASC 250-10-45-22). All other items of profit and loss (including accruals for loss contingencies) shall be included in the determination of net income for the period. The entity must disclose the following (ASC 250-10-50-7, ASC 250-10-50-9):

- The effect of the correction on each financial statement line item and any per-share amounts affected for each prior period presented.
- The gross and net effect (of related income taxes) of prior period adjustments on net income should be disclosed in the year of adjustment and all years presented.
- The cumulative effect of the change on retained earnings or other appropriate components of equity (or net assets in the statement of financial position) as of the beginning of the earliest period presented.

A common practice for business entities is to present historical, statistical-type summaries of financial information for a number of periods, commonly five or 10 years. When error corrections are recorded during any of the periods included in these summaries, the reported amounts of net income and its components, as well as other affected items, shall be restated with disclosure in the first summary published after the correction. (ASC 250-10-50-7A)

INTERIM PERIOD ADJUSTMENTS

An adjustment of prior interim periods of a current fiscal year can include any of the following settlements (ASC 250-10-45-25):

1. Litigation or similar claims
2. Income taxes
3. Renegotiation
4. Utility revenues governed by rate-making processes

In adjusting interim periods of the current year, any adjustment of prior periods is made to the first interim period of the current year. Adjustments to the other interim periods of the current year are related to the interim period affected (ASC 250-10-45-26).

The effects (*a*) on income from continuous operations, (*b*) on net income, and (*c*) on earnings per share of an adjustment to a current interim period must be disclosed fully (ASC 250-10-50-11).

When considering the materiality in reporting the correction of an error, amounts are considered both in relation to the estimated income for the entire fiscal year and the effect on the trend of earnings (ASC 250-10-45-27). Changes that are material with respect to an interim period but not material with respect to the estimated income for the full fiscal year or to the trend in earnings for the entire fiscal year are separately disclosed in the interim period (ASC 250-10-50-12).

CHAPTER 10

ASC 255—CHANGING PRICES

CONTENTS

PART I: GENERAL GUIDANCE

ASC 255-10: OVERALL

OVERVIEW

Financial statements prepared in conformity with U.S. GAAP are based on the assumption of a stable monetary unit. This means that the monetary unit used to convert all financial statement items into a common denominator (e.g., dollars) does not vary sufficiently over time so that distortions in the financial statements are material. In addition, financial statements prepared in conformity with U.S. GAAP place heavy reliance on historical cost. For example, several important financial statement items, including inventory and plant assets, are measured and presented at the historical cost of the item rather than on the current value of the items. However, in the last two decades, some reporting standards have moved away from historical cost and placed increased reliance on current value.

Over the years, two approaches have been proposed and procedures developed to compensate for changes in the monetary unit and changes in the value of assets and liabilities after their acquisition—current value accounting and general price-level accounting. Current value accounting replaces historical cost as the primary measurement upon which the elements of financial statements are based. In contrast, general price-level accounting adheres to historical cost but substitutes a current value of the monetary unit (e.g., dollar) for the historical amount of the monetary unit by using price indexes. *Neither current value accounting nor general price-level accounting is required at the present time,* although specific applications of current or fair value are gradually being incorporated into U.S. GAAP. In ASC 255, the FASB presents disclosure standards that are optional for dealing with the problem of the impact of changing prices on financial statements.

BACKGROUND

Guidance related to financial reporting and changing prices at times in the past required certain large enterprises to disclose the effects of changing prices via a series of supplemental disclosures. These disclosures are now encouraged, but are no longer required (ASC 255-10-15-3).

REPORTING UNDER ASC 255

Net Monetary Position

Assets and liabilities are identified as monetary items if their amounts are fixed or determinable without reference to future prices of specific goods and services. Cash, accounts and notes receivable in cash, and accounts and notes payable in cash are examples of monetary items (ASC Glossary).

Monetary items lose or gain general purchasing power during inflation or deflation as a result of changes in the general price-level index (ASC 255-10-50-51). For example, a holder of a $10,000 promissory note executed 10 years ago and due today will receive exactly $10,000 today, in spite of the fact that $10,000 in cash today is worth less than $10,000 was worth 10 years ago.

Assets and liabilities that are not fixed in terms of the monetary unit are referred to as nonmonetary items. Inventories, investment in common stocks, property, plant, and equipment, and deferred charges are examples of nonmonetary items (ASC 255-10-50-51). A nonmonetary asset or liability is affected (*a*) by the rise or fall of the general price-level index and (*b*) by the increase or decrease of the fair value of the nonmonetary item. Holders of nonmonetary items lose or gain with the rise or fall of the general price-level index if the nonmonetary item does not rise or fall in proportion to the change in the price-level index. For example, the purchaser of 10,000 shares of common stock 10 years ago was subject (*a*) to the decrease in purchasing power of the dollar and (*b*) to the change in the fair value of the stock. Only if the decrease in purchasing power exactly offsets an increase in the price of the stock is the purchaser in the same economic position today as 10 years ago.

The difference between monetary assets and monetary liabilities at any specific date is the net monetary position. The net monetary position may be either positive (monetary assets exceed monetary liabilities) or negative (monetary liabilities exceed monetary assets).

In periods in which the general price level is rising (inflation), it is advantageous for a business to maintain a net liability monetary position. The opposite is true during periods in which the general price level is falling (deflation). In periods of inflation, a business that has a net liability monetary position will experience general price-level gains, because it can pay its liabilities in a fixed number of dollars that are declining in value over time. In periods of inflation, a business that has a net asset monetary position will experience general price-level losses because it holds more monetary assets than liabilities and the value of the dollar is declining.

> ***PRACTICE POINTER:*** Some assets and liabilities have characteristics of both monetary and nonmonetary items. Convertible debt, for example, is monetary in terms of its fixed obligation, but nonmonetary in terms of its conversion feature. Whether an item is monetary or nonmonetary is determined as of the balance sheet date. Therefore, if convertible debt has not been converted as of that date, classify it as a monetary item. Additionally, classify a bond receivable held for speculation as nonmonetary, because the amount that will be received when the bond is sold is no longer fixed in amount, as it would be if the same bond were held to maturity. ASC 255-10-55-1 contains a table that reflects the monetary/nonmonetary classification of most assets and liabilities.

Current Cost Accounting

Current cost accounting is a method of measuring and reporting assets and expenses associated with the use or sale of assets at their current cost or lower recoverable amount at the balance sheet date or at the date of use or sale. Current cost/constant purchasing power accounting is a method of accounting based on measures of current cost of lower recoverable amounts in units of currency that each have the same general purchasing power. For operations for which the U.S. dollar is the functional currency, the general purchasing power of the dollar is used. For operations for which the functional currency is other than the U.S. dollar, the general purchasing power of either (*a*) the dollar or (*b*) the functional currency is used (ASC Glossary).

Determining Current Costs

Current cost, often referred to as current replacement cost, is the current cost to purchase or reproduce a specific asset. Current reproduction cost must contain an allocation for current overhead costs (direct costing is not permitted).

The current cost of inventory owned by an enterprise is the current cost to purchase or reproduce that specific inventory. The current cost of property, plant, and equipment owned by an enterprise is the current cost of acquiring an asset that will perform or produce in a manner similar to the owned asset (ASC 255-10-50-21, 22).

An enterprise may obtain current cost information internally or externally, including independent appraisals, and may apply the information to a single item or to groups of items. An enterprise is expected to select the types of current cost information that are most appropriate for its particular circumstances. The following types and sources of current cost information may be utilized by an enterprise (ASC 255-10-50-23):

- Current invoice prices
- Vendor firms' price lists, quotations, or estimates
- Standard manufacturing costs that reflect current costs
- Revision of historical cost by the use of indexation, based on:
  - — Externally generated price indexes for the goods or services being restated, or
  - — Internally generated indexes for the goods or services being restated

Depreciation Methods

Depreciation methods, useful lives, and salvage values used for current cost purposes are generally the same as those used for historical cost purposes. If historical cost computations already include an allowance for changing prices, then a different method may be used for current cost purposes. However, any material differences shall be disclosed in the explanatory notes to the supplementary information (ASC 255-10-50-29).

Recoverable Amounts

The recoverable amount of an asset is the current worth of cash expected to be recoverable from the use or sale of the asset (ASC Glossary). Recoverable amounts may be determined by reference to fair values or values in use. They reflect write-downs during a current period, from the current cost amount to a lower recoverable amount. These reductions reflect a permanent decline in the value of inventory, or property, plant, and equipment.

Net Realizable Value

Net realizable value (the fair value of an asset less costs to sell the asset) is the expected amount of net cash or other net equivalent to be received from the sale of an asset in the regular course of business. Net realizable value is used only if the specific asset is about to be sold (ASC 255-10-50-36).

Value in Use

Value in use is the total present value of all future cash inflows that are expected to be received from the use of an asset. Value in use is used only if there is no immediate intention to sell or otherwise dispose of the asset. Value in use is estimated by taking into consideration an appropriate discount rate that includes an allowance for the risk involved in the circumstances (ASC Glossary).

Income Tax Expense

Income tax expense and the provision for deferred taxes, if any, are not restated in terms of current cost and are presented in the supplementary information at their historical cost. Disclosure is required in the supplementary information to the effect that income tax expense for the current period is presented at its historical cost.

Optional Supplementary Information under ASC 255

Under ASC 255, an enterprise is encouraged to disclose certain minimum supplementary information for each of its five most recent years. In addition, if income from continuing operations as shown in the primary financial statements differs significantly from income from continuing operations determined on a current cost/constant purchasing power basis, certain additional disclosures relating to the components of income from continuing operations for the current year also should be disclosed (ASC 255-10-50-11).

The minimum supplementary information encouraged by ASC 255 is disclosed in average-for-the-year units of constant purchasing power. The Consumer Price Index for All Urban Consumers (CPI-U) is used to restate the current cost of an item in average-for-the-year units of constant purchasing power. Alternatively, an enterprise may disclose the minimum supplementary information in dollars having a purchasing power equal to that of dollars of the base period used in calculating the CPI-U. The level of the CPI-U used for each of the five most recent years should be disclosed (ASC 255-10-50-7, 8).

An enterprise is encouraged to disclose the following minimum supplementary information for the five most recent years (ASC 255-10-50-3):

- Net sales and other operating revenue
- Income from continuing operations on a current cost basis
- Purchasing power gain or loss on net monetary items
- Increase or decrease in the current cost or lower recoverable amount of inventory and property, plant, and equipment, net of inflation
- Aggregate foreign currency translation adjustment on a current cost basis, if applicable
- Net assets at the end of each fiscal year on a current cost basis
- Income per common share from continuing operations on a current cost basis
- Cash dividends declared per common share
- Market price per common share at year-end

Each of the above disclosures included in the five-year summary of selected financial data is discussed below.

Net Sales and Other Operating Revenue

Net sales and other operating revenue for each of the five most recent years is restated in average-for-the-year units of constant purchasing power using the CPI-U.

Income from Continuing Operations on a Current Cost Basis

Income from continuing operations on a current cost basis for each of the five most recent years is computed in accordance with ASC 255 and then restated in average-for-the-year units of constant purchasing power using the CPI-U. For purposes of the minimum supplementary information, only certain items that are included in income from continuing operations in the primary financial statements have to be adjusted to compute income from continuing operations on a current cost basis. Under ASC 255, these items are adjusted to compare income from continuing operations on a current basis (ASC 255-10-50-39):

- *Cost of goods sold* Determined on a current cost basis or lower recoverable amount at the date of a sale or at the date on which resources are used on or committed to a specific contract
- *Depreciation, depletion, and amortization* Determined based on the average current cost of the assets' service potentials or lower recoverable amounts during the period of use

All other revenue, expenses, gains, and losses that are included in the primary financial statements are not adjusted in computing income from continuing operations on a current cost basis.

Income tax expense that is included in the primary financial statements is not adjusted in computing income from continuing operations on a current cost basis (ASC 255-10-50-41). Disclosure must be made in the minimum supplementary information to the effect that income tax expense for the current period is presented at its historical cost.

Purchasing Power Gain or Loss on Net Monetary Items

The purchasing power gain or loss on net monetary items for each of the five most recent years is computed and then restated in average-for-the-year units of constant purchasing power using the CPI-U. The purchasing power gain or loss on net monetary items is determined by restating in units of constant purchasing power the opening and closing balances of, and transactions in, monetary assets and monetary liabilities (ASC 255-10-50-50).

Increase or Decrease in Inventory, Property, Plant, and Equipment at Current Costs

The increase or decrease in current costs for inventory and property, plant, and equipment for each of the five most recent years must be restated in average-for-the-year units of constant purchasing power using the CPI-U. The increase or decrease in the current cost amounts represents the difference between the measures of the assets at their entry dates for the year and at their exit dates for the year. The entry date is the beginning of the year or the date of acquisition, whichever is applicable. The exit date is the end of the year or the date of use, sale, or commitment to a specific contract, whichever is applicable (ASC 255-10-50-42).

The increase or decrease in the current cost amounts of inventory, property, plant, and equipment for the five-year summary is reported after the effects of each year's general inflation. The increase or decrease in the current cost amounts for the current year is reported both before and after the effects of general inflation (ASC 255-10-50-43).

Aggregate Foreign Currency Translation Adjustment (if Applicable)

The aggregate foreign currency translation adjustment (if applicable) for each of the five most recent years is computed on a current cost basis and then restated in average-for-the-year units of constant purchasing power using the CPI-U.

Current cost information for operations measured in a foreign functional currency is measured either (*a*) after translation and based on the CPI-U (the translate-restate method) or (*b*) before translation and based on a broad measure of the change in the general purchasing power of the functional currency (the restate-translate method). In this event, the same method must be used for all operations measured in foreign functional currencies and for all periods presented. ASC 255-10-55-66, 67-70 and ASC 255-10-55-78, 79-80 contain illustrative calculations of current cost/constant purchasing power information (ASC 255-10-50-45, 46).

Net Assets at End of Each Fiscal Year

For purposes of the minimum supplementary information required by ASC 255, net assets at the end of each fiscal year are equal to all of the net assets appearing in the basic historical cost financial statements except that inventories, property, plant, and equipment are included at their current costs or at a lower recoverable amount. (Total net assets at historical cost less inventories, property, plant, and equipment at historical cost, plus inventories, property, plant, and equipment at current costs or lower recoverable amounts, equals net assets as encouraged by ASC 255.) The amount computed for net assets at end of each fiscal year is then restated in average-for-the-year units of constant purchasing power using the CPI-U (ASC 255-10-50-34).

When comprehensive restatement of financial statements is made in lieu of the minimum supplementary information, net assets for the five-year summary of selected financial data may be reported at the same amount shown in the comprehensive restated financial statements (ASC 255-10-50-35).

Income per Common Share from Continuing Operations on a Current Cost Basis

Income per common share from continuing operations for each of the five most recent years is computed and then restated in average-for-the-year units of constant purchasing power using the CPI-U. Income per common share from continuing operations on a current cost basis is found by dividing the outstanding number of shares of common stock into the total restated income from continuing operations on a current cost basis.

Cash Dividends Declared per Common Share

Cash dividends declared per common share for each of the five most recent years are restated in average-for-the-year units of constant purchasing power using the CPI-U.

Market Price per Common Share at Year-End

Market price per common share at year-end for each of the five most recent years is restated in average-for-the-year units of constant purchasing power using the CPI-U.

Average Level of CPI-U

The average level of CPI-U for each of the five most recent years is disclosed in a note to the minimum supplementary information. If an enterprise presents comprehensive current cost/constant purchasing power financial statements measured in year-end units of purchasing power, the year-end level of the CPI-U for each of the five most recent years is disclosed (ASC 255-10-50-8).

Explanatory Disclosures

An enterprise shall provide an explanation of the disclosures encouraged by ASC 255 and a discussion of their significance in the circumstances of the enterprise. These explanatory statements should be detailed sufficiently so that a user who possesses reasonable business acumen will be able to understand the information presented (ASC 255-10-50-10).

Additional Disclosures for the Current Year

If income from continuing operations as shown in the primary financial statements differs significantly from income from continuing operations determined on a current cost/constant purchasing power basis, certain other disclosures for the current year are encouraged by ASC 255 in addition to the minimum supplementary information.

Income from continuing operations for the current year on a current cost basis is computed in accordance with ASC 255 and then restated in average-for-the-year units of constant purchasing power using the CPI-U. The information for income from continuing operations for the current year on a current cost basis is presented in either a *statement format* or a *reconciliation format*, which discloses all adjustments between the supplementary information and the basic historical cost financial statements (see illustrations in ASC 255-10-55-14, 15-21). The same categories of revenue and expense that appear in the basic historical cost financial statements are used for the presentation of income from continuing operations for the current year on a current cost basis. Account classifications may be combined if they are not individually significant for restating purposes, or if the restated amounts are approximately the same as the historical cost amounts (ASC 255-10-50-12).

Income from continuing operations for the current year on a current cost basis does not include (*a*) the purchasing power gain or loss on net monetary items; (*b*) the increase or decrease in the current cost or lower recoverable amount of inventory and property, plant, and equipment, net of inflation; and (*c*) the translation adjustment (if applicable). However, an enterprise may include this information after the presentation of income from continuing operations for the current year on a current cost basis (ASC 255-10-50-14).

Only certain items that are included in income from continuing operations in the primary financial statements have to be adjusted to compute income from continuing operations for the current year on a current cost basis. Under ASC 255, these items are (ASC 255-10-50-39):

- *Cost of goods sold* Determined on a current cost basis or lower recoverable amount at the date of sale or at the date on which resources are used on or committed to a specific contract
- *Depreciation, depletion, and amortization* Determined based on the average current cost of the assets' service potentials or lower recoverable amounts during the period of use

Other revenues, expenses, gains, and losses that are included in the primary financial statements are not adjusted and may be measured at amounts included in those statements.

Income tax expense that is included in the primary financial statements is not adjusted in computing income from continuing operations for the current year on a current cost basis (ASC 255-10-50-41). Disclosure must be made in the minimum supplementary information to the effect that income tax expense for the current period is presented at its historical cost.

Disclosure must also include (ASC 255-10-50-16):

- Separate amounts for the current cost or lower recoverable amount at the end of the current year of (*a*) inventory and (*b*) property, plant, and equipment.
- The increase or decrease in current cost or lower recoverable amount before and after adjusting for the effects of inflation of (*a*) inventory and (*b*) property, plant, and equipment.
- The principal types and sources of information used to calculate current costs for the current year.
- The differences, if any, in depreciation methods, useful lives, and salvage values used in (*a*) the primary financial statements and (*b*) the disclosure of current cost information for the current year.

Specialized Assets

Timberlands, growing timber, mineral ore bodies, proved oil and gas reserves, income-producing real estate, and motion picture films are classified as specialized assets. Specialized assets are considered unique, and the determination of their current costs frequently is difficult, if not impossible. For example, the current cost of an existing oil field may be difficult to determine because the oil field is one of a kind and cannot be duplicated. Yet, the definition of current cost is the current cost to purchase or reproduce the specific asset, and the current cost of property that is owned is the current cost of acquiring an asset that will perform or produce in a manner similar to that of the owned property.

ASC 255 provides special rules for determining the current costs of specialized assets. As a substitute for the current cost amounts and related expenses, the historical cost amounts of specialized assets may be adjusted for changes in specific prices by the use of a broad index of general purchasing power (ASC 255-10-50-32).

PRACTICE NOTE: ASC 255 provides additional guidance on reporting the effects of changing prices on timber assets and mineral resource assets, but does not provide similar guidance for other types of specialized assets.

Timber Assets

In the event an enterprise estimates the current cost of growing timber and timber harvested by adjusting historical costs for changes in specific prices, the historical costs may include either (*a*) only costs that are capitalized in the primary financial statements or (*b*) all direct costs of reforestation and forest management, even if such costs are not capitalized in the primary financial statements. Reforestation and forest management costs include planting, fertilization, fire protection, property taxes, and nursery stock (ASC 255-10-50-33).

Mineral Resource Assets

The requirements for determining the current cost amounts for mineral resource assets are flexible because there is no generally accepted approach for measuring the current cost of finding mineral reserves. In determining the current cost amounts of mineral resource assets, ASC 255 permits the use of specific price indexes applied to historical costs, market buying prices, and other statistical data to determine current replacement costs. ASC 255 encourages the disclosure of the types of data or information that are used to determine current cost amounts (ASC 255-10-50-30).

ASC 255 contains the following definition for mineral resource assets (ASC Glossary):

> **Mineral resource assets** Assets that are directly associated with and derive value from all minerals extracted from the earth. Such minerals include oil and gas, ores containing ferrous and nonferrous metals, coal, shale, geothermal steam, sulphur, salt, stone, phosphate, sand, and gravel. Mineral resource assets include mineral interests in properties, completed and uncompleted wells, and related equipment and facilities, and other facilities required for purposes of extraction. The definition does not cover support equipment, because that equipment is included in the property, plant, and equipment for which current cost measurements are required.

For enterprises that own significant mineral reserves, the following information on owned mineral reserves, excluding oil and gas, is encouraged to be disclosed for each of the five most recent years (ASC 255-10-50-17):

- The estimated amount of proved or of proved and probable mineral reserves on hand at the end of the year. A date during the year may be used, but the date must be disclosed.
- The estimated quantity of each significant mineral product that is commercially recoverable from the mineral reserves in the item above. The estimated quantity may be expressed in percentages or in physical units.

- The quantities of each significant mineral produced during the year. The quantity of each significant mineral produced by milling or similar processes also must be disclosed.
- The quantity of mineral reserves (proved or proved and probable) purchased or sold in place during the year.
- The average market price of each significant mineral product. If transferred within the enterprise, the equivalent market price prior to further use should be disclosed.

In classifying and detailing the above information, current industry practices should prevail.

The following procedures shall be used in determining the quantities of mineral reserves that should be reported (ASC 255-10-50-18):

- In consolidated financial statements, 100% of the quantities of mineral reserves attributable to both the parent company and all consolidated subsidiaries shall be reported regardless of whether a subsidiary is partially or wholly owned.
- In a proportionately consolidated investment, an investor shall include only its proportionate share of the investor's mineral reserves.
- Mineral reserve quantities attributable to an investment accounted for by the equity method shall not be included at all. If significant, however, the mineral reserve quantities should be reported separately by the investor.

CHAPTER 11

ASC 260—EARNINGS PER SHARE

CONTENTS

PART I: GENERAL GUIDANCE

ASC 260-10: OVERALL

OVERVIEW

Earnings per share (EPS) is an important measure of corporate performance for investors and other users of financial statements. EPS figures are required to be presented in the income statement of publicly held companies and are presented in a manner consistent with the captions included in the income statement. Certain securities, such as convertible bonds, some preferred stocks, and stock options, permit their holders to become common stockholders or add to the number of shares of common stock already held. When potential reduction, called *dilution,* of EPS figures is inherent in a company's capital structure, a dual presentation of EPS is required—basic EPS and diluted EPS.

PRACTICE NOTE: Potential dilution refers to any situation where the reporting entity has sold or otherwise relinquished its authority to issue additional shares of stock. For example, in the case of a convertible bond or preferred stock, the holder of that security has the authority to decide whether additional shares of common stock are issued via the conversion of the convertible security. In the case of stock options, the holder of the options has the authority to decide whether additional shares of stock are acquired. In these cases, when additional shares of stock are issued, the potential exists for EPS to decline, leading to the requirements to disclose both basic and diluted EPS. A useful way to think about the dual presentation is that basic EPS is a historical number based on the actual experience of the company and diluted EPS is a pro-forma amount that reflects what might have been had additional shares of stock been issued in prior periods.

BACKGROUND

EPS figures are used to evaluate the past operating performance of a business in evaluating its potential and in making investment decisions. EPS figures are commonly presented in prospectuses, proxy material, and financial reports to shareholders. They are also used in the compilation of business earnings data for the press, statistical services, and other publications. Stock prices are presented on a per-share basis. EPS figures are believed to be of value in assisting investors in weighing the significance of a corporation's current net income and of changes in its net income from period to period in relation to the shares the investor holds or may acquire.

The U.S. guidance on EPS codified in ASC 260 was issued at the same time as IAS-33 (Earnings per Share) and includes provisions that are substantially the same. ASC 260 applies to entities with publicly held common stock or potential common stock (e.g., financial instruments or contracts that could result in the issuance of additional shares). It simplified existing standards for computing EPS by replacing primary earnings per share with basic EPS and by altering the calculation of diluted EPS, which replaced fully diluted EPS.

SIMPLE AND COMPLEX CAPITAL STRUCTURES

ASC 260 applies to all entities that have issued common stock or potential common stock that trades in a public market (i.e., in a stock exchange or in an over-the-counter market, including securities that trade only locally or regionally). *Potential common stock* consists of other securities and contractual arrangements that may result in the issuance of common stock in the future, such as (ASC 260-10-15-2):

- Options
- Warrants
- Convertible securities
- Contingent stock agreements

Additional guidance on the applicability of ASC 260 includes the following (ASC 260-10-15-3):

- The standard applies in situations in which an entity has made a filing, or is in the process of making a filing, with a regulatory agency in anticipation of selling securities in the future.

- The standard does *not* require the presentation of EPS by investment companies or in financial statements of wholly owned subsidiaries.
- The standard applies to entities that are not required to present EPS but choose to do so.

For purposes of presenting earnings per share, a distinction is made between enterprises with a simple capital structure and those with a complex capital structure.

Simple Capital Structures

A simple capital structure is one that consists of capital stock and includes no potential for dilution via conversions, exercise of options, or other arrangements that would increase the number of shares outstanding. For organizations with simple capital structures, the presentation of EPS using assumed income numbers and 50,000 shares of common stock outstanding in the income statement would appear as follows:

	20X9	*20X8*
Net income	$190,000	$160,000
Earnings per common share:		
Net income per share ($190÷50), ($160÷50)	$3.80	$3.20

Complex Capital Structures

For organizations with complex capital structures, two EPS figures are presented with equal prominence on the face of the income statement. The captions for the two EPS figures are "Earnings per common share" and "Earnings per common share—assuming dilution" (or other similar descriptions).

The first of these captions is commonly referred to as *basic EPS* and the second as *diluted EPS*. The difference between basic EPS and diluted EPS is that basic EPS considers only outstanding common stock, whereas diluted EPS incorporates the potential dilution from all potentially dilutive securities that would have reduced EPS.

Based on the information presented in the previous section and assuming 60,000 shares of stock outstanding for basic EPS and 75,000 for diluted EPS, EPS for a complex capital structure might appear as follows, immediately following net income:

	20X9	*20X8*
Earnings per common share	$ 3.17	$ 2.67
Earnings per share assuming dilution	$ 2.53	$ 2.13

Following are the general principles related to the computation of diluted EPS. These are discussed further and reflected in illustrations that make up the remainder of this chapter.

PRACTICE NOTE: The basic EPS calculation is based on historical numbers as they are reflected in the primary financial statements (e.g., net income, number of outstanding shares). Diluted EPS, on the other hand, incorporates the potential impact on EPS of the issuances of shares that have not occurred at the time of the financial statements. Diluted EPS is a conservative and hypothetical number for EPS that projects the impact of certain transactions that could occur in the future (e.g., issuance of common stock pursuant to convertible preferred stock or bonds, exercise of stock options). Typically, the responsibility for these projected transactions has been transferred to investors and others outside management through previous transactions. Because diluted EPS is based on transactions that have not yet occurred, certain assumptions are required, as reflected in the issuance of shares of stock via convertible instruments, stock options, and other contractual arrangements.

The computation of diluted EPS is similar to basic EPS except that the denominator is increased by the number of additional shares that would have been outstanding if potential common shares had been issued. The numerator is also adjusted to reflect the impact of the issuance of the additional shares. (ASC 260-10-45-16)

Options, Warrants and the Treasury Stock Method—The dilutive effect of outstanding options and warrants is reflected in diluted EPS by applying the treasury stock method in most situations. The treasury stock method involves a three-step process:

1. Exercise of the options and warrants is assumed at the beginning of the period (or at the time of issuance, if later) and common shares are assumed to be issued.
2. The proceeds from the sale of shares are assumed to be used to purchase common stock at the average market price during the period.
3. The incremental shares (i.e., the difference between the number of shares issued in Step 1 and the number of shares purchased in Step 2) are the additional shares included in the denominator of the diluted EPS calculation. (ASC 260-10-45-23)

Applying the Treasury Stock Method in Interim Statements—The number of incremental shares included in quarterly diluted EPS is computed using the average market price during the three months of the reporting period. For year-to-date diluted EPS, the number of incremental shares in the denominator is determined by computing the year-to-date weighted average of the number of incremental shares included in each quarterly diluted EPS computation. (ASC 260-10-55-3)

Åverage Market Price—The average market price of common stock shall represent a meaningful average. Theoretically, every market transaction for an entity's common stock could be included in determining the average. As a practical expedient, a simple average of weekly or monthly prices usually is considered adequate. (ASC 260-20-55-4) Generally, closing market prices are adequate for use in computing average market prices. However, when prices fluctuate widely, an average of high and low prices for the period produces a more representative price. The method used to compute the average market price shall be used consistently unless it is no longer representative because of changed conditions. (ASC 260-10-55-5)

Convertible Securities and the If-Converted Method—The dilutive effect of convertible securities is reflected in diluted EPS by the if-converted method. For convertible preferred stock, the preferred dividends applicable to the convertible preferred stock is added to the numerator. For convertible debt, interest charges applicable to the convertible debt is added back in the numerator. (However, for convertible debt for which the principal is required to be paid in cash, interest charges are not added back in the numerator.) For convertible debt, the numerator adjustment is made on a net-of-tax basis. Convertible instruments are assumed to have been converted at the beginning of the period (or at the time of issuance, if later), and the resulting number of common shares is included in the denominator. (ASC 260-10-45-40)

Variable Denominator—Changes in the entity's share price may affect the exercise price of a financial instrument or the number of shares that would be used to settle the financial instrument. For example, when the principal of a convertible debt instrument is required to be settled in cash but the conversion premium is settled in shares, the number of shares to be included in the diluted EPS denominator is affected by the entity's share price. In applying both the treasury stock and the if-converted method in calculating diluted EPS, the average market price is used for purposes of calculating the denominator for diluted EPS when the number of shares that may be issued is variable. (ASC 260-10-45-21A)

Contingently Convertible Securities—Contingently convertible instruments are included in EPS regardless of whether the market price trigger has been met. There is no substantive economic difference between contingently convertible instruments and convertible instruments with a market price premium. As a result, the treatment in diluted EPS does not differ because of a contingent market price trigger. (ASC 260-10-45-44)

Contracts That May Be Settled in Stock or Cash—The effect of potential shares settlement is included in the diluted EPS calculation for instruments that are otherwise to be settled in cash and that contain a provision that require or permit share settlement. An example of this type of instrument is a written call option that gives the holder a choice of settling in common stock or cash. (ASC 260-10-45-45)

Anti-dilution—The assumption of shares having been issued is not made where the resulting calculation would increase rather than reduce diluted EPS.

CALCULATING EPS

Objectives and General Guidance

The objectives and general approach for measuring basic and diluted EPS are presented in Table 11-1:

Table 11-1: Basic EPS vs. Diluted EPS

	Basic EPS	*Diluted EPS*
Objective	To measure the performance of an entity over the reporting period based on its outstanding common stock	To measure the performance of an entity over the reporting period based on its outstanding common stock and after giving effect to all dilutive potential common shares that were outstanding during the period
Computation	Income attributable to common stock ÷ Weighted average number of common shares outstanding	(Income attributable to common stock + Adjustments for changes in income [loss] that are consistent with the issuance of dilutive potential common shares) ÷ (Weighted average number of common shares outstanding + Dilutive potential common shares)

Additional guidelines for determining *basic EPS* are as follows (ASC 260-10-45-10, 11, 12, 13):

- Shares issued and acquired (e.g., treasury stock) during the period are weighted for the portion of the period they were outstanding.
- The amount of income (or loss) attributable to common stock is reduced (or increased) by dividends declared on preferred stock (whether or not paid) and by dividends on cumulative preferred stock (whether or not declared or paid).
- Contingently issuable shares (i.e., shares that are issuable for little or no cash consideration upon the satisfaction of certain conditions) are treated as outstanding and included in computing basic EPS as of the date that the conditions required for their issuance have been satisfied.

Additional guidelines for computing *diluted EPS* are as follows (ASC 260-10-45-16, 21):

- The denominator is similar to that for basic EPS, except that dilutive potential common shares are added.
- Numerator adjustments are required that are consistent with the assumed issuance of dilutive potential common shares. For example, if shares issuable upon conversion of a convertible bond are added to the denominator, the after-tax interest savings is added to the numerator.
- The denominator of diluted EPS is based on the most advantageous conversion rate or exercise price from the standpoint of the security holder (i.e., the maximum number of shares that would be issued).
- Once EPS figures have been published, they are not retroactively restated for subsequent conversions or changes in the market price of the common stock.

When computing both basic and diluted EPS in consolidated financial statements, if one or more less-than-wholly owned subsidiaries are included in the consolidated group, the income attributable to the noncontrolling interest is excluded from income from continuing operations and net income (ASC 260-10-45-11A).

Illustration of Determining Weighted-Average Shares

Common stock outstanding, 1/1/20X9	200,000 shares
Preferred stock (convertible into 2 shares of common stock) outstanding, 1/1/20X9	50,000 shares
Convertible debentures (convertible into 100 shares of common stock for each $1,000 bond)	$100,000

On March 31, ABC reacquired 5,000 shares of its own common stock.

On May 1, 20,000 shares of ABC preferred stock were converted into common stock.

On July 1, $50,000 of ABC convertible debentures was converted into common stock.

On September 30, ABC reacquired 5,000 shares of its common stock.

Computation of Weighted-Average Shares

1.	Common stock outstanding, 1/1/X9	200,000
2.	Common stock reacquired, 3/31/X9 (5,000 × 9/12)	(3,750)
3.	Conversion of preferred stock on 5/1/X9 (20,000 × 2 × 8/12)	26,667
4.	Conversion of convertible debentures on 7/1/X9 (50 × 100 × 6/12)	2,500
5.	Common stock reacquired on 9/30/X9 (5,000 × 3/12)	(1,250)
	Total weighted average shares, 20X9	224,167

1. **Common stock outstanding** Because the 200,000 shares of common stock were outstanding for the entire year, all the shares are included in the weighted average shares.
2. **Common stock reacquired** On March 31, 20X9, 5,000 shares were reacquired, which means that 9/12 of the year they were not outstanding. Since the 5,000 shares are already included in the 200,000 shares (1. above), that portion which was not outstanding during the full year is deducted. 9/12 of the 5,000 shares, or 3,750 shares, are excluded from the computations, which means that only 196,250 of the 200,000 shares were outstanding for the full year.
3. **Conversion of preferred** On May 1, 20X9, 20,000 shares of the preferred were converted into common stock. Since the conversion rate is 2 for 1, an additional 40,000 shares were outstanding from May 1 to the end of the year. 8/12 of the 40,000 shares, or 26,667 shares, are included in the weighted average shares outstanding for the year.
4. **Conversion of convertible debentures** On July 1, 20X9, $50,000 of the convertible debentures were converted into common stock. The conversion rate is 100 shares for each $1,000 bond, which means that the $50,000 converted consisted of fifty $1,000 bonds, or 5,000 shares of common stock. Since the conversion was on July 1, only 6/12 of the 5,000 shares, or 2,500 shares, are included in the weighted average shares outstanding for the year.
5. **Common stock reacquired** 5,000 additional shares out of the 200,000 shares outstanding at the beginning of the year were reacquired on September 30, which means that for 3/12 of the year they were not outstanding. 3/12 of 5,000 shares, or 1,250 shares, are excluded from the computation of weighted average shares outstanding for the year.

Stock splits or stock dividends (or reverse splits or dividends) are retroactively recognized in all periods presented in the financial statements. A stock split or stock dividend is recognized if it occurs after the close of the period but before issuance of the financial statements. If this situation occurs, it must be disclosed in the statements. Also, the dividends per share must be reported in terms of the equivalent number of shares outstanding at the time the dividend is declared.

Antidilution

The term *antidilution* refers to increases in EPS or decreases in loss per share. Diluted EPS computed in accordance with ASC 260 is intended to be a conservative measure of performance and, accordingly, is intended to reflect the potential reduction in EPS resulting from issuance of additional common shares. Thus, potential issuances that would increase EPS or reduce loss per share generally are excluded from the calculation.

Illustration of Antidilution

A company reports net income of $100,000 and has 50,000 shares of outstanding common stock. Basic EPS is $2.00 ($100,000/50,000 shares). The same company has 15,000 shares of potential common stock.

Situation 1

Assume the numerator adjustment for the potential common shares is +$15,000. Including these potential common shares, EPS is computed as follows:

$$\frac{\$100{,}000 + \$15{,}000}{50{,}000 + 15{,}000} \quad \frac{\$115{,}000}{65{,}000} \quad = \$1.77 \text{ per share}$$

In this situation, the potential common shares are *dilutive* (i.e., they reduce EPS), and diluted EPS is $1.77.

Situation 2

Assume the numerator adjustment for the potential common shares is +$50,000. Including these potential common shares, EPS is computed as follows:

$$\frac{\$100{,}000 + \$50{,}000}{50{,}000 + 15{,}000} \quad \frac{\$150{,}000}{65{,}000} \quad = \$2.31 \text{ per share}$$

In this situation, the potential common shares are *antidilutive* (i.e., they increase EPS), and would not be included in diluted EPS.

In applying the antidilution provisions of ASC 260, the following guidelines are important (ASC 260-10-45-17, 18):

- In determining whether potential common shares are dilutive or antidilutive, each issue or series of issues of potential common shares is considered separately.
- In cases in which multiple issuances of potential common shares exist, one may be dilutive on its own but antidilutive when combined with other potential common shares. To reflect maximum dilution, each issue or series of issues of potential common shares is considered in sequence, starting with the most dilutive and moving to the least dilutive.
- An entity may report more than one income figure in its income statement (e.g., income from continuing operations and net income). For purposes of determining whether potential common stock is dilutive, income from continuing operations is the control number for determining antidilution.

Once an issue or series of issues of potential common shares is determined to be *dilutive* using the appropriate income figure, that issue or series of issues is considered to be outstanding in computing diluted EPS on all income amounts, even if it is *antidilutive* in one or more of those amounts. Similarly, once an issue or series of issues of potential common shares is determined to be antidilutive using the appropriate income figure, that issue or series of issues is omitted in computing diluted EPS on all income amounts, even if it would have been dilutive in one or more of those amounts.

Options and Warrants

The dilutive effect of options and warrants generally is determined by the *treasury stock method* (ASC 260-10-45-23). That method involves three interrelated steps, as follows:

Step 1: Exercise is assumed to have taken place and common shares are assumed to have been issued.

Step 2: The proceeds from the issuance of common stock are assumed to have been used to purchase treasury stock at the average market price for the period.

Step 3: The incremental shares issued (i.e., shares sold in Step 1 reduced by share repurchased in Step 2) are added to the denominator of the diluted EPS computation.

Illustration of Application of the Treasury Stock Method

By dividing its $100,000 net income by 100,000 shares of outstanding common stock, a company determines its basic EPS to be $1. In addition, options are outstanding that permit the purchase of 10,000 shares of common stock at $25. The average market price of the stock is $40. The treasury stock method is applied as follows:

Step 1: 10,000 shares sold at $25: 10,000 × $25 = $250,000 in proceeds

Step 2: $250,000 used to purchase treasury stock at $40: $250,000 / $40 = 6,250

Step 3: Net increase in outstanding shares: 10,000 – 6,250 = 3,750

Diluted EPS is computed as follows:

$$\frac{\$100{,}000}{100{,}000 + 3{,}750} = \$.96$$

Under this method, options and warrants will have a dilutive effect on EPS when the average market price of the stock (used for assumed repurchase in Step 2) exceeds the issuance price (used for assumed sale in Step 1), because of an assumed net increase in the number of outstanding shares. In this situation, options and warrants are described as "in the money." When options and warrants are outstanding for only part of the period, the amount determined by applying the treasury stock method is weighted for the part of the period the options and warrants were outstanding.

The rationale behind the treasury stock method is that any number of shares of common stock that could have been purchased on the open market with the exercised price funds from the options or similar instruments are not additional outstanding stock and have no dilutive effect on EPS.

PRACTICE POINTER: A shortcut method of calculating the net increase in the number of outstanding shares of common stock by the treasury stock method is as follows:

$$\text{Incremental shares outstanding} \quad \frac{M - E}{M} \quad \times \text{ Number of shares obtainable}$$

where M = the market price and E = the exercise price. For example, assume a company has 10,000 options outstanding that permit the purchase of 1 share of common stock each at $16. The average market price is $25. Applying the three-step process of the treasury stock method indicates a net increase of 3,600 shares:

1. Proceeds = 10,000 × $16 = $160,000
2. Repurchase of shares = $160,000/25 = 6,400 shares
3. Net increase = 10,000 – 6,400 = 3,600 shares

The shortcut calculation is as follows:

$$\frac{\$25 - \$16}{\$25} \times \$10{,}000 = 3{,}600$$

When the market price of common stock rises significantly during the year, computation of the weighted average on a quarterly basis is preferred.

Illustration of Computation of Incremental Shares for Stock Options and Similar Instruments

A company has 10,000 stock options outstanding, which are exercisable at $60 each. Given the following market prices, determine the incremental shares by quarters, and the number of shares that are included in diluted EPS.

	Quarters			
	1	*2*	*3*	*4*
Average market price	56	64	70	68
Ending market price	60	68	72	64

Determining the incremental shares by quarters for diluted EPS follows:

1st quarter: no calculation*	=	0
2nd quarter: $10{,}000 - \left[\frac{10{,}000 \times \$60}{\$64}\right]$	=	625
3nd quarter: $10{,}000 - \left[\frac{10{,}000 \times \$60}{\$70}\right]$	=	1,429
4th quarter: $10{,}000 - \left[\frac{10{,}000 \times \$60}{\$68}\right]$	=	1,176
Total incremental shares	=	3,230
Divided by 4 quarters (3,230 ÷ 4)	=	808

* The exercise price of $60 is higher than the average market price.

The total is divided by four quarters because four quarters entered into the computation. The 808 shares are included in the computation of diluted EPS.

Share-Based Payment Arrangements and Awards of Share Options and Nonvested Shares

Fixed awards and nonvested stock to be issued to an employee under a stock-based compensation plan are considered options for purposes of computing diluted EPS. Guidelines for including these arrangements in diluted EPS are (ASC 260-10-45-15):

- They are considered to be outstanding as of the grant date, even though their exercise may be contingent upon vesting.
- They are included even if the employee may not receive the stock until some future date.
- Their impact is determined by applying the treasury stock method, and they are included only if their impact is dilutive.

In applying the treasury stock method, an important determination is the amount of proceeds due the issuing entity. ASC 260 identifies three components of the amount of proceeds from stock-based compensation arrangements:

1. The amount, if any, the employee must pay
2. The amount of compensation cost attributed to future services and not yet recognized
3. The amount of current and deferred tax benefits, if any, that would be credited to additional paid-in capital upon exercise of the options

The dilutive effect of outstanding call options and warrants is reflected in diluted EPS by applying the treasury stock method with certain exceptions. Equivalents of options and warrants include nonvested stock granted under a share-based payment arrangement, stock purchase contracts, and partially paid stock subscriptions. Antidilutive contracts, such as purchased put options and purchased call options, are excluded from diluted EPS. (ASC 260-10-45-22)

Awards of share options and nonvested shares to be issued to a grantee under a share-based payment arrangement are considered options for purposes of computing diluted EPS. Such share-based awards are considered to be outstanding as of the grant date for purposes of computing diluted EPS even though their exercise may be contingent upon vesting. They are included in the diluted EPS computation even if the grantee may not receive or be able to sell the stock until some future date. The dilutive effect of a share-based payment arrangement is computed using the treasury stock method. (ASC 260-10-45-28A) The provisions in ASC 260-10-45-28A through 45-31 apply to share-based awards issued to grantees under a share-based payment arrangement in exchange for goods and services or as consideration payable to a customer. (ASC 260-10-45-28)

If an entity issues a contract that may be settled in common stock or in cash at the election of either the entity or the holder, the determination of whether that contract is reflected in the computation of diluted EPS is made based on facts available each period. It should be presumed that the contract will be settled in common stock and the resulting potential common shares included in diluted EPS if the effect is more dilutive. (ASC 260-10-45-45)

These paragraphs make several other important observations. First, if stock-based compensation arrangements are payable in common stock or in cash at the discretion of either the employee or the employer, the determination of whether they are potential common shares is based on the guidance in ASC 260-10-45-45 (covered below). Second, if the plan permits the employee to choose between types of equity instruments, diluted EPS is computed based on the terms used in the computation of compensation expense for the period. Finally, performance awards and targeted stock price options are subject to ASC 260's provisions on contingently issuable shares (covered below).

Illustration of Application of Treasury Stock Method to a Share-Based Payment Arrangement

Entity H adopted a share option plan on January 1, 20X8, and granted 500,000 at-the-money share options with an exercise price of $25. On that date, the fair value of each share option granted was $16.33. All share options vest at the end of five years (cliff vesting). At the grant date, Entity H assumes an annual forfeiture rate of 2% and therefore expects to receive the requisite service for 451,960 [500,000 × $(.98^5)$] share options. Employees forfeited 8,000 stock options ratably during 20X8. Thus, the weighted average number of share options outstanding in 20X8 equaled 496,000 [(500,000 + 492,000)/2]. The average stock price during 20X8 is $40, and there are 15,000,000 weighted-average common shares outstanding for the year. Net income for the period is $50,000,000 (inclusive of share-based compensation). Entity H's tax rate is 35%.

Entity H has sufficient previously recognized excess tax benefits in additional paid-in capital from prior share-based payment arrangements to offset any write-off of deferred tax assets associated with its grant of share options on January 1, 20X8. All share options are the type that upon exercise give rise to deductible compensation cost for income tax purposes.

Computation of Basic EPS for the Year Ended 12/31/20X8:

Net income	$50,000,000
Weighted-average common shares outstanding	15,000,000
Basic earnings per share	$ 3.33

Computation of average unrecognized compensation cost in 20X8:

Beginning of period:		
Unrecognized compensation cost (500,000 × $16.33)		$8,165,000
End of period:		
Beginning unrecognized compensation cost	$8,165,000	
Annual compensation cost recognized during 20X8, based on estimated forfeitures [(451,960 × $16.33) / 3]	(2,460,169)	
Annual compensation cost not recognized during the period related to outstanding options at 12/31/20X8, for which service is not expected to be rendered [(492,000 – 451,960) × $16.33) / 3]	(217,951)	
Total compensation cost of actual forfeited options (8,000 × $16.33)	(130,640)	
Total unrecognized compensation cost at end of period, based on actual forfeitures		5,356,240
Average total unrecognized compensation, based on actual forfeitures [(8,165,000 + 5,356,240) / 2]		$6,760,620

Computation of tax benefit:

Total compensation cost of average outstanding options (496,000 × $16.33)	$8,099,680
Intrinsic value of average outstanding options for the year ended 12/31/20X8 [496,000 × ($40 – $25)]	(7,440,000)
Excess of total compensation cost over estimated tax deduction	659,680
Tax benefit deficiency ($659,680 × .35)	$ 230,888

Computation of assumed proceeds for diluted earnings per share:

Amount employees would pay if the weighted-average number of options outstanding were exercised using the average exercise price (496,000 × $25)	$12,400,000
Average unrecognized compensation cost in 20X8 (see above calculation)	6,760,620
Tax benefit deficiency that would be offset in paid-in capital (see above calculation)	(230,888)
Assumed proceeds	$18,929,732

Assumed repurchase of shares:

Repurchase shares at average market price during the year ($18,929,732 ÷ $40)	473,243
Incremental shares (496,000 – 473,243)	22,757

Computation of Diluted EPS for the Year Ended 12/31/20X8:

Net income		$50,000,000
Weighted-average common shares outstanding	15,000,000	
Incremental shares	22,757	
Total shares outstanding		15,022,757
Diluted earnings per share ($50,000,000 ÷ 15,022,757)		$ 3.328

Written Put Options and Purchased Options

Certain contracts may require an entity to repurchase its own stock. Examples are written put options and forward purchase contracts other than forward purchase contracts accounted for as a liability according to ASC 480, *Distinguishing Liabilities from Equity*. These contracts are reflected in the calculation of diluted EPS if their effect is dilutive when the *reverse treasury stock method* is applied. As the name implies, that method is the reverse of the treasury stock method for requirements to repurchase, rather than issue, shares of common stock in stock option plans (ASC 260-10-45-35).

The steps in the reverse treasury stock method are analogous to those in the treasury stock method:

Step 1: Assume that enough common shares were issued at the average market price to raise enough proceeds to satisfy the contract.

Step 2: The proceeds are assumed to be used to buy back the shares required in the contract.

Step 3: The increase in number of shares (i.e., shares sold in Step 1 reduced by the shares purchased in Step 2) is added to the denominator of the diluted EPS computation.

Applying the reverse treasury stock method results in dilution of EPS if the options are "in the money" (i.e., the exercise price is above the average market price).

Illustration of the Reverse Treasury Stock Method

Ranalli's Lawn Service International (RLSI) has sold 10,000 put options at an exercise price of $40 per option. The average market price of RLSI's common stock during 20X8 is $25 per share. RLSI would apply the reverse treasury stock method as follows:

Step 1: RLSI needs to raise $400,000 (10,000 × $40) to satisfy its obligation under the put contract. In order to raise $400,000, RLSI must sell 16,000 shares of common stock, given the average market price per share of its stock during 20X8 ($400,000 ÷ $25 = 16,000 shares).

Step 2: It is assumed that the $400,000 will be used to buy back the 10,000 shares, at $40 per share, per the terms of the put options written by RLSI.

Step 3: The 6,000 increase in the number of shares outstanding (16,000 shares issued from Step 1 minus the 10,000 shares repurchased from Step 2) are added to the denominator in calculating diluted EPS.

Contracts held by an entity on its own stock (e.g., purchased put options and purchased call options) are not included in the determination of diluted EPS, because to do so would be antidilutive due to the reduced number of outstanding shares (ASC 260-10-45-37).

Convertible Securities

Incorporating the dilutive effect of convertible securities into EPS figures requires application of the *if-converted method* (ASC 260-10-45-40). The method derives its name from the underlying assumption that both the numerator and the denominator of the EPS calculation are restated to what they would have been if the convertible security had already been converted into common stock for the period. This usually requires the numerator to be adjusted for the amount of the preferred dividend (convertible preferred stock) or the interest expense (convertible debt instrument).

Specific guidelines for applying the if-converted method are as follows:

- For convertible preferred stock, the amount of the preferred dividend deducted in determining income attributable to common stockholders is added back in the numerator.
- For convertible debt securities, the numerator is adjusted for the following:
  - — Interest charges applicable to the security are added back to the numerator.
  - — To the extent nondiscretionary adjustments based on income would have been computed differently if the interest on convertible debt had never been recognized, the numerator is adjusted appropriately (e.g., for profit-sharing and royalty arrangements).
  - — The above adjustments are made net-of-tax.
- Convertible preferred stock and convertible debt are treated as having been converted at the beginning of the period or at the time of issuance, if later.
- Conversion is not assumed if the effect is antidilutive. (This effect occurs when the preferred dividend per common share or the interest net of tax and nondiscretionary adjustments per common share exceeds basic EPS.)

Illustration of the If-Converted Method

A company had $100,000 of net income for the year and 100,000 shares of common stock outstanding. Consider the following two independent situations:

Situation 1

25,000 shares of 6%, $10 par-value convertible preferred stock are outstanding, and are convertible into 25,000 shares of common stock.

Basic EPS: $\frac{\$100,000 - \$15,000^*}{\$100,000 \text{ shares}} = \frac{\$85,000}{100,000} = \$.85$

* Preferred dividend = 25,000 shares × $10 par × .06.

Diluted EPS: $\frac{\$100,000 + \$15,000 - \$15,000}{100,000 + 25,000 \text{ shares}} = \frac{\$100,000}{125,000} = \$.80$

Explanation: The $15,000 preferred dividend is deducted to determine basic EPS. To determine diluted EPS, the preferred dividend is added back to the numerator, and the 25,000 equivalent common shares are added to the denominator. This reduces EPS from $.85 to $.80.

Situation 2

100 convertible bonds, 10%, 1,000 par value, are outstanding, and each is convertible into 150 shares of common stock. The income tax rate is 35%, and interest already has been deducted in determining net income.

Basic EPS: $\frac{\$100,000}{\$100,000 \text{ shares}} = \$1.00$

Diluted EPS: $\frac{\$100,000 + \$6,500^*}{100,000 + (100 \times 150) \text{ shares}} = \frac{\$106,500}{115,000} = \$.93$

* After-tax interest: (100 bonds × $1,000 par × .10) × (1–.35).

Explanation: Basic EPS is calculated based on $100,000 of net income and 100,000 shares of common stock outstanding. To include the dilutive effect of the convertible bonds in diluted EPS, the after-tax effect of the interest is added to the numerator (i.e., interest that would have been avoided and the accompanying increase in income taxes), and the equivalent number of common shares (150 per bond × 100 bonds = 15,000) is added to the denominator. The impact is a reduction in EPS from $1.00 to $.93.

Down Round Feature

An entity may issue a freestanding financial instrument with a down round feature classified as equity. A down round feature reduces the strike price of an issued financial instrument if the issuer sells shares of its stock for an amount less than the currently stated strike price of the issued financial instrument or issues an equity-linked financial instrument with a strike price below the currently stated strike price of the issued financial instrument. A down round feature may reduce the strike price of a financial instrument to the current issuance price or the reduction may be limited by a floor or on the basis of a formula that results in a price that is at a discount to the original exercise price but above the new issuance price of shares, or may reduce the strike price to below the current issuance price.

An entity that presents earnings per share in accordance with ASC 260 shall recognize the value of the effect of a down round feature in an equity-classified freestanding financial instrument and equity-classified convertible preferred stock, if the conversion features have not been bifurcated in accordance with other guidance, when the down round feature is triggered. That effect is treated as a dividend and a reduction in income available to common stockholders in basic earnings per share. (ASC 260-10-25-1)

As of the date that a down round feature is triggered, the entity measures the value of the effect of the feature as the difference between the fair value of the financial instrument and an equity-classified convertible preferred stock (if the conversion feature has not been bifurcated in accordance with other guidance). The value of the effect of the feature is the difference between the following amounts, determined immediately after the down round feature is triggered: (1) the fair value of the financial instrument (without the down round feature) with a strike price corresponding to the current strike price of the issued instrument, and (2) the fair value of the financial instrument (without the down round feature) with a strike price corresponding to the reduced strike price upon the down round feature being triggered. (ASC 260-10-30-1)

The entity shall recognize the value of the effect of a down round feature in an equity-classified convertible preferred stock each time it is triggered, but shall not otherwise subsequently remeasure its value of a feature it has recognized and measured in accordance with the previous requirement. The entity shall not subsequently amortize the amount in additional paid-in capital arising from recognizing the value of the effect of the down round feature. (ASC 260-10-35-1)

For a freestanding equity-classified financial instrument and an equity-classified convertible preferred stock with a down round feature that has not been bifurcated in accordance with other guidance, the value of the effect of the down round feature is deducted in computing income available to common stockholders when that feature has been triggered. (ASC 260-10-45-12B)

Contracts Subject to Settlement in Stock or Cash

Entities may issue a contract that allows either the entity or the holder to elect settlement in either common stock or cash. The impact of this type of arrangement on EPS is determined on the basis of the facts available each period. Usually it will be assumed that the contract will be settled in common stock if the effect of that assumption is more dilutive than an assumption that the contract will be settled in cash. If past experience or stated policy provides a reasonable basis for assuming that the contract will be settled in cash, however, the assumption that it will be settled in common stock may be overcome.

A contract that is reported as an asset or liability in the financial statements may require an adjustment to the numerator for any change in income or loss that would have taken place if the contract had been reported as an equity instrument. This is similar to the numerator adjustment for a convertible security presented earlier (i.e., the if-converted method) (ASC 260-10-45-45).

Contingently Issuable Shares

Contingently issuable shares are shares that must be issued upon the satisfaction of certain conditions. They are considered outstanding and are included in diluted EPS as follows (ASC 260-10-45-48):

- *All conditions for issuance satisfied by the end of the period*—Contingently issuable shares are included as of the beginning of the period in which the conditions were satisfied, or as of the date of the contingent stock agreement, if later.
- *All conditions for issuance not satisfied by the end of the period*—The number of contingently issuable shares included in diluted EPS is based on the number of shares, if any, that would be issuable if the end of the reporting period were the end of the contingency period.

In applying these procedures, the following guidance is provided (ASC 260-10-45-51, 52, 53, 54, 55):

Condition for Issuance of Stock	*Treatment of Contingent Issuance in Diluted EPS, If Dilutive*
Attainment or maintenance of a specified level of earnings, and that amount has been attained	Additional shares that would be issued, based on current earnings, are included in diluted EPS.
Future market price of stock	Additional shares that would be issued, based on the current market price, are included in diluted EPS.
Future earnings and market price of stock	Additional shares that would be issued, based on both current earnings and current market price of stock, are included in diluted EPS only if both conditions are met.
Condition other than earnings and/or market price of stock	Additional shares that would be issued under an assumption that the current status will remain unchanged are included in diluted EPS.
Other contingently issuable potential common shares (e.g., contingently issuable convertible securities)	Additional shares that would be issuable under current conditions based on appropriate sections of ASC 260 for options and warrants, convertible securities, and contracts that may be settled in stock or cash are included in diluted EPS.

INCOME STATEMENT PRESENTATION AND DISCLOSURE

Entities with simple capital structures (i.e., without potential common shares) and entities with complex capital structures (i.e., with potential common shares) are required to present EPS on the face of the income statement as follows (ASC 260-10-45-2):

- *Simple capital structure*—basic EPS on income from continuing operations and net income
- *Complex capital structure*—basic and diluted EPS (with equal prominence) on income from continuing operations and net income

An entity that reports discontinued operations shall include basic and diluted EPS either on the face of the income statement or in related notes. If an entity chooses to present EPS figures on other items, those figures must be in notes to the financial statements, along with an indication of whether the EPS figures are pretax or net-of-tax (ASC 260-10-45-3, 5).

Several other guidelines for the presentation of EPS figures are as follows (ASC 260-10-45-4, 7):

- EPS figures are required for all periods for which an income statement (or summary of earnings) is presented.
- If diluted EPS is presented for one period, it must be presented for all periods presented, even if it is the same as basic EPS for one or more periods.
- The terms "basic EPS" and "diluted EPS" are used in ASC 260, but are not required to be used in financial statements. Alternative titles, such as "earnings per common share" and "earnings per common share—assuming dilution" are acceptable.

PRACTICE POINTER: Per-share amounts that are not required and that an entity chooses to disclose shall be computed as indicated in ASC 260-10 and disclosed only in notes to the financial statements. This disclosure includes whether such per-share amounts are pretax or net of tax. (ASC 260-10-45-5)

In addition to specifying the EPS content on the face of the financial statement, ASC 260 also requires the following disclosures (ASC 260-10-50-1):

- A reconciliation of the numerators and denominators used to compute basic and diluted EPS for income from continuing operations or net income, as appropriate.
- The amount of preferred dividend deducted in arriving at the amount of income attributable to common stockholders.
- Potential common stock that was not included in the calculation of diluted EPS because it is antidilutive in the current period.
- Description of any transaction that occurred after the end of the most recent period that would have materially affected the number of common shares outstanding or potential common shares if the transaction had occurred before the end of the reporting period.

PRACTICE POINTER: Normally, antidilutive potential common stock is omitted in determining diluted EPS. In applying the specific provisions of ASC 260, however, there are some instances in which potential common stock that is antidilutive is required to be included. There are also instances in which potential common stock that appears to be dilutive must be excluded. Take care to include or exclude the potential common stock in determining diluted EPS, even though doing this may seem counter-intuitive to the assumptions and intent underlying diluted EPS.

Two situations in which this is the case are as follows:

Including Antidilution

If the income statement includes more than one income figure [e.g., income (loss) from continuing operations and net income (loss)], the one that appears first in the income statement is the benchmark number for determining whether potential common stock is included. If the potential diluter dilutes that income figure, it is included in determining diluted EPS for both income figures, even though it may be antidilutive in the second income figure presented. For example, a company may report income as follows:

Income from continuing operations	$100,000
Discontinued operations	(125,000)
Net loss	($25,000)

Stock options that would dilute EPS on income from continuing operations are outstanding. Because the market price of the stock exceeds the exercise price of the options, these options are dilutive and are included in computing earnings per share.

In this case, the stock options are considered to be potential common stock in determining earnings (loss) per share on both income from continuing operations and net loss, even though they are dilutive in the first figure and antidilutive in the second.

Excluding Dilution

Where multiple convertible securities exist, test them for dilution in their order of dilutive effect, beginning with the most dilutive and proceeding to the least dilutive. EPS adjusted for previously considered convertible securities becomes the basis for judging the potential of each convertible security in the order considered.

For example, assume a company has basic EPS of $1.00 and has two convertible bond issues outstanding. These two convertibles have ratios of numerator adjustment (interest net of tax) to denominator adjustment (number of shares) as follows:

Bonds A	$.90
Bonds B	$.95

Bonds A are more dilutive than Bonds B ($.90 is less than $.95), so they are considered first. Assume that including Bonds A reduces EPS from $1.00 to $.97. The $.95 figure for Bonds B is compared with $.97, determined to be further dilutive, and included in determining diluted EPS. On the other hand, if including Bonds A had reduced EPS from $1.00 to $.85, Bonds B would have been judged antidilutive and excluded from the determination of diluted EPS, even though they would have been dilutive if considered alone.

Illustration of Basic and Diluted EPS

In 20X8, Stahl, Inc., a calendar-year public company, had 52,500 shares of common stock outstanding at January 1, sold 10,500 shares on March 1, and repurchased 2,000 shares on November 1. Net income for the year was $375,000, and the appropriate income tax rate was 35%. Stahl's common stock sold for an average of $25 during the year and ended the year at $28.

Other financial instruments in the company's capital structure are as follows:

- Preferred stock—10,000 shares outstanding, $50 par, 6% dividend (cumulative)
- Stock options—15,000 options to purchase one share each of common stock at $20 each
- Convertible bonds—$200,000 par, 10%, convertible into 20 shares of common stock per $1,000 bond

Basic and diluted EPS are determined as follows:

Preliminary Calculations

Weighted-average number of common shares outstanding

Jan. 1	52,500	× 2 months	= 105,000
	10,500		
March 1	63,000	× 8 months	= 504,000
	(2000)		= 122,000
Nov. 1	61,000	× 2 months	731,000
	731,000 / 12 months =		60,917

Alternatively, the weighted-average can be calculated as follows:

Jan. 1	Outstanding	=	52,500
March 1	10,500 × 10/12	=	8,750
Nov. 1	2,000 × 2/12	=	(333)
			60,917

Preferred dividend

10,000 shares × $50 par value × .06 = $30,000

Treasury stock method applied to stock options

Sale of common stock	15,000 shares × $20	=	$300,000
Repurchase of common stock	$300,000 / $25	=	12,000
Net increase in outstanding shares	15,000 – 12,000	=	3,000

Alternatively, the effect of applying the treasury stock method may be computed as follows:

	(25 – 20) / 25 × 15,000	=	3,000

If-converted method applied to convertible bonds

Numerator increase	$200,000 × .10 × (1 – .35)	=	$13,000
Denominator increase	20 shares × 200 bonds	=	4,000
Dilutive effect	$13,000 / 4,000 shares	=	3.25

Basic and Diluted EPS

Numerator	Net income	$375,000	
	Preferred income	(30,000)	
		$345,000	Basic
	Impact of potential common shares:		
	Convertible bonds	13,000	
		$358,000	Diluted
Denominator	Weighted-average outstanding shares	60,917	Basic
	Impact of potential common shares:		
	Convertible bonds	4,000	
	Stock options	3,000	
		67,917	Diluted
Basic EPS		$345,000/60,917 = $5.66	
Diluted EPS		$358,000/67,917 = $5.27	

PART II: INTERPRETIVE GUIDANCE

ASC 260-10: OVERALL

ASC 260-10-45-15; ASC 470-50-40-12(a), 40-12A, 40-17 through 40-17A, 40-18A, 40-21; ASC 505-10-60-8; ASC 718-10-15-5; ASC 815-40-35-3, 35-14 through 35-18, 50-6, 55-49 through 55-52, 65-2 Issuer's Accounting for Certain Modifications or Exchanges of Freestanding Equity-Classified Written Call Options (A consensus of the FASB Emerging Issues Task Force)

BACKGROUND

The FASB asked the Emerging Issues Task Force to address the manner in which *issuers* should account for modifications of the terms and conditions or exchanges of freestanding written call options (e.g., warrants) that are classified as equity and continue to be classified in equity subsequent to such transactions. There has been diversity in practice due to a lack of guidance on this subject in the FASB Codification. This guidance only applies to entities that present earnings per share (EPS) in accordance with the guidance in ASC Topic 260.

ACCOUNTING ISSUE

Should an issuer account for a modification or an exchange of a freestanding written call option that is classified in equity and continues to be classified as such after a modification or exchange as (1) an adjustment to equity and, if so, how would EPS be affected, if at all, or (2) an expense, and if so, how would it be recognized?

ACCOUNTING GUIDANCE

The following is guidance applicable to the accounting for such transactions under different Topics in the FASB Codification and under different circumstances:

ASC Topic 260 (Earnings Per Share)

ASC 260-10-45-15 has been added to provide that an entity that modifies or exchanges an equity-classified freestanding written call *option* discussed in ASC 815-40-35-17(d) should deduct the effect of the modification or exchange (as measured in accordance with ASC 815-40-35-16) in its computation of income available to common shareholders when the issuer and the holder or the issuer alone has executed the transaction.

ASC Subtopic 470-50 (Debt—Modifications and Extinguishments)

Guidance under the following circumstances has been added:

- *Modifications and exchanges.* ASC 470-50-40-12A provides accounting guidance for a situation in which a modification or exchange of an equity-classified freestanding written call option held by a creditor is a part of or is directly related to a modification or an exchange of an existing *debt instrument* held by the same creditor (see ASC 815-40-35-14 through 35-15 and ASC 815-40-35-17(c)). It provides that the creditor holding the equity-classified freestanding written call option should include an increase or a decrease in the instrument's fair value, as calculated in accordance with the guidance in ASC 815-40-35-16, in the calculation of the 10% cash flow test discussed in ASC 470-50-40-10.
- *Fees between debtor and creditor.* ASC 470-50-40-17A provides that an increase or a decrease in the fair value of an equity-classified freestanding written call option held by a creditor (calculated in accordance with the guidance in ASC 815-40-35-16) that is modified or exchanged as part of or is directly related to a modification or an exchange of an existing *debt instrument* held by the same creditor (see ASC 815-40-35-14 through 35-15 and ASC 815-40-35-17(c)) should be accounted for in the same manner as fees between the debtor and the creditor as discussed in ASC 470-50-40-17.
- *Third-party costs of exchange or modification.* ASC 470-50-40-18A provides that an increase (not a decrease) in the fair value of an equity-classified freestanding written call option held by a third party (calculated in accordance with the guidance in ASC 815-40-35-16) that is modified or exchanged as part of or is directly related to a modification or an exchange of a debt instrument (see ASC 815-40-35-14 through 35-15 and ASC 815-40-35-17(c)) should be accounted for in the same manner as third-party costs incurred that are directly related to the modification or exchange of a debt instrument discussed in ASC 470-50-40-18.
- *Line-of-credit or revolving-debt arrangements.* The accounting would be as follows:

  In such arrangements, fees between a debtor and a creditor include an increase or a decrease in the fair value of an equity-classified freestanding written call option held by the creditor (calculated in accordance with the guidance in ASC 815-40-35-16) that is modified or exchanged as part of or is directly related to a modification or an exchange of a line-of-credit or a revolving-debt arrangement held by the same creditor (see ASC 815-40-35-14 through 35-15 and ASC 815-40-35-17(c)). Third-party costs include an increase but not a decrease in the fair value of an equity-classified freestanding written call option held by a third party (calculated in accordance with the guidance in ASC 815-40-35-16) that is modified or exchanged as a part of or is directly related to a modification or an exchange of a line-of-credit or revolving-debt arrangement (see ASC 815-40-35-14 through 35-15 and ASC 815-40-35-17(c)).

ASC Topic 505 (Equity)

Financial Instruments

ASC 505-10-60-8 refers readers to ASC Subtopic 815-40 on contracts in an entity's own equity for guidance on accounting for modifications or exchanges of equity-classified freestanding written call options (e.g., warrants) that remain classified in equity after a modification or an exchange.

ASC Topic 718 (Compensation—Stock Compensation)

ASC 718-10-15-5 refers readers to ASC 815-40-35-14 through 35-15, 815-40-35-18, 815-40-55-49, and 815-40-55-52 for guidance on an issuer's accounting for modifications or exchanges of written call options to compensate grantees.

ASC Subtopic 815-40 (Derivatives and Hedging—Contracts in Entity's Own Equity)

Equity Instruments—Permanent Equity

- ASC 815-40-35-15 provides that the circumstances of a modification or exchange of an equity-classified freestanding written call option should be considered to determine whether a modification or an exchange is related to a financing or other arrangement or an arrangement that includes multiple elements, such as an arrangement that includes a debt financing and an equity financing. An entity also should consider all of a modification's or an exchange's terms and conditions, other transactions entered into at the same time or in contemplation of a modification or exchange, other rights and privileges obtained or obligations incurred (including services), due to the modification or exchange. The guidance in ASC 815-40-35-16 through 35-18 should be applied to modifications or exchanges not under the scope of another Topic.
- ASC 815-40-35-16 provides that a modification of the terms or conditions of an exchange of an equity-classified freestanding written call option should be accounted for as an exchange of the original instrument for a new instrument. The substance of that transaction is that the entity repurchases the original instrument by issuing a new instrument. The effect of a modification or an exchange of transactions recognized in accordance with the guidance in ASC 815-40-35-17(c) (discussed below) should be measured as the difference between the fair value of the modified or exchanged instrument and the instrument's fair value immediately before its modification or exchange. The effect of a modification or an exchange in all of the other transactions recognized under the guidance in ASC 815-40-35-17 is measured as the excess, if any, of the fair value of the modified or exchanged instrument over the fair value of the instrument immediately before its modification or an exchange. The total effect of a modification or an exchange of a multiple-element transaction should be allocated to the transaction's respective elements.
- ASC 815-40-35-17 provides guidance for the recognition of the effect of a modification or an exchange (calculated in accordance with the guidance in ASC 815-40-35-16), as if the consideration was paid in cash, as follows:
  1. *Equity issuance.* Recognize as an equity issuance cost the effect of a modification or an exchange that is directly related to a proposed or actual equity offering. See additional guidance in SAB Topic 5.A, Expense of Offering (ASC 340-10-S99-1).
  2. *Debt origination.* Recognize as a debt discount or debt issuance cost the effect of a modification or an exchange that is part of or directly related to an issuance of a debt instrument in accordance with the guidance in ASC Topic 835 on interest.
  3. *Debt modification.* Recognize the effect of a modification or an exchange that is a part of or directly related to a modification or an exchange of an existing debt instrument in accordance with the guidance in ASC Subtopic 470-50 on debt modifications and extinguishments and ASC Subtopic 470-60 on troubled debt restructurings by debtors.
  4. *Other.* Recognize as a dividend the effect of a modification or an exchange that is not related to a financing transaction in items 1 through 3 and is not within the scope of any other Topic (such as ASC Topic 718). Further, an entity that presents earnings per share (EPS) in accordance with the guidance in ASC Topic 260 should recognize the effect of a modification or an exchange of an equity-classified freestanding written call option as a reduction of income available to common stockholders in basic earnings per share in accordance with the guidance in ASC 260-10-45-15.

DISCLOSURE

ASC 815-40-50-6 provides that an entity that has recognized the effects of modifications or exchanges of equity-classified freestanding written call options in accordance with the guidance in ASC 815-40-35-17 during any of the periods presented should disclose the following:

1. Information about the nature of the modification or exchange transaction (see ASC 815-40-35-15)
2. The amount of the effect of the modification or exchange (see ASC 815-40-35-16)
3. The manner in which a modification's or an exchange's effect has been recognized (see ASC 815-40-35-17).

TRANSITION AND EFFECTIVE DATE

ASC 815-40-65-2. The following is the transition and effective date guidance for ASU 2021-04, *Earnings Per Share (Topic 260), Debt—Modifications and Extinguishments (Subtopic 470-50), Compensation—Stock Compensation (Topic 718), and Derivatives and Hedging—Contracts in Entity's Own Equity (Subtopic 815-40): Issuer's Accounting for Certain Modifications or Exchanges of Freestanding Equity-Classified Written Call Options*:

1. The ASU's guidance is effective for all entities for fiscal years that begin after December 15, 2021, including interim periods within those fiscal years. Early application, including early application in an interim period as of the beginning of the fiscal year that includes that interim period, is permitted for all entities.
2. The guidance should be applied prospectively to modifications or exchanges of equity-classified freestanding written call options under the scope of this guidance that occur on or after the date at which an entity first applies the guidance in ASU 2021-04.
3. The following transition disclosures consistent with ASC Topic 250 should be provided:
   a. The nature of and reason for a change in accounting principle
   b. The transition method
   c. A qualitative description of the financial statement line items affected by the change.
4. An entity that issues interim financial statements should provide the disclosures mentioned in item 3 above in the financial statements of both the interim period of the change and the fiscal year of the change.

ASC 260-10-45-61A, 45-68B, 55-76A through 55-76D Determining Whether Instruments Granted in Share-Based Transactions Are Participating Securities

BACKGROUND

Participating securities are defined in ASC 260-10-45-59A as:

> Securities that may participate in dividends with common stocks according to a predetermined formula (for example, two for one) with, at times, an upper limit on participation (for example, up to, but not beyond a specified amount per share).

Further, under the guidance in ASC 260, entities that have participating securities or multiple classes of securities with a different dividend rate for each class of security are required to compute their earnings per share by the two-class method.

The guidance on issue 2 of the Issue that follows, "Participating Securities and the Two-Class Method under FASB Statement No. 128" provides that a participating security is one that may participate in undistributed earnings with common stock in its current form, regardless of whether participation depends on the occurrence of a specific event. However, that guidance applies *only* to share-based payment awards that are *fully* vested and does *not* address whether unvested share-based payment awards are participating securities.

ACCOUNTING ISSUE

Can instruments granted in share-based payment transactions be participating securities before the required service has been rendered?

ACCOUNTING GUIDANCE

The computation of basic earnings per share under the two-class method should include *unvested* share-based payment awards, which include *nonforfeitable* rights to paid or unpaid dividends or dividend equivalents, because securities that include such rights are considered to be participating securities. A share-based payment award that includes a right to receive a dividend that is *not* forfeited regardless of whether the award becomes vested or remains unvested is a participating right, because it is *not* contingent on the performance of additional services after the dividend has been declared. However, an award under which the right to dividends would be forfeited if the award does *not* vest would *not* be treated as a participating right, because it does not meet the definition of a participating security. In addition, an award whose exercise price would be reduced by amounts equivalent to distributions to common shareholders would *not* be treated as a participating right; the transfer of value to the holder of the award is not a nonforfeitable right, because it would occur only if the award is exercised.

Under the guidance in ASC 718-10-55-45, nonrefundable dividends or dividend equivalents paid on awards for which the required service has *not* been or is *not* expected to be rendered and therefore do *not* vest must be recognized as additional compensation cost and dividends or dividend equivalents paid on awards for which the required service has been or is expected to be performed must be recognized in retained earnings. Consequently, dividends or dividend equivalents recognized as compensation cost on unvested share-based payment awards that are *not* expected to or do *not* vest should *not* be included in the earnings allocation for the computation of earnings per share because doing so would result in a double reduction of earnings available to common shareholders—as compensation cost and as a distribution of earnings. However, *undistributed* earnings should be allocated to all share-based payment awards outstanding during the period, including those for which the required service is *not* expected to be performed (or is not performed because of forfeiture during the period if an entity elects to account for forfeitures when they occur in accordance with ASC 718-10-35-3). For calculating EPS under the guidance in this FSP, the estimated number of awards for which it is expected that the required service will *not* be performed should be consistent with an entity's estimate used to recognize compensation cost under the guidance in ASC 718. A change in estimate of the number of awards for which the required service is *not* expected to be performed should be applied in the period in which the change in estimate occurs. Although that change in estimate will affect an entity's current period income, an entity's change in the current period of its expected forfeiture rate would *not* affect its EPS calculations in prior periods.

ASC 260-10-45-60, 45-60A through 45-68; 55-24 through 55-30, 55-71 through 55-75 Participating Securities and the Two-Class Method under FASB Statement No. 128, *Earnings per Share*

BACKGROUND

Under the guidance in ASC 260, entities that have issued participating securities, which are defined in ASC 260-10-45-59A as securities that may participate in dividends with common stock according to a prescribed formula, are required to compute earnings per share (EPS) by the two-class method. ASC 260-10-45-60B states further that the two-class method also should be used for securities that are *not* convertible into a class of common stock.

ACCOUNTING ISSUES

1. Does the two-class method require the presentation of basic and diluted EPS for all participating securities?

1a. When should basic and diluted EPS be presented if the two-class method does not require the presentation of basic and diluted EPS for all participating securities?

2. How should a participating security requiring the application of ASC 260-10-45-60B be defined?

2a. Should all potential common shares, that is, securities or other contracts that may entitle their holders to obtain common stock (such as options, warrants, forwards, convertible debt, and convertible preferred stock), be participating securities?

2b. Do dividends or dividend equivalents paid to the holder of a convertible participating security that are applied to either reduce the conversion price or increase the conversion ratio of the security represent participation rights?

3. How should undistributed earnings be allocated to a participating security?

4. Would an entity that allocated undistributed earnings to a nonconvertible participating security continue to do so in a period of net loss if the effect is anti-dilutive?

5. Would a convertible participating security be excluded from the computation of basic EPS if an entity has a net loss from continuing operations?

6. How should a convertible participating security be included in the computation of diluted EPS?

ACCOUNTING GUIDANCE

The EITF reached the following consensus positions:

1. Under the two-class method, presentation of basic and diluted earnings per share is *not* required for all participating securities.
2. For applying the requirements in ASC 260-10-45-59A, 45-60B, a participating security is defined as one that may participate with common stocks in undistributed earnings without considering (*a*) the form of participation and (*b*) whether participation depends on the occurrence of a specific event.
3. Dividends or dividend equivalents transferred to a holder of a convertible security in the form of a reduction of the conversion price or an increase in the security's conversion ratio are not participation rights. This consensus would also apply to other contracts or securities to issue an entity's common stock if the exercise price would be adjusted

because of an issuer's declaration of dividends. However, this guidance does *not* apply to forward contracts to issue an entity's own equity shares because forward contracts are participating securities.

4. An issuer should consider whether a dividend or dividend equivalent applied to reduce the conversion price or increase the conversion ratio of a convertible security in its financial statements is a contingent beneficial conversion feature. That decision should be made in accordance with the guidance in "Accounting for Convertible Securities with Beneficial Conversion Features or Contingently Adjustable Conversion Ratios" and "Application of Issue No. 98-5 to Certain Convertible Instruments" in Chapter 35, *ASC 470—Debt*.

PRACTICE NOTE: The above guidance will be deleted as the result of the issuance of ASU 2020-6, *Debt-Debt with Conversion and Other Options (Subtopic 470-20) and Derivatives and Hedging-Contracts in an Entity's Own Equity (Subtopic 815-40): Accounting for Convertible Instruments and Contracts in an Entity's Own Equity*, which will be effective as follows:

a. Public business entities that meet the definition of an SEC filer, except for smaller reporting companies as defined by the SEC, will be required to apply the ASU's guidance for fiscal years that begin after December 15, 2021, including interim periods within those fiscal years.

b. All other entities will be required to apply the guidance beginning in fiscal years that begin after December 15, 2023, including interim periods within those fiscal years.

c. All entities are permitted to early adopt the guidance, but not earlier than for fiscal years that begin after December 15, 2020, including interim periods within those fiscal years.

The guidance in ASC 260-10-45-64 will be superseded on the ASU's effective date.

---

5. Undistributed earnings for a period should be allocated based on a security's contractual participation rights to share in current earnings as if all of the earnings for the period had been distributed. Undistributed earnings should *not* be allocated based on arbitrary assumptions if the participating security's terms do *not* state objectively determinable, non-discretionary participation rights. This consensus is based on the guidance in ASC 260-10-45-60B(b) which states that under the two-class method, "the remaining earnings shall be allocated to common stock and participating securities to the extent that each security may share in earnings as if all the earnings for the period had been distributed," even though this is a pro forma allocation and may not represent the economic probabilities of actual distributions to the holders of the participating securities.

6. An entity should allocate losses to a nonconvertible participating security in a period in which the entity has a net loss if the security's contractual terms provide that, in addition to the right to participate in the issuer's earnings, the security also has an obligation to share in the issuer's losses on an objectively determinable basis. A holder of a nonconvertible participating security has an obligation to share in the issuer's losses if either of the following conditions exists:

   a. The holder has an obligation to commit assets in addition to the initial investment to fund the issuing entity's losses without increasing the holder's investment interest in the entity.

   b. The participating security's contractual principal or mandatory redemption amount is reduced by the issuing entity's incurred losses.

7. The basis for the guidance in item 6 (above) also applies to the inclusion of convertible securities in basic EPS when an issuer has a net loss and the security's contractual terms provide that the participating security has an obligation to share in the issuer's losses on an objectively determinable basis. The existence of an obligation to share in an issuer's losses should be determined in the applicable reporting period based on the security's contractual rights and obligations.

8. The computation of basic EPS using the two-class method should include participating securities.

9. All securities that meet the definition of a participating security in item 2 (above) should be included in the computation of basic EPS under the two-class method, regardless of whether they are convertible, nonconvertible, or potential common stock securities.
10. Until options or shares are fully vested, the guidance in this Issue does not apply to stock-based compensation, accounted for under the provisions of ASC 718 (FAS-123(R), Share-Based Payments), such as options and nonvested stock that include a right to receive dividends declared on an issuer's common stock.

ASC 260-10-45-43 through 45-44; 55-78 through 55-79, 55-81 through 55-82, 55-84 through 55-84B The Effect of Contingently Convertible Instruments on Diluted Earnings per Share

BACKGROUND

This issue addresses the question of when to include the dilutive effect of contingently convertible debt instruments (Co-Cos) in diluted earnings per share (EPS). Co-Cos are convertible debt instruments that include a contingent feature and are generally convertible into an issuer's common shares after the stock price of the issuer's common stock exceeds a predetermined amount for a specified period of time, known as the market price trigger. A Co-Co's conversion price usually is higher than the underlying stock's market price when the Co-Co is issued and its market price trigger usually is higher than the conversion price. Because the market price trigger is higher than the conversion price, a Co-Co is less likely to be converted than is a convertible debt instrument without a market price trigger.

The Issue was discussed because some issuers were accounting for Co-Cos differently than for convertible debt without a market price trigger. That is, most issuers of Co-Cos are not including the instrument's dilutive effect in diluted EPS until the market price trigger has been reached. Some issuers, however, are including the dilutive effect of convertible debt without a market price trigger in diluted EPS as of the instrument's issue date.

ACCOUNTING ISSUE

When should the dilutive effect of a contingently convertible instrument be included in diluted earnings per share calculations?

ACCOUNTING GUIDANCE

All financial instruments with embedded contingent conversion features, such as contingently convertible debt and contingently preferred stock should be included in the calculation of diluted earnings per share, if dilutive, without considering whether the market conditions for conversion have been met, because the economics of such instruments do not differ from conventional convertible debt with a market price conversion premium. Instruments with more than one contingency also should be included if at least one of the instrument's contingencies requires the occurrence of a market condition that would trigger conversion, regardless of whether a non-market condition, such as a change in control, has been met. Instruments requiring that both a market trigger *and* a substantive nonmarket-based contingency be met for conversion to occur, however, are *not* included under the scope of this Issue until the non-market-based contingency has occurred. See ASC 260-10-45-45 through 45-46 for guidance on the accounting for contracts that may be settled in stock or in cash after a contingency has been met.

ASC 260-10-05-3 through 05-5; 15-5; 45-72 through 45-73; 55-103 through 55-110 Application of the Two-Class Method under FASB Statement No. 128, *Earnings per Share*, to Master Limited Partnerships

BACKGROUND

Master limited partnerships (MLPs) that are publicly traded may issue several classes of securities with the right to participate in a partnership's distributions based on a formula that is specified in the partnership agreement. Generally, an MLP's capital structure is composed of publicly traded "common units" that are held by its limited partners (LPs), a general partner (GP) interest, and holders of incentive distribution rights (IDRs), which may be a separate class of non-voting LP interests depending on the MLP's capital structure. In some cases, IDRs may initially be held by a GP that may transfer or sell them separately from its general interest, but sometimes IDRs are embedded in a GP's interest so that they cannot be detached and sold separately from the GP's interest in the MLP.

In accordance with the provisions of a partnership agreement, a GP usually is required to distribute 100% of an MLP's "available cash" (as defined in the partnership agreement) to the GP and the LPs at the end of each reporting period. That distribution is based on a schedule referred to as a "waterfall," which stipulates the distributions at each threshold. As certain thresholds are met, available cash is distributed further to holders of IDRs or to a GP whose IDRs are embedded in the GP's interest in the MLP. The timing of a distribution after the end of a reporting period is stipulated in an MLP's contract. "Available cash" is defined as all cash on hand at the end of each reporting period *less* cash retained by the partnership as capital to: (1) operate the business; (2) meet debt obligations and other legal obligations; and (3) provide funds for distribution to the holders of common units, the GP, and the IDR holders for one or more of the following reporting periods. After considering priority income allocations as a result of incentive distributions, a partnership's net income or loss is distributed to its GP's and LPs' capital accounts based on their respective sharing of income and losses stated in the partnership agreement.

Because of their capital structure, MLPs must compute earnings per unit (EPU) under the provisions for the two-class method discussed in ASC 260, which requires that undistributed earnings be allocated to common units and participating securities as if all of the period's earnings had been distributed. However, under the guidance in Issue 3 of "Participating Securities and the Two-Class Method under FASB Statement No. 128" (discussed above), a reporting period's undistributed earnings are allocated to a participating security based on its contractual participation rights to share in the current period's earnings as if *all* of that period's earnings had been distributed. Consequently, the FASB received requests for guidance on the effect of IDRs on the computation of EPU when the two-class method is applied to the interests of an MLP's LPs and its GP.

ACCOUNTING GUIDANCE

The following conclusions were reached:

- *Scope.* The guidance in this Issue applies to MLPs making incentive distributions that are treated as equity distributions when certain thresholds are met. This Issue does *not* provide guidance for determining whether an incentive distribution should be accounted for as an equity distribution or as compensation cost.
- *IDRs that are a separate class of LP interest.* IDRs that are held separately are participating securities because they are entitled to participate in earnings with common equity holders. Consequently, an MLP's earnings for a reporting period should be allocated to the GP, LPs, and IDR holders using the two-class method in ASC 260 to calculate EPU as follows:
  - When the two-class method is used to calculate an MLP's EPU, the current period's net income (or loss) should be reduced (or increased) by the amount of available cash that has been or will be distributed for that period to the GP, LPs, and IDR holders. For example, under the XYZ MLP's partnership agreement, its GP is required to distribute available cash within 60 days after the end of each fiscal quarter. Because XYZ must file its financial statements with a regulatory agency within 45 days after the end of each fiscal quarter, the amount of available cash that will be distributed to the GP, LPs, and IDR holders must be determined in order to calculate the MLP's EPU for the first quarter. Further, XYZ's income or loss must be reduced (or increased) by the amount of available cash to be distributed in order to compute the *undistributed* earnings that must be allocated to the GP, LPs, and IDR holders in the computation of the first quarter's EPU.
  - *Undistributed earnings*, if any, should be distributed to the GP, LPs, and IDR holders based on the terms of the partnership agreement. Although available cash must be distributed for the period presented based on the distribution waterfall specified in the partnership agreement, undistributed earning must be distributed to IDR holders based on an IDR's *contractual participation rights* to share in the current period's earnings. However, if a partnership agreement includes a "specified threshold" for the distribution of undistributed earnings (e.g., 5% of earnings), as discussed in ASC 260-10-55-24, undistributed earnings should *not* be distributed to an IDR holder beyond that specified threshold.
  - To determine whether there is a specified threshold for distributions to IDR holders, it is necessary to evaluate whether such distributions are contractually limited to available cash, as defined in the partnership agreement, if all of a period's earnings have been distributed. In that case, an IDR holder that has received a distribution of available cash up to its specific threshold would *not* be eligible to share *in undistributed* earnings. However, if a partnership agreement's provisions do *not* specifically limit distributions to IDR holders to available cash, undistributed earnings should be distributed to IDR holders based on the partnership agreement's distribution waterfall for available cash.
  - If cash distributions *exceed* current-period earnings, such excess distributions over earnings should be allocated to the GP and LPs based on the partnership agreement's provisions for the allocation of losses to the respective partners' capital accounts. If IDR holders do *not* have a contractual obligation to share in an MLP's losses, *no*

portion of an excess distribution over earnings would be allocated to them. However, if IDR holders have a contractual obligation to share in an MLP's losses on an objectively determined basis, excess distributions, if any, would be allocated to the GP, LPs, and IDR holders based on the partnership agreement's provisions for their respective sharing of losses.

- *IDRs embedded in a GP's interest.* Although IDRs embedded in a GP's interest are not separate participating securities, the two-class method should be used to calculate EPU for the GP's and LPs' interests because those interests are separate classes of equity:
  - — When an MLP's EPU is calculated under the two-class method, the current period's net income (or loss) should be reduced (or increased) by the amount of available cash that has been or will be distributed for that period to the GP (including the embedded IDR's distribution rights) and LPs. For example, under the XYZ MLP's partnership agreement, its GP is required to distribute available cash within 60 days after the end of each fiscal quarter. Because XYZ must file financial statements with a regulatory agency within 45 days after the end of each fiscal quarter, the amount of available cash that will be distributed to the GP and LPs must be determined to calculate the MLP's EPU for the first quarter. Furthermore, XYZ's income or loss should be reduced (or increased) by the amount of available cash to be distributed to compute the *undistributed* earnings that must be allocated to the GP and LPs in the computation of the first quarter's EPU.
- *Undistributed earnings.* Undistributed earnings, if any, should be distributed to the GP (including the embedded IDR's distribution rights) and LPs based on the terms of the partnership agreement. Although *available cash* must be distributed for the period presented based on the distribution waterfall specified in the partnership agreement, undistributed earnings should be distributed to the GP based on an embedded IDR's *contractual participation rights* to share in the current period's earnings. However, if a partnership agreement includes a specified threshold for the distribution of undistributed earnings (e.g., 5% of earnings), as discussed in ASC 260-10-55-24, undistributed earnings should *not* be distributed to the GP for the embedded IDR's distribution rights beyond that specified threshold:
  - — To determine whether there is a specified threshold for distributions to a GP for the embedded IDR's distribution rights, it is necessary to evaluate whether such distributions are contractually limited to available cash, as defined in the partnership agreement, if all of a period's earnings have been distributed. In that case, a GP that has received a distribution of available cash up to its specific threshold for the embedded IDR's distribution rights would *not* be eligible to share in undistributed earnings. However, if a partnership agreement's provisions do *not* specifically limit distributions to a GP for the distribution rights of embedded IDRs to available cash, undistributed earnings should be distributed to the GP for the distribution rights of embedded IDRs based on the partnership agreement's distribution waterfall for available cash.
  - — If cash distributions *exceed* current-period earnings, such excess distributions over earnings would be allocated to the GP and LPs based on the partnership agreement's provisions for their respective sharing of losses for the period.

ASC 260-10-99S-2 The Effect on the Calculation of Earnings per Share for a Period that Includes the Redemption or Induced Conversion of Preferred Stock

The SEC staff's guidance in this announcement has been amended by ASU 2009-8.

The SEC staff's guidance applies to redemptions and induced conversions of preferred stock instruments that are classified in equity. Such transactions should be accounted for as follows:

- An exchange or modification of preferred stock instruments is considered a redemption if the transaction is accounted for as an extinguishment and results in a new basis of accounting for the modified or exchanged preferred stock.
- The guidance in this pronouncement applies to redemptions and induced conversions of preferred stock classified in temporary equity under the guidance in ASR 268 and ASC 480-10-S99-3A (Topic D-98), which are considered to be classified in equity.
- A subsequent reclassification of an equity security to a liability based on guidance in other U.S. GAAP (e.g., if a preferred share becomes mandatorily redeemable under the guidance in ASC 480-10) is considered to be a redemption of equity by means of issuing a debt instrument.

This announcement does not affect the accounting for conversions of preferred stock into other securities classified as equity as a result of conversion privileges included under the terms of instruments at issuance.

The SEC staff believes that on such redemptions or conversions, the difference between the fair value of the consideration transferred to the preferred stockholders and the carrying amount of the preferred stock in the registrant's balance sheet (net of issuance costs) should be subtracted from or added to net income for the calculation of income available to common stockholders used in computing earnings per share. The SEC staff believes that the difference between the fair value of the consideration transferred to the preferred stockholders and the carrying amount of the preferred stock in the registrant's balance sheet represents a return to the preferred shareholder that should be treated similarly to dividends paid on preferred stock whether or not the embedded conversion feature is "in the money" or "out of the money" at redemption. If a redemption includes the reacquisition of a beneficial conversion feature in a convertible preferred stock that had previously been recognized, the fair value of the consideration transferred should be reduced by the intrinsic value of the conversion option at the commitment date.

The SEC Staff believes that if the fair value of securities and other consideration transferred by a registrant to the holders of convertible preferred stock as a result of an offer inducing conversion exceeds the fair value of the securities that would have been issued based on the original conversion terms, the difference should be subtracted from net earnings used to calculate net earnings available to common shareholders in the earnings per share calculation. Registrants should follow the guidance in ASC 470-20-05-10; 40-13 through 40-17; 45-2; 55-2 through 55-9 to determine whether conversion occurred as a result of an inducement offer.

SEC OBSERVER COMMENT

Subsequently, the SEC Observer responded to a question about the accounting for redemption of convertible preferred stock that has appreciated since issuance. He reiterated that the guidance stated above applies to all classes of preferred stock and that the entire redemption amount that exceeds the *carrying amount* of the preferred stock should be deducted from earnings available to common shareholders. (See below in ASC 260-10-S99 and the discussion in ASC 470-20-40-13, "Determining Whether Certain Conversions of Convertible Debt to Equity Securities Are within the Scope of FASB Statement No. 84, *Induced Conversions of Convertible Debt*," in Chapter 35, *ASC 470—Debt*.)

ASC 260-10-50-3, 55-16A, 55-111 Effects on Historical Earnings per Unit of Master Limited Partnership Dropdown Transactions

BACKGROUND

Earnings per unit of a master limited partnership, which is accounted for under the guidance in FASB Accounting Standards Codification® (ASC) 260, *Earnings per Share*, are calculated by using the two-class method because a general partner, limited partners, and holders of incentive distribution rights participate differently in the distribution of available cash based on their contractual rights under the partnership agreement.

Under the existing guidance in ASC 260, a general partner's transfer of net assets (referred to as a dropdown) to a master limited partnership is accounted for as a transaction between entities under common control. In that case, the master limited partnership's operating statement is adjusted *retrospectively*, in essence, pretending that the transaction occurred when the entities first were under common control.

The issue is that ASC 260 does not provide guidance for the presentation of earnings per unit for periods that predate a dropdown transaction that occurs after a master limited partnership has been established. The Emerging Issues Task Force (EITF) considered this issue because reporting entities have addressed that lack of guidance in diverse ways. In their recalculation of previously reported earnings per unit of a master limited partnership: (1) some reporting entities also have been allocating to the general partner, limited partners, and the holders of incentive distribution rights, the earnings (losses) of the business before the general partner transferred it to the master limited partnership in the same manner as those parties' contractual rights to the distribution of the master limited partnership's earnings (losses); or (2) other reporting entities have been allocating the earnings (losses) of the business before the general partner transferred it to the master limited partnership only to the general partner without adjusting the limited partners' previously reported earnings per unit.

ACCOUNTING ISSUE

How should a master limited partnership present information about its earnings per unit for periods after its establishment but before a dropdown transaction that is accounted for under the guidance in ASC 805-50 has occurred?

SCOPE

The guidance applies to all master limited partnerships accounted for under the guidance in ASC 260 that receive net assets through dropdown transactions that are accounted for under the guidance for transactions between entities under common control in ASC 805, *Business Combinations* (ASC 805-50).

ACCOUNTING GUIDANCE

The following guidance applies:

Master glossary. The definition of "dropdown" has been amended to read as follows:

> A transfer of certain net assets from a sponsor or general partner to a master limited partnership in exchange for consideration.

Disclosure: Master limited partnerships. ASC 260-10-50-3 has been added to require that in the period in which a dropdown transaction accounted for under the guidance in ASC 805-50 occurs, a reporting entity should provide a narrative disclosure to explain how a dropdown transaction affects the computation of earnings per unit under the two-class method and how the rights to the earnings (losses) of transferred net assets differ before and after a dropdown transaction has occurred.

Implementation guidance: Prior-period adjustments. ASC 260-10-55-16A has been added to refer to the guidance in ASC 260-10-55-111 on the presentation of prior-period earnings per unit for entities under the scope of the guidance for master limited partnerships that retrospectively adjust their financial statements and financial information for prior periods when a dropdown transaction is accounted for according to the guidance in ASC 805-50 for transactions between entities under common control.

Presentation of historical earnings per unit after a dropdown transaction has been accounted for as a transaction between entities under common control. Under the guidance in ASC 260-10-55-111, a master limited partnership that accounts for a general partner's dropdown transaction according to the guidance in ASC 805-50 for transactions between entities under common control should allocate the total amount of the net earnings (losses) of the transferred net assets before the dropdown date to the general partner's interest in its calculation of historical earnings per unit under the two-class method. Consequently, the earnings (losses) per unit previously reported for the limited partners' interests in periods before the dropdown transaction occurred should be unchanged because of that transaction.

ASC 260-10-55-3A, 55-3B, 55-85 through 55-87 Computing Year-to-Date Diluted Earnings per Share under FASB Statement No. 128

BACKGROUND

A member of the FASB staff discussed their view on the computation of a company's year-to-date diluted EPS if it has a year-to-date loss from continuing operations but has had income from continuing operations in one or more quarters. The question was raised because the guidance in ASC 260-10-45-17; 260-10-55-3 seems to conflict when a company has a year-to-date loss for a period of more than three months but has had income in some quarters during the year. ASC 260-10-55-3 provides the following computational guidance for applying the treasury stock method; the number of incremental shares that will be included in the denominator is determined by computing the year-to-date weighted average of incremental shares included in each quarterly computation of diluted EPS, however, the antidilution rule in ASC 260-10-45-19 states that the conversion, exercise, or contingent issuance of securities should not be assumed if the effect on EPS is antidilutive.

ACCOUNTING GUIDANCE

The FASB staff believes that the guidance in ASC 260-10-45-17 should be followed; therefore, no potential common shares (incremental shares) should be included in the computation of diluted EPS if the result is antidilutive.

Illustration of Quarterly and Year-to-Date Calculation

ABC Company has:

- 20,000 common shares outstanding
- 2,000 shares of preferred stock convertible into 4,000 common shares

- Quarterly income (loss) (same as income from continuing operations) as follows:

	Q1: $20,000	Q2: ($30,000)	Q3: ($8,000)	Q4: $10,000

Quarterly EPS

	Q1	*Q2*	*Q3*	*Q4*
Income	$20,000	$(30,000)	($8,000)	$10,000
Common shares	20,000	20,000	20,000	20,000
Incremental shares	4,000	0*	0*	4,000
Basic EPS	$1.00	($1.50)	($.40)	$.50
Diluted EPS	$.83	($1.50)	($.40)	$.42

Year-to-date EPS

	Q1	*Q2*	*Q3*	*Q4*
Income	$20,000	($10,000)	($18,000)	$(8,000)
Common shares	20,000	20,000	20,000	20,000
Incremental shares	4,000	0*	0*	0*
Basic EPS	$1.00	($.50)	($.90)	($.40)
Diluted EPS	$.83	($.50)	($.90)	($.40)

* Incremental shares are not included because they are antidilutive.

ASC 260-10-45-11 through 45-12 Effect of Preferred Stock Dividends Payable in Common Shares on Computation of Income Available to Common Stockholders

This announcement clarifies the accounting for preferred stock dividends that an issuer has paid or intends to pay in its own common shares when the issuer computes income available to common stockholders. The FASB staff announced that in accordance with the definition of income available to common stockholders in ASC, *Glossary*, and the guidance in ASC 260-10-45-11, issuers should adjust the amount of net income or loss for dividends on preferred stock, regardless of the method of payment. The staff noted that this approach is consistent with the accounting for common stock issued for goods and services. To apply the guidance in this announcement, issuers should restate earnings per share reported in prior periods.

CHAPTER 12

ASC 270—INTERIM REPORTING

CONTENTS

GENERAL GUIDANCE

ASC 270-10: OVERALL

OVERVIEW

Interim financial reports may be issued quarterly, monthly, or at other intervals less than a full year, and may include complete financial statements or summarized information. In addition, they usually include the current interim period and a cumulative year-to-date period, or last 12 months to date, with comparative reports on the corresponding periods of the immediately preceding fiscal year.

BACKGROUND

The majority of U.S. GAAP have been developed for annual financial reporting purposes. These reporting standards generally are also applicable to interim financial reports. Some problems exist, however, in adapting U.S. GAAP intended primarily for annual reporting purposes to financial reporting for shorter periods of time.

Two competing approaches explain the relationship between interim financial reports and annual financial reports. The *discrete* approach, sometimes called the *independent* approach, views an interim period in the same way as an annual period. Within this approach, accounting principles for an annual period are equally appropriate for periods of differing lengths of time and are applied in the same manner. An alternative approach is the *integral* approach, sometimes called the *dependent* approach, which views an interim period as a component, or *integral* part, of the annual period rather than as a separate or discrete period. Within this approach, the purpose of interim financial reporting is to provide information over the course of the annual period that assists in anticipating annual results.

ASC 270 endorses certain aspects of both the discrete and integral approaches, but generally favors the *integral*, or *dependent*, approach to financial reporting for interim periods. Accordingly, certain procedures that are used in reporting for annual periods are modified in reporting for interim periods.

PRACTICE POINTER: That interim period reports should be viewed as an integral part of the annual period and that an important objective of interim reporting is for users to become increasingly informed in successive quarters of the emerging annual results are evidence of the FASB's focus on the dependent or integral approach to interim reporting. This results in some differences in practice in interim reports than in annual reports for the same financial statement elements. Care should be taken in preparing and reviewing interim financial information to not assume that U.S. GAAP appropriate for *annual* financial statements are applied in preparing and interpreting interim reports. Examples where U.S. GAAP may differ are the determination of cost of goods sold where a LIFO inventory layer has been eroded in an early interim period, accounting for income taxes on a cumulative year-to-date basis, and the determination of the materiality of items in interim financial statements.

ACCOUNTING AND REPORTING IN INTERIM PERIODS

Each interim period should generally be viewed as an integral part of the annual period. An important objective of interim reporting is for the user of the information to become progressively better informed about annual information as time passes. Accounting principles and reporting practices generally are those of the latest annual reports of the entity, with limited exceptions, such as a change in an accounting principle (ASC 270-10-45-2). A change in an accounting principle during an interim period is discussed in the chapter covering ASC 250 (Accounting Changes and Error Corrections).

Revenues are recognized as earned on the same basis as fiscal periods (ASC 270-10-45-3).

As closely as possible, product costs are determined as those for the fiscal period with some exceptions for inventory valuation, as follows (ASC 270-10-45-5, 6):

- Companies using the gross profit method to determine interim inventory costs, or other estimation methods different from those used for annual inventory valuation, should disclose the method used at the interim date and any significant adjustments that result from reconciliation(s) with the annual physical inventory.
- A liquidation of a base-period LIFO inventory at an interim date that is expected to be recovered by the end of the annual period is valued at the expected cost of replacement. Cost of sales for the interim period includes the expected cost of replacement and not the cost of the base-period LIFO inventory.
- Inventory losses from market declines resulting from applying lower of cost or market (Subtopic 330-10) shall not be deferred beyond the interim period in which they occur. Recoveries of losses on the same inventory in subsequent interim periods of the same fiscal year shall be recognized as gains in the later interim period, but cannot exceed the losses included in prior interim periods. (*Temporary* market declines that are expected to be made up by the end of the annual period need not be recognized in interim periods.)
- Inventory and product costs computed by the use of a standard cost accounting system are determined by the same procedures used at the end of a fiscal year. Variances from standard costs that are expected to be made up by the end of the fiscal year need not be included in interim-period statements.

PRACTICE POINTER: Although all four of these procedures are acceptable in interim financial statements, they are not considered U.S. GAAP for purposes of annual financial statements. Some may result in material differences in the amount of net income (e.g., using the replacement cost for erosion of a LIFO layer in an early interim period), and care should be taken that a similar procedure is not used in annual financial statements.

The objective is to achieve a fair measure of the results of operations for the annual period and the financial position at the end of that period. Following are specific standards that apply in interim periods in accounting for costs and expenses other than product costs:

- Costs and expenses other than product costs are charged to interim periods as incurred, or are allocated among interim periods based on an estimate of time expired, benefit received, or activity associated with the periods. Procedures for assigning specific cost and expense items to an interim period shall be consistent with the bases followed by the entity in reporting for the annual period. If a specific cost or expense item changed to expense for annual reporting purposes benefits more than one interim period, that cost or expense may be allocated to those interim periods.
- Some costs and expenses incurred in an interim period cannot be readily identified with the activities or benefits of other interim periods and are charged to the interim period in which they occur. Disclosure is required of the nature and amount of such costs.
- Arbitrary assignment of the amount of costs to an interim period is not permitted.
- Gains and losses that arise in any interim period similar to those that would not be deferred at year-end shall not be deferred to later interim periods within the same fiscal year. (ASC 270-10-45-8)
- Companies that have material seasonal revenue variations must take care to avoid the possibility that interim-period financial statements become misleading. Disclosure of such variations should be made in the interim-period financial statements. In addition, it is desirable to disclose results for a full year, ending with the current interim period (ASC 270-10-45-11).

- Material unusual of infrequent transactions reported separately in the interim periods in which they occur (ASC 270-10-45-11A).
- Other pertinent information, such as accounting changes, contingencies, seasonal results, and business combinations, is disclosed to provide the necessary information for the proper understanding of the interim financial statements (ASC 270-10-50-5 and 6).

Interim reports should not contain arbitrary amounts of costs or expenses. Estimates should be reasonable and based on all available information applied consistently from period to period (ASC 270-10-45-10). An effective tax rate is used for determining the income tax provision in interim periods, applied on a cumulative year-to-date basis (ASC 740-270-30-4, 5). Income taxes for interim-period reports are discussed in Chapter 46, *ASC 740—Income Taxes*.

Material contingencies and other uncertainties that exist at an interim date are disclosed in interim reports in the same manner as that required for annual reports. These interim-date contingencies and uncertainties should be evaluated in relation to the annual report. The disclosure for such items must be repeated in every interim and annual report until the contingency is resolved or becomes immaterial (ASC 270-10-50-6).

SUMMARIZED INTERIM FINANCIAL INFORMATION

Publicly traded companies typically report summarized financial information at interim dates in considerably less detail than is provided in annual financial statements. If publicly traded companies report summarized financial information at interim dates, this disclosure should include the following (ASC 270-10-50-1):

- Sales or gross revenues, provision for income taxes, net income, and comprehensive income
- Basic and diluted earnings-per-share data
- Seasonal revenues, costs, and expenses
- Significant changes in estimates or provisions for income taxes
- Disposal of a segment of a business, unusual, or infrequently occurring items
- Contingent items
- Changes in accounting principles or estimates
- Significant changes in financial position
- All of the following about reportable segments determined in accordance with ASC 280, including provisions related to restatement of segment information in previously issued financial statements:
  - — Revenues from external customers
  - — Intersegment revenues
  - — A measure of segment profit or loss
  - — Total assets from which there has been a material change from the amount disclosed in the last annual report
  - — Description of differences from the last annual report in the basis of segmentation or in the measurement of segment profit or loss
  - — Reconciliation of total reportable segments' measures of profit or loss to the entity's consolidated income before income taxes and discontinued operations.

Costs and expenses incurred in an interim period that cannot be readily identified with the activities or benefits of other interim periods are charged to the interim period in which they occur. Disclosure in the notes to the financial statements include the nature and amount of such costs unless items of a comparable nature are included in both the current interim period and in the corresponding interim period of the preceding year. (ASC 270-10-50-1B)

A public business entity, a not-for-profit entity that has issued, or is a conduit bond obligor for, securities that are traded, listed, or quoted on an exchange or an over-the-counter market, or an employee benefit plan that files or furnishes financial statements with or to the Securities and Exchange Commission, shall disclose all of the following about revenues from contracts with customers consistent with ASC 606:

- A disaggregation of revenues for the period.
- The opening and closing balances of receivables, contract assets, and contract liabilities under contracts with customers.

- Revenue recognized in the reporting period that was included in the contract liability balance at the beginning of the period.
- Revenue recognized in the reporting period from performance obligations satisfied, or partially satisfied, in previous periods.
- Information about the entity's remaining performance obligations as of the end of the reporting period. (ASC 270-10-50-1A)

A lessor shall disclose a table of all lease-related income items. Those items are identified in ASC 842-30-50-5 (ASC 270-10-50-6A).

PRACTICE POINTER: In addition to the information items listed above, which are generally applicable to all entities, ASC 270 includes an extensive list of additional required disclosures for defined benefit pension plans and other defined benefit retirement plans. In addition, ASC 270 includes specific required disclosures for a variety of financing-related instruments and transactions (ASC 270-10-50-1, items j through s).

PRACTICE POINTER: To satisfy the ASC 270 interim reporting disclosure requirements, companies may present abbreviated financial statements, separate information items, or both. One commonly used alternative is for a company to present an abbreviated income statement and selected information items from the balance sheet and statement of cash flows. Another alternative is to present abbreviated versions of all financial statements. In all approaches, companies typically omit most of the detailed note disclosures that are required in annual financial statements.

Regardless of the approach taken, when summarized financial information is reported regularly on a quarterly basis, the required information should be furnished for the current quarter, the current year-to-date or the last 12 months to date, with comparable information for the preceding year (ASC 270-10-50-1). (The illustration at the end of this chapter suggests a format for this information.)

PRACTICE POINTER: Summarized interim financial statements based on these minimum disclosures *do not* constitute a fair presentation of financial position and results of operations in conformity with U.S. GAAP. Care should be taken that statements do not imply that interim information is in accordance with U.S. GAAP for annual financial statements unless it is (which is rarely the case).

PRACTICE POINTER: The authors favor presenting the last 12 months for comparative information rather than year-to-date information. Presenting the last 12 months' information is generally more useful in creating the context for the current period being presented and for assessing the current interim period impact on annual results.

In the event that fourth-quarter results are not issued separately, the annual report should include disclosures for the fourth quarter on the aggregate effect of material year-end adjustments, infrequently occurring and/or unusual items, and disposal of business segments that occurred in the fourth quarter (ASC 270-10-50-2).

Illustration of Format for Presenting Interim Financial Information

When quarterly information is regularly reported by publicly held companies, ASC 270 requires (1) minimum disclosure of specific information items for the current quarter and comparable information for the same quarter of the previous year and (2) current year-to-date or twelve-months-to-date information and comparable information for the same period of the previous year.

The following is a suggested format, using illustrative dates and numbers, for the presentation of this information:

Hypothetical Company Interim Financial Information For Quarter Ending June 30, 20X8, and Comparable Periods (in thousands)

	Current Quarter		*Twelve-Months-to-Date*	
	3 months ending 6/30/20X8	*3 months ending 6/30/20X7*	*Year ending 6/30/20X8*	*Year ending 6/30/20X7*
[Information item]	$50	$40	$425	$575

FOURTH QUARTER REPORTING

If interim financial information is not separately reported for the fourth quarter, users of interim information may make inferences about the fourth quarter by subtracting information based on the third quarter interim report from annual results. In the absence of a separate fourth quarter report or disclosure of the results of the fourth quarter in the annual report, disposals of components of the entity and unusual or infrequently occurring items recognized in the fourth quarter, as well as the aggregate effect of year-end adjustments that are material to the results of that quarter, shall be disclosed in the annual report (ASC 270-10-50-2).

CHAPTER 13

ASC 272—LIMITED LIABILITY ENTITIES

CONTENTS

INTERPRETIVE GUIDANCE

ASC 272-10: OVERALL

ASC 272-10-05-1, 05-2, 05-5, 05-6; 45-1 through 45-7; 50-1 through 50-5; ASC 850-10-60-9 Accounting and Reporting by Limited Liability Companies and Limited Liability Partnerships

BACKGROUND

Limited liability companies and limited liability partnerships (referred to hereafter as LLCs) are formed under the laws of individual states and therefore have characteristics that are not uniform. Generally, however, they have the following characteristics:

- They are unincorporated associations of two or more persons.
- Their members have limited personal liability for the obligations of the LLC.
- They are treated as partnerships for federal income tax purposes.
- At least two of the following corporate characteristics are lacking:
  - — Limited liability
  - — Free transferability of interests
  - — Centralized management
  - — Continuity of life

PB-14 provides guidance for U.S. LLCs that prepare financial statements in accordance with generally accepted accounting principles.

ACCOUNTING GUIDANCE

LLCs that are subject to U.S. federal, foreign, state, or local taxes (including franchise taxes) must account for those taxes in accordance with the guidance in ASC 740 (Income Taxes), including accounting for a change in tax status.

Financial Statement Display

- A complete set of financial statements must include the following:
  - — Statement of financial position
  - — Statement of operations
  - — Statement of cash flows
  - — Notes to financial statements
- Disclosure is required of changes in members' equity for the period, either in a separate statement or in notes to the financial statements.

- The equity section of the statement of financial position is referred to as "members' equity." Information about the different classes of members' equity is required, including the amount of each class, stated separately, either in the financial statements (preferable) or in notes to the financial statements (acceptable).
- If the members' equity is less than zero, the deficit should be reported, even though the members' liability may be limited.
- If an LLC maintains separate accounts for components of members' equity (e.g., undistributed earnings, earnings available for withdrawal, unallocated capital), disclosure of these accounts is required in the financial statements or notes.
- If an LLC records amounts due from members for capital contributions, such amounts receivable should generally be presented as deductions from members' equity, with the very limited exception of instances where there is substantial evidence of ability and intent to pay within a reasonably short period.
- Comparative financial statements are encouraged, but not required. Any exceptions to comparability must be disclosed in the notes to the financial statements.
- If the formation of an LLC results in a new reporting entity, the guidance in ASC 250-10-45-21 for a change in reporting entity should be followed. In accordance with an amendment in Accounting Standards Update (ASU) 2010-8, a change should be applied retrospectively to prior periods presented to show financial information for the new reporting entity for those periods.

Disclosures

- The following information should be disclosed:
  - Description of any limitation of members' liability
  - The different classes of members' interests and the respective rights, preferences, and privileges of each class
  - The amount of each class of members' equity included in the statement of financial position
  - If an LLC has a limited life, the date on which the LLC will cease to exist.

ASC 272-10-05-3, 05-4; ASC 323-30-35-3; 15-4 Accounting for Investments in Limited Liability Companies

BACKGROUND

Although limited liability companies (LLCs) are similar both to corporations and to partnerships, LLCs also differ in many ways from those types of entities. LLCs are similar to corporations because their members generally are *not* personally liable for the LLC's liabilities. They differ from corporations in that owners of LLCs control the operations of those entities, whereas the operations of corporations are controlled by their Boards of Directors and their committees rather than by their common shareholders.

LLCs are *similar* to partnerships in the following ways: (*a*) the members of LLCs are taxed on their shares of the LLCs' earnings; (*b*) LLC members generally cannot assign their financial interests without the consent of *all* members; and (*c*) most LLCs are dissolved as a result of a member's death, bankruptcy, or withdrawal.

LLCs *differ* from partnerships in that (*a*) it is *not* necessary for *one* owner to be liable for the LLC's liabilities, such as the general partner in a limited partnership; (*b*) the owners of LLCs control the operations of those entities, unlike limited partnerships, whose operations are managed by the general partner; and (*c*) all partners in a general partnership have *unlimited* liability.

Although the authoritative accounting literature provides no specific guidance regarding the accounting for noncontrolling LLCs, the guidance in ASC 323 (Investments-Equity Method and Joint Ventures) currently is being applied in accounting for those entities. Under the provisions of ASC 323, the equity method should be used to account for investments in which an investor can exercise *significant influence* over an investee's operating and financial policies. It is presumed that investments of at least 20% meet that requirement. Even though that guidance does *not* specifically apply to partnerships, ASC 323-30-15-3; 25-2; 30-1 through 30-2; 35-1 through 35-2; 810-10-45-14 states that many of the provisions would be "appropriate in accounting" for partnerships.

ASC 970-323 states that noncontrolling interests in limited partnerships should be accounted for under the equity method, unless a limited partner's interest is "so minor that the limited partner may have virtually no influence over partnership operating and financial policies." The cost method should be used under those circumstances. Another source of guidance is ASC 323-30-S99-1; S55-1, in which the SEC staff clarifies what percentage is considered minor. It states that investments in limited partnerships of *more* than 3%-5% should be accounted for by the equity method, because they are more than minor investments.

ACCOUNTING ISSUE

To determine whether a *noncontrolling* investment in an LLC should be accounted for by the cost method or by the equity method, should an LLC be considered to be similar to a corporation or to a partnership?

ACCOUNTING GUIDANCE

The following guidance applies when determining how to account for a noncontrolling investment in an LLC: The guidance in this Issue does *not* apply to: Investments in LLCs that must be accounted for as debt securities under the guidance in ASC 860-20-35-2 (Accounting for Transfers and Servicing of Financial Assets and Extinguishments of Liabilities); Equity interests in LLCs that must be accounted for under the guidance in ASC 325-40-05-1 through 05-2, 15-2 through 15-9, 25-1 through 25-3, 30-1 through 30-3, 35-1 through 35-10A, 35-13, 35-16, 45-1, 55-1 through 55-2; ASC 310-20-60-1 through 60-2; ASC 310-30-15-5, 60-1; ASC 320-10-35-38, 55-2; ASC 835-10-60-7 (Recognition of Interest Income and Impairment on Purchased and Retained Beneficial Interests in Securitized Financial Assets); and LLCs that must be accounted for under the guidance in ASC 810-10-15-10, 25-1 through 25-8, 25-10 through 25-14, 55-1 (Investor's Accounting for an Investee When the Investor Has a Majority of the Voting Interest but the Noncontrolling Shareholder or Shareholders Have Certain Approval or Veto Rights) (see Chapter 49, *ASC 810—Consolidation*).

An LLC that maintains a "specific ownership account" for each investor in the LLC is treating its investors in a manner similar to the way partnership capital accounts are structured. Consequently, investments treated in that manner should be considered to be similar to limited partnerships (LPs) when determining the appropriate accounting. Such LLCs should be accounted for under the guidance in ASC 970-323 and the guidance in the SEC's announcement in ASC 323-30-S99-1, S55-1, which is discussed in Chapter 21, *ASC 323—Investments—Equity Method and Joint Ventures*. It was noted that specific ownership accounts may exist in entities organized in another form. The characteristics of those organizations were not considered, but some suggested that it may be appropriate for such entities to analogize to the guidance in this Issue.

CHAPTER 14

ASC 274—PERSONAL FINANCIAL STATEMENTS

CONTENTS

INTERPRETIVE GUIDANCE

ASC 274-10: OVERALL

ASC 274-10-05-1 through 05-3; 15-1, 15-2; 25-1; 35-1 through 35-15; 45-1 through 45-13; 50-1, 50-2; 55-1 through 55-7, 55-9 through 55-14 Accounting and Financial Reporting for Personal Financial Statements

BACKGROUND

The guidance in ASC 274 addresses the preparation and presentation of personal financial statements for individuals or groups of related individuals (e.g., a husband and wife, a family).

The primary focus of personal financial statements is on an individual's assets and liabilities. Users of personal financial statements normally consider estimated current value information to be more relevant to their decision-making than historical cost information. The guidance in ASC 274 explains how the estimated current amounts of assets and liabilities should be determined and applied in a presentation of personal financial statements.

ACCOUNTING GUIDANCE

Form of the Statements

Personal financial statements consist of the following:

- *Statement of financial condition* Presents the estimated current values of assets, estimated current amounts of liabilities, estimated income taxes on the differences between the estimated current values of assets and the estimated current amounts of liabilities and their tax bases, and net worth as of a specified date.

  The term *net worth* is used to designate the difference between total assets and total liabilities, after deduction of estimated income taxes on the differences between the current amounts of those items and their tax bases.

- *Statement of changes in net worth* Presents the major sources of increases and decreases in net worth (e.g., income or (loss)), changes in the estimated current values of assets, changes in the estimated amounts of liabilities, changes in the estimated income tax on the differences between the estimated current value of assets and the estimated current amount of liabilities and their related tax bases).

- *Comparative financial statements* Presents information about the current period and one or more prior periods (optional).

Methods of Presentation

Assets and liabilities should be recognized on the accrual basis rather than on the cash basis. The most useful presentation of assets and liabilities is in their order of liquidity and maturity, respectively, without classification as current and noncurrent.

In personal financial statements for one of a group of joint owners of assets, the statements should include only that individual's interest as a beneficial owner. Business interests that constitute a large part of an individual's total assets should be shown separately from other investments. The estimated current value of an investment in a separate entity should be shown in one amount as an investment if the entity is marketable as a going concern. Assets and liabilities of the separate entity should not be combined with similar personal items.

The estimated current values of assets and the estimated current amounts of liabilities of limited business activities not conducted in a separate business entity (e.g., investment in real estate and a related mortgage) should be presented as separate amounts, particularly if a large portion of the liabilities may be satisfied with funds from sources unrelated to the investment.

Guidelines for Determining Current Values and Amounts

The estimated current value of an asset in personal financial statements is the amount at which the item could be exchanged between a buyer and a seller, each of whom is well informed and willing, and neither of whom is compelled to buy or sell. Costs of disposal should be considered in estimating current values. Recent transactions involving similar assets and liabilities in similar circumstances ordinarily provide a reasonable basis for determining the current value of an asset and the estimated current amount of a liability. In the absence of recent similar transactions, adjustments of historical cost for changes in a specific price index, appraisals, and discounted amounts of projected cash receipts and payments may be appropriate.

Receivables

Receivables should be presented at the amounts of estimated cash that will be collected, using appropriate interest rates at the date of the financial statements.

Marketable Securities

The value of marketable securities should be based on quoted market prices, if available, based on their closing prices on the date of the financial statements if the securities were traded on that date. Bid-and-ask quotations may be used to estimate the current value of securities. An adjustment to market price may be required if an investor owns sufficient amounts of securities that if sold would influence the market price.

Options

If published prices of options are unavailable, their current value should be determined on the basis of the values of the underlying assets, taking into consideration such factors as the options' exercise price and length of the option period.

Investments in Life Insurance

The estimated current value of life insurance is the cash value of a policy less the amount of loans against it, if any. The policy's face value should be disclosed.

Investments in Closely Held Businesses

There is no one generally accepted procedure for determining the estimated current value of an investment in a closely held business. Alternative valuation procedures include the following:

- Multiple of earnings
- Liquidation value
- Reproduction value
- Appraisal
- Discounted amounts of projected cash receipts and payments
- Adjustments of book value or cost of the person's share of equity

The objective should be to approximate the amount at which an investment could be exchanged between a buyer and a seller, each of whom is well informed and willing, and neither of whom is compelled to buy or sell.

Real Estate

Investments in real estate, including leaseholds, should be presented at current value, with consideration given to information such as the following:

- Sales of similar property in similar circumstances
- The discounted amount of projected receipts and payments related to a property or a property's net realizable value, based on planned courses of action
- Appraisals based on an estimated selling price, net of estimated selling costs, provided by an independent real estate agent familiar with similar properties in similar locations.
- Appraisals used to obtain financing
- Assessed value for property taxes

Intangible Assets

Investments in intangible assets should be based on discounted amounts of projected cash receipts and payments based on the planned use or sale of the assets. A purchased intangible asset's cost may be used if no other information is available.

Future Interests and Similar Assets

Rights to receive future sums that will not be forfeited should be presented as assets at their discounted amounts if those rights have all of the following characteristics:

- The rights are for fixed or determinable amounts.
- The rights are not contingent on a holder's life expectancy or the occurrence of a particular event, such as disability or death.
- The rights do not require a holder to perform future services.

Examples of rights that may have those characteristics are guaranteed minimum portions of pensions, deferred compensation contracts, and beneficial interests in trusts.

Payables and Other Liabilities

Payables and other liabilities should be presented at their discounted amounts of cash to be paid. The discount rate should be the rate implicit in the transaction in which the debt was incurred—unless the debtor is able to discharge the debt currently at a lower amount, in which case the debt should be presented at the lower amount.

Noncancelable Commitments

Noncancelable commitments to pay future sums should be presented as liabilities at their discounted amounts if those commitments have all of the following characteristics:

- The commitments are for fixed or determinable amounts.
- The commitments are not contingent on others' life expectancies or on the occurrence of a particular event, such as disability or death.
- The commitments do not require future performance of services by others.

Income Taxes Payable

A liability for income taxes should include unpaid income taxes for completed tax years and an estimate of the amount of accrued income taxes for the elapsed portion of the financial statements' current year.

Estimated Income Taxes on the Difference between the Estimated Current Values of Assets and the Current Amounts of Liabilities and Their Tax Bases

A provision should be made for estimated income taxes on the difference between the estimated current values of assets and the estimated current amounts of liabilities and their tax bases. The estimate should include consideration of negative tax bases of tax shelters, if any. That amount should be presented between liabilities and net worth in the statement of financial condition. Methods and assumptions used to estimate income taxes should be disclosed.

Financial Statement Disclosure

Personal financial statements should include adequate information to make the statements informative. The items in the following list, which is *not* all-inclusive, indicate the nature and type of information that should be disclosed:

- The name(s) of individual(s) covered by the financial statements
- A statement that assets are presented at their estimated current values and liabilities at their estimated current amounts

- The method used to estimate current values of assets and current amounts of liabilities
- If assets are held jointly by the individual and others, the nature of the joint ownership
- If the individual's investment portfolio is material in relation to other assets and is concentrated in one or a few companies, the names of the companies or industries and the current values of the securities
- If the individual has a material investment in a closely held business:
  - The name of the company and the individual's ownership percentage
  - The nature of the business
  - Summarized financial information about the assets, liabilities and results of operations of the business
- Descriptions of intangible assets and their estimated useful lives
- Amount of life insurance
- Nonforfeitable rights (that do not have the characteristics described above)
- The following tax information:
  - The methods and assumptions used to compute the estimated income taxes on the difference between the estimated current values of assets and the estimated current amounts of liabilities and their tax bases
  - Unused operating losses and capital loss carryforwards
  - Other unused deductions and credits and their expiration dates
  - The difference between the estimated current values of major assets and the estimated current amounts of liabilities or categories of assets and liabilities and their tax bases
- Maturities, interest rates, collateral, and other details related to receivables and debt
- Noncancelable commitments (that do not have the characteristics described above)

PRACTICE POINTER: Generally accepted accounting principles other than those described in ASC 274 may apply to the preparation of personal financial statements. For example, ASC 450 and ASC 850 may provide useful guidance in preparing personal financial statements.

CHAPTER 15

ASC 275—RISKS AND UNCERTAINTIES

CONTENTS

INTERPRETIVE GUIDANCE

ASC 275-10: OVERALL

ASC 275-10-05-2 through 05-8; 10-1; 15-3 through 15-6; 50-1 through 50-2, 50-4, 50-6 through 50-21, 50-23; 55-1 through 55-19; 60-3; ASC 205-20-55-80; ASC 330-10-55-8 through 55-13; ASC 814-10-30-55-8 through 55-13; ASC 450-20-50-2; 55-36 through 55-37; ASC 460-10-55-27; ASC 605-35-55-3 through 55-10; ASC 740-10-55-219 through 55-222; ASC 932-360-55-15 through 15-19; ASC 958-205-60-1; ASC 605-55-70; ASC 985-20-55-24 through 5-29 Disclosure of Certain Significant Risks and Uncertainties

BACKGROUND

Volatility and uncertainty in the business and economic environment result in the need for disclosure of information about the risks and uncertainties confronted by reporting entities. Under the guidance in this pronouncement, disclosure is required about significant risks and uncertainties that confront entities in the following areas: nature of operations, use of estimates in the preparation of financial statements, certain significant estimates, and current vulnerability due to certain concentrations.

PRACTICE POINTER: The guidance in ASC 275-10-05-02 and ASC 275-10-50-1 has been amended by the guidance in ASU 2014-10, *Development Stage Entities (ASC 915), Elimination of Certain Financial Reporting Requirements, Including an Amendment to Variable Interest Entities Guidance in Topic 810, Consolidation.* Under that amendment, an entity's disclosure about the nature of its operations should include information about activities in which the entity is "currently" involved but the primary operations of those activities have not yet begun. In addition, new paragraph ASC 275-10-50-2A provides that an entity that has not begun its primary operations should disclose information about the risks and uncertainties related to activities in which the entity is "currently" involved and should explain the objective of those activities. Example 1A in ASC 275-55-3A through 3B illustrates disclosures about activities whose planned operations have not yet begun.

ASC 275-10-05-7 is amended by the conforming amendments in Section B of ASU 2014-09, *Revenue from Contracts with Customers (ASC 606).* The amendment, which provides that estimates in the financial reporting process involve "estimating and constraining estimates of variable consideration to be included in the transaction price for a contract with a customer in accordance with paragraphs 606-10-32-5 through 32-14 and measuring progress toward complete satisfaction of a performance obligation in accordance with paragraphs 606-10-25-31 through 25-37" is inserted in the second sentence of ASC 275-10-05-7 and the existing phrase, "accruing income for the current period under a long term contract requires an estimate of the total profit to be earned on the contract" is deleted. In addition, the existing guidance in ASC 275-10-60-7 is deleted and replaced by a statement that the guidance in ASC 606-10-50-1 through 50-23 should be consulted for disclosures about revenue from contracts with customers.

ACCOUNTING GUIDANCE

Nature of Operations

Financial statements should include a description of the major products or services an entity sells or provides and its principal markets and locations of those markets. Entities that operate in more than one market must indicate the relative importance of their operations in each market. Disclosures concerning the nature of operations are not required to be quantified, and relative importance may be described by terms such as *predominantly, about equally, major,* and *other*.

Illustration of a Nature of Operations Note for a Pharmaceutical Company

Geneca Inc. is a research-driven pharmaceutical company that discovers, develops, manufactures, and markets a broad range of human, animal, and agricultural health products. Human health products include therapeutic and preventive agents, generally sold by prescription, for the treatment of human disorders.

PRACTICE POINTER: Entities that operate in more than one market are required to indicate the relative importance of their operations in each market. Similar to the previous illustration, most companies do not include this disclosure in the "nature of operations" note. Rather, information on the relative importance of operations in different markets is typically found in the business segments note.

Use of Estimates

Financial statements should include a statement that they were prepared in conformity with U.S. GAAP, which requires the application of management's estimates.

Illustration of a Use of Estimates Note—Basic

We prepare our financial statements under generally accepted accounting principles, which require management to make estimates and assumptions that affect the reported amounts or certain disclosures. Actual results could differ from those estimates.

Illustration of a Use of Estimates Note—Detailed

We prepare our financial statements under generally accepted accounting principles, which require management to make estimates and assumptions that affect the reported amounts or certain disclosures. Actual results could differ from those estimates. Estimates are used when accounting for certain items such as long-term contracts, allowance for doubtful accounts, depreciation and amortization, employee benefit plans, taxes, restructuring reserves, and contingencies.

Significant Estimates

Disclosure regarding an estimate is required when *both* of the following conditions are met:

- It is at least reasonably possible that the estimate of the effect on the financial statements of a condition, situation, or set of circumstances that existed at the date of the financial statements will change in the near term due to one or more future confirming events.
- The effect of the change would have a material effect on the financial statements.

The disclosure requirements in ASC 450 for contingencies are supplemented by the following guidance:

- If an estimate requires disclosure under the guidance in ASC 450 or another pronouncement, there should be an indication that it is at least reasonably possible that a change in the estimate will occur in the near term.

- An estimate that does not require disclosure under the guidance in ASC 450 (such as estimates associated with long-term operating assets and amounts reported under profitable long-term contracts) may meet the standards described above and, if so, requires the following:
  - Disclosure of its nature
  - An indication that it is reasonably possible that a change in the estimate will occur in the near term

The following are examples of the types of situations that may require disclosure in accordance with the guidance in this pronouncement, assuming the conditions stated above are met:

- Inventory subject to rapid technological obsolescence
- Specialized equipment subject to technological obsolescence
- Valuation allowances for deferred tax assets based on future taxable income
- Capitalized motion picture film production costs
- Capitalized computer software costs
- Deferred policy acquisition costs of insurance enterprises
- Valuation allowances for commercial and real estate loans
- Environmental remediation-related obligations
- Litigation-related obligations
- Contingent liabilities for obligations of other entities
- Amounts reported for long-term obligations (e.g., pensions and other post-retirement benefits)
- Estimated net proceeds recoverable, the provisions for expected loss to be incurred, etc., on disposition of a business or assets
- Amounts reported for long-term contracts

Vulnerability from Concentrations

Vulnerability from concentrations exists because of an enterprise's greater exposure to risk than would be the case if the enterprise had mitigated its risk through diversification. Financial statements should disclose concentrations if *all* of the following conditions are met:

- The concentration existed at the date of the financial statements.
- The concentration makes the enterprise vulnerable to the risk of a near-term severe impact.
- It is reasonably possible that the events that could cause the severe impact will occur in the near term.

Information sufficient to inform financial statement users of the general nature of the risk associated with the concentration is required for the following specific concentrations:

- Concentrations in the volume of business transacted with a particular customer, supplier, lender, grantor, or contributor
- Concentrations in revenue from particular products, services, or fund-raising events
- Concentrations in the available sources of supply of materials, labor, or services, or of licenses or other rights used in the entity's operations
- Concentrations in the market or geographic area in which an entity conducts its operations

In addition, for concentrations of labor subject to collective bargaining agreements, disclosure shall include both the percentage of the labor force covered by a collective bargaining agreement and the percentage of the labor force covered by a collective bargaining agreement that will expire within one year. For concentrations of operations located outside the entity's home country, disclosure shall include the carrying amounts of net assets and the geographic areas in which they are located.

Illustration of a Note on Concentrations—No Exposure

As of December 31, 20X4, we do not have any significant concentration of business transacted with a particular customer, supplier, or lender that could, if suddenly eliminated, severely impact our operations. We also do not have a concentration of available sources of labor or services that could, if suddenly eliminated, severely impact our operations. We invest our cash with high-quality credit institutions.

Illustration of a Note on Concentrations—Customer Concentration Exposure

The company's five largest customers accounted for approximately 48% of net revenues for 20X4. At December 31, 20X4, these customers accounted for approximately 38% of net accounts receivable.

CHAPTER 16

ASC 280—SEGMENT REPORTING

CONTENTS

PART I: GENERAL GUIDANCE

ASC 280-10: OVERALL

OVERVIEW

The term *segment reporting* refers to the presentation of information about certain parts of an enterprise rather than about the enterprise as a whole. The need for segment information became increasingly important in the 1960s and 1970s as enterprises diversified their activities into different industries and product lines, as well as into different geographic areas. Financial analysts and other groups of financial statement users insisted on the importance of disaggregated information—in order for them to assess risk and perform other types of analyses.

BACKGROUND

The objective of presenting disaggregated information about segments of a business enterprise is to produce information about the different types of activities in which an enterprise is engaged in and the economic environment in which those activities are carried out. Specifically, the FASB believes that segment information assists financial statement users to (ASC 280-10-10-1):

- Understand enterprise performance
- Assess its prospects for future net cash flows
- Make informed decisions about the enterprise

PRACTICE NOTE: The FASB does not specifically identify risk assessment as the objective of segment reporting. Risk assessment, however, is an important dimension of financial analysis and directly relates to the need for segment information. The requirements of ASC 280 include information about products and services, information about activities in different geographic areas, and information about reliance on major customers. All relate to areas of significant risk to an enterprise and to areas where risk may vary considerably from situation to situation, including risks associated with producing and selling different products, operating in different geographic areas, and differing levels of reliance on major customers.

In 1994, the AICPA's Special Committee on Financial Reporting (the "Jenkins Committee") issued its report, which suggested that for users analyzing a company involved in diverse business segments, information about those segments may be as important as information about the company as a whole. That study suggested that standard setters give a high priority to improving segment reporting, and that segment information should be reoriented toward the way management operates the business enterprise. Consistent with this suggestion, in identifying operating segments, ASC 280 requires a management approach that is generally consistent with the AICPA special committee's recommendations.

IDENTIFYING SEGMENTS

Scope

ASC 280 applies to public business enterprises. Any single aspect or combination of the following identifies an enterprise as a public enterprise (ASC 280-10-15-2; ASC Glossary):

- Has issued debt or equity securities or is a conduit bond obligor for conduit debt securities that are traded in a public market (a domestic or foreign stock exchange or an over-the-counter market)
- Is required to file financial statements with the Securities and Exchange Commission
- Provides financial statements for the purpose of issuing securities in a public market

ASC 280 does not apply in the following situations (ASC 280-10-15-3):

- Nonpublic business enterprises
- Not-for-profit enterprises (regardless of whether the entity meets the definition of a public entity)
- The separate financial statements of parents, subsidiaries, joint ventures, or equity method investees if those enterprises' separate statements are consolidated or combined and both the separate company statements and the consolidated or combined statements are included in the same financial report

Although the requirements of ASC 280 are not required for *nonpublic* business enterprises, ASC 280 encourages them to provide the same information as public business enterprises.

Operating Segments

The concept of operating segments is instrumental to understanding ASC 280. Operating segments are components of an enterprise (ASC 280-10-50-1):

- That engage in business activities from which it may recognize revenue and incur expenses; and
- Whose operating results are reviewed by the enterprise's chief operating decision maker for purposes of making decisions with regard to resource allocation and performance evaluation.

ASC 280 includes several guidelines that help implement these general criteria for identifying an enterprise's operating segments, as follows:

- Having recognized revenues is not a requirement for a component of a business to be an operating segment (ASC 280-10-50-3). For example, a start-up component of the business, which has not yet recognized revenue, may be an operating segment.
- Not every component of an enterprise is an operating segment or part of an operating segment (ASC 280-10-50-4). For example, corporate headquarters may not be an operating segment.
- Concerning personnel involved in segments (ASC 280-10-50-5, 7, 8):

- — The term *chief operating decision maker* refers to a function, not a specific position title. The intent is to identify that person who performs two functions: (*i*) makes decisions relative to the allocation of resources and (*ii*) evaluates the performance of the segments of the enterprise. The chief operating decision maker may be an individual (e.g., chief executive officer, chief operating officer) or it may be a group of individuals.

  PRACTICE NOTE: ASC 280 does not designate a specific position title that might mean different things in different enterprises. The term *chief operating decision maker* was developed to apply to whatever position within an enterprise makes decisions relative to the allocation of resources and evaluates the performance of segments of the enterprise.

  — The term *segment manager* is intended to refer to the functions having direct accountability to and regular contact with the chief operating decision maker to discuss operating activities, financial results, forecasts, and similar matters. A segment manager may be responsible for more than one segment. The chief operating decision maker also may be a segment manager for one or more operating segments.

- Other factors that may be important in identifying an enterprise's operating segments are (*a*) the nature of the business activities of each component of the enterprise, (*b*) the way the business is organized in terms of managerial responsibility for components of the enterprise, and (*c*) the manner in which information is presented to the board of directors of the enterprise (ASC 280-10-50-6).
- The three primary characteristics of an operating segment may apply to two or more overlapping components of an enterprise (i.e., a matrix organization). For example, one individual may be responsible for each product and service line and another individual may be responsible for each geographic area in which those product and service lines are distributed. The chief operating decision maker may use information both based on products and services and on geographic areas to make decisions about resource allocation and segment performance. In this situation, the components based on products and services are considered operating segments (ASC 280-10-50-9).

Reportable Segments

Reportable segments are operating segments that meet the criteria for separate reporting under ASC 280. Essentially, a reportable segment is one that accounts for a sufficient amount of an enterprise's activities to warrant disclosure of separate information.

Quantitative Thresholds

A logical starting point is the quantitative thresholds for identifying reportable segments. These criteria state that an operating segment is a reportable segment if any of the following quantitative criteria is met (ASC 280-10-50-12).

- The operating segment's total revenues (both external, such as sales to other enterprises, and intersegment, such as sales between operating segments) make up 10% or more of the combined revenue of all operating segments.
- The absolute amount of the reported profit or loss of the operating segments is 10% or more of the greater (absolute amount) of the total profit of all operating segments reporting a profit or the total loss of all operating segments reporting a loss.
- The operating segment's assets make up 10% or more of the combined assets of all operating segments.

In determining its reportable segments that meet these quantitative criteria, management may combine the activities of two or more operating segments, but only if certain similar economic characteristics are present in both (or all) operating segments. These operating segments' segment characteristics include (ASC 280-10-50-11):

- The nature of their products and services
- The nature of their production processes
- The types of their customers
- Their distribution methods
- The nature of their regulatory environment (if applicable).

Another quantitative criterion is that the identified reportable segments must constitute at least 75% of the total consolidated revenue (ASC 280-10-50-14). If the operating segments that are initially identified as reportable segments do not meet this threshold, additional operating segments must be identified, even if they do *not* meet the quantitative criteria presented earlier. Information about those operating segments for which separate information is not presented can be combined and presented in the aggregate with an appropriate description (e.g., "all other segments").

Comparability

Comparability among years is an important factor in identifying reportable segments, as evidenced by the following requirements that relate to changes in segments meeting the quantitative criteria from one year to the next (ASC 280-10-50-16, 17):

- If a prior year reportable segment fails to meet one of the quantitative criteria but management believes it to be of continuing significance, information about that segment shall continue to be presented.
- If an operating segment meets the criteria as a reportable segment for the first time in the current period, prior-year segment information that is presented for comparative purposes shall be restated to reflect the new reportable segment as a separate segment.

ASC 280 indicates that 10 reportable segments is probably a reasonable maximum number for purposes of disclosing separate segment information (ASC 280-10-50-18). While the maximum of 10 is not stated as an absolute requirement, management is advised that when the number of reportable segments exceeds 10, consideration should be given to whether a practical limit has been reached.

DISCLOSURE OF INFORMATION ABOUT MULTIPLE REPORTABLE SEGMENTS

Segment information is required in four areas (ASC 280-10-50-20):

1. General information
2. Information about segment profit or loss and assets
3. Reconciliation of segment information to aggregate enterprise amounts
4. Interim period information

The information required by ASC 280 must be reported for each period for which an income statement is presented, including prior periods presented for comparative purposes. Reconciliation of segment balance sheet information to enterprise balance sheet amounts is only required when a balance sheet is presented (ASC 280-10-50-20).

The following sections cover the specific disclosure requirements in the four general areas identified above.

General Information

General information is necessary for financial statement users to understand the specific information about segments that is required to be disclosed. The general information logically would precede the information about segment profit or loss and assets and reconciliations, which are identified in the following two sections (ASC 280-10-50-21):

1. Factors used to identify the enterprise's reportable segments
2. Types of products and services that are the basis for revenues from each reportable segment

In identifying the enterprise's reportable segments, an explanation of the basis for organization is required. Management may have used the following organizational alternatives, for example:

- Products and services
- Geographic areas
- Regulatory environment
- Combination of factors

Information about Segment Profit or Loss and Assets

The heart of the segment reporting requirements of ASC 280 is information about segments' profit or loss and assets. A measure of profit or loss and total assets is required for each reportable segment. This amount should be based on the information reported to the chief operating decision maker for making decisions about allocating resources to segments and assessing segment performance.

If the chief operating decision maker uses only one measure of segment profit or loss and only one measure of assets, those are the measures that should be reported. On the other hand, if the chief operating decision maker uses multiple measures of segment profit or loss or segment assets in resource allocation decisions and performance evaluation, the information reported to satisfy ASC 280 should be that which management believes is determined most consistently with that used in the determination of the corresponding amounts in the enterprise's consolidated financial statements (ASC 280-10-50-28).

In presenting segment profit or loss, the following information is required for each segment if the specific amounts are included in the measure of segment profit or loss reviewed by the chief operating decision maker (ASC 280-10-50-22):

- Revenues from transactions with external customers
- Revenues from other operating segments
- Interest revenue
- Interest expense
- Depreciation, depletion, and amortization
- Unusual or infrequently occurring items
- Income recognized on equity-method investments
- Income tax expense or benefit
- Significant noncash items other than depreciation, depletion, and amortization

Following are guidelines included in ASC 280 for the determination of the information items listed above:

- In identifying unusual items, ASC 225-20 is the primary source of authority.
- Interest revenue and expense should be presented separately (i.e., not net) unless the net amount is the figure used by the chief operating decision maker to assess performance and make resource allocation decisions.

Additional information about assets of each reportable segment is required, as follows, if these amounts are considered by the chief operating decision maker in evaluating the assets held by a segment (ASC 280-10-50-25):

- The amount of investment in equity method investees
- Total expenditures for additions to long-lived assets (except financial instruments, long-term customer relationships of a financial institution, mortgage and other servicing rights, deferred policy acquisition costs, and deferred income taxes)

In addition to the specific information items about segment profit or loss and segment assets, enterprises are required to present explanatory information that should assist users of the financial statements in better understanding the meaning of that information, as follows (ASC 280-10-50-29):

- The basis of accounting for transactions between reportable segments
- Differences in the measurement of the reportable segments' profit or loss and the enterprise's consolidated income before income taxes, discontinued operations, and cumulative effect of changes in accounting principle
- Differences in the measurement of the reportable segments' assets and the enterprise's consolidated assets
- Any changes from prior years in the measurement of reported segment profit or loss, and the effect, if any, of those changes on the amount of segment profit or loss
- The nature of any asymmetrical allocations to segments

PRACTICE NOTE: In further explaining the second and third requirements above, ASC 280 points out that the required reconciliation information (explained below) may satisfy this requirement. It also indicates that enterprises should consider whether differences in accounting policies with regard to the allocation of centrally incurred costs are necessary for understanding the segment information and, if so, to explain those allocation policies. In further explaining the fifth requirement above, ASC 280 illustrates an "asymmetrical allocation" as an enterprise allocating depreciation to a segment without allocating the related depreciable asset to that segment.

Reconciliations

Reconciliations of certain segment information to the enterprise's consolidated totals are an important part of the disclosure requirements of ASC 280, as indicated in the following table (ASC 280-10-50-30):

Segment information	*Reconciled to Consolidated information*
1. Reportable segments' revenues	1. Consolidated revenues
2. Reportable segments' profit or loss	2. Consolidated income before income taxes, and discontinued operations
3. Reportable segments' assets	3. Consolidated assets
4. Reportable segments' amounts for other significant items	4. Corresponding consolidated amounts

In presenting these reconciliations, all significant reconciling items must be separately identified and described.

PRACTICE POINTER: Like many authoritative accounting standards, ASC 280 establishes minimum required disclosures. In the case of segment information, the illustration in ASC 280-10-50-30d implies that a decision to disclose information beyond the minimum requirements carries with it a responsibility to provide reconciling information about that item for the segments and for the consolidated enterprise. The following wording in ASC 280-10-50-30d is important: ". . . an enterprise *may choose* to disclose liabilities for its reportable segments, *in which case the enterprise would reconcile* the total of reportable segments' liabilities for each segment to the enterprise's consolidated liabilities if segment liabilities are significant."

Interim Period Information

ASC 280 requires abbreviated segment information in interim financial statements. The following is an abbreviated categorized listing of the information required to be disclosed in condensed interim financial statements (ASC 280-10-50-32):

- Revenue from external customers
- Intersegment revenue
- Segment profit or loss
- Total assets for which there has been a material changes from last annual report
- A description of differences from the last annual report in the basis of segmentation or in the basis of measurement of segment profit or loss
- Reconciliation of segments' profit or loss to enterprise consolidated income before income taxes and discontinued operations.

In meeting the reconciliation of segment profit or loss requirement, enterprises have two alternatives, depending on whether they allocate items such as income taxes to segments. If they do *not* allocate these items, the reconciliation should be from reportable segments' profit or loss to enterprise consolidated income before income taxes, discontinued operations, and the cumulative effect of a change in accounting principle. On the other hand, if the items indicated above are allocated to segments, the reconciliation may be from segments' profit or loss to consolidated income after those items. In either case, significant reconciling items are to be separately identified and described in that reconciliation.

PRACTICE POINTER: If an enterprise allocates items such as income taxes to segments, it would be reasonable to expect fewer reconciling items between the total of the reportable segments' profit or loss and the related consolidated totals than would be the case if these same items were *not* allocated to segments and, therefore, were required to be part of the reconciliation. In other words, the more items that are allocated down to the segments in determining their profit or loss, the closer the total of the reportable segments' profit and loss will be to the consolidated enterprise's net income and the fewer the items required to meet the reconciliation requirement.

Restatement of Previously Reported Information

An enterprise may change the structure of its internal organization in a manner that causes information about its reportable segments to lack comparability with previous period information. In this situation, and where practicable, previous period information presented for comparative purposes should be restated in accordance with the revised organization. This requirement applies to both previous interim and annual periods. In addition to restating the financial information presented, an explanation of the change is required, including that previous period information has been restated (ASC 280-10-50-34).

If restatement of previous period information is not practicable in the year of the internal organization change, disclosure is required of current period information under both the previous and the new organizational structure if it is practicable to do so (ASC 280-10-50-35).

DISCLOSURE OF ENTERPRISE-WIDE INFORMATION

The previous discussion has focused on disclosure of information about multiple reporting segments. An enterprise is required to report certain disaggregated information, even if it functions as a single operating unit.

Enterprise-wide information is required in the following three areas:

1. Information about products and services
2. Information about geographic areas
3. Information about major customers

Enterprises that are organized around reporting segments may have satisfied these requirements already as a result of satisfying the disclosure requirements for multiple reporting segments. If not, they are required to present the enterprise-wide information, as are enterprises that are not subject to the requirements of those enterprises with multiple reportable segments. Information required in the three areas identified above is as follows:

Products and Services (ASC 280-10-50-40)

- Revenues from external customers for each product and service or group of related products and services

Geographic Areas (ASC 280-10-50-41)

- Revenues from external customers:
  - — Attributable to the enterprise's country of domicile
  - — Attributed to all foreign countries in total from which revenue is derived
  - — Revenues from individual foreign countries if the amounts are material
  - — The basis for attributing revenues from external customers to individual countries
- Long-lived assets (not including financial instruments, long-term customer relationships of a financial institution, mortgage and other servicing rights, deferred policy of acquisition costs, and deferred income taxes:
  - — Attributable to the enterprise's country of domicile
  - — Attributable to all foreign countries in total where assets are held
  - — Assets from individual foreign countries if the amounts are material

Major Customers (ASC 280-10-50-42)

- Revenues from a single customer that accounts for 10% or more of revenue
- The segment(s) from which sales to each major customer were made

In preparing the information about products and services and geographic areas, amounts should be based on the same information used to prepare the enterprise's general purpose-financial statements. If this is impracticable, the information is not required, but an explanation should be provided.

In preparing the information about major customers, the following additional guidance is provided:

- Neither the identity of the major customer nor the amount of revenue that each segment reports from that customer is required.
- A group of entities under common control is considered a single customer.
- For purposes of identifying major *governmental* customers, the federal government, a state government, a local government, or a foreign government is considered a single customer.

Illustration—Sample Disclosures of Segment Information

ASC 280 requires the disclosure of extensive information about an enterprise's operating segments. Following are brief examples of how some of these requirements might appear in notes to the financial statements. In all cases, dollar figures (in thousands) are assumed for illustrative purposes.

Management Policy in Identifying Reportable Segments

Company A's reportable business segments are strategic business units that offer distinctive products and services that are marketed through different channels. They are managed separately because of their unique technology, marketing, and distribution requirements.

Types of Products and Services

Company B has four reportable segments: food processing, apparel manufacturing, insurance, and entertainment. Food processing is a canning operating for sales to regional grocery chains. The apparel segment produces mid-price clothing for distribution through discount department stores. The insurance segment provides primarily property insurance for heavy manufacturing enterprises. The entertainment segment includes several theme parks and multiple-screen theaters.

Segment Profit or Loss

Company C's accounting policies for segments are the same as those described in the summary of significant accounting policies. Management evaluates segment performance based on segment profit or loss before income taxes and nonrecurring gains and losses. Transfers between segments are accounted for at market value.

	Segments				*Consolidated*	
	A	*B*	*C*	*D*	*Other*	*Totals*
Revenues from external customers	$200	$200	$300	$400	$100	$1,200
Intersegment revenues		50		60		110
Interest revenue	10	15		40		65
Interest expense	20	10	40	30		100
Depreciation and amortization	50	60	100	120		330
Segment profit	40	75	80	180		375
Segment assets	$180	$220	$280	$450	$250	$1,380
Expenditures for segment assets	20	70	30	80	20	220

Reconciliation of Segment Information to Consolidated Amounts

Information for Company D's reportable segments relates to the enterprise's consolidated totals as follows:

Revenues	
Total revenues for reportable segments	$1,800
Other revenues	250
Intersegment revenues	(200)
Total consolidated revenues	$1,850
Profit or Loss	
Total profit or loss for reportable segments	$250
Other profit or loss	40
Intersegment profits	(35)
General corporate expenses	(50)
Income before income taxes	$205

Assets	
Total assets for reportable segments	$3,000
Assets not attributed to segments	200
Elimination of intersegment receivables	(300)
General corporate assets not attributed to segments	500
Total consolidated assets	$3,400

Geographic Information

Company E attributes revenues and long-lived assets to different geographic areas on the basis of the location of the customer. Revenues and investment in long-lived assets by geographic area are as follows:

	Revenues	*Long-lived Assets*
United States	$1,200	$ 800
Mexico	500	400
Brazil	450	375
Taiwan	300	200
Other	800	720
Total	$3,250	$2,495

Major Customer Information

Company F has revenue from a single customer that represents $800 of the enterprise's consolidated revenue. This customer is served by the automotive parts operating segment.

PART II: INTERPRETIVE GUIDANCE

ASC 280-10: OVERALL

ASC 280-10-55-25 Segment Reporting of Puerto Rican Operations

BACKGROUND

Under the guidance in ASC 280, an entity is required to disclose certain information about its foreign operations and export sales. Further, according to the guidance, foreign operations include an entity's revenue-producing operations that are located outside its home country (e.g., the United States for U.S. enterprises).

ACCOUNTING GUIDANCE

Question: Are Puerto Rican operations and operations in other areas under U.S. sovereignty or jurisdiction (e.g., Virgin Islands, American Samoa) considered foreign for purposes of applying the guidance in ASC 280.

Answer: Puerto Rican operations, as well as those in other non-self-governing U.S. territories, should be considered domestic operations. Factors such as proximity, economic affinity, and similarities of business environments indicate this classification for these operations.

ASC 280-10-50-13 Determining Whether to Aggregate Operating Segments That Do Not Meet the Quantitative Thresholds

BACKGROUND

Under the guidance in ASC 280-10-50-10, entities are required to report separate information about each operating segment that has been identified in accordance with the guidance in ASC 280-10-50-1-9 or that has been created by combining two or more segments in accordance with the guidance in ASC 280-10-50-11 and exceeds the quantitative thresholds in ASC 280-10-50-12. Under the guidance in ASC 280-10-50-11 the combination of two or more operating segments into a single operating segment is permitted if the combination is consistent with the objective and basic principles of ASC 280, the segments have similar economic characteristics, and they are similar in each of the following areas:

- The nature of the products and services
- The nature of the production processes
- The type or class of customer for their products or services
- The methods used to distribute their products or provide their services
- The nature of the regulatory environment, for example, banking, insurance, or public utilities, if applicable.

Segments about which information must be reported separately are referred to as reportable segments.

ACCOUNTING ISSUE

How should an entity evaluate the criteria in ASC 280-10-50-11 that are used to combine two or more operating segments into a single segment when determining whether operating segments that do not meet the quantitative thresholds may be aggregated in accordance with the guidance in ASC 280-10-50-13?

ACCOUNTING GUIDANCE

Operating segments that do *not* meet the quantitative thresholds can be combined only if: (*a*) the combination is consistent with the objective and basic principles of ASC 280 (*b*) the segments have similar economic characteristics, and (*c*) the segments share a majority of the criteria for combination listed in ASC 280-10-50-11.

ASC 280-10-55-12 through 55-14 Questions Related to the Implementation of FASB Statement No. 131

The FASB staff reported on the following technical questions about ASC 280 received from constituents and the staff's responses:

Question 1: Is an entity required to disclose the amount of depreciation and amortization for each reportable segment if the entity's chief operating decision maker uses the amount of earnings before interest, taxes, depreciation, and amortization (EBITDA) to evaluate the performance of the entity's segments but management reports reviewed by the operating decision maker also include summaries of depreciation and amortization expense related to each reportable segment?

Answer: Yes. Based on the guidance in ASC 280-10-50-22 and 50-25 (paragraphs 27 and 28 of FAS-131), depreciation and amortization expense should be disclosed for each reportable segment under the above circumstances. Under the guidance in ASC 280-10-50-22, entities are required to report a measure of profit or loss for each reportable segment, and under the guidance in ASC 280-10-50-22 and 50-25 other amounts must be disclosed about each reportable segment if those amounts are *included* in the measure of profit or loss reviewed by the chief operating decision maker. The FASB staff believes that amortization and depreciation expense should be reported for each reportable segment in the circumstances stated above, even though those amounts are *not* included in the measure of segment profit and loss used by a chief operating decision maker to evaluate each business segment's performance, is based on the guidance in ASC 280-10-50-22 and 50-25, which states that "the amount of each segment item reported shall be the measure reported to the chief operating decision maker for purposes of making decisions about allocating resources to the segment and assessing its performance." The staff noted that this guidance can be applied to other amounts reported to the chief operating decision maker that are not included in the amount of segment profit or loss used to evaluate a segment's performance.

Question 2: ASC 280-10-50-12 provides a choice of three quantitative thresholds to determine whether an entity should report separate information about an operating segment. Specifically, ASC 280-10-50-12 states that separate information should be reported about an operating segment if "the absolute amount of its reported profit or loss is 10% or more of the greater, in absolute amount, of (1) the combined reported profit of all operating segments that did not report a loss or (2) the combined reported loss of all operating segments that did report a loss." If a chief operating decision maker uses different measures of profit or loss to evaluate the performance of separate segments (e.g., the performance of three of seven segments is evaluated based on operating income and the performance of the remaining four segments is evaluated based on net income), how should the quantitative threshold for segment profit or loss be applied?

Answer: The purpose of the guidance in ASC 280-10-50-12 is to identify the segments for which to report separate information. Therefore, the size of each segment's profit or loss must be compared on a consistent basis to the entity's total profit and loss, which should be similar to the amount used in the consolidated financial statements (without reconciling items), because the total amount would include segments and business activities that do not meet the criterion for a reportable segment and consequently are reported in the "all other" classification. The requirement that a reportable segment should be one that makes up 10% or more of the entity's *total* reported profit or loss (or revenue or assets) is similar to previous guidance, which also required as in ASC 280-10-50-14, that reportable segments should account for at least 75% of an entity's total consolidated revenue from *external* sources.

If an entity's chief operating decision maker does not evaluate the performance of all segments based on the same measures of profit and loss, the criterion in ASC 280-10-50-12, nevertheless, should be applied to a consistent measure of segment profit and loss to determine the entity's reportable segments. That procedure does not affect the requirement in ASC 280-10-50-22 that the actual measure of profit or loss used by the chief operating decision maker to evaluate each reportable segment's performance be disclosed.

The staff noted that the above guidance for ASC 280-10-50-12 also applies if the criteria in ASC 280-10-50-12 are used, that is, the 10% threshold of revenue or assets should be applied to total revenues or assets, which should be similar to the amount of consolidated revenues or assets (without reconciling items).

CHAPTER 17

ASC 305—CASH AND CASH EQUIVALENTS

ASC 305 does not provide any unique accounting guidance but rather only provides implementation guidance on cash on deposit at a financial institution (ASC 305-10-05-1).

CHAPTER 18

ASC 310—RECEIVABLES

CONTENTS

PART I: GENERAL GUIDANCE

ASC 310-10: OVERALL

OVERVIEW

Receivables arise from credit sales, loans, and other transactions. Receivables may be in the form of loans, notes, and other types of financial instruments and may be originated by an entity or purchased from another entity. (ASC 310-10-05-4) Accounts receivable are reported at their net realizable value for the purposes of U.S. GAAP. Net realizable value is the total amount of the receivables less an estimated allowance for uncollectible accounts. U.S. GAAP also address how allowances for credit losses related to certain loans should be determined, including how to recognize and measure loan impairment and how to measure income on impaired loans.

In addition to providing general guidance on accounting for receivables, ASC 310 includes accounting for the following:

- Nonrefundable fees and other costs
- Troubled debt restructurings by creditors. (ASC 310-10-05-1)

BACKGROUND

A loan is impaired if, based on current information and events, it is probable that the creditor will be unable to collect all amounts due according to the contractual terms of the loan agreement, including both the contractual interest and the principal receivable. For further discussion of troubled debt restructurings from the perspective of the debtor, see the coverage of ASC 470-60 (Debt—Troubled Debt Restructurings by Debtors).

Debt may be restructured for a variety of reasons. A restructuring of debt is considered a troubled debt restructuring (TDR) if the creditor, for economic or legal reasons related to the debtor's financial difficulties, grants a concession to the debtor that it would not otherwise consider. The concession may stem from an agreement between the creditor and the debtor, or it may be imposed by law or court (ASC Glossary).

GENERAL GUIDANCE ON RECEIVABLES

Receivables generally arise from credit sales, loans, or other transactions. They may be in the form of loans, notes, and other types of financial instruments and may be originated by an entity or purchased from another entity. (ASC 310-10-05-4)

ASC 310 applies to a broad range of financial instruments and transactions, including trade accounts receivable, loans, loan syndications, factoring arrangements, standby letters of credit, and financing receivables. It does not apply to mortgage banking activities or to a contract that is required to be accounted for as a derivative instrument under ASC 815-10. (ASC 310-10-15-2 and 3)

Recognition

For the purposes of U.S. GAAP, accounts receivable are reported at their net realizable value. Net realizable value is the total amount of the receivables less an estimated allowance for uncollectible accounts.

Under ASC 450, an accrual for a loss contingency is charged to income if both of the following conditions are met:

- It is *probable* that as of the date of the financial statements an enterprise does not expect to collect the full amount of its accounts receivable, based on information available before the actual issuance of the financial statements, and
- The amount of loss contingency (uncollectible receivables) can be *reasonably estimated.*

Transfers of receivables under factoring arrangements that meet sale criteria are accounted for by the factor as purchases of receivables. Factoring commissions under these arrangements are recognized over the period of the loan contract. That period begins when a finance company or an entity with financing activities including trade receivables funds a customer's credit and ends when the customer's account is settled. (ASC 310-10-25-3)

Regarding loan syndications and loan participants, each lender accounts for the amount it is owed by the borrower. Repayments by the borrower may be made to a lead lender that then distributes the collections to the other lenders in the syndicate. In this situation, the lead lender is simply functioning as a servicer and does not recognize the aggregate loan as an asset. (ASC 310-10-25-4)

When an entity purchases a credit card portfolio that includes the cardholder relationships at an amount that exceeds the sum of the amounts due under the credit card receivables, the premium between the amount paid and the sum of the balances of the credit card loans at the date of purchase is allocated between the cardholder relationships and the loans acquired. The premium relating to cardholder relationships represents an identifiable intangible asset that is accounted for in accordance with ASC 350. (ASC 310-10-25-7)

Initial Measurement

When a note is received solely for cash and no other rights or privilege is exchanged, the presumption is that the present value at issuance is measured by the cash proceeds exchanged. If cash or some other rights or privileges are exchanged for a note, the value of the rights or privileges is given accounting recognition in accordance with ASC 835-30-25-6. (ASC 310-10-30-2)

Notes exchanged for property, goods, or services are valued and accounted for at the present value of the consideration exchanged between the contracting parties at the date of the transaction in a manner similar to that followed for a cash transaction. (ASC 310-10-30-3) The established exchange price of property, goods, or services acquired for a note may generally be used to establish the present value of the note. If interest is not stated, the stated amount is unreasonable, or the stated face amount of the note is materially different from the current cash price for the same or similar items or from the fair value of the note, the note, the sales price, and the cost of the property, goods, or services exchanged for the note are recorded at the fair value of the property, goods or services or at an amount that reasonably approximates the fair value of the note, whichever is more clearly determinable. In the absence of established exchange prices of the property, goods, or services or evidence of the fair value of the note, the present value of a note that stipulates either no interest or an interest rate that is clearly unreasonable is determined by discounting all future payments on the notes using an imputed rate of interest as described in ASC 835-30. (ASC 310-10-2 through 6)

PRACTICE POINTER: ASC 310-10-35 provides specific guidance on the subsequent measurement of the following specific types of receivables:

- Financial assets subject to prepayment
- Standby commitments to purchase loans
- Loans and trade receivables not held for sale
- Nonmortgage loans held for sale
- Loans not previously held for sale
- Amortization of discount or premium on notes
- Premium allocated to loans purchase in a credit card portfolio
- Hedged portfolios of loans
- Interest income

Presentation Guidance

Loan or trade receivables may be presented on the balance sheet as aggregate amounts. Receivables held for sale shall be in a separate balance sheet category. Major categories of loans or trade receivables shall be presented either in the balance sheet or in notes to the financial statements. (ASC 310-10-45-2)

Current assets are cash and other assets expected to be realized in cash, sold, or consumed during the normal operating cycle of the business. This includes:

- Trade accounts, notes, and acceptances receivable
- Receivables from officers, employees, affiliates, and others, if collectible in the ordinary course of business within one year
- Installment or deferred accounts and notes receivable if they conform generally to normal trade practices and terms within the business. (ASC 310-10-45-9)

Cash receipts from returns on loans and other debt instruments, and equity securities are classified in the statement of cash flows as operating activities. Cash flows from purchases, sales, and maturities of available-for-sale securities are classified as investing activities and reported gross in the statement of cash flows. (ASC 310-10-45-10)

Disclosures

The summary of significant accounting policies shall include the following:

- The basis for accounting for loans and trade receivables;
- The method used in determining the lower of amortized cost basis or fair value of nonmortgage loan held for sale;
- The classification and method of accounting for interest-only strips loans, and other receivables, or retained interest in securitizations that can be contractually prepaid or otherwise settled in a way that the holder would not recover substantially all of the recorded investment; and
- The method for recognizing interest income on loan and trade receivables, including a statement about the entity's policy for treatment of related fees and costs, including the method of amortizing net deferred fees or costs. (ASC 310-10-50-2)

If major categories of loans or trade receivables are not presented separately in the balance sheet, they shall be disclosed in notes to the financial statements. (ASC 310-10-50-3)

The allowance for credit losses and any unearned income, any unamortized premiums and discounts, and any net unamortized deferred fees and costs shall be disclosed in the financial statements. (ASC 310-10-50-4)

PRACTICE POINTER: ASC 310-10-50-3 through 35 include a wide range of disclosures required for different aspects of receivables and loans in specific circumstances. These include assets serving as collateral, foreclosed and repossessed assets, risks and uncertainties, fair value disclosures, modifications, and loans in process of foreclosure.

NONREFUNDABLE FEES AND OTHER COSTS

For each reporting period, to the extent that the amortized cost basis of an individual callable debt security exceeds the amount repayable by the issuer at the next call date, the excess is amortized to the next call date. For this purpose, the next call date is the first call date when a call option at a specified price becomes exercisable. Once that date has passed, the next call date is when the next call option at a specific price becomes exercisable, if applicable. If there is no remaining premium or if there are no further call dates, the entity resets the effective yield using the payment terms of the debt security. Securities within the scope of this requirement are those that have explicit, noncontingent call options that are callable at fixed prices and on preset dates at prices less than the amortized cost basis of the security. (ASC 310-20-35-33)

PRACTICE POINTER: The above is applicable for all public business entities for fiscal years, including interim periods within those fiscal years, beginning after December 15, 2020. For all other entities, the effective date is for fiscal years beginning after December 31, 2021 and for interim periods within fiscal years beginning after December 15, 2022.

TROUBLED DEBT RESTRUCTURINGS BY CREDITORS

A troubled debt restructuring is one in which the creditor grants the debtor certain concessions that would not normally be considered. The concessions are made because of the debtor's financial difficulty, coupled with the creditor's objective to maximize recovery of its investment. Troubled debt restructurings are often the result of legal proceedings or of negotiation between the parties (ASC 310-40-15-5, 6).

Troubled debt restructurings include situations in which (ASC 310-40-15-9):

- The creditor accepts a third-party receivable or other asset(s) of the debtor, in lieu of the receivable from the debtor.
- The creditor accepts an equity interest in the debtor in lieu of the receivable. (This is not to be confused with convertible securities, which are *not* troubled debt restructurings.)
- The creditor accepts modification of the terms of the debt, including but not limited to:
  - Reduction in the stated interest,
  - Extension of maturity at an interest rate below the current market rate,
  - Reduction in face amount of the debt, and
  - Reduction in accrued interest.

The reductions mentioned in the bulleted items above can be either absolute or contingent.

For the purposes of ASC 310-40, troubled debt restructurings do not include the following (ASC 310-40-15-11):

- Changes in lease agreements;
- Employment-related agreements, such as deferred compensation contracts or pension plans;
- A debtor's failure to pay trade accounts that do not involve a restructure agreement; and
- A creditor's legal action to collect accounts that do not involve a restructure agreement.

A troubled debt restructuring by a debtor in bankruptcy proceedings is permitted under ASC 310 provided that the restructuring does *not* constitute a *general restatement* of the debtor's liabilities (ASC 310-40-15-10). ASC 310 requires that a creditor account for all loans that are restructured as part of a TDR involving a modification of terms as an impaired loan.

Not all debt restructuring is considered troubled, even though the debtor is in financial difficulty. Circumstances in which the restructuring is *not* troubled include (ASC 310-40-15-12):

- The debtor satisfies the debt by giving assets or equity with a fair value that at least equals either:
  - The creditor's amortized cost basis, or
  - The debtor's carrying amount of the payable.

- The creditor reduces the interest rate primarily in response to changes in market rates.
- In exchange for the debtor's debt, the debtor issues new debt securities that have an effective interest rate that is at or near the current market interest rate of debt with similar maturity dates and interest rates issued by non-troubled debtors.

PRACTICE NOTE: If the debtor can obtain funds at current market rates and conditions, this provides evidence that the restructuring is not a troubled debt restructuring.

A receivable or payable, referred simply as debt, represents a contractual right to receive money or a contractual obligation to pay money on demand or on fixed or determinable dates that is already included as an asset or liability in the creditor's or debtor's balance sheet at the time of the restructuring. (ASC 310-40-15-4A)

A restructuring is considered a TDR if the creditor for economic or legal reasons related to the debtor's financial difficulties grants a concession to the debtor that it would not otherwise consider. A concession is usually granted by the creditor in an attempt to protect as much of its investment as possible. (ASC 310-40-15-5)

Generally, a debtor that can obtain funds from sources other than the existing creditor at market interest rates at or near those rates for non-troubled debt is *not* involved in a TDR. A TDR may include, but is not limited to, the following:

- Transfers from the debtor to the creditor of receivables from third parties, real estate, or other assets to satisfy fully or partially a debt.
- Issuance or other granting of an equity interest to the creditor by the debtor to satisfy fully or partially a debt unless the equity interest is granted pursuant to existing terms for converting the debt into an equity interest.
- Modification of terms of a debt, such as:
  - — Reduction of the stated interest rate for the remaining original life of the debt.
  - — Extension of the maturity date or dates of a stated interest rate lower than the current market rate for new debt with similar risk.
  - — Reduction of the face amount or maturity amount of the debt as stated in the instrument or other agreement.
  - — Reduction of accrued interest. (ASC 310-40-15-9)

In determining whether a restructuring is a TDR, the creditor must separately conclude that *both* of the following exists:

- The restructuring constitutes a concession.
- The debtor is experiencing financial difficulty.

Granting a Concession

The following additional guidance is provided to assist creditors in determining whether it has granted a concession. If the debtor does not otherwise have access to funds at a below market rate or debt with similar risk characteristics as the restructuring debt, the restructuring is considered to be at a below-market rate and may indicate that the creditor has granted a concession. In that circumstance, the creditor should consider all aspects of the restructuring to determine if it has made a concession. (ASC 310-40-15-15)

A temporary or permanent increase in the contractual interest rate as a result of a restructuring does not preclude the restructuring from being considered a concession because the new contractual interest rate on the restructured debt may still be below the market interest rate for new debt with similar risk characteristics. In this situation, the creditor should consider all aspects of the restructuring to determine whether a concession has been granted. (ASC 310-40-15-16)

A restructuring that results in an insignificant delay in payment is not considered a concession. The creditor should consider various factors in assessing whether a restructuring that results in a delay in payment is insignificant. (ASC 310-40-15-17)

Assessing Financial Difficulty

If a decision is made that the creditor has made a concession, a separate assessment must be made whether the debtor is experiencing financial difficulties to determine whether the restructuring constitutes a TDR.

The following should be considered in making this judgment:

- The debtor is currently in payment default on any if its debt.
- The probability that the debtor will be in payment default on any of its debt in the foreseeable future without the modification.
- The debtor has declared or is in the process of declaring bankruptcy.
- There is substantial doubt as to whether the debtor will continue to be a going concern.
- The debtor has securities that have been delisted, are in the process of being delisted, or are under threat of being delisted from an exchange.
- On the basis of estimates and projections that only encompass the debtor's current capabilities, the creditor forecasts that the debtor's entity-specific cash flows will be insufficient to service any of its debt in accordance with the contractual terms of the existing agreement for the foreseeable future.
- Without the current modification, the debtor cannot obtain funds from sources other than the existing creditors at an effective interest rate equal to the market rate for similar debt for a non-troubled debtor. (ASC 310-40-15-20)

Further guidance to assist the creditor in assessing whether a debtor is experiencing financial difficulties include the following. Payment default is not a necessary criterion for determining that a debtor is having financial difficulties. A creditor should evaluate whether it is probable that the debtor will be in payment default on any of its debt in the foreseeable future without the current modification in its debt.

Transfer of Asset(s)

Guidance on accounting for transfers of financial assets, including receivables, is found in ASC 860-20 (Transfers and Servicing—Sales of Financial Assets).

When the creditor receives assets as full settlement of a receivable, they are accounted for at their fair value at the time of the restructuring. The fair value of the receivable satisfied can be used if it is more clearly determinable than the fair value of the asset or equity acquired. In partial payments the creditor *must* use the fair value of the asset or equity received (ASC 310-40-35-6).

The excess of the amortized cost basis over the fair value of the assets received (less cost to sell if a long-lived asset is received) is recognized as a loss (ASC 310-40-40-3). The creditor accounts for these assets as if they were acquired for cash (ASC 310-40-40-5).

Illustration of Transfer of Assets

A debtor owes $20,000, including accrued interest. The creditor accepts land valued at $17,000 and carried on the debtor's books at its $12,000 cost, in full payment.

Under U.S. GAAP, the debtor recognizes two gains: $5,000 ($17,000 – $12,000) on the transfer of the assets, and $3,000 ($20,000 – $17,000) on the extinguishment of debt.

The creditor recognizes a loss of $3,000 ($20,000 – $17,000).

Transfer of Equity Interest

The creditor records the receipt of an equity interest as any other asset by recording the investment at its fair value and recognizing a loss equal to the difference between the fair value of the equity interest and the amortized cost basis (ASC 310-40-40-3).

Illustration of Transfer of Equity Interest

A debtor grants an equity interest valued at $10,000, consisting of 500 shares of $15 par value stock, to retire a payable of $12,000. Given these facts, the debtor records the issuance of the stock at $10,000 ($7,500 par value and $2,500 additional paid-in capital) and a gain on the extinguishment of debt of $2,000 ($12,000 – $10,000). The creditor records an investment asset of $10,000 and an ordinary loss of $2,000 ($12,000 – $10,000) on the TDR.

PRACTICE POINTER: Determining the fair value of an equity interest of a debtor company involved in a troubled debt restructuring may be difficult. In many cases, the company's stock will not be publicly traded, and there may be no recent stock transactions that would be helpful. Even if a recent market price were available, consider whether that price reflects the financially troubled status of the company that exists at the time the troubled debt restructuring takes place.

Modification of Terms

A creditor in a TDR involving a modification of terms accounts for the restructured loan at the present value of expected future cash flows discounted at the loan's contractual interest rate, the loan's observable market price, or the fair value of collateral if the loan is collateral-dependent.

PRACTICE NOTE: A loan is impaired if it is probable that a creditor will be unable to collect all amounts due according to the contractual terms of the loan agreement. A loan whose terms are modified in a TDR will have already been identified as impaired. A loan is considered collateral-dependent if repayment is expected to be provided solely by the underlying collateral.

Illustration of Modification of Terms

A debtor has a loan to a creditor, details of which are as follows:

Principal	$10,000
Accrued interest	500
Total	$10,500

They agree on a restructuring in which the total future cash payments, both principal and interest, are $8,000. The present value of these payments is $7,500.

Under U.S. GAAP, the debtor recognizes a gain of $2,500 ($10,500 – $8,000) at the time of the restructuring, and all future payments are specified as principal payments. Under U.S. GAAP, the creditor recognizes a loss of $3,000 ($10,500 – $7,500).

Combination of Types

When a restructuring involves combinations of asset or equity transfers and modification of terms, the creditor reduces the recorded investment by the fair value of assets received less cost to sell, including an equity interest in the debtor. Thereafter, the creditor accounts for the TDR in accordance with ASC 310 (ASC 310-40-35-7).

Related Issues

Legal fees and other direct costs resulting from a TDR are expensed by the creditor when incurred (ASC 310-40-25-1).

A receivable obtained by a creditor from the sale of assets previously obtained in a TDR is accounted for in accordance with ASC 835-30 (Interest—Imputation of Interest), regardless of whether the assets were obtained in satisfaction of a receivable to which ASC 835-30 was not intended to apply (ASC 310-40-40-8).

For creditors, a troubled debt restructuring may involve substituting debt of another business enterprise, individual, or governmental unit for that of a troubled debtor. That kind of restructuring should be accounted for according to its substance (ASC 310-40-25-2).

CREDITOR DISCLOSURE REQUIREMENTS FOR TROUBLED DEBT RESTRUCTURINGS

The creditor shall disclose the following regarding troubled debt restructurings (ASC 310-40-50-1):

1. As of the date of each statement of financial position presented, the total recorded investment in the impaired loans at the end of each period, as well as (*a*) the amount of the recorded investment for which there is a related allowance for credit losses, and the amount of that allowance; and (*b*) the amount of the recorded investment for which there is no related allowance for credit losses
2. The creditor's policy for recognizing interest income on impaired loans, including how cash receipts are recorded
3. For each period for which results of operations are presented, the average recorded investment in the impaired loans during each period; the related amount of interest income recognized during the time within that period that the loans were impaired; and, if practicable, the amount of interest income recognized (cash-basis method of accounting) during the time within that period that the loans were impaired
4. Amount(s) of any commitment(s) to lend additional funds to any debtor who is a party to a restructuring

OTHER CLASSIFICATION AND DISCLOSURE ISSUES

ASC 230-10-45-11 states that cash flows from purchases, sales, and maturities of available-for-sale debt securities are classified as cash flows from investment activities and reported gross in the statement of cash flows. ASC 230-10-45-21 states that some loans are similar to debt securities in a trading account in that they are originated or purchased specifically for resale and are held for short periods of time. (ASC 310-10-45-11)

ASC 825-10-50 provides guidance on the required disclosure of fair value of certain assets and liabilities. ASC 825-10-50 explains that, for trade receivables and payables, no disclosure is required if the trade receivable or payable is due in one year or less. (ASC 310-10-50-26)

PART II: INTERPRETIVE GUIDANCE

ASC 310-10: OVERALL

IMPORTANT NOTICE: See the discussion of the future impact of ASU 2016-13, *Financial Instruments—Credit Losses (Topic 326): Measurement of Credit Losses on Financial Instruments*, in Practice Note below.

ASC 310-10-05-9; 15-5; 25-15 through 25-30; 35-55 through 35-61; 40-3 through 40-5; 45-15; ASC 360-10-35-3, 35-9 Purpose and Scope of AcSEC Practice Bulletins and Procedures for Their Issuance

BACKGROUND

The AICPA issued Practice Bulletins to disseminate the views of the AICPA Accounting Standards Executive Committee (AcSEC) (now known as the Financial Reporting Executive Committee) on narrow financial accounting and reporting issues. AcSEC was a senior technical body of the AICPA authorized to represent the AICPA on matters that addressed accounting and financial reporting unique to specific industries. Practice Bulletins addressed issues that were not addressed and are not expected to be addressed by either the FASB or the Governmental Accounting Standards Board (GASB).

ACCOUNTING GUIDANCE

Before 1987, when AcSEC began to issue Practice Bulletins, similar guidance was provided in "Notices to Practitioners," which were published in either *The CPA Letter* or the *Journal of Accountancy*. Unlike Notices to Practitioners, which are not numbered for retrievability, Practice Bulletins are numbered and designed to convey information that will enhance the quality and comparability of financial statements.

Drafts of proposed Practice Bulletins, which have been discussed at AcSEC open meetings, are available to the public as part of the meeting's agenda. However, Practice Bulletins have not been exposed for public comment, and their issuance is not subject to public hearings.

A Practice Bulletin is issued if both of the following conditions are met: (*a*) two-thirds or more of AcSEC's members vote to issue the proposed Bulletin, and (*b*) after reviewing the proposed Bulletin, the FASB and GASB indicate that neither plans to address the particular issue.

Most of the Notices to Practitioners that preceded the issuance of Practice Bulletins have been superseded. Three Notices to Practitioners continue to be in effect, however, and are discussed in the appendix to PB-1, "Purpose and Scope of AcSEC Practice Bulletins and Procedures for Their Issuance." The following is a brief discussion of the three Notices to Practitioners that were not superseded.

ACRS Lives and U.S. GAAP

In most cases, the number of years specified by the ACRS for recovery deductions will not bear any reasonable resemblance to the asset's useful life. In these cases, ACRS recovery deductions cannot be used as the depreciation expense amount for financial reporting purposes. Rather, depreciation for financial reporting purposes should be based on the asset's useful life.

Accounting by Colleges and Universities for Compensated Absences

Note: The following discussion pertains solely to private (nonpublic) colleges and universities.

When ASC 710, *Compensation—General*, and ASC 420, *Exit or Disposal Cost Obligations*, were issued, there was some discussion as to whether the guidance in ASC 710 would apply to colleges and universities. The FASB decided *not* to exempt colleges and universities from the provisions of that standard. A Notice to Practitioners was issued to assist colleges and universities in applying that guidance. The essential conclusions of the Notice were as follows:

- In recognizing the liability, and the associated charge, for compensated absences in the current and prior years, the unrestricted current fund is to be used (use of the plant fund is specifically prohibited).
- In some cases, the liability for compensated absences might be recoverable from future state and federal grants and contracts for funded research. A receivable, and the associated revenue, can be recognized to offset a portion of the liability only in limited situations. More specifically, a receivable can be recognized only if it meets the definition of an *asset* in Statement of Financial Accounting Concepts No. 6 (Elements of Financial Statements of Business Enterprises). In evaluating the receivable, the college or university should consider the measurability and collectibility of the receivable and the institution's legal right to it.
- The reduction in the unrestricted current fund balance caused by recognizing the liability for compensated absences may be reduced by interfund transfers. These interfund transfers may be recognized only if (*a*) unrestricted assets are available for permanent transfer and (*b*) payment (or other settlement) to the unrestricted current fund is expected within a reasonable period.

ADC Arrangements

This Notice to Practitioners addresses the funding provided by financial institutions for real estate acquisition, development, and construction (ADC). In some cases, financial institutions enter into ADC agreements where the institution has essentially the same risks and rewards as an investor or a joint venture participant. In these cases, treating the ADC funding as a loan would not be appropriate.

The notice applies only to ADC arrangements in which a financial institution is expected to receive some or all of the residual profit. Expected residual profit is the amount of funds the lender is expected to receive—whether these funds are referred to as interest, as fees, or as an equity kicker—above a customary amount of interest and fees normally received for providing comparable financing.

The profit participation between the lender and the developer is not always part of the mortgage loan agreement. Therefore, the auditor should be cognizant that such side agreements may exist and should design the audit to detect such profit participation agreements between the lender and the developer.

PRACTICE POINTER: A side agreement may exist to provide the lender with a profit participation in ADC loans. This side agreement may not be referred to in the mortgage agreement between the lender and the developer. The auditor should specifically ask the lender to confirm whether it is party to a profit participation agreement on a particular loan.

A number of characteristics, in addition to the sharing of the expected residual profit, indicate that the ADC arrangement is more akin to an investment or a joint venture than to a loan. These characteristics are as follows:

- The financial institution provides all, or substantially all, of the funds necessary to acquire, develop, and construct the project. The developer has title but little or no equity investment in the project.
- The financial institution rolls into the loan any commitment and/or origination fees.
- The financial institution adds to the loan balance all, or substantially all, interest and fees during the term of the loan.

- The financial institution's only security for the loan is the ADC project. There is no recourse to other assets of the borrower. Also, the borrower does not guarantee the debt.
- The financial institution recovers its investment in one of three ways: (*a*) the project is completed and sold to an independent third party, (*b*) the borrower obtains refinancing from another source, or (*c*) the project is completed and placed in service, and cash flows are sufficient to fund the repayment of principal and interest.
- Foreclosure during the development period due to delinquency is unlikely, because the borrower is not required to make any payments during this period.

In some cases, even though a lender is expected to participate in the residual profit from the project, the facts and circumstances of the borrowing arrangement are consistent with a loan. The following characteristics of an ADC arrangement are consistent with a loan:

- The lender's participation in the expected residual profit is less than 50%.
- The borrower has a substantial equity investment in the project, not funded by the lender. This equity investment can be either in the form of cash or in the form of the contribution of land to the project.
- Either (*a*) the lender has recourse to other substantial, tangible assets of the borrower, which have not already been pledged under other loans, or (*b*) the borrower has secured an irrevocable letter of credit from a creditworthy, independent third party for substantially all of the loan balance and for the entire term of the loan.
- A take-out commitment for the entire amount of the loan has been secured from a creditworthy, independent third party. If the take-out commitment is conditional, the conditions should be reasonable and their attainment should be probable.

Some ADC loans contain personal guarantees from the borrower or from a third party, but such guarantees are rarely sufficient to support classifying an ADC arrangement as a loan.

In evaluating the substance of a personal guarantee, the following factors should be considered: (1) the ability of the guarantor to perform under the guarantee, (2) the practicality of enforcing the guarantee in the applicable jurisdiction, and (3) a demonstrated intent on the part of the lender to enforce the guarantee. Factors that might indicate the ability to perform under the guarantee include placing liquid assets in escrow, pledging marketable securities, and obtaining irrevocable letters of credit from a creditworthy, independent third party.

In the absence of the support discussed above for a guarantee, a guarantor's financial statements should be evaluated. In evaluating a guarantor's financial statements, an auditor should consider both the guarantor's liquidity and net worth. A guarantee has little substance if it is supported only by assets already pledged as security for other debt. Also, guarantees made by a guarantor on other projects should be considered.

If a lender expects to receive more than 50% of the residual profit from a project, the lender should account for the income or loss from the arrangement as a real estate investment. The guidance in ASC 970, Real Estate-General, ASC 360, Property Plant and Equipment, and ASC 976, Real Estate-Retail Land should be followed.

If a lender expects to receive less than 50% of the residual profit from a project, an ADC arrangement should be accounted for as a loan or as a joint venture, depending on the applicable circumstances. If an ADC arrangement is classified as a loan, interest and fees accounted for as a receivable may be recognized as income if they are recoverable. In assessing the recoverability of loan amounts and accrued interest, the guidance in both ASC 974, Real Estate-Real Estate Investment Trusts, and the guidance in ASC 942 (Audit and Accounting Guide, *Banks and Savings Institutions*) might be useful. If an ADC arrangement is classified as a joint venture, the primary accounting guidance may be found in ASC 970 and in ASC 835-20, Interest-Capitalization.

For balance sheet reporting purposes, ADC arrangements classified as investments in real estate or as joint ventures should be combined and reported separately from ADC arrangements accounted for as loans.

In some cases, a lender's share of the expected residual profit is sold before a project is completed. The applicable accounting in those cases hinges on whether the ADC arrangement was treated as a loan, as an investment in real estate, or as a joint venture. If an ADC arrangement was treated as a loan, proceeds received from a sale of the expected residual profit should be recognized as additional interest income over the remaining term of the loan. If an ADC arrangement was treated as a real estate investment or a joint venture, any gain to be recognized upon sale of the expected residual profit is determined based on the guidance ASC 976.

The accounting treatment of an ADC project should be periodically reassessed. For example, an ADC arrangement originally classified as an investment or as a joint venture might subsequently be classified as a loan if a lender is not expected to receive more than 50% of the residual profit and if the risk to the lender has decreased significantly. It is important to note that a change in accounting for an ADC arrangement depends on a change in the facts that were relied upon when the ADC arrangement was initially classified. The absence of, or a reduced participation in, a residual profit is not sufficient to change the categorization of an ADC arrangement. In addition, it is possible for an ADC arrangement initially classified as a loan to be reclassified as a real estate investment or a joint venture. A lender may take on additional risks and rewards of ownership by releasing collateral to support a guarantee and by increasing its percentage of profit participation. An improvement in a project's economic prospects does not justify a change in how an ADC arrangement is categorized. A change in classification is expected to be rare and should be supported by adequate documentation.

Finally, regardless of the accounting treatment for an ADC arrangement, it is necessary to continually assess the collectibility of principal, accrued interest, and fees. Also, ADC financing often entails a heightened risk of related-party transactions. An auditor needs to design the audit accordingly.

ASC 310-10-05-5, 05-7; 25-3, 25-6, 25-8; 25-13; 30-7; 35-41 through 35-43, 35-46 through 35-49; 45-2 through 45-3; 50-2 through 50-11; ASC 310-20-15-3; 50-1; ASC 460-10-35-3; 45-1; ASC 460-605-25-7; ASC 825-10-35-1 through 35-3; ASC 835-30-15-1; ASC 860-20-50-5; ASC 860-50-15-3; ASC 860-50-40-2, 40-6; ASC 860-942-15-2 through 15-3; ASC 942-210-45-1 through 45-2; ASC 942-305-05-2; 45-1; 50-1; ASC 942-310-15-2; ASC 942-320-50-4; ASC 942-325-25-1 through 25-3; 35-1 through 35-4; ASC 942-360-45-2; ASC 942-405-25-1 through 25-4; 35-1; 45-1 through 45-4; 50-1; ASC 942-470-45-1 through 45-2; 50-2 through 50-3; ASC 942-505-50-1H through 50-7; ASC 942-825-50-1 through 50-2; ASC 944-320-50-1; ASC 948-10-15-3; 50-2 through 50-5 Accounting by Certain Entities (Including Entities with Trade Receivables) That Lend to or Finance the Activities of Others

BACKGROUND

This guidance was issued to reduce the variability among financial institutions (including entities with trade receivables) in accounting for similar transactions. It provides accounting guidance for entities that lend to or finance the activities of other parties, including entities that simply extend normal trade credit to customers (i.e., accounts receivable). The guidance does *not* apply to entities that carry loans and trade receivables at fair value, with changes in fair value flowing through the current period's income statement. Examples of such entities include: investment companies, broker-dealers in securities, and employee benefit plans.

PRACTICE NOTE: This guidance applies to all entities that lend to or finance the activities of their customers or other parties, even if an entity is not considered to be a finance company. Therefore, the guidance on the recognition, measurement, and disclosure of loans and trade receivables, credit losses, and other items, applies to manufacturers, retailers, and other non-financial entities. Also, more specific guidance is provided for finance companies.

ACCOUNTING GUIDANCE

The following guidance applies to a number of items, including loans and trade receivables not held for sale, nonmortgage loans held for sale, sales of loans not held for sale, and credit losses—including losses on off-balance-sheet instruments, standby commitments to purchase loans, delinquency fees, prepayment fees, and rebates.

PRACTICE NOTE: The following guidance is based on the amendments of ASC 310-10-35-47 through 35-48 in ASU 2016-13, *Financial Instruments—Credit Losses (Topic 326): Measurement of Credit Losses on Financial Instruments*. The amendments will be effective for public business entities that are SEC filers in fiscal years beginning after December 15, 2019, including interim periods in those fiscal years, and for all other public business entities in fiscal years beginning after December 15, 2020, including interim periods in those fiscal years. For all other entities, including not-for-profit entities and employee benefit plans within the scope of ASC 960 through 965 on plan accounting, in fiscal years beginning after December 15, 2020, and interim periods within fiscal years beginning after December 15, 2021, in accordance with ASU 2016-13. In July 2019, the FASB directed its staff to prepare an exposure draft that would extend the effective date of ASU 2016-13 by one year for entities other than public business entities that are SEC filers. For entities subject to the potential extension, the standard would be effective for fiscal years beginning after December 15, 2022, including interim periods within those fiscal years.

Nonmortgage Loans and Trade Receivables Not Held for Sale

ASC 310-10-35-47A provides that nonmortgage loans, which management intends and is able to hold for the foreseeable future or until maturity or payoff, should be reported on the balance sheet at their amortized cost bases. ASC 326-20 provides guidance on the measurement of credit losses for financial instruments measured at amortized cost basis.

Nonmortgage Loans Held for Sale

A nonmortgage loan held for sale should be reported at the lower of its amortized cost basis or fair value. An excess, if any, of a loan's amortized cost basis over fair value should be accounted for as a valuation allowance, with changes of the valuation allowance included in determining net income of the period in which the changes occur.

Transfers of Nonmortgage Loans Between Classifications

If an entity decides to sell a nonmortgage loan previously classified as not held-for-sale, a previously recorded allowance for credit losses, if any, while the loan was not held for sale should be reversed in earnings on the transfer date. The nonmortgage loan then should be reclassified and transferred into the held-for-sale classification at its amortized cost basis, which is reduced by previous writeoffs, if any, but without an allowance for credit losses. The guidance in ASC 310-10 should be followed to determine whether a valuation allowance is necessary.

When a nonmortgage loan is transferred from the held-for-sale classification to the not held-for-sale classification, a valuation allowance, if any, that was previously recorded on the loan should be reversed in earnings at the transfer date. The nonmortgage loan then should be reclassified and transferred into the not held-for-sale classification at its amortized cost basis, which is reduced by previous writeoffs, if any, but without a valuation allowance. The guidance in ASC 326 should be followed to determine whether an allowance for credit losses is necessary.

Other Presentation Matters

Nonmortgage Loans or Trade Receivables

The guidance in ASC 310-10-45-2 has been amended by ASU 2019-04 to (*a*) include nonmortgage loans in the paragraph's guidance, and (*b*) to require that the amounts reversed or established for a valuation allowance or an allowance for credit losses, whichever applies, related to a transfer of nonmortgage loans (see ASC 310-10-35-48A through 35-48B) be presented on a gross basis in the income statement. Those amounts may be presented in the income statement or in the notes to financial statements.

Credit losses—whether for loans or trade receivables—should be subtracted from the related allowance account. A loan or trade receivable should be written off in the period in which the particular loan or receivable is deemed uncollectible. (This guidance will be superseded by ASU 2016-13 when it becomes effective, as discussed in the Practice Note above. It will be moved to ASC 326-20-35-8, and amended.)

An entity may have credit losses arising from off-balance-sheet exposures. If an entity has such a loss, the loss and a related liability should be recognized. A loss accrual should be recorded separately from any valuation account related to a recognized financial instrument that may exist.

Entities may enter into standby commitments to purchase loans. In return for a fee, the entity stands ready to purchase loans at a stated price. The appropriate accounting treatment depends on whether (1) the settlement date is reasonable and (2) the entity has the intent and ability to accept the loans without selling assets. An example of a reasonable settlement date is one within a normal loan commitment period. If both of those criteria are met, the loan is recorded at cost, less any standby commitment fee received, at the settlement date. If either one of the criteria is not met, the standby commitment is recorded as a written put option.

Delinquency fees should be recognized in income if the entity is allowed to charge a fee (i.e., the conditions necessary for charging delinquency fees have been met). This treatment assumes that the collection of delinquency fees is reasonably assured. Prepayment penalties should not be recognized in income until the loans are prepaid.

Borrowers are sometimes entitled to rebates of previous finance charges paid. The calculation of rebate amounts is typically governed by state law, often using the Rule of 78s, rather than reflecting an entity's internal accounting procedures, which typically follow the interest method. Any differences between rebate calculations and interest income previously recognized are treated as adjustments of previously recognized interest income. The difference should be recognized in income when loans (or receivables) are prepaid or renewed.

Presentation and Disclosure

These presentation and disclosure guidelines are related to (1) accounting policies for loans and trade receivables, (2) accounting policies for credit losses and doubtful accounts, (3) accounting policies for nonaccrual and past due loans and trade receivables, (4) sales of loans and trade receivables, (5) loans or trade receivables, (6) foreclosed or repossessed assets, (7) nonaccrual and past due loans and trade receivables, and (8) assets serving as collateral.

The following are the presentation and disclosure requirements:

- To provide a summary of the entity's significant accounting policies for loans and trade receivables, and its basis of accounting for loans, trade receivables, and lease financings must be disclosed. In addition, an entity must disclose (*a*) whether it uses the aggregate or individual asset basis to determine the lower of cost or fair value of nonmortgage loans held for sale; (*b*) the classification and method of accounting for interest-only strips, loans, other receivables, and certain retained interests in securitizations; and (*c*) its method of recognizing interest income on loan and trade receivables.
- To describe the entity's policies and methodology for determining the allowance for loan losses, allowance for doubtful accounts, and any liability for off-balance-sheet credit losses.
- To disclose its policy and methodology for the recognition and measurement of losses related to loans, trade receivables, and other credit exposures.
- To provide disclosures about its policies for nonaccrual and past due loans and trade receivables.
- To describe its policy for placing loans (or trade receivables) on nonaccrual status, and how payments received on nonaccrual loans (or trade receivables) are treated.
- To disclose its policy for restoring loans (or receivables) to accrual status.
- To disclose its policy for writing off loans and trade receivables as uncollectible.
- To describe whether it evaluates past due (or delinquency) status based on when the most recent payment was received or based on contractual terms.
- To separately disclose its aggregate gains or losses from sales of loans or trade receivables.
- To present major categories of loans and trade receivables separately, either in the financial statements or in the notes.
- To present receivables held for sale as a separate category on the balance sheet.
- To present foreclosed or repossessed assets as a separate line item on the balance sheet or as part of other assets with disclosure of the amounts related to foreclosed or repossessed assets in the notes.

PRACTICE POINTER: The guidance in ASC 310-10-50-11 has been amended by the guidance in ASU 2014-04, *Receivables—Troubled Debt Restructurings by Creditors (Subtopic 310-40): Reclassification of Residential Real Estate Collateralized Consumer Mortgage Loans upon Foreclosure* (discussed below) to require that an entity that has obtained physical possession of foreclosed residential real estate properties should disclose the carrying amount of such properties held at the reporting date in accordance with the guidance in ASC 310-40-40-6 and ASC 310-40-55-10A.

- For nonaccrual and past due loans and receivables, to disclose in the notes to the financial statements (*a*) the entity's recorded investment in nonaccrual loans and trade receivables as of each balance sheet date, and (*b*) its recorded investment in loans (or receivables) that are still accruing interest even though they are past due 90 days or more.
- To disclose the carrying amounts of loans, receivables, securities, and financial instruments that are serving as collateral for borrowings.

ASC 310-10-25-7; 35-52 Difference between Initial Investment and Principal Amount of Loans in a Purchased Credit Card Portfolio

BACKGROUND

An entity has purchased a credit card portfolio for an amount of cash that exceeds the balance of the credit card receivables.

The guidance in ASC 310-20-35-15; 25-22 states that the difference between the amount paid to acquire a loan (initial investment) and the loan's principal amount at acquisition should be recognized over the life of the loan as a yield adjustment. The financial institution should defer and amortize the premium on a straight-line basis over the period the cardholders are entitled to use their cards.

This Issue was addressed because of diversity in practice.

ACCOUNTING ISSUES

- Should the difference (premium) between the amount an entity pays to purchase credit card loans and the sum of the balances of the receivables at the date of purchase be allocated between the loans acquired and identifiable intangible assets acquired, if any?
- Over what period should an entity amortize amounts allocated to loans and identifiable intangible assets acquired?

ACCOUNTING GUIDANCE

The following guidance should be followed:

- The difference (premium) between the amount an entity pays to purchase a credit card portfolio, including the cardholder relationships, and the sum of the balances of the credit card loans at the date of purchase should be allocated between the credit cardholder relationships acquired and loans acquired. (See "Effect of ASC 860" below.)
- The portion of a premium related to credit cardholder relationships is an identifiable intangible asset and should be amortized over the period of estimated benefit under the provisions of ASC 350. The portion allocated to the loans should be amortized over the life of the loans in accordance with the guidance in ASC 310, Receivables. A determination of the life of a credit card loan should consider whether the terms of the agreement permit the loan's repayment period to continue after the expiration date of the credit card if the card is not renewed.

PRACTICE POINTER: Under the guidance in ASC 350, intangible assets should be amortized over their useful lives, unless the life of the intangible asset is considered to be indefinite.

EFFECT OF ASC 860

Under the guidance in ASC 860, Transfers and Servicing, the consensus position in Issue 1, that the difference between the amount paid to purchase credit card loans and the sum of the balances of the receivables at the purchase date should be allocated between the credit cardholder relationships and the loans acquired, is unaffected if the conditions for treatment as a sale in ASC 860-10-40-4 through 40-5 and 55-68A exist. ASC 860-20-30-1 provides that assets obtained and liabilities incurred by a transferee should be measured and recognized at fair value. The subsequent measurement issues discussed in Issue 2 are not addressed in ASC 860 and therefore do not affect the guidance on the amortization of credit cardholder relationships.

ASC 310-10-05-9; ASC 815-15-55-9, 55-10 Application of the AICPA Notice to Practitioners Regarding Acquisition, Development, and Construction Arrangements to Acquisition of an Operating Property

BACKGROUND

Company A, not necessarily a financial institution, makes a 10- to 15-year loan to Company B to acquire an operating property. In addition to paying a market interest rate and fees, Company B agrees that upon sale or refinancing of the loan, it will share with Company A a certain percentage of the property's appreciation, which is calculated as the difference between the original loan balance and the net proceeds from the sale of the property or the property's appraised value. Company B may discontinue paying a portion of accrued interest during the term of the loan but will pay that interest at maturity.

ACCOUNTING ISSUES

- Does ASC 310-10-5-9; 15-5; 25-15 through 25-30; 45-15; 40-3 40-5; 310-35-55-61 apply to financing of acquisitions of operating properties?
- If yes, how should its guidance be applied?

ACCOUNTING GUIDANCE

- The guidance in ASC 310-10-5-9; 15-5; 25-15 through 25-30; 45-15; 40-3 40-5; and ASC 310-35-55-61 should be considered by preparers and auditors in accounting for shared appreciation mortgages, loans on operating real estate properties, and real estate acquisition, development, and construction (ADC) arrangements entered into by entities that are not financial institutions, even though the third Notice discussed only ADC arrangements of financial institutions.

- The nature of expected residual profit should be determined based on the guidance in ASC 310-10-25-15 through 25-17, which discuss various profit-sharing arrangements, such as a specific percentage of the borrower's profit on a sale.
- The guidance in ASC 310-10-5-9; 15-5; 25-15 through 25-30; 45-15; 40-3 40-5; and ASC 310-35-55-61 is the best guidance available to preparers and auditors on this subject.

PRACTICE POINTER: The guidance in ASC 810 requires the consolidation of variable interest entities by an entity that absorbs a majority of a variable entity's expected losses or has the right to receive a greater part of the variable entity's expected residual returns or both.

EFFECT OF ASC 815

The embedded equity kicker discussed in this Issue should be analyzed to determine whether it is a separate derivative under the definition in ASC 815. If not, the guidance above continues to apply.

SEC OBSERVER COMMENT

The SEC Observer stated that *all* SEC registrants are expected to follow the guidance in ASC 310-10-5-9; 15-5; 25-15 through 25-30; 45-15; 40-3 40-5; and ASC 310-35-55-61 for existing and future real estate ADC arrangements.

SUBSEQUENT DEVELOPMENTS

The following events occurred after this guidance was issued:

- The SEC staff issued SAB-71, which incorporates the guidance in ASC 310-10-5-9; 15-5; 25-15 through 25-30; 45-15; 40-3 40-5; and ASC 310-35-55-61 in its discussion of mortgage loans having the economics of a real estate investment or joint venture instead of a loan. The SAB also refers to the guidance in this Issue and was supplemented by SAB-71A.
- The Federal Home Loan Bank Board (FHLBB) issued a notice that requires all financial institutions insured by the Federal Savings and Loan Insurance Corporation (FSLIC) or its affiliates to follow the principles in ASC 310-10-5-9; 15-5; 25-15 through 25-30; 45-15; 40-3 40-5; and ASC 310-35-55-61 in classifying and accounting for ADC arrangements in reports or financial statements filed with the FSLIC and the FHLBB.

ASC 310-10-50-18; 30-05-2 through 05-3; 15-1 through 15-4, 15-6 through 15-10; 25-1; 30-1; 35-2 through 35-3, 35-5 through 35-6, 35-8 through 35-15; 40-1; 45-1; 50-1 through 50-3; 55-2, 55-5 through 55-29; 60-3 Accounting for Certain Loans or Debt Securities in a Transfer

SCOPE

The guidance in this pronouncement applies to all nongovernmental entities that acquire loans, including not-for-profit organizations. Loans under its scope: (1) have had a deterioration in credit quality since origination; (2) have been acquired in a transfer that (*a*) meets the conditions in ASC 860-10-40-4 through 40-5 to be accounted for as a sale or purchase, (*b*) is a business combination, (*c*) is made to a newly created subsidiary if the investor wrote down the loan to its fair value with the intent of transferring the subsidiary's stock as a dividend to the parent company's shareholders, or (*d*) is a contribution receivable or a transfer in satisfaction of a prior promise to give; and (3) it is probable at acquisition, as defined in ASC 860-10-35-3, that all contractually required payments receivable will not be collected, with the following exceptions:

- Loans measured at fair value with all changes in fair value included in earnings or, for not-for-profit organizations, loans measured at fair value with all changes in fair value included in the statement of activities and included in the performance indicator, if one is presented
- Mortgage loans classified as held for sale under the guidance in ASC 948-310-35-1
- Loans acquired in a business combination accounted for at historical cost
- Loans held by liquidating banks
- Revolving credit agreements (e.g., credit cards and home equity loans), if the borrower has revolving privileges at the acquisition date
- Loans that are retained interests

Loans that are derivative instruments accounted for under the provisions of ASC 815 Accounting for also are excluded from the scope. However, if a loan that would normally come under the scope of this guidance has an embedded derivative accounted for under the provisions of ASC 815, the host instrument would be accounted for under the scope of this guidance if it meets the scope requirements.

Recognition, Measurement, and Display

A loan loss allowance should *not* be established at acquisition for loans acquired in a transfer. Loans acquired in a business combination should be initially recognized at the present value of amounts expected to be received. A valuation allowance should be established only for incurred losses at the present value of cash flows that were expected at acquisition but not received.

Income recognition should be based on a reasonable expectation about the timing and amount of cash flows to be collected. If after acquisition, an investor is unable to calculate a yield on a loan because of a lack of information necessary to reasonably estimate the cash flows expected to be collected, the investor is permitted to place the loan on a nonaccrual status and recognize income by the cost recovery method or on a cash basis. If, however, the timing and amount of cash flows expected to be collected, for example, from a sale of a loan into the secondary market or a sale of loan collateral, is reasonably estimable, the cash flows should be used to apply the interest method under the guidance in this pronouncement. Interest income should *not* be recognized if it would cause the net investment in the loan to exceed the payoff amount. Income should *not* be accrued on loans acquired primarily for the rewards of owning the underlying collateral, such as for the use of the collateral in the entity's operations or to improve it for resale.

Changes in Cash Flows Expected to Be Collected

Investors should account for changes in cash flows expected to be collected as follows:

1. For loans accounted for as debt securities, cash flows expected to be collected over the life of a loan should continue to be estimated, unless a subsequent evaluation reveals that:

   a. The debt security's fair value is *less* than its amortized cost basis. In that case, it should be determined whether the decline is other than temporary and the guidance on impairment of securities in ASC 320-20-45-9 should be applied. The timing and amount of cash flows expected to be collected should be considered in determining the probability of collecting all cash flows that were expected to be collected at acquisition as well as additional cash flows as a result of changes in estimates made after acquisition.

   b. It is probable, based on current information and events, that cash flows previously expected to be collected have significantly increased or actual cash flows significantly exceed previously expected cash flows. The amount of the accretable yield for the loan should be recalculated as the excess of the revised cash flows expected to be collected over the sum of (i) the initial investment *less* (ii) cash collected *less* (iii) other-than-temporary impairments *plus* (iv) the yield accreted to date. The amount of accretable yield should be adjusted by reclassifying amounts from the nonaccretable difference. This adjustment should be accounted for as a change in estimate in accordance with the guidance in ASC 250. The amount of periodic accretion should be adjusted over the remaining life of the loan.

2. For loans *not* accounted for as debt securities, cash flows expected to be collected over the life of a loan should continue to be estimated, unless a subsequent evaluation reveals that:

   a. It is probable, based on current information and events, that all cash flows originally expected to be collected and additional cash flows expected to be collected as a result of changes in estimates after acquisition will *not* be collected, in which case, the condition in ASC 450-20-25-2 is met. Therefore, the loan should be considered impaired when applying the measurement and other provisions of ASC 450 or the provisions of ASC 310, if applicable.

   b. It is probable based on current information and events that cash flows originally expected to be collected have increased significantly or actual cash flows significantly exceed cash flows previously expected to be collected. In that case:

      (1) The remaining valuation allowance or allowance for loan losses established after the loan's acquisition should be reduced by the increase in the present value of cash flows expected to be collected; *and*

(2) The amount of the loan's accretable yield should be recalculated as the excess of revised cash flows expected to be collected over the sum of (1) the initial investment *less* (2) cash collected *less* (3) write-downs *plus* (4) the yield accreted to date. The amount of accretable yield should be adjusted by reclassifying the nonaccretable difference. This adjustment should be accounted for as a change in estimate in accordance with the guidance in ASC 250. The amount of periodic accretion should be adjusted over the remaining life of the loan.

Prepayments

The treatment of expected prepayments should be consistent in accounting for cash flows expected to be collected and for projections of contractual cash flows so that the nonaccretable difference will *not* be affected. The nonaccretable difference also should *not* be affected if actual prepayments differ from expected prepayments.

Restructured or Refinanced Loan

A loan that is refinanced or restructured subsequent to acquisition, other than by a troubled debt restructuring, should *not* be accounted for as a new loan. The provisions of this pronouncement, including those related to changes in cash flows expected to be collected, continue to apply.

Variable Rate Loans

Contractually required payments receivable on a loan with a contractual interest rate that varies based on subsequent changes in an independent factor, for example, the prime rate, should be based on the factor as it changes over the life of the loan. The loan's effective interest rate or cash flows expected to be collected should *not* be based on projections of future changes in that factor. At acquisition, the amount of cash flows expected to be collected should be calculated based on the rate in effect at the acquisition date. Increases in cash flows expected to be collected should be accounted for according to the guidance in 1(b) and 2(b), above, in the discussion of changes in cash flows expected to be collected. The amount of cash flows originally expected to be collected and the accretable yield should be reduced if cash flows expected to be collected decrease as a direct result of a change in the contractual interest rate. This change should be accounted for according to the guidance in 1(a) and 2(a), above, in the discussion of changes in cash flows originally expected to be collected and recognized prospectively as a change in accounting estimate according to the guidance in ASC 250. In this case, *no* loss will be recognized, but the future yield will be reduced.

Multiple Loans Accounted for as a Single Asset

Investors are permitted to recognize, measure, and disclose information about loans *not* accounted for as debt securities as a similar single asset if the loans were acquired in the same fiscal year and have similar credit risks or risk ratings, and have one or more common major characteristic, such as financial asset type, collateral type, size, interest rate, date of origination, term, or geographic location, so that a composite interest rate and expectation of cash flows to be collected for the pool can be used. However, each individual loan should meet the scope criteria discussed above. The total cost of the acquired assets should be allocated to the individual assets based on their relative fair values at the acquisition date. The amount by which contractually required payments receivable exceed an investor's initial investment for a specific loan or a pool of loans with common risk characteristics should not be used to offset changes in cash flows expected to be collected from another loan or another pool of loans with different risk characteristics.

Once aggregated, the carrying amounts of individual loans should *not* be removed from the pool unless the investor sells, forecloses, writes off, or pays off the loan in another manner. The percentage yield calculation used to recognize accretable yield on a pool of loans should *not* be affected by the difference between a loan's carrying amount and the fair value of the collateral or other assets received.

Disclosures

The notes to the financial statements should include the following information about loans that meet the scope criteria:

1. How prepayments are considered in determining contractual cash flows and cash flows expected to be collected
2. Disclosures required in ASC 310-10-50-12 through 50-13 and 35-34, if the condition in ASC 320-20-45-9 or ASC 450-20-25-2 related to the discussion of changes in cash flows expected to be collected is met
3. Separate information about loans accounted for as debt securities and those that are *not*, including:
   (a) The outstanding balance, which consists of the undiscounted sum of all amounts, including amounts considered to be principal, interest, fees, penalties, and other amounts under the loan owed to the investor at

the reporting date, except for amounts irrevocably forgiven in a debt restructuring; amounts legally discharged and interest, fees, penalties, and other amounts that would be accrued after the reporting date for loans with a net carrying amount; and the related carrying amount at the beginning and end of the period.

(b) The accretable yield at the beginning and at the end of the period, reconciled for additions, accretion, disposals of loans, and reclassifications to or from the nonaccretable difference during the period.

(c) Contractually required payments receivable, cash flows expected to be collected, and the fair value at the acquisition date of loans acquired during the period.

(d) The carrying amount at the acquisition date of loans under the scope of this guidance not accounted for in accordance with the income recognition model in this pronouncement that are acquired during the period and the carrying amount of all such loans at the end of the period.

4. The following disclosures are required only for loans *not* accounted for as debt securities:

(a) For each period for which an income statement is presented, the amount of (*a*) expenses, if any, recognized in accordance with the guidance in 2(a) of the section on changes in cash flows expected to be collected and (*b*) reductions of the allowance recognized in accordance with the guidance in 2(b)(1) of the section on changes in cash flows expected to be collected.

(b) The amount of the allowance for uncollectible accounts at the beginning and end of the period.

ASC 310-10-35-2, 35-4, 35-6, 35-8, 35-15, 35-19, 35-25, 35-27, 35-34 through 35-36, 35-38; 55-1 through 55-6; 310-40-50-4; 310-45-20-60-3 Application of FASB Statements No. 5 and No. 114 to a Loan Portfolio

The SEC staff issued this announcement in response to inquiries regarding the transition required for companies that change their application of generally accepted accounting principles as a result of the guidance in the FASB staff's Viewpoints article, "Application of FASB Statements 5 and 114 to a Loan Portfolio," which was published in the FASB's April 12, 1999, *Status Report*. The SEC staff noted that the guidance in that article is part of generally accepted accounting principles and should be followed by *all* creditors.

According to the SEC staff, if an SEC registrant's application of the guidance in the Viewpoints article results in a material adjustment, the change should be reported and disclosed in the first quarter ending after May 20, 1999, like a cumulative effect of a change in accounting principles in accordance with the guidance in ASC 250-10-45-5. The SEC staff reported that a March 10, 1999, letter to financial institutions—which was issued jointly by the SEC, Federal Deposit Insurance Corporation, Federal Reserve Board, Office of the Controller of the Currency, and Office of Thrift Supervision (the Agencies)—encourages the FASB and its staff to issue additional guidance on accounting for loan losses. In addition, the letter states that the Agencies support the work of the AICPA's Allowance for Loan Losses Task Force in its effort to develop specific guidance on the measurement of credit losses and how to distinguish probable losses inherent in a portfolio at the balance sheet date from possible or future losses that are not inherent in the balance sheet at that date. The Agencies require that allowances be reported for probable losses. The letter also states that the senior staff of the Agencies are working jointly on guidance for (*a*) documentation to support the allowance in addition to that provided in the SEC Financial Reporting Release No. 28 (Accounting for Loan Losses by Registrants Engaged in Lending Activities) under the heading *Procedural Discipline in Determining the Allowance and Provision for Loan Losses to be Reported* and (*b*) improved disclosures about allowances for credit losses.

The EITF asked that the Viewpoints article and a May 21, 1999, letter from the Board of Governors of the Federal Reserve System, which provides guidance to supervisors and bankers regarding the Viewpoints article, be attached to the announcement. The SEC staff supports that guidance.

ASC 310-20: NONREFUNDABLE FEES AND OTHER COSTS

ASC 310-20-05-3; 35-4, 35-6, 50-4 Amortization Period for Net Deferred Credit Card Origination Costs

BACKGROUND

A credit card issuer normally charges annual fees to its cardholders. Sometimes, as part of a promotion designed to attract new customers, the issuer waives the annual fee or charges no fee. The issuer incurs certain direct costs of issuing credit cards. In addition, the credit card agreement entered into as part of the promotion generally provides the cardholder with an extended period to repay the outstanding balance on the credit card in the event of cancellation or nonrenewal. If a cardholder does not renew the card after a one-year period, for example, the agreement may allow the cardholder to repay the outstanding balance over an additional period, such as two or three years.

The guidance in ASC 310 does not specifically address the amortization of costs associated with credit card originations. The Statement requires that direct loan origination costs be offset against origination fees, with the net amount deferred and recognized as an adjustment to the loan yield.

The Issue applies to the amortization of deferred origination costs on credit cards with fees, without fees, or if fees have been waived for a limited period of time. It does not apply, however, to origination costs for private label credit cards, which are issued by, or on behalf of, an entity for purchases only of that entity's goods or services.

ACCOUNTING ISSUE

Over what period of time should direct credit card origination costs be amortized when the credit card arrangement provides for no fees?

ACCOUNTING GUIDANCE

- Based on the definition of *Direct Loan Origination Costs* in the ASC *Master Glossary*, an issuer of a credit card that is not a private label credit card should net the costs of originating the credit card, which qualify as direct loan origination costs for deferral in accordance with the guidance in ASC 310-20-25-6, against the related credit card fee, if any, and should amortize the net amount on a straight-line basis over the privilege period. If a significant fee is charged, the privilege period is the period over which the cardholder is entitled to use the card. If no significant fee is charged, the privilege period is one year. The significance of the fee should be evaluated based on the relationship of the fee and related costs.
- An entity should disclose its accounting policy, the net amount capitalized at the balance sheet date, and the amortization period of credit card fees and costs for purchased and originated cards that are not private label credit cards.

This guidance applies only to originated credit card accounts, not accounts purchased from third parties. The amortization of a premium, if any, paid on purchases of credit card portfolios is discussed in ASC 310-10-25-7 and 35-52.

SUBSEQUENT DEVELOPMENT

In a discussion of the guidance in ASC 310-20-05-4, 25-18 and 35-8, which is discussed below, a conclusion was reached that credit card accounts acquired individually should be accounted for as originations under the guidance in this Issue.

DISCUSSION

Three approaches for amortization of direct loan origination costs were proposed: (*a*) over the privilege period, or one year; (*b*) over the repayment period, which may extend beyond the privilege period; or (*c*) over the relationship period, which includes renewal periods.

The guidance is based on the first approach. It is consistent with the guidance in ASC 310-20-25-15; 310-20-35-5, which states that "fees that are periodically charged to cardholders shall be deferred and recognized on a straight-line basis over the period the fee entitles the cardholder to use the card." It is also consistent with the guidance in ASC 310-20-35-6 through 35-7 and 25-16 through 25-17, in which the FASB staff repeated the guidance in ASC 310-20-25-15; 35-5 and stated further that "[r]elated origination costs eligible for deferral should be amortized over the same period on a straight-line basis." Proponents of this approach argued that credit card fees and related costs should be netted and amortized over the same period. Additional arguments for amortization of initiation costs over the privilege period included the fact that this approach is simple, conservative, and it enhances comparability among credit card issuers.

ASC 310-20-05-4; 25-18; 35-8 Accounting for Individual Credit Card Acquisitions

BACKGROUND

A credit card issuer can obtain new customer accounts by (*a*) purchasing a portfolio of existing credit card accounts, (*b*) originating the credit card relationship, or (*c*) purchasing individual credit card accounts through a third party. The accounts normally have no outstanding receivable balances at acquisition. The accounting for the cost associated with a bulk purchase of a credit card portfolio was addressed in ASC 310-10-25-7 and 35-52 and internal credit card origination in ASC 310-20-05-3; 35-4, 35-6; and 50-4, both of which were discussed above. However, neither provided guidance for situations in which credit card accounts are purchased individually.

Individual credit card accounts can be obtained three ways:

- *Direct marketing specialist* The credit card issuer hires a marketing company to solicit new credit card customers and usually pays the specialist a fee for each approved credit card agreement.
- *Affinity group* The credit card issuer enters into an arrangement with a company or an organization to solicit credit card accounts from their customers or members. This third-party entity is responsible for the solicitation and related costs and sells the approved credit card accounts to the issuer for a fee.
- *Co-branding* Co-branding is a variation of an affinity group, in which the name of the third party is included on the credit card. The co-branding third party provides additional products and services, such as extended warranties and discounts. In this type of arrangement, the credit card issuer and the third party benefit from increased card usage, an extended cardholder relationship period, and increased sales of the third party's products or services. Whatever the method of acquisition, the credit card issuer incurs a cost in obtaining new accounts.

ACCOUNTING ISSUE

Should a credit card issuer account for acquisitions of individual credit card accounts as purchases in accordance with the guidance in ASC 310-10-25-7 and 35-52 or as self-originations, in accordance with the guidance in ASC 310 and ASC 310-20-05-3; 35-4, 35-6, and 50-4?

ACCOUNTING GUIDANCE

A credit card issuer should:

- Account for credit card accounts acquired individually as self-originations, in accordance with the guidance in ASC 310 and ASC 310-20-05-3; 35-4, 35-6; and 50-4.
- Defer amounts paid to third parties to acquire individual credit card accounts, net those amounts against any related credit card fees, and amortize the net amount on a straight-line basis over the privilege period.

The privilege period is the period during which a cardholder is entitled to use the card, if the credit cardholder is charged a significant fee. The privilege period is one year, if there is no significant fee. The significance of the fee is based on the relationship of its amount to the card's acquisition cost.

DISCUSSION

Alternative methods of accounting for purchases of individual credit card accounts were considered and different criteria to distinguish purchases from self-originations were discussed. Proponents of the final guidance noted that the definition of *Direct Loan Origination Costs* in the ASC *Master Glossary* addresses this third-party activity as follows: "Direct loan origination costs of a completed loan shall include only (*a*) incremental direct costs of loan origination incurred in transactions with independent third parties for that loan and (*b*) certain costs directly related to specified activities performed by the lender for that loan." Further, it was noted that the third-party relationship in this situation is merely a marketing tool in which a credit card issuer is outsourcing its solicitation and origination activities. The risks and costs are still borne, however, by the credit card issuer. Proponents supported their contention that these credit card accounts are self-originations rather than purchases by arguing that the third party only solicits accounts and acts as an agent for the issuer, and the customer cannot use the credit card until it is issued by the issuer. They also argued that purchases of individual credit card accounts are unlike bulk purchases of existing credit card accounts that may have outstanding balances. In the latter transactions, the credit card issuer must accept the account and issue a credit card.

ASC 310-20-35-11 Creditor's Accounting for a Modification or an Exchange of Debt Instruments

BACKGROUND

The authoritative accounting literature provides different guidance to creditors and debtors as to how to determine whether a modification or exchange of a debt instrument should be accounted for as an extinguishment of a debt instrument and its replacement with a new debt instrument or as a continuation of a debt instrument that has been modified. ASC 310 provides such guidance for creditors and ASC 470-50-05-4, 15-3, 40-6 through 40-14, 40-17 through 40-20, 55-1 through 55-9 (EITF Issue 96-19), provides such guidance for debtors. Under the guidance in that Issue, which is discussed below, a debtor is required to account for a modification or exchange of debt as new debt if it is *substantially different* from the original debt. Whereas, under the guidance in ASC 310 (FAS-91), a creditor is not permitted to account for an original debt instrument that has been modified as a new instrument unless the modification is *more than minor*. However, ASC 310 (FAS-91) provides no guidance on how to evaluate what is more than a minor modification.

ACCOUNTING ISSUE

How should a creditor evaluate whether a modification of a debt instrument's terms as a result of a refinancing or restructuring (other than in a troubled debt restructuring) should be considered to be more than *minor* in applying the guidance in ASC 310-20-35-10?

ACCOUNTING GUIDANCE

The following guidance is provided:

- When applying the guidance in ASC 310-20-35-10, a modification or an exchange of debt instruments should be considered *more than minor* if the present value of the cash flows under the new debt instrument differs by at least *10%* from the present value of the remaining cash flows under the terms of the original debt instrument.
- If the difference between the present value of the cash flows of a new and an existing debt instrument differs by *less than* 10%, the creditor should evaluate whether a modification or exchange of debt instruments is *more* than minor based on the facts and circumstances and other relevant information related to the modification.
- Creditors should apply the guidance in ASC 470-50-05-4, 15-3, 40-6 through 40-14, 40-17 through 40-20, 55-1 through 55-9 to calculate a debt instrument's present value of cash flows when applying the 10% test.

ASC 310-30: LOANS AND DEBT SECURITIES ACQUIRED WITH DETERIORATED CREDIT QUALITY

ASC-310-30-35-13, 40-1 through 40-2; ASC 310-40-15-11 Effect of a Loan Modification When the Loan Is Part of a Pool That Is Accounted for as a Single Asset

BACKGROUND

Under the guidance in ASC 310-30-15-6, an entity is permitted to account for acquired assets with "common risk characteristics" in a pool of assets, which becomes a unit of accounting when it is established. Because the purchase discount for loans accounted for in a pool is not allocated to the individual loans, all the loans in a pool are accreted at a rate based on the cash flow projection for the pool. Also, impairment is tested on the total pool and not on the individual loans.

Guidance for evaluating whether a loan modification should be classified as a troubled debt restructuring (TDR) is provided in ASC 310-40-15-4, which states that a restructuring of debt represents a TDR if a creditor grants a concession to the debtor as a result of the debtor's financial difficulties. Questions have been raised about whether TDR accounting applies if acquired loans with credit deterioration are accounted for in a pool. If so, some believe that the troubled loan should be removed from the pool or that the whole pool should be accounted for as a TDR. A loan that is removed from a pool would no longer be accounted for under the guidance in ASC 310-30. However, others believe that such loans should not be removed from the pool.

SCOPE

The guidance in this Issue applies to modifications of loans accounted for as a pool that is established under the provisions of ASC 310-30-15-6. The guidance in this Issue does *not* apply to loans accounted for individually under the guidance in ASC 310-30 or those not under the scope of that guidance.

ACCOUNTING GUIDANCE

TDR accounting should *not* be applied to loans accounted for as a pool under the guidance in ASC 310-30 if those loans had deteriorating credit when they were acquired. The Additional disclosures are not required, because it is expected that as part of its project on loan loss disclosures, the FASB will consider whether additional disclosures should be required about loan modifications, including for loans accounted for within a pool under the guidance in ASC 310-30.

ASC 310-40: TROUBLED DEBT RESTRUCTURINGS BY CREDITORS

ASC 310-40-15-3; 55-4; 470-60-15-3; 55-15 Classification of Debt Restructurings by Debtors and Creditors

BACKGROUND

A *troubled debt restructuring* is defined in ASC 310-40-15-3 through 15-12; 35-2, 35-5 through 35-7; 40-2, 40-5 through 40-6, 40-8; 25-1 through 25-2; 50-1; 55-2; 10-1 through 10-2; and ASC 470-60-15-3 through 15-12; 55-3; 35 through 35-12; 45-1 through 45-2; 50-1 through 50-2; 10-1 through 10-2; and ASC 450-20-60-12 as a restructuring in which a creditor, for economic or legal reasons related to a debtor's financial difficulties, grants a concession to the debtor that the creditor otherwise would *not* consider.

ACCOUNTING GUIDANCE

Question: In applying the guidance in ASC 310-40-15-3 through 15-12; 35-2; 35-5 through 35-7; 40-2, 40-5 through 40-6, 40-8; 25-1 through 25-2; 50-1; 55-2; 10-1 through 10-2; ASC 470-60-15-3 through 15-12; 55-3, 35 through 35-12, 45-1 through 45-2, 50-1 through 50-2, 10-1 through 10-2; and ASC 450-20-60-12, can a debt restructuring be a troubled debt restructuring (TDR) for a debtor but not for a creditor?

Answer: Yes, a debtor may have a TDR even though the creditor does not have a TDR. A debtor and a creditor apply that guidance individually based on their specific facts and circumstances to determine whether a particular restructuring constitutes a TDR. The guidance in ASC 310-40-15-8, 15-12 is especially helpful to creditors in determining whether a particular restructuring is a TDR for debtors or creditors. The guidance in ASC 310-40-15-3 through 15-12, 35-2, 35-5 through 35-7, 40-2, 40-5 through 40-6, 40-8, 25-1 through 25-2, 50-1, 55-2, 10-1 through 10-2; ASC 470-60-15-3 through 15-12, 55-3, 35 through 35-12, 45-1 through 45-2, 50-1 through 50-2, 10-1 through 10-2; and ASC 450-20-60-12 establishes tests for applicability that are not necessarily symmetrical between a debtor and a creditor, especially if a debtor's carrying amount and a creditor's recorded investment differ.

ASC 310-40-40-1 Substituted Debtors in a Troubled Debt Restructuring

BACKGROUND

A creditor and a debtor agree to a troubled debt restructuring on a mortgage loan receivable under which the debtor will make payments to the creditor for the next 30 years. With the creditor's permission, the debtor sells the house, collateralizing the loan on a contract for deed to a third party for less than the creditor's net investment in the loan. The debtor retains title to the house and the creditor retains a lien on the property. The debtor finances the sale of the house to the third party so that the monthly principal and interest payments equal the debtor's required payments on the restructured loan. The third party makes the monthly payments directly to the creditor.

ACCOUNTING ISSUE

Should the sale of the collateral and subsequent payments by the third party to the creditor be considered a settlement of the restructured loan, thus requiring the creditor to recognize a loss for the difference between the carrying amount of the net investment in the restructured loan and the fair value of the payments to be received from the third party purchaser?

ACCOUNTING GUIDANCE

The creditor should recognize an asset for the fair value of the payments to be received from the third-party purchaser and a loss on the settlement of the restructured loan that is measured based on the difference between the creditor's net investment in the loan and the fair value of the asset received to satisfy the loan in accordance with the guidance in ASC 310-40-40-3.

ASC 310-40-40-6, 55-1, 55-10A; ASC 310-10-50-11, 50-35; ASC 270-10-50-1; ASC 360-50-4 Reclassifications of Collateralized Mortgage Loans upon a Troubled Debt Restructuring

OVERVIEW

The EITF was asked to address this issue because of the large number of residential real estate properties held by lenders as a result of the economic downturn and weakness in the real estate market, which resulted in many foreclosures. Lenders refer to such holdings as other real estate owned (OREO), which is not related to a lender's operations. Under the existing guidance in FASB Accounting Standards Codification® (ASC) 310, *Receivables* (ASC 310-40-40-6), which applies to troubled debt restructurings, a creditor is required to derecognize a receivable for a loan and recognize the collateral in "a troubled debt restructuring that is in substance a repossession or foreclosure by the creditor, that is, the creditor receives physical possession of the debtor's assets regardless of whether formal foreclosure proceedings take place . . . ." As a result of the extended timeline of the foreclosure process, some creditors were applying that guidance to residential real estate consumer mortgage loans. That practice caused diversity in the reporting for foreclosed residential real estate because the terms "in substance repossession or foreclosure" and "physical possession" were not defined in the accounting literature. Consequently, creditors have had difficulty in determining when an "in substance repossession" of residential real estate property occurs. The guidance below, which was issued in ASU 2014-04, is intended to clarify how the guidance in ASC 310-40-40-6, which is quoted above applies to the accounting for consumer mortgage loans collateralized by residential real estate properties.

ACCOUNTING ISSUE

When is a creditor considered to have received physical possession of a residential real estate property collateralizing a consumer mortgage loan as a result of an in substance repossession or foreclosure

SCOPE

The guidance applies to all creditors who receive physical possession of residential real estate properties used as collateral for consumer mortgage loans as a result of in substance repossession or foreclosure.

ACCOUNTING GUIDANCE

Physical Possession of Residential Real Estate Collateralizing a Consumer Mortgage Loan

The guidance in ASC 310-40 has been amended by the addition of ASC 310-40-55-10A, which provides that a creditor is considered to have received physical possession of residential real estate property collateralizing a consumer mortgage loan as a result of an in substance repossession or foreclosure only if one of the following two conditions has been met:

1. The creditor has received legal title to the residential real estate property when foreclosure is completed. Legal title to a residential real estate property may be obtained even if a borrower has redemption rights that give the borrower a legal right for a period of time after foreclosure to reclaim the real estate property by paying certain amounts specified by law.
2. The borrower satisfied the loan by conveying all interest in the residential real estate property to the creditor by completing a deed in lieu of foreclosure or a similar legal agreement, after the borrower and the creditor have fulfilled agreed on terms and conditions.

DISCLOSURE

The following disclosures are required:

- ASC 310-10-50-11 has been amended to require an entity to disclose the carrying amounts of foreclosed residential real estate properties collateralizing consumer mortgage loans that are held at the reporting date as a result of receiving "physical possession" of those properties in accordance with the guidance in ASC 310-40-40-6 and ASC 310-40-55-10A.
- Disclosures about loans in the process of foreclosure also is required. ASC 310-10-50-35 has been added to require disclosure about an entity's recorded investment in consumer mortgage loans secured by residential real estate undergoing formal foreclosure proceedings in accordance with the applicable jurisdiction's local requirements.
- The disclosure requirement in ASC 270, *Interim Reporting* (270-10-50-1), has been amended by the addition of subparagraph(s), which provides that a publicly traded company should report, at a minimum, in its summarized interim financial report:
  - — The carrying amount of foreclosed residential real estate property, as required in the last sentence of ASC 310-10-50-11; and
  - — The amount of loans in the process of foreclosure, as required in ASC 310-10-50-35.

ASC 310-40-40-6A, 40-7; 55-12 Valuation of Repossessed Real Estate

BACKGROUND

A seller finances a sale of real estate. Although the buyer's initial investment is insufficient for full accrual profit recognition under the guidance in ASC 360, the transaction qualifies for sales recognition, with profit deferred and recognized on the installment or cost recovery methods. Some time after the sale, the buyer defaults on the seller's mortgage, and the seller forecloses the property. The property's fair value at foreclosure is less than the seller's gross receivable, which includes the cost of the property and deferred profit, but is greater than the net receivable, which consists of principal and interest receivable reduced by deferred profit and related allowances.

ACCOUNTING ISSUE

At what amount should a seller recognize the foreclosed property?

ACCOUNTING GUIDANCE

A seller should recognize a foreclosed property at the lower of the net receivable or the property's fair value. This guidance assumes that under the circumstances, it is appropriate under the circumstances to include any accrued interest income on the financing in the net receivable. It was noted that the guidance in ASC 470, Debt, does *not* apply in this situation, because deferred profit is not considered a valuation allowance account, as contemplated in ASC 470. However, the guidance in ASC 470 would apply, if profit had been recognized on the full accrual method, with recognition of the property at fair value, if appropriate.

PRACTICE POINTER: ASC 360 provides guidance on accounting for long-lived assets held for sale as well as specific criteria on how to determine when a long-lived asset should be classified as held for sale. Under that guidance, a newly acquired foreclosed asset classified as held for sale should be recognized at the lower of its carrying amount or fair value less selling costs.

Illustration of Valuation of Foreclosed Real Estate

	Installment Method	*Cost Recovery Method*
Sales transaction:		
Seller's financing	$475,000	$475,000
Buyer's initial investment	25,000	25,000
Sales value	$500,000	$500,000
Sales value	$500,000	$500,000
Cost	350,000	
Gain	150,000	150,000
Amount recognized	(7,500)	0
Deferred profit	$142,500	$150,000
Foreclosure at end of first year:		
Original principal balance	$475,000	$475,000
Accrued interest in first year at 8%	38,000	38,000
Gross receivable at foreclosure	513,000	513,000
Less: Deferred profit	(142,500)	(150,000)
Net receivable	$370,500	$363,000
Property's fair value at foreclosure	$430,000	$430,000

Under the guidance in this Issue, the foreclosed property would be recognized at $370,500 under the installment method or at $363,000 under the cost recovery method.

DISCUSSION

As stated above, it was noted that the guidance in ASC 470 does not apply in this transaction, because deferred profit is not considered a valuation allowance under the guidance in ASC 470. That comment is based on the guidance in ASC 470-60-15-12, which states that a foreclosure is not considered a troubled debt restructuring if the fair value of the receivable is at least equal to the "recorded investment in the receivable." The primary focus of the guidance in ASC 470 is on transactions that would result in a loss. In the case of a sale on which profit has been deferred—as in the transaction in this Issue—the net receivable, not the gross receivable, should be considered the seller's recorded investment in the receivable and compared to fair value, because it does not include deferred profit on a sale. If profit had been recognized on the full accrual method, the gross receivable would have been compared to fair value.

Recognition of foreclosed real estate at the net receivable amount results in no gain or loss on foreclosure. The original cost of the property is increased or decreased by gains and interest income recognized in prior periods and cash collected on the sale and financing. More cash may be received than recognized as gains and interest income under the installment method if the gain is a small percentage of the sales price. The same may occur under the cost recovery method, because no gain is recognized until the cost has been recovered. In those situations, the property would be recognized at less than its original cost because of the excess cash. In the above Illustration, a $3 gain was recognized on the sale, $15 of interest income was accrued, and $10 cash was received on the down payment. When the property is recognized at foreclosure, the original cost of $140 would be increased by $8 (3 + 15 – 10) to $148, which also equals the $205 receivable less deferred profit of $57.

The journal entry to recognize the foreclosed property would be as follows:

Property	$370,500	
Deferred profit	142,500	
Receivable		$513,000

ASC 310-40-40-6 through 40-7B; ASC 310-10-40-1A Troubled Debt Restructuring by Creditors (ASC 310-40): Classification of Certain Government-Guaranteed Mortgage Loans upon Foreclosure

BACKGROUND

The EITF was asked to address this issue because of diversity in the manner in which creditors classify residential and nonresidential mortgage loans for which repayment of the unpaid balance of a loan is fully guaranteed by the Federal Housing Administration (FHA) of the U.S. Department of Housing and Urban Development (HUD) and the U.S. Department of Veterans Affairs (VA), which guarantees partial repayment of the unpaid principal balance of residential mortgage loans. Qualifying creditors participating in those government-sponsored loan guarantee programs are generally required or permitted to convey real estate property obtained on foreclosure to the government agency that guaranteed the loan.

The guidance on troubled debt restructuring under U.S. generally accepted accounting principles (U.S. GAAP) currently applies only to circumstances under which a creditor satisfies its receivable by obtaining a debtor's assets, including through foreclosure. However, there is no guidance for the classification or measurement of a foreclosed loan that includes a government guarantee under which a creditor is entitled to a loan's full unpaid principle balance if the loan is foreclosed. Some creditors follow the existing guidance by reclassifying the guaranteed loans to real estate, while others reclassify those loans to other receivables. The objective of the following guidance is to provide a consistent accounting treatment for government guaranteed loans in foreclosure, which will provide users with useful information about a creditor's receivables from foreclosed mortgages that are expected to be recovered through government guarantees.

ACCOUNTING GUIDANCE

Scope

The guidance applies to creditors that hold government-guaranteed mortgage loans, including FHA and VA guaranteed loans.

Classification and Measurement of Certain Government-Guaranteed Residential Mortgage Loans upon Foreclosure

ASC 310, *Receivables,* has been amended by the addition of ASC 310-40-40-7A and 40-7B to ASC 310-40, *Troubled Debt Restructuring by Creditors*. Under the guidance in ASC 310-40-40-7A, a guaranteed mortgage loan receivable should be derecognized and a separate other receivable should be recognized on foreclosure, which occurs when a creditor receives physical possession of a real estate property that collateralizes a mortgage loan, as required in ASC 310-40-40-6, if the following conditions are met:

- The loan has a government guarantee that cannot be separated from the loan before foreclosure.
- At foreclosure, the creditor: (1) intends to convey the real estate property to the guarantor; (2) intends to claim the guarantee; and (3) is able to recover the unpaid principal through the guarantee because the creditor determines that it has complied with the guarantee program's required conditions and procedures.
- At foreclosure, the amount of a claim, if any, which is determined based on the real estate's fair value, is fixed.

ASC 310-40-40-7B requires that a separate other receivable should be measured at foreclosure based on the loan's balance of principal and interest expected to be recovered from the guarantor.

ASC 310-40-40-8A, 40-9 Accounting for Conversion of a Loan into a Debt Security in a Debt Restructuring

BACKGROUND

A creditor receives a debt security issued by a debtor in a debt restructuring. The fair value of the debt security differs from the creditor's basis in the loan on the date the debt is restructured because (*a*) there has been a direct write-off against the loan, so the fair value of the security exceeds the basis of the loan, or (*b*) there has been no direct write-off against the loan, so the basis of the loan exceeds the fair value of the security.

ASC 310-35-13 through 35-14, 35-16 through 35-26, 35-28, 35-29, 35-34, 35-37, 35-39; 45-5 through 45-6; 50-15, 50-19; ASC 310-30-30-2; ASC 310-40-35-8, 35-12; 50-2 through 50-3, 50-12 through 50-13 provides guidance to creditors on accounting for impaired loans, while ASC 320-10-05-2; 50-1A through 50-3, 50-5, 50-9 through 50-11; 55-3; 15-5; 30-1; 35-1 through 35-2, 35-4 through 35-5, 35-10 through 35-13, 35-18; 15-2 through 15-4, 15-7; 25-3 through 25-6, 25-9, 25-11 through 25-12, 25-14 through 25-16; 45-1 through 45-2, 45-8 through 45-11, 45-13, provides guidance on accounting for investments in marketable securities and investments in all debt securities. ASC 320-10-15-6, 55-2 states that the provisions of the latter apply to securities received in a debt restructuring.

ACCOUNTING ISSUES

1. At what amount should a creditor recognize a debt security issued by a debtor and received in a debt restructuring?
2. How should a creditor account for a difference, if any, between the creditor's basis in a loan and the fair value of a debt security issued by the debtor at the date of a restructuring?

ACCOUNTING GUIDANCE

- A creditor should recognize a debt security issued by a debtor and received in a debt restructuring at the fair value of the security at the date of the restructuring.
- A creditor should account for the difference between the creditor's basis in a loan and the fair value of a debt security issued by a debtor as follows:
  - — Recognize the difference as a recovery of the loan if the fair value of the debt security exceeds the net carrying amount of the loan.
  - — Recognize the difference as a charge to the allowance for credit losses if the net carrying amount of the loan exceeds the fair value of the debt security.
  - — After a restructuring, account for a debt security issued by the debtor in accordance with the guidance in ASC 320-10-05-2; 50-1A through 50-3, 50-5, 50-9 through 50-11; 55-3; 15-5; 30-1; 35-1 through 35-2, 35-4 through 35-5, 35-10 through 35-13, 35-18; 15-2 through 15-4, 15-7; 25-3 through 25-6, 25-9, 25-11 through 25-12, 25-14 through 25-16; 45-1 through 45-2, 45-8 through 45-11, 45-13.
- If a security is received in a restructuring to settle a claim for past-due interest on a loan, the security should be measured at its fair value at the date of the restructuring and accounted for consistent with the entity's policy for recognizing cash received for past-due interest. After the restructuring, the security should be accounted for based on the guidance in ASC 320-10-05-2; 50-1A through 50-3, 50-5, 50-9 through 50-11; 55-3; 15-5; 30-1; 35-1 through 35-2, 35-4 through 35-5, 35-10 through 35-13, 35-18; 15-2 through 15-4, 15-7; 25-3 through 25-6, 25-9, 25-11 through 25-12, 25-14 through 25-16; 45-1 through 45-2, 45-8 through 45-11, 45-13.

Illustration of the Conversion of a Loan into a Debt Security

Example 1—Conversion of a Loan with a Prior Write-down into a Security

Original recorded investment in the loan	$50,000
Write-down	(5,000)
Recorded investment in the loan as adjusted	$45,000
Fair value of security at restructuring:	
Scenario 1	$47,000
Scenario 2	$45,000
Scenario 3	$40,000

Accounting for a Debt Security Classified as Available-for-Sale

Scenario 1

Investment in debt security	$47,000	
Loan		$45,000
Allowance for credit losses—recovery		2,000

Scenario 2		
Investment in debt security	$45,000	
Loan		$45,000
Scenario 3		
Investment in debt security	$40,000	
Allowance for credit losses	5,000	
Loan		$45,000

Example 2—Conversion of a Loan with a Valuation Allowance into a Security

Recorded investment in the loan	$50,000
Valuation allowance	5,000
Net carrying amount of the loan	$45,000
Fair value of security at restructuring:	
Scenario 1	$47,000
Scenario 2	$45,000
Scenario 3	$40,000

Accounting for a Debt Security Classified as Available-for-Sale

Scenario 1		
Investment in debt security	$47,000	
Valuation allowance	5,000	
Loan		$50,000
Allowance for credit losses—recovery		2,000
Scenario 2		
Investment in debt security	$45,000	
Valuation allowance	5,000	
Loan		$50,000
Scenario 3		
Investment in debt security	$40,000	
Valuation allowance	5,000	
Allowance for credit losses	5,000	
Loan		$50,000

DISCUSSION

- Debt securities are within the scope of ASC 320-10-05-2; 50-1A through 50-3, 50-5, 50-9 through 50-11; 55-3; 15-5; 30-1; 35-1 through 35-2, 35-4 through 35-5, 35-10 through 35-13, 35-18; 15-2 through 15-4, 15-7; 25-3 through 25-6, 25-9, 25-11 through 25-12, 25-14 through 25-16; 45-1 through 45-2, 45-8 through 45-11, 45-13, and must be recognized at fair value, if they are classified as trading or available-for-sale.
- Two alternative approaches were discussed. Under one approach, the difference, if any, between a creditor's basis in a loan and the fair value of the debt security at the date of the restructuring would be accounted for as a fair value adjustment under the guidance in ASC 320.

  The other approach—the one adopted—is that of settlement accounting. Proponents of this approach argued that assets carried at fair value are excluded by the modification-of-terms provisions in ASC 310-40-15-3 through 15-12; 35-2, 35-5 through 35-7; 40-2, 40-5 through 40-6, 40-8; 25-1 through 25-2; 50-1; 55-2; 10-1 through 10-2; ASC 470-60-15-3 through 15-12; 55-3; 35 through 35-12; 45-1 through 45-2; 50-1 through 50-2; 10-1 through 10-2; ASC 450-20-60-12 (FAS-15) as well as from the scope of ASC 310-35-13 through 35-14, 35-16 through 35-26, 35-28, 35-29, 35-34, 35-37, 35-39; 45-5 through 45-6; 50-15, 50-19; ASC 310-30-30-2; ASC 310-40-35-8, 35-12; 50-2 through 50-3, 50-12 through 50-13, because modification-of-terms accounting and allowance for loan losses are unnecessary when an asset is accounted for at fair value. Proponents of this view believed that accounting for a debt security at fair value provides an embedded gain or loss that should be accounted for as a recovery, if there is a gain, or as a write-off, if there is a loss. They noted that recovery accounting is an established practice that measures historical loan loss experience. The gain is a function of the market's evaluation of collectability based on credit considerations instead of market interest rates. Proponents of this view also argued that a gain should not be considered a holding gain, because the gain in that case occurred before the restructuring, whereas here the asset was a loan and it would be misleading to recognize it as a gain on the security. An adjustment of bad debt expense for the loan would therefore best present the economics of the transaction.

- The accounting guidance is based on the notion that a gain on securities received in payment for past-due interest that was never recognized on the balance sheet should be recognized as income, as if those claims were sold for cash.

ASC 310-40-40-10; 35-11; 55-13 through 55-15 Determination of Cost Basis for Foreclosed Assets under FASB Statement No. 15, *Accounting by Debtors and Creditors for Troubled Debt Restructurings*, and the Measurement of Cumulative Losses Previously Recognized under Paragraph 37 of FASB Statement No. 144, *Accounting for the Impairment or Disposal of Long-Lived Assets*

Question: When a long-lived asset is accounted for under the guidance in ASC 360 and ASC 840 after foreclosure, should a valuation allowance related to the loan that was collateralized by that long-lived asset be carried over as a separate element of the asset's cost basis?

Answer: No. When a loan is foreclosed, the lender receives the long-lived asset collateralizing the loan in full satisfaction of the receivable. As required in ASC 310-40-40-3, the asset that collateralized the loan must be measured at its fair value less selling costs, with the amount of that measurement becoming the asset's new cost basis. After foreclosure, when the asset is accounted for under the provisions of ASC 360, the valuation allowance related to the loan before foreclosure should *not* be carried over to the long-lived asset's cost basis because under the guidance in ASC 360-10-35-40 and 40-5, the amount of gain that can be recognized on a long-lived asset is limited to the amount of cumulative impairment losses recognized and measured under the guidance in ASC 360, Property, Plant, and Equipment, previously measured and recognized under the guidance in ASC 450, Contingencies, and ASC 310, Receivables, do *not* enter into the calculation of the impairment of an asset's value under the guidance in ASC 360.

For example, a lender has a $100,000 loan receivable, which is collateralized by a long-lived asset with a fair value of $80,000 and estimated selling costs of $6,000 at the date on which the lender determines that foreclosure is probable. One month later, when the asset is foreclosed, the fair value of the collateral is unchanged. Based on the guidance in ASC 310-40-05-8 and ASC 310-10-35-16 through 35-17, the lender's *loan impairment* loss at the foreclosure date is measured at $26,000, based on the difference between the loan receivable ($100,000) and the fair value of the collateral ($80,000) less selling costs ($6,000). At that date, the new cost basis of the long-lived asset received in full satisfaction of the receivable also is measured at $74,000 under the guidance in ASC 310). Three months later when the asset is tested for impairment under the guidance in ASC 360 its value has declined to $70,000 with estimated selling costs of $4,000. Under the provisions of ASC 360, the lender recognizes an $8,000 asset impairment loss [($80,000 – $6,000) – ($70,000 – $4,000)]. When the asset is sold six months later, its fair value has increased to $84,000, less $7,000 in selling costs. Although the asset's fair value has increased by $11,000 [($84,000 – $7,000) – ($70,000 – $4,000)], the lender can recognize a gain of only $8,000, which is the amount of the asset's impairment loss previously recognized under the guidance in ASC 360. The $26,000 loan impairment loss on foreclosure is *not* included in measuring the cumulative losses recognized under the guidance in ASC 360.

ASC 310-40-50-5; S50-1; S99-1 Applicability of the Disclosures Required by FASB Statement No. 114 When a Loan Is Restructured in a Troubled Debt Restructuring into Two (or More) Loans

BACKGROUND

Under the provisions of ASC 310-35-13 through 35-14, 35-16 through 35-26, 35-28, 35-29, 35-34, 35-37, 35-39; 45-5 through 45-6; 50-15, 50-19; ASC 310-30-30-2; ASC 310-40-35-8, 35-12; 50-2 through 50-3, 50-12 through 50-13, as amended by ASC 310-10-35-40; 50-16 through 50-17, 50-20; ASC 310-40-35-10; 50-6, creditors must disclose information about their investments in impaired loans and related allowances for credit losses. Creditors need not make those disclosures in years subsequent to the year in which a loan is restructured in a troubled debt restructuring that involves a modification of terms if the following two criteria are met: (*a*) the interest rate provided for in the restructuring agreement at least equals the rate the creditor was willing to accept for a new loan with comparable risk at the time the loan was restructured and (*b*) the loan is not impaired under the terms of the restructuring agreement.

Because it was expected that the above criteria would be applied to a single loan resulting from a loan restructuring, some have questioned whether loans resulting from a loan restructuring that involves a loan-splitting or other multiple-loan structure—in which the original loan is restructured into two or more loans—should be considered separately or together for the purpose of impairment disclosures. For example, a lender may restructure a loan by splitting it into two loans: Loan A, which meets the criteria for exemption from the disclosures after the year of the restructuring, and Loan B, which includes the remaining cash flows under the original loan that are not expected to be collected and have been charged off. Here, Loan B does not meet the criteria for exemption from disclosure. Loan B may be forgiven when Loan A is paid off, or the debtor may be required to make payments on Loan B only if its results of operations exceed certain sales levels.

ACCOUNTING ISSUE

Should two or more restructured loans that result from a troubled debt restructuring be considered independently or collectively when assessing whether the disclosures required in ASC 310-10-50-12 through 13, 35-34, apply?

ACCOUNTING GUIDANCE

Two or more loan agreements resulting from a troubled debt restructuring, as defined in ASC 310-40-15-3 through 15-12; 35-2, 35-5 through 35-7; 40-2, 40-5 through 40-6, 40-8; 25-1 through 25-2; 50-1; 55-2; 10-1 through 10-2; ASC 470-60-15-3 through 50-12; 55-3; 35 through 35-12; 45-1 through 45-2; 50-1 through 50-2; 10-1 through 10-2; ASC 450-20-60-12 , should be considered separately when assessing whether the disclosures in ASC 310-10-50-12 through 13, 35-34, should be made in years subsequent to the year of the restructuring, because the loans are legally distinct from the original loan. Nevertheless, a creditor should continue measuring a loan's impairment based on the contractual terms of the *original* loan agreement, in accordance with the guidance in ASC 310-10-35-20 through 35-22, 35-24 through 35-27, 35-32, 35-37; ASC 310-40-35-12; ASC 310-30-30-2.

SEC OBSERVER COMMENT

The SEC Observer stated the staff's concern that disclosures about impaired loans after the loans have been restructured into multiple loans in a troubled debt restructuring may imply under some circumstances that the quality of the loan portfolio has improved merely as result of a troubled debt restructuring. Consequently, the staff believes that registrants should inform users clearly about how multiple loan structures affect the disclosures about impaired loans.

Illustration of Required Disclosure Requirements When a Loan Is Restructured in a Troubled Debt Restructuring into Two (or More) Loans

MHR Corp. restructures a loan into two loans in a troubled debt restructuring. Loan A represents the portion of the contractual cash flows expected to be collected and meets the criteria for exemption from disclosure in the years following the restructuring. Loan B represents the portion of the contractual cash flows *not* expected to be collected and that will be written off.

MHR should disclose information about Loan B in years subsequent to the restructuring in conformity with the requirements of ASC 310-35-13 through 35-14, 35-16 through 35-26, 35-28, 35-29, 35-34, 35-37, 35-39; 45-5 through 45-6; 50-15, 50-19; ASC 310-30-30-2; ASC 310-40-35-8, 35-12; 50-2 through 50-3, 50-12 through 50-13, because the recorded investment in that loan and the related allowance for credit losses would be zero.

DISCUSSION

Loans resulting from a troubled debt restructuring are legally separate loans that should, therefore, be considered separately when assessing whether they should be exempted from disclosure. Although the combined loans meet the definition of an impaired loan and must be measured for impairment purposes based on the terms of the original loan agreement, the loans should be considered new loans for disclosure purposes, because the criteria for exemption from disclosure are based on the terms specified in the restructuring agreement—not on those stated in the original loan agreement.

ASC 310-40-55-6 through 55-10 Use of Zero Coupon Bonds in a Troubled Debt Restructuring

BACKGROUND

A creditor agrees to a troubled debt restructuring on a collateralized loan. Under the terms of the agreement, the debtor liquidates some of the collateral and repays a portion of the loan. The remainder of the loan is restructured. The debtor then liquidates the remainder of the collateral, with the creditor's approval, and invests the proceeds in a series of zero coupon bonds that will mature each year at a value equal to the yearly debt service requirement under the restructured loan. The creditor holds the zero coupon bonds as the only collateral for the restructured loan.

ACCOUNTING ISSUE

Is the sale of collateral and a creditor's receipt of zero coupon bonds with a fair value that is lower than the creditor's net investment in the loan, a debt settlement that requires the creditor to recognize a loss?

ACCOUNTING GUIDANCE

Because the loan is settled with zero coupon bonds, the creditor should recognize (*a*) a loss on the difference between the fair value of the zero coupon bonds and the net investment in the loan and (*b*) an asset for the fair value of the zero coupon bonds.

PRACTICE POINTER: Under the guidance in ASC 310-40-40-3 creditors are required to account for long-lived assets received from a debtor in full satisfaction of a receivable at fair value less cost to sell. A loss should be recognized if the recorded investment in the receivable exceeds the fair value of the assets less selling costs. Such losses are included in the creditor's income for the period, unless all or a part of the loss is offset against the allowance for uncollectible accounts or other valuation accounts.

EFFECT OF ASC 860

ASC 860-30-05-2 through 05-3 provides guidance to debtors and creditors on the accounting for collateral based on whether the secured party has the right to sell or pledge the collateral. Under the circumstances in this Issue, the debtor would reclassify the zero coupon bond held by the creditor as an encumbered asset and report it in the balance sheet separately from other assets that are not encumbered in that manner. That guidance was not reconsidered in ASC 860. Under the guidance ASC 860-50-50-4 a creditor would report the fair value of the collateral and any portion that has been sold or repledged, if the creditor has the right to sell or pledge the collateral. If a creditor does not have that right, the *debtor* should report information about that collateral.

DISCUSSION

The guidance in ASC 310-40-40-6 provides that a creditor must have physical possession of the collateral, regardless of whether it has been legally foreclosed, to account for a loan as in-substance foreclosed and to recognize the fair value of the asset. That is, a creditor should continue to account for a loan for which foreclosure is probable as a loan until the creditor has possession of the collateral.

Although in this Issue, the creditor did not legally foreclose on the loan, the debtor's obligation on the restructured loan was settled with the zero coupon bonds because the creditor had possession of the bonds and was collecting annual payments. The creditor should therefore recognize a loss on that transaction. Under the guidance in ASC 310-40-40-6, this transaction qualifies for accounting as an in-substance foreclosure and would be accounted for under the accounting guidance in this Issue.

CHAPTER 19

ASC 320—INVESTMENTS—DEBT SECURITIES

CONTENTS

PART I: GENERAL GUIDANCE

ASC 320-10: OVERALL

OVERVIEW

ASC 320 addresses accounting and reporting for investments in debt securities. A primary issue in accounting and reporting for debt investments is the appropriate use of market value. It requires that debt securities held as investments be classified in three categories and given specific accounting treatments, as follows:

Trading securities. Measured at fair value in the statement of financial position. Unrealized holding gains and losses are included in earnings.

Available-for-sale securities. Measured at fair value in the statement of financial position. Unrealized gains and losses are excluded from earnings and reported in other comprehensive income until realized. An exception to this general rule is that all or a portion of the unrealized holding gain or loss designated as being hedged in a fair value hedge is recognized in earnings during the period as of the hedge.

Held-to-maturity securities. Measured at amortized cost in the statement of financial position. A transaction gain or loss on a held-to-maturity foreign-currency-denominated debt security is accounted for under ASC Subtopic 830-20. (ASC 320-10-35-1)

PRACTICE POINTER: Guidance in ASC 825 (Financial Instruments) permits companies to account for a variety of financial instruments by the fair value method. To the extent to which an entity selects the fair value method for investments that would otherwise have been accounted for under ASC 320, the following applies: An enterprise shall report its investments in available-for-sale securities and trading securities separately from similar assets that are subsequently measured using another measurement attribute on the face of the statement of financial position. Two options are available for presenting this information: (1) the aggregate of those measured by fair value and those measured by non-fair-value amounts are presented in the same line item and the amount of fair value included in the aggregate amount is parenthetically disclosed; (2) two separate line items are presented, one for the fair value amount and one for the non-fair-value amount. For further discussion of fair value, see Chapter 51, *ASC 820—Fair Value Measurement*, in this *Guide* discussing ASC 820, *Fair Value Measurement*.

Dividend and interest income, including amortization of premium and discount arising at acquisition, for all three categories of investments in debt securities are included in earnings (ASC 320-10-35-4).

BACKGROUND

A *debt security* is any security that represents a creditor relationship with an enterprise. It includes preferred stock that must be redeemed by the issuing enterprise or that is redeemable at the option of the investor. It also includes a collateralized mortgage obligation that is issued in equity form but is required to be accounted for as a nonequity instrument, regardless of how that instrument is classified in the issuer's statement of financial position. Other examples of debt securities are the following:

- U.S. Treasury securities
- U.S. government agency securities
- Municipal securities
- Corporate bonds
- Convertible debt
- Commercial paper
- All securitized debt instruments, such as collateralized mortgage obligations and real estate mortgage investment conduits
- Interest-only and principal-only strips

The following items are *not* debt securities:

- Option contracts
- Financial futures contracts
- Forward contracts
- Lease contracts
- Trade accounts receivable arising from sales on credit by industrial or commercial enterprises
- Loans receivable arising from consumer, commercial, and real estate lending activities of financial institutions

These last two items are examples of receivables that do not meet the definition of *security* unless they have been securitized, in which case they *do* meet the definition.

ACCOUNTING FOR INVESTMENTS

Scope of ASC 320

The guidance in ASC 320 applies to all entities, including the following entities that are not deemed to belong to specialized industries:

- Cooperatives and mutual entities, such as credit unions and mutual insurance entities
- Trusts that do not report substantially all of their securities at fair value (ASC 320-10-15-2)

ASC 320 does not apply to entities whose specialized accounting practices include accounting for all investments in debt securities at fair value, with changes in value recognized in earnings or in the change of net assets. Examples are brokers and dealers in securities, defined benefit or contribution pension and other postretirement plans, and investment companies (ASC 320-10-15-3).

The guidance in ASC 320 does not apply to the following:

- Derivative instruments subject to the requirements of ASC 815
- Investments in consolidated subsidiaries (ASC 320-10-15-7)

Recognition

At acquisition, investments in debt securities are classified in one of the following categories:

Trading. If a security is acquired with the intent of selling it within hours or days, the security is classified as trading. An entity is not precluded from classifying as trading a security it plans to hold for a longer period. Classification of a security as trading is not precluded simply because the entity does not intend to sell it in the near future.

Available-for-sale. Investments in debt securities not classified as trading or as held-to-maturity are classified as available-for-sale. (ASC 320-10-25-1)

Held-to-maturity. Investments in debt securities are classified as held-to-maturity only if the reporting entity has the positive intent and ability to hold those securities to maturity.

The held-to-maturity classification is restricted to those situations where the entity has the intent to hold the security to maturity. It is not appropriate if the entity has the intent to hold the security for only an indefinite period. Held-to-maturity is not appropriate if the entity anticipates that it would sell the security in response to any of the following:

- Changes in market interest rates and related changes in the security's prepayment risk
- Needs for liquidity
- Changes in the availability of and the yield on alternative investments
- Changes in funding sources and terms
- Changes in foreign currency risk

PRACTICE POINTER: In ASC 320, the FASB specifically identifies circumstances that are not consistent with held-to-maturity classification and circumstances that are consistent with held-to-maturity classification. (*See* ASC 320-10-25-4 through 18)

Measurement

Investments in debt securities are measured as follows:

Trading securities. Investments in debt securities classified as trading that have readily determinable fair values are measured subsequently at fair value in the statement of financial position. Unrealized holding gains and losses for trading securities are included in earnings.

Available-for-sale securities. Investments in debt securities that are classified as available-for-sale are measured subsequently at fair value in the statement of financial position. Unrealized holding gains and losses are excluded from earnings and reported in other comprehensive income until realized except as follows. All or a portion of the unrealized holding gain or loss of an available-for-sale security that is designated as being hedged in a fair value hedge is recognized in earnings during the period of the hedge.

PRACTICE POINTER: The accumulated amount of unrealized holding gains and losses on available-for-sale investments that is included in stockholders' equity is *not* a direct adjustment to retained earnings. It is a separate component of stockholders' equity—a positive amount (credit balance) for accumulated unrealized gains and a negative amount (debit balance) for accumulated unrealized losses.

Held-to-maturity securities. Investments in debt securities classified as held-to-maturity are subsequently measured at amortized cost in the statement of financial position (ASC 320-10-35-1).

PRACTICE POINTER: Other than the highly restrictive definition of held-to-maturity securities, ASC 320 provides little guidance on how management should determine the appropriate classification of debt investments. Classification is based primarily on management's intent for holding a particular investment:

- Trading securities provide a source of ready cash when needed, with the hope of gain from holding the investment for a short period of time
- Held-to-maturity investments are positively intended to be retained until maturity
- Available-for-sale investments rest somewhere between these extremes and is the default classification for securities that are neither trading nor held-to-maturity

Management's past patterns of practices with regard to securities are an important consideration in determining appropriate classification, as are projections of cash requirements that may imply a need to liquidate investments.

Dividend and interest income, including amortization of premium and discount arising at acquisition, for all three categories of investment are included in earnings.

Reassessment of Classification and Transfers between Categories

At each reporting date, the appropriateness of the classification of the entity's debt investments shall be assessed (ASC 320-10-35-5).

At the date of a transfer between classifications, the security's unrealized holding gain or loss is accounted for as follows:

- Transfers of a debt security from or into the trading category are accounted for at fair value. The unrealized holding gain or loss at the date of the transfer is accounted for as follows: (*a*) for a security transferred from the trading category, the unrealized holding gain or loss will have already been recognized in earnings and is not reversed, and (*b*) for a security transferred into the trading category, the portion of the unrealized holding gain or loss at the date of transfer that has not been previously recognized in earnings is recognized in earnings immediately. (ASC 320-10-35-10)
- For a debt security that is transferred into the available-for-sale category from the held-to-maturity category: (*a*) reverse in earnings any allowance for credit losses previously recorded, (*b*) reclassify and transfer the debt security at its amortized cost basis, (*c*) determine if an allowance for credit losses is necessary, (*d*) report in other comprehensive income any unrealized gain or loss at the date of transfer, and (*e*) consider whether the transfer calls into question the entity's ability to hold securities that remain in the held-to-maturity category to maturity. (ASC 320-10-35-10A)
- For a debt security that is transferred into the held-to-maturity category from the available-for-sale category: (*a*) reverse in earnings any allowance for credit losses previously recorded, (*b*) reclassify and transfer the debt security at its amortized cost plus or minus the amount of any remaining unrealized holding gain or loss reported in accumulated other comprehensive income, (*c*) evaluate the debt security for an allowance for credit losses, and (*d*) continue to report the unrealized holding gain or loss at the date of the transfer in a separate component of shareholders' equity, but the gain or loss shall be amortized over the remaining life of the security as an adjustment of yield in a manner consistent with the amortization of any premium or discount. (ASC 320-10-35-10B)

Derecognition

With respect to trading securities, because all changes in their fair value are reported in earnings as they occur, the sale does not necessarily give rise to a gain or loss. Generally, cash received is recorded and the security is removed at its fair value. If the entity is not taxed on the changes in fair value, deferred tax accounts are adjusted (ASC 320-10-40-1).

When available-for-sale securities are sold, cash received is recorded and the asset removed at its fair value. The amount recorded in other comprehensive income, representing unrealized gain or loss while the investment is held, is reversed into earnings and deferred tax accounts are adjusted (ASC 320-10-40-2).

Financial Statement Presentation

Available-for-sale securities and trading securities are reported separately from similar assets that are subsequently measured using another measurement attribute on the face of the statement of financial position in one of the following ways:

- Present the aggregate of those fair value and non-fair-value amounts in the same line item and parenthetically disclose the amount of the fair value included in the aggregate amount.
- Present two separate line items that display the fair value and the non-fair value amounts. (ASC 320-10-45-1)

In a statement of financial position, the three categories of debt investments (held-to-maturity, available-for-sale, and trading) are presented as either current or noncurrent, as appropriate (ASC 320-10-45-2).

PRACTICE POINTER: Treating cash flows from trading securities in the operating section of the statement of cash flows is consistent with the fact that trading securities involve active and frequent buying and selling. They represent temporary investment of available funds for purposes of generating short-term profits. Classifying cash flows from held-to-maturity and available-for-sale securities as investing cash flows is consistent with the longer-term nature of those investments. For available-for-sale and held-to-maturity investments, the usual classification in the statement of financial position would be noncurrent, since securities that are held primarily for *liquidity purposes* would be in the trading category. In certain circumstances, however, these investments may qualify for inclusion among current assets. For example, when held-to-maturity (debt) investments are within one year of maturity, they are expected to provide near-term cash and would be classified appropriately as current assets. Similarly, management intent concerning available-for-sale securities that have been held for a period of time may qualify those securities for classification as current, whereas in previous periods they would have been considered noncurrent.

An entity that recognizes a deferred tax asset relating only to a net unrealized loss on available-for-sale securities may at the same time conclude that it is more likely than not that some or all of that deferred tax asset will not be realized. The offsetting entry to the valuation allowance is to the component of other comprehensive income classified as unrealized gains and losses on investments because the valuation allowance is directly related to the unrealized holding loss on the available-for-sale securities (ASC 320-10-45-3).

ASC 320 does not specify the income statement classification of gains and losses for transfers involving trading securities. However, gains or losses that accumulated before the transfer should be classified consistently with realized gains and losses from the category from which security is being transferred, not the category into which the security is being transferred (ASC 320-10-45-7).

All or a portion of the unrealized holding gain and loss of an available-for-sale security that is designated as being hedged in a fair value hedge is recognized in earnings during the period of the hedge (ASC 320-10-45-8).

Cash flows from purchases, sales, and maturities of available-for-sale securities and held-to-maturity securities are classified as investing activities and reported gross for each security classification in the statement of cash flows. Cash flows from purchases, sales, and maturities of trading securities are classified based on the nature and purpose for which the securities were acquired (ASC 320-10-45-11).

ASC 320 does not require the presentation of individual amounts of the three categories of investments on the face of the statement of financial position, provided that information is disclosed in notes (ASC 320-10-45-13).

Disclosure Requirements

For available-for-sale securities, the following information is to be disclosed by major security type as of each date for which a statement of financial position is presented:

- Amortized cost basis
- Total allowance for credit losses
- Aggregate fair value

- Total allowance for credit losses
- Total unrealized gains for securities with net gains in accumulated other comprehensive income
- Total unrealized losses for securities with net losses in accumulated other comprehensive income
- Information about contractual maturities of those securities as of the date of the most recent statement of financial position presented (ASC 320-10-50-2)

If for the purposes of identifying and measuring an impairment, the applicable accrued interest is excluded from both the fair value and amortized cost basis of an available-for-sale debt security, the entity may, as a practical expedient, exclude the applicable accrued interest that is included in the amortized cost basis for the purpose of the disclosure requirements stated above. If an entity elects this practical expedient, it shall disclose the total amount of accrued interest, net of the allowance for credit losses (if any), excluded from the disclosed amortized cost basis (ASC 320-10-50-2A).

Maturity information may be combined in appropriate groupings. The fair value and the net carrying amount are required disclosures in at least the following maturity groups: within one year, after one year through five years, after five years through 10 years, after 10 years (ASC 320-10-50-3).

All reporting entities shall disclose the following information for securities classified as held-to-maturity by major security type:

- Amortized cost basis
- Net carrying amount
- Gross gains and losses in accumulated other comprehensive income for any derivatives that hedged the forecasted acquisition of the held-to-maturity securities
- Information about the contractual maturities of those securities as of the date of the most recent statement of financial position presented. The fair value and the net carrying amount of debt securities on the basis of at least the following maturity groupings are required: within one year, after one year through five years, after five years through 10 years, after 10 years. Securities not due at a single maturity date, such as mortgage-backed securities, may be disclosed separately rather than allocated over several maturity groupings. If allocated, the basis for allocation shall be disclosed (ASC 320-10-50-5)

A public business entity shall disclose the following information for securities classified as held to maturity, by major security type, as of each date for which a statement of financial position is presented: aggregate fair value, gross unrecognized holding gains, and gross unrecognized holding losses (ASC 320-10-50-5A).

A financial institution that is a public business entity shall disclose the fair value of debt securities classified as held to maturity, by major security type, on the basis of at least the following four maturity groupings: within one year, after one year through five years, after five years through 10 years, after 10 years (ASC 320-10-50-5B).

If for the purposes of identifying and measuring an impairment, the applicable accrued interest is excluded from the amortized cost basis of held-to-maturity securities, an entity may, as a practical expedient, exclude the accrued interest receivable balance that is included in the amortized cost basis of the held-to-maturity securities for purposes of the above disclosure requirements. If an entity applies this practical expedient, it shall disclose the total amount of accrued interest, net of allowance for credit losses (if any), exclude from the disclosed amortized cost basis (ASC 320-10-50-5C).

For each period for which the results of operations are presented, the following information is required:

- Proceeds from the sales of available-for-sale securities and the gross realized gains and gross realized losses that have been included in earnings
- The basis on which the cost of a security sold or the amount reclassified out of accumulated other comprehensive income into earnings was determined
- The gross gains and gross losses included in earnings from transfers of securities from the available-for-sale category into the trading category
- The amount of the net unrealized holding gain or loss on available-for-sale securities for the period that has been included in accumulated other comprehensive income and the amount of gains and losses reclassified out of accumulated other comprehensive income into earnings for the period
- The portion of trading gains and losses that relates to trading securities still held at the reporting date (ASC 320-10-50-9)

For any sales of or transfers from securities classified as held-to-maturity, the following information is required to be disclosed for each period for which the results of operations are presented:

- The net carrying amount of the sold or transferred security
- The net gain or loss in accumulated other comprehensive income for any derivative that hedged the forecasted acquisition of the held-to-maturity security
- The related realized or unrealized gain or loss
- The circumstances leading to the decision to sell or transfer the security (ASC 320-10-50-10)

PART II: INTERPRETIVE GUIDANCE

Practice Pointers in the discussion below will note the guidance that will be affected by the amendments in ASU 2016-01, when it will no longer apply to public business entities but will continue to apply to all other entities, including not-for-profit entities and employee benefit plans under the scope of ASC 960 through 965 on plan accounting.

ASC 320-10: OVERALL

ASC 320-10-25-19 through 25-20, 40-3, 55-14 through 55-15, 55-21 Structured Notes Acquired for a Specified Investment Strategy

BACKGROUND

Structured notes are securities that are issued combined with other structured note securities as a unit or a pair to accomplish a strategic investment result for an investor. Under one strategy, two structured notes with opposite reset positions are purchased. (For example, one month after issuance, the interest rate on Bond A resets from 8% to 1% if 10-year Treasury bond rates decreased by one basis point since the Bond's issuance or to 15% if Treasury rates increased by one basis point. The interest rate on Bond B would reset in the opposite direction.) Each structured note's coupon rate or maturity date is determined shortly after issuance based on the movement of market rates. Although the yields on the two structured notes move in opposite directions after the reset date, the average yield of the two securities generally represents the market yield of the combined instruments at issuance.

ACCOUNTING ISSUE

Should an investor account separately for each structured note security or account for the two securities as a unit?

ACCOUNTING GUIDANCE

An investor who purchases structured notes for a specific investment strategy should account for the two structured notes as a unit until one of the securities is sold. Thereafter, the remaining security would be accounted for in accordance with the guidance in Accounting Standards Update No. 2009-16, *Transfers and Servicing (Topic 860): Accounting for Transfers of Financial Assets*.

In making a judgment as to whether the securities were purchased for a specified investment strategy (not all the indicators are required for the securities to be accounted for under the consensus), the Task Force stated that the following indicators should be used:

1. The securities are related because their fair values will move in opposite directions in response to changes in interest rates on a specified date or after a specified period following issuance. Their fair values may change because of changes in their coupon interest rates or changes in their maturities.
2. The securities are issued simultaneously or they are issued separately but the terms for their remaining lives are as discussed in (1) above.
3. The securities are issued by the same counterparty and/or the same issuer. They may also be issued by different issuers but are structured through an intermediary.

4. The investor's *only* reason for purchasing the two securities is to achieve a specific accounting result, because there would be no valid business purpose for entering into the transactions individually. The investor would not purchase the securities otherwise.

The Task Force noted that the substance of the investment strategy in these transactions is that the investor has purchased one market-based security that results in no gain or loss when the interest rate resets and should be accounted for as such. However, the unit's fair value may change as a result of a change in credit ratings or a change in market rates.

PRACTICE NOTE: ASC 860 was amended in 2009 to require that transfers of structured notes that meet the conditions for sale accounting in ASC 860 be accounted for in accordance with the guidance in ASC 860-20-30-1.

ASC 320-10-35-38 through 35-43, 55-10 through 55-12, 55-16 through 55-19; ASC 835-10-60-6 Recognition of Interest Income and Balance Sheet Classification of Structured Notes

BACKGROUND

The guidance in ASC 320 on accounting for debt securities also applies to *structured notes,* which are debt instruments whose cash flows are linked to the movement in one or more indices, interest rates, foreign exchange rates, commodities prices, prepayment rates, or other market variables. Such instruments are issued by enterprises sponsored by the U.S. government, multilateral development banks, municipalities, and private corporations. Interest payments on structured notes may be based on formulas related to the investor's preference for risk and return, and principal payments may be indexed to movements in an underlying market. Structured notes normally include forward or option components, such as caps, calls, and floors, which are not separable or detachable. Consequently, investors that use structured notes to manage financial risks and enhance yield often prefer those debt instruments for administrative reasons over debt securities with fixed interest rates, which may require entering into separate derivatives.

In general, interest income on structured notes is comprised of a stated or coupon interest, acquisition premium or discount amortization, if any, and possible adjustments of the principal based on an index or formula. The following is a list of some common forms of structured notes that are within the scope of this Issue:

- *Index amortizing notes* Principal is repaid based on a predetermined amortization schedule, which is linked to movements in a specific mortgage-backed security or index. Although the investor receives the total principal by the maturity date, it is uncertain when principal payments will be received, because the note's maturity is extended in relation to increasing market interest rates or decreasing prepayment rates. An above-market interest rate is paid on such notes.
- *Inverse floating-rate notes* The coupon rate on such notes changes in an inverse relationship to a specified interest rate level or index.
- *Range bonds* The interest rate on such bonds depends on the number of days a reference rate is between predetermined levels at issuance. No interest or a below-market interest rate is earned when the reference rate is not within the range.
- *Dual index notes* The coupon rate on these notes often is fixed for a short period (the first year) and becomes variable for a longer period. It generally is determined by the spread between two market indices, usually the Constant Maturity Treasury rate and LIBOR.
- *Inflation bonds* The bond's contractual principal is indexed to the inflation rate and its coupon rate is below that for traditional bonds with similar maturity.
- *Equity-linked bear notes* These notes have a fixed coupon rate that is lower than traditional debt. Their principal is guaranteed but may exceed the initial investment based on a decrease in the S&P index.

ACCOUNTING ISSUES

- How should investors in structured notes estimate cash flows that will be received?
- How should changes in cash flow estimates be recognized and measured in interest income?
- Is a held-to-maturity classification permitted for investments in structured notes under the provisions of ASC 320?

ACCOUNTING GUIDANCE

Income on structured note securities that are classified as debt securities under the available-for-sale or held-to-maturity categories of ASC 310 should be measured using the *retrospective interest method.*

Income for a reporting period is measured under the retrospective interest method as the sum of (1) the difference between a security's amortized cost at the end of the period and its amortized cost at the beginning of the period and (2) cash received during the period. A security's amortized cost is based on the present value of estimated future cash flows at an effective yield (the internal rate of return) that equates all past actual and current estimated cash flow streams to the initial investment. If the sum of newly estimated undiscounted cash flows is less than the security's amortized cost, the effective yield is negative. In that case, a zero effective yield is used to compute amortized cost.

All estimates of future cash flows used to determine the effective yield for income recognition under the retrospective interest method either should be based on quoted forward market rates or prices in active markets, if available or should be based on spot rates or prices as of the reporting date if market-based prices are unavailable.

The impairment guidance in ASC 320 continues to apply to *host contracts* from which embedded derivatives have been separated based on the guidance in ASC 310-20-35-9, 35-10 and should be accounted for at fair value.

- Structured notes for which income is recognized using the retrospective method must meet at least one of the following conditions:
  - — The note's contractual principal that will be paid at maturity or the original investment is at risk (other than due to a borrower's failure to pay the contractual amounts due). Principal-indexed notes whose principal repayment is based on movements in the S&P 500 index or notes whose principal repayment is linked to certain events or circumstances are examples of these instruments.
  - — The note's return on investment varies (other than due to changes in a borrower's credit rating) because either:
    - (1) The coupon rate is not stated or a stated coupon rate is not fixed or pre-specified, *and* the variation in coupon rate or the return on investment is not a constant percentage of, or does not move in the same direction as, changes in market-based interest rates or interest rate indices, such as LIBOR or the Treasury Bill Index, or
    - (2) A variable or fixed coupon rate is below market interest rates for traditional notes with comparable maturities and a portion of the potential yield depends on the occurrence of future events or circumstances. Inverse floating-rate notes, dual index notes, and equity-linked bear notes are examples of these instruments.
  - — The note's contractual maturity is based on a specific index or on the occurrence of specific events or circumstances that cannot be controlled by the parties to the transaction, except for the passage of time or events that cause normal covenant violations. Index amortizing notes and notes whose contractual maturity is based on the price of oil are examples of these instruments.
- The following financial instruments are *not* within the scope of the guidance in this Issue:
  - — Mortgage loans or similar debt instruments that are not securities under the guidance in ASC 320; traditional bonds convertible into the issuer's stock; multicurrency debt securities; debt securities classified as trading; debt securities that participate directly in an issuer's operations, such as participating mortgages; reverse mortgages;
  - — Structured notes that are accounted for as trading securities under the guidance in ASC 320, because based on their terms it is reasonably possible that an investor could lose all or substantially all of the investment (other than if a borrower fails to pay all amounts due).
- Entities should determine, based on the provisions of ASC 320, whether the value of an individual structured note has experienced an other-than-temporary decline below amortized cost and should include the change in earnings.

It was noted that after recognizing an other-than-temporary impairment on a structured note, an entity should consider its collectibility in estimating future cash flows for the purpose of determining the effective yield used in the retrospective interest method calculation of income to be recognized on the note. That is, the entity would no longer assume that the contractual interest and the note's principal would be repaid. For example, if an investor has recognized a $30 other-than-temporary loss on a $100 investment whose fair value has decreased to $70, and the investor expects to collect no more than $80 of the principal at maturity, only $80 of principal should be used in estimating future cash flows for the effective yield calculation.

EFFECT OF ASC 815

The impairment guidance in ASC 320 continues to apply to *host contracts* from which embedded derivatives have been separated based on the guidance in ASC 815-15-25-1, 25-14, 25-26 through 25-29 and should be accounted for at fair value.

The guidance on the second Issue is partially nullified by ASC 815, which requires the separation of certain embedded derivatives from the host contract under the conditions discussed in ASC 815-15-25-1. Those derivatives should be accounted for at fair value under the guidance in ASC 815. Although they may not be designated as hedging instruments, contracts with embedded derivatives that cannot be reliably identified for separation from their host contracts should be measured at fair value in their entirety. However, the guidance in this Issue should continue to apply to (1) embedded derivatives that are *not* required to be separated under the guidance in this Issue, and (2) host contracts that meet any of the three conditions above, even though their embedded derivatives have been separated under the guidance in ASC 815. The calculation of the effective yield is not addressed in the Statement.

SUBSEQUENT DEVELOPMENT

During a discussion of ASC 860 at a subsequent meeting, the EITF agreed that the guidance in this Issue should apply to the recognition of interest income from beneficial interests in a securitization structure that holds common stocks.

ASC 320-10-15-7, 35-17, 35-20 through 35-30, 35-32A through 35-35A, 35-45, 35-8A through 35-9A, 50-6 through 50-8B, 55-22 through 55-23 The Meaning of Other-Than-Temporary Impairment and Its Application to Certain Investments

BACKGROUND

The following discussion provides guidance on how to determine when an investment is considered to be impaired, whether the impairment is other than temporary, and how to measure an impairment loss. It also provides guidance on accounting considerations after another-than-temporary impairment has been recognized and requires certain disclosures about unrealized losses that have not been recognized as other-than-temporary impairments. As a result of the issuance of this guidance, certain provisions of ASC 320, ASC 958-320, and ASC 323 are amended.

SCOPE

The following guidance does not apply to:

- Derivatives accounted for under the requirements in ASC 815, including derivatives that have been separated from a host contract under the guidance in ASC 815-15-25. However, if an investment that would usually be accounted for under the guidance in ASC 320 includes an embedded derivative that must be separated under the guidance in ASC 815, the host instrument should be accounted for under the guidance in ASC 320 after separation from the embedded derivative.
- Investments in consolidated subsidiaries.

PRACTICE POINTER: ASU 2016-01 amends the guidance in Topic 320 with the addition of ASC 320-10-15-7A, which refers to ASC 815-10-15-141 that explains that the guidance in the Topic's Subsections on Certain Contracts on Debt and Equity Securities applies to forward contracts and purchased options that are not derivative instruments under the guidance in Topic 815 but that are related to an acquisition of securities that will be accounted for under the guidance in Subtopic 320-10.

The following guidance applies to investments in:

Debt securities under the scope of ASC 320. (*Equity securities* will be accounted for under the guidance in ASC 321, *Equity Securities*, in accordance with the provisions of ASU 2016-01.)

PRACTICE POINTER: The following guidance will be affected by the amendments in ASU 2016-01. It no longer applies to public business entities after December 15, 2017, All other entities, including not-for-profit entities and employee benefit plans under the scope of ASC 960 through 965 on plan accounting, will be required to apply the amendments in ASU 2016-01 for fiscal years that begin after December 15, 2018, and interim periods within fiscal years that begin after December 15, 2019.

The guidance applies to all equity securities held by insurance companies, because those securities must be reported at fair value.

An investment should be evaluated for impairment based on its form (e.g., a mutual fund that primarily invests in debt securities should be evaluated for impairment as an equity security).

The following guidance will be affected by the amendments in ASU 2016-01. It no longer applies to public business entities after December 15, 2017. All other entities, including derivative are accounted for separately. The guidance should be applied to host instruments that meet the scope of this guidance.

Debt securities under the scope of ASC 958-320 held by investors that report a "performance indicator" as defined in ASC 954 are included under the guidance in ASC 320.

Equity securities are *not* under the scope of ASC 320 and ASC 958-320 and not accounted for under the equity method in ASC 323 and related interpretations (i.e., cost-method investments).

ACCOUNTING GUIDANCE

Step 1: Determining Whether an Investment is Impaired

Each debt security (investment) should be evaluated for impairment at the individual security level, which is the level and aggregation method that an entity uses to measure realized and unrealized gains and losses on its debt securities. An investment is impaired if its fair value is less than its cost at the balance sheet reporting date. That evaluation should be made in each reporting period, including interim periods for entities that issue such reports.

Separate contracts, such as a debt security and a guarantee or other credit enhancement, should not be combined for the determination of a debt security's impairment or whether the debt security can be contractually prepaid or settled in manner that would prevent an investor from recovering substantially all of its cost.

Proceed to step 2 if the fair value of an investment is less than its cost.

Step 2: Evaluating Whether an Impairment is Other Than Temporary

An investment's impairment is either temporary or other than temporary if the investment's fair value is less than its amortized cost at the balance sheet date of the reporting period in which the evaluation was made. Other guidance may also be used to determine whether an impairment is other than temporary, such as the guidance in ASC 323-10-35 and ASC 325-40-35, as applicable. Other than temporary does not mean permanent.

If an entity decides to sell a debt security, it should consider whether an other-than-temporary impairment has occurred. If an entity does not intend to sell a debt security but available information indicates that the entity will have to sell the debt security before the security's amortized cost has been recovered, it should consider that an other-than-temporary impairment has occurred.

Accounting for Debt Securities After Recognition of an Other-Than-Temporary Impairment

An investor should account for a debt security after an other-than-temporary impairment has been recognized as if the debt security had been purchased on the measurement date of the other-than-temporary impairment. A discount or reduced premium recorded for the debt security based on the new cost basis should be amortized *prospectively* over the debt security's remaining life based on the amount and timing of future estimated cash flows.

Disclosures

An investor should disclose the following information in its annual financial statements about all investments whose costs exceed their fair value (unrealized loss position), including those disclosed under the guidance in ASC 310-30-15-5; ASC 320-10-35-38, 55-2; ASC 325-40-05-1 through 05-2, 15-2 through 15-9, 25-1 through 25-3, 30-1 through 30-3, 35-1 through 35-13, 35-15 through 35-16, 45-1, 55-1 through 55-25, 60-7, for which other-than-temporary impairments have *not* been recognized:

- Quantitative information about the items in (a) and (b) below should be presented in a table, as of each date on which a balance sheet is presented, by category of investment as required under the guidance in ASC 320 and ASC 958-320 and cost method investments:
  a. The total fair value of investments with unrealized losses;
  b. The total amount of unrealized losses.

That information should be reported separately for investments that have been continuously in an unrealized loss position for *less* than 12 months and those that have been in that position for twelve months or *longer*. To determine how long an investment has been in a continuous unrealized loss position, the balance sheet date of the reporting period in which an impairment has been identified is used as the reference point. The annual balance sheet date of the period in which an impairment is identified should be used as the reference point by entities that do not prepare interim financial information. A continuous unrealized loss position ends in the period in which (*a*) an other-than-temporary impairment is recognized or (*b*) an investment's fair value has been recovered up to or beyond its cost.

- Additional information in a narrative format as of the most recent balance date to help users of the financial statements to understand the quantitative disclosures as well as the rationale for the conclusion that unrealized losses are not other than temporary impairments. Those disclosures may be presented by combined investment categories, but significant unrealized losses should be presented separately. The following information could include:
  - — The nature of the investments;
  - — The causes of impairments;
  - — The number of investment positions in an unrealized position;
  - — Other evidence that an investor considered to reach the conclusion that an investment is not other-than-temporarily impaired, for example, reports of industry analysts, sector credit ratings, the volatility of a security's fair value, and other information considered to be relevant.

The following additional information, if applicable, should be disclosed for investments accounted for on the cost method, as of each date for which a balance sheet is presented in annual financial statements:

- The total carrying amount of all cost-method investments;
- The total carrying amount of cost-method investments that were not evaluated for impairment;
- The fact that the fair value of a cost-method investment is not estimated if no events or changes in circumstances that may have a significant effect on the investment's fair value were identified, and
  - — The investor determined that in accordance with the guidance in ASC 825-10-50-16 through 23 and ASC 958-320-50-4 that it is not practicable to estimate the investment's fair value, or
  - — The investor is exempt from estimating fair value under the guidance in ASC 825.

ASC 320-10-25-18 Impact of Certain Transactions on the Held-to-Maturity Classification under FASB Statement No. 115

BACKGROUND

Under current guidance sales recognition is required if control of a security has been transferred to another entity, unless a concurrent contract to repurchase the security exists. Wash sales and certain bond swaps that do not involve the issuer are accounted for as sales, therefore, under guidance in ASC 860.

Although the guidance in ASC 320 lists changes in circumstances that would result in a change of intent to hold a security to maturity without calling into question the entity's intent to hold other debt securities to maturity, it does not discuss the effect of exchanges not accounted for as sales.

ACCOUNTING ISSUE

Are certain transactions related to held-to-maturity securities that are not accounted for as sales (such as wash sales and bond swaps) inconsistent with an entity's previously stated intent to hold those securities to maturity, and do such transactions therefore call into question the entity's intent to hold other debt securities to maturity?

ACCOUNTING GUIDANCE

If a transaction, such as a wash sale or bond swap, involving held-to-maturity securities is *not accounted for as a sale,* the transaction is not inconsistent with the entity's previously stated intent to hold the security to maturity and, therefore, would *not* call into question the entity's intent to hold other debt securities to maturity.

PRACTICE POINTER: ASC 860-10-40-5, which requires that a wash sale or swap be accounted for as a sale, partially nullifies the guidance in this Issue. Unless there is a concurrent contract to repurchase or redeem the transferred financial assets from the transferee, the transferor does not continue to have effective control over the transferred assets.

However, the guidance would apply to other transactions not accounted for as sales under ASC 860, such as the desecuritization of securities discussed in ASC 320-10-25-18; ASC 860-10-55-34, 55-74 below. This Issue was not reconsidered in ASC 860. Additional guidance on wash sales may be found in ASC 860-10-55-57.

It was noted, however, that an entity's intent to hold other debt securities to maturity would be called into question if the entity does not hold to maturity the debt instrument received or retained as a result of the transaction.

DISCUSSION

The guidance is based on the view that a transaction that is not accounted for as a sale should not be considered a sale when applying the provisions of ASC 320. Proponents of this view argued that a sale has not occurred because the entity is in the same economic position as before the wash sale or swap occurred; the risks and benefits of ownership are not transferred when an entity receives substantially the same security as the security transferred.

ASC 320-10-S35-1, S99-2 Adjustments in Assets and Liabilities for Holding Gains and Losses as Related to the Implementation of FASB Statement No. 115

The SEC staff has been asked about the adjustment of certain assets and liabilities, such as noncontrolling interests, certain life insurance policyholder liabilities, deferred acquisition costs, amortized using the gross-profits method, or and intangible assets acquired in business combination with a corresponding adjustment to other comprehensive income when unrealized holding gains and losses from securities held as available-for-sale are recognized in comprehensive income. In other words, whether an entity should adjust the carrying amounts of those assets and liabilities to the amount at which they would have been reported if those unrealized gains and losses had been realized.

The SEC observer analogized to the guidance in ASC 740-20-45-11, which discusses the classification of deferred tax effects of unrealized holding gains and losses reported in comprehensive income. Under that guidance, entities are required to report the tax effects of those gains and losses as charges or credits to other comprehensive income. In other words, by recognizing unrealized holding gains and losses in equity, temporary differences may be created. Deferred differences would be recognized for those temporary differences and their effect would be reported in accumulated other comprehensive income with the related unrealized holding gains and losses. Consequently, deferred tax assets and liabilities must be recognized for temporary differences related to unrealized holding gains and losses, but their corresponding charges or credits are reported in other comprehensive income as charges or credits to income in the income statement.

By analogy to the guidance in ASC 740-20-45-11, the SEC staff believes that registrants should adjust certain assets and liabilities, such as noncontrolling interests, certain life insurance policyholder liabilities, deferred acquisition costs amortized using the gross-profits method, and intangible assets related to the acquisition of insurance contracts in a business combination that are amortized using the gross-profits method for unrealized holding gains or losses from securities classified as available-for-sale if such adjustments would have been made had the gains or losses actually been realized. Corresponding credits or charges should be made to other comprehensive income. Assets should be adjusted at subsequent balance sheet dates through valuation allowances.

Liabilities, such as certain policyholder liabilities should be adjusted if an insurance policy requires the holder to be charged or credited for a portion or all of the realized gains or losses of specific securities classified as available-for-sale. In addition, assets that are amortized using the gross-profits method, such as deferred acquisition costs accounted for under the guidance in ASC 944-30-35-4 and ASC 944-30-35-11, and certain intangible assets as a result of insurance contracts acquired in a business combination should be adjusted to show the effects that would have been recognized if unrealized gains or losses had actually been realized. However, capitalized acquisition costs related to such insurance contracts under the scope of ASC 944-30-35-1A through 35-3A and 35-17 should not be adjusted for unrealized gains or losses unless there would have been a "premium deficiency" if the gain or loss had been realized.

The guidance in this SEC staff announcement should not affect reported net income.

ASC 320-10-25-18; ASC 860-10-55-34, 55-74 The Applicability of FASB Statement No. 115 to Desecuritizations of Financial Assets

The FASB staff made the following announcements about the applicability of ASC 320 to the accounting for the desecuritization of financial assets: the process by which securities are broken down into their underlying loans or other financial assets.

- The FASB staff addressed the accounting for desecuritizations by analogizing to ASC 860-10-40-5, which addressed the accounting for the securitization of financial assets. The paragraph states that a transfer of financial assets over which the transferor surrenders control should be accounted for as a sale if consideration (other than a beneficial interest in the transferred assets) has been received. (In contrast, sales accounting is not appropriate for a transaction that includes a transfer of securities or a beneficial interest in a securitized pool of financial assets in which the only consideration received by the transferor is the financial assets underlying the securities or the beneficial interest in the transferred securities.) The FASB agreed that this approach should be used for desecuritizations in general.
- The FASB staff believes that the guidance in ASC 320-10-25-18 related to the effect of the held-to-maturity classification of wash sales and bond swaps should also apply to desecuritizations that are not accounted for as sales. The guidance in ASC 320-10-25-18 provides that an entity's intent to hold other debt securities to maturity under the guidance in ASC 320 is not called into question if the entity holds to maturity securities received or retained in a wash sale or bond swap transaction not accounted for as a sale. Similarly, the FASB staff believes that an entity's intent to hold other debt securities to maturity should not be called into question if an entity that transfers beneficial interests classified as held-to-maturity in a desecuritization transaction not accounted for as a sale holds to maturity the financial assets received or retained in the desecuritization.

ASC 320-10-15-2, 15-5, 25-1, 25-5, 25 through 25-8, 25-10, 25-12 through 25-13, 25-16 through 25-18, 30-3 through 30-4, 35-6 through 35-9, 35-13, 35-15 through 35-16, 35-18, 35-32 through 35-33, 40-1 through 40-2, 45-3 through 45-7, 45-12, 50-12, 50-14, 55-2 through 55-6, 55-8 through 55-9, 55-24 through 55-25; ASC 323-30-60-2; ASC 958-320-15-4, 15-6, 55-2 through 55-3, 60-1 A Guide to Implementation of Statement 115 on Accounting for Certain Investments in Debt and Equity Securities

BACKGROUND

The guidance in this section includes responses to 60 specific questions regarding the application of ASC 320.

STANDARDS

Scope

Question 1: Does the guidance in ASC 320 apply to a loan that has been insured, such as a loan insured by the Federal Housing Administration, or to a conforming mortgage loan?

Answer: No. The guidance in ASC 320 applies only to debt securities, including debt instruments that have been securitized. A loan is not a debt security until it has been securitized.

Question 2: For a loan that was restructured in a troubled debt restructuring involving a modification of terms, does the guidance in ASC 320 apply to the accounting by the creditor (i.e., investor) if the restructured loan meets the definition of a *security* in ASC 320?

Answer: Yes. The guidance in ASC 320 applies to all debt securities. See ASC 860; ASC 320-10-15-6; 55-2; and ASC 310-40-40-8A, 40-9 for further guidance on this general topic.

Question 3: Are options on securities covered by ASC 320?

Answer: In some cases. An investment in an option on an equity interest is covered by the guidance in ASC 320 if the option has a fair value that is "currently available on a securities exchange." An equity interest includes any security that gives the holder the right to acquire (e.g., warrants, rights, calls) or to sell (e.g., puts) an ownership interest in an enterprise at a fixed or determinable price. The guidance in ASC 320 does not cover written options, cash-settled options on equity securities, options on equity-based indexes, or options on debt securities.

Question 4: What accounting literature addresses the accounting for equity securities that do not have readily determinable fair values?

Answer: ASC 323 provides guidance in accounting for equity securities that do not have readily determinable fair values. If the investment does not qualify for treatment under the equity method (i.e., typically less than a 20% ownership stake), the investment is accounted for using the cost method. Investments accounted for using the cost method are to be adjusted to reflect other-than temporary declines in fair value. [There is an exception to this general requirement for investments made by insurance companies—see ASC 944] There is currently no authoritative guidance as to the accounting for options and warrants in the absence of a readily determinable fair value.

Question 5: An entity invests in a limited partnership interest (or a venture capital company) that meets the definition of an *equity security* but does not have a readily determinable fair value. However, substantially all of the partnership's assets consist of investments in debt securities or equity securities that have readily determinable fair values. Is it appropriate to "look through" the form of an investment to determine whether the guidance in ASC 320 applies?

Answer: No, an entity should not "look through" its investment to the nature of the securities held by an investee. Therefore, given the lack of a readily determinable market value in this case, the guidance in ASC 320 would not apply. Guidance on accounting for limited partnership investments is provided in ASC 323-30.

Securities Classified as Held-to-Maturity

Question 6: Does ASC 320 apply to certificates of deposit (CDs) or guaranteed investment contracts (GICs)?

Answer: No. Equity investments are discussed in ASC 321 after the effective date of ASU 2016-01.

Question 7: Are short sales of securities (sales of securities that the seller does not own at the time of the sale) under the scope of ASC 320?

Answer: No. A short sale gives rise to an obligation to deliver securities. Short sales are not investments and therefore do not fall under the scope of ASC 320. Various AICPA Industry Audit Guides require obligations due to short sales to be periodically adjusted to market value. Changes in the underlying obligation are reflected in earnings as they occur.

Question 8: Not discussed in the Codification.

Question 9: Does the guidance in ASC 320 apply to preferred stock that is convertible into marketable common stock?

Answer: No. Equity securities are discussed in ASC 321 after the effective date of ASU 2016-01. No.

Question 10: Does the guidance in ASC 320 apply to financial statements issued by a trust?

Answer: It depends. ASC 321, *Equity Securities*, applies if the trust does not report all of its investments at fair value. Some trusts record all investments at fair or market value, with any resulting changes reflected in income or in the change in net assets. ASC 320 does not apply in such cases.

Question 11: ASC 320-20-35-5 states, "At each reporting date, the appropriateness of the [security's] classification shall be reassessed." If the guidance in ASC 320-20-35-5 requires an enterprise to reassess its classification of securities, why do transfers or sales of held-to-maturity securities for reasons other than those specified in ASC 320-10-25-6, 25-9, and 25-14 call into question ("taint") an enterprise's intent to hold other debt securities to maturity in the future?

Answer: The point of ASC 320-20-35-5 is primarily to require a periodic evaluation of an entity's ability to hold a security to maturity. An enterprise's intent to hold a security to maturity should not change; however, the ability of the enterprise to hold the security to maturity may change. Also, while an entity may initially classify a debt security as available-for-sale, subsequent developments may indicate that the entity has the ability to hold the securities to maturity. Assuming management intends to hold the debt securities to maturity, the investment would be reclassified from the available-for-sale portfolio to the held-to-maturity portfolio.

Question 12: What are the consequences of a sale or transfer of held-to-maturity securities for a reason other than those specified in ASC 320-10-25-6, 25-9, and 25-14? In other words, what does it mean to "call into question [the entity's] intent to hold other debt securities to maturity in the future"?

Answer: A sale or transfer of held-to-maturity securities for a reason other than those specified in ASC 320-10-25-6, 25-9, and 25-14 calls into question the appropriateness of continuing to classify any debt securities as held-to-maturity. If the sale represents a material contradiction of the entity's stated intent to hold securities to maturity, any remaining securities classified as held-to-maturity would need to be reclassified as available-for-sale. Also, if a pattern of sales of held-to-maturity securities has occurred, any remaining securities classified as held-to-maturity would need to be reclassified. The reclassification would occur in the reporting period in which the sale occurred.

Question 13: If a sale or transfer of a security classified as held-to-maturity occurs for a reason other than those specified in ASC 320-10-25-6, 25-9, and 25-14, does the sale or transfer call into question ("taint") the enterprise's intent about only the same type of securities (e.g., municipal bonds) that were sold or transferred, or about all securities that remain in the held-to-maturity category?

Answer: All securities that remain in the held-to-maturity category would be tainted.

Question 14: If held-to-maturity securities are reclassified to available-for-sale because sales occurred for reasons other than those specified in ASC 320-10-25-6, 25-9, and 25-14, what amount of time must pass before the enterprise can again classify securities as held-to-maturity?

Answer: This is a matter of judgment. The key issue is whether circumstances have changed sufficiently for management to assert with a greater degree of credibility that it has the intent and ability to hold the debt securities to maturity.

PRACTICE POINTER: No specific guidance is provided on the length of time that must pass before an entity can again classify securities as held-to-maturity when it had previously sold held-to-maturity securities for reasons other than those specified in ASC 320-10-25-6, 25-9, and 25-14. At a minimum, the reasons why management previously sold held-to-maturity securities must have changed. For example, if management previously sold held-to-maturity securities due to a cash shortage brought about by the enterprise's deteriorating financial condition, the financial condition and cash position of the enterprise must have substantially improved. Or, if held-to-maturity securities were sold in the past due to a shortage of capital, the enterprise must have obtained or have ready access to the capital it is likely to need in the future.

In addition, it would seem reasonable for at least one year to pass before an enterprise could again classify securities as held-to-maturity when it had previously sold held-to-maturity securities for reasons other than those specified in ASC 320-10-25-6, 25-9, and 25-14. Finally, a change in top management—particularly financial management—may allow management to credibly assert that it has the intent to hold debt securities to maturity. The ability of the entity to hold such securities to maturity even after new management is hired would still need to be assessed.

Question 15: Is it consistent with the guidance in ASC 320 to have a documented policy to initially classify all debt securities as held-to-maturity but then automatically transfer every security to available-for-sale when it reaches a predetermined point before maturity (e.g., every held-to-maturity security will be transferred to available-for-sale 24 months before its stated maturity) so that an entity has the flexibility to sell securities?

Answer: No. Such a policy would suggest that the entity does not have the intent and ability to hold the security to maturity.

Question 16: May securities classified as held-to-maturity be pledged as collateral?

Answer: Yes. However, the entity must believe that it will be able to satisfy the liability and thereby recover unrestricted access to the debt security that is serving as collateral for the borrowing. However, if sale accounting is used according to the guidance in ASC 860, the securities pledged may not be treated as held-to-maturity.

Question 17: May held-to-maturity securities be subject to a repurchase agreement (or a securities lending agreement)?

Answer: Yes, if the repurchase agreement is accounted for as a secured borrowing. The entity must intend and expect to repay the borrowing and thereby recover unrestricted access to the debt security that is serving as collateral for the borrowing.

Question 18: May convertible debt securities be classified as held-to-maturity?

Answer: Although such treatment is not specifically prohibited, classifying convertible debt securities as held-to-maturity generally would be inappropriate. Convertible debt securities generally carry a lower interest rate than standard debt securities. However, the holder of a debt security stands to profit from the conversion feature if the common stock of the entity issuing the convertible security rises in value. It is implausible to suggest that an entity would not avail itself of such a profit opportunity because it characterized securities as held-to-maturity. If an entity exercises a conversion feature on a security being treated as held-to-maturity, it will call into question the appropriateness of classifying any other securities as held-to-maturity.

Question 19: May a callable debt security be classified as held-to-maturity?

Answer: Yes. The debt instrument's maturity date is viewed as being accelerated if an issuer exercises its call provision. The issuer's exercise of a call feature in no way invalidates the holder's treatment of the security as held-to-maturity. However, per ASC 860, some callable debt securities may not qualify for treatment as held-to-maturity securities. More specifically, this limitation applies to a callable debt security purchased at a significant premium if that security can be prepaid or otherwise settled in such a way that the holder would not recover its full investment.

Question 20: May a puttable debt security be classified as held-to-maturity?

Answer: Yes, if the entity has the intent and ability to hold the puttable debt security to maturity. If the entity exercises the put feature, it will call into question the appropriateness of classifying any other debt securities as held-to-maturity. In addition, some puttable debt securities may not qualify for held-to-maturity treatment per ASC 860-20-35-2.

Question 21: Not included in the Codification.

Question 22: May a mortgage-backed interest-only certificate be classified as held-to-maturity?

Answer: No. ASC 860 amends the guidance in ASC 320 to prohibit held-to-maturity accounting for interest-only strips.

Question 23: If an enterprise holds a debt security classified as held-to-maturity, and that security is downgraded by a rating agency, would a sale or transfer of that security call into question the entity's intent to hold other debt securities to maturity in the future?

Answer: No. A downgrade by a rating agency is an example of a significant deterioration in the issuer's creditworthiness. A sale or transfer that results from such a deterioration does not "taint" the remaining held-to-maturity portfolio (see ASC 320-10-25-6).

Question 24: What constitutes a "major" business combination or a "major" disposition under the guidance in ASC 320-10-25-6?

Answer: A sale or transfer of held-to-maturity securities is permitted under the guidance in ASC 320-10-25-6 as part of a "major" business combination or "major" disposition if necessary to maintain an entity's existing interest rate risk position or credit risk policy. However, the guidance in ASC 320 does not define what constitutes a "major" business combination or disposition. The Statement does state that the sale of a component of an entity qualifies as a major disposition. The purchase or sale of a large pool of financial assets or liabilities would not constitute a major business combination or disposition. In addition, the sale of held-to-maturity securities to fund a business combination is not permitted.

Question 25: Not included in the Codification.

Question 26: May securities classified as held-to-maturity be sold under the exception provided in ASC 320-10-25-6 in anticipation of or otherwise prior to a major business combination or disposition without calling into question the enterprise's intent to hold other debt securities to maturity in the future?

Answer: No. Any such transfers or sales should occur at the same time as or after the business combination or disposition.

Question 27: The guidance in ASC 320-10-25-12 provides that "necessary transfers or sales should occur concurrent with or shortly after the business combination or disposition." How long is *shortly*?

Answer: The term *shortly* is not defined in ASC 320. However, as time elapses it becomes increasingly difficult to justify that any sale or transfer of held-to-maturity securities was necessitated by the combination or disposition, and not by other events and circumstances.

Question 28: If a regulator directs a particular institution (rather than all institutions supervised by that regulator) to sell or transfer held-to-maturity securities (e.g., to increase liquid assets), are those sales or transfers consistent with ASC 320-10-25-6?

Answer: No. The exception provided in ASC 320-10-25-6 pertains only to a change in regulations affecting all entities affected by the legislation or regulator. However, this type of sale does not necessarily "taint" the remainder of the held-to-maturity portfolio. A forced sale by a regulator may qualify as an event that is isolated, nonrecurring, and unusual, and that could not have been reasonably anticipated (see ASC 320-10-25-6).

Question 29: Is a sale of held-to-maturity securities in response to an unsolicited tender offer from the issuer consistent with the guidance in ASC 320-10-25-6?

Answer: No. Such a sale does not fall under one of the specific exceptions outlined in ASC 320-10-25-6. It also does not qualify as an event that is isolated, nonrecurring, and unusual, and that could not have been reasonably anticipated. Therefore, if held-to-maturity securities are sold in response to the tender offer, the remaining held-to-maturity portfolio is tainted.

Question 30: Is it consistent with the guidance in ASC 320 for an insurance company or other regulated enterprise to classify securities as held-to-maturity and also indicate to regulators that those securities could be sold to meet liquidity needs in a defined interest rate scenario whose likelihood of occurrence is reasonably possible but not probable?

Answer: No. Stating that held-to-maturity securities could be sold if a particular interest-rate environment developed is inconsistent with management's intent and ability to hold these securities to maturity.

Question 31: Is it ever appropriate to apply the exceptions in ASC 320-10-25-6 to situations that are similar, but not the same?

Answer: No. The exceptions outlined in ASC 320-10-25-6 are quite specific by design. They should not be extended to similar fact patterns. The guidance in ASC 320-10-25-6 does permit a general exception to the requirement for holding held-to-maturity securities to maturity. That is, held-to-maturity securities can be sold in response to an event that is isolated, nonrecurring, and unusual, and that could not have been reasonably anticipated.

Question 32: What constitutes an event that is "isolated, nonrecurring, and unusual-that could not have been reasonably anticipated" as described in ASC 320-10-25-6?

Answer: This general exception provision involves four elements. Three of these elements are as follows: (1) Was the event isolated? (2) Was the event nonrecurring? (3) Was the event unusual? The fourth element pertains to the extent that the event could have been reasonably anticipated. Very few events will meet all four of these conditions. In general, the types of events that would qualify are extremely remote disaster scenarios. For example, a run on a bank or on an insurance company would qualify.

Question 33: The guidance in ASC 320-10-25-14 allows a sale of a held-to-maturity security to be considered a maturity when the enterprise has collected a substantial portion (at least 85%) of the principal outstanding at acquisition due to scheduled payments on a debt security payable in equal installments (that comprise both principal and interest) over its term. What types of securities would typically qualify or not qualify for this exception?

Answer: This exception applies to (*a*) debt securities that are payable in equal installments, comprising both principal and interest, and (*b*) variable rate debt securities that would be payable in equal installments if there were no change in interest rates. It does not apply to debt securities for which the principal payment is level and the interest amount is based on the outstanding principal balance.

Securities Classified as Trading and as Available-for-Sale

Question 34: How often must sales occur for an activity to be considered "trading"?

Answer: Under the guidance in ASC 320, trading securities are described as securities that will be held for only a short period of time or that will be sold in the near term. Securities that management intends to hold for only hours or days must be classified as trading securities. However, securities that will be held for a longer period of time are not precluded from being classified as trading securities.

Question 35: If an enterprise acquires a security without intending to sell it in the near term, may the enterprise classify the security in the trading category?

Answer: Yes. In general, securities classified as trading will be held for a short period of time or will be sold in the near term. This general requirement is not an absolute. However, the decision to classify a security as trading is to be made at the time the security is acquired. Transfers of securities into or out of the trading category should be rare.

Question 36: If an enterprise decides to sell a security that has been classified as available-for-sale, should the security be transferred to trading?

Answer: No. Securities that will mature within one year or that management intends to sell within one year should not automatically be transferred into the trading category. Similarly, if an entity decides to sell a held-to-maturity security (in response to one of the conditions outlined in ASC 320-10-25-6), such security should not be reclassified as available-for-sale or trading. Refer to ASC 320-10-50-9 and 50-10 for mandated disclosures relating to the sale.

Question 37: What should be the initial carrying amount under ASC 320 of a previously nonmarketable equity security that becomes marketable (i.e., due to a change in circumstances, it now has a fair value that is readily determinable)?

Answer: Equity securities are discussed in ASC 321 after the effective date of ASU 2016-01. In general, the basis for applying the provisions of ASC 320 should be the security's cost. However, if the change in marketability provides evidence that an other-than-temporary impairment has occurred, the impairment loss should be recognized and the writedown recorded prior to applying ASC 320. This treatment assumes that the nonmarketable security had not been accounted for using the equity method.

Question 38: What should be the initial carrying amount under ASC 320 of a marketable equity security that should no longer be accounted for under the equity method (e.g., due to a decrease in the level of ownership)?

Answer: The guidance for equity securities is discussed in ASC 321 after the effective date of ASU 2016-01. The initial carrying amount of the security should be the previous carrying amount of the investment.

Changes in Fair Value—Reporting

Question 39: How is a sale of an available-for-sale security recorded?

Answer: In general, cash or a receivable account should be debited for the amount of the proceeds, and the investment account should be credited for its fair value (i.e., its selling price). Any unrealized gain or loss relating to the investment being sold (recorded in comprehensive income) is reversed into earnings. Deferred tax accounts that relate to any unrealized gain or loss are also adjusted. This general procedure needs to be modified if the entity has not yet recorded all changes in the value of the security being sold (some entities record these changes only at reporting dates), or if a write-down for an other-than-temporary impairment has already been recorded.

Illustration of Sale of Available-for-Sale Securities

Pluto Enterprises purchases 1000 shares of Venus, Inc., common stock for $10 per share on April 1, 20X5. Pluto accounts for these securities as available-for-sale securities. The fair value of Venus' stock at December 31, 20X5, is $12 per share. Therefore, in Pluto's December 31, 20X5, balance sheet, its investment in the Venus securities would be recorded at $12,000. A $2,000 unrealized gain would be recorded in the stockholders' equity section of Pluto. Pluto's effective tax rate is 34%. Pluto sells these shares on June 30, 20X6, at $7 per share. Pluto adjusts the carrying value of securities only at year-end. The journal entry to record the sale would be as follows:

Cash (1,000 shares × $7 per share)	$7,000	
Unrealized gain	2,000	
Deferred tax liability ($2000 × 34%)	680	
Loss on sale of securities	3,000	
Available-for-sale securities		$12,000
Income tax expense		680

Question 40: How is a sale of a trading security recorded?

Answer: For trading securities, changes in fair value are recorded as they occur. Therefore, in most cases, the entry is to debit cash (or a receivables account) for the proceeds received, and to credit the trading securities account for the fair value of the securities sold (i.e., the selling price of the securities). This procedure must be modified if, for example, changes in the fair value of securities are recorded at the end of the day. Also, for those entities not taxed on a marked-to-market basis, the deferred tax accounts would be adjusted.

Questions 41 and 42: Not discussed in the Codification.

Transfer of Securities between Category Types

Question 43: When securities are transferred from available-for-sale to held-to-maturity or vice versa, is the subsequent amortization of a premium or discount based on the amortized cost of the security or on its fair value at the date of transfer?

Answer: The answer to this question depends on whether the transfer is from the available-for-sale category to the held-to-maturity category, or vice versa.

In the case of *transfer from available-for-sale to held-to-maturity,* the difference between the par value of the debt security that is transferred and its fair value on the date of transfer is accounted for as a yield adjustment in accordance with the provisions of ASC 310. The fair value of the debt security on the date of transfer, adjusted for subsequent amortization, serves as the security's amortized cost basis for required disclosures.

In the case of *transfer from held-to-maturity to available-for-sale,* the amortized cost of the security in the held-to-maturity portfolio is transferred to the available-for-sale portfolio for purposes of determining future amortization. In addition, the amortized cost of the security is used for comparing the cost of the security with its fair value (for the purpose of computing unrealized gain or loss) and for disclosure purposes.

Question 44: It is indicated in ASC 320-10-35-10 that for transfers involving the trading category, the unrealized holding gain or loss should be recognized in earnings. How should the gain or loss be classified on the income statement?

Answer: ASC 320-10-35-10 provides that when a security is transferred from the trading category, an unrealized holding gain or loss at the transfer date will have already been recognized in earnings and should not be reversed. At the transfer date of a security into the trading category, the portion of its unrealized holding gain or loss that has not been previously recognized in earnings should be recognized in earnings at the transfer date. Such gains or losses are recognized in a manner consistent with how realized gains and losses for the category from which the security being transferred are treated.

Question 45: How is a transfer from available-for-sale to held-to-maturity accounted for?

Answer: The following is the guidance in ASC 320-10-35-10B, which has been added in ASU 2019-04 for the transfer of a debt security from available-for-sale to held-to-maturity. That guidance will be effective for all entities for fiscal years beginning after December 15, 2019, including interim periods within those fiscal years. Early adoption, including adoption in an interim period, is permitted provided that an entity has adopted all of the pending content that links to ASC 825-10-65-2. If the guidance is adopted in an interim period, adjustments, if any, should be presented as of the beginning of the fiscal year in which the entity adopted all of the pending content that links to ASC 825-10-65-2.

- An allowance for credit losses, if any, previously recorded on an available for sale security should be reversed.
- A debt security transferred to the held-to-maturity category should be reclassified and recorded at its amortized cost basis less previous write-offs, if any, excluding an allowance for credit losses, if any, plus or minus the amount of a remaining unrealized holding gain or loss, if any, reported in accumulated comprehensive income.
- A security should be evaluated for credit losses based on the guidance in ASC 326-20.
- A debt security's unrealized holding gain or loss should be reported at the transfer date in a separate component of shareholders' equity, such as accumulated other comprehensive income, but the gain or loss should be amortized over the security's remaining life as an adjustment of yield in a manner consistent with the amortization of any premium or discount. Amortization of an unrealized holding gain or loss reported in equity will offset or reduce the effect on interest income of the amortization of the premium or discount for that held-to-maturity security. A transfer of a debt security into the held-to-maturity category may create a premium or discount that under amortized cost accounting should be amortized thereafter as an adjustment of yield in accordance with the guidance in ASC 310-20 on receivables—non-refundable fees and costs.

Illustration of Transferring a Security from Available-for-Sale to Held-to-Maturity

Sonic, Inc., has a $1,000 par value bond that it acquired at $1,100 on January 1, 20X4. The bond has a ten-year life. During 20X4, $10 of the bond premium would be amortized. The bond is originally accounted for as available-for-sale. On December 31, 20X4, the fair value of the bond is $1,180. Therefore, at December 31, 20X4, Sonic would have $90 of unrealized gain in stockholders' equity. The $90 of unrealized gain plus the $90 of unamortized premium has the effect of stating the bond at its fair value, $1,180.

On January 1, 20X5, Sonic transfers this debt security into its held-to-maturity category. On the date of transfer, the adjusted bond premium is $180 ($90 of original unamortized premium and the $90 unrealized gain). The remaining life of the debt security is nine years. Each year for the next nine years, Sonic will amortize $20 of the bond investment premium. This has the effect of reducing income. Sonic also will amortize the unrealized gain that existed on the date of transfer at the rate of $10 per year ($90/9 years). This has the effect of increasing income. The net effect of both amortization entries is a reduction in Sonic's income of $10 per year for the next nine years (the remaining life of the bond). This amount, $10, is equal to what would be amortized based on the original unamortized bond premium.

Impairment

Question 46: Not discussed in the Codification.

Question 47: Should an enterprise recognize an other-than-temporary impairment when it decides to sell a specific available-for-sale debt security at a loss shortly after the balance sheet date?

Answer: In most cases, yes. A loss should be recognized if the enterprise does not expect the fair value of the security to recover before the planned sale date. The loss resulting from an other-than-temporary impairment is to be recorded in the period in which the decision to sell the security was made, not in the period when the actual sale occurs.

Question 48: May a valuation allowance be used to recognize impairment on securities subject to ASC 320?

Answer: No. A general allowance for unidentified impairments in an overall portfolio is inappropriate. Other-than-temporary impairments are to be evaluated on a security-by-security basis. When such an impairment is identified, the related security is to be written down to this reduced value, which serves as the security's cost basis going forward. Such a write-down is recognized in earnings when it occurs.

Questions 49 and 50: Not discussed in the Codification.

Presentation of Financial Statements and Disclosure

Question 51: Must the statement of cash flows show purchases, sales, and maturities of securities reported as cash equivalents?

Answer: No. The guidance in ASC 320 does not change the portion of the guidance in ASC 230 that permits showing cash equivalents as a net change within the statement of cash flows. However, ASC 320 does require the disclosure of the amortized cost and fair values of cash equivalents, shown separately by major security type. In addition, a note should explain what portion of each category of securities is shown as cash equivalents in the statement of financial position and the statement of cash flows.

Question 52: Must the disclosures required in ASC 320-10-50-1 through 50-3, 50-5, 50-9 through 50-10 be included in interim financial statements?

Answer: Only if a complete set of financial statements is presented at an interim-period date. If the interim financial statements are limited to summary financial information, per the requirements of APB-28 (Interim Financial Reporting), the above-mentioned disclosure requirements of ASC 320 are not required.

Question 53: ASC 320-10-50-9 requires disclosure of the change in the net unrealized holding gain or loss on trading securities that has been included in earnings during the period. How is that amount calculated?

Answer: ASC 320-10-50-9 requires the disclosure of gains or losses recognized in income during the period that resulted from trading securities still held at the end of the period.

Illustration of Disclosing Unrealized Gains and Losses

Rutledge, Inc., reports $100,000 of net gains and losses from trading securities in its 20X5 income statement. Of this amount, $80,000 resulted from securities that were sold during 20X5. Therefore, to satisfy the disclosure requirement of ASC 320-10-50-9, Rutledge would disclose that $20,000 of gains recognized during 20X5 pertain to trading securities still held at December 31, 20X5.

Deferred Tax Implications

Question 54 and Answer: The guidance has been amended by ASU 2016-01 and moved to ASC 740-20-45-15.

Question 55 and Answer: The guidance has been amended by ASU 2016-01 and moved to ASC 740-20-45-18.

Question 56 and Answer: The guidance has been amended by ASU 2016-01 and moved to ASC 740-20-45-16.

Question 57 and Answer: The guidance has been amended by ASU 2016-01 and moved to ASC 740-20-45-17. See ASC 740-10-45-20; ASC 740-20-45-20; ASC 225-20-60-2; ASC 740-20-45-2 through 45-3, 45-5, 45-8, 45-11 through 45-12, and 45-14; and ASC 740-20-05-2 for additional information.

Questions 58 through 60: Not included in the Codification.

ASC 320-10-15-6, 55-2 Application of Statement 115 to Debt Securities Restructured in a Troubled Debt Restructuring

BACKGROUND

This guidance was issued to clarify a perceived inconsistency between some of the guidance in ASC 310 and ASC 320. This problem came to light during the FASB's discussion of the applicability of the guidance in ASC 320 to Brady bonds that were received in a troubled debt restructuring (TDR). The term *Brady bonds* refers to bonds issued to financial institutions by foreign governments under a program designed by Treasury Secretary Nicholas Brady in the late 1980s to help developing countries refinance their debt to those institutions.

If the guidance in ASC 320 did not apply to a debt security that was restructured in a TDR involving a modification of terms before the effective date of the guidance in ASC 310-10-35-13 through 35-14, 35-16 through 35-26, 35-28, 35-29, 35-34, 35-37, 35-39; 45-5 through 45-6, 50-15, 50-19; ASC 310-30-30-2; ASC 310-40-35-8, 35-12; 50-2 through 50-3, 50-12 through 50-13, the provisions related to impairment under that guidance and the guidance in ASC 320 would not apply. Consequently, such a debt security would be accounted for in accordance with the guidance in ASC 310-40-15-3 through 15-12, 35-2, 35-5 through 35-7, 40-2, 40-5 through 40-6, 40-8, 25-1 through 25-2, 50-1, 55-2, 10-1 through 10-2; ASC 470-60-15-3 through 15-12, 55-3, 35-11 through 35-12, 45-1 through 45-2, 50-1 through 50-2, 10-1 through 10-2; ASC 450-20-60-12, which would not require the recognition of the time value of money or the security's fair value.

STANDARDS

Question: For a loan that was restructured in a TDR involving a modification of terms, does the guidance in ASC 320 apply to the accounting by a creditor if the restructured loan meets the definition of a *security* in ASC 320?

Answer: Generally, yes. The guidance in ASC 320-10-05-2, 50-1A through 50-3, 50-5, 50-9 through 50-11, 55-3, 15-5, 30-1, 35-1 through 35-2, 35-4 through 35-5, 35-10 through 35-13, 35-18, 15-2 through 15-4, 15-7, 25-3 through 25-6, 25-9, 25-11 through 25-12, 25-14 through 25-16, 45-1 through 45-2, 45-8 through 45-11, 45-13 applies to all loans that meet the definition of the term of a *security* under that guidance. Therefore, any loan that was restructured in a TDR involving a modification of terms, including loans restructured before the effective date of the guidance in ASC 310-10-35-13 through 35-14, 35-16 through 35-26, 35-28, 35-29, 35-34, 35-37, 35-39, 45-5 through 45-6, 50-15, 50-19; ASC 310-30-30-2; ASC 310-40-35-8, 35-12; 50-2 through 50-3, 50-12 through 50-13, are subject to the requirements under the guidance in ASC 320-10-05-2, 50-1A through 50-3, 50-5, 50-9 through 50-11, 55-3, 15-5, 30-1; 35-1 through 35-2, 35-4 through 35-5, 35-10 through 35-13, 35-18, 15-2 through 15-4, 15-7, 25-3 through 25-6, 25-9, 25-11 through 25-12, 25-14 through 25-16, 45-1 through 45-2, 45-8 through 45-11, 45-13.

CHAPTER 20

ASC 321—INVESTMENTS—EQUITY SECURITIES

CONTENTS

PART I: GENERAL GUIDANCE

OVERVIEW

The most common accounting for investments in equity securities is fair value with unrealized gains and losses recognized in income in the period in which they occur. Certain exceptions to this general principle are described in this chapter. Disclosure requirements are specified primarily in situations where determining fair value is not practicable and where unrealized gains and losses that have been recognized are on investments in equity securities that are still held by the investing entity at the end of its financial reporting period.

BACKGROUND

An *equity security* is any security representing interest in an entity (e.g., common, preferred, or other capital stock) or the right to acquire (e.g., warrants, rights, forward purchase contracts, call options) or dispose of (e.g., put options, forward sales contracts) an ownership interest in an entity at fixed or determinable prices. This does not include the following:

- Written equity options;
- Cash-settled options on equity securities or options on equity-based indexes; and
- Convertible debt or preferred stock that by its terms either must be redeemed by the issuing entity or is redeemable at the option of the investor (ASC Glossary).

The guidance in ASC 321 establishes standards of financial accounting and reporting for investments in equity securities and other ownership interests, including investments in partnerships, unincorporated joint ventures, and limited liability companies. (ASC 321-10-15-4) It applies to all entities that are not deemed to be specialized industries. It applies to cooperatives and mutual entities, such as credit unions and mutual insurance entities and trusts that do not report substantially all of their securities at fair value. (ASC 321-10-15-2)

ASC 321 does not apply to entities in specialized industries whose accounting practices include accounting for substantially all investments at fair value, with changes in value recognized in income or in the change in net assets. Examples of these entities, and the applicable ASC sections, are brokers and dealers in securities (ASC 940), defined benefit pension, other postretirement, and health and welfare plans (ASC 960, ASC 962, and ASC 965), and investment companies (ASC 946). ASC 321 does not apply to the following specific types of investments:

- Derivative to the requirements of ASC 815;
- Investments accounted for by the equity method (ASC 323);
- Investments in consolidated subsidiaries;
- An exchange membership that has the characteristics specified in ASC 940-340-25-1 for an ownership interest in the exchange; and
- Federal Home Loan Bank and Federal Reserve Bank Stock. (ASC 321-10-15-5)

If an equity security no longer qualifies to be accounted for by the equity method (e.g., due to a decrease in the level of ownership), the security's initial basis for which subsequent changes in fair value are measured shall be the previous amount of the investment. Upon discontinuance of the equity method, the entity shall remeasure the equity security in accordance with ASC 321-10-35-1 or 2, as applicable. For purposes of applying ASC 321-10-35-2 of the investor's retained investment, if the investor identifies observable price changes in orderly transactions for the identical or a similar investment of the same issuer that results in its discontinuing the equity method, the entity shall remeasure its retained investment at fair value immediately after it no longer applies the guidance in ASC 323 (ASC 321-10-30-1).

ACCOUNTING FOR EQUITY INVESTMENTS

Initial Measurement

With certain exceptions, investments in equity securities are measured at fair value in the statement of financial position. Unrealized holding gains and losses on investments in equity securities are included in earnings. (ASC 321-10-35-1)

An entity may elect to measure an equity security without a readily determinable fair value that does not qualify for the practical expedient to estimate fair value at its cost minus impairment, if any. If the entity identifies observable price changes in orderly transactions for the identical or similar investment of the same issuer, it shall measure the equity security at fair value as of the date that the observable transaction occurred. An election to measure an equity security in this manner shall be made for each investment separately. (ASC 321-10-35-2)

Subsequent Measurement

An entity may elect to measure an equity security without a readily determinable fair value that does not qualify for estimating fair value (see ASC 820-10-13-59) at its cost less impairment, if any, plus or minus changes resulting from observable price changes in orderly transactions for the identical or similar investment of the same issuer (ASC 321-10-35-2). An equity investment accounted for in this manner shall be written down to its fair value if a qualitative assessment indicates that the investment is impaired and the fair value of the investment is less than its carrying value. At each reporting period, the entity shall make a qualitative assessment considering impairment to evaluate if the investment is impaired. A non-comprehensive list of factors to consider includes:

- A significant deterioration in the earnings performance, credit ranking, asset quality, or business prospects of the investee.
- A significant adverse change in the regulatory, economic, or technological environment of the investee.
- A significant adverse change in the general market condition of either the geographical area or the industry in which the investee operates.
- A bona fide offer to purchase, an offer by the investee to sell, or a completed auction process for the same or similar investment for an amount less than the carrying amount of the investment.
- Factors that raise significant concerns about the investee's ability to continue as a going concern. (ASC 321-10-35-3)

If an equity investment without a readily determinable fair value is impaired, the investing entity shall include an impairment loss in net income equal to the difference between the (estimated) fair value of the investment and its carrying amount. (ASC 321-10-35-4)

Dividend income from investments in equity securities is included in earnings. (ASC 321-10-35-6)

Derecognition

Because changes in an equity investment's fair value are reported in earnings as they occur, its sale usually does not necessarily give rise to a gain or loss. Assuming fair value of the investment has been recorded up to the point of sale, the entry to record the sale is an increase in cash and a decrease in the investment account to remove the security at its fair value. If the entity is not taxed on the change in fair value, deferred taxes are adjusted. (ASC 321-10-40-1)

Financial Statement Presentation and Disclosure

An entity classifies cash flows from purchases and sales of equity securities on the basis of the nature and purpose for which it acquired the securities. (ASC 321-10-45-2)

For equity securities without readily determinable fair values, the following information is required disclosure:

- The carrying amount of investments without readily determinable fair values.
- The amount of impairments and downward adjustments, if any, both annual and cumulative.
- The amount of upward adjustments, if any, both annual and cumulative.
- As of the date of the most recent statement of financial position, additional information in narrative form that is sufficient to permit users to understand the quantitative disclosures and the information considered in reaching the carrying amounts and upward or downward adjustments resulting from observable price changes. (ASC 321-10-50-3)

For each period for which the results of operations are presented, disclosure is required of the portion of unrealized gains and losses for the period that relates to equity securities still held at the reporting date. (ASC 321-10-50-4)

Illustration of Disclosure When a Portion of Unrealized Gains and Losses Are on Securities Still Held

Watson, Inc. reports $245,000 net gains and losses recognized during the year on investments in equity securities. Included in this amount are $135,000 gains and losses on equity investments that were sold during the year.

In its financial statements, Watson, Inc. should disclose the amount of unrealized gains and losses on investments in equity securities that are still held at year-end of $105,000, calculated as follows:

Net gains and losses recognized during the period	$245,000
Less: Net gains and losses recognized during the period on equity securities sold during the period	(135,000)
Unrealized gains and losses recognized during the period on investments in equity securities still held at the financial reporting date	$110,000

An option to buy an equity security that does not meet the definition of a derivative instrument is within the scope of ASC 321. An investment in an option on securities should be accounted for under the requirements of ASC 815-10 if the option meets the definition of a derivative instrument. This Topic applies to those forward contracts and options that are not derivative instruments subject to ASC 815-10, but that involve the acquisition of securities that will be accounted for under this Topic (ASC 321-10-55-3).

PART II: INTERPRETIVE GUIDANCE

ASC 321-10: OVERALL

ASC 321-10-15-5, 30-1, 55-3; ASC 323-10-35-33, 35-36; ASC 815-10-15-141A, 15-142; ASC 825-10-65-6 Clarifying the Interactions between Topic 321, Topic 323, and Topic 815 (a Consensus of the FASB Emerging Issues Task Force) (ASU 2020-01)

BACKGROUND

ASC 321 (Investments—Equity Securities) was added as a result of the issuance of ASU 2016-01, *Financial Instruments—Overall (Subtopic 825-10): Recognition and Measurement of Financial Assets and Financial Liabilities.* ASC 321-10-35-2 provides a measurement alternative method for the measurement of equity securities that have *no readily determinable fair value* held by entities that do not qualify for the remeasurement of such securities under the practical expedient method discussed in ASC 820-10-35-59 through 35-62. Under the measurement alternative method in ASC 321-10-35-2, an entity is permitted to determine the fair value of an equity security with no readily determinable fair value at its cost less impairment, if any. Further, the entity should remeasure that security's fair value based on "observable" price changes in "orderly" transactions of identical or similar equity securities of the same issuer, as of the date the observable transactions occurred.

The Emerging Issues Task Force took on this project, because stakeholders questioned the implications of the guidance related to the measurement alternative discussed in ASC 321-10-35-2 on the equity method discussed in ASC 323 (Investments—Equity Method and Joint Ventures), and on the guidance in ASC 815 (Derivatives and Hedging) for certain forward contracts and purchased options to purchase securities that would be accounted for as under the equity method after they are settled or exercised.

ACCOUNTING ISSUES

1. How should certain equity securities be accounted for when the equity method is applied or discontinued?
2. What are the scope considerations for forward contracts and purchased options on certain securities?

ACCOUNTING GUIDANCE

ISSUE 1

ASC 323-10-35-33 provides accounting guidance to an investee who qualifies for the equity method as a result of an increase in the level common stock ownership or degree of influence. The paragraph is amended to provide that an investor's current basis for a previously held interest in an investee should be remeasured in accordance with the guidance in ASC 321-10-35-1 or ASC 321-10-35-2, as applicable, immediately before the equity method of accounting is adopted. In addition, if in the process of applying the guidance in ASC 321-10-35-2 , the investor finds that there have been observable price changes in orderly transactions for an issuer's identical or similar investments that result in the application of the guidance in ASC 323, the investor should remeasure its previously held investment at fair value immediately *before* applying ASC 323.

ASC 323-10-35-36 provides accounting guidance for a decrease in an investor's ownership or degree of influence in an investee for various reasons. That guidance is amended to provide that an investor who discontinues accounting for its investment under the equity method should remeasure the investment in accordance with the guidance in ASC 321-10-35-1 or ASC 321-10-35-2, as applicable. If in applying the guidance in ASC 321-10-35-2 to the investor's retained investment, the investor finds that there have been observable price changes in orderly transactions for an issuer's identical or similar investments that result in the issuer's discontinuance of the equity method, the investor should remeasure its previously held investment at fair value immediately *after* discontinuing the equity method.

If accounting for an equity security under the equity method is no longer appropriate, ASC 321-10-30-1 is amended to provide that when the equity method is discontinued, the security should be remeasured in accordance with the guidance in ASC 321-10-35-1 or ASC 321-10-35-2, as applicable. If in applying the guidance in ASC 321-10-35-2 to the entity's retained investment, the entity finds that there have been observable price changes in orderly transactions for an issuer's identical or similar investments that result in the issuer's discontinuance of the equity method, the entity should remeasure its retained investment at fair value immediately *after* it no longer applies the guidance in ASC 323.

ISSUE 2

ASC 815-10-15-141A is added to provide guidance specifically for the financial instruments discussed in ASC 815-10-15-141(a), which applies to forward contracts and purchased options that were entered into to purchase securities that will be accounted for under the guidance in either ASC 320 or ASC 321. That additional guidance provides that upon entering into such transactions, an entity should not consider how it would account for the underlying securities when a settlement of a forward contract or the exercise of a purchased option occurs, individually or with existing investments. That is, whether the entity would account for those underlying securities under (*a*) the equity method in accordance with ASC 323, or (*b*) the fair value option in accordance with ASC 825 if those securities otherwise would have been accounted for under ASC 323.

The guidance in ASC 815-10-15-142 is amended to provide that consideration of the guidance in ASC 815-10-15-141A is necessary to validate that paragraph's existing guidance.

ASC 321-10-15-6 and ASC 321-10-55-3 are amended to state that ASC 815-10-15-141A provides guidance for applying the provisions of ASC 815-10-15-141 to forward contracts and purchased options to purchase securities accounted for under the scope of ASC 321.

TRANSITION AND EFFECTIVE DATE INFORMATION

ASC 825-10-65-6 is added to provide transition and effective date information related to the guidance in ASU 2020-01, which is as follows:

a. *Public business entities* The guidance is effective for fiscal years, and interim periods within those fiscal years that begin after December 15, 2020.

b. *All other entities* The guidance is effective for fiscal years, and interim periods within those fiscal years that begin after December 15, 2021.

c. Early application of the guidance is permitted, including early adoption in an interim period for:

   1. Public business entities for periods for which financial statements have not yet been issued, and

   2. All other entities for periods for which financial statements have not yet been made available for issuance.

d. The guidance should be applied prospectively at the beginning of the interim period that includes the adoption date.

e. The following information should be disclosed in the interim annual periods of the year of adoption:

   1. The nature and reason for the change in accounting principle;

   2. The transition method; and

   3. A qualitative description of the financial statement line items affected by the change.

CHAPTER 21

ASC 323—INVESTMENTS—EQUITY METHOD AND JOINT VENTURES

CONTENTS

PART I: GENERAL GUIDANCE

ASC 323-10: OVERALL

OVERVIEW

The equity method of accounting for investments in common stock is appropriate when an investment enables the investor to influence the operating or financial decisions of the investee. In these circumstances, the investor has a degree of responsibility for the return on its investment, and it is appropriate to include in the investor's results of operations its share of the earnings or losses of the investee. The equity method is not intended as a substitute for consolidated financial statements when the conditions for consolidation are present.

BACKGROUND

Domestic and foreign investments in common stock and corporate joint ventures are presented in financial statements on the *equity basis* by an investor whose investment in the voting stock and other factors give it the ability to *exercise significant influence over the operating and financial policies* of the investment.

Under the equity method of accounting for investments in common stock, net income of the investor during a period includes the investor's proportionate share of the net income reported by the investee for the periods subsequent to acquisition. *The effect of this treatment is that net income for the period and stockholders' equity at the end of the period are the same as if the companies had been consolidated.* Dividends received are treated as adjustments of the amount of the investment under the equity basis.

When appropriate, investors use the equity method to account for investments in common stock, corporate joint ventures, and in other common stock investments (domestic and foreign) in which ownership is less than a majority interest. Generally, an investor measures an investment in the common stock of an investee, including a joint venture, initially at cost in accordance with the guidance in ASC 805-50-30. An exception is that an investor shall initially measure at fair value a retained investment in the common stock of an investee, including a joint venture, in a deconsolidation transaction in accordance with ASC 810-10-40-3A through 40-5.

PRESUMPTION OF SIGNIFICANT INFLUENCE

The equity method is an appropriate means of recognizing increases or decreases measured by U.S. GAAP in the economic resources underlying the investment. The equity method closely meets the objectives of accrual accounting because the investor recognizes its share of the earnings and losses of the investee in the periods in which they are reflected in the accounts of the investee. The equity method also enables investors in corporate joint ventures to reflect the underlying nature of their investment in those ventures (AAC 323-10-05-4).

Evidence that the investor has significant influence over the investee includes the following (ASC 323-10-15-6):

- Investor has representation on the board of directors of the investee.
- Investor participates in the policy-making process of the investee.
- Material intercompany transactions occur between the investor and the investee.
- There is an interchange of managerial personnel between the investor and the investee.
- Technological dependency of the investee on the investor exists.
- There exists significant extent of ownership of the investor in relation to the concentration of other shareholders.

In the absence of evidence to the contrary, an investment (directly or indirectly) of less than 20% of the voting stock of an investee is presumed to indicate lack of significant influence, and the use of the equity method or consolidated statements is not required.

Absent evidence to the contrary, *an investment (directly or indirectly) of 20% or more of the voting stock of an investee is presumed to indicate the ability to exercise significant influence, and the equity method is required for a fair presentation* (ASC 323-10-15-8).

PRACTICE POINTER: There is a presumption that significant influence does not exist in an investment of less than 20%. However, this presumption may be overcome by evidence to the contrary. Significant influence over the operating and financial policies of an investment of less than 20% can occur. The 20% cut-off is intended to be a guideline, subject to individual judgment, rather than a rigid rule.

For example, an investor might own 18% of the voting common stock of an investee, be responsible for a substantial amount of the sales of the investee, and be represented on the investee's board of directors. In this case, the equity method may be the appropriate method of accounting by the investor, even though the investor holds only 15% of the voting stock.

Even with an investment of 20% or more, evidence may exist to demonstrate that the investor cannot exercise significant influence over the operating and financial policies of the investee. The presumption of significant influence in investments of 20% or more may be overcome by sufficient evidence.

The 20% ownership is based on current outstanding securities that have voting privilege. Potential ownership and potential voting privileges should be disregarded (ASC 323-10-15-9).

The following conditions may indicate that an investor is *unable* to exercise significant influence over the operating and financial policies of an investee:

- The investee opposes the investment (e.g., files a lawsuit, complains to government regulatory authorities), challenging the ability of the investee to exercise significant influence (ASC 323-10-15-10).
- An agreement is executed between the investee and the investor that indicates that significant influence does not exist (ASC 323-10-15-10).

PRACTICE POINTER: These types of agreements generally are referred to as *standstill agreements* and frequently are used to settle disputes between an investor and an investee. They may contain information as to whether the investor can or cannot exercise significant influence over the investee. The following are some typical provisions of a standstill agreement:

- The investee agrees to use its best efforts to obtain representation for the investor on its board of directors.
- The investor agrees not to seek representation on the investee's board of directors.
- The investee may agree to cooperate with the investor.
- The investor may agree to limit its ownership in the investee.
- The investor may agree not to exercise its significant influence over the investee.
- The investee may acknowledge or refute the investor's ability to exercise significant influence.

If a standstill agreement contains provisions indicating that the investor has given up some significant rights as a shareholder, the agreement is regarded, under ASC 323, as a factor in determining that the equity method should not be used.

- Significant influence is exercised by a small group of shareholders other than the investor representing majority ownership of the investee (ASC 323-10-15-10).
- The investor attempts, but cannot obtain, the financial information that is necessary to apply the equity method (ASC 323-10-15-10).
- The investor attempts and fails to obtain representation on the investee's board of directors (ASC 323-10-15-10).

PRACTICE POINTER: ASC 323 implies that the investor must actually try to obtain financial information or representation on the investee's board. It seems logical that the same effect should result in the event that the investor had prior knowledge that it would fail in these attempts and, therefore, did not even attempt them.

Many other factors, not listed above, may affect an investor's ability to exercise significant influence over the operating and financial policies of an investee. An investor must evaluate all existing circumstances to determine whether factors exist that overcome the presumption of significant influence in an investment of 20% or more of an investee.

PRACTICE POINTER: On the other hand, an investor must also evaluate existing circumstances in an investment of less than 20% of an investee. The presumption that significant influence does not exist in an investment of less than 20% may be overcome by factors that indicate that significant influence does exist.

If there is not enough evidence to reach a definitive conclusion at the time that the investment is made, it may be advisable to wait until more evidence becomes available.

Change in Significant Influence

Because of the purchase or sale of investment shares, and for other reasons that may affect the assessment of the ability to significantly influence the investee, an investor may be required to change to or from the equity method. The following procedures are applied in these situations:

- An investor with a common stock investment using the equity method may have other investments in the investee. A situation may exist in which previous losses have reduced the common stock investment to zero and the investor is not required to advance additional funds to the investee. In this case, the investor continues to report its share of equity losses to the extent of and as an adjustment to the adjusted basis of the other investments in the investee. The order in which those equity method losses are applied to the other investments follows the seniority of the other investments (i.e., priority in liquidation) (ASC 323-10-35-24).
- An investment in common stock that was previously accounted for by other than the equity method may become qualified for use of the equity method by an increase in the level of ownership. Examples are the acquisition of additional voting stock by the investor and acquisition or retirement of voting stock by the investee. When the investment qualifies for the use of the equity method (i.e., falls within the scope of ASC 323), the entity adds the cost of acquiring the additional interest in the investee, and adopts the equity method of accounting as of the date the investment becomes qualified for equity method accounting. The current basis of the investor's previously held interest in the investee is remeasured in accordance with ASC 321-10-35-1 or ASC 321-10-35-2, immediately before adopting the equity method of accounting (ASC 323-10-35-33).
- An investment in voting stock may fall below the 20% level, or other factors indicate that the investor can no longer exercise significant influence. In this case, the equity method is discontinued and the carrying amount of the investment at the date of discontinuance becomes the cost of the investment. The earnings or losses that relate to the stock retained by the investor that were previously accrued remain as part of the carrying amount of the investment. If the investor identifies observable price changes in orderly transactions for the identical or a similar investment of the same issuer that results in it discontinuing the equity method, the entity shall remeasure its retained investment at fair value immediately after discontinuing the equity method. Subsequent accounting for investments in equity securities is not consolidated or accounted for by the equity method (ASC 323-10-35-36).

APPLYING THE EQUITY METHOD

Under the equity method, the original investment is recorded at cost and is adjusted periodically to recognize the investor's share of earnings or losses after the date of acquisition. *Dividends received reduce the basis of the investment.* Continuing operating losses from the investment may indicate the need for an adjustment in the basis of the investment in excess of those recognized by the application of the equity method.

An investor's share of earnings or losses from its investment usually is shown as a *single amount* (called a *one-line consolidation*) in the income statement. The following procedures are appropriate in applying the equity method (ASC 323-10-35-5, 6, 8, 16):

1. Intercompany profits and losses are eliminated by reducing the investment balance and the income from investee for the investor's share of the unrealized intercompany profits and losses.
2. The investment is shown in the investor's balance sheet as a single amount and earnings or losses are shown as a single amount (one-line consolidation) in the income statement, *except for the investor's share of prior-period adjustments, which are shown separately.*

3. Capital transactions of the investee that affect the investor's share of stockholders' equity are accounted for on a step-by-step basis.
4. Gain or loss is recognized when an investor sells the common stock investment, *equal to the difference between the selling price and the carrying amount of the investment at the time of sale.*
5. If the investee's financial reports are not timely enough for an investor to apply the equity method currently, the investor may use the most recent available financial statements, and the lag in time created should be consistent from period to period.
6. Other than temporary declines, a loss in value of an investment should be recognized in the books of the investor.
7. When the investee has losses, applying the equity method decreases the basis of the investment. The investment account generally is not reduced below zero, at which point the use of the equity method is discontinued, unless the investor has guaranteed obligations of the investee or is committed to provide financial support. The investor resumes the equity method when the investee subsequently reports net income and the net income exceeds the investor's share of any net losses that were not recognized during the period of discontinuance.
8. Dividends for cumulative preferred stock of the investee are deducted before the investor's share of earnings or losses is computed, whether the dividend was declared or not.
9. The investor's shares of earnings or losses from an investment accounted for by the equity method are based on the outstanding shares of the investee without regard to common stock equivalents. (ASC 323-10-35-19)

A difference between the cost of an investment and the amount of the underlying equity in net assets of the investee is to be accounted for as if the investee were a consolidated subsidiary. As a general rule, the portion of the difference that is recognized as goodwill is not to be amortized. However, if the entity elects the accounting alternative for amortizing goodwill (ASC 350-20), the portion of the difference that is recognized as goodwill shall be amortized on a straight-line basis over 10 years or less if the entity demonstrates that a shorter useful life is appropriate. (ASC 323-10-35-13)

Equity method investments shall be reviewed for impairment in accordance with ASC 323-10-35-32.

Illustration of Equity Method

On December 31, 20X8, LKM Corporation acquired a 30% interest in Nerox Company for $260,000. Total stockholders' equity on the date of acquisition consisted of capital stock (common $1 par) of $500,000 and retained earnings of $250,000. During 20X9, Nerox Company had net income of $90,000 and paid a $40,000 dividend. LKM has an income tax rate of 35%.

Entries to record the investment, the dividends and net income of the investee are as follows:

Investment in Nerox	260,000	
Cash		260,000
Cash ($40,000 × 30%)	12,000	
Investment in Nerox		12,000
Investment in Nerox	27,000	
Income from investee		27,000
Income tax expense	5,250	
Deferred income taxes		5,250

The deferred income tax is determined as follows:

($27,000 – $12,000) × 35% = $5,250

On December 31, 20X9, the investment account on the balance sheet would show $275,000 ($260,000 – $12,000 + $27,000) and the income statement would show $27,000 as income from investee. Income tax expense and deferred income tax liability would increase by $5,250. The equity method goodwill at acquisition is determined as follows:

($260,000 – 30% ($500,000 + $250,000)) = $35,000

Assume that the equity method goodwill is not impaired as of December 31, 20X9.

The balance in the investment account equals the investment percentage multiplied by the stockholders' equity of the investee, adjusted for any unamortized goodwill. This reconciliation for the above example is as follows:

Stockholders' equity, beginning of 20X9	$750,000
Add: 20X9 net income	90,000
Deduct: 20X9 dividends	(40,000)
Stockholders' equity, end of 20X9	$800,000
Ownership percentage	30%
Pro rata share of stockholders' equity	$240,000
Investment balance, end of 20X9	$275,000
Less: Equity method goodwill	(35,000)
Investment balance adjusted for equity method goodwill	$240,000

Illustration of Step Acquisition

Roper, Inc. owned common stock in Purple Tiger Co. from 20X8 to 20Y1 as follows: 20X8 and 20X9—10%; 20Y0—17%; 20Y1—25%. Purple Tiger has no preferred stock outstanding. Roper, Inc. carries the investment at cost, which approximates market value.

As part of the audit of the 20Y1 financial statements, the decision was made to change to the equity method for the investment in Purple Tiger Co. The net income and dividends paid by Purple Tiger Co. from 20X8 to 20Y1 were as follows:

	Net Income	*Dividends Paid*
20X8	$72,500	$30,000
20X9	65,000	35,000
20Y0	68,800	38,000
20Y1	85,000	40,000

Dividends received have been properly recorded for 20X8-20Y1 as dividend revenue. All investments were made in amounts approximating the underlying book value acquired.

The general journal entry to record Roper, Inc.'s change from the cost to the equity method, ignoring income taxes, is as follows:

Dividend income	10,000	
Investment in Purple Tiger, Co. ($46,696 – 22,960)	23,736	
Equity in income of Purple Tiger Co.		21,250
Retained earnings ($25,446 – 12,960)		12,486

Analysis of net income and dividends:

	Net Income		*Roper Share*	*Dividends*		*Roper Share*
20X8	$72,500 × 10%	=	$7,250	$30,000 × 10%	=	$3,000
20X9	65,000 × 10%	=	6,500	35,000 × 10%	=	3,500
20Y0	68,800 × 17%	=	11,696	38,000 × 17%	=	6,460
			25,446			12,960
20Y1	85,000 × 25%	=	21,250	40,000 × 25%	=	10,000
			$46,696			$22,960

Joint Ventures

A *joint venture* is an entity that is owned, operated, and jointly controlled by a group of investors. A joint venture might be organized as a partnership or a corporation, or be unincorporated (each investor holding an undivided interest).

Technically, ASC 323 applies only to corporate joint ventures. If the criteria for applying the equity method are met, investments in corporate joint ventures must use the equity method. In 1979, the AICPA Accounting Standards

Executive Committee (AcSEC) published an Issues Paper titled *Joint Venture Accounting,* which made several recommendations regarding accounting for joint ventures:

- The equity method is applied to investments in unincorporated joint ventures subject to joint control.
- Majority interests in unincorporated joint ventures should be consolidated.
- Investments in joint ventures not subject to joint control should be accounted for by proportionate consolidation.
- Additional supplementary disclosures regarding the assets, liabilities, and results of operations are required for all material investments in unincorporated joint ventures.

Income Taxes

Applying the equity method results in the recognition of income based on the undistributed earnings of the investee. If the investee is not an S corporation, the investor has no tax liability for equity method income until those earnings are distributed. Thus, application of the equity method gives rise to temporary differences that should be considered when deferred tax assets and liabilities are measured.

Intercompany Profits and Losses

Intra-entity profits and losses are eliminated until realized by the investor or investee as if the investee were consolidated. Intra-entity profits or losses on assets remaining with an investor or investee shall be eliminated, giving effect to any income taxes on the intra-entity transactions, except for both of the following:

1. A transaction with an investee, including a joint venture investee, that is accounted for as a deconsolidation of a subsidiary or a derecognition of a group of assets in accordance with ASC 810-10-40-3A through 40-5.
2. A transaction with an investee, including a joint venture investee, that is accounted for as a change in ownership transaction in accordance with paragraphs 810-10-45-21A through 45-24.

Illustration of Elimination of Intercompany Profits

An equity method investor sells inventory "downstream" to an investee. At the end of the year, $50,000 of profit remains in inventory from intercompany sales. The investor has a 40% interest in the voting stock of the investee, and the income tax rate is 30%. The entry for the elimination of intercompany profits is made as follows:

Income from investee ($50,000 × 40%)	20,000	
Deferred tax asset ($20,000 × 30%)	6,000	
Investment in investee		20,000
Income tax expense		6,000

If the intercompany sales were "upstream" (i.e., from the investee to the investor), the elimination entry would be as follows:

Income from investee [$20,000 × (1 – .30)]	14,000	
Deferred tax asset	6,000	
Inventory		20,000

DISCLOSURE STANDARDS

Disclosure must be made for investments accounted for by the equity method and include (ASC 323-10-50-3):

- The name of the investment
- The percentage of ownership
- The accounting policies of the investor in accounting for the investment
- The difference between the carrying value of the investment and the underlying equity in the net assets, and the accounting treatment of such difference
- The quoted market price of the investment, except if it is a subsidiary

- If material, a summary of the assets, liabilities, and results of operations presented as a footnote or as separate statements
- The material effect on the investor of any convertible securities of the investee

If the equity method is not used for an investment of 20% or more of the voting stock, disclosure of the reason is required. Conversely, if the equity method is used for an investment of less than 20%, disclosure of the reason is required.

PRACTICE POINTER: In evaluating the extent of disclosure, the investor must weigh the significance of the investment in relation to its financial position and results of operations.

PRIVATE COMPANY COUNCIL ALTERNATIVE GUIDANCE

U.S. GAAP requires that the portion of the difference between the cost of an investment and the amount of underlying equity in net assets that is recognized as goodwill must not be amortized. However, if a private company elects the accounting alternative in ASC 350-20 on goodwill, the portion of the difference recognized as goodwill must be amortized on a straight-line basis over 10 years, or less than 10 years if the entity demonstrates that another useful life is more appropriate (ASC 323-10-35-13).

PART II: INTERPRETIVE GUIDANCE

ASC 323-10: OVERALL

ASC 323-10-15-3 through 15-5, 15-13 through 15-18, 55-1 through 55-18 Whether an Investor Should Apply the Equity Method of Accounting to Investments Other than Common Stock

BACKGROUND

According to the guidance in ASC 323-10-15-3, 15-4, 15-6 through 15-8, the guidance in ASC 323 applies only to an interest in a business entity's voting *common stock.* However, investments in such vehicles as convertible debt, preferred equity securities, options, warrants, interests in unincorporated entities, complex licensing and management arrangements, and other types of financial instruments have been giving investors rights, privileges, or preferences that previously had been limited to investors in common stock. Rights, privileges, or preferences—such as (*a*) the right to vote with common stockholders, (*b*) the right to appoint directors to the company's board, (*c*) important participating and protective rights as discussed in ASC 810-10-15-10, 25-1 through 25-8, 25-10 through 25-14, and 55-1, (*d*) the right to cumulative and participating dividends, and (*e*) liquidation preferences—may enable investors in such financial instruments to exercise significant influence over an investee's operating and financial policies even though they do not own the company's voting common stock.

ACCOUNTING ISSUE

Should an investor who exercises significant influence over an investee by means other than an ownership of the investee's voting common stock account for the investee by the equity method of accounting?

ACCOUNTING GUIDANCE

The following guidance should be applied:

- Investors that have significant influence over their investees' operating and financial policies should apply the equity method of accounting as discussed in ASC 323 only if those investments are in common stock or in-substance common stock.
- The risk and reward characteristics of an entity's in-substance common stock must be substantially the same as those of the entity's common stock. An investment in an entity is in-substance common stock if all of the following characteristics indicate that it is substantially similar to an investment in that entity's common stock:
  - — *Subordination* An investment's subordination characteristics must be substantially similar to those of the entity's common stock. If an investment has a substantive liquidation preference over common stock, it is not substantially similar to the common stock.
  - — *Risks and rewards of ownership* An investment's risk and reward of ownership characteristics must be substantially similar to those of the entity's common stock. For example, an investment that is not expected to participate in an

entity's earnings and losses and capital appreciation and depreciation in substantially the same manner as common stock is not substantially similar to common stock. In contrast, if an investment participates in an investee's dividend payments in a manner that is substantially similar to the participation of common stock in such dividend payments, the investment is substantially the same as common stock. It was noted that the right to convert certain investments to common stock would indicate that those investments can participate in the investee's earnings and losses and in capital appreciation and depreciation in a substantially similar manner as common stock.

— *Obligation to transfer value* If an investee is obligated to transfer substantive value to an investor, but the entity's common stockholders do not participate in the same manner, the investment is not substantially similar to common stock. An example is an investment's substantive redemption provision, such as a mandatory redemption provision or a put option at other than fair value, which is not offered to common shareholders.

An investment is in-substance common stock if its subordination and risk and reward characteristics are substantially similar to an investee's common stock and the investee is *not* required to transfer value to the investor in a manner that differs from the participation of common shareholders. If, based on the characteristics discussed previously, an investor is unable to determine whether an investment in an entity is substantially similar to the entity's common stock, the investor should determine whether it is expected that there will be a high correlation between future changes in the investment's fair value and changes in the fair value of the common stock. The investment is not in-substance common stock if that high correlation is not expected to exist.

An investor that has significant influence over an investee's operating and financial policies should determine whether an investment is substantially similar to common stock on the date on which the investor makes the investment. That determination should be reconsidered if one or more of the following circumstances occur:

- An investment's contractual terms change so that there is a change in any of the characteristics previously discussed.
- The investee's capital structure changes significantly, including the receipt of additional subordinated financing.
- The amount of an existing interest has increased. Consequently, the investor's method of accounting for its cumulative interest should be based on the characteristics of the investment on which the additional investment was made so that one method will be used by the investor to account for the cumulative interest in an investment of the same issuance.

An investee's losses, however, should not cause an investor to reconsider the determination of whether an investment is substantially similar to common stock.

An investor that gains the ability to exercise significant influence over an investee's operating and financial policies after the date on which the investment in the entity was made should determine whether the investment is substantially similar to common stock by considering the characteristics previously discussed and the relevant information existing on the date the investor obtained significant influence.

Investments other than common stock that have a "readily determinable fair value" under the guidance in ASC 320-10-15-5, 35-2 and 30-1 should be accounted for in accordance with the guidance in ASC 320 rather than based on this guidance. It was noted that the equity method of accounting should be applied in all cases under the scope of this guidance if an investor has significant influence over an investee's operating and financial policies and owns an investee's common stock or in-substance common stock.

ASC 323-10-25-2A, 30-2A through 30-2B, 35-14A, 35-32A, 40-1 Equity Method Investment Accounting Considerations

BACKGROUND

The project in which the FASB and the International Accounting Standards Board (IASB) collaborated to converge the guidance on accounting for business combinations and that on accounting and reporting for noncontrolling interests resulted in the issuance of revised guidance in ASC 805 and ASC 810-10-65-1 whose principles are based on the premise that a reporting entity has gained or lost control of a business or a subsidiary. Although it was not the objective of that project to reconsider the accounting for equity method investments, the issuance of that guidance has affected the application of the equity method. Consequently, some constituents asked whether all of the provisions of the revised guidance must be applied when accounting for an equity method investment because an entity's ability to control an investee differs substantially from its ability to exert significant influence on an investee's activities.

SCOPE

The following guidance applies to all investments accounted for under the equity method.

ACCOUNTING GUIDANCE

The accounting guidance is as follows:

Initial measurement. An equity-method investment's initial carrying value should be measured based on the cost accumulation model discussed in ASC 805-50-25-1, 30-1 through 30-3, 35-1 for asset acquisitions. The initial measurement of an equity method investment should include contingent consideration only if doing so is required in specific authoritative guidance other than ASC 805. Nevertheless, if there is an arrangement for contingent consideration in an agreement in which the fair value of an investor's share of an investee's net assets exceeds the investor's initial cost, the entity should recognize a liability for one of the following amounts, whichever is less:

- The maximum amount of consideration not otherwise recognized; or
- The amount by which the investor's share of an investee's net assets exceeds the initial cost measurement that includes contingent consideration otherwise recognized.

If a contingency related to a liability recognized based on the guidance above is resolved and the consideration is issued or becomes issuable, the amount by which the fair value of the contingent consideration exceeds the amount of the recognized liability should be added to the cost of the investment. However, the cost of an investment should be reduced if the recognized liability exceeds the fair value of the consideration.

Decrease in the value of an investment. In accordance with the guidance in ASC 323-10-35-32, an equity method investor should recognize other-than-temporary impairments related to an equity method investment. Although that investor should not perform a separate impairment test of an investee's asset, the investor should recognize its share of an impairment, if any, that is recognized by an investee in accordance with the guidance in ASC 323-10-35-7 and 35-13, and should consider how the impairment, if any, affects the investor's basis difference in the assets that caused the investee to recognize an impairment.

Change in level of ownership or degree of influence. An equity method investor should account for an investee's issuance of shares as if the investor had sold a proportionate share of its investment with a gain or loss recognized in earnings.

ASC 323-10-25-3 through 25-5, 30-3, S45-1, S99-4, 55-19 through 55-20; ASC 718-10-S60-1 Accounting by an Investor for Stock-Based Compensation Granted to Employees of an Equity Method Investee

BACKGROUND

ASC 323 provides guidance to investors on the accounting for gains or losses on investments accounted for under the equity method. It does not, however, provide guidance to investors on how they should account for unreimbursed costs incurred on behalf of an investee, such as the cost of stock-based compensation granted to an investee's employees. Under the circumstances considered in this Issue, the entity's other investors do not contribute a proportionate amount and the investor's relative ownership percentage of the investee does not increase. It is assumed in this Issue that the grant of stock-based compensation to the investee's employees did not occur as a result of the investor's agreement to acquire an interest in the investee.

ACCOUNTING ISSUES

1. Should a contributing investor and an equity method investee capitalize or expense stock-based compensation costs incurred by the investor on behalf of the investee and when should the investee and the contributing investor account for those costs?
2. How should noncontributing equity method investors in an investee account for stock-based compensation costs incurred by a contributing equity method investor on behalf of the investee if they do not fund a proportionate amount of those costs?

ACCOUNTING GUIDANCE

- A contributing investor that incurs stock-based compensation cost on behalf of an equity method investee should expense those costs as incurred (i.e., in the same period in which the investee recognizes those costs) in so far as the investor's claim on the investee's book value does not increase.

An investee should recognize an expense and a corresponding capital contribution for the costs of stock-based compensation incurred on its behalf by a contributing investor as the investor incurs those costs, as if the investor had paid cash to the investee's employees according to the guidance in ASC 505-50-25-4 and 25-9.

- Noncontributing investors should recognize income for an amount that corresponds to their increased interest in the investee's net book value (i.e., their proportionate share of the increase in the investee's contributed capital) because of the contributing investor's funding of stock-based compensation for the investee's employees. They also should recognize their percentage share of the investee's gains or losses, which would include the expense recognized for the cost of stock-based compensation incurred by the contributing investor on the investee's behalf.

SEC OBSERVER COMMENT

The SEC Observer attending the EITF's meeting stated that registrants should classify income or expense, if any, as a result of the consensus in this Issue under the same income statement caption that includes the registrant's equity in the investee's earnings.

ASC 323-10-35-7 through 35-11, 55-27 through 55-29, 15-5; ASC 323-30-15-3, 25-2, 35-1 through 35-2; ASC 810-10-45-14 The Equity Method of Accounting for Investments in Common Stock: Accounting Interpretations of APB Opinion No. 18

BACKGROUND

The following is the guidance for two implementation issues associated with ASC 323: (1) elimination of intercompany profit or loss and (2) its applicability to partnerships and joint ventures.

ACCOUNTING GUIDANCE

Question 1: Under the guidance in ASC 323 and ASC 810, intercompany profits or losses on assets still remaining with an investor or an investee at a reporting date must be eliminated. Should all of the intercompany profit or loss be eliminated, or should only the portion related to the investor's common stock interest in the investee be eliminated?

Answer: The extent of intercompany profits or losses, all or a proportionate amount, that should be eliminated under the equity method depends on the relationship between an investor and its investee. Under certain relationships between an investor and its investee, the investor would recognize no intercompany profits or losses until they have been realized through transactions with third parties. The following are examples of situations in which this accounting treatment would apply:

- An investor owns a majority of an investee's voting shares and enters into a transaction with the investee that is not on an arm's-length basis.
- An investee is established with the investor's cooperation and the investor controls the investee by guarantying the investee's debt, extending credit and making other special arrangements for the benefit of the investee, or through the investor's ownership of warrants or convertible securities issued by the investee. This type of arrangement exists if an investee is established for the purpose of financing and operating or leasing property sold by an investor to an investee.

In other cases, an investor would eliminate intercompany profit based on its percentage ownership of an investee. If so, the percentage of intercompany profit eliminated would be the same regardless of whether the transaction is "downstream" (the investor sells to its investee) or "upstream" (the investee sells to the investor). Intercompany profit should be eliminated on a net-of-tax basis.

Illustration of Upstream Intercompany Profit Elimination

At year-end, an investor that owns 40% of its investee's outstanding common stock holds $800,000 of inventory purchased from the investee during the year. The investee's gross profit rate on sales of inventory is 25%. Thus, at year-end, the investor holds inventory for which the investee recognized $200,000 of gross profit ($800,000 × 25%). Both the investor and the investee are subject to a 36% tax rate.

To compute its equity "pickup," the investor (*a*) deducts $128,000 [$200,000 less 36% income tax] from the investee's net income and (*b*) eliminates $51,200 ($128,000 × 40%), its share of the intercompany after-tax gross profit, from its equity income. The investor's offsetting entry of $51,200 would be made either to its investment account (the most common approach) or to its inventory account.

Question 2: Do the provisions of ASC 323 apply to investments in partnerships and joint ventures?

Answer: Not directly, because the guidance in ASC 323-10 applies only to common stock investments in corporations. It does not pertain to partnerships and unincorporated joint ventures. However, many of the provisions would apply in accounting for investments in unincorporated ventures. For example, partnership profits and losses accrued by investor-partners are generally reflected in their financial statements at a single amount. In addition, and consistent with the guidance in ASC 323-30, the following additional provisions would apply to a partnership: (1) the elimination of intercompany profits and losses, and (2) the accrual of income taxes on the profits accrued by investor-partners regardless of the tax basis used in the partnership return.

Generally, the preceding discussion regarding the applicability of the guidance in ASC 323-10 to partnerships would also apply to unincorporated joint ventures. However, under the guidance in ASC 810-10-45-14, if it is established industry practice, an investor-venturer may present its pro rata share of a venture's assets, liabilities, revenues, and expenses in its financial statements, except in the construction and extractive industries.

PRACTICE NOTE: The G4+1 (standard setters representing Australia, Canada, New Zealand, the United Kingdom, the United States, and the International Accounting Standards Committee (IASC)) released a Special Report titled *Reporting Interests in Joint Ventures and Similar Arrangements*. The Special Report recommends the use of the equity method in accounting for joint ventures. In addition, the Special Report rejects the notion that joint venture participants should depart from the equity method by recognizing their pro rata share of the assets, liabilities, revenues, and expenses of the venture.

ASC 323-10-35-19 Accounting by an Equity Method Investor for Investee Losses When the Investor Has Loans to and Investments in Other Securities of an Investee

This guidance is intended to clarify the guidance in ASC 323-10-35-3 through 35-4, 35-6 through 35-7, 35-13, 35-15 through 35-16, 35-19 through 35-22, 35-20, 35-32 through 35-33 through 35-36, 45-1 through 45-2, 45-12; ASC 225-20-60-1; ASC 250-10-60-2; ASC 460-10-60-1 regarding whether an investor in an investee's common or other voting stock should provide for the investee's operating losses if its common stock investment has been reduced to zero, but in addition, the investor: (*a*) owns the investee's debt securities, which may include mandatorily redeemable preferred stock, (*b*) owns the investee's preferred stock, or (*c*) has made loans to the investee.

The FASB staff believes that the carrying amount of an equity method investor's *total* investment includes additional support committed to or made by the investor in the form of capital contributions, investments in additional common or preferred stock, loans, debt securities, or advances. The investee's losses, therefore, should be reported up to the *total* investment.

The staff believes that this position is consistent with the provisions of ASC 970-323-35-34, 35-5, 35-12. It provides the following examples of circumstances in which an investor would reduce its equity in a real estate venture for losses that exceed the investment:

- The investor is legally obligated because of its position as guarantor or general partner.
- The investor's commitment to provide additional support is implied based on considerations such as the investor's business reputation, intercompany relationships, or the investor's credit standing. A commitment may also be implied by an investor's previous support to the investee or the investor's statements to other investors or third parties about its intentions.

ASC 323-10-35-23 through 35-26, 55-30 through 55-32, 55-34 through 55-47; ASC 320-10-35-3 Accounting by an Equity Method Investor for Investee Losses When the Investor Has Loans to and Investments in Other Securities of the Investee

BACKGROUND

In ASC 323-10-35-19, which is discussed above, the FASB staff clarified the guidance in ASC 323-10-35-23 through 35-28 regarding how an equity method investor in an investee's common or other voting stock should account for the investee's operating losses when the investment has been reduced to zero *and* the investor also has one or more of the following: (*a*) the investee's debt securities, which include mandatory redeemable preferred stock; (*b*) the investee's preferred stock; or (*c*) loans to the investee.

The FASB staff believes that the guidance in ASC 323-10-35-19 indicates that an equity method investor's *total* investment in an investee includes, in addition to its investment in the investee's common stock or other voting stock, the investor's additional support committed to or made to the investee in the form of capital contributions, investments in additional common or preferred stock, loans, debt securities, or advances. The investor should, therefore, report an investee's losses up to the amount of the *total* investment.

This Issue is a follow-up to the FASB staff's guidance in ASC 323-10-35-19. It is intended to clarify the relationship among the guidance in ASC 323, the guidance on impaired loans in ASC 310-10-30-2, 35-13 through 35-14, 35-16 through 35-22, 35-24 through 35-29, 35-32, 35-34, 35-37, 35-39, 45-5 through 45-6, 50-12 through 50-13, 50-15, 50-19; ASC 310-40-35-8 through 35-9, 35-12; 50-2 through 50-3 and that in ASC 320-10 in accounting for an equity method investor's *total* investment in an investee.

ACCOUNTING ISSUE

If the carrying value of an equity method investee's common stock has been reduced to zero, how does the investor's accounting under the guidance in ASC 323 interact with the investor's accounting for its investments in the investee's other securities?

ACCOUNTING GUIDANCE

1. An investor should continue to report its share of equity method losses in an investee in the income statement up to the balance of and as an adjustment of the adjusted basis of the investor's other investments in the investee—such as preferred stock, debt securities, and loans—if (*a*) the investor is not required to advance additional funds to the investee and (*b*) the investment in the investee's common stock has been reduced to zero.

PRACTICE NOTE: See the guidance in ASC 323-10-35-27 and 28, 55-49 through 55-57.

Equity method losses should be distributed to those other investments according to their order of seniority (i.e., priority in liquidation). In each period, an investor should first charge the adjusted basis of other investments with equity method losses incurred during the period, and then should apply the provisions of ASC 310-10-30-2, 35-13 through 35-14, 35-16 through 35-22, 35-24 through 35-29, 35-32, 35-34, 35-37, 35-39, 45-5 through 45-6, 50-12 through 50-13, 50-15, 50-19; ASC 310-40-35-8 through 35-9, 35-12; 50-2 through 50-3 those in ASC 320-10 or ASC 321-10 to those investments, as appropriate.

The *cost basis* of the other investments, as defined under this guidance, is their original cost, which has been adjusted for other-than-temporary write-downs, unrealized gains and losses on debt securities classified as trading in accordance with ASC 320-10, or equity securities accounted for under the guidance in ASC 321-10 and amortization of a discount or premium, if any, on debt securities and loans. The *adjusted basis* of the other investments is the cost basis adjusted for a valuation account under the guidance in ASC 310-10-30-2, 35-13 through 35-14, 35-16 through 35-22, 35-24 through 35-29, 35-32, 35-34, 35-37, 35-39, 45-5 through 45-6, 50-12 through 50-13, 50-15, 50-19 and ASC 310-40-35-8 through 35-9, 35-12; 50-2 through 50-3 for loans to an investee and the cumulative amount of losses under the equity method that have been charged to the other investments. Subsequent income earned on the equity method investment should be attributed to the adjusted basis of the other investments in reverse of the order in which losses were attributed to those other investments (e.g., equity method income should be applied to the most senior investments first.).

---

2. To determine the amount of a loss on the equity method that should be reported at the end of the period, an investor that holds an investee's securities and debt under the scope of the guidance in ASC 310-10-30-2, 35-13 through 35-14, 35-16 through 35-22, 35-24 through 35-29, 35-32, 35-34, 35-37, 35-39, 45-5 through 45-6, 50-12 through 50-13, 50-15, 50-19; ASC 310-40-35-8 through 35-9, 35-12, 50-2 through 50-3 and the guidance in ASC 320-10 should perform the following tasks:
   a. Determine the maximum amount of equity method losses under the provisions of ASC 323.
   b. Account for equity method losses as follows:
      (1) If the adjusted basis of the other investments in the investee is positive, adjust the balance of the other investment for the amount of the loss on the equity method based on that investment's seniority. The

adjusted basis of an investment accounted for in accordance with the guidance in ASC 320-10 becomes the debt security's basis used to measure subsequent fair value changes.

(2) If the adjusted basis of the other investment is zero, further losses on the equity method investment should *not* be reported. However, an investor, should continue to keep track of unrecorded equity method losses in order to apply the guidance in ASC 323-10-35-20. If one of the other investments is sold when its carrying amount is greater than its adjusted basis, the difference between the investment's cost basis and its adjusted basis on sale equals the equity method losses that were attributed to that other investment and that difference should be reversed when the asset is sold. Such amounts are considered unreported equity losses that should be tracked before the investor can report future income on the equity method investment.

c. The provisions in ASC 310-10-30-2, 35-13 through 35-14, 35-16 through 35-22, 35-24 through 35-29, 35-32, 35-34, 35-37, 35-39, 45-5 through 45-6, 50-12 through 50-13, 50-15, 50-19; ASC 310-40-35-8 through 35-9, 35-12; 50-2 through 50-3 and those in ASC 320-10 should be applied to the adjusted basis of the other investments in the investee, if appropriate, after the provisions of ASC 323 have been applied. Other generally accepted accounting principles not within the scope of the guidance in ASC 310-10-30-2, 35-13 through 35-14, 35-16 through 35-22, 35-24 through 35-29, 35-32, 35-34, 35-37, 35-39, 45-5 through 45-6, 50-12 through 50-13, 50-15, 50-19; ASC 310-40-35-8 through 35-9, 35-12; 50-2 through 50-3 and in ASC 320-10 should also be applied to other investments, if appropriate.

PRACTICE POINTER: An entity that has an interest in a variable interest entity and is required to absorb the majority of that entity's expected losses or is entitled to receive most of the entity's expected residual returns, or both, must consolidate that entity in accordance with the guidance in ASC 323-10-45-4; ASC 810-10-05-8 through 05-13, 15-12, 15-13B, 15-14, 15-15 through 15-17, 25-37 through 25-47, 25-55 through 25-57, 30-1 through 30-4, 30-7 through 30-9, 35-3 through 35-5, 45-25, 50-2 through 50-4 through 50-7, 50-9 through 50-10, 55-16 through 55-49, 55-93 through 55-181, 55-183 through 55-205; ASC 860-10-60-2; ASC 954-810-15-3, 45-2; ASC 958-810-15-4; ASC 715-60-60-3; ASC 715-30-60-7; ASC 712-10-60-2; and ASC 460-10-60-13, as amended by the guidance in ASC 810-10-65-2, and 30-7 through 30-9, which also provides guidance on the consolidation of some corporations that investors previously may have accounted for under the equity method.

PRACTICE POINTER: When applying the guidance in ASC 323, the term "common stock" also applies to "in-substance common stock," as defined under the guidance in ASC 323-10-15-3 through 15-5, 15-13 through 15-18, 55-1 through 55-18. Consequently, investors that have significant influence over their investees' operating and financial policies should apply the guidance in ASC 323-10-35-23 through 35-26, 55-30 through 55-32, 55-34 through 55-47; and ASC 320-10-35-3 only to investments in common stock or in-substance common stock.

Illustration of the Application of the Guidance to Equity Method Investments and Other Investments in an Investee

At the beginning of 20X9, Company A has a 45% equity method investment in Company B's common stock, which has been reduced to zero as a result of losses in previous years. On that date, the carrying amounts of Company A's other investments in Company B are as follows:

- Preferred stock at $35,000, which constitutes 45% of Company B's outstanding preferred stock.
- A $60,000 loan, which constitutes 45% of Company B's loan indebtedness.

Company A has no obligation to fund Company B's additional losses.

It is assumed in this illustration that all of Company B's operating income and losses discussed below have been adjusted for intercompany interest on the loan and dividends received on the preferred stock in accordance with ASC 323-10-35-19.

The table on the following pages summarizes the following information about Company A's accounting for income or loss on its equity method investment in Company B and for changes in the value of its other investments in Company B after its common stock investment in Company B has been reduced to zero:

1. *12/31/X9*—Company B has a loss of $50,000. The fair value of the preferred stock is $30,000 and the carrying value of the loan is $54,000.
2. *12/31/Y0*—Company B has a loss of $150,000. The fair value of the preferred stock is $15,000 and the carrying value of the loan is $45,000.
3. *12/31/Y1*—Company B has no income. The fair value of the preferred stock is $29,000 and the carrying value of the loan is $40,000.
4. *12/31/Y2*—Company B has $200,000 income. The fair value of the preferred stock is $30,000 and carrying value of the loan is $55,000.
5. *12/31/Y3*—Company B has no income. The fair value of the preferred stock is $32,000 and the carrying value of the loan is $58,000.
6. *12/31/Y4*—Company B has income of $100,000. Company A sells the preferred stock for $33,000. The carrying value of the loan is $60,000.

Summary of Transactions (Amounts are in thousands)

		Preferred Stock				*Investment in Company B*					
Year	*Inc/Loss (Equity Loss)*	*Fair Value*	*Adjusted Basis*	*Loan*	*Common Stock*	*Carrying Amount*	*Adjusted Basis*	*OCI*	*P&L*	*Cash*	*Unrecognized Loss*
1/1/X9		35.0	35.0	60.0	0.00	95.0	95.0				
20×9	(22.5)	(22.5)	(22.5)			(22.5)	(22.5)		(22.5)		
		17.5[a]				17.5		17.5			
				(6.0)		(6.0)	(6.0)		(6.0)		
		30.0	12.5	54.0		84.0	66.5	17.5	28.5		
20×0	(67.5)	(12.5)	(12.5)	(54.0)		(66.5)	(66.5)[b]		(66.5)		(1.0)[c]
		(2.5)				(2.5)		(2.5)			
		15.0	0.0	0.0		15.0	0.0	15.0	(66.5)		(1.0)
20×1	0.0								0.0		
		14.0				14.0		14.0			
		29.0				29.0		29.0	0.0		
20×2	72.0	17.0	17.0	54.0		71.0	71.0		71.0[d]		1.0
		(16.0)				(16.0)		(16.0)			
				1.0		1.0	1.0				
		30.0	17.0	55.0		85.0	72.0	13.0	71.0		
20×3	0.0										
		2.0				2.0		2.0	0.0		
				3.0		3.0	3.0		3.0		
		32.0	17.0	58.0		90.0	75.0	15.0	3.0		
20×4	45.0				27.0	27.0	27.0		27.0[e]		
		(32.0)	(17.0)			(32.0)	(17.0)	(15.0)	15.0	32.0	
				2.0		2.0	2.0		2.0		
		0.0	0.0	60.0	27.0	87.0	87.0	0.0	44.0	32.0	0.0

---

[a] Because the carrying amount of the preferred stock was reduced to $12,500 when Company B's $22,500 equity method loss was applied against the balance of the preferred stock investment in Company B, an unrealized gain of $17,500 is recognized to adjust the preferred stock to its fair value of $30,000.

[b] A portion of the $67,500 loss is recognized by reducing the $12,500 adjusted cost basis of the preferred stock investment to zero. The $54,000 adjusted basis of the loan is then reduced to zero. Because the equity method loss is limited to Company A's total adjusted basis of its total investments in Company B, the remaining $1,000 of equity method loss is unrecognized but should be tracked.

[c] Because the loan has been reduced to zero, no additional reduction in the value of the loan would be recognized.

[d] In accordance with the guidance in ASC 323, the equity method income of $72,000 must be reduced by the unrecognized $1,000 loss in 20×0 when the preferred stock investment and the loan were reduced to zero. The adjusted cost bases of the other investments are reinstated in reverse of the order in which the equity method loss was applied. That is, the loan is reinstated first to its adjusted amount of $54,000 and the remaining $17,000 is allocated to the preferred stock.

[e] During the previous years, Company A recognized $18,000 in losses related to its investment in Company B's preferred stock ($35,000 cost less $17,000 adjusted basis). Although the $15,000 gain recognized on the sale of the preferred stock investment reverses some of those losses, Company A actually incurred a $3,000 loss on the sale of the investment ($35,000 cost basis less $32,000 proceeds). Therefore, only $27,000 of the equity method income should be recognized ($45,000 less $18,000 losses on the preferred stock). That amount is used to reinstate a portion of the common stock investment in Company B.

ASC 323-10-35-27 and 35-28, 55-49 through 55-57 Percentage Used to Determine the Amount of Equity Method Losses

BACKGROUND

Under the guidance in ASC 323, an investor that is not obligated to provide additional financing after its common stock investment in an equity method investee has been reduced to zero must apply subsequent equity method losses—such as debt securities, preferred stock, and loans—to its other investments in the investee.

ACCOUNTING ISSUE

How should an investor who is *not* obligated to provide additional financing after its common stock investment in an equity method investee has been reduced to zero measure and recognize subsequent equity method losses applied to its other investments in the investee?

ACCOUNTING GUIDANCE

The following example was used in the discussion:

> An investor owns 40% of an investee's outstanding common stock, 50% of the investee's outstanding preferred stock, and has extended loans that represent 60% of the investee's outstanding loans. The investor's common stock investment has been reduced to zero and the investor is not obligated to provide additional funds.

The following accounting guidance applies under the circumstances:

- An investor should *not* recognize equity method losses based exclusively on the investor's percentage ownership of the investee's common stock.
- In a discussion of whether equity method losses should be recognized based on (*a*) the specific ownership percentage of the investment to which the equity method losses are applied or (*b*) the change in the investor's claim on the investee's book value. Although the results were the same under both approaches for the above example, it was not clear whether the results might differ in other situations. It was noted that both approaches would be acceptable and that other approaches not discussed also may be acceptable. However, once the guidance in ASC 323-10-35-23 through 35-26, 55-30 through 55-32, 55-34 through 55-47; ASC 320-10-35-3 has been applied to the other investments, no additional adjustments would be necessary.
- Entities should choose one approach that should be applied entity-wide to distribute equity method losses to the other investments after the common stock investment has been reduced to zero as a result of previous losses. The policy should be disclosed in the notes to the financial statements.

SUBSEQUENT DEVELOPMENT

A conclusion was reached in ASC 323-10-15-13 through 15-5, 15-13 through 15-18, 55-1 through 55-18 (Whether an Investor Should Apply the Equity Method of Accounting to Investments Other Than Common Stock), that when the guidance in ASC 323 is applied, the term "common stock" also applies to "in-substance common stock," as defined under that guidance. Consequently, investors that have significant influence over their investees' operating and financial policies should apply the guidance in ASC 323-10-35-23 through 35-26, 55-30 through 55-32, 55-34 through 55-47; ASC 320-10-35-3 only to investments in common stock or in-substance common stock.

ASC 323-10-35-29, 35-30 Accounting for Subsequent Investments in an Investee after Suspension of Equity Method Loss Recognition

BACKGROUND

According to the guidance in ASC 323-10-35-20 an investor should discontinue applying the equity method of accounting when an investment (and net advances) equal zero. Further, an investor should recognize losses only if the investor has guaranteed an investee's obligations or is committed to provide financial support to an investee. Even after an investee has resumed recognition of net income, an investor should *not* resume applying the equity method until the investor's share of net income equals the amount of net losses not recognized after application of the equity method was suspended.

Although the following guidance applies to related matters, none addresses the question discussed in this Issue:

- In ASC 323-10-35-19, Accounting by an Equity Method Investor for Investee Losses When the Investor Has Loans to and Investments in Other Securities of an Investee, (see above), the FASB staff stated that an equity method investor should report its losses in an investee up to its *total* investment in the investee, which in the staff's view includes additional support to an investee in the form of capital contributions, investments in additional common or preferred stock, loans, debt securities, or advances.

- The guidance in ASC 323-10-35-23 through 35-26, 55-30 through 55-32, 55-34 through 55-47; ASC 320-10-35-3, Accounting by an Equity Method Investor for Investee Losses When the Investor Has Loans to and Investments in Other Securities of the Investee, addresses the interaction of an investor's accounting for an investee under the guidance in ASC 323 with the investor's accounting for its investments in an investee's other securities in accordance with the guidance in ASC 310-10-35, Accounting by Creditors for Impairment of a Loan—An Amendment of FASB Statements Nos. 5 and 15, and ASC 320-10. Under that guidance, an investor should continue reporting its share of equity method losses in an investee up to the balance of and as an adjustment of the adjusted basis of an investor's other investments in an investee, such as preferred stock, debt securities, and loans, if (*a*) the investor is *not* required to advance additional funds to the investee and (*b*) the investment in the investee's common stock has been reduced to zero.
- The guidance in ASC 323-10-35-27 and 28; 55-49 through 57, Percentage Used to Determine the Amount of Equity Method Losses, addresses how an investor that is *not* obligated to provide additional support to an equity method investee after its common stock investment has been reduced to zero should measure and recognize subsequent equity method losses applied to its other investments in an investee. Under that guidance, an investor should *not* recognize equity method losses based exclusively on its percentage ownership of the investee's common stock. Two methods of recognizing equity method losses were discussed: (1) based on an investor's specific ownership percentage of an investment to which the equity method losses are applied or (2) based on a change in an investor's claim on an investee's book value.

ACCOUNTING ISSUE

If an investor that has suspended equity method loss recognition in an investee in accordance with the guidance in ASC 323-10-35-19 and that in ASC 323-10-35-23 through 35-26, 55-30 through 55-32, 55-34 through 55-47; and ASC 320-10-35-3 (see above) subsequently makes an additional investment in an investee but *does not* increase its ownership from significant influence to one of control, should that investor (*a*) account for the transaction as a step acquisition, or (*b*) recognize a loss in the amount of previously suspended losses?

ACCOUNTING GUIDANCE

The EITF reached the following consensus positions on the issues:

- If all or part of an additional investment made by an investor who has appropriately suspended recognition of equity method losses in accordance with the guidance in ASC 323-10-35-19 and in ASC 323-10-35-23 through 35-26, 55-30 through 55-32, 55-34 through 55-47; and ASC 320-10-35-3 is in substance funding earlier losses, the investor should recognize its previously suspended losses only up to the amount that the additional investment is considered to be a funding of earlier losses discussed in (*b*) below.
- Whether the additional investment should be considered to be a funding of previous losses depends on the facts and circumstances of the investment and requires judgment.

The following factors should be considered in making that determination, but no one factor alone should be considered presumptive or determinative:

— *The source of the investment, a third party or the investee* If an investor purchases an additional investment in an investee from a third party and neither the investor nor the third party provide additional funds to the investee, it is unlikely that prior losses are being funded.

— *Whether the amount paid to acquire an additional investment in an investee represents the fair value of the additional ownership interest received* A payment that exceeds the fair value of an additional investment in an investee would indicate that the excess paid over fair value is intended to fund prior losses.

— *Whether an additional investment in an investee increases the investor's ownership percentage of the investee* If an investment is made directly with an investee, the form of the investment should be considered and whether other investors are also making investments proportionate to their interests in the investee. It may be an indication that prior losses are being funded if (*a*) an additional investment in an investee does not increase the investor's ownership or other interests in the investee, or (*b*) if all other existing investors are also making additional pro rata equity investments in the investee.

— *Seniority of an additional investment* If an investor's additional investment in an investee has a *lower* seniority than the investor's existing investment in the investee, it may be an indication that an additional investment is funding previous losses.

It was noted that an investor making an additional investment in an investee should also consider whether as a result of the additional investment the investor becomes "otherwise committed" to provide financial support to the investee as a result of the additional investment.

ASC 323-10-35-37 through 35-39; ASC 323-30-35-4 Accounting by an Investor for Its Proportionate Share of Accumulated Other Comprehensive Income of an Investee Accounted for under the Equity Method in Accordance with APB Opinion No. 18 upon a Loss of Significant Influence

BACKGROUND

Under the guidance in ASC 323-10-35-18, an investor is required to recognize its proportionate share of an investee's equity adjustments in other comprehensive income, such as unrealized gains and losses on available-for-sale securities, minimum pension liability adjustments, and foreign currency items, as increases or decreases in the investment account with corresponding adjustments to equity in accordance with the guidance in ASC 323-10-35-15. Constituents have asked the question below.

Question: How should an investor account for its proportionate share of an investee's adjustments of other comprehensive income (OCI) if the investor has (*a*) lost significant influence in the investee, (*b*) lost control of the investee that results in accounting for the investment under the guidance in ASC 321, or (*c*) has discontinued accounting for a limited partnership under the equity method, because the conditions in ASC 970-323-25-6 for accounting for the investment under the guidance in ASC 321 have been met.

ACCOUNTING GUIDANCE

When an investor loses significant influence over an investee (or under the circumstances in (b) or (c) above), the investor should offset its proportionate share of the investee's equity adjustments of OCI against the investment's carrying value. However, if the offset amount would reduce the investment's carrying value to *less than* zero, the investor should (*a*) reduce the carrying value to zero, and (*b*) recognize the remaining balance in income.

ASC 323-30: PARTNERSHIPS, JOINT VENTURES, AND LIMITED LIABILITY COMPANIES

ASC 323-30-25-1; ASC 910-810-45-1; ASC 810-1-45-14; ASC 930-810-45-1; ASC 932-810-45-1 Investor Balance Sheet and Income Statement Display under the Equity Method for Investments in Certain Partnerships and Other Ventures

BACKGROUND

Although the guidance in ASC 323-10 applies only to corporate entities, partnerships and other unincorporated entities have analogized to that guidance and applied the equity method when accounting for investments in investees over which they can exercise significant influence. Generally, such investments are reported as a single amount in the balance sheet with the investor's share of the investee's earnings or losses displayed as a single amount in the income statement. Even though the guidance in ASC 323-10 does not apply to situations in which an investor has an undivided interest in each asset and a proportionate obligation for the liabilities of a partnership or other venture, which is not a separate legal entity, it has been the practice of companies in some industries (e.g., oil and gas, mining, and construction) to report their investments in other entities by the equity method on a proportionate gross basis. Those entities present a proportionate share of an investee's revenues and expenses under each major revenue and expense category in their income statement and may present their proportionate share of the investee's assets and liabilities separately under each related major caption in the balance sheet.

The pro rata consolidation method is discussed in several pronouncements of the authoritative accounting literature. The guidance in ASC 323-30-15-3, 25-2, 35-1 through 35-2 and ASC 810-10-45-14 provides that in industries in which it is established industry practice, an investor-venturer in an unincorporated joint venture who owns an undivided interest in each asset and is proportionately liable for its share of each liability may account in its financial statements for a pro rata share of the venture's assets, liabilities, revenues, and expenses.

The guidance in ASC 970-323, which is sometimes applied by analogy to non-real estate ventures, also provides guidance on pro rata consolidation. The guidance in ASC 970-810-45-1 provides that an investor/venturer may present its undivided interest in a venture's assets, liabilities, revenues, and expenses if (*a*) decisions related to the venture's financing, development, sale, or operations can be made without the approval of two or more of the owners, (*b*) each investor/venturer is only entitled to its share of the income, (*c*) each is responsible only for its pro rata share of the venture's expenses, and (*d*) each is liable only for liabilities incurred for its proportionate interest in the entity.

Real estate entities under the scope of ASC 970-323 are required to apply the guidance in ASC 970-810-45-1. That is, real property owned by undivided interests that is under joint control should be presented under the equity method, like investments in noncontrolled partnerships.

ACCOUNTING ISSUE

Are there circumstances under the equity method in which it is appropriate to use a proportionate gross presentation in the financial statements of a legal entity?

ACCOUNTING GUIDANCE

- A proportionate gross financial statement presentation may *not* be used to report on investments in unincorporated *legal* entities, which are normally accounted for on the equity method, except by entities in the construction industry or the extractive industries, because that type of reporting has been a longstanding practice in those industries. Under this guidance, entities are considered to be in the extractive industries only if their activities are limited to the extraction of mineral resources, such as those involved in oil and gas exploration and production. This guidance does *not* apply to entities involved in refining, marketing, or transporting extracted mineral resources.
- The guidance in ASC 323-10 applies to common stock investments of *all* corporate entities in which an investor has significant influence over the investee. Consequently, the guidance in ASC 323-10-35-19, which requires the display of a single amount for such investments, should be applied. This guidance does not affect the accounting for undivided interests under the circumstances discussed in the Background section above.

SEC OBSERVER COMMENT

The SEC Observer indicated that the SEC staff expects corporate entities to follow the provisions of ASC 323-10 if an investor has significant influence over its investee. Further, the use of pro rata consolidation by such entities is not acceptable in SEC filings even if under an agreement, the benefits and risks are attributed to the owners as if they held undivided interests in the entity.

ASC 323-30-S99-1, S55-1 Accounting for Limited Partnership Investments

The Acting Chief Accountant of the SEC announced at the May 1995 meeting of the Emerging Issues Task Force that the SEC staff will no longer accept cost method accounting for an investment in a limited partnership, even though the partner has an interest of 20% or less and has no significant influence over an investee. The staff now believes that investors in limited partnerships should follow the guidance in ASC 970-323-25-6 through 25-7 under which limited partners are required to use the equity method to account for such investments, unless their interest is so minor that they have virtually no influence over the partnership's operating and financial policies. According to the SEC staff, investments of more than 3%-5% generally have been considered to be more than minor in practice. The announcement applies to all investments in limited partnerships made after May 18, 1995, not just to those holding real estate.

ASC 323-740: INVESTMENTS-INCOME TAXES

ASC 323-740-05-02 through 05-3, 15-3, 25-1, 25-1A through 25-1C, 25-2, 25-2A, 25-4 through 25-5, 30-1, 35-1 through 35-6, 45-1 through 45-2, 50-1 through 50-2, 55-2 through 55-5, 55-7 through 55-8 Accounting for Investments in Qualified Affordable Housing Projects (ASU 2014-01)

BACKGROUND

Investors in limited liability entities that manage or invest in qualified affordable housing projects benefit from the Low Income Housing Tax Credit (LIHTC) program, which was first enacted in 1986 under Section 42 of the Internal Revenue Code (IRC) and made permanent in 1993 by the Revenue Reconciliation Act of 1993. The purpose of the LIHTC program is to encourage investments of private capital in the construction and rehabilitation of low income housing by providing tax credits to entities that invest in or manage qualified affordable housing projects. Corporate investors generally purchase interests in limited liability entities, which manage or invest in qualified affordable housing projects. Investors in qualified affordable housing projects usually expect to receive most of their return through tax credits and other tax benefits, such as deductions from taxable income for operating losses.

The tax credit is allowed on such an entity's return each year for 10 years if a sufficient number of unit have been rented to qualifying tenants and is subject to restrictions on gross rentals paid by those tenants. The tax credits are subject to recapture over 15 years starting in the first year in which tax credits are earned.

The accounting guidance for such tax credits originated in EITF Issue No. 94-1, "Accounting for Tax Benefits Resulting from Investments in Affordable Housing Projects," which was codified in the FASB Accounting Standards Codification® (ASC) in ASC 323-740, *Investments—Equity Method and Joint Ventures—Income Taxes* (see below). Under that guidance, a reporting entity that had an LIHTC investment was permitted to elect to account for it by the effective yield method if the investment met all of the following conditions:

- The investor obtains a letter of credit, a tax indemnity agreement, or another similar arrangement from creditworthy entity that guarantees the availability of the tax credits to be allocated to the investor.
- There is a positive projected yield based only on the cash flows from the guaranteed tax credits.
- The investor must be a limited partner in the affordable housing project for legal and tax purposes with a liability that is limited to the investor's capital investment.

Before the issuance of the guidance below in ASU 2014-01, if those conditions were not met, an LIHTC investment had to be accounted for under the equity or cost method by applying the guidance in ASC 970-323, *Real Estate—General—Investments—Equity Method and Joint Ventures*. The advantage of accounting for such an investment under the effective yield method was that the net benefit of the tax credit (i.e., net of the amortization of the limited liability entity) allocated to an investor was recognized in the income statement as a component of income taxes ascribed to continuing operations. Generally, no pretax losses were recognized in the financial statements for LIHTC investments accounted for under the effective yield method. In contrast, under the equity method, the performance of an LIHTC investment, which is generally a loss, would be reported in pretax income, and the tax credits would be reported in after-tax income. The loss occurs because qualified affordable housing projects generally operate at breakeven in terms of cash flow while a limited liability entity also recognizes depreciation expense on the affordable housing property and interest expense from other project financing. The income statement presentation under the cost method would result in a gross up (similar to the equity method).

The EITF addressed this issue at the request of constituents who believe that:

- The income statement presentation under the equity and cost methods is distorted and difficult to understand because pretax losses on otherwise profitable LIHTC investments are reported separately from the tax benefits.
- The following requirements to qualify for the use of the effective yield method are too restrictive and should be reconsidered: (1) the examples of creditworthy guarantors set a threshold of creditworthiness that has been obtained by less than 5% of LIHTC investments; and (2) it is difficult to meet the requirement for a positive yield only on the cash flows from guaranteed tax credits because yields on tax credits have declined due to the lower risk profile of LIHTC investments.

ACCOUNTING ISSUE

How should a reporting entity account for an investment in a qualified affordable housing project that is made through a limited liability entity?

SCOPE

The following guidance applies to all reporting entities that invest in or manage qualified affordable housing projects through limited liability entities that are flow-through entities for tax purposes.

RECOGNITION

The EITF has amended the existing guidance in ASC 323-740-25-1 by substituting the proportional amortization method for the effective yield method as the method that entities may elect to use to account for limited liability investments in qualified affordable housing projects because (*a*) those investments differ from debt instruments for which the effective yield method is more appropriate, and (*b*) the proportional amortization method would better represent the economics of the investments and is less complex to apply.

Under the amended guidance in ASC 323-740-25-1, a reporting entity (investor) may elect to account for an investment in a qualified affordable housing project through a limited liability entity by applying the proportional amortization method if all of the following conditions are met:

- It is probable that the tax credits to be allocated to the investor will be available. (25-1a.)
- The investor is unable to exercise *significant influence* over the limited liability entity's operating and financial policies. (25-1aa.)
- Substantially all of the projected benefits are from tax credits and other tax benefits, such as those generated from the investment's operating losses. (25-1aaa.)
- The investor's positive projected yield is based only on cash flows from the tax credits and other tax benefits. (25-1b.)
- The investor is a limited liability investor in the limited liability entity for legal and tax purposes, and its liability is limited to the investor's capital investment. (25-1c.)

Under the proportional amortization method, an investment's initial cost is amortized in proportion to the tax credits and other tax benefits that an investor received. The net investment performance is recognized in the income statement as a component of income tax expense (benefit).

A reporting entity is required to consider the indicators of significant influence in ASC 323-110-15-6 through 15-7 to determine whether it can exercise significant influence over the limited liability entity's operating and financial policies, because this guidance is intended for investments made primarily for the purpose of receiving tax credits and other tax benefits. In addition, a reporting entity does not need to include other transactions with the limited liability entity (e.g., bank loans) in its consideration of whether it meets the conditions in ASC 323-740-25-1 if it meets all of the following conditions:

- The reporting entity's business is to enter into those other transactions (e.g., a financial institution that provides loans to other projects).
- The other transactions' terms are consistent with those of arm's-length transactions.
- The other transactions do not give the reporting entity the ability to exercise *significant influence* over the limited liability entity's operating or financial policies.

When a reporting entity makes its initial investment, it should evaluate based on the existing facts and circumstances whether it meets all of the conditions required to apply the proportional amortization method, as discussed above. Those conditions should be reevaluated if either of the following occur thereafter:

- A change in the nature of an investment (e.g., if the investment is no longer in a flow-through entity for tax purposes).
- A change in the relationship with the limited liability entity as a result of which the reporting entity would no longer meet the conditions discussed above.

An investment in a qualified affordable housing project through a limited liability entity that is not accounted for by the proportional amortization method should be accounted for under the guidance in ASC 970-323. If so, the guidance in ASC 323-740-25-3 through 25-5 and ASC 323-740-50-1 through 50-2, which is not related to the proportional amortization method, applies.

PRACTICE POINTER: Under the guidance in ASU 2016-01, ASC 323-740-25-2A amends the existing guidance to permit using the cost method to account for an investment in a qualified affordable housing project by applying the guidance in ASC 323-740-25-3 through 25-5 and ASC 323-740-50-1 through 50-2, which are not related to the proportional amortization method.

As required in ASC 323-740-25-3, an investor should recognize a liability for delayed equity contributions that are unconditional and legally binding, as well as for equity contributions that are contingent on a future event when it becomes probable that the contingent event will occur. Additional guidance on accounting for delayed equity contributions may be found in ASC 450, Contingencies, and in ASC 840-30-55-15.

An entity that elects to use the proportional amortization method to account for an investment in a qualified affordable housing project through a limited liability entity and meets the conditions in ASC 323-740-25-1 is making an accounting policy decision that should be applied consistently to all such investments that meet the conditions rather than a decision to apply that method to individual investments that qualify for the use of the proportional amortization method (ASC 323-740-25-4).

INITIAL MEASUREMENT

In accordance with the guidance in ASC 323-740-25-5, when making an initial investment in a qualified affordable housing project through a limited liability entity, an investor is not permitted to recognize the benefit of all of the tax credits that will be received during the investment's term. The methodology under the proportional amortization method is discussed below.

SUBSEQUENT MEASUREMENT

An investor that elects to apply the proportional amortization method amortizes the investment's initial cost in proportion to the tax credits and other tax benefits allocated to the investor as follows:

- Reduce the amount of the initial investment by its expected residual value, if any.
- Multiply the resulting amount by the percentage of actual tax credits and other tax benefits allocated to the investor in the current period.
- Divide the resulting amount by the total estimated tax credits and other benefits the investor expects to receive over the investment's life.

A practical expedient, which is discussed in ASC 323-740-35-4, permits an investor to amortize an investment's initial cost in proportion only to the tax credits allocated to the investor if the investor can reasonably expect that the measurement would be substantially similar to the measurement that would result from applying the calculation above for the proportional amortization method.

Cash received from the limited liability entity's operations should be included in earnings when realized or realizable. Gains or losses on the sale of an investment, if any, should be included in earnings when a sale occurs.

An investment in a qualified affordable housing project through a limited liability entity should be tested for impairment if it is indicated by events or changes in circumstances that it is more likely than not that an investment's carrying amount will not be realized. An impairment loss should be measured as the amount by which an investment's carrying amount exceeds its fair value. A previously recognized impairment loss should not be reversed.

OTHER PRESENTATION MATTERS

If the proportional amortization method is used, the amortization of the investment in a limited liability entity is recognized in the income statement as a component of income tax expense (or benefit). The current tax expense (or benefit) should be accounted for under the guidance in ASC 740, *Income Taxes*.

DISCLOSURE

A reporting entity that invests in a qualified affordable housing project is required to disclose the following information to enable financial statement users to understand the following (ASC 323-740-50-1):

- The nature of investments in qualified affordable housing projects.
- How the measurement of investments in qualified affordable housing projects and the related tax credits affect a reporting entity's financial position and results of operations.

To meet those objectives, it is suggested in ASC 323-740-50-2 that a reporting entity may consider making the following disclosures:

- The amount of affordable housing tax credits and other tax benefits recognized during the year;
- The balance of the investment recognized in the balance sheet;
- The amount recognized as a component of income tax expense (benefit) from qualified investments accounted for using the proportional amortization method;
- The amount of investment income or loss included in pretax income from investments accounted for using the equity method;
- Commitments or contingent commitments (e.g., guarantees or commitments to provide additional capital contributions), if any, including the amount of equity contributions that are contingent commitments related to qualified

affordable housing project investments and the year or years in which contingent commitments are expected to be paid; and

- The amount and nature of impairment losses during the year due to the forfeiture or ineligibility of tax credits or other circumstances. For example, the impairment losses may be based on actual property-level foreclosures, loss of qualification as a result of occupancy levels, compliance issues with tax code provisions, or other issues.

ASC 323-740-05-3, S25-1, 25-1 through 25-5, 35-2, 45-2, 55-2 through 55-5, ASC 55-7 through 55-9; S99-2; ASC 325-20-35-5, 35-6 Accounting for Tax Benefits Resulting from Investments in Affordable Housing Projects

BACKGROUND

The affordable housing credit, which had expired after June 30, 1992, is a tax benefit that was retroactively extended and made permanent under the Revenue Reconciliation Act of 1993. Investors commonly receive such tax benefits by purchasing interests in limited liability entities that manage or invest in qualified affordable housing projects, because the tax benefits flow through to the limited partners. Credits are available if a sufficient number of units are rented to qualifying tenants at a rental that does not exceed statutory amounts. The affordable housing credit may be taken on an investor's tax return each year for ten years and is subject to recapture over 15 years, beginning with the first year tax credits are earned.

ACCOUNTING ISSUE

How should investors in qualified affordable housing project limited partnerships account for their investments?

ACCOUNTING GUIDANCE

- A receivable for the entire tax benefits to be received over the term of an investment in a qualified affordable housing project should *not* be recognized when the initial investment is made.
- Income from affordable housing credits should *not* be recognized for financial reporting purposes before they are reported for tax purposes.
- A limited liability entity's investments in qualified affordable housing projects should be tested for impairment when events or changes in circumstances indicate that it is more likely than not that an investment's carrying amount will not be realized (see ASC 323-740-35-6).
- A liability should be recognized for (*a*) unconditional and legally binding delayed equity contributions and for (*b*) equity contributions contingent on a future event when it becomes probable. ASC 450 and ASC 842-50-55-2 provide additional guidance on the accounting for delayed equity contributions.

The Task Force observed that additional guidance on accounting for delayed equity contributions may be found in ASC 450, ASC 840-30-55-15.

PRACTICE NOTE: The guidance in ASU 2014-01, *Accounting for Investments in Qualified Affordable Housing Projects*, which is discussed above, amends certain parts of the guidance in this Issue. The existing guidance in ASC 323-740-25-1 is amended by substituting the proportional amortization method for the effective yield method as the method that entities may elect to use to account for limited liability investments in qualified affordable housing projects because (*a*) those investments differ from debt instruments for which the effective yield method is more appropriate, and (*b*) the proportional amortization method would better represent the economics of the investments and is less complex to apply. Other important changes are included in ASC 323-740-35 in which guidance for subsequent measurement is provided as well as the addition of disclosure requirements about investments in qualified affordable housing projects in ASC 343-740-50 and changes in the implementation guidance.

Equity method

For investments not accounted for on the proportional amortization method or the cost method, the guidance in ASC 970-323 and ASC 323 and other guidance should be followed.

Under the guidance in ASC 970-323 and ASC 323, application of the equity method is generally required to account for limited partnership investments in real estate ventures, unless the limited partner has only a minor interest with practically no influence over the partnership's operating and financial policies.

PRACTICE POINTER: The equity method may be used to account for investments in limited partnerships even if an ownership interest does not meet the 20% presumption of significant influence. See the discussion of the SEC staff's position on the use of the equity method to account for limited partnership investments in ASC 323-30-S99-1, S55-1 above.

Cost method

a. The cost method should be used only if an investment is so minor that there is virtually no influence over operating and financial policies.

b. The difference between the carrying amount of an investment and its estimated residual value should be amortized during the periods in which an investor receives allocated tax credits.

   (1) The estimated residual value is the value of the investment at the end of the last period in which tax credits are allocated to the investor without considering anticipated inflation.

   (2) Annual amortization is calculated based on the ratio of tax credits received in the current year to total estimated tax credits that will be allocated to the investor.

PRACTICE POINTER: Under the guidance in ASC 810, an entity that absorbs a majority of a variable entity's expected losses or has the right to receive a greater part of the variable entity's expected residual returns or both is required to consolidate the variable interest entity.

CHAPTER 22

ASC 325—INVESTMENTS—OTHER

CONTENTS

PART I: GENERAL GUIDANCE

ASC 325-10: OVERALL

OVERVIEW

ASC 325 addresses the circumstances in which the cost method is used to account for investments in voting stock. This includes the following:

- Use of the cost method after the completion of a business combination by each combining entity for cost method investments held in the other entity prior to the business combination.
- Accounting for tax benefits resulting from qualified investments in affordable housing projects through a limited partnership. (ASC 325-20-15-2)

BACKGROUND

Investments are accounted for by one of three methods: the cost method (addressed in this section), the fair value method (addressed in ASC Topics 320 and 321) and the equity method (addressed in Topic 323). While practice varies to some extent, the cost method is generally used for investments in noncontrolled corporations, in some corporate joint ventures and, to a lesser extent, unconsolidated subsidiaries, particularly foreign. (ASC 325-20-05-2)

ACCOUNTING BY THE COST METHOD

Under the cost method, the investor recognizes an investment in stock of an investee as an asset (ASC 325-20-25-1). The investment is measured initially at cost (ASC 325-30-1). Dividends received are the basis for recognizing earnings from the investment, provided the dividends are distributed from net accumulated earnings of the investee since the date of acquisition by the investor.

Subsequent Measurement

The net accumulated earnings of the investee subsequent to the date of investment are recognized by the investor only to the extent distributed by the investee as dividends. Dividends received in excess of earning subsequent to the date of investment are considered a return of investment and recorded as reductions in the cost of the investment. (ASC 325-20-35-1)

Financial statements of an investor with an investment accounted for by the cost method may not reflect substantial changes in the affairs of the investee. For example, a series of operating losses of an investee or other factors may indicate that a decrease in the value of the investment has occurred that is other than temporary and should be recognized. (ASC 325-20-35-2)

The percentage investment in voting stock of an investee may fall below the original level of ownership due to sale of a portion of an investment by the investor, sale of additional shares of stock by the investee to other investors, or other transactions. As a result, the investor may lose the ability to influence policy, and no longer qualifies for the equity method and is required to discontinue accruing its share of the earnings or losses of the investee. In changing to the cost method, the earnings or losses that relate to the stock retained by the investor and that were previously accrued remain as part of the carrying amount of the investment. Dividends received by the investor in subsequent periods that exceed the investor's share of earnings subsequent to change from the equity method are applied to reduce the carrying amount of the investment. (ASC 325-20-35-3)

Disclosure

For cost method investments, the investor shall disclose the following, if applicable, as of the dates for which a statement of financial position is presented in its interim and annual financial statements:

- The aggregate carrying amount of all cost-method investments
- The aggregate carrying amount of cost-method investments that the investor did not evaluate for impairment
- The fact that the fair value of a cost-method investment is not estimated if there are not identified events or changes in circumstances that may have a significant adverse effect on the fair value of the investment, and any of the following:
  - — That the investor determined that it is not practicable to estimate the fair value of the investment
  - — That the investor is exempt from estimating annual fair values under Subtopic 825-10
  - — That the investor is exempt from estimating interim fair values because it does not meet the definition of a publicly traded company. (ASC 325-20-50-1)

PART II: INTERPRETIVE GUIDANCE

ASC 325-20: COST METHOD INVESTMENTS

IMPORTANT NOTICE: Under the provisions of ASU 2016-01, the guidance under ASC 325-20, *Investments—Other—Cost Method Investments*, will be superseded on the effective date: (*a*) for public business entities in fiscal years beginning after December 15, 2017, including interim periods within those fiscal years; and (*b*) for all other entities, including not-for-profit entities and employee benefit plans under the scope of ASC 960 through 965 on plan accounting, in fiscal years beginning after December 15, 2018, and interim periods within fiscal years beginning after December 15, 2019.

ASC 325-20-30-2 through 30-6 Nonmonetary Exchange of Cost-Method Investments

BACKGROUND

A cost-method investor has an investment in the common stock of a company, which is involved in a business combination. The investor will receive either new stock that represents an ownership interest in the combined entity, or the shares currently held by the investor will represent an ownership interest in the combined entity. According to the provisions of ASC 805-10-25-5, the company that will hold a majority interest in the combined entity is considered to be the acquirer. The combined company will continue to be publicly traded.

ACCOUNTING ISSUES

1. Should an investor that uses the cost method to account for an investment in shares of Company B (the *acquiree*) account for an exchange of those shares in a business combination at fair value, thus recognizing a new accounting basis in the investment and a *realized* gain or loss to the extent fair value differs from the investor's cost basis?
2. Should an investor in Company A, which is considered to be the *acquirer* in a business combination, account for a cost-method investment in the same manner as the investor in Issue 1?
3. Would an agreement on Issues 1 and 2 change if before the business combination, an investor in either company also held an investment in the other company that is a party to the transaction?

ACCOUNTING GUIDANCE

1. A cost-method investor in a company considered to be the acquiree should recognize the investment at fair value.

PRACTICE POINTER: At the effective date of ASU 2016-01 (see the Important Notice at the beginning of Part II), ASC 321-10 will provide guidance to entities that report investments in marketable equity securities at fair value. *Realized* gains on securities available for sale (not trading securities) are reported in the financial statements in income. *Unrealized* holding gains and losses are reported in the financial statements in other comprehensive income in accordance with the guidance in ASC 220-10, which amends the guidance in ASC 320, but the total amount of accumulated unrealized gains and losses should continue to be reported in a separate component of shareholders' equity until those amounts are realized. Accordingly, under the guidance on Issue 1, an investor would recognize a new cost basis in the securities of Company B exchanged for securities in the combined entity and report a realized gain or loss in income.

2. A cost-method investor in a company considered to be the acquirer should continue to carry the investment at historical cost.

PRACTICE NOTE: Although an investor would continue carrying the investment at its historical cost, under the provisions of ASC 320, as amended, an investor is required to report the fair value of the investment in its financial statements and to report *unrealized* holding gains or losses in comprehensive income.

PRACTICE NOTE: ASC 805-10-25-5 provides guidance for identifying the acquirer in a business combination, but has no effect on the guidance provided in this issue.

3. The conclusion in Issues 1 and 2 would not change if an investor in either company also held an investment in the other company before the merger.

Illustration of the Accounting Guidance

Company Z has an investment in 1,000 shares of Company T, which it carries at cost ($35,000), and an investment in 1,000 shares of Company A, which it also carries at cost ($50,000). Company T enters into a business combination with Company A. Shareholders of Company T receive 0.5 shares of stock in Company A for each share of Company T. Company A accounts for the transaction as a pooling of interests. After the combination, 1,000,000 shares of the combined entity are outstanding, of which 550,000 (or 55%) are owned by former shareholders in Company A and 450,000 shares are owned by former shareholders in Company T. The fair value of a share in the combined entity is $80.

As a result of the transaction, Company Z would own 1,500 shares of the combined entity (1,000 × .5 shares of Company T plus 1,000 shares of Company A). Based on the consensus in Issue 1, Company Z would change its basis in the 500 shares of Company A received for its stake in Company T to $40,000 (500 × $80) and would realize a gain of $5,000. Under the consensus in Issue 2, Company Z would continue carrying its investment in the combined entity at $50,000, which is the cost basis of its investment in Company A.

DISCUSSION

The underlying question in this Issue is whether the investor's exchange of shares of one entity for shares in the combined entity is an event that culminates the earnings process. That depends on whether the original investment is in the company whose shareholders receive the greater interest in the shares of the combined entity (the acquirer) or in the company whose shareholders receive the lesser interest (the acquiree). The accounting guidance reflects the view that the exchange of shares by the acquiree's shareholders results in the culmination of the earnings process. Those shareholders actually disposed of their investment in Company T (see Illustration) in exchange for shares in the combined entity in which they will not have a controlling interest.

ASC 325-30: INVESTMENTS IN INSURANCE CONTRACTS

ASC 325-30-05-3 through 05-5, 15-2 through 15-3, 25-1, 35-1 through 35-2 Accounting for Purchases of Life Insurance

BACKGROUND

The premium paid by a purchaser of life insurance serves several purposes. Part of it pays the insurer for assumption of mortality risk and provides for recovery of the insurer's contract acquisition, initiation, and maintenance costs. Part of the premium contributes to the accumulated contract value. The relative amounts of premium payment credited to various contract attributes change over time as the age of the insured person increases and as earnings are credited to previous contract values. An insurance contract is significantly different from other investment agreements. The various attributes of the policy could be obtained separately through term insurance and the purchase of separate investments, but the combination of benefits and contract values typically could not be acquired without the insurance contract.

ACCOUNTING GUIDANCE

Question: How should an entity account for an investment in life insurance?

Answer: The amount that could be realized under the contract at the date of the financial statements (i.e., the contract's cash surrender value) should be reported as an asset. The change in that value during the period is an adjustment to the amount of premium paid in recognizing expense or income for that period.

Illustration of the Accounting for a Life Insurance Contract

Roth Enterprises carries a "key-person" life insurance policy on its CEO, Susan Ray. The face value of the policy is $1 million. The cash surrender value of the policy was $50,000 at 1/1/20X4. During 20X4 Roth Enterprises paid premiums of $10,000, and the cash surrender value of the policy was $55,000 at 12/31/20X4. The cash surrender value at 12/31/20X4, $55,000, would be included as an asset on the balance sheet of Roth Enterprises. The insurance premium expense recognized on the income statement, $5,000, is the net of premiums paid, $10,000, and the increase in the policy's cash surrender value, $5,000 [$55,000– $50,000].

ASC 325-30-05-2, 05-6 through 05-9, 15-4, 30-1, 35-3 through 35-7, 50-1, 55-2 through 55-4 Accounting for Purchases of Life Insurance—Determining the Amount That Could Be Realized in Accordance with FASB Technical Bulletin No. 85-4

BACKGROUND

Some entities purchase insurance policies—corporate-owned life insurance (COLI) or bank-owned life insurance (BOLI)—to fund the cost of providing employee benefits; others do so to protect the entity against the loss of "key" employees. COLI and BOLI may be structured as:

- *Individual-life policies,* which have a contract value component and may include a surrender charge and a cash surrender value that represents the amount that could be realized if the policy is surrendered.
- *Multiple individual-life policies,* which are individual-life policies on which an employer has taken a rider at an additional cost so that the surrender charges on individual policies would be waived if all of the individual policies are surrendered at once.

- *Group life policies*, which are legal contracts with an insurance company that enables an employer to cover multiple employees with individual-life insurance. Although separate certificates are issued to the covered individuals, the group policy contract is the controlling document. Under a group life policy, a policyholder receives the full cash surrender value if an individual policy is surrendered separately.

Many policies include provisions to make them more attractive to a policyholder, such as a provision that allows the policyholder to recover certain costs. However, the policies may also include provisions, such as a prohibition against a change of control or a restructuring that occurs within the last 24 months, a prohibition against a planned restructuring within the prior 12 months, or a limit on a policyholder operating a loss carryforward position, that would limit the amount that an entity may be able to recover in cash. Additionally, a policy may require that a policyholder meet certain criteria to recover any amount. Further, the amount due to the policyholder may be received over an extended period after the insurance policy or certificate has been surrendered.

There has been diversity in practice in the calculation of the amount that would be realized on multiple individual policies with a separate group-level rider agreement, multiple individual policies with a contractual requirement in each individual policy referring to the other policies as a group, or a group life policy with multiple certificates in the form of individual life insurance for multiple employees. The issues addressed here are related to an interpretation of the phrase "the amount that could be realized under an insurance contract" in ASC 325-30, which requires that this amount be reported in the balance sheet as an asset. To calculate that amount, it is necessary to assume how the contracts are settled and whether they are surrendered individually or as a group.

ACCOUNTING ISSUES

1. Should a policyholder consider any additional amounts included in an insurance policy's contractual terms, other than its cash surrender value, when calculating the amount of cash into which an insurance policy could be converted under the guidance in ASC 325-30?
2. Should a policyholder consider its contractual ability to surrender all of the individual life insurance policies or certificates in a group policy at once when calculating the amount of cash into which the insurance policy could be converted under the guidance ASC 325-30?

ACCOUNTING GUIDANCE

- In determining the "amount that could be realized under the life insurance contract," policy holders should to take into account any contractual amounts that are included in addition to the policy's cash surrender value. Contractual limitations also should be considered when realizable amounts are determined if it is probable that those terms would limit the amounts that could be realized under an insurance contract. Amounts recoverable at an insurance company's discretion should be *excluded* from the computation of the amount that could be realized under an insurance contract. Amounts that policyholders can recover more than one year after a policy has been surrendered should be discounted based on the guidance in ASC 835-30-15.
- Policyholders should determine the "amount that could be realized under the life insurance contract" by assuming that individual life insurance contracts and individual certificates in group policies will be surrendered individually. In addition, the amount that a policyholder would ultimately realize, if any, on an assumed surrender of a final policy or a final certificate in a group policy should be included in the computation.
- If a policyholder who has made a request to surrender a policy with contractual limitations on the holder's ability to surrender the policy continues to participate in changes in the policy's cash surrender value in the same manner as before making the request, the policyholder should *not* discount the cash surrender value component of the amount that could be realized under the insurance contract. However, a future amount that could be realized under an insurance contract should be discounted under the guidance in ASC 835-30-15 if the policyholder is not permitted to participate in changes to the policy's cash surrender value because of the policy's contractual restrictions. It was noted that Internal Revenue Code Section 1035 exchanges (Sec. 1035 exchanges) do *not* represent a cash surrender as intended in ASC 325-30. A policyholder should determine the amount that could be realized under an insurance contract on a group basis if a group of individual life policies or a group policy only permit that all individual-life policies or certificates be surrendered as a group.

DISCLOSURE

Policyholders should disclose the existence of contractual restrictions on the ability to surrender a policy.

ASC 325-30-05-59A, 25-1A, 30-1B, 40-1 Accounting for Stock Received from the Demutualization of a Mutual Insurance Company

BACKGROUND

A mutual insurance company is not owned by stockholders, but by its policyholders who are members with rights by virtue of their insurance contract, the corporation's bylaws and charter, or its articles of incorporation and various laws. Such rights may include sharing in the mutual's excess capital, participating in corporate governance, receiving the corporation's remaining value on liquidation, and the expectation that the corporation will be operated to benefit the members.

Although policyholders' membership interests in a mutual differ significantly for a number of reasons from stockholders' ownership interests in a corporation, their rights are important when a mutual insurance company is demutualized and there are changes to a corporation owned by its stockholders. In that situation, the mutual entity values each policyholder's membership rights and distributes those amounts to the policyholders in stock, cash, policy enhancements, or in combination. The members' rights are extinguished in a demutualization—the members become customers and perhaps stockholders as well.

U.S. GAAP do not permit policyholders in a mutual insurance company to recognize their membership interests as an asset, because the members receive no information as to the value of those interests. Further, those interests are forfeited if the policy lapses.

ACCOUNTING ISSUE

How should a policyholder account for stock received in a demutualization of a mutual insurance company?

ACCOUNTING GUIDANCE

A member receiving stock in a demutualization of an insurance company should determine the fair value of the stock and recognize it in income as a gain from continuing operations.

ASC 325-30-15-6, 25-2; 30-1C through 30-2, 35-8 through 35-12, 40-1A, 45-1 through 45-5, 50-2 through 50-10 Accounting for Life Settlement Contracts by Third-Party Providers

BACKGROUND

The following is guidance for the initial and subsequent measurement, financial presentation, and disclosure of third-party investors' investments in life settlement contracts, which for the purpose of this guidance are contracts between owners of life insurance policies and third-party investors with the following features:

- The investor does not have the insurable interest (i.e., an interest in the insured's survival) necessary to issue an insurance policy.
- Consideration given by an investor to the policy's owner exceeds the policy's current cash surrender value.
- Under the contract, the investor will be paid the face value of the insurance policy when the insured dies.

Investments in such contracts had been accounted under the guidance in ASC 325-30-15-2 through 15-3, 35-1 through 35-2, 25-1, 05-3 through 05-5 under which investors reported the amount that could be realized on such insurance contracts as assets. As a result, investors recognized the excess of the purchase price of a life settlement contract over the cash surrender value of the underlying insurance policy as an expense.

Owners of life insurance policies enter into life settlement contracts for various reasons, such as for estate planning, compensation arrangements, and for the purpose of investing. Some have questioned whether the guidance in ASC 325-30-15-2 through 15-3, 35-1 through 35-2, 25-1, 05-3 through 05-5 should apply to life settlement contracts entered for investing purposes, because they believe that a policy's cash surrender value does *not* present the economic substance of the investing activity.

The following guidance applies to transactions in which a broker assists in the settlement transaction between a policy owner and an investor and to those that occur without a broker's assistance.

Certain provisions of ASC 325-30-15-2 through 15-3, 35-1 through 35-2, 25-1, 05-3 through 05-5 and of ASC 815 are amended by the following guidance.

ACCOUNTING GUIDANCE

Under this guidance, investors may elect to account for investments in life settlement contracts by the investment method or the fair value method. That election, which is irrevocable, should be made based on the facts of the specific contract and should be supported by contemporaneous documentation or a documented policy permitting an automatic election.

Investment Method

Under the investment method, an investor should account for an investment in a life settlement contract as follows:

- The initial investment is recognized at the price of the transaction plus all initial direct external costs.
- Continuing costs, such as policy premiums and direct external costs, if any, to keep the policy in force should be capitalized.
- No gain should be recognized until the insured has died.
- When an insured has died, an investor should recognize in earnings, or other performance indicators if an entity does not report earnings, the difference between a life settlement contract's carrying amount and the proceeds received from the underlying life insurance policy.
- An investment in a life settlement contract should be tested for impairment whenever an investor becomes aware of new or updated information indicating that, when the insured dies, the carrying amount of the investment plus expected undiscounted future premiums and capitalizable direct external costs, if any, will exceed the expected proceeds from the insurance policy. That information includes, but is not limited to, a change in expected mortality and in the creditworthiness of the underlying insurance policy's issuer. Testing a life settlement contract for impairment is *not* necessary if only a change in interest rates occurs.
- An impairment loss should be recognized if expected undiscounted cash inflows (generally, the insurance proceeds) are less than an investment's carrying amount plus expected undiscounted future premiums and capitalizable direct external costs, if any. If there are expected discounted future premiums and capitalizable direct external costs, the investment should be written down to fair value.
- Current interest rates should be considered in the fair value measurement.

Fair Value Method

Under the fair value measurement method, an investor should account for an investment in a life settlement contract as follows:

- An initial investment in a life settlement contract should be accounted for at its transaction price.
- In subsequent periods, the entire investment should be remeasured at fair value at each reporting period and changes in the investment's fair value should be recognized in earnings in the period in which they occur or by other performance indicators if an entity does not report earnings.
- Premiums paid and life insurance proceeds received should be reported on the same financial reporting line in which changes in fair value are reported.

Financial Statement Presentation

1. *Balance sheet presentation*

Investments that are remeasured at fair value should be reported on the face of the balance sheet separately from investments reported under the investment method. Investors may elect to use one of the following presentation alternatives:

a. Display the carrying amounts of investments accounted for under the fair value method on a separate line from those accounted for under the investment method.

b. Display the total carrying amount of investments accounted for under the fair value method and those accounted for under the investment method and parenthetically disclose separate information about the carrying amounts of the investments accounted for under each method.

2. *Income statement presentation*

Investment income from investments in life settlement contracts that are remeasured at fair value should be presented separately on the face of the income statement from investment income on such investments accounted for under the investment method. Investors may elect one of the following presentation alternatives:

a. Display income from investments in life settlement contracts accounted for under the fair value method and income from such investments accounted for under the investment method as separate line items.
b. Display the total amount of investment income from investments in life settlement contracts accounted for under the fair value method with the investment income from such contracts accounted for under the investment method and parenthetically disclose separate information about the investment income from investments accounted for under each method.

3. *Statement of cash flows presentation*

Cash receipts and cash payments related to life settlement contracts under the guidance in ASC 230 should be classified based on the nature and purpose for which the life settlement contracts were acquired.

4. *Disclosures*

Investors should disclose the following information:

a. The accounting policy for life settlement contracts, including the classification of cash receipts and disbursements in the statement of cash flows.
b. The disclosures required in other U.S. pronouncements of generally accepted accounting principles, including other disclosure requirements regarding the use of fair value.
c. Life settlement contracts accounted for under the investment method:
   (1) Based on the remaining life expectancy for each of the first five succeeding years from the balance-sheet date and thereafter, as well as the total, the number of life settlement contracts, the carrying values, and the death benefits of the underlying insurance policies.
   (2) The nature of new or updated information that causes a change in an investor's expectations on the timing of realization of proceeds from investments in life settlement contracts, including the information in item (1) above. However, investors are *not* required to seek out such information to update the assumptions used to determine the remaining life expectancy of their life settlement contracts.
d. Life settlement contracts accounted for under the fair value method:
   (1) The methods and significant assumptions used to estimate the fair value of investments in life settlement contracts, including mortality assumptions, if any.
   (2) Based on the remaining life expectancy for each of the first five succeeding years from the balance-sheet date and thereafter, the total number of life settlement contracts, the carrying values, and the death benefits of the underlying insurance policies.
   (3) Reasons for changes in the expectation of the timing of realization of investments in life settlement contracts, including significant changes to amounts disclosed in item (2) above.
e. For each period reported in the income statement:
   (1) Gains and losses recognized during the period on investments sold during the period.
   (2) Unrecognized gains or losses recognized during the period on investments still held at the balance sheet date.

ASC 325-30-35-1 Recognition of Insurance Death Benefits

BACKGROUND

Some companies purchase life insurance policies to cover the lives of certain employees, with the company as the beneficiary. Such policies, referred to as corporate-owned life insurance (COLI) policies, are used for various purposes: (*a*) to protect the company if a key employee dies; (*b*) to accumulate funds to finance a shareholder/partner buy/sell agreement in case a shareholder/partner dies or leaves the company; or (*c*) to fund the employer's obligations to certain employee benefit plans, such as pension plans, by borrowing against the policy.

In the past, companies have recognized income on COLI policies when proceeds were received upon the death of an employee. Because companies were taking out policies on certain groups of employees, it was suggested that income from death benefits on COLI policies could be recognized over the estimated period of the employees' lives on an actuarially projected basis.

ACCOUNTING ISSUES

1. Should an entity recognize income on death benefits from COLI policies on an actuarially projected basis or upon the death of the insured?
2. If a company intends to retain COLI policies in force until the death of the insured and to borrow against them, should the company recognize the policy as an asset at the policy's net loan value, which is the maximum amount that the entity can contractually borrow against the policy, or at its cash surrender value?

ACCOUNTING GUIDANCE

1. A purchaser of life insurance should not recognize income from death benefits based on actuarial projections. Under the guidance in ASC 325-30-15-2 through 15-3, 35-1 through 35-2, 25-1, 05-3 through 05-5, a purchaser is required to recognize an asset for the amount at which the policy could be realized on the date of the financial statements. Because a death benefit may not be realized before the insured's actual death, recognition of death benefits on an actuarially projected basis is an inappropriate means of measuring the asset.
2. It was noted that the guidance in ASC 325-30-15-2 through 15-3, 35-1 through 35-2, 25-1, 05-3 through 05-5, specifies that the asset should be measured at its cash surrender value and that changes in that value be used to adjust policy premiums. The issue whether it is appropriate to recognize the difference between the cash surrender value and premiums paid as a temporary difference has been resolved by the guidance in ASC 740-10-25-30, which states that "[t]hat excess is a temporary difference if the cash surrender value is expected to be recovered by surrendering the policy, but it is not a temporary difference if the asset is expected to be recovered without tax consequences upon the death of the insured (there will be no taxable amount if the insurance policy is held until the death of the insured)."

ASC 325-40: BENEFICIAL INTERESTS IN SECURITIZED FINANCIAL ASSETS

ASC 325-40-05-1 through 05-2, 15-2 through 15-9, 25-1 through 25-3, 30-1 through 30-3, 35-1 through 35-13, 35-15 through 35-16, 45-1, 55-1 through 55-25, 60-7; ASC 310-20-60-1 through 60-2; ASC 310-30-15-5; ASC 320-10-35-38, 55-2 Recognition of Interest Income and Impairment on Purchased Beneficial Interests and Transferor's Beneficial Interests in Securitized Financial Assets Obtained in a Transfer Accounted for as a Sale

BACKGROUND

PRACTICE NOTE: In June 2009, the FASB issued the guidance in ASC 860-10-35-4, 35-6, 05-8; ASC 860-20-25-5, 55-46 through 55-48; ASC 460-10-60-35; ASC 860-50-05-2 through 05-4, 30-1 through 30-2, 35-1A, 35-3, 35-9 through 35-11, 25-2 through 25-3, 25-6, 50-5, which has amended the guidance discussed below.

Scope

This guidance applies to beneficial interests that a transferor *acquires as proceeds* in securitization transactions accounted for as sales under the guidance in ASC 860 as amended by ASC 860-10-35-4, 35-6, 05-8; 860-20-25-5, 55-46 through 55-48; 460-10-60-35; 860-50-05-2 through 05-4, 30-1, 30-2, 35-1A, 35-3, 35-9 through 35-11, 25-2 through 25-3, 25-6, 50-5 and to *purchased* beneficial interests in securitized financial assets. This guidance also applies to beneficial interests that are:

- Debt securities accounted for under the guidance in ASC 310 or required to be accounted for like debt securities in accordance with the guidance in ASC 860-20-35-2; ASC 320-35-45, as amended by the guidance in ASC 860-10-35-4, 35-6, 05-8; ASC 860-20-25-5, 55-46 through 55-48; ASC 460-10-60-35; 860-50-05-2 through 05-4, 30-1 through 30-2, 35-1A, 35-3, 35-9 through 35-11; 25-2, 25-3, 25-6, 50-5.
- Securitized financial assets that have contractual cash flows, such as loans, receivables, and guaranteed lease residuals (The guidance in ASC 320-10-35-38 through 35-43, 55-10 through 55-12, 55-16 through 55-19; ASC 835-10-60-6 applies to securitized financial assets that do not involve contractual cash flows, such as common stock equity securities.)
- Financial instruments that do not cause an entity holding the beneficial interests to consolidate the entity that issued the beneficial interests (e.g., a special purpose entity).
- Not included under the scope of AICPA Practice Bulletin 6 (not in ASC), as amended by ASC 310-10-35-12 through 35-14, 35-16 through 35-26, 35-28 through 35-29, 35-32, 35-34, 35-37, 35-39; 45-5 through 45-6, 50-13, 50-15, 50-19; ASC 310-30-30-2; ASC 310-40-35-8 through 45-9, 45-12; ASC 310-40-50-2 through 50-3, 50-12 and ASC 320-10-05-2, 15-2

through 15-5, 15-7, 25-1, 25-3 through 25-6, 25-9, 25-12, 25-14 through 25-16, 25-18, 30-1, 35-1 through 35-2, 35-4 through 35-5, 35-10 through 35-13, 35-18, 45-1 through 45-2, 45-8 through 45-11, 45-13, 50-1A through 50-3, 50-5, 50-9 through 50-11, 55-3; ASC 942-320-50-1 through 50-3 and ASC 310-30-05-2 through 05-3, 15-1 through 15-4, 15-6 through 15-10, 25-1, 30-1, 35-2 through 35-3, 35-6, 35-8 through 35-15, 40-1, 45-1, 50-1 through 50-3, 50-18, 55-5, 55-29; ASC 835-10-60-3.

- (*a*) Not beneficial interests in securitized financial assets with high credit quality (e.g., guaranteed by the U.S. government) so that the possibility of credit loss is remote and (*b*) do not permit a debtor to prepay or settle the obligation so that the holder would not recover substantially all of its recorded investment. Interest income on such beneficial interests should be recognized in accordance with the guidance in ASC 310-20. The guidance in ASC 320-10-35-38 through 35-43; 55-10 through 55-12, 55-16 through 55-19; ASC 835-10-60-6, ASC 320, SEC Staff Bulletin 59, and Statement of Auditing Standards 92, should be followed to determine whether an other-than-temporary impairment of such beneficial assets exists.
- Issued in equity form but meet the definition of a "debt security" in the ASC, Glossary, such as (*a*) a right to receive a future stream of cash flows under specified terms and conditions or (*b*) that must be redeemed by the issuer or must be redeemable at the investor's option. Classified as trading securities under the guidance in ASC 320, because under U.S. GAAP, entities in certain industries, such as banks and investment companies, are required to report investment income as a separate item in the income statement even though those entities report their investments at fair value and report changes in value in earnings. The fact that beneficial interests are classified as held-to-maturity, available-for-sale, or trading should not affect the recognition and measurement of interest income on those instruments.
- The portions of hybrid beneficial interests referred to as host contracts, if they meet the scope requirements. A host contract must be separated from a hybrid instrument's embedded derivative, which must be accounted for separately according to the guidance in ASC 815-15-05-1, 35-2A, 25-1, 25-14, 25-26 through 25-29; ASC 815-10-15-72 through 15-73. Hybrid beneficial interests measured at fair value in accordance with the guidance in ASC 815-15-30-1 are not included under the scope if a transferor does not report interest income from those instruments as a separate item in the income statement.

In accordance with the guidance in ASC 325-40-15-6, as amended by ASU 2016-01 (see effective date information in the Important Notice regarding ASU 2016-01), beneficial interests issued in the form of equity that do not meet the criteria for a debt security in ASC 325-40-15-5 are not under the scope of this issue and should be accounted for under the guidance in ASC 323-10, the applicable consolidation guidance, or ASC 321-10.

ACCOUNTING ISSUE

How should a transferor that retains an interest in securitized financial assets or an entity that purchases a beneficial interest in securitized financial assets account for income and impairment?

ACCOUNTING GUIDANCE

1. The holder of a beneficial interest should estimate at the date the beneficial interest is acquired (the transaction date) the amount by which all cash flows that will be received from the beneficial interest will exceed the initial investment (the accretable yield). The holder should use the effective yield method to recognize that amount as interest income over the life of the beneficial interest. The initial investment is the fair value of the beneficial interest as of the transfer date if the holder also is the transferor as required under the guidance in ASC 860, as amended by the guidance in ASC 860-10-35-4, 35-6, 05-8; ASC 860-20-25-5, 55-46 through 55-48; ASC 460-10-60-35; 860-50-05-2 through 05-4, 30-1 through 30-2, 35-1A, 35-3, 35-9 through 35-11, 25-2 through 25-3, 25-6; 50-5. The accretable yield should not be presented in the balance sheet. According to ASC 325-40-25-2, as amended by ASU 2016-01, if a beneficial interest is issued in the form of equity or is classified as a trading debt security, the difference between its carrying amount and fair value should be recorded through earnings as a gain or a loss.
2. The estimated cash flows should be adjusted over the life of the beneficial interest if:
   a. Based on the estimated fair value of the beneficial interest, using current information and events, it is probable that estimated cash flows will be more or less than the previous projection. An investor should recalculate the amount of the accretable yield for the beneficial interest on that date as the excess of estimated cash flows over the sum of (*a*) the initial investment *less* (*b*) cash received to date *less* (*c*) other-than-temporary impairment recognized to date *plus* (*d*) the yield accreted to date. The adjustment should be recognized prospectively as a change in estimate in accordance with the guidance in ASC 250 and the periodic accretion should be adjusted

over the life of the beneficial interest. Based on cash flows, interest income may be recognized on a beneficial interest, even if accretion of the net investment in the beneficial interest results in an amount that exceeds the amount at which the beneficial interest could be settled if the entire amount were prepaid immediately.

b. A beneficial interest's fair value is less than its reference amount. The guidance on impairment of securities in ASC 320-10-45-9 should be applied to determine whether a decline is other-than-temporary. If based on the holder's best estimate of cash flows, all of the cash flows estimated in accordance with paragraph 2a above will not be collected, an other-than-temporary impairment has occurred and the beneficial interest should be written down to fair value. The change in value should be included in income. However, an other-than-temporary impairment need not be recognized if a change in the interest rate of a *plain vanilla* variable rate beneficial interest occurs without other indicators of impairment. To determine whether a favorable or adverse change in estimated cash flows from the amount previously projected (based on the timing and amount of estimated cash flows) has occurred, the present value of the remaining cash flows estimated at the initial transaction date, or the last date on which the amount was previously revised, should be compared to the present value of estimated cash flows at the current financial reporting date. Cash flows should be discounted at a rate that equals the current yield used to accrete the beneficial interest. A change is considered to be favorable—that is, an other-than-temporary impairment has *not* occurred—if the present value of the current estimated cash flows exceeds the present value of the estimated cash flows at the initial transaction date or the last date at which the amount was previously revised. A change is considered to be adverse—that is, an other-than-temporary impairment has occurred—if the present value of the current estimated cash flows is less than the present value of estimated cash flows at the initial transaction date or the last date at which the amount was previously revised.

3. At the transaction date, estimated cash flows are defined as the estimate of the amount and timing of future cash flows of principal and interest used to determine the purchase price or the holder's fair value for gain or loss recognition under the guidance in ASC 860. Thereafter, estimated cash flows are defined as the holder's estimate of the amount and timing of estimated cash flows from principal and interest payments, based on the holder's best assessment of current information and events a market participant would use to determine the current fair value of a beneficial interest. A favorable or adverse change in estimated cash flows is considered in terms of the timing and amount of estimated cash flows.

4. An entity that intends to sell a retained interest classified as available-for-sale should recognize a loss on an other-than-temporary impairment at the time a decision to sell is made, if the retained interest will be sold at a loss shortly after the balance sheet date, its fair value is less than its carrying amount, and it is not expected to recover before the date of an expected sale. The guidance in SAB-59, SAS-81, and ASC 860 should also be considered in determining whether an other-than-temporary impairment exists.

5. The cost recovery method should be used if a beneficial interest is placed on nonaccrual status or if a holder cannot reliably estimate the security's cash flows.

PRACTICE POINTER: Under the guidance in ASC 810, an entity that absorbs a majority of a variable entity's expected losses or has the right to receive a greater part of a variable entity's expected residual returns or both is required to consolidate that variable interest entity.

PRACTICE POINTER: The guidance in ASC 815 is amended by the guidance in ASC 815-15-25-4 through 25-5, which provides an election for the fair value measurement of certain hybrid financial instruments with embedded derivatives that otherwise would have to be bifurcated. If an entity elects to account for an entire hybrid financial instrument at fair value, that financial instrument should not be used as a hedging instrument in a hedging relationship under the guidance in ASC 815.

PRACTICE POINTER: Although the guidance in ASC 860-50-35-3, 35-6 through 35-7, 50-5 amends the accounting guidance in ASC 860 for separately recognized servicing assets and servicing liabilities, it does not affect the guidance herein. The guidance in ASC 325-40-05-1 through 05-2, 15-2 through 15-9, 25-1 through 25-3, 30-1 through 30-3, 35-1 through 35-13, 35-15 through 35-16, 45-1, 55-1 through 55-25, 60-7; ASC 310-20-60-1 through 60-2; ASC 310-30-15-5; ASC

320-10-35-38, 55-2 represents the FASB's decision in ASC 860-50-35-3, 35-6 through 35-7, 50-5 to replace the term "retained interests" with "interests that continue to be held by a transferor".

PRACTICE POINTER: The guidance in ASC 860-10-35-4, 35-6, 05-8; ASC 860-20-25-5, 55-46 through 55-48; ASC 460-10-60-35; ASC 860-50-05-2 through 05-4, 30-1 through 30-2, 35-1A, 35-3, 35-9 through 35-11, 25-2 through 25-3, 25-6, 50-5 amends the previous guidance in ASC 860 by eliminating the concept of a special-purpose entity and the scope exception that exempted special-purpose entities from following the guidance in ASC 810. Under the guidance in ASC 810, derecognition provisions should be applied to a transfer of an entire financial asset, a group of entire financial assets, or a participating interest in an entire financial asset. In addition, interests acquired by a transferor on completion of a transfer of an entire financial asset or an entire group of financial assets that meet the conditions to be accounted for as a sale should be recognized and measured initially at fair value. The term "interests that continue to be held by a transferor" as it is used in ASC 860, applies only if a transferor retains participating interests on completion of a transfer of participating rights in a transaction that meets the conditions to be accounted for as a sale. Under the guidance in ASC 860-10-35-4, 35-6, 05-8; ASC 860-20-25-5, 55-46 through 55-48; ASC 460-10-60-35; ASC 860-50-05-2 through 05-4, 30-1 through 30-2, 35-1A, 35-3, 35-9 through 35-11, 25-2 through 25-3, 25-6, 50-5, that term should be used only for such retained participation rights.

CHAPTER 23

ASC 326—FINANCIAL INSTRUMENTS—CREDIT LOSSES

CONTENTS

PART I: GENERAL GUIDANCE

ASC 326-10: OVERALL

OVERVIEW

The primary objective of ASC 326 is to provide decision-useful information about the expected credit losses on financial instruments and other commitments to extend credit held by a reporting entity. This guidance replaces the prior incurred loss impairment methodology with a methodology that reflects expected credit losses. It requires consideration of a broad range of reasonable and supportable information to support estimates of credit losses, including more timely and forecasted information believed to be useful to financial statement users. ASC 326 affects entities that hold financial assets and net investments in leases that are not accounted for at fair value through net income. This includes loans, debt securities, trade receivables, net investments in leases, off-balance-sheet credit exposures, reinsurance receivables, and any other financial assets that include the contractual right to receive cash.

ASC 326 provides guidance on how entities should measure expected credit losses on financial instruments:

- Measured at amortized cost and on leases
- That are debt securities, including loans, classified as available-for-sale securities (ASC 326-10-05-2)

BACKGROUND

Assets measured at amortized cost are presented at the net amount expected to be collected. An allowance for credit loss valuation account is deducted from amortized cost to determine the net carrying value at the amount expected to be collected. The income statement reflects the measurement of credit losses from newly recognized financial assets, as well as the expected increase or decrease in the expected credit losses that will have taken place during the period. The expected credit losses is based on relevant information about past events, including historical experience, current conditions, and reasonable and supportable forecasts that affect the collectibility of the reported amount. Judgment is required to determine the relevant information and estimation methods that are appropriate in specific circumstances.

Illustration of Current Expected Credit Loss Model

A company has a pool of loans to builders with similar risk characteristics that it estimates expected credit losses on a collective basis. Amortized cost of this loan pool is $5,000,000 and the historical loss rate on these loans has been 1%. Using the methodology in place before ASC 326, this historical loss rate would have been used to calculate an allowance for credit losses of $50,000.

However, ASC 326 now requires the entity to also consider changes management expects to occur based on reasonable and supportable forecasts. Management expects costs of building supplies to increase substantially in the coming year so it makes adjustments of 0.5% to its loss rate such that the expected credit loss rate is estimated to be 1.5% and the allowance for credit losses should now be reported as $75,000.

The allowance for credit losses for purchased financial assets with a more-than-insignificant amount of credit deterioration since origination that are measured at amortized cost is determined in a similar manner to other financial assets measured at amortized cost. The initial allowance for credit losses, however is added to the purchase price rather than being reported as a credit loss expense. Subsequent changes in the allowance for credit losses are recognized as a credit loss expense. Interest income for these assets is recognized based on the effective interest rate, excluding the discount included in the purchase price that is attributed to the acquirer's assessment of credit losses at acquisition.

Credit losses related to available-for-sale debt securities are recorded through an allowance for credit losses. The amount of the allowance for credit losses is limited to the amount by which fair value is below amortized cost because the classification as available-for-sale is based on the premise of an investment strategy that recognizes the investment could be sold at fair value, if cash collection would result in the realization of an amount less than fair value.

The allowance for credit losses for purchased available-for-sale securities with a more-than-insignificant amount of credit deterioration since origination is determined in a manner similar to other available-for-sale debt securities. The initial allowance for credit losses is added to the purchase price rather than reported as a credit loss expense. Only subsequent changes in the allowance for credit losses are recorded as credit loss expense. Interest income is recognized based on the effective interest rate, excluding the discount embedded in the purchase price that relates to the acquirer's assessment of credit losses at acquisition.

TRANSITION AND EFFECTIVE DATE INFORMATION

For public business entities that are SEC filers, excluding entities eligible as smaller reporting companies, the amendments became effective for fiscal years *beginning* after December 15, 2019, and for interim periods within those fiscal years. The one-time determination of whether an entity is eligible to be a smaller reporting company was based on the entity's most recent determination as of November 15, 2019. For all other entities, the amendments are effective for fiscal years *beginning* after December 15, 2022, including interim periods within those fiscal years. All entities had the option to adopt the amendments earlier as of fiscal years beginning after December 15, 2018, including interim periods within those fiscal years. (ASC 326-01-65-1)

The changes in ASC 326 are applied using a modified-retrospective approach, by a cumulative-effect adjustment to opening retained earnings as of the beginning of the first reporting period in which the guidance is effective. For purchased financial assets with credit deterioration, a prospective approach should be applied, adjusting the amortized cost basis to reflect the addition of the allowance for credit losses. The remaining non-credit discount or premium should be accreted into interest income at the effective interest rate at the adoption date of ASC 326. For debt securities for which an other-than-temporary impairment had been recognized before the adoption date of ASC 326, a prospective approach should be applied to ensure the amortized cost basis and effective interest rate remain unchanged. Amounts previously recognized in accumulated other comprehensive income should continue to be accreted into interest income over the remaining life of the debt security and any recoveries of amounts previously written off should be recorded to income in the period received. (ASC 326-10-65-1)

Targeted transition relief has been provided for entities using the fair value option for newly originated or purchased financial assets that had existing financial assets reported at amortized cost. Entities are permitted to irrevocably elect the fair value option on an instrument-by-instrument basis for all financial instruments described in ASC 326-20-15-2 except for held-to-maturity debt securities. (ASC 326-10-65-1) This transition relief is effective when the entity first applies ASC 326 or, if ASC 326 has already been adopted, for fiscal years beginning after December 15, 2019, including interim periods within those fiscal years. This change should be made by a cumulative-effect adjustment to opening retained earnings as of the beginning of the first reporting period in which the guidance is effective. (ASC 326-10-65-2)

The FASB expects that an entity can leverage its current systems and methods for recording the allowance for credit losses. The inputs used to record the allowance will need to appropriately reflect an estimate of expected credit losses and the use of reasonable and supportable forecasts.

In the period an entity adopts ASC 326, the following disclosures should be made:

- The nature of the change in accounting principle and an explanation of the newly adopted accounting principle
- The method of applying the change
- Any material effects of adoption on line items in the statement of financial position as of the beginning of the first period for which ASC 326 is effective
- The cumulative effect of the change in retained earnings and other equity components in the statement of financial position as of the beginning of the first period for which ASC 325 is effective (ASC 326-10-65-1)

EXPECTED CREDIT LOSSES ON FINANCIAL INSTRUMENTS MEASURED AT AMORTIZED COST

Scope

This guidance (ASC 326-20-15-2) applies to all entities for the following items:

- Financial assets measured at amortized cost including financing receivables; held-to-maturity debt securities; receivables from revenue transactions that fall under the scope of ASC 605, ASC 606, or ASC 610; and repurchase and securities lending agreement receivables within the scope of ASC 860
- Net investments in leases recognized by the lessor in accordance with ASC 842
- Off-balance-sheet credit exposures not accounted for as insurance
- Reinsurance receivables within the scope of ASC 944 (ASC 326-20-15-2)

The guidance in this Subtopic (ASC 326-20-15-3) does not apply to:

- Financial assets measured at fair value through net income
- Available-for-sale debt securities
- Participant loans from defined contribution employee benefit plans
- Insurance policy loan receivables
- Not-for-profit pledges receivable
- Loans and receivables between entities under common control (ASC 326-20-15-3)
- Receivables arising from operating leases accounted for in accordance with Topic 842

Initial Measurement

Estimates of expected credit losses are recorded as an allowance for credit losses, a valuation account presented separately on the statement of financial position and deducted from or added to the amortized cost basis of the financial asset or assets to present the net amount expected to be collected. The allowance should include expected recoveries or write-offs and expected write-offs up to the amount previously written off or expected to be written off. A credit loss expense will be reported in net income for the amount of the adjustment to the allowance for credit losses. If financial assets have similar risk characteristics, they can be reported, and their expected credit losses can be estimated on a pool basis; however, if the financial assets' risk characteristics are unique, any expected credit losses should be evaluated on an individual basis. (ASC 326-20-30-1 through 2)

An entity can choose from various methods to develop an estimate of expected credit losses. If an entity uses a discounted cash flow method, then expected cash flows should be discounted at the financial asset's effective interest rate. If the contractual interest rate of the financial asset changes based on an index or rate, such as the prime rate, then the effective interest rate should be based on that index or rate as it changes over the life of the financial asset. If an entity chooses to project changes in the index or rate to estimate expected future cash flows, those same projections should be used to determine the effective interest rate and the effective interest rate should be adjusted to consider the timing of expected cash flows from expected prepayments. As long as an asset has not been restructured in a troubled debt restructuring, the effective interest rate used to discount expected cash flows may be adjusted on a class of financing receivable or major security-type level to consider the timing of expected cash flows from expected prepayments. The allowance for credit losses that is calculated will then reflect the difference between the amortized cost basis and the present value of the expected cash flows. (ASC 326-20-30-4 through 4A) The change in present value may result from the passage of time and from changes in estimates of the timing or amount of expected cash flows. This entire change may be presented as credit loss expense or the portion of the change due to the passage of time may be reported as interest income. (ASC 326-20-45-3)

If an entity uses a method other than discounted cash flows to estimate expected credit losses, then the allowance for credit losses will reflect the entity's expected credit losses of the amortized cost basis of the financial asset as of the reporting date. Entities may measure the amortized cost basis on a combined basis or by separately measuring its components: the amortized cost basis excluding applicable accrued interest, applicable accrued interest, and any premiums or discounts, foreign exchange, and fair value hedge accounting adjustments. An entity may elect not to measure allowance for credit losses for accrued interest receivables at the class of financing receivable or major security-type level if uncollectible accrued interest receivables are written off in a timely manner. (ASC 326-20-30-5 through 5A)

Estimated prepayments should be considered in future principal and interest cash flows if using a discounted cash flow method and either considered separately or embedded in other credit loss information if using a different method to estimate expected credit losses. The contractual term should not be extended for expected extensions, renewals, and modifications unless the entity has a reasonable expectation of executing a troubled debt restructuring with the borrower or there are extension or renewal options in the contract that are not unconditionally cancellable by the entity. Relevant, available information regarding cash flow collectibility should be considered when developing an estimate of expected credit losses, including both quantitative and qualitative factors. Historical loss experience internal and external to the entity should also be taken into consideration and adjusted as needed to reflect changes management expects given current and forecasted conditions. An entity should include a measure of the expected risk of credit loss in its estimate of expected credit losses, which may be zero in some instances. Credit enhancements that may mitigate expected credit losses on financial assets should be included in the estimate of expected credit losses unless they are freestanding contracts, such as a purchased credit-default swap. (ASC 326-20-30-6 through 12)

PRACTICE POINTER: Unless an entity has a reasonable expectation that it will execute a troubled debt restructuring with a borrower at the reporting date, then the contractual term of the financial asset should not be extended for expected extensions, renewals, or modifications. (ASC 326-20-30-6)

PRACTICE POINTER: For net investment in leases recognized by a lessor in accordance with ASC 842, an entity shall use the lease term as the contractual term rather than applying the guidance in ASC 326-20-30-6.

If an entity has purchased financial assets with credit deterioration, then the allowance for credit losses at the acquisition date should be added to the purchase price to determine the initial amortized cost basis. If there is a pool of purchased financial assets with credit deterioration, any non-credit discount or premium should be allocated to each individual asset. If expected credit losses are estimated using a discounted cash flow method, the discount rate used should equate the asset's purchase price with the present value of the purchaser's estimate of the asset's future cash flows. The allowance for credit losses for purchased financial assets with credit deterioration shall include expected recoveries of amounts previously written off and expected to be written off by the entity and shall not exceed the aggregate of amounts previously written off and expected to be written off. If a method other than a discounted cash flow method is used to estimate expected credit losses, expected recoveries shall not include any amounts that resulted in an acceleration of the noncredit discount. The entity may include increases in expected cash flows after acquisition. (ASC 326-20-30-13 through 14)

Subsequent Measurement

Entities should compare the current estimates of expected credit loss with estimates previously recorded and report a credit loss expense or reversal of credit loss expense in net income for the amount of the adjustment to the allowance for credit losses. The risk characteristics of financial assets should be reevaluated to determine if they remain in the same grouping or need to be moved to another pool or be measured individually. (ASC 326-20-35-1 through 2)

Estimates of expected credit losses of off-balance-sheet credit exposures should also be adjusted and recorded on the financial statements. The estimate of expected credit losses should be presented as a liability in the statement of financial position and should be recorded separately from the allowance for credit losses related to recognized financial instruments. (ASC 326-20-45-2)

To avoid delay in reporting credit losses, if foreclosure of a collateral-dependent financial asset is probable, an entity should remeasure the financial asset and expected credit losses at the reporting date using the fair value of the collateral less estimated selling costs if the asset will be sold and not operated regardless of the measurement method initially used. If a borrower is experiencing financial difficulty, an entity may determine that it expects repayment on a collateral-dependent financial asset to be provided through operation or sale of that asset. In this situation, the entity can use the practical expedient of the fair value of the collateral (adjusted for estimated selling costs if repayment depends on the asset's sale) when recording the net carrying amount and allowance for credit losses of that financial asset. If the fair value of the collateral equals or exceeds the amortized cost basis, an entity should adjust the allowance to present the net amount expected to be collected to the fair value of the collateral so long as the allowance added to the amortized cost basis of the financial asset does not exceed amounts previously written off. (ASC 326-20-35-4 through 5)

For certain financial assets, the borrower may be contractually required to continually adjust the amount of the collateral securing the financial assets as a result of fair value exchanges in the collateral. If the entity reasonably expects the borrower to continue to replenish the collateral to meet the requirements of the collateral, as a practical expedient the entity may use a method that compares the amortized cost basis with the fair value of collateral at the reporting date to measure the estimate of expected credit losses. The expectation of non-payment is zero if the fair value of the collateral is equal to or exceeds the amortized cost basis of the financial asset and the entity reasonably expects the borrower to continue to replenish the collateral to meet the contract requirements. If the fair value of the collateral is less than the amortized cost, and the entity reasonably expects the borrower to continue to replenish the collateral, the entity shall estimate expected credit losses for the unsecured amount of the amortized cost basis. The allowance for credit losses on the financial asset is limited to the difference between the fair value of the collateral at the reporting date and the amortized cost basis of the financial asset. (ASC 326-20-35-6)

PRACTICE POINTER: If a decision is made to sell a loan that was measured at amortized cost, the loan should be transferred to the held-for-sale classification. (ASC 326-20-35-7)

PRACTICE POINTER: If a financial asset is partially or fully written off, the write-offs should be deducted from the allowance in the period the financial asset is deemed uncollectible. An entity may elect to write off accrued interest receivables at the class of financing receivable or major security-type level by reversing interest income, recognizing credit loss expense, or both. (ASC 326-20-35-8 through 8A)

Disclosure Requirements

The disclosure requirements in ASC 326-20 are designed to enable a financial statement user to understand:

- A portfolio's credit risk and how management monitors the portfolio's credit quality
- Management's estimate of expected credit losses
- Changes in the estimate of expected credit losses during the period (ASC 326-20-50-2)

An entity should determine the appropriate amount of detail to provide in disclosures not only to ensure important information is not hidden in overly aggregated disclosures but also to prevent burdening financial statement users with excessive detail. Disclosures should be made by portfolio segment or class for financing receivables and net investment in leases. Disclosures for held-to-maturity debt securities should be made by major security type. (ASC 326-20-50-3)

An entity may present the accrued interest receivable balance net of the allowance for credit losses separately or within another statement of financial position line item, in which case both the amount and statement of financial position line item in which it is included should be disclosed. Entities electing not to measure an allowance for credit losses for accrued interest receivables should disclose what it considers timely for writing off uncollectible accrued interest receivables. Entities electing to write off accrued interest receivables should disclose the amount of accrued interest receivables written off by portfolio segment or major security type. Any accrued interest receivable balance can be excluded from the amortized cost basis disclosures in ASC 326-20-50-4 through 22; if this practical expedient is elected, the total amount of accrued interest excluded should be disclosed. (ASC 326-20-50-3A through 3D)

Credit quality information should be disclosed to enable financial statement users to understand how management monitors credit quality of its financial assets and to assess the quantitative and qualitative risks associated with that credit quality. The quantitative and qualitative credit quality information that should be disclosed by class of financing receivable and major security type includes:

- A description of the credit quality indicators
- Amortized cost basis by credit quality indicator
- The date or range of dates the information for each credit quality indicator was updated (ASC 326-20-50-4 through 5)

Public business entities are required, and other entities are permitted to disclose the amortized cost basis within each credit quality indicator by origination year. If financing receivables or net investment in leases have been purchased, the origination year is the initial date of issuance, not the year of purchase. If an entity has line-of-credit arrangements converted to term loans, the amount should be disclosed by class of financing receivable and the amortized cost basis should be presented in a separate column. Except as previously described, if a financing receivable is modified, extended, or renewed or a lease is modified, the guidance in ASC 310 and ASC 842, respectively, should be used to determine whether that financial asset should be presented as a current-period origination. (ASC-326-20-50-6 through 7)

The information about the allowance for credit losses provided in disclosures should allow financial statement users to understand management's method for developing its allowance for credit losses, the information used to develop the current estimate of expected credit losses, and the circumstances causing changes to the allowance for credit losses reported for the period. To accomplish this, the following information should be disclosed by portfolio segment and major security type:

- A description of how expected loss estimates are developed
- The entity's accounting policies and method used to estimate the allowance for credit losses, including the past events, current conditions, and future forecasts influencing management's current estimate
- Relevant risk characteristics for each portfolio segment
- Changes in factors that influenced management's current estimate of expected credit losses and the reasons for those changes
- Changes to the entity's accounting policies and methodology from the prior period, the rationale for those changes, and their quantitative effect
- Reasons for any significant changes in write-off amounts
- A discussion of the reversion method applied for periods beyond the reasonable and supportable forecast period
- The amount of any significant financial asset purchases, sales, or reclassifications of loans held for sale during the reporting period (ASC 326-20-50-10 through 11)

Quantitative disclosures of the activity in the allowance for credit losses should be disclosed by portfolio segment and major security type, including the beginning balance in the allowance for credit losses; the current-period provision for expected credit losses; the initial allowance for credit losses for any purchased financial assets with credit deterioration; write-offs, recoveries collected; and the ending balance in the allowance for credit losses. (ASC 326-20-50-13)

If an entity has financial assets that are past due, an aging analysis of the amortized cost basis should be disclosed. For any financial assets on nonaccrual status, the entity should include in the summary of significant accounting policies its policies for nonaccrual, determining past-due or delinquency status, and recognizing write-offs in the allowance for credit losses. The following information should be disclosed for financial assets on nonaccrual status:

- The amortized cost basis of at the beginning and end of the reporting period
- The amount of interest income recognized during the period
- The amortized cost basis of financial assets 90 days or more past due but not on nonaccrual status
- The amortized cost basis of financial assets on nonaccrual status for which there is no related allowance for credit losses at the reporting date (ASC 326-20-50-15 through 17)

For purchased financial assets with credit deterioration acquired during the reporting period, a reconciliation of the difference between the purchase price and par value should be presented, including the purchase price, allowance for credit losses at the acquisition date, discount or premium due to other factors, and the par value. (ASC-326-20-50-19)

If repayment of a financial asset is expected to be provided by operation or sale of collateral, the type of collateral, the extent to which the collateral secures the related financial asset, and any significant changes in the extent to which the collateral secures the related financial asset should be disclosed. (ASC-326-20-50-20)

For any off-balance-sheet credit exposures, an entity should disclose in its description of accounting policies the method used to estimate the liability for off-balance-sheet credit exposures and related charges for those credit exposures. This description should identify the factors management used and discuss the relevant risk elements to particular categories of financial instruments. (ASC 326-20-50-21)

EXPECTED CREDIT LOSSES ON FINANCIAL INSTRUMENTS CLASSIFIED AS AVAILABLE-FOR-SALE DEBT SECURITIES

Impairment

An investment is impaired if its fair value is less than its amortized cost basis. Impairment should be assessed at the individual security level so it is identifiable, not as a general allowance in a portfolio of debt securities. Likewise, an entity should not combine separate contracts to determine whether a debt security is impaired. For individual debt securities classified as available-for-sale, an entity should determine whether fair value has declined below the amortized cost basis due to a credit loss or other factors. An identified impairment due to credit losses should be recorded through an allowance for credit losses limited to the difference in fair value and amortized cost basis. Any impairment not recorded in the allowance for credit losses should be recorded in other comprehensive income. (ASC 326-30-35-1 through 5)

If the applicable accrued interest is excluded from the fair value and amortized cost basis of an available-for-sale debt security, the entity can do one of two things. The estimate of expected credit losses can be determined by measuring the applicable accrued interest amount separately from the other amortized cost basis components or on a combined basis. Alternatively, the entity can elect at the major security-type level not to measure an allowance for credit losses for accrued interest receivables if uncollectible accrued interest receivables are written off in a timely manner. (ASC 326-30-30-1A through 1B)

To determine whether a credit loss exists, an entity should consider the following indicators:

- The extent to which fair value is less than amortized cost
- Adverse conditions specifically relating to the security, industry, or location
- Payment structure of the debt security and the probability the issuer will be able to make increasing future payments
- Failure of the issuer to make scheduled interest or principal payments
- Any changes to a security's rating by a rating agency.

Other factors to be considered include information about the collectibility of the security based on past events, current conditions, and future forecasts such as the remaining payment terms, prepayment speeds, the issuer's financial condition, expected defaults, and the value of any underlying collateral. Industry reports, credit ratings, and other market data relevant to the collectibility of the security should be included in this consideration. (ASC 326-30-55-1 through 4)

An entity should develop an estimate of the present value of cash flows expected to be collected from the security using all the factors described above and compare that to the amortized cost basis of the security. A credit loss exists when the present value of expected cash flows is less than the amortized cost basis of the security and that loss is recorded to the allowance for credit losses limited by the amount that fair value is less than the amortized cost basis. Credit losses on impaired securities should continue to be measured using the present value of expected future cash flows. (ASC 326-30-35-1 through 2)

PRACTICE POINTER: If an entity intends to sell or more likely than not will be required to sell a debt security before its amortized cost basis is recovered, any allowance for credit losses should be written off and the amortized cost basis should be written down to the debt security's fair value with any incremental impairment reported in earnings. (ASC

326-30-35-10) The new amortized cost basis should not be adjusted for subsequent recoveries in fair value, but these changes should be included in other comprehensive income. (ASC 326-30-35-15)

Once a debt security has been identified as having a credit loss, an entity should reassess the amount of that credit loss each reporting period if there is an allowance for credit losses. Subsequent changes should be recorded to the allowance for credit losses with a corresponding adjustment to credit loss expense. If the security's contractual interest rate varies based on an index or rate, the entity can calculate the security's effective interest rate as that index or rate changes or is projected to change over the life of the security or it can fix the rate as of the date the credit loss was determined. This choice should be applied consistently within an entity across all securities that have a contractual interest rate tied to an index or rate. If applicable accrued interest is excluded from the fair value and amortized cost basis of the available-for-sale debt security an entity may elect to write off accrued interest receivables at the major security-type level by reversing interest income, recognizing credit loss expense, or both. (ASC 326-30-35-11 through 13A)

A purchased debt security classified as available-for-sale should be considered a purchased financial asset with credit deterioration when the indicators of a credit loss have been met. The allowance for credit losses for purchased financial assets with credit deterioration should be measured at the individual security level and the amortized cost basis should be measured as the purchase price plus any allowance for credit losses. The discount rate for estimated credit losses is the rate that equates the purchase price with the present value of the purchaser's estimate of the asset's future cash flows. Changes in the allowance for credit losses should be reported in net income as credit loss expense. Holding gains and losses should be recorded net of taxes in other comprehensive income. (ASC 326-30-30-1 through 4)

Disclosure Requirements

The disclosure requirements in ASC 326-30 are designed to enable a financial statement user to understand:

- Credit risk inherent in available-for-sale debt securities
- Management's estimate of expected credit losses
- Changes in the estimate of expected credit losses during the period (ASC 326-30-50-2)

An entity should determine the appropriate amount of detail to provide in disclosures not only to ensure important information is not hidden in overly aggregated disclosures but also to prevent burdening financial statement users with excessive detail. (ASC 326-30-50-3)

Available-for-sale debt securities should be presented on the statement of position at fair value with the amortized cost basis and allowance for credit losses presented parenthetically. Amounts related to available-for-sale debt securities for which an allowance for credit losses has been recorded to other comprehensive income should be presented separately in the appropriate financial statement. When an entity reports changes in the present value of cash flows expected to be collected on a debt security, the entire change can be reported as a credit loss expense or the change in present value due to changes in estimates can be reported as a credit loss expense with any change in present value due to the passage of time reported as interest income. (ASC 326-30-45-1 through 3)

An entity may present the accrued interest receivable balance net of the allowance for credit losses separately or within another statement of financial position line item, in which case both the amount and statement of financial position line item in which it is included should be disclosed. Entities electing not to measure an allowance for credit losses for accrued interest receivables should disclose what it considers timely for writing off uncollectible accrued interest receivables. Entities electing to write off accrued interest receivables should disclose the amount of accrued interest receivables written off by portfolio segment or major security type. Any accrued interest receivable balance can be excluded from the amortized cost basis disclosures in ASC 326-30-50-4 through 10; if this practical expedient is elected, the total amount of accrued interest excluded should be disclosed. (ASC 326-30-50-3A through 3D)

An entity should disclose the following information for available-for-sale debt securities in its interim and annual financial statements:

- As of each date for which a statement of financial position is presented, quantitative information in tabular form aggregated by each major security type and disaggregated by investments that have been in a continuous unrealized loss position for less than one year and longer than one year:
  - The aggregate related fair value of investments with unrealized losses
  - The aggregate amount of unrealized losses

- As of the date of the most recent statement of financial position, additional information to allow a financial statement user to understand the quantitative disclosures and the information the entity considered in reaching the conclusion that an allowance for credit losses is unnecessary. This information could include:
  - — Nature of the investments
  - — Causes and severity of the impairments
  - — Number of investments in an unrealized loss position
  - — Other relevant evidence considered (ASC 326-30-50-4 through 5)

The information about the allowance for credit losses provided in disclosures should allow financial statement users to understand the method and significant inputs used to measure the amount related to credit loss, including its accounting policy for recognizing write-offs of uncollectible available-for-sale debt securities. To accomplish this, the following information should be disclosed by major security type:

- Performance indicators of the security's underlying assets, including default rates, delinquency rates, and percentage of nonperforming assets
- Debt-to-collateral-value ratios
- Third-party guarantees
- Current levels of subordination
- Vintage
- Geographic concentration
- Industry analyst reports and forecasts
- Credit ratings
- Other market data relevant to the collectibility of the security (ASC 326-30-50-7)

Quantitative disclosures of the activity in the allowance for credit losses on available-for-sale debt securities should be disclosed by major security type, including:

- The beginning balance in the allowance for credit losses
- Additions to the allowance for credit losses on securities for which credit losses were not previously recorded
- Additions to the allowance for credit losses for any purchases of available-for-sale debt securities accounted for as purchased financial assets with credit deterioration
- Reductions for securities sold during the period
- Reductions in the allowance for credit losses for securities intended to be sold or more likely than not required to be sold prior to recovery of the amortized cost basis
- Increases or decreases to the allowance for credit losses on securities with an allowance recorded in a prior period
- Write-offs charged against the allowance
- Recoveries of previously written-off amounts
- The ending balance in the allowance for credit losses (ASC 326-30-50-9)

For purchased financial assets with credit deterioration acquired during the reporting period, a reconciliation of the difference between the purchase price and par value should be presented, including the purchase price, allowance for credit losses at the acquisition date, discount or premium due to other factors, and the par value. (ASC-326-20-50-10)

CHAPTER 24

ASC 330—INVENTORY

CONTENTS

PART I: GENERAL GUIDANCE

ASC 330-10: OVERALL

OVERVIEW

The preparation of financial statements requires careful determination of an appropriate dollar amount of inventory. Inventory is usually presented as a current asset in the balance sheet and is a direct determinant of cost of goods sold in the income statement; as such, it has a significant impact on the amount of net income. The valuation of inventories is of primary importance in the determination of a company's net income as well as its financial position.

BACKGROUND

Inventories of goods must periodically be compiled, measured, and recorded in the books of accounts of a business. Inventory usually is classified as (*a*) finished goods, (*b*) work in process, or (*c*) raw materials (ASC Glossary). Inventories exclude long-term assets that are subject to depreciation.

PRACTICE POINTER: Inventories are normally classified as current assets. However, when there are excessive quantities that may not reasonably be expected to be used or sold within the normal operating cycle of a business, excess inventory should be classified as noncurrent. Unusually high levels of excess inventory may raise the question of whether the recorded amount of the inventory will be realized in the future and could require the write down or write off of inventory.

The basis of accounting for inventories is cost, which is the price paid or consideration given to acquire the asset. In inventory accounting, cost is the sum of the expenditures and charges, direct and indirect, in bringing goods to their existing condition or location (ASC 330-10-30-1).

While the principle of measuring inventory at cost can be easily stated, the application of the principle, particularly to work-in-process items and finished goods, is difficult because of the required allocation of various costs and charges. For example, idle factory expense, excessive spoilage, double freight, and rehandling costs can be so abnormal that they may have to be charged to the current period, rather than being included in the cost of inventory. Selling expenses are not part of inventory costs. *The exclusion of all overhead from inventory costs* (direct or variable costing) *is an unacceptable accounting procedure* (ASC 330-10-30-2, 8).

General and administrative expenses are presented as period charges as a general rule with the exception of the portion of such expenses that are clearly related to production and constitute a part of inventory (product) costs. The exclusion of all overhead from inventory costs is not an acceptable practice. The exercise of judgment in individual situations requires a consideration of the adequacy of the procedures of the cost accounting system in use, the soundness of the principles being applied, and their consistent application (ASC 330-10-30-10).

INVENTORY SYSTEMS

Periodic System

The amount of inventory is determined by a physical count as of a specific date. As long as the count is made frequently enough for reporting purposes, it is not necessary to maintain extensive inventory records on a continuous basis as inventory is purchased and sold. The inventory shown in the balance sheet is determined by the physical count and is priced in accordance with the inventory costing method used. The net change between the beginning and ending inventories enters directly into the computation of the cost of goods sold.

Perpetual System

In a perpetual system, inventory records are maintained and updated continuously as items are purchased and sold. The system has the advantage of providing inventory information on a timely basis but requires the maintenance of a full set of inventory records. Theoretically, physical counts are not necessary, but they are normally taken to verify the inventory records. U.S. GAAP require that a physical check of perpetual inventory records be made periodically.

SUBSEQUENT MEASUREMENT OF INVENTORY

Accounting for inventory subsequent to purchase depends on the cost method and can generally be described in two categories:

1. Inventory measured using any method other than last-in, first-out (LIFO) or the retail inventory method.
2. Inventory measured using LIFO or the retail inventory method. (ASC 330-10-35-1A)

PRACTICE NOTE: As part of the FASB's initiative to simplify financial reporting, ASU 2015-11, *Inventory (Topic 330): Simplifying the Measurement of Inventory*, removed the previous requirement to determine a ceiling and floor for purposes of determining market in applying lower of cost or market.

In the case of inventory measured using methods other than LIFO and the Retail Inventory method, inventory is measured at the lower of cost or net realizable value, which is defined as estimated selling price in the ordinary course of business, less predictable costs of completion, disposal, and transportation. (Master Glossary) When evidence exists that the net realizable value is lower than cost, the difference shall be recognized as a loss in earnings in the period in which it occurs. That loss may be required due to damage, physical deterioration, obsolescence, changes in price level, and other causes. (ASC 330-10-35-1B)

When inventory is measured using LIFO or the Retail Inventory method, a departure from cost is required when the utility of the goods is no longer as great as their cost. Where evidence indicates that the utility of goods, in their disposal in the ordinary course of business, will be less than cost, the difference is recognized as a loss of the current period. This is generally accomplished by stating such goods at the lower level commonly referred to as market. (ASC 330-10-35-1C)

The cost basis of recording inventory usually achieves the objective of proper matching of costs and revenues. However, under certain circumstances, cost may not be the amount properly charged against revenues of future periods. Cost is the appropriate measure of inventory only if the utility of the goods has not diminished since their acquisition.

In accounting for inventory, a loss is recognized when the utility is impaired by damage, deterioration, obsolescence, changes in price levels, or other causes. The measurement of such losses is accomplished by accounting for inventory at the lower of cost or market (LCM). LCM provides a practical means for measuring utility and thereby determining the amount of loss that should be recognized and accounted for in the current period. (ASC 330-10-35-2)

LCM is intended to provide a means of measuring the residual usefulness of an inventory expenditure. Market is interpreted as indicating utility on the inventory date and may be thought of in terms of the equivalent expenditure that would be required to procure the same utility at that date. (ASC 330-10-35-3) When evidence indicates that cost will be recovered with an approximately normal profit upon sale in the ordinary course of business, no loss is recognized, even though replacement or reproduction costs are lower. (ASC 330-10-35-5)

Due to the many variations in circumstances encountered in inventory pricing, the definition of market is intended as a guide rather than an absolute rule. It should be applied realistically in light of the objectives stated above with regard to the form, content, and composition of the inventory. (ASC 330-10-35-7)

Depending on the character and composition of the inventory, the guidance described above may be applied directly to each item, to the total of the inventory, or to the components of each category of inventory. (ASC 330-10-35-8)

Substantial and unusual losses that result from the subsequent measurement of inventory shall be disclosed in the financial statements. (ASC 330-10-50-2)

INVENTORY COST METHODS

For inventory purposes, cost may be determined by specific identification or by the association of the flow of cost factors—first-in, first out (FIFO), last-in, first-out (LIFO), and average cost.

In selecting an inventory cost method, an important objective is the selection of the method that under the circumstances most clearly reflects periodic income. When similar goods are purchased at different times, it may not be possible or practical to identify and match the specific costs of the item sold. Frequently, the identity of goods and their specific related costs are lost between the time of acquisition and the time of use or sale. This has resulted in the general acceptance of several assumptions with respect to the flow of cost factors to provide practical bases for the measurement of periodic income (ASC 330-10-30-9).

First-In, First-Out Method (FIFO)

The FIFO method of identifying inventory is based on the assumption that costs are charged against revenue in the order in which they occur. The inventory remaining on hand is presumed to consist of the most recent costs.

Theoretically, FIFO approximates the results that would be obtained by the specific identification method if items were sold in the order in which they were purchased.

Last-In, First-Out Method (LIFO)

The LIFO method matches the most recent costs incurred with current revenue, leaving the first cost incurred to be included as inventory. LIFO requires that records be maintained as to the base-year layer and additional layers that may be created or used up. An additional LIFO layer is created in any year in which the quantity of ending inventory is more than the beginning inventory and is priced at the earliest or average costs of the year in which it was created.

When the quantity of ending inventory is less than the beginning inventory, one or more LIFO layers may be used up. Once a LIFO layer is used up, any future new LIFO layer is priced at the cost of the year in which it is created, and not by reinstating a prior LIFO layer cost.

In addition to the disclosure of significant accounting policies required by ASC 235 (Notes to Financial Statements) disclosing the basis of stating inventories (ASC 330-10-50-1), a business using the LIFO method of reporting inventory must disclose the following, if it reports to the SEC:

- Current replacement value of the LIFO inventories at each balance sheet date presented
- The effect on the results of operations for any reduction of a LIFO layer

---

PRACTICE POINTER: While the LIFO inventory method is sometimes justified on the basis of a superior matching of current revenues and current costs, the primary catalyst for using LIFO is its acceptance for income tax purposes and the lower taxable income that it produces. The LIFO conformity requirement that is included in income tax law requires a company that uses LIFO for tax purposes to also use LIFO for financial reporting purposes. In changing from another inventory cost method to the LIFO method for financial reporting purposes, the company must present a justification. Changing an accounting method for financial reporting purposes because of its preferability for tax purposes generally is not an acceptable justification. Therefore, changing to LIFO usually is justified by reasons such as higher quality earnings that result from matching current revenues with current costs, and bringing the company into conformity with normal industry practice.

Weighted-Average Method

The weighted-average method of inventory valuation assumes that costs are charged against revenue based on an average of the number of units acquired at each price level. The resulting average price is applied to the ending inventory to find the total ending inventory value. The weighted average is determined by dividing the total costs of the inventory available, including any beginning inventory, by the total number of units.

Illustration of Application of FIFO, LIFO, and the Weighted-Average Methods of Inventory Valuation

Assume the following facts:

	Units Purchased During the Year		
Date	*Units*	*Cost per Unit*	*Total Cost*
January 15	10,000	$5.10	$ 51,000
March 20	20,000	5.20	104,000
May 10	50,000	5.00	250,000
June 8	30,000	5.40	162,000
October 12	5,000	5.30	26,500

	Units Purchased During the Year		
Date	*Units*	*Cost per Unit*	*Total Cost*
December 21	5,000	5.50	27,500
Totals	120,000		$621,000

Beginning inventory consisted of 10,000 units at $5.

Ending inventory consisted of 14,000 units.

Under *FIFO*, the first units in stock are the first units out, which means that the ending inventory is of the units purchased last. Since the ending inventory is 14,000 units and December purchases were only 5,000 units, go back to October purchases for another 5,000 units and to June purchases for another 4,000 units, as follows:

December purchases	5,000 units	@	$5.50	=	$27,500
October purchases	5,000 units	@	5.30	=	26,500
From June purchases	4,000 units	@	5.40	=	21,600
Ending inventory using FIFO	14,000 units				$75,600

Under *LIFO*, the last units in stock are the first units out, which means that the ending inventory is composed of the units purchased first. Using LIFO, go back to the earliest inventory to start the calculations. The earliest inventory available is the *beginning inventory* of 10,000 units at $5, but the ending inventory is 14,000 units. Thus, go to the next earliest purchase, which is January, and use 4,000 units at the January price to complete the ending inventory valuation, as follows:

Beginning inventory	10,000 units	@	$5.00	=	$50,000
From January purchase	4,000 units	@	5.10	=	20,400
Ending inventory using LIFO	14,000 units				$70,400

Under the *weighted-average* method, multiply the weighted-average cost per unit by the 14,000 units in the ending inventory, thus:

	Units	*Cost per Unit*	*Total Cost*
Beginning inventory	10,000	$5.00	$50,000
Purchases:			
January 15	10,000	5.10	51,000
March 20	20,000	5.20	104,000
May 10	50,000	5.00	250,000
June 8	30,000	5.40	162,000
October 12	5,000	5.30	26,500
December 21	5,000	5.50	27,500
Totals	130,000		$671,000

Weighted average	=	Total costs divided by total units
	=	$671,000 divided by 130,000
	=	$5.1615 per unit
Ending inventory	=	14,000 × $5.1615 per unit = $72,261

Comparison of the Three Methods

Ending inventory, FIFO	$75,600
Ending inventory, LIFO	70,400
Ending inventory, weighted average	72,261

In periods of inflation, the FIFO method produces the highest ending inventory, resulting in the lowest cost of goods sold and the highest gross profit. LIFO produces the lowest ending inventory, resulting in the highest cost of goods sold and the lowest gross profit. The weighted-average method yields results between those of LIFO and FIFO.

Moving-Average Method

The moving-average method can be used only with a perpetual inventory. A revised cost per unit is recomputed after every addition to the inventory.

Illustration of Moving-Average Method

	Total Units	*Total Cost*	*Unit Cost*
Beginning inventory	1,000	$ 5,000	$5.00
Sales of 200 units	800	4,000	5.00
Purchase of 1,200 @ $6	2,000	11,200*	5.60
Sales of 1,000 units	1,000	5,600	5.60
Purchase of 1,000 @ $5	2,000	10,600**	5.30

Note: Only purchases change the unit price; sales are taken out at the prior moving-average unit cost.

* $4,000 + (1,200 @ $6) = $11,200; $11,200/2,000 units = $5.60/unit
** $5,600 + (1,000 @ $5) = $10,600; $10,600/2,000 units = $5.30/unit

Under the moving-average method, the ending inventory is costed at the last moving-average unit cost for the period.

Dollar-Value LIFO Method

A variation of the conventional LIFO method is the dollar-value LIFO method. Under the regular LIFO method, units of inventory are priced at unit prices. Under the dollar-value LIFO method, the base-year inventory is priced in dollars; for inventories of all subsequent years, price indices are used, with the base year as 100.

Illustration of Dollar-Value LIFO Method

Year	*Inventory at Base-Year Prices*	*Price Index*	*LIFO Inventory Amount*
1	$100,000	100	$100,000
2	20,000	105	21,000
3	10,000	110	11,000
4	20,000	120	24,000
5	20,000	125	25,000
Totals	$170,000		$181,000

Retail Inventory Method

Because of the great variety and quantity of inventory in some types of businesses, the reversed markup procedure of inventory pricing, such as the retail inventory method, may be both practical and appropriate.

The retail inventory method requires the maintenance of records of purchases at both cost and selling price. A ratio of cost to retail is calculated and applied to the ending inventory at retail to compute the approximate cost.

Illustration of Basic Retail Inventory Method

	Cost	*Retail*
Inventory, at beginning of period	$ 100,000	$150,000
Purchases during the period	1,100,000	1,850,000
Totals (ratio of cost to retail 60%)	$1,200,000	$2,000,000
Sales during the period		(1,800,000)
Estimated ending inventory at retail		$ 200,000
Estimated ending inventory at cost (60% × $200,000)		$ 120,000

Physical inventories measured by the retail method should be taken periodically as a check on the accuracy of the estimated inventories.

Original selling prices may be modified, thus necessitating an understanding of the following terminology:

- *Original retail*—the first selling price at which goods are offered for sale
- *Markup*—the selling price raised above the original selling price
- *Markdown*—the selling price lowered below the original selling price
- *Markup cancellation*—markup selling price decreased, but not below the original selling price
- *Markdown cancellation*—markdown selling price increased, but not above the original selling price
- *Net markup*—markup less markup cancellation
- *Net markdown*—markdown less markdown cancellation
- *Markon*—difference between the cost and the original selling price, plus any net markups

Illustration of Markups and Markdowns

Original cost	$100
Original selling price ($50 markon)	$150
Markup	50
Original selling price plus markup	200
Markup cancellation	(25)
Original selling price plus net markup	175
Markdown (consists of $25 markup cancellation and a $25 markdown)	(50)
Original selling price less markdown	125
Markdown	(25)
Original selling price less markdown	100
Markdown cancellation	25
Original selling price less net markdown	125
Markup (consists of a $25 markdown cancellation and a $25 markup)	50
Original selling price plus net markup	$175

Theoretically, the last selling price consists of:

$50	Markup
(25)	Markup cancellation
(25)	Markup cancellation
(25)	Markdown
(25)	Markdown
25	Markdown cancellation
25	Markdown cancellation
25	Markup
$25	net plus change

Now the goods are priced at the original selling price plus a net markup of $25, or a total of $175.

The purpose of the conventional retail inventory method is to produce an inventory valuation closely approximating what would be obtained by taking a physical inventory and pricing the goods at the lower of cost or market.

The basic assumption of the retail inventory method is that there exists an equal distribution of goods (high-cost ratio and low-cost ratio) between sales, beginning inventory, and ending inventory. In instances in which this basic premise does not prevail, cost ratios should be determined by departments or small units. This requires keeping separate sales, purchases, markups, markdowns, and beginning and ending inventories by departments.

Lower-of-Cost-or-Market Application

To approximate the lower of cost or market in the computations, *markdowns and markdown cancellations are excluded in calculating the ratio of cost to retail and are added to the retail inventory after the ratio is determined.*

In calculating the cost-to-retail ratio, any adjustment to the retail value will necessarily affect the ratio and the resulting cost figure. Adjustments that decrease the denominator of the ratio increase the ratio and the value for ending inventory at cost, increasing gross profit. In the interest of conservatism, as well as for other reasons, adjustments that decrease the retail figure should be avoided. Markups, which increase the denominator, however, are included *net* of cancellations.

Net markdowns (markdowns less markdown cancellations) are an example of adjustments that decrease the denominator. Including them in the retail figure violates the lower-of-cost-or-market rule. As shown below, net markdowns are not included in the calculation of the ratio but *are* included in the determination of ending inventory after computing the ratio. The rationale for this is that the cost-to-retail ratio is presumed to be based on normal conditions, and markdown is not a normal condition. When *applying* the ratio, however, to conform to the lower-of-cost-or-market rule, the retail value must be reduced by the amount of the markdowns.

Employee discounts apply only to goods sold, not those remaining on hand. A sale at less than normal retail price to an employee does not represent a valid reduction to lower of cost or market, nor does it represent a valid adjustment of the cost-to-retail ratio or the value of the ending inventory. Therefore, employee discounts should not enter into any of the calculations, but are deducted from retail in the same way as markdowns after the computation of the cost-to-retail ratio.

Inventory spoilage and shrinkage affect the ending inventory figure but do not enter into the cost-to-retail ratio calculation. When arriving at the final figure for inventory at cost, the amount of shrinkage is deducted either at cost or at retail depending upon whether shrinkage is stated at cost or at retail.

Illustration of Retail Method/Lower-of-Cost-or-Market Application

	Cost	*Retail*
Inventory, at beginning of period	$ 200,000	$ 300,000
Purchases	550,000	800,000
Transportation-in	50,000	
Markups		100,000
Markup cancellations		20,000
Markdowns		70,000
Markdown cancellations		10,000

The calculations are as follows:

	Cost	Retail
Inventory, at beginning of period	$200,000	$ 300,000
Purchases	550,000	800,000
Transportation-in	50,000	
Markups		100,000
Markup cancellations		(20,000)
Totals (ratio of cost to retail 67.8%)	$800,000	$1,180,000
Markdowns		(70,000)
Markdown cancellations		10,000
Total goods at retail		$1,120,000
Less: Sales during the period		(860,000)
Inventory, ending (at retail)		$ 260,000
Inventory, ending (67.8% × $260,000)*		$ 176,280

* At estimated lower cost or market.

LIFO Application

The LIFO method of evaluating inventory can be estimated via the retail inventory method by using procedures somewhat different from the conventional retail method. Basically, two differences have to be taken into consideration:

1. Because the LIFO method produces a valuation approximating cost, and the conventional retail method produces a valuation approximating the lower of cost or market, to apply the LIFO concept to the conventional retail method it is necessary to include all markdowns as well as markups in determining the ratio of cost to retail.
2. With the LIFO method, the quantity of inventory on hand is from the earliest purchases during the year or from prior years' LIFO layers. The cost-to-retail ratio considers the current relationship between cost and selling price. Therefore, the beginning inventory is omitted from the cost-to-retail ratio, because it may cause a distortion.

Illustration of Retail Method/LIFO Application

Information from the previous example is restated on a LIFO basis, as follows:

	Cost	Retail
Inventory, beginning of period	Omitted	Omitted
Purchases	$550,000	$ 800,000
Transportation-in	50,000	
Markups		100,000
Markup cancellations		(20,000)
Markdowns		(70,000)
Markdown cancellations		10,000
Totals (ratio of cost to retail 73.2%)	$600,000	$ 820,000

	Cost	Retail
Add: Inventory, beginning of period		300,000
Total goods at retail		$1,120,000
Less: Sales during period		(860,000)
Inventory, ending of period (at retail)		$ 260,000

Because the $260,000 ending LIFO inventory (at retail) is less than the $300,000 beginning LIFO inventory (at retail), a prior LIFO layer was partially depleted:

	Retail
Beginning inventory	$300,000
Ending inventory	(260,000)
LIFO layer depleted	$ 40,000

The $40,000 difference is multiplied by the beginning inventory cost-to-retail ratio ($200,000/$300,000 = 66.7%) and then subtracted from the beginning inventory at cost, as follows:

	Cost
Beginning inventory	$200,000
$40,000 × 66.7%	(26,680)
Ending inventory (at cost)	$173,320

If the ending LIFO inventory (at retail) had been greater than the beginning LIFO inventory (at retail), a new LIFO layer would have been created which would have been costed at the new cost-to-retail ratio (73.2%).

MISCELLANEOUS INVENTORY ISSUES

Title to Goods

Legal title to merchandise usually determines whether or not it is included in the inventory of an enterprise. Title to goods passes from the seller to the buyer in any manner and on any conditions explicitly agreed on by the parties. If no conditions are explicitly agreed on, title to goods passes from the seller to the buyer at the time and place at which the seller completes its performance with reference to the physical delivery of the goods. Title passes to the buyer at the time and place of shipment if the seller is required only to send the goods. If the contract requires delivery at destination, however, title passes when the goods are tendered at the destination.

Commonly encountered terms are *F.O.B. (free on board) Destination* and *F.O.B. Shipping Point*. In the former case, the seller is responsible for the goods during shipment; title passes when the goods are received by the buyer. In the latter case, the buyer is responsible for the goods during shipment; title passes when the goods leave the seller's location.

Abnormal Facility and Other Costs

ASC 330 also provides guidance in accounting for abnormal amounts of idle facility expense, freight, handling costs, and spoilage. The basic principle for accounting for inventory is that inventories are to be accounted for at cost, meaning acquisition and production costs. Although this principle may be easily stated, it is difficult to apply because of the variety of considerations inherent in the allocation of costs and charges. Guidelines for applying these principles can be summarized as follows:

- Variable production overhead costs are allocated to each unit of production on the basis of the actual use of the production facilities.
- The allocation of fixed production overheads to the costs of conversion is based on the normal capacity of the production facilities.

- "Normal capacity" refers to a range of production levels and is the production expected to be achieved over a number of periods or seasons under normal circumstances, taking into account the loss of capacity resulting from planned maintenance.
- Some variation in production levels from period to period is expected and establishes the range of normal production. This range will vary based on business-related and industry-related factors.
- Judgment is required to determine when a production level is abnormally low (i.e., outside the range of expected variation in production).
- Examples of factors that might be anticipated to cause an abnormally low production level include significantly reduced demand, labor and materials shortages, and unplanned facilities or equipment downtime.
- The actual level of production may be used if it approximates normal capacity.
- In periods of abnormally high production, the amount of fixed overhead allocated to each unit of production is decreased so that inventories are not measured above cost. The amount of fixed overhead allocated to each unit of production is not increased as a consequence of abnormally low production or an idle plant.

Unallocated overhead costs are recognized as an expense in the period in which they are incurred. Other costs, such as abnormal handling costs, are treated as a current period expense, as are general and administrative costs, except for the portion that clearly relates to production and constitutes a part of inventory costs. Selling expenses are not included in inventory costs. The exclusion of all overhead costs from inventory costs is not an accepted accounting procedure.

PRACTICE POINTER: The exercise of judgment in individual situations involves a consideration of the adequacy of the procedures of the cost accounting system in use, the soundness of the principles on which that system is based, and the consistency of the application of those principles.

Standard Costs

The use of standard costs is a management tool that identifies favorable or unfavorable variances from predetermined estimates established by past performance or time and motion studies. Inventory valuation by the use of standard costs is acceptable, if adjusted at reasonable intervals to reflect the approximate costs computed under one of the recognized methods, and adequate disclosure is made in the financial statements.

At the end of the reporting period, the physical inventory is costed at LIFO, FIFO, or some other generally accepted method. Any variation between this result and the carrying value of the inventory at standard cost must be closed out to cost of goods sold and ending inventory such that the reported figure represents that which the generally accepted method would yield.

Relative Sales Value Costing

Determining the relative sales cost of inventory items is used when costs cannot be determined individually. Joint products, lump-sum purchase of assets (basket purchase), and large assets that are subdivided (real estate tracts) are examples of items that would be costed by their relative sales value.

Illustration of Relative Sales Value Costing

ABC Company purchases inventory consisting of four large pieces of machinery for $100,000. At the time of purchase, an appraisal discloses the following fair values:

Machine #1	$ 12,000
Machine #2	28,000
Machine #3	40,000
Machine #4	30,000
Total	$110,000

The cost of each machine is an allocated amount, based on relative fair values, as follows:

Machine #1	12/110 × $100,000	=	$ 10,909
Machine #2	28/110 × $100,000	=	25,455
Machine #3	40/110 × $100,000	=	36,364
Machine #4	30/110 × $100,000	=	27,272
	Total cost allocated		$100,000

Alternatively, a percentage of total cost to the appraised value can be computed: $100,000/$110,000 = 90.91%. That percentage is then applied to the value of each item to determine its cost. For example, cost for Machine #1 is $12,000 × 90.91% = $10,909.

Firm Purchase Commitments

Losses on firm purchase commitments for inventory goods are measured in the same manner as inventory losses and, if material, recognized in the accounts and disclosed separately in the income statement (ASC 330-10-50-5).

The recognition of losses, which are expected to arise from firm, noncancelable commitments and which arise from the decline in the utility of a cost expenditure, should be disclosed in the current period income statement. In addition, all significant firm purchase commitments must be disclosed in the financial statements or in footnotes, whether or not any losses are recognized.

Discontinued Operations

Inventories used in a component of a business entity should be written down to their fair value less cost to sell and the amount of write-down included as part of the gain or loss recognized on the disposal of the component of the business entity (ASC 360-10-35-40). Such a write-down, however, should not be attributable to any inventory adjustment that should have been recognized prior to the measurement date of the loss on disposal. In this event, the loss on the write down is included in the operating results of the component of the business entity in accordance with ASC 205-20 (Presentation of Financial Statements—Discontinued Operations) (ASC 205-20-45-3).

Interim Financial Reporting

Generally, the same principles and methods are used to value inventories for interim financial statements as are used for annual reports. For practical purposes, however, ASC 270 specifies certain exceptions (ASC 270-10-45-6):

- An estimated gross profit frequently is used to determine the cost of goods sold during an interim period. This is acceptable for U.S. GAAP, as long as periodic physical inventories are taken to adjust the gross profit percentage used. Companies using the gross profit method for interim financial statements should disclose that fact and any significant adjustments that may occur in amounts determined by a physical count.
- When the LIFO method is used for interim financial statements and a LIFO layer is depleted, in part or in whole, that is expected to be replaced before the end of the fiscal period, it is acceptable to use the expected cost of replacement for the depleted LIFO inventory in determining cost of goods sold for the interim period.
- Inventory losses from market declines, other than those expected to be recovered before the end of the fiscal year, are included in the results of operations of the interim period in which the loss occurs. Subsequent gains from market price recovery in later interim periods are included in the results of operation in which the gain occurs, but only to the extent of the previously recognized losses.
- Standard costs are acceptable in determining inventory valuations for interim financial reporting. Unplanned or unanticipated purchase price, volume, or capacity variances should be included in the results of operations of the interim period in which they occur. Anticipated and planned purchase price, volume, or capacity variances that are expected to be recovered by the end of the fiscal year are deferred at interim dates. In general, the same procedures for standard costs used at the end of the fiscal year should be used for interim financial reporting.

PRACTICE POINTER: All of these procedures, which are acceptable in interim financial statements, are not considered U.S. GAAP for purposes of annual financial statements. They generally represent procedures that are necessary for interim statements to articulate with the annual period of which the interim periods are a part. Some may have a material impact on the amount of net income (e.g., using the replacement cost for erosion of a LIFO layer in an early interim period), and care must be taken that a similar procedure is not used in annual financial statements.

Terminated Contracts

When inventory is acquired for a specific customer contract that is subsequently terminated for any purpose, the carrying value of such inventory should be adjusted to reflect any loss in value.

Research and Development

ASC 730 (Research and Development) contains U.S. GAAP relevant to inventory expense allocation. Inventories of supplies used in research and development activities are charged to expense unless they clearly have an alternative use or can be used in future research and development projects.

When research and development activities consume goods, supplies, or materials from other sources within an organization, the carrying value of such inventory is charged to research and development expense. Goods produced by research and development activities that may be used in the regular inventory of the organization may be transferred physically to regular inventory, at which time a credit in the amount of the costs assigned to the goods should be made to research and development.

Intercompany Profits

Regardless of any noncontrolling interest, all intercompany profits in inventory are eliminated for consolidated financial statements and investments in common stocks accounted for by the equity method.

Long-Term Construction-Type Contracts

The construction in progress account used in both the completed contract and percentage-of-completion methods of accounting for long-term construction-type contracts is an inventory account.

Income Taxes

Inventories accounted differently for financial accounting and tax purposes may create temporary differences for which the recognition of deferred taxes may be necessary.

Accounting Change

An accounting change involving inventories in interim or annual reports necessitates accounting for the cumulative effect of the change and/or restatement of prior-period reports, including certain required pro forma information in accordance with ASC 250 (Accounting Changes and Error Corrections).

Nonmonetary Exchanges

A nonmonetary exchange of inventory held for sale in the ordinary course of business for similar property to be held for the same purpose does not complete the earnings process and no gain or loss is recognized. The inventory received in the nonmonetary exchange should be recorded at the book value of the inventory surrendered, unless cash is also involved in the transaction, in accordance with ASC 845 (Nonmonetary Transactions).

Capitalization of the Service Cost Component into Inventory

The service cost component of net periodic pension costs and net periodic postretirement benefit costs is the only component directly arising from employees' services provided in the current period. When it is appropriate to capitalize employee compensation into the construction or production of an asset, the service cost component applicable to the pertinent employees for the period is the relevant amount to be considered for capitalization (ASC 330-10-55-6A).

Inventory Profits

Profits from the sale of inventory, whose cost and selling price have increased significantly since acquisition, may include *ghost profits* or *inventory profits*. These profits are abnormal, because the cost to replace the inventory has increased significantly and the normal gross profit on the inventory is considerably less than the gross profit containing the ghost or inventory profits.

During periods of rapid inflation, a significant portion of reported net income of a business may actually be ghost or inventory profits. The use of the LIFO method for pricing inventories may offset part or all of any ghost or inventory profits, because current purchases or production costs are matched against current revenue, leaving the earliest inventory on hand.

Certain publicly held companies are encouraged by the SEC to disclose in a supplemental statement the current replacement cost for cost of goods sold, inventories, and resulting ghost or inventory profits.

DISCLOSURE

The general disclosure requirements for inventories are:

- A description of accounting principles used and the methods of applying those principles (ASC 235-10-50-3).
- Any accounting principles or methods that are peculiar to a particular industry (ASC 235-10-50-3).
- Classification of inventories (ASC 330-10-50-1).
- Basis of pricing inventories (ASC 330-10-50-1).

Businesses that depend on a limited number of sources for raw material or inventory or upon precarious sources (labor problems, foreign governments, etc.) should disclose the pertinent facts in their financial statements or footnotes thereto.

CHANGES IN DISCLOSURE REQUIREMENTS FOR INVENTORY

IMPORTANT NOTICE FOR 2022

The FASB has outstanding a proposed ASU that can be expected to have an important impact related to disclosures of information about inventories when issued as a final ASU. This exposure draft is a part of the disclosure framework project whose objective and primary focus is to improve the effectiveness of notes to financial statements by facilitating clear communication of information required by U.S. GAAP. This proposed ASU has been outstanding since 2017.

This amendment to the Accounting Standards Codification would apply to all entities that are required to follow Topic 330. The following additional disclosures would be added to those that are already required:

(1) Inventory disaggregated by components (e.g., raw materials, work-in-process, finished goods, and supplies);

(2) Inventory disaggregated by measurement basis;

(3) Changes in inventory that are not specifically related to the purchase, manufacture, or sale of inventory in the ordinary course of business;

(4) A qualitative description of the types of costs capitalized into inventory;

(5) The effect of LIFO liquidations on income; and

(6) The replacement cost of LIFO inventory.

Entities that report some or all of their inventory by the retail inventory method would be required to provide qualitative and quantitative information about the critical assumptions used in the calculation of inventory under that method.

Entities that are subject to segment information requirements (ASC 280) would be required to disclose inventory by reportable segment and by components for each reportable segments to the extent that information is regularly provided to the chief operating decisionmaker. This requirement would apply to both annual and interim reports.

This proposed ASU is in the deliberations stage. An expected issuance and effective date are not indicated.

PART II: INTERPRETIVE GUIDANCE

ASC 330-10: OVERALL

ASC 330-10-55-2 Recognition of Inventory Market Declines at Interim Reporting Dates

BACKGROUND

A company has inventory whose market price has declined below its cost in an interim period. Although economic projections indicate that prices will not recover in the near term, there is considerable uncertainty about the accuracy of such projections.

ACCOUNTING ISSUE

Should a company account for a decline in the market price of its inventory below cost during an interim period if it is uncertain whether the market price will recover in the near term?

ACCOUNTING GUIDANCE

Under the provisions of ASC 270, the value of inventory should be reduced to the lower of cost or market during an interim period unless (1) there is strong evidence that market prices will recover before the inventory is sold or that (2) inventory accounted for by the LIFO method will regain its value by year-end unless a decline in market prices is the result of seasonal price fluctuations, the value of the inventory generally should be reduced.

DISCUSSION

This Issue was raised in an attempt to clarify the language in ASC 270-20-45-6 related to the recognition of market declines in interim periods if there is a *reasonable* expectation that prices will recover in the fiscal year. It states that "*[t]emporary* market declines need not be recognized at the interim date since no loss is expected to be incurred in the fiscal year." This referred to SEC SAB-59 (Views on Accounting for Noncurrent Marketable Equity Securities), which states that the SEC staff does not believe that the term *other than temporary,* as used in the guidance in ASC 320 should be interpreted to mean *permanent impairment* as used elsewhere in accounting practice. The conclusion on this Issue appears to indicate that the Emerging Issues Task Force was unwilling to interpret the language in ASC 270 to mean anything other than what it says, and that positive evidence of recovery is necessary to avoid a write-down rather than uncertainty that the decline will be permanent

ASC 330-10-55-3 through 55-4 Uniform Capitalization Rules for Inventory under the Tax Reform Act of 1986

BACKGROUND

Under the Tax Reform Act of 1986, manufacturers of products and wholesalers and retailers of goods for resale are required to capitalize certain direct costs and a portion of indirect costs related to the inventory produced or acquired for resale. Examples of such costs are excess tax depreciation over depreciation for financial reporting purposes, warehousing costs, insurance premiums, certain personnel costs, and costs related to accounting and data services operations for inventory. Previously, such costs were charged to expense for financial reporting and tax purposes.

ACCOUNTING ISSUES

- Are the types of costs required to be allocated to inventories for tax purposes capitalizable for financial reporting purposes under generally accepted accounting principles?
- If so, would a new costing method be a preferable method for justifying a change in accounting method?

ACCOUNTING GUIDANCE

It may not be preferable or appropriate to capitalize costs for reporting purposes that are capitalizable for tax purposes. However, some costs capitalized for tax purposes also may qualify to be capitalized for financial reporting purposes, depending on such factors as the nature of an entity's operations and industry practice. An entity should decide whether to capitalize or expense such costs based on an analysis of the individual facts and circumstances.

ASC 330-10-S35-2; ASC 420-10-S45-2, S99-3 Classification of Inventory Markdowns and Other Costs Associated with a Restructuring

BACKGROUND

A previous pronouncement, which was superseded by ASC 420 provided guidance on the timing of liability recognition related to exit or restructuring costs. It also provided guidance on the types of costs that could be accrued when an exit or restructuring plan is adopted. It did not specifically address asset impairments that might result from an exit plan, nor did it provide guidance as to whether a liability for such costs should be presented in the income statement with restructuring charges.

ACCOUNTING ISSUE

Should inventory markdowns associated with an exit plan or a restructuring activity be classified in the income statement as a cost of goods sold or as an exit or restructuring cost?

ACCOUNTING GUIDANCE

Although no guidance was provided on this Issue, it was noted that disclosure of the amount of inventory markdowns related to an exit plan or restructuring activity may be appropriate, regardless of how the inventory markdowns are classified.

SEC OBSERVER COMMENT

During the discussion of this Issue, the SEC Observer stated that the SEC staff prefers classification of such inventory markdowns as a cost of goods sold in the income statement. Subsequently, the SEC Observer reiterated that the staff's preference is based on the view that (*a*) it is difficult to distinguish inventory markdowns due to a decision to restructure a business or to exit an activity from markdowns caused by external market conditions that are independent of that decision, and (*b*) decisions about the timing, method, and pricing of inventory dispositions are normal recurring activities related to the management of an ongoing business.

CHAPTER 25

ASC 340—DEFERRED COSTS AND OTHER ASSETS

CONTENTS

PART I: GENERAL GUIDANCE

ASC 340-10: OVERALL

BACKGROUND

Guidance in ASC 340 covers accounting for prepaid expenses and certain deferred costs, specifically preproduction costs related to long-term supply arrangements. The specific guidance for many other costs that are deferred is included in various other ASC topics.

Prepaid expenses are assets that are typically used up or expire within the normal operating cycle of an entity. Some expenses are paid prior to receipt of the benefit, while others are paid after the benefit is received. The term *prepaid expenses* defines those expenses that are paid in advance of their use or consumption. Prepaid expenses include such items as insurance, interest, rents, taxes, unused royalties, currently paid advertising not yet received, and operating supplies. (ASC 340-10-5-2 through 5)

Preproduction costs related to long-term supply arrangements result from manufacturers incurring cost related to products they will supply to their customers under long-term supply arrangements. While practice varies from industry to industry, the supplier may be contractually guaranteed reimbursement of design and development costs, implicitly guaranteed reimbursement of design and development costs through the pricing of the product or other means, or not guaranteed reimbursement of the design and development costs incurred under the long-term supply arrangement. (ASC 340-10-5 through 6)

PART II: INTERPRETIVE GUIDANCE

IMPACT OF ASU 2014-09: REVENUE FROM CONTRACTS WITH CUSTOMERS

On May 28, 2014, the FASB issued ASU 2014-09, *Revenue from Contracts with Customers,* with an original effective date for annual reporting periods beginning after December 15, 2016, including interim periods within that reporting period, for public business entities, certain not-for- profit (NFP) entities, and certain employee benefit plans. The original effective date for all other entities was for annual reporting periods beginning after December 15, 2017, and interim periods within annual periods beginning after December 15, 2018.

In August 2015, the FASB issued ASU 2015-14, *Revenue from Contracts with Customers (Topic 606): Deferral of the Effective Date.* The amendments in that ASU deferred the effective date of ASU 2014-09 for all entities by one year. Public business entities, certain NFP entities, and certain employee benefit plans were required to apply the guidance in ASU 2014-09 to annual reporting periods beginning after December 15, 2017, including interim reporting periods within that reporting period. All other entities were required to apply the guidance in ASU 2014-09 to annual reporting periods beginning after December 15, 2018, and interim reporting periods within annual reporting periods beginning after December 15, 2019. Early adoption was permitted.

The Coronavirus Disease 2019 (COVID-19) pandemic has adversely affected the global economy and has caused widespread disruptions to business and capital markets. The FASB received feedback that many private companies and NFP organizations are experiencing challenges with finalizing their transition to ASU 2014-09 because of the unique challenges resulting from the COVID-19 pandemic. As a result, in June, 2020, the FASB issued ASU 2020-05, *Revenue from Contracts with Customers (Topic 606) and Leases (Topic 842): Effective Dates for Certain Entities,* as a limited deferral of the effective date of ASU 2014-09. ASU 2020-05 defers, for one year, the required effective date of ASU 2014-09 for certain entities that have not yet issued their financial statements (or made financial statements available for issuance) reflecting the adoption of ASU 2014-09. Those entities may elect to adopt the guidance for annual reporting periods beginning after December 15, 2019, and for interim reporting periods within annual reporting periods beginning after December 15, 2020. Instead, those entities may elect to follow the earlier stated effective date of annual reporting periods beginning after December 15, 2018, and interim reporting periods within annual reporting periods beginning after December 15, 2019.

The relatively long transition period between the original issuance of ASU 2014-09 and its revised effective dates results in both the guidance under ASU 2014-09 (ASC 606) and the previous guidance from multiple sources (ASC 605) being in effect for several years. While ASC 606 is already in effect for some entities, the previous guidance (ASC 605) continues in effect for other entities. Consistent with the policy of retaining guidance that has been replaced until it is no longer applicable to all entities, the 2022 *GAAP Guide* continues to include coverage of both ASC 606 and ASC 605. When the guidance in ASC 606 becomes effective for all entities, it will become the sole content of chapter 38 and the guidance in ASC 605 will be removed and no longer presented as supplemental guidance.

ASC 340-10: OVERALL

ASC 340-10-05-6, 25-1 through 25-3, S50-1, 55-2 through 55-5, S99-3; ASC 460-10-60-2; ASC 730-10-60-1 Accounting for Pre-Production Costs Related to Long-Term Supply Arrangements

BACKGROUND

Manufacturers that supply parts to original equipment manufacturers (OEMs), such as manufacturers of automobiles, often incur pre-production costs associated with the design and development of products they will manufacture for their customers. They incur pre-production engineering costs—for example, in designing, developing, and building molds, dies, and other tools—which will be used in manufacturing parts such as seats and instrument panels for automobiles. Those costs are referred to in the Issue as *tooling costs.*

Eligibility to be awarded a contract to supply *production parts* to the automotive industry includes the capability to produce the tooling used to manufacture the parts. Although suppliers begin pre-production activities and incur tooling costs several years before actual production begins, they do so only after they have been awarded a contract to produce specific parts for a specific car or model, approximately two to five years before production begins.

Suppliers recover tooling costs in several ways. An OEM may be contractually obligated to pay the supplier a guaranteed amount for tooling costs, which is included in the price of each part purchased; the OEM may agree to pay the supplier a lump sum for those costs; or if there is no specific agreement for reimbursement, the supplier may include those costs in the price of each part. Even if there is no contractual reimbursement arrangement, OEMs have historically compensated their suppliers for tooling costs if a program terminates early or the number of units purchased is less than expected.

Although this Issue is discussed in terms of the automotive industry, a consensus would also apply to other industries with similar production arrangements.

ACCOUNTING ISSUES

1. How should an entity account for costs incurred to design and develop products sold under long-term supply arrangements?
2. How should an entity account for costs incurred to design and develop molds, dies, and other tools used in producing products sold under long-term supply arrangements?
3. Should customer reimbursement for design and development costs affect the supplier's accounting for such costs?

ACCOUNTING GUIDANCE

1. Suppliers should expense design and development costs for products sold under long-term supply contracts as they are incurred.
2. Design and development costs for molds, dies, and other tools used in producing products under long-term supply contracts should be accounted for as follows:
   a. Capitalize as part of the cost of molds, dies, and other tools (subject to the impairment test in ASC 360-10), that are *owned* by the supplier and will be used to produce products under long-term supply arrangements.
   b. Capitalize as part of the cost of molds, dies, and other tools (subject to impairment test in ASC 360-10) that are *not owned* by the supplier and will be used to produce products under long-term supply arrangements if the supplier has a *noncancelable* right under the arrangement (as long as the supplier is performing under the terms of the arrangement) to use the molds, dies, and other tools during the supply arrangement.
   c. Expense design and development costs of *nonowned* molds, dies, and other tools as incurred if the supplier does *not* have a noncancelable right to use the molds, dies, and other tools during the supply arrangement.
   d. Expense as incurred in accordance with the guidance in ASC 730-10-05-1, 05-25, 05-50. 05-55 if design and development costs are for owned or not owned molds, dies, and other tools that involve new technology.
3. Recognize design and development costs as assets as incurred if the supplier has a *contractual guarantee* for reimbursement of those costs. That is, the guarantee is included in a legally enforceable supply arrangement that provides criteria (e.g., a maximum total amount or a specific amount per part) for the objective measurement and verification of the reimbursement.

ASC 340-20: CAPITALIZED ADVERTISING COSTS

IMPORTANT NOTICE: All of the guidance in ASC 340-20, will be superseded when the guidance in ASU 2014-09, *Revenue from Contracts with Costumers*, which will reside in ASC 606, Revenue from Contracts with Customers, becomes effective for public entities for annual reporting periods that begin after December 15, 2017, and after December 15, 2018, for nonpublic entities. However, the guidance in ASC 340-20-25-4 through 25-18, which applies to insurance contracts discussed under the scope of ASC 944, will be amended and relocated to the industry specific guidance for insurance contracts in ASC 944-30-25-1AA and ASC 944-30-25-1C through 25-1P.

ASC 340-20-05-2, 15-3 through 15-4, 25-1 through 25-4, 25-6, 25-8 through 25-16, 30-2, 35-1 through 35-6, 45-1, 50-1, 55-1; ASC 720-35-05-1 through 05-5, 15-2 through 15-4; 25-1 through 25-6, 35-1, 50-1, 55-1; ASC 958-720-25-5 Reporting on Advertising Costs

BACKGROUND

Before the issuance of the guidance in ASC 340, there was no broad authoritative guidance on the treatment of advertising costs. Entities accounted for these costs in diverse ways. Some entities charged advertising expenditures to expense as incurred. Other entities, believing that advertising created a probable future economic benefit that was sufficiently measurable, capitalized these costs and amortized them against future revenues.

Advertising is defined as the promotion of an industry, company, brand, product name, or specific product or service for the purpose of improving an entity's image and/or increasing future revenues. Advertising is typically distributed via one or more media outlets (e.g., television, radio, magazines, direct mail).

ACCOUNTING GUIDANCE

In most cases, the costs of advertising should be expensed as incurred or the first time the advertisement appears. There are two exceptions to this general rule. First, entities are to capitalize certain direct-response advertising. Second, expenditures for advertising costs that are made subsequent to the recognition of revenues related to those costs are to be capitalized and charged to expense when the related revenues are recognized. For example, some entities enter into an arrangement whereby they are responsible for reimbursing some or all of their customers' advertising costs. In most cases, revenues related to the transactions creating these obligations are earned before the reimbursements are made. The entity responsible for reimbursing advertising expenditures would recognize a liability and the related advertising expense concurrently with the recognition of revenue.

There are two general types of advertising costs: the costs of producing advertisements and the costs of communicating them. Costs of communicating advertisements should not be expensed until the dissemination service has been received. For example, the costs of purchasing television or radio airtime should not be expensed until the advertisement is aired (the costs of communicating certain direct-response advertisements will be charged to expense as the advertising benefit is received).

Illustration of Expensing Advertising Costs

Ace Motor Company plans to introduce a series of new cars (the A series). Ace Motor agrees to reimburse dealerships for advertising costs they incur during January of 20X5 to promote this new series of cars. The reimbursement rate is set at 20% of the value of orders placed by the dealership for cars in the A series (up to 50% of the advertising costs incurred by the dealership). Russell Ace, a dealership in Waterbury, Connecticut, incurs $100,000 of advertising costs during January 20X5 and places $300,000 of orders for cars from the A series during that month. When the automobiles are shipped, Ace Motor will record $300,000 of revenue. Concurrently with recognizing the revenue, Ace Motor is to record a liability and a charge to advertising expense for $50,000 (Ace's reimbursement obligation to the Russell Ace dealership).

Direct-Response Advertising

Direct-response advertising must meet two conditions in order to be capitalized. First, the primary purpose of the advertising must be to generate sales, and these sales must be capable of being traced specifically to the advertising. Second, the direct-response advertising must result in probable future economic benefits.

Generation of Sales and Traceability to Direct-Response Advertising

In order for the costs of direct-response advertising to be capitalized, sales derived therefrom must be traceable directly to the advertising. The entity must maintain records that identify customers making purchases and the advertisement that customers responded to. Acceptable documentation includes the following examples:

- Files indicating customer names and the applicable direct-response advertisement
- A coded order form, coupon, or response card, included with an advertisement that includes the customer name
- A log of customers placing phone orders in response to a number appearing in an advertisement, linking those calls to the advertisement

---

Illustration of Direct-Response Advertising

Fantastic Systems, Inc., has developed a new product—an aerobic exercise machine called the Air Flyer. In order to elicit sales of this product, Fantastic Systems produces a 30-minute infomercial. Fantastic Systems has obtained a unique toll-free telephone number to facilitate sales that result from the airing of this infomercial. This toll-free number is displayed frequently throughout the infomercial. Assuming this infomercial results in probable future economic benefits to Fantastic Systems (discussed below in the section titled "Probable Future Economic Benefits of Direct-

Response Advertising"), the cost of producing and airing this infomercial would be capitalizable as direct-response advertising. Given the targeted toll-free number used, the resultant sales and the customer names can be traced to a specific advertisement (i.e., the infomercial).

Certain advertising costs may be related to a direct-response advertising campaign and yet still not be capitalizable. If the subsequent sale cannot be traced to the direct-response advertising, the related advertising costs cannot be capitalized.

Illustration of Advertising Costs Not Capitalized

Fleet Foot, Inc., a large athletic-shoe manufacturer, incurs costs to produce and air a television advertisement for a new running shoe. The commercial states that order forms, with discount coupons, will soon be distributed to certain consumers (this is the direct-response advertisement). The costs of producing and airing the television commercial are not capitalizable, since there is no link between subsequent sales and the television commercial. However, the cost of producing and distributing the order forms would be capitalizable (assuming this direct-response advertisement provided Fleet Foot with future economic benefits).

Probable Future Economic Benefits of Direct-Response Advertising

Probable future economic benefits are expected future revenues from direct-response advertising minus the costs to be incurred in generating those revenues. In order for the costs of direct-response advertising to be capitalized, there must be *persuasive evidence* that the effect of the current advertising campaign will be similar to that of previous advertising campaigns that generated future economic benefits. In terms of probable future benefits, attributes to consider in evaluating the similarity between the current direct-response advertising campaign and prior campaigns include audience demographics, the advertising method, the product, and economic conditions.

A specific entity needs to base its decision about whether to capitalize direct-response advertising costs on its past results with other direct-response advertising campaigns. In the absence of prior experience with direct-response advertising, an entity cannot rely on industry statistics as support for capitalizing advertising costs. The most persuasive type of evidence in support of the capitalization of direct-response advertising costs is a prior history of similar advertising for similar products that resulted in future economic benefits. Although an entity may not have a prior history of advertising a similar product, it may have used direct-response advertising to promote a related product or service. An entity may be able to support the capitalization of direct-response advertising for the new product or service if it can document that the results from a prior advertising campaign for a related product or service are likely to be highly correlated with the current advertising campaign. Test market results may suggest that the reaction of prospective consumers to the advertising campaign for a new product or service is likely to be similar to consumer reaction to a similar campaign for a different product or service.

PRACTICE POINTER: In the absence of a high degree of correlation between a current campaign and previous advertising campaigns for other products, a success rate based on the historical ratio of successful products or services to total products or services introduced to the marketplace would not be sufficient to support capitalization.

Illustration of Capitalizing Costs of Subsequent Products

As discussed in a previous illustration, Fantastic Systems, Inc., marketed a new fitness product, the Air Flyer, via a direct-response television campaign. This product was introduced in 20X4, and the costs of the campaign were capitalized as direct-response advertising. Fantastic Systems plans to introduce a new product, the Magic Club, in 20X5. The Magic Club, which is a new type of golf club, clearly represents a different product than the Air Flyer. On the basis of test market results, however, Fantastic Systems believes that there will be a high degree of correlation between the response of consumers to the ads for the Air Flyer and the response to the ads for the Magic Club. Therefore, Fantastic Systems can capitalize the costs of producing and distributing an infomercial for the Magic Club.

Direct-response advertising that is not capitalized, because future economic benefits are uncertain, should not be retroactively capitalized if future results indicate that the advertisement did produce economic benefits.

Measurement of the Costs of Direct-Response Advertising

Each separate direct-response advertising campaign that meets the capitalization criteria represents a *separate stand-alone cost pool.*

The costs of direct-response advertising that should be capitalized include both of the following:

- Incremental direct costs of direct-response advertising incurred in transactions with independent third parties (e.g., idea development, writing advertising copy, artwork, printing, magazine space, and mailing).
- Payroll and payroll-related costs for the direct-response advertising activities of employees who are directly associated with and devote time to the advertising reported as assets (e.g., idea development, writing advertising copy, artwork, printing, and mailing). The costs of payroll and fringe benefits for these employees should be capitalized only to the extent of the time spent working on the particular advertising project (i.e., if 10% of an employee's time is spent working on a direct-response advertising campaign that is subject to capitalization, 10% of that employee's compensation and fringe benefit costs would be included among the costs to be capitalized).

If the criteria for capitalization are met, the entire cost of the direct-response campaign, not just a pro rata share of the cost based on the expected response rate of consumers to the campaign, is capitalizable. For example, an entity distributes one million order forms and coupons to target customers and expects to receive 10,000 orders as a result of this mailing. In this case, orders can be directly traced to the advertisement. If this advertising campaign is likely to generate future economic benefits, the cost of the entire mailing campaign should be capitalized (not just the cost of mailing to the 10,000 individuals who are likely to place an order).

Amortization of Capitalized Advertising Costs

Amortization of direct-response advertising costs for a particular cost pool is as follows: Current Period Revenues Attributable to the Direct-Response Advertising Cost Pool/(Current Period Revenues Attributable to the Direct-Response Advertising Cost Pool + Estimated Future Revenues Attributable to the Direct-Response Advertising Cost Pool). Estimated future revenues may change over time, and the amortization ratio is to be recalculated each period.

Direct-response advertising costs are typically amortized over a period of not more than one year or one operating cycle. This suggests that future revenues attributable to the advertisement are limited to those likely to result within the next year (or within the next operating cycle). This recommendation is based on the view that the reliability of future revenue estimates decreases as the length of time for which such estimates are made increases. However, a possible exception to this general recommendation is illustrated below.

Illustration of Amortizing Advertising Costs

An entity undertakes a direct-response advertising campaign, via a series of television commercials and a dedicated toll-free number, to sell classic works of literature (e.g., *Moby Dick* and *A Tale of Two Cities*). Because sales can be tied directly to the advertisement, the costs of this campaign will be capitalized if the campaign is likely to generate probable future economic benefits. For this entity such benefits exist. Customers who buy the first book are sent a response card on a monthly basis thereafter, asking them if they would like to order another book in the set (there are 24 books in the collection). These future advertising efforts (mailing the response card on a monthly basis) are viewed as minimal. The entity also knows that a certain percentage of the customers who buy the first book will buy a quantifiable percentage of the remaining books. In this case, the amortization ratio used will include total revenues expected from all sales, including an estimate of future book sales. If a significant advertising effort was necessary for each book sold, however, each of these advertising efforts would be treated separately—in terms of both initial capitalization and subsequent amortization.

Assessment of Realizability of Capitalized Advertising Costs

The realizability of capitalized direct-response advertising costs should be evaluated at each reporting date on a cost-pool-by-cost-pool basis. The unamortized direct-response advertising costs are to be compared to probable future *net* revenues that are expected to be generated directly from such advertising. *Net revenues* are gross revenues less costs to be incurred in generating those revenues, excluding the amortization of advertising costs. Examples of costs to be included in making this evaluation are cost of goods sold, sales commissions, and payroll and payroll-related costs.

If the carrying amount of unamortized direct-response advertising exceeds probable future net revenues, the difference should be charged to advertising expense in the current period.

Illustration of Write-Off of Unamortized Advertising Costs

MMX Enterprises has $400,000 of unamortized direct-response advertising costs at December 31, 20X5; probable future net revenues are $300,000. This difference—$100,000—would be reported as advertising expense in 20X5.

Any later-period increase in probable future net revenue cannot be used to increase the carrying amount of the unamortized advertising costs (i.e., the write-down cannot be reversed on the basis of a subsequent increase in probable net revenues).

Miscellaneous Issues

Certain tangible assets (e.g., blimps and billboards) may be used in a number of different advertising campaigns. These tangible assets should be capitalized and depreciated over their estimated useful lives. The related depreciation charge is a cost of advertising to the extent that the tangible asset has been used for an advertising-related purpose.

Costs to produce a film, audio, or a video that is used as a vehicle for an advertisement do not constitute tangible assets under this guidance. Sales materials, such as brochures and catalogs, should be classified as prepaid supplies until they are no longer owned or expected to be used. At that point, the related cost would be considered a cost of advertising.

Disclosures

The notes to the financial statements should contain the following disclosures:

- The accounting policy selected for non-direct-response advertising costs. The two choices are to (*a*) expense these costs as incurred or (*b*) expense them the first time the advertising takes place.
- A description of the direct-response advertising reported as assets (if any), the related accounting policy, and the amortization period.
- The total amount charged to advertising expense for each income statement presented, with a separate disclosure (if any) of amounts representing a write-down to net realizable value.
- The total amount of advertising expenditures reported as an asset for each balance sheet presented.

ASC 340-20-25-17 through 25-18, 35-7 Direct-Response Advertising and Probable Future Benefits

BACKGROUND

Under the provisions of ASC 340 and ASC 720, a direct-response advertisement must provide an entity with probable future economic benefits in order for the related advertising costs to be capitalized. In determining whether an advertisement provides an entity with probable future economic benefits, an entity estimates future revenues (derived from the advertisement) less costs incurred in generating those revenues. There has been diversity in practice as to which revenues are considered in making this determination.

Some entities have limited their consideration of future revenues to primary revenues, that is, revenues derived from sales to customers receiving and responding to a direct-response advertisement. Other entities have taken a more expansive view of the appropriate revenues to consider. Those entities consider both primary and secondary revenues in evaluating whether an advertisement provides probable future economic benefits. Secondary revenues are revenues other than those derived from sales to customers receiving and responding to a direct-response advertisement. For example, revenues that publishers receive from magazine subscriptions are considered primary revenues. Revenues resulting from advertisements placed in the magazine are considered secondary revenues.

ACCOUNTING GUIDANCE

In determining probable future revenues, an entity should consider only primary revenues—that is, revenues expected from customers who receive and respond to a direct-response advertisement. In addition, only primary revenues should be considered for the purpose of amortizing capitalized direct-response advertising costs and for assessing whether those costs, which are reported as assets, will be realized.

CHAPTER 26

ASC 350—INTANGIBLES—GOODWILL AND OTHER

CONTENTS

PART I: GENERAL GUIDANCE

ASC 350-10: OVERALL

OVERVIEW

Intangible assets are long-lived assets used in the production of goods and services. They are similar to property, plant, and equipment except for their lack of physical properties. Examples of intangible assets include copyrights, patents, trademarks, and goodwill. Intangible assets with finite lives are subject to amortization over their estimated useful lives. As a general rule, assets with indefinite useful lives are not amortized. Each period these assets are tested for impairment and also to determine whether the assumption of an indefinite useful life is still valid. If the asset's life is determined to have become limited, it is amortized prospectively over its remaining useful life.

BACKGROUND

The term *intangible asset* refers to non-financial assets that lack physical substance and that provide the entity with various benefits. Intangible assets differ considerably in their characteristics, useful lives, and relationship to operations of an enterprise.

ASC 350 requires the separation of intangible assets into two categories—those with finite useful lives, which are amortized, and those with indefinite useful lives, which are not amortized.

The following are some of the basic principles upon which accounting for intangible assets in accordance with ASC 350 is based.

Identifiability

Patents, copyrights, franchises, trademarks, and other similar intangible assets can be specifically identified with reasonably descriptive names. Other types of intangible assets lack specific identification, the most common being goodwill.

Manner of Acquisition

Intangible assets may be purchased or developed internally and may be acquired singly, in groups, or in business combinations.

Determinate or Indeterminate Life

Patents, copyrights, and most franchises are examples of intangible assets with determinate lives, established by law or by contract. Other intangible assets, such as secret processes and goodwill, have no established term of existence, and the expected period of benefit may be indeterminate at the time of acquisition.

Transferability

The rights to a patent, copyright, or franchise can be identified separately and bought or sold. Goodwill, on the other hand, is inseparable from a business and is transferable only as an inseparable intangible asset of an enterprise.

PRACTICE POINTER: While some of the attributes that underlie purchased goodwill may be developed internally, only goodwill purchased as part of a business combination is recorded as an intangible asset. Examples of such items include customer loyalty, superior reputation, and other similar characteristics.

Cost of Intangibles

A company records as assets the costs of intangible assets acquired from other enterprises or individuals. The cost of an intangible asset is measured by (*a*) the amount of cash disbursed or the fair value of other assets distributed, (*b*) the present value of amounts to be paid for liabilities incurred, and (*c*) the fair value of consideration received for stock issued.

Scope

ASC 350-30-15-3 covers the following aspects of accounting and reporting for intangible assets:

- Intangible assets acquired individually or with a group of assets other than in a business combination or an acquisition by a not-for-profit entity
- Intangible assets (other than goodwill) recognized in accordance with ASC 805 (Business Combinations) or ASC 958 (Not-for-Profit Entities), subsequent to their acquisition
- Cost of internally developing identifiable intangible assets that an entity recognizes as assets

Intangible assets acquired in a business combination are covered in ASC 805. ASC 350 does not change accounting that is prescribed in the following pronouncements (ASC 350-10-15-4):

- ASC 730 (Research and Development)
- ASC 740 (Income Taxes)
- ASC 860 (Transfers and Servicing)
- ASC 920 (Entertainment—Broadcasters)
- ASC 928 (Entertainment—Music)
- ASC 932 (Extractive Industries—Oil and Gas)
- ASC 950 (Financial Services—Title Plant)
- ASC 980 (Regulated Operations)
- ASC 985 (Software)

ASC 350-20: GOODWILL

ACCOUNTING FOR GOODWILL

An entity may incur internal costs that are similar to acquired intangible assets, including goodwill. These costs, as well as the costs of maintaining or restoring intangible assets that have indeterminate lives or that are inherent in a continuing business or nonprofit activity and related to the entity as a whole, are expensed as incurred (ASC 350-20-25-3).

Goodwill is not amortized and is tested for impairment at a level of reporting referred to as a reporting unit (ASC 350-20-35-1). A reporting unit is an operating segment or one level below an operating segment (also known as a component) (ASC Master Glossary). See ASC 280 (Segment Reporting) for additional guidance on the definition of an operating segment. A component of an operating segment is a reporting unit if the component constitutes a business or nonprofit activity for which discrete financial information is available and segment management (as defined in ASC 280-10-50-7) regularly reviews the operating results of that component. Two or more components of an operating segment shall be aggregated and treated as a single reporting unit if the components have similar operating characteristics. An operating segment is deemed to be a reporting unit if (1) all of its components are similar, (2) none of its components is a reporting unit, or (3) if it comprises only a single component (ASC 350-20-35-34, 35, 36).

Fair Value Measurements

The fair value of a reporting unit refers to the price that would be received to sell the unit, as a whole in an orderly transaction between market participants at the measurement date. Quoted market prices in active markets are the best evidence of fair value and shall be used as the basis for the measurement. However, the market price of an individual equity security may not be representative of the fair value of the reporting unit as a whole (ASC 350-20-35-22). If quoted market prices are not available, an estimate of fair value should be based on the best information available. This may involve prices of similar assets and liabilities and the use of other valuation techniques, such as a present value technique. An estimate of fair value may be based on multiples of earnings or revenue or another similar performance measure if that technique is consistent with the objectives of measuring fair value (ASC 350-20-35-24).

Testing for Impairment

Goodwill is tested for impairment on an annual basis, or more frequently if events and circumstances change (ASC 350-20-35-28). The annual test may be performed at any time during the fiscal year but must be performed at the same time each year. Different reporting units may be tested for impairment at different times (ASC 350-20-35-28, 30).

An entity should use a two-step impairment test to identify potential goodwill impairment. However, before applying the two-step impairment test, an entity may first consider qualitative factors to determine if the two-step test is even necessary (ASC 350-20-35-3). This optional qualitative assessment is used to determine whether it is more likely than not (i.e., a likelihood of more than 50%) that the fair value of a reporting unit is less than its carrying amount, including goodwill. In making this determination, an entity must assess relevant events and circumstances including, but not limited to, the following (ASC 350-20-35-3C):

1. Macroeconomic conditions
   a. Deterioration in general economic conditions
   b. Limitations on accessing capital
   c. Fluctuations in foreign exchange rates
   d. Other developments in equity and credit markets
2. Industry and market considerations
   a. Deterioration in the environment in which an entity operates
   b. Increased competitive environment
   c. Decline in market-dependent multiples or metrics
   d. Change in the market for an entity's products or services
   e. Regulatory or political development
3. Cost factors such as increases in raw materials, labor, or other costs that have a negative effect on earnings or cash flows
4. Overall financial performance
   a. Negative or declining cash flows
   b. Decline in actual or planned revenue or earnings
5. Other relevant entity-specific events
   a. Changes in management, key personnel, strategy, or customers
   b. Contemplation of bankruptcy
   c. Litigation
6. Events affecting a reporting unit
   a. Change in the composition or carrying amount of its net assets
   b. A more-likely-than-not expectation of selling or disposing all, or a portion, of a reporting unit
   c. Testing for recoverability of a significant asset group within a reporting unit
   d. Recognition of a goodwill impairment loss in the financial statements of a subsidiary that is a component of a reporting unit
7. If applicable, a sustained decrease in share price

These examples of events to be considered are not all-inclusive and an entity must consider the extent to which each of the adverse events identified could affect the comparison of a reporting unit's fair value with its carrying amount. An entity should also consider positive and mitigating events that may affect the determination of whether it is more likely than not that an impairment exists (ASC 350-20-35-3F).

If, after considering the totality of the events and circumstances such as those listed above, an entity determines that it is not more likely than not that the fair value of a reporting unit is less than its carrying amount, then the two-step impairment test is not necessary. However, if an entity determines that it is more likely than not that the fair value of the reporting entity is less than its carrying amount, the entity must perform the two-step impairment test as follows (ASC 350-20-35-4, 9):

Step 1: Identify potential impairment by comparing the fair value of a reporting unit with its carrying amount, including goodwill.

Step 2: Measure the amount of goodwill loss by comparing the implied fair value of the reporting unit goodwill with the carrying amount of that goodwill and recognize a loss by the excess of the latter over the former.

The implied fair value of goodwill is determined in the same way that goodwill is recognized in a business combination or in an acquisition involving a not-for-profit entity. The entity assigns the fair value of a reporting unit to all the assets and liabilities of that unit as if the reporting unit had been acquired in a business combination or in an acquisition involving a not-for-profit entity. The excess of the fair value of the unit over the amounts assigned to its other assets and its liabilities is the implied fair value of goodwill. That process is performed only for purposes of testing goodwill for impairment. The entity shall neither write up nor write down a recognized asset or liability, nor should it recognize a previously unrecognized intangible asset as a result of the allocation process (ASC 350-20-35-14, 17).

If the determination of the amount of loss due to the impairment of goodwill is not complete when the financial statements are issued and a goodwill impairment loss is considered probable and can be reasonably estimated, the best estimate of that loss shall be recognized in the financial statements (ASC 350-20-35-18).

A private company or not-for-profit entity may make an accounting policy election to apply the accounting alternative for a goodwill triggering event evaluation to goodwill only as of the end of each reporting period. This applies to both interim and annual reporting periods. The entity would not evaluate goodwill impairment triggering events and measure any related impairment during the reporting period. (ASC 350-20-35-84) This accounting alternative does not change the requirement to assess other assets for impairment. If the impairment test related to other assets would have resulted in a goodwill impairment triggering event, the entity electing this accounting alternative should consider the results of an impairment test related to other assets in connection with its goodwill impairment test only as of the end of its annual goodwill impairment and reporting date. (ASC 350-20-35-85)

PRACTICE POINTER: This alternative was made available in ASU 2021-03, *Intangibles—Goodwill and Other (Topic 350)*. It provides private companies and not-for-profit entities an accounting alternative to perform the goodwill impairment triggering event evaluation only at the end of the reporting period rather than continuously throughout the period. Certain stakeholders expressed concern regarding the cost and complexity of private companies being required to evaluate triggering events and potentially measuring a goodwill impairment throughout the reporting period. This issue became more apparent during COVID-19 because of the uncertainty in the economic environment and the significant changes in facts and circumstances in successive quarters of the annual period. An entity that does not elect the accounting alternative of amortizing goodwill and that performs its annual impairment evaluation as of a date other than the annual reporting date should perform a triggering event evaluation only as of the end of the reporting period. This alternative is effective on a prospective basis for fiscal years beginning after December 15, 2019. Early adoption is permitted for financial statements that have not been issued or made available for issuance as of March 30, 2021. The amendment also includes an unconditional one-time option to adopt the alternative prospectively after its effective date without assessing preferability under ASC 250 (Accounting Changes and Error Corrections).

Assigning Assets and Liabilities to Reporting Units

For purposes of testing goodwill impairment, acquired assets and assumed liabilities are assigned to a reporting unit if both of the following criteria are met:

- The asset will be employed in, or the liability relates to, the operations of a reporting unit.
- The asset or liability will be considered in determining the fair value of the reporting unit.

Assets and liabilities may be employed in the operations of more than one reporting unit. The method used to determine the amount of such assets and liabilities to be assigned to a reporting unit must be reasonable and supported, and applied consistently (ASC 350-20-35-39, 40).

Assigning Goodwill to Reporting Units

For purposes of testing goodwill for impairment, all goodwill that is acquired in a business combination or in an acquisition involving a not-for-profit entity must be assigned to one or more reporting units as of the acquisition date. Goodwill is assigned to reporting units on the basis of expected benefits from the synergies of the combination, even though other assets or liabilities of the acquired entity may not be assigned to those reporting units. Goodwill may be divided among multiple reporting units, and the method of allocating goodwill must be reasonable and supportable, and applied consistently (ASC 350-20-35-41).

Subsidiary Goodwill

Goodwill recognized by a public or nonpublic subsidiary in its separate financial statements prepared in accordance with U.S. GAAP shall be accounted for in accordance with ASC 350. Such subsidiary goodwill shall be tested for impairment in accordance with ASC 350 using the subsidiary's reporting unit. If a goodwill impairment loss is recognized at the subsidiary level, goodwill of the reporting unit(s), at which the subsidiary resides, must be tested for impairment if the event that gave rise to the loss at the subsidiary level would more likely than not reduce the fair value of the reporting unit below its carrying amount (ASC 350-20-35-48).

Disposal of a Reporting Unit

When a reporting unit is to be disposed of in its entirety, goodwill of that unit shall be included in the carrying amount of the reporting unit in determining any gain or loss on disposal. When a portion of a reporting unit that constitutes a business is to be disposed of, goodwill associated with that business or nonprofit activity shall be included in the carrying amount of the business or nonprofit activity in determining the gain or loss on disposal. The amount of goodwill included is based on the relative fair value of the business activity to be disposed of and the portion of the reporting unit that will be retained (ASC 350-20-40-1, 2, 3).

Testing for Impairment and Disposal of a Reporting Unit When the Reporting Unit Is Less than Wholly Owned

If a reporting unit is less than wholly owned, any impairment loss shall be attributed to the parent and the noncontrolling interest on a rational basis. Similarly, when all or a portion of a less-than-wholly-owned reporting unit is disposed of, the gain or loss on disposal shall be attributed to both the parent and the noncontrolling interest (ASC 350-20-35-57, A).

Financial Statement Presentation and Disclosure of Goodwill

For each period for which a statement of financial position is presented the change in the carrying amount of goodwill during the period shall be disclosed (ASC 350-20-50-1), showing separately:

- The gross amount and accumulated impairment losses at the beginning and ending of the period
- Additional goodwill recognized during the period (except goodwill included in a disposal group that, on acquisition, meets the criteria to be classified as held for sale (see ASC 360-10-45-9)
- Adjustments resulting from the subsequent recognition of deferred tax assets during the period (see ASC 805-740-25-2 through 25-4 and 45-2)
- Impairment losses recognized during the period and net foreign exchange differences arising during the period
- Any other changes in the carrying amounts during the period.

For each goodwill impairment loss recognized, the following information is required to be disclosed (ASC 350-20-50-2):

- A description of the facts and circumstances leading to the impairment
- The amount of the impairment loss and the method of determining the fair value of the associated reporting unit
- If a recognized impairment loss is an estimate that has not yet been finalized, that fact and the reasons therefore and, in subsequent years, the nature and amount of any significant adjustments made to the initial estimate of the impairment loss

The quantitative disclosures about Level 3 unobservable inputs used in fair value measurements, which are required by ASC 820-10-50-2(bbb), are not required for fair value measurements related to financial accounting and reporting for goodwill after its initial recognition in a business combination (ASC 350-20-50-3).

PRIVATE COMPANY COUNCIL ALTERNATIVE GUIDANCE

PRACTICE POINTER: A number of specific ASC sections provide guidance for an entity electing the accounting alternative in this subsection (ASC 350-20-15-3A).

The general guidance in ASC Subtopic 350-20 indicates that goodwill must not be amortized, but rather should be tested for impairment on an annual basis (ASC 350-20-35-1). However, ASC Subtopic 350-20 also includes alternative guidance that a private company can elect to follow that permits the amortization of goodwill. A private company or a not-for profit entity can elect to apply this alternative guidance for the following transactions or activities (ASC 350-20-15-4):

- Goodwill recognized in a business combination or in an acquisition of a not-for-profit entity after it has been initially recognized and measured
- Amounts recognized as goodwill in applying the equity method of accounting for investments
- The excess reorganization value recognized by entities that adopt fresh-start reporting in accordance with ASC 852 on reorganizations

An entity that elects to follow this alternative guidance must also apply all of the related guidance regarding subsequent measurement, derecognition, other presentation matters, and disclosures. Further, once an entity has elected to apply this alternative guidance, it must be applied to existing goodwill and to all additions to goodwill recognized in future transactions within the scope of the alternative guidance (ASC 350-20-15-5).

Subsequent Measurement

Under the alternative guidance for private companies, goodwill must be amortized on a straight-line basis over a period not to exceed ten years (ASC 350-20-35-63). An entity may revise the estimated remaining useful life of goodwill if certain events or circumstances occur that warrant such a change. However, the cumulative amortization period used cannot exceed 10 years (ASC 350-20-35-64). The alternative guidance also allows a private company to test its goodwill for impairment at the entity level rather than the reporting unit level (ASC 350-20-35-65).

Goodwill of an entity shall be tested for impairment if events or circumstances change that indicate that the fair value of the entity may be below its carrying amount (i.e., a triggering event). For entities that have elected the accounting alternative for a goodwill impairment triggering event (see above discussion), a goodwill impairment evaluation is performed only at the end of each reporting period. (ASC 350-20-35-66) Qualitative factors may be assessed to determine whether it is more likely than not (i.e., a probability of more than 50%) that the fair value of the entity is less than its carrying value, including goodwill. (ASC 350-20-35-67)

PRACTICE POINTER: An entity may choose to forgo the qualitative assessment of the likelihood of an impairment and instead proceed directly to a quantitative assessment by comparing the entity's fair value with its carrying amount (ASC 350-20-35-70).

In making this determination, an entity must assess relevant events and circumstances including, but not limited to, the following (ASC 350-20-35-3C):

1. Macroeconomic conditions
   a. Deterioration in general economic conditions
   b. Limitations on accessing capital
   c. Fluctuations in foreign exchange rates
   d. Other developments in equity and credit markets
2. Industry and market considerations
   a. Deterioration in the environment in which an entity operates
   b. Increased competitive environment
   c. Decline in market-dependent multiples or metrics
   d. Change in the market for an entity's products or services
   e. Regulatory or political development

3. Cost factors such as increases in raw materials, labor, or other costs that have a negative effect on earnings or cash flows
4. Overall financial performance
   a. Negative or declining cash flows
   b. Decline in actual or planned revenue or earnings
5. Other relevant entity-specific events
   a. Changes in management, key personnel, strategy, or customers
   b. Contemplation of bankruptcy
   c. Litigation
6. Events affecting a reporting unit
   a. Change in the composition or carrying amount of its net assets
   b. A more-likely-than-not expectation of selling or disposing all, or a portion, of a reporting unit
   c. Testing for recoverability of a significant asset group within a reporting unit
   d. Recognition of a goodwill impairment loss in the financial statements of a subsidiary that is a component of a reporting unit
7. If applicable, a sustained decrease in share price

These examples of events to be considered are not all-inclusive and an entity must consider the extent to which each of the adverse events identified could affect the comparison of a reporting unit's fair value with its carrying amount. An entity should also consider positive and mitigating events that may affect the determination of whether it is more likely than not that an impairment exists (ASC 350-20-35-68).

If, after considering the totality of the events and circumstances such as those listed above, an entity determines that it is not more likely than not that the fair value of the entity is less than its carrying amount, then further testing is unnecessary and no quantitative analysis is required. However, if an entity determines that it is more likely than not that the fair value of the entity is less than its carrying amount, or if the entity elected to bypass the optional qualitative assessment discussed above, the entity must perform a quantitative assessment to determine the fair value of the entity. This fair value amount of then compared to the entity's carrying amount, including goodwill, and a goodwill impairment loss must be recognized if the fair value of the entity is less than its carrying amount (ASC 350-20-35-71, 72). After a goodwill impairment loss is recognized, the remaining carrying amount of goodwill must be amortized over the remaining useful life of goodwill (ASC 350-20-35-78).

If goodwill and another asset (or asset group) of an entity are being tested for impairment at the same time, the entity should first test the other asset for impairment before testing goodwill. If the other asset is impaired, the impairment loss related to that asset should be recognized before testing goodwill for impairment (ASC 350-20-35-79).

PRACTICE NOTE: Under this alternative guidance, the portion of the difference between the cost of an investment and the amount of underlying equity in net assets of an equity method investee that is recognized as goodwill (i.e., equity method goodwill) must also be amortized on a straight-line basis over a period not to exceed ten years. However, equity method goodwill must not be reviewed for impairment in accordance with ASC Subtopic 350-20, but rather shall be reviewed for impairment in accordance with ASC 323-10-35-32 (ASC 350-20-35-81, 82).

Derecognition

When a portion of an entity is to be disposed of, the related goodwill must be included in the carrying amount of the entity to determine the gain or loss on disposal. An entity must use a reasonable and rational approach to determine the amount of goodwill to allocate to the portion of the entity to be disposed of (ASC 350-20-40-9).

Disclosure

The following information shall be disclosed in the notes to the financial statements for any additions to goodwill in each period for which a statement of financial position is presented (ASC 350-20-50-4):

- The amount assigned to goodwill in total and by major business combinations or by reorganization event resulting in fresh-start reporting
- The weighted average amortization period in total and the amortization period by major business combination or by reorganization event resulting in fresh-start reporting

The following information must be disclosed in the financial statements or the notes to the financial statements for each period for which a statement of financial position is presented (ASC 350-20-50-5):

- The gross carrying amounts of goodwill, accumulated amortization, and accumulated impairment loss
- The aggregate amortization expense for the period
- Goodwill included in a disposal group classified as held for sale and goodwill derecognized during the period without having previously been reported in a disposal group classified as held for sale

When a goodwill impairment loss is recognized, the following information must be disclosed in the notes to the financial statements that include the period in which the impairment loss is recognized (ASC 350-20-50-6):

- A description of the facts and circumstances leading to the impairment
- The amount of the impairment loss and the method used to determine the fair value of the entity
- The caption in the income statement in which the impairment loss is included
- The method of allocating the impairment loss to the individual amortizable units of goodwill

ASC 350-30: GENERAL INTANGIBLES OTHER THAN GOODWILL

ACCOUNTING FOR INTANGIBLE ASSETS OTHER THAN GOODWILL

Initial Recognition and Measurement

Intangible assets that are acquired individually, or as part of a group of assets, are initially recorded at their fair value. The cost of a group of assets acquired in a transaction is allocated to the individual assets based on their relative fair values. Goodwill does not arise in such a transaction. Intangible assets, including related goodwill, that are acquired in a business combination are accounted for in accordance with ASC 805 (ASC 350-30-25-1, 2), and goodwill arising in connection with an acquisition of a nonprofit activity by a not-for-profit entity is accounted for in accordance with ASC 958 (ASC 350-30-05-1).

Accounting Subsequent to Acquisition

Intangible Assets Subject to Amortization

Intangible assets with finite useful lives are amortized over those lives. Intangible assets with indefinite useful lives are not amortized. Guidelines for determining the useful lives of intangible assets are (ASC 350-30-35-3):

- The expected use of the asset by the entity
- The expected useful life of another asset or group of assets to which the useful life of the asset in question may relate
- Legal, regulatory, or contractual provisions that may limit the asset's useful life
- Legal, regulatory, or contractual provisions that enable renewal or extension of the useful life without significant cost
- The effects of obsolescence, demand, competition, and other economic factors
- The level of maintenance expenditures required to obtain the expected future cash flows from the asset

As asset for which no legal, regulatory, contractual, competitive, economic, or other factors limit the useful life is considered to have an indefinite, but not infinite, useful life (ASC 350-30-35-4).

The cost of a recognized intangible asset, less its residual value to the reporting entity, should be amortized over its useful life unless that life is determined to be indefinite (ASC 350-30-35-6).

The remaining amortization period, for those assets being amortized, should be evaluated at each reporting period (ASC 350-30-35-9). If the life is finite, but the precise length of that life is not known, the best estimate of the asset's useful life shall be used for amortization purposes. The method of amortization shall be the pattern in which the economic benefits are consumed or otherwise used up. If that pattern cannot be reliably determined, the straight-line method shall be used. An intangible asset should not be written off in the period of acquisition unless it is determined to be impaired during that period (ASC 350-30-35-6, 7).

An intangible asset that is subject to amortization shall be reviewed for impairment in accordance with the guidance in ASC 360.

PRACTICE POINTER: For example, an entity acquires a copyright that has a remaining legal life of 40 years. The entity expects to receive cash flows from the copyright for the next 20 years. The copyright will be amortized over the next 20 years, in a manner consistent with the benefits received from the copyright. The copyright will be reviewed for impairment using the provisions of ASC 360.

Intangible Assets Not Subject to Amortization

If an intangible asset is determined to have an indefinite useful life, it shall not be amortized until its useful life is determined to be no longer indefinite. An assessment of the useful life of an intangible asset that is not being amortized is required each reporting period to determine whether events and circumstances continue to support an indefinite useful life. If such an asset is determined to have a finite useful life, the asset shall be tested for impairment in accordance with ASC 350-30-35-18, 19. Intangible assets acquired in a business combination or in an acquisition involving a not-for-profit entity that are used in research and development activities shall be considered to have an indefinite life until the related research and development efforts end (ASC 350-30-35-15, 16, 17).

All intangible assets not subject to amortization (those with indefinite useful lives) shall be tested for impairment annually, and more frequently if events and circumstances indicate that it is more likely than not that the asset may be impaired.

However, before conducting a quantitative impairment test, an entity may first consider qualitative factors to determine if the quantitative test is even necessary. This optional qualitative assessment is used to determine whether it is more likely than not (i.e., a likelihood of more than 50%) that an indefinite-lived intangible asset is impaired (ASC 350-30-35-18). In making this determination, an entity must assess relevant events and circumstances including, but not limited to, the following (ASC 350-30-35-18B):

1. Cost factors such as increases in raw materials, labor, or other costs that have a negative effect on earnings or cash flows
2. Overall financial performance
   a. Negative or declining cash flows
   b. Decline in actual or planned revenue or earnings
3. Legal, regulatory, contractual, political, business, or other factors, including asset-specific factors
4. Other relevant entity-specific events
   a. Changes in management, key personnel, strategy, or customers
   b. Contemplation of bankruptcy
   c. Litigation
5. Industry and market considerations
   a. Deterioration in the environment in which an entity operates
   b. Increased competitive environment
   c. Decline in market-dependent multiples or metrics
   d. Change in the market for an entity's products or services
6. Macroeconomic conditions
   a. Deterioration in general economic conditions
   b. Limitations on accessing capital
   c. Fluctuations in foreign exchange rates
   d. Other developments in equity and credit markets

These examples of events to be considered are not all-inclusive and an entity must consider all relevant events and circumstances that could affect significant inputs used to determine the fair value of the indefinite-lived intangible asset. An entity should also consider the following to determine whether it is more likely than not that the indefinite-lived intangible asset is impaired (ASC 350-30-35-18C):

1. Positive and mitigating events and circumstances that could affect the significant inputs.
2. If an entity has made a recent fair value calculation for an indefinite-lived intangible asset, the difference between that fair value and the then carrying amount.
3. Whether there have been any changes to the carrying amount of the indefinite-lived intangible asset.

If, after considering the totality of events and circumstances such as those listed above, an entity determines that it is not more likely than not that the indefinite-lived asset is impaired, then the entity does not need to calculate the fair value of the asset and conduct the quantitative impairment test. However, if an entity determines that it is more likely than not that the indefinite-lived asset is impaired, the entity must calculate the fair value and conduct the quantitative impairment test (ASC 350-30-35-18E, F).

If impaired, an impairment loss is recognized in an amount equal to the excess of the asset's carrying value over its fair value. After such a loss is recognized, the adjusted carrying amount of the asset is its new accounting basis. Subsequent reversal of a previously recognized impairment loss is prohibited (ASC 350-30-35-19, 20).

PRACTICE POINTER: The remaining useful life of an intangible asset subject to amortization is reviewed each reporting period, as is the continuing status of intangible assets viewed to have an indefinite life. Conversely, unless certain events or circumstances suggest otherwise, the impairment status of intangible assets are only tested on an annual basis.

PRACTICE POINTER: Assume an entity has the rights to a broadcast license that can be renewed indefinitely. Based on a review of the relevant facts and circumstances, it appears likely that the entity will continue to renew its license for the foreseeable future and that the license will continue to have economic value and will generate positive cash flows for the entity holding the license. The cost of the broadcast license will not be amortized because the expected useful life of the license is indefinite. The broadcast license will be reviewed for impairment using the guidance in ASC 350 (ASC 350-30-35-18, 19).

PRACTICE POINTER: An entity acquired a trademark associated with a product in 20X8. At acquisition, based on the relevant facts and circumstances, the trademarked product appeared to have an indefinite life. Therefore, the cost of the trademark was not amortized. In 20Y1, the entity decided to phase out production of the trademarked product over a period of five years. The entity would first evaluate whether the trademark is impaired using the guidance in ASC 350. The carrying amount of the trademark, after any necessary impairment-related adjustment, would be amortized over the next five years. During each of the next five years, the trademark would be reviewed for impairment using the provisions of ASC 360 (since the intangible asset is now subject to periodic amortization).

Internal-Use Software

Entities often license internal-use software from third parties. A software license is generally accounted for as the acquisition of an intangible asset and the incurrence of a liability to the extent that all or a portion of the software licensing fees are not paid on or before the acquisition date by the licensee. The intangible asset acquired shall be recognized and measured in accordance with ASC 350-30-25-1 and ASC 350-30-30-1.

Financial Statement Presentation and Disclosure

At a minimum, all intangible assets shall be combined and presented as a separate line item in the statement of financial position (balance sheet). This is not intended to preclude separate presentation of individual intangible assets or classes of intangible assets. Amortization expense and impairment losses on intangible assets are required to be presented in the income statement (statement of activities) as separate items within continuing operations (or a similar caption). An impairment loss is not recognized as a change in accounting principle (ASC 350-30-45-1, 2, 3).

In the period of acquisition, the following information is required for intangible assets acquired, whether acquired individually or as part of a group of assets (ASC 350-30-50-1):

- For intangible assets subject to amortization:
  - The total amount assigned and the amount assigned to any major intangible asset class
  - The amount of any significant residual value, in total and by major intangible asset class
  - The weighted-average amortization period in total and by major intangible asset class
- For intangible assets not subject to amortization, the total amount assigned and the amount assigned to any major intangible asset class
- The amount of research and development assets acquired in a transaction other than a business combination and written off in the period, and the line item in the income statement in which the amounts written off are aggregated
- For intangible assets with renewal or extension terms, the weighted-average period before the next renewal or extension period (both explicit and implicit), by major intangible asset

The following information is required in the financial statements or related notes for each period for which a statement of financial position (balance sheet) is presented (ASC 350-30-50-2):

- The gross carrying amount and accumulated amortization, in total and by major intangible asset class
- The aggregate amortization expense for the period
- The estimated aggregate amortization expense for each of the five succeeding years
- For intangible assets not subject to amortization, the total carrying amount and the carrying amount for each major intangible asset class
- The entity's accounting policy on the treatment of costs incurred to renew or extend the term of a recognized intangible asset
- Changes in the carrying amount of goodwill during the period showing separately (ASC 350-20-50-1):
  - The gross amount and accumulated impairment losses at the beginning of the period
  - Additional goodwill recognized during the period
  - Adjustments resulting from the subsequent recognition of deferred tax assets
  - Goodwill included in a disposal group classified as held for sale
  - Impairment losses recognized during the period
  - Net exchange differences recognized during the period in accordance with ASC 830 (Foreign Currency Matters)
  - Any other changes in the carrying amounts during the period
  - The gross amount and accumulated impairment losses at the end of the period

For each impairment loss recognized related to an intangible asset, the following information is required to be disclosed (ASC 350-30-50-3):

- A description of the impaired intangible asset, and the facts and circumstances leading to the impairment
- The amount of the impairment loss and the method of determining fair value
- The caption in the income statement (or the statement of activities) in which the impairment loss is aggregated
- The segment in which the impaired intangible asset is reported under ASC 280, if applicable

PART II: INTERPRETIVE GUIDANCE

INTANGIBLES—GOODWILL AND OTHER

ASC 350-20: GOODWILL

ASC 350-20-35-7, 35-25 through 35-26, 55-10 through 55-16, 55-18 through 55-23 Deferred Income Tax Considerations in Applying the Goodwill Impairment Test in ASC 350, Intangibles—Goodwill and Other

OVERVIEW

As a result of the guidance in ASC 350, there has been a drastic change in the way that companies account for goodwill acquired in a business combination. Under that guidance, an entity must allocate goodwill acquired in a business combination to one or more reporting units. In addition, corporate assets and liabilities also must be allocated to reporting units if (*a*) an asset is employed or a liability is related to a reporting unit's operations, and (*b*) the asset or liability will be taken into account in determining the reporting unit's fair value.

Under the guidance in ASC 350, goodwill must be tested for impairment at the reporting level at least annually using the following procedure: (1) a reporting unit's fair value is compared to its carrying amount to determine whether the carrying amount exceeds its fair value (an excess, if any, may be a goodwill impairment), and (2) the *implied* fair value of goodwill, which is determined in the same way as the measurement of goodwill in a business combination under the provisions of ASC 805, Business Combinations, an acquisition of a business, or a nonprofit activity acquired by a not-for-profit entity under the guidance in ASC 958-805, which is compared with the carrying amount of goodwill.

ACCOUNTING ISSUES

- In estimating a reporting unit's fair value, should it be assumed that it would be bought or sold in a *nontaxable* rather than in a *taxable* transaction?
- Should deferred income taxes be included in a reporting unit's carrying amount when comparing the reporting unit's fair value to its carrying amount?
- When measuring deferred tax assets and liabilities for the purpose of determining the implied fair value of a reporting unit's goodwill for the ASC 350 goodwill impairment test, should an entity use the existing income tax bases or assume new income tax bases for a reporting unit's assets and liabilities?

ACCOUNTING GUIDANCE

The following guidance was provided:

- Judgment based on the relevant facts and circumstances should be used in determining whether the fair value of a reporting unit should be estimated based on the assumption that the reporting unit could be bought or sold in a nontaxable transaction rather than in a taxable transaction. That decision should be made on a case-by-case basis by considering whether (*a*) the assumption is consistent with those that others in the marketplace would include in fair value estimates, (*b*) the assumed structure is practicable, and (*c*) the assumed structure provides a seller with the highest and best use and would provide the maximum value for the reporting unit, including consideration of related tax implications. Members noted that in determining whether a nontaxable transaction is practicable, an entity should consider whether the reporting unit could be sold in a nontaxable transaction; and whether the entity's ability to treat a sale as a nontaxable transaction would be impeded by income tax laws and regulations or corporate governance requirements.
- Deferred income taxes should be included in a reporting unit's carrying amount for Step 1 of the goodwill impairment test, regardless of the tax structure (taxable or nontaxable) on which the reporting unit's fair value will be determined based on an assumption that it would be bought or sold in a taxable or nontaxable transaction.
- The income tax bases of a reporting unit's assets and liabilities inherent in the tax structure (taxable or nontaxable) assumed in an entity's estimate of the reporting unit's fair value in Step 1 of the impairment test should be used in determining the implied fair value of the reporting unit's goodwill in Step 2 of the impairment test. If a *nontaxable* transaction is assumed, the entity's existing income tax bases should be used. New income tax bases should be used if a *taxable* transaction is assumed. It was noted that in Step 2 of the test, the implied fair value of a reporting entity's goodwill is determined in the same way as the amount of goodwill recognized in a business combination under the guidance in ASC 805-30-30-5. This method is also used to determine the amount of goodwill recognized in an acquisition of a business or the acquisition of a nonprofit activity by a not-for-profit entity under the guidance in ASC 958-805.

ASC 350-20-55-1 through 55-9 Clarification of Reporting Unit Guidance in ASC 350-20-35-33 through 35-35

To clarify the guidance in ASC 350-20-35-33 through 35-35, the FASB staff has provided the following guidance on how to determine whether a component of an operating segment is a reporting unit:

- Judgment should be used based on the specific facts and circumstances related to the entity.
- No single characteristic or factor among those listed in ASC 350-20-35-33 through 35-35 is determinative.

The way an entity's operations are managed and the way it has integrated an acquired entity with its own operations are significant.

The guidance in ASC 350-20-35-33 through 35-35 states that "[a] component of an operating segment is a reporting unit if the component constitutes a business for which discrete financial information is available and segment management regularly review the operating results of the component." Judgment based on the specific facts and circumstances is necessary to determine whether a component is a business. The guidance in ASC 805, Business Combinations, should be used to determine whether a group of assets represents a business.

This pronouncement has been amended by the guidance in ASC 958-805, which states that any references to a "business or businesses" likewise refer to a "nonprofit activity" and "nonprofit activities," respectively.

ASC 350-30: GENERAL INTANGIBLES OTHER THAN GOODWILL

ASC 350-30-15-5, 25-5, 35-5A through 35-5B, 55-1 through 55-1B, 55-28H through 55-28I, 55-28K through 55-28L Accounting for Defensive Intangible Assets

BACKGROUND

A "defensive asset" or "locked-up asset" is an intangible asset that has been acquired in a business combination or in an asset acquisition that an entity does *not* intend to actively use but intends to keep others from using it. Although the entity does not actively use the asset, its existence probably increases the value of other assets owned by the acquiring entity. In the past, entities have attributed little or no value to acquired intangible assets that they did not intend to actively use, regardless of whether they might have been actively used by another acquirer.

However, as a result of the issuance of ASC 805 and ASC 820, Fair Value Measurement, intangible assets must be recognized at a value that represents an asset's *highest and best use* based on assumptions about other entities in the market. When those Statements become effective, entities will generally assign a greater value to defensive intangible assets than they previously would have assigned under the guidance in ASC 805. Consequently, constituents have asked how defensive assets should be accounted for after their acquisition, including the assignment of an estimated useful life.

SCOPE

This guidance applies to all acquired intangible assets that an entity does *not* intend to use actively but intends to hold to keep competitors from gaining access to those assets, except if an intangible asset is used in research and development activities, which are accounted for in accordance with the guidance in ASC 350-30-35-15 through 35-17A. Whether an asset is a defensive asset depends on the entity's intentions for its use. The accounting for such assets may change if an entity decides to begin to actively use the asset.

The identification of market participants, market participants' assumptions, or valuation issues related to defensive intangible assets are not discussed in this Issue.

ACCOUNTING GUIDANCE

The following guidance applies:

Recognition. A defensive intangible asset should be accounted for as a separate unit of accounting and should not be included in the cost of an entity's existing intangible assets because defensive intangible assets are identified separately.

Subsequent measurement. A defensive asset's benefit to an entity that holds it is represented by the direct or indirect cash flows that result from preventing others from realizing value from that asset. The useful life assigned to a defensive intangible asset, in accordance with the guidance in ASC 350-30-35-1 through 35-3 should represent an entity's consumption of the expected benefits related to the asset by estimating the period over which the asset's fair value will diminish. That period is a surrogate for the period over which an entity expects that the defensive asset will contribute indirectly to the entity's future cash flows.

Defensive intangible assets rarely have an indefinite useful life because their fair value generally diminishes over time due to a lack of market exposure or as a result of competitive or other factors. In addition, an acquired intangible asset that meets the definition of a defensive intangible asset cannot be considered as immediately abandoned.

ASC 350-30-35-21 through 35-28, 35-30 through 35-32, 35-34 through 35-35, 35-37 through 35-38 Unit of Accounting for Testing Impairment of Indefinite-Lived Intangible Assets

BACKGROUND

Under the provisions of ASC 350, intangible assets that are not required to be amortized must be evaluated for impairment at least annually. If an intangible asset's carrying amount exceeds its fair value, an impairment loss should be recognized. Recognized losses should not be restored in the future.

Constituents asked for guidance regarding the unit of accounting to be used when evaluating the impairment of intangible assets with indefinite lives. That is, (*a*) whether identical or similar indefinite-lived intangible assets may be combined for the purpose of testing impairment, for example, contiguous easements that were purchased in separate transactions but that are used as one asset, and (*b*) whether different indefinite-lived intangible assets, for example, a trade name and an easement, may be tested for impairment on a combined basis.

ACCOUNTING ISSUE

What unit of accounting should be used when testing indefinite-lived intangible assets for impairment under the guidance in ASC 350-30-35-18 through 35-20?

ACCOUNTING GUIDANCE

Acquired or internally developed *intangible* assets with indefinite lives that have been separately recognized and are inseparable from each other because they are operated as a single unit should be combined in one accounting unit when testing impairment. Judgment, depending on the relevant facts and circumstances, is required to determine whether several such intangible assets are inseparable. Although the indicators discussed below should be considered in making that determination, they should not be considered to be presumptive or determinative.

Indicators that two or more indefinite-lived intangible assets should be combined as a single unit of accounting when testing for impairment

- The assets were purchased to construct or improve a single asset and will be used together.
- The assets would have been recognized as one asset if they had been acquired at the same time.
- The assets represent the highest and best use when considered as a group, because (*a*) it is unlikely that a substantial portion of the assets would be sold separately or (*b*) if a substantial portion of the assets were sold individually, the fair value of the remaining assets as a group would be significantly lower.
- An entity's marketing or branding strategy indicates that the assets are complementary, as that term is used in ASC 805-20-55-18.

Indicators that two or more indefinite-lived intangible assets should not be combined as a single unit of accounting for impairment testing purposes

- The assets generate cash flows independently of one another.
- Each asset is likely to be sold separately. Previous separate sales of such assets are an indicator that combining them is not appropriate.
- The entity has a plan or is considering one to dispose of one or more of those assets separately.
- The assets are used exclusively by different asset groups referred to in ASC 360.
- Economic and other factors that might limit the useful economic life of one of the assets would not necessarily be the same for other assets combined in the unit of accounting.

The following was noted about the unit of accounting used to test indefinite-lived intangible assets for impairment:

- Indefinite-lived intangible assets should be in a separate unit of accounting, not tested with goodwill or finite-lived assets.
- A unit of accounting cannot consist of indefinite-lived assets that together represent a business.
- A unit of accounting may consist of indefinite-lived intangible assets presented in the separate financial statements of consolidated subsidiaries. Consequently, a loss recognized in consolidated financial statements may differ from total impairment losses, if any, recognized in the subsidiaries' separate financial statements.

- A unit of accounting and associated fair value used to test impairment of indefinite-lived intangible assets contained in a single reporting unit also should be used to measure a goodwill impairment loss in accordance with the guidance in ASC 350-20-35-9 through 13.
- If, because of a change in the way its intangible assets are used, a company combines those assets with assets that were previously tested separately for impairment to constitute a unit of accounting for the purpose of testing for impairment, the assets that were accounted for separately should be tested for impairment in accordance with the guidance in ASC 350-30-35-18 through 20 before they are combined as a unit of accounting.

ASC 350-30-50-4 through 50-5, 55-1(c); ASC 275-10-50-15A Determination of the Useful Life of Intangible Assets

BACKGROUND

Under the guidance in ASC 350-30-35-3, the "legal, regulatory, or contractual provisions that enable renewal or extension of the asset's legal or contractual life without substantial cost" must be considered, but only if renewal or extension of an asset's useful life is supported by evidence and can be achieved without "material modifications of the existing terms and conditions."

The problem is that the useful life of an intangible asset recognized under the guidance in ASC 350 frequently differs from the period of expected cash flows used to measure an asset's fair value under the guidance in ASC 805, Business Combinations, if the underlying arrangement includes terms related to the renewal or extension of the asset's useful life (i.e., the useful life of an asset accounted for under the guidance in ASC 350 is usually shorter than the expected period of cash flows under the guidance in ASC 805). That difference may occur, especially if material modifications are required for renewal or extension of a long-lived intangible asset's useful life, even though the likelihood of renewal or extension is high. The FASB was asked to consider whether the difference between an intangible asset's useful life and the period of expected cash flows used to measure its fair value is justified. This following guidance does *not* address the *initial measurement* of recognized intangible assets, the *amortization method* to be used, and the accounting for costs incurred to renew or extend a recognized intangible asset's term.

ACCOUNTING GUIDANCE

This guidance applies to recognized intangible assets accounted for under the guidance in ASC 350, regardless of how they were acquired.

Subsequent Measurement—Determining Useful Life

To determine the useful life of a recognized intangible asset, an entity is required to develop assumptions about the renewal or extension of an arrangement based on its own historical experience related to the renewal or extension of similar arrangements, which should be adjusted for entity-specific factors discussed in ASC 350-30-35-3. An entity that has no historical experience should consider assumptions that other participants in the market would use about an arrangement's renewal or extension that are (1) consistent with the asset's highest and best use and (2) adjusted for factors in ASC 350-30-35-3 that specifically apply to the entity.

Before this discussion, the guidance in ASC 350-30-35-3 did not permit an entity to base its assumptions on its own past experience related to the renewal or extension of an arrangement if it was likely that doing so would require incurring a substantial cost or making material modifications to an arrangement, because of a concern that entities might lengthen the useful lives of intangible assets inappropriately. The FASB staff believes that the guidance related to the fair value measurement of intangible assets and the requirement to test intangible assets for impairment along with the disclosure requirements would reduce that concern. As a result of this amendment of the guidance in ASC 350-30-35-3, an entity is permitted to base its assumptions on its *own* past experience even if it would result in a substantial cost or would require material modifications to an arrangement.

Entities that measure a recognized intangible asset's fair value by the *income approach* should determine the asset's useful life for amortization purposes by considering the period of expected cash flows used to measure the intangible asset's fair value adjusted for the entity's specific circumstances in accordance with the guidance in ASC 350-30-35-3. Those factors include, but are not limited to, an entity's expected use for the asset and its past experience in renewals and extensions of such arrangements.

If the useful life of a recognized intangible asset differs from the expected cash flows used to measure the asset's fair value, it is usually because the assumptions used by the entity to measure the asset's fair value are specific to the entity and thus differ from those used by other entities in the market to determine the asset's price. In that case, the entity should use its own assumptions because its amortization of a recognized intangible asset should be based on the period over which the asset will contribute, directly or indirectly, to the entity's future cash flows.

DISCLOSURES

Entities are required to disclose information about recognized intangible assets that would help users of financial statements to determine how the entity's intent or ability to renew or extend an arrangement affects the entity's expected cash flows associated with the asset.

Disclosure of the following information is required, if applicable, in addition to the disclosures required in ASC 350-20-50-1 through 50-2:

- The entity's accounting policy for costs incurred to renew or extend a recognized intangible asset's term;
- For each class of major intangible assets, the weighted-average period at acquisition or renewal before the next explicit or implicit renewal or extension;
- If renewal or extension costs are capitalized, the total cost incurred to renew or extend the term of a recognized intangible asset disclosed by major class of intangible assets for each period for which a balance sheet is presented.

The criterion in ASC 275-10-50-8, which provides guidance on when an entity should disclose information about an estimate, has been met if the effect of a change in either an intangible asset's (*a*) useful life, or (*b*) the expected likelihood of its renewal or extension would be material to the financial statements, either individually or in total by major class of intangible assets.

ASC 350-40: INTERNAL-USE SOFTWARE

ASC 350-40-05-1C through 05-1F, 05-10, 15-1 through 15-4D, 15-8 and 15-9. 25-18, 30-4 and 30-5, 35-11 through 35-17, 45-1 through 45-3, 50-1 through 50-3, 65-3, ASC 350-10-05-3 Customer's Accounting for Implementation Costs Incurred in a Cloud Computing Arrangement That Is a Service Contract (EITF Consensus)

BACKGROUND

In response to stakeholders' requests for guidance on the accounting for the costs an entity incurs to implement and setup, and other upfront costs related to a cloud computing arrangement (hosting arrangement) in which a customer enters into a service contract rather a software license, the FASB issued Accounting Standard Update No. 2018-15, which extends the scope of Subtopic 350-40 to include such arrangements. Guidance previously included in ASC 350-40-50-1 through 50-1B is amended in ASU 2018-15 and moved to become ASC 350-40-05-1D through 05-1F.

GLOSSARY

The definition of a hosting arrangement has been amended to read as follows:

> In connection with accessing and using software products, an arrangement in which the customer of the software does not currently have possession of the software; rather the customer accesses and uses the software on an as-needed basis.

ACCOUNTING GUIDANCE

A hosting arrangement in the form of a service contract should be accounted for as follows:

- Implementation costs of a hosting arrangement that do not meet both criteria in ASC 350-40-15-4A should be accounted for in accordance with the guidance for a hosting arrangement that is a service contract.
- A customer in a hosting arrangement that is a service contract is required to follow the accounting guidance for internal-use software to determine which costs of implementing a service contract should be capitalized and which costs should be expensed.
- If an entity enters into a hosting arrangement that includes multiple elements, the cost of each individual element should be allocated based on its relative standalone price under a contract.
- Hosting fees should be expensed as the service is provided.
- A customer in a hosting arrangement that is a service contract should determine to which project stage an implementation activity is related. Significant costs incurred to implement such a hosting arrangement should be capitalized if it is determined that they may provide a future benefit to the entity in subsequent periods. Such costs should be amortized over the term of the related hosting arrangement based on the guidance in ASC 350-40-35-17,

which provides that amortization of capitalized implementation costs should start when a module or component of a hosting arrangement is ready for its intended use, regardless of whether the overall hosting arrangement will be placed in service in planned stages that may extend beyond a reporting period. A module or component of a hosting arrangement is ready for its intended use after all substantial testing is completed. Amortization should be on a straight-line basis, or on another systematic and rational basis that better represents an entity's expected benefit from access to the hosting arrangement.

- The term of a hosting arrangement that is a service contract should be determined to be a fixed noncancelable term, including all of the following:
  - Periods covered by an option to extend the arrangement if it is reasonably certain that the customer will exercise the option
  - Periods covered by an option to terminate the arrangement if it is reasonably certain that the customer will not exercise the option
  - Periods covered by an option to extend (or not terminate) the arrangement when exercising the option is under the vendor's control.
- An entity should periodically reassess a hosting arrangement's estimated term and should account for a change, if any, as a change in an accounting estimate in accordance with the guidance in Topic 250. The effects of the following should be considered in that assessment:
  - Obsolescence
  - Technology
  - Competition
  - Other economic factors
  - Rapid changes that may be occurring in the development of hosting arrangements or hosted software
  - Significant implementation costs expected to have a significant economic value for a customer when an option to extend or terminate a hosting arrangement becomes exercisable.
- The impairment of capitalized implementation costs related to a hosting arrangement that is a service contract should be recognized and measured in accordance with the provisions in ASC 360-10-35 as if they were a long-lived asset. That guidance applies, for example, if there is a question about the recoverability of the carrying amount of a related implementation cost due to the occurrence of one of the following events or changes in circumstances related the hosting arrangement:
  - Expectation that a hosting arrangement will not provide potential substantive service
  - Significant change in the extent or manner in which a hosting arrangement is used currently or in the future
  - Significant change made or to be made to a hosting arrangement
  - An asset that is not used must be accounted for as abandoned under the guidance in ASC 360-10-35-47 through 35-49. However, capitalized implementation costs related to each module or component of a hosting arrangement that is a service contract should be evaluated separately to determine when their use has ceased.
- Costs of training and certain data conversion should be expensed, as in the case of developing internal use software.

Presentation

Information related to implementation costs related to a hosting arrangement that is a service contract should be presented as follows:

- Amortization of capitalized implementation costs discussed in ASC 350-40-35-13 should be presented in an income statement in the same line item as the expense for fees for the related hosting arrangement.
- Capitalized implementation costs discussed in ASC 350-40-25-18 should be presented in the balance sheet in the same line item in which an entity presents a prepayment of fees for the related hosting arrangement.
- Cash flows from capitalized implementation costs discussed in ASC 350-40-25-18 should be classified in the same manner as cash flows for fees for the related hosting arrangement.

Disclosure

An entity should disclose the following information about a hosting arrangement that is a service contract:

- Disclosures required in Topics 275 and 235 as well as those required in Subtopic 730-10 and Subtopic 360-10 should be made about capitalized implementation costs of an entity's hosting arrangements. The disclosures required in Subtopic 360-10 should be made as if the capitalized implementation costs were a separate major class of depreciable asset.
- The nature of hosting arrangements that are service contracts.

TRANSITION AND OPEN EFFECTIVE DATE INFORMATION

The following is the transition and effective date for ASU 2018-15:

- The guidance is effective for public business entities for annual periods, including interim periods in those annual periods, that begin after December 15, 2019.
- The guidance is effective for all other entities for annual periods that begin after December 15, 2020, and interim periods in those annual periods that begin after December 15, 2021.
- Earlier application of the guidance is permitted, including adoption in any interim period for:
  - — Public business entities for periods for which financial statement have not yet been issued
  - — All other entities for periods for which financial statements have not yet been made available for issuance.
- The guidance should be applied using one of the following two methods:
  - — Prospectively to costs for activities performed on or after the date that an entity first applies the guidance
  - — Retrospectively in accordance with the guidance on accounting changes in ASC 250-10-45-5 through 45-10.
- Public business entities that elects to apply the guidance prospectively or retrospectively should disclose the following information in the interim and annual periods of adoption:
  - — The nature of and reason for the change in accounting principle
  - — The transition method
  - — A qualitative description of the financial statement items affected by the change.
- A public business entity that elects to apply the guidance retrospectively also should disclose quantitative information about the effects of the change.
- All other entities should disclose the required information discussed in the preceding two bullets for prospective transition and retrospective transition, respectively, in the annual period in which the guidance is adopted. However, an entity that has elected early adoption of the guidance in an interim period should disclose that information in the interim period in which the guidance is adopted.

ASC 350-40-05-2 through 350-40-05-6, 05-8, 05-9, 15-2 through 15-7, 25-1 through 25-15, 30-1 through 30-4, 35-1 through 35-10, 50-1, 55-1 through 55-4; ASC 350-10-05-6; ASC 730-10-60-2; ASC 985-20-60-1 Accounting for Costs of Computer Software Developed or Obtained for Internal Use

BACKGROUND

> ***PRACTICE NOTE:*** The guidance in ASC 350-40-35-8 will be affected by the guidance in ASU 2014-09, *Revenue from Contracts with Customers*, when the ASU's guidance becomes effective for public business entities in annual reporting periods beginning after December 15, 2017, and for other entities in annual reporting periods beginning after December 15, 2018, and interim reporting periods beginning after December 15, 2019.

This guidance has been provided as a result of diversity in practice in accounting for costs associated with software purchased for internal use. Some entities have been capitalizing the costs of software purchased for internal use, while other entities have been expensing those costs if the software was developed internally.

ACCOUNTING GUIDANCE

Internal-use software has the following characteristics: (1) the software is acquired, internally developed, or modified solely to meet an entity's internal requirements; or (2) the entity has no substantive plan to externally market internally developed or modified software. If an entity has a history of developing software internally and marketing it externally, there is a rebuttable presumption that any software developed by that entity is intended for sale, lease, or other marketing. In that case, ASC 986-20 provides the applicable authoritative guidance.

Software that becomes part of a product or a process that is sold (e.g., software designed for and embedded in a semiconductor chip) should be accounted for under the provisions of ASC 986-20, not under the guidance in this pronouncement. However, software used in the production of a product or the provision of a service but not acquired by the customer (e.g., software embedded in a switch used by a telecommunications company to provide telephone service) should be accounted for under the guidance in this pronouncement.

The guidance in this Issue does *not* apply to internal-use software that meets the criteria in ASC 350-40-15-4A through 15-4C, which apply to software for internal use that an entity can access through a cloud hosting arrangement.

Stages of Computer Software Development

The three stages of computer software development are (1) preliminary project stage, (2) application development stage, and (3) post-implementation/operation stage. The preliminary project stage includes the conceptual formulation of alternatives, evaluation of alternatives, determination of the existence of needed technology, and the final selection of alternatives. The application development stage includes the design of chosen paths, including software configuration and software interfaces, coding, installation of hardware, and testing (including the parallel processing phase). The post-implementation/operation stage includes training and application maintenance.

Internal-Use Computer Software Costs as R&D

Internal-use computer software costs may be incurred for research and development purposes. Such costs, which are accounted for in accordance with the guidance in ASC 730-20, include the following:

- Purchased or leased computer software used in R&D activities if the software does not have alternative future uses.
- All internally developed internal-use computer software if (*a*) the software developed represents a pilot project or (*b*) the software is used in a particular R&D project, regardless of whether the software has alternative future uses.

Capitalizing or Expensing Internal-Use Computer Software Costs

The accounting treatment of internal-use computer software costs (i.e., capitalize or expense) largely depends on the nature of the cost incurred. Internal and external costs incurred during the preliminary project stage should be expensed as incurred. Internal and external costs incurred during the application development stage should be capitalized. Software costs that allow for access or conversion of old data by new systems also should be capitalized. Internal and external training costs and maintenance costs should be expensed as incurred.

Upgrades and Enhancements

Upgrades and enhancements are defined as modifications to existing internal-use software that result in additional functionality (e.g., modifications to enable software to perform tasks that it was previously incapable of performing). In order for the costs of upgrades or enhancements to be capitalized, it must be probable that these expenditures will result in additional software functionality. Internal costs of upgrades or enhancements should be expensed if the activity relates to the preliminary project stage or the post-implementation/operation stage; costs incurred during the application development stage should be capitalized. External costs of upgrades or enhancements should be expensed if the activity relates to the preliminary project stage or the post-implementation/operation stage; costs incurred during the application development stage should be capitalized.

Applying the Capitalization Criteria

Capitalization of costs should begin when both of the following occur:

- The preliminary project stage is complete.
- Management with applicable authority authorizes, implicitly or explicitly, the project's funding, and it is probable that the project will be completed and the software will be used to perform the intended function.

Capitalization should cease no later than when the software project is substantially complete and ready for its intended use. The software is ready for its intended use after all substantial testing is completed.

The development of new software that is intended to replace existing internal-use software affects the accounting for any unamortized costs. First, the remaining useful lives of software that will be replaced should be reconsidered. Second, when new software that is replacing the existing software is ready for its intended use, the unamortized cost of the software that is being replaced should be charged to expense.

The following types of costs, incurred during the application development stage, are eligible for capitalization:

- External direct costs of materials and services consumed in developing or obtaining the software (e.g., fees paid to third-party developers, costs incurred to obtain software from third parties, and travel expenses incurred by employees in their duties directly associated with developing software)
- Payroll and payroll-related costs (e.g., employee benefits) for employees who are directly associated with and who devote time to the internal-use computer software project, to the extent of time spent directly on the project
- Interest costs incurred while developing internal-use computer software (see ASC 835-20).

General and administrative costs and overhead costs should *not* be capitalized.

Software Purchased for Internal Use with Multiple Elements

In some cases, the purchase price of a software package includes multiple elements. For example, a software product may be purchased from an external vendor for a lump sum that includes the software itself, training, a maintenance agreement, data conversion services, reengineering, and rights to future upgrades and enhancements. The total purchase price should be allocated among all the individual elements based on objective evidence of the fair values of the contract components. Such fair values may differ from prices stated within the contract for each element.

Impairment

Impairment of internal-use computer software costs should be recognized and measured in accordance with the provisions of ASC 360. If it is no longer probable that the software being developed will be completed and placed in service, the asset should be reported at the lower of its carrying amount or its fair value less costs to sell. The rebuttable presumption is that such uncompleted software has a fair value of zero. Indications that the software may not be completed and placed in service include the following:

- A lack of expenditures budgeted or incurred for the project
- Programming difficulties that cannot be resolved on a timely basis
- Significant cost overruns
- Management plans to purchase third-party software rather than completing the internally developed software; costs of internally developed software will significantly exceed the cost of comparable software from a third-party vendor
- Management plans to purchase third-party software rather than completing the internally developed software; third-party software has more advanced features
- The business segment or unit to which the software relates is unprofitable or has been or will be discontinued

Amortization

The costs of software developed for internal use should be amortized on a straight-line basis unless another systematic and rational basis is more representative of the software's use. The amortization period should be relatively short.

External Marketing of Internal-Use Computer Software

In some cases, the entity decides to market software developed for internal use to external parties. Proceeds received from the sale of such software, net of direct incremental costs of marketing, should be applied against the carrying amount of the internal use software. Direct incremental costs of marketing include commissions, software reproduction costs, warranty and service obligations, and installation costs. No profit should be recognized until the proceeds received from the sale of the internal use software and amortization charges reduce the carrying amount of the software to zero. Subsequent proceeds should be recognized in revenue as earned.

ASC 350-50: WEBSITE DEVELOPMENT COSTS

ASC 350-10-05-7; ASC 350-50-15-2 through 15-3, 25-2 through 25-17, 55-2 through 55-9 Accounting for Web Site Development Costs

BACKGROUND

Web sites are developed by different kinds of companies. Many are "brick and mortar" companies; others are start-up companies that will be conducting their business operations only on the Internet. There are three broad categories of Internet web sites: (1) sites that provide information only, (2) sites that provide information and a service, and (3) sites that provide information and enter into transactions with customers over the Internet. In addition, Internet web sites can be accessed by the general public, extranet sites can be accessed only by subscribers, and intranet sites can be accessed only by individuals within a specific company.

The stages of web site development include (*a*) planning, (*b*) web application and infrastructure development, (*c*) graphics and content, and (*d*) production. Because there is no specific guidance on the accounting for web site development costs, the accounting for those costs has been diverse.

This Issue does not apply to costs of hardware, such as servers, necessary to support a web site. It also does not apply to costs incurred under web site development contracts for others. Such costs are accounted for under contract accounting.

ACCOUNTING ISSUE

How should an entity account for costs incurred to develop a web site?

ACCOUNTING GUIDANCE

Planning Stage Activities

All costs of web site planning activities should be expensed, regardless of whether they are related to software. Those costs include, but are not limited to, a business plan, a project plan, or both; identification of specific goals; determining the web site's functions (e.g., order placement, shipment tracking); identifying necessary hardware and web applications; determining whether the technology necessary to achieve the site's intended functions exists; alternative means of achieving the site's functions; identifying software tools; and legal costs to address copyright issues.

Web Site Application and Infrastructure Development Stage

During the web site application and infrastructure development stage, the necessary hardware is acquired and software is developed. This guidance does *not* apply to costs of hardware acquired. It is assumed that all costs related to software development are incurred for the purpose of operating the web site (internal-use software). Those costs should be accounted for according to the guidance in ASC 350-10-05-6; ASC 350-40-05-2 through 05-6, 05-8, 05-9, 15-2 through 15-7, 25-1 through 25-16, 30-1 through 30-4, 35-1 through 35-10, 50-1, 55-1 through 55-4; ASC 730-10-60-2; ASC 985-20-60-1. That is, the costs generally should be *capitalized* under the guidance in ASC 350-40-25-2 through 25-15, 05-8 through 5-9, 15-2, 30-1. An entity that has a plan or is developing a plan to market the software to others should account for those costs under the guidance in ASC 985-20-05-1 through 05-2, 15-2 through 15-4, 25-1 through 25-4, 25-6 through 25-11, 35-1 through 35-4, 50-1 through 50-2; ASC 985-330-40-1; ASC 730-10-60-4, 55-1. Costs of obtaining or registering an Internet name would be capitalized in accordance with the guidance in ASC 350. In addition, fees paid periodically to an Internet service provider for hosting a web site on its servers, generally, should be *expensed* over the benefit period.

Graphics Development Costs

Graphics involve the design of a web page and do not change with content. Because they are part of the software, they should be *capitalized* according to the guidance in ASC 350-40-25-2 through 25-4 for internal-use software. If those costs are related to software to be sold to others, they should be accounted for based on the provisions of ASC 985-20-05-1 through 05-2, 15-2 through 15-4, 25-1 through 25-4, 25-6 through 25-11, 35-1 through 35-4, 50-1 through 50-2; ASC 985-330-40-1; ASC 730-10-60-4, 55-1. Changes to a web site's graphics after the site has been launched may be related to web site maintenance or enhancements. The accounting for such changes is discussed in 5(b) below.

Content Development Costs

A web site's content may consist of articles, pictures, maps, and so forth and may be presented as text or in graphical form. (The graphics discussed above are not included here.) The accounting is not addressed here, because the accounting guidance for costs of web site content, which may be acquired from others or developed internally, may not be limited to forms of content found only on web sites.

Costs Incurred to Operate a Web Site

Costs incurred to operate a web site should be accounted for as follows:

- *Costs with no future benefit*. Expense operating costs with no future benefit as incurred (e.g., training, administration, maintenance, and other web site operating costs) because the costs of operating a web site should be accounted for in the same way as the costs of operating other kinds of entities.
- *Costs with a future benefit*. Costs incurred to develop upgrades and enhancements that increase the functions of web site software should be accounted for in the same way as the costs of developing new software according to the guidance in ASC 350-10-05-6; ASC 350-40-05-2 through 05-6, 05-8, 05-9, 15-2 through 15-7, 25-1 through 25-16, 30-1 through 30-4, 35-1 through 35-10, 50-1; 55-1 through 55-4; ASC 730-10-60-2; ASC 985-20-60-1. Similar costs incurred for upgrades or enhancements to software to be sold to others should be accounted for based on the guidance for product enhancements in ASC 985-20-05-1 through 05-2, 15-2 through 15-4, 25-1 through 25-4, 25-6 through 25-11, 35-1 through 35-4, 50-1 through 50-2; ASC 985-330-40-1; ASC 730-10-60-4; 55-1. Determining whether a change to web site software is an upgrade or enhancement (product enhancement) or maintenance requires judgment based on the specific facts and circumstances. In addition, it was noted that the guidance in ASC 350-10-05-6; ASC 350-40-05-2 through 05-6, 05-8 through 05-9, 15-2 through 15-7, 25-1 through 25-16, 30-1 through 30-4, 35-1 through 35-10, 50-1; 55-1 through 55-4; ASC 730-10-60-2; ASC 985-20-60-1 provides that if it is not cost-effective to separate internal costs incurred for maintenance from those incurred for minor upgrades and enhancements, the total amount should be expensed as incurred.

CHAPTER 27

ASC 360—PROPERTY, PLANT, AND EQUIPMENT

CONTENTS

PART I: GENERAL GUIDANCE

ASC 360-10: OVERALL

OVERVIEW

Primary issues addressed in ASC 360 are the acquisition, depreciation, and impairment of property, plant, and equipment. These assets are often referred to as simply plant or fixed assets. In addition, guidance in recognizing and measuring the impairment of property, plant, and equipment is included in this section. Finally, ASC 360 provides guidance in accounting for certain real estate sales.

The general basis of accounting for plant assets is historical cost which includes all costs leading up to the asset being in the location and condition for use. Recognition of depreciation is required in general-purpose financial statements that present financial position, cash flows, and results of operations. Depreciation is an area of accounting where a variety of methods are available in practice. Depreciation is a process of cost allocation, not valuation.

Impairment of a long-lived asset exists when the asset's fair value is less than its carrying amount, which is defined as cost less accumulated depreciation and is often referred to as book value. Recognition of an impairment loss is required in this circumstance because the carrying amount will not be recovered in the future. This general principle underlies accounting for impairment losses of all long-lived assets, but it is applied differently for those assets that are expected to be held and used and for assets to be disposed of by sale or otherwise.

A significant financial reporting issue encountered in accounting for real estate transactions is the timing of revenue recognition. Promulgated U.S. GAAP address this important issue by classifying real estate transactions into the following three categories:

1. Real estate sales, except retail land sales
2. Sale-leasebacks involving real estate
3. Retail land sales

ASC 360 addresses real estate sales and retail land sales. ASC 840 (Leases) addresses sale-leasebacks involving real estate.

BACKGROUND

Property, plant, and equipment, often referred to as *fixed or plant assets,* are used in production, distribution, and services by all enterprises. Examples include land, buildings, furniture, fixtures, machinery, equipment, and vehicles. The nature of the assets employed by a particular enterprise is determined by the nature of its activities. For example, a manufacturing business would require significantly different plant assets than would a transportation or service business.

Property, plant, and equipment have two distinct characteristics:

1. They are acquired for use in operations and enter into the revenue-generating stream indirectly. They are held primarily for use, not for sale.
2. They have relatively long lives.

U.S. GAAP generally require property, plant, and equipment to be recorded at cost, which is subsequently reduced by depreciation or amortization as the asset's cost is gradually transferred to the income statement in a manner that allocates the cost to expense over the useful life of the asset. Commonly used depreciation methods include straight-line, units of production, sum-of-the-years'-digits, and declining balance, although other methods may meet the criteria of *systematic* and *rational.* This process focuses primarily on the determination of income rather than the valuation of the asset. In fact, the resulting carrying amount or book value of the asset, which is included in the balance sheet, is not intended to represent the current or fair value of the asset, but is appropriately described as that portion of the historical cost of the asset that is awaiting allocation to income in future periods.

Historically, the practice of systematically allocating the cost of a long-lived asset to expense as a part of determining net income was modified in some circumstances in which the value of the asset was believed to be impaired, defined as its future value being less than its book value or carrying amount. A loss was recognized for the amount of this excess, although this practice was not consistently followed.

ASC 360 applies to long-lived assets (i.e., plant or fixed assets), to intangible assets being amortized, and to long-lived assets to be disposed of. ASC 360's scope includes capital leases of lessees, long-lived assets of lessors under operating leases, proved oil and gas properties accounted for under the successful efforts method, and long-term prepaid assets (ASC 360-10-15-4). ASC 360 applies to all entities. It does not apply to the following types of assets (ASC 360-10-15-5):

- Goodwill
- Intangible assets not being amortized that are to be held and used
- Financial instruments, including cost- or equity-method investments
- Deferred policy acquisition costs
- Deferred tax assets
- Unproved oil and gas properties under the successful efforts method

Certain sections of the Codification establish separate standards of accounting for specific long-lived assets in specialized situations. Specifically, assets whose accounting is prescribed in other sections of the Codification are (ASC 360-10-15-5):

- ASC 928 (Entertainment—Music)
- ASC 920 (Entertainment—Broadcasters)
- ASC 985 (Software)
- ASC 980 (Regulated Operations)

U.S. GAAP require that the realization of revenue be recognized in the accounting period in which the earning process is substantially completed and an exchange has taken place. If revenue is deferred to a future period, the associated costs of that revenue are also deferred. Frequently, it may be necessary to estimate revenue and/or costs to achieve a proper matching.

In addition, revenue usually is recognized at the amount established by the parties to the exchange, except for transactions in which collection of the receivable is not reasonably assured. In the event that collection of the receivable is not reasonably assured, the installment method or cost-recovery method may be used. Alternatively, collections may be recorded properly as deposits in the event that considerable uncertainty exists as to their eventual collectibility.

ASC 360 addresses the recognition of revenue from real estate sales and contains specialized accounting and reporting principles and practices.

ASC 360 establishes U.S. GAAP for the recognition of revenue on all real estate transactions for any type of accounting entity. It provides separate criteria for the recognition of revenue on (*a*) all real estate transactions except retail land sales and (*b*) retail land sales. The following items are expressly excluded from the provisions of ASC 360:

- Exchanges of real estate for other real estate
- Sales and leasebacks

PRINCIPLES OF ACCOUNTING FOR DEPRECIABLE ASSETS

Asset Cost

The basis of accounting for depreciable assets is cost, and all normal expenditures of readying an asset for use are capitalized. However, unnecessary expenditures that do not add to the utility of the asset are charged to expense. For example, an expenditure for repairing a piece of equipment that was damaged during shipment should be charged to expense.

Razing and removal costs (less salvage value) of structures located on land purchased as a building site are added to the cost of the land. Land itself is never depreciated.

Salvage Value

Salvage or *residual value* is an estimate of the amount that will be realized through the sale or other disposal at the end of the useful life of a depreciable asset. Generally, the depreciable amount of a plant asset is its cost less its salvage or residual value.

PRACTICE POINTER: Depreciable assets may have little or no salvage value, net of the cost of removal and disposal, at the end of their estimated useful lives. If this amount is immaterial or highly uncertain, the amount(s) may be ignored for purposes of determining depreciation.

Estimated Useful Life

The *estimated useful life* of a depreciable asset is the period over which services are expected to be rendered by the asset (ASC 360-10-35-4). An asset's estimated useful life may differ from company to company or industry to industry. A company's maintenance policy may affect the longevity of a depreciable asset.

PRACTICE NOTE: Total utility of an asset, expressed in time, is often referred to as its *physical life*. The utility of an asset to a specific owner, expressed in time, is referred to as its *service life*.

Valuation of Assets

Under specific circumstances, assets may be valued in the following ways:

Historical Cost

The amount paid at the date of acquisition, including all normal expenditures of readying an asset for use.

Replacement Cost

The amount that it would cost to replace an asset. Frequently, replacement cost is the same as fair value.

Fair Market Value

The price at which a willing seller would sell to a willing buyer, neither of them being under any compulsion to buy or to sell.

Present Value

The value today of something due in the future.

General Price-Level Restatement

The value of an asset restated in terms of current purchasing power.

Leasehold Improvements

Leased assets may provide the lessee (i.e., party acquiring use of the assets) with many of the benefits of ownership. The lessee may invest in improvements on leased assets to enhance their usefulness. These investments are referred to as *leasehold improvements*.

Leasehold improvements frequently are made to property for which the lease extends over a relatively long period. For example, improvements to a leased building might range from relatively inexpensive improvements to extensive remodeling to prepare the leased asset for the intended use of the lessee.

Leasehold improvements are established in a separate account at cost and amortized over the shorter of the life of the improvement or the length of the lease. Amortization or depreciation policy is usually the same as similar expenditures for owned assets. If no similar assets are owned, amortization or depreciation must employ a method that is systematic and rational (as discussed above) and based on reasonable assumptions.

PRACTICE POINTER: Leasehold improvements generally are depreciated over the estimated useful lives of the improvements or the remaining lease term, whichever is shorter. For example, if the lessee constructs a street, curbs, and lighting on land leased for 15 years, those improvements should be depreciated over their estimated useful lives or 15 years, whichever is less. The method of depreciation (most likely straight-line) should generally be that of similar assets (i.e., streets, curbs, lighting) that the company has installed on owned land. Because improvements will revert to the lessor at the end of the lease term, the period of depreciation should not exceed the term of the lease.

Some leases contain renewal options, and a number of entities (particularly retailers) have depreciated leasehold improvements over the remaining lease term plus the term of the renewal period (assuming that this period is less than the estimated economic life of the leasehold improvement). The SEC addressed the appropriateness of this accounting treatment in a letter from the Chief Accountant's office to the AICPA in February 2005. Leasehold improvements should only be depreciated over a term that includes the renewal option period when the exercise of the renewal option is "reasonably assured." A renewal option is only "reasonably assured" if the rent available at renewal is sufficiently less than the property's fair rental value as to reasonably assure that the renewal option will be exercised. Many public companies were routinely including the renewal option period in determining the depreciable life of the leasehold improvement, even if the renewal rental amount was not below fair value. In addition, companies should disclose the depreciation (amortization) period of material leasehold improvements and the relationship of this period to the initial lease term.

Some lessors provide incentives or allowances under operating leases to fund leasehold improvements. These incentives or allowances are to be accounted for as leasehold improvements and depreciated as discussed above. The proper accounting treatment for incentives or allowances received from lessors is discussed in Chapter 56, *ASC 842—Leases*.

Self-Constructed Depreciable Assets

A business may construct a depreciable asset for its own use, in which case the following procedures are appropriate:

- All *direct costs* are included in the total cost of the asset.
- *Fixed overhead costs* are not included unless they are increased by the construction of the asset.
- *Interest costs* may or may not be capitalized as part of construction cost of the fixed assets.

PRACTICE POINTER: Interest costs that are material must be capitalized on certain qualifying assets under the provisions of ASC 835.

Illustration of Self-Constructed Depreciable Assets

A company takes advantage of excess capacity to construct its own machinery. Costs associated with the construction are as follows:

Direct material	$100,000
Direct labor	50,000
Overhead—Variable	25,000
—Fixed	35,000
	$210,000

The machinery has an estimated useful life of five years, with an expected salvage value of 10% of its cost.

The cost of the machine is $175,000, which includes all of the scheduled costs above except fixed overhead. Because fixed overhead is not increased by the construction of the machinery, to capitalize fixed overhead as part of the cost would relieve operations of expenses that would otherwise be charged to them.

The amount subject to depreciation is computed as follows:

$$\$175,000 - .10\ (\$175,000) = \$157,500$$

Improvement of Depreciable Assets

Expenditures that increase the capacity or operating efficiency or extend the useful life of an asset, if they are substantial, are capitalized. Minor expenditures usually are treated as period costs even though they may have the characteristics of capital expenditures. When the cost of improvements is substantial or when there is a change in the estimated useful life of an asset, depreciation charges for future periods are revised based on the new book value and the new estimated remaining useful life.

The revision of an asset's estimated useful life is measured prospectively and accounted for in the current and future periods. No adjustment is made to prior depreciation.

Illustration of Improvement of Depreciable Assets

A machine that originally cost $100,000 was being depreciated (no salvage value) over ten years, using the straight-line method. At the beginning of the fifth year, $20,000 was expended, which improved the operating efficiency of the machine and extended its useful life two years.

Original cost	$100,000
Less: Four years' depreciation	(40,000)
Book value	$ 60,000
New expenditures	20,000
New depreciable base	$ 80,000
Divided by: Revised useful life (6 + 2) in years	8
Amount of annual depreciation	$ 10,000

DEPRECIATION

Types of Depreciation

Physical depreciation is related to a depreciable asset's wear and deterioration over a period.

Functional depreciation arises from obsolescence or inadequacy of the asset to perform efficiently. Obsolescence may arise when there is no further demand for the product that the depreciable asset produces or from the availability of a new depreciable asset that can perform the same function for substantially less cost.

Depreciation Methods

The goal of depreciation methods is to provide for a reasonable, consistent matching of revenue and expense by allocating the cost of the depreciable asset systematically over its estimated useful life.

The accumulation of depreciation in the books is accomplished by using a contra account, called accumulated depreciation or allowance for depreciation.

The amount subject to depreciation—*depreciable base*—is the difference between cost and estimate of residual or salvage value.

Straight-Line Method

Straight-line depreciation is determined by the formula:

$$\frac{\textit{Cost less salvage value}}{\text{Estimated useful life in years}}$$

The straight-line method of depreciation is appropriate when the asset use is expected to be relatively even over its estimated useful life or there is no discernible pattern of decline in service potential.

Illustration of Straight-Line Method of Depreciation

A machine with an invoice price of $500,000 has an expected useful life of eight years. Costs to transport, install, and test the machine were $25,000. The salvage value of the machine at the end of its eight-year life is estimated to be $50,000.

Straight-line depreciation is the same each year. It is computed by adding the $25,000 costs to prepare the asset for its intended use to the $500,000 invoice price, reducing that amount by the estimated salvage value of $50,000, and dividing by the estimated years of useful life:

$$\frac{(\$500{,}000 + \$25{,}000) - \$50{,}000}{8 \text{ years}} = \$59{,}375$$

Units-of-Production Method

The *units-of-production method* relates depreciation to the estimated production capability of an asset and is expressed in a rate per unit or hour. The formula is:

$$\frac{\textit{Cost less salvage value}}{\text{Estimated units or hours}}$$

Illustration of Units-of-Production Method of Depreciation

A machine is purchased at a cost of $850,000 and has a salvage value of $100,000. It is estimated that the machine has a useful life of 75,000 hours.

$$\frac{\$850{,}000 - \$100{,}000}{75{,}000} = \$10 \text{ per hour depreciation}$$

In an accounting period during which the machine was used 12,500 hours, depreciation would be $125,000 (12,500 × $10).

The units-of-production method is used in situations in which the usage of the depreciable asset varies considerably from period to period, and in those circumstances in which the service life is more a function of use than passage of time.

Sum-of-the-Years'-Digits Method

The *sum-of-the-years'-digits method* is an accelerated method of depreciation that provides higher depreciation expense in the early years and lower charges in later years.

To find the sum of the years' digits, the digit of each year is progressively numbered and then added up. For example, the sum of the years' digits for a five-year life would be:

$$5 + 4 + 3 + 2 + 1 = 15$$

The sum of the years' digits becomes the denominator, and the digit of the highest year becomes the first numerator. For example, the first year's depreciation for a five-year life would be 5/15 of the depreciable base of the asset, the second year's depreciation would be 4/15, and so on.

When dealing with an asset with a long life, it is helpful to use the following formula for finding the sum of the years' digits, *S*, where *N* is the number of years in the asset's life.

$$S = \frac{N\,(N + 1)}{2}$$

To find the sum of the years' digits for an asset with a 50-year life:

$$S = \frac{50\,(50 + 1)}{2}$$

$$S = 50\,(25\ 1/2)$$

$$S = 1{,}275$$

Illustration of Sum-of-the-Years'-Digits Method of Depreciation

Assume that an asset costing $11,000 has a salvage value of $1,000 and an estimated useful life of four years.

The first step is to determine the depreciable base:

Cost of asset	$11,000
Less: Salvage value	1,000
Depreciable base	$10,000

The sum of the years' digits for four years is: 4 + 3 + 2 + 1 = 10

The first year's depreciation is 4/10, the second year's 3/10, the third year's 2/10, and the fourth year's 1/10, as follows:

4/10 of $10,000	=	$ 4,000
3/10 of $10,000	=	3,000
2/10 of $10,000	=	2,000
1/10 of $10,000	=	1,000
Total depreciation		$10,000

Declining-Balance Methods

The declining-balance method is an example of one of the methods that meets the requirements of being systematic and rational. If the expected productivity of the asset is to generate revenue that is greater during the earlier years of its estimated useful life, or maintenance charges tend to increase during later years, the declining-balance method may provide the best allocation of cost (ASC 360-10-35-7).

A frequently used variation of the declining-balance method is *double-declining-balance*, although other alternative (lower than double) methods are acceptable. Under double-declining balance, depreciation is computed at double the straight-line rate and this percentage is applied to the remaining book value. No allowance is made for salvage until the book value (cost less accumulated depreciation) reaches estimated salvage value. At that time, depreciation recognition ceases.

Illustration of Double-Declining-Balance Method of Depreciation

An asset costing $10,000 has an estimated useful life of ten years. Using the double-declining-balance method, depreciation expense is computed as follows.

First, the regular straight-line method percentage is determined, which in this case is 10% (10-year life). This amount is doubled to 20% and applied each year to the remaining book value, as follows:

Year	*Percentage*	*Remaining book value*	*Depreciation expense*
1	20	$10,000	$2,000
2	20	8,000	1,600
3	20	6,400	1,280
4	20	5,120	1,024
5	20	4,096	819
6	20	3,277	655
7	20	2,622	524
8	20	2,098	420
9	20	1,678	336
10	20	1,342	268
Salvage value		1,074	

In this example, a book value (i.e., portion of cost not depreciated) of $1,074 remains after recognizing ten years of depreciation. Should the asset remain in service, depreciation would continue to be recognized until the asset is no longer used or the book value approaches zero. Should the salvage value be a greater amount (e.g., $1,500), depreciation would cease to be recognized when a total of $8,500 is reached ($10,000 cost – $8,500 accumulated depreciation = $1,500 book value). In the above example, under this assumption, only $178 of depreciation would be recognized in the ninth year, leaving a book value of $1,500. No depreciation would be recognized in the tenth year.

Had the preceding illustration been 150% of declining balance, the rate would have been 15% of the remaining book value (i.e., 150% of 10%). The declining-balance method meets the requirements of being systematic and rational. If the expected productivity or revenue-earning power of the asset is relatively greater during the early years of its life, or where maintenance charges tend to increase during later years, the declining-balance method may provide the most satisfactory allocation of cost.

Partial-Year Depreciation

When an asset is placed in service during the year, the depreciation expense is taken only for the portion of the year that the asset is used. For example, if an asset (of a company on a calendar-year basis) is placed in service on July 1, only six months' depreciation is taken.

Alternatively, a company may adopt a simplifying assumption concerning partial-year depreciation which, applied consistently, usually is considered a reasonable approximation of depreciation computed to the nearest month. For example, the following policies are sometimes encountered:

- A half year of depreciation in the year of purchase and in the year of disposal
- A full year of depreciation taken in the year of purchase and none taken in the year of sale (or the opposite)

These policies are particularly appropriate when a large number of similar fixed assets are placed in service and removed from service on a constant basis. In such cases, calculating depreciation to the nearest full month or other refinement may not be cost-efficient and an assumption like the above may result in similar results.

Illustration of Partial-Year Depreciation

A calendar-year company purchased a machine on March 7. The machine cost $64,000, and at the end of its expected five-year life it will have a salvage value of $10,000.

Depreciation on a yearly basis is calculated as follows:

$$\frac{\$64{,}000 - \$10{,}000}{5 \text{ years}} = \$10{,}800$$

Depreciation for the year of purchase under three different policies is as follows:

$$\frac{\$10{,}800}{12 \text{ months}} = \$900 \text{ per month}$$

Policy	*Depreciation for Year of Purchase*
Computed to nearest full month	10 months × $900 = $9,000
Full year's depreciation in year of purchase; none in last year of asset's useful life	$10,800
Half year's depreciation in first and last years of asset's life	$10,800 × 1/2 = $5,400

Other Types of Depreciation

U.S. GAAP require that depreciation be determined in a manner that systematically and rationally allocates the cost of an asset over its estimated useful life. Straight-line, units-of-production, sum-of-the-years'-digits, and declining-depreciation methods are considered acceptable, provided they are based on reasonable estimates of useful life and salvage value. Other methods that are used less frequently are:

Replacement Depreciation

The original cost is carried on the books, and the replacement cost is charged to expense in the period the replacement occurs.

Retirement Depreciation

The cost of the asset is charged to expense in the period it is retired.

Present-Value Depreciation

Depreciation is computed so that the return on the investment of the asset remains constant over the period involved.

PRACTICE POINTER: For financial accounting purposes, companies should not use depreciation guidelines or other tax regulations issued by the IRS, but should estimate useful lives and calculate depreciation expense according to generally accepted accounting procedures. Only when the difference between a U.S. GAAP depreciation method and a tax depreciation method is immaterial is the latter acceptable in financial statements. When property, plant, and equipment write-offs for tax purposes differ from depreciation for financial accounting purposes, deferred income taxes are recognized.

In periods of inflation, depreciation charges based on historical cost of the original fixed asset may not reflect current price levels, and hence may not be an appropriate matching of revenues and expenses for the current period. In 1953, promulgated U.S. GAAP took the position that it was acceptable to provide an appropriation of retained earnings for replacement of fixed assets, but not acceptable to depart from the traditional cost method in the treatment of depreciation, because a radical departure from the generally accepted procedures would create too much confusion in the minds of the users of financial statements. Although inflation has become quite serious from time to time, depreciation based on historical cost remains the official, promulgated accounting principle.

IMPAIRMENT

Long-Lived Assets to Be Held and Used

Impairment is defined in ASC 360 as the condition that exists when the carrying amount of a long-lived asset exceeds its fair value. An impairment loss is recognized only if the carrying amount of a long-lived asset is not recoverable and exceeds its fair value. This circumstance exits if the carrying amount of the asset in question exceeds the sum of the undiscounted cash flows expected to result from the use and eventual disposition of the asset. The impairment loss is measured as the amount by which the carrying amount of a long-lived asset exceeds its fair value (ASC 360-10-35-17).

The guidance for impairment or disposal of long-lived assets applies to the following transactions and activities:

- Right-of-use assets of lessees.
- Long-live assets of lessors subject to operating leases.
- Proved oil and gas properties that are being accounted for using the successful-efforts method of accounting.
- Long-term prepaid assets. (ASC 360-10-15-4)

Not-for-profit entities that hold collections of art, historical treasures, or similar assets shall follow the accounting and disclosure requirements of ASC 958-360 on not-for-profit entities—property, plant, and equipment. (ASC 360-10-15-6) Collections generally are held by museums, botanical gardens, libraries, aquariums, arboretums, historical sites, planetariums, zoos, art galleries, and similar educational, research, and public service entities.

If a long-lived asset is part of a group that includes other assets and liabilities not covered by the Impairment or Disposal of Long-Lived Assets ASC Subsections, the guidance in the Impairment or Disposal of Long-Lived Assets subsections applies to the group. In this situation, the unit of accounting for the long-lived asset is its group. For a long-lived asset to be held and used, that group is referred to as an asset group. For a long-lived asset to be disposed of by sale or otherwise, that group is referred to as a disposal group. The guidance in the Impairment or Disposal of Long-Lived Assets subsections does not change U.S. GAAP applicable to those other individual assets and liabilities not covered by the Impairment or Disposal of Long-Lived Assets subsections that are included in such groups (ASC 360-10-15-4).

Testing Assets for Recoverability

A long-lived asset must be tested for recoverability when events or changes in circumstances indicate that the carrying amount of the asset may not be recoverable. Examples of such events or changes in circumstances are (ASC 360-10-35-21):

- A significant decrease in the market price of a long-lived asset.
- A significant adverse change in the extent or manner in which a long-lived asset is used, or in its physical condition.

- A significant adverse change in legal factors or in the business climate that could affect the value of a long-lived asset.
- An accumulation of costs significantly in excess of the amount originally expected for the acquisition or construction of a long-lived asset.
- A current period operating or cash flow loss, combined with a history of operating or cash flow losses or a projection or forecast that demonstrates continuing losses associated with the use of a long-lived asset.
- A current expectation that it is more likely than not that a long-lived asset will be sold or otherwise disposed of significantly before the end of its previously estimated useful life.

Testing a long-lived asset for recoverability may require a review of depreciation estimates and method as required by ASC 250 (Accounting Changes and Error Corrections) or the amortization period required by ASC 350 (Intangibles—Goodwill and Other). Any revision in the remaining useful life of a long-lived asset resulting from that review shall be considered in developing the estimates of future cash flows that are used to test the asset for recoverability (ASC 360-10-35-22).

PRACTICE NOTE: The approach identified in ASC 360 requires the investigation of potential impairments on an **exception basis.** The requirement to compare undiscounted future cash flows with the carrying amount of the asset represents a "trigger mechanism" to assist in identifying those assets that require further analysis. In explaining its conclusions, the FASB states that an asset must be tested for recoverability only if there is reason to believe that the asset is impaired.

Grouping Assets

For purposes of recognizing and measuring an impairment loss, a long-lived asset shall be grouped with other assets and liabilities at the lowest level for which identifiable cash flows are largely independent of the cash flows of other assets and liabilities. In limited circumstances, a long-lived asset may not have identifiable cash flows that are largely independent of the cash flows of other assets and liabilities. In this situation, the asset group for the long-lived asset that is being evaluated for an impairment loss includes all assets and liabilities of the entity. An example of this circumstance is a corporate headquarters facility (ASC 360-10-35-23, 24).

When fair value is estimated on the basis of the present value of expected future cash flows, assets should be grouped at the lowest level for which there are identifiable cash flows that are largely independent of the cash flows of other groups of assets. For example, assume a company has four long-lived assets identified as A, B, C, and D. Evidence suggests that the value of Asset A is impaired. If the cash flows of the four assets can be separately identified, those associated with Asset A alone are used to measure the fair value of that asset. On the other hand, if the cash flows of Assets A and B are intermingled such that separate identification of cash flows of each asset is impossible, the joint cash flows of these two assets must be considered in measuring the fair value of Assets A and B combined, even though evidence does not suggest that the value of Asset B is impaired.

PRACTICE POINTER: As the level of aggregation of assets in applying ASC 360 goes up, the likelihood that a loss will be recognized goes down. This is because when assets are aggregated, the impairment loss that may exist within one asset is offset by the excess of fair value over carrying amount for the other assets that are part of the aggregation. For example, if impairment appears to exist for Asset A, and if Asset A can be valued independently, a loss is recognized. On the other hand, if the fair value of Asset A cannot be determined independently of Assets B and C, the excess of fair value over carrying amount of these two assets must be overcome by the impairment loss of Asset A before a loss is recognized. When assets are aggregated in applying ASC 360, it is reasonable to conclude that some—perhaps many—impairment losses are never recognized, because they are offset against the fair value in excess of carrying amount of other assets.

Goodwill is included in an asset group to be tested for impairment under ASC 360 only if the asset group is or includes a reporting unit. A reporting unit is defined in ASC 350 as one level below an operating segment. ASC 350 requires goodwill to be tested for impairment at the reporting unit level. Goodwill shall not be included in a lower level asset group that includes only part of a reporting unit. Estimates of future cash flows used to test that lower-level asset group for recoverability shall not be adjusted for the effect of excluding goodwill from the group (ASC 360-10-35-26).

Other than goodwill, the carrying amounts of any assets and liabilities not covered by ASC 360 that are included in an asset group shall be adjusted in accordance with other applicable generally accepted accounting principles prior to testing the asset group for recoverability (ASC 360-10-35-27).

An impairment loss for an asset group reduces only the carrying amounts of a long-lived asset or assets of the group. The loss is allocated to the long-lived assets of the group on a pro rata basis using the relative carrying amounts of the assets, except that the loss allocated to an individual long-lived asset of the group shall not reduce the carrying amount of that asset below its fair value whenever that fair value is determinable without undue cost and effort (ASC 360-10-35-28).

New Cost Basis

When an impairment loss has been recognized, the adjusted carrying amount of the long-lived asset becomes its new cost basis. This basis is used to depreciate the asset over its remaining useful life. Restoration of previously recognized impairment losses is prohibited, even though circumstances subsequent to the loss recognition indicate that the earlier carrying amount of the asset is recoverable (ASC 360-10-35-20).

Estimating Future Cash Flows

Estimates of future cash flows used to test the recoverability of a long-lived asset shall include only the future cash flows that are directly associated with, and that are expected to arise, as a direct result of using and eventually disposing of the asset. Estimates of future cash flows used to test recoverability shall incorporate the entity's own assumptions about its use of the asset and shall consider all available evidence (ASC 360-10-35-29, 30).

Estimates of future cash flows used to test recoverability shall be made for the remaining useful life of the asset to the entity. The remaining useful life, where recoverability is evaluated at an asset group level, is based on the remaining useful life of the primary asset in the group. The primary asset is the asset group's most significant cash-flow-generating tangible asset being depreciated or intangible asset being amortized. These estimates are based on the existing service potential of the asset to the entity. Estimates of future cash flows used to test the recoverability of a long-lived asset that is in use, including a long-lived asset for which development is substantially complete, are based on the existing service potential of the asset at the date it is tested. This encompasses its remaining useful life, cash flow generating capacity and, for tangible assets, physical output capacity. Those estimates include cash flows associated with future expenditures necessary to maintain the existing service potential of a long-lived asset, including those that replace the service potential of a component part of a long-lived asset. Those estimates exclude cash flows associated with future capital expenditures that would increase the potential of a long-lived asset (ASC 360-10-35-31, 32, 33).

Estimates of future cash flows used to test the recoverability of a long-lived asset that is under development shall be based on the expected service potential of the asset when it is substantially complete, including cash flows associated with all future expenditures necessary to develop a long-lived asset and including interest payments that will be capitalized as part of the cost of the asset (ASC 360-10-35-34).

Fair Value

Fair value is best estimated using an expected present value technique. This is especially true when the long-lived assets have uncertainties as to both timing and amount.

Illustration of Recognizing an Impairment Loss on Assets to Be Held and Used

Zeta Company has machinery for which circumstances indicate a potential impairment in value. The machinery cost $100,000 and has accumulated depreciation of $35,000, resulting in a carrying amount of $65,000. The first step is to determine how the undiscounted future cash flows compare with $65,000. Assuming that those cash flows are estimated to be $50,000, an impairment loss is evident. The next step is to determine the fair value of the asset by the appropriate method (i.e., quoted market price, estimate based on similar assets, estimate based on an appropriate valuation technique). If the fair value is determined to be $40,000, the result is an impairment loss of $25,000, computed as follows:

Asset cost	$100,000
Less: Accumulated depreciation	35,000
Carrying amount	$ 65,000
Less: Fair value	40,000
Impairment loss	$ 25,000

An impairment loss of $25,000 is recognized, and $40,000 is now considered the cost of the asset for future accounting and depreciation purposes. Notice that the undiscounted future cash flow of $50,000 is used only to identify the need to measure the amount of the impairment loss. That amount is not used directly to determine the amount of the loss, although it may be useful if the fair value is determined by estimating the present value of future cash flows.

Long-Lived Assets to Be Disposed Of

In addition to covering assets to be held and used, ASC 360 also specifies accounting standards for assets to be disposed of. Assets to be disposed of other than by sale (e.g., by abandonment or in an exchange for a similar productive asset) shall continue to be classified as held and used until disposition. An asset to be abandoned is considered disposed of when it ceases to be used. If an entity commits to a plan to abandon a long-lived asset before the end of its estimated useful life, depreciation estimates shall be revised in accordance with ASC 250 to reflect the use of the asset over a shorter useful life than originally expected. A temporarily idle asset is not considered abandoned. An asset to be exchanged for a similar productive asset is considered disposed of when it is exchanged. Similarly, an asset that is to be distributed to owners in a spin-off is considered to have been disposed of when it is distributed (ASC 360-10-45-15; 360-10-35-47).

Disposal by Sale

A long-lived asset to be sold is classified as held for sale in the period in which all of the following criteria are met (ASC 360-10-45-9):

- Management, having the authority to approve the action, commits to a plan to sell the asset or asset group.
- The asset (asset group) is available for immediate sale in its present condition.
- An active program to locate a buyer has been initiated.
- The sale of the asset (asset group) is probable, and transfer of the asset (asset group) is expected to qualify for recognition as a completed sale within one year. ASC 360 provides certain exceptions to this one-year requirement (ASC 360-10-45-11).
- The asset (asset group) is being actively marketed for sale at a price that is reasonable in relation to its fair value.
- Actions required to complete the plan indicate that it is unlikely that significant changes in the plan will be made or that the plan will be withdrawn.

A long-lived asset (asset group) that is newly acquired and that will be held for sale rather than for use should be classified as held for sale as of the acquisition date only if the sale is expected within one year and the other requirements stated in the previous paragraph that are not met are probable of being met within a short period from the acquisition date (ASC 360-10-45-12).

PRACTICE POINTER: ASC 360 indicates that in applying this requirement, the term "short period" should be interpreted as within three months.

If the criteria for considering an asset as held for sale are met after the financial statement date, but before the financial statements are issued, that asset shall be treated as held and used in the financial statements. Information concerning the intent to sell the asset is required to be presented in notes to the financial statements (ASC 360-10-45-13).

A long-lived asset (asset group) classified as held for sale shall be measured at the lower of its carrying amount or fair value less cost to sell. If the asset (asset group) is newly acquired, the carrying amount of the asset (asset group) shall be based on its fair value less cost to sell at the acquisition date. A long-lived asset shall not be depreciated once it is classified as held for sale (ASC 360-10-35-43).

Costs to sell are the incremental direct costs to transact a sale. These are the costs that result directly from and are essential to a sale transaction and that would not have been incurred if the decision to sell had not been made. These costs include:

1. Broker commissions
2. Legal and title transfer fees
3. Closing costs that must be incurred before legal title can be transferred

These costs exclude expected future losses associated with the operations of the asset (asset group) while it is classified as held for sale (ASC 360-10-35-38).

A loss shall be recognized for any initial or subsequent write-down to fair value less cost to sell. A gain shall be recognized for any subsequent increase in fair value less cost to sell, but not in excess of the cumulative loss previously recognized. The loss or gain shall adjust only the carrying amount of a long-lived asset, whether classified as held for sale individually, or as part of a disposal group (ASC 360-10-35-40).

Figure 27-1: Impairment of Assets Held and Used

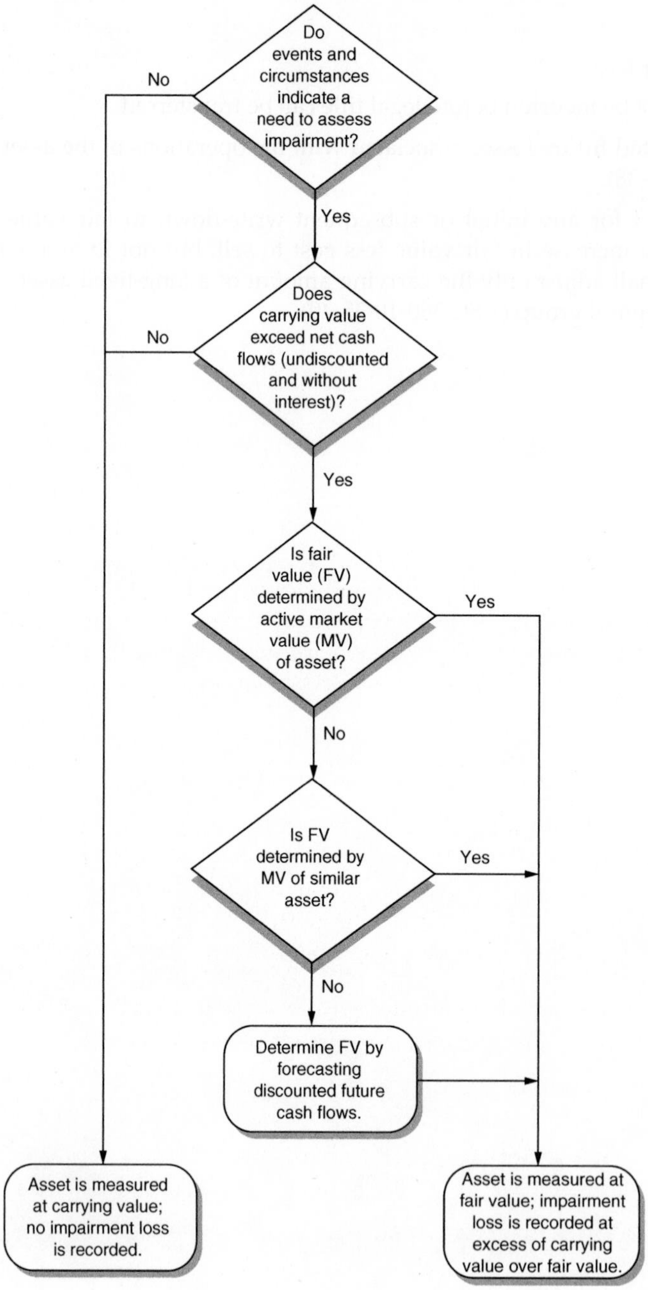

Illustration of Impairment of Asset to Be Disposed Of

Wampler, Inc. has a piece of specialized machinery that is no longer efficiently usable for its operations as a result of technological advances that require replacement. The machine cost Wampler $500,000 and has an accumulated depreciation (based on double-declining balance) of $275,000. Estimates of the selling price and the cost to sell, including solicitation and execution of a sales agreement, are $185,000 and $25,000, respectively. Wampler should record an impairment loss in the current period, as follows:

Asset cost		$500,000
Accumulated depreciation		(275,000)
Asset carrying amount		$225,000
Less: Estimated selling price	$185,000	
Cost to sell	(25,000)	(160,000)
Impairment loss		$ 65,000

Changes in a Plan to Sell

Circumstances may arise that cause an entity to decide not to sell a long-lived asset (asset group) that was previously classified as held for sale. In this instance the asset (asset group) should be reclassified as to be held and used. An asset (asset group) that is so reclassified should be measured individually at the lower of (1) its carrying amount before the asset (asset group) was classified as held for sale, adjusted for any depreciation or amortization expense that would have been recognized had the asset (asset group) been continuously classified as held and used, or (2) the fair value at the date of the decision not to sell the asset (ASC 360-10-35-44). Any adjustment required by this process is included as an element of income from continuing operations in the period of the decision to not sell the asset (ASC 360-10-45-7).

DEPLETION

Depletion is the process of allocating the cost of a natural resource over its estimated useful life in a manner similar to depreciation. An estimate is made of the amount of natural resources to be extracted, in units or tons, barrels, or any other measurement. The estimate of total recoverable units is then divided into the total cost of the depletable asset, to arrive at a depletion rate per unit. Estimated costs to restore the property should be added, and estimated residual value should be subtracted. The annual depletion expense is the rate per unit times the number of units extracted during the fiscal year. If at any time there is a revision of the estimated number of units that are expected to be extracted, a new unit rate is computed. The cost of the natural resource property is reduced each year by the amount of the depletion expense for the year. This process is similar to the units-of-production depreciation method explained earlier.

DISCLOSURE

Accumulated depreciation and depletion are deducted from the assets to which they relate. The following disclosures of depreciable assets and depreciation are required in the financial statements or notes thereto (ASC 360-10-50-1).

- Depreciation expense for the period
- Balances of major classes of depreciable assets by nature or function
- Accumulated depreciation allowances by classes or in total
- The methods used, by major classes, in computing depreciation

PRACTICE NOTE: Practice varies on whether these disclosures are made in the aggregate for all categories of depreciable assets or separately for each category. Presentation in the aggregate seems to be the dominant practice, despite the fact that separate disclosure provides more useful information.

PRACTICE POINTER: ASC 360-10-50-1 requires that the above disclosures be made in the financial statements or in the notes. In addition, ASC 250 (Accounting Changes and Error Corrections) requires disclosure of the effect of a change from one depreciation method to another (ASC 250-10-50-4).

Reporting on impairment losses depends on whether the assets are to be held and used or disposed of. An impairment loss on long-lived assets to be held and used shall be included in income from continuing operations before income taxes in the income statement of a business enterprise and in income from continuing operations in the statement of activities of a not-for-profit organization (ASC 360-10-45-4).

The following information shall be disclosed in the period in which an impairment loss on an asset to be held and used is recognized (ASC 360-10-50-2):

- Description of the impaired long-lived asset and the facts and circumstances leading to the impairment.
- The amount of the impairment loss and the caption of the income statement or statement of activities that includes the loss.
- The method(s) of determining fair value.
- If applicable, the segment in which the impaired long-lived asset is reported under ASC 280 (Segment Reporting).

The following disclosures must be made in the notes to the financial statements in any period in which a long-lived asset has either been disposed of or has been classified as held for sale (ASC 360-10-50-3):

- Description of the circumstances leading to the disposal.
- Expected manner and timing of the disposal.
- Gain or loss recognized on the disposal.
- The caption in the statement where net income is reported that includes the gain or loss, if not separately presented on the face of that statement.
- The carrying amount(s) of the major classes of assets and liabilities included as part of a disposal group classified as held for sale, if not separately presented on the face of the statement of financial position.
- If applicable, the segment in which the long-lived asset is reported under ASC 280 (Segment Reporting).

For further coverage of the reporting requirements for assets to be disposed of, see the discussion in Chapter 2, *ASC 205—Presentation of Financial Statements*.

ASC 360-20: REAL ESTATE SALES

RECOGNITION OF SALES

The guidance in this subtopic does not apply to the following:

- The sale of only property improvements or integral equipment without a concurrent sale of the underlying land, except for sales of property improvements or integral equipment with the concurrent lease of the underlying land to the buyer.
- The sale of the stock or net assets of a subsidiary or a segment of a business if the assets of that subsidiary or that segment contain real estate, unless the transaction is, in substance, the sale of real estate.
- Exchanges of real estate for other real estate (see ASC 845).
- The sale of securities that are accounted for in accordance with ASC 320 or ASC 321.
- Retail land sales.
- Natural assets such as those that have been extracted from the land, such as oil, gas, coal, and gold. (ASC 360-20-15-10)

Real Estate Sales (Except Retail Land Sales)

In a real estate sale, a significant portion of the sales price usually is represented by a long-term receivable, which is not backed by the full faith and credit of the buyer. Usually, the seller can recover the property only in the event of default by the buyer. Another unusual facet of real estate sales is the seller's possible continuing involvement in the property. For instance, the seller may be legally bound to make certain improvements to the property or to adjacent property.

To ensure the collection of the long-term receivable, which usually is part of a real estate transaction, ASC 360 requires minimum down payments for all real estate sales before a seller is permitted to recognize a profit. ASC 360 emphasizes the timing of the recognition of profits but does not cover other aspects of real estate accounting.

Real estate transactions that are *not* considered "retail land sales" include the following:

1. Sales of homes, buildings, and parcels of land
2. Sales of lots to builders
3. Sales of corporate stock or a partnership interest in which the substance of the transaction is actually a sale of real estate
4. Sales of options to acquire real estate
5. Sales of time-sharing interests in real estate

As stated above, sales of time-sharing interests in real estate are to be accounted for as nonretail land sales. For a seller to report the total profit on a sale of real estate (other than a retail land sale) by the full accrual method, ASC 360 requires that the transaction meet specific criteria, as follows (ASC 360-20-40-5):

- A sale must be completed (consummated).
- The buyer's initial and continuing payments (investment) must be adequate.
- The seller's receivable is not subject to future subordination, except to (*a*) a primary lien on the property existing at the date of sale or (*b*) a future loan or an existing permanent loan commitment the proceeds of which must first be applied to the payment of the seller's receivable.
- All of the benefits and risks of ownership in the property are substantially transferred to the buyer by the seller.
- The seller does not have a substantial continued involvement with the property after the sale.

If a sale of real estate, other than a retail land sale, meets all of the above criteria, the seller must recognize the entire profit on the sale in accordance with the full accrual method of accounting. If a real estate sale fails to meet all of the above criteria, profit on the sale is recognized by (*a*) the deposit method, (*b*) the installment sales method, (*c*) the cost-recovery method, (*d*) the reduced profit method, or (*e*) the percentage-of-completion method. The method that is used is determined by the specific circumstances of each real estate sale.

PRACTICE NOTE: For sale-leaseback transactions, the sale portion of such a transaction involving real estate is accounted for as a sale only if it qualifies as a sale under the provisions of ASC 360. In addition, ASC 840 prohibits a lease involving real estate from being classified as a sales-type lease unless the lease agreement provides for the title of the leased property to be transferred to the lessee at or shortly after the end of the lease term. Additional coverage of the accounting for sale-leaseback transactions can be found in our discussion of ASC 840 (Leases).

When a Real Estate Sale Is Consummated

ASC 360 contains four criteria that must be met for a sale of real estate to be considered "consummated" (ASC 360-20-40-7):

1. The contracting parties are legally bound by the contract.
2. All consideration required by the terms of the contract has been paid.
3. If the seller is responsible by the terms of the contract to obtain permanent financing for the buyer, the seller must have arranged for such financing.
4. The seller has performed all of the acts required by the contract to earn the revenue.

As a general rule, the above criteria are met at the time of, or after, the closing of the real estate sale. These criteria rarely are met before closing or at the time a sales agreement is executed.

An exception to the "consummation rule" may occur if, after the date of sale, the seller has continued involvement with the property to construct office buildings, condominiums, shopping centers, or other similar improvements on the land that take a long time to complete. As will be discussed later, ASC 360 permits some profit recognition under certain circumstances even if the seller has this type of substantial continued involvement with the property.

Buyer's Initial and Continuing Investment

In determining whether the buyer's minimum initial investment is adequate under the provisions of ASC 360, the *sales value* of the property—not the stated sales price in the contract—is used. The *sales value* is defined as the stated sales price of the property, increased or decreased for other considerations included in the sale that clearly represent greater or smaller proceeds to the seller on the sale. Thus, any payments made by the buyer that are not included in the stated sales price in the contract and that represent additional proceeds to the seller are included as part of the buyer's minimum investment. These additional proceeds enter into the determination of both the buyer's minimum investment and the sales value of the property. Examples of additional proceeds to the seller are (*a*) the exercise price of a real estate option to purchase the property, (*b*) management fees, (*c*) points to obtain financing, (*d*) prepaid interest and principal payments, (*e*) payments by the buyer to third parties that reduce previously existing indebtedness on the property, and (*f*) any payments made by the buyer to the seller that will be applied at a future date against amounts due the seller (ASC 360-20-40-8). However, payments by the buyer to third parties for improvements to the property or payments that are not verifiable are not considered as additional proceeds to the seller (ASC 360-20-40-13). See ASC 970 for a discussion of other real estate costs a buyer or seller may incur such as preacquisition costs, postacquisition costs, and costs to sell or rent real estate.

Decreases in the stated sales price that are necessary to arrive at the sales value of the property may include, but are not limited to, the following (ASC 360-20-40-8):

- The amount of discount, if any, necessary to reduce the receivable from the buyer to its present value. Thus, if the buyer's receivable does not bear interest or if the rate of interest is less than the prevailing rate, a discount would be required to reduce it to its present value.
- The present value of services that the seller agrees to perform without compensation or, if the seller agrees to perform services at less than prevailing rates, the difference between (*a*) the present value of the services at prevailing rates and (*b*) the present value of the agreed-upon compensation.

Illustration of Computation of Sales Value

XYZ, Inc. agrees to build improvements for ABC Company for a total price of $1,750,000. The improvements are to be built on land leased by ABC from a third party. The payments on the land lease are $18,000 per year, payable monthly in advance, and the lease term is for 45 years. ABC Company will pay for the improvements as follows:

Cash down payment	$ 250,000
10% unsecured note payable in five annual payments of $20,000 plus interest	100,000
Primary loan from insurance company secured by improvements to the property, payable in equal monthly payments over 28 years at 8 1/2% interest	1,400,000
Total stated sales price of improvements	$1,750,000

The computation of the *sales value*, as required by ASC 360, is as follows:

Present value of land lease payments for 28 years, payable $1,500 monthly, discounted at 8 1/2% interest	$ 193,361
Primary loan from insurance company	1,400,000
Total equivalent primary debt	$1,593,361
Unsecured note from buyer to seller	100,000
Cash down payment	250,000
Sales value*	$1,943,361

* The adequacy of the buyer's minimum initial investment in the property is based on the *sales value* of the property and not on the stated sales price.

As indicated in the previous illustration, the effects of an underlying land lease must also be included in computing the sales value of the property. If a seller sells improvements to a buyer that are to be built on property subject to an underlying land lease, the present value of the lease payments must be included in the sales value of the property. The present value of the lease payments is computed over the actual term of the primary indebtedness of the improvements, if any, or over the usual term of primary indebtedness for the type of improvements involved. The present value of the land lease payments is tantamount to additional indebtedness on the property. If the land lease is not subordinated, the discount rate to determine the present value of the land lease payments should be comparable to interest rates on primary debt of the same nature. If the land lease is subordinated, however, a higher discount rate comparable to secondary debt of the same nature should be used.

If a land lease exists between the buyer and a third party, its effects on the sales value of the property are used only to determine the adequacy of the buyer's initial investment. When the seller of the improvements is also the lessor of the land lease, however, the computation of the profit on the sale of the improvements is also affected. Because it is impossible to separate the profits on the improvements from the profits on the underlying lease, ASC 360 requires a special computation limiting the amount of profit that can be recognized. The amount of profit that can be recognized on the improvements is equal to the sales value of the property, less the cost of improvements and the cost of the land. However, the present value of the lease payments in the sales value may not exceed the actual cost of the land (ASC 360-20-40-57).

The result of limiting the amount of profit that can be recognized on the sale of improvements is to defer any residual profit on the land from being recognized until the land is sold or the future rental payments actually are received (ASC 360-20-40-59).

If a land lease between a buyer and a seller of improvements on the land is for a term of less than 20 years or does not substantially cover the economic life of the improvements being made to the property, the transaction should be accounted for as a single lease of land and improvements (ASC 360-20-40-56).

The buyer's minimum initial investment must be made in cash or cash equivalency at or before the time of sale. A buyer's note does not qualify for the minimum initial investment unless payment of the note is unconditionally guaranteed by an irrevocable letter of credit from an established unrelated lending institution. A permanent loan commitment by an independent third party to replace a loan made by the seller is not included in the buyer's initial investment. Any funds that have been loaned or will be loaned, directly or indirectly, to the buyer by the seller are deducted from the buyer's initial investment (down payment) to determine whether the required minimum has been met. For the purposes of this provision, the seller must be exposed to a potential loss as a result of the funds loaned to the buyer. For example, if a buyer made an initial cash investment of $200,000 in a real estate transaction, $25,000 of which was a loan from the seller, the buyer's minimum initial investment under the provisions of ASC 360 would be $175,000. However, if an unrelated banking institution unconditionally guaranteed the timely repayment of the $25,000 to the seller, the entire $200,000 would be eligible as the buyer's initial investment (ASC 360-20-40-10, 13).

A direct relationship exists between the amount of a buyer's first investment (down payment) and the probability that the seller eventually will collect the balance due. The larger the down payment, the more likely it is that the buyer will pay the balance due. A reasonable basis for establishing the amount of a buyer's initial investment is the prevailing practices of independent lending institutions. Thus, the difference between the amount of primary mortgage an independent lending institution would lend on a particular parcel of real estate and the sales value of the property is a realistic guide to figure the amount of the buyer's initial investment (ASC 360-20-40-18).

To apply the full accrual method of accounting to a real estate transaction (other than a retail land sale), ASC 360 provides that the minimum initial investment (down payment) of the buyer should be the *greater* of 1 or 2 below:

1. The percentage of the sales value of the property as indicated in the following (ASC 360-20-55-1):

	Minimum Down Payment (% of Sales Value)
Land:	
Held for commercial, industrial, or residential development to commence within two years after sale	20%
Held for commercial, industrial, or residential development after two years	25%
Commercial and Industrial Property:	
Office and industrial buildings, shopping centers, etc.:	
Properties subject to lease on a long-term lease basis to parties having satisfactory credit rating; cash flow currently sufficient to service all indebtedness	10%
Single tenancy properties sold to a user having a satisfactory credit rating	15%

	Minimum Down Payment (% of Sales Value)
All other	20%
Other Income-Producing Properties (hotels, motels, marinas, mobile home parks, etc.):	
Cash flow currently sufficient to service all indebtedness	15%
Start-up situations or current deficiencies in cash flow	25%
Multi-Family Residential Property:	
Primary residence:	
Cash flow currently sufficient to service all indebtedness	10%
Start-up situations or current deficiencies in cash flow	15%
Secondary or recreational residence:	
Cash flow currently sufficient to service all indebtedness	15%
Start-up situations or current deficiencies in cash flow	25%
Single Family Residential Property (including condominium or cooperative housing):	
Primary residence of the buyer	5%*
Secondary or recreational residence	10%*

* If collectibility of the remaining portion of the sales price cannot be supported by reliable evidence of collection experience, a higher down payment is called for and should not be less than 60% of the difference between the sales value and the financing available from loans guaranteed by regulatory bodies, such as FHA or VA, or from independent financial institutions. This 60% test applies when independent first-mortgage financing is not utilized and the seller takes a receivable from the buyer for the difference between the sales value and the initial investment. When independent first-mortgage financing is utilized, the adequacy of the initial investment on sales of single-family residential property should be determined in accordance with ASC 360.

2. The *lesser* of the following (ASC 360-20-55-1):
   a. The difference between the sales value of the property and 115% of the maximum permanent mortgage loan or commitment on the property recently obtained from a primary independent lending institution, or
   b. Twenty-five percent (25%) of the sales value of the property.

Illustration of Determination of Buyer's Minimum Initial Investment

The sales value of property being sold is $200,000, and the maximum permanent mortgage loan recently placed on the property from an independent lending institution is $150,000. The property being sold is commercial land, which will be developed by the buyer within two years after the date of sale. For the full accrual method of accounting to be applied to this real estate transaction, ASC 360 provides that the minimum initial investment (down payment) of the buyer should be the greater of (1) or (2) below:

1. The percentage of the sales value of the property as indicated on the table is $40,000 (20% of $200,000).
2. a. The difference between the sales value of the property and 115% of the recently placed permanent mortgage loan is $27,500 (115% of $150,000 = $172,500 and the difference between $200,000 [sales value] and $172,500 is $27,500).

   b. 25% of the sales value ($200,000) is $50,000.

   The lesser of 2a ($27,500) and 2b ($50,000) = $27,500.

   The greater of 2a ($27,500) and 1 ($40,000) = $40,000.

   Thus, the minimum down payment of the buyer is $40,000.

PRACTICE POINTER: Even if the buyer makes the required minimum initial investment, make a separate assessment to determine the collectibility of the receivable. In other words, there must be reasonable assurance that the receivable will be collected after the seller receives the minimum initial investment; if there is not, do not record the sale by the full accrual method. The buyer must make the minimum initial investment, and the seller must be reasonably assured that the balance of the sales price will be collected, before the real estate sale is recorded and any profits are recognized. The assessment of the receivable by the seller should include credit reports on the buyer and an evaluation of the adequacy of the cash flow from the property.

In addition to an adequate initial investment, ASC 360 requires that the buyer maintain a continuing investment in the property by increasing his or her investment each year. The buyer's total indebtedness for the purchase price of the property must be reduced each year in equal amounts, which will extinguish the entire indebtedness (interest and principal) over a specified maximum period. The specified maximum period for land transactions is 20 years. The specified maximum period for all other real estate transactions is no more than that offered by independent financial institutions at the time of sale for first mortgages (ASC 360-20-40-19).

The buyer's commitment to pay the full amount of his or her indebtedness to the seller becomes doubtful if the total indebtedness is not to be paid within the specified maximum period.

A buyer's payments on his or her indebtedness must be in cash or cash equivalency. Funds provided directly or indirectly by the seller cannot be considered in determining the buyer's continuing investment in the property (ASC 360-20-40-20).

Release Provisions

Real estate agreements involving land frequently provide for the periodic release of part of the land to the buyer. The buyer obtains the released land free of any liens. The conditions for the release usually require the buyer to have previously paid sufficient funds to cover the sales price of the released land, and often an additional sum is required to effectuate the release. In these types of transactions involving released land, the requirements for a buyer's initial and continuing investment must be determined based on the sales value of property not released or not subject to release (ASC 360-20-40-21). In other words, for a seller to recognize profit at the time of sale, a buyer's investment must be enough to pay any amounts for the release of land and still meet the specified initial and continued investment required by the provisions of ASC 360 (ASC 360-20-40-22). If the buyer's initial and continuing investment is not sufficient, then each release of land should be treated as a separate sale and profit recognized at that time (ASC 360-20-40-23).

Future Subordination

If, at the time of sale, a seller's receivable is subject to future subordination, other than (*a*) to a primary (first mortgage) lien on the property existing at the date of sale or (*b*) to a future loan or existing permanent loan commitment the proceeds of which must first be applied to the payment of the seller's receivable, no profit should be recognized, because the effect of future subordination on the collectibility of a receivable cannot be evaluated reasonably. The cost-recovery method should be used to recognize profit at the time of sale if the seller's receivable is subject to future subordination, other than the exceptions (*a*) and (*b*) noted above (ASC 360-20-40-25).

Nontransfer of Ownership and Seller's Continued Involvement

Real estate transactions must be analyzed carefully to determine their economic substance. Frequently, the economic substance of a real estate sale is no more than a management fee arrangement or an indication that the risks and benefits of ownership have not really been transferred in the agreement. Accounting for a real estate transaction can become quite complicated because of the many types of continuing relations that can exist between a buyer and a seller. The substance of the real estate transaction should dictate the accounting method that should be used.

PRACTICE POINTER: As a general rule, before a profit is recognized, a sale must occur, collectibility of the receivable must be reasonably assured, and the seller must perform all of the acts required by the contract to earn the revenue. Profit also may be recognized—at the time of the sale—on contracts that provide for the continued involvement of the seller if the maximum potential loss of the seller is expressly limited and defined by the terms of the contract. In this event, recognize the total profit on the sale, less the maximum potential loss that could occur because of the seller's involvement, at the time of the sale.

Two important factors in evaluating the economic substance of a real estate sale are (1) the transfer of the usual risks and rewards of ownership in the property and (2) the full performance by the seller of all acts required by the contract to earn the revenue. Generally, both of these factors must be accomplished before full profit can be recognized on the sale of real estate. The more common types of real estate transactions and how they should be accounted for are discussed in the following paragraphs.

Profit Recognition Other Than Full Accrual Basis

If a sale of real estate, other than a retail land sale, meets all of the ASC 360 criteria discussed earlier, the seller must recognize the entire profit on the sale in accordance with the full accrual basis of accounting.

When one (or more) of the ASC 360 criteria is not met in a real estate sale, an alternative method of recognizing revenue from the sale must be used. The alternative method selected may be required by ASC 360 or may be a matter of professional judgment. The four accounting methods recommended by ASC 360 are (1) the deposit method, (2) the cost-recovery method, (3) the installment sales method, and (4) the reduced profit method.

Deposit Accounting

The uncertainty about the collectibility of the sales price in a real estate transaction may be so great that the effective date of the sale is deferred and any cash received by the seller is accounted for as a deposit. However, cash received that is designated by contract as nonrefundable interest may be applied as an offset to existing carrying charges on the property, such as property taxes and interest, instead of being accounted for as a deposit.

All cash received, except that appropriately used as an offset to the carrying charges of the property, must be reflected in the seller's balance sheet as a liability (deposit on a contract for the sale of real estate). No change is made in accounting for the property subject to the contract and its related mortgage debt, if any. However, the seller's financial statements should disclose that these items are subject to a sales contract. Depreciation expense should continue as a period cost, in spite of the fact that the property has been sold legally. Until the requirements of ASC 360 are met for profit recognition, the seller does not report a sale and continues to report all cash received (including interest received) either as a deposit or, in the case of nonrefundable interest, as an offset to the carrying charges of the property involved (ASC 360-20-55-17). If the buyer forfeits a nonrefundable deposit, or defaults on the contract, the seller should reduce the deposit account appropriately and include such amounts in income of the period (ASC 360-20-55-19).

Cost-Recovery Method

If a seller's receivable is subject to subordination that cannot be reasonably evaluated, or if uncertainty exists as to the recovery of the seller's cost on default by the buyer, the cost recovery method should be used. Even if cost has been recovered by the seller but additional collections are highly doubtful, the cost-recovery method is appropriate. Frequently, the cost recovery method is used initially for transactions that would also qualify for the installment sales method.

PRACTICE NOTE: Both the cost recovery method and the installment sales method defer the recognition of profit on the sale until collections actually are received.

Under the cost recovery method, all collections (including interest received) are applied first to the recovery of the cost of the property; only after full cost has been received is any profit recognized (ASC Glossary). The only expenses remaining to be charged against the profit are those relating to the collection process. When the cost recovery method is used, the total sales value is included in the income statement for the period in which the sale is made (ASC 360-20-55-14). From the total sales value in the income statement, the total cost of the sale and the deferred gross profit on the sale are deducted. On the balance sheet, the deferred gross profit is reflected as a reduction of the related receivable. Until full cost is recovered, principal payments received are applied to reduce the related receivable, and interest payments received are added to the deferred gross profit. At any given time, the related receivable, less the deferred gross profit, equals the remaining cost that must be recovered. After all cost is recovered, subsequent collections reduce the deferred gross profit and appear as a separate item of revenue on the income statement.

Installment Sales Method

Promulgated U.S. GAAP prohibit accounting for sales by installment accounting except under exceptional circumstances in which collectibility cannot be assured or estimated reasonably. Collectibility can be in doubt because of the length of an extended collection period or because no basis of estimation can be established.

PRACTICE NOTE: The installment sales method frequently is more appropriate for real estate transactions in which collectibility of the receivable from the buyer cannot be reasonably assured because defaults on loans secured by real estate usually result in the recovery of the property sold.

Under the installment sales method of accounting, each payment collected consists of part recovery of cost and part recovery of gross profit, in the same ratio that these two elements existed in the original sale. In a real estate transaction, the original sale is equal to the sales value of the property. Thus, under the installment sales method, profit is recognized on cash payments made by the buyer to the holder of the primary debt assumed and on cash payments to the seller. The profit recognized on the cash payments is based on the percentage of total profit to total sales value (ASC 360-20-55-7).

Illustration of Installment Sales Method

Jones Company sells real property to Smith for $2,000,000. Smith will assume an existing $1,200,000 first mortgage and pay $300,000 in cash as a down payment. The $500,000 balance will be in the form of a 12% second mortgage to Jones Company payable in equal payments of principal and interest over a ten-year period. The cost of the property to Jones is $1,200,000.

Computation of Sales Value and Gross Profit

Cash	$ 300,000
Second mortgage	500,000
First mortgage	1,200,000
Total sales value (which is the same as the stated sales price)	$2,000,000
Less: Cost of property sold	1,200,000
Total gross profit on sale	$ 800,000
Gross profit percentage ($800,000/$2,000,000)	40.0%
Profit to be recognized on down payment (40% of $300,000)	$ 120,000

Assuming that the $300,000 down payment is not sufficient to meet the requirements of full profit recognition on the sale, Jones recognizes $120,000 gross profit at the time of sale. Several months later Smith makes a cash payment of $100,000 on the first mortgage and $50,000 on the second mortgage. The amount of gross profit that Jones recognizes on these payments would be as follows:

Payment on first mortgage	$100,000
Payment on second mortgage	50,000
Total cash payments	$150,000
Gross profit realized (40% of $150,000)	$ 60,000

Even though Jones does not receive any cash on Smith's payment on the first mortgage, gross profit is still realized because the gross profit percentage was based on the total sales value, which included the first mortgage liability.

When the installment sales method is used, the total sales value is included in the income statement of the period in which the sale is made. From the total sales value in the income statement, the total cost of the sale and the deferred gross profit are deducted (ASC 360-20-55-10). On the balance sheet, the deferred gross profit on the sale is deducted from the related receivable. As cash payments are received, the portion allocated to realized gross profit is presented as a separate item of revenue on the income statement and deferred gross profit is reduced by the same amount. At any given time, the related receivable, less the deferred gross profit, represents the remaining cost of the property sold (ASC 360-20-55-9). Since realized gross profit is recognized as a portion of each cash collection, a percentage relationship will always exist between the long-term receivable and its related deferred gross profit. This percentage relationship will be the same as the gross profit ratio on the initial sales value.

Reduced Profit Method

The buyer's receivable is discounted to the present value of the lowest level of annual payments required by the sales contract. The discount period is the maximum allowed under the provisions of ASC 360, and all lump-sum payments are excluded in the calculation. The discount rate cannot be less than that stated in the sales contract, if any, or than the prevailing interest rate in accordance with existing U.S. GAAP. The buyer's receivable discounted as described above is used in determining the profit on the sale of real estate and usually results in a "reduced profit" from that which would be obtained under normal accounting procedures. Lump sum and other payments are recognized as profit when the seller receives them (ASC 360-20-55-16).

Change to Full Accrual Method

After the cost-recovery method or the installment sales method is adopted for a real estate transaction, the receivable should be evaluated periodically for collectibility. When it becomes apparent that the seller's receivable is reasonably assured of being collected, the seller should change to the full accrual accounting method. The change is a change in accounting estimate. When the change to the full accrual accounting method is made, any remaining deferred gross profit is recognized in full in the period in which the change is made (ASC 360-20-55-12, 15). If the change creates a material effect on the seller's financial statements, full disclosure of the effects and the reason for the change should be appropriately made in the financial statements or notes thereto.

Profit Recognition When Sale Is Not Consummated

If a real estate sale has not been consummated in accordance with the provisions of ASC 360, the deposit method of accounting is used until the sale is consummated (ASC 360-20-40-28).

As mentioned previously, an exception to the "consummation rule" occurs if the terms of the contract require the seller to sell a parcel of land and also construct on the same parcel a building that takes an extended period to complete. In other words, the seller is still involved with the property after the sale because he or she must construct the building. In most jurisdictions a "certificate of occupancy" must be obtained, indicating that the building or other structure has been constructed in accordance with the local building regulations and is ready for occupancy. Thus, a certificate of occupancy usually is necessary to consummate the real estate transaction. However, ASC 360 contains a special provision for profit recognition when a sale of real estate requires the seller to develop the property in the future. If the seller has contracted (*a*) for future development of the land; (*b*) to construct buildings, amenities, or other facilities on the land; or (*c*) to provide offsite improvements, partial recognition of profit may be made if future costs of development can be estimated reasonably at the time of sale (ASC 360-20-40-28). In this event, profit can be recognized for any work performed and finished by the seller when (*a*) the sale of the land is consummated and (*b*) the initial and continuing investments of the buyer are adequate. In other words, if the sale of the land meets the first two criteria for the use of the full accrual method of accounting, any profit allocable to (*a*) the work performed before the sale of the land and (*b*) the sale of the land can be recognized by the percentage of-completion method. Thus, the total profit on the sale may be allocated to work performed before the sale of the land and before future construction and development work. The allocation of the total profit is based on the estimated costs for each activity using a uniform rate of gross profit for all activities. If significant uncertainties exist or if costs and profits cannot be reasonably estimated, however, the completed contract method should be used (ASC 360-20-40-62, 63).

If a buyer has the right to defer until completion payments due for developmental and construction work, or if the buyer is financially unable to pay these amounts as they come due, care should be exercised in recognizing any profits until completion or satisfactory payment.

The terms of a real estate transaction accounted for by the deposit method may indicate that the carrying amount of the property involved is more than the sales value in the contract and that a loss has been incurred. Because the seller is using the deposit method, no sale is recorded and thus no loss. However, the information indicates an impairment of an asset that should be appropriately recorded by the seller in the period of discovery by a charge to income and the creation of a valuation allowance account for the property involved (ASC 360-20-40-29).

Profit Recognition When Buyer's Investment Is Inadequate

If all of the criteria for the full accrual method of accounting are met except that the buyer's initial investment is inadequate, the seller accounts for the sale by the installment sales method, provided the seller is reasonably assured of recovering the cost of the property if the buyer defaults. If the seller is not reasonably assured of recovering the cost of the property, or if cost recovery has been made but future collections are uncertain, the seller uses the cost-recovery method or the deposit method to account for the sale (ASC 360-20-40-31).

If all of the criteria for the full accrual method of accounting are met except that the buyer's continuing investment is inadequate, the seller shall account for the sale by the reduced profit method, provided the buyer's periodic payments cover both of the following items (ASC 360-20-40-33):

- Amortization of principal and interest based on the maximum primary mortgage that could be obtained on the property
- Interest, at an appropriate rate, on the excess amount, if any, of the total actual debt on the property over the maximum primary mortgage that could be obtained on the property

If both of the above conditions are not met, the seller shall not use the reduced profit method. Instead, the seller should account for the sale by either the installment sales method or the cost-recovery method, whichever is more appropriate under the specific circumstances (ASC 360-20-40-34).

Profit Recognition—Subordinated Receivable

As mentioned previously, the cost-recovery method is used to recognize profit at the time of sale if the seller's receivable is subject to future subordination (ASC 360-20-40-25).

This restriction does not apply in the following circumstances (ASC 360-20-40-25):

- A receivable is subordinate to a first mortgage on the property existing at the time of sale.
- A future loan, including an existing permanent loan commitment, is provided for by the terms of the sale, and the proceeds of the loan will be applied first to the payment of the seller's receivable.

Profit Recognition—Seller's Continued Involvement

In some real estate transactions, the seller does not transfer the benefits and risks of ownership to the buyer, or the seller maintains a substantial continued involvement with the property after the date of sale. These types of real estate transactions require careful examination to determine the appropriate method of accounting to be applied.

In legal form a real estate transaction may be a sale, but if in substance the contract is a profit sharing, financing, or leasing arrangement, no sale or profit is recognized. If a real estate contract contains any of the following provisions, it should be accounted for as a profit sharing, financing, or leasing arrangement:

- The return of the buyer's investment in the property is guaranteed by the seller (ASC 360-20-40-41).
- The buyer can compel the seller to repurchase the property (ASC 360-20-40-38).
- An option or obligation exists for the seller to repurchase the property (ASC 360-20-40-38).
- The seller is required to operate the property at its own risk for an extended period (ASC 360-20-40-42).
- The seller, as general partner, holds a receivable from the limited partnership as a result of a real estate sale. The collection of the receivable depends on the successful operation of the limited partnership by the general partner, who is also the seller and holder of the receivable (ASC 360-20-40-40).
- The seller guarantees a specific return on the buyer's investment for an extended period of time (ASC 360-20-40-41).
- The sale includes a leaseback to the seller of all or part of the property.

In real estate transactions in which the seller guarantees for a limited period (*a*) to return the buyer's investment or (*b*) to give the buyer a specific rate of return, the seller shall account for the sale by the deposit method of accounting. After the operations of the property become profitable, the seller may recognize profit based on performance. After the limited period has expired and all of the criteria for the full accrual method of accounting are met in accordance with ASC 360, the seller may recognize in full any remaining profit on the sale of real estate.

Initiating and Supporting Operations

As part of a real estate transaction, the seller may be required to initiate or support the operations of the property for a stated period of time or until a certain level of operations has been achieved. In other words, the seller may agree to operate the property for a certain period or until a certain level of rental income has been reached.

Even if there is no agreement, there is a presumption that a seller has an obligation to initiate and support operations of the property he or she has sold in any of the following circumstances (ASC 360-20-40-43):

- The seller sells to a limited partnership an interest in property in which he or she is a general partner.
- The seller retains an equity interest in the property sold by the seller.
- A management contract between the buyer and seller provides for compensation that is significantly higher or lower than comparable prevailing rates and that cannot be terminated by either the buyer or the seller.
- The collection of the receivable from the sale held by the seller is dependent on the operations of the property and represents a significant portion of the sales price. (A *significant receivable* is defined as one in excess of 15% of the maximum primary financing that could have been obtained from an established lending institution.) (ASC 360-20-40-40)

If the seller has agreed to the initiating and supporting operations for a limited period, the seller may recognize profit on the sale based on the performance of the required services. The measurement of performance shall be related to the cost incurred to date and the total estimated costs to be incurred for the services. However, profit recognition may not start until there is reasonable assurance that estimated future rent receipts will cover (*a*) all operating costs, (*b*) debt service, and (*c*) any payments due the seller under the terms of the contract. For this purpose, the estimated future rental receipts shall not exceed the greater of (*a*) leases actually executed or (*b*) two-thirds of the estimated future rent receipts. The difference between the estimated future rent receipts and the greater of (*a*) or (*b*) shall be reserved as a safety factor (ASC 360-20-40-44).

If the sales contract does not specify the period for which the seller must initiate and support operations of the property, a two-year period shall be presumed. The two-year period shall commence at the time of initial rental, unless rental receipts cover all operating cost, debt service, and other commitments before the end of the two-year period (ASC 360-20-40-43).

Services without Compensation

As part of the contract for the sale of real estate, the seller may be required to perform services related to the property sold without compensation or at a reduced rate. In determining profit to be recognized at the time of sale, a value should be placed on such services at the prevailing rates and deducted from the sales price of the property sold. The value of the compensation should then be recognized over the period in which the services are to be performed by the seller (ASC 360-20-40-43).

Sale of Real Estate Options

Proceeds from the sale of real estate options shall be accounted for by the deposit method. If the option is not exercised by its expiration date, the seller of the option shall recognize profit at that time. If an option is sold by the owner of the land and subsequently exercised, the proceeds from the sale of the option are included in determining the sales value of the property sold (ASC 360-20-40-45).

Sales of Partial Interests in Property

A seller may continue to be involved in property sold by retaining an interest in the property and by giving the buyer preference as to profits, cash flow, return on investment, or some other similar arrangement. In this event, if the transaction is in substance a sale, the seller shall recognize profit to the extent that the sale proceeds, including receivables, exceed the seller's total cost in the property (ASC 360-20-40-49).

A seller may retain a partial interest in the property sold, such as an undivided interest or some other form of equity. If a seller sells a partial interest in real estate property and the sale meets all of the criteria for the full accrual method, except for the seller's continued involvement related to the partial interest in the property, the seller shall recognize the proportionate share of the profit that is attributable to the outside interests in the property. If the seller controls the buyer, however, profit on the sale shall not be recognized until realized from transactions with outside individuals, or through the sale of the property to outside parties (ASC 360-20-40-47).

A seller may sell single-family units in a condominium project. If the units or time sharing interests are sold individually, the seller shall recognize profit on the sales by the percentage-of-completion method, provided all of the following conditions are met (ASC 360-20-40-50):

- Construction has progressed beyond the preliminary stage, which means that the engineering and design work, execution of construction contracts, site clearance and preparation, and excavation or completion of the building foundation have all been completed.
- The buyer cannot obtain a refund, except for nondelivery.
- The property will not revert to rental property, as evidenced by the number of units or interests that have been sold. In determining the sufficiency of the number of units or interests sold, reference shall be made to local and state laws, the provisions of the condominium or time-sharing contract, and the terms of the financing agreements.
- Total sales and costs can be estimated reasonably in accordance with the percentage-of-completion method of accounting.
- Sales prices are collectible.

Until all of the above conditions are met, the seller shall account for the sales proceeds from the single-family units or time-sharing interests by the deposit method of accounting (ASC 360-20-40-54).

Disclosures

ASC 360 does not contain any specific disclosure requirements for the sale of real estate, other than retail land sales. However, professional judgment may require that a significant sale of real estate be disclosed appropriately in the financial statements.

If interest is imputed on a receivable arising out of a real estate sale, certain disclosures are required by ASC 835 (Interest). In addition, if commitments or contingencies arise in a real estate sale, disclosure may be required by ASC 450 (Contingencies).

Retail Land Sales

The development of a large tract of land, usually over several years, is typical for a company in the retail land sales industry. Master plans are drawn for the improvement of the property, which may include amenities, and all necessary regulatory approvals are obtained. Large advertising campaigns are held at an early stage, frequently resulting in substantial sales before significant development of the property. In most retail land sales, a substantial portion of the sales price is financed by the seller in the form of a long-term receivable secured by the property. Interest and principal are paid by the buyer over an extended number of years. In the event of default, the buyer usually loses his or her entire equity and the property reverts back to the seller. Frequently, the retail land sales contract or existing state law provides for a period in which the purchaser may receive a refund of all or part of any payments made. In addition, the seller may be unable to obtain a deficiency judgment against the buyer because of operation of the law. Finally, many project-wide improvements and amenities are deferred until the later stages of development, when the seller may be faced with financial difficulties.

Because of small down payments, frequent cancellations and refunds, and the possibility that the retail land sales company may not be financially able to complete the project, certain specific conditions must be met before a sale can be recognized. ASC 976 (Real Estate - Retail Land) provides guidance regarding profit recognition for retail land sales.

PART II: INTERPRETIVE GUIDANCE

ASC 360-10: OVERALL

ASC 360-10-25-2 through 25-4, 30-3, 30-4, 30-13 through 30-14; ASC 840-30-35-21, 35-53 Accounting for an Interest in the Residual Value of a Leased Asset

BACKGROUND

This guidance responds to five questions related to accounting for the residual value of a leased asset.

PRACTICE NOTE: The guidance in Accounting Standards Update 2016-02, *Leases*, will not affect the guidance in this Issue.

ACCOUNTING GUIDANCE

Question 1: How should an entity account for (*a*) the acquisition from a lessor of an unconditional right to own and possess, at the end of a lease term, an asset subject to the lease; and (*b*) the acquisition of a right to receive all or a portion of the proceeds from the sale of a leased asset at the end of the lease?

Answer: At the date the rights are acquired, both transactions involve a right to receive, at the end of the lease term, all or a portion of the future benefit included in a leased asset. That right should be accounted for as the acquisition of an asset.

Question 2: How should an entity acquiring an interest in the residual value of a leased asset determine the cost at acquisition?

Answer: The cost is the amount of cash disbursed, the fair value of other consideration given (which could include noncash assets or services rendered), and the present value of liabilities assumed. The fair value of the interest in the residual value at the date of the agreement should be used to measure the cost of the interest if that fair value is more clearly evident than the fair value of the assets surrendered, services rendered, or liabilities assumed.

Question 3: How does an entity that acquires an interest in the residual value of a leased asset account for that asset during the lease term?

Answer: An entity that acquires an interest in the residual value of a leased asset should not recognize increases in the asset's estimated value over the remaining term of the lease. The asset should be reported at no more than its acquisition cost until sale or disposition. If the value of the asset declines below its carrying amount and that decline is considered other than temporary, the asset should be written down to fair value and the amount of the write-down should be recognized as a loss. Subsequent increases in fair value before sale or disposition should not be recorded.

Question 4: Do the provisions indicated in the answer to Question 3 apply to lease brokers?

Answer: Yes.

Question 5: If a lessor sells substantially all of the minimum rental payments associated with a sales-type, direct financing, or leveraged lease and retains an interest in the residual value of the leased asset, how should the lessor account for that asset over the remaining lease term?

Answer: The lessor should not recognize increases in the leased asset's residual value over the remaining lease term. However, if the fair value of the residual declines, that decline should be recognized as a loss if the decline is considered other than temporary. Subsequent recoveries in fair value should not be recorded.

ASC 360-10-25-5, 45-1; ASC 340-10-25-5; ASC 908-360-45-2 Accounting for Planned Major Maintenance Activities

BACKGROUND

ASC 908 provides guidance regarding the accounting for planned major maintenance activities in the airline industry that is also followed by entities in other industries. Under the guidance in ASC 908, the following four alternative methods of accounting for planned major maintenance activities are permitted: (1) direct expense; (2) built-in overhaul; (3) deferral; and (4) accrual in advance. The FASB believes that liabilities for planned major maintenance activities recognized under the accrual-in-advance method do *not* meet the definition of a liability in FASB Concepts Statement No. 6 (Elements of Financial Statements) (not in ASC), because an expense is recognized in a period before a transaction or event obligating the entity has occurred. Future costs to be incurred for maintenance to improve an asset's operating efficiency, comply with regulatory operating guidelines, or extend an asset's useful life do *not* represent an entity's current duty or responsibility before an obligating transaction or event has occurred. Therefore, the guidance in ASC 908 regarding the accounting for planned major maintenance activities is being amended by the guidance in this FSP, which applies to *all* industries.

ACCOUNTING GUIDANCE

Application of the accrual-in-advance method to account for planned major maintenance activities is prohibited in annual and interim financial reporting periods. Major maintenance activities should be accounted for based on the direct expense, built-in overhaul, or deferral method, which should be applied in the same manner in annual and interim financial reporting periods.

ASC 360-20: REAL ESTATE SALES

IMPORTANT NOTICE

The guidance in ASU 2014-09, *Revenue from Contracts with Customers* (ASC 606), will supersede the guidance in ASC 360-20 related to real estate sales, because revenue from real estate contracts with customers will be accounted for the same as other contracts with customers under the guidance in ASC 606, rather than based on specific-industry guidance, when the guidance in the ASU becomes effective for public business entities for annual reporting periods that begin after December 15, 2017, including interim reporting periods within those reporting periods, and a year later for nonpublic entities. The guidance in ASC 610-20, Other Income-Gains and Losses from the Derecognition of Nonfinancial Assets, and that in ASC 810-10, Consolidation-Overall, may apply to transactions that are not with customers. However, the existing guidance in ASC 360-20 related to sale-leaseback transactions of real estate under the scope of ASC 840-40 will remain until the guidance in ASU 2016-02, *Leases,* becomes effective for fiscal years that begin after December 15, 2018, including interim periods within those fiscal years, for public business entities; not-for-profit entities that have issued, or are conduit bond obligors for, securities that are traded, listed, or quoted on an exchange or an over-the-counter market; and employee benefit plans that file financial statements with the U.S. Securities and Exchange Commission (SEC). For all other entities, the amendments in the ASU are effective for fiscal years that begin after December 15, 2019, and interim periods within fiscal years that begin after December 15, 2020.

ASC 360-20-15-3 Accounting for Transfers of Investments That Are in Substance Real Estate

PRACTICE NOTE: The guidance in this Issue will apply only to assets that are part of sale-leaseback transactions under the scope of ASC 840-40 when the guidance in ASU 2014-09 becomes effective for public business entities in annual reporting periods that begin after December 15, 2017, and for all other entities in annual periods that begin after December 15, 2018. That guidance will remain in a section whose title will be: Property, Plant and Equipment—Real Estate Sales—Sale-Leaseback Accounting, until the guidance in ASU 2016-02, *Leases,* becomes effective for public business entities for fiscal years that begin after December 15, 2018.

BACKGROUND

The guidance in ASC 860 on accounting for transfers of financial assets differs substantially from the guidance in ASC 360 on the accounting for sales of real estate. This Issue was raised because some believe that sales or exchanges of financial assets, such as corporate stock of enterprises with substantial real estate assets, partnership interests, and time-sharing interests, that are in substance real estate should be accounted for under the guidance in ASC 360, not under the guidance in ASC 860 (FAS-140).

Under the guidance in ASC 860, a transfer of financial assets is accounted for as a sale if it meets the criteria in ASC 860-10-40-4, 40-5. The requirements for profit recognition on sales of real estate assets are discussed in ASC 360-20-40-5. Although both pronouncements require a transferor to relinquish control over the asset by prohibiting a transferor from maintaining a continuing involvement with the asset, the requirements for sales recognition and for subsequent accounting for transactions that do not meet their respective criteria are different.

ACCOUNTING ISSUE

Should sales or transfers of financial assets that are in substance real estate be accounted for under the provisions of ASC 360 or the provisions of ASC 860?

ACCOUNTING GUIDANCE

Sales or transfers of investments in the form of financial assets that are in substance real estate should be accounted for under the provisions of ASC 360.

It was noted that the guidance would apply to transfers of acquisition, development, and construction loans (ADC loans), which are considered to be investments that are in substance real estate according to ASC 810-10-25-59. However, this guidance would not apply to marketable investments in real estate investment trusts (REITs) accounted for under the provisions of ASC 320, because they are not considered to be investments that are in substance real estate. Sales or exchanges of such investments should be accounted for under the guidance in ASC 860.

PRACTICE POINTER: The guidance in ASC 860-10-15-4 provides that transfers of ownership interests that are in substance real estate are not under its scope. Such transactions should be accounted for under the guidance in ASC 360. That provision affirms the above guidance.

ASC 360-20-15-3(f), 55-68 through 55-77; ASC 810-10-40-3B Derecognition of In-Substance Real Estate—a Scope Clarification

PRACTICE NOTE: The guidance in this Issue will be superseded when the guidance in ASU 2014-09 becomes effective.

BACKGROUND

During 2010, the FASB issued ASU 2010-2, *Consolidation (Topic 810): Accounting and Reporting for Decreases in Ownership of a Subsidiary—a Scope Clarification*. That guidance, which has been incorporated in the Codification in ASC 810-10-40-3A, 40-4 through 40-5, 45-21A, 50-1B, 65-3; ASC 845-10-15-20, 30-22, 30-25 through 25A; ASC 323-10-30-2, 35-7; and ASC 805-10-50-2, requires an entity that gives up control of a subsidiary to deconsolidate the subsidiary and to recognize a profit or a loss under the transaction. However, if an entity reduces its ownership interest in a subsidiary but there is no change in control, the transaction is accounted for as a change in the entity's equity in the subsidiary. In addition, that guidance applies only if such transactions are consummated by a business entity or a nonprofit activity.

That guidance does *not* apply to sales of in substance real estate, which should be accounted for under the guidance in ASC 360, *Property, Plant, and Equipment* (ASC 360-20). A subsidiary that is in substance real estate is an entity that has been established by an investor (parent) for the sole purpose of purchasing real estate that is capitalized with nonrecourse debt. There has been diversity in practice because some practitioners have questioned whether the criteria in ASC 360-20 related to continuing involvement must be met for a parent to deconsolidate a subsidiary that is in substance real estate. Others have expressed concern that the guidance in ASC 810, *Consolidation* (ASC 810-10), would apply if the derecognition is not due to a sale of the real estate, but rather occurs because the subsidiary has defaulted on its nonrecourse debt.

ACCOUNTING ISSUE

Does the accounting guidance in ASC 360-20 apply to a parent (reporting entity) that no longer has a controlling financial interest in substance real estate subsidiary?

SCOPE

The following guidance applies only to situations in which has lost its controlling financial interest (as discussed in ASC 810-10) in a wholly owned in substance real estate subsidiary as a result of the subsidiary's default on its nonrecourse debt.

ACCOUNTING GUIDANCE

A parent should apply the guidance in ASC 360 to determine whether an in substance real estate subsidiary should be derecognized. That is, if a parent of an in-substance real estate subsidiary no longer has a controlling financial interest in the subsidiary, as discussed in ASC 810-10, because the subsidiary has defaulted on its nonrecourse debt, the reporting entity should apply the guidance in ASC 360-20-40-5 to determine whether it should derecognize real estate owned by its in-substance real estate subsidiary. In addition:

- The requirements for derecognition in ASC 360-20-40-5 apply regardless of whether a reporting entity owns the real estate directly or indirectly through its in-substance real estate subsidiary;
- A two-step impairment approach required under the guidance in ASC 360-20 does not permit the consideration of nonrecourse debt when a real estate asset is evaluated for impairment; and
- It would be inappropriate for a parent to derecognize the substance subsidiary's nonrecourse debt until it has been legally released from that obligation by the lender.

ASC 360-20-15-4 through 15-8; 55-58 through 55-59 Determining Whether Equipment Is "Integral Equipment" Subject to ASC 360

BACKGROUND

The guidance in ASC 360-20-15-2 through 15-3, 15-10, 55-4 through 55-5, which concludes that sales of "integral equipment" should be accounted for under the guidance in ASC 360, defines that term as ". . . any physical structure or equipment attached to the real estate that cannot be removed and used separately without incurring significant cost." An office building, a manufacturing facility, a power plant, and a refinery are cited as examples. Some are concerned that in applying the provisions of ASC 840 and ASC 360 there will be diversity in determining which assets are considered "integral equipment," because the accounting literature on real estate sales and leasing transactions does not provide guidance on how to interpret the phrase ". . . cannot be removed and used separately without incurring significant cost."

ACCOUNTING ISSUE

How should entities determine whether equipment is "integral equipment"?

ACCOUNTING GUIDANCE

- The phrase "cannot be removed and used separately without incurring significant cost" raises the following two questions: (*a*) whether the equipment can be removed without incurring significant cost and (*b*) whether the equipment can be moved to another location to be used by another entity without significantly diminishing its fair value or usefulness.
- To determine whether an asset should be considered to be integral equipment, it is necessary to know (*a*) the significance of the cost of removing the equipment from its existing location, including the cost of repairing damage caused by its removal, and (*b*) the diminution in the equipment's fair value due to its removal. The cost of shipping and reinstalling equipment at a new location should be considered the minimum amount of diminution in the fair value of equipment due to its removal. To determine whether there is additional diminution in fair value, it is necessary to consider the nature of the equipment and its likely use by other potential users.
- Equipment should be considered to be "integral equipment" if the combined cost of removal and the equipment's decrease in value exceeds 10% of the fair value of the installed equipment. For leasing transactions, estimates of the costs of removal, the decrease in the equipment's value, as well as its fair value should be based on information as of the inception of the lease.

ASC 360-20-40-11 through 40-12 and 55-3 Profit Recognition on Sales of Real Estate with Insured Mortgages or Surety Bonds

BACKGROUND

Sellers financing residential or other properties may require mortgage insurance on a portion of the loan. They often accept surety bonds instead of letters of credit to support the buyer's notes. Under the guidance in ASC 360-20-40-10, one of the conditions for a buyer's initial investment under the full accrual method is that the buyer's notes be accompanied by a letter of credit from an independent lending institution.

ACCOUNTING ISSUES

1. Can a financial instrument, such as a surety bond, that meets the following conditions be considered equivalent to an irrevocable letter of credit in determining whether a buyer's notes should be included in the buyer's initial investment, so profit can be recognized on the full accrual method, if:
   a. The seller has the same rights of collection as under an irrevocable letter of credit;
   b. The surety has the same obligation to the seller as under an irrevocable letter of credit; or
   c. The surety has the same recourse to the buyer in the case of default as under an irrevocable letter of credit?
2. Can government or private insurance covering part of the balance of a mortgage be considered equivalent to an irrevocable letter of credit and included in a buyer's initial and continuing investment, in determining whether to recognize profit on a sale using the full accrual method?
3. Do the minimum down payment percentages stated in ASC 360-20-55-1, 55-2 apply, or should the loan limits in governmental programs be used if a buyer of a single-family residential property qualifies for a loan from the Federal Housing Administration (FHA) or Veterans Administration (VA), which insure or guarantee a part or the full amount of the mortgage, but require no down payments or down payments of less than 5%?

ACCOUNTING GUIDANCE

- A seller may consider an irrevocable financial instrument, such as a surety bond from an independent insurer that meets the conditions stated in Issue 1 above, to be equivalent to an irrevocable letter of credit that can be used to support a buyer's notes, which are included in the buyer's initial investment in determining whether profit can be recognized under the full accrual method. The buyer's commitment to pay is an important criterion in ASC 360 that must be met for full profit recognition.

- Mortgage insurance is not considered equivalent to an irrevocable letter of credit in determining whether the full accrual method is appropriate, because purchasing mortgage insurance does not demonstrate the buyer's commitment to meet the obligation to pay for the property.
- Under the guidance in ASC 360-20-55-3, the normal down payment requirements or loan limits under FHA or VA government-insured programs may be used by a seller for sales of owner-occupied single-family residential homes financed and insured under those programs as surrogates for the minimum initial investment guidance in ASC 360-20-55-1 through 55-2 in determining whether the seller may recognize profit on the full accrual method. Because government insurance transfers the risk on the mortgage receivable to the governmental agency, all loans insured by the VA or FHA qualify for full accrual profit recognition. However, that guidance does not apply to private mortgage insurance for which the minimum initial investment criteria in ASC 360-20, *Property, Plant, and Equipment-Real Estate Sales*, continue to apply.

DISCUSSION

1. A surety bond differs from mortgage insurance, because the bond exposes the buyer to the same risk of loss as under an irrevocable letter of credit. If a buyer defaults on the notes, the surety has recourse to the buyer's general assets for the amount of the bond. Those who believed that a surety bond is equivalent to an irrevocable letter of credit and should therefore qualify under the requirements of the guidance in ASC 360 argued that it (*a*) demonstrates the buyer's commitment to pay for the property and (*b*) increases the likelihood that the seller will collect the receivable supported by the bond.
2. Mortgage insurance should not be considered equivalent to an irrevocable letter of credit, because it does not demonstrate the buyer's commitment to pay for the property—a requirement of ASC 360 even though it increases the likelihood that the sales price will be collected.

ASC 360-20-40-14 through 40-17, 40-32; 55-55 through 55-56 Effect of Various Forms of Financing under ASC 360

BACKGROUND

Real estate sales are financed in various ways. The financing may be provided by independent third parties, by the seller, or both. Also, the financing may be nonrecourse to the buyer; that is, the lender's only recourse in the event the buyer defaults is to foreclose on the property. The financing also may involve the buyer's assumption of the seller's preexisting recourse or nonrecourse mortgage obligations.

The guidance in ASC 360 establishes accounting standards for recognizing profit or loss on sales of real estate. It is unclear, however, as to how various forms of financing affect a seller's profit recognition.

The guidance in ASC 360-20-40-3 states that a seller recognizes profit on the full accrual method if *both* of the following conditions are met:

1. The profit can be determined; there is reasonable assurance that the sales price is collectible; and it is possible to estimate the amount that will not be collectible.
2. The earnings process is essentially complete; the seller has no obligation to perform significant activities after the sale.

In applying condition 1, collectibility is demonstrated by a buyer's initial and continuing investments, which must be adequate to demonstrate a commitment to pay for the real estate. A sufficient investment puts the buyer at risk of loss through default and motivates the buyer to pay on the debt. Unless both conditions are met, the seller must defer all or a part of the profit. Deferred profit would be recognized in the future on the installment, cost-recovery, or the reduced-profit method.

ACCOUNTING ISSUE

How should profit be recognized on sales of real estate that involve various forms of financing?

ACCOUNTING GUIDANCE

- The initial and continuing investment requirements of ASC 360 apply. However, a seller can recognize profit on the full accrual method if consideration received by the seller for the *full* sales value of the property consists of the following:
  — Cash, as long as the seller has no contingent liability on debt the buyer might incur or assume,
  — The seller's existing nonrecourse debt on the property is assumed by the buyer,
  — Recourse debt on the property is assumed by the buyer with the seller's *complete release* from those obligations, or
  — Any combination of the above.
- In determining the adequacy of a buyer's initial investment for purposes of recognizing profit by the full accrual method, *neither* of the following forms of financing should be included as part of a buyer's initial investment:
  — Debt secured by the property, whether borrowed directly from the seller or others or indirectly by the buyer's assumption of the seller's existing debt, and
  — Payments to the seller from the proceeds of debt secured by the property.

  The buyer's commitment to pay for the property is demonstrated only by the payment of a sufficient amount of cash or other qualifying form of investment, not by a borrowing secured by the property. Items included or excluded from the initial investment are discussed in ASC 360-20-40-10 and 40-13.
- Neither of the following should be considered a buyer's cash payments in the seller's computation of the amount of profit that can be recognized initially under the installment, cost recovery, or reduced-profit method:
  — A buyer's debt secured by the property, either incurred directly from the seller or others or indirectly by assuming the seller's existing debt, and
  — Cash paid to the seller from the proceeds of a buyer's debt secured by the property.

  A seller may, however, recognize as income deferred profit in excess of the total amount of (*a*) the seller's financing and (*b*) the buyer's outstanding debt secured by the property for which the seller is contingently liable.

Illustration of Profit Recognition When Buyer's Initial Investment Is Inadequate

Assumptions		
Sales price		$250,000
Seller's basis in property sold		$187,500
Seller's profit		$62,500
Initial investment requirement		20%
Continuing investment test is met.		
a.	Buyer's initial cash investment	0
	Seller's recourse mortgage assumed*	$250,000
	No profit recognized	
b.	Buyer's initial cash investment	0
	Seller financing	$250,000
	No profit recognized	
c.	Buyer's initial cash investment	0
	Seller financing	$50,000
	Seller's recourse mortgage assumed*	$200,000
	No profit recognized	
d.	Buyer's initial cash investment	0
	First mortgage from independent lender	$200,000
	Seller financing	$50,000
	Profit recognized on cost recovery or installment method on excess over seller financing	*$12,500*
e.	Buyer's initial cash investment	$25,000
	Seller financing	$225,000
	Profit recognized on the installment method ($25,000 × .25)	*$ 6,250*

f.	Buyer's initial cash investment	$25,000
	Seller's recourse mortgage assumed*	$225,000
	Profit recognized on the installment method ($25,000 ×.25)	*$6,250*
g.	Buyer's initial cash investment	$25,000
	First mortgage from independent lender	$200,000
	Seller financing	$25,000
	Profit recognized on cost recovery or installment method on excess of seller financing ($62,500 – $25,000)	*$37,500*
h.	Buyer's initial cash investment	$25,000
	Seller's nonrecourse mortgage assumed	$200,000
	Seller financing	$25,000
	Profit recognized on cost recovery or installment method on excess of seller financing	*$37,500*
i.	Buyer's initial cash investment	$25,000
	Seller's recourse mortgage assumed*	$200,000
	Seller financing	$25,000
	Profit recognized on the installment method ($25,000 × .25)	*$6,250*

* The seller remains contingently liable on the mortgage.

ASC 360-20-40-35 Profit Recognition on Sales of Real Estate with Graduated Payment Mortgages or Insured Mortgages

BACKGROUND

A sale of real estate is financed by a graduated payment mortgage. Such mortgages may have negative amortization of principal in the early years and may be partially or fully insured.

ACCOUNTING ISSUES

- Do graduated payment mortgages meet the requirements for the buyer's initial and continuing investment under the full accrual method?
- Can government or private mortgage insurance be considered part of the buyer's initial and continuing investment?

ACCOUNTING GUIDANCE

- A graduated payment mortgage with negative amortization of principal does not meet the continuing investment test in ASC 360. Therefore, profit should not be recognized based on the full accrual method.
- See the guidance in ASC 360-20-40-11 through 40-12 and 55-3, Profit Recognition on Sales of Real Estate with Insured Mortgages or Surety Bonds, above.

DISCUSSION

The guidance in ASC 360 is based on AICPA accounting guides that were issued in the 1970s to curb profit recognition abuses in the real estate industry. The purpose of the buyer's initial and continuing investment requirements is to demonstrate that the buyer has an economic commitment to the property. Under the guidance in ASC 360-20-40-10, 40-19 through 40-20, which provide guidance on those requirements, a buyer must be contractually obligated to make sufficient annual payments to *reduce* the indebtedness on the property. In contrast, a negative amortization mortgage *increases* the buyer's indebtedness, because the balance of the loan increases.

ASC 360-20-40-39 Antispeculation Clauses in Real Estate Sales Contracts

BACKGROUND

An antispeculation clause is included in some land sales contracts to assure that a buyer develops the land according to a master plan. Under such contracts, the buyer is required to develop the land within a specified period of time and may be prohibited from developing it for certain uses. If the buyer does not comply with the contract, the seller has the right, but not the obligation, to repurchase the property, which represents a potential penalty to the buyer for not complying with the sales contract. The buyer does not, however, have the right to put the property back to the seller.

According to the guidance in ASC 360-20-40-38, a seller should not recognize profit on a sale on the full accrual method, if a sales contract includes a repurchase option. Such a transaction should be accounted for as a financing, leasing, or profit-sharing arrangement instead of as a sale.

ACCOUNTING ISSUE

Is a seller precluded from recognizing a sale if a real estate sales contract includes an antispeculation clause?

ACCOUNTING GUIDANCE

A seller is not precluded from recognizing a sale if there is only a *remote probability* that the buyer will not comply with a sales contract's antispeculation clause.

However, a probability test is not appropriate if a seller has an option to repurchase the property that is not contingent on the buyer's compliance with a specific requirement.

DISCUSSION

The following factors that would indicate that there is only a remote probability that the buyer will not comply with the contract's antispeculation clause were discussed:

- The buyer has the ability and intent to follow the provisions of the sales contract. If the buyer is a substantive party and the seller does not expect to have a right to repurchase the property, no option exists on sale.
- The risks and rewards of ownership have been transferred to the buyer. The buyer will benefit from the appreciation of the property if it is developed according to the contract, while the seller has no obligation and would have no incentive to repurchase the property if its value depreciates. The seller does not share in the appreciation or depreciation of the property.
- There are business reasons for the option. The seller includes the antispeculation clause in the contract only to enforce the buyer's promise to develop the property as agreed in the contract. The clause is more like a restriction in a deed than a repurchase option. In practice, deed restrictions in retail land sales that limit the type of home that can be built on a property do not preclude full accrual profit recognition.

ASC 360-20-40-50 through 40-55 Applicability of the Assessment of a Buyer's Continuing Investment under ASC 360 for Sales of Condominiums

BACKGROUND

Developers of condominium units usually sell individual units during a project's construction phase. Under the guidance in ASC 360-20-40-5 on accounting for real estate sales, one of the requirements for the seller to recognize profit under the full accrual method is that the buyer must demonstrate a commitment to pay by having an adequate continuing investment in the property. However, that requirement may not be met during a condominium's construction phase, because of the length of time it takes to complete such a project. In addition, because the risks and rewards of ownership have *not* been transferred to the buyer during the construction phase, the developer's continuing involvement is discussed further in ASC 360-20-40-50.

Under the guidance in ASC 360-20-40-50, a developer may recognize profit on individual condominium units using the percentage-of-completion method during a project's construction phase, if certain criteria are met. One of those criteria is the collectibility of the sales price. ASC 360-20-40-4 states that a buyer that makes a substantial initial and continuing investment in a property demonstrates a commitment to pay the remainder of the sales price, because the buyer will not want to lose that investment through a default. Additional factors to consider in an evaluation of collectibility are the buyer's credit standing, the property's age and location, and the adequacy of cash flow from the property. Some have questioned whether a developer needs to apply the continuing investment test discussed in ASC 360-2-40-19 through 40-20 in order to conclude that the sales price is collectible and profit may be recognized on the percentage-of-completion method.

ACCOUNTING ISSUES

1. Does an entity that recognizes profit on the percentage-of-completion method need to evaluate the adequacy of a buyer's continuing investment under the guidance in ASC 360-20-40-19, 40-20?
2. When the criteria in ASC 360-20-40-50 are applied to reassess whether profit may be recognized on the percentage-of-completion method, should the initial and continuing investment tests be applied on a cumulative basis (*a*) from the date the seller and the buyer entered into a contract or (*b*) prospectively from the date on which a reassessment is made to determine whether profit may be recognized on the percentage-of-completion method on a transaction that previously did *not* meet the criteria in ASC 360-20-40-50 for profit recognition on that method?

ACCOUNTING GUIDANCE

1. When evaluating the collectibility of the sales price of an individual condominium unit under the guidance in paragraph ASC 360-20-40-50, a seller's conclusion should be based on whether the buyer's initial and continuing investment is adequate. It was noted that just as for other types of real estate sales, a buyer's initial and continuing investment should be made in the form required in ASC 360-20-40-10 and that only the nonrefundable portion of such investments should be counted toward the buyer's initial and continuing investment. The continuing investment criterion in ASC 360-20-40-19 through 40-20 has been met if a buyer is required to either (1) pay additional amounts during the construction term that are at least equal to the level annual payments required to fund principal and interest on an amortizing customary mortgage for the property's remaining purchase price, which is the difference between the purchase price and the buyer's initial investment; or (2) increase the minimum initial investment by an equivalent total amount. The remaining purchase price is calculated based on the property's sales price. This test should be performed by using a hypothetical loan between a seller and a buyer for the amount of the purchase price *less* the buyer's initial investment. Using the remaining purchase price is consistent with the guidance in ASC 360-20-40-19 through 40-20, because it refers to a buyer's "debt for the purchase price of the property."
2. The deposit method discussed in ASC 360-20-55-17, 55-19 through 55-20 should be used until a buyer's payments meet the criteria in ASC 360-20-40-50, including an assessment of collectibility using the initial and continuing investment tests discussed in ASC 360-20-40-9, 40-10, 40-13, 40-18 40-20. When an entity reevaluates whether profit should be recognized under the percentage-of-completion method, all of the criteria in ASC 360-20-40-50 should be reevaluated.
3. The initial and continuing investment tests should be applied *prospectively* from the date on which the collectibility of the sales price is reevaluated, as if the deposit was received on that date.

ASC 360-20-55-66 through 55-67 Transfer of Ownership Interest as Part of Down Payment under ASC 360

BACKGROUND

An income-producing property is owned in a partnership by two parties. One of the parties, which holds a 75% interest in the property, sells its interest to the party holding a 25% interest in the property. The seller receives a 10% down payment and a note for the balance secured by 100% of the property, which has no outstanding debt. ASC 360-20-55-66 specifies a minimum initial investment of 15% of the sales value of the property as an initial investment for this type of transaction.

ACCOUNTING ISSUES

- Does the buyer's pledge of 100% of the purchased property as security for a note meet the requirements for the buyer's initial investment in determining whether profit may be recognized on the full accrual method?
- If yes, can a note collateralized by assets other than the purchased property, such as other real estate or marketable securities, be included as part of the buyer's initial investment in determining whether profit can be recognized on the full accrual method?

ACCOUNTING GUIDANCE

Under the provisions of ASC 360 full accrual profit recognition is not permitted for this transaction, because the buyer's initial investment should not include the purchased property or other assets pledged as security for a note.

DISCUSSION

Under the criteria stated in ASC 360-20-40-10, only a buyer's cash down payment in this transaction qualifies to be included in the buyer's initial investment. A note would have to be supported by an irrevocable letter of credit from an independent lending institution. Under the guidance in ASC 360-20-40-11 through 40-12 and 55-3, which is discussed above, a surety bond meeting certain conditions could be substituted for an irrevocable letter of credit, but mortgage insurance is not acceptable because it does not demonstrate a buyer's commitment to pay for the property. Under a strict interpretation of ASC 360-20-40-10, a note collateralized by the property or other assets would not qualify.

In addition, this transaction would not qualify for full accrual profit recognition, because the 10% down payment does not meet the minimum down payment required in ASC 360-20-55-2 for an income-producing property, which is 15% of the sales value.

ASC 360-20-60-1; 55-2 through 55-6, 55-8, 55-13 through 55-18 The Treatment of Certain Site Restoration/Environmental Exit Costs When Testing a Long-Lived Asset for Impairment

BACKGROUND

This Issue addresses the accounting for environmental exit costs that have not been recognized for accounting purposes and that are incurred when operations cease (even if the asset is retained) or if the asset is sold or abandoned. Such costs can include an environmental audit or assessment; a feasibility study or other assessment; actual remediation and/or site restoration; monitoring activities; legal costs; costs to change permits or licenses; costs related to equipment shutdown; and fines and penalties. An entity may incur environmental exit costs if certain assets are sold, abandoned, or cease operations. Funds for such costs may not be expended for some time if the costs are not incurred until the end of the asset's life or if the costs are deferred indefinitely, because the asset has not been sold or abandoned.

Under the provisions of ASC 360, future cash flows from using or eventually disposing of an asset must be estimated when the recovery of the asset's carrying amount is reviewed because events or changes in circumstances suggest that it may be impaired. An impairment loss is recognized based on the asset's fair value if its carrying amount exceeds the sum of the asset's expected undiscounted future cash flows, excluding interest charges.

The environmental exit costs considered generally are not accrued over the life of an asset, and it is unclear whether those costs should be included in undiscounted future cash flows used in the impairment calculation. Because such costs might not be incurred for many years, the amount would be small on a discounted basis but might be very large on an undiscounted basis. Consequently, including such costs in the undiscounted cash flow test would result in more frequent measurement of asset impairment and asset revaluation to fair value.

ACCOUNTING ISSUE

Should undiscounted expected future cash flows used to test the recoverability of the carrying amount of a long-lived asset under the guidance in ASC 360 include exit costs related to environmental matters that may be incurred if a long-lived asset is sold, abandoned, or ceases operations?

ACCOUNTING GUIDANCE

PRACTICE POINTER: ASC 410 provides guidance for the initial recognition and measurement of asset retirement obligations and subsequent accounting for such obligations. It applies to all *legal* obligations related to the retirement of tangible long-lived assets and requires that the fair value, if estimable, of such obligations be recognized in the period in which the liability is incurred. If the fair value is not estimable at that time, recognition is required when a reasonable estimate of fair value can be made. Previous guidance in this Issue related to liabilities that have not been recognized has been partially nullified by the guidance in ASC 410.

Previous guidance reached in this Issue based on the guidance in (*a*) ASC 360 and (*b*) ASC 410, has been modified as follows:

- The guidance in ASC 410 nullifies the original guidance that future cash flows for environmental exit costs that have been *recognized* as a liability be excluded from undiscounted expected future cash flows used to test an asset's recoverability under the guidance in ASC 360 even though under the guidance in ASC 410 future cash flows for a liability that has been recognized for an asset's retirement obligation should be excluded from undiscounted cash flows used to test the asset for recoverability.
- The guidance in ASC 360 affects the guidance regarding management's intent for an asset by requiring that the likelihood of possible outcomes be considered if (*a*) a range of possible future cash flows is estimated or (*b*) management intends to recover an asset's carrying amount by alternative means instead of by selling or abandoning the asset, or ceasing its operations.

The FASB staff developed examples of situations in which environmental exit costs either would be included in or excluded from undiscounted cash flows, based on management's intent for the asset. Environmental exit costs would be *included* in the ASC 360 recoverability test in the following situations:

- The asset's useful life is expected to be limited because of actual or expected technological advances, contractual provisions, or regulatory restrictions, and management intends to sell, abandon, or close the asset at the end of its useful life and will incur environmental exit costs in doing so.

- Although management expects the asset to become profitable in the future, the asset has a negative cash flow from operations in the current period, and a forecast or projection anticipates continuing losses. Management is uncertain whether it can continue funding future cash outflows until the asset begins generating net cash inflows. Under a forced liquidation, management would have to sell, abandon, or close the asset and would incur environmental exit costs.
- Management's intent to sell or abandon the asset in the future will result in remediation costs to conform with applicable laws or regulations.

Environmental exit costs would be *excluded* from undiscounted expected future cash flows in the following situations:

- The asset has an indefinite useful life; management intends to operate the asset indefinitely and has the ability to do so; and based on all available information the asset will continue to be profitable. Expected future cash flows for repair, maintenance, and capital expenditures required to obtain future cash flows would be included in the recoverability test under the guidance in ASC 360, however.
- Management intends to operate the asset at least during its remaining depreciable life. Total undiscounted future cash flows expected from operating the asset during that period exceed its carrying amount, including related goodwill, and there is no reason for management to believe that disposal of the asset would result in a net cash outflow.
- Environmental exit costs related to an asset that has a finite life would be incurred only if it is sold or abandoned. To avoid the cost of remediating the asset, management intends to close the asset permanently at the end of its useful life or to idle it by reducing production to a minimal level. The recoverability test should consider the entity's assumptions for the use of the asset. Expected future cash flows required to (*a*) maintain or protect the asset after it has been closed or (*b*) to fund losses incurred after the asset has been idled should nevertheless be included in the recoverability test under the guidance in ASC 360.
- Management expects to sell the asset in the future without incurring environmental exit costs. The effect of environmental exit costs on the asset's fair value should be considered in estimating net proceeds from a future sale to be used in the recoverability test under the guidance in ASC 360.

DISCUSSION

The accounting guidance is based on the premise that the environmental exit costs discussed in this Issue generally are not accrued over the life of the asset, either because they are considered avoidable or because in some jurisdictions, they are considered deferrable indefinitely as long as the asset is in operation or is not sold or abandoned, even if its operations cease. It was agreed that the trigger should be based on management's plans for the asset. However, management's intention to operate an asset indefinitely or to idle it, but not sell or abandon it, would have to be supported by cash flow estimates demonstrating an entity's ability to do so.

The FASB staff's scenarios—under which exit costs would be included or excluded from the calculation under the provisions of ASC 360 are intended to provide facts and circumstances for the application of the consensus, but they also provide some specific guidance. For example, the second and fourth situations—under which environmental exit costs would *not* be included in undiscounted cash flows—nevertheless specify certain costs that *would be included* in the recoverability test under the guidance in ASC 360.

CHAPTER 28

ASC 405—LIABILITIES

CONTENTS

PART I: GENERAL GUIDANCE

ASC 405-10: OVERALL

ASC 405-10 does not provide any accounting guidance but rather only provides a link to guidance on liabilities in other ASC subtopics (ASC 405-10-05-1).

ASC 405-20: EXTINGUISHMENTS OF LIABILITIES

BACKGROUND

Liabilities may be settled by either transferring assets to the creditor or by otherwise obtaining an unconditional release from the creditor. Alternatively, an entity may choose to set aside certain assets dedicated to the eventual settlement of a liability. However, this alternative approach of setting aside assets dedicated for eventual settlement has raised issues about when a liability should be considered extinguished. This subtopic provides guidance for resolving those issues. The guidance in this subtopic applies to the extinguishment of all liabilities, including both financial and nonfinancial liabilities.

DERECOGNITION

Unless addressed by other guidance (e.g., ASC 405-20-40-3, 4), a liability must be derecognized (i.e., removed from the balance sheet) only if it has been extinguished. A liability has been extinguished if either of the following conditions is met (ASC 405-20-40-1):

1. The debtor pays the creditor and is relieved of its obligation for the liability.

2. The debtor is legally released from being the primary obligor under the liability, either by the courts or by the creditor.

If a debtor is released by the creditor from being the primary obligor for a liability under the condition that a third party assumes the role of primary obligor and the original debtor becomes secondarily liable, that release is considered to have extinguished the original debtor's liability. However, the original debtor becomes a guarantor, and must recognize a guarantor obligation. The guarantor obligation is initially measured at fair value and that amount reduces the gain or increases the loss that the debtor recognizes on the extinguishment of the original liability (ASC 405-20-40-2).

PART II: INTERPRETIVE GUIDANCE

ASC 405-20: LIABILITIES-EXTINGUISHMENT OF LIABILITIES

ASC 405-20-15-2, 40-1, 40-3 through 40-4, 50-2, 65-1 Recognition of Breakage for Certain Prepaid Stored-Value Products

BACKGROUND

There are different kinds of prepaid stored-value products, which are essentially prepaid credit cards that have a monetary value that may be redeemed for goods and services, cash, or both. One kind of prepaid stored-value product is issued by leading consumer brands (branded cards), such as national retailers, restaurants, and various telecom service providers that can only be redeemed at the issuing merchants' business establishments. Another kind of prepaid stored-value product, which may be redeemed at third-party merchants (content providers) that accept those products, is issued by credit card companies (leading payment network card associations, e.g., Visa, MasterCard, American Express, or Discover). Consumers may purchase branded prepaid stored-value products directly from an entity or at distribution outlets (e.g., grocery stores or other retail outlets). Prepaid stored-value products issued by credit card companies also are sold at those venues.

An entity that issues its own branded prepaid stored-value products recognizes a liability for the amount of each prepaid stored-value product that is sold. That liability is extinguished as a customer redeems a portion or the total amount of a prepaid stored-value product for goods, services, cash or both. If a customer redeems only a portion of a prepaid stored-value product's value, a portion of the liability is extinguished, but the unused portion of the stored-value product's value remains as a liability. An entity that issues prepaid stored-value products that are redeemable at third-party merchants recognizes a liability for the obligation to provide a product holder with the ability to purchase goods or services at third-party merchants. That liability is extinguished fully, or partially, when the prepaid stored-value product's holder purchases goods or services from a third-party merchant. When that occurs, the issuing entity incurs a liability to the merchant that is commonly settled in cash through a settlement process. However, some prepaid stored-value products may be used only partially and some may remain unused indefinitely.

U.S. generally accepted accounting principles (U.S. GAAP) do not provide specific guidance for the derecognition of liabilities related to amounts on prepaid stored-value products that are not redeemed for an extended period of time after issuance. Some entities believe that the liability on prepaid stored-value products that have been sold but not yet redeemed is a financial liability, while others believe that it is a nonfinancial liability. ASC 405-20 includes derecognition guidance for financial and nonfinancial liabilities, but there is diversity in the method used to derecognize the nonrefundable value of prepaid credit cards that are never redeemed (breakage). But under its guidance, derecognition of a liability is prohibited before the value of a prepaid stored-value product is redeemed, has expired, or becomes subject to unclaimed property laws. The guidance in ASC 606, *Revenue from Contracts with Customers*, which is effective for business entities in fiscal years that begin after December 15, 2017, includes authoritative guidance for breakage, but only for nonfinancial liabilities. The objective of this guidance is to resolve the diversity in practice related to the derecognition of prepaid stored-value products.

ACCOUNTING ISSUE

How should an issuer account for amounts remaining on prepaid stored-value products that are not redeemed for an extended period of time after issuance?

SCOPE AND SCOPE EXCEPTIONS

The guidance applies to entities that issue prepaid stored-value products (e.g., prepaid gift cards issued on a specific payment network, such as Visa, MasterCard, Discover, and redeemable at merchants those cards, telecommunication cards, and traveler's checks). ASC 405-20-15-2 has been amended to exclude from the scope of ASC 405-20 the derecognition of nonfinancial liabilities for which guidance is provided elsewhere in U.S. GAAP, such as the derecognition guidance for gaming chips discussed in ASC 924, *Entertainment—Casinos* (924-405), or the breakage guidance in ASC 606, *Revenue from Contracts with Customers.*

ACCOUNTING GUIDANCE

The derecognition guidance in ASC 405-20-40-1 has been amended to provide that the situations addressed in ASC 405-20-40-3 through 40-4 or ASC 606-10-55-46 through 55-49 are an exception to the guidance in that paragraph, which provides guidance for the derecognition of a liability that has been extinguished.

A separate subsection has been added to ASC 405-20 for a discussion of the accounting for prepaid stored-value products in ASC 405-20-40-3 through 40-4. As discussed in ASC 405-20-40-3, prepaid stored-value products may be purchased by consumers in digital or physical form for use as payment for goods or services. Although holders of such prepaid stored-value products may be permitted to redeem those products for cash, none can be redeemed only for cash (e.g., nonrecourse debt, bearer bonds, or trade payables). ASC 405-20-40-3 provides that the derecognition guidance in ASC 405-20-40-4 does not apply to liabilities for prepaid stored-value products under the following circumstances:

- If the portion of the dollar value of prepaid stored-value products (or portions thereof) that ultimately is not redeemed for cash or used to purchase products or services (breakage) must be remitted in accordance with unclaimed property laws
- If prepaid stored-value products are attached to segregated bank accounts like customer depository accounts

ASC 405-20-40-3 also provides that customer loyalty programs or transactions under the scope of other topics, such as Topic 606, *Revenue from Contracts with Customers,* are excluded from the guidance in ASC 405-20-40-4.

ASC 405-20-40-4 provides the following guidance for the recognition of breakage as a result of the sale of a prepaid stored-value product under the scope of ASC 405-20-40-3:

- An entity that expects to be entitled to an amount of breakage should derecognize the expected breakage amount in proportion to the pattern of rights that a holder is expected to exercise only to the magnitude that it is probable that a significant amount of the breakage recognized will not be subsequently reversed.
- An entity that does not expect to be entitled to an amount of breakage should derecognize an amount related to breakage when the likelihood becomes remote that a product holder will exercise its remaining rights.

An entity that issues prepaid stored-value products is required to update the estimated breakage amount at the end of each period to faithfully represent the circumstances at the end of that period and the changes during the period. An entity is required to account for changes in its estimated amount of breakage as a change in accounting estimate under the guidance in ASC 250-10-45-17 through 45-20.

The disclosure guidance in ASC 402-20 has been amended to include a separate subsection for prepaid stored-valued cards. ASC 405-20-50-2 has been added to require that an entity that recognizes breakage in accordance with the guidance in ASC 405-20-40-4 should disclose the method used to recognize breakage and the significant judgments made in its application.

TRANSITION AND EFFECTIVE DATE

ASC 405-20-65-1 requires the following:

1. A public business entity, a not-for-profit entity that has issued, or is a conduit bond obligor for, securities that are traded, listed, or quoted on an exchange or an over-the-counter market, and an employee benefit plan that files or provides financial statements with or to the Securities and Exchange Commission should apply the new guidance for prepaid stored-value cards discussed above for financial statements issued for fiscal years that begin after December 15, 2017, and interim periods within those fiscal years. All other entities should apply the guidance for financial statements issued for fiscal years that begin after December 15, 2018, and interim periods within fiscal years that begin after December 15, 2019.
2. Earlier application of the guidance is permitted, including adoption in an interim period.
3. An entity that adopts the guidance must do so by electing to use one of the following two methods:
   a. Retrospective application to each prior period presented in accordance with the guidance on accounting changes in ASC 250-10-45-5 through 45-10.
   b. Retrospective application by making a cumulative-effect adjustment to beginning retained earnings as of the beginning of the fiscal year in which the guidance is adopted.
4. The disclosures in ASC 250-10-50-1(a) and (b)(3) and ASC 250-10-50-2 should be provided, as applicable, in the period in which an entity adopts the guidance. An entity that elects to apply the guidance retrospectively in accordance with the first method under the bullet above should provide the disclosure required in ASC 250-10-50-1(b)(1).

AMENDMENTS TO SUBTOPIC 825-10

The list in ASC 825-10-50-8, which applies to financial instruments to which the fair value disclosure requirements in ASC 825-10-50-10 through 50-16 do not apply, is amended by the addition of item (o), liabilities as a result of a sale of prepaid stored-value products under the scope of ASC 405-10-40-3.

ASC 405-40: OBLIGATIONS RESULTING FROM JOINT AND SEVERAL LIABILITY ARRANGEMENTS

ASC 405-40-50-1 through 50-2, 30-1 through 30-2, 15-1 through 15-2, 25-1 through 25-2, 05-1, 35-1 Obligations Resulting from Joint and Several Liability Arrangements for Which the Total Amount of the Obligation is Fixed at the Reporting Date

BACKGROUND

There has been diversity in practice in accounting for obligations that result from joint and several liability obligations that have a fixed amount at the reporting date because U.S. generally accepted accounting principles (U.S. GAAP) has provided no accounting guidance for the recognition, measurement, and disclosure of such obligations. The scope of this ASU includes debt arrangements, other contractual obligations, settled litigation, and judicial rulings. Some entities have been recording the total amounts under such arrangements based on the existing guidance for liability extinguishment in Financial Accounting Standards Board (FASB) Accounting Standards Codification™ (ASC) 405, *Liabilities* (ASC 405-20), while others have been following the guidance for contingent liabilities in ASC 450, *Contingencies* (ASC 450-20), or ASC 410, *Asset Retirement and Environmental Obligations* (ASC 410-30), by recognizing a lower amount that may be based on an allocation, an amount equal to proceeds received, or the portion of an obligation that an entity has agreed to pay as a co-obligor.

ACCOUNTING GUIDANCE

ASC 405-40 has been added to ASC 405 to address the recognition, measurement, and disclosure of obligations incurred in joint and several liability arrangements that have a fixed amount at the reporting date. That guidance is as follows:

- *ASC 405-40-15-1* through 15-2 provide the *scope* of the guidance in ASC 405-40, *Obligations Resulting from Joint and Several Liability Arrangements*. Under this guidance, the total amount of such an arrangement must be fixed at the reporting date. That is, the total amount of the obligation incurred by the co-obligors in an arrangement must be fixed to be accounted for under the guidance in ASC 405-40, but the amount that an entity expects to pay on behalf of the co-obligors may be uncertain at that date. The amount of an obligation may be considered to be fixed at a reporting date only if there is no measurement uncertainty about its total amount. However, the total amount may differ in subsequent reporting periods as a result of factors other than an uncertainty about an obligation's measurement (e.g., because an additional amount was borrowed under a line of credit or due to a change in an arrangement's interest rate). The guidance in ASC 405-40 does not apply to obligations accounted for under the guidance in: (1) ASC 410 for asset retirements; (2) ASC 450 for contingencies; (3) ASC 460 for guarantees; (4) ASC 715 for compensation-retirement benefits; and (5) ASC 740 for income taxes.
- *ASC 405-40-25-1 and 25-2* provide *recognition* guidance for obligations as a result of joint and several liability arrangements under the scope of ASC 405. For example, the guidance applies at the inception of debt arrangements, but it applies to other arrangements after their inception, such as when an obligation's total amount becomes fixed after an arrangement's inception. Corresponding entries should depend on an obligation's facts and circumstances. The following are examples of corresponding entries:
  - — Cash for proceeds from a debt arrangement;
  - — An expense for a legal settlement;
  - — A receivable (that is assessed for impairment) for a contractual right; or
  - — An equity transaction with an entity under common control.
- *ASC 405-30-1 and 30-2* provide *initial measurement* guidance for such liability arrangements, which would initially be measured as the sum of the following:
  - — The amount a reporting entity agreed to pay based on an arrangement among its co-obligors; and
  - — An additional amount that a reporting entity expects to pay on behalf of its co-obligors. If a reporting entity believes that a certain amount within a range that it expects to pay is a better estimate than other amounts within

the range, it should include it as the additional amount in the obligation's measurement. The minimum amount in a range should be included as the additional amount in measuring an obligation if no other amount within a range is a better estimate. The corresponding entry or entries should be based on the facts and circumstances.

- *ASC 405-40-35-1* provides that the *subsequent* measurement of obligations as a result of joint and several liability arrangements under the scope of ASC 405 should be based on the guidance in ASC 405-40-30.
- *ASC 405-40-50-1 and 50-2* provide the following guidance for the required *disclosures* about each obligation, or each group of similar obligations, as a result of joint and several liability arrangements:
  - — The nature of an arrangement, including how the liability was incurred, the entity's relationship with the co-obligors, and the arrangement's terms and conditions;
  - — An arrangement's total outstanding amount, which should not be reduced by the effect of amounts, if any, that may be recovered from other entities;
  - — An entity's carrying amount of a liability, if any, and the carrying amount of a recognized receivable, if any;
  - — The nature of recourse provisions, if any, that would enable the entity to recover from other entities amounts that it paid, including limitations, if any, on the amounts that may be recovered; and
  - — In the period in which an entity first recognizes and measures the liability or in a period in which the liability changes significantly, the corresponding entry and its location in the financial statements.

The disclosures discussed above should be made in addition to the required disclosures about related parties in ASC 850, *Related Party Disclosures*.

CHAPTER 29

ASC 410—ASSET RETIREMENT AND ENVIRONMENTAL OBLIGATIONS

CONTENTS

PART I: GENERAL GUIDANCE

ASC 410-10: OVERALL

The purpose of ASC 410-10 is to differentiate between asset retirement obligations and environmental obligations (ASC 410-10-05-2). ASC 410-20 provides guidance on accounting for asset retirement obligations, including asset retirement costs, including environmental remediation liabilities resulting from the normal use of a long-lived asset (ASC 410-10-05-2). ASC 410-30 provides guidance on accounting for environmental remediation liabilities (ASC 410-10-05-2).

ASC 410-20: ASSET RETIREMENT OBLIGATIONS

OVERVIEW

ASC 410-20 requires accounting recognition and measurement of a liability for an asset retirement obligation and associated asset retirement costs. It was issued to narrow areas of differences in the ways entities previously accounted for obligations related to the retirement of long-lived assets. Some entities recognized liabilities as they were incurred, while others did not recognize liabilities until the assets were retired. Also, practices varied in terms of how asset retirement obligations were measured and presented in financial statements.

ASC 410 applies to all entities, including rate-regulated entities that meet the criteria for applying ASC 980 (Regulated Operations) (ASC 410-20-15-1). It applies to the following transactions and activities (ASC 410-20-15-2):

1. All legal obligations associated with the retirement of tangible long-lived assets that result from an acquisition, construction, or development. (A legal obligation is defined as an obligation that a party is required to settle as a result of an existing or enacted law, statute, ordinance, or written or oral contract, or by legal construction of a contract under the doctrine of promissory estoppel.)
2. An environmental remediation liability that results from the normal operation of a long-lived asset and that is associated with the retirement of that asset.
3. A conditional obligation to perform a retirement activity.
4. Obligations of a lessor in connection with an underlying asset.
5. The costs associated with the retirement of specified assets that meet the definition of historical waste equipment.

ASC 410 does not apply to the following transactions or activities (ASC 410-20-15-3):

1. Obligations that arise solely from a plan to dispose of a long-lived asset as defined in ASC 360-10.
2. An environmental remediation liability that results from the improper operation of a long-lived asset.
3. Activities necessary to prepare an asset for an alternative use.
4. Historical waste held by private households.
5. Certain obligations of a lessee in connection with an underlying asset.
6. An obligation for asbestos removal that results from other-than-normal operation of an asset.
7. Cost associated with complying with funding or assurance provisions.
8. Obligations associated with the maintenance, rather than the retirement, of a long-lived asset and the cost of the replacement of a component of a ling-lived asset.
9. The cost of a replacement part that is a component of a long-lived asset.

Initial Recognition and Measurement

Recognition of a liability for the fair value of an asset retirement obligation is required in the period in which it is incurred, if a reasonable estimate of fair value can be made. If such an estimate cannot be made in the period the obligation is incurred, the liability shall be recognized when a reasonable estimate of fair value can be made (ASC 410-20-25-4).

PRACTICE NOTE: The FASB indicates that this requirement is consistent with the definition of a liability in the FASB's conceptual framework, which states that liabilities are probable future sacrifices of economic benefits arising from present obligations of a particular entity to transfer assets or provide services to other entities in the future as a result of past transactions or events. The term "probable" is used with its general meaning and refers to that which can be reasonably expected or believed on the basis of available evidence or logic, but is neither certain nor proved. It is intended to reflect the fact that business and other economic activities occur in an environment in which few outcomes are certain. This is in contrast to the use of the word "probable" in ASC 450 (Contingencies), which requires a high degree of expectation.

The fair value of a liability for an asset retirement obligation will typically be determined using an expected present value technique. Cash flows are discounted using a credit-adjusted risk-free rate. This results in the effect of an entity's credit standing affecting the discount rate rather than affecting expected cash flows.

The obligation may be incurred over more than one financial reporting period if the events that lead to the obligation occur over more than one period. An incremental liability incurred in a subsequent reporting period is considered an additional layer of the original liability, with each layer measured at fair value and combined with the original layer(s) (ASC 410-20-35-1).

Accounting Subsequent to Initial Recognition

When the initial liability is recognized, the asset cost is increased by the amount equal to the same amount as the liability. That cost shall subsequently be allocated to expense using a systematic and rational method over the asset's useful life. This process does not preclude the entity from capitalizing an amount of asset retirement cost and allocating an equal amount to expense in the same accounting period (ASC 410-20-35-2).

In applying the provisions of ASC 360 in asset impairment situations, the carrying amount of the asset being tested for impairment includes the amounts of capitalized asset retirement costs. Estimates of future cash flows related to the liability for an asset retirement obligation that has been recognized in the financial statements are excluded from the undiscounted cash flows used to test the asset for recoverability and from the discounted cash flows used to measure the asset's fair value. If the fair value of the asset is based on a quoted market price and that price considers the costs that will be incurred in retiring the asset, the quoted market price shall be increased by the fair value of the asset retirement obligation when measuring the amount of impairment (ASC 360-10-35-18, 19).

In subsequent periods, changes in the liability for an asset retirement obligation resulting from the passage of time and revisions to either the timing or amount of the original estimate of undiscounted cash flows shall be recognized. In so doing, changes due to the passage of time shall first be incorporated before measuring changes resulting from a revision of either the timing or the amount of estimated cash flows (ASC 410-20-35-3, 4). Changes in the liability due to the passage of time are determined by applying an interest method of allocation to the liability at the beginning of the period using the credit-adjusted risk-free interest rate that existed when the liability was initially measured. That amount is recognized as an increase in the carrying amount of the liability and the expense shown as an operating item in the income statement (referred to as accretion expense) (ASC 410-20-35-5). Changes resulting from revisions in the amount and/or timing of the original estimate of undiscounted cash flows are recognized as an increase or decrease in the carrying amount of the liability and the related asset retirement cost capitalized. Upward revisions are discounted using the current credit-adjusted risk-free rate. Downward revisions shall be discounted using the credit-adjusted risk-free rate that existed when the original liability was recognized. When the asset cost changes as a result of revisions to estimated cash flows, the amount of the asset retirement cost allocated to expense in the period of change and subsequent periods, as appropriate, shall be adjusted (ASC 410-20-35-8).

Illustration of Accounting for an Asset Retirement Obligation—Obligation Incurred in a Single Reporting Period

This example illustrates (*a*) initial measurement of a liability for an asset retirement obligation using an expected present value technique, (*b*) subsequent measurement assuming that there are no changes in expected cash flows, and (*c*) settlement of the asset retirement obligation (ARO liability) at the end of its term.

Ocaxet Inc. completes construction of and places into service an offshore oil platform on January 1, 20X8. The entity is legally required to dismantle and remove the platform at the end of its useful life, which is estimated to be five years. Ocaxet Inc. develops the following estimates of costs to dismantle and remove the platform.

Labor costs are based on current, relevant marketplace wages and Ocaxet Inc. estimates the probability of a range of cash flow estimates as follows:

Cash Flow Estimate	*Estimated Probability*	*Expected Cash Flows*
$ 125,000	20%	$ 25,000
150,000	60	90,000
200,000	20	40,000
		$ 155,000

Ocaxet Inc. estimates allocated overhead and equipment charges to be 70% of labor costs.

Ocaxet Inc. understands that the contractor typically adds a markup on labor and allocated internal costs to provide a profit margin on the job and estimates this markup rate to be 15%. Ocaxet Inc. also estimates the market risk premium to be 5% of the estimated inflation-adjusted cash flows. The risk-free rate of interest is 4%, and Ocaxet Inc. adjusts that rate by 3% to reflect the effect of its credit standing. Thus, the credit-adjusted risk-free rate used to compute expected present value is 7%. Ocaxet Inc. also assumes an annual inflation rate of 3.5% annually over the five-year period.

Initial measurement of the ARO liability at January 1, 20X8:

	Expected Cash Flows
Expected labor costs	$ 155,000
Allocated overhead and equipment charges (.70 × $155,000)	108,500
Contractor's markup [.15 × ($155,000 + $108,500)]	39,525

	Expected Cash Flows
Expected cash outflows before inflation adjustment	303,025
Inflation factor (1.035^5)	1.1877
Expected cash flows adjusted for inflation	359,903
Market-risk premium (.05 × $359,903)	17,995
Expected cash flows adjusted for market risk	$377,898
Expected Present value using credit-adjusted risk-free rate of 7% for 5 years [$(1/(1 + .07^5)$ × $377,898]	$269,436

On December 31, 20Y2, Ocaxet Inc. settles its asset retirement obligation by using its internal workforce at a cost of $357,000. Assuming no changes during the five-year period in the cash flows used to estimate the obligation, the entity would recognize a gain of $20,898 on settlement of the obligation:

Labor	$210,000
Allocated overhead and equipment charges (70% of labor)	147,000
Total costs incurred	357,000
ARO liability	377,898
Gain on settlement of obligation	$ 20,898

Interest Method of Allocation

Year	*Liability Balance 1/1*	*Accretion (7%)*	*Liability Balance 12/31*
20X8	269,436	18,861	288,297
20X9	288,297	20,181	308,478
20Y0	308,478	21,593	330,071
20Y1	330,071	23,105	353,176
20Y2	353,176	24,722	377,898

Schedule of Expenses

Year-End	Accretion Expense	Depreciation Expense*	Total Expense
20X8	18,861	53,887	72,748
20X9	20,181	53,887	74,068
20Y0	21,593	53,887	75,480
20Y1	23,105	53,887	76,992
20Y2	24,722	53,887	78,609

* Assume straight-line deprecation ($269,436/5)

Journal Entries:

January 1, 20X8:

Long-lived asset (asset retirement cost)	269,436	
ARO liability		269,436
To record the initial fair value of the ARO liability		

December 31, 20X8-20Y2:

Depreciation expense (asset retirement cost)	53,887	
Accumulated depreciation		53,887
To record straight-line depreciation on the asset retirement cost		
Accretion expense	Per schedule	
ARO liability		Per schedule
To record accretion expense on the ARO liability		

December 31, 20Y2:		
ARO liability	377,898	
Wages payable		210,000
Allocated overhead and equipment charges		147,000
Gain on settlement of ARO liability		20,898
To record settlement of the ARO liability		

Illustration of Accounting for an Asset Retirement Obligation—Obligation Incurred over Multiple Reporting Periods

This example highlights the recognition and measurement provisions for an ARO liability that is incurred over more than one reporting period.

Asem Inc. places a nuclear utility plant into service on December 31, 20X8. The entity is legally required to decommission the plant at the end of its useful life, which is estimated to be ten years.

The following schedule reflects the expected cash flows and respective credit-adjusted risk-free rates used to measure each portion of the liability through December 31, 20Y0, at which time the plant is 90% contaminated:

Date	*Expected Cash Flows*	*Credit-Adjusted Risk-Free Rate*
12/31/X8	$30,000	8.0%
12/31/X9	2,250	7.3
12/31/Y0	2,775	7.7

On December 31, 20Y0, Asem Inc. increases by 10% its estimate of expected cash flows that were used to measure those portions of the liability recognized on December 31, 20X8, and December 31, 20X9. Because the change results in an upward revision to the expected cash flows, the incremental estimated cash flow is discounted at the current credit-adjusted risk-free rate of 7.7%. As a result, the total incremental cash flows of $6,000 [($30,000 + $2,250) × 10%) + $2,775] are discounted at the then current credit-adjusted risk-free rate of 7.7% and recorded as a liability on December 31, 20Y0.

	Date Incurred		
	12/31/X8	12/31/X9	12/31/Y0
Initial measurement of the ARO liability:			
Expected labor cost	$30,000	$2,250	$2,775
Credit-adjusted risk-free rate	8.0%	7.3%	7.7%
Discount period in years	10	9	8
Expected present value	$13,896	$1,193	$1,533
Measurement of incremental expected cash flows occurring on 12/31/Y0:			
Increase in expected cash flows of 10% [($30,000 + 2,250) × 10%]			$3,225
Credit-adjusted risk-free rate at December 31, 2010			7.7%
Discount period remaining in years			8
Expected present value [$3,225 × (1/(1.077⁸)]			$1,782

Carrying Amount of Liability Incurred in 20X8

Year	*Liability Balance 1/1*	*Accretion (8.0%)*	*New Liability*	*Liability Balance 12/31*
20X8			13,896	13,896
20X9	13,896	1,112		15,008
20Y0	15,008	1,201		16,209

Carrying Amount of Liability Incurred in 20X9

Year	*Liability Balance 1/1*	*Accretion (7.3%)*	*New Liability*	*Liability Balance 12/31*
20X9			$1,193	$1,193
20Y0	$1,193	$87		1,280

Carrying Amount of Liability Incurred in 20Y0 Plus Effect of Change in Expected Cash Flows

Year	*Liability Balance 1/1*	*Accretion (7.7%)*	*Change in Cash Flow Estimate*	*New Liability*	*Liability Balance 12/31*
20Y0			$1,782	$1,533	$3,315

Carrying Amount of Total Liability

Year	*Liability Balance 1/1*	*Accretion*	*Change in Cash Flow Estimate*	*New Liability*	*Liability Balance 12/31*
20X8				$13,896	$13,896
20X9	$13,896	$1,112		1,193	16,201
20Y0	16,201	1,288	$1,782	1,533	20,804

Journal Entries:

December 31, 20X8:		
Long-lived asset (asset retirement cost)	13,896	
ARO liability		13,896
To record the initial fair value of the ARO liability incurred in this period		
December 31, 20X9:		
Depreciation expense ($13,896/10)	1,390	
Accumulated depreciation		1,390
To record straight-line depreciation on the asset retirement cost		
Accretion expense	1,112	
ARO liability		1,112
To record accretion expense on the ARO liability		
Long-lived asset (asset retirement cost)	1,193	
ARO liability		1,193
To record the initial fair value of the ARO liability incurred in this period		
December 31, 20Y0:		
Depreciation expense [($13,896/10) + ($1,193/9)]	1,523	
Accumulated depreciation		1,523
To record straight-line depreciation on the asset retirement cost		
Accretion expense	1,288	
ARO liability		1,288
To record accretion expense on the ARO liability		
Long-lived asset (asset retirement cost)	1,782	
ARO liability		1,782
To record the change in liability resulting from a revision in expected cash flows		
Long-lived asset (asset retirement cost)	1,533	
ARO liability		1,533
To record the initial fair value of the ARO liability incurred in this period		

CONDITIONAL ASSET RETIREMENT OBLIGATIONS

ASC 410 provides guidance on measuring the liability associated with an asset retirement obligation when there is uncertainty associated with the timing or method of the asset retirement. Although ASC 410 requires entities to recognize the fair value of an asset retirement obligation in the period in which the obligation is incurred, differences in practice have arisen because of differences in interpretation as to when a reasonable estimate of fair value can be made. In particular, although an entity may be legally required to retire a fixed asset, there may be uncertainties associated with the timing and/or method of the asset retirement. The timing and/or method may be conditional on a future event, and the entity may or may not control this future event. Some entities recognize a liability at the time the asset retirement obligation is incurred, and consider the uncertainties associated with the timing and/or method of retiring the asset in estimating the liability's fair value. Other entities only recognize a liability when the date and method of asset retirement are essentially fixed. ASC 410 is designed to reduce these differences in practice.

Interpretive Guidance

An asset can be retired by, among other ways, sale, abandonment, recycling, and disposal. A liability exists if an entity has a legal obligation to retire a fixed asset, even if the timing and/or method of retiring the asset is conditional on a future event. That is, the obligation to retire the asset is unconditional, even though the timing and/or method of retiring the asset may be uncertain. Because a liability exists, that liability should be recognized if its fair value can be reasonably estimated (ASC 410-20-25-7).

An asset retirement obligation is considered to be reasonably estimable if (1) the purchase price of the asset reflects the costs associated with the legally mandated obligation to retire the fixed asset, (2) the entity could transfer the asset retirement obligation to another party because an active market for such transfers exists, and (3) enough information exists to apply an expected present value technique (ASC 410-20-25-6). In many instances, the fair value of the asset retirement obligation will not be transparent in the purchase price, nor will an active market for the transfer of the obligation exist. Therefore, very commonly, the fair value of an asset retirement obligation is determined using an expected present value technique.

Assuming the use of an expected present value technique, the fair value of an asset retirement obligation is reasonably estimable if either of two conditions exists (ASC 410-20-25-8):

1. The settlement date and the method of settlement have been determined by the party that created the legal obligation (e.g., the legislative, executive, or private body that created the law, regulation, or contract giving rise to the legal obligation).

PRACTICE POINTER: The only uncertainty remaining if the date and method of settlement have been determined is whether the entity will be required to retire the asset by the party that created the legal obligation. The entity will either be required to retire the asset or it will not. If no information exists as to which outcome is more likely, the entity is to assign a 50% probability to each outcome.

---

2. Information is available that enables the entity to estimate the settlement date or range of possible settlement dates, and to assign probabilities to these potential settlement dates, and estimate the settlement method or potential settlement alternatives, and to assign probabilities to these potential settlement methods. This information should be developed from the entity's past practice, industry practice, the intent of management, and the asset's economic life.

PRACTICE POINTER: In some cases, the entity still may be able to arrive at a reasonable estimate of the fair value of the asset retirement obligation even if the entity cannot assign probabilities to the potential settlement dates or methods of settlement. For example, the potential settlement dates may be close in time to each other and the alternative settlement methods may involve similar cash outflows. In this instance, differences in the assigned probabilities would not have a material effect on the computed fair value of the asset retirement obligation.

Notwithstanding the above guidance, there will be some instances where although a legal obligation to retire the asset exists (i.e., a liability exists), the liability will not be recognized because the entity cannot reasonably estimate the fair value of the liability. A liability must be recorded in a latter period, however, when information becomes available to estimate the fair value of the liability. And, if a liability is not recognized because it cannot be reasonably estimated, the entity must disclose that fact and must disclose the reasons the fair value of the liability cannot be reasonably estimated (ASC 410-20-25-10).

Illustration of Accounting for a Conditional Asset Retirement Obligation

A company constructs manufacturing, distribution, and sales facilities that contain a building material that is non-toxic in its present state, but which is toxic if disposed of without following special procedures. There is no legal requirement to dispose of the building material. If any building is destroyed or substantially remodeled, however, the entity must follow legally mandated disposal procedures for the toxic material.

The company is able to estimate dates on which it is likely to destroy (raze) or substantially remodel each building, the methods that are likely to be used, and the associated probabilities. Therefore, at the date that each building is constructed, the company is able to estimate the asset retirement obligation using an expected present value technique. The recorded value of each building would be increased by the estimated present value of the asset retirement obligation, and a liability for the asset retirement obligation would be recognized as well.

DISCLOSURE

Following are disclosures required about asset retirement obligations (ASC 410-20-50-1):

- General description of the asset retirement obligation and the associated long-lived asset
- Fair value of assets that are legally restricted for purposes of settling asset retirement obligations
- A reconciliation of the beginning and ending carrying amounts of asset retirement obligations showing separately:
  - — Liabilities incurred in the current period
  - — Liabilities settled in the current period
  - — Accretion expense
  - — Revisions in estimated cash flows where there is a significant change in the current period

If the fair value of an asset retirement obligation cannot be reasonably estimated, that fact and the reasons should be disclosed (ASC 410-20-50-2).

PART II: INTERPRETIVE GUIDANCE

ASC 410-30: ENVIRONMENTAL OBLIGATIONS

IMPORTANT NOTICE: All of the guidance in ASC 410-30, will be superseded when the guidance in ASU 2014-09, *Accounting for Revenue from Contracts with Costumers*, which will reside in ASC 606, Revenue from Contracts with Customers, becomes effective for public entities, certain not-for-profit entities, and certain employee benefit plans for annual reporting periods that begin after December 15, 2017 and after December 15, 2018 for nonpublic entities.

ASC 410-30-05-1 through 3, 05-5 through 05-25; 10-1; 15-1 through 15-3; 25-1 through 25-15, 25-17, 25-20 through 25-23; 30-1 through 30-19; 35-1 through 35-5, 35-8 through 35-12, 35-12A; 45-1 through 45-2, 45-4 through 45-5; 50-1 through 50-17; 55-1 through 55-6, 55-14 through 55-17, 55-27 through 55-51; 60-3, 60-8 Environmental Remediation Liabilities

BACKGROUND

ASC 410-30 provides accounting guidance for environmental remediation liabilities that relate to pollution resulting from some past act. Generally, these liabilities result from one of the following (ASC 410-30-10-1):

- Superfund provisions
- The corrective-action provisions of the Resource Conservation and Recovery Act (RCRA)
- State and non-U.S. laws and regulations that are analogous to the RCRA

ASC 410-30 applies to all entities that prepare financial statements in conformity with generally accepted accounting principles applicable to nongovernmental entities. The provisions of ASC 410-30 are intended to be applied on a site-by-site basis (ASC 410-30-15-2).

ASC 410-30 is written in the context of operations taking place in the United States, although the guidance provided is applicable to all of a reporting entity's operations (ASC 410-30-05-1; ASC-410-30-15-1). It is *not* intended to provide guidance for the following (ASC 410-30-15-3):

- Environmental contamination incurred in the normal operation of a long-lived asset.
- Accounting for pollution control costs with respect to current operations.
- Accounting for costs of future site restoration or closure that are required upon the cessation of operations or sale of facilities.

- Accounting for environmental remediation actions that are undertaken at the sole discretion of management and that are not induced by the threat of litigation or of assertion or by a claim of assessment by governments or other parties.
- Natural resource damages and toxic torts.
- Recognizing liabilities of insurance companies for unpaid claims.
- Asset impairment issues.

PRACTICE POINTER: Guidance on the accounting for costs of future site restoration or closure that are required upon the cessation of operations or sale of facilities is provided in ASC 410-20; ASC 450-20; ASC 835-20; ASC 360-10-35; ASC 840-40 and ASC 840-10; ASC 980-410. In addition, guidance on asset impairment issues is provided in ASC 360-10; ASC 840-30; ASC 840-20; ASC 205-10, ASC 205-20; ASC 958-225-45, ASC 958-360; ASC 855-10; ASC 225-20.

The following discussion is intended to provide guidance for the accounting for "cleanup" activities rather than preventative or other activities. For example, it does not discuss situations in which remediation is required only when a property is for sale. The discussion focuses on the document's detailed guidance on accounting and disclosure for environmental remediation liabilities.

ACCOUNTING GUIDANCE

Recognition of Environmental Remediation Liabilities

The guidance for the recognition of environmental remediation liabilities is based on the recognition criteria in ASC 450 by requiring the accrual of a liability when *both* of the following conditions are met (ASC 410-30-25-1):

- Information available before the financial statements are issued or are available for issuance (as discussed in ASC 855-10-25) indicates that it is probable that an asset has been impaired or a liability has been incurred at the date of the financial statements.
- The amount of the loss can be reasonably estimated.

A liability related to environmental remediation often results over a period of time rather than as a distinct event (ASC 410-30-25-2). The underlying cause of such a liability is the past or present ownership or operation of a site, or the contribution or transportation of waste to a site, at which remedial actions must be made. To meet the criteria for recognizing a liability, the underlying cause must have occurred on or before the date of the financial statements (ASC 410-30-25-3).

Probability That a Liability Has Been Incurred

Applying the criteria in ASC 450-20-25-2 to environmental remediation liabilities requires that it has been asserted (or it is probable that it will be asserted) that the entity is responsible for participating in a remediation process because of a past event and available evidence indicates that the outcome of such litigation, claim, or assessment will be unfavorable (i.e., the entity will be held responsible for participating in a remediation process because of the past event). This usually means that litigation has begun, a claim or an assessment has been asserted, or commencement of litigation or assertion of a claim or assessment is considered probable.

In recognition of the legal framework in which most environmental remediation liabilities occur, the guidance is based on a presumption that if litigation has commenced (or a claim or an assessment has been asserted or is considered probable), and the reporting entity is associated with the site, the outcome will be unfavorable for the entity (ASC 410-30-25-4).

Ability to Make a Reasonable Estimate

Developing an estimate of environmental remediation liabilities involves a consideration of many factors, such as the following (ASC 410-30-25-7):

1. The extent and types of hazardous substances at the site
2. The range of technologies that can be used for remediation
3. Evolving standards of what constitutes acceptable remediation
4. The number and financial condition of other potentially responsible parties and the extent of their responsibility for the remediation

---

Illustration of Estimating an Environmental Remediation Liability

Foster, Inc., has determined that its environmental remediation obligation meets the recognition criteria in ASC 410-30 The company is in the process of estimating the amount of the obligation that will be recognized. The company has further determined that the liability consists of four components, described as follows:

Component	*Description*
A	Estimated at $750,000
B	Estimated to be within a range of $500,000 to $900,000, with the most likely amount at $625,000
C	Estimated to be within a range of $275,000 to $400,000, with no amount within that range more likely than any other amount
D	Unable to estimate

The environmental remediation liability that should be recognized at this time, subject to adjustment in the future as additional information becomes available, is determined as follows:

Component A	$ 750,000
Component B	625,000
Component C	275,000
Component D	None
	$1,650,000

The guidance in ASC 450-20-25-5, 30-1, 05-5, 55-23 through 55-34 is particularly important in estimating the amount of an environmental remediation liability. In the early stages of the remediation process, liabilities are not easily quantified. This fact should not preclude the recognition of a liability (ASC 410-30-25-10). The range and ultimate amount of the liability will be determined as events occur over time. The range of an environmental remediation liability typically is estimated by first estimating the various components of the liability—which may themselves be in the form of a range. As suggested under the guidance in ASC 450-20-25-5, 30-1, 05-5, 55-23 through 55-34, if an amount within a range is a better estimate than any other amount within the range, that amount should be used. If no amount within a range is a more reliable estimate than any other, the minimum amount in the range should be used. Thus, the amount of an environmental remediation liability will be a combination of most likely amounts and minimum amounts of the components of the liability. Even if a range for certain components of the liability cannot be estimated, a liability still should be recognized and recorded at the appropriate amount for the components that can be estimated. A complexity that arises in estimating environmental remediation liabilities is the assignment and allocation among the various potentially responsible parties (PRPs). The final allocation may not be known until the remediation effort is substantially complete and may depend on factors such as the PRPs' willingness to negotiate a cost allocation. This fact should not preclude an entity from recognizing its best estimate of its share of a liability if the probability criterion is met (ASC 410-30-25-12). A change, if any, in estimating an environmental remediation liability, including those due to negotiations with other PRPs, is accounted for as a change in accounting estimate in accordance with the guidance in ASC 250.

Measurement of Environmental Remediation Liabilities

Once an entity determines that it is probable that an environmental remediation liability has been incurred, it must estimate the amount of that liability based on available evidence. The liability's estimate includes the allocable share of the liability for a specific site, and the share of amounts related to the site that will not be paid by other PRPs or the government (ASC 410-30-30-8).

The following four issues that must be addressed in the measurement of an entity's environmental remediation liability are identified (ASC 410-30-30-9):

- Costs that should be included in the measurement
- Whether the measurement should consider the effects of expected future events or developments
- How the measurement should be affected by the existence of other PRPs
- How the measurement should be affected by potential recoveries

Costs to Be Included

Costs to be included in the measurement of an environmental remediation liability include (*a*) incremental direct costs of the remediation effort and (*b*) costs of compensation and benefits for employees who are expected to devote a significant amount of time on the remediation effort (e.g., in-house lawyers and engineers) (ASC 410-30-30-10).

The remediation effort is considered on a site-by-site basis and includes the following (ASC 410-30-30-11):

- Pre-cleanup activities (e.g., the performance of a remedial investigation, risk assessment, or feasibility study and the preparation of remedial action plan)
- Performance of remedial actions under Superfund, corrective actions under RCRA, and analogous actions under state and non-U.S. laws
- Government oversight and enforcement activities
- Operation and maintenance of the remedy

The following are examples of incremental direct costs of a remediation effort:

- Fees paid to outside law firms for work related to remedial actions
- Costs related to completing the remedial investigation/feasibility study
- Fees to outside engineering and consulting firms for site investigations and the development of remedial action plans and designs
- Costs of contractors performing remedial actions
- Government oversight costs
- Costs of machinery and equipment related to the remedial effort that do not have alternative uses
- The PRP's assessments of the costs it incurred in dealing with a site
- Operating costs and remedial action maintenance

The costs of the following are included in the measurement of the remediation liability (ASC 410-30-30-12):

- Determining the extent of the remedial actions that are required
- Determining the types of remedial actions to be used
- Allocating the costs among PRPs

The costs of routine environmental compliance matters and litigation costs involved with potential recoveries are *not* part of the remediation effort. Further, including the cost of defense against assertions of liability in the measurement of the environmental remediation liability is not required (ASC 410-30-30-13, 14). Practice is diverse: some include legal defense costs in the measurement of a liability under the guidance in ASC 450, while most entities treat litigation costs as period costs (ASC 410-30-30-14).

Effects of Expected Future Events or Developments

Remediation of a site may extend over several years. As a result, the laws that govern the remediation process and the technology available may change during the remediation process. Other factors that may affect estimates of costs to be incurred are the effect of inflation and productivity improvements.

Enacted laws and adopted regulations and policies should provide the basis for measuring a remediation liability. Changes in those factors should not be anticipated, and the effect of changes that are enacted or adopted should be recognized only when they occur. The remediation plan should be based on the methodology that is expected to be approved, and the liability should be based on that methodology and remediation technology, which should continue to be the basis for the liability until it is probable that a revised methodology will be accepted (ASC 410-30-35-5).

The measurement of environmental remediation liabilities should be based on the reporting entity's estimate of what it will cost to perform each of the elements of the remediation effort (identified earlier) when those elements are expected to be performed. As such, an entity should take into account productivity improvements due to experience, as well as inflation. If it is not practicable to estimate inflation, a cost estimate should include the minimum in the range of the liability until the costs can be estimated more reasonably (ASC 410-30-30-17).

If the amount and timing of cash payments is (reasonably) fixed or reliably determinable, the measurement of the liability, or a component of the liability, may be discounted to reflect the time value of money. The discount rate that should be used is that rate (*a*) that will produce an amount at which the environmental liability theoretically could be settled in an arm's-length transaction with a third party and (*b*) that does not exceed the interest rate on monetary assets that are essentially risk-free and have maturities comparable to that of the environmental liability.

Allocation of the Liability Among PRPs

The environmental remediation liability recorded by an entity should be based on the entity's estimate of its allocable share of the joint and several remediation liability. This requires an identification of the PRPs for the site, an assessment of the likelihood that other PRPs will pay their share of the liability, and a determination of the portion of the liability that will be allocated to the entity (ASC 410-30-30-1).

Identification of PRPs The guidance identifies five categories of PRPs:

1. *Participating PRPs* PRPs that acknowledge their potential involvement with the site. These PRPs also are referred to as "players."
2. *Recalcitrant PRPs* PRPs that adopt an attitude of nonresponsibility, even though evidence suggests their involvement in the site. Typically, parties in this category must be sued in order for their allocable share of the remediation liability to be collected.
3. *Unproven PRPs* Parties that have been identified as PRPs by the Environmental Protection Agency (EPA) but that do not acknowledge their potential involvement because no substantive evidence currently links them to the site. These PRPs eventually will be reclassified based on evidence that is later discovered.
4. *Unknown PRPs* Parties that have liability with respect to a Superfund site but as of yet have not been identified as a PRP by the EPA. As the investigation progresses, additional PRPs may be identified. These PRPs will later be reclassified to the participating category or the recalcitrant category.
5. *Orphan Share PRPs* Identified PRPs that cannot be identified or have no assets PRPs from which no contributions will be received because they are not found or have no assets (are insolvent).

Over the duration of the remediation project, individual entities may move from one PRP category to another (ASC 410-30-30-3).

Allocation process The environmental remediation liability is allocated only among participating PRPs. There are several ways to allocate the liability among PRPs. The following are the four principal factors that are considered in a typical allocation process:

1. *Elements of fair share* Examples are the amount of waste based on volume, mass, type, and toxicity and the length of time the site was used.
2. *Classification of PRP* Examples are site operator, transporter of waste, and generator of waste.
3. *Limitations on payments* Any statutory or regulatory limitations on contributions.
4. *Degree of care* Refers to the degree of care exercised in selecting the site or in selecting a transporter.

The environmental remediation liability may be allocated according to any of the following methods: (1) PRPs may agree among themselves as to the allocation, (2) PRPs may hire an allocation consultant whose conclusions may or may not be binding, or (3) PRPs may request a nonbinding allocation of responsibility from the EPA. The allocation method or percentages may change as the project moves forward (ASC 410-30-30-5).

An entity should determine its allocable share of the remediation liability based on its estimate of the allocation method and its percentage of the amount that will ultimately be used for the entire remediation effort. Sources for this estimate should be the allocation method and the percentages that the PRPs have agreed to, the method and percentages that have been assigned by a consultant, or the method and percentages determined by the EPA, depending on the method that is chosen (as described in the preceding paragraph). If the entity's estimate of the ultimate liability differs significantly from the method or percentage from these primary sources, the entity's estimate should be based on objective, verifiable evidence, such as the following (ASC 410-30-30-6):

- Existing data about the kinds and quantities of waste at the site
- Experience with allocation approaches in comparable situations
- Reports of environmental specialists
- Internal data refuting EPA allegations about the entity's contribution of waste to the site

A consideration in estimating an entity's allocable share of the liability is the financial condition of the participating PRPs, including their ability to pay. The entity should include in its liability its share of amounts that are not expected to be paid by other PRPs or by the government (ASC 410-30-30-7).

Impact of potential recoveries Potential recoveries may come from a number of sources, such as insurers, PRPs other than participating PRPs, and government or third-party funds. The environmental remediation liability should be determined without regard to potential recoveries. An asset related to recoveries should be separately recognized only when realization is considered probable. If the claim is subject to litigation, the realization of the recovery claim is not considered probable.

The amount that may be recovered should be determined based on the available information and the specific circumstances (see ASC 410-30-30-15). The transaction costs of receiving a potential recovery also should be considered in measuring the potential amount. In addition, the time value of money should be considered in measuring the amount of a potential recovery if the time value of money has been considered in measuring the liability.

Financial Statement Presentation and Disclosure

The following are guidelines for financial statement presentation and disclosure related to environmental remediation obligations. Entities that are subject to the rules and regulations of the Securities and Exchange Commission (SEC) also are required to adhere to various SEC rules that apply to environmental matters.

Financial Statement Presentation

Several assets may result from an environmental remediation obligation, including the following (ASC 410-30-45-1):

- Receivables from other PRPs that are not providing initial funding
- Anticipated recoveries from insurers
- Anticipated recoveries from prior owners as a result of indemnification agreements

ASC 210-20, ASC 815-10 specifies that offsetting assets and liabilities is appropriate only if a right of setoff exists, which requires *all* of the following:

- Each of the two parties owes the other party a determinable amount.
- The reporting entity has the right to set off the amounts owed with the amount owed by the other party.
- The reporting entity intends to set off.
- The right of setoff is enforceable at law.

Although those conditions would apply to assets and liabilities related to an environmental remediation, it would be rare for the facts and circumstances surrounding environmental remediation liabilities and related assets to meet those conditions (ASC 410-30-45-2).

Recording an environmental remediation liability usually results in a charge to income. It is difficult to substantiate the classification of environmental remediation costs as a component of nonoperating expenses, because the events underlying the obligation are part of the entity's operations. Thus, environmental remediation-related expenses should be reported as a component of operating income in an income statement that separates operating and nonoperating items. Credits (i.e., gains or loss recoveries) recognized in an entity's financial statements should be presented in the income statement in the same manner. Any earnings on assets that are reflected in an entity's balance sheet and are reserved for its environmental liabilities should be reported as investment income (ASC 410-30-45-4).

Environmental remediation-related expenses and recoveries that are attributable to discontinued operations that were accounted for as such in accordance with ASC 205-20 shall be classified as discontinued operations.

DISCLOSURE

Accounting policies ASC 235-10-05-3 through 05-4, 50-1 through 50-6 provides guidance concerning information that must be disclosed about the accounting policies used by an entity in the preparation of its financial statements. With regard to environmental remediation liabilities, that disclosure should include an indication of whether the accrual is measured on a discounted basis (ASC 410-30-50-4).

Environmental remediation liabilities are increasingly significant and involve subjective judgment. As a result, entities are encouraged, but not required, to disclose the event, situation, or set of circumstances that generally triggers recognition of loss contingencies that arise out of the entity's environmental remediation-related obligations. Entities also are encouraged to disclose their policy regarding the timing of recognition of recoveries (ASC 410-30-50-8). An example of an accounting policy note is presented in the following Illustration.

Illustration of Accounting Policy Note

Environmental remediation costs Company X accrues losses associated with environmental remediation obligations when they are probable and reasonably estimable, which usually is no later than the time of completion of the remedial feasibility study. These accruals are adjusted as additional information is available or if circumstances change. Costs of future expenditures for environmental remediation obligations are [not] discounted to their present value. Expected recoveries of environmental remediation costs from other parties are recognized as assets when their receipt is judged to be probable.

Loss contingencies The disclosure requirements in ASC 450 and in ASC 275-10-05-2 through 05-8, 10-1, 15-3 through 15-6, 50-1 through 50-2, 50-4, 50-6 through 50-21, 50-23, 55-1 through 55-19, 60-3; ASC 205-20-55-80; ASC 330-10-55-8 through 55-13; ASC 814-10-30-55-8 through 55-13; ASC 450-20-50-2; 55-36 through 55-37; ASC 460-10-55-27; ASC 605-35-55-3 through 55-10; ASC 740-10-55-219 through 5-22; ASC 932-360-55-15 through 15-19; ASC 958-205-60-1; ASC 605-55-70; ASC 985-20-55-24 through 55-29 are particularly important for environmental remediation liabilities. The guidance in ASC 450 requires that the following disclosures be made about loss contingencies:

- If accrual is possible, the nature of an accrual for a loss contingency and, in some circumstances, the amount accrued to keep financial statements from being misleading
- If no accrual is possible because the loss is either not probable or estimable, or if an exposure to loss exists in excess of the accrued amount, the reasonable possibility of loss, the nature of the loss, and an estimate of the possible range of loss, or a statement that such an estimate cannot be made

The disclosure requirements in ASC 275-10-50-6 through 50-15 that are particularly important for an environmental remediation liability are the following:

- Estimates used in determining the carrying amount of assets or liabilities or gain or loss contingencies
- Information regarding an estimate when information known before issuance of the financial statements indicates that both of the following are met:
  - — It is at least reasonably possible that the estimate of the effect on the financial statements of a condition, situation, or set of circumstances that existed at the date of the financial statements will change in the near term due to one or more future confirming events.
  - — The effect of the change would be material to the financial statements.
- Information regarding the nature of the uncertainty and an indication that it is at least reasonably possible that a change in the estimate will occur in the near term. (If the estimate involves a loss contingency covered by ASC 450, the disclosure also should include an estimate of the possible loss or range of loss or state that such an estimate cannot be made.)

Uncertainties associated with environmental remediation loss contingencies are pervasive and may result in wide ranges of reasonably possible loss contingencies. Those contingencies may occur over many years. As a result, additional specific disclosures related to environmental remediation loss contingencies that would contribute to a better understanding of an entity's financial statements are encouraged but are not required.

Related to Recorded Accruals

The following information is must be disclosed:

1. The nature of an accrual (if required to keep financial statements from being misleading), including the total amount accrued
2. If any portion of an accrued obligation is discounted, the undiscounted amount of the obligation and the discount rate used in the present value calculation (ASC 410-30-50-7)
3. If the criteria ASC 275-10-50-8 are met with respect to the accrued obligation or to any recognized asset for third-party recoveries, an indication that it is at least reasonably possible that a change in the estimate, obligation, or asset will occur in the near term

Related to Reasonably Possible Loss Contingencies

1. The nature of the reasonably possible loss contingency; also, an estimate of the possible loss exposure, or the fact that such an estimate cannot be made
2. If the criteria in ASC 275-10-50-8 regarding estimated gain or loss contingencies are met, it is an indication that it is at least reasonably possible that a change in the estimate will occur in the near term

Disclosures Encouraged But Not Required (ASC 410-30-50-10)

1. The estimated time frame of disbursements for recorded amounts if expenditures are expected to continue over a long period of time
2. The estimated time frame for realization of recognized probable recoveries if those recoveries are not expected in the near term
3. If an estimate of the probable or reasonably possible loss or range of loss cannot be made, the reasons why
4. If information about the reasonably possible loss or the recognized and additional reasonably possible loss for an environmental remediation obligation related to an individual site is relevant to an understanding of the financial statements, the following with respect to that site:
    a. The total amount accrued for the site
    b. The nature of any reasonably possible loss contingency or additional loss, and an estimate of the possible loss or the fact that such an estimate cannot be made and why
    c. Whether other PRPs are involved, and the entity's estimated share of the obligation
    d. The status of regulatory proceedings
    e. The estimated time frame for resolution of the contingency

Probable But Not Reasonably Estimable Losses

1. If the environmental remediation liability may be material, a description of the remediation obligation and the fact that a reasonable estimate cannot be made
2. Disclosure of the estimated time frame for resolution of the uncertainty about the amount of the loss (encouraged, but not required) (ASC 410-30-50-11)

Unasserted Claims

1. If an entity is required by existing laws and regulations to report the release of hazardous substances and to begin a remediation study, or if assertion of a claim is considered probable, the matter represents a loss contingency subject to the disclosure requirements for unasserted claims under the guidance in ASC 450.

Environmental Remediation Costs Currently Recognized (ASC 410-30-50-12)

Entities are encouraged, but not required, to disclose the following details concerning environmental remediation costs:

1. The amount recognized for environmental remediation loss contingencies for each period
2. The amount of any recovery from third parties that is credited to environmental remediation costs in each period
3. The income statement caption in which environmental remediation costs and credits are included.

ASC 410-30-15-3, 25-16, 25-18, 25-19, 35-14, 55-19 through 55-26; ASC 410-20-15-2 Capitalization of Costs to Treat Environmental Contamination

BACKGROUND

Companies may incur environmental contamination treatment costs such as removal costs, containment costs, neutralization costs, and costs to prevent current or future contamination. Examples of those costs include: costs to remove contamination (e.g., cleaning up a disposal site); costs to acquire tangible property (e.g., air pollution control equipment); costs of environmental studies; and costs of fines. Such costs may be incurred voluntarily or be required by law.

This issue does not address the following:

- When to recognize liabilities resulting from environmental contamination
- How to measure such liabilities
- Whether to report costs of treating environmental contamination as an unusual or extraordinary item

ACCOUNTING ISSUE

Should costs of treating environmental contamination be capitalized or expensed?

ACCOUNTING GUIDANCE

Environmental cleanup costs should generally be expensed as incurred. In accordance with the guidance in ASC 410-30-25-18, some costs may be capitalized if they are recoverable and meet *one* of the following criteria:

- The cost extends the life, increases the capacity, or improves the safety or efficiency of existing owned property. To determine whether this criterion has been met, the condition of the property after making the expenditure must be compared to its condition when first constructed or acquired. Its condition must be improved to qualify for capitalization.

  For example, reinforcement of an oil tanker's hull would be a qualifying expenditure. Reinforcing the hull makes the tanker safer than it was when originally acquired. Removing toxic waste from a site would not qualify under this criterion, because the expenditure only restores the property to its original condition. (See the third criterion for an exception.)
- The cost prevents or reduces future environmental contamination that may result from an entity's operations or activities (e.g., installing air scrubbers in a factory's smokestack).
- The cost is incurred to treat property currently held for sale (e.g., removing toxic waste from a site would qualify under this criterion, if the property is held for sale).

DISCUSSION

Proponents of using specific criteria to distinguish between environmental cleanup costs that should be capitalized and those that should be expensed believed that such costs generally should be expensed, but realized that under certain circumstances, it may be appropriate to capitalize those costs. They noted that by establishing specific criteria for capitalization, the predominant practice of expensing environmental cleanup costs would be retained. For example, cleaning up a gasoline station's contaminated soil does not create an asset because it does not increase the station's capacity or improve its safety or efficiency over its condition when it was first constructed. Rather, the soil is restored to its original condition.

If the criterion of improvement rather than repair is applied, some believed it would be appropriate to capitalize asbestos cleanup costs based on the premise that a building containing asbestos was unsafe even when it was built and that removal made it safer.

ASC 410-30-45-6; ASC 410-20-15-3 Accounting for the Cost of Asbestos Removal

NOTE: The original guidance in this Issue has been updated to conform with the requirements in ASC 410-30.

BACKGROUND

Many jurisdictions require that "dangerous asbestos" found in buildings be treated by removal or containment. In addition, many companies have voluntarily treated asbestos in buildings they own.

ACCOUNTING ISSUES

- Should costs incurred to treat an asbestos problem in an existing property that was identified after acquiring the property be capitalized or recognized as an expense?
- Should those costs be charged to expense, and if so, should they be reported as an extraordinary item?

ACCOUNTING GUIDANCE

- Costs incurred to treat asbestos problems in an existing property may be *capitalized* if they are recoverable and meet at least one of the following criteria in ASC 410-30-25-18:
  - — The property's useful life is extended, its capacity is increased or its safety or efficiency improves. That is, the property's condition must be better than it was before the costs were incurred.
  - — Incurring those costs will mitigate or prevent environmental contamination that has not yet occurred and that otherwise may occur as a result of operations and activities. The property's condition must be better than it was before the costs were incurred.
  - — The costs are incurred to prepare a property currently held for sale.
- The costs of asbestos treatment generally should be treated as expenses. They do not qualify for treatment as extraordinary items in accordance with the guidance in ASC 225-20 (ASC 410-30-45-6).

SEC OBSERVER COMMENT

The SEC Observer noted that registrants should discuss significant exposure to asbestos treatment costs in "Management's Discussion and Analysis" regardless of the treatment of such costs in the financial statements.

DISCUSSION

Issue 1 The threshold question in Issue 1 is whether costs of treating asbestos that are incurred while owning a building improve the property and extend its useful life, or whether they are incurred to repair the property. Those who supported capitalization argued that the nature and extent of the costs influence the decision whether to capitalize or expense the costs of asbestos treatment. They contended that treatment extends the building's useful life because it cannot continue to be occupied unless the hazardous condition was remedied.

Others noted that if the fair value of the building after asbestos treatment exceeds its book value by more than the cost of treatment, the owner has an economic incentive to incur the cost.

Issue 2 Classification as an extraordinary item requires an event or transaction to be unusual and infrequent. Some argued that although asbestos treatment may not meet both criteria for an extraordinary item, such events occur infrequently. Consequently, related costs might qualify under the guidance in ASC 225-20-45-16 to be classified as a separate component of income from continuing operations. Although it was agreed that expenses related to asbestos treatment are not extraordinary, the conclusion does not address whether such costs may be accounted for as infrequent items.

SUBSEQUENT DISCUSSION

The discussion of related issues in ASC 410-30-15-3, 25-16, 25-18, 25-19, 35-14, 55-19 through 55-26: ASC 410-20-15-2 through 15-3 (discussed below) and the conclusion on the first Issue provides additional guidance for the capitalization of asbestos treatment costs.

The guidance in ASC 410-20 applies only to *legal* obligations related to the retirement of tangible long-lived assets that result from the acquisition, construction, or development and the normal operation of those assets. That guidance does *not* apply to an obligation to remove asbestos resulting from other than the normal operation of an asset. However, the guidance in ASC 410-30-05, 05-15, 05-25, 05-30, 05-35, 05-55 (discussed below) may apply in those circumstances. Asset retirement obligations under the scope of ASC 410-20 must be recognized at the fair value of the liability in the period incurred. The associated costs should be capitalized as part of a long-lived asset's carrying amount and amortized to expense using a systematic and rational method over the asset's useful life. A liability should be recognized on the acquisition date for an existing retirement obligation related to acquired tangible long-lived assets as if the obligation had been incurred on that date.

CHAPTER 30

ASC 420—EXIT OR DISPOSAL COST OBLIGATIONS

CONTENTS

PART I: GENERAL GUIDANCE

ASC 420-10: OVERALL

OVERVIEW

ASC 420 addresses financial accounting and reporting for costs associated with exit or disposal activities. The objective of this ASC Topic is to improve financial reporting by requiring that a liability for a cost related to exit or disposal activities be recognized and measured initially at fair value only when the liability is incurred.

BACKGROUND

ASC 420 applies to costs associated with an exit activity including exit activities associated with an entity newly acquired in a business combination (or in an acquisition involving a not-for-profit entity), or with a disposal activity covered by ASC 360 (Property, Plant, and Equipment). The costs covered by ASC 420 include, but are not limited to (ASC 420-10-15-3):

- Termination benefits provided to current employees that are voluntarily terminated under the terms of a benefit arrangement that is, in substance, not an ongoing benefit arrangement or an individual deferred compensation contract.
- Costs to terminate a contract that is not a lease.
- Costs to consolidate facilities or relocate employees.

ASC 420 does not apply to costs associated with the retirement of a long-lived asset covered by ASC 410 (Asset Retirement and Environmental Obligations) or to the following (ASC 420-10-05-4):

- Postemployment benefits provided through a pension or postretirement benefit plan
- Stock compensation plans
- Individual deferred compensation arrangements

- Certain other nonretirement postemployment benefits
- Certain special or contractual benefits

PRACTICE NOTE: Exit activities include, but are not limited to, restructurings. Examples of restructurings are (1) sale or termination of a line of business, (2) closing business activities in a particular location, (3) relocation of business activities, (4) change in management structure, and (5) a reorganization that fundamentally changes the entity's operating nature and focus.

ACCOUNTING FOR COSTS ASSOCIATED WITH EXIT OR DISPOSAL ACTIVITIES

Recognition and Measurement

ASC 420 requires liability recognition for a cost associated with an exit or disposal activity, measured at fair value, in the period in which the liability is incurred (with limited exceptions). In the unusual circumstance in which fair value cannot be reasonably estimated, liability recognition is delayed until such an estimate can reasonably be made (ASC 420-10-25-1).

A liability for a cost associated with an exit or disposal activity is incurred when the CON-6 (Elements of Financial Statements) definition of a liability is met:

> Liabilities are probable future sacrifices of economic benefits arising from present obligations of a particular entity to transfer assets or provide services to another entity in the future as a result of past transactions or events.

Only present obligations to others are liabilities under this definition. An obligation becomes a present obligation when a transaction or event occurs that leaves the entity little or no discretion to avoid the future transfer or use of an asset to settle the liability. An exit or disposal plan, in and of itself, does not create a present obligation, although it may lead to one in the future if the criteria for liability recognition are met (ASC 420-10-25-2).

The objective of initial measurement of a liability for a cost associated with an exit or disposal activity is fair value. A present value technique is often the best available valuation technique for estimating the fair value of a liability for a cost associated with an exit or disposal activity. For a liability that has uncertainties both in timing and amount, an expected present value technique generally is the appropriate technique.

PRACTICE POINTER: In many cases, a quoted market price for the restructuring liability will not be available and the most appropriate valuation technique will be a present value technique. An expected present value technique is generally preferred to a traditional present value technique. In an expected present value technique, the entity weighs multiple cash flow outcomes, based on their probability of occurrence, and then discounts these cash flows using a credit-adjusted (for the entity's credit standing), risk-free discount rate. The discounted cash flows are then added together to compute the expected present value of the restructuring liability. Conversely, a traditional present value technique subjectively adjusts the discount rate to reflect uncertainty in the amount and timing of the most likely cash flow pattern associated with the restructuring liability. Because a restructuring liability often has uncertainty associated with the amount and timing of the relevant cash flows, ASC 420 expresses a preference for the expected present value technique. CON-7 (Using Cash Flow Information and Present Value in Accounting Measurements) provides a detailed discussion of present value techniques available.

Once a liability for an exit or disposal activity has been recognized, in subsequent periods changes in the liability are measured using the credit-adjusted, risk-free rate that was used to measure the liability initially. The cumulative effect of a change resulting from a revision to either the timing or the amount of estimated cash flows is recognized as an adjustment to the liability in the period of the change and reported in the income statement in the same line item that was used when the related costs were recognized initially and recorded as liabilities. Changes due to the passage of time are recognized as an increase in the carrying amount of the liability and as an expense (e.g., accretion expense) (ASC 420-10-35-1, 2, 4).

PRACTICE NOTE: Accretion expense is not interest cost eligible for capitalization under the provisions of ASC 835 (Interest).

Recognition and Measurement of Certain Costs

One-time termination benefits are benefits provided to current employees who are involuntarily terminated under a one-time benefit arrangement. A one-time benefit arrangement is an arrangement established by a plan or termination that applies for a specified termination event or for a specified future period. A one-time termination benefit arrangement exists at the date the plan termination meets all of the following criteria and has been communicated to employees (ASC 420-10-25-4):

- Management, having the authority to approve the action, commits to a plan of termination.
- The plan identifies the number of employees to be terminated, their job classifications or functions, their locations, and the expected completion date.
- The plan establishes the terms of the benefit arrangement, including the benefits that employees will receive, in sufficient detail to enable employees to determine the type and amount of benefits they will receive if they are involuntarily terminated.
- Actions required to complete the plan indicate that it is unlikely that significant changes to the plan will be made or that the plan will be withdrawn.

The timing of recognition and related measurement of a liability for one-time termination benefits depends on whether employees are required to render service until they are terminated in order to receive the termination benefits and, if so, whether employees will be retained to render services beyond a minimum retention period. The minimum retention period shall not exceed the legal notification period or, if none exists, 60 days (ASC 420-10-25-6, 7).

If employees are not required to render service until they are terminated in order to receive the termination benefits or if employees will not be retained to render services beyond the minimum retention period, a liability for the termination benefits shall be recognized (measured at fair value) at the communication date (ASC 420-10-25-8).

Illustration of One-Time Termination Benefits—No Future Employee Service Required

On May 1, 20X9, Gardial, Inc., announces plans to close its operations in Bakersfield, California. Gardial, Inc., notifies all of its 300 employees that they will be terminated within 75 days. Each employee will receive a cash payment of $10,000 when that employee ceases providing service during the 75-day period. Because no future employee service is required to receive the one-time termination benefits, Gardial, Inc., will recognize the fair value of its termination liability on the date the plan is communicated to the employees (assuming that the termination benefit plan meets the ASC 420 criteria for recognizing a liability). A liability of $3,000,000 will be recorded on the communication date (given the short discount period, the gross value of the liability is not likely to differ materially from the fair value of the liability).

If employees are required to render service until they are terminated in order to receive the termination benefits and will be retained to render service beyond the minimum retention period, a liability for the termination benefits shall be measured initially at the communication date, based on the fair value of the liability as of the termination date, but recognized ratably over the future service period (ASC 420-10-25-9). A change resulting from a revision to either the timing or the amount of estimated cash flows over the future service period shall be measured using the credit-adjusted, risk-free rate that was used initially to measure the liability, and the cumulative effect of the change shall be recognized as an adjustment to the liability in the period of change (ASC 420-10-35-3).

Illustration of One-Time Termination Benefits—Future Employee Service Required

On October 1, 20X5, Miller, Inc., announces plans to close its plant in San Antonio, Texas, in 24 months. Employees who remain with Miller until the plant closes will receive a $15,000 cash retention bonus. The bonus will be paid one year after the termination date. An employee who leaves voluntarily before the plant closes will not be eligible for any of the retention bonus.

Miller has 1,000 employees on October 1, 20X5. Miller develops a number of scenarios associated with its likely employee retention over the next 24 months. These are:

- Most likely scenario (70% probability)—600 employees stay with Miller until 9/30/X7
- Optimistic scenario (20% probability)—800 employees stay with Miller until 9/30/X7
- Pessimistic scenario (10% probability)—300 employees stay with Miller until 9/30/X7

Miller announces its restructuring and communicates the employee retention plan to its employees on October 1, 20X5 (assume that Miller meets the ASC 420 criteria for recognizing a liability).

Miller measures what the fair value of the liability will be on the *termination date* (9/30/X7) on the *communication date*. This computation is as follows:

600 employees × $15,000 × 0.70	=	$6,300,000
800 employees × $15,000 × 0.20	=	2,400,000
300 employees × $15,000 × 0.10	=	450,000
Expected payment		$9,150,000

Miller's best estimate on 10/1/X5 (the communication date) of the undiscounted amount of its liability at 9/30/X7 (the termination date) is $9,150,000. Miller's credit-adjusted, risk-free interest rate is 10%. Therefore, the expected present value of Miller's liability on the termination date is computed as follows:

$9,150,000 × .909090 (present value interest factor = $8,318,174 for $1 at 10% for 1 year)

The expected present value of Miller's termination liability, $8,318,174, is recognized ratably over the next 24 months (i.e., the future service period).

The following journal entry will be made each month for the next 24 months:

Restructuring Expense (8,318,174 / 24)	346,590.48	
Liability for Termination Benefits		346,590.58

During the 12 months from 9/30/X7 (the termination date) until 9/30/X8 (the date of payment of the retention bonus), the liability will increase due to the passage of time and accretion expense will be recognized. The following journal entry will be made each month from 10/1/X7 through 9/30/X8:

Accretion Expense [(9,150,000 – 8,318,174)/12]	69,318.83	
Liability for Termination Benefits		69,318.83

By 9/30/X8, Miller will have a balance of $9,150,000 in the "Liability for Termination Benefits" account. The following journal entry will be recorded on 9/30/X8 for the payment of the retention bonuses:

Liability for Termination Benefits	9,150,000	
Cash		9,150,000

Some termination plans offer both voluntary and involuntary benefits. A voluntary benefit, which is more than the involuntary benefit, is offered to employees who voluntarily terminate their employment. An involuntary benefit is provided to all employees losing their jobs. In this case, a liability for the involuntary benefits is recognized when the restructuring and the benefits under the termination plan are communicated to employees (ASC 420-10-25-10). A liability and an expense, for the difference between the voluntary benefit and the involuntary benefit, are recognized when the employee voluntarily resigns (i.e., at that time the employee accepts the employer's offer and a liability exists). ASC 715 (Compensation—Retirement Benefits) provides additional details on the required accounting.

A liability for costs to terminate a contract before the end of its term shall be recognized and measured at its fair value when the entity terminates the contract in accordance with the contract terms. A liability for costs that will continue to be incurred under a contract for its remaining term without economic benefit to the company shall be recognized and measured at its fair value when the entity ceases using the right conveyed by the contract (e.g., the right to used leased property) (ASC 420-10-25-11, 12, 13).

Other costs associated with an exit or disposal activity include, but are not limited to, costs to consolidate or close facilities and relocate employees. A liability for costs of this type are recognized and measured at fair value in the period in which the liability is incurred, which generally is when goods or services associated with the activity are received. The liability shall not be recognized before it is incurred, even if the costs are incremental to other operating costs and will be incurred as a direct result of a plan (ASC 420-10-25-14, 15).

PRACTICE POINTER: Note that many costs associated with a restructuring (e.g., costs of consolidating facilities, closing facilities, and relocating employees) are not recognized until the period when the cost is incurred. Generally, this is the period when the goods or services associated with the restructuring activity are received. This treatment differs from the treatment afforded one-time termination benefits and that afforded the costs associated with terminating a contract. The liability associated with one-time termination benefits is either recorded on the communication date or gradually recognized over the interval between the communication date and the termination date (see the two illustrations of one-time termination benefits, preceding). The liability associated with terminating a contract is recognized on the contract termination date. Note that by limiting those costs that can be recognized as a liability before the period when goods or services are received, the judgment required in establishing reserves for restructuring activity is reduced, which is designed to limit management's ability to manage income by establishing overly large restructuring reserves and then reversing these reserves in future periods with the effect of increasing income.

Reporting and Disclosure

Costs associated with an exit or disposal activity that does not involve a discontinued operation shall be included in income from continuing operations before taxes in the income statement of a business enterprise and in income from continuing operations in the statement of activities of a not-for-profit organization. If a subtotal "Income from Operations" is presented, it shall include the amounts of those costs. Costs associated with an exit or disposal activity that is presented as a discontinued operation are included in the results of discontinued operations (ASC 420-10-45-3).

If an event or circumstance occurs that discharges an entity's previously recognized liability for an exit or disposal activity, then the liability shall be reversed and the related costs reversed through the same line item in the income statement (statement of activities) used when the liability was previously recognized (ASC 420-10-40-1).

The following information shall be disclosed in notes to financial statements in the period in which an exit or disposal activity is initiated, and in future periods until the exit or disposal activity is completed (ASC 420-10-50-1):

- A description of the exit or disposal activity, including the facts and circumstances leading to the expected activity and the expected completion date
- For each major type of costs associated with the activity:
  - The total amount expected to be incurred in connection with the activity, the amount incurred in the period, and the cumulative amount incurred to date
  - A reconciliation of the beginning and ending liability balances showing separately the changes during the period attributable to costs incurred and charged to expense, costs paid or otherwise settled, and adjustments to the liability with an explanation of the reasons for those adjustments
- The line item in the income statement (statement of activities) in which the costs described above are aggregated
- For each reportable segment, the total amount of costs expected to be incurred in connection with the activity, the amount incurred in the period, and the cumulative amount incurred to date, net of any adjustments to the liability with an explanation of the reason(s) therefore
- If a liability for a cost associated with the activity is not recognized because fair value cannot be reasonably determined, that fact and the reasons therefore

PART II: INTERPRETIVE GUIDANCE

ASC 420-10: EXIT OR DISPOSAL COST OBLIGATIONS

ASC 420-10-55-1, 55-16, 55-19; ASC 715-30-60-4 Evaluating Whether a One-Time Termination Benefit Offered in Connection with an Exit or Disposal Activity Is Essentially an Enhancement to an Ongoing Benefit Arrangement

Question: Under what circumstances are additional termination benefits offered in connection with an exit or disposal activity considered, in substance (*a*) enhancements to an ongoing benefit arrangement and, therefore, subject to the provisions of ASC 715, and ASC 712, or (*b*) one-time termination benefits subject to the guidance in ASC 420?

Answer: Certain companies offer postretirement (e.g., pension and health care) and other postemployment benefits to employees under the terms of an ongoing employee benefit plan. Those types of benefit plans are accounted for under the terms discussed in ASC 715, and ASC 712. The issue is whether a one-time termination benefit should be accounted for under the terms discussed in ASC, or ASC 712 or under the terms of ASC 420. The guidance in ASC 715, or ASC 712, applies if an additional termination benefit amends the terms of an existing pension, other postretirement, or postemployment benefit arrangement. For example, if a company has an employee benefit plan providing that employees who are terminated for reasons other than cause will receive one week of salary for every year of service, the provisions of ASC 712 would apply if, as part of an exit or disposal activity, that plan is revised to provide that each involuntarily terminated employee will receive *two* weeks of salary for every year of service, and the revised terms of the employee benefit plan would apply to future exit or disposal activities. If, however, the terms of the ongoing employee benefit arrangement are *not* revised, and an additional termination benefit only applies to an exit or disposal activity that occurs in the current year, the provisions of ASC 420 would apply.

ASC 420-10-60-3; ASC 450-10-60-7; ASC 710-10-60-4; ASC 712-10-60-1; ASC 715-60-60-2; ASC 805-20-55-50, 55-51
Recognition of Liabilities for Contractual Termination Benefits or Changing Benefit Plan Assumptions in Anticipation of a Business Combination

BACKGROUND

The timing of liability recognition for termination benefits paid to involuntarily terminated employees for a plan that is governed by an *existing contractual agreement* that will be implemented only if a business combination occurs is addressed in this Issue.

The guidance applies, but is not limited to, the following types of agreements, which are referred to here as *contractual termination benefits:*

- Golden parachute employment agreements that require payment if control changes in a business combination
- Union agreements requiring payment of termination benefits for involuntary terminations when a plant closes as a result of a business combination
- Postemployment plans requiring payments for involuntary terminations due to a business combination

Curtailment losses also may be incurred as a result of the write-off of unrecognized prior service costs and a change in the projected benefit obligation from a significant reduction in the expected years of future service of current employees. Payments under the above-mentioned agreements are addressed.

Guidance on loss recognition for curtailments and liabilities is provided in ASC 450-20-25-1 to 25-7, ASC 715-30, ASC 715-20, ASC 715-60, 715-70, and ASC 712-10. To recognize a loss under ASC 450, which is the primary source of guidance on loss accruals, it must be probable before the financial statements are issued that an asset has been impaired or a liability has been incurred at the date of the financial statements and the amount of the loss is reasonably estimable. The guidance in ASC 715-30 provides that a loss and a liability should be recognized for a pension plan curtailment and for contractual termination benefits when it is probable that a curtailment will occur or that employees will be entitled to contractual benefits and the amount can be reasonably estimated. Comparable guidance for other postretirement curtailment losses is provided under the guidance in ASC 715-60. Costs related to the termination of employees under a postemployment benefit plan may result in curtailment losses or accruals for contractual termination benefits under the guidance in ASC 712-10.

In the situation addressed below, a transaction in which an entity has agreed to a business combination is discussed. The entity's management believes that the combination is probable and has developed a plan under which certain employees will be terminated if the combination is consummated. Termination benefits will be paid under a preexisting plan or contractual relationship.

ACCOUNTING ISSUE

Should a liability for contractual termination benefits and curtailment losses under an employee benefit plan that will be triggered when a business combination is consummated be recognized when it is probable that the business combination will occur or when the business combination is consummated?

ACCOUNTING GUIDANCE

An entity should recognize a liability for contractual termination benefits and curtailment losses under employee benefit plans that are triggered by a business combination only when the business combination is consummated.

DISCUSSION

The guidance is based on the view that a business combination is not merely a confirming event—it is the necessary event that triggers a contractual obligation to pay termination benefits when an entity undergoes a business combination. Proponents argued that an entity can avoid liability recognition until a business combination has been consummated. In addition, the FASB staff believes that if a business combination is considered a discrete event, a liability for contractual termination benefits should be recognized only when the business combination has been consummated, because the effects of a business combination should not be recognized until it has occurred.

CHAPTER 31

ASC 430—DEFERRED REVENUE AND CONTRACT LIABILITIES

ASC 430 does not provide any unique guidance but rather only provides a link to guidance on deferred and contract liabilities in other ASC subtopics (ASC 430-10-05-1).

CHAPTER 32

ASC 440—COMMITMENTS

CONTENTS

GENERAL GUIDANCE

ASC 440-10: OVERALL

OVERVIEW

The authoritative accounting literature contains disclosure requirements for many types of long-term obligations. These include unrecorded obligations (e.g., unrecorded unconditional purchase obligations), as well as recorded obligations (e.g., recorded purchase obligations, debt maturities, required stock redemptions).

Other pronouncements cover disclosure requirements for specific types of obligations (e.g., ASC 842 (Leases)).

For unrecorded unconditional purchase obligations, ASC 440 requires disclosure of the nature and terms of the obligation, amounts of the obligation as of the latest balance sheet date, and for each of the next five years, a description of any variable portion of the obligation and amounts purchased under the obligation for each period for which an income statement is presented. Similar disclosures are required for recorded obligations, including purchase obligations, debt maturities, and capital stock redemption requirements.

BACKGROUND

Enterprises and/or individuals frequently acquire assets or liabilities by written contract. A contract may contain unconditional rights and obligations or conditional rights and obligations. A right or obligation is unconditional when only the passage of time is necessary for it to mature. A conditional right or obligation is one that matures only on the occurrence of one or more events that are specified in the contract.

If a significant period elapses between the execution and subsequent performance of a contract, an issue may arise as to when, if at all, the assets and/or liabilities created by the contract should be recognized by the contracting parties. Under existing accounting practices, assets and/or liabilities that are created by a contract may not be recognized at all, or may be either recognized in the accounts or disclosed in a note to the financial statements.

Under existing accounting principles, exchanges between enterprises or individuals usually are recorded when the transfer of resources, services, and/or obligations occurs. Unfulfilled purchase commitments for the future exchange of resources, services, and/or obligations, however, are not recorded until the commitment is at least partially fulfilled by one of the contracting parties. Exceptions to the general rule for unfulfilled purchase commitments are certain leases and losses on firm noncancelable purchase commitments, which are recorded under existing accounting principles.

PRACTICE POINTER: The disclosure of certain contractual rights or obligations is sometimes confused with the disclosure of a contingency. The disclosure of a contingency is necessary only when a contingent *gain* or *loss* exists in accordance with the provisions of ASC 450 (Contingencies). If there is no contingent *gain* or *loss*, disclosure is not required. On the other hand, the disclosure of information on certain contractual rights or obligations may be required by U.S. GAAP to avoid financial statements that are misleading.

A situation may arise in which the disclosure of a contractual obligation is required by U.S. GAAP and—at the same time—a *loss contingency* may exist involving the same contractual obligation. In this event, disclose the information concerning both the obligation and the contingency in accordance with U.S. GAAP.

PURCHASE OBLIGATIONS

Unconditional Purchase Obligations

For the purposes of ASC 440, an *unconditional purchase obligation* is one in which one party is required to transfer funds in the future to another party in return for delivery of specified quantities of goods or services at fixed or minimum prices (ASC Glossary).

PRACTICE NOTE: In contrast, an unconditional purchase obligation to transfer assets other than funds to another party in return for specified quantities of goods or services at specified prices is not considered an unconditional obligation and, apparently, would not be covered by ASC 440.

For ASC 440 disclosure requirements to apply, an unconditional purchase obligation must be associated with the financing arrangements (*a*) for the facilities that will provide the contracted goods or services or (*b*) relating to the costs of the contracted goods or services (such as carrying costs). Unconditional purchase obligations that have a remaining term of one year or less are excluded from the provisions of ASC 440 (ASC 440-1-50-2). An unconditional purchase obligation qualifies for disclosure even though it is cancelable because of (ASC 440-10-50-2):

- A remote contingency
- Permission of the other party
- A replacement agreement between the same parties
- A provision for a penalty payment in an amount that reasonably assures the continuation of the agreement

The provisions in ASC 440 dealing with unrecorded purchase obligations are primarily directed to take-or-pay contracts and throughput contracts.

PRACTICE POINTER: In a *take-or-pay contract,* a buyer agrees to pay certain periodic amounts for certain products or services. The buyer must make the specified periodic payments, even though it does not take delivery of the products or services.

In a *throughput contract,* one party agrees to pay certain periodic amounts to another party for the transportation or processing of a product (e.g., an oil pipeline). The periodic payments must be made, even though the minimum quantities specified in the agreement in each period have not been sent to the other party for transporting or processing.

In take-or-pay contracts and throughput contracts, the periodic payments are unconditional and are not dependent on the occurrence of a specified event or the fulfillment of a condition.

Disclosure of Unrecorded Unconditional Purchase Obligations

ASC 440 requires disclosure of information for unrecorded unconditional purchase obligations that are (*a*) substantially noncancelable, (*b*) associated with the financing arrangements for the facilities that will provide the contracted goods or services or related to the costs of the contracted goods or services (such as carrying costs), and (*c*) for a remaining term in excess of one year. The following information is to be disclosed (ASC 440-10-50-4):

- A description of the nature and term of the obligation
- The total fixed and determinable amount of unrecorded unconditional purchase obligations as of the latest balance sheet date, and the total determinable amount of unrecorded unconditional purchase obligations for each of the five years after the latest balance sheet date
- A description of the nature of any variable component of the unrecorded unconditional purchase obligations
- For each income statement presented, the amounts actually purchased under the unconditional purchase obligations

---

PRACTICE POINTER: An unconditional obligation may consist of a determinable portion and a variable portion. The determinable portion is quantified and disclosed in accordance with item (2) above. The variable portion need not be quantified, but the nature of such amounts must be disclosed in accordance with item (3) above.

Similar or related obligations may be combined and disclosures are not required if the aggregate commitment of all unrecorded unconditional purchase obligations is immaterial.

ASC 842 (Leases) requires the disclosure of certain lease payments. Lease payments that are not required to be disclosed in accordance with ASC 842, however, must be disclosed if they meet the requirements for disclosure outlined in ASC 440 (ASC 440-10-50-3).

PRACTICE NOTE: Apparently, ASC 440 requires the disclosure of certain leases that were specifically excluded from ASC 842, if such leases are (*a*) substantially noncancelable, (*b*) part of the financing arrangements for the facilities that will provide specified goods or services, or related to the costs of the specified goods or services, and (*c*) for a remaining term in excess of one year. The following types of leases and similar agreements were expressly excluded from ASC 842 and may require disclosure under the provisions of ASC 440:

1. Natural resource leases, including oil, gas, minerals, and timber
2. Leases involving services only
3. Licensing agreements, including motion picture films, plays, manuscripts, patents, and copyrights

---

ASC 440 does not require, but does encourage, the disclosure of the present value of the total determinable amounts of unrecorded unconditional purchase obligations for each of the five years after the latest balance sheet date (item 2 above). In computing the present value of an obligation, the discount rate usually is the effective interest rate at the inception of the borrowings that (*a*) financed the project or (*b*) are associated with the unrecorded unconditional purchase obligations. If it is not practical to determine the discount rate, or if there are no borrowings associated with the obligations, the discount rate is the purchaser's incremental borrowing rate. The purchaser's incremental borrowing rate is the rate the purchaser would have incurred at the inception of the obligation to borrow funds, on similar terms, to discharge the unconditional purchase obligation (ASC 440-10-50-5).

DISCLOSURE OF RECOGNIZED COMMITMENTS

In addition to requiring disclosure of information about unrecognized commitments, ASC 440 requires disclosure of similar information for recognized commitments. A purchaser shall disclose for each of the five years following the date of the latest balance sheet presented the aggregate amount of payments for recognized unconditional purchase obligations that meet the criteria stated above for unrecognized commitments. The information to be disclosed is the same as that stated above for unrecognized commitments (ASC 440-10-50-6, 7).

PRACTICE NOTE: The requirement to disclose the payments due in each of the next five years on recorded obligations is sometimes overlooked, according to several studies of disclosure deficiencies in financial statements. This may be because ASC 440 is erroneously thought of as requiring disclosure only for unrecorded obligations. While it does cover unrecorded obligations, it also applies to recorded obligations.

Illustration of Take-or-Pay, Throughput, and Similar Contracts

During 20X5, Memphis Company entered into a long-term contract to purchase all of the widgets produced by a supplier. The contract expires in 20Y3, and Memphis Company must make minimum annual payments to the supplier, whether or not it takes delivery of the widgets. The minimum total payments for each of the five and later years succeeding December 31, 20X5, are as follows:

Year	*Total Payments (in thousands)*
20X6	$ 4,000
20X7	12,000
20X8	14,000
20X9	10,000
20Y0	12,000
Subsequent years	28,000
Total	80,000
Less: Imputed interest	(30,000)
Present value of payments	$50,000

Illustration of Maturities and Sinking Fund Requirements

Maturities of long-term debt and sinking fund requirements on long-term debt for each of the five years* succeeding December 31, 20X5, are as follows:

Year	*Long-Term Debt and Sinking Fund Requirements*
20X6	$50,000
20X7	50,000
20X8	100,000
20X9	100,000
20Y0	50,000

Illustration of Redemption of Capital Stock

Mandatory redemption requirements for all classes of capital stock for each of the five years* succeeding December 31, 20X5, are as follows:

Year	*4% Preferred*	*7% Preferred*
20X6	$ 200,000	$ 400,000
20X7	200,000	400,000
20X8	200,000	400,000
20X9	none	400,000
20Y0	none	400,000

ASC 440 requires a statement about the nature and term of the obligation, and may be the appropriate place for an enterprise to describe the associated benefits, if any. The lack of explicit requirements to disclose associated benefits does not preclude an enterprise from describing those benefits.

PRACTICE NOTE: ASC 440 contains specific disclosure requirements for recorded and unrecorded take-or-pay and throughput contracts (ASC 440-10-50-4). Both of these types of contracts are considered unconditional obligations under the provisions of ASC 440. However, a take-or-pay or throughput contract may, in substance, be a product financing arrangement. A product financing arrangement may also require unconditional periodic payments that are not dependent on the occurrence of a specified event or the fulfillment of a specified condition. Product financing arrangements are covered in this Guide in the chapter covering ASC 470-40 (Debt—Product Financing Arrangements).

* ASC 440 does *not* require the disclosure of the above information for periods subsequent to the fifth year.

* ASC 440 does *not* require the disclosure of the above information for periods subsequent to the fifth year.

CHAPTER 33

ASC 450—CONTINGENCIES

CONTENTS

PART I: GENERAL GUIDANCE

ASC 450-10: OVERALL

OVERVIEW

Contingencies are an important aspect of financial reporting in accordance with U.S. GAAP due to uncertainties surrounding many elements of the financial statements. Significant judgment is required in presenting information that assists financial statement users in assessing the amount, timing, and uncertainty of future cash flows. Standards governing accounting for loss contingencies require accrual and/or note disclosure when specified recognition and disclosure criteria are met. Gain contingencies generally are not recognized in financial statements but may be disclosed.

ASC 275 (Risks and Uncertainties) contains material that is closely related to the material on contingencies in ASC 450 and has broad applicability, particularly in four areas:

1. Nature of an entity's operations
2. Use of certain information in the preparation of financial statements
3. Certain significant estimates
4. Current vulnerability to concentrations

For coverage of ASC 275, see Chapter 15, *ASC 275—Risks and Uncertainties.*

BACKGROUND

A *contingency* is an existing condition, situation, or set of circumstances involving uncertainty that may, through one or more related future events, result in the acquisition or loss of an asset or the incurrence or avoidance of a liability, usually with the concurrence of a gain or loss. The resulting gain or loss is referred to as a *gain contingency* or a *loss contingency.*

The existence of a loss contingency may be established on or before the date of the financial statements, or after the date of the financial statements but prior to the issuance of the financial statements. When a loss contingency is determined to exist as a result of a past transaction, the probability of one or more future events confirming that loss must be evaluated. In addition to the future event confirming the loss, it may also be important in appropriately measuring the amount of that loss. Accounting for a loss contingency is based on the degree of probability that one or more future events will occur that will confirm that a loss has already occurred as a result of one or more past transactions or events. Gain contingencies are ordinarily not recorded until they are actually realized, although note disclosure in the financial statements may be necessary.

PRACTICE POINTER: Two important judgments are required in accounting for loss contingencies. First is whether a past event has already occurred that will be confirmed, or not confirmed, by one or more future events. Second is the ability to estimate the dollar amount of any potential loss. These two judgments essentially drive the accounting for loss contingencies (i.e., whether a loss should be accrued and/or disclosed). Disclosures of certain risks and uncertainties are subject to a lower threshold and may not be directly tied to past events in the same manner as contingencies.

Loss contingencies may arise from the risk of exposure resulting from items such as the following (ASC 450-20-05-3):

- Collectibility of receivables
- Property loss by fire, explosion, or other hazards
- Expropriation of assets
- Pending or threatened litigation, claims, or assessments
- Guarantees of indebtedness of others
- Obligations relating to product warranties or defects
- Risk of loss from catastrophic losses of property

PRACTICE POINTER: Not all uncertainties in the accounting process are *contingencies*, as that term is used in ASC 450. Many estimates that are inherent in the financial reporting process are *not* contingencies, and the authoritative literature covered in this section does *not* apply. For example, depreciable assets have a reasonably estimated life, and depreciation expense is used to allocate the cost of the asset systematically over its estimated useful life. The uncertainty regarding the useful life of the asset is not considered to be a contingency under ASC 450.

PRACTICE NOTE: ASC 450 does not apply to accounting for income taxes. ASC 740 addresses the uncertainty associated with income taxes. Also, ASC 450 does not apply to the measurement of credit losses for instruments within the scope of ASC 326 on measurement of credit losses.

ASC 450-20: LOSS CONTINGENCIES

LOSS CONTINGENCIES

Classification

A loss contingency is determined to be an actual loss only upon the occurrence of one or more future events, whose likelihood of occurring may vary significantly. The likelihood that future events will confirm a loss are classified as (*a*) probable (likely to occur), (*b*) reasonably possible (between *probable* and *remote*), or (*c*) remote (low chance of occurring) (ASC 450-20-25-1).

The accounting treatment for loss contingencies flows logically from the three ranges of probability described in the previous paragraph. Figure 33-1 provides the general structure of accounting that is required.

Accounting and Reporting

Depending upon the probability that future events(s) will confirm the loss, loss contingencies are classified as probable, reasonably possible, or remote. This leads to three possible accounting outcomes: (*a*) accrue the contingent loss as a charge to income as of the date of the financial statements, (*b*) disclose the contingent loss in a note to the financial statements, or (*c*) neither accrue nor disclose the loss.

The following two conditions must be met for a *loss contingency* to be accrued as a charge to income as of the date of the financial statements (ASC 450-20-25-2):

1. It is *probable* that, as of the date of the financial statements, an asset has been impaired or a liability incurred, based on information available before the actual issuance date of the financial statements. Implicit in this condition is that it is *probable* that one or more future events will occur to confirm the loss.
2. The amount of loss can be estimated reasonably.

PRACTICE POINTER: If a loss contingency is classified as *probable* and only a range of possible loss (similar to a minimum-maximum) can be established, then the **minimum** amount in the range is accrued, unless some other amount within the range appears to be a better estimate (ASC 450-20-30-1). The range of possible loss must also be disclosed.

Loss contingencies that are accrued ordinarily also require note disclosure so that the financial statements are not misleading. This disclosure ordinarily consists of the nature of the contingency and, in some circumstances, the amount accrued. The term *reserve* should only be used for an amount of unidentified or unsegregated assets held for a specific purpose (ASC 450-20-50-1).

Illustration of Accrued Contingent Liability

Following is a pro forma illustration of disclosure of a loss contingency for which the probability of future events confirming a loss is high and for which an amount can be reasonably estimated:

> During 20X8, the Company became aware of past circumstances (describe nature of contingency) that management believes are likely to require recognition of a loss(es) in future year(s). While the exact amount of this (these) loss(es) is not known, a reasonable estimate, based on information currently available, is $XXX. This amount has been recognized as a loss in the current year and appears as a contingent liability (provide title) in the 20X8 statement of financial position. Recognition of this loss had the impact of reducing net income and earnings per share by $XX and $XX, respectively, in 20X8.

If one or both conditions for the accrual of a loss contingency is/are not met and the likelihood of loss is considered either *probable* or *reasonably possible*, financial statement disclosure of the loss contingency is required. The disclosure shall contain a description of the nature of the loss contingency and the range of possible loss, or include a statement that an estimate of the loss cannot be made (ASC 450-20-50-3, 4). However, these disclosures are not required for credit losses on instruments within the scope of ASC 326 on measurement of credit losses (ASC 450-20-50-2A).

Figure 33-1: Probability That Future Event(s) Will Confirm Loss

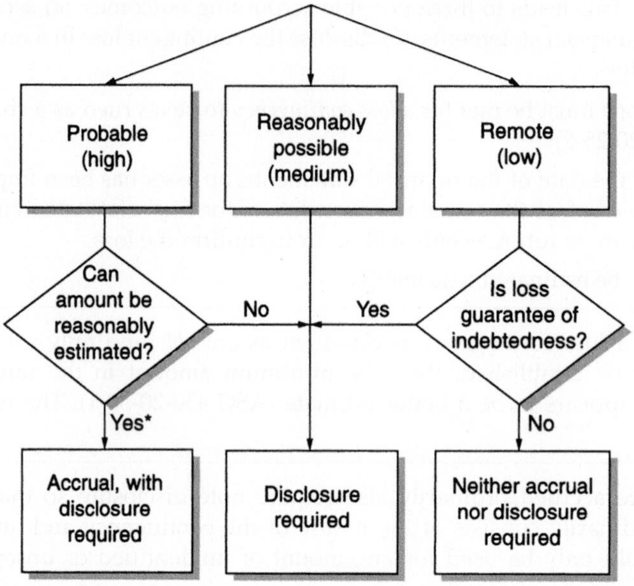

* Includes estimation of a range of loss, in which case the minimum amount is accrued and the amount of the range is disclosed.

Litigation, Claims, or Assessments

If both conditions for the accrual of a loss contingency are met, an accrual for the estimated amount of pending or threatened litigation and actual or possible claims or assessments is required. Factors that should be considered in determining whether the conditions for accrual have been met include (*a*) the nature of the litigation, claim, or assessment, (*b*) progress of the case, including progress after the date of the financial statements but before the issuance date of the financial statements, (*c*) opinions of legal counsel, and (*d*) management's intended response to the litigation, claim, or assessment (ASC 450-20-55-12).

Illustration of Disclosed Loss Contingency

Following is a pro forma illustration of disclosure of a loss contingency for which the probability of future events confirming the loss is reasonably possible and for which the outcome is sufficiently uncertain that accrual is not appropriate:

During 20X8, a suit was filed against the company by a former employee alleging that the company engaged in discriminatory employment practices. The suit requests damages of $1,000,000. Management has indicated its plans to vigorously contest this suit and believes that the loss, if any, resulting from the suit will not have a material impact on the company's financial position, results of operations, or cash flows in future years.

Product or Service Warranty Obligation

A product or service warranty obligation is a contingency under the provisions of ASC 450, because of the potential claims that may result from the warranty. If both of the conditions for the accrual of a loss contingency are met, an accrual for the estimated amount of a warranty obligation must be made even if the warranty obligation cannot be identified specifically. An enterprise may base its estimate of a warranty obligation on its prior experience, the experience of other enterprises in the same industry, and/or an appraisal of current economic conditions. If an enterprise is unable to estimate reasonably the amount of its warranty obligation and the range of possible loss is wide, significant uncertainty exists as to whether a sale should be recorded before the expiration of the warranty period or until sufficient experience has been gained to permit a reasonable estimate of the obligation (ASC 460-10-25-6).

Loss Contingencies Arising after the Date of the Financial Statements

A loss contingency that is classified as *probable* or *reasonably possible*, that occurs after the balance sheet date but before the issuance date of the financial statements, may have to be disclosed to avoid misleading financial statements. If professional judgment deems this type of disclosure necessary, the disclosure shall contain a description of the nature of the loss contingency and the range of possible loss, or include a statement that no estimate of the loss can be made. It may be desirable to disclose this type of loss contingency by supplementing the historical financial statements with pro forma statements reflecting the loss as if it occurred at the date of the financial statements (ASC 450-20-50-10).

PRACTICE POINTER: Disclosing loss contingencies that arise after the date of the financial statements may require either adjustment to the financial statements or note disclosure, depending on the nature of the loss contingency. If the subsequent event confirms or provides additional information on a condition that existed at the financial statement date, make an adjustment to the financial statements. Otherwise, disclose the loss contingency, which, in some cases, may be made best by presenting pro forma restated financial information as a part of the note disclosure.

Unasserted Claims or Assessments

An *unasserted claim* is one that has not been asserted by the claimant because the claimant has no knowledge of the existing claim or has not elected to assert the existing claim. If it is *probable* that an unasserted claim will be asserted by the claimant and it is *probable* or *reasonably possible* that an unfavorable outcome will result, the unasserted claim must be disclosed in the financial statements. If these conditions are not met, however, disclosure is not required for unasserted claims or assessments in which the potential claimant apparently has no knowledge of the claim's existence (ASC 450-20-55-14, 15).

Disclosure of Noninsured Property

An enterprise may be underinsured or not insured at all against the risk of future loss or damage to its property by fire, explosion, or other hazard. The fact that an enterprise's property is underinsured or not insured constitutes an existing uncertainty as defined by ASC 450. The absence of insurance does not mean, however, that an asset has been impaired or a liability incurred as of the date of the financial statements (ASC 450-20-55-5). ASC 450 does not require financial statement disclosure of noninsurance or underinsurance of possible losses, but specifically states that it does not discourage this practice (ASC 450-20-50-7).

PRACTICE POINTER: The removal of insurance does not, in and of itself, mean that a loss has already been incurred and that a contingent liability should be recorded. While the uninsured enterprise assumes greater risk than an insured one, a contingent loss results from a past event and the removal of insurance does not qualify for such an event.

Appropriations of Retained Earnings

ASC 450 does not prohibit an enterprise from appropriating specific amounts of retained earnings for potential loss contingencies. The amount of appropriated retained earnings, however, must be reported within the stockholders' equity section of the balance sheet and clearly identified as an appropriation of retained earnings. In addition, the following rules must be observed (ASC 505-10-45-3, 4):

- No costs or losses shall be charged against the appropriated retained earnings and no part of the appropriated retained earnings may be transferred to income or in any way used to affect the determination of net income for any period.
- The appropriated retained earnings shall be restored intact to retained earnings when the appropriation is no longer considered necessary.

ACQUISITION CONTINGENCIES

Measurement at the Acquisition Date

The acquirer *does not apply* the guidance in ASC 450 in determining which assets and liabilities arising from contingencies to recognize as of the acquisition date. ASC 805 provides this guidance and further details are provided in our discussion of ASC 805.

In addition, ASC 450 does not apply to contingent gains and losses that are recognized at the acquisition or merger date if the acquisition or merger involves not-for-profit entities. Guidance on the subsequent accounting for contingent gains and losses recognized at the acquisition or merger date is provided in ACC 958. However, ASC 450 does apply to contingent gains and losses that existed at the acquisition or merger date but were not recognized because they did not meet the recognition criteria in ASC 958.

Subsequent Measurement and Accounting

In general, the assets acquired, liabilities assumed or incurred, and equity instruments issued in a business combination shall be subsequently measured and accounted for by the acquirer in accordance with other applicable U.S. GAAP.

An asset or liability arising from a contingency recognized as of the acquisition date, that would be in the scope of ASC 450 if not acquired or assumed in a business combination, shall continue to be recognized by the acquirer at its acquisition-date fair value unless new information is obtained about the possible outcome of the contingency. When new information is obtained, the acquirer must evaluate that information and measure an asset at the *lower* of its acquisition-date fair value or the best estimate of its future settlement amount, while a liability is measured at the *higher* of its acquisition-date fair value or the amount that would be recognized under ASC 450. An asset or liability arising from a contingency shall only be derecognized by the acquirer when the contingency is resolved.

ASC 450-30: GAIN CONTINGENCIES

GAIN CONTINGENCIES

As a general rule, gain contingencies may be disclosed in the financial statements by note, but should not be reflected in income, because doing so may result in recognizing revenue prior to its realization. Care should be exercised in disclosing gain contingencies to avoid misleading implications concerning the recognition of revenue prior to its realization (ASC 450-30-25-1; 450-30-50-1).

PART II: INTERPRETIVE GUIDANCE

ASC 450-20: LOSS CONTINGENCIES

ASC 450-20-S25-1, S50-2, S99-2 Accounting for Legal Costs Expected to Be Incurred in Connection with a Loss Contingency

The accounting for legal costs expected to be incurred in connection with a loss contingency under the guidance in ASC 450 was discussed. It was noted that practice is to expense such costs, but some suggested that accounting practice for such costs is mixed. Although the Emerging Issues Task Force decided not to discuss this matter any further, the SEC Observer stated that the SEC staff expects registrants to apply their accounting policies consistently and to disclose material accounting policies and the methods of applying those policies in accordance with the requirements in ASC 235-10-05 and 10-50.

CHAPTER 34

ASC 460—GUARANTEES

CONTENTS

PART I: GENERAL GUIDANCE

ASC 460-10: OVERALL

OVERVIEW

Guarantees are a relatively common business transaction. Examples include (1) the guarantee of the indebtedness of another party, (2) obligations of commercial banks under "standby letters of credit," and (3) guarantees to repurchase receivables that have been sold. The FASB observed differences in how companies interpret the need for issuers of guarantees to recognize a liability and the disclosures required by issuers of guarantees. ASC 460 clarifies these issues.

BACKGROUND

ASC 460 does not specify the subsequent accounting for guarantees that have been recognized. If a guarantee represents a derivative financial instrument, appropriate accounting is in conformity with ASC 815 (Derivatives and Hedging). For guarantees within the scope of ASC 326-20, the expected credit loss (i.e., the contingent aspect) of the guarantee must be accounted for in accordance with that Subtopic in addition to and separately from the fair value (i.e., noncontingent aspect) of the guarantee liability accounted for in accordance with ASC 460-10-30-5. If the guarantee does not qualify for derivative accounting under ASC 815 and is not within the scope of ASC 326-20 on financial instruments measured at amortized cost, guidance is provided by ASC 460 (ASC 460-10-35-4).

ACCOUNTING FOR GUARANTEES

ASC 460 applies to guarantees that have any of the following characteristics:

- Contracts that contingently require the guarantor to make payments in cash, financial instruments, other assets, shares of its stock, or provision of services to the guaranteed party based on changes in the *underlying* that is related to an asset, liability, or an equity security of the guaranteed party (ASC 460-10-15-4).

PRACTICE NOTE: ASC 815 uses the term *underlying* to denote a specified interest rate, security price, commodity price, foreign exchange rate, index of price or rate, or other variable. An underlying may be a price or rate of an asset or liability but is not the asset or liability itself.

- Contracts that contingently require the guarantor to make payments to the guaranteed party based on another entity's failure to perform under an obligating agreement (ASC 460-10-15-4).
- Indemnification agreements that contingently require the indemnifying party to make payments to the indemnified party based on changes in an underlying that is related to an asset, liability, or equity security of the indemnified party (ASC 460-10-15-4).
- Indirect guarantees of the indebtedness of others (ASC 460-10-15-4).

Commercial letters of credit or other loan commitments that are commonly thought of as guarantees of funding are not included in the scope of ASC 460 because they do not meet the characteristics of guarantees as previously stated. Similarly, the scope of ASC 460 does not include indemnifications or guarantees based on an entity's own future performance (ASC 460-10-55-16). Exceptions to the disclosure requirements listed above apply to all items listed in ASC 460-10-15-7.

The provisions of ASC 460 related to recognizing a liability do *not* apply to the following, but the disclosure requirements of ASC 460 do apply in these circumstances (ASC 460-10-25-1):

- Product warranties or other guarantees for which the underlying is related to performance (regarding function, not price) of nonfinancial assets that are owned by the guaranteed party
- Guarantees that are accounted for as derivatives
- Guarantees that represent contingent consideration in a business combination (or an acquisition involving a not-for-profit entity)
- Guarantees for which the guarantor's obligation would be reported by an equity item (i.e., rather than a liability) under U.S. GAAP
- An original lessee's guarantee of lease payments when the lessee remains secondarily liable in conjunction with being relieved from being the primary obligor under a lease restructuring
- Guarantees issued between either parents and their subsidiaries or corporations under common control
- A parent's guarantee of a subsidiary's debt to a third party, and a subsidiary's guarantee of the debt owed to a third party by either its parent or another subsidiary of the parent

Disclosure of Guarantees

ASC 460 clarified that a guarantor is required to disclose the following information (ASC 460-10-50-4):

- The nature of the guarantee, including the approximate term of the guarantee, how it arose, and the events or circumstances that would require the guarantor to perform under the guarantee
- The maximum potential amount of future payments under the guarantee
- The carrying amount of the liability, if any, for the guarantor's obligations under the guarantee
- The nature and extent of any recourse provisions or available collateral that would enable the guarantor to recover the amounts paid under the guarantee

For product warranties, the guarantor is required to disclose its accounting policy and method of determining its liability under the warranty rather than disclosing the maximum potential amount for future payments under the guarantee. In addition, a tabular reconciliation of the changes in the guarantor's product warranty liability for the reporting period is required (ASC 460-10-50-8).

Recognition of a Guarantee Liability

In addition to specifying the disclosure requirements for guarantee liabilities, ASC 460 clarifies that a guarantor is required to recognize, at the inception of a guarantee, a liability for the obligations it has undertaken, including its ongoing obligations to perform under the terms of a guarantee in the event the specified triggering events or conditions occur. The initial recording of the liability should be the fair value of the guarantee at its inception (ASC 460-10-25-4; 460-10-30-2).

When a liability due to the issuance of a guarantee is recorded, the nature of the offsetting debit depends on the nature of the original transaction giving rise to the guarantee (ASC 460-10-55-23). If the guarantee is issued in a standalone transaction *for consideration*, cash or a receivable is recognized. If the guarantee is issued in a standalone transaction to an unrelated party *for no consideration*, an expense is recognized. If the guarantee is issued as part of a sale of assets, a product, or a business, the consideration received in the sale is allocated between the guarantee and the assets, product, or business sold. If the guarantee relates to the formation of a partially owned business or joint venture, an increase in the value of the investment account is recognized.

The FASB states that some entities may not recognize liabilities for a guarantee because (1) the recognition requirements in ASC 450 related to loss contingencies have not been met at the inception of the guarantee, and (2) the premium for the guarantee was not separately identified because it was embedded in purchase or sales agreements, service contracts, joint venture agreements, or other commercial agreements. ASC 460 requires the entity to record the fair value of a guarantee at inception, even if it is *not* probable that payments will be required under the guarantee (ASC 460-10-25-3). ASC 460 also indicates that where the premium for the guarantee is not separately identified, it must be estimated. The party issuing the guarantee should consider what the premium would be if the guarantee had been issued on a standalone basis in a transaction with an unrelated party as a practical expedient (ASC 460-10-30-2).

Indirect Guarantees

Indirect guarantees arise under an agreement that obligates one entity to transfer funds to a second entity upon the occurrence of specified events under conditions whereby the funds become legally available to the creditors of the second entity and those creditors may enforce the second entity's claim against the first entity under the agreement (ASC Glossary). Although the risk of loss may be remote, indirect guarantees of the indebtedness of others are required to be disclosed in the financial statements (ASC 460-10-50-2).

PART II: INTERPRETIVE GUIDANCE

ASC 460-10: OVERALL

ASC 460-10-35-2 Whether FASB Interpretation No. 45, *Guarantor's Accounting and Disclosure Requirements for Guarantees, Including Indirect Guarantees of Indebtedness of Others*, Provides Support for Subsequently Accounting for a Guarantor's Liability at Fair Value

Question: Is a guarantor that wishes to report its liability for obligations under a guarantee (including a seller's recourse obligations, if any, included in ASC 460-10-15-4, 25-34, 55-2, 55-5, 55-12 through 55-13 at fair value after initial recognition permitted to cite the guidance in ASC 460 to justify using that accounting method for *subsequent measurement* of the liability?

Answer: No. A guarantor may *not* cite ASC 460 to justify measuring the guarantor's liability for its obligations at fair value after a guarantee has been issued. The guidance in ASC 460 applies only to the measurement of a guarantor's liability for the guarantee when it is initially recognized.

The FASB staff has noted that although ASC 460-10-35-1 through 35-2, 35-4 discusses three methods that are used in practice to measure a liability *after* initial recognition, the discussion is *not* intended to imply that a guarantor can choose any of those methods to subsequently account for a liability. A guarantor should *not* account for a liability for its obligation under a previously issued guarantee at fair value in subsequent periods unless doing so can be justified under generally accepted accounting principles, for example, accounting for a guarantee as a derivative under the guidance in ASC 815. Subsequent to initial recognition, a guarantor that is using fair value to measure its obligations under a guarantee, other than one under the scope of ASC 815, and relying on the guidance in ASC 460 to justify that treatment should reconsider the appropriateness of that treatment.

ASC 460-10-55-1, 55-10 through 55-11; ASC 954-460-55-1 Application of FASB Interpretation No. 45 in Minimum Revenue Guarantees Granted to a Business or Its Owners

BACKGROUND

The guidance below, which has amended the guidance in ASC 460, was issued in response to questions raised by constituents regarding the applicability of the guidance in ASC 460 to a guarantee granted to a business or its owner under which the business or the owner is guaranteed a specified minimum amount of revenue for a specified period of time. For example, a not-for-profit health care facility that recruits a nonemployee physician to establish a practice in a certain area guarantees to make a payment to the physician if the physician's gross revenues do not equal or exceed a specified dollar amount during a specified period of time. In another example, a corporation that wants a daycare center to open a facility next to its plant guarantees to the daycare center that it will earn a minimum amount of revenue per month over a specified period of time (e.g., during the first 12 months). If the daycare center does not earn the guaranteed minimum amount during any month in the first 12 months, the corporation guarantees to make up the shortfall.

ACCOUNTING GUIDANCE

The guidance in ASC 460-10-15-4, 25-34, 50-2, 50-5, 50-12 through 50-13 was amended to provide the following:

- Except as provided in ASC 460-10-15-7, the following provisions of apply to guarantee contracts with the following characteristics, if any:
  - Contracts under which a guarantor is contingently required to make payments (either in cash, financial instruments, other assets, shares of stock, or provision of services) to the guaranteed party based on changes in an *underlying* (as defined in ASC, *Glossary*, that is related to a *guaranteed* party's asset, liability, or equity security).
  - Contracts under which a guarantor is contingently required to make payments to a guaranteed party if another entity does not perform under an obligating agreement (a performance guarantee). Contracts under which a guarantor is contingently required to make payments (either in cash, financial instruments, other assets, shares of its stock, or provision of services) to the guaranteed party based on changes in an *underlying* (as defined in ASC, *Glossary*) that is related to an indemnified party's asset, liability, or equity security.
  - Indirect guarantees of others' indebtedness, even if a payment to a guaranteed party is not based on changes related to a guaranteed party's asset, liability, or equity security.

A guarantor should recognize a liability in its balance sheet at the inception of a guarantee.

The examples in the Background discussion above are codified as an example of a financial guarantee in ASC 460-10-55-2e as follows:

> A guarantee to a business or its owner(s) that revenue earned by a business (or a specific portion of the business) will be at least a specified amount for a specified period of time.

FASB BASIS FOR CONCLUSION

The FASB reached a conclusion that the guarantee discussed under this guidance meets the characteristics discussed in ASC 460-10-55-2, because the guarantee's *underlying,* which, in this case, is the gross revenues of a business or of a business owner, is related to an asset or equity security belonging to the party receiving the guarantee. A business' revenues change as result of transactions with customers. Because the gross revenues of a business are related to changes in its assets or liabilities, a guarantee made to a business meets the characteristics in ASC 460-10-55-2. In addition, a guarantee made to an owner of a business meets the characteristics in ASC 460-10-55-2, because the gross revenues of the business are related to changes in the owner's investment in the business. The FASB further believes that guarantors should account for minimum revenue guarantees under the provisions in ASC 460 because a minimum revenue guarantee granted to a business or its owners does *not* meet any of the scope exceptions in ASC 460-10-15-7, 15-9, 15-10, 25-1, and 30-1.

The FASB noted that the list of examples under the guidance in ASC 460-10-55-23 (FIN-45, paragraph 11) is not a comprehensive all-inclusive list of contracts that would meet the provisions of that paragraph. In addition, minimum revenue guarantees granted to physicians should be accounted for under the provisions of this FSP regardless of whether the physician's practice is considered to be a business under the guidance in ASC 718-10-55-85A; ASC 810-10-05-15 through 05-16, 15-19 through 15-22, 25-61 through 25-64, 25-66 through 25-72, 25-74 through 25-79, 25-81, 55-90, 55-91, and 55-92.

ASC 460-10-55-17 Impact of FASB Interpretation No. 45, *Guarantor's Accounting and Disclosure Requirements for Guarantees, Including Indirect Guarantees of Indebtedness of Others,* on EITF Issue No. 95-1, *Revenue Recognition on Sales with a Guaranteed Minimum Resale Value*

BACKGROUND

The guidance in ASC 460-10-55-17, 60-22; ASC 605-50-60-1; ASC 840-10-55-12 through 55-25, addresses whether a manufacturer should recognize a sale on equipment sold with a resale value guarantee. Under that guidance, a manufacturer should *not* recognize a sale on a transfer of equipment if the buyer receives a resale value guarantee. A conclusion was also reached that the transaction should be accounted for as a lease, based on the guidance in ASC 840, because the buyer has the right to use the equipment from the sales date to the date on which the manufacturer guarantees a minimum resale value for the equipment. Further, classification as a sales-type lease or an operating lease should be based on the calculation of the minimum lease payments, as defined in ASC 840-10-25-4, which would be the difference between the proceeds on the initial transfer of the equipment to the buyer (the selling price) and the manufacturer's residual value guarantee at the first date on which the buyer can exercise the guarantee.

When ASC 460 was issued, the FASB staff determined that the guidance for sales-type leases should be nullified by the guidance in ASC 460 because the guarantee would be related to an asset removed from the manufacturer's books under that type of lease. Some constituents questioned that decision, because under a sales-type lease, a manufacturer would be required to recognize two guarantees for the same asset, that is, once when a sales-type lease transaction is recorded with the amount of the residual value of the equipment remaining on the manufacturer's books and again in accordance with the requirements of ASC 460, at the fair value of the guarantee at inception.

ACCOUNTING ISSUE

How does the guidance in ASC 460 affect the conclusion in ASC 460-10-55-17, 60-22; ASC 605-50-60-1; ASC 840-10-55-12 through 55-25?

ACCOUNTING GUIDANCE

The guidance in ASC 460-10-55-17, 60-22; ASC 605-50-60-1; ASC 840-10-55-12 through 55-25 applies to a sales-type lease, under which a manufacturer guarantees the residual value of equipment transferred under the lease and continues to recognize an asset for the residual value of the guaranteed equipment. A conclusion was reached that the provisions of ASC 460 do *not* affect the guidance in ASC 460-10-55-17, 60-22; ASC 605-50-60-1; ASC 840-10-55-12 through 55-25 related to sales-type leases, because the guidance in ASC 460 does *not* apply to a guarantee for an asset related to an underlying lease recorded on a guarantor's books.

ASC 460-10-55-31 through 55-34 Accounting for Intellectual Property Infringement Indemnification under FIN-45

Question: A software vendor-licensor may include an indemnification clause in a software licensing agreement that indemnifies a licensee against liability and damages arising from any claims of patent, copyright, trademark, or trade secret infringement by the software vendor's software. Does an indemnification of that type constitute a guarantee subject to the scope of ASC 460?

Answer: Yes. An infringement indemnification arrangement requires a guarantor to make a payment to the guaranteed party if an infringement claim against the licensee results in a liability or damage, if any, related to the licensed software. However, because an infringement claim can impair a licensee's ability to use the software, the occurrence of an infringement claim is related to the licensed software's performance. Therefore, an infringement indemnification arrangement falls under the scope of ASC 460 and a liability need not be recognized at the inception of the guarantee (i.e., the product scope exception applies). The disclosure requirements of ASC 460 related to guarantees under product warranties would apply to guarantees related to infringement indemnification arrangements.

CHAPTER 35

ASC 470—DEBT

CONTENTS

PART I: GENERAL GUIDANCE

OVERVIEW

ASC 470 establishes U.S. GAAP for the current/noncurrent classification in the debtor's balance sheet of obligations that are payable on demand or callable by the creditor. This includes guidance regarding when a short-term obligation can be excluded from current liabilities. ASC 470 also addresses convertible debt, product financing, debt modifications and extinguishments, and the accounting by debtors for a troubled debt restructuring.

Debt may be issued with a conversion feature or a feature that permits the separate purchase of other securities, usually common stock of the issuing company. These "hybrid" debt/equity securities generally derive some portion of their value from the equity component (i.e., the conversion feature or the separate purchase option) that is included in the issue price. A significant accounting question that arises is the recognition, if any, of the equity feature when a hybrid security is issued. That treatment, in turn, affects the subsequent accounting when the conversion feature or separate purchase option is exercised.

A *product financing arrangement* is a transaction in which an enterprise sells and agrees to repurchase inventory at a purchase price equal to the original sale price plus carrying and financing costs, or other similar transaction. In certain circumstances, a transaction labeled a *sale* is, in substance, a product financing arrangement and should be treated as such.

An *extinguishment of debt* is the reacquisition of debt, or removal of debt from the balance sheet, prior to or at the maturity date of that debt. Gain or loss on the extinguishment is the difference between the total reacquisition cost of the debt to the debtor and the net carrying amount of the debt on the debtor's books at the date of extinguishment.

The authoritative literature carefully defines when debt has been extinguished and generally requires any gain or loss on extinguishments of debt to be included in the determination of net income in the period of the extinguishment transaction.

Debt may be restructured for a variety of reasons. A restructuring of debt is considered a troubled debt restructuring (TDR) if the creditor, for economic or legal reasons related to the debtor's financial difficulties, grants a concession to the debtor that it would not otherwise consider. The concession may stem from an agreement between the creditor and the debtor, or it may be imposed by law or court (ASC Glossary).

A loan is impaired if, based on current information and events, it is probable that the creditor will be unable to collect all amounts due according to the contractual terms of the loan agreement, including both the contractual interest and the principal receivable. For a discussion of troubled debt restructurings from the creditor's perspective, see the coverage in ASC 310-40 (Troubled Debt Restructurings by Creditors).

BACKGROUND

Convertible Debt

Convertible debt is convertible into the equity of the issuer or an affiliated enterprise. Common characteristics of convertible debt are (ASC 470-20-25-11).

- The interest rate is lower than the interest rate the issuer could establish for nonconvertible debt.
- The initial conversion price is greater than the fair value of the underlying security at time of issuance.
- The conversion price does not decrease (except pursuant to certain antidilutive considerations).
- The security usually is callable by the issuer.
- The debt usually is subordinate to the nonconvertible debt of the issuer.

Conversion of the convertible debt requires the holders to relinquish their status as debt holders to become stockholders.

Debt also may be issued with detachable purchase warrants that usually permit the holders to purchase shares of common stock at a set price for a specified period. The holders of the detachable warrants are not required to relinquish their status as debt holders to become stockholders.

Product Financing Arrangements

Product financing arrangements usually provide for one entity to obtain inventory or product for another entity (the sponsor), which agrees to purchase the inventory or product at specific prices over a specific period. The agreed-upon prices usually include financing and holding costs. The following are examples of common types of product financing arrangements in which a sponsor (the entity seeking to finance the product pending its future use or resale) (ASC 470-40-05-2):

- Sells inventory or product to another entity (the entity through which the financing flows) and in a related arrangement agrees to repurchase the product (or a substantially identical product).
- Arranges for another entity to purchase a product or inventory on the behalf of a sponsor, who, in a related arrangement, agrees to buy the product or inventory from the other entity.
- In accordance with the arrangement described above, controls the disposition of the product or inventory purchased or held by another entity.

In all of the above examples of product financing arrangements, the sponsor agrees to purchase, over a specified period, the product or inventory from the other entity at prearranged prices. The substance of a product financing arrangement, regardless of its legal form, is that of a financing arrangement rather than a sale or purchase by the sponsor.

PRACTICE NOTE: Distinguishing a product financing arrangement from the outright sale of products may require careful professional judgment. Usually it will require an analysis and consideration of two related transactions rather than a single transaction. For example, if a sponsor sells inventory or product to another entity and in a separate agreement contracts to buy the inventory or product back, the initial transaction may appear to be a sale. Only when the two transactions (i.e., the "sale" and the later repurchase) are combined is the true substance of the transaction apparent. In applying U.S. GAAP for product financing arrangements, an important dimension is the follow-through analysis and understanding of the subsequent transaction.

Other factors that may be present in a product financing arrangement are (ASC 470-40-05-4):

- The entity that provides the financing arrangement to the sponsor is an existing trust, nonbusiness entity or credit grantor, or was formed for the sole purpose of providing the financing arrangement to the sponsor.
- Small quantities of the product involved in the financing arrangement may be sold by the financing entity, but most of the product is ultimately used or sold by the sponsor.
- The product is stored on the sponsor's premises.
- The sponsor guarantees the debt of the other entity.

For purposes of the guidance in ASC 470, unmined or unharvested natural resources and financial instruments are not considered products. They are not covered by the provisions of ASC 470 (ASC 470-40-15-3).

PRACTICE NOTE: No mention is made in ASC 470-40 as to how a product financing arrangement involving unmined or unharvested natural resources should be accounted for. For example, X Company enters into a financing arrangement with Y Company wherein Y Company acquires 10,000 acres of unharvested timberlands for the sole benefit of X Company. X Company guarantees the bank loan that was necessary to acquire the timberlands and agrees to purchase the processed timber from Y Company at specified prices over a specified period. The specified prices include (*a*) the cost of the timber, (*b*) processing costs, (*c*) interest costs on the bank loan, and (*d*) a handling fee. Only the standing timber was purchased and not the land.

It appears that the provisions of ASC 470-40 are appropriate for this type of transaction, but ASC 470-40 does not expressly cover this situation.

In a product financing arrangement, the specified prices that the sponsor must pay cannot be subject to change except for fluctuations because of finance and holding costs. The specified prices may be stated or determinable by reference to the substance of the arrangement, such as (*a*) resale price guarantees or (*b*) options that, in substance, compel or require the sponsor to purchase the product. In addition, the cost of the product and related costs to the other entity must be covered substantially by the specified prices that the seller must pay for the product. Related costs include interest, holding costs, and other fees charged by the other entity (ASC 470-40-15-2).

Modifications and Extinguishments of Debt

Prior to the establishment of U.S. GAAP for extinguishment of debt, differences in practice existed with regard to the recognition of gains and losses from refunding of debt issues. ASC 470 requires that gains and losses from early extinguishment of debt be included in net income of the period of extinguishment.

Troubled Debt Restructuring

A troubled debt restructuring is one in which the creditor grants the debtor certain concessions that would not normally be considered. The concessions are made because of the debtor's financial difficulty, and the creditor's objective is to maximize recovery of its investment. Troubled debt restructurings are often the result of legal proceedings or of negotiation between the parties (ASC 310-40-15-5, 6).

Troubled debt restructurings include situations in which (ASC 310-40-15-9):

- The creditor accepts a third-party receivable or other asset(s) of the debtor, in lieu of the receivable from the debtor.
- The creditor accepts an equity interest in the debtor in lieu of the receivable. (This is not to be confused with convertible securities, which are *not* troubled debt restructurings.)
- The creditor accepts modification of the terms of the debt, including but not limited to:
  - — Reduction in the stated interest
  - — Extension of maturity at an interest rate below the current market rate
  - — Reduction in face amount of the debt
  - — Reduction in accrued interest.

The reductions mentioned in the bulleted item above can be either absolute or contingent.

PRACTICE NOTE: If the debtor can obtain funds at current market rates and conditions, this provides evidence that the restructuring is not a troubled debt restructuring.

ASC 470-10: OVERALL

LIABILITY CLASSIFICATION ISSUES

Disclosure of Long-Term Obligations

The combined aggregate amount of maturities and sinking fund requirements for all long-term borrowings shall be disclosed for each of the five years following the date of the latest balance sheet presented. ASC 505-10-50-11 provides specific disclosure guidance on redeemable securities. (ASC 470-50-1)

Current Obligations Expected to Be Refinanced

A short-term obligation shall be excluded from current liabilities only if the company intends to refinance it on a long-term basis and the intent is supported by the ability to refinance that is demonstrated in one of the following ways (ASC 470-10-45-14):

- A long-term obligation or equity security whose proceeds are used to refinance the short-term obligation is issued after the date of the balance sheet but before the financial statements are issued or available to be issued.
- Before the financial statements are issued or available to be issued, the company has entered into an agreement that enables it to refinance a short-term obligation on a long-term basis. The terms of the agreement must be clear and unambiguous and must contain the following provisions:
  - — The agreement may not be canceled by the lender or investor, and it must extend beyond the normal operating cycle of the company.
  - — At the balance sheet date and at its issuance, the company was not in violation, nor was there any information that indicated a violation, of the agreement.
  - — The lender or investor is expected to be financially capable of honoring the agreement.

PRACTICE POINTER: If the company has no operating cycle or the operating cycle occurs more than once a year, then the one-year rule is used.

The amount of short-term obligation that can be reclassified as non-current cannot exceed the actual proceeds received from the issuance of the new long-term obligation or the amount of available refinancing covered by the established agreement (ASC 470-10-45-16). The amount must be adjusted for any limitations in the agreement that indicate the full amount obtainable will not be available to retire the short-term obligation (ASC 470-10-45-17). In addition, if the agreement indicates that the amount available for refinancing will fluctuate, then the most conservative estimate must be used. If no reasonable estimate can be made, then the agreement does not fulfill the necessary requirements and the full amount of current liabilities must be presented (ASC 470-10-45-18).

An enterprise may intend to seek alternative financing sources besides those in the established agreement when the short-term obligation becomes due. If alternative sources do not materialize, however, the company must intend to borrow from the source in the agreement (ASC 470-10-45-20).

PRACTICE POINTER: If the terms of the agreement allow the prospective lender or investor to set interest rates, collateral requirements, or similar conditions that are unreasonable to the company, the intent to refinance may not exist.

ASC 470 addresses the issue of a short-term obligation that is repaid and is subsequently replaced with a long-term debt obligation or equity securities. Because cash is temporarily required to retire the short-term obligation, the obligation should be classified as a current liability in the balance sheet (ASC 470-10-45-15).

Any *rollover agreements* or *revolving credit agreements* must meet the above provisions to enable a company to classify the related short-term obligations as noncurrent (ASC 470-10-45-21). The financial statements must contain a note disclosing the amount excluded from current liabilities and a full description of the financial agreement and new obligations incurred or expected to be incurred or the equity securities issued or expected to be issued (ASC 470-10-50-4).

Callable Obligations

ASC 470 establishes U.S. GAAP for the current/noncurrent classification in the debtor's balance sheet of obligations that are payable on demand or callable by the creditor.

ASC 470 is applied to a classified balance sheet to determine whether the obligation should be classified as current or noncurrent for balance sheet purposes. ASC 470 is applied to both classified and unclassified balance sheets to determine the maturity dates of obligations disclosed by notes. For example, an unclassified balance sheet may contain a note disclosure of the maturity dates of obligations, despite the fact that the obligations are not classified in the unclassified balance sheet, or may not be identified separately from other obligations in the unclassified balance sheet.

At the debtor's balance sheet date, an obligation may, by its terms, be payable on demand. This includes long-term obligations that are callable because a violation of an objective acceleration clause in a long-term debt agreement may exist at the date of the debtor's balance sheet. Such callable obligations must be classified as a current liability at the debtor's balance sheet date unless (ASC 470-10-45-11):

- The creditor has waived the right to demand payment for a period that extends beyond one year (or the debtor's normal operating cycle if longer), or
- The debtor has cured the violation after the balance sheet date, but prior to the issuance date of the financial statements, and the obligation is not callable for a period that extends beyond one year (or the debtor's normal operating cycle if longer).

A long-term debt agreement may provide for a grace period that commences after the occurrence of a violation of an objective acceleration clause. ASC 470 requires that such an obligation be classified as a current liability at the debtor's balance sheet date, unless the two criteria above are met and, in addition, the unexpired grace period extends beyond one year (or the debtor's normal operating cycle if longer) (ASC 470-10-45-11).

PRACTICE NOTE: ASC 470 requires that an obligation be classified as current or noncurrent, based solely on whether the legal terms of the loan agreement require payment within one year (or the operating cycle if longer).

A creditor may have waived the right to demand payment on a specific obligation for a period that extends beyond one year (or the operating cycle if longer). In this event, the debtor shall classify the obligation as a noncurrent liability.

Acceleration Clauses

An *objective acceleration clause* in a long-term debt agreement is one that contains objective criteria that the creditor must use as the basis for calling part or all of the loan, such as a specified minimum amount of working capital or net worth requirement.

In the event of a violation of an objective acceleration clause, most long-term obligations become immediately callable by the creditor, or become callable after a grace period that is specified in the loan agreement. When this occurs, the creditor can demand payment of part or all of the loan balance, in accordance with the terms of the debt agreement.

A subjective acceleration clause is one that permits the lender to unilaterally accelerate part or all of a long-term obligation. For example, the debt agreement might state that "if, in the opinion of the lender, the borrower experiences recurring losses or liquidity problems, the lender may at its sole discretion accelerate part or all of the loan balance . . . ."

Acceleration clauses are accounted for in the same manner as other loss contingencies. If it is *probable* that the subjective acceleration clause will be exercised by the creditor, the amount of the long-term obligation that is likely to be accelerated shall be classified as a current liability by the debtor. On the other hand, if it is only *reasonably possible* that the subjective acceleration clause will be exercised by the creditor, note disclosure may be all that is required. Finally, if the possibility of subjective acceleration is *remote*, no disclosure may be required.

ASC 470-20: DEBT WITH CONVERSION AND OTHER OPTIONS

ASC 470-20-50-1 provides accounting and reporting guidance for debt (including certain preferred stock) with specific conversion features and other options, as follows:

- Debt instruments with detachable warrants
- Convertible debt instruments
- Interest forfeitures
- Induced conversions
- Conversion upon issuer's exercise of call option
- Own-share lending arrangements issued in contemplation of convertible debt issuance or other financing

CONVERTIBLE DEBT

A convertible debt instrument is a complex hybrid instrument that includes an option, the alternative choices of which cannot exist independently of one another. That is, the two choices are mutually exclusive and the instrument will either be converted or redeemed. (ASC 470-20-05-4) A convertible debt instrument may offer certain advantages to the issuer and the purchaser. For the issuer, convertible debt has a lower interest rate than does nonconvertible debt. The issuer may view convertible debt as essentially a way of raising equity capital. (ASC 470-20-05-5) The purchaser obtains an option to receive either the face or redemption amount of the instrument or the number of shares into which the instrument is convertible. (ASC 470-20-05-6)

Following are some of the unique characteristics that may be embedded in convertible debt instruments:

- Some convertible debt instruments may be convertible into common stock at the lower of a conversion rate fixed at the time of issuance and a fixed discount to the market price of the common stock at the date of conversion. (ASC 470-20-05-7)
- Entities may issue convertible debt instruments that may be settled in cash or other assets upon conversion. (ASC 470-20-05-7A)
- Certain convertible debt instruments may have a contingently adjustable conversion ratio (i.e., a conversion price that is variable based on future events). (ASC 470-20-05- 8)

- Certain convertible debt instruments may become convertible only upon the occurrence of a future event that is outside the control of the issuer or holder. (ASC 470-20-05-8A)
- When a convertible debt instrument is converted to equity securities, the terms of the conversion may provide that any accrued but unpaid interest at the date of conversion is forfeited by the former debt holder. This occurs either because the conversion date falls between interest payment dates, or because there are no interest payment dates, as in the case of a zero coupon convertible debt instrument. (ASC 470-20-05-9)

PRACTICE POINTER: The guidance on convertible debt instruments in ASC 470-20 is to be considered after considering the guidance in Subtopic 815-15 on bifurcation of embedded derivatives for an embedded conversion option or other embedded feature. Also, this guidance does not apply to a convertible debt instrument issued to a grantee that is subject to the guidance in ASC 718 on stock compensation unless the instrument is modified as described in and no longer subject to the guidance in that topic. Also, this guidance does not apply to stock-settled debt that is subject to other ASC subtopics unless the stock-settled debt also contains a substantive conversion feature for which all relevant guidance in this ASC section shall be considered in addition to the relevant guidance in other ASC subtopics. (ASC 470-20-15-2C, 2D)

Convertible preferred stock is considered a convertible debt instrument if it is mandatorily redeemable and it is classified as a liability under ASC 480-10. (ASC 470-20-15-2D)

Issuance

Under current U.S. GAAP, a debt with an embedded conversion feature is accounted entirely as a liability at the time of issuance. No portion of the proceeds from issuance is accounted for as attributable to the conversion feature. At the time of issuance, the debt issue is treated entirely as debt unless the conversion feature is required to be accounted for separately as an embedded derivative under ASC 815-15, or the conversion feature results in a premium that is subject to the guidance in ASC 470-20-25-13. That guidance requires that a substantial premium be treated as paid-in capital. (ASC 470-20-25-12, 13)

PRACTICE NOTE: In considering alternative methods of accounting for convertible debt, some believe that the value inherent in the conversion feature should be formally recognized at the time the convertible debt is issued; others believe that the instrument should be accounted for entirely as debt until conversion occurs. Existing U.S. GAAP state that the most important reason for accounting for convertible debt solely as debt at the time of issuance is that the alternatives available to the debt holder are mutually exclusive. The holder must give up rights as a debt holder to become a stockholder.

If the issuance of a convertible debt instrument includes other rights and privileges, stated or unstated, in addition to the convertible debt instrument, a portion of the initial proceeds attributable to those rights and privileges shall be recognized based on guidance in other applicable U.S. GAAP (ASC 470-20-25-15).

Illustration of Convertible Bond Issuance

Alpha Company issues $1,000,000 of convertible bonds at 98% of par value. Each $1,000 bond is convertible into 10 shares of the company's common stock. The bond issue is recorded as if there were no conversion feature, as follows:

Cash ($1,000,000 × 98%)	980,000	
Discount on bonds payable	20,000	
Bonds payable		1,000,000

Disclosure of the features of the bond, including the conversion option, is required. The entry above, however, is the same as it would be had the bonds not been convertible.

Conversion

When a convertible debt security with an inseparable conversion feature is converted into equity securities of the debtor in accordance with the original conversion terms, the convertible debt security is surrendered by the holder and the debt is retired by the debtor. The issuer substitutes equity for debt in its balance sheet. The following is an illustration of such a transaction.

Illustration of Convertible Debt Security Converted into Equity Security

Blue Corporation has outstanding $20,000,000 of 8% convertible bonds, with an unamortized bond premium balance of $800,000. Each $1,000 bond is convertible into ten shares of Blue Corporation's $5 par value common stock. On April 1, 20X8, all of the convertible bonds were converted by the bondholders.

8% convertible bonds payable	20,000,000	
Unamortized bond premium	800,000	
Common stock ($5 par × 200,000)		1,000,000
Capital in excess of par (common stock)		19,800,000

Under current accounting practice, no gain or loss is recognized on the conversion of convertible bonds to common stock if the conversion is made in accordance with the original conversion terms.

Generally, convertible debt is issued in anticipation that it will be converted into equity securities, and that the issuer will repay the face amount of the debt at its maturity date. Although most convertible debt issues provide for the issuance of common equity shares upon conversion, the terms of a convertible debt security may provide for the issuance of preferred or other type of equity security upon conversion. When an enterprise converts debt to common equity shares, the liability for the debt is eliminated and the number of common equity shares outstanding is increased, which may affect the computation of earnings per share (EPS). When debt is converted to common equity shares, the pretax net income of the enterprise also increases by the amount of interest expense that was previously paid on the convertible debt.

PRACTICE POINTER: Convertible debt generally is converted by a holder when the market value of its underlying equity securities into which the debt can be converted exceeds the face amount of the debt. If a convertible bondholder does not convert, the issuer may exercise the call provision in the debt to force conversion.

Convertible debt usually is not converted when the fair value of its underlying equity securities is less than the face amount of the debt. Under this circumstance, the issuer may (*a*) exercise the call provision in the debt and pay the bondholders the face amount of the convertible debt, (*b*) offer the bondholders an inducement to convert that exceeds the original conversion terms, or (*c*) not pay off the debt until the scheduled maturity date (ASC 470-20-05-5).

Induced Conversion

ASC 470 applies to conversions of convertible debt in which the original conversion terms are changed by the debtor to encourage the holder of the convertible debt to convert to equity securities of the debtor. Changes in the original conversion terms may include (*a*) the reduction of the original conversion price to increase the number of shares of equity securities received by the bondholder, (*b*) the issuance of warrants or other securities, or (*c*) the payment of cash or some other type of consideration (ASC 470-20-40-15).

ASC 470-20-40-16 applies to induced conversions of convertible debt to equity securities pursuant to terms that reflect changes made by the debtor to the conversion privileges provided in the terms of the debt at issuance. Such conversions have the following characteristics: (*a*) are exercisable for a limited period of time and (*b*) include the issuance of all the equity securities issuable pursuant to conversion privileges included in the terms of the debt at issuance for each debt instrument that is converted, regardless of the party that initiates the offer or whether the offer relates to all debt holders. (ASC 470-20-40-13)

If a convertible debt instrument is converted to equity securities of the debtor pursuant to an inducement offer, the debtor recognizes an expense equal to the fair value of all securities and other consideration transferred in the transactions in excess of the fair value of securities issuable in the original conversion terms. The fair value of the securities or other consideration is measured as of the date the inducement offer is accepted by the convertible debt holder. (ASC 470-20-40-16)

PRACTICE POINTER: If individual bondholders accepted an inducement offer on many different days during the "limited period of time" allowed by existing U.S. GAAP, a separate computation of the fair value of the incremental consideration would be required if the fair value of the debtor's common stock changes from day to day.

Illustration of Induced Conversion

Black Corporation has outstanding 100 10% convertible bonds, issued at par value and due on December 31, 20X8. Each $1,000 bond is convertible into 20 shares of Black Corporation $1 par value common stock. To induce bondholders to convert to its common stock, Black Corporation increases the conversion rate from 20 shares per $1,000 bond to 25 shares per $1,000 bond. This offer was made by Black Corporation for a limited period of 60 days commencing March 1, 20X9.

On April 1, when the market price of Black's common stock was $60, one bondholder tendered a $1,000 convertible bond for conversion. Under ASC 470, the amount of incremental consideration is equal to the fair value of the additional five shares of Black Corporation's common stock on April 1. The amount of incremental consideration is $300 (5 shares × $60 per share).

The journal entry to record the transaction is:

Convertible bonds payable	1,000	
Debt conversion expense	300	
Common stock ($1 par value) ($1 × 25 shares)		25
Capital in excess of par (common stock)		1,275

The incremental consideration paid or issued by a debtor may also be calculated as the difference between (*a*) the fair value of the equity securities and/or other consideration required to be issued under the original terms of the conversion privilege and (*b*) the fair value of the equity securities and/or other consideration that is actually issued.

Market value of securities based on inducement (25 × $60)	$1,500
Market value of securities based on original terms (20 × $60)	(1,200)
Fair value of incremental consideration	$ 300

PRACTICE NOTE: There is a significant difference between extinguishment accounting and conversion accounting. As a rule, gain or loss is recognized in extinguishment accounting, while no gain or loss is recognized in conversion accounting. Extinguishment accounting results in the *extinguishment* of a debt, while conversion accounting results in the issuance of equity securities and the *retirement* of a debt.

Disclosure of Convertible Debt Instruments

ASC 470-20-50 requires extensive disclosure for convertible debt instruments. The objective of these disclosures is to provide users of financial statements with the following:

- Information about the terms and features of convertible debt instruments
- An understanding of how these instruments have been reported in the entity's statement of financial position and statement of financial performance
- Information about events, conditions, and circumstances that can affect the assessment of the amount or timing of an entity's future cash flows related to those instruments (ASC 470-20-50-1A)

This objective requires disclosure of the rights and privileges of each convertible debt instrument outstanding, including the following:

- Principal amount
- Coupon rate
- Conversion or exercise prices or rates and the number of shares into which the instrument is potentially convertible
- Pertinent dates (e.g., conversion date(s) and maturity date)

- Parties that control the conversion rights
- Manner of settlement upon conversion, including any alternative settlement methods
- Terms that may changes conversion prices, the number of shares to be issued, and other conversion rights and the timing of those rights
- Liquidation preference and any unusual voting rights
- Other material terms and features of the instruments not covered above (ASC 470-20-50-1B)

For contingently convertible instruments, the following information shall be disclosed:

- Events or changes in circumstances that would adjust or change the contingency or would cause the contingency to be met
- Information on whether the shares that would be issued if the contingently convertible securities were converted are included in the calculation of diluted EPS and reasons as to why or why not
- Other information that is helpful in understanding the nature and the potential impact of conversion (ASC 470-20-50-1C)

For each date for which a statement of position is presented, the following disclosures are required:

- The unamortized premium, discount or issues costs and, if applicable the premium amount recorded as paid-in capital
- The net carrying amount
- For public business entities, the fair value of the entire instrument and the level of the fair value hierarchy (ASC 470-20-50-1D)

As of the date of the latest statement of financial position, the following information shall be provided:

- Changes to conversion or exercise prices that occurred during the reporting period other than changes due to standard antidilution provisions
- Events or changes in circumstances that occurred during the reporting period that cause conversion contingencies to be met or conversion terms to be significantly changed
- Number of shares issued upon conversion, exercise, or satisfaction of required conditions during the reporting period
- Maturities and sinking fund requirements for convertible debt instruments for each of the five years following the date of the most recent statement of financial position (ASC 470-20-50-1E)

Finally, the entity shall disclose the following information about interest recognized for each period for which a statement of financial performance is presented:

- The effective interest rate for the period
- The amount of interest recognized for the period disaggregated by both the contractual interest expense and the amortization of the premium discount, or issue costs (ASC 470-20-50-1F)

PRACTICE POINTER: Following the above requirements, ASC 470-20-50 provides cross-references to ASC 815 for convertible debt instruments that are accounted for as derivatives in accordance with ASC 815.

DEBT WITH DETACHABLE PURCHASE WARRANTS

Issuance

In contrast to accounting for convertible debt, when detachable purchase warrants are issued in conjunction with debt, separate amounts are allocated to the debt and the purchase warrants and accounting recognition is required to be given to each component. The allocation to the two components of the hybrid debt/equity security is based on the relative fair values of the two instruments at the time of issuance (ASC 470-20-30-1).

PRACTICE NOTE: This conclusion is based primarily on the fact that the options available to the debt holder are *not* mutually exclusive—bondholders can become stockholders while retaining their status as bondholders.

Illustration of Issuance of Debt with Detachable Warrants

Xeta Corporation issues 100 $100-par-value, 5% bonds with a detachable common stock warrant to purchase one share of Xeta's common stock at a specified price. At the time of issuance, the quoted market price of the bonds was $97, and the stock warrants were quoted at $2 each. The proceeds of the sale to Xeta Corporation were $9,900. The transaction is accounted for as follows:

Cash	9,900	
Discount on 5% bonds payable (100 × $3)	300	
5% bonds payable		10,000
Paid-in capital (stock warrants) (100 × $2)		200

The bonds and warrants are recorded separately at their market values:

Bonds:	$10,000 × 97% = $9,700, recorded at $10,000 par value, less $300 discount
Warrants:	100 × $2 = $200

Exercise of Warrants

Once a separate purchase feature, such as a detachable stock purchase warrant, is issued, it usually is traded separately from its related convertible debt security. The separate purchase feature has its own market price, and conversion requires (*a*) the surrender of the purchase option and (*b*) the payment of any other consideration required by the terms of the warrant.

Under current accounting practice (ASC 470), when a separate purchase feature is exercised in accordance with the original purchase terms, no gain or loss is recognized on the transaction. The amount previously credited to paid-in capital for the purchase feature at issuance is eliminated, the amount of cash received, if any, is recorded, and the par value of the capital stock issued and the appropriate amount of capital stock in excess of par is recorded. The following is an illustration of such a transaction.

Illustration of Exercise of Separate Purchase Feature

Ace Corporation previously issued debt securities with detachable stock purchase warrants. A credit of $10 for each warrant was recorded in paid-in capital at the date of issuance, representing the relative market value of each warrant. There was no discount or premium on the issuance of the related debt with detachable stock purchase warrants. Each stock purchase warrant permitted the purchase of 50 shares of Ace's $1 par value common stock, upon the payment of $200 and the surrender of the warrant. Assuming that one warrant was exercised, the journal entry would be:

Cash	200	
Paid-in capital (stock warrants)	10	
Capital stock ($1 par value)		50
Capital in excess of par (common stock)		160

The conversion of a separate conversion feature, such as a detachable stock purchase warrant, is accounted for solely as an equity transaction, and no gain or loss is recorded.

PRACTICE POINTER: The accounting described in this section applies to "detachable" stock purchase warrants and other similar instruments, meaning that the stock purchase warrant can be exercised without affecting the other security from which it is detachable. Occasionally, a stock purchase warrant is encountered that is inseparable from another security (i.e., a nondetachable stock purchase warrant), and the related security must be surrendered to effect the stock purchase. In this case, although the name may imply otherwise, the stock purchase warrant effectively is part of a convertible security and should be accounted for as such.

PRACTICE NOTE: ASC 470 recognizes that it is not practical to discuss all possible types of debt with conversion features and debt issued with purchase warrants, or debt issued with a combination of the two. It states that securities not explicitly dealt with in ASC 470 should be accounted for in accordance with the substance of the transaction in a manner consistent with existing U.S. GAAP (ASC 470-20-25-13).

ASC 470-40: PRODUCT FINANCING ARRANGEMENTS

ACCOUNTING FOR PRODUCT FINANCING ARRANGEMENTS

If an entity buys a product for a sponsor's benefit and the sponsor agrees, in a related arrangement, to buy the product, or a processed product containing the original product, back from the other entity, an asset and the related liability are recorded by the sponsor at the time the other entity acquires the product (ASC 470-40-25-2).

Excluding processing costs, the difference between the cost of the product and the cost the sponsor actually pays under the terms of the product financing arrangement is accounted for by the sponsor as financing and holding costs. These financing and holding costs are recorded on the books of the sponsor in accordance with its regular accounting policies for such costs, even though the costs are incurred and paid directly by the other entity (ASC 470-40-25-3).

Separately identified interest costs that the sponsor pays as part of the specified prices may qualify for interest capitalization under ASC 835. If not, the separately identified interest costs actually paid by the sponsor are included in the total interest costs incurred during the period (ASC 470-40-25-4).

Illustration of Accounting for Product Financing Arrangements

Assume that each of the following situations meets the definition of a product financing arrangement (PFA) in accordance with ASC 470. In each situation, Walsh is the sponsor and Foster is the purchaser. Following are the appropriate journal entries for Walsh.

Case 1: Walsh arranges for Foster to purchase inventory costing $1,000 from a third party and agrees to purchase that inventory from Foster for $1,050 in 30 days.

Inventory under PFA	1,000	
Due to Foster under PFA		1,000

Case 2: Walsh arranges for Foster to acquire inventory from an outside party for $750 and guarantees the resale price to outside parties for $850.

Inventory under PFA	750	
Due to Foster under PFA		750

ASC 470-50: MODIFICATIONS AND EXTINGUISHMENTS

WHEN DEBT IS EXTINGUISHED

Debt is extinguished and is derecognized in, or removed from, the debtor's financial statements only in the following circumstances (ASC 405-20-40-1):

- The debtor pays the creditor and is relieved of its obligations for the liability. This includes (*a*) the transfer of cash, other financial assets, goods, or services or (*b*) the debtor's reacquisition of its outstanding debt securities, whether the securities are cancelled or held as treasury bonds.
- The debtor is legally released from being the primary obligor under the liability, either judicially or by the creditor. If a third party assumes nonrecourse debt in conjunction with the sale of an asset that serves as sole collateral for that debt, the sale and related assumption effectively accomplish a legal release of the seller-debtor for purposes of applying ASC 405.

When a refunding is desired because of lower interest rates or some other reason, the old debt issue may not be callable for several years. This is the usual circumstance for an advance refunding. In an advance refunding, a new debt issue is sold to replace the old debt issue that cannot be called. The proceeds from the sale of the new debt issue are used to purchase high grade investments, which are placed in an escrow account. The earnings from the investments in the escrow account are used to pay the interest and/or principal payments on the existing debt, up to the date that the existing debt can be called. On the call date of the existing debt, whatever remains in the escrow account is used to pay the call premium, if any, and all remaining principal and interest due on the existing debt. This process is frequently referred to as an in-substance defeasance. An in-substance defeasance is *not* considered an extinguishment of debt.

ACCOUNTING FOR EXTINGUISHMENTS OF DEBT

Under ASC 470, all extinguishments of debt are basically alike, and accounting for such transactions is the same, regardless of the method used to achieve the extinguishment. Therefore, in terms of gain or loss recognition, there is no difference in accounting for an extinguishment of debt by (*a*) cash purchase, (*b*) exchange of stock for debt, (*c*) exchange of debt for debt, or (*d*) any other method.

Gain or loss on the extinguishment of debt is the difference between the reacquisition price and the net carrying amount of the debt on the date of the extinguishment (ASC 470-50-40-2). In the event of an extinguishment of debt for which the fair value option has been elected, the net carrying amount of the extinguished debt equals its fair value at the reacquisition date, and the entity must include in net income the cumulative amount of the gain or loss previously recorded in other comprehensive income for the extinguished debt that resulted from changes in instrument-specific credit risk. (ASC 470-50-40-2A)

Reacquisition Price

This is the amount paid for the extinguishment. It includes call premium and any other costs of reacquiring the portion of the debt being extinguished (ASC Glossary). When extinguishment is achieved through the exchange of securities, the reacquisition price is the total present value of the new securities being issued.

Net Carrying Amount

This is the amount due at the maturity of the debt, adjusted for any unamortized premium or discount and any other costs of issuance (legal, accounting, underwriter's fees, etc.) (ASC Glossary).

Illustration of Reacquisition Loss on Extinguishment

On December 31, 20X8, a corporation decides to retire $500,000 of an original issue of $1,000,000 8% debentures, which were sold on December 31, 20X3, for $98 per $100 par-value bond and are callable at $101 per bond. Legal and other expenses for issuing the debentures were $30,000. Both the original discount and the issue costs are being amortized over the 10-year life of the issue by the straight-line method.

Amount of original expenses of issue	$30,000
Amount of original discount (2% of $1,000,000)	$20,000
Amount of premium paid for redemption (debentures callable at 101, 1% of $500,000)	$ 5,000
Date of issue	12/31/20X3
Date of maturity	12/31/20Y3
Date of redemption	12/31/20X8

Because that the original expenses of $30,000 are being amortized over the ten-year life of the issue and five years have elapsed since the issue date, half of these expenses have been amortized, leaving a balance of $15,000 at the date of reacquisition. Only half of the outstanding debentures are being retired, however, which leaves $7,500 to account for in the computation of gain or loss.

The original discount of $20,000 (debentures sold at $98) is handled the same as the legal and other expenses. Because half of the discount has already been amortized, leaving a $10,000 balance at the date of redemption, and because only half of the issue is being reacquired, $5,000 is included into the computation of gain or loss.

Based on the above information, the loss on reacquisition is computed as follows:

Reacquisition price:		
$500,000 × 101%		$505,000
Net carrying amount:		
Face value	$500,000	

Discount	(5,000)	
Legal and other expenses	(7,500)	
		(487,500)
Loss on reacquisition		$ 17,500

The general journal entry to record the reacquisition of the bonds is as follows:

Bond payable	500,000	
Loss of retirement of bonds payable	17,500	
Discount on bonds payable		5,000
Deferred legal and other expenses		7,500
Cash		$505,000

ASC 470-60: TROUBLED DEBT RESTRUCTURINGS BY DEBTORS

ACCOUNTING FOR TROUBLED DEBT RESTRUCTURINGS

Debtors account for troubled debt restructurings by the type of restructuring. Types of restructuring include:

- Transfer of asset(s) in full settlement.
- Transfer of an equity interest in full settlement.
- Modification of terms of the debt.
- Combinations of the above three types.

Transfer of Asset(s)

The debtor recognizes a gain equal to the excess of the carrying amount of the payable (including accrued interest, premiums, etc.) over the fair value of the asset(s) given up. The difference between the fair value and the carrying amount of the asset(s) given up is the gain or loss on the transfer of asset(s), which is also included in net income in the period the transfer occurs (ASC 470-60-35-2, 3).

PRACTICE POINTER: Determine fair value either by the assets given up or by the amount payable, whichever is more clearly evident. In the case of a partial settlement, however, use the value of the asset(s) given up. This eliminates the need to allocate the fair value of the payable between the settled portion and the remaining outstanding balance.

Illustration of Transfer of Assets

A debtor owes $20,000, including accrued interest. The creditor accepts land valued at $17,000 and carried on the debtor's books at its $12,000 cost, in full payment.

Under U.S. GAAP, the debtor recognizes two gains: $5,000 ($17,000 – $12,000) on the transfer of the assets, and $3,000 ($20,000 – $17,000) on the extinguishment of debt.

The creditor recognizes a loss of $3,000 ($20,000 – $17,000).

Transfer of Equity Interest

The difference between the fair value of the equity interest and the carrying amount of the payable is recognized as a gain by the debtor (ASC 470-60-35-4).

Illustration of Transfer of Equity Interest

A debtor grants an equity interest valued at $10,000, consisting of 500 shares of $15 par value stock, to retire a payable of $12,000. Given these facts, the debtor records the issuance of the stock at $10,000 ($7,500 par value and $2,500 additional paid-in capital) and a gain on the extinguishment of debt of $2,000 ($12,000 – $10,000). The creditor records an investment asset of $10,000 and an ordinary loss of $2,000 ($12,000 – $10,000) on the TDR.

PRACTICE POINTER: Determining the fair value of an equity interest of a debtor company involved in a troubled debt restructuring may be difficult. In many cases, the company's stock will not be publicly traded, and there may be no recent stock transactions that would be helpful. Even if a recent market price were available, consider whether that price reflects the financially troubled status of the company that exists at the time the troubled debt restructuring takes place.

Modification of Terms

A restructuring that does not involve the transfer of assets or equity often involves the modification of the terms of the debt. The debtor accounts for the effects of the restructuring prospectively and does not change the carrying amount unless the carrying amount exceeds the total future cash payments specified by the new terms. The *total future cash payments* are the principal and interest, including any accrued interest at the time of the restructuring that will be payable by the new terms. *Interest expense* is computed by a method that results in a constant effective rate (such as the interest method). The new effective rate of interest is the discount rate at which the carrying amount of the debt is equal to the present value of the future cash payments (ASC 470-60-35-5).

When the total future cash payments are less than the carrying amount, the debtor reduces the carrying amount accordingly and recognizes the difference as a gain. When there are several related accounts (e.g., discount, premium), the reduction may need to be allocated among them. All cash payments after the restructuring go toward reducing the carrying amount and *no* interest expense is recognized after the date of restructure (ASC 470-60-35-6).

When there are indeterminate future payments, or any time the future payments might exceed the carrying amount, the debtor recognizes no gain. The debtor assumes that the future contingent payments will have to be made at least to the extent necessary to obviate any gain. In estimating future cash payments, it is assumed that the maximum amount of periods (and interest) is going to occur (ASC 470-60-35-7).

Illustration of Modification of Terms

A debtor has a loan to a creditor, details of which are as follows:

Principal	$10,000
Accrued interest	500
Total	$10,500

They reach an agreement to restructure the total future cash payments, both principal and interest, to $8,000. The present value of these payments is $7,500.

Under U.S. GAAP, the debtor recognizes a gain of $2,500 ($10,500 – $8,000) at the time of the restructuring, and all future payments are specified as principal payments. Under U.S. GAAP, the creditor recognizes a loss of $3,000 ($10,500 – $7,500).

Combination of Types

When a restructuring involves combinations of asset or equity transfers and modification of terms, the debtor first uses the fair value of any asset or equity to reduce the carrying amount of the payable. The difference between the fair value and the carrying amount of any asset(s) transferred is recognized as gain or loss. The remainder of the restructuring is accounted for as a modification of terms in accordance with ASC 470 (ASC 470-60-35-8).

Related Issues

Amounts contingently payable in future periods are recognized as payable and as interest expense in accordance with the treatment of other contingencies. The criteria for recognizing a loss contingency are the following:

- It is probable that the liability has been incurred.
- The amount can be reasonably estimable.

If any contingently payable amounts were included in the total future cash payments, they must now be deducted from the carrying amount of the restructured payable to the extent they originally prevented recognition of a gain at the time of the restructuring (ASC 470-60-35-10).

In estimating future payments subject to fluctuation, estimates are based on the interest rate in effect at the time of restructure. A change in future rates is treated as a change in accounting estimate. The accounting for these fluctuations cannot result in an immediate gain. Rather, the future payments will reduce the carrying amount, and any residual value is considered gain (ASC 470-60-35-11).

Legal fees and other direct costs that a debtor incurs in granting an equity interest to a creditor reduce the amount otherwise recorded for that equity interest. All other direct costs that a debtor incurs to effect a TDR are deducted in measuring the gain on restructuring of payables or are included in expense for the period, if no gain on restructuring is recognized (ASC 470-60-35-12).

DISCLOSURE REQUIREMENTS FOR TROUBLED DEBT RESTRUCTURINGS

Debtors

The debtor must disclose the following regarding any debt restructuring during a period (ASC 470-60-50-1):

- Description of the terms of each restructuring
- Aggregate gain on the restructuring
- Aggregate net gain or loss on asset transfer
- Per share amount of aggregate gain on the restructuring

The debtor should disclose contingently payable amounts included in the carrying amount of restructured payables and the total of contingently payable amounts and the conditions under which the amounts become payable or are forgiven (ASC 470-60-50-2).

PRACTICE POINTER: In response to COVID-19, in fall of 2020, the FASB issued a staff educational paper to help stakeholders apply debt restructuring and modification guidance during the COVID-19 pandemic. In the media coverage of the release of this document, the observation is made that many stakeholders have either had to apply guidance on debt restructurings or modifications for the first time, or have had to do so more frequently. The educational paper is intended to help these entities successfully navigate accounting guidance at this difficult time. The educational paper provides an overview of accounting guidance for debt restructurings and modifications and provides examples of common restructurings and modifications. This resource is available at the COVID-19 web portal on the FASB web site.

PART II: INTERPRETIVE GUIDANCE

ASC 470-10: OVERALL

ASC 470-10-25-1 through 25-2, 35-3 Sales of Future Revenues

BACKGROUND

Company G enters into an agreement with Company H (an investor) to receive a sum of cash in exchange for a specified percentage or amount of Company G's future revenues or another measure of income, such as gross margin or operating income, for a particular product line, business segment, trademark, patent, or contractual right, for a specified period. The future revenue or income may be from a foreign contract, transaction, or operation denominated in a foreign currency.

ACCOUNTING ISSUES

- Assuming the proceeds received from a sale of future revenues are appropriately accounted for as a liability, should the liability be characterized as debt or deferred income?
- How should debt or deferred income be amortized? How should foreign currency effects, if any, be recognized?

PRACTICE POINTER: The distinction between recognizing a liability as debt or as deferred income is significant, because (1) liabilities characterized as deferred income are generally ignored in the calculation of the debt-to-equity ratio and (2) under the provisions of ASC 830, Foreign Currency Matters, the effects on debt of changes in foreign currency exchange rates are accounted for differently from the effects of such changes on deferred income.

ACCOUNTING GUIDANCE

- A liability's characterization depends on the specific facts and circumstances of the underlying transaction.
- The existence of any one of the following factors would result in a rebuttable presumption that a liability should be characterized as debt:
  - Based on its form, the transaction is intended as a borrowing, not a sale.
  - The company has a significant, continuing involvement in generating cash flows that will be paid to an investor.
  - The company or an investor may cancel the transaction, with the company paying a lump sum of cash or transferring other assets to the investor.
  - The terms of the transaction implicitly or explicitly limit an investor's return. (The limitation may be stated explicitly; for example, a rate of return not to exceed 10%. Or the limitation may be implicit in the agreement; for example, if revenues for a particular period do not meet certain expectations, the payment to the investor is calculated in an alternate manner that limits the investor's return.)
  - An investor's rate of return is not significantly affected by variations in the company's measure of performance on which the transaction is based.
  - The investor has recourse to the company for payments due.
- If the proceeds are classified as debt, they should be amortized under the interest method.
- If the proceeds are recognized as revenue, they should be amortized under the units-of-revenue method.
- Amortization for a period under the units-of-revenue method is calculated based on the ratio of the proceeds received from an investor to the total payments expected to be made to the investor over the term of the agreement. That ratio is applied to the cash payment for the period.

ASC 470-10-35-1 through 35-2, 45-7 through 45-8; ASC 835-10-60-9 Increasing-Rate Debt

BACKGROUND

Increasing-rate debt is a financial instrument consisting of notes that mature three months from the original issue date, for example, and that can be extended at the issuer's option for another period of the same duration at each maturity date. The interest rate on the notes increases each time their maturity is extended.

Whether to classify increasing-rate debt as a current or long-term liability is a secondary issue in this discussion, which addresses primarily how to determine interest expense on such debt.

ACCOUNTING ISSUE

- How should an issuer determine interest expense on increasing-rate debt, and what maturity date should be used in that determination?
- How should an issuer account for an excess interest accrual if interest expense is determined by the interest method and the debt is paid earlier than estimated?
- How should the note be classified in the balance sheet?

ACCOUNTING GUIDANCE

- An issuer should determine periodic interest expense on increasing-rate debt by the interest method based on an estimate of the outstanding term of the debt. That estimate should consider the issuer's plans, ability, and intent to service the debt.
- If an issuer repays increasing-rate debt at par before its estimated maturity date, interest expense should be adjusted for excess accrued interest, if any.

- Increasing-rate debt should be classified as current or noncurrent based on whether the borrower anticipates repaying the notes with current assets or noncurrent assets. For example, the debt would be classified as current if repayment were from current assets or from a new short-term borrowing. It would be classified as long-term if repayment were financed by a long-term financing arrangement or from the issuance of equity securities.

EFFECT OF ASC 815

Provisions that extend the term of a debt instrument should be analyzed to determine whether they represent a derivative that should be accounted for separately under the guidance in ASC 815.

PRACTICE POINTER: The guidance in ASC 815 has been amended by the guidance in ASC 815-15-25-4 through 25-5, which permits an entity to elect to measure at their fair value certain hybrid financial instruments with embedded derivatives that otherwise would have to be bifurcated. If an entity elects to measure an entire hybrid instrument at its fair value, that financial instrument *cannot* be used as a hedging instrument in hedging relationship under the guidance in ASC 815.

SUBSEQUENT DEVELOPMENT

ASC 340-10-S99-2 states the view of the SEC staff that the above guidance should be followed in accounting for "bridge financing" that consists of increasing-rate debt.

DISCUSSION

The above guidance is consistent with the guidance in ASC 310-45-13; ASC 505-10-25-1; ASC 605-10-25-1, 25-3, 25-5; ASC 850-10-50-2 (which states that liabilities that are expected to be satisfied with current assets should be classified as current liabilities). Based on the provisions of ASC 470 however, if an entity intends to repay a short-term obligation scheduled to mature within one year of the balance sheet date with (1) proceeds from a long-term obligation, (2) the issuance of equity securities, or (3) by renewing, extending, or replacing it with short-term obligations for an uninterrupted period extending beyond one year (or the operating cycle) from the balance sheet date, the obligation should be classified as a long-term liability, subject to certain criteria.

ASC 470-10-45-1, 55-3 through 55-6 Classification of Obligations When a Violation Is Waived by the Creditor

BACKGROUND

Under Company F's loan agreement with a financial institution, the company must comply with certain covenants that, for example, require maintaining a minimum current ratio or debt-to-equity ratio on a quarterly basis. If Company F violates a covenant at specified dates, quarterly or semiannually, the lender may call the loan. However, the lender may waive the right to call the loan for longer than one year while retaining the right to require the company to comply with the covenant requirement during that period.

ACCOUNTING ISSUE

Under such circumstances, can Company F continue to classify the debt as a noncurrent liability or should the debt be reclassified as a current liability?

ACCOUNTING GUIDANCE

Unless the facts and circumstances indicate otherwise (e.g., the borrower violates a covenant after the balance sheet date but before the financial statements are issued), noncurrent classification is appropriate unless:

- A covenant was violated at the balance sheet date or would have been violated without a loan modification, and
- It is probable that the borrower will not be able to comply with a loan covenant on measurement dates within the next 12 months.

Further, borrowers that classify debt as noncurrent should disclose the negative effects of probable future noncompliance with debt covenants.

DISCUSSION

Resolving how to classify debt when a lender has waived the right to call the debt, but has retained the right to require compliance with debt covenants at interim dates, involves a determination of whether the lender's waiver of the right to call the debt can be considered a grace period as contemplated in ASC 470-10-45-12. Under that guidance in a grace period is a specified period of time during which a lender has waived the right to call the debt, giving the borrower time to cure the violation. For example, if an agreement provides that a borrower who has violated a covenant at the balance sheet date has a three-month grace period to cure a violation, the lender does not have the right to call the debt at the balance sheet date. The guidance in ASC 470-10-45-12 provides that the debt can continue to be classified as noncurrent if it is probable (as defined in ASC 450) at the balance sheet date that the borrower can comply with the covenant within the grace period, thus preventing the lender from calling the debt. If the concept of a grace period in ASC 470-10-45-12 is extended to this issue, it would be necessary to assess the probability that the borrower can comply with the covenant by the next measurement date.

The following five scenarios were discussed:

1. The debt covenants apply only after the balance sheet date, and it is probable that the borrower will not be able to comply with the covenants as required three months after the balance sheet date.
2. The borrower complies with the debt covenants at the balance sheet date, but it is probable that the borrower will fail the requirements three months after the balance sheet date.
3. The borrower complies with the debt covenants at the balance sheet date, but it is probable that the borrower will not meet a more restrictive covenant three months later at the next compliance date.
4. On the compliance date, which occurred three months before the balance sheet date, the borrower had complied with the loan covenants. Before the balance sheet date, the borrower negotiates with the lender to modify the loan agreement by eliminating a compliance requirement at the balance sheet date or by modifying a requirement that the borrower would otherwise fail. The borrower must, however, meet the same requirement or a more restrictive requirement three months later at the next compliance date, and it is probable that the borrower will fail the requirement at that time.
5. The borrower has violated the covenant at the balance sheet date, but obtained a waiver from the lender before issuing the financial statements. The borrower must, however, meet the same or a more restrictive covenant three months later. It is probable that the borrower will not meet the requirement at that date.

Applying the accounting guidance above to those five scenarios, it appears that the debt classification should be based on existing circumstances at the balance sheet date rather than based on expectations. Thus, the debt in scenarios 1, 2, and 3 can continue to be classified as noncurrent, because in each case the borrower complied with the loan covenants at the balance sheet date. In scenarios 4 and 5, however, in which the borrower failed to comply at the balance sheet date, current classification would be required even though the borrower negotiated a waiver in both cases. Noncurrent classification would, nevertheless, be permitted if the borrower expects to repay the debt with noncurrent assets and meets the conditions in ASC 470.

PRACTICE NOTE: Although it is not stated specifically, the presumption is that the waiver of the lender's right to call the debt while retaining the right to require compliance with the debt covenants is, in substance, a grace period, because the probability test in in ASC 470-10-45-12 is applied.

ASC 470-10-S45-1, S99-4; ASC 810-10-S45-1 Classification of a Subsidiary's Loan Payable in Consolidated Balance Sheet When Subsidiary's and Parent's Fiscal Years Differ

BACKGROUND

Company A, which has a February 28, 20X5, year-end, issues consolidated financial statements that include its subsidiary, Company B, which has a December 31, 20X0, year-end. Company B has a material loan payable with a January 31, 20X6, maturity.

Under the guidance in ASC 810-10-45-12, a parent company is permitted to consolidate a subsidiary's financial statements if the difference between their year-ends is no more than three months.

ACCOUNTING ISSUE

How should Company A classify Company B's loan payable in its February 28, 20X5, consolidated financial statements?

SEC STAFF COMMENT

The SEC Observer stated that the SEC staff would expect registrants to classify the loan as current under those circumstances.

ASC 470-10-45-2, 50-3 Subjective Acceleration Clauses in Long-Term Debt Agreements

ACCOUNTING GUIDANCE

Question: Should long-term debt that includes a subjective acceleration clause be classified as a current liability?

Answer: The classification of debt as long-term or current depends on the circumstances. If a borrower has recurring losses or liquidity problems, long-term debt should be classified as current. Otherwise, only disclosure of the acceleration clause would be required. If the likelihood that the debt's due date will be accelerated is remote, neither reclassification nor disclosure would be required.

ASC 470-10-45-3 through 45-6 Balance Sheet Classification of Borrowings Outstanding under Revolving Credit Agreements That Include both a Subjective Acceleration Clause and a Lock-Box Arrangement

BACKGROUND

An entity has a revolving credit agreement with a note due in three years. The borrowing, which is collateralized, includes a subjective acceleration clause and is evidenced by a note signed on entering into the agreement. Under the agreement, the borrower is *required* to maintain a lock-box with the lender, to which the borrower's customers must remit their payments. The lender applies the outstanding payments to reduce the debt.

The effect of an acceleration clause on balance sheet classification for long-term obligations is determined based on the guidance in ASC 470-10-45-2 and 50-3. However, if a borrowing considered to be a short-term obligation has a subjective acceleration clause, it has been classified in the balance sheet as a current liability, under the guidance in ASC 470-10-05-4, 15-2 through 15-3, 45-5, 45-12A through 45-14, 45-16 through 45-21, 50-4, 55-14 through 55-32. The following accounting guidance does not apply if maintaining a lock-box is at a borrower's discretion.

The following guidance also addresses the balance sheet classification of a borrowing with a subjective acceleration clause and a "springing" lock-box arrangement under which amounts paid by a borrower's customers are deposited in the *borrower's* general bank account and are not used by the bank to reduce the debt without the lender's activation of a subjective acceleration clause. However, if a lender exercises the subjective acceleration clause, the lender has the right to redirect all of the lock-box's receipts to the lender's loan account and to apply them against the outstanding debt.

ACCOUNTING ISSUES

1. Should a borrowing under a revolving credit agreement be considered a short-term borrowing if it includes a subjective acceleration clause and requires the borrower to maintain a lock-box with the lender so that customers' payments are remitted directly to the lender and applied to reduce the outstanding debt?
2. Does the answer to question (1) apply to a revolving credit arrangement with a springing lock and a subjective acceleration clause?

ACCOUNTING GUIDANCE

A revolving credit agreement under which borrowings are due at the end of a specified period, such as at the end of three years, not when short-term notes under that agreement roll over, for example, every 90 days, may be classified as long-term debt.

The effect of a subjective acceleration clause on a revolving-credit agreement that is classified as long-term debt should be determined based on the guidance in ASC 470-10-45-2. That is, the classification of a revolving credit agreement as long-term or current under those circumstances depends on the circumstances. If a borrower has recurring losses or liquidity problems, long-term debt should be reclassified as current. Otherwise, only disclosure of a subjective acceleration clause would be required. However, neither reclassification nor disclosure would be required if the likelihood that the lender will accelerate the debt's due date is remote.

Some lenders require borrowers with revolving credit agreements to maintain a lock box with the lender to which customers remit their payments. A revolving credit agreement should be classified as a short-term borrowing if it includes *both* a subjective acceleration clause and a requirement for the borrower to maintain a lock-box with the lender to which customers remit payments that are used to reduce the debt.

The balance sheet classification of debt that includes a subjective acceleration clause should be based on the guidance in ASC 470-10-05-4, 15-2 through 15-3, 45-5, 45-12A through 45-14, 45-16 through 45-21, 50-4, 55-14 through 55-32 or that in ASC 470-10-05-4, 15-2 through 15-3, 45-5, 45-12A through 45-14, 45-16 through 45-21, 50-4, and 55-14 through 55-32, which requires short-term debt with an acceleration clause to be classified as a current liability. An obligation may be classified as a long-term obligation, however, if it is refinanced after the balance sheet date on a long-term basis, thus meeting the conditions in ASC 470-10-45-14, based on an agreement other than a revolving credit agreement.

The term *lock-box arrangement* as it is used in this guidance applies to situations in which a debt agreement requires that a borrower's cash receipts be used in the ordinary course of business to repay the debt without the occurrence of another event. Therefore, because a borrower has no alternative but to use working capital to repay the obligation, under those circumstances a revolving credit agreement should be classified as a *short-term* obligation

Debt in an arrangement with a springing lock box should be classified as a *long-term* obligation, because the customers' payments are *not* used automatically to reduce the debt unless another event has occurred. Because the debt is classified as a long-term obligation, the guidance in ASC 470-10-45-2 (discussed above) should be used to determine the effect of a subjective acceleration clause on the classification of the arrangement discussed.

DISCUSSION

The deciding factor in the first conclusion—the borrowing is a short-term obligation—was the fact that the agreement requires the borrower to maintain a lock-box, enabling the lender to use the proceeds to repay the borrowing and then lend the money back to the borrower under the revolving credit agreement, which results in a new borrowing. Those who supported this view argued that because of the lock-box requirement, the borrowing is repaid with current assets.

ASC 470-10-45-9 through 45-10 Classifying Demand Notes with Repayment Terms

BACKGROUND

In addition to specifying repayment terms, some loan agreements also may include language that enables a creditor to call a loan on demand. For example, an agreement may state that "the term note shall mature in monthly installments as set forth therein *or on demand, whichever is earlier*," or "principal and interest shall be due *on demand, or if no demand is made*, in quarterly installments beginning on . . . ."

ACCOUNTING ISSUES

- How should a loan agreement that allows a creditor to demand payment at the creditor's discretion be classified in a classified balance sheet?
- What disclosures should be made about maturities of a long-term obligation that includes such a clause?

ACCOUNTING GUIDANCE

Debt under an agreement that enables the creditor to demand payment at the creditor's discretion should be classified as a current liability, in accordance with the guidance in ASC 470-10-45-10. A demand provision is not the same as a subjective acceleration clause, which is discussed in ASC 470-10-45-2; ASC 470-10-50-3.

DISCUSSION

The guidance in ASC 470-10-45-10 deals specifically with the classification of an obligation that by its terms can be called by a lender on demand within one year from the balance sheet date (or operating cycle, if longer). It provides that such an obligation should be classified as a current liability, even if the obligation is not expected to be liquidated during that period unless (*a*) the creditor has waived or lost the right to call the debt or (*b*) it is probable that the debtor will cure the violation during the grace period. This issue was addressed, because some had been treating the "due on demand clause" as a subjective acceleration clause under the guidance in ASC 470-10-45-2, 50-3.

ASC 470-10-55-1 Subjective Acceleration Clauses and Debt Classification

The FASB staff discussed its response to an inquiry as to whether the treatment of subjective acceleration clauses under the guidance in (*a*) ASC 470-10-45-2, 50-3 and that in (*b*) ASC 470-10-45-13 through 45-20 is inconsistent. Under the guidance in (*b*), short-term obligations can be classified as noncurrent if an entity has the ability and intent to refinance the obligation on a long-term basis. That ability can be demonstrated by an existing financial agreement. However, under that guidance, an agreement would only qualify if it has no subjective acceleration clauses that enable the lender to accelerate the debt. Conversely, under the guidance in (*a*), as long as acceleration of the due date is remote, there is no need to reclassify a noncurrent liability and disclose the existence of a subjective acceleration clause.

The FASB staff explained that the circumstances discussed in the two pronouncements differ. The guidance in (*a*) deals with loans made initially on a long-term basis; thus, continuing that classification requires a judgment about the likelihood that the loan's due date will be accelerated. Conversely, the guidance in (*b*) deals with circumstances under which a short-term obligation may be excluded from classification as a current liability by getting a new loan or refinancing the debt with long-term debt based on conditions at date refinancing date. The FASB staff justified the higher standard required in (*b*) because it deals with a refinancing of a short-term obligation as long-term rather than with the likelihood that existing long-term debt will be accelerated.

ASC 470-10-55-7 through 9 Classification by the Issuer of Redeemable Instruments That Are Subject to Remarketing Agreements

The FASB staff reported that it received inquiries about the balance sheet classification of debt instruments with the following characteristics:

- The debt has a long maturity (e.g., 30 to 40 years).
- The debt can be put to the issuer for redemption on short notice (within 7 to 30 days).
- The issuer has a remarketing agreement with an agent who agrees to resell redeemed bonds on a best efforts basis under which the agent is required to buy only securities that the agent can sell to the public. The issuer must pay off any debt the agent is unable to resell.
- A short-term letter of credit is used to secure the debt to protect the holder if the redeemed debt cannot be remarketed. The issuer of the redeemable debt must repay the issuer of the letter of credit for amounts drawn down on the same day.

According to the guidance in ASC 470-10-45-10, obligations that are due on demand within one year of the balance sheet should be classified as current liabilities, even if they will not be repaid during that period. The following two conditions are specified in ASC 470-10-45-14 for a short-term liability to be classified as noncurrent if a debtor intends to refinance the liability:

1. The liability will be refinanced on a long-term basis.
2. Either of the following two events occurs before the issuance of the balance sheet to confirm the debtor's ability to refinance short-debt debt on a long-term basis:
   a. A long-term obligation or equity securities have been issued.
   b. The debtor entered into a *financing agreement* based on readily determinable terms meeting all of the following conditions:
      (1) The agreement does not expire within one year (or the entity's operating cycle) from the balance sheet date and cannot be canceled by the lender or investor (obligations incurred cannot be called) during the period except if the debtor violates a provision with which compliance can be determined or measured objectively.
      (2) The debtor had not violated any of the provisions at the balance sheet date and there is no indication that any violations occurred after that date but before the balance sheet was issued. Alternatively, the lender has waived any violation that had occurred at the balance sheet date or before the balance sheet was issued.
      (3) The lender or investor is expected to be financially viable to honor the agreement.

The FASB staff believes that, in accordance with the guidance in ASC 470-1-45-12 issuers should classify as current liabilities debt instruments that can be redeemed by the holder on demand or within one year, even if a best efforts remarketing agreement exists. In that situation, classification as a long-term liability would be acceptable only if a letter-of-credit arrangement meets the requirements in ASC 470-10-45-14 for a financing agreement, as discussed above.

ASC 470-20: DEBT WITH CONVERSION AND OTHER OPTIONS

ASC 470-20-05-1, 05-12A through 12C, 15-2, 25-1, 25-20A, 30-26A, 35-11A, 45-2A, 50-2A through 50-2C, 65-3; ASC 260-10-45-70B Accounting for Own-Share Lending Arrangements in Contemplation of Convertible Debt Issuance

BACKGROUND

Under certain market conditions, entities that need financing find it easier to place convertible debt rather than straight debt; issuing such debt may also be more attractive to the issuer because it has a lower interest rate. Investors that purchase convertible debt frequently use a hedging technique called "delta neutral" hedging to hedge changes in the value of an option to buy shares, such as the one embedded in convertible debt, with a "short" position on the shares. By using a hedge, an investor offsets gains on the conversion option if the price of the stock increases and offsets losses on the conversion option if the stock's price decreases.

Many issuers of convertible debt have also been entering into separate arrangements with the investment bank that underwrites their offering under which the entity issues legally outstanding shares of its own common stock and lends those shares to the investment bank in exchange for a loan processing fee that usually equals the par value of the common stock. Even though the holders of the shares are legally entitled to receive dividends and to vote, such arrangements require that during the period that the shares are loaned to the investment bank, it must reimburse the issuer for dividends paid on the shares even if those shares have been sold in the market. In addition, as long as the investment bank is the owner of record, it is precluded from voting on matters submitted to the issuer's shareholders for a vote. Some agreements include a provision requiring the investment bank to post collateral during the loan term. However, issuers usually do not enforce that requirement.

Investment banks use those shares to enter into equity derivative contracts, such as options, forwards, and total return swaps, on their own behalf with investors in the issuers' convertible debt instruments. Those equity derivative contracts enable the investors to hedge the long position in the issuer's stock that they hold through the convertible debt's embedded conversion option. The investment bank may also sell the loaned shares in equity markets.

Investment banks enter into share loan arrangements, which create a short position, to hedge their own market risk related to their long position as a result of the equity derivative contracts entered into with the investors. By borrowing issuers' shares and the sale of derivatives to investors, investment banks eliminate their own exposure to changes in the issuers' stock prices and create a short position that hedges the investors' conversion option in the convertible debt instruments.

When the convertible debt matures, the investment bank generally must return the loaned shares to the issuer without additional consideration. An issuer may be entitled to a cash payment for the fair value of its common stock if an investment bank does not return the loaned shares.

SCOPE

This guidance applies to an equity-classified share-lending arrangement on an entity's own shares that is executed in contemplation of a convertible debt offering or other financing.

ACCOUNTING GUIDANCE

- *Measurement.* An entity that plans to issue convertible debt instruments or other financing should: (1) measure a share-lending arrangement of its own shares at the fair value of the shares at the date of issuance; and (2) recognize the arrangement in its financial statements as an issuance cost with an offset to additional paid-in capital.
- *Subsequent measurement.* If the default of a counterparty to a share-lending arrangement becomes probable, the issuer of the share-lending arrangement should recognize an expense that equals the then fair value of the unreturned shares, net of the fair value of probable recoveries, with an offset to additional paid-in capital. An issuer of a share-lending arrangement should remeasure the fair value of unreturned shares each reporting period through earnings until consideration on the arrangement payable by the counterparty becomes fixed. Subsequent changes in the amount of probable recoveries also should be recognized in earnings.
- *Earnings per share presentation.* Loaned shares should be excluded from the basic and diluted earnings-per-share calculations unless there is a default of the share-lending arrangement. In that case, the loaned shares would be included in the calculation of basic and diluted earnings per share. If dividends on the loaned shares are not reimbursed to the entity, amounts, if any, including contractual (accumulated) dividends and participation rights in undistributed earnings that may be attributed to the loaned shares should be deducted in the computation of income available to common shareholders, as required in the "two-class" method discussed in ASC 260-10-45-60B.

DISCLOSURE

The following disclosures should be made by entities that enter into a share-lending arrangement on their own shares in contemplation of a convertible debt offering or other financing arrangement. The information should be disclosed in the interim and annual financial statements, in any period in which a share-lending arrangement is outstanding:

- A description of outstanding share-lending arrangements, if any, on an entity's own stock and all significant terms of such arrangements, including the number of shares, the term, the circumstances under which cash settlement would be required, and requirements, if any, for the counterparty to provide collateral.
- The entity's reason for entering into a share-lending arrangement.
- The fair value of outstanding loaned shares as of the balance sheet date.
- How the share-lending arrangement is treated in the earnings per share calculation.
- The unamortized amount and classification of issuance costs related to the share-lending arrangement at the balance sheet date.
- The amount of interest cost recognized in conjunction with the amortization of the issuance costs related to the share-lending arrangement for the reporting period.
- The amounts of dividends, if any, paid for loaned shares that will not be reimbursed.

The disclosures required in ASC 470-10-50-5; ASC 505-10-15-1, 50-3 through 50-5, 50-11 apply to entities that enter into share lending arrangements on their own shares in contemplation of a convertible debt offering or other financing and should disclose:

- The amount of expense reported in the income statement that is related to a default in the period the entity concludes that it is probable that a counterparty to its share-lending arrangement will default.
- In any subsequent period, material changes, if any, in the amount of expense as a result of changes in the fair value of the entity's shares or the probable recoveries.
- If a default is probable but has not yet occurred, the number of shares related to a share-lending arrangement that will be shown in basic and diluted earnings per share when the counterparty's default occurs.

ASC 470-20-05-7 through 05-8, 25-4 through 25-6, 30-3, 30-6, 30-8, 30-10 through 30-11, 30-15, 35-2, 35-7, 40-2 through 40-3, 55-30 through 55-33, 55-35 through 55-38, 55-40 through 55-43, 55-45 through 50-48, 55-50 through 55-54A, 55-56 through 55-60A, 55-62 through 55-66, 55-69; ASC 505-10-50-8 Accounting for Convertible Securities with Beneficial Conversion Features or Contingently Adjustable Conversion Ratios

Notice: As a result of the issuance of ASU 2020-06, *Debt-Debt with Conversion and Other Options (Subtopic 470-20) and Derivatives and Hedging-Contracts in Entity's Own Equity (Subtopic 815-40): Accounting for Convertible Instruments and Contracts in an Entity's Own Equity*, the following guidance will be superseded when that guidance becomes effective in accordance with ASC 815-40-65-1:

a. For public business entities that meet the definition of an SEC filer, except for smaller reporting companies, as defined by the SEC, for fiscal years that begin after December 15, 2021, including interim periods within those fiscal years.

b. For all other entities, for fiscal years that begin after December 15, 2023, including interim periods within those fiscal years.

c. All entities are permitted to apply the guidance early, but not earlier than for fiscal periods that begin after December 15, 2020, including interim periods within those fiscal years.

BACKGROUND

This Issue was addressed because some entities were issuing convertible debt securities and convertible preferred stock with a nondetachable conversion feature that are in-the-money at the commitment date (a beneficial conversion feature), which is the date on which there is an agreement on the terms of the transaction and an investor has committed to purchase the convertible securities based on those terms. The securities may be converted into common stock at a conversion rate that is fixed on the commitment date or at a fixed discount from the common stock's market price at the conversion date, whichever is lower. The conversion price of some convertible securities may vary based on future events—for example, subsequent financing at a lower price than the original conversion price, the company's liquidation or a change of control, or an initial public offering that has a lower price per share than the agreed upon amount.

This guidance applies to convertible debt securities with beneficial conversion features that must be settled in stock and convertible shares with beneficial conversion features that allow an issuer to choose whether to satisfy the obligation in stock or in cash. It also applies to instruments in which the beneficial conversion features are convertible into more than one instrument, such as convertible preferred stock that can be converted into common stock and detachable warrants. The guidance does *not* apply to instruments under the scope of *Accounting for Convertible Debt Instruments That May be Settled in Cash,* which is discussed in this chapter.

ACCOUNTING ISSUES

1. Should a beneficial conversion feature embedded in a convertible security be valued separately at the commitment date?
2. If an embedded beneficial conversion feature should be valued separately, how should it be recognized and measured?
3. How should convertible securities issued with conversion ratios that are adjusted as a result of the occurrence of future events be accounted for?

ACCOUNTING GUIDANCE

Beneficial conversion features embedded in convertible securities should be valued *separately* at the commitment date. (See "Effect of ASC 815," below.)

PRACTICE POINTER: For a revised definition of a commitment date, see the guidance on Issue 5 in *Application of Issue No. 98-5 to Certain Convertible Instruments*, which is discussed below:

1. The *commitment* date is defined here as the date on which an entity has reached an agreement with an unrelated party that is binding on both parties and is usually legally enforceable. The agreement has the following two features:
   a. It includes specific information about all significant terms, including the quantity to be exchanged, a fixed price, and the timing of the transaction. The price may be stated as a specific amount of an entity's functional currency or of a foreign currency. In addition, a specified interest rate or specified effective yield may be stated.
   b. It includes a disincentive for nonperformance that is large enough to make performance probable. For the purpose of applying the definition of a firm commitment, the existence of statutory rights in the legal jurisdiction governing the agreement, such as remedies for default that equal the damages suffered by the counterparty to the agreement, would be a sufficiently large disincentive for nonperformance that makes performance probable.

      It was noted that the commitment date of an agreement that includes subjective provisions permitting either party to rescind its commitment to consummate the transaction should *not* occur until the provisions expire or the convertible instrument is issued, whichever occurs first. For example, an investor may be allowed to rescind its commitment to purchase a convertible instrument if a material adverse change occurs in the issuer's operations or financial condition, or the commitment is conditional on customary due diligence or shareholder approval.

      If the securities are purchased by several investors, such as a group of lenders that participate in a syndicate, the commitment date is the latest commitment date for the group or the issuance date for each individual security, whichever comes first.
2. Embedded beneficial conversion features should be *recognized* and *measured* as follows:
   a. Allocate a portion of the proceeds equal to the intrinsic value of the embedded beneficial conversion feature to additional paid-in capital at the commitment date. The intrinsic value is calculated as the difference between the *conversion price* and the *fair value* of the common stock or other securities into which the security can be converted multiplied by the *number* of shares into which the security can be converted. Fair value is determined at the market price, if available, or at the best estimate of fair value, without adjustments for transferability restrictions, large block factors, avoided underwriter's fees, or time value discounts. To allocate an amount to the beneficial conversion feature of convertible securities issued with detachable warrants or with another security, such as common stock, the

proceeds are first allocated between the convertible instruments and the detachable warrants based on the relative fair value method in ASC 470-20-05-2 through 05-6, 25-2 through 25-3, 25-10 through 25-13, 30-1 through 30-2; ASC 505-10-60-3.

b. If the *intrinsic value* of the beneficial conversion feature is *greater* than the proceeds from the sale of the convertible instrument, the discount assigned to the beneficial conversion feature should *not* exceed the amount of the proceeds allocated to the convertible instrument. *(This guidance has been partially nullified by the guidance in ASC 815.)*

   A discount as a result of the recognition of a beneficial conversion option of a convertible instrument that has a stated redemption date should be amortized from the issuance date to the convertible instrument's stated redemption date regardless of when the instrument's earliest conversion date occurs. However, a discount as a result of the recognition of a beneficial conversion option of a convertible instrument with *no* stated redemption date, such as perpetual preferred stock, should be amortized from the issuance date to the earliest conversion date. (Updated based on the guidance in Issue 6 of *Application of Issue No. 98-5 to Certain Convertible Securities*, which is discussed in this chapter. Also see the Subsequent Development section.) SEC registrants should account for other discounts on perpetual preferred stock with no stated redemption date but with the requirement that it be redeemed upon the occurrence of a future event outside the issuer's control (such as a change in control) based on the guidance in ASC 480-10-S99.

   The issuer should disclose the terms of the transaction in the notes to the financial statements in accordance with the guidance in ASC 470-10-50-5; ASC 505-10-15-1, 50-3 through 50-5, 50-11. That disclosure also should include information about the amount in excess of the instruments' total fair value to be received by the holder at conversion over the proceeds received by the issuer and the amortization period of the discount.

   A discount on convertible *preferred* securities resulting from the allocation of proceeds to a beneficial conversion feature is analogous to a *dividend*, which should be recognized as a return to the preferred shareholders by the effective yield method. (Updated based on the guidance on Issue 6 of *Application of Issue No. 98-5 to Certain Convertible Securities*. Also see the Subsequent Development section.) A discount on convertible *debt* securities as a result of the allocation of proceeds to the beneficial conversion feature should be recognized as *interest expense* using the effective yield method. (Updated based on the guidance on Issue 6 of *Application of Issue No. 98-5 to Certain Convertible Instruments*. See the discussion of the effect of that guidance.)

c. The basic accounting model is modified if an instrument has a multiple-step discount to the market price that increases over time (e.g., 10% at three months, 15% at six months, 20% at nine months, and 25% at one year). The beneficial conversion feature's intrinsic value should be calculated based on the conversion terms that are most beneficial to an *investor*. The resulting discount is amortized over the shortest period during which an investor can recognize that return (e.g., in the above example, 25% over one year).

   A discount on a convertible instrument with a stated redemption date should be amortized from the instrument's issuance date to its stated redemption date, regardless of when the earliest conversion date occurs. In the example above, the discount would be 25% and the amortization period would be from the issuance date to the redemption date. (Updated based on the guidance in Issue 6 of *Application of Issue No. 98-5 to Certain Convertible Instruments*. Also see the Subsequent Development section.)

   A discount on a convertible instrument that has *no* stated redemption date should be amortized over the minimum period in which the investor can recognize that return. In the example above, the discount would be 25% and the amortization period would be one year. (Updated based on the guidance in Issue 6 of *Application of Issue No. 98-5 to Certain Convertible Instruments*. Also see the Subsequent Development section.) However, the amortized portion of the discount may have to be adjusted so that, at any point in time, the discount at least equals the amount the investor could obtain if the security were converted at that date. In the example above, a discount of at least 10% should have been recognized at the end of three months. Under this method, the cumulative amortization should equal the *greater of* (*a*) the amount obtained by using the effective yield method based on the conversion terms most beneficial to an investor or (*b*) the amount of discount that an investor can realize at that interim date.

If the instrument is converted *before* the discount has been fully amortized, the unamortized portion of the discount at the conversion date should be recognized immediately as interest expense or as a dividend, whichever is appropriate (Updated based on the guidance in Issue 6 of *Application of Issue No. 98-5 to Certain Convertible Instruments*. Also see the Subsequent Development section.) However, no adjustment should be made to amounts previously amortized if the amortized discount is greater than the amount realized by the holder because the instrument was converted at an earlier date. The portion of the discount already amortized need not be adjusted, however, if that amount exceeds the amount the holder realized on an early conversion.

d. If an instrument with an embedded beneficial conversion feature is extinguished before its conversion, a portion of the price to reacquire the security includes a repurchase of the beneficial conversion feature. The amount of the price that is allocated to the beneficial conversion feature should be measured based on the intrinsic value of the beneficial conversion feature at the date of extinguishment. An excess, if any, is allocated to the convertible security. A gain or loss on the extinguishment of *debt* should be classified in accordance with the guidance in ASC 470-50-45-1 through 45-2. A gain or loss on a *preferred security* should be accounted for based on the guidance in ASC 260-10-S99-2 and ASC 260-10-S99-3.

The guidance in ASC 835-10-60-10, *Accrued Interest Upon Conversion of Convertible*, which is discussed in this chapter, provides that a convertible debt's carrying amount, including an unamortized premium or discount, if any, should be credited to equity on conversion, continues to apply to convertible debt that does not include a beneficial conversion option.

3. A *contingent* beneficial conversion feature of a security that (*a*) becomes convertible only if a future event not under the holder's control occurs and (*b*) is convertible from inception with conversion terms that change if a future event occurs is *measured* at the stock price on the commitment date, but *recognized* in earnings only when the contingency is *resolved*.

EFFECT OF ASC 815

The guidance in ASC 815 partially nullifies the consensus Issue 1. An issuer and a holder of a security with an embedded conversion feature should analyze the terms of the entire embedded conversion feature to determine whether the guidance in ASC 815-15-25-1 from the host contract for separation and accounting of embedded derivatives applies. Although instruments that meet the criteria under ASC 815-10-15-74 may not be considered derivatives for the purpose of the issuer's accounting and, therefore, would be exempted from the requirements in ASC 815, this exemption does not apply to a holder's accounting for a security that is convertible into an issuer's stock. In addition, a holder will generally find that the conversion feature can be separated from the instrument if it meets the requirement for separation in ASC 815-15-25-1—that is, its economic characteristics and risks are not clearly and closely related to those of the host contract.

Under the guidance in ASC 815-15-25-4 through 25-5, which amends the guidance in ASC 815 entities are permitted to measure at fair value certain hybrid financial instruments with embedded derivatives that otherwise would have to be separated. A hybrid financial instrument that is accounted for entirely at fair value cannot be used as a hedging instrument in a hedging relationship under the guidance in ASC 815. During the discussion of this Issue, some stated that an issuer of such securities would usually be unable to make a reliable measurement of the fair value of an embedded conversion feature. Similarly, that also would apply to the holder of such securities. Under the guidance in ASC 815-15-25-52, however, it would be unusual for an entity to conclude that it cannot reliably separate an embedded derivative from its host contract.

EFFECT OF ASC 480

ASC 480-10-05-1 through 05-6, 10-1, 15-3 through 15-5, 15-7 through 15-10, 25-1 through 25-2, 25-4 through 25-15, 30-1 through 30-7, 35-3 through 35-5, 45-1 through 45-4, 50-1 through 50-4, 55-1 through 55-12, 55-14 through 55-28, 55-34 through 55-41, 55-64; ASC 835-10-60-13; ASC 260-10-45-70A establishes classification and measurement guidance for certain financial instruments that have the characteristics of both liabilities and equity. An issuer is required to classify a financial instrument under the scope of that guidance as a liability or as an asset in some circumstances.

SUBSEQUENT DEVELOPMENT

If the commitment date defined under this guidance did not occur before November 16, 2000, the guidance *Application of Issue 98-5 to Certain Convertible Instruments* (discussed below) should be applied to all instruments issued after that date. See that guidance for the SEC Observer's comments, which provide specific guidance for SEC registrants.

Illustrations of the Accounting for a Beneficial Conversion Feature of a Convertible Security

Example 1—Instruments that are convertible at issuance

A. *Fixed dollar conversion terms*—Convertible debt issued at a $600,000 face value is convertible at issuance into the issuer's common stock at $20 a share. The redemption date is on the fifth anniversary of issuance. The fair value of each share is $25 on the commitment date. The accounting for such instruments is as follows:

1. Calculate the number of shares into which the debt will be converted at the conversion price: $600,000/$20 = 30,000 shares.
2. Calculate the intrinsic value of the beneficial conversion feature at the commitment date: fair value of $25 – $20 conversion price at the commitment date = $5 × 30,000 shares = $150,000.
3. The debt is recognized at $600,000, with the $150,000 intrinsic value of the debt credited to additional paid-in capital.
4. The debt discount should be amortized over a period of five years from the issuance date to the redemption date, because the debt has a stated redemption on the fifth anniversary of the issuance date.
5. Entry at issuance date:

Cash	$600,000	
Debt discount	150,000	
Debt		$600,000
Additional paid-in capital		150,000

(Examples B and C were deleted because they were superseded by later guidance.)

D. *Instrument with fixed terms that change when a future event occurs*—Convertible debt issued at a $600,000 face value is convertible at issuance and redeemable on the fifth anniversary of issuance. The instrument is convertible into the issuer's common stock at $24, 80% of the stock's $30 fair value at the commitment date. However, if the company has an IPO, the convertible debt can be converted at 80% of the fair value of the IPO price or the fair value on the commitment date, whichever is less. Such debt instruments should be accounted for as follows:

1. The instrument includes a "basic" beneficial conversion feature that does not depend at issuance on the occurrence of a future event; its intrinsic value is calculated as follows: (600,000/24) = 25,000 × (30 – 24) = $150,000, which is calculated at the commitment date and recognized at the issuance date. The debt discount (equal to the intrinsic value of the beneficial conversion feature) should be amortized over a five year period from the issuance date to the stated redemption date. (For guidance on recognition and measurement of the contingent beneficial conversion feature, see the guidance on issues 3 and 7 of ASC 470-20-25-8 through 25-9, 25-20, 30-1, 30-5, 30-7, 30-9 through 30-10, 30-12 through 30-13, 30-16 through 30-21, 35-1, 35-4, 35-7 through 35-10, 40-1, 40-4, 45-1, 55-11 through 55-12, 55-14 through 55-17, 55-19 through 55-21, 55-23 through 55-24, 55-26 through 55-27; ASC 505-10-50-7. ASC 260-10-50-1, Application of Issue No. 98-5 to Certain Convertible Instruments.)
2. The accounting entry at issuance date:

Cash	$600,000	
Debt discount	150,000	
Debt		$600,000
Additional Paid-in Capital		150,000

Under the terms of the convertible debt instrument, a calculation of the number of shares that would be received on conversion if an IPO occurs is not permitted at the commitment date.

E. *Instrument with variable terms that depend on the occurrence of a future event*—Convertible debt issued at $600,000 face value is redeemable on the fifth anniversary of the issuance date. The instrument is convertible at issuance into the issuer's common stock at 80% of the $30 stock price at the commitment date. However, if the price of each common share has increased by at least 20% one year after an IPO, the debt can be converted at 60% of the stock price. Such instruments should be accounted for as follows:

1. The intrinsic value of the beneficial conversion feature is measured based on the terms at issuance. Calculated at the commitment date, it equals $150,000 (calculated in the same manner as in example D above) and is recognized at issuance. The debt discount is amortized over the five-year redemption period.
2. The accounting entry is the same as the one in example D above.
3. Under the terms of the convertible debt instrument, a calculation of the number of shares that would be received on conversion if an IPO occurs is not permitted at the commitment date. (For guidance on recognition and measurement of the contingent beneficial conversion feature, see the guidance on issues 3 and 7 of *Application of Issue No. 98-5 to Certain Convertible Instruments*.)

(Example F has been superseded by subsequent guidance.)

Example 2—Instruments that are *not* convertible at issuance

A. *Fixed dollar conversion terms*—(This Example, formerly Example A, has been modified as a result of the guidance in *Application of Issue No. 98-5 to Certain Convertible Instruments*.)

Convertible debt with a $600,000 face value redeemable on the fifth anniversary of issuance is convertible any time after one year into the issuer's common stock at $24 per share. The fair value of each share is $30 at the commitment date. The accounting for such instruments is as follows:

1. Calculate the intrinsic value of the beneficial conversion feature as in the previous examples.
2. A portion of the proceeds from the issuance of the convertible debt, equal to the intrinsic value is allocated to additional paid-in capital.
3. The debt discount should be amortized over the five-year redemption period.
4. The accounting entry is the same as above.

(Example B has been superseded by subsequent guidance.)

Example 3—Extinguishment of convertible debt with a beneficial conversion feature before conversion

(This example has been modified as a result of the guidance in *Application of Issue No. 98-5 to Certain Convertible Instruments*.)

Proceeds from the issuance of zero coupon debt	$600,000
The intrinsic value of the beneficial conversion feature	$540,000

The issuer recognizes $540,000 at the commitment date as a discount on the debt. The offsetting entry is a credit to additional paid-in capital. The remaining $60,000 is recognized as debt and is accreted to its full face value of $600,000 over the five-year redemption period of the debt. The debt is extinguished one year after the issuance date.

Facts at the extinguishment date:

Reacquisition price	$700,000
Intrinsic value of beneficial conversion feature	432,000
Carrying value of debt	140,000

At the extinguishment date, the proceeds from the extinguishment first should be allocated to the beneficial conversion feature ($432,000) with the remainder allocated to the extinguishment of the convertible debt security.

The accounting entry to record the extinguishment is as follows:

*Debt	$140,000	
Additional paid-in capital	432,000	
Loss on extinguishment	128,000	
Cash		$700,000

---

* The net carrying amount of the debt one year after issuance is calculated using the effective interest method to amortize the debt discount over the five-year redemption period.

PRACTICE NOTE: See Chapter 37, *ASC 505—Equity,* for a discussion of Disclosure of Information about Capital Structure Relating to Contingently Convertible Securities (formerly FASB Statement No. 129).

ASC 470-20-05-9, 35-11, 40-11; ASC 835-10-60-10 Accrued Interest upon Conversion of Convertible Debt

BACKGROUND

The conversion terms of some convertible debt instruments provide that former debt holders will forfeit interest accrued but unpaid at the conversion date if they convert zero coupon bonds, which do not pay interest, or other convertible debt securities into the issuer's equity securities between interest payment dates.

ACCOUNTING ISSUES

1. Should interest expense be accrued or imputed on such debt instruments to the date of conversion when it is forfeited?
2. If interest should be accrued to the date of conversion, how should it be recognized when the debt is converted into common stock?

ACCOUNTING GUIDANCE

1. Accrue or impute interest to the date the debt instrument is converted to equity securities.
2. Interest accrued from the last payment date, if applicable, to the date of conversion should be charged to interest expense and credited to capital as part of the cost of securities issued, net of related income tax effects, the same as the converted debt principal and unamortized issue discount or premium on the debt, if any.

ASC 470-20-05-11; 40-4A through 40-10; 55-68 Accounting for the Conversion of an Instrument That Becomes Convertible upon the Issuer's Exercise of a Call Option

BACKGROUND

Contingently convertible debt instruments (CoCos), which were discussed in *The Effect of Contingently Convertible Instruments on Diluted Earnings per Share,* are convertible debt instruments that include a contingent feature and generally are convertible into an issuer's common shares after the stock price of the issuer's common stock exceeds a predetermined amount, known as a market price trigger, for a specified period of time. A CoCo's conversion price usually is higher than the underlying stock's market price when the CoCo is issued and its market price trigger usually is higher than the conversion price.

Since the issuance of the guidance in *The Effect of Contingently Convertible Instruments on Diluted Earnings per Share,* some have asked whether CoCos also may include embedded call options under which issuers can call such debt instruments when they would not be otherwise convertible. Holders would have the option to receive cash for the call price or a specified number of shares of the issuer's stock. For example, a CoCo with a $1,000 par amount matures on September 30, 2012. The holder can convert the debt to the issuer's securities if the price of the debt security exceeds $1,500. The issuer has the option to call the debt between 2008 and the debt's maturity date. The holder may choose to receive cash for the call amount or a fixed number of shares, regardless of whether the price trigger of $1,500 has been met.

SCOPE

This guidance applies only to the accounting for the issuance of equity securities to settle a debt instrument that has become convertible because the issuer has exercised a call option included in the original terms of the debt instrument and that otherwise would *not* have been convertible at the conversion date. Conversions based on terms that include changes made by a debtor to conversion privileges under the terms of the debt at issuance in order to encourage conversion are accounted for according to the guidance in ASC 470-20-05-10, 40-13 through 40-17, 45-2, 55-2 through 55-9, and guidance for modifications to embedded conversion options is discussed in ASC 470-50-40-12, 40-15 through 40-16 *(Debtor's Accounting for a Modification (or exchange) of Convertible Debt)*. That guidance does *not* apply to convertible debt instruments accounted for under the scope of *Accounting for Convertible Debt Instruments That May Be Settled in Cash upon Conversion (Including Partial Cash Settlement)*.

ACCOUNTING ISSUE

How should an issuer account for the conversion of a debt instrument that becomes convertible when the issuer exercises its call option under the original terms of the debt instrument?

ACCOUNTING GUIDANCE

- Equity securities issued on the conversion of a debt instrument that include a *substantive* conversion feature at the issuance date should be accounted for as a *conversion* if the debt instrument becomes convertible because the issuer has exercised a call option based on the debt instrument's original conversion terms. *No* gain or loss should be recognized on the issuance of equity securities to settle the debt instrument.
- Equity securities issued on the conversion of a debt instrument that does *not* include a *substantive* conversion feature at the issuance date should be accounted for as a *debt extinguishment* if the debt instrument becomes convertible because the issuer has exercised a call option based on the debt instrument's original conversion terms. In that case, the equity securities' fair value should be considered a part of the price of reacquiring the debt.
- A convertible debt instrument's issuance date is its *commitment* date, as defined in Issue 4 of *Application of EITF Issue 98-5, Accounting for Convertible Securities with Beneficial Conversion Features or Contingently Adjustable Conversion Ratios,* to Certain Convertible Instruments. The determination as to whether a conversion feature is substantive should be based on the assumptions, considerations, and information about the marketplace available as of the issuance date, although that determination may be made *after* the issuance date.

The guidance above should be applied as follows:

- A conversion feature is considered to be *substantive* if it is at least *reasonably possible*, as defined in ASC 450, that the conversion feature will be exercisable in the future without the issuer's exercise of its call option. The holder's intent need not be evaluated to make such a determination.
- It was noted that for the purpose of this guidance, a conversion feature would *not* be considered to be substantive if the debt instrument's conversion price at issuance is so high that it would *not* be regarded at least *reasonably possible* at the date of issuance that a conversion would occur—even if the instrument includes a feature that would permit conversion *before* the maturity date. Further, a debt instrument does *not* include a substantive conversion feature if a conversion can only occur if the issuer exercises its call option.
- The determination as to whether a debt instrument's conversion feature is *substantive* should be based solely on assumptions, considerations, and marketplace information that were available as of the instrument's *issuance* date, even though that determination may be made *after* the debt instrument has been issued.

The following guidance, which is *not* all inclusive, may be useful in determining whether a conversion feature is substantive—that is, that it is at least reasonably possible that the conversion feature will exercised in the future:

- Compare the fair value of the conversion feature to the fair value of the debt instrument.
- Compare the effective annual interest rate based on the terms of the debt instrument to the estimated effective annual rate that an issuer estimates it could get on a similar nonconvertible debt instrument with an equivalent expected term and credit risk.
- Compare the fair value of the debt instrument to the fair value of an identical convertible instrument that has a *noncontingent* conversion option to determine the effect of a contingency. Similarity in the fair value of the two instruments may indicate that the conversion feature is substantive. To use this approach, it must be clear that the conversion feature, without considering the contingencies, is substantive.
- Consider the nature of the conditions required for the instrument to become convertible by a qualitative evaluation of the conversion provisions. For example, if it is likely that a contingent event will occur *before* an instrument's maturity date, it may indicate that a conversion feature is substantive. To use this approach, it must be clear that the conversion feature, without considering the contingencies, is substantive.

It was noted that guidance on this Issue does *not* address the accounting for a contingently convertible debt instrument when the guidance in ASC 260, Earnings per Share, and related interpretive guidance, including the guidance in *The Effect of Contingently Convertible Instruments on Diluted Earnings per Share*, is applied.

ASC 470-20-10-1 through 10-2, 15-2, 15-4 through 15-6, 25-21 through 25-27, 30-27 through 30-31, 35-12 through 35-20, 40-19 through 40-26, 45-3, 50-3 through 50-6, 55-70 through 55-82, 65-1; ASC 815-15-55-76A; ASC 825-10-15-5 Accounting for Convertible Debt Instruments That May Be Settled in Cash upon Conversion (Including Partial Cash Settlement)

Notice: As a result of the issuance of ASU 2020-06, *Debt-Debt with Conversion and Other Options (Subtopic 470-20) and Derivatives and Hedging-Contracts in Entity's Own Equity (Subtopic 815-40): Accounting for Convertible Instruments and Contracts in an Entity's Own Equity*, the following guidance will be superseded when that guidance becomes effective in accordance with ASC 815-40-65-1:

a. For public business entities that meet the definition of an SEC filer, except for smaller reporting companies, as defined by the SEC, for fiscal years that begin after December 15, 2021, including interim periods within those fiscal years.

b. For all other entities, for fiscal years that begin after December 15, 2023, including interim periods within those fiscal years.

c. All entities are permitted to apply the guidance early, but not earlier than for fiscal periods that begin after December 15, 2020, including interim periods within those fiscal years.

BACKGROUND

The type of convertible debt instruments discussed below are settled (*a*) in cash on conversion for the accreted value of the obligation, and (*b*) in cash or stock for the conversion spread, which is the excess conversion value over the accreted value. Those debt instruments have been accounted for as a convertible debt instruments in accordance with the guidance in ASC 470-20-05-2 through 05-6, 25-2 through 25-3, 25-11 through 25-13, 30-1 through 30-2; ASC 505-10-60-3. Diluted earnings per share on such instruments have been calculated in the same manner as debt issued with detachable warrants. Because the accounting for those instruments has a less dilutive effect on the calculation of diluted earnings per share than convertible debt instruments for which earnings per share must be calculated by the if-converted method, the issuance of such convertible debt instruments has become very popular and has caused some practitioners to question whether the accounting for those debt instruments properly represents their economic effects. In addition, the FASB staff believes that the accounting for those debt instruments results in an inappropriate expansion of the guidance in ASC 470-20-25-12 which initially did not apply to convertible debt instruments settled in cash or partial cash, and that the manner in which those debt instruments are accounted for misleads investors.

ACCOUNTING GUIDANCE

Scope

The convertible debt instruments under the scope of this guidance are *not* discussed in ASC 470-20-25-12. This guidance applies only to convertible debt instruments that, in accordance with their terms, must be settled at conversion in cash or partially in cash, unless an instrument includes an embedded conversion option that must be accounted for separately as a derivative under the provisions of ASC 815. In addition, mandatorily convertible preferred shares classified as liabilities under the provisions of ASC 480-10-05-1 through 05-6, 10-1, 15-3 through 15-5, 15-7 through 15-10, 25-1 through 25-2, 25-4 through 25-15, 30-1 through 30-7, 35-3 through 35-5, 45-1 through 45-4, 50-1 through 50-4, 55-1 through 55-12, 55-14 through 55-28, 55-34 through 55-41, 55-64; ASC 835-10-60-13; and ASC 260-10-45-70A, which include an unconditional obligation requiring an issuer to settle the face amount of the instruments in cash at a specified date are considered to be convertible debt instruments for the purpose of determining whether the instruments should be accounted for under the scope of this guidance. However, convertible preferred shares accounted for as equity or as temporary equity are *not* included under the scope of this guidance.

The following guidance also does *not* apply to convertible debt instruments that:

- Require or permit settlement in cash or other assets on conversion only if the holders of the underlying shares receive the same form of consideration in exchange for their shares.
- Require issuers to settle their obligations for fractional shares on conversion in cash, but otherwise do *not* require or permit settlement on conversion in cash or other assets.

Recognition

The underlying principle of the approach of this guidance is that interest costs related to convertible debt instruments recognized in periods *after* their initial recognition should represent the borrowing rate an entity would have incurred had it issued a comparable debt instrument *without* the embedded conversion option. That goal is accomplished by requiring issuers to separately account for the liability and equity components of convertible debt instruments.

Initial Measurement

Issuers should apply the following guidance for the *initial* measurement of convertible debt:

- First, determine the carrying amount of an instrument's liability component based on a fair value measurement of a similar liability (including embedded features, if any, other than the conversion option) that has *no* related equity component.
- Next, determine the carrying amount of the instrument's equity component corresponding to the embedded conversion option by deducting the liability component's fair value from the initial proceeds attributed to the total convertible debt instrument.
- For the purpose of the determinations made in the two bullets above and for the purpose of subsequent measurement, evaluate in the context of a total convertible debt instrument whether its embedded features, other than the conversion option (including an embedded prepayment feature) are *substantive* at the issuance date. If, at issuance, an entity has concluded that it is *probable* that a convertible instrument's embedded feature will *not* be exercised, that embedded feature is deemed to be *nonsubstantive* and would *not* affect the initial measurement of an instrument's liability component.
- Attribute a portion of the initial proceeds of a convertible debt instrument to additional unstated (or stated) rights or privileges, if any, included in the transaction based on guidance in other applicable U.S. generally accepted accounting principles (GAAP).
- Apply the guidance in ASC 815 first if embedded features *other* than the conversion option (e.g., prepayment options) are embedded in a convertible debt instrument accounted for under this guidance to determine whether any of those features should be accounted for separately from the liability component as derivative instruments under the guidance in ASC 815 and its related interpretations. As stated above, this guidance does *not* apply if *no* equity component exists because the conversion option is accounted for separately as a derivative under the guidance in ASC 815. The following steps provide guidance to issuers of convertible debt instruments on how to apply the guidance in ASC 815 and its related interpretations to the accounting for embedded derivatives:

  Step 1: Identify the embedded features, other than the embedded conversion option, that should be evaluated under the guidance in ASC 815 and its related interpretations.

  Step 2: Apply the guidance in ASC 815 and its related interpretations to determine whether any of the embedded features identified in Step 1 should be accounted for separately as derivative instruments. This guidance does *not* affect the determination of whether an embedded feature needs to be accounted for separately as a derivative.

  Step 3: Apply the guidance in the first two bullets above to separate the liability component, including embedded features, if any, other than the conversion option, from the equity component.

  Step 4: If applicable, split embedded features, if any, which must be accounted for separately as derivatives based on the evaluation in Step 2, from the convertible debt instrument's liability component in accordance with the guidance in ASC 815 and its related interpretations. An embedded derivative's separation from the liability component would *not* affect the accounting for the equity component.

Transaction costs incurred with third parties other than the investors that are directly related to the issuance of convertible debt instruments accounted for under this guidance should be allocated to the liability and equity components in the same proportion as the allocation of proceeds and accounted for as costs of issuing debt and equity, respectively.

Because of the separate recognition of a liability component and an equity component for convertible debt instruments accounted for under this guidance, a temporary basis difference related to the liability component may occur when the provisions of ASC are applied. Additional paid-in capital should be adjusted when deferred taxes are initially recognized for the tax effect of that temporary difference.

The fair value option under the scope exception in ASC 825-10-15-5 does *not* apply to convertible debt instruments under the scope of this guidance.

Subsequent Measurement

Under this guidance, the excess of the principal amount of the liability component *over* its initial fair value must be amortized to interest cost based on the interest method discussed in ASC 835-30-35-2. In accordance with the interest method, debt discounts must be amortized over the expected life of a similar liability that does *not* have a related equity component (considering the effects of embedded features other than the conversion option). An issuer that initially measured the fair value of the liability component based on a valuation technique consistent with an income approach is required to consider the periods of cash flows used initially to determine the appropriate period over which to amortize the debt discount.

A liability component's expected life is *not* affected by embedded features that were determined to be *nonsubstantive* at the time the convertible debt instrument is issued. The third bullet under the discussion related to initial measurement above provides guidance for determining whether or not an embedded feature, other than the conversion option, is substantive.

An equity component that continues to meet the conditions for equity classification in ASC 460-10-60-14; ASC 480-10-55-63; ASC 505-10-60-5; ASC 815-10-15-78, 55-52; ASC 815-15-25-15; ASC 815-40-05-1 through 50-4, 05-10 through 05-12, 25-1 through 25-5, 25-7 through 25-20, 25-22 through 25-24, 25-26 through 25-35. 25-37 through 25-40, 30-1, 35-1 through 35-2, 35-4 through 35-6, 35-8 through 35-13, 40-1 through 40-2, 50-1 through 50-5, 55-1 through 55-18, *Accounting for Derivative Financial Instruments Indexed to, and Potentially Settled in, a Company's Own Stock*, need *not* be remeasured in subsequent periods. If in accordance with the provisions of that guidance a conversion option must be reclassified from stockholders' equity to a liability measured at fair value, the difference between the amount that had been recognized in equity and the fair value of the conversion option at the reclassification date should be accounted for as an adjustment to stockholders' equity. However, if a conversion option that had been accounted for in stockholders' equity is reclassified as a liability, gains or losses recognized to account for that conversion option at fair value while classified as a liability should *not* be reversed if subsequently the conversion option is reclassified back to stockholders' equity. Reclassifications of a conversion option do *not* affect the accounting for the liability component.

Derecognition

An issuer that derecognizes an instrument under this guidance should allocate the consideration transferred and the related transaction costs incurred to the extinguishment of the liability component and the reacquisition of the equity component.

Instruments accounted for under this guidance should be derecognized as follows, regardless of the form of consideration transferred at settlement, which may include cash or other assets, stock, or any combination of the two:

- Measure the fair value of the consideration transferred to the holder. In the case of a modification or exchange that results in the original instrument's derecognition, measure the new instrument at fair value (including both the liability and equity components if the new instrument also is accounted for under the provisions of this guidance).
- Allocate the fair value of the consideration transferred to the holder between the liability and equity components of the original debt instrument as follows:
  1. Allocate a portion of the settlement consideration to the liability component's extinguishment at its fair value immediately *before* the extinguishment. Recognize a gain or loss on debt extinguishment in the income statement for a difference, if any, between consideration allocated to the liability component and the sum of (*a*) the net carrying amount of the liability component, and (*b*) unamortized debt issuance costs, if any.
  2. Allocate the remaining settlement consideration to the equity component's reacquisition and recognize that amount as a reduction of stockholders' equity.

Allocate a portion of the settlement consideration to other unstated (or stated) rights or privileges, if any, included in the derecognition transaction in addition to the settlement of the convertible debt instrument based on guidance in other applicable U.S. GAAP.

Allocate to the liability and equity components transaction costs incurred with third parties other than the investor(s) that are directly related to the settlement of a convertible debt instrument accounted for under this guidance in proportion to the allocation of consideration transferred at settlement and accounted for as debt extinguishment costs and equity reacquisition costs, respectively.

Modifications and Exchanges

To determine whether a modification or an exchange of an original instrument accounted for under the scope of this guidance should be accounted for as an extinguishment of that instrument or as a modification to the original instrument's terms, an issuer should apply the guidance in ASC 470-50-40-12, 40-15, 40-16 (Debtor's Accounting for a Modification (or Exchange) of Convertible Debt Instruments) and ASC 470-50-05-4, 15-3, 40-6 through 40-14, 40-17 through 40-20, 55-1 through 55-9 (Debtor's Accounting for a Modification or Exchange of Debt Instruments). An issuer of an original instrument that is a modified or exchanged instrument, but *not* derecognized, should reevaluate the liability component's expected life under the section for subsequent measurement in this guidance, and determine a new effective interest rate for the liability component in accordance with the guidance in ASC 470-50-40-12, 40-15, 40-16 and ASC 470-50-05-4, 15-3, 40-6 through 40-14, 40-17 through 40-20, 55-1 through 55-9.

The components of an instrument under the scope of this guidance that has been modified to no longer require or permit cash settlement on conversion should continue to be accounted for separately, unless the original instrument must be derecognized under the guidance in ASC 470-50-40-12, 40-15, 40-16 and ASC 470-50-05-4, 15-3, 40-6 through 40-14, 40-17 through 40-20, 55-1 through 55-9. Accounting in accordance with *other* GAAP (e.g., ASC 470-20-25-12), not this guidance, is required for a new convertible debt instrument that was issued after the original convertible debt instrument was derecognized under the guidance in ASC 470-50-40-12, 40-15, 40-16 and ASC 470-50-05-4, 15-3, 40-6 through 40-14, 40-17 through 40-20, 55-1 through 55-9 and that may *not* be settled in cash on conversion.

An issuer should apply the guidance in ASC 470-50-40-12, 40-15, 40-16 and ASC 470-50-05-4, 15-3, 40-6 through 40-14, 40-17 through 40-20, 55-1 through 55-9. to determine whether extinguishment accounting is required if a convertible debt instrument *not* originally under the scope of this guidance is modified so that it qualifies to be accounted for under the scope of this guidance. If the modification is *not* accounted for as an extinguishment, the guidance discussed above should be applied *prospectively* from the date of the modification and the liability component should be measured at its fair value as of the date of the modification. The fair value of the liability component should be deducted from the total carrying amount of the convertible debt instrument to determine the carrying amount of the equity component represented by the embedded conversion option. A portion of the unamortized debt issuance costs, if any, should be reclassified at the modification date and accounted for as equity issuance costs based on the proportion of the overall carrying amount of the convertible debt instrument allocated to the equity component.

Induced Conversions

The terms of an instrument under the scope of this guidance may be amended to bring about early conversion (e.g., by offering a more favorable conversion ratio or paying an additional amount for conversions that occur *before* a specific date). In that case, an issuer should recognize a loss equal to the fair value of all securities and other amounts transferred in the transaction that exceed the fair value of the consideration that would have been issued under the instrument's original conversion terms. The instruments would be derecognized based on this guidance for derecognition using the fair value of the consideration that would have been issued in accordance with the instrument's original conversion terms. This guidance does *not* apply if the holder does not exercise the embedded conversion option.

Balance Sheet Classification of the Liability Component

An issuer's determination whether to classify the liability component as a current or a long-term liability is *not* affected by this guidance. All of a convertible debt instrument's terms (including the equity component) should be considered in making that determination by applying other applicable U.S. GAAP. The liability component's balance sheet classification also has *no* effect on that component's measurement in accordance with this measurement guidance.

Disclosure

The objective of the disclosure requirements under this guidance is to provide information to financial statement users about the terms of convertible debt instruments within the scope of those financial statements and how information about those debt instruments is presented in an issuer's balance sheet and income statement. In addition to the disclosures required in other applicable GAAP, entities should provide the following information in their annual financial statements about convertible debt instruments under the scope of this guidance that were outstanding during any of the periods presented.

An entity should disclose the following information as of each date for which a balance sheet is presented:

a. The carrying amount of the equity component.
b. The principal amount of the liability component, its amortized discount, and its net carrying amount.

The following information should be disclosed as of the most recent balance sheet presented:

a. The remaining period over which a discount on the liability component, if any, will be amortized
b. The conversion price and the number of shares used to determine the total consideration to be delivered on conversion
c. The amount by which the instrument's if-converted value exceeds its principal amount, regardless of whether the instrument is currently convertible. This disclosure is required only for public entities, as defined in ASC, *Glossary*
d. Information about derivative transactions entered into in connection with the issuance of instruments within the scope of this guidance, including the terms of those derivative transactions, how they relate to the instruments under the scope of this guidance, the number of shares underlying the derivative transactions, and the reasons for entering into those derivative transactions. The purchase of call options that are expected to substantially offset changes in the conversion option's fair value is an example of a derivative transaction entered into in connection with the issuance of an instrument under the scope of this guidance. That disclosure is required regardless of whether the related derivative transactions are accounted for as assets, liabilities, or equity instruments.

An entity should disclose the following information for each period for which an income statement is presented:

a. The effective interest rate on the liability component for the period
b. The amount of interest cost related to both the contractual interest coupon and amortization of the discount on the liability component recognized for the period.

ASC 470-20-25-8 through 25-9, 25-20, 30-1, 30-5, 30-7, 30-9 through 30-10, 30-12 through 30-13, 30-16 through 30-21, 35-1, 35-4, 35-7 through 35-10, 40-1, 40-4, 45-1, 55-11 through 55-12, 55-14 through 55-17, 55-19 through 55-21, 55-23 through 55-24, 55-26 through 55-27; ASC 505-10-50-7; ASC 260-10-50-1 Application of Issue No. 98-5 to Certain Convertible Securities

Notice: As a result of the issuance of ASU 2020-06, *Debt-Debt with Conversion and Other Options (Subtopic 470-20) and Derivatives and Hedging-Contracts in Entity's Own Equity (Subtopic 815-40): Accounting for Convertible Instruments and Contracts in an Entity's Own Equity*, the following guidance will be superseded when that guidance becomes effective in accordance with ASC 815-40-65-1:

a. For public business entities that meet the definition of an SEC filer, except for smaller reporting companies, as defined by the SEC, for fiscal years that begin after December 15, 2021, including interim periods within those fiscal years.
b. For all other entities, for fiscal years that begin after December 15, 2023, including interim periods within those fiscal years.
c. All entities are permitted to apply the guidance early, but not earlier than for fiscal periods that begin after December 15, 2020, including interim periods within those fiscal years.

BACKGROUND

Under the guidance in *Accounting for Convertible Securities with Beneficial Conversion Features or Contingently Adjustable Conversion Ratios* (formerly EITF Issue 98-5, which is discussed above), an in-the-money nondetachable beneficial conversion features embedded in convertible securities should be valued separately at the issue date. Under that guidance, embedded beneficial conversion features are recognized and measured based on their intrinsic value at the commitment date. Guidance is also provided on the measurement and recognition of beneficial conversion features *contingent* on future events. That guidance has been reconsidered because certain practice questions have been raised about the application of that guidance.

PRACTICE NOTE: See Chapter 46, *ASC 740—Income Taxes*, for a discussion of ASC 740-10-55-51 (Income Tax Consequences of Issuing Convertible Debt with a Beneficial Conversion Feature).

ACCOUNTING ISSUES

1. Is the intrinsic value model discussed in *Accounting for Convertible Securities with Beneficial Conversion Features or Contingently Adjustable Conversion Ratios* sufficiently operational to address practice Issues or should embedded beneficial conversion options be measured based on a fair value method?

2. If the intrinsic value model is retained, in determining whether an instrument includes a beneficial conversion feature, should an issuer calculate the intrinsic value of a conversion option based on (*a*) a conversion price specified in the instrument or (*b*) an effective conversion price based on the proceeds received for or allocated to the convertible instrument?
3. Under the guidance in the ASC references in Issue 1, above, if a convertible instrument includes an embedded *contingent* conversion option, the intrinsic value of the contingent conversion option is measured based on the fair value of the underlying stock at the commitment date, but that amount is not recognized unless an event occurs that causes the contingency to be resolved. In applying the model under that guidance, which conversion option should be considered an "initial" conversion option and which should be considered a "contingent" conversion option?
4. Is a contingent conversion feature that will reduce the conversion price if the fair value of the underlying stock declines after the commitment date to or below a specified price that is lower than the fair value of the underlying stock at the commitment date, a beneficial conversion option even under both of the following conditions: (*a*) the initial active conversion price equals or exceeds the fair value of the underlying stock at the commitment date; and (*b*) at the future date on which the adjustment of the conversion price is triggered, the *contingent* conversion price exceeds the fair value of the underlying stock at the commitment date?
5. When does a commitment date occur for the purpose of determining the fair value of an issuer's common stock used to measure an embedded conversion option's fair value?
6. Should the commitment date, as defined in Issue 5 above, also be the date on which the assumptions, including the fair value of an issuer's stock, are determined for the purpose of allocating the proceeds, in accordance with the guidance in ASC 470-20-05-2 through 05-6, 25-2 through 25-3, 25-10 through 25-13, 30-1 through 30-2; ASC 505-10-60-3 on a relative fair value basis to separate instruments in a financing transaction that includes a convertible instrument with an embedded conversion feature?
7. Is it appropriate to accrete (*a*) a discount that results from an allocation of proceeds on a relative fair value basis to a transaction's separate instruments over the convertible instrument's life and (*b*) a discount from recording a beneficial conversion option under the guidance in the ASC references in Issue 1 above over the period to the first date the convertible instrument may be converted?
8. How should an issuer apply the guidance in the ASC references in Issue 1 above if a contingent conversion option's terms do not permit calculation at the commitment date of the number of shares a holder would receive when the price is adjusted on the occurrence of a contingent event until the contingent event actually occurs?
9. How should the guidance in the ASC references in Issue 1 above be applied if a beneficial conversion option terminates after a specified period of time and the instrument is mandatorily redeemable at a premium at that date?
10. How should a convertible instrument issued to a provider of goods or services be accounted for?
11. Is a commitment date for convertible instruments issued as paid-in-kind (PIK) interest or dividends (*a*) the commitment date of the original convertible instrument to which the PIK issuance relates or (*b*) the date on which interest is recognized as a liability or a dividend is declared?
12. How should an issuer account for the issuance of a convertible instrument to repay its debt on a nonconvertible instrument when the nonconvertible instrument's matures, including whether the model under the guidance in the ASC references in Issue 1 above applies to the embedded conversion option in the instrument issued as payment of the matured debt?

ACCOUNTING GUIDANCE

1. The intrinsic value model in *Accounting for Convertible Securities with Beneficial Conversion Features or Contingently Adjustable Conversion Ratios*(Issue 98-5) should be retained.
2. The intrinsic value, if any, of an embedded conversion option should be computed using the effective conversion price based on the proceeds received for, or allocated to, the convertible instruments. Consequently, an issuer would account for a financing transaction that includes a convertible instrument as follows: (*a*) allocate the proceeds received on a fair value basis to the convertible instrument and other detachable instruments, such as detachable warrants, if any, included in the exchange, and (*b*) apply the model in *Accounting for Convertible*

Securities with Beneficial Conversion Features or Contingently Adjustable Conversion Ratios to the amount allocated to the convertible security and calculate an effective conversion price, which will be used to measure an embedded conversion option's intrinsic value, if any.

3. The intrinsic value of an embedded conversion option should be measured using the most favorable conversion price that would be in effect at the conversion date assuming that the current circumstances will not change, except for the passage of time. An issuer should account for changes to conversion terms that would be triggered by future events not under the Issuer's control as contingent conversion options of which the intrinsic value is not recognized until the triggering event occurs.

   Excess amortization should not be reversed if the amortized amount of a discount on a convertible security as a result of an initial measurement of a conversion option's intrinsic value (before the conversion option is adjusted due to the occurrence of a future event) is greater than the remeasured amount of the conversion option's intrinsic value after the conversion option has been adjusted. In contrast, a debit should be recognized in paid-in-capital to adjust an amount initially recognized inequity for the conversion option's intrinsic value if the unamortized portion of an original discount is greater than the amount required for the total discount (amortized and unamortized) to equal the adjusted conversion option's intrinsic value if the unamortized portion of an original discount is greater than the amount required for the total discount (amortized and unamortized) to equal the adjusted conversion option's intrinsic value. An adjusted unamortized discount, if any, should be amortized based on the interest method and the guidance in Issue 8 below.

4. A beneficial conversion amount must be recognized if a conversion price is reduced (reset) under the circumstances discussed in Issue 4 above as a result of a contingent conversion feature, because the holder realizes the instrument's enhanced economic value when the price is reset. A convertible instrument should be considered to be debt settled in stock if the price of the security's conversion option is continuously reset based on price increases or decreases of the underlying stock so that the value of the common stock to the holder is fixed at any conversion date. In that case, the guidance in *Accounting for Convertible Securities with Beneficial Conversion Features or Contingently Adjustable Conversion Ratios* would apply only to the initial accounting for the convertible security, including an initial active beneficial conversion feature, if any, but the provisions related to the contingent beneficial conversion option apply only the first time the option price is reset.

5. For consistency with the definition of a firm commitment in ASC 815 and in ASC 815-25-55-84, the definition of a commitment date in *Accounting for Convertible Securities with Beneficial Conversion Features or Contingently Adjustable Conversion Ratios* is replaced by the following definition:

   A legally enforceable agreement reached with an unrelated party that is binding on both parties has the following characteristics:

   a. All significant terms are specified, including the quantity to be exchanged in the transaction, a fixed price in the entity's functional currency or a foreign currency or as a specified interest or specified effective yield, and its timing.

   b. Performance is probable because there is a sufficiently large disincentive for nonperformance. The existence of statutory rights in the legal jurisdiction governing the agreement under which the nondefaulting party can pursue remedies equivalent to the damages suffered provides, in and of itself, a sufficiently large disincentive for nonperformance to apply the definition of a firm commitment.

   It was noted that a commitment date would *not* occur until an agreement's subjective provisions that would permit either party to rescind its commitment to consummate a transaction have expired or the convertible security has been issued, whichever occurs earlier.

6. The same measurement date should be used in applying the guidance in ASC 470-20-05-2 through 05-6, 25-2 through 25-3, 25-10 through 25-13, 30-1 through 30-2; 505-10-60-3 and in *Accounting for Convertible Securities with Beneficial Conversion Features or Contingently Adjustable Conversion Ratios* so that (*a*) the proceeds from a transaction are allocated to the separable components and (*b*) the intrinsic value of a conversion option is measured based on measurement attributes as of the same point in time. Therefore, when the proceeds of a convertible security are allocated under the guidance in ASC 470-20-05-2 through 05-6, 25-2 through 25-3, 25-10 through 25-13, 30-1 through 30-2; ASC 505-10-60-3 to the separate securities issued together with it, the allocation should be determined based on the relative fair values of all the securities at the commitment date defined in Issue 5 above.

7. The following is guidance for the accretion of discounts:
   a. The model discussed in *Accounting for Convertible Securities with Beneficial Conversion Features or Contingently Adjustable Conversion Ratios* should be modified to require that issuers of convertible securities that have a *stated* redemption date be required to recognize a discount when they recognize a beneficial conversion option that will be accreted from the date of issuance to the stated convertible security's redemption date, regardless of the earliest conversion date. The guidance in *Accounting for Convertible Securities with Beneficial Conversion Features or Contingently Adjustable Conversion Ratios* should continue to apply to convertible securities without a stated redemption date.
   b. At the date of conversion, interest expense or a dividend, as appropriate, should be immediately recognized for the remaining unamortized discount due to (*a*) an allocation of proceeds under the guidance in ASC 470-20-05-2 through 05-6, 25-2 through 25-3, 25-10 through 25-13, 30-1 through 30-2; ASC 505-10-60-3 to other separable securities included in securities with beneficial conversion features and (*b*) the discount that results from the accounting for the beneficial conversion.
   c. The calculation of an embedded conversion option's intrinsic value is not affected by costs of issuing convertible securities. Such costs should also not be offset in the calculation of the conversion option's intrinsic value against proceeds received from the issuance. The Task Force noted that issuance costs in this consensus are limited to incremental and direct costs incurred with parties other than the investor in the convertible security. Amounts paid to an investor when the transaction is consummated should be accounted for as a reduction in the issuer's proceeds, not as issuance costs, they do affect the calculation of an embedded option's intrinsic value.

   All discounts should be accounted for based on their nature, i.e., a discount that occurs as a result of the accounting for a beneficial conversion option is amortized from the date on which a security was issued to the earliest conversion date. SEC registrants should account for other discounts on perpetual preferred stock that has no redemption date but that must be redeemed upon the occurrence of a future event not under the issuer's control based on the guidance in ASC 480-10-S99.
8. If under the terms of a contingent conversion option, an issuer is not permitted to calculate the number of shares the holder would receive when the price is adjusted on the occurrence of a contingent event, the issuer should calculate the number of shares that the holder would receive based on the new conversion price. That number of shares should be compared to the number that would have been received before the contingent event occurred. The incremental intrinsic value from the resolution of the contingency and the adjustment to the conversion price, which is recognized when the contingent event occurs, equals the difference between the number of shares in the two calculations multiplied by the stock price at the commitment date. The discount would be accreted in accordance with the guidance in Issue 5 above.

PRACTICE POINTER: This guidance applies to convertible securities with a beneficial conversion feature that ends after a specified period of time. A convertible security under the scope of this guidance that was issued in the form of equity shares and whose terms require the holder to redeem the shares if the conversion feature expires becomes a liability under the guidance in ASC 480-10-05-1 through 05-6, 10-1, 15-3 through 15-5, 15-7 through 15-10, 25-1 through 25-2, 25-4 through 25-15, 30-1 through 30-7, 35-3 through 35-5, 45-1 through 45-4, 50-1 through 50-4, 55-1 through 55-12, 55-14 through 55-28, 55-34 through 55-41, 55-64; ASC 835-10-60-13; ASC 260-10-45-70A when the conversion feature expires. Under the guidance in ASC 480-10-30-2, a security that becomes redeemable and is reclassified as a liability should be measured at its fair value. A corresponding reduction should be made to equity by adjusting paid-in capital if the fair value of the liability is different from the amount at which the convertible debt was reported. No gain or loss should be recognized. If a convertible security in the form of shares is convertible into a variable number of shares based mainly or exclusively on one of the conditions stated in ASC 480-10-25-14 but must be redeemed by transferring assets if the security is *not* converted, the convertible security becomes a liability under the guidance in ASC 480-10-25-14 because the outstanding shares represent an unconditional obligation to be redeemed. That security is no longer accounted for under the scope of this guidance.

---

9. If a beneficial conversion option terminates after a specified time period and the security becomes mandatorily redeemable at a premium, the guidance in *Accounting for Convertible Securities with Beneficial Conversion Features or*

Contingently Adjustable Conversion Ratios should be applied with the discount accreted to the mandatory redemption amount, because a holder who received an in-the-money embedded conversion option is entitled to receive a premium when the instrument is redeemed.

10. See ASC 470-20-05-12, 25-17 through 25-19; ASC 470-30-22-26 below. ASC 480-10-05-1 through 05-6, 10-1, 15-3 through 15-5, 15-7 through 15-10, 25-1 through 25-2, 25-4 through 25-15, 30-1 through 30-7, 35-3 through 35-5, 45-1 through 45-4, 50-1 through 50-4, 55-1 through 55-12, 55-14 through 55-28, 55-34 through 55-41, 55-64; ASC 835-10-60-13; ASC 260-10-45-70A provide guidance to issuers on the classification and measurement of certain financial instruments with the characteristics of both liabilities and equity and requires issuers to classify financial instruments under the scope of that guidance as liabilities or as assets, under certain circumstances.
11. The original commitment date for convertible securities on which interest or dividends must be paid-in-kind (PIK) with the same convertible securities as those originally issued is the commitment date for the convertible securities issued to satisfy the agreement if the issuer or holder cannot choose another form of payment, and the holder will always receive the number of shares on conversion as if all accumulated dividends or interest have been PIK, even if the original security or a portion of it has been converted before accumulated dividends or interest were declared or accrued. If so, the fair value of the issuer's underlying stock at the commitment date for the original issuance is used to measure the intrinsic value of the embedded conversion option in the PIK securities. In other situations, the date that interest is recognized as a liability or a dividend is declared is the commitment date for convertible securities issued as PIK interest or dividends with the intrinsic value of the conversion option embedded in such PIK securities being measured based on the fair value of the issuer's underlying stock at that date.
12. The fair value of a convertible security issued to repay a nonconvertible security at maturity should be equal to the redemption amount owed on the nonconvertible debt if the old debt has matured and the Issuer's exchange of debt securities is *not* a troubled debt restructuring under the guidance in ASC 310; ASC 470. The fair value of the convertible debt should not exceed the amount at which the nonconvertible debt must be redeemed, because the issuer could have paid that amount in cash. The intrinsic value, if any, of the new debt's embedded conversion option should be measured and accounted for after the exchange under the model in *Accounting for Convertible Securities with Beneficial Conversion Features or Contingently Adjustable Conversion Ratios* based on the fair value of the proceeds received. It was noted that the guidance in ASC 470-50-05-4, 15-3, 40-6 through 40-14, 40-17 through 40-20, 55-1 through 55-9 (Debtor's Accounting for a Modification or Exchange of Debt Securities) should be applied first if the original instrument is extinguished before its maturity.

SEC OBSERVER COMMENT

The SEC Observer stated that registrants are expected to apply the guidance in Issue 2 to all transactions accounted for under the guidance in *Accounting for Convertible Securities with Beneficial Conversion Features or Contingently Adjustable Conversion Ratios* including those for which a commitment date occurred before November 16, 2000. Registrants should report the initial application of that guidance to all existing, terminated, and converted transactions subject to the guidance in *Accounting for Convertible Securities with Beneficial Conversion Features or Contingently Adjustable Conversion Ratios* as of the beginning of the registrant's quarter that includes November 16, 2000, in a manner similar to a cumulative effect of a change in accounting principle in accordance with the guidance in ASC 250 (FAS-154). A cumulative effect, if any, should be recognized and accounted for in accordance with the guidance in Issue 98-5 before recognizing the effect of other consensus positions in this Issue.

ASC 470-20-05-12; 25-17 through 25-19; 30-22 through 30-26 Accounting for a Convertible Security Granted or Issued to a Nonemployee for Goods or Services or as Consideration Payable to a Customer

Notice: As a result of the issuance of ASU 2020-06, *Debt-Debt with Conversion and Other Options (Subtopic 470-20) and Derivatives and Hedging-Contracts in Entity's Own Equity (Subtopic 815-40): Accounting for Convertible Instruments and Contracts in an Entity's Own Equity*, the following guidance will be superseded when that guidance becomes effective in accordance with ASC 815-40-65-1:

a. For public business entities that meet the definition of an SEC filer, except for smaller reporting companies, as defined by the SEC, for fiscal years that begin after December 15, 2021, including interim periods within those fiscal years.
b. For all other entities, for fiscal years that begin after December 15, 2023, including interim periods within those fiscal years.
c. All entities are permitted to apply the guidance early, but not earlier than for fiscal periods that begin after December 15, 2020, including interim periods within those fiscal years.

BACKGROUND

In addition to the FASB's guidance in ASC 470, the EITF issued the guidance on accounting for convertible securities with beneficial conversion features in *Accounting for Convertible Securities with Beneficial Conversion Features or Contingently Adjustable Conversion Ratios* (formerly Issue 98-5), and in *Application of EITF Issue 98-5 to Certain Convertible Securities* (formerly Issue 00-27), (both Issues are discussed above). In addition, ASC 718, *Compensation—Stock Compensation*, and ASC 505-50-05-3, 05-8, 15-2 through 15-3, 25-2, 25-4, 25-9, 30-2 through 30-7, 30-11 through 30-14, 30-21 through 30-23, 30-25 through 30-28, 30-30 through 30-31, 35-3, 35-5 through 35-10, 55-2 through 55-11, 55-13 through 55-17, 55-20 through 55-24, 55-28, 55-31 through 55-40; ASC 440-10-60-4 (formerly Issue 96-18, Accounting for Equity Securities That Are Issued to Other Than Employees for Acquiring, or in Conjunction with Selling, Goods or Services) have provided guidance on accounting for equity securities (including convertible securities) that are issued in exchange for goods or services. However, neither the FASB nor the EITF has provided guidance for the recognition and measurement of transactions in which convertible securities are issued to nonemployees in exchange for goods or services or combined with cash. The convertible securities discussed below include a nondetachable conversion option that allows a holder to convert the security into the issuer's stock.

ACCOUNTING ISSUES

1. Should the intrinsic value of the conversion option of a convertible security issued in exchange for goods or services or combined with cash be measured under the model in *Accounting for Convertible Securities with Beneficial Conversion Features or Contingently Adjustable Conversion Ratios*, as interpreted by *Application of EITF Issue 98-5 to Certain Convertible Securities* (formerly Issue 00-27), at (*a*) the security's commitment date as defined in Issue 00-27, (*b*) the measurement date under Issue 96-18, or (*c*) the later of the two dates?

2. How should the fair value of the convertible security be measured?

3. Should distributions paid or payable on such convertible securities be recognized as a financing cost (interest expense or dividend) or as a cost of the goods or services received from the counterparty?

4. Should a purchaser of a convertible security with a beneficial conversion option for cash account for goods or services provided (received) as an adjustment to the consideration for the convertible security if the purchaser also provides (receives) goods or services to (from) the issuer under a different contract?

ACCOUNTING GUIDANCE

It was noted that the existing guidance should be applied as follows:

1. To determine the fair value of a convertible equity or debt security issued in exchange for goods or services (or combined with cash) that can be converted into the issuer's equity securities, apply the guidance in ASC 718, as interpreted by ASC 505-50-05-3, 05-8, 15-2 through 15-3, 25-2, 25-4, 25-9, 30-2 through 30-7, 30-11 through 30-14, 30-21 through 30-23, 30-25 through 30-28, 30-30 through 30-31, 35-3, 35-5 through 35-10, 55-2 through 55-11, 55-13 through 55-17, 55-20 through 55-24, 55-28, 55-31 through 55-40; ASC 440-10-60-4 (EITF Issue 96-18).

2. To determine whether a convertible security includes a beneficial conversion option, apply the requirements of Issue 98-5 and Issue 00-27 so that the fair value determined in (1) above is considered the proceeds from issuing the security.

3. To measure the intrinsic value, if any, of the conversion option under Issue 98-5, as interpreted by Issue 00-27, compare the proceeds received for the security (fair value calculated under (1) above) to the fair value of the common stock the counterparty would receive when the option is exercised.

The following guidance was provided on the Issues:

1. The fair value of a convertible security issued in exchange for goods or services and the intrinsic value, if any, of a conversion option under the guidance in (formerly EITF Issue 98-5) should be determined using the *measurement date* in ASC 505-50-05-3, 05-8, 15-2 through 15-3, 25-2, 25-4, 25-9, 30-2 through 30-7, 30-11 through 30-14, 30-21 through 30-23, 30-25 through 30-28, 30-30 through 30-31, 35-3, 35-5 through 35-10, 55-2 through 55-11, 55-13 through 55-17, 55-20 through 55-24, 55-28, 55-31 through 55-40; ASC 440-10-60-4 (formerly Issue 96-18), not the commitment date in ASC 470-20-25-8 through 25-9, 25-20, 30-1, 30-5, 30-7, 30-9 through 30-10, 30-12 through 30-13, 30-16 through

30-21, 35-1, 35-4, 35-7 through 35-10, 40-1, 40-4, 45-1, 55-11 through 55-12, 55-14 through 55-17, 55-19 through 55-21, 55-23 through 55-24, 55-26 through 55-27; ASC 505-10-50-7; ASC 260-10-50-1 (formerly EITF Issue 00-27).

2. The following guidelines should be used to determine the fair value of a convertible security:
   a. The fair value of the goods or services received should be used if that amount can be determined with reliability and the issuer has not recently issued similar convertible securities.
   b. The best evidence of a convertible security's fair value may be found in recent issuances of similar convertible securities for cash to parties having only an investor relationship with the issuer.
   c. The fair value of a convertible security should not be less than the fair value of equity shares to which it would be converted if reliable information about (a) or (b) above does not exist.
3. Distributions paid or payable under a convertible security should be accounted for as a cost of goods or services received unless the security is considered to have been issued under the guidance in ASC 718 and ASC 505-50-S25-1; S99-1 (formerly Topic D-90, Grantor Balance Sheet Presentation of Unvested, Forfeitable Equity Securities Granted to a Nonemployee), which provides that forfeitable equity securities are considered unissued until future services have been provided. Thereafter, distributions under such securities should be accounted for as financing costs. A discount on a convertible security as a result of a beneficial conversion feature should not be accreted until the securities are considered to have been issued for accounting purposes.
4. To determine whether the fair value of goods and services and that of a convertible security equal the separately stated pricing of an agreement for goods or services and of a convertible security, it is necessary to evaluate the terms of both. If the fair value and separately stated pricing are not equal, the terms of those transactions should be adjusted by recognizing the fair value of the convertible security and adjusting the fair value of the purchase or sales price of the goods or services. To determine the fair value of a convertible security issued to a provider of goods or service that is part of a larger issuance, evidence of the fair value of that convertible security may be found in the amount paid by unrelated investors making a substantive investment in the issuance.

ASC 470-50: MODIFICATIONS AND EXTINGUISHMENTS

ASC 470-50-05-1, 15-2 through 15-3, 40-3 Early Extinguishment of Debt through Exchange for Common or Preferred Stock

BACKGROUND

Under the guidance in ASC 470-50-05-1, 15-3 through 15-4, 40-2, 40-4; ASC 850-10-60-3, a conversion of debt into common or preferred stock is not an extinguishment if the conversion represents the exercise of a conversion right contained in the terms of the debt issue. Other exchanges of common or preferred stock for debt would constitute an extinguishment.

ACCOUNTING GUIDANCE

Question: Does the guidance in ASC 470-50-05-1, 15-3 through 15-4, 40-2, 40-4; ASC 850-10-60-3, apply to extinguishments of debt effected by the issuance of common or preferred stock, including redeemable and fixed-maturity preferred stock?

Answer: All extinguishments of debt must be accounted for in accordance with the guidance in ASC 310-40-15-3 through 15-12, 10-1 through 10-2, 25-1 through 25-2, 35-2, 35-5, 35-7, 40-2 through 40-6, 40-8, 50-1 through 50-2, 55-2; ASC 470-60-15-3 through 15-12, 35-1 through 35-12, 45-1 through 45-2, 55-3, 10-1 through 10-2; ASC 450-20-60-12 as amended by the guidance in ASC 470-50-45-1. The guidance in ASC 470-50-05-1, 15-3 through 15-4, 40-2, 40-4; ASC 850-10-60-3 applies to all extinguishments except those subject to the requirements of ASC 310-40-15-3 through 15-12, 10-1 through 10-2, 25-1 through 25-2, 35-2, 35-5, 35-7, 40-2 through 40-6, 40-8, 50-1 through 50-2, 55-2; ASC 470-60-15-3 through 15-12, 35-1 through 35-12, 45-1 through 45-2, 55-3, 10-1 through 10-2; ASC 450-20-60-12, which applies to extinguishments in troubled debt restructurings. In accordance with the guidance in ASC 470-50-05-1, 15-3 through 15-4 40-2, 40-4; ASC 850-10-60-3, the difference between the net carrying amount of the extinguished debt and the reacquisition price is recognized currently in income of the period of extinguishment. In this situation, the reacquisition price of the extinguished debt is the value of the common or preferred stock issued or the value of the debt, whichever is more clearly evident.

ASC 470-50-05-4, 15-3, 40-6 through 40-14, 40-17 through 40-20, 55-1 through 55-9 Debtor's Accounting for a Substantive Modification and Exchange of Debt Securities

PRACTICE NOTE: The guidance in ASC 860, which superseded the guidance in FAS-125, did not change that pronouncement's guidance on the extinguishment of liabilities. The guidance in this Issue was not reconsidered in ASC 860-10-35-4, 35-6, 05-8; ASC 860-20-25-5, 55-46 through 55-48; ASC 860-50-05-2 through 05-4, 30-1 through 30-2, 35-1A, 35-3, 35-9 through 35-11, 25-2 through 25-3, 25-6, 50-5; ASC 460-10-60-35 which amended the guidance in ASC 860.

PRACTICE NOTE: The guidance in this Issue has been amended by the guidance in *Debtor's Accounting for a Modification (or Exchange) of Convertible Debt Instruments*, which is discussed below.

PRACTICE NOTE: ASU 2020-03, *Codification Improvements to Financial Instruments*, amends (*a*) ASC 470-50-40-17 (Fees Between Debtor and Creditor) and (b) ASC 470-50-40-18 (Third-Party Costs of Exchange or Modification) to include a reference to ASC 470-50-40-21 (Line-of-Credit or Revolving-Debt Arrangements).

BACKGROUND

Under the provisions of ASC 405-20-40-1, which superseded existing guidance on extinguishment of debt, a liability is extinguished and derecognized only if one of the following two conditions exists:

- The debtor is relieved of the obligation by paying the creditor in cash, other financial assets, goods, or services, or the debtor has reacquired the outstanding debt securities, which are either canceled or held as treasury bonds, *or*
- The debtor obtains a legal release from being primarily liable on the obligation.

Exchanges of debt or modifications of debt that have a substantive effect on the amount and timing of the future cash flows of the debt securities are not treated as extinguishments under the guidance in ASC 860, which does not address the accounting for such transactions.

ACCOUNTING ISSUES

- How should a debtor account for an exchange of debt securities with substantially different terms?
- How should a debtor account for a substantial modification of terms of an existing debt agreement that is not a troubled debt restructuring?

ACCOUNTING GUIDANCE

- An *exchange* of debt securities with substantially different terms is accounted for as a debt extinguishment, with the liability for the existing debt derecognized in accordance with the guidance in ASC 405-20-40-1.
- A substantial modification of the terms of existing debt is accounted for and reported as an extinguishment the same as an exchange of debt with substantially different terms, because the debtor can achieve the same economic result in the two transactions.
- From a debtor's perspective, if the present value of the cash flows under the terms of a new debt security differ by at least 10% from the present value of the cash flows remaining under the original debt security, the exchange of debt securities with the creditor or the modification of debt in a nontroubled debt restructuring is achieved with substantially different debt securities. Present value is calculated based on the following guidance:
  - — The new debt security's cash flows include all cash flows stated in the terms of the new debt security as well as amounts paid by the debtor to the creditor less amounts received by the debtor from the creditor in the exchange or modification.
  - — For debt securities (original or new) that have a floating interest rate, the variable rate effective on the date of the exchange or modification is used to calculate the security's cash flows.
  - — For debt securities (original or new) that are callable or puttable, cash flows are analyzed separately assuming exercise and nonexercise of the put option. Cash flow assumptions that result in a smaller change are used to determine whether the 10% difference for substantially different securities is met.

— Judgment should be used to determine the appropriate cash flows of debt securities with contingent payment terms or unusual interest rate terms.

— For accounting purposes, the effective interest rate of the original debt security is used as the discount rate to calculate the present value of cash flows.

— If debt exchanged or modified within one year before the current transaction was determined not to be substantially different, the debt terms existing before that exchange are used to determine whether the current exchange or modification is substantially different.

- Changes in the amount of principal, interest rates, or maturity of the debt can affect cash flow. Fees exchanged between a debtor and a creditor for the purpose of changing any of the following features or provisions of the debt also can affect cash flows:
  — Recourse or nonrecourse features
  — Priority of the obligation
  — Collateralization (including changes in collateral) or noncollateralization features
  — A guarantor or elimination thereof
  — Option features

  Debt securities are *not* substantially different if a debt security is changed or modified as discussed above, but the effect on the present value of cash flow is less than 10%.
- New debt securities as a result of exchanges or modifications of old debt that are considered to be substantially different (the old debt is extinguished) are recognized initially at fair value. That amount is used to determine the gain or loss on extinguishment and the effective interest rate of the new debt security.
- New debt securities as a result of exchanges or modifications of old debt that are *not* considered to be substantially different are *not* accounted for as extinguishments of the old debt. A new effective interest rate is calculated on the date of the exchange or modification based on the carrying amount of the original debt security and the revised cash flows.
- For exchanges or modifications that result in an extinguishment of the old debt and the new debt is initially recognized at fair value:
  — Fees paid by a debtor to a creditor or received by a debtor from a creditor (e.g., to cancel the debtor's call option or to extend a no-call period) in the exchange or modification are associated with the extinguishment transaction and included in determining the gain loss on the extinguishment.
  — Amounts paid to third parties as a result of an exchange or modification (such as legal fees) are associated with the new or modified debt securities and amortized over the term of the new or modified debt based on the interest method similar to debt issue costs.
- For exchanges or modifications that do *not* result in an extinguishment of the old debt:
  — Fees paid by the debtor to the creditor or received by the debtor from the creditor (e.g., to cancel the debtor's call option or to extend a no-call period) in the exchange or modification are associated with the new or modified debt securities and amortized with existing unamortized discount or premium to adjust interest expense over the remaining term of the new or modified debt based on the interest method.
  — Amounts paid to third parties as a result of the exchange or modification, such as legal fees, are expensed as incurred.

The following guidance applies to a transaction in which a borrower, who instead of acquiring debt securities directly, loans money to a third party to acquire the borrower's debt securities. The borrower and third party agree to offset the payments of their payables and receivables as they become due as long as the third party retains the borrower's debt. Under those circumstances, the original debt securities should not be extinguished and the securities should not be offset in the borrower's financial statements against the receivable from the third party.

Because the above guidance contemplates only single debtors and creditors and does not consider how actions taken by a third-party intermediary acting as an agent or a principal would affect a debtor's accounting, the following implementation guidance is provided:

1. A transaction in which a debtor pays cash to a creditor to extinguish its current debt and the creditor issues new debt in exchange should be accounted for as an extinguishment of the current debt only if the new debt security has substantially different terms, as defined in the Issue. This guidance does *not* apply to exchanges of cash between debtors and creditors, because such transactions already meet the requirement for debt extinguishment in ASC 405-20-40-1.
2. In determining whether there has been an exchange of debt securities or a modification of the terms of an existing debt security between a debtor and a creditor, the actions of a third-party intermediary acting as an *agent* for a debtor should be considered in the same manner as if they had been taken by the debtor.
3. In determining whether there has been an exchange of debt securities or a modification of the terms of an existing debt security between a debtor and a creditor, the actions of a third-party intermediary acting as a *principal* should be considered to be those of a third-party creditor in the same manner as the actions of any other creditor.
4. A debtor's accounting for a debt is not affected by transactions among debt holders, because such actions do not cause a modification of the terms of the original debt or an exchange of debt securities between a debtor and the debt holders.
5. To determine whether a gain or loss should be recognized on transactions between a debtor and a third-party creditor, the guidance in ASC 405-20-40-1 and the guidance in this Issue should apply.

When applying the guidance, it may be necessary to determine whether a third-party intermediary is acting as an agent or as a principal. Legal definitions of those terms and an evaluation of the facts and circumstances related to a third-party intermediary's involvement may be useful. The following indicators should be considered:

- If an intermediary is only required to place or reacquire debt for a debtor but does not risk its own funds, it is an indicator that the third-party intermediary is acting as an *agent* for the debtor. For example, an intermediary that uses its own funds is acting as an agent if the debtor will compensate the intermediary for any incurred losses. However, an intermediary is acting as a *principal* if the intermediary risks losing its own funds.
- If an intermediary places notes issued by a debtor in accordance with a best-efforts agreement under which the intermediary agrees to buy only securities that can be sold to others and otherwise the debtor must repay the debt, it is an indicator that the intermediary is acting as an *agent* for the debtor. An intermediary can be deemed to be acting as a *principal* if the intermediary acts on a firmly committed basis and must hold debt that is not sold.
- An indicator that an intermediary is acting as an *agent* is an arrangement in which the intermediary can act only on an exchange of debt or a modification of debt terms based on the debtor's instructions. However, an intermediary that acquires debt from or exchanges debt with another debt holder in the market and the transaction exposes the intermediary to the risk of loss may be deemed to be acting as a *principal*.
- If an intermediary is paid only a specified fee to act for the debtor, it is an indicator that the intermediary is acting as an *agent*. An intermediary's ability to realize a gain on the transaction based on the value of the security issued by the debtor is an indicator that the intermediary is acting as a *principal*.

Debtors can recognize gains or losses on transactions related to a modification or exchange of debt securities only for transactions meeting the conditions in ASC 405-20-40-1 or the requirements for extinguishment under this guidance.

Illustrations of Debtor's Accounting for a Substantive Modification and Exchange of Debt Securities

Identification of Debtor and Creditor

- XYZ Bank (lead bank/creditor) makes a $10 million loan to ABC Construction Co. (debtor). The debt instrument is a contract between the bank and the debtor. Subsequently, the bank transfers a $1 million undivided interest in the debt to each of nine banks that have a participating interest in the loan, as evidenced by a certificate of participation, but are not direct creditors. The debtor would apply this guidance only if the debtor and the lead bank agree to exchange the debt or to modify its terms.
- A syndicate of ten banks (creditors) jointly funds a $10 million loan to ABC Construction Co. (debtor). In this transaction, each member of the syndicate individually loans $1 million to the debtor and issues a separate debt instrument. After one year, the debtor asks the creditors to modify the terms of the debt instruments. Six creditors agree to the modification, but four do not. Because each of the creditors has a separate right to repayment under the provisions of ASC 860-10-55-4 and ASC 310-10-25-4, the debtor accounts for the modified

loans in accordance with the guidance in this Issue. The loans from creditors who would not modify the terms of the debt instruments are unaffected.

- IHT Manufacturing Corp. issues identical debt instruments to an underwriter who sells them in the form of securities to the public. Each investor (creditor) holding a security (debt instrument) is considered to be a separate creditor for the purpose of applying the guidance in this Issue. If IHT asks the holders of the securities for a modification in the terms of the debt instruments (or an exchange of debt instruments), the debtor applies the guidance only to debt instruments held by creditors that agree to an exchange or modification. Debt instruments held by the other security holders are unaffected.

Exchanges or Modifications of Debt Involving a Third-Party Intermediary

1. In the following three scenarios, the actions of an investment banker acting in the capacity of a third-party intermediary for a debtor (*agent*) are viewed as the actions of the debtor:
   a. The investment banker acquires debt instruments from holders for cash and later transfers debt instruments with the same or different terms to the same or different investors. The debtor accounts for the cash transaction as an extinguishment of the debt, because it meets the criterion in ASC 405-20-40-1.
   b. The investment banker redeems the debtor's outstanding debt instruments in exchange for new debt instruments. The debtor must account for that transaction under the guidance in this Issue. The transaction would be accounted for as an extinguishment only if the terms of the new debt are substantially different from those of the debt exchanged.
   c. The investment banker acquires debt instruments from holders for cash and at the same time issues new debt instruments for cash. This transaction is also accounted for under the guidance in this Issue; the original debt is extinguished only if the terms of the new debt are substantially different from those of the original debt.
2. In this transaction, a third-party investment banker acts as a *principal* and is treated the same as other debt holders. If the investment banker acquires debt instruments from other debt holders, the transaction does not affect the debtor's accounting. Exchanges and modifications between the investment banker and the debtor are accounted for under the guidance in this Issue based on whether the terms of the new or modified debt instrument differ substantially from those of the original debt instrument.

Transactions among Debt Holders

An investment banker intermediary acting as a *principal* for a debt holder exchanges a debt instrument for cash with another party in the marketplace. Because the funds do not pass through the debtor or its agent, the debtor's accounting is not affected by that transaction. However, if the cash exchanged by the debt holders passes through the debtor, the debtor would account for the transaction as an extinguishment.

Gain or Loss Recognition

A debtor cannot recognize a gain or loss in the following situations until the debt has been extinguished under the provisions of ASC 405-20-40-1 and the consensus in this Issue:

1. A debtor announces it intends to call a debt instrument at the first call date. (The SEC Staff Accounting Bulletin No. 94 (Recognition of a Gain or Loss on Early Extinguishment of Debt) states that the staff would object to gain or loss recognition in a period other than the period in which the debt is extinguished.)
2. A debtor places amounts equal to the principal, interest, and prepayment penalties of the debt instrument in an irrevocable trust established for the benefit of the creditor. (Under the guidance in ASC 860, debt is not extinguished in an in-substance defeasance.)
3. The debtor and a creditor agree that the debtor will redeem a debt instrument issued by the debtor from a third party.

SUBSEQUENT DEVELOPMENT

The guidance in ASC 470-50-40-12, 40-15 through 40-16 *(Debtor's Accounting for a Modification (or Exchange) of Convertible Debt Instruments)*, which was issued in 2006, amends the guidance discussed above and provides the following guidance:

- If a debt instrument is exchanged or its terms are modified, the resulting change in the embedded conversion option's fair value should *not* be included in the cash flow test used under the guidance in this Issue to determine whether a new debt instrument's terms are *substantially* different from those in the original debt instrument. If the results of the cash flow test under the guidance in this Issue are inconclusive as to whether a *substantial* modification or an exchange has occurred, a separate analysis should be performed. Debt extinguishment accounting is required if:
  - A *substantial* modification or an exchange is deemed to have occurred based on the results of a separate analysis, because the change in the embedded conversion option's fair value that is calculated as the difference between the fair value of the embedded conversion option immediately *before* and *after* a modification or exchange has occurred equals at least 10% of the carrying amount of the *original* debt instrument immediately *before* the modification or exchange occurred.
  - A modification or exchange is considered to be substantial if a *substantive* conversion option is *added* or a conversion option that was substantive at the date of a modification or exchange of a convertible debt instrument is *eliminated.* To determine whether an embedded conversion option is substantive on the date it is added to or eliminated from a debt instrument, the guidance in ASC 470-20-05-11. 40-4A through 40-10. 55-68 (Accounting for Conversion of an Instrument That Became Convertible upon the Issuer's Exercise of a Call Option), which is discussed above.
- If a modification or exchange of a convertible debt instrument is *not* accounted for as a debt extinguishment, the debt instrument's carrying amount should be reduced by an *increase* in the embedded conversion option's fair value, which is calculated as the difference between the fair value immediately *before* and *after* the modification or exchange, by increasing a debt discount or reducing a debt premium. A corresponding increase should be made to additional paid-in capital. However, a decrease in an embedded conversion option's fair value should *not* be recognized. Further, if a modification or exchange of a convertible debt instrument is *not* accounted for as a debt extinguishment, the issuer should *not* recognize a beneficial conversion feature or reevaluate an existing one as a result of that transaction.

DISCUSSION

This guidance is based on a determination of whether the economics of an exchanged or modified debt instrument differ substantially from those of the original debt instrument. The decision whether to account for an exchange or modification of debt instruments as an extinguishment should be based on whether the instruments exchanged or modified are substantially different and the debtor is in a different *economic* position after an exchange or modification than before the transaction.

A cutoff of 10% rather than 5% was used to determine whether debt instruments are substantially different to compensate for using the historical effective interest rate instead of a market rate in computing the present value of cash flows. The difference in the present value of cash flows is used as the primary test. A working group suggested that negotiated fees exchanged between a debtor and a creditor to change debt terms other than the principal amount, interest rate, or maturity of the debt should be used as a surrogate for measuring the significance of the other changes.

ASC 470-50-40-5, 15-3; ASC 470-20-40-4 Early Extinguishment of Debt: Accounting Interpretations of APB Opinion No. 26

BACKGROUND

The guidance in ASC 470-50-40-5, 15-3; ASC 470-20-40-4 clarifies the applicability of ASC 470-50-05-1, 15-3 through 15-4, 40-2, 40-4; ASC 850-10-60-3 to debt tendered to exercise warrants.

ACCOUNTING GUIDANCE

Question: The guidance in ASC 470-50-05-1, 15-3 through 15-4, 40-2, 40-4; ASC 850-10-60-3 indicates that a gain or loss should be recognized currently in income when a debt security is reacquired by the issuer except through conversion by the holder. Does that guidance apply to debt tendered to exercise warrants that were originally issued with that debt, but which were detachable?

Answer: The guidance in ASC 470-50-05-1, 15-3 through 15-4, 40-2, 40-4; ASC 850-10-60-3 does not apply to debt tendered to exercise detachable warrants that were originally issued with that debt if the debt is permitted to be tendered toward the exercise price of the warrants under the terms of the securities at issuance. In this circumstance, the debt is considered a conversion. The guidance in ASC 470-50-05-1, 15-3 through 15-4, 40-2, 40-4; ASC 850-10-60-3 does not apply to a conversion of debt. In practice, however, the carrying amount of the debt, including any unamortized premium or discount, is transferred to capital accounts when the debt is converted. No gain or loss is recognized.

Illustration of Debt Tendered to Exercise Detachable Warrants

DeVries Chemical originally issued a $100 million bond issue at par. In addition, each bond contained two detachable warrants, enabling the holder to purchase DeVries stock at $50 per warrant. DeVries allocated $3 million of the purchase price to the detachable stock warrants. Therefore, the net carrying amount of the bonds at issuance was $97 million.

The terms of the indenture permitted holders to tender their bonds toward the exercise price of the warrants. The carrying value of the $100 million bond issue on 7/15/20X4 was $98.5 million. Given a decline in interest rates since the bonds were issued, the market price of DeVries's bonds on 7/15/20X4 had risen to $100 million.

Institutional Equities International holds 20% of the DeVries bond issue. On 7/15/20X4 Institutional Equities exercises all of its warrants, 40,000 [($20,000,000 / $1,000) × 2], by tendering bonds with a market value of $2 million (40,000 × $50). The par value of DeVries's common stock is $1 per share.

DeVries Chemical would prepare the following journal entry to record the issuance of its stock as the result of Institutional Equities exercising its warrants and tendering bonds with a market value of $2 million.

Bonds payable		2,000,000
Discount on bonds payable	30,000	
Common stock	40,000	
Additional paid-in capital	1,930,000	

ASC 470-50-40-12, 40-15 through 40-16 Debtor's Accounting for a Modification (or Exchange) of Convertible Debt Instruments

BACKGROUND

The need for the following guidance arose because of concerns about the accounting for modifications that *decrease* the value of or *eliminate* an embedded conversion option.

ACCOUNTING ISSUES

1. How should an issuer consider a modification of a debt instrument (or an exchange of debt instruments) that affects an embedded conversion option's terms in analysis to determine whether debt extinguishment accounting applies?
2. How should an issuer account for a debt instrument's modification or an exchange of debt instruments that affects an embedded conversion option's terms if extinguishment accounting does *not* apply?

SCOPE

This guidance applies to modifications and exchanges of debt instruments that (*a*) add or eliminate an embedded conversion option or (*b*) affect an existing embedded conversion option's fair value. No accounting guidance is provided for a modification or exchange of a debt instrument if its embedded conversion option is separately accounted for as a derivative under the guidance in ASC 815 before a modification occurs, after the modification, or in both instances.

ACCOUNTING GUIDANCE

1. If a debt instrument is exchanged or its terms are modified, the resulting change in the embedded conversion option's fair value should *not* be included in the cash flow test used under the guidance in ASC 470-50-05-4, 15-3, 40-6 through 40-14, 40-17 through 40-20, 55-1 through 55-9 to determine whether a new debt instrument's terms are substantially different from those in the original debt instrument. If the results of the cash flow test under the guidance in ASC 470-50-05-4, 15-3, 40-6 through 40-14, 40-17 through 40-20, 55-1 through 55-9 are inconclusive as to whether a *substantial* modification or an exchange has occurred, a separate analysis should be performed. Debt extinguishment accounting is required if:

a. A *substantial* modification or an exchange is deemed to have occurred based on the results of a separate analysis, because the change in the embedded conversion option's fair value that is calculated as the difference between the fair value of the embedded conversion option immediately *before* and *after* a modification or exchange has occurred equals at least 10% of the carrying amount of the *original* debt instrument immediately *before* the modification or exchange occurred.

b. A modification or exchange is considered to be substantial if a *substantive* conversion option is *added* or a conversion option that was substantive at the date of a modification or exchange of a convertible debt instrument is *eliminated*. To determine whether an embedded conversion option is substantive on the date it is added to or eliminated from a debt instrument, the guidance in ASC 470-20-05-11, 40-4A through 40-10, 55-68 (Accounting for the Conversion of an Instrument That Became Convertible upon the Issuer's Exercise of a Call Option) should be considered.

2. If a modification or exchange of a convertible debt instrument is *not* accounted for as a debt extinguishment, the debt instrument's carrying amount should be reduced by an *increase* in the embedded conversion option's fair value, which is calculated as the difference between the fair value immediately *before* and *after* the modification or exchange, by increasing a debt discount or reducing a debt premium. A corresponding increase should be made to additional paid-in capital. However, a decrease in an embedded conversion option's fair value should *not* be recognized. Further, if a modification or exchange of a convertible debt instrument is not accounted for as a debt extinguishment, the issuer should *not* recognize a beneficial conversion feature or reevaluate an existing one as a result of that transaction.

ASC 470-50-40-21 through 40-22, 55-11 through 55-13 Debtor's Accounting for Changes in Line-of-Credit or Revolving-Debt Arrangements

BACKGROUND

A line-of-credit or a revolving-debt arrangement enables a debtor to borrow up to an agreed amount, to repay some of the indebtedness, and to borrow additional amounts. Such arrangements may include amounts borrowed by the debtor and a lender's commitment to make additional funds available under specified terms. Usually, a debtor incurs a cost to establish a line-of-credit or a revolving-credit arrangement. Such costs are usually deferred and amortized over the term of an arrangement. The guidance in ASC 470-50-05-4, 15-3, 40-6 through 40-14, 40-17 through 40-20, 55-1 through 55-9 did not specifically address modifications or exchanges of revolving debt arrangements or lines of credit on which amounts have been drawn. It specifically excluded those on which no funds had been drawn because of their unique characteristics.

Application of the guidance in ASC 470-50-05-4, 15-3, 40-6 through 40-14, 40-17 through 40-20, 55-1 through 55-9 to *revolving-debt* arrangements and to *lines of credit* is unclear, because of the difficulty of determining whether a change is substantial when there is an outstanding balance and a lender has committed to lend additional amounts. The guidance in ASC 470-50-40-21 through 40-22, 45-2, 55-11 through 55-13 applies to modifications and exchanges of lines-of-credit and revolving-debt arrangements.

ACCOUNTING ISSUE

How should a debtor account for modifications to or exchanges of line-of-credit or revolving-debt arrangements, including the accounting for unamortized costs at the time of the change, fees paid to or received from the creditor, and third-party costs incurred?

ACCOUNTING GUIDANCE

A modification to or exchange of a line-of-credit or a revolving debt arrangement that results in a new line-of-credit or revolving-debt arrangement or in a traditional term debt arrangement should be evaluated as follows:

> A debtor should compare the product of the remaining term and the maximum available credit of the *old* arrangement (referred to as the borrowing capacity) with the borrowing capacity under the *new* arrangement and should account for related costs in the following manner:
>
> - *Fees paid to the creditor, and third-party costs incurred, if any* Associate those costs with the *new* arrangement, regardless whether the borrowing capacity of the new arrangement is *greater* than, *equal* to, or *less* than under the old arrangement, by deferring and amortizing those costs over the term of the new arrangement.
> - *Unamortized deferred costs of the old arrangement* Account for the unamortized, deferred costs of the *old* arrangement as follows:
>   (1) *Borrowing capacity of the new arrangement is greater than or equal to the new arrangement* Amortize over the term of the *new* arrangement.

(2) *Borrowing capacity of the new arrangement is less than that under the old arrangement* Write off the unamortized deferred costs of the *old* arrangement at the time of the change in proportion to the decrease in borrowing capacity. Defer and amortize the remaining amount related to the *old* arrangement over the term of the *new* arrangement.

The scope of this guidance is limited to modifications of or exchanges of line-of-credit or revolving-debt arrangements in *nontroubled* situations involving a debtor and creditor who were involved in the original arrangement.

PRACTICE NOTE: ASU 2020-03, *Codification Improvements to Financial Instruments*, notes that ASC 470-50-40-17 through 40-18 provide guidance related to fees between a debtor and a creditor or third-party costs not related to exchanges of or modifications to a line-of-credit or revolving-debt arrangements resulting in either a new line-of-credit or revolving-debt arrangement.

Illustration of a Debtor's Accounting for Changes in a Line-of-Credit or Revolving Credit Arrangement

On 1/1/X9 Company M has a revolving credit arrangement with Bank X that has a 6-year term with 4 years remaining and a $12 million commitment. The company's borrowing capacity under this arrangement is $48 million (4 years × $12 million commitment).

On 4/1/X9, the company renegotiates its credit arrangement with Bank X. At that time, $250,000 in unamortized costs relating to the company's current credit arrangement remain on its balance sheet. To change the credit arrangement, the company will have pay a $150,000 fee to the bank and will also incur $250,000 in third-party costs. The company can choose among the following changes to its current arrangement:

- **Terms** (1) Increase the amount of the bank's commitment to $18 million with the term remaining at 4 years, or (2) replace the original revolving agreement with a 4-year, $12 million term loan on which the principal is due at the end of 4 years. Thus, the loan has a $48 million borrowing capacity.

  Accounting Result (1) The company's borrowing capacity increases from $48 million to $72 million. The $250,000 of unamortized costs of the original arrangement is amortized over the 4-year term of the new arrangement. The $400,000 in fees to the bank and third parties is deferred and amortized over 4 years. (2) The company's borrowing capacity is unchanged. The accounting for unamortized deferred costs of the old arrangement and costs of the new arrangement is the same as in (1).

- **Terms** Decrease the amount of the bank's commitment to $6 million and increase the term to 5 years.

  Accounting Result The company's borrowing capacity decreases from $48 million to $30 million, a reduction of 37.5%. Therefore, $93,750 ($250,000 × .375) of the unamortized costs of the original arrangement is written off. The remaining $156,250 is amortized over the 5-year term of the new arrangement. The $400,000 in fees to the bank and third parties is deferred and amortized over 5 years.

- **Terms** Replace the bank's revolving credit arrangement with a $6 million term loan on which the principal is due at the end of 3 years.

  Accounting Result The company's borrowing capacity decreases from $48 million to $18 million, a reduction of 62.5%. Therefore, $156,250 ($250,000 × .625) of the unamortized costs of the original arrangement is written off. The remaining $93,750 is amortized over the 3-year term of the new arrangement. The $400,000 in fees to the bank and third parties is deferred and amortized over 3 years.

ASC 470-60: TROUBLED DEBT RESTRUCTURINGS BY DEBTORS

ASC 470-60-15-10, 55-1, 55-2 Applicability of Statement 15 to Debtors in Bankruptcy Situations

BACKGROUND

Some confusion arose over the applicability of ASC 310-40-15-3 through 15-12, 35-2, 35-5 through 35-7, 40-2 through 40-6, 40-8, 25-1 through 25-2, 50-1, 55-2, 10-1 through 10-2; ASC 470-60-15-3 through 15-12, 55-3, 35-1 through 35-12, 45-1 through 45-2, 50-1 through 50-2, 10-1 through 10-2; ASC 450-20-60-12 to bankruptcy situations, prompting the issuance of ASC 470-60-15-10, 55-1 through 55-2. On the one hand, the guidance in ASC 310-40-15-3 through 15-12, 35-2, 35-5 through 35-7, 40-2, 40-5 through 40-6, 40-8, 25-1 through 25-2, 50-1, 55-2, 10-1 through 10-2; ASC 470-60-15-3 through 15-12, 55-3, 35-1 through 35-12, 45-1 through 45-2, 50-1 through 50-2, 10-1 through 10-2; ASC 450-20-60-12 indicates that it applies to troubled debt restructurings (TDRs) consummated under a reorganization arrangement, other provisions of the Federal Bankruptcy Act or other federal statutes. On the other hand, the guidance indicates that it does not apply to situations in which liabilities are generally restated under federal statutes, a quasi-reorganization, or corporate adjustment.

ACCOUNTING GUIDANCE

Question: Does the guidance in ASC 310-40-15-3 through 15-12, 10-1 through 10-2, 25-1 through 25-2, 35-2, 35-5, 35-7, 40-2 through 40-6, 40-8, 50-1 through 50-2, 55-2; ASC 470-60-15-3 through 15-12, 35-1 through 35-12, 45-1 through 45-2, 55-3, 10-1 through 10-2; ASC 450-20-60-12 apply to TDRs of debtors involved in bankruptcy proceedings?

Answer: That guidance does not apply to debtors who, in connection with bankruptcy proceedings, enter into a TDR that results in a general restatement of a debtor's liabilities.

ASC 470-60-55-4 through 55-14, 15-13 Debtor's Accounting for a Modification or an Exchange of Debt Instruments in accordance with FASB Statement No. 15, *Accounting by Debtors and Creditors for Troubled Debt Restructurings*

OVERVIEW

ASC 310-40-15-3 through 15-12, 10-1 through 10-2, 25-1 through 25-2, 35-2, 35-5 through 35-7, 40-2 through 40-6, 40-8, 50-1 through 50-2, 55-2; ASC 470-60-15-3 through 15-12, 35-1 through 35-12, 45-1 through 45-2, 50-1, 10-1 through 10-2; ASC 450-20-60-12 provides some guidance on determining whether a modification or exchange of debt constitutes a troubled debt restructuring. The guidance in ASC 470-60-15-9 includes a list of factors that may exist in a troubled debt restructuring and ASC 470-60-15-12 lists factors that *may* indicate that a modification or exchange of debt does *not* "necessarily" constitute a troubled debt restructuring. However, it appears that further clarification is required. For example, some question whether a reduction in the face amount of a debt instrument should always be accounted for as a troubled debt restructuring based on the guidance in ASC 470-60-15-9, and whether the guidance in ASC 310-40-15-3 through 15-12, 10-1 through 10-2, 25-1 through 25-2, 35-2, 35-5, 35-7, 40-2 through 40-6, 40-8, 50-1 through 50-2, 55-2; ASC 470-60-15-3 through 15-12, 35-1 through 35-12, 45-1 through 45-2, 50-1, 10-1 through 10-2; ASC 450-20-60-12 applies to a transaction in which a debtor exchanges its existing debt by issuing new marketable debt that meets the criterion in ASC 470-60-15-12 for a nontroubled debt restructuring. In the latter situation, the new debt's effective interest rate is based on a market price that approximates the price of debt with similar maturity dates and stated interest rates that has been issued by a nontroubled borrower.

ACCOUNTING ISSUE

Does any single characteristic or factor, taken alone, determine whether a debtor should account for a modification or exchange as a troubled debt restructuring under the guidance in ASC 310-40-15-3 through 15-12, 10-1 through 10-2, 25-1 through 25-2, 35-2, 35-5, 35-7, 40-2 through 40-6, 40-8, 50-1 through 50-2, 55-2; ASC 470-60-15-3 through 15-12, 35-1 through 35-12, 45-1 through 45-2, 55-3, 10-1 through 10-2; ASC 450-20-60-12?

ACCOUNTING GUIDANCE

When determining whether a modification or an exchange of debt instruments is within the scope of the guidance in ASC 310-40-15-3 through 15-12, 10-1 through 10-2, 25-1 through 25-2, 35-2, 35-5, 35-7, 40-2 through 40-6, 40-8, 50-1 through 50-2, 55-2; ASC 470-60-15-3 through 15-12, 35-1 through 35-12, 45-1 through 45-2, 50-1, 10-1 through 10-2; ASC 450-20-60-12, a debtor should consider (*a*) whether the entity is experiencing financial difficulty and (*b*) whether the creditor has granted a concession to the debtor. A debtor would follow that guidance if both questions are answered affirmatively. If the answer to either question is negative, a debt modification or exchange should *not* be accounted for under that guidance.

The following factors are irrelevant in determining whether the guidance in ASC 310-40-15-3 through 15-12, 10-1 through 10-2, 25-1 through 25-2, 35-2, 35-5, 35-7, 40-2 through 40-6, 40-8, 50-1 through 50-2, 55-2; ASC 470-60-15-3 through 15-12, 35-1 through 35-12, 45-1 through 45-2, 55-3, 10-1 through 10-2; ASC 450-20-60-12 applies to a debt modification or exchange:

- The amount that current creditors had invested in the old debt.
- A comparison of the fair value of new debt at issuance to the fair value of the old debt immediately before a modification or exchange.
- Transactions among debt holders.

The length of time that current creditors have held an investment in an old debt is also irrelevant in determining whether a modification or exchange is under the scope of that guidance *unless* all the current creditors recently acquired the debt from the previous debt holders in what is, effectively, a planned refinancing.

Determining Whether a Debtor Is Experiencing Financial Difficulties

A debtor should evaluate whether it is experiencing financial difficulties if its creditworthiness has deteriorated since the debt was first issued. A debtor is experiencing financial difficulties if the following indicators exist:

- The debtor is currently in default on any of its debt.
- The debtor has declared or is declaring bankruptcy.
- Significant doubt exists whether the debtor will continue as a going concern.
- The debtor's securities have been delisted, are in the process of being delisted, or are under the threat of being delisted from an exchange.
- The debtor forecasts that based on estimates covering only its current business capabilities, the debtor's entity-specific cash flows will be insufficient to service interest and principal on the debt through maturity in accordance with the contractual terms of the existing agreement.
- The debtor cannot obtain funds from other sources at an effective interest rate that equals the current market interest rate for similar debt for a non-troubled debtor.

Despite the criteria listed above, if *both* of the following factors exist, there is determinative evidence that a debtor is *not* experiencing financial difficulties and a modification or exchange would *not* be under the scope of the guidance in ASC 310-40-15-3 through 15-12, 10-1 through 10-2, 25-1 through 25-2, 35-2, 35-5, 35-7, 40-2 through 40-6, 40-8, 50-1 through 50-2, 55-2; ASC 470-60-15-3 through 15-12, 35-1 through 35-12, 45-1 through 45-2, 55-3, 10-1 through 10-2; ASC 450-20-60-12:

- The debtor is servicing its old debt on a current basis and can obtain funds to repay the old debt from sources other than the current creditors at an effective interest rate that equals the current market interest rate for a non-troubled debtor; *and*
- The creditors agree to restructure the old debt only to show a decrease in current interest rates for the debtor or positive changes in the debtor's creditworthiness since the original issuance of the debt.

Determining Whether a Creditor Granted a Concession

- A creditor has granted a concession if the debtor's effective borrowing rate on restructured debt is less than the effective borrowing rate of the old debt immediately *before* it was restructured. To calculate the effective borrowing rate of restructured debt, after considering all the terms including new or revised options or warrants, if any, and new or revised guarantees or letters of credit, if any, all cash flows under the new terms should be projected and the discount rate that equates the present value of the cash flows under the *new* terms to the debtor's current carrying amount of the *old* debt should be computed.
- Although this is rare, if persuasive evidence exists that a decrease in the borrowing rate is attributed exclusively to a factor that is not depicted in the computation, such as additional collateral, a creditor may not have granted a concession and the modification or exchange should be evaluated based on the substance of the modification.

Despite the guidance provided above, an entity that is currently restructuring its debt after having done so recently should calculate the effective borrowing rate of the restructured debt, after considering all the terms including new or revised options or warrants, if any, and new or revised guarantees or letters of credit, if any, by projecting all cash flows under the new terms and determining the debtor's previous carrying amount of the debt immediately before the previous restructuring. To determine whether the effective borrowing rate has decreased and therefore the creditor has granted a concession, the debtor should compare the new effective borrowing rate to that related to the debt immediately before the previous restructuring.

CHAPTER 36

ASC 480—DISTINGUISHING LIABILITIES FROM EQUITY

CONTENTS

PART I: GENERAL GUIDANCE

ASC 480-10: OVERALL

OVERVIEW

ASC 480 defines the distinction between liabilities and equity. The approach taken is to specifically define liabilities and require that all other financial instruments be classified as equity in the balance sheet. The FASB states that ASC 480 is generally consistent with its definitions of the various elements of the statement of financial position (balance sheet), income statement, and statement of cash flows.

ASC 480 establishes standards for issuers of financial instruments with characteristics of both liabilities and equity related to the classification and measurement of those instruments. It requires the issuer to classify a financial instrument as a liability, or asset in some cases, which was previously classified as equity. The classification standards are generally consistent with the definition of liabilities in FASB conceptual framework and with the FASB's proposal to revise that definition to encompass certain obligations that a reporting entity can or must settle by issuing its own equity shares.

LIABILITIES AND EQUITY

Distinction between Liabilities and Equity

ASC 480 requires an issuer to classify the following instruments as liabilities, or assets in certain circumstances:

- A financial instrument issued in the form of shares that is mandatorily redeemable in that it embodies an unconditional obligation that requires the issuer to redeem the shares by transferring the entity's assets at a specified or determinable date(s) or upon an event that is certain to occur.
- A financial instrument other than an outstanding share that, at its inception, embodies an obligation to repurchase the issuer's equity shares, or is indexed to such an obligation, and that requires or may require the issuer to settle the obligation by transferring assets (ASC 480-10-25-8).
- A financial instrument other than an outstanding share that embodies an unconditional obligation that the issuer must or may settle by issuing a variable number of equity shares if, at inception, the monetary value of the obligation is based solely or predominantly on any of the following (ASC 480-10-25-14):
  - A fixed monetary amount known at inception (e.g., a payable to be settled with a variable number of the issuer's equity shares).
  - Variations in something other than the fair value of the issuer's equity shares (e.g., a financial instrument indexed to the S&P 500 and settleable with a variable number of the issuer's equity shares).
  - Variables inversely related to changes in the fair value of the issuer's equity shares (e.g., a written put option that could be net share settled).

ASC 480 applies to issuers' classification and measurement of freestanding financial instruments, including those that comprise more than one option or forward contract. It does not apply to features that are embedded in a financial instrument that is not a derivative in its entirety. In applying the classification provisions of ASC 480, nonsubstantive or minimal features are to be disregarded.

Required Disclosures

Issuers of financial instruments are required to disclose the nature and terms of the financial instruments and the rights and obligations embodied in those instruments. That disclosure shall include information about any settlement alternatives in the contract and identify the entity that controls the settlement alternatives (ASC 480-10-50-1).

For all outstanding financial instruments within the scope of ASC 480, and the settlement alternative(s), the following information is required to be disclosed by issuers (ASC 480-10-50-2):

- The amount that would be paid, or the number of shares that would be issued and their fair value, determined under the conditions specified in the contract if the settlement were to occur at the reporting date.
- How changes in the fair value of the issuer's equity shares would affect those settlement amounts.
- The maximum amount that the issuer could be required to pay to redeem the instrument by physical settlement, if applicable.
- The maximum number of shares that could be required to be issued, if applicable.
- That a contract does not limit the amount that the issuer could be required to pay or the number of shares that the issuer could be required to issue, if applicable.
- For a forward contract or an option indexed to the issuer's equity shares, the forward price or option strike price, the number of the issuer's shares to which the contract is indexed, and the settlement date(s) of the contract.

Mandatorily Redeemable Financial Instruments—Applicability and Implementation

The classification, measurement, and disclosure guidance in subtopic ASC 480-10 does not apply to mandatorily redeemable financial instruments that meet both of the following: (1) they are issued by nonpublic entities *that are not registered with the SEC*, and (2) they are mandatorily redeemable but not on fixed dates for fixed amounts, or if the amount due is not tied to an interest rate index, currency index, or other external index (ASC 480-10-15-7A).

In addition, ASC 480's guidance does not apply to mandatorily redeemable noncontrolling interests if the interest would not be classified as a liability by the subsidiary (under the "only upon liquidation" exception in ASC 480) but would be classified as a liability by the parent in the consolidated financial statements. In addition, the *measurement* provisions of ASC 480 do not apply to other mandatorily redeemable noncontrolling interests issued before November 5, 2003, both for the parent company and the subsidiary that issued the noncontrolling interests (ASC 480-10-15-7E).

Illustration of Applying ASC 480

Mandatorily redeemable financial instruments. Financial instruments issued in the form of shares that embody unconditional obligations of the issuer to redeem the instruments by transferring its assets at a specified or determinable date(s) or upon an event that is certain to occur are required to be classified as liabilities. This includes certain forms of trust-preferred securities and stock that must be redeemed upon the death or termination of the individual who holds them. Although some mandatorily redeemable instruments are issued in the form of shares, those instruments are classified as liabilities under ASC 480 because of the embodied obligation on the part of the issuer to transfer its assets in the future:

Example:

Statement of Financial Position	
Total assets	$5,000,000
Liabilities other than shares	$4,200,000
Shares subject to mandatory redemption	800,000
Total liabilities	$5,000,000

Notes to Financial Statements	
Shares subject to mandatory redemption:	
Common stock	$600,000
Retained earnings attributed to those shares	200,000
	$800,000

Certain obligations to issue a variable number of shares.ASC 480 requires liability classification if, at inception, the monetary value of an obligation to issue a variable number of shares is based solely or predominantly on any of the following:

- A fixed monetary amount known at inception.
- Variations in something other than the fair value of the issuer's equity shares.
- Variations inversely related to changes in the fair value of the issuer's equity shares.

Example: An entity may receive $500,000 in exchange for a promise to issue a sufficient number of shares of its own stock to be worth $525,000 at a specified future date. The number of shares to be issued to settle the obligation is variable, depending on the number required to meet the $525,000 obligation, and will be determined based on the fair value of the shares at the settlement date. The instrument is classified as a liability under ASC 480.

Freestanding financial instruments.ASC 480 requires that certain of its provisions to be applied to a freestanding instrument in its entirety:

Example: An issuer has two freestanding instruments with the same counterparty: (1) a contract that combines a written put option at one strike price and a purchased call option at another strike price on its equity shares; and (2) outstanding shares of stock. The primary requirements of ASC 480 are applied to the entire freestanding instrument that includes both a put option and a call option. It is classified as a liability and is measured at fair value. The outstanding shares of stock are not within the scope of ASC 480.

PART II: INTERPRETIVE GUIDANCE

ASC 480-10: OVERALL

ASC 480-10-15-8 Issuers' Accounting for Employee Stock Ownership Plans under FASB Statement No. 150, *Accounting for Certain Financial Instruments with Characteristics of both Liabilities and Equity*

BACKGROUND

Employee Stock Ownership Plans (ESOPs) are employee benefit plans under the Employee Retirement Income Security Act of 1974 (ERISA) and the Internal Revenue Code (IRC) of 1986. Employers that sponsor ESOPs are required by law to provide employees with a put option or another means of redeeming shares that cannot be readily traded. ESOPs often require that shares be sold back to the employer at fair value when an employee dies, retires, or reaches a certain age. Shares that must be redeemed meet the definition of mandatorily redeemable shares in ASC 480, which does *not* apply to obligations under stock-based compensation arrangements accounted for under certain of the guidance ASC 718, ASC 460, and ASC 505. But other applicable guidance under Subtopic 718-40 continues to apply to ESOP shares that are mandatorily redeemable or freestanding under agreements to repurchase shares.

ACCOUNTING GUIDANCE

Question: Does the guidance in Subtopic 480-10 apply to mandatorily redeemable ESOP shares or freestanding agreements to repurchase ESOP shares?

Answer: No. The guidance in Subtopic 480-10 does *not* apply to mandatorily redeemable ESOP shares or freestanding agreements to repurchase those shares, that are accounted for under the guidance in Topic 718-40 until they are redeemed or under the guidance in Subtopic 505-50. Nevertheless, freestanding financial instruments issued under a share-based compensation arrangement that are no longer subject to the guidance in Topic 718 or Subtopic 505-50, would be accounted for under the guidance in Subtopic 480-10, for example, when a mandatorily redeemable share is issued as a result of an employee's exercise of an employee share option.

ASC 480-10-25-9, 25-13, 55-33 Issuer's Accounting under FASB Statement No. 150 for Freestanding Warrants and Other Similar Instruments on Shares That Are Redeemable

BACKGROUND

This guidance applies to freestanding financial instruments that are *not* outstanding shares, such as warrants. They are issued with an obligation to repurchase the issuer's equity shares and require or may require settlement by a transfer of assets. Such financial instruments, therefore, are accounted for as liabilities under the guidance in ASC 480-10-25-9 through 25-12. In ASC 480-10-55-29 through 55-32, 40-42 through 40-52, there is an example of a warrant that may be put to the issuer at a fixed price immediately after the warrant has been exercised. Constituents have raised the following question.

QUESTION

Does the timing of the redemption feature or the redemption price, which may be at fair value or a fixed amount, affect whether the guidance in ASC 480-10-25-9 through 25-12 should be applied to warrants for shares that can be put to the issuer?

ACCOUNTING GUIDANCE

Because freestanding warrants and other similar instruments on shares that are puttable or mandatorily redeemable include obligations to transfer assets, they should be accounted for as liabilities (under the guidance in ASC 480-10-25-9 through 25-12) regardless of when they are redeemed or their redemption price.

The phrase "requires or may require" is used in ASC 480-10-25-9 through 25-12 to refer to financial instruments under which an issuer is conditionally or unconditionally obligated to transfer assets. For puttable shares, the issuer would be *conditionally* obligated to transfer assets if the warrant is exercised and the shares are put to the issuer. In the case of mandatorily redeemable shares, the issuer would be *conditionally* obligated to transfer assets if the holder exercises the warrant. In both cases, the warrant should be accounted for as a liability.

ASC 480-10-45-2A through 45-2B Accounting for Mandatorily Redeemable Shares Requiring Redemption by Payment of an Amount That Differs from the Book Value of Those Shares, under FASB Statement No. 150, *Accounting for Certain Financial Instruments with Characteristics of both Liabilities and Equity*

Question: Some companies have outstanding shares, all of which are subject to mandatory redemption on the occurrence of events that are certain to occur. Assume that on the date of adoption, the redemption price of the shares is more than their book value. On the date of adoption, the company would recognize a liability for the redemption price of the shares that are subject to mandatory redemption, reclassifying the amounts previously classified as equity. Any difference between the redemption price on the date of adoption and the amounts previously recognized in equity is reported in income as a cumulative effect transition adjustment loss. The redemption price may be a fixed amount or may vary based on specified conditions. How should the cumulative transition adjustment and subsequent adjustment to reflect changes in the redemption price of the shares be reported if they exceed the company's equity balance?

Answer: The cumulative adjustment amount and any subsequent adjustments to it should be reported as an excess of liabilities over assets (i.e., as a deficit). If the redemption price of the mandatorily redeemable shares is less than the book value of those shares, the excess of that book value over the liability reported for the mandatorily redeemable shares should be reported as an excess of assets over liability (i.e., as equity).

For example, assume that Company X adopts the guidance in ASC 480 when both the fair value and redemption value of the mandatorily redeemable shares is $20 million and the book value of those shares is $15 million of which $10 million is paid-in capital. On the date that guidance is adopted, the company would recognize a liability of $20 million by transferring $15 million from equity and recognizing a cumulative transition adjustment loss of $5 million. Assume further that net income attributable to the mandatorily redeemable share is $1 million for the year and the fair value of the shares at the end of the year is $21.2 million. No cash dividends are paid. The following is the presentation in the statement of financial position at the end of the year, assuming assets of $26 million and other liabilities of $10 million (all numbers in millions):

Assets	$26,000
Liabilities other than shares	$10,000
Shares subject to mandatory redemption	21,200
Total liabilities	$31,200
Excess of liabilities over assets	(5,200)
Total	$26,000

ASC 480-10-S45-5; S99-4 Sponsor's Balance Sheet Classification of Capital Stock with a Put Option Held by an Employee Stock Ownership Plan

BACKGROUND

Federal income tax regulations require employer securities held by an ESOP to have a put option, referred to as a liquidity put, allowing the employee to demand redemption if the securities are not readily marketable. The employer may have the option to satisfy the demand for redemption with cash, marketable securities, or both. Under the provisions of some ESOPs, the ESOP may substitute for the employer in redeeming the employees' shares.

Companies may also issue to their ESOPs convertible preferred stock, which is convertible into the company's common stock. Such stock is not publicly traded and therefore has a put option. The holder generally has the option of when to convert the stock, but under the terms of some convertible stock the issuer/employer is permitted to convert the shares. In some cases, the stock is converted or put to the employer when there is a takeover attempt or a merger. The convertible stock may have the following features:

- It has a "floor put" feature that guarantees the participant a minimum value, and is exercised if the convertible is "out of the money." The employer may have the option of redeeming the stock for cash, giving the participant common stock that would be issuable on conversion plus additional shares, or giving the participant common stock that would be issuable on conversion plus cash. The participant may have the option of receiving cash, common shares, or a combination of both.
- After a certain period of time, the employer may have the option to call the stock at a stipulated price. The ESOP can hold callable stock if it provides for a reasonable period of time after calling for the stock to be converted to common shares instead of cash, if participants so desire.
- The convertible stock can be held only by the ESOP and is automatically converted to common stock when distributed to participants leaving the plan. However, a floor put feature enables participants to require the trustee to put the convertible stock even before it has been distributed to participants if the convertible stock is "out of the money."

SEC Staff Accounting Series Release (ASR) 268 (Presentation in Financial Statements of "Redeemable Preferred Stocks") requires public companies to classify mandatorily redeemable preferred stock or stock whose redemption is outside the issuer's control outside of stockholders' equity.

In a leveraged ESOP, the employer records the ESOP's debt as a liability. The liability is offset by a contra-equity account referred to as "unearned ESOP shares," which is recorded as a debit in equity. (Before the issuance of ASC 718-40

(Employers' Accounting for Employee Stock Ownership Plans), such an account was referred to as *loan to ESOP or deferred* compensation.) When the employer issues stock to the ESOP, this contra-equity account is credited and there is no effect on equity.

ACCOUNTING ISSUES

- Under what circumstances should all or a portion of convertible preferred stock with put options held by an ESOP be classified outside of equity?
- If convertible preferred stock with put options issued to a leveraged ESOP is classified outside of stockholders' equity, should the contra-equity account, unearned ESOP shares, be classified in the same manner?

ACCOUNTING GUIDANCE

- Publicly held companies should classify convertible preferred stock issued to ESOPs in accordance with the provisions of ASR-268, which requires that mandatorily redeemable preferred stock be classified as a separate item between liabilities and equity, commonly referred to as the "mezzanine."
- A proportional amount of the contra-equity account in the employer's balance sheet should be similarly classified.

  For example, if $7,500,000 of $10,000,000 of preferred stock issued to an ESOP is convertible and therefore is classified outside of stockholders' equity, 75% of the balance of the contra-equity account would be classified in the same manner. Thus, if the remaining ESOP debt is $8,000,000, 75% (or $6,000,000) of the contra-equity account, unearned ESOP shares, would be classified outside of stockholders' equity.

PRACTICE POINTER: Under the guidance in ASC 460-10-55-5, a put option issued by an ESOP may be a guarantee. If a put is a guarantee that is not accounted for under the provisions of ASC 815-10-15, the ESOP sponsor's obligations under that guarantee would be reported as a liability under U.S. GAAP; the sponsor would be required to recognize a liability for the fair value of the put at its inception and provide the disclosures specified in ASC 460. The requirement in ASC 460 that a put be recognized as a liability at its inception and the requirement to disclose additional information change the sponsor's reporting and, therefore, partially nullify the guidance above.

ASC 480-10 provides guidance to issuers on the classification and measurement of financial instruments with characteristics of both liabilities and equity, except for mandatorily redeemable financial instruments of nonpublic entities. Financial instruments under the scope of ASC 480-10 should be classified as liabilities or, in some cases, as assets. Because ESOP shares with embedded repurchase features or freestanding instruments to repurchase ESOP shares are covered under the guidance in ASC 718-40 (Employers' Accounting for Employee Stock Ownership Plans) and related guidance, the guidance in ASC 480-10 does not apply to those shares. However, the requirement in the SEC's ASR-268 that ESOP shares be reported in temporary equity continues to apply.

EFFECT OF ASC 815

Put options discussed in this Issue should be analyzed to determine whether they meet the definition of a derivative in ASC 815. Contracts classified in temporary equity may qualify for the exception in ASC 815-10-15-74, because temporary equity is considered to be stockholders' equity.

SEC STAFF COMMENT

The SEC Observer stated that under ASR-268, the maximum possible cash obligation related to equity securities that give a holder the option to demand redemption in cash, regardless of the probability of occurrence, should be reported outside of equity. Consequently, employers should report outside of equity all allocated and unallocated convertible preferred securities held by an ESOP that are redeemable in cash. However, if a cash obligation is related only to the market-value guarantee feature of some convertible securities, the SEC staff would not object if a registrant reports outside of equity only amounts representing the maximum cash obligation based on the market price of the underlying securities at the reporting date. The entire guaranteed amount of such securities may, nevertheless, be reported outside of equity at the registrant's option to recognize the uncertainty of the ultimate cash obligation resulting from possible declines in the market value of the underlying security.

DISCUSSION

- In this Issue, arguments for classification outside stockholders' equity focused on the fact that redemption may be outside the control of the employer as a result of the put and the employer's potential cash obligation.
- Some supported classifying all or a portion of the contra-equity account outside of equity because that account, unearned ESOP shares, resulted from a transaction in which the employer issued the securities and incurred the liability. They argued that the purpose of the contra-equity account is to offset shares that have not been paid for, as in a stock subscription. Thus, if shares not paid for are reclassified, the contra-equity account should be treated in the same manner.

ASC 480-10-55-29 through 55-32, 40-42 through 40-52 Issuer's Accounting for Freestanding Financial Instruments Composed of More Than One Option or Forward Contract Embodying Obligations under FASB Statement No. 150, *Accounting for Certain Financial Instruments with Characteristics of both Liabilities and Equity*

Question 1: How does ASC 480-10-25-8 through 25-12 apply to freestanding financial instruments composed of more than one option or forward contract embodying obligations that require or that may require settlement by transfer of assets? An example of this type of financial instrument is a puttable warrant that allows the holder to purchase a fixed number of the issuer's shares at a fixed price that also is puttable by the holder at a specified date for a fixed monetary amount that the holder could require the issuer to pay.

Answer: ASC 480-10-15-3 through 15-4 states that the guidance applies to freestanding financial instruments, including those that are composed of more than one option or forward contract. The guidance in ASC 480-10-25-4 through 25-14 applies to a freestanding financial instrument in its entirety. Under the guidance in ASC 480-10-25-8 through 25-12, if a freestanding instrument is composed of a written call option and a written put option, the existence of the call option does not affect the instrument's classification. Thus, a puttable warrant is a liability because it includes an obligation indexed to an obligation to repurchase the issuer's shares and may require a transfer of assets. It is a liability even if the repurchase feature is conditional on a defined contingency in addition to the level of the issuer's share price. The warrant is *not* an outstanding share and does *not* meet the exception for outstanding shares in ASC 480-10-25-8 through 25-12 and, unlike the application of ASC 480-10-25-14 does *not* involve making any judgments about whether it is predominant among the entity's obligations or contingencies.

For example, Company X issues a puttable warrant to Investor Y. Under the warrant's terms, Investor Y is permitted to purchase one equity share at a strike price of $10 on a specified date. The put feature permits Investor Y to put the warrant back to Company X on that date for $2 and to require settlement in cash. If the share price on the settlement date exceeds $12, Investor Y would be expected to exercise the warrant, obligating Company X to issue a fixed number of shares in exchange for a fixed amount of cash. That feature of the financial instrument does *not* result in a liability. However, if the share price is equal to or less than $12, Investor Y would be expected to put the warrant back to Company X and could choose to obligate Company X to pay $2 in cash. That feature does result in a liability, because the financial instrument includes an obligation that is indexed to an obligation to repurchase the issuer's shares and may require a transfer of assets. Therefore, under the guidance in ASC 480-10-25-8 through 25-12, Company X would be required to classify the financial instrument as a liability.

Question 2: How does the guidance in ASC 480-10-25-14 apply to freestanding financial instruments composed of more than one option or forward contract that include obligations? For example, a puttable warrant that allows the holder to purchase a fixed number of the issuer's shares at a fixed price that also is puttable by the holder at a specified date for a fixed monetary amount to be paid, at the issuer's discretion, in cash or in a variable number of shares. Does such a financial instrument include an obligation for the issuer that is a liability in accordance with the guidance in ASC 480-10?

Answer: The answer depends on the circumstances. A financial instrument that is composed of more than one option or forward contract including obligations to issue shares must be analyzed to determine whether the obligations under any of the instrument's components have one of the characteristics discussed in ASC 480-10-25-14 and, if so, whether those obligations are predominant relative to other obligations. The analysis involves two steps.

Step 1: Identify any component obligations that, if freestanding, would be liabilities under the guidance in ASC 480-10-25-14 and, also, identify other component obligations of the financial instrument.

Step 2: Assess whether the monetary value of any freestanding components are collectively predominant over the collective monetary value of any other component obligations. If so, the entire financial instrument is accounted for under the guidance in ASC 480-10-25-14. If not, the financial instrument is not included under the scope of ASC 480-10.

For example, Company X issues a puttable warrant to Investor Y. The warrant allows Investor Y to purchase one equity share at a strike price of $10 at a specified date. The put feature allows Investor Y to put the warrant back to Company X on that date at $2, and can be settled in fractional shares. If the share price on the settlement date exceeds $12, Investor Y would be expected to exercise the warrant and obligate Company X to issue a fixed number of shares in exchange for a fixed amount of cash. The monetary value of the shares varies directly with changes in the share price above $12. If the share price is equal to or less than $12, Investor Y would most likely put the warrant back to Company X, obligating it to issue a variable number of shares with a fixed monetary value (known at inception) of $2. Thus, at inception, the number of shares that the puttable warrant obligates Company X to issue can vary, and the financial instrument must be examined as described previously. The facts and circumstances are used to make a judgment whether the monetary value of the obligation to issue a number of shares that varies is predominantly based on a fixed monetary amount that is known at inception and, if so, it is a liability under the guidance in ASC 480-10-25-14.

In the previous example, if Company X's share price is well below the $10 exercise price of the warrant at inception, the warrant has a short life, and Company X's stock is determined to have low volatility, the circumstances would suggest that the monetary value of the obligation to issue shares is based predominantly on a fixed monetary amount known at inception and the instrument should be classified as a liability.

ASC 480-10-S99-3A Classification and Measurement of Redeemable Securities

The SEC Observer stated the views of the SEC staff about the application of Accounting Series Release (ASR) No. 268, *Presentation in Financial Statements of* "Redeemable Preferred Stocks."

SCOPE

Under the guidance in ASR 268, SEC registrants are required to classify outside permanent equity redeemable preferred securities that can be redeemed (*a*) at a fixed or determinable price on a fixed or determinable date, (*b*) at the holder's option, or (*c*) when an event occurs that is not completely under the issuer's control. The SEC staff believes that the above guidance can be applied by analogy to other equity instruments, such as common stock, derivatives instruments, noncontrolling interests if the redemption feature is not considered to be a freestanding option under the scope of ASC 480-10, equity securities held by and employee stock ownership plan with terms allowing an employee to put the securities to the sponsor for cash or other assets, and redeemable instruments classified in equity granted under a share-based payment arrangement with employees as discussed in ASC 718-10-S99.

The guidance in ASR 268 does *not* apply to the following instruments:

- Freestanding financial instruments that are classified as assets or liabilities under the guidance in ASC 480-10 or other GAAP;
- Freestanding derivative instruments classified in stockholders' equity under the guidance in ASC 815-40, which applies to embedded derivatives indexed to, and potentially settled in, a company's own stock;
- Equity instruments subject to registration payment arrangements as defined in ASC 825-20-15-3;
- Share-based payment awards;
- Convertible debt instruments that contain an equity component that is classified separately. A convertible debt instrument may be required to be separated into a liability and an equity component under other GAAP. A convertible debt instrument that is not redeemable at the balance sheet date, but that may become redeemable based on the passage of time or the occurrence of an event is not considered to be redeemable at the balance sheet date;
- Certain redemptions that occur as a result of a liquidation event. However, deemed liquidation events under which a holder is required or permitted to redeem only one or more equity instruments of a specific class for cash or other assets would require the application of ASR 268; and
- Certain redemptions covered by proceeds from insurance, for example, an equity instrument that becomes redeemable on the holder's or disability.

CLASSIFICATION

PRACTICE NOTE: ASC 480 provides guidance for issuers on the classification and measurement of financial instruments with the characteristics of both liabilities and equity. Financial instruments under the scope of ASC 480 must be classified as liabilities, or as assets in some situations, because they represent an issuer's obligations.

SEC OBSERVER COMMENT

The SEC Observer clarified the SEC staff's position regarding the interaction of the staff's guidance on this announcement with the guidance in ASC 480 when accounting for *conditionally* redeemable preferred shares. The guidance in ASC 480 does *not* apply to the accounting for such shares if they are conditionally redeemable at a holder's option or when an uncertain event *not* under the issuer's control occurs, because there is no unconditional obligation to redeem the shares by a transfer of assets at a specified or determinable date or when a certain event occurs. The condition is resolved when an uncertain event occurs. Once it becomes certain that such an event will occur, the shares should be accounted for under the provisions of ASC 480, which requires that the shares be measured at fair value and reclassified as a liability. As a result, stockholders' equity would be reduced by an equivalent amount with no gain or loss recognition. The reclassification is similar to a redemption of shares by issuing debt. As in the redemption of preferred shares discussed in ASC 260-10-99S-2 ("The Effect on the Calculation of Earnings per Share for the Redemption or Induced Conversion of Preferred Stock"), when calculating earnings per share, the difference between the fair value of the liability and the carrying amount of the preferred debt at reclassification should be deducted from or added to net earnings available to common shareholders.

The SEC staff believes that an issuer of a redeemable equity security should evaluate separately all the events that could trigger redemption if some of the security's redemption features are not under the issuer's control. A security should be classified outside of permanent equity if *any* event not under the issuer's sole control, regardless of the probability of occurrence, could trigger its redemption. Although a change in classification is not required if an event occurs that would cause a potential ordinary liquidation that would require cash payment only if the company is totally liquidated, the occurrence of events that could cause the redemption of one or more particular classes or types of equity securities would require that those securities be classified outside of permanent equity. The classification of equity securities whose redemption is not solely under the issuer's control should be based on the individual facts and circumstances.

For example, the SEC Observer noted that a redeemable security with a provision that requires the issuer to obtain the approval of the board of directors to call the security may not necessarily be under the issuer's control, because the board of directors may be controlled by the holders of the particular redeemable security. In contrast, classification in permanent equity would continue to be appropriate in a situation in which a preferred stock agreement includes a provision stating that the issuer's decision to sell all or substantially all of the company's assets and a subsequent distribution to common stockholders triggers redemption of the preferred equity security, because the decision to sell all or substantially all of the issuer's assets is solely under the issuer's control. That is, a distribution to common stockholders cannot be *triggered* or required by the preferred stock holders as a result of their representation on the board of directors.

One exception to the requirement in this announcement that should *not* be analogized to other transactions occurs when there is a provision that the equity securities become redeemable as a result of the holder's death or disability. Under that circumstance, the redemption of the securities would be funded by the proceeds of an insurance policy that is in force and that the issuer intends to and is able to maintain in force. Consequently, the securities continue to be classified in permanent equity.

MEASUREMENT

The SEC staff believes the *initial* amount of a redeemable equity security included in temporary equity in accordance with the guidance in ASR 268 should be its fair value on the issue date, except in the following circumstances:

- *Share-based payment arrangements with employees.* Measure the initial amount recognized in temporary equity based on the instrument's redemption provisions and the proportion of consideration received as employee services.
- *Employee stock ownership plans.* If the cash redemption option is related only to a market value guarantee feature, a registrant's accounting policy for temporary equity may be to present (*a*) the amount of the total guaranteed market value of the equity securities, or (*b*) the maximum cash obligation based on the fair value of the underlying equity securities at the balance sheet date.

- *Noncontrolling interests.* Present in temporary equity the initial carrying amount of a noncontrolling interest in accordance with the guidance in ASC 805-20-30.
- *Convertible debt instruments that include a separately classified equity component.* Present an amount in temporary equity only if the instrument is currently redeemable or convertible at the issuance date for cash or other assets. If a portion of a component classified as equity is included in temporary equity, present the amount of cash or other assets that would be paid to a holder on conversion or redemption at the issuance date in excess of the component classified as a liability on the issuance date.
- *Host equity contracts.* Present in temporary equity the initial carrying amount of the host contract in accordance with the guidance in ASC 815-15-30.
- *Preferred stock with a beneficial conversion feature or that is issued with other instruments.* Include in temporary equity the total amount allocated to the instrument in accordance with the guidance in ASC 470-20 *less* the amount of the beneficial conversion feature recognized at the issuance date.

The following are the views of the SEC staff about the *subsequent measurement* of a redeemable equity instrument subject to the requirements of ASR 268:

- The amount of securities currently redeemable at a holder's option should be adjusted to their maximum redemption amount at each balance sheet date. If the maximum amount is contingent on an index or similar variable, the amount in temporary equity should be calculated based on the existing conditions at the balance sheet date, such as the instrument's current fair value. At each balance sheet date, the amount of dividends *not* currently declared or paid but that will be paid under the redemption features or if their ultimate payment is *not* under the registrant's control should be included. If an instrument is not currently redeemable, an adjustment is unnecessary if it is not probable that the instrument will become redeemable, such as when redemption will occur only based on the passage of time.
- If it is probable that an equity instrument will become redeemable, the SEC staff will not object if either of the following accounting methods are applied consistently for securities that will become redeemable at a future *determinable* date but whose redemption amount is *variable* (e.g., they are redeemable at fair value):
  a. Accrete changes in the redemption value from the date of issuance or when redemption becomes probable (if later) to the security's earliest redemption date using an appropriate method, usually the interest method. Changes in redemption value are considered to be changes in accounting estimates and accounted for, and disclosed, in accordance with the guidance in ASC 250.
  b. Recognize changes in the redemption value (e.g., fair value) immediately as they occur and adjust the security's carrying amount to equal the redemption value at the end of each reporting period. Under this method, the end of the reporting period would be viewed as if it were also the security's redemption date.

The following is additional guidance provided by the SEC staff on subsequent measurement under the following circumstances:

- *Share based payment arrangements with employees.* At each balance sheet date, base the amount included in temporary equity on the instrument's redemption provisions considering the proportion of consideration received in the form of employee services (the pattern of recognition of compensation cost in accordance with the guidance in ASC 718).
- *Employee stock ownership plans.* If a cash redemption obligation is related only to a market value guarantee feature, a registrant's accounting policy for temporary equity may be to present (*a*) the amount of the total guaranteed market value of the equity securities, or (*b*) the maximum cash obligation based on the fair value of the underlying equity securities at the balance sheet date.
- *Noncontrolling interests.* Determine the adjustment of the carrying amount in temporary equity after attributing the subsidiary's net income or a loss according to the guidance in ASC 810-10.
- *Convertible debt instruments that include a separately classified equity component.* Present an amount in temporary equity only if the instrument is currently redeemable or convertible at the issuance date for cash or other assets. If a portion of a component classified as equity is included in temporary equity, present the amount of cash or other assets that would be paid to a holder on conversion or redemption at the issuance date in excess of the component classified as a liability on the issuance date.

- *Fair value option*. Redeemable equity instruments included in temporary equity in accordance with the requirements in ASR 268 should not be measured at fair value through earnings instead of applying the SEC staff's measurement guidance. Also see the guidance in ASC 825-10-15-5(f), which prohibits the use of the fair value option for financial instruments that are wholly or partially classified in stockholder's equity, including temporary equity.

The SEC staff believes that regardless of which of the above accounting methods is used to account for a redeemable equity security, that security's carrying amount should be reduced only to the extent that the registrant had previously increased the security's carrying amount as a result of the application of the guidance in this Topic.

The SEC staff expects registrants to apply the accounting method selected consistently and to disclose the selected policy in the notes to the financial statements. In addition, registrants that elect to accrete changes in redemption value over the period from the date of issuance to the earliest redemption date should disclose the security's redemption value as if it were redeemable.

RECLASSIFICATION INTO PERMANENT EQUITY

If temporary classification of a redeemable equity security is no longer required, its carrying amount should be reclassified from temporary to permanent equity at the date of the occurrence of the event causing reclassification. Prior financial statements should *not* be adjusted. The SEC staff also believes that reversal of previously recorded adjustments to the security's carrying amount would be inappropriate when a reclassification occurs.

DECONSOLIDATION OF A SUBSIDIARY

An entity that deconsolidates a subsidiary recognizes a gain or loss on that transaction in net income based on the measurement guidance in ASC 810-10-40-5. The carrying amount of a noncontrolling interest, if any, in the former subsidiary affects that gain or loss calculation. The SEC staff believes that because adjustments to a noncontrolling interest's carrying amount from the application of the guidance in this SEC staff announcement have not entered into the determination of the entity's net income, the noncontrolling interest's carrying amount should likewise *not* include any adjustments made to the noncontrolling interest as a result of the application of the guidance in this SEC staff announcement. Previous adjustments to the noncontrolling interest's carrying amount from the application of the guidance in this SEC staff announcement should be eliminated by recording a credit to the parent entity's equity.

EARNINGS PER SHARE

Preferred Securities Issued by a Parent or Single Reporting Entity

Increases or decreases in the carrying amount of a redeemable security should be treated like dividends on nonredeemable stock by charging retained earnings, or if no retained earnings exist, by charging paid-in capital, regardless of the method used to account for the security or whether the security is redeemable at a fixed price or at fair value. In calculating earnings per share and the ratio of earnings to combined fixed charges and preferred stock dividends, income available to common stockholders should be reduced or increased as a result of increases or decreases in a preferred security's carrying amount. Guidance related to the accounting at the date of a redemption or induced conversion of a preferred equity security may be found in ASC 260-10-S99-2 ("The Effect on the Calculation of Earnings per Share for the Redemption or Induced Conversion of Preferred Stock").

Common Securities Issued by a Parent or a Single Reporting Entity

Increases or decreases in the carrying amount of a redeemable security should be treated like dividends on nonredeemable stock by charging retained earnings, or if no retained earnings exist, by charging paid-in capital, regardless of the method used to account for the security or whether the security is redeemable at a fixed price or at fair value. But those increases or decreases in a redeemable common stock's carrying amount should *not* affect income available for common stock holders. The SEC staff believes that in so far as a common shareholder has a contractual right to receive an amount other than the fair value of those shares at redemption, a common shareholder has, in substance, received a different distribution than the other common shareholders. Entities whose capital structures include a class of common stock with dividend rates that differ from those of another class of common shareholders but without senior rights, are required to calculate their earnings per share based on the two-class method discussed in ASC 260-10-45-59A. As a result, increases or decreases in the carrying amount of a class of common stock that is redeemable at other than fair value should be considered in the calculation of earnings per share using the two-class method. In footnote 8 of this Topic, the SEC staff states that if a common security is redeemable at other than fair value, it is acceptable to allocate earnings under the two-class method using one of the following two methods:

- Treat the total periodic adjustment to the security's carrying amount as a result of the application of the guidance in this Topic like an actual dividend, or
- Treat like an actual dividend only the portion of the periodic adjustment to the security's carrying amount as a result of the application of the guidance in this Topic that represents a redemption in excess of fair value.

The SEC staff does not expect the two-class method to be used in the calculation of earnings per share if a class of common stock is redeemable at fair value, because the dividend distribution to those shareholders does not differ from that made to other common shareholders. The SEC staff believe that common stock redeemable based on a specified formula is considered redeemable at fair value if the formula is intended to equal or reasonably approximate fair value. However, a formula based only on a fixed multiple of earnings or a similar measure would *not* qualify.

The SEC staff also believe that likewise, the two-class method need *not* be used if share-based payment awards in the form of common shares or options or common shares granted to employees are redeemable at fair value. However, the two-class method may still apply to such share-based payment awards under the guidance in ASC 260-10-45-59A and ASC 260-10-45-60, 45-60A through 45-68, 55-24 through 55-30, 55-71 through 55-75 (*Participating Securities and the Two-Class Method under Statement No. 128*).

Noncontrolling Interests

In accordance with the guidance in ASC 810-10-45-23, (*a*) changes in a parent's ownership interest accounted for by the equity method while a parent retains control of the subsidiary and (*b*) an adjustment to a noncontrolling interest as a result of the application of the guidance in this SEC staff announcement, have no effect on net income or comprehensive income in the consolidated financial statements. Instead, such adjustments are accounted for like a repurchase of a noncontrolling interest, although they may be recognized in retained earnings rather than in paid-in capital. The SEC staff requires that the above earnings per share guidance for preferred securities and common shares issued by a parent should be applied to noncontrolling interests as follows:

- *Noncontrolling interest in the form of preferred securities.* If a redemption feature of a noncontrolling interest in the form of preferred securities was issued or guaranteed by a parent, an adjustment to the security's carrying amount reduces or increases income available to common stockholders. If not, the adjustment is attributed to the parent and the noncontrolling interest in accordance with the guidance in ASC 260-10-55-64 through 55-67.
- *Noncontrolling interest in the form of common securities.* Adjustments to the carrying amount of a noncontrolling interest issued in the form of common stock to represent a fair value redemption feature do *not* affect earnings per share. However, if a noncontrolling interest was issued in the form of common stock to represent a non-fair value redemption feature, adjustments to the noncontrolling interest's carrying amount affect earnings per share, but the way those adjustments reduce or increase income available to common stockholders may differ. Application of the two-class method is unnecessary if the terms of the redemption feature are fully considered when net income is attributed under the guidance in ASC 810-10-45-21. But if they are not fully considered, the two-class method must be applied at the level of the subsidiary to determine net income available to the parent's common stockholders.

Convertible Debt Instruments that Include a Separately Classified Equity Component

There should be no incremental earnings per share accounting from the application of the SEC staff's guidance in this announcement for convertible debt instruments to the requirements of ASR 268. The earnings per share accounting is addressed in ASC 260-10.

DISCLOSURES

Certain disclosures about redeemable equity instruments are required under the guidance in ASC 268 and SEC Regulation S-X. The SEC staff expects registrants to provide the following additional disclosures in the notes to the financial statements:

- The accounting method used to adjust the amount to be redeemed on a redeemable equity instrument.
- The redeemable amount of an equity instrument as if it were currently redeemable if a registrant chooses to accrete changes immediately in the amount at which a redeemable equity instrument would be redeemed (method b. discussed for equity instruments if it is probable that the equity instrument would be redeemed).
- If a redeemable equity instrument is not adjusted to the amount at which it would be redeemed, the reasons why it is not probable that the instrument will be redeemed.
- A reconciliation between net income and income available to common stockholders if charges or credits related to preferred stock instruments issued by a parent and those related to a noncontrolling interest in the form of a preferred stock instrument, as discussed above, are material.
- The amount credited to a parent's equity when a subsidiary is deconsolidated, as discussed above.

CHAPTER 37

ASC 505—EQUITY

CONTENTS

PART I: GENERAL GUIDANCE

OVERVIEW

The various elements that constitute stockholders' equity in the statement of financial position are classified according to source. Stockholders' equity may be classified broadly into four categories: (1) legal capital, (2) additional paid-in capital, (3) noncontrolling interests in subsidiaries, and (4) retained earnings. Detailed information is presented in the body of the statement, in related notes, or in some combination thereof.

ASC 505-10: OVERALL

BACKGROUND

Stockholders' equity represents the interest of the owners of a corporation in the corporation's assets. It represents the residual interest in the enterprise's assets, after liabilities have been subtracted, arising from the investment of owners and the retention of earnings over time.

In the balance sheet, stockholders' equity usually is displayed in two broad categories—*paid-in* or *contributed capital* and *retained earnings*. Paid-in or contributed capital represents the amount provided by stockholders in the original purchase of shares of stock or resulting from subsequent transactions with owners, such as treasury stock transactions. Retained earnings represent the amount of previous income of the corporation that has not been distributed to owners as dividends or transferred to paid-in or contributed capital.

PRACTICE POINTER: A business may be able to eliminate an accumulated deficit in retained earnings in situations where the business has been struggling but reaches a turnaround point where profitable operations seem likely by going through a quasi-reorganization. For guidance as to when a quasi-reorganization would be appropriate and coverage of the accounting and reporting for a quasi-reorganization, see Chapter 60, *ASC 852—Reorganizations*.

Illustration of Balance Sheet Presentation of Stockholders' Equity December 31, 20X5

Preferred stock, $50 par value, 10,000 shares authorized, 7,000 shares authorized and outstanding	$ 350,000
Common stock, $25 par value, 100,000 shares authorized, 75,000 shares issued	1,875,000
Paid-in capital in excess of par value on common stock	500,000
Common stock dividend to be distributed	262,500
Total paid-in capital	$2,987,500
Retained earnings	1,000,000
Total paid-in capital and retained earnings	$3,987,500
Treasury stock, 10,000 shares of common stock at cost	(300,000)
Total stockholders' equity	$3,687,500

STOCKHOLDERS' EQUITY TERMINOLOGY AND RELATIONSHIPS

Legal (or *stated*) *capital* usually is defined by state law. It refers to the amount of capital that must be maintained by a corporation for the protection of its creditors. Legal capital may consist of common or preferred shares. Preferred shares may be participating or nonparticipating as to the earnings of the corporation, may be cumulative or noncumulative as to the payment of dividends, may have a preference claim on assets upon liquidation of the business, and may be callable for redemption at a specified price. Usually, preferred stock does not have voting rights.

Common stock usually has the right to vote, the right to share in earnings, a preemptive right to a proportionate share of any additional common stock issued, and the right to share in assets on liquidation.

Stock is usually issued with a par value. No-par value stock may or may not have a stated value. *Par* or *stated value* is the amount that is established in the stock account at the time the stock is issued. When stock is issued above or below par value, a premium or discount on the stock is recorded, respectively. A discount reduces paid-in or contributed capital; a premium increases paid-in or contributed capital. A premium on stock is often referred to as "paid-in capital in excess of par value." Because the issuance of stock at a discount is not legal in many jurisdictions, discounts on stock are not frequently encountered.

A corporation's charter contains the types and amounts of stock that it can legally issue, which is called the *authorized capital stock*. When part or all of the authorized capital stock is issued, it is called *issued capital stock*. Since a corporation may purchase its own capital stock in the form of treasury stock, the amount of issued capital stock in the hands of stockholders is called *outstanding capital stock*.

A corporation may sell its capital stock by subscriptions. An individual subscriber becomes a stockholder upon subscribing to the capital stock. Upon full payment of the subscription, a stock certificate evidencing ownership in the corporation is issued. When the subscription method is used to sell capital stock, a subscription receivable account is debited and a capital stock subscribed account is credited. On payment of the subscription, the subscription receivable account is credited and cash or other assets are debited. On the actual issuance of the stock certificates, the capital stock subscribed account is eliminated and the regular capital stock account is increased.

Illustration of Capital Stock Relationships

A company has the following capital stock structure: The numbers below represent shares of a particular class of stock (e.g., common stock) and indicate the relationships among the various components of authorized stock. The number of shares authorized is 10,000, of which 8,000 have been issued and 2,000 are unissued. Of the 8,000 issued shares, 7,000 are outstanding (i.e., in the hands of investors) and 1,000 represent treasury shares (i.e., shares that were issued and outstanding at one time, but have been reacquired by the company). Of the 2,000 unissued shares, 500 have been subscribed and 1,500 are unsubscribed. The 500 subscribed shares have been partially paid and are considered unissued until they are fully paid, at which time they will be issued and thereafter are outstanding shares.

Following are examples of how the numbers of shares change for several independent common capital stock transactions:

1. *Sale of 700 shares of previously unissued stock*—Unsubscribed stock declines by 700 shares, as does the number of unissued shares. Outstanding shares and issued shares both increase by 700. As a result, unissued shares number 1,300 (2,000 – 700) and issued shares number 8,700 (8,000 + 700), of which 7,700 (7,000 + 700) are outstanding.
2. *Sale of 100 shares of treasury stock*—Treasury stock declines to 900 (1,000 – 100) shares and outstanding increases to 7,100 (7,000 + 100) shares. The total number of unissued and issued shares remains unchanged.
3. *Subscribed shares (500) are paid in full*—Subscribed shares become zero (500 – 500), reducing unissued shares to 1,500 (2,000 – 500). Outstanding and issued shares increase to 7,500 and 8,500, respectively.

PRACTICE POINTER: While rarely encountered in practice, an additional source of stockholders' equity is donated capital. This occurs when capital is donated to a company, such as a return of capital stock in the settlement of an estate by the company's founder, without the company paying anything in return.

DISCLOSURE OF INFORMATION ABOUT STOCKHOLDERS' EQUITY

When financial statements are prepared in conformity with U.S. GAAP, capital changes must be disclosed in a separate statement(s) or note(s) to the financial statement. This requirement is in addition to disclosure of the changes in retained earnings, although all capital changes may be included in one statement. Capital accounts may have to be disclosed because of changes during the year in capital stock, additional paid-in capital accounts, retained earnings, treasury stock, and other capital accounts (ASC 505-10-50-2).

ASC 505 establishes standards for disclosing information about an entity's capital structure. Three terms are particularly important in understanding and applying ASC 505—securities, participating rights, and preferred stock (ASC Glossary). These terms are defined as follows:

- **Securities**—evidence of debt or ownership or a related right, including options and warrants as well as debt and stock
- **Participating rights**—contractual rights of security holders to receive dividends or returns from the issuer's profits, cash flows, or returns on investments
- **Preferred stock**—a security that has preferential rights over common stock

ASC 505 requires information about capital structure to be disclosed in three separate categories—information about securities, liquidation preference of preferred stock, and redeemable stock.

Information about Securities

The entity shall provide within its financial statements a summary explanation of the pertinent rights and privileges of the various securities that are outstanding (ASC 505-10-50-3). Information that is to be disclosed includes:

- Dividend and liquidation preferences
- Participating rights
- Call prices and dates
- Conversion or exercise prices or rates and dates
- Sinking-fund requirements
- Unusual voting rights
- Significant terms of contracts to issue additional shares or terms that may change conversion or exercise prices (excluding standard antidilution provisions)

In addition to the information about rights and privileges associated with securities, the number of shares issued upon conversion, exercise, or satisfaction of required conditions during the most recent annual fiscal period and any subsequent interim period shall be disclosed. An entity must also disclose actual changes to conversion or exercise prices that occur during the reporting period.

Liquidation Preference of Preferred Stock

Preferred stock or other senior securities may have a preference in involuntary liquidation that is in excess of the security's par or stated value. In this situation, the issuing entity shall disclose the liquidation preference of the stock (i.e., the relationship of the liquidation preference and the par or stated value of the shares). Under the following guidelines, this disclosure should be (ASC 505-10-50-4):

- Presented within the equity section, either parenthetically or "in short" (i.e., included in the body of the financial statement, but not added in the total of stockholders' equity).
- Presented as an aggregate amount.

PRACTICE POINTER: Take care not to overlook the requirement that the liquidation preference of preferred stock must be presented in the aggregate and *in the body of the equity section of the balance sheet* rather than in notes to the financial statements. This is an unusual requirement and could be easily overlooked.

Other disclosures, which may be made either in the financial statements or in related notes, are:

- The aggregate *or* per share amounts at which preferred stock may be called or are subject to redemption through sinking fund operations or otherwise
- The aggregate *and* per share amounts of cumulative preferred dividends in arrears

Redeemable Stock

Redeemable stock *must be repurchased* by the issuing entity. In this situation, the issuing entity is required to disclose the amount of redemption requirements, separately by issue or combined, for all issues of stock for which the redemption prices and dates are fixed or determinable. This information is required for each of the next five years following the date of the latest statement of financial position that is presented (ASC 505-10-50-11).

Illustration of Capital Structure Disclosures

Following are examples of the disclosures required by ASC 505. Disclosures of information about securities, the liquidation preference of preferred stock, and redeemable stock are the direct result of specific circumstances that exist within the reporting entity. No example can include all possible information that may require disclosure. Care should be taken in relying on these or other examples because of differences that may exist among reporting entities.

Information about Securities

ABC Company's capital structure includes common and preferred stock that is described as follows in its statement of financial position and in a note to the financial statements:

Statement of financial position:

Convertible preferred stock—$40 par value, 5 million shares authorized, 4 million shares and 3.8 million shares issued and outstanding in 20X6 and 20X5, respectively

Common stock—$10 par value, 10 million shares authorized, 6 million shares issued and outstanding in 20X6 and 20X5

Note to the financial statements:

Each share of ABC preferred stock is convertible into four shares of ABC common stock at any time through December 31, 20X9. The preferred stock is entitled to a cumulative annual dividend of $2.50.

Liquidation Preference of Preferred Stock

DEF Company has preferred stock outstanding, as described below in the body of the statement of financial position:

Preferred stock—$10 per share par value, 1 million shares authorized, issued and outstanding: 20X6 and 20X5—.8 million and .75 million shares, respectively. Aggregate liquidation preference: 20X6 and 20X5—$12 million and $11.25 million, respectively.

Redeemable Stock

GHI Company has redeemable preferred stock outstanding, as described below in notes to the financial statements:

Preferred stock—Each share of GHI preferred stock is convertible into four shares of GHI common stock. On December 31, 20X8, the preferred shares are redeemable at the company's option at $50 per share. Based on the current market price of the stock, the company expects the majority of the preferred shares to be converted into common stock prior to December 31, 20X8.

CONVERTIBLE PREFERRED STOCK

Entities may issue convertible preferred stock that may be convertible into common stock at the lower of a conversion rate fixed at the time of issuance and fixed discount to the market price of the common stock at the date of issuance (ASC 505-10-05-5). Certain convertible preferred stock becomes convertible only upon the occurrence of a future event that is outside the control of the holder (ASC 505-10-05-7).

If convertible preferred stock is required to be redeemed once the conversion feature expires, the financial instrument is a liability (ASC 480) upon expiration of the conversion feature, and the issuer is required to reclassify the instrument as a liability, measured initially at fair value with a corresponding reduction of equity. No gain or loss is recognized. Thereafter, the financial instrument is accounted for under ASC 480. (ASC 505-10-35-1)

Disclosure

The objective of disclosure about convertible preferred stock is to provide users with information about:

- The terms and features of convertible preferred stock
- How convertible preferred stock has been reported in the statement of financial position (balance sheet) and statement of financial performance
- The events, conditions, and circumstances that can affect how to assess the amount or timing of an entity's future cash flows related to its convertible preferred stock (ASC 505-10-50-12)

To comply with the general disclosure requirements, the entity shall explain the pertinent rights and privileges of each outstanding instrument, including the following:

- Number of shares issued and par value
- Dividends
- Conversion or exercise prices or rates and number of shares into which the instrument is potentially convertible
- Pertinent dates (e.g., conversion dates)
- Parties that control the conversion rights
- Manner of settlement upon conversion and any alternative settlement methods (e.g., cash, shares, or a combination of these)
- Terms that may change conversion or exercise prices, number of shares issued, and other conversion rights and the timing of those rights
- Liquidation preference
- Other material terms and features of the instrument that are not included above (ASC 505-10-50-13)

Additional disclosures for contingently convertible instruments are stated in ASC 505-10-50-15.

The amount of dividends declared for each period for which a statement of financial performance is presented is required. Also, the entity shall disclose the following as of the date of the statement of financial position:

- Changes to conversion or exercise prices that occur during the reporting period other than changes due to standard antidilution provisions
- Events or changes in circumstances that occur during the reporting period that cause conversion contingencies to be met or conversion terms to be significantly changed
- The number of shares issued upon conversion, exercise, or satisfaction of required conditions during the reporting period (ASC 505-10-50-16)

If a conversion option is accounted for as a derivative in accordance with ASC 815-15, the entity shall provide disclosures in accordance with that topic for the conversion option in addition to the disclosures required in this section. The entity shall disclose the following information about derivative transactions entered into in connection with convertible preferred stock:

- The terms of those derivative transactions, including terms of settlement
- How those derivative transactions relate to the derivative transactions
- The reasons for entering into those derivative transactions (ASC 505-10-50-18)

ADDITIONAL PAID-IN CAPITAL

All stockholders' equity that is not classified as legal capital, noncontrolling interests in subsidiaries, or retained earnings usually is designated as additional paid-in capital. The common sources of additional paid-in capital are:

- Excess of par or stated value paid for capital stock
- Sale of treasury stock
- The issuance of detachable stock purchase warrants (ASC 470-20-25-2)
- Donated assets
- Capital created by a corporate readjustment or quasi-reorganization

If capital stock is issued for the acquisition of property and it appears that, at about the same time and pursuant to a previous agreement or understanding, some portion of the stock so issued is donated to the corporation, the par value of the stock is not an appropriate basis for valuing the property. Generally, donated stock should be recorded at fair value at the time it is received. Fair value may be determined by the value of the stock or the value of the asset, services, or other consideration received.

Charges that are properly chargeable to income accounts of the current or future years should not be made to paid-in capital (ASC 505-10-25-1).

NONCONTROLLING INTERESTS

In the presentation of consolidated financial statements, a noncontrolling interest (formerly referred to as *minority interest*) is that portion of equity (net assets) in a subsidiary company that is not attributable, directly or indirectly, to the parent company. The noncontrolling interest in the subsidiary is part of the equity of the consolidated group (ASC 810-10-45-15).

A noncontrolling interest is reported in the consolidated statement of financial position within equity, clearly labeled as being separate from the parent's equity. For example, the following title might be used: *Noncontrolling interest in subsidiary.* An entity with noncontrolling interests in more than one subsidiary may present those interests in the aggregate in the consolidated statement of financial position (ASC 810-10-45-16).

ASC 505-20: CASH DIVIDENDS, STOCK DIVIDENDS AND STOCK SPLITS

Definition

A *dividend* is a pro rata distribution by a corporation, based on shares of a particular class, and usually represents a distribution based on earnings.

CASH DIVIDENDS

Cash dividends are the most common type of dividend distribution. Preferred stock usually pays a fixed dividend, expressed in dollars or a percentage of par or stated value. Three dates usually are involved in a dividend distribution:

1. *Date of declaration*: The date the board of directors formally declares the dividend to the stockholders
2. *Date of record*: The date the board of directors specifies that stockholders of record on that date are entitled to the dividend payment
3. *Date of payment*: The date the dividend is actually disbursed by the corporation or its paying agent

Cash dividends are recorded on the books of the corporation as a liability (dividends payable) on the date of declaration. Dividends are paid only on authorized, issued, and outstanding shares, thereby eliminating any dividend payment on treasury stock.

STOCK DIVIDENDS

Stock dividends are distributions of a company's own capital stock to its existing stockholders in lieu of cash. Stock dividends are accounted for by transferring an amount equal to the fair value of the stock from retained earnings to paid-in capital. The dividend is recorded at the date of declaration by reducing retained earnings and establishing a temporary account, such as "Stock Dividend to Be Distributed." Because no asset distribution is required for a stock dividend, that account is part of stockholders' equity, in contrast to a cash dividend payable account, which is a liability. When the stock is distributed, the stock dividend account is eliminated and permanent capital accounts (e.g., common stock and paid-in capital in excess of par [stated] value) are increased (ASC 505-20-30-3).

Illustration of Stock Dividends

LPS Corporation declares a 5% stock dividend on its 1,000,000 shares of outstanding $10 par common stock (5,000,000 authorized). On the date of declaration, LPS stock is selling for $25 per share.

Total stock dividend (5% of 1,000,000)		50,000 shares
Value of 50,000 shares @ $25 per share (market)		$1,250,000
Entry or date of declaration:		
Retained earnings	1,250,000	
Stock dividend to be distributed		1,250,000
Entry or date of distribution:		
Stock dividend to be distributed	1,250,000	
Common stock (50,000 × $10)		500,000
Paid-in capital in excess of par value		750,000

STOCK SPLITS

When a stock distribution is more than 20% to 25% of the outstanding shares immediately before the distribution, it is considered a stock split, sometimes referred to as a "stock split-up" (ASC 505-20-25-3) or a "stock split in the form of a stock dividend." A stock split increases the number of shares of capital stock outstanding, and a reverse stock split decreases the number of shares of capital stock outstanding.

PRACTICE POINTER: While the 20-25% distribution is often used to distinguish between stock dividends and stock splits, the underlying distinction is whether the distribution affects the market price in approximately the same proportion as the percentage distribution indicates. As a general rule, distributions in relatively small percentages (e.g., 5 %-10%) have little, if any, impact on the stock's market price. Larger distributions, whether labeled a large stock dividend or a stock split, generally have a significant impact on the stock's market price.

In both straight and reverse stock splits, the total dollar amount of stockholders' equity does not change. The par or stated value per share of capital stock, however, decreases or increases in proportion with the increase or decrease in the number of shares outstanding. For example, in a stock split of 4 for 1 of $40 par value capital stock, the new stock has a par value of $10 ($40 ÷ 4) and the number of shares outstanding increases to four shares for each share of stock previously outstanding. In a reverse stock split of 1 for 4 of $40 par value capital stock, the new stock has a par value of $160 per share ($40 × 4) and the number of shares outstanding decreases to one share for each four shares of stock previously outstanding.

A stock split is used by a corporation to reduce the market price of its capital stock to make the market price of the stock more attractive to buyers (ASC Glossary). Thus, in a 4 for 1 straight stock split, the new shares would probably sell for about one-fourth of the previous market price of the old shares prior to the split. Reverse stock splits are unusual and are used to increase the market price of a corporation's stock. For example, a reverse stock split of 1 for 4 of stock selling for $3 would be expected to increase the market price of the new shares to about $12 per share.

No journal entry is required to record a stock split except a memorandum entry in the capital stock account to indicate the new par or stated value of the stock and the number of new shares outstanding after the split. Stock splits should not be referred to as dividends (ASC 505-20-25-2; 505-20-30-6; 505-20-50-1).

A stock split may, however, be accomplished in the form of a stock dividend. In this case, the distribution of stock is called *a stock split issued in the form of a stock dividend*, and the percentage distribution is large enough (i.e., in excess of 20% to 25% of the outstanding stock) that the market value of the stock reacts accordingly. Accounting in this situation is similar to a stock dividend, except that only the par or stated value of the stock, rather than the market value, is transferred from retained earnings to paid-in capital.

PRACTICE NOTE: Stock dividends and stock splits are similar in that they result in increased numbers of outstanding shares of stock for which existing stockholders make no payment. They differ, however, in size, in their impact on the stock's market price, and, most important, in managerial intent. In the case of a stock dividend, management intent usually is to make a distribution to owners while preserving present cash; in the case of a stock split, management intent is to affect (reduce) market price. Accounting for stock dividends and stock splits is summarized in Figure 37-1. A key point in this illustration is that the accounting is driven by the impact on the market price of the stock.

Figure 37-1: Accounting for Stock Dividends and Stock Splits

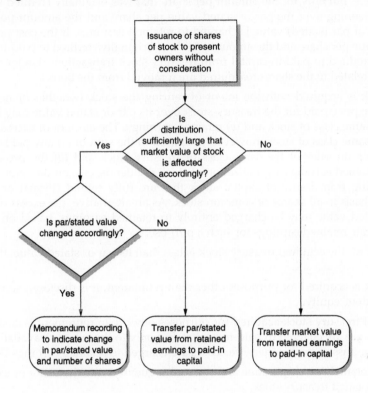

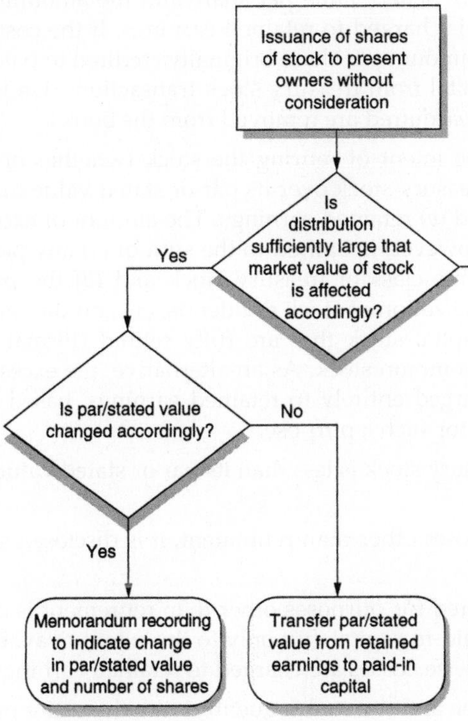

STOCK RIGHTS

No accounting entry is necessary for an entity issuing the stock right or warrant, except for detachable stock purchase warrants or similar rights, which are accounted for separately and assigned a value.

ASC 505-30: TREASURY STOCK

TREASURY STOCK

Treasury stock is a company's own capital stock that has been issued and subsequently reacquired. It is ordinarily presented as a reduction in the amount of stockholders' equity. Treasury stock is not considered an asset, because it is widely held that a corporation cannot own part of itself. The status of treasury stock is similar to that of authorized but unissued capital stock. Restrictions on the availability of retained earnings for the payment of dividends or any other restrictions required by state law are disclosed in the financial statements.

Accounting and Reporting

Under U.S. GAAP, both the cost method and the par value method of accounting for treasury stock are acceptable. Under the cost method, each acquisition of treasury stock is accounted for at cost, that is the amount the company paid to acquire its own stock. Separate records are maintained to reflect the date of purchase of the treasury stock, the number of shares acquired, and the reacquisition cost per share. Treasury stock may be kept based on an acceptable inventory method, such as FIFO or average cost basis. Upon the sale or other disposition, the treasury stock account is credited for an amount equal to the number of shares sold, multiplied by the cost per share and the difference between this amount and the cash received is treated as paid-in capital in excess of par (stated) value. The cost method of accounting for treasury stock is more commonly used in practice than the par value method.

Under the par value method of accounting for treasury stock, the treasury stock account is increased by the par or stated value of each share reacquired. Any excess paid per share over the par or stated value reduces paid-in capital in excess of par (stated) value, but only for the amount per share that was originally credited when the stock was issued. Any excess cost per share remaining over the par or stated value per share and the amount per share originally recognized as paid-in capital in excess of par (stated) value is charged to retained earnings. If the cost per share of treasury stock is less than the par or stated value per share and the amount per share originally credited to paid-in capital in excess of par (stated) value, the difference is credited to paid-in capital from treasury stock transactions. Under the par value method, all of the original capital balances related to the shares reacquired are removed from the books.

When treasury stock is acquired with the intent of retiring the stock (whether or not retirement is actually accomplished), the excess of the price paid for the treasury stock over its par or stated value may be allocated between (*a*) paid-in capital arising from the same class of stock and (*b*) retained earnings. The amount of excess that can be allocated to paid-in capital arising from the same class of stock, however, is limited to the sum of (*a*) any paid-in capital arising from previous retirements and net gains on sales of the same class of treasury stock and (*b*) the pro rata portion of paid-in capital, voluntary transfers of retained earnings, capitalization of stock dividends, etc., on the same class of stock. For this purpose, any paid-in capital arising from issues of capital stock that are fully retired (formal or constructive) is deemed to be applicable on a pro rata basis to all shares of common stock. As an alternative, the excess of the price paid for the treasury stock over its par or stated value may be charged entirely to retained earnings, based on the fact that a corporation can always capitalize or allocate retained earnings for such a purpose.

When the price paid for the acquired treasury stock is less than its par or stated value, the difference is credited to paid-in capital.

When treasury stock is acquired for purposes other than retirement, it is disclosed separately in the balance sheet as a deduction from stockholders' equity.

A gain on the sale of treasury stock acquired for purposes other than retirement is credited to paid-in capital from the sale of treasury stock. Losses are charged to paid-in capital, but only to the extent of available net gains from previous sales or retirements of the same class of stock; otherwise, losses are charged to retained earnings (ASC 505-30-30-8).

If treasury stock is donated to a corporation and then subsequently sold, the entire proceeds shall be credited to paid-in capital from the sale of donated treasury stock.

PRACTICE POINTER: Under the cost and par value methods, adjustments to paid-in capital from treasury stock transactions are recognized at different times and determined in different ways. Under the cost method, base adjustments to paid-in capital on the relationship between the purchase price and the subsequent selling price; they are recognized at the time of the sale of the treasury stock is sold. Under the par value method, base adjustments to paid-in capital on the relationship between the original selling price of the stock and the purchase price; they are recognized at the time the treasury stock is purchased.

These relationships are summarized as follows:

	Cost Method	*Par Value Method*
Timing of adjustment to paid-in capital	Point of sale	Point of purchase
Paid-in capital increased	Selling price greater than purchase price	Purchase price less than original selling price
Paid-in capital decreased	Selling price less than purchase price	Purchase price greater than original selling price
Retained earnings decreased	Loss on sale greater than paid-in capital from previous treasury stock transactions	Purchase price is so high that all paid-in capital from previous treasury stock transactions is eliminated

The cost method is much more widely used in practice than the par value method.

Purchase Price of Treasury Stock

If treasury shares are reacquired for a purchase price significantly in excess of their current market price, it is *presumed* that the total purchase price includes amounts for stated or unstated rights or privileges. Under this circumstance, the total purchase price is allocated between the treasury shares and the rights or privileges that are identified with the purchase of the treasury shares based on the fair value of the rights or privileges, or the fair value of the treasury shares, whichever is more clearly evident.

PART II: INTERPRETIVE GUIDANCE

ASC 505-10: OVERALL

ASC 505-10-15-2, 50-6, 50-8A, 50-9 through 50-10; ASC 470-10-60-2 Disclosure Requirements under FASB Statement No. 129, *Disclosure of Information about Capital Structure,* Relating to Contingently Convertible Securities

Question: How do the disclosure requirements in ASC 505-10-50-3, which requires entities to explain the significant rights and privileges of their outstanding securities, including (*a*) conversion or exercise prices and rates and relevant dates, (*b*) sinking-fund requirements, (*c*) unusual voting rights, and (*d*) significant terms of contracts to issue additional shares, apply to contingently convertible securities, such as instruments with contingent conversion requirements that have not been met and that are not otherwise required to be included in computing diluted earnings per share (EPS)?

Answer: The FASB staff believes that the provisions of ASC 505 apply to all contingently convertible securities, including those with contingent conversion requirements that have not been met and that otherwise would not be included in the computation of EPS under the provisions of ASC 260, Earnings per Share. To help users of financial statements understand the conditions of a contingency, entities should disclose the significant terms of the conversion features of contingently convertible securities and the possible effect of conversion in accordance with the guidance in ASC 505-10-50-3. Disclosing the following quantitative and qualitative terms of contingently convertible securities would be useful to users:

- A description of (i) events or changes in circumstances under which a contingency causing conversion would be met and (ii) significant features of a security necessary to understand the conversion rights and their timing, for example, the periods in which a contingency might be met and in which securities might be converted
- The conversion price and the number of shares into which the security might be converted
- A description of events or changes in circumstances, if any, that might result in an adjustment or change in a contingency, the conversion price, or the number of shares, including the significant terms of those changes
- The manner in which a transaction will be settled when conversion occurs or alternative settlement methods, such as settlement in cash, shares, or a combination of the two.

The following disclosures also may be useful to users:

- Whether a diluted EPS calculation includes shares that would be issued if contingently convertible securities were to be converted if the contingency is met, and if it does not, why
- As required under the guidance in ASC 460-10-60-14; ASC 480-10-55-63; ASC 505-10-60-5; ASC 815-10-15-78, 55-52, 15-25-15; ASC 815-40-05-1 through 05-4, 05-10 through 05-12, 25-1 through 25-5, 25-7 through 25-20, 25-22 through 25-24, 25-26 through 25-35, 25-37 through 25-40, 30-1 35-1 through 35-2, 35-6, 35-8 through 35-13, 40-1 through 40-2, 50-1 through 50-5, 55-1 through 55-18 (Accounting for Derivative Financial Instruments Indexed to, and Potentially Settled in, a Company's Own Stock), information about derivative transactions entered into as a result of the issuance of contingently convertible securities, such as the terms of derivative transactions, including the settlement terms, how the transactions are related to contingently convertible securities, the number of shares underlying the derivatives, and the possible effect of the issuance of contingently convertible securities. A purchase of a call option with terms that presumably would substantially offset changes in the value of a written call option embedded in a convertible security is an example of such a transaction.

ASC 505-10-45-1 through 45-2; ASC 310-10-45-14; ASC 850-10-60-4 Classifying Notes Received for Capital Stock

BACKGROUND

A contribution to an entity's equity is made by a noncontrolling shareholder(s), controlling majority shareholder(s), or an entity's majority or sole owner in the form of a note, rather than in cash. The transaction may occur because a new company is being formed, a company needs additional capital for credit or other purposes, or a parent company wants to make its wholly owned subsidiary more self-sufficient by increasing its equity. Such transactions may be in the form of a sale of stock or a contribution to paid-in capital.

ACCOUNTING ISSUE

Should the note always be classified as a reduction of equity, or are there any circumstances under which it can be classified as an asset?

ACCOUNTING GUIDANCE

Recognizing such a note receivable as an asset, even though generally inappropriate, would be permitted only in the following very limited circumstances:

- There is substantial evidence of intent and ability to pay.
- The note will be repaid within a reasonably short period of time, for example, as discussed in ASC 210-10-S99-1. Under the SEC's rules, a public entity is required to deduct the receivable from equity.
- The note must be collected in cash before the financial statements are available or issued as discussed in ASC 855-10-25.

SEC STAFF COMMENT

The SEC Observer reiterated that exceptions from the SEC's rule would be very rare for registrants.

DISCUSSION

This Issue is one of the rare instances in which an issue that would apply only to privately held companies was discussed. Although there is no guidance on this matter in U.S. GAAP, the SEC has developed guidance for its registrants. Rule 5-02.30 of SEC Regulation S-X requires registrants to deduct from equity notes receivable when common stock transactions involve the company's common stock. This rule is restated in SEC Staff Accounting Bulletins, Topics 4E and 4G (ASC 310-10-S99-2, S99-3). In all cases, the presumption is that such notes are seldom paid.

Proponents of asset recognition suggested that a note should meet the following criteria to qualify as an asset:

- A scheduled repayment date
- Collection within a short period of time (five years suggested as the maximum)
- A market interest rate
- Collateralization by tangible assets with an adequate margin or a letter of credit
- The debtor's representation of intent to pay.

ASC 505-20: STOCK DIVIDENDS AND STOCK SPLITS

ASC 505-20-15-3A Accounting for Distributions to Shareholders with Components of Stock and Cash

BACKGROUND

Real estate investment trusts (REITs) are required by the Internal Revenue Service (IRS) to distribute at least 90% of their taxable income. REITS occasionally issue a "special" dividend distribution above the REIT's recurring quarterly dividend in periods in which a REIT has had large nonrecurring earnings. Frequently, those special dividends have been issued in cash and stock subject to IRS approval in a private letter ruling. In 2008, the IRS issued a ruling that permits REITS to make their annual required distributions in cash and stock if shareholders are permitted to elect to receive their total distribution in cash or in stock equal to the amount of the cash distribution. If too many shareholders elect to receive their distribution in cash, those electing to receive cash must receive a pro rata amount of cash that corresponds to their proportionate interest in the distribution. However, shareholders making that election cannot receive less than 10% of their total distribution in cash. The guidance in that ruling has also been extended to closed-end investment funds, which also must distribute at least 90% of their taxable income. Entities that want to declare regular or special dividends in cash and stock must obtain a private letter ruling from the IRS.

As a result of this IRS ruling, the following diversity in practice developed:

1. Some entities were accounting for the portion of a dividend issued in stock as a new stock issuance, which is included in earnings per share (EPS) *prospectively*. Others who considered it to be a stock dividend followed the guidance in ASC 260-10-55-12, and *retrospectively* restated shares outstanding and EPS.
2. Some believed that a stock dividend should be included in EPS on the date the dividend is declared, while others believed that a stock dividend should be included in EPS when the shares' trading price has been adjusted to include the effects of the stock dividend or when a dividend is settled.

ACCOUNTING GUIDANCE

The stock portion of a distribution to shareholders that contains components of cash and stock and allows shareholders to select their preferred form of distribution should be considered to be an issuance of stock in applying the EPS provisions of ASC 260. This guidance is based on the view that under this type of distribution a shareholder's ownership position changes unlike in the case of a stock dividend in which a shareholder is left in the same ownership position as before the transaction had occurred. Such a distribution should be classified as a liability when an entity becomes obligated to make the distribution in accordance with the guidance in ASC 480-10-25-14. Further, a distribution classified as a liability would be included in diluted EPS in accordance with the guidance in ASC 260-10-45-45 through 45-47 for contracts that may be settled in stock or in cash.

DISCLOSURE

In accordance with the guidance in ASC 260-10-50-2, an entity should disclose any transaction that occurs *after* the end of the most recent period but *before* the financial statements are issued or are available to be issued that would cause a material change in the number of common shares or potential common shares outstanding at the end of the period had that transaction occurred *before* the end of the period.

ASC 505-30: TREASURY STOCK

ASC 505-30-25-3 through 25-4, 30-2, 30-4, 50-3 through 50-4, 60-1; ASC 225-20-55-4 Accounting for a Purchase of Treasury Shares at a Price Significantly in Excess of the Current Market Price of the Shares and the Income Statement Classification of Costs Incurred in Defending against a Takeover Attempt

BACKGROUND

Most treasury stock transactions engaged in by an enterprise are solely capital transactions and do not involve recognition of revenue and expense. In some cases, however, treasury stock transactions may involve the receipt or payment of consideration in exchange for rights or privileges, which may require recognition of revenue or expense. The following guidance was issued to clarify this and other issues that may arise in a takeover attempt.

PRACTICE POINTER: A number of states do not recognize the concept of treasury stock and may treat reacquired shares as issued, but not outstanding.

ACCOUNTING GUIDANCE

Purchase Price in Excess of Market Price

Question 1: How should a company account for a purchase of treasury shares at a price that is significantly in excess of the current market price of the shares?

Answer: This situation creates an assumption that the purchase price includes amounts attributable to items other than the shares purchased. The price paid in excess of the current market price of the shares should be attributed to the other elements in the transaction. If the fair value of those other elements is more clearly evident than the market value of the stock, the former amount should be assigned to those elements and the difference should be recorded as the cost of the treasury shares. If no stated or unstated consideration in addition to the capital stock can be identified, the entire purchase price should be assigned to the treasury stock.

Illustration of the Accounting for "Greenmail" Payments

Saul Rainwood buys 1 million shares of Old Steel Inc. over a period of time at prices ranging from $10 to $19 per share. On May 29, 20X5, shares of Old Steel Inc. close at $15 per share. On May 30, 20X5, Old Steel reacquires all of Rainwood's shares at $30 per share, and Rainwood enters into an agreement to not reacquire more than 5% of Old Steel's common stock for a period of three years. As a result of this transaction, Old Steel would recognize treasury stock of $15 million and record a $15 million expense for the excess purchase price over the stock's closing market price on May 29th. The $15 million charged to expense is the consideration Rainwood received, over and above the stock's market price, for disposing of his shares and agreeing not to reacquire a substantial ownership stake for a period of time (i.e., a greenmail payment).

Agreements with a Shareholder or Former Shareholder Not to Purchase Additional Shares

Question 2: Should amounts that an entity pays to a shareholder (or former shareholder) that are attributed to an agreement precluding that shareholder (or former shareholder) from purchasing additional shares be capitalized as assets and amortized over the period of the agreement?

Answer: No, such payments should be expensed as incurred.

Costs of Defense and "Standstill" Agreement in a Takeover Attempt

Question 3: Should the costs a company incurs to defend itself in a takeover attempt or the costs of a "standstill" agreement be classified as extraordinary?

Answer: No. Neither meets the criteria for an *extraordinary* item discussed in ASC 225-20.

ASC 505-30-25-5 through 25-6, 55-1, 55-3, 55-5 through 55-6, 60-2; ASC 260-10-55-89 Accounting for an Accelerated Share Repurchase Program

BACKGROUND

In an accelerated share repurchase program, an entity purchases a specified number of shares immediately, but the purchase price for those shares is based on the average market price of the shares over a specified period of time. Such programs combine the benefits of an immediate share retirement of a tender offer with the price benefits of repurchases on the open market. They may be structured as a treasury stock purchase or a forward contract:

1. *Treasury stock purchase* An investment banker who is an unrelated third party borrows 1 million shares of Company A's common stock from investors, becomes the shares' owner of record, and sells the shares short to Company A on July 1, 20X9 at the fair value of $50 a share and is paid $50 million in cash on that date. Company A has legal title to the shares, which are held as treasury stock, and no other party can vote those shares.

2. *Forward contract* Company A enters into a forward contract with an investment banker on 1 million shares of Company A's common stock. If the volume-weighted average daily market price during the contract period from July 1, 20X9, to October 1, 20X9, exceeds the $50 initial purchase price (net of the investment banker's commission), the Company has the option to deliver to the investment banker on October 1, 20X9, cash or shares of common stock equal to the price difference times 1 million. If the volume-weighted average daily market price during the contract period is less than the $50 purchase price, the investment banker delivers to Company A on October 1, 20X9, cash or shares of common stock equal to the price difference times 1 million.

ACCOUNTING ISSUE

How should accelerated share repurchase programs be accounted for?

ACCOUNTING GUIDANCE

Accelerated repurchase programs should be accounted for as two separate transactions as follows:

1. As a treasury stock transaction in which shares of the company's stock are acquired and recognized on the acquisition date (e.g., July 1, 20X9)

2. As a forward contract that is indexed to its own common stock

According to the guidance in ASC 815-40, the forward contract in the example discussed above would be classified as an equity instrument, because the entity would receive cash if there is a gain on the contract, but has the option to pay in cash or stock if there is a loss on the contract. Therefore, no fair value changes of the contract would be recognized and the contract's settlement would be recognized in equity.

In calculating basic and diluted earnings per share (EPS), the number of shares used to calculate the weighted-average common shares outstanding would be reduced by the shares repurchased as treasury stock. The guidance in ASC 260-10-55-88 should be used to measure the effect of the forward contract on EPS.

ASC 505-50: EQUITY-BASED PAYMENTS TO NONEMPLOYEES

ASC 505-50-05-1, 05-4 through 05-5, 25-5, 30-18 through 30-19, 30-29, 35-13 through 35-15, 50-2, 55-25 through 55-27; ASC 845-10-50-2 Accounting by a Grantee for an Equity Instrument to Be Received in Conjunction with Providing Goods or Services

> *PRACTICE NOTE:* The guidance in this Issue will be superseded by the guidance in ASC 2014-09, *Accounting for Revenue from Contracts with Customers*, when it becomes effective on December 15, 2017, for public entities, and on December 15, 2018, for nonpublic entities.

BACKGROUND

The following is guidance for grantors regarding the accounting for equity instruments issued to other than employees in exchange for products or services. Previous guidance addressed the amount at which such equity instruments should be recognized and the date on which recognition should occur. However, a *grantee's* accounting for such transactions, which may span over more than one reporting period and may contain terms contingent on the grantee's performance, is currently not addressed in the authoritative literature.

ACCOUNTING ISSUES

1. On what date should a *grantee* measure the fair value of revenue received in the form of equity instruments in exchange for goods or services provided to a grantor?
2. If the terms of equity instruments received by a *grantee* for goods or services provided to a grantor can be adjusted after the measurement date based on the resolution of a contingency, such as performance above a level to which the grantee has committed, performance after the instrument was earned, or market conditions, how should a grantee account for an increase in the fair value of revenue received in the form of equity instruments after the contingency has been resolved?

ACCOUNTING GUIDANCE

1. A grantee should measure the fair value of equity instruments received in exchange for providing goods or services to a grantor based on the stock price and other measurement assumptions on either of the following dates, whichever is earlier (the measurement date):
   a. When the parties agree on the terms of the compensation arrangement in the form of equity instruments and on the grantee's performance commitment to earn the equity instruments
   b. When the grantee's performance required to earn the equity instruments is completed (i.e., the vesting date)
2. The accounting is as follows if on the measurement date, the quantity or any of the terms of the equity instruments depend on:
   a. **Achieving a market condition** Revenue is measured based on the fair value of the equity instruments, including the adjustment provisions. The fair value of the equity instruments is used without considering the market condition plus the fair value of the commitment to change the quantity or terms of the equity instruments if the market condition is met.
   b. **Additional grantee performance** Changes in fair value as a result of an adjustment to the instrument for a condition requiring additional grantee performance should be measured as additional revenue based on the guidance in ASC 718-20-35-3 through 35-4 for modification accounting. At the date on which the quantity or terms of the equity instrument are revised, the adjustment is measured as the difference between (*a*) the current fair value on the date of the revised equity instrument using the known quantity and terms, and (*b*) the current fair value on that date of the old equity instrument before the adjustment. If the fair value of the equity instruments changes after the measurement date for reasons that are unrelated to the achievement of performance conditions, those fair value changes should be accounted for in accordance with the relevant guidance on accounting and reporting for investments in equity instruments, such as the guidance in ASC Topics 320, 323, 325, 825, and 855. For example, on July 1, 2000, the date on which the parties agreed on the grantee's performance commitment, the fair value of an equity instrument granting options to the contractor is $500,000. On July 1, 2001, the amount of the original instrument is adjusted because the grantee has met a condition for additional performance. The equity instrument's fair value is $1 million on that date. If the fair value of the

original instrument is $650,000 on July 1, 2001, the increase in its fair value due to the performance condition is $350,000 ($1 million less $650,000). The $150,000 increase in the fair value of the original instrument from $500,000 to $650,000 is unrelated to the grantee's performance and should be accounted for based on other relevant literature.

It was noted that although the Issue does not address the timing of revenue recognition, a grantee would recognize deferred revenue or revenue in the same periods and in the same manner as cash, rather than equity instruments, received for goods or services.

DISCLOSURE REQUIREMENTS

In accordance with the guidance in ASC 845-10-50-1, the amount of gross operating revenue recognized as a result of the nonmonetary transactions discussed in this Issue should be disclosed in the financial statements of each reporting period. In addition, the SEC Observer reminded registrants about the requirements in Item 303(a)(3)(ii) of Regulation S-K under which an entity must disclose known trends or uncertainties that have had or that are reasonably expected to have a materially favorable or unfavorable effect on revenues.

ASC 505-50-05-3, 05-8, 15-2 through 15-3, 25-2, 25-4, 25-9, 30-2 through 30-7, 30-11 through 30-14, 30-21 through 30-23, 30-25 through 30-28, 30-30 through 30-31, 35-3, 35-5 through 35-10, 55-2 through 55-11, 55-13 through 55-17, 55-20 through 55-24, 55-28, 55-31 through 55-40; ASC 440-10-60-4 Accounting for Equity Instruments That Are Issued to Other Than Employees for Acquiring, or in Conjunction with Selling, Goods or Services

BACKGROUND

Before the issuance of ASC 505 (FAS-123(R)), there was no guidance on the *measurement date* for *nonemployee* stock options, nor whether the measurement date guidance established for employee stock options should be used as a model. Also, no guidance was provided for the issuance of nonemployee stock options involving the *sale* of goods and services, such as stock options used as sales incentives.

Compensation cost for equity instruments issued to *employees* was generally measured based on the fair value of the award at the grant date, but there was an exception for certain situations in which it would be impossible to "reasonably estimate" the fair value of a stock option or other equity instrument on that date, for example, if the option exercise price changes by a specified amount based on a change in the price of the underlying security. Under such circumstances, the award's fair value had to be measured based on the stock price and other relevant information on the "first date at which it is reasonably possible to estimate that value." However, it required using the intrinsic value of the award at the grant date to estimate compensation cost in those situations. ASC 505 which was issued in 2004 as a revision of FAS-123, also did not provide guidance on the accounting for share-based payment transactions with *nonemployees* but referred readers to this Issue for such guidance.

This Issue provides guidance on the measurement date and the recognition of *all* stock-option transactions with *nonemployees*. It does not apply, however, to equity instruments issued in a business combination or to equity instruments issued to lenders or investors providing financing to an issuer.

ACCOUNTING ISSUES

1. What date should an issuer use to measure the fair value of equity instruments in all transactions under the scope of this Issue?
2. In what period(s) and in what manner (capitalize or expense) should an issuer recognize the fair value of equity instruments in all transactions under the scope of this Issue?
3. How should the cost of equity instruments be recognized *before the measurement date* if the quantity and terms are all known in advance, because they do not depend on the counterparty's performance or market conditions?
4. If the quantity or terms of the equity instruments are not all known in advance, because they are based on the counterparty's performance or market conditions:
   a. How should the equity instruments be measured *at the measurement date*?
   b. How should the cost of the equity instruments be recognized *before the measurement date*?
   c. How should the equity instruments be accounted for *after the measurement date* if the quantity or terms of the equity instruments change as a result of the counterparty's performance or market conditions?

ACCOUNTING GUIDANCE

1. The fair value of equity instruments in all awards to nonemployees should be measured based on the stock price and other measurement assumptions on one of the following dates (the measurement date), whichever occurs first:
   a. The date on which an issuer and a counterparty reach a commitment for the counterparty's performance to earn the equity instruments. The counterparty's performance is considered probable (there is a performance commitment) because of a strong enough disincentive for nonperformance (in addition to forfeiture of the equity instruments) resulting from the relationship between the issuer and the counterparty. However, performance is not assured merely because an issuer can sue the counterparty for nonperformance. That action was not considered to be a large enough disincentive, because the option to sue for nonperformance always exists. In addition, there may not be sufficient assurance that damages will be collected.
   b. The date on which the counterparty's performance is concluded, because the counterparty has delivered or purchased, as appropriate, the goods or services, even though on that date, the quantity and all the terms of the equity instruments may still depend on other events, such as a target stock price. (This date is used if the counterparty made no performance commitment.) In some cases, a counterparty may be required to perform over a period of time, such as over several years; the equity award is fully vested, cannot be forfeited, and can be exercised on the date the parties enter into the contract. It was noted that this fact pattern would be rare, because usually there is a required vesting period. However, there was agreement if that situation occurs, the fair value of an award could be measured on the date the parties enter into a contract even if the services are yet to be performed.
2. The period(s) in which an entity should recognize the fair value of instruments that will be issued or whether the amounts should be expensed or capitalized was not discussed. However, the following conclusions were reached on the period and manner of recognition for all transactions:
   a. An asset, expense, or sales discount should be recognized (or previous recognition reversed) in the same period(s) and in the same manner as if the issuer had paid for the goods or services in cash or used cash rebates as a sales discount instead of paying with equity instruments.
   b. An asset, expense, or sales discount that had been recognized should *not* be reversed, if a counterparty does not exercise a stock option and the option expires unexercised.
3. Equity instruments should be measured at their current fair values at each interim financial reporting date, if the quantity and terms of the transaction are known and it is appropriate under U.S. GAAP for an issuer to recognize costs related to that transaction during financial periods preceding the measurement date. The methods illustrated in ASC 505-50-55-28 should be used to ascribe the changes in fair values to interim reporting dates.
4. If the quantity or any of the transaction's terms are unknown initially, the equity instruments should be accounted for as follows:
   a. The fair value of the equity instruments should be recognized as follows at the measurement date:
      (1) The issuer should recognize the equity instruments at their fair value on the measurement date, if the quantity or any of the transaction's terms depend on the achievement of market conditions, which are related to achieving a specified market target, such as a specified stock price or intrinsic value of a stock option. The fair value of the equity instruments should be computed without considering the market condition plus the fair value of the issuer's commitment to change the quantity or terms of the equity instruments, based on whether the market condition is met.
      (2) The issuer should recognize, on the measurement date, the lowest total amount (i.e., the variable terms multiplied by the applicable number of equity instruments) within a range of total fair values for the equity instruments based on different possible outcomes, if the quantity or any terms of the equity instruments on that date depend on the achievement of performance conditions by the counterparty, such as increasing market share for a specified product by a specified amount. The amount recognized may be zero.
      (3) The consensus in 4(a)(2) above applies, if the transaction requires the counterparty to meet performance conditions and market conditions.

b. If the quantity or the terms of a transaction are unknown and it is appropriate for the issuer to recognize the cost of the transaction in reporting periods *before* the measurement date, the equity instruments should be accounted for as follows:
   (1) The equity instruments should be recognized at their fair value on the date of recognition, as in the consensus on Issue 3 above, if the outcome of a transaction depends only on market conditions (see ASC 505-50-30-28 for application guidance).
   (2) The equity instruments should be recognized at the lowest total fair value at each interim date, if the outcome depends only on the counterparty's performance. The method illustrated in ASC 505-50-55-28, and 55-33 through 40 should be used to ascribe the changes in fair values between interim reporting dates (ASC 505-50-30-25).
   (3) The guidance in 4(a)(2) above also applies, if the outcome of a transaction depends both on the counterparty's performance and on market conditions (ASC 505-50-30-26).

c. If the quantity or any of the terms of a transaction are unknown initially, the accounting after the measurement date should be as follows:
   (1) For transactions that depend only on market conditions, ASC 505-50-35-6 provide that after measuring the current fair value of the issuer's commitment related to a market condition, in accordance with 4(a)(1) above, the issuer should, if necessary, recognize and classify future changes in the fair value of the commitment in accordance with accounting guidance on financial instruments, such as the guidance in ASC 815-40.
   (2) For transactions that depend only on a counterparty's performance, the lowest total fair value measured, based on the guidance in 4(a)(2) above, should be adjusted to recognize the additional cost of the transaction using the method for modification accounting in ASC 718-20-35-3 through 35-4 as each quantity and term of the transaction becomes known and until all such information becomes known as a result of the counterparty's performance. Under that method, the adjustment is measured at the date the quantity or terms of the equity instruments are known as the difference between (*a*) the current fair value of the *revised* instruments, using the current known quantity or term, and (*b*) the fair value of the equity instruments before knowing the revised quantity or term. The current fair value is calculated using the assumptions that result in the lowest total fair value, if the quantity or any terms are still unknown (ASC 505-50-35-7).
   (3) For transactions that depend on a counterparty's performance and on market conditions, an issuer should apply the method discussed in ASC 718-20-35-3 through 35-4 until the last condition related to the counterparty's performance has been met. The issuer should measure the current fair value of the commitment to issue additional equity instruments or change the terms of the equity instruments, based on whether the market condition is met, if the counterparty has met the last performance condition but one or more market conditions remain unresolved. This amount is an additional cost of the transaction. An issuer should, if necessary, recognize and classify future changes in the fair value of a commitment in accordance with accounting guidance on financial instruments, such as that in ASC 815-40, after measuring the current fair value of the issuer's commitment related to market conditions (ASC 505-50-35-8 through 35-10).

5. In accordance with the guidance in ASC 505-50-25-7, the measurement date is the date on which the two parties enter into a contract under which Company X grants to Company Y fully vested and nonforfeitable equity instruments, even though Company Y's performance will occur over a period of time (e.g., over several years).

EFFECT OF ASC 815

The terms of the stock options in this Issue should be analyzed to determine whether they meet the definition of a derivative in ASC 815. Although paragraph ASC 815-10-15-74 exempts *issuers* of contracts related to stock-based compensation arrangements under the provisions in ASC 718 from accounting for those contracts as derivatives the guidance in ASC 815-10-55-49 through 55-51, 55-53 through 55-55, 15-75 provides that the exception in ASC 815-10-15-74 does not apply to nonemployee *holders* of derivatives who receive the options as compensation for goods or services. Those parties are required to account for the options as derivatives under the guidance in ASC 815. However, all or a portion of the contract may be exempt if the underlying is a specified volume of sales or service revenue of one of the counterparties in the arrangement. The guidance in ASC 815-10-15-122, 15-125 through 15-127 and ASC 815-10-15-133 through 15-138 may also be relevant.

Illustration of Accounting for Nonemployee Stock Options with Variable Terms

1. In the following arrangement, the counterparty's commitment to perform is made before performance is completed. However, the quantity of the equity instruments to be issued is unknown. On 8/1/X7, Gary and Harry Real Estate Corp. (the Company) enters into an agreement with APEX Painters, Inc., under which APEX would paint five of the Company's office buildings beginning on 9/1/X7. The agreement provides that, in exchange for its services, the Company will pay APEX $50,000 and will issue to APEX 5,000 stock options that are exercisable over five years at an exercise price of $10, if APEX completes the project by 12/31/X7. No stock options will be issued if the project is completed after that date, and the contract price will be reduced by $10,000 for each week completion is delayed. The project is completed on time. Assuming the total fair value of the award on 8/1/X7—the date the agreement is reached—is $50,000, the Company should measure the fair value of the award on the commitment date—8/1/X7—in accordance with the consensus in 1(a), because it is probable that APEX will perform. In accordance with the consensus in paragraph 4(a)(ii), the Company should recognize a fair value of zero at the commitment date, because that is the lowest total fair value if the project is not completed by the deadline. The fair value of the award should be measured at the award's current fair value on 12/31/X7, when the project is completed.

2. In the following example, there is no commitment to perform until the counterparty has completed performance:

   A manufacturer of a new type of oven offers its customers 5,000 shares of its stock as an incentive to purchase a minimum of 500 ovens over the following two years. For every additional 100 ovens purchased, the manufacturer offers its customers an additional 1,000 shares. Customers have no performance commitment, because they are not required to purchase the ovens. The manufacturer will recognize the fair value of the 5,000 shares on the date the customer has purchased the minimum number of ovens as discussed in paragraph 4(a)(ii). The cost of the incentive should be adjusted for each additional 100 ovens purchased by a customer in accordance with paragraph 4(c)(ii) using modification accounting.

3. In the following example, the guidance on the measurement date is applied to a transaction that has a market condition:

   On 7/1/98, the XYZ Insurance Co. hires ABC Software Company to modify the company's software to comply with the requirements for the year 2000. XYZ will pay ABC $50,000 in cash and will issue 500 stock options if the modifications are completed by 6/30/99. There is a performance commitment, because ABC will incur a substantial penalty, which is considered to be a "sufficiently large disincentive for nonperformance," if the software modifications are not completed by that date. XYZ and ABC agreed on the quantity and terms of the stock options when the contract was signed on 7/1/98. The fair value of the stock options is $50,000 on the commitment date. However, if ABC completes the project by 6/30/99 and the fair value of XYZ's shares is less than $50,000 on 12/31/01, XYZ will issue an additional five stock options for each dollar that the stock price is below $100 per share, up to 125 stock options. Initially, XYZ will measure the 500 stock options (one option per share) at their fair value on 7/1/98, the day ABC made a commitment to perform. The fair value of the shares on that date is $40,000. In addition, XYZ would also recognize an additional $10,000 for the fair value of the additional stock options that could potentially be issued, regardless of whether the commitment is in-the-money. The total cost to be recognized for the options would be $50,000. After the initial recognition on the commitment date, XYZ would account for the 125 stock options that may be issued in accordance with existing authoritative guidance on financial instruments, including EITF Issue 96-13.

ASC 505-50-05-6 through 05-7, 25-7 through 25-8, 30-15 through 30-16, 35-11 through 35-12, S25-2, S99-2, 45-1 Accounting Recognition for Certain Transactions Involving Equity Instruments Granted to Other Than Employees

BACKGROUND

The guidance in ASC 505-50-05-3, 05-8, 15-2 through 15-3, 25-2, 25-4, 25-9, 30-2 through 30-7, 30-11 through 30-14, 30-21 through 30-23, 30-25 through 30-28, 30-30 through 30-31, 35-3, 35-5 through 35-10, 55-2 through 55-11, 55-13 through 55-17,

55-20 through 55-24, 55-28, 55-31 through 55-40; ASC 440-10-60-4 applies to a grantor's measurement of the fair value of equity instruments granted to other than employees. The guidance in ASC 505-50-05-1, 05-4 through 05-5, 25-5, 30-18 through 30-19, 30-29, 35-13 through 35-15, 50-2, 55-25 through 55-27; ASC 845-10-50-2 applies to a grantee's measurement of the fair value of such equity instruments for revenue recognition purposes. However, that guidance provides only that recognition should occur in the same period and in the same manner as if cash had been exchanged, but it does not provide guidance on the period or manner in which to recognize the fair value of a transaction.

Under that guidance, the measurement date occurs when a performance commitment is reached or if there is no performance commitment, on the vesting date when performance is complete, whichever occurs earlier. As a result, some grantors were structuring equity instruments as nonforfeitable instruments under which a grantee was fully vested at the date the parties entered into a contract, thereby establishing the measurement date. Those arrangements did not require a grantee to achieve a specific future performance to earn or retain the equity instruments. That is, a grantee could exercise the instruments immediately or at a specified future date whether or not future performance was met. Because instruments with such provisions were issued for accounting purposes under the guidance in ASC 718, a grantor recognized their issuance as a credit in equity at the fair value of the instrument measured in accordance with the guidance in ASC 505-50-05-3, 05-8, 15-2 through 15-3, 25-2, 25-4, 25-9, 30-2 through 30-7, 30-11 through 30-14, 30-21 through 30-23, 30-25 through 30-28, 30-30 through 30-31, 35-3, 35-5 through 35-10, 55-2 through 55-11, 55-13 through 55-17, 55-20 through 55-24, 55-28, 55-31 through 55-40 and ASC 440-10-60-4.

Although the equity instruments could not be forfeited, under many arrangements, they could not be exercised until a future date. Instruments with such provisions provided, however, that they could be exercised if a grantee met certain performance requirements. Some questioned whether a grantee's rights under those instruments were truly vested before the grantee's performance, which accelerated exercisability. In addition, some equity instruments were structured with sufficiently large disincentives to nonperformance. That also raised the question whether it is appropriate for a grantee to recognize equity instruments with such provisions as assets at the measurement date.

ACCOUNTING ISSUES

1. In what period and manner should a *grantor* recognize the measured cost of a transaction if a grantor issues a fully vested, exercisable, nonforfeitable equity instrument at the date a grantor and a grantee enter into an agreement for goods or services and no specific performance is required of the grantee?

1a. When, if ever, should a grantor present an asset in the balance sheet as contra-equity, if the grantor believes that an asset (other than a note or a receivable) has been received in return for fully vested, nonforfeitable equity instruments issued at the date the grantor and grantee enter into an agreement for goods or services under which the grantee retains the equity instruments without a specific performance requirement?

2. How should a *grantor* that issues a fully vested, exercisable, nonforfeitable equity instrument that can be exercised only after a specific period of time, measure and recognize the equity instrument at the date of the arrangement, and thereafter, if the grantee achieves a performance condition that accelerates exercisability under the terms of the instrument?

ACCOUNTING GUIDANCE

1. No specific guidance was provided on the period and manner in which a grantor should recognize the measured cost of fully vested, nonforfeitable equity instruments issued at the date a grantor and grantee enter into an agreement for goods or services. However, the guidance in ASC 505-50-25-7 provides that a grantor may recognize a prepaid asset or an immediate expense for the issuance of such financial instruments based on the circumstances.

1a. A grantor that issues fully vested, nonforfeitable equity instruments in exchange for an asset (other than a note or a receivable) should *not* report the acquired asset as a contra-equity in the balance sheet. This conclusion applies only to a grantor that issues equity instruments to *nonemployees* in exchange for goods or services. (ASC 505-50-45-1)

2. For nonforfeitable equity instruments that can be exercised only after a specified time period, but that a grantee may exercise earlier if specified performance conditions are achieved:

a. Measure the fair value of the equity instruments at the *grant* date and recognize the measured cost in the same period and manner as if it has been paid for in cash or the grantor had used cash rebates as sales discounts rather than granting equity instruments.
b. At the acceleration date, account for the incremental cost, if any, of the equity instruments issued, as the difference between (i) the current fair value of the *revised* equity instruments at the date they are exercisable and (ii) the

current fair value of the *old* equity instruments immediately before their exercisability is accelerated. If acceleration of a grantee's ability to exercise the option is the only change in terms, a significant additional charge will only occur if the expected dividend on the underlying instrument is greater than the sum of (i) the effect of discounting the exercise price and (ii) a loss in the time value of money, without the discounting, because the equity instrument has been exercised early.

SEC OBSERVER'S COMMENTS

The SEC Observer stated that grantees and grantors should use the same commitment date and similar values for such transactions, or the staff would challenge their accounting.

ASC 505-50-S25-1; S99-1 Grantor Balance Sheet Presentation of Unvested, Forfeitable Equity Instruments Granted to a Nonemployee

The SEC Observer discussed the following guidance, which addresses the balance sheet classification of unvested forfeitable equity instruments granted to nonemployees for future services instead of cash. Under such arrangements, a grantor has the right to recover the consideration paid as well as to impose a large penalty as damages for nonperformance. The guidance in ASC 505-50-05-3, 05-8, 15-2 through 15-3, 25-2, 25-4, 25-9, 30-2 through 30-7, 30-11 through 30-14, 30-21 through 30-23, 30-25 through 30-28, 30-30 through 30-31, 35-3, 35-5 through 35-10, 55-2 through 55-11, 55-13 through 55-17, 55-20 through 55-24, 55-28, 55-31 through 55-40; ASC 440-10-60-4 (Accounting for Equity Instruments That Are Issued to Other Than Employees for Acquiring, or in Conjunction with Selling, Goods or Services) provides that the commitment and measurement date for such instruments is the date that equity instruments were issued to a grantee if the grantee has a large enough disincentive for nonperformance.

Because practice is diverse as to the recognition of such transactions on the measurement date, the SEC staff will require registrants that receive a right to receive future services in exchange for unvested, forfeitable equity instruments to consider such instruments as *unissued* for accounting purposes until the instruments vest, which occurs when the future services have been received. Therefore, there is no recognition at the measurement date and the transaction is not recorded.

This announcement does not apply to arrangements under which fully vested, nonforfeitable, equity instruments are exchanged for future services, which are addressed in ASC 505-50-05-6 through 05-7, 25-7 through 25-8, 30-15 through 30-16, 35-11 through 35-12, S25-2, S99-2, 45-1 (Accounting Recognition for Certain Transaction Involving Equity Instruments Granted to Other Than Employees).

ASC 505-60: SPINOFFS AND REVERSE SPINOFFS

ASC 505-60-05-2 through 05-4, 15-2, 25-2, 25-4 through 25-5, 25-7 through 25-8, 45-1, 55-2, 55-5, 55-7 through 55-12 Accounting for Reverse Spinoffs

BACKGROUND

A *spinoff* is a transaction in which a company (a *spinnor*) transfers assets (usually a subsidiary) into a new legal entity (the *spinnee*) and distributes the shares in that entity to its shareholders, who do *not* give up any shares held in the spinnor. Spinoff transactions benefit companies in several ways. For example, neither the spinnor nor its shareholders recognize a gain on the distribution of shares if the spinoff qualifies as a nontaxable reorganization. A spinoff also avoids the double taxation that would result from a sale of a subsidiary and distribution of the proceeds to the company's shareholders.

ASC 845-10-30-10 provides guidance on accounting for spinoff transactions, which are nonreciprocal transfers to owners. It requires that a spinoff be accounted for based on the carrying value of the assets distributed to its shareholders. The transaction should *not* be accounted for as a sale of a spinnee followed by a distribution of the proceeds.

Some companies have been accounting for spinoffs based on the form of the transaction rather than on its substance—that is, the spinnee becomes the continuing entity. It is important to determine which entity will be treated as the spinnee for accounting purposes, because under the provisions of ASC 205, a spinnor must report a spinnee as a discontinued operation if the spinnee is a discontinued operation and meets the conditions in ASC 205-20-45-1A through 45-1C for such reporting.

ACCOUNTING ISSUE

Should a spinoff that treats a spinnee as the continuing entity be accounted for as a *reverse* spinoff, in which the spinnee is treated as the spinnor for accounting purposes based on the substance rather than the form of the transaction?

ACCOUNTING GUIDANCE

1. A transaction should be accounted for as a *reverse* spinoff if the substance of the transaction is most accurately depicted for shareholders and other users of financial statements by treating a legal spinee as the accounting spinnor. Judgment based on an evaluation of the relevant facts and circumstances should be used to determine whether a transaction should be accounted for as a reverse spinoff.
2. Although it should be presumed that the *legal* spinnor is also the spinnor for *accounting* purposes, that presumption may be tested by considering the following indicators, neither of which should be considered presumptive or determinative:
   a. The accounting spinnor (legal spinnee) is larger than the accounting spinnee (legal spinnor) based on assets, revenues, and earnings.
   b. The fair value of the accounting spinnor (legal spinnee) exceeds that of the accounting spinnee (legal spinnor).
   c. The former combined entity's senior management remains with the accounting spinnor (legal spinnee).
   d. The accounting spinnor (legal spinnee) has been held longer than the accounting spinnee (legal spinnor).

CHAPTER 38

ASC 606/605—REVENUE RECOGNITION

CONTENTS

PART I: GENERAL GUIDANCE

IMPACT OF ASU 2014-09: REVENUE FROM CONTRACTS WITH CUSTOMERS

On May 28, 2014, the FASB issued ASU 2014-09, *Revenue from Contracts with Customers,* with an original effective date for annual reporting periods beginning after December 15, 2016, including interim periods within that reporting period, for public business entities, certain not-for-profit (NFP) entities, and certain employee benefit plans. The original effective date for all other entities was for annual reporting periods beginning after December 15, 2017, and interim periods within annual periods beginning after December 15, 2018.

In August 2015, the FASB issued ASU 2015-14, *Revenue from Contracts with Customers (Topic 606): Deferral of the Effective Date.* The amendments in that ASU deferred the effective date of ASU 2014-09 for all entities by one year. Public business entities, certain NFP entities, and certain employee benefit plans were required to apply the guidance in ASU 2014-09 to annual reporting periods beginning after December 15, 2017, including interim reporting periods within that reporting period. All other entities were required to apply the guidance in ASU 2014-09 to annual reporting periods beginning after December 15, 2018, and interim reporting periods within annual reporting periods beginning after December 15, 2019. Early adoption was permitted.

The Coronavirus Disease 2019 (COVID-19) pandemic has adversely affected the global economy and has caused widespread disruptions to business and capital markets. The FASB received feedback that many private companies and NFP organizations are experiencing challenges with finalizing their transition to ASU 2014-09 because of the unique challenges resulting from the COVID-19 pandemic. As a result, in June 2020, the FASB issued ASU 2020-05, *Revenue from Contracts with Customers (Topic 606) and Leases (Topic 842): Effective Dates for Certain Entities,* as a limited deferral of the effective date of ASU 2014-09. ASU 2020-05 defers, for one year, the required effective date of ASU 2014-09 for certain entities that have not yet issued their financial statements (or made financial statements available for issuance) reflecting the adoption of ASU 2014-09. Those entities may elect to adopt the guidance for annual reporting periods beginning after December 15, 2019, and for interim reporting periods within annual reporting periods beginning after December 15, 2020. Instead, those entities may elect to follow the earlier stated effective date of annual reporting periods beginning after December 15, 2018, and interim reporting periods within annual reporting periods beginning after December 15, 2019.

The relatively long transition period between the original issuance of ASU 2014-09 and its revised effective dates results in both the guidance under ASU 2014-09 (ASC 606) and the previous guidance from multiple sources (ASC 605) being in effect for several years. **While ASC 606 is already in effect for some entities, the previous guidance (ASC 605) continues in effect for other entities.** Consistent with the policy of retaining guidance that has been replaced until it is no longer applicable to all entities, the 2022 *GAAP Guide* continues to include coverage of both ASC 606 and ASC 605. When the guidance in ASC 606 becomes effective for all entities, it will become the sole content of this chapter and the guidance in ASC 605 will be removed and no longer presented as supplemental guidance.

ASC 606: REVENUE FROM CONTRACTS WITH CUSTOMERS

(Replaces ASC 605)

ASC 606-10: OVERALL

OVERVIEW

Revenue is generally regarded as one of the most important numbers in evaluating a company's performance and financial position. Not only is the amount of revenue itself of great importance, revenue drives other elements of the financial statements. U.S. GAAP and IFRS concerning revenue recognition differ, and both were considered in need of improvement. As a result, the two standard-setting boards worked in conjunction to address the major changes reflected in ASU 2014-09. This project is now almost 20 years in the making.

ASC 606 replaces a number of diverse standards by requiring revenue to be recognized with a five-step process:

Step 1: Identify the contract with a customer
Step 2: Identify the performance obligations in the contract
Step 3: Determine the transaction price
Step 4: Allocate the transaction price to the performance obligations in the contract
Step 5: Recognize revenue as the entity satisfies a performance obligation

BACKGROUND

In 2002, the FASB and IASB initiated a joint project that was intended to clarify the principles for revenue recognition and share a common revenue recognition standard that would meet the following criteria:

- Remove inconsistencies and weaknesses in revenue recognition requirements.
- Provide a more robust framework for addressing revenue issues as they arise.
- Improve comparability of revenue recognition practices across entities, industries, jurisdictions and capital markets.
- Improve financial statement disclosures related to revenue recognition.
- Simplify the preparation of financial statements by reducing the number of requirements to which an entity must refer.

PRACTICE NOTE: Following are quotes from the chairs of FASB and IASB reflecting their reactions to the completion of the revenue recognition standards, as reported by the AICPA in its News Update quoting a *Journal of Accountancy* article:

"The revenue recognition standard represents a milestone in our efforts to improve and converge one of the most important areas of financial reporting. It will eliminate a major source of inconsistency in GAAP, which currently consists of numerous disparate, industry-specific pieces of revenue recognition guidance." (Russell Golden, FASB Chair)

"The successful completion of this project is a major achievement for both boards. Together, we have improved the revenue requirements of both IFRS and U.S. GAAP, while managing a fully converged standard." (Hans Hoogervorst, IASB Chair)

Prior to ASC 606, revenue recognition standards in U.S. GAAP were numerous and many involved industry-specific and transaction-specific guidance. These requirements were developed on a piecemeal basis and many addressed narrow issues or transactions without reference to a common recognition framework. As a result, issues about revenue recognition were often difficult to resolve. Also, economically similar transactions sometimes resulted in differing revenue recognition practices.

Guidance regarding revenue recognition in IFRS was limited and lacked cohesion. General disclosure requirements were generally limited to the entity's accounting policies and the effect of revenue on those policies. IFRS lacked guidance on specific topics that were challenging to address in practice, resulting in difficulty in accounting for complex transactions. In many cases, in applying IFRS, the absence of specific guidance led entities to use, or analogize, to U.S. GAAP.

The FASB believes that the new guidance provided by ASC 606 will significantly improve financial reporting by enhancing comparability of revenue recognition practices across entities, industries, jurisdictions, and capital markets. The approach, which is largely principles-based, provides a framework for addressing revenue recognition issues comprehensively for entities that apply U.S. GAAP, as well as those that apply IFRS. It applies to contracts with customers across a wide range of industries and transactions and is expected to remain relevant as markets and transactions evolve.

PRACTICE NOTE: Much has been said about the significance of ASU 2014-09 and its impact on companies. To support these statements, consider the following:

- The time for completion was one of the longest in the history of standard-setting in the United States. The project was added to the FASB's agenda in June 2002, and ASU 2014-09 was approved in May 2014. Since then, several amendments, beyond the delays in effective dates described above, have been made.
- The standard is one of the longest in history—700 pages, of which 500 represent changes in the Accounting Standards Codification. Subsequent to ASU 2014-09, several additional standards that amend the original standard have been issued.
- The number of sections of the ASC affected is among the highest ever—one entirely new section (ASC 606), one new subsection (ASC 340-40), and changes affecting many other Topics and Subtopics throughout the ASC.
- The number of examples included in ASU 2014-09 is 63. This is unprecedented in U.S. authoritative literature.
- The transition period was one of the longest in history, and the delays in the effective date were intended to provide additional time for the FASB to clarify implementation and for companies to prepare for the significant changes required.

Amendments to the FASB Accounting Standards Codification®

The amendments to the ASC resulting from ASU 2014-09 are so comprehensive and so numerous that they require almost 500 pages of text to cover. The FASB presents these changes in two categories, as follows:

Section A—Revenue from Contracts with Customers: Amendments to the Accounting Standards Codification

Section B—Conforming Amendments Related to Revenue from Contracts with Customers: Amendments to the Accounting Standards Codification

Section A includes two new sections of the ASC: Topic 606, Revenue from Contracts with Customers, and Subtopic 340-40, Other Assets and Deferred Costs—Contracts with Customers. Section B includes the changes required in the remainder of the ASC in three categories: direct changes, conforming changes, and editorial changes.

In addition to the above, ASU 2014-09 includes background information and the basis for conclusions and amendments to the XBRL taxonomy.

Important Terminology

The ASC Glossary includes a number of terms that are important in understanding ASU 2014-09. Following are abbreviated definitions of some of the more important terms. For more complete definitions, as well as terms not presented here, the reader is referred to the ASC Glossary.

Contract

An agreement between two or more parties that creates enforceable rights and obligations.

Performance Obligation

A promise in a contract with a customer to transfer to the customer a good or service, including a bundle of goods or services, that is distinct, or a series of distinct goods or services that are substantially the same and that have the same pattern of transfer to the customer.

Public Business Entity

A public business entity is a business entity that meets any one of the following criteria. Neither a not-for-profit entity nor an employee benefit plan is considered a business entity.

- The entity is required by the SEC to file or furnish financial statements, or does file or furnish financial statements, including voluntary filers, with the SEC.
- The entity is required by the Securities Exchange Act of 1934, including rules or regulations under the Act, to file or furnish financial statements with a regulatory agency other than the SEC.
- The entity is required to file or furnish financial statements with a foreign or domestic regulatory agency in preparation for the sale of or for purposes of issuing securities that are not subject to contractual restrictions on transfer.
- The entity has issued, or is a conduit bond obligator for, securities that are traded, listed, or quoted on an exchange or an over-the-counter market.
- The entity has one or more securities that are not subject to contractual restrictions on transfer, and is required by law, contract, or regulation to prepare U.S. GAAP financial statements and make them publicly available on a periodic basis.

Revenue

Inflows or other enhancements of assets of an entity or settlements of its liabilities from delivering or producing goods, rendering services, or other activities that constitute the entity's ongoing major or central operations.

Standalone Selling Price

The price at which an entity would sell a promised good or service separately to a customer.

Transaction Price

The amount of consideration to which an entity expects to be entitled in exchange for transferring promised goods or services to a customer. This excludes amounts collected on behalf of third parties.

SUMMARY OF REVENUE RECOGNITION UNDER ASC 606

The objective of the guidance in ASC 606 is to establish principles that an entity applies to report useful information to users of financial statements about the nature, amount, timing, and uncertainty of revenue and cash flows arising from a contract with a customer. (ASC 606-10-10-1) The core principle is that an entity recognizes revenue to depict the transfer of promised goods or services to customers in an amount that reflects the consideration to which the entity expects to be entitled in exchange for those goods or services. (ASC 606-10-10-2)

The ASC 606 guidance is written for an individual contract with a customer. As a practical expedient, the entity may apply the guidance to a portfolio of contracts with similar characteristics if the entity expects that the effects on the financial statements of applying the guidance in this manner would not differ materially from applying the guidance to individual contracts within the portfolio. In applying ASC 606 guidance to a portfolio, use of estimates and assumptions that reflect the size and composition of the portfolio is appropriate. (ASC 606-10-10-4)

Scope

ASC 606 guidance applies to all contracts with customers *except* those covered by the indicated ASC Topic:

- Lease contracts within the scope of ASC 842 (Leases).
- Insurance contracts within the scope of ASC 944 (Financial Services—Insurance).
- Financial instruments and other contractual rights:
  - Receivables (ASC 310)
  - Investments—Debt Securities (ASC 320)
  - Investments—Equity Securities (ASC 321)
  - Investments—Equity Method and Joint Ventures (ASC 323)
  - Investments—Other (ASC 325)
  - Liabilities (ASC 405)
  - Debt (ASC 470)
  - Derivatives and Hedging (ASC 815)
  - Financial Instruments (ASC 825)
  - Transfers and Servicing (ASC 860).
- Guarantees within the scope of ASC 460.
- Nonmonetary exchanges between entities in the same line of business to facilitate sales to customers or potential customers. (ASC 606-10-15-2)

An entity shall apply the guidance in this ASC to a contract, other than to a contract listed above, only if the counterparty to the contract is a customer. A customer is a party that has contracted with the entity to obtain goods or services that are an output of the entity's ordinary activities in exchange for consideration. (ASC 606-10-15-3)

Application of Core Principle

The core principle of ASC 606 is that an entity recognizes revenue in an amount that reflects the consideration to which the entity expects to be entitled in exchange for goods or services. (ASC 606-10-05-3)

Applying this core principle involves the following five-step process:

Step 1: Identify the contract(s) with a customer—A contract is an agreement between two or more parties that creates enforceable rights and obligations.

Step 2: Identify the performance obligations in the contract—A contract includes promises to transfer goods or services to a customer. If those goods or services are distinct, the promises are performance obligations and are accounted for separately.

Step 3: Determine the transaction price—The transaction price is the amount of consideration in a contract to which an entity expects to be entitled in exchange for transferring promised goods or services to a customer.

Step 4: Allocate the transaction price to the performance obligations in the contract—An entity typically allocates the transaction price to each performance obligation on the basis of the relatively standalone selling price of each distinct good or service promised in the contract.

Step 5: Recognize revenue when the entity satisfies a performance obligation—The entity recognizes revenue when it satisfies a performance obligation by transferring a promised good or service to a customer. The amount of revenue recognized is the amount allocated to the satisfied performance obligation. (ASC 606-10-05-4)

Recognition and Measurement of the Five-Step Process

An entity shall account for a contract with a customer within the scope of ASC 606 only when all of the following criteria are met:

- The parties to the contract have approved the contract.
- The entity can identify each party's rights regarding the goods or services to be transferred.
- The entity can identify the payment terms for the goods or services to be transferred.
- The contract has commercial substance.
- It is probable that the entity will collect substantially all of the consideration to which it will be entitled in exchange for goods or services that will be transferred to the customer. (ASC 606-10-25-1)

Step 1: Identify the contracts with a customer

The initial step in the revenue recognition process is to identify one or more contracts with a customer. ASC 606 defines a contract as an agreement between two or more parties that creates enforceable rights and obligations. An entity shall apply the requirement to all contracts that meet the following criteria:

1. Approval and commitment of the parties.
2. Identification of the rights of the parties.
3. Identification of the payment terms.
4. Has commercial substance.
5. Is probable that the entity will collect the consideration to which it is entitled in exchange for the goods or services that will be transferred.

In some cases, the entity should combine contracts and account for them as a single contract. There is also guidance provided on how to account for contract modifications.

Step 2: Identification of the performance obligations

Once the existence of a contract is determined, the second step is to identify the performance obligation(s) inherent in the contract. A performance obligation is a promise in a contract with a customer to transfer a good or service to the customer. If an entity promises to transfer more than one good or service to the customer, the entity should account for each promised good or service as a performance obligation only if it is distinct or it is a series of distinct goods or services that are substantially the same and have the same pattern of transfer.

A good or service is considered distinct if both of the following criteria are met:

1. The customer can benefit from the good or service either on its own or together with other resources that are available to the customer (i.e. the good or service is *capable of being distinct*).
2. The promise to transfer the good or service is separately identifiable from other promises in the contract (i.e., the good or service is *distinct within the context of the contract*).

A good or service that is not distinct is combined with other promised goods or services until the entity identifies a bundle of goods or services that is distinct.

Step 3: Determine the transaction price

The third step in the process to recognize revenue is to determine the transaction price. In determining the transaction price, the following guidelines are offered in ASC 606:

- Where variable consideration is involved, the amount to include in the transaction price is estimated as either the expected value or the most likely amount.

- In determining the transaction price, variable consideration should be included only to the extent it is probable that a significant reversal in the amount of revenue recognized will not occur when the uncertainty of the variable consideration is resolved.
- The promised amount of consideration should be adjusted for the effects of the time value of money if the timing of payments provides the customer with a significant benefit of financing for the transfer of goods or services to the customer.
- Noncash consideration should be measured at fair value. If a reasonable direct estimate of the fair value of any noncash consideration cannot be made, the value should be estimated indirectly by reference to the standalone selling price of the goods or services promised in exchange for the consideration.
- If the entity pays, or expects to pay, consideration to the customer that the customer can apply against amounts owed, the transaction price should be reduced by the amount of the expected payment.

PRACTICE POINTER: In applying the guidelines listed above, ASC 606 provides additional guidance. For example, in applying the third guideline, as a practical matter, an entity is not required to assess whether a contract has a significant financing component if the entity expects at contract inception that the period between payment and the transfer of the goods or services will be one year or less. In applying the fifth guideline, if the consideration payable to a customer is variable, the entity should consider the guidance on constraining estimates of variable consideration.

Step 4: Allocate the transaction price to the performance obligations in the contract

For a contract with more than one performance obligation, the fourth step in the process is to allocate the transaction price to the performance obligations in the contract. The transaction price must be allocated between or among the performance obligations so that the amount of consideration depicts the amount of consideration the entity expects to be entitled to as each performance obligation is satisfied.

Allocating consideration to each performance obligation requires the entity to determine the standalone selling price at the inception of the contract of the distinct goods or services underlying each performance obligation. Allocation would then be made to each performance obligation on a relative standalone selling price basis. If a standalone selling price is not observable, the amount must be estimated.

Subsequent changes in the transaction price should be allocated to the performance obligations on the same basis as at the inception of the contract. Amounts allocated to a satisfied performance obligation are recognized as revenue, or as a reduction in revenue, in the period in which the transaction price changes.

Step 5: Recognize revenue when or as the entity satisfies a performance obligation

The final step, and the ultimate goal, of the revenue recognition process is to recognize revenue. This is appropriate when the entity satisfies a performance obligation by transferring the promised good or services to a customer. Transfer is considered to have occurred when the customer obtains control of the good or service.

PRACTICE POINTER: An important determination that must be made is whether the entity satisfies performance obligations over time or at a point in time. If the entity satisfies a performance obligation over time, it is appropriate to recognize revenue in different reporting periods. If the performance obligation is satisfied at a single point in time, the revenue associated with that performance obligation would be recognized entirely in a single reporting period. For example, some long-term construction projects may be structured in a manner that includes multiple performance obligations that may be met during the project, leading to revenue recognition at multiple times during the contract. Others may be structured with a single performance obligation, resulting in revenue being recognized entirely when that obligation is satisfied.

Transfer of control is deemed to have occurred if any one of the following criteria is met:

1. The customer receives and consumes the benefits provided by the entity's performance.
2. The entity's performance creates or enhances an asset that the customer controls as the asset is created or enhanced.
3. The entity's performance does not create an asset with an alternative use to the entity, and the entity has an enforceable right to payment for the performance that is completed.

Performance obligations that are not satisfied over time are satisfied at a point in time. Determining the point in time at which the customer obtains control of the promised asset requires consideration of factors such as the following (not a comprehensive list):

- The entity has a right to payment for the asset.
- The customer has legal title to the asset.
- The entity has transferred physical possession of the asset.
- The customer has the risks and rewards of ownership.
- The customer has accepted the asset.

Contracts

An entity shall account for a contract with a customer in accordance with ASC 606 when all of the following criteria are met:

- The parties have approved the contract and are committed to perform their respective obligations.
- The entity can identify each party's rights regarding the goods and services to be transferred.
- The entity can identify the payment terms.
- The contract has commercial substance (i.e., the risk, timing, or amount of the entity's future cash flows is expected to change as a result of the contract).
- It is probable that the entity will collect the consideration to which it is entitled in exchange for the goods or services to be transferred to the customer. (ASC 606-10-25-1)

The contract is an agreement between two or more parties that creates enforceable rights and obligations. The contract may be written, oral, or implied by an entity's customary business practices. Practices and processes for establishing contracts with customers may vary across legal jurisdictions, industries, and entities (ASC 606-10-25-2). Some contracts have no fixed duration and can be terminated or modified at any time. Other contracts automatically renew on a periodic basis that is specified in the contract (ASC 606-10-25-3). A contract does not exist if each party has the unilateral enforceable right to terminate an unperformed contract without compensating the other party (ASC 606-10-25-4).

Depending on details of a contract, promised goods or services may include, but are not limited to, the following:

- Sale of goods produced by an entity.
- Resale of goods purchased by an entity.
- Resale of rights to goods or services purchased by an entity.
- Performing a contractually agreed-upon task.
- Providing a service of standing ready to provide goods or services or of making goods or services available to a customer to use as and when the customer desires.
- Providing a service of arranging for another party to transfer goods or services to a customer.
- Granting rights to goods or services to be provided in the future that a customer can resell or provide to its customer.
- Constructing, manufacturing, or developing an asset on behalf of a customer.
- Granting licenses.
- Granting options to purchase additional goods or services. (ASC 606-10-25-18)

Two or more contracts entered into at or near the same time with the same customer shall be combined and accounted for as a single contract if one or more of the following criteria is/are met:

- The contracts are negotiated as a package with a single commercial objective.
- The consideration to be paid in one contract depends on the price or performance of the other contract(s).
- The goods or services promised in the contracts are a single performance obligation. (ASC 606-10-24-9)

A contract modification is a change in the scope, price, or both of a contract that is approved by both parties to the contract (ASC 606-10-25-10). A contract modification is accounted for as a separate contract if both of the following conditions are met:

- The scope of the contract increases because of the addition of promised goods or services that are distinct.
- The price of the contract increases by an amount of consideration that reflects the entity's standalone selling prices of the promised good or service and any appropriate adjustments to that price to reflect circumstances of the particular contract. (ASC 606-10-25-12)

If a contract modification is not accounted for as a separate contract, the entity shall account for the promised goods or services not yet transferred at the date of the modification in whichever of the following is applicable:

- If the remaining goods or services are distinct from the goods or services transferred on or before the date of the modification, the modification is accounted for as if it were a termination of the existing contract and the creation of a new contract.
- If the remaining goods or services are not distinct and, therefore, form a part of a single performance obligation that is partially satisfied at the date of the modification, the modification is accounted for as if it were a part of the existing contract.
- If the remaining goods and services are a combination of the above, the entity shall account for the effects of the modification on the unsatisfied performance obligations in a manner that is consistent with the above. (ASC 606-10-25-13)

Illustration of Modification of Contract Terms

April, Inc. (the entity) contracts to sell 100 products to a customer for $15,000 ($150 per product). The products are transferred to the customer over a four-month period. After 70 products have been delivered, the contract is modified to require April to deliver an additional 25 products to the customer at $140 per product.

Case A: Additional products for a price that reflects the standalone selling price

When the contract is modified, the price of the contract modification for the additional products is $3,500 (25 additional products × $140). Assume that the price of the additional products reflects the standalone selling price of the products at the time of the modification and the additional products are distinct from the original products.

In this case, the contract modification for the additional 25 products is a new and separate contact that does not affect accounting for the initial contract. The entity would recognize revenue of $150 per product for the 100 products in the original contract and $140 per product for the 25 additional products in the new contract ($140 × 25 = $3,500).

Case B: Additional products for a price that does not reflect the standalone selling price

During the course of negotiating the additional 25 products, the parties agree to a price of $140 per product. However, the customer discovers a defect in the delivered products and the parties agree to a $1,000 credit on the price the entity charges for the additional 25 products. Consequently, the contract modification specifies that the price of the additional products is $2,500 ($3,500 – $1,000 credit).

At the time of the modification, the entity recognizes the $1,000 credit as a reduction of the revenue for the initial 70 products. In accounting for the sale of the additional 25 products, the negotiated price of $140 per product does not reflect the standalone selling price of the additional products. The contract modification does not meet the conditions to be accounted for as a separate contract. Consequently, the amount of revenue recognized for the remaining products is a blended price of $145.45, determined as follows:

Original contract (30 products × $150)	$4,500
Modification (25 products × $140)	3,500
	$8,000
Remaining products (30 + 25)	55
Blended price ($8,000 / 55 products)	$145.45

Performance Obligations

At the inception of a contract, the entity shall assess the goods or services promised in the contract and identify as a performance obligation each promise to transfer either of the following:

- A good or service, including a bundle of either, that is distinct.
- A series of distinct goods or services that are substantially the same and have the same pattern of transfer to the customer. (ASC 606-10-25-14)

Generally, a contract with a customer explicitly states the goods or services that are promised to be transferred to a customer. The promised goods or services identified in a contract with a customer may not be limited to the goods or services that are explicitly stated in the contract. A contract may include promises that are implied by customary business practices, published policies, or specific statements made at the time of entering into the contract (ASC 606-10-25-16).

Depending on the contract, promised goods or services do not include activities that an entity must undertake to fulfill a contract unless those activities transfer a good or service to the customer (ASC 606-10-25-17).

Promised goods or services may include, but at not limited to, the following:

- Sale of goods produced by an entity.
- Resale of goods purchased by an entity.
- Resale of rights to goods or services purchased by an entity.
- Performing a contractually agreed-upon task.
- Providing a service to provide goods or services or of making goods or services available for a customer to use as and when the customer decides.
- Providing a service of arranging for another party to transfer goods and services to a customer.
- Granting rights to goods or services to be provided in the future.
- Constructing, manufacturing, or developing an asset on behalf of a customer.
- Granting licenses.
- Granting options to purchase additional goods or services. (ASC 606-10-25-18)

An entity that promises a good to a customer also might perform related shipping and handling. If the shipping and handling activities are performed before the customer obtains control of the goods, then the shipping and handling activities are not a promised service to the customer and are activities to fulfill the entity's promise to transfer the good (ASC 606-10-25-18A). If the shipping and handling are performed after a customer obtains control of the good, then the entity may elect to account for shipping and handling as activities to fulfill the promise to transfer the good. The policy election should be followed consistently to similar types of transactions (ASC 606-10-25-1B).

A good or service that is promised to a customer is considered distinct if the customer can benefit from the good or service either on its own or together with other resources, or the entity's promise to transfer the good or service is separately identified from other promises in the contract (ASC 606-10-25-19).

Revenue is recognized when the entity satisfies a performance obligation by transferring a promised good or service to a customer. An asset is considered to have been transferred when the customer obtains control of the asset (ASC 606-10-25-23). Performance obligations may be satisfied over time or at a point in time.

A performance is considered satisfied, and revenue recognized, when one of the following is met:

- The customer simultaneously receives and consumes the benefits provided by the entity's performance.
- The entity's performance creates or enhances an asset that the customer controls.
- The entity's performance does not create an asset with an alternative use to the entity and the entity has an enforceable right to payment for performance completed. (ASC 606-10-25-27)

A performance obligation is considered satisfied at a point when a customer obtains control of a promised asset. Determining the point in time when a customer takes control requires the entity to consider various factors which include, but are not limited to, the following:

- The entity has a right to payment for the asset, that is the customer is obligated to pay for the asset.
- The customer has legal title to the asset.
- The entity has transferred physical possession of the asset.
- The customer has the significant risks and rewards of ownership of the asset.
- The customer has accepted the asset. (ASC 606-10-25-30)

A performance obligation satisfied over time requires an entity to recognize revenue over time by measuring the progress toward complete satisfaction of that performance obligation. An objective when measuring progress is to depict an entity's performance in transferring control of goods or services to a customer (ASC 606-10-25-31). An entity shall apply a single method of measuring progress for each performance obligation over time. That method shall be applied consistently to similar performance obligations and similar circumstances. At the end of each reporting period, the entity shall remeasure its progress toward complete satisfaction of a performance obligation (ASC 606-10-25-32).

PRACTICE POINTER: Appropriate methods for measuring progress are classified as output methods and input methods. These are described in greater detail in ASC 606-10-55-16 through 55-21. Generally, output methods recognize revenue on the basis of direct measurements of the value to the customer of the goods or services transferred to date relative to the remaining goods or services promised under the contract. These methods include surveys of performance completed, appraisals of results achieved, milestones reached, time elapsed, and units produced or delivered. In contrast, input methods recognize revenue on the basis of the entity's efforts to satisfy a performance obligation. Examples of input methods are resources consumed, labor hours expended, costs incurred, time elapsed, and machine hours used.

Illustration of Identifying Performance Obligations

Foster, Inc. (the entity), an automobile dealer, contracts with a customer to deliver an automobile, provide designated service for a two-year period, and provide a warranty for 60,000 miles or five years whichever comes first.

The entity assesses the goods and services promised to determine if they are distinct. The entity observes that the automobile is delivered before the other services are delivered and the automobile is functional without the service or warranty. The entity concludes that the customer benefits from each of the goods and services either on their own or together with the other goods and services. The entity determines that the promise to transfer goods and services to the customer is separate for each good and service. On the basis of this assessment, the entity identifies three performance obligations in the contract for the following goods or services:

1. Automobile
2. Service
3. Warranty

Revenue is recognized on the automobile at the point of delivery, on the service agreement as service is provided, and on the warranty as warranty work is completed.

Transaction Price

The transaction price is the amount of consideration to which an entity expects to be entitled in exchange for transferring promised goods or services to a customer. This excludes amounts collected on behalf of third parties (e.g., sales taxes). This may include fixed amounts, variable amounts or both (ASC 606-10-32-2). The nature, timing, and amount of consideration promised by a customer affect the estimate of the transaction price. In determining the transaction price, an entity shall consider the effects of all of the following:

- Variable consideration
- Constraining estimates of variable consideration
- The existence of a significant financing component in the contract
- Noncash consideration
- Consideration payable to a customer (ASC 606-10-32-3)

If a contract includes variable consideration, an estimate is made of the amount of consideration to which the entity will be entitled in exchange for transferring the promised goods or services. (ASC 606-10-32-4) Factors included in estimating the amount of consideration include discounts, rebates, refunds, credits, price concessions, incentives, performance bonuses, penalties, and other similar items. The promised consideration may vary if an entity's entitlement to consideration is contingent on the occurrence or nonoccurrence of a future event (ASC 606-10-32-5, 6).

Two methods are available for estimating the amount of variable consideration. The method that is expected to better predict the amount of consideration should be used. The expected value method is the sum of probability-weighted amounts in a range of possible consideration amounts. An expected value may be an appropriate estimate of the amount of variable consideration if an entity has a large number of contracts with similar characteristics. The most likely method is the single most likely amount in a range of possible consideration amounts. The most likely may be an appropriate estimate of the amount of consideration if the contract has only two possible outcomes (ASC 606-10-32-8). The method used shall be applied consistently throughout the contract when estimating the effect of an uncertainty on an amount of variable consideration. The entity shall consider all information reasonably available, including historical, current, and forecast. The information used to estimate the amount of variable consideration typically is similar to the information used by management during the bid-and-proposal process and in establishing prices for promised goods or services (ASC 606-10-32-9).

Constraining estimates of variable consideration refers to the fact that the amount of variable consideration is included only to the extent that it is probable that a significant reversal in the amount of cumulative revenue recognized will not occur when the uncertainty associated with the variable consideration is subsequently resolved (ASC 606-24-32-11). Factors to be considered in making this judgment are:

- Whether the consideration is highly susceptible to factors outside the entity's influence.
- The uncertainty about the amount of consideration is expected to require a long period of time.
- The entity's experience with similar types of contracts is limited or has limited predictive value.
- The entity has a practice of either offering a broad range of price concessions or changing the payment terms and conditions of similar contracts.
- The contract has a large number and broad range of possible consideration amounts. (ASC 606-10-32-12)

Consideration payable to a customer includes: (*a*) cash amounts that an entity pays, or expects to pay, to the customer, (*b*) credit or other items that can be applied against amounts owed to the entity's customer, and (*c*) equity instruments granted in conjunction with selling goods or services. An entity shall account for consideration payable to a customer as a reduction of the transaction price and, therefore, of revenue unless the payment to the customer is for a distinct good or service that the customer transfers to the entity. If the consideration payable to the customer includes a variable amount, the entity shall estimate the transaction price in accordance with ASC 606-10-32-5 through 32-13. (ASC 606-10-32-25)

Equity instruments granted by an entity in conjunction with selling goods and services shall be measured and classified under ASC 718 on stock compensation. The equity instrument is measured at the grant date in accordance with ASC 718. Changes in the measurement of the equity instrument after the grant date that are due to the form of the consideration are not included in the transaction price. Changes due to the form of the consideration are reflected elsewhere in the grantor's income statement (ASC 606-10-32-25A).

If consideration payable to a customer is a payment for a distinct good or service from the customer, an entity shall account for the purchase of the good or service in the same way it accounts for other purchase from supplies. If the amount of consideration payable to the customer exceeds the fair value of the distinct good or service that the entity receives from the customer, the entity shall account for the excess as a reduction of the transaction price. If the entity cannot reasonably estimate the fair value of the good or service received from the customer, it shall account for all of the consideration payable to the customer as a reduction of the transaction price (ASC 606-10-32-26).

Allocating the Transaction Price to Performance Obligations

The entity allocates the transaction price to each performance obligation in an amount that depicts the amount of consideration to which the entity expects to be entitled in exchange for transferring the promised goods or services to the customer (ASC 606-10-32-28). Generally, the allocation of the transaction price to performance obligations identified in the contract is based on the relative standalone selling price. This requires the entity to determine the standalone selling price at contract inception of the distinct goods or services underlying each performance obligation in the contract and allocate the transaction price in proportion to those standalone selling prices (ASC 606-10-32-31). If a standalone selling price is not directly observable, the entity estimates the standalone selling price, considering all information that is reasonably available, maximizing the use of observable inputs and applying estimation methods consistently in similar circumstances. Several methods are available for estimating the standalone selling price (ASC 606-10-32-34).

Illustration of Allocating the Transaction Price to Performance Obligations

Weller, Inc. (the entity) enters into a contract to sell three products (X, Y, and Z) to a customer for a total of $1,000. The entity will satisfy the performance obligations for each of the products at different points in time. Product X is a standard product of Weller, Inc. and has a directly-observable $500 price. The prices of Products Y and Z are not directly observable.

Because the prices of Products Y and Z are not directly observable, Weller must estimate them. To estimate the standalone selling price, the entity uses the adjusted market assessment approach for Product Y and the expected cost plus margin approach for Product Z. By these methods, the estimated standalone prices for Products Y and Z are $400 and $300, respectively.

The customer receives a discount for purchasing the products as a bundle. The total of the standalone prices for the three products is $1,200: $500 + $400 + $300. Consequently, the total price of $1,000, which includes the discount, is allocated proportionately to the three products as follows:

Product A ($500/$1200)	$417
Product B ($400/$1,200)	333
Product C ($3,000/$1,200)	250
	$1,000

Equity Instruments Granted as Consideration Payable to a Customer

Equity instruments granted in conjunction with an entity selling goods or services are measured and classified under ASC 718 on stock compensation. If the number of equity instruments is variable due to a service condition or a performance condition that affects the vesting of an award, the entity should estimate the number of equity instruments that it will be obligated to issue to its customer and update that estimate until the award ultimately vests. The entity should include the effect of any market conditions and services or performance conditions that affect factors other than vesting. Changes in the grant date fair value of an award due to revisions in the expected outcome of a service condition or a performance condition are not deemed to be changes due to the form of the consideration and, therefore, should be reflected in the transaction price (ASC 606-10-55-88A).

Equity instruments granted by an entity in conjunction with selling goods or services are required to be measured and classified under ASC 718 at the grant date of the instrument. When an estimate of the fair value of an equity instrument is required before the grant date, the estimate should be based on the fair value of the award at the reporting dates that occur before the grant date. The entity should change the transaction price for the cumulative effect of measuring the fair value at each reporting period after the initial estimate until the grant date occurs. In the period in which the grant date occurs, the entity should change the transaction price for the cumulative effect of measuring the fair value at the grant date rather than the fair value previously used at any prior reporting date (ASC 606-10-55-88B).

Disclosure

The objective of the disclosure requirements in ASC 606 is for an entity to disclose sufficient information to enable users of financial statements to understand the nature, amount, timing, and uncertainty of revenue and cash flow from contracts with customers. To achieve this overall objective, qualitative and quantitative information is required about the following:

- Its contracts with customers.
- The significant judgments and changes in judgments made in applying ASC 606 to those contracts.
- Any assets recognized from the costs to obtain or fulfil a contract with a customer. (ASC 606-10-50-1)

The entity shall consider the level of detail necessary to satisfy the disclosure objective and how much emphasis to place on each of the various requirements. The entity may aggregate or disaggregate disclosures so that useful information is not obscured by either the inclusion of a large amount of insignificant detail or the aggregation of items that have substantially different characteristics. (ASC 606-10-50-2)

Amounts disclosed are for each reporting period for which a statement of comprehensive income is presented and as of each reporting period for which a statement of financial position is presented. (ASC 606-10-50-3)

PRACTICE POINTER: ASC 606 identifies a significant number of disclosures that are required in addition to the general disclosures identified above. Disclosure requirements are stated for each of the following areas: contracts with customers, disaggregation of revenue, contract balances, performance obligations, transaction price allocated to the remaining performance obligations, significant judgments in the application of ASC 606, determining the timing of satisfaction of performance obligations, determining the transaction price, and the amounts allocated to performance obligations. (ASC 606-10-50-4 through 50-21)

Particularly important is disclosure of information regarding performance obligations. An entity shall disclose information about its performance obligations in contracts with customers, including all of the following:

- When the entity typically satisfies its performance obligations, including when performance obligations are satisfied in a bill-and-hold arrangement.
- The significant payment terms.
- The nature of the goods or services that the entity has promised to transfer, highlighting any performance obligations to arrange for another party to transfer goods or services.
- Obligations for returns, refunds, and other similar obligations.
- Types of warranties and related obligations. (ASC 606-10-50-12)

The entity shall disclose the following information about remaining performance obligations:

- The aggregate amount of the transaction price allocated to the performance obligations that are unsatisfied as of the end of the reporting period.
- An explanation of when the entity expects to recognize as revenue the amount disclosed above. This information may be disclosed in either of the following ways:
  - On a quantitative basis using the time bands that would be most appropriate for the duration of the remaining performance obligations; or
  - By using qualitative information. (ASC 606-10-50-13)

This information is not required to be disclosed if the performance obligation is part of a contract that has an original expected duration of one year or less, or if the entity recognizes revenue from the satisfaction of the performance obligation in accordance with ASC 606-10-55-18. (ASC 606-10-50-13)

This information is also not required for variable consideration for which either of the following conditions is met:

- The variable consideration is a sales-based or usage-based royalty promised in exchange for a license of intellectual property accounted for in accordance with ASC 606-10-55-65 through 55-65B.
- The variable consideration is allocated entirely to a wholly unsatisfied performance obligation or to a wholly unsatisfied promise to transfer a distinct good or service that forms part of a single performance obligation in accordance with ASC 606-10-25-14. (ASC 606-10-50-14A)

PRACTICE POINTER: The implementation guidance in ASC 606 is organized in the following categories:

- Assessing collectibility
- Performance obligations satisfied over time
- Methods for measuring progress toward satisfaction of a performance obligation
- Sale with a right of return
- Warranties
- Principal versus agent considerations
- Customer options for additional goods or services
- Customers' unexercised rights
- Nonrefundable upfront fees
- Licensing

- Repurchase agreements
- Consignment arrangements
- Bill-and-hold arrangements
- Customer acceptance
- Equity instruments granted as consideration payable to a customer
- Disclosure of disaggregated revenue.

ASC 606 also includes a significant number of examples, perhaps the most in the history of standard-setting in the U.S. ASU 2014-09 is so pervasive and has so many diverse elements that the FASB apparently felt that it was necessary to illustrate how many of the aspects of the standard are to be applied. Following is a list of the 63 examples in ASU 2014-09 that are organized in 21 categories (ASC 606-10-55-93):

1. Identifying the Contract
   Example 1—Collectibility of the Consideration
   Example 2—Consideration Is Not the Stated Price—Implicit Price Concession
   Example 3—Implicit Price Concession
   Example 4—Reassessing the Criteria for Identifying a Contract
2. Contract Modifications
   Example 5—Modification of a Contract for Goods
   Example 6—Change in the Transaction Price after a Contract Modification
   Example 7—Modification of a Services Contract
   Example 8—Modification Resulting in a Cumulative Catch-Up Adjustment to Revenue
   Example 9—Unapproved Change in Scope and Price
3. Identifying Performance Obligations
   Example 10—Goods and Services Are Not Distinct
   Example 11—Determining Whether Goods or Services Are Distinct
   Example 12—Explicit and Implicit Promises in a Contract
4. Performance Obligations Satisfied Over Time
   Example 13—Customer Simultaneously Receives and Consumes the Benefits
   Example 14—Assessing Alternative Use and Right to Payment
   Example 15—Asset Has No Alternative Use to the Entity
   Example 16—Enforceable Right to Payment for Performance Completed to Date
   Example 17—Assessing Whether a Performance Obligation Is Satisfied at a Point in Time or Over Time
5. Measuring Progress toward Complete Satisfaction of a Performance Obligation
   Example 18—Measuring Progress When Making Goods or Services Available
   Example 19—Uninstalled Materials
6. Variable Consideration
   Example 20—Penalty Gives Rise to Variable Consideration
   Example 21—Estimating Variable Consideration
7. Constraining Estimates of Variable Consideration
   Example 22—Right of Return
   Example 23—Price Concessions
   Example 24—Volume Discount Incentive
   Example 25—Management Fees Subject to the Constraint
8. The Existence of a Significant Financing Component in the Contract
   Example 26—Significant Financing Component and Right of Return
   Example 27—Withheld Payments on a Long-Term Contract
   Example 28—Determining the Discount Rate
   Example 29—Advance Payment and Assessment of the Discount Rate
   Example 30—Advance Payment

ASC 605: REVENUE RECOGNITION (Replaced by ASC 606)

OVERVIEW

U.S. GAAP, as well as recognized industry practices, generally call for revenue recognition at the point of sale. One aspect of a sale that complicates this generally simple rule is a right of return on the part of the buyer. Revenue from sales in which a right of return exists is recognized at the time of sale only if certain specified conditions are met. If those conditions are met, sales revenue and cost of sales are reduced to reflect estimated returns and costs of those returns. If they are not met, revenue recognition is postponed.

PRACTICE NOTE: Much of existing U.S. GAAP is highly transaction specific (e.g., franchise fee revenue, revenue recognition when right of return exists). The most generic guidance on revenue recognition currently in force is the Securities and Exchange Commission's Staff Accounting Bulletins on revenue recognition (SAB 101, SAB 104). SAB 101 is largely modeled after the guidance in ASC 985 (Software). A reader interested in understanding U.S. GAAP for recognizing revenue is advised to consult SAB 101 and SAB 104. SAB 104 is useful as conceptual guidance in areas where no other authoritative literature exists.

Long-term construction contracts present a difficult financial reporting problem, primarily because of their large dollar amounts and their relatively long duration (i.e., they typically span more than one accounting period, sometimes beginning and ending several years apart). U.S. GAAP, in the area of revenue recognition for long-term construction contracts, deal with this situation by permitting two methods—the *percentage-of-completion method* and the *completed-contract method*—although the two are not alternatives for the same situation. The percentage-of-completion method is required in situations in which reliable estimates of the degree of completion are possible, in which case a pro rata portion of the income from the contract is recognized in each accounting period covered by the contract. In those situations where reliable estimates are not possible, the completed-contract method is used, in which income is deferred until the end of the contract period.

The installment sales method of accounting defers the recognition of gross profit on installment sales until cash is collected. It is commonly used for income tax purposes, but is acceptable for purposes of financial reporting in limited situations.

BACKGROUND

Generally, the broad principle underlying revenue recognition is that revenue must be earned before it is recognized. Revenue usually is recognized when an exchange has taken place which signifies that the earning process is complete. The earning process is not complete until collection of the sales price is complete or is reasonably assured. The authoritative accounting literature to date reflects a series of pronouncements on specific situations related to revenue recognition but lacks a broad, over-arching standard upon which accounting for specific situations is based. Revenue recognition situations that are specifically covered in promulgated standards include installment sales (including alternatives to the installment sales method), right of return, contract income, and the involuntary conversation of assets.

The installment sales method is acceptable only in unusual circumstances in which collectibility cannot be reasonably estimated or assured. The doubtfulness of collectibility can be caused by the length of an extended collection period or because no basis for estimating the probability of collection can be established. In such cases, a company may consider using either the installment sales method or the even more conservative cost recovery method (ASC 605-10-25-3).

In some industries, dealers and distributors of personal property have the right to return unsold merchandise. The right to return merchandise usually is an industry practice but may also occur as a result of a contractual agreement. The return period can last for a few days, as in the perishable food industry, or it can extend for several years, which is not infrequent for some types of publishers. The rate of return of some companies may be high, while in other industries, such as perishable foods, the rate of return may be insignificant.

As long as a right of return exists and the returns could be significant, the seller is exposed to reacquiring the ownership of the property. The risks and rewards of ownership have not, in substance, been passed on to the buyer. Because the earning process is not complete until collection of the sales price is assured reasonably, certain accounting problems arise in recognizing revenue when the right to return exists.

Because of the length of time involved in long-term construction contracts, a problem exists as to when income should be recognized. The completed-contract method and the percentage-of-completion method generally are followed to account for these long-term contracts.

PRACTICE NOTE: The specialized accounting and auditing practices for construction contractors that previously appeared in the AICPA Industry Audit and Accounting Guide titled "Construction Contractors" is now codified in ASC 605.

Involuntary conversion occurs when an asset that is not intended for sale is involuntarily converted to a monetary asset, such as in the case of fire or other destruction, theft, or condemnation by a governmental authority. In these situations, gains or losses may occur that require recognition.

INSTALLMENT SALES METHOD

The installment sales method of accounting recognizes gross profit only to the extent that cash has been collected. Each payment collected consists of *part* recovery of cost and *part* gross profit, in the same ratio that these two elements existed in the original sale.

PRACTICE POINTER: Because gross profit ratios are different for many products and departments and may vary from year to year, it is necessary to keep a separate record of sales by year, product line, and department. This requires keeping separate accounts and records for receivables, realized gross profit, unrealized gross profit, and repossessions for each category of product.

Generally, the seller protects its interest in an installment sale by retaining title to the goods through a conditional sales contract, lease, mortgage, or trustee. In the event of a default on an installment sales contract, the related account receivable and unrealized gross profit are written off. In many cases of default, the goods are repossessed by the seller. The loss (or gain) on a default of an installment sales contract is determined as follows:

When goods are repossessed, one of the major problems is determining the value of these inventory goods. Some of the methods of determining their value include:

- Fair value
- Unrecovered cost (results in no gain or loss)
- Resale value less reconditioning costs plus a normal profit (net realizable value)
- No value—a good method when no other method is appropriate, particularly when the actual value is minor

PRACTICE POINTER: Care should be taken in valuing repossessed goods at unrecovered cost because a loss that should be recorded may be overlooked.

Illustration of Installment Sales Method

A furniture dealer sells for $1,000 a chair that cost $700. The gross profit percentage for this sale is 30%. Under the installment sales method, the dealer would recognize 70% of each payment as a recovery of cost and 30% as realized gross profit.

The entries to record the initial sale, assuming the use of a perpetual inventory system and no down payment, are:

Accounts receivable—installment sales	1,000	
Installment sales		1,000
Cost of installment sales	700	
Inventory		700

At the end of the accounting period, the company closes out the installment sales account and the cost of installment sales to unrealized gross profit on installment sales account, which in this example is $300. The entry is:

Installment sales	1,000	
Cost of installment sales		700
Unrealized gross profit on installment sales		300

In the period that the company collects $400, the entries are:

Cash	400	
Accounts receivable—installment sales		400
Unrealized gross profit on installment sales	120	
Realized gross profit on installment sales		120

The $400 collected includes $280 recovery of cost and $120 of realized gross profit on installment sales (a 70%/30% relationship).

If the first payment of $400 was the only payment the company received and the goods were not repossessed, the journal entry to record the default and loss would be:

Unrealized gross profit	180	
Loss on installment sales	420	
Accounts receivable—installment sales		600

If the goods were repossessed and had an inventory value of $250, the journal entry would be:

Unrealized gross profit	180	
Loss on installment sales	170	
Inventory	250	
Accounts receivable—installment sales		600

COST RECOVERY METHOD

The cost recovery method is used in very unusual situations in which recovery of cost is undeterminable or extremely questionable. The procedure is simply that all cost is recovered before any profit is recognized. Once all cost has been recovered, any other collections are recognized as profit. The only expenses remaining to be charged against such revenue are those relating to the collection process.

Illustration of Cost Recovery Method

If a company sells for $100 an item that cost $40 and receives no down payment, the first $20 collected, regardless of the year collected, is considered recovery of half the cost. The next $20 collected is recovery of the balance of the cost, regardless of the year collected. The remaining $60 (all gross profit) is recognized as income when received. The only additional expenses that are charged against the remaining $60 are those directly related to the collection process.

DEFERRED INCOME TAXES

The installment sales method is generally acceptable for income tax purposes, because the government attempts to collect taxes when the taxpayer has the cash available rather than basing collection on a theoretical analysis of accounting principles. The use of installment accounting for tax purposes and the accrual method for financial reporting purposes often results in a temporary difference and creates a deferred tax liability.

DISCLOSURE

Accounts receivable on installment sales are shown separately in the balance sheet. They are classified as current assets in accordance with the normal operating cycle of the entity, which may extend for more than one year. The amounts maturing each period for each class of installment receivable should also be disclosed.

Unrealized gross profit is presented in the balance sheet as a separate caption, usually as a contra account to the related installment receivable.

ASC 605-15: PRODUCTS

REVENUE RECOGNITION FOR RETURNABLE MERCHANDISE

When a buyer has the right to return merchandise purchased, the seller may recognize income from the sale when, *all* of the following conditions are met (ASC 605-15-25-1):

- The price between the seller and the buyer is substantially fixed, or determinable at the date of sale.
- The seller has received full payment, or the buyer is indebted to the seller and the indebtedness is not contingent on the resale of the merchandise.
- Physical destruction, damage, or theft of the merchandise would not change the buyer's obligation to the seller.
- The buyer has economic substance and is not a front, straw party, or conduit, existing for the benefit of the seller.
- No significant obligations exist for the seller to help the buyer resell the merchandise.
- A reasonable estimate can be made of the amount of future returns.

If all of the above conditions are met, revenue is recognized on sales for which a right of return exists, provided that an appropriate provision is made for costs or losses that may occur in connection with the return of merchandise from the buyer (ASC 605-15-25-2).

PRACTICE NOTE: An exchange of one item for a similar item of the same quality and value is not considered a return for the purposes of ASC 605.

If all of the conditions of ASC 605 are met, an appropriate provision for costs or losses that may occur in connection with the return of merchandise from the buyer must be made by the seller. The provision for costs or losses must be in accordance with ASC 450 (Contingencies) (ASC 605-15-45-1). Under ASC 450, a provision for a loss contingency is accrued, by a charge to income, provided that both of the following conditions exist:

- It is *probable* that at the date of the financial statements, an asset has been impaired or a liability incurred, based on information available prior to the issuance of the financial statements.
- The amount of loss can be estimated reasonably.

The requirement for the accrual of a loss contingency is satisfied when all of the conditions of ASC 605-15-25 are met. Thus, if returns are *probable* and all of the conditions of U.S. GAAP are met, accrual of a loss is required. This accrual results in a reduction in sales revenue and the related cost of sales in the income statement.

PRACTICE POINTER: If all of the conditions of ASC 605-15-25 are not met, the seller cannot recognize the sales revenue until the right of return privilege has substantially expired or the applicable provisions are subsequently met (ASC 605-15-25-1). The seller has several alternatives in accounting for these transactions: First, do not record the transaction on the books at all and maintain a **memorandum account** for these types of transactions. Second, record the transaction as a debit to a deferred receivable account and a credit to a deferred sales account. Last, handle the transaction as a consignment. In any event, maintain control for these types of transactions, particularly if they are a part of recurring business activities.

Reasonable Estimates of Returns

Reasonable estimates of returns depend on individual circumstances. An enterprise must take into consideration its individual customers and the types of merchandise involved in determining the estimated amount of returns that may occur. The following factors may impair the ability to make a reasonable estimate of returns (ASC 605-15-25-3):

- Possible technological obsolescence or changes in demand for the merchandise
- A long return period
- Little or no past experience in determining returns for similar types of sales of similar merchandise
- An inability to apply past experience due to changing circumstances
- A limited number of similar transactions

PRACTICE POINTER: The above factors are to be considered in conjunction with the past experience with a specific customer and the individual product involved in the sale. One or more of these factors may or may not impair the ability of an enterprise to make a reasonable estimate of the amount of future returns.

Illustration of Reasonable Estimates of Returns

The right to return merchandise to a seller may apply to only a portion of a total sale. For example, X Company sells 100,000 widgets to Y Company on January 1 for $1 per widget (cost $0.65). In the sales agreement, X Company grants to Y Company the right to return up to a maximum of 30% of the widgets within six months from the date of sale. Under these circumstances, ASC 605 would only apply to the 30% of the widgets that can be returned by Y Company. Assuming that all of the conditions imposed by ASC 605 are met and it is probable that one-half (50%) of the widgets subject to return will actually be returned and the estimated cost that X Company expects to incur in connection with the returns is $1,000, the computations would be as follows:

Total sale	$100,000
Less: Portion of the sale not subject to ASC 605	70,000
Balance of the sale subject to ASC 605	$ 30,000
Less: Provision for estimated returns (50% of $30,000)	15,000
Balance of sale which is recognized	$ 15,000
Balance of sale not subject to ASC 605	70,000
Total revenue recognized at date of sale	$ 85,000

Under ASC 605, X Company reports $84,000 of revenue on the date the title to the widgets passes to Y Company. X Company also sets up a provision for returnable merchandise and related costs of $16,000. Sales and related cost of sales are reported at their gross amounts in the income statement and the sales and related cost of sales for the *probable* returns are deducted from the gross amounts. The journal entries to record the transactions on the books of X Company are as follows:

Accounts receivable	100,000	
Sales		100,000
(To record the gross sales to Y Company.) Cost of sales	65,000	
Inventory		65,000
(To record cost of sales for Y Company order.) Estimated sales returns	15,000	
Deferred cost of sales ($0.65 per widget)	9,750	
Cost of sales		9,750
Provision for estimated returns		15,000

(To defer sales of $15,000 and the related cost of sales of $9,750.)

The provision for estimated returns is a contra accounts to accounts receivable. The deferred cost of sales represents the cost of inventory that is expected to be returned; it is most logically classified as inventory.

ASC 605-35: CONSTRUCTION-TYPE AND PRODUCTION-TYPE CONTRACTS

COMPLETED-CONTRACT METHOD

The completed-contract method recognizes income only on completion or substantial completion of the contract. *A contract is regarded as substantially complete if the remaining costs are insignificant* (ASC 605-35-25-88).

Any excess of accumulated costs over related billings is reflected in the balance sheet as a current asset; any excess of accumulated billings over related costs is reflected as a current liability. In the case of more than one contract, the accumulated costs or liabilities should be stated separately on the balance sheet. The preferred terminology for the balance sheet presentation is *(Costs) (Billings) of uncompleted contracts in excess of related (billings) (costs)* (ASC 605-35-45-4).

In some cases, it is preferable to allocate general and administrative expenses to contract costs rather than to period income. In years in which no contracts are completed, a better matching of costs and revenues is achieved by carrying general expense as a charge to the contract. If a contractor has many jobs, however, it is more appropriate to charge these expenses to current periods (ASC 605-35-25-99).

Although income is not recognized until completion of the contract, a provision for an expected loss should be recognized when it becomes evident that a loss will occur (ASC 605-35-25-89).

Illustration of the Completed-Contract Method

A construction company has a balance in its construction-in-progress account of $500,000, representing the costs incurred to date on a project. While the project was initially expected to be profitable, management now expects a loss on the project at completion of $75,000. At the time of this determination, the following entry should be made:

Estimated loss on construction project	75,000	
Construction in progress		75,000

This entry reduces the construction (inventory) account by $75,000 and recognizes the loss in income of the period in which the determination of the loss is estimable. Assuming the estimate of the loss is accurate, future costs will be charged to the construction account as incurred and the balance in that account will equal the revenue on the contract.

The primary advantage of the completed-contract method is that it is based on final results rather than on estimates. The primary disadvantage of this method is that it does not reflect current performances when the period of the contract extends over more than one accounting period (ASC 605-35-05-12).

Accounting for the Completed-Contract Method

The following are important points in accounting for contracts under the completed-contract method:

1. Overhead and direct costs are charged to a construction-in-progress account (an asset).
2. Billings and/or cash received are charged to advances on the construction-in-progress account (a liability).
3. At completion of the contract, gross profit or loss is recognized as follows:

   Contract price – total costs = gross profit or loss
4. At balance sheet dates that occur during the contract period, the excess of either the construction-in-progress account or the advances account over the other is classified as a current asset or a current liability. It is a *current* asset or a *current* liability because of the *normal operating cycle concept.*
5. Expected losses are recognized in full in the year they are identified. An expected loss on the total contract is determined by:
   a. Adding estimated costs to complete to the recorded costs to date to arrive at total contract costs
   b. Adding to advances any additional revenue expected to arrive at total contract revenue
   c. Subtracting b from a to arrive at total estimated loss on contract

PERCENTAGE-OF-COMPLETION METHOD

Revenues generally are recognized when (*a*) the earning process is complete or virtually complete and (*b*) an exchange has taken place.

Accounting for long-term construction contracts by the percentage-of-completion method is a modification of the general practice of realization at the point of sale. Realization is based on the evidence that the ultimate proceeds are available and the consensus that the result is a better measure of periodic income (matching-of-revenue-and-cost principle).

The principal merits of the percentage-of-completion method are the reflection of the status of the uncompleted contracts and the periodic recognition of the income currently rather than irregularly as contracts are completed. The principal disadvantage of this method is the necessity of relying on estimates of the ultimate costs (ASC 605-35-05-7).

The percentage-of-completion method recognizes income as work progresses on the contract. The method is based on an estimate of the income earned to date, less income recognized in earlier periods. Estimates of the degree of completion usually are based on one of the following (ASC 605-35-25-52):

- The relationship of costs incurred to date to expected total costs for the contract
- Other measures of progress toward completion, such as engineering estimates

During the early stages of a contract, all or a portion of items such as material and subcontract costs may be excluded if it appears that the results would produce a more meaningful allocation of periodic income (ASC 605-35-25-53).

When current estimates of the total contract costs indicate a loss, a provision for the loss on the entire contract should be made. When a loss is indicated on a total contract that is part of a related group of contracts, however, the group may be treated as a unit in determining the necessity of providing for losses (ASC 605-35-25-5, 46).

PRACTICE POINTER: Income to be recognized under the percentage-of-completion method at various stages ordinarily should not be measured by interim billings.

Accounting for the Percentage-of-Completion Method

The following are important points in accounting for contracts under the percentage-of-completion method:

- Journal entries and balance sheet treatment are the same as for the completed-contract method, *except* that the amount of estimated gross profit earned in each period is recorded by charging the construction-in-progress account and crediting realized gross profit.
- Gross profit or loss is recognized in each period by the following formula:

$$\left[\text{percentage of completion} \times \text{total estimated gross profit or loss}\right] - \text{gross profit recognized to date} = \text{current period realized gross profit}$$

- An estimated loss on the total contract is recognized immediately in the year it is discovered. Any gross profit (or loss) reported in prior years, however, must be added (or deducted) from the total estimated loss.

PRACTICE POINTER: The completed-contract and percentage-of-completion methods are *not* intended to be alternative methods of accounting for the same contract. Each is appropriate in certain circumstances, but do *not* consider them *equally appropriate in the same circumstances.* Where reasonable estimates of the percentage of completion are possible, the percentage-of-completion method constitutes U.S. GAAP and should be used. On the other hand, if reasonable estimates of the percentage are *not* possible, the completed-contract method constitutes U.S. GAAP and should be used.

Illustration of Accounting for the Completed-Contract and Percentage-of-Completion Method

The following data pertain to a $2,000,000 long-term construction contract:

	20X5	*20X6*	*20X7*
Costs incurred during the year	$500,000	$700,000	$300,000
Year-end estimated costs to complete	1,000,000	300,000	—
Billing during the year	400,000	700,000	900,000
Collections during the year	200,000	500,000	1,200,000

The journal entries for both the completed-contract method and the percentage-of-completion method for the three years are as follows, assuming the degree of completion is determined based on costs incurred:

20X5	*Completed Contract*		*% of Completion*	
Construction in progress	500,000		500,000	
Cash or liability		500,000		500,000

20X5	*Completed Contract*		*% of Completion*	
Accounts receivable	400,000		400,000	
Advance billings		400,000		400,000
Cash	200,000		200,000	
Accounts receivable		200,000		200,000
Construction in progress	no entry		166,667	
Realized gross profit (P&L)				166,667
20X6	*Completed Contract*		*% of Completion*	
Construction in progress	700,000		700,000	
Cash or liability		700,000		700,000
Accounts receivable	700,000		700,000	
Advance billings		700,000		700,000
Cash	500,000		500,000	
Accounts receivable		500,000		500,000
Construction in progress	no entry		233,333	
Realized gross profit (P&L)				233,333
20X7	*Completed Contract*		*% of Completion*	
Construction in progress	300,000		300,000	
Cash or liability		300,000		300,000
Accounts receivable	900,000		900,000	
Advance billings		900,000		900,000
Cash	1,200,000		1,200,000	
Accounts receivable		1,200,000		1,200,000
Construction in progress	no entry		100,000	
Realized gross profit (P&L)				100,000
Advance billings	2,000,000		2,000,000	
Construction in progress		1,500,000		2,000,000
Realized gross profit (P&L)		500,000		—

At the end of each year during which the contract is in progress, the excess of the construction-in-progress account over the advance billings account is presented as a current asset:

20X5: ($500,000 + $166,667) – $400,000 = $266,667

20X6: ($500,000 + $166,667 + $700,000 + $233,333)

– ($400,000 + $700,000) = $500,000

In this illustration, the estimated gross profit of $500,000 was the actual gross profit on the contract. If changes in the estimated cost to complete the contract had been appropriate at the end of 20X5 and/or 20X6, or if the actual costs to complete had been determined to be different when the contract was completed in 20X7, those changes would have been incorporated into revised estimates during the contract period. For example, if at the end of 20X6 the costs to complete were estimated to be $400,000 instead of $300,000, the 20X6 gross profit of $133,333 would have been determined as follows:

$$\left(\frac{\$1{,}200{,}000}{\$1{,}600{,}000^*}\right) \times (2{,}000{,}000 - \$1{,}6000{,}000) = \$300{,}000$$

$$\$300{,}000 - \$166{,}667 = \$133{,}333$$

*$500,000 (20X5) + $700,000 (20X6) + $400,000 (20X6 estimated) = $1,600,000

ASC 605-40: GAINS AND LOSSES

INVOLUNTARY CONVERSION OF NONMONETARY ASSETS TO MONETARY ASSETS

When a nonmonetary asset is involuntarily converted to a monetary asset, a monetary transaction results, and ASC 605 requires that a gain or loss be recognized in the period of conversion (ASC 605-40-25-3). The gain or loss is the difference between the carrying amount of the nonmonetary asset and the proceeds from the conversion.

Examples of involuntary conversion are the total or partial destruction of property through fire or other catastrophe, theft of property, or condemnation of property by a governmental authority (eminent domain proceedings).

Gain or loss from an involuntary conversion of a nonmonetary asset to a monetary asset is classified as part of continuing operations, disposal of a segment, etc., according to the particular circumstances (ASC 605-40-45-1). In addition, a gain or loss recognized for tax purposes in a period different from that for financial accounting purposes creates a temporary difference, for which recognition of deferred taxes may be necessary (ASC 740-10-55-66).

The involuntary conversion of a LIFO inventory layer at an interim date is not required if the proceeds from involuntary conversion are expected to be reinvested in replacement inventory by the end of the fiscal year (ASC 605-40-25-3).

PRACTICE NOTE: This is the same treatment afforded a temporary liquidation at interim dates of a LIFO inventory layer that is expected to be replaced by the end of the annual period.

In the event the proceeds from an involuntary conversion of a LIFO inventory layer are not reinvested in replacement inventory by the end of the fiscal year, gain for financial accounting purposes need not be recognized, providing the taxpayer does not recognize such gains for income tax reporting purposes and provided that replacement is intended but not yet made by year-end (ASC 605-40-25-3).

PART II: INTERPRETIVE GUIDANCE

IMPORTANT NOTICE: As stated above in the discussion of the effect of the guidance in ASU 2014-09 (as amended by ASU 2015-14, which amends the ASU's effective date), most of the guidance in ASC 605 will be superseded by the guidance in the ASU when it becomes effective for public entities, certain not-for-profit entities, and certain employee benefit plans for annual reporting periods that begin after December 15, 2017, including interim reporting periods within those periods. Earlier application is permitted only as of annual reporting periods that begin after December 15, 2016, including interim reporting periods within that annual reporting period. The guidance in ASU 2014-09 (as amended by 2015-14) is effective for all other entities for annual reporting periods that begin after December 15, 2018, and interim reporting periods within annual reporting periods that begin after December 15, 2019. Earlier application is permitted only as of annual reporting periods that begin after December 15, 2016, including interim reporting periods within that annual reporting period, or an annual reporting period that begins after December 15, 2016, and interim reporting periods within annual reporting periods that begin one year after the annual period in which the guidance in ASU 2014-09 was first applied. However, some of the guidance in ASC 605 will be retained for certain contracts entered into under the industry specific-guidance for the following industries: agriculture, insurance, health care entities, not-for-profit entities, and regulated operations, some of which are discussed in the Appendices of the *GAAP Guide*. The guidance for loss contracts discussed in ASC 605-20 for separately priced warranties on services, and the guidance in ASC 605-35 for loss provisions for construction-type and production-type contracts will be amended. Under the guidance in ASU 2014-09, a new Topic, ASC 610 (Other Income) will be added to the FASB Accounting Standards Codification® (ASC) to provide guidance for the recognition of gains or losses. It will codify new guidance on the sale or transfer of nonfinancial assets that are not under the scope of ASC 606 because the counterparty is not a customer. The guidance in ASC 610-30 (Other Income—Gains and Losses on Involuntary Conversions) will consist of guidance moved from ASC 605-40 (Revenue Recognition—Gains and Losses).

ASC 605-15: PRODUCTS

IMPORTANT NOTICE: All of the guidance in ASC 605-15 will be superseded when the guidance in ASU 2014-09, *Accounting for Revenue from Contracts with Costumers*, which will reside in ASC 606 (Revenue from Contracts with Customers), becomes effective.

ASC 605-15-05-6, 15-2, 25-5; ASC 840-10-60-3 Products Sold and Subsequently Repurchased Subject to an Operating Lease

BACKGROUND

Finished products are sold by a manufacturer to an independent dealer that sells those products to customers, who may be individuals or other independent entities. Customers may purchase such products by (*a*) paying cash, (*b*) using their own financing sources, or (*c*) using traditional consumer financing or lease financing arranged by the dealer and provided by unrelated commercial banks, other finance companies, or by the manufacturer's wholly owned subsidiary.

ACCOUNTING ISSUE

Should a manufacturer recognize a sale on a product sold to an independent dealer if the dealer's customer subsequently enters into an operating lease with the manufacturer or its finance subsidiary, which acquires title to the product subject to the lease?

ACCOUNTING GUIDANCE

A manufacturer can recognize a sale when a product is transferred to a dealer if *all* of the following conditions exist:

- The dealer is a substantive and independent entity whose business with the manufacturer and retail customers is conducted separately.
- The manufacturer has delivered the product and passed the risks and rewards of ownership to the dealer, including responsibility for the ultimate sale of the product and for insurability, theft, or damage. The dealer cannot return the product to the manufacturer if the customer does not enter into a lease with the manufacturer or its finance subsidiary.
- At the time the product is delivered to the dealer, the manufacturer or its finance affiliate has no legal obligation to provide a lease to the dealer's potential customer.
- Other financing alternatives are available to the customer from sources that are not affiliated with the manufacturer, and the customer makes the selection from the financing alternatives.

DISCUSSION

The guidance is based on the following views:

- A manufacturer's sale of the product to the dealer is a legal sale. Because the manufacturer has no further obligation related to the product, other than warranty obligations, the dealer's transaction with the retail customer is a separate transaction.
- The sale to the dealer meets the criteria for revenue recognition in paragraph 83 of CON-5 (not included in the ASC), because revenue was earned when the manufacturer sold the product to the dealer. The manufacturer has no obligation related to future sales to retail customers.
- The manufacturer's involvement in financing alternatives is not a primary issue in the dealer's sales process as long as the customer can choose between financing from the manufacturer's subsidiary and alternative financing sources from unaffiliated parties.
- The manufacturer does not guarantee the dealer's recovery of its investment in the product.
- The economic substance of the operating lease is independent of the manufacturer's sale to the dealer, because title, risks, and rewards of ownership have been transferred to the dealer, including the product's ultimate sale and disposition in case of theft or damage.

ASC 605-20: SERVICES

IMPORTANT NOTICE: Most of the guidance in ASC 605-20 will be superseded when the guidance in ASU 2014-09, which will reside in ASC 606 (Revenue from Contracts with Customers), becomes effective. However, the guidance in ASC 605-20-25-1 and ASC 605-20-25-6 that is related to separately priced extended warranty and product maintenance contracts will be retained and amended. Consequently, ASC 605-20 will be renamed as follows: Revenue Recognition—Provision for Losses on Separately Priced Extended Warranty and Product Maintenance Contracts. ASC 605-20-25-8 will be moved to ASC 942-825-50-2.

ASC 605-20-25-1 through 25-6; ASC 460-10-15-9; 60-41 Separately Priced Extended Warranty and Product Maintenance Contracts

BACKGROUND

An *extended warranty* is an agreement to provide warranty protection in addition to that covered in the manufacturer's original warranty, if any, or to extend the period of coverage beyond that provided by the manufacturer's warranty. A *product maintenance contract* is an agreement to perform certain agreed-upon services to maintain a product for a specified period. Some contracts cover both an extended warranty and product maintenance. A *separately priced contract* is one in which a customer has the option to purchase the services provided under the contract for a stated amount that is separate from the price of the product.

ACCOUNTING GUIDANCE

Question: How should revenue and costs from a separately priced extended warranty or a product maintenance contract be recognized?

Answer: Revenue should be deferred and recognized over the contract period on a straight-line basis, except when sufficient historical evidence indicates that the costs of performing under the contract are incurred in a pattern other than straight-line. In those circumstances, revenue should be recognized over the contract period in proportion to the costs expected to be incurred in performing the services required under the contract.

Costs that are directly related to the acquisition of a contract and that would not have been incurred if the contract had not existed should be deferred and charged to expense in proportion to the revenue recognized. All other costs should be charged to expense as incurred.

A loss exists if the total expected costs of providing services under the contract and unamortized acquisition costs exceed the related unearned revenue. A loss is recognized by (*a*) charging any unamortized acquisition costs to expense, and (*b*) recognizing a liability for excess costs, if any.

Illustration of Recognition of Revenue and Costs on a Separately Priced Extended Warranty Contract—Warranty Costs Not Incurred on a Straight-Line Basis

Dorf Motors sells a separately priced extended warranty contract for $1,200 on 1/1/20X4 in conjunction with the sale of its Spitfire model. The extended warranty contract extends the manufacturer's warranty (three years, 36,000 miles) by an additional three years and 36,000 miles. Dorf has sufficient warranty experience to predict claim costs under the extended warranty as follows: year 1: $0 (manufacturer's warranty in effect), year 2: $0, year 3: $0, year 4: $100, year 5: $200, and year 6: $300. Dorf incurred $200 of costs directly related to the sale of the extended warranty contract that would not have been incurred if the contract had not been sold.

On 1/1/X4, Dorf would record a liability for deferred revenue of $1,200. None of this deferred revenue would be recognized in X4, X5, and X6, since any warranty work performed by Dorf in those years falls under the manufacturer's warranty, not under the extended warranty. Revenue, and amortization of direct costs, would be recognized as follows during X7–X9:

	Revenue Recognized	*Amortization of Direct Costs*
X7	$200 [($100 / $600) × $1,200]	$33 [($200 / $1,200)] × $200

	Revenue Recognized	Amortization of Direct Costs
X8	$400 [($200 / $600) × $1,200]	$67 [($400 / $1,200)] × $200
X9	$600 [($300 / $600) × $1,200]	$100 [($600 / $1,200)] × $200

ASC 605-20-15-3, 25-8 through 25-12; ASC 460-10-60-8; ASC 310-10-60-4 Fees for Guaranteeing a Loan

BACKGROUND

An entity, usually a financial institution or insurance company, guarantees the debt of another entity and is paid a fee for doing so. The guarantee may be in the form of (*a*) a general guarantee to ensure that the funds will be repaid or (*b*) a pledge of assets that could be claimed by a lender if the borrower defaults. Such guarantees are usually used by entities that would otherwise be unable to borrow or would have to pay a very high interest rate.

The following are examples of such transactions:

- An entity issues three-to-six-year notes, which are guaranteed with a surety bond issued by an insurance company. The entity pays an annual premium to the insurance company based on the entity's annual debt service and pledges assets valued at 110% of the debt as collateral to the insurance company.
- A developer issues tax-exempt industrial bonds to finance a project. A financial institution guarantees the debt by pledging specific assets.
- A guarantor and an investment banker establish a special-purpose entity that issues commercial paper for borrowers who would be unable to do so themselves. The guarantor provides a surety bond for each borrower to guarantee repayment of the funds. The investment banker sells the commercial paper and lends the funds to the borrower at a spread above the commercial paper interest rate. The loan and the commercial paper have the same maturity dates.

ACCOUNTING ISSUES

How should a guarantor account for initial and continuing fees received?

ACCOUNTING GUIDANCE SCOPE

The following guidance does not apply to:

- Guarantees accounted for as derivatives under the guidance in ASC 815-10-15;
- Product warranties; and
- Guarantees that must be accounted for as financial guarantee insurance contracts under the guidance in ASC 944.

RECOGNITION

A loan guarantee generally consists of two sets of fees—an initial fee when a transaction is consummated and an annual fee over the term of a loan. A guarantor should recognize income from such fees over the term of the guarantee. Direct costs associated with a guarantee should be accounted for in a manner related to the recognition of income from the fee.

Guarantee contracts that are only intended to reimburse a guaranteed party for a loss because a debtor defaults on a loan are excluded from the guidance in ASC 815-10-15-58. However, if a guarantee meets the definition of a derivative because it is triggered by changes in an underlying, such as a decrease in a borrower's creditworthiness, the guarantee should be accounted for under the guidance in ASC 815-10.

DISCUSSION

A guarantor of a loan usually receives two fees: (*a*) an initial fee, which is paid when the transaction is closed, and (*b*) an annual fee, which is paid over the term of the loan. This Issue addresses the accounting for the initial fee. The guidance is based on the notion that the initial fee cannot be separated from annual fees and should thus be recognized over the term of the loan. The guarantor does not earn the total initial fee when the transaction is closed, but rather over the period during which the guarantor will be at risk.

ASC 605-20-25-13; S25-1, S99-2 Services for Freight-in-Transit at the End of a Reporting Period

BACKGROUND

Motor carriers provide a variety of services to their customers. The services can be (*a*) limited, involving only pickup and delivery (usually of a full trailer loaded by a customer—known as "truckload carriers"), or (*b*) extensive, including pickup of small loads, consolidation of loads from different customers, transportation to the motor carrier's terminal, transfer at hub terminals, and final delivery.

Revenue is recognized when customers are billed, usually at the time freight is received from a customer (shipper). Direct expenses are incurred throughout the freight service process from pickup to delivery and completion.

This Issue addresses revenue and expense recognition at the balance sheet date for freight that has been received but has not yet been delivered.

At the time this Issue was discussed, the following five alternative methods of revenue recognition were used in practice:

1. Revenue was recognized when freight was received from the shipper (or when freight left the carrier's terminal), and expenses were recognized when incurred.
2. Revenue was recognized when freight was received from the shipper (or when freight left the carrier's terminal), and estimated costs to complete were accrued at the end of each reporting period.
3. Revenue and direct costs were recognized when a shipment was completed, and the expense was recognized as incurred.
4. Revenue was recognized when the shipment was completed, and an expense was recognized as incurred.
5. Revenue was allocated between reporting periods based on the relative transit time in each reporting period, and an expense was recognized as incurred.

ACCOUNTING ISSUE

How should motor carriers recognize revenue and expense for freight services in process at the balance sheet date?

ACCOUNTING GUIDANCE

Alternative 1 is not an acceptable method of revenue recognition for freight carriers. This guidance is not limited to motor carriers.

SEC OBSERVER COMMENT

The SEC Observer indicated that a change from Alternative 1 to Alternative 2 would not be acceptable, because under Alternative 2, revenue would be recognized before performance has occurred, and liabilities would be recognized before they have been incurred.

DISCUSSION

The following illustration shows the potential income statement effect of revenue and expense recognition under the five alternatives. However, because only one shipment in one reporting period is considered, the results are not as extreme as for companies that have a large number of shipments and report revenue and expense over a number of periods.

Illustration of Revenue and Expense Recognition by Motor Carriers

Assumptions	
Amount billable for shipment A	$2,000
Total expected direct costs associated with shipment A	$1,400
Date freight is received from shipper	June 29, 20X1
Date of final delivery	July 2, 20X1
Reporting date	June 30, 20X1
Direct costs (expenses) incurred through June 30, 20X1	$800
Amount billable and billed at June 30, 20X1	$2,000

Revenue and expense recognition at June 30, 20X1

	Alternative				
	1	*2*	*3*	*4*	*5*
Revenue	$2,000	$2,000	$0	$0	$1,000
Expense	800	1,400	0	800	800
Gross profit (loss)	$1,200	$ 600	$ 0	$(800)	$ 200

When this Issue was discussed, predominant industry practice was to recognize revenue based on Alternative 1. The appeal of that method was its simplicity; other methods could involve extensive record keeping. Proponents believed that because of the short-term nature of the service (normally no more than five days), using Alternative 1 would not lead to abuse or distortion. Opponents argued that the earnings process is not complete when the shipment is picked up, because the carrier still must perform significant services, including final delivery.

Paragraph 83 of CON-5 (not included in ASC) refers to two factors for revenue recognition: (*a*) revenues must be realized and realizable and (*b*) revenues must be earned. Alternative 1 does not conform to that guidance.

Although Alternative 2 attempts to match expenses to revenues recognized, it is unacceptable because revenue is recognized before delivery of the shipment. Thus, it does not meet the revenue recognition criteria in CON-5 (not included in ASC). In addition, direct operating expenses are accrued before they have been incurred and the benefits consumed.

Proponents of Alternative 3 believed that the act of delivering the freight is significant because it indicates performance of the service. They believed that revenue is not earned until performance.

Alternative 4 is the most conservative method. Under this alternative, revenue is recognized the same as in Alternative 3, but there is no deferral (or matching) of expenses. There are also no onerous record-keeping requirements. Those who supported this alternative agreed with the revenue recognition criteria in Alternative 3, but believed that direct costs should not be deferred but treated as period costs. In addition, they argued that the cost of estimating and allocating direct costs to different periods is not warranted. Those who supported Alternative 3 argued that revenues and expenses would not be matched properly under Alternative 4.

Proponents of Alternative 5 argued that it provides the best measure of revenue earned during the period and is most faithful to the revenue recognition criteria in CON-5 (not included in ASC), because revenue recognized under that alternative is based on proportional performance, i.e., relative transit time in each reporting period. In addition, an attraction of this alternative was that direct costs are charged to expense as incurred and not allocated between reporting periods. Proponents believed that allocation of such costs would be too subjective. Opponents of the proportional performance alternative argued that there is no reliable way to estimate the degree of performance.

ASC 605-20-25-14 through 25-18, 50-1 Accounting for Advertising Barter Transactions

OVERVIEW

In the late 1990s, a number of internet companies were entering into barter transactions with other internet companies under which the two companies advertised each other's products or services on their respective web sites without additional compensation. The transactions had no effect on net income or cash flow from operations because the companies generally accounted for the transactions by recognizing equal amounts of barter advertising revenue and barter advertising expense in their income statements.

Some accountants were concerned that this accounting treatment does not conform with the guidance on the recognition of revenues and expenses in Statement of Financial Accounting Concepts No. 6 (not in ASC), guidance on accounting for nonmonetary transactions in ASC 845 (formerly, APB-29) and ASC 845-10-05-11 through 05-12, 15-12 through 15-15, 15-17, 15-20, 25-3, 25-6 through 25-11, 30-12 through 30-14, 30-21 through 30-27, 55-2, 55-28, 55-30 through 55-37, 60-3, S99-3; and ASC 810-10-55-1A (formerly, EITF Issue 01-2, Interpretations of APB 29, see Chapter 57, *ASC 845—Nonmonetary Transactions*). Further, some contended that recognition of barter advertising revenue that results in no income or cash flows may mislead investors who use information about revenues to evaluate companies that have net operating *losses* and net cash *outflows*. The scope of this Issue is *not* limited to internet companies.

ACCOUNTING ISSUE

Should revenues and expenses related to nonmonetary exchanges involving barter transactions of advertising be recognized at the readily determinable fair values of the advertising provided or received in the exchange?

ACCOUNTING GUIDANCE

The following guidance was provided:

- Revenues and expenses related to advertising barter transactions should be recognized at their fair value only if the fair value of the advertising provided to the counterparty can be determined based on the entity's own known amount of cash received for similar advertising from other buyers that are unrelated to the counterparty in the current barter transaction. A swap of offsetting consideration between the parties to the barter transaction, such as exchanging checks for the same amount, does not provide evidence of the fair value of a transaction. If the fair value of an advertising barter transaction cannot be determined based on the above, the transaction should be recognized based on the carrying amount of the advertising provided to the counterparty, which most likely will be zero.
- An entity's historical practice of receiving cash or marketable securities for similar advertising provided should be based on a period no longer than six months before the current barter transaction. A shorter and more representative period should be used if as a result of economic changes, similar transactions that occurred during the previous six months are not representative of the fair value of the advertising provided. Cash transactions that occur after advertising was provided in a barter transaction should not be used to determine the fair value of the advertising provided in the barter transaction (i.e., no look back is permitted to value previous barter transactions).
- Advertising provided for cash may be considered to be similar to advertising provided in a barter transaction if the cash transaction was in the same medium and used the same advertising vehicle, such as the same publication, same web site, or the same broadcast channel, as the barter transaction. Further, the characteristics of advertising provided for cash and that provided in a barter transaction should be reasonably similar in the following respects:
  - Circulation, exposure, or saturation in an intended market
  - Timing in terms of time of day, day of week, daily, weekly, 24 hours a day/7 days a week, and the season
  - Prominence in terms of page on web site, section of periodical, location on page, and size of advertisement
  - Demographics of readers, viewers, or customers
  - Length of time advertising will be shown.
- The quantity or volume of advertising provided in a past cash or near-cash transaction that meets the criteria in this Issue can be used as evidence of fair value for a subsequent barter transaction only if the latter provides an equal quantity or volume of advertising. That is, a past cash transaction can be used as evidence for the recognition of revenue on a barter transaction only up to the dollar amount of the cash transaction. In addition, a cash transaction that has been used to support an equivalent quantity and dollar amount of barter revenue, within the limits of this Issue, cannot be used as evidence of fair value of other barter transactions.
- The amount of revenue and expense recognized from advertising barter transactions should be disclosed for each income statement period presented. Entities providing advertising in barter transactions that do not qualify for recognition at fair value should disclose for each income statement period presented the volume and type of advertising provided and received, such as the number of equivalent pages, number of minutes, or the overall percentage of advertising volume.

ASC 605-20-S25-2, S99-1 Accounting for Management Fees Based on a Formula

Certain fee-based arrangements, which are common in the investment advisory and real estate management businesses, include an incentive fee related to performance in addition to a base fee—for example, based on cost savings generated by a real estate management company. Under such arrangements, the amount of the fee generally is not confirmed until the end of a contractual time period. This announcement states the views of the SEC staff on the accounting for revenue from incentive fees at interim dates before the final amount has been confirmed. The SEC staff has been asked to address this Issue because sometimes performance that exceeds the required target in the early part of a measurement period may be reversed if the performance target is not achieved in a later measurement period. The SEC staff provided the following example:

> An investment advisor managing a mutual fund is paid a monthly base fee. However, the advisor is also paid an incentive fee equal to 20% of the Fund's returns that exceed the S&P 500's return for the year. The contract can be terminated by each party with reasonable notice at the end of each quarter. At termination, the Advisor's incentive fee will be calculated based on the Fund's returns to date compared to those of the S&P 500 during that period. If the Fund's return exceeds the S&P 500's returns by $200,000 in the first quarter, $100,000 in the second quarter, and $50,000 in the fourth quarter, but is $75,000 less than the S&P 500's returns in the third quarter, the Fund's total return for the year would exceed the S&P 500's return by $275,000. The Advisor's total incentive fee for the year would be $55,000 in the fourth quarter.

An informal survey conducted by the SEC staff indicated that a majority of investment advisors and property managers recognize no income from incentive fees until the end of the contract period. Under that method, $55,000 would be recognized as incentive fee revenue at the end of the fourth quarter. However, others recognize the amount of revenue from incentive fees that would be receivable at a point in time as if the contract were terminated at that date. Under this second method, the advisor would recognize $40,000 as an incentive fee at the end of the first quarter ($200,000 × .2) and $20,000 at the end of the second quarter ($100,000 × .2). At the end of the third quarter, the advisor would reduce previously recognized revenue by $15,000 ($75,000 × .2) and would recognize $10,000 ($50,000 × .2) at the end of the fourth quarter.

Although the SEC Staff prefers the first method, because it believes it is more consistent with the guidance in SEC Staff Accounting Bulletin (SAB) Topic 13A, the staff would not object if companies use the second method, which provides better information about a manager's actual performance during each interim period.

The SEC Staff objects, however, to the use of another method under which revenue recognized under the second method discussed above would be reduced by an amount that management believes will be lost as a result of future performance. The Staff believes that method is inconsistent with the guidance in SAB Topic 13A and the requirement that the fee be fixed or determinable.

The following are the views of the SEC Staff on some variations of the methods discussed above:

- Unless an arrangement has been terminated, revenue should not be recognized based on amounts that would be receivable at termination as a result of provisions for penalties or liquidated damages in addition to the amount payable under the incentive fee formula.
- Revenue recorded at an interim date should not exceed the amount a customer would be required to pay on termination if a customer can terminate an arrangement at will and thus avoid paying all or some of the fee due to the manager.
- Revenue should be recognized in interim periods under the second method for a *fixed* incentive fee (e.g., a fixed amount for exceeding the S&P 500) only if the target has been exceeded and should be limited to a proportionate amount of the fixed payment due.
- The SEC Staff's views apply even if a manager or adviser has no termination rights during the contract term.

The SEC Staff encourages registrants to submit to the Staff for preclearance any questions regarding revenue accounting for such arrangements.

DISCLOSURE

The accounting policy for such arrangements should be disclosed in accordance with ASC 235-10-50, SAB Topic 13. Disclosure is required about previously recognized revenue that may be lost due to future performance contingencies, as well as disclosure of the nature of the contracts causing the contingencies, and the amount of revenue that would be affected, if material.

ASC 605-25: MULTIPLE-ELEMENT ARRANGEMENTS

IMPORTANT NOTICE: All of the guidance in ASC 605-25 will be superseded when the guidance in ASU 2014-09, which will reside in ASC 606 (Revenue from Contracts with Customers), becomes effective.

ASC 605-25-15-3A, 25-2, 30-2, 30-5, 30-6A through 30-6B, 30-7, 50-1 through 50-2, 55-1, 55-3, 55-7, 55-12, 55-25, 55-29, 55-32, 55-34, 55-36 through 55-47, 55-52, 55-54, 55-6A through 55-57, 55-61, 55-69, 55-75 through 55-6B, 55-93, 65-1; (ASU 2009-13) Revenue Arrangements with Multiple Deliverables

BACKGROUND

The following accounting guidance addresses practice issues related to: (1) the determination of the unit of accounting for arrangements under which a vendor performs multiple activities that generate revenue (e.g., the delivery of multiple products or the performance of multiple services under arrangements that consist of products that cannot function separately and for which evidence of the separate fair values of the deliverables is unavailable); and (2) issues related to allocation methods used in revenue recognition under the guidance in ASC 605, *Revenue Recognition*, ASC 605-25-05-1 and 05-02. Although paragraph 83 of Financial Accounting Standards Board (FASB) Concepts Statement No. 5, Recognition and Measurement in Financial Statements of Business Enterprises (CON-5) (not included in the ASC), provides guidance on the fundamental factors to consider regarding the timing of revenue recognition, many issues encountered by entities in practice are not addressed in the current accounting literature.

SCOPE

The following accounting guidance, which amends the guidance in ASC 605-25, Multiple-Element Arrangements, applies to all deliverables under contractually binding arrangements, regardless of their form (i.e., written, oral, or implied), in all industries, if a vendor will perform multiple revenue-generating activities unless it is stated otherwise in ASC 605-25-15-3A and 15-4, which is the scope section of ASC 605-25.

The guidance in another ASC Topic or the guidance in ASC 605-25 should be applied as follows in determining how to: (1) separate units of accounting; and (2) allocate consideration to each unit of accounting in an arrangement:

- If guidance on determining separation and allocation is provided under another ASC Topic, the arrangement should be accounted for under the guidance in that Topic (ASC 605-25-15-3A(a)).
- If guidance on determining separation but not allocation is provided in another ASC Topic, the allocation of consideration to separate units, some of which may be accounted for under the guidance in that other ASC Topic and others under the guidance in ASC 605-25, should be based on the relative selling price of a deliverables under the scope of the other ASC Topic and the selling prices of the deliverables not under the scope of that ASC Topic. To allocate consideration for deliverables accounted for under the guidance of another ASC Topic and those accounted for not under the guidance of that ASC Topic, the selling prices of the deliverables should be determined based on the guidance in ASC 605-25-30-6A and 30-7. Thereafter, the guidance in ASC 605-25 would apply to the identification of separate units of accounting and the allocation of consideration under an arrangement should be allocated to deliverables not subject to the guidance in the other ASC Topic (ASC 605-25-15-3A(b)).
- If no guidance for determining separation or allocation exists under another ASC Topic, the guidance in ASC 605-25 should be followed to determine the separation of units of accounting and the allocation of consideration. However, if a deliverable subject to the guidance of another ASC Topic does not meet the criteria in ASC 605-25-25-5, as amended (criterion b., which required "objective and reliable evidence of the fair value of the undelivered item(s)" is superseded by the guidance in ASC 605-25) for a deliverable to be considered a separate unit of accounting, consideration allocated to that deliverable should be combined with the amount allocated to other undelivered items under the arrangement. Revenue for those combined deliverables should be recognized as one unit of accounting (ASC 605-25-15-3A(c)).

ACCOUNTING ISSUES

The following issues have been raised regarding the model of revenue recognition when there are multiple payment streams:

- How should an entity determine whether an arrangement with multiple deliverables consists of more than one unit of accounting?
- How should consideration be allocated among separate units of accounting in an arrangement that consists of more than one unit of accounting?

ACCOUNTING GUIDANCE

The following principles and application guidance should be used to determine: (1) how to measure consideration on an arrangement; (2) whether to divide an arrangement into separate units of accounting; and (3) how consideration on an arrangement should be allocated to separate units of accounting.

Units of Accounting

The following principles apply:

- Divide revenue arrangements with multiple deliverables into separate units of accounting if a deliverable meets the criteria ASC 605-25-25-5 to be considered a separate unit of accounting.

- Allocate consideration on an arrangement among separate units of accounting based on their relative selling prices, except as specified in ASC 605-25-30-4. However, the amount to be allocated to a delivered unit of accounting is limited under the guidance in ASC 605-25-30-5.
- Consider recognition criteria separately for each unit of accounting. (ASC 605-25-25-2)

At the inception of an arrangement and as each item is delivered, a vendor should evaluate all of the deliverables in an arrangement to determine whether they are separate units of accounting. For an arrangement with multiple deliverables, a delivered item should be considered to be a separate unit of accounting if it meets both of the following criteria, which should be applied consistently to arrangements with similar characteristics and in similar circumstances:

- A delivered item has value to the customer on its own (i.e., the item can be sold separately by any vendor or the customer can resell it on its own). An observable market for a deliverable is not required in the case of a customer's resale of a deliverable.
- If an arrangement includes a general right of return for a delivered item, the delivery or performance of an undelivered item is considered probable and substantially under the vendor's control. (ASC 605-25-25-5)

A delivered item under an arrangement that does not meet those two criteria should be combined with other applicable undelivered items under the arrangement. Revenue on such an arrangement should be allocated and recognized for the combined deliverables as a single unit of accounting (ASC 605-25-25-6).

Measurement and Allocation of Consideration Received on an Arrangement

The total amount of consideration on an arrangement should be fixed and determinable, except for the effect of: (1) a customer's right to a refund, if any, or other concessions; or (2) performance bonuses to which a vendor may be entitled (ASC 605-25-30-1).

At the inception of an arrangement, consideration should be allocated to all of the deliverables under an arrangement based on their relative selling prices, except as discussed in ASC 605-25-30-4 and 30-5. To apply the relative selling price method, it is necessary to determine the selling price for a deliverable by using vendor-specific objective evidence (VSOE) of the selling price, if available. Otherwise, evidence of a third party's selling price should be used, as discussed in ASC 605-25-30-6B. If information about neither of those selling prices exists, a vendor should use its best estimate of a deliverable's selling price when applying the relative selling price method as discussed in ASC 605-25-30-6C. When a vendor decides whether to use VSOE or third-party evidence of a deliverable's selling price, the vendor should not overlook information that is reasonably available without excessive cost or effort (ASC 605-25-30-2).

If a separate unit of accounting in an arrangement must be recognized at fair value under the guidance in another ASC Topic and marked to market in each subsequent period, the amount allocated to that deliverable should be its fair value. In that case, all other consideration on an arrangement should be allocated to other units of accounting based on the guidance in ASC 605-25-30-2 (ASC 605-25-30-4).

The amount that may be allocated to a delivered unit(s) of accounting should not exceed an amount that is not contingent on: (1) the delivery of additional items; or (2) meeting other specified performance conditions. That is, the amount allocated to a delivered unit or units is the lesser of the amount that would be allocated under the guidance in ASC 605-25-30-2 and 605-25-30-4, or the noncontingent amount. Although the guidance in ASC 605-15 may affect the amount of revenue recognized, the allocated amount is not adjusted for the effect of a general right of return under ASC 605-25-30-5.

Revenue recognized in a period should not exceed an amount that has been measured based on the assumption that the arrangement will not be canceled. An asset recognized for amounts in excess of revenue that has been recognized under an arrangement for cash payments or other consideration that a vendor has received from a customer since the arrangement's inception should not exceed all of the consideration to which the vendor is legally entitled, including cancellation fees if a customer cancels the order. However, a vendor's intent to enforce its contractual right if a customer cancels an order should be considered in determining the amount of asset recognition (ASC 605-25-30-6).

The VSOE of a selling price should not exceed the price charged for a deliverable: (1) sold separately; or (2) not yet sold separately if it is probable that the established price will not change before the product is introduced (ASC 605-25-30-6A).

Third-party evidence of a selling price consists of the price the vendor or a competitor would charge for interchangeable products or services sold separately to customers under similar circumstances (ASC 605-25-30-6B).

A vendor's best estimate of a selling price should be consistent with the objective of determining VSOE of a deliverable's selling price. Market conditions and factors specifically related to an entity should be considered in estimating a selling price (ASC 605-25-30-6C).

It should not be presumed that prices for individual products or services under an arrangement with multiple deliverables that are stated in a contract represent VSOE or third-party evidence of a selling price or a vendor's best estimate of a selling price (ASC 605-25-30-7).

Disclosure

The objective of the following disclosures is to provide financial statement users with qualitative and quantitative information about: (1) a vendor's revenue arrangements, and (2) significant judgments made in applying the guidance on revenue allocation and how changes in those judgments or in the application of the guidance may significantly affect the timing or amount of revenue recognized. Consequently, to comply with this requirement, a vendor should disclose other qualitative and quantitative information, as necessary, in addition to the required disclosures (ASC 605-25-50-1).

The following information should be disclosed by similar types of arrangements:

1. The nature of a vendor's arrangements for multiple-deliverables;
2. All significant deliverables under the arrangements;
3. The general timing of delivery or performance of a service for deliverables under those arrangements;
4. Provisions related to performance, cancellation, and refunds;
5. A discussion of the significant factors, inputs, assumptions, and methods used to determine a selling price, based on VSOE, third-party evidence, or an estimated selling price, for significant deliverables;
6. Whether significant deliverables under an arrangement qualify as separate units of accounting, and, if applicable, the reasons why they do not qualify;
7. The general timing of revenue recognition for significant units of accounting; and
8. Separate information about the effect of changes in either the selling price or the method or assumptions used to determine the selling price of a specific unit of accounting if either one of those changes significantly affects the allocation of consideration for an arrangement. (ASC 605-25-50-2)

ASC 605-28: MILESTONE METHOD

IMPORTANT NOTICE: All of the guidance in ASC 605-28 will be superseded when the guidance in ASU 2014-09, which will reside in ASC 606 (Revenue from Contracts with Customers), becomes effective.

ASC 605-28-05-1, 15-1 through 15-4, 25-1 through 25-3, 50-1 through 50-2, 65-1; 605-10-05-1, 25-2A; ASC 605-25-15-2A; (ASU 2010-17) Milestone Method of Revenue Recognition

BACKGROUND

One of the practice issues raised during the discussion of the guidance in ASC 605-25, Multiple Element Arrangements, was the need for guidance for the application of the milestone method as a means of allocating contingent consideration when revenue becomes fixed or determinable.

SCOPE

The following guidance, which applies to all entities, may be applied to arrangements under which (1) a vendor's obligations to a customer are satisfied over a period of time; and (2) all or a portion of the consideration under an arrangement is contingent on the achievement of one or more milestones, unless this guidance conflicts with other guidance in ASC 605.

Guidance related to the milestone method of revenue recognition should be used to account for research or development arrangements under which a vendor satisfies its performance obligation to provide deliverables or units of accounting over a period of time and a portion or all of the consideration to the vendor is contingent on the achievement of uncertain future events and circumstances (i.e., milestones), such as the successful completion of phases in a drug study or a specific result from research or development endeavors, except if this guidance conflicts with other guidance in ASC 605. The milestone method is not the only acceptable method of accounting for a vendor's revenue that is contingent on the achievement of milestones. However, regardless of the method used to attribute revenue that depends on the achievement of milestones, a vendor's revenue recognition policy should be applied consistently to similar deliverables or units of accounting.

ACCOUNTING GUIDANCE

- The guidance in ASC 605-28 may be applied to arrangements under which: (1) a vendor's obligations to a customer are satisfied over a period of time; and (2) all or a portion of revenue under an arrangement is contingent on the achievement of one or more milestones, unless the guidance conflicts with other guidance in ASC 605.
- A milestone is an event: (1) for which, at the date an arrangement is entered into there is a substantive uncertainty that the event will be achieved; (2) that can only be achieved based in whole or in part as result of a vendor's performance or a specific outcome as a result of a vendor's performance; and (3) that if achieved, will result in additional payments being made to the vendor. Further, a milestone is *not* an event that is contingent only on the passage of time or on a counterparty's performance.

To recognize all of the revenue in the period in which a milestone has been achieved, a vendor should account for a deliverable or unit of accounting that depends on the complete achievement of a *substantive* milestone according to the guidance in ASC 605-28. A vendor may not elect to follow another accounting method under which the vendor would recognize all of the revenue on a milestone in the period in which the milestone has been achieved. However, a vendor that meets the requirements of that guidance is not prohibited from electing to apply a different accounting policy under which revenue related to a portion of the revenue for achieving a milestone would be deferred.

Although determining whether a milestone is *substantive* at the inception of an arrangement is based on judgment, for a milestone to be considered substantive, revenue earned by achieving a milestone must meet all of the following principles: (1) It corresponds with either (*a*) the vendor's performance to achieve the milestone, or (*b*) the value of the delivered item(s) has been improved by the vendor's performance to achieve the milestone; (2) it is related only to *past* performance; and (3) it is reasonable relative to all of the deliverables and payment terms under the arrangement, including revenue on other potential on milestones.

A milestone is *not* considered to be substantive if any portion of the revenue received for achieving a milestone does *not* apply exclusively to *past* performance but is related to the remaining deliverables in a unit of accounting under an arrangement. If so, not all of the consideration received for reaching a milestone should be recognized as revenue. Further, since recognition of all revenue earned when a milestone is achieved must be related to a *substantive* milestone; a milestone cannot be separated into substantive and nonsubstantive portions. Further, if a portion of revenue earned on achieving a milestone is subject to a refund or an adjustment based on a vendor's future performance through a penalty or clawback, that revenue also is *not* considered to be related to past performance and, therefore, the milestone would not be considered to be substantive. However, a vendor would *not* be precluded from applying the milestone method to other milestones under an arrangement if revenue from an individual milestone is *not* related exclusively to past performance.

The attribution model in ASC 605-28 for revenue recognition on an arrangement that is contingent on the achievement of a milestone is *not* the only acceptable, revenue recognition method regardless of whether the milestone is considered to be substantive. However, a vendor's revenue recognition policy for arrangements under which revenue recognition is contingent on a vendor's achievement of a milestone should be applied *consistently* to similar deliverables or units of accounting.

DISCLOSURE

Entities that elect to apply the guidance in ASC 605-28 should disclose the following information in the notes to their financial statements for each arrangement that includes a milestone payment:

- A description of the overall arrangement;
- A description of the individual milestones and related contingent consideration;
- Whether the milestones are considered to be substantive;
- The factors considered in determining whether a milestone is substantive; and
- The amount of revenue recognized on milestones during the period.

ASC 605-35: CONSTRUCTION-TYPE AND PRODUCTION-TYPE CONTRACTS

IMPORTANT NOTICE: Most of the guidance in ASC 605-35 will be superseded when the guidance in ASU 2014-09, which will reside in ASC 606 (Revenue from Contracts with Customers), becomes effective. However, because the guidance related to loss provisions for construction-type and production-type contracts in ASC 605-35-05-1, 15-1 through 15-6, 25-7, 25-10, 25-45 through 25-49, 45-1 through 45-2, will be retained and amended, the title of ASC 605-35 will be changed to Revenue Recognition—Provision for Losses on Construction-Type and Production-Type Contracts.

ASC 605-35-05-1 through 05-13, 15-6, 25-1 through 25-50, 25-54 through 25-88, 25-90 through 25-98, 45-1 through 45-2, 50-1 through 50-10, 55-1; ASC 210-10-60-2; ASC 460-1-60-10; ASC 910-20-25-5; ASC 912-20-25-1 Accounting for Performance of Construction-Type and Certain Production-Type Contracts

BACKGROUND

ASC 605-35 provides guidance on the application of U.S. GAAP in accounting for the performance of contracts for which a customer provides specifications for any of the following:

- Construction of facilities
- Production of goods
- Provision of related services

The basic accounting issue for contract accounting is the point(s) at which revenue should be recognized as earned and costs should be recognized as expenses. Accounting for contracts involves the measurement and the allocation of revenues and expenses of relatively long-term events over relatively short-term accounting periods. To deal with the uncertainties inherent in the performance of contracts, the allocation process often requires contractors to rely on estimates of revenues, costs, and the extent of progress to completion.

Guidance for the following two generally accepted methods of accounting for long-term construction contracts, which should be applied in specified circumstances and should not be used as alternatives, is provided in ASC 605-35:

- *Percentage-of-completion* Revenue is recognized as work progresses on a contract.
- *Completed-contract* Revenue is recognized only when work on a contract is complete.

Under the units-of-delivery method, which is a modification of the percentage-of-completion method, revenue is recognized on a contract as deliverable products are completed.

The following three key estimates are required to account for long-term construction contracts:

- The extent of progress toward completion
- Contract revenues
- Contract costs

PRACTICE POINTER: If estimates of costs to complete work on a contract and the extent of progress toward completion are reasonably dependable, using the percentage-of-completion method is preferable. If those estimates are unreliable, the completed-contract method should be used. The two methods are not considered alternatives for the same circumstances.

ACCOUNTING GUIDANCE

Scope

The guidance in ASC 605-35 applies to all contractors. It is not limited to long-term contracts, nor is it limited to construction contracts. Contracts covered are binding agreements between a buyer and a seller in which a seller agrees, to perform a service to a buyer's specifications for compensation under a contract, which is a legally enforceable agreement. Performance often will extend over long periods, and a seller's right to receive payment depends on performance in accordance with the agreement. Contracts that are under the scope of this guidance include the following:

- Construction industry contracts (e.g., general building and heavy earthmoving);
- Contracts to design and build ships and transport vessels;
- Contracts to design, develop, manufacture, or modify complex aerospace or electronic equipment;
- Contracts for construction consulting services;
- Contracts for services performed by architects, engineers, or architectural or engineering design firms; and
- Contracts to design and deliver computer software or a software system, either alone or with other products or services that require significant production, modification, or customization. (See the guidance in ASC 985-605-25-88 through 25-107 for additional guidance on the application of ASC 605-35 to software contracts.)

Contracts under the scope of ASC 605-35 may be classified into four broad types based on their pricing method:

1. *Fixed-price* An agreement to perform all activities under a contract for a stated price;
2. *Cost-type (including cost-plus)* An agreement to perform under a contract for a price to be determined on the basis of a defined relationship to the costs to be incurred, e.g., costs of all activities required plus a fixed fee or a fixed percentage of incurred costs;
3. *Time-and-material* An agreement to perform all activities required under a contract for a price based on fixed hourly rates for some measure of the labor hours required;
4. *Unit-price* An agreement to perform all activities required under a contract for a specified price for each unit of output.

Each of those types of contracts may include provisions for incentives, penalties, or other provisions to modify a contract's basic pricing terms.

The term *contractor* refers to a person or entity that enters into a contract to construct facilities, produce goods, or to render services based on a buyer's specifications by acting as a general or prime contractor, a subcontractor, or a construction manager. The term *profit center* refers to a measurement unit designated for the accumulation of revenues and costs and the measurement of income on a contract. Revenues, costs, and income are usually determined for a single contract, but under specified circumstances they may be determined for a combination of two or more contracts, a segment of a contract, or a group of combined contracts.

Basic Accounting Policy

The basic accounting policy decision made in contract accounting under U.S. GAAP is between the percentage-of-completion method and the completed-contract method. As stated previously, the determination of which is preferable depends on a careful evaluation of circumstances, because the two methods are not alternatives for the same situation. The basic policy followed should be disclosed in a note to the financial statements.

The use of the percentage-of-completion method depends on the ability to make reasonably dependable estimates of the extent of completion, contract revenues, and contract costs. Entities with significant contracting operations generally have the ability to produce reasonably reliable estimates and, accordingly, the percentage-of-completion method is preferable in most circumstances. If estimating the final outcome of a contract would be impractical, except to assure that no loss will be incurred, a contractor should use a zero estimate of profit, and equal amounts of revenues and costs should be recognized until results can be estimated more precisely.

Under the completed-contract method, income is recognized only when a contract is completed or substantially completed. During the period of performance, billings and costs are accumulated on the balance sheet as inventory, but no profit or income is recorded until the contract is complete or substantially complete. The completed-contract method is appropriate if reasonably dependable estimates of the extent of completion, contract revenues, and/or contract costs cannot be made, or if a contractor's financial position and results of operations would not vary materially if the percentage-of-completion method were used. If there is assurance that no loss will be incurred on a contract, the percentage-of-completion method based on a zero profit margin is preferable until more precise estimates can be made.

Profit Center

The basic assumption is that each contract is a profit center for revenue recognition, cost accumulation, and income measurement. However, if a group of contracts is so closely related, that they are effectively parts of a single project with an overall profit margin, combining the contracts for purposes of profit recognition should be considered.

Contracts may be combined for accounting purposes if the following criteria are met:

(1) Negotiated as a package in the same economic environment with an overall profit margin.

(2) Essentially, constitute an agreement to perform a single project.

(3) Require performance of closely interrelated construction activities with common costs.

(4) In substance, represent an agreement with a single customer.

A single contract or a group of contracts that otherwise meet the test for combining may include several elements or phases, each of which was negotiated separately without regard to performance on the others. A contract may be segmented for accounting purposes if the following steps were taken and are documented and verifiable:

- The contractor submitted bona fide proposals on the separate components of the project and on the entire project.
- The customer had the right to accept the proposals either on the separate components of the project or on the entire project.
- The aggregate amount of the proposal on the separate components approximated the amount of the proposal on the entire project.

Measuring Progress on Accounts

Progress toward completion may be measured in terms of costs, units of work, or value added. All are acceptable in appropriate circumstances. The method or methods selected should be applied consistently.

Several approaches can be described as based on input measures. Those methods are based on costs and on other efforts expended. An example is the efforts-expended approach, in which a measure of work, such as labor hours, machine hours, or materials quantities, is used as a measurement of the extent of progress. Output methods, on the other hand, measure progress in terms of results achieved. Estimating the extent of progress toward completion based on units completed is an example of an output method.

Income Determination—Revenue Elements

The major factors that must be considered in determining total estimated revenues are the basic contract price, contract options and additions, change orders, and claims.

Basic Contract Price

The estimated revenue from a contract is the total amount that a contractor expects to realize from a contract. It is determined primarily based on the terms of the contract. The contract may be relatively fixed or highly variable and, as a result, subject to a great deal of uncertainty. One problem peculiar to cost-type contracts is the determination of reimbursable costs that should be reflected as revenue.

Contract Options and Additions

An option or an addition to an existing contract is treated as a separate contract in any of the following circumstances:

- The product or service to be provided differs significantly from the product or service provided under the original contract.
- The price of the new product or service is negotiated without regard to the original contract and involves different economic judgments.
- The product or service to be provided under an exercised option or amendment is similar to that under the original contract, but the contract price and anticipated contract cost relationship are significantly different.

If none of these circumstances is present, the option or addition may be combined with the original contract for purposes of revenue recognition.

Change Orders

Change orders are modifications of an original contract that effectively change the provisions of the contract without adding new provisions. Change orders may have a significant effect on the amount of contract revenue to be recognized.

Claims

Claims are amounts in excess of the agreed contract price that a contractor seeks to collect from customers or others as a result of customer-caused delays, errors in specifications and designs, contract terminations, change orders in dispute, and other similar causes. Recognition of such claims is appropriate only if it is probable that the claim will result in additional contract revenue and if the amounts can be reliably estimated.

Income Determination—Cost Elements

At any point in the contract, estimated contract costs consist of two components: costs incurred to date and estimated costs to complete the contract. Costs incurred to date generally can be determined with reasonable certainty, depending on the adequacy and effectiveness of the cost accounting system. Estimating the costs to complete a contract generally involves greater uncertainty.

Contract costs are accumulated in the same manner as inventory and are charged to operations as the related revenue from the contract is recognized. General principles for accounting for production costs are as follows:

- All direct costs (e.g., materials, labor, subcontracting costs) are included in contract costs.
- Indirect costs, such as indirect labor, contract supervision, tools and equipment, and supplies, may be allocated to contracts as indirect costs if otherwise allowable under U.S. GAAP.
- General and administrative costs ordinarily should be charged to expense, but may be included as contract costs under certain circumstances.
- Selling costs are generally excluded from contract costs.
- Costs under cost-type contracts are charged to contract costs in conformity with U.S. GAAP in the same manner as costs under other types of contracts.
- In computing estimated gross profit or in providing for losses on contracts, estimates of costs to complete should reflect all the types of costs included in contract costs.
- Inventoriable costs should not be carried at amounts that, when added to the estimated costs to complete, are greater than the estimated realizable value of the contract.

Estimating the costs to complete a contract should result from the following:

- Systematic and consistent procedures that are correlated with the cost accounting system to provide a basis for periodically comparing actual and estimated amounts.
- Quantities and prices of all significant elements of costs.
- Estimation procedures that include the same elements of cost that are included in actual accumulated costs.
- The effects of future wage and price escalations.
- Periodic review and revision, as appropriate, to reflect new information.

Revised Estimates

Adjustments to the original estimates of the total contract revenue, total contract cost, and extent of progress toward completion may be required as work progresses under the contract and as experience is gained. Such revisions should be accounted for by the cumulative catch-up method in accordance with the guidance in ASC 250, Accounting Changes and Error Corrections.

Provisions for Anticipated Losses

If current estimates indicate that the total contract revenues and costs will result in a loss, a provision of the entire loss on the contract should be made. This is true for both the percentage-of-completion method and the completed-contract method. A provision for loss should be made in the accounting period in which it becomes evident.

A provision for a loss on a contract should be shown separately as a liability on the balance sheet—unless related costs are accumulated in the balance sheet, in which case the loss provision may be offset against the related accumulated costs. In a classified balance sheet, a provision shown as a liability should be classified as a current liability.

ASC 605-45: PRINCIPAL AGENT CONSIDERATIONS

IMPORTANT NOTICE: All of the guidance in ASC 605-45 will be superseded when the guidance in ASU 2014-09, which will reside in ASC-606 (Revenue from Contracts with Customers), becomes effective.

ASC 605-45-05-1 through 05-2, 15-3 through 15-5, 45-1 through 45-18, 50-1, 55-2 through 55-3, 55-5 through 55-6, 55-8 through 55-9, 55-11 through 55-14, 55-16, 55-18, 55-20, 55-22, 55-24 through 55-25, 55-27 through 55-31, 55-33 through 55-34, 55-36 through 55-38, 55-40 through 55-45 Reporting Revenue Gross as a Principal versus Net as an Agent

BACKGROUND

As a result of the proliferation of sales of goods and services over the Internet, the SEC staff noted diversity in registrants' revenue recognition practices. Frequently, a vendor that does not stock merchandise sold on its Internet site arranges for a supplier to ship the merchandise directly to a buyer. Similarly, services sold on an Internet site are frequently performed by a third party, not by the Internet vendor. In some cases, a vendor's profit on a transaction consists of a commission or fee for selling a third party's products or services. The importance of a company's revenue recognition method has increased in the current economic environment because some investors value Internet companies—especially start-ups that may show losses or very little net income in the early years—based on multiples of revenues instead of multiples of gross profit or earnings.

SEC Staff Accounting Bulletin (SAB) Topic 13 addresses the question whether Company A, which sells Company T's products on the Internet, should recognize (*a*) both the gross amount of a sale and the related costs or (*b*) the net revenue earned on a sale. In determining how a company should recognize revenue, the SEC staff considers whether an entity

1. Is acting as a principal in the transaction
2. Takes title to the merchandise
3. Has the risks and rewards of ownership, such as risks of loss for collection, delivery, or returns
4. Is acting as an agent or broker (including performing services as an agent or broker) and is compensated by a commission or fee

The SEC also requires an entity that performs as an agent or broker to report sales on a net basis if no risks and rewards of ownership of the goods are assumed.

Because the SEC staff believes that additional factors may exist, the staff asked the EITF to develop an accounting model that is consistent with the requirements of SAB Topic 13. The following guidance is not limited to Internet transactions, but also may apply to transactions with travel agents, magazine subscription brokers, and sales of products through catalogs, consignment sales, or special-order retail sales.

The following guidance does not address the timing of revenue recognition and whether revenue should be deferred if the earnings process is not complete.

ACCOUNTING ISSUE

Under what circumstances should an entity report revenue based on (*a*) the *gross* amount billed to a customer for the sale of a product or service on which the company earns revenue or (*b*) the *net* amount retained (the amount billed less the amount paid the supplier), because the supplier or service provider paid the company a commission or fee?

ACCOUNTING GUIDANCE

The decision whether to report revenue at (*a*) the *gross* amount billed to a customer, because an entity earned the revenue from a sale of goods or services, or (*b*) the *net* difference between the amount billed to a customer less the amount paid to the supplier, because an entity earned a commission or a fee, requires judgment based on the facts and circumstances. The following factors, which should not be considered to be presumptive or determinative, should be considered in that decision based on their strength:

- Indicators of Gross Revenue Reporting
  - — *Acting as the primary obligor* The fact that an entity is responsible for fulfilling a customer's order, including whether the product or service is acceptable to the customer, is a strong indicator that an entity has the risks and rewards of a principal and should report revenue at the *gross* amount billed to the customer. An entity's marketing representations and the terms of a sales contract indicate whether the entity or a supplier is fulfilling the order.
  - — *General inventory risk before the order is placed or on product return* If an entity (*a*) takes title to a product before it is ordered by a customer who has the right of return and (*b*) takes title to a product if it is returned, the company has general inventory risk, which indicates that it has the risk and rewards of a principal in the transaction and is

a strong indicator that it should report revenue at the gross amount. The entity and the supplier should have no arrangement to reduce or mitigate inventory risk, for example, the right to return unsold products to a supplier.

— *Latitude in establishing the price* An entity's ability, within economic constraints, to establish the price of a product or service charged to a customer may indicate that an entity is acting as a principal in the transaction.

— *Addition of meaningful value to a product or service* The fact that an entity adds meaningful value (the selling price is greater because of the addition) to a product or provides a significant portion of a service ordered by a customer may indicate that the entity has primary responsibility for fulfillment, including customer satisfaction with the component of the product or portion of total services provided by the supplier.

— *Discretion in selecting the supplier* The fact that an entity can select a supplier among several to provide a product or service ordered by a customer may indicate that the entity has primary responsibility for fulfillment.

— *Involvement in determining product or service specifications* The requirement for an entity to determine the nature, type, characteristics, or specifications of a product or service ordered by a customer may indicate that it has primary responsibility for fulfillment.

— *Retention of the risk of physical loss of inventory after a customer's order or during shipping* The risk of physical loss of inventory exists (*a*) from the time an entity takes title to a product at the point of shipment (e.g., the supplier's facilities) until the product is transferred to a customer on delivery or (*b*) from the time an entity takes title to a product after a customer's order has been received until the product is delivered to a carrier for shipment to the customer. This indicator provides less persuasive evidence than general inventory risk that the gross amount of revenue should be reported.

— *Assumption of credit risk* An entity assumes credit risk if it is responsible for collecting the sales price from the customer and has to pay the supplier regardless of whether it collects the full sales price. An entity's assumption of credit risk for the amount billed to a customer may provide weak evidence that the entity has the risks and rewards of a principal in the transaction and should report revenue gross. No credit risk is assumed if an entity collects the full sales price before delivering a product or service to a customer.

- Indicators of Net Revenue Reporting

— *The supplier is the primary obligor* The fact that a supplier is responsible for fulfillment, including whether the product or services ordered or purchased by the customer are acceptable, may indicate that an entity does not have the risks and rewards as a principal in the transaction and should report revenue based on the amount retained after paying the supplier. An entity's representations while marketing a product and the sales contract generally provide evidence of whether the entity or a supplier is required to fulfill the order or service.

— *The entity earns a fixed amount* The fact that an entity earns a fixed amount on a transaction regardless of the amount billed for a product or service indicates that the entity is acting as an agent for a supplier.

— *The supplier assumes the credit risk* The fact that a supplier assumes the credit risk, because the full sales price has not been collected before a product or service is delivered to a customer, indicates that the entity is acting as an agent for the supplier.

Disclosure

Voluntary disclosures of an entity's gross volume of transactions that are reported may be useful to users of financial statements. The information could be disclosed parenthetically in the income statement or in the notes to the financial statements. Gross amounts disclosed on the face of the income statement should not be described as revenues and should not be reported in a column that is included in the sum of net income or loss. Such amounts may be described as gross billings.

ASC 605-45-15-2, 15-4, 45-22 through 45-23 Reimbursements Received for "Out-of-Pocket" Expenses Incurred

BACKGROUND

The following guidance applies to the accounting for reimbursements received from customers for a service provider's "out-of-pocket" expenses incurred, such as expenses related to mileage, airfare, hotel stays, out-of-town meals, photocopies, and telecommunication and facsimile charges. Reimbursements may be based on actual amounts incurred or are included in a negotiated flat fee for professional services provided and out-of-pocket expenses incurred.

This Issue does not apply to the following transactions for which other guidance already exists:

- Sales of financial assets, including debt and equity securities, loans, and receivables
- Lending transactions
- Insurance and reinsurance premiums
- Broker-dealer transactions under the scope of ASC 940, *Financial Services—Brokers and Dealers*, and reimbursements received for expenses incurred by entities that follow the guidance for other specialized industries, which provide accounting guidance for reimbursements.

ACCOUNTING GUIDANCE

Service providers should present reimbursements for out-of-pocket expenses incurred as revenue in the income statement.

ASC 605-45-15-2, 50-3 through 50-4 Taxes Collected from Customers and Remitted to Governmental Authorities

BACKGROUND

Entities are assessed for taxes by various governmental authorities on all kinds of transactions—from sales taxes on a broad range of goods and services to excise taxes on specific kinds of transactions. Because such taxes are calculated, remitted to the governmental authority, and administered differently, there is no one model to follow in accounting and reporting for them. In addition, some taxes (such as sales taxes) are collected from customers and transmitted by vendors to the appropriate governmental agencies, and other taxes (such as income taxes) are paid by the entity.

The SEC staff has received questions regarding the income tax presentation of various taxes. In response to questions regarding how changes in the party responsible for paying state and local sales taxes would affect a vendor's presentation on the income statement, the SEC staff has recommended that pass-through taxes be accounted for in accordance with the guidance in ASC 605-45. The SEC staff continues to hold that view.

ACCOUNTING ISSUES

1. Should the scope of this Issue include all nondiscretionary amounts assessed by governmental authorities in connection with a transaction with a customer, or only sales, use, and value-added taxes?
2. Should taxes assessed by a governmental authority under the scope of Issue 1 be presented in the income statement on a gross or net basis?

ACCOUNTING GUIDANCE

1. The scope of this guidance includes any tax assessed by a governmental authority that is both imposed on and that occurs at the same time as a specific revenue-producing transaction between a seller and a customer and may include, but is not limited to, sales, use, value added, and some excise taxes. Tax schemes based on gross receipts and taxes imposed while acquiring inventory are *excluded* from the scope of this Issue.
2. An entity's decision to present taxes discussed under the scope of ASC 605-45 in revenues and costs (a gross basis) or to exclude them from revenues and costs (a net basis) should be disclosed as an accounting policy under the guidance in ASC 235-10-05-3 through 05-4; 50-1 through 50-6. However, existing policies related to taxes assessed by a governmental authority as a result of this guidance need *not* be reevaluated. If an entity reports its taxes on a gross basis, the amounts of those taxes should be disclosed in interim and annual financial statements for each period for which an income statement is presented, if the amounts are significant. Taxes reported on a gross basis may be disclosed as a total amount.

ASC 605-45-05-2, 15-2, 15-4, 45-19 through 45-21, S45-1, 50-2, S99 Shipping and Handling Fees and Costs

BACKGROUND

The income statement classification of amounts charged to customers for shipping and handling and related costs differs among companies. Some report charges to customers in revenue and report costs incurred as expenses, but others report only the net amount of costs and revenues. In addition, the costs included in the shipping and handling category also differ by entity. Some include only amounts paid to third-party shippers, but others may also include internal costs, such as salaries and overhead related to the preparation of the goods for shipment. Some charge customers for shipping costs incurred and direct incremental handling costs. Many charge amounts for shipping and handling that are not a direct reimbursement of costs incurred.

The following guidance applies only to shipping and handling fees and costs reported by companies that report revenue at the gross amount billed.

ACCOUNTING ISSUES

1. How should a seller of goods classify in the income statement amounts billed to a customer for shipping and handling?
2. How should a seller of goods classify in the income statement costs incurred for shipping and handling?

ACCOUNTING GUIDANCE

1. An entity that reports the gross amount of shipping and handling fees based on the indicators in ASC 605-45-45 through 45-18 for gross revenue reporting should classify as revenue all amounts billed to customers for shipping and handling fees in sales transactions.
2. Netting shipping and handling costs against shipping and handling revenues is prohibited.
3. Application of the consensus in 1 above is subject to the SEC Observer's comments, which are discussed below.

SEC OBSERVER COMMENT

The SEC Observer stated that registrants are expected to evaluate the significance of shipping and handling costs so that the accounting guidance above is applied based on the significance of such costs to (*a*) each line item on the income statement in which they are included and (*b*) the total gross margin.

ASC 605-50: CUSTOMER PAYMENTS AND INCENTIVES

IMPORTANT NOTICE: The existing guidance in ASC 605-50 provides revenue recognition guidance for consideration given by a vendor to a customer from the vendor's standpoint and the customer's standpoint. All of the guidance in ASC 605-50 from the vendor's standpoint will be superseded when the guidance in ASU 2014-09 Section A, which will reside in ASC 606 (Revenue from Contracts with Customers), becomes effective. However, the guidance from the customer's standpoint in ASC 605-50-45-15 through 45-21 and ASC 605-50-25-10 through 25-12, will be amended and moved to ASC 705-20 (Cost of Sales and Services—Accounting for Consideration Received from a Vendor) (ASC 705-20-25-3 through 25-12).

ASC 605-50-05-1, 15-2 through 15-3, 25-1 through 25-9, 45-1 through 45-11, S45-1, 55-1, 55-3, 55-5, 55-8 through 55-12, 55-14 through 55-15, 55-17 through 55-22, 55-24 through 55-25, 55-27 through 55-28, 55-30 through 55-31, 55-33 through 55-37, 55-40 through 55-44, 55-46 through 55-47, 55-49 through, 55-50, 55-52, through 55-53, 55-55 through 55-69, 55-71 through 55-72, 55-74 through 55-77, 55-79 through 55-95, 55-97 through 55-107, S99-1 ASC 330-10-35-13; ASC 908-360-55-1 Vendor's Income Statement Characterization of Consideration Given to a Customer (Including a Reseller)

BACKGROUND

The objective of the following discussion is to provide guidance on how a vendor, which is a manufacturer or distributor, should report in its income statement consideration, including sales incentives, given to a customer, which may be a reseller or an entity that purchases the vendor's products from a reseller. Consideration from a vendor to a customer may be in the form of cash, but it can also be in the form of discounts, coupons, free products or services, or rebates that a customer can apply against amounts owed to the vendor. The guidance also applies to a service provider's consideration to a manufacturer or a reseller of equipment.

ACCOUNTING ISSUES

Income Statement Presentation

1. When an incentive or other consideration is given by a vendor to a customer (*a*) should an adjustment of the vendor's selling price for products sold be deducted from revenue in the vendor's income statement or (*b*) should costs a vendor incurs for assets or services that a customer provides to the vendor be accounted for as an expense in the vendor's income statement?
2. Should a vendor that has "negative revenue" as a result of a revenue deduction for consideration given to customers based on the guidance provided recharacterize that amount as an expense in the income statement?

Recognition and Measurement

3. When should a vendor recognize as an asset upfront nonrefundable consideration that the vendor gives to a customer instead of immediately recognizing a cost in the income statement?

4. When should a vendor recognize and how should the vendor measure the cost of sales incentives offered voluntarily to customers at no charge that customers can exercise in a single transaction if *no* loss is incurred on the sale of the product or service?

5. When should a vendor recognize and how should the vendor measure the cost of sales incentives discussed in Issue 4 if a loss is incurred on the sale of the product or service?

6. How should a vendor account for an offer to a customer to rebate or refund a specified amount of cash that may be redeemed only if the customer completes a specified cumulative level of revenue transactions or remains a customer for a specified period of time?

ACCOUNTING GUIDANCE

Scope

The guidance applies to the following kinds of arrangements:

1. Slotting fees, which are fees that a vendor pays to a customer for shelf space for the vendor's products and other product placement arrangements, such as brand development or new product introduction arrangements, for which a vendor pays fees for the right to display its products in favorable locations in a store, for end-cap placement, and for additional shelf space. A vendor may incur slotting fees (*a*) before selling any of the products to the customer, (*b*) on a regular schedule to maintain a shelf space allocation, or to continue being a regular vendor, or (*c*) periodically as negotiated. The vendor may or may not receive stated rights for those fees.

2. Cooperative advertising arrangements, in which a vendor reimburses a customer for a portion of the costs incurred to advertise the vendor's products. The vendor is generally required to participate in advertising costs based on the actual cost. The customer may be reimbursed for an amount limited to a specified percentage of its purchases from the vendor. In other arrangements, the amount of reimbursement is based on a percentage of the customer's purchases from the vendor during a specific time period, regardless of actual costs incurred by the customer to advertise the vendor's products.

3. Buydowns are arrangements under which a vendor agrees to reimburse a customer up to a specified amount for shortfalls in the sales price received by the customer for the vendor's products over a specified time period. Under such arrangements, the vendor reimburses, compensates, or issues credit memos to the customer for a decrease in revenue per product unit during a specified promotion period for a product. The customer is not required to make any expenditures for advertising or promotions. Other related arrangements in which a vendor reduces the net price paid by the customer for the vendor's products include factory incentives, dealer holdbacks, price protection, and factory-to-dealer incentives.

The scope of this Issue does *not* include the following:

- Coupons, rebates, and other forms of rights for free or significantly discounted products or services that a customer received in an earlier exchange transaction and that the vendor accounted for as a separate element of that transaction.
- Offers for free or significantly discounted products or services that a customer can exercise in the future without an additional exchange with the vendor as a result of a current revenue transaction.

Recognition and Measurement

The following guidance for the measurement and timing of cost recognition of sales incentives applies only to arrangements that meet *both* of the following conditions:

- An incentive is linked to a single sales transaction; multiple sales transactions are not required to exercise an incentive.
- A vendor does not receive a benefit that can be identified from the customer in exchange for a sales incentive.

Vendors should recognize the cost of sales incentives offered voluntarily and without charge to customers that can be used or exercised as a result of a single exchange transaction if such incentives do *not* result in a loss on a sale or service on either of the following dates, whichever occurs later:

a. The date on which the vendor recognizes the related revenue.

b. The date on which a sales incentive is offered. (That is, if a vendor offers the sales incentive after having recognized revenue on the sale, for example, if a manufacturer offers discount coupons to customers after the sale of the products.)

A liability or deferred revenue should be recognized at the later of the above dates based on an estimated amount of refunds or rebates that will be claimed if customers must submit a form to receive refunds or rebates of specific amounts for prior purchases. A maximum potential liability or deferred revenue should be recognized for refunds or rebates if it is not possible to make a reasonable and reliable estimate of the amount of *future* refunds or rebates. Although that estimate depends on many factors, a vendor's ability to make a reasonable and reliable estimate may be impaired as a result of the following:

(1) The period during which refunds or rebates can be claimed is relatively long.

(2) A vendor has no historical experience with similar types of sales incentives or is unable to apply that experience because circumstances have changed.

(3) The volume of relatively homogeneous transactions is insufficient.

A vendor that offers sales incentives voluntarily at no cost to its customers that can be used or exercised as a result of a single exchange transaction and that will result in a loss on the sale of the products or services should *not* recognize a liability for the sales incentives before the date on which revenue is recognized on the transactions.

A sales incentive that will result in a loss on the sale of a product may indicate that existing inventory is impaired under the guidance in ASC 330.

The above guidance also applies to the accounting for an excess of the fair value of a sales incentive a vendor has provided to a customer over the fair value of an identifiable benefit received by the vendor in exchange for the sales incentive.

A vendor should *reduce* revenue by the amount recognized as an obligation for a rebate or refund to a customer. The cost of honoring claims for rebates or refunds should be allocated on a rational and systematic basis to each underlying revenue transaction with a customer that will enable the customer to reach a cumulative level at which a rebate or refund will be earned. The total rebate or refund obligation should be measured based on an estimated number of customers that will earn and claim refunds under the offer. "Breakage" should be included if the amount of future rebates can be reasonably estimated. Otherwise, the vendor should recognize a liability for the maximum rebate or refund, without a reduction for breakage. Although the ability to make that estimate may vary on a case-by-case basis, a vendor's ability to make a reasonable estimate may be affected by the following factors:

a. The period during which a rebate or refund can be claimed is relatively long.

b. The vendor has no historical experience with similar types of sales incentives for similar products or is unable to use that experience because the circumstances differ.

c. The volume of homogenous transactions is not large enough to make a reasonable estimate.

Under some programs, the amount of a cash rebate or refund may increase, based on the customer's volume of purchases. If a vendor can reasonably estimate the volume of a customer's future purchases, a liability should be recognized for the *estimated* amount of the cash rebate or refund. Otherwise, the vendor should recognize a liability for the maximum potential refund or rebate under the program.

Changes in the estimated amounts of cash rebates or refunds from a previous offer, such as a retroactive increase or decrease in the amount of the rebate, should be recognized immediately as a cumulative catch-up adjustment to adjust the balance of the rebate obligation. Revenue on future sales should be reduced based on the *revised* rate of the refund.

Income Statement Presentation

Vendors account for sales incentives or other consideration given to customers under the following methods:

- As a reduction of revenue in the vendor's income statement by adjusting the selling prices of the vendor's products or services;
- As a cost or expense in the vendor's income statement by accounting for a sales incentive or other compensation as a cost incurred.

It is presumed that a vendor's consideration to a customer in the form of cash or sales incentives related to the vendor's products is a reduction of the vendor's prices that results in a reduction of revenue in the income statement. However, that presumption may be overcome, and the vendor should account for the consideration as a cost if the vendor has received or will receive from the customer a benefit that meets the following two conditions:

a. In return for the consideration, the vendor has received or will receive an identifiable benefit from the customer in the form of goods or services. The benefit should be one for which the vendor would have entered into an exchange transaction with a third party that is separate from the vendor's sales of goods or services to the customer.
b. The fair value of the benefit can be reasonably estimated. Otherwise, an excess of consideration paid by the vendor over the fair value of the benefit, if any, should be deducted from revenue presented in the vendor's income statement.

A vendor should report as an *expense* in its income statement the cost of consideration consisting of a free product or service, such as a gift from a vendor or a free airline ticket to be honored by an unrelated entity, and other noncash consideration in the form of equity instruments, because the free item is a deliverable in the exchange transaction and *not* a refund or rebate of a portion of the sales price obligation.

The effect of the requirement for separability in (*a*) above would generally result in the recognition of slotting fees or similar fees related to product development or placement as a reduction of revenue. For example, a vendor's agreement to reimburse a customer for a reduction in a product's sales price would always be recognized as a revenue reduction. Buydowns, which would never meet criterion (*a*), should always be accounted for as reductions of revenue.

In addition, this guidance also applies to consideration from a vendor to a customer that resells the product in another format or uses the product as a component of another product, for example, a payment for cooperative advertising from a fabric manufacturer to a clothing manufacturer.

Revenue reductions that result in negative revenue. Negative revenue may result from the application of this guidance to cash consideration given by a vendor to a customer or from transactions or changes in estimates under the application of guidance in other topics of the ASC that require a reduction of revenue. Although it is presumed that no portion of amounts accounted for under this guidance as a reduction of revenue should be reclassified as an expense, a vendor may be permitted to reclassify a cumulative shortfall of revenue from doing business with a particular customer, as an expense if the vendor can demonstrate that accounting for amounts under this and other guidance in the ASC have resulted in negative revenue for the specific customer. To provide that information, a vendor that sells products directly to resellers, which subsequently sell the products to other resellers, such as retailers, down the distribution chain, must perform a customer analysis to identify the specific reseller or distributor from which retailers purchased the vendor's products.

Reclassification of negative revenue as an expense would be permitted if a vendor gives cash consideration to a *new* customer before the customer has purchased any products or placed or committed to place any orders and that consideration exceeds cumulative revenue from that customer at the time that consideration is recognized in the income statement. Reclassification as an expense would *not* be permitted if a vendor has an existing supply arrangement with a customer under which (*a*) the vendor is an exclusive supplier of a specific product for a certain period of time and it is probable that the customer will place an order, or (*b*) the customer is required to order a minimum amount of the vendor's products in the future.

Revenue earned by a vendor from a particular customer also may include revenue earned from other entities in a consolidated group that includes the customer. Also, the *inception of an overall relationship* with a customer may occur when a new relationship is established or when a relationship is reestablished with a customer with whom the vendor previously had a business relationship that had been terminated.

Each financial reporting period should stand on its own when applying this guidance on the recharacterization of "negative revenue." Amounts presented as an expense in one period should not be reclassified in a later period even if a credit to expense results. A credit up to the expense previously recognized should be presented in the income statement as a reduction of expense if a reduction in the measured fair value of consideration occurs due to changes in estimates or other factors. A remaining credit, if any, should be presented as an increase in revenue.

ASC 605-50-05-1, 15-2, 25-10 through 25-12, 45-12 through 45-15, 55-116 through 55-117, 55-119 through 55-120, 55-122 through 55-123 Customer's Characterization of Certain Consideration Received from a Vendor

BACKGROUND

In ASC 605-50, *Accounting for Consideration Given by a Vendor to a Customer (Including a Reseller of the Vendor's Products)*, guidance is provided on (*a*) how *vendors* should account for consideration given to customers that are resellers of their products and entities that purchase their products from a reseller, and (*b*) how to measure and when to recognize such consideration in the income statement. The following guidance addresses how *resellers* of a vendor's products should account for cash consideration received from vendors.

ACCOUNTING ISSUES

1. Under what circumstances should a reseller account for cash consideration received from a vendor as (*a*) an adjustment of the vendor's prices for its products or services and presented as a reduction of cost of sales in the reseller's income statement, (*b*) an adjustment of a cost incurred by the reseller and presented as a reduction of that cost in the reseller's income statement, or (*c*) a payment received for assets or services delivered to a vendor and presented as revenue in the reseller's income statement?
2. How should a reseller measure the amount of and when should a reseller recognize a vendor's offer of a rebate or refund of a specific amount of cash consideration payable only if the reseller makes a specified amount of purchases or remains a reseller for a specified time period?

ACCOUNTING GUIDANCE

Scope

The following guidance applies to a customer's accounting for:

- Cash consideration received from a vendor;
- Sales incentives offered to consumers by manufacturers.

Customer's Accounting for Consideration Received from a Vendor

If a vendor's rebate or refund for a specified amount of cash consideration payable under a binding arrangement will occur only if a reseller achieves a cumulative level of purchases or remains a customer for a specified time period, a reseller should reduce its cost of sales based on a systematic and rational allocation of the cash consideration related to each of the underlying transactions resulting in the reseller's progress toward earning the rebate or refund only if receipt of the rebate or refund is *probable* and reasonably estimable. Otherwise, the consideration should be recognized as milestones are achieved.

Although making a reasonable estimate of the amount of future cash rebates or refunds depends on many factors and circumstance that may vary on a case-by-case basis, the existence of the following factors may impair a customer's ability to determine the probability and to reasonably estimate the amount of a rebate or refund:

- The purchases will occur over a relatively long period.
- No historical experience with similar products exists or such experience cannot be applied because of changing circumstances.
- In the past, expected cash rebates or refunds needed significant adjustments.
- The product is affected by significant external factors, such as technological obsolescence or changes in demand.

Changes in estimates of cash rebates or refunds and a vendor's retroactive changes of a previous offer, such as a retroactive increase or decrease in a rebate's amount, are changes in estimates that should be accounted for with a cumulative catch-up adjustment. That is, the cumulative balance of rebates would be revised immediately. Entities should consider whether any portion of such an adjustment would affect inventory, thus requiring that only a portion of the adjustment be reported in the income statement.

It is presumed that cash consideration received by a customer from a vendor is a *reduction* of the vendor's prices for its products or services and should be reported as a reduction of cost of sales in the customer's income statement.

That presumption may be overcome, however, if a vendor's cash consideration to a customer is (*a*) a payment for assets or services delivered to the vendor that should be presented as revenue or other income in the customer's income statement, depending on the circumstances, or (*b*) a reimbursement of the customer's costs to sell the vendor's products or services that should be reported as a reduction of the customer's selling costs in the income statement.

Payment for assets or services. If a vendor receives or will receive in exchange for its cash consideration an identifiable benefit (e.g., goods or services) that is sufficiently separable from the customer's purchases of the vendor's products, the customer should report the payment as revenue in its income statement. Indicators supporting that treatment include (*a*) the fact that the reseller could have entered into an exchange transaction with another party to provide the benefit and (*b*) the fair value of the benefit provided can be reasonably estimated. A customer should reduce its cost of sales reported in the income statement if the vendor's cash consideration for the benefit received exceeds the benefit's estimated fair value.

Reimbursement of customer's costs. If cash consideration paid by a vendor to a reseller is a reimbursement of the customer's specific, incremental, identifiable costs incurred to sell the vendor's products or services, that amount should be reported in the customer's income statement as a reduction of that cost. Cash consideration in excess of a customer's cost, if any, should be reported in the customer's income statement as a reduction of cost of sales.

ASC 605-50-15-2, 25-13 through 25-18, 50-1, 55-108, 55-110 through 55-114 Service Provider's Accounting for Consideration Given to a Manufacturer or Reseller of Equipment

BACKGROUND

Frequently, the customers of a service provider must purchase equipment produced by a manufacturer and sold by a third-party reseller that distributes the equipment without having a direct involvement with the service provider. To increase demand for its service, a service provider, may induce third-party manufacturers or resellers to reduce the price of the equipment.

ACCOUNTING ISSUES

1. Should consideration given by a service provider to a third-party manufacturer or reseller of equipment (*not* the service provider's customer) that provides a benefit to a service provider's customer be described as "cash consideration" or as "other than cash" consideration?
2. If a customer needs certain equipment in order to receive a service from a service provider, is consideration given by the service provider to a third-party manufacturer or a reseller of equipment that benefits a customer of both the service provider and the equipment manufacturer or reseller, in substance, the same as if the service provider had given the consideration directly to the end-customer?
3. Should consideration given by a service provider to a manufacturer or a reseller of equipment (*not* the service provider's customer) be accounted for under the model in ASC 605-50-05-1, 15-2 through 15-3, 25-1 through 25-9, 45-1 through 45-11 if the customer needs the equipment in order to receive a service from a service provider and the consideration can be linked to the benefit received by the service provider's customer?

ACCOUNTING GUIDANCE

If consideration given by a service provider to a third-party manufacturer or reseller that is *not* the service provider's customer can be linked contractually to the benefit that the service provider's customer receives, the service provider should account for that consideration under the ASC 605-50-45-2 through 45-3 as cash or as other than cash.

This guidance is based on the view that consideration given by a service provider to a third-party manufacturer or a reseller that can be linked contractually to the service provider's customer is in substance the same as if the service provider had given the consideration directly to its customer.

There is a presumption that cash consideration should be accounted for as a *reduction* of revenue unless *both* of the following two conditions are met: (*a*) the vendor receives or will receive an identifiable benefit in exchange for the consideration, and (*b*) the vendor can make a reasonable estimate of the fair value of the benefit in condition (*a*). Under the guidance ASC 605-50-45-3, "other than cash consideration" should be accounted for as an expense.

A service provider that gives consideration to a third-party manufacturer or a reseller that provides a benefit to the service provider's customer should describe that consideration based on the form in which the service provider has instructed the third-party manufacturer or reseller that it be given. That is, if a service provider requires that consideration given to its customer by a third-party manufacturer or reseller be in a form other than "cash consideration," as defined in

605-50-45-3, the service provider should describe that consideration as "other than cash" in its application of that guidance. A service provider also should describe such consideration as "other than cash" if the service provider does *not* control the form in which the consideration is given to its customer. If a reseller or third-party manufacturer uses the consideration to reduce a customer's price on equipment purchased, the service provider should describe the consideration given to the third-party manufacturer or reseller as "other than cash."

Disclosure

The following information should be disclosed about such incentive programs:

- The program's features, and
- Amounts recognized in the income statement for such incentive programs and how they were classified in each period presented, if significant.

ASC 605-50-45-16 through 45-20, 55-124 through 55-127 Reseller's Characterization of Sales Incentives Offered to Consumers by Manufacturers

BACKGROUND

The guidance in ASC 605-50-25-10 through 25-12 and 45-12 through 45-14, *Customer Accounting for Certain Consideration Received from a Vendor*, provides that a customer receiving cash from a vendor should reduce its cost of sales in the income statement based on the presumption that the vendor's price is reduced by the cash received. That presumption may be overcome, however, if the cash received is (*a*) a payment for assets or services received from the customer that should be accounted for as revenue or other income in the customer's income statement, or (*b*) a payment to reimburse the customer for costs incurred to sell the vendor's products that should be accounted for as a reduction of those costs in the customer's income statement.

The following guidance addresses a reseller's accounting for sales incentives, such as coupons, offered by manufacturers (vendors) directly to consumers for products that will be purchased from resellers. Depending on the form of the incentive, some are tendered by a consumer directly to a reseller for a reduction in the sales price of a product, while others are sent by the consumer to the manufacturer for a rebate after the product has been purchased from a reseller. In either case, the reseller's gross margin for the product is unaffected. A reseller that agrees to accept an incentive as partial payment of a product's sales price will be reimbursed by the vendor for the amount of the incentive.

ACCOUNTING ISSUE

Should consideration received by a reseller from a vendor as a reimbursement for honoring the vendor's sales incentives offered directly to consumers be recognized as a reduction of the cost of the reseller's purchases from the vendor and, therefore, be accounted for as a reduction of cost of sales under the guidance in ASC 60-50-45-12 through 45-14?

ACCOUNTING GUIDANCE

The term "vendors' sales incentives offered directly to consumers" is limited to a vendor's incentive that meets all of the following criteria (*a*) consumers can use the incentives at any reseller that accepts the manufacturer's incentive as partial payment of the reseller's price for the vendor's product, (*b*) the vendor reimburses resellers directly for the face amount of the incentive, (*c*) the terms governing a reseller's reimbursement for the vendor's sales incentive offered to consumers may be determined only based on the terms of that incentive and must not be influenced by or negotiated in connection with any other incentive arrangement between the vendor and the reseller, and (*d*) the reseller is subject to an expressed or implied agency relationship with the vendor regarding the sales incentive transaction between the vendor and the consumer.

Sales that meet all of the above criteria are *not* covered under the guidance in ASC 605-50-45-12 through 45-14. Sales incentives that do *not* meet all of those criteria should be accounted for under the guidance in (*a*) ASC 605-50-45-2 through 45-3, which provide that a sales incentive should be accounted for as a reduction of revenue (paragraph 45-2) or as an expense (paragraph 45-3), or under the guidance in ASC 605-50-45-12 through 45-14, that is, as a reduction of cost of sales (paragraphs 45-12 and 45-13(b)), or as revenue (paragraphs 45-13(a) and 45-14, as applicable).

The following example illustrates a transaction that meets the above criteria:

- A reseller that purchases a box of cereal from a manufacturer for $3 sells it for $4. The reseller recognizes $4 as revenue and $3 as a cost of the sale of a box of cereal.
- The cereal's manufacturer offers a $.50 coupon to consumers for a limited period of time. The consumer pays $3.50 in cash for the box of cereal and presents a $.50 coupon that the reseller remits to a clearinghouse, which reimburses the $.50 to the reseller.
- Since the guidance in ASC 605-50-45-12 through 45-14 does *not* apply to the transaction discussed in this Issue, the reseller is in the same position as if the consumer had purchased the box of cereal without the coupon. Therefore, the reseller would recognize revenue of $4 and a cost of $3 for the sale of a box of cereal.

CHAPTER 39

ASC 705—COST OF SALES AND SERVICES

CONTENTS

PART I: GENERAL GUIDANCE

ASC 705-10: OVERALL

ASC 705-10 does not provide any unique guidance but rather only provides a link to guidance on accounting for the cost of sales and services in other ASC subtopics.

PART II: INTERPRETIVE GUIDANCE

ASC 705-20: COST OF SALES AND SERVICES—ACCOUNTING FOR CONSIDERATION RECEIVED FROM A VENDOR

IMPORTANT NOTICE: The following two Issues were moved here and amended as a result of the FASB's issuance of ASU 2014-09, *Revenue from Contracts with Customers,* which will supersede most of the guidance in ASC 605 (Revenue Recognition) when it becomes effective for the annual financial reporting periods of public business entities that begin after December 15, 2017, and for the annual financial reporting periods of nonpublic entities that begin after December 15, 2018. However, the original versions of the Issues may be found in Chapter 38, *ASC 605—Revenue Recognition* (ASC 605-50: Overall).

ASC 705-20-25-10 through 25-12, ASC 705-20-25-1 through 25-3 Accounting for Certain Consideration Received from a Vendor (Supplier)

BACKGROUND

The following guidance addresses how entities should account for cash consideration received from vendors under various circumstances.

ACCOUNTING ISSUES

1. Under what circumstances should a reseller account for cash consideration received from a vendor as *(a)* an adjustment of the vendor's prices for its products or services and presented as a reduction of cost of sales in the reseller's income statement, *(b)* an adjustment of a cost incurred by the reseller and presented as a reduction of that cost in the reseller's income statement, or *(c)* a payment received for assets or services delivered to a vendor and presented as revenue in the entity's income statement?
2. How should a reseller measure the amount of, and when should a reseller recognize a vendor's offer of, a rebate or refund of a specific amount of cash consideration payable only if the reseller makes a specified amount of purchases or remains a reseller for a specified time period?

ACCOUNTING GUIDANCE

Scope

The following guidance applies to an entity's accounting for cash consideration received from a vendor under the following circumstances:

- A binding arrangement to achieve a certain cumulative level of purchases or remain a customer for a specified time period
- Consideration in exchange for a good or product
- A reimbursement for costs incurred to sell the vendor's products

ASC 705-20-25-10 provides that if a vendor's rebate or refund for a specified amount of cash consideration payable under a binding arrangement depends on the entity's achievement of a cumulative level of purchases or requires that the entity will remain a customer for a specified time period, the entity should reduce its cost of sales based on a systematic and rational allocation of the cash consideration related to each of the underlying transactions resulting in the entity's progress toward earning the rebate or refund only if receipt of the rebate or refund is *probable* and reasonably estimable. If it is not probable that the entity will receive a rebate or refund and the amount cannot be reasonably estimated, the consideration should be recognized as milestones are achieved.

Consideration from a vendor may be in the form of cash that an entity receives or expects to receive from a vendor or in the form of credit or other items, such as coupons or vouchers, that an entity can apply against amounts that it owes to the vendor. An entity should account for such consideration as a reduction of the purchase price of goods or services purchased from the vendor, except if the consideration consists of one of the following:

- Payment for a distinct good or service (as discussed in ASC 606-10-25-19 through 25-22) that the entity transfers to the vendor.
- A reimbursement for costs that the entity incurred to sell the vendor's products.
- Consideration for sales incentives that manufacturers offer to customers (ASC 705-20-25-1).
- If an entity receives consideration from a vendor for a distinct good or service (see ASC 606-10-25-19 through 25-22) that it transferred to the vendor, the entity should account for that consideration as a sale in accordance with the guidance in ASC 606. If the consideration received exceeds the item's standalone selling price, which is defined as "the price at which an entity would sell a promised good or service separately to a customer," the entity should account for the excess as a reduction of the purchase price of goods or services purchased from the vendor, if any. If the standalone selling price is not directly available, it should be estimated based on the guidance in ASC 606-10-32-33 through 32-35 (ASC 705-20-25-2).
- An entity that receives cash consideration from a vendor as a reimbursement for "specific, incremental, identifiable" costs incurred to sell the vendor's products or services should recognize that amount as a reduction of those costs in the income statement. Any amount of the reimbursement that exceeds the costs being reimbursed should be presented as a reduction of the cost of sales in the entity's income statement (ASC 705-20-25-3).

Although making a reasonable estimate of the amount of future cash rebates or refunds depends on many factors and circumstances that may vary on a case-by-case basis, the existence of the following factors may impair an entity's ability to determine the probability of receiving a rebate or refund and reasonably estimating the amount:

- The related purchases will occur over a relatively long period.
- The entity has no historical experience with similar products or such experience cannot be applied because of changing circumstances.
- In the past, expected cash rebates or refunds needed significant adjustments.
- The product is affected by significant external factors, such as technological obsolescence or changes in demand (ASC 705-20-25-11).

Changes in estimates of cash rebates or refunds and a vendor's retroactive changes of a previous offer, such as a retroactive increase or decrease in a rebate's amount, are changes in estimates that should be accounted for with a cumulative catch-up adjustment. That is, the cumulative balance of recognized rebates would be adjusted to the revised cumulative estimate immediately. Entities should consider whether any portion of such an adjustment would affect other accounts, such as inventory, thus requiring that only a portion of the adjustment be reported in the income statement (ASC 705-20-25-12).

ASC 705-20-25-1 through 25-9 Accounting for Consideration Received from a Vendor (Supplier)

BACKGROUND

The following guidance addresses an entity's (reseller's) accounting for sales incentives, such as coupons, offered by manufacturers (vendors) directly to consumers for products that will be purchased from resellers. Depending on the form of the incentive, some are presented by a consumer directly to a reseller for a reduction in a product's sales price, while others are sent by the consumer to the manufacturer for a rebate after having purchased the product. In either case, the entity's gross margin for the product is unaffected, because a reseller that agrees to accept an incentive as partial payment of a product's sales price will be reimbursed by the vendor for the amount of the incentive.

ACCOUNTING ISSUE

Should consideration received by an entity from a vendor as a reimbursement for honoring a vendor's sales incentives offered directly to consumers be recognized as a reduction of the cost of the reseller's purchases from the vendor and, therefore, be accounted for as a reduction of cost of sales under the guidance in ASC 705-20-25-1 through 25-2? (ASC 705-20-25-6)

ACCOUNTING GUIDANCE

Vendors that sell their products to entities for resale to consumers may offer sales discounts and incentives, such as rebates or coupons, directly to consumers. An entity that has direct contact with consumers may agree to accept those incentives when it sells the products to consumers by reducing the product's price. The entity is reimbursed by the manufacturer for the incentives that it has accepted. In some circumstances, for example, a mail-in rebate, the manufacturer reimburses the consumer directly for a discount or incentive. When a manufacturer reimburses an entity for a discount or incentive that reduces the price that a consumer pays to the entity for a product, the entity's gross margin on the sale of that product is not affected (ASC 705-20-25-4 through 25-5).

For the purpose of applying the guidance in this Issue, a *vendor's sales incentive offered directly to consumers* must meet all of the following criteria:

- A consumer can present the incentive to any entity that sells the vendor's product as partial payment of the price charged.
- The vendor (or a clearinghouse authorized by the vendor) reimburses the entity directly based on the incentive's face value.
- The terms under which a vendor reimburses an entity for an incentive offered to consumers must be determined only by the incentive's terms and must not be influenced or negotiated by the vendor and the entity in conjunction with arrangements between them for other incentives.
- The entity is in an expressed or implied agency relationship with the vendor in the sales incentive transaction between the vendor and the consumer (ASC 705-20-25-7).

If an entity's sales incentive arrangements meet all of the criteria listed in ASC 705-20-25-7, it should not account for consideration received from a vendor as a reduction of the purchase price of the goods or services acquired from the vendor and should consider the guidance in ASC 606, *Revenue from Contracts with Customers*. However, sales incentive arrangements that do not meet all of the criteria in ASC 705-20-25-7 should be accounted for as a reduction of the purchase price of the goods or services that the entity acquired from the vendor.

CHAPTER 40

ASC 710—COMPENSATION—GENERAL

CONTENTS

PART I: GENERAL GUIDANCE

ASC 710-10: OVERALL

OVERVIEW

Deferred compensation contracts are accounted for individually on an accrual basis. Such contracts ordinarily include certain requirements such as continued employment for a specified period of time, availability for consulting services, and agreements not to compete after retirement. The estimated amounts to be paid under each contract are accrued in a systematic and rational manner over the period of active employment from the initiation of the contract, unless it is evident that future services expected to be received by the employer are commensurate with the payments or a portion of the payments to be made. If elements of both current and future services are present, only the portion applicable to the current services is accrued.

BACKGROUND

The main source of U.S. GAAP for deferred compensation contracts is ASC 710 and ASC 715 (Compensation—Retirement Benefits). If individual deferred compensation contracts, as a group, are tantamount to a pension plan, they are accounted for in accordance with the U.S. GAAP for pension plans, discussed in ASC 715-30 (Defined Benefit Plans—Pension).

If individual deferred compensation contracts are, as a group, equivalent to a plan for postretirement benefits other than pensions, they are accounted for in accordance with the U.S. GAAP on postretirement benefits, discussed in ASC 715-60 (Defined Benefit Plans—Other Post-Retirement).

PRACTICE NOTE: Professional judgment is required to determine whether individual contracts are equivalent to a pension or postretirement plan.

ACCOUNTING STANDARDS

According to ASC 710, deferred compensation contracts are accounted for on an individual basis for each employee. If a deferred compensation contract is based on current and future employment, only the amounts attributable to the current portion of employment are accrued (ASC 710-10-25-9, 10).

If a deferred compensation contract contains benefits payable for the life of a beneficiary, the total liability is based on the beneficiary's life expectancy or on the estimated cost of an annuity contract that would provide sufficient funds to pay the required benefits (ASC 710-10-30-1).

The total liability for deferred compensation contracts is determined by the terms of each individual contract. The amount of the periodic accrual, computed from the first day of the employment contract, must total no less than the then present value of the benefits provided for in the contract. The periodic accruals are made systematically over the active term of employment.

Illustration of Calculating Deferred Compensation

A deferred compensation contract provides for the payment of $50,000 per year for five years, beginning one year after the end of the employee's ten-year contract. A 10% interest rate is appropriate.

The present value for the five $50,000 payments at the end of ten years is determined as follows:

Present value of $50,000 in five years	$ 31,045
Present value of $50,000 in four years	34,150
Present value of $50,000 in three years	37,565
Present value of $50,000 in two years	41,320
Present value of $50,000 in one year	45,455
Total present value of benefits at end of employment	$189,535

In order to have available the funds required to pay the benefits in accordance with the contract, $189,535 must be accumulated over ten years. To find the amount of the annual accrual that earning 10% interest will total $189,535 at the end of ten years, assuming that payments are made at the beginning of each year over the 10-year period, the following formula for the value of an annuity due may be used:

$$\$189{,}535 = R\,(17.531^{*})$$

$$R = \$10{,}811$$

* Amount of an annuity due at 10% for 10 periods.

COMPENSATED ABSENCES

Compensated absences arise from employees' absences from employment because of illness, holiday, vacation, or other reasons. ASC 420 establishes U.S. GAAP for employees' compensated absences. When an employer expects to pay an employee for compensated absences, a liability for the estimated probable future payments must be accrued if all the following conditions are met (ASC 710-10-25-1):

- The employee's right to receive compensation for the future absences is attributable to services already performed by the employee.
- The employee's right to receive the compensation for the future absences is vested, or accumulates.
- It is probable that the compensation will be paid.
- The amount of compensation is reasonably estimable.

If no accrual is made because the fourth criterion is not met, the fact that the employer meets the first three conditions and not the fourth condition must be disclosed in the financial statements.

Vested rights are those that have been earned by the employee for services already performed. They are not contingent on future services by the employee and are an obligation of the employer even if the employee leaves the employer. Rights that accumulate are nonvesting rights to compensated absences that are earned and can be carried forward to succeeding years. Rights that accumulate increase an employee's benefits in one or more years subsequent to the year in which they are earned. An employer does not have to accrue a liability for nonvesting rights to compensated absences that expire at the end of the year in which they are earned, because they do not accumulate (ASC 710-10-25-3).

Nonvesting sick pay benefits that accumulate and can be carried forward to succeeding years are given special treatment by ASC 710. If payment of nonvesting accumulating sick pay benefits depends on the future illness of the employee, an employer is not required to accrue a liability for such payments. The reasons cited in ASC 710 for this exception are (*a*) cost/benefit, (*b*) materiality, and (*c*) the reliability of estimating the days an employee will be sick in succeeding years. This exception does not apply in circumstances in which the employer pays the sick pay benefits even though the employee is not actually sick. An employer's general policy for the payment of nonvesting accumulating sick pay benefits should govern the accounting for such payments (ASC 710-10-25-7).

PRACTICE POINTER: One issue that must be resolved in recognizing the expense and liability for compensated absences is the rate of compensation to use—the current rate or the rate expected to apply when the compensated absence is taken by the employee. In situations in which the rate of compensation increases rapidly and/or a long period of time lapses between the time the compensated absence is earned and taken by the employee, the rate of compensation used may be significant. U.S. GAAP does not provide guidance on this issue. Other authoritative standards may provide some help in making this decision. For example, net periodic pension cost is determined based on the projected benefit obligation, which includes expected future increases in compensation. If the difference in the amount of liability for compensated absences, when measured by the current and expected future rates of compensation, is material, the latter more faithfully measures the obligation and expense of the employer.

Once a total amount of liability for compensated absences is determined, the amount expected to require the use of current assets should be classified as a current liability. The remaining balance should be presented as a noncurrent liability.

PART II: INTERPRETIVE GUIDANCE

ASC 710-10: OVERALL

ASC 710-10-05-8 through 05-9, 15-8 through 15-10, 25-15 through 25-18; 35-2 through 35-4, 45-2 through 45-4; ASC 260-10-60-1; ASC-810-15-10 Accounting for Deferred Compensation Arrangements Where Amounts Earned Are Held in a Rabbi Trust and Invested

---

PRACTICE POINTER: Under the guidance in ASC 810-10-05-8 through 05-8A, 15-12 through 15-17, 25-37 through 25-44, 30-1 through 30-4, 30-7 through 30-9, 35-3 through 35-5, 45-25, 50-2AA through 50-7, 50-9 through 50-10, 55-16 through 55-49, 55-93 through 55-181, 55-183 through 55-205, 60-13; ASC 323-10-45-4; ASC 712-10-60-2; ASC 715-10-60-3, 60-7; ASC 860-10-60-2; ASC 954-810-15-3, 45-2; ASC 958-810-15-4, an entity is required to consolidate a variable interest entity if the entity has a controlling interest in the variable entity. ASC 810-10-25-38 through 25-38G provides guidance for determining whether an entity has a controlling financial interest in a variable interest entity.

BACKGROUND

Some employers have set up deferred compensation arrangements under which amounts—such as bonuses earned by a select group of management or highly compensated employees—are placed in a grantor trust, which is commonly referred to as a "rabbi trust." Amounts placed in a rabbi trust are *not* tax deductible to the employer, and the employee is *not* taxed on deferred amounts until that compensation is paid. A rabbi trust qualifies for income tax purposes only if its terms state explicitly that the employer can use assets held by the trust to satisfy the claims of its creditors in bankruptcy.

The following are the types of deferred compensation plans in which a Rabbi Trust may be held:

- Plan A—Diversification of the trust's assets is *not* permitted. The funds must be invested in an employer's stock and settlement must be in a fixed number of shares of the employer's stock.
- Plans B—Diversification of the trust's assets is *not* permitted. The funds must be invested in an employer's stock and settlement may be in cash or shares of the employer's stock.

- Plan C—Diversification of the trust's assets into the securities of other entities is permitted after a certain time period (e.g., six months), but an employee has elected *not* to diversify the trust's assets, so the funds are invested only in the employer's stock and would be settled in cash, shares of the employer's stock, or diversified assets.
- Plan D—Diversification of the trust's assets is permitted after a certain time period (e.g., six months) and an employee *has* elected to diversify the trust's assets. Settlement may be in cash, shares of the employer's stock, or diversified assets.

The following accounting guidance does not apply to stock appreciation rights (SARs), even if they are funded through a rabbi trust.

ACCOUNTING ISSUES

- Should an employer be required to consolidate the accounts of a rabbi trust in its financial statements?
- How should an employer report investments in a rabbi trust?
- How does an employee's election to diversify the assets held by a rabbi trust into nonemployer securities affect the accounting for the trust's assets and for the deferred compensation obligation?

ACCOUNTING GUIDANCE

1. Employers should consolidate in their financial statements the accounts of rabbi trusts in all plans.
2. Assets held by a rabbi trust should be accounted for as follows:
    a. Employer stock held in a rabbi trust under Plans A, B, and C should be classified in equity and accounted for similar to treasury stock and reported in an employer's consolidated financial statements at acquisition cost without adjustment for changes in the fair value of the employer's stock
    b. If diversification is prohibited and the obligation must be settled in a fixed number of an employer's shares, as under Plan A, the employer's deferred compensation obligation should be classified as an equity instrument without adjustment for changes in the fair value of the employer's stock. However, a deferred compensation obligation for a rabbi trust under Plans B and C, which can be settled in cash, should be classified as a liability that should be adjusted for changes in the fair value of the employer's stock by a corresponding charge (or credit) to compensation cost.
    c. Diversified assets held by a rabbi trust under Plan D should be accounted for in accordance with generally accepted accounting principles appropriate for each specific asset; for example, debt securities should be accounted for in accordance with the guidance in Subtopic 320-10, *Investments-Debt Securities;* and equity securities should be accounted for based on the guidance in Subtopic 321-10, *Investments-Equity Securities.* A deferred compensation obligation under Plan D should be classified as a liability. Debt securities held by a rabbi trust may be classified as trading at acquisition.
    d. If diversification is permitted (Plans C and D) and the obligation is not required to be settled in a fixed number of the employer's shares, the deferred compensation obligation should be adjusted for changes in its fair value. Deferred compensation cost should be adjusted by a corresponding charge (or credit) to compensation cost. Changes in the fair value of the deferred compensation obligation should *not* be recognized in comprehensive income even if changes in the fair value of the assets held by the rabbi trust are recognized in comprehensive income in accordance with the guidance in ASC 320. Diversified assets held by a rabbi trust may be classified in the trading category at acquisition.

The following is guidance for *earnings per share* (EPS) calculations:

1. Treat employer shares held by a rabbi trust in the same manner as treasury stock in EPS calculations and exclude the amount from the denominator in the calculation of basic and diluted EPS.
2. Include the deferred compensation obligation in the denominator of the EPS calculation in accordance with the guidance in ASC 260-1-45.
3. Include employer shares in Plan A in the basic and diluted EPS calculations, because ASC 260-10-45-13 requires that treatment if an obligation must be settled by delivering the employer's shares.
4. Include employer shares in the diluted EPS calculation only for rabbi trusts held under Plans B, C, or D, because according to the guidance in ASC 260-10-45-30, and 45-45 through 45-46, that treatment is required if an obligation can be settled by delivery of cash, shares of employer stock, or diversified assets.

DISCUSSION

- A rabbi trust should be consolidated, because it is not bankruptcy proof. That is, an employer can use the trust's assets to settle the claims of general creditors in bankruptcy. Consolidation of rabbi trusts is common practice and is consistent with the treatment implied in the discussion in ASC 715-60-55-26; ASC 710-10-60-2, Plan Assets under FASB Statement 106.
- A consolidated entity holding a parent's stock must treat it as treasury stock in consolidation and subtract it from equity.
- The decision to classify a deferred compensation obligation as an equity instrument under plan A, which does not permit diversification and must be settled in the employer's shares, was made, because that treatment conforms to the framework established in ASC 815-10-15-78, 15-25-15, 55-52; ASC 815-40-05-1 through 05-4, 05-10 through 05-12, 25-1 through 25-5, 25-7 through 25-20, 25-22 through 25-24, 25-26 through 25-35, 25-37 through 25-40, 30-1, 35-1 through 35-2, 35-6, 35-8 through 35-13, 40-1 through 40-2; 50-1 through 50-5, 55-1 through 55-18; ASC 460-10-60-14; ASC 480-10-55-63; ASC 505-10-60-5, Accounting for Derivative Financial Instruments Indexed to, and Potentially Settled in, a Company's Own Stock (see Chapter 50, *ASC 815—Derivatives and Hedging*). Subsequent changes in the fair value of an employer's stock are not recognized for the same reason.
- The decision to recognize changes in the fair value of the deferred compensation obligation in income by adjusting compensation cost even if the diversified assets are recognized as available-for-sale securities is based on the view of the FASB staff that the award is a stock-based compensation award and that authoritative literature, such as ASC 840-40-25-4 through 25-5, 35-4, 55-79 through 55-80, 55-82 through 55-84, 55-86 through 55-88, 55-90 through 55-92, and 55-94, requires that changes in the value of such awards subsequent to an employee's service period be recognized in income as an adjustment of compensation cost.

ASC 710-10-15-3, 25-12 through 25-14, S15-1, S25-1, S99-1 Lump-Sum Payments under Union Contracts

BACKGROUND

In connection with the signing of a new union contract, a company might give employees one or more lump-sum payments instead of, or in addition to, a base wage rate increase. Typically, employees are not required to refund any portion of such lump-sum payments if they leave the company before the contract period ends. In addition, employees who leave the company generally are replaced by other union members at the same base wage rate but replacements receive no lump-sum payments.

ACCOUNTING ISSUE

Should lump-sum payments made to employees in connection with the signing of a new union contract be (1) charged to expense immediately or (2) deferred and amortized over the contract period or some portion of the contract period?

ACCOUNTING GUIDANCE

Lump-sum payments made to employees in connection with the signing of a new union contract may be deferred provided that the payments clearly will benefit future periods in the form of lower base wage rates. The deferred charge should be amortized over periods clearly benefited, but not longer than the contract period.

It was noted that the terms and conditions of those types of arrangements vary and must be reviewed to determine how to account for the lump-sum payments.

DISCUSSION

Those who supported deferral argued that lump-sum payments that result in lower wage costs over the contract period provide a future economic benefit to the entity. They believed that such payments represent a cost of the contract, which will benefit the entity over the entire contract period and consequently should be deferred and recognized in the periods in which services are performed.

Proponents also referred to certain pronouncements that recommend recognition of compensation costs over the periods during which an employee performs services. For example, the goal of recognizing pension costs over the periods in which employees provide services are discussed in ASC 715, Compensation - Retirement Benefits. Under the guidance in ASC 710-10-15-4 through 15-5, 25-9 through 25-11, 30-1 through 30-2; ASC 310-10-45-4, 50-14; ASC 360-10-50-1, ASC 715-20-60-1; ASC 505-10-50-2; and ASC 835-30-35-3, employers are required to accrue and amortize amounts to be paid to employees under deferred compensation contracts for current services in a systematic and rational manner over the period of active employment beginning when the employer enters into the contract.

To refute the argument of those who compare lump-sum payments to bonuses for past services, proponents of deferral also argued that such payments had not been promised to the employees before the union contract negotiation; all contractually required payments have already been made to the employees; and the only reason for making those payments is to obtain a lower base wage rate over the contract period.

ASC 710-10-15-3, 25-5 Accounting for Sabbatical Leave and Other Similar Benefits Pursuant to FASB Statement No. 43, *Accounting for Compensated Absences*

BACKGROUND

Some entities, such as colleges and universities, provide a benefit to their employees, known as a sabbatical leave. Under sabbatical leave, employees are entitled to a compensated absence for a specified period of time, such as three months, after having worked for the employer for a specified period of time (e.g., seven years). An employee is compensated during a sabbatical but is not required to perform any duties for the employer. Employees are not entitled to compensation for unused sabbatical leave if their employment terminates before having worked for the full eligibility period. Further, employees that have worked for the specified period but did not avail themselves of the benefit are not entitled to the benefit if their employment is terminated.

The guidance in ASC 710-10-25-1 provides that employers should accrue a liability for employees' compensation for future absences if certain conditions are met. Condition 6b states that "the obligation relates to rights that vest or accumulate." In addition, the guidance in ASC 710-10-25-1(b) defines *accumulate* to mean "that earned but unused rights to compensated absences may be carried forward to one or more periods subsequent to that in which they are earned even though there may be a limit to the amount that can be carried forward." Based on that guidance, some question whether a sabbatical benefit should be accrued even though the benefit does not vest.

ACCOUNTING ISSUE

Does an employee's right to a compensated absence under a sabbatical or similar benefit accumulate in accordance with the guidance in ASC 710-10-25-1 if the employee must complete a minimum service period and if the benefit does not increase with additional years of service?

SCOPE

The following guidance is limited to sabbatical or similar arrangements under which an employee is *not* required to perform direct or indirect services for or on behalf the employer during that absence. It does *not* apply to public colleges or universities, even those that have adopted GASB-20, because the guidance in ASC 710 conflicts with that in GASB-16.

ACCOUNTING GUIDANCE

Compensation costs associated with an employee's right to a sabbatical or other similar arrangement should be accrued over the required service period if, under that arrangement, (*a*) the employee is required to complete a minimum period of service, and (*b*) the benefit does *not* increase with additional years of service accumulated in accordance with the guidance in ASC 710-10-25-1(b) for arrangements under which an employee is *not* required to perform duties for the employer during a compensated absence. All of the other conditions in ASC 710-10-25-1 also must be met.

CHAPTER 41

ASC 712—COMPENSATION—NONRETIREMENT POSTEMPLOYMENT BENEFITS

GENERAL GUIDANCE

ASC 712-10: OVERALL

OVERVIEW

The FASB has established accounting standards for employers that provide benefits for former or inactive employees after employment, but before retirement (*postemployment benefits*). Employers are required to recognize the obligation to provide postemployment benefits in accordance with ASC 712 if the criteria for accrual established in that pronouncement are met. If the ASC 712 criteria are not met, the employer must account for postemployment benefits when it is probable that a liability has been incurred and the amount of that liability can be reasonably estimated, in accordance with ASC 450 (Contingencies).

TERMINATION BENEFITS

Termination benefits are classified as either *special* or *contractual*. Special termination benefits are those that are offered to employees for a short period in connection with the termination of their employment. Contractual termination benefits are those that are required by the terms of an existing plan or agreement and that are provided only on the occurrence of a specified event, such as early retirement or the closing of a facility (ASC 712-10-05-2).

POSTEMPLOYMENT BENEFITS

Accrual is required for an obligation for postemployment benefits that meet the following criteria in ASC 710-10-25-1 (ASC 712-10-25-4):

- The employer's obligation relating to employees' rights to receive compensation for future compensated absences is attributable to employees' services already rendered.
- The obligation relates to rights that vest or accumulate.
- Payment of the compensation is probable.
- The amount can be estimated reasonably.

If an obligation for postemployment benefits is not accrued in accordance with either ASC 712 or ASC 450 only because the amount cannot be estimated, the financial statements shall disclose that fact (ASC 712-10-50-2).

CHAPTER 42

ASC 715—COMPENSATION—RETIREMENT BENEFITS

CONTENTS

PART I: GENERAL GUIDANCE

ASC 715-10: OVERALL

OVERVIEW

U.S. GAAP for employers' accounting for pension plans emphasizes the determination of annual pension expense (identified as net periodic pension cost) and the presentation of the funded status of the pension plan. Net periodic pension cost is made up of several components that reflect different aspects of the employer's financial arrangements, as well as the cost of benefits earned by employees.

ASC 715 requires the accrual of postretirement benefits other than pensions in a manner similar to the recognition of net periodic pension cost in accounting for pension plan costs. The accounting requirements for postemployment and postretirement benefit plans are similar to the accounting requirements for pension plans and differ only where there are compelling reasons for different treatments.

In applying principles of accrual accounting for pension plans and postretirement benefits, the FASB emphasizes three fundamental features:

1. *Delayed income statement recognition*—Changes in the pension and postretirement benefit obligations and changes in the value of pension and plan assets are recognized on the balance sheet as they occur, through changes in the pension and postretirement benefit assets and/or liabilities; however, on the income statement these changes are not recognized as they occur, but rather systematically and gradually over subsequent periods. Items recognized on the balance sheet immediately but deferred for income statement recognition are included in accumulated other comprehensive income.
2. *Net cost*—The recognized consequences of events and transactions affecting a pension or postretirement benefit plan are reported for each type of plan as a single net amount in the employer's financial statements. This approach results in the aggregation of items that would be presented separately for any other part of the employer's

operations: the compensation cost of benefits, the interest cost resulting from deferred payment of those benefits, and the results of investing pension or plan assets.

3. *Offsetting*—Pension plan assets and liabilities are shown net in the employer's statement of financial position, even though the liability has not been settled. Also, the return on plan assets reduces postretirement benefit cost in the employer's statement of income. The assets may still be controlled and substantial risks and rewards associated with both are clearly borne by the employer.

Employers may cancel (settle) or reduce (curtail) a pension plan. A *settlement of a pension plan* is an irrevocable action that relieves the employer (or the plan) of primary responsibility for an obligation and eliminates significant risks related to the obligation and the assets used to effect the settlement. Examples of transactions that constitute a settlement include (*a*) making lump-sum cash payments to plan participants in exchange for their rights to receive specified pension benefits and (*b*) purchasing nonparticipating annuity contracts to cover vested benefits.

Curtailment is a significant reduction in, or an elimination of, defined benefit accruals for present employees' future services. Examples of curtailments are (*a*) termination of employees' services earlier than expected, which may or may not involve closing a facility or discontinuing a segment of a business, and (*b*) termination or suspension of a plan so that employees do not earn additional defined benefits for future services.

The FASB also has established accounting standards for employers that provide benefits for former or inactive employees after employment, but before retirement (*postemployment benefits*). Employers are required to recognize the obligation to provide postemployment benefits in accordance with ASC 712 (Compensation—Nonretirement Postemployment Benefits) if the criteria for accrual established in that pronouncement are met. If ASC 710 criteria are not met, the employer must account for postemployment benefits when it is probable that a liability has been incurred and the amount of that liability can be reasonably estimated, in accordance with ASC 450 (Contingencies).

BACKGROUND

Employment is based on an explicit or implicit exchange agreement. The employee agrees to provide services for the employer in exchange for a current wage, a pension benefit, and frequently other benefits such as death, dental, disability. Although pension benefits and some other benefits are not paid currently, they represent deferred compensation that must be accounted for as part of the employee's total compensation package.

Pension benefits usually are paid to retired employees or their survivors on a periodic basis, but may be paid in a single lump sum. Other benefits, such as death and disability, may also be provided through a pension plan. Most pension plans also provide benefits upon early retirement or termination of service.

A pension plan may be contributory or noncontributory; that is, the employees may be required to contribute to the plan (contributory), or the entire cost of the plan may be borne by the employer (noncontributory). A pension plan may be funded or unfunded; that is, the employees and/or the employer may make cash contributions to a pension plan trustee (funded), or the employer may make only credit entries on its books reflecting the pension liability under the plan (unfunded).

PRACTICE NOTE: A qualified pension plan under the Employee Retirement Income Security Act (ERISA) has to be funded. Every year the plan actuary must determine the minimum funding for the defined benefit pension plan. If the plan fails to meet the minimum funding requirement, a penalty tax is imposed on the employer on the funding deficiency.

Although interest cost on the pension liability and the expected return on a pension plan's assets increase or decrease net periodic pension cost, they are considered financial costs rather than employee compensation costs. Financial costs can be controlled by the manner in which the employer provides financing for the pension plan. An employer can eliminate interest cost by funding the plan completely or by purchasing annuity contracts to settle all pension obligations. The return on plan assets can be increased by the contribution of more assets to the pension fund.

Pension Plan Accounting

The assets of a pension plan usually are kept in a trust account, segregated from the assets of the employer. The employer makes periodic contributions to the pension trust account and, if the plan is contributory, so do employees. The plan assets are invested in stocks, bonds, real estate, and other types of investments. Plan assets are increased by contributions and earnings and gains on investments and are decreased by losses on investments, payment of pension benefits, and administrative expenses. The employer usually cannot withdraw plan assets placed in a trust account. An exception arises, however, when the plan assets exceed the pension obligation and the plan is terminated. In this event, the pension plan agreement may permit the employer to withdraw the excess amount of plan assets, providing that all other existing pension plan obligations have been satisfied by the employer. Under U.S. GAAP, pension plan assets that are not effectively restricted for the payment of pension benefits or segregated in a trust are not considered pension plan assets.

Accounting and reporting for a pension plan (defined benefit plan) as a separate reporting entity are covered by ASC 960 (Plan Accounting—Defined Benefit Pension Plans).

Deferred Compensation Plan

A deferred compensation plan is a contractual agreement that specifies that a portion of the employee's compensation will be set aside and paid in future periods as retirement benefits. ASC 715 covers deferred compensation plans that are in substance pension plans.

Postemployment and postretirement benefits generally are considered a form of deferred compensation to an employee because an employer provides these types of benefits in exchange for an employee's services. Thus, these benefits must be measured properly and recognized in the financial statements and, if the amount is material, financial statement disclosure may be required. For convenient discussion, this chapter uses the term *postretirement benefits* to mean postretirement benefits other than pensions. Practice sometimes uses the abbreviation "OPEB" (other postretirement employee benefits) with the same meaning.

POSTEMPLOYMENT BENEFITS

ASC 715 also specifies U.S. GAAP for postemployment benefits and generally applies to benefits provided to former or inactive employees, their beneficiaries, and covered dependents after employment, but before retirement. Benefits may be provided in cash or in kind and may be paid as a result of a disability, layoff, death, or other event. Benefits may be paid immediately upon cessation of active employment, or over a specified period of time.

Postemployment benefits that meet the following requirements are accounted for in accordance with Subtopic 710-10 (ASC 712-10-25-4):

- The employer's obligation relating to employees' rights to receive compensation for future compensated absences is attributable to employees' services already rendered.
- The obligation relates to rights that vest or accumulate.
- Payment of the compensation is probable.
- The amount can be estimated reasonably.

Postemployment benefits that are covered by ASC 715 but do not meet the above criteria are accounted for in accordance with ASC 450. ASC 450 requires recognition of a loss contingency, including a liability for postemployment benefits, when the following conditions are met (ASC 712-10-25-5):

- Information available prior to issuance of the financial statements indicates that it is probable that an asset has been impaired or a liability incurred at the date of the financial statements.
- The amount of loss can be reasonably estimated.

If an obligation for postemployment benefits is not accrued in accordance with either ASC 712 (Compensation—Nonretirement Postemployment Benefits) or ASC 450 only because the amount cannot be estimated, the financial statements shall disclose that fact (ASC 712-10-50-2).

ASC 715 amends ASC 710 with regard to the method of accruing an employer's obligation under deferred compensation contracts that are not tantamount to a plan for pension or other postretirement benefits. ASC 715 requires the employer to make periodic accruals, so that the cost of the deferred compensation is attributed to the appropriate years of an employee's service, in accordance with the terms of the contract between the employer and that employee.

PRACTICE NOTE: The employer must make the attribution in a systematic and rational manner. By the time an employee becomes fully eligible for the deferred compensation specified in the contract, the accrued amount should equal the then present value of the expected future payments of deferred compensation.

Illustrations of Accruals Required by ASC 715

Example 1: *Employee must remain in service for a number of years to be eligible for the deferred compensation.*

A deferred compensation contract with a newly hired employee provides for a payment of $100,000 upon termination of employment, provided the employee remains in service for at least four years.

The employer makes annual accruals during each of the first four years of this employee's service, to recognize the portion of deferred compensation cost attributable to each of these years. To make these annual accruals, the employer starts by making reasonable assumptions about (*a*) the employee's anticipated retirement date and (*b*) the discount rate for making computations of present value.

If the employer assumes that the employee will remain in service for a total of nine years (including five years after becoming fully eligible for the deferred compensation), and the discount rate is 8%, the present value of the $100,000 deferred compensation at the end of the fourth year will be $68,058 (present value of $100,000 payable at the end of five years at 8% discount).

Accruals are made for each of the first four years, so that the balance in the accrued liability account at the end of the fourth year will be $68,058. The simplest way to accomplish this is on a straight-line basis, as follows:

Accrued amount anticipated at end of fourth year	$68,058
Annual accrual during each of first four years (1/4 of $68,058)	$17,015

This computation results in the recognition of $17,015 deferred compensation cost during each of the first four years of the employee's service. The balance in the accrued liability account at the end of the fourth year, when the employee is eligible to terminate and collect the deferred compensation, is $68,058, the present value of the $100,000 deferred compensation payable five years later. (The five years represent the anticipated total service of nine years, less the four years already served.)

Next, assume the employee remains in service throughout the fifth year and is still expected to complete the nine-year term originally anticipated. The accrued liability is adjusted as of the end of the fifth year to reflect the present value of the deferred compensation, which is $73,503 (present value of $100,000 payable at the end of four years at 8% discount).

The cost recognized for the fifth year will therefore be $5,445, determined as follows:

Accrued amount at end of fifth year	$ 73,503
Accrued amount at end of fourth year	(68,058)
Cost recognized in fifth year	$ 5,445

Example 2: *Employee is eligible in the same year the contract is signed.*

An employee is hired on January 1, 20X8. The contract provides for a payment of $20,000 upon termination of employment, provided the employee remains in service for at least six months. The employer anticipates that the employee will remain in service for three years. The assumed discount rate is 8%.

The employee is still in service at the end of calendar year 20X8. Having completed at least six months of service, the employee is eligible to terminate and collect the deferred compensation. The accrual as of December 31, 20X8, is $17,147, the present value of $20,000 payable at the end of two years at 8% discount. (The two years represent the originally anticipated service of three years, less the one year of 20X8 already served.) The entire amount of the accrual is recognized as a deferred compensation cost in 20X8, since the employee achieved full eligibility by the end of the year.

If the employee remains in service throughout 20X9 and all assumptions remain unchanged, the amount of the accrued liability as of December 31, 20X9, is adjusted to $18,519, the present value of $20,000 at the end of one year at 8% discount.

The cost recognized in 20X9 is therefore $1,372, determined as follows:

Accrued amount at end of 20X9	$18,519
Accrued amount at end of 20X8	(17,147)
Cost recognized in 20X9	$1,372

ASC 715-20: DEFINED BENEFIT PLANS—GENERAL

FINANCIAL STATEMENT DISCLOSURE

Disclosures by Public Entities about Pension Plans and Other Postretirement Plans

ASC 715 requires the following information to be provided for each period for which an income statement is presented (ASC 715-20-50-1):

- Reconciliation of beginning and ending balances of the benefit obligation showing separately the effects of service cost, interest cost, contributions by plan participants, actuarial gains and losses, changes in foreign currency exchange rates, benefits paid, plan amendments, business combinations, divestitures, curtailments, settlements, and special termination benefits
- Reconciliation of beginning and ending balances of the fair value of plan assets, showing separately the effects of actual return on plan assets, changes in foreign currency exchange rates, contributions by the employer, contributions by plan participants, benefits paid, business combinations, divestitures, and settlements
- Funded status of the plan, and the amounts recognized in the statement of financial position, with separate disclosure of assets, current liabilities, and noncurrent liabilities
- Information about plan assets:
  - Narrative description of investment policies and strategies
  - For each class of plan assets, the percentage of the fair value of total plan assets held as of the financial statement date
  - Narrative description of the basis used to determine the overall expected long-term rate-of-return-on-asset assumption
  - Information that enables users of financial statements to assess the inputs and valuation techniques used to develop fair value measurements of plan assets at the reporting date
  - Additional asset categories and additional information about specific assets within a category are encouraged if they are expected to be useful in understanding the risks associated with each asset category and its expected long-term rate of return
- For defined benefit pension plans, the accumulated benefit obligation
- The benefits expected to be paid in each of the next five fiscal years and in the aggregate for the five fiscal years thereafter
- The employer's best estimate of contributions expected to be paid to the plan during the next fiscal year beginning after the date of the latest statement of financial position
- The amount of net periodic benefit cost recognized, showing separately the service cost component, the interest cost component, the expected return on plan assets, the transition asset or obligation component, the gain or loss component, the prior service cost or credit component, and amount of gains or losses recognized due to a plan settlement or curtailment
- The net gain or loss and prior service cost or credit included in other comprehensive income during the period

- The net gain or loss, prior service cost or credit, and transition asset or obligation included in net periodic benefit cost during the period and removed from accumulated other comprehensive income via an entry to other comprehensive income
- Amounts included in accumulated other comprehensive income and not yet recognized as a component of net periodic benefit cost, separately showing the net gain or loss, net prior service cost or credit, and net transition asset or obligation
- On a weighted-average basis, the following assumptions: discount rates, rates of compensation increase, expected long-term rates of return on plan assets, and interest crediting rates
- Assumed health care cost trend rates for the next year used to determine expected cost of benefits covered by the plan, and a general description of the direction and pattern of change in the assumed trend rates thereafter
- Amounts and types of securities of the employer and related parties included in the plan assets
- Any alternative method used to amortize prior service amounts or net gains and losses
- Any substantive commitments used as the basis for accounting for the benefit obligation
- The cost of providing special or contractual termination benefits recognized during the period and a description of the nature of the event
- Explanation of the following information: (1) reasons for significant gains and losses related to changes in the defined benefit obligation for the period, and (2) any other significant change in the benefit obligation or plan assets not otherwise apparent in the other required disclosures
- If applicable, the election to measure plan assets and benefit obligations using the month-end that is closest to the employer's fiscal year end in accordance with ASC 715-30-35-63A or ASC 715-60-35-123A and the month-end measurement date

---

PRACTICE NOTE: If an employer determines the measurement date of plan assets in accordance with ASC 715-30-35-63A or ASC 715-60-35-123A and the employer contributes assets to the plan between the measurement date and its fiscal year-end, the employer must not adjust the fair value of each class of plan assets for the effects of the contribution. However, the employer must disclose the amount of the contribution to permit reconciliation of the total fair value of all the classes of plan assets to the ending balance of the fair value of plan assets, as well as to permit reconciliation of the total fair value of all plan assets in the fair value hierarchy to the ending balance of the fair value of plan assets (ASC 715-20-50-1).

Disclosures by Employers with Two or More Plans

Employers with two or more plans shall aggregate information for all defined benefit pension plans and for all other defined benefit postretirement plans unless disaggregating in groups is considered to provide more useful information (ASC 715-20-50-2). If aggregate disclosures are presented, the following information, as of the date of each statement of financial position presented, is required (ASC 715-20-50-3):

- For pension plans, the projected benefit obligation and fair value of plan assets for plans with projected benefit obligations in excess of plan assets, and the accumulated benefit obligation and fair value of plan assets for plans with accumulated benefit obligations in excess of plan assets.
- For other postretirement benefit plans, the accumulated postretirement benefit obligation and fair value of plan assets for plans with accumulated postretirement benefit obligations in excess of plan assets.

The liability presented is current to the extent that the actuarial present value of benefits to be paid within the next year, or operating cycle if longer, exceeds the fair value of plan assets. This determination is to be made on a plan-by-plan basis. Otherwise, the liability is noncurrent (ASC 715-20-45-3).

Multiemployer Plan Disclosures

[See the *Multiple-Employer Plans* main section in this chapter for the disclosure requirements related to their plans.]

Reduced Disclosures for Nonpublic Companies

A nonpublic entity is not required to present the complete set of information identified earlier as being required for public entities. The required disclosures for a nonpublic entity are as follows (ASC 715-20-50-5):

- The benefit obligation, fair value of plan assets, and funded status of the plan.
- Employer contributions, participant contributions, and benefits paid.
- Information about plan assets:
  - — A narrative description of investment policies and strategies.
  - — For each class of plan assets (e.g., equity securities, debt securities, real estate), the percentage of the fair value of total plan asset held as of the measurement date used for each statement of financial position presented.
  - — A narrative description of the basis used to determine the overall expected long-term rate-of-return-on-assets assumption.
  - — Information that enables users of financial statements to assess the inputs and valuation techniques used to develop fair value measurements of plan assets at the reporting date.
  - — Disclosure of additional asset categories and additional information about specific assets within a category is encouraged if that information is expected to be useful in understanding the risks associated with each asset category and the overall expected long-term rate of return on assets.
- For defined benefit pension plans, the accumulated benefit obligation.
- The benefits expected to be paid in each of the next five fiscal years, and in the aggregate for the five fiscal years thereafter.
- The employer's best estimate of contributions expected to be paid to the plan during the next fiscal year.
- The amounts recognized in the statements of financial position.
- The amount of net periodic benefit cost recognized, showing separately the service cost component, the interest cost component, the expected return on plan assets, the gain or loss component, the prior service cost or credit component, the transition asset or obligation component, and gain and loss from settlements or curtailments.
- Amounts included in accumulated other comprehensive income and not yet recognized as a component of net periodic benefit cost, separately showing the net gain or loss, net prior service cost or credit, and net transition asset or obligation.
- On a weighted-average basis, the following assumptions used in the accounting for the plan: discount rates, rates of compensation increase, expected long-term rates of return on plan assets, and interest crediting rates.
- The assumed health care trend rates for the year used to measure the expected cost of benefits covered by the plan, and a general description of the direction and pattern of change in the assumed trend rates thereafter, and the ultimate trend rates and when those rates are expected to be achieved.
- If applicable, the amounts and types of securities of the employer and related parties included in plan assets.
- The nature and effect of significant nonroutine events, such as amendments, combinations, divestitures, curtailments, and settlements.
- If applicable, the election to measure plan assets and benefit obligations using the month-end that is closest to the employer's fiscal year end in accordance with ASC 715-30-35-63A or ASC 715-60-35-123A and the month-end measurement date.
- The amount of net periodic benefit cost recognized. In addition, if the components other than the service cost component are not presented in a separate line item or items in the income statement, the amount of the other components and the line item(s) used in the income statement to present them must be disclosed.
- An explanation of the reasons for significant gains and losses related to changes in the benefit obligation for the period.

PRACTICE NOTE: If an employer determines the measurement date of plan assets in accordance with ASC 715-30-35-63A or ASC 715-60-35-123A and the employer contributes assets to the plan between the measurement date and its fiscal year-end, the employer must not adjust the fair value of each class of plan assets for the effects of the contribution. However, the employer must disclose the amount of the contribution to permit reconciliation of the total fair value of all the classes of plan assets to the ending balance of the fair value of plan assets, as well as to permit reconciliation of the total fair value of all plan assets in the fair value hierarchy to the ending balance of the fair value of plan assets (ASC 715-20-50-1).

A nonpublic entity that has more than one defined benefit pension plan or more than one other defined benefit postretirement plan shall provide the required information separately for pension plans and other postretirement benefit plans.

Disclosures in Interim Financial Reports

A publicly traded entity shall disclose the following information in its financial statements that include an income statement (ASC 715-50-6):

- The amount of net periodic benefit cost recognized for each period for which an income statement is presented with separate disclosure of the components of net periodic benefit cost
- The total amount of the employee's contributions paid, or expected to be paid, during the current year if significantly different from amounts previously disclosed

A nonpublic entity is required to disclose its best estimate of its contributions expected to be paid to the plan during the next fiscal year beginning after the date of the latest statement of financial position presented. In addition, a nonpublic entity shall disclose in interim periods for which a complete set of financial statements are presented the total amount of the employer's contributions paid and expected to be paid if significantly different from its disclosure in the immediately preceding annual report (ASC 715-50-6).

ASC 715-30: DEFINED BENEFIT PLANS—PENSION

OVERVIEW OF PENSION PLAN ACCOUNTING

Scope and Applicability

Most of the provisions of ASC 715 address *defined benefit pension plans* of single employers. A defined benefit pension plan is one that contains a pension benefit formula, which generally describes the amount of pension benefit that each employee will receive for services performed during a specified period of employment (ASC 715-30-05-4). The amount of the employer's periodic contribution to a defined benefit pension plan is based on the total pension benefits (projected to employees' normal retirement dates) that could be earned by all eligible participants.

In contrast, a *defined contribution pension plan* does not contain a pension benefit formula, but generally specifies the periodic amount that the employer must contribute to the pension plan and how that amount will be allocated to the eligible employees who perform services during that same period. Each periodic employer contribution is allocated among separate accounts maintained for each employee, and pension benefits are based solely on the amount available in each employee's account at the time of his or her retirement.

For the purposes of ASC 715, any plan that is not a defined contribution pension plan is considered a defined benefit pension plan (see definition of *defined benefit pension plan* in ASC Glossary).

ASC 715 requires that its provisions be applied to any arrangement, expressed or implied, that is similar in substance to a pension plan, regardless of its form or method of financing. Thus, a pension plan arrangement does not have to be in writing if the existence of a pension plan is implied by company policy. A qualified plan, however, has to be in writing under ERISA, as well as for federal and state tax purposes. Frequently, defined contribution pension plans provide for some method of determining defined benefits for employees, as may be the case with some *target benefit* plans. A target benefit plan is a defined contribution plan. The benefit defined in the document is only for the purpose of determining the contribution to be allocated to each participant's account. It is not intended to promise any benefit in the future. If, in substance, a plan does provide defined benefits for employees, it is accounted for as a defined benefit pension plan.

Actuarial Assumptions

Actuarial assumptions are factors used to calculate the estimated cost of pension plan benefits. Employee mortality, employee turnover, retirement age, administrative expenses of the pension plan, interest earned on plan assets, and the date on which a benefit becomes fully vested are some of the more important actuarial assumptions (ASC Glossary).

Under ASC 715, each significant actuarial assumption must reflect the best estimate for that particular assumption. In the absence of evidence to the contrary, all actuarial assumptions are made on the basis that the pension plan will continue in existence (going-concern concept) (ASC 715-30-35-42).

Discount rates used in actuarial valuations reflect the rates at which the pension benefits could be settled effectively. In selecting appropriate interest rates, employers should refer to current information on rates used in annuity contracts that could be purchased to settle pension obligations, including annuity rates published by the Pension Benefit Guaranty Corporation (PBGC), or the rates of return on high-quality fixed-income investments that are expected to be available through the maturity dates of the pension benefits (ASC 715-30-35-43).

The chosen discount rate should produce a liability amount that would generate the necessary future cash flows to pay pension benefits as they become due, if such amount was invested at the financial statement date in a portfolio of high-quality fixed-income investments. This liability amount is theoretically equal to the market value of a portfolio of high-quality zero coupon bonds, where each bond matches the amount and maturity of future payments due under the pension plan. However, reinvestment risk exists to the extent that the pension plan's assets include interest-bearing debt instruments (rather than only zero coupon bonds) and to the extent that plan investments have a maturity date less than some of the anticipated pension payments. In such cases, the assumed discount (interest) rate needs to consider expected reinvestment rates extrapolated using the existing yield curve at the financial statement date. The discount rate should be reevaluated at each measurement (financial statement) date (ASC 715-30-35-44).

PRACTICE POINTER: The discount rate used to determine the pension liability and the interest cost component of net periodic pension cost should change in accordance with changes in market interest rates—if interest rates rise the discount rate should increase, if interest rates fall the discount rate should decline. In addition, the determination of the discount rate is separate from the determination of the expected return on plan assets.

An actuarial gain or loss is the difference between an actuarial assumption and actual experience. Under ASC 715, actuarial gains and losses that are not included in determining net periodic pension cost in the year in which they arise are included in other comprehensive income, and they may be included as a component of net periodic pension cost in subsequent periods if certain criteria are met (ASC 715-30-35-18, 19).

PRACTICE POINTER: In accounting for pension plans—particularly defined benefit plans—the CPA relies heavily on the expertise of actuaries. Actuaries are educated in mathematics, modeling, and other areas that permit them to deal with the many uncertainties required to make estimates related to an enterprise's pension plan that are necessary for both funding and financial reporting. Actuarial assumptions are one area where the CPA is particularly vulnerable, because of the significant impact that different actuarial assumptions may have on the elements of the financial statements. Essentially, the CPA's responsibility is to be generally familiar with the actuary's work and to approach the results of the actuary's work with the professional skepticism that is typical of the CPA's work in many areas. The guidance in Wolters Kluwer's *GAAS Guide* AU Section 336 "Using the Work of a Specialist" is particularly germane when the CPA needs to rely on the work of an actuary.

Pension Plan Assets

The resources of a pension plan may be converted into (*a*) plan assets that are invested to provide pension benefits for the participants of the plan, such as stocks, bonds, and other investments (ASC Glossary) or (*b*) plan assets that are used in the operation of the plan, such as real estate, furniture, and fixtures (ASC 715-30-35-52). Plan assets must be segregated in a trust or otherwise effectively restricted so that the employer cannot use them for other purposes. Under ASC 715, plan assets do not include amounts accrued by an employer as net periodic pension cost, but not yet paid to the pension plan. Plan assets may include securities of the employer if they are freely transferable (ASC Glossary).

Pension plan assets that are held as investments to provide pension benefits are measured at fair value (ASC Glossary). (Additional guidance on determining fair values can be found in Chapter 51, *ASC 820—Fair Value Measurement.*) Pension plan assets that are used in the operation of the plan are measured at cost, less accumulated depreciation or amortization (ASC 715-30-35-52). For the purposes of ASC 715, plan liabilities that are incurred, other than for pension benefits, may be considered reductions of plan assets (ASC Glossary).

Recording Pension Events

Under ASC 715, an enterprise makes three primary types of entries in its records each accounting period:

1. To record net periodic pension cost
2. To record funding of the pension plan
3. To recognize the funded status of the pension plan

Illustration of Basic Entries to Record Pension Events

Maddux Co. determines its net periodic pension cost to be $10,000 for 20X7, its first year of operation. An equal amount is funded by transferring cash to the insurance company that administers the plan. The fair value of Maddux's pension plan assets equals the pension liability at year end. The applicable tax rate is 35%. The entries to record these events areas follow:

Net periodic pension cost	10,000	
Deferred tax asset	3,500	
Deferred tax benefit—net income		3,500
Liability for pension benefits		10,000
Liability for pension benefits	10,000	
Cash		10,000

In this case, the fair value of the pension plan assets and liabilities are equal so there is no need for a third journal entry, to recognize a pension plan asset (overfunded plan) or a pension plan liability (underfunded plan).

As this illustration shows, the transfer of cash to the plan administrator is treated as a retirement of the pension liability. Most of the provisions of ASC 715 pertain to the computation of the amount to be recorded in the first journal entry type in the above illustration as net periodic pension cost. This computation requires numerous worksheet calculations, which are illustrated throughout ASC 715.

Pension Plan Terminology

Key terms that are important for an understanding of accounting for pensions in accordance with ASC 715 are discussed below.

Projected Benefit Obligation

Projected benefit obligation is the actuarial present value, as of a specified date, of the total cost of all employees' vested and nonvested pension benefits that have been attributed by the pension benefit formula to services performed by employees to that date.

The projected benefit obligation includes the actuarial present value of all pension benefits (vested and nonvested) attributed by the pension benefit formula, *including consideration of future employee compensation levels* (ASC Glossary). Vested benefits are pension benefits that an employee has an irrevocable right to receive at a date specified in the pension agreement, even if the employee does not continue to work for the employer (ASC Glossary). In the event a pension plan is discontinued, a vested benefit obligation remains a liability of the employer.

Payments of pension benefits decrease both the projected benefit obligation and the fair value of plan assets, while contributions to a plan decrease cash and the financial statement liability.

The projected benefit obligation does not appear on the books of the employer, but the difference between the projected benefit obligation and the fair value of the pension plan's assets (i.e., the funded status of the plan) is recognized as a pension plan asset or liability. In addition, the employer maintains a record of the projected benefit obligation.

Accumulated Benefit Obligation

Accumulated benefit obligation is an alternative measure of the pension obligation; it is calculated like the projected benefit obligation, except that current or past compensation levels instead of projected future compensation levels are used to determine pension benefits (ASC Glossary). In the event a pension plan is discontinued, the balance of any unfunded accumulated benefit obligation remains a liability of the employer.

PRACTICE NOTE: Basically, there are two types of pension benefit formulas: pay-related benefit and non-pay-related benefit. For a non-pay-related benefit formula, the accumulated benefit obligation and the projected benefit obligation are the same.

Fair Value of Plan Assets

Fair value of plan assets is determined in accordance with the guidance in ASC 820 (Fair Value Measurements and Disclosures). (Additional guidance on determining fair values can be found in the Chapter 51, *ASC 820—Fair Value Measurement.*) The fair value of pension plan investments should be reduced by brokerage commissions and other selling costs if these are likely to be significant (ASC 715-30-35-50). Plan assets that are used in the operation of the pension plan (building, equipment, furniture, fixtures, etc.) are valued at cost less accumulated depreciation or amortization (ASC 715-30-35-52).

Pension plan assets are recorded on the books of the pension plan. However, an employer maintains records of the cost and fair value of all pension plan assets.

Funded Status of Plan

For the employer's accounting purposes, *funded status of plan* is the difference between the projected benefit obligation and the fair value of plan assets as of a given date (ASC Glossary). If the projected benefit obligation exceeds the fair value of the plan assets, a pension plan liability exists. If the fair value of plan assets exceeds the projected benefit obligation, a pension plan asset exists. ASC 715 requires that the employer recognize a pension plan asset or liability in its statement of financial position.

Prior Service Cost or Credit

Unrecognized prior service cost is the cost of retroactive benefits granted in a plan amendment. Upon the initial adoption of a pension plan or through a plan amendment, certain employees may be granted pension benefits for services performed in prior periods. These retroactive pension benefits are referred to as *prior service costs,* and usually are granted by the employer with the expectation that they will produce future economic benefits, such as reducing employee turnover, improving employee productivity, and minimizing the need to increase future employee compensation. If retroactive benefits are granted in a plan amendment the employer debits other comprehensive income and credits the liability for pension benefits. In addition, an employer is required to amortize any prior service cost in equal amounts over the future periods of active employees who are expected to receive the benefits (ASC 715-30-35-10). The amortization of prior service cost is included as a component of net periodic pension cost.

An employer may amend a pension plan to reduce pension benefits. This results in a prior service credit and is recorded by reducing the liability for pension benefits and increasing other comprehensive income. Any prior service credit is first applied to reduce any prior service cost remaining in accumulated other comprehensive income. Any balance remaining is amortized as a component of net periodic pension cost in a similar manner to the amortization of prior service cost (ASC 715-30-35-17).

An employer does not establish a general ledger account for prior service cost—rather any increase in this amount directly affects other comprehensive income and the liability for pension benefits, but the employer does maintain worksheet records of such amounts.

Gain or Loss

Gain or loss results in a change in either plan assets or the projected benefit obligation as a result of actual results that differ from expectations or changes in actuarial assumptions. For example, gains or losses arise from the difference between (*a*) the actual and expected amount of projected benefit obligation at the end of a period and/or (*b*) the actual and expected amount of the fair value of pension plan assets at the end of the period. Gains and losses are recognized by adjusting other comprehensive income and the liability for pension benefits. In addition, gains and losses may be recognized as a component of net periodic benefit cost in subsequent periods if certain criteria are met (ASC 715-30-35-18, 19, 21).

A gain or loss that, as of the beginning of the year, exceeds 10% of the greater of (*a*) the projected benefit obligation or (*b*) the market-related value of plan assets is subject to recognition. Recognition for the year is equal to the amount of the gain or loss in excess of 10% of the greater of the projected benefit obligation or the value of plan assets, divided by the average remaining service period of active employees expected to receive benefits under the plan. This frequently is referred to as the *corridor test* in applying ASC 715 (ASC 715-30-35-24). The gain or loss that is subject to the corridor test is included in the balance of accumulated other comprehensive income and, if recognized, is removed from accumulated other comprehensive income (through recognition in other comprehensive income in the current period) with the offsetting entry affecting net periodic pension cost.

An employer does not establish general ledger accounts for pension gains and losses. Rather, any changes in these amounts directly affect other comprehensive income and the liability for pension benefits; however, the employer does maintain worksheet records of such amounts.

NET PERIODIC PENSION COST

The employer's *net periodic pension cost* represents the net amount of pension cost for a specified period that is charged against income. Under ASC 715, the components of net periodic pension cost are (*a*) service cost, (*b*) interest cost on the projected benefit obligation, (*c*) actual return on plan assets, (*d*) amortization of prior service cost or credit (if any), (*e*) recognition of gain or loss (if required by ASC 715), and (*f*) amortization of any transition obligation or asset that remains and that is included in accumulated other comprehensive income (ASC 715-30-35-4).

All of the components of net periodic pension cost are not necessarily recognized in determining income in the year when they arise. For example, the total prior service cost that results from a plan amendment is determined in the period in which it arises. Under the provisions of ASC 715, however, the employer recognizes cost in equal amounts over the future service periods of each active employee who is expected to receive the benefits of the plan amendment that gave rise to the prior service cost (ASC 715-30-35-10).

Net periodic pension cost is estimated in advance at the beginning of a period based on actuarial assumptions relating to (*a*) the discount rate on the projected benefit obligation, (*b*) the expected long-term rate of return on pension plan assets, and (*c*) the average remaining service periods of active employees covered by the pension plan. At the end of the period, adjustments are made to account for the differences (actuarial gains or losses), if any, between the estimated and actual amounts.

The actuarial assumptions used to calculate the previous year's net periodic pension cost are used to calculate that cost in subsequent interim financial statements, unless more current valuations of plan assets and obligations are available or a significant event has occurred, such as a plan amendment, which usually would require new valuations (ASC 715-30-35-68).

The following illustration shows how the different components of net periodic pension cost are estimated.

Illustration of Computing Net Periodic Pension Cost

Service cost component	$2,000
Interest cost component	3,000
Return on plan assets	(2,500)
Amortization of prior service cost	1,000
Amortization of (gain) or loss	1,000
Amortization of transition obligation (asset)	1,500
Total net periodic pension cost	$6,000

For simplicity, an assumption is made that there are no differences (actuarial gains or losses) between the estimated and actual amounts at the end of the period, and that the employer made no contributions to the pension fund during the period.

		Beginning of period	*End of period*
(a)	Projected benefit obligation	$(115,000)	$(120,000)
(b)	Fair value of plan assets	65,000	67,500
(c)	Funded status of plan	$ (50,000)	$ (52,500)
(d)	Prior service cost	10,000	9,000
(e)	(Gain) or loss	5,000	4,000
(f)	Transition obligation or asset at date of initial application of pension plan accounting	35,000	33,500
(g)	Balance in accumulated other comprehensive income related to the pension plan	$ 50,000	$ 46,500
(h)	Reduction in net income during the period related to the pension plan		$ (6,000)

The following journal entries are recorded to record the initial funded status of the pension plan and to recognize net periodic pension cost during the year (and to transfer amounts out of accumulated other comprehensive income) (tax effects are not considered):

Accumulated other comprehensive income	50,000	
Liability for pension benefits		50,000
Net periodic pension cost	2,500	
Liability for pension benefits		2,500
Net periodic benefit cost	3,500	
Other comprehensive income		3,500

The following explains the changes in the accounts that were affected by the net periodic pension cost accrual.

(a) *Projected benefit obligation* An increase in the projected benefit obligation of $5,000, representing the service cost component of $2,000 and interest cost component of $3,000 for the period. The projected benefit obligation is not recorded in the employer's books, but is important information in accounting for pension cost.

(b) *Fair value of plan assets* The $2,500 increase in the fair value of plan assets, between the beginning and end of the period, represents the increase in the fair value of plan assets for the period. The fair value of plan assets is not recorded in the employer's books, but is important information in accounting for pension cost.

(c) *Funded status of plan* The $2,500 decrease in the funded status of the plan, between the beginning and end of the period, is the difference between the $5,000 increase in the projected benefit obligation for the period and the $2,500 increase in the fair value of plan assets for the period.

(d) *Prior service cost* The $1,000 decrease in prior service cost, between the beginning and end of the period, is the amount of amortization of prior service cost that has been recognized by the employer as a component of net periodic pension cost.

Prior service cost is not recorded on the books of the employer, but records are maintained for such amounts. Thus, the employer reduces the balance of the unrecognized prior service cost by $1,000. However, prior service cost is included in accumulated other comprehensive income until it is recognized as a component of net periodic pension cost.

(e) *Gain or loss* The $1,000 decrease in the gain or loss (actuarial gain or loss), between the beginning and end of the period, is the amount of amortization that has been recognized by the employer as a component of net periodic pension cost.

Gain or loss (actuarial gain or loss) is not recorded on the books of the employer, but records are maintained for such amounts. Thus, the employer reduces the balance of the unrecognized net gain or loss by $1,000. As above, the gain or loss is included in accumulated other comprehensive income until it is recognized as a component of net periodic pension cost.

(f) *Transition obligation or transition asset at date of initial application of pension plan accounting* The $1,500 decrease in the transition obligation, between the beginning and the end of the period, is the amount of amortization that has been recognized by the employer as a component of net periodic pension cost for the period.

The transition obligation or asset is not recorded on the books of the employer, but records are maintained for such amounts. Thus, the employer reduces the balance of the unrecognized net obligation or net asset by $1,500. As above, the transition obligation or asset is included in accumulated other comprehensive income until it is recognized as a component of net periodic pension cost.

(g) *Balance in accumulated other comprehensive income related to the pension plan* At the beginning of the year, the entire unfunded status of the pension plan is due to amounts for prior service cost, gain or loss, and transition obligation that have not yet been recognized as a component of net periodic benefit cost. By the end of the year, the balance in accumulated other comprehensive income is reduced to $46,500 because $3,500 of these amounts were included in net periodic pension cost during the year.

(h) *Reduction in net income during the period related to the pension plan* Net income is reduced during the year by the amount of net periodic pension cost, $6,000. The unfunded status of the pension plan, $52,500, now comprises two components: amounts for prior service cost, gain or loss, and transition obligations that have not yet been recognized as a component of net periodic benefit cost equal $46,500. The remaining $6,000 represents the pension cost for the period, none of which has been funded (i.e., the employer made no contributions to the plan during the period).

Service Cost Component

In a defined benefit pension plan, ASC 715 requires that a pension benefit formula be used to determine the amount of pension benefit earned by each employee for services performed during a specified period. Under ASC 715, attribution is the process of assigning pension benefits or cost to periods of employee service, in accordance with the pension benefit formula (ASC Glossary).

The service cost component of net periodic pension cost is defined as the actuarial present value of pension benefits attributed by the pension benefit formula to employee service during a specified period (ASC Glossary). For example, a pension benefit formula may state that an employee shall receive, at the retirement age stated in the plan, a pension benefit of $20 per month for life, for each year of service. To compute the total future value of the pension benefit for the year, the monthly benefit is multiplied by the number of months in the employee's life expectancy at retirement age. This number of months is determined by reference to mortality tables. The actuarial present value of all employees' future pension benefits that are earned during a period is computed and included as the service cost component of the net periodic pension cost for the same period (ASC 715-30-35-36).

If the terms of the pension benefit formula provide for benefits based on estimated future compensation levels of employees, estimates of those future compensation levels are used to determine the service cost component of net periodic pension cost. For example, if the pension benefit formula states that an employee's benefit for a period is equal to 1% of his or her final pay, an estimate of the employee's final pay is used to calculate the benefit for the period. Assumed compensation levels should reflect the best estimate of the future compensation levels of the employee involved and be consistent with assumed discount rates to the extent that they both incorporate expectation of the same future economic conditions. Thus, future compensation levels in final-pay plans or career-average-pay plans are reflected in the service cost component of net periodic pension cost. Assumed compensation levels also shall reflect changes because of general price levels, productivity, seniority, promotion, and other factors (ASC 715-30-35-31).

Changes resulting from a plan amendment that has become effective and automatic benefit changes specified by the terms of the pension plan, such as cost-of-living increases, are included in the determination of service cost for a period (ASC 715-30-35-35).

An employer's substantive commitment to make future plan amendments in recognition of employees' prior services may indicate pension benefits in excess of those reflected in the existing pension benefit formula. Such a commitment may be evidenced by a history of regular increases in non-pay-related benefits, benefits under a career-average pay plan, or other evidence. In this event, ASC 715 requires that the pension plan be accounted for based on the employer's substantive commitment, and that appropriate disclosure be made in the employer's financial statements (ASC 715-30-35-34).

A plan's pension benefit formula might provide no benefits for the first 19 years of an employee's service and a vested benefit of $1,000 per month for life in the 20th year of an employee's service. This benefit pattern is no different than providing a benefit of $50 per month for 20 years and requiring 20 years before the benefits vest. If a pension plan benefit formula attributes all or a disproportionate portion of total pension benefits to later years, the employee's *total projected benefit* is calculated and used as the basis of assigning the total pension benefits under the plan. In this event, the employee's total projected benefit is assumed to accumulate in proportion to the ratio of the total completed years of service to date to the total completed years of service as of the date the benefit becomes fully vested (ASC 715-30-35-38). An employee's total projected benefit from a pension plan is the actuarial present value of the total cost of pension benefits that the employee is likely to receive under the plan. If the pension benefit formula is based on future compensation, future compensation is used in calculating the employee's total projected benefit.

PRACTICE NOTE: Under current pension law, the longest a single employer can make an employee wait before receiving vested benefits is five years. For a multiemployer plan, the longest period is ten years.

In the event a pension benefit formula does not indicate the manner in which a specific benefit relates to specific services performed by an employee, the benefit shall be assumed to accumulate as follows (ASC 715-30-35-38):

- *If the benefit is includable in vested benefits* The benefit is accumulated in proportion to the ratio of total completed years of service to date to the total completed years of service as of the date the benefit becomes fully vested. A vested benefit is a benefit that an employee has an irrevocable right to receive. For example, an employee is entitled to receive a vested benefit whether or not he or she continues to work for the employer.
- *If the benefit is not includable in vested benefits* The benefit is accumulated in proportion to the ratio of completed years of service to date to the total projected years of service. (An example of a benefit that is not includable in vested benefits is a death or disability benefit that is payable only if death or disability occurs during the employee's active service.)

Interest Cost Component

The two factors used to determine the actuarial present value of a future pension benefit are (1) the probability that the benefit will be paid to the employee (through the use of actuarial assumptions) and (2) the time value of money (through the use of discounts for interest cost). The probability that a pension benefit will be paid is based on actuarial assumptions such as employee mortality, employee turnover, and the date the benefits become vested. An employer's liability for a retirement fund of $56,520 that is due in ten years is not equal to a present liability of $56,520. At an 8% discount rate the $56,520 has a present value of only $26,179. The $26,179 increases each year by the employer's interest cost of 8%, and in ten years grows to $56,520, if the 8% interest rate does not change.

ASC 715 requires an employer to recognize, as a component of net periodic pension cost, the interest cost on the projected benefit obligation. The interest cost is equal to the increase in the amount of the projected benefit obligation because of the passage of time (ASC Glossary).

PRACTICE NOTE: ASC 715 specifies that the interest cost component of net periodic pension cost shall **not** be considered to be interest for the purposes of applying the provisions of ASC 835 (Interest).

Actual Return on Plan Assets Component

The actual return on plan assets is equal to the difference between the fair value of plan assets at the beginning and end of a period, adjusted for employer and employee contributions (if a contributory plan) and pension benefit payments made during the period (ASC Glossary). *Fair value* is the amount that a pension plan could reasonably be expected to receive from a current sale of an investment in an orderly, nonforced transaction (ASC Glossary). Plan assets that are used in the operation of the pension plan (building, equipment, furniture, fixtures, etc.) are valued at cost, less accumulated depreciation or amortization (ASC 715-30-35-52).

A return on plan assets decreases the employer's cost of providing pension benefits to its employees, while a loss increases pension cost. Net periodic pension income can result from a significantly high return on pension plan assets during a period.

ASC 715 requires an employer to recognize, as a component of net periodic pension cost, the actual return (or loss) on pension plan assets (ASC 715-30-35-4).

Amortization of Prior Service Cost or Credit Component

Upon the initial adoption of a pension plan or as the result of a plan amendment, employees may be granted pension benefits for services performed in prior periods. These retroactive pension benefits are assumed to have been granted by the employer in the expectation that they will produce future economic benefits, such as reducing employee turnover, improving employee productivity, and minimizing the need for increasing future employee compensation. The cost of pension benefits that are granted retroactively to employees for services performed in prior periods is referred to as *prior service cost* (ASC 715-30-35-10).

Under ASC 715, only a portion of the total amount of prior service cost arising in a period, including retroactive benefits that are granted to retirees, is included in net periodic pension cost. ASC 715 requires that the total prior service cost arising in a period from an adoption or amendment of a plan be amortized in equal amounts over the future service periods of *active* employees who are expected to receive the retroactive benefits (ASC 715-30-35-10).

PRACTICE POINTER: Because retirees are not expected to render future services, the cost of their retroactive benefits cannot be recognized over their remaining service periods. ASC 715 requires that the total prior service cost arising from a plan adoption or amendment, including the cost attributed to the benefits of retirees, amortized in equal amounts over the future service periods of only the active employees who are expected to receive benefits.

If substantially all of the participants of a pension plan are inactive, the prior service cost attributed to the benefits of the inactive participants are amortized over the remaining life expectancy of those participants (ASC 715-30-35-11).

PRACTICE NOTE: ASC 715 addresses the method of amortizing that portion of the cost of retroactive plan amendments that affect benefits of inactive participants of a plan composed of substantially all inactive participants, but does not address the method of amortizing the portion of the cost of the same retroactive plan amendments that affect benefits of the active participants of the same plan (ASC 715-30-35-11). Two alternatives appear to be available. The first is that the cost of the active participants' benefits is charged to income of the period of the plan amendment. The second is that the cost of the **active** participants' benefits is amortized in the same manner as if the plan were not composed of substantially all inactive participants. In this event, the cost attributed to the retroactive benefits of the **active** participants of a plan composed of substantially all **inactive** participants is amortized in equal amounts over the future service periods of each active employee who is expected to receive the retroactive benefits.

ASC 715 permits the consistent use of an alternative approach that more rapidly amortizes the amount of prior service cost. For example, straight-line amortization of prior service cost over the average future service period of active employees who are expected to receive benefits under the plan is acceptable. If an alternative method is used to amortize prior service cost, it must be disclosed in the financial statements (ASC 715-30-35-13).

Some companies have a history of increasing pension benefits through regular plan amendments. In these cases, the period in which an employer expects to realize the economic benefits from retroactive pension benefits that were previously granted is shorter than the entire remaining future service period of all active employees. Under this circumstance, ASC 715 requires that a more rapid rate of amortization be applied to the remaining balance of the prior service cost to reflect the earlier realization of the employer's economic benefits and to allocate properly the cost to the periods benefited (ASC 715-30-35-14).

An amendment to a pension plan usually increases the cost of employees' pension benefits and increases the amount of the projected benefit obligation. However, a pension plan amendment may decrease the cost of employees' pension benefits, which results in a decrease in the amount of the projected benefit obligation and is referred to as a prior service credit. Any decrease resulting from a pension plan amendment is applied to reduce the balance of any existing prior service cost in accumulated other comprehensive income and any excess is amortized on the same basis as increases in prior service cost (ASC 715-30-35-17).

Gains and Losses Component

Gains and losses are changes in the amount of either the projected benefit obligation or pension plan assets, resulting from the differences between estimates or assumptions used and actual experience. A gain or loss can result from the difference between (*a*) the expected and actual amounts of the projected benefit obligation at the end of a period and/or (*b*) the expected and actual amounts of the fair value of pension plan assets at the end of a period. Technically, both of these types of gains and losses are considered *actuarial gains and losses.* Under ASC 715, however, a gain or loss resulting from a change in the projected benefit obligation is referred to as an *actuarial gain or loss*, while a gain or loss resulting from a change in the fair value of pension plan assets is referred to as a *net asset gain or loss.* For the purposes of ASC 715, the sources of these gains and losses are not distinguished separately, and they include amounts that have been realized as well as amounts that are unrealized (ASC 715-30-35-18).

Under ASC 715, the gains and losses component of net periodic pension cost consists of (*a*) the difference between the expected and actual returns on pension plan assets (net asset gain or loss) and (*b*) if required, amortization of any net gain or loss from previous periods and included in accumulated other comprehensive income (ASC 715-30-35-26).

As discussed in a previous section, the actual return on pension plan assets is equal to the difference between the fair value of pension plan assets at the beginning and end of a period, adjusted for any contributions and pension benefit payments made during that period. Fair value is the amount that a pension plan could reasonably be expected to receive from a current sale of an investment in an orderly, nonforced transaction (ASC Glossary).

The expected return on pension plan assets during the period is computed by multiplying the *market-related value* of plan assets by the *expected long-term rate of return.* The expected long-term rate of return is an actuarial assumption of the expected long-term rate of return that will be earned on plan assets during the period. Under ASC 715, the current rate of return earned on plan assets and the likely reinvestment rate of return should be considered in estimating the long-term rate of return on plan assets. The expected long-term rate of return on plan assets should reflect the average rate of earnings expected on plan investments (ASC 715-30-35-47).

To reduce the volatility of changes in the fair value of pension plan assets and the resulting effect on net periodic pension cost, ASC 715 requires the use of a market-related value for plan assets to compute the expected return on such assets during a period. Market-related value is used only to compute the expected return on pension plan assets for the period (expected return = market-related value × expected long-term rate of return) (ASC Glossary).

Under ASC 715, the market-related value of a plan asset can be either (*a*) the actual fair value of the pension plan asset or (*b*) a calculated value that recognizes, in a systematic and rational manner, the changes in the actual fair value of the pension plan asset over a period of not more than five years (ASC Glossary). In computing the market-related value of a pension plan asset, an enterprise may use actual fair value or a calculated value based on a five-year moving average of the changes in the actual fair value of the pension plan asset. In this event, the calculated market-related value would include only 20% of the total changes in the actual fair value of the pension plan asset that have occurred during the past five years. For example, if the actual fair value of a plan asset at the end of each of the last six years was $8,000, $10,000, $12,000, $14,000, $16,000, and $13,000, the net gain for the most recent five years is $5,000 ($2,000 + $2,000 + $2,000 + $2,000 – $3,000 = $5,000). In this event, only 20% of the $5,000 gain ($1,000) is included in computing the calculated market-related value of the pension plan asset for the current year.

The difference between the actual fair value of a pension plan asset and its calculated market-related value is the amount of net gain or loss from previous years that has not yet been recognized in the calculated market-related value.

Market-related value may be computed differently for each class of plan assets, but the method of computing it must be applied consistently from year to year for each class of plan assets. For example, fair value may be used for bonds and other fixed income investments, and a calculated market-related value for stocks and other equities (ASC Glossary).

Illustration of Computing Market-Related Value

For computing the market-related value of a particular class of plan assets as of the end of each period, an employer uses a calculated value that includes 20% of the gains and losses on the plan assets that have occurred over the last five years. The total market-related value of this particular class of plan assets at the beginning of calendar year 20X5 was $100,000. The total fair value of the plan assets was $120,000 at the beginning of 20X5 and $130,000 at the end of 20X5. Actual gains and losses for the past five years as of the beginning of 20X5 were: 20X0 $10,000; 20X1 $(8,000); 20X2 $12,000; 20X3 $10,000; 20X4 $(4,000); the result is a net gain of $20,000 for these five years. Employer's contributions to the plan for 20X5 are estimated at $2,000 and benefit payments expected to be paid from the plan in 20X5 are also $2,000. The expected long-term rate of return on plan assets for 20X5 is 10%. The computation of the estimated market-related value as of December 31, 20X5, for this particular class of plan assets is determined as follows:

Market-related value at the beginning of period	$100,000
Add:	
Expected return on assets for 20X5 (market-related value, multiplied by expected long-term rate of return ($100,000 × 10%)	10,000

20% of the net gain or loss for the last five years (20% × $20,000)	4,000
Employer's contribution	2,000
Benefit payments made from plan	(2,000)
Estimated market-related value, Dec. 31, 20X5	$114,000

Note: The difference between the fair value ($130,000) and market-related value ($114,000) of plan assets at the end of 20X5 is $16,000. This difference represents the amount of net gain from the five years to the beginning of 20X5 that has not yet been recognized in the market-related value of plan assets.

The expected return on plan assets is based on market-related values, which do not include all of the net asset gains and losses from previous years (unless market-related values are equal to fair values). Thus, net asset gains and losses may include both (*a*) gains and losses of previous years that have been included in market-related value and (*b*) gains and losses of previous years that have not yet been included in market-related value (ASC 715-30-35-22, 23).

As mentioned above, ASC 715 does not require the recognition of any gains and losses as components of net periodic pension cost of the period in which they arise, except to the extent that the net asset gain or loss for the period offsets or supplements the actual return of pension plan assets for the period. However, gains and losses are recognized as a component of other comprehensive income as they occur. In subsequent years, however, all gains and losses, except those which have not yet been recognized in the market-related values of pension plan assets, are subject to certain minimum amortization provisions of ASC 715. Gains and losses that are amortized as a component of net periodic pension cost are removed from the beginning balance of accumulated other comprehensive income.

ASC 715 requires recognition of net gains or losses based on beginning-of-the-year balances. A net gain or loss that, as of the beginning of the year, exceeds 10% of (*a*) the projected benefit obligation or (*b*) the market-related value of plan assets, whichever is greater, is subject to recognition. The minimum recognition for the year is calculated by dividing the average remaining service period of active employees who are expected to receive benefits under the plan into the amount of net gain or loss that, as of the beginning of the year, exceeds 10 % of (*a*) the projected benefit obligation or (*b*) the market-related value of plan assets, whichever is greater. If substantially all of a plan's participants are inactive, however, the average remaining life expectancy of the inactive participants is divided into the excess net gain or loss subject to amortization. The computation of the minimum amortization required by ASC 715 is made each year based on beginning-of-the-year balances of unrecognized net gains or losses (ASC 715-30-35-24).

In lieu of the minimum amortization of net gains and losses specified by ASC 715, an employer may use an alternative method provided that the method (*a*) is systematic and applied consistently, (*b*) is applied to both gains and losses similarly, (*c*) reduces the unamortized balance included in accumulated other comprehensive income by an amount greater than the amount that would result from the minimum amortization method provided by ASC 715, and (*d*) is disclosed in the financial statements (ASC 715-30-35-25).

Illustration of Gains and Losses Component of Net Periodic Pension Cost

ABC Corporation has a remaining transition obligation of $400 on January 1, 20X5. ABC Corp. amortized $40 of this transition obligation in 20X5. The net asset (gain) or loss for 20X5, resulting from changes in actuarial assumptions, was a loss of $400, which was recognized in other comprehensive income. The market-related value of pension plan assets at the beginning of 20X6 is $1,600 and the average remaining service life of active employees is ten years.

The expected net periodic pension cost for 20X6 is $340, determined as follows: the sum of service cost $200, interest cost $240 (10%), amortization of unrecognized net asset loss $20, and amortization of the transition obligation $40, less a 10% expected return on plan assets of $160 (expected return = market-related value of plan assets of $1,600 × expected long-term rate of return of 10%). No contributions were made to the pension plan in 20X6.

	Actual 12/31/X5	*Expected 12/31/X6*	*Actual 12/31/X6*
(a) Projected benefit obligation	$(2,400)	$(2,840)	$(2,900)
(b) Fair value of plan assets	1,640	1,800	1,750
Funded status of plan	$ (760)	$(1,040)	$(1,150)
Prior service cost	0	0	0

	Actual 12/31/X5	Expected 12/31/X6	Actual 12/31/X6
Net (gain) or loss	400	380	490
Transition obligation existing at 12/31/X5	360	320	320

(a) The difference between the actual projected benefit obligation for 20X5 and the expected projected benefit obligation for 20X6 is $440, which consists of the expected service cost of $200, and the expected interest cost of $240. However, the actual projected benefit for 20X6 increased $500 over the actual projected benefit for 20X5. The difference between the expected increase in the projected benefit obligation of $440 and the actual increase of $500 represents a $60 actuarial loss. The $60 loss occurred because the actuarial assumptions used were different from actual experience.

The $40 amortization of the transition obligation does not affect the projected benefit obligation because the full amount of the transition obligation was recognized in the projected benefit obligation as of the date of the initial application of pension plan accounting.

(b) The difference between the actual fair value of plan assets for 20X5 and the expected fair value of plan assets for 20X6 is $160, which represents the 10% expected return on plan assets (market-related value of plan assets of $1,600 × 10%). However, the actual fair value of plan assets for 20X6 of $1,750 increased only $110 over the actual fair value of plan assets of $1,640 for 20X5. The difference between the expected increase in the fair value of plan assets of $160 and the actual increase of $110 represents a $50 net asset loss for the period. The loss occurred because the actual rate of return on pension plan assets was less than the expected rate of return.

Cost Components of Net Periodic Pension Cost for 20X6

ASC 715 requires financial statement disclosure of the amount of net periodic pension cost for the period. The disclosure shall indicate separately the service cost component, the interest cost component, the expected return on plan assets for the period, the amortization of the transition obligation or asset, gains and losses recognized, prior service cost recognized, and gain or loss recognized due to a settlement or curtailment (ASC 715-20-50-1).

Service cost	$200
Interest cost	240
Expected return on plan assets	(160)
Amortization of transition obligation	40
Amortization of prior service cost	0
Recognized net actuarial loss	20
Net periodic pension cost	$340

Note: A net asset gain or loss is not recognized in income in the period in which it arises (ASC 715-30-35-19). In this case, the net asset loss is $50—the difference between the expected return on plan assets, $160, and the actual return on plan assets, $110. The expected return on plan assets is included as a component of net periodic pension cost. Recognition of the net asset loss is deferred to future periods. However, the net asset gain or loss is included as a component of other comprehensive income.

Computation of the Amortization of the Net Gain or Loss for 20X6

Net (gain) or loss 1/1/X6	$400
Add asset gain or subtract asset loss not yet recognized in market-related values at 1/1 [difference between fair value of plan assets ($1,640) and market-related value ($1,600)]	40
Net (gain) or loss subject to the minimum amortization provisions of ASC 715	440
10% of the greater of the projected benefit obligation or market-related value at 1/1	(240)
Net (gain) or loss subject to amortization	$200
Amortization for 20X6 (over the ten-year average remaining service life of active employees)	$ 20

Note: The net (gain) or loss at 1/1 must be adjusted to exclude asset gains and losses not yet reflected in market-related values, because gains and losses are not required to be amortized (ASC 715-30-35-22).

Note: The $60 loss that occurred in 20X6 as a result of the difference between the expected and actual projected benefit obligation for 20X6, and the $50 loss that occurred in 20X6 as a result of the difference between the expected and actual fair value of plan assets for 20X6, will become subject to the minimum amortization provisions of ASC 715 as of 1/1/X7. The computation of the amount of net (gain) or loss as of 1/1/X7, is as follows:

Net asset (gain) or loss 1/1/X6		$400
Less: Amortization for 20X6		20
Net asset (gain) or loss 12/31/X6		380
Add: Actuarial net (gain) or loss for 20X6	$60	
Net asset (gain) or loss for 20X6	50	110
Net (gain) or loss as of 1/1/X7		$ 490

Amortization of the Transition Obligation or Transition Asset (as of the Date of Initial Application of Pension Plan Accounting)

The *funded status* of a pension plan for employer accounting purposes is equal to the difference between the projected benefit obligation and the fair value of pension plan assets. The funded status indicates whether the employer has underfunded or overfunded the pension plan.

The transition obligation or transition asset of a pension plan is determined by the employer as of the date of its financial statements of the beginning of the year in which pension plan accounting is initially applied. The transition obligation or transition asset is equal to the difference between the projected benefit obligation and fair value of pension plan assets, plus previously recognized unfunded accrued pension cost or less previously recognized prepaid pension cost.

A transition obligation or asset is amortized by the employer on a straight-line basis over the average remaining service period of employees expected to receive benefits under the plan, as of the date of initial application of the guidance that preceded the adoption of the ASC (i.e., FAS-87), except under the following circumstances:

- If the amortization period is less than 15 years, an employer may elect to use 15 years.
- If the plan is composed of all or substantially all inactive participants, the employer shall use those participants' average remaining life expectancy as the amortization period.

The above amortization method is also used to recognize any unrecognized net obligation or net asset of a defined contribution pension plan.

RECOGNITION OF FUNDED STATUS OF PENSION PLAN

An employer is required to recognize the overfunded or underfunded status of a defined benefit pension plan as an asset or a liability in its statement of financial position. If the fair value of a pension plan's assets exceeds the plan's projected benefit obligation the plan is overfunded and an asset is recognized. If the plan's projected benefit obligation exceeds the fair value of the plan's assets the plan is underfunded and a liability is recognized (ASC 715-30-25-1). When the funded status of the pension plan is first recognized in the statement of financial position, the offsetting entry is to accumulated other comprehensive income (net of tax). The recognition of a pension plan asset or liability may result in temporary differences under ASC 740 (Income Taxes). Deferred tax effects are to be recognized for these temporary differences as a component of income tax expense or benefit in the year in which the differences arise, and allocated to various financial statement components (ASC 715-30-25-3).

Asset and liability gains and losses, and prior service costs or credits, that occur in periods after recognition of the funded status of the plan and that are not immediately included as a component of net periodic pension cost are included in other comprehensive income. As gains and losses, prior service costs and credits, and the transition asset or obligation are included in net periodic pension cost they are recognized as an adjustment to other comprehensive income (ASC 715-30-25-4).

All pension plans that are overfunded are aggregated and a noncurrent asset presented in the statement of financial position. All pension plans that are underfunded are aggregated and a liability presented in the statement of financial position. The liability is current to the extent that the actuarial present value of benefits to be paid within the next year, or operating cycle if longer, exceeds the fair value of plan assets. This determination is made on a plan-by-plan basis.

Otherwise, the liability is noncurrent (ASC 715-30-25-2). The employer should not reduce a liability resulting from an underfunded pension plan because another pension plan is overfunded (ASC 715-30-25-6).

MISCELLANEOUS CONSIDERATIONS

Measurement Dates

All pension plan assets that are held as investments to provide pension benefits are measured generally at their fair values as of the date of the financial statements. There are two exceptions to this general rule. If a subsidiary sponsors a pension plan and the subsidiary has a different year end than its parent, the fair value of the subsidiary's pension plan assets is measured at the date of the subsidiary's financial statements. If an investee accounted for by the equity method sponsors a pension plan and the investee has a different year-end than the investor, the fair value of the investee's pension plan assets is measured at the date of the investee's financial statements (ASC 715-30-35-62).

A reporting entity that has a fiscal year-end that does not coincide with a month-end may incur additional costs to measure the fair value of plan assets, since the information about the fair value of plan assets obtained from a third-party service provider is typically reported as of a month-end and must be adjusted to reflect the fair values as of the fiscal year-end. A reporting entity in this situation may elect to measure the plan assets and benefit obligations using the month-end that is closest to the entity's fiscal year-end. The reporting entity must apply this election consistently from year to year and consistently to all of its defined benefit plans (ASC 715-30-35-63A).

If a contribution or significant event caused by the employer (such as a plan amendment, settlement, or curtailment that calls for a remeasurement) occurs between the month-end date used to measure plan assets and benefit obligations and the employer's fiscal year-end, the employer must adjust the fair value of plan assets and the actuarial present value of benefit obligations to recognize those contributions or significant events in the period in which they occurred. Such an adjustment is not made for other events occurring during this time that were not caused by the employer, for example, changes in market prices or interest rates (ASC 715-30-35-63B).

Unless more current amounts are available for both the obligation and plan assets, the funded status of the pension plan reported in interim financial statements is the same amount as reported by the employer in its previous year-end statement of financial position, adjusted for subsequent accruals of service cost, interest cost, return on plan assets, contributions, and benefit payments (ASC 715-30-35-65).

If an employer causes a significant event that requires the employer to remeasure both plan assets and benefit obligations and the date of the significant event does not coincide with a month-end, the employer may remeasure plan assets and benefit obligations using the month-end that is closest to the date of the significant event (ASC 715-30-35-66A). In these cases, the employer must adjust the fair value of plan assets and the actuarial present value of benefit obligations for any effects of the significant event that may or may not be captured in the month-end measurement (ASC 715-30-35-66B).

The same assumptions used to calculate the previous year-end net periodic pension cost are used to calculate the net periodic pension cost in subsequent interim financial statements, unless more current valuations of plan assets and obligations are available or a significant event has occurred, such as a plan amendment that usually would require new valuations (ASC 715-30-35-68).

Employers with Two or More Pension Plans

If an employer sponsors more than one defined benefit pension plan, the provisions of ASC 715 are applied separately to each plan. An employer shall not apply the assets of one plan to reduce or eliminate the underfunding of another plan, unless the employer clearly has the right to do so (ASC 715-30-25-6).

Annuity Contracts

All or part of an employer's obligation to provide pension plan benefits to individuals may be transferred effectively to an insurance company by the purchase of annuity contracts. An annuity contract is an irrevocable agreement in which an insurance company unconditionally agrees to provide specific periodic payments, or a lump-sum payment to another party, in return for a specified premium. Thus, by use of an annuity contract, an employer can effectively transfer to an insurance company its legal obligation to provide specific employee pension plan benefits. For the purposes of ASC 715, a contract is not considered an annuity contract if the insurance company is a captive insurer or there is reasonable doubt that the insurance company will meet its obligation. A captive insurer is one that does business primarily with the employer and its related parties (ASC 715-30-35-54).

An annuity contract may be participating or nonparticipating. In a participating annuity contract, the insurance company's investing activities with the funds received for the annuity contract generally are shared, in the form of dividends, with the purchaser (the employer or the pension fund). An annuity contract is not considered an annuity contract, for the purposes of ASC 715, unless all the risks and rewards associated with the assets and obligations assumed by the insurance company are actually transferred to the insurance company by the employer (ASC 715-30-35-57).

The cost incurred for currently earned benefits under an annuity contract is the cost of those benefits, except for the cost of participating rights of participating annuity contracts, which must be accounted for separately (see below). The service cost component of net periodic pension cost for the current period is the cost incurred for nonparticipating annuity contracts that cover all currently earned benefits (ASC 715-30-35-53). Pension benefits not covered by annuity contracts are accounted for in accordance with the provisions of ASC 715 that address accounting for the cost of pension benefits not covered by annuity contracts (ASC 715-30-35-55).

The projected benefit obligation and the accumulated benefit obligation do not include the cost of benefits covered by annuity contracts. Except for the cost of participation rights (see below), pension plan assets do not include the cost of any annuity contracts (ASC 715-30-35-53).

The difference in cost between a nonparticipating annuity contract and a participating annuity contract usually is attributable to the cost of the participation right. The cost of a participation right, at the date of its purchase, is recognized as a pension plan asset. In subsequent periods, a participation right is included in plan assets at its fair value, if fair value is reasonably determinable. If fair value is not reasonably determinable, a participation right is included in plan assets at its amortized cost and systematically amortized over the expected dividend period stated in the contract. In this event, amortized cost may not exceed the net realizable value of the participation right (ASC 715-30-35-57, 58).

Other Contracts with Insurance Companies

The purchase of insurance contracts that are, in substance, annuity contracts, is accounted for in accordance with the provisions of ASC 715 (see previous section). The purchase of other types of insurance contracts shall be accounted for as pension plan assets and reported at fair value. The best evidence of fair value for some insurance contracts may be their contract values. Under ASC 715, the cash surrender value or conversion value of an insurance contract is presumed to be its fair value (ASC 715-30-35-60).

Multiple-Employer Plans

Some pension plans to which two or more unrelated employers contribute are not multiemployer plans, but are groups of single-employer plans combined to allow participating employers to pool assets for investment purposes and to reduce the cost of plan administration. Under ASC 715, multiple-employer plans are considered single-employer plans and each employer's accounting shall be based on its respective interest in the plan (ASC 715-30-35-70).

Non-U.S. Pension Plans

ASC 715 does not make any special provision for non-U.S. pension plans. In some foreign countries, it is customary or required for an employer to provide benefits for employees in the event of a voluntary or involuntary severance of employment. In this event, if the substance of the arrangement is a pension plan, it is subject to the provisions of ASC 715 (e.g., benefits are paid for substantially all terminations) (ASC 715-30-15-3).

Business Combinations

When a single-employer defined benefit pension plan is acquired as part of a business combination accounted for by the acquisition method, the acquirer shall recognize an asset or a liability representing the funded status of the plan. When determining the funded status of the plan, the acquirer shall exclude the effects of expected plan amendments, terminations, or curtailments that at the acquisition date it has no obligation to make. If an acquiree participates in a multiemployer plan, and it is probable that it will withdraw from that plan, the acquirer shall recognize as part of the business combination a withdrawal liability in accordance with ASC 450 (ASC 805-20-25-23).

DEFINED CONTRIBUTION PENSION PLANS

A defined contribution pension plan provides for employers' contributions that are defined in the plan, but does not contain any provision for defined pension benefits for employees. Based on the amount of the employer's defined contributions, however, pension benefits are provided in return for services performed by employees.

Under ASC 715, a defined contribution pension plan provides for individual accounts for each plan participant and contains the terms that specify how contributions are determined for each participant's individual account. Each periodic employer contribution is allocated to each participant's individual account in accordance with the terms of the plan, and pension benefits are based solely on the amount available in each participant's account at the time of his or her retirement. The amount available in each participant's account at the time of his or her retirement is the total of the amounts contributed by the employer, plus the returns earned on investments of those contributions, and forfeitures of other participants' benefits that have been allocated to the participant's account, less any allocated administrative expenses.

Under ASC 715, the net periodic pension cost of a defined contribution pension plan is the amount of contributions made or due in a period on behalf of participants who performed services during that same period. Contributions for periods after an individual retires or terminates shall be estimated and accrued during periods in which the individual performs services.

SETTLEMENTS AND CURTAILMENTS

In connection with the operation of a defined benefit pension plan, ASC 715 provides for the delayed recognition of actuarial gains and losses, prior service costs, and the net obligation or asset that arises at the date of the initial application of pension plan accounting. As a result, at any given date, an employer's pension plan records may reflect a balance of a (*a*) net gain or loss, (*b*) prior service cost, and/or (*c*) net transition obligation or net asset. These amounts are included in accumulated other comprehensive income until they are recognized as a component of net periodic pension cost. Part or all of these amounts may be recognized in a settlement or curtailment of a pension plan.

In a settlement of a defined benefit pension plan, the employer or the pension plan is released irrevocably from its primary responsibility for all or part of its pension plan obligation, and all significant risks relating to the settlement are eliminated. For example, through the purchase of nonparticipating annuity contracts or cash payments to some or all of the plan participants in exchange for their pension benefits, an employer may be released irrevocably from the pension plan obligation related to the benefits involved in the exchange. After the settlement of a pension plan, an employer may continue to provide pension benefits in the same pension plan or a new plan.

In a curtailment of a defined benefit pension plan, some of the future pension benefits for present employees are reduced, generally resulting in a net decrease (gain) or increase (loss) in the projected benefit obligation. For example, if employees are terminated as a result of a plan curtailment, some or all of their pension benefits based on future compensation levels may cease to be an obligation of the employer or pension plan. In this event, the projected benefit obligation is decreased (a gain) by the amount of the pension benefits that are no longer an obligation of the plan. On the other hand, if terminated employees who are eligible for subsidized early retirement benefits accept the benefits at a date earlier than expected, there is an increase (loss) in the projected benefit obligation. Gain or loss on a plan curtailment is based on the net decrease (gain) or increase (loss) in the projected benefit obligation.

An employer may have to recognize an additional loss that is not included in the gain or loss on a plan curtailment, but is recognized as part of the total effects of a plan curtailment. This loss is equal to the amount of decrease in the unrecognized prior service cost of the pension benefits that are reduced by the plan curtailment. A separate loss computation is necessary for the prior service cost of each plan amendment.

The pension benefits that are reduced or eliminated in a plan curtailment may have been granted to some or all of the employees who were working for the employer as of the date of the initial application of pension plan accounting. For this reason, any transition *net obligation* that arose at the date of the initial application of pension plan accounting and that remains unamortized at the date of the plan curtailment is also treated as a separate prior service cost.

A pension plan settlement and a pension plan curtailment may occur simultaneously or separately. If the expected years of future service for some employees are reduced but the pension plan continues in existence, a curtailment has occurred, but not a settlement. If an employer settles all or a portion of its pension obligation and continues to provide defined benefits to employees for future services, either in the same plan or in a successor plan, a settlement has occurred, but not a curtailment. If an employer terminates its defined benefit pension plan without replacing it with another defined benefit pension plan, and settles its present pension plan obligation in full, a curtailment and settlement has occurred. Under these circumstances, it makes no difference whether or not some or all of the employees continue to work for the employer.

Employers frequently offer termination benefits as part of an overall plan to reduce employment levels, to increase productivity, or generally to decrease payroll costs. To induce certain groups of employees to terminate employment, many employers offer attractive termination benefits. This is particularly true for those employees who are close to, or have reached, the early retirement age specified in the employer's existing pension plan. Termination benefits may consist of periodic future payments, lump-sum payments, or a combination of both. The payment of termination benefits may be made from a new or existing employee benefit plan, from the employer's existing assets, or from a combination of these sources.

Under ASC 715, termination benefits are classified either as *special* or *contractual*. Special termination benefits are those that are offered to employees for a short period of time in connection with their termination of employment. Contractual termination benefits are those that are required by the terms of an existing plan or agreement and are provided only on the occurrence of a specified event, such as early retirement or the closing of a facility.

The cost of termination benefits is recognized by an employer as a loss and a corresponding liability. The recognition date depends on whether the benefits are special or contractual.

SETTLEMENTS OF DEFINED BENEFIT PENSION PLANS

Under ASC 715, a settlement of a defined benefit pension plan is an irrevocable transaction that (*a*) releases the employer or the pension plan from its primary responsibility for the payment of all or a portion of the pension plan obligation and (*b*) eliminates all of the significant risks associated with the assets and obligations used to effectuate the settlement (ASC 715-30-15-6). A settlement of a defined benefit pension plan does not require that the plan be completely terminated.

All or a part of an employer's obligation to provide pension plan benefits to individuals may be transferred effectively to an insurance company by the purchase of annuity contracts. An annuity contract is an irrevocable agreement in which an insurance company unconditionally agrees to provide specific periodic payments or a lump sum payment to another party in return for a specified premium. For the purposes of ASC 715, this definition of an annuity contract is not met if the insurance company is a *captive insurer* or there is reasonable doubt that the insurance company will meet its obligation. A captive insurer is one that does business primarily with the employer and its related parties (ASC 715-30-35-54).

An annuity contract may be participating or nonparticipating. In a participating annuity contract, the insurance company's investing returns are shared generally, in the form of dividends, with the purchaser of the contract (the employer or the pension fund). An annuity contract is not considered an annuity contract unless all the risks and rewards associated with the assets and obligations assumed by the insurance company are actually transferred to the insurance company by the employer (ASC 715-30-35-57).

Gain or loss on a plan settlement is based on pension plan records that have been updated as of the day before the settlement. Under ASC 715, the maximum gain or loss on a settlement of a defined benefit pension plan is equal to the total balance of (*a*) any net gain or loss that remains in accumulated other comprehensive income the date of the plan settlement and (*b*) any transition asset that arose at the date of the initial application of pension plan accounting that remains in accumulated other comprehensive income (ASC 715-30-35-79).

If the total pension plan obligation is settled by the employer, the maximum gain or loss is recognized. If part of the pension benefit obligation is settled, the employer must recognize a pro rata portion of the maximum gain or loss, equal to the percentage reduction in the projected benefit obligation, unless the transaction qualifies as a "small settlement" (discussed below). Thus, if 40% of the pension plan obligation is settled, 40% of the maximum gain or loss on the settlement is recognized, and if 100% of the pension benefit obligation is settled, 100% of the maximum gain or loss is recognized (ASC 715-30-35-79).

If the employer purchases a participating annuity contract to settle a pension obligation, the cost of the contract must be allocated between the cost of the pure annuity feature and the cost of the participation right. The amount of cost allocated to the participation rights reduces gain (but not loss) that would otherwise be recognized on a plan settlement. However, the participation rights do not affect the determination of the amount of loss that is recognized on a plan settlement (ASC 715-30-35-79).

Reporting Gain or Loss on a Plan Settlement

Gain or loss on a plan settlement is reported as an ordinary gain or loss.

Small Settlements for the Year

Part or all of a pension plan's obligation to an employee may be settled by the payment of cash or the purchase of an annuity contract.

The cost of a cash settlement of a pension plan obligation is the amount of cash paid to the employee. The cost of a settlement of a pension plan obligation involving a nonparticipating annuity contract is the cost of the contract. The cost of a settlement involving a participating annuity contract is the cost of the contract less the amount attributed to the participation rights (ASC 715-30-35-83).

If the total cost of all plan settlements for the year is small or insignificant, gain or loss recognition may not be required. ASC 715 provides that an employer is not required, but is permitted, to recognize the gain or loss on all plan settlements for the year if the cost of all such settlements does not exceed the sum of the service cost and interest cost components of the net periodic pension cost for the current year. Once an accounting policy is adopted for small or insignificant settlements, it must be applied consistently from year to year. Thus, an employer that initially elects nonrecognition of gain or loss on all small settlements during a year must continue that same accounting policy from year to year (ASC 715-30-35-82).

PRACTICE POINTER: If the total cost of all plan settlements for the year is small or insignificant, the employer has discretion to decide whether or not to recognize gain or loss, provided only that the accounting policy is followed consistently from year to year.

CURTAILMENT OF DEFINED BENEFIT PENSION PLANS

Under ASC 715, a curtailment of a defined benefit pension plan results from an event in which (*a*) the expected years of future service arising from a prior plan amendment are *significantly* reduced for present employees who are entitled to receive pension benefits from that prior plan amendment or (*b*) the accrual of defined pension benefits is eliminated for some or all of the future services of a *significant* number of employees (ASC Glossary).

The total effects of a plan curtailment consist of (1) the decrease (loss) in the prior service cost (or unrecognized transition obligation) remaining in accumulated other comprehensive income that results from the significant reduction of the expected years of future service for present employees (see (*a*) above), and (2) the net decrease (gain) or increase (loss) in the projected benefit obligation that results from the elimination of the accrual of defined pension benefits for some or all of the future services of a significant number of employees (see (*b*) above). Each of these two components that comprise the total effects of a plan curtailment are discussed separately below (ASC 715-30-35-92, 93).

Decrease (Loss) in Prior Service Cost

Retroactive pension benefits are sometimes granted by an employer, upon adoption of a plan or through a plan amendment, based on employees' services in prior periods. The costs of these retroactive pension benefits are referred to as prior service costs. Retroactive pension benefits are granted by an employer in expectation of future economic benefits, such as reduced employee turnover and higher productivity. ASC 715 requires that the prior service cost relating to a specific plan amendment be amortized in equal amounts over the expected years of future service of each active employee who is expected to receive benefits from the plan amendment. Periodic amortization for each expected year of future service is calculated by dividing the total expected years of future service into the total amount of unrecognized prior service cost. The total amount of prior service cost represents the total cost of pension benefits that have been granted under the provisions of the plan amendment. If the expected years of future service are reduced as a result of a plan curtailment, the related prior service cost also must be reduced and recognized as a loss by the employer.

The expected years of future service for present employees may be reduced significantly by the termination or suspension of pension benefits for future services so that employees are no longer allowed to earn additional benefits. In addition, the termination of some of the present employees earlier than expected may also result in a significant reduction in their total expected years of future service. As a result of the significant reduction in the expected years of future service, a loss is incurred by the employer in the amount of the decrease in the balance of the related unamortized unrecognized prior service cost at the date of the plan curtailment. To compute the loss, the percentage reduction in the total remaining expected years of future service at the date of the plan curtailment first must be calculated (number of expected years of future service that are reduced, divided by the total number of remaining expected years of future service before reduction). To determine the amount of the loss, the balance of the related prior service cost amount at the date of the plan curtailment is multiplied by the percentage reduction in the total number of expected years of future service. For example, if the total remaining expected years of future service at the date of the plan curtailment is 1,000, and the number of years of future service that is reduced is 400, the percentage reduction is 40%. The balance of the related prior service cost at the date of the plan curtailment is reduced by 40%, which represents the loss that the employer must recognize as part of the total effects of the plan curtailment.

For the purposes of ASC 715, the balance of any transition *net obligation* that arose at the date of the initial application of pension plan accounting, which is included in accumulated other comprehensive income at the date of a subsequent plan curtailment, also is treated as a separate prior service cost amount (ASC 715-30-35-92). Thus, if the expected years of future service are reduced significantly for those employees employed at the date of the initial application of pension plan accounting, a separate loss must be calculated and recognized by the employer. This loss equals the amount by which the *transition obligation* included in accumulated other comprehensive income is reduced when multiplied by the percentage reduction resulting from the expected years of future service that are significantly reduced for those employees who were employed at the date of the initial application of pension plan accounting.

The total of all decreases (losses) in prior service costs and/or transition net obligation is included in the total effects of a plan curtailment, but is not included in the gain or loss on the plan curtailment.

The following steps are necessary to compute each decrease (loss) in the balance of the prior service cost amount at the date of a plan curtailment arising from a significant reduction in the expected years of employees' future service:

Step 1: Compute the percentage reduction in the total remaining expected years of future service, at the date of the plan curtailment, resulting from the expected years of future service that are significantly reduced. For example, if the expected years of future service that are reduced are 600 and the total remaining expected years of future service at the date of the plan curtailment is 1,000, the percentage reduction is 60%.

Step 2: Multiply the balance of the prior service cost included in accumulated comprehensive income (or transition obligation) of each plan amendment affected by the plan curtailment by the percentage calculated in Step 1. The result is the amount of loss that the employer must recognize as part of the total effects of the plan curtailment. The balance of the prior service cost amount (or transition obligation) is also reduced by the same amount. (From a practical standpoint, the dollar amount of amortization for each expected year of future service can be multiplied by the total number of expected years of future service that is reduced.)

Step 3: The amount of loss recognized on the decrease in the balance of the prior service cost amount (or transition obligation) is not part of the gain or loss on the plan curtailment, but is included in the total effects of the plan curtailment.

Illustration of Computation of Expected Years of Future Service and Loss from the Decrease in Prior Service Cost Resulting from the Expected Years of Future Service That Are Significantly Reduced by a Plan Curtailment

Company X had 50 employees who were expected to receive pension benefits under a new pension plan amendment, which became effective January 1, 20X5. In the computation of the expected years of future service for each employee who was entitled to receive benefits under the new plan amendment, the company assumed that five employees would either quit or retire each year during the next ten years. The total amount of prior service cost arising from the new pension plan amendment was $27,500.

		Year									
Employee Number	*Expected Years of Future Service*	*X5*	*X6*	*X7*	*X8*	*X9*	*Y0*	*Y1*	*Y2*	*Y3*	*Y4*
1-5	5	5									
6-10	10	5	5								
11-15	15	5	5	5							
16-20	20	5	5	5	5						
21-25	25	5	5	5	5	5					

		Year									
Employee Number	*Expected Years of Future Service*	*X5*	*X6*	*X7*	*X8*	*X9*	*Y0*	*Y1*	*Y2*	*Y3*	*Y4*
26-30	30	5	5	5	5	5	5				
31-35	35	5	5	5	5	5	5	5			
36-40	40	5	5	5	5	5	5	5	5		
41-45	45	5	5	5	5	5	5	5	5	5	
46-50	50	5	5	5	5	5	5	5	5	5	5
Service years rendered	275	50	45	40	35	30	25	20	15	10	5
Amortization fraction		50/27	45/275	40/275	35/275	30/275	25/275	20/275	15/275	10/275	5/275

Amortization for each expected year of future service equals $100 ($27,500 prior service cost divided by 275 years of expected future service).

Assume, at the beginning of X7, that 15 employees are terminated, resulting in a reduction of 90 years (given) of expected future service. The percentage reduction of expected future service years is 50%, determined as follows:

Expected years of future service, beginning of X7, before terminations (275, less amortization of 50 for X5 and 45 for X6)	180
Reduction due to terminations (given)	90
Percentage reduction: 90/180	50%

The remaining balance of prior service cost relating to the new plan amendment at the beginning of year 3 was $18,000 (180 remaining years of expected future service multiplied by the $100 amortization rate per year). Thus, the pension plan curtailment, relating to the expected years of future service that were significantly reduced by the termination of 15 employees, results in a loss of $9,000 (50% of $18,000).

Decrease (Gain) or Increase (Loss) in the Projected Benefit Obligation

A plan curtailment may result in a net decrease (gain) or net increase (loss) in the projected benefit obligation. For example, if employees are terminated as a result of a plan curtailment, some or all of their pension benefits based on future compensation levels may cease to be an obligation of the employer or pension plan. In this event, the projected benefit obligation is decreased (a gain) by the amount of the benefits that are no longer an obligation of the plan. On the other hand, if terminated employees who are eligible for subsidized early retirement benefits accept those benefits at an earlier date than expected, there usually is an increase (loss) in the projected benefit obligation. Gain or loss on a plan curtailment is based on the net decrease (gain) or increase (loss) in the projected benefit obligation (ASC 715-30-35-93).

The following steps are necessary to compute the gain or loss on a plan curtailment:

Step 1: Determine the total net gain (decrease) or net loss (increase) in the projected benefit obligation resulting from the plan curtailment. Do not include any increase (loss) in the projected benefit obligation that arises in connection with termination benefits (ASC 715-30-35-93).

Step 2: Determine whether a net gain or net loss exists. Combine the remaining balance of any unrecognized *net obligation* that arose at the date of the initial application of pension plan accounting and remains in accumulated other comprehensive income at the date of the plan curtailment, with the balance of any unrecognized net gain or loss that arose after the initial application of pension plan accounting and also remains unamortized at the date of the plan curtailment. (**Note:** The remaining balance of any transition obligation that arose at the date of the initial application of pension plan accounting and remains in accumulated other comprehensive income at the date of the plan curtailment is treated as part of prior service cost.) (ASC 715-30-35-92).

The amount of gain or loss on the plan curtailment is recognized as follows:

1. *If the change in the projected benefit obligation is a net gain (Step 1) and there is a net gain included in accumulated other comprehensive income (Step 2)* Curtailment gain is recognized in the amount of the net gain in the projected benefit obligation. (The unrecognized net gain computed in Step 2 is not used.)

2. *If the change in the projected benefit obligation is a net gain (Step 1) and there is an unrecognized net loss (Step 2)* If the net gain in the projected benefit obligation does not exceed the net loss included in accumulated other comprehensive income, no curtailment gain or loss is recognized. If the net gain exceeds the net loss included in accumulated other comprehensive income, curtailment gain is recognized in the amount of the excess of the net gain in the projected benefit obligation over the net loss included in accumulated other comprehensive income.

3. *If the change in the projected benefit obligation is a net loss (Step 1) and there is a net gain included in accumulated other comprehensive income (Step 2)* If the net loss in the projected benefit obligation does not exceed the net gain, no curtailment gain or loss is recognized. If the net loss exceeds the net gain included in accumulated other comprehensive income, curtailment loss is recognized in the amount of the excess of the net loss in the projected benefit obligation over the net gain in accumulated other comprehensive income.

4. *If the change in the projected benefit obligation is a net loss (Step 1) and there is a net loss in accumulated other comprehensive income (Step 2)* Curtailment loss is recognized in the amount of the net loss in the projected benefit obligation. (The unrecognized net loss computed in Step 2 is not used.)

Recognition of the Total Effects of a Plan Curtailment

The total effects of a plan curtailment consist of (*a*) the decrease (loss) in the prior service cost amount and/or transition net obligation, resulting from the significant reduction of the expected years of future service for present employees, and (*b*) the net decrease (gain) or increase (loss) in the projected benefit obligation that results from the elimination of the accrual of defined pension benefits for some or all of the future services of a significant number of employees.

If the total effects of a plan curtailment result in a loss, the loss is recognized when it is *probable* that the curtailment will occur and the effects of the curtailment can be *reasonably estimated*. If the total effects of a plan curtailment result in a gain, the gain is recognized only when the related employees terminate or the plan suspension or amendment is adopted (ASC 715-30-35-94).

Reporting Total Effects of a Plan Curtailment

Gain or loss on the total effects of a pension plan curtailment is reported as an ordinary gain or loss.

TERMINATION BENEFITS

Under ASC 715, termination benefits are classified as either *special* or *contractual*. Special termination benefits are those that are offered to employees for a short period in connection with the termination of their employment. Contractual termination benefits are those that are required by the terms of an existing plan or agreement and that are provided only on the occurrence of a specified event, such as early retirement or the closing of a facility (ASC 712-10-05-2).

ASC 715 requires the recognition of the cost of termination benefits as a loss and corresponding liability. The recognition date depends on whether the benefits are special or contractual.

Special Termination Benefits

The recognition date on which the employer records the loss and corresponding liability for special termination benefits occurs when (*a*) the employees accept the offer of the special termination benefits and (*b*) the amount of the cost of the benefits can be reasonably estimated (ASC 715-30-25-10).

Contractual Termination Benefits

The recognition date on which the employer records the loss and corresponding liability for contractual termination benefits occurs when (*a*) it is probable that employees will be entitled to the benefits and (*b*) the amount of the cost of the benefits can be estimated reasonably (ASC 715-30-25-10).

Reporting a Loss on Termination Benefits

A loss on termination benefits is reported as an ordinary loss.

FINANCIAL STATEMENT DISCLOSURE

The disclosure requirements for settlements and curtailments of plans are incorporated into a general set of disclosure requirements for all pension and other postretirement plans. They are covered earlier in this chapter in the discussion of subtopic ASC 715-20.

Illustration of Curtailment and Settlement of a Pension Plan

The updated records of a defined benefit pension plan reflect the following:

Vested benefits	$ (30,000)
Nonvested benefits	(50,000)
Accumulated benefit obligation	$ (80,000)
Effects on benefits as a result of considering future compensation levels	(20,000)
Projected benefit obligation	$(100,000)
Fair value of plan assets	95,000
Funded status of plan, recognized as a liability on the balance sheet	$ (5,000)
Prior service cost	1,000
Net (gain) or loss	(1,000)
Transition net obligation or (net asset) at date of initial application of pension plan accounting	2,000

Assume that the above plan is completely terminated without a successor plan. Under this circumstance, the effects on benefits as a result of considering future compensation levels are no longer an obligation of the employer or the plan, since all of the plan participants have been terminated. Assume also that the total projected benefit obligation was settled by the purchase of nonparticipating annuity contracts for $80,000, and the excess plan assets in the amount of $15,000 were withdrawn by the employer.

Computation of the total effects of a plan curtailment

The total effects of a plan curtailment consist of (*a*) the total loss resulting from the decreases in the balances of any unamortized unrecognized prior service costs and/or the transition net obligation included in accumulated other comprehensive income relating to the expected years of future service that were significantly reduced for present employees and (*b*) the net decrease (gain) or increase (loss) in the projected benefit obligation resulting from the elimination of the accrual of defined pension benefits for some or all of the future services of a significant number of employees.

The loss resulting from the decrease in the balance of any prior service costs (or transition net obligation) is computed as follows:

Step 1. The percentage reduction, if any, in the balances of any prior service cost and/or the transition net obligation must be calculated (each loss must be computed separately, unless the pension plan is completely terminated). In the above illustration, the percentage reduction resulting from the significant reduction in the expected years of future service is 100%, because the plan is completely terminated. As a result, no separate computation is necessary.

Step 2. Multiply the balance of the prior service cost and transition net obligation by its percentage reduction, if any. In the above illustration, the balance of the prior service cost of $1,000 is multiplied by 100%, and the balance of the transition net obligation of $2,000 is multiplied by 100%; the sum of the resulting amounts is a total loss of $3,000.

Step 3. The $3,000 computed in Step 2 is treated as an effect of the plan curtailment, not as part of the gain or loss on the plan curtailment.

The net decrease (gain) or increase (loss) in the projected benefit obligation is computed as follows:

Step 4. Calculate the net decrease (gain) or net increase (loss) in the projected benefit obligation resulting from the plan curtailment. Do not include any increase (loss) in the projected benefit obligation that arose in connection with termination benefits. In the above illustration, the effects on benefits as a result of considering future compensation levels of $20,000 are no longer an obligation of the employer or the plan. This results in a $20,000 net decrease (gain) in the projected benefit obligation, because there are no other decreases or increases.

Step 5. Compute the total of (*a*) the balance of any net gain or loss that remains in accumulated other comprehensive income at the date of the plan curtailment and (*b*) the balance of any transition net asset that remains in accumulated other comprehensive income at the date of the plan curtailment. In the above illustration, the total is a gain of $1,000 (net gain of $1,000 and no net asset).

Step 6. Compute the gain or loss on the plan curtailment, as follows:

- If Step 4 (projected benefit obligation) is a gain and Step 5 is also a gain, curtailment gain is recognized in the amount of Step 4 (the amount of gain in Step 5 is ignored).
- If Step 4 (projected benefit obligation) is a loss and Step 5 is also a loss, curtailment loss is recognized in the amount of Step 4 (the amount of loss in Step 5 is ignored).
- If Step 4 (projected benefit obligation) is a gain and Step 5 is a loss, curtailment gain is recognized in the amount by which the gain in Step 4 exceeds the loss in Step 5. If Step 5 exceeds Step 4, no gain or loss is recognized.
- If Step 4 (projected benefit obligation) is a loss and Step 5 is a gain, curtailment loss is recognized in the amount by which the loss in Step 4 exceeds the gain in Step 5. If Step 5 exceeds Step 4, no gain or loss is recognized.

In the above illustration, the net decrease (gain) in the projected benefit obligation was $20,000 (Step 4) and the total net gain or loss is a gain of $1,000 (Step 5). Since both steps result in a gain, a gain on the plan curtailment in the amount of Step 4 is recognized, which is $20,000.

Settlement gain or loss

As in Step 5 above, compute the total of (*a*) the balance of any net gain or loss that remains in accumulated other comprehensive income at the date of the plan settlement and (*b*) the balance of any transition net asset that remains in accumulated other comprehensive income at the date of the plan settlement.

If part of the pension obligation is settled, the employer must recognize a pro rata portion of the maximum gain or loss, equal to the total of the net gain or loss and/or the transition net asset multiplied by the percentage reduction in the projected benefit obligation. In the above illustration, there was a net gain of $1,000 and no transition net asset. Since the pension plan was terminated, the pension obligation completely settled, and the decrease in the projected benefit obligation was 100%, the pro rata portion that must be recognized is 100%, or $1,000. Thus, the gain on the settlement of the pension plan is $1,000.

Summary

The loss on the decrease in the prior service cost amount and transition net obligation is $3,000, which was computed in Step 3. This loss is reported as a "Loss on Effects of Curtailment of Pension Plan." The net gain on the decrease in the projected benefit obligation is $20,000, which was computed in Step 6. This gain is reported as a "Gain on the Curtailment of Pension Plan." The "Gain on the Settlement of Pension Plan" is $1,000, which was computed separately above. Thus, the net gain on the pension plan curtailment and settlement was $18,000 ($3,000 loss, $20,000 gain, and $1,000 gain).

Journal entry

The journal entry and suggested financial statement presentation of the net gain on pension plan curtailment and settlement of $18,000 is as follows:

Cash (excess plan assets)	15,000	
Liability for pension benefits	3,000	
Gain from termination of pension plan		18,000

Suggested financial statement presentation:	
Gain on curtailment of pension plan	$20,000
Loss on effects of curtailment of pension plan	(3,000)
Total effects of plan curtailment	$17,000
Gain on settlement of pension plan	1,000
Net gain on pension plan curtailment and settlement	$18,000

ASC 715-60: DEFINED BENEFIT PLANS—OTHER POST-RETIREMENT

U.S. GAAP REQUIREMENTS

ASC 715 establishes *accounting* standards for employers with postretirement benefit plans. *Postretirement benefits* consist of all forms of benefits other than retirement income provided by an employer to retired workers, their beneficiaries, and their dependents (ASC 715-60-15-3). The term does not include benefits paid after employment but before retirement, such as layoff benefits. Postemployment benefits are also covered by ASC 715, which is the subject of a later section in this chapter.

Postretirement benefit payments may begin immediately on employees' termination of service or may be deferred until retired employees reach a specified age. Benefits such as health care, tuition assistance, or legal services are provided to retirees as the need arises. Other benefits, such as life insurance, are provided on the occurrence of specified events (ASC 715-10-05-7).

A *postretirement benefit plan* is one in which an employer agrees to provide certain postretirement benefits to current and former employees after they retire. A postretirement benefit plan may be *contributory* (employees may be required to contribute to the plan) or *noncontributory* (the entire cost of the plan is borne by the employer).

A postretirement benefit plan may be *funded* or *unfunded*—that is, the employees and/or the employer may make cash contributions to a postretirement benefit plan trustee (i.e., funded), or the employer may make only credit entries on its books reflecting the postretirement benefit liability under the plan and pay all benefits from its general assets (i.e., unfunded).

General Approach—Deferred Compensation

According to ASC 715, postretirement benefits are a type of *deferred compensation* that is accounted for as part of an employee's total compensation package. A *deferred compensation plan* is an agreement specifying that a portion of an employee's compensation will be set aside and paid in future periods. ASC 715 requires employers to account for postretirement benefit plans on the accrual basis.

Comparison of Pension Accounting to Postretirement Benefit Accounting

Although there are some important differences, the accounting for postretirement benefits is very similar to the accounting for pension benefits.

In accounting for postretirement benefits under ASC 715, an employer makes at least two types of journal entries to record its cost of these benefits—one to record the annual expense and related liability and a second to record the payment or funding of the liability, if any.

Illustration of Basic Entries for Recording Postretirement Benefits

Assuming a company determines its annual expense for postretirement benefits is $10,000 and funds that amount, the following entries are made (assume a 30% tax rate):

1.	Net periodic postretirement benefit cost	10,000	
	Deferred tax asset	3,000	
	Deferred tax benefit—net income		3,000
	Liability for postretirement benefits		10,000
	(To accrue postretirement benefit cost of $10,000 for a specific period.)		

2.	Liability for postretirement benefits	10,000	
	Cash		10,000
	(To record cash contribution to postretirement plan trust or to pay benefits of $10,000.)		

These entries are similar to those required for pension accounting, except for differences in the titles of the accounts.

Most of the provisions of ASC 715 pertain to the computation of the amount to be recorded in journal entry type (1) above. This computation requires numerous worksheet calculations, which are illustrated throughout ASC 715.

Use of Reasonable Approximations

ASC 715 allows an employer to use estimates, averages, or computational shortcuts, provided that the employer reasonably expects that the results will not be materially different from those which would have been reached by a fully detailed application of the requirements in ASC 715 (ASC 715-60-35-1).

Scope and Applicability

The requirements of ASC 715 related to postretirement benefits affect:

1. Types of benefits
2. Types of beneficiaries
3. General rather than selective coverage of employees
4. Source and form of payment
5. Nature of the employer's undertaking

Types of Benefits

ASC 715 applies to an employer's undertaking to provide various types of nonpension benefits to employees after they retire. The benefits may commence immediately upon termination of the employee's active service, or may be deferred until the retired employee reaches a specified age.

The benefits include health care, life insurance outside of a pension plan, tuition assistance, day care, legal services, housing subsidies, and other types of postretirement benefits (ASC 715-60-15-4). If an employer has established a plan to provide benefits to active employees as well as to retired employees, ASC 715 requires the employer to divide the plan into two parts for accounting purposes; one part covering benefits to active employees and the other part covering benefits to retired employees. The employer should use the accounting standards of ASC 715 only for the part covering benefits to retired employees (ASC 715-60-15-7).

Types of Beneficiaries

The beneficiaries may be retired employees, disabled employees, any other former employees who are expected to receive benefits, or retirees' beneficiaries and covered dependents, pursuant to the terms of an employer's undertaking to provide such benefits. The beneficiaries may also be individuals who (*a*) have ceased permanent active employment because of disability, (*b*) have not yet completed formal procedures for retirement, or (*c*) are carried on nonretired status under the disability provisions of the plan so that they can continue accumulating credit for pensions or other postretirement benefits (ASC 715-60-35-44).

General Rather Than Selective Coverage of Employees

The plan should cover employees in general, rather than selected individual employees. An employer's practice of providing postretirement benefits to selected employees under individual contracts with specific terms determined on an individual basis does not constitute a postretirement benefit plan under ASC 715. ASC 715 does apply to contracts with individual employees if these contracts, taken together, are equivalent to a plan covering employees in general (ASC 715-10-15-5).

PRACTICE NOTE: An employer's commitment to selected individual employees is accrued in accordance with the terms of the individual contracts (see the section in the ASC 715-10 discussion titled *Illustrations of Accruals Required by ASC 715*). Professional judgment is required whenever contracts with individual employees may be equivalent to a general plan.

Source and Form of Payment

A plan is covered by ASC 715 if it provides reimbursement or direct payment to providers for the cost of specified services as the need for those services arises, or if it provides lump sum benefits, such as death benefits. The plan may be either funded or unfunded (ASC 715-10-15-2).

PRACTICE NOTE: If the plan is funded, the assets of a postretirement benefit plan usually are kept in a trust account, segregated from the assets of the employer. Contributions to the postretirement benefit plan trust account are made periodically by the employer and, if the plan is contributory, by the employees. The plan assets may be invested in stocks, bonds, real estate, and other types of investments. Plan assets are increased by earnings, gains on investments, and contributions by the employer (and employees if the plan is contributory), and are decreased by losses on investments and the payment of benefits and any related administrative expenses.

Nature of the Employer's Undertaking

ASC 715 applies to any arrangement that is in substance a plan for providing postretirement benefits, regardless of its form (ASC 715-10-15-3).

PRACTICE NOTE: When it is not clear that a plan exists, professional judgment is required in determining whether a plan exists "in substance." ASC 715 provides little guidance on this issue.

ASC 715 applies not only to written plans, but also to unwritten plans if the existence of these plans can be perceived based on (*a*) the employer's practice of paying benefits or (*b*) the employer's oral representations to current or former employees. Once an employer pays benefits or promises to pay benefits, ASC 715 presumes that the employer has undertaken to provide future benefits as indicated by the past payments or promises, unless there is evidence to the contrary (ASC 715-10-15-3).

PRACTICE NOTE: To indicate the existence of a plan, it appears that the employer's oral representations (*a*) should refer to a plan that is general in its scope and (*b*) should be communicated to current or former employees in general, or to individual employees as representatives of the employees in general.

One issue is whether ASC 715 applies only to legally enforceable obligations, or to a broader range of commitments including those that cannot be legally enforced.

PRACTICE NOTE: The Employee Retirement Income Security Act (ERISA) gives substantial legal protection to the expectations of employees under pension plans, but does not give the same level of protection to employee expectations of nonpension benefits. Courts have upheld the right of employers to terminate or curtail benefits under nonpension plans, unless the employers have entered into legally binding commitments to maintain benefits, such as collective bargaining agreements.

PRACTICE NOTE:

- Accountants should obtain expert advice before (*a*) advising employers on the applicability of ASC 715 to existing plans, (*b*) advising employers on the structuring of new plans or the restructuring of existing plans if the structure of the plan may determine whether the plan is within the scope of ASC 715, or (*c*) auditing the financial statements of an employer if there is a serious question as to whether the employer's plan is within the scope of ASC 715.
- If a plan is covered by ASC 715, the next question is whether the plan is a defined benefit plan or a defined contribution plan. ASC 715 prescribes significantly different accounting and reporting requirements for these two types of plans. ASC 715 deals primarily with defined benefit plans. For the distinctive accounting and

reporting requirements applicable to defined contribution plans, see the section titled "Defined Contribution Plans" in this chapter. When considering the structuring or restructuring of a plan, the employer and its advisors should consider whether the plan is covered by ASC 715 and, if so, whether the plan is governed by the accounting and reporting requirements for defined benefit plans or for defined contribution plans.

SINGLE-EMPLOYER DEFINED BENEFIT POSTRETIREMENT PLANS

ASC 715 deals primarily with an employer's accounting for a single-employer plan that provides defined benefits. ASC 715 also briefly covers multiemployer plans, multiple-employer plans, and defined contribution plans. Each is discussed later in this chapter.

PRACTICE NOTE: The accounting and reporting requirements for defined contribution plans differ significantly from those for defined benefit plans. If a plan has some characteristics of each type, ASC 715 calls for careful analysis of the substance of the plan. The difference in the accounting and reporting requirements, depending on whether the plan is a defined benefit plan or a defined contribution plan, may be a significant factor to be considered by employers attempting to structure or restructure their plans.

In a defined benefit plan, the benefit may be defined in terms of a specified monetary amount (such as a life insurance benefit), or a specified type of benefit (such as all or a percentage of the cost of specified surgical procedures). The benefits may be subject to a maximum (or *cap*), either per individual employee or for the plan as a whole, or the employer may agree to pay the full amount of benefits without regard to any maximum amount (ASC 715-60-15-8).

The employee's entitlement to benefits is expressed in the benefit formula, which specifies the years of service to be rendered, age to be attained while in service, or a combination of both, which must be met for an employee to be eligible to receive benefits under the plan. The benefit formula may also define the beginning of the period of service during which the employee earns credit toward eligibility, as well as the levels of benefits earned for specific periods of service (ASC 715-60-05-2).

The total amount of benefits depends not only on the benefit formula but also on actuarial factors, such as the longevity of the retired employee (and the longevity of the retiree's beneficiaries and covered dependents), and the occurrence of specific events entitling the individuals to benefits (such as illnesses) (ASC 715-60-35-2).

Because of these factors, the employer cannot precisely calculate the amount of benefits to be paid in the future to any retired employee (or to the retiree's beneficiaries and covered dependents). The FASB is satisfied, however, that employers can make reasonable estimates useful for accounting purposes.

Accumulated Postretirement Benefit Obligation

ASC 715 requires the employer to accrue the accumulated postretirement benefit obligation. Once an employee has attained full eligibility, the amount of this obligation is the same as the employee's *expected* postretirement benefit obligation. Until then, the *accumulated* amount is the portion of the expected amount attributed to employee service rendered to a particular date (ASC Glossary).

The accumulated and the expected amounts represent the actuarial present value of the anticipated benefits. Measurement of these amounts is based on assumptions regarding such items as the expected cost of providing future benefits and any cost-sharing provisions under which the employee, the government, or others will absorb part of these costs. If the benefits or cost-sharing provisions are related to the employee's salary progression, the calculation of benefits and cost-sharing reflects the anticipated impact of this progression (ASC 715-60-35-2).

PRACTICE NOTE: The accounting for postretirement benefits differs from the accounting for pensions in this respect, because the accounting for pensions does not anticipate salary progression in determining the accumulated pension benefit obligation.

Illustration of Relationship between Expected and Accumulated Postretirement Benefit Obligations

A plan provides postretirement health care benefits to all employees who render at least ten years of service and attain age 65 while in service. A 60-year-old employee, hired at age 45, is expected to terminate employment at the end of the year in which the employee attains age 67 and is expected to live to age 77. A discount rate of 8% is assumed.

At December 31, 20X5, the employer estimates the expected amount and timing of benefit payments for that employee as follows:

Age	Expected Future Claims	Present Value at Age	
		60	65
68	$ 2,322	$ 1,255	$ 1,843
69	2,564	1,283	1,885
70	2,850	1,320	1,940
71	3,154	1,353	1,988
72	3,488	1,385	2,035
73	3,868	1,422	2,090
74	4,274	1,455	2,138
75	4,734	1,492	2,193
76	5,240	1,530	2,247
77	7,798	2,108	3,097
	$40,292	$14,603	$21,456

At December 31, 20X5, when the employee's age is 60, the *expected* postretirement benefit obligation is $14,603, and the *accumulated* postretirement benefit obligation is $10,952 (15/20 of $14,603 because the employee has worked 15 of the 20 years needed to attain age 65 while in service and thus become fully eligible for benefits).

Assuming no changes in health care costs or other circumstances, the obligations at later dates are as follows:

- December 31, 20Y0 (age 65), the expected and the accumulated postretirement benefit obligations are both $21,456. These amounts are the same, because the employee is fully eligible.
- December 31, 20Y1 (age 66), the expected and the accumulated postretirement benefit obligations are both $23,172 ($21,456 the previous year, plus interest at 8% for 1 year).

Measurement of Cost and Obligations

In discussing the measurement of cost and obligations of single-employer defined benefit plans, ASC 715 addresses the following issues:

- Accounting for the substantive plan
- Assumptions
- Attribution

Accounting for the Substantive Plan

According to ASC 715, the accounting and reporting should reflect the substantive plan; that is, the plan as understood by the employer and the employees. Generally, the substantive plan is accurately reflected in writing. The employer's past practice or communications of intended future changes, however, may indicate that the substantive plan differs from the written plan (ASC 715-60-35-48).

PRACTICE NOTE: If an independent auditor is faced with a situation in which the substantive plan appears to be different from the written plan, the auditor should (*a*) seek expert advice, (*b*) consult with the highest levels of the employer's management, and (*c*) fully document the matter in the audit files.

ASC 715 discusses the following areas in which the substantive plan may differ from the written plan:

- Cost sharing
- Benefit changes
- Plan amendments

Cost Sharing

In general, the employer's cost-sharing policy is regarded as part of the substantive plan if (*a*) the employer has maintained a consistent level of cost-sharing with retirees, (*b*) the employer consistently has increased or decreased the share of the cost contributed by employees or retirees, or (*c*) the employer has the ability to change the cost-sharing provisions at a specified time or when certain conditions exist, and has communicated to plan participants its intent to make such changes (ASC 715-60-35-51).

An employer's past practice regarding cost sharing, however, is not regarded as the substantive plan if (ASC 715-60-35-52):

- The cost sharing was accompanied by offsetting changes in other benefits or compensation.
- The employer was subjected to significant costs, such as work stoppages, to carry out that policy.

Along similar lines, an employer's communication of its intent to change the cost-sharing provisions is not regarded as the substantive plan if (ASC 715-60-35-54):

- The plan participants would be unwilling to accept the change without adverse results to the employer's operations.
- The plan participants would insist on other modifications of the plan that would offset the change in cost sharing, to accept the proposed change.

In estimating the amount of contributions to be received by the plan from active or retired employees, the employer should consider any relevant substantive plan provisions, such as the employer's past practice of consistently changing the contribution rates. If the employer is obliged to return contributions to employees who do not become eligible for benefits (together with interest, if applicable), the estimated amount of this obligation is (*a*) included in the employer's total benefit obligation and (*b*) factored into calculations of the contributions needed by the plan (ASC 715-60-35-57).

Benefit Changes

The measurement of the obligation under the plan includes automatic benefit changes specified by the plan. An example is a plan that promises to pay a benefit in kind, such as health care benefits, instead of a defined dollar amount. The obligation to pay the benefit automatically changes in amount when the cost of the benefit changes (ASC 715-60-35-58, 59).

Plan Amendments

Measurement also includes plan amendments as soon as they have been contractually agreed upon, even if some or all of the provisions become effective in later periods (ASC 715-60-35-60).

PRACTICE NOTE: Even if a plan amendment has not been contractually agreed upon, it appears that an employer should reflect the amendment if it can be regarded as a change in the substantive plan. In general, a substantive plan may differ from the written plan in either of two cases: (1) when the employer has communicated its intention to adopt the amendment and certain conditions are met or (2) when the employer has engaged in consistent past practice.

Assumptions

An employer has to make numerous assumptions to apply ASC 715. Each assumption should reflect the best estimate of the future event to which it relates, without regard to the estimates involved in making other assumptions. ASC 715 describes this as an explicit approach to assumptions (ASC 715-60-35-71).

PRACTICE NOTE: The FASB finds the use of **explicit** assumptions preferable to **implicit** assumptions, under which the reliability of assumptions would be judged in the aggregate, not individually.

All assumptions should be based on the expectation that the plan will continue in the absence of evidence that it will not continue (ASC 715-60-35-72). Some of the assumptions discussed in ASC 715 apply generally to all types of benefits, while other assumptions are unique to health care benefits.

ASC 715 discusses the following general assumptions:

- Time value of money (discount rates)
- Expected long-term rate of return on plan assets
- Future compensation levels
- Other general assumptions

Time Value of Money (Discount Rates)

One of the essential assumptions relates to discount rates. Assumed discount rates are used in measuring the expected and accumulated postretirement benefit obligations and the service cost and interest cost components of net periodic postretirement benefit cost. Assumed discount rates should reflect the time value of money at the measurement date, as indicated by rates of return on high-quality fixed-income investments currently available with cash flows corresponding to the anticipated needs of the plan. If the employer could settle its obligation under the plan by purchasing insurance (e.g., nonparticipating life insurance contracts to provide death benefits), the interest rates inherent in the potential settlement amount are relevant to the employer's determination of assumed discount rates (ASC 715-60-35-79).

The chosen discount rate should produce a liability amount that would generate the necessary future cash flows to pay postretirement benefits as they become due if such amount was invested at the financial statement date in a portfolio of high-quality fixed-income investments. This liability amount is theoretically equal to the market value of a portfolio of high-quality zero coupon bonds, where each bond matches the amount and maturity of future payments due under the postretirement benefit plan. However, reinvestment risk exists to the extent that the plan's assets include interest-bearing debt instruments (rather than only zero coupon bonds) and to the extent that plan investments have a maturity date that is sooner than some of the anticipated postretirement benefit payments. In such cases, the assumed discount (interest) rate needs to consider expected reinvestment rates extrapolated using the existing yield curve at the financial statement date. The discount rate should be reevaluated at each measurement (financial statement) date (ASC 715-60-35-80, 81).

PRACTICE POINTER: The discount rate used to determine the postretirement benefit liability and the interest cost component of net periodic postretirement benefit cost should change in accordance with changes in market interest rates: if interest rates rise, the discount rate should increase; if interest rates fall, the discount rate should decline. In addition, the determination of the discount rate is separate from the determination of the expected return on plan assets.

Expected Long-Term Rate of Return on Plan Assets

Assumptions are also required in determining the expected long-term rate of return on plan assets. In general, plan assets are investments that have been segregated and restricted, usually in a trust, for the exclusive purpose of paying postretirement benefits.

The expected long-term rate of return on plan assets should reflect the anticipated average rate of earnings on existing plan assets and those expected to be contributed during the period (ASC 715-60-35-84).

PRACTICE NOTE: This factor is used, together with the *market-related value* of plan assets, in computing the *expected return* on plan assets. The difference between the actual return and the expected return on plan assets is defined in ASC 715 as "plan asset gain or loss," discussed later.

If the return on plan assets is taxable to the trust or other fund under the plan, the expected long-term rate of return shall be reduced to reflect the related income taxes expected to be paid (ASC 715-60-35-86).

When estimating the rate of return on plan assets, the employer should consider the rate of return on (*a*) assets currently invested and (*b*) assets that will be reinvested. If the income from plan assets is taxable, the anticipated amount of taxes should be deducted to produce a net-of-tax rate of return. If a plan is unfunded or has no assets that qualify as plan assets under ASC 715, the employer has no basis or need to calculate an expected long-term rate of return on plan assets (ASC 715-60-35-84).

Future Compensation Levels

If the benefit formula provides for varying amounts of postretirement benefits based on the compensation levels of employees, the employer has to make further assumptions about the impact of anticipated future compensation levels on the cost of benefits and the obligation to pay them (ASC 715-60-35-75).

Estimates of future compensation are based on anticipated compensation of individual employees, including future changes arising from general price levels, productivity, seniority, promotion, and other factors. All assumptions should be consistent with regard to general factors such as future rates of inflation. The assumptions should also include any indirect effects related to salary progression, such as the impact of inflation-based adjustments to the maximum benefit provided under the plan (ASC 715-60-35-75, 88).

Other General Assumptions

Other general assumptions involved in applying ASC 715 include the following:

- Participation rates for contributory plans
- The probability of payment (such as turnover of employees, dependency status, and mortality)

PRACTICE POINTER: As is the case in pension accounting, the CPA is not expected to be an expert in actuarial science. In fact, accounting for pensions and other retirement benefits is an area where the CPA relies heavily on the expertise of actuaries. However, the CPA still must have a general understanding of the work of the actuary, including the reasonableness of the underlying assumptions the actuary is using to prepare information that may have a significant impact on an enterprise's funding of benefit plans, as well as its financial statements.

Assumptions Unique to Postretirement Health Care Benefits

Many postretirement benefit plans include health care benefits. Measurement of an employer's postretirement health care obligation requires the use of special types of assumptions that will affect the amount and timing of future benefit payments for postretirement health care, in addition to the general assumptions required by all postretirement benefit plans.

ASC 715 discusses the following assumptions unique to postretirement health care benefits:

- Per capita claims cost
- Assumptions about trends in health care costs

Per Capita Claims Cost

An employer should estimate the net incurred claims cost at each age at which a participant is expected to receive benefits. To estimate this net cost, the employer first estimates the assumed per capita gross claims cost at each age, and then subtracts the effects of (*a*) Medicare and other reimbursements from third parties and (*b*) cost-sharing provisions that cause the participant to collect less than 100% of the claim. If plan participants are required to make contributions to the plan during their active service, the actuarial present value of the participants' future contributions should be subtracted from the actuarial present value of the assumed net incurred claims costs (ASC 715-60-35-91).

The *assumed per capita claims cost* is the annual cost of benefits from the time at which an individual's coverage begins, for the remainder of that person's life (or until coverage ends, when sooner). The annual benefit cost is based on the best possible estimate of the expected future cost of benefits covered by the plan that reflects age and other appropriate factors such as gender and geographical location. If the employer incurs significant costs in administering the plan, these costs should also be considered part of the assumed per capita claims cost (ASC 715-60-35-92, 93).

If an employer does not have a reliable basis for estimating the assumed per capita claims cost by age, the employer may base its estimate on other reliable information. For example, the estimate may be based on the claims costs that have actually been incurred for employees of all ages, adjusted by factors to reflect health care cost trends, age of the covered population, and cost sharing (ASC 715-60-35-95).

A number of assumptions are based on the estimated effects of inflation. The employer should use consistent methods of estimating inflation, whether the assumption relates to discount rates, compensation levels, or health care cost trend rates.

If the history of the plan is reliable enough to provide a basis for future estimates, the past and present claims data of the plan are considered in calculating the assumed per capita claims cost. If the plan does not provide any reliable data, the employer may base its estimates on other employers' claims information, as assembled by insurance companies, actuarial firms, or employee benefits consulting firms (ASC 715-60-35-95).

PRACTICE NOTE: The independent auditor should verify that any outside information comes from reliable and independent sources, and that the audit files fully identify these sources.

The estimates derived from the experience of other employers should, however, be adjusted to reflect the demographics of the specific employer and the benefits available under its plan, to the extent they differ from those of the other employers. Relevant factors include, for example, health care utilization patterns, expected geographical locations of retirees and their dependents, and significant differences among the nature and types of benefits covered (ASC 715-60-35-95).

Assumptions about Trends in Health Care Cost Rates

Assumptions about the trend in health care cost rates represent the expected annual rate of change in the cost of health care benefits currently provided under the plan (because of factors other than changes in the demographics of participants) for each year from the measurement date until the payment of benefits. The trend rates are based on past and current cost trends, reflecting such factors as health care cost inflation, changes in utilization or delivery patterns, technological advances, and changes in the health status of plan participants. Examples include the possible future use of technology that is now being developed or the reduction of the need for benefits resulting from participation in wellness programs (ASC 715-60-35-99).

Different cost trend rates may be required for different types of services. For example, the cost trend rate for hospital care may differ from that for dental care. Further, the cost trend rates may fluctuate at different rates during different projected periods in the future. For example, there may be a rapid short-term increase, with a subsequent leveling off in the longer term.

Absent information to the contrary, the employer should assume that governmental benefits will continue as provided by existing law, and that benefits from other providers will continue in accordance with their existing plans. Future changes in the law are not anticipated (ASC 715-60-35-102).

Attribution

Once the expected postretirement benefit obligation for an employee has been determined, an equal amount of that obligation is attributed to each year of service in the attribution period, unless the benefit formula of the plan is frontloaded and thus necessitates attribution on a different basis (ASC 715-60-35-62).

The attribution period starts when the employee begins earning credit toward postretirement benefits. This generally occurs on the date of hire, but may be at a later date if the benefit formula requires a waiting period before the employee can earn credit. In any event, the attribution period ends when the employee reaches full eligibility for benefits. The cost of providing the benefits is attributed to the period during which the employee builds up full eligibility. The employer does not attribute any of the service cost to any period after the employee has achieved full eligibility (ASC 715-60-35-66, 68).

Illustration of Attribution Period

Under the postretirement benefit plan of Company Q, employees qualify by rendering at least five years of service and reaching age 65 while in service. The company hires an employee at age 61. Assume the expected postretirement benefit obligation for this employee is $10,000. The attribution period is five years. (Note that the employee will not become eligible at age 65, because the employee will not yet have completed five years of service.) For each of the first five years of service, the annual service cost will be $2,000 (1/5 of $10,000). No service cost will be attributed after the first five years, even if the employee remains in service.

Illustration of Attribution under a Frontloaded Plan

A "frontloaded" plan is one in which a disproportionate share of the benefit obligation is attributed to the early years of an employee's service.

A life insurance plan provides postretirement death benefits of $200,000 for 10 years of service after age 45 and additional death benefits of $10,000 for each year of service thereafter until age 65. (The maximum benefit is therefore $300,000, consisting of the basic $200,000 plus 10 additional years @ $10,000.)

In this situation, the benefit obligation is attributed to periods corresponding to the benefit formula, as follows:

- The actuarial present value of a death benefit of $20,000 (1/10 of $200,000) is attributed to each of the first 10 years of service after age 45.
- The actuarial present value of an additional $10,000 death benefit is attributed to each year of service thereafter until age 65.

RECOGNITION OF NET PERIODIC POSTRETIREMENT BENEFIT COST

The amount of net periodic postretirement benefit cost is derived from the net change in the amount of the accumulated postretirement benefit obligation, after ignoring those components of the net change that do not pertain to the cost of benefits (ASC 715-60-35-7).

The net periodic postretirement benefit cost recognized for a period consists of the following components (ASC 715-60-35-9):

- Service cost
- Interest cost
- Actual return on plan assets, if any
- Amortization of prior service cost or credit included in accumulated other comprehensive income
- Gain or loss (to the extent recognized)
- Amortization of the transition obligation or asset at the date of initial application of the accounting requirements for postretirement benefit plans (if the full amount was not immediately recognized upon initial adoption of these requirements) and still remaining in accumulated other comprehensive income

---

PRACTICE NOTE: The employer makes one entry to accrue the net periodic postretirement benefit cost, the amount of which is the total of the components listed above, determined by worksheet calculations.

Illustration of Basic Transactions and Adjustments

Company A's date of transition to the accounting requirements for postretirement benefit plans was the beginning of Year 1. At that time, the accumulated postretirement benefit obligation was $300,000. The plan was unfunded.

At the end of Year 1, Company A paid $65,000 of postretirement benefits. Service cost attributed to Year 1 was $60,000. The assumed discount rate was 10%.

Worksheets as of the end of Year 1 are as follows:

	Postretirement Benefit Cost	*Accumulated Postretirement Benefit Obligation*	*Transition Obligation*
Beginning of year	$NA	$(300,000)	$300,000
Recognition of components of net periodic postretirement benefit cost:			
Service cost	(60,000)	(60,000)	
Interest cost[(a)]	(30,000)	(30,000)	

	Postretirement Benefit Cost	Accumulated Postretirement Benefit Obligation	Transition Obligation
Amortization of transition obligation[(b)]	(15,000)		(15,000)
	$(105,000)	(90,000)	(15,000)
Benefit payments		65,000	
Net change		(25,000)	(15,000)
End of year		$(325,000)	$285,000

[(a)] 10% (assumed discount rate) of $300,000 (accumulated postretirement obligation at beginning of year)
[(b)] 20-year straight-line amortization of transition obligation (discussed later in this chapter)

The amounts on this worksheet are reflected in the reconciliation of the funded status of the plan with the amounts shown on the statement of financial position, as follows:

	Beginning of Year 1	Net Change	End of Year 1
Accumulated postretirement benefit obligation	$(300,000)	$(25,000)	$(325,000)
Plan assets at fair value	-0-		-0-
Funded status—Recognized as a liability on the balance sheet[(a)]	(300,000)	(25,000)	(325,000)
Transition obligation included in other comprehensive income	300,000	(15,000)	285,000

[(a)] The liability for postretirement benefits is $300,000 at the beginning of Year 1. It increases during Year 1 by the amount that service cost, interest cost, and expected return on plan assets exceed the cash contributions during the year ($90,000 – $65,000).

Basic Transactions and Adjustments

Service Cost Component

The *service cost component* of net periodic postretirement benefit cost is defined as the portion of the expected postretirement benefit obligation attributed to employee service during a specified period, based on the actuarial present value of the expected obligation (ASC Glossary).

A *defined benefit* postretirement benefit plan contains a benefit formula that defines the benefit an employee will receive for services performed during a specified period (service cost). ASC 715 requires that the terms of the benefit formula be used to determine the amount of postretirement benefit earned by each employee for services performed during a specified period. Under ASC 715, attribution is the process of assigning postretirement benefits or cost to periods of employee service, in accordance with the postretirement benefit formula.

Interest Cost Component

ASC 715 requires an employer to recognize as a component of net periodic postretirement benefit cost the interest cost on the accumulated postretirement benefit obligation. The interest cost is equal to the increase in the amount of the obligation because of the passage of time, measured at a rate equal to the assumed discount rate. ASC 715 specifies that the interest cost component of net periodic postretirement benefit cost is not considered interest expense for purposes of capitalizing interest as required by ASC 835 (Interest) (ASC Glossary).

Actual Return on Plan Assets Component

If a plan is funded, a component of periodic postretirement benefit cost is the actual return on plan assets. The amount of the actual return on plan assets is equal to the difference between the fair value of plan assets at the beginning and end of a period, adjusted for employer contributions, employee contributions (if the plan is contributory) and postretirement benefits paid during the period.

Fair value is the amount that reasonably could be expected to result from a current sale of an investment between a willing buyer and a willing seller, that is, a sale other than a forced liquidation. Plan assets that are used in the operation of the postretirement benefit plan (e.g., building, equipment, furniture, fixtures) are valued at cost less accumulated depreciation or amortization. The actual return on plan assets is shown net of tax expense if the fund holding the plan assets is a taxable entity (ASC Glossary).

A return on plan assets decreases the employer's cost of providing postretirement benefits to its employees, while a loss on plan assets increases postretirement benefit cost. Net periodic postretirement benefit income can result from a significantly high return on plan assets during a period.

Illustration of Actual Return on Plan Assets

An employer may determine its actual gain or loss on plan assets as follows:

Plan assets, beginning of year, at fair value	$ 200,000
Add: Amounts contributed to plan	750,000
Less: Benefit payments from plan	(650,000)
	300,000
Less: Plan assets, end of year, at fair value	340,000
Actual (return) loss on plan assets	$ (40,000)

PRACTICE NOTE: Actual return on plan assets is one of the components of net periodic postretirement benefit cost. As discussed later in this chapter, ASC 715 requires this component to be disclosed in the notes to the financial statements. Another component of net postretirement benefit cost is gains and losses (discussed later in this chapter). The "gains and losses" component includes, among other items, "plan asset gains and losses," defined as the difference between the actual return and the expected return on plan assets.

The following example illustrates the combined effect on net periodic postretirement benefit cost of (*a*) actual return on plan assets and (*b*) plan asset gains and losses: If the actual return on plan assets is $1,000,000 and the expected return is $700,000, the plan asset gain is the $300,000 difference between the actual return and the expected return. This $300,000 plan asset gain is part of the "gains and losses" component of net periodic postretirement benefit cost, while the $1,000,000 actual return on plan assets is another component. The combined effect is a net decrease of $700,000 in net periodic postretirement benefit cost, the result of offsetting the $300,000 plan asset gain against the $1,000,000 actual return. This $700,000 is equal to the expected return on plan assets. The total amount of net periodic postretirement benefit cost includes the $700,000 as well as other components, including service cost, interest cost, etc. The $300,000 plan asset gain is taken into account in computing in future years (*a*) the expected return on plan assets and (*b*) amortization of deferred gains and losses. (See discussion and illustration later in this chapter.)

Amortization of Prior Service Cost or Credit Component

When a postretirement benefit plan is initially adopted or amended, employees may be granted benefits for services performed in prior periods. The cost of postretirement benefits that are granted retroactively to employees is referred to as *prior service cost* (ASC 715-60-35-13).

Under ASC 715, only a portion of the total amount of prior service cost arising in a period is included in net periodic postretirement benefit cost. ASC 715 requires that the total prior service cost arising in a period from the adoption or amendment of a plan be amortized in a systematic manner. *Amortization* of prior service cost is a component of net periodic postretirement benefit cost.

Initiation of a Plan, or Amendment that Improves Benefits in an Existing Plan

When an employer initiates a plan or adopts an amendment that improves the benefits in an existing plan, the amount of prior service cost is the amount of increase in the accumulated postretirement benefit obligation that can be attributed to service of employees in prior periods.

Methods of Amortizing Prior Service Cost

ASC 715 provides a number of rules regarding the amortization of prior service cost, as follows:

- General rule
- Special rule if all or most employees are fully eligible
- Simplified computation
- Accelerated amortization

Illustration of Plan Amendment Increasing Benefits

At the beginning of Year 2, Company A amended its plan, causing the accumulated postretirement benefit obligation to increase by $84,000. Active plan participants had an average of 12 remaining years of service before reaching full eligibility for benefits.

At the end of Year 2, the employer paid $60,000 in benefits. Service cost was $50,000.

The worksheets as of the end of Year 2 are as follows:

	Postretirement Benefit Cost	*Accumulated Postretirement Benefit Obligation*	*Transition Obligation*	*Prior Service Cost*
Beginning of year	NA	$(325,000)	$285,000	$ -0-
Plan amendment		(84,000)		84,000
Recognition of components of net periodic postretirement benefit cost:				
Service cost	(50,000)	(50,000)		
Interest cost[(a)]	(40,900)	(40,900)		
Amortization of transition obligation[(b)]	(15,000)		(15,000)	
Amortization of prior service cost[(c)]	(7,000)			(7,000)
	(112,900)	(174,900)	(15,000)	77,000
Benefit payments		60,000		
Net change		(114,900)	(15,000)	77,000
End of year[(d)]		$(439,900)	$270,000	$77,000

[(a)] 10% (assumed discount rate) of $325,000 (accumulated postretirement benefit obligation at beginning of year), plus 10% of $84,000 (increase in obligation by plan amendment)
[(b)] 20-year amortization of original $300,000 transition obligation
[(c)] Straight-line amortization of prior service cost, based on average remaining years of service (12 years) of active plan participants before reaching full eligibility
[(d)] The liability on the balance sheet at the end of year 2 ($439,900) equals the liability at the beginning of the year ($325,000) increased by the plan amendment ($84,000) and by the excess of service cost, interest cost, and expected return on plan assets ($90,900) over cash contributions ($60,000) during the year.

Analysis of postretirement benefit accounts:

	End of Year 1	*Net Change*	*End of Year 2*
Accumulated postretirement benefit obligation	$(325,000)	$(114,900)	$(439,900)
Plan assets at fair value	-0-		-0-
Funded status—Recognized as a liability on the balance sheet	(325,000)	(114,900)	(439,900)
Prior service cost	-0-	77,000	77,000
Transition obligation	285,000	(15,000)	270,000

- *General rule*: The general rule requires amortization of prior service cost in equal installments during each employee's remaining years of service until that employee reaches full eligibility under the new or amended plan (ASC 715-60-35-15).

- *Special rule if all or most employees are fully eligible*: If all or almost all employees are already fully eligible for benefits when the plan is initiated or amended, the employer amortizes prior service cost over the remaining life expectancy of those employees (ASC 715-60-35-17).

- *Simplified computation*: ASC 715 allows a simplified form of computation, provided it amortizes prior service cost more quickly than the methods described above. For example, instead of basing its amortization on the period during which each individual employee reaches full eligibility, an employer may amortize prior service cost over the *average* remaining years of service of all active plan participants until they reach full eligibility (ASC 715-60-35-18).
- *Accelerated amortization*: An enterprise uses an accelerated method of amortization if a history of plan amendments and other evidence indicates that the employer's economic benefits from the initiation or amendment of the plan will be exhausted before the employees reach full eligibility for postretirement benefits. In this situation, amortization should reflect the period during which the employer expects to receive economic benefits from the existence of the plan (ASC 715-60-35-19).

Plan Amendments that Reduce Obligation

If a plan amendment reduces the accumulated postretirement obligation, the reduction (a negative prior service cost) is recognized as a credit to other comprehensive income. The prior service credit is amortized in accordance with the above rules after it is applied (*a*) to reduce any existing (positive) prior service cost included in accumulated other comprehensive income and (*b*) to reduce any transition obligation included in accumulated other comprehensive income (ASC 715-60-35-20).

Gain or Loss Component

The approach to gains and losses in ASC 715 is similar to that required for pension plan accounting. Gains or losses consist of certain types of changes in (*a*) the accumulated postretirement benefit obligation and (*b*) the plan assets. The changes may result from either (*a*) experience different from that assumed or (*b*) changes in assumptions (ASC 715-60-35-23).

Gains and losses include amounts that have been realized (e.g., the sale of a security) and amounts that have not been realized (e.g., changes in the market value of plan assets) (ASC 715-60-35-23). Gains or losses that are not recognized immediately are included in other comprehensive income in the year they occur.

Elements of the Gain or Loss Component

The gain or loss component of net periodic postretirement benefit cost is the combination of three elements (ASC 715-60-35-36; ASC Glossary):

1. The difference between the actual return on plan assets and the expected return on plan assets.
2. Other gains and losses immediately recognized, or the amortization of net gain and loss included in accumulated other comprehensive income.
3. Any amount immediately recognized as a gain or loss pursuant to a decision to temporarily deviate from the substantive plan (ASC Glossary).

PRACTICE POINTER: The gain or loss component of net postretirement benefit cost does not include the actual return on plan assets during the period, which is another component of net periodic postretirement benefit cost, discussed earlier in this chapter.

The gain or loss component does include, among other items, the difference between the actual return and the expected return on plan assets, since this difference falls within the general concept of gains and losses according to ASC 715—changes resulting from experience different from that assumed or from changes in assumptions.

Plan Asset Gains and Losses

Plan asset gains and losses are the difference between the actual return (including earnings and holding gains/losses) and the expected return for the same period (ASC Glossary).

The computation of plan asset gains and losses starts with determining the expected return on plan assets, which is the difference between: (1) the expected long-term rate of return on plan assets and (2) the market-related value of plan assets (ASC 715-60-35-26; ASC Glossary). Plan asset gains and losses include both changes reflected in the market-related value of plan assets and changes not yet reflected in the market-related value of plan assets (ASC 715-60-35-27).

The market-related value may be either fair market value or a calculation that recognizes changes in fair market value systematically over a period of five years or less. The employer may use different methods of calculating market-related value for different categories of assets, but each category must be treated consistently during successive periods (ASC Glossary). ASC 715 requires plan asset gains and losses during the period to be included as a component of net periodic postretirement benefit cost.

PRACTICE NOTE: Plan asset gains and losses (excluding amounts not yet reflected in the market-related value of plan assets) are taken into account in computing the future expected return on plan assets. This year's plan asset gains and losses will therefore be reflected, in the computation of the expected return on plan assets, in future years' net periodic postretirement benefit cost. Plan asset gains and losses (excluding amounts not yet reflected in the market-related value of plan assets) are also taken into account in computing amortization of net gains and losses included in accumulated other comprehensive income.

Other Gains and Losses Immediately Realized

Immediate recognition of other types of gains and losses is required in some situations and permitted in others.

An employer recognizes an immediate gain or loss if it decides to deviate temporarily from its substantive plan, either by (*a*) forgiving a retrospective adjustment of the current or prior years' cost-sharing provisions as they relate to benefit costs already incurred by retirees or (*b*) otherwise changing the employer's share of benefit costs incurred in the current or prior periods (ASC 715-60-35-34).

If immediate recognition of gains and losses is not required, an employer may elect to use a method that consistently recognizes gains and losses immediately, provided: (*a*) any gain that does not offset a loss previously recognized in income must first offset any transition obligation included in accumulated other comprehensive income and (*b*) any loss that does not offset a gain previously recognized in income must first offset any transition asset included in accumulated other comprehensive income (ASC 715-60-35-32).

	Postretirement Benefit Cost	*Cash*	*Transition Obligation*	*Net Loss*	*Liability for Postretirement Benefit Plan*	*MEMO ACCT Accumulated Postretirement Benefit Obligation*	*MEMO ACCT Plan Assets*
Beginning of year	NA	NA	$2,700,000	$302,500	($2,596,500)	($3,625,000)	($1,028,500)
Recognition of components of net periodic postretirement benefit cost:							
Service cost	180,000					(180,000)	
Interest cost	326,250					(326,250)	
Amortization of transition obligation	150,000	(150,000)					
Amortization of unrecognized net loss							
Expected return on plan assets[(a)]	(96,850)						96,850
Assets contributed to plan		(956,250)					956,250
Benefit payments from plan						450,000	(450,000)
Net expense or net change	559,400	(956,250)	(150,000)		(546,850)	(56,250)	603,100
End of year—projected	NA	NA	$2,550,000	$302,500	($2,049,650)	($3,681,250)	$1,631,600

(a) See Schedule 1.

Amortization of deferred gains and losses from previous periods Any gains and losses not recognized immediately as a component of net periodic benefit cost are immediately recognized in other comprehensive income. ASC 715 establishes a special formula to determine (*a*) whether an employer is required to amortize gains and losses included in accumulated other comprehensive income and (*b*) if amortization is required, the minimum amount of periodic amortization. ASC 715 allows other methods instead of those provided by the formula, if certain qualifications are met.

ASC 715 requires amortization of net gains and losses included in accumulated other comprehensive income if the beginning-of-year balance of net unrecognized gain or loss (with a modification noted below) is more than a base figure used for comparison purposes (ASC 715-60-35-29).

The base figure is 10% of the greater of the accumulated postretirement benefit obligation or the market-related value of plan assets as of the beginning of the year (ASC 715-60-35-29).

For purposes of this comparison, the gain or loss included in accumulated other comprehensive income is modified, so as to exclude any plan asset gains or losses that have not yet been reflected in market-related value.

PRACTICE POINTER: If gains or losses included in accumulated other comprehensive income are not greater than the base figure, they come within the 10% "corridor" and the employer need not recognize them. This procedure is similar to the corridor test for recognizing gains and losses on pensions.

If amortization is required under the formula, the amount to be amortized is the difference between the beginning-of-year balance of net gain or loss (adjusted to exclude any plan asset gains or losses that have not yet been reflected in the market-related value) and the base figure.

The minimum amortization is the amount to be amortized, determined as above, divided by the average remaining service period of active plan participants. If all or almost all of the plan's participants are inactive, divide instead by the average remaining life expectancy of the inactive participants (ASC 715-60-35-29).

Instead of using the minimum amortization method, an employer may use any other systematic method of amortization, provided that (*a*) the amortization for each period is at least as much as the amount determined by the minimum amortization method, (*b*) the method is used consistently, (*c*) the method applies consistently to gains and losses, and (*d*) the method is disclosed (ASC 715-60-35-31).

Illustration of Gains and Losses

At the beginning of 20X5, Company L prepared the following projection of changes during that year:

As of the end of 20X5, Company L prepared the following worksheet and supporting schedules to reflect actual changes during the year:

	Projected 12/31/X5	*Net Gain (Loss)*	*Actual 12/31/X5*
Accumulated postretirement benefit obligation	$(3,681,250)	$ 118,630[b]	$(3,562,620)
Plan assets at fair value	1,631,600	(110,180)[c]	1,521,420
Funded status—liability	(2,049,650)	8,450	(2,041,200)
Net (gain) loss	302,500	(8,450)	294,050
Transition obligation	2,550,000	—	2,550,000

[b] Liability at year-end was $118,630 less than projected, because of changes in assumptions not detailed here.
[c] See Schedule 1.

	Net Periodic Postretirement Benefit Cost
Service cost	$180,000
Interest cost	326,250
Expected return on plan assets[d]	(96,850)
Amortization of transition obligation	150,000
Net periodic postretirement benefit cost	$559,400

[d] See Schedule 3.

Schedule 1—Plan Assets

Expected long-term rate of return on plan assets	10%
Beginning balance, market-related value(f)	$968,500
Contributions to plan (end of year)	956,250
Benefits paid by plan	(450,000)
Expected return on plan assets	96,850
	1,571,600
20% of each of last five years' asset gains (losses)	(7,036)
Ending balance, market-related value	$ 1,564,564
Beginning balance, fair value of plan assets	$ 1,028,500
Contributions to plan	956,250
Benefits paid	(450,000)
Actual return (loss) on plan assets(g)	(13,330)
Ending balance, fair value of plan assets	$ 1,521,420
Deferred asset gain (loss) for year(h)	$ (110,180)
Gain (loss) not included in ending balance market-related value(i)	$ (43,144)

(f) This example adds 20% of each of the last five years' gains or losses.
(g) See Schedule 3.
(h) (Actual return on plan assets) – (expected return on plan assets).
Note: The term *deferred asset gain (loss) for year* follows the terminology in the illustrations attached to ASC 715, although the text of ASC 715 refers to the same item as *plan asset gains and losses*.
(i) (Ending balance, fair value of plan assets) – (ending balance, market-related value of plan assets).

Schedule 2—Amortization of Unrecognized Net Gain or Loss

10% of beginning balance of accumulated postretirement benefit obligation	$ 362,500
10% of beginning balance of market-related value of plan assets(j)	96,850
Greater of the above	$ 362,500
Unrecognized net (gain) loss at beginning of year	$ 302,500
Asset gain (loss) not included in beginning balance of market-related value(k) ($1,028,500 – $968,500)	60,000
Amount subject to amortization	$ 362,500
Amount in excess of the corridor subject to amortization	None
Required amortization	None

(j) See Schedule 1.
(k) See Schedule 1.

Schedule 3—Actual Return or Loss on Plan Assets

Plan assets at fair value, beginning of year	$1,028,500
Plus: Assets contributed to plan	956,250
Less: Benefit payments from plan	(450,000)
	1,534,750
Less: Plan assets at fair value, end of year	(1,521,420)
Actual (return) loss on plan assets	$ 13,330

Amortization of Transition Obligation/Asset Component

The final component of net periodic postretirement benefit cost is amortization of the transition obligation or asset at the date of initial application of ASC 715 that remains in accumulated other comprehensive income. At the beginning of the fiscal year in which ASC 715 is first applied, the funded status of the plan was computed by comparing the difference between (1) the accumulated postretirement benefit obligation and (2) the fair value of plan assets plus any recognized accrued postretirement benefit cost less any recognized prepaid postretirement benefit cost. The resulting difference, either a transition asset or transition obligation, can either be recognized immediately in net income or on a delayed basis as a component of net periodic postretirement benefit cost.

If delayed recognition is chosen, the transition asset or obligation is generally recognized over the average remaining service period of active plan participants (ASC 715-60-35-39). However, there are a number of exceptions to this general requirement:

- If the average remaining service period of active plan participants is less than 20 years, the transition asset or obligation can be amortized over 20 years.
- If all or almost all of the plan's participants are inactive, the transition asset or obligation can be amortized over the average remaining life expectancy of these plan participants.
- Amortization of the transition obligation (not transition asset) must be accelerated if cumulative benefit payments subsequent to the transition date exceed cumulative postretirement benefit cost accrued subsequent to the transition date. Additional amortization of the transition obligation is recognized to the extent that cumulative benefit payments exceed cumulative accrued postretirement benefit cost. Cumulative benefit payments include any payments related to a plan settlement and cumulative benefit payments are to be reduced by: (1) plan assets and (2) any recognized accrued postretirement benefit obligation, both measured as of the transition date.

RECOGNITION OF FUNDED STATUS OF POSTRETIREMENT BENEFIT PLANS

An employer is required to recognize the overfunded or underfunded status of a defined postretirement benefit plan as an asset or a liability in its statement of financial position. If the fair value of a postretirement benefit plan's assets exceeds the plan's accumulated postretirement benefit obligation, the plan is overfunded and an asset is recognized. If the plan's accumulated postretirement benefit obligation exceeds the fair value of the plan's assets, the plan is underfunded and a liability is recognized (ASC 715-60-35-5). When the funded status of the postretirement benefit plan is first recognized in the statement of financial position, the offsetting entry is to accumulated other comprehensive income (net of tax). The recognition of a postretirement benefit plan asset or liability may result in temporary differences under ASC 740 (Income Taxes). Deferred tax effects are to be recognized for these temporary differences as a component of income tax expense or benefit in the year in which the differences arise, and allocated to various financial statement components.

Asset and liability gains and losses as well as prior service costs or credits that occur in periods after recognition of the funded status of the plan and that are not immediately included as a component of net periodic postretirement benefit cost are included in other comprehensive income. As gains and losses, prior service costs and credits, and the transition asset or obligation are included in net periodic postretirement benefit cost, they are recognized as an adjustment to other comprehensive income.

MEASUREMENT OF PLAN ASSETS

Plan assets generally are stocks, bonds, and other investments. Such assets may include the participation rights in participating insurance contracts, but not other rights in insurance contracts. The employer's own securities may be included as plan assets, but only if they are transferable and otherwise meet the conditions under ASC 715 (ASC Glossary).

Plan assets are increased by various means, including the employer's contributions, employees' contributions if the plan is contributory, and earnings from investing the contributed amounts. Plan assets are decreased by benefit payments, income taxes, and other expenses (ASC Glossary).

All plan assets should be segregated and restricted for paying postretirement benefits. Usually, the assets are in a trust. Plan assets may be withdrawn only for the stated purposes of the plan. In limited circumstances, the plan may permit withdrawal when the plan's assets exceed its obligations and the employer has taken appropriate steps to satisfy existing obligations (ASC Glossary).

If assets are not segregated or restricted effectively in some other way, they are not plan assets even though the employer intends to use them for paying postretirement benefits. Contributions that are accrued but not yet paid into the plan are not regarded as plan assets (ASC Glossary).

For purposes of disclosure, ASC 715 requires the employer to use fair value as the measurement for all plan investments, including equity or debt securities, real estate, and other items (ASC 715-60-35-107). Fair value is determined in accordance with the guidance in ASC 820 (Fair Value Measurements and Disclosures). (Additional guidance on determining fair values can be found in the Chapter 51, *ASC 820—Fair Value Measurement*.)

Plan assets used in plan operations, such as buildings, equipment, furniture and fixtures, and leasehold improvements, are measured at cost less accumulated depreciation or amortization (ASC 715-60-35-107).

Insurance Contracts

Benefits covered by insurance contracts (defined below) are excluded from the accumulated postretirement benefit obligation. Insurance contracts are also excluded from plan assets, except for the amounts attributable to participation rights in participating insurance contracts.

Definition of Insurance Contracts

ASC 715 defines an *insurance contract* as a contract in which the insurance company unconditionally undertakes a legal obligation to provide specified benefits to specific individuals in return for a fixed premium. The contract must be irrevocable and must involve the transfer of significant risk from the employer (or the plan) to the insurance company. A contract does not qualify as an insurance contract if (*a*) the insurance company is a *captive insurer* doing business primarily with the employer and related parties or (*b*) there is any reasonable doubt that the insurance company will meet its obligations under the contract (ASC 715-60-35-110).

Participating Insurance Contracts

Some contracts are *participating insurance contracts*, in which the purchaser (either the plan or the employer) participates in the experience of the insurance company. The purchaser's participation generally takes the form of a dividend that effectively reduces the cost of the plan. If, however, the employer's participation is so great that the employer retains all or most of the risks and rewards of the plan, the contract is not regarded as an insurance contract for purposes of ASC 715 (ASC 715-60-35-114, 117).

The purchase price of a participating contract ordinarily is higher than the price of a similar contract without the participation right. The difference between the price with and without the participation right is considered to be the cost of the participation right. The employer should regard this cost as an asset when purchased. At subsequent dates, the employer measures the participation right at its fair value if fair value can be estimated reasonably. Otherwise, the participation right is measured at its amortized cost, but this amount should not exceed the participation right's net realizable value. The cost is amortized systematically over the expected dividend period (ASC 715-60-35-115, 116).

Cost of Insurance

Insurance contracts, such as life insurance contracts, may be purchased during a period to cover postretirement benefits attributed to service by employees in the same period. In this situation, the cost of the benefits equals the cost of purchasing the insurance (after adjusting for the cost of any participation rights included in the contract) (ASC 715-60-35-118).

Accordingly, if all postretirement benefits attributed to service by employees in the current period are covered by nonparticipating insurance contracts purchased during the same period, the cost of the benefits equals the cost of purchasing the insurance. If the benefits are only partially covered by nonparticipating insurance contracts, the uninsured portion of the benefits is accounted for in the same way as benefits under uninsured plans (ASC 715-60-35-118, 119).

Insurance Company Not Fully Bound

If the insurance company does not unconditionally undertake a legal obligation to pay specified benefits to specific individuals, the arrangement does not qualify as an insurance contract for purposes of ASC 715. The arrangement is accounted for as an investment at fair value (ASC 715-60-35-120).

Fair value is presumed to equal the cash surrender value or conversion value, if any. In some cases, the best estimate of fair value is the contract value.

MEASUREMENT DATE

All postretirement benefit plan assets that are held as investments to provide postretirement benefits are generally measured at their fair values as of the date of the employer's fiscal year-end statement of financial position. There are two exceptions to this general rule. First, if a subsidiary sponsors a postretirement benefit plan and the subsidiary has a different year-end than its parent, the fair value of the subsidiary's postretirement benefit plan assets is measured at the date of the subsidiary's financial statements. Second, if an investee, accounted for using the equity method, sponsors a postretirement benefit plan and the investee has a different year-end than the investor, the fair value of the investee's postretirement benefit plan assets is measured at the date of the investee's financial statements (ASC 715-60-35-121).

A reporting entity that has a fiscal year-end that does not coincide with a month-end may incur additional costs to measure the fair value of plan assets, since the information about the fair value of plan assets obtained from a third-party service provider is typically reported as of a month-end and must be adjusted to reflect the fair values as of the fiscal year-end. A reporting entity in this situation may elect to measure the plan assets and benefit obligations using the month-end that is closest to the entity's fiscal year-end. The reporting entity must apply this election consistently from year to year and consistently to all of its defined benefit plans (ASC 715-60-35-123A).

If a contribution or significant event caused by the employer (such as a plan amendment, settlement, or curtailment that calls for a remeasurement) occurs between the month-end date used to measure plan assets and benefit obligations and the employer's fiscal year-end, the employer must adjust the fair value of plan assets and the actuarial present value of benefit obligations to recognize those contributions or significant events in the period in which they occurred. Such an adjustment is not made for other events occurring during this time that were not caused by the employer, for example, changes in market prices or interest rates (ASC 715-60-35-123B).

Unless more current amounts are available for both the obligation and plan assets, the funded status of the postretirement benefit plan reported in interim financial statements shall be the same amount as reported by the employer in its previous year-end statement of financial position, adjusted for subsequent accruals of service cost, interest cost, and return on plan assets, contributions, and benefit payments (ASC 715-60-35-125).

If an employer causes a significant event that requires the employer to remeasure both plan assets and benefit obligations and the date of the significant event does not coincide with a month-end, the employer may remeasure plan assets and benefit obligations using the month-end that is closest to the date of the significant event (ASC 715-60-35-126A). In these cases, the employer must adjust the fair value of plan assets and the actuarial present value of benefit obligations for any effects of the significant event that may or may not be captured in the month-end measurement (ASC 715-60-35-126B).

DISCLOSURES

The disclosure requirements relating to postretirement benefit plans are covered in the discussion of subtopic ASC 715-20.

EMPLOYERS WITH TWO OR MORE PLANS

ASC 715 deals with the questions of measurement and disclosure separately for an employer with two or more plans and for employers with one plan.

Aggregate Measurement

ASC 715 generally requires an employer with two or more plans to measure each plan separately. An employer may measure its plans as an aggregate rather than as separate plans, however, if the plans meet the following criteria (ASC 715-60-35-129, 130):

1. The plans provide postretirement health care benefits
2. The plans provide either of the following:
   a. Different benefits to the same group of employees
   b. The same benefits to different groups of employees
3. The plans are unfunded (without any plan assets)
4. The employer aggregates all of its plans that meet the preceding three tests.

An employer may make a separate aggregation of plans providing welfare benefits (i.e., postretirement benefits other than health care), if requirements (2) through (4) above are met. However, a plan that has plan assets should not be aggregated with other plans, but should be measured separately (ASC 715-60-35-130).

MULTIPLE-EMPLOYER PLANS

A multiple-employer plan is distinct from a multiemployer plan. In a *multiple-employer* plan, individual employers combine their single-employer plans for pooling assets for investment purposes, or for reducing the costs of administration. The participating employers may have different benefit formulas; each employer's contributions to the plan are based on that employer's benefit formula. These plans generally are not the result of collective bargaining agreements.

An employer shall apply the provisions of ASC 450 to its participation in a multiemployer plan if it is probable or reasonably possible that either of the following would occur (ASC 715-80-50-2):

1. An employer would withdraw from the plan under circumstances that would give rise to an obligation.
2. An employer's contribution to the fund would be increased during the remainder of the contract period to make up for a shortfall in the funds necessary to maintain the negotiated level of benefit coverage.

An employer that participates in a multiemployer plan that provides pension benefits shall disclosure information prescribed in ASC 715-80-50-4 through 715-80-50-10. The disclosures of the employer's contributions to the plan include all items recognized as net pension costs and are based on the most recently available information through the date at which the employer has evaluated subsequent events. (ASC 715-80-50-3)

- Narrative description of both the general nature of the multi-employer plans that provide pension benefits and the employer (ASC 715-80-50-4).
- The employer's participation in the plans that would indicate how the risks of participation are different from single-employer plans. (ASC 715-80-50-4)
- When feasible, present in a tabular form, supplemented with greater narrative outside the table (ASC 715-80-50-5):
  - Legal name of the plan.
  - The plan's Employer Identification Number and, if available, its plan number.
  - For each statement of financial position, the most recently available certified zone status provided by the plan, specifying the date of the plan's year-end and whether the plan has utilized any extended amortization provisions that affect the calculation of the zone status.
  - If the zone status is not available, as of the most recent date available, the total plan assets and accumulate benefit obligation and whether the plan was less than 65% funded, between 65% and 80% funded, at least 80% funded.
  - The expiration dates of the collective-bargaining agreements requiring contributions to the plan. If more than one collective-bargaining agreement applies, a range of the expiration dates, supplemented with a qualitative description that identifies the significant collective-bargaining agreements within that arrange as well as other information to help investors understand the significance of the agreements and when they expire.
  - For each period for which a statement of income (statement of activities for not-for-profits) is presented the employer's contributions to the plan, whether the contributions represent more than 5% of total contributions to the plan.
  - As of the most recent annual period, whether a funding improvement plan or rehabilitation plan has been implemented, whether the employer paid a surcharge to the plan, and a description of any minimum contributions required for future periods by the collective-bargaining agreement, statutory obligation, or other contractual obligations.

- A description of the nature and effect of any significant changes that affect comparability of total employer contributions from period to period, such as a business combination or divestiture, a change in the contractual employer contribution rate, and a change in the number of employees covered by the plan during each year. (ASC 715-80-50-6)
- If information is not available in the public domain, in addition to the above requirements:
  - A description of the nature of the plan benefits.
  - A qualitative description of the extent to which the employer could be responsible for the obligations of the plan, including benefits earned by employees during employment with another employer.
  - Other quantitative information as of the most recent date available to help users understand the financial information about the plan. (ASC 715-80-50-7)
- In a tabular form for each annual period for which a statement of income or statement of activities is presented, the total contributions made to all plans that are not individually significant and the total contributions to all plans. (ASC 715-80-50-9)

An employer that participates in multiemployer plans that provide postretirement benefits other than pensions shall disclose the amount of contributions to those plans for each annual period for which a statement of income (or statement of activities) is presented. This disclosure shall include a description of the nature and effect of any changes that affect comparability of total employer contributions from period to period, such as a business combination or divestiture, a change in the contractual employer contribution rate, and a change in the number of employees covered by the plan during each year. The disclosure shall include a description of the nature of the benefits and the types of employees covered by these benefits, such as medical benefits provided to active and employees and retirees. (ASC 715-80-50-11)

PRACTICE POINTER: The above represents a highly summarized version of the information required to be disclosed regarding multiemployer plans from ASC 715. Entities subject to these requirements are encouraged to consult ASC 715-80-50-1 through ASC 715-80-55-8 for more detailed guidance and illustrations.

PLANS OUTSIDE THE UNITED STATES

ASC 715 applies to plans outside as well as inside the United States. If the accumulated postretirement obligation of the plans outside the United States is significant in proportion to the total of all the employer's postretirement benefit plans, the employer should make separate disclosure of the plans outside the United States. Otherwise, the employer may make combined disclosure of plans outside and inside the United States (ASC 715-10-15-6).

PRACTICE NOTE: ASC 715 does not define *outside the United States*. The following factors, among others, may be relevant: (*a*) where all or most of the employees and beneficiaries are located and (*b*) which country's law governs the relationships among employees, beneficiaries, and the employer.

BUSINESS COMBINATIONS

When a single-employer defined benefit postretirement plan is acquired as part of a business combination accounted for by the acquisition method, the acquirer recognizes an asset or a liability representing the funded status of the plan. When determining the funded status of the plan, the acquirer shall exclude the effects of expected plan amendments, terminations, or curtailments that at the acquisition date it has no obligation to make. If an acquiree participates in a multiemployer plan, and it is probable that it will withdraw from that plan, the acquirer recognizes as part of the business combination a withdrawal liability in accordance with ASC 450 (ASC 805-20-25-25).

SETTLEMENT AND CURTAILMENT OF A POSTRETIREMENT BENEFIT OBLIGATION

According to ASC 715, a *settlement* is a transaction that has the following characteristics (ASC Glossary):

- Is an irrevocable action
- Relieves the employer (or the plan) of primary responsibility for pension or postretirement benefit obligation
- Eliminates significant risks related to the obligation and the assets used to put the settlement into effect

Settlements take place, for example, in the following situations (ASC 715-60-15-16):

- The employer makes lump-sum cash payments to plan participants, in exchange for their rights to receive future specified postretirement benefits.
- The employer purchases long-term nonparticipating insurance contracts to cover the accumulated postretirement benefit obligation for some or all of the participants in the plan (but the insurance company cannot be under the employer's control).

Settlements do *not* take place, however, in the following situations (ASC 715-60-55-105):

- The employer purchases an insurance contract from an insurance company controlled by the employer. This does not qualify as a settlement because the employer is still exposed to risk through its relationship with the insurance company.
- The employer invests in high-quality fixed-income securities with principal and income payment dates similar to the estimated due dates of benefits. This does not qualify as a settlement because (*a*) the investment decision can be revoked, (*b*) the purchase of the securities does not relieve the employer or the plan of primary responsibility for the postretirement benefit obligation, and (*c*) the purchase of the securities does not eliminate significant risks related to the postretirement benefit obligation.

Accounting for a Plan Settlement

Maximum Gain or Loss

When a postretirement benefit obligation is settled, the maximum gain or loss recognized in income is the gain or loss plus any transition asset included in accumulated other comprehensive income. This maximum gain or loss includes any gain or loss resulting from the remeasurement of plan assets and of the accumulated postretirement benefit obligation at the time of settlement (ASC 715-60-35-151).

Settlement Gain or Loss When Entire Obligation Is Settled

If an employer settles the entire accumulated postretirement benefit obligation, a further distinction is made depending on whether the maximum amount subject to recognition is a gain or a loss.

If the maximum amount is a gain, the amount of this gain first reduces any transition obligation remaining in accumulated other comprehensive income and any excess gain is recognized in income. If the maximum amount is a loss, the full amount of this loss is recognized in income (ASC 715-60-35-153).

Settlement Gain or Loss When Only Part of Obligation Is Settled

If an employer settles only part of the accumulated postretirement benefit obligation, the employer recognizes in income a pro rata portion of the amount of gain or loss that would have been recognized if the entire obligation had been settled. The pro rata portion equals the percentage by which the partial settlement reduces the accumulated postretirement benefit obligation (ASC 715-60-35-135).

Participating Insurance

If an employer settles the obligation by purchasing a participating insurance contract, the cost of the participation right is deducted from the maximum gain but not from the maximum loss, before the employer determines the amount to be recognized in income (ASC 715-60-35-156).

Settlements at Lower Cost Than Current Cost of Service and Interest

ASC 715 defines the *cost of a settlement* as follows (ASC 715-60-35-157).

- If the settlement is for cash, its cost is the amount of cash paid to plan participants.
- If the settlement uses nonparticipating insurance contracts, its cost is the cost of the contracts.
- If the settlement uses participating insurance contracts, its cost is the cost of the contracts, less the amount attributed to participation rights.

If the cost of all settlements during a year is no more than the combined amount of service cost and interest cost components of net postretirement benefit cost for the same year, ASC 715 permits but does not require the employer to recognize gain or loss for those settlements. The employer should apply a consistent policy each year (ASC 715-60-35-158).

Accounting for a Plan Curtailment

A *curtailment* is an event that either (*a*) significantly reduces the expected years of future service of active plan participants or (*b*) eliminates the accrual of defined benefits for some or all of the future services of a significant number of active plan participants. The following events are examples of curtailments (ASC Glossary; 715-60-15-17):

- Termination of employees' services earlier than anticipated. (This may or may not relate to the closing of a facility or the discontinuation of a segment of the employer's business.)
- Termination or suspension of a plan, so that employees no longer earn additional benefits for future service. (If the plan is suspended, future service may be counted toward eligibility for benefits accumulated based on past service.)

Gain and Loss Recognition

Under the general provisions of ASC 715 for plans that continue without curtailment, the employer should recognize prior service cost on an amortized basis, on the theory that the employer receives economic benefits from the future services of employees covered by the plan.

When a plan is curtailed, the employer's expectation of receiving benefits from future services of its employees is reduced. Accordingly, curtailment requires the employer to recognize as a loss all or part of the remaining balance of prior service cost included in accumulated other comprehensive income. In this context, prior service cost includes the cost of plan amendments and any transition obligation remaining in accumulated other comprehensive income (ASC 715-60-35-164).

Curtailment Resulting from Termination of Employees

If a curtailment occurs as the result of the termination of a significant number of employees who were plan participants, the curtailment loss consists of the following components (ASC 715-60-35-165):

- The portion of the remaining prior service cost included in accumulated other comprehensive income (relating to this and any prior plan amendment) attributable to the previously estimated number of remaining future years of service of all terminated employees, **plus**
- The portion of the remaining transition obligation included in accumulated other comprehensive income attributable to the previously estimated number of remaining future years of service, but only of the terminated employees who were participants in the plan at the date of the initial application of the accounting guidance on postretirement benefit plans.

Curtailment Resulting from Terminating Accrual of Additional Benefits for Future Services

If a curtailment results from terminating the accrual of additional benefits for the future services of a significant number of employees, the curtailment loss consists of the following components (ASC 715-60-35-166):

- *The **pro rata** amount of the remaining prior service cost included in accumulated other comprehensive income*—This amount is based on the portion of the remaining expected years of service in the amortization period that originally was attributable to the employees (*a*) who were plan participants at the date of the plan amendment and (*b*) whose future accrual of benefits has been terminated, **plus**
- *The **pro rata** amount of the remaining transition obligation included in accumulated other comprehensive income*—This amount is based on the portion of the remaining years of service of all participants who were active at the date of transition to the accounting requirements for postretirement benefit obligations, that originally was attributable to the remaining expected future years of service of the employees whose future accrual of benefits has been terminated.

Changes in Accumulated Postretirement Benefit Obligation

A curtailment may cause a gain by decreasing the accumulated postretirement benefit obligation, or a loss by increasing that obligation.

If a curtailment decreases the accumulated obligation, the gain from this decrease is first used to offset any net loss included in accumulated other comprehensive income and the excess is a curtailment gain. If a curtailment increases the accumulated obligation, the loss from this increase is first used to offset any net gain included in accumulated other comprehensive income and the excess is a curtailment loss. In this context, any remaining transition asset is regarded as a net gain, and is combined with the net gain or loss included in accumulated other comprehensive income (ASC 715-60-35-169).

If a curtailment produces a net loss as the combined effect of the above calculations regarding prior service cost and the accumulated postretirement benefit obligation, this combined net loss is recognized in income when it is *probable* that a curtailment will occur and the net effect of the curtailment is reasonably estimable. If the sum of these effects results in a net gain, however, the net gain is recognized in income when the affected employees terminate or the plan suspension or amendment is adopted (ASC 715-60-35-171).

Illustration of Curtailment

Company B reduced its workforce, including a significant number of employees who had accumulated benefits under the postretirement benefit plan. An analysis of the terminated employees revealed:

1. At the time of curtailment, the terminated employees represented 22% of the *remaining years of expected service* of all employees who had been plan participants at the employer's date of transition.
2. At the time of curtailment, the terminated employees represented 18% of the *remaining years of service prior to full eligibility* of all employees who had been plan participants at the date of a prior plan amendment.

Company B's worksheet computation of the curtailment gain or loss is as follows:

	Before Curtailment	*Curtailment*	*After Curtailment*
Accumulated postretirement benefit obligation	$(514,000)	$108,000	$(406,000)
Plan assets at fair value	146,000		146,000
Funded status	(368,000)	108,000	(260,000)
Net gain	(89,150)		(89,150)
Prior service cost[(a)]	66,000	(11,880)	54,120
Transition obligation[(b)]	390,000	(85,800)	304,200

[(a)] Effect of curtailment is 18% of $66,000 (prior service cost).
[(b)] Effect of curtailment is 22% of $390,000 (transition obligation).

Relationship of Settlements and Curtailments to Other Events

An event may be either a settlement, or a curtailment, or both at the same time (ASC 715-60-35-172).

A curtailment occurs, but not a settlement, if the expected future benefits are eliminated for some plan participants (e.g., because their employment is terminated), but the plan continues to exist, to pay benefits, to invest assets, and to receive contributions.

A settlement occurs, but not a curtailment, if an employer purchases nonparticipating insurance contracts to cover the accumulated postretirement benefit obligation, while continuing to provide defined benefits for future service (either in the same plan or in a successor plan).

A termination, or in effect both a settlement and curtailment, occurs if an employer settles its obligation and terminates the plan without establishing a successor defined benefit plan to take its place. This occurs whether the employees continue to work for the employer or not.

Illustration of Partial Settlement and Full Curtailment Resulting from Sale of Line of Business

Company C sold a line of business to Company D. Company C has a separate postretirement benefit plan that provides benefits to retirees of the division that is sold. In connection with the sale:

1. Company C terminated all employees of the sold division (a full curtailment).
2. Company D hired most of the employees.

3. Company D assumed the accumulated postretirement benefit obligation of $160,000 for postretirement benefits related to the former employees of Company C hired by Company D, and Company C retained the obligation for its current retirees (a partial settlement).
4. The plan trustee transferred $200,000 of plan assets to Company D, consisting of $160,000 for the settlement of the accumulated postretirement benefit obligation and $40,000 as an excess contribution.
5. Company C determined that its gain on the sale of the division was $600,000, before considering any of the effects of the sale on the postretirement benefit plan.

Company C's accounting policy is to determine the effects of a curtailment before determining the effects of a settlement when both events occur simultaneously.

For Company C, the net loss from the curtailment is $456,000, which is recognized with the $600,000 gain resulting from the disposal of the division. The effect of the curtailment is determined as follows:

	Before Curtailment	*Curtailment-Related Effects Resulting from Sale*	*After Curtailment*
Accumulated postretirement benefit obligation	$(514,000)	$ (20,000)[(a)]	$(534,000)
Plan assets at fair value	220,000		220,000
Funded status	(294,000)	(20,000)	(314,000)
Net gain	(99,150)	20,000[(a)]	(79,150)
Prior service cost	66,000	(66,000)[(b)]	—
Transition obligation	390,000	(390,000)[(c)]	—

(a) Loss from earlier-than-expected retirement of fully eligible employees (not detailed here)
(b) 100% (reduction in remaining years for service to full eligibility) of the unrecognized prior service cost
(c) 100% (reduction in remaining years for service to full eligibility) of the unrecognized transition obligation

The $16,255 loss related to the settlement and transfer of plan assets that is recognized with the gain from the sale is determined as follows:

	After Curtailment	*Settlement and Transfer of Plan Assets*	*After Settlement*
Accumulated postretirement benefit obligation	$(534,000)	$160,000	$(374,000)
Plan assets at fair value	220,000	(200,000)	20,000
Funded status	(314,000)	(40,000)	(354,000)
Net gain	(79,150)	23,745[(d)]	(55,405)
Prior service cost	—	—	—
Transition obligation	—	—	—
	—		
Computation of loss on settlement and transfer	$(393,150)	$ (16,255)	$(409,405)

(d) The unrecognized net gain is computed as follows:
Step 1. Compute the percentage of the accumulated postretirement benefit obligation settled to the total accumulated postretirement benefit obligation ($160,000/$534,000 = 30%).
Step 2. Maximum gain is measured as the transition asset, plus any net gain included in other comprehensive income ($79,150 + $0 = $79,150).
Step 3. The settlement gain is 30% of $79,150 = $23,745.

MEASUREMENT OF THE EFFECTS OF TERMINATION BENEFITS

If an employer offers postretirement benefits as special termination benefits that are not required by any preexisting contract, the employer recognizes a liability and a loss when the employees accept the offer and the amount is reasonably estimable. If the employer is contractually obliged to provide postretirement benefits as termination benefits, the employer recognizes a liability and a loss when it is probable that benefits will be paid and the amount is reasonably estimable (ASC 715-60-25-4, 5).

If an employer offers special or contractual termination benefits and curtails the postretirement benefit plan at the same time, ASC 715 requires the employer to account separately for the termination benefits and the curtailment (ASC 715-60-25-4, 5).

The amount of the liability and loss to be recognized when employees accept an offer of termination benefits in the form of postretirement benefits is determined by taking the following steps (ASC 715-60-25-6):

Step 1.	Determine the accumulated postretirement benefit obligation for those employees (without including any special termination benefits), on the assumption that (*a*) any of those employees who are not yet fully eligible for benefits will terminate as soon as they become fully eligible, and (*b*) any of those employees who are fully eligible will retire immediately.
Step 2.	Adjust the accumulated postretirement benefit obligation as computed in Step 1 to reflect the special termination benefits.
Step 3.	Subtract the amount in Step 1 from the amount in Step 2.

ASC 715-70: DEFERRED CONTRIBUTION PLANS

DEFINED CONTRIBUTION PLANS

A *defined contribution plan* provides an individual account for each participant, and specifies how to determine the amount to be contributed to each individual's account. The plan does not specify the amount of postretirement benefits to be received by any individual. This amount is determined by the amount of contributions, the return on the investment of the amount contributed, and any forfeitures of the benefits of other plan participants that are allocated to the individual's account (ASC 715-70-05-3).

Accounting for Contributions

A defined contribution plan may require the employer to contribute to the plan only for periods in which an employee renders services, or the employer may be required to continue making payments for periods after the employee retires or terminates employment. To the extent an employer's contribution is made in the same period as the employee renders services, the employer's net periodic postretirement benefit cost equals the amount of contributions required for that period. If the plan requires the employer to continue contributions after the employee retires or terminates, the employer should make accruals during the employee's service period of the estimated amount of contributions to be made after the employee's retirement or termination (ASC 715-70-35-1).

Disclosure

The disclosure requirements for defined contribution plans are consolidated with disclosure requirements for both pension and other postretirement plans in the discussion on subtopic ASC 715-20.

ASC 715-80: MULTI-EMPLOYER PLANS

MULTIEMPLOYER PLANS

A multiemployer plan is one to which two or more unrelated employers contribute. Multiemployer plans generally result from *collective bargaining agreements*, and are administered by a joint board of trustees representing management and labor of all contributing employers. Sometimes these plans are called *joint trusts, Taft-Hartley*, or *union plans*. An employer may participate in a number of plans; for example, the employees may belong to a number of unions. Numerous employers may participate in a multiemployer plan. Often the employers are in the same industry, but sometimes the employers are in different industries, and the only common element among the employers is that their employees belong to the same labor union (ASC Glossary).

The assets contributed by one employer may be used to provide benefits to employees of other employers, since the assets contributed by one employer are not segregated from those contributed by other employers (ASC 715-80-05-1; ASC Glossary). Even though the plan provides defined benefits to employees of all the employers, the plan typically requires a defined contribution from each participating employer, but the amount of an employer's obligation may be changed by events affecting other participating employers and their employees.

A multiemployer plan can exist even without the involvement of a labor union. For example, a national not-for-profit organization may organize a multiemployer plan for itself and its local chapters.

Accounting for Multiemployer Plans

Distinctive accounting requirements apply to an employer that participates in a multiemployer plan. The employer recognizes as net periodic pension cost or net postretirement benefit cost the contribution required for the period, including cash and the fair value of noncash contributions. The employer recognizes as a liability any unpaid contributions required for the period (ASC 715-80-35-1).

PRACTICE NOTE:

- This accounting resembles that required for the single employer that has a *defined contribution plan* (see section covering subtopic ASC 715-70 titled "Defined Contribution Plans").
- By participating in a multiemployer plan, an employer that has a *defined benefit plan* accounts for it essentially as if it were a *defined contribution plan.* The financing of the plan is, in effect, off-balance-sheet.

Withdrawal from Multiemployer Plans

When an employer withdraws from a multiemployer plan, the employer may be contractually liable to pay into the plan a portion of its unfunded accumulated postretirement benefit obligation.

PRACTICE NOTE: Contractual obligations are the only ones facing the employer that withdraws from a multiemployer *postretirement* benefit plan. In contrast, an employer that withdraws from a multiemployer *pension* plan is subject not only to contractual obligations, but also to statutory obligations under the Multiemployer Pension Plan Amendments Act of 1980.

An employer should apply ASC 450 if withdrawal from the plan is probable or reasonably possible, and the employer will incur an obligation as a result (ASC 715-70-50-1).

Obligation under "Maintenance of Benefits" Clause

An employer should also apply ASC 450 if it is probable or reasonably possible that the employer's contribution to the multiemployer plan will increase during the remainder of the contract period under a "maintenance of benefits" clause, to make up for a shortfall in the funding of the plan to assure the full level of benefits described in the plan.

PART II: INTERPRETIVE GUIDANCE

ASC 715-20: DEFINED BENEFITS PLANS—GENERAL

ASC 715-20-25-1 through 25-4 Accounting for Cash Balance Plans

BACKGROUND

A survey conducted in 2002 indicated that 32 of the Fortune 100 companies have changed their traditional defined benefit plans to cash balance plans. The IRS defines a cash balance plan as follows:

> A defined benefit plan that defines benefits for each employee by reference to the employee's hypothetical account. An employee's hypothetical account is determined by reference to hypothetical allocations of contributions and earnings to an employee's account under a defined contribution plan.

The benefits in most cash balance plans are reported to employees as accumulated cash balances. Although most plans offer members the option to receive a lump-sum distribution of the account balance in settlement of the full obligation, to maintain a plan's tax-qualified status, such plans are required to offer members the option to receive their benefits in the form of a life annuity. The IRS requires that cash balance plans be funded similar to defined benefit plans, but employers report the benefits to employees as principal credits and interest credits as in 401(k) plans and other defined contribution plans. Nevertheless, cash balance plans have some features of defined benefit plans, such as the option of a life annuity, interest credits not based on plan assets' performance, joint and survivor options, and grandfathered or transitional defined benefit formulas. The existence of prior-service costs, deferred gains or losses, and an inability to divide the assets into defined contribution and defined benefit components makes it impractical to account for cash balance plans as defined contribution plans. Further, most employers classify cash balance plans as defined benefit plans, because (*a*) under the IRS definition of a defined contribution plan, employers are required to report individual funded account balances, and (*b*) according to ASC 715-30, a plan is a defined benefit plan if it is *not* a defined contribution plan.

ACCOUNTING ISSUE

- Should a cash balance pension plan be considered a defined benefit plan?

ACCOUNTING GUIDANCE

The following guidance on the accounting for cash balance plans in ASU 2020-10, Codification Improvements, supersedes the previous guidance in ASC 715-30-35-71 through 35-72:

- ASC 715-20-25-1 provides that a cash balance plan is a defined benefit plan.
- ASC 715-20-25-2 provides that a cash balance plan informs employees about a pension benefit in the form of a current account balance that is based on principal credits and future interest credits based on those principal credits.
- ASC 715-25-3 provides that individual account balances of a cash balance plan are determined by reference to a hypothetical account rather than specific assets, and the benefit depends on credits to the account at the employer's promised interest rate, not the actual return on the plan assets. An employer's obligation to the plan is not met by making required principal and interest contributions to participants' accounts for the period. Rather, over a period of time an employer must fund amounts that can accumulate to the actuarial present value of the benefit due at the distribution time to participants based on the plan's terms. An employer's contributions to a cash balance plan trust and the earnings on the invested plan assets may be unrelated to the principal and interest credits to participants' hypothetical accounts.
- ASC 715-20-25-4 states that determining whether a plan is pay-related and the appropriate attribution approach for a cash balance plan with other characteristics or for other types of defined benefit pension plans requires an evaluation of the specific features of those benefit arrangements. (See ASC 715-30-35-36 through 35-39, ASC 715-30-55-7 through 55-15, and 715-30-55-127A (Example 8) for guidance on attribution approaches.

ASC 715-20-S50-1, S99-2; ASC 715-30-35-40 through 35-41 Determination of Vested Benefit Obligation for a Defined Benefit Pension Plan

BACKGROUND

A projected benefit obligation (PBO) is defined in the ASC *Glossary* as "the actuarial present value as of a date of all benefits attributed by the pension benefit formula to employee service rendered prior to that date." The only difference between a PBO and an accumulated benefit obligation (ABO) is that the PBO considers assumptions about future compensation levels. The PBO and the ABO are both affected by the vested benefit obligation (VBO), which is the actuarial present value of benefits for which an employee is entitled to receive a pension currently or in the future without the requirement for continued employment.

Under some defined benefit pension plans, such as foreign plans, most or all of the benefits to which an employee is entitled upon termination is based on service to date. If the employee is terminated, the vested benefit would be payable to the employee immediately or indexed for inflation, if it were payable at a future date. For example, the Italian severance pay statute usually requires that the accrued benefit paid to an employee on separation be based on service to date. The undiscounted value of the amount paid immediately would be greater than the actuarial present value of the benefits the employee has a right to receive based on service to date. Similarly, legislation in the United Kingdom requires that deferred vested benefits of terminated employees be revalued from the separation date to the normal retirement age. In that situation, the VBO based on termination at the measurement date could be greater than the ABO if the calculation of the ABO considers the statutory revaluation only after the employee's expected termination date.

The difficulty in applying the guidance in ASC 715-30 to such plans is in determining whether the VBO should be calculated based on the presumption that the employee is terminated immediately (Approach 1) or the employee continues to provide service to the termination or retirement date with the maximum amount discounted to its present value (Approach 2). If the VBO exceeds the PBO, the ABO, or both in Approach 1, those amounts would have to be adjusted.

ACCOUNTING ISSUE

Should the VBO be the actuarial present value of the vested benefits to which an employee is entitled, based on service to date as if the employee were separated immediately (Approach 1), or to which an employee is currently entitled, based on the employee's expected separation or retirement date (Approach 2)?

ACCOUNTING GUIDANCE

The VBO may be based on either approach for situations that are not specifically considered in ASC 715-30 if the facts and circumstances are analogous to those discussed above.

A FASB staff representative reported that when responding to technical inquiries, the FASB staff recommended that the VBO be determined using Approach 1, because the staff believes that the VBO is not contingent on future service under that approach. Some believe that Approach 2 is more consistent with the intent of ASC 715-30 (FAS-87), because pension obligations are measured based on actuarial expectations.

SEC STAFF COMMENT

The SEC Observer noted that registrants should disclose the method used.

DISCUSSION

The following is the rationale for the two approaches.

Approach 1 Vested benefits are defined in the ASC's *Glossary* as "benefits for which the employee's right to receive a *present* or future pension benefit is no longer contingent on remaining in the service of the employer." (Emphasis added.) Those who supported this approach argued that the *present* benefit that the employee is entitled to should be measured at the *present* time. They believed that the value of the vested benefit is the actuarial value at the present, which should not be discounted. Supporters also believed that the employer's liability for the VBO should be based on the concept that it is a measure of the employer's obligation if the plan were discontinued. Proponents believed that if the vested benefit is an obligation, it should not be discounted to a lesser amount than the employer's current obligation. Rather, it should be measured based on service to date using the plan's benefit formula. They argued further that discounting the obligation assumes that the employee will perform future services for the employer. That conflicts with the definition of vested benefits, which do not depend on future services. Others argued for measuring the obligation at its current value, because some plans permit employees to take advances against their vested benefits while still employed.

Approach 2 Proponents of this approach noted that the PBO, ABO, and VBO are defined in FAS-87 in terms of actuarial present value, which is based on estimates of death, disability, withdrawal, or retirement in determining the probability and timing of payment. That amount is discounted from the expected payment date to the present. Others argued that even if the VBO under Approach 1 were greater than the PBO or the ABO or both, those amounts need not be adjusted, because they believed that the VBO does not represent a minimum value for the ABO and the PBO.

Background papers discussed the application of the two approaches to the Italian Termination Indemnity Plan and the U.K. Plan as follows:

Italian Termination Indemnity Plan Under the Italian plan, an employee's benefit generally is paid on termination. The amount equals a total of the following: (*a*) the prior year's balance, (*b*) the prior year's balance times 75% of the increase in the consumer price index, plus 1.5%, and (*c*) one-month service accrual for the current year.

Under Approach 1, the VBO must equal the balance payable to the employee on immediate separation. The VBO will usually be greater than the PBO, which discounts the benefits of expected payment. If so, the PBO is adjusted so the two amounts are equal. As a result, net periodic pension cost equals the change in the balance of the VBO and PBO from the beginning to the end of the year, adjusted for payments to employees actually terminated during the year. This method is the same as the method by which pension costs were measured before the issuance of ASC 715-30. If the PBO is greater than the VBO, net periodic pension cost is based on the PBO and the usual application of ASC 715.

Under Approach 2, the VBO is calculated by projecting out to the date when benefits to which the employee is currently entitled would be paid and discounting that amount to the present. The VBO would thus be the same as the usual calculation of the PBO. ASC 715 would be applied as for U.S. plans.

U.K. Plan Under government regulations in the U.K., an employee who reaches a certain age is entitled to a guaranteed minimum pension of a specified amount based on salary and service to date. Legislation enacted near the time this Issue was discussed required that benefits for an employee's services after the date of the legislation be revalued from the date of separation to the normal retirement date based on changes in price indices. Some plans were amended to provide such increases for all of an employee's service. Consequently, the VBO often would be greater than the ABO when vested benefits are revalued. Because the PBO includes salary escalation, it would still be greater than the VBO.

Under Approach 1, the ABO would have to be adjusted to equal the VBO, because the ABO should not be less than the benefit to which an employee is currently entitled.

Under Approach 2, the VBO would be measured based on the discounted value of the benefit receivable at the date of expected separation. It would not exceed the ABO and would not require adjustment.

Although periodic pension cost is unlikely to be affected by the different ABO amounts under the two approaches, the minimum liability as calculated under FAS-87 could be affected.

ASC 715-20-S55-1, S99-1 Selection of Discount Rates Used for Measuring Defined Benefit Pension Obligations and Obligations of Postretirement Plans Other Than Pensions

The SEC Observer announced that registrants should use the guidance in ASC 715-30-35-44 to select the discount rate for measuring the pension benefit obligation in a defined benefit pension plan and the guidance in ASC 715-60-35-80 for obligations of postretirement benefit plans other than pensions. That paragraph states in part that "the objective of selecting assumed discount rates to measure the single amount that, if invested at the measurement date in a portfolio of high-quality debt instruments, would provide the necessary future cash flows to pay the accumulated benefits. The SEC Observer stated that the staff expects that discount rates used by registrants at each measurement date to measure obligations for pension benefits and postretirement benefits other than pensions would reflect the current level of interest rates. He stated that the SEC staff suggests that high-quality, fixed-income debt securities are those that receive one of the two highest ratings from a recognized ratings agency, such as a rating of Aa or higher from Moody's Investors Service, Inc.

ASC 715-30: DEFINED BENEFIT PLANS PENSION

ASC 715-30-35-73 Accounting for the Transfer of Excess Pension Assets to a Retiree Health Care Benefits Account

Under the Revenue Reconciliation Act of 1990 (the Act), an employer can transfer excess pension assets of a defined benefit pension plan (other than a multiemployer plan) to a health care benefits account that is part of the pension plan without including that amount in gross taxable income and without incurring penalties. The Act provides that such transfers be made beginning after December 31, 1990, and before the employer's 1996 tax year, and that amounts transferred not exceed the amount reasonably expected to be paid for "qualified current retiree health liabilities." Transfers are limited to one per year.

The FASB staff announced that such transfers should be recognized as a negative contribution or withdrawal from the pension plan and a positive contribution to the retiree health care plan. The transfer does not result in a gain or loss.

ASC 715-30-35-89 through 35-91 Accounting for Pension Benefits Paid by Employers after Insurance Companies Fail to Provide Annuity Benefits

BACKGROUND

Based on the guidance in ASC 715-30, a company purchases annuity contracts from an insurance company to settle its obligation under a defined benefit pension plan; the company may or may not terminate the plan. The insurance company subsequently becomes insolvent and is unable to meet its obligation under the annuity contracts. The company decides to make up some or all of the shortfall in payments to the plan's retirees.

ACCOUNTING ISSUE

How should a company account for the cost of making up the shortfall of payments to retirees caused by an insurance company's failure to fulfill its obligation under annuity contracts?

ACCOUNTING GUIDANCE

An employer's assumption of the cost of making up a shortfall in payments to retirees as a result of an insurance company's failure to meet its obligations under annuity contracts should be recognized as a loss to the extent of a gain, if any, and recognized on the original settlement. The loss recognized would be the lesser of (*a*) a gain recognized on the original settlement and (*b*) the amount of the benefit obligation assumed by the employer. The excess of the obligation assumed by the employer over the loss recognized should be accounted for as a plan amendment or a plan initiation in accordance with the provisions of ASC 715-30-35-10 through 35-11, 35-13 through 35-14, and 35-17. Thereafter, the provisions of ASC 715-30 should be applied.

ASC 715- 30-55-70 through 55-78, 55-171; 715-20-50-10 Accounting for the Transfer to the Japanese Government of the Substitutional Portion of Employee Pension Fund Liabilities

BACKGROUND

Many large Japanese corporations have Employee Pension Fund (EPF) plans that are defined benefit pension plans established under the Japanese Welfare Pension Insurance Law (JWPIL). Those plans consist of the following:

- A substitutional portion based on the part of the old-age pension benefits set by JWPIL based on pay (similar to social security benefits).
- A corporate portion based on a contributory defined benefit pension arrangement established by employers with benefits based on a formula determined by each employer and its EPF.

Corporations that have an EPF—and their employees—need not contribute to Japanese Pension Insurance (JPI), which would be required if the substitutional portion of the benefit were not funded through the EPF. As a result, the corporate and substitutional benefits are paid to retired beneficiaries out of the EPF's assets. All of an EPF's assets are invested and managed as a single portfolio and are not separately segregated to the substitutional and corporate portions. The percentage of the substitutional portion relative to the total EPF is not predetermined and varies by employer.

In June 2001, the JWPIL was amended to allow employers and their EPFs to separate the substitutional portions of their pension plans and transfer the obligations and related assets to the government. The separation process will be completed in four phases. After completion of that process, employers and their EPFs will be released from making further payments of the substitutional portion to beneficiaries. In addition, employers and their employees will be required to contribute periodically to the JPI; the Japanese government will be responsible for making all benefit payments earned under JWPIL. The remaining part of the EPF will be a corporate defined benefit plan (CDBP), which employers will be able to transfer to a defined contribution plan.

ACCOUNTING ISSUE

How should Japanese companies that report on U.S. securities exchanges and consequently account for EPFs as single-employer defined benefit plans using a single-plan approach account for (*a*) the separation of the substitutional portion of the benefit obligation of an EPF from the corporate portion and (*b*) the transfer of the substitutional portion and related assets to the Japanese government?

ACCOUNTING GUIDANCE

When the transfer of the substitutional portion of the pension benefit obligation and the related assets (phase 4) to the Japanese government has been completed, employers should account for that process as the conclusion of a single settlement transaction consisting of a series of steps. The following guidance applies only to this specific situation.

The guidance should be applied as follows:

- A transaction should be accounted for as a settlement when it is complete, that is, when the total substitutional portion of the benefit obligation has been eliminated because enough assets to complete the separation process have been transferred to the Japanese government.
- In accordance with the guidance in ASC 715-30, immediately before the separation, the total projected benefit obligation should be remeasured at fair value, including the effects of changes in actuarial assumptions (such as expected future salary increases), if any, and actual experience since the previous measurement date. This remeasurement should include only benefits earned under the substitutional arrangement *before* the government accepts responsibility for all substitutional payments.
- A settlement of the substitutional portion of the obligation should be accounted for as follows:
  - — Recognize as a gain or loss on settlement a proportionate amount of the ASC 715-30 net gain or loss included in accumulated other comprehensive income related to the total EPF as a gain or loss on settlement.
  - — Determine the proportionate amount of the net gain or loss that should be recognized based on the proportion of the projected benefit obligation settled to the total projected benefit obligation, but exclude previously accrued salary progression from that calculation.

— After separation, continue accounting for the EPF's remaining assets and obligation as well as for both prior-service costs included in accumulated other comprehensive income and gains and losses, if any, in accordance with the guidance in ASC 715-30 and ASC 715-20.

— Account for and disclose the difference between the settled obligation and the assets transferred to the government, which were determined based on the government's formula, as a subsidy from the government separately in accordance with generally accepted accounting principles.

— In accordance with this consensus, account for and disclose the derecognition of previously accrued salary progression at the time of settlement *separately* from the government's subsidy.

OBSERVATION: Under the guidance in ASC 715-30, employers are required to recognize in the financial statements the amount of obligations related to single-employer defined benefit pension plans, retiree health care, and other postretirement plans.

Minimum pension liability adjustments are eliminated under the Statement. Gains or losses, prior service costs or credits, and transition assets and obligations must be recognized in accumulated other comprehensive income if they have not yet been recognized as components of net periodic benefit cost.

ASC 715-30-55-81 through 55-86 Accounting for Early Retirement or Postemployment Programs with Specific Features (Such as Terms Specified in Altersteilzeit Early Retirement Arrangements)

BACKGROUND

The German government has established an early retirement program, referred to as the Altersteilzeit (ATZ) arrangement, under which employees that meet certain age and other requirements transition from full or part-time employment to retirement before their legal retirement age. The German government reimburses employers that participate in the program for bonuses paid to participating employees and for additional contributions paid into the German government's pension program under an ATZ arrangement for a maximum of six years. The program, which was developed in 1996, will expire in 2009.

Typical features of ATZ arrangements include the following:

- Type I: Participants work 50% of a normal full-time schedule during each year of the ATZ period and receive 50% of their salaries each year.
- Type II: Participants work full time for half of the ATZ period (the active period) and do not work for the other half of the ATZ period (the inactive period). They receive 50% of their salary each year of the ATZ period.
- For both Type I and Type II arrangements: The participants receive an annual bonus. Although the amount of the bonus may vary by employer, it generally equals 10-15% of the employee's most recent regular pay before the ATZ period. Therefore, during the ATZ period, employees generally receive 60-65% of their regular pay before the ATZ period. Employers also make additional contributions for the participants into the German government's pension program.

ACCOUNTING ISSUES

- How should a termination/retirement benefit under a Type II ATZ arrangement be accounted for?
- How should a government subsidy under Type I and Type II ATZ arrangements be accounted for?

ACCOUNTING GUIDANCE

- For Type II ATZ arrangements, employers should account for the bonus feature and additional contributions into the German government's pension program as postemployment benefits under the guidance in ASC 712. Additional compensation should be recognized from the time an employee signs an ATZ contract until the end of the employee's active service period.
- Under Type I and Type II arrangements, employers should recognize the government's subsidy when they meet the necessary criteria and are entitled to receive it.

The FASB staff noted that employers should recognize the salary components of Type I and Type II ATZ arrangements, other than the bonus and additional contributions to the German government's pension arrangement, from the beginning of the ATZ period to the end of the active service period. Under Type II arrangements, the deferred portion of an employee's salary should be discounted if it is expected that the payment will be deferred for longer than a year. The EITF agreed with the FASB staff's view.

ASC 715-60: DEFINED BENEFIT PLANS—OTHER POST-RETIREMENT

ASC 715-60-05-8 through 05-11, 15-11 through 15-13, 35-133 through 35-148, 50-2B, 50-4, 50-6, 55-103; ASC 715-740-10-55 through 10-57, 10-166 through 10-167 Accounting and Disclosure Requirements Related to the Medicare Prescription Drug Improvement and Modernization Act of 2003

BACKGROUND

The Medicare Prescription Drug Improvement and Modernization Act (the Act) will provide Medicare participants with a prescription drug benefit under Medicare Part D. In addition, sponsors of retiree health care benefit plans providing prescription drug benefits that are at least "actuarially equivalent" to those provided under Medicare Part D will be entitled to receive a federal subsidy.

Under the guidance in ASC 715-60-35-91, plan sponsors are required to consider Medicare in measuring a plan's accumulated postretirement benefit obligation (APBO) and net periodic postretirement benefit cost.

New Features of Medicare under the Act

Two new features have been added to Medicare as a result of the Act: (1) plan sponsors will receive subsidies based on 28% of the annual prescription drug costs between $250 and $5,000 incurred by individual beneficiaries (subject to indexing and the Act's provisions regarding *allowable retiree costs*) and (2) retirees will have the option to decide whether to enroll in a prescription drug benefit under Medicare Part D.

The amount of a plan sponsor's subsidy will depend on how many of the plan's beneficiaries that are eligible for Medicare decide *not* to enroll in Medicare Part D, which is voluntary. The Secretary of Health and Human Services has not yet issued detailed regulations on how to implement the Act, including how to determine whether a plan's prescription drug benefit is "actuarially equivalent" to the benefit under Medicare Part D, the evidence needed to demonstrate actuarial equivalency, documentation requirements for the subsidy, and the manner in which the subsidy will be paid by the appropriate agency.

The per capita claims cost of a plan that has been providing a prescription drug benefit to retirees will depend on (*a*) the extent that current and future retirees will voluntarily enroll in Medicare Part D and pay a monthly premium, which initially will be $35, and (*b*) how the Act will affect the trend in health care costs and consumers' behavior.

Other Effects of the Act

Under the Act, plan sponsors will be able to exclude the federal subsidy from their taxable income for federal income tax purposes, which means that the temporary difference related to the APBO that results in a deferred tax asset under ASC 740 (FAS-109, Accounting for Income Taxes) will be affected, depending on how the subsidy is accounted for.

In addition, the Act provides for a two-year transition period during which plan sponsors may amend existing plans or establish new ones in response to the legislation in order to maximize the financial benefit to the entity or improve employee relations. Changes in the benefit formula as a result of plan amendments will affect the APBO.

ACCOUNTING GUIDANCE

Question 1: How should the effect of the subsidy on the following matters be accounted for?

1. Benefits attributable to past service
2. Current measures of net periodic postretirement benefit cost
3. Changes in estimates
4. Plan amendments
5. Income tax accounting

Answer: The subsidy's effect should be accounted for as follows:

- On initial application of the guidance in this FSP, the effect of the subsidy on the APBO should be accounted for as an actuarial experience gain in accordance with the guidance in ASC 715-60-35-23, 35-25, 35-29 through 35-30.
- The subsidy should be included in measuring the cost of benefits attributable to current service because it affects the sponsor's share of the plan's costs. By including the subsidy in the calculation of net periodic postretirement benefit cost, the sponsor's service cost—which is defined in ASC 715-60-35-10—is reduced.

- A change in estimate is an actuarial experience gain in accordance with the guidance in ASC 715-60-35-23 through 35-25, if the amount of the estimated expected subsidy changes because of changes in regulations or legislation, changes in the underlying estimates of postretirement prescription drug costs, or other changes that are *not* plan amendments.
- Sponsors that amend a plan to make it actuarially equivalent to Medicare Part D should combine the direct effect on the APBO and the effect on the APBO from the subsidy that the sponsor expects to receive. If actuarial equivalency under the Act of a plan's prescription drug benefits is disqualified as the result of a subsequent plan amendment that *reduces* the coverage, there is *no* effect on an actuarial experience gain, if any, that was previously recognized. Nevertheless, the combined net effect on the APBO of the plan's loss of (i) actuarial equivalency under the Act as a result of the plan amendment reducing coverage and (ii) the subsidy's elimination should be accounted for as a prior service cost or credit as of the date on which the amendment is adopted.
- Because the subsidy is exempt from federal taxation, it has *no* effect on temporary differences, if any, under the guidance in ASC 740 that are related to the plan.

Question 2: What disclosures are required?

Answer: Sponsors that have not yet determined whether the prescription drug benefits are actuarially equivalent to Medicare Part D under the Act should disclose the following information in their interim or annual financial statements:

- The Act's existence
- The fact that a subsidy has not been considered in amounts presented for the APBO or net periodic postretirement benefit cost because it has not been determined whether the benefits under the plan are actuarially equivalent to Medicare Part D under the Act

The following disclosures should be made in the financial statements of the first interim or annual period in which the effects of the subsidy are included in measuring the APBO and in the first period in which the effects of the subsidy are included in measuring net periodic postretirement benefit cost:

- The amount by which the APBO is reduced for the subsidy related to benefits attributed to past service
- The subsidy's effect on the measurement of net periodic postretirement benefit cost in the current period, including the(i) amortization of the actual experience gain, if any, as a component of the net amortization under the guidance in ASC 715-60-35-29 through 35-30 (ii) reduction in current period service cost as a result of the subsidy; and (iii) consequent reduction in interest cost on the APBO due to the subsidy
- Other disclosures under the guidance in ASC 715-20-50-1, which requires an explanation of significant changes, if any, in a plan's benefit obligation or assets that would *not* be obvious in the Statement's other required disclosures

Question 3: After this guidance has been adopted, how should an employer determine a plan's actuarial equivalence without a plan amendment?

Answer: A sponsor that was unable to determine whether its plan is actuarially equivalent to Medicare Part D when this guidance was adopted may receive new information about the Act, such as regulations clarifying actuarial equivalency or interpretive information. If after reconsideration of actuarial equivalency of the plan's benefits the sponsor concludes that there is actuarial equivalence, that conclusion may be a significant event under the guidance in ASC 715-60-35-126. If the effects of the subsidy on the plan are significant, the plan's assets and obligations should be measured as of the date that actuarial equivalency was determined. The subsidy's effect on the APBO should be presented as an actuarial gain in accordance with the guidance in paragraph (a) of the answer to Question 1 of this FSP. The amount of net periodic postretirement benefit cost in later periods should include the effects of those measurements. However, prior financial statements should *not* be retroactively adjusted. A cumulative effect for prior periods also should *not* be recognized in income.

ASC 715-60-05-14 through 05-15, 15-20 through 15-21, 35-177 through 35-179, 55-176 through 55-177, 55-179 Accounting for Deferred Compensation and Postretirement Benefit Aspects of Endorsement Split-Dollar Life Insurance Arrangements

BACKGROUND

A company may purchase life insurance to protect against a loss of "key" employees, to fund deferred compensation and postretirement benefit obligations, and to provide investment return. Split-dollar life insurance, the structure of which may be complex and varied, is one type of life insurance that may be purchased by a company. The most common types of such arrangements are *endorsement split-dollar* life insurance (owned and controlled by the company) and *collateral assignment split-dollar* life insurance (owned and controlled by the employee).

There is diversity in practice in accounting for the deferred compensation and postretirement features of *endorsement* split-life insurance policies, the terms of which may be as follows:

- The employer pays a single premium at the inception of a policy to insure an employee's life.
- The insurer may charge or credit the policyholder based on negative or positive experience for a specific risk (e.g., mortality risk). The insurer usually realizes an additional premium by adjusting the policy's cash surrender value.
- The employer and an employee enter into a separate agreement whereby the policy's benefits are split between the employer and the employee with the employer endorsing a portion of the death benefits to the employee.
- The employer owns and controls the policy and may terminate the arrangement at will.
- Upon the death of an employee, the employee's beneficiary receives the portion of the death benefits designated to the employee and the employer keeps the remainder.
- An employee's beneficiary may receive the benefit directly from the insurance company or from the employer.

An employee's portion of the death benefits is commonly based on (*a*) the amount by which the employee's portion of the death benefits exceeds the gross premiums, (*b*) the amount by which the employee's portion of the death benefits exceeds the gross premiums plus an additional fixed or variable investment return on those premiums, (*c*) the face amount of the death benefit under the policy less the employee's portion of the policy's cash surrender value, or (*d*) an amount equal to a multiple of the employee's base salary at retirement or death (e.g., twice the employee's base salary).

SCOPE

This Issue applies only to the recognition of a liability and the related compensation costs for endorsement split-life insurance arrangements that are owned and controlled by an employer. It does *not* apply to split-dollar life insurance arrangements that provide a specific benefit to an employee only during the period that the employee is the employer's active employee. The question is how employers should account for the aspects of those policies that are related to deferred compensation, postretirement, or postemployment benefits.

ACCOUNTING ISSUE

When an employer and an employee enter into a split-dollar life insurance arrangement, should the postretirement benefit associated with the arrangement be accounted for in accordance with the guidance in ASC 715-60 or that in ASC 710?

ACCOUNTING GUIDANCE

An employer should recognize a liability for future benefits associated with an *endorsement* split-dollar life insurance arrangement that is based on a substantive agreement with an employee in accordance with the guidance in ASC 715-60 if a substantive postretirement benefit plan exists. If an arrangement is in substance an individual deferred compensation contract with an employee, the guidance in ASC 710 should be followed based on the substantive arrangement with an employee. The purchase of a standard endorsement split-dollar life insurance policy does *not* settle an employer's liability for a benefit obligation under the provisions of ASC 715 or ASC 710-10-25-9 through 25-11. For example, an employer that agrees to maintain a life insurance policy during an employee's retirement should accrue the cost of the insurance policy under the guidance in ASC 715-60 or ASC 710-10-25-9 through 25-11. Likewise, an employer that has agreed to provide an employee with a death benefit should accrue a liability in accordance with the guidance in ASC 715-60 or ASC 710-10-25-9 through 25-11 over the employee's service period for the actuarial present value of the future death benefit as of the employee's expected retirement date.

It was noted that the substance of an arrangement should be determined based on the available evidence, such as an arrangement's explicit written terms, communications from the employer to an employee, and the conclusion as to who is the primary obligor for the postretirement benefit, the employer or the insurance company. For example, an employer's promise to pay a postretirement death benefit even if the insurance company defaults on a payment indicates that the employer has promised to provide a postretirement benefit and is the primary obligor. In addition, if the amount of a death benefit is *not* explicitly related to the insurance policy, the amount of the postretirement benefit should be the amount of the death benefit promised to the employee. In contrast, if under the terms of an arrangement, an employer has *no* obligation to pay a death benefit if the insurance company defaults on a payment, it is an indication that the employer has promised to maintain a life insurance policy during the employee's retirement. Employers should follow the guidance in ASC 715-60 and ASC 710-10-25-9 through 25-11, as applicable, to determine how to measure and attribute their cost or obligation under an arrangement.

ASC 715-60-05-15, 35-180 through 35-185, 55-178, 55-180 through 55-181 Accounting for Deferred Compensation and Postretirement Benefit Aspects of Collateral Assignment Split-Dollar Life Insurance Arrangements

BACKGROUND

A company may purchase life insurance to protect against a loss of "key" employees, to fund deferred compensation and postretirement benefit obligations, or to provide an investment return. Two types of split-dollar life insurance arrangements exist: *endorsement* split-dollar life insurance, which is owned and controlled by the company, and *collateral assignment* split-dollar life insurance, which is owned and controlled by the employee.

Under existing guidance, an employer is required to recognize a liability for future benefits associated with an *endorsement* split-dollar life insurance arrangement that is based on a substantive agreement with the employee in accordance with the guidance in ASC 715-60 if a substantive postretirement benefit plan exists. If an arrangement is, in substance, an individual deferred compensation contract with an employee, the guidance in ASC 710 should be followed based on a substantive arrangement with an employee.

The following guidance addresses how an employer should account for *collateral assignment* split-dollar life insurance arrangements. Under this type of arrangement, although an employee owns and controls the policy, the employer usually pays all of the premiums and in turn, the employee irrevocably assigns all or a portion of the death benefits to the employer as collateral for the employer's payment of the premiums, which are considered to be a loan. Usually, the employer is entitled to receive a portion of the death benefits equal to the amount of premiums paid by the employer or that amount plus an additional fixed return on the premiums. An employee that retires may have the option or be required to transfer the policy to the employer to satisfy the outstanding loan. Under the Sarbanes Oxley Act of 2002, all public and private entities are required to account for such arrangements as employer loans in accordance with the provisions of ASC 835-30.

Interest on Receivables and Payables. The employer must recognize a receivable from the employee at a discounted amount for the premiums paid.

ACCOUNTING ISSUES

- Based on a substantive agreement with an employee, should an employer recognize a liability for a postretirement benefit related to a *collateral assignment* split-dollar life insurance arrangement in accordance with the guidance in ASC 715 (FAS-106), if, in substance, a postretirement benefit exists, or in accordance with the guidance in APB-12, if an arrangement is, in substance, an individual deferred compensation contract?
- How should an employer recognize and measure the asset in a *collateral assignment* split-dollar life insurance arrangement?

ACCOUNTING GUIDANCE

1. If a substantive postretirement benefit plan exists, an employer should recognize a liability for a postretirement benefit associated with a *collateral assignment* split-dollar life insurance arrangement in accordance with the guidance in ASC 715-60. The guidance in ASC 710-10-25-9 through 25-11 should be followed for an arrangement that is, in substance, an individual deferred compensation contract with an employee and if, based on that contract, the employer has agreed to maintain a life insurance policy during the employee's retirement or to provide the employee with a death benefit. If in the past an employer has had a stated or implied commitment to provide an employee with a loan to pay premiums on an insurance policy during an employee's retirement or is currently promising to provide loans in the future, it may be presumed that the employer has in effect agreed to maintain the life insurance policy, unless there is opposing evidence. An employer that has committed to maintain a life insurance policy or to provide a death benefit after an employee's retirement should account for those obligations as follows:
   - Accrue the estimated cost of maintaining the life insurance policy after an employee's retirement in accordance with the guidance in ASC 715-60, or

- Accrue a liability for the actuarial present value of a future death benefit as of an employee's expected retirement date in accordance with the guidance in ASC 710-10-25-9 through 25-11.

  To determine whether an arrangement is substantive, all relevant information should be considered, such as the explicit written terms of an arrangement, an employer's communications to the employee, an employer's past administrative procedures for the same or similar arrangements, and whether an employer has the primary obligation for an employee's postretirement benefit. For example, if under the terms of an arrangement, an employer has *no* stated or implied obligation to provide loans to an employee to pay for premiums on a life insurance policy, the employer may have *no* postretirement obligation. In contrast, if under a collateral assignment arrangement with an employee, an employer has a stated or implied obligation to provide an employee with loans to cover the insurance company's gains or losses, the employer may have a postretirement obligation. The guidance in ASC 715-60 or ASC 710-10-25-9 through 25-11, as applicable, should be consulted to determine how to measure and assign the cost of the obligation under an arrangement.

  Collateral assignment split-dollar insurance arrangements should be reevaluated in periods after their inception based on the guidance in ASC 715-60 to determine whether the substance of an arrangement has changed as a result of a change in facts and circumstances, such as an amendment to an arrangement or a change from an employer's past practice, and may require that a liability be recognized or that a previously recognized liability for a postretirement obligation be adjusted.

2. An employer should recognize and measure an asset based on the nature and substance of a collateral assignment split-dollar life insurance arrangement. To determine the nature and substance of an arrangement, an employer should evaluate (*a*) future cash flows to which the employer is entitled, if any, and (*b*) an employee's obligation and ability to repay the employer. For example, at the balance sheet date, an employer's asset would be limited to the cash surrender value of an insurance policy, if the amount the employer could recover from an employee or retiree is limited to the amount of the insurance policy's cash surrender value, even if the employer's loan to the employee or retiree exceeds that amount. In contrast, an employer should recognize the value of a loan, including accrued interest, if applicable, based on the guidance in ASC 835-30, if under the arrangement, an employee or retiree is required to repay the employer regardless of the collateral assigned and the employer (*a*) has determined that the employee's or retiree's loan is collectible and (*b*) intends to try to recover the amount by which the loan exceeds the insurance policy's cash surrender value. To determine the nature and substance of a collateral assignment split-dollar life insurance arrangement, an employer should consider all the available information.

ASC 715-60-15-5 through 15-6, 25-4, 35-21, 35-33, 35-64 through 35-65, 35-96, 35-111 35-113, 35-168, 55-1 through 55-25, 55-27 through 55-30, 55-32 55-34, 55-106 through 55-111, 55-140, 55-142 through 55-175; ASC 715-20-55-1 through 55-2; ASC 715-70-55-2 through 55-3; ASC 715-80-55-3 through 55-5; ASC 710-10-55-2, 55-5 through 55-6, 60-3 Guide to Implementation of ASC 715-60 on Employers' Accounting for Postretirement Benefits Other Than Pensions

ACCOUNTING GUIDANCE

Scope

Question F1: Does this Statement apply to long-term disability benefits paid to former employees on disability retirement under an employer's postretirement benefit plan?

Answer: Yes, if the benefits provided are postretirement benefits. Disability benefits paid to former or inactive employees who are not on disability retirement should be accounted for in accordance with guidance in ASC 712. Similarly, if disability income benefits are paid pursuant to a pension plan, the applicable accounting guidance is found in ASC 715-30.

Question F2: If some employees, upon their retirement, voluntarily elect under the provisions of the Consolidated Omnibus Budget Reconciliation Act of 1985 (COBRA), as amended, to continue their health care coverage provided through the active employee health care plan and the cost to the employer of their continuing coverage exceeds the retirees' contributions, should the employer account for that cost under the guidance in ASC 715-60?

Answer: No. The right to continue health care coverage under COBRA is not based on employee retirement. This right generally is available to any terminated employee. Therefore, employers should follow the guidance in ASC 712 when the cost of continuing health care coverage under COBRA exceeds the former employees' contributions.

Question F3: A collectively bargained defined benefit postretirement health care plan of a single employer may stipulate that the benefits will be provided for the duration of the collective-bargaining agreement, or the plan may imply or explicitly state that benefits are subject to renegotiation upon the expiration of the current collective-bargaining agreement. Past negotiations have resulted in the continuation of the plan, although the plan has been amended at various times. Should the accumulated postretirement benefit obligation (APBO) be measured based only on benefits expected to be paid during the period in which the current agreement will be in force?

Answer: No. The APBO should be measured assuming that the defined benefit postretirement health care plan will continue after the expiration of the existing collective-bargaining agreement. Unless there is evidence to the contrary, a postretirement benefit plan that currently exists is expected to continue in the future.

Contracts Involving Deferred Compensation

Question F4: How should an employer account for a deferred compensation contract that does not provide a vested benefit for the employee's prior service at the date the contract is entered into? For example, an employee must render 30 years of service to receive benefits under a deferred compensation contract and has rendered 16 years of service at the date of entering into the contract. Credit is granted for that prior service in determining eligibility for the benefit to be provided. Should the total obligation be accrued over the remaining 14 years of service, or should the employer immediately recognize the portion related to the 16 years of service already rendered?

Answer: The total obligation under the deferred compensation contract should be accrued over the remaining 14 years of service. An obligation related to the prior service would be accrued only if the employee was entitled to part of the benefit without regard to future service (i.e., if the credit for prior service results in a vested benefit).

Question F5: An employee becomes fully eligible for benefits under a deferred compensation contract five years after entering into the contract. The contract states, however, that if the employee dies or becomes disabled, benefits will be payable immediately. The contract is not one of a group of contracts that possess the characteristics of a pension plan. What is the attribution period?

Answer: If the employee is expected to provide service over the five-year period, the obligation should be accrued over this time period. If the employee dies or becomes disabled before the five-year period expires, any remaining unrecognized cost would be recognized in the period in which the death or disability occurred. No accrual is required if the employee is not expected to work for the employer for the next five years.

Substantive Plan

Question F6: Can future amendments to a written postretirement health care plan that change the amount of a defined dollar cap be anticipated as part of the substantive plan?

Answer: Yes, if the employer's past practices indicate that plan amendments are a common occurrence. For example, the employer may have a history of regularly increasing (or decreasing) the defined dollar cap under a postretirement health care plan.

Question F7: Is a postretirement health care plan with a defined dollar cap considered to be a plan that provides benefits defined in terms of monetary amounts as discussed in ASC 715-60-35-56?

Answer: No. In this scenario, the benefit is reimbursement of specified eligible medical claims. The fact that the employer's reimbursement of these claims is limited to a specific dollar amount (i.e., the dollar cap) does not indicate that the benefits are defined in monetary amounts.

Measurement

Question F8: Should the assumed discount rates used to measure an employer's postretirement benefit obligation be the same rates used to measure its pension obligation under the guidance in ASC 715-30?

Answer: Not necessarily. As under the guidance in ASC 715-30, the discount rate chosen to measure the liability for postretirement benefit obligations should reflect the interest rate on high-quality debt instruments of a duration comparable to that of the benefit obligation. However, a different discount rate may be appropriate, because the timing of expected payments under the postretirement benefit plan may differ from the expected timing of pension payments.

Question F9: An employer sponsors a health care plan that provides benefits to both active employees and retirees under age 65. The plan requires active employees and retirees to contribute to the plan. Can the contributions of active employees ever be used to reduce the employer's cost of providing benefits to retirees?

Answer: Yes, but only if contributions by active employees exceed the cost of providing health care benefits for this group over its working life and the employer has no obligation to refund the excess contributions. The cost of providing health care coverage for active employees should be measured on the assumption they are the only group covered by the plan (i.e., retirees would be excluded in this computation).

Question F10: An employer has a contributory health care plan covering active employees and retirees under which retirees pay 100% of the average cost of benefits determined based on the combined experience of active employees and retirees. The employer pays all of the remaining cost. The active employees do not contribute to the plan. Under this arrangement, does the employer have an obligation under this Statement?

Answer: Yes, if the actual cost of providing health care benefits to retirees exceeds their contributions. If this is the case, the employer is subsidizing the retirees' health care benefits. The employer has an obligation for the difference between the expected cost of the retirees' benefits and the expected contribution amounts.

Question F11: Are there any circumstances under which an employer may measure its postretirement health care benefit obligation by projecting the cost of premiums for purchased health care insurance?

Answer: Yes, if the postretirement benefit plan provides that the benefit to be received by retirees is a payment of their future health care insurance premiums.

Question F12: If an employer has measured its postretirement health care benefit obligation by projecting the cost of premiums for purchased health care insurance, does that reduce or eliminate the applicability of any provisions of this Statement, for example, the calculation and disclosure of service and interest cost?

Answer: No. All of the provisions in this Statement, including the disclosure of service and interest cost, still apply.

Question F13: Should employers assume a trend of decreasing (or increasing) Medicare reimbursement rates if Medicare has consistently reduced (or increased) the portion of benefits it will cover? For example, certain health care costs may have increased by 15% last year but Medicare may have covered only a smaller increase, which increased the employer's or retirees' share of the cost of benefits. When determining its postretirement benefit obligation, should an employer assume that such a reduction in Medicare coverage would continue?

Answer: Generally, not. Changes in Medicare coverage should be projected only if they result from currently enacted legislation or regulations. Future changes in Medicare legislation or regulations should not be anticipated even if past experience indicates that such changes are likely.

Attribution

Question F14: An employer modifies the eligibility requirements under its postretirement benefit plan by changing the plan's credited service period from "25 years of service after age 40" to "15 years of service after both (*a*) reaching age 50 and (*b*) rendering 10 years of service." What is the beginning of the attribution period?

Answer: The credited service period for this pension plan is undefined. Therefore, the attribution period begins on the date of hire. The net effect of the above change is to lengthen the attribution period for employees under age 40.

Question F15: An employer provides retiree health care and life insurance benefits under one plan. Employees are eligible for health care and death benefits upon attaining age 55 and having rendered 20 years of service; however, the life insurance benefits are based on final pay. Does basing the life insurance benefits on final pay extend the full eligibility date to a plan participant's expected retirement date? For example, if an employee is expected to fulfill the 20-year service requirement before age 55 and is expected to retire at age 62 with salary increases in all years of service, is the employee's full eligibility date the date he or she reaches age 62?

Answer: Yes, assuming the additional life insurance benefits earned between age 55 and the employee's expected retirement date are not trivial in relation to the total benefit to be received. This postretirement benefit plan has an indefinite credited service period. Therefore, the attribution period begins on the date of hire and ends on the full eligibility date. The full eligibility date is the date on which an employee has earned all of the benefits that he or she will receive under the postretirement benefit plan. In this case, the full amount of life insurance benefits to be received will not be known until the employee retires.

Question F16: Would the answer to the question in paragraph F15 be different if the benefits were provided and accounted for under two separate plans, one providing life insurance benefits and the other providing health care benefits?

Answer: Yes. If health care and life insurance benefits are provided under separate plans, the full eligibility date would be determined separately for each plan.

Question F17: If the terms of the plan in the question in paragraph F15 specified which 20-year service period constituted the credited service period—for example, the first 20 years after date of hire, or the first 20 years of service after age 35—would basing life insurance benefits on final pay still extend the full eligibility date to the expected date of retirement?

Answer: Yes, assuming the additional life insurance benefits earned between age 55 and the employee's expected retirement date are not trivial in relation to the total benefit to be received.

Question F18: Under what conditions would a plan be considered a frontloaded plan?

Answer: A plan is considered frontloaded if all, or a disproportionate portion of, expected benefits to be received under the plan are attributed to employees' early years of service. If a plan is frontloaded, the expected postretirement benefit obligation (EPBO) should not be attributed ratably to each year of credited service in the credited service period but should be attributed in accordance with the plan benefit formula. The employee group as a whole is evaluated in determining whether the plan is frontloaded.

Illustration of a Frontloaded Plan

TWR, Inc., offers a postretirement benefit plan that provides both health care and life insurance benefits. Employees are eligible for health care and death benefits upon attaining age 55 and after having completed 20 years of service. Life insurance benefits are based on final pay, and employees are expected to receive annual pay raises between age 55 and their expected retirement age, 62. An employee named Jane Doe is hired at age 20 at a starting salary of $30,000. TWR assumes annual pay increases of 4%, a life expectancy of 75 years, and a discount rate of 7%.

Assume that the EPBO for Jane Doe at age 40 is $43,091 ($28,500 for health care benefits and $14,591 for life insurance benefits). A ratable allocation of the EPBO over her expected working life, 42 years, would result in an accumulated postretirement benefit obligation (APBO) of $20,519 at the end of year 20 ($13,571 for health care benefits and $6,948 for life insurance benefits; both of these amounts are 20/42 of the applicable EPBO). Based on the respective benefit formulas, assume that the APBO at the end of 20 years is $28,500 for health care benefits and $6,157 for life insurance benefits. Because the APBO based on the benefit formulas of $34,657 is a significantly greater amount than a ratable allocation of the EPBO of $20,519, the postretirement plan is considered to be frontloaded. For frontloaded benefit plans, benefits should be attributed using the respective benefit formulas. Therefore, TWR would report an APBO of $34,657 for Jane Doe at the end of year 20.

Question F19: An employer has a retiree health care plan that bases benefits on length of service; to be eligible for any benefits under it, employees must render a minimum of ten years of service after they reach age 45. However, upon attaining age 45, employees receive credit for 3% of the maximum benefit for each year of service before age 45. For example, at age 45 an employee hired at age 25 receives credit for 60% (3% × 20 years) of the plan's postretirement health care benefits. When does the credited service period begin?

Answer: The credited service period begins at the date of hire. The total benefits to be received are a function of the total years of service, including service before age 45.

Question F20: An employer requires that, to be eligible to participate in its retiree health care plan, an employee must participate in its contributory active health care plan. An employee can join the active plan at any time before retirement but must have worked 10 years and attained age 55 while in service to be eligible for benefits under the retiree plan. When does the attribution period begin?

Answer: At the date of hire if the employee is expected to participate in the active health care plan. This is because the plan does not specify which ten years of service must be worked in order to qualify for benefits under the plan. If an employee is not expected to participate in the active health care plan, the employee would not be considered a plan participant for purposes of the postretirement benefit plan.

Question F21: Should an employer's annual accrual for the service cost component of net periodic postretirement benefit cost relate to only those employees who are in their credited service periods?

Answer: In most cases, yes. However, in some cases a plan will establish a nominal service period in relation to the employee's expected total years of service. For example, an employee is hired at age 25 and is expected to work until age 62.

The plan may specify that the credited service period begins at age 55 and runs until retirement. In this case, the credited service period according to the plan would be nominal in relation to the total expected years of service. In such instances, the attribution period, and the recognition of service cost, would begin at the date of hire.

Question F22: In determining the attribution period, what is considered a nominal credited service period?

Answer: Judgment is required in determining what qualifies as a nominal credited service period. Generally, the service period would be considered nominal if it is very short in relation to the total expected years of employee service before full eligibility for benefits.

Curtailments and Negative Plan Amendments

Question F23: An employer's previous accounting for postretirement benefits has considered the written plan to be the substantive plan. On July 1, 20X4, its Board of Directors approves a negative plan amendment (i.e., an amendment that reduces benefits attributable to prior service) that will be effective on January 1, 20X6. The employer intends to announce the negative plan amendment to plan participants on July 1, 20X5. When should the effects of the negative plan amendment be considered for accounting purposes?

Answer: July 1, 20X5, the date on which the negative plan amendment is communicated to employees. It would have been appropriate to account for the effects of the negative plan amendment on July 1, 20X4, the date the amendment was approved by the Board, if the amendment had been communicated to employees at that time or within a reasonable period of time thereafter. A reasonable period of time would be the time it would normally take to prepare information about the amendment and to distribute it to employees and retirees. A one-year period is excessive for this purpose.

Question F24: Is it important to distinguish between a reduction in the accumulated postretirement benefit obligation (APBO) caused by a negative plan amendment and a reduction caused by a curtailment?

Answer: Yes. A reduction in the APBO caused by a curtailment is potentially recognizable as a current component of income. Conversely, a reduction in the APBO caused by a negative plan amendment that exceeds any prior service cost or transition obligation included in accumulated other comprehensive income is *not* immediately recognized as a reduction of current postretirement benefit costs.

Question F25: What is the difference between a negative plan amendment and a curtailment that reduces the APBO?

Answer: A negative plan amendment is a change in the terms of the plan that reduces or eliminates benefits for employee services already rendered. A curtailment reduces the APBO by reducing the number of employees covered under the plan and/or by eliminating the benefits attributable to future service for some or all plan participants.

Illustration of a Negative Plan Amendment and a Curtailment That Reduces the APBO

Company A sponsors a postretirement health care plan that previously was noncontributory. A plan amendment requiring current and future retirees to contribute $200 per month toward the cost of benefits provided would be a negative plan amendment because this change reduces the APBO for employee service already rendered.

Company B sponsors a postretirement life insurance plan. Life insurance benefits previously were defined based on final pay. Company B changes this plan on December 31, 20X4, to fix the life insurance benefits payable based on salaries in effect on that date. This change qualifies as a curtailment because the accrual of additional death benefits based on future employee service has been eliminated.

Question F26: Company B sponsors a postretirement life insurance plan. Life insurance benefits previously were defined based on final pay. Company B changes this plan on December 31, 20X4, to fix the life insurance benefits payable based on salaries in effect on that date. Before this change, the APBO at December 31, 20X4, included an amount—$400,000—based on projected future employee pay levels. Thus, the APBO at December 31, 20X4, decreases by $400,000 as a result of the plan amendment because increases in employees' future pay levels will no longer increase their death benefits under the plan. Why is the $400,000 a "potentially" currently recognizable curtailment gain?

Answer: Whether any or all of the $400,000 curtailment gain should be recognized currently as a component of net periodic postretirement benefit cost depends on the existence and amount of a net loss included in accumulated other comprehensive income for prior service cost, or a transition obligation included in accumulated other comprehensive income that must be offset before a curtailment gain can be recognized.

Question 27: Should the accounting for a curtailment always consider any prior service cost included in accumulated other comprehensive income or a transition obligation included in accumulated other comprehensive income?

Answer: Yes. The theoretical reason for not immediately recognizing prior service cost as a current component of postretirement benefit cost is that amendments of the postretirement benefit plan will result in a positive future economic benefit (e.g., a more motivated and committed workforce). A curtailment raises doubt about the existence of these future economic benefits. Therefore, this Statement requires recognition in net periodic postretirement benefit cost of any prior service cost included in accumulated other comprehensive income. In the case of a curtailment, any transition obligation remaining in accumulated other comprehensive income is considered to be a prior service cost.

Question F28: Does a curtailment result only from events that occur outside a postretirement benefit plan?

Answer: No. Although many curtailments result from events that occur outside the postretirement benefit plan—for example, (*a*) closing a plant, (*b*) selling a division or subsidiary, or (*c*) laying off a number of employees—a curtailment can also result from events that occur inside—for example, from a negative plan amendment that has the effect of eliminating the accrual of some or all of the future benefits for a significant number of plan participants.

Question F29: Does a gain result if, at the time of a curtailment, there exists negative prior service cost included in accumulated other comprehensive income due to a previous plan amendment that reduced benefits under the plan?

Answer: Yes. In accounting for a curtailment, a (negative) prior service cost included in accumulated other comprehensive income that results from a reduction in benefits (a negative plan amendment) is treated the same as a prior service cost that results from an increase in benefits. Therefore, any *negative* prior service cost included in accumulated other comprehensive income associated with future years of service that are affected by the curtailment is a gain. To the extent that this gain is not offset by any other curtailment losses, it is recognized currently as a component of income.

Question F30: What are examples of the accounting for a negative plan amendment that results in a curtailment?

Answer: The first illustration that follows is an example of a negative plan amendment that results in a curtailment gain. The second illustration is an example of a negative plan amendment that results in a curtailment loss.

Illustration of Negative Plan Amendment—Curtailment Gain

X, Inc., sponsors a defined benefit postretirement benefit plan. The only benefit provided under the plan is a life insurance benefit. The amount of life insurance provided under the plan is based on final pay levels. On December 31, 20X8, X, Inc., eliminates this benefit for employees who are not age 45 or older. This group constitutes a significant portion of the workforce of X, Inc. This change in the postretirement benefit plan results in two separate reductions in the APBO. First, benefits earned by employees under age 45, based on prior pay levels, are eliminated (resulting in a $300,000 reduction in the APBO). Second, the APBO had been calculated based on assumptions about the future of those employees' pay levels. Because employees under age 45 will no longer be plan participants, the future pay levels of those employees, who were considered in calculating the APBO, are no longer relevant (resulting in a $500,000 reduction in the APBO). This change in the postretirement benefit plan results in the elimination of future benefit accruals for that group of employees. As such, the $500,000 reduction in the APBO is potentially recognizable as a current curtailment gain. This curtailment would be accounted for in the following manner:

			December 31, 20X8		
	Before Negative Plan Amendment	*Negative Plan Amendment*	*After Negative Plan Amendment*	*Curtailment*	*After Curtailment*
(APBO)	$(1,500,000)	$ 300,000	$(1,200,000)	$ 500,000	$(700,000)
Recognized liability					
Prior service cost	100,000	(100,000)	-0-		
Transition obligation	140,000	(140,000)	-0-		
Net loss	200,000		200,000	(200,000)	
Negative prior service cost		(60,000)	(60,000)		(60,000)
	$ 440,000	$ (300,000)	$ 140,000	$ (200,000)	$ (60,000)

The journal entry to record the negative plan amendment is as follows:

Postretirement benefit liability	$300,000	
Other comprehensive income		$300,000

The journal entry to record a curtailment gain is as follows:

Postretirement benefit liability	$500,000	
Other comprehensive income		$200,000
Curtailment gain		$300,000

The following facts should be noted about the above accounting:

- Any decrease in the APBO as a result of a negative plan amendment is used first to reduce any existing prior service cost included in accumulated other comprehensive income and then to reduce any transition obligation included in accumulated other comprehensive income. Any amount that remains from the negative plan amendment is treated as "negative prior service cost." The negative prior service cost, $60,000, is recognized by amortization over future periods beginning January 1, 20X8. The negative prior service cost is amortized and recognized in net periodic postretirement benefit cost by assigning an equal amount to each remaining year of service up to the full eligibility date for each plan participant who was active at the date of the amendment but was not yet fully eligible for benefits at that date. Only participants who are over age 45 and who do not yet qualify for plan benefits qualify under this definition.
- The decrease in the APBO as a result of the curtailment is used first to reduce any net loss included in accumulated other comprehensive income on the curtailment date. Any remaining curtailment amount is recognized currently in income. The curtailment gain currently recognized is *not* a component of net periodic postretirement benefit cost and should be disclosed separately.

Illustration of Negative Plan Amendment—Curtailment Loss

Crown Color, Inc., sponsors an unfunded postretirement health care plan covering employees at three locations. On December 1, 20X8, Crown Color amends its benefit plan. Any employee of its Butte, Montana, plant who does not retire by December 31, 20X8, is not entitled to receive benefits under the plan. Employees of the Butte plant who retire by December 31, 20X8, will receive benefits under the terms of the postretirement health care plan. Crown Color's employees at its other two locations are not affected by this change in the postretirement benefit plan.

As a result of the above, Crown Color's accumulated postretirement benefit obligation is reduced by $200,000. This reflects an elimination of benefits attributed to years of service already rendered by employees who are not yet eligible to retire and to service rendered by eligible employees who choose not to retire (this reduction represents the results of the negative plan amendment). As a result of the early retirement of other (eligible) employees at the Butte plant, Crown Color's APBO increases by $100,000 (this represents a curtailment).

Before these changes, Crown Color's transition obligation included in accumulated other comprehensive income was $400,000. At the date of transition to this Statement, the remaining expected years of service of employees at the Butte location represented 35% of the total remaining expected years of service of all of Crown Color's employees. This will be accounted for in the following manner:

	December 31, 20X8				
	Before Negative Plan Amendment	*Negative Plan Amendment*	*After Negative Plan Amendment*	*Curtailment*	*After Curtailment*
(APBO) Recognized liability	$(475,000)	$ 200,000	$ (275,000)	$(100,000)	$(375,000)
Amounts recognized in accumulated other comprehensive income:					
Prior service cost	50,000	(50,000)	-0-		
Transition obligation	400,000	(150,000)	250,000	(87,500)	162,500
Net gain	(75,000)				
	$375,000	$(200,000)	$175,000	$(12,500)	$162,500

The journal entry to record the negative plan amendment is:

Postretirement benefit liability	$200,000	
Other comprehensive income		$200,000

The journal entry to record the curtailment loss is:

Curtailment loss	$100,000	
Other comprehensive income	$12,500	
Postretirement benefit liability		$112,500

The following facts should be noted about the above accounting:

- The increase in the APBO as a result of the curtailment is used first to reduce any net gain recognized in accumulated other comprehensive income at the date of the curtailment.
- As a result of the plan amendment, 35% of the total expected remaining years of service, for all of Crown Color's locations, have been eliminated. Therefore, Crown Color should accelerate the recognition of 35% of the transition obligation remaining in accumulated other comprehensive income *after* the negative plan amendment is recorded (i.e., 35% of $250,000, the transition obligation remaining in accumulated other comprehensive income after the negative plan amendment becomes effective, is immediately recognized).
- The curtailment loss is not a component of net periodic postretirement benefit cost and therefore should be disclosed separately.

Question F31: An employer adopts an amendment to its postretirement health care plan that has the dual effect of expanding the plan's coverage and increasing the deductible. Should the increase in the deductible be measured and recognized separately from the benefit improvement?

Answer: No. It is not unusual for numerous plan changes to be made at the same time. Some of the changes may increase benefits; other changes may decrease benefits. All of the changes should be considered together to determine whether there has been a net increase in benefits (a positive plan amendment) or a net decrease in benefits (a negative plan amendment).

Gains and Losses

Question F32: In applying the provisions of ASC 715-60-35-29, 35-32 for the recognition of gains and losses as a component of net periodic postretirement benefit cost is it appropriate for an employer to elect annually a new method of amortization of gains and losses included in accumulated other comprehensive income?

Answer: No. The employer should choose a method of amortizing gains and losses and follow the chosen method consistently from period to period. Any change in the method of recognizing gains and losses would fall within the scope of ASC 250 and would need to meet the preferability requirement of ASC 250 for an accounting change. Although the employer has some discretion in choosing how to recognize gains and losses, the amortization of these items must equal or exceed the minimum amortization as set forth in ASC 715-60-35-29, 35-30.

Question F33: An employer sponsors a contributory postretirement health care plan that has an annual limitation on the dollar amount of the employer's share of the cost of benefits (a defined dollar-capped plan). The cap on the employer's share of annual costs and the retirees' contribution rates are increased 5% annually. Any amount by which incurred claims costs exceed the combined employer and retiree contributions is initially borne by the employer but is passed back to retirees in the subsequent year through supplemental retiree contributions for that year. In 20X8, incurred claims costs exceed the combined employer and retiree contributions, requiring a supplemental retiree contribution in 20X9. If the employer decides in 20X9 to absorb the excess that arose in 20X8 rather than pass it on to the retirees, when should the employer recognize as a component of net periodic postretirement benefit cost the loss due to that temporary deviation from the substantive plan?

Answer: The loss should be recognized as a component of net periodic postretirement benefit cost at the time the employer makes the decision to deviate from the substantive plan. In this case, the loss would be recognized in 20X9.

Question F34: If an employer previously projected that health care costs under a defined dollar capped plan would exceed the cap in 20X8, but actual claims in that year do not exceed the cap, should a gain be recognized immediately as a component of net periodic postretirement benefit cost in 20X8 in accordance the guidance in ASC 715-60-35-34 through 35-35?

Answer: No. The above situation represents a situation where the experience of the benefit plan is better than expected. This situation gives rise to an unrealized gain. Under the provisions of ASC 715-60-35-23 and 35-25, this type of gain should be recognized in accumulated other comprehensive income (see question in paragraph F59). A gain is recognized immediately as a component of net periodic postretirement benefit cost only when the employer deviates, on a temporary basis, from the provisions of the substantive plan and, as a result, there is a reduction in the APBO.

Question F35: What situation would result in a gain that would be recognized immediately as a component of net periodic postretirement benefit cost in accordance with ASC 715-60-35-34, 35-35?

Answer: A gain would be recognized immediately as a component of net periodic postretirement benefit cost if plan participants agreed to make a one-time voluntary contribution to the plan that exceeds the amount called for under the terms of the substantive plan, and future contributions by plan participants are expected to revert to the level specified by the substantive plan.

Plan Assets

Question F36: May an employer include in plan assets the assets of a "rabbi trust" (so named because the first grantor trust to receive a favorable ruling from the Internal Revenue Service was one formed for a rabbi)?

Answer: No. Plan assets held in a rabbi trust are *explicitly* available to an employer's creditors in the event of bankruptcy. Under the guidance in ASC 715-60, assets must be segregated and restricted (typically in a trust) to qualify as plan assets. The guidance in ASC 715-60-55-26; and ASC 710-10-60-2 states that a trust does not have to be "bankruptcy-proof" for the trust assets to qualify as plan assets under the guidance in ASC 715-60. However, the EITF believes that trust assets would *not* qualify as plan assets if such assets were *explicitly* available to the employer's general creditors in the event of bankruptcy.

Question F37: An insurance contract with a captive insurance company does not qualify as a plan asset. However, can an investment contract with a captive insurance company qualify as a plan asset if it meets the criteria in the ASC's *Glossary*?

Answer: Yes, assuming the investment contract with the captive insurance company is segregated and restricted for the payment of plan benefits (see ASC 944-20-15-16 through 15-19). An investment contract with a captive insurance company represents an obligation of the employer to pay cash to the benefit plan to be used for the purpose of providing postretirement benefits. Since an accrued liability of the employer to pay cash is not considered a plan asset, the investment contract should be considered a debt security of the employer. This debt security must be currently transferable to be included in plan assets.

Question F38: If an employer issues its own debt or equity securities directly to its postretirement benefit trust, may those securities be included in plan assets under the guidance in this Statement?

Answer: Yes, provided there are no restrictions on the transfer of these assets. The plan trustee must have the unilateral right to unconditionally sell, transfer, or otherwise dispose of the securities. Assets that are not currently transferable but that can be converted into transferable assets should not be considered plan assets. For example, nontransferable convertible preferred stock does not qualify as a plan asset even if it can be converted into transferable common stock.

Disclosures

Question F39: This question has been deleted.

Question F40: Should an employer's disclosure of the weighted average of the assumed discount rates for its postretirement benefit obligation be the same as its disclosure for its pension benefit obligation?

Answer: Not necessarily (see the answer to the question in paragraph F8 for additional discussion). Even if the assumed discount rates are the same, the weighted average of those rates may differ between the timing and pattern of benefits to be provided and may be different for a postretirement benefit plan than for a pension plan. A pension plan typically provides a fixed yearly benefit, which is not expected to change over time. However, a postretirement health care plan is likely to pay more of its benefits as retirees age (since health typically deteriorates with age). If the timing or pattern of postretirement benefits differs from the timing or pattern of pension benefits because of the expected cost of health care, the difference should be considered in the weighting of the assumed discount rates.

Multiple Plans—Employers

Question F41: An employer has two legally separate postretirement benefit plans. Both plans are unfunded (defined benefit) plans covering the same employees. One plan provides postretirement medical care and the other provides postretirement dental care. May the employer account for the two plans as one plan?

Answer: Yes. The guidance in ASC 715-60-35-130, allows an employer to combine unfunded (defined benefit) postretirement health care plans if either (*a*) different benefits are provided to the same group of employees or (*b*) the same benefits are provided to different groups of employees. However, if either of these plans were funded (i.e., if they held plan assets), they could not be combined but must be measured separately.

Question F42: When is it appropriate for the employer in the question in paragraph F4 to change from one-plan accounting to two-plan accounting—that is, to accounting for each plan separately?

Answer: The employer must move to two-plan accounting if the provisions of ASC 715-60-35-130 are no longer met. For example, two-plan accounting would become mandatory if either (*a*) different benefits were provided to different groups of employees or (*b*) one or both of the plans became funded (i.e., held plan assets). If the conditions of ASC 715-60-35-130 continue to be met, the employer would have to meet the preferability requirement of ASC 250 to support a voluntary change from one-plan accounting to two-plan accounting.

Multiemployer Plans

Question F43: An employer that has a single-employer postretirement benefit plan decides to provide health care benefits to its retirees by participating with several unrelated employers in a group postretirement health care benefit arrangement that does not result from collective bargaining. The arrangement is administered by an independent board of trustees and provides a uniform level of benefits to all retirees by utilizing group medical insurance contracts. Each participating employer is assessed an annual contribution for its share of insurance premiums, plus administrative costs. Employers may require their respective retirees to pay a portion of the annual assessment. Retirees whose former employer stops paying the annual assessment have the right to continue participation if they assume the cost of the annual premiums needed to maintain their existing benefits. Should the employer account for this arrangement as a multiemployer plan?

Answer: No. The key factor is that in a multiemployer plan the obligation to retirees does not depend on the former employer's continued participation. This feature is lacking from the above example.

Question F44: May a multiemployer plan be considered a substantially equivalent replacement plan (a successor plan) for an employer that terminates its single-employer defined benefit postretirement plan in such a way that acceleration of the recognition of prior service cost included in accumulated other comprehensive income as a component of net periodic postretirement benefit cost is not required?

Answer: No. Multiemployer plans and single-employer plans are sufficiently different from each other that either one is precluded from being a successor plan for the other. In a multiemployer plan, the employer promises to make a defined contribution. A single employer plan that gives rise to prior service cost is a defined benefit plan. The nature of the employer's promise—to make a defined contribution or to provide defined benefits—is fundamentally different between these two types of plans.

Question F45: This question has been deleted.

Plan Settlements

Question F46: An employer that immediately recognized its transition obligation in income upon adopting the guidance in this Statement subsequently amends its plan to eliminate its obligation for postretirement benefits and partially compensates affected participants by increasing their pension benefits. How should those events be accounted for?

Answer: In this case, the employer has terminated its postretirement benefit plan and has effectively settled its postretirement benefit obligation by increasing the pension benefits that it will provide. The cost to the employer in providing enhanced pension benefits is the cost of settling the postretirement benefit plan. This increase in pension benefits results in an increase in pension liability (or a decrease in pension assets). The obligation for the postretirement benefit plan should be eliminated. The difference between the reduction in the postretirement benefit liability and the increase in the pension liability benefits equals the gain on the plan termination that should be recognized in accordance with the guidance in ASC 715-60.

Illustration of Immediate Termination of Plan

GPP, Inc., sponsors a postretirement benefit plan and a pension plan. On December 31, 20X8, GPP terminates its postretirement benefit plan. As partial compensation to the employees who are affected, GPP amends its pension plan so that current and future retirees will receive a pension benefit equal to 2% of final salary for each year of employment (GPP's previous pension benefit formula was 2% of an employee's salary over the employee's last five years of service).

GPP's postretirement benefit liability on December 30, 20X8, is $4,400,000; the expected benefit obligation on that date is $7,800,000. As a result of the change in the pension plan formula, GPP's pension liability increases by $750,000. GPP wants to determine the gain on the plan termination.

The gain on the plan termination is the difference between the reduction in the accumulated postretirement benefit obligation and the increase in the expected benefit obligation. Therefore, GPP would recognize a gain of $3,650,000 ($4,400,000 – $750,000).

Special Termination Benefits

Question F47: What is the intent of the guidance in ASC 715-60-25-6 on special termination benefits?

Answer: ASC 715-60-25-6 provides guidance for an employer's accounting for special termination benefits offered to employees in exchange for early retirement.

Question F48: How should an employer measure the postretirement benefit incentive that employees are to receive in exchange for their early termination of employment?

Answer: The termination incentive typically is measured as the difference between (1) the actuarial present value of the accumulated benefits for the terminating employees considering the enhanced benefits (it is assumed that the employees retire immediately) *and* (2) the actuarial present value, based on benefits attributable to prior service, of the accumulated benefits for the terminating employees without the enhanced benefits. (It is assumed that the employees retire at the earliest date on which they would be eligible for postretirement benefits.)

Defined Contribution Plans

Question F49: An employer has two legally separate postretirement benefit plans: (1) a defined benefit plan and (2) a defined contribution plan. The terms of the defined benefit plan specify that the employer's obligation under that plan is reduced to the extent that a participant's account balance in the defined contribution plan will be used to pay incurred health care costs covered by the defined benefit plan. For purposes of applying the guidance in this Statement, should those plans be considered a single plan or two plans?

Answer: Two plans. The nature of the promises under each plan, the way those promises are satisfied, the availability of plan assets to pay benefits, and the respective accounting for each type of plan are all so dissimilar as to preclude accounting for a defined benefit and a defined contribution plan as a single plan for the purposes of applying the guidance in this Statement.

Question F50: If any assets of the defined contribution plan described in the question in paragraph F49 have not yet been allocated to participants' individual accounts, do they reduce the accumulated postretirement benefit obligation of the defined benefit plan?

Answer: No. The employer's intent to allocate these assets to the accounts of individual employees in the future is not sufficient to reduce the employer's present obligation under the defined benefit plan. Under such an arrangement, the assets of individual employees in the defined contribution plan would be used to pay health care costs incurred in the future (the employer's obligation under the defined benefit plan is limited to covering health care costs in excess of amounts held in individual defined contribution accounts). When unallocated assets are assigned to the accounts of individual employees, the employer's obligation under the defined benefit plan is reduced. This reduction is recognized immediately as a component of net periodic postretirement benefit cost.

ASC 715-60-55-26; ASC 710-10-60-2 Plan Assets under ASC 715-60

BACKGROUND

According to Title I of the Employee Retirement Income Security Act (ERISA), the assets of a pension, profit-sharing, or stock bonus plan must be held in a trust created or organized in the United States. ERISA specifically provides that plan assets held in a trust are protected from the claims of general creditors and are considered bankruptcy-proof. This protection does not appear to extend to assets held to fund other postretirement employee benefits (OPEBs), which are addressed in under the guidance in ASC 715-60.

The guidance in ASC 715-60 sets standards for accounting for other postretirement benefit costs, specifically health care benefit costs. It requires entities to report their obligations to provide postretirement benefits at the time employees render services necessary to earn benefits. For example, Company X has a policy that all employees with 20 years of service are guaranteed lifetime health insurance coverage. In accordance with the guidance in ASC 715-60, the company must currently accrue the expected cost of providing health insurance to match the cost to each employee's actual service period.

Accounting for OPEB plans is similar to accounting for pension plans. Like pension and profit-sharing plans, OPEB plans must maintain sufficient plan assets to fund the expected costs of a postretirement plan. According to the ASC's *Glossary*, a plan's assets include stocks, bonds, and other investments that are segregated in a trust and restricted for the purpose of providing postretirement benefits. In accordance with the guidance in ASC 715-60, many employers have established trusts to fund OPEB plans. However, some of those trusts are not protected from general creditors in the event of a bankruptcy. Therefore, some have questioned whether a trust established to fund postretirement plans must be bankruptcy-proof.

ACCOUNTING ISSUE

Does a trust established to pay postretirement benefits in accordance with the provisions of ASC 715-60 have to be protected from the claims of general creditors in bankruptcy for the trust's assets to qualify as plan assets?

ACCOUNTING GUIDANCE

- It is not necessary to determine that a trust is bankruptcy-proof for the trust's assets to qualify as plan assets under the guidance in ASC 715-60.
- Assets held by a trust that explicitly provides that its trust assets are available to the employer's general creditors if the employer declares bankruptcy would *not* qualify as plan assets under the guidance in ASC 715-60.

DISCUSSION

Even though the guidance in ASC 715 (FAS-106) is clear that plan assets must be restricted solely to the provision of postretirement benefits and to the payment of retirees' benefits, and that the requirement is consistent with pension accounting, the guidance above confirms the view that plan assets do not have to be maintained in a bankruptcy-proof trust to qualify as plan assets. Furthermore, proponents of this view argued that accounting is generally based on the "going concern" notion—the possibility of an employer's bankruptcy is remote and protection in bankruptcy is not relevant. Also, in the event of a bankruptcy, an employer would no longer control plan assets, so the issue of proper asset segregation and usage would no longer apply.

Nevertheless, even though an explicit protection of plan assets in bankruptcy is not required under the guidance, the second conclusion prohibits an explicit statement that plan assets are available to creditors.

ASC 715-70: DEFERRED CONTRIBUTION PLANS

ASC 715-70-55-4 through 55-9 Measurement of Excess Contributions to a Defined Contribution Plan or Employee Stock Ownership Plan

Note: The conclusions below in Issues 1d, 1e, and 2a to 2e relating to employers' accounting for unallocated shares contributed to an ESOP as a result of a pension reversion have been nullified by the guidance in ASC 718-40. However, under the transition provisions of that guidance, employers may elect not to apply the provisions of ASC 718-40 to shares purchased in a pension reversion that occurred before December 31, 1992. The guidance below continues to apply to such shares if an employer so elects. In addition, the guidance related to employers' accounting for unallocated shares contributed to defined contribution plans are not affected by the guidance in ASC 718-40.

BACKGROUND

An employer terminates a defined benefit pension plan and contributes the withdrawn assets to a defined contribution plan or to an employee stock ownership plan (ESOP). If the amount contributed exceeds the employer's required (or maximum) annual contribution to the plan, the excess assets are held in a suspense account until they are allocated to plan participants. The employer retains the risks and rewards of ownership related to those assets while they are held in the suspense account. Excess contributions made to an ESOP must either be converted to the employer's stock within 90 days of the asset reversion or be used to retire debt incurred to acquire the employer's stock.

ACCOUNTING ISSUES

1. Contributions to a defined contribution plan
    a. How should an employer initially account for the excess contribution not allocated to individual participants?
    b. If an employer recognizes the unallocated amount as an asset, how should it be measured and classified in subsequent periods, until it is allocated to individual participants?

c. How should an employer measure compensation expense?
d. How should an employer account for its own common stock?
e. How should an employer account for its own debt securities and third-party debt securities?

2. Contributions to an ESOP
    a. How should an employer initially account for the excess contribution not allocated to individual participants?
    b. How should an employer measure compensation expense?
    c. How should an employer account for its own common stock and debt securities and third-party debt securities?
    d. How should an employer account for dividends on unallocated shares?
    e. How should an employer treat its own unallocated common stock in determining EPS?

ACCOUNTING GUIDANCE

The following guidance applies to *defined contribution plans* only:

1a. Recognize an excess contribution as an asset regardless of whether the excess unallocated contribution results from a plan reversion or from another source.

1b. Account for unallocated contributions in subsequent periods as follows:

a. Recognize an unallocated amount as an asset and treat it as if it were part of the employer's investment portfolio. For example, an unallocated amount that consists of equity securities should be accounted for in accordance with the guidance in ASC 321-10. Employers such as investment companies and broker-dealers, which are subject to specialized industry accounting rules, as indicated in ASC 320-10-15-3 for debt securities and in ASC 321-10-15-3 for equity securities, should apply the specialized industry rules. Income from such securities, including dividends, interest, and realized gains and losses, should be reported in a manner consistent with the employer's reporting of similar items.

1c. Recognize compensation expense at the time of plan allocation based on the assets' fair market value at that time.

The following guidance applies to both *defined contribution plans* and *ESOPs:*

1d. In the employer's financial statements, recognize as treasury stock the portion of the plan's unallocated assets consisting of the employer's common stock.

1e. Account for unallocated assets consisting of employer debt securities as follows:

a. Recognize the portion of the plan's unallocated assets consisting of the employer's debt securities as an asset, not as an extinguishment of debt.

b. Measure employer debt securities or debt securities issued by a third party that are included in the plan's unallocated assets at fair value, and recognize unrealized gains or losses in a separate component of equity in accordance with ASC 320 (FAS-115).

The following guidance applies only to employer debt securities included in the unallocated assets of a defined contribution plan or an ESOP and does *not* apply in other circumstances in which an entity reacquires its own debt securities.

The following guidance applies to *ESOPs* only:

2a. Reduce shareholders' equity for unallocated shares in the employer's own stock, as if they were treasury stock.

2b. Recognize compensation expense at the date of allocation based on the then-current market price of the stock, and recognize the difference between the purchase price and the current market price as an increase or decrease to shareholders' equity.

2c. Same as Issues 1d and 1e above.

2d. Account for dividends on an employer's own common stock as follows:

a. Increase treasury stock for dividends on employer common stock that are invested in additional employer common stock. Such dividends are not considered income and should not reduce retained earnings. In conformity with the 1986 Tax Reform Act, an ESOP's sponsor receives a tax deduction for cash dividends paid to participants within 90 days or that are used to repay the ESOP's loan in a leveraged ESOP.

b. Charge compensation expense for dividends paid to participants on unallocated shares.

c. Charge dividends on allocated shares to retained earnings.

d. Charge prepayments on ESOP debt as compensation expense, and account for dividends on unallocated shares as treasury stock.

e. Follow the guidance in SOP 76-3 for other dividends (see Chapter 43, *ASC 718 —Compensation—Stock Compensation*).

OBSERVATION: The guidance in SOP 76-3 is not included in the FASB Accounting Standards Codification® but has been grandfathered for existing ESOPs and, therefore, is included in Chapter 43, *ASC 718—Compensation—Stock Compensation.*

2e. Unallocated shares of employer common stock should not be considered outstanding in the earnings-per-share computation.

It was noted that this accounting differs from that required in paragraph 11 of SOP 76-3. The Task Force reached this conclusion because they believed that unallocated employer common stock resulting from a pension reversion differs sufficiently from unallocated employer shares contemplated in the discussion of leveraged ESOPs in SOP 76-3.

DISCUSSION

The guidance in this Issue applies to two vehicles used for a similar purpose to compensate employees. The generic term *defined contribution plan* is used to describe plans under which employers make regular periodic awards to participants' accounts, which are subject to vesting provisions. A defined contribution plan—as contemplated in this Issue—is a type of pension plan, which is accounted for under the guidance in ASC 715-30. While an ESOP meets the definition of a defined contribution plan, it may be established for a variety of reasons, such as to raise new capital, create a market for the employer's stock, or to replace benefits lost on the termination of a defined benefit plan. ESOPs differ from other defined contribution plans because they invest only in shares of the employer's stock, whereas defined contribution plans invest primarily in debt and equity securities of other entities. Special accounting applies to ESOPs because of their specialized nature; they were accounted for under SOP 76-3 until the issuance of the guidance in ASC 718-40. The differences between those plans are considered in the guidance above.

1a. Two alternative methods of accounting for the excess contribution to defined contribution plans were suggested. One was to recognize that amount as prepaid pension cost, consistent with the requirement in ASC 715-30-25-1 for a defined benefit pension plan. Another was to recognize the entire contribution as net periodic pension cost. The conclusion that the employer should recognize the unallocated contribution as an asset was based on the view that the employer retains the risks and benefits of the excess contribution until it is actually allocated to participants. Because the employer will use the excess contributions to make future contributions to the plan, a gain or loss on those funds will determine whether the employer has to contribute additional assets in future years.

1b. This conclusion is consistent with the EITF's conclusion on Issue 1a. If the excess contribution is recognized as the employer's asset, it should be accounted for the same as other such assets held by the employer.

1c. This conclusion is a further extension of the view that the employer retains the risks and rewards of the excess contribution, which ultimately should be reflected in compensation expense. That is, the difference between the carrying amount of the unallocated shares and their market value is recognized as a realized gain or loss.

1d. The guidance on this Issue is the same as that in Issue 2a for ESOPs, which hold shares only in the employer's own stock. The rationale for treating an ESOP's unallocated shares in the employer's own stock as treasury stock in the employer's financial statements was that the shares were under the employer's control and that such shares do not differ from treasury stock held for the purpose of meeting the requirements of other employee stock plans. Those who supported this view argued that although the plans may differ, the substance of the transaction is the same.

1e. The recognition of unallocated assets consisting of employer debt securities as assets was supported rather than as an extinguishment of debt, because of the view that the conditions for an extinguishment of debt have not been met. That is, a debtor/creditor relationship continues to exist because control over the debt instrument has not been returned to the debtor (employer); the ESOP's trustee continues to control the debt instrument.

ASC 715-80: MULTIEMPLOYER PLANS

ASC 715-80-55-2 Accounting for Employers' Obligations for Future Contributions to a Multiemployer Pension Plan

BACKGROUND

A multiemployer pension plan is a pension plan established by two or more unrelated entities to provide pension benefits to employees of those participating employers. To qualify as a multiemployer plan, assets contributed by employers are not segregated into separate accounts and may be used by the multiemployer plan to provide pension benefits to any employer's employees. All employers share in the plan's gains and losses.

When an employer enters a plan initially or elects to improve employees' pension benefits, the employer must sign a written agreement and make an unconditional promise to make certain future contributions to the plan. The contributions will be used to liquidate the past service cost associated with initiating the plan or increasing benefits. In return, the plan agrees unconditionally to pay pension benefits to the employer's employees covered under the plan.

ACCOUNTING ISSUE

Should an employer recognize a liability to a multiemployer plan for the total amount of future payments related to prior service cost, as required under an agreement executed when an employer begins participating in a multiemployer plan or increases benefits to employees under the plan?

ACCOUNTING GUIDANCE

An employer that agrees to make future contributions to a multiemployer plan to liquidate prior service cost associated with initiating a defined benefit pension plan or increasing its benefits is not required to recognize a liability for more than unpaid contributions that are due.

DISCUSSION

In discussing the accounting for single-employer defined benefit pension plans, ASC 715-30-35-10 provides guidance on how to account for prior service cost related to initiation of a plan and plan amendments that provide for increased benefits based on prior service. It states that related costs should be recognized over the future service periods of active employees when a plan is amended who are expected to benefit under the plan.

This Issue was discussed because of diversity in views on the timing of recognition of prior service costs under an agreement in a multiemployer defined benefit plan. Such agreements provide that an employer has an "unconditional obligation" to make future installment payments for past service costs, and the plan has an unconditional obligation to make future benefit payments to participants. The problem was that although ASC 715-30-35-10 provides for delayed recognition of prior service costs, the discussion of multiemployer plans in ASC 715-80-05-1, does not specifically address the recognition of such costs. Some believed that an employer participating in a multiemployer plan should recognize a liability for the total obligation under the employer's agreement with the multiemployer plan. Proponents of recognition argued that the delayed recognition concept in ASC 715-30 does not apply to multiemployer plans, because of the bilateral agreement between the parties.

Opponents of immediate recognition of the total liability for prior service costs at the date of the agreement argued that a multiemployer plan does not differ from other defined benefit pension plans and that the agreement provides for a bilateral unconditional obligation to comply with federal pension laws. In addition, they argued that ASC 715-30 did not intend to change previous practice for multiemployer pension plans under which a prior service liability was not accrued.

CHAPTER 43

ASC 718—COMPENSATION—STOCK COMPENSATION

CONTENTS

PART I: GENERAL GUIDANCE

OVERVIEW

An entity may pay for goods or services by issuing its stock. Although stock can be issued as compensation for many types of goods or services, the accounting treatment of stock issued in exchange for employee services, especially stock options, has been particularly controversial. In some instances, the stock issued to employees does not include compensation (noncompensatory plan); in other instances, the stock issued to employees includes compensation (compensatory plan). A *compensatory plan* is one in which services rendered by employees are partially compensated for by the issuance of stock. The measurement of compensation expense included in compensatory plans is the primary issue encountered in accounting for stock issued to employees.

ASC 718-10: OVERALL

BACKGROUND

U.S. GAAP for issuances of stock as compensation to grantees is found in ASC 718. ASC 718 applies to all share-based payment transactions, including both employee and nonemployee awards, in which an entity compensates grantees by issuing its shares, share options, or other equity instruments or by issuing liabilities to a grantee in amounts based, at least in part, on the price of the entity's shares or other equity instruments or that require or may require settlement by issuing the entity's equity shares or other equity instruments. Guidance referencing grantees is applicable to both employee and nonemployee awards, while guidance referencing employees or nonemployees is only applicable to those specific types of awards. In addition, ASC 805 (Business Combinations) provides guidance on whether a share-based payment award issued as part of an acquisition is part of the acquisition price or is for continued service. If the share-based payment award is part of the consideration transferred then the applicable accounting guidance is ASC 805; otherwise, the guidance in ASC 718 is applicable (ASC 718-10-15-6).

ASC 718 provides guidance in accounting for the issuance of stock options, restricted stock, performance-based stock issuances, stock appreciation rights, and employee stock purchase plans. Descriptions of the more common types of plans follow.

Stock Option Plan

In a stock option plan, a grantee is granted the right to purchase a fixed number of shares at a certain price during a specified period (ASC Glossary).

Restricted Stock Plan

Shares that have been issued under a restricted stock plan cannot be sold for a period of time due to a contractual or governmental restriction. A limitation on the ability to sell the shares typically results from the shares not yet being vested. The grantee may be prohibited (restricted) from selling the shares until the grantee meets a service or performance condition (ASC Glossary).

Performance-Based Stock Plan

A stock award where a pertinent provision of the award (e.g., vesting, exercisability, exercise price) is affected by whether one or more performance targets are achieved (ASC Glossary).

Stock Appreciation Rights

Under a stock appreciation rights plan, grantees receive an amount equal to the increase in the value of a specified number of shares over a specified period of time. This amount usually is paid in cash, although it can be issued in the form of stock.

Employee Stock Purchase Plan

Employee stock purchase plans are a type of employee benefit permitted by the Internal Revenue Code. These types of plans are typically established as either a stock bonus plan or a stock bonus plan combined with a money purchase pension plan and are designed to invest in the employer's stock (ASC Glossary).

COMPENSATORY PLANS

Compensatory plans give rise to compensation, usually out of an offer or agreement by a corporation to issue shares to one or more officers or employees at a stated price that is less than the prevailing market price. Under ASC 718, the issuance of equity instruments (stock and options) in exchange for employee services is recognized at the instruments' fair value in an entity's primary financial statements. ASC 718 addresses the accounting for the issuance of equity instruments in exchange for employee services and the resulting recognition of compensation expense.

PRACTICE NOTE: SEC Staff Accounting Bulletin No. 107 (SAB 107), *Share-Based Payment*, is designed to provide guidance to public companies in applying U.S. GAAP related to share-based payments to employees and non-employees. Although SEC pronouncements typically are not covered in the *GAAP Guide,* this edition is covering selected excerpts of SAB 107 because of the complexity of U.S. GAAP related to the accounting for share-based payments and because SAB 107 provides detailed and specific guidance in accounting for these types of payments.

Public companies are required to recognize compensation cost for equity instruments based on the grant-date fair value of those instruments. The resulting compensation cost is recognized as an expense over the period that the employee must work in order to be entitled to the award. The grant-date fair value of the equity instrument is estimated using an option-pricing model (e.g., the Black-Scholes model, a binomial model), adjusted to reflect the unique characteristics of the equity instrument. Nonpublic companies also must recognize compensation expense based on the grant-date fair value of the equity instrument issued, though some variation in how this principle is applied may be required due to the inability to determine the fair value of the equity instrument at its date of issuance.

PRACTICE POINTER: SAB 107 indicates that compensation expense for share-based payment arrangements with employees should appear in the same income statement line item as cash-based compensation paid to employees. Some companies may want to highlight the non-cash portion of employee compensation expense (i.e., the expense as a result of a share-based payment arrangement). SAB 107 indicates that companies could make this disclosure as a parenthetical notation to the appropriate income statement line item, in the cash flow statement, in the financial statement notes, or in the MD&A.

Recognition and Measurement Principles

The cost of goods obtained or services received in exchange for awards of share-based compensation generally is measured at the fair value of the equity instruments issued or the fair value of the liabilities incurred. The fair value of the liabilities incurred in share-based transactions is remeasured at the end of each reporting period until settlement (ASC 718-10-30-3).

Share-based payments awarded to a grantee by a related party or other holder of an economic interest in the entity as compensation for goods or services provided to the reporting entity are share-based transactions to be accounted for under ASC 718 unless the transfer is clearly for a purpose other than compensation for goods or services to the reporting entity. The substance of such a transaction is that the economic interest holder makes a capital contribution to the reporting entity and that entity makes a share-based payment to the grantee in exchange for services rendered or goods received (ASC 718-10-15-4).

Measurement of Awards Classified as Equity—Public Company

For equity instruments awarded to grantees, the measurement objective is to estimate the fair value at the grant date of the equity instruments that the entity is obligated to issue when grantees have delivered the good or rendered the service and have satisfied any other conditions required to earn the right to benefit from the instruments. To satisfy this measurement objective, the restrictions and conditions inherent in equity instruments awarded are treated differently depending on whether they continue in effect after the employee's requisite service period or the nonemployee's vesting period. A restriction that continues in effect (e.g., the inability to transfer vested equity share options to third parties or inability to sell vested shares for a period of time) is considered in estimating the fair value of the instruments at the grant date. For equity share options and similar instruments, the effect of nontransferability is taken into account by reflecting the effects of expected exercise by grantees and post-vesting termination behavior in estimating the option's expected term, and the option's expected term affects the estimate of the option's fair value (ASC 718-10-30-6, 10).

In contrast, a restriction that results from the forfeitability of instruments to which grantees have not yet earned the right (e.g., the inability to exercise a nonvested equity share option or to sell nonvested shares) is *not* reflected in estimating the fair value of the related instruments at the grant date. Rather, those restrictions are taken into account by recognizing compensation cost only for awards for which grantees deliver the good or render the service (ASC 718-10-30-11).

Ordinarily, awards and share-based compensation specify a performance and/or service condition that must be satisfied for a grantee to earn the right to benefit from the award. No compensation cost is recognized for instruments forfeited because a service condition or performance condition is not satisfied. Some awards contain a market condition. The effect of a market condition is reflected in the grant-date fair value of the award. Compensation cost is recognized for an award with a market condition provided that the good is delivered or the service is rendered, regardless of whether the market condition is satisfied (ASC 718-10-30-12, 14).

The effects on grant-date fair value of service and performance conditions that apply only during the employee's requisite service period or a nonemployee's vesting period are reflected based on the outcomes of those conditions (ASC 718-10-30-13).

A nonvested equity share or nonvested equity share unit is measured at its fair value as if it were vested and issued on the grant date. A restricted share awarded to a grantee (i.e., a share that will be restricted after the grantee has a vested right to it) is measured at its fair value, which is the same amount for which a similarly restricted share would be issued to a third party (ASC 718-10-30-17, 19).

The fair value of an equity share option or similar instrument is measured based on the observable market value of an option with the same or similar terms and conditions if one is available. Otherwise, the fair value of an equity share option or similar instrument is estimated using a valuation technique such as an option-pricing model (ASC 718-10-30-7, 9). The valuation technique used should possess all of the following characteristics (ASC 718-10-55-11):

- It is applied in a manner consistent with the fair value measurement objective and other requirements of ASC 718;
- It is based on established principles of financial economic theory and generally applied in that field; and
- It reflects all substantive characteristics of the instrument.

The estimated fair value of the instrument at grant date does not take into account the effect on fair value of vesting conditions and other restrictions that apply only during the employee's requisite service period or the nonemployee's vesting period. Under the fair-value-based method required by ASC 718, the effect of vesting restrictions that apply only during the employee's requisite service period or the nonemployee's vesting period is reflected by recognizing compensation cost only for instruments for which the good is delivered or the service is rendered (ASC 718-10-55-12).

PRACTICE NOTE: SAB 107 indicates that only rarely will there be only one acceptable method of determining the fair value of a share-based payment arrangement. SAB 107 also indicates that estimates of fair value are not intended to predict future events. As long as a reasonable and appropriate process is used to estimate fair value, a difference (no matter how significant) between the estimate of fair value and actual future events does not necessarily reflect on the reasonableness of the original estimates.

Valuation Techniques for Share Options and Other Similar Instruments

A lattice model (e.g., a binomial model) and a closed-form model (e.g., the Black-Scholes-Merton formula) are among the valuation techniques that meet the criteria required by ASC 718 for estimating the fair values of share options and similar instruments granted in share-based payment transactions. ASC 718 does not specify a preference for a particular valuation technique or model for estimating the fair value of share options and similar instruments granted in share-based payment transactions (ASC 718-10-55-16, 17).

Illustration of Application of Lattice Model to Valuing an Employee Stock Option

This example illustrates the valuation of stock options using the binomial model, a lattice-based option-pricing model. Aqua Resources Inc. grants fully vested stock options with an exercise price of $25 and a term of five years. The owner of the option can therefore purchase shares of stock for $25 for the next five years until the option expires. There is a 75% probability that the price of the security will increase by 16% each year and a 25% probability that the price will decline by 14% each year. Aqua Resources uses a discount rate of 6%. The bold numbers indicate the expected share prices, and the corresponding numbers below are the option value calculations.

If the share price exceeds $25 by Year 5, the option holder realizes a gain of the net amount upon exercise of the option. For example, if the share price increases all five years, the holder will net $27.51 ($52.51 – $25) upon exercise. If the share price falls below $25 by Year 5, the option holder will not exercise since the share price is less than the exercise price.

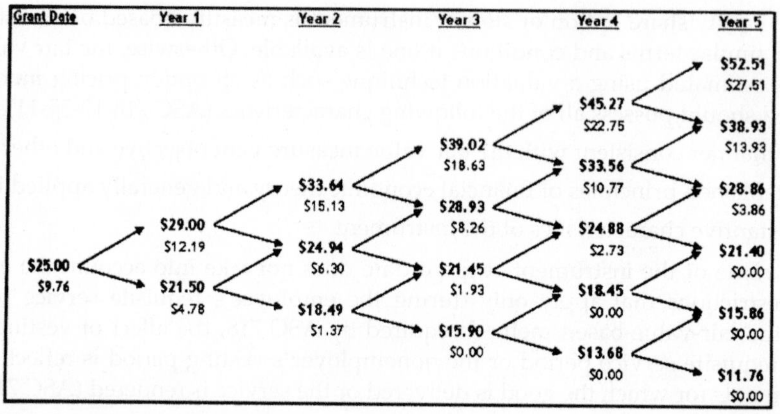

To calculate the option value at the time of grant, we first determine the option value at the expiration period and then works backward to the date of the grant. For example, assume that in Year 4, the share price has increased to $45.27 based on the aforementioned estimates. In this case, the option holder has an asset that will either rise to a share price of $52.51 (total five-year net increase of $27.51) or fall to a share price of $38.93 (total five-year net increase of $13.93). The respective probability of these outcomes is 75% and 25%. Using a discount rate of 6%, the value of the option in Year 4 will be $22.75, as calculated below:

Year 4: [(75% × $27.51)/1.06] + [(25% × $13.93)/1.06] = $22.75

Continuing to work backward, the option value at the grant date is determined as follows:

Year 3: [(75% × $22.75)/1.06] + [(25% × $10.77)/1.06] = $18.63

Year 2: [(75% × $18.63)/1.06] + [(25% × $8.26)/1.06] = $15.13

Year 1: [(75% × $15.13)/1.06] + [(25% × $6.30)/1.06] = $12.19

Grant Date: [(75% × $12.19)/1.06] + [(25% × $4.78)/1.06] = **$ 9.76**

Thus, the value of the option is based on the expected share price at each node of the lattice. Note that when the share price does not exceed the exercise price at Year 5, the option has no value since the option would simply expire unexercised. Accordingly, there is no real risk of loss to the owner; the higher the probability of an increase in stock price, the higher the value of the option. Also note that one of the advantages of the binomial model is that it can use different volatility estimates for different time periods; however, different volatilities are not used in this illustration.

Illustration of Application of Lattice Model—Early Exercise of Fully Vested Options

Using the same information as in the previous example, we allow for the early exercise of the options. Assume that there is an expectation of early exercise when the underlying share price reaches 1.3 times the exercise price. As shown, when the price exceeds $32.50 ($25 × 1.3), employees will exercise their options, stopping the binomial tree from expanding. The underlined share prices indicate where early exercise takes place. The shaded areas represent the portion of the binomial tree that is no longer relevant due to early exercise.

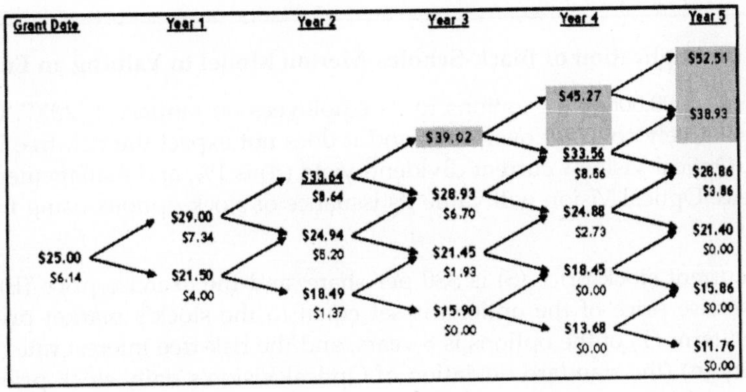

For example, if the share price increases in Years 1 and 2, the value of the option would be $33.64 in Year 2. Because the price now exceeds $32.50, the option holder is assumed to exercise the option early, and no further increases in share value are possible. Therefore, the total net increase is calculated as $8.64 ($33.64 – $25), and the option value at grant date falls from $9.76 to $6.14 as a result of early exercise:

Year 1: [(75% × $8.64)/1.06] + [(25% × $5.2)/1.06] = $7.34

Grant Date: [(75% × $7.34)/1.06] + [(25% × $4.00)/1.06] = **$6.14**

Illustration of Application of Lattice Model—Early Exercise and Cliff Vesting

Using the same information as in the previous examples, we now assume three-year cliff vesting. This extends the life of the option and increases its value from $6.14 to $7.57. Early exercise cannot occur in Year 2 even though the share price may exceed $32.50 by that time, as indicated by the double-underlined share price. The single-underlined share prices indicate where early exercise is allowed and does take place, and the shaded areas represent the portion of the binomial tree that is no longer relevant due to early exercise. The option value at grant date is calculated in the same manner as illustrated previously.

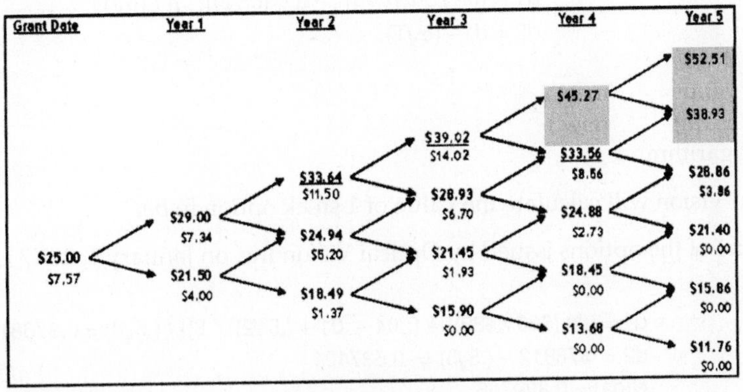

The Black-Scholes-Merton formula assumes that option exercises occur at the end of an option's contractual term and that expected volatility, expected dividends, and risk-free interest rates are constant over the option's term. This formula must be adjusted to take into account certain characteristics of share options and similar instruments that are not consistent with the formula's assumptions (e.g., exercising before the end of the option's contractual term when estimating expected term) (ASC 718-10-55-18).

PRACTICE NOTE: A closed-form model (e.g., Black-Scholes-Merton) is not always appropriate for valuing a share option. For example, if an option's exercise is conditional on the entity's stock price rising a certain amount, SAB 107 indicates that a closed-form model would not be appropriate.

Illustration of Application of Black-Scholes-Merton Model to Valuing an Employee Stock Option

Optical Vision Inc. issues 100,000 stock options to its employees on January 1, 20X7. Optical Vision expects its stock price volatility to be relatively constant over time, and it does not expect the risk-free interest rate to fluctuate greatly from its present level. Optical Vision's current dividend yield (d) is 1%, and management plans to maintain a relatively constant dividend yield. Optical Vision will value its issuance of stock options using the Black-Scholes-Merton option pricing method.

Optical Vision's current stock price (S) is $30 per share, and the exercise price (E) of the option is $30 (i.e., as is often the case, the exercise price of the options is set equal to the stock's market price on the date the options are granted). The expected term (T) of the options is 8 years, and the risk-free interest rate (r) is 4%. Optical Vision expects its stock price volatility (σ) (the standard deviation of Optical Vision's daily stock price) to be 50% over the expected term of the option.

The Black-Scholes-Merton formula to value this option is:

$C = (Se^{-dT}N(d1)) - (Ee^{-rT}N(d2))$ where :
C = the computed value of 1 option
e = the base of the natural logarithm (2.7182818)

N(d1 or d2) = the cumulative normal density function – the probability that a particular number falls at or below d1 or d2, respectively

where:

$$d1 = \{(\ln (S/E)) + ((r - d + (\sigma^2/2))^*T)\} / (\sigma\sqrt{T})$$
$$d2 = d1 - (\sigma\sqrt{T})$$

ln = the natural logarithm

Therefore, Optical Vision will calculate the value of 1 stock option to be:

Therefore, the fair value of the options issued by Optical Vision Inc. on January 1, 20X7 is $1,599,000 ($15.99 × 100,000).

$$d1 = \{(\ln (\$30 / \$30)) + ((.04 - .01 + (.5^2/2)) * 8)\} / (.5\sqrt{8}) = 0.876812$$
$$d2 = .876812 - (.5\sqrt{8}) = -0.537401$$
$$N(d1) = 0.809706$$
$$N(d2) = 0.295495$$
$$C = (\$30\ e^{-.01*8}\ 0.809706) - (\$30\ e^{-.04*8}\ 0.295495) = \$15.99$$

In contrast to the Black-Scholes-Merton formula, a lattice model can be designed to accommodate dynamic assumptions of expected volatility and dividends over the option's contractual term and estimates of expected option exercise patterns during the option's contractual term. This includes the effect of black-out periods. As a result, a lattice model more fully reflects the substantive characteristics of particular share options or similar instruments (ASC 718-10-55-18).

An entity should change the valuation technique it uses to estimate fair value if it concludes that a different technique is likely to result in a better estimate of fair value (ASC 718-10-55-20).

PRACTICE POINTER: Some entities may not initially use a lattice model because they have not previously captured the data necessary to apply such a model. However, after changing their systems to capture the needed data, such an entity should change to a lattice model from the Black-Scholes-Merton model if the entity concludes that a lattice model provides a better estimate of fair value.

Selecting Assumptions for Use in an Option-Pricing Model

If an observable market price is not available for a share option or similar instrument with the same or similar terms and conditions, the fair value of the instrument is estimated using a valuation technique or model that meets the criteria of ASC 718 (discussed previously) and takes into account at least the following (ASC 718-10-55-21):

- The exercise price of the option;
- The expected term of the option, considering the option's contractual term and grantees' expected exercise behavior and post-vesting termination behavior;
- The current price of the underlying share;
- The expected volatility of the price of the underlying share for the expected term of the option;
- The expected dividends on the underlying share for the expected term of the option; and
- The risk-free interest rate(s) for the expected term of the option.

There may be a range of reasonable estimates of expected volatility, dividends, and term of the option. If no amount within the range is more or less likely than any other amount, the average of the amounts within the range, referred to as the expected value, should be used (ASC 718-10-55-23).

PRACTICE NOTE: SAB 107 indicates that a company may appropriately conclude that its past experience with the exercise of options by employees is the best estimate of future exercise behavior. In this instance, it is appropriate to use the company's historical exercise experience in estimating the option's expected term.

In certain circumstances, historical information may not be available. If this is the case, the entity may base expectations about future volatility on the average volatilities of similar entities for an appropriate period following their going public (ASC 718-10-55-25).

The valuation technique an entity selects to estimate fair value for a particular type of instrument should be used consistently and should not be changed unless a different valuation technique is expected to produce a better estimate of fair value. Assumptions used to estimate the fair value of instruments granted in share-based payment transactions also should be determined in a consistent manner from period to period (ASC 718-10-55-27).

PRACTICE NOTE: SAB 107 indicates that a change in the model or technique used to determine fair value would *not* be considered a change in accounting principle. However, the SEC indicates that companies should not change valuation models or techniques frequently.

A U.S. entity issuing an option on its own shares must use as the risk-free interest rate the implied yields currently available from the U.S. Treasury zero-coupon yield curve over the contractual term of the option if the entity is using a lattice model incorporating the option's contractual term. If the entity is using a closed-form model, the risk-free interest rate is the implied yield currently available on U.S. Treasury zero-coupon issues with a remaining term equal to the expected term used in the model to value the options (ASC 718-10-55-28).

The expected term of an employee share option or similar instrument is the period of time for which the instrument is expected to be outstanding. In most cases, the expected term is shorter than the option's contractual term because employees typically exercise options before the end of the contractual period (ASC 718-10-55-29). The expected term is an assumption in the closed-form model. If an entity uses a lattice model that has been modified to take into account an option's contractual term and employees' expected exercise and post-vesting employment termination behavior, the expected term is estimated based on the resulting output of the lattice (ASC 718-10-55-30).

PRACTICE POINTER: SAB 107 indicates that the expected term can be estimated based on (1) the company's historical option exercise experience, (2) exercise patterns of employees in similar industries, or (3) as an output of a lattice model where the expected term can then be used as an input into the Black-Scholes-Merton model. (Note that a lattice model could also be used to value the option itself.)

Other factors that may affect expectations about employees' exercise and post-vesting employment termination behavior include (ASC 718-10-55-31):

- The vesting period of the award (the expected term of the award cannot be less than this);
- Employees' historical exercise and post-vesting employment termination behavior for similar grants;
- Expected volatility of the price of the underlying share;
- Blackout periods and other coexisting arrangements, such as agreements that allow for exercise to automatically occur during blackout periods if certain conditions are satisfied; and
- Employees' ages, lengths of service, and home jurisdictions.

Aggregating individual awards into relatively homogeneous groups with respect to exercise and post-vesting employment termination behaviors and estimating the fair value of the options granted to each group separately reduces potential misstatement. An entity shall aggregate individual awards into relatively homogeneous groups with respect to exercise and post-vesting employment termination behaviors regardless of the valuation technique or model used to estimate fair value (ASC 718-10-55-34).

PRACTICE NOTE: SAB 107 indicates that a reasonable estimate of fair value can be developed using as few as two groups. Groups should be identified based on differences in expected exercise behavior. Two possible groups where exercise behavior will likely differ are executives and non-executives.

Volatility is a measure of the amount by which a financial variable, such as share price, has fluctuated (i.e., historical volatility) or can be expected to fluctuate (i.e., expected volatility) during a period. Option-pricing models require expected volatility as an assumption because an option's value is dependent on potential share returns over the option's term. The higher the volatility, the more the returns on the shares can be expected to vary. An entity's estimate of expected volatility should be reasonable and supportable (ASC 718-10-55-36).

Factors that are to be considered in estimating expected volatility include (ASC 718-10-55-37):

- Volatility in the share price, including potential changes in the entity's share price in the future (e.g., as a result of reversion to the average level of volatility of other similar companies);
- Implied volatility of the share price determined by the market prices of traded options or other traded financial instruments, such as outstanding convertible debt;
- For public companies, the length of time an entity's shares have been publicly traded;
- Appropriate and regular intervals for price observations; and
- Corporate and capital structure, recognizing that entities with greater levels of debt tend to have higher volatility.

PRACTICE POINTER: Some entities have exchange-traded financial instruments (e.g., exchange-traded options) that can be used to derive implied (stock price) volatility. SAB 107 encourages public companies to consider such implied volatility in estimating expected volatility. For example, the SEC indicates that a company with exchange-traded options could rely heavily, possibly even exclusively, on the implied volatility in these options, as evidenced by the option's price, in estimating expected volatility for the purpose of applying ASC 718.

PRACTICE NOTE: SAB 107 indicates that daily, weekly, or monthly price observations may provide a sufficient basis to estimate expected volatility. The SEC also indicates that weekly or monthly price observations are more appropriate than daily price observations if the stock is thinly traded. A public company listed on an organized stock exchange would generally use daily price observations to estimate volatility.

Consideration of Market, Performance, and Service Conditions

Analysis of the market, performance, or service conditions that are explicit or implicit in the terms of an award is required to determine the employee's requisite service period or the nonemployee's vesting period over which compensation cost is recognized and whether recognized compensation cost may be reversed if an award fails to vest or become exercisable (ASC 718-10-55-61).

Vesting or exercisability may be conditional on satisfying two or more types of conditions: a market condition and a performance or service condition. Alternatively, vesting may be conditional on satisfying one of the two or more types of conditions. Regardless of the nature and number of conditions that must be satisfied, the existence of a market condition requires recognition of compensation cost if the good is delivered or the service is rendered, even if the market condition is never satisfied (ASC 718-10-55-62).

Market, performance, and service conditions may affect an award's exercise price, contractual term, quantity, conversion ratio, or other pertinent factors that are relevant in measuring an award's fair value. For instance, an award's quantity may double, or an award's contractual term may be extended, if a company-wide revenue target is achieved. Market conditions that affect an award's fair value are included in the estimate of grant-date fair value. Performance or service conditions that only affect vesting are excluded from the estimate of grant-date fair value, but all other performance or service conditions that affect an award's fair value are included in the estimate of grant-date fair value (ASC 718-10-55-64).

Illustration of Accounting for a Stock Option with a Market Condition

Beta Company grants share options whose exercise price varies with an index of the share prices of a group of entities in the same industry. This qualifies as a market condition per ASC 718. Assume that on January 1, 20X7, Beta grants 50 share options on its common stock with an initial exercise price of \$20 to each of 500 employees. The share options have a maximum term of ten years. The exercise price of the share options increases or decreases on December 31 of each year by the same percentage that the index has increased or decreased during the year. For example, if the peer group index increased by 10% in 20X7, the exercise price of the share options during 20X8 would increase to \$22 (\$20 × 1.10). Assume that, on January 1, 20X7, the peer group index is 500 and the dividend yield on the index is 1%.

Each indexed share option may be analyzed as a share option to exchange 0.04 (20/500) "shares" of the peer group index for a share of Beta stock—that is, to exchange one noncash asset for another. The intrinsic value of a share option to exchange .04 "shares" of the peer group index for a share of Beta stock also equals the difference between the prices of the two assets exchanged.

To illustrate the equivalence of an indexed share option and the share option above, assume that an employee exercises the indexed share option when Beta's share price has increased 100% to \$40 and the peer group index has increased 70% from 500 to 850. Thus, the exercise price of the indexed share option is \$34 (\$20 × 1.70).

Price of Beta share	\$40.00
Less: Exercise price of share option	34.00
Intrinsic value of indexed share option	\$ 6.00

That is the same as the intrinsic value of a share option to exchange .04 shares of the index for 1 share of Beta stock:

Price of Beta share	\$40.00
Less: Price of a share of the peer group index (.04 × \$850)	34.00
Intrinsic value at exchange	\$ 6.00

Option-pricing models can be extended to value a share option to exchange one asset for another. The volatility of a share option to exchange two noncash assets is based on their cross-volatility, the relationship between the volatilities of the prices of the assets to be exchanged. In a share option with an exercise price payable in cash, the amount of cash to be paid has zero volatility, so only the volatility of the stock needs to be considered in estimating that option's fair value. In contrast, when two noncash assets are involved, the fair value of a share option depends on possible movements in the prices of both assets. In this example, fair value depends on the cross-volatility of a share of the peer group index and a share of Beta stock. Historical cross-volatility can be computed directly based on measures of Beta's share price in shares of the peer group index. For example, Beta's share price was 0.04 shares at the grant date and 0.0471 (40/850) shares at the exercise date. Those share amounts then are used to compute crossvolatility. Cross-volatility can also be computed indirectly based on the respective volatilities of Beta stock and the peer group index and the correlation between them.

In a share option with an exercise price payable in cash, the assumed risk-free interest rate (discount rate) represents the return on cash that will not be paid until exercise. In this example, an equivalent share of the index, rather than cash, is what will not be "paid" until exercise. Therefore, the dividend yield on the peer group index of 1% is used in place of the risk-free interest rate as an input to the option-pricing model.

The initial exercise price for the indexed share option is the value of an equivalent share of the peer group index, which is $20 (0.04 × $500). The fair value of each share option would be based on relevant inputs.

The indexed share options have a three-year explicit service period. The market condition affects the grant-date fair value of the award and its exercisability; however, vesting is based solely on the explicit service period of three years. The at-the-money nature of the award makes the derived service period irrelevant in determining the requisite service period in this example; therefore, the requisite service period of the award is three years based on the explicit service period. The accrual of compensation cost would be based on the number of options for which the requisite service is expected to be rendered, and that cost would be recognized over the requisite service period.

An award may be indexed to a factor in addition to the entity's share price. If that factor is not a market, performance, or service condition, that award is classified as a liability for purposes of ASC 718. An example of this is an award of options whose exercise prices are indexed to the market price of a commodity (ASC 718-10-55-65).

The employee's requisite service period for an award that has only a service condition is presumed to be the vesting period unless there is clear evidence to the contrary. An employee's share-based payment award becomes vested at the date that the employee's right to receive or retain equity shares, other equity instruments, or cash under the award is no longer contingent on satisfaction of either a performance condition or a service condition. Any unrecognized compensation cost shall be recognized when an award becomes vested. If the award includes no market, performance, or service conditions, the entire amount of compensation cost is recognized when the award is granted (ASC 718-10-55-67, 68).

A requisite service period for an employee may be explicit, implicit, or derived. An explicit service period is one that is stated in the terms of the share-based payment award. An implicit service period is one that may be inferred from an analysis of an award's terms. A derived service period is based on a market condition in a share-based payment award that affects exercisability, exercise price, or the employee's ability to retain the award. A derived service period is inferred from the application of certain techniques used to estimate fair value (ASC 718-10-55-69, 70, 71).

An award with a combination of market, performance, or service conditions may contain multiple explicit, implicit, or derived service periods. For such an award, the estimate of the requisite service period is based on an analysis of (1) all vesting and exercisability conditions; (2) all explicit, implicit, and derived service periods; and (3) the probability that performance or service conditions will be satisfied. For example, if vesting or exercisability is based on satisfying *both* a market condition and a performance or service condition and it is probable that the performance or service condition will be satisfied, an initial estimate of the requisite service period generally is the *longest* of the explicit, implicit, or derived service periods. If vesting or exercisability is based on satisfying *either* a market condition or a performance or service condition and it is probable that the performance or service condition will be satisfied, the initial estimate of the requisite service period generally is the *shortest* of the explicit, implicit, or derived service periods (ASC 718-10-55-72, 73).

Compensation cost ultimately recognized is equal to the grant-date fair value of the award based on the actual outcome of the performance or service condition. The proper accounting for a change in the initial estimate of the requisite service period depends on whether that change would affect the grant date fair value of the award that is to be recognized as compensation. For example, if the quantity of instruments for which the requisite service is expected to be rendered changes because a vesting condition becomes probable of satisfaction or if the grant-date fair value of an instrument changes because another performance or service condition becomes probable of satisfaction, the cumulative effect on current and prior periods of those changes in estimates is recognized in the period of change. In contrast, if compensation cost is already being attributed over an initially estimated requisite service period and that period changes because another market, performance, or service condition becomes the basis for the requisite service period, any unrecognized compensation cost at the time of the change is recognized prospectively over the revised requisite service period, if any (ASC 718-10-55-77, 78).

Illustration of Accounting for a Stock Option with Performance Conditions

This example illustrates the computation of compensation cost if Alpha Company grants an award of share options with multiple performance conditions. Under the award, employees vest in differing numbers of options depending on the amount by which the market share of one of Alpha's products increases over a three-year period (the options cannot vest before the end of the three-year period).

On January 1, 20X7, Alpha grants to each of its 500 employees an award of up to 150 ten-year-term share options on its common stock. If market share increases by at least 4% by December 31, 20X9, each employee vests in at least 50 share options at that date. If market share increases by at least 8%, another 50 share options vest, for a total of 100. If market share increases by more than 16%, all 150 share options vest. Assume that Alpha's share price on January 1, 20X7, is $20, and the grant-date fair value per share option is $15.

The compensation cost of the award depends on the estimated number of options that will vest. Alpha must determine whether it is probable (as defined in ASC 450) that any performance condition will be achieved, that is, whether market share growth will be at least 4% over the three-year period. Accruals of compensation cost are initially based on the probable outcome of the performance conditions—in this case, different levels of market share growth over the three-year vesting period—and adjusted for subsequent changes in the estimated or actual outcome. If Alpha determines that no performance condition is probable of achievement (i.e., market share growth is expected to be less than 4%), then no compensation cost is recognized; however, Alpha is required to reassess at each reporting date whether achievement of any performance condition is probable and would begin recognizing compensation cost if and when achievement becomes probable.

Accruals of cost must be based on the probable outcome of performance conditions. Accordingly, Alpha cannot base accruals of compensation cost on an amount that is not a possible outcome (and thus cannot be the probable outcome). For example, if Alpha estimates a 90%, 45%, and 15% likelihood that market share growth will be at least 4%, 8%, and 16%, respectively, it would not try to determine a weighted average of the possible outcomes because that number of shares is not a possible outcome.

The table below shows the compensation cost that would be recognized in 20X7, 20X8, and 20X9, if Alpha estimates at the grant date that it is probable that market share will increase at least 4 but less than 8% (i.e., each employee would receive 50 share options). That estimate remains unchanged until the end of 20X9, when Alpha's market share has actually increased over the three-year period by more than 8%. Thus, each employee vests in 100 share options.

Through 20X7, Alpha's estimated and actual forfeiture rate is 5%. Alpha therefore estimates that 429 employees ($500 \times .95^3$) will remain in service until the vesting date. (If actual forfeiture rates differ from estimated forfeiture rates, Alpha would adjust its estimate of expected forfeiture rates which would affect the recognition of compensation cost.) The compensation cost of the award is initially estimated based on the number of options expected to vest, which in turn is based on the expected level of performance and the fair value of each option. The amount of compensation cost recognized (or attributed) when achievement of a performance condition is probable depends on the relative satisfaction of the performance condition based on performance to date. Alpha determines that recognizing compensation cost ratably over the three-year vesting period is appropriate with one-third of the value of the award recognized each year.

Share Option with Performance Condition—Number of Share Options Varies

Year	Total Value of Award	Pretax Cost for Year	Cumulative Pretax Cost
20X7	$321,750 ($15 × 50 × 429)	$107,250 ($321,750 × 1/3)	$107,250
20X8	$321,750 ($15 × 50 × 429)	$107,250 [($321,750 × 2/3)- $107,250]	$214,500
20X9	$643,500 ($15 × 100 × 429)	$429,000 ($643,500 – $214,500)	$643,500

Reload Options

Some companies issue new options to employees when an employee uses existing shares of the company's stock to exercise a stock option rather than paying in cash. Additional options are issued equal to the number of shares used to pay for the shares purchased under a previous stock option grant (ASC Glossary). The effect of a reload feature in terms of an award shall not be included in estimating the grant-date fair value of the award. A subsequent grant of reload options shall be accounted for as a separate award when the reload options are granted (ASC 718-10-30-23).

Measurement of Awards Classified as Equity—Nonpublic Company

As was the case for a public company, stock or options issued by a nonpublic company in exchange for goods or services are recorded at fair value. In determining the fair value of a stock option, the volatility of the underlying stock needs to be estimated. This can often be difficult for a nonpublic company, given the lack of trading of these shares and their illiquid market. Therefore, a nonpublic entity must exercise judgment in selecting a method to estimate expected volatility and might do so by basing its expected volatility on the average volatilities of similar public entities (ASC 718-10-55-25).

In other instances, a nonpublic entity may not be able to reasonably estimate the fair value of its equity share options and other instruments because it is not practicable to estimate the expected volatility of its share price. In this circumstance, the entity accounts for the equity share options and similar instruments based on a value calculated using the historical volatility of an appropriate industry sector index. If the complexity of the terms of an equity share option or other equity instrument precludes making a reasonable estimate of fair value, the option or instrument shall be accounted for based on its intrinsic value, remeasured at each reporting date through the date of exercise or other settlement. The intrinsic value method continues to be used, even if the entity subsequently concludes that a reasonable estimate of fair value can be made (ASC 718-10-55-25, 27).

As discussed previously, if it is not practicable for a nonpublic entity to estimate its stock price volatility, the entity may estimate its stock price volatility using an industry-sector index (the calculated value method) (ASC 718-10-55-52). For purposes of applying ASC 718, it is not practicable for a nonpublic entity to estimate the expected volatility of its share price if it is unable to obtain sufficient historical information about past volatility, or other information on which to base a reasonable and supportable estimate of expected volatility at the grant date of the award without undue cost and effort. In that situation, ASC 718 requires the nonpublic entity to estimate a value of its equity share options and similar instruments by substituting the historical volatility of the appropriate industry sector index for the expected share price volatility as an assumption in its valuation model. There are many different indices available to consider in selecting an appropriate industry sector index. An appropriate index is one that is representative of the industry sector in which the nonpublic entity operates and that also reflects, if possible, the size of the entity. In *no* circumstance shall a nonpublic entity use a broad-based market index, such as the S&P 500, Russell 3000®, or Dow Jones Wilshire 5000, because these indices are sufficiently diversified as to be *not* representative of the industry sector(s) in which the nonpublic entity operates (ASC 718-10-55-55, 56).

For an award that meets certain conditions, a nonpublic entity may make an entity-wide accounting policy election to estimate the expected term using the following practical expedient (ASC 718-10-30-20A):

- If vesting is based only on a service condition, estimate the expected term as the midpoint between the employee's requisite service period or the nonemployee's vesting period and the contractual term of the award.
- If vesting is based on a performance condition, the nonpublic entity must first determine whether it is probable that the performance condition will be met.
  - — If probable, estimate the expected term as the midpoint between the employee's requisite service period or the nonemployee's vesting period and the contractual term.
  - — If not probable, estimate the expected term as either:
    - The contractual term if the service period is implied, or
    - The midpoint between the employee's requisite service period or the nonemployee's vesting period and the contractual term if the requisite service period is stated explicitly.

Awards that have all of the following characteristics are eligible for the practical expedient to be used buy a nonpublic entity (ASC 718-10-30-20B):

- Share option is granted at the money
- Grantee only has a limited time to exercise the award (usually 30-90 days) if the grantee no longer provides goods, terminates service after vesting, or ceases to be a customer
- Grantee can only exercise the award (i.e., cannot sell or hedge)
- Award does not include a market condition

Illustration of Accounting for a Stock Option Award by a Private Company—Company Unable to Estimate Its Expected Stock Price Volatility

Talisman Inc. is a small, private company that develops, markets, and distributes computer software. On January 1, 20X6, Talisman issues 200 stock options to each of its 75 employees. Talisman's share price on January 1, 20X6, is valued at $5, and the exercise price is $5 on that date. The options cliff vest in three years, and the contractual term of the options is seven years. Although the contractual term of the options is seven years, Talisman expects the term of the options to be four years (i.e., Talisman expects the options to be exercised early). Talisman assumes no forfeitures over the next three years (a simplifying assumption for this example), and expects to pay no dividends. We assume away income taxes.

> ***PRACTICE POINTER:*** The AICPA issued a practice aid, *Valuation of Privately-Held-Company Equity Securities Issued as Compensation*, that may be helpful in valuing equity securities of privately-held companies where these securities are issued as compensation.

Talisman does not maintain an internal market for its shares, and its shares are rarely traded privately. The last time Talisman issued equity shares was in 20W7, and it has never issued convertible debt securities. In addition, Talisman is unable to identify any similar public companies. As such, Talisman is unable to estimate the expected volatility of its share price—a key input to valuing its employee stock options on January 1, 20X6. Therefore, Talisman will value the options it has issued using the *calculated value method*.

Under the calculated value method, the historical volatility of an appropriate industry sector index is used instead of the company's own stock price volatility. Talisman operates exclusively in the software industry. Using the Dow Jones Indexes Web site and the Industry Classification Benchmark tab on this Web site, Talisman determines that its operations fit within the software subsector of the software and computer services sector. Talisman, based on its share price and contributed capital, would be classified as a small-cap company within the index. Talisman therefore selects the small-cap version of the software index as an appropriate industry sector index. Again, using the Dow Jones Indexes Web site, Talisman obtains the daily closing total return values from the index from January 1, 20X1, through December 31, 20X5 (five years of daily total return values). Using the five years of daily total return values, Talisman computes the annualized historical volatility of the software index to be 30%. This 30% volatility is an input to the option pricing model used by Talisman, and the computed value of the options granted by Talisman is $3.25 per share.

Talisman would make the following journal entries at December 31, 20X6, 20X7, and 20X8:

Compensation cost [(200 × 75 × $3.25) / 3]	16,250	
Additional paid-in capital		16,250
—To recognize compensation cost.		

All of the stock options are exercised on December 31, 20X9. Talisman would record the following entry (Talisman issues no-par common stock).

Cash (200 × 75 × $5)	75,000	
Additional paid-in capital	48,750	
Common stock		123,750
—To record the issuance of common stock upon exercise of stock options and to reclassify previously recorded additional paid-in capital.		

Recognition of Nonemployee Compensation Cost

An entity must recognize the goods acquired or services received in a share-based payment transaction with nonemployees when it obtains the goods or as services are received. The entity may recognize an asset before it actually receives the goods or services if it has first exchanged a share-based payment for an enforceable right to receive the goods or services (ASC 718-10-35-1A).

The total amount of compensation cost recognized for share-based payment awards to nonemployees must be based on the total number of instruments for which a good has been delivered or a service has been rendered. To determine the amount of compensation cost to be recognized each period, an entity must make an entity-wide accounting policy election for all nonemployee share-based payment awards, including share-based payment awards granted to customers, to do either of the following (ASC 718-10-35-1D):

1. Estimate the number of forfeitures expected to occur. The entity must base initial accruals of compensation cost on the estimated number of nonemployee share-based payment awards for which a good is expected to be delivered or a service is expected to be rendered. That estimate must be revised if subsequent information indicates that the actual number of instruments is likely to differ from the previous estimate. The cumulative effect on current and prior periods of a change in the estimates must be recognized as compensation cost in the period of the change.
2. Recognize the effect of forfeitures in compensation cost when they occur. Previously recognized compensation cost for a nonemployee share-based payment award is reversed in the period that the award is forfeited.

An entity must recognize an increase in equity or a liability, depending on whether the instruments granted satisfy the equity or liability classification criteria (ASC 718-10-35-1F).

Recognition of Employee Compensation Cost over the Requisite Service Period

Compensation cost associated with an award of share-based employee compensation classified as equity is recognized over the requisite service period with a corresponding credit to equity (usually paid-in capital). The requisite service period is that period during which the employee is required to provide service in exchange for the award (i.e., the vesting period). The service period is estimated based on an analysis of the terms of the share-based payment award. The requisite service period for employee awards may be explicitly stated or it may be implicit, being inferred from analysis of other terms of the award (ASC 718-10-35-2, 5).

The total amount of compensation cost recognized at the end of the requisite service period for an award of share-based compensation is based on the number of instruments for which the requisite service has been rendered. Previously recognized compensation costs should not be reversed if an employee share option expires unexercised if the requisite service has been rendered. An entity must make an entity-wide accounting policy election for all employee share-based payment awards to do either of the following to determine the amount of compensation costs to be recognized in each period (ASC 718-10-35-3):

- An entity must base initial accruals of compensation cost on the estimated number of instruments for which the requisite service is expected to be rendered. That estimate must be revised if subsequent information indicates that the actual number of instruments is likely to differ from the previous estimate. The cumulative effect on current and prior periods of a change in the estimated number of instruments for which the requisite service period is expected to be or has been rendered must be recognized as compensation cost in the period of the change.
- An entity may recognize the effect of forfeitures in compensation cost when they occur. Previously recognized compensation cost for an award is reversed in the period that the award is forfeited.

Accruals of compensation cost for an award with a performance condition is based on the probable outcome of that performance condition. Compensation cost is accrued if it is probable that the performance condition will be achieved and is not accrued if it is not probable that the performance condition will be achieved. Previously recognized compensation is not reversed if an employee share option for which the requisite service has been rendered expires unexercised (ASC 718-10-25-20; 718-10-35-3).

The entity makes its best estimate of the requisite service period at the grant date and bases accruals of compensation cost on that period. That initial estimate is adjusted in light of changes in facts and circumstances. If an award requires satisfaction of one or more market, performance, or service conditions (or a combination of these), compensation cost is recognized if the requisite service is rendered. No compensation cost is recognized if the requisite service is not rendered (ASC 718-10-30-25, 26).

Performance or service conditions that affect vesting are not reflected in estimating the fair value of an award at the grant-date because those conditions are restrictions that result from the forfeitability of instruments to which grantees have not yet earned the right. The effect of a market condition is reflected, however, in estimating the fair value of an award at the grant date. Market, performance, and service conditions (or a combination of these) may affect the award's exercise price, contractual term, quantity, conversion ratio, or other factors that are considered in measuring an award's grant-date fair value. That fair value is estimated for each possible outcome of such a performance or service condition, and the final measure of compensation shall be based on the amount estimated at the grant date for the condition or outcome that is actually satisfied (ASC 718-10-30-27).

ASC 718-20: AWARDS CLASSIFIED AS EQUITY

MODIFICATIONS OF AWARDS OF EQUITY INSTRUMENTS

A modification of the terms or conditions of an equity award shall be treated as an exchange of the original award for a new award. Except as described in ASC 718-20-35-2A, the effects of a modification are measured as follows (ASC 718-20-35-3):

- Incremental compensation cost is measured as the excess, if any, of the fair value of the modified award over the fair value of the original award immediately before its terms are modified, based on the share price and other pertinent factors as of that date. The effect of the modification on the number of instruments expected to vest also shall be reflected in determining incremental compensation cost.
- Total recognized compensation cost for an equity award shall at least equal the fair value of the award at the grant-date unless at the date of the modification the performance or service conditions of the original award are not expected to be satisfied. Total compensation cost measured at the date of the modification is (1) the portion of the grant-date fair value of the original award for which the promised good is expected to be delivered (or has already been delivered) or the service is expected to be rendered (or has already been rendered) at that date plus (2) the incremental cost resulting from the modification.
- A change in compensation cost for an equity award measured at intrinsic value is measured by comparing the intrinsic value of the modified award, if any, with the intrinsic value of the original award, if any, immediately before the modification.

An entity that has elected to account for forfeitures as they occur must assess at the modification date whether the performance or service conditions of the original award are expected to be met when measuring the effects of the modification. The entity shall then apply its accounting policy to account for forfeitures as they occur when subsequently accounting for the modified award (ASC 718-20-35-3A).

Except as described in ASC 718-20-35-2A, the cancellation of an award accompanied by the concurrent grant of a replacement award or other valuable consideration is accounted for as a modification of the terms of the cancelled award. Incremental compensation cost is measured as the excess of the fair value of the replacement award or other valuable consideration over the fair value of the cancelled award at the cancellation date (ASC 718-20-35-8).

A cancellation of an award that is not accompanied by the concurrent grant of a replacement award or issuance of other valuable consideration is accounted for as a repurchase for no consideration. Any previously unrecognized compensation cost is recognized at the cancellation date (ASC 718-20-35-9). In other circumstances, the entity may pay cash to repurchase an equity award. The cash payment is charged against equity as long as the amount paid does not exceed the fair value of the equity instruments on the date of payment. Additional compensation cost is recognized if the cash payment exceeds the fair value of the equity instruments. Also, any previously unrecognized compensation cost is recognized at the repurchase date (ASC 718-20-35-7).

ASC 718-30: AWARDS CLASSIFIED AS LIABILITIES

MEASUREMENT OF AWARDS CLASSIFIED AS LIABILITIES

In determining whether an instrument is classified as a liability or equity, the entity applies generally accepted accounting principles applicable to financial instruments issued in transactions that do not involve share-based payments. ASC 480 (Distinguishing Liabilities from Equity) provides guidance for making this determination (ASC 718-10-25-6, 7).

An award may be indexed to a factor in addition to the entity's share price. If the additional factor is not a market, performance, or service condition, the award is classified as a liability for purposes of applying ASC 718, and the additional factor is reflected in estimating the fair value of the award (ASC 718-10-25-13).

The determination of whether a share-based payment award is accounted for as an equity instrument or as a liability shall reflect the substance of the award and any related arrangement. Generally, the written terms provide the best evidence of the substantive terms of an award, but an entity's past practice may indicate that the substantive terms differ from its written terms (ASC 718-10-25-15).

The measurement objective for liabilities incurred under share-based compensation arrangements is the same as the measurement objective for equity instruments awarded to grantees as described previously. The measurement date for liability instruments, however, is the date of settlement. Liabilities incurred under share-based payment arrangements are remeasured at the end of each reporting period until they are settled (ASC 718-30-30-1).

A public entity measures a liability award under a share-based payment arrangement based on the award's fair value remeasured at each reporting date until settlement. Compensation cost for each period is based on the change in the fair value of the instrument for each reporting period. A nonpublic entity shall make a policy decision regarding whether to measure all of its liabilities incurred under share-based payment arrangements (for employee and nonemployee awards) issued in exchange for distinct goods or services at fair value or at intrinsic value. However, a non-public entity must initially and subsequently measure awards determined to be consideration payable to a customer (per ASC 606-10-32-25) at fair value (ASC 718-30-30-2). Regardless of the method selected, a nonpublic entity shall remeasure its liabilities under share-based payment arrangements at each reporting date until settlement (ASC 718-30-35-3, 4).

Changes in the fair value (or intrinsic value for a nonpublic entity that elects that method) of a liability incurred under a share-based payment arrangement issued in exchange for goods or services that occur during the employee's requisite service period or the nonemployee's vesting period shall be recognized as compensation cost over that period. The percentage of the fair value (or intrinsic value) that is accrued as compensation cost at the end of each period shall equal the percentage of the requisite service that has been rendered for an employee award or the percentage that would have been recognized had the grantor paid cash for the goods or services instead of paying with a nonemployee award at that date. Changes in the fair value (intrinsic value) of a liability issued in exchange for goods or services that occur after the end of the employee's requisite service period or the non-employee's vesting period are compensation cost of the period in which the changes occur (ASC 718-30-35-2).

Illustration of the Accounting for Stock Appreciation Rights to be Settled in Cash—Recognition of a Liability

Ultimate Metrics International is a public company that grants 750,000 share appreciation rights (SARs) to its employees on January 1, 20X8. Each holder of an SAR is to receive in cash the increase in Ultimate Metrics stock price above $15 per share (Ultimate Metrics' stock price on January 1, 20X8). Ultimate Metrics determines the fair value of the SAR grant on January 1, 20X8, in the same manner as if it had issued 750,000 stock options (i.e., an option-pricing model is used). Using an acceptable option-pricing model, Ultimate Metrics computes the fair value of each SAR as $7.50. The SARs cliff vest at the end of three years. Ultimate Metrics expects forfeitures of 7% of the SARs each year, and actual forfeitures equal expected forfeitures. Ultimate Metrics has made a policy election to estimate the number of forfeitures expected to occur and includes that estimate in its initial accrual of compensation costs. As a result, Ultimate Metrics expects 603,268 (750,000 × .933) of the SARs to vest, and the fair value of the SAR award on January 1, 20X8, is $4,524,510 [(603,268 × $7.50]. Ultimate Metrics' tax rate is 35%.

Because the SARs are to be settled in cash, Ultimate Metrics must record a liability. In addition, ASC 718 requires the liability to be remeasured at each reporting date through the date of settlement of the SARs (this period includes the vesting period and any period after the vesting date until the SARs are settled).

The fair value of the SARs is $11.25 at December 31, 20X8, and the resulting fair value of the award is $6,786,765 (603,268 × $11.25). Ultimate Metrics will recognize $2,262,255 ($6,786,765 ÷ 3), one-third of the total fair value, as compensation cost during 20X8. The journal entries recorded at December 31, 20X8, are:

Compensation cost ($6,786,765 ÷ 3)	2,262,255	
Share-based compensation liability		2,262,255
—To recognize compensation cost.		
Deferred tax asset ($2,262,255 × .35)	791,789	
Deferred tax benefit		791,789
—To recognize a deferred tax asset for the temporary difference.		

The fair value of the SARs is $6.75 at December 31, 20X9, and the resulting fair value of the award is $4,072,059 (603,268 × $6.75). Ultimate Metrics will recognize two-thirds of this amount, $2,714,706, as a liability at December 31, 20X9. Compensation cost recognized during 20X9 is $2,714,706 less the amount of compensation cost recognized during 20X8. The journal entries recorded at December 31, 20X9, are:

Compensation cost ($2,714,706 – $2,262,255)	452,451	
Share-based compensation liability		452,451
—To recognize compensation cost.		

Deferred tax asset ($452,451 × .35)	158,358	
Deferred tax benefit		158,358
—To recognize a deferred tax asset for the temporary difference.		

The fair value of the SARs is $12.50 at December 31, 20Y0, and the resulting fair value of the award is $7,540,850 (603,268 × $12.50). The liability at December 31, 20Y0, is this entire amount because the award is now fully vested. Compensation cost recognized during 20Y0 is $7,540,850 less the amounts recognized in 20X8 and 20X9. The journal entries recorded at December 31, 20Y0, are:

Compensation cost ($7,540,850 – $2,262,255 – 452,451)	4,826,144	
Share-based compensation liability		4,826,144
—To recognize compensation cost.		
Deferred tax asset ($4,826,144 × .35)	1,689,150	
Deferred tax benefit		1,689,150
—To recognize a deferred tax asset for the temporary difference.		

All of the SARs are exercised on December 31, 20Y0, and Ultimate Metrics International settles its $7,540,850 liability by making a cash payment. The journal entries are:

Share-based compensation liability (2,262,255 + 452,451 + 4,826,144)	7,540,850	
Cash		7,540,850
—To record the cash payment to employees upon the exercise of the SARs.		
Deferred tax benefit (791,789 + 158,358 + 1,689,150)	2,639,297	
Deferred tax asset		2,639,297
—To write off the deferred tax asset related to the SARs.		
Income taxes payable	2,639,297	
Income taxes expense		2,639,297
—To record the current tax benefit provided by the exercise of the SARs.		

Disclosure Requirements

An entity with one or more share-based payment arrangements must disclose information that enables users of the financial statements to understand:

- The nature and terms of such arrangements that existed during the period and the potential effects of those arrangements on shareholders;
- The effect of compensation cost arising from share-based payment arrangements on the income statement;
- The method of estimating the fair value of the equity instruments granted, during the period; and
- The cash flow effects of share-based payment arrangements. (ASC 718-10-50-1)

The minimum information needed to achieve ASC 718's disclosure objectives is (ASC 718-10-50-2, 2A):

- A description of the share-based payment arrangements, including the general terms of the awards under the arrangements. This includes the method used for measuring compensation cost from share-based payment arrangements.
- For the most recent year for which an income statement is presented:
  - The number and weighted-average exercise prices for each of the following groups of share options or share units:
    - Those outstanding at the beginning of the year.
    - Those outstanding at the end of the year.
    - Those exercisable or convertible at the end of the year.
    - Those granted during the year.
    - Those exercised or converted, forfeited, or expired during the year.

- The number and weighted-average grant-date fair value (or calculated value or intrinsic value for a nonpublic entity that uses either of those approaches) for instruments not covered by the disclosures in the previous paragraph (e.g., nonvested stock). The following disclosures should be made:
  - Nonvested shares at the beginning of the year.
  - Nonvested shares at the end of the year.
  - Shares granted, vested, and forfeited during the year.

- For each year for which an income statement is presented:
  - The weighted-average grant-date fair value (or calculated value or intrinsic value for a nonpublic entity that uses either of those approaches) of equity options or other equity instruments granted during the year.
  - The total intrinsic value of options exercised, share units converted, share-based liabilities paid, and the total fair value of shares vested during the year.
- For fully vested share options (units) and share options (units) expected to vest (or unvested share options for which the employee's requisite service period or the nonemployee's vesting period has not been rendered but that are expected to vest based on a performance condition being met, if an entity accounts for forfeitures as they occur) at the date of the latest balance sheet:
  - The number, weighted-average exercise price (conversion ratio), aggregate intrinsic value, and weighted-average remaining contractual term of options (units) outstanding.
  - The number, weighted-average exercise price (conversion ratio), aggregate intrinsic value (only for public companies), and weighted-average remaining contractual term of options (units) currently exercisable (or convertible)
- For each year for which an income statement is presented (these disclosures are not required for a nonpublic company using the intrinsic value method):
  - A description of the method used during the year to estimate the fair value (calculated value) of awards under share-based payment arrangements.
  - A description of the significant assumptions used during the year to estimate the fair value (calculated value) of share-based compensation awards, including:
    - Expected term of share options and similar instruments and the method used to incorporate the contractual term for the instruments and employees' expected exercise and post-vesting employment termination behavior into the fair value of the instrument.
    - Expected volatility of the entity's shares and the method used to estimate it. A nonpublic company using the calculated value method must disclose why it could not estimate the volatility of its stock, the industry sector index used, why that index was chosen, and how the index was used to calculate volatility.
    - Expected dividends.
    - Risk-free rate(s).
    - Any discount, and how it was estimated, for post-vesting restrictions on the sale of stock received.
- An entity that grants equity or liability instruments under multiple share-based payment arrangements shall provide the information specified above separately for different types of awards (including nonemployee versus employee) to the extent that differences in the characteristics of awards make separate disclosure important for an understanding of the entity's use of share-based compensation.
- For each year for which an income statement is presented:
  - Total compensation cost for share-based payment arrangements recognized in income as well as the total recognized tax benefit related thereto, and the total compensation cost capitalized as part of the cost of an asset.
  - A description of significant modifications, including the terms of the modifications, the number of grantees affected, and the total incremental compensation cost resulting from the modifications.
- As of the latest balance sheet date, the total compensation cost related to nonvested awards not yet recognized and the weighted-average period over which this compensation cost is expected to be recognized.

- If not separately disclosed elsewhere, the amount of cash received from the exercise of share options and similar instruments granted under share-based payment arrangements and the tax benefit from stock options exercised during the year.
- If not separately disclosed elsewhere, the amount of cash used to settle equity instruments granted under share-based payment arrangements.
- A description of the entity's policy for issuing shares upon share option exercise, including the source of those shares (e.g., newly issued shares or treasury stock). If the entity expects to repurchase shares in the following annual period, the entity shall disclose an estimate of the amount of shares (or range) to be repurchased during that period.
- If not separately disclosed elsewhere, the policy for estimating expected forfeitures or recognizing forfeitures as they occur.

PRACTICE NOTE: Given that many companies buy back stock in order to offset the potential earnings per share dilution that would otherwise result from the issuance of stock when options are exercised, the required disclosure of the amount of shares to be repurchased during the next year is likely to be closely followed by financial analysts.

ASC 718-50: EMPLOYEE SHARE PURCHASE PLANS

NONCOMPENSATORY PLANS

Certain stock purchase plans are not intended to compensate employees. For example, a corporation may intend to raise additional capital or to diversify its ownership to include employees and officers. A plan is *noncompensatory* if the cash received per share is very close to the amount of cash that would be received if the same deal were offered to all shareholders. In these types of transactions, a company generally does not recognize any compensation cost.

An employee share purchase plan that satisfies all of the following criteria does not give rise to recognizable compensation cost (ASC 718-50-25-1):

- The plan satisfies at least one of the following conditions:
  - — The terms of the plan are no more favorable than those available to all holders of the same class of shares.
  - — Any purchase discount from the market price does not exceed the per-share amount of share issuance costs that would have been incurred to raise a significant amount of capital by a public offering. (A purchase discount of 5% or less from the market price is considered to comply with this condition without justification. A purchase discount greater than 5% that cannot be justified under this condition results in compensation cost for the entire amount of the discount.)
- Substantially all employees that meet limited qualifications may participate on an equitable basis.
- The plan incorporates no option features, other than the following:
  - — Employees are permitted a short time (not over 31 days) after the purchase price has been fixed to enroll in the plan.
  - — The purchase price is based solely on the market price of the shares at the date of purchase, and employees are permitted to cancel participation before the purchase date and obtain a refund of amounts previously paid.

A provision that establishes the purchase price as an amount based on the lesser of the equity share's market price at date of grant or its market price at date of purchase is an example of an option feature that causes the plan to be compensatory. Similarly, a plan in which the purchase price is based on the share's market price at the grant date and that permits a participating employee to cancel participation before the purchase date and obtain a refund of amounts previously paid contains an option feature that causes the plan to be compensatory (ASC 718-50-25-2).

The requisite service period for any compensation cost resulting from an employee share purchase plan is the period over which the employee participates in the plan and pays for the shares (ASC 718-50-25-3).

The portion of the fair value of an instrument attributed to goods obtained or services received is net of any amount that a grantee pays for that instrument when it is granted. For example, if a grantee pays $25 at the grant date for an option with a fair value at that date of $100, the amount attributed to goods or services provided by the grantee is $75. An entity must apply the guidance in ASC 606-10-32-26 when determining the amount of the equity instrument's fair value that is attributed to goods obtained or services received from the customer (ASC 718-10-30-3).

Illustration of an Employee Share Purchase Plan

Stein Inc. plans to adopt an employee share purchase plan on January 1, 20X6. Stein wants its employee share purchase plan to be noncompensatory. Under the terms of the plan, all employees who have completed six months of service will be eligible to participate in the plan. Employees will be able to purchase up to $8,000 of Stein Inc.'s common stock each year at an eight percent discount from its market price at the date of purchase. The per share amount of share issuance costs to raise a significant amount of capital by selling stock through a public offering is five percent of Stein's share price. Stein is considering three different alternatives for offering a share discount to existing holders of its common stock.

Alternative 1 Stein Inc. would allow its current common stockholders to purchase up to $8,000 of its stock on a yearly basis at a three percent discount from its market price on the date of purchase. The employee stock purchase plan would be compensatory because the discount offered to employees (eight percent) is larger than the discount offered to existing stockholders (three percent). Therefore, the entire eight percent discount offered to employees would be viewed as compensatory (i.e., compensation expense would be recognized for the full amount of the eight percent discount when employees purchase shares under the plan).

Alternative 2 Stein Inc. would allow its current common stockholders to purchase up to $8,000 of its stock on a yearly basis at an eight percent discount from its market price on the date of purchase. The employee stock purchase plan would be non-compensatory because the discount offered to employees is the same as the discount offered to existing stockholders.

Alternative 3 Stein Inc. would allow its current common stockholders to reinvest dividends received in new shares of common stock. Existing stockholders could buy up to $8,000 of new shares of common stock using dividends received at a discount of eight percent. Since Stein Inc.'s common stock is widely-held, very few existing shareholders would receive dividends equal to $8,000. Therefore, most shareholders would not be able to get the benefit of purchasing $8,000 of stock at an eight percent discount, whereas all employees meeting minimal eligibility requirements would receive this benefit. As a result, this plan would be viewed as compensatory and compensation expense would be recognized for the full amount of the eight percent discount when employees purchase shares under the plan.

ASC 718-740: INCOME TAXES

ACCOUNTING FOR TAX EFFECTS OF SHARE-BASED COMPENSATION AWARDS

Tax deductions generally arise in different amounts and in different periods from compensation costs recognized in financial statements. The cumulative effect of compensation cost recognized for instruments classified as equity that ordinarily would result in a future tax deduction are considered to be deductible temporary differences in applying ASC 740 (Income Taxes). ASC 740 requires a deferred tax asset to be evaluated for future realization and to be reduced by a valuation allowance if it is more likely than not that some portion or all of the deferred tax asset will not be realized. Differences between the deductible temporary difference computed pursuant to ASC 718 (described previously) and the tax deduction that would result based on the current fair value of the entity's shares shall not be considered in measuring the gross deferred tax asset or determining the need for a valuation allowance for a deferred tax asset recognized under ASC 718 (ASC 718-740-05-04; 718-740-25-2; 718-740-30-2).

If a deduction for compensation expense reported on a tax return for an award of equity instrument differs from the cumulative compensation cost for those instruments recognized for financial reporting (referred to in ASC 718 as the excess tax benefit), any resulting difference must be recognized as income tax expense or benefit in the income statement in the period in which the amount of the deduction is determined, which typically is when an award is exercised or expires, in the case of share options, or vests, in the case of nonvested stock awards. (ASC 718-740-35-2, 3)

Illustration of Accounting for a Stock Option with a Service Condition—Including Treatment of Income Tax Effects

Diaz Inc. is a public company that awards 2,000,000 stock options to 4,000 different employees (each employee received 500 options) on January 1, 20X6. The term of the options is seven years, and they vest in full in three years (cliff vesting). These options are not classified as incentive tax options for tax purposes. Diaz Inc.'s tax rate is 35%. Diaz Inc.'s stock price on January 1, 20X6, is $50 per share, and the option's exercise price is also $50. Diaz expects that 5% of the options will be forfeited (due to turnover) in each of the next three years. Using a lattice-based valuation model, the fair value of the options on January 1, 20X6, is $24.75.

Diaz Inc. expects 1,714,750 of the options to vest over the three-year period (2,000,000 × $.95^3$). Under ASC 718 compensation cost is only recognized for those share options where a performance or service condition is met. In this case, the service condition is that each of the 4,000 employees that receive options must work through December 31, 20X8. Estimated total compensation cost is $42,440,062 ($1,714,750 × $24.75).

During 20X6, Diaz experienced only a four percent employee turnover rate. However, at 12/31/X6 Diaz still expects the employee turnover rate to average five percent over the X6-X8 period (i.e., the estimate of total compensation cost developed at 1/1/X6 is not changed). Diaz Inc. would prepare the following journal entries at December 31, 20X6:

Compensation cost ($42,440,062 / 3)	14,146,687	
Additional paid-in capital		14,146,687
—To recognize compensation cost in 20X6.		
Deferred tax asset ($14,146,687 × .35)	4,951,340	
Deferred tax benefit		4,951,340
—To recognize deferred tax benefit for the temporary difference related to compensation cost.		

Note that the net effect of the above entries is that Diaz Inc.'s net income in 20X6 is reduced by $9,195,347 ($14,146,687 – $4,951,340).

During 20X7 employee turnover again runs at a 4% annual rate. Diaz Inc. now expects an average employee turnover of four percent over the X6-X8 period. As such, Diaz computes a new estimate of total compensation cost which is $43,794,432 [(2,000,000 × $.96^3$) × $24.75]. Diaz Inc. will recognize compensation cost in 20X7 so that the sum of compensation cost recognized in 20X6 and 20X7 will equal two-thirds of $43,794,432. Diaz Inc. would prepare the following journal entries at December 31, 20X7:

Compensation cost [($43,794,432 × 2/3) – $14,146,687]	15,049,601	
Additional paid-in capital		15,049,601
—To recognize compensation cost in 20X7.		
Deferred tax asset ($15,049,601 × .35)	5,267,360	
Deferred tax benefit		5,267,360
—To recognize deferred tax benefit for the temporary difference related to compensation cost.		

The turnover during 20X8 is 4%. Diaz Inc. would prepare the following journal entries at December 31, 20X8:

Compensation cost ($43,794,432 / 3)	14,598,144	
Additional paid-in capital		14,598,144
—To recognize compensation cost in 20X8.		
Deferred tax asset ($14,598,144 × .35)	5,109,351	
Deferred tax benefit		5,109,351
—To recognize deferred tax benefit for the temporary difference related to compensation cost.		

All 1,769,472 (2,000,000 × $.96^3$) vested options are exercised on December 31, 20Y1. Diaz Inc.'s stock price is $120 on December 31, 20Y1. Diaz Inc. would prepare the following journal entry (Diaz issues no par common stock):

Cash (1,769,472 × $50)	88,473,600	
Additional paid-in capital ($14,146,687 + $15,049,601 + $14,598,144)	43,794,432	
Common stock		132,268,032
—To record the issuance of common stock upon the exercise of the stock options and to reclassify previously recorded additional paid-in capital.		

Income Tax Effects

Diaz Inc. is able to deduct the difference between the market price of the stock on the date the options are exercised, $120, and the exercise price of the option, $50, on its federal income tax return. The tax benefits from deductions in excess of compensation cost recognized are recorded as credits to income tax expense. The tax deductible amount is $123,863,040 [($120 − $50) × 1,769,472]. The tax benefit realized by Diaz Inc. is $43,352,064 ($123,863,040 × .35) (assuming sufficient taxable income to fully realize the tax deduction). Diaz Inc. would make the following journal entry at December 31, 20Y1, to record the tax consequences related to the exercise of the stock options:

Deferred tax expense ($4,951,340 + $5,267,360 + $5,109,351)	15,328,051	
Deferred tax asset		15,328,051
—To write off the deferred tax asset related to stock options exercised.		
Income taxes payable ($123,863,040 × .35)	43,352,064	
Income tax expense		43,352,064
—To adjust taxes currently payable and current tax expense to recognize the current tax benefit from deductible compensation cost when the options are exercised.		

STOCK COMPENSATION

IMPORTANT NOTICE FOR 2022

As Wolters Kluwer's 2022 *GAAP Guide* goes to press, the FASB has outstanding an Exposure Draft of an Accounting Standards Update (ASU), *Stock Compensation—Determining the Current Price of an Underlying Share for Equity-Classified Share-Option Awards*, that may have an important impact on the preparation of financial statements in the future. The proposed ASU is a proposal of the Private Company Council and is in response to private company stakeholders' concerns about the cost and complexity associated with determining the fair value of private company stock-option awards. Determining the fair value for these awards is sometimes difficult because private company equity shares are often not actively traded, thus there is not always a readily observable market price.

The proposed ASU would provide all nonpublic companies that issue equity-classified share-option awards with a practical expedient to determine the current price of a share underlying an equity-classified share-option award using a valuation method performed in accordance with Section 409A of the U.S. Internal Revenue Code. This would include any one of the following methods:

- A valuation determined by an independent appraisal within 12 months preceding the grant date
- A valuation based on a formula that, if used as part of a nonlapse restriction with respect to the share, would be considered the fair market value of the share
- A valuation made reasonably and in good faith and evidenced by a written report that considers the relevant factors of the illiquid stock of a start-up corporation

It is expected that an independent appraisal will often be the method used by nonpublic entities who elect to apply the practical expedient in this proposed ASU. The effective date for this proposed ASU has not been determined. Early adoption will be permitted.

PART II: INTERPRETIVE GUIDANCE

ASC 718-10: OVERALL

ASC 718-10-25-3 Accounting for Payroll Taxes Associated with Stock Option Exercises

The FASB staff was asked to clarify the accounting for payroll taxes paid by an employer under the Federal Insurance Contributions Act (FICA) and Medicare taxes that the employer pays when an employee exercises stock options.

The FASB staff believes that because the difference between the exercise price paid by an employee and the fair value of the acquired stock on the exercise date is treated as if it were compensation paid to the employee, payroll taxes on those amounts should be recognized as operating expenses and included in the income statement.

ASC 718-10-25-5 Practical Accommodation to the Application of Grant Date as Defined in ASC 718

BACKGROUND

The *grant date* of a share-based payment award is defined in Appendix E of ASC 718 based on certain criteria, one of which is the concept that an employer and employee have a "mutual understanding" of a share-based payment award's most important terms. That concept was initially included in the definition of the grant date in FAS-123 (Accounting for Stock-Based Compensation).

In practice, an award's grant date is the date on which an award is approved in accordance with an entity's corporate governance provisions if the approved grant is communicated to the entity's employees within a short period of time after the award's approval. Communicating the key terms and conditions of an award to employees receiving share-based payments immediately after the board of directors' approval or the approval of management with the relevant authority may be difficult for many companies with large numbers of employees that are located in different geographic locations, because the companies prefer to communicate with their employees personally.

To address those concerns, the FASB believes that there should be a *practical* solution to the manner in which the concept of "mutual understanding" is applied. Because this solution is unique to the circumstances described, the concepts in this FSP should *not* be applied by analogy to other concepts in ASC 718 or other generally accepted accounting principles.

ACCOUNTING GUIDANCE

It is presumed that there is a mutual understanding of the key terms and conditions of an award made to an individual employee at the date an award is approved by the board of directors or management with the relevant authority if all the other criteria in the definition of the grant date *and* the following two conditions have been met:

1. The award was made unilaterally so that a recipient is *unable* to negotiate its key terms and conditions with the employer.
2. It is expected that the employer will communicate the award's key terms and conditions to the individual recipients within a short period of time from the date on which the award was approved (i.e., within a reasonable period of time in which an entity could communicate information about the awards to the recipients in accordance with the entity's customary human resource practices).

ASC 718-10-25-14A Effect of Denominating the Exercise Price of a Share-Based Payment Award in the Currency of the Market in Which the Underlying Equity Security Trades

OVERVIEW

Guidance on the classification of share-based payment awards as equity or a liability is provided in ASC 718, *Compensation—Stock Compensation.* The exercise price of employee stock options granted by a public company to its employees is usually denominated in the currency in which the underlying equity securities trade. Such awards are usually classified in equity. However, ASC 718-10-25-13 provides that if an award is indexed to a factor that is "not a market, performance, or service condition, the award should be classified as a liability . . . ."

Share-based awards of public companies that regularly raise capital in a country other than their home country and whose securities trade on an exchange in that foreign country frequently are denominated in the foreign country's functional currency, which may differ from the issuer's functional currency, the functional currency of the subsidiary that has issued the share-based payment awards, or the currency in which the employees receiving the awards are paid. Under the guidance in ASC 718-10-25-13, if an award is indexed "to a factor in addition to the entity's share price" and that "additional factor is not a market, performance, or service condition, the award shall be classified as a liability." Because there is no guidance in ASC 718 regarding which currency is considered the "ordinary" currency of a share-based payment award that qualifies for classification in equity, some believe that it is the issuer's functional currency, while others believe that it is the functional currency of the country in which the shares are traded. Therefore, the question has been raised whether awards denominated in the currency of the market in which the underlying equity security trades should be classified as equity or as liability awards.

SCOPE

The following guidance applies to share-based payment awards accounted for under the scope of ASC 718.

ACCOUNTING GUIDANCE

Equity treatment of an employee share-based payment award is appropriate if an award is denominated in the currency of a market in which a substantial portion of the entity's equity securities are traded and all of the other criteria for classification in equity have been met

An employee share-based payment award denominated in a currency other than the functional currency of the foreign operation or in the currency in which the employee is paid should *not* be classified in equity because it contains a condition that is *not* a market, performance, or service condition. Such an award should be accounted for as a liability.

ASC 718-10-25-22 Recognition and Measurement of Employer Payroll Taxes on Employee Stock-Based Compensation

BACKGROUND

As a result of the increased use of employee stock options as a means of compensating employees and the rapid growth of the market value of stock in certain sectors of the economy, the significance of payroll taxes incurred by employers on employee stock-based compensation is increasing. Under the guidance in ASC 718-10-25-23, employers are required to recognize an expense for payroll taxes incurred in connection with stock-based compensation. There is no guidance, however, on when the employer should recognize that expense. Currently, employers recognize a cost when an event, such an employee's exercise of a stock option, results in a payment to the taxing authority. Some question whether the timing of cost recognition for an employer's payroll taxes on stock-based compensation under the guidance in ASC 718 is appropriate.

ACCOUNTING ISSUE

When should an employer recognize a liability and the corresponding cost for employer payroll taxes on employee stock-based compensation?

ACCOUNTING GUIDANCE

Employers should recognize a liability for payroll taxes on an employee's stock-based compensation on the date that the measurement and payment of the tax to the taxing authority is triggered. For example, in the case of a nonqualified option in the United States, a liability would generally be recognized on the exercise date.

ASC 718-10-S25-1, S99-2; ASC 505-50-S25-3 Escrowed Share Arrangements and the Presumption of Compensation

As a result of requests for clarification of the SEC staff's position regarding the presumption that escrowed share arrangements represent compensation for certain shareholders, the SEC Staff Observer made the following announcement regarding such arrangements.

Sometimes when an entity has an initial public offering or enters into another transaction to raise capital, some of the entity's shareholders may agree to put a portion of their shares in escrow. An escrowed share arrangement can occur between a company and its shareholders or between the shareholders and new investors. Under the terms of some escrowed share arrangements, the shares are released back to the shareholders only if specified criteria related to performance are met.

In the past, the SEC staff has held the view that there is a presumption that an escrowed share arrangement that involves the release of shares to certain shareholders when those shareholders have met certain criteria related to performance is compensatory and that it is like a reverse stock split under which shareholders subsequently receive a restricted stock award under a plan based on performance.

To determine whether the presumption of compensation has been overcome, a registrant should consider the substance of an arrangement and whether a shareholder has entered into the arrangement for a purpose that is not related to, or contingent on, continued employment. For example, as a condition of a financing transaction, an investor may request that specific shareholders who own a significant portion of an entity's shares and who also may be the entity's officers or directors participate in an escrowed share arrangement. Under those circumstances, if the shares are released or cancelled, regardless of whether a shareholder's employment will continue, the facts and circumstances may indicate that the arrangement was entered into by the shareholders to make the financing transaction possible and *not* for the purpose of compensation. The SEC staff believes that if the presumption that an escrow arrangement is compensatory has been overcome based on the facts and circumstances, the arrangement should be recognized and measured based on its nature and accounted for as a reduction of proceeds allocated to newly issued securities.

The SEC staff also believes that consistent with the principle stated in ASC 805-10-55-25, if shares in an escrowed share arrangement are automatically forfeited on the termination of employment of a participant in the arrangement, such an arrangement is considered to be compensatory.

ASC 718-10-30-28, 55-88 Accounting for Share-Based Payments When the Terms of an Award Provide That a Performance Target Could be Achieved after the Requisite Service Period

BACKGROUND

The issue here concerns the accounting for a situation in which an entity issues share-based payment awards to employees that require the achievement of specific performance targets in order for the employees to benefit from the awards. Although under most share-based payment awards, a performance target must be achieved during an employee's service period, under the terms of the awards in question, an employee may benefit from an award even if a performance target is achieved after the employee's required service period has ended. An example of such a performance target may be a nonpublic entity's issuance of awards to management as an incentive to sell the entity's shares in an initial public offering.

There has been diversity in the accounting for such awards in practice because the existing guidance under U.S. generally accepted accounting principles (U.S. GAAP) does not address whether a performance target that can be achieved after an employee's required service period has been completed is a performance condition that affects vesting or a condition that affects an award's fair value at the grant date.

The term "performance condition" is defined in the Glossary of the FASB Accounting Standards Codification® (ASC) as:

> A condition affecting the vesting, exercisability, exercise price, or other pertinent factors used in determining the fair value of an award that relates to both of the following:
>
> a. An employee's rendering service for a specified (either explicitly or implicitly) period of time.
>
> b. Achieving a specified performance target that is defined solely by reference to the employer's own operations (or activities).

Some reporting entities have accounted for a performance target that can be achieved after an employee has completed the required service period as a performance condition that affects only an award's vesting and is not included in an award's estimated fair value at the grant date. Others have referred to ASC 718-10-30-6, which states that "the measurement objective for equity instruments awarded to employees is to estimate the fair value at the grant date of the equity instruments that the entity is obligated to issue when employees have rendered the requisite service and satisfied any other conditions necessary to earn the right to benefit from the instruments," because they believe that this guidance states one of the main principles of accounting for share-based payments. The proponents of that view also argue that if the measurement period of a performance target exceeds the required service period, the performance target should be treated as a nonvesting condition that affects the fair value of the awards at the grant date.

ACCOUNTING ISSUE

How should a share-based payments award be accounted for if the award's terms provide that an employee is eligible to benefit from the award even when a performance target is achieved after the employee's required service period has ended?

ACCOUNTING GUIDANCE

Scope

The following guidance applies to all reporting entities that grant to their employees share-based payment awards with terms that permit the achievement of a performance target after an employee's required service period has been completed.

Initial Measurement

Under the guidance in ASC 718-10-30-27, a performance or service condition that affects vesting should not be included in an estimate of a share-based payment award's fair value at the grant date and there is no specific requirement that an employee has to provide services to an employer until a performance target has been achieved. To amend U.S. GAAP for awards under the scope of this issue, the guidance in ASC 718 is amended by the addition of ASC 718-10-30-28, which provides how an entity should account for share-based payment awards under whose terms an employee is eligible to vest in an award even if the award's performance target is achieved after the employee's required service period has been completed, and regardless of whether the employee continues to be employed by the entity.

Under that guidance, the achievement of a performance target that affects vesting and may occur after an employee has completed the required service period should be accounted for as a performance condition, as discussed in ASC 718-10-30-27. Consequently, the performance target should not be included in estimating an award's fair value at the grant date. Rather, an entity should recognize compensation cost in the period in which it becomes probable that a performance target will be achieved. The amount recognized should correspond to the compensation cost related to the periods in which the employees have already performed the required services. If the achievement of a performance target becomes probable during an employee's required service period, the amount of unrecognized compensation cost should be recognized prospectively over the employee's remaining required service period. The total amount of compensation cost that an entity recognizes during and after the employees' required service periods should represent the number of awards expected to vest based on the performance target and should be adjusted to account for the number of awards that eventually vest. If an entity has an accounting policy to account for forfeitures as they occur in accordance with the guidance in ASC 718-10-35-3, it should reverse compensation cost previously recognized, in the period in which the award is forfeited before the required service period has been completed.

An employee's required service period ends when an employee can stop rendering services to an entity and is still eligible to vest in an award when a performance target is achieved. The definition of the term *vest* clarifies that a vesting period, which includes the period in which a performance target could be achieved, may not be the same as the required service period.

ASC 718-10-35-9, 35-10, 35-11 Classification and Measurement of Freestanding Financial Instruments Originally Issued in Exchange for Employee Services under ASC 718

BACKGROUND

This guidance was issued for the following reasons:

- To defer the requirement in ASC 718 that freestanding financial instruments accounted for under the guidance in ASC 718 that were conveyed to a holder by an employer and linked to the holder's employment should be accounted for in accordance with the recognition and measurement guidance in other applicable generally accepted accounting principles (GAAP) if the instrument's rights no longer are linked to the holder's employment.
- To supersede the guidance in FSP EITF 00-19-1 (Application of EITF Issue No. 00-19 to Freestanding Financial Instruments Originally Issued as Employee Compensation).
- To amend the guidance in ASC 815-10-15-74 and Statement 133 Implementation Issue No. C3 (Scope Exceptions: Exception Related to Share-Based Payment Arrangements) by adding a footnote to both documents stating that this guidance defers the guidance in ASC 718-10-35-13 under certain circumstances for employee awards and provides additional guidance for awards that no longer are within the scope of ASC 718. Such awards should be analyzed to determine whether they should be accounted for under the guidance in ASC 815.

Entities that offer stock-based compensation to employees and nonemployees are required to account for such arrangements under the guidance in ASC 718. However, the guidance in ASC 718 provides that the rights conveyed by freestanding instruments issued under those arrangements are *excluded* from the scope of ASC 718 if the holder's rights under the instruments no longer are linked to the holder's employment by the issuer. According to the guidance in ASC 718-10-35-13, those instruments should be accounted for under the measurement and recognition guidance in other applicable GAAP. The guidance in ASC 718-10-35-14 and the related footnotes 123 and 124 provide guidance as to when an award no longer is linked to employment.

ACCOUNTING GUIDANCE

In accordance with the amendment of ASC 718-10-35-10 in ASU 2019-08, *Compensation-Stock Compensation (Topic 718) and Revenue from Contracts Customers (Topic 606): Codification Improvements-Share-Based Consideration Payable to a Customer*, the recognition and measurement guidance in ASC 718 for freestanding financial instruments issued to a grantee under the initial recognition and measurement guidance in ASC 718 should continue to apply for the life of those instruments, unless an instrument's terms are modified after any of the following occur:

a. A grantee vests in the award and is no longer providing goods or services.

b. A grantee vests in the award is no longer a customer.

c. A grantee is no longer an employee.

Other modifications should be accounted for in accordance with the guidance in ASC 718-10-35-14. After an instrument has been modified, it should be accounted for in accordance with the recognition and measurement guidance of other applicable GAAP.

ASC 718-10-35-15 Classification of Options and Similar Instruments Issued as Employee Compensation That Allow for Cash Settlement upon the Occurrence of an Event

BACKGROUND

The subject of this guidance is the classification of options and similar instruments issued to employees as compensation that can be settled in cash when a contingent event occurs. ASC 718-10-25-11 is amended by this guidance.

This issue was addressed because under some share-based payment plans, cash settlement of an option or similar instrument is required if a contingent event occurs. Settlement of an option in cash is required or permitted, at a holder's option, if the issuer has a change in control or another event affecting its liquidity occurs or if the holder dies or becomes disabled. Under the guidance in ASC 718-10-25-11, options or similar instruments must be classified as liabilities if settlement in cash or other assets is required "under any circumstances." Because cash settlement of an entity's options or similar instruments issued as employee compensation *may* be required on the occurrence of a change in control, those instruments would have to be classified as liabilities under the guidance in ASC 718-10-25-11.

ACCOUNTING GUIDANCE

This guidance amends the guidance in ASC 718-10-25-11 to incorporate the notion that the conditions in those paragraphs would *not* be met until the occurrence of a contingent event requiring cash settlement that is *not* under an employee's control, such as an initial public offering, becomes *probable.*

An option or similar instrument should be accounted for as a modification from equity to a liability award if that instrument is reclassified from equity to a liability, because it becomes *probable* that an event requiring cash settlement will occur. On the date it becomes probable that a contingent event will occur, the issuer should:

- Recognize a share-based liability equal to the portion of the award attributed to past service (considering a provision, if any, for accelerated vesting) multiplied by the award's fair value on that date.
- Charge an offsetting debit to equity if the liability is equal to or less than the amount previously recognized in equity.
- Recognize compensation cost for an amount, if any, by which the liability exceeds the amount previously recognized in equity.

Total compensation cost recognized for an award that has a contingent cash settlement feature must be at least equal to the award's fair value at the grant date.

This guidance, which applies only to options or similar instruments issued in connection with employee compensation arrangements, should *not* be applied by analogy to instruments that are *not* related to employee share-based arrangements.

AMENDMENT OF ASC 718-10-25-11

The following footnotes are being added to ASC 718-10-25-11:

- "A cash settlement feature that can be exercised only upon the occurrence of a contingent event that is outside the employee's control (such as an initial public offering) would not meet condition (b) until it becomes probable that event will occur."
- "SEC registrants are required to consider the guidance in ASR 268. Under that guidance, options and similar instruments subject to mandatory redemption requirements or whose redemption is outside the control of the issuer are classified outside permanent equity."

ASC 718-40: EMPLOYEE STOCK OWNERSHIP PLANS

ASC 718-40-05-2 through 05-4, 15-2 through 15-4, 25-2 through 25-6, 25-9 through 25-17, 25-19 through 25-21, 30-1 through 30-5, 35-1, 40-2 through 40-7, 45-2 through 45-9, 50-1, 55-1 through 55-38 Employers' Accounting for Employee Stock Ownership Plans

BACKGROUND

An employee stock ownership plan (ESOP) is an employee benefit plan described by the Employee Retirement Income Security Act (ERISA) of 1974 and the Internal Revenue Code of 1986. An ESOP can be either a qualified stock bonus plan or a combination of a qualified stock bonus plan and a money purchase pension plan. In both cases, the ESOP is expected to invest primarily in stock of the sponsoring employer.

SOP 76-3, which was issued in December 1976, primarily provided accounting and reporting guidance for leveraged ESOPs. ASC 718-40, which supersedes it, must be applied for ESOP shares acquired after December 30, 1992, but at the company's discretion, it also may be applied to ESOP shares acquired before December 31, 1992. Alternatively, companies are permitted to continue to apply the guidance in SOP 76-3, which was grandfathered when the FASB issued the Accounting Standards Codification™ and is included at the end of this chapter, to ESOP shares acquired before December 31, 1992. A number of changes affecting ESOPs occurred between the release of SOP 76-3 and the issuance of the guidance below. For instance, Congress passed a number of laws affecting ESOPs, and numerous regulatory changes in this area have emanated from the Internal Revenue Service and from the U.S. Department of Labor. A number of these changes sparked a substantial growth in the number of ESOPs. Not only has the number of ESOPs grown, but also their complexity has increased. ESOPs are now formed for a number of different purposes:

- To fund a matching program for one or more employee benefit plans of the sponsor (e.g., 401(k) savings plan, formula-based profit-sharing plan)
- To raise new capital or to create a market for the existing stock
- To replace benefits lost from the termination of other employee benefit plans (e.g., retirement plans, other postretirement benefit plans)
- To help finance a leveraged buy-out
- To be used by owners to terminate their ownership interests in the entity on a tax-advantaged basis
- To be used as a deterrent against hostile takeovers

The financing of ESOPs also has changed significantly since SOP 76-3 was issued. When SOP 76-3 was issued, ESOP borrowing was typically from an outside lender. In today's environment, it is not unusual for an ESOP to be internally leveraged (the ESOP borrows from the employer sponsoring the ESOP, with or without an outside loan to the employer). In addition, some ESOPs use dividends on shares held by the ESOP largely to fund required debt payments. When SOP 76-3 was issued, most debt repayments were funded through employer contributions.

Finally, the guidance in ASC 718-40 was issued to resolve some continuing controversies regarding the measurement of compensation cost and how dividends on shares held by an ESOP should be treated. Those two issues had been problematic since the issuance of SOP 76-3.

ACCOUNTING GUIDANCE

The provisions of ASC 718-40 provide guidance to employers that sponsor ESOPs and apply to all ESOPs, both leveraged and nonleveraged. The accounting for leveraged and nonleveraged ESOPs is discussed separately on the following pages. In addition, pension reversion ESOPs and the disclosures required by the guidance in ASC 718-40 are discussed.

Accounting for Leveraged ESOPs

A leveraged ESOP borrows money to acquire shares of the employer sponsoring the ESOP. An ESOP may borrow either from the employer sponsor or directly from an outside lender. The shares acquired from the debt proceeds initially are held in a suspense account (i.e., they are not immediately allocated to the accounts of employees participating in the ESOP). The ESOP's debt is liquidated through (*a*) contributions of the employer to the ESOP and (*b*) dividends on the employer's stock held by the ESOP. As the ESOP's debt is repaid, shares are released from the suspense account. Released shares must be allocated to participants' accounts by the end of the ESOP's fiscal year.

Purchase of Shares

An ESOP may purchase either newly issued shares or treasury shares from the employer. The employer should record the issuance or sale of shares to the ESOP at the time it occurs, based on the fair value of its shares at that time. The offsetting debit is to unearned ESOP shares, a contra-equity account, which is to be shown as a separate line item on the employer's balance sheet.

In some cases, the ESOP may acquire shares of the employer through secondary market purchases. Even in this case, the employer should debit unearned ESOP shares for the cost of the shares purchased by the ESOP. If the ESOP is internally leveraged (i.e., the ESOP has borrowed from the employer), the offsetting credit recorded by the employer is to cash. If the ESOP is externally leveraged (i.e., the ESOP has borrowed directly from an outside lender), the offsetting credit recorded by the employer is to an appropriately titled debt account.

Illustration of Issuance of ESOP Shares as a Form of Employee Compensation

Pfeiffer, Bryant & Co. sponsors an ESOP for its employees. During the first quarter of 20X4, the employees of Pfeiffer, Bryant & Co. earn the right to receive 10,000 shares. The ESOP holds 25,000 shares of Pfeiffer Bryant's stock, acquired at an average cost of $20 per share. Pfeiffer Bryant's stock price was $22 at 1/1/X4, $29 at 3/31/X4, and was $25 on average during the first quarter of 20X4. Pfeiffer Bryant would record this transaction as follows:

Compensation cost (10,000 × $25)	$250,000	
Unearned ESOP shares (10,000 × $20)		$200,000
Additional paid-in capital		50,000

Release of ESOP Shares—General

ESOP shares are released for one or more of three purposes: (1) to compensate employees directly, (2) to settle a liability for other employee benefits, and (3) to replace dividends on allocated shares when these dividends are used to pay debt service.

The allocation of shares to employees typically is based on employee service. The number of shares to be released for each period (quarter or year) of employee service is usually specified in ESOP documents. As employees provide services, the release of ESOP shares is earned (hence they are committed to be released whether or not they have yet to be legally released). ESOP shares are legally released for distribution to participant accounts when debt payments are made.

When shares are committed to be released (which may occur before the shares are legally released), unearned ESOP shares should be credited for the cost of the shares to be released. The offsetting debit, which is based on the fair value of the shares, depends on the purpose for which the ESOP shares are being released. If the committed-to-be-released shares relate to employee compensation, the debit is to compensation cost. If the committed-to-be-released shares relate to the settlement of a liability for other employee benefits, the debit is to employee benefits payable. If the committed-to-be-released shares are to replace dividends on allocated shares, the debit is to dividends payable. Therefore, in most cases, the debit for committed-to-be-released shares, which is based on fair value, will differ from the credit for these same shares, which is based on cost. This difference is accounted for as a debit or credit to shareholders' equity, typically through the use of the additional paid-in capital account.

Release of ESOP Shares—Direct Compensation of Employees

As employees provide services over the accounting period (quarter or year), they ratably earn the right to receive ESOP shares. In essence, the commitment to release shares occurs ratably throughout the period. Therefore, compensation cost should be measured based on the average fair value of the stock over the relevant time period. Compensation cost recognized in previous interim periods should not be changed to reflect changes in the stock's fair value in later interim periods in the same fiscal year.

Release of ESOP Shares—Satisfaction of Other Employee Benefits

In some cases, an employer will settle its liability to provide other employee benefits by allocating shares of stock held by the ESOP to participant accounts. For example, some employers may allocate ESOP shares to satisfy a commitment to fund a 401(k) plan or a profit-sharing plan. The employer should recognize the expense and the liability for employee benefits (e.g., 401(k) contributions, profit-sharing contributions) in the same manner as if the ESOP was not used to fund the benefit. The employer should debit the liability account (for employee benefits) when ESOP shares are committed to be released to settle the liability. The number of shares to be released depends on the amount of the liability and the fair value of the ESOP shares at the time the liability is settled.

Release of ESOP Shares—Replacement of Dividends on Allocated Shares When Such Dividends Are Used to Service Debt

Dividends on shares of stock already allocated to participants' accounts can be used to service debt. However, if dividends on allocated shares are used in this manner, unallocated shares with a fair value equal to the dividends diverted must be allocated to participants' accounts.

When shares are committed to be released to replace the dividends on allocated shares used for debt service, the employer should debit dividends payable. In addition, only those dividends that pertain to shares already allocated are charged to retained earnings.

Determination of Fair Value

A number of the provisions of ASC 718-40 require the use of the fair value of the ESOP shares.

Dividends on Unallocated ESOP Shares

Dividends declared on unallocated ESOP shares are not charged against retained earnings by the employer. If dividends on unallocated shares are used for debt service, the employer debits debt and/or interest payable (the credit is to cash). In some cases, dividends on unallocated shares may be paid to participants or added to participants' accounts. In these cases, the offsetting debit is to compensation cost.

Dividends on Allocated ESOP Shares

Dividends declared on allocated ESOP shares are charged against retained earnings by the employer. The employer can satisfy its liability for the distribution of dividends in one of three ways: (1) by contributing cash to participant accounts; (2) by contributing additional shares, with a fair value equal to the amount of the dividends, to participant accounts; or (3) by releasing ESOP shares held in suspense, with a fair value equal to the amount of the dividends, to participant accounts.

Redemption of ESOP Shares

Employers are required to offer a put option to holders of ESOP shares that are not readily tradable (required for both leveraged and nonleveraged ESOPs). The employer is required to purchase the employee's stock at its fair value at the time the put option is exercised. The employer would record its purchase of the employee's stock in a manner identical to the purchase of treasury shares.

Reporting of Debt and Interest—General

The employer's accounting for ESOP-related debt and interest depends on the type of ESOP debt. The three types of ESOP-related debt can be described as follows:

1. *Direct loan* The loan is from an outside lender to the ESOP.
2. *Indirect loan* The loan is from the employer to the ESOP, and the employer borrows a comparable sum from an outside lender.
3. *Employer loan* The loan is from the employer to the ESOP. There is no related outside borrowing by the employer.

Reporting of Debt and Interest—Direct Loan

The ESOP's liability to the lender should be recorded by the employer (in essence, the ESOP's debt is treated as the debt of the employer). In addition, accrued interest payable on the loan is recorded by the employer. Cash payments that the employer makes to the ESOP, which are to be used to service debt payments, are recorded as a reduction in the related debt and the accrued interest payable amounts. The employer should record the reduction in these two liability accounts when the ESOP remits a loan or interest payment to the lending institution. The source of the cash contribution from the employer to the ESOP does not affect this accounting treatment (i.e., the accounting treatment is as specified above, regardless of whether the source of cash is an employer contribution or dividends on ESOP stock).

Recording of Debt and Interest—Indirect Loan

Because the employer borrows from an outside lender, the employer obviously records this borrowing as a liability. In addition, in the case of an indirect loan, the ESOP has borrowed from the employer (typically an amount equal to what the employer has borrowed from an outside lender). Although the employer has a loan receivable from the ESOP, the employer does not recognize this asset in its financial statements. Because the employer does not record the loan receivable, the employer also does not recognize interest income. The employer may make a cash contribution to the ESOP for the purpose of funding the ESOP's debt repayments—concurrent payments from the ESOP back to the employer. Neither the cash contribution from the employer to the ESOP nor the concurrent debt repayment from the ESOP to the employer is recognized in the employer's financial statements.

Recording of Debt and Interest—Employer Loan

The employer has made a loan to the ESOP, and the employer has not borrowed a comparable amount from an unrelated lender. Although the employer has a note receivable, it is not recognized in the employer's financial statements. Therefore, interest income also is not recognized. (The ESOP's note payable and related interest cost also are not recognized in the employer's financial statements.)

Earnings per Share

Shares that are committed to be released are treated as outstanding in computing both basic and diluted EPS. Shares not committed to be released are not treated as outstanding in either computation.

ESOPs holding convertible preferred stock may encounter the following unique EPS issues (however, some complexity in this area has been reduced by the issuance of ASC 260-10):

- How to compute the number of shares outstanding for the application of the if-converted method
- How earnings applicable to common stock in if-converted computations should be adjusted for the effects of dividends on allocated shares used for debt service
- Whether prior periods' EPS should be restated for a change in the conversion ratio

Convertible preferred stock—Number of common shares outstanding The number of common shares that would be issued on conversion of preferred stock, where the convertible preferred stock is committed to be released, should be considered outstanding for the purpose of applying the if-converted method. This treatment applies to the computation of both basic and diluted EPS (assuming the effects are dilutive).

A participant's account balance may contain convertible preferred stock when it is withdrawn. The participant may be entitled to receive either (*a*) common stock or (*b*) cash with a value equal to (1) the fair value of convertible preferred stock or (2) a stated minimum value per share. The common stock that would have been issuable (upon conversion) may have a fair value that is less than the fair value of the convertible preferred stock or less than the stated minimum value per share. If this is the case, the participant will receive common stock or cash with a value greater than the fair value of the common stock that would have been issuable given the stated conversion rate. The presumption is that any shortfall will be made up by the issue of additional shares of common stock. However, this assumption can be overcome if past experience or a stated policy indicates that any shortfall will be paid in cash.

When the employee applies the if-converted method, the number of common shares issuable on assumed conversion is the greater of:

- The shares issuable at the stated conversion rate *or*
- The shares issuable if participants were to withdraw the convertible preferred shares from their accounts.

The shares issuable, if participants were to withdraw the convertible preferred shares from their accounts, are to be computed as the ratio of:

- The average fair value of the convertible stock or, if greater, its stated minimum value *to*
- The average fair value of the common stock.

Convertible preferred stock—Adjustment to earnings If employers use dividends on allocated shares to pay debt service, earnings applicable to common shares should be adjusted for the purpose of applying the if-converted method. Earnings applicable to common stock would be adjusted for the difference (net of tax) between:

- The amount of compensation cost reported *and*
- The amount of compensation cost that would have been reported if the allocated shares had been converted to common stock at the beginning of the period.

Convertible preferred stock—Changes in conversion rates Earnings per share for prior periods should not be restated for changes in conversion rates.

Accounting for income taxes Differences between book ESOP-related expense and the ESOP-related expense allowed for tax purposes may result from the following:

- The fair value of committed-to-be-released shares is different from the cost of these shares *and/or*
- The timing of expense recognition is different for book purposes than for tax purposes.

In either case, the guidance in ASC 740, Income Taxes, should be followed. The tax effects of differences between book and tax reporting are to be recognized as a component of stockholders' equity (i.e., these differences do not give rise to deferred tax assets and liabilities).

If the cost of shares committed to be released exceeds their fair value, the expense deductible for tax purposes will exceed the book expense. The tax effect of this difference should be credited to stockholders' equity. If the cost of shares committed to be released is less than their fair value, the expense deductible for book purposes will exceed the expense deductible for tax purposes. The tax effect of this difference should be charged to stockholders' equity to the extent that prior credits to stockholder's equity that are related to cost exceeding the fair value of shares that were committed to be released in previous years.

Dividends paid on ESOP shares frequently result in a tax deduction. The tax-advantaged nature of ESOPs is a contributing factor behind their growth. The tax benefit of tax-deductible dividends on allocated ESOP shares is to be recorded as a reduction in income tax expense from continuing operations.

Accounting for terminations If an ESOP is terminated, either in whole or in part, all outstanding debt related to the shares terminated must be repaid or refinanced. The ESOP may repay the debt through one or more of the following sources:

- Employer contributions
- Dividends on ESOP shares
- Proceeds from selling suspense shares, either to the employer or to another party

The number of suspense shares the employer may purchase is limited. The employer can purchase only those shares that have a fair value equal to the applicable unpaid debt. Any shares that remain must be allocated to participants' accounts.

For example, if the ESOP sells suspense shares and uses the proceeds to repay the debt, the employer would account for this transaction as follows:

- Debit the book value of the debt and the accrued interest payable that relate to the shares being terminated.
- Credit unearned ESOP shares for the cost of the shares being terminated.
- Debit or credit any resulting difference to paid-in capital.

If the employer reacquires the suspense shares, the employer should account for the purchase in a manner similar to the purchase of treasury stock. The employer debits treasury stock based on the fair value of the suspense shares acquired (on the date the employer reacquires them). The employer credits unearned ESOP shares based on their cost. Any difference between the cost and the fair value of the suspense shares reacquired is assigned to paid-in capital.

If the fair value of the suspense shares on the termination date of the ESOP is greater than the ESOP's unpaid debt, the remaining suspense shares are released to participants. The release of these remaining suspense shares to participants is charged to compensation cost. The charge is equal to the fair value of the shares released to participants, determined as of the date the ESOP-related debt is extinguished.

Accounting for Nonleveraged ESOPs

A nonleveraged ESOP is less complex than a leveraged ESOP, and the accounting guidance on it is less complex and less voluminous. An employer contributes shares of its stock or cash to the ESOP for the benefit of employees. If the employer's contribution is cash, the ESOP uses the cash contribution to purchase employer securities. The employer shares that are donated or acquired by the ESOP may be outstanding shares, treasury shares, or newly issued shares. The shares held by the ESOP are allocated to participants' accounts; they are held by the ESOP and are distributed to employees at a future date (e.g., termination, and retirement). Shares obtained by the ESOP must be allocated to individual accounts by the ESOP's fiscal year-end.

Purchase of Shares

The employer records compensation cost based on the contribution that the terms of the plan require the employer make to the ESOP in the reporting period. Compensation cost includes the fair value of shares contributed, the fair value of shares committed to be contributed, cash contributed, and cash committed to be contributed.

Dividends

The employer should record a charge to retained earnings for dividends declared on shares held by a nonleveraged ESOP, with one exception to this requirement: Dividends on suspense account shares held by a pension reversion ESOP are to be accounted for in a manner similar to dividends on suspense account shares held by a leveraged ESOP.

Redemptions

As was the case with leveraged ESOPs, the employer is required to provide ESOP participants with put options if the employer shares held by the ESOP are not readily tradable. If a participant exercises his or her put option, the employer is to record the reacquisition of its stock from the participant in a manner similar to the purchase of treasury stock.

Earnings per Share

In general, all shares held by a nonleveraged ESOP are to be treated as outstanding by the employer in computing its EPS, with one exception: Suspense account shares of a pension reversion ESOP should not be treated as outstanding until they are committed to be released to participants' accounts.

Income Taxes

Compensation cost for financial reporting purposes may be accrued earlier than it is deductible for tax purposes, which creates a FAS-109 temporary difference.

Accounting for Pension Reversion ESOPs

An employer may terminate a defined benefit pension plan and recapture excess pension plan assets, although such a reversion of pension plan assets exposes the employer to an excise tax on the reversion of the pension assets. The employer may avoid some of the excise tax by transferring the pension assets to an ESOP (either new or existing, either leveraged or nonleveraged). The ESOP uses the (reverted) pension plan assets to acquire shares of the employer or to retire ESOP-related debt.

The ESOP may use the pension assets it receives to acquire shares of the employer. If the shares are acquired from the employer (either new shares or treasury shares), the employer would debit unearned ESOP shares (the offsetting credit is to common stock or treasury stock). If the shares are acquired on the secondary market, the employer would still debit unearned ESOP shares (the offsetting credit is to cash).

The ESOP may use the pension plan assets received on the reversion to repay debt. If this is the case, ESOP shares will be committed to be released from the suspense account. The guidance for leveraged ESOPs should be followed in determining the appropriate accounting. For instance, the employer will record the reduction in debt as it is repaid. The employer also will reduce the account "unearned ESOP shares" as these shares are committed to be released. How these committed-to-be-released shares are used determines the offsetting debit (see the earlier discussion on this issue for leveraged ESOPs).

Disclosures

An employer that sponsors an ESOP (both for leveraged and nonleveraged plans) is required to make the following disclosures:

1. A description of the ESOP, employee groups covered, the method of determining contributions, and the nature and effects of any significant changes that would affect comparability across periods
2. The accounting policies followed by the ESOP, which include the method of determining compensation, the classification of dividends on ESOP shares, and the treatment of ESOP shares for EPS computations
3. The amount of compensation cost for the period
4. As of the balance sheet date, the number of (*a*) allocated shares, (*b*) committed-to-be-released shares, and (*c*) suspense shares
5. As of the balance sheet date, the fair value of unearned ESOP shares
6. The existence and nature of any repurchase obligation (if such an obligation exists, the fair value of shares already allocated that are subject to the repurchase obligation)

Shares of an ESOP acquired before December 31, 1992, can continue to be accounted for under the provisions of SOP 76-3. For employers that elect to continue to account for these "old shares" under SOP 76-3, the disclosures required by items 2 and 4 above need to be made separately for shares accounted for under SOP 93-6 and SOP 76-3. Also, the fair value of unearned ESOP shares as of the balance sheet date (item 5) does not have to be disclosed for "old shares."

For leveraged and pension reversion ESOPs only, the following additional disclosures are required:

- The basis for releasing shares
- How dividends on allocated and unallocated shares are used

Illustrations

A number of detailed examples on the application of the above guidance are included in ASC 718-40-55. The accounting is illustrated for the following types of ESOPs: (1) a common-stock leveraged ESOP with a direct loan, (2) a common-stock leveraged ESOP used to fund the employer's match of a 401(k) savings plan with an indirect loan, (3) a common-stock nonleveraged ESOP, (4) a convertible-preferred-stock leveraged ESOP with a direct loan, and (5) a convertible, preferred stock, leveraged ESOP used to fund a 401(k) savings plan with an employer loan. The guidance in ASC 718-40 includes an example of an ESOP termination and of the required ESOP note disclosures. The first illustration that follows is a simplified example of the accounting for a common-stock leveraged ESOP with a direct loan; the second illustration is for a common-stock nonleveraged ESOP.

Illustration of a Common-Stock Leveraged ESOP with a Direct Loan

Neal and Neel (N&N) established a common-stock leveraged ESOP with a direct loan on January 1, 20X4. Relevant information regarding the ESOP is as follows:

1. The ESOP borrows $2,500,000 from an outside lender at 8% for four years. The proceeds are used to purchase 50,000 shares of newly issued N&N stock that has a market value of $50 per share.
2. The ESOP will fund the debt service with cash contributions from N&N and with dividends on the employer stock it holds.
3. Dividends on all shares of stock held by the ESOP, allocated and unallocated, are used for debt service.
4. N&N makes cash contributions to the ESOP at the end of each year.
5. The average market price of N&N's common stock during each year is as follows: 20X4, $54; 20X5, $47; 20X6, $56; 20X7, $60.
6. At the end of each quarter, N&N pays dividends of $.50 per share on its common stock. Therefore, dividends on ESOP shares are $100,000 per year (50,000 shares × $.50 dividend per share per quarter × 4 quarters per year). Because dividends on allocated shares are used for debt service, N&N must provide the ESOP with additional shares of common stock. The number of additional shares of common stock required is determined by dividing the dividends on allocated shares by the average market price of N&N's stock.
7. Both principal and interest payments on the ESOP's debt are due in equal annual installments at the end of each year. Yearly debt service is as follows:

Table 1—Debt Service

Year	*Principal*	*Interest*	*Total Debt Service*
20X4	$554,802	$200,000	$754,802
20X5	599,186	155,616	754,802
20X6	647,121	107,681	754,802
20X7	698,891	55,911	754,802
Total	$2,500,000	$519,208	$3,019,208

8. The number of shares of N&N stock released to participants' accounts each year is as follows:

Table 2—Shares Released for Compensation and Dividends

Year	*Dividends*	*Compensation*	*Total*
20X4	0	12,500	12,500
20X5	532	11,968	12,500
20X6	893	11,607	12,500
20X7	1250	11,250	12,500

The number of shares released for dividends is determined by dividing the amount of dividends on allocated shares (which are being used for debt service) by the average market price of the common stock during the year in question. For example, in the year 20X5, 12,500 shares of common stock were allocated (see Table 3 below). Dividends on these 12,500 shares are $25,000 (12,500 shares × $2 per year). Dividing $25,000 by $47 (the average market price of N&N's common stock during 20X5) results in the issuance of 532 shares during 20X5 to replace the dividends on allocated shares used for debt service. In this example, the remaining shares are released as compensation to ESOP participants.

9. Shares released and allocated are based on total debt service payments made during the year (both principal and interest). Because 25% of debt service payments are made in each year, 25% of the shares (12,500) are released each year. Shares released in a particular year are allocated to participants' accounts during the next year. See Table 3.

Table 3—Shares Released and Allocated

	Cumulative Number of Shares		*Average Shares*	*Year-End Suspense*
Year	*Released*	*Allocated*	*Released*	*Shares*
20X4	12,500	0	6,250	37,500
20X5	25,000	12,500	18,750	25,000
20X6	37,500	25,000	31,250	12,500
20X7	50,000	37,500	43,750	0

10. N&N's income before giving effect to the ESOP is as follows: 20X4, $2,600,000; 20X5, $2,800,000; 20X6, $3,100,000; 20X7, $3,200,000.

11. All interest cost and compensation cost are charged to expense each year.

12. Excluding ESOP shares, the weighted average equivalent number of shares outstanding is 2,000,000 each year.

13. N&N's combined statutory tax rate is 36% each year.

14. The only book/tax difference is that associated with the ESOP.

15. No valuation allowance is necessary for any deferred tax asset.

The following tables and journal entries illustrate the results of applying ASC 718-40.

Table 4—Summary of the Effects of Applying ASC 718-40

Year	*Principal*	*Unearned ESOP Shares*	*Paid-In Capital*	*Dividends*	*Interest Expense*	*Compensation Expense*	*Cash*
Notes:	(1)	(2)	(3)	(4)	(1)	(5)	(6)
20X4	$ 554,802	$ (625,000)	$ (50,000)	$ 0	$200,000	$ 675,000	$(754,802)
20X5	599,186	(625,000)	37,500	25,000	155,616	562,496	(754,802)
20X6	647,121	(625,000)	(75,000)	50,000	107,681	649,992	(754,802)
20X7	698,891	(625,000)	(125,000)	75,000	55,911	675,000	(754,802)
Total	$2,500,000	$(2,500,000)	$(212,500)	$150,000	$519,208	$2,562,488	$(3,019,208)

Notes:

(1) Principal paid and interest expense from Table 1.
(2) The credit to unearned ESOP shares is calculated by multiplying the number of ESOP shares released each year (12,500) by the cost of these shares to the ESOP ($50 per share).
(3) The debit or credit to paid-in capital is computed by multiplying the number of ESOP shares released each year (12,500) by the difference between the average market price per share (for the particular year) and the cost per share ($50). For example, in 20X4 this calculation resulted in a $50,000 credit [($54 – $50) × 12,500].
(4) The dividend amount is calculated by multiplying the cumulative number of shares allocated (see Table 3) by the dividend per share, $2 per year.
(5) Compensation expense is computed by multiplying the number of shares released for compensation (see Table 2) by the average market price per share (for the particular year).
(6) The cash disbursed each year comprises a yearly contribution of $654,802 and $100,000 of dividends. Also note that this amount equals the yearly debt service.

Table 5—Tax Computations

	20X4	*20X5*	*20X6*	*20X7*
Current provision:				
Income before ESOP	$2,600,000	$2,800,000	$3,100,000	$3,200,000
ESOP contribution	(654,802)	(654,802)	(654,802)	(654,802)
ESOP dividends	(100,000)	(100,000)	(100,000)	(100,000)
Taxable income	$1,845,198	$2,045,198	$2,345,198	$2,445,198
Multiplied by 36%	664,271	736,271	844,271	880,271
Deferred provision:				
Reduction in unearned ESOP shares for financial reporting	$625,000	$625,000	$625,000	$625,000
Related tax deduction(1)	554,802	599,186	647,121	698,891
Difference	$(70,198)	$(25,814)	$22,121	$73,891
Tax rate	36%	36%	36%	36%
Deferred tax expense (benefit)	$(25,271)	$(9,293)	$7,964	$26,601

Notes:

(1) The tax deduction in computing the deferred income tax provision is equal to the amount of the principal repayment.

Table 6—Reconciliation of Effective Tax Rate to Provision for Income Taxes

	20X4	*20X5*	*20X6*	*20X7*
Pretax income(1)	$1,725,000	$2,081,888	$2,342,327	$2,469,089
Tax at 36% (statutory rate)	621,000	749,480	843,238	888,872
Benefit of ESOP dividends(2)	0	(9,000)	(18,000)	(27,000)
Effect of difference between average fair value and cost of released shares(3)	18,000	—	13,500(4)	45,000
Provision as reported	$639,000	$740,480	$838,738	$906,872

Notes:

(1) See Table 7 for the computation of the pretax income.

(2) Computed by multiplying the yearly ESOP dividend amount (see Table 4) by the statutory tax rate, 36%.

(3) Computed by multiplying the number of shares released during the year (12,500 each year) by the difference between the average market value during the year and the cost of the ESOP shares and then multiplying this amount by the statutory tax rate. This computation is as follows for 20X4: [12,500 × ($54 – $50) × 36%]. This amount cannot be negative; therefore, this amount is zero during any year in which the cost of the ESOP shares exceeds the average market value during the year (e.g., year 20X5).

(4) Computed as explained in item 3 minus the excess cost of the ESOP shares released in year 20X5 over their fair value multiplied by the tax rate. The entire computation is [(($56 – $50) × 12,500) × 36%] – [(($50 – $47) × 12,500) × 36%].

Table 7—Tax and EPS Computations

	20X4	*20X5*	*20X6*	*20X7*
Income before ESOP	$2,600,000	$2,800,000	$3,100,000	$3,200,000
Interest expense	(200,000)	(155,616)	(107,681)	(55,911)
Compensation expense	(675,000)	(562,496)	(649,992)	(675,000)
Pretax income	$1,725,000	$2,081,888	$2,342,327	$2,469,089
Provision for income tax:				
Currently payable	$664,271	$736,273	$844,271	$880,271
Deferred	(25,271)	(9,293)	7,964	26,601
Shareholders' equity(1)	0	13,500	(13,500)	0
Total	$639,000	$740,480	$838,735	$906,872
Net income	$1,086,000	$1,341,408	$1,503,592	$1,562,217

	20X4	20X5	20X6	20X7
Average shares outstanding(2)	2,006,250	2,018,750	2,031,250	2,043,750
Earnings per share	$0.54	$0.66	$0.74	$0.76

Notes:

(1) Calculated by multiplying the shares released during the year (12,500) by the excess of ESOP cost over the average market value of the stock ($50 – $47) and then multiplying this amount by the statutory tax rate (36%). This amount reverses in full in 20X6 since the fair value of the N&N stock in that year, $56, is more than $3 above the cost of N&N's stock to the ESOP, $50.

(2) Calculated by adding the cumulative average number of shares released in each year (see Table 3) to the weighted average number of common shares otherwise outstanding.

Journal Entries

January 1, 20X4 (Date N&N Establishes the ESOP)

Cash	$2,500,000	
Debt		$2,500,000
[To record the ESOP loan]		
Unearned ESOP shares (contra-equity)	$2,500,000	
Common stock and paid-in capital		$2,500,000
[To record the issuance of 50,000 shares to the ESOP at $50 per share—the fair value of the stock at the time it is issued]		

December 31, 20X4

Interest expense	$200,000	
Accrued interest payable		$200,000
[To record interest expense]		
Accrued interest payable	$200,000	
Debt	554,802	
Cash		$754,802
[To record the debt payment. The cash disbursement consists of $100,000 of dividends (none of which is charged to retained earnings in 20X4, because none of the shares has yet to be allocated) and $654,802 of additional employer contributions to the ESOP.]		
Compensation expense	$675,000	
Paid-in capital		$ 50,000
Unearned ESOP shares		625,000
[To record release of 12,500 shares at average fair value of $54. The ESOP's cost is $50.]		
Deferred tax asset	$ 25,271	
Provision for income taxes	639,000	
Income taxes payable		$664,271
[To record income taxes for 20X4; see Tables 5-7 for the computations of these amounts]		

December 31, 20X5

Interest expense	$155,616	
Accrued interest payable		$155,616
[To record interest expense]		
Accrued interest payable	$155,616	
Debt	599,186	
Cash		$754,802
[To record the debt payment. The cash disbursement consists of $100,000 of dividends ($25,000 of which is charged to retained earnings in 20X5 (see Table 4)) and $654,802 of additional employer contributions to the ESOP.]		
Retained earnings	$25,000	
Dividends payable		$25,000
[To record declaration of a $2.00-per-share dividend on 12,500 allocated shares]		
Compensation expense	$562,500*	
Dividends payable	25,000	
Paid-in capital	$37,500	
Unearned ESOP shares		$625,000

[To record the release of 12,500 shares (11,968 for compensation and 532 for dividends) at an average fair value of $47 per share. The per-share cost is $50.]

---

* $4 rounding difference

Deferred tax asset	$9,293	
Provision for income taxes	740,480	
Paid-in capital		$13,500
Income taxes payable		736,273

[To record income taxes for the year 20X5; see Tables 5-7 for the computations of these amounts.]

December 31, 20X6

Interest expense	$107,681	
Accrued interest payable		$107,681

[To record interest expense]

Accrued interest payable	$107,681	
Debt	647,121	
Cash		$754,802

[To record the debt payment. The cash disbursement consists of $100,000 of dividends ($50,000 of which is charged to retained earnings in 20X6 (see Table 4)) and $654,802 of additional employer contributions to the ESOP.]

Retained earnings	$50,000	
Dividends payable		$50,000

[To record declaration of a $2.00-per-share dividend on 25,000 allocated shares]

Compensation expense	$650,000*	
Dividends payable	50,000	
Paid-in capital		$75,000
Unearned ESOP shares		625,000

[To record the release of 12,500 shares (11,607 for compensation and 893 for dividends) at an average fair value of $56 per share. The per-share cost is $50.]

---

* $8 rounding difference

Provision for income taxes	$838,735	
Paid-in capital	13,500	
Deferred income taxes		$ 7,964
Income taxes payable		844,271

[To record income taxes for 20X6; see Tables 5-7 for the computations of these amounts.]

December 31, 20X7

Interest expense	$55,911	
Accrued interest payable		$55,911

[To record interest expense]

Accrued interest payable	$ 55,911	
Debt	698,891	
Cash		$754,802

[To record the debt payment. The cash disbursement consists of $100,000 of dividends ($75,000 of which is charged to retained earnings in 20X7 (see Table 4)) and $654,802 of additional employer contributions to the ESOP.]

Retained earnings	$75,000	
Dividends payable		$75,000

[To record declaration of a $2.00-per-share dividend on 37,500 allocated shares]

Compensation expense	$675,000	
Dividends payable	75,000	
Paid-in capital		$125,000
Unearned ESOP shares		625,000

[To record the release of 12,500 shares (11,250 for compensation and 1,250 for dividends) at an average fair value of $60 per share. The per-share cost is $50.]

Provision for income taxes	$906,872	
Deferred income taxes		$ 26,601
Income taxes payable		880,271

[To record income taxes for 2002; see Tables 5-7 for the computations of these amounts]

Illustration of a Common-Stock Nonleveraged ESOP

Melton, Inc. established a common-stock nonleveraged ESOP on January 1, 20X4. Melton is to contribute 15% of its pretax profit before ESOP-related charges as of the end of each of the next four years. The ESOP will use this contribution to purchase newly issued shares at the current market price (the year-end price, since contributions to the ESOP are made at year-end). Melton's stock price at December 31 of each year is as follows: 20X4, $52; 20X5, $49; 20X6, $54; 20X7, $63. With the exception of these new facts, all of the relevant facts are identical to the assumptions used in the previous illustration. The following table and journal entries illustrate the results of applying ASC 718-40.

Table 1—Summary of the Effects of Applying ASC 718-40

Year	*Compensation Expense*	*Dividends*	*Number of ESOP Shares Purchased*	*Cumulative ESOP Shares*
Notes:	(1)	(2)	(3)	(4)
20X4	$390,000	$ —	7,500	7,500
20X5	420,000	15,000	8,571	16,071
20X6	465,000	32,142	8,611	24,682
20X7	480,000	49,364	7,619	32,301

Notes:

(1) Compensation expense is equal to pretax profit before ESOP-related charges multiplied by 15%.

(2) Dividends are equal to cumulative ESOP shares, as of the beginning of the year, multiplied by the annual dividend per share, $2.

(3) The number of ESOP shares purchased is computed by dividing the yearly employer contribution (i.e., compensation expense) by the year-end market price of Melton's common stock. For example, in 20X4, 7,500 shares are purchased ($390,000/$52 per share).

(4) Cumulative ESOP shares are shares held at the beginning of the year plus shares purchased during the year.

Journal Entries

December 31, 20X4

Compensation expense	$390,000	
Common stock and paid-in capital		$390,000

[To record Melton's contribution, the sale of shares to the ESOP, and compensation expense]

Provision for income taxes	$795,600	
Income taxes payable		$795,600

[To record income taxes at 36% on taxable income of $2,210,000 ($2,600,000 of pre-ESOP income less $390,000 of compensation expense)]

December 31, 20X5

Compensation expense	$420,000	
Retained earnings	15,000	
Common stock and paid-in capital		$420,000
Dividends payable		15,000

[To record Melton's contribution, the sale of shares to the ESOP, declaration of dividends, and compensation expense]

Dividends payable	$15,000	
Cash		$15,000

[To record the payment of dividends]

Provision for income taxes	$856,800	
Income taxes payable		$856,800

[To record income taxes at 36% on taxable income of $2,380,000 ($2,800,000 of pre-ESOP income less $420,000 of compensation expense)]

December 31, 20X6

Compensation expense	$465,000	
Retained earnings	32,142	
Common stock and paid-in capital		$465,000
Dividends payable		32,142

[To record Melton's contribution, the sale of shares to the ESOP, declaration of dividends, and compensation expense]

Dividends payable	$32,142	
Cash		$32,142

[To record the payment of dividends]

Provision for income taxes	$948,600	
Income taxes payable		$948,600

[To record income taxes at 36% on taxable income of $2,635,000 ($3,100,000 of pre-ESOP income less $465,000 of compensation expense)]

December 31, 20X7

Compensation expense	$480,000	
Retained earnings	49,364	
Common stock and paid-in capital		$480,000
Dividends payable		49,364

[To record Melton's contribution, the sale of shares to the ESOP, declaration of dividends, and compensation expense]

Dividends payable	$49,364	
Cash		$49,364

[To record the payment of dividends]

Provision for income taxes	$979,200	
Income taxes payable		$979,200

[To record income taxes at 36% on taxable income of $2,720,000 ($3,200,000 of pre-ESOP income less $480,000 of compensation expense)]

ASC 718-50: EMPLOYEE SHARE PURCHASE PLANS

ASC 718-50-30-1 through 30-3, 35-1 through 35-2, 55-2 through 55-9, 55-22 through 55-33 Accounting under ASC 718-50 for Certain Employee Stock Purchase Plans with a Look-Back Option

BACKGROUND

ASC 718 states that the objective of the fair value method of accounting for stock-based compensation is to estimate the fair value of the equity instrument—based on the stock price and other measurement assumptions at the grant date—that is issued in exchange for employee services. This objective also applies to the fair value measurement of grants under a compensatory employee stock purchase plan (ESPP).

A *look-back option* is a feature that provides the employee a choice of purchasing stock at two or more times (e.g., an option to purchase stock at 85% of the stock price at the grant date or at a later exercise date). Section 423 of the Internal Revenue Code provides that the employee will not be immediately taxed on the difference between the fair value of the stock and a discounted purchase price if the following requirements are met:

- The option price is not less than 85% of the market price when the option is granted or when the option is exercised.
- The choice does not have a term in excess of 27 months.

The criteria for evaluating whether an ESPP qualifies for noncompensatory treatment are established in ASC 718-50-25-1; if it does, the employer is not required to recognize compensation expense. If an ESPP satisfies *all* of the following criteria, the discount from market price to the employee is not stock-based compensation and simply reduces the proceeds from issuing the shares of stock:

- The plan incorporates no option features.
- The discount from the market prices does not exceed the greater of (*a*) a per-share discount that would be reasonable in an offer of stock to stockholders or others or (*b*) the per-share amount of stock issuance costs avoided by not having to raise a significant amount of capital by a public offering of the stock.
- Substantially all full-time employees meeting limited employment qualifications may participate on an equitable basis.

A look-back option is one feature that causes an ESPP to be considered compensatory. In reaching this conclusion, the FASB observed that a look-back option can have substantial value, because it enables the employee to purchase the stock for an amount that *could be* significantly less than the fair value at the date of purchase. A look-back option is not an essential element of a plan aimed at promoting broad employee stock ownership; a purchase discount also provides incentive for participation. Based on these observations, the FASB concluded that broad-based plans that contain look-back options cannot be treated as noncompensatory.

ACCOUNTING GUIDANCE

The following guidance responds to three questions concerning the different types of ESPP plans with look-back options described above. The following is a recap of the illustration in ASC 718-50-55-10 through 55-20 and the FASB's responses to the questions.

Illustration of Look-Back Option without Dividends

On January 1, 2004, Company S offered employees the opportunity to purchase its stock at either 85% of the current price ($50) or 85% of the price at the end of the year when the options expire. For purposes of valuing the option, expected volatility is assumed to be .30, and the risk-free interest rate for the next 12 months is 6.8%.

The value of this look-back option can be estimated at the grant date by combining its two components, as follows:

1. 15% of a share of nonvested stock
2. 85% of a 1-year call option held with an exercise price of $50

The option holder will receive value of at least 15% of a share of stock upon exercise, regardless of the stock price after the grant date. In this example, the stock price is $50 when the grant is made. If the price falls to $40 and the option is exercised at that price, the holder pays $34 ($40 × .85) and receives value of $6, which is 15% of the market price at the date of exercise. On the other hand, if the market price increases to $60, the holder can purchase stock at only $42.50 ($50 × .85) and receive value of $17.50 ($60 – $42.50).

Using an option-pricing model to value the look-back option under the stated assumptions (e.g., .30 expected volatility and 6.8% risk-free interest rate) results in the following:

15% of a share of nonvested stock ($50 × .15)	$7.50
Call on 85% of a share of stock with an exercise price of $50 ($7.56 × .85)	6.43
Total grant date value	$13.93

This calculation is based on the idea that the value of the look-back option consists of two components: (1) the 15% reduction from a $50 market value ($7.50) and (2) 85% of a call option with an exercise price of $50. The $7.56 figure in the second component is the value of the call option as computed by an option-pricing model.

Illustration of Look-Back Option with Dividends

This example assumes the same facts as in the previous case, except that Company S pays a 2.5% annual dividend quarterly (i.e., .625% per quarter). Calculation of the value of the look-back option is similar to the calculation in the previous illustration, except that the components are *reduced to reflect the dividends that the holder of the option does not receive* during the term of the option. The value of the two components of the option is calculated as follows:

15% of a share of nonvested stock ($50 × .15 × .9754)	$7.32
Call on 85% of a share of stock, $50 exercise price, 2.5% dividend yield ($6.78 × .85)	5.76
Total grant date value	$13.08

The first component is the minimum benefit to the holder, regardless of the price of the stock at the exercise date. The second component is the additional benefit to the holder if the stock price exceeds $50 at the exercise date. The $6.78 in the second component is the value of the call option as computed by an option-pricing model.

Questions and Answers

Question 1: ASC 718-50-55-10 through 55-20 provides the only specific guidance on measuring the compensation cost associated with an award under a compensatory ESPP with a look-back option. Is the fair value measurement technique described in that illustration applicable to all types of ESPPs with a look-back option?

Answer: No. The measurement approach in ASC 718-50-55-10 through 55-20 was intended to illustrate how the fair value of an award under a basic type of ESPP with a look-back option could be determined at the grant date by focusing on the substance of the arrangement and valuing each feature of the award separately. The fundamental components of a look-back option may differ from plan to plan, affecting the individual calculations. For example, it is assumed in the illustration that the number of shares that may be purchased is fixed at the grant date based on the grant date stock price and the amount the employee elects to have withheld (Type A plan). Some plans (e.g., Type B plans) do not fix the number of shares that the employee is permitted to purchase, requiring modification to the determination of fair value.

Question 2: How should measurement approach in ASC 718-50-55-10 through 55-20 be modified to determine the fair value of an ESPP award plan with a Type B look-back option (i.e., the plan does *not* fix the number of shares that an employee is permitted to purchase)?

Answer: In a Type A plan, the number of shares an employee is permitted to purchase is limited to the number based on the price of the stock at the origin of the agreement. For example, if an employee had $4,250 withheld from salary, and the plan permitted him or her to purchase shares at 85% of the $50 current stock price, he or she could purchase 100 shares, as follows:

$ 4,250 / (85% × $50) = 100 shares

In a Type B plan, the employee is permitted to purchase as many shares as the $4,250 withheld will permit. If, for example, the market price falls to $30, the employee is not limited to purchasing 100 shares and may actually purchase 167 shares, determined as follows:

$ 4,250 / (85% × $30) = 167 shares

Following the approach in ASC 718-50-55-10 through 55-20 of combining the components of the plan, and using the same underlying assumptions as in that illustration, the value of the Type B option is calculated at the grant date as follows:

15% of a share of nonvested stock ($50 × 15%)	$7.50
One-year call on 85% of a share of stock, exercise price of $50 ($7.56 × 85%)	6.43
One-year put on 15% of a share of stock, exercise price of $50 ($4.27 × 15%)	.64
	$14.57

This Illustration is the same as that presented earlier (the "no dividend" case) with the addition of a third component: a one-year put option on the employer's stock, valued with a standard option-pricing model. The same assumptions are applied. This has the effect of adding $.64 to the value of the option, raising the total to $14.57 ($7.50 + $6.43 + $.64).

Total compensation is measured at the grant date based on the number of shares that can be purchased using the total withholdings and the grant date market price, rather than on the potentially greater number of shares that may be purchased if the market price falls. For example, in the above Illustration, an employee who had $1,275 withheld could purchase 30 shares based on the grant date price [$1,275/($50 × .85)], and total compensation expense recognized for that employee would be $437 (30 × $14.57).

Question 3: The characteristics of Type A and Type B plans are incorporated into other types of ESPP plans with a look-back option. The measurement approach in ASC 718-50-55-10 through 55-20 for a Type A plan, as modified by Question 2 for a Type B plan, forms the basis for determining the fair value of the award under the other types of ESPP with a look-back option. What additional modifications are necessary to determine the fair value of awards under other types of ESPPs?

Answer: The fair value of an award under an ESPP plan with a look-back option with multiple purchase periods (Type C plan) should be determined in the same manner as an award under a graded vesting stock option plan. Such awards under a two-year plan with purchase periods at the end of each year would be valued as having two separate options, both starting with the initial grant date and having different lives (12 and 24 months, respectively).

This same approach should be used to value ESPP awards with multiple purchase periods that incorporate reset or rollover mechanisms (Type D and Type E plans). At the date the reset or rollover mechanism becomes effective, the terms of the award have been modified. This is, in substance, an exchange of the original award for a new award with different terms. Similarly, an election by an employee to increase withholdings (Types F, G, and H plans) is a modification of the terms of the award, which is similar to an exchange of the original award for a new award with different terms.

The guidance in ASC 718-50 indicates that a modification of the terms of an award that makes it more valuable should be treated as an exchange of the original award for a new award. In substance, the employer repurchases the original instrument by issuing a new instrument of greater value and incurs additional compensation cost for that incremental value.

A Type I plan permits an employee to increase withholdings retroactively. An employee may elect not to participate, or to participate at a minimal level, until just before the exercise date. This makes it difficult to determine when there is a mutual understanding of the terms of the award and, thus, when the grant date actually occurs. In this situation, the later date when the employee remits an amount to the company should be considered the grant date for purposes of valuing the option.

Changes in compensation resulting from salary increases, commissions, or bonus payments are not plan modifications and do not represent changes in the terms of the plan. The only incremental compensation cost is that which results from the additional shares that may be purchased with the additional amounts withheld.

ASC 718-740: INCOME TAXES

ASC 718-740-45-8 Accounting for Income Tax Benefits of Dividends on Share-Based Payment Awards

BACKGROUND

A share-based payment arrangement may include a "dividend protection" provision under which employees may be entitled to receive, for example, (*a*) dividends or dividend equivalents on *nonvested* equity shares and *nonvested* equity share units during the vesting period, (*b*) payments equal to dividends on equity shares underlying an outstanding option, or (*c*) exercise price reductions of share options based on dividends paid on the underlying equity shares while an option is outstanding.

Under the guidance in ASC 718, employers charge the payment of dividends or dividend equivalents to employees on nonvested shares to retained earnings, but in some cases, those amounts are treated as deductible compensation cost for income tax purposes. The FASB staff has received questions regarding the accounting for income tax benefits related to the dividend payments discussed above.

SCOPE

The guidance in this Issue applies to share-based payment arrangements with dividend protection features under which employees have a right receive: (1) dividends or dividend equivalents during the vesting period on awards of nonvested shares and nonvested share units, all of which are classified as equity; or (2) equity share options until the awards are exercised. Some entities have been treating those dividends, nonvested equity units, and outstanding equity share options as deductible compensation for income tax purposes while charging those dividends to retained earnings under the provisions in ASC 718, Share-Based Payment (Revised December 2004), thus providing employers with an income tax deduction.

ACCOUNTING ISSUE

How should an entity recognize an income tax benefit it receives on dividends or dividend equivalents that are: (1) paid to employees that hold nonvested shares, nonvested share units, or outstanding share options, all of which are classified as equity; and (2) charged to retained earnings under the provisions of ASC 718?

ACCOUNTING GUIDANCE

An income tax benefit from dividends or dividend equivalents that have been charged to retained earnings and paid to employees for nonvested equity shares, nonvested equity share units, and outstanding equity share options that are classified as equity should be recognized as income tax expense or benefit in the income statement.

ISSUES GRANDFATHERED UNDER THE CODIFICATION

NOTE: The guidance in ASC 718-40 superseded the guidance in SOP 76-3 and nullified the consensus positions in that Issue. However, under the transition provisions of ASC 718-40, employers that elect *not* to apply the guidance in ASC

718-40 to shares purchased before December 31, 1992, can continue to apply the provisions of SOP 76-3 and the applicable guidance in the EITF Issues that follow to those shares.

EMPLOYEE STOCK OWNERSHIP PLANS

SOP 76-3 Accounting Practices for Certain Employee Stock Ownership Plans

BACKGROUND

An employee stock ownership plan (ESOP) is an employee benefit plan sponsored under the provisions of the Employee Retirement Income Security Act (ERISA) of 1974. An ESOP can be either a qualified stock bonus plan or a combination of a qualified stock bonus plan and a money purchase pension plan. In both cases, the ESOP is expected to invest primarily in "qualifying employer securities."

At the time SOP 76-3 was issued, there were two essential differences between an ESOP and other qualified stock bonus plans. First, the ESOP generally is permitted to borrow money for the purpose of purchasing the employer's stock. Second, the allowable investment tax credit percentage that the employer can claim may increase by as much as 1.5% if that amount is contributed to the ESOP.

In borrowing money for the purpose of purchasing the employer's stock, the ESOP typically borrows from a bank or another commercial lender. The employer shares purchased can be outstanding shares, treasury shares, or newly issued shares. The ESOP holds these shares until they are distributed to employees. The shares may be allocated to individual employees even though the actual shares may not be distributed until a later date. In some cases, the ESOP issues notes to existing shareholders in exchange for their stock.

The employer typically collateralizes the ESOP debt by pledging the stock (purchased from the debt proceeds), and by either guaranteeing or committing to make ESOP contributions sufficient to service the related debt. The employer's annual contribution to the ESOP is tax-deductible (subject to certain limitations). The employer's annual contribution is used to fund (1) amortization of the debt principal, (2) interest payments on the debt, (3) working capital needs, and (4) other expenses. If the employer's annual ESOP contribution exceeds items 1 through 4, the excess can be used to purchase additional employer securities.

SOP 76-3 was issued because several accounting questions arose relating to ESOPs that borrowed money from a bank or other lender to acquire shares, or that issued notes directly to existing shareholders in exchange for their shares.

ACCOUNTING GUIDANCE

The provisions of SOP 76-3 were largely superseded by SOP 93-6 (Employers' Accounting for Employee Stock Ownership Plans). However, shares acquired by an ESOP before December 31, 1992, or shares acquired after that date that were committed to be released before the beginning of the year in which SOP 93-6 was adopted, can continue to be accounted for under the guidance in SOP 76-3.

If the employer has either guaranteed or committed to funding the ESOP in a manner sufficient to cover debt service payments, the related debt (i.e., obligation of the ESOP) is to be recorded as a liability on the employer's balance sheet. AcSEC concluded that the employer's guarantee or commitment was in substance the assumption of the ESOP's debt; as such, the related debt amount should be shown as a liability in the employer's financial statements.

The offsetting debit that the employer records upon recognizing a liability for the ESOP's debt is to shareholders' equity. The employer does not recognize the assets of the ESOP; employees of the ESOP—not the employer—own these assets.

As the ESOP makes payments on its debt, the employer is to reduce its liability. As the employer reduces its liability, the offsetting credit is to shareholders' equity. Symmetry should exist between the liability for ESOP-related debt and the corresponding entry to shareholders' equity.

The annual ESOP contribution (or contribution commitment) that the employer makes is recognized as an expense. This requirement applies to all ESOPs—whether the ESOP has borrowed money from a bank or another lender or has issued a note directly to existing shareholders for their shares. The employer's contribution or contribution commitment is recognized in the year it was made, regardless of whether such contribution is concurrently used to reduce the ESOP's debt.

The expense is to be divided between interest expense and compensation expense, and the employer should disclose the interest rate and terms of the ESOP's debt in its financial statements (since SOP 76-3 essentially views such debt as that of the employer).

The employer should treat all shares held by the ESOP as outstanding for the purpose of calculating the employer's EPS (whether or not the shares have been allocated to individual employees). The employer should charge all dividends pertaining to shares held by the ESOP to retained earnings.

If the employer receives any additional investment tax credit (ITC) as a result of an ESOP contribution, such incremental ITC is to be recorded as a reduction in income tax expense in the year that the applicable ESOP contribution is made. This accounting treatment applies, regardless of the method generally utilized by the employer in accounting for the ITC (flow-through or deferral) for property acquisitions.

EITF Issue 89-8 Expense Recognition for Employee Stock Ownership Plans

BACKGROUND

An employer may establish a leveraged employee stock ownership plan (ESOP) to benefit its employees by granting them shares of its stock. The employer also realizes tax benefits on its contributions to the ESOP.

A leveraged ESOP is established by forming a trust that borrows money to acquire shares of the employer's stock, which are restricted to common stock and convertible preferred stock. Usually, the ESOP borrows from a financial institution and pledges the stock as security. Alternatively, the employer may borrow from a financial institution, and, in turn, lend the money to the trust to purchase the employer's stock. When the employer recognizes the ESOP debt as a liability, an equivalent amount is recognized as a debit in shareholders' equity, similar to unearned compensation, as discussed in paragraph 14 of APB-25. In both cases, the debt is serviced with proceeds from employer contributions to the ESOP and dividends on unallocated shares of the employer's stock. As payments are made on the debt, shares are released and allocated to employees' individual accounts, and the debit in shareholders' equity is reduced. The amount of shares to be released and allocated to employees is based on a percentage of the total number of shares the ESOP purchased. The percentage may be determined in one of two ways:

1. The ratio of principal and interest paid in the current period to the total principal and interest to be paid.
2. The ratio of principal paid in the current period to the total debt principal.

SOP 76-3 was the primary source of guidance when this Issue was discussed. It viewed a leveraged ESOP as a deferred compensation plan and provided that annual expense be based on the amount contributed or committed to be contributed for the year. Because the structure of ESOPs had changed since the issuance of the SOP in 1976, the guidance on expense recognition needed to be updated. Specifically, because loan repayment terms had changed, loan repayments on ESOPs were not always level over the term of the loan, with some repayment schedules tied to an employer's expected cash flow or compensation costs. Other repayment schedules required only interest payments in early years, with principal payments delayed for a number of years, or otherwise had nonlevel repayment terms. Some debt agreements permitted voluntary prepayments or required prepayments if the employer's cash flow exceeded certain amounts. Some questioned whether such changes in repayment terms should affect an employer's expense recognition for contributions to a plan.

ACCOUNTING ISSUE

How should an employer recognize expense for contributions to an ESOP?

EITF CONSENSUS

1. Expense recognition for contributions to an ESOP should be as follows for shares acquired after December 14, 1989:
   a. Recognize contributions to an ESOP as expense in accordance with the shares-allocated method, discussed below, for shares with level and nonlevel repayment terms.
   b. Under the shares-allocated method, interest expense is recognized each period as incurred. Expense related to the principal portion (the compensation element) is recognized based on the cost of shares allocated for the period.
   c. It is computed as follows:

$$\frac{\text{Shares allocated for the period}}{\text{Total shares purchased}} \times \text{Original principal}$$

+ Interest incurred for the period = Expense related to the principal

d. Reduce compensation expense recognized each period by dividends used to service the ESOP debt.

2. Expense recognition for contributions to an existing ESOP for shares acquired before December 15, 1989, should be as follows:
   a. The current method may continue to be used if cumulative expense, before dividends are deducted, is at least equal to 80% of cumulative expense under the shares-allocated method before dividends are deducted.
   b. Recognize an additional amount in the current period if cumulative expense under the current method is less than 80% of cumulative expense under the shares-allocated method (total cumulative expense should equal 80% of expense under the shares-allocated method).
   c. Expense recognition should not be reduced if the cumulative amount under the current method exceeds 80% of the amount under the shares-allocated method.
3. Report the effect of initial application of this consensus as a cumulative effect of a change in accounting principle, in accordance with APB-20.
4. Adjust the debit in shareholders' equity related to the ESOP loan for the difference between the periodic expense and cash contributions, if any, in each period.

SEC OBSERVER COMMENT

The SEC Observer stated that SEC registrants should fully disclose their method of accounting for ESOPs in accordance with the pension plan disclosure requirements in paragraph 65 of FAS-87. Accordingly, the following information should be disclosed:

- A description of the plan, including employee groups covered
- The basis for determining contributions
- The nature and effect of significant matters affecting comparability of information for all periods presented
- The cost of contributions to the ESOP recognized during the period

In addition, the SEC staff expects the following information to be disclosed for each period presented:

- Actual interest incurred on ESOP debt
- Amount contributed to the ESOP
- Amount of dividends paid by the ESOP on shares held by the ESOP for ESOP debt service

The SEC Observer suggested that registrants consider the need to discuss the potential effect of leveraged ESOPs in the results of operations and liquidity sections of "Management's Discussion and Analysis of Financial Condition and Results of Operations," as required by Item 303 of Regulation S-K. An example is a large scheduled increase in contributions to an ESOP.

At a meeting subsequent to the issuance of SOP 93-6, the SEC Observer stated that the above disclosure requirements should continue to be made by registrants for shares grandfathered from the accounting provisions of that SOP.

DISCUSSION

The Task Force believed that the shares-allocated method is consistent with the guidance in paragraph 9 of SOP 76-3, which required the employer's expense to be the amount contributed or committed to be contributed to the ESOP for the year. (The employer is committed to the extent that interest is accrued and shares are allocated.) Task Force members noted that if shares are allocated based on principal, expense recognition is the same whether the cash payments or shares-allocated methods are used.

The Task Force noted that sometimes the debt payments, the allocation of related shares to participants, and the period over which participants earned those shares may not occur in the same reporting period. If this is the case, the employer may have to accrue or defer compensation expense recognition. The cost of shares should be recognized in the period in which they were earned, regardless of whether debt payments were made in that period. However, expense recognition for prepaid debt should not be deferred for more than one period. Accruals and deferrals should be consistent. Interest should be charged as incurred.

EITF Issue 89-12 Earnings-per-Share Issues Related to Convertible Preferred Stock Held by an Employee Stock Ownership Plan

BACKGROUND

An employer sponsoring an ESOP issues high-yield convertible preferred stock to the ESOP, which finances that purchase with debt. The ESOP repays the debt by using the dividends from the convertible preferred stock and the employer's contributions. In accordance with the guidance in SOP 76-3, the employer charges such dividends to retained earnings.

The employer may redeem the convertible preferred stock in common stock, cash, or a combination of both at a redemption price that equal's the stock's initial value. Each share may be converted into a fixed number of shares of common stock. The employer also may guarantee ESOP participants that on retirement or termination they will receive at least the redemption price in common stock, cash, or a combination of both.

ACCOUNTING ISSUES

The EITF discussed the following issues related to the calculation of EPS under the if-converted method:

1. Should convertible preferred shares issued to an ESOP be considered common stock equivalents?
2. Should net income be reduced by the additional ESOP contribution that would be necessary to meet the debt service requirement if the preferred stock is assumed to be converted, thus eliminating the availability of dividends on the convertible preferred stock?
3. If the employer guarantees that participants will receive at least the redemption price of the preferred stock on retirement or termination, should the number of shares assumed to be outstanding be increased, and if so, to what extent, if the market price of the underlying common stock is less than the redemption price of the preferred stock?
4. What would be the effect on the answer in Issue 3 if the redemption price guarantee can be paid in cash?

EITF CONSENSUS

The EITF reached the following consensus positions, which apply regardless of how the convertible stock is classified in the employer's balance sheet. (Publicly held companies must classify convertible shares as temporary equity. In addition, the if-converted method should not be applied if it is antidilutive.)

1. FAS-128 nullified the consensus in Issue 1.
2. If the preferred stock is assumed to be converted, dividends on those shares would no longer be paid and the ESOP would receive only dividends on the common stock into which the shares were converted. As a result, the employer would have to make an additional contribution to the ESOP for debt service. The employer should therefore adjust net income for the difference between the current dividends on the convertible preferred stock and the dividends on the common stock considered outstanding under the if-converted method. EITF members noted that under the provisions of some employee benefit plans, an employer may be required to make other nondiscretionary adjustments related to the conversion of preferred stock and the additional ESOP contribution.
3. The calculation of EPS in paragraph 63 of APB-15 and FAS-128, which requires using the market price at the end of the reporting period to determine the number of shares to be issued, applies if the market price of the underlying common stock is less than the guaranteed value of the convertible stock. The number of common shares to be used in calculating EPS under the if-converted method is the sum of the following: for unallocated shares—the number of common shares based on the stated conversion, *plus* for allocated shares—the number of common shares equivalent to the redemption value, but not less than the number of shares at the stated conversion rate for convertible preferred stock allocated as of the reporting date. As required in paragraph 63 APB 15, EPS for prior periods should be restated if the number of shares issued or contingently issuable changes as a result of changes in the market price.
4. An employer that is required or has the ability and intent to satisfy a guarantee in cash should use the stated conversion rate for all shares in calculating EPS; the employer need not assume the issuance of additional shares for the guarantee feature.

> *OBSERVATION:* The disclosure requirements in FIN-45 (Guarantor's Accounting and Disclosure Requirements for Guarantees, Including Indirect Guarantees of Indebtedness to Others) apply to guarantees of the value of the preferred stock by employers that continue to apply the guidance in SOP 76-3 to shares acquired before January 1, 1993. The other provisions of FIN-45 do *not* affect the consensuses in this Issue.

SEC OBSERVER COMMENT

The SEC Observer noted that registrants should not analogize these consensus positions to other situations involving the calculation of EPS. In addition, registrants should apply the consensus positions retroactively to EPS calculations for all periods presented in SEC filings subsequent to the consensus. Although the SEC staff would accept the calculations required in the consensus, the SEC staff will deal with unusual situations based on the specific case.

FASB STAFF COMMENT

The FASB staff stated that consensus positions 2, 3, and 4 apply to basic (referred to as "primary" when this Issue was discussed) and diluted EPS calculations if the convertible preferred stock is a common stock equivalent.

DISCUSSION

Issue 2 In computing diluted EPS under the provisions of APB-15 (and FAS-128) a convertible security is assumed to have been converted at the beginning of the period, thus requiring appropriate adjustments to net income. In the case of convertible preferred stock held by an ESOP, if it is assumed that the stock has been converted to common stock, the ESOP will receive dividends on the common stock, but dividends from preferred shares would no longer be available to the ESOP for debt service. Consequently, the employer's contribution for debt service would increase to compensate for a potential deficiency resulting from the difference between dividends on the preferred stock and on the common stock. To illustrate, assume that an ESOP has an annual debt service requirement of $2,000,000, and dividends on the employer's preferred stock held by the ESOP are $1,000,000. The employer would thus contribute $1,000,000 for debt service. However, if it is assumed that (*a*) the ESOP converts the preferred stock, (*b*) dividends from the common stock are only $600,000, and (*c*) there is no change in the debt service requirement, the employer would have to increase the debt service contribution by $400,000 to make up the deficiency.

The EITF's consensus was based on the view that regardless of the source of the proceeds (i.e., whether from dividends on the preferred stock or from an additional employer contribution), the ESOP made debt service payments during the year. Because dividends on the preferred stock would not have been available during the year—as a result of the assumed conversion of the preferred stock at the beginning of the year—it is assumed that the deficiency between the higher dividends on the preferred stock and the dividends on the common stock into which it is converted is made up by an additional employer contribution, which is considered a nondiscretionary adjustment to net income in accordance with paragraph 51 of APB-15.

Issue 3 Sometimes an ESOP that invests in the employer's convertible securities guarantees that the value the employee would receive at the time of conversion would not be less than a specified amount per share of preferred stock. To illustrate, assume the following: A preferred stock that is convertible into common stock on a one-for-one basis has a guarantee that the employee would receive at least $12 for each share of preferred stock at the date of conversion. If an employee converts 100 shares of preferred stock when the fair value of the common stock is more than $12 per share, the employee would receive 100 shares of common stock. If, however, the common stock's fair value is less than the $12 per share guaranteed minimum value, the employee would receive additional shares or cash so that the total value received is equal to the guaranteed amount. For example, at $10 per share, the employee would receive 120 shares of common stock, 100 shares of common stock plus $200, or a combination of common stock and cash worth $1,200.

The following illustrates the EITF's consensus on Issue 3. An ESOP holds 100,000 shares of convertible preferred stock, of which 60,000 shares are allocated to participants and 40,000 shares are unallocated. One share of preferred stock is convertible into two shares of common stock, and participants are guaranteed a market value of common stock equivalent to $10 per preferred share. On December 31, 1989, the market price per share of common stock is $4. The number of shares to be included in diluted EPS is calculated as follows:

Unallocated shares:		
40,000 shares × 2		80,000
Allocated shares:		
Guaranteed value (60,000 shares × $10)	$600,000	
Market price per share	$ 4	
Shares required to satisfy guarantee ($600,000/$4)	150,000	
Shares based on conversion rate (60,000 shares × 2)	120,000	
Shares used:		150,000
		230,000

Issue 4 The consensus reached by the Task Force analogized to the guidance in paragraph 6 of FIN-31, which dealt with whether stock appreciation rights that are payable in stock or in cash should be considered common stock equivalents. Under the Interpretation, the decision was made based on "the terms most likely to be elected based on the facts available each period." FAS-128 carried forward that guidance but provides that it should be presumed that settlement will be in common stock. The potential common shares would, therefore, be included in diluted EPS. The presumption that the rights will be paid in stock may be overcome based on past experience and on the company's stated policy that the rights will be paid partially or wholly in cash. Similarly, this consensus depends on the requirement or the employer's ability and expressed intent to satisfy the guarantee in cash.

EITF Issue 92-3 Earnings-per-Share Treatment of Tax Benefits for Dividends on Unallocated Stock Held by an Employee Stock Ownership Plan

BACKGROUND

Under current federal income tax laws, an employer that sponsors an employee stock ownership plan (ESOP) is entitled to deduct dividends on stock held by the ESOP in computing the employer's corporate taxable income. When this Issue was discussed in March 1992, ASC 740 had just been issued but its application was not required until 1993. Consequently, companies were accounting for income taxes based on earlier guidance, or had early adopted the guidance in ASC 740. Under the guidance in ASC 740-20-45-3, tax benefits related to dividends on unallocated ESOP shares must be credited directly to retained earnings.

ACCOUNTING ISSUES

- In computing EPS, should entities applying the provisions of FAS-109 adjust net income for tax benefits related to dividends on unallocated common stock held by an ESOP?
- Should the same treatment apply to convertible preferred stock ESOPs when computing EPS under the if-converted method?

EITF CONSENSUS

- In computing EPS, companies applying the guidance in ASC 740 should not adjust net income for tax benefits related to dividends on unallocated common stock held by an ESOP, because under the guidance in ASC 740, tax benefits on such shares must be charged to retained earnings.
- The same treatment applies to convertible preferred stock ESOPs in computing EPS under the if-converted method.

DISCUSSION

The Task Force's consensus positions on this Issue were based on the view that the amount used in EPS computations should be consistent with the calculation of net income based on the provisions of ASC 740.

This consensus was nullified by the guidance in ASC 718-40-05-2 through 05-4, 15-2 through 15-4, 25-2 through 25-6, 25-9 through 25-17, 25-19 through 25-21, 30-1 through 30-5, 35-1, 40-2 through 40-7, 45-2 through 45-9, 50-1, 55-1 through 55-38 for shares acquired by an ESOP *after* December 31, 1992.

CHAPTER 44

ASC 720—OTHER EXPENSES

CONTENTS

PART I: GENERAL GUIDANCE

ASC 720-25: CONTRIBUTIONS MADE

OVERVIEW

The guidance in ASC 720-25 applies to contributions of cash and other assets, including unconditional promises to give made by resource providers (ASC 720-25-15-2). The guidance in ASC 720-25 does not apply to the following transactions and activities specified in ASC 958-605-15-6: (1) exchange transactions where each party transfers assets and other consideration of equal value, (2) transfers where the entity is an agent, trustee, or intermediary rather than a donor or donee, (3) tax exemptions, incentives, or abatements, (4) asset transfers from a government to a business, and (5) transfers of assets that are part of an existing exchange transaction between a recipient and an identified customer (ASC 720-25-15-3).

A contribution made to an entity shall be recorded at fair value, whether the contribution is of assets or is the settlement or cancellation of a liability (ASC 720-25-30-1). A gain or loss is recognized if the fair value of the asset contributed differs from its recorded value (ASC 720-25-25-2). If the unconditional promise to give is expected to be paid within one year, it can be recorded at net settlement value (ASC 720-25-30-2).

A contribution is recognized as an expense in the period it is made. If the contribution is an asset, assets are decreased; if the contribution is an unconditional promise to give, a liability is increased (ASC 720-25-25-1).

ASC 720-30: REAL AND PERSONAL PROPERTY TAXES

OVERVIEW

Generally, the basis for recognizing expense for property taxes is monthly accrual on the taxpayers' books over the fiscal period of the taxing authority for which the taxes are levied. At the end of the accounting period, the financial statements will show the appropriate accrued or prepaid amount.

BACKGROUND

FASB Concepts Statements (CONs) constitute the FASB's conceptual framework. In CON-6 (Elements of Financial Statements), *liabilities* are defined as probable future sacrifices of economic benefits arising from present obligations of a particular entity to transfer assets or provide services to other entities in the future as a result of past transactions or events. A liability has three essential characteristics:

- It embodies a present duty or responsibility to one or more other entities that entails settlement by probable future transfer of assets at a specified or determinable date, on occurrence of a specific event, or on demand.
- The duty or responsibility obligates a particular entity, leaving it little or no discretion to avoid the future sacrifice.
- The transaction or other event obligating the entity has already happened.

Unlike excise tax, income tax, and Social Security tax, which are directly related to particular business events, real and personal property taxes are based on an assessed valuation of property as of a given date, as determined by law. For this reason, the legal liability for such taxes generally is considered to accrue when a specific event occurs, rather than over a period of time. Following are several dates that have been suggested as the point in time in which property taxes legally accrue (ASC 720-30-25-1):

- Assessment date
- Beginning of the taxing authority's fiscal year
- End of the taxing authority's fiscal year
- Date on which the tax becomes a lien on the property
- Date the tax is levied
- Date(s) the tax is payable
- Date the tax becomes delinquent
- Tax period appearing on a tax bill

The date most widely accepted as obligating the entity is the date of assessment of the taxes by the appropriate taxing authority.

ACCOUNTING AND REPORTING STANDARDS

Although many states have different laws or precedents as to when the legal liability accrues for real and personal property taxes, the general rule is that it accrues on the date the taxes are assessed (ASC 720-30-25-1). The exact amount of tax may not be known on the assessment date, however, and a reasonable estimate must be made. The inability to determine the exact amount of real and personal property taxes is not an acceptable reason for not recognizing an existing tax liability (ASC 720-30-25-6).

In those cases in which the accrued amount is subject to a great deal of uncertainty, the liability should be described as estimated. Whether the amount of the accrued tax liability for real and personal property taxes is known or estimated, it should be reported as a current liability in the balance sheet (ASC 720-30-45-1).

A monthly accrual over the fiscal period of the taxing authority is considered the most acceptable basis for recording real and personal property taxes. This results in the appropriate accrual or prepayment at any closing date (ASC 720-30-25-7). An adjustment to the estimated tax liability of a prior year is made when the exact amount is determined. This adjustment is made in the income statement of the period in which the exact amount is determined, either as an adjustment to the current year's provision or as a separate item on the income statement.

In most circumstances, however, real and personal property taxes are considered an expense of doing business and are reported in the appropriate income statement (*a*) as an operating expense, (*b*) as a separate deduction from income, or (*c*) allocated to several expense accounts, such as manufacturing overhead and general and administrative expenses (ASC 720-30-45-3).

PRACTICE POINTER: In interim financial reports, estimate the end-of-period liability in order to estimate the expense for the year. Reflect adjustments to the amount of the estimate in the interim period during which the adjustment becomes known.

Property taxes on property held for resale to customers or under construction are typically capitalized.

PRACTICE NOTE: The promulgated U.S. GAAP do not describe the criteria for capitalizing or not capitalizing real estate taxes.

Illustration of Accounting and Reporting Standards for Property Taxes

On October 1, 20X5, the City assesses $12,000 of property taxes on Wilson, Inc., for the fiscal year, October 1, 20X5-September 30, 20X6. Wilson records the assessment as follows:

	Oct. 1, 20X5	
Deferred property taxes	12,000	
Property taxes payable		12,000

At December 31, 20X5, the end of Wilson's financial reporting year, Wilson adjusts the deferred property taxes account by recognizing three months of expense, as follows:

	Dec. 31, 20X5	
Property tax expense	3,000	
Deferred property taxes		3,000

At February 1, 20X6, Wilson pays the property taxes and makes the following entry:

	Feb. 1, 20X6	
Property taxes payable	12,000	
Cash		12,000

Throughout, or at the end of 20X6, the remaining nine months of property taxes are recognized as expense:

	Various dates, 20X6	
Property tax expense	9,000	
Deferred property taxes		9,000

PART II: INTERPRETIVE GUIDANCE

ASC 720-15: STARTUP COSTS

ASC 720-15-15-1 through 15-5, 25-1, 55-1, 55-3, 55-5, 55-7, 55-9, 55-10 Reporting on the Costs of Start-Up Activities

---

IMPORTANT NOTICE: The guidance in ASC 720-15-15-4 and 55-7 in this Issue will be amended as a result of the FASB's issuance of the ASU 2014-09, *Accounting for Revenue from Contracts with Customers*. For public business entities, its guidance became effective for annual financial reporting periods that began after December 15, 2017, and for nonpublic entities, it will be effective for annual financial reporting periods that begin after December 15, 2018.

BACKGROUND

"Reporting on the Costs of Start-Up Activities," was the second in a series of projects under which the AICPA's former Accounting Standards Executive Committee (AcSEC), now known as the Financial Reporting Executive Committee, considered how to report on costs of activities that are undertaken to create future economic benefits. The first project resulted in the issuance of the Statement of Position, "Reporting on Advertising Costs" (see Chapter 25, *ASC 340—Deferred Costs and Other Assets*).

Start-up activities are defined broadly as onetime activities related to all of the following:

- Opening a new facility
- Introducing a new product or service
- Conducting business in a new territory
- Conducting business with a new class of customer or beneficiary
- Initiating a new process in an existing facility
- Commencing some new operation
- Organizing a new entity (i.e., organization costs)

In practice, start-up costs are referred to in different ways, including preoperating costs and organization costs.

Certain costs are not considered start-up costs and should be accounted for in accordance with existing authoritative accounting pronouncements. They include the following:

- Costs of acquiring or constructing long-lived assets and getting them ready for their intended use
- Costs of acquiring or producing inventory
- Costs of acquiring intangible assets
- Costs related to internally developed assets
- Costs under the guidance in ASC 730
- Costs of fund-raising incurred by not-for-profit organizations
- Costs of raising capital
- Costs of advertising
- Learning or start-up costs incurred in connection with existing contracts with customers and in anticipation of follow-on contracts for the same goods or services (see Subtopic 340-40 on other assets and deferred costs)
- Costs incurred in connection with acquiring a contract with a customer (see Subtopic 340-40)

ACCOUNTING GUIDANCE

Costs of start-up activities, including organization costs should be expensed as incurred.

PRACTICE POINTER: This guidance continues a general trend (begun with ASC 730-10) of expensing costs with uncertain amounts, timing, or future cash flows. The costs associated with start-up activities, although clearly incurred with the expectation of generating future benefits, may not meet the definition of an asset or may not be measurable with sufficient accuracy because of the following:

- The expenditure fails to generate future benefits (i.e., no asset).
- The timing of any future benefits that might be generated is uncertain (i.e., measurement difficulties in valuing the resulting asset).
- The amount of such future benefits may not exceed the costs of generating those benefits (i.e., no asset).

The conclusion that costs of start-up activities should be expensed as incurred has been incorporated in the following guidance:

- ASC 605-35, Accounting for Performance of Construction-Type and Certain Production-Type Contracts;
- ASC 908-720-25-1 through 25-4, Accounting for Developmental and Preoperating Costs, Purchases and Exchanges of Take-off and Landing Slots, and Airframe Modifications;
- ASC 910, Construction Contractors;
- ASC 912, Audits of Federal Government Contractors;
- ASC 924, Audits of Casinos;

- ASC 946, Foreign Currency Accounting and Financial Statement Presentation for Investment Companies;
- ASC 946, Audits of Investment Companies.

ASC 720-20: INSURANCE COSTS

ASC 720-20-05-2 through 05-8, 15-4 through 15-6, 15-8, 25-2 through 25-12, 25-14, 30-2; 35-2 through 35-5, 35-8 through 35-10, 45-1, 50-1, 55-3 through 55-12, 55-14 through 55-20; ASC 450-30-60-4; ASC 954-720-25-4A Accounting for Claims-Made Insurance and Retroactive Insurance Contracts by the Insured Entity

BACKGROUND

Companies generally purchase claims-made policies to cover product, directors and officers (D&O), and malpractice liabilities. Such coverage insures an entity for claims reported during the policy's term, depending on the policy's retroactive date. Two categories of claims are covered: (*a*) retroactive claims for incidents that occurred *before* the policy's term and reported during its term or (*b*) *prospective* claims for incidents that occur and are reported during the policy's term.

Claims-made policies are generally renewed annually. If a company ceases its operations, it can purchase tail insurance, which insures the entity against claims made *after* the policy has terminated. By renewing its policy annually and purchasing tail insurance, if needed, a company can convert a claims-made policy to one based on occurrence so that the company is covered for any claims made against it. Because the date of occurrence is usually irrelevant in determining whether a claim is covered, a claims-made policy is usually the only form of insurance that covers exposures for which it is difficult to determine the date of occurrence and occurrences that may extend over long periods of time. Some companies that purchase such insurance are frequently unaware of outstanding unasserted claims of liabilities that do not meet the recognition criteria in ASC 450 or other generally accepted accounting principles (GAAP). Consequently, no liability has been recognized for such claims, including incurred but not reported (IBNR) claims. Other companies that purchase claims-made coverage may know about potential claims related to specific incidents, and may choose to specifically include those unasserted claims under the coverage or to exclude them.

The following guidance does *not* apply to reinsurance transactions.

ACCOUNTING ISSUES

1. How should an insured entity, such as a manufacturer, retailer, service company, or financial institution, including an insurance company that purchases insurance *not* related to its core insurance operations, account for a purchased retroactive insurance policy to cover a liability for a *past* event recognized in accordance with ASC 450, and does that transaction result in a gain being recognized?

2. Does a claims-made insurance policy correspond to a purchased retroactive insurance policy covered by the consensus in Issue 1?

3a. Should an insured entity recognize a liability at the balance sheet date for IBNR claims?

3b. If it is impossible to reasonably estimate the probable losses from IBNR claims and the number of incidents cannot be reasonably estimated, may a liability be accrued based on the estimated cost of purchasing tail coverage to insure the entity for events that occur during the period of the claims-made policy but that are *not* reported to the insurance carrier in that period?

4a. If an entity's fiscal year and the term of a prospective policy are the same, how should both of the following be accounted for: (*a*) the IBNR liability in subsequent periods in which the entity purchases another claims-made insurance policy that covers a portion of losses included in the IBNR liability, and (*b*) the premiums for the subsequent claims-made insurance policy?

4b. What is the accounting effect on a conclusion reached on Issue 4(a) if a prospective claims-made policy's term is *not* the same as the entity's fiscal year?

5. What disclosures should be made by companies insured under claims-made policies?

ACCOUNTING GUIDANCE

1. The guidance below applies only to retroactive insurance contracts that (*a*) do not legally extinguish an entity's liability, (*b*) meet the conditions in ASC 450 for indemnification against loss or liability, (*c*) indemnify the insured against loss or

liability for liabilities that were incurred as a result of a past event, for example, environmental remediation liabilities, and (*d*) are not reinsurance transactions.

Under the guidance in ASC 450-20-05-3, entities are required to determine whether an insurance contract results in a transfer of insurance risk. The guidance for insurance enterprises in ASC 944-20 may be useful in making that determination. Under that guidance, reinsurance contracts that do *not* transfer insurance risk should be accounted for as deposits.

Although ASC 944-20 applies only to insurance companies, purchased retroactive insurance contracts that indemnify an insured should be accounted for in a manner similar to that provided in ASC 944-20 for retroactive reinsurance contracts. The guidance in ASC 944-605-25-35 should be applied, if appropriate, based on the facts and circumstances of the specific transaction.

Amounts paid for retroactive insurance should be expensed immediately, and a receivable should be recognized at the same time for expected recoveries related to the underlying event. If a receivable exceeds the amount paid for the insurance, there is a deferred gain, which should be amortized using the interest method over the estimated period that the entity expects to recover substantially all amounts due under the terms of the insurance contract, provided the amount and timing of the insurance recoveries can be reasonably estimated. If not, a deferred gain should be amortized based on the proportion of actual recoveries to total estimated recoveries.

A gain should *not* be recognized and a related liability should *not* be derecognized immediately, because the liability has not been completely extinguished. Amounts receivable on an insurance policy should *not* be offset against a liability for a past insurable event, because those amounts do *not* meet the criteria in ASC 210-20-45-1 for offsetting. Legal and other costs covered under purchased insurance contracts should be accounted for in a consistent manner in the related asset and liability accounts. For example, if the costs are covered under the term of the insurance contracts and the entity's policy is to accrue such costs, they should also be included in the insurance receivable.

2. A claims-made insurance policy contains a retroactive provision if it provides coverage for specific, known claims that were reportable by an insured entity to the insurance carrier before the period of the policy, such as asserted claims, unasserted claims, or known previous events and circumstances, if any, that might result in a specific asserted or unasserted claim.

Retroactive and prospective provisions of such policies should be accounted for separately, if practicable. Otherwise, an entire policy should be accounted for as a retroactive contract in accordance with the guidance in ASC 944-605-25-35. Claims-made insurance policies that do *not* include retroactive provisions should be accounted for on a *prospective* basis based on the guidance in 4(a) and 4(b) below.

ASC 944-20-15-34B states that under a claims-made policy, an *insured event* is the act of *reporting* to an insurer a loss covered by a policy during the period stated in the policy. Therefore, *prospective* claims-made insurance policies cover only losses reported to an insurer during the term of a policy. A policy with a retroactive provision covers insured events that occurred or were reportable *before* the term of the policy and, therefore, covers claims for specific, known claims that were reportable before the policy's effective date. The fact that a liability for IBNR claims has been recognized is *not* a conclusive factor in determining whether a claims-made insurance policy does or does not contain a retroactive provision.

All the relevant facts and circumstances should be considered in determining whether a claims-made policy includes a retroactive provision. The following are indicators that a policy does *not* contain a retroactive provision (i.e., it does not cover previously reportable claims) and should be accounted for on a prospective basis, but no one indicator is conclusive:

a. The insured always purchases claims-made insurance policies for the type of risk that is insured, and tail coverage for prior periods and prior policies can be easily obtained at a reasonable cost compared to tail coverage that does not contain retroactive provisions offered to similar companies.

b. The claims-made policy covers unknown risks for a finite or limited time period, because (*a*) the claims are incurred during the policy's period and paid shortly after the end of the policy's period, (*b*) the policy covers a limited time period, (*c*) claims-made insurance is the most easily available coverage for this type of insurance risk, and (*d*) it is difficult to determine the date on which the type of risk covered under the policy will occur.

c. The claims-made insurance policy has clear indicators *not* subject to interpretation, negotiation, or manipulation, that a claim is covered under the policy, such as, a provision requiring an insured (*a*) to notify the insurance carrier of an asserted claim or that an incident occurred during the policy term, or (*b*) to represent that it was not aware of such an incident when the claims-made policy was purchased.

d. The claims-made policy's premium is *not* significantly higher than that for a policy that could be purchased by a similar entity with similar insurance risks that does not know of any circumstances or events that would result in claims, except for a typical number of claims incurred but not reported (IBNR).

e. The policy's premium may be based on estimates and predictions based on the insured's past experience, but not on estimates of settlements of specific, known events expected to be recovered under the policy.

f. The current year's premium does *not* significantly exceed the amount charged in previous years, except for increases in the amount or type of coverage.

g. The policy is purchased primarily to cover insurance risk, *not* as a financing arrangement. Such claims-made policies usually include (*a*) no adjustments based on experience, and (*b*) coverage of the final loss from a claim once it has been made, regardless of when the claim is settled.

h. If a claims-made insurance policy has a specified retroactive date before the relationship with the insurer begins, the period from the specified retroactive date to the date the claims-made relationship with the insurer begins is short or is covered by other insurance.

The guidance in 1 above is *not* intended to preclude prospective accounting for claims-made policies or portions of those policies that contain only prospective provisions even though the guidance applies in situations in which an insured entity uses the policy to finance known losses that occurred or were reportable *before* entering into the insurance contract. In addition, an insured entity that enters into multiple claims-made insurance contracts at the same time should consider whether to combine the insurance contracts so it can determine how to account for them. ASC 944-20-15-40 provides guidance on those matters.

3a. Under the guidance in ASC 450-20-25-2, entities that insure certain risks using a claims-made approach are required to recognize a liability for probable losses from IBNR claims and incidents if a loss is *probable* and *reasonably estimable*. ASC 450-20-55-10 through 55-17 provides implementation guidance for litigation, claims, and assessments.

3b. If an entity has not purchased tail insurance coverage, the estimated cost of such coverage is irrelevant in determining a loss accrual, because netting an insurance receivable against a claim liability is prohibited under the guidance in ASC 210-20-45-1. However, if an insured entity had a unilateral option to purchase tail coverage at a premium that does not exceed a specified fixed maximum amount, the entity could record a receivable for expected insurance recoveries (after considering deductibles and the policy's limits) for the insurable portion of the IBNR liability under the tail coverage. The cost of the expected premium for tail coverage should be recorded. Nevertheless, the need to determine whether an additional liability should be accrued as a result of policy limits and other factors is *not* eliminated by purchasing tail coverage.

4a. If an entity's fiscal year and the policy's year are the same, it should recognize the expense of the annual premium based on a combination of any of the following:

a. Accruing the IBNR liability;
b. Accruing expected increases in insurance recoveries;
c. Amortizing the insurance premium on a pro rata basis over the year.

A liability for unusual claims or incidents and related insurance recoveries should be recognized in the interim period in which they become known.

Under this approach, usual recurring losses are accounted for in the interim period as part of annual reporting, so that expected changes, if any, in the IBNR liability and related insurance recoveries not related to specific events can be spread over the whole year. But unusual material losses should be accounted for as separate items and recognized as they occur. It is assumed under this approach that the purchase of a one-year term claims-made insurance policy is a recurring event and that the premium will be paid on the first day of each policy year.

If an entity's fiscal year and the policy's term are the same, an entity's liability at year-end for IBNR is related to the entity's obligation for claims and incidents that were incurred *before* the year-end but that will be reportable after year-end. Policyholders that purchase claims-made policies consisting of *prospective* provisions should account for those policies as follows:

a. At the *beginning* of the fiscal year, a prepaid expense should be recognized for the total premium paid for the new policy.

b. At the *beginning* of the fiscal year, the IBNR liability as of the end of the fiscal year should be estimated by considering claims and incidents that occurred before the year-end but that will *not* be reportable until after the year-end. That amount should be roughly the IBNR liability at the beginning of the year plus adjustments to the IBNR liability for relevant historical patterns and possible adjustments, if any, due to new factors that have been identified, such as major changes in products, manufacturing processes, or risk management systems.

c. The estimated annual expense should be computed as the sum of (*a*) the premium paid for the claims-made policy, (*b*) the difference between the IBNR liability at the beginning of the year and the estimated amount at the end of the year, and (*c*) the difference between the beginning insurance recoverable related to the IBNR liability and estimated amount at the end of the year.

   That estimated amount should be recognized in interim periods using a method that best represents the manner in which the benefits of the insurance coverage are used up and the IBNR liability is incurred. Liabilities for specific claims incurred during the year not included in the estimated IBNR liability should be recognized as an expense in interim periods in which they are incurred. The method used should be selected by considering the relevant facts and circumstances and should be applied consistently.

d. The estimated year-end IBNR liability should be reviewed at interim reporting dates. Routine adjustments of the estimated liability should be recognized ratably in each of the remaining interim periods. But significant adjustments of the year-end IBNR liability should be recognized in an interim period in which events and circumstances indicate that unusual claims and incidents occurred *before* the end of that interim period but that will probably not be reported until after year-end and, therefore, will *not* be covered under the existing claims-made policy.

e. Unusual claims and incidents that have occurred *before* the end of an interim period but that will probably be reported *before* the year-end do *not* affect net income if they are covered under an existing policy. The asset under the insurance claim and the liability for the incident should be presented on the balance sheet.

f. An entity should evaluate recognized insurance recoverables, if any, that are related to IBNR liabilities or to specific incurred claims and adjust them, if necessary, based on changes in circumstances. See ASC 410-30-35-8 for guidance on the recognition of receivables for expected insurance recoveries

Prepaid insurance should *not* be offset against a recognized IBNR liability or a liability incurred as a result of a past insurable event unless the conditions in ASC 210-20 are met.

4b. If an entity's fiscal year and policy year are *not* the same, the accrual in interim periods should be based on the entity's estimated premium for the claims-made policy expected to be purchased later in that fiscal year. At year-end, the entity should recognize the following: (*a*) an IBNR *liability* for the obligation for claims and incidents that occurred *before* year-end but that will be reported *after* year-end, (*b*) an insurance recoverable for outstanding claims, if any, that are reimbursable under an existing claims-made policy, and (*c*) an *asset* for prepaid insurance premiums for coverage of claims and incidents that will occur *after* year-end, but will be reported *before* the current policy expires. Policyholders that purchase claims-made policies with terms that are *not* the same as the entity's fiscal year should account for those policies as follows:

a. The estimated premium for a new claims-made policy expected to be purchased during the fiscal year should be estimated at the *beginning* of the fiscal year. The portion of the future premium relating to coverage for claims or incidents that will occur *after* the end of the fiscal year but that will be reported *before* the new claims-made policy expires should also be estimated. That amount is the estimated prepaid asset at end of the fiscal year. An estimate of the future premium considers the effect of past claims and incidents that are expected to affect the amount of the premium and the effect of historical patterns and relevant new factors, such as a major change in products, manufacturing processes, or risk management systems.

b. At the *beginning* of the fiscal year, the IBNR liability as of the end of the fiscal year should be estimated by considering claims and incidents that will be incurred before the year-end but that will not be reportable until after the year-end. That amount should be roughly the IBNR liability at the beginning of the year plus adjustments for relevant historical patterns and possibly additional adjustments if the entity has identified new factors that would affect the IBNR liability, such as major changes in products, manufacturing processes, or risk management systems.

c. The estimated annual expense should be computed as the sum of (*a*) the balance of the premium cost of the claims-made policy that expires during the year, (*b*) the difference between the estimated premium cost for a new claims-made policy, (*c*) the difference between the beginning IBNR liability and the estimated IBNR liability at year-end, and (*d*) the difference between the beginning and estimated ending insurance receivable related to the IBNR liability. That estimated annual expense should be recognized ratably in interim periods using a method that best represents the manner in which the benefits of the insurance coverage are used up and the IBNR liability is incurred. That method should be appropriate based on the relevant facts and circumstances and should be applied consistently. Liabilities for specific claims incurred during the year that are not included in the estimated IBNR liability should be recognized as an expense in the period in which they are incurred.

d. The estimated year-end IBNR liability should be reviewed at interim reporting dates. Routine adjustments of the estimated liability, such as adjustments of the estimated future premium to reflect the actual cost should be recognized ratably in the remaining interim periods. But significant adjustments of the year-end IBNR liability should be recognized in an interim period in which events and circumstances indicate that unusual claims and incidents occurred before the end of that interim period but that will probably not be reportable until after the subsequent interim period.

e. An entity should evaluate assets related to insurance recoverables, if any, that are related to an IBNR liability or to specific incurred claims and should adjust them, if necessary, based on changes in circumstances. See ASC 410-30-35-8 through 35-11 for guidance related to the recognition of receivables for expected insurance recoveries.

f. Unusual claims and incidents incurred before the end of an interim period but that will probably be reported before the new claims-made policy expires do *not* affect net income if they will be covered by insurance. Both the asset under an insurance claim and the liability for an incident should be presented in the balance sheet.

5. If an entity changes from occurrence-based insurance to claims-made insurance or elects to significantly reduce or eliminate its insurance coverage, disclosure is required under the guidance ASC 450-20-50-3 if it is at least reasonably possible that a loss has been incurred. That paragraph also includes a discussion of disclosures for unasserted claims.

ASC 720-40: ELECTRONIC EQUIPMENT WASTE OBLIGATIONS

ASC 720-40-05-1 through 05-4, 15-1, 25-1 through 25-3, 35-1, 55-2 through 55-3; ASC 410-20-15-2 through 15-3, 55-23 through 55-30, 55-64 through 55-67 Accounting for Electronic Equipment Waste Obligations

BACKGROUND

The following guidance addresses the accounting for obligations related to the European Union's Directive 2002/96/EC on Waste Electrical and Electronic Equipment (the Directive). The Directive refers to two types of waste: (1) "new waste," the term used for products put on the market *after* August 13, 2005, and (2) "historical waste" equipment, the term used for all products that have been on the market on or *before* August 13, 2005. For the purpose of financing the cost of historical waste, the Directive differentiates between such waste from households and from commercial users.

The guidance discussed here applies only to *historical* waste. The guidance in ASC 720-40 applies to historical waste from private households, while the guidance in ASC 410-20 applies to historical waste from commercial users. Under the Directive the costs related to new waste will be assumed by the producers of such equipment. The following two questions are addressed under the guidance that follows: (1) should commercial users of electronic equipment or producers of such equipment that sell to private households and to commercial users recognize the Directive's effects on historical waste management under U.S. GAAP and (2) if so, when and how should those effects be accounted for?

ACCOUNTING GUIDANCE

Historical Waste Equipment Held by Commercial Users

The Directive provides that a commercial user retains a waste management obligation for historical waste until it replaces the equipment. At the time of replacement, that obligation may be transferred to the entity that has produced the newly acquired equipment, subject to the laws adopted by applicable EU-member countries. A commercial user that does not replace the equipment retains the obligation until the equipment's disposition. Under the Directive, however, EU-member countries have the option of requiring commercial users to retain an obligation for a portion of or all costs associated with historical waste even if the equipment is replaced. In that case, a commercial user may retain a portion or all of the obligation until disposing of the equipment. Therefore, for all intents and purposes, commercial users may be obligated to incur the costs of retiring assets that meet the definition of historical waste equipment.

Commercial users should apply the provisions ASC 410-20 and the related guidance in ASC 410-20-25 and 20-55 to obligations related to historical waste because they are, in effect, asset retirement obligations. The guidance in ASC 410-20-25-1-5, 30-1, 35-1 through 35-2; ASC 360-10-35-18 through 35-19 applies to the initial recognition and measurement of a liability and the cost of asset retirement. Recognition of that obligation is required regardless of a commercial user's intent and ability to replace the equipment and transfer the obligation. The obligation may be transferred to the producer of replacement equipment, depending on the laws of the applicable EU-member country, and if so, would be reflected in the asset's purchase price.

The cost related to an asset's retirement should be capitalized when a liability related to historical waste is initially recognized by increasing the related asset's carrying amount by the same amount as the liability. The guidance in ASC 410-20-35-3 through 35-8, which requires recognition of changes in the amount of an obligation as a result of the passage of time and changes in the timing or amount of the original estimate of undiscounted cash flows, should be applied in periods following the initial accounting for the liability.

A commercial user that subsequently replaces equipment and transfers its obligation for historical waste to the producer of the newly acquired equipment should determine, based on the fair value of the asset retirement obligation, how much of the purchase price is related to the newly acquired equipment and how much is related to the transferred asset retirement obligation. The cost basis of the newly acquired equipment should equal the difference between the amount paid and the fair value of the obligation transferred. The transferred liability should be removed from the commercial user's balance sheet and a gain or loss should be recognized for the difference between the carrying amount of the liability at the date that replacement equipment was purchased and the portion of the purchase price related to the transferred obligation. Producers of replacement equipment that accept the transfer of and obligation related to historical waste and for whom recycling of electronic waste equipment is *not* a revenue-producing activity should recognize revenue on a net basis based on the amount received less the fair value of the transferred liability for historical waste. The producer should derecognize the transferred obligation when it is settled. Producers that do conduct such recycling as a revenue-producing activity should measure revenue earned on the sale of replacement equipment and the assumption of the obligation based on the guidance in ASC 605-25-05; 05-15, 05-25, 05-30, 05-50, 05-55. In EU countries where commercial users retain their historical waste obligations when purchasing replacement equipment, *no* portion of the purchase price of newly acquired equipment should be allocated to the liability, which remains on the commercial user's balance sheet until it is settled.

Historical Waste Held by Private Households

The guidance in this section is not related to the guidance for asset retirement in ASC 410-20. Under the Directive, historical waste held by private households should be financed collectively by producers that are sellers in the market during each measurement period, which should be defined by each EU member. The amount to be financed is not affected by the volume of equipment qualifying as historical waste sold by electronic equipment producers in the market before the measuring period. Producers will be required to contribute proportionate amounts based on their shares of the market by type of equipment. Each EU-member country will determine the exact method of computation. For example, if the amount of the liability of each producer in the market is computed based on its respective share of the market by type of equipment sold during a measurement period, a producer would recognize a liability for its obligation and an offsetting amount as an expense over the measurement period based on its portion of the estimated total costs of the waste management program to be allocated and its estimated market share. Each producer is required to adjust its liability as information about the actual cost of the program and the producer's actual respective market share becomes available. Because an obligation is triggered by participation in the market during the measurement period, a producer should *not* recognize an obligation *before* that period begins.

ASC 720-45: BUSINESS AND TECHNOLOGY REENGINEERING

ASC 720-45-05-2 through 05-3; 15-2; 25-1 through 25-4; 30-1; 55-1 Accounting for Costs Incurred in Connection with a Consulting Contract or an Internal Project That Combines Business Process Reengineering and Information Technology Transformation

BACKGROUND

Many companies are installing advanced software packages that will improve their ability to participate in electronic commerce and take advantage of new computer technology. Because the software is often not compatible with the company's existing business processes, the project also involves reengineering the company's business processes to work with the new software. Such projects may be carried out through a contract with an outside consulting firm or performed by the company's own personnel. As part of the total project, the company may install new computer hardware, reconfigure work areas, and purchase new furniture, office equipment, and workstations.

A business process reengineering project consists of the following activities:

- Documenting the current business processes (not the current software structure), which may be referred to as mapping, developing an "as-is" baseline, flow charting, or determining the current business structure.
- Reengineering business processes for greater efficiency and effectiveness, which may be referred to as analysis, developing "should-be" processes, or improving profit/performance.
- Determining the composition of the workforce required to operate the reengineered business processes.

The issue whether to capitalize or expense business process reengineering was excluded from the scope of ASC 350-10-05-6; 350-40-05-2 through 05-6, 05-8, 05-9; 15-2 through 15-7; 25-1 through 25-16; 30-1 through 30-4; 35-1 through 35-10; 50-1; 55-1 through 55-4; 730-10-60-2; 985-20-60-1 (SOP 98-1, Accounting for Computer Software Developed or Obtained for Internal Use), and it is not addressed in ASC 720-15-15-1 through 15-5; 25-1; 55-1, 55-3 through 55-54, 55-6 through 55-7, 55-9 through 55-10 (SOP 98-5, Reporting on the Costs of Start-Up Activities). However, guidance is provided in ASC 350-20-25-3 (paragraph 10 of FAS-142, Goodwill and Other Intangible Assets) which states that "costs of internally developing, maintaining, or restoring intangible assets (including goodwill) that are not specifically identifiable, that have indeterminate lives, or that are inherent in a continuing business and related to an enterprise as a whole shall be recognized as an expense when incurred."

ACCOUNTING ISSUES

1. How should the costs of a project to transform a company's information technology and to reengineer its business processes be accounted for if the project is carried out by internal personnel or through a consulting contract with a third party?
2. How should a company allocate the total costs of a business reengineering consulting contract to a project's various activities?

ACCOUNTING GUIDANCE

1. Costs of business process reengineering activities (such as those described in the Overview) should be *expensed as incurred*, regardless of whether they are performed by internal personnel or through a consulting contract with a third party. This guidance also applies if such activities are included in a project to acquire, develop, or implement internal-use software. However, this guidance does not affect the accounting for internal-use software development costs or for the acquisition of property and equipment.

   It was noted that although personnel involved in a business process reengineering project also may have expertise in information technology and software application, the project's effort is focused on the reengineering process, not on software systems.
2. The total price of a business process reengineering project performed under a consulting contract with a third party should be allocated to each activity based on the relative fair value of the separate activities. Objective evidence of the fair value of the different elements of the contract should be used to make the allocation, rather than basing the allocation it solely on the separate prices stated for the various elements of the contract.

APPLICATION GUIDANCE

The FASB staff provided the following application guidance for the recognition of internal costs or costs of work performed by third parties:

- Business process reengineering and information technology transformation costs that should be expensed as incurred in accordance with this guidance:
  - — Preparation of request for proposal
  - — Current state assessment
  - — Process reengineering
  - — Workforce restructuring
- Costs of preliminary software project stage activities that should be expensed as incurred in accordance with ASC 350-10-05-6; 350-40-05-2 through 05-6, 05-8, 05-9; 15-2 through 15-7; 25-1 through 25-16; 30-1 through 30-4; 35-1 through 35-10; 50-1; 55-1 through 55-4; 730-10-60-2; 985-20-60-1 on internal-use software:

— Conceptual formulation of alternatives

— Evaluation of alternatives

— Determination of existence of needed technology

— Final selection of alternatives

- Costs of software application development stage activities that should be capitalized in accordance with the guidance in ASC 350-10-05-6; 350-40-05-2 through 05-6, 05-8, 05-9; 15-2 through 15-7; 25-1 through 25-16; 30-1 through 30-4; 35-1 through 35-10; 50-1; 55-1 through 55-4; 730-10-60-2; 985-20-60-1:

  — Design of chosen path, including software configuration and software interface

  — Coding

  — Installation to hardware

  — Testing, including parallel processing phase

  — Data conversion costs to develop or obtain software allowing the new system to access old data

- Costs of software application development stage activities that should be expensed as incurred in accordance with the guidance in ASC 350-10-05-6; 350-40-05-2 through 05-6, 05-8, 05-9; 15-2 through 15-7; 25-1 through 25-16; 30-1 through 30-4; 35-1 through 35-10; 50-1; 55-1 through 55-4; 730-10-60-2; 985-20-60-1:

  — All data conversion processes not included above

  — Training

- Costs of post-implementation/operation stage activities that should be expensed as incurred in accordance with the guidance in ASC 350-10-05-6; 350-40-05-2 through 05-6, 05-8, 05-9; 15-2 through 15-7; 25-1 through 25-16; 30-1 through 30-4; 35-1 through 35-10; 50-1; 55-1 through 55-4; 730-10-60-2; 985-20-60-1:

  — Training

  — Application maintenance

  — Ongoing support

- Costs of acquiring fixed assets accounted for in accordance with a company's existing policy:

  — New computer equipment, office furniture, and workstation purchases

  — Reconfiguration of work area, including architect fees and hard construction costs

(The FASB staff included the information related to the application of the guidance in ASC 350-10-05-6; 350-40-05-2 through 05-6, 05-8, 05-9; 15-2 through 15-7; 25-1 through 25-16; 30-1 through 30-4; 35-1 through 35-10; 50-1; 55-1 through 55-4; 730-10-60-2; 985-20-60-1 for illustrative purposes only. In addition, capitalization of costs under that guidance requires that other criteria be met.)

ASC 720-50: FEES PAID TO THE FEDERAL GOVERNMENT BY PHARMACEUTICAL MANUFACTURERS AND HEALTH INSURERS

ASC 720-50-05-1 through 05-4, 15-1, 25-1, 45-1, 65-1 through 65-2 Fees Paid to the Federal Government by Pharmaceutical Manufacturers and Health Insurers

BACKGROUND

Under the requirements of the Patient Protection and Affordable Care Act and the Health Care and Education Reconciliation Act (the Acts), which were signed into law in March 2010, companies in the pharmaceutical manufacturing industry will be required to pay an annual fee for each calendar year beginning on or after January 1, 2011. Health insurers will be required to pay an annual fee beginning on or after January 1, 2014.

The pharmaceutical industry's total fee, which ranges between $2.5 and $4.1 billion, will be allocated to individual entities in the industry based on the amount of their branded prescription drug sales for the preceding year as a percentage of the industry's total branded prescription drug sales during that period. A portion of an entity's payments to the U.S. Treasury department become payable when an entity has a gross receipt from branded prescription drug sales to any specified government program or based on coverage under any government program within each calendar year that begins on or after January 1, 2011. Subject to when the pharmaceutical manufacturing industry becomes obligated to pay the fee, it is expected that entities in that industry will recognize their prorated portion of the fee in the annual period in which the fee is due. Entities in the industry generally consider the fee to be an annual cost of participating in the government programs for the year in which the payment is due and that the amount of sales in the prior year is used only as a means of allocating the fee among the entities in the industry based on their market share in the government programs. The SEC staff has indicated that it would not object if entities in the industry recognize the annual fee over the calendar year when it is paid by allocating the fee on a straight-line basis or based on another method that provides a better allocation of the cost or revenue reduction over the benefit period.

The annual fee that will be paid by entities in the health insurance industry will be allocated to individual health insurers based on the ratio of the amount of net premiums that an entity has written during the preceding year to the amount of health insurance for any U.S. health risk written during the preceding calendar year. A portion of a health insurance entity's annual fee becomes payable to the U.S. Treasury department when that entity provides health insurance for any U.S. health risk for each calendar year beginning on or after January 1, 2014.

Although there is agreement on the annual periods in which those fees will be recognized, there are different opinions about: (1) how to classify those annual fees in reporting entities' income statements; and (2) whether to expense the entire annual fees when a liability is recognized for those fees or whether to recognize an asset for the fees that would be amortized over the calendar year.

SCOPE

The guidance herein applies to all entities in the pharmaceutical manufacturing industry and to health insurers subject to the annual fee, as defined under the Acts. Before analogizing to the following accounting guidance, the facts and circumstances of other fee arrangements should be considered

ACCOUNTING GUIDANCE

Pharmaceutical manufacturers should estimate and recognize a liability for the full amount of the annual fee discussed in ASC 720-50-05-1 through 05-2 when the first qualifying sale has been made. Likewise, health insurers should estimate and recognize a liability for the full amount of the annual fee discussed in ASC 720-50-05-3 through 05-4 once the entity has provided qualifying health insurance in the applicable calendar year in which the fee is payable. Pharmaceutical manufacturers and health insurers should recognize a corresponding amount as a deferred cost that should be amortized to expense on a straight line basis unless another method provides a better allocation of the fee over the year in which it is payable. The annual fee paid to the U.S. Treasury does not correspond to a cost related to the acquisition of policies that conforms with the definition of an *acquisition cost* in ASC 944-30. Pharmaceutical manufacturers and health insurers should account for the annual fee as an operating expense.

Transition Method and Disclosures

1. Pharmaceutical entities—The above guidance should be effective for calendar years that begin after December 31, 2010. Entities are not required to evaluate their existing policies related to similar fees assessed by governmental authorities.
2. Health insurers—The above guidance should be effective for calendar years that begin after December 31, 2013. Entities are not required to evaluate their existing policies related to similar fees assessed by governmental authorities.

CHAPTER 45

ASC 730—RESEARCH AND DEVELOPMENT

CONTENTS

PART I: GENERAL GUIDANCE

ASC 730-10: OVERALL

OVERVIEW

Research and development (R&D) cost is carefully defined in the authoritative accounting literature. Once R&D costs are appropriately identified, U.S. GAAP require that they be expensed in the period incurred. Some costs related to R&D activities, however, are appropriately capitalized and carried forward as assets if they have alternative future uses. R&D-related assets typically include items of property, plant, and equipment and intangible assets used in the ongoing R&D effort of the enterprise.

> *PRACTICE NOTE:* Assets related to R&D are presented in financial statements in appropriate asset categories, but not as R&D assets, a common practice prior to the establishment of the current standards of accounting for R&D. As indicated later in this chapter, depreciation on R&D-related assets is included in R&D expense.

BACKGROUND

Research is the planned efforts of a company to discover new information that will help create a new product, service, process, or technique or vastly improve one in current use. *Development* takes the findings generated by research and formulates a plan to create the desired item or to improve an existing one. Development in the context of this area of U.S. GAAP does not include normal improvements in existing operations (ASC Glossary). The following specific activities, amongst others, are *not* covered by the provisions of ASC 730-10-15-4:

- Activities that are unique to the extractive industries, such as prospecting, exploration, drilling, mining, and similar functions. Research and development activities of companies in extractive industries that are comparable in nature to other companies, such as the development or improvement of techniques and processes, *are* covered.
- Research and development performed under contract for others, including indirect costs that are specifically reimbursable under a contract.

PRACTICE POINTER: R&D does not include market research and testing, because these items specifically relate to the selling and marketing operations of a company. In addition, general and administrative expenses not *directly* related to the R&D activities are not included in R&D.

Because of the high degree of uncertainty of any resulting future benefit, the underlying basic principle in accounting for R&D is conservatism. Because at the time of performing R&D there is uncertainty concerning future success, the most conservative approach is to expense the item in the period incurred.

ASC 730 does not apply if research and development assets are acquired in a business combination, or if they are acquired in an acquisition of a business or nonprofit activity by a not-for-profit entity (ASC 730-10-25-1). ASC 805 applies to accounting for these assets and requires that tangible and intangible assets used in research and development are measured at fair value, regardless of whether they have an alternative future use. In future periods, tangible assets acquired in a business combination that are used in research and development activities are accounted for as are other similar tangible assets. In future periods, intangible assets acquired in a business combination that are used in research and development activities are accounted for in a similar manner to other intangible assets (ASC 730-10-15-4).

ACCOUNTING AND REPORTING RESEARCH AND DEVELOPMENT—GENERAL STANDARDS

All R&D costs covered by U.S. GAAP are expensed in the period when they are incurred (ASC 730-10-25-1). Assets used in R&D activity, such as machinery, equipment, facilities, and patents that have alternative future uses either in R&D activities or otherwise are capitalized. Depreciation and amortization on such capitalized R&D-related assets is charged to R&D expense. All expenditures in conjunction with an R&D project, including personnel costs, materials, equipment, facilities, and intangibles, for which the company has no alternative future use beyond the specific project for which the items were purchased, are expensed. Indirect costs, including general and administrative expenses, which are *directly* related to the R&D project also are expensed when incurred (ASC 730-10-25-2).

Illustration of Determining R&D Expense

Lambert, Inc. develops new products and, therefore, engages in extensive research and development activities. Following is a description of current period expenditures related to a current Lambert project:

1.	Material and labor directly related to the project	$150,000
2.	Purchase of machinery and equipment required to carry out the project:	
	a. Useful only for this project	75,000
	b. Useful for this and other R&D projects over an estimated five-year period	90,000
3.	Contract services acquired	15,000
4.	Overhead and administration allocation	50,000

Assuming the overhead and administration allocation is for activities closely related to the project, and assuming depreciation of machinery and equipment by the straight-line method with no expected salvage value, the R&D expense for the year is:

Material and labor	$150,000
Machinery and equipment	75,000
Depreciation of machinery and equipment ($90,000/5 years)	18,000
Contract services	15,000
Overhead and administration	50,000
R&D expense	$308,000

The machinery and equipment with alternative future uses ($90,000 – $18,000 = $72,000 book value) is considered an asset available for use in future periods.

PRACTICE POINTER: ASC 730 does not require assets related to R&D that have alternative future uses in R&D, production, or other activities to be expensed in the period incurred. Typical assets with alternative future uses include machinery, equipment, facilities, patents, and copyrights. Include amortization and depreciation of these assets in R&D

expense as long as the assets are used in R&D activities. No asset described as "research and development" should appear in the balance sheet. Present R&D-related assets that are included in the balance sheet in the normal asset categories they represent—plant assets, intangible assets, etc.

Research and development costs acquired by the acquisition method in a business combination are assigned their fair values, if any, in accordance with ASC 805 (Business Combinations).

Disclosure

The amount of R&D charged to expense for the period must be disclosed in the financial statements for each period presented (ASC 730-10-50-1).

ASC 730-20: RESEARCH AND DEVELOPMENT ARRANGEMENTS

RESEARCH AND DEVELOPMENT ARRANGEMENTS

ASC 730 also covers an enterprise's research and development arrangements that are partially or completely funded by other parties. In this respect, a typical arrangement is for the parties to set up a limited partnership through which the R&D activities related to a specific project are funded. Although the limited partnership arrangement is used in ASC 730 for illustrative purposes, the legal structure of an R&D arrangement may take a variety of forms and is sometimes influenced by income tax implications and securities regulations (ASC 730-20-05-10).

In a typical R&D arrangement, an enterprise that has the basic technology for a particular project is the general partner and manages the R&D activities. The limited partners, who may or may not be related parties, provide all or part of the funds to complete the project. If the funds are not sufficient, the arrangement may allow or require the general partner to either (*a*) sell additional limited partnership interest or (*b*) use its own funds to complete the project. In addition, some funds may be provided in the form of loans or advances to the limited partnership. The repayment of the loans or advances may be guaranteed by the partnership (ASC 730-20-05-2, 3).

Contract

The actual R&D activities usually are performed by the enterprise or a related party, under a contract with the limited partnership. The contract price is either fixed or cost plus a fixed or percentage fee and is performed on a *best efforts* basis, with no guarantee of ultimate success. The legal ownership of the results of the project vests with partnership (ASC 730-20-05-4). Frequently, the enterprise has an option to acquire the partnership's interest in the project or to obtain exclusive use of the results of the project (ASC 730-20-05-5). If the project is a success, the enterprise will usually exercise its option to acquire the project. Under some circumstances, however, even if the project is unsuccessful, the enterprise may still have reason to acquire the project, in spite of the fact that it is not legally required to do so. For example, the enterprise may want to prevent the final results of the project becoming available to a competitor (ASC 730-20-05-7).

Many of the liabilities and obligations that an enterprise undertakes in an R&D project that is funded by others are specified in the agreements. Some liabilities and obligations, however, may exist in substance but may not be reduced to writing. For example, future payments by the enterprise to other parties for royalties or the acquisition of the partnership's interest in the project may, in substance, represent (*a*) the repayment of a loan or (*b*) the purchase price of a specific asset (ASC 730-20-05-9).

Nature of Obligation

In R&D arrangements that are partially or completely funded by other parties, accounting and reporting for R&D costs depend upon the nature of the obligation that an enterprise incurs in the arrangement. The nature of the obligation in such R&D arrangements can be classified in one of the following categories:

- The obligation is solely to perform contractual services.
- The obligation represents a liability to repay all of the funds provided by the other parties.
- The obligation is partly to perform contractual services and partly a liability to repay some, but not all, of the funds provided by the other parties.

If the nature of the obligation incurred by an enterprise is solely to perform contractual services, all R&D costs are charged to *cost of sales*. If the nature of the obligation represents a liability to repay all of the funds provided by the other parties, all R&D costs are charged to *expense* when incurred.

If the nature of the obligation incurred by an enterprise is partly a liability and partly the performance of contractual services, R&D costs are charged partly to expense and partly to cost of sales. The portion charged to cost of sales is related to the funds provided by the other parties that do not have to be repaid by the enterprise. The portion charged to expense is related to the funds provided by the other parties that *are* likely to be repaid by the enterprise. Under ASC 730, the portion charged to expense is referred to as the enterprise's portion of the R&D costs. Under the provisions of ASC 730, an enterprise shall charge its portion of the R&D costs to expense in the same manner as the liability is incurred. Thus, if the liability arises on a pro rata basis, the enterprise's portion of the R&D costs shall be charged to expense in the same manner. If the liability arises as the initial funds are expended, the enterprise's portion of the R&D costs shall be charged to expense in the same manner (ASC 730-20-25-7).

ASC 730 provides guidance in determining the nature of the obligation that an enterprise incurs in R&D arrangements that are partially or completely funded by other parties. An enterprise is required to report in its financial statements the estimated liability to repay other parties, if any, incurred in an R&D arrangement that is partially or completely funded by other parties. The estimated liability shall include any contractually defined obligations and any obligations not contractually defined but otherwise reasonably evident (ASC 730-20-25-3, 5).

An important criterion in determining an enterprise's obligation is whether the financial risk involved in an R&D arrangement has been substantively transferred to other parties. To the extent that the enterprise is committed to repay any of the funds provided by the other parties regardless of the outcome of the research and development, all or part of the risk has not been transferred (ASC 730-20-25-4).

Under the provisions of ASC 730, if significant evidence exists that the enterprise is *likely* to repay any funds, it is presumed that a liability has been incurred. This presumption can be overcome only by substantial evidence to the contrary. Circumstances in which significant evidence exists that the enterprise is likely to repay funds and a liability is presumed are as follows (ASC 730-20-25-6):

- Regardless of the success of the R&D project, the enterprise has indicated the intent to repay all or part of the funds provided by other parties.
- If it failed to repay any of the funds, the enterprise would suffer a *severe economic penalty*. Under ASC 730, an economic penalty is *severe* if an enterprise would probably elect, under normal business circumstances, to repay the funds rather than to incur the penalty.
- At the inception of the R&D arrangement, a material related party relationship, as defined in ASC 850 (Related Party Disclosures), exists between the enterprise and any of the parties funding the R&D project.
- At the inception of the R&D arrangement, the project is substantially complete. Under this circumstance, the financial risks involved in the R&D project are already known to all parties.

An obligation may represent a liability whether it is payable in cash, securities, or by some other means (ASC 730-20-25-3).

Obligation for Contractual Services

If substantially all of the financial risks of the R&D project are transferred to the other parties and the enterprise is not committed to repay any of the funds provided by the other parties, the enterprise shall account for its obligation as contractual R&D services (ASC 730-20-25-8). If repayment by the enterprise of any of the funds provided by the other parties depends on the availability of a future economic benefit to the enterprise, the enterprise shall also account for its obligation as contractual R&D services. In these circumstances, the financial risks of the R&D arrangement have clearly been transferred to others and the enterprise is only obligated to perform contractual R&D services.

Frequently, an enterprise makes a loan or advance to the other parties that is designated to be repaid as a reduction of the purchase price for the results of the project, or as a reduction of future royalty payments from the enterprise. In this event, the portion of the loan or advance that is designated to be repaid as a reduction of the purchase price for the results of the project, or as a reduction of future royalties, shall be accounted for by the enterprise as R&D expense, unless it can be attributed to activities other than R&D, such as marketing or advertising (ASC 730-20-25-11).

At or before the completion of the R&D project, the enterprise may elect to exercise its option to purchase the partnership's interest, or to obtain exclusive rights to the results of the project. The enterprise shall account for the purchase of the partnership's interest, or the exclusive rights, in accordance with existing U.S. GAAP. Thus, any asset that results from the R&D project shall be assigned its fair value, and intangible assets shall be accounted for in accordance with ASC 350 (Intangibles—Goodwill and Other) (ASC 730-20-25-9, 10).

If an enterprise is required to issue warrants or similar instruments in connection with the R&D arrangement, a portion of the funds provided by the other parties shall be recorded as paid-in capital. The amount capitalized as paid-in capital shall be equal to the fair market value of the warrants or other instruments at the date the R&D arrangement is consummated (ASC 730-20-25-12).

Financial Statement Disclosure

Notes to the financial statements shall include the following disclosures for R&D arrangements that are accounted for as contracts to perform R&D services for others (ASC 730-20-50-1):

- The terms of the significant agreements relating to the R&D arrangement, including purchase provisions, license agreements, royalty arrangements, and commitments to provide additional funds as of the date of each balance sheet presented
- The amount of R&D costs incurred and compensation earned during the period for such R&D arrangements for each income statement presented

PART II: INTERPRETIVE GUIDANCE

ASC 730-20: RESEARCH AND DEVELOPMENT ARRANGEMENTS

ASC 730-20-25-13 through 25-14, 35-1, 65-1; ASC 730-10-55-3 Accounting for Nonrefundable Advance Payments for Goods or Services to Be Used in Future Research and Development Activities

BACKGROUND

The following guidance addresses the accounting for *nonrefundable* portions of prepayments made by entities involved in research and development activities (R&D entities) related to purchases of goods and services that will be used in an entity's future activities, such as prepayments to contract research organizations (CROs), which perform clinical trial management services. Prepayments to CROs are generally for activities, such as for per-patient clinical trial treatment costs and travel costs of a CRO's personnel. In addition, CROs often enter into contracts with third parties to deliver goods or services to an R&D entity and must pay those third parties even if the R&D activities are terminated. Advance payments are usually made three to six months *before* an R&D entity's activities begin.

R&D entities usually purchase goods and services for a specific project and can not use them for another future project. A portion of the prepayment may sometimes be refundable, but usually some portion of an advance payment is nonrefundable.

There is diversity in the way that R&D entities account for the nonrefundable portion of advance payments. Some defer those prepayments until the R&D activities have been performed while others expense them as the payments are made.

SCOPE

The guidance herein applies only to *nonrefundable* advance payments for goods and services to be used or rendered in future R&D activities under executory contractual arrangements. The accounting guidance in ASC 730, Research and Development, applies to nonrefundable advance payments for materials, equipment, facilities, and purchased intangible assets having an alternative future use in an entity's future R&D activities.

ACCOUNTING ISSUE

Should *nonrefundable* advance payments for goods or services that will be used or rendered for research and development activities be expensed when the advance payment is made or when the research and development equity has been performed?

ACCOUNTING GUIDANCE

R&D entities should defer and capitalize as assets *nonrefundable* advance payments for goods and services that will be used or rendered in an entity's future R&D activities under an executory contractual arrangement.

Nonrefundable advance payment for materials, equipment, facilities, and purchased intangible assets that have an alternative future use in future research and development projects or for other purposes should be accounted for according to the guidance in ASC 730-10. Nonrefundable advance payments that have been capitalized should be recognized as an expense when the related goods have been delivered or the services have been performed.

Entities should continue to evaluate whether they expect that purchased goods will be delivered and purchased services will be rendered. If the goods and services will *not* be used in an entity's future R&D activities, capitalized advanced payments for those goods or services should be expensed.

The above guidance does not apply to *refundable* advance payments for future R&D activities and should *not* be applied by analogy to other types of advance payments.

CHAPTER 46

ASC 740—INCOME TAXES

CONTENTS

PART I: GENERAL GUIDANCE

OVERVIEW

The income tax consequences of many transactions recognized in the financial statements are included in determining taxes currently payable in the same accounting period. Sometimes, however, tax laws differ from the recognition and measurement requirements of financial reporting standards. Differences arise between the tax bases of assets or liabilities and their reported amounts in the financial statements. These differences are called *temporary differences* and they give rise to deferred tax assets and liabilities.

Temporary differences ordinarily reverse when the related asset is recovered or the related liability is settled. A *deferred tax liability* or *deferred tax asset* represents the increase or decrease in taxes payable or refundable in future years as a result of temporary differences and carryforwards at the end of the current year.

The objectives of accounting for income taxes are to recognize:

- The amount of taxes payable or refundable for the current year.
- The deferred tax liabilities and assets that result from future tax consequences of events that have been recognized in the enterprise's financial statements or tax returns.

BACKGROUND

Accounting for income taxes is strongly influenced by the fact that some transactions are treated differently for financial reporting purposes and for income tax purposes. Other transactions are treated the same way in financial reporting and for income tax purposes, but in different accounting periods. Differences in timing are referred to as temporary differences and are reconciled in the financial statements by the recognition of deferred tax assets and liabilities.

For several decades, deferred tax assets and liabilities were recognized in the financial statements by the deferred method which placed primarily emphasis on determining net income by matching of revenues and expenses. Income tax expense was determined by applying the current tax rate to pretax accounting income. Any differences between the resulting expense and the amount of income taxes payable in the current period were adjustments to deferred income taxes. The deferred method focused first on the income statement, and adjustment to balance sheet elements were determined by the measurement of income tax expense.

The Financial Accounting Standards Board significantly changed this approach when it changed accounting for income taxes to the asset/liability method, frequently referred to as simply the liability method. This method places primary emphasis on the valuation of the elements of the balance sheet—deferred tax assets and liabilities. The amount of income tax expense currently payable or refundable, plus or minus the changes in deferred tax assets and liabilities, is the income tax expense that is recognized in the income statement for a financial reporting period. The asset/liability method focuses first on the balance sheet, and the amount of income tax expense is determined by changes in the elements of the balance sheet.

ASC 740-10: OVERALL

THE ASSET/LIABILITY METHOD

ASC 740 requires income taxes to be accounted for by the asset/liability method. Its main effects on financial statements include the following:

- Emphasis is on the recognition and measurement of deferred tax assets and liabilities. Deferred income tax expense is determined residually (i.e., as the difference between the beginning and required ending balances in deferred tax assets and liabilities for the period).
- Deferred tax asset and liability amounts are remeasured when tax rates change to approximate more closely the amounts at which those assets and liabilities will be realized or settled.
- Deferred tax assets are recognized for operating loss and other carryforwards. Deferred tax assets are subject to reduction by a valuation allowance if evidence indicates that it is *more likely than not* that some or all of the deferred tax assets will not be realized. Determining this valuation allowance is similar to accounting for reductions in receivables to net realizable value.
- Disclosure requirements result in the presentation of a significant amount of information in the notes to the financial statements.

PRACTICE NOTE: The asset/liability method is commonly referred to as the liability method, although it results in both deferred tax assets and deferred tax liabilities. Because of the popularity of the liability method terminology, we primarily use that terminology in this chapter.

GENERAL PROVISIONS OF ASC 740

Scope

ASC 740 requires what traditionally has been referred to as "comprehensive income tax allocation," as opposed to partial allocation or nonallocation. This means that the income tax effects of all revenues, expenses, gains, losses, and other events that create differences between the tax bases of assets and liabilities and their amounts for financial reporting are required to be recognized (ASC 740-10-05-1).

ASC 740 is applicable to:

- Domestic federal income taxes and foreign, state, and local taxes based on income (ASC 740-10-15-3).
- An enterprise's domestic and foreign operations that are consolidated, combined, or accounted for by the equity method. ASC 740 provides guidance for determining the tax bases of assets and liabilities for financial reporting purposes (ASC 740-10-15-3).
- Foreign enterprises in preparing financial statements in accordance with U.S. GAAP. (ASC 740-10-15-2).

ASC 740 does not apply to the following transactions/activities (ASC 740-10-15-4):

1. A franchise or similar tax to the extent it is based on capital or a non-income based amount and there is no portion of the tax based on income. If a franchise or similar tax is partially based on income, deferred tax assets and liabilities are recognized and accounted for in accordance with this Topic, with deferred tax assets and liabilities measured using the applicable statutory income tax rate. The entity shall not consider the effect of potentially paying a non-income-based tax in future years when evaluating the realizability of its deferred tax assets. The current tax expense based on income is accounted for in accordance with this Topic, and any incremental amount incurred accounted for as a non-income-based tax.
2. A withholding tax for the benefit of recipients of a dividend.

Three important financial statement issues are specifically set aside and not covered by ASC 740:

1. Accounting for the investment tax credit (ITC)
2. Accounting for income taxes in interim periods
3. Discounting deferred income taxes

Accounting for the ITC and accounting for income taxes in interim periods are covered by other authoritative pronouncements. Discounting of deferred income taxes is not permitted.

Basic Principles of the Liability Method

The objectives of accounting for income taxes are identified in terms of elements of the balance sheet (ASC 740-10-10-1):

- To recognize the amount of taxes payable or refundable for the current year
- To recognize the deferred tax assets and liabilities for the future tax consequences of events that have been recognized in the financial statements or in tax returns

This emphasis on the balance sheet is consistent with the liability method of accounting for income taxes incorporated ASC 740.

Accounting for income taxes under ASC 740 is based on the following basic principles at the date of the financial statements:

- A tax liability or asset is recognized for the estimated taxes payable or refundable on tax returns for the current and prior years.
- A deferred tax liability or asset is recognized for the estimated future tax effects attributable to temporary differences and carryforwards. (ASC 740-10-25-2)

PRACTICE POINTER: The reader is encouraged to consult ASC 740-10-25-2 for exceptions to these basic requirements in certain specialized situations (e.g., foreign subsidiaries or corporate joint ventures, undistributed earnings of a domestic subsidiary or corporate joint venture that is essentially permanent in duration, bad debt reserves of U.S. savings and loan associations, policyholders' surplus of stock life insurance entities, deposits in statutory reserve funds by U.S. steamship entities, leveraged leases, goodwill for which amortization is not deductible for tax purposes, inventory in the buyer's tax jurisdiction where the carrying value as reported in the consolidated financial statements as a result of an intra-entity transfer of inventory from one tax-paying component to another tax-paying component of the same consolidated group, assets and liabilities remeasured from the local currency into the functional currency using historical exchange rates and that result from changes in exchange rates or indexing for tax purposes. Many of these include certain specific time parameters for application.

Temporary Differences

Deferred tax assets and liabilities that result from temporary differences are based on the assumption that assets and liabilities in an entity's balance sheet eventually will be realized or settled at their recorded amounts (ASC 740-10-25-20).

The following categories of temporary differences refer to events that result in differences between the tax bases of assets and liabilities and their reported amounts in the financial statements (ASC 740-10-25-20):

- Revenues or gains that are taxable after they are recognized in accounting income (e.g., receivables from installment sales)
- Expenses or losses that are deductible for tax purposes after they are recognized in accounting income (e.g., a product warranty liability)
- Revenues or gains that are taxable before they are recognized in accounting income (e.g., subscriptions received in advance)
- Expenses or losses that are deductible for tax purposes before they are recognized in accounting income (e.g., depreciation expense)
- A reduction in the tax basis of depreciable assets because of tax credit
- Investment tax credits accounted for by the deferred method
- An increase in the tax basis of assets because of indexing when the local currency is the functional currency
- Business combinations accounted for by not-for-profit entities by the acquisition method
- Intra-entity transfers of an asset other than inventory

Taxable and Deductible Temporary Differences

Temporary differences that will result in taxable amounts in future years when the related asset or liability is recovered or settled are referred to as *taxable temporary differences.* Temporary differences that will result in deductible amounts in future years are referred to as *deductible temporary differences.* (ASC 740-10-25-23) Table 46-1 provides examples of some of the more common taxable and deductible temporary differences.

Temporary differences include some items that do not appear in the company's balance sheet. For example, a company may expense organization costs when they are incurred but recognize them as a tax deduction in a later year. Between the two events, no balance-sheet item exists for this type of temporary difference (ASC 740-10-25-25, 26).

The identification of temporary differences may require significant professional judgment. Similar items may be temporary differences in one instance and not in another. For example, the excess of the cash surrender value of life insurance over premiums paid is a temporary difference and results in deferred taxes if the cash surrender value is expected to be recovered by surrendering the policy, but it is not a temporary difference and does not result in deferred taxes if the asset is expected to be recovered upon the death of the insured (ASC 740-10-25-30). Management intent and professional judgment are important factors in making the appropriate determination of the nature of assets and liabilities of this type.

PRACTICE POINTER: Developing a system for identifying and tracking the amounts of all temporary differences and carryforwards is an important implementation issue for ASC 740. Theoretically, differences should be identified by comparing items and amounts in the entity's balance sheets for accounting purposes and for tax purposes. Many companies do not maintain tax-basis balance sheets, though this may be the most logical way to identify and track temporary differences in relatively complex situations.

Table 46-1: Examples of Taxable and Deductible Temporary Differences

Nature of Temporary Difference	*Explanation*	*Deferred Tax*
	Taxable Temporary Differences	
Depreciable assets	Use of modified accelerated cost recovery system (MACRS) for tax purposes and straight-line for accounting purposes makes the tax basis of the asset less than the accounting basis	Liability, to be paid as MACRS deduction becomes less than straight-line depreciation
Installment sale receivable	Sales recognized for accounting purposes at transaction date and deferred for tax purposes until collection, resulting in a difference between the tax and accounting basis of the installment receivable	Liability, to be paid when the sale is recognized for tax purposes
	Deductible Temporary Differences	
Warranty liability	Expense recognized on accrual basis for accounting purposes and on cash basis for tax purposes, resulting in a liability that is recognized for financial reporting purposes but has a zero basis for tax purposes	Asset, to be recovered when deduction is recognized for tax purposes
Accounts receivable allowance for doubtful accounts	Expense recognized on an accrual basis for accounting purposes and deferred for tax purposes	Asset, to be recovered when uncollectible account is written off for tax purposes

Certain differences between the tax basis and the accounting basis of assets and liabilities will not result in taxable or deductible amounts in future years, and no deferred tax asset or liability should be recognized (ASC 740-10-05-9). These differences are often referred to as permanent differences, although that term is not used in ASC 740.

Recognizing and Measuring Deferred Tax Assets and Liabilities

The emphasis placed on the balance sheet by the asset/liability method of accounting for income taxes is evident from the focus on the recognition of deferred tax liabilities and assets. The change in these liabilities and assets is combined with the income taxes currently payable or refundable to determine income tax expense (ASC 740-10-30-3).

Five steps are required to complete the annual computation of deferred tax liabilities and assets (ASC 740-10-30-5):

1. Identify the types and amounts of existing temporary differences and the nature and amount of each type of operating loss and tax credit carryforward and the remaining length of the carryforward period.
2. Measure the total deferred tax liability for taxable temporary differences using the applicable tax rate.
3. Measure the total deferred tax asset for deductible temporary differences and operating loss carryforwards using the applicable tax rate.
4. Measure deferred tax assets for each type of tax credit carryforward.
5. Reduce deferred tax assets by a valuation allowance if it is more likely than not that some or all of the deferred tax assets will not be realized.

Valuation Allowance and Tax-Planning Strategies

A basic requirement is to reduce the measurement of deferred tax assets not expected to be realized (ASC 740-10-30-16) All available evidence is considered to determine whether a valuation allowance for deferred tax assets is needed and, if so, at what amount (ASC 740-10-30-17).

Determining the need for and calculating the amount of the valuation allowance involves the following steps at the end of each accounting period:

1. Determine the amount of the deferred tax asset recognized on each deductible temporary difference, operating loss, and tax credit carryforward. (These are not offset by the deferred tax liability on taxable temporary differences.)
2. Assess the sources of future taxable income which may be available to recognize the deductible differences and carryforwards by considering the following (ASC 740-10-30-18):
   a. Taxable income in prior carryback year(s) if carryback is permitted under tax law
   b. Future reversals of existing taxable temporary differences
   c. Tax planning strategies that would make income available at appropriate times in the future that would otherwise not be available
   d. Future taxable income exclusive of reversing differences and carryforwards

> *PRACTICE POINTER:* The four sources of future taxable income (listed above) are organized differently here than in ASC 740 in order to emphasize the implementation of the standard. In identifying income to support the recognition of deferred tax assets (and thereby supporting a case that an allowance is not required), a logical approach is to consider sources of income in order from the most objective to the least objective. Income in prior carryback years is most objective, followed by the income from the reversal of taxable temporary differences, income resulting from tax planning strategies, and finally, future income from other sources.

3. Based on all available evidence, make a judgment concerning the realizability of the deferred tax asset.
4. Record the amount of the valuation allowance, or change in the valuation allowance (the example below assumes that the allowance is being recorded for the first time or is being increased for $100,000).

Income tax expense	$100,000	
Allowance to reduce deferred tax asset to lower recoverable value		$100,000

PRACTICE NOTE: ASC 740 relaxes the criteria for recognizing deferred tax assets by requiring the recognition of deferred tax assets for all deductible temporary differences and all operating loss and tax credit carryforwards. An important adjunct to this provision, however, is the requirement to determine the need for, and amount of, a valuation allowance to reduce the deferred tax asset to its realizable value. The valuation allowance aspects of U.S. GAAP require significant judgment on the part of accountants and auditors of financial statements. A valuation allowance is required if it is more likely than not that some or all of the deferred tax assets will not be realized. *More likely than not* is defined as a likelihood of more than 50%.

Applicable Tax Rate

Reference to the applicable tax rate is made in the four steps identified above. The *applicable tax rate* is that rate expected to apply to taxable income in the periods in which the deferred tax liability or asset is expected to be settled or realized based on enacted tax law. If the entity's taxable income is low enough to make the graduated tax rates a significant factor, the entity uses the average graduated tax rate applicable to the amount of estimated annual taxable income in the periods in which the deferred tax liability or asset is expected to be settled or realized (ASC 740-10-10-3). For example, if a company has taxable temporary differences of $20,000 that are expected to reverse in a year when no other income is expected, the applicable tax rate under current tax law is 15% and the deferred tax liability is:

$20,000 × 15% = $3,000

If the taxable temporary differences total $60,000, graduated tax rates become a factor (the tax rate changes at $50,000); deferred taxes are $10,000:

$50,000 × 15%	=	$ 7,500
$10,000 × 25%	=	2,500
		$10,000

The average applicable tax rate is 16.67%.

$10,000/$60,000 = 16.67%

PRACTICE POINTER: Determining the applicable tax rate may be relatively straightforward, or it may require careful analysis and professional judgment. When an entity has been consistently profitable at sufficiently high levels that graduated tax rates are not a significant factor, use the single flat tax rate at which all income is used to compute the amount of deferred taxes on cumulative temporary differences. If a company experiences intermittent tax loss and tax income years, or if the company is consistently profitable at a level low enough that the graduated tax rates are a significant factor, greater judgment is required to determine the applicable tax rate.

Deferred tax assets and liabilities are remeasured at the end of each accounting period and adjusted for changes in the amounts of cumulative temporary differences and for changes in the applicable income tax rate, as well as for other changes in the tax law (ASC 740-10-35-4). As a result of this procedure, the deferred tax provision is a combination of two elements:

1. The change in deferred taxes because of the change in the amounts of temporary differences
2. The change in deferred taxes because of a change in the tax rate caused by new enacted rates or a change in the applicability of graduated tax rates (or other changes in the tax law)

Treating the change in income tax rates in this manner is consistent with accounting for a change in estimate under ASC 250 (Accounting Changes and Error Corrections).

Tax Planning Strategies

Consideration of tax planning strategies is required by ASC 740. Tax planning strategies are an important part of determining the need for, and the amount of, the valuation allowance for deferred tax assets. Tax-planning strategies are actions that (ASC 740-10-30-19):

- Are prudent and feasible
- The entity might not ordinarily take, but *would* take to prevent an operating loss or tax credit carryforward from expiring before it is used
- Would result in the realization of deferred tax assets

Examples include actions the entity could take to accelerate taxable income to utilize expiring carryforwards, to change the character of taxable or deductible amounts from ordinary income or loss to capital gain or loss, and to switch from tax-exempt to taxable investments.

Negative Evidence

Negative evidence, such as cumulative losses in recent years, supports a conclusion that a valuation allowance is necessary. Other examples of negative evidence are (ASC 740-10-30-21):

- A history of operating loss or tax credit carryforwards expiring before they are used
- Losses expected in early future years (by a presently profitable entity)
- Unsettled circumstances that, if unfavorably resolved, would adversely affect future operations and profit levels on a continuing basis in future years
- A carryback or carryforward period that is so short that it significantly limits the probability of realizing deferred tax assets

Positive Evidence

Positive evidence supports a conclusion that a valuation allowance is *not required*. Examples of positive evidence are (ASC 740-10-30-22):

- Existing contracts or firm sales backlog that will produce more than enough taxable income to realize the deferred tax asset based on existing sales prices and cost structures
- An excess of appreciated asset value over the tax basis of the entity's net assets in an amount sufficient to realize the deferred tax asset
- A strong earnings history exclusive of the loss that created the future deductible amount, coupled with evidence indicating that the loss is an aberration rather than a continuing condition (e.g., an unusual or infrequent item)

PRACTICE POINTER: Projecting the reversal of temporary differences for each future year individually is commonly referred to as "scheduling." Does ASC 740 require scheduling? On the one hand, the requirement to recognize deferred tax assets and liabilities for all taxable and deductible temporary differences, as well as for all carryforwards, seems to diminish or eliminate the need to schedule. Also, using a flat tax rate in determining the amount of deferred tax assets and liabilities, as described earlier, diminishes the need to schedule individual future years. On the other hand, scheduling may help determine the need for, and amount of, a valuation allowance, including the consideration of tax-planning strategies. To determine the availability of taxable income in the appropriate years—to take advantage of deferred tax assets and to make the judgments concerning the valuation allowance—projecting taxable income from known or estimated sources by year, or scheduling, may still be important.

Professional judgment is required in considering the relative impact of negative and positive evidence to determine the need for, and amount of, the valuation allowance for deferred tax assets. The weight given the effect of negative and positive evidence should be commensurate with the extent to which it can be objectively verified. The more negative evidence exists, the more positive evidence is needed to conclude that a valuation allowance is not required (ASC 740-10-30-23).

The effect of a change in the valuation allowance that results from a change in circumstances, which in turn causes a change in judgment about the realizability of the related deferred tax asset, is included in income from continuing operations with limited exceptions (ASC 740-10-42-20).

SPECIALIZED APPLICATIONS OF ASC 740

Several specialized applications of ASC 740 are summarized briefly below.

Change in Tax Status

An enterprise's tax status may change from nontaxable to taxable or taxable to nontaxable. A deferred tax liability or asset is recognized for temporary differences at the date that a nontaxable enterprise becomes a taxable enterprise. An existing deferred tax liability or asset is eliminated at the date an enterprise becomes a nontaxable enterprise (ASC 740-10-25-32).

Reclassification of Certain Tax Effects

PRACTICE POINTER: The following amendments to the ASC are effective for all entities for fiscal years beginning after December 15, 2018, and for interim periods within those fiscal years.

ASU 2018-02, *Income Statement—Reporting Comprehensive Income (Topic 220): Reclassification of Certain Tax Effects from Accumulated Other Comprehensive Income,* deals with the reclassification of certain tax effects from accumulated other comprehensive income that results from the Tax Cuts and Jobs Act of 2017. This amendment allows a reclassification from accumulated other comprehensive income to retained earnings from stranded tax effects resulting from this Act. See Chapter 5, *ASC 220—Comprehensive Income,* of the 2022 *GAAP Guide* for more coverage of this topic.

Regulated Enterprises

Regulated enterprises are *not* exempt from the requirements of ASC 740. Specifically, ASC 740 (ASC 740-10-25-1):

- Prohibits net-of-tax accounting and reporting
- Requires recognition of a deferred tax liability for tax benefits that flow through to customers when temporary differences originate and for the equity component of the allowance for funds used during construction
- Requires adjustment of a deferred tax liability or asset for an enacted change in tax laws or rates

As a result of an action by a regulator, if it is probable that the future increase or decrease in taxes payable for the second and third items above will be restored from or returned to customers through future rates, an asset or a liability is recognized for that probable future revenue or reduction in future revenue in accordance with ASC 980 (Regulated Operations). That asset or liability is a temporary difference for which a deferred tax liability or asset is required.

Business Combinations

A deferred tax asset or liability is recognized as of the acquisition date for an acquired entity's taxable or deductible temporary differences or operating loss or tax credit carryforwards. Taxable or deductible temporary differences occur when there are differences between the tax bases and the recognized values of assets acquired and liabilities assumed in a business combination. The acquirer must assess the need for a valuation allowance related to any acquired deferred tax asset (ASC 805-740-25-3).

A change in a valuation allowance for an acquired entity's deferred tax asset that occurs during the measurement period and results from new information about fact and circumstances that existed at the acquisition date is recognized with a corresponding reduction to goodwill. Once goodwill is reduced to zero, any additional change in the valuation allowance is recognized as a bargain purchase. All other changes to the valuation allowance are reported as a reduction or increase to income tax expense (ASC 805-740-45-2).

Quasi-Reorganizations

The tax benefits of deductible temporary differences and carryforwards as of the date of a quasi-reorganization ordinarily are reported as a direct addition to contributed capital if the tax benefits are recognized in subsequent years. The only exception is for enterprises that previously adopted ASC 740 and affected a quasi-reorganization involving only the elimination of a deficit in retained earnings by a reduction in contributed capital prior to adopting ASC 740. For those enterprises, subsequent recognition of the tax benefit of prior deductible temporary differences and carryforwards is included in income, reported as required by ASC 740, and then reclassified from retained earnings to contributed capital (ASC 852-740-45-3).

Separate Financial Statements of a Subsidiary

The allocation of income taxes among the members of a group of entities that file a consolidated tax return must be based on a method that is systematic, rational, and consistent with the broad principles established in ASC 740, although ASC 740 does not require a single allocation method. A method that allocates deferred taxes to members of the group by applying ASC 740 to each member as if it were a separate taxpayer meets the above criteria (ASC 740-10-30-27). Examples of methods that are *not* consistent with the broad principles of ASC 740 include (ASC 740-10-30-28):

- A method that allocates only current taxes payable to a member of the group that has taxable temporary differences
- A method that allocates deferred taxes to a member of the group using a method fundamentally different from the asset and liability method
- A method that allocates no deferred tax expense to a member of the group that has taxable income because the consolidated group has no deferred tax expense

An entity is not required to allocate the consolidated amount of current and deferred tax expense to legal entities that are not subject to tax. The entity may elect to allocate the consolidated amount of current and deferred tax to legal entities that are both not subject to tax and disregarded by the taxing authority (e.g., single-member limited liability companies). The election is not required for all members of a group that files a consolidated tax return. The entity shall not make the election to allocate the consolidated amount of current and deferred tax expense for legal entities that are partnerships or are other pass-through entities that are not wholly owned (ASC 740-10-30-27A).

Miscellaneous Topics

ASC 740 indicates that deferred taxes should not be discounted (ASC 740-10-30-8), and that offsetting of assets and liabilities (including tax assets and liabilities) is prohibited unless a legal right of setoff exists (ASC 210-20-05-1).

ASC 740-30 indicates several situations in which deferred taxes are not recognized for certain temporary differences unless it becomes apparent that those differences will reverse in the foreseeable future.

ASC 740 guides the accounting for the tax effects of share-based compensation awards which are accounted for under ASC 718 (Compensation—Stock Compensation).

Accounting for Tax Effects of Share-Based Compensation Awards

Tax deductions generally arise in different amounts and in different periods from compensation costs recognized in financial statements. The cumulative effect of compensation cost recognized for instruments classified as equity that ordinarily would result in a future tax deduction are considered deductible temporary differences in applying ASC 740. ASC 740 requires a deferred tax asset to be evaluated for future realization and reduced by a valuation allowance if it is more likely than not that some portion or all of the deferred tax asset will not be realized. Differences between the deductible temporary difference computed pursuant to ASC 718 and the tax deduction that would result based on the current fair value of the entity's shares are not considered in measuring the gross deferred tax asset or determining the need for a valuation allowance for a deferred tax asset recognized under ASC 718 (ASC 718-740-05-04; 718-740-25-2; 718-740-30-2).

If a deduction reported on a tax return for an award of equity instrument exceeds the cumulative compensation cost for those instruments recognized for financial reporting (referred to in ASC 718 as the excess tax benefit), any resulting realized tax benefits that exceed the previously recognized deferred tax asset for those instruments are recognized as paid-in capital (ASC 718-740-35-3).

The amount deductible on the employer's tax return may be less than the cumulative compensation cost recognized for financial reporting purposes. The write-off of a deferred tax asset related to that deficiency, net of any related valuation allowance, is first offset to the extent of any remaining additional paid-in capital from excess tax benefits from previous awards accounted for in accordance with the requirements under previous U.S. GAAP. Any remaining balance of the write-off of a deferred tax asset related to a tax deficiency shall be recognized in the income statement (ASC 718-740-35-5; 718-740-45-04).

PRACTICE NOTE: The special applications discussed in this section illustrate the pervasive nature of accounting for income taxes. Income tax considerations affect many parts of the financial statements and many kinds of business transactions. This dimension of accounting for income taxes makes ASC 740 a very important pronouncement and accounts, at least partially, for the long and difficult process of making the transition from the deferred method to the asset/liability method.

Leveraged Leases

For the specific requirements for accounting for income taxes related to leveraged leases, see ASC 842-50.

Unrecognized Gains or Losses from Involuntary Conversions

Gains or losses that result from an involuntary conversion of a nonmonetary asset to a monetary asset that are not recognized for income tax purposes in the same period in which the gain or loss is recognized for financial reporting purposes are considered temporary differences for which a deferred tax liability or deferred tax asset should be recognized. (ASC 740-10-55-66)

FINANCIAL STATEMENT PRESENTATION AND DISCLOSURE ISSUES

ASC 740 requires deferred tax assets and liabilities to be presented in a classified balance sheet as noncurrent amounts (ASC 740-10-45-4).

PRACTICE NOTE: This represents a departure from past practice in which deferred tax assets and liabilities were presented in net current and net noncurrent amounts. As part of the FASB's simplification project, the previous requirement to separate deferred tax assets and liabilities into current and noncurrent amounts has been eliminated. For public business entities, this new presentation is effective for financial statements issued for annual periods beginning after December 15, 2016, and interim periods within those annual periods. For all other entities, the effective date is for financial statements issued for annual periods beginning after December 15, 2017, and for interim periods within annual periods beginning after December 15, 2018. Earlier application is permitted for all entities as of the beginning of an interim or annual reporting period. The change required may be accounted for either prospectively or retroactively with appropriate disclosure of the nature of the change and whether prior period information has been retrospectively adjusted.

For a particular tax-paying component of an entity and within a particular tax jurisdiction, all deferred tax liabilities and assets shall be offset and presented as a single noncurrent amount. However, an entity shall not offset deferred tax liabilities and assets attributable to different tax-paying components of the entity or to different tax jurisdictions (ASC 740-10-45-6).

Disclosures

The following components of the net deferred tax liability or asset recognized in an enterprise's balance sheet must be disclosed (ASC 740-10-50-2):

- The total of all deferred tax liabilities for taxable temporary differences
- The total of all deferred tax assets for deductible temporary differences and loss and tax credit carryforwards
- The total valuation allowance recognized for deferred tax assets
- The net change during the year in the total valuation allowance

Disclosure of significant components of income tax expense attributable to continuing operations for each year presented is required in the financial statements or related notes (ASC 740-10-50-9):

- Current tax expense or benefit
- Deferred tax expense or benefit
- Investment tax credit
- Government grants (to the extent recognized as reductions in income tax expense)
- Tax benefits of operating loss carryforwards
- Tax expense that results from allocating tax benefits
- Adjustments to a deferred tax liability or asset for enacted changes in tax laws or rates or for a change in the tax status of the enterprise
- Adjustments of the beginning balance of the valuation allowance because of a change in circumstances that causes a change in judgment about the realizability of the related deferred tax asset in the future

---

PRACTICE NOTE: The effect of two unique features of the asset/liability method can be seen in the disclosure requirements listed above. The seventh item requires disclosure of the amount of the adjustment to deferred tax assets and liabilities for enacted changes in tax laws or rates. The eighth item requires disclosure of the amount of the adjustment of the beginning balance of the valuation allowance on deferred tax assets made as a result of a change in judgment about the realizability of that item.

The amount of income tax expense or benefit allocated to continuing operations and amounts separately allocated to other items shall be disclosed for each year for which those items are presented.

Several distinctions are made in the disclosures required by public enterprises and those required by nonpublic enterprises. The two most significant ones are summarized as follows (ASC 740-10-50-6, 8, 12, 13):

	Public/Nonpublic Company Disclosures	
	Public	*Nonpublic*
Temporary Differences and Carryforwards	Approximation of tax effect of each type	Description of types
Statutory Reconciliation	Reconciliation in percentages or dollars	Description of major reconciling items

Companies with operating loss and tax credit carryforwards must disclose the amount and expiration dates. Disclosure is also required for any portion of the valuation allowance for deferred tax assets for which subsequently recognized tax benefits will be credited directly to contributed equity (ASC 740-10-50-3).

An entity that is a member of a group that files a consolidated tax return must disclose the following in its separately issued financial statements (ASC 740-10-50-17):

- The aggregate amount of current and deferred tax expense for each statement of earnings presented and the amount of any tax-related balances due to or from affiliates as of the date of each statement of financial position presented
- The principal provisions of the method by which the consolidated amount of current and deferred tax expense is allocated to members of the group and the nature and effect of any changes in that method during the year.

An entity that is both not subject to tax and disregarded by the taxing authority that elects to include the allocated amount of current and deferred tax expense in its separately issued financial statements shall disclose that fact and provide the disclosures required in ASC 740-10-50-17.

Illustration of Major Provisions of ASC 740

This illustration considers Power Company for three consecutive years, with the objective of preparing the year-end income tax accrual and income tax information for the company's financial statements. Power Company's first year of operations is 20X8. During that year, the company reported $160,000 of pretax accounting income. Permanent and temporary differences are combined with pretax financial income to derive taxable income, as follows:

Pretax financial income	$160,000
Permanent difference:	
Interest on municipal securities	(5,000)
Pretax financial income subject to tax	$155,000
Temporary differences:	
Depreciation	(28,000)
Warranties	10,000
Revenue received in advance	7,000
Taxable income	$144,000

The $5,000 interest on municipal securities represents nontaxable income, and the $28,000 depreciation temporary difference represents the excess of accelerated write-off for tax purposes over straight-line depreciation for financial reporting purposes. Warranties are expensed at the time of sale on an estimated basis, but are deductible for income tax purposes only when paid. In 20X8, $10,000 more was accrued than paid. Revenue received in advance is taxable at the time received, but is deferred for financial reporting purposes until earned. In 20X8, $7,000 was received that was not earned by year-end. Depreciation is a *taxable temporary difference* that reduces current tax payable and gives rise to a deferred tax liability. The warranties and revenue received in advance are *deductible temporary differences* that increase current tax payable and give rise to deferred tax assets.

Exhibit A presents analyses that facilitate the preparation of the year-end tax accrual, as well as information for the financial statements. Similar analyses are used for each of the three years in this Illustration. The analysis in the upper portion of Exhibit A "rolls forward" the amount of the temporary differences from the beginning to the end of the year. Because 20X8 is the first year for Power Company, the beginning balances are all zero. The change column includes the amounts used in the earlier calculation to determine taxable income from pretax accounting income. The numbers without parentheses are deductible temporary differences; those in parentheses are taxable temporary differences. The company is in a net taxable temporary difference position at the end of the year because the net amount of temporary differences is $(11,000), due to the large amount of the depreciation difference.

EXHIBIT A: Analysis of Cumulative Temporary Differences and Deferred Taxes, 20X8

Cumulative Temporary Differences (TD)

	Beginning Balance 20X8	*Change*	*Ending Balance 20X8*
Deductible TD:			
Warranties	0	$ 10,000	$ 10,000
Revenue received in advance	0	7,000	7,000
(Taxable) TD:			
Depreciation	0	(28,000)	(28,000)
	0	$(11,000)	$(11,000)

Deferred Income Taxes

	Beginning Balance @—%	*Ending Balance @34%*	*Change*
Assets:			
Warranties	0	$3,400	$ 3,400
Revenue receivedin advance	0	2,380	2,380
(Liabilities):			
Depreciation	0	(9,520)	(9,520)
	0	$(3,740)	$(3,740)

The lower portion of Exhibit A converts these temporary differences to amounts of deferred income taxes based on those differences. Again, the beginning balances are all zero and the ending balances are computed at 34%, the assumed income tax rate for 20X8 in this Illustration. The amounts in parentheses are deferred tax liabilities, based on taxable temporary differences. The numbers without parentheses are deferred tax assets, based on deductible temporary differences.

The December 31, 20X8, entry to record the income tax accrual for Power Company is as follows:

Dec. 31, 20X8		
Income tax expense ($48,960 + $3,740)	$52,700	
Deferred income tax asset ($3,400 + $2,380)	5,780	
Income tax payable ($144,000 × 34%)		$48,960
Deferred income tax liability		9,520

The amounts of deferred income taxes are taken from the lower analysis in Exhibit A. The income tax payable is determined by multiplying the $144,000 taxable income by the 34% tax rate. An important point is that income tax expense is determined last: It is the net of the other three numbers and can be computed only after the remaining elements of the entry have been determined. This illustrates the priority on first establishing the tax elements in the balance sheet, followed by the impact that changes in those elements have on the determination of net income.

An important step to complete before moving to 20X9 is a proof of the numbers obtained, commonly referred to as a *statutory rate reconciliation*. For 20X8, this calculation is as follows:

Pretax financial income @ statutory rate ($160,000 × 34%)	$54,400
Less: Permanent differences ($5,000 × 34%)	(1,700)
Income tax expense	$52,700

Effects of these calculations on the balance sheet and income statement will be considered after all three years of analysis are completed.

Power Company's second year of operations is 20X9, in which pretax financial income is $150,000. Municipal interest is $12,000 and temporary differences for depreciation and warranties are $(35,000) and $12,000, respectively. Of the revenue received in advance in 20X8, $5,000 is earned and an additional $9,000 is received in 20X9 that is expected to be earned in 20Y0. A new temporary difference is the litigation loss that results from the $10,000 accrual on an estimated basis for accounting purposes. This loss will be deductible for tax purposes when the suit is settled, which is expected to occur in 20Y0.

Taxable income for 20X9 is determined as follows:

Pretax financial income	$150,000
Permanent difference:	
Interest on municipal securities	(12,000)
Pretax financial income subject to tax	$138,000
Temporary differences:	
Depreciation	(35,000)
Warranties	12,000
Revenue received in advance ($9,000 – $5,000)	4,000
Litigation loss	10,000
Taxable income	$129,000

Exhibit B includes a 20X9 analysis similar to the 20X8 analysis in Exhibit A. During 20X9, new tax legislation increases the income tax rate for 20X9 and all future years to 40%. The amounts in 20X9 simply are moved forward from the end of 20X8. In the lower portion of Exhibit B, the change column is calculated by determining the change required to move the beginning balance to the desired ending balance.

The entry to record income taxes at the end of 20X9 is as follows:

Dec. 31, 20X9		
Income tax expense ($51,600 + $4,260)	55,860	
Deferred income tax asset	11,420	
Income tax payable ($129,000 × 40%)		51,600
Deferred income tax liability		15,680

Notice that the adjustments to the deferred income tax asset and liability are calculated as the changes in those accounts. It is not necessary to deal with that consideration in 20X8 because it was the company's first year. The desired ending balances of the deferred income tax asset and liability from Exhibit B are compared with the balances from Exhibit A and the differences are debited or credited into the deferred tax accounts, as appropriate, to produce the desired ending balances. For example, the deferred income tax liability must have a credit (liability) balance of $25,200 at the end of 20X9. The account began with a credit balance of $9,520, requiring a credit of $15,680 ($25,200 – $9,520) in the year-end tax accrual. Similarly, the required debit (asset) balance for the deferred income tax asset is $17,200 ($8,800 + $4,400 + $4,000); with a debit balance of $5,780 at the end of 20X8, the adjustment is $11,420. This illustrates the basic approach of the liability method of accounting for income taxes: The desired balance sheet figures are determined first and the expense is recognized in the amount required to meet the balance sheet objective.

EXHIBIT B: Analysis of Cumulative Temporary Differences and Deferred Taxes, 20X9

Cumulative Temporary Differences (TD)

	Beginning Balance 20X9	*Change*	*Ending Balance 20X9*
Deductible TD:			
Warranties	$ 10,000	$12,000	$ 22,000
Revenue received in advance	7,000	4,000	11,000
Litigation	0	10,000	10,000
(Taxable) TD:			
Depreciation	(28,000)	(35:000)	(63,000)
	$(11,000)	$ (9,000)	$(20,000)

Deferred Income Taxes

	Beginning Balance @34%	*Ending Balance @40%*	*Change*
Assets:			
Warranties	$ 3,400	$ 8,800	$ 5,400
Revenue received in advance	2,380	4,400	2,020
Litigation loss	0	4,000	4,000
(Liabilities):			
Depreciation	(9,520)	(25,200)	(15,680)
	$(3,740)	$ (8,000)	$ (4,260)

The statutory rate reconciliation has an additional component in 20X9, because of the tax rate change from 34% to 40%. This change has the effect of increasing deferred taxes and, therefore, tax expense, as indicated in the following reconciliation:

Pretax financial income at statutory rate ($150,000 × 40%)	$ 60,000
Less: Permanent differences ($12,000 × 40%)	(4,800)
Plus: Tax increase on beginning cumulative temporary differences [$11,000 × (40% – 34%)]	660
Income tax expense	$ 55,860

Notice that the adjustment for the increase in the tax rate is calculated only for the beginning balance of cumulative temporary differences. The temporary differences originating in 20X9 have already been taxed at 40%. As indicated earlier, the balance sheet and income statement presentation of deferred tax information will be considered after the analysis for 20Y0.

During the third year of this Illustration, Power Company's activities took a significant downturn. Because of negative economic trends and a loss of several important contracts, the company reported a pretax financial *loss* of $275,000.

An analysis of the pretax financial loss, permanent and temporary differences, and the amount of loss for tax purposes are analyzed as follows:

Pretax financial (loss)	$(275,000)
Permanent difference:	
Interest on municipal securities	(15,000)
Pretax financial (loss) subject to tax	$(290,000)
Temporary differences:	
Depreciation	(40,000)
Warranties	18,000
Revenue received in advance ($15,000 – $10,000)	5,000
Litigation loss	(10,000)
Taxable (loss)	$(317,000)

This analysis is similar to those for 20X8 and 20X9, except for the negative amount of pretax financial loss. Revenue of $10,000 received in advance that was previously taxed was recognized in accounting income and an additional $15,000 was received that was deferred for accounting purposes, but taxed currently. The litigation of 20X9 was completed and the $10,000 loss was deducted for tax purposes.

Notice that the loss for tax purposes is $317,000. Assume that Power Company decides to carry back the loss to the extent possible and receive a refund for income taxes paid in the carryback period. Under current tax law, the loss can be carried back only two years, the entire life of Power Company. The amount of the refund to be received is $100,560:

20X8: $144,000 × 34%	=	$ 48,960
20X9: $129,000 × 40%	=	51,600
		$100,560

The determination of deferred tax balances in Exhibit C is similar to those in the two previous exhibits with modifications necessary to include the loss carryforward of $44,000, which is determined by subtracting the amount of loss that is carried back from the total loss for tax purposes for 20Y0:

$317,000 – ($144,000 + $129,000) = $44,000

EXHIBIT C: Analysis of Cumulative Temporary Differences and Deferred Taxes, 20Y0

Cumulative Temporary Differences (TD)

	Beginning Balance20 Y0	*Change*	*Ending Balance 20Y0*
Deductible TD:			
Warranties	$ 22,000	$ 18,000	$ 40,000
Revenue received in advance	11,000	5,000	16,000
Litigation	10,000	(10,000)	0
(Taxable) TD:			
Depreciation	(63,000)	(40,000)	(103,000)
Loss Carryforward:			
20Y0 Loss*	0	44,000	44,000
	$(20,000)	$ 17,000	$ (3,000)

Deferred Income Taxes

	Beginning Balance @40%	*Ending Balance @40%*	*Change*
Assets:			
Warranties	$ 8,800	$16,000	$ 7,200
Revenue received in advance	4,400	6,400	2,000
Litigation loss	4,000	0	(4,000)
Loss carryforward	0	17,600	17,600
(Liabilities):			
Depreciation	(25,200)	(41,200)	(16,000)
	$(8,000)	$(1,200)	$6,800

* [$317,000–($144,000 + $129,000)]

A category for the $44,000 loss carryforward has been added to the analysis at the top of Exhibit C. The loss carryforward results in a deferred tax asset, as indicated in the analysis at the bottom of Exhibit C.

PRACTICE POINTER: Accumulating the information required to implement ASC 740 is facilitated by preparing a workpaper like those in Exhibits A, B, and C. Such a workpaper includes the following major components:

- A record of the cumulative temporary differences and carryforwards, including:
  - Separation of temporary differences into taxable and deductible categories
  - Beginning balances, the increase or decrease in the cumulative temporary differences, and the ending balances
- A record of cumulative amounts of carryforwards identified by year
- A record of deferred income taxes, including:
  - Separate classifications of deferred tax liabilities and assets
  - Beginning balances, ending balances, and the resulting changes in deferred taxes for the year

---

The journal entry to record income taxes at the end of 20Y0 is as follows:

Dec. 31, 20Y0		
Receivable for past income taxes [($144,000 × 34%) + ($129,000 × 40%)]	$100,560	
Deferred income tax asset ($40,000 – $17,200)	22,800	
Deferred income tax liability ($41,200 – $25,200)		$ 16,000
Income tax benefit ($100,560 + $6,800)		107,360

As shown in the change column of Exhibit C, the balances of both the deferred income asset and liability increased significantly from 20X9 to 20Y0. The two most significant differences are the reversal of the temporary difference from the litigation loss and the inclusion of the loss carryforward, both of which are relatively large amounts.

In the journal entry above, income tax expense has been replaced by the account income tax benefit, which indicates the positive impact (loss reduction) of using the 20Y0 loss to receive the refund of 20X8 and 20X9 income taxes and to offset income taxes that would otherwise have to be paid after 20Y0.

The 20Y0 statutory rate reconciliation can now be prepared as follows:

Pretax financial (loss) at statutory rate [($275,000) × 40%]	$(110,000)
Less: Permanent differences ($15,000 × 40%)	(6,000)
Plus: Loss carryback at 34% [$144,000 × (40% – 34%)]	8,640
Income tax (benefit)	$(107,360)

The last item in the reconciliation, identified as "loss carryback at 34%," is required because the 20X8 part of the carryback was determined at 34%, the 20X8 income tax rate, rather than the current (20Y0) rate of 40%.

Now that the three-year analysis of the cumulative temporary differences and the loss carryforward, the related deferred tax asset and liability, and the year-end journal entries to record income taxes is completed, attention can be focused on the amounts that will be presented in the balance sheet and income statements. That information is presented in Exhibit D. For each year, the deferred tax asset and liability appear in the noncurrent asset section of the balance sheet. In addition, in 20Y0, a current asset is presented for the $100,560 receivable of 20X8 and 20X9 taxes resulting from the 20Y0 carryback. For 20X8 and 20X9, a current liability is presented for income taxes payable—$48,960 and $51,600 in 20X8 and 20X9, respectively.

The income statement presentation for each year displays pretax financial income (loss), followed by income tax expense (benefit), separated into current and deferred components. In 20X8 and 20X9, income tax expense reduces the amount of net income reported, as would be expected given the profitability reported by the company in those years. In 20Y0, however, the benefit of the carryback and carryforward results in a reduction in the amount of loss that would otherwise have been reported because of the refund of past taxes and the anticipation of reduced taxes in the future, when the carryforward is realized.

EXHIBIT D: Financial Statement Presentation of Income Taxes, 20X8-20Y0

Balance Sheet

	20X8	20X9	20Y0
Current assets:			
Receivable: for past income taxes	—	—	$100,560

Balance Sheet

	20X8	*20X9*	*20Y0*
Noncurrent asset:			
Deferred income tax asset	$5,780	$7,200	40,000
Current liabilities:			
Income taxes payable	48,960	51,600	—
Noncurrent liabilities:			
Deferred income tax liability	9,520	25,200	41,200

Income Statement

Income (loss):			
Before income tax	$160,000	$150,000	$(275,000)
Income tax expense (benefit):			
Current	48,960	51,600	(100,560)
Deferred	3,740	4,260	(6,800)
	52,700	55,860	(107,360)
Net income (loss)	$107,300	$ 94,140	$(167,640)

To examine the accounting procedures required when a valuation allowance is established for deferred tax assets, return to Exhibit C. Assume that, after careful consideration, management determines it is more likely than not that 25% of the deferred tax assets will not be realized. This requires a valuation allowance of $10,000 based on the information from Exhibit C: Total deferred tax asset of $6,400 + $16,000 + $17,600 = $40,000 × 25% = $10,000.

The journal entry to record income taxes at the end of 20Y0 under these revised assumptions, and including the valuation allowance, is as follows:

Dec. 31, 20Y0		
Receivable for past income taxes [($144,000 × 34%) + ($129,000 × 40%)]	$100,560	
Deferred income tax asset	22,800	
Allowance to reduce deferred tax assets to lower recoverable value		$10,000
Deferred income tax liability		16,000
Income tax benefit ($100,560 + $6,800 – $10,000)		97,360

The statutory rate reconciliation for 20Y0, including the recognition of the valuation allowance, is as follows:

Pretax financial income (loss) at statutory rate [($275,000) × 40%]	$(110,000)
Less: Permanent differences ($15,000 × 40%)	(6,000)
Plus: Loss carryback at 34% [$144,000 × (40% – 34%)]	8,640
Increase in valuation allowance	10,000
Income tax (benefit)	$ (97,360)

The valuation allowance is evaluated at the end of each year, considering positive and negative evidence about whether the asset will be realized. At that time, the allowance will either be increased or reduced; reduction could result in the complete elimination of the allowance if positive evidence indicates that the value of the deferred tax assets is no longer impaired and the allowance is no longer required.

UNCERTAIN TAX POSITIONS

ASC 740 recognizes that the ultimate deductibility of positions taken on tax returns is often uncertain. Guidance is provided on when tax positions claimed by an entity can be recognized (recognition) and guidance on the dollar amount at which those positions are recorded (measurement). Differences between tax positions taken in a tax return and recognized in accordance with ASC 740 will generally result in an increase in income taxes currently payable or a reduction in an income tax refund receivable or an increase in a deferred tax liability or a decrease in a deferred tax asset.

Scope

Because income taxes primarily affect business enterprises, ASC 740 is most applicable to for-profit businesses. However, ASC 740 also applies, assuming income taxes are an issue, to not-for-profit entities and pass-through entities (e.g., real estate investment trusts and investment companies).

A tax position is a position taken in a tax return already filed or to be filed in the future and that affects the determination of deferred income tax assets or liabilities (in either annual or quarterly financial statements). The effects of a tax position can result in either a permanent reduction in taxes payable or a reduction in the deferral of taxes payable to a future period, or can increase the realizability of deferred tax assets. Examples of tax positions include shifting income from one tax jurisdiction to another, the inclusion and characterization of income, and the recognition of deductions (ASC Glossary).

Recognition

The definition of the appropriate unit of account for analyzing uncertain tax positions is judgmental. In exercising this judgment, the entity must consider both how it prepares and supports its tax return, as well as the likely approach taken by the relevant taxing authority in defining the unit of account for the entity (ASC 740-10-25-13).

The entity initially recognizes the effects on the financial statements of a tax position when it is more likely than not (i.e., greater than a 50% likelihood) that the claimed tax position will be upheld by the relevant taxing authority, including any appeals or litigation. The evaluation of whether the tax position is more likely than not to be upheld should be based on the facts, circumstances and information regarding the technical merits of the position (ASC 740-10-25-6). In making this evaluation, the entity should:

- Presume that the tax position will be evaluated by the relevant taxing authority, and that this authority will have full knowledge of the facts and circumstances surrounding the position (ASC 740-10-25-7).
- Evaluate the technical merits of a tax position based on tax legislation, statutes, and related legislative intent (implementing regulations and rulings and case law) (ASC 740-10-25-7).
- Consider each tax position on its own—that is, do not consider the possibility of offset or aggregation (ASC 740-10-25-7).

The benefits associated with tax positions that are not more-likely-than-not to be upheld are not recognized in the financial statements. Rather, a liability for the additional tax that taxing authorities are likely to assess is recognized in the financial statements.

Measurement

Before the financial statement effects of a tax position are recognized, the entity must conclude that it is more-likely-than-not that the tax position will be upheld by the relevant taxing authority. For each tax position, the entity is to consider the possible dollar amounts that might be realized upon settlement with the appropriate taxing authority (i.e., there is an implicit assumption that the tax return will be audited and that all tax positions will be evaluated). The entity is to estimate the probabilities associated with each possible settlement of the tax position. The amount recognized in the financial statements is the largest amount where the probability of ultimate receipt exceeds 50% (ASC 740-10-30-7).

PRACTICE POINTER: Relatively few tax disputes are litigated and even fewer are litigated to the court of "last resort." Therefore, assuming the tax position is more-likely-than-not to be upheld, the amount recognized related to the tax position is often the amount that the entity would settle for in a negotiation with taxing authorities ASC 740-10-55-4.

Effect of ASC 740 on Evaluation of Deferred Tax Assets

To realize a deferred tax asset, an entity must have taxable income in the future. Some entities plan to use one or more tax-planning strategies to provide taxable income in the future. ASC 740 is to be applied in evaluating the amount of any future taxable income as a result of using a tax-planning strategy (ASC 740-10-30-20).

PRACTICE POINTER: To the extent that future taxable income as a result of applying a tax-planning strategy is not more-likely-than-not to be realized, the entity may have to increase the valuation allowance associated with any recognized deferred tax asset.

Subsequent Recognition

A tax position may not be more-likely-than-not to be upheld at the time the position is initially taken, but circumstances may change in the future such that the tax position becomes more-likely-than-not to be upheld. The financial statement effects of the tax position are to be recognized in the first interim period that any of the following conditions occur (ASC 740-10-25-8): (1) it is now more-likely-than-not that the tax position will be upheld by the relevant taxing authority, (2) the entity has negotiated a settlement of the tax position with the taxing authority, or (3) the statute of limitations for the taxing authority to challenge the claimed tax position has expired.

Any such change in the evaluation of the realizability of a tax position must result from the receipt of new information, not from a new evaluation of information that existed at the time the tax position was originally taken (ASC 740-10-25-14).

Derecognition

If circumstances change and an unrecognized tax position is no longer more-likely-than-not to be recognized, the financial statement effects of the tax position are to be derecognized in the first period when this change occurs. An entity cannot use a valuation allowance account as a substitute for derecognizing the financial statement effects of the tax position (ASC 740-10-40-2).

Treatment of Interest and Penalties

An entity may take a tax position in its return that does not even meet the minimum statutory threshold for the avoidance of penalties. In this case, the entity recognizes an expense for the amount of the statutory penalty in the period in which the tax position is taken. If circumstances change and the more-likely-than-not threshold is met, a settlement with the taxing authorities is reached, or the statute of limitations for examining prior tax returns lapses, than previously recognized interest and penalties is derecognized (ASC 740-10-25-57).

The recognition of interest that result from the application of ASC 740 can be treated as either income tax expense or interest expense, and penalties can be treated as either income tax expense or in another expense classification. The entity is given discretion in categorizing interest and penalties. However, the categorization of interest and penalties must be consistently applied (ASC 740-10-45-25). In addition, the entity must disclose its policy on how it treats interest and penalties in its financial statements (ASC 740-10-50-19).

Financial Statement Classification

An unrecognized tax benefit exists for the difference between a position taken on a tax return and the amount recognized under the provisions of ASC 740. Essentially, tax positions that are unlikely to be upheld are not recognized in the financial statements and are labeled as unrecognized tax benefits. An unrecognized tax position creates a liability for financial reporting purposes (or reduces an income tax refund receivable or a net operating loss carryforward). The liability reflects the fact that an entity is paying a taxing authority less (based on the filed tax return) than is likely to eventually be owed because certain tax positions are unlikely to be upheld (ASC 740-10-25-16; 740-10-45-11).

The application of ASC 740 also may affect the recognition of deferred tax assets and liabilities. Taxable and deductible temporary differences result from the difference between the book basis of assets and liabilities and the tax basis of those same assets and liabilities. Taxable and deductible temporary differences, formerly based on the tax treatment used in the tax return, are based on the tax treatment that is likely to ultimately be upheld by the relevant taxing authorities (ASC 740-10-25-17).

Disclosure Requirements

A table reconciling the total amounts of unrecognized tax benefits from the beginning to the end of the year must be included for each annual reporting period. At a minimum, this table must include (ASC 740-10-50-15A):

- The gross amounts of increases and decreases in unrecognized tax benefits as a result of tax positions taken in the current and prior periods. An unrecognized tax benefit results from a tax position claimed on a tax return that is not given financial statement effect because it is not more-likely-than-not that the tax position will be upheld by taxing authorities.
- The gross amounts of decreases in unrecognized tax benefits resulting from settlements with taxing authorities.
- The gross amounts of decreases in unrecognized tax benefits resulting from a lapse in the statute of limitations.

In addition to the above, the entity must disclose the total amount of unrecognized tax benefits that would affect the entity's tax rate if they were recognized and the total amount of interest and penalties included in the income statement and the balance sheet (ASC 740-10-50-15). Moreover, if the entity has any unrecognized tax benefits where the amount of these unrecognized benefits may significantly increase or decrease over the next year, the entity must disclose (ASC 740-10-50-15):

- A description of the uncertainty.
- A description of the event that could change the amount of unrecognized tax benefits.
- An estimate of the amount by which the unrecognized tax benefit may change (range) or a statement that an estimate of this range cannot be developed.

The entity also must disclose the tax years that are still subject to examination by the taxing authorities (ASC 740-10-50-15).

Implementation Guidance

Subsequent to the issuance of ASC 740-10, the FASB issued implementation guidance on accounting for uncertainty in income taxes and amend disclosures for nonpublic entities (ASC 740-10).

Following are the key provisions of this guidance:

- If income taxes paid by the entity are attributable to the entity, the transaction should be accounted for consistent with the guidance for uncertainty in income taxes in ASC 740-10. If income taxes paid by the entity are attributable to the owners, the transaction should be recorded as a transaction with the owners. The determination of attribution should be made for each jurisdiction where the entity is subject to income taxes and is determined on the basis of laws and regulations of each jurisdiction.
- Management determination of the taxable status of the entity, including its status as a pass-through entity or tax-exempt not-for-profit entity, is a tax position subject to the standards required for accounting for uncertainty in income taxes.
- A reporting entity must consider the tax positions of all entities within a related group of entities regardless of the tax status of the reporting entity.
- The disclosures required by ASC 740-10-15(a)-(b) are eliminated for nonpublic entities. These disclosures require a tabular reconciliation of the total amount of unrecognized tax benefits at the beginning and end of the period and disclosure of the total amount of unrecognized tax benefits that, if recognized would affect the effective tax rate.

PRACTICE NOTE: The elimination of the disclosure requirements above resulted from users of private company financial statement indicating that these disclosures do not provide decision-useful information. Their elimination reduces the cost of preparing private company financial statements without eliminating information useful to decision makers. The elimination of these disclosures does not apply to public companies.

Illustration—Measuring Benefit of a Tax Position

Hust and Jacony Inc. have taken a tax position that results in a $80 million tax benefit. Hust and Jacony conclude that it is more-likely-than-not (more than a 50% likelihood) that its claimed tax position will be upheld by the relevant taxing authority and, as such, the benefit associated with the tax position should be recognized. However, Hust and Jacoby believe that it may not receive the full $80 million tax benefit. In determining the amount of tax benefit to record in its financial statements, Hust and Jacoby estimate potential outcomes and the probabilities associated with those outcomes. Hust and Jacoby develop the following schedule:

Estimated Outcome	*Individual Probability*	*Cumulative Probability*
$80 million	10%	10%
60 million	15%	25%
50 million	40%	65%
40 million	20%	85%
20 million	15%	100%

Hust and Jacoby would record a benefit associated with this tax position of $50 million because this is the largest benefit that has more than a 50% cumulative probability of being received.

Illustration—Measurement when Uncertainty Exists Surrounding the Timing of Tax Deductibility

Neel and Neal Inc. (N&N) purchase a separately identifiable intangible asset for $4.5 million on 1-1-X7. The intangible asset has an indefinite life for financial reporting purposes and is therefore not being amortized. The tax treatment related to the timing of the deductibility of the intangible asset is ambiguous—there is some support for an immediate expensing of the intangible asset, but other sources suggest that the intangible is to be amortized over 15 years. N&N deduct the entire cost of the intangible asset in 20X7 for tax purposes.

N&N conclude that realization of the tax benefit associated with deducting the cost of the intangible asset is more-likely-than-not and, therefore, a tax benefit is to be recognized in the financial statements. The only uncertainty is whether the entire tax benefit is recognizable in 20X7 or ratably over the next 15 years.

N&N estimates that it has a 35% likelihood of being able to deduct the entire cost of the intangible asset in 20X7. If immediate expensing is not allowed, deductibility through periodic amortization over the next 15 years would be allowed. The tax benefit that is more than 50% likely of being realized is associated with amortization over 15 years (the probability of immediate expensing being supported is only 35%). Therefore, the tax benefit is the tax savings associated with a $300,000 ($4.5 million ÷ 15 years) in 20X7.

N&N would recognize the following on its 12-31-X7 financial statements:

- A deferred tax liability related for the tax effects of the difference between the book basis of the intangible asset ($4.5 million) and the tax basis of the intangible asset ($4.2 million) (The tax basis of the intangible asset is computed based on the provisions of ASC 740, not on the amount deducted in the tax return.)
- An income tax liability for the tax effects of the difference between the deduction claimed on the tax return ($4.5 million) and the appropriate deduction determined based on the provisions of ASC 740 ($300 thousand)

In addition, N&N must evaluate whether to accrue interest and penalties because the amount claimed on the tax return exceeds the amount that is supportable under the provisions of ASC 740 (i.e., the amount that has a greater than 50% likelihood of being ultimately realized).

ASC 740-20: INTRAPERIOD TAX ALLOCATION

INTRAPERIOD TAX ALLOCATION

Income tax expense or benefit for the year shall be allocated among continuing operations, discontinued operations, and items charged or credited directly to shareholders' equity. The amount allocated to continuing operations is the tax effect of the pretax income or loss from continuing operations that occurred during the year, plus or minus income tax effects of (ASC 740-20-45-10):

- Changes in circumstances that cause a change in judgment about the realization of deferred tax assets
- Changes in tax laws or rates
- Changes in tax status
- Tax deductible dividends paid to shareholders

The remainder is allocated to items other than continuing operations (ASC 740-20-45-2).

The tax effects of the following items are charged or credited directly to the related components of stockholders' equity (ASC 740-20-45-11):

- Adjustments of the opening balance of retained earnings for certain changes in accounting principles or to correct an error.
- Gains and losses included in comprehensive income but excluded from net income.
- An increase or decrease in contributed capital.
- Deductible temporary differences and carryforwards that existed at the date of a quasi-reorganization.
- All changes in the tax bases of assets and liabilities caused by transactions among or with shareholders shall be included in equity, including the effect of valuation allowances initially required upon recognition of any related deferred tax assets. Changes in valuation allowances occurring in subsequent periods shall be included in the income statement.

Generally, the tax benefit of an operating loss carryforward or carryback is reported in the same manner as the source of the income or loss in the current year, and not in the same manner as (*a*) the source of the operating loss carryforward or taxes paid in a prior year or (*b*) the source of expected future income that will result in realization of deferred tax assets for an operating loss carryforward from the current year. Exceptions to this general rule are:

- Tax effects of deductible temporary differences and carryforwards that existed at the date of a purchase business combination and for which a tax benefit is recognized initially in subsequent years in accordance with ASC 805-740-25-3.
- Tax effects of deductible temporary differences and carryforwards that are allocated to shareholders' equity in accordance with ASC 740-20-45-11. (See previous list.)

If there is only one item other than continuing operations, the portion of income tax expense or benefit that remains after the allocation to continuing operations is allocated to that item. If there are two or more items, the amount that remains after the allocation to continuing operations is allocated among those other items in proportion to their individual effects on income tax expense or benefit for the year (ASC 740-20-45-14).

ASC 740-30: OTHER CONSIDERATIONS OR SPECIAL AREAS

INCOME TAXES IN SPECIAL AREAS

A deferred tax liability is not recognized for the following temporary differences, unless it becomes apparent that they will reverse in the foreseeable future (ASC 740-10-25-3):

- An excess of the amount for financial reporting over the tax basis of an investment in a foreign subsidiary or a foreign corporate joint venture as defined in the ASC Glossary that is essentially permanent in nature
- For a domestic subsidiary or a domestic corporate joint venture that is essentially permanent in duration, undistributed earnings that arose in fiscal years beginning on or before December 15, 1992
- "Bad debt reserves" for tax purposes of U.S. savings and loan associations and other qualified thrifts that arose in tax years beginning before December 31, 1987
- Policyholders' surplus of stock life insurance companies that arose in fiscal years beginning on or before December 15, 1992

Whenever a deferred tax liability is not recognized because of one of these exceptions, the following information is required to be disclosed (ASC 942-740-50-1):

1. A description of the types of temporary differences for which a deferred tax liability has not been recognized and the types of events that would cause those temporary differences to become taxable
2. The cumulative amount of each type of temporary difference
3. The amount of the unrecognized deferred tax liability for temporary differences related to investments in foreign subsidiaries and foreign corporate joint ventures that are essentially permanent in duration if determination of that liability is practicable, or a statement that determination is not practicable
4. The amount of the deferred tax liability for temporary differences other than those in item (3) above that is not recognized

A deferred tax liability is recognized for the following types of taxable temporary differences (ASC 740-30-25-2; 942-740-25-2):

- An excess of the amount of accounting basis over the tax basis of an investment in a domestic subsidiary that arises in fiscal years beginning after December 15, 1992
- An excess of the amount for accounting purposes over the tax basis of an investment in a 50%-or-less-owned investee except as provided in ASC 740 for a foreign corporate joint venture that is essentially permanent in nature
- "Bad debt reserves" for tax purposes of U.S. savings and loan associations and other qualified thrifts that arise in tax years beginning after December 31, 1987

Whether an excess of the amount for accounting purposes over the tax basis of an investment in a more-than-50%-owned domestic subsidiary is a taxable temporary difference must be assessed. It is not a taxable temporary difference if the tax law provides a means by which the reported amount of that investment can be recovered tax free and the enterprise expects that it will ultimately use that means (ASC 740-30-25-7).

A deferred tax asset is recognized for an excess of the tax basis over the amount for accounting purposes of an investment in a subsidiary or corporate joint venture that is essentially permanent in duration only if it is apparent that the temporary difference will reverse in the foreseeable future (ASC 740-30-25-9).

An investment in the common stock of a subsidiary may change so that it is no longer a subsidiary because the parent sells a portion of the investment, the subsidiary sells additional stock, or other transactions affect the investment. If a parent did not recognize income taxes on its equity in undistributed earnings of a subsidiary, it shall accrue in the current period income taxes on the temporary difference related to its remaining investment in accordance with the guidance in ASC 740-10 (ASC 740-30-25-15).

If a parent entity did not recognize income taxes on its equity in undistributed earnings of a subsidiary for the reasons cited in ASC 740-30-25-17 and the entity in which the investment is held ceases to be a subsidiary, it shall accrue in the current period income taxes on the temporary difference related to its remaining investment in common stock in accordance with ASC 740-10 (ASC 740-30-45-3).

ASC 740-270: INTERIM REPORTING

ACCOUNTING FOR INCOME TAXES IN INTERIM PERIODS

ASC 740 provides guidance in accounting for income taxes in interim periods in accordance with the provisions of ASC 270. Generally, an entity is required to estimate the annual effective tax rate to use to determine the interim period income tax provision, applied on a cumulative year-to-date basis (ASC 740-270-30-4-5). The estimated annual income tax rate may change between quarters within the year as the ability to estimate the annual rate improves (ASC 740-270-30-6).

Following is guidance on the determination of the estimate of the annual effective tax rate:

- The effects of new tax legislation are not recognized prior to enactment. The tax effect of a change in tax laws or rates on taxes currently payable or refundable for the current year are reflected in the computation of the annual effect tax rate beginning in the first interim period that includes the enactment date of the new legislation (ASC 740-270-25-5).
- The effects of changes in judgment about beginning-of-year valuation allowances and effects of changes in tax laws or rates on deferred tax assets or liabilities and taxes payable or refundable for prior years are excluded from the estimated annual effective tax rate calculation (ASC 740-270-30-11).
- If an entity has an ordinary loss for the year to date at the end of an interim period and anticipates an ordinary loss for the fiscal year, the interim period tax benefit is computed in accordance with ASC 740-270-30-5. The estimated tax benefit for the fiscal year used to determine the estimated annual effective tax rate shall not exceed the tax benefit determined in accordance with ASC 740-270-30-30 through 30-33 (ASC 740-270-30-28).

Investment tax credits related to leases that are accounted for as leveraged leases are deferred and accounted for as return on the net investment in the leveraged leases in the years in which the net investment is positive. The use of the term *years* is not intended to preclude application of the accounting described in shorter periods. If an entity accounts for investment tax credits related to leveraged leases in this manner, those investment tax credits are not taken into account in estimating the annual effective tax rate (ASC 740-270-30-15).

Illustration of Quarterly Income Tax Calculation

Valentine, Inc. reports pretax income for the first two quarters of 20X9 as follows: January-March, $500,000; April-June, $450,000. At the end of the first quarter, management estimates that its effective annual income tax rate will be 40%. At the end of the second quarter, this estimate had been revised to 38%.

Income tax expense for the first quarter is calculated as follows:

$$\$500{,}000 \times 40\% = \$200{,}000$$

Income tax expense for the second quarter is determined by applying the revised estimate of the effective annual income tax rate to the cumulative pretax income to date and subtracting the amount recognized as income tax expense in the first quarter:

$$[(\$500{,}000 + \$450{,}000) \times 38\%] - \$200{,}000 = \$161{,}000$$

This same process is followed for the remaining quarters of the year: cumulative income to date × the estimated annual income tax rate – previous quarters' tax expense = current quarter expense.

If an entity has a significant unusual or infrequently occurring loss or a loss from discontinued operations, the tax benefit of that loss shall be recognized in an interim period when the tax benefit is expected to be either (*a*) realized during the year, or (*b*) recognizable as a deferred tax asset at the end of the year. Realization would appear to be more likely than not if future taxable income from (ordinary) income during the current year is expected based on an established seasonal pattern of loss in early interim periods offset by income in later interim periods (ASC 740-270-25-12).

CHANGES IN DISCLOSURE REQUIREMENTS FOR INCOME TAXES

IMPORTANT NOTICE FOR 2022

A proposed ASU is outstanding which can be expected to expand income tax information disclosed in notes to the financial statements. This proposed ASU is a revision of a former proposal issued in 2016. It is a part of the FASB's disclosure framework project whose objective is to improve the effectiveness of financial statement disclosures by facilitating clear communication of information that is important to financial statement users.

The proposed changes would modify the current disclosures for income taxes. The term "public entity" would be replaced with the term "public business entity." The following additional disclosures to those currently required would apply to all entities:

- Income (or loss) from continuing operations before income tax expense (or benefit) and before intra-entity eliminations disaggregated between domestic and foreign.
- Income tax expense (or benefit) from continuing operations disaggregated between federal, state, and foreign.
- Income taxes paid disaggregated between federal, state, and foreign.

In addition to the above, public business entities would be required to disclose the following:

- The line items in the statement of financial position in which the unrecognized tax benefits are presented and related amounts of such unrecognized tax benefits.
- The amount and explanation of the valuation allowance recognized and/or released during the reporting period.
- The total amount of unrecognized tax benefits that offsets the deferred tax assets for carryforwards.

The FASB states that the proposed update would reduce diversity in practice, remove disclosures that no longer are considered cost beneficial or relevant, and would add disclosure requirements identified as relevant. The amendments would be applied prospectively. The effective date and transition requirements will be determined after the FASB considers stakeholder feedback on the proposed amendments.

PART II: INTERPRETIVE GUIDANCE

ASC 740-10: OVERALL

ASC 740-10-25-9 Definition of *Settlement* in FASB Interpretation No. 48

BACKGROUND

The FASB directed the FASB staff to draft this guidance, which amends the guidance in ASC 740-10, because constituents have asked the staff whether an entity may recognize a tax benefit that it previously had decided should not be recognized if the only change that has occurred is the completion of a tax authority's examination or audit. Constituents have also asked for clarification of the following information in ASC 740-10:

- The meaning of the term *ultimate settlement* in ASC 740-10-30-7;
- The meaning of the terms *ultimately settled* and *negotiation* in ASC 740-10-40-3;
- The concept stated in ASC 740-10-35-2 that "a tax position need not be legally extinguished and its resolution need not be certain to subsequently recognize or measure the position."

This guidance amends the guidance in ASC 740 by clarifying that a taxing authority's examination effectively could result in the settlement of a tax position. Judgment is required in determining whether a tax position is effectively settled, because examinations occur in different ways. That determination should be made separately for each individual tax position, but an entity may conclude that all its tax positions in a specific tax year have effectively been settled.

ACCOUNTING GUIDANCE

In applying the guidance in ASC 740-10-40-3, the benefit of a tax position should be recognized when it is considered to be effectively settled. All of the following conditions should be evaluated to determine whether an effective settlement has occurred:

1. The taxing authority's examination procedures have been completed, including all appeals and administrative reviews related to the tax position that the taxing authority is required or expected to perform;
2. The entity does *not* intend to appeal or litigate any aspect of the tax position included in the completed examination;
3. Assuming that the taxing authority has full knowledge of all the relevant information, the entity believes that the possibility that the taxing authority would reexamine any aspect of the tax position is remote based on the taxing authority's commonly understood policy on reopening closed examinations and the tax position's specific circumstances.

Further, to be considered effectively settled through examination, the taxing authority need not have specifically reviewed or examined the tax position in the tax years under examination. Nevertheless, a tax position's effective settlement as a result of an examination does not mean that it is an effective settlement of a similar or identical tax position that has *not* been examined.

If at a later date, an entity becomes aware that a tax position that it had considered effectively settled may be examined or reexamined, the entity should reevaluate the tax position in accordance with the guidance in ASC 740-10, because the tax position should no longer be considered to be effectively settled.

Based on information obtained during the examination process, an entity may change its judgment about the technical merits of a tax position and wish to apply that view to similar tax positions taken in other periods. However, an entity should not change its judgment about the technical merits of a tax position in other periods based exclusively on the conditions for effective settlement stated above.

A number of changes are made to the terms *ultimate settlement* or *ultimately settled,* in ASC 740-10 to conform to this guidance. The term *effectively settled* replaces the term *ultimately settled* when it is used in the Interpretation to describe recognition. Likewise, the terms *settlement* or *settled* replace the terms *ultimate settlement* or *ultimately settled* when they are used in the Interpretation to describe measurement.

ASC 740-10-25-34, 50-4, 55-2 through 55-6, 55-15 through 55-22, 55-25, 55-40 through 55-41, 55-48, 55-59 through 55-65, 55-79 through 55-80, 55-163 through 55-164, 55-168 through 55-169, 55-213 through 55-216; ASC 740-20-55-1 through 55-7; ASC 942-740-35-1 through 35-3; ASC 942-852-55-2 through 55-6; ASC 855-10-60-2 A Guide to Implementation of ASC 740 on Income Taxes

ACCOUNTING GUIDANCE

Scheduling

Question 1: When is it necessary to schedule reversal patterns of existing temporary differences?

Answer: Scheduling individual years in terms of reversals of temporary differences is required under ASC 740 in the following circumstances:

- Deferred taxes that do not relate to a specific asset or liability are classified as current or noncurrent based on the timing of their reversal.

PRACTICE POINTER: The guidance in the preceding bullet will be superseded by the guidance in ASU 2015-17, *Income Taxes (Topic 740): Balance Sheet Classification of Deferred Taxes,* when the ASU becomes effective for the financial statements of public business entities issued for annual periods that begin after December 15, 2016, and interim periods within those annual periods. For all other entities, the amendments in the ASU are effective for financial statements issued for annual periods that begin after December 15, 2017, and interim periods within annual periods that begin after December 15, 2018. Early adoption of the guidance is permitted.

- When deferred tax assets are recognized without consideration of offsetting, after which an assessment is required concerning the need for a valuation allowance. The timing of reversal of temporary differences may be an important consideration in determining the need for and amount of a valuation allowance on deferred tax assets.
- When tax rate changes are phased in, which will often require scheduling.

In scheduling the reversal of temporary differences, consistency and minimizing complexity are particularly important considerations. The same methods should be used for all temporary differences in a particular category for a particular tax jurisdiction.

Question 2: The guidance in ASC 740 states that future originating temporary differences for existing depreciable assets and their subsequent reversals are a factor in assessing the likelihood of future realization of a tax benefit of deductible temporary differences and carry forwards. Should future originating and reversing temporary differences always be scheduled for purposes of determining the need for a valuation allowance for deferred tax assets related to existing deductible temporary differences and carryforwards?

Answer: Not necessarily. There are four possible sources of taxable income to support the realizability of deferred tax assets. When it can easily be demonstrated that future taxable income will be sufficient, scheduling is generally not necessary. However, if reversal of taxable temporary differences is the basis for a realization assumption for deferred tax assets, the timing of reversal is important and may require scheduling.

Question 3: Does ASC 740 require separate deferred tax computations for each state or local tax jurisdiction?

Answer: As a general rule, the answer is "yes," if there are significant differences between the tax laws of the different jurisdictions involved. In the United States, however, many state and local income taxes are based on U.S. federal income tax, and aggregate computations of deferred tax assets and liabilities may be appropriate.

Question 4: An enterprise may have a basis under the tax law for claiming certain deductions (e.g., repair expense) on its income tax return. It may have recognized a liability (including interest) for the probable disallowance of that deduction that, if disallowed, would be capitalized for tax purposes and deductible in future years. How should an item like this be considered in the scheduling of future taxable or deductible differences?

Answer: If expenses are disallowed, taxable income of that year is higher, which provides a source of taxable income for purposes of assessing the need for a valuation allowance for deductible temporary differences. Taxable income after the year of disallowance will be lower because of annual deductions attributable to those capitalized amounts. A deductible amount for the accrued interest is scheduled for the future year in which that interest is expected to be deductible (i.e., when the underlying issues are expected to be settled with the tax authority).

Question 5: A change in tax law may require a change in accounting method for tax purposes (e.g., the uniform cost capitalization rules required by the Tax Reform Act of 1986). For calendar-year taxpayers, inventories on hand at the beginning of 1987 are revalued under the new rules, and the initial catch-up adjustment is deferred and taken into taxable income over not more than four years. Does the deferral of the initial catch-up adjustment for a change in accounting method for tax purposes give rise to a temporary difference?

Answer: Yes. The uniform cost capitalization rules initially resulted in two temporary differences—one related to the additional amounts initially capitalized into inventory for tax expense and one related to the deferred income for tax purposes that results from the initial catch-up adjustment.

Question 6: The Omnibus Budget Reconciliation Act of 1987 requires family-owned farming businesses to use the accrual method of accounting for tax purposes. The initial catch-up adjustment to change from the cash method to the accrual method is deferred and included in taxable income if the business ceases to be family-owned. It also is included in taxable income if gross receipts from farming activities in future years drop below certain 1987 levels. Does the deferral of the initial catch-up adjustment for that change in accounting method for tax purposes give rise to a temporary difference?

Answer: Yes. The entire amount of the catch-up adjustment is a temporary difference.

Question 7: State income taxes are deductible for U.S. federal income tax purposes. Does a deferred state income tax liability or asset give rise to a temporary difference for purposes of determining a deferred U.S. federal income tax liability or asset?

Answer: Yes. A deferred state income tax liability or asset gives rise to a temporary difference for purposes of determining deferred taxes for U.S. federal income tax purposes.

Recognition and Measurement

Question 8: The temporary difference for the "base-year tax reserve" of a savings and loan association is one of the exceptions to comprehensive recognition of deferred taxes under the guidance in ASC 740. If a deferred tax liability is not recognized for that temporary difference, should a savings and loan association anticipate future percentage-of-taxable-income (PTI) bad-debt deductions in determining the deferred tax liability for other types of temporary differences?

Answer: No. Deferred tax assets and liabilities for temporary differences are measured based on enacted tax rates expected to apply to taxable income when the deferred tax asset or liability is expected to be realized or settled. For the same reason that other special deductions may not be anticipated, it is not permissible to reduce a deferred tax liability by anticipating future PTI bad-debt reductions.

Question 9: An enterprise charged losses directly to contributed capital in a quasi-reorganization. At that time, the deferred tax asset for the enterprise's deductible temporary differences and carryforwards was offset by a valuation allowance. Part of those deductible temporary differences were related to losses that were included in determining income in prior years, and the remainder were attributable to losses that were charged directly to contributed capital. When recognized by reducing or eliminating the valuation allowance, how should the tax benefit of such deductible temporary differences and carryforwards be reported?

Answer: All unrecognized tax benefits of deductible temporary differences and carryforwards that existed at the time of a quasi-reorganization (except as provided in ASC 852-740-45-3 should be reported as a direct addition to contributed capital when recognized at a date after the quasi-reorganization. The benefit of an operating loss or tax credit carryforward that existed at the date of a quasi-reorganization should not be included in the determination of income of the "new" enterprise, regardless of whether they were charged to income before the quasi-reorganization or were charged directly to contributed capital as part of the quasi-reorganization. A charge to income is appropriate only if, subsequent to a quasi-reorganization, the enterprise determines that due to a change in circumstances it should recognize or increase a valuation allowance to reduce the tax benefits that were recognized in recording the quasi-reorganization.

Question 10: Some enterprises have credited a net gain directly to contributed capital at the date of a quasi-reorganization. Does the answer to Question 9 change for those enterprises?

Answer: No. The accounting for any subsequently recognized tax benefit of deductible temporary differences and carryforwards that exist at the time of a quasi-reorganization should not change based on whether gains were credited or losses charged directly to contributed capital.

Change in Tax Status

Question 11: What disclosure is required if a change in an enterprise's tax status becomes effective after year-end but before financial statements are issued?

Answer: This change should not be reflected in the financial statements of the previous year, but disclosure should include the change in the enterprise's tax status for the following year and the effects of that change, if material.

Question 12: Should an enterprise that changes from taxable C corporation status to nontaxable S corporation status eliminate its entire U.S. federal deferred tax liability?

Answer: The enterprise should continue to recognize a deferred tax liability to the extent that it would be subject to a corporate-level tax on net unrealized "built-in gains."

Illustration of Change in Tax Status

Company M's assets are as followed when its S corporation election becomes effective:

	Tax Basis	*Reported Amount*	*Temporary Difference*	*Built-In Gain (Loss)*
Marketable Securities	$100	$ 80	$(20)	$(8)
Inventory	50	100	50	20

If the enterprise has no tax loss or tax credit carryforwards available to offset the built-in gain and if marketable securities and inventory will both be sold in the same year, the $20 built-in gain on the inventory is offset by the $8 built-in loss on the marketable securities, and the $12 difference would be shown as a deferred tax liability.

Business Combinations

Questions 13-17a to c were nullified by the guidance in FAS-141(R).

Disclosure

Question 18: ASC 740 requires disclosure of the significant components of income tax expense attributable to continuing operations. Should the total of the amounts disclosed for the components of tax expense equal the amount of income tax expense that is reported in the statement of earnings? Should the amounts for current and deferred tax expense be disclosed before or after reduction for the tax benefit of operating loss carryforwards and tax credits?

Answer: The total of the amounts disclosed for the components of tax expense should be the amount of tax expense reported in the statement of earnings for continuing operations. Separate disclosure is required of (*a*) the tax benefit of operating loss carryforwards and (*b*) tax credits and tax credit carryforwards that were recognized.

Allocation of Tax Expense

Question 19: How should income tax expense be allocated between pretax income from continuing operations and other items when the enterprise has temporary differences?

Answer: The guidance in ASC 740 states that the amount of income tax expense or benefit allocated to continuing operations is the tax effect of pretax income or loss from continuing operations that occurred during the year (subject to certain adjustments). Income tax expense allocated between pretax income from continuing operations and other items should include deferred taxes.

Questions 20 and 24 are deleted because the effective date of FAS-109 has passed.

Tax-Planning Strategies

Question 25: The guidance in ASC 740 indicates that tax-planning strategies include elections for tax purposes. What are some examples of those elections?

Answer: Examples are as follows:

- Election to file a consolidated tax return
- Election to claim either a deduction or a tax credit for foreign taxes paid
- Election to forego carrying an operating loss back and only carry that loss forward

Question 26: An enterprise might identify several qualifying tax-planning strategies that would either reduce or eliminate the need for a valuation allowance for its deferred tax assets. May the enterprise recognize the effect of one strategy in the current year and postpone recognition of the effect of the other strategies to a later year?

Answer: No. The enterprise should recognize the effect of all tax-planning strategies that meet the criteria of ASC 740 in the current year.

Illustration of Multiple Tax Planning Strategies

Amber Co. has determined that its allowance on deferred tax assets should be $60,000, without regard to tax-planning strategies. The company has identified two income tax-planning strategies that would reduce its allowance on deferred tax assets by $10,000 (Strategy 1) and by $15,000 (Strategy 2), respectively. Both qualify as tax-planning strategies under FAS-109. Amber cannot recognize the effect of only Strategy 1 or only Strategy 2 but, rather, must recognize the impact of both and report an allowance on deferred tax assets of $35,000 [$60,000 – ($10,000 + $15,000)].

Question 27: Because the effects of known qualifying tax strategies must be recognized, is management required to make an extensive effort to identify all tax-planning strategies that meet the criteria for tax-planning strategies?

Answer: Management is required to make a reasonable effort to identify significant tax-planning strategies. If evidence indicates that other sources of taxable income will be adequate to eliminate the need for a valuation allowance, consideration of tax-planning strategies is not required.

Question 28: Under current U.S. federal income tax law, approval of a change from taxable C corporation status to nontaxable S status is automatic if the enterprise meets the criteria for S corporation status. If an enterprise meets those criteria but has not changed to S corporation status, would a strategy to change to nontaxable S corporation status be a qualifying tax-planning strategy that would permit an enterprise to not recognize deferred taxes?

Answer: No. The effect of a change in tax status should be recognized on the date when the change in tax status occurs.

ASC 740-10-25-39 through 25-40, 30-14 Accounting for Tax Credits Related to Dividend Payments in Accordance with ASC 740

BACKGROUND

In certain foreign jurisdictions, such as Germany, corporate income tax rates depend on whether the income is distributed to shareholders. In Germany, undistributed profits are taxed at a 45% rate, but distributed income is taxed at a 30% rate. If a corporation pays dividends from undistributed income that was taxed at the undistributed rate, it receives a tax credit or tax refund for the difference between (*a*) the tax calculated at the *undistributed rate* effective in the year the income was earned for tax purposes and (*b*) the tax calculated at the *distributed rate* effective in the year in which a dividend was paid. Germany also has an integrated tax system, under which shareholders are taxed on the pretax dividend and receive a credit for taxes previously paid by the corporation on that income. For example:

Corporate Tax before Distribution	
Taxable income	€ 500,000
Corporate tax (45%)	(225,000)
Retained earnings	275,000
Corporate Tax at Distribution	
Retained earnings	€ 275,000
Tax credit received on distribution [500,000 × (45% – 30%)]	75,000
Tax basis of dividend declared	350,000
Withholding tax (25%)	(87,500)
Cash distributed to shareholder	€ 262,500
Shareholder Taxation	
Cash received	€ 262,500
Tax withheld	87,500
	350,000

Add: Net corporate tax paid (30%)	150,000
Taxable income	500,000
Tax rate (maximum individual rate)	53%
Tax liability before credits	265,000
Tax credit for corporate tax	(150,000)
Credit for withholding tax	(87,500)
Net tax due	€ 27,500
Net cash to shareholder (262,500DM – 27,500DM)	€ 235,000

Because German companies are permitted to consider dividends declared from the current year's earnings and paid in a subsequent year in the tax provision, a blended tax rate between 45% and 30% is used. Some German companies also use a blended rate when calculating deferred tax assets and liabilities. Others use the undistributed rate and recognize the effect of the tax credit, which has no time limit, in the period in which dividends are paid. The effective tax rate for that year would be less than 30% to the extent that distributions are greater than earnings in that year.

PRACTICE NOTE: This guidance applies only to the accounting in the German entity's separate financial statements.

ACCOUNTING ISSUE

Should a corporate entity recognize in its separate financial statements a deferred tax asset for the tax benefit of future tax credits that will be realized when it distributes income that was previously taxed at the undistributed rate (thus measuring the tax effect of temporary differences at the distributed rate), or should the entity recognize the tax credit in the period in which it is realized on the tax return (thus measuring the tax effects of temporary differences at the undistributed tax rate)?

ACCOUNTING GUIDANCE

- A corporate entity paying dividends subject to a tax credit should *not* recognize a deferred tax asset for tax benefits related to future tax credits that it will realize when it distributes income that was previously taxed.
- The entity should reduce income tax expense in the period that these tax credits are included in the entity's tax return.

Consequently, the tax effects of temporary differences should be measured using the *undistributed* tax rate.

DISCUSSION

The approach supported is similar to the one discussed in ASC 740-10-25-37 for a special deduction, under which tax expense is recognized in the current period based on an estimate of the liability reported for tax purposes. The tax provision is reduced in the period in which the tax credit is realized for tax purposes. Proponents of this view argued that this approach avoids an overstatement of net assets by anticipating a refund that will occur only if earnings are distributed. The declaration and payment of dividends is the event that would trigger the recognition of a deferred tax asset in this Issue. Proponents also argued that because the company must distribute cash to realize the tax credits, a potential credit does not represent an asset that would be available to the entity's general creditors and that would be reported for an extended time period if the entity does not pay dividends. Another argument to support this view was that under FAS-109, deferred tax assets are recognized only for future deductible temporary differences and for tax credit and loss carryforwards; the tax credit in this Issue is not a basis difference or a carryforward.

PRACTICE POINTER: Under this guidance, entities with net operating loss carryforwards would recognize the deferred asset at the 45% undistributed rate.

ASC 740-10-25-41 Measurement in the Consolidated Financial Statements of a Parent of the Tax Effects Related to the Operations of a Foreign Subsidiary That Receives Tax Credits Related to Dividend Payments

OVERVIEW

Other guidance, which only applies to the accounting in the foreign entity's separate financial statements, states that a deferred tax asset should not be recognized for the tax benefits of future tax credits that will be realized when earnings taxed at the undistributed tax rate are subsequently distributed to shareholders. Thus, the tax effects of temporary differences would be measured at the undistributed tax rate in a foreign subsidiary's separate financial statements. This Issue applies to the accounting in the parent's consolidated financial statements.

ACCOUNTING ISSUE

Should the tax effects related to the operations of a foreign subsidiary eligible to receive a tax credit for dividends paid be measured based on the undistributed or distributed tax rate of the applicable foreign jurisdiction in the consolidated financial statements of a parent company that has not taken advantage of the exception in APB-23 for foreign unremitted earnings?

ACCOUNTING GUIDANCE

- The *distributed* rate should be used to measure a future tax credit that will be received when dividends are paid. The deferred tax effects related to a foreign subsidiary's operations should be measured at the distributed rate in a parent company's consolidated financial statements if the entity does not apply the exception for foreign unremitted earnings in ASC 740-30.
- The undistributed rate should be used in a parent company's consolidated financial statements to the extent that deferred taxes have not been provided for unremitted earnings as a result of the application of the exception in ASC 740-30.

DISCUSSION

Proponents of using the distributed rate in the parent's consolidated financial statements noted that, under this guidance, the transfer of cash is within the entity, while dividends discussed in other guidance would be paid to outside shareholders. An argument supporting the distributed rate was that a corporation's income will eventually be distributed to its shareholders for whose benefit it is earned. In addition, the tax credit is available to German corporations for an unlimited time once income has been taxed at the undistributed rate. When a dividend is distributed to the parent by a German subsidiary, the tax credit will be realized at the distributed rate. Some proponents of this view also analogized the distributed tax rate to the regular tax system and the undistributed tax rate to the alternative tax system as used in the discussion of the recognition of a deferred tax asset for alternative minimum tax credit carryforwards in ASC 740-10-25-3.

ASC 740-10-25-43; ASC 840-30-35-48 through 35-52 Tax Reform Act of 1986: Issues Related to the Alternative Minimum Tax

BACKGROUND

Under the Tax Reform Act of 1986 (the Act), an entity computes its federal income tax liability based on the regular tax system or on the alternative minimum tax (AMT) system, whichever tax amount is greater. An entity may earn an AMT credit for tax paid under the AMT system that exceeds the amount that would have been paid under the regular tax system. An AMT credit can be carried forward indefinitely to reduce the regular tax in future years, but not below the AMT for that year.

ACCOUNTING ISSUES

- Should the AMT system be considered a separate but parallel tax system that can generate a credit for use in future years, or should the AMT amount paid in excess of the regular tax that results in an AMT credit be considered a prepayment of the regular tax in a future year?
- Should leveraged lease calculations consider the effect of the AMT on cash flows and, if so, how? (Discussed in Chapter 56, *ASC 842—Leases*.)

ACCOUNTING GUIDANCE

The AMT system should be considered a separate but parallel tax system that may result in a tax carryforward. Because the AMT credit can only be used to reduce regular tax in excess of AMT in a future year, it should not be considered a prepayment of the regular tax in a future year.

SUBSEQUENT DEVELOPMENT

The guidance in ASC 740-10-30-10 states that, for federal tax purposes, the applicable tax rate is the regular tax rate. The applicable tax rate in other jurisdictions is determined based on the tax law after considering any interaction between the two systems. A deferred tax asset is recognized for AMT carryforwards in accordance with the Statement's requirements for the computation of deferred tax assets and the provision of a valuation allowance.

DISCUSSION

The decision to treat the AMT as a separate tax system was based on the fact that the AMT system included many items considered to be "permanent" tax differences under the provisions of APB-11, which was the authoritative pronouncement on accounting for income taxes at the time this Issue was discussed. Some argued that because the AMT credit could be carried forward only to offset the regular tax in excess of the AMT in future years, its realizability was not assured and amounts that would otherwise be excluded from taxation would be taxed under the AMT system.

Under the guidance in ASC 740, the AMT credit is treated as a deferred tax asset that may require a valuation allowance. To simplify the calculation of deferred taxes, the recognition of deferred taxes for regular tax temporary differences at the enacted regular tax rate is required. Thus, an entity that can offset taxable differences with tax-deductible differences can realize the tax benefit at the regular tax rate. However, if an entity expects to be taxed indefinitely under the AMT system, has no reversals available, and must use regular tax-deductible differences against future taxable income, it may need to establish a valuation allowance to reduce its deferred tax asset to an amount that is realizable under the AMT system. In addition, under the provisions of ASC 740, an entity's deferred tax liability may build up beyond an amount that can be reversed, because deferred taxes continue to be provided on deferred tax liabilities at the regular rate, which exceeds the AMT rate. Nevertheless, an entity that continues paying taxes based on the AMT system will eventually have a deferred tax asset from AMT credit carryforwards sufficient to reduce the deferred tax liability to the AMT rate applied to AMT differences. Because of these anomalous results, some now believe that the AMT credit is a prepayment of regular taxes.

ASC 740-10-25-48 Effect of a Retroactive Change in Enacted Tax Rates That Is Included in Income from Continuing Operations

OVERVIEW

The Omnibus Budget Reconciliation Act of 1993 (OBRA) was enacted on August 10, 1993. OBRA increased the top corporate tax rate from 34% to 35% retroactively to January 1, 1993. ASC 740-10-35-4; 45-15 requires adjusting deferred tax liabilities and assets for the effect of a change in tax rates and including the adjustment in income from continuing operations in the period that includes the date the new tax law was enacted.

ACCOUNTING ISSUES

- If an enacted change in tax rates has a retroactive effective date, how should the tax effect on current and deferred tax assets and liabilities be measured on the date of enactment?
- How should the reported tax effect among items not included in income from continuing operations, such as discontinued operations (see the guidance in ASU 2014-08, *Presentation of Financial Statements (ASC 205) and Property, Plant, and Equipment (ASC 360): Reporting Discontinued Operations and Disclosures of Disposals of Components of an Entity*), cumulative effects of changes in accounting principles, and items charged or credited directly to shareholders' equity, be measured and recognized?

ACCOUNTING GUIDANCE

- The tax effect of a retroactive change in enacted tax rates on current and deferred tax assets and liabilities should be measured on the date of enactment (August 10, 1993), based on temporary differences and currently taxable income existing at the date of enactment. The cumulative tax effect should be included in income from continuing operations.
- An entity should measure the reported tax effect of items not included in income from continuing operations, such as discontinued operations (see the guidance in ASU 2014-08), cumulative effects of changes in accounting principles, and items charged or credited directly to shareholders' equity, that occurred during the current fiscal year but before the date of enactment based on the enacted rate at the time the transaction was recognized for financial reporting purposes. The tax effect of a retroactive change in enacted tax rates on current or deferred tax assets and liabilities related to such items should be included in income from continuing operations in the period in which the change was enacted.

Illustration Using Guidance in ASC 740-10-25-48

Income from January 1, 19X3, through August 9, 19X3	
Pretax income from continuing operations	$5,000,000
Pretax income from extraordinary gain on June 30, 19X3	500,000
Total pretax income on August 9, 19X3	$5,500,000
Temporary differences	
Balance on January 1, 19X3	$8,000,000
Extraordinary gain on June 30, 19X3	500,000
Balance on August 10, 19X3	$8,500,000
Total 19X3 tax expense	
Current ($5,000,000 × .35)	$1,750,000
Deferred [($8,500,000 × .35) – ($8,000,000 × .34)]	255,000
Total 19X3 tax expense	$2,005,000
Allocation of 19X3 tax expense	
Continuing operations	
Current	$1,750,000
Rate change ($8,500,000 × .01)	85,000
Extraordinary item	
Tax effect on extraordinary gain ($500,000 × .34)	170,000
Total 19X3 tax expense	$2,005,000
Effect of change in rates enacted August 10, 19X3	
Increase in tax on income from continuing operations ($5,000,000 × .01)	$ 50,000
Increase in tax on balance of temporary differences on August 10, 19X3 ($8,500,000 × .01)	85,000
Adjustment included in continuing operations in period of enactment	$ 135,000
Tax adjustment allocated to extraordinary gain in period of enactment*	0

* The tax adjustment is included in the rate change on $8,500,000, which is allocated to continuing operations.

ASC 740-10-25-50 through 25-54, 35-5, 45-22 through 45-24, S25-1, S99-3, 55-171 through 55-191, 55-199 through 55-201, 55-203 through 55-204, 55-76 Accounting for Acquired Temporary Differences in Certain Purchase Transactions That Are Not Accounted for as Business Combinations

BACKGROUND

The guidance in ASC 740-10-25-29 provides that a deferred tax liability or deferred tax asset be recognized for all temporary differences between the reported amount of an asset or liability and its tax basis in accordance with the measurement guidance in ASC 740-10-30-5. The guidance in ASC 805-740-25-3 provides specific guidance for the accounting of deferred taxes in business combinations. Under the guidance in ASC 740, an acquiring entity is required to recognize a deferred tax liability or a deferred tax asset, or both, for differences among the assigned values and the tax bases of assets and liabilities acquired in a business combination. Deferred tax assets and deferred tax liabilities recognized as a result of a business combination are included in the calculation of the purchase price of the acquisition in accordance with the guidance in ASC 805-740-55-3, rather than in income in the period in which the combination occurred.

This Issue was raised because ASC 740 did not provide guidance on how to account for a deferred tax asset or deferred tax liability that results from the purchase of a single asset that is *not* a business combination. The Issue applies to the following four types of transactions:

- A company imports an asset into a foreign jurisdiction. The asset costs $100 but its tax basis is reduced to $80 as a result of a penalty imposed by the jurisdiction on imported goods.
- A foreign jurisdiction is encouraging companies in certain industries to purchase certain kinds of equipment. A company purchases an asset that costs $100, but its tax basis has been increased to $150. The additional tax deduction cannot be recaptured on sale of the asset.

- A subsidiary of a U.S. company acquires a shell company that has no assets to take advantage of its net operating losses (NOLs). The NOLs are acquired at a discount from their undiscounted face value. For example, NOLs with a $5 million deferred tax benefit are acquired for $2 million.
- Corporate taxpayers in a foreign country can elect to step up the tax basis of certain fixed assets to fair value if they immediately pay the authorities 3% of the step-up. A company would make this election if it believes it's likely that it will use the additional deductions (at the U.S. corporate 22% tax rate) to reduce future taxable income and the current payment is justified by the timing and amount of future tax savings.

ACCOUNTING ISSUES

- How should an entity account for the tax effect of an acquisition of assets not in a business combination if the acquisition cost and tax basis differ?
- How should an entity account for a net-tax benefit as a result of a purchase of future tax benefits from a nongovernmental third party that is not a taxing authority?
- How should an entity account for all direct transactions with a government acting as a taxing authority?

ACCOUNTING GUIDANCE

1. If the amount paid for an asset acquired individually, not in a business combination, differs from its tax basis, the tax effect of the purchase should *not* be recognized in income immediately. The asset's assigned value and the related deferred tax asset or liability should be determined by using the simultaneous equations method, which is illustrated in Example 1 below. The following guidance should be applied:
   a. Recognize (1) a *financial asset* at its fair value, (2) an *acquired asset held for disposal* at fair value less cost to sell, and (3) deferred tax assets as required in ASC 740.
   b. Allocate the excess of amounts assigned to acquired assets over the amount paid pro rata to reduce the assigned values of acquired noncurrent assets, except those discussed in (a) above. If noncurrent assets have been reduced to zero, classify a remainder, if any, as a deferred credit, which is not a temporary difference under the guidance in ASC 740.
   c. Adjust the purchase price in accordance with the guidance in ASC 805-740-30-3, for a reduction in the acquiring company's valuation allowance directly related to the asset acquisition. After the acquisition, account for an acquired valuation allowance in accordance with the guidance in ASC 805-740-25-3 through 25-4; 45-2.
   d. Amortize to income tax expense deferred credits resulting from the application of the guidance in proportion to the tax benefits realized by recognizing those deferred credits, which should not be classified as deferred tax liabilities or offset against deferred tax assets.
   e. Subsequent to the acquisition, account for the effect of the adjustments as follows: (1) recognize in continuing operations as part of income tax expense, if it becomes more likely than not that some or all of an acquired deferred tax asset will not be realized, and (2) offset against income tax expense the proportionate share of any unamortized balance of the deferred credit.
   f. Account for income tax uncertainties that exist at the acquisition date in accordance with the guidance in ASC 740-10-45-23.
2. An entity purchasing future tax benefits from a nongovernmental third party should account for the net tax benefit using the same model as discussed above in the guidance above.
3. Recognize in income transactions directly between a taxpayer and a governmental entity acting in its capacity as a taxing authority, in a manner similar to the accounting for changes in tax laws, rates, or other tax elections under the guidance in ASC 740.

PRACTICE POINTER: ASC 740-10-25-54, on which the following paragraph was originally based, has been amended in ASU 2019-12, *Income Taxes (Topic 740): Simplifying the Accounting for Income Taxes*. The paragraph, as amended, is shown below. The amendment is effective for public business entities for fiscal years that begin after December 15, 2020, and interim periods within those fiscal years. The guidance is effective for all other entities for fiscal years that begin after December 15, 2021, and interim periods within fiscal years that begin after December 15, 2022. Early adoption is permitted for public business entities for periods for which financial statements have not yet been issued, and for other entities for periods for which financial statements have not yet been made available for issuance.

If a step up in the tax basis of goodwill is related to a separate transaction, a deferred tax asset would be recognized for the total amount of the newly created tax goodwill.

In addition, if inventory was transferred by one of a group's tax-paying components to another of the group's tax-paying components, the prohibition in ASC 740-10-25-3(e) against the recognition of a deferred tax asset for the difference between the basis of the inventory in the buyer's tax jurisdiction and the inventory's reported carrying value in the consolidated group's financial statements would apply. That prohibition also applies to intercompany purchases of tax benefits by one component of a consolidated group from one of its other components.

SEC OBSERVER COMMENT

The SEC Observer reported that unless the SEC staff clearly understands the specific fact pattern, the staff would object if the guidance in this Issue were applied to adjust the basis of acquired assets in situations other than those discussed in the following examples.

Illustrations of the Guidance on Accounting for Temporary Differences in Certain Purchases That Are Not Accounted for as Business Combinations

Example 1—Tax basis exceeds purchase price

A. A company purchases a building for $500,000 in a foreign jurisdiction that permits tax deductions to exceed the cost of the asset. The tax basis of the building is $600,000 and the tax rate is 40%. The additional tax deduction is not recaptured when the asset is sold.

The following simultaneous equations should be used to determine the amounts at which to recognize the building and the deferred tax asset:

FBB = Final Book Basis

CPP = Cash Purchase Price

DTA = Deferred Tax Asset

To determine the amount of the building's FBB:

$\text{FBB} - (\text{Tax Rate} \times (\text{FBB} - \text{Tax Basis})) = \text{CPP}$

$\text{FBB} - (.40 \times (\text{FBB} - \$600{,}000)) = \$500{,}000$

$\text{FBB} = \$433{,}333$

To determine the amount of DTA:

$(\text{Tax Basis} - \text{FBB}) \times \text{Tax Rate} = \text{DTA}$

$(\$600{,}000 - \$433{,}333) \times .40 = \text{DTA}$

$\text{DTA} = \$66{,}667$

The company would make the following entry for the transaction:

Building	$433,333	
Deferred Tax Asset	66,667	
Cash		$500,000

B. The same situation as in A above, but the purchase price is $250,000 and the tax basis is $1,000,000.

Use the formulas above to calculate the FBB and DTA.

FBB = ($250,000)

Because FBB is a negative amount, zero is used for FBB in the second equation.

DTA = $400,000

When recording the transaction, the difference between the deferred tax asset and the amount of cash paid to acquire the building is recognized as a deferred credit as follows:

Building	$0	
Deferred tax asset	$400,000	
Deferred credit		$150,000
Cash		$250,000

C. In this example the acquisition of a financial asset results in a deferred credit. Company X acquires the stock of Company Y for $900,000. Company Y's principal asset is a marketable equity security with a fair value of $750,000 and a tax basis of $1,250,000. The tax rate is 40%. The acquisition of Company Y's stock is accounted for as an asset acquisition, not a business combination, because Company Y has no operations.

In recording this transaction, the acquired financial asset is recognized at its fair value and the deferred tax asset is calculated based on the guidance in ASC 740. A deferred credit is recognized for the difference between the total of the fair value of the stock plus the amount of the deferred asset and the amount paid for the stock.

Marketable equity security	$750,000	
Deferred tax asset ($500,000 × .40)	200,000	
Deferred credit		$ 50,000
Cash		900,000

D. In this example, Company Z acquires future tax benefits by purchasing the net operating loss carryforwards (NOLs) of Company P, which is a shell company without operations. The shell entity is acquired for $7 million, which is substantially less than the $15 million gross amount of the deferred tax asset for the NOLs. It is more likely than not that the deferred tax asset will be realized. The tax rate is 40%.

In recording the transaction, Company Z recognizes the deferred tax asset at its gross amount and records a deferred credit for the amount by which the deferred tax asset exceeds the amount paid.

Deferred tax asset	$15,000,000	
Deferred credit		$8,000,000
Cash		7,000,000

Example 2—Purchase price exceeds tax basis

A company in a foreign jurisdiction imports a machine, which costs $25,000. Its tax basis is reduced, however, to $20,000, because the jurisdiction imposes a 20% penalty on imported goods. A deferred tax liability has to be recognized for the temporary difference related to the machine. The tax rate is 40%.

The amount of the machine's final book basis (FBB) and the deferred tax liability (DTL) are calculated by the simultaneous equations used in Example 1.

FBB – .40 × (FBB – $20,000) = $25,000

FBB = $28,333

($28,333 – $20,000) .40 = DTL

DTL = $3,333

The company recognizes the following amount:

Machine	$28,333	
Deferred tax liability		$3,333
Cash		25,000

Example 3—A transaction with a governmental taxing authority

Under the tax laws of country X, Company A elects to step up the tax basis of fixed assets with a current tax basis of $4 million to their $8 million fair value. To do so, the company must pay the government $200,000, which is 5% of the $4 million step-up. The company believes that at the U.S. 22% corporate tax rate, it is likely that it will be able to use the additional deductions from the stepped up tax basis of certain fixed assets, which would justify the $80,000 payment.

Company A would record the tax effects of the transaction as follows:

Deferred tax asset ($4 million × 22%)	$880,000	
Deferred income tax benefit		680,000
Cash		200,000

ASC 740-10-45-10A through 45-13, 65-3; ASC 210-10-15-3, 65-3 Presentation of an Unrecognized Tax Benefit When a Net Operating Loss Carryforward, a Similar Tax Loss, or a Tax Credit Carryforward Exists

OVERVIEW

Until the issuance of ASU 2013-11, ASC 740 (Income Taxes) did not include guidance for the balance sheet presentation of an unrecognized tax benefit when an entity has a net operating loss carryforward, a similar tax loss, or a tax credit carryforward. As a result, there was diversity in practice in the balance sheet presentation of unrecognized tax benefits under those circumstances. Some entities presented an unrecognized tax benefit as a liability, unless it was directly related to a tax position in a tax year that results in, or that resulted in, the recognition of a net operating loss carryforward for that year that had not been used. Under certain circumstances, other entities presented unrecognized tax benefits as reductions of deferred tax assets for net operating loss carryforwards or tax credit carryforwards. The following guidance is intended to reduce those diverse practices.

ACCOUNTING ISSUE

How should an entity that has a net operating loss carryforward, a similar tax loss, or a tax credit carryforward present an unrecognized tax benefit in its financial statements?

SCOPE

The guidance applies to all entities that have an unrecognized tax benefit when the entity has a net operating loss carryforward, a similar tax loss, or a tax credit carryforward at the reporting date.

ACCOUNTING GUIDANCE

Unrecognized Tax Benefits

ASC 740-10-45-10A provides that an unrecognized tax benefit, or a portion of it, should be presented in the balance sheet as a reduction of a deferred tax asset for a net operating loss carryforward, a similar tax loss, or a tax credit carryforward, except as stated in ASC 740-10-45-10B and 45-12.

ASC 740-10-45-10B provides that an unrecognized tax benefit should be recognized as a liability in the balance sheet and should not be combined with deferred tax assets, if under the applicable tax jurisdiction's tax laws, any amount of a net operating loss carryforward, a similar tax loss, or a tax credit carryforward is not available at the reporting date for the settlement of additional income taxes: (1) due to the disallowance of a tax position; or (2) because the applicable jurisdiction's tax law does not require the entity to use the deferred tax asset, and the entity does not intend to use it for that purpose. An entity's judgment whether a deferred asset is available should be based on the unrecognized tax benefit and deferred tax asset that exist at the reporting date and should include the presumption that the tax position would be disallowed at the reporting date.

The guidance in ASC 740-10-45-11 has been amended to require that an unrecognized tax benefit should be classified as a current liability in a classified balance sheet if the entity anticipates paying or receiving cash within one year or the operating cycle, if longer, in accordance with the guidance in ASC 740-10-45-10A and 45-10B. The remainder of the paragraph has been deleted.

ASC 740-10-45-13, which discusses offsetting, is amended to include a reference to ASC 740-10-45-10A and 45-10B.

TRANSITION AND EFFECTIVE DATE

ASC 740-10-65-3 provide the following guidance:

- The guidance discussed above is effective for fiscal years and interim periods within those years that begin after December 15, 2013, for public entities, and after December 15, 2014, for nonpublic entities. Early application of the guidance is permitted.
- The guidance should be applied prospectively to all existing unrecognized tax benefits at the effective date. However, entities are permitted to apply the guidance retrospectively.
- The disclosures in ASC 250-10-50-1 through 50-3 should be made in the period in which an entity adopts the guidance.

BALANCE SHEET—OFFSETTING

Income Taxes

The reference to ASC 740-30 in ASC 210-20-15-3d has been replaced by ASC 740-10. That change also applies to the same reference in ASC 210-20-60-3.

ASC 740-10-45-21; ASC 740-20-45-11 Accounting by a Company for the Income Tax Effects of Transactions among or with Its Shareholders under ASC 740

BACKGROUND

Under U.S. tax laws, the following transactions among shareholders or between a company and its shareholders may have tax consequences.

Transactions that result in a change in expectations about the future realization of deferred tax assets

If the ownership of more than 50% of a company's stock changes within a certain time period, the company may be prohibited from using an existing net operating loss (NOL) carryforward or the amount available to offset future income may be limited. Consequently, the NOL deferred tax asset would have to be written off or a valuation allowance, which was not previously required, would have to be recognized to reduce the deferred tax asset. The following are examples of such transactions:

- An investor purchases more than 50% of the shares in the open market and consolidates the company but does not use pushdown accounting for financial reporting purposes.
- The company converts debt into equity in a troubled debt restructuring.

Transactions that result in changes in tax bases of an entity's assets or liabilities for tax purposes

- One hundred percent of a company's shares are purchased by a privately held company. The company accounts for the transaction as a purchase business combination and consolidates the subsidiary, but because it is a private company it need not push down the fair value of the assets to the subsidiary. The company, however, adjusts the bases of the subsidiary's assets and liabilities for tax purposes.
- A company merges with another company and accounts for the business combination as a pooling of interests. The entity treats the transaction as a purchase of assets for tax purposes.

This Issue does not apply to transactions among or with a subsidiary's minority shareholders or to transactions with shareholders requiring a change in a company's tax status (e.g., a change from a nontaxable S corporation to a taxable C corporation).

ACCOUNTING ISSUES

- Should an entity charge changes in the *valuation allowance* as a result of transactions among or with shareholders to the income statement or directly to equity?
- Should write-offs of deferred tax assets that result from transactions among or with shareholders be charged to the income statement or directly to equity?
- Should the tax effects of changes in the *tax bases of assets (and liabilities)* that result from transactions among or with shareholders be charged (or credited) to the income statement or directly to equity?
- Should a subsequent reduction in the valuation allowance that was initially established when deferred tax assets were created from changes in the tax bases of assets and liabilities in transactions among or with shareholders be credited to income or directly to equity?

ACCOUNTING GUIDANCE

- Changes in the *valuation allowance* caused by changes in expectations about the realization of deferred tax assets that result from transactions among or with shareholders should be included in the *income statement*.
- Write-offs of preexisting deferred tax assets that will not be realized that result from a transaction with or among an entity's shareholders should be included in the *income statement*.

  The net effect is the same whether a deferred tax asset is eliminated or the valuation allowance is increased to equal 100% of the related deferred tax asset.
- The tax effects of all changes in the *tax bases of assets and liabilities* that result from transactions among or with shareholders should be included *in equity*. Also included in equity is the effect of a valuation allowance initially

required on the recognition of deferred tax assets because of changes in the tax bases of assets and liabilities from transactions with or among shareholders.

- Changes in the valuation allowance initially required on the recognition of deferred tax assets that result from changes in the tax bases of assets and liabilities because of transactions with or among shareholders should be included in the *income statement* in subsequent periods.

DISCUSSION

This guidance was developed in response to requests for a framework that could be used to categorize the tax effects of transactions among shareholders and between a company and its shareholders in a consistent manner.

- Proponents of recognizing changes in the valuation allowance as a result of an entity's transactions with shareholders or among shareholders in the income statement argued that the model for intraperiod tax allocation in ASC 740 generally requires allocating the tax expense or benefit to income from continuing operations, unless the incremental portion of the tax expense or benefit is not directly related to continuing operations. Because there is no pretax charge or credit to equity for transactions among shareholders, the tax expense or benefit would not be allocated to equity under the guidance in ASC 740. Further, they argued that changes in the valuation allowance as a result of an entity's transactions with shareholders are only indirectly related to the equity transaction, such as an initial public stock offering. The effects of the change should, therefore, also be included in the income statement.
- Proponents of this view believed that the treatment of a write-off of a deferred tax asset should be the same as that for an increase in the valuation allowance in Issue 1, because the end result is the same. In both cases, the company expects that a deferred tax asset will not be realized because of a transaction with or among shareholders.
- The rationale for charging equity with the tax effects of changes to the tax bases of assets and liabilities as a result of transactions with or among shareholders is that such transactions are similar to a taxable business combination accounted for as a pooling of interests, which is discussed in ASC 740-10-25-3, 25-18. It provides that the deferred tax consequences of temporary differences resulting from an increase in the tax basis of assets in the transaction be recognized in equity. Proponents of this view believe that a taxable pooling does not differ from other transactions among shareholders that result in a change in the tax bases of assets and liabilities.
- Proponents of this view also refer to ASC 740-10-25-3, 25-18, which requires that tax benefits resulting from increases in the tax bases of assets after the date of a taxable business combination should be recognized in the income statement.

ASC 740-10-45-18, 25-47 Adjustment Due to Effect of a Change in Tax Laws or Rates

Questions received by the FASB staff on proposed changes in tax rates, which were eventually enacted on August 10, 1993, retroactive to January 1, 1993 were addressed. The questions dealt with when such a change should be recognized, especially if a company is adopting a new accounting standard at the same time. In addition to referring to the requirements of ASC 740-10-35-4, the FASB staff stated that the effect of a change in tax rates should be recognized on the date it is enacted. Thus, if a company adopts a new accounting standard before the date of enactment, the cumulative effect of adopting that standard would not include the change in tax rates, which would be recognized in income from continuing operations in the period of enactment, even if the change in tax rates is retroactive to the date on which a new standard was adopted.

ASC 740-10-55-26, 55-140 through 55-144, 15-4, 05-5 Application of ASC 740 to a State Tax Based on the Greater of a Franchise Tax or an Income Tax

BACKGROUND

PRACTICE POINTER: The guidance below has been amended in ASU 2019-12, *Income Taxes (Topic 740): Simplifying the Accounting for Income Taxes*, as is shown below. The amendment is effective for public business entities for fiscal years that begin after December 15, 2020, and interim periods within those fiscal years. The guidance is effective for all other entities for fiscal years that begin after December 15, 2021, and interim periods within fiscal years that begin after December 15, 2022. Early adoption is permitted for public business entities for periods for which financial statements have not yet been issued, and for other entities for periods for which financial statements have not yet been made available for issuance.

The state of Texas revised its corporate franchise tax in August 1991 to include a tax on income apportioned to Texas. The tax is based on federal taxable income and became effective January 1, 1992. The corporate tax is computed as follows:

- 0.25% of net taxable capital at the beginning of the year, *or*
- 4.5% of net earned surplus (a term used in the Texas tax code to refer to federal taxable income apportioned to Texas), whichever is greater.

ACCOUNTING ISSUE

What portion of the tax is based on income, and how should deferred taxes be calculated under ASC 740?

ACCOUNTING GUIDANCE

- ASC 740-10-55-26, as amended, provides that a tax based on capital is not an income tax.
- For example, a state's franchise tax on each corporation is set at the greater of 0.25% of the corporation's net taxable capital and 4.5% of the corporation's net taxable earned surplus, which is the term defined by statute for federal taxable income.
- Under the guidance in ASC 740, an entity should recognize a deferred tax asset and liability for temporary differences that exist as of the of the balance sheet date using the tax rate to be applied to the corporation's net taxable earned surplus (e.g., 4.5%).
- The portion of the total computed franchise tax that exceeds the amount equal to the tax on the corporation's net taxable earned surplus should not be presented as a component of income tax expense during any period in which the total computed franchise tax exceeds the amount equal to the tax on the corporation's earned surplus.

The EITF's discussion implied that the above guidance would apply to other states or jurisdictions with essentially the same tax structures.

Illustration of the Calculation of Texas State Tax and Deferred Tax Liability

- Company A is a Texas corporation whose business is conducted only in Texas.
- The company's net taxable income in 20X5 is $75,000, and net taxable income is expected to be $100,000 and $50,000 in 20X6 and 20X7, respectively.
- Company A has taxable temporary differences of $100,000 in 20X5 that are expected to reverse as follows: $75,000 in 20X6 and $25,000 in 20X7.
- Net taxable capital is $1,075,000 in 20X5 and is estimated to be $1,171,625 in 20X6 and $1,217,125 in 20X7.
- The following computation of the deferred tax liability for state franchise taxes at the end of 20X5 ignores the effects of federal income taxes.

State Franchise Tax—20X5

Tax based on net taxable capital (.0025 × $1,075,000)	= $2,687
Tax based on net taxable income (.045 × $75,000)	= $3,375

In 20X5, Company A's state franchise tax of $3,375 is based on net taxable income. Based on the consensus, that tax consists of the following components:

Tax related to net taxable capital (.0025 × $1,075,000)	$2,687
Tax related to net taxable income [$75,000 – (.05555 × $1,075,000) = .045 × $15,283]	688*
Total tax	$3,375

---

* If the franchise tax payable is based on net taxable income, a simpler method of determining the amount related to income is to calculate the difference between the tax based on net taxable capital and the tax based on net taxable income.

Income tax expense in 20×5 is $688, the amount related to net taxable income.

Estimated State Franchise Tax—20X6

Tax based on net taxable capital (.0025 × $1,171,625)	= $2,929
Tax based on net taxable income (.045 × $100,000)	= $4,500

The deferred tax liability on the $75,000 taxable temporary difference expected to reverse in 20X6 would be (.045 × $75,000) $3,375, but based on the consensus, the amount is limited to $1,571, the excess of net taxable income over net taxable capital ($4,500 X $2,929).

Estimated State Franchise Tax—20X7

Tax based on net taxable capital (.0025 × $1,217,125)	= $3,043
Tax based on net taxable income (.045 × $50,000)	= $2,250

No deferred tax liability is recognized for the $50,000 of temporary tax differences expected to reverse in 20X7, because the tax based on net taxable capital exceeds the tax based on net taxable income.

ASC 740-10-55-27 through 55-30, 55-146 through 55-148 Application of ASC 740 (Income Taxes) to the Tax Deduction on Qualified Production Activities Provided by the American Jobs Creation Act of 2004

BACKGROUND

Under the American Jobs Creation Act (the Job Act), which was signed into law on October 22, 2004, employers will be able to deduct up to 9% of (1) income from qualified production activities, as defined in the Job Act or (2) taxable income after the deduction for net operating loss carryforwards, if any, whichever is less. Up to 50% of W-2 wages paid by an employer qualify for the deduction. The FASB directed the FASB staff to provide guidance on the application of ASC 740 in accounting for this deduction.

QUESTION

Should the tax deduction related to income from qualified production activities be accounted for under the guidance in ASC 740 as a special deduction or as a tax-rate reduction?

ACCOUNTING GUIDANCE

The FASB staff believes that the characteristics of the Job Act's deduction for qualified production activities are similar to the special deductions illustrated in ASC 740-10-25-37, because this deduction depends on the performance of specific activities and the level of wages in the future. Consequently, the deduction under the Job Act should be accounted for as a special deduction under the provisions of ASC 740. The FASB staff also noted that an entity should take this special deduction into account in (1) measuring deferred taxes if graduated taxes are a significant factor and (2) determining whether a valuation allowance is required in accordance with ASC 740-10-25-37.

ASC 740-10-55-50, 25-31 Temporary Differences Related to LIFO Inventory and Tax-to-Tax Differences

The following responses to inquiries related to LIFO temporary differences were discussed:

- A deferred tax liability should be recognized in accordance with FAS-109 for LIFO inventory temporary differences resulting from excess financial reporting basis over tax basis.
- A deferred tax liability should be recognized for LIFO inventory belonging to a parent company or its subsidiary even if that temporary difference is not "settled" because the subsidiary will be sold before that difference reverses.

Paragraph 72 of FAS-96 required recognition of a tax benefit for the difference between (1) the tax basis of a parent company in an acquired company's stock and (2) the acquired company tax basis of its net assets. Such differences are referred to as *tax-to-tax* differences. Although that requirement was eliminated in ASC 740, the FASB staff was asked whether recognition of a deferred tax asset for a tax-to-tax difference is *permitted*. The staff responded that under ASC 740, deferred tax assets may be recognized *only* for deductible temporary differences and carryforwards, which are book-tax differences.

ASC 740-10-55-51 Income Tax Consequences of Issuing Convertible Debt with a Beneficial Conversion Feature

OVERVIEW

Under the guidance in ASC 470-20, nondetachable conversion features of convertible securities are not accounted for separately. However, under previous guidance, a nondetachable conversion feature of a convertible debt security that is "in-the-money" should be accounted separately, because it is considered a beneficial conversion feature that is recognized and measured separately by allocating a portion of the proceeds equal to the intrinsic value of the conversion feature to additional paid-in capital. At the commitment date, as defined in EITF Issue 00-27, the intrinsic value of the beneficial conversion feature is calculated as the difference between the conversion price and the fair value of the common stock or other securities into which the security can be converted multiplied by the number of shares into which the security can be converted. A convertible security is recognized at par if no discount or premium is associated with it at issuance and a discount is recognized for the amount allocated to additional paid-in capital. A convertible instrument's debt discount should be accreted from the instrument's issuance date to a stated redemption date or through the earliest conversion date if the instrument does not have a stated redemption date as discussed in EITF Issue 00-27. Under the U.S. Federal Income Tax Code, a convertible debt security's tax basis equals the total proceeds received when the debt is issued.

ACCOUNTING ISSUES

1. Does the issuance of convertible debt with a beneficial conversion feature result in a basis difference when applying the guidance in ASC 740?
2. If issuance of convertible debt with a beneficial conversion feature results in a basis difference, is that difference a temporary difference under the guidance in ASC 740?
3. If issuance of convertible debt with a beneficial conversion feature results in a temporary difference under the guidance in ASC 740, should a deferred tax liability for the temporary difference of the convertible debt be recognized as an adjustment to additional paid-in capital or by recognizing a deferred charge by analogy to the accounting model in Example 4 of Issue 98-11 (Accounting for Acquired Temporary Differences in Certain Purchase Transactions That Are Not Accounted for as Business Combinations)?

ACCOUNTING GUIDANCE

1. Convertible debt issued with a beneficial conversion feature results in a basis difference when the guidance in ASC 740 is applied. By recognizing a beneficial conversion feature, two separate instruments, a debt instrument and an equity instrument, are created for financial reporting purposes and are accounted for as a single debt instrument under the Federal Income Tax Code. As a result, the debt instrument's book basis and tax basis differ.
2. The basis difference resulting from the issuance of convertible debt with a beneficial conversion feature should be treated as a temporary difference under the guidance in ASC 740 This guidance is consistent with the definition of a temporary difference in ASC 740d because the amount recognized as a liability for the difference between the book basis and the tax basis of debt with a beneficial conversion feature becomes taxable when the liability's reported amount is settled.
3. Deferred taxes recognized for a temporary difference of debt with a beneficial conversion feature should be recognized as an adjustment of additional paid-in capital. The EITF noted that because additional paid-in capital was adjusted for the basis difference created when the beneficial conversion feature of the convertible debt was recognized, additional paid-in capital should be adjusted when the deferred tax liability caused by the basis difference is established in accordance with the guidance in ASC 740-20-45-11 that requires an adjustment to be made to "the related components of shareholders' equity."

ASC 740-10-55-53, 25-31 Intraperiod Tax Allocation of the Tax Effect of Pretax Income from Continuing Operations

In response to several inquiries about *intraperiod* tax allocation, the FASB staff stated at the July 1993 EITF meeting that ASC 740 generally requires determining the tax effect of pretax *income* from continuing operations without considering the tax effect of items not included in continuing operations. For example, an entity has income from continuing operations of $1,000 and a loss from discontinued operations of $1,000 in the current year. The entity also has a $2,000 net operating loss carryforward from a previous year. The deferred tax asset is zero, because it is offset by a valuation allowance that has not been reduced during the year. According to the FASB staff, tax expense from continuing operations should be offset by the loss carryforward with no tax benefit allocated to the loss from discontinued operations.

The staff noted, however, that the guidance in ASC 740-20-45-7 is an exception to the Statement's approach to intraperiod tax allocation. Under the approach discussed in that paragraph, items not included in income from continuing operations in the current year are considered, nevertheless, in calculating the amount of tax benefit that results from a *loss* from continuing operations and that should be allocated to continuing operations. The Board made that exception for consistency with the Statement's approach, under which the tax consequences of future taxable income are considered in evaluating whether deferred tax assets are realizable.

ASC 740-10-55-69, 55-70, 55-71 Classification of Payment Made to IRS to Retain Fiscal Year

BACKGROUND

The Revenue Act of 1987 changed the requirements of the Tax Reform Act of 1986 by permitting partnerships and S corporations to elect to either retain their fiscal year or adopt a calendar year for tax purposes. If an entity elects to retain its fiscal year, it is required to make one annual deposit that approximates the income tax the partners would have paid on the short-period income tax return had the entity adopted a calendar year.

The election and the deposit are made by the partnership or S Corporation rather than by the partners. The deposit is adjusted annually based on the entity's income in the previous year so the entity either makes a payment to the IRS or receives a refund.

ACCOUNTING ISSUE

Should an entity report the annual payment in the financial statements as a period expense, an asset in the form of a deposit, or as a debit to partners' equity?

ACCOUNTING GUIDANCE

The payment should be reported as an asset.

DISCUSSION

The authoritative literature provides no specific guidance for the resolution of this issue, except for the definition and discussion of the characteristics of assets and expenses in CON-5 (Recognition and Measurement in Financial Statements of Business Enterprises) (not in ASC) and CON-6 (Elements of Financial Statements—A Replacement of FASB Concepts Statement No. 3) (not in ASC).

To support their view that the payment should not be reported as a debit to the partners' equity accounts, proponents argued that the payment was made on behalf of the entity so it could retain the fiscal year for tax purposes. In addition, the IRS does not associate the individual partners with the payment, which is not offset against their actual individual tax liabilities. The argument for recognizing the payment as an asset rather than as a current expense was based on the view that it will not be realized by the entity currently but only if the entity is liquidated, its income declines to zero, or it converts to a calendar year-end.

ASC 740-10-55-73 through 55-74, 15-4 Accounting for Tax Effects of Dividends in France in Accordance with ASC 740

BACKGROUND

To eliminate double taxation on dividends at the shareholder level, French shareholders who receive dividends from French corporations automatically receive a tax credit for taxes paid by the corporation under that country's integrated tax system. To achieve such integration, when a French corporation distributes dividends to its shareholders, it is required to pay a tax known as *precompte mobilier* (precompte), which is equal to the tax credit available to shareholders (50% of the dividend received) but is limited to the difference between the tax calculated by applying the regular corporate tax rate (currently, 33%) to the dividend declared and taxes already paid by the corporation on the income distributed to shareholders. However, taxes previously paid on income retained for five years or longer are not considered in this calculation. An example of a precompte calculation is as follows:

Income Distributed within Five Years		*Income Distributed after Five Years*	
	Corporate Taxation When Income Is Earned		
Taxable income	€ 600,000	Taxable income	€ 600,000
Corporate tax	(200,000)	Corporate tax	(200,000)
Available for dividends	€ 400,000	Available for dividends	€ 400,000
	Corporate Taxation When Income Is Distributed		
Earnings to be distributed	€ 400,000	Earnings to be distributed	€ 400,000
Precompte*	0	Precompte*	(133,000)
Amount distributed	€ 400,000	Amount distributed	€ 267,000
	Shareholder Taxation		
Cash dividend	€ 400,000	Cash dividend	€ 267,000

Income Distributed within Five Years

Imputed amount for corporate tax paid (50% of dividend)	200,000
Taxable income	€ 600,000
Shareholder tax rate**	60%
Tax liability before credit	360,000
Tax credit (50% of dividend)	(200,000)
Tax payable by shareholder	160,000
Net dividend to shareholder (€ 400,000 – € 160,000)	€ 240,000

Income Distributed after Five Years

Imputed amount for corporate tax paid (50% of dividend)	133,000
Taxable income	€ 400,000
Shareholder tax rate**	60%
Tax liability before credit	240,000
Tax credit (50% of dividend)	(133,000)
Tax payable by shareholder	107,000
Net dividend to shareholder (€ 267,000 – € 107,000)	€ 160,000

* Precompte paid by the corporation on distribution equals the regular corporate tax rate applicable to the amount distributed (€ € 400,000 × .33) less corporate taxes previously paid on that amount. The credit for previously paid corporate taxes is unavailable if earnings are not distributed within five years. The precompte is equal to zero in this example, because earnings are distributed within five years and the corporate rate on distributions is the same as the regular corporate tax previously paid on earnings.

** A 60% shareholder tax rate is assumed.

ACCOUNTING ISSUE

Should a distributing corporation record a tax assessed on dividends distributed to shareholders, such as the French precompte tax, as (*a*) an income tax recorded as tax expense or (*b*) a withholding tax for shareholders receiving dividends that would be recorded in equity and included in dividends paid?

ACCOUNTING GUIDANCE

The EITF reached a consensus that a tax such as precompte is a withholding tax that should be included with the dividend and recorded in equity in the corporation's *separate* financial statements if both of the following conditions are met:

- The corporation is required to pay the tax only if a dividend is distributed to shareholders and the corporation's future income taxes are not reduced by that tax.
- Recipients of dividends receive (*a*) a credit for at least the amount of corporate taxes paid on amounts distributed that can be used to reduce taxes due, regardless of the recipient's tax status, or (*b*) a refund (if the shareholder's marginal tax rate is less than 33% or a foreign shareholder with ownership in excess of 5%-15% is from a country having a tax treaty with France).

DISCUSSION

The guidance is based on the arguments that the precompte is considered a withholding tax under the French tax system and that a corporation incurs this tax only when it distributes earnings. Although the precompte is equal to the tax credit available to shareholders to avoid double taxation, which is 50% of the dividend received, it cannot exceed the difference between the regular tax on the dividend paid and the amount previously paid by the corporation on that income. Thus, if a corporation is taxed at less than the 33% rate, the tax credit received by shareholders would be overstated. Through the precompte, the excess is withheld at the source, rather than by reducing the tax payer's credit. That approach treats all dividends in the same manner and is more convenient administratively. Another argument to support the view that the precompte is a withholding tax is that shareholders can receive a refund on overpayments of the tax.

This accounting treatment would only be appropriate in the freestanding financial statements of a French company. In consolidation, the withholding tax could not be charged to equity, but would be recognized as an expense and charged to the subsidiary's retained earnings.

ASC 740-30: OTHER CONSIDERATIONS OR SPECIAL AREAS

ASC 740-30-25-10 Recognition of Deferred Tax Assets for a Parent Company's Excess Tax Basis in the Stock of a Subsidiary That Is Accounted for as a Discontinued Operation

OVERVIEW

A company decides to sell a subsidiary, which can be accounted for and reported as a discontinued operation. It is expected that the subsidiary's operations will break even between the date the company decides to dispose of the subsidiary (the measurement date) and the disposal date, and the company expects no pretax gain or loss on the disposal. Because the company's tax basis in the subsidiary's stock exceeds its basis in the subsidiary for financial reporting, the decision to sell the subsidiary makes it more likely than not that the deductible temporary difference will reverse in the near future and the company will realize the deferred tax asset.

ACCOUNTING ISSUE

Should the company recognize a deferred tax asset at the measurement date in accordance with the guidance in ASC 740-30-25-9?

ACCOUNTING GUIDANCE

A tax benefit should be recognized for the excess of the entity's outside tax basis over its financial reporting basis in the subsidiary in accordance with the guidance in ASC 740-30-25-9, when it becomes apparent that the temporary difference will reverse in the foreseeable future. This criterion should also be applied to situations in which the financial reporting basis exceeds the company's outside tax basis in its investment in the subsidiary by recognizing a deferred tax liability.

CHAPTER 47

ASC 805—BUSINESS COMBINATIONS

CONTENTS

PART I: GENERAL GUIDANCE

ASC 805-10: OVERALL

OVERVIEW

A business combination occurs when two or more entities combine to form a single entity. An *asset combination* results when one company acquires the assets of one or more other companies, or when a new company is formed to acquire the assets of two or more existing companies. In an asset combination, the target companies cease to exist as operating entities and may be liquidated or become investment companies. An *acquisition of stock combination* occurs when one company acquires more than 50% of the outstanding voting common stock of one or more target companies, or when a new company is formed to acquire controlling interest in the outstanding voting common stock of two or more target companies.

In an acquisition method combination, the acquirer is required to measure the identifiable assets acquired, the liabilities assumed, and any noncontrolling interests in the acquiree at their acquisition-date fair values. Any excess of the fair value of the consideration given over the fair value of the net assets acquired is reported as goodwill. If the fair value of the consideration given is less than the fair market value of the net assets acquired, the resulting excess of fair value of acquired net assets over the cost of the acquired entity is recognized in earnings as a gain on the acquisition date. The operating statements for acquisition method combinations report combined results only for the period subsequent to the combination.

BACKGROUND

Business combinations are accounted for using the acquisition method of accounting. While the primary source of authoritative guidance on business combinations is ASC 805, other pronouncements also address issues related to business combinations. For example:

- ASC 740 (Income Taxes) requires that a liability or asset be recognized for the deferred tax consequences of differences between the assigned values and the tax bases of the assets and liabilities (other than nondeductible goodwill and leveraged leases) recognized in a purchase business combination.
- ASC 715 (Compensation—Retirement Benefits) requires that assets and liabilities recorded under the acquisition method include an asset or a liability representing the funded status of the plan.

THE ACQUISITION METHOD OF ACCOUNTING FOR BUSINESS COMBINATIONS

Scope

ASC 805 applies to any transaction or event in which an acquirer obtains control of one or more businesses. This includes combinations that are achieved without any consideration being transferred as well as to combinations involving mutual entities. ASC 805 does not apply to (ASC 805-10-15-4):

- The formation of a joint venture.
- The acquisition of an asset or a group of assets that does not constitute a business.
- A combination between entities or businesses under common control.
- A combination between not-for-profit organizations or the acquisition of a for-profit business by a not-for-profit organization.
- Financial assets and financial liabilities of a consolidated variable interest entity that is a "collateralized financing entity" (as defined).

The Acquisition Method

All business combinations subject to the requirements of ASC 805 are to be accounted for by the acquisition method (ASC 805-10-25-1). Application of the acquisition method requires the following (ASC 805-10-05-4):

- Identifying the acquirer
- Determining the acquisition date
- Recognizing and measuring the identifiable assets acquired, the liabilities assumed, and any noncontrolling interests in the acquiree (discussed in ASC 805-20)
- Recognizing and measuring goodwill or a gain from a bargain purchase (discussed in ASC 805-30).

Identifying the Acquirer

ASC 805 defines the acquirer as the entity that obtains control of one or more businesses in the business combination.

ASC 805 also provides additional guidance for identifying the acquirer in a business combination in which a variable interest entity is acquired. The acquirer is always the primary beneficiary of the variable interest entity (ASC 805-10-25-5).

Determining the Acquisition Date

The acquirer must identify the acquisition date as the date on which it obtains control of the acquiree (ASC 805-10-25-6). This is usually the date on which the acquirer legally transfers the consideration for the combination, although in certain instances the acquirer may obtain control on an earlier or later date (ASC 805-10-25-7).

Additional Guidance for Applying the Acquisition Method to Particular Types of Business Combinations

A Business Combination Achieved in Stages. An acquirer may obtain control over another business in which it already owns a noncontrolling equity interest. ASC 805 refers to this as a *business combination achieved in stages*, but also as a step acquisition. In these cases, the acquirer must remeasure its previously held equity interest in the acquiree to reflect its acquisition-date fair value, with any resulting gain or loss recognized in earnings. The acquirer must also reclassify any amounts that it had recognized in previous reporting periods with respect to its previously held equity method investment in other comprehensive income and include that amount in the calculation of gain or loss as of the acquisition date (ASC 805-10-25-10).

PRACTICE POINTER: If the previously held equity interest is in a foreign entity, the amount included in the calculation of the gain or loss must also include any foreign currency translation adjustment related to that previously held investment (ASC 805-10-25-10).

A Business Combination Achieved without a Transfer of Consideration. As a result of the broader scope of ASC 805, the acquisition method of accounting for business combinations applies to those combinations that are achieved without a transfer of consideration by the acquirer. Examples of such combinations include (ASC 805-10-25-11):

a. The acquiree repurchases a sufficient number of its own shares for an existing investor (the acquirer) to obtain control.

b. Noncontrolling veto rights lapse that previously kept the acquirer from controlling an acquiree in which the acquirer held a majority voting interest.

c. The acquirer and acquiree agree to combine their businesses by contract alone

Measurement Period

In some business combinations, the end of the reporting period occurs before the acquirer can complete the initial accounting for the combination. In these cases, the acquirer must report provisional amounts in its financial statements for those items for which the accounting is incomplete. ASC 805 provides a measurement period that allows the acquirer to obtain additional information that is needed to complete the accounting for the combination. This includes the information necessary to identify and measure the following as of the acquisition date (ASC 805-10-25-15):

a. The identifiable assets acquired, liabilities assumed, and any noncontrolling interests in the acquiree

b. The consideration transferred for the acquiree

c. In a business combination achieved in stages, the equity interest in the acquiree previously held by the acquirer

d. The resulting goodwill recognized for the business combination or the gain recognized on a bargain purchase.

If during the measurement period the acquirer obtains new information about facts and circumstances that existed at the acquisition date that, if known, would have affected the measurement of amounts recognized as of that date, the acquirer must retrospectively adjust the provisional amounts that were recognized at the acquisition date. Further, the acquirer must recognize additional assets or liabilities if it obtains new information about facts or circumstances that existed as of the acquisition date and that, if known, would have resulted in the recognition of those assets and liabilities as of that date. The measurement period must not exceed one year and will end as soon as the acquirer receives the information it was seeking or learns that additional information is not obtainable (ASC 805-10-25-14).

Measurement period adjustments are not included in earnings, but rather are recognized as an offset to goodwill. For example, if an acquirer recognizes an increase in the provisional amount recognized for an identifiable asset, there must be a corresponding decrease in goodwill. Adjustments made by the acquirer during the measurement period must be recognized with a corresponding adjustment to goodwill in the reporting period in which the adjustments to the provisional amounts are determined. Thus, the acquirer must adjust its financial statements as needed, including recognizing in its current-period earnings the full effect of changes in depreciation, amortization, or other income, as a result of the change to the provisional amounts calculated as if the accounting had been completed at the acquisition date. After the measurement period ends, the accounting for a business combination shall only be revised by the acquirer to correct an error in accordance with the guidance on accounting changes (ASC 805-10-25-16, 17, 19).

Determining What Is Part of the Business Combination Transaction

In some cases, the acquirer and the acquiree may have preexisting or additional business arrangements that must be separated from the business combination. When applying the acquisition method to account for a business combination, the acquirer must recognize only the consideration transferred for the acquiree and the assets acquired and liabilities assumed in the exchange for the acquiree. All separate transactions must be accounted for in accordance with the relevant GAAP.

Transactions entered into before the business combination by the acquirer or primarily for the benefit of the acquirer or the combined entity, rather than primarily for the benefit of the acquiree, are likely to be separate transactions and not part of the business combination transaction. The following are examples of separate transactions that shall not be included as part of the business combination (ASC 805-10-25-21):

a. A transaction that in effect settles preexisting relationships between the acquirer and acquiree

b. A transaction that compensates employees or former owners of the acquiree for future services

c. A transaction that reimburses the acquiree or its former owners for paying the acquirer's acquisition-related costs

ASC 805 requires the acquirer to recognize acquisition-related costs as expenses in the periods in which the costs are incurred and the services are received. The costs to issue debt and equity securities are to be recognized in accordance with other relevant GAAP (ASC 805-10-25-23).

Tax Issues Related to Business Combinations

A deferred tax asset or liability is recognized as of the acquisition date for an acquired entity's taxable or deductible temporary differences or operating loss or tax credit carryforwards. Taxable or deductible temporary differences occur when there are differences between the tax bases and the recognized values of assets acquired and liabilities assumed in a business combination. The acquirer must assess the need for a valuation allowance related to any acquired deferred tax asset (ASC 805-740-25-3).

A change in a valuation allowance for an acquired entity's deferred tax asset that occurs during the measurement period and results from new information about fact and circumstances that existed at the acquisition date shall be recognized with a corresponding reduction to goodwill. Once goodwill is reduced to zero, any additional change in the valuation allowance shall be recognized as a bargain purchase. All other changes to the valuation allowance shall be reported as a reduction or increase to income tax expense (ASC 805-740-45-2).

Financial Statement Disclosures

General Information

The acquirer shall disclose the following information for each business combination that transpires during the current reporting period (ASC 805-10-50-2; ASC 805-20-50-1; ASC 805-30-50-1):

- The name and a description of the acquiree
- The acquisition date
- The percentage of voting interests acquired
- The primary reasons for the acquisition
- A description of how the acquirer obtained control of the acquiree
- The acquisition-date fair value of the total consideration transferred and of each class of consideration transferred (e.g., cash, equity interests, liabilities incurred)
- The amounts recognized as of the acquisition date for each major class of assets acquired and liabilities assumed
- The fair value of any noncontrolling interests in the acquiree at the acquisition date, including a description of how the fair value of the noncontrolling interests was measured
- For acquired receivables not subject to the requirements of ASC 326-30:
  - — The fair value of the receivables (unless the receivables arise from sales-type or direct financing leases by the lessor for which the acquirer must disclose the amounts recognized as of the acquisition date)
  - — The gross contractual amounts receivable
  - — The best estimate at the acquisition date of the expected uncollectible amount of the receivables
- In a bargain purchase:
  - — The amount of gain recognized and the line item in the income statement in which the gain is recognized
  - — A description of the reasons why the transaction resulted in a gain
- In a business combination achieved in stages:
  - — The acquisition-date fair value of the equity interest in the acquiree held by the acquirer immediately before the acquisition date
  - — The amount of gain or loss recognized as a result of remeasuring to fair value the equity interest in the acquiree held by the acquirer before the business combination, and the line item in the income statement in which that gain or loss is recognized
  - — The valuation technique(s) used to measure acquisition date fair value of the equity interest in the acquiree held by the acquirer immediately before the business combination
  - — Information that enables the user of the acquirer's financial statements to assess inputs used to develop the fair value measurement of the equity interest in the acquiree held by the acquirer immediately before the business combination

Transactions Recognized Separately from the Business Combination

In addition to the foregoing, the acquirer shall disclose the following information regarding transactions that are not part of the exchange for the acquiree, but rather are accounted for separately from the business combination (ASC 805-10-50-2):

- A description of each transaction
- How the acquirer accounted for each transaction
- The amounts recognized for each transaction and the line item in the financial statements in which each amount is recognized
- The method used to determine the settlement amount when the transaction is the effective settlement of a preexisting relationship
- The amount of acquisition-related costs, including the amount recognized as an expense and the line item(s) in the income statement in which those expenses are recognized
- The amount of issuance costs that are not recognized as an expense and a description of how they are recognized

Special Disclosures for Public Companies

In addition to the foregoing, if the acquirer is a public company, it shall disclose the following information (ASC 805-10-50-2):

- The amounts of revenue and earnings of the acquiree since the acquisition date included in the consolidated income statement for the reporting period
- If comparative financial statements are not presented, the revenue and earnings of the combined entity for the current reporting period as though the acquisition date for all business combinations that occurred during the year had been as of the beginning of the annual reporting period (supplemental pro forma information)
- If comparative financial statements are presented, the revenue and earnings of the combined entity as though the business combination(s) that occurred during the current year had occurred as of the beginning of the comparable prior annual reporting period (supplemental pro forma information)
- The nature and amount of any material, nonrecurring pro forma adjustments directly attributable to the business combination(s) included in the reported pro forma revenue and earnings (supplemental pro forma information)

ASC 805-20: IDENTIFIABLE ASSETS AND LIABILITIES, AND ANY NONCONTROLLING INTEREST

Recognizing and Measuring the Identifiable Assets Acquired, the Liabilities Assumed, and Any Noncontrolling Interests in the Acquiree

Recognition Principle

The acquirer must recognize, as of the acquisition date, the identifiable assets acquired, the liabilities assumed, and any noncontrolling interests in the acquiree separately from goodwill (ASC 805-20-25-1). To be recognized under the acquisition method, the assets acquired and liabilities assumed must meet the definitions of assets and liabilities in FASB Concepts Statement No. 6 (Elements of Financial Statements), at the acquisition date. For example, expected future costs for which the acquirer is not obligated at the acquisition date, such as relocation of acquiree's employees, are not liabilities at the acquisition date and, therefore, are not recognized when applying the acquisition method (ASC 805-20-25-2).

In some cases, the appropriate accounting treatment for a particular asset or liability depends on how the asset or liability has been classified or designated by the entity. ASC 805 requires the acquirer, at the acquisition date, to classify or designate the identifiable assets acquired and liabilities assumed as necessary to permit the subsequent application of other relevant GAAP. Some examples of these classifications and designations include (ASC 805-20-25-7):

- Classification of particular investments in securities as trading, available for sale, or held to maturity in accordance with ASC 320 (Investments—Debt Securities) and ASC 321 (Investments—Equity Securities).
- Designation of a derivative instrument as a hedging instrument in accordance with ASC 815 (Derivatives and Hedging).
- Assessment of whether an embedded derivative is required to be separated from the host contract in accordance with ASC 815.

Measurement Principle

The acquirer is required to measure the identifiable assets acquired, the liabilities assumed, and any noncontrolling interests in the acquiree at their acquisition-date fair values (ASC 805-20-30-1). The acquirer will not recognize a separate valuation allowance for an asset that has related uncertainty regarding cash flows, because the effects of the cash flow uncertainty are included in the fair value measure, unless the assets acquired are financial assets for which the acquirer must apply the guidance in ASC 805-20-30-4A, 4B. (ASC 805-20-30-4) The guidance for acquired financial assets depends on whether or not the assets are purchased financial assets with credit deterioration. For assets that are accounted for as purchased financial assets with credit deterioration, an acquirer must recognize an allowance in accordance with ASC 326 with a corresponding increase to the amortized cost basis of the financial assets as of the acquisition date. (ASC 805-20-30-4B) For acquired financial assets that are not purchased financial assets with credit deterioration, the acquirer must record the purchased financial assets at the acquisition date fair value. In addition, for these assets within the scope of ASC 326, an allowance must be recorded with a corresponding charge to credit loss expense as of the reporting date. (ASC 805-20-30-4A) In some cases, the acquirer may not intend to use a particular acquired asset, or may intend to use the asset in a way other than its highest and best use. Nevertheless, the acquirer must measure the asset at fair value reflecting its highest and best use in accordance with ASC 820 (Fair Value Measurements and Disclosures), both initially and for purposes of subsequent impairment testing (ASC 805-20-30-6). This includes research and development assets that must be measured and recognized at their acquisition-date fair values.

Exception to the Recognition Principle

An exception to the recognition principle is made for assets and liabilities arising from contingencies. The acquirer **does not apply** the guidance in ASC 450 (Contingencies) in determining which assets and liabilities arising from contingencies to recognize as of the acquisition date. Rather, ASC 805 requires the acquirer to recognize as of the acquisition date all of the assets acquired and liabilities assumed that arise from *contractual contingencies*, measured at their acquisition-date fair values (ASC 805-20-25-19), par. 24a). For *non-contractual contingencies* the acquirer must assess whether it is **more likely than not** that as of the acquisition date the contingency gives rise to an asset or liability as defined in Concepts Statement No. 6, and will recognize the asset or liability at its acquisition-date fair value if that definition is met. If that definition is not met, the acquirer must account for the non-contractual contingency in accordance with other GAAP, including ASC 450 as appropriate (ASC 805-20-25-19).

Exceptions to Both the Recognition and Measurement Principles

Deferred tax assets and liabilities arising from the assets acquired and liabilities assumed in a business combination are to be recognized in accordance with ASC 740 (Income Taxes) (ASC 805-740-25-2). The acquirer shall also recognize a liability (or asset, if any) related to the acquiree's employee benefit plans in accordance with other relevant GAAP (ASC 805-20-25-22).

The acquiree may in some cases contractually indemnify the acquirer for the outcome of an asset or liability arising from a contingency. As a result, the acquirer obtains an indemnification asset, which shall be recognized at the same time the acquirer recognizes the indemnified item, measured on the same basis as the indemnified item (ASC 805-20-25-27).

Exceptions to the Measurement Principle

As part of a business combination, an acquirer may reacquire a right that it had previously granted to the acquiree. This may include, for example, the right to use the acquirer's trade name under a franchise agreement or a right to use certain of the acquirer's technology. A reacquired right is an identifiable intangible asset that is recognized by the acquirer separately from goodwill. The determination of the acquisition-date fair value of the reacquired right is based on the remaining term of the contract to which the reacquired right relates, even if market participants would consider potential contractual renewals in determining its fair value (ASC 805-20-30-20).

An acquirer may also recognize a liability or an equity instrument related to the replacement of an acquiree's share-based payment awards with share-based payment awards of the acquirer. In this case, the acquirer must measure the liability or equity instrument in accordance with ASC 718 (Compensation—Stock Compensation) (ASC 805-20-30-21).

Leases

Assets and liabilities arising from leases of an acquiree must be recognized in accordance with ASC 842. If the acquirer is the lessee, the acquirer may elect not to recognize assets or liabilities at the acquisition date for leases that, at the acquisition date, have a remaining lease term of 12 months or less. This includes not recognizing an intangible asset if the terms of an operating lease are favorable relative to market terms or a liability if the terms are unfavorable relative to market returns (ASC 805-20-25-28A, B).

For leases in which the acquiree is the lessee, the acquirer must record a lease liability at the present value of the remaining lease payments, as if the acquired lease were a new lease of the acquirer at the acquisition date. The acquirer must also measure the right-of-use asset at the same amount as the lease liability, adjusted to reflect favorable or unfavorable terms of the lease when compared with market terms (ASC 805-20-30-24).

For leases in which the acquiree is a lessor of a sales-type lease or a direct financing lease, the acquirer must measure its net investment in the lease as the sum of both of the following (ASC 805-20-30-25):

- The lease receivable at the present value of the following:
  - The remaining lease payments.
  - The amount of any residual value in the underlying asset that is guaranteed by the lessee or any other third party unrelated to the lessor.
- The unguaranteed residual value of the underlying asset.

Subsequent Measurement and Accounting

In general, the assets acquired, liabilities assumed or incurred, and equity instruments issued in a business combination shall be subsequently measured and accounted for by the acquirer in accordance with other applicable GAAP. However, ASC 805 provides specific guidance for the subsequent measurement and accounting for the following assets acquired, liabilities assumed or incurred, and equity instruments issued in a combination (ASC 805-10-35-1):

a. Reacquired rights

b. Assets and liabilities arising from contingencies recognized as of the acquisition date

c. Indemnification assets

d. Contingent consideration.

Reacquired Rights

A reacquired right recognized as an intangible asset as of the acquisition date must be amortized over the remaining contractual period of the contract in which the right was granted (ASC 805-20-35-2).

Assets and Liabilities Arising from Contingencies

An asset or liability arising from a contingency recognized as of the acquisition date, that would be in the scope of ASC 450 if not acquired or assumed in a business combination, shall continue to be recognized by the acquirer at its acquisition-date fair value unless new information is obtained about the possible outcome of the contingency. When new information is obtained, the acquirer must evaluate that information and measure an asset at the *lower* of its acquisition-date fair value or the best estimate of its future settlement amount, while a liability is measured at the *higher* of its acquisition-date fair value or the amount that would be recognized under ASC 450 (ASC 805-20-35-3). An asset or liability arising from a contingency shall only be derecognized by the acquirer when the contingency is resolved.

Indemnification Assets

The acquirer must subsequently measure an indemnification asset on the same basis as the indemnified liability or asset. If the indemnification asset is not measured at its fair value, the collectibility of the asset must be assessed. Indemnification assets shall only be derecognized by the acquirer when it collects the asset, sells it, or otherwise loses the right to it (ASC 805-20-35-4; 805-20-40-3).

Contingent Consideration

Some changes in the fair value of contingent consideration are measurement period adjustments and are accounted for in accordance with ASC 805-10. However, other changes in the fair value of contingent consideration result from events that occur after the acquisition date such as meetings a specified earnings target or reaching a specified share price. These changes are not measurement period adjustments, and the acquirer must account for them as follows (ASC 805-30-35-1):

a. Contingent consideration classified as equity shall not be remeasured and its subsequent settlement shall be accounted for within equity.

b. Contingent consideration classified as an asset or a liability is remeasured to fair value at each reporting date until the contingency is resolved. The changes in fair value are recognized in earnings unless the contingency involves a hedging instrument that is required by ASC 815 to recognize the changes in other comprehensive income.

Financial Statement Disclosures Related to Contingencies

The acquirer shall disclose the following information regarding contingencies:

- For contingent consideration arrangements (ASC 805-20-50-1a):
  - The amount recognized as of the acquisition date
  - A description of the arrangement and the basis for determining the amount of the payment
  - An estimate of the range of outcomes (undiscounted) or, if a range cannot be estimated, that fact and the reasons why a range cannot be estimated
- For assets and liabilities arising from contingencies (ASC 805-20-50-1d):
  - The amounts recognized at the acquisition date or an explanation of why no amount was recognized
  - The nature of recognized and unrecognized contingencies

ASC 805-30: GOODWILL OR GAIN FROM BARGAIN PURCHASE, INCLUDING CONSIDERATION TRANSFERRED

Recognizing and Measuring Goodwill or a Gain from a Bargain Purchase

Goodwill

The acquirer shall recognize goodwill as of the acquisition date, measured as the excess of (a) over (b) below (ASC 805-30-30-1):

a. The aggregate of:

   1. The consideration transferred, which is usually the acquisition-date fair value.
   2. The fair value of any noncontrolling interests in the acquiree.
   3. In a business combination achieved in stages, the acquisition-date fair value of the acquirer's previously held equity interest in the acquiree.

b. The net of the acquisition-date amounts of the identifiable assets acquired and the liabilities assumed.

In a business combination involving two mutual entities, the acquisition-date fair value of the acquiree's equity interests may be more readily measurable than the acquisition-date fair value of the acquirer's equity interests. If so, the acquirer shall use the acquisition-date fair value of the acquiree's equity interests in determining the amount of goodwill to be recognized. In a business combination in which no consideration is transferred, the acquirer must use a valuation technique to determine the acquisition-date fair value of the acquirer's interest in the acquiree. The value derived from this valuation technique is then used in place of the acquisition-date fair value of the consideration transferred when determining the amount of goodwill to be recognized (ASC 805-30-30-3).

Gain from a Bargain Purchase

Occasionally, an acquirer will make a bargain purchase, which is a business combination in which the amount of net assets acquired exceeds the value of the consideration transferred plus the fair value of any noncontrolling interests in the acquiree plus the fair value of the acquirer's previously held equity interest in the acquiree. ASC 805 requires the acquired assets and assumed liabilities to be recorded at their acquisition-date fair values with limited exceptions. This requirement results in the acquired assets and assumed liabilities being recognized at their fair value, while the amount of the bargain is recognized by the acquirer in earnings on the acquisition date (ASC 805-30-25-2).

However, before recognizing a gain from a bargain purchase, the acquirer is required by ASC 805 to reassess whether it has correctly identified all of the acquired assets and assumed liabilities, and to recognize any additional assets or liabilities that are discovered during this review. The acquirer must also review the procedures it used to measure the following amounts as of the acquisition date (ASC 805-30-30-5):

a. The identifiable assets acquired and liabilities assumed

b. The noncontrolling interests in the acquiree, if any

c. For a business combination achieved in stages, the acquirer's previously held equity interest in the acquiree

d. The consideration transferred.

Consideration Transferred

The consideration transferred in a business combination must be measured at fair value, and equals the sum of the acquisition-date fair values of the assets transferred by the acquirer, the liabilities incurred by the acquirer to former owners of the acquiree, and the equity interests issued by the acquirer. The consideration transferred may include assets and liabilities of the acquirer that have acquisition-date fair value that differ from their carrying amounts. If so, the acquirer must remeasure the transferred assets and liabilities to their fair values as of the acquisition date and recognize a gain or loss in earnings, unless the transferred assets and liabilities remain with the combined entity after the combination. In that case, the acquirer will continue to measure the transferred assets and liabilities at their carrying amounts immediately prior to the acquisition date and not recognize any gain or loss in earnings, since the acquirer controls the assets and liabilities both before and after the business combination (ASC 805-30-30-7, 8).

In some business combinations, the acquirer has an obligation to make additional payments based on the occurrence of future events (often called "contingent consideration"). Any such obligation must be recognized by the acquirer at its acquisition-date fair value as a part of the total consideration transferred (ASC 805-30-25-5). Another type of consideration is share-based payment awards that are awarded by the acquirer to replace awards held by grantees of the acquiree. If the acquirer is obligated to issue these awards as a replacement for the acquiree's awards, then at least some, if not all, of the fair value of the acquirer's replacement awards are included in the amount of consideration transferred in the business combination (ASC 805-30-30-9). However, if the acquirer is not obligated to replace the acquiree awards but chooses to do so anyway, then all of the fair-value-based measure of the replacement awards must be recognized as compensation expense by the acquirer in the post-combination financial statements (ASC 805-30-30-10).

Financial Statement Disclosures Related to Goodwill

The acquirer shall disclose the following information regarding goodwill (ASC 805-30-50-1):

- A qualitative description of the factors that make up for the goodwill recognized. For example:
  - — Expected synergies from combining the operations of the acquiree and the acquirer
  - — Intangible assets that do not qualify for separate recognition
- The amount of goodwill that is expected to be deductible for tax purposes
- The amount of goodwill by reportable segment (assuming the entity is required to disclose segment information in accordance with ASC 280 (Segment Reporting))

ACQUISITION METHOD: IMPLEMENTATION GUIDANCE

Types of Business Combinations

A business combination may be accomplished in one of two ways. The acquiring company may purchase the assets (asset acquisition) of the target company. In this instance, normally the target company is liquidated and only one entity continues. Alternatively, the acquiring company may purchase more than 50% (up to 100%) of the outstanding voting common stock of the target company. In this instance, the financial statements of the two entities are consolidated in accordance with ASC 810.

Asset Acquisition

In an asset acquisition, entries are made to record the assets and assume the liabilities of the target company on the books of the acquiring company. These assets and liabilities are recorded at their acquisition-date fair values, with limited exceptions. If the purchase price exceeds the fair market value of the net assets, goodwill is recorded in the acquisition entry. If the fair market value of identifiable assets exceeds the purchase price, the resulting excess of fair value of acquired net assets over cost is recognized as a gain in earnings on the acquisition date (ASC 805-30-25-2).

Illustration of Asset Acquisition

On July 1, 20X8, S Company sold all its net assets and business to P Company for $430,000 cash. The following is S Company's balance sheet as of July 1, 20X8:

Balance Sheet

Cash	$ 20,000
Accounts receivable	72,000
Allowance for doubtful accounts	(8,000)
Inventory	120,000
Plant and equipment (net)	260,000
Total assets	$464,000
Accounts payable	$ 60,000
Accrued expenses	5,000
Mortgage payable—plant	120,000
Common stock	200,000
Retained earnings	79,000
Total liabilities and equity	$464,000

Additional Information:

Confirmation of the accounts receivable revealed that $10,000 was uncollectible.

The physical inventory count was $138,000 (fair value).

The fair value of the plant and equipment was $340,000.

S Company has in-process research and development costs that have a fair value of $15,000.

The journal entry to record the investment on the books of P Company is:

Cash	$20,000	
Accounts receivable	62,000	
Inventory	138,000	
Plant & equipment	340,000	
In-process R&D	15,000	
Goodwill	40,000	
Accounts payable		$ 60,000
Accrued expenses		5,000
Mortgage payable		120,000
Cash		430,000

The computation of goodwill involved in the transaction is:

Computation of Goodwill

Assets (book value)	$ 464,000
Liabilities ($60,000 + $5,000 + $120,000)	(185,000)
Total net assets (book value)	$ 279,000
Adjustments to fair value:	
Additional uncollectibles	(2,000)
Increase in inventory	18,000
Increase in plant and equipment	80,000
In-process R&D	15,000
Adjusted net assets (fair value)	$ 390,000

Consideration transferred	$ 430,000
Adjusted net assets (fair value)	(390,000)
Goodwill	$ 40,000

Had the purchase price been only $365,000, the excess of fair value of acquired net assets over consideration transferred would have been computed as follows.

Adjusted net assets (fair value)	$ 390,000
Consideration transferred	(365,000)
Excess of fair value of acquired net assets over consideration transferred	$ 25,000

The $25,000 excess of fair value of acquired net assets over consideration transferred represents the "bargain" for this business combination that the acquirer must recognize in earnings as a gain on the acquisition date. The journal entry to record the investment on the books of P Company is:

Cash	$20,000	
Accounts receivable	62,000	
Inventory	138,000	
Plant & equipment	340,000	
In-process R&D	15,000	
Accounts payable		$ 60,000
Accrued expenses		5,000
Mortgage payable		120,000
Cash		365,000
Gain on bargain purchase		25,000

Stock Acquisition

In an acquisition of stock, entries are made to record the investment in the stock of the investee. An analysis of the difference between the underlying book value and the sum of the consideration transferred plus fair value of any noncontrolling interests is required to prepare consolidated financial statements for the parent and subsidiary to reflect the fair market value of the identifiable assets and goodwill as of the date of acquisition. Using data from the previous example in which the consideration transferred was $430,000, the only entry required to record the combination is:

Investment in S Company	$430,000	
Cash		$430,000

At the financial statement date, consolidated financial statements will be prepared that combine the assets and liabilities of the parent and subsidiary companies. At that time, the account "Investment in S Company" is eliminated from the statements along with the stockholders' equity in S Company. In addition, the identifiable assets of S Company are adjusted to fair market value and the goodwill of $40,000 is recorded in the consolidated balance sheet. Operating expenses, depreciation, and amortization of the combined entities are adjusted to reflect the revised asset values.

In a stock acquisition in which the acquirer purchases less than 100% of the outstanding voting common stock of the target company, the acquirer must recognize any noncontrolling interests at its fair value as of the acquisition date. Measuring the noncontrolling interests at its fair value results in the recognition of goodwill attributable to the noncontrolling interests in addition to the goodwill attributable to the acquirer. In the case of a bargain purchase, the recognition of the noncontrolling interests at its acquisition-date fair value may not result in any goodwill being recognized, but rather may reduce the amount of the bargain reported by the acquirer in its current income statement.

Illustration of Stock Acquisition

On July 1, 20X8, P Company acquires 90% of the equity interests of S Company for $540,000 cash. The following is S Company's balance sheet as of July 1, 20X8:

Balance Sheet

Cash	$ 40,000
Accounts receivable	65,000

Balance Sheet

Allowance for doubtful accounts	$ (5,000)
Inventory	175,000
Plant and equipment (net)	210,000
Total assets	$485,000
Accounts payable	$ 85,000
Accrued expenses	15,000
Common stock	260,000
Retained earnings	125,000
Total liabilities and equity	$485,000

Additional Information:

Confirmation of the accounts receivable revealed that $10,000 was uncollectible.

The physical inventory count was $230,000 (fair value).

The fair value of the plant and equipment was $275,000.

The fair value of the 10% noncontrolling interests in S Company is $60,000.

The journal entry to record the investment on the books of P Company is:

Investment in S Company	$540,000	
Cash		$540,000

P Company would record its acquisition of S Company in its consolidated financial statements as follows:

Cash	$40,000	
Accounts receivable	55,000	
Inventory	230,000	
Plant & equipment	275,000	
Goodwill	100,000	
Accounts payable		$ 85,000
Accrued expenses		15,000
Cash		540,000
Equity—noncontrolling interests in S Company		60,000

The computation of goodwill involved in the transaction is:

Computation of Goodwill

Assets (book value)	$ 485,000
Liabilities ($85,000 + $15,000)	(100,000)
Total net assets (book value)	$ 385,000
Adjustments to fair value:	
Additional uncollectibles	$(5,000)
Increase in inventory	55,000
Increase in plant and equipment	65,000
Adjusted net assets (fair value)	$ 500,000
Consideration transferred	$ 540,000
Fair value of noncontrolling interests in S Company	60,000
Adjusted net assets (fair value)	(500,000)
Goodwill	$ 100,000

Assume the former owners of S Company had to dispose of their investments in S Company by a specified date and did not have time to market S Company to multiple potential buyers. Therefore, the purchase price paid by P Company for its 90% ownership was only $425,000. In this case, the amount of gain on this bargain purchase that would be recognized by P Company in its income statement on the acquisition date is computed as follows.

Adjusted net assets (fair value)	$ 500,000
Consideration transferred	(425,000)
Fair value of noncontrolling interests in S Company	(60,000)
Excess of fair value of acquired net assets over consideration transferred plus noncontrolling interests	$ 15,000

The $15,000 excess of fair value of acquired net assets over consideration transferred plus noncontrolling interests represents the "bargain" for this business combination that the acquirer must recognize in earnings as a gain on the acquisition date. P Company would record its acquisition of S Company in its consolidated financial statements as follows:

Cash	$40,000	
Accounts receivable	55,000	
Inventory	230,000	
Plant & equipment	275,000	
Accounts payable		$ 85,000
Accrued expenses		15,000
Cash		425,000
Equity—noncontrolling interests in S Company		60,000
Gain on bargain purchase		15,000

ASC 805-40: REVERSE ACQUISITIONS

A reverse acquisition is an acquisition in which the entity that issues securities is identified as the acquiree for accounting purposes based on guidance in 805-10-55-11 through 55-15. The entity whose equity interests are acquired must be the acquirer for accounting purposes for a transition to be considered a reverse acquisition.

Measuring Consideration

In a reverse acquisition, the accounting acquirer usually issues no consideration for the acquiree. Instead, the accounting acquiree usually issues its equity shares to the owners of the accounting acquirer. The acquisition-date fair value of the consideration transferred by the accounting acquirer for its interest in the accounting acquiree is based on the number of equity interests the legal subsidiary would have had to issue to give the owners of the legal parent the same percentage interests in the combined entity that results from the reverse acquisition (ASC 805-40-30-2).

Non-Controlling Interest

The assets and liabilities of the legal acquiree are measured and recognized in the consolidated financial statements at their pre-combination carrying amounts. Therefore, in a reverse acquisition the controlling interest reflects the noncontolling shareholders' proportionate interest in the pre-combination carrying amounts of the legal acquiree's net assets. This is true even though the noncontrolling interests in the other acquisition are measured at fair values at the acquisition date (ASC 805-40-30-3).

Other Presentation Matters

Consolidated financial statements following a reverse acquisition are issued under the name of the legal parent (accounting acquiree) but described in notes to the financial statements as a continuation of the financial statements of the legal subsidiary (accounting acquirer) with the following adjustment. The legal acquirer's legal capital is adjusted to reflect the legal capital of the accounting acquiree. This adjustment is required to reflect the capital of the legal parent (accounting acquiree). Comparative-year information is retroactively adjusted to reflect the legal capital of the legal parent (accounting acquiree) (ASC 805-40-45-1).

Information accompanying the financial post-refer-acquisition financial statements should disclose the following (ASC 805-40-45-2):

- The assets and liabilities of the legal subsidiary (accounting acquirer) recognized and measured at their pre-combination carrying amounts.

- The assets and liabilities of the legal parent (the accounting acquiree) recognized and measured as applicable with the guidance on business combinations.
- The retained earnings and other equity balances of the legal subsidiary (accounting acquirer) before the business combination.
- The amount recognized as issued equity interests in the consolidated financial statements determined by adding the issued equity interest of the legal subsidiary (accounting acquirer) outstanding immediately before the business combination to the fair value of the legal parent (accounting acquiree) in accordance with guidance applicable to business combinations.
- The noncontrolling interest's proportionate share of the legal subsidiary's (accounting acquirer's) pre-combination carrying amounts of retained earnings and other equity interests.

ASC 805-50: RELATED ISSUES

Acquisition of Assets Rather Than a Business

Assets are usually acquired in exchange transactions that trigger the initial recognition of the assets acquired and liabilities assumed. If the consideration given in exchange for assets, or net assets, acquired is in the form of assets surrendered (e.g., cash), the assets surrender shall be derecognized at the date of the acquisitions. If the consideration given is in the form of liabilities incurred or equity interests issued, the liabilities incurred and equity interests issued are initially recognized at the date of acquisition. However, if the assets surrendered are nonfinancial assets or in substance nonfinancial assets within the scope of ASC 610-20 on gains and losses from the derecognition of nonfinancial assets, the assets surrendered must be derecognized in accordance with the guidance in ASC 610-20 and the assets acquired must be treated as noncash consideration (ASC 805-50-25-1).

Assets are recognized based on their cost to the acquiring entity, which generally includes the transaction costs of the asset acquisition, and no gain or loss is recognized unless the fair value of the noncash assets given as consideration differs from the assets' carrying amounts on the acquiring entity's books. Asset acquisitions in which the consideration is given in cash are measured by the amount of cash paid, which generally includes the transactions costs of the asset acquisition. If the consideration given is not in the form of cash and no other GAAP apply (e.g., ASC 845 on nonmonetary transactions or ASC 610-20), measurement is based on either the cost, measured based on the fair value of the consideration given, or the fair value of the assets acquired, whichever is more reliably measured (ASC 805-50-30-2).

Transactions Between Entities Under Common Control

In accounting for a transfer of assets or exchange of shares between entities under common control, the entity that receives the net assets or the equity interests initially recognizes the assets and liabilities transferred at the date of transfer (ASC 805-50-25-2).

When accounting for a transfer of assets or exchange of shares between entities under common control, the entity that receives the net assets or the equity interest initially measures the recognized assets and liabilities transferred measured at their carrying amounts in the accounting of the transferring entity at the date of transfer. If the carrying amounts of the assets and liabilities transferred differ from the historical cost of the parent of the entities under common control (e.g., because pushdown accounting had not been applied), the financial statements of the receiving entity shall reflect the transferred assets and liabilities at the historical cost of the parent of the entities under common control (ASC 805-50-30-5).

Financial statements of the receiving entity shall report results of operations for the period in which the transfer occurs as if the transfer had occurred at the beginning of the period (ASC 805-50-45-2).

Pushdown Accounting

An acquiree shall have the option to apply pushdown accounting in its separate financial statements when an acquirer obtains control of the acquiree. An acquirer might obtain control of an acquiree in a variety of ways, including any of the following (ASC 805-50-25-4):

- By transferring cash or other assets
- By incurring liabilities
- By issuing equity interests

- By providing more than one type of consideration
- Without transferring consideration, including by contract alone

The option to apply pushdown accounting can be elected each time there is a change-in-control event in which an acquirer obtains control of the acquiree. If the acquiree elects the option to apply pushdown accounting, it must apply the accounting as of the acquisition date (ASC 805-50-25-6). If the acquiree does not elect to apply pushdown accounting upon a change-in-control event, it can elect to apply pushdown accounting to its most recent change-in-control event in a subsequent reporting period as a change in accounting principle in accordance with ASC 250 on accounting changes and error corrections (ASC 805-50-25-7). The decision to apply pushdown accounting to a specific change-in-control event if elected by an acquiree is irrevocable (ASC 805-50-25-9).

Because of factors like the consideration of common ownership and changes in control, a new basis of accounting is not appropriate for the following transactions that create a master limited partnership (ASC 805-50-30-7):

- A rollup in which the general partner of the new master limited partnership was also the general partner of some or all of the predecessor limited partnerships and no cash is involved in the transactions.
- A dropdown in which the sponsor receives 1% of the units in the master limited partnership as the general partner and 24% of the units as a limited partner, the remaining 75% of the units are sold to the public, and a 2/3 vote of the limited partners is required to replace the general partner.
- A rollout.
- A reorganization.

If an acquiree elects the option to apply pushdown accounting in its separate financial statements, it must disclose information that enables users of financial statements to evaluate the effect of pushdown accounting (ASC 805-50-50-5). Information to evaluate the effect of pushdown accounting may include the following (ASC 805-50-50-6):

- The name and a description of the acquirer and a description of how the acquirer obtained control of the acquiree
- The acquisition date
- The acquisition-date fair value of the total consideration transferred by the acquirer
- The amounts recognized by the acquiree as of the acquisition date for each major class of assets and liabilities as a result of applying pushdown accounting
- A qualitative description of the factors that make up the goodwill recognized
- In a bargain purchase, the amount of the bargain purchase recognized in additional paid-in capital and a description of the reasons why the transaction resulted in a gain
- Information to evaluate the financial effects of adjustments recognized in the current reporting period that relate to pushdown accounting that occurred in the current or previous reporting periods

PRIVATE COMPANY COUNCIL ALTERNATIVE GUIDANCE

Under U.S. GAAP, an acquirer must recognize, separately from goodwill, the identifiable assets acquired, the liabilities assumed, and any noncontrolling interest in the acquiree as of the acquisition date (ASC 805-20-25-1). However, ASC 805 now includes alternative guidance that allows a private company to avoid recognizing certain identifiable intangible assets separately from goodwill. This alternative guidance for private companies reduces the cost and complexity associated with the measurement of certain identifiable intangible assets without significantly diminishing decision-useful information to users of private company financial statements and will generally result in those companies separately recognizing fewer intangible assets in a business combination.

Under this alternative guidance provided to private companies, an acquirer shall not recognize separately from goodwill the following intangible assets (ASC 805-20-25-30):

- Customer-related intangible assets unless they are capable of being sold or licensed independently from other assets of a business
- Noncompetition agreements

Customer-related intangible assets that may still require separate recognition (i.e., because they are capable of being sold or licensed independently of other assets) include but are not limited to (ASC 805-20-25-31):

- Mortgage servicing rights
- Commodity supply contracts
- Core deposits
- Customer information (e.g., names and contact information)

An entity that elects this alternative guidance must also adopt the alternative accounting guidance available to private companies for amortizing goodwill (ASC 805-20-15-4).

Neither contract assets (see ASC Topic 606) nor leases are considered to be customer-related intangible assets for purposes of applying this accounting alternative. Therefore, they are not eligible to be subsumed into goodwill and must be recognized separately (ASC 805-20-25-32, 33).

BUSINESS COMBINATIONS

IMPORTANT NOTICE FOR 2022

As Wolters Kluwer's 2022 *GAAP Guide* goes to press, the FASB has outstanding an Exposure Draft of an Accounting Standards Update (ASU), *Business Combinations—Accounting for Contract Assets and Contract Liabilities from Contracts with Customers*, that may have an important impact on the preparation of financial statements in the future. The proposed ASU was issued in response to stakeholders' concerns regarding how to apply ASC 805 (Business Combinations) to a contract with a customer acquired in a business combination after the acquirer has adopted ASC 606. Although current GAAP provides guidance on when to recognize and how to measure assets and liabilities in a business combination, it does not provide guidance specific to contract assets and contract liabilities arising from revenue contracts with customers that are accounted for in accordance with ASC 606. The proposed ASU would provide guidance on how to recognize and measure those contract assets and contract liabilities in a business combination.

The proposed ASU also provides guidance to resolve inconsistencies in the post-acquisition recognition of revenue that may occur due to differences in the timing of payment of a revenue contract. The effective date for this proposed ASU has not been determined. Early adoption will be permitted.

PART II: INTERPRETIVE GUIDANCE

ASC 805-10: OVERALL

ASC 805-10-35-1, 20-25-15A, 25-18A, 25-19 through 20B, 30-9 through 30-9A, 30-23, 35-3 through 35-4A, 50-1; ASC 805-30-35-1A Accounting for Assets Acquired and Liabilities Assumed in a Business Combination That Arise from Contingencies

BACKGROUND

Under the guidance in ASC 805, an acquirer in a business combination must recognize the fair value on the acquisition date of all *contractual* contingencies and all *noncontractual* contingencies that more likely than not will result in an asset or liability, as defined in CON-6 (Elements of Financial Statements) (not in ASC). However, *noncontractual* contingencies that are *not* more than likely to result in an asset or a liability as of the acquisition date, would be accounted for in accordance with other U.S. generally accepted accounting principles (U.S. GAAP), including ASC 450.

In accordance with the guidance in ASC 805 such assets and liabilities would continue to be reported at their fair values as of the acquisition date until there is new information about the related contingency's possible outcome. At that time, the resulting liability would be measured at its fair value at acquisition or an amount based on the guidance in ASC 450, whichever is *lower*. An asset would be measured at its fair value at acquisition or at the best estimate of the amount at which it would be settled in the future. An acquirer would continue to report assets and liabilities that resulted from preacquisition contingencies until the related contingencies have been resolved.

Constituents raised issues related to the application of its guidance, which includes guidance to:

- Determine the fair value at acquisition of a contingency related to litigation;
- Support the measurement and recognition of liabilities related to legal contingencies if supporting information is unavailable due to attorney-client privilege;

- Distinguish between contractual and noncontractual contingencies;
- Address a situation in which an acquiree that intends to settle a contingent liability out of court wants to recognize a loss contingency based on the guidance in ASC 450, but cannot do so because the liability does *not* meet the more-likely-than-not threshold for a noncontractual contingency, as required in ASC 805;
- Derecognize a liability that results from a contingency recognized as of the acquisition date;
- Disclose information in financial statements that is potentially prejudicial;
- Determine whether an acquiree's arrangements for contingent consideration assumed in a business combination should be accounted for in accordance with the guidance for contingent consideration or in accordance with guidance for the accounting of other assets and liabilities resulting from contingencies.

The following guidance amends the guidance in ASC 805 and clarifies its guidance on initial recognition and measurement, subsequent measurement and accounting, and disclosure of assets and liabilities that result from contingencies in business combinations.

ACCOUNTING GUIDANCE

Scope

The following guidance applies to all of a business combination's acquired assets and assumed liabilities that have resulted from contingencies that would be accounted for under the guidance in ASC 450. That is, in the same manner as contingencies that were *not* acquired or assumed in a business combination. The guidance in this pronouncement does *not* apply to assets or liabilities that result from contingencies for which there is specific accounting guidance in ASC 805).

Initial Measurement and Recognition

An asset acquired or a liability assumed in a business combination that has resulted from a contingency should be recognized at the acquisition date at its fair value if that amount can be determined during the measurement period, such as the fair value of an obligation under a warranty. If that fair value cannot be determined during the measurement period, the following two criteria must be met for such assets and liabilities to be recognized at the acquisition date based on the guidance in ASC 450 and in ASC 450, for the application of similar criteria in ASC 450-20-25-2:

- Based on information available *before* the end of the measurement period, it is probable that an asset existed and that a liability had been incurred at the acquisition date. This condition intended to imply that it is probable at the acquisition date that one or more future events will occur to confirm the existence of the recognized asset or liability.
- It is possible to reasonably estimate the amount of the asset or liability.

An asset or a liability resulting from a contingency should *not* be recognized as of the acquisition date if the criteria for measurement and recognition discussed above are *not* met at that date based on information available during the measurement period. After the acquisition date, assets and liabilities that result from contingencies that did *not* meet the criteria for recognition at the acquisition date should be accounted for *after* the acquisition date based on other applicable GAAP, including ASC 450, whichever is appropriate.

An acquirer should initially recognize at fair value an acquiree's arrangements for contingent consideration assumed in a business combination by applying the guidance in ASC 805 for such arrangements.

Subsequent Measurement and Accounting

Subsequent to an acquisition, an acquirer should:

- Measure and account for assets and liabilities that result from a contingency using a systematic and rational approach based on the nature of the contingency,
- Measure contingent consideration arrangements assumed from an acquiree in a business combination based on the guidance in ASC 805-30-35-1.

Disclosures

Information disclosed by an acquirer in a business combination should enable financial statement users to evaluate the nature of the business combination and how it affects the entity financially during the reporting period in which it occurs or after the reporting period but before financial statements are issued. An acquirer should disclose the following information in the notes to the financial statements about each business combination that occurs during a reporting period:

1. For assets and liabilities as a result of contingencies recognized at the acquisition date:
    a. Amounts recognized at the acquisition date and the basis used for recognition, that is, fair value or an amount based on the guidance in ASC 450.
    b. The nature of the contingencies.
2. For contingencies not recognized at the acquisition date, disclose information required in ASC 450, if the criteria for making those disclosures are met.

ASC 805-10-50-2, 50-8 through 50-9, 55-49 through 55-50 Disclosure of Supplementary Pro Forma Information for Business Combinations

OVERVIEW

Under the existing guidance in ASC 805-10-50-2(h), an acquirer that is a public entity is required to provide the following information:

- The amounts of revenue and earnings of an acquiree since the acquisition date included in the consolidated income statement for the reporting period;
- The revenue and earnings of the combined entity for the current reporting period as though the acquisition date for all business combinations that occurred during the year had been as of the beginning of the annual reporting period (supplemental pro forma information); and
- If comparative financial statements are presented, the revenue and earnings of the combined entity for the comparable prior reporting period as though the acquisition date for all business combinations that occurred during the current year had occurred as of the beginning of the comparable prior annual reporting period (supplemental pro forma information).

The Securities and Exchange Commission (SEC) also requires pro forma financial information to be included in a Form 8-K filing under the requirements of Article 11 of Regulation S-X. That information is intended to inform investors about how a transaction that has occurred in the current period might affect future financial statements by showing how it might have affected the historical financial statements had the transaction occurred at the beginning of a comparable prior period.

This Issue was discussed because the guidance in ASC 805-10-50-2(h)(2) and 50-2(h)(3) has been interpreted differently by preparers in practice. Some preparers have interpreted that guidance to mean that pro forma information should be prepared as if the business combination has occurred at the beginning of the current annual period and the beginning of the prior annual period. Others have interpreted the guidance to mean that pro forma information is required only as if the business combination had occurred at the beginning of the prior annual period.

ACCOUNTING ISSUE

How should a public entity prepare pro forma information in a business combination?

ACCOUNTING GUIDANCE

Scope

The following guidance applies to all public entities, as defined in ASC 805, that have entered into a material business combination or a series of immaterial business combinations that are material in their totality.

- A *public* entity that presents comparative financial statements is required to disclose pro forma information about the combined entity's revenue and earnings as if an acquisition that occurred during the current year had occurred as of the beginning of the comparable prior annual reporting period.
- To provide users of financial statements with additional useful information, the supplemental pro forma disclosures under ASC 805 are expanded to require a narrative description of the nature and amount of material, nonrecurring pro forma adjustments directly as a result of a business combination.

ASC 805-20: IDENTIFIABLE ASSETS AND LIABILITIES, AND ANY NONCONTROLLING INTEREST

ASC 805-20-S30-1, S35-1, S99-3 Use of the Residual Method to Value Acquired Assets Other Than Goodwill

Under current guidance on accounting for business combinations in ASC 805-20-55-2, intangible assets that result from contractual or legal rights must be recognized separately from goodwill. The SEC Observer reported at the EITF's

September 2004 meeting that, in some circumstances, SEC registrants had claimed that they are unable to value a legal or contractual right directly or separately from goodwill in a business combination because the asset's characteristics made it indistinguishable from goodwill. Examples cited were cellular/spectrum licenses and cable franchise agreements. Some of those entities had assigned a purchase price to all other identifiable assets and liabilities and had assigned the remaining residual amount to the "indistinguishable" intangible asset without recognizing goodwill or recognizing goodwill based on a technique other than that specified in ASC 805-30-30-1, 25-1.

Entities in the telecommunications, broadcasting, and cable industries had been using the residual method to value intangible assets. That method was similar to the allocation methods used to account for business combinations accounted for under the purchase method in APB-16 (Business Combinations), before that guidance was superseded by FAS-141 and later ASC 805 (FAS-141(R)). The SEC Observer stated that proponents of that approach claimed that the residual method resulted in a value that approximates the value that would have been arrived at under a direct value method or that, under the circumstances, it would have been impracticable to use other methods. Some believed that the value obtained under the residual method for indistinguishable intangible assets was an acceptable surrogate for fair value because it was very difficult to determine fair value by using a direct value method. Entities that used the residual method to assign the purchase price to indistinguishable intangible assets often also used it to test for impairment.

SEC OBSERVER COMMENT

The SEC Observer stated that registrants must follow the guidance in 805-30-30-1 under which intangible assets meeting the criteria for recognition should be recognized at fair value. Goodwill differs from other recognized assets because it is specifically stated in ASC 805-30-30-1 that goodwill is the residual of the cost of an acquisition "over the net amounts assigned to assets acquired and liabilities assumed" and is, therefore, defined and measured as an excess. Other recognized intangible assets must be measured at fair value.

The SEC staff does not believe that it can be assumed that using the residual method to value intangible assets will result in amounts that represent the fair value of those assets. In addition, the fact that it is difficult to value certain intangible assets is not an excuse for not following the guidance in paragraphs ASC 805-20-55-2 through 45, under which the fair value of intangible assets must be determined separately from goodwill. In addition, the SEC Observer noted that some entities are valuing the same intangible assets by the direct value method. Consequently, entities should use a direct value method rather than the residual value method to determine the fair value of intangible assets other than goodwill. Further, impairment should be tested in accordance with the guidance in ASC 350.

ASC 805-20-35-4, 35-48 Subsequent Accounting for an Indemnification Asset Recognized at the Acquisition Date as a Result of a Government-Assisted Acquisition of a Financial Institution

BACKGROUND

Under the guidance in ASC 805, *Business Combinations*, if an acquirer in a business combination is indemnified by the seller against a specific contingency or uncertainty related to all or part of a specific asset or liability acquired in the transaction, the acquirer must recognize an indemnification asset at the same time as the recognition of the indemnified item. Therefore, the indemnification asset and the indemnified item are initially measured on the "same basis," but the indemnified item is subject to a valuation allowance for uncollectible amounts. ASC 805-20-35-4, which provides guidance on how to measure an indemnification asset subsequent to a business combination, also provides that an indemnification asset should be measured "on the same basis" as the indemnified asset or liability, subject to "any contractual limitation" on its amount. It states further that an indemnification asset not measured at fair value should be measured based on management's "assessment" of the indemnification asset's collectability.

When the Federal Deposit Insurance Corporation (FDIC) facilitates the sale of a certain failing financial institution's assets and the assumption of certain of its liabilities, it frequently enters into a loss sharing agreement (LSA) with the acquirer to indemnify the acquirer for certain losses incurred on assets covered under the LSA.

This guidance has been issued due to diversity in practice in the subsequent measurement of an indemnification asset that has been recognized in accordance with the guidance in ASC 805-20-25-27 and 25-28 in a government-assisted acquisition when the amount of the cash flows expected to be collected on an indemnification asset have decreased. That diversity in practice appeared to be due to different interpretations of the phrases "on the same basis" and "contractual limitations" found in ASC 805-20-35-4. Some interpreted those terms to mean that a loss on an indemnification asset should be amortized over the indemnification asset's term. Others interpreted that guidance to mean that a loss should be amortized over the remaining life of the assets subject to indemnification. Still others were writing off an indemnification asset immediately if the expected cash flows on the assets subject to indemnification increase.

SCOPE

The following guidance applies to all entities that recognize an indemnification asset, in accordance with the guidance in ASC 805-20, due to a government-assisted acquisition of a financial institution.

ACCOUNTING GUIDANCE

Business Combinations—Identifiable Assets and Liabilities, and Any Noncontrolling Interest

The amendment of the guidance in ASC 805 moves the existing guidance in ASC 805-20-35-4A to 35-4C, provides new guidance in ASC 805-20-35-4B, and includes a reference to that paragraph in ASC 805-20-35-4. ASC 805-20-65-1 provides transition guidance.

Indemnification Assets Arising from Government-Assisted Acquisitions of a Financial Institution

ASC 805-20-35-4B provides the following guidance:

An indemnification asset acquired in connection with a government-assisted acquisition of a financial institution that (1) includes an indemnification agreement and (2) was recognized at acquisition in accordance with the guidance in ASC 805-20-25-27 and 25-28 should be measured in future periods on the same basis as the item that is indemnified. In certain circumstances, the effect of a change in the expected cash flows related to an indemnification agreement should be amortized as follows:

- Limit the amortization of changes, if any, in the value of an indemnification asset based on its contractual limitations on the amount and term of the agreement.
- Limit the amortization period to the term of the indemnification agreement or the remaining life of the indemnified assets, whichever is less.

Indemnified assets accounted for under the guidance in ASC 310-30-35-10 should be amortized as follows:

- If expected cash flows on indemnified assets increase and there is no previously recorded impairment allowance, a related decrease in the indemnification asset should be amortized over the term of the indemnification agreement or the remaining life of the indemnified assets.
- If the expected cash flows on indemnified assets increase reversing all or a portion of a previously recorded valuation allowance, the related decrease in the indemnification asset should be recognized immediately in earnings. A remaining decrease in the indemnification asset, if any, should be amortized over the term of the indemnification agreement or the remaining life of the indemnified assets.

ASC 805-50: RELATED ISSUES

ASC 805-50-15-7, 15-10 through 15-11, 25-4 through 25-9, 30-10 through 30-12, 35-2, 50-5 through 50-6 Pushdown Accounting

BACKGROUND

Before the issuance of ASU 2014-17, *Pushdown Accounting,* there was only limited guidance in U.S generally accepted accounting principles (U.S. GAAP) regarding when, if ever, an entity that is acquired by another entity can use the acquirer's accounting basis to establish a new accounting and reporting basis (pushdown) in its separate financial statements. Guidance for applying the pushdown basis of accounting is provided for Securities and Exchange Commission (SEC) registrants in FASB Accounting Standards Codification® (ASC) 805, *Business Combinations* (ASC 805-50-S99-1 through S99-4), which codifies the guidance in SEC Staff Accounting Bulletin (SAB) Topic No. 5.J, *New Basis of Accounting Required in Certain Circumstances,* EITF Topic No. D-97, "Push-Down Accounting," and other comments made by the SEC Observer at meetings of the Emerging Issues Task Force (EITF).

The EITF had previously reached consensus positions on pushdown accounting for non-SEC registrants in EITF Issue No. 86-9, "IRC Section 338 and Pushdown Accounting," and in EITF Issue No. 87-21, "Change of Accounting Basis in Master Limited Partnership Transactions," which applied to certain transactions that create a master limited partnership. Because there was diversity in practice in the application of pushdown accounting by entities that are not SEC registrants, issues related to comparability occurred as a result of the option in the SEC guidance to apply pushdown accounting when

80% to 95% of an entity has been acquired. Consequently, guidance was needed regarding whether and at what threshold an acquired entity that is a business or a not-for-profit activity can establish a new accounting basis in its separate financial statements. This ASU provides guidance for those kinds of entities.

The guidance for pushdown accounting under ASU 2014-17 applies to the separate financial statements of an acquired entity and its subsidiaries, which is a public or a nonpublic business entity or a not-for-profit activity when an event occurs under which an acquirer (i.e., an individual or an entity) obtains the ability to control an acquired entity.

ACCOUNTING GUIDANCE

Master Glossary

The definition of Pushdown Accounting in the Master Glossary is amended to read as follows: "Use of the **acquirer's** basis in the preparation of the **acquiree's** separate financial statements."

Business Combinations—Related Issues

General. ASC 805-50-05-1 is superseded by ASU 2014-17. ASC 805-50-05-2(d), which is one of the listed subsections, is amended by substituting the title, "Formation of a Master Limited Partnership," for the existing title, "New Basis of Accounting (Pushdown)." The subsection title "Pushdown Accounting" is added to the list in ASC 805-50-05-2(e).

Formation of a master limited partnership. The first sentence of ASC 805-50-05-6 under this subsection is amended by substituting the title of this subsection for the previously used title, "New Basis of Accounting (Pushdown)." The second sentence is amended to state that this section provides guidance on "when" a master limited partnership may record a new basis of accounting for a master limited partnership's assets and liabilities. The last sentence of ASC 805-50-05-6 is deleted. The new subsection title is substituted for the existing one in the last sentence of ASC 805-50-05-7. ASC 805-50-05-8 is superseded by ASU 2014-17.

Pushdown accounting. ASC 805-50-05-9 is added to state that this subsection provides guidance on "whether and at what threshold an **acquiree** that is a business or **nonprofit activity** can apply **pushdown accounting** in its separate financial statements."

Scope

Formation of a master limited partnership. This subsection has its own scope, which is separate from the scope stated in ASC 805-10-15. ASC 805-50-15-7, which addresses "entities," is amended to provide that the guidance on "Formation of a Master Limited Partnership" applies to a publicly traded master limited partnership formed from assets of existing businesses. It refers to a statement in ASC 805-50-05-7, that usually a master limited partnership's general partner is associated with the existing business. ASC 805-50-15-8 and 15-9 are superseded by ASU 2014-17.

Pushdown accounting. ASC 805-50-15-10 provides that the guidance applies to the separate financial statements of an acquiree and its subsidiaries. ASC 805-50-15-11, which addresses "transactions," provides that the guidance in the Pushdown Accounting subsections does not apply to transactions listed in ASC 805-10-15-4, which are not subject to the guidance on business combinations in ASC 805.

Recognition

The guidance in ASC 805-50-25-3 is superseded by the guidance in ASU 2014-17.

Pushdown accounting. Under the amended guidance in ASC 805-50-25-4, an acquired entity can elect to apply pushdown accounting in its separate financial statements when an acquirer gains control of an acquired entity by one of the following ways, among others:

- Transferring cash or other assets;
- Incurring liabilities;
- Issuing equity interests;
- Providing more than one type of consideration; or
- Entering into a contractual agreement, without transferring consideration, as discussed in ASC 805-10-25-11.

ASC 805-50-25-5 provides that the General guidance on Consolidation in ASC 810-10 for determining whether a controlling financial interest exists should be applied to identify the acquirer. Further, in the case of a business combination, the guidance in ASC 805-10-55-11 through 55-15 should be considered to identify an acquirer if it is unclear which of the combining entities is the acquirer. If an acquiree is a variable interest entity (VIE), an acquiree's primary beneficiary is always the acquirer. Determining which party, if any, is a VIE's primary beneficiary should be based on the guidance in the subsections for VIEs in ASC 810-10, not the General guidance related to a controlling financial interest or the guidance in ASC 805-10-55-11 through 55-15.

The guidance in ASC 805-50-25-6 provides that acquirees that file with the SEC and conduit bond obligors for conduit debt securities that are traded in a public market should make their election to apply pushdown accounting in their separate financial statements before their financial statements are issued. Other entities should make the election before their financial statements are available to be issued for the reporting period in which the change-in-control event occurred. Each time there is a change-in-control event in which an acquirer gains control of an acquiree, the election to apply pushdown accounting should be evaluated and may be elected. An acquiree that elects to apply pushdown accounting should apply that accounting as of the acquisition date.

If an acquiree does not elect to apply pushdown accounting when a change-in-control event occurs, ASC 805-50-25-7 provides that it can elect to apply pushdown accounting related to that event in a subsequent reporting period. In that case, a change in accounting principle should be recognized in accordance with the guidance in ASC 250, *Accounting Changes and Error Corrections*. Pushdown accounting should be applied as of the acquisition date of the change-in-control event.

Under the guidance in ASC 805-50-25-8, an acquiree's subsidiary is eligible to elect to apply pushdown accounting to its separate financial statements in accordance with the guidance in ASC 805-50-25-4 through 25-7, regardless of whether or not the acquiree has elected to do so.

ASC 805-50-25-9 provides that once an entity has elected to apply pushdown accounting to a change-in-control event, it cannot be revoked.

Initial Measurement

Pushdown accounting. The guidance for the initial measurement of pushdown accounting is included in ASC 805-50-30-10 through 30-12. Those paragraphs provide that an acquiree that elects to apply pushdown accounting in its separate financial statements should present the acquirer's new basis of accounting for the acquiree's individual assets and liabilities established under the guidance in ASC 805. If an acquirer is not required to apply the guidance in ASC 805 and consequently has not established a new basis of accounting for an acquiree's individual assets and liabilities, an acquiree should present in its separate financial statements the new basis of accounting that the acquirer would have established if the guidance in ASC 805 had been applied.

ASC 805-50-30-11 provides that although an acquiree is required to recognize in its separate financial statements goodwill that occurs as a result of the application of the guidance in ASC 805, an acquiree's income statement should not include bargain purchase gains, if any. However, an acquiree's separate financial statements should include an acquirer's bargain purchase gains, if any, as an adjustment to additional paid-in capital (or net assets of a not-for-profit acquiree).

Subsequent Measurement

Pushdown accounting. Under the guidance in ASC 805-50-35-2, an acquiree is required to follow the subsequent measurement guidance in ASC 805 or other guidance in the ASC for the subsequent measurement and accounting of the applicable assets, liabilities, and equity instruments.

Disclosure

Pushdown accounting. Under the guidance in ASC 805-50-50-5, an acquiree that elects to apply pushdown accounting in its separate financial statements should disclose information in the period in which pushdown accounting was applied (or the current period if an acquiree recognizes adjustments related to pushdown accounting) to helps financial statement users to evaluate the effect of pushdown accounting. Presentation of the required disclosures in ASC 805, as applicable, would satisfy that requirement.

Disclosure of the following information is suggested in ASC 805-50-50-6, but disclosure of additional information may be necessary to meet the objective in ASC 805-50-50-5 (above):

- An acquirer's name and description and how the acquirer gained control.
- The acquisition date.
- The fair value of the acquirer's total consideration on the acquisition date.

- The amounts of each major class of assets and liabilities recognized by an acquiree on the acquisition date by using pushdown accounting. If the initial pushdown accounting is incomplete for amounts, if any, recognized by the acquiree, the reasons why the initial accounting is incomplete.
- A qualitative description of the factors that constitute the amount of goodwill recognized, such as expected synergies from an acquiree's and acquirer's combined operations, or intangible assets that do not qualify for separate recognition, or other factors. In a bargain purchase, the amount of the bargain purchase recognized in additional paid-in capital (or net assets of a not-for-profit acquire) and a description of the reasons why the transaction resulted in a gain.
- Information to evaluate the financial effects of adjustments recognized in the current reporting period related to pushdown accounting that occurred in the current or a previous reporting period (including adjustments made as result of the initial accounting for pushdown accounting being incomplete (see ASC 805-50-25-13 through 25-14)).

ASC 805-50-05-7, 30-7 through 30-9 Change of Accounting Basis in Master Limited Partnership Transactions

BACKGROUND

The enactment of the Tax Reform Act of 1986 resulted in the formation of an increasing number of Master Limited Partnerships (MLPs), which are partnerships whose interests are traded publicly. MLPs may be formed to realize the value of undervalued assets; to pass income and deductible losses through to its shareholders; to raise capital; to enable companies to sell, spin off, or liquidate operations; or to combine partnerships. They are generally formed from assets in existing businesses operated in the form of limited partnerships and in connection with a business in which the general partner is also involved.

The following are different methods of creating an MLP:

- In a *roll-up,* two or more legally separate limited partnerships are combined into one MLP.
- In a *drop-down*, units of a limited partnership that was formed with a sponsor's assets (usually a corporate entity) are sold to the public.
- In a *roll-out*, a sponsor places certain assets into a limited partnership and distributes its units to shareholders.
- In a *reorganization*, an entity is liquidated by transferring all of its assets to an MLP.

EFFECTS OF ASC 805 (FAS-141(R))

FAS-141, which superseded APB-16, applies to transactions in which all entities transfer net assets, or the owners of those entities transfer their equity interests to a newly formed entity in a transaction that is referred to as "roll-up." Its scope excludes, however, transfers of net assets or exchanges of equity interests between entities under common control. All the facts and circumstances should be analyzed to determine the nature of the transaction and the appropriate method of accounting for it.

FAS-141 has been replaced by ASC 805 (FAS-141(R)), which was issued in December 2007. Although, its scope continues the exclusion of transfers of net assets or exchanges of equity interests between entities under common control, guidance on the accounting for those transactions is included in Appendix D, "Continuing Authoritative Guidance," of the Statement.

ACCOUNTING ISSUES

1. Can new-basis accounting ever be used for the assets and liabilities of an MLP?
2. How should an MLP account for transaction costs in a roll-up?

ACCOUNTING GUIDANCE

1. A new basis is not appropriate in the following circumstances:
    a. The MLP's general partner in a roll-up was also the general partner of the predecessor limited partnerships, and no cash has been exchanged in the transaction.
    b. A sponsor in a drop-down receives 1% of the units of the MLP as its general partner and 24% of the units as a limited partner, with the remaining 75% of the units sold to the public. The general partner can be replaced by a two-thirds vote of the limited partners.
    c. An MLP is created as a roll-out.

d. An MLP is created as a reorganization.

In addition, the conclusion on a roll-up would not change even if the general partner was the general partner of only some of the predecessor limited partnerships. Task Force members noted that if a general partner of predecessor limited partnerships who will not be a general partner of the MLP receives MLP units in settlement of management contracts or for other services that will not carry over to the MLP, those units have the characteristics of compensation rather than equity, and should be accounted for as such by the MLP. The Task Force did not reach a consensus on situations in which new-basis accounting would be appropriate, but did not preclude the possibility.

2. A roll-up's transaction costs should be charged to expense.

ASC 805-50-S30-3, S99-4 Changes of Ownership Resulting in a New Basis of Accounting

OVERVIEW

Entity A has acquired the voting common stock of Entity B in a business combination accounted for as a purchase transaction. Under the guidance in ASC 805, Entity A is required to account for the assets and liabilities acquired in the transactions at their fair values. However, the accounting literature provides no guidance as to whether Entity B should report its assets and liabilities on the same basis as Entity A, thus adopting a "new basis of accounting."

ACCOUNTING ISSUES

1. At what level of change in ownership should an entity adopt a new basis of accounting to report its assets and liabilities?
2. How should the new basis of accounting be computed?
3. At what amount should minority interests be reported?

ACCOUNTING GUIDANCE

No conclusion was reached on those issues. However, the SEC Observer stated the view of the SEC staff.

SEC OBSERVER COMMENT

The SEC Observer stated that SEC registrants are required to adopt pushdown accounting only if virtually 100% of the stock has been acquired and there is no outstanding publicly held debt or preferred stock. The SEC Observer stated further that net assets (in a business combination) or long-lived assets transferred between companies under common control or between a parent and subsidiary should be reported at their historical cost in the subsidiary's separate financial statements.

CHAPTER 48

ASC 808—COLLABORATIVE ARRANGEMENTS

CONTENTS

INTERPRETIVE GUIDANCE

ASC 808: COLLABORATIVE ARRANGEMENTS

ASC 808-10: OVERALL

ASC 808-10-10-1, 15-2 through 15-13, 45-1 through 45-5, 50-1, 55-1 through 55-19, 65-1 Accounting for Collaborative Arrangements

BACKGROUND

The following discussion addresses the accounting for arrangements entered into by entities in a number of industries, such as the pharmaceutical, biotechnology, motion picture, software, and computer hardware industries, under which intellectual property is jointly developed and commercialized with other entities; usually, without creating a separate legal entity for that activity. All of the activities are conducted by the parties to the arrangement using their own employees and facilities. For example, one of the participants may be responsible for performing the research and development of a product while the other participant may be responsible for the product's commercialization. Because the accounting for such arrangements is diverse (i.e., arrangements may be accounted for on a gross basis or a net basis), accounting and disclosure guidance was developed to improve the comparability of financial statements.

The following guidance applies to collaborative arrangements conducted by parties that participate in such arrangements without creating a separate legal entity for that purpose. This guidance is *not* limited to specific industries or to intellectual property. However, arrangements for which specific guidance exists under other current authoritative literature are excluded from the scope of this guidance and should be accounted for according to the existing guidance. In addition, the following guidance does *not* apply to arrangements that involve a financial investor.

ACCOUNTING GUIDANCE

Scope

A contractual arrangement under which the parties are involved in a joint operating activity and are exposed to significant risks and rewards that depend on the activity's ultimate success is referred to as a "collaborative arrangement." Although for the most part the activities of a collaborative arrangement under the scope of this guidance are *not* conducted through a separate legal entity created for that purpose, the existence of a specific legal entity for specific activities related to *part* of an arrangement or for a specific geographic location for part of an arrangement's activities would *not* exclude an arrangement from the definition of a *collaborative arrangement* in the ASC Glossary. However, the guidance in ASC 810, ASC 323-10, or other related literature should be applied to account for any part of a collaborative arrangement performed in a separate legal entity. The disclosure requirements under this guidance apply to the total arrangement, regardless of the parts that are conducted in a separate legal entity.

Participants should determine at the inception of an arrangement whether it is a collaborative arrangement based on the facts and circumstances at that time. However, a collaborative arrangement may begin at any time during an activity on which the participants have been collaborating. If the facts or circumstances of the participants' roles or their exposure to risks and rewards change, the arrangement should be reevaluated. Exercising an option is an example of a situation that might change a participant's role in a collaborative arrangement.

> ***PRACTICE NOTE:*** The FASB has issued ASU 2018-18, *Collaborative Arrangements (Topic 808): Clarifying the Interaction between Topic 808 and Topic 606*, to clarify how the guidance in ASC 606, *Revenue from Contracts with Customers*, interacts with the guidance in ASC 808. The following paragraphs have been inserted:
>
> - ASC 808-15-5A provides that a portion of a collaborative arrangement under the scope of ASC 808 may also be accounted for under the guidance in other Topics in addition to ASC 606.
> - ASC 808-10-15-5B provides that the recognition, measurement, presentation, and disclosure requirements in ASC 606 should partially apply based on the guidance in ASC 606-10-15-4 and ASC 606-10-25-19 through 25-22 to a distinct unit of account within a collaborative arrangement with a customer for a promised good or service (or bundle of goods or services).
> - ASC 808 10-15-5C provides that the accounting for a unit of account, recognition, and measurement of a collaborative arrangement that is partially or totally outside the scope of other Topics, including ASC 606, should be based by analogy on the authoritative accounting literature. If no appropriate analogy exists, an entity should elect to follow a reasonable, rational, and consistent accounting policy.

The amendments in ASU 2018-08 are effective for public business entities for fiscal years beginning after December 15, 2019, and interim periods within those fiscal years. For all other entities, the amendments are effective for fiscal years beginning after December 15, 2020, and interim periods within fiscal years beginning after December 15, 2021. Early adoption is permitted, including adoption in any interim period (1) for public entities for periods for which financial statements have not yet been issued and (2) for all other entities for periods for which financial statement have not yet been made available for issuance. An entity may not adopt the amendments earlier than its adoption of ASC 606.

Joint Operating Activity

Participants in a collaborative arrangement may jointly develop and bring to market intellectual property, pharmaceutical products, software, computer hardware, or a motion picture. One participant may be primarily responsible for a specific activity or two or more participants may be jointly responsible for certain activities. Joint operating activities may include research and development, marketing, general and administrative activities, manufacturing, and distribution. A joint operation of a hospital is an example of a collaborative arrangement.

Active Participation

Active participation in a collaborative arrangement may consist of, but may not be limited to:

- Significant involvement in directing and carrying out joint activities;
- Participation on a steering committee or other means of oversight or governance; or
- Holding a contractual or other legal right to underlying intellectual property.

However, if an entity's only responsibility is to provide financial resources to a venture, that entity generally is *not* an active participant in a collaborative arrangement under the scope of this guidance.

Significant Risks and Rewards

To determine whether participants in a collaborative arrangement are exposed to significant risks and rewards that depend on a joint operating activity's commercial success, an arrangement's specific facts and circumstances, including, but not limited to, the arrangement's terms and conditions, should be considered. Based on an arrangement's terms and conditions, participants in an arrangement may *not* be exposed to *significant risks and rewards* if:

- Services are performed for fees at fair market value rates.
- A participant can leave an arrangement without cause and recover a significant portion or all of its cumulative economic participation to date.
- Only one participant receives an initial allocation of profits.
- The amount of a reward that a participant can receive is limited.

The following factors should be considered in an evaluation of risks and rewards:

- The stage of the endeavor's life cycle in which collaboration begins.
- The expected time period or financial commitment that participants will devote to the arrangement as it relates to an endeavor's total life span or expected value.

Consideration exchanged for a license related to intellectual property may *not* be an indicator that the participants are *not* exposed to risks or rewards on the ultimate success of their effort. Judgment is necessary to determine whether the participants are exposed to risks and rewards.

Other Presentation Matters

PRACTICE NOTE: ASU 2014-09, *Revenue from Contracts with Customers (Topic 606)*, superseded the guidance related to reporting revenue as a principal versus an agent in ASC 605, *Revenue Recognition*. That guidance has been amended and moved to ASC 606-10-55-36 through 55-40. Participants in a collaborative arrangement should report costs incurred and revenues generated from transactions with entities that do not participate in the arrangement (third parties) in an appropriate line item in the participants' respective financial statements in accordance with the guidance in ASC 606-10-55-36 through 55-40, Principal versus Agent Consideration.

A participant in a collaborative arrangement who is considered to be the principal participant in a specific revenue or cost transaction with a third party, should report that transaction on a gross basis in its financial statements based on the guidance in ASC 606-10-55-36 through 55-40. Collaborative arrangements should *not* be accounted for by the equity method of accounting in ASC 323-10 and 323-30.

The parts of a collaborative arrangement accounted for under the scope of other authoritative literature, as discussed above in ASC 808-10-15-5A, should be presented in accordance with that literature's provisions. The presentation of parts of a collaborative arrangement should be evaluated based on the arrangement's nature and contractual terms, and the nature of its business operations. An entity should not present transactions in a collaborative arrangement together with revenue from contracts with customers under ASC 606, except in accordance with the guidance in ASC 808-10-5B if a transaction is with a customer for a distinct unit of account within a collaborative arrangement for a promised good or service (or bundle of goods or services).

Disclosure

Participants in a collaborative arrangement should disclose the following information in the initial reporting period and annually thereafter:

- The nature and purpose of collaborative arrangements.
- The entity's rights and obligations under a collaborative arrangement.
- The entity's accounting policy for collaborative arrangements.
- Income statement classification and amounts related to transactions as a result of the collaborative arrangement between participants for each period in which an income statement is presented.

Separate disclosure should be made about information related to collaborative arrangements that are significant individually.

Transition and Open Effective Date Information

The following is the transition and effective date information in ASU 2018-18, *Collaborative Arrangements (Topic 808): Clarifying the Interaction between Topic 808 and Topic 606,* in ASC 808-10-65-2 of the ASU. The amendments of the guidance above will be effective as follows:

1. For public business entities for fiscal years that begin after December 15, 2019, including interim periods within those fiscal years.
2. For all other entities, for fiscal years that begin after December 15, 2020, and interim periods within fiscal years that begin after December 15, 2021.

3. Earlier application of the guidance in ASU 2018-18 is permitted for entities that also adopted the pending content linked to ASC 606-10-65-1, including adoption in any interim period for:
   a. Public business entities for periods for which financial statements have not yet been issued, and
   b. All other entities for periods for which financial statements have not yet been made available for issuance.
4. The pending guidance in ASU 2018-18 should be applied retrospectively to the date in which it initially applied the pending guidance in ASC 606-10-65-1. The cumulative effect of initially applying that guidance should be recognized as an adjustment to the opening balance of retained earnings of the earliest annual period presented or the annual period that includes the date that the guidance in ASC 606-10-65-1 was adopted, whichever is later.
5. An entity may elect to apply the pending content in ASU 2018-18 retrospectively either to all contracts or only to uncompleted contracts at the initial application date of the pending guidance in ASC 606-10-65-1. A completed contract is one for which all (or substantially all) of the revenue and expenses were recognized in accordance with the guidance that was in effect on the initial application of the guidance. Whether an entity has applied the guidance to all contracts or only to uncompleted contracts should be disclosed.
6. In accordance with the requirement in ASC 606-10-65-1(g), application of the practical expedient for contract modification in ASC 606-10-65-1(f)(4) may be elected.
7. The disclosures in ASC 250-10-50-1 through 50-2 (except for the disclosure in ASC 250-10-50-1(b)(2)) are required in the period in which the pending content that links to ASC 808-10-65-2(g) is adopted.

CHAPTER 49

ASC 810—CONSOLIDATION

CONTENTS

PART I: GENERAL GUIDANCE

ASC 810-10: OVERALL

OVERVIEW

Consolidated financial statements represent the results of operations, statement of cash flows, and financial position of a single entity, even though multiple, separate legal entities are involved. Consolidated financial statements are presumed to present more meaningful information than separate financial statements and must be used in substantially all cases in which a parent directly or indirectly controls the majority voting interest (over 50%) of a subsidiary. Consolidated financial statements should not be used in those circumstances in which there is significant doubt concerning the parent's ability to control the subsidiary.

> ***PRACTICE NOTE:*** There are two primary models for determining whether consolidation is appropriate—the voting interest entity model and the variable interest entity model. Under the voting interest entity model, the usual condition for a controlling financial interest for legal entities other than limited partnerships is ownership by one reporting entity, directly or indirectly, of more than 50% of the outstanding voting shares of another entity. Under the variable interest entity model, a controlling financial interest requires both (*a*) the power to direct the activities that most significantly impact the variable interest entity's economic performance, and (*b*) the obligation to absorb losses of or the right to receive benefits from the variable interest entity that could potentially be significant to the variable interest entity.

BACKGROUND

It is desirable to present comparative financial statements in annual reports, because such a presentation is likely to provide much more information than noncomparative statements. A consolidated financial statement presents the results of operations, statement of cash flows, and financial position of a single entity. With few exceptions, a parent company is to consolidate all of its majority-owned subsidiaries. A company must consolidate the assets, liabilities, revenues, and expenses of a variable interest entity if the company has a controlling financial interest in that entity. ASC 810 established accounting and reporting standards to ensure consistency in the reporting and disclosure of noncontrolling interests in consolidated financial statements, including the deconsolidation of a subsidiary. ASC 958 provides guidance on the application of ASC 810 for not-for-profit entities. ASC 810 discusses the requirements for determining whether an entity is a variable interest entity, as well as the requirements for determining the primary beneficiary of a variable interest entity.

Retained earnings of a subsidiary at the date of acquisition are not treated as part of consolidated retained earnings (ASC 810-10-45-2). The retained earnings, other capital accounts, and contributed capital at the date of acquisition represent the book value that is eliminated in preparing consolidated statements.

A parent company should not exclude a majority-owned subsidiary from consolidation because it has a different fiscal year. For consolidation purposes, a subsidiary usually can prepare financial statements that correspond with its parent's fiscal period. If a subsidiary's fiscal year is within three months or less of its parent's fiscal year, it is acceptable to use those fiscal-year financial statements for consolidation purposes, provided that adequate disclosure is made of any material events occurring within the intervening period (ASC 810-10-45-12).

MAJORITY-OWNED SUBSIDIARIES

Investments in which a parent company has a controlling financial interest represented by the direct or indirect ownership of a majority voting interest (more than 50%) generally must be consolidated, except those in which significant doubt exists regarding the parent's ability to control the subsidiary (ASC 810-10-15-8). For limited partnerships, the usual condition for consolidation is ownership by one limited partner, directly or indirectly, of more than 50% of the limited partnership's kick-out rights through voting interests (ASC 810-10-15-8A). In addition, in some cases the existence of noncontrolling interests can prevent the owner of a more than 50% voting interest from having a controlling financial interest. For example, the majority owner may need the approval of the noncontrolling shareholder to control the operations or assets of the investee, or the noncontrolling shareholder may have veto rights over the actions of the majority owner, and these restrictions may be so substantive as to prevent the majority owner from having control (ASC 810-10-15-10).

PRACTICE POINTER: In determining whether consolidated financial statements are required in a particular situation, a reasonable starting point is to assume that if majority ownership exists, consolidation is appropriate. For that point, consider those rare circumstances in which a majority ownership interest does exist but consolidation would not be appropriate. However, such circumstances are clearly intended to be exceptions to a policy of consolidation in most situations of majority ownership.

ASC 810 requires that the exchange restrictions or other governmental controls in a foreign subsidiary be so severe that they "cast significant doubt on the parent's ability to control the subsidiary" (ASC 810-10-15-10). This amendment narrows the exception for a majority-owned foreign subsidiary from one that permits exclusion from consolidation of any or all foreign subsidiaries to one that effectively eliminates distinctions between foreign and domestic subsidiaries. Thus, a majority-owned subsidiary must be consolidated unless significant doubt exists regarding the parent's control of the subsidiary. ASC 830 contains special rules for translating foreign currency financial statements of foreign subsidiaries that operate in countries with highly inflationary economies.

PRACTICE NOTE: ASC 810 comes close to requiring that all majority-owned subsidiaries be consolidated. A limited exception is a situation where control does not rest with the majority owner, as when a subsidiary is in legal reorganization or bankruptcy. ASC 323, on the other hand, is amended to eliminate the requirement that unconsolidated subsidiaries be accounted for by the equity method. In the rare instance indicated above, where (majority-owned) subsidiaries are not consolidated, the authoritative literature apparently does not specify a particular method of accounting, although the equity method may be judged the appropriate method to use in the circumstances.

ACCOUNTING AND REPORTING ON SUBSIDIARIES

The identifiable assets acquired, the liabilities assumed, and any non-controlling interests in the subsidiary must be measured at their acquisition-date fair values (ASC 805-20-30-1). Any excess of the fair market value of the consideration given over the fair market value of the net assets acquired is reported as goodwill (ASC 805-30-30-1). If the fair market value of the consideration given is less than the fair market value of the net assets acquired, the resulting excess of fair value of acquired net assets over the cost of the acquired entity is recognized in earnings as a gain on the acquisition date (ASC 805-30-25-2).

When a subsidiary is initially consolidated during the year, the consolidated financial statements shall include the subsidiary's revenues, expenses, gains, and losses only from the date the subsidiary is initially consolidated (ASC 810-10-45-4).

CONSOLIDATION ISSUES

Combined Financial Statements

Consolidated financial statements usually are justified on the basis that one of the consolidating entities exercises control over the affiliated group. When there is no such control, combined financial statements may be used to accomplish the same results. For example, a group of companies controlled by an individual shareholder, or a group of unconsolidated subsidiaries that could otherwise not be consolidated, should utilize combined financial statements. Combined financial statements are prepared on the same basis as consolidated financial statements, except that no company in the group has a controlling interest in the other (ASC 810-10-55-1B).

Comparative Financial Statements

Comparative financial statements reveal much more information than noncomparative statements and furnish useful data about differences in the results of operations for the periods involved or in the financial position at the comparison dates (ASC 205-10-45-1).

Consistency is a major factor in creating comparability. Prior-year amounts and classifications must be, in fact, comparable with the current period presented, and exceptions must be disclosed clearly (ASC 205-10-45-2, 4).

Consolidation versus Equity Method

The income and balance sheet effects of intercompany transactions are eliminated in equity method adjustments as well as in the financial statements of consolidated entities (ASC 810-10-45-1). In consolidated financial statements, the details of all entities to the consolidation are reported in full. In the equity method, the investment is shown as a single amount in the investor balance sheet, and earnings or losses generally are shown as a single amount in the income statement. This is the reason the equity method is frequently referred to as *one-line consolidation*.

PRACTICE POINTER: While their impact on reporting income is the same, the equity method and consolidation differ in the extent of detail each reflects in the financial statements. The authoritative literature clearly states that the equity method is not necessarily an appropriate alternative to consolidation, or vice versa. Generally, consolidation is appropriate where majority interest exists, and the equity method is appropriate where the investor has the ability to exert significant influence over the investee but lacks majority ownership.

Consolidated Work Papers and Intercompany Transactions

The preparation of consolidated financial statements is facilitated by the preparation of a consolidated statements work-sheet. Traditionally, this worksheet was prepared by hand and the adjustments and eliminations required for consolidation were not posted to the books of the individual companies. Computerization of accounting processes, including the preparation of worksheets to assist in the preparation of consolidated financial statements, has modernized this process and all eliminations and adjustments are posted.

Following is a brief discussion of some of the most frequently encountered intercompany transactions.

Sales and Purchases

The gross amount of all intercompany sales and/or purchases is eliminated on the consolidated work papers. When the adjustment has already been made in the trial balance for ending inventory, the eliminating entry is made by debiting sales and crediting cost of sales. When no adjustment has been made for ending inventory, the eliminating entry is made by crediting the purchases account. In this latter case, a more straightforward approach is to make an adjusting entry establishing the cost of sales and then eliminating intercompany sales by crediting cost of sales.

Receivables and Payables

Intercompany receivables and payables include:

- Accounts receivable and accounts payable.
- Advances to and from affiliates.
- Notes receivable and notes payable.
- Interest receivable and interest payable.

The gross amounts of all intercompany receivables and payables are eliminated on the consolidated work papers. Care must be exercised when a receivable is discounted with one of the consolidated companies (no contingent liability). If the balance sheet reflects a discounted receivable with another affiliate, the amount must be eliminated by a debit to discounted receivables and a credit to receivables. If one affiliate discounts a receivable to another affiliate, who in turn discounts it to an outsider, a real contingent liability still exists, and must be shown on the consolidated balance sheet.

Unrealized Profits in Inventory

Regardless of any noncontrolling interests, all (100%) of any intercompany profit in ending inventory is eliminated on the consolidated workpapers. In addition, the cost of sales account must be adjusted for intercompany profit in beginning inventory arising from intercompany transactions in the previous year. If the adjustment for intercompany profits in inventories is not made, consolidated net income will be incorrect and consolidated ending inventory will be overstated.

Illustration of Profit in Inventory

P Company purchased $200,000 and $250,000 of merchandise in 20X8 and 20X9, respectively, from its subsidiary S at 25% above cost. As of December 31, 20X8, and 20X9, P had on hand $25,000 and $30,000 of merchandise purchased from S. The following is the computation of intercompany profits:

Computation of Intercompany Profits

Beginning inventory	$25,000	=	125%
Cost to S	(20,000)	=	(100%)
Intercompany profit	$ 5,000		25%
Ending inventory	$30,000	=	125%
Cost to S	(24,000)	=	(100%)
Intercompany profit	$ 6,000		25%

The adjustment is different for a consolidated balance sheet than for a consolidated income statement and balance sheet. If intercompany profit adjustments have not been recorded in equity method entries on P Company's books, for a consolidated balance sheet only the elimination entry is:

Retained earnings	$6,000	
Inventory		$6,000

Assuming no equity method adjustments are made, and a perpetual inventory system is used, for a consolidated income statement and balance sheet the following adjustments are necessary:

Sales	$250,000	
Costs of sales		$250,000
To eliminate intercompany sales.		
Consolidated retained earnings	5,000	
Cost of sales		5,000
To reverse consolidated adjustment of 12/31/X8.		
Cost of sales	6,000	
Inventory		6,000
To eliminate intercompany profit in ending inventory.		

The adjustment to consolidated retained earnings is necessary because the intercompany profit was eliminated on the prior year's consolidated work papers. (Consolidated adjustments and eliminations are not posted to the books of the individual companies. Therefore, the beginning inventory for P still reflected the prior year's intercompany inventory profits from S.)

If merchandise containing an intercompany inventory profit is reduced from the purchase price to market value and the reduction is equal to, or more than, the actual intercompany inventory profit, no deferral of profit entry is required in consolidation. For example, if merchandise costing one affiliate $10,000 is sold to another affiliate for $12,000, who reduces it to market value of $11,000, the consolidated work paper adjustment for unrealized intercompany inventory profits should be only $1,000.

Noncontrolling interests do not affect the adjustment for unrealized intercompany profits in inventories. Consolidated net income and noncontrolling interests in the net income of a subsidiary are affected by the adjustment, however, because the reduction or increase in beginning or ending inventory of a partially owned subsidiary does affect the determination of net income.

Unrealized intercompany losses in inventory are accounted for in the same manner as unrealized profits, except that they have the opposite effect. Profits or losses on sales and/or purchases prior to an affiliation are not recognized as a consolidated adjustment.

Unrealized Profits in Long-Lived Assets

Regardless of any noncontrolling interests, all (100%) of any intercompany profits on the sale and/or purchase of long-lived assets between affiliates are eliminated on the consolidated workpapers.

When one affiliate constructs or sells a long-lived asset to another affiliate at a profit, the profit is eliminated on the consolidated work-papers. As with unrealized intercompany profits or losses in inventory, noncontrolling interests do not affect any consolidated adjustment for profits in intercompany sales of long-lived assets between affiliates. Net income of the subsidiary involved in the intercompany profit on a long-lived asset is affected by the adjustment, however, which in turn affects consolidated net income and noncontrolling interests.

If a nondepreciable asset is involved in an intercompany profit on a long-lived asset, the profit is eliminated by a debit to either retained earnings, in the case of an adjusted consolidated balance sheet, or to gain on sale, in the case of a consolidated income statement.

Depreciable assets require the same adjustment for intercompany profit as nondepreciable long-lived assets, and an adjustment must also be made for any depreciation recorded on the intercompany profit.

Illustration of Profit in Long-Lived Assets

S Company, an 80%-owned subsidiary, sells to P Company for $100,000 a piece of machinery that cost $80,000. The sale was made on July 1, 20X8, and consolidated statements are being prepared for December 31, 20X8. P Company depreciates machinery over ten years on a straight-line basis and records one-half year's depreciation on the purchased machinery.

The first entry eliminates the $20,000 of intercompany profit, as follows:

Gain on sale of machinery	$20,000	
Machinery		$20,000

Since P Company has recorded one-half year's depreciation on the machinery, the following additional entry is made:

Accumulated depreciation	$1,000	
Depreciation expense		$1,000

Because consolidated eliminations and adjustments are never posted to any books, additional entries are required in the following year. Assuming that intercompany profit adjustments were not made under the equity method on P Company's books, the following eliminations are needed:

Retained earnings—P Company	$16,000	
Retained earnings—S Company	$4,000	
Machinery		$20,000
To eliminate intercompany profit on prior year's sale of machinery.		
Accumulated depreciation	3,000	
Retained earnings—P Company		800
Retained earnings—S Company		200
Depreciation expense		2,000
To eliminate the $2,000 depreciation expense on intercompany profit on the sale of machinery and to eliminate the $1,000 depreciation expense for prior year's depreciation.		

If the intercompany sale had been made from P Company to S Company, the retained earnings adjustments would have been made only to P Company's accounts.

The process of eliminating the depreciation expense on the intercompany profit on the sale of long-lived assets continues until the asset is fully depreciated. Thereafter, until the asset is disposed of or retired, adjustments are needed to the machinery and accumulated depreciation accounts. In the example, the following entry would be made every year on the consolidated work papers after the asset is fully depreciated and before it is disposed of or retired.

Accumulated depreciation	$20,000	
Machinery		$20,000

An affiliate that makes an intercompany profit on the sale of long-lived assets to another affiliate may pay income taxes on the gain. This occurs usually when the affiliated group does not file consolidated tax returns and the gain cannot be avoided for tax purposes. In such cases, the intercompany profit on the sale should be reduced by the related tax effects in computing the consolidated adjusting entry.

Intercompany Bondholdings

Intercompany bonds purchased by an affiliate are treated in the year of acquisition as though they have been retired. Any gain or loss is recognized in the consolidated income statement for the year of acquisition.

The amount of gain or loss on an intercompany bond purchase is the difference between the unamortized bond premium or discount on the books of the issuer and the amount of any purchase discount or premium.

An intercompany gain or loss on bonds does not occur when an affiliate makes the purchase directly from the affiliated issuer, because the selling price will be exactly equal to the cost.

Illustration of Intercompany Bonds

An affiliate purchases $20,000 face value 6% bonds from an affiliated issuer for $19,500.

On the affiliated investor's books, the following entry is made:

Investment in bonds	$19,500	
Cash		$19,500
On the affiliated issuer's books the entry is:		
Cash	19,500	
Discount on bonds payable	500	
Bonds payable		20,000
The consolidated elimination is:		
Bonds payable	20,000	
Discount on bonds payable		500
Investment in bonds		19,500

An intercompany gain or loss on bonds does not occur when the purchase price is exactly the same as the carrying value on the books of the affiliated issuer.

The following conditions must exist for an affiliated investor to realize a gain or loss on intercompany bondholdings:

- The bonds are already outstanding.
- The bonds are purchased from outside the affiliated group.
- The price paid is different from the carrying value of the affiliated issuer.

Illustration of Intercompany Bonds with Gain/Loss

Company S acquires $50,000 of face amount 6% bonds from an outsider. These bonds were part of an original issue of $300,000 made by the parent of Company S. The purchase price was $45,000, and the bonds mature in four years and nine months (57 months). Interest is payable on June 30 and December 31, and the purchase was made on March 31.

The journal entry on the books of Company S to record the purchase is:

Investment in bonds	$45,000	
Accrued interest receivable	750	
Cash		$45,750

On the consolidated workpapers at the end of the year, the following entries are made:

Investment in bonds	$5,000	
Gain on intercompany bondholdings		$5,000
To adjust the investment in bonds to face amount and record the gain.		
Bonds payable—Co. P	50,000	
Investment in bonds—Co. S		50,000
To eliminate intercompany bondholdings.		
Interest income—Co. S	2,250	
Interest expense—Co. P		2,250
To eliminate intercompany interest on bonds that was actually paid.		
Interest income—Co. S	789	
Investment in bonds		789
To eliminate amortization of $5,000 discount on bonds recorded on Co. S's books. (9/57 of $5,000 = $789)		
Accrued interest payable	1,500	
Accrued interest receivable		1,500
To eliminate accrued interest payable on Dec. 31 by Co. P, and the accrued interest receivable on Dec. 31 by Co. S.		

This example contains all the possible adjustments except for an issuer's premium or discount. Assume the following additional information on the original issue:

Face amount	$300,000
Issued at 96	288,000
Date of issue	1/1/X1
Maturity date	1/1/Y0

Company S had purchased its $50,000 face amount when the issue had four years and nine months left to maturity.

On the parent company's books, this discount is being amortized over the life of the bond issue at the rate of $1,200 per year ($12,000 discount divided by 10 years). An adjustment is made on the consolidated workpapers to eliminate the portion of the unamortized bond discount existing at the date of purchase that is applicable to the $50,000 face amount purchased by Company S.

Total discount on issue	$12,000
1/6 applicable to Co. S's purchase	$ 2,000
Amount of discount per month ($2,000 divided by 120 months)	$ 16.67
Four years and nine months equal 57 months × $16.67	$ 950

The amount of unamortized bond discount on Co. P's books applicable to the $50,000 purchase made by Company S was $950 at the date of purchase. This $950 would have entered into the computation of the gain or loss on intercompany bondholdings. In the example, the gain or loss on intercompany bondholdings of $5,000 would have been reduced by $950 ($4,050) and the following additional consolidated elimination would have been made:

Gain or loss on intercompany bondholdings	$950	
Unamortized bond discount		$950

In addition, the amortization on the intercompany portion of the bond discount would be reversed in the consolidated worksheet (9 months × $16.67):

Unamortized bond discount	$150	
Interest expense		$150

Intercompany Dividends

Intercompany dividends are eliminated on the consolidated work-papers. Consolidated retained earnings should reflect the accumulated earnings of the consolidated group arising since acquisition that have not been distributed to the shareholders of, or capitalized by, the parent company. In the event that a subsidiary capitalizes earnings arising since acquisition by means of a stock dividend, or otherwise, a transfer to paid-in capital is not required in consolidating (ASC 810-10-45-9).

Intercompany Stockholdings

Shares of the parent held by a subsidiary should not be treated as outstanding stock in the consolidated balance sheet. Such shares are treated as "treasury stock" on the consolidated balance sheet and subtracted from consolidated stockholders' equity.

Income Tax Considerations

Income taxes are deferred on any intercompany profits where the inventory still exists within the consolidated group (ASC 810-10-45-8). If consolidated tax returns are filed, however, no adjustment need be made for deferred income taxes, because intercompany profits are eliminated in computing the consolidated tax liability.

Nature of Classification of the Noncontrolling Interest in the Consolidated Statement of Financial Position

A noncontrolling interest is defined as a portion of equity in a subsidiary that is not attributable to a parent company, and thus clarifies a noncontrolling interest in a subsidiary as part of the equity of the consolidated group (ASC 810-10-45-15). Furthermore, a noncontrolling interest is limited to a parent's ownership of a financial instrument issued by a subsidiary that is classified as equity in the subsidiary's financial statements. A financial instrument that is classified as a liability in the subsidiary's financial statements based on the guidance in other standards does not represent an ownership interest and, therefore, is not a noncontrolling interest (ASC 810-10-45-17).

Prior to ASC 810, there was limited guidance related to the classification and reporting of noncontrolling interests. This resulted in considerable diversity in practice with noncontrolling interests reported either as liabilities or in the mezzanine section between liabilities and equity. This diversity has been eliminated and comparability improved by requiring a noncontrolling interest to be reported in the consolidated statement of financial position within equity (net assets), separately from the parent's equity or net assets (ASC 810-10-45-16).

Attributing Net Income and Comprehensive Income to the Parent and the Noncontrolling Interest

Revenues, expenses, gains, losses, net income or loss, and other comprehensive income (and similar amounts reported by not-for-profit entities) attributable to the noncontrolling interest shall be included in the amount reported in consolidated net income (ASC 810-10-45-19). The amounts of consolidated net income attributable to the parent and to the noncontrolling interest also must be disclosed on the face of the consolidated statement of income.

ASC 958 modified how a subsidiary's losses are attributed to the parent and the noncontrolling interest in the unusual case in which losses attributable to the parent and the noncontrolling interest exceed their interests in the subsidiary's equity. Prior to ASC 958 such excess losses attributable to the noncontrolling interest were charged against the parent. Such excess losses attributable to the parent and the noncontrolling interest are now charged to those interests, respectively. In other words, the noncontrolling interest must continue to be attributed its share of losses even if doing so results in a deficit noncontrolling interest balance (ASC 810-10-45-21).

Changes in a Parent's Ownership Interest in a Subsidiary

ASC 958 established a single method of accounting for changes in a parent's ownership interest in a subsidiary when the parent retains its controlling financial interest in the subsidiary. Such a change in the parent's ownership interest in a subsidiary could include (ASC 810-10-45-22):

- the parent purchases additional ownership interests in its subsidiary,
- the parent sells some of its ownership interests in its subsidiary,
- the subsidiary reacquires some of its ownership interests, or
- the subsidiary issues additional ownership interests.

ASC 958 clarified that changes in a parent's ownership while retaining a controlling financial interest in the subsidiary must be accounted for as equity transactions, and, therefore, no gain or loss shall be recognized in consolidated net income or comprehensive income (changes in net assets). ASC 958 required the noncontrolling interest carrying amount to be adjusted to reflect the change in its ownership interest in the subsidiary, and any difference between the fair value of the consideration received or paid and the amount by which the noncontrolling interest is adjusted to be recognized in the equity (net assets) attributable to the parent (ASC 810-10-45-23). Similarly, if a change in a parent's ownership interest occurs in a subsidiary that has accumulated other comprehensive income, the carrying amount of accumulated other comprehensive income shall be adjusted to reflect the change in ownership interest with a corresponding charge or credit to the equity (net assets) attributable to the parent (ASC 810-10-45-24).

ASC 810-10 was amended by ASU 2010-02 in 2010 to clarify the scope of the decrease in ownership provisions of the subtopic and related guidance. Situations to which this guidance applies are the following (ASC 810-10-40-3A):

1. A subsidiary that is a business or nonprofit activity.
2. A group of assets that is a business or nonprofit activity.
3. A subsidiary that is not a business or nonprofit activity if the substance of the transaction is not addressed directly by guidance in other ASC Topics.

The decrease in ownership guidance in ASC 810-10 does *not* apply to the following transactions if they involve businesses or nonprofit activities (ASC 810-10-45-21A1):

1. Conveyances of oil and gas mineral rights. (Entities should apply the mineral property conveyance and related transactions guidance in ASC 932-360 (Oil and Gas—Property, Plant, and Equipment) to these transactions.)
2. A transfer of a good or service in a contract with a customer within the scope of ASC 606.

If a decrease in ownership occurs in a subsidiary that is not a business or nonprofit activity, the entity first must consider whether the substance of the transaction causing the decrease is addressed in other U.S. GAAP, such as transfers of financial assets, revenue recognition, exchanges of nonmonetary assets, sales of in substance real estate, or conveyances of oil and gas mineral rights, and apply the applicable guidance for those transactions. If no other guidance exists, ASC 810-10 applies.

Illustration of Changes in a Parent's Ownership Interest in a Subsidiary

Example 1

Subsidiary A has 50,000 shares of common stock outstanding, all of which are owned by its parent, ABC Co. The carrying amount of Subsidiary A's equity is $800,000. ABC Co. sells 10,000 of its shares in Subsidiary A to an unrelated entity for $200,000 in cash, reducing its ownership interest from 100 percent to 80 percent. That transaction is accounted for by recognizing a noncontrolling interest in the amount of $160,000 ($800,000 × 20 percent). The $40,000 excess of the cash received ($200,000) over the adjustment to the carrying amount of the noncontrolling interest ($160,000) is recognized as an increase in additional paid-in capital attributable to ABC Co. The sale of Subsidiary A's shares by ABC Co. is accounted for as an equity transaction in the consolidated financial statements as follows:

Cash	$200,000	
Noncontrolling interest		$ 160,000
Additional paid-in capital (ABC Co.)		40,000

Example 2

Subsidiary A has 50,000 shares of common stock outstanding. Of those shares, 45,000 are owned by its parent, ABC Co., and 5,000 are owned by other shareholders (a noncontrolling interest in Subsidiary A). The carrying amount of Subsidiary A's equity is $1,200,000. Of that amount, $1,080,000 is attributable to ABC Co., and $120,000 is a noncontrolling interest in Subsidiary A. Subsidiary A issues 10,000 previously unissued shares to a third party for $480,000 in cash, reducing ABC Co.'s ownership interest in Subsidiary A from 90 percent to 75 percent (45,000 shares owned by ABC Co. / 60,000 issued shares).

Even though the percentage of ABC Co.'s ownership interest in Subsidiary A is reduced when Subsidiary A issues additional shares to a third party, ABC Co.'s investment in Subsidiary A increases to $1,260,000, calculated as 75 percent of Subsidiary A's equity of $1,680,000 ($1,200,000 + $480,000). Therefore, ABC Co. recognizes a $180,000 increase in its investment in Subsidiary A ($1,260,000-$1,080,000) and a corresponding increase in its additional paid-in capital (i.e., the additional paid-in capital attributable to ABC Co.). In addition, the noncontrolling interest is increased to $420,000, calculated as 25 percent of $1,680,000. The sale of additional shares by Subsidiary A is accounted for as an equity transaction in the consolidated financial statements as follows:

Cash	$480,000	
Noncontrolling interest		$ 300,000
Additional paid-in capital (ABC Co.)		180,000

Example 3

Subsidiary A has 50,000 shares of common stock outstanding. Of those shares, 40,000 are owned by its parent, ABC Co., and 10,000 are owned by other shareholders (a noncontrolling interest in Subsidiary A). The carrying amount of the noncontrolling interest is $240,000, which includes $20,000 of accumulated other comprehensive income. ABC Co. pays $150,000 in cash to purchase 5,000 shares held by the noncontrolling shareholders (50 percent of the noncontrolling interest), increasing its ownership interest from 80 percent to 90 percent. That transaction is recognized by reducing the carrying amount of the noncontrolling interest by $120,000 ($240,000 × 50 percent). The $30,000 excess of the cash paid ($150,000) over the adjustment to the carrying amount of the noncontrolling interest ($120,000) is recognized as a decrease in additional paid-in capital attributable to ABC Co. In addition, ABC Co.'s share of accumulated other comprehensive income is increased by $10,000 ($20,000 × 50 percent) through a corresponding decrease in additional paid-in capital attributable to ABC Co. The purchase of shares from the noncontrolling shareholders is accounted for as an equity transaction in the consolidated financial statements as follows:

Noncontrolling interest	$120,000	
Additional paid-in capital (ABC Co.)	40,000	
Accumulated other comprehensive income (ABC Co.)		$ 10,000
Cash		150,000

Deconsolidation of a Subsidiary

A parent is required to deconsolidate a subsidiary as of the date the parent ceases to have a controlling financial interest in the subsidiary. For example, the following events would result in the deconsolidation of a subsidiary (ASC 810-10-55-4A):

- A parent sells some or all of its ownership interest in the subsidiary, and as a result, the parent no longer has a controlling financial interest in the subsidiary
- A contractual agreement expires, and the parent's control of the subsidiary is dependent on that agreement
- The subsidiary issues additional shares, thereby reducing the parent's ownership interest in the subsidiary to a point that does not result in the parent having a controlling financial interest
- The subsidiary becomes under the control of a government, court, administrator, or regulator

When deconsolidating a subsidiary, the parent shall measure any noncontrolling interest it retains in the former subsidiary at its fair value and recognize a gain or loss in net income attributable to the parent, measured as the difference between (ASC 810-10-40-5):

a. The aggregate of:
   1. The fair value of any consideration received
   2. The fair value of any retained noncontrolling investment in the former subsidiary at the date the subsidiary is deconsolidated
   3. The carrying amount of any noncontrolling interest in the former subsidiary held by any party other than the former parent (including any accumulated other comprehensive income attributable to the noncontrolling interest) at the date the subsidiary is deconsolidated
b. The carrying amount of the former subsidiary's assets and liabilities

Illustration of Gain or Loss on the Deconsolidation of a Subsidiary

Sub Co. has 10,000 shares of common stock outstanding. Of those shares, 8,000 are owned by its parent, ABC Co., and 2,000 are owned by other shareholders (a noncontrolling interest in Sub Co.). The carrying amount of Sub Co.'s equity is $1,000,000. ABC Co. sells 4,000 of its shares in Sub Co. to an unrelated entity for $600,000 in cash, reducing its ownership interest from 80 percent to 40 percent. Therefore, ABC Co. no longer has a controlling interest in Sub Co., and would recognize a gain of $400,000 on the deconsolidation of Sub Co., calculated as follows:

Fair value of consideration received	$ 600,000
Fair value of retained noncontrolling investment in Sub Co.	600,000
Carrying amount of noncontrolling interest in Sub Co. held by parties other than ABC Co.	200,000
	$1,400,000
Less: carrying amount of Sub Co.'s net assets	– 1,000,000
Gain on deconsolidation of Sub Co.	$ 400,000

Note that the guidance provided in ASC 845-10 applies to the deconsolidation of a subsidiary through a nonreciprocal transfer to owners, such as a spinoff (ASC 810-10-40-5).

Disclosures

The consolidation policy should be disclosed fully on the financial statements or in footnotes thereto (ASC 810-10-50-1).

ASC 810 requires expanded disclosures in the consolidated financial statements that clearly identify and distinguish between the interests of the parent and the interests of the noncontrolling owners of a subsidiary. A parent with one or more less-than-wholly-owned subsidiaries shall disclose for each reporting period (ASC 810-10-50-1A):

- Separately, on the face of the consolidated financial statements, the amounts of consolidated net income and consolidated comprehensive income, including the amounts of each that are attributable to the parent and the noncontrolling interest
- Either in the notes or on the face of the consolidated income statement, amounts attributable to the parent for the following, if reported in the consolidated financial statements:
  — Income from continuing operations
  — Discontinued operations
- Either in the consolidated statement of changes in equity, if presented, or in the notes to the consolidated financial statements, a reconciliation at the beginning and the end of the period of the carrying amount of total equity (net assets), including the amounts attributable to the parent and to the noncontrolling interest. The reconciliation must separately disclose:
  — Net income
  — Transactions with owners acting in their capacity as owners, showing separately contributions from and distributions to owners
  — Each component of other comprehensive income
- In the notes to the consolidated financial statements, a separate schedule that shows the effects of any changes in a parent's ownership interest in a subsidiary on the equity attributable to the parent

Additional disclosures are required for a not-for-profit entity if it has one or more consolidated subsidiaries with noncontrolling interests. A schedule of changes in net assets attributable to the parent and the noncontrolling interests must appear either on the face of the financial statements or in the notes. The schedule reconciles the beginning and ending balances of the parent's controlling interest, as well as the beginning and ending balances for each class of net assets for which a noncontrolling interest exists. This schedule must include:

- A performance indicator (if the entity is subject to the AICPA Audit and Accounting Guide, *Health Care Organizations*)
- Discontinued operations
- Changes in a subsidiary's ownership interests, including transactions with owners acting in their capacity as owners with contributions from and distributions to owners being shown separately
- The aggregate amount of all other changes in unrestricted net assets

If a subsidiary is deconsolidated, the parent is required to disclose (ASC 810-10-50-1B):

- The amount of any gain or loss recognized
- The portion of any gain or loss related to the remeasurement of any retained investment in the former subsidiary to its fair value
- The caption in the income statement in which the gain or loss is recognized unless separately presented on the face of the income statement
- The valuation technique used to measure the fair value of any retained investment in the former subsidiary or group of assets and information that enables users of its financial statements to assess the inputs used to develop the measurement
- The nature of continuing involvement with the subsidiary or entity acquiring the group of assets after it has been deconsolidated or derecognized
- Whether the transaction that resulted in the deconsolidation of the subsidiary or the derecognition of the group of assets was with a related party or whether the former subsidiary or entity acquiring the group of assets will be a related part after deconsolidation

---

Illustration of Computing Noncontrolling Interest and Consolidated Net Income

Computing noncontrolling interests in a complex father-son-grandson affiliation may be demonstrated by using the following diagram (dollar amounts are income figures for the separate entities):

The computations of noncontrolling interests and consolidated net income follow:

	E	D	C	B	A
Net income	$60,000	$50,000	$80,000	$40,000	$100,000
75% to D	(45,000)	45,000			
		$95,000			
90% to A		(85,500)			85,500
85% to B			(68,000)	68,000	
				$108,000	
80% to A				(86,400)	86,400
Noncontrolling interests	$15,000	$9,500	$12,000	$21,600	
Consolidated net income					$271,900

In a situation in which a subsidiary owns shares of the parent company, consolidated net income may be found algebraically, as the following depicts:

Company	*Unconsolidated Income (excluding income from investees)*	
A	$40,000	A, the parent, owns 80% of B
B	20,000	B owns 70% of C
C	10,000	C owns 20% of A

The figures and relationships can be put into algebraic form so as to compute *consolidated net income.*

Solving for *A*, we have:

Company A's income on an equity basis, which equals consolidated income, is determined by multiplying by the 80% interest outstanding (i.e., the remaining 20% is held within the consolidated entity):

$69,369 × 0.8 = $55,495 consolidated net income

The noncontrolling interests in the two subsidiaries are determined as follows:

VARIABLE INTEREST ENTITIES

ASC 810 addresses consolidation by business enterprises of variable interest entities that have certain specified characteristics. If a business enterprise has a controlling financial interest in a variable interest entity, the assets, liabilities, and results of activities of that entity should be included in the consolidated financial statements of the business enterprise.

PRACTICE NOTE: ASC 810 was issued because transactions involving variable interest entities have become increasingly common, and the authoritative accounting literature related to these transactions is fragmented and incomplete.

ASC 810 clarifies the accounting for certain entities in which equity investors do not have sufficient equity at risk for the entity to finance its activities without additional subordinated financial support or, as a group, the equity investors lack any one of the following characteristics that provide an enterprise with a controlling financial interest in a variable interest entity (ASC 810-10-05-8):

1. The power to direct the activities of an entity that most significantly impact the entity's economic performance
2. The obligation to absorb the expected losses of the entity
3. The right to receive the expected residual returns of the entity.

Consolidated financial statements usually are required for a fair presentation when one of the companies in the group directly or indirectly has a controlling financial interest in the other companies. For legal entities other than limited partnerships, the usual condition for a controlling financial interest is a majority voting interest. For limited partnerships, the usual condition for a controlling financial interest is ownership of a majority of the limited partnership's kick-out rights through voting interests. For certain types of entities, however, application of the majority voting interest and kick-out rights requirements may not identify the party with a controlling interest because the control may be achieved through arrangements that do not involve voting interests or kick-out rights (ASC 810-10-05-8).

Key Definitions

Variable interest in a variable interest entity refers to a contractual, ownership, or other pecuniary interest in an entity that changes with changes in the fair value of the entity's net assets excluding variable interests. Equity interests with or without voting rights are considered variable interests if the entity is a variable interest entity, only to the extent that the investment is at risk. Entity is used to refer to any legal structure used to conduct activities or hold assets. This includes corporations, partnerships, limited liability companies, grantor trusts, and other trusts (ASC Glossary).

PRACTICE POINTER: Examples of variable interests in a variable interest entity often include (1) equity investments that are at risk, (2) investments in subordinated beneficial interests, (3) investments in subordinated debt instruments, (4) guarantees, (5) written put options, (6) forward purchase and sale contracts, (7) derivatives and total return swaps that reduce the exposure of the entity to risks that cause variability, and (8) leases with a residual value guarantee and options to acquire the underlying assets at the lease's termination at specified prices (ASC 810-10-55).

Fees paid to a decision maker could be a variable interest, but if *all* of the following conditions are met, such fees would *not* be considered a variable interest: (1) the fees represent fair compensation for the services provided; (2) the decision maker (and its related parties) do not hold interests that would result in the decision maker absorbing more than a trivial amount of expected losses or receiving more than a trivial amount of expected returns; and (3) the service arrangement does not include any unusual terms, conditions, or amounts (ASC 810-10-55-37).

Scope

ASC 810 applies to all entities except (1) not-for-profit (NFP) organizations, unless the NFP organization is used by a business enterprise to circumvent the provisions of ASC 810; and (2) separate accounts for life insurance enterprises (ASC 810-10-15-17).

In addition to the above exceptions contained in the original ASC 810, four more exceptions have been added. These exceptions pertain to situations in which the data needed to apply ASC 810-10-55 is unavailable, where the entity to be evaluated qualifies as a *business*, where the entity to be evaluated is a governmental organization, and for certain investment funds (ASC 810-10-15-12, 17).

ASC 810 does not have to be applied to variable interest entities (or potential variable interest entities) created before December 31, 2003, if the reporting enterprise does not have the necessary information to (1) determine whether the entity is a variable interest entity, (2) determine whether the enterprise is the primary beneficiary of the variable interest entity, and (3) apply the consolidation provisions to a variable interest entity where the enterprise is the primary beneficiary. However, this exception is available only to those enterprises that lack the necessary information after making an *exhaustive effort* to obtain the needed information, and the exception lasts only as long as the needed information cannot be obtained (ASC 810-10-15-17).

PRACTICE POINTER: The FASB does not define what it means by an *exhaustive effort*. Therefore, companies and their auditors should exercise significant judgment in claiming a scope exception to (ASC 810-10-55) under this provision.

In most circumstances, an entity that qualifies as a *business* does not have to be evaluated by a reporting enterprise to determine whether it is a variable interest entity (ASC 810-10-15-17). The FASB defines a business as an integrated set of activities and assets that is capable of being conducted and managed for the purpose of providing a return in the form of dividends, lower costs, or other economic benefits directly to investors or other owners, members, or participants (ASC Glossary). However, if *one or more* of the following conditions exist, an entity that qualifies as a business must be evaluated by the reporting enterprise to determine whether the consolidation criteria apply (ASC 810-10-15-17):

- The reporting enterprise (or its related parties) designed or redesigned the entity (with the exception of operating joint ventures under joint control and franchisees).
- Substantially all of the entity's activities involve or are conducted on behalf of the reporting enterprise (or its related parties).
- The reporting enterprise (and its related parties) provides more than half of the entity's equity, subordinated debt, and other forms of subordinated financial support.
- The entity's primary activities are securitizations, asset-backed financings, or single-lessee leasing arrangements.

The consolidation criteria of ASC 810 generally are not applicable to governmental organizations or financing entities established by a governmental organization. The exception to this rule is if the governmental organization is used by a business enterprise to circumvent the provisions of ASC 810.

Finally, the provisions of ASC 810 do not apply to entities that are required to comply with requirements that are similar to those included in Rule 2a-7 of the Investment Company Act of 1940 for registered money market funds.

Consolidation Criteria

An entity is subject to consolidation if *at least one* of the following three conditions exists, as a result of the manner in which the entity was originally structured (ASC 810-10-15-14):

1. The total equity investment at risk is not sufficient to permit the entity to finance its activities without additional subordinated financial support from any party, including equity holders. The total equity investment at risk:
   a. Includes only equity investments in the entity that participate significantly in profits and losses, even if those investments have no voting rights.
   b. Does *not* include equity interests that the entity issued in exchange for subordinated interests in other variable interest entities.

c. Does *not* include amounts provided to the equity investor directly or indirectly by the entity or by other parties involved with the entity unless the provider is a parent, subsidiary, or affiliate of the investor that is required to be included in the same set of consolidated financial statements as the investor.

d. Does *not* include amounts financed for the equity investor directly by the entity or by other parties involved with the entity unless that party is a parent, subsidiary, or affiliate of the investor that is required to be included in the same set of consolidated financial statements as the investor.

2. As a group, the holders of the equity investment at risk *lack any one* of the following characteristics:

a. The power to direct the activities of an entity that most significantly impact the entity's economic performance through voting rights or similar rights. (For legal entities other than limited partnerships, the investors lack that power through voting rights or similar rights if no owners hold voting rights or similar rights. For limited partnerships, partners lack that power if neither (1) a simple majority or lower threshold of limited partners with equity at risk is able to exercise substantive kick-out rights through voting interests over the general partner(s), nor (2) limited partners with equity at risk are able to exercise substantive participating rights over the general partner(s).)

b. The obligation to absorb the expected losses of the entity. (The investors do not have that obligation if they are directly or indirectly protected from the expected losses or are guaranteed a return by the entity itself or by other parties involved with the entity.)

c. The right to receive the expected residual returns of the entity. (The investors do not have that right if their returns are capped by the entity's governing documents or by arrangements with other variable interest holders or with the entity.)

3. Equity investors are considered to lack the direct or indirect ability to make decisions about an entity's activities if:

a. The voting rights of some investors are not proportional to their rights to receive returns or absorb losses. In applying this requirement, the enterprise is to consider each party's obligations to absorb losses or receive returns related to all of each party's interests in the entity, not only to the equity investment at risk.

b. Substantially all of the legal entity's activities (e.g., providing financing or buying assets) either involve or are conducted for an investor that has disproportionately few voting rights.

A *variable interest entity* is an entity subject to ASC 810-10-55. *Variable interests* are the investments or other interests that will absorb portions of a variable interest entity's expected losses or receive portions of the entity's expected residual returns. The initial determination of whether an entity is a variable interest entity is made when an enterprise becomes involved with the entity, based on the circumstances on that date and including future changes that are required in existing governing documents and contractual arrangements (ASC 810-10-25-37). The initial determination of whether an entity is a variable interest entity is reconsidered only if one or more of the following occurs (ASC 810-10-35-4):

- The entity's governing documents or the contractual arrangements among the parties involved change and the change affects the characteristics or the adequacy of the entity's equity investment at risk.
- The equity investment or a portion thereof is returned to equity investors, and other interests become exposed to expected losses.
- The entity undertakes additional activities or acquires additional assets—beyond those envisioned when the entity was formed or at the most recent reconsideration event—that increase the entity's expected losses.
- An additional at-risk equity investment is received by the entity, or the entity's activities are changed in a manner as to reduce its expected losses.
- Circumstances change such that the holders of the equity investment at risk, as a group, lose the power to direct the activities that most significantly impact the entity's economic performance.

Expected Losses and Expected Residual Returns

Expected losses (expected residual returns) are a function of expected negative (positive) variability in the fair value of the entity's net assets, excluding variable interests (ASC Glossary).

PRACTICE NOTE: Variable interests held by the potential variable interest entity are excluded in computing expected losses (expected residual returns) because a variable interest is expected to absorb volatility and expected losses, rather than to create them.

An equity investment at risk of less than 10% of the entity's total assets is considered insufficient to permit the entity to finance its activities without subordinated financial support in addition to the equity investment, unless the equity investment can be demonstrated to be sufficient. ASC 810 establishes a hierarchy for evaluating the sufficiency of the equity investment: a qualitative assessment first; then a quantitative assessment if a conclusion about the adequacy of the equity investment at risk cannot be made after diligent effort; and finally, if neither analysis taken alone is conclusive, both the qualitative and quantitative analyses should be considered (ASC 810-10-25-45). The two qualitative factors that should be considered are whether (1) the entity has demonstrated that it can finance its activities without additional subordinated financial support (ASC 810-10-25-45) and (2) the entity has at least as much equity invested as other entities that hold only similar assets of similar quality in similar amounts and operate with no additional subordinated financial support (ASC 810-10-25-45). If the adequacy of the equity investment at risk cannot be determined based on the qualitative assessment, the one quantitative factor that should be considered is whether the amount of equity invested in the entity exceeds the estimate of the entity's expected losses based on reasonable quantitative evidence (ASC 810-10-25-45).

Some entities may require an equity investment at risk of greater than 10% of their assets to finance their activities, especially if they are involved in high-risk activities, hold high-risk assets, or have exposure to risks that are not reflected in the reported amounts of the entities' assets or liabilities (ASC 810-10-25-46).

Variable Interests and Interests in Specified Assets

A variable interest in specified assets of a variable interest entity is deemed to be a variable interest in the entity only if the fair value of the specified assets is more than half of the total fair value of the entity's assets or if the holder has another variable interest in the entity as a whole. The expected losses and expected residual returns applicable to variable interests in specified assets of a variable interest entity are deemed to be expected losses and expected residual returns of the entity only if that variable interest is deemed to be a variable interest in the entity. Expected losses related to variable interests in specified assets are not considered part of the expected losses of the entity for purposes of determining the adequacy of the equity at risk or identifying the primary beneficiary in the entity unless the specified assets constitute a majority of the assets of the entity (ASC 810-10-25-55).

A reporting entity with a variable interest in specified assets of a variable interest entity shall treat a portion of the entity as a separate variable interest entity if the specified assets are essentially the only source of payment for specified liabilities or specified other interests. This requirement does not apply unless the entity has been determined to be a variable interest entity (ASC 810-10-25-57).

Consolidation Based on Variable Interests

An enterprise shall consolidate a variable interest entity when that enterprise has a variable interest (or combination thereof) that provides the enterprise with a controlling financial interest. The determination of a controlling financial interest includes an assessment of the characteristics of the enterprise's variable interest (including involvement of related parties) in the variable interest entity, as well as the involvement of other variable interest holders. An enterprise is considered to have a controlling financial interest in a variable interest entity if it has both (1) the power to direct the activities of the variable interest entity that are most important to the entity's economic performance and (2) the obligation to absorb losses and the right to receive benefits from the entity that could potentially be significant to the variable interest entity (ASC 810-10-05).

An enterprise is identified as the primary beneficiary of a variable interest entity if the enterprise is determined to have a controlling financial interest and, thus, is required to consolidate the variable interest entity. Ongoing reassessments are required of whether an enterprise is the primary beneficiary of a variable interest entity. Although more than one enterprise may share in the obligation to absorb losses and the right to receive benefits of the variable interest entity, only one enterprise, if any, will have the power to direct the activities that are most important to the variable interest entity's economic performance. Therefore, only one enterprise, if any, is expected to be identified as the primary beneficiary of a variable interest entity (ASC 810-10-25-38A).

PRACTICE NOTE: When determining whether a reporting entity has the right to receive benefits from a variable interest entity that could potentially be significant to the variable interest entity, fees paid to the reporting entity (other than those included in arrangements that expose the reporting entity to risk of loss as described in ASC 810-10-25-38J) are excluded if both of the following conditions are met (ASC 810-10-25-38H):

- The fees are compensation for services provided and are commensurate with the level of effort required to provide those services.
- The service arrangement includes only terms, conditions, or amounts that are customarily present in arrangements for similar services negotiated at arm's length.

The determination of which enterprise, if any, has the power to direct the variable interest entity's most important activities requires judgment. For example, there may be kick-out rights and participating rights that are held by other parties. Kick-out rights are the ability to remove an enterprise with the power to direct the variable interest entity's most important activities, and participating rights are the ability to block the actions through which an enterprise would exercise such power. An enterprise's determination of whether it has the power to direct the most important activities of a variable interest entity is not affected by the existence of kick-out rights or participating rights held by other parties unless a single party (including its related parties) has the unilateral ability to exercise the kick-out rights or participating rights (ASC 810-10-25-38C).

If an enterprise determines that the power to direct a variable interest entity's most important activities is shared among multiple unrelated parties such that no one party has such power, then no party shall be considered the primary beneficiary. Power is shared if decisions about those activities require the consent of each of the parties sharing power. If an enterprise concludes that power is not shared but that the activities that most significantly impact the variable interest entity's economic performance are directed by multiple unrelated parties and the nature of the activities that each party is directing is the same, then the party, if any, with the power over the majority of those activities shall be considered to have the power to direct the variable interest entity's most important activities (ASC 810-10-25-38D).

The Effect of Related Parties

When a single reporting entity, which is a single decision maker, is determining whether or not it is the primary beneficiary of a variable interest entity, the single decision maker must include all of its direct variable interests in the entity and, on a proportionate basis, its indirect variable interests in the entity held through related parties. For example, if the single decision maker owns a 20% interest in a related party and that related party own a 40% interest in the entity being evaluated, the single decision maker's indirect interest in the variable interest entity held through the related party would be equivalent to an 8% direct interest in the variable interest entity (ASC 810-10-25-42).

A related party includes not only those entities meeting the ASC 850 requirement but also those parties acting as de facto agents for the entity holding the variable interest. Examples of de facto agents of the enterprise include (1) a party that is dependent on the enterprise for the financing of its operations; (2) a party whose interest in the variable interest entity results from a contribution or loan from the enterprise; (3) an officer, director, or employee of the enterprise; (4) a party that cannot sell, transfer, or encumber its interest in the entity without the approval of the enterprise; and (5) a party that has a close business relationship (ASC 810-10-25-43).

If there does not exist a single decision maker that is determined to have a controlling financial interest in a variable interest entity, but there are two or more related parties that would qualify as the primary beneficiary if their interests were combined, then the party within the related party group that is most closely associated with the variable interest entity is the primary beneficiary. Significant judgment must be exercised in making this determination (ASC 810-10-25-44).

Initial Measurement

The primary beneficiary of a variable interest entity that is under common control with the variable interest entity shall initially measure the assets, liabilities, and noncontrolling interests of a variable interest entity at the amounts at which they are carried in the accounts of the enterprise that controls the variable interest entity (ASC 810-10-30-1).

If the primary beneficiary and the variable interest entity are not under common control, then the initial measurement depends on whether or not the variable interest entity is a *business*. The initial consolidation of a variable interest entity that is a *business* is a business combination and shall be accounted for in accordance with the provisions of (ASC 810-10-30-3).

If the variable interest entity is not a business, then the primary beneficiary initially shall measure and recognize the assets (except goodwill) and liabilities of the variable interest entity in accordance with ASC 805-20-25 and ASC 805-20-30. However, the primary beneficiary of a variable interest entity shall initially measure assets and liabilities that it has transferred to that entity at the same amounts at which the assets and liabilities would have been measured had they not been transferred. No gain or loss is recognized on the transfer (ASC 810-10-30-3).

PRACTICE NOTE: This provision applies to transfers at, after, or shortly before the enterprise became the primary beneficiary (ASC 810-10-30-3).

The primary beneficiary shall recognize a gain or loss for the difference between (1) the fair value of any consideration paid, the fair value of any noncontrolling interests, and the reported amount of any previously held interests and (2) the net amount of the variable interest entity's identifiable assets and liabilities recognized and measured in accordance with the guidance in ASC 810. No goodwill shall be recognized if the variable interest entity is not a business (ASC 810-10-30-4).

Accounting after Initial Measurement

The principles of consolidated financial statements apply to the primary beneficiaries' accounting for consolidated variable interest entities. After initial measurement, accounting shall be as if the entity were consolidated based on voting interests. Any specialized accounting requirements applicable to the type of business of the variable interest entity shall be applied as they would for a consolidated subsidiary. Intercompany balances and transactions are eliminated. Fees and other sources of income or expense between a primary beneficiary and a consolidated variable interest entity are eliminated against the related expense or income of the variable interest entity. The effect of this elimination on net income or expense of the variable interest entity is attributed to the primary beneficiary in the consolidated financial statements (ASC 810-10-35-3). If an enterprise is required to deconsolidate a variable interest entity, the enterprise must follow the guidance for deconsolidating subsidiaries in ASC 810-10-40.

Disclosures Related to Variable Interest Entities

The principal objectives of the disclosure requirements in ASC 810 are to provide financial statement users with an understanding of the following (ASC 810-10-50-8):

- The significant judgments and assumptions made by an enterprise in determining whether it must consolidate a variable interest entity
- The nature of restrictions on a consolidated variable interest entity's assets and on the settlement of its liabilities reported by an enterprise
- The nature of, and changes in, the risks associated with an enterprise's involvement with the variable interest entity
- How an enterprise's involvement with the variable interest entity affects enterprise's financial position, financial performance, and cash flows.

Disclosures may be reported in the aggregate for similar entities if separate reporting would not provide more useful information. An enterprise must disclose how similar entities are aggregated and must distinguish between variable interest entities that are consolidated and variable interest entities that are not consolidated because the enterprise is not the primary beneficiary but has a variable interest (ASC 810-10-50-9).

An enterprise that is a primary beneficiary of a variable interest entity or an enterprise that holds a variable interest in a variable interest entity but is not the entity's primary beneficiary must disclose the following (in addition to the disclosures required by other standards) (ASC 810-10-50-12):

- Its methodology for determining whether the enterprise is the primary beneficiary of a variable interest entity, including significant judgments and assumptions made
- If circumstances change such that the determination of whether to consolidate a variable interest entity has changed, the primary reasons for the change and the effect on the enterprise's financial statements

- Whether the enterprise has provided support to the variable interest entity that it was not required to provide, or whether the enterprise intends to provide such support, including:
  - — The type and amount of support
  - — The reasons for proving the support
- Qualitative and quantitative information about the enterprise's involvement with the variable interest entity, including the nature, purpose, size, and activities of the variable interest entity, and how the entity is financed.

If the variable interest entity is a business, the primary beneficiary shall provide the disclosures required by ASC 805. If the variable interest entity is not a business, the primary beneficiary shall disclose the amount of gain or loss recognized on the initial consolidation of the variable interest entity. The primary beneficiary shall disclose the following (in addition to the disclosures required by other standards) (ASC 810-10-50-14):

- The carrying amounts and classification of the variable interest entity's assets and liabilities that are consolidated in the statement of financial position
- Lack of recourse if creditors of a consolidated variable interest entity have no recourse to the general credit of the primary beneficiary
- Terms of arrangements that could require the enterprise to provide financial support to the variable interest entity.

An enterprise that holds a significant variable interest in a variable interest entity but is not the primary beneficiary shall disclose the following (ASC 810-10-50-15):

- The carrying amounts and classification of the assets and liabilities in the enterprise's statement of financial position that relate to the enterprise's variable interest in the variable interest entity
- The enterprise's maximum exposure to loss as a result of its involvement with the variable interest entity
- A tabular comparison of the carrying amounts of the assets and liabilities and the enterprise's maximum exposure to loss
- A public entity is encouraged to disclose information about any liquidity arrangements, guarantees, and/or other commitments by third parties that may affect the fair value or risk of the enterprise's variable interest in the variable interest entity is encouraged

An enterprise that does not apply ASC 810 because the enterprise, after exhaustive effort, does not have the information necessary to (1) determine whether the entity is a variable interest entity, (2) determine whether the enterprise is the primary beneficiary of the variable interest entity, and (3) apply the consolidation provisions of ASC 810 to a variable interest entity where the enterprise is the primary beneficiary must make additional disclosures. These disclosures are as follows (ASC 810-10-50-16):

- The number of entities that ASC 810 is not being applied to and why the necessary information is not available.
- The nature, purpose, entity activities, size (if available), and the relation between the enterprise and entity or entities that ASC 810 is not applied to.
- The maximum amount of loss that the reporting enterprise is exposed to because of its involvement with the entity or entities.
- For all periods presented, the amount of income, expense, purchases, sales, or other activity measures between the reporting enterprise and the entity or entities. This information does not have to be disclosed for prior periods if it is unavailable.

PRIVATE COMPANY COUNCIL ALTERNATIVE GUIDANCE

The general guidance in U.S. GAAP requires a reporting entity to consolidate an entity in which it has a controlling financial interest. The determination of whether an entity has a controlling financial interest can be made using either the voting interest model or the variable interest entity model. The voting interest model generally considers there to be a controlling financial interest when the reporting entity owns a majority of an entity's voting interests. The variable interest entity model requires the reporting entity to first determine whether the entity being evaluated for consolidation is a variable interest entity, and if they are, then the reporting entity is considered to have a controlling financial interest when it has both:

- The power to direct the activities that most significantly affect the economic performance of the entity; and
- The obligation to absorb losses or the right to receive benefits of the entity that could potentially be significant to the entity.

In response to concerns about the costs and complexity of private firms applying the variable interest entity model, ASC Subtopic 810-10 includes alternative guidance that a reporting entity can elect to follow that, when certain conditions exist, would not require the reporting entity to apply variable interest entity guidance to a legal entity under common control. Specifically, a reporting entity that elects this alternative guidance does not have to evaluate a legal entity under the guidance for variable interest entities if all of the following criteria are met (ASC 810-10-15-17AD):

1. The reporting entity and the legal entity are under common control.
2. The reporting entity and the legal entity are not under common control of a public business entity.
3. The legal entity under common control is not a public business entity.
4. The reporting entity does not directly or indirectly have a controlling financial interest in the legal entity.

Disclosure

A reporting entity that neither consolidates nor elects the alternative guidance and does not apply the guidance for variable interest entities to one or more legal entities must disclose the following (ASC 810-10-50-2AG):

- The nature and risks associated with a reporting entity's involvement with the legal entity under common control.
- How a reporting entity's involvement with the legal entity under common control affects the reporting entity's financial position, financial performance, and cash flows.
- The carrying amounts and classification of the assets and liabilities in the reporting entity's statement of financial position resulting from its involvement with the legal entity under common control.
- The reporting entity's maximum exposure to loss resulting from its involvement with the legal entity under common control.
- If the reporting entity's maximum exposure to loss exceeds the carrying amount of assets and liabilities, qualitative and quantitative information to allow users of financial statements to understand the excess exposure.

When providing the above disclosures regarding the reporting entity's exposures, the reporting entity must also consider exposures through implicit guarantees. The facts and circumstances that will determine whether an implicit guarantee exists will include, but are not limited to, the following (ASC 810-10-50-2AH):

- Whether there is an economic incentive for the reporting entity to act as a guarantor or to make funds available.
- Whether the reporting entity has acted as a guarantor for or has made funds available to the legal entity in the past.

PART II: INTERPRETIVE GUIDANCE

ASC 810-10: OVERALL

ASC 810-10-05-14 through 05-16, 15-18 through 15-22, 25-60 through 25-79, 25-81, 55-206 through 55-209; ASC 718-10-55-85A Consolidation of Entities Controlled by Contract

---

PRACTICE NOTE: The accounting guidance below applies only to physician practices that are *not* variable interest entities.

BACKGROUND

Changes in the delivery of medical services, such as the proliferation of health management organizations (HMOs) and preferred provider organizations (PPOs), have caused an increasing number of physician practices to enter into contractual arrangements, under which a physician practice management (PPM) entity acquires and manages the physician practice (medical entity) and may enter into employment and noncompete agreements with the physicians who become its employees. Because a PPM may be precluded from acquiring the physician practice's equity instruments for legal or business reasons (some states restrict ownership of medical practices to physicians), the PPM entity may acquire some or all of the physician practice's net assets, assume all of its contractual rights and responsibilities, and enter into a long-term management agreement with the physician owners to operate the physician practice in exchange for consideration. To reduce its exposure to malpractice suits, the PPM entity may acquire the physician practice's shares and transfer them to a physician shareholder of the PPM entity who has incorporated a nominally capitalized new medical practice and acts as a nominee shareholder of the PPM entity. The PPM entity can change the nominee at any time. The following are examples of such arrangements:

Company A—Existing physician practice

Company B—New physician practice

Company C—PPM entity

Company D—The PPM entity's subsidiary

Dr. Friendly—A physician who acts as nominee shareholder of Company C

- Physicians who are the shareholders of Company A exchange their shares in Company A for shares of Company C and also enter into a long-term management agreement with Company C. Because state law does not permit a non-physician-owned practice to enter into contractual arrangements between physicians and hospitals and between physicians and HMOs, the physicians form Company B concurrently with the merger and transfer their patient contracts to it. The physicians thus become the owners and employees of Company B under an employment contract with Company B.
- Company C creates a wholly owned subsidiary, Company D, which acquires all of Company A's net assets in exchange for some of its shares of voting common stock. At the same time, Company A enters into a long-term management agreement with Company D. The physicians who continue as the owners of Company A enter into new employment agreements with Company D.
- Company C issues shares to the shareholders of Company A, which simultaneously delivers the shares in Company A to Dr. Friendly and enter into a management agreement with Company C. The management agreement gives the rights to the residual interest in Company A to Company C, although the shares held by Dr. Friendly have only a nominal value. The physicians enter into employment agreements with the existing physician practice, which is now owned by Dr. Friendly.

This issue was raised for the following reasons:

- Although ASC 805 provides guidance on the accounting for combinations of business entities or their net assets, it does not address whether an ownership interest in an entity can be acquired by acquiring the target's tangible assets and entering into a long-term service agreement with the target, rather than by ownership of its outstanding equity instruments.
- Under the guidance in ASC 840-10-45-4 and ASC 810-10-60-4, entities are required to consolidate in their financial statements the financial statements of other entities in which they have a controlling financial interest as evidenced by a majority voting interest. That guidance states, however, that the majority owner may not always control the entity. In addition, the phrase *controlling financial interest* is not defined under that guidance, which also does not address the question of when a contract provides an entity with a controlling financial interest.

ACCOUNTING ISSUE

Can a PPM entity obtain a controlling financial interest (as discussed in ASC 840-10-45-4 and ASC 810-10-60-4) in a physician practice through a contractual management agreement without owning a majority of the physician practice's outstanding voting equity instruments?

SCOPE

The accounting guidance discussed below applies to contractual management relationships with both of the following characteristics:

1. Entities in the health care industry, such as practices of medicine, dentistry, veterinary science, and chiropractic medicine, which are collectively referred to here as physician practices.
2. Entities in which the PPM entity does not own a majority of the outstanding equity instruments of the physician practice, because the PPM entity is not permitted to own the equity instruments under the law or the PPM entity has chosen not to own them.

The accounting guidance that follows also may apply to entities in industries other than the health care industry if the circumstances are similar to those discussed here.

ACCOUNTING GUIDANCE

A PPM entity has a controlling financial interest in a physician practice through a contractual management agreement if the following requirements are met:

1. The term of the contractual arrangement between the PPM entity and the physician practice has the following characteristics:
   a. It spans over the physician practice's remaining legal life or over a period of ten years or longer.
   b. The physician practice cannot terminate the agreement, except if the PPM entity commits gross negligence, fraud, other illegal acts, or declares bankruptcy.
2. The PPM entity's control is evidenced by its exclusive decision-making authority over both of the following:
   a. The physician practice's ongoing, major, or central operations, including the scope of services, patient acceptance policies and procedures, pricing, negotiation and execution of contracts, approval of operating and capital budgets, and issuance of debt in cases in which the physician practice uses debt financing as an ongoing, major, or primary source of financing, except for the authority to dispense medical services.
   b. Decisions related to (*a*) total compensation of the practice's licensed medical professionals, and (*b*) establishing and implementing guidelines for selecting, hiring, and firing those employees.
3. The PPM entity's financial interest in the physician practice must be significant and must meet both of the following requirements:
   a. The PPM entity has the unilateral ability to sell or transfer its financial interest.
   b. The PPM entity has the right to receive income from ongoing fees and the sale of its interest in the physician practice, based on the practice's operating performance and changes in its fair value.

The following requirements should be considered to determine whether a PPM entity controls a physician practice by contract:

Documentation of a Management Agreement

The management agreement between a PPM entity and a physician practice should be reviewed to determine whether it documents the existence of a controlling financial interest. If such documentation is available, it also should be reviewed to determine whether the requirements in the following accounting guidance are met, regardless of whether the parties are acting in accordance with the document's provisions.

If the existence of a controlling interest is not documented in the agreement, the relevant facts and circumstances (such as the legal rights and obligations of each party and the reasons for undocumented arrangements) should be evaluated to determine whether the requirements of the following accounting guidance have been met. For example, a controlling financial interest may be undocumented, because the shareholders of the physician practice have not transferred ownership of their outstanding equity interests to the PPM entity or its nominee. Documentation also may be unavailable in cases in which the PPM entity and the nominee own the shares collectively, because documentation may not seem necessary when there are no third-party physician practice owners.

Term of the Agreement

The term of the management agreement should be evaluated based on its substance, rather than on its form, by considering the original stated contract term and renewal or cancellation provisions. For example, an arrangement that specifies an initial five-year term and that provides for a single five-year renewal option that can be exercised unilaterally by the PPM entity is considered to have an adequate term, because a contract that spans over an initial five-year term and a five-year renewal is effectively a ten-year contract.

The adequacy of the term generally should be based on the facts and circumstances of the specific arrangement. The requirement that the term of an arrangement be for at least ten years is intended to imply that the arrangement has an unlimited life. However, that requirement is not intended to apply to all consolidations. Specifically, in other situations involving consolidation, a ten-year term is not necessarily required for a relationship to be considered "other than temporary."

Control

1. Nominee shareholder situations
   a. *More than 50% ownership.* There is a rebuttable presumption that the physician practice is under the PPM entity's control, if the PPM entity's nominee shareholder or the PPM entity and the nominee shareholder *together* own a *majority* of the physician practice's outstanding voting equity instruments. That presumption may be rebutted, however, if the PPM entity does *not* have *exclusive authority* over the decisions that constitute the control requirement, because others, such as other physician practice shareholders and physicians employed by the physician practice, were granted decision-making rights by either (*a*) the PPM entity under the management agreement or through the nominee, or (*b*) by the physician practice under its corporate governance provisions. The presumption cannot be rebutted if the PPM entity's exclusive decision-making authority is pursuant to a management agreement, the physician practice's corporate governance provisions, or obtained through its nominee.
   b. *Less than 50% ownership.* There is no presumption of control if a PPM entity's nominee shareholder or a PPM entity and a nominee together own less than a majority of a physician practice's outstanding voting equity instruments. In that case, a PPM entity must demonstrate that it meets the control requirements as a result of a combination of its rights under the management agreement, the power of its nominee shareholder, and the physician practice's provisions for corporate governance.
2. *Provisions for binding arbitration.* The existence of a provision requiring binding arbitration to settle disagreements between a PPM entity and a physician practice without overriding a PPM entity's exclusive decision-making authority, such as disputes about the meaning of contract terms, does not necessarily indicate that the arrangement does not meet the requirement of control. In contrast, the control requirement is not met if binding arbitration can affect a PPM entity's exclusive decision-making authority.
3. *Powers limited by law.* A PPM entity's exclusive decision-making authority over a matter is not precluded under the control requirement, if federal, state, or corresponding non-U.S. laws limit its powers or the discretion of any party over a particular decision. For example, a PPM entity's ability to control patient acceptance policies and procedures within the law is unaffected by "antidumping" statutes that prohibit physicians from refusing to treat certain types of patients.
4. *Scope of service decisions.* A PPM entity is considered to have exclusive decision-making authority over the scope of a physician practice's services, if the PPM entity and the physician practice agree on the practice's range of medical disciplines, such as cardiology, neurology, or obstetrics, in the initial negotiations of the management agreement. If a PPM entity does not have exclusive decision-making authority over the initial and ongoing decisions about a practice's scope of services, the PPM entity does not control the physician practice. Scope-of-service decisions include those about the range of services to be provided within the selected disciplines.
5. *Physician cosigning provisions*
   a. *Perfunctory provisions.* A perfunctory provision requiring a PPM entity's physicians to sign contracts with the practice's customers, in addition to a PPM entity's execution of the contracts, does not affect a PPM entity's exclusive decision-making authority over the execution of customer contracts. A physician's signature is considered to be perfunctory, if the obligations under a contract are no greater than if only the PPM entity had signed a contract and if either of the following conditions is met:
      (1) A physician is required to sign a contract under state law, or a payor on a contract requested a physician's signature.
      (2) A management agreement or a physician's employment contract provides that a physician's approval is not needed to execute contracts negotiated by a PPM entity.
   b. *Nonperfunctory provisions.* A physician's signature is *not* considered to be perfunctory and the first control requirement is not met if any one of the following exists:
      (1) A PPM entity gave signatory authority to the physicians (other than a PPM entity's nominee shareholder).
      (2) A physician's signature creates obligations in addition to those that would be incurred if only the PPM entity had signed a contract.
      (3) The physicians can decide which customer contracts the PPM entity will execute (e.g., whether the physicians alone or together with the PPM entity decide the terms of an acceptable contract).

Financial Interest

Because a significant financial interest is not defined, what is significant must be determined based on the facts and circumstances of the particular situation. The following guidance should be applied to determine whether a PPM arrangement or a similar contractual management arrangement meets the requirement of a controlling financial interest:

1. *Nominee shareholder situations*
   a. *Presumption of financial interest.* Without citing a PPM entity's current compliance with the financial interest requirement, there is a presumption that a PPM entity has a significant financial interest in a physician practice, if
      (1) A PPM entity's nominee shareholder or a PPM entity together with its nominee own a majority a physician practice's outstanding equity instruments, and
      (2) Based on a PPM entity's and its nominee shareholder's rights and obligations to others, such as other shareholders of the physician practice and the practice's employees, a PPM entity or its shareholder nominee can change the terms of the PPM entity's financial interest in the physician practice at its own discretion with or without nominal consideration.

      That presumption is rebutted only if a PPM entity is *not* permitted to change the terms of its financial interest in a physician practice so that it meets the financial interest requirement, which would be very unlikely.
   b. *No presumption of financial interest.* There is no presumption that a PPM entity has a significant financial interest in a physician practice, if its nominee shareholder holds less than a majority of the physician practice's outstanding voting equity instruments. If so, a PPM entity would have to demonstrate that it has a significant financial interest, in accordance with the requirements discussed above, due to a combination of its rights under a management agreement and the powers of its nominee shareholder.
2. *Type and level of a PPM entity's participation in a practice's fair value*

   A PPM entity's financial interest in a physician practice gives it a right to share in a change, any, in the practice's fair value that must be economically similar to a shareholder's right. A change in a physician practice's fair value is composed of (*a*) a change in its current operating results and (*b*) an amount available only if the physician practice were to be sold or liquidated.

   A PPM entity must be able to share in both amounts, which must represent a significant portion of a change in the practice's total fair value. If a PPM entity's relationship with a physician practice ends before a sale or liquidation occurs, to meet the requirement in (b) in the paragraph above, the PPM entity would need to have the right to share in a change in the physician practice's fair value during the period that the PPM entity was associated with the physician practice. To comply with that requirement, the calculation of ongoing fees and sales proceeds should be evaluated based on their substance rather than on their form. Judgment is required to determine whether the financial interest requirements are met for specific management fee structures.

Period in which consideration is recorded

A PPM entity's consideration to a physician practice for modifying its arrangement with a physician practice should be accounted for in the financial reporting period in which an arrangement has been modified and should be recognized under generally accepted accounting principles according to the nature of that consideration.

Share-based compensation—identifying a PPM entity's employees

Under the guidance in ASC 718-10-55-85A, employees of a physician practice that is consolidated by a PPM entity are considered to be the PPM entity's employees for the purpose of determining how to account for each employee's share-based payment compensation. Employees of a physician's practice that is not consolidated by a PPM entity are not considered to be the PPM entity's employees for that purpose.

SEC OBSERVER COMMENT

The SEC Observer stated that because no unique industry characteristics were identified in connection with the above guidance, it is not unique to physician practices. Therefore, the conclusions reached above may apply to arrangements in other industries in which one entity has a controlling financial interest in another entity through a contractual arrangement or a nominee structure. The SEC staff will consider the guidance discussed above when evaluating the accounting for such arrangements.

ASC 810-10-15-10, 25-1 through 25-8, 25-10 through 25-14, 55-1 Investor's Accounting for an Investee When the Investor Has a Majority of the Voting Interest but the Noncontrolling Shareholder or Shareholders Have Certain Approval or Veto Rights

BACKGROUND

Under the guidance in ASC 810-10-15-10, an entity that holds a direct or indirect controlling financial interest in an investee, which is evidenced by ownership of a majority voting interest, is required to consolidate the investee in its financial statements. There are circumstances, however, under which noncontrolling shareholders are granted certain approval or veto rights, referred to as noncontrolling shareholder rights, that restrict the powers of a shareholder with a majority voter interest or a limited partner with a majority of kick-out rights through voter interests to control an entity's operations or its assets.

The following guidance does *not* apply to the accounting by entities, such as investment companies, which are required under U.S. GAAP to present substantially all of their assets at fair value, including investments in controlled entities, and that report changes in value in a statement of net income or financial performance. Investments in noncorporate entities and variable interest entities (VIEs) also are outside the scope of this Issue.

ACCOUNTING ISSUES

1. Which rights held by noncontrolling shareholders overcome the presumption in ASC 840-10-45-4 that all majority-owned investments should be consolidated?
2. Does the extent of a majority shareholder's financial interest—50.1% versus 99.9%—affect the conclusion to Issue 1?
3. Would the conclusions in the above Issues apply in other circumstances under which a corporate investee would otherwise have been consolidated under the guidance in ASC 810-15-10?

ACCOUNTING GUIDANCE

Scope

The following guidance applies only to investments with majority voting interests in corporations or similar entities, such as limited liability companies that are equivalent to regular corporations as a result of their governing provisions. That guidance also should be used to evaluate the effect of noncontrolling shareholder's or limited partner's approval or veto rights in other situations in which consolidation of an investee would normally be required under U.S. GAAP (e.g., a 49% ownership with 100% control of the board of directors).

PRACTICE NOTE: ASC 272-10-05-3, through 05-4; 323-30-15-4; 35-3, which provide guidance for determining whether a noncontrolling investment in an LLC should be accounted for by the cost or the equity method, does not affect the guidance in this Issue.

Framework for Evaluating the Rights of Noncontrolling Shareholders

Noncontrolling shareholders' or limited partners' rights should be evaluated based on the following framework if a noncontrolling interest is obtained and should be reassessed whenever the terms of those rights or their exercisability has been changed significantly:

1. Judgment, which depends on the facts and circumstances, should be used to determine whether a noncontrolling investor's rights overcome the presumption that an investor with a majority voting interest or a limited partner with a majority of kick-out rights through voting interests should consolidate an investee.
2. The facts and circumstances should be evaluated based on whether noncontrolling shareholders' rights, individually or in combination, provide the noncontrolling investors or limited partners with effective participation in certain significant financial and operating decisions made by an investee in the "ordinary course of business."
3. A noncontrolling investor that has *effective participation* rights can block significant decisions proposed by an investor with a majority voting interest or a general partner. A noncontrolling investor's ability to block a majority investor from making an investee take a significant action in the ordinary course of business deprives the majority investor of the ability to control the investee. In the case of limited partnerships, a limited partner with kick-out

rights through voting interests cannot require a general partner to take a significant action in the ordinary course of business if other limited partners vetoed it.

4. Noncontrolling rights should be assessed when a majority voting interest or a majority of kick-out rights has been obtained and should be reassessed if there is a significant change in the terms or a noncontrolling shareholder's or limited partner's ability to exercise the rights.

All noncontrolling shareholders' rights are intended to protect the investments of noncontrolling investors or limited partners in an investee (protective rights). Such noncontrolling shareholders' rights do not overcome the presumption in ASC 840-10-45-4 that a shareholder holding a majority voting interest or a limited partner with a majority of kick-out rights through voting interests should consolidate an investee. However, noncontrolling shareholders or limited partners may have substantive rights (participating rights) that permit them to block certain actions proposed by the majority investor or a limited partner with a majority of kick-out rights through voting interests regarding an investee's financial and operating decisions made in the ordinary course of business. For the purpose of applying this guidance, decisions made *in the ordinary course of business* are defined as those normally made to address matters that are encountered in the current operations of a business. Although it may not necessarily be expected that the events or transactions requiring such decisions to be made will occur in the near term, it must be at least reasonably possible that events or transactions that require making such decisions will occur. This ordinary course of business definition *does not* apply to self-dealing transactions with controlling shareholders.

Participating rights enable noncontrolling shareholders or limited partners to participate in significant decisions, because those holding a majority voting interest are prevented from making certain decisions in the ordinary course of business without the noncontrolling shareholder's or limited partner's agreement. The existence of noncontrolling shareholders' or limited partners' participating rights does not overcome the presumption that a majority-owned investee should be consolidated by an investor with a majority of the voting rights or a limited partner with a majority of kick-out rights through a majority voting interest but should be determined based on the facts and circumstances.

Protective Rights

Contractual or legal rights that enable noncontrolling shareholders to block the following corporate actions are considered to be protective rights that would *not* overcome the presumption that a shareholder with a majority voting interest or a limited partner with a majority of kick-out rights through a majority voting interest should consolidate an investee:

- Amendments to an investee's articles of incorporation or partnership agreement
- Pricing of transactions between an owner of a majority voting interest or a limited partner with a majority of kick-out rights through a majority voting interest and the investee and related self-dealing transactions
- An investee's liquidation in the context of ASC 852 on reorganizations or a decision that an investee should file for bankruptcy or other receivership
- Acquisitions and dispositions of assets *not* expected to be undertaken in the ordinary course of business. Noncontrolling shareholders' rights related to acquisitions and dispositions made in the ordinary course of business are considered to be *participating* rights. Therefore, judgment based on the specific facts and circumstances should be used to determine whether such rights are substantive (see ASC 810-10-25-13 and ASC 810-10-55-1).
- Issuance or repurchase of equity interests

That list illustrates some, but not all, corporate actions that may be blocked as a result of a noncontrolling shareholder's or limited partner's protective rights.

Participating Rights

Contractual or legal rights that enable noncontrolling shareholders to effectively participate in the following corporate decisions are considered to be substantive participating rights that would overcome the presumption that a shareholder with a majority voting interest should consolidate an investee:

- Hiring, terminating, *and* decisions related to the compensation of management implementing an investee's policies and procedures.
- Establishing an investee's operating *and* capital decisions, including budgets, in the ordinary course of business.

Those items illustrate some, but not all, substantive participating rights that may be granted to noncontrolling shareholders or limited partners. They are considered to be participating rights, because in their entirety they permit noncontrolling shareholders or limited partners to effectively participate in certain significant financial and operating decisions required to conduct an investee's business activities in the ordinary course of business. It is necessary to consider the facts and circumstances in determining whether a noncontrolling investor's individual right, such as the ability to prevent a majority investor from firing management responsible for implementing an investee's policies and procedures, should be considered in and of itself a substantive participating right. Nevertheless, the presumption that an investor with a majority voting interest or a limited partner with a majority of kick-out rights through voting interests should consolidate its investee would not be overcome by noncontrolling shareholders' rights that appear to be participating rights but that are not substantive individually. A determination whether a noncontrolling shareholder's or a limited partner's right is a substantive participating right should *not* be based on the likelihood of whether a noncontrolling investor or a limited partner would exercise that right.

Determination of Noncontrolling Shareholders' Rights Based on Facts and Circumstances

Not all noncontrolling shareholders' rights that appear to be participating rights are substantive. The following factors should be considered in determining whether certain rights that enable noncontrolling shareholders to effectively participate in significant decisions made in an investee's ordinary course of business substantive participating rights:

- *The significance of a majority owner's interest in an investee* The greater the difference between the noncontrolling shareholders' or limited partners' ownership interests and that of a majority owner's interest or that of a limited partner with a majority of kick-out rights through voting interests in an investee, the more likely that the noncontrolling shareholders' rights are protective rights, not substantive rights. The greater the extent of the noncontrolling shareholder's or limited partner's interest in an investee, the greater the skepticism about a majority owner's ability to control an investee.
- *Whether corporate decisions are made by the shareholders or the board of directors, and the rights of each level* For matters that can be decided by a shareholders' vote, it is necessary to determine whether other shareholders, individually or as a whole, have substantive participating rights as a result of their ability to vote on matters submitted for a vote of the shareholders.
- *Whether relationships between the majority and noncontrolling shareholders are between related-parties, as defined in ASC 850-10* For example, if noncontrolling shareholders are members of a majority shareholder's immediate family, it is likely that noncontrolling shareholders' rights would *not* overcome the presumption that a majority investor should consolidate an investee.
- *The significance of noncontrolling shareholders' rights to make operating or capital decisions in an entity's ordinary course of business* Noncontrolling shareholders' or limited partners' rights related to operating or capital decisions, such as the location of an investee's headquarters or the selection of its auditors, which do not significantly affect an investee's ordinary course of business, are not considered to be substantive participating rights and would not overcome the presumption that a majority investor should consolidate the investee.
- *The chance that significant decisions under noncontrolling shareholders' or limited partners' participating rights will occur* If there is only a remote possibility, which is defined in ASC 450 as a slight chance, that the noncontrolling shareholders' or limited partners' approval will be required in making certain decisions in the ordinary course of business, the presumption that the majority owner should consolidate an investee is not overcome.
- *The feasibility that a majority owner would exercise a contractual right to acquire the noncontrolling shareholders' interest in an investee at fair value or less* If a majority investor's acquisition of the noncontrolling shareholders' or limited partners' interest in an investee is prudent, feasible, and within the majority owner's control, it demonstrates that the noncontrolling shareholders' or limited partners' participating rights are not substantive. However, that presumption would not be true if the noncontrolling shareholders or limited partners control critical technology or are the entity's principal source of funding. A majority owner's call option on the noncontrolling shareholders' interests overrides the noncontrolling shareholders' rights to veto the majority shareholder's or general partner's actions, but does not result in an additional ownership interest for a majority shareholder.

Implementation Guidance

The following implementation guidance is provided in addition to the factors discussed above to assist in evaluating whether noncontrolling shareholders' rights, individually or in combination, should be considered protective rights or substantive participating rights, which enable noncontrolling shareholders to be involved in significant decisions expected to be made in the ordinary course of business:

- Noncontrolling shareholders' or limited partners' rights to approve acquisitions or dispositions of assets that are expected to be made in the ordinary course of business may be substantive participating rights. The presumption that a majority investor or a limited partner with a majority of kick-out rights through voting interests should consolidate an investee would not be overcome by rights that affect acquisitions that are unrelated to an investee's existing business. Those rights are usually protective rights. Noncontrolling shareholders' or limited partner's rights to approve an investee's additional indebtedness to finance an acquisition not in the ordinary course of business would be considered a protective right.
- Noncontrolling shareholders' or limited partners' rights to approve the incurrence of additional debt should be evaluated based on existing facts and circumstances. If it is reasonably possible or probable that the noncontrolling shareholders' or limited partners' approval will be required to incur debt in the ordinary course of business, those rights would be considered a substantive participating right.
- Noncontrolling shareholders' or limited partners' rights to approve dividends or other distributions may be protective or participating and should be evaluated based on the facts and circumstances. Rights to block normal or expected dividend distributions may be substantive participating rights, whereas rights to block extraordinary dividends or distributions would be protective.
- Rights related to a specific action, such as leasing property, may be participating or protective and should be evaluated based on the specific facts and circumstances. If an investee could purchase instead of lease property without the noncontrolling shareholder's approval, the right to block a lease is not substantive.
- Rights related to negotiations of collective-bargaining agreements with unions may be participating or protective and should be evaluated based on the specific facts and circumstances. A noncontrolling shareholder's or limited partner's right to approve or veto a new or broader collective bargaining agreement is not substantive if an investee has no collective-bargaining agreement or the union does not represent a substantial number of an investee's employees.
- Determining whether a noncontrolling shareholder's or limited partner's right to block a majority owner's action is substantive requires consideration of the provisions in the shareholder agreement that state what happens if a noncontrolling investor or limited partner has exercised its right. For example, if a shareholder agreement provides that if a noncontrolling shareholder or limited partner blocks an operating budget's approval, the budget will default to the previous year's budget adjusted by inflation. If the investee is a mature company whose operating budgets do not vary significantly from one year to the next, the noncontrolling investor's or limited partner's right to block the budget's approval is not substantive and does not allow the noncontrolling investor or limited partner to effectively participate.
- Noncontrolling shareholders' or limited partner's rights related to the initiation or resolution of a lawsuit may be participating or protective and should be evaluated based on the specific facts and circumstances. Such rights would be substantive participating rights if participating in law-suits is commonly a part of the entity's ordinary course of business, as it is for some insurance companies.
- If a noncontrolling investor or a limited partner has the right to block an investee's operating budget for a specified number of years, that right may be a substantive participating right during that specified time period, based on the facts and circumstances. However, if the noncontrolling investor's or limited partner's ability to exercise its right changes after that time period, for example, the right terminates, that right is no longer a substantive participating right from that date forward and the presumption that the majority investor should consolidate the investee can no longer be overcome.

ASC 810-10-15-14, 25-21 through 25-29, 25-31 through 25-33, 25-35 through 25-36, 55-55 through 55-56, 55-58 through 55-86 Determining the Variability to Be Considered

BACKGROUND

Applying the guidance related to the accounting for a variable interest entity (VIE) in ASC 810-10-05-8 through 05-13, 15-13 through 15-17, 15-20, 25-37 through 25-38G, 25-42 through 25-44, 30-1 through 30-4, 30-7 through 30-9, 35-3 through 35-4, 45-25, 50-2AA through 50-4, 50-5A through 50-6, 50-9 through 50-10, 55-16 through 55-32, 55-37 through 55-89, 55-93 through 55-205, 69-30; ASC 323-10-45-4; ASC 712-10-60-2; ASC 715-10-60-3, 60-7; ASC 860-10-60-2; ASC 954-810-15-3, 45-2; ASC 958-810-15-4 requires determining the variability to be considered in order to establish (*a*) whether an entity is a VIE, (*b*) the interests in an entity that are variable interests, and (*c*) which party, if any, is a VIE's primary beneficiary. Calculations of expected losses, if any, and expected returns are affected by that variability.

Reporting entities are determining the variability to be considered in a variety of ways. Some reporting entities have been considering only variability caused by changes in cash flows under the *cash flow method*; others have been considering only variability caused by changes in fair value under the *fair value method*. Regardless of the method used, entities applying the guidance referred to above should reach the same conclusion as to whether an entity is a VIE and which interests should be considered variable interests. However, this is not always the case.

To protect certain equity and liability holders from exposure to (*a*) variability caused by certain assets and operations held by an entity or (*b*) divergence in the overall profile of an entity's assets and liabilities, reporting entities may enter into arrangements, such as derivative contracts that reduce or eliminate those types of variability. During the life of any entity, it may treat those arrangements as recorded or unrecorded assets or liabilities. Application of the cash flow method or the fair value method does not resolve the variety of opinions as to whether such arrangements should be treated as variable interests or should be considered *creators* of variability.

ACCOUNTING GUIDANCE

A VIE's design should be analyzed based on the following steps to determine its variability:

Step 1. Analyze the *nature* of an entity's risks.

Step 2. Determine (*a*) the *purpose* for which an entity was established and (*b*) the variability created by the risks identified in Step 1 that the entity has been designed to create and pass on to its interest holders, including all of an entity's potential variable interest holders (contractual, ownership, or other financial interests).

Once the variability to consider has been determined, the interests designed to absorb that variability may be identified. Although the cash flow and fair value methods are examples of methods that may be used to measure the amount of an entity's variability in the form of expected losses and expected residual returns, the FASB staff believes that such methods do *not* provide an appropriate means for determining which variability should be considered when accounting for VIEs.

In Step 1, risks that *cause* variability are considered. They include, but are not limited to, credit risk; interest rate risk, including prepayment risk, foreign currency exchange risk; commodity price risk; equity price risk; and operations risk.

In Step 2, which is intended to determine the *purpose* for which an entity was created and the variability it was designed to create and pass on to its interest holders, the relevant facts and circumstances that should be considered include, but are not limited to, the activities of the entity; the terms of contracts into which the entity has entered into; the nature of interests the entity has issued; the manner in which the interests were negotiated and marketed to potential investors; and the parties that participated in the design and redesign of an entity.

Assets are *not* variable interests. Rather, an entity's assets and operations *cause* variability, which is absorbed by the entity's liabilities and equity interests. Some contracts or arrangements appear to have the attributes of creating *and* absorbing variability because, at different times in an entity's life, they may be represented as assets or as liabilities that may or may not be recorded. As stated in ASC 810-10-55-19, a conclusion about whether a contract or arrangement *creates* or *absorbs* variability should be based on the arrangement's *role* in the entity's design, regardless of the arrangement's legal form or its classification as an asset or liability.

How to Determine Variability

A review of the terms of contracts into which an entity has entered should include an analysis of other documents, such as the original documents prepared to establish the entity, governing documents, marketing materials, and other contractual arrangements into which the entity has entered and has provided to potential investors or other parties with which it is associated. To determine variability, the following should be considered:

- Whether the *terms of interests issued*, regardless of their legal form or accounting designation, transfer to the interest holders all or a portion of the risk or return, or both, of a legal entity's certain assets or operations. A transfer of variability to interest holders strongly indicates that the entity has been designed to create that variability and to pass it on to its interest holders.
- If a legal entity issues both senior interests and subordinated interests, whether *subordination* (i.e., the priority on claims to an entity's cash flows) is substantive, often affects the determination of which variability should be considered. Because expected losses generally are first absorbed by subordinated interests and then by senior

interests, the latter have a higher credit rating and a lower interest rate than subordinated interests. The primary factor in determining whether a subordinated interest is substantive is the relationship of its amount to the legal entity's overall *expected* losses and residual returns. Absorption of variability by a substantively subordinated interest strongly indicates that the legal entity was designed to create such variability and pass it on to its interest holders. A subordinated interest that is considered equity-at-risk, as the term is used in ASC 810-10-15-14, may be considered substantive for the purpose of determining the variability that should be considered, even if it is not regarded to be sufficient under the guidance in ASC 810-10-15-14(a), and ASC 810-10-25-45.

- Periodic interest receipts or payment should be excluded from the variability to consider whether a legal entity was not *designed* to create and pass on interest rate risk associated with such interest receipts or payments to its interest holders. However, cash proceeds received from anticipated sales of fixed-rate investments in an actively managed portfolio or those held in a static pool that, by design, will be required to be sold before maturity to satisfy the legal entity's obligations also may vary as a result of interest rate fluctuations. That kind of variability strongly indicates that the legal entity was designed to create that variability and to pass it on to its interest holders.

The existence of the following two characteristics strongly indicates that a derivative instrument *creates* variability:

- The underlying is an observable market rate, price, index of prices or rates, or other market observable, which includes the occurrence or nonoccurrence of a specified market observable event.
- The derivative counterparty is *senior* in priority in relation to the entity's other interest holders.

An entity's design should be analyzed further to determine whether a derivative instrument having the two characteristics discussed above creates variability or is a variable interest if changes in the derivative instrument's fair value or cash flows are expected to offset all, or nearly all, of the risk or return, or both, related to a majority of an entity's assets, excluding the derivative instrument, or the entity's operations.

A qualitative analysis of an entity's design performed in accordance with this guidance and other accounting guidance for VIEs often will result in a conclusive determination of the variability that should be considered when accounting for a VIE—that is, the determination as to which interests are variable interests and the ultimate determination of which variable interest holder, if any, is the primary beneficiary.

ASC 810-10-15-17D, 30-10 through 30-16, 35-6 through 35-9, 50-20 through 50-22, 55-205J through 55-205K, 65-6; ASC 805-10-15-4; ASC 820-10-15-3 Measuring the Financial Assets and the Financial Liabilities of a Consolidated Collateralized Financing Entity

BACKGROUND

Under the guidance in ASU 2009-17, *Improvements to Financial Reporting by Enterprises Involved with Variable Interest Entities,* which amended the guidance in FASB Accounting Standards Codification (ASC) 810, *Consolidation*, a reporting entity that has a controlling financial interest in a variable interest entity (VIE) because it (1) has the power to direct the activities that significantly affect the VIE's economic performance, and (2) is obligated to absorb the VIE's losses, if any, and has the right to receive significant benefits from the VIE, is the primary beneficiary of the VIE and must consolidate it in its financial statements.

A collateralized financing entity (CFE) is a VIE that holds financial assets and issues beneficial interests in those financial assets that have recourse to the related financial assets and are classified as financial liabilities. An entity that manages a CFE may be required to consolidate the CFE if it is the primary beneficiary because it holds some beneficial interests issued by the CFE, or even if it does not own any beneficial interests in a CFE's financial assets (e.g., it may be considered to be a primary beneficiary because of a subordinated fee structure). A CFE may also hold nonfinancial assets temporarily as a result of a debtor's default on the CFE's underlying debt instruments held as assets as well as financial assets and financial liabilities that approximate fair value and are incidental to the CFE's operations (e.g., cash, broker receivables, or broker payables).

Before the issuance of this guidance in ASU 2014-13, some entities elected to measure a CFE's eligible financial assets and financial liabilities at fair value under the guidance in ASC 825, *Financial Instruments* (825-10). The Emerging Issues Task Force (EITF) was asked to address this issue because of diversity in practice in accounting for the difference between the fair value of a CFE's financial assets and the fair value of its financial liabilities at initial consolidation. In addition, there was diversity in the accounting for subsequent gains or losses as a result of changes in the fair value of a CFE's financial assets and financial liabilities.

ACCOUNTING GUIDANCE

Master Glossary

The ASC's Master Glossary includes the following definition of a CFE, which may be a collateralized debt obligation (CDO) or a collateralized loan obligation (CLO) entity:

A variable interest entity that holds financial assets, issues beneficial interests in those financial assets, and has no more than nominal equity. The beneficial interests have contractual recourse only to the related assets of the collateralized financing entity and are classified as financial liabilities. A collateralized financing entity may hold nonfinancial assets temporarily as a result of default by the debtor on the underlying debt instruments held as assets by the collateralized financing entity or in an effort to restructure the debt instruments held as assets by the collateralized financing entity. A collateralized financing entity also may hold other financial assets and financial liabilities that are incidental to the operations of the collateralized financing entity and have carrying values that approximate fair value (for example, cash, broker receivables, or broker payables).

ACCOUNTING GUIDANCE

Scope

The guidance in ASC 810-10-15-17D provides that all reporting entities that consolidate a collateralized financing entity may use the measurement alternative discussed below instead of the fair value measurement guidance in ASC 820, *Fair Value Measurement*, if both of the following conditions exist:

- All of a CFE's financial assets and financial liabilities are measured at fair value in an entity's consolidated financial statements under other applicable guidance in the ASC, except for financial assets and financial liabilities with carrying values that approximate fair value that are incidental to a CFE's operations.
- Changes in the fair value of those financial assets and financial liabilities are included in earnings.

Initial Measurement

If an entity meets the scope requirements ASC 810-10-15-17D when it initially consolidates a CFE, it may elect to measure the CFE's financial assets and financial liabilities using the measurement alternative, which is discussed in ASC 810-10-30-10 through 30-16 as follows:

- A CFE's financial assets and financial liabilities should be measured using the fair value of the financial assets or the fair value of the financial liabilities, whichever is more observable. A gain or loss as a result of the initial application of the measurement alternative should be included in a reporting entity's earnings in its consolidated income (loss) statement.
- If the fair value of a CFE's financial assets is more observable, the financial assets should be measured at fair value. A CFE's financial liabilities should be measured as the difference between the following two amounts:
  (1) The sum of: (*a*) the fair value of the CFE's financial assets (including the carrying values of financial assets, if any, that are incidental to the CFE's operations), and (*b*) the carrying value of nonfinancial assets, if any, held temporarily by the CFE; and
  (2) The sum of: (*a*) the fair value of a reporting entity's retained beneficial interests, if any (other than beneficial interests representing compensation for services), and (*b*) the reporting entity's carrying value of beneficial interests, if any, representing compensation for services.
- If the fair value of a CFE's financial liabilities is more observable, the financial liabilities should be measured at fair value. A CFE's financial assets should be measured as the difference between the following two amounts:
  (1) The sum of: (*a*) the fair value of the CFE's financial liabilities (other than a reporting entity's retained beneficial interests, but including the carrying values of financial liabilities, if any, that are incidental to the CFE's operations); (*b*) the fair value of a reporting entity's retained beneficial interests, if any (other than those representing compensation for services); and (*c*) the reporting entity's carrying value of beneficial interests, if any, representing compensation for services, and
  (2) The carrying value of nonfinancial assets held temporarily, if any. The amounts that result from either of the above calculations should be allocated to the financial assets or financial liabilities, whichever is less observable (other than a reporting entity's retained beneficial interests), as applicable, using a reasonable and consistent method.

- The carrying value of beneficial interests representing compensation for services (e.g., the right to receive management fees or servicing fees) and the carrying value of nonfinancial assets held temporarily, if any, should be measured based on other guidance in the ASC.
- An entity that does not elect to apply the measurement alternative to a CFE that meets the scope requirements in ASC 810-10-15-17D is required to measure the fair value of a CFE's financial assets and financial liabilities under the requirements of ASC 820. If so, an initial difference, if any, in the fair values of a CFE's financial assets and financial liabilities should be included in a reporting entity's earnings in the consolidated income (loss) statement.

Subsequent Measurement

Under the guidance in ASC 810-10-35-6 through 35-9, an entity that meets the scope requirements ASC 810-10-15-17D and elects to apply the fair value measurement alternative on the initial consolidation of a CFE should apply that guidance consistently for a CFE's subsequent measurement as long as the scope requirements in ASC 810-10-15-17D are met. However, application of the alternative guidance should cease if a CFE no longer meets those scope requirements. In that case, a CFE's financial assets and financial liabilities should be measured using the guidance in ASC 820.

A reporting entity that applies the alternative measurement guidance should recognize in earnings amounts that represent its economic interests in a consolidated CFE, including:

(1) changes in the fair value of its retained beneficial interests, if any (except for those representing compensation for services); and

(2) beneficial interests that represent compensation for services (e.g., management fees or servicing fees).

In subsequent reporting periods, an entity that measures the fair value of a CFE's financial assets and financial liabilities under the requirements of ASC 820, even though it meets the scope requirements in ASC 810-10-15-17D to apply the measurement alternative, should include subsequent changes in the fair values of a CFE's financial assets and financial liabilities in the reporting entity's earnings in the consolidated income (loss) statement.

Disclosure

Under the guidance in ASC 810-10-50-20 through 50-22, a reporting entity that consolidates a CFE and measures the CFE's financial assets and financial liabilities using the alternative measurement guidance initially and in subsequent reporting periods is required to disclose the following:

- The information required in ASC 820 and ASC 825, related to the fair value measurements of a consolidated CFE's financial assets and financial liabilities.
- The amount of the financial assets or the financial liabilities, whichever is less observable, that was measured based on the fair value that is the more observable of the two.
- The above disclosures do not apply to financial assets and financial liabilities that are incidental to a CFE's operations and have carrying values that approximate fair value.

Transition and Effective Date

The following is the transition guidance in ASC 810-10-65-6:

- The guidance is effective for public business entities for annual periods, and interim periods within those annual periods, that begin after December 15, 2015. For all other entities, the guidance is effective for annual periods that end after December 15, 2016, and interim periods that begin after December 15, 2016.
- When adopted, the measurement alternative in ASC 810-10-30-10 through 30-15 and ASC 810-10-35-6 through 35-8 may be applied to existing consolidated CFEs that meet the scope requirements in ASC 810-10-15-17D using a modified retrospective approach by remeasuring an existing consolidated CFE's financial assets or financial liabilities as of the beginning of the annual period of adoption and recording a cumulative-effect adjustment for the remeasurement to equity. A reporting entity that does not elect to apply the measurement alternative should reclassify accumulated differences, if any, in the fair value of the financial assets and the fair value of the financial liabilities of its CFE to retained earnings if those differences were previously presented in another caption within equity (e.g., appropriated retained earnings).
- A reporting entity may elect to apply the guidance retrospectively to all relevant prior periods that begin with the annual period in which the amendments to ASU 2009-17 were initially adopted.

- If a reporting entity consolidates a CFE that does not meet the scope requirements in ASC 810-10-15-17D because it had not elected the fair value option in ASC 825 to measure a CFE's eligible financial assets, eligible financial liabilities, or both when it initially consolidated the CFE, it may elect at the adoption date to apply the measurement alternative discussed above to a consolidated CFE's financial assets and financial liabilities or to continue using the other guidance in the ASC to measure a consolidated CFE's financial assets and financial liabilities. However, under the circumstances discussed above, a reporting entity that does not elect to apply the measurement alternative at the adoption date is not permitted to begin applying the fair value measurement requirements in ASC 820 or to change its basis for measuring a consolidated CFE's financial assets and financial liabilities.
- Earlier application of the guidance is permitted as of the beginning of an annual period.
- The disclosures in ASC 250-10-50-1 through 50-3 are required in the period in which an entity adopts the ASU's guidance.

ASC 810-10-25-15; ASC 946-10-65-1 Retention of Specialized Accounting for Investments in Consolidation

BACKGROUND

Some operating companies have subsidiaries that are venture capital investment companies, which provide financing to companies in various stages of development by investing in their securities. Venture capital investment companies generally follow the specialized accounting principles for investment companies and carry their investments at market value.

ACCOUNTING ISSUE

Should an operating company report the investments of its venture capital subsidiary in consolidated financial statements at market value based on the subsidiary's specialized accounting principles, or should the investments be reported in the same manner as the parent's investments?

ACCOUNTING GUIDANCE

A subsidiary's specialized industry accounting principles should be retained in consolidation if they are appropriate at the subsidiary's level.

ASC 810-10-25-49 through 25-54 Implicit Variable Interests

PRACTICE NOTE: The guidance below applies to public as well as nonpublic reporting entities.

BACKGROUND

There has been diversity in practice in accounting for situations in which a reporting entity, Entity A, has an interest in or other involvement that is *not* a variable interest with Entity B, which is a variable interest entity (VIE) or a potential VIE. In addition, Entity C, which is *not* a VIE, is a related party to Entity A that also has a variable interest in Entity B. Questions have been raised as to whether the reporting entity (Entity A) should consider whether an *implicit* variable interest has been created between it and the VIE (Entity B). A reporting entity's interest in or other financial involvement with a VIE may be in the form of a lessee under a leasing arrangement, as a party to a supply contract, service contract, derivative contract, or in other forms of involvement.

An *implicit* variable interest is an indirect financial interest in an entity that changes as a result of changes in the fair value of the entity's net assets, not including variable interests. Such variable interests may result from transactions with related parties and other parties. *Explicit* variable interests in an entity *directly* absorb or receive the entity's variability, while *implicit* variable interests act the same as explicit variable interests but they absorb or receive variability *indirectly* from the entity.

The question addressed is whether a reporting entity should consider if it has an *implicit* variable interest in a VIE or a potential VIE under specific conditions. Information about implicit and explicit variable interests is necessary in the application of the accounting guidance for VIEs in ASC 810-10-05-8 through 05-13; 15-13 through 15-17; 15-20 through 25-38G; 25-42 through 25-44; 30-1 through 30-4; 30-7 through 30-9; 35-3 through 35-4; 45-25; 50-2AA through 50-4, 50-5A through 50-6; 50-9 through 50-10; 55-16 through 55-32; 55-37 through 55-89, 55-93 through 55-205, because it may affect (*a*) whether a potential VIE should be considered to be a VIE, (*b*) the calculation of expected losses and residual returns, and (*c*) which party, if any, is a VIE's primary beneficiary.

ACCOUNTING GUIDANCE

Question: Should a reporting entity consider whether it has an *implicit* variable interest in a VIE or potential VIE under the following conditions:

- A reporting entity has an interest in, or other involvement with, a VIE or potential VIE that is *not* considered a variable interest in the VIE under the *explicit* terms of the reporting entity's interest in or involvement with the VIE. Therefore, the entity has *no* explicit variable interest in the VIE. Further, without considering related party relationships, the reporting entity would have *no* implicit variable interest in the entity.
- The reporting entity's related party has a variable interest in the same entity.

Answer: A reporting entity should consider whether it has an *implicit* variable interest in a VIE or potential VIE based on all the facts and circumstances when the reporting entity determines whether it may absorb the VIE's or a potential VIE's variability. If a reporting entity determines that it holds an implicit variable interest in a VIE and it is a related party, as defined in ASC 810-10-25-43, to other holders of variable interests in an entity, it should determine whether it is the VIE's primary beneficiary based on the guidance in ASC 810-10-25-42 through 25-44B. The guidance in ASC 810-10-25-49 through 25-54 applies to related parties as defined in ASC 810-10-25-43. Judgment based on all the facts and circumstances is required to determine which party in a related party group is most closely associated with a VIE. The factors stated in ASC 810-10-25-44 that should be considered include (*a*) whether a principal-agency relationship exists between parties in a related party group; (*b*) the VIE's relationship to and significance of its activities with parties in a related party group; (*c*) exposure to a VIE's expected variability; and *(d)* a VIE's design.

If a reporting entity that holds an implicit variable interest in a VIE is not the primary beneficiary, the entity should disclose the information required in ASC 810-10-50-4.

ASC 810-10-25-58 Reporting Variable Interests in Specified Assets of Variable Interest Entities as Separate Variable Interest Entities

Question: Should a variable interest entity (Entity A) treat a specified asset (or a group of assets) and a related liability that is secured only by the specified asset or group of assets as a separate variable interest entity (Entity B), as discussed in the ASC 810-10-25-57, if other parties have rights or obligations related to the specified asset or to residual cash flows from the specified asset?

Answer: A separate variable interest entity does not exist under the circumstances discussed above. Entity B should be treated as a separate variable interest entity for accounting purposes only if all of its assets, liabilities, and equity are separate from those of Entity A and can be identified separately. Under those circumstances, Entity A would not be able to use returns on Entity B's assets and Entity B would not be able to use Entity A's assets to settle its liabilities.

ASC 810-10-40-1 through 40-2A; ASC 505-10-60-4 Early Extinguishment of a Subsidiary's Mandatorily Redeemable Preferred Stock

---

PRACTICE POINTER: Under the guidance in ASC 480, Distinguishing Liabilities from Equity, a financial instrument that is mandatorily redeemable at a specified or determinable date, or on the occurrence of a certain event, should be accounted for as a liability, except if a redemption occurs when a reporting entity is being liquidated or terminated. Consequently, that guidance nullifies the guidance in this Issue related to mandatorily redeemable preferred stock. In addition, under the guidance in ASC 480, amounts paid to holders of those contracts in excess of the initial amount at which they were measured should be accounted for as an interest cost rather than as a charge to a noncontrolling interest in the entity. The guidance in this Issue continues to apply to a financial instrument with a redemption feature that is *not* considered a mandatorily redeemable financial instrument under the guidance in ASC 480.

BACKGROUND

Company X acquires Company Z in a purchase business combination. Subsequent to the business combination, Company Z issues mandatorily redeemable preferred stock with a fixed dividend and no voting rights. The carrying amount of that stock is $75 million. Eighteen months after the redeemable stock is issued, its market value declines. Company X purchases the subsidiary's redeemable preferred stock for $60 million on the open market and holds it until it is due to be redeemed.

ACCOUNTING ISSUE

How should Company X account for the purchase of its wholly owned subsidiary's mandatorily redeemable preferred stock?

ACCOUNTING GUIDANCE

The company should treat the acquisition of the subsidiary's mandatorily redeemable preferred stock as a capital transaction. Thus, the company should recognize no gain or loss from the acquisition in its consolidated financial statements.

ASC 810-10-45-13, 50-2 Reporting a Change in (or the Elimination of) a Previously Existing Difference between the Fiscal Year-End of a Parent Company and That of a Consolidated Entity or between the Reporting Period of an Investor and That of an Equity Method Investee

OVERVIEW

Under the guidance in the ASC 810, *Consolidations* and ASC 323, *Investments—Equity Method and Joint Ventures,* a parent company's reporting year-end is permitted to be different from that of a consolidated entity's year-end for the purpose of consolidating the entity's operations; and an investor's reporting year-end is permitted to be different from its equity-method investee's year-end for the purpose of recognizing a change in an equity investment's net assets. Parent companies and investors that want to obtain financial results that are more consistent with, or the same as, their respective entity's results have asked for guidance on how to account for a change in or an elimination of a previously existing difference (lag period) in a consolidated entity's or equity method investee's reporting year-end.

SCOPE

This guidance applies to all entities that change or eliminate an existing difference between a parent company's reporting year-end and that of a consolidated entity or that of an investor and its equity method investee. This guidance does *not* apply if a parent company changes its fiscal year-end.

ACCOUNTING ISSUE

How should a parent company recognize the effect of a change to or the elimination of an existing difference between a parent company's reporting period and a consolidated entity's reporting period or between an investor's reporting period and an equity-method investee's reporting period?

ACCOUNTING GUIDANCE

A change or elimination of an existing difference between a parent company's reporting period and that of an entity consolidated in its financial statements or between an investor's reporting period and the reporting period of an equity method investee should be accounted for in a parent company's or an investor's financial statements as a change in accounting principle in accordance with the guidance in ASC 250-10-05, 10-15, 10-45, 10-50, 10-55, 10-60. That guidance is based on the view that a change to or elimination of a lag period is a change in accounting principle. Although voluntary changes under the guidance in ASC 250, *Accounting Changes and Error Corrections,* must be required to be reported retrospectively, according to the guidance in ASC 250-10-45-9 through 45-10, retrospective application is *not* required if applying the effects of a change in accordance with that guidance would be impracticable.

DISCLOSURE

The information required under the guidance in ASC 250-10-50 for a change in accounting principle should be disclosed.

ASC 810-10-55-2 through 55-4 Elimination of Profits Resulting from Intercompany Transfers of LIFO Inventories

BACKGROUND

This guidance was issued as a reminder concerning inventory transfers between or from LIFO pools, either within a company or between a reporting entity's subsidiaries or divisions. A LIFO liquidation or decrement occurs when the number of units (or total base year cost if the dollar-value LIFO method is used) in a LIFO pool is less at the end of the year than at the beginning of the year, causing prior-year costs, rather than current-year costs, to be charged to current-year income.

ACCOUNTING STANDARDS

According to the guidance in ASC 810-10-10-1, the purpose of consolidated financial statements is to present the results of operations and the financial position of a parent company and its subsidiaries as if the group were a single company.

Intercompany profits on assets remaining within a group should be eliminated in the preparation of consolidated financial statements so that the results of operations and financial position are not affected by inventory transfers within a reporting entity. Inventory transferred between or from LIFO pools may cause LIFO inventory liquidations that could affect the amount of intercompany profit to be eliminated.

Different approaches are used to eliminate such profit in the preparation of consolidated financial statements. Each reporting entity should adopt an approach that, if consistently applied, defers reporting intercompany profits from transfers within a reporting entity until those profits are realized by the reporting entity through sales outside the consolidated group of entities. The approach selected should be one that is suited to the reporting entity's circumstances.

ASC 810-10-55-50 through 55-54 Calculation of Expected Losses if There is no History, nor Future Expectation of, Net Losses

Question: Should an entity be accounted for as a variable interest entity if it has no history of net losses and expects to continue to be profitable in the foreseeable future?

Answer: An entity should be treated as a variable interest entity under those circumstances because even entities that expect to be profitable will have expected losses. The term "expected losses" is used to refer to negative variability in the fair value of a variable interest entity's net assets, without its variable interests, and does *not* apply to the expected amount of variability of its net income or loss. A variable interest entity's expected losses are defined in ASC 810-10-20, *Glossary,* as the expected negative variability in the fair value of the entity's net assets without the variable interests, not an expected amount of variability in net income or loss.

Example: Entity A is formed on January 1, 200X, to purchase a building that is financed with 95% debt and 5% equity. If Entity A does not make the required debt payments, its lenders have recourse only to the building. On the same day, Entity A leases the building to Entity B under a five-year market-rate lease that includes a guarantee of a portion of the building's residual value. The present value of the minimum lease payments, including the residual value guarantee, is less than 90% of the building's fair value. No other entities have interests in Entity A. The appropriate discount rate is assumed to be 5%.

In accordance with the definitions of expected losses and expected residual returns in ASC 810-10-20 *Glossary,* the entity's estimated annual results in the above example include estimated cash flows and the estimated fair value of Entity A's assets that will be distributed to variable interest holders instead of cash, regardless of cash flows or flows of other assets to and from variable interests. The guarantee constitutes a variable interest in Entity A, because it is an interest in assets with a fair value that is more than half of the total fair value of Company A's assets. Consequently, losses absorbed by the residual value guarantee are Company A's losses and are included in the results used to calculate expected losses. To simplify the calculation, it is assumed that (*a*) the estimated results, which include both cash flows and changes in the fair value of Company A's net assets, and related probabilities are the same each year of the five-year lease and (*b*) the carrying value of the building at the end of the lease is its fair value.

The illustration below demonstrates the calculation at January 1, 200X, of the expected results identified as a variable interest at the inception of the guarantee. It is assumed that the fair value of the expected result will be equal to the sum of the present values of probability-weighted estimated annual results for the five-year lease term, without the effects of the residual value guarantee. A variation in the estimated results, if any, as compared to the expected result, is a change in the value of the entity's net assets, without the variable interests, from the value of those net assets on the calculation date.

Illustration of Expected Results at Inception of Guarantee Identified as Variable Interest (amounts in thousands)

Estimated Annual Results[(a)]	*Probability*	*Expected Annual Results*	*Fair Value of Expected Five-Year Results*[(b)]
$(10,000)	5.0%	$(500)	$(2,165)
(5,000)	10.0	(500)	(2,165)
0	20.0	0	0
10,000	50.0	5,000	21,648

Estimated Annual Results[(a)]	*Probability*	*Expected Annual Results*	*Fair Value of Expected Five-Year Results*[(b)]
50,000	15.0	7,500	32,471
	100.0	$11,500	$49,789

(a) Estimated annual results include estimated cash flow, excluding cash flow or flows of other assets to and from variable interests, and the estimated fair value of Company A's assets to be distributed to holders of variable interests instead of cash.
(b) It is assumed that the fair value of expected five-year results is the sum of the present values of the expected results for each year in the five-year period. In the present value calculations to determine the fair value of the five-year expected results, the expected annual results are treated as level annuities because to simplify the calculation it is assumed that the annual estimated results and probabilities are the same for each year of the five-year period.

The illustration below demonstrates the calculation of expected losses as the negative variability from the fair value of the expected results. It shows that an estimated annual result of $0 and one of $10,000 can contribute to expected losses even though neither is a negative amount, because a company's value will be less relative to its value based on the expected results if a positive estimated result is less than the expected results. The calculation of an expected loss shows that the expected loss is the fair value of the probability-weighted negative variation from the expected results. Expected losses include all negative variations.

Illustration of Calculation of Expected Losses as Negative Variability from Fair Value of Expected Results (amounts in thousands)

Estimated Annual Result	*Present Value of Estimated Five-Year Result*[(a)]	*Positive Fair Value of Expected Five-Year Results (from above)*	*(Negative) Variation Expected from Value*	*Probability*	*Expected Losses*	*Residual Returns*
$(10,000)	$(43,294)	$49,789	$(93,083)	5.0%	$(4,654)	
(5,000)	(21,648)	49,789	(71,437)	10.0	(7,144)	
0	0	49,789	(49,789)	20.0	(9,958)	
10,000	43,294	49,789	(6,495)	50.0	(3,247)	
50,000	216,473	49,789	166,684	15.0		25,003
				100.0%	$(25,003)	$25,003

(a) The estimated annual results are treated as level annuities in calculating the present value of the estimated five-year results because, in order to simplify the calculation, it is assumed that the annual estimated results are the same for each year of the five-year periods.

ASC 810-30: RESEARCH AND DEVELOPMENT ARRANGEMENTS

ASC 810-30-15-2, 15-3, 25-1, 25-3; 30-1, 35-1, 45-1, 45-2, 55-1 through 55-4 Accounting for Transactions with Elements of Research and Development Arrangements

BACKGROUND

The following guidance applies only to certain new transactions, such as the one in this example. A Sponsor capitalizes a *wholly owned* subsidiary (Newco) with $110 million in cash and the right to technology developed by the Sponsor, which has no book value, in exchange for shares in Class A and Class B common stock in Newco, which have a nominal fair value. Simultaneously, the Sponsor and Newco enter into agreements that include a *development contract* and a *purchase option.* Thereafter, the Sponsor distributes the Class A common shares in Newco, which have a fair value of $80 million, to its shareholders. The Sponsor continues to hold all of the Class B common shares that give the Sponsor no financial interest and no voting interest except for certain blocking rights. Newco, which has no employees—except for a CEO—and has only nominal office facilities, is required to spend all of the cash contributed by the Sponsor on R&D, which will be performed by the Sponsor under a cost plus 10% development contract with Newco. The Sponsor will be paid $55 million for each of two years, at the end of which all of the cash will have been expended.

The Sponsor has the right to exercise the option to purchase all of Newco's Class A common shares at any time during the term of the development contract at a price that approximates the fair value of the shares. During that two-year period, Newco is not permitted to change the Sponsor's rights under the purchase option without the Sponsor's previous approval. Newco also is prohibited from merging, liquidating, selling a substantial portion of its assets, or amending its certificate of incorporation to change the purchase option, Newco's authorized capitalization, or the certificate of incorporation's provisions regarding Newco's board of directors without the Sponsor's previous approval.

The following guidance does not apply to: (*a*) arrangements in which funds are provided by third parties, because those arrangements generally would be accounted for under the guidance in ASC 730, *Research and Development,* and (*b*) legal special-purpose entities that must be consolidated under the guidance for variable interest entities (VIEs) in ASC 810-10.

Under the provisions of ASC 730, an entity should account for an R&D arrangement that gives it the right to the results of R&D funded partially or entirely by others based on the nature of the obligation incurred under that arrangement. An entity that must repay funds provided by others, regardless of the results of the R&D, is required to estimate and recognize that liability. However, if the financial risk related to the R&D has been transferred to that entity, because its obligation to repay funds provided by others depends totally on whether the R&D's results have a future economic benefit, the entity would account for its obligation as a contract to perform R&D for others.

ACCOUNTING ISSUE

How should a Sponsor account for a research and development arrangement under the scope of this Issue?

ACCOUNTING GUIDANCE

- A Sponsor should account for an R&D arrangement under the scope of this guidance as follows:
  - On distribution of Newco's Class A common stock, reclassify cash contributed to Newco as restricted cash and recognize R&D expense as those activities are performed.
  - Account for the distribution of the Class A common stock as a dividend to the Sponsor's common stockholders.
  - Calculate the amount of the dividend based on the fair value of Newco's Class A common stock and recognize the transaction when the Sponsor distributes the stock to its stockholders.
  - Present Newco's Class A common stock as a noncontrolling interest in the Sponsor, classified in equity separately from the parent's equity.
- In determining the amount of net income or earnings available to the Sponsor's common stockholders for the EPS calculation, the Sponsor should *not* allocate any portion of R&D expense to Newco's Class A common stock. It was noted that the accounting result under this guidance is in essence the same as it would be in consolidation with the incurred R&D costs allocated to Newco's Class B common stock held by the Sponsor, because the value of the Class A common stock is related to the value of the purchase option, *not* to the Sponsor's original funding of the arrangement.
- The Sponsor should account for a purchase option, if any, as follows:
  - *Purchase option is exercised* Account for the exercise of the option to acquire the Class A common stock like an acquisition of a noncontrolling interest by allocating the excess of the option's exercise price over its carrying amount to the assets acquired (in-process or completed R&D) and liabilities assumed, if any.
  - *Purchase option is* not *exercised* If an option expires, reclassify Newco's Class A common stock to additional paid-in capital as an adjustment to the initial dividend.

CHAPTER 50

ASC 815—DERIVATIVES AND HEDGING

CONTENTS

PART I: GENERAL GUIDANCE

OVERVIEW

Other chapters within this *Guide* discuss pronouncements that specifically address other types of financial instruments. For ease of reference, the table below summarizes current accounting pronouncements related to financial instruments; relevant discussions of these topics can be found in the specific chapters covering these ASC pronouncements.

Pronouncement	*Title*
ASC 210	Balance Sheet
ASC 310	Receivables
ASC 320	Investments—Debt Securities
ASC 321	Investments—Equity Securities
ASC 460	Guarantees
ASC 470	Debt
ASC 480	Distinguishing Liabilities from Equity
ASC 505	Equity
ASC 810	Consolidation

Pronouncement	*Title*
ASC 825	Financial Instruments
ASC 835	Interest
ASC 848	Reference Rate Reform
ASC 860	Transfers and Servicing

PRACTICE POINTER: The accounting for financial instruments has become increasingly complex in recent years. Readers also should refer to Wolters Kluwer's *Financial Instruments* for comprehensive accounting guidance for each major type of financial instrument or transaction. Practitioners who encounter these areas should seek the assistance of experts in analyzing the applicable accounting literature.

BACKGROUND

Significant financial innovation and the rapid development of complex financial instruments prompted the FASB to undertake an involved and lengthy project to develop guidance for financial instruments in 1986. Many financial instruments were described as *off-balance-sheet* instruments because they failed to meet one or more of the criteria for recognition. Before addressing the difficult recognition and measurement issues associated with financial instruments, the FASB developed guidance to improve disclosures surrounding financial instruments.

The FASB issued considerable guidance in the early and mid-1990s that addressed the recognition and measurement of financial instruments. A significant milestone in the FASB's financial instrument project was reached in 1998 with the issuance of guidance on accounting for derivative instruments and hedging activities. This guidance was the result of extensive discussion and debate by the FASB on the subject of accounting for derivative instruments; it overhauled the fragmented preexisting accounting model for derivative instruments by establishing recognition and measurement standards for all derivatives, regardless of their use, based on fair value. For guidance on the disclosure of information about the fair value of financial instruments, see Chapter 52, *ASC 825—Financial Instruments*.

ASC 815-10: OVERALL

ACCOUNTING FOR DERIVATIVE INSTRUMENTS AND HEDGING ACTIVITIES

ASC 815 establishes accounting and reporting standards for derivative instruments, including derivative instruments that are embedded in other contracts, and hedging activities. The guidance in ASC 815 is based on the following fundamental principles (ASC 815-10-10-1):

- Derivative instruments represent rights or obligations that meet the definitions of assets and liabilities and, therefore, should be reported in the financial statements.
- Fair value is the most relevant measure for financial instruments and the only relevant measure for derivative instruments.
- Only items that are assets or liabilities should be reported as such in the financial statements.
- Special accounting for items designated as being hedged should be provided only for qualifying items. One aspect of qualification is an assessment of the expectation of effective offsetting of changes in fair value or cash flows during the term of the hedge for the risk being hedged.

Definition of a Derivative and Scope Issues

A derivative instrument is defined as a financial instrument or other contract with all of the following characteristics (ASC 815-10-15-83):

- It has (1) one or more underlyings and (2) one or more notional amounts or payment provisions, or both. (An *underlying* is a specified interest rate, security price, commodity price, foreign exchange rate, index of prices or rates or other variable including the occurrence or nonoccurrence of a specified event. A *notional amount* is a number of currency units, shares, bushels, pounds, or other unit specified in the contract.) The interaction of the underlying and notional amount determines the amount of the settlement and, in some cases, whether or not a settlement is required;

- It requires no initial investment or an initial investment that is smaller than would be required for other types of contracts that would be expected to have a similar response to changes in market factors; and
- Its terms require or permit net settlement, it can be readily settled net by a means outside the contract, or it provides for delivery of an asset that puts the recipient in a position not substantially different from net settlement.

ASC 815 contains a number of exceptions to the definition of a derivative. Some of the scope exceptions were granted because the FASB recognized established accounting models already existed for certain instruments that would meet the definition of a derivative. Other scope exceptions were granted in order to simplify application of the standard. The following is a partial list of those scope exceptions (ASC 815-10-15-13):

- "Regular-way" security trades (i.e., security trades that require delivery of an existing security within a timeframe established by regulations in the marketplace or exchange in which the transaction is executed), if they cannot be net settled; purchases and sales of "when-issued" securities or other securities that do not yet exist that meet certain specified conditions; and all security trades that are required to be recognized on a trade-date basis by other GAAP
- Normal purchases and normal sales (i.e., contracts that provide for the purchase or sale of something other than a financial instrument or derivative instrument that will be delivered in quantities expected to be used or sold by the reporting entity over a reasonable period in the normal course of business) (ASC 815-10-15-15)
- Certain insurance contracts and market risk benefits
- Certain financial guarantee contracts
- Certain contracts that are not traded on an exchange
- Derivatives that serve as impediments to sales accounting
- Investments in life insurance (in specific circumstances)
- Certain investment contracts (in specific circumstances)
- Loan commitments for origination of any type of loan that are held by a potential borrower
- Loan commitments issued to originate mortgage loans that will be classified as held for investment under ASC 948 (Financial Services—Mortgage Banking) (however, loan commitments issued to originate mortgage loans that will be classified as held for sale under ASC 948 are subject to ASC 815) (ASC 815-10-15-69, 71)
- Contracts issued or held by the reporting entity that are both indexed to the entity's own stock and classified in stockholders' equity
- Contracts issued by the entity in connection with stock-based compensation arrangements (should be analyzed to determine if subject to ASC 815)
- Contracts between a buyer and a seller to enter into a business combination at a future date

A contract that qualifies for a scope exception under ASC 815 should be accounted for in accordance with relevant GAAP.

PRACTICE POINTER: The definition of a derivative and the scope exceptions in ASC 815 are complicated and highly interpretive. Practitioners encountering complex instruments that may be subject to ASC 815 should seek the advice of experts in the area of accounting for derivatives.

General Disclosures

An entity with derivative instruments shall disclose information to allow financial statement users to understand how and why the entity uses the derivative instruments as well as how the derivative instruments are accounted for and how they affect the entity's financial position, financial performance, and cash flows. An entity that holds or issues derivative instruments must make the following disclosures (ASC 815-10-50-1, 2):

- Objectives for holding or issuing the instruments
- The context needed to understand these objectives
- The entity's strategies for achieving these objectives
- Information about these instruments in the context of each instrument's primary underlying risk exposure (e.g., interest rate, credit, foreign exchange rate, overall price)

- Distinction between those instruments used for risk management purposes and those used for other purposes
- Information that allows users of its financial statements to understand the volume of its derivative activity
- For instruments designated as hedging instruments, a distinction between derivative instruments designated as fair value hedges, cash flow hedges, or hedges of the foreign currency exposure of a net investment in a foreign operation
- For instruments not designated as hedging instruments, the purpose of the derivative activity

ASC 815 requires the following quantitative disclosures for all derivative instruments and nonderivative instruments that qualify as hedging instruments (ASC 815-10-50-4A, 4B, 4C):

- The location and fair value amounts of derivative instruments reported in the statement of financial position
  - Fair value shall be presented on a gross basis even when the derivative instruments qualify for net presentation in accordance with ASC 210-20 (Balance Sheet—Offsetting)
  - Fair value amounts shall be presented as separate asset and liability values segregated between derivatives that are designated and qualify as hedging instruments and those that are not. Within these two broad categories, fair values amounts shall be presented separately by type of derivative contract (e.g., interest rate contracts, foreign exchange contracts, commodity contracts)
  - The disclosure shall identify the line item(s) in the statement of financial position in which the fair value amounts are included
- The location and amount of gains and losses on derivative instruments and related hedged items reported in the statement of financial performance, or when applicable the statement of financial position (e.g., gains and losses initially recognized in other comprehensive income). Gains and losses must be presented separately for:
  - Fair value hedges and related hedged items
  - Gains and losses in cash flow hedges included in the assessment of effectiveness that were recognized in other comprehensive income during the current period
  - Amounts excluded from the assessment of effectiveness that were recognized in other comprehensive income
  - Gains and losses in cash flow hedges that are included in the assessment of effectiveness and recorded in accumulated other comprehensive income during the term of the hedging relationship and reclassified into earnings during the current period
  - The portion of gains and losses in fair value and cash flow hedges representing the amount, if any, excluded from the assessment of hedge effectiveness that is recognized in earnings.
  - The amount of gains and losses reclassified into earnings as a result of the discontinuance of cash flow hedges, because it is probable that the original forecasted transactions will not occur by the end of the originally specified time period.
  - The amount of net gain or loss recognized in earnings when a hedged firm commitment no longer qualifies as a fair value hedge.
  - For qualifying net investment hedges, an entity must present the gains and losses separately for all of the following by type of contract:
    - The gains and losses on derivative instruments designated and qualifying in net investment hedges that were recognized in the cumulative translation adjustment section of other comprehensive income during the current period.
    - The gains and losses on derivative instruments designated and qualifying in net investment hedges recorded in the cumulative translation adjustment section of accumulated other comprehensive income during the term of the hedging relationship and reclassified into earnings during the current period.
    - The portion of gains and losses on derivative instruments designated and qualifying and qualifying in net investment hedges representing the amount, if any, excluded from the assessment of hedge effectiveness.
  - The total amount of each income and expense line item presented in the statement of financial performance in which the results of fair value or cash flow hedges are recorded.

The quantitative disclosures listed above must be presented by type of derivative contract and in tabular format. For items designated and qualifying as hedged items in fair value hedges, an entity must disclose the following in tabular format:

- The carrying amount of hedged assets and liabilities recognized in the statement of financial position.
- The cumulative amount of fair value hedging adjustments to hedged assets and liabilities included in the carrying amount of the hedged assets and liabilities recognized in the statement of financial position.
- The line item in the statement of financial position that includes the hedged assets and liabilities.
- The cumulative amount of fair value hedging adjustments remaining for any hedged assets and liabilities for which hedge accounting has been discontinued.

Derivative instruments often include contingent features that can result in an immediate payment to a counterparty or a posting of additional collateral on an agreement that is in a liability position. ASC 815 requires disclosures about credit-risk-related contingent features that could affect an entity's liquidity. Specifically, an entity must disclose (ASC 815-10-50-4H):

- The existence and nature of credit-risk-related contingent features and the circumstances that would trigger these features in derivative instruments that are in a net liability position at the end of the reporting period
- The aggregate fair value amounts of derivative instruments that contain credit-risk-related contingent features and are in a net liability position at the end of the reporting period
- The aggregate fair value of assets already posted as collateral at the end of the reporting period and:
  - The aggregate fair value of additional assets that would be required to be posted as collateral if the contingent features were triggered
  - The aggregate fair value of assets needed to settle the instruments immediately if the contingent features were triggered

Disclosures about derivative instruments are typically scattered throughout multiple footnotes to the financial statements, which can make them difficult to understand and follow. ASC 815 requires an entity to cross-reference from the derivative footnote to any other footnotes in which derivative-related information is disclosed (ASC 815-10-50-4I).

Reporting Cash Flows of Derivative Instruments That Contain Financing Elements

An instrument accounted for as a derivative under ASC 815 that at its inception includes off-market terms, requires an up-front cash payment, or both, often contains a financing element. If a significant financing element is present at inception, other than a financing element inherently included in an at-the-market derivative instrument with no prepayments, then the borrower shall report all cash inflows and outflows associated with that derivative instrument as a financing activity as described in ASC 230 (Statement of Cash Flows) (ASC 815-10-45-11, 12).

ASC 815-15: EMBEDDED DERIVATIVES

EMBEDDED DERIVATIVES

Contracts that do not in their entirety meet the definition of a derivative instrument (e.g., bonds, insurance policies, leases) may contain embedded derivative instruments as a result of implicit or explicit terms that affect some or all of the cash flows or the value of other exchanges required by the contract in a manner that makes them similar to a derivative instrument.

ASC 815 also applies to interests in securitized financial assets. That is, an entity must now evaluate whether an interest in securitized financial assets contains an embedded derivative that would be required to be separated from the host contract and accounted for separately (ASC 815-10-15-11).

Interest-only and principal-only strips are not subject to the provisions of ASC 815-10 if the interest-only or principal-only strips represent the rights to receive only a specified proportion of the contractual interest cash flows or contractual principal cash flows of a particular debt instrument and do not include any terms not in the original debt instrument. This exemption applies if some portion of the interest or principal cash flows is stripped to provide compensation to either a servicer or to the entity that stripped the debt instrument. However, this exemption does not apply if a portion of the interest or principal cash flows is stripped to guarantee payments, to pay for servicing in excess of adequate compensation, or for any other purpose (ASC 815-10-15-72, 73).

Other than the limited exemption provided above, a holder of an interest in a securitized financial asset must determine whether the interest represents a freestanding derivative or whether it contains an embedded derivative. The analysis requires the entity to understand the contractual terms of the interest in the securitized financial assets. The entity must analyze the nature and amounts of assets, liabilities, and other financial instruments that comprise the entire securitization transaction. The holder of an interest in securitized financial assets must understand the interest's payoff structure and its payment priority to determine whether the instrument contains an embedded derivative (ASC 815-15-25-11, 12, 13). An embedded derivative must be separated from the host contract and accounted for as a derivative instrument assuming the following conditions are met (ASC 815-15-25-1):

- The economic characteristics and risks of the embedded derivative instrument are not clearly and closely related to the economic characteristics of the host contract.
- The hybrid instrument that embodies the embedded derivative instrument and the host contract is not remeasured at fair value under otherwise applicable generally accepted accounting principles.
- A separate instrument with the same terms as the embedded instrument would be a derivative subject to the requirements of ASC 815.

PRACTICE POINTER: ASC 815 contains implementation guidance and illustrations related to the assessment of whether an embedded derivative is considered clearly and closely related to a host contract. For a more in-depth discussion of the application of ASC 815 and related interpretations to instruments with embedded derivatives, see Wolters Kluwer's *Financial Instruments*.

Under ASC 815, entities are permitted, but not required, to irrevocably elect to measure financial instruments with an embedded derivative at fair value. Rather than bifurcating the instrument with the embedded derivative accounted for at fair value and the host contract accounted for separately under whatever U.S. GAAP requirements pertain to that instrument, the entire instrument can be accounted for at fair value (ASC 815-15-25-4). However, a hybrid financial instrument that is not bifurcated between the embedded derivative and the underlying host, but rather is accounted for as one combined instrument at fair value, *cannot* be designated as a hedging instrument (ASC 815-20-25-71(a)(3)).

The hybrid financial instrument can be either an asset or a liability, and it can either have been issued by or acquired by the entity. The election as to whether to record a hybrid financial instrument at fair value can be made on an instrument-by-instrument basis. Once an entity chooses to measure a hybrid financial instrument at fair value, it cannot change this measurement basis for that particular instrument in the future. Changes in the fair value of the hybrid financial instrument are recognized in earnings as they occur (ASC 815-15-25-5).

An entity that chooses to measure a hybrid financial instrument at fair value must support the decision with concurrent documentation. Alternatively, an entity can have a policy to automatically elect to measure hybrid financial instruments at fair value, but any such preexisting policy must be documented (ASC 815-15-25-5).

At the inception of a hybrid financial instrument, the transaction price and the instrument's fair value would normally be the same. However, in some circumstances, the transaction price may differ from the instrument's fair value. In these situations, the difference between the transaction price and fair value can only be recognized in earnings if the entity chooses the fair value election and if fair value is determined by a quoted market price in an active market, comparison to other observable current market transactions, and a valuation technique that uses observable market data.

As clarified by ASC 815, the requirements in ASC 815-10-15-11 and ASC 815-15-25 do not apply to a transfer of credit risk that is only in the form of subordination of one financial instrument to another. However, only the embedded credit derivative feature created by the subordination is exempt from these requirements. Other embedded credit derivative features are subject to these requirements even if their effects are allocated to interests in tranches of securitized financial instruments in accordance with those subordination provisions (ASC 815-15-15-9).

Entities may have some hybrid financial instruments measured at fair value under ASC 815 and other hybrid financial instruments measured using another measurement attribute. Hybrid financial instruments with different measurement bases must be separately grouped and presented on the balance sheet. The entity can include separate line items on the balance sheet for the fair-value/non-fair-value carrying amounts or combine the amounts, with parenthetical disclosure, on the face of the balance sheet, of the fair value amount included in the combined total (ASC 815-15-45-1).

Entities that choose to measure hybrid financial instruments at fair value under ASC 815 must provide information to allow users to understand the effect of changes in fair value on earnings (ASC 815-15-50-2).

ASC 815-20: HEDGING—GENERAL

RECOGNITION AND MEASUREMENT OF DERIVATIVES

ASC 815 requires the recognition of all derivatives (both assets and liabilities) in the statement of financial position and the recognition of their measurement at fair value. In accordance with ASC 815, each derivative instrument is classified in one of the following four categories: (1) no hedge designation, (2) fair value hedge, (3) cash flow hedge, and (4) foreign currency hedge. Changes in the fair value of derivative instruments in each category are accounted for as indicated in the following table (ASC 815-20-35-1):

Derivative Designation	*Accounting for Changes in Fair Value*
No hedge designation	Included in current income
Fair value hedge	Included in current net income (with the offsetting gain or loss on the hedged item attributable to the risk being hedged)
Cash flow hedge	Included in other comprehensive income (outside net income)
Foreign currency hedge of a net investment in a foreign operation	Included in comprehensive income (outside of net income) as part of the cumulative translation adjustment

Derivatives Designated in Hedging Relationships

Fair Value Hedges

Certain instruments are designated as hedging the exposure to changes in the fair value of an asset or liability or an identified portion thereof that is attributed to a particular risk. A fair value hedge must meet all of the following criteria:

- At the inception of the hedge, there is formal documentation of the hedging relationship and the entity's risk management objective and strategy for undertaking the hedge. This must include identification of *(a)* the hedging instrument, *(b)* the hedged item or transaction, *(c)* the nature of the risk being hedged, and *(d)* how the hedging instrument's effectiveness in offsetting the exposure to changes in the fair value of the hedged item will be assessed (ASC 815-20-25-3).
- Both at the inception of the hedge and on an ongoing basis, the hedging relationship is expected to be highly effective in achieving offsetting changes in fair value attributed to the hedged risk during the period that the hedge is designated. An assessment is required whenever financial statements or earnings are reported, and at least every three months (ASC 815-20-25-75).
- If a written option is designated as hedging a recognized asset or liability or an unrecognized firm commitment, the combination of the hedged item and the written option provides at least as much potential for gains as the exposure to losses from changes in the combined fair values (ASC 815-20-25-94).

An asset or liability is eligible for designation as a hedged item in a fair value hedge if all of the following criteria are met (ASC 815-20-25-12):

- The hedged item is specifically identified as either all or a specified portion of a recognized asset or a recognized liability or an unrecognized firm commitment. The hedged item is a single asset or liability (or specified portion thereof) or is a portfolio of similar assets or a portfolio of similar liabilities (or a specified portion thereof).
- The hedged item presents an exposure to changes in fair value attributable to the hedged risk that could affect reported earnings. (The reference to affecting reported earnings does not apply to an entity that does not report earnings as a separate caption in a statement of financial performance, such as a not-for-profit organization.)
- The hedged item is not *(a)* an asset or liability that is remeasured with the changes in fair value attributable to the hedged risk reported currently in earnings, *(b)* an investment accounted for by the equity method, *(c)* a noncontrol-

ling interest in one or more consolidated subsidiaries, *(d)* an equity investment in a consolidated subsidiary, *(e)* a firm commitment either to enter into a business combination or to acquire or dispose of a subsidiary, a noncontrolling interest, or an equity method investee, or *(f)* an equity instrument issued by the entity and classified as stockholders' equity in the statement of financial position (ASC 815-20-25-43b).

- If the hedged item is all or a portion of a debt security that is classified as held-to-maturity in accordance with ASC 320 (Investments—Debt Securities), the designated risk being hedged is the risk of changes in its fair value attributable to credit risk, foreign exchange risk, or both. If the hedged item is an option component of a held-to-maturity security that permits its prepayment, the designated risk being hedged is the risk of changes in the entire fair value of that option component.
- If the hedged item is a nonfinancial asset or liability other than a recognized loan servicing right or a nonfinancial firm commitment with financial components, the designated risk being hedged is the risk of changes in the fair value of the entire hedged asset or liability.
- If the hedged item is a financial asset or liability, a recognized loan servicing right, or a nonfinancial firm commitment with financial components, the designated risk being hedged is *(a)* the risk of changes in the overall fair value of the entire hedged item, *(b)* the risk of changes in its fair value attributable to changes in the designated benchmark interest rate (i.e., interest rate risk), *(c)* the risk of changes in its fair value attributable to changes in the related foreign currency exchange risk (i.e., foreign exchange risk), or *(d)* the risk of changes in its fair value attributable to both changes in the obligor's creditworthiness and changes in spread over the benchmark interest rate with respect to the hedged item's credit section at inception (i.e., credit risk).

Cash Flow Hedges

A derivative instrument may be designated as hedging the exposure to variability in expected future cash flows attributed to a particular risk. That exposure may be associated with an existing recognized asset or liability (e.g., variable rate debt) or a forecasted transaction (e.g., a forecasted purchase or sale). Designated hedging instruments and hedged items or transactions qualify for cash flow hedge accounting if all of the following criteria are met:

- At the inception of the hedge, there is formal documentation of the hedging relationship and the entity's risk management objective and strategy for undertaking the hedge. This must include identification of *(a)* the hedging instrument, *(b)* the hedged transaction, *(c)* the nature of the risk being hedged, and *(d)* how the hedging instrument's effectiveness hedges the risk to the hedged transaction's variability in cash flows attributable to the hedged risk will be assessed (ASC 815-20-25-3).
- Both at the inception of the hedge and on an ongoing basis, the hedging relationship is expected to be highly effective in achieving offsetting cash flows attributable to the hedged risk during the term of the hedge. An assessment is required when financial statements or earnings are reported, and at least every three months (ASC 815-20-25-75).
- If a written option is designated as hedging the variability in cash flows for a recognized asset or liability, the combination of the hedged item and the written option provides at least as much potential for favorable cash flows as the exposure to unfavorable cash flows (ASC 815-20-25-94).
- If a hedging instrument is used to modify the contractually specified interest receipts or payments associated with a recognized financial asset or liability from one variable rate to another variable rate, the hedging instrument must be a link between an existing designated asset with variable cash flows and an existing designated liability with variable cash flows and must be highly effective in achieving offsetting cash flows (ASC 815-20-25-50).

A forecasted transaction is eligible for designation as a hedged transaction in a cash flow hedge if all of the following additional criteria are met (ASC 815-20-25-15):

- The forecasted transaction is specifically identified as a single transaction or a group of individual transactions. If a group, the individual transactions within the group must share the same risk exposure that is being hedged.
- The occurrence of the forecasted transaction is probable.
- The forecasted transaction is with a party external to the reporting entity and it presents an exposure to variations in cash flows for the hedged risk that could affect reported earnings.

- The forecasted transaction is not the acquisition of an asset or incurrence of a liability that will subsequently be remeasured with changes in fair value attributed to the hedged risk reported currently in earnings.
- If the forecasted transaction relates to a recognized asset or liability, the asset or liability is not remeasured with changes in fair value attributable to the hedged risk reported currently in earnings.
- If the variable cash flows of the forecasted transaction relate to a debt security that is classified as held-to-maturity under ASC 320, the risk being hedged is the risk of changes in its cash flows attributable to credit risk, foreign exchange risk, or both.
- The forecasted transaction does not involve a business combination subject to the provisions of ASC 805 (Business Combinations), or a combination of not-for-profit entities subject to the provisions of ASC 958 (Not-for-Profit Entities), and is not a transaction involving *(a)* a parent company's interest in consolidated subsidiaries, *(b)* a noncontrolling interest in a consolidated subsidiary, *(c)* an equity-method investment, or *(d)* an entity's own equity instruments.
- If the hedged transaction is the forecasted purchase or sale of a nonfinancial asset, the designated risk being hedged is *(a)* the risk of changes in the functional-currency-equivalent cash flows attributable to changes in the related foreign currency exchange rates, *(b)* the risk of changes in the cash flows relating to all changes in the purchase price or sales price of the asset, regardless of whether that price and the related cash flows are stated in the entity's functional currency or a foreign currency, or *(c)* the risk of variability in cash flows attributable to changes in a contractually specified component.
- If the hedged transaction is the forecasted purchase or sale of a financial asset or liability, the interest payments on that financial asset or liability, or the variable cash inflow or outflow of an existing financial asset or liability, the designated risk being hedged is *(a)* the overall risk of changes in the hedged cash flows related to the asset or liability, *(b)* for forecasted interest receipts or payments on an existing variable-rate financial instrument, the risk of changes in its cash flows attributable to changes in the contractually specified interest rates, *(c)* the risk of changes in the functional currency-equivalent cash flows attributable to changes in the related foreign currency exchange rates, or *(d)* the risk of changes in cash flows attributable to default, changes in the obligor's creditworthiness, and changes in the spread over the contractually specified interest rate or benchmark interest rate.

Assessing Ongoing Hedge Effectiveness

If a fair value or cash flow hedge initially qualifies for hedge accounting, the entity must continue to assess whether the hedge remains effective. Such an analysis of effectiveness may be done on either a quantitative or a qualitative basis (ASC 815-20-35-2).

Quantitative Analysis of Effectiveness

Quantitative assessments can be based on regression or other statistical analysis of past changes in fair values or cash flows as well as on other relevant information (ASC 815-20-35-2G). If the hedge fails the effectiveness test at any time, the hedge ceases to qualify for hedge accounting. At least quarterly, the hedging entity must determine whether the hedging relationship has been highly effective in having achieved offsetting changes in fair value or cash flows through the date of the periodic assessment (ASC 815-20-35-2).

PRACTICE POINTER: A hedging relationship is considered to be highly effective if the ratio of the change in the fair value of the hedging instrument to the change in the fair value of the hedged item is in the range from 0.80 to 1.25.

Qualitative Analysis of Effectiveness

An entity may elect to use a qualitative approach to testing hedge effectiveness if both of the following criteria are met (ASC 815-20-352A):

- The entity performed a quantitative analysis of effectiveness at the inception of the hedge and the results of that quantitative analysis demonstrate that the hedge is highly effective.
- At the inception of the hedge, the entity can reasonably expect high effectiveness on a qualitative basis in subsequent periods.

If an entity elects to use a qualitative approach to testing hedge effectiveness, the entity must verify and document whenever financial statements or earnings are reported and at least every three months that the hedging relationship has not changed such that it can assert qualitatively that the hedge continues to be highly effective (ASC 815-20-35-2C).

ASC 815-25: FAIR VALUE HEDGES

ACCOUNTING FOR FAIR VALUE HEDGES

Changes in the fair value of derivative instruments that qualify as fair value hedges are recognized currently in earnings, except for amounts excluded from the assessment of effectiveness. The excluded amounts are recognized in earnings through an amortization approach (see ASC 815-20-25-83A). However, the entity may alternatively elect to instead record changes in the fair value of the excluded component currently in earnings (ASC 815-20-25-83B). The gain or loss on the hedged item attributable to the hedged risk adjusts the carrying amount of the hedged item and is recognized currently in earnings (ASC 815-25-35-1).

PRACTICE NOTE: Although ASC 815 generally requires accounting for derivative instruments at fair value, those qualifying as fair value hedges are the only types of hedges for which the change in value is included currently in determining net income. This accounting distinguishes fair value hedges from cash flow hedges and foreign currency hedges and can be expected to result in some volatility in reported income.

PRACTICE NOTE: The application of hedge accounting procedures will typically require a departure from U.S. GAAP when accounting for the hedged item.

An entity shall discontinue prospectively accounting for a fair value hedge if *any* of the following occurs (ASC 815-25-40-1):

- Any criterion of a fair value hedge, or hedged item, is no longer met.
- The derivative expires, or is sold, terminated, or exercised.
- The entity removes the designation of the fair value hedge.

An asset or liability that is designated as a fair value hedge is subject to the applicable U.S. GAAP requirement for assessment of impairment or credit losses (asset) or recognition of an increased obligation (liability) (ASC 815-25-35-10).

ASC 815-30: CASH FLOW HEDGES

ACCOUNTING FOR CASH FLOW HEDGES

If the hedging relationship is highly effective at offsetting changes in cash flows attributable to the hedged risk, an entity must record in other comprehensive income the entire change in the fair value of the designated hedging instrument that is included in the assessment of hedge effectiveness. Similar to fair value hedges, the gain or loss related to a component of the hedge that is excluded from the assessment of hedge effectiveness must be recognized in earnings either through an amortization approach (see ASC 815-20-25-83A), or alternatively in current earnings. Amounts in accumulated other comprehensive income are reclassified into earnings (net income) in the same period in which the hedged forecasted transaction affects earnings (ASC 815-30-35-3).

PRACTICE NOTE: Changes in the fair value of cash flow hedges are not included currently in determining net income as they are with fair value hedges. Rather, they are included in "other comprehensive income," outside the determination of net income.

An entity shall discontinue prospectively accounting for cash flow hedges as specified above if *any* of the following occurs (ASC 815-30-40-1):

- Any criterion for a cash flow hedge, or the hedged forecasted transaction is no longer met.
- The derivative expires, or is sold, terminated, or exercised.
- The entity removes the designation of the cash flow hedge.

If cash flow hedge accounting is discontinued, the accumulated amount in other comprehensive income remains and is reclassified into earnings when the hedged forecasted transaction affects earnings, assuming the forecasted transaction is still probable to occur by the end of the originally specified time period (as documented at hedge inception) or within an additional two-month period of time thereafter. In rare cases, there may be extenuating circumstances that are related to the nature of the forecasted transaction and that are beyond the control of the reporting entity that may permit the entity to keep the balance in other comprehensive income beyond the additional two-month period of time (ASC 815-30-40-4).

However, if it is probable that the forecasted transaction will not occur either by the end of the originally specified time period or within the additional two-month period of time and the hedge does not qualify for the extension due to extenuating circumstances, the gain or loss reported in other comprehensive income must be immediately reclassified into earnings (ASC 815-30-40-5).

PRACTICE NOTE: Due to the economic impact of the COVID-19 pandemic, the cash flow hedges of some forecasted transactions have been discontinued because the forecasted transactions have been determined to no longer be probable of occurring by the originally specified time period or within the additional two-month time period thereafter. In these cases, the postponement or cancellation of the forecasted transactions were considered to be caused by the impact of the COVID-19 pandemic. In response to stakeholders' concerns regarding these discontinued cash flow hedges, the FASB issued a Staff Q&A to provide some additional guidance on the issue, including the following:

Question 1: When cash flow hedge accounting has been discontinued, may delays in the timing of the forecasted transactions related to the effects of the COVID-19 pandemic be considered rare cases caused by extenuating circumstances outside the control or influence of an entity?

FASB Response: Yes. An entity may apply the exception for extenuating circumstances if those delays are related to the effects of the COVID-19 pandemic. When applying the exception, the entity should consider whether the forecasted transactions remain probable over a time period that is reasonable, given the nature of the entity's business, the nature of the forecasted transaction, and the magnitude of the disruption to the entity's business related to the effects of the COVID-19 pandemic.

Question 2: If an entity must reclassify gains and losses from other comprehensive income into earnings because of missed forecasts related to the effects of the COVID-19 pandemic, should those missed forecasts be considered when determining whether the entity has a history of missing forecasts that would call into question the entity's ability to accurately predict forecasted transactions and the propriety of using cash flow hedge accounting in the future for similar transactions?

FASB Response: No. Missed forecasts related to the effects of the COVID-19 pandemic need not be considered when determining whether an entity has a pattern of missing forecasts.

Cash Flow Hedge Disclosures

The following disclosures are required for derivatives that have been designated and qualify as cash flow hedging instruments and the related hedged transactions (ASC 815-30-50-1):

- A description of the transactions or other events that will result in the reclassification into earnings of gains or losses that are reported in accumulated other comprehensive income and the estimated net amount of the existing gains or losses at the reporting date that is expected to be reclassified into earnings within the next 12 months.
- The maximum length of time over which the entity is hedging its exposure to the variability in future cash flows for forecasted transactions excluding those forecasted transactions related to the payment of variable interest on existing financial instruments.

Reporting Changes in Components of Comprehensive Income

Changes in components of comprehensive income are the following:

- Within other comprehensive income, entities must display a separate classification of the net gain or loss on derivative instruments designated and qualifying as fair value or cash flow hedging instruments that are reported in comprehensive income (ASC 815-20-45-3)

- As part of the disclosure of accumulated other comprehensive income in accordance with ASC 220 (Comprehensive Income), entities must disclose the beginning and ending accumulated derivative gain or loss, the related net change associated with current period hedging transactions, the net amount of any reclassification into earnings, and the difference between the change in fair value of an excluded component and the initial value of that excluded component recognized in earnings under an amortization approach in accordance with ASC 815-20-25-83A (ASC 815-30-50-2)

ASC 815-35: NET INVESTMENT HEDGES

FOREIGN CURRENCY HEDGES

If the hedged item is denominated in a foreign currency, ASC 815 indicates that an entity may designate the following types of hedges as hedges of foreign currency exposure (ASC 815-10-05-4):

- A fair value hedge of an unrecognized firm commitment or a recognized asset or liability (including an available-for-sale debt security)
- A cash flow hedge of a forecasted transaction, an unrecognized firm commitment, the forecasted functional-currency equivalent cash flows associated with a recognized asset or liability, or a forecasted intercompany transaction
- A hedge of a net investment in a foreign operation

Foreign currency fair value hedges and cash flows hedges are generally subject to the fair value and cash flow hedge accounting requirements, respectively, covered earlier.

The change in fair value of a derivative instrument that qualifies as a hedge of net investment of a foreign operation is reported in other comprehensive income (outside net income) as part of the cumulative translation adjustment in accordance with ASC 830 (Foreign Currency Matters) (ASC 815-35-35-1).

PRACTICE POINTER: Foreign currency hedges build on the guidance for fair value and cash flow hedges presented earlier, and (for foreign currency hedges of net investments in foreign operations) on accounting for the cumulative translation adjustment requirements of ASC 830. If a foreign currency hedge satisfies the ASC 815 criteria as a fair value or cash flow hedge, it is treated accordingly. If the foreign currency hedge is a hedge of net investment in a foreign operation, it is treated as a part of the cumulative translation adjustment. In this latter case, changes in fair value are included in other comprehensive income (much like a cash flow hedge), and are included in the cumulative translation adjustment rather than separately disclosed.

OFFSETTING DERIVATIVE ASSETS AND LIABILITIES

Offsetting of assets and liabilities in the balance sheet is improper except when the right of setoff exists. ASC 210-20 (Balance Sheet—Offsetting) establishes four criteria that must be satisfied to in turn establish a valid right of setoff. Generally, for an asset and liability to be offset and displayed as a net position, all four of the following criteria must be satisfied (ASC 210-20-45-1):

1. Each party owes the other party determinable amounts.
2. The reporting party has the right to set off the amount payable, by contract or other agreement, with the amount receivable.
3. The reporting entity intends to net settle.
4. The right of setoff is enforceable at law.

Chapter 3, *ASC 210—Balance Sheet*, discusses the guidance related to offsetting of assets and liabilities in greater detail.

An exception to the general offsetting rule exists for derivative contracts executed with the same counterparty under a master netting agreement. A master netting agreement is a contractual agreement entered into by two parties to multiple contracts that provides for the net settlement of all contracts covered by the agreement in the event of default under any one contract. For such derivative contracts, assets and liabilities may be offset and presented as a net amount even if the reporting entity does not meet the requirement in ASC 210 that the reporting entity has the intent to net settle. Offsetting derivative assets and liabilities under this exception is an election and the reporting entity must apply the election consistently.

PRIVATE COMPANY COUNCIL ALTERNATIVE GUIDANCE

Private companies that find it difficult to obtain fixed-rate borrowing may enter into a receive-variable, pay-fixed interest rate swap to economically convert their variable-rate borrowing into a fixed-rate borrowing. Under U.S. GAAP such a swap would be considered a derivative instrument and the entity would be required to recognize the swap at its fair value on their balance sheet as an asset or a liability. Although the entity could elect to apply hedge accounting to mitigate the income statement volatility of recording a swap's change in fair value, many private companies find it difficult to comply with the requirements to qualify for hedge accounting and, therefore, choose to not apply hedge accounting, which results in income statement volatility. However, ASC 815 now includes alternative guidance that allows a private company to apply a 'simplified hedge accounting approach' for certain types of swaps that are entered into for the purpose of economically converting a variable-rate borrowing into a fixed-rate borrowing. This alternative hedge accounting guidance acts as a practical expedient to qualify for cash flow hedge accounting under ASC 815 if certain conditions are met.

Recognition

ASC 815-20-25-3 requires certain documentation to be completed at the hedge inception in order to quality for hedge accounting. However, for private companies that elect to apply the simplified hedge accounting approach, such documentation must be completed by the date on which the first annual financial statements are available to be issued after hedge inception rather than concurrently at hedge inception (ASC 815-20-25-136).

A private company, except for a financial institution as described in ASC 942-320-50-1, may elect the simplified hedge accounting approach for a cash flow hedge of a variable-rate borrowing with a receive-variable, pay-fixed interest rate swap if all of the following conditions are met (ASC 815-20-25-137):

- Both the variable rate on the swap and the borrowing are based on the same index and reset period.
- The terms of the swap are typical (i.e., it is a "plain vanilla swap"), and there is no floor or cap on the variable interest rate of the swap unless the borrowing has a comparable floor or cap.
- The repricing and settlement dates for the swap and the borrowing match or differ by no more than a few days.
- The swap's fair value at inception is at or near zero.
- The notional amount of the swap matches the principal amount of the borrowing being hedged.
- All interest payments occurring on the borrowing during the term of the swap are designated as hedged whether in total or in proportion to the principal amount of the borrowing being hedged.

If all of the above conditions are met, a private company that elects the simplified hedge accounting approach can assume perfect effectiveness in a cash flow hedging relationship involving a variable-rate borrowing and a receive-variable, pay-fixed interest rate swap (ASC 815-20-25-134).

Subsequent Measurement

There have also been questions raised about the relevance and cost associated with measuring a swap at its fair value if the swap is entered into for the purpose of economically converting a variable-rate borrowing to a fixed-rate borrowing. In response to these concerns, the alternative guidance allows a private company that elects to apply the simplified hedge accounting guidance to subsequently measure a receive-variable, pay-fixed interest rate swap at settlement value instead of fair value. The main difference in measuring based on settlement value versus fair value is that nonperformance risk is not included in the calculation of settlement value (ASC 815-10-35-1A, 1B).

Disclosure

If the simplified hedge accounting guidance is used to for a qualifying interest rate swap, the settlement value of that swap may be used in place of fair value when disclosing the information required by ASC 815 (Derivatives and Hedging), or when providing other fair value disclosures such as those required under ASC 820 (Fair Value Measurement). However, any amounts disclosed at settlement value will be subject to all of the same disclosure requirements as amounts disclosed at fair value, and those amounts disclosed at settlement value must be clearly stated as such and disclosed separately from amounts disclosed at fair value (ASC 815-10-50-3).

CODIFICATION IMPROVEMENTS TO HEDGE ACCOUNTING

IMPORTANT NOTICE FOR 2022

As Wolters Kluwer's 2022 *GAAP Guide* goes to press, the FASB has outstanding an Exposure Draft of an Accounting Standards Update (ASU), *Codification Improvements to Hedge Accounting,* that may have an important impact on the preparation of financial statements in the future. The proposed ASU is intended to provide clarification to stakeholders as they implement ASU 2017-12, *Derivatives and Hedging (Topic 815): Targeted Improvements to Accounting for Hedging Activities.* The amendments in this proposed ASU will affect entities that elect to apply hedge accounting in accordance with ASC 815.

This proposed ASU provides clarification on the following issues encountered by stakeholders in the implementation of ASU 2017-12:

- A change in hedged risk in a cash flow hedge
- Contractually specified components in cash flow hedges of nonfinancial forecasted transactions
- Foreign-currency-denominated debt instrument as hedging instrument and hedged item (dual hedge)
- Using the term "prepayable" under the shortcut method

The proposed amendments would be effective for all entities for fiscal years beginning after December 15, 2020. For public business entities, the proposed amendments would be effective for interim periods within fiscal years beginning after December 15, 2020. For all other entities, the proposed amendments would be effective for interim periods within fiscal years beginning after December 15, 2021.

FAIR VALUE HEDGING—PORTFOLIO LAYER METHOD

IMPORTANT NOTICE FOR 2022

As Wolters Kluwer's 2022 *GAAP Guide* goes to press, the FASB has outstanding an Exposure Draft of an Accounting Standards Update (ASU), *Fair Value Hedging—Portfolio Layer Method,* that may have an important impact on the preparation of financial statements in the future. The proposed ASU is intended to provide clarification to stakeholders as they implement ASU 2017-12, *Derivatives and Hedging (Topic 815): Targeted Improvements to Accounting for Hedging Activities.* The amendments in this proposed ASU will affect entities that elect to apply the portfolio layer method that is created by this new guidance.

In response to stakeholder concerns regarding the difficulty of achieving fair value hedge accounting of interest rate risk for portfolios of prepayable financial assets, ASU 2017-12 added the last-of-layer method to make portfolio fair value hedge accounting more accessible for those types of assets. For a closed portfolio of prepayable financial assets, the last-of-layer method allows an entity to hedge a stated amount of the asset or assets in the closed portfolio that is anticipated to be outstanding for the period hedged.

The proposed guidance renames the last-of-layer method as the portfolio layer method and allows multiple-layer hedging relationships to be designated for a single closed portfolio of prepayable financial assets. In applying hedge accounting to multiple-layer strategies, an entity could choose to use different types of derivatives and structures that work best with their individual circumstances. The proposed guidance would require an entity to perform an analysis to support its expectation that the aggregate amount of the hedged layers is anticipated to be outstanding for the periods hedged. Furthermore, all assets in the closed portfolio must have a contractual maturity date after the earliest-ending hedge period and become prepayable before the latest-ending hedge period.

The effective date for the proposed guidance will be determined once a final ASU has been issued.

PART II: INTERPRETIVE GUIDANCE

ASC 815-10: OVERALL

ASC 815-10-15-36A, 15-45(a)(1) Application of the Normal Purchases and Normal Sales Scope Exception to Certain Electricity Contracts within Nodal Energy Markets

OVERVIEW

Under the guidance in FASB Accounting Standards Codification® (ASC) 815, *Derivatives and Hedging,* derivative contracts should be measured at fair value. However, that requirement may be overcome if a contract qualifies for the "normal purchases and normal sales" scope exception discussed in ASC 815-10-15-35 and 15-36. Such contracts involve the purchase or sale of goods or commodities, not financial or derivative instruments, which an entity will use or sell in the normal course of business. Two sets of criteria for the normal purchases and normal sales scope exception are discussed in ASC 815-10-15-22 through 15-44 and in ASC 815-10-15-45 through 15-50. Both sets of criteria require physical delivery and prohibit net settlement to qualify.

For example, a forward contract under which an entity purchases a stated volume of electricity at a fixed price from a company that generates power for delivery to a liquid hub location in an interconnected electricity grid operated by an independent system operator that has established price points at each node or hub location (a nodal energy market) often meets ASC 815's definition of a derivative.

The Emerging Issues Task Force (EITF) addressed this Issue because of diversity in practice. Some stakeholders believed that a forward contract for the sale of electricity may qualify for the normal purchases and normal sales scope exception if electricity is physically delivered to a location within an interconnected electricity grid and one of the parties to the contract incurs charges (or credits) for the subsequent transmission of the electricity based partially on marginal pricing differences at the grid's various locations payable to (or receivable from) an independent system operator. However, others believed that the physical delivery criterion is not met, because they argued that the party that receives the electricity under a forward contract sells the electricity to the independent system operator at the grid entry point at the marginal price at that location and at the same time must purchase the same quantity of electricity from the grid's independent system operator at the marginal price at the exit point; that transaction may result in a charge or a credit if the prices at the two locations differ. Consequently, they believed that the sale of electricity under a forward contract to an independent system operator results in a net settlement of the forward contract, which does not meet the requirements for the normal purchases and normal sales scope exception.

SCOPE

The guidance applies to all entities that enter into forward contracts for the purchase or sale of electricity that will be transmitted or delivered to a location in a nodal energy market. Under such a contract, one of the parties to the contract (an independent system operator) incurs charges (or credits) for the subsequent transmission of the electricity that are partially based on locational marginal price differences payable to (or receivable from) an independent system operator.

ACCOUNTING GUIDANCE

Scope Exceptions—Probable Physical Settlement

ASC 815-10-15-36A has been added to clarify which types of forward contracts for the purchase or sale of electricity and for transmission services under the scope of the guidance qualify for the scope exception and should not be considered to be a series of sequential contracts entered into with the intent to ultimately acquire or sell a commodity as discussed in ASC 815-10-15-41. Those contracts may involve the transmission or delivery of electricity to a location (e.g., a hub location) that differs from the point at which the electricity is ultimately consumed or the point at which the electricity ultimately exits the electricity grid for transmission to a customer load zone. Delivery to those points would be activated by a grid's independent system operator. ASC 815-10-15-36A also provides that the use of locational marginal pricing to determine the transmission charge (or credit) should not be considered to be a net settlement, even if legal title to the related electricity is transferred to the independent system operator during transmission.

Application to Power Purchase or Sale Agreements

ASC 815-10-15-45(a)(1) has been amended to include the criteria that both parties to a contract must meet in order to qualify for the normal purchases and normal sales scope exception. It repeats the information in the discussion above under the scope of the guidance and the discussion of the new guidance in ASC 815-10-15-36A.

ASC 815-10-15-58, 55-45; ASC 815-15-15-9, 15-11, 25-8; ASC 460-10-50-4 through 50-6 Disclosures about Credit Derivatives and Certain Guarantees: An Amendment of ASC 815 and ASC 460

BACKGROUND

As a result of the expansion of the market in credit derivatives, concerns have been raised that the information about derivative instruments and certain guarantees presented in financial reports do not include an adequate discussion of how potential unfavorable changes in credit risk would affect a reporting entity's financial position, financial performance, and the cash flows of sellers of credit derivatives and certain guarantees. As a result of the issuance of this guidance, (*a*) the guidance in ASC 815 has been amended to require that sellers of credit derivatives make such disclosures, including information about derivatives embedded in hybrid instruments, and (*b*) the guidance in ASC 460-10-05-1, 05-2, 10-1, 15-4 through 15-7, 15-9, 15-10, 25-1 through 25-4, 30-1 through 30-4, 35-1 through 35-2, 35-4, 50-2, 50-4 through 50-6, 50-8, 55-2 through 55-3, 55-5 through 55-9, 55-12 through 55-13, 55-15 through 55-18, 55-20 through 55-24, 55-28 through 55-29; ASC 840-10-25-34, 60-2, is amended to require an additional disclosure about the current status of a guarantee's payment and/or performance risk.

ACCOUNTING GUIDANCE

Scope

This pronouncement provides guidance for disclosures about credit derivatives accounted for under the guidance in ASC 815, hybrid instruments that have embedded credit derivatives, and guarantees accounted for under the scope of ASC 460-10.

> A credit derivative is defined under this guidance as follows:
>
> A credit derivative is a derivative instrument (a) in which one or more of its underlyings are related to the credit risk of a specified entity (or a group of entities) or an index based on the credit risk of a group of entities and (b) that exposes a seller to potential loss from credit-risk-related events specified in the contract.

The following guidance applies to credit derivatives, which include credit default swaps, credit spread options, and credit index products, among others. The amendment to ASC 815 also applies to hybrid instruments that have embedded credit derivatives, such as credit-linked notes.

Amendment to Disclosure Requirements of ASC 815

The following guidance applies to sellers of credit derivatives that are defined as "a party that assume financial risk." That party, which is sometimes called a *writer of a contract*, might be "a guarantor in a guarantee-type contract, and any party that provides the credit protection in an option-type contract, a credit default swap, or any other credit derivative contract." ASC 815 is amended to require that sellers of credit derivatives disclose information about their credit derivatives and hybrid instruments that have embedded credit derivatives so that users of financial statements can evaluate the possible effect of those financial instruments on their sellers' financial position, financial performance, and cash flows.

A seller of a credit derivative is required to disclose the following information in its balance sheet about each credit derivative or group of similar credit derivatives, even if there is only a remote likelihood that the seller will have to make any payments under the credit derivative. Disclosures for groups of similar derivatives may be presented by (1) separating the information by major types of contracts, such as single-name credit default swaps, traded indexes, other portfolio products, and swaptions, and (2) further separating the information into additional subgroups for major types of referenced/underlying asset classes, such as corporate debt, sovereign debt, and structured finance. The following information should be disclosed:

a. The nature of the credit derivative, including its approximate term; the reason for entering into it; events or circumstance under which a seller would have to perform under a credit derivative; the balance sheet date of the payment/performance risk of a credit derivative, which could be based on either credit ratings issued by an external source or current internal groupings that the seller uses to manage its risk, and if so, how those internal groupings are determined and used to manage risk.

b. The maximum potential amount of undiscounted future payments that a seller could be required to make under a credit derivative that would not be reduced by the effect of amounts, if any, that may possibly be recovered under provisions in the credit derivative providing for recourse or collateralization (see (d) below). If the maximum potential payments under a credit derivative's terms are unlimited, that fact should be disclosed. In addition, a seller that is unable to estimate the maximum potential amount of future payments under a contract should disclose the reasons for the inability to estimate that amount.

c. A credit derivative's fair value as of the balance sheet date.

d. The nature of (1) recourse provisions, if any, that would enable a seller to recover payments made under a credit derivative from a third party, and (2) assets, if any, held as collateral or by a third party that a seller can obtain and liquidate to recover all or a portion of an amount that would be paid under a credit derivative if a payment is triggered by the occurrence of a specified event or condition. If possible, a seller should estimate the approximate portion of the maximum potential amount under a credit derivative that would be expected to be covered by proceeds from the liquidation of those assets. A seller of credit protection should consider the effect of purchased credit protection with identical underlyings in estimating potential recoveries.

A seller of credit derivatives that are embedded in hybrid instruments should disclose the required information for the total hybrid instruments, not solely for the embedded credit derivatives.

Amendment to Disclosure Requirement of ASC 460

The disclosures required under this guidance are substantially similar to those for guarantors under the guidance' in ASC 460-10-50-4, except for the disclosure about the current status of the payment/performance risk of the credit derivative. Therefore, ASC 460-10-50-4 is amended by to require that the current status of a payment/performance risk of a guarantee be disclosed so that similar disclosures will be made for instruments with similar risks and rewards. That is, a guarantor that uses internal groupings to manage its risk is also required to disclose how those groupings are determined and used to manage risk.

ASC 815-10-15-141 through 15-142, 25-17, 30-5, 35-5, 35-6, 50-9; ASC 320-10-55-5 Accounting for Forward Contracts and Purchased Options to Acquire Securities Covered by ASC 320 and ASC 321

BACKGROUND

An entity enters into forward contracts or purchased options to acquire securities that will be accounted for under the guidance in ASC 320. The forward contracts, purchased options, and underlying securities are denominated in the same currency as the entity's functional currency. A period of time elapses between the date the forward contracts are entered into or the options are purchased and the acquisition date of the underlying securities. This guidance applies only to transactions that involve physical settlement of the securities.

ACCOUNTING ISSUE

How should an entity account for forward contracts and purchased options having no intrinsic value at acquisition that are entered into to purchase securities that will be accounted for under the guidance in ASC 320 or ASC 321 during the time the forward contract or option is outstanding and when the securities are acquired?

ACCOUNTING GUIDANCE

An entity entering into forward contracts and purchased options on debt securities with no intrinsic value at acquisition in order to acquire securities that will be accounted for under the guidance in ASC 320 should designate the forward contracts or purchased options at inception as held-to-maturity, available-for-sale, or trading securities. Those financial instruments should be recognized based on the guidance for the applicable category in ASC 320. Those forward contracts and purchased options should not be used as hedging instruments.

Forward contracts and purchased options on equity securities under the scope of ASC 815-10-15 should be recognized at inception in a manner that is consistent with the guidance in ASC 321 for equity securities. Those forward contracts and purchased options should not be used as hedging instruments.

Forward contracts and purchased options on debt securities that are designated as held to maturity, available for sale, or trading should be measured initially in accordance with the guidance in ASC 320 for that category of security. Forward contracts and purchased options on equity securities should be measured initially according to the guidance in ASC 321.

PRACTICE POINTER: The forward contracts and purchased options discussed above would meet the definition of a derivative in ASC 815 if the asset underlying the derivative contract is convertible to cash. Contracts that permit net settlement would be accounted for in the same manner. Forward contracts and purchased options that are derivatives should be recognized as assets or liabilities and accounted for at fair value in accordance with the guidance in ASC 815.

An entity's accounting policy for the premium paid to acquire an option classified as held-to-maturity or available-for-sale should be disclosed.

After inception, the guidance should be applied to the three categories of debt securities as follows:

1. **Held-to-maturity**
   a. Recognize *no* changes in the fair value of the forward contract or purchased option; recognize a loss in earnings, however, if a decline in the fair value of the underlying securities is other than temporary.
   b. Record debt securities purchased under a forward contract at the forward contract price on the settlement date.
   c. Record debt securities purchased by exercising an option at the option strike price plus the option premium's remaining carrying amount, if any.
   d. If an option to purchase a security expired worthless, record the purchase of the same debt security in the market at its market price plus the option premium's remaining carrying amount, if any.
   e. If an entity does not take delivery under a forward contract or does not purchase the same security in the market if option expires worthless, an entity's intent to hold other debt securities to maturity will be called into question.
2. **Available-for-sale**
   a. Recognize changes in the fair value of a forward contract or purchased option as part of the separate component of shareholders' equity under ASC 320 as they occur; unless a decline in the fair value of the underlying securities is other than temporary
   b. Record debt securities purchased under a forward contract at their fair values on the settlement date.
   c. Record debt securities purchased by exercising an option at the option strike price plus the fair value of the option at the exercise date.
   d. Record the purchase of the same debt security in the market at its market price plus the option premium's remaining carrying amount, if any, if the option to purchase a security expired worthless.
3. **Trading**
   a. Recognize changes in the fair value of a forward contract or purchased option in earnings as they occur.
   b. Record debt securities purchased under a forward contract or by exercising an option at the fair value of the securities at the settlement date.

According to the guidance in ASC 815-10-35-6, changes in the fair value of forward contracts and purchased options on equity securities under the Subsection, "Certain Contracts on Debt and Equity Securities," should be recognized as they occur. Changes in the observable price or impairment of such financial instruments on equity securities that have no readily determinable fair value and are measured under the guidance in ASC 321-10-35-2 should be recognized in earnings as they occur. However, equity securities under the scope of this Subsection that are purchased under a forward contract or by exercising an option should be recorded at their fair value at the settlement date.

PRACTICE POINTER: Because ASC 220 requires that unrealized gains and losses on available-for-sale securities be reported in other comprehensive income, changes in the fair value of forward contracts or purchased options would be reported in that manner. Accumulated changes in value continue to be reported in a separate component of equity.

Illustration of Accounting for Forward Contracts and Purchased Options to Acquire Securities Covered by ASC 320

Example 1

On December 1, 20X5, Rolling Ridge Realty Corp., an entity with a 12/31 year-end, entered into a forward purchase contract to purchase a debt security on February 28, 20X6, at $5,000. The forward purchase contract has no cost. Assume that on December 31, 20X5, the fair value of the debt security declined to $4,500, but the decline is *not* considered to be other than temporary. The fair value of the debt security was $4,000 on the settlement date. The entity should account for the transaction as follows if the debt security is classified as (*a*) held-to-maturity, (*b*) available-for-sale, or (*c*) trading:

(a) Held-to-maturity

December 1, 20X5

A forward contract having no cost is not recognized.

December 31, 20X5

A change in the fair value of the forward contract is not recognized.

February 29, 20X6

The debt security is recognized at the forward contract price on the settlement date.

Debt security	$5,000	
Payable		$5,000

(b) Available-for-sale

December 1, 20X5

A forward contract having no cost is not recognized.

December 31, 20X5

A decline in the fair value of the forward contract is recognized in a separate component of equity and also is reported in comprehensive income in the financial statements.

Equity (separate component)	$500	
Payable		$500

February 29, 20X6

A debt security purchased under a forward contract is recognized at the fair value of the underlying security at the settlement date.

Debt security	$4,000	
Loss on forward contract	1,000	
Payable		$4,500
Equity (separate component)		500

(c) Trading

December 1, 20X5

A forward contract having no cost is not recognized.

December 31, 20X5

A decline in the fair value of the forward contract is recognized in earnings.

Loss on forward contract	$500	
Payable		$500

February 29, 20X6

A debt security purchased under a forward contract is recognized at the fair value of the security on the settlement date.

Debt security	$4,000	
Loss on forward contract	500	
Payable		$4,500

Example 2

On December 1, 20X5, Rolling Ridge Realty Corp., an entity with a 12/31 year-end, purchases an option at a $50 premium to purchase a debt security at $5,000. The option, which has no intrinsic value at acquisition, expires on February 29, 20X6. Assume that the price of the debt security and the fair value of the option are as follows: (*a*) $5,100 and $100, respectively, on December 31, 20X5, and (*b*) $5,200 and $200, respectively, on February 29, 20X6, the settlement date.

The entity should account for the transaction as follows if the debt security is classified as (*a*) held-to-maturity, (*b*) available-for-sale, or (*c*) trading:

(a) Held-to-maturity

December 1, 20X5

The cost of the option is recognized as an asset.

Option	$50	
Cash		$50

December 31, 20X5

A change in the fair value of the option is not recognized.

February 29, 20X6

On the settlement date, the debt security is recognized at the strike price plus the cost of the option.

Debt security	$5,050	
Payable		$5,000
Option		50

(b) Available-for-sale

December 1, 20X5

The cost of the option is recognized as an asset.

Option	$50	
Cash		$50

December 31, 20X5

An unrealized increase in the fair value of the option is recognized in a separate component of equity and also is reported in comprehensive income in the financial statements.

Option	$50	
Equity (separate component)		$50

February 29, 20X6

On settlement, the debt security is recognized at the option strike price plus the fair value of the option on the exercise date.

Debt security	$5,200	
Equity (separate component)	50	
Payable		$5,000
Option		100
Gain on option		150

(c) Trading

December 1, 20X5

The option is recognized as an asset.

Option	$50	
Cash		$50

December 31, 20X5

An increase in the fair value of the option is recognized in earnings.

Option	$50	
Gain on option		$50

February 29, 20X6

On settlement, the debt security is recognized at its fair value.

Debt security		$5,200	
	Payable		$5,000
	Option		100
	Gain on option		100

ASC 815-10-45-2 Offsetting Foreign Currency Swaps

BACKGROUND

An entity has entered into a debt agreement with principal and interest payable in a foreign currency. The entity's functional currency is the U.S. dollar. To avoid fluctuations in the value of the debt resulting from changes in exchange rates, the entity enters into a currency swap contract under which periodically it will receive foreign currency equivalent to its principal and interest payments on the debt (which is denominated in the foreign currency) for which the entity will pay a stipulated amount in U.S. dollars. The swap thus creates a foreign currency receivable and a U.S. dollar payable. If the terms of the swap contract require settlement only of the net change in the contract value, the entity calculates and recognizes that amount at each balance sheet date. Some believe, as a result of these transactions, the U.S. dollar debt replaces the foreign currency debt.

ACCOUNTING ISSUE

How should the effect of a change in exchange rates on a foreign currency swap contract be displayed in the balance sheet?

ACCOUNTING GUIDANCE

The effect of a change in exchange rates (the difference between the accrued receivable and payable) on a foreign currency swap should *not* be netted against foreign currency debt, because a swap and debt are unrelated transactions without the legal right of setoff in ASC 220.

ASC 815-10-45-9; ASC 932-330-35-1 Issues Involved in Accounting for Derivative Contracts Held for Trading Purposes and Contracts Involved in Energy Trading and Risk Management Activities

BACKGROUND

The following guidance was developed because some have questioned whether entities should be permitted to report unrealized gains or losses at the *inception* of energy trading contracts if *no* quoted market prices or other current market transactions with similar terms and counterparties exist. The FASB staff believes that the guidance related to dealer profit indicates that quoted market prices or information about other market conditions is *required* to recognize unrealized gains or losses at the inception of a contract. In addition, there were questions about how the application of the guidance on disclosures in ASC 235-10-05-3 through 05-4; 50-1 through 50-6; 275-10-05-2 through 05-8; 10-1; 15-3 through 15-6; 50-1, 50-2, 50-4, 50-6 through 50-21, 50-23; 55-1 through 55-19; 60-3; 330-10-55-8 through 55-13; 410-30-55-8 through 55-13; 450-20-50-2; 55-36, 55-37; 460-10-55-27; 740-10-55-219 through 55-222; 958-205-60-1; 985-20-55-24 through 5-29, applies to energy trading contracts.

ACCOUNTING ISSUES

1. Should gains and losses on energy trading contracts be reported gross or net in the income statement?
2. Is recognition of unrealized gains and losses at the inception of an energy trading contract appropriate if no quoted market prices or current market transactions for contracts with similar terms exist?
3. What information should companies be required to disclose about energy trading activities?

ACCOUNTING GUIDANCE

Realized and unrealized gains or losses should be presented on a *net* basis for *all* securities accounted for as *derivatives* under the provisions of ASC 815 that are part of a trading activity or held for trading purposes. To clarify the meaning of *trading purposes,* the FASB staff observed that whether derivatives are held for trading purposes depends on an issuer's or holder's intent as discussed in ASC 320-10-25-1—that is, whether the instruments are bought and sold frequently to produce profits on short-term price differences. It was noted that other commodity derivatives, such as gold, are presented net in the financial statements.

SUBSEQUENT DEVELOPMENTS

- The following is a clarification regarding the determination of fair value when a quoted market price is unavailable. The FASB staff believes that the price used in a transaction is the best information available on which to estimate the fair value of a transaction at the inception of an arrangement if there are *no (a) quoted* market prices in an active market, (*b*) *observable* prices of other current market transactions, or (*c*) other *observable data* to use in making a valuation. Consequently, unrealized gains or losses should be recognized on derivative instruments only if the fair value of an instrument can be obtained from quoted market prices in active markets, from observable evidence of comparable market transactions, or based on valuation techniques using observable market data.
- Mark-to-market accounting for energy trading contracts that are not derivative instruments under the guidance in ASC 815 is prohibited. In addition, gains and losses on all derivative instruments under the guidance in ASC 815 that are held for trading purposes should be presented *net* in the income statement, regardless of the method of settlement. Some have questioned whether the guidance regarding the meaning of *trading purposes* in the context of that guidance contradicts the hedge criteria in ASC 815 so that a derivative held for trading purposes could not be designated as a hedge. The FASB staff reported that the clarification regarding the meaning of *trading purposes* was not intended to limit the designation of a derivative as a hedge under the provisions of ASC 815. Therefore, a derivative held for trading purposes may be designated *prospectively* as a hedge if it meets all the related requirements in ASC 815.

PRACTICE POINTER: Derivatives and other financial instruments accounted for under the guidance in ASC 815 should be measured at fair value on initial recognition and in subsequent periods under the guidance in ASC 820-10. The provisions of ASC 820-10 should be applied *retrospectively* in the year in which that guidance is first applied to a financial instrument that was measured at fair value when initially recognized under the provisions of ASC 815 using the transaction price in accordance with the FASB staff's guidance.

SEC OBSERVER COMMENT

The SEC Observer stated that the guidance prohibiting mark-to-market accounting for energy trading contracts that are not derivatives also applies to brokers and dealers in securities, because the guidance applicable to those entities does not provide for specialized accounting in that area.

The SEC Observer also reminded registrants about the required disclosures in Item 303 of Regulations S-K and S-B, which addresses the requirements for Management's Discussion and Analysis, and the guidance in Financial Reporting Release (FRR) 61.

ASC 815-10-45-10, 55-46 through 55-48 Accounting for Options Granted to Employees in Unrestricted, Publicly Traded Shares of an Unrelated Entity

BACKGROUND

This guidance addresses how an employer that grants to its employees stock option awards in the publicly traded shares of an unrelated entity should account for those awards.

ACCOUNTING ISSUE

How should an employer account for stock option awards issued to employees in unrestricted, publicly traded shares of an unrelated entity?

ACCOUNTING GUIDANCE

- Option awards granted to employees in the stock of an unrelated entity that require employees to remain employed for a specified time period and specify the exercise price meet the definition of a derivative in ASC 815 that should be accounted for at its fair value at inception. Subsequent changes in the derivative's fair value should be included in determining net income. The options should continue to be accounted for as a derivative after the award has vested.
- Before an award has vested, an employer should present changes in an option award's fair value as *compensation* expense in the income statement.

After an award has vested, an employer may present changes in an option award's fair value elsewhere in the income statement.

ASC 815-10-55-62 Reporting Realized Gains and Losses on Derivative Instruments That Are Subject to ASC 815 and Not "Held for Trading Purposes" as Defined in ASC 815-10-45-9; ASC 932-330-35-1

> *IMPORTANT NOTICE:* The guidance in ASC 815-10-55-62 will be amended to show that the guidance in ASC 605-45 related to gross versus net indicators will be replaced by the guidance related to principal versus agent considerations in ASC 606-10-55-36 through 55-40 when the guidance in ASU 2014-09, *Accounting for Revenue from Contracts with Costumers*, which will reside in ASC 606 (Revenue from Contracts with Customers), becomes effective for public entities for annual reporting periods that begin after December 15, 2017, and the interim periods therein, and for nonpublic entities for annual reporting periods that begin after December 15, 2018 and interim reporting periods beginning after December 15, 2019.

BACKGROUND

During its discussion of the guidance in ASC 815-10-45-9; ASC 932-330-35-1 (Issues Involved in Accounting for Derivative Contracts Held for Trading Purposes and Contracts Involved in Energy Trading and Risk Management Activities) (see above), the EITF reached a consensus that *all* derivatives instruments held for trading purposes that are accounted for under the provisions of ASC 815 should be reported *net* in the income statement, regardless of whether or not they are settled physically.

ACCOUNTING ISSUE

Should realized gains and losses on contracts *not* held for trading purposes (as defined in ASC 932-330-35-1; 815-10-45-9) that are accounted for as derivatives under the guidance in ASC 815 be reported gross or net in the income statement, regardless of whether the derivative is designated as a hedging instrument?

ACCOUNTING GUIDANCE

- Judgment based on the facts and circumstances, considering the context of the entity's various activities rather than solely on the terms of the contract, should be used to determine whether realized gains and losses on *physically* settled derivative contracts *not* held for trading purposes should be reported in the income statement gross or net; and
- The economic substance of the transaction, the guidance in ASC 845-10 for nonmonetary exchanges, and the gross versus net reporting indicators in ASC 605-45-05-1, 05-2; 15-3 through 15-5; 45-1, 45-2, 45-4 through 45-14, 45-6 through 45-18; 50-1; 55-2, 55-3, 55-5, 55-6, 55-8, 55-9, 55-11 through 55-14, 55-16, 55-18, 55-20, 55-22, 55-24, 55-25, 55-27 through 55-31, 55-33, 55-34, 55-36 through 55-38, 55-40 through 55-45, should also be considered in that decision.

ASC 815-15: EMBEDDED DERIVATIVES

ASC 815-15-25-16 through 25-17D, 25-20 Determining Whether the Host Contract in a Hybrid Financial Instrument Issued in the Form of a Share Is More Akin to Debt or to Equity

BACKGROUND

The guidance in FASB Accounting Standards Codification (ASC) 815, *Derivatives and Hedging* (ASC 815-15-25-1), provides that an embedded derivative should be separated from its host contract if it meets three conditions, one of which is that the embedded derivative's economic characteristics are not "clearly and closely related" to the host contract's economic characteristics. The provisions of ASC 815-15-25-16 through 25-18 are intended to help reporting entities to determine: (1) whether the nature of a host contract in a hybrid financial instrument is more like debt or like equity; (2) whether an embedded derivative's economic characteristics and risks are "clearly and closely related" to the host contract; and (3) whether or not an embedded derivative should be separated from the host contract.

The Emerging Issues Task Force (EITF) was asked to consider this issue because there was diversity in practice in applying that guidance to hybrid financial instruments issued in the form of shares (e.g., shares of preferred stock that give their holders certain preferences or rights over other shareholders). Examples of those rights or preferences may include conversion rights, redemption rights, voting powers, and liquidation and dividend payment preferences. Issuers and investors were using one of the following two methods to determine whether a host contract in a hybrid financial instrument issued as a share is more like equity or more like debt: (1) all of a hybrid financial instrument's terms and features, including those of an embedded derivative, were considered; or (2) all of a hybrid financial instrument's terms and features were considered, but the terms and features of an embedded derivative were excluded. As a result, some hybrid financial instruments that were economically similar were accounted for differently. Also, a hybrid financial instrument's redemption features were considered differently from other features in determining whether the character of a host contract is more like debt or like equity. That is, some believed that a host contract in the form of a share of preferred stock is similar to a debt instrument if it includes a fixed-price, noncontingent redemption option. Others did not believe that the existence of that feature is the only factor in determining whether a host contract is more like a debt or an equity instrument. The objective of the following guidance is to clarify the existing guidance and consequently eliminate diversity in practice.

ACCOUNTING ISSUE

How should an entity determine whether a host contract in a hybrid financial instrument issued in the form of a share is more similar to debt instrument or to an equity instrument?

SCOPE

The following guidance applies to all entities that issue hybrid financial instruments in the form of shares or invest in such financial instruments.

ACCOUNTING GUIDANCE

The following guidance is provided:

Derivatives and Hedging—Embedded Derivatives

Recognition. ASC 815-15-25-17A provides that an entity should determine the nature of a hybrid financial instrument issued in the form of a share by considering:

- All of an instrument's stated and implied substantive terms and features;
- Each term and feature based on the relevant facts and circumstances;
- The economic characteristics and risks of an entire hybrid financial instrument, including the embedded derivative feature that is being considered for potential bifurcation;
- That the existence or omission of a single term or feature, if any, does not necessarily determine a host contract's economic characteristics in the evaluation of its stated and implied substantive terms and features;
- The necessity of using judgment based on an evaluation of all the relevant terms and features, even though an individual term or feature may be weighted more heavily in an evaluation based on the facts and circumstances;
- That the existence of a fixed price, noncontingent redemption option held by an investor in a convertible preferred stock contract, would not, in and of itself, lead to a presumption that a host contract's nature is more similar to a debt instrument or to an equity instrument; and
- That a host contract's nature depends on an entire hybrid financial instrument's economic characteristics and risks.

ASC 815-15-25-17B clarifies that the guidance in ASC 815-15-25-17A for determining whether a host contract in a hybrid financial instrument issued in the form of a share is more like an equity instrument or a debt instrument should be used to evaluate one or more features of an embedded derivative for bifurcation under the guidance in ASC 815-15-25-1(a). The guidance in ASC 815-15-25-17A is not intended to address: (1) when an embedded derivative feature should be bifurcated from a host contract; or (2) the accounting under the guidance if bifurcation is required. It also is not intended to specify how to determine the nature of a host contract in a hybrid instrument that is not issued in the form of a share.

ASC 815-15-25-17C provides that in applying the guidance in ASC 815-15-25-17A, an entity also should consider the substance of a hybrid financial instrument's terms and features relative to their equity-like or debt-like strength in view of the facts and circumstances. The following may be part of an entity's assessment of the relative importance of each term and feature among others:

- The characteristics of the relevant terms and features (e.g., contingent vs. noncontingent or in-the-money vs. out-of-the-money);
- The circumstances under which a hybrid financial instrument was issued or acquired (e.g., characteristics specific to the issuer, such as an issuer is thinly capitalized or well capitalized and profitable); and
- The potential results of a hybrid financial instrument (e.g., an issuer settles by issuing a fixed number of shares, an issuer settles by transferring a specified amount of cash, or an instrument remains a legal-form equity) and the likelihood of the result. The nature of an assessment of potential results may be qualitative.

ASC 815-15-25-17D provides the following examples of common terms and features included in hybrid financial instruments issued in the form of a share and the types of information and indicators that an issuer or an investor may consider in assessing the terms and conditions' substance for determining a host contract's nature, as discussed in ASC 815-15-25-17C.

Redemption rights. An issuer's or investor's ability to redeem a hybrid financial instrument at a fixed or determinable amount is generally considered to be a debt-like characteristic. Not all redemption rights have equal importance. For example, a noncontingent redemption option may have more relative importance in an analysis than a contingent redemption option. The weight given to redemption rights among a hybrid financial instrument's other terms and features may be evaluated based on the following facts and circumstances:

- Are redemption rights held by an issuer or investors;
- Is redemption mandatory;
- Is a redemption right contingent or noncontingent;
- Is a redemption right in-the-money or out-of-the-money (and to what degree);
- Would any laws restrict an issuer or investors from exercising a redemption right (e.g., if redemption would cause an issuer's insolvency);
- Considerations specific to an issuer (e.g., is a hybrid financial instrument essentially a residual interest in an issuer because the issuer is thinly capitalized or the issuer's common equity has already incurred losses or is the issuer a profitable well capitalized entity); and
- If a hybrid financial instrument also contains a conversion right, to which extent is a redemption price or formula more or less favorable than a conversion price or formula, in terms of the economics of the redemption price or formula and the conversion price or formula, not just the form of the settlement at redemption or conversion.

Conversion rights. An investor's ability to convert a preferred share into a fixed number of common shares is generally an equity-like characteristic, but not all conversion rights are equally important. For example, a noncontingent conversion option or one that is deeply in-the-money may carry more weight in an analysis than a conversion option that is contingent on a remote event or is deeply out-of-the-money. The relative weight of conversion rights among a hybrid financial instrument's other terms and features may be evaluated based on information about the following (among other relevant) facts and circumstances:

- Is a conversion right held by an issuer or investors;
- Is conversion mandatory;
- Is a conversion right contingent or noncontingent;
- Is a conversion right in-the-money or out-of-the-money (and to which degree); and
- If a hybrid financial instrument also contains a redemption right held by investors, is conversion more likely to occur before redemption (e.g., an initial public offering or a change in control event is expected before the ability to exercise the right to redemption).

Voting rights. A class of stock's ability to exercise voting rights is generally considered to be an equity-like characteristic, but not all voting rights carry the same weight. For example, voting rights that permit a class of stock to vote on all significant matters may carry more weight in an analysis than voting rights that are only protective. The weight of voting rights among a hybrid financial instrument's other terms and features may be evaluated based on information about the following (among other relevant) facts and circumstances:

- The matters on which an investor's class is permitted to vote (compared to common shareholders); and
- The amount of influence an investor's class of stock can exercise because of its voting rights.

Dividend rights. Dividends can be considered to be a debt-like or equity-like characteristic. For example, mandatory fixed dividends are generally considered to be a debt-like characteristic, but discretionary dividends based on earnings generally are considered to be an equity-like characteristic. The weight of dividend terms among a hybrid financial instrument's other terms and features may be based on information about the following (among other relevant) facts and circumstances:

- Are dividends mandatory or discretionary;
- The basis on which dividends are determined and whether they are stated or participating; and
- Are the dividends cumulative or noncumulative.

Protective covenants. Protective covenants are generally considered to be a debt-like characteristic, but not all protective covenants carry the same weight. Protective covenants that are substantive may carry more weight than covenants that provide only limited protective rights. The weight of protective covenants among a hybrid financial instrument's other terms and features may be evaluated based on information about the following (among other relevant) facts and circumstances:

- Are any collateral requirements like collateralized debt;
- In a hybrid financial instrument that includes a redemption option held by an investor, does the issuer's parent guarantee the issuer's performance on redemption; and
- Does a hybrid financial instrument provide an investor with certain rights like creditor rights (e.g., the right to force bankruptcy or a preference in liquidation).

ASC 815-15-25-37, 25-41 through 21-42, 55-35(c), 55-37(c), 55-39(a), 55-43(b), 55-45(c), 55-47(c), 55-124, 65-3 Contingent Put and Call Options in Debt Instruments

BACKGROUND

The Emerging Issues Task Force (EITF) undertook this project because of diversity in practice in the application of the four-step decision sequence, which was devised by the Derivatives Implementation Group (DIG) to address interpretive questions related to the guidance in the FASB Accounting Standards Codification (ASC). As a result of different interpretations of what the four-step decision sequence is intended to accomplish, two different approaches were being used in practice to determine whether an embedded contingent call (put) option that can accelerate the repayment of principal on debt instruments meets the criterion that its economic characteristics and risks are clearly and closely related to those of the host debt instrument. Under the first approach, only the four-step decision sequence was used as follows to consider whether: (1) the payoff is adjusted based on changes in an index, (2) the payoff is indexed to an underlying other than interest rates or credit risk, (3) the debt involves a substantial premium or discount, and (4) the call (put) option can be exercised contingently. The second approach consisted of an assessment of whether the event that triggers the ability to exercise the call (put) option is indexed only to interest rates, or whether consideration of credit risk is required in addition to the four-step decision sequence. Because the conclusions reached under the two approaches may differ regarding whether a contingent embedded call (put) option is clearly and closely related to its debt host, they may result in different conclusions about whether an embedded call (put) option should be bifurcated and accounted for separately.

ACCOUNTING ISSUE

How does the four-step decision sequence interact with the existing guidance in ASC 815 in assessing whether an embedded contingent call (put) option that can accelerate the repayment of principal on debt instruments meets the criterion that its economic characteristics and risks are clearly and closely related to those of the host debt instrument?

SCOPE

The guidance applies to all entities that invest in or debt instruments (or hybrid financial instruments that are determined to have a debt host) that have been determined to have a debt host with embedded call (put) options.

ACCOUNTING GUIDANCE

The EITF has clarified the existing guidance in ASC 815 for determining whether contingent call (put) options that can accelerate the payment of principal on debt instruments are clearly and closely related to their debt hosts by reaching a consensus that the assessment should be based solely on the four-step decision sequence in ASC 815-15-25-42. Consequently, the existing guidance in Topic 815 has been amended as follows:

- ASC 815-15-25-40. Superseded by the ASU's guidance.
- ASC 815-15-25-41. Deleting the first sentence through "In contrast," in the second sentence, which now begins with "Call."
- ASC 815-15-25-42. The four-step decision sequence is amended as follows:
  - — Step 1: In the first sentence, deleting "(rather than simply being the repayment of principal at par, together with any unpaid accrued interest)."

 — Step 2: In the last sentence, deleting "as well as under the provisions of paragraphs 815-15-25-1 and 815-15-25."
 — Step 3: Rewriting the third sentence to state: "If no, further analysis of the contract under paragraph 815-15-25-26 is required, if applicable."
 — Step 4: "If not contingently exercisable, further analysis of the contract under paragraph 815-15-25-26 is required, if applicable."

- ASC "815-15-25-40," which has been superseded, is replaced by "815-15-25-41" in the following paragraphs: ASC 815-15-25-37, 55-35(c), 55-37(c), ASC 815-15-55-39(a) and 55-39(b), 55-43(b), 55-45(c), 55-47(c), and 55-124.

TRANSITION AND EFFECTIVE DATE

The following is the transition and effective date guidance in ASC 815-15-65-3:

- The amended guidance is effective for financial statements issued by public business entities for fiscal years that begin after December 15, 2016, and interim periods within those fiscal years.
- All other entities will be required to apply the guidance in financial statements issued for fiscal years that begin after December 15, 2017, and in interim periods within fiscal years that begin after December 15, 2018.
- The amended guidance should be applied to existing debt instruments on a modified retrospective basis as of the beginning of the fiscal year for which the guidance is effective. An entity that had bifurcated an embedded derivative but is no longer required to do so as a result of applying the amended guidance should account for the debt instrument's carrying amount at the adoption date at the debt host contract's carrying amount plus the fair value of the previously bifurcated embedded derivative. A premium or discount that results from applying the amended guidance should not affect the entity's assessment of whether the call (put) option is clearly and closely related to the debt instrument. In other words, for the purpose of analyzing an embedded derivative, upon adoption, an entity should consider the host contract's and call (put) option's economic characteristics and risks as they existed at the date of the instrument's initial recognition (at issuance or acquisition). No cumulative-effect adjustment to beginning retained earnings for the period of adoption is necessary.
- An entity that had bifurcated an embedded derivative but is no longer required to do so as a result of applying the amended guidance has a one-time option, as of the beginning of the fiscal year for which the guidance is effective, to irrevocably elect to measure the entire debt instrument at fair value with changes in fair value recognized in earnings, if the instrument is under the scope of ASC 825-10-15-4 through 15-5. If a fair value election is made, the effects of initially complying with the amended guidance should be reported as a cumulative-effect adjustment directly to retained earnings as of the beginning of the fiscal year in which the amended guidance is adopted.
- Earlier application of the amended guidance is permitted, including adoption in an interim period. An entity that early adopts the amended guidance in an interim period should show adjustments as of the beginning of the fiscal year that includes the interim period.
- An entity should provide the disclosures in ASC 250-10-50-1(a), 50-1(b)(3), and 50-2, as applicable, in the period in which the amended guidance is adopted.

ASC 815-15-35-4, 40-1 through 40-2, 40-4, 50-3; ASC 470-20-25-16 Issuer's Accounting for a Previously Bifurcated Conversion Option in a Convertible Debt Instrument When the Conversion Option No Longer Meets the Bifurcation Criteria in ASC 815

BACKGROUND

Under the guidance in ASC 815, convertible debt with an embedded conversion option must be bifurcated to separate the conversion option from its host contract and accounted for separately as a derivative if the three conditions discussed in ASC 815-15-25-1 are met. Because under the guidance in ASC 815 an entity must reassess in each reporting period whether an embedded conversion option meets the conditions for bifurcation, sometimes an embedded conversion option that has been separated from its host contract no longer meets the conditions for separate accounting as a derivative. This Issue was undertaken because opinions vary as to how to account for the change. Some believe that the change should be recognized by combining the liability related to the derivative with the liability on the debt instrument. Proponents of this view believe that a premium resulting from the change should be amortized over the remaining term of the debt. Others reclassify the carrying value of the liability on the derivative and combine it with the liability on the debt instrument only as long as the future amortization of a premium that results from the transaction does *not* result in a negative effective yield.

ACCOUNTING ISSUE

How should an issuer account for a previously bifurcated conversion option in a convertible debt instrument if that conversion option no longer meets the criteria for bifurcation in ASC 815?

ACCOUNTING GUIDANCE

- An issuer should reclassify the carrying amount of a liability related to an embedded conversion option in a convertible debt instrument that had been bifurcated but that no longer meets the criteria for bifurcation in FAS-133 to shareholders' equity at its fair value on the date the liability is reclassified. Amortization of a debt discount, if any, recognized when a conversion option was originally bifurcated from a convertible debt instrument should continue.
- An issuer should immediately recognize as interest expense the unamortized amount of a discount, if any, which remains at the conversion date, if a holder exercises a conversion option whose carrying amount had been reclassified to shareholders' equity under the guidance in this Issue.
- If a convertible debt instrument with a conversion option whose carrying amount had been reclassified to shareholders' equity according to the guidance in this Issue is extinguished for cash or other assets before its stated maturity date, the issuer should allocate the reacquisition price as follows: (*a*) allocate to equity the portion that equals the fair value of the conversion option at the extinguishment date, and (*b*) allocate the remaining amount to the debt extinguishment to determine the amount of a gain or loss.

This guidance is *not* inconsistent with the guidance in ASC 470-20-05-2 through 05-6; 25-2, 25-3, 25-10 through 25-13; 30-1, 30-2; 505-10-60-3, because *(a)* the instrument was bifurcated initially in accordance with the guidance in ASC 815, and *(b)* the guidance in ASC 470-20 applies to convertible debt instruments only at issuance, not to subsequent changes.

DISCLOSURE

Issuers should disclose the following information for the period in which an embedded conversion option that was previously accounted for as a derivative under the guidance in ASC 815 no longer meets the criteria for bifurcation:

- A description of the principal changes as a result of which an embedded conversion option is no longer required to be bifurcated under the guidance in FAS-133.
- The amount of a liability that is reclassified to stockholders' equity.

ASC 815-20: HEDGING—GENERAL

ASC 815-20-25-3 Documentation of the Methods Used to Measure Hedge Ineffectiveness under ASC 815

The guidance below was based on a FASB staff announcement at a meeting of the Emerging Issues Task Force (EITF) to clarify the guidance in ASC 815 related to the required documentation at the beginning of fair value, cash flow, and net investment hedges. According to the FASB staff, the guidance in ASC 815-20-25-3 and ASC 815-30-35-11 through 35-32, 55-91 through 55-93 requires formal documentation, at the beginning of a hedge, about the hedging relationship, and the entity's risk management objective for entering into the hedge. The following information was required:

- The hedging instrument.
- The hedged item or transaction.
- The nature of the hedged risk.
- The method used to retrospectively and prospectively evaluate whether the hedging instrument will be effective in offsetting the exposure to changes in an item's fair value or variability in cash flows attributed to the hedged risk. An entity should plan to assess a hedged instrument's effectiveness on a reasonable basis.

PRACTICE NOTE: ASU 2017-12, *Derivatives and Hedging (Topic 815): Targeted Improvements to Hedging Activities*, amends the guidance in ASC 815-20-25-3 to require the following additional information:

- An initial prospective assessment of hedge effectiveness on a quantitative basis by a dollar-offset test or a statistical method unless one of the following apply:
  - — Cash flow or fair value hedge—If the shortcut method in ASC 815-20-25-102 through 25-117 is used or it is determined that the hedging instrument's and the hedged item's critical terms match in accordance with ASC 815-20-25-84 through 25-85.

  - Cash flow hedge—(*a*) The hedging instrument is an option meeting the conditions in ASC 815-20-25-129 through 25-129A; (*b*) a **private company** that is not a financial institution is applying the simplified hedge accounting approach in ASC 815-20-25-133 through 25-138; (*c*) hedge effectiveness is assessed under the change in variable cash flow methods in ASC 815-30-35-16 through 35-29 and all the hedging instrument's and the hedged item's critical terms are the same.
  - Net investment hedge—Hedge effectiveness is assessed using a method based on changes in: (*a*) spot exchange rates and the conditions in ASC 815-35-35-5 (for derivatives) or ASC 815-35-35-12 (for non-derivatives) are met; or (*b*) forward exchange rates and the conditions in ASC 815-35-35-17A are met.
- An initial prospective quantitative assessment of hedge effectiveness based on information as of a hedge's inception date is considered to be performed at that time if it is completed by the earliest of the following:
  - The date of the first quarterly hedge effectiveness assessment.
  - The availability for issuance of financial statements including the hedged transaction.
  - The date that any criterion in ASC 815-20-25 no longer is met.
  - The date that the hedging instrument expires, is sold, terminated, or exercised.
  - The date a hedging relationship is dedesignated.
  - The date that a cash flow hedge of a forecasted transaction (in accordance with the guidance in ASC 815-20-25-13(b)) occurs.
- At the inception of a hedge, an entity is required to document whether it elects to subsequently perform retrospective and prospective hedge effectiveness assessments based on qualitative information and how. An entity also is required to document which quantitative method it would use if a hedge relationship's facts and circumstances change so that hedge effectiveness must be assessed quantitatively in accordance with ASC 815-20-35-3D. In addition, an entity should document that it will use the same quantitative method to assess hedge effectiveness initially and subsequently. ASC 815-20-55-55 through 55-56 provide guidance regarding a change in quantitative method after an initial quantitative effectiveness assessment was performed.
- If an entity applies the short cut method in ASC 815-20-25-102 through 25-117, it may elect to document at the inception of a hedge a quantitative method that it would use to assess hedge effectiveness and to measure a hedge's results if it determines a point during the hedge relationship's term that it is no longer appropriate to use the shortcut method.
- ASC 815-20-25-3(b)(2)(v) has been superseded by ASU 2017-12, *Derivatives and Hedging (Topic 815): Targeted Improvements to Accounting for Hedging Activities*.
- An entity is required to support its expectation that a hedged item in a hedging relationship that is designated under the last-of-layer method will be outstanding as of the hedged item's maturity date (see ASC 815-20-25-12A(a)).
- ASC 815-20-25-3A has been added to direct users of the information in ASC 815-20-25-3 to ASC 815-20-25-133 through 25-142 for guidance on the documentation of hedge relationships by private companies that are not financial institutions and by entities using the simplified hedge accounting approach.

- The method to be used to measure hedge ineffectiveness (including when the change in fair value method discussed in Issue G7 of the Implementation Guide is used).

ASC 815-20-25-6 through 25-6A Inclusion of the Fed Funds Effective Swap Rate (or Overnight Index Swap Rate) as a Benchmark Interest Rate for Hedge Accounting

BACKGROUND

ASC 815 (Derivatives and Hedging) provides guidance related to the risks that an entity is permitted to hedge in a fair value or cash flow hedge. Interest rate risk is the risk that the fair value of a recognized asset or liability or a transaction's cash flows may change as a result of a change in the interest rate of a designated benchmark interest rate, which is defined in the ASC's Glossary as, "A widely quoted rate in an active financial market that is broadly indicative of the overall level of interest rates attributable to high-credit-quality obligors in that market." Until the issuance of ASU 2013-10, the use of only two benchmark interest rates was permitted under the guidance in ASC 815: (1) the interest rate on direct Treasury obligations of the U.S. government (UST); and, for practical reasons, (2) the London Interbank Offered Rate (LIBOR) swap rate.

Since the 2008 financial crisis, entities have experienced increased exposure to the Fed Funds Effective Swap Rate (also known as the Overnight Index Rate or OIS) and there has been a significant increase in demand for the ability to hedge that rate. In part, it has occurred as a result of an increase of overnight interbank trading by depository institutions that hold balances at the Federal Reserve and lend surplus funds to other banks that need to increase the overnight balances of their accounts. The weighted average of this rate from all such transactions on any particular day is referred to as the daily Fed Funds rate. The related Fed Funds Effective Swap Rate (which represents the Overnight Index Swap Rate or OIS in the United States) is the fixed rate swapped in exchange for a floating overnight rate, which is the Fed Funds Effective Rate. Other reasons for the increased importance of the OIS rate is the greater, and sometimes volatile, spread between LIBOR and OIS, and new regulations to restrict systemic risks, such as a requirement for increased collateralization of derivatives. Respondents on the exposure draft of the proposed ASU, which proposed that OIS should be a permitted U.S. benchmark interest rate, were very supportive of the proposal.

SCOPE

The guidance in ASU 2013-10 applies to all entities, public and nonpublic, that elect to hedge a benchmark interest rate in transactions accounted for under the guidance in ASC 815.

ACCOUNTING ISSUE

Should the use of the Fed Funds Effective Swap Rate (OIS) be permitted in addition to the interest rate on direct Treasury obligations of the U.S. government (UST), and, for practical reasons, the London Interbank Offered Rate (LIBOR) swap rate?

ACCOUNTING GUIDANCE

The following is the definition of the "Fed Funds Effective Swap Rate (or Overnight Index Swap Rate)," which has been added to the Master Glossary of the ASC:

> The fixed rate on a U.S. dollar, constant-notional interest rate swap that has its variable-rate leg referenced to the Fed Funds effective rate with no additional spread over the Fed Funds effective rate on that variable-rate leg. That fixed rate is the derived rate that would result in the swap having a zero fair value at inception because the present value of fixed cash flows, based on that rate, equates to the present value of the variable cash flows.

Benchmark Interest Rates

ASC 815-20-25-6A has been amended to include the Fed Funds Effective Swap Rate (also referred to as the Overnight Index Swap Rate or OIS) as a benchmark interest rate in addition to the UST rate and LIBOR. In addition, the Fed Funds rate also may be used as a benchmark rate in the United States.

PRACTICE NOTE: ASU 2017-12 has amended ASC 815-20-25-6A to include the Securities Industry and Financial Markets Association (SIFMA) Municipal Swap Rate to the rates considered to be benchmark rates. The last sentence of ASC 815-20-25-6A, which prohibited the use of the Prime Rate, the Federal National Mortgage Association (FNMA or Fannie Mae) Par Mortgage Rate, and the Securities Industry and Financial Markets Association Swap Index (formerly the Bond Market Association index) as a benchmark interest rate in the United States, has been deleted.

PRACTICE NOTE: ASU 2018-16, *Derivatives and Hedging (Topic 815): Inclusion of the Secured Overnight Financing Rate (SOFR) Overnight Index Swap (OIS) Rate as a Benchmark Interest Rate for Hedge Accounting Purposes*, has amended ASC 815-20-25-16A, which lists the benchmark rates for direct Treasury Obligations of the U.S. government by revising the "Fed Funds Effective Swap Rate" to be the "Fed Funds Effective Rate Overnight Index Swap Rate" and deleted "(referred to as the Overnight Index Swap Rate)," and inserted "the Secured Overnight Financing Rate (SOFR) Overnight Index Swap Rate." Entities that have not already adopted the amendments in ASU 2017-12 are required to adopt the amendments in this ASU concurrently with those in ASU 2017-12. The amendments are effective for fiscal years beginning after December 15, 2018, and interim periods within those fiscal years for public business entities that have already adopted the amendments in ASU 2017-12. For all other entities that have already adopted the amendments in ASU 2017-12, the amendments are effective for fiscal years beginning after December 15, 2019, and interim periods within those fiscal years. Early adoption is permitted in any interim period upon issuance of this ASU if an entity has already adopted ASU 2017-12.

ASC 815-25: FAIR VALUE HEDGES

ASC 815-25-35-14, 55-52; ASC 815-30-35-45 Effect of Derivative Gains and Losses on the Capitalization of Interest

BACKGROUND

According to the guidance in ASC 835-20, the purpose of capitalizing interest costs of an acquired asset is to measure interest cost incurred to finance an asset acquisition that would otherwise not have been incurred. Under that guidance, interest that is eligible for capitalization on qualified assets includes interest on borrowings and obligations with explicit interest rates, interest imputed in accordance with the guidance in ASC 835-30 on certain types of payables. If the specific interest on a new borrowing can be associated with the eligible portion of the asset, that rate should be used for interest capitalization purposes. Otherwise, a weighted average of the rates on borrowings is applied to expenditures not related to specific new borrowings. Interest capitalization during a period is limited to the amount of interest incurred during the period.

This Issue has been raised because there is diversity in practice when the guidance in ASC 835-20 is applied in connection with the guidance in ASC 815 to interest costs in a fair value hedge accounting model.

ACCOUNTING ISSUE

Should the interest rate used to capitalize interest costs according with the guidance in ASC 835-20 on the historical cost of certain assets be the effective yield after gains and losses have been recognized on the effective portion of a derivative instrument that qualifies as a fair value hedge of fixed interest rate debt or should the original effective interest rate on that debt be used?

ACCOUNTING GUIDANCE

An entity that elects to begin amortizing adjustments of the carrying amount of a hedged liability under the guidance in ASC 815-25-55-66 should include those amounts in interest costs used to determine the capitalization rate under the guidance in ASC 835-20. Interest costs related to the ineffective portion of a fair value hedge should *not* be included in the capitalization rate.

In the example in ASC 815-25-55-46, 55-48, the entity decides to immediately begin amortizing the adjustments of the carrying amount of the fixed rate debt while the hedge is still in place. If the entity in that example recognizes as interest expense the fair value change attributed to the passage of time, the amounts recognized as expenses in ASC 815-25-55-48 would be eligible for capitalization under the guidance in ASC 835-20.

Under the guidance in ASC 815, a gain or loss on the hedging instrument in a cash flow hedge is not permitted to be capitalized as a basis adjustment of the qualifying assets. Under the guidance in ASC 815-30-35-3, 35-7, 35-38 through 35-41, amounts accumulated in other comprehensive income must be reclassified into earnings in the period in which the forecasted transaction affects earnings. Because an asset's depreciable life coincides with the amortization period of the capitalized interest on the debt, the FASB staff believes that amounts accumulated in comprehensive income that are related to a cash flow hedge of the fluctuations in the variable interest rate on a specific borrowing associated with an asset under construction for which interest costs are capitalized as a cost of that asset should be reclassified into earnings over the depreciable life of the constructed asset.

ASC 815-25-40-1A, ASC 815-30-40-1A, ASC 815-20-55-56 through 55-56A, ASC 815-20-65-2 Effect of Derivative Contract Novations on Existing Hedge Accounting Relationships

BACKGROUND

A novation of a derivative contract occurs when one of the parties to a derivative contract is replaced with a different party. Novations of derivative contracts may occur as a result of mergers of financial institutions, intercompany novations, an entity's exit from a particular derivatives business relationship, an entity's management against internal credit limits, and in response to laws or regulatory requirements. A derivative instrument undergoing a novation may be the hedging instrument in a hedge accounting relationship that was designated under the guidance in ASC 815.

The Emerging Issues Task Force (EITF) addressed the Issue of the novation of a derivative instrument that had been designated as a hedging instrument under the guidance in ASC 815 because the guidance in ASC 815 did not specifically address how a change in the counterparty to a derivative instrument may affect an existing hedge accounting relationship. In addition, there was diversity in practice in the application of the limited existing guidance.

ACCOUNTING ISSUE

Would a change in the counterparty to a derivative instrument that had been designated as a hedging instrument under the guidance in ASC 815 trigger the requirement that the hedge accounting relationship be dedesignated, thus, discontinuing the application of hedge accounting?

ACCOUNTING GUIDANCE

The following guidance clarifies that a change in the counterparty to a derivative instrument that was designated as a hedging instrument under the guidance in ASC 815 would not, "in and of itself," result in the requirement that the hedge accounting relationship be dedesignated if all the other criteria for hedge accounting, including those in ASC 815-20-35-14 through 35-18 continue to be met.

The following are the related amendments:

- *Derivatives and Hedging—Fair Value Hedges.* ASC 815-25-40-1 lists three conditions under which hedge accounting would have to be discontinued for a fair value hedge. ASC 815-25-40-1A has been added to clarify the guidance in ASC 815-25-40-1 by providing that "a change in the counterparty to a derivative instrument that has been designated as the hedging instrument in an existing hedging relationship would not, in and of itself, be considered a termination of the derivative instrument."
- *Derivatives and Hedging—Cash Flow Hedges.* ASC 815-30-40-1 lists three conditions under which hedge accounting would have to be discontinued for a cash flow hedge. ASC 815-30-40-1A has been added to clarify the guidance in ASC 815-30-40-1 by providing that "a change in the counterparty to a derivative instrument that has been designated as the hedging instrument in an existing hedging relationship would not, in and of itself, be considered a termination of the derivative instrument."
- *Derivative and Hedging—Hedging—General.* ASC 815-20-55-56 provides general implementation guidance regarding the dedesignation of an original hedging relationship when an entity changes any of that relationship's critical terms that were documented at the relationship's inception. ASC 815-20-55-56A has been added to clarify the guidance in ASC 815-20-55-56 by providing that "a change in the counterparty to a derivative instrument that has been designated as the hedging instrument in an existing hedging relationship would not, in and of itself, be considered a change in a critical term of the hedging relationship."

TRANSITION AND EFFECTIVE DATE

The following guidance is included in ASC 815-20-65-2:

- The guidance is effective for public business entities for fiscal years that begin after December 15, 2016, and interim periods within those fiscal years.
- The guidance is effective for all other entities for fiscal years that begin after December 15, 2017, and interim periods within fiscal years that begin after December 15, 2018.
- The guidance should be applied prospectively or on a modified retrospective basis.
- Entities that elect to apply the guidance prospectively should apply it to all existing hedging relationships in which the counterparty to a derivative instrument changed after the guidance has been adopted.
- Entities that elect to apply the guidance using a modified retrospective approach should apply it to all derivative instruments meeting all of the following conditions:
  - — The derivative instrument was outstanding during all or a portion of the periods presented in the financial statements.
  - — The derivative instrument was previously designated as a hedging instrument in a hedging relationship.
  - — The hedging relationship was dedesignated only as a result of a novation of the derivative instrument, and all other hedge accounting criteria would have otherwise continued to be met (including those in ASC 815-20-35-14 through 35-18).
- Under the modified retrospective approach, an entity should not revise its financial statements for derivative instruments that are no longer outstanding as of the beginning of the earliest period presented in the financial statements.

- Under the modified retrospective approach, the effect of the hedge designation of derivative instruments that were dedesignated from hedging relationships during a period presented in the financial statements should be removed from each period presented.
- Under the modified retrospective approach, for derivative instruments that were dedesignated from hedging relationships before the beginning of the earliest period presented but that remain outstanding during all or a portion of the periods presented:
  - — The effect of the hedge dedesignation should be removed from the financial statements for each period presented; and
  - — Beginning retained earnings should reflect a cumulative-effect adjustment for effects to financial statements before the beginning of the earliest period presented.
- Under the modified retrospective approach, assessments of effectiveness and measurements of ineffectiveness required under the original hedge documentation should be performed for all periods between the date on which the hedging relationship was dedesignated as a result of a novation and the date on which this guidance was adopted.
- Early application of the guidance is permitted for all entities, including in an interim period.
- The disclosures in ASC 250-10-50-1(a) and 50-2, as applicable, should be provided in the period in which the guidance is adopted.
- An entity that elects to apply the guidance using the modified retrospective approach also should provide the disclosures in ASC 250-10-50-1(b)(1) and (b)(3), as applicable, in the period in which this guidance is adopted.

ASC 815-40: CONTRACTS IN ENTITY'S OWN EQUITY

ASC 815-40-05-1 through 05-4, 05-10 through 05-12, 25-1 through 25-5, 25-7 through 25-20, 25-22 through 25-24, 25-26 through 25-35, 25-37 through 25-40, 30-1, 35-1 through 35-2, 35-6, 35-8 through 35-13, 40-1 through 40-2, 50-1 through 50-5, 55-1 through 55-18, 55-52; ASC 815-15-25-15; ASC 815-10-15-78; ASC 460-10-60-14; ASC 480-10-55-63; ASC 505-10-60-5
Accounting for Derivative Financial Instruments Indexed to, and Potentially Settled in, a Company's Own Stock

BACKGROUND

PRACTICE POINTER: ASC 480-10 (formerly FAS-150) provides guidance for issuers on the classification and measurement of financial instruments with the characteristics of both liabilities and equity. Financial instruments under the scope of that guidance must be classified as liabilities or as assets in some situations.

The guidance in this Issue has been *partially nullified* as follows:

- Free-standing instruments under the scope of ASC 480-10 (FAS-150), such as forward purchase contracts, written put options, and certain other instruments that can be settled with the issuer's equity shares, must be classified as liabilities and measured in accordance with that guidance.
- Nonpublic entities are no longer permitted to classify proceeds from put warrants as equity. In accordance with the provisions ASC 480-10, a liability should be recognized for a put warrant that includes an obligation to repurchase an issuer's equity shares, or one that is indexed to such an obligation, which requires or may require a transfer of assets. Put warrants that include an obligation to issue a variable number of shares if the value of that obligation is primarily based on (*a*) a fixed sum of money at inception, (*b*) variations based on something different than the fair value of the issuer's shares, or (*c*) variations inversely related to changes in the fair value of the issuer's equity shares are also included under the scope of ASC 480-10 Put warrants *not* under the scope of ASC 480-10 should be accounted for under the guidance in this Issue. (See ASC 480-10-55-29 through 55-32; 40-42 through 40-52 for additional guidance on put warrants.)
- The guidance in ASC 480-10 (FAS-150) *nullifies* the requirement under this Issue (which is analogous to the SEC's guidance in ASR-268) that public companies account as temporary equity for the cash redemption amounts of obligations to deliver cash in exchange for the entity's own shares in physical settlements of freestanding financial instruments classified as equity. Such amounts should be classified as liabilities under the guidance in ASC 480-10

(FAS-150) and measured at their fair value or at the present value of the redemption amount, unless the Statement requires a different valuation or other accounting guidance applies.

- The guidance in this Issue continues to apply when financial instruments embedded in other financial instruments that are *not* derivatives in their entirety are evaluated for bifurcation under ASC 815 (FAS-133), such as written put options embedded in nonderivative host contracts, because the guidance in ASC 480-10 (FAS-150) does *not* apply to such financial instruments. That is, an embedded written option that would have been classified in equity under this Issue before the guidance in ASC 480-10 (FAS-150) was issued would continue to be considered an equity instrument when evaluating whether an embedded derivative could be bifurcated under the guidance in ASC 815-15-25-1 (paragraph 12 of FAS-133).

An entity may enter into contracts that are indexed to and settled in its own stock for various economic reasons, for example, to hedge share dilution from existing written call options, to hedge the effect of existing written option positions on earnings, to hedge planned future purchases of treasury stock, to hedge a planned future issuance of shares, or to hedge the cost of a business combination. The following are such contracts:

- *Forward sale contract* A contract requiring an entity to sell a specific number of its shares of stock at a specific price on a specific future date. For example, an entity enters into a contract to sell 500 shares of its common stock at $50 per share on June 30, 20X8. The entity has a loss if the market price of the stock is more than $50 per share on that date. Conversely, the entity has a gain if the market price of the stock is less than $50 per share on that date.
- *Forward purchase contract* A contract requiring an entity to purchase a specific number of shares of its stock at a specific price on a specific future date. For example, an entity enters into a contract to purchase 500 shares of its common stock at $50 per share on June 30, 20X8. The entity has a gain if the market price of the stock is more than $50 per share on that date. Conversely, the entity has a loss if the market price of the stock is less than $50 per share on that date.
- *Purchased put option* A contract giving an entity a right to, but not requiring it to, sell a specific number of its shares of stock at a specific price on a specific future date. For example, an entity may purchase a right to sell 500 shares of its common stock at $50 per share on June 30, 20X8. The entity has a gain if the market price of the stock is less than $50 per share on that date. The contract is worthless if the market price of the stock is more than $50 per share on that date because the entity would not exercise the option if it can sell shares for more elsewhere.
- *Purchased call option* A contract giving an entity the right to, but not requiring it to, buy a specific number of its shares of stock at a specific price on a specific future date. For example, an entity may purchase a right to buy 500 shares of its common stock at $50 per share on June 30, 20X8. The entity has a gain if the market price of the stock is more than $50 per share on that date. The contract is worthless if the market price of the stock is less than $50 per share on that date because the entity would not exercise the option if it can buy shares for less elsewhere.
- *Written put option* A contract sold by an entity giving the holder the right, but not the obligation, to sell to the entity a specific number of the entity's shares of stock at a specific price on a specific future date. For example, an entity may sell put options giving the holder the right to sell to the entity 500 shares of its common stock at $50 per share on June 30, 20X8. If the market price is less than $50, the option will expire unexercised because the holder can buy the shares for less on the open market. The entity's gain will be limited to the option premium received.
- *Written call option (and warrant)* A contract sold by an entity giving the holder the right, but not the obligation, to purchase a specific number of the entity's shares of common stock at a specific price on a specific future date. For example, an entity may sell a call option giving the holder the right to purchase 500 shares of the entity's common stock at $50 per share on June 30, 20X8. If the market price is less than $50 per share on that date, the option will expire unexercised, because the holder can purchase the shares for less on the option market. The entity's gain will be limited to the option premium. If the market price is more than $50 on that date, the holder will exercise the option and the entity will have a loss.

Such contracts may be settled as follows:

- *Physical settlement.* The buyer delivers the full stated amount of cash and the seller delivers the full stated number of shares.
- *Net share settlement.* The party incurring a loss delivers to the party realizing a gain shares equal to the current fair value of the gain.
- *Net cash settlement.* The party incurring a loss pays cash to the party realizing a gain in an amount equal to the gain; no shares are exchanged.

The contracts may be freestanding, that is, they are entered into separately from the entity's other financial instruments or equity transactions, or they are entered into with another action, but the contract can be detached legally and exercised separately. Although such contracts may be embedded, that is, be an integral part of a debt security (see ASC 480-10-55-29 through 55-32; 40-42 through 40-52 for an example of such a security), the contracts discussed in this Issue are freestanding.

The EITF discussed the initial recognition of written put options in Issue 87-31, which is codified in this Issue. Under that consensus, proceeds received on the sale of written put options were recognized as equity transactions. Changes in the market value of the options were not recognized. Although the consensus in Issue 87-31 did not specify the method of settlement, it is clear that the Task Force expected such transactions would be settled in shares, not in net cash nor based on a choice of settlement in cash or shares. The consensus analogized the transactions to those contemplated under SEC Accounting Series Release (ASR) No. 268 (Presentation in Financial Statements of "Redeemable Preferred Stock"), thus requiring public companies to transfer from permanent equity to temporary equity an amount equal to the redemption price of the common stock, regardless of whether the put options can be exercised immediately or are "in the money" when issued. Under that consensus, permanent equity would not be adjusted until the options are redeemed, exercised, or expire.

Although ASC 470-20 (APB-14), and Issue 86-35 (codified in this Issue), provided guidance on accounting for freestanding written call options or warrants on an entity's own stock, they did not specifically address the accounting for freestanding written call options or warrants that must be settled in either net shares or net cash or that permit the entity to choose the method of settlement.

ACCOUNTING ISSUE

How should an entity classify and measure freestanding contracts that are indexed to, and potentially settled in, the entity's own stock?

ACCOUNTING GUIDANCE

The Framework for Accounting (the Model)

Scope

The EITF developed a framework of accounting ("the Model"), which only applies to freestanding derivative financial instruments that are indexed to and settled in an entity's own stock, such as forward contracts, options, and warrants.

The Model does *not* apply to the accounting for:

- A derivative or a financial instrument if the derivative is embedded in the financial instrument and cannot be detached from it
- Contracts issued to compensate employees or to acquire goods and services from nonemployees *before* performance has occurred (the Issue does apply after performance has occurred)
- Contracts indexed to and settled in a consolidated subsidiary's stock (see Issues 00-4 and 00-6)

Initial and Subsequent Balance Sheet Classification and Measurement

Under the Model, freestanding contracts that are indexed to, and potentially settled in, an entity's own stock are classified in the balance sheet based on the concept that contracts that must be settled in net cash are assets or liabilities, and that contracts that must be settled in shares are equity instruments. It is assumed under the Model that if given a choice between settlement in shares or in cash, an entity would choose to settle a contract in its own stock in shares or in net shares, whereas the counterparty would choose to settle the same contract in cash or in net cash. The Model does not apply, however, if the settlement alternatives do not have the same economic value or if one of the settlement alternatives is fixed or has caps or floors. If this is the case, the accounting is based on the instrument's (or combination of instruments') economic substance. If the number of shares an entity is required to deliver under a contract is limited in accordance with a net-share settlement alternative, the Model applies even though the settlement alternatives may have different economic values.

Freestanding contracts are measured initially at fair value. At each subsequent balance sheet date before settlement, they are accounted for based on the initial classification and the required or assumed settlement method. For example, if a contract that is classified as an equity instrument gives the entity a choice between net share settlement or physical settlement requiring the entity to deliver cash, it is assumed that the entity would choose to settle the contract in net shares.

Conversely, it is assumed that given the choice, the counterparty would require the entity to settle the contract by physical delivery of cash.

The contracts are classified based on their economic substance and measured as follows:

1. Contracts Classified as Equity Instruments
   a. *Contracts that require physical settlement in shares or settlement in net shares* Reported in *permanent* equity (see the following discussion on equity instruments classified as temporary equity) and measured initially at fair value. Fair value is not adjusted for subsequent changes for contracts classified in equity.
   b. *Contracts under which an entity can choose to settle in (a) its own shares (physical settlement in shares or net share settlement) or in net cash or (b) in net shares or by physical settlement requiring the entity to deliver cash* Reported in *permanent* equity and measured initially at fair value, which is not adjusted for subsequent changes. Amounts paid or received for contracts settled in cash are included in contributed capital.
   c. ASR 268 provides guidance by analogy to *public* companies for the transactions discussed in this Issue. Consequently, for the following contracts, which are generally reported in permanent equity, public companies must transfer to *temporary equity* an amount equal to the cash redemption amount in a physical settlement:
      (1) Contracts under which physical settlement in cash is required (e.g., an entity must buy back its share from the holder of a written put option)
      (2) Contracts under which an entity chooses settlement in net cash or by physical settlement requiring the entity to deliver cash
      (3) Contracts under which a counterparty can choose to settle in net shares or by physical settlement requiring the entity to deliver cash
2. Contracts Classified as Assets or Liabilities
   a. *Contracts that must be settled in net cash* Measured initially and subsequently at fair value.
   b. *Contracts under which a counterparty can choose to settle in net cash or in shares (physical settlement or in net shares)* Measured initially and at fair value.

Gains and losses on contracts classified as assets or liabilities are reported in income and disclosed in the financial statements. Gains or losses continue to be included in income even if the contract is ultimately settled in shares.

DISCUSSION

- Those who believe that contracts requiring physical settlement in shares should be classified in equity argue that classifying such contracts as assets or liabilities, and thus including gains and losses in income, would be inconsistent with the guidance in ASC 225-10-15-3; 45-1; 225-20-05-1; 250-10-05-5; 45-22, 45-24, 45-28; 50-8 through 50-9; 505-10-25-2 (APB-9) and that in ASC 310-10-45-14; 505-10-45-1 through 45-2; and 850-10-60-4 (EITF Issue 85-1). Such classification also would be inconsistent with the guidance in ASR-268 (Presentation Financial Statements of "Redeemable Preferred Stocks"), which requires an entity to transfer an amount that equals the contracted purchase price of the stock under financial instruments (such as forward purchase contracts and purchased call options) from permanent equity to temporary equity. In addition, a transaction settled in the entity's shares was considered to be a classic equity transaction.
- The EITF agreed that because contracts in which an *entity* chooses whether to settle the obligation with the entity's shares or in cash are under the entity's control, such contracts should be accounted for as equity transactions.
- Contracts that require net cash settlement should be classified as assets or liabilities because the right to receive or pay cash is a future economic benefit or future economic sacrifice that meets the definition of an asset or a liability in CON-6 (Elements of Financial Statements) (not in ASC). In addition, because no shares are exchanged, the transaction does not have the characteristics of an equity transaction, even if the amount of cash to be exchanged is indexed to the price of the entity's stock.
- Contracts giving a counterparty the right to demand payment in cash or in shares should be recognized as an asset or a liability because the transaction is not under the entity's control. For example, a liability may be incurred if the counterparty demands a cash settlement when a forward contract is in a loss position.
- Proponents of the view that gains and losses on contracts recognized as assets or liabilities should be recognized currently in income argue that ASC 250-10-45-22; 225-10-45-1 (paragraph 17 of APB-9, *Reporting the Results of*

Operations) requires that treatment. They believe that because the entity does not transfer its shares, the transaction does not qualify for the exemption in ASC 505-10-25-2 (paragraph 28 of APB-9), which states that charges or credits resulting from transactions in the entity's capital stock may be excluded from the determination of net income.

Additional Requirements for Equity Classification

The guidance in ASC 815-10-15-74; 815-15-25-1 (paragraphs 11(a) and 12(c) of FAS-133) provides that embedded derivatives indexed to a reporting entity's *own* stock and classified in stockholders' equity should *not* be considered to be derivatives for the purposes of ASC 815 (FAS-133), even if they were freestanding. The additional requirements for equity classification discussed in this section do *not* apply under the provisions of ASC 815 (FAS-133) when evaluating whether derivative financial instruments, such as forward contracts, options, or warrants, indexed to an entity's own stock that are embedded in a *debt* instrument would be classified in stockholders' equity if they were freestanding.

The requirements in this Issue used to determine whether an embedded derivative indexed to an entity's own stock should be classified in stockholders' equity if it were freestanding do not apply to *conventional convertible debt instruments* if the value of the conversion option can be realized only when the holder exercises that option and receives all of the proceeds in a fixed number of shares or in an equivalent amount of cash, at the issuer's option. Issuers should apply the requirements of this Issue, however, when evaluating whether other embedded derivatives are equity instruments not covered under the scope of ASC 815 (FAS-133).

Equity derivative contracts that include a provision under which an entity could be required to settle a contract in net cash should be accounted for as an asset or liability under the Model, *not* as the issuer's equity.

SEC registrants should classify equity contracts as temporary equity in accordance with the SEC's Accounting Series Release (ASR) No. 268 (Presentation in Financial Statements of "Redeemable Preferred Stocks") if the contract includes a provision that could require the issuer to pay cash to the counterparty in a *physical settlement* for the issuer's shares. A contract that permits the counterparty to require a *net cash settlement* should be classified as an *asset* or *liability*. This consensus does *not* require an evaluation of the likelihood that an event causing a cash settlement (net cash or physical) would occur. However, the potential outcome need not be considered when the provisions of ASR-268 are applied if cash payment is required only in the case of the issuer's final liquidation.

A derivative indexed to, and potentially settled in, a company's own stock should be classified in equity *only* if all of the following conditions are met:

- The entity is permitted to settle the contract in registered or unregistered shares.
- The entity has enough authorized but unissued shares available to settle the contract, after considering all of its other commitments that may require issuing stock during the period the contract is outstanding.
- The contract specifically limits the number of shares to be delivered in a share settlement, even if the contract terminates when the stock price is at a stated trigger price.
- The contract does not require the entity to post collateral for any reason.
- The issuer is not required to pay cash to the counterparty if the counterparty has sold the shares initially delivered to it and the proceeds are less than the total amount due.
- The counterparty's rights under a contract are no greater than those of the underlying stock's shareholders.

An entity may be required under a contract's provisions to settle in net shares or to physically deliver cash and receive its own shares, such as in a forward purchase contract or a written put option. Therefore, an entity that does not control settlement in net shares under the above conditions or the Issues discussed below would continue to account for the contract as an equity instrument. SEC registrants, however, would be required to transfer to temporary equity the amount due in cash on settlement.

The conditions discussed above apply to the following guidance:

- A contract that requires an issuer to settle by delivering only registered shares in a net-share or physical settlement, or cash in a net-cash settlement, should be accounted for as an *asset or liability*, because (*a*) events or actions necessary to deliver registered shares are *not* within the entity's control and (*b*) under the model discussed above, it is assumed that the entity will be required to settle in net cash.
- Delivery of unregistered shares in a *private placement* is within an entity's control if during the six months before the classification assessment date, the entity did not file a statement with the SEC that was later withdrawn (a failed

registration statement). However, if the entity did have a failed registration during the previous six months, there should be a legal determination as to whether the entity can deliver unregistered shares in a settlement in shares or in net shares. An entity, therefore, should classify a contract as permanent equity if the entity (*a*) has not had a failed registration statement, (*b*) is permitted under the contract to deliver unregistered shares to settle a contract in net shares, and (*c*) meets other conditions in this Issue.

- Settlement in shares or net shares is *not* within an entity's control if the shareholders' approval is required to increase the number of authorized shares for such settlement. To control settlement, an entity must determine whether it will have a sufficient number of authorized and unissued shares at the date on which a contract's classification is determined. To make this determination, an entity should compare (*a*) the number of authorized but unissued shares, less the number of shares the entity could be required to deliver during the contract period to satisfy existing commitments, with (*b*) the maximum number of shares that the entity could be required to deliver in a net-share or physical settlement under the contract. An entity controls settlement in shares if the number of shares in (*a*) is greater than the number of shares in (*b*) and meets the entity conditions above. If settlement is *not* under the entity's control, the contract should be classified as an *asset* or *liability*.
- If the number of shares an entity may need to settle a contract cannot be determined at the classification date, net-share settlement is *not* under the entity's control because the entity cannot determine whether it has sufficient authorized shares for settlement. If a contract limits the number of shares delivered at the contract's expiration in a net-share settlement, the entity *can* determine whether such settlement is within its control by comparing the maximum number of shares needed with the available authorized but unissued shares. That comparison would determine whether a sufficient number of shares are available to settle a contract in net shares after delivering shares to satisfy other existing commitments as well as for top-off or make-whole provisions discussed below.
- A derivative contract must be classified as an *asset* or *liability* if net-share settlement is permitted, but net-cash settlement is *required* if an entity does not make timely SEC filings because doing so is not within the entity's control.
- If a contract requires net-cash settlement on the occurrence of an event that results in a change of control, the contract should be classified as an *asset* or *liability,* because the occurrence of such an event would not be under the entity's control. However, classification in permanent equity would be acceptable if, under a contract's change of control provision, the counterparty can receive or deliver on settlement the same form of consideration as to the shareholders of the security underlying the contract. For example, the counterparty to the contract and the shareholders would both receive cash in the transaction. Further, a contract's classification would not be affected if it includes a provision related to a change in control that specifies that if all stockholders receive the acquiring entity's stock, the contract will be indexed to the purchaser's stock (or the issuer's in a business combination accounted for as a pooling of interests).
- A contract that grants a counterparty the rights of a creditor in case the entity declares bankruptcy should *not* be classified as equity, unless the contract includes a statement that the counterparty's rights are not senior to the claims of the common shareholders of the underlying stock in case of bankruptcy. However, equity classification would be permitted for a contract that requires net-cash settlement in case of bankruptcy if it is possible to demonstrate that the counterparty's claims in bankruptcy could be settled in net shares or would not have a higher rank in bankruptcy than those of the underlying stock's common shareholders.
- Equity classification is permitted if a contract requires net-cash settlement in case of nationalization, because the counterparty and the underlying stock's common shareholders, who would receive cash as compensation for the expropriated assets, would receive the same form of compensation.
- *Top-off* or *make-whole* provisions are sometimes included in contracts to reimburse a counterparty for losses incurred, or to transfer to the entity gains the counterparty recognized on the difference between the value of the contract at the settlement date and the value the counterparty realized in a sale of the securities after the settlement date. A contract that includes such a provision may be classified as equity only if (*a*) the provision can be settled in net shares and (*b*) the maximum number of shares that could be delivered is fixed and is less than the number of available authorized shares after meeting other commitments settled in shares.
- Equity classification is *not* permitted if a contract includes a provision requiring an issuer to post collateral if certain events occur (e.g., a drop in the price of the underlying stock), because the requirement to post collateral is not consistent with the concept of equity. However, equity classification is permitted if the equity securities to be delivered under a contract are placed in trust.

Contract Reclassification

A contract's classification should be reassessed at each balance sheet date. If necessary, a contract should be reclassified as of the date on which an event causing a change in classification has occurred. Contracts may be reclassified an unlimited number of times.

A contract's change in classification should be accounted for as follows:

- A change in the fair value of a contract that is reclassified from permanent or temporary equity to an asset or liability classification should be accounted for as an adjustment to stockholders' equity for the period between the date of the contract's last classification as equity to the date of reclassification to an asset or a liability. In addition, after a contract is reclassified from permanent or temporary equity to an asset or a liability, all changes in the contract's fair value should be recognized in income.
- Conversely, gains or losses recognized in accounting for the fair value of a contract that has been properly classified as an asset or a liability should not be reversed if the contract is reclassified to equity.
- If the total notional amount of a contract that can be partially settled in net shares can no longer be classified in permanent equity, the portion that could be settled in net shares as of the balance sheet date would continue to be classified in permanent equity while the other portion would be reclassified in temporary equity, or as an asset or liability, as appropriate.

If more than one of an entity's derivative contracts may be partially settled, and some or all of those contracts are *required* to be partially settled, different methods can be used to determine which contracts, or portions thereof, should be reclassified.

Determining how to partially reclassify such contracts is an accounting policy decision that should be disclosed in accordance with ASC 235-10-05-3 through 05-4, 50-1 through 50-6. However, the reclassification method should be systematic, rational, and consistent. Under acceptable methods, an entity might (*a*) partially reclassify all contracts proportionately, (*b*) reclassify contracts with the *earliest inception* date first, (*c*) reclassify contracts with the *earliest maturity* date first, (*d*) reclassify contracts with the *latest inception* date first, or (*e*) reclassify contracts with the *latest maturity* date first.

Disclosures

The following disclosures required under the guidance in ASC 505-10-15-1, 50-3 through 50-5, 50-11; ASC 470-10-50-5 apply to *all* contracts under the scope of this Issue:

- For an option or forward contract indexed to the issuer's equity, disclose the forward rate, option strike price, number of issuer's shares to which the contract is indexed, the settlement date or dates of the contract, and whether the issuer accounts for the contract as an asset, a liability, or equity.
- For contracts with terms that *state* alternative settlement methods, disclose the alternatives, including who controls the alternatives and the *maximum* number of shares that *could be required to be issued* to settle a contract with net shares. Under the guidance in ASC 505-10-15-1; 50-3 through 50-5, 50-11; 470-10-50-5 additional disclosures about actual issuances and settlements that occurred during the accounting period also are required.
- For contracts that *do not* state a fixed or determinable maximum number of shares that may be required to be issued, disclose the fact that an infinite number of shares potentially could be issued to settle the contract.
- Disclose the contract's current fair value for each settlement alternative, denominated in monetary amounts or number of shares, and the effect of changes in the price of the issuer's equity instruments on settlement amounts.
- For equity instruments under this Issue that are classified as temporary equity, disclose the amount of redemption requirements, by issue or combined for all issues, that are redeemable at fixed or determinable prices on fixed or determinable dates in each of the five years after the date of the latest balance sheet presented.
- For contracts classified as assets or liabilities that meet the definition of a derivative under the guidance in ASC 815, disclose information regarding the objective for holding or issuing those instruments based on the guidance in ASC 815-10-50-1 through 50-5, as well as the disclosures required in ASC 815-30-50-1, regarding fair value hedges, cash flow hedges, and hedges of net investments in foreign operations.

Issuers should disclose information about contract reclassifications in or out of equity during the life of an instrument, the reason for reclassification, and the effect on the issuer's financial statements. In addition, the entity's accounting policy regarding the method used to partially reclassify contracts under this Issue should be disclosed in accordance with the guidance in ASC 235-10-50-1 through 50-6.

Application Guidance for Specific Instruments

The following guidance represents the Task Force's consensus positions on the application of the Model to the following types of freestanding derivative financial instruments that are indexed to, and potentially settled in, an entity's own stock.

1. Forward Sale Contracts, Written Call Options or Warrants, and Purchased Put Options

BACKGROUND

An entity enters into a contract to sell a specific number of its shares of common stock to the holder at a specified price on a specified future date. The contract may be settled by delivery of shares to the counterparty (physical settlement), in net shares, in net cash, or based on the entity's or counterparty's choice of settlement method.

ACCOUNTING GUIDANCE

Based on the Model, the contracts are accounted for as follows:

- *Contracts requiring physical settlement in shares or settlement in net shares* The contracts are *equity* instruments recognized in permanent equity and measured initially at fair value. Fair value is not adjusted for subsequent events.
- *Contracts requiring net cash settlement* The contracts are reported as *assets* or *liabilities* and measured initially and subsequently at fair value. Subsequent changes in fair value, if any, are reported in income and disclosed in the financial statements.
- *Contracts giving an entity the choice of settlement method*
  - — Settlement in net shares or by physical settlement in shares. The contracts are *equity* instruments recognized in permanent equity and measured initially at fair value, which is not adjusted for subsequent changes.
  - — Settlement in net shares or net cash, or settlement in net cash or physical settlement in shares. The contracts are *equity* instruments reported in permanent equity and measured initially at fair value, which is not adjusted for subsequent changes. If cash is paid or received in a net cash settlement, that amount is reported in contributed capital.
- *Contracts giving the counterparty the choice of settlement method*
  - — Settlement in net shares or by physical settlement in shares. The contracts are *equity* instruments reported in permanent equity and measured initially at fair value, which is not adjusted for subsequent changes.
  - — Settlement in net shares or net cash, or settlement in net cash or physical settlement in shares. The contracts are reported as *assets* or *liabilities* and measured initially and subsequently at fair value. Subsequent changes in fair value, if any, are reported in earnings and disclosed in the financial statements. Gains or losses are included in income and disclosed in the financial statements, even if the contract is ultimately settled in shares.

Illustration of the Accounting for a Purchased Put Option Indexed to, and Potentially Settled in, an Entity's Own Stock

On 7/15/X5, Preston Company (a public entity with a 12/31 year-end) purchases a put option that is indexed to 100 common shares of the entity's own stock at $25 per share, when the fair value of the stock is $25 per share. The option expires on 10/13/X5. The option premium is $150. Assume that the price of each common share and the fair value of the option are $23 and $225 on 9/30/X5. The price of each share of common stock on 10/13/X5, the settlement date, is $20. Under the following two scenarios, Preston accounts for the contract at each date as follows: (*a*) 7/15/X5, (*b*) 9/30/X5, and (*c*) 10/13/X5.

Scenario 1: The entity can choose to settle in net shares or net cash

(a) At initiation of the contract—7/15/X5

Because the entity can choose the method of settlement, the indexed option is an equity transaction.

Additional paid-in capital	$150	
Cash		$150

(b) At interim dates—9/30/X5

Contracts recorded as equity transactions are not adjusted to fair value at interim dates.

(c) At settlement—10/13/X5

The entity chooses to settle in net cash. Because the price per share is $20 on the settlement date, the option is worth $500 [($25 – $20) × 100]. The counterparty pays the entity $500 to settle the contract.

Cash	$500	
Additional paid-in capital		$500

Scenario 2: The counterparty can choose to settle in net cash or in net shares

(a) At initiation of the contract—7/15/X5

Because the counterparty decides on the method of settlement, the indexed option is recognized as an asset.

Indexed option	$150	
Cash		$150

(b) At interim dates—9/30/X5

The per share price has increased to $23. The entity reduces the carrying amount of the option to its fair value of $225 and recognizes a loss of $105 ($330 – $225).

Loss on indexed option	$105	
Indexed option		$105

(c) At settlement—10/13/X5

The counterparty chooses to settle in net shares. Because the price per share is $20 on the settlement date—$5 less than the reference price of $25—the option is worth $500. The entity, therefore, had a total gain recognized on settlement is $275 ($500 less the $225 recorded amount of the option).

Treasury stock	$500	
Indexed option		$225
Gain on indexed option		275

SUBSEQUENT DEVELOPMENT

SEC registrants that have entered into forward equity sales transactions after May 1, 1998, should classify those transactions as debt. Such transactions combine the issuance of common stock with a forward contract that requires the issuer to give the holder a guaranteed return.

2. Written Put Options and Forward Purchase Contracts

BACKGROUND

An entity enters into a contract under which it agrees to purchase a specified number of the entity's shares of common stock at a specified price on a specified future date. The contract may be settled by physical settlement, in net shares, in net cash, or the issuing entity or the counterparty may have the right to choose the settlement method. (This discussion also applies to shareholder rights (SHARPs) issued by an entity to its shareholders, which give them the right to sell a specified number of common shares to the entity for cash.)

ACCOUNTING GUIDANCE

Based on the Model, the contracts are accounted for as follows:

- *Contracts requiring physical settlement in cash* The contracts are *equity* instruments reported in permanent equity, but because the option writer is required to settle the contract in cash, *public* companies must transfer to temporary equity an amount equal to the redemption amount. The instruments are measured initially at fair value without subsequent adjustment for changes in fair value.
- *Contracts requiring net share settlement* The contracts are equity instruments reported in permanent equity and measured initially at fair value, without subsequent adjustment for changes in fair value.

- *Contracts requiring net cash settlement* The contracts are *liabilities* that are measured initially at fair value and adjusted for changes in fair value, which are reported in earnings and disclosed in the financial statements.
- *Contracts giving the entity the choice of settlement method*
  - — Settlement in net shares or physical settlement in cash, or settlement in net shares or net cash. The contracts are equity instruments that are reported in permanent equity. The instruments are measured initially at fair value without subsequent adjustment for changes in fair value. Cash paid or received in a physical settlement in cash or a net cash settlement is recognized in contributed capital. (It is assumed that the entity will settle in net shares.)
  - — Settlement in net cash or by physical settlement in cash. The contracts are *equity* instruments that are reported in permanent equity, but because the option writer is required to settle the contract in cash, *public* companies must transfer to temporary equity an amount equal to the redemption amount. The instruments are measured initially at fair value without subsequent adjustment for changes in fair value. If the contract is ultimately settled in net cash or in net shares, the amount reported in temporary equity is transferred and reported as an addition to permanent equity.
- *Contracts giving the counterparty the choice of settlement method*
- Settlement in net cash or by physical settlement in cash. The contracts are *equity* instruments that are reported in permanent equity, but because the option writer is required to settle the contract in cash, *public* companies must transfer to temporary equity an amount equal to the redemption amount. The instruments are measured initially at fair value without subsequent adjustment for changes in fair value. If the contract is ultimately settled in net cash or in net shares, the amount reported in temporary equity is transferred and reported as an addition to permanent equity.
- Settlement in net cash or net shares, or in net cash or physical settlement in cash. The contracts are liabilities that should be measured at fair value and adjusted for changes in fair value. Gains or losses are included in earnings and disclosed in the financial statements, even if the contract is ultimately settled in shares.

PRACTICE POINTER: Under the provisions of ASC 460-10-05-1, 05-2, 10-1, 15-4 through 15-7, 15-9, 15-10; 25-1 through 25-4, 30-1 through 30-4, 35-1 through 35-2, 35-4, 50-2, 50-4 through 50-6, 50-8, 55-2 through 55-3, 55-5 through 55-9, 55-12 through 55-13, 55-15 through 55-18, 55-20 through 55-24, 55-28, 55-29; ASC 840-10-25-34; ASC 840-10-60-2, guarantors are required to recognize a liability at the inception of a guarantee for the obligation assumed. Contracts under the guidance in this Issue that also meet the definition of a guarantee in ASC 460, such as physically settled written puts, are initially valued at fair value, as required in ASC 460. Although the accounting is *not* affected, the guarantee should be disclosed under the requirements in ASC 460.

DISCUSSION

- A written put option or forward purchase contract that requires settlement in net cash is a liability because it represents an obligation to sacrifice assets in the future. Proponents of this view argued that the transaction should not be recognized in equity because no shares will be exchanged. They also referred to the treatment of purchased options or purchased forward contracts settled in cash. Recognition of gains or losses is based on the view that such recognition is required by ASC 250-10-45-22; ASC 225-10-45-1 for items treated as assets or liabilities and is consistent with the Model.
- A written put option that permits the *counterparty* to choose the settlement method should also be recognized as a liability, because the entity cannot control whether it will be required to transfer cash to the counterparty. Proponents of this approach also referred to the treatment of purchased put options and purchased forward contracts when the counterparty can choose the method of settlement. Recognition of a gain or loss is based on the view that such recognition is required by ASC 250-10-45-22; ASC 225-10-45-1 for items treated as assets or liabilities and is consistent with the Model.
- Written put options giving the entity the choice of settlement method should be accounted for as equity transactions because the entity can choose to settle the option in shares of stock rather than in cash.

Illustration of the Accounting for the Sale of Written Put Options on an Issuer's Stock That Require or Permit Cash Settlement

On 12/15/X5, Preston Company (a public entity with a 12/31 year-end) sells a put option that is indexed to 100 common shares of the entity's own stock at a price of $25 per share when the fair value of the stock is $25 per share. The option expires on 3/14/X6. The option premium is $150. Assume that the price of each common share and the fair value of the option is as follows: *(a)* $22 and $330, respectively, on 12/31/X5. The price of each share of common stock on 3/14/X6, the settlement date, is $20.

Under the following two scenarios, Preston accounts for the contract as follows at each date: (*a*) 12/15/X5, (*b*) 12/31/X5, and (*c*) 3/14/X6.

Scenario 1: The entity can choose to settle in net cash or by physical settlement in cash.

(a) At initiation of the contract—12/15/X5

Because the entity chooses the method of settlement, the indexed option is treated as an equity transaction.

Cash	$150	
Additional paid-in capital		$150

Because the entity's stock is publicly traded, the entity must transfer to temporary equity an amount equal to 100 shares at the settlement price.

Additional paid-in capital	$2,500	
Cost of settling put options		$2,500

(b) At year-end—12/31/X5 (interim date)

Contracts recorded as equity transactions are not adjusted to fair value at interim dates.

(c) At settlement of the contract in net shares—3/14/X6

Because the price per share is $20 on the settlement date, the option contract is worth $500 [($25 – $20) × 100]. The entity chooses to settle in net cash and pays the counterparty $500 to settle the contract.

Cost of settling put options	$2,500	
Additional paid-in capital		$2,000
Cash		500

Scenario 2: The counterparty can choose to settle in net cash or in net shares

(a) At initiation of the contract—12/15/X5

Because the counterparty can choose to settle in net cash or net shares, the option is treated as a liability.

Cash	$150	
Indexed option contract payable		$150

(b) At year-end—12/31/X5 (interim date)

The per share price of $22 is $3 less than the $25 per share price on settlement. The entity adjusts the liability to the option's fair value of $330 and recognizes a loss of $180.

Loss on indexed option contract	$180	
Indexed option contract payable		$180

(c) At settlement—3/14/X6

The counterparty chooses to settle in net shares. Because the price per share is $20 on the settlement date—$5 less than the reference price of $25—the option is worth $500. The entity, therefore, has a total loss of $350 on the contract ($500 less $150 premium). The entity settles the contract by delivering 25 shares ($500/$20) to the counterparty to settle the contract. The loss recognized on settlement is $275 ($500 less the $225 recorded liability).

Loss on indexed option contract	$275	
Indexed Option payable	225	
Treasury shares		$500

3. Purchased Call Option

BACKGROUND

An entity purchases a call option giving it the right, but not the obligation, to purchase from the option's seller a specific number of the entity's shares of common stock at a specified price on a specified future date. The contract may be settled by physical settlement, in net shares, in net cash, or based on the settlement method chosen by the entity or the counterparty.

ACCOUNTING GUIDANCE

Purchased call options are accounted for the same as forward sale contracts, written call options or warrants, and purchased put options as previously discussed.

4. Detachable Stock Purchase Warrants

BACKGROUND

An entity issues senior subordinated notes with a detachable warrant giving the holder the right to purchase 5,000 shares of the issuer's stock for $50 per share at any time and the right to require the entity to repurchase all or some of the warrants for at least $1,000 per share several months after the notes mature in about five years.

ACCOUNTING GUIDANCE

The issuer should account for the notes as follows:

- The proceeds should be allocated between the liability for the debt and the warrant. The resulting discount should be amortized over the term of the notes in accordance with the guidance in ASC 835-30.
- The warrants are considered to be, in substance, a debt instrument and are accounted for as a liability, because the alternatives for settling the warrants do not have the same economic value. The put gives the holder a guaranteed return in cash (5,000 shares × $1,000 = $5,000,000) that significantly exceeds the value of the share settlement (5,000 shares × $ 50 = $ 250,000) without the put at the date of issuance.

DISCUSSION

This Issue deals with the balance sheet classification of a detachable stock purchase warrant with a put option at a fixed price. Under the provisions of ASC 470-20-05-2 through 05-6; 25-2 through 25-3, 25-10 through 25-11, 25-13; 30-1 through 30-2; and 505-10-60-3, the proceeds would be allocated between the debt and the warrant. However, the treatment of the warrant as a liability is more appropriate because, based on the economics of the transaction, it is probable that it will be put to the issuer at the fixed price, which substantially exceeds the price of the stock.

5. Put Warrants

BACKGROUND

Put warrants, which generally are issued with debt instruments, combine the characteristics of warrants and put options. They are detachable from the debt and can be exercised under specified conditions by (*a*) using the warrant feature to acquire the issuer's stock at a specified price, (*b*) using the put feature to receive cash from the issuer, or (*c*) using both the warrant and put features to acquire stock and receive cash from the issuer. The put feature may be exercisable only for a specified time period and may expire under certain conditions. The put feature is canceled if the warrant is exercised and, likewise, exercising the put feature cancels the warrant feature. APB-14 requires that a portion of the proceeds from the issuance of debt with detachable warrants be allocated to the warrants.

ACCOUNTING GUIDANCE

Public companies should report the proceeds from the issuance of put warrants as liabilities because the counterparty has the choice of settling the contract in cash or in shares. In subsequent periods, the put warrants are measured at fair value; changes in fair value are reported in earnings.

6. Contracts with Multiple Settlement Alternatives

- Account as *equity instruments* for contracts under the Model if the contract has several alternatives under which the issuer is required to *receive* net cash when the contract is in a *gain* position, but is required to choose between *paying* in net cash or in net stock when the contract is in a *loss* position.

This guidance does not apply if a contract is primarily a purchased option under which the amount of cash that could be received when the contract is in a gain position would significantly exceed the amount that could be paid when the contract is in a *loss* position—for example, if the amount of loss is contractually limited to a small amount. Such contracts should be accounted for as assets or liabilities.

Account as *assets* or *liabilities* for contracts under the Model, if a contract has several alternatives under which an issuer is required to *pay* net cash when the contract is in a *loss* position, but is required to choose between receiving net cash or net stock when the contract is in a *gain* position.

7. Earnings per Share

The guidance in ASC 480-10-05-1 through 05-6, 10-10-1, 15-3 through 15-5, 15-7 through 15-10, 25-1 through 25-2, 25-4 through 25-15, 30-1 through 30-7, 35-3 through 35-5, 45-1 through 45-4, 50-1 through 50-4, 55-1 through 55-12, 55-14 through 55-28, 55-34 through 55-41, 55-64; ASC 835-10-60-13; ASC 260-10-45-70A amends the guidance in ASC 260 for forward-purchase contracts that must be physically settled by repurchasing a fixed number of the issuer's equity shares of common stock for cash. Diluted earnings per share can no longer be computed by the reverse treasury stock method for those contracts. Therefore, common shares subject to the forward-purchase contracts should be excluded from the calculation of basic and diluted earnings per share (EPS).

BACKGROUND

An entity sells put options that are publicly traded and expire two years from the date of issuance. The puts obligate the entity to purchase from the holder one share of the entity's stock at a fixed price, which is lower than the market price of the entity's stock at the date of issuance. The entity may repurchase the puts in the open market at any time during the redemption period.

ACCOUNTING ISSUE

Although none of the issues specifically addresses the calculation of EPS, one of the Task Force's consensus positions provides related guidance.

ACCOUNTING GUIDANCE

An issuer should use the reverse treasury stock method to calculate the potential dilutive effect of put options having a higher exercise price than the market price of the stock ("in the money") during the reporting period. Under the reverse treasury stock method, the number of additional shares to be included in the calculation of EPS is equal to the number of shares the entity must issue for cash at the current market price to satisfy the put obligation minus the number of shares repurchased from the holder of the puts.

To calculate the *dilutive* effect of written put options and similar contracts when the contract's exercise price *exceeds* its market price during the reporting period (the contract is in the money), the *average* market price of the contract *during the period* should be used in calculating the incremental number of shares that would have to be issued to obtain the cash to satisfy a *put* obligation under the reverse treasury method.

PRACTICE POINTER: It is assumed that company shares will be issued if an entity can choose the settlement method. However, that presumption may be overcome if an entity has a stated policy that requires contracts to be settled in cash or has historically settled contracts wholly or partially in cash. If a counterparty can choose the settlement method, the more dilutive method should be used in computing EPS.

DISCUSSION

The treasury stock method discussed in ASC 260-10-45-23 is used to calculate the incremental number of shares to be issued for options under which the holder can purchase an entity's stock at less than its market price. This calculation assumes that the entity receives cash, satisfies a portion of its obligation by repurchasing an equivalent number of shares in the open market, and satisfies the remainder of the obligation by issuing stock. The guidance requires using the *reverse treasury stock method* in ASC 260-10-45-35, under which it is assumed that the entity (1) finances the cash payment to the holder of the put option by issuing new shares at the market price (in this case, a lower price than the amount at which the put will be exercised), and (2) sells the shares obtained by redeeming the put options at the market price for cash. The difference between (1) and (2) is the *incremental number of shares,* for example:

Number of puts outstanding	$1,000
Exercise price	$50
Market price at 12/31/X4	$40
Shares to be sold to satisfy puts ($50,000/$40)	1,250
Less: Treasury shares obtained from satisfaction of put options	1,000
Incremental shares	250

ASC 815-40-15-5 through 15-8D, 55-26 through 55-48; ASC 815-10-65-3; ASC 718-10-60-1B Determining Whether an Instrument (or Embedded Features) Is Indexed to an Entity's Own Stock

PRACTICE NOTE: The following guidance, which is relevant to this Issue, has been added as a result of the issuance of ASU 2017-11, *Earnings Per Share (Topic 260); Distinguishing Liabilities from Equity (Topic 480); Derivatives and Hedging (Topic 815):*

- ASC 815-40-15-5D paragraph requires that entities classifying financial instruments that include a *down round feature* exclude that feature when they consider whether the instrument is indexed to the entity's own stock in accordance with the guidance in ASC 815-40-15-7C through 15-7I (Step 2).
- The existing guidance ASC 815-40-55-34(b) for Step 2 is deleted and the guidance in 815-40-15-5D is added, as well as a statement that "[t]he instrument does not contain any other features to be assessed under Step 2."
- ASC 815-40-55-34A is added to call readers' attention to ASC 260-10-45-12B, related to earnings per share considerations; ASC 260-10-25-1 related to recognition considerations; and ASC 505-10-50-3 through 50-3A related to disclosure considerations.

BACKGROUND

Under the guidance in ASC 815-10-15-74(a), a freestanding contract, such as a stock purchase warrant, that is (1) indexed to its own stock *and* (2) classified in an entity's balance sheet as equity is *not* considered to be a derivative.

Although under the guidance in ASC 815-15-25-1, a derivative instrument embedded in a host contract must be separated and accounted for separately as a derivative, under the guidance in ASC 815-15-25-1, an embedded instrument's terms must be the same as those of the host instrument in order for that instrument to be accounted for separately as a derivative. Therefore, an embedded derivative that meets the exception in ASC 815-10-15-74 would *not* be separated from its host instrument and accounted for as a derivative.

The purpose of this discussion is to develop guidance on how to determine whether an instrument or an embedded feature is indexed to an entity's own stock, which is the first part of the exception in ASC 815-10-15-74. However, the second requirement in ASC 815-10-15-74 (i.e., whether an instrument or an embedded feature that has the characteristics of a derivative, as discussed in ASC 815-10-15-83, 15-85, 15-88 through 15-89, 15-92 through 15-96, 15-99 through 15-100, 15-110, 15-119 through 15-120, 15-128, ASC 440-10-60-10, is classified in an entity's stockholder's equity or would be classified that way if it were a freestanding instrument) is not addressed because other authoritative accounting guidance, including that in ASC 460-10-60-14; ASC 480-10-55-63; ASC 505-10-60-5; ASC 815-10-15-78, 55-52, 15-25-15, 40-05-1 through 05-4, 05-10, 05-11 through05-12; 25-1 through 25-5, 25-7 through 25-20, 25-22 through 25-24, 25-26 through 25-35, 25-37 through 25-40, 30-1, 35-1 through 35-2, 35-6, 35-8 through 35-13, 40-1 through 40-2, 50-1 through 50-5, 55-1 through 55-18 and ASC 815-40-25-4 through 25-42 address that question.

The purpose of this guidance is to help users to evaluate whether certain freestanding instruments that do *not* have all of the characteristics of a derivative under the guidance in ASC 815, but are potentially settled in an entity's own equity shares, should be accounted for under the guidance in ASC 460-10-60-14; ASC 480-10-55-63; ASC 505-10-60-5; ASC 815-10-15-78, 55-52; ASC 815-15-25-15; ASC 815-40-05-1 through 05-4, 05-10 through 05-12; 25-1 through 25-5, 25-7 through 25-20, 25-22 through 25-24, 25-26 through 25-35, 25-37 through 25-40, 30-1, 35-1 through 35-2, 35-6, 35-8 through 35-13, 40-1 through 40-2, 50-1 through 50-5, 55-1 through 55-18. For example, a physically settled forward contract to issue an entity's own equity shares for cash does *not* meet the net settlement characteristic of a derivative discussed in ASC 815-10-15-83,

15-85, 15-88 through 15-89, 15-92 through 15-96, 15-99 through 15-100, 15-110, 15-119 through 15-120, 15-128, ASC 440-10-60-10 if the underlying equity shares are *not* readily convertible to cash. However, if that forward contract is *not* considered to be indexed to an entity's own stock, the contract would *not* be accounted for under the guidance in ASC 460-10-60-14; ASC 480-10-55-63; ASC 505-10-60-5; ASC 815-10-15-78, 55-52; ASC 815-15-25-15; ASC 815-40-05-1 through 05-4, 05-10 through 05-12, 25-1 through 25-5, 25-7 through 25-20, 25-22 through 25-24, 25-26 through 25-35, 25-37 through 25-40, 30-1, 35-1 through 35-2, 35-6, 35-8 through 35-13, 40-1 through 40-2, 50-1 through 50-5, 55-1 through 55-18, which applies only to instruments indexed to, and potentially settled in, an issuer's own stock.

The following guidance should be applied to a unit of accounting based on the requirements in other U.S. generally accepted accounting principles (U.S. GAAP). That is, an issuer that had issued two freestanding financial instruments should apply the guidance in this Issue separately to each instrument if that treatment is required under other U.S. GAAP. However, an issuer that had issued two freestanding financial instruments would apply this guidance to a *single combined* financial instrument if under other U.S. GAAP, the two instruments must be *linked* and accounted for as one financial instrument.

ACCOUNTING GUIDANCE

Scope

The following guidance applies to: (1) freestanding financial instruments or embedded features with all of the characteristics of derivatives in ASC 815-10-15-83, 15-85, 15-88 through 15-89, 15-92 through 15-96, 15-99 through 15-100, 15-110, 15-119 through 15-120, 15-128, ASC 440-10-60-10 when determining whether those instruments qualify for the first part of the scope exception in ASC 815-10-15-74 and (2) freestanding financial instruments that are potentially settled in an entity's own stock, regardless of whether they have all of the characteristics of a derivative in ASC 815-10-15-83, 15-85, 15-88 through 15-89, 15-92 through 15-96, 15-99 through 15-100, 15-110, 15-119 through 15-120, 15-128, ASC 440-10-60-10, when determining whether an instrument should be accounted for under the guidance in ASC 460-10-60-14; ASC 480-10-55-63; ASC 505-10-60-5; ASC 815-10-15-78, 55-52; ASC 815-15-25-15; ASC 815-40-05-1 through 05-4, 05-10 through 05-12; 25-1 through 25-5, 25-7 through 25-20, 25-22 through 25-24, 25-26 through 25-35, 25-37 through 25-40, 30-1, 35-1 through 35-2, 35-6, 35-8 through 35-13, 40-1 through 40-2, 50-1 through 50-5, 55-1 through 55-18.

This guidance does *not* apply to share-based payment awards under the scope of ASC 718, when determining whether those instruments are classified as liability awards or equity awards under the guidance in ASC 718. However, because equity-linked financial instruments issued to investors in order to establish a market-based measure of the fair value of employee options at the grant date are *not* covered under the guidance in ASC 718, the guidance in this Issue applies when determining whether an instrument or an embedded feature: (1) is indexed to an entity's own stock; or (2) should be accounted for under the guidance in ASC 460-10-60-14; ASC 480-10-55-63; ASC 505-10-60-5; ASC 815-10-15-78, 55-52; ASC 815-15-25-15; ASC 815-40-05-1 through 05-4, 05-1 through 05-12; 25-1 through 25-5, 25-7 through 25-20, 25-22 through 25-24, 25-26 through 25-35, 25-37 through 25-40, 30-1, 35-1 through 35-2, 35-6, 35-8 through 35-13, 40-1 through 40-2; 50-1 through 50-5; 55-1 through 55-18.

Accounting Issue

How should an entity determine whether an equity-linked financial instrument or an embedded feature is indexed to the entity's own stock?

Recognition

For accounting purposes, the financial instruments discussed in this Issue are always considered to have been issued, except when parties to a business combination exchange contingently exercisable options (i.e., lock-up options) to purchase the other entity's equity securities at favorable prices in order to encourage a merger's completion. Under the terms of such options, if a specified event interferes with a merger's completion, it may trigger the exercise of those options. However, such options are *not* exercised and expire if a merger is completed as planned. For accounting purposes, lock-up options are *not* considered to have been issued. The guidance in this paragraph applies to both the issuer and the holder of instruments under the scope of this Issue.

An "exercise contingency," as the term is used in this Issue, is a provision that gives the right to an entity or its counterparty to exercise an equity-linked financial instrument or an embedded feature based on changes in an "underlying," which is defined in ASC 815 as a specific interest rate, security price, commodity price, foreign exchange rate, index of prices or rates, or other variable, such as a requirement that a specific event should or should *not* occur. For example, an instrument may include a provision that accelerates an entity's or counterparty's ability to exercise an instrument or a provision that extends the time period during which an entity or its counterparty can exercise an instrument. Both are exercise contingencies. An exercise contingency that would result in an adjustment to an instrument's strike price or to the number of shares used to calculate the amount of a settlement should be evaluated under Step 1 (below) and the potential adjustment of the settlement amount should be evaluated under Step 2 (below).

The following two-step approach should be used to determine whether an equity-linked financial instrument or an embedded feature is indexed to an entity's own stock:

- *Step 1.* Evaluate the instrument's contingent exercise provisions, if any. A financial instrument or an embedded feature that is subject to an exercise contingency may be considered to be indexed to an entity's own stock if the index triggering the instrument's contingent exercise provisions is *not* based on: (1) an observable market, except for the market for the issuer's stock, if applicable; or (2) an observable index, except for one that is calculated or measured exclusively by referring to the issuer's own operations, such as its sales revenues; earnings before interest, taxes, depreciation, and amortization (EBITDA); net income; or total equity. Proceed to Step 2 if (as a result of the evaluation in Step 1) an instrument is *not* prohibited from being considered to be indexed to an entity's own stock.
- *Step 2.* Evaluate the instrument's settlement provisions. An instrument should be considered to be indexed to an entity's own stock if the amount of the settlement will be equal to the difference between the fair value of a *fixed* number of the entity's equity shares and a *fixed* monetary amount or a *fixed* amount of a debt instrument issued by the entity. For example, an issued share option that gives a counterparty the right to buy a *fixed* number of the issuer's shares for a *fixed* price or for a *fixed* stated principal amount of a bond to be issued by the entity should be considered to be indexed to the issuing entity's own stock.

If an instrument's strike price or the number of shares used to calculate the amount to settle may be adjusted under an instrument's provisions, they are *not* fixed—regardless of the probability that an adjustment will occur or whether an adjustment is under the entity's control. However, an instrument or an embedded feature whose strike price or number of shares used to calculate the settlement amount are *not* fixed may still be considered to be indexed to an entity's own stock if inputs to the fair value of a "fixed-for-fixed" forward or option on equity shares are the only variables that could affect the amount of a settlement, which is equal to the difference between the price of a *fixed* number of equity shares and a *fixed* strike price. Such fair value inputs may include an entity's stock price and additional variables, such as: (1) the instrument's strike price; (2) its terms; (3) expected dividends or other dilutive activities; (3) stock borrow cost; (4) interest rates; (5) stock price volatility; (6) an entity's credit spread; and (7) an entity's ability to maintain a standard hedge position in the underlying shares. The determination and adjustments of the settlement amount, including a determination of an entity's ability to maintain a standard hedge position must be commercially reasonable.

Nevertheless, an instrument or an embedded feature should *not* be considered to be indexed to an entity's own stock if the *calculation* of the amount at which a fixed-for-fixed option or forward on equity shares would be settled: (1) is affected by variables that are *not* pertinent to the option's or forward contract's pricing; (2) include variables other than those used to determine the forward's or option's fair value; or (3) includes a feature, such as a leverage factor, that increases the instrument's exposure to the additional variables related to fair value inputs discussed above in a manner that is inconsistent with a fixed-for-fixed forward or option on equity shares.

The following two types of provisions related to equity-linked financial instruments also should *not* prevent an instrument from being considered to be indexed to an entity's own stock:

1. Provisions permitting adjustments that would neutralize the effects of events that may cause stock price irregularities. For example, provisions that adjust a financial instrument's terms to offset a net gain or loss incurred by an instrument's holder as a result of differences between changes in: (1) the fair value of an equity-linked instrument; and (2) the fair value of an offsetting hedge position in the underlying shares caused by a merger announcement or a similar event.
2. Provisions that enable an entity to unilaterally modify a financial instrument's terms at any time, as long as that modification benefits the counterparty. An issuer's ability to reduce the conversion price of a convertible debt instrument at anytime to induce conversion is an example of such a provision.

Strike Price Denominated in a Foreign Currency

An issuer of an equity-linked financial instrument having a strike price denominated in a functional currency that differs from the issuer's is exposed to changes in currency exchange rates. If the strike price of an equity-linked financial instrument is valued in a currency other than the issuer's functional currency, including a conversion option that is embedded in a convertible debt instrument valued in a currency other than the issuer's functional currency, an equity-linked financial instrument would *not* be considered to be indexed to the issuing entity's own stock. However, the currency in which the underlying shares trade does *not* affect the determination of whether an equity-linked instrument is indexed to an entity's own stock.

ASC 815-40-25-41 through 42 The Meaning of "Conventional Convertible Instrument" in EITF Issue No. 00-19, "Accounting for Derivative Financial Instruments Indexed to, and Potentially Settled in, an Entity's Own Stock"

BACKGROUND

ASC 815-10-15-74 provides that contracts issued or held by a reporting entity should *not* be considered to be derivative instruments if they are (*a*) indexed to that entity's *own* stock and (*b*) reported in the entity's balance sheet in stockholders' equity. In ASC 460-10-60-14; ASC 480-10-55-63; ASC 505-10-60-5; ASC 815-10-15-78, 55-52; ASC 815-15-25-15; ASC 815-40-05-1 through 50-4, 05-10 through 05-12, 25-1 through 25-5, 25-7 through 25-20, 25-22 through 25-24, 25-26 through 25-35, 25-37 through 25-40, 30-1, 35-1 through 35-2, 35-4 through 35-6, 35-8 through 35-13, 40-1 through 40-2, 50-1 through 50-5, 55-1 through 55-18, which applies only to *freestanding* derivatives such as forward contracts, options, and warrants, the guidance is provided for determining whether an embedded derivative would be classified in stockholders' equity in accordance with the guidance in ASC 815-10-15-74 if it were freestanding. However, that guidance provides that a *conventional convertible debt instrument* should be exempted from the evaluation of whether it contains an embedded derivative indexed to the entity's own stock that would require bifurcation if the holder of that debt instrument can realize the value of the conversion option only by exercising the option and receiving the proceeds, at the issuer's discretion, in a fixed number of shares or an equivalent amount of cash.

Because the guidance in ASC 460-10-60-14; ASC 480-10-55-63; ASC 505-10-60-5; ASC 815-10-15-78, 55-52; ASC 815-15-25-15; ASC 815-40-05-1 through 50-4, 05-10 through 05-12; 25-1 through 25-5, 25-7 through 25-20, 25-22 through 25-24, 25-26 through 25-35, 25-37 through 25-40, 30-1, 35-1 through 35-2, 35-4 through 35-6, 35-8 through 35-13, 40-1 through 40-2, 50-1 through 50-5, 55-1 through 55-18 does not specifically define the term *conventional convertible debt*, there has been diversity in practice in determining which convertible debt instruments qualify for the exemption.

ACCOUNTING ISSUE

Should the exemption for applying the Accounting Model discussed in paragraphs 12 to 32 of Issue 00-19 for "conventional convertible debt instruments" be deleted from the Issue or clarified?

ACCOUNTING GUIDANCE

- The exemption for conventional convertible debt instruments should be *retained*.
- A convertible debt instrument should be considered to be *conventional* for the purpose of applying the guidance in ASC 460-10-60-14; ASC 480-10-55-63; ASC 505-10-60-5; ASC 815-10-15-78, 55-52; ASC 815-15-25-15; ASC 815-40-05-1 through 05-4, 05-10 through 05-12, 25-1 through 25-5, 25-7 through 25-20, 25-22 through 25-24, 25-26 through 25-35, 25-37 through 25-40, 30-1; 35-1, 35-2, 35-4 through 35-6, 35-8 through 35-13, 40-1 through 40-2; 50-1 through 50-5, 55-1 through 55-18 if the holder has an option under the debt instrument's provisions to convert it into a fixed number of shares or an equivalent amount of cash at the issuer's discretion based on the passage of time or the occurrence of a contingent event. The existence of a standard antidilution provision does *not* prohibit the conversion of an instrument into a fixed number of shares.
- Convertible preferred stock having a mandatory redemption date may qualify for the exemption provided in Issue 00-19 (see ASC references above) for conventional convertible debt if the instrument's economic characteristics are more similar to debt than equity.

The applicable information required in ASC 505-10-15-1, 50-3 to 50-5, 50-11, should be disclosed for instruments under the scope of this Issue.

ASC 815-45: WEATHER DERIVATIVES

ASC 815-45-15-2, 25-1, 25-5, 25-6, 30-1 through 3A, 35-1 through 35-2, 35-4, 35-7, 55-1 through 55-8, 55-10, through 55-11, 50-1; ASC 460-10-60-15 Accounting for Weather Derivatives

BACKGROUND

Weather derivative contracts, which are contracts indexed to climactic or geological variables, are new types of derivatives seen in the market. An increasing number of entities are entering into such contracts for a number of business reasons.

Current accounting practices are diverse, because it is unclear whether the contracts should be accounted for under accrual accounting, settlement accounting, or insurance accounting. Some believe that changes in the fair value of those contracts should be recognized in earnings at each reporting date.

Under the guidance in ASC 815, contracts that are not traded on an exchange are not covered by the Statement if they are settled based on a climactic or geological variable or another physical variable. However, if derivatives settled based on a physical variable eventually become exchange-traded, they will be covered under the guidance in ASC 815.

Contracts written by insurance companies to compensate their holders for an insurable event that causes the holder to incur a liability or that adversely affects the value of a specific asset or liability for which the holder is at risk are *not* covered by the scope of this Issue.

ACCOUNTING ISSUES

1. How should an entity account for a weather derivative that is nonexchange-traded or forward-based (risk is two-directional)?

2. How should an entity account for a purchased weather derivative that is nonexchange-traded and option-based (risk is one-directional)?

3. How should an entity account for a written weather derivative that is nonexchange-traded and option-based?

ACCOUNTING GUIDANCE

1. Use the *intrinsic value method* to account for nonexchange-traded, forward-based weather derivatives that are entered into for nontrading purposes. Under that method, the value of the derivative is computed as follows: (*a*) determine the difference between the expected results of an allocation of the cumulative strike price at inception and the actual results during the period; (*b*) multiply that amount by the contract price, such as dollars per heating degree day; (*c*) allocate the cumulative strike price based on information from external statistical sources, such as the National Weather Service, to individual periods within the contract's term based on a reasonable expectation at the inception of the term of normal or expected experience under the contract. At interim periods, calculate the intrinsic value of the contract based on the cumulative difference between actual experience and the allocation through that date. The allocation of the cumulative strike price at inception should *not* be adjusted when actual results are known.

2. Amortize the premium paid or due on a nonexchange-traded, option-based weather derivative purchased for nontrading purposes to expense in a rational and systematic manner. Measure the contract at interim balance-sheet dates using the intrinsic value method as discussed above.

3. Account for all weather derivatives entered into for trading or speculative purposes at *fair value* and report subsequent fair value changes in period earnings.

4. Under this Issue, entering into weather derivative contracts for the purpose of earning a profit on an exposure to changes in climactic or geological conditions indicates that an entity may be involved in trading or speculative activities. Judgment based on the relevant facts and circumstances must be used in evaluating whether or when an entity's involvement in weather derivative contracts should be considered a trading or speculative activity. That evaluation should consider the entity's various activities rather than merely considering the terms of the contract. The entity's intent for entering into weather derivative contracts is another consideration. The following factors or indicators should be considered in evaluating whether an operation's (subsidiary, division, or unit) weather derivative contracts are entered into for trading or speculative purposes. Affirmative answers to the questions in Category A are strong indicators that the operation is not engaged in trading activities. Although affirmative answers only to the questions in Category B may indicate that the operation is engaged in trading activities, negative answers to any or all of the questions in either category may not by themselves indicate that the operation is not engaged in trading activities. All available information should be used to reach a conclusion:

   a. Fundamental indicators

      (1) Is the operation's primary business exposed to weather related risk covered by the contracts held?

      (2) Is the volume of weather derivative contracts reasonable in relation to the operation's primary business?

(3) Is the contract's change in value expected to move in a direction that would mitigate or offset the risk of the underlying exposure?

(4) Does the operation price the contract offers or trades based on externally developed price models?

b. Secondary indicators—management and controls

(1) Are compensation or performance measures or both related to short-term profits on weather derivative contracts?

(2) Do internal communications discuss the operation's business activities in terms of the operation's trading strategy?

(3) Does the operation's business name include the term *trading?*

(4) Are the operation's employees referred to as *traders?*

(5) Are net market positions determined regularly?

(6) Is the operation's infrastructure segregated by back office processing functions and front office trading function as in a trading operation or an investment bank?

(7) Is the operation's infrastructure equipped to determine price and other risks on a real-time basis?

(8) Does the operation manage its activities on a portfolio or book basis?

Although it is easier to determine whether an operation is engaged in trading activities when those activities are segregated within the organization or by legal entity, only the portion of an operation that is determined to be engaged in trading activities, based on an evaluation of the indicators discussed above, should be required to account for its activities at fair value. Entities whose trading activities are not segregated from their other activities should identify their trading and nontrading contracts at inception using the above indicators.

Because weather derivative contracts under the scope of this Issue are financial instruments, entities that enter into such contracts should make the required disclosures for financial instruments in ASC 825-10-50-2A, 50-3 through 50-4, 50-8 through 50-23, 50-26; 55-3 through 55-5.

PRACTICE POINTER: Under the guidance in ASC 460, at the inception of a guarantee, a guarantor is required to recognize a liability for the obligation assumed by issuing the guarantee. Weather derivatives are option-based contracts under which the party receiving the guarantee is paid based on whether a specific event related to the weather does or does not occur at a specified location within a specified time period, such as 20 inches of snow in New York City during the first week of February. Under the guidance in ASC 460, which requires that payments be based on a change in an underlying related to an asset or liability of the party to whom the guarantee was given, a weather derivative is *not* a guarantee, because an event related to the weather is not an asset or liability of the party to whom the guarantee was given.

SEC OBSERVER COMMENT

The SEC Observer stated that because weather derivative contracts under the scope of this guidance are financial instruments, the SEC staff believes that registrants should make the disclosures about those contracts required in Item 305 of SEC Regulation S-K, if applicable.

CHAPTER 51

ASC 820—FAIR VALUE MEASUREMENT

CONTENTS

PART I: GENERAL GUIDANCE

ASC 820-10: OVERALL

OVERVIEW

The early years of the 21st century have introduced a new era in which fair value measurement is gradually replacing historical cost as the primary measurement approach for certain assets and liabilities. Evidence suggests that fair value measurement and reporting will be extended to a wide range of balance sheet items as experience with developing and auditing fair value information becomes more widespread.

The Codification has two primary Topics on fair value: ASC 820 (Fair Value Measurement) and ASC 825 (Financial Instruments). For a discussion of the fair value option for financial assets and liabilities, see the Chapter 52, *ASC 825—Financial Instruments*. In addition, fair value is currently required in accounting for a wide range of financial instruments under other FASB standards. Guidance related to financial reporting and changing prices was issued in 1979 during a period of the highest inflation in the United States in recent history. That guidance, which required companies that met a specified size criterion to report supplemental information on current value basis, was later eliminated as a requirement owing to a reduction in inflation and the belief that the information required was of limited value to users of financial statements. This guidance is technically still in effect, although application of it is on a voluntary basis and rarely, if ever, implemented. For coverage of this guidance, see Chapter 10, *ASC 255—Changing Prices*.

BACKGROUND

For many years, historical cost was the primary basis by which assets and liabilities were accounted. The advantage of historical cost over alternative measurement methods was primarily due to its objectivity. That is, the cost of an item at its origin (i.e., its historical cost) to the reporting entity was generally believed to be more readily determined by objective means than were other measures of value, such as current replacement cost, current exit or sales price, or fair value. Notable exceptions were situations in which the historical cost exceeded the current value of an item, leading to the application of the lower of cost or market for inventories and some investments. More recently, however, standards have been developed that require an assessment of the impairment of value where evidence suggests that an item's current worth is less than its recorded amount.

FAIR VALUE MEASUREMENT

ASC 820 defines fair value, establishes a framework for measuring fair value in generally accepted accounting principles, and requires disclosures about fair value measurements. Fair value is based on market prices or market inputs; fair value is not based on entity-specific measurements. The objective of fair value measurement is to estimate the price at which an asset could be sold, or a liability settled, in an orderly transaction between market participants at the measurement date (i.e., fair value measures exit prices) (ASC 820-10-05-1B).

When available, fair value should be determined by referring to market prices for identical assets and liabilities. If market prices are not available, fair value is to be estimated using a valuation technique that maximizes the use of relevant observable market inputs and minimizes the use of unobservable market inputs. Assumptions used in determining fair value should be consistent with the assumptions that market participants would use (ASC 820-10-05-1C).

Scope

The guidance in ASC 820 applies in situations where other accounting pronouncements require or permit fair value measurements with the following exceptions:

- ASC 820 does not apply under accounting principles that address share-based payment transactions, such as ASC 718, *Compensation—Stock Compensation,* except for ASC 718-40 which is within the scope of ASC 820 (ASC 820-10-15-2).
- ASC 820 does not eliminate the practicability exceptions to fair value measurements that are included in accounting pronouncements within the scope of ASC 820 (ASC 820-10-15-3).
- ASC 820 does not apply to the recognition and measurement of revenue from contracts in accordance with ASC 606 (Revenue from Contracts with Customers) or to the recognition and measurement of gains and losses upon the derecognition of nonfinancial assets in accordance with ASC 610-20 (Gains and Losses from the Derecognition of Nonfinancial Assets) (ASC 820-10-15-2).

In addition, ASC 820 does not apply under accounting pronouncements that require or permit measurements that are similar to fair value but that are not intended to measure fair value (e.g., ASC 330 (Inventory)) (ASC 820-10-15-2).

Measurement

Fair value is the price that would be received to sell an asset or paid to transfer a liability in an orderly transaction between market participants at the measurement date (ASC 820-10-35-2). In determining the fair value of an asset or liability, the characteristics of the asset or liability should be considered if these characteristics would be considered by the market. Examples of potentially relevant characteristics are the condition and location of the asset, as well as any restrictions on the sale or use of the asset (ASC 820-10-35-2B).

The asset or liability may be a standalone asset or liability or a group of assets or liabilities, depending on its unit of account (ASC 820-10-35-2D). The unit of account determines what is being measured by reference to the level at which the asset or liability is aggregated for purposes of applying other ASC topics that require or permit fair value measurement (ASC 820-10-35-2E).

Fair value measurement assumes that the asset or liability is exchanged in an orderly transaction between market participants to sell the asset or transfer the liability at the measurement date under current market conditions. The term "orderly transaction" refers to a transaction that assumes exposure to the market for a period prior to the measurement date to allow for market activities that are usual and customary for transactions involving such assets or liabilities. It is not a forced transaction. The objective of a fair value measurement is to determine the price that would be received to sell the asset or paid to transfer the liability at the measurement date (referred to as the exit price) (ASC 820-10-35-3).

PRACTICE POINTER: The Securities and Exchange Commission's Division of Corporate Finance indicates that actual market prices are relevant in determining fair value even when the market is less liquid than its historical norm (i.e., reduced trading volume). However, actual market prices should not be used in determining fair value if they reflect a forced liquidation or distress sale.

Principal or Most Advantageous Market

A fair value measurement assumes that the transaction to sell the asset or transfer the liability occurs in the principal market for the asset or liability or, in the absence of a principal market, the most advantageous market for the asset or liability (ASC 820-10-35-5). The principal market is the market in which the reporting entity would normally sell the asset or transfer the liability. The most advantageous market is the market in which the reporting entity would sell the asset or transfer the liability at a price that maximizes the amount that would be received for the asset or minimizes the amount that would be paid to transfer the liability. An exhaustive search does not have to be performed to identify the principal or most advantageous market (ASC 820-10-35-5A). However, the reporting entity must have access to the principal (or most advantageous) market at the measurement date. Since different entities have access to different markets, the principal (or most advantageous market) for a particular asset or liability may differ across entities (ASC 820-10-35-6A). Although a reporting entity must have access to the principal (or most advantageous) market, the entity does not need to be able to sell the asset or transfer the liability on the measurement date in order to estimate fair value using the principal (or most advantageous) market (ASC 820-10-35-6B).

PRACTICE POINTER: Assuming a principal market (i.e., market with the greatest volume of activity for the asset or liability), fair value is determined by reference to the price in that market even if the price in another market is more advantageous for the company (ASC 820-10-35-6).

The price in the principal or most advantageous market used to measure the fair value of the asset or liability should not be adjusted for transaction costs. Transaction costs represent the incremental direct costs to sell the asset or transfer the liability in the principal or most advantageous market for the asset or liability. These costs are not an attribute of the asset or liability. Transaction costs do not include the costs that would be incurred to transport the asset or liability to its principal or most advantageous market. The price in the principal or most advantageous market used to measure the fair value of the asset or liability shall be adjusted for the costs that would be incurred to transport the asset or liability to its principal or most advantageous market (ASC 820-10-35-9B, 9C).

PRACTICE POINTER: In some cases, there may not be a market price available for the asset or liability on the measurement date. In this case, the reporting entity must still assume that a transaction to sell the asset or transfer the liability could take place. A reporting entity will have to determine fair value using a model when market prices do not exist (ASC 820-10-35-6C).

Illustration of Determining the Highest and Best Use of an Asset

Hogan Company (Hogan) has recently acquired land in a business combination. The land hosts a manufacturing facility. Similar parcels of land have recently been sold and converted to residential use. Hogan determines that it could sell its land for residential use. The fair value of the manufacturing operation is $2.5 million. It would cost Hogan $500,000 to demolish the manufacturing operation and to otherwise convert the land to a vacant site suitable for residential development. The value of a vacant site if sold for such a development is $2.7 million. The fair value of the land if used to host the manufacturing operation (i.e., in-use value), $2.5 million, exceeds the fair value of the land if readied and sold for residential development (i.e., in-exchange value), $2.2 million (i.e., $2.7 million – 0.5 million). Therefore, the highest and best use of the land is its in-use value, $2.5 million.

Market Participants

Market participants are buyers and sellers in the principal or most advantageous market for the asset or liability that meet the following criteria:

- They are independent of the reporting entity.
- They are knowledgeable, having a reasonable understanding about the asset or liability and the transaction based on all available information.
- They are able to transact for the asset or liability.
- They are willing to transact for the asset or liability (i.e., willing, but not forced or otherwise compelled to do so).

The fair value of the asset or liability is determined based on the assumptions market participants would use in pricing the asset or liability, assuming that market participants will act in their own best interests. In developing the assumptions, the reporting entity is not required to identify specific market participants. Rather, it should identify characteristics that distinguish market participants generally, considering factors specific to the asset or liability, the principal or most advantageous market for the asset or liability, and market participants with whom the reporting entity would transact in that market (ASC 820-10-35-9).

Application to Nonfinancial Assets

A fair value measurement assumes the highest and best use of the nonfinancial asset by market participants, considering the use of the asset that is physically possible, legally permissible, and financially feasible at the measurement date. The highest and best use of the nonfinancial asset determines the valuation premise that is used to measure the fair value of the asset (ASC 820-10-35-10A, 10B).

PRACTICE NOTE: The reporting entity's current use of a nonfinancial asset is assumed to be the asset's highest and best use absent evidence to the contrary (ASC 820-10-35-10C).

In-Use Assets The highest and best use of the nonfinancial asset is in use if the asset would provide maximum value to market participants principally in combination with other assets or with other assets and liabilities. In this instance, the fair value of the nonfinancial asset is determined based on the price that would be received in a current transaction to sell the asset assuming that the asset would be used with other assets or with other assets and liabilities and that the assets would be available to market participants (ASC 820-10-35-10E).

PRACTICE NOTE: If a nonfinancial asset's highest and best use is in-use, the assumption is that other market participants already own the other assets and liabilities that the asset to be measured is used in combination with (ASC 820-10-35-11A).

An entity must measure the fair value of a nonfinancial asset at its highest and best use, from the perspective of market participants, even if the reporting entity doesn't plan to use the asset in that manner (ASC 820-10-35-10D).

Standalone Assets A nonfinancial asset might provide maximum value to market participants if the asset is used on a standalone basis. In this instance, the fair value of the nonfinancial asset is measured based on the price that would be received in a current transaction to sell the nonfinancial asset standalone (ASC 820-10-35-10E).

Application to Liabilities and Instruments Included Within Shareholders' Equity

Fair value measurement assumes that the liability or instrument included within shareholders' equity (e.g., equity instruments issued as consideration in a business combination) is transferred to a market participant at the measurement date and that the nonperformance risk related to the liability is the same before and after its transfer. Nonperformance risk refers to the risk that the obligation will not be fulfilled and affects the value at which the liability is transferred. The fair value of the liability shall reflect the nonperformance risk relating to that liability. The credit risk of the reporting entity is one factor in determining the nonperformance risk. Nonperformance risk should be the same after the assumed transfer as it was before the transfer (ASC 820-10-35-16, 17, 18). Some liabilities include a third-party credit enhancement (e.g., credit default insurance, other guarantees, etc.). When that third-party enhancement is accounted for separately, it should not be considered in determining the fair value of the liability (ASC 820-10-35-18A).

A fair value measurement assumes that a liability is exchanged in an orderly transaction between market participants. However, most liabilities have contractual or legal restrictions that prevent the liabilities from being transferred, although some liabilities are traded in the marketplace as assets. If a quoted market price for an identical liability exists, then that price would represent a Level 1 measurement. However, if no such quoted price exists for an identical liability, a reporting entity must measure fair value using one or more of the following approaches (ASC 820-10-35-16B, 16BB):

- A valuation approach that uses:
  - — The quoted price in an active market of an identical item when that item is held by another entity as an asset
  - — The quoted price in a non-active market of an identical item when that item is held by another entity as an asset
  - — Quoted prices for similar liabilities or similar liabilities when traded as assets
  - — A valuation approach—for example, an income approach that would be used to value the item if it was held as an asset

When measuring the fair value of a liability or an equity instrument held by another party as an asset, a reporting entity must adjust the quoted price of the asset only if there are factors that are specific to the asset but are not applicable to the fair value measurement of the liability or shareholders' equity instrument. If the asset includes a characteristic restricting its sale, then the fair value of the asset should also include the effect of the restriction. For example, a reporting entity must consider whether the quoted price of the asset should be adjusted if the quoted price for the asset relates to a similar (but not identical) liability or shareholders' equity instrument traded as an asset, or if the unit of account for the asset is not the same as for the liability or shareholders' equity instrument (ASC 820-10-35-16D).

There are some liabilities and shareholders' equity instruments without a readily determinable market value and where the identical item is not held by another party as an asset (e.g., an asset retirement obligation). In this case, fair value is determined using a valuation technique from the perspective of a market participant that owes the liability or has issued the claim on equity (ASC 820-10-35-16H). For example, the present value of a liability in this case would include estimates of future cash outflows to settle the liability and the compensation that the market participant would require to assume the obligation. The compensation required to assume the obligation includes payment both for assuming the obligation given that resources can be used for other purposes, and includes a premium for the risk that the actual cash outflows will exceed the expected cash outflows (ASC 820-10-35-16J). In adjusting for risk, either future cash outflows can be increased or the discount rate used to determine present value can be reduced, but not both (ASC 820-10-35-16L).

Application to Financial Assets and Financial Liabilities with Offsetting Positions

Generally, the fair value of financial instruments is to be measured at the level of the individual asset or liability (i.e., the fair values of assets and liabilities are presented gross and are not netted). Some entities hold groups of financial assets, financial liabilities, nonfinancial items accounted for as derivatives in accordance with ASC 815, or combinations of these items that are exposed to common risks. These common risks might be interest rate risk, currency risk, or credit risk. An entity might manage its exposure to these types of risks on a net basis, rather than on a group basis. When an entity manages its exposure to market and credit risk on a net basis, the entity can determine the fair value of the net position—either the price that would be received for selling a net asset position, or the price that would be paid to transfer a net liability position. However, this exception to the normal guidance in ASC 820 is only available when the risks to be offset are substantially the same (ASC 820-10-35-18D, 18J). The reporting entity must make an accounting policy decision to avail itself of the exception that allows certain financial instruments to be measured on a net basis rather than on a gross basis (ASC 820-10-35-18G).

PRACTICE NOTE: The exception that allows certain financial instruments to be measured on a net rather than on a gross basis only applies to financial assets and financial liabilities within the scope of ASC 815 or ASC 825 and nonfinancial items accounted for as derivatives in accordance with ASC 815. (ASC 820-10-35-18H)

Although an entity may be able to measure fair value on a net basis given the guidance in the preceding paragraph, the exception does not pertain to financial statement presentation. That is, financial instruments may need to be presented on a gross basis in the financial statements even though they are measured on a net basis (ASC 820-10-35-18F).

Fair Value at Initial Recognition

When an asset is acquired or a liability assumed in an exchange, the transaction price represents the price paid to acquire the asset or received to assume the liability. In contrast, the fair value of the asset or liability represents the price that would be received to sell the asset or paid to transfer the liability (i.e., an exit price) (ASC 820-10-30-2).

In many cases, the transaction price equals the exit price and, therefore, represents the fair value of the asset or liability at initial recognition. In determining whether a transaction price represents the fair value of the asset or liability at initial recognition, the reporting entity must consider factors specific to the transaction and to the specific asset or liability. Examples of situations in which the transaction price might not represent the fair value of an asset or liability at initial recognition are when (ASC 820-10-30-3A):

- The transaction is between related parties.
- The transaction occurs under duress or the seller is forced to accept the price in the transaction.
- The unit of account represented by the transaction price is different from the unit of account of the asset or liability measured at fair value (e.g., the asset is one element in the transaction that includes multiple elements).
- The market in which the transaction occurs is different from the market in which the reporting entity would sell the asset or transfer the liability.

Illustration of Using Observable Market Inputs in the Most Advantageous Market

Daves Incorporated (Daves) owns 50,000 shares of the common stock of Fauver Company (Fauver). The stock of Fauver is traded on two different markets, A and B. The price of Fauver on A is $17 per share and transaction costs are $2. The price of Fauver on B is $16 per share and transaction costs are $0.50. Neither market is the principal market for Fauver. Because neither market is the principal market, fair value is determined using the market that maximizes the amount that would be received after considering transaction costs. The net amount received on Market A would be $15 and it would be $15.50 on Market B. Therefore, the fair value of Fauver stock is determined using the price in that market—$16. Note that although transaction costs are considered in determining the most advantageous market, these costs are not considered in determining the fair value of the asset.

Valuation Techniques

Valuation techniques are classified in ASC 820 in three categories: (1) market approach; (2) income approach; and (3) cost approach. Following are brief descriptions of each approach.

Market approach The market approach uses prices and other relevant information generated by market transactions involving identical or comparable assets or liabilities. These approaches often use market multiples derived from a set of comparables. Multiples might lie in ranges with a different multiple for each comparable. The selection of where within the range the appropriate multiple falls requires judgment. Matrix pricing is a valuation technique that is consistent with the market approach.

Income approach The income approach uses valuation techniques to convert future amounts to a single present amount. The measurement is based on the value indicated by current market expectations about those future amounts. Examples include present value techniques, option pricing models, such as the Black-Scholes-Merton formula, and a binomial model.

Cost approach The cost approach is based on the amount that currently would be required to replace the service capacity of an asset (sometimes referred to as current replacement cost). The price that would be received for the asset is determined on the basis of the cost to a buyer to acquire or construct a substitute asset of comparable utility, adjusted for obsolescence.

Valuation techniques that are appropriate in the circumstances and for which sufficient data are available shall be used to measure fair value. A combination of valuation techniques may be appropriate, and valuation techniques used to measure fair value shall be applied consistently. A change in the valuation technique or its application is appropriate if the change results in a measurement that is equally or more representative of fair value in the circumstance. Revisions from a change in the valuation technique or its application are accounted for as changes in accounting estimate in accordance with ASC 250 (Accounting Changes and Error Corrections).

The term "inputs" refers to the assumptions that market participants use in pricing the asset or liability. Observable inputs reflect the assumptions market participants would use in pricing the asset or liability based on market data obtained from sources independent of the reporting entity. Unobservable inputs reflect the reporting entity's own assumptions about the assumptions market participants would use in pricing the asset or liability developed on the basis of the best information available in the circumstances. Valuation techniques should maximize the use of observable inputs and minimize the use of unobservable inputs (ASC 820-10-35-24, 36).

Valuation techniques used to measure fair value shall be applied consistently. A change in a valuation technique or its application is appropriate if the change results in a measurement that is equally or more representative of the fair value in the circumstances. Revisions resulting from a change in the valuation technique or its application shall be accounted for as a change in accounting estimate (ASC 820-10-35-25, 26).

Premiums or discounts in determining fair value are not to be considered when a quoted price in an active market is available. However, if a quoted price in an active market is not available, premiums or discounts are to be considered in determining fair value if they would be considered by market participants in pricing the asset or liability. Any premium or discount considered needs to be related to the underlying asset or liability—for example, a control premium would be considered. Conversely, features that describe an entity's asset holding—for example, the size of the reporting entity's ownership stake in another entity's equity securities (sometimes referred to as a blockage factor)—is not to be considered in determining fair value (ASC 820-10-35-36B).

Illustration of Use of Multiple Techniques to Estimate Fair Value

Cochran Incorporated (Cochran) completes a business acquisition on July 1, 20X8. Among the assets acquired is an internally developed, custom software program that is licensed to external customers. Cochran must estimate the fair value of this software program in assigning the purchase price to the individual assets and liabilities acquired. Cochran determines that the asset has a higher value in use than in exchange. Cochran cannot determine the fair value of the asset using a market approach because transactions for comparable software assets are not available given the customized nature of the software. Cochran estimates the fair value of the software using both the income and cost approach. Cochran applies the income approach by determining the present value of expected license fees over the software's useful life; the estimated fair value using this approach is $7 million. The cost of writing a substitute software program of comparable utility is $5 million. Because the software program was developed using proprietary information, Cochran concludes that it is not possible to directly replace the existing program. Therefore, Cochran estimates the fair value of the software program as $7 million.

Fair Value Hierarchy

ASC 820 contains a fair value hierarchy that is intended to increase consistency and comparability in fair value measurements and related disclosures (ASC 820-10-5-37). This hierarchy prioritizes the inputs to valuation techniques used to measure fair value into three levels: Level 1 (highest priority), Level 2, and Level 3 (lowest priority):

1. Quoted Market Prices in Active Markets (Level 1):
   a. Level 1 inputs are quoted market prices in active markets for identical assets or liabilities that are accessible at the measurement date (ASC 820-10-35-40).
   b. An active market for the asset or liability is a market in which transactions for the asset or liability occur with sufficient frequency and volume to provide pricing information on an ongoing basis (ASC Glossary).
   c. A quoted market price in an active market provides the most reliable evidence of fair value and should be used whenever available (ASC 820-10-35-41).
   d. For liabilities, a quoted price in an active market for the identical liability is a Level 1 input. A quoted price for the identical liability when traded as an asset is also a Level 1 input if no adjustments are required to the quoted price of the asset. Any adjustment required to the quoted price of the asset will result in a lower level measurement (ASC 820-10-35-41C).
2. Other Than Quoted Market Inputs (Level 2) (ASC 820-10-35-47, 48):
   a. Level 2 inputs are from other than quoted market prices included in Level 1 that are observable for the asset or liability, either directly or indirectly.
   b. Level 2 inputs include the following:
      (1) Quoted market prices of similar assets or liabilities in active markets;
      (2) Quoted market prices for identical or similar assets or liabilities in markets that are not active;

(3) Inputs other than quoted prices that are observable for the asset or liability (e.g., interest rates and yield curves observable at commonly quoted intervals, volatilities, prepayment speeds, loss severities, credit spreads, and default rates); and

(4) Inputs that are derived principally from or corroborated by observable market data by correlation or other means.

3. Unobservable Inputs (Level 3) (ASC 820-10-35-53, 54A):

   a. Level 3 inputs are unobservable and shall be used to measure fair value to the extent that observable inputs are not available.

   b. Unobservable inputs are allowed in situations where there is little, if any, market activity for the asset or liability at the measurement date.

   c. Unobservable inputs reflect the assumptions that market participants would use in pricing the asset or liability.

   d. Unobservable inputs shall be developed based on the best information available under the circumstances. The entity is not required to consider all possible efforts to obtain information about market participant assumptions, but the entity shall not ignore information about market participant assumptions that is reasonably available without undue cost and effort.

PRACTICE POINTER: In some cases both observable and unobservable inputs may be used to estimate fair value. When the use of an unobservable input has a significant effect on the fair value estimate, the measurement would be categorized as having been made within Level 3 of the fair value hierarchy (ASC 820-10-35-38A).

Fair Value Given a Decline in the Volume or Level of Activity

The fair value of an asset or liability may be affected when there is a significant decline in the volume or level of activity for the asset or liability. Items to consider in evaluating the significance of any decline in the volume or level of activity include: (1) the number of recent transactions; (2) whether price quotations are based on current information; (3) wide variations in price quotations, either compared to the past or across different market makers; (4) indices that historically were correlated with fair value measurements are no longer highly correlated; (5) a significant increase in implied liquidity risk premiums or yields; (6) a wide bid-ask spread or a significant increase in the bid-ask spread; (7) a significant decrease in new issuances of securities; and (8) a lack of information about transactions in principal-to-principal markets (ASC 820-10-35-54C).

A significant decrease in the volume or level of activity does not automatically indicate that market prices do not represent fair value or that transactions in the market are not orderly. However, if the entity determines that the transaction (market) price does not represent fair value, an adjustment to the entity's fair value determination must be made. Moreover, any such adjustment may be significant to the entity's estimate of fair value. Generally, a reduction in the volume or level of activity in a market indicates heightened risk. As a result, in determining fair value, the risk premium that would be assessed by market participants needs to be considered in determining fair value (ASC 820-10-35-54E). When there is a significant decline in the volume or level of activity, the entity may want to use multiple valuation techniques in determining fair value (ASC 820-10-35-54F).

Transactions that Are Not Orderly

Just because the volume or level of activity for an asset or liability has declined does not automatically indicate that transactions are not orderly. Indicators that a transaction may not be orderly include: (1) the asset or liability was exposed to the market for too short a time before the financial statement date to adequately market the asset or liability, (2) the seller only marketed the asset or liability to a single buyer, (3) the seller is distressed, (4) the seller was forced to sell by a regulator or to meet legal requirements, (5) the transaction price differs greatly from the prices of other recent transactions (ASC 820-10-35-54I).

If the transaction is not orderly, very little weight should be placed on the transaction in determining fair value. If the entity cannot determine whether the transaction was orderly, the transaction price is one input in determining fair value but it would receive less weight than when the transaction is known to have been orderly. The entity does not have to undertake exhaustive efforts to determine if the transaction is orderly; however, the entity cannot ignore evidence that is reasonably available (ASC 820-10-35-54J).

PRACTICE POINTER: An entity can use quoted prices provided by third parties (e.g., pricing services and brokers) in determining fair value. However, these third parties must determine fair value in accordance with the guidance in ASC 820 (ASC 820-10-35-54L). Moreover, not all quotes from third parties are created equal—binding offers should be afforded greater weight in determining fair value than indicative prices (ASC 820-10-35-54M).

Illustration of Using a Level 2 Input to Estimate Fair Value

King Company (King) acquires a recently developed and unoccupied office building. King needs to estimate the fair value of the building in assigning the purchase price to the individual assets and liabilities acquired. As the building is new and has not yet been occupied, King cannot determine the fair value of the building using a Level 1 input—a quoted price in an active market for the identical asset. However, it can determine a fair value for the building using a Level 2 input. King determines the price per square foot received in rent for similar buildings in similar locations based on actual transactions. Using this price per square foot, King can determine the likely rental income the building will generate and thereby estimate the fair value of the building using an income approach.

Disclosures

For assets and liabilities that are measured at fair value in the statement of financial position or disclosed in the notes to the financial statements, the reporting entity shall disclose the following information (ASC 820-10-50-1C):

- The valuation techniques and inputs used to arrive at its measures of fair value, including judgments and assumptions that the entity makes
- The uncertainty in the fair value measurements as of the reporting date
- How changes in fair value measurements affect an entity's performance and cash flows

In deciding whether this disclosure objective is met, the reporting entity shall consider: (1) how detailed its disclosures need to be, (2) which disclosures to emphasize, (3) the appropriate level of aggregation vs. disaggregation, and (4) whether users need additional information to be able to properly evaluate the quantitative information disclosed (ASC 820-10-50-1D).

To meet these requirements, the following information is required to be disclosed for each class of assets and liabilities measured at fair value in the statement of financial position after initial recognition. These disclosure requirements do not apply to investments within the scope of ASC 820-10-15-4 through 15-5 that measure fair value using net asset value per share as a practical expedient, in accordance with ASC 820-10-35-59 (ASC 820-10-50-2):

- The fair value measurement at the end of the reporting period, for both recurring and nonrecurring fair value measurements. The reasons for any nonrecurring fair value measurements need to be disclosed (e.g., a long-lived asset held for sale measured at fair value less cost to sell).
- The level within the fair value hierarchy in which the fair value measurement in its entirety falls, segregating the fair value measurement using quoted prices in active markets (Level 1), significant other observable inputs (Level 2), and significant unobservable inputs (Level 3), separately for both recurring and nonrecurring fair value measurements. These disclosures are not required for nonpublic entities (ASC 820-10-50-2F).
- A description of the valuation techniques and inputs to determine fair value for recurring and nonrecurring fair value measurements categorized within Level 2 or 3 of the hierarchy. In addition, any change in either or both a valuation approach and a valuation technique, and the reason therefor, need to be disclosed.
- Quantitative information about significant unobservable inputs for recurring and nonrecurring fair value measurements determined using Level 3 of the hierarchy.
- For recurring fair value measurements based on Level 3 of the hierarchy, a reconciliation as of the beginning and ending balances, separately presenting changes during the period from each of the following:
  - — Total gains or losses for the period recognized in earnings (or changes in net assets), and the line item of where those gains or losses are included in earnings (or changes in net assets);

  - Total gains or losses for the period recognized in other comprehensive income, and the line item of where those gains and losses are included in other comprehensive income;
  - Purchases, sales, issues, and settlements (each type disclosed separately); and
  - Transfers in and/or out of Level 3 and the reasons for those transfers. These disclosures must separately identify significant transfers into Level 3 from transfers out of Level 3. A reporting entity must consistently follow its policy for determining which transfers are significant and when those transfers between levels are recognized. A reporting entity's policy as to the timing of recognizing transfers must be the same for transfers into Level 3 as that for transfers out of Level 3. The timing of this recognition could be, for example: (1) the actual date of the event or change in circumstances that caused the transfer, (2) the beginning of the reporting period, or (3) the end of the reporting period (ASC 820-10-50-2C).
- For recurring fair value measurements based on Level 3 of the hierarchy, the amount of the total gains or losses for the period included in earnings (or changes in net assets) that is attributable to the change in unrealized gains or losses relating to those assets and liabilities held at the end of the reporting period and the line item of where those unrealized gains or losses are reported in the statements of comprehensive income (or activities).
- For recurring fair value measurements based on Level 3 of the hierarchy, a description of the uncertainty of the fair value measurement due to the use of significant unobservable inputs if those inputs reasonably could have been different at the reporting date. In addition, if other significant unobservable inputs interrelate with other highly sensitive unobservable inputs, these interrelationships and their possible effects must be disclosed. These disclosures are not required for nonpublic entities.
- For recurring and nonrecurring fair value measurements, disclose if the highest and best use of a nonfinancial asset differs from its current use, and explain why a nonfinancial asset is being used in a manner different from its highest and best use.

An entity must determine the appropriate classes of assets and liabilities—these classes determine the relevant groupings for which fair value information is reported. In determining the appropriate classes of assets and liabilities, the entity is to consider: (1) nature, characteristics, and risks of the assets and liabilities; and (2) the level of the hierarchy used to determine fair value (ASC 820-10-50-2B).

PRACTICE POINTER: Determining the appropriate classes of assets and liabilities for which to disclose fair value information requires judgment. Notwithstanding this fact, the number of classes of assets and liabilities disclosed when fair value is determined using Level 3 of the hierarchy is likely to be greater due to the greater degree of uncertainty and subjectivity associated with Level 3 measurements (ASC 820-10-50-2B).

The fair value of certain assets and liabilities may be required to be disclosed but the asset or liability may not be measured at fair value in the financial statements. In that case, limited disclosures are required for public companies. However, public companies are not required to disclose information about significant unobservable inputs (ASC 820-10-50-2E). No disclosures are required for nonpublic companies (ASC 820-10-50-2F).

For derivative assets and liabilities, an entity must present both of the following (ASC 820-10-50-3):

- The fair value disclosures required by ASC 820-10-50-2(a) through (b) on a gross basis.
- The reconciliation disclosure required by ASC 820-10-50-2(c) through (d) on either a gross or a net basis.

The quantitative disclosures required by ASC 820 are required to be presented using a tabular format (ASC 820-10-50-8). In addition, a change in the valuation technique used to determine fair value is not considered a change in accounting estimate under ASC 250 (ASC 820-10-50-7).

PART II: INTERPRETIVE GUIDANCE

ASC 820-10: OVERALL

ASC 820-10-05-3, 55-23C through 55-23D, 25-1 through 25-2, 50-4A, 55-8 through 55-9 Liability Issued with an Inseparable Third-Party Enhancement

BACKGROUND

Issuers of debt securities sometimes issue their securities combined with a financial guarantee made by an unrelated third party (i.e., a credit enhancement), which the issuer purchases to guarantee its credit obligations. The guarantee gives investors additional assurance that the debt will be paid by the issuer or the guarantor and usually enables the issuer to: (1) pay a lower interest rate on the debt securities; (2) receive higher proceeds; or (3) both.

Generally, if an issuer that has issued debt securities with a credit enhancement defaults on its debt, the issuer is *not* released from its obligation, because the issuer is required to reimburse the guarantor for payments made to investors. Consequently, if an issuer of debt securities defaults on its obligation, that obligation still exists but the investor has been paid by a different creditor.

Under the guidance in ASC 825, which was effective for fiscal years that began after November 15, 2007, an entity is permitted to measure its financial assets and liabilities at fair value depending on certain requirements. Therefore, an entity is permitted to measure the liability discussed below at fair value. In addition, under the guidance in ASC 825 requires entities to disclose the fair value of all financial instruments (with some exceptions). Because under the guidance in ASC 820, the fair value of a liability must include the risk that an obligation will *not* be satisfied, some have questioned whether a debt instrument that includes an *inseparable* credit enhancement should be accounted for as one unit of accounting or as two if the debt instrument is measured at fair value.

ACCOUNTING ISSUE

Should a debt instrument that includes an *inseparable* credit enhancement be accounted for as one unit of accounting or as two if the debt instrument is measured at fair value?

SCOPE

The guidance in this Issue applies to the accounting for a debt instrument measured at fair value that is issued with a contractual guarantee from a third party (i.e., credit enhancement) that cannot be separated from the debt instrument. It does *not* apply to the accounting for guarantees, such as deposit insurance, provided by a government or a government agency.

ACCOUNTING GUIDANCE

Measurement

An issuer's fair value measurement of its liability for a debt instrument issued with a credit enhancement purchased from an unrelated third party should *not* include the effect of the credit enhancement in the liability's fair value measurement, which is not the issuer's asset but was purchased by the issuer for the investor's benefit. By purchasing a credit enhancement, an issuer transfers its debt obligation from the investor to the guarantor. Proceeds received by the issuer from an investor who has purchased the liability with the credit enhancement should be allocated to the premium paid for the credit enhancement and to the issued liability.

Disclosure

An issuer should disclose the existence of a credit enhancement on its issued debt that the issuer purchased from an unrelated third party.

ASC 820-10-35-54C through 35-54M Determining Fair Value When the Volume and Level of Activity for the Asset or Liability Have Significantly Decreased

BACKGROUND

With the issuance of the guidance in ASC 820 in September 2006, the FASB established a single definition of fair value and a framework for measuring fair value under U.S. generally accepted accounting principles (U.S. GAAP) for the purpose of increased consistency and comparability of fair value measurements. The following guidance was issued, because constituents asked for additional guidance on determining when a market for a financial asset is no longer active and whether a transaction is not orderly.

ACCOUNTING GUIDANCE

To determine whether there has been a significant decrease in the volume and level of activity for an asset or liability, a reporting entity should evaluate, the significance and relevance of the following factors, among others, based on the available evidence:

- Few recent transactions;
- Price quotations based on outdated information;
- Substantial variance in price quotations either over time or among market makers;

- Lack of correlation between indices and recent indications of the fair value of assets and liabilities that previously were highly correlated;
- Based on all available market data about credit and other nonperformance risk for an asset or liability, a significant increase in implied liquidity risk premiums, yields, or performance indicators (e.g., delinquency rates or loss severities) for observed transactions or quoted prices as compared to a reporting entity's estimate of expected cash flows;
- Wide bid-ask spread or significant increase in bid-ask spread;
- Significant decline or lack of a market for new issuances (i.e., a primary market) for an asset or liability or similar assets or liabilities; and
- Limited public information available (e.g., for transactions in a principal-to-principal market).

A reporting entity that concludes that the volume and level of activity for an asset or liability has significantly decreased in comparison to normal market activity for that asset or liability should perform further analysis of the transactions or quoted prices. A decrease in the volume or level of activity may not by itself indicate that a transaction price or quoted price does not represent fair value or that a transaction in that market is not orderly. However, if a reporting entity determines that a transaction price or quoted price does not represent fair value, the transaction prices or quoted prices need adjustment if the reporting entity uses that information to measure fair value and that adjustment may be significant to the entire fair value measurement. Significant adjustments to fair value estimates also may be necessary if the price of a similar asset requires significant adjustment for comparability to the asset being measured or if a price is out-of-date.

No guidance is provided in this discussion on how to make significant adjustments to transactions or quoted prices in the process of estimating fair value. Valuation techniques used to measure fair value are discussed in ASC 820-10-35-24 through 35-27 and 55-3A through 55-3G. Regardless of the valuation technique used, risk adjustments should be included, including a risk premium, which represents the amount that market participants would require to compensate them for uncertainty inherent in an asset's or liability's cash flows. A risk adjustment should represent an orderly transaction between market participants at the measurement date under current market conditions.

Using a different valuation technique or multiple techniques may be appropriate if there has been a significant decrease in the volume of an asset's or liability's activity. A range of fair value estimates may result when multiple valuation techniques are used to estimate fair value. The reasonableness of the range of fair values should be considered with the objective of determining the amount in the range that best represents the fair value of an asset or liability under the existing conditions. Further analysis may be required if a wide range of fair value estimates results from the use of multiple valuation techniques.

The objective of a fair value measurement does *not* change, regardless of the circumstances or the valuation techniques used. Under the guidance in ASC 820-10-35-54G:

> Fair value is the price that would be received to sell an asset or paid to transfer a liability in an orderly transaction (that is, not a forced liquidation or distressed sale) between market participants at the measurement date under current market conditions.

Estimating the price at which willing market participants would enter into a transaction considering the conditions that exist at the measurement date if there has been a significant decrease in the volume and level of activity for an asset or liability depends on the facts and circumstances and requires using significant judgment. It is irrelevant in estimating fair value whether a reporting entity intends to hold an asset or to settle a liability, because under the guidance in ASC 820-10-35-54H "[f]air value is a market-based measurement, not an entity-specific measurement."

The fact that there has been a significant decrease in the volume and level of activity for an asset or liability should not lead to a presumption that all transactions are distressed or forced (i.e., not orderly). The following circumstances, among others, may indicate that a transaction is *not* orderly:

- The lack of an adequate period of market exposure before the measurement date to carry out the usual and customary marketing activities for transactions related to such assets or liabilities under current market conditions.
- The asset or liability was marketed only to one market participant during the usual and customary marketing period.

- The seller is in or close to bankruptcy or receivership, or the sale was forced to meet regulatory or legal requirements.
- The transaction price is outside the range of fair value estimates in comparison to other recent transactions for the same or similar asset or liability.
- The seller was forced to sell because of regulatory or legal requirements.

To determine whether a transaction is orderly, an entity should evaluate the circumstances based on the weight of the evidence.

If there has been a significant decrease in the volume or level of activity for an asset or liability, an entity should consider the following guidance in its determination of whether a transaction is or is not orderly:

- Little, if any, significance, as compared to other indicators of fair value, should be placed on a transaction price in an entity's estimate of fair value or market risk premiums if the weight of the evidence indicates that the transaction is *not* orderly.
- A transaction price should be considered in an entity's estimate of fair value or market risk premiums if there is significant evidence to indicate that a transaction is orderly. The importance of a transaction price as compared to other indicators of fair value depends on the facts and circumstance, such as the volume of the transaction, comparability of the transaction to the asset or liability being measured at fair value, and the period of time between the transaction and the measurement date.
- An entity should consider a transaction price in estimating fair value or market risk premiums even if the information is insufficient to indicate whether the transaction was orderly. However, that transaction price should *not* be used as the only or primary basis for making that estimate. Less significance should be placed on transactions for which the reporting entity has insufficient information to reach a conclusion about whether the transaction is orderly in comparison to other known orderly transactions.

Although a reporting entity should *not* ignore information that is easily accessible at a reasonable cost, it need not make all possible efforts to determine whether a transaction is orderly. If a reporting entity is a party to a transaction, it is expected to have sufficient evidence as to whether a transaction is orderly.

Under the guidance in ASC 820, fair value may be estimated by using quoted prices from third parties, such as pricing services or brokers, if a reporting entity finds that those amounts were determined in accordance with the guidance in ASC 820. However, if there is a significant decrease in the volume or level of activity for an asset or liability, the reporting entity needs to evaluate whether the information is based on current orderly transactions or on a valuation technique that represents the assumptions of market participants, including assumptions about risk. Less significance should be placed on quoted prices that are not related to transactions. In addition, the nature of a quote (i.e., whether it is an indicative price or a binding offer) should be considered in determining the significance of available evidence. Binding offers should be considered to be more significant.

ASC 820-10-35-54B, 50-6A, 55-100, 55-107; ASC 230-10-15-4; ASC 715-20-50-1, 50-5 Disclosures for Investments in Certain Entities That Calculate Net Asset Value per Share (or Its Equivalent)

BACKGROUND

ASC 820-10-35-59 through 35-62 provide guidance to reporting entities that are permitted, as a practical expedient, to estimate the fair value of an investment using an investment's net asset value per share (or its equivalent), if that calculation is made in accordance with the principles in ASC 946, *Financial Services—Investment Companies*, as of the entity's measurement date. A reporting entity is eligible to measure an investment's fair value using the practical expedient if it meets the following two criteria in ASC 820-10-15-4:

1. The investment's fair value is not readily determinable.
2. The investment is in an entity that has all of the characteristics of an investment company stated in ASC 946-10-15-2 (i.e., has investment activity, has unit ownership, pools its funds, and is a reporting entity) or if an investment is in an entity that does not have all of the characteristics of an investment company, but the entity is following the industry practice of issuing financial statements based on the measurement principles used in ASC 946 (e.g., certain investments in real estate funds).

Under current U.S. generally accepted accounting principles (U.S. GAAP), entities that meet the criteria in ASC 820-10-15-4 for applying the practical expedient to measure the fair value of certain investments at net asset value per share (or its equivalent) are required to follow the guidance in ASC 820-10-35-54B regarding the categorization of those investments in the fair value hierarchy. Under that guidance, such investments that are redeemable at the measurement date at net asset value per share (or its equivalent) are categorized in Level 2, while investments that will never be redeemable at net asset value per share (or its equivalent) are categorized in Level 3. In addition, if such an investment is not redeemable at the measurement date, but will be redeemable at a future date, a reporting entity has to consider the length of time until the investment becomes redeemable in determining whether the investment should be categorized in Level 2 or Level 3 of the fair value hierarchy. Because there has been diversity in practice in determining the categorization of investments that will be redeemable in the future, the EITF addressed this issue.

ACCOUNTING ISSUE

How should an entity that elects to measure the fair value of an investment at its net asset value per share (or its equivalent) as a practical expedient under the guidance in ASC 820-10-35-59 categorize in the fair value hierarchy an investment that will be redeemable in the future?

SCOPE

The guidance applies to reporting entities electing to measure the fair value of investments under the scope of the guidance in ASC 820-10-15-4 and 15-5 by using an investment's net asset value per share (or its equivalent) as a practical expedient under the guidance in ASC 820-10-35-59.

ACCOUNTING GUIDANCE

The following is the applicable accounting guidance:

Subsequent measurement. ASC 820-10-35-54B has been amended to state that investments under the scope of ASC 820-10-15-4 and 15-5 for which fair value is measured at net asset value per share (or its equivalent) by using the practical expedient in ASC 820-10-35-59 should not be categorized under the fair value hierarchy. That guidance is also amended to state that the disclosure requirements in ASC 820-10-50-2 do not apply to such investments, but that the applicable disclosures are discussed in ASC 820-10-50-6A. Nevertheless, reporting entities are required to disclose the amount of an investment measured using the net asset value per share (or its equivalent) as a practical expedient so that the fair value of investments included in the fair value hierarchy can be reconciled to the line items presented in the balance sheet in accordance with the requirement in ASC 820-10-50-2B. Items (a) through (c) of ASC 820-10-35-54B have been superseded.

Disclosure. ASC 820-10-50-6A is amended to apply only to investments under the scope of ASC 820-10-15-4 and 15-5 for which the practical expedient has been applied. ASC 820-10-50-6A(g) has been superseded.

PRACTICE POINTER: The guidance in ASC 820-10-50-6A(b) applies to disclosures about "classes of investments that include investments that can never be redeemed with the investees, but the reporting entity receives distributions through the liquidation of the underlying assets of the investees." The requirement that an entity disclose the period of time over which the investees are expected to liquidate the underlying assets has been amended in ASU 2018-13, *Fair Value Measurement (Topic 820): Disclosure Framework—Changes to the Disclosure Requirements for Fair Value Measurement*, to require that such disclosure be made "if the investee has communicated the timing to the reporting entity or announced the timing publicly. If the timing is unknown, the reporting entity shall report that fact." The amendments in ASU 2018-13 are effective for all entities for fiscal years and interim periods within those fiscal years beginning after December 15, 2019. Early adoption is permitted upon issuance of this ASU.

Implementation guidance and illustrations. ASC 820-10-55-100 is amended to require that sufficient information be provided about assets and liabilities measured at fair value at the reporting date to enable users to reconcile to the line items presented in the balance sheet. A reference to ASC 820-10-50-2B has been added as a source of required disclosures for the fair value of assets.

Case A: Disclosure—Assets Measured at Fair Value, which is a table of fair value measurements at the end of the reporting period categorized by levels in the fair value hierarchy, has been amended by the addition of a line item for "Hedge fund investments measured at net asset value" under the "Hedge fund investments" heading and the addition of a line item "Other investments measured at net asset value" under the "Other investments" heading. Both items include an amount only in the measurement date column. Both items include a footnote reference stating that the items were measured at net asset value per share (or its equivalent) as a practical expedient and that they were not classified in the fair value hierarchy. The footnote also states that the fair value of those items was included to facilitate reconciliation of the fair value hierarchy to the line items presented in the balance sheet.

As a result of the issuance of ASU 2016-01, the table has been amended as follows:

- The subheading "Trading Securities" has been changed to "Equity Securities";
- The line item "Equity – other" and the amount have been deleted;
- The line items "Equity securities-financial services industry," "Equity securities-healthcare industry," and "Equity securities-other" have been added with related amounts in the first two columns;
- "Total trading securities" has been changed to "Total equity securities"; and
- The subheading "Available-for-sale equity securities" and the line items below it have been deleted as well as the lines for "Total available-for-sale equity securities" and "Total available-for-sale securities."

Case D: The title of Case D has been amended to apply to investments that are measured at net asset value per share (or its equivalent) as a practical expedient. ASC 820-10-55-107 is amended in the same manner, including deletion of the reference in the first sentence to the disclosures required in ASC 820-10-50-1 and 50-2. The line item for "private equity funds—international" in the table has been deleted as well as footnote (f) to that line item.

CHAPTER 52

ASC 825—FINANCIAL INSTRUMENTS

CONTENTS

PART I: GENERAL GUIDANCE

ASC 825-10: OVERALL

OVERVIEW

ASC 825 defines the term "financial instrument" as cash, evidence of an ownership interest in an entity, or a contract that both (ASC Glossary):

- Imposes on one entity a contractual obligation (1) to deliver cash or another financial instrument to a second entity or (2) to exchange other financial instruments on potentially unfavorable terms with the second entity
- Conveys to the second entity a contractual right (1) to receive cash or another financial instrument from the first entity or (2) to exchange other financial instruments on potentially favorable terms with the first entity

The Codification contains various Topics that provide guidance on accounting for different financial instruments. This chapter focuses on principles governing only fair value disclosures for all financial instruments. The term *fair value* is defined as the price that would be received to sell an asset or paid to transfer a liability in an orderly transaction between market participants at the measurement date (ASC Glossary).

ASC 825 requires disclosure of fair value information about financial instruments, whether or not those instruments are recognized in the statements of financial position, with certain exceptions. It applies to all entities. It does not change requirements for recognition, measurement, or classification of financial instruments in financial statements (ASC 825-10-50-8).

FAIR VALUE OPTION FOR FINANCIAL ASSETS AND LIABILITIES

ASC 825 provides companies with an option to report selected financial assets and liabilities at fair value. This is hereafter referred to as the "fair value option." The fair value option reduces both the complexity in accounting for financial instruments and the volatility in earnings caused by measuring related assets and liabilities differently. ASC 825 contains presentation and disclosure requirements that are designed to facilitate comparisons between companies that choose different measurement attributes for similar types of assets and liabilities.

ASC 825 requires companies to provide additional information that is intended to help investors and other users of financial statements to more easily understand the effects on reported earnings of the company's choice to use fair value. It also requires companies to display the fair value of those assets and liabilities for which the company has chosen to use fair value in the primary financial statements.

ASC 825 permits all entities to elect to measure eligible items at fair value. Under this standard, a business entity shall report unrealized gains and losses at each subsequent reporting date. Upfront costs and fees related to items for which the fair value option is elected are recognized in earnings as incurred and are not deferred.

Eligibility

The following items are eligible to be accounted for by the Fair Value Option under ASC 825 (ASC 825-10-15-4):

- A recognized financial asset or liability (with certain specified exceptions).
- A firm commitment that would otherwise not be recognized at inception and that involves only financial instruments.
- A written loan commitment.
- The rights and obligations under an insurance contract that is not a financial instrument but whose terms permit the insurer to settle by paying a third party to provide those goods or services.
- The rights and obligations under a warranty that is not a financial instrument but whose terms permit the warrantor to settle by paying a third party to provide those goods or services.
- A host of financial instruments resulting from the separation of an embedded nonfinancial derivative instrument from a nonfinancial hybrid instrument under ASC 815-15-25-1.

On the other hand, no entity can elect the Fair Value Option for (ASC 825-10-15-5):

- An investment in a subsidiary that the entity is required to consolidate.
- An interest in a variable interest entity that the entity is required to consolidate.
- Employers' and plans' obligations for pension benefits, other postretirement benefits, postemployment benefits, employee stock options and stock purchase plans, and other forms of deferred compensation.
- Financial assets and financial liabilities recognized under leases.
- Deposit liabilities, withdrawable on demand, of banks, savings and loan associations, credit unions, and other similar depository institutions.
- Financial instruments that, in whole or in part, are classified by the issuer as a component of stockholders' equity.

Election Dates

The choice of whether to elect the fair value option is made on each eligible item's election date, which is when one of the following occurs (ASC 825-10-25-4):

- The entity first recognizes the eligible item.
- The entity enters into an eligible firm commitment.
- Financial assets that have been reported at fair value with unrealized gains and losses included in earnings because of specialized accounting principles cease to qualify for that specialized accounting.
- The accounting treatment for an investment in another entity changes because the investment becomes subject to the equity method of accounting.

- An event that requires an eligible item to be measured at fair value at the time of the event but does not require fair value measurement at each subsequent reporting date (excluding the recognition of impairment under lower-of-cost-or-market accounting or accounting for securities in accordance with either ASC 321 or ASC 326).

Some additional events that require the remeasurement of eligible items at fair value, initial recognition of eligible items, or both, and thereby create an election date for the fair value option are (1) business combinations; (2) consolidation or deconsolidation of a subsidiary or variable interest entity; and (3) significant modifications of debt (ASC 825-10-25-5).

Applying the Fair Value Option

The fair value option may be elected for a single eligible item without electing it for other identical items with the following exceptions (ASC 825-10-25-7):

- If multiple advances are made to one borrower pursuant to a single contract, and the individual advances lose their identity as a part of a larger loan balance, the fair value option must be applied only to the larger balance and not to each advance individually.
- If the fair value option is applied to an investment that would otherwise be accounted for by the equity method, it is applied to all of the investor's financial interests in the same entity that are eligible items.
- If the fair value option is applied to an eligible insurance or reinsurance contract, it shall be applied to all claims and obligations under the contract.
- If the fair value option is elected for an insurance contract for which integrated or unintegrated contract features or coverages are issued, the fair value option must also be applied to those features or coverages.

The fair value option is not required to be applied to all instruments issued or acquired in a single transaction. A financial instrument that is legally a single contract may not be separated into parts for the purposes of applying the fair value option. In contrast, a loan syndication arrangement may result in multiple loans to the same borrower by different lenders, each of which is a separate instrument for which the fair value option may be elected or not elected. An investor in an equity security may elect the fair value option for its entire investment in that security, including any fractional shares issued by the investee (ASC 825-10-25-10, 11-12).

In the statement of financial position or the accompanying notes to the financial statements, an entity shall separately present financial assets and financial liabilities by measurement category and form of financial asset. Entities shall report assets and liabilities that are presented by the fair value option in a manner that separates those reported fair values from the carrying amounts of similar assets and liabilities measured using another measurement attribute in either of the following ways (ASC 825-10-45-1A, 1B, 2):

- Present the aggregate of fair value and non-fair-value amounts in the same line item and parenthetically disclose the amount measured at fair value included in that aggregate amount; or
- Present two separate line items to display fair value and non-fair-value carrying amounts.

In the statement of cash flows, receipts and cash payments related to items measured at fair value are classified according to their nature and purpose as required by ASC 230 (Statement of Cash Flows) (ASC 825-10-45-3).

DISCLOSURE OF INFORMATION ABOUT FAIR VALUE OF FINANCIAL INSTRUMENTS

General Disclosure Requirements

ASC 825 includes extensive disclosures in the financial statements. The primary objectives of these disclosures are to facilitate comparisons between (1) entities that choose different measurement attributes for similar assets and liabilities; and (2) assets and liabilities in the financial statements of an entity that selects different measurement attributes for similar assets and liabilities.

As of each date for which a statement of financial position is presented, the following information is required to be disclosed (ASC 825-10-50-28):

1. Management's reason for electing a fair value option for each eligible item or for a group of eligible items
2. If the fair value option is elected for some, but not all, eligible items within a group:
    a. A description of those items and the reason for partial election
    b. Information to enable users to understand how the group of similar items relates to individual line items on the statement of financial position

3. For each line item in the statement of financial position that includes an item or items for which the fair value option has been elected:
    a. Information to enable users to understand how each line item in the statement of financial position relates to major categories of assets and liabilities presented in accordance with the fair value disclosure requirements in ASC 820
    b. The aggregate carrying amount of items included in each line item in the statement of financial position that are not eligible for the fair value option
4. The difference between the aggregate fair value and the aggregate unpaid principal balance of:
    a. Loans and long-term receivables that have contractual principal amounts and for which the fair value option has been elected
    b. Long-term debt instruments that have contractual principal amounts and for which the fair value option has been elected
5. For loans held as assets for which the fair value option has been elected:
    a. The aggregate fair value of loans that are 90 days or more past due
    b. If the entity's policy is to recognize interest income separately from other changes in fair value, the aggregate fair value of loans in nonaccrual status
    c. The difference between the aggregate fair value and the aggregate unpaid principal balance for loans that are 90 days or more past due, in nonaccrual status, or both
6. For investments that would have been accounted for under the equity method if the entity had not chosen the fair value option, the information required by ASC 323-10-50-3 with certain specified exclusions.

For each period for which an interim or annual income statement is presented, the following information is required (ASC 825-10-50-30):

1. For each line item in the statement of financial position, the amounts of gains and losses from fair value changes included in earnings during the period and in which line item in the income statement those items are reported
2. A description of how interest and dividends are measured and where they are reported in the income statement
3. For loans and other receivable held as assets:
    a. The estimated amount of gains or losses included in earnings during the period attributable to changes in instrument-specific credit risk
    b. How the gains or losses attributed to changes in instrument-specific credit risk were determined
4. For liabilities, all of the following about the effects of the instrument-specific credit risk and changes in it:
    a. The amount of change, during the period and cumulatively, of the fair value of the liability that is attributed to changes in the instrument-specific credit risk
    b. If a liability is settled during the period, the amount, if any, recognized in other comprehensive income that was recognized in net income at settlement
    c. How the gains and losses attributed to changes in instrument-specific credit risk were determined.

Other disclosure requirements are as follows:

1. In annual periods only, an entity shall disclose the methods and significant assumptions used to estimate the fair value of items for which the fair value option has been elected (ASC 825-10-50-31).
2. If an entity elects the fair value option at the time of the events described in ASC 825-10-25-4(d) and 4(e) (see explanation below), the following information is required ASC 825-10-50-32:
    a. Qualitative information about the nature of the event
    b. Quantitative information by line item in the statement of financial position indicating which line items in the income statement include the effect on earnings of initially electing the fair value option for an item.

ASC 825-10-25-4(d) and 4(e) permit the fair value option to be elected when the accounting treatment of an investment changes because the investment becomes subject to the equity method of accounting. ASC 825-10-25-5 also indicates that a business combination, consolidation or deconsolidation of a subsidiary, and significant modifications of debt are options that would trigger this disclosure.

3. An entity shall disclose, either in the body of the financial statements or in the accompanying notes, the fair value of financial instruments and the level of the fair value hierarchy within which the fair value measurements are categorized in their entirety (Level 1, 2, or 3). For financial instruments recognized at fair value in the statement of financial position, the disclosure requirements of ASC 820 (Fair Value Measurements and Disclosures) also apply (ASC 825-10-50-10).

PRACTICE POINTER: ASC 825 indicates that fair value information disclosed in the notes shall be presented with the related carrying value in a form that makes it clear whether the fair value and the carrying value represent assets or liabilities and how the carrying amounts relate to information reported in the statement of financial position. If disclosure of fair value information is in more than one note, one of the notes must include a summary table that contains cross-referenced locations(s) of the remaining disclosures (ASC 825-10-50-10, 11, 12).

---

4. In estimating the fair value of deposit liabilities, a financial entity shall not take into account the value of its long-term relationships with depositors, commonly known as core deposit intangibles, which are separate intangible assets, not financial instruments. For deposit liabilities with no defined maturities, the fair value to be disclosed is the amount payable on demand at the reporting date. An entity is not prohibited from disclosing separately the estimated fair value of any of its nonfinancial intangible and tangible assets and nonfinancial liabilities (ASC 942-470-50-1).
5. For trade receivables and payables, no disclosure is required under ASC 825 when the carrying amount approximates fair value (ASC 310-10-50-26).
6. In disclosing the fair value of a financial instrument, amounts of instruments shall not be netted, even if the instruments are of the same class or otherwise related except as permitted by ASC 210.

Disclosures about Concentrations of Credit Risk

An entity shall disclose all significant credit risks from all financial instruments. Group concentrations of credit risk exist if a number of counterparties are engaged in similar activities and have similar economic characteristics that would cause their ability to meet contractual obligations to be affected in a similar way by changes in economic or other conditions (ASC 825-10-50-20). Following is information required to be disclosed about each significant concentration of credit risk (ASC 825-10-50-21):

- Information about the shared activity, region, or economic characteristic that identifies the concentration
- The maximum amount of loss due to credit risk (i.e., the loss that would result to parties to the financial instrument if the parties failed completely to perform and any security proved to be of no value)
- The entity's policy of requiring collateral to support financial instruments subject to credit risk, information about the entity's access to the collateral, and the nature and a brief description of collateral
- The entity's policy of entering into master netting arrangements to mitigate credit risk of financial instruments, information about the arrangements for which the entity is a party, and a description of the terms of those agreements.

Encouraged Disclosures about Market Risk of All Financial Instruments

Entities are encouraged, but not required, to disclose quantitative information about the market risks of financial instruments that are consistent with the way it manages or adjusts those risks (ASC 825-10-50-23).

Methods of disclosure are expected to vary among reporting entities. Possible ways of disclosing this information include (ASC 825-10-50-23):

- Details about current positions and activity during the period
- The hypothetical effects on comprehensive income or net income of possible changes in market value
- A gap analysis of interest rate repricing or maturity dates

- The duration of the financial instruments
- The entity's value at risk from derivatives and from other positions at the end of the reporting period and the average value of the risk during the period.

Situations Not Covered by ASC 825

While ASC 825 is intended to require disclosure of fair value information about a wide spectrum of financial instruments, a number of instruments and other items are exempt. These exemptions fall into three categories (ASC 825-10-50-8):

- Items subject to reporting and disclosure requirements of other authoritative pronouncements (e.g., pensions, extinguished debt, insurance contracts other than financial guarantees and investment contracts, leases, and equity method investments). ASC 825 does not change existing disclosure requirements for these items.
- Other items explained in terms of certain definitional problems that the FASB was unable to resolve at the time (e.g., insurance contracts other than those mentioned above, lease contracts, warranty obligations, and unconditional purchase obligations that may have both financial and nonfinancial components). The FASB believes that definitional and valuation difficulties for these contracts and obligations require further consideration before decisions can be made about the appropriateness of fair value disclosure requirements.
- The ASC 825 disclosures are intended to apply only to financial assets and liabilities, thereby excluding items such as noncontrolling interests in consolidated subsidiaries and an entity's own equity instruments included in stockholders' equity.

Applying the Fair Value Option to Not-for-Profit Organizations

The following modifications are required in applying the fair value option to not-for-profit organizations (ASC 825-10-15-7):

1. References throughout ASC 825 to the income statement are replaced with references to the statement of activities, statement of changes in net assets, or statement of operations. Similarly, references to earnings are replaced with references to changes in net assets.
2. Health care organizations subject to ASC 954 (Health Care Organizations), shall report unrealized gains and losses on items for which the fair value option has been elected within the performance indicator or a part of discontinued operations, as appropriate.
3. Certain disclosure requirements (presented in ASC 825-10-50-30) apply not only with respect to the effect on performance indicators or other measures of operations, if presented, but also with respect to the effect on the change in each of the net asset classes (without donor restrictions or with donor restrictions), as appropriate.

Optional Disclosures for Nonpublic Entities

ASC 825 makes the fair value disclosures optional for nonpublic entities, except for disclosures required by ASC 825-10-50-20 through 50-23. However, for interim periods, the disclosure guidance in ASC 825-10-50-20 through 50-23 is optional for nonpublic entities (ASC 825-10-50-2A).

PART II: INTERPRETIVE GUIDANCE

IMPORTANT NOTICE: The Financial Accounting Standards Board (FASB) issued ASU 2016-01, *Financial Instruments—Overall (Subtopic 825-10): Recognition and Measurement of Financial Assets and Financial Liabilities*, on January 5, 2016. The ASU amends some of the existing guidance related to the recognition, measurement, presentation, and disclosure of financial instruments. The guidance will be effective for public business entities for fiscal years that begin after December 15, 2017, including interim periods within those fiscal years. For all other entities, including not-for-profit entities and employee benefit plans under the scope of ASC 960 through 965 on plan accounting, the amendments in this ASU are effective for fiscal years that begin after December 15, 2018, and interim periods within fiscal years that begin after December 15, 2019.

ASC 825-10: OVERALL

ASC 825-10-50-2A, 50-8, 50-10 through 50-12; ASC 320-10-35-26; ASC 270-10-50-1(m) Interim Disclosures about Fair Value of Financial Instruments

BACKGROUND

The following guidance was issued to address the concerns of constituents regarding a lack of comparability between the financial statements of entities that report the values of their financial instruments based on different measurement attributes, for example, at fair value or at amortized cost. Although the FASB and the International Accounting Standards Board (IASB) had undertaken a joint project to address the recognition and measurement of financial instruments, the FASB decided that the clarity and quality of financial information in financial statements would be improved if reporting entities disclose the information about fair value more frequently. In addition, the FASB believes that such disclosures about fair value would stimulate the discussion between financial statement users and preparers regarding the current valuations of financial instruments.

This guidance amends the guidance in ASC 825 by requiring that publicly traded companies disclose information about the fair value of financial instruments for interim periods in addition to those in their annual financial statements. The guidance in ASC 270 is also amended to require that the disclosures be made in summarized financial information at interim reporting periods.

ACCOUNTING GUIDANCE

Scope

The following guidance applies to all financial instruments under the scope of ASC 825 that are held by publicly traded companies.

PRACTICE POINTER: ASC 825-10-50-8 was amended by Accounting Standards Update (ASU) 2014-03, *Derivatives and Hedging (Topic 815): Accounting for Certain Receive-Variable, Pay-Fixed Interest Rate Swaps—Simplified Hedge Accounting Approach*, to state that the fair value disclosure requirements in ASC 825-10-50-10 through 50-16 do not apply to receive-variable, pay-fixed interest rate swaps for which the simplified hedge accounting approach in ASC 815 is applied.

PRACTICE POINTER: Because it was unclear to stakeholders whether entities other than public business entities are required to provide the fair value option disclosures in ASC 825-10-50-24 through 50-32, ASU 2020-03, *Codification Improvements to Financial Instruments,* amends the existing guidance by inserting ASC 825-10-50-23A to clarify that the disclosure requirements in those paragraphs apply "to all entities that have elected the fair value option." This guidance is effective for public business entities at issuance, and prospectively for all other entities for fiscal years that begin after December 15, 2019, and interim periods within fiscal years that begin after December 15, 2020. Early application is permitted.

Amendment to Disclosure Requirements of ASC 825 and ASC 260

Disclosures about the fair value of a publicly traded company's financial instruments, if it is practicable to estimate that value, should be included in the body or the accompanying notes of an entity's summarized financial information issued for interim periods and its financial statements issued for annual periods.

As required in ASC 825, the disclosures should be made, regardless of whether the financial instruments are recognized in the entity's balance sheet. The manner in which information about the fair value and carrying amount of financial instruments is disclosed in the notes to the financial statements should be unambiguous as to whether the instruments are assets or liabilities and should clarify how the carrying amounts are related to the information reported on the balance sheet.

- The methods and significant assumptions used to estimate the fair value of financial instruments should be disclosed and should describe changes in methods and significant assumptions, if any, made during the period.

The following are amendments made by ASU 2016-01:

- ASC 825-10-50-2A is amended to provide that the disclosure guidance in ASC-825-10-50-20 through 50-23 applies to all entities and that for interim reporting periods, the disclosures in those paragraphs are optional for entities that do not meet the definition of a public business entity.
- ASC 825-10-50-8, which provides a list of items for which the disclosures about fair value in ASC 825-10-50-10 through 50-16 are not required has been amended by the addition of the following items:
  - — Item l - Investments in equity securities accounted for under the measurement guidance for equity securities without readily determinable fair values (ASC 321);
  - — Item m - Trade receivables due in one year or less; and
  - — Item n - Deposit liabilities with no defined or contractual maturities.
- ASC 825-10-50-10 is amended to require that an entity disclose the fair value of financial instruments and the level of the fair value hierarchy within which the fair value measurements are categorized in their entirety (level 1, 2, or 3). Subparagraphs (a) through (d) are superseded by the ASU.

ASC 825-10-55-1 through 55-2; ASC 310-10-50-25 Terms of Loan Products That May Give Rise to a Concentration of Credit Risk

BACKGROUND

The following guidance was issued in response to questions from constituents and as a result of discussions with the staff of the SEC and with regulators of financial institutions. Those questions are related to loan products that have contractual terms and features that may cause the originator, holder, investor, guarantor, or servicer of the loan to experience a greater exposure to nonpayment or realization. The following terms or loan features may increase credit risk:

- The ability to defer principal repayment or to make payments that are smaller than interest accrual and result in negative amortization
- High loan-to-value ratio
- Using the same collateral for multiple loans that result in a high loan-to-value ratio when combined
- Adjustable-rate mortgages (option ARMs) under which a borrower may choose to pay a different amount each month for a specified period of the loan term but eventually may be subject to future increases in repayments that exceed increases solely from increased market interest rates—for example, if a loan to reach a maximum limit for accrual of principal because of negative amortization
- A below market interest rate during the initial period of a loan term that may increase significantly thereafter
- Interest-only loans

Information about credit losses on loans that have reduced payment requirements in the early part of the loans' terms may not be known to creditors until a loan's payment terms change. This delays a creditor's ability to determine that a loss accrual should be recognized and a loan loss allowance should be established under the guidance in ASC 450 and ASC 310-10-30-2, 35-13 through 35-14, 35-16 through 35-22, 35-24 through 35-29, 35-32, 35-34, 35-37, 35-39; 45-5 through 45-6; 50-12 through 50-13, 50-15, 50-19; ASC 310-40-35-8 through 35-9, 35-12, 50-2 through 50-3.

Loan products with initial payment requirements for amounts less than or equal to the contractual interest, such as option ARMs, negative amortizing, deferred interest, or interest-only loans, can increase the loan-to-value ratio and reduce a borrower's equity. A borrower's contractually required repayments on such loans may increase in the future as a result of increases in interest rates, a step-up from the initial interest rate, or required amortization of the principal amount. The borrower's ability to repay a loan may be affected by those payment increases and may lead to default and losses. The risk of loss on loans with high loan-to-value ratios that are based on appreciation of the collateral may increase if the expected appreciation does not occur.

The purpose of this guidance is to emphasize the requirement to assess the adequacy of disclosures for secured and unsecured loans and how changes in market and economic conditions affect the adequacy of those disclosures.

ACCOUNTING GUIDANCE

Question 1: Under what circumstances, if any, do the terms of loan products cause a *concentration of credit risk* as the term is used in ASC 825-10-50-2A through 50-3, 50-8 through 50-23, 55-3 through 55-5, 60-1; ASC 942-470-50-1; ASC 310-10-50-26; ASC 958-320-50-4?

Answer: A reporting entity's *concentration of credit risk* may be caused by the terms of certain loan products, either as individual products or as a group of products with similar features. Under the guidance in ASC 958-320-50-4; ASC 825-10-50-20 through 50-21, disclosures are required about each significant concentration, including "information about the (shared) activity, region, or economic characteristic that identifies the concentration." Shared characteristics that may be used to determine significant concentrations may include, but are not limited to:

- Borrowers subject to significant increases in payments
- Loan terms permitting negative amortization
- Loans with high loan-to-value ratios

Judgment should be used in determining whether a loan's terms cause a concentration of credit risk.

Under the guidance in ASC 825-10-50-23, entities are encouraged to disclose "quantitative information about the market risks of financial instruments that is consistent with the way it manages or adjusts those risks." In addition, entities may disclose information about how their underwriting procedures deal with controlling credit risk that may occur as a result of future payment increases on loans.

Question 2: What disclosures or other accounting considerations apply for entities that originate, hold, guarantee, service, or invest in loan products whose terms may give rise to a concentration of credit risk?

Answer: Disclosures in addition to those required in Question 1 should be considered. The type of disclosures and their extent should be influenced by the type of entity making the disclosures and how significant the loan products are to the reporting entity. Under the guidance in ASC 275-10-50-1, disclosure is required about the existence of risks and uncertainties as of the date of the financial statements in the following areas:

- Nature of operations
- Estimates used in preparing the financial statements
- Certain significant estimates
- Current exposure as a result of certain concentrations

The contractual terms of certain loan products cause entities to be vulnerable to risks and uncertainties in one or more of those areas. Under the guidance in ASC 275-10-50-18, revenue concentrations from particular products should be disclosed. Disclosure of other concentrations is required if they meet the following requirements in ASC 275-20-50-16:

- A concentration that exists at the date of the financial statements
- The entity is exposed to the risk of a near-term severe impact as a result of that concentration
- There is at least a reasonable possibility that the events that could cause the severe impact will occur in the near term

Disclosure about a possible change in estimate is required under ASC 275-10-50-8 if information available before the issuance of financial statements suggests both that "it is at least reasonably possible that the estimate of the effect on the financial statements of a condition, situation, or set of circumstances that existed at the date of the financial statements will change in the near term because of one or more future confirming events" and "the effect of the change would be material to the financial statements."

If significant, noncash interest income recognized as a result of negative amortization that is added to the principal balance of an outstanding loan before it is received in cash should be included in the reconciliation of an entity's net income to net cash flows from operating activities under the provisions of ASC 230.

An entity should consider whether the principal risk characteristics of a recognized servicing asset related to loan products with terms that may cause a concentration of credit risk would result in a separate stratum when impairment is determined. Disclosure of the risk characteristics used to stratify recognized servicing assets for the measurement of impairment is required under the provisions of ASC 860, as amended by ASC 860-10-40-5 through 40-6A. Originators and servicers that have provided guarantees on those loan products also should consider the specific risk characteristics when they estimate the guarantees' fair value. Each product's characteristics should be considered when estimating the fair value of loan products than an entity classifies a held for sale and when fair value is determined for the disclosures required under ASC 825-10-50-2A through 50-3, 50-8 through 50-23, 55-3 through 55-5, 60-1; ASC 942-470-50-1; ASC 310-10-50-26; ASC 958-320-50-4.

Entities are reminded that interest income must be recognized by the interest method as discussed in ASC 310. If, during the term of a loan, the loan's stated interest rate increases so that interest accrued under the interest method in early periods would exceed interest at the stated rate, interest income should *not* be recognized if the net investment in the loan would increase to such an extent that it would exceed the amount at which the borrower could settle the obligation. The guidance in ASC 310-20-35-18 and the related implementation guidance should be applied if interest income is recognized on loans with interest rates that increase during the term of the loan, such as loans with a reduced initial interest rate.

SEC Rules and Regulations, such as Item 303 of Regulation S-K (Management's Discussion and Analysis of Financial Conditions and Results of Operations), may require public entities to make additional disclosures. Additional disclosures also may be required of banks and bank holding companies that are subject to the requirements of SEC Regulation S-X, rule 9-03, and SEC Industry Guide 3.

ASC 825-20: REGISTRATION PAYMENT ARRANGEMENTS

ASC 825-20-05-1, 15-1 through 15-2, 15-4 through 15-2, 25-2 through 25-3, 30-1, 30-4 through 30-5, 35-1, 50-1 through 50-2, 55-2 through 55-8, 55-10 through 55-14; ASC 815-10-25-16; ASC 815-40-25-21, 25-43; ASC 470-20-30-23 Accounting for Registration Payment Arrangements

BACKGROUND

An entity may issue equity shares, warrants, or debt instruments that are conditional on a *registration payment arrangement,* which has the following characteristics:

- The agreement states that the issuer agrees to try to use its "best efforts" or apply "commercially reasonable efforts" to (*a*) file a registration statement for the resale of specified financial instruments or equity shares that will be issued when specified financial instruments are exercised or converted and to have the Securities and Exchange Commission (SEC) or another securities regulator (if the registration statement is filed in a foreign jurisdiction) declare the registration statement effective within a specified grace period, and (*b*) to maintain the registration statement's effectiveness for a specified time period or indefinitely.
- The issuer must transfer consideration, which may be significant, to the counterparty if the issuer fails to take those actions within the grace period or the registration statement's effectiveness is not maintained. The consideration may be required to be transferred in a lump sum of cash or in periodic cash payments, equity instruments, or as adjustments to the financial instrument conditional to the registration payment arrangement.

This guidance addresses the accounting under such arrangements for financial instruments that are accounted for under the guidance in ASC 460-10-60-14; ASC 480-10-55-63; ASC 505-10-60-5; ASC 815-10-15-78, 55-52; ASC 815-15-25-15; 40-05-1 through 05-4, 05-10 through 05-11, 05-12, 25-1 through 25-5, 25-7 through 25-20, 25-22 through 25-24, 25-26 through 25-35; 25-37 through 25-40, 30-1, 35-1 through 35-2, 35-6, 35-8 through 35-13, 40-1, 40-2, 50-1 through 50-5, 55-1 through 55-18.

ACCOUNTING GUIDANCE

The following guidance applies to:

- Issuers' accounting for registration payment arrangements having the characteristics discussed above in the Background section, regardless of whether the arrangement is included as a provision of a financial instrument or other agreement or is issued as a separate agreement.
- Arrangements under which an issuer is required to obtain or maintain a listing on a stock exchange, instead of, or in addition to, obtaining or maintaining an effective registration statement, are accounted for under the scope of ASC 825-20, Financial Instruments—Registration Payment Arrangements, as long as the remaining characteristics of the definition of the term *registration payment arrangement* discussed in the Background section are met.

This guidance does *not* apply to:

- Contracts that are *not* registration payment arrangements that have the characteristics discussed in the Overview, such as a building contract with a provision that requires a contractor to obtain a certificate of occupancy by a specific date or pay a penalty every month until it is obtained.
- Arrangements requiring registration or listing of convertible debt instruments or convertible preferred stock if the form of consideration that would be transferred to a counterparty is an adjustment to the conversion ratio. (For

accounting guidance, see ASC 470-20-05-7 through 05-08, 25-4 through 25-5; 30-3, 30-6, 30-8, 30-10, 30-15; 35-2 through 35-3, 35-7, 40-2 through 40-3, 55-30 through 55-33, 55-35 through 55-38, 55-45 through 55-48, 55-50 through 55-52, 55-54 through 55-54A, 55-56 through 55-58, 55-60 through 55-60A, 55-62 through 55-66, 55-69; ASC 505-10-50-8 ("Accounting for Convertible Securities with Beneficial Conversion Features or Contingently Adjustable Conversion Ratios") and ASC 260-10-50-1; ASC 470-20-25-8, 25-9, 25-20, 30-1, 30-5, 30-7, 30-9 through 30-10, 30-12 through 30-13, 30-16 through 30-21, 35-1, 35-4, 35-7 through 35-10, 40-1, 40-4, 45-1, 55-11 through 55-12, 55-14 through 55-17, 55-19 through 55-21, 55-23 through 55-24, 55-26 through 55-27; ASC 505-10-50-7.)

- Arrangements in which an observable market, other than the market for the issuer's stock, or an observable index must be consulted to determine the amount of consideration that should be transferred to a counterparty, for example, if consideration transferred to a counterparty when an issuer cannot obtain an effective registration statement is determined based on the price of a commodity.
- Arrangements in which the financial instrument or instruments conditional on the registration payment arrangement are settled when consideration is transferred, for example, if a warrant can be put to the issuer when an effective registration statement is not declared within the grace period for the resale of equity shares that would be issued when the warrant is exercised.

Recognition and Measurement

The following recognition and measurement guidance is provided:

- A contingent obligation to make future payments or to transfer consideration in another manner under a registration payment arrangement should be recognized and measured *separately* in accordance with the guidance in ASC 450 and ASC 450-20.
- A financial instrument conditional on a registration payment arrangement should be recognized and measured in accordance with other guidance in generally accepted accounting principles, such as ASC 835-30, ASC 815, and ASC 825-20-05-1, 15-1 through 15-5, 25-2 through 25-3, 30-1, 30-4 through30-5, 35-1, 50-1 through 50-2, 55-2 through 55-8, 55-10 through 55-14; ASC 815-10-25-16; ASC 815-40-25-21, 25-43; ASC 470-20-30-23, without considering the contingent obligation to transfer consideration under a registration payment arrangement. In other words, the registration payment arrangement should be recognized and measured separately from the financial instrument conditional on the arrangement.
- A contingent liability under a registration payment arrangement should be included in the allocation of proceeds for a related financing transaction in accordance with the measurement guidance in ASC 450 if it is *probable* that consideration under a registration payment arrangement will be transferred. The guidance in other applicable GAAP should be applied to allocate the remaining proceeds to financial instruments issued along with the registration payment arrangement. For example, after a liability for a registration payment arrangement has been recognized and measured under the guidance in ASC 450, the remaining proceeds of a debt instrument and a warrant classified as equity that are issued along with the registration payment arrangement would be allocated based on their relative fair values of the debt and the warrant under the guidance in ASC 470-20-25-2, 25-3. Under this allocation method, a financial instrument issued along with a registration payment arrangement might initially be measured at a discount to its principal amount. To determine whether a convertible instrument includes a beneficial conversion feature under the guidance in ASC 470-20-05-7 through 05-08, 25-4 through 25-5, 30-3, 30-6, 30-8, 30-10, 30-15, 35-2 through 35-3, 35-7, 40-2 through 40-3, 55-30 through 55-33, 55-35 through 55-38, 55-45-through 55-48, 55-50 through 55-52, 55-54 through 55-54A, 55-56 through 55-58, 55-60 through 55-60A, 55-62 through 55-66, 55-69; ASC 505-10-50-8 and ASC 260-10-50-1; ASC 470-20-25-8 through 25-9, 25-20, 30-1, 30-5, 30-7, 30-9, through 30-10, 30-12 through 30-13, 30-16 through 30-21, 35-1, 35-4, 35-7 through 35-10, 40-1, 40-4, 45-1, 55-11 through 55-12, 55-14 through 55-17, 55-19 through 55-21, 55-23 through 55-24, 55-26 through 55-27; ASC 505-10-50-7, an entity should use the effective conversion price based on the proceeds allocated to the convertible instrument to calculate the embedded conversion option's intrinsic value, if any.
- If it becomes probable that consideration will be transferred under a registration payment arrangement or if the amount of a previously recognized contingent liability increases or decreases in a subsequent period, the initial recognition of the contingent liability or the change in the amount of a previously recognized contingent liability should be recognized as income.

- An issuer's share price at the reporting date should be used to measure a contingent liability under ASC 450, if:
  - — The entity would be required to deliver shares under a registration payment arrangement,
  - — It is probable that consideration will be transferred, and
  - — It is possible to reasonably estimate the number of shares that will be delivered.

DISCLOSURES

In addition to the required disclosures under other applicable GAAP, an issuer of a registration payment arrangement is required to disclose the following information about each registration payment arrangement or each group of similar arrangements, even if there is only a *remote* likelihood that the issuer will be required to transfer consideration under an arrangement:

- The features of a registration payment arrangement, including its term, the financial instrument conditional on the arrangement, and the events or circumstances under which an issuer would be required to transfer consideration.
- Settlement alternatives, if any, stated in a registration payment arrangement, including the party controlling the settlement alternatives.
- The maximum potential undiscounted amount of consideration that an issuer would be required to transfer under a registration payment arrangement, including the maximum number of shares that may be required to be issued or, if applicable, that the potential amount of the consideration to be transferred is *unlimited*.
- The current carrying amount of an issuer's liability under a registration payment arrangement and the income statement classification of gains or losses, if any, as a result of changes in that liability's carrying amount.

AMENDMENTS TO OTHER PRONOUNCEMENTS

This following guidance is amended:

- ASC 815-10-15-82. The following guidance has been added:

  Registration payment arrangements. Registration payment arrangements within the scope of ASC 825-20 are not subject to the requirements of this Subtopic. The exception in this subparagraph applies to both the issuer that accounts for the arrangement pursuant to that Subtopic and the counterparty.
- ASC 480-10-15-7. The following guidance has been added:

  This Statement does not apply to registration payment arrangements within the scope of ASC 825-20.
- ASC 460-10-15-7. The following guidance has been added: A registration payment arrangement within the scope of the guidance in ASC 825-20-05-1 15-1 through 15-5, 25-2 through 25-3, 30-1, 30-4 through 30-5, 35-1, 50-1 through 50-2, 55-2 through 55-8, 55-10 through 55-14; ASC 815-10-25-16; ASC 815-40-25-21, 25-43; ASC 470-20-30-23.

CHAPTER 53

ASC 830—FOREIGN CURRENCY MATTERS

CONTENTS

PART I: GENERAL GUIDANCE

OVERVIEW

There are two primary areas in accounting for foreign operations:

1. Translation of foreign currency financial statements for purposes of consolidation, combination, or reporting on the equity method (one-line consolidation)
2. Accounting and reporting of foreign currency transactions, including forward exchange contracts

BACKGROUND

Business transactions and foreign operations that are recorded in a foreign currency must be restated in U.S. dollars in accordance with generally accepted accounting principles.

Transactions occur at various dates and exchange rates tend to fluctuate considerably. Before an attempt is made to translate the records of a foreign operation, the records should be in conformity with U.S. GAAP. In addition, if the foreign statements have any accounts stated in a currency other than their own, they must be converted into the foreign statement's currency before translation into U.S. dollars or any other reporting currency.

A brief summary of ASC 830 follows:

- Foreign currency financial statements must be in conformity with U.S. GAAP before they are translated.
- Assets, liabilities, and operations of an entity must be expressed in the functional currency of the entity. The functional currency of an entity is the currency of the primary economic environment in which the entity operates.
- The current rate of exchange is used to translate the assets and liabilities of a foreign entity from its functional currency into the reporting currency.
  - — The weighted-average exchange rate for the period is used to translate revenue, expenses, and gains and losses of a foreign entity from its functional currency to the reporting currency.
  - — The current rate of exchange is used to translate changes in financial position other than those items found in the income statement, which are translated at the weighted average exchange rate for the period.
- Gain or loss on the translation of foreign currency financial statements is not recognized in current net income but is reported as a separate component of stockholders' equity. If remeasurement from the recording currency to the functional currency is necessary prior to translation, however, gain or loss on remeasurement is recognized in current net income.
- The amounts accumulated in the separate component of stockholders' equity are realized on the sale or substantially complete liquidation of the investment in the foreign entity.
- The financial statements of a foreign entity in a country that has had cumulative inflation of approximately 100% or more over a three-year period (highly inflationary) must be remeasured into the functional currency of the reporting entity.
- A foreign currency transaction is one that requires settlement in a currency other than the functional currency of the reporting entity.

- Gains or losses from foreign currency transactions are recognized in current net income, except for:
  - Gain or loss on a designated and effective economic hedge of a net investment in a foreign entity
  - Gain or loss on certain long-term intercompany foreign currency transactions
  - Gain or loss on a designated and effective economic hedge of a firm, identifiable, foreign currency commitment that meets certain conditions
- Taxable foreign exchange gains or losses that do not appear in the same period in taxable income and either (*a*) financial accounting income (books) or (*b*) a separate component of stockholders' equity (books) are temporary differences for which deferred taxes must be provided in accordance with existing U.S. GAAP.
- Certain specific disclosures are required by ASC 830.

PRACTICE NOTE: ASC 815 (Derivatives and Hedging) addresses accounting for freestanding foreign currency derivatives and certain foreign currency derivatives embedded in other instruments. ASC 830 does not address accounting for derivative instruments.

ASC 830-10: OVERALL

TRANSLATION OBJECTIVES

ASC 830 establishes accounting and reporting standards for (*a*) foreign currency transactions and (*b*) translation of foreign currency financial statements that are included by consolidation, combination, or the equity method in a parent company's financial statements. Foreign financial statements must conform to U.S. generally accepted accounting principles before they can be translated into the currency in which the reporting entity prepares its financial statements (ASC 830-10-10-1; ASC 830-10-15-3). Translation of financial statements for any other purpose is beyond the scope of ASC 830.

PRACTICE NOTE: If the functional currency of a foreign operation is the same as that of its parent, there is no need for translation. A translation adjustment occurs only if the foreign operation's functional currency is a functional currency different from that of its parent.

An important objective in translating foreign currency is to preserve the financial results and relationships that are expressed in the foreign currency. This is accomplished by using the *functional currency* of the foreign entity. The functional currency is then translated into the *reporting currency* of the reporting entity. ASC 830 assumes that the reporting currency for an enterprise is U.S. dollars. The reporting currency may be a currency other than U.S. dollars, however.

PRACTICE NOTE: The ultimate objective of translating foreign transactions and financial statements is to produce the same results that each individual underlying transaction would have produced on the date it occurred, if it had then been recorded in the reporting currency.

FUNCTIONAL CURRENCY

ASC 830 requires that the assets, liabilities, and operations of an entity be measured in terms of the functional currency of that entity. The functional currency is the currency of the primary economic environment in which an entity generates and expends cash. The functional currency generally is the currency of the country in which the entity is located (ASC 830-10-45-2).

PRACTICE POINTER: In some instances, two levels of translation are required. For example, if a foreign entity's books of record are kept in Euros and the functional currency is the British pound, the books of record are remeasured into British pounds before the financial statements are translated into the currency of the reporting entity. Any translation gain or loss from Euros to British pounds is included in the remeasured net income. If the functional currency of the foreign entity is the Euro, only translation to the reporting currency is necessary. If the functional currency of the foreign entity is that of the reporting entity, only remeasurement from Euros to the reporting currency is required.

For the purposes of determining functional currency under ASC 830, foreign operations may be separated into two models. The first model is the self-contained foreign operation, located in a particular country, whose daily operations are not dependent on the economic environment of the parent's functional currency. This type of foreign operation primarily generates and expends local currency; the net cash flows that it produces in local currency may be reinvested, or converted and distributed to its parent company. The functional currency for this type of foreign operation is its local (domestic) currency.

The second model of foreign operation usually is a direct and integral component or extension of the parent company's operation. Financing usually is in U.S. dollars and frequently is supplied by the parent. The purchase and sale of assets usually are made in U.S. dollars. In other words, the daily operations of this type of foreign operation are dependent on the economic environment of the parent's currency. In addition, the changes in the foreign operation's individual assets and liabilities directly affect the cash flow of the parent company. The functional currency for this type of foreign operation is the U.S. dollar.

In the event that the facts in a given situation do not clearly identify the functional currency, the determination rests on the judgment of management. The FASB has developed guidelines based on certain indicators discussed below that should be considered in determining the functional currency of a foreign operation (ASC 830-10-55-5).

Cash Flow Indicators

The foreign operation's cash flows are mostly in foreign currency that does not directly affect the parent company's cash flows. Under these circumstances, the functional currency is the local currency.

The foreign operation's cash flows directly affect the parent company's cash flows on a current basis and usually are available for remittance through intercompany account settlement. Under these circumstances, the functional currency is the parent company's currency.

Sales Price Indicators

The foreign operation's sales prices for its products are primarily determined (on a short-term basis) by local competition or local government regulation, and not by exchange rate changes. Under these circumstances, the functional currency is the local currency.

The foreign operation's sales prices for its products are mostly responsive (on a short-term basis) to exchange rate changes, such as worldwide competition and prices. Under these circumstances, the functional currency is the parent company's currency.

Sales Market Indicators

The foreign operation has an active local sales market for its products, although there also may be significant amounts of exports. Under these circumstances, the functional currency is the local currency.

The foreign operation's sales market is mostly in the parent's country, or sales contracts are mostly made in the parent company's currency. Under these circumstances, the functional currency is the parent company's currency.

Expense Indicators

The foreign operation's costs of production (e.g., labor or material) or service are mostly local costs, although there also may be imports from other countries. Under these circumstances, the functional currency is the local currency.

The foreign operation's costs of production or service, on a continuing basis, are primarily costs for components obtained from the parent's country. Under these circumstances, the functional currency is the parent company's currency.

Financing Indicators

Financing for the foreign operation is in local currency, and funds generated by the foreign operation are sufficient to service debt obligations. Under these circumstances, the functional currency is the local currency.

Financing for the foreign operation is provided by the parent company or is obtained in U.S. dollars. Funds generated by the foreign operation are insufficient to service its debt. Under these circumstances, the functional currency is the parent company's currency.

Intercompany Transactions

There is little interrelationship between the operations of the foreign entity and the parent company, except for competitive advantages, such as trademarks, patents, etc. Intercompany transactions are of a low volume. Under these circumstances, the functional currency is the local currency.

There is an extensive interrelationship between the operations of the foreign entity and the parent company. Intercompany transactions are numerous. Under these circumstances, the functional currency is the parent company's currency.

The functional currency of a foreign entity must be used consistently from one fiscal year to another, unless significant changes in economic facts and circumstances dictate a change (ASC 830-10-45-7).

PRACTICE POINTER: Once an entity determines its functional currency, the entity should not change that determination unless significant changes in economic facts and circumstances indicate that the functional currency has changed. If there is a change in the functional currency of a foreign entity, that change is accounted for as a change in accounting estimate. Thus, the change is accounted for in the period of the change and/or future periods (prospectively).

If a change in functional currency occurs, do not remove the translation adjustments for prior periods from the separate component of stockholders' equity. Thus, the translated amounts of nonmonetary assets at the end of the period prior to the change in functional currency become the accounting basis for subsequent periods (ASC 830-10-45-10).

REMEASURING FINANCIAL STATEMENTS TO THE FUNCTIONAL CURRENCY

The following is a brief review of the translation provisions of ASC 830 for the remeasurement process from the recording currency to the functional currency, prior to translation from the functional currency to the reporting currency. (For further explanation, see the practice pointer under the "Functional Currency" section, above.)

Two categories of exchange rates are used in remeasuring financial statements. Historical exchange rates are those that existed at the time of the transaction, and the current exchange rate is the rate that is current at the date of remeasurement.

Monetary assets and liabilities are those that are fixed in amount, such as cash, accounts receivable, and most liabilities. Monetary assets and liabilities are translated at the current rate of exchange. All other assets, liabilities, and stockholders' equity are remeasured by reference to the following four money price exchanges based on the type of market and time:

1. *Past purchase exchange*—the historical or acquisition cost, because it is based on the actual past purchase price
2. *Current purchase exchange*—the replacement cost, because it is measured by the current purchase price of a similar resource
3. *Current sale exchange*—the market price, because it is based on the current selling price of the resource
4. *Future exchange*—the present value of future net money receipts, discounted cash flow, or the discounted net realizable value, because it is based on a future resource

All other assets, liabilities, and stockholders' equity are remeasured based on the four money price exchanges, as follows:

- Accounts based on past purchase exchanges (historical or acquisition cost) are remeasured at historical exchange rates.
- Accounts based on current purchase, current sale, and future exchanges are remeasured at the current exchange rate.

Revenue and expense transactions are remeasured at the average exchange rate for the period, except those expenses related to assets and liabilities, which are remeasured at historical exchange rates. For example, depreciation and amortization are remeasured at historical exchange rates, the rate that existed at the time the underlying related asset was acquired.

The following is a list of assets, liabilities, and stockholders' equity items and their corresponding remeasurement rates per ASC 830:

	Remeasurement Rates	
	Current	*Historical*
Cash (in almost all forms)	X	
Marketable securities—at cost		X
Marketable securities—at market	X	
Accounts and notes receivable	X	
Allowance for receivables	X	
Inventories—at cost		X
Inventories—at market, net realizable value, selling price	X	
Inventories—under fixed contract price	X	
Prepaid expenses		X
Refundable deposits	X	
Advances to subsidiaries	X	
Fixed assets		X
Accumulated depreciation		X
Cash surrender value—life insurance	X	
Intangible assets (all)		X
Accounts and notes payable	X	
Accrued expenses	X	
Accrued losses on firm commitments	X	
Taxes payable	X	
All long-term liabilities	X	
Unamortized premium or discount on long-term liabilities	X	
Obligations under warranties	X	
Deferred income		X
Capital stock		X
Retained earnings		X
Noncontrolling interests		X

Revenue and expenses not related to any balance sheet items are remeasured at the average currency exchange rate for the period. The average may be based on a daily, weekly, monthly, or quarterly basis or on the weighted-average rate for the period, which will probably result in a more meaningful conversion. Revenue and expense items that are related to a balance sheet account, such as deferred income, depreciation, and beginning and ending inventories, are remeasured at the same exchange rate as the related balance sheet item.

In remeasuring the lower-of-cost-or-market rule, the remeasured historical cost is compared to the remeasured market, and whichever is lower in functional currency is used. This may require a write-down in the functional currency from cost to market, which was not required in the foreign currency financial statements. On the other hand, if market was used on the foreign statements and in remeasuring to the functional currency market exceeds historical cost, the write-down to market on the foreign statements will have to be reversed before remeasuring, which would then be done at the historical rate. Once inventory has been written down to market in remeasured functional currency statements, the resulting carrying amount is used in future translations until the inventory is sold or a further write-down is necessary. This same procedure is used for assets, other than inventory, that may have to be written down from historical cost.

PRACTICE POINTER: The reason for the above procedure in applying the lower-of-cost-or-market rule in remeasuring foreign financial statements is that exchange gains and losses are a consequence of remeasurement and not of applying the lower-of-cost-or-market rule. This means that remeasured market is equal to replacement cost (market) in the foreign currency remeasured at the current exchange rate, except that:

- Remeasured market cannot exceed net realizable value in foreign currency translated at the current exchange rate.
- Remeasured market cannot be less than (1) above, reduced by an approximate normal profit translated at the current exchange rate.

For remeasurement purposes, the current exchange rate is the one in effect as of the balance sheet date of the foreign statements. Therefore, if the parent company's financial statements are at a date different from the date(s) of its foreign operation(s), the exchange rate in effect at the date of the foreign subsidiary's balance sheet is used for remeasurement and translation purposes.

Any translation adjustment arising from the remeasurement process is included in remeasured net income. In other words, any gain or loss resulting from the remeasurement process that is required by ASC 830 is included in net income in the remeasured financial statements (ASC 830-10-45-17).

After the foreign entity's financial statements are remeasured in the functional currency, they are ready for translation. If the functional currency of a foreign entity is the U.S dollar and the reporting currency of the parent is also the U.S. dollar, there will be no translation adjustment.

TRANSLATION OF FOREIGN OPERATIONS—HIGHLY INFLATIONARY ECONOMIES

ASC 830 defines a highly inflationary economy as one in which the cumulative inflation over a three-year consecutive period approximates 100%. In other words, the inflation rate in an economy must be rising at the rate of about 30 to 35% per year for three consecutive years to be classified as highly inflationary.

For the purposes of ASC 830, a foreign entity in a highly inflationary economy does not have a functional currency. The functional currency of the reporting entity is used as the functional currency of the foreign entity in a highly inflationary economy. Thus, the financial statements for a foreign entity in a highly inflationary economy are remeasured into the functional currency of the reporting entity. The remeasurement process required by ASC 830 is the same as that required for a foreign entity's financial statements that are not expressed in the functional currency (ASC 830-10-45-11).

PRACTICE NOTE: Apparently, exchange adjustments resulting from the remeasurement process for foreign entities in highly inflationary economies are included in the determination of remeasured net income, rather than reported as a separate component of stockholders' equity.

The International Monetary Fund (IMF) publishes monthly statistics on international inflation rates. After the financial statements of a foreign entity in a highly inflationary economy are expressed in the functional currency of the reporting entity, they are ready for translation. Since the financial statements are now expressed in the reporting currency, however, there will be no translation adjustment.

ASC 830-20: FOREIGN CURRENCY TRANSACTIONS

FOREIGN CURRENCY TRANSACTIONS

A foreign currency transaction is one that requires settlement in a currency other than the functional currency of the reporting entity. Generally, gains and losses on foreign currency transactions are recognized in current net income (ASC 830-20-40-1). The following transactions, however, may require different treatment (ASC 820-20-35-3, 4):

- Gain or loss resulting from a foreign currency transaction that is designated as an economic hedge of a net investment in a foreign entity
- Gain or loss resulting from intercompany foreign currency transactions of a capital nature or long-term financing nature, between an investor and investee where the investee entity is consolidated, combined, or accounted for by the equity method by the investor
- Forward exchange contracts

If the exchange rate changes between the time a purchase or sale is contracted for and the time actual payment is made, a foreign exchange gain or loss results.

Illustration of Foreign Currency Transaction

Alex Co. purchased goods for 100,000 pesos when the exchange rate was 10 pesos to a dollar. The journal entry in dollars is:

Purchases	10,000	
Accounts payable		10,000

Assuming that when the goods are paid for, the exchange rate is 12:1, the journal entry in dollars is:

Accounts payable	10,000	
Cash		8,333
Foreign exchange gain		1,667

At a 12:1 exchange rate, the $8,333 can purchase 100,000 pesos. The difference between the $8,333 and the original recorded liability of $10,000 is a foreign exchange gain. If payment is made when the exchange rate is less than 10 pesos to a dollar, a foreign exchange loss would result.

For example, if the exchange rate when the payment is made in only eight pesos to one dollar, a loss of $2,500 would result because $12,500 would be required to satisfy the payable of 100,000 pesos. In this case, the entry to record the payment would be:

Accounts payable	10,000	
Foreign exchange loss	2,500	
Cash		12,500

A foreign exchange gain or loss is computed at each balance sheet date on all recorded foreign transactions that have not been settled. The difference between the exchange rate that could have been used to settle the transaction at the date it occurred, and the exchange rate that can be used to settle the transaction at a subsequent balance sheet date, is the gain or loss recognized in current net income. Generally, the current exchange rate is the rate that is used to settle a transaction on the date it occurs, or on a subsequent balance sheet date (ASC 830-20-25-1).

Deferred Foreign Currency Transactions

Certain gains and losses on forward exchange contracts and certain types of foreign currency transactions are not included in current net income but are either (*a*) reported in the separate component of stockholders' equity, along with translation adjustments, or (*b*) included in the overall gain or loss of the related foreign currency transaction. These deferred gains and losses may be classified as follows (ASC 830-20-35-3, 5):

- Gain or loss on a designated and effective economic hedge of a net investment in a foreign entity
- Gain or loss on certain long-term intercompany foreign currency transactions
- Gain or loss on a designated and effective economic hedge of a firm, identifiable, foreign currency commitment

---

PRACTICE POINTER: As an example of a foreign currency transaction intended to be an economic hedge of a net investment in a foreign entity, take the case of a U.S. parent company with a net investment in a Greek subsidiary that borrows Greek currency in the amount of its net investment in the Greek subsidiary.

The U.S. company designates the loan as an economic hedge of its net investment in the Greek subsidiary. In other words, the U.S. parent computes its net investment in the foreign currency of its foreign subsidiary and then borrows the same amount of foreign currency as the amount of its net investment. In this event, if the net investment in the foreign subsidiary declines because of a change in exchange rates, the change is made up in the foreign currency loan. The U.S. company can buy a larger amount of the subsidiary's foreign currency with fewer U.S. dollars. When the net investment in the foreign subsidiary and the loan in the foreign currency of the foreign subsidiary are both translated into U.S. dollars, the change in the net investment in the foreign subsidiary (an asset) should be approximately equal to the change in the foreign currency loan, except for taxes, if any. Thus, the foreign currency loan acts as a hedge against any increase or decrease in the net foreign investment that is attributable to a change in the exchange rate.

ASC 830 requires that both translated amounts be recorded and reported in a separate component of stockholders' equity. If the translated amount of the foreign currency loan (after taxes, if any) exceeds the translated amount of the net investment in the foreign subsidiary that was hedged, however, the gain or loss that is allocable to the excess must be included in net income, and not recorded and reported as a separate component of stockholders' equity.

Gains or losses on intercompany foreign currency transactions of a capital or long-term nature are not included in current net income, but are reported in the separate component of stockholders' equity, along with translation adjustments. The entities involved in the intercompany foreign currency transactions reported in this manner must be consolidated, combined, or accounted for by the equity method. Gain or loss on intercompany foreign currency transactions that are not of a permanent nature are included in net income (ASC 830-20-35-3).

Accounting for a gain or loss on a foreign currency transaction that is intended to hedge an identifiable foreign currency commitment is addressed by ASC 815 (Derivative and Hedging). An example is an agreement to purchase or sell equipment.

Deferred Taxes

ASC 830 requires that deferred taxes be recognized on taxable foreign currency transactions and taxable translation adjustments of foreign currency financial statements, regardless of whether the exchange gain or loss is charged to current net income or recorded and reported as a separate component of stockholders' equity. Thus, all taxable foreign exchange gains or losses that do not appear in the same period in taxable income and either (*a*) financial accounting income or (*b*) the separate component of stockholders' equity are temporary differences, for which deferred taxes must be provided (ASC 830-20-05-3). The amount of the deferred taxes should be determined in accordance with existing U.S. GAAP (ASC 830-30-45-21).

PRACTICE NOTE: Historically, there has been a presumption in U.S. GAAP that all undistributed earnings of a subsidiary (domestic or foreign) would eventually be transferred to the parent company. Hence, U.S. GAAP have always considered undistributed income from foreign and domestic subsidiaries to be a temporary difference, requiring a provision for deferred income taxes. ASC 740 (Income Taxes) does not require deferred taxes to be provided for the excess of the book basis over the tax basis of an investment in a foreign subsidiary, if the excess is considered to be relatively permanent. An important reason that such an excess might exist is undistributed income from foreign subsidiaries. ASC 740 indicates:

> A deferred tax liability is not recognized for the following types of temporary differences, unless it is apparent that those temporary differences will reverse in the foreseeable future:
>
> In the basis for conclusions of ASC 740, the FASB states that the hypothetical nature of the tax allocation calculations for undistributed income from foreign subsidiaries "introduces significant implementation issues." Thus, tax allocation is not required for undistributed income of foreign subsidiaries that is essentially permanent in nature or for any other difference between the book basis and tax basis of investments of permanent nature.

Intraperiod income tax allocation is also required in the preparation of financial statements. The total income tax expense for a period should be allocated properly to (*a*) income from continuing operations, (*b*) discontinued operations, (*c*) adjustments of prior periods, and (*d*) direct entries to other stockholders' equity accounts. Therefore, the portion of income tax expense for a period that is attributable to items in the separate component of stockholders' equity is allocated to the separate component of stockholders' equity, and does not appear as an increase or decrease of income tax expense for the period. In other words, deferred taxes related to items in the separate component of stockholders' equity account are charged or credited to the separate component of stockholders' equity account (ASC 830-20-45-5). The illustration at the end of the chapter demonstrates this concept.

PRACTICE NOTE: All aspects of income tax allocation are complicated, and these provisions of ASC 830 require careful application to the specific facts of each situation. In particular, intercompany transactions of a long-term nature and the discontinuation of a foreign operation may present peculiar problems.

Foreign Currency Transaction Disclosures

The aggregate transaction gain or loss that is included in determining net income for the period, including gain or loss on forward exchange contracts, shall be presented in the financial statements or disclosed in the notes thereto (ASC 830-20-45-1).

Disclosure of exchange rate changes and related effects on foreign currency transactions that occur subsequent to the balance sheet date should be disclosed, if the effects are material. No adjustment should be made to the financial statements for exchange rate changes that occur subsequent to the balance sheet date (ASC 830-20-50-2; 830-20-35-8).

ASC 830-30: TRANSLATION OF FINANCIAL STATEMENTS

TRANSLATION OF FOREIGN CURRENCY STATEMENTS

The translation of foreign currency financial statements to the functional currency of the reporting entity does not produce realized exchange gains or losses. Instead, the gains or losses are considered unrealized and are recorded and reported in other comprehensive income (ASC 830-30-45-12).

PRACTICE POINTER: Although ASC 830 generally requires translation using the current exchange rate, not all financial statement elements are converted at this rate. For example, common stock, paid-in capital, donated capital, retained earnings, and similar items are not translated at the current exchange rate. Translation of these elements of the financial statements is made as follows:

Capital accounts are translated at their historical exchange rates when the capital stock was issued, or at the historical exchange rate when the capital stock was acquired.

Retained earnings are translated at the translated amount at the end of the prior period, plus the translated amount of net income for the current period, less the translated amount of any dividends declared during the current period.

Assets and liabilities are translated from the foreign entity's functional currency to the reporting entity's functional currency using the current exchange rate at the balance sheet date of the foreign entity (ASC 830-30-45-3). If a current exchange rate is not available at the balance sheet date of the foreign entity being translated, the first exchange rate available after the balance sheet date is used (ASC 830-20-30-2).

Revenue, expenses, and gains and losses are translated from the foreign entity's functional currency to produce the approximate results that would have occurred if each transaction had been translated using the exchange rate in effect on the date that the transaction was recognized. Since the separate translation of every transaction is impractical, an appropriate weighted-average exchange rate for the period should be used (ASC 830-30-45-3; 830-10-55-10).

Gains or losses on the translation of foreign currency financial statements for the purposes of consolidation, combination, or reporting on the equity method are not included in current net income. All adjustments resulting from the translation of foreign currency financial statements are recorded and reported as a separate component of stockholders' equity. These adjustments are treated as unrealized gains and losses, similar to unrealized gains and losses of available-for-sale debt securities (ASC 320 [Investments-Debt Securities]).

To summarize, the translation process embodied in ASC 830 includes the following steps:

1. Financial statements must be in conformity with U.S. GAAP prior to translation.
2. The functional currency of the foreign entity is determined.
3. The financial statements are expressed in the functional currency of the foreign entity. Remeasurement of the financial statements into the functional currency may be necessary. Gains or losses from remeasurement are included in remeasured current net income.
4. If the foreign entity operates in a country with a highly inflationary economy, its financial statements are remeasured into the functional currency of the reporting entity.
5. The functional currency financial statements of the foreign entity are translated into the functional currency of the reporting entity using the current rate of exchange method. Gains or losses from translation are not included in current net income.

Illustration of Foreign Currency Translation When Euro Is Functional Currency

On December 31, 20X8, Gardial Inc. (a U.S. company) created a 100%-owned subsidiary in Prague, investing $15,000,000 in equity at that time when the direct exchange rate was $1.20. Gardial used this investment to purchase $13,200,000 of fixed assets on that date. The direct exchange rates were $1.30 at December 31, 20X9, and $1.25 for 20X9 as an average. No dividends were declared or paid in 20X9.

During 20Y0, the dollar strengthened so that the direct exchange rate at December 31, 20Y0, was $1.26. The average rate for 20Y0 was $1.28. Cash dividends of $1,000 were declared and paid on November 29, 20Y0, when the direct exchange rate was $1.27.

Assume that (1) the subsidiary is a self-contained foreign operation that uses the euro as its functional currency, (2) the statements have already been adjusted so that they conform to U.S. GAAP, (3) all intercompany adjustments have been made, and (4) all sales, costs, and expenses occurred evenly throughout the year.

Illustration of Foreign Currency Translation When U.S. Dollar Is Functional Currency

Assume the same monetary facts as in the previous illustration. In addition, all ending inventory existing on December 31, 20X9, was purchased when the exchange rate was $1.29, and all ending inventory existing on December 31, 20Y0, was purchased when the exchange rate was $1.27. Also, the ending inventory cost was always below market. All fixed assets were acquired in prior years when the direct exchange rate was $1.20, and no fixed assets were retired in 20X9 or 20Y0.

Also assume that (1) the subsidiary is a direct and integral component of the parent company's operation and uses the U.S. dollar as its functional currency, (2) the statements have already been adjusted so that they conform to U.S. GAAP, (3) all intercompany adjustments have been made, and (4) all sales, costs, and expenses occurred evenly throughout the year.

PRACTICE NOTE: Total assets and total equity are both slightly higher under the current translation method than under the monetary/nonmonetary translation method. This difference is the result of using historical exchange rates for inventory and fixed assets rather than the current rate. Thus, under certain circumstances, these two methods can produce significantly different reporting results.

REALIZATION OF SEPARATE COMPONENT OF STOCKHOLDERS' EQUITY

Upon part, complete, or substantially complete sale or upon complete liquidation of an ownership interest in an equity method investment in a foreign entity, a *pro rata* portion of the accumulated translation adjustments attributable to that foreign entity, which has been recorded as a separate component of stockholders' equity, is included in determining the gain or loss on the sale or other disposition of that foreign investment (ASC 830-30-40-2). Thus, if an enterprise sells a 50% ownership interest in a foreign investment, 50% of the accumulated translation adjustments related to that foreign investment is included in determining the gain or loss on the sale of the interest.

PRACTICE NOTE: Any required provision for the permanent impairment of a foreign investment is determined before translation and consolidation. Apparently, this means that the amounts accumulated in the separate component of stockholders' equity for a specific foreign investment are not included in determining whether the investment has become permanently impaired.

ELIMINATION OF INTERCOMPANY PROFITS

The exchange rate to be used to eliminate intercompany profits is the rate that existed on the date of the intercompany transaction. The use of approximations and/or averages is permitted as long as they are reasonable (ASC 830-30-45-10).

PRACTICE POINTER: Intercompany profits occur on the date of sale or transfer. Thus, the exchange rate on the date of sale or transfer is used to determine the amount of intercompany profit to be eliminated.

EXCHANGE RATES

The balance sheet date of the foreign entity that is consolidated, combined, or accounted for by the equity method is used for translation purposes, if different from the balance sheet date of the reporting entity. Thus, the current exchange rate for the translation of foreign currency financial statements is the rate in effect on the balance sheet date of the foreign entity that is being translated (ASC 830-30-45-8). If a current exchange rate is not available at the foreign entity's balance sheet date, the first exchange rate available after the balance sheet date is used. The current rate used for the above translations is the rate applicable to currency conversion for the purpose of dividend remittances (ASC 830-30-45-6).

Conditions may exist when it will be prudent to exclude a foreign entity from financial statements that are consolidated, combined, or accounted for by the equity method. Disruption of a foreign operation caused by internal strife or severe exchange restrictions may make it impossible to compute meaningful exchange rates. Under these circumstances, earnings of a foreign operation should be included only to the extent that cash has been received in unrestricted funds. Disclosure should be made of any foreign subsidiary or investment that is excluded from the financial statements of the parent or investor. This may be accomplished by separate supplemental statements or a summary describing the important facts and information.

Financial Statement Translation Disclosures

An analysis of the changes in the separate component of stockholders' equity account for cumulative translation adjustments for the period shall be disclosed in either (*a*) a separate financial statement or (*b*) notes to the financial statements, or (*c*) be included as part of a stockholders' equity or a similar statement. The following is the minimum information that must be disclosed in the analysis (ASC 830-30-45-20).

- Beginning and ending cumulative balances
- The aggregate increase or decrease for the period from translation adjustments and gains and losses from (*a*) hedges of a net investment in a foreign entity and (*b*) long-term intercompany transactions (ASC 815 specifies additional disclosures for instruments designated as hedges of the foreign currency exposure of a net investment in a foreign operation.)
- The amount of income taxes for the period allocated to translation adjustments
- The amount of translation adjustment transferred to net income during the period as a result of a sale or complete or substantially complete liquidation of a foreign investment

Illustration of How an Enterprise Determines the Beginning Balance of the Separate Component of Stockholders' Equity

	Beginning of the Year			*Beginning of the Year*		
Current Assets	*Functional currency*	*FAS-52 exchange rates*	*U.S. dollars*	*Functional currency*	*Current exchange rates*	*U.S. dollars*
Cash	F 1,000	C*1.25	$ 800	F 1,000	C 1.25	$ 800
Accounts receivable	4,000	C 1.25	3,200	4,000	C 1.25	3,200
Inventory	10,000	H†2.00	5,000	10,000	C 1.25	8,000
Total	F15,000		$ 9,000	F15,000		$12,000
Property, plant, & equipment	F75,000	H 1.50	$50,000	F75,000	C 1.25	$60,000
Total assets	F90,000		$59,000	F90,000		$72,000
Current Liabilities	F20,000	C 1.25	$16,000	F20,000	C 1.25	$16,000
Deferred income taxes	5,000	H 2.00	2,500	5,000	C 1.25	4,000
Long-term obligations	20,000	C 1.25	16,000	20,000	C 1.25	16,000
Total liabilities	F45,000		$34,500	F45,000		$36,000
Net assets (equals stockholders' equity)	F45,000		$24,500	F45,000		$36,000

Computation of the Beginning Balance of the Separate Component of Stockholders' Equity

Net assets at beginning of the year at current exchange rate	$36,000
Net assets at beginning of the year at Specified in ASC 830	($24,500)
Beginning balance of separate component of stockholders' equity	$11,500

*C = Current exchange rate. †H = Historical exchange rate.

PART II: INTERPRETIVE GUIDANCE

ASC 830-10: OVERALL

ASC 830-10-45-1 through 45-5, 55-13 through 55-14 Accounting for a Change in Functional Currency When an Economy Ceases to Be Considered Highly Inflationary

BACKGROUND

Company A has a subsidiary operating in an economy that was considered highly inflationary during the previous five years. A *highly inflationary economy* is defined in ASC 830 (FAS-52) as one that has experienced a cumulative inflation rate of 100% or more for the most recent three-year period. In accordance with the guidance in ASC 830, the subsidiary used Company A's reporting currency rather than the local (foreign) currency as its functional currency. Based on the criteria in ASC 830, except for the inflationary environment, the subsidiary would have used the local currency as its functional currency. In 20X6, the inflation rate had declined sufficiently that the cumulative rate for the three most recent years was less than 100%; the economy was no longer considered highly inflationary. Accordingly, Company A decided to use the local currency as the subsidiary's functional currency.

PRACTICE POINTER: When the local currency is not the functional currency, a subsidiary's financial statements must be **remeasured** into the functional currency using **current** exchange rates for monetary items and **historical** exchange rates (exchange rate at acquisition) for nonmonetary items. When the local currency is also the functional currency, all assets and liabilities are **translated** at current exchange rates.

ACCOUNTING ISSUE

How should an entity account for a change in a subsidiary's functional currency from the reporting currency to the local currency solely because the economy in which the subsidiary operates is no longer considered to be highly inflationary?

ACCOUNTING GUIDANCE

The EITF reached a consensus in ASC 830-10-45-9 through 45-10, which provides guidance on the treatment of a change in functional currency from the reporting currency to the local currency, does not apply to situations in which the functional currency changes solely because the economy has ceased to be highly inflationary. The functional currency bases of nonmonetary assets and liabilities should be restated at the date of change by translating reporting currency amounts into the local currency at their current exchange rates. Those translated amounts become the new accounting bases for the nonmonetary assets and liabilities in the entity's new functional currency (the local currency).

The difference between the new accounting bases in the functional currency and their tax bases in that currency is considered a temporary difference under ASC 740. The guidance in ASC 830-740-25-2; 45-2 addresses how related deferred taxes should be recognized.)

DISCUSSION

The issue arose because in cases in which the local currency becomes the functional currency, the bases of nonmonetary assets and liabilities must be established in the new functional currency (local currency). Those functional currency bases are then translated into the reporting currency at current rates in accordance with ASC 830. The following two methods were suggested for determining the bases of nonmonetary assets and liabilities in the newly established functional currency:

Method 1 The historical bases in the *local currency* become the functional currency bases for nonmonetary items.

Method 2 Historical bases in the *reporting currency* are translated into the local currency at current rates to establish the new functional currency bases for nonmonetary items. (This method was adopted.)

Illustration of Two Methods Considered for Determining New Functional Currency Bases of Nonmonetary Items

- Company A's Subsidiary F operated in a highly inflationary economy from 1/1/X1 to 12/31/X5.
- On 1/1/X2, Subsidiary F purchased equipment costing LC10,000 (local currency) with a useful life of 20 years.
- On 1/1/X6, the economy in which Subsidiary F operated ceased to be considered highly inflationary. As of this date, under the consensus, a new functional currency basis needs to be established.

- The exchange rates used in this illustration are as follows:

1/1/X2	$1 = LC2
1/1/X6	$1 = LC10
19X6 average	$1 = LC11
12/31/X6	$1 = LC12

On 12/31/X5, the equipment has a net book value of LC8,000 (LC10,000 less accumulated depreciation of LC2,000) in Subsidiary F's financial statements. The equipment is presented in Company A's financial statements at a net book value of $4,000 [$5,000 original remeasured cost (LC10,000 × $1/LC2) less $1,000 accumulated depreciation].

Effect of Using Methods 1 and 2

Method 1	
Net book value in local currency	LC8,000
Current exchange rate	LC10 to $1
Translation at current rate—New reporting currency basis	$800
Prior reporting currency basis	$4,000
Cumulative translation adjustment	$3,200
Method 2 (Adopted in the Consensus)	
Reporting currency basis	$4,000
Translation back to local currency at current rate	LC10 to $1
New local currency basis	LC40,000

	Comparison of Methods	
	Method 1	*Method 2*
Local currency basis	LC8,000	LC40,000
Reporting currency basis	$800	$4,000
Prior reporting currency basis	$4,000	$4,000
Adjustment to cumulative		
Translation adjustments account	$3,200	0
Effect on 20X6 Earnings		
Book value 1/1/X6	$800	$4,000
20X6 depreciation expense		
Functional currency basis	LC8,000	LC40,000
Remaining useful life	16 years	16 years
Depreciation in LC	500	2,500
Average exchange rate	LC11 to $1	LC11 to $1
Depreciation expense	$45	$227
Book value 12/31/X6	$755	$3,773

The principal argument for Method 2 was that it is stated in the discussion in ASC 830 that financial information presented in the local currency of a highly inflationary economy is not meaningful, because the local currency is too unstable to provide a reliable measurement of an entity's financial position and results of operations. Accordingly, the reporting currency provides a better basis for establishing the new measurement basis of nonmonetary assets and liabilities. In the same vein, opponents to Method 1 argued that using the historical local currency basis would deem the local currency a reliable measuring unit during a highly inflationary period, thus reintroducing the effects of inflation and negating the intent of ASC 830.

ASC 830-10-45-10, 45-16 Accounting for a Change in Functional Currency and Deferred Taxes When an Economy Becomes Highly Inflationary

The FASB staff announced that a change in the functional currency of an economy that is determined to be highly inflationary in accordance with the provisions in ASC 830 should be accounted for based on the guidance in ASC 830-10-45-9, 45-10. According to that guidance "translation adjustments for prior periods should not be removed from equity and the translated amounts for nonmonetary assets at the end of the prior period become the accounting basis for those assets in the period of the change and subsequent periods."

The FASB staff also announced its view on the recognition of deferred tax benefits when the functional currency changes to that of the reporting entity. Under the guidance in ASC 740-10-25-3, recognition of deferred tax benefits is not permitted for assets and liabilities indexed for tax purposes, if those assets are remeasured into the reporting currency using historical exchange rates. Consequently, no deferred tax benefits should be recognized as a result of tax indexing that occurs after a functional currency becomes the reporting currency until those benefits are realized on the tax return. Nevertheless, deferred tax benefits that are recognized before the functional currency changes to the reporting currency should be eliminated only when the related indexed amounts are realized as deductions for tax purposes.

ASC 830-10-45-12; 55-24 through 55-26 Determining a Highly Inflationary Economy under ASC 830

The FASB staff made an announcement interpreting the guidance in ASC 830 on how to determine whether an economy is highly inflationary. It is stated in ASC 830-10-45-11 that an economy is highly inflationary if its cumulative inflation rate is 100% or more over a three-year period. The role of judgment in making that determination is discussed in ASC 830-10-45-13.

The FASB staff believes that an economy should always be considered highly inflationary if the cumulative inflation rate for the previous three-year period exceeds 100%. However, the staff gave the following examples in which historical trends and other factors would be considered to determine whether an economy is highly inflationary if the cumulative inflation rate is *less* than 100%:

- An economy would continue being considered highly inflationary if it was so in the past, even though its cumulative three-year inflation rate is close to but less than 100% as a result of a decrease in the rate during the last one or two years, unless evidence suggests that the drop is not temporary.
- An economy that was highly inflationary in the prior year should *not* be considered highly inflationary in the current year, if its cumulative three-year inflation rate is close to but less than 100%, even though the inflation rate was very high in one isolated year, which was atypical in comparison to the economy's historical inflation rates and the rate in the current year.

ASC 830-20: FOREIGN CURRENCY TRANSACTIONS

ASC 830-20-35-6 through 35-7; ASC 320-10-35-36 through 35-37; Accounting for the Effects of Changes in Foreign Currency Exchange Rates on Foreign-Currency-Denominated Available-for-Sale Debt Securities

BACKGROUND

The *available-for-sale* (AFS) category of securities was established in ASC 320-10. Unrealized holding gains or losses on securities in that category are reported in a separate component of stockholders' equity and recognized in income when realized.

This Issue addresses the accounting for available-for-sale securities denominated in a foreign currency. Under the guidance in ASC 830-20-35-1, foreign currency transaction gains or losses occur when *monetary* assets and liabilities are denominated in a currency other than the entity's functional currency and the exchange rate between the currencies changes. Some have questioned whether available-for-sale debt securities should be considered to be non-monetary with no recognition of gains and losses on remeasurement, because such securities, which are not held to maturity, are carried at fair value, so their amounts are not fixed. Gains or losses on hedges of net investments in foreign entities and hedges of identifiable foreign currency commitments also are exempted from recognition in earnings under the guidance in ASC 830-20-35(a).

A change in the fair value of available-for-sale (AFS) debt securities denominated in a foreign currency consists of the following two components: (*a*) a change in the market price of the security in the local currency as a result of such factors as changes in interest rates and credit risk and (*b*) a change in exchange rates between the local currency and the entity's functional currency.

ACCOUNTING ISSUE

Should both components of a change in the fair value of available-for-sale debt securities be reported in a separate component of stockholders' equity, or should the component related to the change in exchange rates (component b) be reported in earnings as a foreign currency transaction gain or loss, with changes due to other factors (component a) reported in stockholders' equity?

ACCOUNTING GUIDANCE

Entities should report both components of a change in the fair value of foreign-currency-denominated available-for-sale debt securities in other comprehensive income in accordance with the guidance in ASC 220.

Based on the guidance in ASC 320, changes in market interest rates and foreign exchange rates since acquisition should be considered when determining whether an AFS debt security denominated in a foreign currency has experienced an other-than-temporary impairment.

EFFECT OF ASC 815

The guidance in Issue 1 is not affected by the guidance in ASC 815, which applies only to AFS debt securities that are designated in fair value hedging relationships. A gain or loss on a currency derivative in a fair value hedge of an AFS security is reported in earnings under the guidance in ASC 815, instead of in other comprehensive income as required under this guidance, together with the gain or loss on the AFS security related to changes in the foreign currency's exchange value.

Illustration of a Change in Market Value of an Available-for-Sale Debt Security Denominated in a Foreign Currency

On 7/1/X6, a company whose functional currency is the U.S. dollar acquires a debt security denominated in a foreign currency (FC) and classifies it as available for sale. How would the company compute the change in market value at 9/30/X6?

At 7/1/X6

- Purchase price = FC500
- Exchange rate = $2.50 per FC1
- Historical cost basis = $1,250

At 9/30/X6

- Fair market value = FC600
- Exchange rate = $2.00 per FC1
- U.S. dollar fair market value = $1,200

Components of the Change in Market Value at 9/30/X6

(a) Change in market value Change in fair market value at historical exchange rate

(FC600 – FC500) × $2.50	$250

(b) Effect of exchange rates Current fair market value less historical cost basis plus change in fair market value at historical exchange rates

(FC600 × $2.00) – ($1,250 + $250)	(300)
Net effect	($ 50)

ASC 830-20-55-1 through 55-3 Foreign Debt-for-Equity Swaps

OVERVIEW

In a foreign debt-for-equity swap, a U.S. company that has a subsidiary in Mexico purchases a U.S. dollar-denominated loan in the secondary market at less than the loan's face amount. The loan is due from the Mexican government or an entity operating in Mexico. The company in turn enters into an agreement to sell the loan to the Mexican government for an amount denominated in Mexican pesos that exceeds the amount the company paid for the loan. Under the agreement, which is designed to keep the pesos within Mexico's economy, the company must invest the proceeds in its subsidiary, which is required to use the proceeds for a specified purpose, such as capital expenditures. When the Mexican government purchases the loan, it transmits the pesos directly to the subsidiary, which issues capital stock to the U.S. parent. The agreement restricts the U.S. parent from redeeming the shares, receiving dividends on those shares, or selling the shares within Mexico for a stated period of time. For example, a U.S. company purchases a loan with remaining principal of $15 million for $7.5 million. The Mexican government purchases the loan from the company for $11 million in pesos translated at the official exchange rate, which the company invests in its Mexican subsidiary and receives stock.

ACCOUNTING ISSUE

How should the U.S. company report in its consolidated financial statements the difference between the amount paid to purchase the dollar-denominated loan and the local currency proceeds from the sale of the loan invested in its foreign subsidiary?

ACCOUNTING GUIDANCE

Note: ASC 805 provides guidance on accounting for a bargain purchase, which was previously referred to as negative goodwill.

The excess proceeds in local currency from the sale of a loan translated at the official exchange rate over the cost to purchase the loan should be reported as follows in the parent company's consolidated financial statements:

- Reduce the basis of long-lived assets acquired or constructed under the agreement.
- Reduce the carrying amounts of existing long-lived assets other than goodwill by a corresponding amount, if the agreement does not specifically require the acquisition or construction of long-lived assets, or if the excess is greater than the cost of such assets.

The excess should be applied first to fixed assets with the longest remaining lives until they have been reduced to zero. A remainder, if any, after the carrying amounts of all fixed assets have been reduced to zero should be reported as a bargain purchase as required in ASC 805-30.

This guidance applies to a debt-to-equity swap of a foreign branch that has (1) an accumulated deficit and no significant assets or liabilities other than the local currency debt, and (2) used the proceeds from the foreign debt-for-equity currency swap to extinguish the debt. The excess should be reported as a bargain purchase as required in ASC 805-30.

DISCUSSION

Because the excess in a foreign debt-for-equity swap does not result from a change in exchange rates, it does not meet the criteria to be reported as a transaction gain or loss or a translation adjustment under the provisions of ASC 830. The issue here was whether the U.S. company should report the excess of the proceeds invested in the subsidiary over the purchase price of the loan in income in its consolidated financial statements. Proponents of the consensus argued that because the foreign government required the company to invest the total proceeds in the subsidiary and restricted its use of the proceeds, the earnings process was not complete. Any excess that cannot be identified with assets is accounted for similarly to an unallocated excess in a purchase method business combination, which would be reported as a bargain purchase.

ASC 830-30: TRANSLATION OF FINANCIAL STATEMENTS

ASC 830-30-40-1A through 40-3, 65-1; ASC 805-10-25-10; ASC 810-10-40-4A Parent's Accounting for the Cumulative Translation Adjustment upon Derecognition of Certain Subsidiaries or Groups of Assets within a Foreign Entity or of an Investment in a Foreign Entity

BACKGROUND

The guidance below resolves the diversity in practice that occurred under the following circumstances:

- A parent entity that holds a group of assets, which may be a nonprofit activity or a business (as defined in ASC 805 (Business Combinations)), within a consolidated foreign entity sells or transfers those assets to an independent third party, thus relinquishing its financial control in those assets, but continues to hold an ownership interest in the foreign subsidiary after the disposal of those assets; or
- The foreign entity sells the subsidiary or group of assets directly. The foreign entity may or may not distribute the proceeds to the parent.

According to the guidance in ASC 830 (Foreign Currency Matters), the cumulative translation adjustment (CTA) related to assets that have been sold or transferred to an independent third party would be released into earnings only if the parent entity sells or "completely or substantially" liquidates its ownership interest in the foreign subsidiary. That guidance does not address how a parent of a consolidated foreign entity should account for the CTA if the parent liquidates a portion, but not all, of its ownership interest in a foreign subsidiary.

As a result of the lack of guidance in ASC 830 regarding the accounting for the release of the CTA if a parent does not liquidate all of its ownership interest in a foreign subsidiary, the following two approaches were applied in practice:

1. *ASC 810 approach.* As a result of the FASB's issuance of ASU No. 2010-2, *Consolidation (Topic 810): Accounting and Reporting for Decreases in Ownership of a Subsidiary*, the scope of the accounting guidance for a decrease in ownership and related guidance in ASC 810-10 was expanded to apply to a subsidiary and groups of assets that may be a nonprofit activity or a business (other than a sale of in-substance real estate or a conveyance of oil and gas mineral rights). However, under that guidance, a sale or transfer of an entity's investment in a foreign entity (as defined in ASC 830) is treated the same as a sale or transfer of a subsidiary or group of assets *within* a consolidated foreign entity. Some entities that released a portion of the CTA into earnings upon the disposition of a group of assets of a nonprofit activity or a business (other than a sale of in-substance real estate or conveyance of oil and gas mineral rights) held by a foreign subsidiary analogized that treatment to the amended guidance in ASC 810-10-40-3A and ASC 810-10-40-5.
2. *ASC 830 approach.* Although the FASB expanded the scope of ASC 810-10 for the guidance in ASU No. 2010-2, it did not amend the guidance in ASC 830-30-40 to provide for the release of a portion of the CTA if a parent entity disposes of a group of assets related to a nonprofit activity or to a business (other than a sale of in-substance real estate or of oil and gas mineral rights) held by a consolidated foreign subsidiary, but retains an ownership interest in the subsidiary. As a result, those who believe that the guidance in ASC 830-30-40-1 applies have not released any of the CTA into earnings as long as the entity had not liquidated all of its ownership interest in a foreign subsidiary.

SCOPE

The guidance in Accounting Standards Update (ASU) 2013-05 applies to:

- An entity that no longer has a controlling financial interest in a subsidiary or a group of assets *within* a consolidated foreign entity if: (1) the subsidiary or group of assets is a nonprofit activity or business (other than a sale of in-substance real estate or a conveyance of oil and gas mineral rights), and (2) a CTA balance is associated with the consolidated foreign entity;
- A entity that loses a controlling financial interest in an investment *in* a foreign entity as a result of a sale or other event; and
- An entity that acquires a business in stages (i.e., a step acquisition) by increasing its investment *in* a foreign entity from an investment accounted for under the equity method to one accounted for as a consolidated investment.

ACCOUNTING GUIDANCE

The following definition of a "foreign entity" has been added to the ASC Glossary:

> An operation (for example, subsidiary, division, branch, joint venture, and so forth) whose financial statements are both:
>
> a. Prepared in a currency other than the reporting currency of the reporting entity
>
> b. Combined or consolidated with or accounted for on the equity basis in the financial statements of the reporting entity.

The following guidance is provided in ASU No. 2013-05.

ASC 805-10: Business Combinations—Overall, Recognition. ASC 805-10-25-10 is amended to require that in the case of a business combination related to a previously held equity investment in a foreign entity that is completed in stages, accumulated other comprehensive income (AOCI) that is reclassified and included in the calculation of a gain or loss should include a foreign currency translation adjustment, if any, that is related to the previously held equity investment. The guidance in ASC 830-30-40 applies to the derecognition of foreign currency translation adjustments recorded in AOCI.

ASC 810-10: Consolidation—Overall, Derecognition. ASC 810-10-40-4A has been added to provide that a parent/subsidiary relationship no longer exists after a parent entity has deconsolidated a subsidiary or derecognized a group of assets under the scope of ASC 810-10-40-3A because the parent no longer controls the subsidiary's assets and liabilities or a group of assets. Under those circumstances, the parent must derecognize the related assets, liabilities, and equity components, which should include a noncontrolling interest, if any, and amounts previously recognized in AOCI. If the amount of AOCI that is reclassified and included in the calculation of gain or loss is related to a "foreign entity" (as defined in the ASC Glossary) or to the complete or substantially complete liquidation of the foreign entity in which it existed, a foreign currency translation adjustment, if any, should be included in the amount of AOCI. ASC 830-30-40 provides guidance for the derecognition of foreign currency translation adjustments recorded in accumulated comprehensive income.

ASC 830-30: Foreign Currency Matters—Translation of Financial Statements, Derecognition. ASC 830-30-40-1A has been added to provide that a sale or liquidation of an investment in a foreign entity should include transactions in which: (1) an entity loses a controlling financial interest in a foreign entity as a result of circumstances considered in ASC 810-10 (ASC 810-10-55-4A provides implementation guidance); or (2) an acquirer that gains control of an entity in a business combination completed in stages has held an equity interest in an investment that is a foreign entity, which was accounted for under the equity method immediately before the date of the business combination.

ASC 830-30-40-2, which applies to a reporting entity's sale of a partial ownership interest in an equity method investment in a foreign entity, is amended to provide that if an entity that sells a part of an equity investment in a foreign entity loses significant influence, the pro rata portion of the accumulated translation adjustment component of equity related to the remaining investment should be accounted for under the guidance in ASC 323, *Investments—Equity Method and Joint Ventures* (ASC 323-10-35-37 through 35-39). The guidance in ASC 810-10-45-23 through 45-24 applies if an entity sells a noncontrolling interest in a consolidated foreign entity while retaining a controlling interest in the consolidated foreign entity.

ASC 830-30-40-3 provides that a parent entity's partial liquidation of a foreign entity's net assets should not result in a release of the CTA into income until the entity has met the criteria in ASC 830-30-40-1, which require a sale or the complete or substantial liquidation of an entity's investment in a foreign entity.

TRANSITION

ASC 830-30-65-1 provides the following transition and effective date guidance for the application of the requirements in ASU 2013-5:

- The guidance is effective for fiscal years, and interim periods within those years, that begin after December 15, 2013. Nonpublic entities are required to apply the guidance in fiscal years that begin after December 15, 2014, and subsequent interim and annual periods.
- The guidance should be applied *prospectively* to:
  - — A sale or transfer of a subsidiary or a group of assets that is a nonprofit activity or a business under the scope of ASC 810-10-40-3A *within* a consolidated foreign entity after the effective date;
  - — A sale or transfer of ownership interests *in* a foreign entity after the effective date; and
  - — A business combination completed in stages after the effective date. Prior periods should not be adjusted.
- Early application of the guidance is permitted. If elected, the guidance should be applied from the beginning of the fiscal year in which it is adopted to account for the release of the CTA in the same manner within the fiscal year for all events that result in: (1) disposition and deconsolidation; and (2) step acquisitions.
- The disclosures in ASC 250-10-50-1 through 50-3 are required in the period in which an entity adopts the guidance.

ASC 830-30-45-13 through 45-15 Application of ASC 830 to an Investment Being Evaluated for Impairment That Will Be Disposed Of

BACKGROUND

Under the provisions of ASC 830, translation adjustments that result when a foreign entity's financial statements are translated into a parent company's or an investor's reporting currency are reported separately from the entity's earnings in other comprehensive income. Foreign currency translation adjustments (CTA) that are accumulated in other comprehensive income are reclassified to income only when they are realized if the investment in the foreign entity is sold or is substantially or completely liquidated. This Issue does not apply to foreign investments that are held for use or to transactions related to foreign investments in which CTA will not be reclassified when the transaction is consummated.

ACCOUNTING ISSUES

1. Should an entity include CTA in the carrying amount of its investment in evaluating the impairment of an *equity* method investment in a foreign entity that has committed to a plan to dispose of an investment that will result in the reclassification of CTA to earnings?
2. Should an entity include CTA in the carrying amount of its investment in evaluating the impairment of a *consolidated* investment in a foreign entity that has committed to a plan to dispose of an investment that will result in the reclassification of CTA to earnings?

3. Should an entity that has committed to a plan to dispose of a net investment in a foreign operation (accounted for as an equity investment or as a consolidated subsidiary) include the portion of CTA representing a gain or a loss from an effective hedge of that net investment in the carrying amount of the investment when evaluating the investment for impairment?

ACCOUNTING GUIDANCE

When the impairment of a foreign investment is evaluated, an entity that has committed to a plan to dispose of an equity method investment in a foreign operation or a consolidated foreign subsidiary should *include* in the investment's carrying amount (1) foreign currency translation adjustments that will be reclassified to earnings on the foreign entity's disposal and (2) the portion of CTA related to a gain or loss from an effective hedge of the entity's net investment in the foreign operation.

ASC 830-30-55-1 Foreign Currency Translation—Selection of Exchange Rate When Trading Is Temporarily Suspended

The FASB staff discussed an inquiry from a U.S. company, which had a significant subsidiary in Israel, about the appropriate exchange rate for translating financial statements at year-end. In this case, foreign currency trading was suspended between December 30, 1988, and January 2, 1989. The Israeli government had announced on December 30 that the Israeli shekel, which traded at 1.68 shekel to $1 on December 29, would be devalued on January 2. Although trading resumed on January 2, the new exchange rate of 1.81 shekel to $1 was not established until January 3, 1989. The issue was how to select an exchange rate for year-end reporting when trading is temporarily suspended.

The FASB staff announced that, based on the guidance in ASC 830-30-45-9, the exchange rate on January 3, 1989, would be appropriate for translating the year-end financial statements. ASC 830-30-45-9 states that "[i]f exchangeability between two currencies is *temporarily* lacking at the transaction date or balance sheet date, the first subsequent rate at which exchanges could be made shall be used for purposes of this Statement." [Emphasis added.] The FASB staff noted that the SEC staff agrees with that guidance.

ASC 830-740: INCOME TAXES

ASC 830-740-25-2, 45-2 Accounting for the Income Tax Effects under Topic 740 of a Change in Functional Currency When an Economy Ceases to Be Considered Highly Inflationary

BACKGROUND

When applying the guidance in ASC 830-740-25-2, 45-2 (Issue 92-4), the functional currency bases of nonmonetary assets generally will exceed their local currency tax bases. This difference represents a temporary difference under the guidance in ASC 740, for which a deferred tax liability normally must be recognized.

ACCOUNTING ISSUE

Should an entity account for the income tax effects of a change in functional currency when an economy ceases to be considered highly inflationary by charging income tax expense or the cumulative adjustments component of shareholders' equity?

ACCOUNTING GUIDANCE

When an economy ceases to be considered highly inflationary, deferred taxes associated with a temporary difference resulting from a change in functional currency should be presented as an adjustment to the cumulative translation adjustments component of shareholders' equity.

PRACTICE POINTER: ASC 830 has been amended by ASC 220 to require that translation adjustments be reported in other comprehensive income. Therefore, deferred taxes would be recognized in other comprehensive income. However, it does not change the reporting for accumulated translation adjustments that are reported in a separate component of equity until a foreign investment is sold or liquidated.

DISCUSSION

The guidance is supported by the following arguments:

- Differences between the local currency tax bases of nonmonetary assets and their financial reporting currency bases result from inflation in a highly inflationary economy. Proponents referred to paragraph 119 of FAS-109 (not in ASC), which stated that it is inappropriate to recognize the difference between the foreign currency equivalent of the U.S. dollar cost of nonmonetary assets and their local tax bases as a temporary difference in calculating deferred taxes while an economy is highly inflationary, because that would result in recognition of deferred taxes on exchange gains and losses not recognized in the financial statements under the guidance in ASC 830. They believe that the same rationale should be used if the functional currency is changed from the reporting currency to the local currency in cases in which the local economy is no longer considered highly inflationary. Although deferred taxes must be provided for that difference, they should be charged to the cumulative translation adjustments component because they are related to the net investment in the foreign entity.

- The guidance in ASC 830-10-45-9 through 45-10, which requires charging the effect of a change in functional currency to the cumulative translation adjustments account, should be applied to this situation by analogy. The EITF did not adopt the approach in ASC 740-10-50-10 in their consensus in ASC 830-10-45-9 through 45-10 because they believed that it does not apply to a change in functional currency when an economy ceases to be highly inflationary. Nevertheless, proponents argued that the effect on net income should not differ based on the reason for changing the functional currency.
- The deferred tax effects discussed in this Issue are not caused by an economic effect on the entity when a foreign economy ceases to be considered highly inflationary, but rather by the results of the consensus in ASC 830-10-45-9 through 45-10 and the difference between the way basis differences are normally treated under in the guidance ASC 740 and those caused by highly inflationary economies. Opponents of recognition in income argued that it would be difficult to explain to users why such a change should result in a charge to income.

ASC 830-740-25-4 through 25-5, 30-1 through 30-2, 55-1 through 55-3 Application of ASC 740 in Foreign Financial Statements Restated for General Price-Level Changes

BACKGROUND

Company M, which is located in a country with a highly inflationary economy, prepares price-level-adjusted financial statements in accordance with U.S. GAAP that present changes in the local currency's general purchasing power. In addition, the tax bases of Company M's assets and liabilities are indexed to consider the effects of inflation. Because the adjustments may not be the same for tax and financial statement purposes, the financial reporting and tax bases of assets and liabilities may differ.

Under the guidance in ASC 840, the difference between an asset and liability's financial reporting basis and tax basis is a temporary difference that generally requires the provision of deferred taxes. However, ASC 740-10-25-3 prohibits recognizing a deferred tax liability or asset for differences related to the bases of assets or liabilities that are remeasured under the provisions of ASC 830 from the local currency used in the country in which the entity operates to the functional currency at historical exchange rates and that result from changes in exchange rates or from indexing for tax purposes. ASC 740 states that to do so would result in recognition of deferred taxes on exchange gains or losses not recognized for financial reporting purposes.

Because of that prohibition in paragraph ASC 740-10-25-3, it was unclear whether deferred taxes should be provided for differences in the bases of assets and liabilities that occur as a result of tax indexing when comprehensive, general price-level-adjusted financial statements are prepared using the guidance in APB-3.

ACCOUNTING ISSUES

1. Should paragraph ASC 740-10-25-3 apply to temporary differences between the bases of assets and liabilities for financial reporting in general price-level-adjusted financial statements and their indexed tax bases?
2. If paragraph ASC 740-10-25-3 does not apply, how should deferred income tax expense or benefit for the year be determined?

ACCOUNTING GUIDANCE

1. The guidance in ASC 740-10-25-3 should not be applied to general price-level-adjusted financial statements. Temporary differences in financial statements restated for general price-level changes using end-of-current-year units of purchasing power should be calculated based on the difference between the indexed tax basis amounts of assets and liabilities and the related amounts reported in general price-level-adjusted financial statements.

2. The deferred tax expense or benefit should be calculated as the difference between (*a*) the deferred tax asset or liability reported at the end of the current year based on the above calculation and (*b*) the deferred tax asset or liability reported at the end of the prior year remeasured in end-of-current-year units of purchasing power. Remeasurement of deferred tax assets and liabilities at the end of the prior year should be reported with the remeasurement of all other assets and liabilities as a restatement of beginning equity.

Illustration of the Guidance in ASC 830-740-25-4 through 25-5

Assumptions

- Company M has land that was purchased in 20X0 for FC10,000 (local currency).
- The general price-level-adjusted financial reporting amount of the land at December 31, 20X4, is CFC48,384 (current purchasing power units).
- The indexed basis for tax purposes at December 31, 20X4, is CFC36,456.
- The enacted tax rate is 50%.
- Company M has a taxable temporary difference of CFC11,928 (CFC48,384 – CFC36,456) at December 31, 20X4.
- The related deferred tax liability in current purchasing power units at December 31, 20X4, is CFC5,964 (CFC11,928 × .5).
- During 20X5, general price levels increased by 40% and indexing for tax purposes was 30%.
- The following is the calculation of the deferred tax liability and deferred tax expense at December 31, 20X5:

	20X5
Land—financial reporting basis (CFC48,384 × 1.4)	CFC67,738
Land—tax basis (CFC36,456 × 1.3)	CFC47,393
Taxable temporary difference	CFC20,345
Tax rate	× .5
Deferred tax liability, end of year	CFC10,173
Deferred tax liability restated, at beginning of year (CFC5,964 × 1.4)	CFC 8,350
Deferred tax expense for 20X5	CFC 1,823

Company M should report CFC2,386 (CFC8,350 – CFC5,964) as a restatement of beginning equity for 20X5.

ASC 830-740-25-6 through 25-8; 740-30-25-17 Application of ASC 740 to Basis Differences within Foreign Subsidiaries That Meet the Indefinite Reversal Criterion of ASC 740-30

OVERVIEW

Under the guidance in ASC 740 and ASC 740-30, entities do not recognize a deferred tax liability on temporary differences related to the financial reporting and tax bases of investments in foreign subsidiaries or foreign joint ventures that are not expected to reverse in the foreseeable future. Such differences are referred to as outside basis differences. However, foreign subsidiaries may have other temporary differences, referred to as inside basis differences that also may not reverse in the foreseeable future.

In this particular situation, an Italian subsidiary of a U.S. company uses the Italian lira as its functional currency. The tax basis of the company's fixed assets has been increased to compensate for the effects of inflation, and an equivalent amount has been credited to an account referred to as "revaluation surplus," which is a component of equity established for tax purposes. That amount becomes taxable only if the Italian entity is liquidated or if earnings associated with the revaluation surplus are distributed. Because that amount would not be taxable if the asset is sold, the tax related to the surplus may be deferred indefinitely. However, for discussion purposes, it was assumed that there was no strategy within the entity's control under which it could avoid triggering the tax on the revaluation surplus if it were to realize the carrying amounts of its assets and transfer the net assets to its shareholders.

ACCOUNTING ISSUES

1. Should the indefinite reversal criterion in APB-23, as amended by FAS-109, apply only to outside basis differences, or should it also apply to the revaluation surplus related to inside basis differences of foreign subsidiaries in the consolidated financial statements of the U.S. parent and its foreign subsidiaries?

2. If the indefinite reversal criterion does not apply to inside basis differences, how should the provisions of ASC 740 be applied?

ACCOUNTING GUIDANCE

1. The indefinite reversal criterion in ASC 740-30, does not apply to a revaluation surplus related to *inside* basis differences of foreign subsidiaries. A deferred tax liability should be provided on the balance of the revaluation surplus. This guidance was analogized to the guidance in ASC 740-10-05-10, which discusses temporary differences that have balances only on the income tax balance sheet and that cannot be related to specific assets or liabilities in the financial statements. Deferred taxes are nevertheless provided for such differences, which will result in taxable or deductible amounts in the future. Similarly, based on Italian law, a revaluation surplus related to inside basis differences will be taxable in the future and thus qualifies as a temporary difference, even though it is a component of equity for tax purposes. In addition, the guidance in ASC 740-10-25-3 specifically limits the indefinite reversal criterion in ASC 740-30 to the situations discussed in that paragraph and prohibits applying it by analogy to other types of temporary differences.

2. Entities should recognize a deferred tax liability for inside basis differences that originated in fiscal years beginning *after* December 15, 1992. Therefore, recognition of a deferred tax liability is not required for existing inside basis differences that originated in fiscal years beginning *before* December 16, 1992 and for which no deferred tax liability was recognized on adoption of the guidance in ASC 740. However, the information required in ASC 942-740-50-1 should be disclosed in those situations.

CHAPTER 54

ASC 832—GOVERNMENT ASSISTANCE

CONTENTS

GENERAL GUIDANCE

GOVERNMENT ASSISTANCE

IMPORTANT NOTICE FOR 2022

As Wolters Kluwer's 2022 *GAAP Guide* goes to press, the FASB has outstanding an Exposure Draft of an Accounting Standards Update (ASU), *Government Assistance*, that may have an important impact on the preparation of financial statements in the future. The FASB is issuing the proposed ASU to increase transparency about government assistance arrangements including the types of arrangements, the accounting for government assistance, and their effect on an entity's financial statements. Under current GAAP, there is no explicit guidance on the accounting for, or the disclosure of, government assistance received by business entities.

The proposed guidance would apply to an entity or entities, other than not-for-profit entities within the scope of ASC 958 (Not-for-Profit Entities), that have entered into a legally enforceable agreement with a government to receive value. The scope of the proposed guidance would not apply to transactions in which the government is (1) legally required to provide a nondiscretionary level of assistance to an entity, or (2) solely a customer.

The proposed guidance would result in entities providing information on existing government assistance agreements for annual reporting periods that would enable a user to better assess all of the following:

- The nature of the assistance, related accounting policies used to account for government assistance, and the effect of government assistance on an entity's financial statements.
- Significant terms and conditions of the legally enforceable agreement.

The new guidance would also require the following disclosures about material existing government assistance agreements for annual reporting periods:

- Information about the nature of the assistance;
- Which line items on the balance sheet and income statement are affected by government assistance and the amounts applicable to each line item;
- Significant terms and conditions of the agreement, including commitments and contingencies; and
- Unless impracticable, the amount of government assistance received but not recognized directly in the financial statements.

The effective date for this proposed ASU will be determined when the final ASU is issued. Note that this proposed ASU has been outstanding since 2015. Given the length of time this Exposure Draft has been outstanding, the future of this project is uncertain.

CHAPTER 55

ASC 835—INTEREST

CONTENTS

PART I: GENERAL GUIDANCE

ASC 835-10: OVERALL

OVERVIEW

Under certain conditions, interest is capitalized as part of the acquisition cost of an asset. Interest is capitalized only during the period of time required to complete and prepare the asset for its intended use, which may be either *sale or use within the business*. Capitalization of interest is based on the principle that a better measure of acquisition cost is achieved when certain interest costs are capitalized. This results in a better matching of revenue and costs in future periods.

Business transactions may involve the exchange of cash or other assets for a note or other instrument. When the interest rate on the instrument is consistent with the market rate at the time of the transaction, the face amount of the instrument is assumed to be equal to the value of the other asset(s) exchanged. An interest rate that is different from the prevailing market rate, however, implies that the face amount of the instrument may not equal the value of the other asset(s) exchanged. In this case, it may be necessary to impute interest that is not stated as part of the instrument, or to recognize interest at a rate other than that stated in the instrument.

BACKGROUND

The basis of accounting for depreciable fixed assets is cost, including all normal expenditures of readying an asset for use are capitalized as part of acquisition cost. Unnecessary expenditures that do not add to the utility of the asset should be charged to expense.

ASC 835 covers the promulgated U.S. GAAP on the capitalization of interest costs on certain qualifying assets that are undergoing activities to prepare them for their intended use. ASC 835 requires that the same materiality tests applied by regular U.S. GAAP be applied to the materiality of capitalizing interest cost.

ASC 835 applies to the capitalization of interest cost on equity funds, loans, and advances made by investors to certain investees that are accounted for by the equity method as described in ASC 323 (Investments—Equity Method and Joint Ventures).

ASC 835 provides special treatment in capitalizing interest costs on qualifying assets that are acquired with (*a*) the proceeds of tax-exempt borrowings and (*b*) gifts or grants that are restricted for the sole purpose of acquiring a specific asset.

PRACTICE POINTER: The basis of capitalizing certain interest costs is that the cost of an asset should include all costs necessary to bring the asset to the condition and location for its intended use. The requirements of ASC 835 to capitalize interest cost may result in a lack of comparability among reporting entities, depending on their method of financing major asset acquisitions. For example, Company A and Company B both acquire an identical asset for $10 million that requires three years to complete for its intended use. Company A pays cash, and at the end of three years, the total cost of the asset is $10 million. In addition, assume that Company A also had net income of $2 million a year for each of the three years and had no interest expense. Assume also that Company B had $1.5 million net income for each of the three years after deducting $500,000 of interest expense per year. If Company B qualifies for capitalized interest costs under ASC 835, it would reflect $2 million per year net income and not show any interest expense. On the balance sheet of Company B at the end of three years, the identical asset would appear at a cost of $11.5 million. Future depreciation charges will vary between the two companies by a total of $1.5 million. Although the interest cost may be necessary to Company B, it does not add to the utility of the asset.

ASC 835 is also the main source of U.S. GAAP on imputing interest on receivables and payables. However, ASC 835 guidance does not apply under the following conditions (ASC 835-30-15-3):

1. Payables that arise in the ordinary course of business and are due in approximately one year or less.
2. Amounts do not require repayment in the future, but rather will be applied to the purchase price of the property, goods, or services to which they relate rather than requiring a transfer of cash.
3. Amounts represent security or retainage deposits.
4. Amounts arise in the ordinary course of business of a lending institution.
5. Amounts arise from transactions between a parent and its subsidiaries, or between subsidiaries of a common parent.
6. The interest rate is affected by the tax attributes or legal restrictions prescribed by a governmental agency.
7. The application of the present value measurement (valuation) techniques to estimates of contractual or other obligations assumed in connection with the sale of property, goods or services.
8. Receivables, contract assets, and contract liabilities in contracts with customers.

Receivables and payables that are not specifically excluded from the provisions of ASC 835 and that are contractual rights to receive or pay money at a fixed or determinable date must be recorded at their present value if (*a*) the interest rate is not stated or (*b*) the stated interest rate is unreasonable (ASC 310-10-30-6).

PRACTICE NOTE: This is an application of the basic principle of substance over form in that the substance of the instrument (interest-bearing), rather than the form of the instrument (noninterest-bearing or bearing interest at an unreasonable rate), becomes the basis for recording.

ASC 835-20: CAPITALIZATION OF INTEREST

QUALIFYING ASSETS

Acquisition Period

In concept, interest cost must be capitalized for all assets that require an *acquisition period* to get them ready for their intended use (ASC 835-20-15-2). *Acquisition period* is defined as the period commencing with the first expenditure for a qualifying asset and ending when the asset is substantially complete and ready for its intended use. Thus, before interest costs can be capitalized, expenditures must have been made for the qualifying asset, providing an investment base on which to compute interest, and activities that are required to get the asset ready for its intended use must actually be in progress.

The usual rules of materiality embodied in U.S. GAAP must be followed in determining the materiality for the capitalization of interest costs. Thus, in applying the provisions of ASC 835, all the usual materiality tests used in applying other promulgated U.S. GAAP should also be used in determining the materiality for capitalization of interest costs.

Intended Use

Capitalization of interest cost is applicable for assets that require an acquisition period to prepare them for their intended use. Assets to which capitalized interest must be allocated include both (1) assets acquired for a company's own use, (2) assets intended for sale or lease that are acquired as discrete projects in the ordinary course of business, and (3) certain of an investor's investments in an investee accounted for under the equity method (ASC 835-20-15-5). Thus, inventory items that require a long time to produce, such as a real estate development, qualify for capitalization of interest costs. However, interest costs are not capitalized for inventories that are routinely produced in large quantities on a repetitive basis (ASC 835-20-15-6).

PRACTICE POINTER: The FASB concluded that the benefit of capitalizing interest costs on inventories that are routinely produced in large quantities does not justify the cost. Thus, interest costs should not be capitalized for inventories that are routinely produced in large quantities.

Capitalization of interest cost is not permitted (*a*) for assets that are ready for their intended use or that are actually being used in the earning activities of a business and (*b*) for assets that are not being used in the earning activities of a business and that are not undergoing the activities required to get them ready for use (ASC 835-20-15-6).

COMPUTING INTEREST COST TO BE CAPITALIZED

The amount of interest cost that may be capitalized for any accounting period may not exceed the actual interest cost (from any source) that is incurred by an enterprise during that same accounting period (ASC 835-20-30-6). In addition to interest paid and/or accrued on debt instruments, interest imputed in accordance with ASC 835-30 (Imputation of Interest) and interest recognized on finance leases in accordance with ASC 842 (Leases) are available for capitalization. ASC 835 specifically prohibits imputing interest costs on any equity funds. In consolidated financial statements, this limitation on the maximum amount of interest cost that may be capitalized in a period should be applied on a consolidated basis.

PRACTICE NOTE: ASC 715 (Compensation—Retirement Benefits) requires that the interest cost component of net periodic pension cost shall not be considered to be interest for purposes of applying ASC 835.

Similarly, the interest cost component of postretirement benefit cost shall not be considered interest for purposes of applying ASC 835.

PRACTICE POINTER: A logical starting point for applying ASC 835 and related pronouncements is to determine the total amount of interest that was incurred and that is available for capitalization as a cost of a qualifying asset. If a company incurs little or no qualifying interest on debt instruments, interest imputed in accordance with ASC 835-30, or interest on finance leases, the requirement to capitalize interest may not be effective, even though the company may have invested in assets that would otherwise require interest capitalization.

Average Accumulated Investment

To compute the amount of interest cost to be capitalized for a particular accounting period, the average accumulated investment in a qualifying asset during that period must be determined. To determine the average accumulated investment, each expenditure must be *weighted* for the time it was outstanding during the particular accounting period.

Illustration of Computing Average Accumulated Investment

In the acquisition of a qualifying asset, a calendar year company expends $225,000 on January 1, 20X8; $360,000 on March 1, 20X8; and $180,000 on November 1, 20X8. The average accumulated investment for 20X8 is computed as follows:

Amount of Expenditure	*Period from Expenditure to End of Year*	*Average Investment*
$225,000	12 months (12/12)	$225,000
360,000	10 months (10/12)	300,000
180,000	2 months (2/12)	30,000
$765,000		$555,000

Identification of Interest Rates

If a specific borrowing is made to acquire the qualifying asset, the interest rate incurred on that borrowing may be used to determine the amount of interest costs to be capitalized. That interest rate is applied to the average accumulated investment for the period to calculate the amount of capitalized interest cost on the qualifying asset. Capitalized interest cost on average accumulated investments in excess of the amount of the specific borrowing is calculated by the use of the weighted-average interest rate incurred on other borrowings outstanding during the period (ASC 835-20-30-3).

If no specific borrowing is made to acquire the qualifying asset, the weighted-average interest rate incurred on other borrowings outstanding during the period is used to determine the amount of interest cost to be capitalized. The weighted-average interest rate is applied to the average accumulated investment for the period to calculate the amount of capitalized interest cost on the qualifying asset. Judgment may be required to identify and select the appropriate specific borrowings that should be used in determining the weighted-average interest rate. The objective should be to obtain a reasonable cost of financing for the qualifying asset that could have been avoided if the asset had not been acquired (ASC 835-20-30-4).

PRACTICE POINTER: In determining the weighted average interest rate for purposes of capitalizing interest, take care not to overlook interest that is available for capitalization even though it has another specific purpose. For example, a company might have interest on mortgage debt on buildings and plant assets. Unless that interest already is being capitalized into a different asset under ASC 835, it is available for capitalization despite the fact that it was incurred specifically to finance the acquisition of a different asset.

Progress payments received from the buyer of a qualifying asset are deducted in the computation of the average amount of accumulated expenditures during a period. Nonetheless, the determination of the average amount of accumulated expenditures for a period may be reasonably estimated (ASC 835-20-30-5).

Illustration of Calculating Weighted-Average Interest Rate

A company has the following three debt issues outstanding during a year in which interest must be capitalized as part of the cost of plant assets:

$1,000,000 par value, 8% interest rate

$1,500,000 par value, 9% interest rate

$1,200,000 par value, 10% interest rate

The weighted-average interest rate is computed as follows:

$1,000,000 × 8%	=	$80,000
1,500,000 × 9%	=	135,000
1,800,000 × 10%	=	180,000
$4,300,000	=	$395,000
$395,000/$4,300,000	=	9.19%

Interest available for capitalization is $395,000. Assuming none of the debt issues relates directly to the asset for which interest is being capitalized, interest is charged to the cost of the asset at a 9.19% interest rate applied to the average investment made on the asset during the year. If, instead, one of the debt issues relates directly to the asset for which interest is being capitalized, interest may be charged at the interest rate applicable to that debt issue on the investment equal to the amount of that debt. Interest on any remaining investment is calculated at the weighted-average interest rate for the remaining debt.

Capitalization Period

The interest capitalization period starts when three conditions are met (ASC 835-20-25-3):

1. Expenditures have occurred.
2. Activities necessary to prepare the asset (including administrative activities before construction) have begun.
3. Interest cost has been incurred.

Interest is not capitalized during delays or interruptions initially by the entity, except for brief interruptions, that occur during the acquisition of the qualifying asset. However, interest continues to be capitalized during externally imposed delays or interruptions (e.g., strikes) (ASC 835-20-25-4).

When the qualifying asset is substantially complete and ready for its intended use, the capitalization of interest ceases. The qualifying asset may be completed in independent parts (i.e., the parts can be used separately from the rest of the project, like units in a condominium) or in dependent parts (i.e., parts that, although complete, cannot be used until other parts are finished, like subassemblies of a machine). Interest capitalization ceases for an independent part when it is substantially complete and ready for its intended use. For dependent parts of a qualifying asset, however, interest capitalization does not stop until all dependent parts are substantially complete and ready for their intended use (ASC 835-20-25-5).

SPECIAL APPLICATIONS

Equity Method Investments

An investor's qualifying assets, for the purposes of capitalizing interest costs under ASC 835, include equity funds, loans, and advances made to investees accounted for by the equity method. Thus, an investor must capitalize interest costs on such qualifying assets if, during that period, the investee is undergoing activities necessary to start its planned principal operations and such activities include the use of funds to acquire qualifying assets for its operations. The investor does not capitalize any interest costs on or after the date that the investee actually begins its planned principal operations.

For the purposes of applying the above guidance, the term *investor* means both the parent company and all consolidated subsidiaries. Thus, all qualifying assets of a parent company and its consolidated subsidiaries that appear in the consolidated balance sheet are subject to the interest capitalization provisions of ASC 835. Capitalization of interest cost in the investee's separate financial statements is unaffected by this guidance.

Capitalized interest costs on an investment accounted for by the equity method are included in the carrying amount of the investment. Up to the date on which the planned principal operations of the investee begin, the investor's carrying amount of the investment, which includes capitalized interest costs (if any), may exceed the underlying equity in the investment. If the investor cannot relate the excess carrying amount of the investment to specific identifiable assets of the investee, the difference is considered goodwill (ASC 323-10-35-34).

Any interest cost capitalized is not changed in restating financial statements of prior periods. Thus, if an unconsolidated investee is subsequently consolidated in the investor's financial statements as a result of increased ownership or a voluntary change by the reporting entity, interest costs capitalized are not changed if restatement of financial statements is necessary.

Tax-Exempt Borrowings and Gifts and Grants

Under the provisions of ASC 835, capitalized interest cost for a qualifying asset is determined by applying either a specific interest rate or a weighted-average interest rate to the average accumulated expenditures during a particular period for the qualifying asset. An underlying premise in ASC 835 is that borrowings usually cannot be identified with specific qualifying assets. The financing policies of most enterprises are planned to meet general funding objectives, and the identification of specific borrowings with specific assets is considered highly subjective.

U.S. GAAP concludes that different circumstances are involved in the acquisition of a qualifying asset with tax-exempt borrowings, such as industrial revenue bonds and pollution control bonds. The tax-exempt borrowings, temporary interest income on unused funds, and construction expenditures for the qualifying asset are so integrated that they must be accounted for as a single transaction (ASC 835-20-30-10). Thus, capitalization of interest cost for any portion of a qualifying asset that is acquired with tax-exempt borrowings is required, as follows (ASC 835-20-30-11).

Capitalization Period

Interest cost is capitalized from the date of the tax-exempt borrowings to the date that the qualifying asset is ready for its intended use.

Amount of Capitalized Interest Cost

The amount of capitalized interest cost allowable is equal to the total actual interest cost on the tax-exempt borrowing, less any interest income earned on temporary investments of the tax exempt funds. The net cost of interest on the tax-exempt borrowing is capitalized and added to the acquisition cost of the related qualifying asset (ASC 835-20-30-11).

External Restriction Requirement

The above guidance only applies when the qualifying asset is financed by tax-exempt borrowing, in which the use of the borrowed funds is restricted to acquiring the assets or servicing the related debt. The restriction must be *external*, that is, imposed by law, contract, or other authority outside the enterprise that borrows the funds. This guidance does not permit the capitalization of interest cost on any portion of a qualifying asset that is acquired with a gift or grant that is restricted to the acquisition of the specified qualifying asset. Restricted interest income on temporary investment of funds is considered an addition to the restricted gift or grant.

PRACTICE POINTER: No interest cost should be capitalized on qualifying assets acquired by restricted gifts or grants, because there is no economic cost of financing involved in acquiring an asset with a gift or grant. In addition, any interest earned on temporary investment of funds from a gift or grant is, in substance, part of the gift or grant.

Disposition of Capitalized Interest

If capitalized interest costs are added to the overall cost of an asset, the total cost of the asset, including capitalized interest, may exceed the net realizable or other lower value of the asset that is required by U.S. GAAP. In this event, ASC 835 requires that the provision to reduce the asset cost to the lower value required by U.S. GAAP be increased. Thus, the total asset cost, including capitalized interest, less the provision, will equal the lower value for the asset that is required by U.S. GAAP (ASC 835-20-25-7).

Capitalized interest costs become an integral part of the acquisition costs of an asset and should be accounted for as such in the event of disposal of the asset (ASC 835-20-40-1).

DISCLOSURE REQUIREMENTS

The total amount of interest costs incurred and charged to expense during the period and the amount of interest costs, if any, which has been capitalized during the period, should be disclosed in the financial statements or notes thereto (ASC 835-20-50-1).

Illustration of the Application of ASC 835

On January 1, 20X8, Poll Powerhouse borrowed $300,000 from its bank at an annual rate of 12%. The principal amount plus interest is due on January 1, 20Y0. The funds from this loan are specifically designated for the construction of a new plant facility. On February 1, 20X8, Poll paid $15,000 for architects' fees and for fees for filing a project application with the state government.

On March 1, 20X8, Poll received state approval for the project and began construction. The following summarizes the costs incurred on this project.

20X8	
February 1 (architects' and filing fees)	$ 15,000
April 1	150,000
September 1	60,000
20X9	
January 1	1,000
March 1	360,000
November 1	180,000
Total Project Cost	$766,000

The $1,000 is a miscellaneous cost and was expensed in 20X9, since it was determined by Poll to be immaterial.

The following schedule summarizes the additional borrowings of Poll as of December 31, 20X9:

Borrowing Date	*Amount*	*Maturity Date*	*Annual Interest Rate*
Mar. 1, 20X8	$1,000,000	Feb. 28, 20Y0	13%
Oct. 1, 20X9	$ 500,000	Sept. 30, 20Y1	14%

From February 1, 20X9, to March 31, 20X9, a major strike of construction workers occurred, halting all construction activity during this period.

In August 20X9, Poll voluntarily halted construction for the entire month because the chief executive officer did not want construction to continue without her supervision during her scheduled vacation.

Calculation of Interest

Poll's new plant facility is a qualifying asset under the provisions of ASC 835 and is subject to interest capitalization. The interest capitalization period begins on the first date that an expenditure is made by Poll, which was for architects' fees, February 1, 20X8.

To compute the interest capitalization for 20X8, the average accumulated expenditures for 20X8 are first calculated as follows:

Amount of Expenditure	*Period from Expenditure to End of Year*	*Average Investment*
$ 15,000	11 months (11/12)	$ 13,750
150,000	9 months (9/12)	112,500
60,000	4 months (4/12)	20,000
$225,000		$146,250

Next, the average investment amounts are multiplied by the interest rate on the borrowing (12%). This rate is used because Poll has specifically associated the borrowing with the construction of the new plant facility, and the average accumulated investment ($146,250) does not exceed the amount of the borrowing ($300,000). Therefore, the interest capitalized for 20X8 is computed as follows:

Average accumulated investment	$146,250
Interest rate	12%
Capitalizable interest cost—20X8	$17,550

Since Poll incurred $144,333 of interest costs [($300,000 × 12%) + ($1,000,000 × 13% × 10/12)], the full $17,550 must be capitalized.

The investment in the asset for 20X8 ($225,000 + $17,550 capitalized interest = $242,550) is included as part of the base to compute 20X9 capitalizable interest cost. One further adjustment is necessary to calculate the average accumulated expenditures for 20X9. The plant facility was completed on December 31, 20X9, but there were two interruptions in construction in 20X9. Interest is capitalized during delays or interruptions that are externally imposed, or during delays inherent in acquiring the qualifying asset. However, interest is not capitalized during delays or interruptions that are caused internally by an enterprise, unless they are brief. Thus, in this problem, interest capitalization continues during the externally imposed strike. However, interest capitalization ceases during August 20X9, because the CEO's vacation is a voluntary interruption.

The average accumulated investment for 20X9 is computed as follows:

Amount of Expenditure	*Period from Expenditure to End of Year, Less One Month of Interruption*	*Average Investment*
$242,550	11 months (11/12)	$222,338
360,000	9 months (9/12)	270,000
180,000	2 months (2/12)	30,000
$782,550		$522,338

Note: The $180,000 was expended on November 1, 20X9, after the interruption, so no adjustment need be made to the average expenditure of $30,000 for the interruption.

The $1,000 miscellaneous cost is not included, since Poll decided that this amount was immaterial and expensed it.

If the average accumulated investment for the qualifying asset exceeds the amount of the specific borrowing made to construct the asset, the capitalization rate applicable to the excess is the weighted-average interest rate incurred on other borrowings. In this problem, the computation of the excess investment over the original loan amount is as follows:

Average investment through December 31, 20X9	$522,338
Less: Amount of original loan	300,000
Excess investment	$222,338

Thus, in 20X9, interest on $222,338 of the $522,338 average investment is capitalized using the weighted-average borrowing rate, whereas interest on the balance of $300,000 is capitalized using the interest rate on the original loan made specifically to acquire the qualifying asset. The weighted-average rate on the other borrowings is computed as follows:

Amount	*Weighted Amount*	*Rate*	*Annual Interest*
$1,000,000	$1,000,000	13%	$130,000
500,000	125,000 (3 mos.)	14%	$17,500
$1,500,000	$1,125,000		$147,500

$$\frac{\$147{,}500}{\$1{,}125{,}000} = 13.11\% \text{ weighted-average interest rate.}$$

The interest cost to be capitalized for 20X9 is computed as follows:

$300,000	×	12.00%	=	$36,000
222,338	×	13.11%	=	29,149
$522,338				$65,149

Since Poll incurred $183,500 [($300,000 × 12%) + ($1,000,000 × 13%) + ($500,000 × 14% × 3/12)] of interest, the full $65,149 is capitalizable as part of the acquisition cost of the asset in 20X9.

The total interest capitalized on the asset is $82,699 ($17,550 in 20X8 plus $65,149 in 20X9). The total asset cost at the end of 20X9 is as follows:

Expenditures other than interest	$765,000
Interest cost capitalized	$82,699
	$847,699

PRACTICE NOTE: In this illustration, interest capitalized in 20X9 was based on an investment amount from 20X8 that included the amount of interest capitalized in 20X8. The authors have not found specific authoritative guidance that supports the inclusion of previously capitalized interest in the investment base, but believes this is consistent with the inclusion of interest in other situations and is logical in the circumstances.

ASC 835-30: IMPUTATION OF INTEREST

CIRCUMSTANCES REQUIRING IMPUTED INTEREST

A note issued or received in a noncash transaction contains two elements to be valued: (1) the principal amount for the property, goods, or services exchanged and (2) an interest factor for the use of funds over the period of the note. These types of notes must be recorded at their present value. Any difference between the face amount of the note and its present value is a discount or premium that is amortized over the life of the note.

PRACTICE POINTER: The interest rate on a note that results from a business transaction entered into at arm's length is generally presumed to be fair. If no interest is stated or if the interest stated appears unreasonable, however, record the substance of the transaction. Further, if rights or privileges are attached to the note, evaluate them separately.

For example, a beer distributor lends $5,000 for two years at no interest to a customer who wishes to purchase bar equipment. There is a tacit agreement that the customer will buy the distributor's products. In this event, a present value must be established for the note receivable, and the difference between the face of the note ($5,000) and its present value must be considered an additional cost of doing business for the beer distributor.

Circumstances requiring interest to be imputed as specified in ASC 835 are summarized in Figure 55-1.

The present value techniques used in ASC 835 should not be applied to estimates of a contractual property or other obligations that are assumed in connection with a sale of property, goods, or services such as an estimated warranty for product performance.

PRACTICE NOTE: Interest that is imputed on certain receivables and payables in accordance with ASC 835-30 is eligible for capitalization under the provisions of ASC 835-20 (Capitalization of Interest).

APPLYING ASC 835-30 PRINCIPLES

Determining Present Value

There is no predetermined formula for determining an appropriate interest rate. *However, the objective is to approximate what the rate would have been, using the same terms and conditions, if it had been negotiated by an independent lender.* The following factors should be considered (ASC 835-30-25-12):

- Credit rating of the borrower
- Restrictive covenants or collateral involved
- Prevailing market rates
- Rate at which the debtor can borrow funds

The appropriate interest rate depends on a combination of the above factors.

Figure 55-1: Circumstances Indicating a Need to Impute Interest

```
          ┌─────────────────────────┐
          │ Note exchanged for      │
          │ property, goods, or     │
          │ services                │
          └─────────────────────────┘
                      │
                      ▼
                 ◇ Is interest ◇ ─────────── No ──────────┐
                 ◇   stated?   ◇                          │
                      │                                   │
                     Yes                                  │
                      │                                   │
                 ◇ Is stated  ◇                           │
                 ◇ interest rate ◇ ─────── No ────────────┤
                 ◇ reasonable? ◇                          │
                      │                                   │
                     Yes                                  │
                      │                                   │
                 ◇ Is face    ◇                           │
                 ◇ amount of note ◇                       │
                 ◇ materially different from ◇ ── Yes ────┤
                 ◇ value inherent in the ◇                │
                 ◇ transaction?* ◇                        │
                      │                                   │
                      No                                  │
                      │                                   │
          ┌─────────────────────────┐   ┌─────────────────────────┐
          │ • Record exchange at    │   │ • Record exchange at    │
          │   face value of note    │   │   value inherent in     │
          │ • Recognize interest at │   │   transaction           │
          │   stated rate           │   │ • Recognize interest at │
          │                         │   │   imputed rate          │
          └─────────────────────────┘   └─────────────────────────┘
```

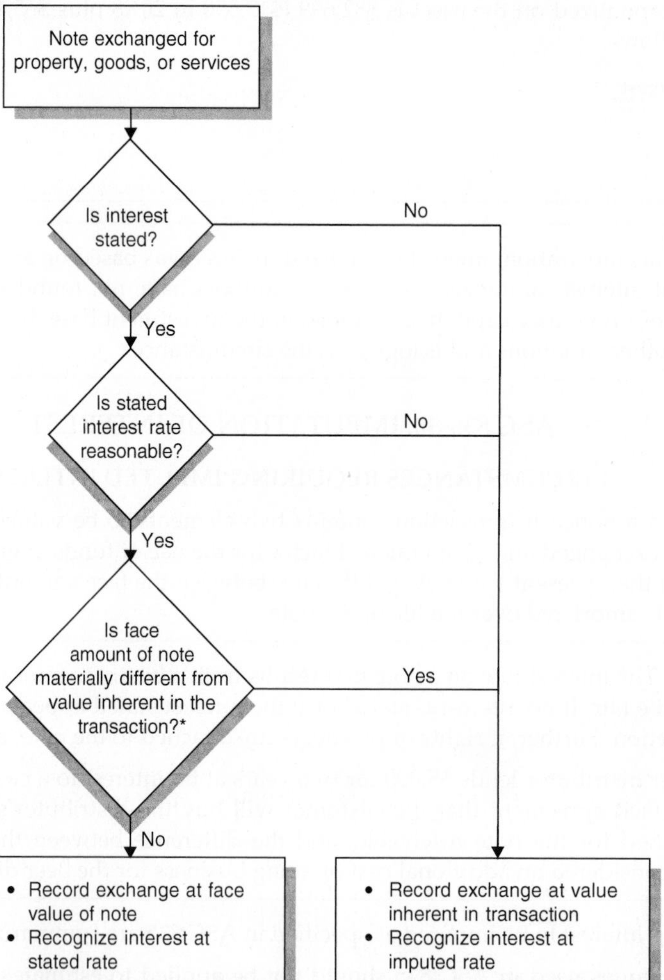

* Value inherent in transaction is the fair value of the property, goods, or services or the market value of the note, whichever is more readily determinable.

PRACTICE POINTER: In determining an appropriate interest rate for purposes of imputing interest for the purchaser in a transaction, a starting point might be the most recent borrowing rate. The more recent the borrowing, the more appropriate that rate may be. Even if the borrowing rate is recent, however, give consideration to the impact that the additional debt from the earlier borrowing would likely have on the company's next borrowing. The size of the transaction for which interest is being imputed relative to other outstanding debt also may be an important factor in determining an appropriate rate.

Discount and Premium

The difference between the present value and the face amount of the receivable or the payable represents the amount of premium or discount. A discount exists if the present value of the total cash flow of the note (face amount plus stated interest), using the appropriate rate of interest, is *less* than the face amount of the note. A premium exists if the present value of the total proceeds of the note (face amount plus stated interest), using the appropriate rate of interest, is *more* than the face amount of the note.

The premium or discount is amortized over the life of the note as interest expense or income, using a constant rate on any outstanding balance (ASC 835-30-35-2). This method is called the *interest method* and is illustrated at the end of this chapter.

The premium or discount that arises from the use of present values on cash and noncash transactions is inseparable from the related asset or liability. Therefore, premiums and discounts are added to or deducted from their related asset or liability in the balance sheet. Similarly, debt issuance costs related to a note must be reported in the balance sheet as a direct deduction from the face amount of that note. The discount, premium, or debt issuance costs resulting from imputing interest are not classified as deferred charges or credits (ASC 835-30-45-1A).

Disclosure

A description of the receivable or payable, the effective interest rate, and the face amount of the note should be presented in the financial statements or disclosed in the notes thereto. The amortization of a discount or premium must be reported as interest expense in the case of liabilities or as interest income in the case of assets. The amortization of debt issuance costs must also be reported as interest expense (ASC 835-30-45-2, 3).

Illustration of Interest Imputed and Accounted for on a Noninterest-Bearing Note

A manufacturer sells a machine for $10,000 and accepts a $10,000 note receivable bearing no interest for five years; 10% is an appropriate interest rate. The initial journal entry would be:

Note receivable	10,000.00	
Sales (present value at 10%)		6,209.00
Unamortized discount on note		3,791.00

The manufacturer records the note at its face amount but records the sale at the present value of the note because that is the value of the note today. The difference between the face amount of the note and its present value is recorded as *unamortized discount on note.*

The *interest method* is used to produce a constant rate, which is applied to any outstanding balance. In the above example, the present value of $6,209 was recorded for the $10,000 sale using the appropriate interest rate of 10% for the five-year term of the note. The difference between the $10,000 sale and its present value of $6,209 is $3,791, which was recorded as unamortized discount on note. The 10% rate, when applied to each annual outstanding balance for the same five years, will result in amortization of the discount on the note, as follows:

		Amortization of Discount on the Note
Original balance	$ 6,209.00	$3,791.00
Year 1, 10%	620.90	(620.90)
Remaining balance	$ 6,829.90	$3,170.10
Year 2, 10%	682.99	(682.99)
Remaining balance	$ 7,512.89	$2,487.11
Year 3, 10%	751.29	(751.29)
Remaining balance	$ 8,264.18	$1,735.82

		Amortization of Discount on the Note
Year 4, 10%	826.42	(826.42)
Remaining balance	$ 9,090.60	$ 909.40
Year 5, to clear accounts	909.40	(909.40)
Remaining balance	$10,000.00	$-0-

Following are the journal entries to record imputed interest at the end of each year and the final collection of the note.

End of 1st year:		
Unamortized discount on note	620.90	
Interest income		620.90
End of 2nd year:		
Unamortized discount on note	682.99	
Interest income		682.99
End of 3rd year:		
Unamortized discount on note	751.29	
Interest income		751.29
End of 4th year:		
Unamortized discount on note	826.42	
Interest income		826.42
End of 5th year:		
Unamortized discount on note	909.40	
Interest income		909.40
Cash	10,000.00	
Note receivable		10,000.00

Illustration of Recording a Note with an Unreasonable Rate of Interest

A company purchases a $10,000 machine and issues for payment a $10,000 four-year note bearing 2% compound interest per year; 10% is considered an appropriate rate of interest. The entire amount due, including all interest, is payable at the maturity date of the note. The initial journal entry is:

Machine (present value of $10,824 @ 10% for 4 periods)	7,393	
Unamortized discount on note	3,431	
Note payable		10,000
Deferred interest payable		824
First year:		
Interest expense	739	
Unamortized discount on note (10% on $7,393)		739
Second year:		
Interest expense	813	
Unamortized discount on note [10% on ($7,393 + $739)]		813
Third year:		
Interest expense	895	
Unamortized discount on note [10% on ($7,393 + $739 + $813)]		895
Fourth year:		
Interest expense	984	
Unamortized discount on note [10% on ($7,393 + $739 + $813 + $895)]		984

In the fourth year, when the note and the 2% interest are paid, the following journal entry is made:

Note payable	$10,000	
Deferred interest payable	824	
Cash		$10,824

The future amount of the note is $10,824 ($10,000 × 1.0824, which compounds the 2% for four periods). The company records a note payable ($10,000) and the deferred interest ($824). The machine is recorded at the present value of this amount ($7,393), determined by discounting the $10,824 at 10% (the reasonable interest rate) for four years. This is because today the $10,824 is worth only $7,393, which is the amount at which the sale is recorded. The difference between the total amount due in four years ($10,824) and its present value ($7,393) is deferred interest ($3,431) for the use of the seller's funds and is amortized by the interest method over the term of the note.

PART II: INTERPRETIVE GUIDANCE

ASC 835-30: IMPUTATION OF INTEREST

ASC 835-30-55-2 Required Use of Interest Method in Recognizing Interest Income

Because the discussion in ASC 310-20 is related to the application of the interest method to nonrefundable loan fees and costs, not to interest income, some have questioned whether the interest method must be used to determine interest income. Using the interest method to recognize interest income is required under GAAP. Alternative methods, such as the Rule of 78s, sum of the years' digits, and straight-line methods, should *not* be used to impute interest income unless the results do not differ materially from those based on the interest method.

CHAPTER 56

ASC 842—LEASES

CONTENTS

PART I: GENERAL GUIDANCE

FUTURE IMPACT OF ASU 2016-02, *LEASES*

In February 2016, the FASB issued ASU 2016-02, *Leases,* as Topic 842 of the FASB Accounting Standards Codification (ASC). The most significant change to U.S. GAAP contained in ASU 2016-02 is lessee recognition of lease assets and liabilities for leases classified as operating leases under previous guidance. The effective dates for the guidance in ASU 2016-02 have been revised by subsequent ASUs issued by the FASB. Specifically, ASU 2019-10, *Financial Instruments—Credit Losses (Topic 326), Derivatives and Hedging (Topic 815), and Leases (Topic 842): Effective Dates,* was issued in November 2019 and extended the effective date by one year for entities other than public business entities that are SEC filers (i.e., "all other" entities). Then in response to the impact of the COVID-19 pandemic, the FASB issued ASU 2020-05, *Revenue from Contracts with Customers (Topic 606) and Leases (Topic 842): Effective Dates for Certain Entities,* in June 2020. This ASU extended the effective date by an additional year for entities in the "all other" category, as well as for public not-for-profit entities that have not yet issued their financial statements (or made financial statements available for issuance) reflecting the adoption of ASU 2016-02. After considering the extensions granted in ASU 2019-10 and ASU 2020-05, the modifications to the ASC brought about by ASU 2016-02 are effective for reporting periods beginning after December 15, 2018, including interim periods within that reporting period for public companies, not-for-profit entities that have issued or are conduit bond obligors for traded, listed, or quoted securities (with an exception for those entities that have not yet issued their financial statements or made financial statements available for issuance as of June 3, 2020, reflecting the adoption of ASU 2016-02), and employee benefit plans that file financial statements with the U.S. Securities and Exchange Commission. For not-for-profit entities that have not yet issued their financial statements or made financial statements available for issuance as of June 3, 2020, reflecting the adoption of ASU 2016-02, the guidance will be effective for fiscal years beginning after December 15, 2019, and interim periods within those fiscal years. For all other entities, the guidance will be effective for fiscal years beginning after December 15, 2021, and interim periods within fiscal years beginning after December 15, 2022. Earlier application is permitted for all entities (ASC 842-10-65-1).

In applying the new lease guidance, an entity may choose to apply practical expedients to leases that began prior to the effective date of the guidance as long as the expedients are applied consistently to all leases for which the entity is lessee or lessor. These expedients are that an entity does not need to reassess: whether existing contracts contain leases, the lease classification applied to existing leases, the initial direct costs associated with existing leases, or land easements that were not previously accounted for as leases (ASC 842-10-65-1). If the practical expedient is not selected, refer to ASC 842-10-65-1 for further details. To assist in the implementation of the new guidance, ASU 2016-02 includes over 40 implementation examples.

Due to the long transition period for ASU 2016-02 and because early application of ASC 842 is permitted, the 2022 *GAAP Guide* includes coverage in this chapter of both the previous guidance on leases (ASC 840), as well as the new guidance under ASC 842. In the 2022 *GAAP Guide,* the guidance under ASC 842 is the primary content of this chapter and the guidance in ASC 840 that will eventually be replaced is included as the last section of the General Guidance of this chapter. The impact of ASU 2016-02 (ASC 842) on other chapters is also reflected in the 2022 *GAAP Guide*. Future editions of the *GAAP Guide* will continue to cover both sets of guidance during the transition period in which both previous reporting guidance and ASC 842 are permitted. In subsequent editions of the *GAAP Guide,* the previous guidance under ASC 840 will be removed once it is no longer applicable.

ASC 842-10: OVERALL

OVERVIEW AND BACKGROUND

A *lease* is a contract that conveys the right to control the use of an asset for a period of time in exchange for consideration (ASC Glossary). Leases typically involve two parties: the party contracting to provide the right to use the asset (lessor) and the party contracting to use the asset (lessee). This topic establishes the principles lessors and lessees should use to provide useful information to financial statement users. Because of certain tax, cash flow, and other advantages, leases have become an important alternative to the outright purchase of property by which companies (lessees) acquire the resources needed to operate.

The term *lease,* as used in promulgated U.S. GAAP, does *not* include the following (ASC 842-10-15-1):

- Leases of intangible assets
- Leases concerning the right to explore for or exploit natural resources such as oil, gas, minerals, and timber

- Leases of inventory
- Leases of assets under construction
- Leases of biological assets, including timber.

In determining whether a contract contains a lease, the customer considers several factors. First, in order for a contract to contain a lease there must be an identified asset. An identified asset is generally explicitly specified but can be implicitly specified. If the customer can readily determine that the supplier of the asset has substantive substitution rights, then there is not an identified asset. This determination is made based on the facts and circumstances at inception of the contract and does not include future events considered unlikely to occur at the time. A supplier has substantive substitution rights if it has the practical ability to substitute alternative assets throughout the period of use and there would be an economic benefit to the supplier for making this substitution (ASC 842-10-15-9 through 15-15).

Next, the customer assesses whether the contract conveys the right to obtain substantially all of the economic benefits from use of the identified asset. If this right is not conveyed, the contract does not contain a lease. The economic benefits could be direct through use of an asset or indirect by subleasing an asset. The customer should only consider the economic benefits of use of the asset within the scope of its right to use the asset in the contract, which may be limited. If the customer is required to pay the supplier or a third party a portion of the cash flows derived from the asset as consideration, this does not prevent the customer from having the right to substantially all of the economic benefits from use of the identified asset (ASC 842-10-15-17 through 15-19).

Finally, the customer determines whether it has the right to direct the use of the identified asset throughout the period of use. If the customer does not have this right, the contract does not contain a lease. The customer has the right to direct the use of the identified asset if it has the right to direct how and for what purpose the asset is used throughout the period. Decision-making rights that affect the economic benefits to be derived from use of the asset are considered in making this determination. If the customer has decision-making rights to change the output type produced by the asset, change when or where the output is produced, or change whether output is produced and its quantity, these could all convey the right to direct use of the asset. Decision-making rights related to asset maintenance and operations do not grant the right to direct use of the asset (ASC 842-10-15-24 through 15-26).

The customer also has the right to direct the use of the identified asset if the relevant decisions about how and for what purpose the asset is used are predetermined, whether through asset design or contract restrictions and (ASC 842-10-15-20):

- The customer has the right to operate the asset throughout the period of use without the supplier having the right to change those operating instructions; or
- The customer designed the asset, predetermining how and for what purpose the asset will be used throughout the period of use.

Protective rights established through contract restrictions may define the customer's scope of use but do not necessarily prevent the customer from having the right to direct the use of the asset (ASC 842-10-15-23).

If it is determined that a contract contains a lease, the separate lease components within the contract should be identified. In order for the right to use an asset to be a separate lease component (ASC 842-10-15-28):

- The lessee should be able to benefit from the right of use on its own or with other resources readily available to the lessee; and
- The right of use should not be highly dependent on or interrelated with the other rights to use underlying assets in the contract.

Once the separate lease components are identified, the consideration in the contract should be allocated to each lease and nonlease contract component. Contract components should transfer a good or service to the lessee; therefore, some items such as administrative expenses to set up or initiate a lease and reimbursement or payment of the lessor's costs are not contract components (ASC 842-10-15-30).

Lessees should allocate the consideration in the contract and any initial direct costs to the separate lease and nonlease components in the contract. However, lessees may make the accounting policy election by class of underlying asset to not separate nonlease and lease components and to account for each lease component along with its associated nonlease components together (ASC 842-10-15-37). The lessee allocates the consideration by the relative standalone price of each contract component. This price is based on observable prices or estimates if observable standalone prices are not available (ASC 842-10-15-33). Consideration in the contract should be remeasured and reallocated when there is remeasurement of the lease liability or a contract modification not accounted for as a separate contract (ASC 842-10-15-36).

Lessors should allocate (unless the lessor makes the accounting policy election in accordance with ASC 842-10-15-42A) the consideration in the contract and any capitalized costs such as initial direct costs or contract costs to the separate lease and nonlease components in the contract according to the requirements in ASC 606-10-32-28 through 32-41 (ASC 842-10-15-38). If there are variable payments other than those described in ASC 842-10-15-35 that are related to a lease component, the lessor must not recognize those payments before the factors determining the payment amount occur. When the changes in facts and circumstances on which the variable payment is based occur, the lessor must allocate those payments to the lease and nonlease components of the contract (ASC 842-10-15-40). Consideration in the contract should be remeasured and reallocated according to the guidance in ASC 606-10-32-42 through 32-45 when there is a contract modification not accounted for as a separate contract (ASC 842-10-15-41).

TERMINOLOGY

The authoritative literature includes many terms that are important for an understanding of lease accounting. Several of these terms are explained below.

Commencement Date

The commencement date is the date on which a lessor makes an underlying asset available for use by a lessee.

Consideration in the Contract

Consideration for lessees includes fixed payments, variable lease payments that depend on an index or rate, the exercise price of an option to purchase the asset if purchase is reasonably certain, penalties for lease termination if reflected in the lease term, fees paid to owners of a special-purpose entity for structuring the transaction, and probable residual value guarantees (ASC 842-10-15-35).

For lessors, consideration includes the lessee consideration factors as well as any other variable payment amounts included in the transaction price related to the lessor's efforts to transfer or successful transfer of non-lease goods or services (ASC 842-10-15-39).

Delayed Equity Investment

Delayed equity investments are equity contributions the lessor agrees to make to service nonrecourse debt when the lessee's rent payments in a leveraged lease transaction do not begin until one to two years after lease inception (ASC Glossary).

Direct Financing Lease

A direct financing lease is a type of finance lease that does *not* transfer ownership to the lessee at the end of the lease term, grant the lessee an option to purchase that is likely to be exercised, have a lease term for the majority of the remaining economic life of the asset, or have minimum lease payments and a residual value guarantee by the lessee such that the present value of the sum of the payments is greater than or equal to substantially all of the fair value of the asset. The lease should have minimum lease payments and a residual value guarantee by the lessee and/or any third party unrelated to the lessor such that the present value of the sum of the payments is greater than or equal to substantially all of the fair value of the asset and it should be probable that these payments are collectible (ASC 842-10-25-3).

Separately identifying sales-type and direct financing leases is an accounting issue for the lessor only, who accounts for the two types of finance leases differently, as described later in this chapter. Both types of leases are treated as a finance lease by the lessee.

Discount Rate

The discount rate for the lessor is the rate implicit in the lease. For the lessee, the discount rate is the rate implicit in the lease or the lessee's incremental borrowing rate if the implicit rate cannot be readily determined.

Economic Life

Estimated economic life is the estimated remaining useful life of the property for the purpose for which it was intended, regardless of the term of the lease (ASC Glossary).

Fair Value

Fair value is the price that would be received to sell an asset or paid to transfer a liability in an orderly transaction between market participants at the measurement date (ASC Glossary).

For the manufacturer or dealer, fair value usually is the normal selling price less trade or volume discounts. Fair value may be less than the normal selling price, however, and sometimes less than the cost of the property.

For others, fair value usually is cost less trade or volume discounts. Fair value may be less than cost, however, especially in circumstances in which a long period elapses between the acquisition of the property by the lessor and the inception of a lease.

Finance Lease

A finance lease meets one or more of the following conditions for the lessee: transfers ownership to the lessee at the end of the lease term, grants the lessee an option to purchase that is likely to be exercised, has a lease term for the majority of the remaining economic life of the asset, or has minimum lease payments and a residual value guarantee such that the present value of the sum of the payments is greater than or equal to substantially all of the fair value of the asset (ASC 842-10-25-2).

Incremental Borrowing Rate

The lessee's incremental borrowing rate is the rate of interest that the lessee would have had to pay at the inception of the lease to borrow the funds, on similar terms, to purchase the leased property (ASC Glossary).

Initial Direct Costs

Initial direct costs are the incremental lease costs that would not have been incurred if the lease had not been obtained (ASC Glossary).

Lease

A lease is a contract conveying the right to control the use of the identified property, plant, or equipment for a period of time in exchange for consideration (ASC Glossary).

Lease Inception

The lease inception is the earlier of the date of the lease agreement or written, executed commitment that sets forth all of the principal provisions of the transaction (ASC Glossary).

Lease Modification

A lease modification is a change to contract terms and conditions that changes the lease scope or consideration (ASC Glossary).

Lease Receivable

The lessor has a lease receivable measured on a discounted basis for its right to receive lease payments from a sales-type or direct financing lease plus any residual value guarantee (ASC Glossary).

Lease Term

The lease term includes all of the following (ASC Glossary):

- The noncancelable term.
- The period covered by an extension option that is reasonably certain to be exercised.
- The period covered by a termination option that is reasonably certain not to be exercised.
- The period covered by an option to extend or not to terminate in which the lessor controls the option.

Leveraged Lease

For the lessor, a leveraged lease is a lease that commenced before the effective date of ASC 842 and was classified as a leveraged lease in accordance with ASC 840 (ASC Glossary).

Market Participants

Market participants are buyers and sellers with the following characteristics (ASC Glossary):

- They are independent, non-related parties.
- They are knowledgeable and have a reasonable understanding of the asset or liability and transaction using information that is readily available and that is obtained through any customary due diligence efforts.
- They are able to enter into the transaction.
- They are willing to enter into the transaction.

Minimum Lease Payments

Minimum lease payments are the payments the lessee is obligated to or can be required to make on the leased property except for contingent rentals, any lessee guarantees of the lessor's debt, and the lessee's obligation to pay executory costs.

In leases with a bargain purchase option, minimum lease payments are only required to include the minimum rental payments over the lease term and the bargain purchase option payment. Otherwise, minimum lease payments include all of the following:

- Minimum rental payments over the lease term.
- Any residual value guarantee. If the lessor can require the lessee to purchase the property at lease termination, the purchase amount is considered a lessee residual value guarantee. If the lessee agrees to make up any deficiency below a stated residual value amount, the minimum lease payments should include the stated residual value, not an estimate of the deficiency.
- Any payment the lessee must make or can be required to make upon failing to renew or extend the lease at the end of its term.
- Payments made before the beginning of the lease term using the same interest rate used to discount lease payments during the lease term.
- Fees paid by the lessee to owners of a special-purpose entity for structuring the lease transaction.

Lease payments dependent on an existing index or rate should be included in minimum lease payments based on the index or rate at lease inception. Lease payments dependent on a factor directly related to the future, such as sales volume, are considered contingent rentals and are excluded from minimum lease payments (ASC Glossary).

Net Investment in the Lease

The net investment in the lease is the sum of the lease receivable and the unguaranteed residual asset, net of any deferred selling profit in a direct financing lease (ASC Glossary).

Operating Lease

An operating lease is any lease other than a finance lease for a lessee and any lease other than a sales-type lease or direct financing lease for a lessor.

Penalty

The term *penalty* refers to any outside factor or provision of the lease agreement that does or can impose on the lessee the requirement to disburse cash, incur or assume a liability, perform services, surrender or transfer an asset or rights to an asset or otherwise forego an economic benefit, or suffer an economic detriment (ASC Glossary).

Rate Implicit in the Lease

The implicit interest rate in the lease is the rate that, at a given date, causes the aggregate present value of the lease payments plus the amount a lessor can expect from the underlying asset at the end of the lease term to equal the fair value of the underlying asset less any realizable investment tax credit that was retained plus any deferred initial direct costs of the lessor (ASC Glossary).

Related Parties

Related parties include (ASC Glossary):

- Entity affiliates.
- Entities for which investments in their equity securities are required to be accounted for by the equity method by the investing entity.
- Trusts for the benefit of employees.
- The entity's principal owners and management and their immediate families.
- Other parties the entity may deal with if one party has control or significant influence over the management or operating policies of the other party.
- Other parties that have control or significant influence over the management or operating policies or have an ownership interest in one of the transacting parties.

Residual Value Guarantee

A residual value guarantee is a guarantee made to the lessor regarding the minimum value of an underlying asset when it is returned at the end of a lease (ASC Glossary).

Sales-Type Lease

A sales-type lease is a type of finance lease that meets one or more of the following criteria: transfers ownership to the lessee at the end of the lease term, grants the lessee an option to purchase that is likely to be exercised, has a lease term for the majority of the remaining economic life of the asset, or has minimum lease payments and a residual value guarantee such that the present value of the sum of the payments is greater than or equal to substantially all of the fair value of the asset (ASC 842-10-25-2).

Separately identifying sales-type and direct financing leases is an accounting issue for the lessor only, who accounts for the two types of finance leases differently, as described later in this chapter. Both types of leases are treated as a finance lease by the lessee.

Selling Profit or Selling Loss

At the commencement date, selling profit or selling loss equals (ASC Glossary):

- The lower of the fair value of the underlying asset or the sum of the lease receivable and any lease payments prepaid by the lessee, minus
- The carrying amount of the underlying asset net of any unguaranteed residual asset, minus
- Any deferred initial direct costs of the lessor.

Short-Term Lease

A short-term lease has a term of 12 months or less and no option to purchase that is reasonably certain to be exercised (ASC Glossary).

Unguaranteed Residual Asset

An unguaranteed residual asset is the discounted amount a lessor expects to derive from the underlying asset at the end of the lease term that is not guaranteed by either the lessee or a third party unrelated to the lessor (ASC Glossary).

Variable Lease Payments

Variable lease payments are those that vary due to changes in facts or circumstances other than the passage of time occurring after the commencement date (ASC Glossary).

LEASE CLASSIFICATION

Lease components are classified separately at the commencement date of the lease. Lease classifications are not reassessed unless the contract is modified but a separate contract is not created, or, for the lessee, if the lease term or assessment of whether the lessee is reasonably certain to exercise an option to purchase the asset changes (ASC 842-10-25-1).

If one or more of the following criteria is present at the inception of a lease, it is classified as a finance lease by the lessee and a sales-type lease by the lessor (ASC 842-10-25-2):

1. Ownership of the asset is transferred to the lessee by the end of the lease term.
2. The lease contains an option to purchase the asset that the lessee is reasonably certain to exercise.
3. The lease term is for the majority of the remaining economic life of the asset. If the lease term begins near the end of the economic life of the asset, this criterion does not apply.
4. The present value of the lease payments plus any residual value guaranteed by the lessee not reflected in the lease payments equals or exceeds substantially all of the fair value of the asset.
5. The asset is specialized such that it is not expected to have an alternative use to the lessor at the end of the lease term.

If none of the criteria above are met, the lease is classified as an operating lease by the lessee and either an operating lease or direct financing lease by the lessor. The lessor classifies the lease as an operating lease unless the following two criteria are met, in which case the lessor classifies the lease as a direct financing lease (ASC 842-10-25-3):

1. The present value of the lease payments plus any residual value guaranteed by the lessee not reflected in the lease payments and/or any other third party unrelated to the lessor equals or exceeds substantially all of the fair value of the asset.
2. It is probable the lessor will collect the lease payments plus any residual value guarantee.

In assessing the above criteria, there are some reasonable thresholds that could be applied. Seventy-five percent or more could be considered the majority of the economic life of the asset; likewise, if a lease begins during the last 25%, it could be considered to be near the end of the economic life of the asset. When comparing the payment amounts to the fair value of the asset, 90% could be considered to be substantially all of the fair value of the asset (ASC 842-10-55-2). Sometimes it is not practicable for an entity to determine the fair value of an asset; in these circumstances, a lease should be classified without using the criterion comparing the lease payments to the asset's fair value (ASC 842-10-55-3). The fair value calculated should be reduced by any investment tax credits retained and expected to be realized by the lessor (ASC 842-10-55-8).

A lessor uses the rate implicit in the lease to assess the present value of the lease payments and residual value guarantees. It should be assumed that initial direct costs are not deferred if the fair value of the asset is different from its carrying amount at the lease commencement date (ASC 842-10-25-4).

When determining if ownership of the asset is transferred at the end of the lease term, an option to purchase the asset does not satisfy this criterion. Examples of situations where ownership is transferred include leases where the lessor delivers documents releasing and transferring ownership of the asset to the lessee provided the lessee performs in accordance with the lease terms or leases where the lessee pays a nominal amount to transfer ownership of the asset (ASC 842-10-55-4 through 55-6).

To assess whether an asset has an alternative use at the end of the lease term, an entity should consider whether there are substantive, enforceable contractual restrictions preventing the asset from having an alternative use to the lessor. The lessor should also consider whether there are practical limitations such as significant economic losses or unique design specifications that would prevent the lessor from being able to redirect use of the asset (ASC 842-10-55-7).

If a lease is acquired through a business combination or acquisition by a not-for-profit entity, the lease classification should remain the same unless there is a lease modification not accounted for as a separate contract (ASC 842-10-55-11).

Related Party Leases

Related party leases should be classified and accounted for as if the parties were unrelated (ASC 842-10-55-12).

PRACTICE NOTE: Specific financial statement disclosures pertaining to related parties are required by ASC 850 (Related Party Disclosures).

Leases Involving Governmental Units

Leases with governmental units often lack fair values, have indeterminable economic lives, and cannot provide for transfer of ownership. These special provisions usually prevent their classification as any other than operating leases (ASC 842-10-55-13).

Leases involving governmental units, however, are subject to the same criteria as any other lease unless all of the following conditions exist; and in that event, these leases are classified as operating leases (ASC 842-10-55-13):

- A governmental unit or authority owns the leased property.
- The leased property is operated by or on behalf of a governmental unit or authority and is part of a larger facility, such as an airport.
- The leased property cannot be moved to another location because it is a permanent structure or part of a permanent structure.
- The governmental unit or authority can terminate the lease agreement at any time under the terms of the lease agreement, existing statutes, or regulations.
- Ownership is not transferred to the lessee and the lessee cannot purchase the leased property.
- Equivalent property in the same area as the leased property cannot be purchased or leased from anyone else.

Lease Modifications

A lease modification should be accounted for as a separate contract if both of the following conditions apply:

- The modification grants the lessee an additional right of use not included in the original lease.
- The lease payments increase proportionally with the standalone price of the additional right of use, given the circumstances of the original contract.

PRACTICE NOTE: Due to the economic impact of the COVID-19 pandemic, many lessors provided lease concessions to lessees for a significant number of lease contracts. The most common concessions are payment forgiveness or deferral of payments. The guidance in ASC 842 and ASC 840 would require entities to account for many of these lease concessions as a modification of the existing leases. In response to stakeholders' concerns regarding these concessions, the FASB issued a Staff Q&A to provide some additional guidance on the issue, including the following:

Question 1: Are lease concessions related to the effects of the COVID-19 pandemic required to be accounted for in accordance with the lease modification guidance in ASC 842 and ASC 840?

FASB Response: No. Entities do not have to account for these lease concessions as a lease modification.

Question 2: Is an entity precluded from accounting for these lease concessions by applying the lease modification guidance in ASC 842 and ASC 840?

FASB Response: No. The COVID-19 exception for accounting for these lease concessions is optional. Entities may still apply the guidance for lease modifications in ASC 842 and ASC 840.

Question 3: Does an entity have to account for all COVID-19-related lease concessions in the same manner (i.e., elect the exception for all or none)?

FASB Response: No. However, entities should apply ASC 842 consistently to leases with similar characteristics and in similar circumstances.

Question 4: Should an entity provide disclosures about these lease concessions?

FASB Response: Yes. Entities should provide disclosures about material concessions granted and the accounting effects to allow users to understand the nature and financial effect of the lease concessions.

If a lease modification does not require that it be accounted for as a separate contract, then reassessment of the lease classification should be as of the effective date of the modification (ASC 842-10-25-8, 9).

If, before expiration of the lease term, a change in a lease occurs as a result of a refunding by the lessor of tax-exempt debt, it should be accounted for in the same manner as any other lease modification (ASC 842-10-55-16).

When considering whether a master lease agreement should be treated as a lease modification, if the lessee is allowed to use additional assets during the lease term but is not required to do so, the lessee taking control over any such additional asset should be accounted for as a lease modification (ASC 842-10-55-18). If, however, the master lease agreement states additional assets the lessee will gain control over during the lease term, the separate lease components should be identified and consideration in the contract should be allocated across those components (ASC 842-10-55-17).

Lessees

Lessees should reallocate the remaining consideration in a contract and remeasure the lease liability using a discount rate determined at the effective date of the lease modification if a contract modification does any of the following (ASC 842-10-25-11):

- Grants the lessee an additional right of use not included in the original contract.
- Extends or reduces the term of an existing lease other than through exercising a contractual option in the lease.
- Changes only the consideration in the contract.
- Fully or partially terminates an existing lease.

If one of the first three changes has occurred, the lessee recognizes the amount of change in the lease liability from the remeasurement as an adjustment to the corresponding right-of-use asset. If the change was full or partial termination of an existing lease, the lessee decreases the carrying amount of the right-of-use asset proportionately to the change in the lease and any difference in that change and the reduction of the lease liability should be recognized as a gain or loss at the modification date (ASC 842-10-25-12, 13).

If the lease modification changes a finance lease to an operating lease, any difference in the carrying amount of the right-of-use asset after recording the adjustment and the amount that would have occurred if operating right-of-use asset measurement guidance had been used should be accounted for in the same manner as a rent prepayment or lease incentive (ASC 842-10-25-14).

Lessors

If an operating lease is modified and not accounted for as a separate contract, the lessor should treat this as termination of the existing lease and creation of a new lease commencing on the effective date of the modification. If the modified lease is an operating lease, the lessor should include any prepaid or accrued lease rentals relating to the original lease as part of the lease payments in the modified lease. If the modified lease is a direct financing or sales-type lease, the lessor should derecognize any deferred rent liability or accrued rent asset and adjust the selling profit or loss as needed (ASC 842-10-25-15).

If a direct financing lease is modified and not accounted for as a separate contract, the lessor should account for the modified lease as follows (ASC 842-10-25-16):

- If the modified lease is a direct financing lease, adjust the discount rate so the initial net investment in the modified lease equals the carrying amount of the net investment in the original lease prior to the modification.
- If the modified lease is a sales-type lease, use the guidance in ASC 842-30. To calculate selling profit or loss, the fair value of the asset is its fair value at the modification date and its carrying amount is the carrying amount of the net investment in the original lease prior to the modification.
- If the modified lease is an operating lease, the carrying amount is the carrying amount of the net investment in the original lease prior to the modification.

If a sales-type lease is modified and not accounted for as a separate contract, the lessor should account for the modified lease as follows (ASC 842-10-25-17):

- If the modified lease is a direct financing or sales-type lease, adjust the discount rate so the initial net investment in the modified lease equals the carrying amount of the net investment in the original lease prior to the modification.
- If the modified lease is an operating lease, the carrying amount is the carrying amount of the net investment in the original lease prior to the modification.

Contract Combinations

An entity can consider two or more contracts entered into near the same time, at least one of which is a lease, as a single transaction if any of the following apply (ASC 842-10-25-19):

- The contracts are negotiated as a package with the same commercial objectives.
- The consideration in one contract depends on the price or performance of the other contract.
- The contractual rights to use underlying assets are a single lease component.

MEASUREMENT OF A LEASE

Lease Term and Purchase Options

An entity initially determines the lease term as the noncancelable period of the lease along with periods covered by an option to extend the lease if the lessee is reasonably certain to exercise the option or the option right is controlled by the lessor, and periods covered by an option to terminate if the lessee is reasonably certain not to exercise the option or the option right is controlled by the lessor (ASC 842-10-30-1). If there is a fiscal funding clause in the lease and the possibility of it being exercised is more than remote, the lease term should only include periods for which funding is reasonably certain (ASC 842-10-55-27).

All factors creating an economic incentive for the lessee should be considered when determining the lease term. These factors may include comparing the contractual terms for the optional periods with current market rates, significant leasehold improvements expected when the option becomes exercisable, costs of terminating the lease and signing a new lease, and the importance of the asset to the lessee's operations (ASC 842-10-55-26).

The lease term begins at the commencement date and includes any rent-free periods provided to the lessee (ASC 842-10-55-25). In the case of a master lease agreement covering several underlying assets, there may be multiple commencement dates if the assets are made available for use on different dates (ASC 842-10-55-22). The noncancelable period is defined as the period during which the contract is enforceable. If the lessee and lessor both have the right to terminate the lease without permission from the other party and without significant penalty, the lease is no longer enforceable (ASC 842-10-55-23).

In some contracts, the lessee may have possession or control over an asset prior to making lease payments. The timing of when lease payments begin does not affect the commencement date of the lease (ASC 842-10-55-20). If an entity has a building or ground lease, the right to use the asset is the same during any construction period as it is after construction so any lease costs or income associated with the lease incurred or earned during a construction period should be recognized according to the guidance for lessees and lessors (ASC 842-10-55-21).

The lessee should only reassess the lease term or option to purchase the asset if one of the following occurs (ASC 842-10-35-1):

- A significant event or change in circumstances occurs that directly affects the lessee's probability of exercising an option to extend or terminate the lease or purchase the asset.
- An event is written into the contract requiring the lessee to exercise or not exercise an option to extend or terminate the lease.
- The lessee exercises an option it was previously determined it would not be reasonably certain of exercising.
- The lessee does not exercise an option it was previously determined it would be reasonably certain of exercising.

Significant events that might cause a lessee to reassess the lease term or option to purchase the asset could include construction of significant leasehold improvements, significant modification or customization of the asset, making a business decision directly relevant to the lessee's ability to exercise an option, or subleasing the asset beyond the exercise date of the option. Market factors would generally not qualify as a significant event that would require reassessment of the lease term or purchase option (ASC 842-10-55-28, 29).

The lessor should only reassess the lease term or lessee option to purchase the underlying asset if the lease is modified and not accounted for as a separate contract (ASC 842-10-35-3).

Measurement of Lease Payments

As of the commencement date, lease payments consist of the following (ASC 842-10-30-5):

- Fixed payments less any lease incentives paid or payable to the lessee.
- Variable payments that depend on an index or rate and measured at that index or rate at the commencement date.
- The exercise price of an option to purchase the asset if purchase is reasonably certain.
- Penalties for lease termination if reflected in the lease term.
- Fees paid to owners of a special-purpose entity for structuring the transaction.
- For the lessee, probable residual value guarantees.

Payments that are in substance fixed payments are treated as fixed payments. In substance fixed payments may appear to be variable but are not, for example, if the lessee has a choice about which of two sets of payments to make but is required to make at least one set of payments (ASC 842-10-55-31). Lease incentives included in the lease payments include payments made to or on behalf of the lessee and losses the lessor incurs by assuming a lessee's pre-existing lease with a third party (ASC 842-10-55-30).

The lessee includes a residual value guarantee in its lease payments if the lessor has the right to require the lessee to purchase the asset at the end of the lease term. However, if there is a lease provision requiring the lessee to pay a residual value deficiency if there is damage, extraordinary wear and tear, or excessive usage, this does not constitute a residual value guarantee. If a lessee obtains a residual value guarantee from a third party, it should not reduce the lessee's calculation of lease payments unless the lessor releases the lessee from its obligation (ASC 842-10-55-34 through 55-36).

Lease payments do not include (ASC 842-10-30-6):

- Any other variable lease payments.
- Lessee guarantee of the lessor's debt.
- Amounts allocated to nonlease components.

Obligations to return an asset to its original condition at the end of the lease term if modified by the lessee generally would not be considered lease payments and would instead be accounted for following the guidance in ASC 410 (Asset Retirement and Environmental Obligations). However, costs incurred from lease requirements to dismantle and remove an asset at the end of the lease term would generally qualify as lease payments (ASC 842-10-55-37).

Indemnification clauses that indemnify lessors for tax benefits that may be lost if tax law changes would generally qualify as variable lease payments (ASC 842-10-55-38).

Lease payments should be remeasured by the lessee if (ASC 842-10-35-4):

- The lease is modified and not accounted for as a separate contract.
- A contingency related to the variable lease payments is resolved such that those payments are now considered lease payments.
- There is a change in: lease term, the assessment of the probability of the lessee exercising an option to purchase the underlying asset, or the amounts probable of being owed by the lessee under residual value guarantees.

A lessor should not remeasure lease payments unless the lease is modified and not accounted for as a separate contract (ASC 842-10-35-6).

Initial Direct Costs

A lessee or lessor's initial direct costs may include commissions or payments made to encourage an existing tenant to terminate its lease (ASC 842-10-30-9). Costs that would be incurred whether or not the lease was obtained are not initial direct costs; examples of these costs are fixed employee salaries, general overhead expenses, advertising, and tax and legal expenses incurred prior to obtaining the lease (ASC 842-10-30-10).

ASC 842-20: LESSEE

LESSEE

Asset and Liability Recognition

The lessee recognizes a right-of-use asset and a lease liability at the commencement date of the lease (ASC 842-20-25-1).

Short-Term Leases

For short-term leases, the lessee can elect not to apply the recognition requirements in ASC 842-20. This accounting policy election can be made by class of underlying asset. If elected, lease payments are recognized in profit and loss on a straight-line basis over the lease term. Variable lease payments are recognized in the period in which the obligation for those payments occurs or becomes probable (ASC 842-20-25-2, ASC 842-20-55-1).

If the lease changes and the lease term is extended by more than 12 months from the end of the prior lease term or the lessee becomes reasonably certain of exercising an option to purchase, the lease is no longer a short-term lease. The date of this change in circumstance serves as the effective commencement date in this instance (ASC 842-20-25-3).

Finance Leases

Unless the following costs are included in the carrying amount of another asset, the lessee should recognize in profit and loss (ASC 842-20-25-5):

- Amortization of the right-of-use asset.
- Interest on the lease liability.
- Variable lease payments not included in the lease liability.
- Any impairment of the right-of-use asset.

Operating Leases

Unless the following costs are included in the carrying amount of another asset, the lessee should recognize in profit and loss (ASC 842-20-25-6):

- Single lease costs allocating the remaining cost of the lease over the remaining lease term on a straight-line basis unless there is another method more representative of the benefit expected from the right to use the asset.
- Variable lease payments not included in the lease liability.
- Any impairment of the right-of-use asset.

If the right-of-use asset is determined to be impaired, the single lease costs should be calculated by adding: (1) amortization of the remaining asset after impairment on a straight-line, or other more representative basis; and (2) increase of the lease liability in the amount that produces a constant discount rate over each remaining period of the lease term on the remaining liability balance (ASC 842-20-25-7).

For operating leases without impairment, the remaining cost throughout the lease term consists of (ASC 842-20-25-8):

- The total lease payments, paid and future, reflective of any remeasurement or lease modification adjustment; plus
- Total initial direct costs attributable to the lease; less
- The periodic lease costs recognized in prior periods.

Lessee Measurement

The lessee measures both a lease liability and a right-of-use asset.

Lease Liability

At the commencement date, the lease liability is the present value of the lease payments to be paid using the discount rate for the lease at commencement. The rate implicit in the lease should be used if it is readily determinable; otherwise, the lessee's incremental borrowing rate should be used. If the entity is not public, it may elect to use a risk-free discount rate for a period comparable with the lease term for all of its leases (ASC 842-20-30-1 through 30-3). The lease liability should continue to be measured in the same manner for an operating lease unless the rate has changed since commencement (ASC 842-20-35-3).

After the commencement date of a finance lease, the lessee measures the lease liability by decreasing the carrying amount by any lease payments made and increasing the carrying amount by interest on the lease liability. The interest is the amount producing a constant periodic discount rate on the remaining lease liability and is recognized in the entity's profit and loss (ASC 842-20-35-1).

If lease payments are remeasured after lease commencement, the entity should recognize the remeasurement as an adjustment to the right-of-use asset, with any additional adjustment required after the asset's carrying amount is zero reflected in the entity's profit or loss (ASC 842-20-35-4). The discount rate should be adjusted in these situations to reflect the remaining lease payments over the lease term at the date of remeasurement unless the remeasurement occurred due to a change in (ASC 842-20-35-5):

- Lease term.
- The assessment of whether the lessee will exercise a purchase option.
- Amount probable of being owed under a residual value guarantee.
- Lease payments due to resolution of a contingency upon which variable lease payments are based.

Right-of-Use Asset

At lease commencement, the right-of-use asset consists of (ASC 842-20-30-5):

- The amount of the initial measurement of the lease liability.
- Any lease payments paid to the lessor on or before the commencement date less any lease incentives received.
- Any initial direct costs incurred.

After the commencement date of a finance lease, the lessee measures the right-of-use asset at cost less any accumulated amortization and impairment losses (ASC 842-20-35-1).

After the commencement date of an operating lease, if the right-of-use asset has not been impaired, it is measured at the amount of the lease liability, adjusted for (ASC 842-20-35-3):

- Prepaid or accrued lease payments.
- The remaining balance of any lease incentives received and not yet recognized in the lease cost.
- Unamortized initial direct costs.
- Impairment of the right-of-use asset.

Right-of-use assets for finance leases should be amortized on a straight-line basis unless there is another systematic basis more representative of the lease. If the lease liability is remeasured and the right-of-use asset adjusted, amortization should be adjusted from the date of remeasurement forward (ASC 842-20-35-7). The amortization term should be from the commencement date to the earlier of the end of the useful life of the right-of-use asset or the end of the lease term unless the lessee is expected to exercise a purchase option, in which case amortization should extend to the end of the useful life of the underlying asset (ASC 842-20-35-8).

If a right-of-use asset may be impaired, use the guidance in ASC 360-10-35 (Property, Plant, and Equipment) to determine if the asset is impaired and to recognize any impairment loss. If it is determined that a right-of-use asset is impaired, it should be measured at its carrying amount after impairment less any accumulated amortization (ASC 842-20-35-10).

Leasehold Improvements

The amortization term for any leasehold improvements should end with the earlier of the useful life of the improvements or the lease term, unless the lessee is expected to exercise a purchase option, in which case amortization should extend to the end of the useful life of the improvements (ASC 845-20-35-12).

Subleases

If the original lessee is not relieved of its primary obligation under the original lease, it becomes a sublessor and accounts for the sublease as follows (ASC 842-20-35-14):

- If the sublease is an operating lease, continue accounting for the original lease in the same manner. If the lease cost for the sublease term exceeds the expected sublease income, this indicates the carrying amount of the right-of-use asset may not be recoverable.
- If the original lease was a financing lease and the sublease is a sales-type or direct financing lease, derecognize the original right-of-use asset and continue to account for the lease liability in the same manner as the original lease. Evaluate the investment in the sublease for impairment.
- If the original lease was an operating lease and the sublease is a sales-type or direct financing lease, derecognize the original right-of-use asset and account for the original lease liability from the sublease commencement date in accordance with the guidance for lease liability measurement for a finance lease. Evaluate the investment in the sublease for impairment.

If the sublease is a sales-type or direct financing lease, use the rate implicit in the lease to determine the sublease classification and measure the net investment in the sublease. If the implicit rate is not readily determined, the discount rate of the original lease may be used (ASC 842-20-35-15).

If the sublease relieves the original lessee of its primary obligation under the original lease, it is considered a termination of the original lease. Any termination payment paid outside of lease payments should be included in determining the profit or loss to be recognized. If the original lessee remains secondarily liable for the original lease, it should recognize the guarantee obligation remaining using the guidance in ASC 405-20-40-2 (Liabilities) (ASC 842-40-3).

Lease Termination

If a lease is terminated prior to the end of the lease term, the lessee should remove the right-of-use asset and lease liability, recognizing any difference as profit and loss (ASC 842-20-40-1).

Purchase of the Underlying Asset

If a lease is terminated because the lessee purchases the underlying asset, any difference between the purchase price and carrying amount of the lease liability prior to purchase should be recorded as an adjustment of the carrying amount of the asset (ASC 842-20-40-2).

Maintenance Deposits

A lease may contain requirements for the lessee to maintain and repair the underlying asset throughout the lease term. The lessor may require a maintenance deposit to protect the lessor if the asset is not properly maintained; this deposit may also be called a maintenance reserve or supplemental rent. The lessor is contractually required to reimburse the lessee for the maintenance costs it incurs from this deposit, to the extent of the amount deposited. If there is a deposit amount remaining at the end of the lease term, the contract should contain a stipulation as to whether the deposit is refundable to the lessee (ASC 842-20-55-4 through 55-6).

If the maintenance deposit is only refunded if the lessee performs specific maintenance activities, the lessee should account for the deposit as an asset. At the lease commencement date, the lessee should determine if it is less than probable that the entirety of the maintenance deposit will be used during the lease term. If it is less than probable that all of the deposit will be returned, the lessee should account for that amount in the same manner as variable lease expense and expense or capitalize maintenance costs as they are incurred (ASC 842-20-55-7 through 55-9).

Illustration of Operating Lease (Lessee)

A lessee enters into a 5-year operating lease for office space with a $20,000 annual lease payment due in arrears that escalates 3% annually. There are $10,000 of initial direct costs and the lessee's incremental borrowing rate is 5%. The lessee receives a $5,000 cash payment from the lessor at commencement that the lessee accounts for as a lease incentive.

The lease liability is measured at the present value of the five lease payments discounted at the lessee's borrowing rate ($91,678). The right-of-use asset is measured at the lease liability plus initial direct costs less the lease incentive ($91,678 lease liability + $10,000 initial direct costs – $5,000 lease incentive = $96,678).

At the commencement date, the lessee accounting is as follows:

Right-of-use asset	$96,678	
Lease liability		$91,678
Cash		5,000

PRACTICE POINTER: The entries recorded by the lessee at the inception of the lease are generally the same for both operating and financing leases.

During each period of the lease term, the lessee will recognize single lease cost of the total of the lease payments less the lease incentive plus the initial direct costs divided by the number of periods in the lease term ($106,183 lease payments – $5,000 lease incentive + $10,000 initial direct costs = $111,183/5 years = $22,237). The single lease cost only changes if there are remeasurements of the lease liability or lease modifications.

At the end of the first year, the lessee accounting is as follows:

Lease expense	$22,237	
Lease liability		$4,584
Right-of-use asset		17,653
Lease Liability	$20,000	
Cash		$20,000

At the end of each period, the carrying amount of the lease liability is the sum of the remaining lease payments discounted at the lessee's incremental borrowing rate ($76,262). The carrying amount of the right-of-use asset is the lease liability adjusted for:

- Accrued lease payments (Year 1: $21,237 single lease cost – $20,000 lease payment = $1,237).
- Unamortized initial direct costs (Year 1: $10,000 initial direct costs – $2,000 initial direct costs recognized as part of single lease cost = $8,000).
- The remaining balance of the lease incentive (Year 1: $5,000 lease incentive – $1,000 lease incentive recognized as part of single lease cost = $4,000).

Financial Statement Presentation and Disclosure

Statement of Financial Position

Finance lease right-of-use assets and operating lease right-of-use assets should be presented separately from each other and from other assets in the statement of financial position or should disclose which line items contain these assets in the notes. Finance lease liabilities and operating lease liabilities should be presented separately from each other and from other liabilities in the statement of financial position or should disclose which line items contain these liabilities in the notes (ASC 842-29-45-1, 2).

The lessee is prohibited from presenting finance and operating lease right-of-use assets in the same line in the statement of financial position. Likewise, the lessee is prohibited from presenting finance and operating lease liabilities in the same line in the statement of financial position (ASC 842-20-45-3).

Statement of Comprehensive Income

For operating leases, lease expense should be included in the lessee's income from continuing operations. For finance leases, interest expense on the lease liability and amortization of the right-of-use asset are not required to be presented as separate line items and should be presented consistently with how the entity presents other interest expense and depreciation or amortization of similar assets, respectively (ASC 842-20-45-4).

Statement of Cash Flows

The lessee should classify all of the following in the statement of cash flows (ASC 842-20-45-5):

- Operating activities include variable lease payments and short-term lease payments not included in the lease liability, payments from operating leases, and interest on the lease liability for finance leases.
- Investing activities include operating lease payments that represent costs to bring another asset to the condition and location necessary for its intended use.
- Financing activities include repayments of the principal portion of the lease liability for finance leases.

Disclosure

Lessee disclosures should include qualitative and quantitative information about its leases, significant judgments made in applying ASC 842 to those leases, and the amounts recognized in the financial statements relating to those leases. Professional judgment should be used to determine the level of detail, aggregation, and emphasis necessary to satisfy these requirements (ASC 842-20-50-1, 2).

The following information about its leases should be disclosed (ASC 842-20-50-3):

- The nature of the leases and any subleases including:
  - A general description.
  - The basis, terms and conditions on which variable lease payments are determined.
  - The existence, terms, and conditions of extension or termination options. Options recognized as part of the right-of-use assets and lease liabilities and those that are not.
  - The existence, terms, and conditions of residual value guarantees.
  - Lease restrictions or covenants.
- Information about leases not yet commenced that create significant rights and obligations for the lessee, including any involvement with construction or design of the underlying asset.
- Significant assumptions and judgments made in applying ASC 842. Examples include determination of whether a contract contains a lease, allocation of consideration among lease and nonlease components, and determining the discount rate for the lease.

The following amounts relating to a lessee's total lease cost for each period presented should be disclosed, including amounts recognized in profit or loss, capitalized, and cash flows (ASC 842-20-50-4):

- Finance lease costs with amortization of the right-of-use asset and interest on the lease liabilities disclosed separately.
- Operating lease costs.
- Short-term lease costs, excluding those for leases with a term of one month or less.
- Variable lease costs.
- Gross sublease income disclosed separately from the finance or operating lease expense.
- Net gain or loss recognized from sale and leaseback transactions.
- Separate disclosure for finance and operating leases of cash paid for lease liabilities in the financing and operating sections of the cash flows respectively, supplemental noncash information on lease liabilities arising from obtaining right-of-use assets, weighted-average remaining lease term, and weighted-average discount rate.

The weighted-average remaining lease term should be calculated on the basis of the remaining lease term and lease liability balance for each lease as of the reporting date. The weighted-average discount rate should be calculated based on the discount rate for the lease used to calculate the lease liability balance and the remaining balance of the lease payments for each lease as of the reporting date (ASC 842-20-55-11, 12).

Following is an illustration of a lessee's financial statement disclosure of total lease cost (using assumed numbers).

Illustration of Lessee's Financial Statement Disclosure of Total Lease Cost

Schedule of Total Lease Cost (in thousands)

	Year Ending December 31,	
	20X2	20X1
Finance lease cost		
Amortization of right-of-use assets	$ 450	$ 500
Interest on lease liabilities	350	400

Operating lease costs	700	600
Short-term lease cost	100	100
Variable lease cost	100	200
Sublease income	(200)	(200)
Total lease cost	$ 1,500	$ 1,600
Other information		
(Gains) and losses on sale and leaseback transactions, net	$ (100)	$ 50
Cash paid for amounts included in the measurement of lease liabilities		
Operating cash flows from finance leases	150	150
Operating cash flows from operating leases	300	400
Financing cash flows from finance leases	250	200
Right-of-use assets obtained in exchange for new finance lease liabilities	75	0
Right-of-use assets obtained in exchange for new operating lease liabilities	20	50
Weighted-average remaining lease term—finance leases	5.2 years	4.7 years
Weighted average remaining lease term—operating leases	3.0 years	3.5 years
Weighted-average discount rate—finance leases	5.6%	5.2%
Weighted-average discount rate—operating leases	7.9%	8.0%

A maturity analysis of finance and operating leases should be presented separately showing undiscounted cash flows for a minimum of the first five years and a total of the amounts for the remaining years. A reconciliation of the undiscounted cash flows to the finance and operating lease liabilities recognized in the statement of financial position should be presented (ASC 842-20-50-6).

Lease transactions with related parties should be disclosed (ASC 842-20-50-7). If a lessee has made the election to not apply the recognition requirements in ASC 842 to its short-term leases, this fact should be disclosed. If the short-term lease expense does not reasonably reflect the entity's commitments, that fact and the amount of its short-term lease commitments should be disclosed (ASC 842-20-50-8). If a lessee has elected the practical expedient of not separating lease and nonlease components, this election and which classes of underlying assets the election has been applied to should be disclosed (ASC 842-20-50-9).

ASC 842-30: LESSOR

LESSOR

Asset and Liability Recognition

At lease commencement, the lessor should derecognize any carrying amount of the underlying asset. If the lease is a sales-type lease and collectability of lease payments is not probable, the asset should not be derecognized (ASC 842-30-40-1).

Sales-Type Leases

The lessor should recognize the following at the commencement date (ASC 842-30-25-1):

- The net investment in the lease.
- Selling profit or loss arising from the lease.
- Initial direct costs:
  - — If the fair value and carrying amount of the asset are different, recognize as an expense.
  - — If the fair value equals the carrying amount of the asset, defer initial direct costs and they will be included in the measurement of the net investment in the lease.

After the lease commencement date, the lessor should recognize (ASC 842-30-25-2):

- Interest income on the net investment in the lease.
- Variable lease payments not included in the net investment in the lease should be recognized as income in profit or loss in the period when changes on which the payments are based occur.
- Credit losses on the net investment in the lease.

If collectibility of lease payments and any residual value guarantee amount is not probable at the commencement date, lease payments and any variable lease payments received should be recognized as a deposit liability until one of the following occurs (ASC 842-30-25-3):

- Collectibility of lease payments and any residual value guarantee becomes probable.
- The contract has been terminated and the lease payments received are nonrefundable.
- The lessor has repossessed the underlying asset, has no further contractual obligation to the lessee, and lease payments received are non-refundable.

If collectibility of lease payments and any residual value guarantee becomes probable, the lessor should derecognize the carrying amount of the underlying asset and any deposit liability recognized, recognize a net investment in the lease based on the remaining lease payments and term using the implicit rate determined at the commencement date, and recognize selling profit or loss. The selling profit or loss should be calculated as the lease receivable plus the carrying amount of the deposit liability minus the carrying amount of the underlying asset, net of the unguaranteed residual asset (ASC 842-30-25-4).

If the contract has been terminated and the lease payments were nonrefundable, the carrying amount of the deposit liability should be derecognized and that amount should be recognized as lease income (ASC 842-30-25-5).

If collectibility is not probable, the lessor should continue to assess collectibility to determine if collectibility becomes probable. However, if collectibility is probable, the lessor should not reassess collectibility as any changes in the credit risk of the lessee will be accounted for using credit loss guidance (ASC 842-30-25-6).

Direct Financing Leases

The lessor should recognize the following at the commencement date (ASC 842-30-25-7):

- The net investment in the lease.
- Any selling loss arising from the lease.

Selling profit and initial direct costs are deferred at lease commencement and included in the measurement of the net investment in the lease (ASC 842-30-25-8).

After the lease commencement date, the lessor should recognize (ASC 842-30-25-9):

- Interest income on the net investment in the lease.
- Variable lease payments not included in the net investment in the lease should be recognized as income in profit or loss in the period when changes on which the payments are based occur.
- Credit losses on the net investment in the lease.

Operating Leases

At lease commencement, the lessor should defer initial direct costs (ASC 842-300-25-10). After lease commencement, the lessor should recognize the following (ASC 842-30-25-11):

- Lease payments as income in profit or loss over the lease term on a straight-line basis unless there is another systematic basis more representative of the lease.
- Variable lease payments as income in profit or loss in the period when changes on which the payments are based occur.
- Initial direct costs as an expense over the lease term on the same basis as lease income.

If collectibility of lease payments and any residual value guarantee by the lessee or any other third party is not probable at lease commencement, lease income should be limited to the lesser of the income recognizable from lease payments and variable lease payments as described in the above paragraph or the lease payments and variable lease payments already collected. If the assessment of collectibility changes after lease commencement, any difference in these amounts should be recognized as a current-period adjustment to lease income (ASC 842-30-25-12, 13).

Lessor Measurement

Net Investment in the Lease

At the commencement date for a sales-type lease or a direct financing lease, the lessor measures the net investment in the lease to include (ASC 842-30-30-1, 2):

- The lease receivable of the lease payments not yet received and any residual value guarantee the lessor expects to receive from the lessee or any other third party, measured at the present value discounted using the rate implicit in the lease.
- The amount of the unguaranteed residual asset the lessor expects to receive from the underlying asset at the end of the lease term, measured at the present value discounted using the rate implicit in the lease.
- For direct financing leases, reduce the net investment in the lease by any selling profit.

If the underlying asset has a carrying amount, it should be derecognized at lease commencement except in the case of a sales-type lease when lease payment collectibility is not probable (ASC 842-30-40-1).

After lease commencement, the net investment in a sales-type or direct financing lease should be measured by (ASC 842-30-35-1):

- Increasing the carrying amount to reflect interest income on the net investment in the lease. The interest income for each period of the lease term should be the amount that produces a constant periodic discount rate on the remaining balance of the net investment in the lease.
- Reducing the carrying amount to reflect the lease payments collected during the period.

Unless the lease is modified and not accounted for as a separate contract, the lessor should not remeasure net investment in the lease after the commencement date (ASC 842-30-35-2).

Operating leases should continue to measure the underlying asset, including testing for impairment in accordance with other ASC Topics (ASC 842-30-30-4, ASC 842-30-35-6).

At the end of the lease term, the net investment in the lease should be reclassified to the appropriate asset category at its carrying amount in accordance with other ASC Topics (ASC 842-30-35-5).

Illustration of Sales-Type Lease (Lessor)

A lessor enters into a 10-year equipment lease with a $20,000 annual lease payment due in arrears and a residual value guarantee by the lessee of $25,000. The equipment has a 12-year estimated remaining economic life, a carrying amount of $160,000, a fair value of $200,000 at the commencement date, and the lessor expects the residual value to be $40,000 at the end of the lease term. Collectibility is probable, asset ownership is not transferred, and there is no purchase option. The lessor incurs $5,000 in initial direct costs and none are prepaid by the lessee. The rate implicit in the lease is 3.1249%. The sum of the present value of the lease payments and residual value guaranteed by the lessee are substantially all of the fair value of the equipment so the lease is classified as a sales-type lease.

The net investment in the lease is measured at fair value of $200,000 at lease commencement, which consists of the lease receivable ($188,570, which equals the present value of the annual payments and residual value guarantee discounted at the implicit rate of the lease) and the present value of the unguaranteed residual value ($11,430 = discounted present value of $40,000 – $25,000).

The selling profit on the lease is calculated as the difference between the lease receivable and the carrying amount of the equipment net of the unguaranteed residual asset ($188,570 – ($160,000 – $11,430) = $40,000).

At the commencement date, the lessor derecognizes the equipment and recognizes the net investment in the lease and the selling profit. The lessor also pays and recognizes the initial direct costs as an expense:

Net investment in the lease	$200,000	
Equipment		$160,000
Selling profit		40,000
Initial direct costs	5,000	
Cash		5,000

During each period of the lease term, the lessor will recognize receipt of a lease payment of $20,000 and interest on the net investment in the lease ($6,250, which is the beginning balance of the net investment in the lease of $200,000 times the rate implicit in the lease), resulting in a balance in the net investment of the lease after Year 1 of $186,250.

The lessor also calculates the components of the net investment in the lease for disclosures. After Year 1, the lease receivable equals $174,463, the beginning balance of the lease receivable of $188,570 less the annual lease payment of $20,000 plus the interest income on the lease receivable for the year of $5,893. The unguaranteed residual asset equals $11,787, the beginning balance of the unguaranteed residual asset of $11,430 plus the interest income on the unguaranteed residual asset for the year of $357.

At the end of the lease term, the lessor reclassifies the net investment in the lease of $40,000, the estimated residual value, to equipment.

Illustration of Direct Financing Lease (Lessor)

A lessor enters into a 10-year equipment lease with a $20,000 annual lease payment due in arrears and a residual value guarantee by a third party of $25,000. The equipment has a 12-year estimated remaining economic life, a carrying amount of $160,000, a fair value of $200,000 at the commencement date, and the lessor expects the residual value to be $40,000 at the end of the lease term. Collectibility is probable, asset ownership is not transferred, and there is no purchase option. The lessor incurs $5,000 in initial direct costs and none are prepaid by the lessee. The rate implicit in the lease is 2.6774%. The sum of the present value of the lease payments and residual value guaranteed by the third party are substantially all of the fair value of the equipment so the lease is classified as a direct financing lease.

The net investment in the lease is measured at the carrying amount of the equipment plus initial direct costs ($165,000 = $160,000 carrying amount + $5,000 initial direct costs). The net investment in the lease consists of the lease receivable ($193,168, which equals the present value of the annual payments and residual value guarantee discounted at the implicit rate of the lease), the present value of the unguaranteed residual value ($11,832 = discounted present value of $40,000 – $25,000) and the deferred selling profit.

The deferred selling profit on the lease is calculated as the lease receivable less the carrying amount of the equipment net of the unguaranteed residual asset less the initial direct costs included in the measurement of the net investment in the lease ($193,168 – ($160,000 – $11,832) – $5,000 = $40,000).

At the commencement date, the lessor derecognizes the equipment and recognizes the net investment in the lease of $165,000, the $160,000 carrying amount plus the $5,000 of initial direct costs:

Net investment in the lease	$165,000	
Equipment		$160,000
Cash		5,000

During each period of the lease term, the lessor will recognize receipt of a lease payment of $20,000 and interest on the net investment in the lease ($11,342, which is the beginning balance of the net investment in the lease of $165,000 times the rate implicit in the lease), resulting in a balance in the net investment of the lease after Year 1 of $156,342. The interest income on the net investment equals the beginning balance of the net investment in the lease times the discount rate (6.87385%) that would have resulted in the sum of the lease receivable and the unguaranteed residual asset equaling the net investment in the lease.

The lessor also calculates the components of the net investment in the lease for disclosures. After Year 1, the lease receivable equals $178,340, the beginning balance of the lease receivable of $193,168 less the annual lease payment of $20,000 plus the interest income on the lease receivable for the year of $5,172. The unguaranteed residual asset equals $12,149, the beginning balance of the unguaranteed residual asset of $11,832 plus the interest income on the unguaranteed residual asset for the year of $317. The deferred selling profit equals $34,147, the initial deferred selling profit of $40,000 less $5,853, the interest income recognized on the net investment in the lease for the year less the sum of the interest income earned on the lease receivable and unguaranteed residual asset during the year.

At the end of the lease term, the lessor reclassifies the net investment in the lease of $40,000, the estimated residual value, to equipment.

Credit Losses

Any credit losses on the net investment in the lease should be recorded using the guidance in ASC 326-20. In determining the loss allowance for the net investment in the lease, the collateral or cash flows the lessor would expect to receive from the lease receivable and the unguaranteed residual asset during and following the end of the remaining lease term should be considered (ASC 842-30-35-3).

Sale of the Lease Receivable

A lessor may sell substantially all of the lease receivable associated with a sales-type or direct financing lease and retain the unguaranteed residual asset. In this situation, the lessor should report any remaining unguaranteed residual asset at its carrying amount as of the date of the sale of the lease receivable and determine if the asset is impaired using the guidance in ASC 360 (ASC 842-30-35-4).

Lease Termination

If a sales-type or direct financing lease is terminated prior to the end of the lease term, a lessor should, using the guidance in other ASC Topics (ASC 842-30-40-2):

- Measure the net investment in the lease for credit losses in accordance with ASC 326-20 on financial instruments measured at amortized cost and record any credit loss identified.
- Reclassify the net investment in the lease to the appropriate asset category at the carrying amount of the residual asset and the lease receivable less any remaining amounts expected to be received.
- Account for the underlying asset of the lease.

Subleases

If the original lease agreement is sold or transferred by the lessee to a third party or the original lessee enters into a sublease, the original lessor continues to account for the lease as it did before. However, if the original lease agreement is replaced by a new agreement with a new lessee, the lessor should account for the termination of the original lease and classify and account for the new lease separately (ASC 842-30-35-7, ASC 842-30-40-3).

Financial Statement Presentation and Disclosure

Statement of Financial Position

For a sales-type or direct financing lease, the lessor should present the aggregate of its net investment in sales-type and direct financing leases separately from other assets (ASC 842-30-45-1). For an operating lease, the lessor should present the underlying asset using the guidance in other ASC Topics (ASC 842-30-45-6).

Statement of Comprehensive Income

Income arising from sales-type or direct financing leases should either be presented separately in the statement of comprehensive income or disclosed in the notes stating which line items in the statement of comprehensive income include lease income (ASC 842-30-45-3).

Profit or loss on the lease should be recognized at the commencement date in the manner most reflective of the lessor's business model. If a lessor uses leases to provide finance, the lessor should present the profit or loss in a single line item. If a lessor uses leases as a means to realize value from goods it would otherwise sell, leasing revenue and cost of goods sold should be presented separately. Leasing revenue should be recognized as the lesser of the fair value of the underlying asset at the commencement date or the sum of the lease receivable and any prepaid lease payments. Cost of goods sold should be recognized as the carrying amount of the underlying asset at the commencement date less the unguaranteed residual asset (ASC 842-30-45-4).

Statement of Cash Flows

All cash receipts from leases should be presented in the operating activities section of the statement of cash flows (ASC 842-30-45-5, ASC 842-30-45-7).

Disclosure

Lessor disclosures should include qualitative and quantitative information about its leases, significant judgments made in applying ASC 842 to those leases, and the amounts recognized in the financial statements relating to those leases. Professional judgment should be used to determine the level of detail, aggregation and emphasis necessary to satisfy these requirements (ASC 842-30-50-1, 2).

The following information about leases should be disclosed (ASC 842-30-50-3):

- The nature of the leases including:
  - — A general description.
  - — The basis, terms, and conditions on which variable lease payments are determined.
  - — The existence, terms, and conditions of extension or termination options.
  - — The existence, terms, and conditions of underlying asset purchase options for the lessee.
- Significant assumptions and judgments made in applying ASC 842. Examples include determination of whether a contract contains a lease, allocation of consideration among lease and nonlease components (unless a lessor elects the practical expedient in ASC 842-10-15-42A and all nonlease components in the contract qualify for that practical expedient), and determination of the amount the lessor expects to derive from the underlying asset following the end of the lease term.
- An entity that elects the practical expedient in ASC 842-10-15-42A must disclose the following, by class of underlying asset:
  - — Its accounting policy election and the class or classes of underlying assets for which it has elected to apply the practical expedient.
  - — The nature of the lease components and nonlease components combined as a result of applying the practical expedient.
  - — The nature of the nonlease components, if any, that are accounted for separately from the combined component because they do not qualify for the practical expedient.
  - — The ASC Topic the entity applies to the combined component (ASC 606 or ASC 842).

Lease income recognized in each annual and interim period should be disclosed in a tabular format and include the following (ASC 842-30-50-5):

- For sales-type and direct financing leases, profit or loss recognized at the commencement date and interest income, either in aggregate or separately by the components of the net investment in the lease.
- For operating leases, lease income relating to lease payments.
- Variable lease payment income not included in the lease receivable.

Any lease transactions between related parties should be disclosed (ASC 842-30-50-4).

Information about how the lessor manages its risk associated with the residual value of its leased assets should be disclosed and include the following (ASC 842-30-50-7):

- Its risk management strategy for residual assets.
- The carrying amount of residual assets covered by residual value guarantees that are not considered to be lease payments.
- Any other means used to reduce residual asset risk, such as buyback agreements.

There are additional disclosures to be made for sales-type and direct financing leases. The components of the net investment in the lease should be disclosed: the carrying amount of lease receivables, unguaranteed residual assets, and for direct financing leases, any deferred selling profit (ASC 842-30-50-6). The lessor should explain significant changes in its unguaranteed residual asset balances and, for direct financing leases, in deferred selling profit. A maturity analysis of lease receivables showing the undiscounted cash flows for a minimum of the first five years and a total of the amounts for the remaining years should be presented. A reconciliation of the undiscounted cash flows to the lease receivables recognized in the statement of financial position should be presented (ASC 842-30-50-9, 10).

Operating leases require additional disclosures. A separate maturity analysis of lease payments showing the undiscounted cash flows for a minimum of the first five years and a total of the amounts for the remaining years should be presented. Disclosures required by ASC 360 should be presented separately for underlying assets under operating leases and owned assets (ASC 842-30-50-12, 13).

Equipment Sale with Guaranteed Minimum Resale Amount

A manufacturer may sell equipment to a purchaser and contractually guarantee the purchaser will receive a minimum resale amount at the time of equipment disposal. The manufacturer may make this guarantee by agreeing to reacquire the equipment at a guaranteed price at specified time periods. In this situation, the guidance in ASC 606-10 (Revenue from Contracts with Customers) should be used to determine if the guarantee constitutes a lease, in which case the guidance in ASC 842 would apply (ASC 842-30-55-2, 3).

The lease payments used to determine the type of lease are generally the difference between the proceeds when the equipment is initially transferred and the residual value guarantee amount as of the first exercise date. If it is determined that the transaction is an operating lease, net proceeds from initial transfer of the equipment should be recorded as a liability. The liability should then be reduced on a pro rata basis to the guaranteed residual value as of the first exercise date with offsetting revenue recorded. If the purchaser decides to use the equipment past the first exercise date, further reduction in the guaranteed residual value should be recorded in the same manner. The equipment should be recorded and depreciated on the manufacturer's balance sheet. Any potential impairment should be accounted for using the guidance in ASC 360 (ASC 842-30-55-5 through ASC 842-30-55-9).

If the purchaser exercises the residual value guarantee by selling the equipment to the manufacturer or another party, the liability should be reduced by any amount paid to the purchaser and any remaining liability should be included in income in the period of sale. If the purchaser sells the equipment to another party, the remaining undepreciated carrying amount of the equipment should also be removed and included in income in the period of sale (ASC 842-30-55-10, 11).

Alternatively, the manufacturer may make this guarantee by agreeing to pay the purchaser for any deficiency between the sales proceeds and the guaranteed minimum resale value. In this circumstance, the guaranteed minimum resale value should be accounted for using the guidance in ASC 460 (Guarantees) and ASC 606 (ASC 842-30-55-4).

ASC 842-40: SALE AND LEASEBACK TRANSACTIONS

SALE AND LEASEBACK TRANSACTIONS

A sale and leaseback is a transaction in which an owner sells property and then leases back part or all of the same property. Such an owner is referred to as the seller-lessee. The buyer-lessor is the party that purchases the property and leases back the same property to the seller-lessee.

Determining Whether the Asset Transfer Is a Sale

To determine whether the asset transfer is a sale, apply the guidance in ASC 606 (Revenue from Contracts with Customers) paragraphs ASC 606-10-25-1 through 25-8 on the existence of a contract and ASC 606-10-25-30 on when an entity satisfies a performance obligation by transferring control of an asset. Indicators that control of an asset has been transferred include: the entity has a present right to payment for the asset and has transferred physical possession of the asset; and the customer has legal title to the asset, has the significant risks and rewards of ownership of the asset, and has accepted the asset (ASC 842-40-25-1).

The buyer-lessor is not prevented from obtaining control of the asset by the existence of a leaseback. However, if the leaseback would be classified as a sales-type or finance lease, the buyer-lessor is not considered to have obtained control of the asset (ASC 842-40-25-2).

If the seller-lessee has an option to repurchase the asset, the asset transfer is not a sale unless the option exercise price is the fair value of the asset at the time the option is exercised and there are readily available, similar assets in the marketplace (ASC 842-40-25-3).

If a lessee obtains legal title to and control of the underlying asset before it is transferred to the lessor, the transaction is a sale and leaseback transaction. However, if the lessee obtains legal title but does not obtain control prior to the asset being transferred to the lessor, the transaction is not a sale and leaseback transaction but is accounted for as an asset purchase by the lessor and a lease between the lessor and lessee (ASC 842-40-55-1, 2).

Transfer of the Asset Is a Sale

If an asset transfer is determined to be a sale, the seller-lessee should recognize the transaction price for the sale when the buyer-lessor obtains control of the asset using the guidance in ASC 606-10-32-2 through 32-7, derecognize the carrying amount of the underlying asset, and account for the lease as follows. The buyer-lessor should account for the purchase using the guidance in other ASC Topics and account for the lease as follows (ASC 842-40-25-4).

The fair value of the transaction should be determined based on the difference between the more easily determinable of the following: the sale price and fair value of the asset; or the present value of the lease payments and the present value of the market rental payments. Variable payments reasonably expected to occur should be included in determining whether the transaction is at fair value. If the transaction is not at fair value, the sale price of the asset should be adjusted using the same method used to determine the transaction was not at fair value. The entity should account for any increase to the sale price as prepayment of rent and any decrease to the sale price as additional financing provided by the buyer-lessor to the seller-lessee. If the transaction is between related parties, these adjustments to the sale price should not be made (ASC 842-40-30-1 through 30-4).

The seller-lessee should follow lessee disclosure requirements and the buyer-lessor should follow lessor disclosure requirements. In addition, the seller-lessee should also disclose the main terms and conditions of the transaction and any transaction gains and losses separately from gains and losses on other asset disposals (ASC 842-50-1, 2).

Illustration of Sale and Leaseback Transaction

A seller sells land with a carrying value of $500,000 to an unrelated buyer for $1 million cash and at the same time enters into a contract (leaseback) with the buyer to use the land for 10 years with annual payments of $60,000. The transaction is determined to be a sale because:

- Seller has a present right to payment of the $1 million sales price.
- Buyer obtains legal title to the land.
- Buyer has the significant risks and rewards of ownership of the land because it can sell the land if the property value increases and must absorb any losses if the property value declines.

The fair value of the land is $700,000, which is observable at the date of sale. The seller and buyer use the fair value to determine that the sale is not at fair value and make accounting adjustments for the difference. The seller recognizes a gain of $200,000 on the sale of the land ($700,000 – $500,000) and recognizes the excess sale price of $300,000 ($1 million – $700,000) as additional financing from the buyer to seller. The seller's incremental borrowing rate is 5% and the leaseback is classified as an operating lease.

At the commencement date, the seller accounting is as follows:

Cash	$1,000,000	
Carrying amount of the land		$500,000
Gain on sale of the land		200,000
Buyer financing liability		300,000
Right-of-use-asset	163,304	
Lease liability		163,304

During each period of the lease term, the seller will decrease the financing obligation for the amount of each lease payment allocated to the obligation and increase its carrying amount for interest accrued at the seller's incremental borrowing rate of 5%. The seller will also recognize the interest expense on the financing obligation and operating lease expense. At the end of the lease term, the financing obligation and lease liability should be zero.

Year 1

Buyer financing liability	$38,851	
Operating lease expense	21,149	
Cash		$60,000
Interest expense	15,000	
Buyer financing liability		15,000

At the commencement date, the buyer accounting is as follows:

Land	$700,000	
Financing asset	300,000	
Cash		$1,000,000

During each period of the lease term, the buyer will decrease the financial asset for the amount of each lease payment received that is allocated to the obligation and increase its carrying amount for interest accrued on the financial asset using the seller's incremental borrowing rate of 5%. The buyer will also recognize the interest income on the financing obligation and operating lease income. At the end of the lease term, the carrying asset of the financing amount should be zero and the land continues to be recognized.

Year 1

Cash	$60,000	
Financing asset		$38,851
Operating lease income		21,149
Financing asset	15,000	
Interest income		15,000

Transfer of the Asset Is Not a Sale

If an asset transfer is determined not to be a sale, the seller-lessee should not recognize the transferred asset and should account for any amounts received as a financial liability using the guidance in other ASC Topics. The buyer-lessor should not recognize the transferred asset and should account for any amounts paid as a receivable using the guidance in other ASC Topics (ASC 842-40-25-5).

The seller-lessee should adjust the interest rate on its financial liability if needed to make sure the following both apply (ASC 842-40-30-6):

- The interest does not exceed payments on the financial liability over the shorter of the lease term and term of the financing.
- The asset carrying amount does not exceed the carrying amount of the financial liability at the earlier of the end of the lease term or the date at which control of the asset transfers to the buyer-lessor.

Lessee Construction or Design Costs

Prior to the commencement date, if a lessee incurs construction or design costs for an underlying asset, these costs should be accounted for using the guidance in other ASC Topics. Any payment for the right to use the underlying asset should be considered lease payments, regardless of payment form or timing (ASC 842-40-55-4).

If the lessee controls the asset prior to the commencement date, the sale and leaseback guidance should be used. The following are some of the potential indicators that the lessee controls the asset under construction prior to lease commencement (ASC 842-40-55-5):

- The lessee has the right to obtain the partially constructed asset at any point during construction.
- The owner-lessor has an enforceable right to payment for its performance to date and does not have an alternative use for the asset.
- The lessee legally owns the land and property improvements under construction or the non-real estate asset under construction.
- The lessee controls or leases the land on which property improvements will be constructed and does not enter into a lease or sublease, respectively, prior to construction that with renewal options would permit the lessor or a third party to lease or sublease the land for substantially all of the economic life of the property improvements.

Sale Subject to a Preexisting Lease

An entity may own an interest in an underlying asset, possibly through an investment in a partnership, and also be a lessee of all or a portion of the underlying asset under an operating lease. If the entity sells its interest in the asset or the asset is sold to an independent third party and the lease is between parties not under common control, the lease is considered a preexisting lease. If the scope or price of the preexisting lease is modified in connection with the sale, the sale and leaseback guidance should be used. If the scope or price of the preexisting lease is not modified, the sale should be accounted for using the guidance in other ASC Topics (ASC 842-40-55-8 through 55-10).

Transfer of Tax Benefits

A U.S. entity may purchase an asset, enter into a contract with a foreign investor providing some ownership right in the asset to the investor, and enter into a leaseback contract for the ownership right of the asset with the foreign investor. In this situation, the entity should determine whether transfer of the ownership right is a sale (ASC 842-40-55-11, 12).

If the leaseback is a finance lease or the entity has an option to repurchase the ownership right at a price other than fair value of that right, the transfer is not a sale and the cash received from the foreign investor should be accounted for as a financial liability using the guidance in other ASC Topics. If the transfer is a sale, income recognized on the cash received should be determined based on the facts and circumstances; and immediate income recognition is not appropriate if there is a more than remote possibility that cash received will be lost due to indemnification or other contingencies (ASC 842-40-55-15 through 55-17).

ASC 842-50: LEVERAGED LEASE ARRANGEMENTS

LEVERAGED LEASE ARRANGEMENTS

Leveraged lease accounting is eliminated for new leases or those modified on or after the effective date of ASC 842 and the lessor should apply the guidance in ASC 842-10 and 842-30. Leveraged leases that commenced prior to the effective date of ASC 842 and were considered leveraged leases under ASC 840 should follow the guidance in ASC 842-50 (ASC 842-10-65-1(z)).

PRACTICE POINTER: To qualify for leveraged lease accounting under ASC 840, a lease had to meet *all* of the following specific criteria:

1. The lease is a direct financing lease.
2. The lease involves three parties, a lessee, lessor, and a long-term creditor, rather than the normal two.
3. The lease provides the lessor with substantial leverage.
4. The pattern of the lessor's investment declines and then rises.

Asset and Liability Recognition and Measurement

A lessor records its investment in a leveraged lease and its initial and continuing investment in the lease is measured as the net of the following accounts (ASC 842-50-30-1):

- Rentals receivable, net of the portion applicable to principal and interest on the nonrecourse debt.
- Receivable for the investment tax-credit to be realized.
- Estimated residual value of the leased asset, which should not exceed the amount estimated at lease inception unless minimum lease payments could escalate during a construction or preacquisition period. In this case, any increases that occurred should be included in determining the estimated residual value at lease inception.
- Unearned and deferred income, which consists of the estimated pretax lease income or loss reduced by initial direct costs and the investment tax credit remaining to be allocated to income over the lease term.

If a leveraged lease is acquired through a business combination or acquisition by a not-for-profit entity, the acquirer should keep the lessor investment in a leveraged lease on the books. The net investment of the acquired leveraged lease should be disaggregated into net rentals receivable, estimated residual value, and unearned income including discount to adjust other components to present value (ASC 842-50-25-2). The guidance in ASC 805 (Business Combinations) should be used to initially assign an amount to the acquired net investment in the leveraged lease based on the remaining future cash flows and recognizing the estimated future tax effects of those cash flows (ASC 842-50-30-2). Subsequent measurement of this investment should be accounted for using the guidance in this Subtopic (ASC 842-50-35-1).

Income Recognition

The investment in a leveraged lease, less applicable deferred taxes, represents the lessor's net investment for purposes of computing periodic net income from the leveraged lease. The following method is used to compute periodic net income (ASC 842-50-35-2):

- A projected cash flow analysis is prepared for the lease term.
- The rate of return on net investment in the years it is positive is computed (usually by trial and error).
- Every year the net investment is increased or decreased by the difference between the net cash flow and the amount of income recognized, if any.

The amount of net income that is recognized each year consists of (ASC 842-50-35-3):

- Pretax lease income or loss (allocated from the unearned income portion of the net investment).
- Investment tax credit (allocated from the deferred income portion of the net investment).
- Tax effect of the pretax lease income or loss recognized (which is reflected in tax expense for the year).

Any tax effect on the difference between pretax accounting income or loss and taxable income or loss is charged or credited to deferred taxes (ASC 842-50-35-4).

If, at the inception or at any time during the lease, the projected net cash receipts over the initial or remaining lease term are less than the lessor's initial or current investment, the resulting loss is immediately recognized (ASC 842-50-35-5).

Changes in Assumptions

All the important assumptions affecting the estimated net income from the leveraged lease, including any estimated residual values, should be reviewed at least annually. Rate of return and income allocation should be recalculated from lease inception if any of the following occur (ASC 842-50-35-6):

- The estimated residual value is determined to be excessive and the decline in residual value is not temporary.
- Another important assumption is revised that changes the estimated total net income from the lease.
- The projected timing of cash flows is revised.

If the lease is being recalculated, the lessor should update all assumptions used to calculate total and periodic income. Actual cash flows prior to the recalculation date and projected cash flows after the recalculation date should be included (ASC 842-50-35-7). Accounts comprising the net investment balance should be adjusted to the recalculated balances and any change should be recognized as a gain or loss in the year the assumption was changed. Pretax gain or loss should be included in the same line as leveraged lease income in income from continuing operations and the tax effect of the gain or loss should be included in the income tax line item. No upward adjustments of the estimated residual value should be made (ASC 842-50-35-8).

The projected timing of income tax cash flows is an important assumption that should be reviewed annually or more frequently if events and circumstances indicate the timing has or will change. The income effect of a change in income tax rate should be recognized in the first accounting period ending on or after the date on which the legislation changing the rate becomes law (ASC 842-50-35-9). Revisions of the projected timing of income tax cash flows only apply to changes directly related to the leveraged lease transaction, such as the following (ASC 842-50-35-10):

- Tax law interpretation.
- Change in the lessor's assessment of the likelihood of succeeding in a challenge by the taxing authority.
- Change in the lessor's expectations about settlement with the taxing authority.

If a lessor expects to settle a tax position for a leveraged lease with a taxing authority, the cash flows after recalculation should be projected to the date of the projected settlement and end with the projected settlement amount and date and should not include interest and penalties. Advance payments and deposits made with a taxing authority should be included in the projected settlement amount (ASC 842-50-35-13 through 35-16).

The entity's assumptions about alternative minimum tax should be included in leveraged lease computations. If there is a change to the entity's tax assumptions that changes total estimated after-tax net income, the rate of return on the lease should be recalculated from inception, accounts comprising the lessor's net investment should be adjusted, and a gain or loss should be recognized in the year the assumption is changed. However, if an entity's tax position frequently changes between alternative minimum tax and regular tax, recalculation each year is not required unless original assumptions about total after-tax net income from the lease are no longer valid (ASC 842-50-35-19, 20).

Financial Statement Presentation and Disclosure

The lessor's balance sheet should present the deferred taxes from a leveraged lease separately from the remainder of the net investment. In the income statement or the notes thereto, separate presentation (from each other) shall be made of (1) pretax income from leveraged leases, (2) the tax effect of pretax income, and (3) the amount of investment tax credit recognized as income during the period (ASC 842-50-45-1).

If leveraged leasing is a significant business activity for the lessor, the components of the net investment balance in leveraged leases should be disclosed in the notes to the financial statements. The components include: rentals receivable, investment-tax-credit receivable, estimated residual value of the leased asset, and unearned and deferred income (ASC 842-50-50-1).

Delayed Equity Investment

In a delayed equity investment, the lessor is often obligated to make up the difference between rent and debt service in the first few years of the transaction. This obligation should be recorded as a liability at present value at lease inception. This liability increases the lessor's net investment, therefore increasing its income; however, it may be offset by accrual of interest on the liability (ASC 842-50-55-2, 3).

Income Taxes

Income tax accounting in this Subtopic is not consistent with the guidance in ASC 740 (Income Taxes). Integrating the results of accounting for income taxes for leveraged leases with other income tax accounting is an issue if all of the following exist (ASC 842-50-55-5):

- Leveraged lease accounting requires recognition of deferred tax credits.
- The guidance in ASC 740 limits recognition of a tax benefit for deductible temporary differences and carryforwards not related to the leveraged lease.
- Resulting unrecognized tax benefits could offset taxable amounts resulting from future recovery of the net investment in the leveraged lease.

ASC 840-10: OVERALL

OVERVIEW

A *lease* is an agreement that conveys the right to use property, usually for a specified period (ASC Glossary). Leases typically involve two parties: the owner of the property (lessor) and the party contracting to use the property (lessee). Because of certain tax, cash flow, and other advantages, leases have become an important alternative to the outright purchase of property by which companies (lessees) acquire the resources needed to operate.

Leases include agreements that, while not nominally referred to as leases, have the characteristic of transferring the right to use property (e.g., heat supply contracts), and agreements that transfer the right to use property even though the contractor may be required to provide substantial services in connection with the operation or maintenance of the assets (ASC 840-10-15-8).

The term *lease*, as used in promulgated U.S. GAAP, does *not* include the following (ASC 840-10-15-10, 15):

- Agreements that are contracts for services that do not transfer the right to use property from one contracting party to another;
- Agreements that concern the right to explore for or exploit natural resources such as oil, gas, minerals, and timber; and
- Agreements that represent licensing agreements for items such as motion picture films, plays, manuscripts, patents, and copyrights.

A central accounting issue associated with leases is the identification of those leases that are treated appropriately as sales of the property by lessors and as purchases of the property by lessees (*capital leases*). Those leases that are not identified as capital leases are called *operating leases* and are not treated as sales by lessors and as purchases by lessees. Rather, they are treated on a prospective basis as a series of cash flows from the lessee to the lessor.

Following is a brief overview of U.S. GAAP for leases.

A lease is an agreement that conveys the right to use assets (tangible or intangible) for a stated period. A lease that transfers substantially all the benefits and risks inherent in the ownership of property is called a *capital lease.* Such a lease is accounted for by the lessee as the acquisition of an asset and the incurrence of a liability. The lessor accounts for such a lease as a sale (sales-type lease) or financing (direct financing lease). All other leases are referred to as *operating leases.*

If the leased property is yet to be constructed or acquired by the lessor at the inception of the lease, the lessor's criterion pertaining to "no important uncertainties of unreimbursable costs yet to be incurred by the lessor" is applied at the date that construction of the property is completed or the property is acquired. Any increases in the minimum lease payments that have occurred during the preacquisition or preconstruction period as a result of an escalation clause are to be considered in determining the fair value of the leased property at the inception of the lease. The amount that can be recorded by the lessor for the residual value of leased property is limited to an amount not greater than the estimate as of the inception of the lease.

A lessor is required to classify a renewal or an extension of a sales-type or direct financing lease as a sales-type lease if the lease would otherwise qualify as a sales-type lease and the renewal or extension occurs at or near the end of the lease term. Otherwise, ASC 840 prohibits the classification of a renewal or extension of a sales-type or direct financing lease as a sales-type lease at any other time during the lease term.

The appropriate accounting for sale-leaseback transactions depends on the percentage amount of the property that the seller-lessee leases back (substantially all of the property, a minor portion of the property, or more than a minor portion of the property but less than substantially all) and whether the lease is classified as a capital lease or an operating lease.

ASC 840-10-20 (Glossary) defines *contingent rentals* as those that cannot be determined at the inception of the lease because they depend on future factors or events (other than just the passage of time). Rental payments based on future sales volume, future machine hours, future interest rates, and future price indexes are examples of contingent rentals. Contingent rentals can either increase or decrease lease payments.

ASC 310 establishes accounting and reporting standards for nonrefundable fees and costs associated with lending, committing to lend, or purchasing a loan or group of loans. Under ASC 310, direct loan origination fees and costs, including initial direct costs incurred by a lessor in negotiating and consummating a lease, are offset against each other and the net amount is deferred and recognized over the life of the loan as an adjustment to the yield on the loan. The provisions of ASC 310 apply to all types of loans, including debt securities, and to all types of lenders, including banks, thrift institutions, insurance companies, mortgage bankers, and other financial and nonfinancial institutions. However, ASC 310 does not apply to nonrefundable fees and costs that are associated with originating or acquiring loans that are carried at market value.

ASC 840 defines *penalty* and *lease term* for all leasing transactions. In addition, it specifies the appropriate accounting for a seller-lessee in a sale-leaseback transaction involving real estate, including real estate with equipment, such as manufacturing facilities, power plants, furnished office buildings, etc. It also establishes the appropriate accounting for a sale-leaseback transaction in which property improvements or integral equipment is sold to a purchaser-lessor and leased back by the seller-lessee who retains the ownership of the underlying land. Finally, it provides the appropriate accounting for sale-leaseback transactions involving real estate with equipment that include separate sale and leaseback agreements for the real estate and the equipment (*a*) with the same entity or related parties and (*b*) that are consummated at or near the same time, suggesting that they were negotiated as a package.

BACKGROUND

Some lease agreements are such that an asset and a related liability should be reported on the balance sheet of the lessee enterprise. The distinction is one of *substance over form* when the transaction actually *transfers substantially all the benefits and risks inherent in the ownership of the property.*

Established in U.S. GAAP are criteria to determine whether a lease transaction is in substance a transfer of the incidents of ownership. If, *at its inception*, a lease meets one or more of the following four criteria, the lease is classified as a capital lease (ASC 840-10-25-1):

1. By the end of the lease term, ownership of the leased property is transferred to the lessee.
2. The lease contains a bargain purchase option.

3. The lease term is substantially (75% or more) equal to the estimated useful life of the leased property.
4. At the inception of the lease, the present value of the minimum lease payments, with certain adjustments, is 90% or more of the fair value of the leased property.

These criteria are examined in more detail later in this chapter.

TERMINOLOGY

The authoritative literature includes many terms that are important for an understanding of lease accounting. Several of these terms are explained below.

Capital Lease

A capital lease transfers the benefits and risks inherent in the ownership of the property to the lessee, who accounts for the lease as an acquisition of an asset and the incurrence of a liability (ASC 840-10-25-1).

Sales-Type Lease

A sales-type lease is a type of capital lease that results in a manufacturer's or dealer's profit or loss to the lessor and transfers substantially all the benefits and risks inherent in the ownership of the leased property to the lessee; in addition, (*a*) the minimum lease payments are reasonably predictable of collection and (*b*) no important uncertainties exist regarding costs to be incurred by the lessor under the terms of the lease (ASC 840-10-25-43).

In a sales-type lease, the *fair value* of the leased property at the inception of the lease differs from the cost or carrying amount because a manufacturer's or dealer's profit or loss exists. Fair value usually is the *normal selling price* of the property.

Direct Financing Lease

A direct financing lease is a type of capital lease that does *not* result in a manufacturer's or dealer's profit or loss to the lessor, but does transfer substantially all the benefits and risks inherent in the ownership of the leased property to the lessee; in addition, (*a*) the minimum lease payments are reasonably predictable of collection and (*b*) no important uncertainties exist regarding costs to be incurred by the lessor under the terms of the lease (ASC 840-10-25-43).

Separately identifying sales-type and direct financing leases is an accounting issue for the lessor only, who accounts for the two types of capital leases differently, as described later in this chapter. Both types of leases transfer substantially all the benefits and risks inherent in the ownership of the leased property to the lessee, who records the transaction as a *capital lease.*

Fair Value

Fair value is the price for which the leased property could be sold between unrelated parties in an arm's-length transaction at the measurement date (ASC 840-10-55-43).

For the manufacturer or dealer, fair value usually is the normal selling price less trade or volume discounts. Fair value may be less than the normal selling price, however, and sometimes less than the cost of the property.

For others, fair value usually is cost less trade or volume discounts. Fair value may be less than cost, however, especially in circumstances in which a long period elapses between the acquisition of the property by the lessor and the inception of a lease.

Fair Rental

Fair rental is the rental rate for similar property under similar lease terms and conditions.

Related Parties

Related parties are one or more entities subject to the significant influence over the operating and financial policies of another entity (ASC 840-10-55-27).

Executory Costs

Executory costs are items such as insurance, maintenance, and taxes paid in connection with the leased property (ASC 840-10-25-1).

Bargain Purchase Option

A bargain purchase option is a lessee's option to purchase the leased property at a sufficiently low price that makes the exercise of the option relatively certain (ASC 840-10-25-1; ASC Glossary).

Bargain Renewal Option

A bargain renewal option is a lessee's option to renew the lease at a sufficiently low rental that makes the exercise of the option relatively certain (ASC Glossary).

Estimated Economic Life

Estimated economic life is the estimated remaining useful life of the property for the purpose for which it was intended, regardless of the term of the lease (ASC 840-10-25-1; ASC Glossary).

Estimated Residual Value

Estimated residual value is the estimated fair value of the leased property at the end of the lease term. The estimated residual value shall not exceed the amount estimated at the inception of the lease except for the effect of any increases that result during the construction or preacquisition period, because of escalation provisions in the lease (ASC Glossary).

Unguaranteed Residual Value

Unguaranteed residual value is the estimated fair value of the leased property at the end of the lease term that is not guaranteed by either the lessee or a third party unrelated to the lessor. A guarantee by a third party related to the lessee is considered a lessee guarantee (ASC Glossary).

Incremental Borrowing Rate

The lessee's incremental borrowing rate is the rate of interest that the lessee would have had to pay at the inception of the lease to borrow the funds, on similar terms, to purchase the leased property (ASC Glossary).

Lease Inception

The inception of the lease is the date of the lease agreement *or* the date of a written commitment (if earlier) signed by the parties involved that sets forth the principal provisions of the lease transaction. A written commitment that does not contain all of the principal provisions of the lease transaction does not establish the inception date (ASC Glossary).

Interest Rate Implicit in the Lease

The interest rate implicit in the lease is the rate that, when applied to certain items (enumerated below), results in an aggregate present value equal to the fair value of the leased property at the beginning of the lease term, less any investment credit expected to be realized and retained by the lessor. The discount rate is applied to (*a*) the minimum lease payments, excluding executory costs such as insurance, maintenance, and taxes (including any profit thereon) that are paid by the lessor and (*b*) the estimated fair value of the property at the end of the lease term, exclusive of any portion guaranteed by either the lessee or a third party unrelated to the lessor (unguaranteed residual value) (ASC Glossary).

Initial Direct Costs

The definition of *initial direct costs* is as follows (ASC 840-20-25-17):

> *Initial direct costs.** Only those costs incurred by the lessor that are (*a*) costs to originate a lease incurred in transactions with independent third parties that (i) result directly from and are essential to acquire that lease and (ii) would not have been incurred had that leasing transaction not occurred and (*b*) certain costs directly related to specified activities performed by the lessor for that lease. Those activities are: evaluating the prospective lessee's financial condition; evaluating and recording guarantees, collateral, and other security arrangements; negotiating lease terms; preparing and processing lease documents; and closing the transaction. The costs

* Initial direct cost shall be offset by nonrefundable fees that are yield adjustments.

directly related to those activities shall include only that portion of the employees' total compensation and payroll-related fringe benefits directly related to time spent performing those activities for that lease and other costs related to those activities that would not have been incurred but for that lease. Initial direct costs shall not include costs related to activities performed by the lessor for advertising, soliciting potential lessees, servicing existing leases, and other ancillary activities related to establishing and monitoring credit policies, supervision, and administration. Initial direct costs shall not include administrative costs, rent, depreciation, any other occupancy and equipment costs, and employees' compensation and fringe benefits related to activities described in the previous sentence, unsuccessful origination efforts, and idle time.

In determining the net amount of initial direct costs in a leasing transaction under ASC 840, a lessor shall apply the provisions of ASC 310 relating to loan origination fees, commitment fees, and direct loan origination costs of completed loans. Initial direct costs are accounted for by lessors as part of the investment in a direct financing lease.

Contingent Rentals

Contingent rentals are those that cannot be determined at the inception of the lease because they depend on future factors or events. Rental payments based on future sales volume, future machine hours, future interest rates, and future price indexes are examples of contingent rentals. Contingent rentals can either increase or decrease lease payments (ASC Glossary).

Increases in minimum lease payments that occur during the preacquisition or construction period as a result of an escalation clause in the lease are not considered contingent rentals (ASC Glossary).

Lease Term

The lease term includes all of the following (ASC Glossary):

- Any fixed noncancelable term
- Any period covered by a bargain renewal option
- Any period in which penalties are imposed in an amount that at the inception of the lease reasonably assures the renewal of the lease by the lessee
- Any period covered by ordinary renewal options during which a guarantee by the lessee of the lessor's debt that is directly or indirectly related to the leased property is expected to be in effect or a loan from the lessee to the lessor that is directly or indirectly related to the leased property is expected to be outstanding

  Note: The phrase *indirectly related to the leased property* is used to cover situations that in substance are guarantees of the lessor's debt or loans to the lessor by the lessee that are related to the leased property, but are structured in such a manner that they do not represent a direct guarantee or loan.
- Any period covered by ordinary renewal options preceding the date on which a bargain purchase option is exercisable
- Any period representing renewals or extensions of the lease at the lessor's option.

A lease term does not extend beyond the date a bargain purchase option becomes exercisable.

Noncancelable Lease Term

A noncancelable lease term is a provision in a lease agreement that specifies that the lease may be canceled only (*a*) on some remote contingency, (*b*) with permission of the lessor, (*c*) if the lessee enters into a new lease with the same lessor, or (*d*) any period in which penalties are imposed in an amount that at the inception of the lease reasonably assures the renewal of the lease by the lessee (ASC Glossary).

Penalty

The term *penalty* refers to any outside factor or provision of the lease agreement that does or can impose on the lessee the requirement to disburse cash, incur or assume a liability, perform services, surrender or transfer an asset or rights to an asset or otherwise forego an economic benefit, or suffer an economic detriment (ASC 840-10-25-6; ASC Glossary):

MINIMUM LEASE PAYMENTS

Normal minimum lease payments for the lessee include (ASC 840-10-25-6):

- The minimum rent called for during the lease term
- Any payment or guarantee that the lessee must make or is required to make concerning the leased property at the end of the lease term (residual value), including:

— Any amount stated to purchase the leased property
— Any amount stated to make up any deficiency from a specified minimum
— Any amount payable for failure to renew or extend the lease at the expiration of the lease term

When a lease contains a *bargain purchase option,* the minimum lease payments include only (*a*) the *minimum rental payments over the lease term* and (*b*) *the payment required to exercise the bargain purchase option.*

The following are excluded in determining minimum lease payments (ASC 840-10-25-5):

- A guarantee by the lessee to pay the lessor's debt on the leased property
- The lessee's obligation (separate from the rental payments) to pay executory costs (insurance, taxes, etc.) in connection with the leased property
- Contingent rentals

PRACTICE POINTER: Guidance on lessee guarantee of the residual value of the leased property is as follows:

- A guarantee by a lessee to make up a residual value deficiency caused by damage, extraordinary wear and tear, or excessive usage is similar to a contingent rental, since the amount is not determinable at the inception of the lease. Therefore, this type of lessee guarantee does not constitute a lessee guarantee of residual value for purposes of computing the lessee's minimum lease payments (ASC 840-10-25-9).
- A lessee's guarantee to make up a residual value deficiency at the end of a lease term is limited to the specified maximum deficiency called for by the lease (ASC 840-10-55-9).
- Unless the lessor explicitly releases the lessee, a guarantee of residual value by an unrelated third party for the benefit of the lessor does not release the obligation of the lessee. Therefore, such a guarantee by an unrelated third party shall not be used to reduce the lessee's minimum lease payments. Costs incurred in connection with a guarantee by an unrelated third party are considered executory costs and are not included in computing the lessee's minimum lease payments (ASC 840-10-55-10).

The minimum lease payments to a lessor are the sum of (ASC 840-10-25-7):

- The minimum lease payments under the lease terms
- Any guarantee by a third party, unrelated to the lessee and lessor, of the residual value or rental payments beyond the lease term, providing such guarantor is financially capable of discharging the potential obligation

LEASE CLASSIFICATION

Lessees

If one or more of the following four criteria is present at the inception of a lease, it is classified as a capital lease by the lessee (ASC 840-10-25-1, 29):

1. Ownership of the property is transferred to the lessee by the end of the lease term.
2. The lease contains a bargain purchase option.
3. The lease term, at inception, is substantially (75% or more) equal to the estimated economic life of the leased property, including earlier years of use. (*Exception:* This criterion cannot be used for a lease that begins within the last 25% of the original estimated economic life of the leased property. *Example:* A jet aircraft that has an estimated economic life of 25 years is leased for five successive five-year leases. If the first four five-year leases were classified as operating leases, the last five-year lease cannot be classified as a capital lease, because the lease would commence within the last 25% of the estimated economic life of the property and would fall under this exception.)
4. The present value of the minimum lease payments at the beginning of the lease term, excluding executory costs and profits thereon to be paid by the lessor, is 90% or more of the fair value of the property at the inception of the lease, less any investment tax credit retained and expected to be realized by the lessor. (*Exception:* This criterion cannot be used for a lease that begins within the last 25% of the original estimated economic life of the leased property.)

A lessee's incremental borrowing rate is used to determine the present value of the minimum lease payments, except that the lessor's implicit rate of interest is used if it is known and it is lower (ASC 840-10-25-31).

PRACTICE POINTER: While the criteria for identifying a capital lease appear very specific, significant professional judgment must be exercised in implementing them. For example:

- Except in the simplest cases, determining the lease term may involve judgment.
- Several of the criteria include terms that require judgment when they are applied to a specific lease. These include "bargain purchase option," "estimated useful life of the property," and "fair value of the property."
- The lease term and the present value of minimum lease payments criteria are not available for leases that begin within the last 25% of the asset's estimated useful life, which is subject to judgment.
- Determining the minimum lease payments for the lessee may require use of that party's incremental borrowing rate, which may involve judgment.

Lessors

If, at inception, a lease meets any one (or more) of the four criteria indicating that substantially all the benefits and risks of ownership have been transferred to the lessee, and it *meets both the following conditions*, the lease is classified by the lessor as a sales-type or direct financing lease, whichever is appropriate (ASC 840-10-25-42):

- *Collection of the minimum lease payments is reasonably predictable.* A receivable resulting from a lease subject to an estimate of uncollectibility based on experience is not precluded from being classified as either a sales-type or a direct financing lease.
- *No important uncertainties exist for unreimbursable costs yet to be incurred by the lessor under the lease.* Important uncertainties include extensive warranties and material commitments beyond normal practice. *Executory costs*, such as insurance, maintenance, and taxes, are not considered important uncertainties.

  Note: In the event the leased property is not acquired or constructed before the inception of the lease, this condition is not applied until such time as the leased property is acquired or constructed by the lessor.

In applying the fourth basic capitalization criterion—the present value of the lease equals or exceeds 90% of the fair value of the property—a *lessor* computes the present value of the minimum lease payments, using the interest rate *implicit in the lease* (ASC 840-10-25-41).

A lease involving real estate is not classified by the lessor as a sales-type lease unless the title to the leased property is transferred to the lessee at or shortly after the end of the lease term.

Classification of a lease as a capital or operating lease is summarized in Figure 56-1.

CHANGING A PROVISION OF A LEASE

If at any time the lessee and lessor agree to a change in the provisions of a lease, other than by renewing the lease or extending its term, that results in a different lease classification at the inception of the lease because it meets different criteria, a new lease agreement is created that must be reclassified according to its different criteria. Renewal, extension, or a new lease under which the lessee continues to use the same property is not considered a change in a lease provision (ASC 840-10-35-4).

Any action that extends the lease term, except to void a residual guarantee, or a penalty for failure to renew the lease at the end of the lease term, is considered a new lease agreement that is classified according to the different criteria (ASC 840-10-35-4).

Changes in estimates or circumstances do not cause a reclassification.

LEASES INVOLVING REAL ESTATE

Leases involving real estate are categorized as follows:

- Land only
- Land and building(s)
- Land, building(s), and equipment
- Only part of a building(s)

Review of Classification of Leases by Lessees

A review of the classifications of leases by lessees is necessary because accounting for leases involving real estate depends primarily on the criteria for classifying leases.

If one or more of the following four criteria are present at the inception of a lease, it is classified as a capital lease by the lessee (ASC 840-10-25-1):

1. Ownership of the property is transferred to the lessee by the end of the lease term.
2. The lease contains a bargain purchase option.
3. The lease term, at inception, is substantially (75% or more) equal to the estimated economic life of the leased property, including earlier years of use. (*Exception:* This criterion cannot be used for a lease that begins within the last 25% of the original estimated economic life of the leased property.)
4. The present value of the minimum lease payments at the beginning of the lease term, excluding executory costs and profits thereon to be paid by the lessor, is 90% or more of the fair value of the property at the inception of the lease, less any investment tax credit retained and expected to be realized by the lessor. (*Exception*: This criterion cannot be used for a lease that begins within the last 25% of the original estimated economic life of the leased property.)

These criteria are referred to by number in the following discussion.

Leases Involving Land Only

A *lessee* accounts for a lease involving land only as a capital lease if either criterion 1 or criterion 2 is met. All other leases involving land only are classified as operating leases by the lessee (ASC 840-10-25-37).

A *lessor* classifies a lease involving land only as a sales-type lease and applies the guidance in ASC 606 on revenue from contracts with customers or ASC 610-20 on gains and losses from the derecognition of nonfinancial assets, if the lease gives rise to a manufacturer's or dealer's profit (or loss) and criterion 1 is met (ASC 840-10-25-55). A lessor classifies a lease involving land only as a direct financing lease or a leveraged lease, whichever is applicable, if the lease does not give rise to a manufacturer's or dealer's profit (or loss), criterion 1 is met, and (*a*) the collection of the minimum lease payments is reasonably predictable and (*b*) no important uncertainties exist regarding costs yet to be incurred by the lessor under the lease (ASC 840-10-25-56). A lessor classifies a lease involving land only as a direct financing lease, a leveraged lease, or an operating lease, whichever is applicable, if criterion 2 is met, and (*a*) the collection of the minimum lease payments is reasonably predictable and (*b*) no important uncertainties exist regarding costs yet to be incurred by the lessor under the lease (ASC 840-10-25-57). All other leases involving land only are classified as operating leases by the lessor (ASC 840-10-25-58).

PRACTICE POINTER: The criteria for recognition of a sale under ASC 360 (Property, Plant, and Equipment) are quite similar to the additional criteria that must be met by lessors under ASC 840 in order for the lease to qualify as a capital lease. That is, under ASC 360, two criteria must be met in order for profit to be recognized in full at the time of the sale: (1) the sales price is reasonably predictable of collection and (2) the lessor of the land is not obligated to perform significant activities under the terms of the lease (ASC 360-20-40-3). Collectibility is assessed by evaluating the adequacy of the lessee's initial and continuing investment (ASC 360-20-40-4). For land to be developed within (after) two years of the sale, the lessee's initial investment should be at least 20% (25%) of the land's sales value (ASC 360-20-55-2). The lessee's continuing investment must be at least an amount equal to the level annual payment required to liquidate the unpaid balance (both interest and principal) over no more than 20 years for a lease involving land (ASC 360-20-40-19).

Leases Involving Land and Building(s)

Leases involving land and building(s) may be categorized as follows:

- Leases that meet criterion 1 or criterion 2
- Leases in which the fair value of the land is less than 25% of the total fair value of the leased property at the inception of the lease
- Leases in which the fair value of the land is 25% or more of the total fair value of the leased property at the inception of the lease

Leases That Meet Criterion 1 or Criterion 2

Leases that meet either criterion 1 or criterion 2 are accounted for as follows:

- *Lessee* The present value of the minimum lease payments, less executory costs and profits thereon (to be paid by the lessor), is allocated between the land and building(s) in proportion to their fair value at the inception of the lease. The present value assigned to the building(s) is amortized in accordance with the lessee's normal depreciation policy (ASC 840-10-25-38).
- *Lessor* If a lease gives rise to a manufacturer's or dealer's profit (or loss) and criterion 1 is met, a lessor classifies a lease involving land and building(s) as a sales-type lease and applies the guidance in ASC 606 (Revenue from Contracts with Customers) on revenue from contracts with customers or ASC 610-20 (Gains and Losses from the Derecognition of Nonfinancial Assets) on gains and losses from the derecognition of nonfinancial assets in the same manner as a seller of the same property. If a lease does not give rise to a manufacturer's or dealer's profit (or loss) and criterion 1 is met, a lessor classifies a lease involving land and building(s) as a direct financing lease or a leveraged lease, whichever is applicable, providing that (*a*) collection of the minimum lease payments are reasonably predictable and (*b*) no important uncertainties exist regarding costs yet to be incurred by the lessor under the lease (ASC 840-10-25-61).

If a lease gives rise to a manufacturer's or dealer's profit (or loss) and criterion 2 is met, a lessor classifies a lease involving land and building(s) as an operating lease. If the lease does not give rise to a manufacturer's or dealer's profit (or loss) and criterion 2 is met, a lessor classifies a lease involving land and building(s) as a direct financing lease or a leveraged lease, whichever is applicable, providing that (*a*) collection of the minimum lease payments is reasonably predictable and (*b*) no important uncertainties exist regarding costs yet to be incurred by the lessor under the lease (ASC 840-10-25-62).

All other leases involving land and building(s) are classified as operating leases by the lessor.

Fair Value of the Land Is Less Than 25% of the Total Fair Value of the Leased Property at the Inception of the Lease

When applying criteria 3 and 4, both the lessee and the lessor consider the land and building(s) as a single unit, and the estimated economic life of the building(s) is the estimated economic life of the single unit. This type of lease is accounted for as follows:

- *Lessee* The land and building(s) are accounted for as a single capitalized asset and amortized in accordance with the lessee's normal depreciation policy over the lease term if either criterion 3 or criterion 4 is met (ASC 840-10-25-38).
- *Lessor* If a lease gives rise to a manufacturer's or dealer's profit (or loss) and criterion 3 or criterion 4 is met, a lessor classifies a lease involving land and building(s), in which the fair value of the land is less than 25% of the total fair value of the leased property at the inception of the lease as an operating lease. If the lease does not give rise to a manufacturer's or dealer's profit (or loss) and criterion 3 or criterion 4 is met, a lessor classifies a lease involving land and building(s) in which the fair value of the land is less than 25% of the total fair value of the leased property at the inception of the lease as a direct financing lease or a leveraged lease, whichever is applicable, providing that (*a*) collection of the minimum lease payments is reasonably predictable and (*b*) no important uncertainties exist regarding costs yet to be incurred by the lessor under the lease. All other leases involving land and building(s) are classified as operating leases by the lessor (ASC 840-10-25-63, 64, 65).

Fair Value of the Land Is 25% or More of the Total Fair Value of the Leased Property at the Inception of the Lease

When applying criteria 3 and 4, both the lessee and the lessor shall consider the land and building(s) separately. To determine the separate values of the land and building(s), the lessee's incremental borrowing rate is applied to the fair value of the land to determine the annual minimum lease payments applicable to the land. The balance of the minimum lease payments remaining is attributed to the building(s). This type of lease is accounted for as follows (ASC 840-10-25-66, 67):

- *Lessee* The building(s) portion is accounted for as a capital lease and amortized in accordance with the lessee's normal depreciation policy over the lease term if the building(s) portion meets either criterion 3 or criterion 4. The land portion is accounted for separately as an operating lease.
- *Lessor* If a lease gives rise to a manufacturer's or dealer's profit (or loss) and criterion 3 or criterion 4 is met, a lessor classifies a lease involving land and building(s) in which the fair value of the land is 25% or more of the total fair value of the leased property at the inception of the lease as an operating lease. If the lease does not give rise to a manufacturer's or dealer's profit (or loss) and criterion 3 or 4 is met, a lessor shall classify the building(s) portion of a lease in which the fair value of the land is 25% or more of the total fair value of the leased property at the inception of the lease as a direct financing lease or a leveraged lease, whichever is applicable, providing that (*a*) collection of the minimum lease payments is reasonably predictable and (*b*) no important uncertainties exist regarding costs yet to be incurred by the lessor under the lease. The land portion is accounted for separately as an operating lease.

All other leases involving land and building(s) are classified as operating leases by the lessor.

Leases Involving Land, Building(s), and Equipment

Equipment values, if material, should not be commingled with real estate values in leases. The minimum lease payments attributed to the equipment shall, if necessary, be estimated appropriately and stated separately. The criteria for the classification of leases are applied separately to the equipment to determine proper accountability (ASC 840-10-25-19, 20).

Leases Involving Only Part of a Building(s)

If the cost and fair value of a lease involving only part of a building(s) can be determined objectively, the lease classification and accounting are the same as for any other land and building(s) lease. An independent appraisal of the leased property or replacement cost can be made as a basis for the objective determination of fair value (ASC 840-10-25-23). In the event that cost and fair value cannot be determined objectively, leases involving only part of a building(s) are classified and accounted for as follows (ASC 840-10-25-39, 69):

Lessee

The lessee classifies the lease only in accordance with criterion 3 as follows: The lease term, at inception, is substantially (75% or more) equal to the estimated economic life of the leased property, including earlier years of use. (*Exception*: This particular criterion cannot be used for a lease that begins within the last 25% of the original estimated economic life of the leased property.)

In applying the above criterion, the estimated economic life of the building(s) in which the leased premises are located is used.

In the event the above criterion is met, the leased property is capitalized as a single unit and amortized in accordance with the lessee's normal depreciation policy over the lease term. In all other cases, the lease is classified as an operating lease.

Lessor

In all cases in which the cost and fair value are indeterminable, the lessor accounts for the lease as an operating lease.

OTHER LEASE ACCOUNTING ISSUES

Subleases and Similar Transactions

Unless the original lease agreement is replaced by a new agreement, the original lessor continues to account for the lease as before (ASC 840-10-35-10).

A termination of a lease is recognized by a lessor in the income of the period in which termination occurs, as follows (ASC 840-10-40-3; ASC 840-30-40-7):

- The remaining net investment is eliminated from the accounts.
- The leased property is recorded as an asset using the lower of the (*a*) original cost, (*b*) present value at termination, or (*c*) present carrying amount at termination.

When an original lessee subleases property, the new lessee is either (1) substituted under the *original* lease agreement or (2) substituted through a new lease agreement. In either case, the original lessee is relieved of the primary obligation under the original lease. The accounting for the termination of the original lease agreement depends on whether the original lease was for property other than real estate or whether it was for real estate.

If the original lease was a capital lease for property other than real estate, the termination of the lease agreement is accounted for as follows:

- Remove the asset and liability pertaining to the capital lease from the books.
- Recognize a gain or loss for the difference between the lease asset and lease liability, and consider any consideration received or paid upon lease termination in computing the gain or loss.
- If the original lessee remains secondarily liable, recognize this guarantee obligation under the provisions specified in ASC 860 (Transfers and Servicing).

If the original lease was a capital lease for real estate, the termination of the lease agreement is accounted for as follows:

- The lease asset and liability are to be removed from the books if the ASC 360 criteria for sale recognition are met.
- If the ASC 360 sales criteria are met, treatment of (1) the lease asset and liability, (2) any consideration received or paid, and (3) any guarantees are all accounted for as immediately above (the same as if the original lease was a capital lease for property other than real estate).
- Any gain should be recognized by the full accrual method if the ASC 360 criteria for the use of this method are met; otherwise, gain should be recognized using one of the other revenue recognition methods discussed in ASC 360 (installment, cost recovery, deposit, or reduced-profit methods).
- Any loss is recognized immediately.

Finally, the original lessee is to recognize its guarantee obligation (per ASC 860) if it remains secondarily liable on a lease that was originally classified as an operating lease.

When a lessee subleases leased property, the original lease continues and a simultaneous new lease is created in which the lessee becomes a sublessor. The results are that the original lessee is both a lessee in the original lease and, at the same time, a sublessor in the new lease. In situations like this, the original lease continues to be accounted for as if nothing happened, but the new lease is classified and accounted for separately.

If an original lessee is not relieved of the primary obligation under an original lease, the transaction is accounted for by the original lessee-sublessor as follows (ASC 840-30-35-12):

- If the criterion for the original lease was criterion (1) (ownership of the property is transferred before the end of the lease term) or (2) (lease contains a bargain purchase option), the new lease is classified based on its own new criteria. If the new lease qualifies for capitalization, it is accounted for as a sales-type or a direct financing lease, whichever is appropriate, and the unamortized balance of the asset under the original lease is treated as the cost of the leased property to the sublessor (original lessee).

  In the event that the new lease does not qualify for capitalization, it is treated as an operating lease.
- If the criterion for the original lease was criterion (3) (lease term is substantially—75% or more—equal to the estimated economic life of the leased property at the inception of the lease) or (4) (present value of the minimum lease payments—excluding executory costs—is 90% or more of the fair value at inception), the new lease is capitalized only if it meets criterion (3) and (*a*) the collection of the minimum lease payments is reasonably predictable and (*b*) no important uncertainties exist regarding costs yet to be incurred by the lessor under the lease. If the new lease meets the criteria above, it is accounted for as a direct financing lease, with the amortized balance of the asset under the original lease as the cost of the leased property.

  If the new lease does not meet the specific conditions above, it is accounted for as an operating lease.

In any event, if the original lease is an operating lease, the sublease also is accounted for as an operating lease (ASC 840-20-25-14).

Even though the sublessor (original lessee) remains primarily obligated under an original lease, a loss may be recognized on a sublease. The loss is measured as the difference between the unamortized cost of the leased property (net carrying amount) and the present value of the minimum lease payments that will be received under the terms of the sublease.

ASC 360 provides guidance on the accounting treatment of long-term leases (including related sublease revenue) terminated as part of the disposal of a component of a business entity. ASC 360 requires that the assets in the component of the business entity being disposed of be carried at the lower of the asset's carrying amount or fair value less cost to sell. Although explicit guidance on this topic no longer appears in the literature, the authors believe that the fair value of the component of the business entity to be disposed of will be (implicitly) reduced by the present value of future rental receipts to be paid on the original lease in excess of the present value of future rental receipts that will be collected on the operating sublease.

Leases Involving Governmental Units

Leases with governmental units usually lack fair values, have indeterminable economic lives, and cannot provide for transfer of ownership. These special provisions usually prevent their classification as any other than operating leases (ASC 840-10-25-25).

Leases involving governmental units, however, are subject to the same criteria as any other lease unless all of the following conditions exist; and in that event, these leases are classified as operating leases (ASC 840-10-25-25):

- A governmental unit or authority owns the leased property.
- The leased property is operated by or on behalf of a governmental unit or authority and is part of a larger facility, such as an airport.
- The leased property cannot be moved to another location because it is a permanent structure or part of a permanent structure.
- Any governmental unit or authority can terminate the lease agreement at any time under the terms of the lease agreement, existing statutes, or regulations.
- Ownership is not transferred to the lessee and the lessee cannot purchase the leased property.
- Equivalent property in the same area as the leased property cannot be purchased or leased from anyone else.

Related Party Leases

Except in cases in which the substance of a lease transaction indicates clearly that the terms and conditions have been significantly influenced by the related parties, related party leases are classified and accounted for as if the parties were unrelated (ASC 840-10-25-26).

It is important to note that, generally, a subsidiary whose principal business activity is leasing property to its parent must be consolidated with the parent's financial statements (ASC 840-10-45-1).

PRACTICE NOTE: Specific financial statement disclosures pertaining to related parties are required by ASC 850 (Related Party Disclosures).

Leveraged Leases

A lessee classifies and accounts for *leveraged* leases in the same manner as *nonleveraged* leases. *Only a lessor* must classify and account for leveraged leases in the specific manner prescribed herein (ASC 840-10-25-33).

ASC 840 defines a *leveraged lease* as a lease having all the following characteristics (ASC 840-10-25-43):

- A leveraged lease meets the definition of a *direct financing lease* as follows:

  A direct financing lease is a lease that does not result in a manufacturer's or dealer's profit or loss because the fair value of the leased property at the inception of the lease is the same as the cost or carrying amount. In a direct financing lease, substantially all the benefits and risks inherent in the ownership of the leased property are transferred to the lessee. In addition, the following requirements must be met:

  — The minimum lease payments are reasonably predictable of collection.

  — No important uncertainties exist regarding costs to be incurred by the lessor under the terms of the lease.
- It involves at least three parties: (*a*) a lessee, (*b*) a lessor, and (*c*) a long-term creditor. (**Note:** The lessor is sometimes referred to as the *equity participant*.)

- The financing is sufficient to provide the lessor with substantial leverage in the transaction and is nonrecourse as to the general credit of the lessor.
- Once the lessor's net investment is completed, it declines in the early years and rises in later years before being liquidated. These fluctuations in the lessor's net investment can occur more than once in the lease term.

PRACTICE POINTER: Leveraged leases are complex contracts that meet very specific criteria. Accounting for leveraged leases is unique in certain ways (e.g., offsetting assets and liabilities) and, therefore, determining whether a given lease is a leveraged lease is particularly important. A lease must meet *all* of the following specific criteria (taken from the definition of a leveraged lease) to be accounted for as a leveraged lease:

1. The lease is a direct financing lease.
2. The lease involves three parties rather than the normal two.
3. The lease provides the lessor with substantial leverage.
4. The pattern of the lessor's investment declines then rises.

Only when all four of these criteria are met is the lease subject to leveraged lease accounting.

If the investment tax credit is accounted for as provided herein and a lease meets the preceding definition, it is classified and accounted for as a leveraged lease (ASC 840-10-25-43).

Lessor's Existing Asset in a Leveraged Lease

Only a direct financing lease may qualify as a leveraged lease (ASC 840-10-25-43). One of the requirements of a direct financing lease is that it may not result in a manufacturer's or dealer's profit or loss. It is difficult for an existing asset of a lessor to qualify for leveraged lease accounting because the carrying amount (cost less accumulated depreciation) of an asset previously placed in service is not likely to be the same as its fair value. An existing asset of a lessor may qualify for leveraged lease accounting, however, if its carrying amount is equal to its fair value, without any write-down or other adjustment to its fair value.

GENERAL DISCLOSURES

General disclosures: A general description of the lessee's leasing arrangements, including (*a*) basis of contingent rental payments; (*b*) terms of renewals, purchase options, and escalation clauses; and (*c*) restrictions imposed by lease agreements, such as additional debt, dividends, and leasing limitations, must be disclosed (ASC 840-10-50-2).

General disclosures for leases of lessors whose significant business activity is leasing: A general description of the lessor's leasing arrangements (ASC 840-10-50-4).

ASC 840-20: OPERATING LEASES

OPERATING LEASES

Accounting and Reporting by the Lessee

Leases that do not qualify as capital leases in accordance with the provisions of ASC 840 are classified as operating leases. The cost of property covering an operating lease is included in the lessor's balance sheet as property, plant, and equipment. ASC 840 requires that rental income and expense relating to an operating lease be recognized over the periods in which the lessee derives benefit from the physical usage of the leased property. Thus, rental expense is recognized over the lease term on a straight-line basis, unless some other systematic and rational basis is more representative of the time pattern in which the benefits of the leased property are derived by the lessee (ASC 840-20-25-1).

PRACTICE POINTER: Use care when implementing accounting standards for sales-type leases involving real estate. A lessor shall not classify a lease involving real estate as a sales-type lease unless title to the leased property is transferred to the lessee at or shortly after the end of the lease term. As a result, a lessor may be required to classify a lease involving real estate as an operating lease, instead of a sales-type lease, because the lease agreement does not provide for the transfer of the leased property to the lessee by the end of the lease term. In this event, the lessor must recognize a loss at the inception of an operating lease involving real estate if the fair value of the leased property is less than its cost or carrying amount, whichever is applicable. The amount of loss is equal to the difference between the fair value of the leased property and its cost or carrying amount at the inception of the lease.

Contingent Rental Expense

Some operating lease agreements provide for rental increases or decreases based on one or more future conditions, such as future sales volume, future machine hours, future interest rates, or future price indexes. These types of rental increases or decreases are classified as *contingent rentals.* Contingent rentals are defined as those that cannot be determined at the inception of the lease because they depend on future conditions or events. A lessee's contingent rental payments are deducted as an expense in the period in which they arise.

Scheduled Rent Increases or Decreases

To accommodate the lessee, a lessor may structure an operating lease agreement to provide for smaller rental payments in the early years of the lease and higher rental payments toward the end of the lease. *Example:* A six-year operating lease agreement may provide for rental payments of $1,000 per month for the first two years; $1,500 per month for the next two years; and $2,000 per month for the last two years; for a total rental payment of $108,000 for the six years. Under this circumstance, ASC 840 requires that the $108,000 total rental payments be amortized over the six-year lease term on a straight-line basis. The monthly amortization for the first two years of the lease term is $1,500, even though only $1,000 per month is paid by the lessee under the terms of the lease (ASC 840-20-25-1).

PRACTICE NOTE: A reasonable argument can be made that in the early years of the above type of lease agreement, the lessee receives not only the use of the leased property, but also the temporary use of cash, equal to the excess of the fair rental value of the leased property over the actual rental payments. Theoretically, to recognize the economic substance of this lease transaction, both the lessee and the lessor should record imputed interest on the difference between the actual amount of rental payments and the computed amount of level rental payments. ASC 840, however, precludes the use of the time value of money as a factor in recognizing rentals under operating leases.

Leasehold Improvements

Leasehold improvements in an operating lease should be amortized by the lessee over the shorter of the economic life of the improvement or the lease term. An assumption of lease renewal where a renewal option exists is appropriate only when the renewal has been determined to be "reasonably assured," as that term is contemplated in ASC 840.

Leasehold improvements made by a lessee that are funded by landlord incentives or allowances under an operating lease should be recorded by the lessee as leasehold improvement assets and should be amortized over a term consistent with the above-stated guidance. The incentives should be recorded as deferred rent and amortized as reductions to lease expense over the lease term. It is inappropriate to net the deferred rent against the leasehold improvements. Further, the statement of cash flows should reflect cash received from the lessor that is accounted for as a lease incentive within operating activities and the acquisition of leasehold improvements for cash within investing activities.

Rent Holidays

Rent holidays in an operating lease should be recognized by the lessee on a straight-line basis over the lease term (including any rent holiday period), unless another systematic and rational allocation is more representative of the time pattern in which leased property is physically employed.

Accounting and Reporting by Lessors

Leases that do not qualify as capital leases in accordance with the provisions of ASC 840 are classified as operating leases. The cost of the property leased to the lessee is included in the lessor's balance sheet as property, plant, and equipment. The lessor's income statement will normally include the expenses of the leased property (unless it is a net lease), such as depreciation, maintenance, taxes, insurance, and other related items. Material initial direct costs (those directly related to the negotiation and consummation of the lease) are deferred and allocated to income over the lease term (ASC 840-20-45-2; 840-20-25-16).

ASC 840 requires that rental income from an operating lease be amortized over the periods in which the lessor's benefits in the leased property are depleted. Thus, rental income is amortized over the lease term on a straight-line basis, unless some other systematic and rational basis is more representative of the time pattern in which the benefits of the leased property are depleted (ASC 840-20-25-1).

ASC 840 requires that a lease involving real estate not be classified by the lessor as a sales-type lease unless title to the leased property is transferred to the lessee at or shortly after the end of the lease term. As a result, an enterprise may be required to classify a lease involving real estate as an operating lease, instead of a sales-type lease, because the lease agreement does not provide for the transfer of the leased property to the lessee by the end of the lease term. In this event, the lessor recognizes a loss at the inception of an operating lease involving real estate if the fair value of the leased property is less than its cost or carrying amount, whichever is applicable. The amount of loss is equal to the difference between the fair value of the leased property and its cost or carrying amount at the inception of the lease.

Contingent Rental Income

Contingent rental income is defined as that which cannot be determined at the inception of the lease because it depends on future conditions or events. A lessor's contingent rental income is accrued in the period in which it arises (ASC Glossary).

Lease Sale or Assignment to Third Parties

Sale or assignment of a sales-type or a direct financing lease does not negate the original accounting treatment. The transfer of minimum lease payments under a sales-type or direct financing lease are accounted for in accordance with ASC 860 (Transfers and Servicing). The accounting for transfers of residual values depends on whether the residual value is guaranteed. If the residual value is guaranteed, its transfer is accounted for in accordance with ASC 860. Transfers of unguaranteed residual values are not subject to the guidance in ASC 860.

If a sale to a third-party purchaser is not recorded as a sale because the entity has not transferred control over the promised asset to the third party, it is accounted for as a *borrowing*. The proceeds from the "sale" are recorded as an obligation on the books of the seller. Rental payments made by the lessee under the operating lease are recorded as revenue to the seller, even if the rentals are paid to the third party. Each rental payment shall consist of imputed interest, and the balance of the payment shall be applied as a reduction of the obligation. Any sale or assignment of lease payments under an operating lease is accounted for as a borrowing (ASC 840-20-35-4).

Financial Statement Disclosures

The following financial statement disclosures are required for all operating leases of lessees having noncancelable lease terms in excess of one year (ASC 840-20-50-1, 2):

- Minimum future rental payments in total and for each of the next five years
- Minimum sublease income due in future periods under noncancelable subleases
- Schedule of total rental expense showing the composition by minimum rentals, contingent rentals, and sublease income (excluding leases with terms of a month or less that were not renewed)

Following is an illustration of a lessee's financial statement disclosures for operating leases (using assumed numbers).

Illustration of Lessee's Financial Statement Disclosure

Operating Leases
Schedule of Minimum Future Rental Payments
(in thousands)

Year Ended December 31	
20X7	$ 815
20X8	2,400
20X9	320
20Y0	250

Year Ended December 31	
20Y1	200
After 20Y1	900
Total minimum future rental payments	$ 4,885

In addition to the above information on operating leases, a note should be included describing minimum sublease income due in the future under noncancelable subleases.

Operating Leases
Schedule of Minimum Future Rental Payments
(in thousands)

	December 31	
	20X6	20X5
Minimum Rentals	$1,100	$1,050
Contingent Rentals	100	125
Less: Sublease rental income	(200)	(150)
Total rental expense, net	$1,000	$1,025

Note: The above schedule of total rental expense excludes leases with terms of one month or less that were not renewed.

In addition to the foregoing information, a footnote describing the general disclosure policy for the lessee's leases should be included, containing (*a*) general leasing arrangements, (*b*) basis of contingent rental payments, (*c*) terms of renewals, purchase options, and escalation clauses, and (*d*) restrictions imposed by lease agreements, such as additional debt, dividends, and leasing limitations.

The following financial statement disclosures are required for operating leases for lessors whose significant business activity is leasing (ASC 840-20-50-4):

- A schedule of the investment in property on operating leases, and property held for lease, by major categories, less accumulated depreciation, as of each balance sheet presented
- A schedule of future minimum rentals on noncancelable operating leases, in total and for each of the next five years
- The amount of contingent rentals included in each income statement presented

Following is an illustration of a lessor's financial statement disclosures for operating leases (using assumed numbers).

Illustration of Lessor's Financial Statement Disclosure

Lessor's Balance Sheet
(in thousands)

	December 31	
	20X6	20X5
Noncurrent assets:		
Property on operating leases and property held for leases (net of accumulated depreciation of $450 and $400 for 20X6 and 20X5, respectively) (Note:_____)	$1,800	$1,600

Schedule of Investment in Property on Operating Leases
and Property Held for Lease (by Major Class Categories)
(in thousands)

Data-processing equipment	$ 900
Transportation equipment	700
Construction equipment	400
Other	200
Total	$2,200

Less: Accumulated depreciation	400
Net investment	$1,800

Schedule of Future Minimum Rentals on Noncancelable Operating Leases
(in thousands)

Year Ended December 31	
20X7	$ 200
20X8	175
20X9	165
20Y0	125
20Y1	110
After 20Y1	200
Total future minimum rentals	$ 975

A footnote should be included for contingent rentals.

ASC 840-30: CAPITAL LEASES

CAPITAL LEASES

Accounting and Reporting by Lessees

Initial Recording

The lessee records a capital lease as an asset and a corresponding liability (ASC 840-30-25-1). The initial recording value of a lease is the *lesser* of the fair value of the leased property or the present value of the minimum lease payments, excluding any portion representing executory costs and profit thereon to be paid by the lessor. Fair value is determined as of the inception of the lease, and the present value of the minimum lease payments is computed at the beginning of the lease term. The inception of the lease and the beginning of the lease term are not necessarily the same dates (ASC 840-30-30-1).

Because the lessee's minimum lease payments *exclude* a lessee's obligation to pay executory costs, executory costs paid by the lessee are expensed as paid or appropriately accrued. If such costs are included in the rental payments and are not identified separately (which is the most likely case), an estimate of the amount is necessary.

A lessee's incremental borrowing rate is used to determine the present value of the minimum lease payments unless the lessor's implicit rate of interest is known and is lower (ASC 840-10-25-31).

Leases with Escalation Clauses

In lease agreements or written commitments in which the leased property is to be acquired or constructed by the lessor, there may be a provision for the escalation of the minimum lease payments during the construction or preacquisition period. Usually, the escalation is based on increased costs of acquisition or construction of the leased property. A provision to escalate the minimum lease payments during the construction or preacquisition period can also be based on other measures of cost or value, including general price-level changes or changes in the consumer price index.

The relationship between the total amount of minimum lease payments and the fair value of a lease is such that when one increases so does the other. For example, assume that the total minimum lease payments of a particular lease are $100,000 payable in five equal annual installments, and the fair value of the same lease is $350,000. If the minimum lease payments are increased 20% to $120,000, it is likely that the fair value of the lease will increase correspondingly, because the lease is then worth more to an investor.

Increases in the minimum lease payments that occur during the preacquisition or construction period as a result of an escalation clause be considered in determining the fair value of the leased property at the inception of the lease for the purposes of the initial recording of the lease transaction by the lessee, or where fair value is used as a basis of allocation.

The initial recording value of a lease transaction by the lessee, which is required by ASC 840, is the lesser of the fair value of the leased property or the present value of the minimum lease payments. For leases that contain escalation clauses, fair value includes the effects of any escalation clauses.

PRACTICE POINTER: The question arises as to when leases of this type should be recorded on the books of the lessee. The initial recording should be made only after the effects of the escalation clause on the fair value of the leased property are determined. Otherwise, ASC 840 is silent in all respects as to when the lease transaction should be recorded. In the case of significant amounts of leases, it appears illogical to wait several years to record the transaction. If this is the only viable alternative, however, full disclosure of all pertinent facts pertaining to the lease agreement or commitment should be made in a prominent footnote.

The other alternative is to record these types of lease transactions immediately at the inception of the lease, utilizing whatever information is available and subsequently adjusting the recorded amounts when the effects of the escalation clauses are known. This alternative does not appear to be viable because of the difficulties mentioned in the following paragraphs.

The last-enumerated criterion in ASC 840 for capitalizing a lease is when the present value of the minimum lease payments is 90% or more of the fair value of the leased property at the inception of the lease. When this criterion is considered for capitalizing a lease in conjunction with the alternative of recording lease transactions at the inception of the lease and then subsequently adjusting the recorded amounts when the effects of the escalation clauses become known, the following problems arise, which are not addressed by ASC 840.

- If we assume that ASC 840 requires that the fair value of leases with escalation clauses be determined at a future date, what fair value should be used to determine whether the lease is or is not a capital lease in accordance with the criterion of whether the present value of the minimum lease payments is 90% or more of the fair value of the leased property at the inception of the lease?
- What if a lease of this type is capitalized in accordance with the criterion that the present value of the minimum lease payments is 90% or more of the fair value at inception of the lease, and subsequently, as a result of the escalation clause, the present value becomes less than 90% of the fair value, so that the lease should not have been capitalized?
- Suppose a lease with an escalation clause is properly classified as an operating lease at inception of the lease and subsequently, as a result of the escalation clause, the lease qualifies as a capital lease.

The above are just a few of the complications that could arise in applying the provisions relating to escalation clauses to lease transactions.

ASC 840 also permits increases in the estimated residual value (see definition) that occur as a result of escalation provisions in leases in which the leased property is to be acquired or constructed by the lessor. For example, if the estimated residual value is 10% of the fair value at the inception of a lease and during the construction or preacquisition period of the leased property the effects of the escalation clause increase the fair value, then the estimated residual value also is allowed to increase above the amount that was estimated at the date of the inception of the lease.

Amortization

The asset recorded under a capital lease is amortized in a manner consistent with the lessee's normal depreciation policy for other owned assets. The period for amortization is either (*a*) the estimated economic life or (*b*) the lease term, depending on which criterion was used to classify the lease. If the criterion used is either of the first two criteria (ownership of the property is transferred to the lessee by the end of the lease term or the lease contains a bargain purchase option), the asset is amortized over its estimated economic life. In all other cases, the asset is amortized over the lease term. Any *estimated residual value* is deducted from the asset to determine the amortizable base (ASC 840-30-35-1).

PRACTICE POINTER: Determining the appropriate amortization period for capital leases is an important issue where the lease term is significantly less than the expected useful life of the asset. A simple rule of thumb is simply to determine which party to the lease is expected to have use of the property during the period between the end of the lease period and the end of the expected life of the asset. If the lease is capitalized by the first or second capitalization criteria (transfer of title and bargain purchase option), the underlying assumption is that the lessee will become the legal owner of the asset by the end of the lease term and will have use of it for the remainder of the asset's expected life. Thus, the estimated life of the asset is the logical period of amortization. On the other hand, an assumption of the transfer of legal title does not underlie the lease if it is capitalized because of the third or fourth criteria (lease term and the present value of minimum lease payments). In either of these circumstances, the lease term is the logical period for amortization of the leased asset. Generally, if the same lease satisfies one or both of the first two criteria and one or both of the second criteria, use the expected life of the asset as the period of amortization.

Interest Expense: Interest Method

The interest method, sometimes referred to as the *effective interest method*, is used to produce a constant rate of interest on the remaining lease liability. A portion of each minimum lease payment is allocated to interest expense and/or amortization, and the balance is applied to reduce the lease liability. Any *residual guarantee(s)* by the lessee or penalty payments are automatically taken into consideration by using the interest method and will result in a balance at the end of the lease term equal to the amount of the guarantee or penalty payments at that date (ASC 840-30-35-6, 7, 8).

Illustration of Interest Method

Jones Company leases a tractor-trailer for $8,000 per year on a noncancelable five-year lease. The yearly lease payment is due at the beginning of the year. Jones guarantees to the lessor that the tractor-trailer will have a residual value of at least $5,000 at the end of the lease term.

Assume that a 12% interest rate is used.

Present value of $8,000 payments for five years at 12% =	$32,299*
Present value of $5,000 guaranteed residual value in five years at 12% =	2,837**
Total asset and lease obligation	$35,136

* $8,000 × 4.03735
** $5,000 × .56743

A schedule of interest expense, amortization, and reduction of the lease obligation of $35,136 to the $5,000 residual guarantee using the interest method follows:

Book Value Lease Obligation Beginning of Year	*Rental Payment/Reduction in Lease Obligation*	*Outstanding Balance During Year*	*Interest @ 12%*	*Book Value Lease Obligation End of Year*
$35,136	$8,000	$27,136	$3,256	$30,392
30,392	8,000	22,392	2,687	25,079
25,079	8,000	17,079	2,049	19,128
19,128	8,000	11,128	1,335	12,463
12,463	8,000	4,463	537	5,000

Change in Lease Terms

If a guarantee or penalty is rendered inoperative because of a renewal or other extension of the *lease term*, or if a new lease is consummated in which the lessee continues to lease the same property, an adjustment must be made to the asset and lease obligation for the difference between the present values of the old and the revised agreements. In these cases, the present value of the future minimum lease payments under the new or revised agreement is computed using the original rate of interest on the initial lease (ASC 840-30-35-8).

Other lease changes are accounted for as follows:

- If a lease change results in revised minimum lease payments, but also is classified as a capital lease, an adjustment is made to the asset and lease obligation for the difference between the present values of the old and the new or revised agreement. The present value of the future minimum lease payments under the new or revised agreement is computed using the original rate of interest used on the initial lease (ASC 840-30-35-19).
- A capital lease may be modified in such a way that the new lease agreement is treated as an operating lease (ASC 840-30-35-20). ASC 840 required that the lease asset and obligation (liability) be removed from the accounts and any

resulting gain or loss be recognized in determining current period income. The new lease agreement was accounted for as an operating lease.

The FASB concluded that the economic effects of the above transaction are similar to those of a sale-leaseback. However, ASC 840 does not require sale-leaseback accounting. Sale-leaseback accounting is required when a capital lease is modified such that the revised lease agreement is classified as an operating lease.

- A renewal, extension, or new lease under which the lessee continues to use the same property, except when a guarantee or penalty is rendered inoperative (see above), is accounted for as follows:
  - *Renewal or extension classified as a capital lease:* An adjustment is made for the difference between the original and revised present values, using the original discount rate (ASC 840-30-35-8).
  - *Renewal or extension classified as an operating lease:* The existing lease continues to be accounted for as a capital lease to the end of its lease term, and the renewal or extension is accounted for as an operating lease (ASC 840-30-17-b).

When leased property under a capital lease is purchased by the lessee, it is accounted for as a renewal or extension of a capital lease. Thus, any difference between the carrying amount and the purchase price on the date of purchase is treated as an adjustment of the carrying amount of the property (ASC 840-30-35-14).

Termination of a Lease

Gain or loss, if any, is recognized on the termination of a capital lease, and the asset and lease liability is removed from the books (ASC 840-30-40-1).

Illustration of Capital Lease (Lessee)

Paine Corporation leases a computer under a noncancelable five-year lease for annual rental payments of $10,000. The yearly lease payment is due at the beginning of the year. The fair value of the computer at the inception of the lease is $40,373, and the incremental borrowing rate of Paine is 10%. There are no executory costs. The annual rent of $10,000 is considered a fair rental as opposed to a bargain rental. The estimated economic life of the computer is 10 years.

Classification of Lease

A review is made of the criteria involved in the provisions of the lease to determine its classification.

1. Criterion (1) is not met, because there is no transfer of the ownership of the leased property before the end of the lease term.
2. Criterion (2) is not met, because the lease does not contain a bargain purchase option.
3. Criterion (3) is not met, because the lease term (five years) is not equal to 75% or more of the estimated economic life (10 years) of the leased property. (*Note:* There are no other provisions affecting the lease term other than the five-year noncancelable term.)
4. Criterion (4) is met, because the present value ($41,699) of the minimum lease payments, excluding executory costs and profits thereon paid by the lessor, is 90% or more of the fair value ($40,373 × .9 = $36,336) of the leased property. [*Note:* The present value of the lease is $41,699, computed as follows: $10,000 × 4.16987, the present value factor for an annuity due, 5 periods, 10%.]

Paine Corporation should record the transaction as a capital lease.

Accounting for the Lease

The initial recording value of the leased property, at the beginning of the lease term, is the lesser of the fair value of the leased property or the present value of the minimum lease payments, excluding any portion that represents executory costs and profit thereon to be paid by the lessor.

The discount rate used by the lessee to find the present value of the minimum lease payments is its incremental borrowing rate of 10%, unless the lessee has knowledge of the lessor's implicit interest rate in the lease, and that rate is lower.

The lessor's interest rate implicit in the lease in this example is 12%. As a rule, the interest rate implicit in the lease is equal to the discount rate that, when applied to the minimum lease payments of $10,000 per year for five years and, if any, the unguaranteed residual value of the leased property, results in a present value equal to the fair value of the leased property at the inception of the lease. (For simplicity, this definition excludes any unusual factors that a lessor might recognize in determining its rate of return.)

This means that Paine must use its incremental borrowing rate of 10% to discount the minimum lease payments to their present value, which is $41,699.

The initial recording value of the leased property is the lesser of the fair value of the leased property at inception or the present value of the minimum lease payments using the lower interest rate. Therefore, the $40,373 fair value is less than the minimum lease payments of $41,699 (computed by using the lower incremental borrowing rate) and is used to initially record the lease, as follows:

Lease property, capital leases	$40,373	
Obligations, capital leases		$40,373

Amortization by Lessee

The asset(s) recorded under a capital lease is amortized in a manner consistent with the lessee's normal depreciation policy for other owned assets. The period for amortization is either (*a*) the estimated economic life or (*b*) the lease term, depending on which criterion was used to classify the lease. If the criterion used to classify the lease as a capital lease was either criterion (1) (ownership of the property is transferred to the lessee by the end of the lease term) or criterion (2) (lease contains a bargain purchase option), the asset is amortized over its economic life. In all other cases, the asset is amortized over the lease term. Any residual value is deducted from the asset to determine the amortizable base.

Because the Paine Corporation's lease qualified under criterion (4) (present value of the minimum lease payments, excluding executory costs and profit thereon paid by the lessor, is 90% or more of the fair value of the leased property), the amortization period is over the lease term.

A schedule of amortization, interest expense, and lease obligation payments for Paine Corporation's computer lease, using the interest method, follows:

Book Value Lease Obligation Beginning of Year	*Rental Payment/Reduction in Lease Obligation*	*Outstanding Balance During Year*	*Interest @ 12%*	*Book Value Lease Obligation End of Year*
$40,373	$10,000	$30,373	$3,645	$34,018
34,018	10,000	24,018	2,882	26,900
26,900	10,000	16,900	2,028	18,928
18,928	10,000	8,928	1,072	10,000
10,000	10,000	-0-	-0-	-0-

Note: The interest rate used is 12%, which is the interest rate implicit in the lease.

Accounting and Reporting by Lessors

Leases are classified for the lessor as either (*a*) sales-type, (*b*) direct financing, or (*c*) operating. Both sales-type and direct financing are forms of capital leases.

Sales-type leases usually are used by sellers of property to increase the marketability of expensive assets. The occurrence of a manufacturer's or dealer's profit or loss generally is present in a sales-type lease.

Direct financing leases do not give rise to a manufacturer's or dealer's profit or loss, and the fair value usually is the cost or the carrying amount of the property.

Recording Sales-Type Leases

The lessor's *gross investment* in the lease is the sum of (*a*) the minimum lease payments to be received less any executory costs and profit thereon to be paid by the lessor and (*b*) any unguaranteed residual value accruing to the benefit of the lessor (this is the estimated fair value of the leased property at the end of the lease term, which is not guaranteed). (**Note:** If the residual value is guaranteed, it is included in the minimum lease payments.) (ASC 840-30-30-6).

The estimated residual value used to compute the unguaranteed residual value accruing to the benefit of the lessor shall not exceed the amount estimated at the inception of the lease (ASC 840-30-30-6).

Using the interest rate implicit in the lease, the lessor's gross investment in the lease is discounted to its present value. The present value of the lessor's gross investment in the lease represents the sales price of the property that is included in income for the period. (**Note:** When using the interest rate implicit in the lease, the present value will always be equal to the fair value.) (ASC 840-30-30-10).

The cost or carrying amount of the property sold plus any initial direct costs (costs incurred by the lessor to negotiate and consummate the lease, such as legal fees and commissions), less the present value of the unguaranteed residual value (if any) accruing to the benefit of the lessor is charged against income in the period in which the corresponding sale is recorded (ASC 840-30-25-6).

The difference between the lessor's gross investment in the lease and the sales price of the property is recorded as unearned income, which is amortized to income over the lease term by the interest method. The unearned income is included in the balance sheet as a deduction from the related gross investment, which results in the net investment in the lease (ASC 840-30-35-22).

A lease involving real estate is not classified by the lessor as a sales-type lease unless the title to the leased property is transferred to the lessee at or shortly after the end of the lease term.

Recording Direct Financing Leases

The lessor's *gross investment* in the lease is computed, which is equal to the sum of (*a*) the minimum lease payments to be received by the lessor, less any executory costs and profit thereon to be paid by the lessor, and (*b*) any unguaranteed residual value accruing to the benefit of the lessor (this is the estimated fair value of the lease property at the end of the lease term, which is not guaranteed). If the residual value is guaranteed, it is included in the minimum lease payments.

Under ASC 310, loan origination fees and direct loan origination costs, including initial direct costs incurred by the lessor in negotiating and consummating the lease, are offset against each other and the resulting net amount is deferred and recognized over the life of the loan as an adjustment to the yield on the loan (ASC 310-20-30-2; 310-20-35-2).

The difference between the lessor's gross investment in the lease and the cost or carrying amount of the leased property, if different, is recorded as unearned income, which is amortized to income over the lease term by the interest method. The unearned income is included in the balance sheet as a deduction from the related gross investment, which results in the net investment in the lease.

Balance Sheet Classification

The resulting net investment in both sales-type and direct financing leases is subject to the same treatment as other assets in classifying as current or noncurrent.

Annual Review of Residual Values

The unguaranteed residual values of both sales-type and direct financing leases should be reviewed at least annually to determine whether a decline, other than temporary, has occurred in their estimated values. If a decline is not temporary, the accounting for the transaction should be revised using the new estimate, and the resulting loss should be recognized in the period that the change is made. *Upward adjustments are not allowed* (ASC 840-30-35-25).

Accounting for Lease Changes

The definition of *lease term* includes any periods in which penalties are imposed in an amount that reasonably assures the renewal of the lease by the lessee. The definition of *minimum lease payments* includes any payments or guarantees that the lessee is required to make concerning the leased property, including any amount (*a*) to purchase the leased property, (*b*) to make up any deficiency from a specified minimum, and (*c*) for failure to renew or extend the lease at the expiration of the lease term. Guarantees and penalties such as these usually are canceled and become inoperative in the event the lease is renewed or extended or a new lease for the same property is consummated.

If a sales-type or direct financing lease contains a residual guarantee or a penalty for failure to renew and is rendered inoperative as a result of a lease renewal or other extension of the lease term, or if a new lease is consummated in which the lessee continues to lease the same property, an adjustment must be made to the unearned income account for the difference between the present values of the old and the revised agreements. The present value of the future minimum lease payments under the new agreement is computed by using the original rate of interest used for the initial lease (ASC 840-30-35-23).

In sales-type and direct financing leases that do not contain residual guarantees or penalties for failure to renew, an adjustment is made to account for lease changes, renewals, or other extensions, including a new lease in which the lessee continues to lease the same property. If the classification of the lease remains unchanged or is classified as a direct financing lease and the amount of the remaining minimum lease payments is changed, an adjustment is made to unearned income to account for the difference between the present values of the old and the new agreements (ASC 840-30-35-30). If a new classification results in a sales-type lease, it is classified and treated as a direct financing lease, unless the transaction occurs within the last few months of the original lease, in which case it is classified as a sales-type lease.

If the classification of a lease is changed to an operating lease, the accounting treatment depends upon whether the operating lease starts immediately or at the end of the existing lease. If the operating lease starts immediately, the remaining net investment is eliminated from the accounts and the leased property is recorded as an asset using the lower of (*a*) original cost, (*b*) present fair value, or (*c*) present carrying amount. The difference between the remaining net investment and the new recorded value of the asset is charged to income in the period of change (ASC 840-30-40-6).

If the operating lease starts at the end of the existing lease, the existing lease continues to be accounted for as a sales-type or direct financing lease until the new operating lease commences, at which time the accounting treatment is the same as if the operating lease started immediately. Renewals and extensions usually commence at the end of the original sales-type or direct financing lease. Under these circumstances there should not be any remaining investment to eliminate from the books and the leased property is not recorded as an asset (ASC 840-30-35-28).

Termination of a Lease

Termination of a lease is recognized in the income of the period in which the termination occurs by the following journal entries (ASC 840-30-40-7).

- The remaining net investment is eliminated from the accounts.
- The leased property is recorded as an asset using the lower of the (*a*) original cost, (*b*) present fair value, or (*c*) present carrying amount.

Financial Statement Disclosure

Assets, accumulated amortization, and liabilities from capital leases are reported separately in the balance sheet by the lessee and classified as current or noncurrent in the same manner as other assets and liabilities (ASC 840-30-45-1, 2, 3).

The lessee must clearly disclose current amortization charges to income, along with the following additional information (ASC 840-30-50-1):

- Gross assets as of each balance sheet date presented, in aggregate and by major property categories (this information may be combined with comparable owned assets)
- Minimum future lease payments in total and for each of the next five years, showing deductions for executory costs, including any profit thereon, and the amount of imputed interest to reduce the net minimum lease payments to present values
- Minimum sublease income due in future periods under noncancelable subleases
- Total contingent rentals actually incurred for each period for which an income statement is presented

Following is an illustration of a lessee's financial statement disclosures for capital leases (using assumed numbers).

Illustration of Lessee's Financial Statement Disclosure

Lessor's Balance Sheet
(in thousands)

	December 31	
	20X6	20X5
Assets:		
Leased property:		
Capital leases, less accumulated amortization (Note: ____)	$2,200	$1,600
Liabilities:		
Current:		
Obligations under capital leases (Note: ____)	$365	$340
Noncurrent:		
Obligations under capital leases (Note: ____)	$1,368	$1,260

Capital Leases
Gross Assets and Accumulated Amortization
(in thousands)

	December 31	
	20X6	20X5
Type of Property		
Manufacturing plants	$1,500	$1,100
Retail stores	1,200	840
Other	300	210
Total	$3,000	$2,150
Less: Accumulated amortization	800	550
Capital leases, net	$2,200	$1,600

Capital Leases
Minimum Future Lease Payments and Present Values
of the Net Minimum Lease Payments
(in thousands)

Year Ended December 31	
20X7	$ 406
20X8	1,232
20X9	160
20Y0	125
20Y1	100
After 20Y1	450
Total future minimum rentals	$ 2,473
Less: Executory costs (estimated)	250
Net minimum lease payments	$2,223
Less: Imputed interest	490
Present value of net minimum lease payments	$1,733

In addition to the foregoing statements and schedules, footnotes describing minimum sublease income and contingent rentals should be included, if required.

The following financial statement disclosures are required by lessors whose *significant business activity is leasing* (not including *leveraged* leasing) for sales-type and direct financing leases (ASC 840-30-50-4):

- A schedule of the components of the *net investment* in leases, as of each balance sheet date, including:
  - — Future minimum lease payments, with separate deductions for executory costs and the allowance for uncollectibles
  - — Unguaranteed residual values accruing to the benefit of the lessor
  - — Initial direct costs (direct financing leases only)
  - — Unearned income
- A schedule of the minimum lease payments, in total and for the next five years
- Contingent rentals included in income

Following is an illustration of a lessor's financial statement disclosures for capital losses (using assumed numbers).

Illustration of Lessor's Financial Statement Disclosure

Lessor's Balance Sheet
(in thousands)

	December 31	
	20X6	*20X5*
Assets:		
Current assets:		
Net investment in sales-type and direct financing leases (Note:)	$208	$200
Noncurrent assets:		
Net investment in sales-type and direct financing leases (Note:)	$972	$830

Schedule of Components—Net Investment in Leases Sales-Type and Direct Financing Leases
(in thousands)

	20X6	*20X5*
Total minimum lease payments receivable	$1,450	$1,250
Less: Estimated executory costs, including profit thereon	150	125
Minimum lease payments	$1,300	$1,125
Less: Allowance for uncollectibles	65	60
Net minimum lease payments receivable	$1,235	$1,065
Add: Estimated unguaranteed residual values of leased properties	240	215
	$1,475	$1,280
Less: Unearned income	295	250
Net investment in sales-type and direct financing leases	$1,180	$1,030

A footnote should be included for contingent rentals.

Schedule of Minimum Lease Payments
(in thousands)

Year Ended December 31	
20X7	$ 260
20X8	195
20X9	156
20Y0	132
20Y1	125
After 20Y1	432
Total minimum lease payments receivable, net of executory costs	$1,300

LEASE MODIFICATIONS

Under the provisions of ASC 840, a capital lease may be modified in such a way that the new lease agreement is treated as an operating lease. ASC 840 requires that the lease asset and obligation (liability) be removed from the accounts and any resulting gain or loss be recognized in determining current period income. The new lease agreement is accounted for as an operating lease.

The FASB concluded that the economic effects of the above transaction are similar to those of a sale-leaseback accounting when a capital lease is modified such that the revised lease agreement is classified as an operating lease.

Refunding of Tax-Exempt Debt

If, before the expiration of the lease term, a change in a lease occurs as a result of a refunding by the lessor of tax-exempt debt and *(a)* the lessee receives the economic advantages of the refunding and *(b)* the revised lease qualifies and is classified either as a capital lease by the lessee or as a direct financing lease by the lessor, the change in the lease shall be accounted for on the basis of whether or not an extinguishment of debt has occurred, as follows (ASC 840-30-35-10).

Figure 56-1: Classification of a Lease as a Capital or Operating Lease

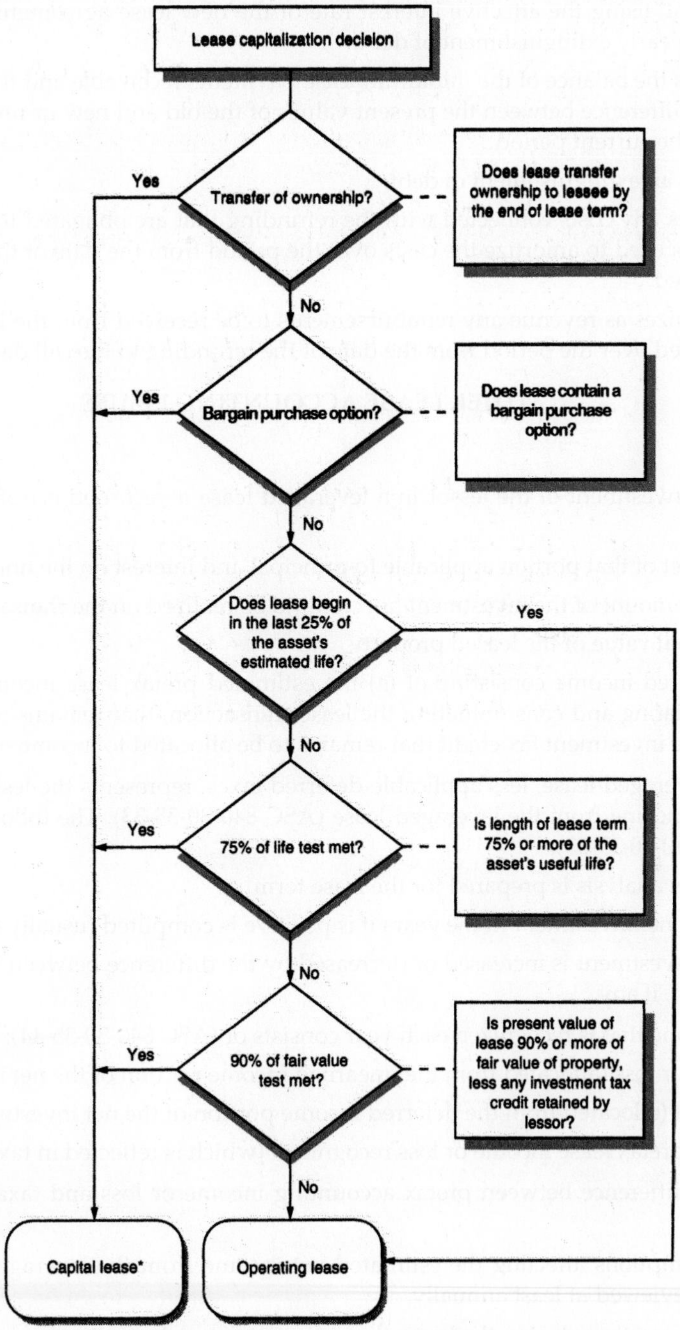

*Lessor must determine that two additional criteria are met to account for the lease as a capital lease:

1. Collection of minimum lease payments is reasonably predictable.
2. No important uncertainties exist for unreimbursable costs to be incurred by the lessor.

- Accounted for as an extinguishment of debt:
  - The lessee adjusts the lease obligation to the present value of the future minimum lease payments under the revised agreement, using the effective interest rate of the new lease agreement. Any gain or loss is treated as a gain or loss on an early extinguishment of debt.
  - The lessor adjusts the balance of the minimum lease payments receivable and the gross investment in the lease (if affected) for the difference between the present values of the old and new or revised agreement. Any gain or loss is recognized in the current period.
- Not accounted for as an extinguishment of debt:
  - The lessee accrues any costs connected with the refunding that are obligated to be reimbursed to the lessor. The interest method is used to amortize the costs over the period from the date of the refunding to the call date of the debt to be refunded.
  - The lessor recognizes as revenue any reimbursements to be received from the lessee for costs paid related to the debt to be refunded over the period from the date of the refunding to the call date of the debt to be refunded.

OTHER LEASE ACCOUNTING ISSUES

Leveraged Leases

The initial and continuing investment of the lessor in a leveraged lease is recorded *net* of the nonrecourse debt, as follows (ASC 840-30-30-14):

- Rentals receivable, net of that portion applicable to principal and interest on the nonrecourse debt
- A receivable for the amount of the investment tax credit to be realized on the transaction
- The estimated residual value of the leased property
- Unearned and deferred income consisting of (*a*) the estimated pretax lease income or loss, after deducting initial direct costs of negotiating and consummating the lease transaction, that remains to be allocated to income over the lease term and (*b*) the investment tax credit that remains to be allocated to income over the lease term

The investment in a leveraged lease, less applicable deferred taxes, represents the lessor's net investment for purposes of computing periodic net income from the leveraged lease (ASC 840-30-35-33). The following method is used to compute periodic net income (ASC 840-30-35-33):

- A projected cash flow analysis is prepared for the lease term.
- The rate of return on net investment in the years it is positive is computed (usually by trial and error).
- Every year the net investment is increased or decreased by the difference between the net cash flow and the amount of income recognized, if any.

The amount of net income that is recognized each year consists of (ASC 840-30-35-44):

- Pretax lease income or loss (allocated from the unearned income portion of the net investment)
- Investment tax credit (allocated from the deferred income portion of the net investment)
- The tax effect of the pretax lease income or loss recognized (which is reflected in tax expense for the year)

Any tax effect on the difference between pretax accounting income or loss and taxable income or loss is charged or credited to deferred taxes.

All the important assumptions affecting the estimated net income from the leveraged lease, including any estimated residual values, should be reviewed at least annually.

If, at the inception or at any time during the lease, the projected net cash receipts over the initial or remaining lease term are less than the lessor's initial or current investment, the resulting loss is immediately recognized (ASC 840-30-25-9).

Upward adjustments of the estimated residual value are not permitted (ASC 840-30-35-40).

The lessor's financial statement disclosure for leveraged leases shall include the amount of deferred taxes stated separately. In the income statement or the notes thereto, separate presentation (from each other) shall be made of (1) pretax income from leveraged leases, (2) the tax effect of pretax income, and (3) the amount of investment tax credit recognized as income during the period (ASC 840-30-45-5).

Business Combinations

A business combination (or an acquisition by a not-for-profit entity), in itself does not affect the classification of a lease. If as a result of a business combination, however, a lease is revised or modified to the extent that under ASC 840 it is considered a new agreement, it is reclassified based on its revision or modification. Ordinarily, a lease retains its previous classification under ASC 840 and is accounted for in the same manner as it was prior to the combination.

The acquiring company in a business combination accounts for a leveraged lease by assigning a fair value (present value, net of tax) to the net investment in a leveraged lease based on the remaining future cash flows with appropriate recognition for any future estimated tax effects. After the fair value (present value, net of tax) of the net investment is determined, it is allocated to net rentals receivable, estimated residual value, and unearned income. Thereafter, a company accounts for the leveraged lease by allocating the periodic cash flow between the net investment and the lease income (ASC 840-30-30-15; 840-30-25-10).

In a business combination in which an acquired lease has not been conformed to ASC 840, the acquiring company classifies such a lease to conform retroactively to ASC 840.

ASC 840-40: SALE-LEASEBACK TRANSACTIONS

SALE-LEASEBACK TRANSACTIONS

A sale-leaseback is a transaction in which an owner sells property and then leases back part or all of the same property. Such an owner is referred to as the seller-lessee. The purchaser-lessor is the party who purchases the property and leases back the same property to the seller-lessee.

Non-Real Estate

Profit or loss on the sale is the amount that would have been recognized on the sale by the seller-lessee, assuming there was no leaseback.

Recognition of profit or loss from the sale-leaseback by the seller-lessee is determined by the degree of rights in the remaining use of the property the seller-lessee retains, as follows:

- Substantially all
- Minor
- More than minor but less than substantially all

Substantially All or Minor

Under the terms of the lease, the seller-lessee may have a *minor* portion or *substantially all* of the rights to the remaining use of the property. This is determined by the present value of a total *reasonable rental* for the rights to the remaining use of the property retained by the seller-lessee. The seller-lessee has transferred *substantially all* of the rights to the remaining use of the property to the purchaser-lessor if the present value of the total *reasonable rental* under the terms of the lease is 10% or less of the fair value of the property sold at the inception of the lease. The seller-lessee has transferred a *minor* portion of the remaining rights to the purchaser-lessor if the terms of the leaseback include the entire property sold and qualify as a capital lease under ASC 840.

PRACTICE NOTE: ASC 840 does not define *reasonable rental* or *fair value*. However, it defines *fair value* as the price the leased property could be sold for between unrelated parties in an arm's length transaction. ASC 840 defines *fair rental* as the rental rate for similar property under similar lease terms and conditions.

Whether the lease is recorded as a capital lease or an operating lease, any profit or loss on the sale by the seller-lessee must be deferred and amortized as follows:

- *Capital lease* For a capital lease, the deferred profit or loss on the sale is amortized in proportion to the amortization of the leased property.
- *Operating lease* For an operating lease, the deferred profit or loss on the sale is amortized in proportion to the gross rental charged to expense over the lease term.

Whether a capital lease or an operating lease, if the leased asset is land only, the amortization of the deferred profit or loss on the sale must be on a straight-line basis over the lease term.

If the seller-lessee retains the rights to a *minor* portion of the remaining use in the property, the seller-lessee accounts for the sale and leaseback as two independent transactions based on their separate terms. The lease must provide for a reasonable amount of rent, however, considering prevailing market conditions at the inception of the lease. The seller-lessee must increase or decrease the profit or loss on the sale by an amount, if any, which brings the total rental for the leased property to a reasonable amount. Any amount created by this adjustment is amortized, as follows:

- *Capital lease* For a capital lease, the deferred or accrued amount is amortized in proportion to the amortization of the leased property.
- *Operating lease* For an operating lease, the deferred or accrued amount is amortized in proportion to the gross rental charged to expense over the lease term.

Whether a capital lease or an operating lease, if the leased asset is land only, the amortization of the deferred or accrued amount must be on a straight-line basis over the lease term.

PRACTICE POINTER: If the total rental on the lease is less than a reasonable amount compared to prevailing market conditions at the inception of the lease, increase a profit on the sale and decrease a loss on the sale.

For an operating lease, the journal entry is a debit to prepaid rent and a credit to profit or loss. Amortize the prepaid rent in an amount that increases the periodic rental expense over the lease term to a reasonable amount. Conversely, if the total rental on the lease is more than a reasonable amount compared to prevailing market conditions at the inception of the lease, decrease a profit on the sale and increase a loss on the sale. The journal entry is a debit to profit or loss and a credit to deferred rent. Amortize the deferred rent in an amount that decreases the periodic rental expense over the lease term to a reasonable amount.

For a capital lease, make no debit to prepaid rent or credit to deferred rent. Instead, the debit or credit increases or decreases the amount that is recorded for the leased property. Then, amortize the leased property in the usual manner.

More Than Minor but Less Than Substantially All

If the seller-lessee retains the rights to more than minor but less than substantially all of the remaining use in the property, the seller-lessee shall recognize any excess profit (not losses) determined at the date of sale as follows:

- *Capital lease* The excess profit (if any) on a sale-leaseback transaction is equal to the amount of profit that exceeds the seller-lessee's recorded amount of the property as determined under the provisions of ASC 840 (the lesser of the fair value of the leased property or the present value of the minimum lease payments). For example, if the seller-lessee's recorded amount of the sale-leaseback property is $100,000 as determined under the provisions of ASC 840, and the amount of profit on the sale-leaseback transaction is $120,000, the excess profit that is recognized by the seller-lessee is $20,000. The balance of the profit ($100,000) is deferred and amortized in proportion to the amortization of the leased property.
- *Operating lease* The excess profit (if any) on a sale-leaseback transaction is equal to the amount of profit that exceeds the present value of the minimum lease payments over the term of the lease. The amount of profit on the sale-leaseback transaction that is not recognized at the date of the sale is deferred and amortized over the lease term in proportion to the gross rentals charged to expense.

Whether a capital lease or an operating lease, if the leased property is land only, the amortization of the deferred profit (if any) must be on a straight-line basis over the lease term.

Profit Recognition Other Than by the Full Accrual Method

A sale-leaseback transaction must qualify under the provisions of ASC 840 and under most of the provisions of ASC 360 before the full amount of the profit on the sale portion of the transaction can be recognized by the sale-leaseback accounting method (full accrual method).

When one (or more) of the criteria for recognizing the full amount of profit on the sale portion of a sale-leaseback transaction is not met, an alternative method of recognizing revenue from the sale must be used. The alternative method selected may be required by ASC 360 or may be a matter of professional judgment. The four accounting methods recommended by ASC 360 are (1) the deposit method, (2) the cost-recovery method, (3) the installment sales method, and (4) the reduced profit method. (The four alternative methods are discussed earlier in this chapter.)

The collectibility of the receivable should be evaluated periodically. When it becomes apparent that the seller's receivable is reasonably assured of being collected, the seller should change to the full accrual accounting method. (Change to the full accrual method is discussed thoroughly earlier in this chapter.)

Real Estate

Standards of accounting for sale-leaseback transactions involving real estate include transactions including real estate with equipment, such as a manufacturing facility, power plant, and an office building with furniture and fixtures. A sale-leaseback transaction involving real estate with equipment includes any sale-leaseback transaction in which the equipment and the real estate are sold and leased back as a package without regard to the relative value of the equipment and real estate elements of the transaction.

Criteria for Sale-Leaseback Accounting

Sale-leaseback accounting shall be used by a lessor-lessee only if the transaction meets all of the following criteria (ASC 840-40-25-9):

- The leaseback is a normal leaseback (see discussion below).
- Payment terms and provisions adequately demonstrate the buyer-lessor's initial and continuing investment in the property.
- Payment terms and provisions transfer all of the other risks and rewards of ownership as demonstrated by the absence of any continuing involvement by the seller-lessee.

A *normal leaseback* is one in which the seller-lessee actively uses substantially all of the property in consideration for payment of rent, including contingent rentals that are based on the future operations of the seller-lessee (ASC Glossary). The phrase "actively uses the property" refers to the use of the property during the lease term in the seller-lessee's trade or business, provided that subleasing of the property is minor. The term "minor" means that the present value of the sublease is not more than 10% of the fair value of the asset sold. Active use of the property may involve providing services where the occupancy of the property is generally transient or short-term and is integral to the ancillary services being provided. Ancillary services may include, but are not limited to, housekeeping inventory control, entertainment, bookkeeping, and food services. For example, the use of property by a seller-lessee engaged in the hotel or bonded warehouse business or the operation of a golf course or parking lot is considered active use.

Adequate Initial and Continuing Investment by the Purchaser-Lessor

To qualify for sale-leaseback accounting under ASC 840, the purchaser-lessor's initial and continuing investment in the property must be adequate as prescribed by ASC 360. In determining whether the purchaser's minimum initial investment is adequate under the provisions of ASC 360, the sales value of the property is used and not the stated sales price that appears in the sales contract.

In addition to an adequate initial investment, ASC 360 requires that the purchaser maintain a continuing investment in the property by increasing the investment each year. The purchaser's total indebtedness for the purchase price of the property must be reduced each year in equal amounts that will extinguish the entire indebtedness (interest and principal) over a specified maximum period. The specified maximum period for land transactions is 20 years. The specified maximum period for all other real estate transactions is no more than that offered at the time of sale for first mortgages by independent financial institutions.

Terms of the Sale-Leaseback Transaction

Terms of the sale-leaseback transaction that are substantially different from terms that an independent third-party would accept represent an exchange of some stated or unstated rights or privileges. Those rights or privileges are considered in evaluating the seller-lessor's continuing involvement (described below). Those terms or conditions include, but are not limited to, the sales price, interest rate, and other terms of any loan from the seller-lessee to the buyer-lessor (ASC 840-40-25-10). The fair value of the property used in making that evaluation is based on objective evidence, such as an independent third-party appraisal or recent sales of comparable property.

Continuing Involvement

A sale-leaseback transaction that does not qualify for sale-leaseback accounting because of continuing involvement by the seller-lessee other than a normal leaseback shall account for the transaction by the deposit method or the financing method, whichever is appropriate. Two examples of continuing involvement that are frequently found in sale-leaseback transactions are (ASC 840-40-25-13):

- The seller-lessee has an obligation or an option to repurchase the property so that the buyer-lessor can compel the seller- lessee to repurchase the property.
- The seller-lessee guarantees the buyer-lessor's investment or a return on that investment for a limited or extended period of time.

Other provisions or conditions that represent guarantees and that do not transfer all of the risks of ownership and that constitute continuing involvement for purposes of these standards include (ASC 840-40-25-14):

- The seller-lessee is required to pay the buyer-lessor at the end of the lease term a decline in the fair value of the property below the estimated residual value on some basis other than excess wear and tear of the property.
- The seller-lessee provides nonrecourse financing to the buyer-lessor for any portion of the sales proceeds or provides recourse financing in which the only recourse is to the leased asset.
- The seller-lessee is not relieved of the obligation under any existing debt related to the property.
- The seller-lessee provides collateral on behalf of the buyer-lessor other than the property directly involved in the sale-leaseback transaction, the seller-lessee or a related party guarantees the buyer-lessor's debt, or a related party to the seller-lessee guarantees a return of or on the buyer-lessor's investment.
- The seller-lessee's rental payment is contingent on some predetermined or determinable level of future operations by the buyer-lessor.

Examples of provisions or conditions that are considered continuing involvement for purposes of determining proper accounting for sale-leaseback transactions of real estate are as follows (ASC 840-40-25-17):

- The seller-lessee enters into a sale-leaseback transaction involving property improvements or integral equipment without leasing the underlying land to the buyer-lessor.
- The buyer-lessor is obligated to share with the seller-lessee any portion of the appreciation on the property.
- Any other provision or circumstance that allows the seller-lessee to participate in any future profits of the buyer-lessor or the appreciation of the leased property.

Financial Statement Presentation

In addition to disclosure requirements presented earlier for leases in general, the financial statements of a seller-lessee shall include a description of the terms of sale-leaseback transactions, including future commitments, obligations, provisions, or circumstances that require or result in the seller-lessee's continuing involvement (ASC 840-40-50-1).

The financial statements of a seller-lessee that has accounted for a sale-leaseback transaction by the deposit method or as a financing shall disclose the following information (ASC 840-40-50-2):

- The obligation for future minimum lease payments as of the date of the latest balance sheet presented in the aggregate and for each of the five succeeding fiscal years.
- The total minimum sublease rentals, if any, to be received in the future under noncancelable subleases in the aggregate for each of the five succeeding fiscal years.

PRACTICE NOTE: Additional guidance concerning profit recognition and sale-leaseback transactions involving real estate can be found in Appendix H, *ASC 970—Real Estate—General.*

WRAP LEASE TRANSACTIONS

In a wrap lease transaction, a lessor leases equipment to a lessee and obtains nonrecourse financing from a financial institution using the lease receivable and the asset as collateral. The lessor sells the asset subject to the lease and the nonrecourse financing to a third-party investor and then leases the asset back. Thus, the original lessor remains the principal lessor, who continues to service the lease. The transaction with the third-party investor may or may not occur at the same time that the original lease is executed with the original equipment user. As a matter of fact, it is not unusual in a wrap lease transaction for the subsequent nonrecourse financing or sale to a third party to occur up to six months after the original lease agreement is executed.

In exchange for the sale of the asset to a third-party investor, the lessor may receive a combination of cash, a note, an interest in the residual value of the leased asset, and certain other rights or contingent rights, such as the right to remarket the asset at the end of the lease term. Depending on the terms of the specific transaction, (*a*) the lessor may or may not be liable for the leaseback payments if the primary lessee defaults, (*b*) the lessor may or may not receive a fee for servicing the lease, (*c*) payments under the leaseback may or may not approximate collections under the note, and (*d*) the terms of the leaseback may or may not correspond with the terms of the original equipment lease.

Under sale-leaseback accounting, the sale portion of a sale-leaseback transaction is recorded as a sale by the seller-lessee. The property sold and all of its related liabilities are eliminated from the seller-lessee's balance sheet. Gain or loss on the sale portion of the sale-leaseback transaction is recognized by the seller-lessee. The lease portion of the sale-leaseback transaction should be classified as a capital lease or an operating lease.

The purchaser-lessor records a sale-leaseback transaction as a purchase and a direct financing lease if the lease portion of the sale-leaseback meets the criteria of a capital lease under ASC 840. Otherwise, the purchaser-lessor records the transaction as a purchase and an operating lease (ASC 840-40-25-8).

In reporting a wrap lease transaction, an enterprise's statement of financial position should include (*a*) the amount of the retained residual interest in the leased property, (*b*) the amount of the gross sublease receivable, (*c*) the amount of the nonrecourse third-party debt, (*d*) the amount of the leaseback obligation, and (*e*) the amount of the note receivable from the investor.

Illustration of Wrap Lease Transactions

Assume that a lessor leases an asset with an undepreciated cost of $1,000 to a lessee for five years at $19.12 a month. The residual value of the leased asset at the end of the lease term is estimated to be $164.53 and the interest rate implicit in the lease is 10%. The lessor would classify the lease as a direct financing lease under the provisions of ASC 840 and record the following journal entry:

Lease receivable (60 × $19.12)	$1,147.20	
Residual value of leased asset	164.53	
Asset		$1,000.00
Unearned income—lease receivable		247.20
Unearned income—residual		64.53

Note: For financial reporting purposes, ASC 840 requires that the lease receivable and residual value of the leased asset be combined and reported as the gross investment in the lease. In addition, the unearned income amounts must also be combined.

Using the lease receivable and the asset as collateral, the lessor enters into a nonrecourse financing arrangement with a financial institution for $900.00 (the present value of the $19.12 monthly lease payment for 60 months discounted at 10%) at a rate of 10%. The lessor would record the following journal entry to reflect the liability for the nonrecourse debt:

Cash	$900	
Nonrecourse debt		$900

The lessor then sells the asset subject to the lease and the nonrecourse debt to a group of equity partners and leases the asset back for five years at $19.12 a month (for simplicity, assume that the lease, the nonrecourse financing, and the sale to the equity partners occur at the same time). The lessor is now the lessee-sublessor and remains the obligor with the financial institution that financed the nonrecourse debt. In return for the asset, the lessor receives the following:

1. Cash of $50, representing the sale of 50% of the residual value of the leased asset
2. An additional $103.66 in cash, representing the transfer of tax benefits
3. A note receivable for $900.00 bearing interest at 10% with 60 monthly payments of $19.12 (60 payments at $19.12 represent a gross note of $1,147.20 and unearned income of $247.20)

4. The right to receive a fee of $82.27 for remarketing the asset at the end of the initial lease term (the present value of an $82.27 payment 60 months in the future discounted at 10% equals $50.00)
5. In addition, the lessor retains a 50% interest in the proceeds of the residual value of the leased asset at the end of the lease term.

LEASES

IMPORTANT NOTICE FOR 2022

As Wolters Kluwer's 2022 *GAAP Guide* goes to press, the FASB has outstanding an Exposure Draft of an Accounting Standards Update (ASU), *Leases*, that may have an important impact on the preparation of financial statements in the future. The proposed ASU is in response to stakeholders' concerns about certain aspects of the current guidance in ASC 842. Specifically, the proposed guidance would address stakeholders' concerns regarding having to recognize an immediate loss on sales-type leases with variable lease payments that do not depend on a reference index or rate (lessor only) by amending the lease classification requirements. Lessors would be required to classify and account for such leases as operating leases, which would remove the need to immediately recognize a selling profit or loss.

The proposed guidance would also address stakeholders' concerns regarding inconsistencies between the guidance in ASC 842 and IFRS 16 as it relates to remeasuring the lease liability when a change in a reference index or rate causes a change in subsequent lease payments. The proposed ASU would provide an entity with the option to remeasure their lease liability in these cases. An entity electing the option to remeasure lease liabilities due to changes in a reference index or rate would be required to disclose that fact.

Finally, the proposed guidance would address stakeholders' concerns regarding the current requirement to apply modification accounting for the remaining lease components if one or more separate lease components are terminated early. The proposed ASU would exempt entities from applying modification accounting to the remaining lease components in such a lease if the early termination does not economically affect the remaining lease components.

The effective date for this proposed ASU has not been determined.

DISCOUNT RATE FOR LESSEES THAT ARE NOT PUBLIC BUSINESS ENTITIES

IMPORTANT NOTICE FOR 2022

As Wolters Kluwer's 2022 *GAAP Guide* goes to press, the FASB has outstanding an Exposure Draft of an Accounting Standards Update (ASU), *Leases—Discount Rate for Lessees That Are Not Public Business Entities*, that may have an important impact on the preparation of financial statements in the future. The current guidance in ASC 842 provides lessees that are not a public business entity with a practical expedient to elect, as an accounting policy, to use a risk-free rate as the discount rate for all leases. The proposed guidance in this exposure draft would allow those lessees to make the election to use the risk-free rate practical expedient by class of underlying asset rather than on an entity-wide level. An entity that elects the risk-free rate expedient would be required to disclose for which asset classes it has elected to apply a risk-free rate.

The effective date for this proposed ASU will differ depending on whether or not an entity has already adopted ASC 842. For entities that have not yet adopted ASC 842 as of the date a final ASU is issued, the proposed guidance would be effective at the same time they adopt ASC 842. For entities that have adopted ASC 842 as of the date a final ASU is issued, the proposed guidance would be effective for fiscal years beginning after December 15, 2021, and interim periods within fiscal years beginning after December 15, 2022. Earlier application would be permitted.

PART II: INTERPRETIVE GUIDANCE

ASC 840-10: OVERALL

ASC 840-10-05-7 through 05-8, 25-12 through 25-13, 25-14; ASC 840-40-15-2, 25-13; ASC 958-840-55-4; ASC 450-20-60-16; ASC 460-10-60-23 Implementation Issues in Accounting for Lease Transactions

BACKGROUND

The following guidance addresses questions related to a lessee's balance sheet classification of leases that (1) require a lessee to accept responsibility for certain risks that normally are the responsibility of the property's legal owner, such as environmental contamination that occurred before the inception of the lease, or (2) include default covenants for nonperformance—for example, if a lessee does not maintain certain financial ratios. Under such provisions, lessor may have the right to require a lessee to acquire the property or to pay the lessor.

Questions 1 and 2 apply to all leasing transactions.

PRACTICE NOTE: Under the provisions of ASC 460, a guarantor is required to recognize a liability for an obligation assumed by issuing a guarantee. Guidance also is provided on appropriate disclosures that should be made by a guarantor. If a guarantee or indemnification included in an *operating lease* meets any of the characteristics in ASC 460-10-15-4, a lessee may be required to recognize a liability at the inception of a lease. The disclosure requirement in ASC 450 also would apply to the guarantee. Capital leases accounted for under the guidance in ASC 840 are excluded from the scope of that guidance.

Under the guidance in ASC 810-10 consolidation of variable interest entities by an entity that absorbs a majority of a variable interest entity's expected losses or has the right to receive a greater part of the variable interest entity's expected residual returns or both is required.

Lessee's Responsibility for Environmental Risk

BACKGROUND

Under the provisions of a certain leases, a lessee may be required to indemnify the lessor or the lessor's lender against loss or damage from the lessee's environmental contamination during the term of the lease and for environmental contamination that occurred before the inception of the lease. Alternatively, a lessee may be required to acquire the property.

ACCOUNTING ISSUE

How should a lease with such provisions be classified in a lessee's balance sheet?

ACCOUNTING GUIDANCE

- Lease provisions requiring indemnification for a lessee's environmental contamination during the term of the lease do *not* affect a lessee's balance sheet classification of the lease.
- If a lessee is required under the terms of a lease to indemnify the lessor or its lender for environmental contamination that existed before the lease term, the lessee should at the inception of the lease term evaluate the likelihood of a loss (without recoveries from third parties) based on enacted environmental laws and existing regulations and policies and whether the lessee may be considered the owner of the property.
  - — If the likelihood of a loss is remote, the lease's classification would be unaffected;
  - — If the likelihood of a loss is at least reasonably possible the lessee should account for the lease in accordance with the sale-leaseback provisions under the guidance in ASC 840-40 as if the lessee had purchased, sold, and leased back the property.

DISCUSSION

If a lessee agrees to pay for remediation of environmental contamination that occurred before the term of a lease, the lessee is taking on a risk of ownership of a property, which is beyond the responsibility of a lessee. The lessee reflects that additional risk by classifying the lease as a capital rather than as an operating lease.

Non-Performance-Related Default Covenants

BACKGROUND

If a lease contains default provisions unrelated to the lessee's use of the property, such as financial covenants that require the lessee to maintain certain financial ratios, the lessee may be required to make a payment to the lessor or acquire the property to remedy a default.

ACCOUNTING ISSUE

How should a lessee classify a lease containing a default provision that is unrelated to the lessee's performance on the lease?

ACCOUNTING GUIDANCE

1. The classification of a lease containing a default provision is unaffected if it meets *all* the following conditions:
   a. The default covenant is customary in financing arrangements.
   b. The occurrence of default can be determined objectively (acceleration clauses would not meet this condition).

c. Default would be determined based on specific criteria that apply only to the lessee and its operations.

d. Based on the facts and circumstances existing at the inception of the lease, it is reasonable to assume that a default will not occur.

Recent trends in a lessee's operations should be considered in applying condition (d) above. If one of the above conditions is absent, a lessee should include the maximum required payment under the default covenant in the amount of minimum lease payments when applying the guidance in ASC 840-10-25-1(d).

2. A lease with a default provision that is part of a sale-leaseback transaction and thus covered by the provisions of ASC 840-40 should be accounted for by the deposit method or as a financing transaction based on the guidance in ASC 360, regardless of whether all the conditions in (1) above are met. This is so because a default remedy that allows a buyer-lessor to require a seller-lessee to acquire the property violates the continuing involvement criteria in ASC 840-40. That default remedy is equivalent to a purchase option under which the seller-lessee can compel the buyer-lessor to sell back the property, for example, by missing scheduled lease payments to the lessor.

ASC 840-10-05-9A through 05-9C, 25-39A through 25-39B, 35-9A Accounting by Lessees for Maintenance Deposits under Lease Agreements

BACKGROUND

Under the terms of certain agreements for leased *equipment,* a lessee is required to repair and maintain the leased asset during the lease term. To protect a lessor if a lessee does *not* properly maintain the leased equipment, some lease agreements include a requirement that the lessee give the lessor a deposit, which is commonly referred to as a "maintenance reserve" or "supplemental rent." Usually, the deposit is calculated based on a performance measure, such as the number of hours a leased asset has been used. Under the terms of the lease, the lessor must use the deposit to reimburse the lessee, up to the amount of the deposit, for costs incurred for maintenance activities that the lessee is contractually obligated to perform under the lease agreement.

If at the end of the lease term of some agreements, the deposit exceeds the total cumulative cost of maintaining the equipment over the lease term, the lessor is required to return the remainder of the deposit to the lessee. Lessees generally account for such refundable maintenance deposits as deposits. However, under the terms of other lease agreements, at the end of the lease term, the lessor is permitted to retain an excess of a deposit, if any, over the lessee's maintenance expenditures if the lessee has not performed the required maintenance activities. There is diversity in practice in the way that lessees account for the portion of a deposit that has *not* been refunded.

Under some contracts, the lessee is required to return the leased asset in a certain condition at the end of the lease term. In that case, a lessee should consult other generally accepted accounting principles (GAAP) to determine when and whether to recognize a liability related to that requirement.

ACCOUNTING ISSUE

How should lessees account for maintenance deposits?

ACCOUNTING GUIDANCE

Scope

The following guidance addresses a lessee's accounting for a maintenance deposit under an arrangement providing that the remainder of the deposit will be refunded only if the lessee has performed specified maintenance activities. The guidance does *not* apply to a lessee's payments to a lessor that are *not* substantively and contractually related to the maintenance of a leased asset.

Recognition

At the inception of a lease, a lessee that determines that it is *less than probable* (as defined in paragraph 25 of CON-6 (Elements of Financial Statements—a Replacement of FASB Concepts Statement No. 3 (incorporating an amendment of FASB Concepts Statement No. 2)) (not in the Codification) that a lessor will return to a lessee the total amount of payments as a reimbursement of maintenance activities, the lessee should consider that fact in determining the portion of each payment that is not accounted for under the scope of this guidance. Lessees should account for maintenance deposits under the scope of this guidance as deposit assets. After the inception of a lease agreement, a lessee should continue to evaluate the probability that the lessor will return the deposit to the lessee through reimbursements for the costs of maintenance activities incurred by the lessee. A lessee should recognize a deposit as additional expense if it is determined that it is less than probable that the lessor will return the deposit. A lessee should expense or capitalize the cost of maintenance activities when the underlying maintenance is performed in accordance with its accounting policy for maintenance activities.

ASC 840-10-15-3 through 15-6, 15-10 through 15-20, 35-2 through 35-3, 55-26, 55-30 through 55-37; ASC 840-20-25-9, 25-22, 40-2, 40-6; ASC 840-30-25-4, 30-5, 40-2 through 40-3, 40-6; ASC 440-10-25-1, 25-3; ASC 815-10-15-79 Determining Whether an Arrangement Is a Lease

BACKGROUND

Determining whether an arrangement includes a lease that should be accounted for under the guidance in ASC 840 should be based on the substance of an arrangement. Under the definition of a lease in the ASC Glossary, a lease is an agreement under which the *right to use* property, plant, or equipment transfers from one party to another, usually for a stated period of time. The following guidance should be used to determine whether an arrangement includes a lease under the guidance in ASC 840.

ACCOUNTING ISSUE

How should an entity determine whether an arrangement is a lease that should be accounted for under the guidance in ASC 840?

ACCOUNTING GUIDANCE

Application Guidance

The determination as to whether or not an arrangement includes a lease, which is accounted for under the guidance in ASC 840, should be made based on the facts and circumstances in accordance with the following application guidance at the time an entity enters into an arrangement:

1. An arrangement transfers the *right to use* property, plant, or equipment if a purchaser/lessee has the right to control how the property, plant, or equipment is used. A right to use has been transferred if a purchaser/lessee is able to, or has the right to do, any one of the following:
    a. Operate the property, plant, or equipment or instruct others to do so at will during the time the purchaser/lessee obtains and controls more than a minor amount of the property, plant, or equipment's output or other function,
    b. Control physical access and obtain and control more than a minor amount of the property, plant, or equipment's output or other function, or
    c. Take the output produced or other function of the property, plant, or equipment during the term of the arrangement and if, based on the facts or circumstances, it is a remote possibility that other parties will take more than a minor amount of the output or other function of the property, plant, or equipment. The price paid per unit of output does not equal the current market price per unit at the time the output is delivered.
2. Under the guidance in ASC 840, the phrase *property, plant, and equipment* refers only to land and *depreciable* assets. Therefore, any inventory, as well as minerals, precious metals, or other natural resources—all of which are *not* depreciable assets—cannot be subject to a lease under the definition of a lease. Similarly, intangible assets, such as motion picture film licensing rights and rights to minerals, precious metals, or other resources, which are amortized or depleted but not depreciated, would *not* qualify for lease accounting.
3. Although an arrangement may explicitly refer to a transfer of specific property, plant, or equipment, it contains a lease only if the transferred property, plant, or equipment—*not* other available property, plant, or equipment—is used to fulfill the purpose of the arrangement.
4. An arrangement qualifies as a lease even if the property, plant, or equipment is *not* explicitly identified, if the owner/seller owns or leases only one asset with which the obligation can be fulfilled and it is not possible for the owner/seller to fulfill its obligation with alternative property, plant, or equipment.
5. Lease accounting is permitted (*a*) if an owner/seller has the right to substitute other property, plant, or equipment because the owner/seller has a warranty obligation under the arrangement, (*b*) until a substitution occurs, if an

owner/seller has an obligation or the ability, which may be contingent, to substitute other property, plant, or equipment for any reason on or after a specified date.

Reevaluating an Arrangement

1. The judgment that an arrangement is a lease, which was made when entering into the arrangement, should be reevaluated only under the following circumstances:
   a. *Contractual terms change* The arrangement should be reevaluated under the application guidance in this Issue unless a change is due to a renewal or extension of the arrangement.
   b. *A renewal option or an extension of the arrangement is exercised* Only the renewal or extension period of an arrangement should be reevaluated if the original terms of an arrangement are not modified. The accounting for the remaining term of the arrangement should not be modified. Exercising a renewal option included in the *lease term*, as defined in the ASC Glossary, is *not* considered a renewal that requires a reevaluation of a lease.
   c. *Dependence on specific property, plant, or equipment exists* An arrangement should be reevaluated to determine whether it contains a lease *prospectively* if there is a change in the position as to whether or not fulfillment depends on specified property, plant, or equipment.
   d. *There is a physical change of specific property, plant, or equipment* An arrangement should be reevaluated to determine whether it includes a lease prospectively if a physical change in specified property, plant, or equipment occurs. For example, replacement of a machine specified in the original arrangement with one that has a higher or lower production capacity would require a reevaluation. However, a physical change of property, plant, or equipment that does not affect the productivity of the property, plant, or equipment specified in the original arrangement does not require such a reevaluation.
2. The following guidance should be applied to account for an arrangement if its classification, or that of a portion of the arrangement, changes, because a modification or another change in the arrangement discussed previously causes the arrangement to be classified as a lease or ends its classification as a lease:
   a. *A supply arrangement becomes an operating lease for a Purchaser/Lessee* A recognized asset for a purchase contract, such as a prepaid asset or a derivative instrument, should be considered part of minimum lease payments and recognized initially as prepaid rent. A recognized liability for a purchase contract, such as a payable or a derivative, should be considered a reduction of minimum lease payments and recognized initially as a lease payable.
   b. *A supply arrangement becomes an operating lease for a Seller/Lessor* A recognized liability for a sales contract, such as deferred revenue or a derivative instrument, should be part of minimum lease payments and recognized initially as deferred rent. A recognized asset, if any, for a sales contract, such as a receivable or a derivative instrument, should be considered a *reduction* of minimum lease payments and recognized initially as a lease receivable if the asset can be recovered from future receipts.
   c. *A supply arrangement is no longer an operating lease but becomes a capital lease for a Purchaser/Lessee* A recognized asset or liability for the purchase contract, such as a prepaid asset, a payable, or a derivative instrument should be included in the basis of the leased asset or lease obligation.
   d. *A supply arrangement becomes a sales-type lease for a Seller/Lessor* If the criteria for treatment as a sale in ASC 840-10-25-42 are met, (i) the property, plant, or equipment should be derecognized, and (ii) an asset or liability for a supply arrangement, if any, should be recognized in earnings as an adjustment of minimum lease payments. Otherwise, (i) a recognized asset or liability for the supply arrangement, if any, should be considered as a reduction of, or part of, minimum lease payments, and (ii) a lease should be recognized in accordance with the guidance in ASC 840.
   e. *A supply arrangement is no longer an operating lease for a Purchaser/Lessee* Previously recognized prepaid rent or rent payable, if any, should be recognized initially as an asset or a liability related to the purchase contract.
   f. *A supply arrangement is no longer an operating lease for a Seller/Lessor* Previously recognized deferred rent or rent receivable, if any, should be recognized initially as a liability or an asset related to the sales contract, subject to a recoverability test.
   g. *A supply arrangement is no longer a capital lease for a Purchaser/Lessee,* Leased property, plant, or equipment that is real estate, including integral equipment, should be derecognized based on the guidance in ASC 360-20. Leased

property, plant, or equipment, and the related lease obligation, other than real estate, including integral equipment, also should be derecognized. Before a sale is recognized, an asset subject to a capital lease should be evaluated for impairment under the guidance in ASC 360-10 The terms of the changes in the arrangement that cause a reevaluation of the lease arrangement must be considered in that evaluation. After an asset is reduced for impairment, if any, the difference between the capital lease asset and the obligation, if any, is recognized initially as an asset or a liability associated with the supply arrangement.

h. *A direct-financing, or sales-type lease becomes a supply arrangement for a Seller/Lessor* The remaining net investment should be removed from the accounts with the leased asset being recognized at the lower of its (1) original cost, (2) current fair value, or (3) current carrying amount. The net adjustment should be charged to income in the period in which the change is made. The lessor should account for a new lease entered into thereafter as an operating lease.

Multiple-Element Arrangements That Include a Lease

IMPORTANT NOTICE: The guidance in ASC 840-10-15-19(b), which is discussed below, will be amended to replace the term "fair value" with "standalone selling price" in accordance the guidance in ASC 606-10-15-4 and ASC 606-10-32-28 through 32-41 when the guidance in ASU 2014-09, *Revenue from Contracts with Costumers*, which will reside in ASC 606 (Revenue from Contracts with Customers), becomes effective for public entities in annual reporting periods that begin after December 15, 2016, and interim periods within those annual periods and in annual reporting periods that begin after December 15, 2017, for nonpublic entities.

A purchaser and a supplier to a lease element of an arrangement should apply the classification, recognition, measurement, and disclosure requirements of ASC 840 if an arrangement includes a lease and related executory costs as well as other nonlease elements. Elements of an arrangement not under the scope of ASC 840 should be accounted for in accordance with other applicable GAAP. When the guidance in ASC 840 is applied, payments and other consideration required under an arrangement should be separated at the inception of an arrangement or when it is reevaluated into (*a*) payments for the lease, including related executory costs and profits, and (*b*) payments for other services based on their relative fair value in accordance with the guidance in ASC 605-25-15-3A(b).

ASC 840-10-15-20; ASC 815-10-15-80 through 15-81; ASC 460-10-60-20 The Impact of the Requirements of ASC 815 on Residual Value Guarantees in Connection with a Lease

BACKGROUND

The following guidance is the result of an attempt to resolve a scope overlap between the guidance ASC 815, *Derivatives and Hedging*, and ASC 840, *Leases*, related to the accounting for residual value guarantees (*a*) for transactions accounted for under the guidance in ASC 840, (*b*) that meet the definition of a derivative in ASC 815, and (*c*) that are either not explicitly excluded from the scope of ASC 815 or do not meet one of its scope exceptions. Although the guidance in ASC 815 did not amend the guidance in ASC 840, ASC 815 does not explicitly exclude residual value guarantees included in lease transactions, except as provided in ASC 815-10-15. The scope overlap does not apply, however, to third-party guarantors' accounting for obligations related to residual guarantees or to contracts not accounted for under the scope of the guidance in ASC 840.

ACCOUNTING ISSUES

1. How should the scope overlap between ASC 840 and ASC 815 related to residual value guarantees be resolved?
2. Should third-party residual value guarantors account for residual value guarantees under the requirements in ASC 815?

ACCOUNTING GUIDANCE

1. Residual value guarantees subject to the guidance in ASC 840 are not subject to the guidance in ASC 815-10.
2. Third-party residual value guarantors should consider the guidance in ASC 815-10 for *all* residual value guarantees provided to determine whether those guarantees are derivatives and whether they qualify for one of the scope exceptions in ASC 815.

PRACTICE POINTER: Under the provisions of ASC 460 (Guarantees), a guarantor is required to recognize a liability for an obligation assumed by issuing a guarantee. ASC 460 also provides guidance on appropriate disclosures that should be made by a guarantor. However, residual value guarantees related to capital leases accounted for under the guidance in ASC 840 are excluded from the scope of ASC 460. In addition, residual value guarantees accounted for as derivative instruments under the guidance in ASC 815 also are exempted from the initial measurement and recognition requirements in ASC 460 and are only subject to the disclosure requirements in ASC 460. However, the initial recognition, initial measurement, and disclosure requirements in ASC 460 would apply to the guarantees discussed under the accounting guidance above.

ASC 840-10-25-3 Fiscal Funding Clauses in Lease Agreements

BACKGROUND

Fiscal funding clauses are frequently found in lease agreements in which the lessee is a governmental entity. The clause generally provides for the lease to be cancelable if the legislature or other funding authority does not appropriate the funds necessary for the governmental unit to fulfill its obligations under the lease agreement.

ACCOUNTING GUIDANCE

Question: What effect, if any, does the existence of a fiscal funding clause in a lease agreement have on the classification of a lease under the guidance in ASC 840?

Answer: The existence of a fiscal funding clause in a lease agreement requires making an assessment of the likelihood that the lease will be canceled by exercising the agreement's fiscal funding clause. If the likelihood that the agreement will be exercised is remote, the lease should be considered to be noncancelable. If the probability is considered other than remote, the lease is considered cancelable and, therefore, is classified as an operating lease.

PRACTICE POINTER: The term *remote* is used in this guidance in the same manner as in ASC 450 (i.e., the chance of the future event or events occurring is slight).

ASC 840-10-25-46, 25-48 through 25-50 Lessors' Evaluation of Whether Leases of Certain Integral Equipment Meet the Ownership Transfer Requirements of ASC 840

IMPORTANT NOTICE: The guidance in ASC 840-10-25-46, which is discussed below, will be amended to change the reference to ASC 360-20 to ASC 978-10-15-7, when the guidance in ASU 2014-09, *Revenue from Contracts with Costumers*, which will reside in ASC 606 (Revenue from Contracts with Customers), becomes effective for public business entities in annual reporting periods that begin after December 15, 2017, and interim periods within those annual periods and in annual reporting periods that begin after December 15, 2018, for nonpublic entities.

BACKGROUND

The guidance in ASC 360-20-15-2 through 15-4, 15-10, 55-4 through 55-5 provides that lease transactions involving integral equipment, as defined under that guidance, are considered to be leases of real estate. Under the guidance in ASC 840-10-25-1, classification as a sales type lease requires that *ownership* of the property be transferred to the lessee by the end of the lease term.

Article 2 of the Uniform Commercial Code (UCC) provides guidelines to be used in determining whether title to personal property has passed. However, unlike transfers of real property, which are recorded in accordance with state law as evidence that ownership has been transferred, there is no system under which title to personal property is recorded. Consequently, questions have been raised about how to provide evidence of a transfer of ownership in integral equipment (without a transfer of the real property) to a lessee by the end of the lease term.

ACCOUNTING ISSUES

- Should integral equipment under a lease be evaluated as real estate in accordance with the guidance in ASC 840?
- If so, how should the requirement in ASC 840-10-25-1(a) regarding the transfer of ownership be evaluated if there is no statutory registration system for leased integral equipment?

ACCOUNTING GUIDANCE

- Equipment subject to a lease that is attached to real property (integral equipment) should be evaluated as real estate using the guidance in ASC 840.
- Without the existence of a statutory system of title registration to integral equipment, the requirement in ASC 840-10-25-1(a) that ownership to equipment be transferred to a lessee by the end of the lease term is met if, under the lease agreement, the lessor is required to deliver the necessary documents (including a bill of sale, if applicable) that will release the integral equipment from the lease and will transfer ownership of the equipment to the lessee. The requirement in ASC 840-10-25-1(a) would also be met if an agreement requires a nominal payment on the transfer of ownership. However, the requirement in ASC 840-10-25-1(a) would *not* be met if a lease agreement states that a transfer of ownership to a lessee would not occur if the lessee chooses not to pay the specified fee, regardless of the amount, because that requirement would be considered a *purchase option*.

ASC 840-10-25-6; ASC 840-20-25-8, 25-12 through 25-13, 30-1, 35-1; ASC 840-40-55-42 through 55-47; ASC 958-810-25-9, 55-7 through 55-16; ASC 958-840-55-2 through 55-3; ASC 460-10-60-24 Implementation Issues in Accounting for Leasing Transactions

Lessee Payments Made before the Beginning of the Lease Term

BACKGROUND

Lessees may sometimes be required to make payments (known as construction period lease payments) to the lessor before construction is completed and the lease term has begun in build-to-suit transactions.

ACCOUNTING ISSUES

1. Should construction period lease payments be included in the minimum lease payments when applying the 90% of fair value recovery test specified in ASC 840-10-25-1?
2. How should a lessee account for such payments if the lease is classified as an operating lease?

ACCOUNTING GUIDANCE

1. Payments made before the lease term begins should be considered to be part of the minimum lease payments, and they should be included in the 90% test at their future value at the beginning of the lease term. The interest rate used to compute the future value of payments to be made before the beginning of the lease term should be the same as that used to discount lease payments to be made during the lease term.
2. If a lease is classified as an operating lease, lease payments made before the lease term begins should be accounted for as prepaid rent and included in total rent costs, which generally should be allocated on a straight-line basis over the term of the lease, in accordance with the guidance in ASC 840-20-25-3 through 25-7, 55-1 through 55-3; ASC 840-10-55-45 through 55-46; ASC 840-30-55-14, 55-19 through 55-20; ASC 840-40-55-17 through 55-21.

Fees Paid to an SPE's Owners

BACKGROUND

Under some lease agreements, a lessee is required to pay an SPE's owner certain fees, which are referred to as structuring or administrative fees, for arranging the lease.

ACCOUNTING ISSUE

How should a lessee and an SPE account for structuring or administrative fees paid to the SPE's owner of record?

ACCOUNTING GUIDANCE

A lessee should include such fees in the minimum lease payments—but not in the fair value of the property—for the purpose of applying the 90% test in paragraph ASC 840-10-25-1.

Costs Incurred by Lessees before Entering into a Lease

BACKGROUND

In build-to-suit lease transactions, a lessee sometimes incurs certain development costs before entering into a lease with a developer-lessor.

The costs may be soft costs, such as architectural fees and zoning fees, or hard costs, such as site preparation and construction costs.

ACCOUNTING ISSUE

What kinds of costs (and in what amount) can a lessee incur before entering a lease agreement without being considered the owner of the property and therefore subject to the requirements of ASC 840-40 for sale-leaseback transactions?

ACCOUNTING GUIDANCE

A lessee that begins construction activities should recognize construction in progress as an asset and account for it under the guidance in ASC 840-40, as discussed below. Construction activities are deemed to have begun if any of the following activities have occurred:

- The lessee has begun construction (broken ground).
- The lessee has incurred hard costs, whether those costs are insignificant or not to the fair value of the property to be constructed.
- The lessee has incurred soft costs that amount to more than 10% of the expected fair value of the leased property. In a build-to-suit lease, soft costs would include the fair value of the lessee's option to acquire real property that is transferred to the securitization entity. Off-balance-sheet purchase commitments at market would not be included, however.

DISCUSSION

A lessee that is involved in more than an insignificant aspect of the construction process and has incurred hard costs or significant soft costs on a project assumes the risks of ownership.

Accounting under the Guidance in ASC 840-40 for Construction-in-Process Transferred to a Lessor

BACKGROUND

A lessee begins construction activities, as discussed above, and subsequently transfers the property to a lessor in a transaction deemed to be within the scope of ASC 840-40-05-9 through 05-10, 15-4, 15-9 through 15-10, 25-9 through 25-14, 25-17, 50-1 through 50-2, 55-36, 55-49 through 55-77; ASC 980-840-25-1 through 25-3, 35-1 through 35-2.

ACCOUNTING ISSUE

How should the lessee apply the provisions of ASC 840-40 to the transaction?

ACCOUNTING GUIDANCE

The transaction would be evaluated as a sale-leaseback under the provisions of ASC 840-40, because the lessee is considered the owner of the project. The lessee should account for the property as follows:

- Recognize a sale and profit or loss if the transaction qualifies as a sale under the guidance in ASC 360 and 840-40.
- Continue reporting construction-in-progress as an asset and recognize proceeds received from the lessor as a liability; if the transaction does *not* qualify for sale-leaseback accounting, the lessee would:
  - — Report additional amounts spent by the lessor on construction as construction-in-progress and as a liability to the lessor.
  - — Depreciate the property after the property is placed in service and account for the lease payments as debt service on the liability.

Interest-only Payments

BACKGROUND

Rental payments on real estate leases that involve a securitization entity often consist of the total interest on the securitization entity's debt plus a return on the securitization entity's equity. The lessee also frequently guarantees that the value of the property will be a specified amount at the end of the lease term. The lease is classified as an operating lease, because the present value of the minimum lease payments, including the maximum deficiency under the residual value guarantee that the lessee is required to pay, does not meet the 90% test under the guidance in ASC 840-10-25-1.

ACCOUNTING ISSUE

How should a lessee account for an interest-only lease that otherwise qualifies as an operating lease?

ACCOUNTING GUIDANCE

In accordance with the guidance in ASC 460-10-30-2(b), a guarantor-lessee should recognize the fair value of a residual value guarantee at the inception of a lease even though the likelihood that a deficiency will occur is *not* probable at that time. A lessee should recognize rent expense on a straight-line basis, in accordance with the guidance in ASC 840-20-25-1. Payments related to a deficiency would not be included in that calculation until it becomes probable that the value of the property at the end of the lease term will be less than the guaranteed amount (even though the maximum deficiency under the residual value guarantee is included in minimum lease payments for the 90% test). When a deficiency becomes probable, the lessee should accrue the amount of the expected deficiency and recognize it on a straight-line basis over the remainder of the lease term. The deficiency must be accrued even if the lessee expects to exercise a purchase or renewal option at the end of the lease term.

ASC 840-10-25-10 through 25-11, 25-53, 50-3; ASC 460-10-55-23A Tax Indemnifications in Lease Agreements

BACKGROUND

Some lessors include tax indemnification clauses in lease agreements that would require a lessee to indemnify the lessor, on an after-tax basis, for tax benefits that may be lost as a result of changes in tax laws.

ACCOUNTING ISSUE

Should lessors and lessees account for tax indemnification payments as (1) contingent rent, (2) replacement of tax benefits, (3) ratably as income/expense, or (4) a revision of the lease?

ACCOUNTING GUIDANCE

Although tax indemnification payments may appear to meet the definition of a contingent rental in ASC 840, they are not the type of payments normally expected to occur under continuing rent provisions. Because they can be closely associated with specific aspects of the tax law, such payments should be accounted for in a manner that recognizes that association. The transaction should not affect the lease's original classification.

Lessors should recognize tax indemnification payments related to tax effects, other than the investment tax credit, in income based on a lease's classification as follows:

a. Capital lease—Adjust the lessor's investment.

b. Operating lease—Recognize ratably over the lease term.

Under the guidance in ASC 460-10-25-4, a lessee (guarantor) should recognize a liability at the inception of a lease for a tax indemnification to a lessor. The liability should be measured in accordance with the guidance in ASC 460-10-30-2 at the fair value of the lessee's obligation under the tax indemnification agreement.

Lessees should make the disclosures about guarantees required under the guidance in ASC 460-10-50-4.

DISCUSSION

The decision to account for tax indemnification payments as a replacement of tax benefits is based on the view that this approach is consistent with the economics of the transaction and allows the parties to continue accounting for a lease without revising the agreement.

ASC 840-10-25-21 through 25-22; ASC 460-10-60-19 Allocation of Residual Value or First-Loss Guarantee to Minimum Lease Payments in Leases Involving Land and Building(s)

BACKGROUND

Real estate leases for land and buildings often include a clause guaranteeing the property's residual value (guarantee) that transfers some risks to a lessee and ensures that a lessor will receive an appropriate return of and on the investment in the property. Under the guidance in ASC 840-10-55-15, a guarantee must be included in minimum lease payments in determining whether to classify a lease as an operating or as a capital lease.

A lease should be classified as a capital lease if any of the following criteria in ASC 840-10-25-1 are met:

1. Ownership of the property is transferred to the lessee by the end of the lease term.
2. The lease contains a bargain purchase option.

3. The lease term is 75% or more of the estimated economic life of the leased property.
4. The present value of minimum lease payments (as defined) is 90% or more of the estimated fair value of the leased property.

ASC 840 distinguishes between real estate leases involving only land and those that involve land and buildings for the purpose of lease classification. Under the guidance in ASC 840-10-25-55 through 55-59, which applies to leases of land only, a lease is classified as a capital lease if it meets one of the above criteria. Thus, a guarantee, which is a component of minimum lease payments and is considered in the calculation in ASC 840-10-25-1(d), is excluded from the calculation in determining the lease classification of land.

Under the provisions of ASC 840-10-25-38, a lease involving land and buildings should be classified and accounted for as a capital lease if either criterion (*a*) or criterion (*b*) is met. If neither of those criteria is met, and the fair value of the land is less than 25% of the total value of the leased property at inception of the lease, ASC 840-10-25-38(b)(1) provides that the land and building be considered as a unit and treated essentially the same as a building.

However, if the fair value of the land is greater than 25% of the total fair value of the property at inception of the lease, paragraph ASC 840-10-25-38(b)(2) requires that the land and building be evaluated *separately* in applying the guidance in ASC 840-10-25-1(c) to determine whether to classify the building as an operating or as a capital lease. Because a guarantee is not considered in the classification of land only, as discussed above, a literal interpretation of paragraph ASC 840-10-25-38(b)(2) would include a guarantee solely in minimum lease payments attributed to the building in this separate evaluation.

Some have questioned that interpretation of the treatment of a guarantee in an economic environment in which land may no longer retain its value. A literal interpretation of paragraph ASC 840-10-25-38(b)(2) often provides anomalous results. For example, if a guarantee equals or exceeds a building's fair value, a separate evaluation of the land and building may indicate that the lessee should classify the lease on the building as a capital lease; an evaluation of the land and building as a unit would result in an operating lease classification. Consequently, alternative methods have been used in practice.

ACCOUNTING ISSUE

How should a residual value guarantee be treated when applying the criterion in ASC 840-10-25-1(d) to a real estate lease involving land and a building if the fair value of the land is 25% or more of the total fair value of the leased property?

ACCOUNTING GUIDANCE

A literal interpretation of ASC 840-10-25-38(b)(2) should be followed. Thus, the lessee and the lessor should determine the amount of annual minimum lease payments to be attributed to the portion of the lease related to the land by multiplying the fair value of the land by the lessee's incremental borrowing rate. The remaining minimum lease payments, including the full amount of the guarantee, should be attributed to the portion of the lease related to the building.

PRACTICE NOTE: The embedded guarantee discussed in this Issue is not a derivative under the guidance in ASC 815.

DISCUSSION

Under the model followed in ASC 840, the value of land does not depreciate and therefore does not require a guarantee.

ASC 840-10-25-35, 40-1, 50-5; ASC 450-20-60-15; ASC 450-30-60-5 Accounting for Contingent Rent

BACKGROUND

Under some lease agreements, a lessee may be required to pay the lessor a contingent amount in addition to a fixed monthly rental payment. Contingent rental payments are usually related to the lessee's use of the property and may be based on machine hours of use or on sales volume during the lease term. For example, a manufacturer may be required to pay contingent rent of $1 per machine hour over 600,000 machine hours per year. A *contingent rental* is defined in the ASC Glossary as "[t]he increases or decreases in lease payments that result from changes occurring after lease inception in the factors (other than the passage of time) on which lease payments are based . . . ."

Some lessors and lessees were accruing amounts related to contingent rent in interim periods based on estimates of the final amount while others waited for recognition until the actual amount was determined.

ACCOUNTING ISSUES

1. How should a *lessor* account in interim periods for contingent rental revenue that is based on future specified targets to be met by the lessee during the lessor's fiscal year?
2. How should a *lessee* account in interim periods for contingent rental expense that is based on future specified targets to be met during the lessee's fiscal year?

ACCOUNTING GUIDANCE

A lessee should recognize contingent rental expense in annual periods and interim periods before having reached specified targets that trigger contingent rental expense if it is *probable* that the target will be reached. If at any time thereafter it becomes probable that a specified target will *not* be reached, the lessee should reverse the expense into income.

A lessor should disclose its accounting policy for contingent rental income. If a lessor accrues contingent rental income before the lessee has achieved the specified target and achievement of the target is probable, the lessor should disclose the effect of the contingent rental income on its rental income as if the lessor's accounting policy were to defer that income until the lessee has met the specified target.

SUBSEQUENT DEVELOPMENT

The SEC staff has issued SAB-101 (Revenue Recognition in Financial Statements), which applies to the accounting by lessors. It provides that contingent rental income *accrues* when changes in the factors on which contingent lease payments are based actually occur (e.g., when a lessee's sales volume reaches an amount that triggers contingent rental income). Because it is inappropriate to recognize revenue based on a probability that an event will occur, registrants should recognize contingent rental income only in the period in which the contingency is resolved.

Illustration of a Lessee's Recognition of Contingent Rental Expense in Interim Periods

Barr Stationary and Supplies, Inc., a retail store, has a 3/31 year-end. The company has entered into a three-year lease at a new location beginning 1/1/X8. The lease specifies a monthly rental of $10,000. In addition, at the end of each year during the term of the lease, the company is obligated to pay the lessor an additional $1,000 rent for each month the company's revenues were equal to or exceeded $50,000 and if the company's total annual sales revenues during that year of the lease were at least $600,000 or more. During the past three years, Barr's monthly revenues ranged between $50,000 and $60,000.

Barr moved into its new location on 2/15/X8. Revenues during January 20X8 were $35,000. Revenues during February were $35,000. Because it was not probable that Barr would meet its monthly target in March, no contingent rental income was accrued for the last quarter of 20X8. Therefore, Barr will accrue contingent rent expense in interim periods beginning in the first quarter of fiscal 20X9.

ASC 840-10-35-6 through 35-9; ASC 805-20-35-6 Determining the Amortization Period for Leasehold Improvements Purchased After Lease Inception or Acquired in a Business Combination

BACKGROUND

A *lease term* is defined in the ASC Glossary as a predetermined period of time during which a lessee cannot cancel a lease as well as periods of time covered by bargain renewal options or periods during which renewal is reasonably assured because the lessee would incur a large penalty if the lease is not renewed. The guidance in ASC 840-30-35-1 states that assets, such as leasehold improvements, under capital leases that do *not* transfer ownership of those assets to a lessee and do not contain a bargain renewal option should be amortized over the assets' useful life or a period limited to the term of a lease, whichever is shorter. Although the amortization of leasehold improvements under capital leases was not discussed in ASC 840, practitioners analogized to the guidance in ASC 840-30-35-1 for operating leases, because as in capital leases, a lessee would not control the use of leasehold improvements if there is no assurance that the lease will be renewed.

Some practitioners questioned whether the amortization period of leasehold improvements acquired a period of time after a lease term begins can extend beyond the lease term. The guidance in ASC 840-10-35-4 provides that the term of a lease for purposes of lease classification cannot be changed unless (*a*) a lease's provisions are modified so that the lease is considered a new agreement or (*b*) a lease is extended or renewed beyond the existing lease term.

The same question was raised regarding the amortization of leasehold improvements acquired as a result of the assumption of existing lease agreements in a business combination, i.e., whether leasehold improvements acquired in a business combination can be amortized over a period that extends beyond the term determined at the inception of a lease by the acquired entity. Under the guidance in paragraphs ASC 840-10-35-5, the acquiring entity is required to retain the lease classification used by the acquired entity, unless one of the conditions in ASC 840-10-35-4 has been met.

ACCOUNTING ISSUES

1. What period should be the amortization period for leasehold improvements acquired in a business combination?
2. What period should be the amortization period for leasehold improvements in operating leases that were *not* considered at the beginning of a lease term but purchased a significant period of time after the inception of a lease?

ACCOUNTING GUIDANCE

The following guidance applies:

1. Under the guidance in ASC 805-20-35-6, leasehold improvements acquired in a business combination or an acquisition by a not-for-profit entity should be amortized over (*a*) the useful life of the assets or (*b*) a term that includes required lease periods and renewals that are considered to be "reasonably assured" at the acquisition date, according to the definition of a *lease term* in the ASC Glossary, whichever is shorter.
2. Leasehold improvements in operating leases *not* considered at or near the beginning of a lease and placed in service a significant period of time after a lease's inception should be amortized over (*a*) the assets' useful life or (*b*) a term that includes required lease periods and renewals that are considered to be "reasonably assured," under the definition of a "lease term" in the ASC Glossary, at the date the leasehold improvements are purchased, whichever is shorter.

The guidance above does not apply to preexisting leasehold improvements and should not be used to justify a reevaluation of the amortization period of preexisting leasehold improvements for additional renewal periods when new leasehold improvements that were not considered before are placed into service significantly after the beginning of a lease term.

That guidance also does not address the amortization of intangible assets that may be recognized in a business combination or an acquisition by a not-for-profit entity for a lease's favorable or unfavorable terms.

ASC 840-10-45-2 through 45-3 Applicability of ASC 840 to Current Value Financial Statements

BACKGROUND

The following guidance was provided as a result of uncertainty concerning the applicability of ASC 840 in current value financial statements.

ACCOUNTING GUIDANCE

Question: Are financial statements prepared on a current value basis subject to the provisions of ASC 840?

Answer: A lessor should classify a lease in financial statements that are prepared on a current value basis as a sales-type or direct financing lease, as appropriate, if it meets any of the criteria in ASC 840-10-25-1 and both of the criteria in ASC 840-10-25-42. In subsequent periods, the lessor should adjust its investment in the lease payments receivable on the lease based on the valuation technique used to prepare its current value financial statements.

ASC 840-10-55-12 through 55-25; ASC 460-10-55-17, 60-22; ASC 605-50-60-1 Sales with a Guaranteed Minimum Resale Amount

---

IMPORTANT NOTICE: The guidance in ASC 840-10-55-14, which is discussed below, will be amended and a new paragraph 840-10-55-14A will be added to clarify that contractually guaranteed resale values should not always be accounted for as leases. Rather, in some circumstances, the repurchase guidance in ASC 606 would apply, while in other circumstances, a guarantee of a minimum amount of proceeds when an asset is resold may require a guarantee measured under the guidance in ASC 460. Those amendments will occur when the guidance in ASU 2014-09, *Revenue from Contracts with Costumers*, which will reside in ASC 606 (Revenue from Contracts with Customers), becomes effective for public business entities in annual reporting periods that begin after December 15, 2017, and interim periods within those annual periods and in annual reporting periods that begin after December 15, 2018, for nonpublic entities.

BACKGROUND

Some manufacturers selling equipment to end users offer an incentive program, under which the manufacturer contractually guarantees the purchaser a minimum resale value on disposition of the equipment, which has an expected useful life of several years. If the equipment meets certain conditions, such as no excess wear and tear, manufacturers may guarantee the resale price in one of two ways: the equipment will be reacquired at a guaranteed price at specified times periods, or the purchaser will be paid for any difference between the proceeds received on the sale of the equipment at the guaranteed minimum resale value. The purchaser is not required, however, to resell the asset to the manufacturer under the incentive program.

Although equipment dealers may be involved in those transactions, the manufacturer is the party responsible for the resale value guarantee. Manufacturers using such programs have been recognizing revenue on the sale of the equipment to independent dealers and have considered the resale protection as a sales incentive. They have recorded the estimated cost of the incentive as a sales discount in the period in which the equipment is sold to the dealer based on historical data, such as amounts realized on resale at auction.

ACCOUNTING ISSUE

Should manufacturers recognize a sale on equipment sold to purchasers with a resale value guarantee?

ACCOUNTING GUIDANCE

- A manufacturer should not recognize a sale on a transfer of equipment if purchasers receive a resale value guarantee.
- The transaction should be accounted for as a lease, based on the guidance in ASC 840.
- The difference between the proceeds on the initial transfer of equipment to a purchaser (the selling price) and the manufacturer's residual value guarantee at the first date on which the purchaser can exercise the guarantee should be used as the amount of minimum lease payments in determining whether the lease should be classified as an operating or as a sales-type lease.

A manufacturer should account for a transfer of equipment under an operating lease as follows:

- Record a liability for the net proceeds received when the equipment is transferred.
- Reduce the liability on a pro rata basis to the guaranteed amount on the first date on which the buyer can exercise the guarantee, and credit revenue for corresponding amounts.
- Continue reducing the liability in a similar manner if a buyer decides to use the equipment beyond the first exercise date.
- Report the equipment in the balance sheet and depreciate it based on the entity's customary depreciation policy.
- Account for potential impairment of the equipment based on the guidance in ASC 360-10.
- Account for a buyer's exercise of the resale value guarantee as follows:
  - If a buyer exercises the resale value guarantee by selling the equipment to another party, (*a*) reduce the liability by any amount paid to the purchaser, (*b*) remove the undepreciated carrying amount of the equipment and any remaining liability from the balance sheet, and (*c*) include the amounts in (*a*) and (*b*) in determining income for the period in which the buyer sells the equipment.
  - If a buyer exercises the resale value guarantee by selling the equipment back to the manufacturer at the guaranteed amount, (*a*) reduce the liability by the amount paid to the purchaser and (*b*) include remaining liability, if any, in determining income for the period in which the guarantee is exercised.

PRACTICE NOTE: ASC 460, which requires a guarantor to recognize the fair value of a liability at the inception of a guarantee, does *not* affect the guidance. Because a manufacturer continues to carry the residual value of equipment (which is guaranteed) as an asset, the guarantee does *not* meet the characteristics in ASC 460-10-15-4 and is not under the scope of the guidance in ASC 460.

DISCUSSION

The FASB staff and the SEC staff both believed that the transactions discussed above should be accounted for under the guidance in ASC 840, because the manufacturer has retained the risk of reselling the equipment. In effect, the purchaser has the right to use the equipment for a predetermined period of time without the risk of resale at the end of that period.

Illustration of Revenue Recognition on Sales with a Guaranteed Minimum Resale Value

On June 1, 20X4, ABC Motor Co. enters into an agreement with Affordable Auto Rental Co. under which ABC sells ten automobiles to Affordable for $15,000 cash per automobile. ABC conditionally guarantees Affordable either (*a*) a maximum resale value (residual value guarantee) of $7,500 per automobile sold back to ABC starting on December 1, 20X5, the first exercise date (subject to wear and tear), or (*b*) the difference between the residual value guarantee and the amount Affordable receives in a sale to an unrelated party. ABC's inventory cost of each automobile is $12,000. ABC, which accounts for the transaction as an operating lease under the consensus in EITF Issue 95-1, depreciates the automobiles over an estimated economic life of five years on a straight-line basis. The company has a November 30th year-end.

Under the two scenarios below, ABC should account for the transaction initially, during the term of the lease, and when Affordable exercises the residual value guarantee as follows:

Scenario 1 On December 1, 20X5, Affordable sells nine automobiles (one was destroyed in a fire) to another party for $60,000 and exercises ABC's residual value guarantee for the nine automobiles.

Scenario 2 On December 1, 20X5, Affordable exercises the residual value guarantee by selling nine automobiles back to ABC.

At June 1, 20X4—Date of Transfer with Residual Value Guarantee

Under both scenarios, ABC recognizes the leased automobiles as an asset at its inventory cost and recognizes a liability (deferred revenue) for the net proceeds it received from Affordable on the transfer. (Net proceeds are assumed to be the cash payment received.)

Cash	$150,000	
Leased automobiles	120,000	
Deferred revenue		$150,000
Inventory—automobiles		120,000

At November 30, 20X4

Under both scenarios, ABC reduces the residual value guarantee by a proportionate amount and recognizes a corresponding amount of revenue [$75,000 × (6/18)]. Six months of depreciation is recognized for the automobiles [$120,000 × (6/60)].

Deferred revenue	$25,000	
Depreciation expense	12,000	
Revenue		$25,000
Accumulated depreciation		12,000

At November 30, 20X5

Under both scenarios, ABC reduces the residual value guarantee by a proportionate amount and recognizes a corresponding amount of revenue [$75,000 × (12/18)]. Six months of depreciation is recognized for the automobiles [$120,000 × (12/60)].

Deferred revenue	$50,000	
Depreciation expense	24,000	
Revenue		$50,000
Accumulated depreciation		24,000

Scenario 1: Exercise of the Residual Value Guarantee

On December 1, 20X5, Affordable sells nine automobiles to an unrelated party for $60,000 and exercises the residual value guarantee. ABC pays Affordable $7,500 (the difference between the guaranteed amount of $67,500 for nine automobiles and $60,000). ABC removes the remaining residual value guarantee and the undepreciated carrying amount of the asset from its balance sheet and uses those amounts to determine income for the quarter ending February 29, 20X6.

Deferred revenue	$75,000	
Accumulated depreciation	36,000	
Cost of sales—automobiles	84,000	
Sale—automobiles		$ 67,500
Leased automobiles		120,000
Cash		7,500

Scenario 2: Exercise of the Residual Value Guarantee

On December 1, 20X5, Affordable exercises the residual value guarantee by selling nine automobiles back to ABC. ABC pays Affordable $67,500 and credits revenue for the amount of the remaining residual value guarantee after the payment.

Deferred revenue	$75,000	
Cash		$67,500
Revenue		$7,500

ASC *Glossary—Incremental Borrowing Rate* Interest Rate Used in Calculating the Present Value of Minimum Lease Payments

BACKGROUND

Under the guidance in ASC 840, a lessee is required to use its incremental borrowing rate (or the lessor's implicit interest rate in certain circumstances) to calculate the minimum lease payments on a lease. The *incremental borrowing rate* is defined as the interest rate that a lessee would have incurred over a similar term to borrow funds it required to purchase a leased asset.

ACCOUNTING GUIDANCE

Question: Is a lessee permitted to use its secured borrowing rate to calculate the present value of minimum lease payments in accordance with the guidance in ASC 840?

Answer: The definition of the *incremental borrowing rate* in the ASC Glossary states that a lessee is not precluded from using a secured borrowing rate as its incremental borrowing rate "if that rate is determinable, reasonable, and consistent with the financing that would have been used in the particular circumstances."

ASC 840-20: OPERATING LEASES

ASC 840-20-25-2 Accounting for Operating Leases with Scheduled Rent Increases

BACKGROUND

The guidance in ASC 840 specifies that rent income generally should be recognized by lessors and lessees as it becomes receivable or payable. If rental payments vary from a straight-line pattern, the income or expense should be recognized on a straight-line basis, unless another systematic and rational method is more representative of the time pattern in which a benefit from the use of an asset was diminished (lessor) or received (lessee). It has been suggested that, under certain circumstances, rentals should be recognized on a basis that is neither straight-line nor representative of the time pattern of an asset's physical use. Examples of situations in which another pattern of recognition might be appropriate are (*a*) rent reductions in the early periods to induce a lessee to sign a lease and (*b*) scheduled rent increases that anticipate inflation.

ACCOUNTING GUIDANCE

Question: If an operating lease includes a scheduled rent increase, is it ever permissible for lessees and lessors to recognize rent expense or income on a basis other than straight-line?

Answer: The following guidance in ASC 840-20-25-2 differentiates between scheduled rent increases that depend on future events from contingent rentals:

- Scheduled rent increases that do *not* depend on future events. The effects of scheduled rent increases, which are included in the calculation of minimum lease payments, should be recognized on a straight-line basis over the lease term, unless some other systematic and rational allocation basis is more representative of the time pattern in which a leased property is used. Factors such as the time value of money, anticipated inflation, and expected future revenues to allocate scheduled rent increases are inappropriate, because they do not relate to the time pattern of the physical use of the leased asset. These factors may affect the amount of rent, however, if they affect the amount of contingent rentals that are not part of the minimum lease payment amount.

Contingent rentals. Increases or decreases in the amount of rental income or expense that depend on the occurrence of future events, such as changes in sales volume, inflation, or property taxes, are considered to be contingent rentals, which affect the measurement of the amount of income or expense accrued under the guidance in ASC 840-10-25-4. The accounting for contingent rentals should reflect the different circumstances if the lessee and the lessor agree to implement scheduled rent increases that will eliminate the risk of variable payments inherent in contingent rentals.

ASC 840-20-25-3 through 25-7, 55-1 through 55-3; ASC 840-10-55-45 through 55-46; ASC 840-30-55-14, 55-19 through 55-20; ASC 840-40-55-17 through 55-21 Issues Relating to Accounting for Leases

BACKGROUND

The guidance below responds to five questions related to the following issues in lease accounting:

- Time pattern of the physical use of the property in an operating lease
- Lease incentives in an operating lease
- Applicability of leveraged lease accounting to a lessor's existing assets
- Money-over-money lease transactions
- Wrap lease transactions

ACCOUNTING GUIDANCE

Question 1: Under the guidance in ASC 840, how should a lessee and a lessor recognize a lessee's rental payment obligation for an operating lease that includes scheduled rent increases designed to accommodate the lessee's projected physical use of a leased property?

Answer: Both the lessee and the lessor should recognize those lease payments as follows:

- If rent escalates in contemplation of a lessee's physical use of a leased property, but the lessee takes possession of or controls the physical use of the property at the beginning of the lease term, the lessee should recognize all rental payments, including the escalated rental payments, as rental expense and the lessor should recognize revenue on a straight-line basis. Under this guidance, the right to control the use of a leased property is treated the same as the physical use of a property. Consequently, the extent to which a property is used does not affect the recognition of rental expense or revenue.
- If rent is escalated under a master leasing agreement because a lessee gains access to and control over additional leased property at the time of the escalation, (*a*) the lessee should consider the escalated rents as additional rental expense and (*b*) the lessor should consider the escalated rents as additional revenue, attributable to the additional leased property. The lessee and the lessor should recognize the escalated rental payments in proportion to the additional property's relative fair value.

Illustration of an Operating Lease with Scheduled Rent Increases

Reeve & Sons is a construction company. Reeve leases a number of pieces of heavy equipment on 1/1/20X4 by entering into a ten-year operating lease. The fair value of this equipment is $600,000 at lease inception, and the yearly lease payment is $50,000. In addition, Reeve's yearly lease payment will increase to $100,000 on 1/1/20X9. On 1/1/20X9, Reeve will also gain access to and control over additional leased property. This additional leased property has a fair value of $300,000 on 1/1/20X4.

Reeve will recognize rental expense of approximately $58,333 during the years 20X4-20X8, and approximately $91,667 during the years 20X9-20Y3. These amounts are computed as follows:

Absolute (relative) fair value of equipment Reeve gains access to on 1/1/20X4	$600,000 (66.67%)
Absolute (relative) fair value of equipment Reeve gains access to on 1/1/20X9	$300,000 (33.33%)
Total lease payments over the ten-year lease	$750,000 [($50,000 × 5) + ($100,000 × 5)]
Portion of $100K annual lease payment from X9-Y3 attributable to the additional leased property	$33,334 ($100K × .3333, rounded)
Total lease payments attributable to the additional leased property	$167,667 ($33,334 × 5, rounded)
Total lease payments attributable to the original leased property	$583,333 [$750K – $167.667K]
Portion of lease payment attributable to original leased property, X4-Y3	$58,333 ($583,333 / 10)
Lease expense recognized, X4-X8	$58,333
Lease expense recognized, X9×Y3	$91,667 ($58,333 + $33,334)

Question 2: For operating leases that include an incentive for a lessee to sign (e.g., up-front cash payment to the lessee), should the lessee or lessor ever recognize rental expense or revenue other than on a straight-line basis?

Answer: Incentive payments to a lessee represent reductions in a lessee's rent expense and a lessor's rental revenue that should be recognized by both on a straight-line basis over the lease term.

Question 3: To be classified as a direct financing lease, the cost or carrying amount of the asset, if different, must be the same as its fair value at the inception of the lease. For a lease to qualify for leveraged lease accounting, the lease must be a direct financing lease. How should a lessor apply those requirements to a lease on an asset that the lessor has owned and previously had placed in service?

Answer: The carrying amount of an asset previously placed in service may not be significantly different from its fair value, but the two are not likely to be the same. Therefore, leveraged lease accounting is not appropriate, except if the lessor acquired the asset to be leased. If a lessor's existing asset's carrying amount is the same as its fair value before a write-down, the asset could qualify for leveraged lease accounting. However, any write-down to an existing asset's fair value in contemplation of leasing the asset precludes the transaction from being accounted for as a leveraged lease.

Question 4: An entity manufactures or purchases an asset, leases the asset to a lessee, and obtains nonrecourse financing in excess of the asset's cost by using the leased asset and the future lease rentals as collateral (referred to as a money-over-money lease transaction). Should an entity ever recognize a gain on a transaction in which cash received plus the present value of any estimated retained residual exceeds the carrying amount of the leased asset at the beginning of the lease term? If not, how should a lessor account for that transaction?

Answer: Other than recognizing a manufacturer's or dealer's profit in a sales-type lease, an entity should never recognize the proceeds from a borrowing in a money-over-money lease as income at the beginning of the lease term. The entity should account for the transaction as (1) the manufacture or purchase of an asset; (2) the leasing of the asset under an operating, direct financing, or sales-type lease; and (3) the borrowing of funds. The asset and the liability for the nonrecourse financing should *not* be offset in the entity's balance sheet unless a legal right of setoff exists.

Question 5: A lessor purchases an asset, leases it to a lessee, obtains nonrecourse financing using the lease rentals or the lease rentals and the asset as collateral, sells the asset and the nonrecourse debt to a third-party investor, and leases the asset back while remaining the principal lessor under the original lease (referred to as a wrap-lease transaction). How should an entity account for that kind of transaction?

Answer: If the leased asset is real estate, the guidance in ASC 840-40 applies to a sale-leaseback transaction. If the property is not real estate, an entity should account for that kind of transaction as a sale-leaseback transaction in accordance with the guidance in ASC 840-40-25-2 through 25-3, 25-8, 30-1 through 30-3, and 35-1 through 35-2, and the lease to the end user should be accounted for as a sublease under the guidance in ASC 840-10-35-10.

ASC 840-20-25-10 through 25-11, 45-1 Accounting for Rental Costs Incurred During a Construction Period

Under some operating leases for land and buildings, a lessee may be able to control the leased property even *before* beginning its operations or beginning to pay rent under a lease's terms. A lessee usually uses a leased asset during that period to construct an asset, such as leasehold improvements. A lessee begins its operations *after* construction is completed and it is then that the lessee begins paying rent under the lease's terms. However, under some leases, a lessee may be required to begin paying rent as soon as the lessee controls the property.

Under the guidance in ASC 840-10-55-45 through 55-46; 840-20-25-3 through 25-7, 55-1 through 55-3; ASC 840-30-55-14, 55-19 through 55-20; and ASC 840-40-55-17 through 55-21, Issues Relating to Accounting for Leases, which is discussed above, rental costs related to operating leases are required to be allocated on a straight-line basis over the term of a lease beginning on the date that a lessee is given control of a leased property, in accordance with the guidance in ASC 840-20-25-2, Accounting for Operating Leases with Scheduled Rent Increases, which is also discussed above. For example, a lessee enters into an operating lease on January 1, 200X, and is given control of the leased property on that date for the purpose of constructing leasehold improvements. The lessee expects to begin its operations on July 1, 200X, and, therefore, must begin paying rent on that date. In that case, the lessee would begin *allocating* rental costs on January 1, 200X, on a straight-line basis over the term of the lease.

The question addressed here is whether a lessee is permitted to *capitalize* rental costs related to ground and building operating leases that are incurred during a construction period.

ACCOUNTING GUIDANCE

A lessee's right to use a leased asset during the construction period or thereafter does *not* differ. Therefore, rental costs incurred on ground or building operating leases during and after the construction period should be accounted for in the same the same manner (i.e., they should be recognized as rental expense and included in income from continuing operations). Rental costs should be allocated over the lease term based on the guidance in ASC 840-20-25-1 through 25-2, discussed above. However, this guidance does *not* affect the application of the maximum guarantee test discussed in ASC 840-40-55-2.

ASC 840-20-25-14 through 25-15; ASC 840-30-35-13 Accounting for Loss on a Sublease Not Involving the Disposal of a Segment

BACKGROUND

The general principle of recognizing a loss on transactions is well established, and extends to contracts that are expected to result in a loss. The following guidance addresses the recognition of a loss on a lease contract.

ACCOUNTING GUIDANCE

Question: Should a loss on a sublease not involving a disposal of a segment be recognized, and how is that loss determined?

Answer: If costs such as executory costs and either amortization of a leased asset or rental payments expected to be incurred on an operating sublease exceed anticipated revenue on a sublease, the sublessor should recognize a loss. Similarly, a loss should be recognized on a direct financing sublease if the carrying amount of the investment in the sublease exceeds (1) the total of rentals expected to be received, and (2) the property's estimated residual value. An exception to that requirement exists if as sublessor, the original lessee's tax benefits from the transaction are sufficient to offset that loss.

ASC 840-20-55-4 through 55-6 Determining Whether a Lease Modification Involves a Termination Penalty

BACKGROUND

An operating lease on real estate is modified before the lease term expires by shortening the lease term and increasing lease payments during that period. As a result, lease payments exceed comparable market rents. The lease classification is unaffected by this modification, which involves no other changes to the lease.

ACCOUNTING ISSUE

Should the amount of lease payments under a modified lease that exceeds the amount of lease payments that would have been required during the shortened lease period under the original lease be considered a modification of future lease payments, or is the excess, in substance, a termination penalty?

ACCOUNTING GUIDANCE

Lease payments under a modified lease that exceed payments that would have been required during the shortened lease period under the original lease should be accounted for as follows, based on the relevant facts and circumstances:

- Excess payments considered to be a modification of future lease payments should be accounted for prospectively over the modified lease term.
- Excess payments considered to be, in substance, a termination penalty should be charged to income in the period of the modification.

The following factors should be considered in determining the nature of the modification:

- *The relationship of the modified lease term to the remaining term on the original lease* The likelihood that the excess is a termination penalty is increased the shorter the term of the modified lease compared to the remaining original lease term.
- *The difference between the modified lease payments and market rents* The likelihood that the excess is a modification of future lease payments is increased the closer the amount of modified lease payments is to market rentals for comparable property.

The charge to income for an increase in lease payments considered to be a *termination penalty* is calculated as the amount by which the modified lease payments exceed the required lease payments under the original lease for the shortened period. Actual or discounted amounts may be recognized consistent with the entity's accounting policy and should be disclosed in accordance with the guidance in ASC 235, if material.

Illustration of the Accounting for Modifications on an Operating Lease That Do Not Change the Lease Classification

Morningstar, Inc. has a lease for office space that expires on February 28, 20X9, with monthly rental payments of \$10,000. On February 20, 20X6, Morningstar and the lessor agree to modify the lease term: it will terminate on February 28, 20X7, with modified monthly lease payments of \$18,000 as of March 1, 20X6. Monthly rentals for comparable space are \$12,000.

Morningstar should account for the modification in the lease by recognizing a termination penalty of \$96,000 [(\$18,000 – \$10,000) × 12 months] in income in the quarter ended March 31, 20X6. The excess payments are considered a termination penalty because (*a*) the shortened lease term of 12 months is only one third of the remaining lease term of 36 months, and (*b*) the modified monthly rental payment of \$18,000 exceeds market rents by 50%.

DISCUSSION

This Issue was raised because of the lack of guidance in ASC 840 for such lease modifications. Proponents of accounting for the excess payments prospectively as a modification of future lease payments believed that under the guidance in ASC 840-10-35-4, that approach is required if the lease classification is unchanged. They also believed that the excess lease payments do not qualify for immediate recognition as a termination penalty, because they are associated with continuing operations and thus do not qualify for accrual as an exit cost, because the activity is not terminated. Conversely, those who believed the excess payments represent a termination penalty argued that the entity receives no future benefit from those payments. They believed that the modification of a lease to a shorter term is analogous to a termination or exit activity.

The EITF's views on this Issue were mixed. Many members believed that the excess payments should be accounted for as a cost of canceling a portion of the lease term and recognized currently as an exit cost. One member suggested another approach, under which termination costs would equal the excess of the present value of rents under the modified lease over rents on the original lease. The EITF was unable to decide, however, whether such costs represent an exit cost in all situations. As a result, they concluded that neither approach may be applicable to all situations and decided to account for such costs prospectively or in the current period, based on the facts and circumstances.

ASC 840-30: CAPITAL LEASES

ASC 840-30-35-25 Upward Adjustment of Guaranteed Residual Values

BACKGROUND

Under the guidance in ASC 840, a lessor is required to periodically review the estimated residual value of sales-type, direct-financing, and leveraged leases. However, under the guidance in ASC 840, an upward adjustment of residual values is prohibited.

ACCOUNTING GUIDANCE

Question: Does the prohibition of upward adjustments of estimated residual values in ASC 840 also apply to upward adjustments that result from renegotiations of the guaranteed portions of residual values?

Answer: The prohibitions against upward adjustments of residual values of leased assets under the guidance in ASC 840 also apply to the guaranteed portion of residual values.

ASC 840-30-35-41, 50-6 Effect of a Change in Income Tax Rate on the Accounting for Leveraged Leases

BACKGROUND

When an important assumption changes, a recalculation of the rate of return and allocation of income from the inception of the lease is required under the guidance in ASC 840. A change in the recalculated balances of net investment is recognized as a gain or loss in the year in which the assumption changes.

ACCOUNTING GUIDANCE

Question: What effect, if any, does a change in income tax rate have on the accounting for leveraged leases under the guidance in ASC 840?

Answer: A lessor's income tax rate is an important assumption in accounting for a leveraged lease. Accordingly, the effect of a change in income tax rate should be recognized in the first accounting period ending on or after the date on which the legislation affecting the change becomes law. If such a change results in a significant variation in the normal relationship between income tax expense and pretax accounting income, the reasons for that variation should be disclosed if they are not otherwise apparent, in accordance with the guidance in ASC 740-10-50-12 through 50-14.

ASC 840-30-35-48 through 35-52; ASC 740-10-25-43 Issues Related to the Alternative Minimum Tax

BACKGROUND

Under the Tax Reform Act of 1986 (the Act), an entity computes its federal income tax liability based on the regular tax system or on the alternative minimum tax (AMT) system, whichever tax amount is greater. An entity may earn an AMT credit for tax paid under the AMT system that exceeds the amount that would have been paid under the regular tax system. An AMT credit can be carried forward indefinitely to reduce the regular tax in future years, but not below the AMT in the current year.

ACCOUNTING ISSUE

Should leveraged lease calculations consider the effect of the AMT on cash flows and if so, how?

ACCOUNTING GUIDANCE

An entity's leveraged lease tax computations should include assumptions about the effect of the AMT by considering the entity's overall tax position. Under the guidance in ASC 840-30-35-38 through 35-40, entities with leveraged leases are required to evaluate important assumptions that affect total net income from the lease at least annually. If total after-tax net income changes as a result of a change in tax assumptions, the lessor should:

- Recalculate the rate of return on the leveraged lease from inception,
- Adjust accounts that constitute the lessor's net investment, *and*
- Recognize a gain or loss in the year in which an assumption is changed.

However, if an entity's tax position changes frequently between the AMT and the regular tax, such a recomputation is not required unless there is an indication that the original assumptions about total after-tax income are no longer valid. In that case, the entity should revise the leveraged lease computations in any period in which total net income from the leveraged lease changes because of the effect of the AMT on the lease's cash flows.

According to the guidance in ASC 840-30-35-33 through 35-35, a lessor is required to allocate income from a leveraged lease among years in which the net investment in the leveraged lease is positive based on projected after-tax cash flows at the inception of the lease. Important assumptions in a leveraged lease calculation include a lessor's income tax rate and the amount of taxes paid or tax benefits received. A difference, if any, between AMT depreciation and tax depreciation assumed in a leveraged lease calculation or between income recognition for financial reporting and AMT income could—depending on a lessor's overall tax situation—result in AMT or utilization of AMT credits. An AMT payment or use of an AMT credit could change total cash flows from the leveraged lease and affect the lessor's income recognition.

ASC 840-30-55-15 through 55-16 Leveraged Leases: Real Estate Leases and Sale-Leaseback Transactions, Delayed Equity Contributions by Lessors

BACKGROUND

Lessors finance leveraged leases of real estate and equipment with debt that is nonrecourse to the general credit of the lessor as required under guidance in ASC 840-10-25-43(c)(3). Rental payments in leveraged lease transactions usually are equal to or greater than payments to service the nonrecourse debt. Depreciation deductions in typical leveraged lease transactions exceed the net amount of rental income and interest expense and provide lessors with tax savings during the early periods of the lease term. Lessors thus recover equity investments quickly. Excess cash accumulated in the middle periods of a leveraged lease's term is used in later periods to pay for taxes due on amounts deferred in earlier periods.

When this question was discussed in 1985, some leveraged lease transactions were being structured so that the lessee began making payments from one to two years after the inception of a lease, thus obligating the lessor to make up the deficiency between rent payments and debt service during that period. In such cases, the lessor agreed, in the lease agreement or in a separate binding agreement, to service the nonrecourse debt with equity contributions limited to a specific amount during the period. Such contributions, which are referred to as *delayed equity investments,* were limited to the specified amount and could be measured at the inception of the lease. Although the debt was nonrecourse to the lessor, long-term creditors frequently had recourse to the lessor's general credit for debt service contributions.

ACCOUNTING ISSUES

The following are issues related to accounting for delayed equity contributions by lessors:

1. Does paragraph ASC 840-10-25-43(c)(3) preclude leveraged lease accounting if a delayed equity investment is considered to be recourse debt?
2. If leveraged lease accounting is not precluded, should a lessor recognize a liability for a delayed equity investment at the inception of a lease?

ACCOUNTING GUIDANCE

- Leveraged lease accounting is not precluded if a delayed equity investment is considered to be recourse debt, because such debt does not contradict the notion of nonrecourse debt under the guidance in ASC 840-10-25-43(c)(3).
- A lessor should recognize a liability for the present value of the obligation at the inception of the lease. The liability increases a lessor's net investment on which the lessor's pattern of income recognition is based. Although an increase in the net investment would result in additional income, the accrual of interest on the liability would offset that amount.

DISCUSSION

A delayed equity investment is part of a lessor's initial investment and does not differ in substance from debt incurred to finance the initial investment. Although a lessor uses such contributions to service the debt, the agreement limits a lessor's payments, which are measurable at the inception of a lease. Further, based on the economics of the transaction, leveraged lease accounting should not be precluded if the substantial leverage criterion in ASC 840-10-25-43(c)(3) has been met and the transaction conforms with the investment phases stipulated in ASC 840-10-25-43(d).

ASC 840-40: SALE-LEASEBACK TRANSACTIONS

ASC 840-40-05-5, 15-5, 25-4, 35-3, 55-2 through 55-16, S55-2, S99-2 ASC 460-10-60-28 through 60-31 The Effect of Lessee Involvement in Asset Construction

BACKGROUND

The following guidance addresses the effect of a lessee's involvement in the construction of an asset by discussing a build-to-suit lease transaction in which a lessee is actively involved with an asset's construction and may assume some or all of the construction risk. The property may be owned by a developer, a Real Estate Investment Trust (REIT), or an institutional investor. Frequently, a securitization entity is established to hold the real estate and becomes the owner-lessor of the property. The SPE's activities include constructing, owning, and leasing the land and buildings to a lessee.

Although a lessee may be actively involved in the asset's construction by entering into an agreement with the owner-lessor to act as the construction manager or general contractor, the owner-lessor retains title to the land and improvements during construction and during the lease period. Sometimes, an affiliate of a lessee enters into a fixed-price construction contract to perform those duties. The lessee leases the property from the owner-lessor when construction is completed. Some have questioned whether a lessee is, in substance, the owner of a project rather than an agent for the owner-lessor if the lessee assumes some or all of the following obligations during the construction period:

- Makes lease payments before construction is completed
- Guarantees construction debt or provides financing, directly or indirectly
- Assumes primary or secondary obligation on construction contracts
- Acts as an agent for the owner-lessor in the construction, financing, or sale of the asset
- Acts as a developer or in the capacity of a general contractor
- Assumes the obligation to purchase the asset if construction is not completed by a specific date
- Assumes the obligation to fund cost overruns

Although the discussion below refers to the construction of a build-to-suit real estate project, the accounting guidance applies to all projects involving the construction of an asset, such as a project to build or lease a ship. However, the guidance would *not* apply if a lessee's (or a party that has an option to become a lessee) maximum obligation, including guaranteed residual values, is only a minor amount, as defined in ASC 840-40, relative to the asset's fair value.

ACCOUNTING ISSUE

How should an entity involved in the construction of an asset that it plans to lease when completed determine whether it should be considered the asset's owner while the asset is under construction?

PRACTICE NOTE: See the guidance in "Accounting for Rental Costs Incurred during a Construction Period," discussed above under ASC 840-20, Operating Leases.

ACCOUNTING GUIDANCE

1. A lessee that has *substantially* all of the construction period risks should be considered the owner of a real estate project during the construction period and should follow the guidance in ASC 840-40. A 90% *maximum guarantee test* similar to the recovery-of-investment test discussed in ASC 840-10-25-1(d) should be used to evaluate whether a lessee has substantially all of the risks during the construction period. All payments associated with the construction project that a lessee is obligated to or can be required to make are included in the lessee's maximum guarantee.

   The following are some items that should be included in a lessee's maximum guarantee, unless modified by other guidance:

   a. Lease payments on a "date certain" lease that must be made whether or not the project is complete;

   b. Construction financing guarantees, which can only be made to the owner-lessor as specified in ASC 840-40-55-15(d);

   c. Existing equity investments in the owner-lessor or in a party related to the owner-lessor or an obligation to make such investments;

   d. Existing loans or advances (or an obligation to makes loans or advances) to the owner-lessor or a party related to the owner-lessor;

   e. Payments made in the capacity of developer, general contractor, or construction manager or agent that are reimbursed more infrequently than normal or customary in the real estate construction industry for transactions with parties not involved in the project in any other capacity;

   f. Payments as the primary or secondary obligor for project costs under construction contracts;

   g. Obligations as a result of the lessee's activities in the capacity of developer or general contractor;

   h. An obligation to purchase the real estate project under any circumstances;

   i. An obligation to pay for construction cost overruns;

j. An obligation to pay to the lessor, or on behalf of the lessor, rent or fees, such as transaction costs, during the construction period;

k. Payments that may be made for indemnities or guarantees to the owner-lessor.

A lessee is considered to have substantially all of the construction period risks and to be the owner of the real estate project during the construction period, if it is determined at the inception of the lease or the date on which the parties agree to the terms of the construction arrangement, whichever is earlier, that the lessee could be required, under the governing documents, to pay at least 90% of the project's total costs (other than the costs of land acquisition) under any circumstances at any time during the construction period.

Although the evaluation of whether the lessee is the owner of the construction project should be made only once, it is necessary to determine whether, at each point during the construction period, the *sum* of the following *two* amounts is *less* than 90% of the total costs incurred on the project to date, other than the costs of acquiring the land:

1. The accreted value of the lessee's previous payments, if any; and
2. The present value of the maximum amount the lessee can be required to pay as of that point in time, regardless of whether construction is complete.

If the test is not met, a lessee is considered to be the real estate project's owner during construction. The lessee also is permitted to provide guarantees in an amount that does not exceed the acquisition cost of the land, but any unused portion of that guarantee may not be used to cover a shortfall in the guarantee of total project costs. To accrete and discount the cash flows in this calculation, the lessee should use (*a*) the interest rate used to discount the lease payments for lease classification purposes, if it is known, or (*b*) the construction borrowing rate. The probability that a lessee will be required to make such payments is *not* considered in the maximum guarantee test.

2. A lessee would be considered the owner of a real estate project even if the present value of the maximum guarantee is *less than 90%* of the project's total costs under the following conditions:

a. The lessee or any party related to the lessee associated with the construction project makes or is required to make on behalf of the lessee an equity investment in the owner-lessor that would be considered to be in substance an investment in real estate according ASC 976-10-15-4, which includes examples of equity investments that are in substance real estate. Based on the guidance in ASC 840-40-55-45, the fair value of an option to acquire real property transferred by a lessee to a lessor would be considered a soft cost that a lessee incurred before entering into a lease agreement. A lessee's loans, such as those discussed in ASC 310-10 regarding Acquisition, Development, and Construction Arrangements, made during the construction period, which in substance are an investment in the real estate project, would be another indicator that a lessee is a real estate project's owner during the construction period,

b. The lessee must pay directly, instead of through rent payments under the lease, for project costs other than

(1) Costs reimbursed under a contract (as discussed under the first consensus above),

(2) Preexisting environmental risks with a remote risk of loss, or

(3) Costs of normal tenant improvements, except for the following:

(a) Costs of structural elements, even if those costs were incurred specifically for the lessee

(b) Equipment that would be a necessary improvement for any lessee, such as the costs of elevators, air conditioning systems, or electrical wiring

(c) Amounts included in the project's original budget that the owner-lessor agreed to pay for on the date the contract was negotiated, regardless of the character of those costs

c. The lessee indemnifies the owner-lessor or its lenders for preexisting environmental risks for which the risk of loss is more than remote. (See the guidance in ASC 840-10-25-12 through 25-13.)

d. Except as permitted in (c) above, the lessee provides indemnities or guarantees to parties other than the owner-lessor or agrees to indemnify the owner-lessor for costs as a result of claims for damages made by third parties, but not for claims made by third parties as a result of the lessee's own actions or lack of action while possessing or controlling the construction project. (See the discussion in ASC 840-40-55-9(d) on the maximum guarantee test, which should include any indemnification of or guarantee to the owner-lessor against third-party claims related to completion of construction. For example, a lessee is not permitted to provide indemnities or guarantees for acts not under the lessee's control, such as condemnation proceedings or casualties.) A lessee who acts in the capacity of a general contractor is responsible for the actions or failure to act of its subcontractors.

e. The lessee takes title to the real estate during the construction period or provides supplies or other materials used in the construction other than those purchased after the lease term began (or the date of the construction agreement, whichever is earlier) that can be reimbursed as discussed above. Materials provided by the lessee are considered "hard costs," which are discussed in ASC 840-40-55-42.

f. The lessee (i) owns the land but does not lease it, or (ii) leases the land but does not sublease it (or provides an equivalent interest in the land, such as a long-term easement) to the owner-lessor before construction begins. A lessee's sale of the land to the owner-lessor must occur before construction begins. If that transaction occurs and the lessee subsequently leases the land back with improvements, the sale of the land would be accounted for under the requirements of ASC 840-40, even if that guidance would not apply to the lease or the improvements under this guidance.

3. A lessee involved in the transactions discussed above should defer its profit, if any, realized during construction—for example, from rental income received under a ground lease or from fees for construction or development services—and amortize it to income based on the guidance in ASC 840-40-55-26 through 55-28.

4. This guidance should be used to determine whether an entity is the owner of a project during the construction period if the entity has an option to or is required to lease the asset after construction is completed.

SEC OBSERVER COMMENT

The SEC Observer stated that the SEC staff believes that a lessee's loan to a lessor should be treated as an Acquisition, Development, and Construction (ADC) arrangement under the scope of AICPA Practice Bulletin (PB) No. 1, Exhibit I, if the lessee can participate in expected residual profit. The staff further believes that a lessee that has an option to purchase a leased asset at a fixed price would be considered to be entitled to participate in expected residual profit. Under the guidance in ASC 310-25-27(a), a loan is, in substance, an investment if the lessee is expected to receive more than 50% of the residual profit. Under the guidance in ASC 310-10-25-27(b), the classification of the loan depends on the circumstances if the lender/lessee receives 50% or less of the residual profit. Under the guidance in ASC 310-10-25-20(b), a borrower that has a substantial investment in a project not funded by a lender may classify the borrowing as a loan. To determine whether a borrower has a sufficient equity investment, the SEC staff will apply the guidance in ASC 360-20-55-1 through 55-2. A lessee would also be considered the owner of a real estate project if the lessor is a special-purpose entity and the lease gives the lessee a fixed-price option to purchase the property or a remarketing agreement under which the lessee would be entitled to the majority of the sales proceeds in excess of the leased asset's original cost.

ASC 840-40-15-2 Application of the Guidance in ASC 840-40-55-2 through 55-16 and ASC 840-10-25-25 to Entities That Enter into Leases with Governmental Entities

BACKGROUND

As discussed in ASC 840-40-05-5, 15-5, 25-4, 35-3, 55-2 through 55-16, S55-2, S99-2 ASC 460-10-60-28 through 60-31, The Effect of Lessee Involvement in Asset Construction, discussed above, a lessee who is involved with a property during the construction period may be considered the owner of the property for financial reporting purposes depending on the circumstances. For example, a lessee that guarantees the construction debt during the construction period is automatically deemed to be the owner of the property.

Although that guidance was initially intended to apply to the private sector, some have questioned whether it also should apply to projects involving major real estate improvements funded by governmental entities, such as airports and other transit facilities. A governmental entity generally finances such projects by issuing tax-exempt bonds that are repaid from rental payments made by lessees. A lessee, such as an airline, is usually the general contractor of the project and is reimbursed by the bond trustee for costs incurred during the project.

Some believe that depending on the arrangement, a lessee involved in the construction of such a project may be required to account for the property under the guidance in ASC 840-40-55-2 through 55-16. Some projects may be accounted for as financings or as deposits, because they do not qualify for lease accounting under the guidance in ASC 840-40, Sale-Leaseback Transactions. However, under the guidance in ASC 840-10-25-25 leases meeting certain criteria must be accounted for as operating leases.

ACCOUNTING ISSUE

Should projects that involve the construction and lease of properties owned by governmental entities that would be accounted for as operating leases under the provisions in ASC 840-10-25-25 (FIN-23) be excluded from the scope of the guidance in ASC 840-40-05-5, 15-5, 25-4, 35-3, 55-2 through 55-16, S55-2, S99-2 ASC 460-10-60-28 through 60-31, The Effect of Lessee Involvement in Asset Construction?

ACCOUNTING GUIDANCE

Government-owned properties under construction that will be leased by others after completion should be included under the scope of ASC 840-40-05-5, 15-5, 25-4, 35-3, 55-2 through 55-16, S55-2, S99-2 ASC 460-10-60-28 through 60-31, The Effect of Lessee Involvement in Asset Construction. That is, a lessee that has substantially all of the risk during the construction period, as defined under that guidance, should be considered the property's owner for accounting purposes. The guidance in ASC 840-40 would apply to a subsequent sale-leaseback transaction.

ASC 840-40-25-14; ASC 460-10-60-33 Impact of an Uncollateralized Irrevocable Letter of Credit on a Real Estate Sale-Leaseback Transaction

BACKGROUND

A buyer-lessor may require a seller-lessee to provide an irrevocable letter of credit to secure all or a portion of the lease payments in connection with a sale-leaseback of real estate. If a seller-lessee pledges assets as collateral for a letter of credit, sale-leaseback accounting for the transaction is precluded under the guidance in ASC 840-40, because there is a continuing involvement. It is unclear, however, whether an *uncollateralized* letter of credit would constitute continuing involvement.

ACCOUNTING ISSUE

Does the existence of an uncollateralized, irrevocable letter of credit preclude sale-leaseback accounting for a transaction that otherwise would qualify?

ACCOUNTING GUIDANCE

Sale-leaseback accounting is not precluded if an uncollateralized, irrevocable letter of credit is provided, because that kind of guarantee is not a form of continuing involvement under the guidance in ASC 840-40-25-14(d). Although a lessee is not precluded from accounting for a transaction as a sale-leaseback under the that guidance while providing an independent third-party guarantee of the lease payments, such transactions should be analyzed carefully to ensure that they are uncollateralized in form and substance. For example, a financial institution's right to offset amounts on deposit against payments on a letter of credit would be considered to be a form of collateral and, therefore, a continuing involvement that would preclude sale-leaseback accounting.

DISCUSSION

The following arguments were made in support of sale-leaseback accounting:

- An uncollateralized letter of credit does not increase the lessee's commitment beyond the obligation to pay rent. It is not a guarantee of return of the buyer's investment.
- A buyer-lessor could achieve almost the same protection by purchasing a surety bond to secure the lease payments. The lessee would not be involved in that transaction and sale-leaseback accounting would not be precluded. If an equivalent level of security could be achieved without a seller-lessee's consent, the seller-lessee would not be providing additional collateral or a guarantee by obtaining an uncollateralized letter of credit.
- Letters of credit and lease guarantees are only promises to pay obligations under a lease agreement. If a seller-lessee has provided a letter of credit and subsequently defaults on the lease payments, the seller-lessee has the same unsecured obligation, but to another party.

ASC 840-40-25-15 through 25-16; ASC 460-10-60-26 through 60-27 Unsecured Guarantee by Parent of Subsidiary's Lease Payments in a Sale-Leaseback Transaction

BACKGROUND

A wholly owned subsidiary enters into a sale-leaseback transaction for a building. In connection with the sale-leaseback, the buyer-lessor requires the subsidiary's parent to guarantee the subsidiary's obligations under the lease. Under the guidance in ASC 840-40-25-12 through 25-14 the use of sale-leaseback accounting is prohibited if there is continuing involvement with a real estate property other than a normal leaseback involving the active use of the property by the seller-lessee. A guarantee is one example of continuing involvement mentioned in ASC 840-40, Sale-Leaseback Transactions. Except for the lease guarantee, the transaction meets all the requirements for sale-leaseback accounting under the guidance in ASC 840-40.

ACCOUNTING ISSUE

If one member of a consolidated group guarantees another member's lease payments in a sale-leaseback of real estate, can the transaction be accounted for as a sale-leaseback in the seller-lessee's separate financial statements and in the entity's consolidated financial statements?

ACCOUNTING GUIDANCE

The following guidance addresses the effect on sale-leaseback accounting if one member of a consolidated group provides an unsecured guarantee of a lease obligation incurred by another member of the consolidated group:

- Sale-leaseback accounting is *not* precluded in the consolidated financial statements if one member of a consolidated group guarantees the lease payments of another member of that group. This conclusion is based on the rationale that an entity's unsecured guarantee of its own lease does not provide a lessor with additional collateral, except if the lessee declares bankruptcy. Thus, such a guarantee does not constitute a continuing involvement that would preclude sale-leaseback treatment under the guidance in ASC 840-40.
- Sale-leaseback accounting *is precluded*, however, in a seller-lessee's separate financial statements, because an unsecured guarantee of the seller-lessee's lease payments by another member of the consolidated group provides the buyer-lessor with additional collateral that reduces its risk of loss and thus constitutes a form of continuing involvement.

ASC 840-40-25-18, 55-48 Sale-Leaseback Transactions with Continuing Involvement

The following guidance is a response to questions on the accounting for sale-leaseback transactions in which a seller has a continuing involvement with the property:

- Sale-leaseback accounting is *precluded* in transactions in which a seller retains a partial ownership in a property.

  Sale-leaseback accounting is *precluded* if a seller-lessee can require the buyer-lessor to refinance debt related to the property and pass the interest savings to the seller-lessee in the form of reduced leaseback payments. Sale-leaseback accounting is *permitted,* however, if leaseback payments, which are considered contingent rentals under the provisions of ASC 840-40, change because they are indexed to an interest rate.

ASC 840-40-30-5 through 30-6 Consideration of Executory Costs in Sale-Leaseback Transactions

BACKGROUND

Executory costs on a lease include such items as maintenance, insurance, and taxes. Those costs may be included in each rental payment, paid separately by a seller-lessee, or paid by a buyer-lessor and billed to the seller-lessee.

Although minimum lease payments, as defined in ASC 840-10-25-6, include executory costs but exclude such costs if they are paid separately, minimum lease payments exclude executory costs in certain lease calculations. For example, executory costs are excluded from minimum lease payments when determining lease classification or in accounting for capital, sales-type, or direct financing leases.

Under the guidance in ASC 840-40-25-4 through 25-5, 35-4, 55-79 through 55-80, 55-82 through 55-84, 55-86 through 55-88, 55-90 through 55-92, 55-94, profit equal to the present value of minimum lease payments in certain sale-leaseback transactions should be deferred. That guidance is silent, however, on whether executory costs should be included or excluded from minimum lease payments when making that calculation.

ACCOUNTING ISSUE

Should the calculation of profit to be deferred on a sale-leaseback transaction include or exclude executory costs?

ACCOUNTING GUIDANCE

Executory costs should be excluded from the calculation of deferred profit on a sale-leaseback transaction, regardless of how executory costs are paid or whether a lease is a capital or operating lease.

ASC 840-40-55-22 through 55-24 Accounting for the Sale and Leaseback of an Asset That Is Leased to Another Party

BACKGROUND

Company A sells equipment to Company B and then leases it back from Company B. The sale and leaseback of the asset is subject to an operating lease and is intended to be leased by Company A to another entity under an operating lease. Company A has thus become a seller, lessee, and sublessor. The question here addresses the accounting treatment of a sale-leaseback transaction in which a seller-lessee retains substantial risks of ownership in a property through the terms of a leaseback.

ACCOUNTING ISSUE

Should a sale-leaseback transaction in which a seller-lessee retains substantial risks of ownership in personal property through a leaseback be accounted for as a borrowing or as a sale-leaseback transaction, if personal property not under the scope of the real estate guidance in ASC 840-40 is subject to an operating lease, is subleased, or is intended to be subleased by a seller-lessee to a third party at the time of a sale?

ACCOUNTING GUIDANCE

A seller-lessee should account for the transaction described above as a sale-leaseback in accordance with the guidance ASC 840-40-25-2 through 25-3, 30-1 through 30-3, and 35-1 through 35-2. Thus, a seller-lessee should recognize a sale, remove the asset from the balance sheet, and classify the leaseback in accordance with the guidance in ASC 840-10-25-43. A gain, if any, on the transaction should be recognized or deferred and amortized in accordance with the guidance in ASC 840-40-25-3.

DISCUSSION

The guidance in ASC 840-20-40-3 states that "the sale of property subject to an operating lease, or of property that is leased by or intended to be leased by the third-party purchaser to another party, shall not be treated as a sale if the seller or any party related to the seller retains substantial risks of ownership of the leased property. A seller may by various arrangements assure recovery of the investment by the third-party purchaser in some operating lease transactions and thus retain substantial risks in connection with the property." The question discussed above was raised because it was unclear whether and how the provisions of ASC 840-20-40-3 through 40-4 apply to sale-leaseback transactions that include assets under an operating lease or that are intended to be subleased by a seller-lessee to another party.

Under one view, the provisions of ASC 840-20-40-3 through 40-4 and of ASC 840-40-25-2 through 25-3 do not apply to the same transactions. That is, transactions that do not qualify as sale-leasebacks under the definition in ASC 840-40-25-2 fall under the provisions of ASC 840-20-40-3 through 40-4 and are accounted for as borrowings in accordance with the provisions of ASC 840-20-35-4. ASC 840-40-25-3 would apply to the accounting for transactions that qualify as sale-leaseback transactions. This view, referred to as the "mutually exclusive" approach, represented predominant practice.

Under a second view, referred to as the "sequential approach," the provisions of ASC 840-20-40-3 through 40-4 and 25-2 through 25-3 do apply to the same transactions. Following this approach, the provisions of a sale-leaseback agreement of property subject to an operating lease or intended to be subleased to an unrelated party after a sale-leaseback are evaluated to determine whether the transaction qualifies for sales recognition under the provisions of ASC 840-20-40-3 through 40-4. Transactions that do not are accounted for as borrowings under the guidance in ASC 840-20-35-4.

Although unstated, the accounting guidance provided above indicates support for the mutually exclusive approach, which applies only the provisions of ASC 840-40-25-2 through 25-3 in accounting for a sale-leaseback transaction of property other than real estate that is subject to an operating lease or a sublease of the property.

ASC 840-40-55-26 through 55-28; ASC 460-10-55-17, 60-32 Deferred Profit on Sale-Leaseback Transaction with Lessee Guarantee of Residual Value

BACKGROUND

A seller-lessee in a sale-leaseback transaction guarantees to a buyer-lessor that a property's residual value will be a stated amount at the end of the lease term. The lease agreement stipulates that the seller-lessee will indemnify the buyer-lessor for a deficiency, if any, in the property's residual value up to a specified amount. The lease does not meet any of the criteria for a capital lease in ASC 840-10-25-1. Hence, it is classified as an operating lease. More than a minor portion of the property, but less than substantially all of it, is covered by the leaseback.

ACCOUNTING ISSUES

If a residual value guarantee affects the determination of profit on a sale-leaseback transaction in accordance with the guidance in ASC 840-40-25-4 through 25-5, 35-4, 55-79 through 55-80, 55-82 through 55-84, 55-86 through 55-88, 55-90 through 55-92, 55-94, should a seller-lessee use the gross amount or the present value of the guarantee in making that calculation?

ACCOUNTING GUIDANCE

A seller-lessee should defer profit equal to the present value of the periodic rents plus the *gross* amount of the residual value guarantee at the date of sale and should account for the components as follows:

- Defer profit equal to the gross amount of the guarantee until the guarantee is resolved at the end of the lease term.
- Amortize profit equal to the present value of the periodic rents in proportion to total gross rental expense over the lease term.

PRACTICE NOTE: This guidance applies only to sale-leasebacks *other than* real estate. Under the provisions in ASC 360 that are related to real estate, sale-leaseback accounting would be precluded if a seller-lessee has any kind of continuing involvement with the property, such as a guarantee of the buyer's investment.

Illustration of Calculation of Profit at the Sale Date and Amortization of Deferred Profit

Assumptions	
Sales price of property	$150,000
Seller's basis in the property	$ 50,000
Annual rent (payable at beginning of year)	$ 16,000
Maximum amount of guarantee	$ 27,000
Leaseback term	5 years
Incremental borrowing rate	12% per year
Date of sale	12/31/X4
Profit to Be Recognized at Date of Sale	
Sales price	$150,000
Less: Basis in property	50,000
Profit on sale	$100,000
Present value of annual rents	$ 64,598
Residual value guarantee—Gross amount	27,000
Profit to be deferred	$ 91,598
Profit to be recognized at date of sale	$ 8,402
Amortization of Deferred Profit	
Total deferred profit at 12/31/X4	$ 91,598

			$.8074
Present value of total rent at date of sale / Total annual rents	$64,598 / 80,000	=	amortized for each $1 of rent
Annual amortization of deferred profit:	$16,000 × .8074	=	$12,918
Deferred profit at 12/31/X9	$ 27,000		

DISCUSSION

Although the guidance in ASC 840-40-25-4 through 25-5, 35-4, 55-79 through 55-80, 55-82 through 55-84, 55-86 through 55-88, 55-90 through 55-92, 55-94 is clear that a seller-lessee should defer profit on a sale-leaseback transaction equal to the present value of the minimum lease payments over the lease term and that such an amount should be amortized in proportion to rental expense over the lease term, it is unclear whether that amount should include a guarantee. In addition, even if a guarantee is included in deferred profit, it is unclear whether it should be included at its gross amount or at its present value. Those who supported including a guarantee at its gross amount, rather than reducing it to its present value, argued that because a guarantee is a contingent gain that is not resolved until the end of the lease term, it should not result in additional profit recognition at the inception of the lease term. Under the guidance in ASC 450, a contingent gain is not recognized until realized.

ASC 840-40-55-29 through 55-34 Accounting for Cross Border Tax Benefit Leases

BACKGROUND

Sale-leaseback transactions can be arranged so that both the seller-lessee and the buyer-lessor are entitled to tax deductions for the same depreciable asset. To accomplish that, the seller-lessee and the buyer-lessor must be located in different countries whose income tax laws differ as to which party is entitled to the deduction for a depreciable asset.

A typical example involves a U.S. entity as the seller-lessee and a foreign investor as the buyer-lessor. The transaction usually is structured as follows:

- A U.S. entity purchases a depreciable asset from a manufacturer and thus obtains title and tax benefits to be used in filing its U.S. taxes.
- The U.S. entity, which also is a manufacturer, enters into an agreement in the form of a leaseback for the ownership right with a foreign investor. The lease agreement includes a purchase option under which the U.S. entity will acquire the foreign investor's ownership right in the asset at the end of the lease term.
- The foreign investor pays the U.S. entity an amount of cash based on the asset's appraised value. The U.S. entity immediately transfers a portion of the cash to a third party trustee, which assumes the U.S. entity's obligation to make future payments on the lease, include payments for the purchase option. The cash retained by the U.S. entity is consideration for the foreign investor's tax benefits in the foreign tax jurisdiction. The U.S. entity may also agree to indemnify the third party trustee against certain events.
- The U.S. company agrees to indemnify the foreign investor only for a loss of tax benefits as a result of certain events such as the sale, loss, or destruction of the equipment or bankruptcy of the U.S. company, which can settle the obligation by buying a letter of credit from a bank in favor of the foreign investor.
- As a result of that transaction, the U.S. entity and the foreign investor have a tax basis in the same depreciable asset.

There were two views on the accounting for the net proceeds retained by the U.S. entity. Some viewed the net proceeds as income that should be recognized immediately. Others viewed the net proceeds as an adjustment of the cost of the equipment or as deferred income.

ACCOUNTING ISSUE

Should net proceeds retained by the U.S. entity (seller-lessee) in a tax benefit sale-leaseback transaction be reported as income immediately or as deferred that is amortized to income?

ACCOUNTING GUIDANCE

The timing of income recognition for cash received by the U.S. entity should be accounted for based on the individual facts and circumstances. However, immediate recognition is not appropriate if there is more than a remote possibility of a loss of the cash consideration as a result of contingencies, such as indemnification clauses.

The total consideration received by the U.S. entity is compensation for the foreign investor's tax benefits and the indemnification of the foreign investor or the third-party trustee. If the possibility of a loss is remote, the amount of income for the tax benefits that the seller-lessee recognizes immediately would be reduced as a result of the recognition of a liability in accordance with the requirement in ASC 460 for the indemnification agreement at inception.

ASC 840-40-55-37 through 55-41 Accounting for the Sale of Property Subject to the Seller's Preexisting Lease

BACKGROUND

A lessee under an operating lease of all or a portion of a property also may own an interest in that property. This might occur if, for example, the lessee has an investment in a partnership that owns the leased property. The lessee might have acquired the equity interest at or near the time the lease agreement was consummated.

The existence of both an operating lease and an equity interest in a property raises a question about whether a gain should be recognized if the lessee sells its equity interest in the property (or the partnership sells the property), but the lessee continues to lease the property under a preexisting operating lease. The question arises because a portion of the gain is deferred in other transactions in which owned property is sold and leased back.

ACCOUNTING ISSUES

1. Should the sale of a lessee's equity interest in a property be accounted for as a sale-leaseback transaction?
2. Should the amount of profit to be deferred be affected by the seller-lessee's prior ownership interest in the property?
3. Should the guidance in ASC 840-40-05-9 through 05-10, 15-4, 15-9 through 15-10, 25-9 through 25-14, 25-17, 50-1 through 50-2, 55-36, 55-49 through 55-77; ASC 980-840-25-1 through 25-3, 35-1 through 35-2 for sale-leaseback transactions apply to transactions involving real estate or real estate and equipment if a seller-lessee vacates and intends to sublease a property or exercises a renewal option subject to provisions in a preexisting lease?
4. Should the sale-leaseback guidance apply to transactions that involve property under the scope of ASC 840-40 if a preexisting lease is between parties under a seller's common control?

EITF CONSENSUS

1. a. A sale of an equity interest in a leased property should be accounted for as a sale-leaseback if the lease is modified in connection with the sale, excluding insignificant modifications.
   b. The sale-leaseback guidance in ASC 840-40 should be followed for all transactions that involve real estate and real estate.
   c. Profit on a sales transaction in which the preexisting lease is not modified significantly should be deferred and amortized into income in accordance with the guidance in ASC 840-40-25-3.
   d. A seller's prior ownership in a property should not affect the calculation of the amount of deferred profit, *regardless* of lease modifications.
2. The accounting for a transaction should not be affected by a seller-lessee's exercise of (*a*) a sublease provision contained in the preexisting lease or (*b*) a renewal option for a period within the original minimum lease term. However, a renewal option for a period not part of the original lease term is a new lease. The guidance in ASC 840-40 applies to such transactions. For example, if a lease has an initial term of ten years and a bargain renewal for an additional five years, the original minimum lease term would be 15 years, and the exercise of the renewal option would not affect the accounting. If, however, the renewal option were a fair value rental option, the minimum lease term would be ten years, and the exercise of the renewal would make the transaction subject to the guidance in ASC 840.
3. A lease between parties under common control should not be considered a preexisting lease. The guidance in ASC 840-40 thus applies to such transactions, with one exception. If the guidance in ASC 980, *Regulated Operations*, applies—that is, if one of the parties to the lease is a regulated enterprise and the lease has been approved by the appropriate regulatory agency—a lease between parties under common control is treated as a preexisting lease.

CHAPTER 57

ASC 845—NONMONETARY TRANSACTIONS

CONTENTS

PART I: GENERAL GUIDANCE

ASC 845-10: OVERALL

OVERVIEW

As a general rule, U.S. GAAP require that both monetary and nonmonetary exchanges be recorded based on the fair value inherent in the transaction. Certain exceptions exist, however, for nonmonetary transactions. Different accounting bases may be required for these transactions, depending on the unique characteristics of the exchange transaction.

BACKGROUND

Business transactions usually involve cash or monetary assets or liabilities that are exchanged for goods or services. These are identified as monetary transactions. Monetary assets or liabilities are fixed in terms of currency and usually are contractual claims to fixed amounts of money. Examples of monetary assets and liabilities are cash, accounts and notes receivable, and accounts and notes payable.

Some business transactions involve the exchange or transfer of nonmonetary assets or liabilities that are not fixed in terms of currency. These are identified as *nonmonetary transactions*. Nonmonetary assets and liabilities are those other than monetary assets and liabilities. Examples are inventory, investments in common stock, property, plant, and equipment, liability for advance rent collected, and common stock.

PRACTICE POINTER: Under certain circumstances, management's intent may affect the monetary/nonmonetary classification of an asset or liability. For example, a marketable bond being held to maturity qualifies as a monetary asset because its face amount is fixed in terms of currency. If the same bond were being held for speculation, however, it would be classified as a nonmonetary asset, because the amount that would be received when sold would not be determinable and therefore not fixed in terms of currency.

ACCOUNTING FOR NONMONETARY EXCHANGES AND TRANSACTIONS

An *exchange* (or *exchange transaction*) is a reciprocal transfer between an enterprise and another entity that results in the enterprise's acquiring assets or services or satisfying liabilities by surrendering other assets or services or incurring other obligations (ASC Glossary). A reciprocal transfer of a nonmonetary asset is considered an exchange only if the transferor has no substantial continuing involvement in the transferred asset such that the usual risks and rewards of ownership of the asset are transferred.

A *nonreciprocal transfer* is a transfer of assets or services in one direction, either from an enterprise to its owners or another entity, or from owners or another entity to the enterprise (ASC Glossary). Examples of nonreciprocal transfers are:

- Declaration and distribution of a dividend
- Acquisition of treasury stock
- Sale of capital stock
- Conversion of convertible debt
- Charitable contributions

Basic Principle

In general, ASC 845 requires that accounting for nonmonetary transactions be based on the fair values of the assets or services involved, which is the same basis that ordinarily would be used for monetary transactions. The cost of a nonmonetary asset acquired in exchange for another nonmonetary asset is the fair value of the asset surrendered to obtain it. A gain or loss may be recognized in the exchange. The fair value of the asset received should be used to measure the cost if that amount is more clearly evident than the fair value of the asset surrendered. Similarly, a transfer of a nonmonetary asset to a stockholder or to another entity in a nonreciprocal transfer is recorded at the fair value of the asset transferred, and a gain or loss is recognized on the disposition of the asset (ASC 845-10-30-1).

Fair value is determined by referring to estimated realizable values in cash transactions of the same or similar assets, quoted market prices, independent appraisals, estimated fair values of assets or services received in exchange, and other available evidence. If one of the parties in a nonmonetary transaction could have elected to receive cash instead of the nonmonetary asset, the amount of cash that could have been received may be evidence of the fair value of the nonmonetary assets exchanged. For guidance on fair value measurement, see Chapter 51, *ASC 820—Fair Value Measurement*.

Fair value should be regarded as not determinable if major uncertainties exist about the realizability of the value that would be assigned to an asset received in a nonmonetary transaction. If the fair value of either the asset surrendered or the asset received is not determinable within reasonable limits, the recorded amount of the nonmonetary asset transferred from the enterprise may be the only available measure of the transaction (ASC 845-10-30-8).

If one of the parties in a nonmonetary transaction could have elected to receive cash instead of the nonmonetary asset, the amount of cash that could have been received may be evidence of the fair value of the nonmonetary assets exchanged.

ASC 845 involves accounting for the transfer of nonmonetary assets in a reciprocal transfer between an entity and another party. A reciprocal transfer qualifies as an exchange if the transferor has no substantial continuing involvement with the assets transferred. The risks and rewards of ownership must be transferred for an exchange transaction to take place.

While exchanges of nonmonetary assets generally are to be accounted for at fair value, there are three circumstances when an exchange is to be recorded based on the book value (less any reduction for impairment) of the net asset transferred. These are when (ASC 845-10-30-3):

- The fair value of the asset transferred or received is not determinable.
- The exchange is to facilitate a sale to a customer and it involves the exchange of a product held for sale in the ordinary course of business for another product to be sold in the same line of business.
- The exchange transaction lacks commercial substance.

An exchange has commercial substance if the entity's future cash flows are expected to change as a result of the transaction. An entity's future cash flows are expected to change if either (1) the amount, timing, or uncertainty of the future cash flows from the asset received differs significantly from the amount, timing, or uncertainty of the future cash flows from the asset transferred or (2) there is a significant difference between the entity-specific value of the asset received and the entity-specific value of the asset transferred. An asset's entity-specific value is its value to a particular entity, given the entity's intended use for that asset, rather than the asset's value as determined by the marketplace.

An exchange would not have commercial substance if such substance were based solely on cash flows as a result of achieving certain tax benefits, if the tax benefits arise solely from achieving a certain financial reporting result.

Gain or Loss

Gain or loss, when applicable, is recognized in nonmonetary transactions. A difference in the gain or loss for tax purposes and that recognized for accounting purposes may constitute a temporary difference in income tax provision (ASC 845-10-30-9).

The process of determining the appropriate amount of gain or loss, if any, to be recognized in nonmonetary exchanges is summarized in Figure 57-1.

Illustration of the Major Provisions of ASC 845

In all of the following cases, an enterprise is giving up nonmonetary Asset A, which has a recorded amount of $10,000.

Case 1: Asset A is exchanged for dissimilar nonmonetary Asset B, which is valued at $12,000. Entry to record:

Asset B	$12,000	
Asset A		$10,000
Gain on exchange		2,000

Explanation: Nonmonetary transaction is recorded at fair value and any gain or loss is recognized.

Case 2: Asset A is exchanged for similar productive (nonmonetary) Asset C, which is valued at $9,500. Entry to record:

Asset C	$9,500	
Loss on exchange	500	
Asset A		$10,000

Explanation: Exchange of similar assets is recorded at fair value; loss is recognized.

Case 3: Asset A is exchanged for similar productive (nonmonetary) Asset D, which is valued at $15,000. Entry to record:

Asset D	$15,000	
Asset A		$10,000
Gain on exchange		5,000

Explanation: Exchange of similar assets is recorded at fair value; gain is recognized.

Case 4: Asset A is exchanged for a similar productive (nonmonetary) Asset E, which is valued at $13,000; the transaction lacks commercial substance because it does not significantly alter future cash flows. Entry to record:

Asset E	$10,000	
Asset A		$10,000

Explanation: Exchange of similar assets is recorded at book value of asset surrendered because the transaction lacks commercial substance.

Case 5: Asset A is exchanged for a similar productive (nonmonetary) Asset F in a transaction that has commercial substance, but for which the fair value of neither asset can be reasonably determined. Entry to record:

Asset F	$10,000	
Asset A		$10,000

Explanation: Because fair value cannot be reasonably determined for either Asset A or Asset F, the acquired asset is recorded at the book value of the asset surrendered.

Figure 57-1: Accounting for Nonmonetary Exchanges

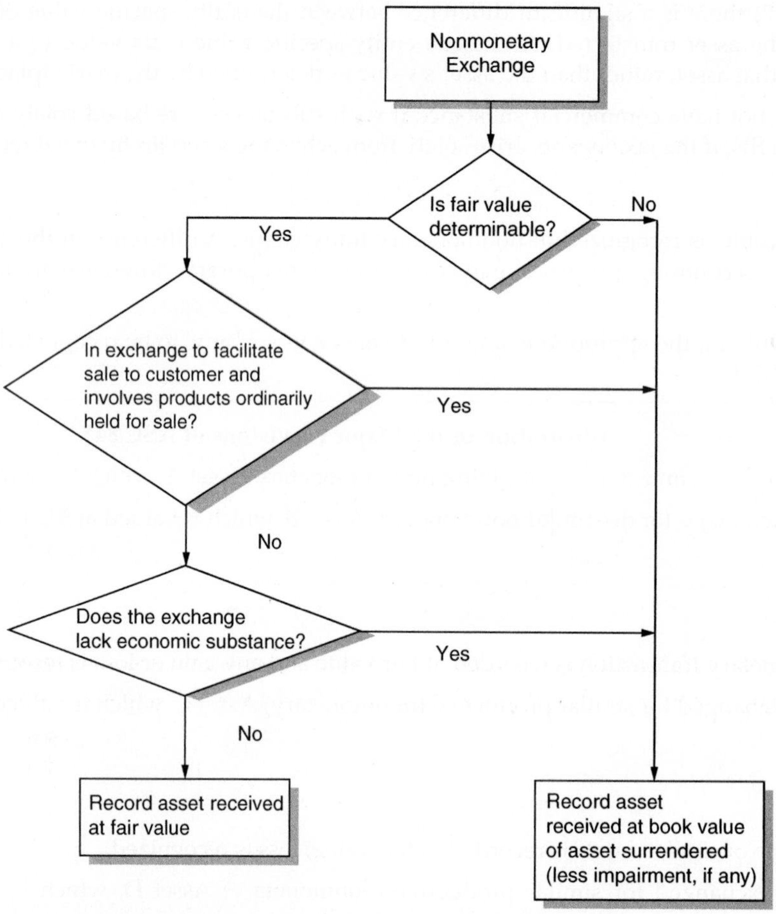

Involuntary Conversion of Nonmonetary Assets to Monetary Assets

When a nonmonetary asset is involuntarily converted to a monetary asset, a monetary transaction results, and ASC 610 (Other Income) requires that a gain or loss be recognized in the period of conversion. The gain or loss is the difference between the carrying amount of the nonmonetary asset and the proceeds from the conversion (ASC 610-30-25-2, 3).

Examples of involuntary conversion are the total or partial destruction of property through fire or other catastrophe, theft of property, or condemnation of property by a governmental authority (eminent domain proceedings).

Gain or loss from an involuntary conversion of a nonmonetary asset to a monetary asset is classified as part of continuing operations, disposal of a segment, etc., according to the particular circumstances (ASC 610-30-45-1). In addition, a gain or loss recognized for tax purposes in a period different from that for financial accounting purposes creates a temporary difference, for which recognition of deferred taxes may be necessary (ASC 740-10-55-66).

The involuntary conversion of a LIFO inventory layer at an interim reporting date does not have to be recognized if the proceeds are reinvested in replacement inventory by the end of the fiscal year (ASC 610-30-25-3).

PRACTICE NOTE: This is the same treatment afforded a temporary liquidation at interim dates of a LIFO inventory layer that is expected to be replaced by the end of the annual period.

In the event the proceeds from an involuntary conversion of a LIFO inventory layer are not reinvested in replacement inventory by the end of the fiscal year, gain for financial accounting purposes need not be recognized, providing the taxpayer does not recognize such gains for income tax reporting purposes and provided that replacement is intended but not yet made by year-end (ASC 610-30-25-3).

Disclosure

Disclosure of the nature of the nonmonetary transaction, the basis of accounting for assets transferred, and gains or losses recognized are required in the financial statements for the period in which the transaction occurs (ASC 845-10-50-1).

PART II: INTERPRETIVE GUIDANCE

ASC 845-10: OVERALL

ASC 845-10-05-8, 15-5 through 15-9, 25-4 through 25-5, 30-15 through 30-16, 45-1, 50-3, 55-10, 55-12 through 55-17, 55-19 through 55-22, 55-24 through 55-26 Purchases and Sales of Inventory with the Same Counterparty

IMPORTANT NOTICE: The guidance in ASC 845-10-15-8, which is discussed below, will be amended to delete the scope exception for exchanges of software and of real estate, which should be accounted for under the guidance in ASC 606 on noncash consideration for contracts with customers when the guidance in ASU 2014-09, *Revenue from Contracts with Customers*, which will reside in ASC 606 (Revenue from Contracts with Customers), becomes effective for public entities in annual reporting periods that begin after December 15, 2017, and interim periods within those annual periods and in annual reporting periods that begin after December 15, 2018, for nonpublic entities.

BACKGROUND

Companies sometimes enter into transactions to buy inventory from companies in the same line of business and to sell inventory in the form of raw materials, work-in-process (WIP), or finished goods to the same companies. Such purchase and sale arrangements may be structured under a single contract or under separate contracts.

The following guidance does *not* apply to inventory purchases and sales arrangements (*a*) accounted for as derivatives under the guidance in ASC 815 or (*b*) related to exchanges of software real estate. No guidance is provided as to whether transactions reported at fair value qualify for revenue recognition.

ACCOUNTING ISSUES

- To determine the effect of the guidance in ASC 845 on sale and purchase transactions of inventory with the same counterparty in the same line of business, under what circumstances should two or more inventory exchange transactions be considered to be one transaction?
- Are there circumstances under which nonmonetary exchanges of inventory in the same line of business should be recognized at fair value?

SCOPE

The following guidance applies to all inventory purchase and sale arrangements, including the following:

- Two or more inventory purchase and sale transactions between the same counterparties that are entered into with the intent of combining the transactions
- One inventory transaction that is legally dependent on the performance of another inventory transaction with the same counterparty. Such transactions are considered to have been made in contemplation of one another and would be considered to be a single exchange under the scope of the following guidance

An exchange of offsetting cash payments on invoices issued by counterparties in inventory purchase and sale transactions is not a factor in the determination whether those transactions should be considered as a single exchange transaction under the guidance in ASC 845-10.

ACCOUNTING GUIDANCE

For the purpose of determining the effect of the guidance in ASC 845 on sale and purchase transactions of inventory between two parties in the same line of business, two or more such transactions should be combined and accounted for as one transaction, because those purchase and sale transactions between the same two parties are entered into in contemplation of one another. The same guidance applies if an inventory transaction, such as a sale to a counterparty, legally depends on the counterparty's performance of another inventory transaction, such as a purchase from the same counterparty.

An inventory transaction that does *not* legally depend on the performance of another inventory transaction with the same counterparty should be evaluated based on the following factors, which are *not* determinative individually or all inclusively, to determine whether those transactions were entered into in contemplation of one another:

— *The counterparties have a specific legal right of offset related to the inventory purchase and sale transactions.* The ability to offset transactions indicates there is a connection between them. It indicates that transactions that were entered into separately, actually were entered into in contemplation of one another. This indicator is more important for net settlement provisions related to specific inventory transactions identified by the counterparties than for those that are netted as part of a master netting agreement for all the transactions between the counterparties.

— *The counterparties have entered into the inventory purchase and sale transactions at the same time.* This indicates that the transactions were entered into in contemplation of one another.

— *The terms of inventory sale and purchase transactions between two counterparties are at off-market rates at the inception of the agreement.* Inventory transactions entered into under such terms indicate they are related to one another, and have been entered into in contemplation of another inventory transaction between the counterparties. This indicator is more important if the products' market prices are readily determinable, such as exchange traded commodities, than if the prices for those products are more flexible.

— *Relative certainty that reciprocal inventory transactions with the same party will occur.* If an entity enters into a sale transaction with a counterparty and the counterparty may, but is not obligated to, deliver an agreed amount of inventory. If that counterparty chooses to deliver its product to the entity, the entity is obligated to purchase the product. The more certain it becomes that the counterparty will deliver the agreed amount of inventory the more likely it becomes that the two transactions have been entered into in contemplation of one another.

Nonmonetary exchange transactions of finished goods inventory for raw materials or WIP inventory in the same line of business are *not* exchange transactions that will result in sales to customers other than the parties to the exchange in accordance with the guidance in ASC 845-10-30-3(b). Such a transaction should be accounted for at *fair value*, if (*a*) its fair value can be determined within reasonable limits *and* (*b*) the transaction has commercial substance. All other nonmonetary exchanges of inventory in the same line of business, such as an exchange of raw materials or WIP inventory for raw materials, WIP, finished goods inventory, or finished goods inventory for finished goods inventory, should be recognized at the *carrying amount* of the transferred inventory.

Inventory accounted for under the guidance for "purchases and sales of inventory with the same counterparty" should be classified as raw materials, WIP, or finished goods, in the same manner as it would be classified in the entity's external financial reporting

The amount of revenue and costs or gains and losses related to inventory exchanges recognized at fair value should be disclosed.

ASC 845-10-05-10, 15-11, 30-17 through 30-20 Barter Transactions

---

IMPORTANT NOTICE: The guidance in ASC 840-10-30-17 through 13-18, which is discussed below, will be superseded when the guidance in ASU 2014-09, *Revenue from Contracts with Customers*, which will reside in ASC 606 (Revenue from Contracts with Customers), becomes effective for public business entities in annual reporting periods that begin after December 15, 2017, and interim periods within those annual periods and in annual reporting periods that begin after December 15, 2018, for nonpublic entities.

BACKGROUND

Entities sometimes exchange nonmonetary assets—equipment, for example—for barter credits. Such transactions may be entered into by the parties to the transaction directly, or the transactions may be arranged by a third party (a barter company) whose business is to match buyers with sellers.

Entities can use barter credits obtained in an exchange to purchase goods or services, such as advertising time, from the other party to the transaction, the barter company, or members of the barter company's exchange network. A barter contract may specify the goods and services that may be purchased, which can be limited to those available from the barter exchange network. Some barter transactions also require a payment of cash in addition to barter credits. Barter credits may expire on a specific date on which they lose their value.

ACCOUNTING ISSUES

- Should exchanges of nonmonetary assets for barter credits be accounted for in accordance with the provisions of ASC 845?
- If so, how should a gain or loss, if any, be determined and recognized?

ACCOUNTING GUIDANCE

1. The provisions of ASC 845 apply to exchanges of nonmonetary assets for barter credits. That guidance should be applied as follows:
   (1) It is assumed that the fair value of a nonmonetary asset exchanged for barter credits is more clearly evident than the fair value of the barter credits received. Therefore, barter credits should be reported at the fair value of the asset exchanged. That assumption may be overcome if:
      (a) The barter credits can be converted into cash in the near future as evidenced by past transactions, *or*
      (b) Independent quoted market prices can be used to determine the fair value of items to be received in exchange for barter credits.
   (2) Assume that the nonmonetary asset's fair value does not exceed its carrying amount unless persuasive evidence supports a higher value.
   (3) Recognize an impairment loss on barter credits if after the exchange it becomes apparent that:
      (a) The remaining value of the barter credits is less than their carrying amount.
      (b) It is probable that the entity will not use some, or all, of its barter credits before they expire.
   (4) If an operating lease is exchanged for barter credits, the lease's impairment should be measured as the excess of remaining lease costs (total of discounted rental payments and unamortized leasehold improvements) over the discounted amount of sublease rentals for the remaining term of the lease.

DISCUSSION

Because of concerns that barter transactions were being used to defer losses that should have been recognized before an exchange occurred, an evaluation of (1) the impairment of a nonmonetary asset exchanged and (2) loss recognition prior to an exchange is required, if the fair value of the nonmonetary asset to be exchanged for barter credits is less than its carrying amount.

The presumption that the fair value of a nonmonetary asset exchanged be more clearly evident than the fair value of barter credits is required due to concerns about the objectivity of the valuation of barter credits.

ASC 845-10-05-11 through 05-12, 15-12 through 15-17, 15-20, 25-6 through 25-12, 30-12 through 30-14, 30-21 through 30-27, S30-2, 55-2, 55-27 through 55-37, 60-3, S99-3 Exchanges Involving Monetary Consideration

---

IMPORTANT NOTICE: The guidance discussed below will be amended as follows: (1) the guidance in ASC in ASC 845-10-15-14 will be amended to state that it does not apply to transfers between a joint venture and its owners and subparagraphs (a) and (b) will be superseded; (2) ASC 845-10-15-15 through 15-17 will be superseded; (3) ASC 845-10-15-20(c) will be superseded; (4) ASC 845-10-25-7 through 25-8 will be superseded; (4) ASC 845-10-30-23 will be superseded; (5) ASC 845-10-30-25 will be amended and partially superseded; (6) ASC 845-10-30-25A will be amended and moved to 30-25C; (7) ASC 845-10-30-25B will be added; (8) the Table in ASC 845-10-55-2 will be amended (9) ASC 845-10-55-29 through 55-37 will be superseded; and (10) the guidance in ASC 845-10-60-3 will be superseded by the guidance in ASU 2014-09, *Revenue from Contracts with Customers,* which will reside in ASC 606 (Revenue from Contracts with Customers), becomes effective for public entities in annual reporting periods that begin after December 15, 2017, and interim periods within those annual periods and in annual reporting periods that begin after December 15, 2018, for nonpublic entities.

BACKGROUND

The accounting guidance below applies to three types of exchange transactions of nonmonetary nonfinancial assets and monetary consideration (boot) for the following kinds of assets:

- Other nonmonetary nonfinancial assets;
- Real estate; and
- A noncontrolling ownership interest in another entity.

SCOPE

The following guidance does not apply to:

- Transfers between a joint venture and its owners;
- Capital contributions of real estate for an unconsolidated real estate investment (see ASC 970-323);
- Transfers of real estate in exchange for nonmonetary assets other than real estate (see ASC 976-605 and ASC 360-20-40);
- A deconsolidation of a subsidiary that is a business or a nonprofit activity under the scope of ASC 810-10; or
- A derecognition of a group of assets that is a business or nonprofit activity under the scope of ASC 810-10.

ACCOUNTING ISSUES

Exchanges Involving Monetary Consideration

1. How much monetary consideration in a nonmonetary exchange would cause an entire transaction to be accounted for as a monetary exchange, which is not included under the scope of ASC 845?

Exchanges of Real Estate Involving Monetary Consideration

2. How should an exchange of similar real estate that is considered to be monetary because it includes boot in excess of 25% of the fair value of an exchange be accounted for?

Monetary Exchange of a Nonfinancial Asset for a Noncontrolling Ownership Interest

3. If a nonmonetary exchange must be accounted for at fair value, should a full or partial gain be recognized if Entity A transfers a nonfinancial asset to Entity B in exchange for a noncontrolling ownership interest in Entity B?

ACCOUNTING GUIDANCE

Exchanges Involving Monetary Consideration

1. If an exchange of nonmonetary assets that would normally be recognized at historical cost includes boot, it should be accounted for as follows:
   a. As a monetary exchange at fair value by both parties if boot is significant (i.e., at least 25% of the fair value of an exchange).
   b. If boot is less than 25% of the fair value of an exchange, the recipient of boot should follow the guidance on pro rata gain recognition in ASC 845-10-30-6; the payer of boot does *not* recognize a gain. Fair value should be used only if it can be measured satisfactorily.

Exchanges of Real Estate Involving Monetary Consideration

2. An exchange of similar real estate with boot equivalent to 25% or more of the fair value of an exchange that is considered to be a monetary exchange under the guidance in Issue 1 above, should be allocated between the monetary and nonmonetary components of the transaction based on the relative fair values of the real estate assets exchanged at the time of the transaction.

Illustration of Accounting for an Exchange of Real Estate with Boot

Company A transfers real estate with a fair value of $500,000 and a net book value of $100,000 to Company B for $120,000 in cash, a note for $100,000, and real estate having a fair value of $280,000 and a net book value of $240,000. The initial investment requirement for full accrual profit recognition under ASC 360 is 20%. The terms of the note from Company B satisfy the continuing investment provisions necessary to apply the full accrual method. Interest on the note, which is considered fully collectible, is at a market rate. The fair values of the real estate transferred by both parties are readily determinable and realizable at the date of the exchange. Neither party has any continuing involvement with the real estate exchanged.

Allocation to Monetary and Nonmonetary Portions

Monetary portion:

$$\frac{\text{Total monetary consideration}}{\text{Total fair value of the exchange}} = \frac{\$220{,}000}{\$500{,}000} = 44\%$$

The monetary portion of the exchange is $120,000 in cash and a note for $100,000.

Nonmonetary portion:

$$\frac{\text{Fair value of real estate exchanged}}{\text{Total fair value of the exchange}} = \frac{\$280{,}000}{\$500{,}000} = 56\%$$

The nonmonetary portion of the exchange is real estate with a fair value of $500,000 for similar real estate with a fair value of $280,000 ($500,000 × .56).

Company A (Receiver of boot)

Because the monetary portion of $120,000 in cash (more than 20% of the total consideration) and the $100,000 note meet the requirements for the buyer's initial and continuing investment, full accrual profit recognition is permitted on the monetary portion under the guidance in ASC 360. Company A would recognize a gain as follows:

Monetary consideration	$220,000
Less: Company A's book value ($100,000) × .44	44,000
Profit recognized	$176,000

No gain is recognized on the nonmonetary portion, because two similar assets are exchanged. The basis for the new asset is as follows:

Net book value of real estate exchanged	$100,000
Pro rata portion of net book value retired ($100,000 × .44)	44,000
	$56,000

Company B (Payer of boot)

Company B accounts for the monetary portion of the exchange at the amount of boot, $220,000, which represents an acquisition of real estate. No gain is recognized on the nonmonetary portion, because two similar assets are exchanged. The basis for the new asset is as follows:

Net book value of real estate exchanged	$240,000
Boot	220,000
	$460,000

Monetary Exchange of a Nonfinancial Asset for a Noncontrolling Ownership Interest

3. A monetary exchange of a financial asset for a noncontrolling ownership interest in the counterparty to an exchange should be accounted for as follows:

   a. Full or partial gain recognition is required in a monetary exchange that must be accounted for at fair value in which Entity A transfers a nonfinancial asset to entity B in exchange for a noncontrolling ownership interest in Entity B.

   b. If Company A has no actual or implied financial or other commitment to support Company B's operations, the amount of the gain recognized by Entity A, if applicable, may exceed the amount computed under (a) above. A commitment exists if the parties to the exchange have signed a binding, written agreement that specifies the agreement's principal provisions. A preliminary agreement does not qualify as a commitment for the purpose of this guidance if the principal provisions have not yet been negotiated, or are subsequently changed.

c. The following transactions should be accounted for as a deconsolidation in accordance with the guidance in ASC 810-10-40-3A, except for a sale of in substance real estate, which should be accounted for based on the guidance in ASC 360-20 or ASC 976-605, or is a conveyance of oil and gas mineral rights, which should be accounted for based on the guidance in AC 932-60.
   (1) Entity A transfers a subsidiary that is a business or a nonprofit activity to Entity B in exchange for a noncontrolling interest in Entity B
   (2) Entity A transfers a group of assets that is a business or a nonprofit activity to Entity B in exchange for a noncontrolling interest in Entity B.
d. Exchanges of nonmonetary assets, other than those discussed in (c) above, for a noncontrolling ownership interest in another entity should be accounted for at fair value with recognition of a full or partial gain on the transaction.
e. If the fair value of a transferred asset is greater than its carrying value either of the following applies:
   (1) A *gain* for the difference should be recognized if the entity accounts for the ownership received using the guidance in ASC 321.
   (2) A *partial gain* should be recognized if the equity method in ASC 323 is used to account for the ownership interest received.

   That partial gain should be calculated using the amount under (1) above reduced by a portion of the gain that is related to the economic interest retained in the transferred asset. For example, if Entity A exchanged an asset with a fair value of $500,000 and a carrying value of $200,000 for a 20% economic interest in Entity B, the calculation of Entity A's gain would be $500,000 – $200,000 = $300,000 × .2 = $60,000. The gain would be $300,000 – $60,000 = $240,000. The amount that Entity A records for the ownership interest received in the exchange is partially based on its fair at the exchange date and partially based on the carryover amount of the asset surrendered.
f. If the fair value of an exchanged nonfinancial asset is less than its carrying value, the difference should be recognized as a *loss*.

CHAPTER 58

ASC 848—REFERENCE RATE REFORM

CONTENTS

PART I: GENERAL GUIDANCE

ASC 848-10: OVERALL

OVERVIEW AND BACKGROUND

The FASB issued ASU 2020-04, *Reference Rate Reform (Topic 848): Facilitation of the Effects of Reference Rate Reform on Financial Reporting*, in March 2020 to provide optional guidance for a limited period of time for companies impacted by recent reference rate reforms. These reforms were in response to concerns about structural risks associated with interbank offered rates, especially the risk of cessation of the London Interbank Offered Rate (LIBOR). The goal of the reference rate reforms was to identify alternative reference rates that would be more observable or transactions based and less susceptible to manipulation (ASC 848-10-05-2).

Stakeholders expressed concerns related to challenges caused by replacing references to discontinued rates with references to replacement rates for a significant volume of contracts and other arrangements, such as debt agreements, lease agreements, and derivative instruments. Under existing guidance, such changes in reference rates would require entities to evaluate whether the modifications result in the creation of new contracts or the continuation of existing contracts. Stakeholders expressed concerns about the time and costs required to perform these evaluations, and also indicated that financial reporting results should reflect the intended continuation of such contracts and arrangements during the period in which the market transitions to the alternative reference rates.

Stakeholders also raised additional concerns specific to hedge accounting. In particular, changes to an alternative reference rate could disallow the application of certain hedge accounting guidance, and certain hedging relationships may no longer qualify as highly effective during the rate transition period. The inability to apply hedge accounting guidance because of reference rate reform could result in financial reporting outcomes that are not an accurate reflection of entities' intended hedging strategies.

The revised guidance in ASU 2020-04 applies to all entities, subject to meeting certain criteria, that have contracts, hedging relationships, and other transactions that reference LIBOR or another reference rate expected to be discontinued because of reference rate reform (ASC 848-10-15-3).

PRACTICE NOTE: ASU 2020-04 also allows an entity to make a one-time election to sell or transfer certain debt securities classified as held to maturity to available for sale or trading. At the time of applying the one-time election, an entity can sell, transfer, or both sell and transfer debt securities classified as held to maturity that both (1) reference a rate that is expected to be discontinued as a result of reference rate reform, and (2) were classified as held to maturity before January 1, 2020 (ASC 848-10-35-1).

As the market transitions to new reference rates, certain derivative instruments may be modified to use a different rate for margining, discounting, or contract price realignment (ASC 848-10-05-02). The FASB subsequently released ASU 2021-01, *Reference Rate Reform (Topic 848): Scope*, in January 2021. This new ASU was issued to respond to stakeholders' concerns that the existing guidance in ASC 848 did not address the discounting transition effects of certain derivative instruments indexed to a wide variety of interest rates, including rates that would not be discontinued as a result of rate reform. This new guidance expands the scope of ASC 848 to include these derivative instruments that do not meet the scope of ASC 848-10-15-3 (ASC 848-10-15-3A).

Effective Date of Reference Rate Reform Guidance

The guidance in ASU 2020-04 is intended to be applied for a relatively short period of time. Generally, this guidance is effective for all entities as of March 12, 2020 through December 31, 2022. This guidance should not be applied to contract modifications made after December 31, 2022, nor to new hedging relationships entered into after December 31, 2022. The guidance also should not be applied to hedging relationships evaluated for periods after December 31, 2022, except for hedging relationships existing as of December 31, 2022, that apply certain optional expedients in ASC 848-30 and ASC 848-40 that are to be retained through the end of the hedging relationship (including for periods evaluated after December 31, 2022) (ASC 848-10-65-1).

ASC 848-20: CONTRACT MODIFICATIONS

OPTIONAL EXPEDIENTS FOR CONTRACT MODIFICATIONS

The guidance in ASC 848-20, if elected, applies to contracts that meet the scope criteria of ASC 848-10-15-3 if either or both of the following occur (ASC 848-20-05-1; ASC 848-20-15-2):

1. Contract modifications that replace a reference rate affected by reference rate reform (including rates referenced in fallback provisions) and contemporaneous modifications of other contract terms related to the replacement of the reference rate (including contract modifications to add or change fallback provisions).
2. The interest rate used for margining, discounting, or contract price alignment is modified due to reference rate reform.

Certain optional expedients provided in ASC 848-20, if elected, shall apply to derivative instruments that meet the scope criteria of ASC 848-10-15-3A (ASC 848-20-15-2A).

The following optional expedients are permitted for contracts that are modified because of reference rate reform and that meet certain scope guidance:

1. Modifications of contracts within the scope of ASC 310 (Receivables) and ASC 470 (Debt) should be accounted for by prospectively adjusting the effective interest rate.
2. Modifications of contracts within the scope of ASC 840 (Leases) and ASC 842 (Leases) should be accounted for as a continuation of the existing contracts with no reassessments of the lease classification and the discount rate or remeasurements of lease payments that would otherwise be required for modifications not accounted for as separate contracts (ASC 848-20-35-11).
3. Modifications of contracts do not require an entity to reassess its original conclusion about whether that contract contains an embedded derivative that is clearly and closely related to the economic characteristics and risks of the host contract (ASC 848-20-35-14).

For other topics within the Codification, ASU 2020-04 includes a general principle that allows an entity to consider contract modifications due to reference rate reform to be an event that does not require contract remeasurement at the modification date or reassessment of a previous accounting determination (ASC 848-20-35-4). An entity that elects these optional expedients for contract modifications must apply them consistently for all eligible contracts or eligible transactions within the relevant topics of the Codification that contain guidance that would otherwise be required to be applied, with the exception of derivative instruments that change the interest rate used for margining, discounting, or contract price realignment (ASC 848-20-35-1).

ASC 848-30: HEDGING—GENERAL

CHANGES IN CRITICAL TERMS OF A HEDGING RELATIONSHIP

The guidance in ASU 2020-04 provides exceptions to the guidance in ASC 815 related to changes to the critical terms of a hedging relationship due to reference rate reform. Certain optional expedients provided in ASC 848-30, if elected, shall apply to hedging instruments that meet the scope criteria of ASC 848-10-15-3A (ASC 848-30-15-1). Specifically, the following changes should not result in the dedesignation of a hedging relationship if certain criteria are met:

1. Certain changes in the critical terms of a designated hedging instrument, a hedged item, or a forecasted transaction in a fair value hedge, a cash flow hedge, or a net investment hedge (ASC 848-30-25-5).
2. A change to rebalance or adjust the hedging relationship as follows (ASC 848-30-25-9):
    a. In a fair value hedge, a change in the proportion of the derivative designated as the hedging instrument or in the proportion of the designated hedged item or both.
    b. In a fair value hedge or a cash flow hedge, a change in the designated hedging instrument to add one or more additional derivatives.
3. For a cash flow hedge, a change in the method used to assess hedge effectiveness when initially applying an optional expedient method and when reverting to the requirements in ASC 815-20 (ASC 848-30-25-8).

OPTIONAL EXPEDIENTS FOR EXCLUDED COMPONENTS

The guidance in ASU 2020-04 provides the following optional expedients for fair value hedging relationships, cash flow hedging relationship, and net investment hedging relationships for which the component excluded from the assessment of hedge effectiveness is affected by reference rate reform (ASC 848-30-25-12, 25-13):

1. An entity may change the systematic and rational method it currently uses to recognize the excluded components in earnings.
2. A change in the fair value of an excluded component due to changes in the hedging instrument's contractual terms may be recognized in current earnings.

The optional expedients for excluded components may be elected on an individual hedging relationship basis (ASC 848-30-25-2).

ASC 848-40: FAIR VALUE HEDGES

OPTIONAL EXPEDIENTS FOR FAIR VALUE HEDGES

The guidance in ASU 2020-04 provides the following optional expedients for fair value hedging relationships for which the derivative designated as the hedging instrument is affected by reference rate reform if certain conditions are met:

1. An entity may change the designated benchmark interest rate documented at hedge inception to a different eligible benchmark interest rate. The method used to change the benchmark interest rate must be reasonable and must be used consistently across similar fair value hedging relationships (ASC 848-40-25-2).
2. An entity may disregard certain conditions required to apply the shortcut method that are not met because of the impact of reference rate reform and may continue to disregard those conditions for the remainder of the fair value hedging relationship (including for the remainder of the hedging relationships that end after December 31, 2022) (ASC 848-40-25-8).

ASC 848-50: CASH FLOW HEDGES

OPTIONAL EXPEDIENTS FOR CASH FLOW HEDGES

The guidance in ASU 2020-04 provides the following optional expedients for cash flow hedging relationships affected by reference rate reform if certain criteria are met:

1. If the designated hedged interest rate risk is a rate that is affected by reference rate reform:
    a. An entity should disregard the change in the designated hedged interest rate risk caused by reference rate reform when the entity assesses whether the hedged forecasted transaction is probable in accordance with ASC 815 (ASC 848-50-25-2).

b. An entity may continue hedge accounting for a cash flow hedge for which the hedged interest rate risk changes if either the hedge is highly effective under an assessment method in ASC 815-20 and ASC 815-30 or if the entity has elected an optional expedient method provided in ASU 2020-04 (ASC 848-50-25-3).

2. For cash flow hedges for which the shortcut method or another method that assumes perfect hedge effectiveness has been applied, an entity may disregard certain conditions required to apply those methods that are not met because of reference rate reform and may continue to apply the shortcut method (ASC 848-50-25-6).
3. For cash flow hedges for which either the hedging instrument or the hedged forecasted transactions reference a rate that is expected to be impacted by reference rate reform, an entity may adjust how it assesses hedge effectiveness (including the shortcut method and other assessment methods that assume perfect hedge effectiveness) to disregard certain mismatches between the designated hedging instrument and the hedged item (ASC 848-50-35-5).
4. An entity may elect to use a qualitative method to assess hedge effectiveness, effectively suspending subsequent hedge effectiveness assessments that would otherwise be required by ASC 815-20 and ASC 815-30 (ASC 848-50-35-10).
5. For cash flow hedges of portfolios of forecasted transactions that reference a rate that is expected to be affected by reference rate reform, an entity may disregard the guidance in ASC 815-20 requiring the group of individual transactions to share the same risk exposure for which they are designated as being hedged (ASC 848-50-25-14).

The optional expedients for cash flow hedging relationships may be elected on an individual hedging relationship basis (ASC 848-50-25-1). After electing an optional expedient method, an entity may revert to hedge accounting requirements in ASC 815-20 and ASC 815-30 without dedesignating the hedging relationship (ASC 848-50-35-20).

CHAPTER 59

ASC 850—RELATED PARTY DISCLOSURES

CONTENTS

GENERAL GUIDANCE

ASC 850-10: OVERALL

OVERVIEW

Financial statement disclosure of related party transactions is required by U.S. GAAP in order for those statements to fairly present financial position, cash flows, and results of operations.

BACKGROUND

A *related party* is one that can exercise control or significant influence over the management and/or operating policies of another party, to the extent that one of the parties may be prevented from fully pursuing its own separate interests.

Related parties consist of all affiliates of an enterprise, including (*a*) their management and their immediate families, (*b*) their principal owners and their immediate families, (*c*) their investments accounted for by the equity method (absent the election of the fair value option under ASC 825, Financial Instruments), (*d*) beneficial employee trusts that are managed by the management of the enterprise, and (*e*) any party that may, or does, deal with the enterprise and has ownership of, control over, or can significantly influence the management or operating policies of another party to the extent that an arm's-length transaction may not be achieved (ASC 850-10-05-3).

Transactions among related parties generally are accounted for on the same basis as if the parties were not related, unless the *substance* of the transaction is not arm's length. Substance over form is an important consideration when accounting for transactions involving related parties.

Common related party transactions include the following (ASC 850-10-05-4):

- Sales, purchases, and transfers of realty and personal property
- Services received or furnished (e.g., accounting, management, engineering, and legal services)
- Use of property and equipment by lease
- Borrowings and lendings
- Maintenance of bank balances as compensating balances for the benefit of another
- Intercompany billings based on allocation of common costs
- Filing of consolidated tax returns

PRACTICE NOTE: The Enron Corp. engaged in a number of related party transactions. These transactions were related to the financial improprieties that caused Enron's failure. Related party transactions are more likely when an entity is dealing with partnerships, particularly when these partnerships are located in tax havens and where there appears to be little economic justification for the partnership's existence. Regulators and standard-setters are focusing more resources on the proper disclosure of related party transactions; auditors and preparers of financial statements need to be aware of this heightened focus.

REPORTING AND DISCLOSURE STANDARDS

ASC 850 requires that material related party transactions that are not eliminated in consolidated or combined financial statements be disclosed in the financial statements of the reporting entity. Related party transactions involving compensation arrangements, expense allowances, and similar items incurred in the ordinary course of business, however, do not have to be disclosed (ASC 850-10-50-1).

If separate financial statements of an entity that has been consolidated are presented in a financial report that includes the consolidated financial statements, duplicate disclosure of the related party transactions is not necessary. Disclosure of related party transactions is required, however, in separate financial statements of (*a*) a parent company, (*b*) a subsidiary, (*c*) a corporate joint venture, or (*d*) an investee that is 50% owned or less (ASC 850-10-50-4).

Information required to be disclosed for material related party transactions is as follows (ASC 850-10-50-1):

- The nature of the relationship of the related parties
- A description of the transactions, including amounts and other pertinent information necessary for an understanding of the effects of the related party transactions, for each period in which an income statement is presented (related party transactions of no or nominal amounts must also be disclosed)
- The dollar amount of transactions for each period in which an income statement is presented; also, the effects of any change in terms between the related parties from terms used in prior periods
- If not apparent in the financial statements, (*a*) the terms of related party transactions, (*b*) the manner of settlement of related party transactions, and (*c*) the amount due to or from related parties

If the operating results or financial position of a reporting entity can be altered significantly by the effects of common ownership or management control of the reporting entity and one or more other entities, even if there are no transactions among any of the entities, the nature of the ownership or management control must be disclosed in the financial statements (ASC 850-10-50-6).

PRACTICE POINTER: The amount of detail disclosed for related party transactions must be sufficient for the user of the financial statements to be able to understand the related party transaction and its impact on the financial statements. Thus, all that is necessary may be disclosure of the total amount of a specific type of material related party transaction or of the effects of the relationship between the related parties. In other circumstances, however, more details may be required for the reader of the financial statements to have a clear understanding of the transaction.

One cannot assume that a related party transaction is consummated in the same manner as an arm's-length transaction. Disclosures or other representations of a material related party transaction in financial statements should not imply that the transaction was made on the same basis as an arm's-length transaction, unless the disclosures or representations can be substantiated (ASC 850-10-50-5).

Illustrations of Related Party Disclosures

Transaction between company and officers/directors During 20X5, the company purchased land and buildings adjoining one of its plants from two company directors for $750,000. The board of directors unanimously approved the purchase, with the two directors involved in the transaction abstaining.

Transaction between company and profit-sharing plan During 20X5, the company purchased land from one of its profit-sharing plans for $750,000. Department of Labor exemption was received prior to the transaction.

Lease between company and officer/owner Several years ago, the company leased land in upstate New York from John Doe, an officer and principal owner. The company constructed and furnished a residence on the property for use by the company's customers and distributors. The annual lease payment to Doe is $12,500, and the lease continues through December 31, 20X5. At that time, Doe has an option to purchase the residence and furnishings for $50,000 or to renew the lease at $10,000 per year for an additional five years.

Salary advance to officer During 20X5, the company made a $100,000 salary advance to John Doe, an officer, as part of a new employment contract that required Doe to relocate to Atlanta, Georgia. According to the terms of the contract, Doe is required to repay the loan at $20,000 per year for the next five years, beginning in 20X8.

CHAPTER 60

ASC 852—REORGANIZATIONS

CONTENTS

PART I: GENERAL GUIDANCE

ASC 852-20: QUASI-REORGANIZATIONS

OVERALL

When a struggling business reaches a turnaround point and profitable operations seem likely, a quasi-reorganization may be appropriate to eliminate an accumulated deficit from past unprofitable operations. The resulting financial statements have more credibility and may make it possible for the company to borrow money for its profitable operations. In addition, by eliminating the deficit in retained earnings, the possibility of paying dividends in the foreseeable future becomes more likely.

BACKGROUND

The specific criteria that must be met for a quasi-reorganization to be appropriate are:

- Assets are overvalued in the balance sheet.
- The company can reasonably expect to be profitable in the future if a restructuring occurs so that future operations are not burdened with the problems of the past.
- Formal shareholder consent is obtained.

Stockholders' equity usually is made up of the following:

- Capital contributed for stock, to the extent of the par or stated value of each class of stock presently outstanding
- Additional paid-in or contributed capital:
  - — Capital contributed in excess of par or stated value of each class of stock, whether as a result of original issues, any subsequent reductions of par or stated value, or transactions by the corporation in its own shares
  - — Capital received other than for stock, whether from shareholders or others (such as donated capital)
- Retained earnings (or deficit), which represents the accumulated income or loss of the corporation.

Generally, items properly chargeable to current or future years' income accounts may *not* be charged to contributed capital accounts. An exception to this rule occurs in accounting for quasi-reorganizations, in which case a one-time adjustment to contributed capital is appropriate.

Although the corporate entity remains unchanged in a quasi-reorganization, a new basis of accountability is established. Net assets are restated downward to their fair values, and stockholders' equity is reduced. Retained earnings (deficit) is eliminated by charging any deficit accumulated from operations and the asset adjustments to either (*a*) capital contributed in excess of par or (*b*) capital contributed other than for capital stock. Contributed capital accounts must be large enough to absorb the deficit in retained earnings, including adjustments made as part of the quasi-reorganization.

PRACTICE POINTER: Although the capital stock account may not be used to directly absorb a deficit in retained earnings, a corporation may reduce the par value of its existing capital stock and transfer the resulting excess to a capital contributed in excess of par account. This procedure frequently is used in a quasi-reorganization.

QUASI-REORGANIZATION

Accounting and Reporting

If a corporation restates its assets and stockholders' equity through a quasi-reorganization, it must make a clear report of the proposed restatements to its shareholders and obtain their formal consent (ASC 852-20-25-3).

Assets are written down to their fair values; if fair values are not readily determinable, conservative estimates are used (ASC 852-20-35-2). Estimates may also be used to provide for known probable losses prior to the date of the quasi-reorganization, when amounts are indeterminable (ASC 852-20-30-4).

PRACTICE POINTER: Determination of the fair value of assets is a subjective process, requiring the use of different valuation and appraisal techniques for different asset categories.

If estimates are used and the amounts subsequently are found to be excessive or insufficient, the difference should be charged or credited to the capital account previously charged or credited and not to retained earnings (ASC 852-20-35-2).

The steps in the accounting procedure are as follows:

Step 1. All asset amounts to be written off are charged to retained earnings (ASC 852-20-25-4).

Step 2. After all amounts to be written off are recognized and charged to retained earnings, the negative (debit) balance is transferred to paid-in capital (ASC 852-20-25-4).

Paid-in capital may have existed prior to the quasi-reorganization, or it may have been created as a result of a reduction of par value in conjunction with the quasi-reorganization.

Step 3. When a deficit in retained earnings is transferred to an allowable capital account, any subsequent balance sheet must disclose, by dating the retained earnings, that the balance in the retained earnings account has accumulated since the date of reorganization (ASC 852-20-50-2). For example:

Retained earnings, since July 1, 20X0 $1,234,567

The dating of retained earnings following a quasi-reorganization would rarely, if ever, be of significance after a period of ten years. There may be exceptional circumstances that could justify a period of less than ten years (ASC 852-20-50-2).

Step 4. Additional paid-in capital originating in a reorganization adjustment is restricted in the same manner as that of a new corporation (ASC 852-20-25-6).

Step 5. Corporations with subsidiaries should follow the same procedures so that no credit balance remains in consolidated retained earnings after a quasi-reorganization in which losses have been charged to allowable capital accounts (ASC 852-20-25-4).

In those cases in which losses have been charged to the allowable capital accounts, instead of a credit balance in a subsidiary's retained earnings, the parent company's interest in such retained earnings is regarded as capitalized by the quasi-reorganization in the same way retained earnings of a subsidiary are capitalized by the parent on the date of its acquisition (ASC 852-20-25-4).

Step 6. The effective date of the quasi-reorganization from which income of the corporation is thereafter determined should be as close as possible to the date of formal stockholders' consent and ordinarily not before the close of the last completed fiscal year (ASC 852-20-25-5).

Adjustments made pursuant to a quasi-reorganization should not be included in the determination of net income for any period.

Accounting for a Tax Benefit

Careful consideration must be given to the proper accounting for any tax attributes in a quasi-reorganization. Under ASC 740 (Income Taxes), tax benefits of deductible temporary differences and carryforwards as of the date of the quasi-reorganization must be reported as a direct addition to capital contributed if the tax benefits are recognized in subsequent years (ASC 852-740-45-3). An exception may exist for entities that have previously adopted the predecessor standard to ASC 740 and effected a quasi-reorganization; in that instance, subsequent recognition of tax benefits may be included in income and then reclassified from retained earnings to capital contributed in excess of par (ASC 852-740-45-1).

Disclosure

Adequate disclosure of all pertinent information must be made in the financial statements. A new retained earnings account dated as of the date of the quasi-reorganization is established and reflected in subsequent financial statements.

Illustration of Accounting for a Quasi-Reorganization

The Centrex Company experienced losses in each of its first six years of operation. In May 20X5, the company acquired two patents on an advanced solar heating unit, which soon became the standard for the industry. The quarter ended September 30, 20X5, was profitable, and the patent and accompanying licensing agreements indicate that continuing profitability is quite likely.

Centrex is closely held and the stockholders have agreed in principle to a quasi-reorganization. Negotiations have been held with various creditors regarding capitalizing debts.

The balance sheet of Centrex at December 31, 20X5, appears as follows:

Assets:	
Cash	$ 25,000
Accounts receivable (net)	410,000
Plant and equipment (net)	1,670,000
Other assets	80,000
Total assets	$2,185,000
Liabilities and Equity:	
Accounts payable	$ 840,000
Notes payable—other	300,000
Equipment notes payable	240,000
Common stock	500,000
Paid-in capital in excess of par value—common stock	1,017,000
Retained earnings	(712,000)
Total liabilities and equity	$2,185,000

The stockholders and creditors have approved the following plan of informal reorganization effective January 1, 20X6:

1. The current shareholders will exchange their 100,000 shares of $5 par stock for 100,000 shares of $1 par stock.
2. The creditors have agreed to accept a new issue of 5% preferred stock valued at $300,000 for an equal amount of accounts payable.
3. The plant and equipment will be written down to its fair value of $1,100,000.
4. Accounts receivable of $70,000 will be written off as uncollectible.
5. Other assets will be written down to their fair value of $50,000.

The first step in a quasi-reorganization is to write down all assets to their fair values. In the example, the journal entry would be:

Retained earnings	670,000	
Plant and equipment ($1,670,000 – $1,100,000)		570,000
Accounts receivable		70,000
Other assets ($80,000 – $50,000)		30,000

Next, the change in the par value of the common stock is recorded:

Common stock	400,000	
Paid-in capital in excess of par value—common stock		400,000

The following journal entry records the new preferred stock issued for $300,000 of accounts payable:

Accounts payable	300,000	
5% Preferred stock		300,000

After all the quasi-reorganization adjustments are made, the deficit in retained earnings ($1,382,000) is eliminated against the paid-in capital—common stock—leaving a zero balance in retained earnings:

Paid-in capital—common stock	1,382,000	
Retained earnings ($712,000 + $670,000)		1,382,000

The Centrex Company balance sheet, after giving effect to the reorganization, appears as follows:

Assets:	
Cash	$25,000
Accounts receivable (net)	340,000
Plant and equipment (net)	1,100,000
Other assets	50,000
Total assets	$1,515,000
Liabilities and Equity:	
Accounts payable	$540,000
Notes payable—other	300,000
Equipment notes payable	240,000
5% Preferred stock	300,000
Common stock ($1 par)	100,000
Paid-in capital in excess of par value—common stock ($1,017,000 + $400,000 -$1,382,000)	35,000
Retained earnings since January 1, 20X5	-0-
Total liabilities and equity	$1,515,000

PART II: INTERPRETIVE GUIDANCE

ASC 852-10: OVERALL

ASC 852-10-05-3 through 05-16, 10-1, 15-1 through 15-3, 25-1, 30-1, 45-1 through 45-2, 45-4 through 45-21, 45-26 through 45-27, 45-29, 50-2 through 50-4, 50-6A, 50-7, 55-3, 55-5 through 55-11, ASC 852-20-15-3; ASC 740-45-1; ASC 210-10-60-3 Financial Reporting by Entities in Reorganization under the Bankruptcy Code

BACKGROUND

Entities experiencing severe financial distress may file for protection from creditors under Chapter 11 of the Bankruptcy Code. An entity filing for protection under Chapter 11 seeks to reorganize and to emerge from bankruptcy as a viable business. The primary objective of the reorganization is to maximize the recovery of creditors and shareholders by preserving the going concern value of the entity.

Legal Summary of the Reorganization Process

To begin the process of bankruptcy reorganization, an entity would file a petition with the Bankruptcy Court, an adjunct of the United States District Courts. The entity filing the bankruptcy petition typically prepares a reorganization plan, which it submits to the Court for confirmation. This plan specifies the treatment of the entity's assets and liabilities, and it may result in debt being forgiven. For the reorganization plan to be confirmed, the consideration to be received by parties in interest under the plan must exceed what would be received if the entity liquidated under Chapter 7 of the Bankruptcy Code. In most cases, the debtor has the exclusive right to file a reorganization plan during the first 120 days after the bankruptcy filing (this right is lost if the Court appoints a trustee).

In general, the provisions of a confirmed reorganization plan bind all parties connected with the entity. This includes (1) the entity itself (i.e., the debtor); (2) any entity issuing securities under the plan; (3) any entity acquiring assets under the plan; and (4) any creditor, stockholder, or general partner of the debtor. This is the case regardless of whether the claim of any of these parties is impaired by the reorganization plan and irrespective of whether the party accepted the plan.

The requirements that must be met for the Bankruptcy Court to approve a reorganization plan include the following:

- The technical requirements of the Bankruptcy Code have been met.
- In soliciting acceptance of the plan, the entity has provided adequate disclosures.
- A class of individuals whose claims are impaired might consent to the plan and yet have some individual members who dissent from this action. These dissenting members must receive at least as much under the plan as they would receive in a Chapter 7 liquidation.
- Priority claims under the terms of the Bankruptcy Code will be paid in cash.
- If the plan is confirmed, it is not likely to be followed by liquidation or further reorganization.
- At least one class of impaired claims, not including insiders, has accepted the plan.
- The plan proponent, typically the debtor, has obtained the consent of all parties with impaired claims or equity securities, or the plan proponent can comply with the "cram-down" provisions of the Bankruptcy Code. (This means that the plan can be forced on nonassenting creditors by the Bankruptcy Court.) The court can confirm a plan even if one or more parties with impaired claims or equity securities do not accept it. In order for the court to confirm a plan under these circumstances, the plan cannot unfairly discriminate against a nonconsenting class impaired by the plan, and it must treat nonconsenting classes in a fair and equitable manner.
  - — A secured claim is treated in a fair and equitable manner if it remains adequately collateralized and if the present value of the payments it is to receive equals the amount of the secured claim when the plan becomes effective.
  - — An unsecured claim is treated in a fair and equitable manner if the discounted assets it is to receive equal the allowed amount of the claim or if any claim junior to it will not receive or retain any assets.
  - — An equity interest is treated in a fair and equitable manner if the discounted assets it is to receive equal the greatest of (1) any fixed liquidation preference, (2) any fixed redemption price, or (3) the value of such interest. Alternatively, the equity interest is treated fairly and equitably if no junior equity security interest will receive or retain any assets under the plan.

ACCOUNTING GUIDANCE

Accounting and Financial Aspects of the Reorganization Process

A central feature of the reorganization plan is to determine the reorganization value of the entity that seeks to emerge from Bankruptcy Court protection. The reorganization value is designed to approximate the fair value of the entity's assets, and it should conform with the amount that a willing buyer would pay for these assets.

The reorganization value is generally determined through the following steps:

Step 1: Consideration of the amount to be received for assets that will not be needed by the reconstituted business

Step 2: Computation of the present value of cash flows that the reconstituted business is expected to generate for some period into the future

Step 3: Computation of the terminal value of the reconstituted business at the end of the period for which future cash flows are estimated

---

Illustration of Estimating Reorganization Value

ERT, Inc., is a debtor-in-possession operating under the protection of Chapter 11 of the Bankruptcy Code. In order to prepare a reorganization plan, ERT needs to estimate its reorganization value. ERT has $150,000 of cash above its likely needs as an ongoing business. (It is not unusual for entities operating under Chapter 11 protection to accumulate excess cash; these entities do not pay most claims during the period of time they are operating under Chapter 11 protection.) Also, ERT is expected to generate $40,000 of net cash flows per month, each year, during the first five years after it emerges from Chapter 11. ERT's terminal value is estimated to be $1,091,456. ERT's reorganization value of approximately $2,816,667 represents the $150,000 of excess cash on hand, the present value of receiving $40,000 per month for the next five years ($1,575,211 discounted at 18%), and the terminal value of the enterprise.

After the entity's reorganization value is determined, it is allocated in interest to parties in accordance with their respective legal priorities. Secured claims have first priority, to the extent of the value of their collateral. Following secured claims are those claims specifically granted priority under the provisions of the Bankruptcy Code. Finally, distributions are made to various classes of unsecured debt and equity interests in accordance with their respective legal priorities, or otherwise as the parties may agree.

Before the reorganization plan is submitted to creditors, equity holders, etc., these groups are provided with a disclosure statement. The disclosure statement must be approved by the Court, and it should contain adequate information for interested parties to make an informed decision as to the appropriateness of the reorganization plan.

The disclosure statement typically contains (1) a description of the reorganization plan, (2) historical and prospective financial information, and (3) a pro forma balance sheet that presents the reorganization value and the capital structure of the new entity. A valuation of the emerging entity is not required for the disclosure statement to be approved by the Bankruptcy Court. Normally, however, such a valuation would be performed unless (1) the reorganization value of the emerging entity exceeds its liabilities or (2) holders of existing voting shares will own a majority of the emerging entity.

Need for and Scope of Guidance

Before the issuance of the guidance in ASC 852-10-05-3 through 05-16, 10-1, 15-1 through 15-3, 25-1, 30-1, 45-1 through 45-2, 45-4 through 45-21, 45-26 through 45-27, 45-29; 50-2 through 50-4, 50-7; 55-3, 55-5 through 55-11; ASC 852-20-15-3; ASC 740-45-1 ASC 210-10-60-3; (SOP 90-7), there was no specific guidance for entities operating in reorganization proceedings. This led to wide diversity in practice.

That guidance applies to both (1) entities that are operating under Chapter 11 protection and that expect ultimately to emerge from such protection as a going concern and (2) entities that have emerged from Chapter 11 protection under a confirmed reorganization plan. It does not apply to (1) entities that restructure their debt outside of the Chapter 11 process, (2) entities that liquidate or that plan to do so, and (3) governmental entities.

Financial Reporting—Entity Operating under Chapter 11 Protection

For the most part, filing for Chapter 11 protection does not change the application of generally accepted accounting principles. One difference is that transactions or events that are directly associated with the reorganization proceedings should be kept separate from ongoing operations.

Balance Sheet Reporting

Prepetition liabilities (i.e., liabilities incurred by the enterprise before the Chapter 11 filing) may be subject to compromise. A liability is compromised when it ultimately is settled for less than its allowed amount. The *allowed* amount is that which is permitted by the Bankruptcy Court, even though such liabilities may not be paid in full. Prepetition liabilities subject to compromise should be separated from prepetition liabilities not subject to compromise (e.g., fully secured liabilities) and from postpetition claims. These two latter amounts are combined and reported as one amount. All liabilities should be reported at the amount allowed by the Bankruptcy Court, even though they ultimately may be settled for less than the allowed amount.

Some secured liabilities may be undersecured. An undersecured liability exists when the fair value of the collateral may be less than the allowed liability. In this case, the entire liability should initially be classified as a prepetition claim subject to compromise. The liability would not be reclassified unless it became clear that the secured claim in question would not be compromised. Certain prepetition liabilities may not become known until after the bankruptcy petition is filed. Those liabilities should be reported at the expected amount of the allowed claims (based on the framework of ASC 450-20. If the existence of the liability is at least reasonably possible, this information should be disclosed in the notes to the financial statements even if the amount of the prepetition liability cannot be estimated.

In certain cases, the allowed amount of a prepetition liability may differ from its recorded amount. When this circumstance occurs, the carrying amount of the liability should be adjusted to the allowed amount. If unamortized debt discounts, premiums, or debt issue costs exist, these accounts are used in making the adjustment to record the liability at its allowed amount. Any resulting gain or loss is classified as a reorganization item and, as such, will be reported separately in the income statement.

Details of claims subject to compromise are to be reported in the financial statement notes. Finally, if a classified balance sheet is presented, claims not subject to compromise are to be categorized as current or noncurrent.

Illustration of Balance Sheet Presentation

Hale & Carter filed for protection from creditors under Chapter 11 of the Bankruptcy Code on February 15, 20X4. Its first set of annual financial statements prepared after this date is prepared on December 31, 20X4. The details of Hale & Carter's liabilities and stockholders' equity are as follows:

Prepetition liabilities subject to compromise	
Secured debt, 12%, secured by a first mortgage on equipment (the fair value of the collateral is less than the claim)	$200,000
Senior subordinated secured notes, 16%	300,000
Subordinated debentures, 19%	200,000
Trade and other miscellaneous claims	100,000
Priority tax claims	50,000
Prepetition liabilities not subject to compromise	
Secured debt, 11%, secured by a first mortgage on a building ($50,000 of principal due on 6/30/X5)	$700,000
Postpetition claims	
Accounts payable—trade	$120,000
Short-term borrowings	180,000
Stockholders' equity	
Preferred stock	$150,000
Common stock	100,000
Retained earnings (deficit)	(500,000)

In its December 31, 20X4, balance sheet, Hale & Carter reports total assets of $1,600,000. (The presentation of the asset side of the balance sheet for an entity operating under Chapter 11 does not present any unique issues.) The right-hand side of Hale & Carter's balance sheet would look as follows:

Liabilities and Shareholders' Deficit	
Liabilities Not Subject to Compromise	
Current liabilities:	
Short-term borrowings	$ 180,000
Accounts payable	120,000
Total current liabilities	$ 300,000

Noncurrent liabilities:	
11%, Long-term note (see Note xx)	$ 700,000
Liabilities Subject to Compromise	$ 850,000[(a)]
Total liabilities	$1,850,000
Shareholders' (deficit):	
Preferred stock	$ 150,000
Common stock	100,000
Retained earnings (deficit)	(500,000)
Total liabilities & shareholders' deficit	$1,600,000

(a) Liabilities subject to compromise consist of the following:

Secured debt, 12%, secured by a first mortgage on equipment (the fair value of the collateral is less than the claim)	$200,000
Senior subordinated secured notes, 16%	300,000
Subordinated debentures, 19%	200,000
Trade and other miscellaneous claims	100,000
Priority tax claims	50,000
	$850,000

Income Statement

Items of revenue, expense, gain, or loss that occur because the entity is operating in reorganization proceedings are to be reported separately. However, under the provisions in ASC 225-20-45 as amended by ASC 360-10 and ASC 470-50-45-1, this requirement does not apply to an item required to be reported separately as a discontinued operation or as an unusual or infrequent item.

The guidance in this pronouncement specifically addresses the treatment of three items on the income statement. First, professional fees related to the reorganization are to be recognized as incurred and categorized as a reorganization expense. Before this guidance was issued, some entities established a liability for professional fees upon filing for bankruptcy; other entities capitalized these fees when incurred and ultimately offset them against debt discharge when the reorganization plan was confirmed. Neither of those treatments is now acceptable. Second, interest expense is *not* a reorganization item. It should be reported only to the extent that interest is paid during the reporting period or to the extent that it will be an allowed claim. In many cases, the interest expense reported will be significantly less than contractual interest. Any difference between reported interest expense and contractual interest is to be disclosed. SEC registrants must disclose this difference on the face of the income statement. Third, any interest income above that which would normally be earned on invested working capital is to be reported as a reorganization item. Entities operating under Chapter 11 protection often generate large amounts of interest income. The entity continues to generate cash flows from operations, and payments under many liabilities are stayed by the bankruptcy proceedings.

Statement of Cash Flows

The guidance in this pronouncement provides that the most beneficial information that can be provided about an entity operating under Chapter 11 protection is the information presented in the statement of cash flows. Cash flows from operating, investing, and financing activities that relate to the reorganization should be shown separately. That treatment is more useful if an entity uses the direct method of preparing the statement. If the indirect method is used, a supplementary schedule (or a note) containing information on operating cash flows due to the reorganization proceedings must be provided.

Disclosure

ASC 852-10-50-6A provides that an entity in reorganization that prepares its Statement of Cash Flows by the indirect method is required to disclose details of its operating cash receipts and payments in a supplementary schedule or in the notes to the financial statements.

Other Issues

A company presenting consolidated results may have one or more entities in reorganization proceedings. Assuming that this hypothetical company also has other entities that are not operating under Chapter 11 protection, condensed combined financial statements for the units operating under Chapter 11 must accompany the consolidated financial statements. Those units operating under Chapter 11 must present intercompany receivables and payables in the condensed combined financial statements. In addition, those entities that are not in reorganization proceedings must evaluate the propriety of reporting an intercompany receivable from a unit that is operating in Chapter 11.

In general, earnings per share for entities in reorganization are calculated in a manner similar to the calculation for any other entity. However, if it is probable that additional shares of stock or common stock equivalents will be issued under the reorganization plan, that fact should be disclosed.

Fresh-Start Reporting—Emergence from Chapter 11

For an entity emerging from Chapter 11 protection to employ fresh-start reporting, two conditions must exist. First, the value of the emerging entity's assets immediately before the reorganization plan is confirmed must be less than the amount of postpetition liabilities and prepetition allowed claims. Second, persons holding existing voting shares immediately before the reorganization plan is confirmed must receive less than 50% of the voting shares of the new entity. Note that the loss of control experienced by the former shareholders must be substantive and not temporary. Fresh-start reporting is to be applied as of the confirmation date, or at a later date when all material conditions precedent to the reorganization plan becoming binding have been resolved.

If an entity emerging from reorganization proceedings does not meet *both* of the criteria outlined in the previous paragraph, the entity is precluded from adopting fresh-start reporting. However, even in this case, the entity needs to ensure that (1) liabilities adjusted as a result of a confirmed reorganization plan are stated at present value and (2) any debt forgiveness received is reported as an unusual or infrequent item.

Implementing Fresh-Start Reporting

In implementing fresh-start reporting, the reorganization value of the emerging entity should be assigned among the tangible and specifically identifiable intangible assets and liabilities of the entity in conformity with the guidance in ASC 805, Business Combinations Any excess of reorganization value over that which can be assigned to tangible and specifically identifiable intangible assets is reported as, if any, goodwill in accordance with the guidance in ASC 350-20-25-2. Goodwill as a result of the implementation of fresh-start reporting is not amortized, but is periodically evaluated for impairment in accordance with the guidance in ASC 350 (Intangibles—Goodwill and Other).

Deferred income taxes should be reported in conformity with GAAP. If deferred taxes cannot be recognized at the date of a plan's confirmation by eliminating the valuation allowance, tax benefits from preconfirmation net operating loss carryforwards and deductible temporary differences should be reported as a reduction of income tax expense.

An entity emerging from bankruptcy that applies fresh start reporting should follow the guidance in accounting standards that are *effective* when fresh-start reporting is adopted.

Transitioning to Fresh-Start Reporting

Before the confirmation date of the reorganization plan, the accounting should follow that which is required when an entity is operating under Chapter 11 protection. Any adjustments to the recorded asset and liability amounts that result from the adoption of fresh-start reporting would be reported in the predecessor entity's final statement of operations. Also, the effects of debt forgiveness are to be reported in the predecessor entity's final statement of operations. The adoption of fresh-start reporting gives rise to a new reporting entity, which has no retained earnings nor deficit when it begins operations. Any deficit of the predecessor entity would be eliminated before the new entity begins operations.

Disclosures Required by Fresh-Start Reporting

A number of disclosures are required for entities that are exiting Chapter 11 proceedings and are adopting fresh-start reporting. These disclosures are as follows:

- Adjustments to the historical amounts of assets and liabilities.
- The amount of debt that has been forgiven.
- The amount of prior retained earnings or deficit that is eliminated.
- Significant matters in determining reorganization value. These include the following:

- *The method or methods used to determine reorganization value* This includes disclosing information such as discount rates, tax rates, the number of years for which cash flows are projected, and the method of determining terminal value.
- *Sensitive assumptions* These are assumptions made where there is a reasonable possibility of divergence from the assumption that could materially affect the estimate of reorganization value.
- *Assumptions about anticipated conditions that are expected to be different from current conditions (unless these differences are already apparent)*

Other Issues

If, for example, a calendar-year-end entity has its reorganization plan confirmed on June 30, 20X5, and adopts fresh-start reporting on July 1, 20X5, on December 31, 20X5, this new entity should not prepare comparative financial statements. The financial statements presented would be limited to capturing the activity of the new entity for the latter half of 20X5. It was believed that presenting comparative financial statements that straddle a confirmation date would be misleading; therefore, such statements should not be presented.

Illustration of Fresh-Start Reporting

Background

Edison, Inc., filed for protection from creditors under Chapter 11 of the Bankruptcy Code on March 1, 20X5. Edison's reorganization plan was confirmed by the applicable Bankruptcy Court on May 1, 20X5.

Reorganization Value

Edison's reorganization value immediately before the confirmation of the reorganization plan was as follows:

Cash in excess of normal operating requirements generated by operations	$ 85,000
Net realizable value expected from asset dispositions	130,000
Present value of discounted cash flows of the emerging entity	525,000 (1)
Terminal value	1,250,000 (2)
Reorganization value	$1,990,000

(1) The present value of discounting estimated yearly cash flows, $250,000, over the forecast period, 3 years, by the appropriate interest rate, 20%.
(2) Terminal value is determined via an independent business valuation.

Applicability of Fresh-Start Reporting

Holders of Edison's existing voting shares before the confirmation of the reorganization plan will receive less than 50% of the voting shares in the emerging entity (in fact, these former shareholders will have no interest in the new entity). This meets the first requirement for use of fresh-start reporting. The second requirement, that reorganization value must be less than total postpetition liabilities and allowed claims, is also met, as illustrated below:

Postpetition current liabilities	$ 400,000
Liabilities deferred pursuant to Chapter 11 proceeding	1,700,000
Total postpetition liabilities and allowed claims	$2,100,000
Reorganization value	(1,990,000)
Excess of liabilities over reorganization value	$ 110,000

Computing the Total Assets of the Emerging Entity

Total assets of the emerging entity are computed by subtracting assets that will be distributed before or simultaneously with the confirmation of the reorganization plan—in this case, the $85,000 of excess cash—from the new entity's reorganization value. Therefore, the total assets of Edison-New Entity at May 1, 20X6, are $1,905,000 ($1,990,000 – $85,000).

Beginning Capital Structure—Emerging Entity

After consideration of the emerging entity's debt capacity, projected earnings to fixed charges, earnings before interest and taxes to interest, free cash flow to interest, etc., the following capital structure for the new entity has been agreed upon:

Capital Structure for the Emerging Entity

Postpetition current liabilities	$400,000
IRS note	75,000
Senior debt	610,000[(1)]
Subordinated debt	420,000
Common stock	400,000

[(1)] $100,000 due each year for the next five years, at 14% interest; $110,000 due in the sixth year.

Distributions to Be Received by Parties in Interest

Secured Debt—The company's $600,000 of secured debt was exchanged for $85,000 in cash, $400,000 of new senior debt, and $115,000 of subordinated debt. The senior debt carries an interest rate of 14%, and principal payments of $65,574 are due during each of the next five years (the first payment is due on June 30, 20X6). The final payment of $72,130 is due in the sixth year.

Priority Tax Claims—Payroll and withholding taxes of $75,000 are payable in five equal annual installments, with the first payment due on May 31, 20X7. The annual interest rate is 11%.

Senior Debt—The company's $400,000 of senior debt was exchanged for $150,000 of new senior debt, $175,000 of subordinated debt, and 15% of the new issue of voting common stock. The senior debt carries an interest rate of 14%, and principal payments of $24,590 are due during each of the next five years (the first payment is due on June 30, 20X6). The final payment of $27,050 is due in the sixth year. Payments under the subordinated debentures are due in equal annual installments over seven years. The first payment is due September 30, 20X7, and the interest rate is 17%.

Trade and Other Claims—The holders of $200,000 of trade and other claims received the following for their stake: (*a*) $60,000 of senior debt, (*b*) $70,000 of subordinated debentures, and (*c*) 10% of the new issue of voting common stock. The senior debt carries an interest rate of 14%, and principal payments of $9,836 are due during each of the next five years (the first payment is due on June 30, 20X6). The final payment of $10,820 is due in the sixth year. Payments under the subordinated debentures are due in equal annual installments over seven years. The first payment is due September 30, 20X7, and the interest rate is 17%.

Subordinated Debentures—The company's $425,000 of subordinated debt was exchanged for $60,000 of new subordinated debentures and 75% of the new issue of voting common stock. Payments under the subordinated debentures are due in equal annual installments over seven years. The first payment is due September 30, 20X7, and the interest rate is 17%.

Common Stock—Edison had 200,000 shares of $1 par value common stock outstanding immediately before the confirmation of its reorganization plan. None of these stockholders will have any interest in the emerging entity. Four hundred thousand shares of new voting common stock, $1 par value, will be issued. These shares will be issued as follows: (*a*) 60,000 shares to holders of the former entity's senior debt, (*b*) 40,000 shares to holders of trade and other claims from the former entity, and (*c*) 300,000 shares to holders of the former entity's subordinated debentures.

Plan of Reorganization—Recovery Analysis

It is necessary to prepare a schedule detailing what the claims of the parties in interest are, and how and to what extent these claims are being satisfied. This schedule facilitates the preparation of the journal entries necessary to implement fresh-start reporting. This type of schedule is included either as a note to the financial statements or as supplementary information to the financial statements.

The following points should be noted about this schedule:

1. All of Edison's liabilities, both prepetition and postpetition, and shareholders' equity accounts are listed in column (a) of the table.
2. Column (b), elimination of debt and equity, represents the difference between the claim held (column (a) amount) and the consideration received for the claim (total recovery listed in column (j)).

3. Columns (c)-(g) represent the book value, which at the date of fresh-start reporting would also equal fair value, of the various items of consideration issued to settle the Chapter 11 claims (e.g., surviving debt, cash, new secured debt).
4. Column (h), common stock percentage, represents the percentage of the voting shares of the emerging entity issued to various parties.
5. Column (i), the value of the common stock issued, is computed by multiplying the net assets of the emerging entity by the percentage of voting shares of common stock received. For instance, the emerging capital structure for Edison will have only $400,000 of common stock (a deficit or retained earnings is always eliminated as part of the fresh-start process). Multiplying this amount by the percentage of common stock received produces the common stock value. Also, although this is not the case for Edison, some entities will have a beginning balance in additional paid-in capital as a result of the fresh-start process.
6. Column (j), total recovery, represents the total of the various types of consideration received.
7. Column (k), total recovery percentage, is computed by dividing the total recovery amount (column (j)) by the amount of the claim.

Journal Entries—Needed to Implement Fresh-Start Reporting

Entry to record debt discharge:

Liabilities subject to compromise	$1,700,000	
Cash		$ 85,000
IRS note		75,000
Senior debt—current		100,000
Senior debt—long-term		510,000
Subordinated debt		420,000
Common stock—new		400,000
Gain on debt discharge		110,000 (1)

(1) The gain on debt discharge can be calculated as follows:

Using the recovery analysis schedule, column (b)—elimination of debt and equity, add the amounts in this column for liabilities that have been compromised. In the case of Edison, the $400,000 of senior debt was settled for $385,000, a $15,000 gain. In a similar fashion, there were $30,000 and $65,000 gains on the settlement of trade claims and subordinated debentures, respectively. The sum of these three amounts is $110,000.

EDISON, INC. PLAN OF REORGANIZATION RECOVERY ANALYSIS

	(a)	(b)	(c)	(d)	(e)	(f)	(g)	(h)	(i)	(j)	(k)
		Elimination of Debt and Equity	*Surviving Debt*	*Cash*	*IRS Note*	*Senior Debt*	*Subordinated Debt*	*Common Stock Percentage*	*Common Stock value*	*Total Recovery*	*Total Recovery Percentage*
Postpetition liabilities	$ 400,000		$400,000							$ 400,000	100
Claim/ Interest											
Secured debt	600,000			$85,000		$400,000	$115,000			600,000	100
Priority tax claim	75,000				$75,000					75,000	100
Senior debt	400,000	$ (15,000)				150,000	175,000	15%	$ 60,000	385,000	96
Trade and other claims	200,000	(30,000)				60,000	70,000	10%	40,000	170,000	85
Subordinated debentures	425,000	(65,000)					60,000	75%	300,000	360,000	85
	1,700,000	(110,000)									
Common shareholders	200,000	(200,000)									
									0	0	0
Deficit	(535,000)	535,000									
	$1,765,000	$225,000	$400,000	$85,000	$75,000	$610,000	$420,000	100%	$400,000	$1,990,000	

Entry to retire Edison's (old) common stock:

Common stock—old	200,000	
Additional paid-in capital		200,000

Entry to record the adoption of fresh-start reporting and to eliminate the deficit in retained earnings:

Inventory	50,000(1)	
Property, plant, and equipment	200,000(1)	
Reorganization value in excess of amounts allocable to identifiable assets	375,000(2)	
Gain on debt discharge	110,000(3)	
Additional paid-in capital	200,000(4)	
Goodwill		400,000(2)
Deficit		535,000(2)

---

(1) The fair values of inventory and property, plant, and equipment immediately before the confirmation of Edison's reorganization plan have increased by $50,000 and $200,000, respectively. To implement fresh-start reporting, the recorded values of these assets are written up to their fair values. Note that the staff of the SEC, in their interpretation of *Financial Reporting Release* Section 210 (ASR-25), believes that the recognition of reorganization value in the balance sheet of an emerging entity that meets the criteria for fresh-start reporting should be limited to no net write-up of assets.

(2) To eliminate goodwill and the deficit of the predecessor entity and to record the excess of the emerging entity's reorganization value over amounts allocated to tangible and identifiable intangible assets. These amounts are obtained from the Balance Sheet Worksheet (see next page).

(3) This amount represents the difference between Edison's allowed liabilities of $2,100,000 (see column (a) of Edison's plan of reorganization—recovery analysis) and the amount paid to settle these same liabilities, $1,990,000 (see column (j) of Edison's plan of reorganization—recovery analysis).

(4) The entry to additional paid-in capital is used to balance the entry. In this case, it represents the book value of Edison's former stockholders that is being forfeited as part of the reorganization plan.

Balance Sheet Analysis—Needed to Implement Fresh-Start Reporting

The table that follows illustrates the implementation of Edison's reorganization plan and the preparation of Edison's initial balance sheet as a reorganized entity.

	Preconfirmation	Adjustments to Record Confirmation of Plan: Debt Exchange	Adjustments to Record Confirmation of Plan: Discharge of Stock	Adjustments to Record Confirmation of Plan: Fresh Start	Edison, Inc.'s Reorganized Balance Sheet
ASSETS					
Current Assets					
Cash	$ 120,000	$(85,000)		$50,000	$ 35,000
Receivables	250,000				250,000
Inventory	350,000				400,000
Assets to be disposed of valued at market, which is lower than cost	30,000				30,000
Other current assets	15,000				15,000
Total current assets	$ 765,000	$(85,000)		$50,000	$ 730,000
Property, plant, and equipment	500,000			200,000	700,000
Assets to be disposed of valued at market, which is lower than cost	100,000				100,000
Goodwill	400,000			(400,000)	0
Reorganization value in excess of amounts allocable to identifiable assets				375,000	375,000
Total assets	$1,765,000	$(85,000)		$225,000	$1,905,000
LIABILITIES AND SHAREHOLDERS' DEFICIT					
Current Liabilities Not Subject to Compromise Short-term borrowings	$ 250,000				$ 250,000
Current maturities of senior debt		$ 100,000			100,000
Accounts payable-trade	150,000				150,000
Total current liabilities	$ 400,000	$ 100,000			$ 500,000
Liabilities Subject to Compromise					
Prepetition liabilities	1,700,000	(1,700,000)			0
IRS note		75,000			75,000
Senior debt, less current maturities		510,000			510,000
Subordinated debt		420,000			420,000
Total Liabilities	$2,100,000	$ (595,000)			$1,505,000
Shareholders' Deficit					
Common stock-old	200,000		(200,000)		-0-
Common stock-new		400,000			400,000
			200,000	(200,000)	-0-
Additional paid-in capital Retained earnings (deficit)	(535,000)	110,000		425,000[(1)]	-0-
Total liabilities in shareholders' deficit	$ (335,000)	$ 510,000	$-0-	$ 225,000	$ 400,000
Total liabilities and shareholders' deficit	$1,765,000	$ (85,000)	$-0-	$ 225,000	$1,905,000

[(1)] Represents the net effect of the elimination of the deficit in retained earnings, via a $535,000 credit to this account, and the debt to retained earnings to eliminate the $110,000 gain on debt discharge.

ASC 852-10-45-20 An Amendment of AICPA Statement of Position 90-7

OVERVIEW

ASC 852-10-05-3 through 05-16, 10-1, 15-1 through 15-3, 25-1, 30-1, 45-1 through 45-2, 45-4 through 45-21, 45-26 through 45-27, 45-29, 50-2 through 50-4, 50-7, 55-3, 55-5 through 55-11, ASC 852-20-15-3; ASC 740-45-1; ASC 210-10-60-3 (Financial Reporting by Entities in Reorganization under the Bankruptcy Code) provides the primary guidance on financial reporting for entities that file for bankruptcy and expect to reorganize as a going concern under Chapter 11 of Title 11 of the United States Code. Under that guidance, entities in Chapter 11 that meet certain criteria are required to adopt fresh-start reporting. In addition, when such an entity first adopts fresh-start reporting, it is required under the guidance in ASC 852-10-45-20 to early adopt at that time changes in accounting principles, if any, that the emerging entity will be required to apply in its financial statements within the 12 months after having adopted fresh-start reporting.

Although new pronouncements issued in 1990 encouraged early adoption of those standards, the FASB has prohibited the early adoption of several recently issued standards. As a result, some have noted that the guidance in ASC 852-10-45-20 related to the early adoption of changes in accounting principles conflicts with the FASB's guidance regarding the adoption date of some recent pronouncements.

The issue is, therefore, whether entities emerging from bankruptcy that apply fresh-start reporting should be permitted to continue following the guidance related to the early adoption of changes in accounting standards or whether such entities should be required to adopt new pronouncements based on their stated effective dates.

ACCOUNTING GUIDANCE

Entities emerging from bankruptcy that use fresh-start reporting should follow only accounting standards that are effective at the date the entity adopts fresh-start reporting, including standards eligible for early adoption, if an entity elects to adopt early.

CHAPTER 61

ASC 853—ACCOUNTING FOR SERVICE CONCESSION ARRANGEMENTS

CONTENTS

INTERPRETIVE GUIDANCE

ASC 853-10: OVERALL

ASC 853-10-05-1 through 05-2, 15-1 through 15-4, 25-1 through 25-2; ASC 840-10-15-9A

Service Concession Arrangements

BACKGROUND

A service concession arrangement is a contract entered into by a public sector entity (i.e., grantor) and a private entity (i.e., operating entity) under which a grantor grants an operating entity the right to operate and maintain existing infrastructure assets (e.g., airports, roads, bridges, tunnels, prisons, and hospitals) or to construct them for a grantor during the term of a service concession arrangement. As part of such an arrangement, an operating entity may be required to provide significant upgrades to the infrastructure (ASC 853-10-05-1).

In exchange for maintaining and operating an infrastructure asset that will be used to provide a service to the public, a grantor may pay an operating entity to perform the service as the services are performed over an extended period of time. Or a grantor may give an operating entity the right to charge the public for using the infrastructure. Under the contract, a grantor may also provide an unconditional guarantee under which an operating entity would be paid a guaranteed minimum amount if fees collected from the public do not reach a specified minimum level. A grantor generally controls and can modify or approve the services that an operating entity must provide using the infrastructure, to whom the services will be provided, and at what price. Performance standards, pricing mechanisms, and arrangements to arbitrate disputes may be set in the contract. A contract may require that an operating entity make an upfront cash payment to a grantor for the right to operate and use the grantor's infrastructure. If so, an operating entity generally is given the right to charge a fee to the infrastructure's users. A residual interest in the assets, if any, at the end of an arrangement is controlled by the grantor. Such arrangements are known as public-to-private service concession contracts (ASC 853-10-05-2).

A fundamental feature of a service concession contract is the public nature of an operating entity's obligation. Under a service concession contract's other common provisions:

- An operating entity constructs infrastructure for a grantor, provides significant upgrades to a grantor's infrastructure, makes a cash payment to a grantor, or provides a combination of those kinds of features.
- An operating entity that provides services to the public on behalf of a grantor must meet minimum performance standards.
- A grantor controls the residual interest in the infrastructure at the end of a contract's term and may specify the minimum condition in which the infrastructure must be at that time.

Because the accounting for service concession arrangements was not specifically addressed in U.S. GAAP, entities that concluded that the terms of an arrangement do not meet the criteria for lease accounting in FASB Accounting Standards

Codification® (ASC) 840 (Leases) were accounting for their rights over the infrastructure as an intangible asset, a financial asset, or both under the guidance in International Financial Reporting Interpretations Committee (IFRIC) 12 (Service Concession Arrangements).

ACCOUNTING ISSUE

How should an operating entity account for its rights over infrastructure in a service arrangement with a grantor?

ACCOUNTING GUIDANCE

Scope

The following guidance applies to an operating entity's accounting for a public-to-private service concession arrangement with a grantor if both of the following conditions exist:

- The grantor controls or has the ability to modify or approve the services an operating entity is required to provide with the infrastructure, to whom the services must be provided, and at what price; and
- The grantor controls the residual interest in the infrastructure, if any, at the end of the arrangement's term, through its ownership, beneficial entitlement, or otherwise.

If a service concession arrangement meets the scope criteria in ASC 980 (Regulated Entities) it should be accounted for under that guidance.

Recognition

The Operating Entity's Rights over the Infrastructure

ASC 853-10-25-1 provides that various aspects of a service concession arrangement may be accounted for under other topics in the ASC. For example, revenue and costs related to construction, upgrade, or operation services should be accounted for under the guidance in ASC 605 (Revenue Recognition).

IMPORTANT NOTICE: The FASB has issued Accounting Standards Update 2014-09, *Revenue from Contracts with Customers*, which will be included in newly established ASC 606. That guidance will supersede the guidance in ASC 605 (Revenue Recognition) and will be effective for public business entities, not-for-profit entities that have issued, or are conduit bond obligors for, securities that are traded, listed, or quoted on an exchange or an over-the-counter market, and employee benefit plans that file or provide financial statements with or to the SEC for annual reporting periods that begin after December 15, 2017, including interim reporting periods within those reporting periods. Earlier application is prohibited. All other entities will be required to apply the guidance in ASC 606 for annual reporting periods that begin after December 15, 2018, and interim reporting periods within annual reporting periods that begin after December 15, 2019.

Although an operating entity may have wide managerial discretion in operating the infrastructure, it does not control the infrastructure's use because the grantor determines what services the reporting entity provides with the infrastructure, to whom it must provide them, and at what price. The grantor also controls any residual interest in the infrastructure at the end of the arrangement. Therefore, ASC 853-10-25-2 provides that an operating entity should NOT recognize the infrastructure of a service concession arrangement as property, plant, and equipment. In addition, because an operating entity does not have the right to control the use of a grantor's infrastructure, service concession arrangements under the scope of this guidance should not be accounted for under the guidance in ASC 840, *Leases*, which is amended by the addition of ASC 840-10-15-9A stating that service concession arrangements under the scope of ASC 853 (Service Concession Arrangements) are not within the scope of ASC 840.

ASC 853-10-25-4, 65-2 Determining the Customer of the Operation Service

BACKGROUND

The Emerging Issues Task Force (EITF) considered this issue because of diversity in practice regarding the determination of who is the customer in a service concession arrangement under which a government entity grantor enters into an agreement with an operating entity that will operate the grantor's infrastructure, for example, an airport, a bridge, a road, or a hospital, for a specified period of time. Some stakeholders considered the government entity to be the customer, while others considered an infrastructure's third-party users to be the operating entity's customers. The objective of the following amendments is to clarify that the government entity grantor is the operating entity's customer.

ACCOUNTING GUIDANCE

ASC 853-10-25-1 has been amended to require that a service concession arrangement be accounted for under the guidance in ASC 605, *Revenue Recognition*, or ASC 606, *Revenue from Contracts with Customers*. Under that guidance, an operating entity should consider the grantor to be the customer of its operation services in all cases for service concession arrangements under the scope of ASC 853. An operating entity should account for other aspects of a service concession arrangement under the guidance in other Topics of the Accounting Standards Codification®.

TRANSITION AND EFFECTIVE DATE

The following transition guidance is included in ASC 853-10-65-2:

a. If an entity has not yet adopted the guidance that links to ASC 606-10-65-1, it is required to adopt the amended guidance that is linked to ASC 853-10-65-2 at the same time as it adopts the guidance linked to ASC 606-10-65-1, unless the entity decides to early adopt the guidance in this pronouncement as discussed in (c) below. If an entity adopts the guidance that links to ASC 606-10-65-1 and ASC 853-10-65-2 at the same time, it is required to apply the same transition method elected (including the same practical expedients, if applicable), and to provide the same transition disclosures required under the guidance linked to ASC 606-10-65-1.

b. Entities that have already adopted the guidance linked to ASC 606-10-65-1 before adopting the guidance linked to ASC 853-10-65-2, should apply the guidance linked to ASC 853-10-65-2 as follows, except for entities that have elected to early adopt the guidance that is linked to ASC 853-10-65-2, as permitted in (c) below:

    1. Public business entities and not-for-profit entities that have issued, or are conduit bond obligors, for securities that are traded, listed, or quoted on an exchange or an over-the-counter market, and employee benefit plans that file or provide financial statements with or to the Securities Exchange Commission, for fiscal years that begin after December 15, 2017, including interim financial statements;

    2. All other entities, for fiscal years that begin after December 15, 2018, and interim periods within fiscal years that begin after December 15, 2019.

c. All entities are permitted to early adopt the guidance that is linked to ASC 853-10-65-2, including in an interim period, subject to the transition guidance in (d) through (i).

d. For the purposes of the transition guidance in (d) through (i):

    1. The initial application date is the beginning of the fiscal year in which the guidance that links to ASC 853-10-65-2 is first adopted, regardless of whether adoption occurs at the beginning of the fiscal year or at the beginning of an interim period other than the first interim period.

    2. A contract is completed if all, or substantially all, of the revenue was recognized in accordance with revenue guidance that is in effect before the initial application date.

e. An entity discussed in (a) that has early adopted the guidance that links to ASC 853-10-65-2 or an entity discussed in (b), regardless of whether it has early adopted the guidance that links to ASC 853-10-65-2 or at the effective date should apply the guidance in this pronouncement using one of the following two methods:

    1. Retrospectively to each prior reporting period presented in accordance with the guidance on accounting changes in ASC 250-10-45-5 through 45-10, subject to the guidance in (f) and (i).

    2. Retrospectively with a cumulative effect of initially applying the guidance that links to ASC 853-10-65-2 recognized at the date of initial application in accordance with the guidance in (g) through (i).

f. An entity that elects to apply the guidance that links to ASC 853-10-65-2 retrospectively in accordance with (e)(1), is required to provide the disclosures in ASC 250-10-50-1 through 50-2 in the period of adoption, except as follows. An entity is not required to disclose the effect of the changes on the current period, which otherwise is required by ASC 250-10-50-1(b)(2). But an entity is required to disclose the effect of the changes on prior periods that were retrospectively adjusted.

g. An entity that elects to apply the amended guidance retrospectively in accordance with (e)(2) is required to recognize the cumulative effect of applying the guidance that links to this paragraph as an adjustment to the opening balance of retained earnings (or other appropriate components of equity or net assets in the balance sheet) of the annual period that includes the initial application date. Under this transition method, an entity may elect to apply the guidance that links to this paragraph retrospectively either to all contracts at the initial application date or only to contracts that are not completed contracts at the initial application date or only to uncompleted contracts at the application date. An entity is required to disclose whether the guidance that links to this paragraph has been applied to all contracts at the initial application date or only to contracts that are not completed at that date.

h. For reporting periods that include the initial application date, an entity applying the guidance that links to this paragraph retrospectively in accordance with (e)(2) is required to disclose the nature of and reason for a change in accounting principle as well as both of the following:
    1. The amount by which the application of the guidance applying that links to this paragraph affects each line item in the financial statement in the current reporting period in comparison to the previous guidance.
    2. An explanation of the reasons for significant changes identified in (h)(1).

i. ASC 606-10-65-1(f) includes several practical expedients for transition.
    1. An entity that early adopts the guidance that links to ASC 853-10-65-2 before adopting the guidance that is linked to AC 606-10-65-1 is prohibited from applying any of the practical expedients provided in ASC 606-10-65-1(f).
    2. An entity discussed in (b) that adopts the guidance that links to ASC 853-10-65-2 at the required effective date or earlier is required to use the same practical expedients that the entity used when it initially applied the guidance that links to ASC 606-10-65-1, if applicable with the transition guidance in ASC 606-10-65-1(g).

CHAPTER 62

ASC 855—SUBSEQUENT EVENTS

CONTENTS

PART I: GENERAL GUIDANCE

ASC 855-10: OVERALL

OVERVIEW

The current authoritative guidance on disclosure of subsequent events (ASC 855) was derived primarily from the existing authoritative auditing guidance on subsequent events. The FASB standard on subsequent events states that financial statement preparation, including the consideration of subsequent events, is the responsibility of the entity and its management.

BACKGROUND

ASC 855 provides guidance on the accounting for events that occur after the balance sheet date but before the financial statements are issued or are available for issuance (ASC 855-10-05-1). First, this guidance includes defining the length of the period after the balance sheet date where events should be evaluated for possible recognition or disclosure in the financial statements. Second, the guidance indicates when events or transactions occurring after the balance sheet date should be recognized in the financial statements. Third, guidance is provided on the disclosures that should be made related to subsequent events.

The guidance in ASC 855 applies to evaluating all subsequent events, unless other applicable U.S. GAAP addresses subsequent events in a particular area. Examples of areas where other authoritative literature addresses subsequent events are contingencies, earnings per share, and uncertainty income taxes (ASC 855-10-15-5).

DISCLOSURE OF SUBSEQUENT EVENTS

Terminology

A subsequent event is an event or transaction that occurs after the balance sheet date but before the financial statements are issued or are available for issuance. Financial statements are issued when they are distributed to shareholders and other financial statements users and their form and format comply with U.S. GAAP (ASC Glossary). Financial statements are available to be issued when their form and format comply with U.S. GAAP, and all approvals necessary for release of the financial statements have been obtained. These approvals may be from management, the board of directors, and from significant shareholders (ASC Glossary).

PRACTICE NOTE: The SEC staff views financial statements as being issued at the earlier of when they are widely distributed to all shareholders or are filed with the SEC (ASC 855-10-S99-2).

There are two types of subsequent events. The first type (recognized, or Type I, subsequent events) provides additional evidence related to conditions that existed at the balance sheet date, including additional evidence relating to estimated amounts in the financial statements. The second type (nonrecognized, or Type II, subsequent events) provides evidence about conditions that did *not* exist at the balance sheet date but that arose before the financial statements were issued or available for issuance (ASC Glossary).

An entity that is an SEC filer or is a conduit bond obligor for conduit debt securities that are traded in a public market must evaluate subsequent events through the date the financial statements are issued. All other entities are to evaluate subsequent events through the date the financial statements are available to be issued (ASC 855-10-25-2).

Recognition

Subsequent events that provide additional evidence about events or conditions that existed at the balance sheet date, including additional evidence relating to estimated amounts in the financial statements, are to be recognized (recognized subsequent events, or Type I subsequent events). For example, the bankruptcy of a customer due to a deteriorating financial condition in the subsequent events period in an example of a Type I subsequent event. The entity would consider the customer's bankruptcy in establishing the year-end balance in the allowance for doubtful accounts. Also, settlement of litigation that existed at the balance sheet date during the subsequent event period would be considered in estimating any loss and liability related to the litigation in the year-end financial statements (ASC 855-10-55-1).

Subsequent events that provide evidence about conditions that arose after the balance sheet date but before the financial statements are issued or are available for issuance are not recognized in the financial statements; however, these events may be disclosed in the financial statements (nonrecognized subsequent events, or Type II subsequent events) (ASC 855-10-25-3). These events, assuming they occurred after the balance sheet date and before the financial statements are issued or available for issuance, are examples of nonrecognized subsequent events: (1) issuance of capital stock or debt, (2) a business combination, (3) settlement of litigation (where the litigation began after the balance sheet date), (4) a casualty loss, (4) changes in the fair value of assets or liabilities, (5) changes in foreign exchange rates, and (6) entering into significant commitments (ASC 855-10-55-2).

Disclosure

An entity that is an SEC filer is not required to disclose the date through which subsequent events were evaluated. If an entity is not an SEC filer, then the entity must disclose the date through which subsequent events were evaluated, and whether that date is the date the financial statements were issued or the date the statements were available to be issued (ASC 855-10-50-1). Certain nonrecognized (Type II) subsequent events may be of such significance that they must be disclosed in order to prevent the financial statements from being misleading. The determination of which nonrecognized subsequent events need to be disclosed is a management judgment decision. If the entity decides to disclose a nonrecognized subsequent event, both the nature of the event and an estimate of its financial effect, or a statement that an estimate of the financial effect is not possible, are to be disclosed (ASC 855-10-50-2).

If a nonrecognized subsequent event is disclosed, the entity should consider providing pro-forma financial data related to the event. And, if the nonrecognized subsequent event is very significant (e.g., a material acquisition), pro-forma data may be needed to adequately convey the nature and impact of the event. Pro-forma data should reflect the event as if it happened on the balance sheet date, and the optional form of the pro-forma presentation may be an additional column on the face of the balance sheet presenting pro-forma amounts (ASC 855-10-50-2).

Other Issues

Entities are sometimes required by the SEC or other regulatory agencies to issue revised financial statements. Unless required by U.S. GAAP or regulatory requirements, events occurring between the date the financial statements were issued (or were available to be issued) and the reissuance date are not to be included in the reissued statements. Unless the entity is an SEC filer, an entity must disclose in the revised financial statements the dates through which subsequent events have been evaluated in both the issued or available-to-be-issued statements and in the revised financial statements (ASC 855-10-25-4 and ASC 855-10-50-4).

PART II: INTERPRETIVE GUIDANCE

ASC 855: SUBSEQUENT EVENTS

ASC 855-10: OVERALL

ASC 855-10-S25-1, S99-2 Issuance of Financial Statements

In response to inquiries as to when financial statements are considered to have been issued, the SEC staff announced that financial statements are issued as of the date they are distributed for "general use and reliance" in a form and format that complies with GAAP. Annual financial statements should include an audit report stating that the auditors complied with Generally Accepted Auditing Standards (GAAS) in completing the audit. Financial statements would be considered to have been issued when the annual or quarterly financial statements are widely distributed to a registrant's shareholders and other users of financial statements or filed with the Commission, whichever is earlier. The SEC staff's position is based on the view that in accordance with Rule 10b-5 12b-20 under the Securities Exchange Act of 1934 and General Instruction C(3) to Form 10-K, registrants and their auditors have a responsibility to issue financial statements that are not misleading as of the date they are filed with the Commission.

If a registrant that has widely distributed its financial statements or its auditor become aware that a transaction that existed at the date of the financial statements causes those financial statements to be materially misleading, the financial statements must be amended so that they are free of material misstatement or omissions before they are filed with the SEC. Registrants should also disclose information about the subsequent events, which should be evaluated by the auditors to determine how the events or transactions affect the auditor's report.

In addition, the SEC staff noted that the issuance of an earnings release should not be considered the issuance of financial statements, because its form and format do not comply with Generally Accepted Accounting Standards (GAAP) and Generally Accepted Auditing Standards (GAAS).

CHAPTER 63

ASC 860—TRANSFERS AND SERVICING

CONTENTS

PART I: GENERAL GUIDANCE

ASC 860-10: OVERALL

OVERVIEW

Transfers of financial assets take many forms and, depending on the nature of the transaction, the transferor may have a continuing interest in the transferred asset. Accounting for transferred assets in which the transferor has no continuing involvement with the transferred asset or with the transferee has been relatively straight forward and not controversial. Transfers of financial assets in which the transferor has some continuing interest, however, have raised issues about the circumstances in which the transfer should be considered a sale of all or part of the assets or a secured borrowing, and how transferors and transferees should account for sales of financial assets and secured borrowings.

ASC 860 establishes accounting and reporting standards for transfers and servicing of financial assets and extinguishments of liabilities based on the consistent application of the financial-components approach. For each party to a transfer, this approach requires the recognition of financial assets and servicing assets that are controlled by the reporting entity, the derecognition of financial assets when control is surrendered, and the derecognition of liabilities when they are extinguished. Specific criteria are established for determining when control has been surrendered in the transfer of financial assets. ASC 860 also contains specific guidance with respect to the accounting for separately recognized servicing assets and servicing liabilities. Finally, ASC 860 provides guidance with respect to the requirements for derecognizing financial assets and the initial measurement by the transferor of interests related to transferred financial assets.

PRACTICE POINTER: This chapter provides an overview of ASC 860. Because transfers of financial assets can be extremely complex transactions, practitioners encountering these transactions should seek the assistance of experts in analyzing the applicable accounting literature.

BACKGROUND

Definitions

The term *financial asset* is defined in ASC 860 as cash, evidence of an ownership interest in an entity, or a contract that conveys to one entity a right (*a*) to receive cash or another financial instrument from a second entity or (*b*) to exchange other financial instruments on potentially favorable terms with the second entity (ASC Glossary).

The term *financial liability* refers to a contract that imposes a contractual obligation on one entity (*a*) to deliver cash or another financial instrument to a second entity or (*b*) to exchange other financial instruments on potentially unfavorable terms with the second entity (ASC Glossary).

The term *transfer* refers to the conveyance of a noncash financial asset to someone other than the issuer of that financial asset. Examples are selling a receivable, putting it into a securitization trust, or posting it as collateral. It excludes the origination of the receivable, the settlement of the receivable, or the restructuring of the receivable into a security in a troubled debt restructuring. The *transferor* is the party that transfers a financial asset (or part of a financial asset or a group of financial assets) that it controls to another entity. The *transferee* is the entity that receives a financial asset from the transferor (ASC Glossary).

The term *servicing asset* refers to a contract to service financial assets under which the estimated future revenues from contractually specified servicing fees, late charges, and other ancillary revenues are expected to more than adequately compensate the servicer for performing the servicing. A service contract is either (1) undertaken in conjunction with selling or securitizing the financial assets being serviced or (2) purchased or assumed separately (ASC Glossary).

The term *servicing liability* refers to a contract to service financial assets under which the estimated future revenues from contractually specified servicing fees, late charges, and other ancillary revenues are not expected to adequately compensate the servicer for performing the servicing (ASC Glossary).

Transfers of Financial Assets

Transfers of financial assets may take many forms, and accounting for those transfers in which the transferor has no continuing involvement with the transferred financial asset or with the transferee is uncontroversial. Accounting for transfers of financial assets in which the transferor has a continuing involvement with the assets or with the transferee, however, is less straightforward. Examples of continuing involvement include (ASC 860-10-05-4):

- Recourse or guarantee arrangements
- Servicing arrangements
- Guarantee arrangements
- Agreements to purchase or redeem transferred financial assets
- Options written or held
- Pledges of collateral
- Arrangements to provide financial support
- Derivatives entered into contemporaneously with, or in contemplation of, the transfer
- The transferor's beneficial interests in the transferred financial assets

Issues raised by these types of transactions include the circumstances in which the transfers should be considered as sales of part or all of the assets or as secured borrowings and the accounting by transferors and transferees for sales and secured borrowings. However, financial assets and liabilities may be disaggregated into components, which become separate assets and liabilities, as a result of a sale or transfer (ASC 860-10-05-5).

Some entities use derivative financial instruments to offset the risks associated with changes in the value of the servicing assets and servicing liabilities. Those derivative instruments are required to be accounted for at fair value, with changes in their fair value being reported in current earnings.

ASC 860 provides guidance for determining whether or not financial assets can be derecognized when those assets are transferred. A transferor's beneficial interests are to be initially recognized at fair value when the transfer is accounted for as a sale.

CONTROL CRITERIA AND TRANSFEROR ACCOUNTING

ASC 860 provides guidance to determine whether the transferor has surrendered control over transferred financial assets. This determination requires the use of judgment and must consider the transferor's continuing involvement in the transferred assets as well as all arrangements or agreements made in connection with the transfer, even if they were not entered into at the time of the transfer (ASC 860-10-40-4).

PRACTICE POINTER: The consideration of the transferor's continuing involvement in the transferred assets and arrangements made in connection with the transfer do not apply to a transfer of financial assets and a related repurchase financing. In transactions involving a contemporaneous transfer of a financial asset and a repurchase financing of that transferred asset with the same counterparty, the initial transfer of the financial asset and the related repurchase agreement must be separately accounted for by the transferor and transferee (ASC 860-10-40-4C).

Transferred financial assets may include the transfer of an entire financial asset, the transfer of a group of entire financial assets, or the transfer of a participating interest in an entire financial asset. A participating interest has the following characteristics (ASC 860-10-40-6A):

1. From the date of transfer, it represents proportionate ownership rights in an entire financial asset.
2. From the date of transfer, all cash flows received from the entire financial asset are divided proportionately based on the ownership shares of each participating interest holder (the priority does change in the event of bankruptcy or other receivership).
3. The priority of each participating interest holder is equal, and no participating interest holder's interest is subordinated to the interest of another participating interest holder. Thus, no participating interest holder is entitled to receive cash before any other participating interest holder.
4. No party can pledge or exchange the entire financial asset without the agreement of all participating interest holders.

If a transfer of a portion of an entire financial asset does not meet the criteria for a participating interest, the transferor and transferee must account for the transfer as a secured borrowing (ASC 860-10-40-4E).

A transfer of an entire financial asset, a group of entire financial assets, or a participating interest in an entire financial asset is accounted for as a sale if the transferor surrenders control over those financial assets. The transferor has surrendered control if all of the following conditions are met (ASC 860-10-40-5):

1. The transferred financial assets have been isolated from the transferor (i.e., they are beyond the reach of the transferor and its creditors, even in bankruptcy).
2. Each transferee (or, if the transferee's sole purpose is to engage in securitization or asset-backed financing activities and is not allowed to pledge or exchange the assets it receives, each third-party holder of its beneficial interests) has the right to pledge or exchange the assets (or beneficial interests) it received, and no condition both (*a*) constrains the transferee (or third-party holder of beneficial interests) from taking advantage of its right to pledge or exchange and (*b*) provides more than a trivial benefit to the transferor.
3. The transferor, its consolidated affiliates, or its agents do not maintain effective control over the transferred assets or third-party beneficial interests related to the transferred assets. Examples of a transferor's effective control over the transferred financial assets include the following:
    a. An agreement that obligates the transferor to repurchase or redeem the assets before their maturity.
    b. An agreement that gives the transferor the unilateral ability to cause the holder to return specific financial assets other than through a cleanup call. (A cleanup call is an option held by the servicer or its affiliate to purchase the remaining transferred financial assets if the amount of outstanding financial assets or beneficial interests becomes burdensome in relation to the benefits of servicing (ASC Glossary).
    c. An agreement that permits the transferee to require the transferor to repurchase the transferred assets at a price that is so favorable to the transferee that it is probable that the transferee will require the transferor to repurchase them.

A repurchase-to-maturity transaction involves a repurchase agreement with a settlement date that is at the maturity date of the transferred financial asset. Thus, the repurchase agreement would not actually require the transferor to reacquire the financial asset (ASC Glossary). A repurchase-to-maturity transaction must be accounted for as a secured borrowing as if the transferor maintains effective control (ASC 860-10-40-5A).

SECURITIZATIONS

Securitization refers to the process by which financial assets (such as loans and other receivables) are transformed into securities (ASC Glossary). Securitizations typically involve a transfer of assets to a securitization entity, through which the characteristics of those assets are changed (e.g., by credit enhancements or derivatives that alter the interest rate or currency characteristics of the original cash flows of the assets). The securitization entity issues beneficial interests in those assets to third-party investors. Entities enter into securitization transactions for a variety of reasons, for example, to obtain funding more economically or to change the characteristics of the assets transferred to achieve different regulatory or accounting treatment.

Transfers to a securitization entity should be evaluated under the control criteria, taking into consideration the nature of the entity, the transferor's rights under the arrangement, and the extent of interests that continue to be held by the transferor. For example, a transferor's right to reacquire specific assets held by the securitization entity indicates that the transferor has not relinquished effective control over the assets. Accordingly, the transferor may not account for the transfer of assets as a sale. If the criteria for a sale are not met, then both the transferor and transferee(s) should account for the transaction as a secured borrowing.

In situations where a transfer of assets in a securitization transaction qualifies as a sale, the transferor must recognize any interests it continues to hold (such as subordinated interests or servicing rights). Interest only strips, loans, other receivables, or other beneficial interests that can contractually be prepaid or otherwise settled in a manner that the holder would not recover substantially all of its recorded investment are measured like investments in debt securities and classified as either available-for-sale or trading in accordance with ASC 320 (ASC 860-20-35-2).

PRACTICE POINTER: The evaluation of control criteria for the transfer of assets to a securitization entity and the determination of the gain or loss to be recognized by the transferor are highly technical and much interpreted areas. Practitioners encountering these areas should seek the advice of experts.

Consolidation of Securitization Entities

ASC 810 establishes the term *variable interest entity,* which refers to an entity that has insufficient equity at risk or lack of a controlling financial interest. Specific conditions in ASC 810 must be evaluated to establish whether an entity is a variable interest entity and must therefore be consolidated by the entity determined to be the primary beneficiary. Many securitization entities are variable interest entities subject to ASC 810; however, the guidance in ASC 810 encompasses other types of entities as well. For more detail about this topic, see our discussion of ASC 810.

DISCLOSURES

ASC 860-10 includes various disclosure requirements related to continuing involvement in transferred assets. The principal objectives of these required disclosures are to provide financial statement users with an understanding of all of the following (ASC 860-10-50-3):

- A transferor's continuing involvement, if any, with transferred financial assets
- The nature of any restrictions on assets reported by an entity in its statement of financial position that relate to a transferred financial asset, including the carrying amounts of those assets
- How servicing assets and servicing liabilities are reported under Subtopic 860-50
- How the transfer of financial assets affects an entity's financial position, financial performance, and cash flows for both:
  - — Transfers accounted for as sales; and
  - — Transfers accounted for as secured borrowings

The objectives listed above apply regardless of whether the Topic requires specific disclosures. The specific disclosures required by this Topic are minimum requirements, and an entity may need to supplement the required disclosures depending on any of the following (ASC 860-10-50-4):

- The facts and circumstances of a transfer,
- The nature of an entity's continuing involvement with the transferred financial assets, and
- The effect of an entity's continuing involvement on the transferor's financial position, financial performance, and cash flows.

The disclosures required by ASC 860 may be reported in the aggregate for similar transfers if separately reporting each transfer would not provide more useful information. A transferor must disclose how similar transfers are aggregated and must distinguish transfers that are accounted for as sales from those accounted for as secured borrowings (ASC 860-10-50-4A).

ASC 860-20: SALES OF FINANCIAL ASSETS

RECOGNITION OF ASSETS OBTAINED OR LIABILITIES INCURRED

Upon completion of a transfer of financial assets that meets the conditions required to be accounted for as a sale, the transferor must recognize any assets obtained or liabilities incurred in the sale, including the following (ASC 860-20-25-1):

1. Cash
2. Servicing assets
3. Servicing liabilities
4. In a sale of an entire financial asset or a group of entire financial assets, any of the following:
    a. The transferor's beneficial interest in the transferred financial assets
    b. Put or call options held or written
    c. Forward commitments
    d. Swaps

DERECOGNITION OF ASSETS AND LIABILITIES

Sale of a Participating Interest

Upon completion of a transfer of a participating interest that meets the conditions required to be accounted for as a sale, the transferor must (ASC 860-20-40-1A):

1. Allocate the previous carrying amount of the entire financial asset between the participating interest sold and the participating interest maintained by the transferor, based on their relative fair values at the transfer date
2. Derecognize the participating interest(s) sold
3. Recognize and initially measure at fair value servicing assets, servicing liabilities, and any other assets obtained and liabilities incurred in the sale
4. Recognize any gain or loss on the sale in income
5. Report any participating interest(s) that continue to be held by the transferor as the difference between the previous carrying amount of the entire financial asset and the amount derecognized at the transfer date

Sale of an Entire Financial Asset Group or Group of Entire Financial Assets

Upon completion of a transfer of an entire financial asset or a group of entire financial assets that meets the conditions required to be accounted for as a sale, the transferor must (ASC 860-20-40-1B):

1. Derecognize the transferred financial assets
2. Recognize and initially measure at fair value servicing assets, servicing liabilities, and any other assets obtained (including a transferor's beneficial interest in the transferred financial assets) and liabilities incurred in the sale
3. Recognize any gain or loss on the sale in income

If the transferred financial asset had previously been accounted for as an available-for-sale security under ASC 320, the amount in other comprehensive income must be recognized in earnings when the transferred financial assets are derecognized on the transfer date.

DISCLOSURES

ASC 860-20 provides guidance on disclosures for securitizations, asset-backed financing arrangements, and similar transfers that both (1) are accounted for as a sale, and (2) result in the transferor maintaining a continuing involvement with the transferred financial assets. For each income statement presented, the entity must disclose all of the following (ASC 860-20-50-3):

1. The characteristics of the transfer including the following:
   a. A description of the transferor's continuing involvement
   b. The nature and initial fair value of the assets obtained and liabilities incurred in the transfer
   c. The gain or loss from sale of transferred financial assets
2. The level within the fair value hierarchy in ASC 820 in which the initial fair value measurements fall
3. The key inputs and assumptions used in measuring the initial fair values
4. The valuation techniques used to measure fair value
5. Cash flows between a transferor and transferee

For each statement of financial position presented, regardless of when the transfer occurred, an entity must disclose all of the following (ASC 860-20-50-4):

1. Sufficient qualitative and quantitative information about the transferor's continuing involvement with the transferred financial assets to permit financial statement users to assess the reasons for the continuing involvement and the risks related to the transferred financial assets
2. The entity's accounting policies for subsequently measuring assets and liabilities related to the continuing involvement with the transferred financial assets
3. The key inputs and assumptions used in measuring the fair value of assets or liabilities related to the transferor's continuing involvement
4. A sensitivity analysis or stress test that shows the hypothetical change in the calculated fair values as a result of two or more unfavorable variations in the key assumption made in measuring fair values
5. A description of the objectives, methodology, and limitations of the sensitivity analysis or stress test
6. Information about the asset quality of transferred financial assets and any other financial assets that the entity manages together with them

An entity must disclose the following for outstanding transactions at the reporting date by type of transaction (e.g., repurchase agreement, securities lending transaction, and sale and total return swap) (ASC 860-20-50-4D):

1. The carrying amount of assets derecognized as of the date of derecognition.
2. The amount of gross cash proceeds received by the transferor for the assets derecognized as of the date of derecognition.
3. Information about the transferor's ongoing exposure to the economic return on the transferred financial assets:
   a. As of the reporting date, the fair value of assets derecognized by the transferor.
   b. Amounts reported in the statement of financial position arising from the transaction.
   c. A description of the arrangements that result in the transferor retaining substantially all of the exposure to the economic return on the transferred financial assets and the risks related to those arrangements.

These disclosure requirements in ASC 860-20-50-4D apply to transactions accounted for as a sale that are both (ASC 860-20-50-4A):

1. A transfer of financial assets to a transferee; and
2. An agreement entered into in contemplation of the initial transfer with the transferee that results in the transferor retaining substantially all of the exposure to the economic return on the transferred financial asset.

ASC 860-30: SECURED BORROWING AND COLLATERAL

SECURED BORROWING AND COLLATERAL

A debtor may grant a security interest in assets to a lender (identified below as the secured party) as collateral for its obligation under a borrowing. If collateral is transferred to the secured party, the arrangement is often referred to as a *pledge*. In some circumstances, a secured party is permitted to sell or repledge collateral it holds under a pledge.

Accounting for collateral by the debtor and the secured party depends on whether the secured party has the right to sell or repledge the collateral and whether the debtor has defaulted under the secured contract.

The following summarizes the accounting by both the debtor and the secured party for noncash collateral transferred in a secured borrowing under several scenarios (ASC 860-30-25-5):

Scenario	*Accounting Requirements*
The secured party is permitted to sell or repledge the collateral.	*Debtor*—Reclassifies the asset and reports it separately from other assets not so encumbered. *Secured party*—Does not recognize the collateral as its asset.
The secured party sells or repledges the collateral.	*Debtor*—Continues to carry the collateral as its asset. *Secured party*—Recognizes the proceeds from the sale of the collateral and records an obligation to return the collateral.
The debtor defaults under the contract secured by the collateral and is no longer entitled to the return of the collateral.	*Debtor*—Derecognizes the collateral. *Secured party*—Recognizes the collateral as its asset at fair value (or, if the collateral has already been sold, derecognizes the obligation to return the collateral).

DISCLOSURES

ASC 860 includes various disclosure requirements related to secured borrowing and collateral. These disclosures are summarized as follows (ASC 860-30-50-1A):

Condition Requiring Disclosure	*Information Required to Be Disclosed*
Collateral	
1. Entity has entered into repurchase agreements or securities lending transactions.	Policy for requiring collateral or other security
2. Assets have been pledged and they are not reclassified and separately reported in the balance sheet.	The carrying amounts of both the assets and associated liabilities and their classifications
3. Collateral that can be sold or pledged has been accepted by the entity.	The fair value of the collateral. Any amount of the collateral that has been sold or pledged A description of the sources and uses of the collateral

ASC 860 also includes disclosure requirements related to financial assets and financial liabilities that are either offset or subject to an enforceable master netting arrangement (ASC 860-30-50-8). An entity must provide financial statement users with sufficient information to permit them to evaluate the effect or potential effect of the netting arrangements on its financial position.

An entity must also disclose the following information for each interim and annual period about the collateral pledged and the associated risks to which the transferor continues to be exposed after the transfer (ASC 860-30-50-7):

1. A disaggregation of the gross obligation by the class of collateral pledged.
2. The remaining contractual maturity of the repurchase agreements, securities lending transactions, and repurchase-to-maturity transactions.
3. A discussion of the potential risks associated with the agreements and related collateral pledged, including obligations arising from a decline in the fair value of the collateral pledged and how those risks are managed.

ASC 860-40: TRANSFERS TO QUALIFYING SPECIAL PURPOSE ENTITIES

TRANSFERS TO QUALIFYING SPECIAL PURPOSE ENTITIES

The FASB has eliminated this ASC subtopic because of the perceived abuse of special purpose entities during the previous financial crisis.

ASC 860-50: SERVICING ASSETS AND LIABILITIES

ACCOUNTING FOR SERVICING ASSETS AND LIABILITIES

Initial Measurement of Servicing Assets and Servicing Liabilities

Servicing assets and servicing liabilities that are required to be separately recognized shall be initially measured at fair value. An entity is required to recognize a servicing asset or servicing liability each time it undertakes an obligation to service a financial asset by entering into a servicing contract in either of the following situations (ASC 860-50-25-1):

- A servicer's transfer of an entire financial asset, a group of entire financial assets, or a participating interest in an entire financial asset that meets the requirements for sale accounting.
- An acquisition or assumption of a servicing obligation that does not relate to financial assets of the servicer or its consolidated affiliates.

An entity that transfers financial assets to an unconsolidated entity in a transfer that qualifies as a sale and that classifies its retained securities as debt securities held-to-maturity in accordance with ASC 320 may either separately recognize its servicing assets or servicing liabilities or report those servicing assets or servicing liabilities together with the asset being serviced.

Subsequent Measurement of Servicing Assets and Servicing Liabilities

An entity may choose between two alternative methods of subsequent measurement for each class of separately recognized servicing assets and servicing liabilities—the amortization method and the fair value measurement method. Using the amortization method, servicing assets and servicing liabilities are amortized over the estimated service period and assessed for impairment or increased obligation based on fair value at each reporting period. Using the fair value measurement method, servicing assets and servicing liabilities are measured at their fair value each reporting date with changes in their fair value reported in earnings in the period in which the changes occur.

An entity must separately select, at the beginning of a fiscal year, either the amortization method or the fair value method for subsequent measurement for each class of servicing assets and servicing liabilities and must then apply the selected method to every servicing asset and servicing liability in a class. Classes of servicing assets and servicing liabilities are identified based on (*a*) the availability of market inputs used in determining the fair values, (*b*) an entity's method for managing the risks of its servicing assets and servicing liabilities, or (*c*) both (*a*) and (*b*). An election to use the fair value method for subsequent measurement for a class of servicing assets and servicing liabilities cannot be later reversed (ASC 860-50-35-3).

One-Time Option to Reclassify Available-for-Sale Debt Securities

An entity may make a one-time election to reclassify available-for-sale debt securities as trading securities without calling into question the treatment of those securities under ASC 320. This election is limited to those available-for-sale securities that an entity intended to use to mitigate the income statement effects of changes in the fair value of servicing assets and servicing liabilities for which the entity has elected the fair value method of subsequent measurement.

DISCLOSURES

ASC 860 includes various disclosure requirements related to transfers and servicing of financial assets. These disclosures are summarized as follows (ASC 860-50-50-2, 3, 4):

	Condition Requiring Disclosure	*Information Required to Be Disclosed*
1.	The entity has servicing assets or servicing liabilities.	Management's basis for determining its classes Description of risks and, if applicable, the instruments used to mitigate the income statements effect of changes in their fair value Amount of contractually specified servicing fees recognized for each period Quantitative and qualitative information about the assumptions used to estimate the fair value
2.	Servicing assets and servicing liabilities are subsequently measured at fair value.	For each class, the activity in the balance of servicing assets and the activity in the balance of servicing liabilities

	Condition Requiring Disclosure	*Information Required to Be Disclosed*
3.	Servicing assets and servicing liabilities are subsequently amortized.	For each class, the activity in the balance of servicing assets and the activity in the balance of servicing liabilities
		For each class, the fair value at the beginning and end of the period
		Risk characteristics used to stratify for purposes of measuring impairment
		Activity by class in any valuation allowance for impairment of recognized servicing assets

EXTINGUISHMENT OF LIABILITIES

A liability is considered extinguished if: (1) the debtor is relieved of its obligations as a result of having paid the creditor or (2) the debtor is legally released from its obligation. A liability must be extinguished before the debtor is permitted to derecognize the liability (ASC 405-20-40-1).

IMPLEMENTATION GUIDANCE

Appendix A of ASC 860 describes certain provisions of the standard in more detail and describes how they apply to certain types of transactions.

The specific areas for which implementation guidance is provided are as follows:

- Unit of account
- Participating interests in an entire financial asset
- Isolation beyond the reach of the transferor and its creditors
- Conditions that constrain a transferee
- Effective control over transferred financial assets or beneficial interests
- Changes that result in the transferor's regaining control of financial assets sold
- Measurement of interests held after a transfer of financial assets
- Participating interests in financial assets that continue to be held by a transferor
- Servicing assets and liabilities
- Securitizations
- Removal-of-accounts provisions
- Sales-type and direct financing lease receivables
- Securities lending transactions
- Repurchase agreements and "wash sales"
- Loan syndications
- Loan participations
- Banker's acceptances and risk participations in them
- Factoring arrangements
- Transfers of receivables with recourse
- Extinguishments of liabilities

The following illustrations highlight two of the most important aspects of ASC 860 for which implementation guidance is provided. These illustrations also provide a flavor of the type of implementation guidance included in ASC 860 for all of the areas listed above.

Measurement of Interests Held after a Transfer of Financial Assets

The financial-components approach recognizes that financial assets and liabilities are divisible into a variety of components. The approach requires accounting recognition of these different components, rather than treating a financial asset as an inseparable unit that has been entirely sold or entirely retained. This approach is applied in the following illustration, in which the primary transaction is the sale of loans for cash, but in which a separate financial asset is recognized for an interest rate swap, and a separate financial liability is recognized for the recourse obligation.

Illustration of Recording Transfers with Proceeds of Cash, Derivatives, and Other Liabilities

Fowler Company receives $2,610 in cash by selling loans with a fair value of $2,590 and a carrying amount of $2,500, undertaking no servicing responsibility. Fowler Company assumes a recourse obligation (valued at $120) to purchase delinquent loans. Fowler Company simultaneously enters into an interest rate swap agreement (valued at $100) with the transferee in which it receives fixed interest at an above-market rate and pays a floating rate.

The net proceeds and gain on the sale are determined as follows:

Net proceeds:		
Cash received	$2,610	
Plus: Interest rate swap	100	
Less: Recourse obligation	(120)	
		$2,590
Carrying amount of loans		(2,500)
Gain on sale		$ 90

The general journal entry to record the transfer and recognize related assets and liabilities is:

Cash	$2,610	
Interest rate swap	100	
Loans		$2,500
Recourse obligation		120
Gain on sale		90

Participating Interests in Financial Assets That Continue to Be Held by a Transferor

Interests in financial assets that continue to be held by the transferor are not included as part of the proceeds from the transfer and are measured at the date of the transfer by allocating the previous carrying amount to the components based on their relative fair values. The following illustration demonstrates these procedures in a situation in which a company sells loans with a recourse obligation, agrees to service the loans, and continues to hold an interest in the loans via an interest-only strip receivable.

Illustrations of Recording Transfers with Interests That Continue to Be Held by a Transferor

Anderson Company sells loans with a carrying amount of $2,600 to another entity for cash. Anderson Company agrees to service the transferred loans for the other entity and incurs a recourse obligation to repurchase any delinquent loans. Anderson Company also continues to hold an interest in the loans via an interest-only strip receivable.

Fair values are as follows: servicing asset, $90; recourse obligation, $150; interest-only strip receivable, $100. Anderson received $2,905 in cash.

The net proceeds are determined as follows:

Cash received	$2,905
Plus: Servicing assets	90
Less: Recourse obligation	(150)
Net proceeds	$2,845

This carrying amount is allocated to the loans sold and the servicing asset based on relative fair values as follows:

	Fair Value	*Percentage of Total Fair Value*	*Allocated Carrying Amount*
Loans sold	$2,845	97	$2,522
Interest-only strip-receivable	100	3	78
Total	$2,945	100	$2,600

The general journal entry to record the transfer is as follows:

Cash	$2,905	
Servicing asset	90	
Interest-only strip receivable	78	
Loans		$2,600
Recourse obligation		150
Gain		323

PART II: INTERPRETIVE GUIDANCE

ASC 860-10: OVERALL

ASC 860-10-05-12 through 05-13, 05-22, 10-9, 10-12 through 10-13, 10-22, 15-4, 35-5, 35-8, 35-10 through 35-12, 40-7, 40-9, 40-11 through 40-12, 40-14, 40-24, 40-26 through 40-27, 40-29, 40-31, 40-33, 40-40, 55-3 through 55-4, 55-7 through 55-18, 55-24A, 55-25A, 55-27 through 55-33, 55-38 through 55-42; 55-46, 55-51, 55-54, 55-58 through 55-59, 55-62 through 55-64, 55-66 through 55-70, 55-75 through 55-79; ASC 860-20-25-6, 35-2 through 35-3, 35-5, 35-7, 35-8, 55-3 through 55-9, 55-11 through 55-16, 55-24, 55-25, 55-28, 55-31, 55-34 through 55-39, 55-60 through 55-61, 55-101 through 55-107; ASC 860-30-15-2 through 15-3, 25-9, 35-2 through 35-3, 45-2 through 45-3; ASC 860-40-05-6, 15-11, 15-15, 15-19 through 15-28, 40-11, 45-2, 45-4, 55-3, 55-11 through 55-12, 55-14 through 55-16, 55-18 through 55-20, 55-23 through 55-25, 55-27 through 55-29; ASC 860-50-25-7 through 25-9, 30-2 through 30-9, 35-11 through 35-15, 50-5; 55-4 through 55-11, 55-13 through 55-18; ASC 320-10-25-5, 25-18; ASC 405-20-55-5 through 55-9
A Guide to Implementation of ASC 860 on Accounting for Transfers and Servicing

IMPORTANT NOTICE: The guidance in this Issue will be amended as follows: (1) ASC 860-10-15-4(e) will be amended by replacing "real estate" with "nonfinancial assets" and replacing "Topics 845 and 976" with "Subtopic 610-20"; (2) ASC 860-10-55-3(b) will be amended by replacing "investment that is in substance a sale of real estate, as defined in Subtopic 320-20" with "in substance nonfinancial asset (see Subtopic 610-20)," as a result of the issuance of ASU 2014-09, *Revenue from Contracts with Customers*, which will reside in ASC 606 (Revenue from Contracts with Customers). That guidance becomes effective for public business entities in annual reporting periods that begin after December 15, 2017, and interim periods within those annual periods and in annual reporting periods that begin after December 15, 2018, for nonpublic entities.

ACCOUNTING GUIDANCE

Scope

Question 1: If a right to receive the minimum lease payments to be obtained under an operating lease is transferred, could that right be considered a financial asset within the scope of ASC 860?

Answer: No. The guidance in ASC 860 does not apply to an unrecognized financial asset.

Question 2: Is a transfer of servicing rights that are contractually separated from the underlying serviced assets within the scope of ASC 860? For example, does the guidance in ASC 860 apply to an entity's conveyance of mortgage servicing rights that have been separated from an underlying mortgage loan portfolio that the entity intends to retain?

Answer: No. ASC 860-10-15-4 states that transfers of nonfinancial assets, for example, servicing assets are not addressed in ASC 860. See the discussion in ASC 860-50-40-3 through 40-5 (Determination of What Risks and Rewards, If Any, Can Be Retained and Whether Any Unresolved Contingencies May Exist in a Sale of Mortgage Loan Servicing Rights) for the treatment of servicing rights that have been separated from the underlying serviced assets.

Question 3: Is a debtor's conveyance of cash or noncash financial assets in full or partial settlement of an obligation to a creditor considered a transfer under the guidance in ASC 860?

Answer: No. A transfer involves the conveyance of a noncash financial asset by and to someone other than the originator of the financial asset.

Question 4: Does the guidance in ASC 860 address a reacquisition by an entity of its own securities by exchanging noncash financial assets (e.g., U.S. Treasury bonds or shares of an unconsolidated investee) for its common shares?

Answer: No. The guidance in ASC 860 does not address either investments by, or distributions to, owners.

Question 5: Do the provisions of ASC 860 apply to "desecuritizations" of securities into loans or other financial assets?

Answer: No. See the discussion in ASC 320-10-25-18; ASC 860-10-55-34, 55-74 (The Applicability of FAS-115 to Desecuritizations of Financial Assets) for additional information.

Question 6: Are securitized stranded costs of a utility company a financial asset, and would the transfer of the asset be within the scope of ASC 860?

Answer: No. Securitized stranded costs do not meet the definition of a financial asset. The cash flows that arise from securitized stranded costs are the result of government regulation; they do not flow from a contract between two or more parties.

Question 7: Would a transfer of beneficial interests in a securitization trust that holds nonfinancial assets, such as securitized stranded costs or other similar rights by third-party investors, be within the scope of ASC 860?

Answer: Yes. In general, the beneficial interests in such a trust would be considered financial assets by third-party investors.

Question 8: Is a judgment from litigation a financial asset?

Answer: Generally not. However, a financial asset exists when a court judgment is reduced to contractually specified payment terms.

Question 9: Is a judgment from litigation a financial asset if it is transferred to an unrelated third party (i.e., would the transfer be within the scope of ASC 860)?

Answer: Yes, if the judgment is enforceable and has been reduced to a contractually specified payment schedule.

Question 10: Does the guidance in ASC 860 apply to a transfer of an ownership interest in a consolidated subsidiary by its parent if that consolidated subsidiary holds nonfinancial assets?

Answer: No. An ownership interest in a consolidated subsidiary denotes an interest in individual assets and liabilities. Some of these assets are nonfinancial in nature.

Question 11: This question was deleted because the concept of temporary control was eliminated by the guidance in ASC 360-10.

Question 12: Would the guidance in ASC 860 apply to a transfer of an investment in a controlled entity that has not been consolidated because that entity accounts for its investment at fair value (e.g., a broker-dealer or an investment company)?

Answer: Generally, yes. An entity that carries an investment in a subsidiary at fair value will realize its investment by transferring that investment, which is a financial asset, rather than by the realization of the underlying assets and liabilities, which might include nonfinancial assets.

Question 13: Is a transfer of an equity method investment within the scope of ASC 860?

Answer: Yes, unless the transfer is in substance a sale of real estate, as defined in ASC 360-20-15-2 through 15-3, 15-10, 55-4 through 55-5. The guidance in ASC 360, *Property, Plant and Equipment*; ASC 976, *Real Estate—Retail Land*, ASC 845, *Nonmonetary Transactions*), and ASC 845-10-05-11, 15-12 to 15-17, 15-20, 35-3 25-6 through 25-12, 30-12 through 30-14, 30-21 through 30-23, S30-2, 55-2, 55-27 through 55-37, 60-3, S99-3 (Exchanges Involving Monetary Consideration) for guidance.

Question 14: Is a forward contract on a financial instrument that must be (or may be) physically settled by the delivery of that financial instrument in exchange for cash a financial asset or liability, the transfer (or extinguishment in the case of a liability) of which would be within the scope of ASC 860?

Answer: Yes.

Question 15: Is a transfer of a recognized financial instrument that may be a financial asset or a financial liability at any point in time, such as during a forward or swap contract, subject to the provisions of both ASC 860-10-40-4 through 40-5 and ASC 405-20-40-1?

Answer: Yes. Certain financial instruments (e.g., forwards or swaps) may ultimately prove to be either financial assets or liabilities. Therefore, transfers of these types of financial instruments must meet the requirements of both ASC 860-20-40-4 through 40-5 (regarding assets) and ASC 405-20-40-1 (regarding liabilities) to be derecognized.

Question 16: Does the guidance in ASC 860 apply to a transfer of a recognized derivative instrument that is not a financial instrument?

Answer: Yes. The guidance in ASC 860 does apply if a derivative involves a nonfinancial liability (e.g., a written commodity option) at the date of transfer, because the guidance in ASC 860 applies to the extinguishments of all liabilities. Some derivatives have characteristics of both nonfinancial assets and nonfinancial liabilities (e.g., a commodity forward contract). In such cases, the guidance in ASC 860 does apply, but it does *not* apply if a derivative involves a nonfinancial asset (e.g., an option to purchase a commodity) at the date of transfer. However, the transfer of nonfinancial derivative instruments, subject to the requirements in ASC 815, should be accounted for using the guidance in ASC 860 (see ASC 815-10-40-2, 40-3; 860-10-15-5; 40-40 (Accounting for Transfers of Assets That Are Derivative Instruments but That Are Not Financial Assets) for additional discussion of this issue).

Control Criteria—Isolation

Question 17: What type of evidence is sufficient to provide reasonable assurance that transferred financial assets are isolated beyond the reach of the transferor and its consolidated affiliates under the guidance in ASC 860?

Answer: There must be reasonable assurance that the transferred financial assets could not be reached by creditors in bankruptcy or other receiver for the transferor or its consolidated affiliates, if any, included in the financial statements being presented and its creditors. The Audit Issues Task Force has issued guidance on evaluating legal interpretations in support of management's assertion that the isolation criterion has been met.

> *PRACTICE POINTER:* Evaluating whether transferred assets are isolated beyond the reach of the transferor (and the transferor's creditors, even in bankruptcy) is primarily a legal judgment. Therefore, the auditor will typically not be able to evaluate management's assertion that transferred assets are appropriately isolated in the absence of a legal letter. The legal letter must not (1) restrict the auditor's reliance on the letter, (2) disclaim an opinion, (3) restrict its scope to facts and circumstances not applicable to the particular transfer, and (4) express its conclusions using conditional language, such as that contained in the Audit Issues Task Force's interpretation (e.g., "In our opinion, the transfer should be considered a sale . . . ").

> *PRACTICE POINTER:* In evaluating whether transferred assets are isolated beyond the reach of the transferor (and the transferor's creditors, even in bankruptcy), a legal specialist should consider the following factors: (1) the structure of the transfer, (2) the nature of the transferor's continuing involvement, if any, with the transferred assets, (3) the type of insolvency or other receivership proceedings applicable to the transferor if it fails, and (4) other applicable legal factors.

Question 18: Is the requirement in ASC 860-10-40-5 (i.e., the isolation requirement) satisfied if the likelihood of bankruptcy is remote?

Answer: No. The focus is not on whether bankruptcy is remote, but whether the transferred financial assets would be isolated from the transferor in the event of bankruptcy.

Question 19: Are transferred financial assets isolated from the transferor in those cases in which the Federal Deposit Insurance Corporation (FDIC) would act as a receiver if the transferor failed?

Answer: Generally, yes. The FDIC cannot recover, reclaim, or recharacterize financial assets transferred by an insured depository institution if the transfer met all the requirements in ASC 860 for sale accounting treatment, except the requirement that the transferred assets be legally isolated for the transferor's creditors. Finally, the Auditing Interpretation (The Use of Legal Interpretations As Evidential Matter to Support Management's Assertion that a Transfer of Financial Assets Has Met the Isolation Criterion in ASC 860-10-40-5) was issued to help auditors assess when transferred assets would be beyond the reach of the FDIC.

Question 19A: Can financial assets transferred by an entity subject to possible receivership by the FDIC be considered isolated from the transferor (i.e., can the transfer meet the condition in ASC 860-10-40-4 through 40-5 if circumstances arise under which *the FDIC or another creditor* can require their return?

Answer: Yes. If an entity subject to possible receivership by the FDIC transfers financial assets, they are isolated from the transferor if the FDIC or another creditor cannot require that the financial assets be returned or can only require a return in receivership, after a default, and in exchange for payment of, at a minimum, principal and interest earned at the contractual yield to the date that investors paid. See Question 19C for guidance if a transferor can require that the transferred financial assets be returned.

Question 19B: Does the answer to Question 19A also apply to financial assets that an entity transferred subject to the U.S. Bankruptcy Code?

Answer: No. According to the guidance in ASC 860-10-55-19 through 55-23, transfers of financial assets by entities subject to the U.S. Bankruptcy Court meet the condition in ASC 860-10-40-4 and 40-5 if the transferred financial asset have been "put presumptively beyond the reach of the transferor and its creditors, even in bankruptcy . . . " That treatment differs from the treatment for receivership under the FDIC.

Question 19C: Can financial assets transferred by any entity be considered isolated from *the transferor* (i.e., can the transfer meet the condition in ASC 860-10-40-4 and 40-5 if circumstances can arise under which *the transferor* can require their return, only in exchange for payment of principal and interest earned (at the contractual yield) to the date investors are paid?

Answer: No, unless the transferor has the ability to require the return of the transferred financial assets solely from a contract with the transferee.

Question 19D: Which of the answers in questions 19A-19C applies to entities subject to possible receivership under jurisdictions other than the FDIC or the U.S. Bankruptcy Code?

Answer: It depends on the circumstances that apply to those entities. Under the guidance in ASC 860-10-55-24 and 55-25A, judgments about the isolation of transferred financial assets of entities that are subject to other possible bankruptcy, conservatorship, or other receivership procedures should be made in comparison to the powers of bankruptcy courts or trustees, conservators, or receivers in those jurisdictions. The same types of judgments may need to be made about the powers of a transferor and its creditors.

Question 20: Could a transfer from one subsidiary (the transferor) to another subsidiary (the transferee) of a common parent be accounted for as a sale for each subsidiary's separate-company financial statements?

Answer: Yes, if two conditions are met. First, the requirements of ASC 860-10-40-4 and 40-5, including the isolation requirement, must be met. Second, the financial statements of the transferee cannot be consolidated with the separate-company financial statements of the transferor.

Question 21: This question has been deleted because ASC 860-10-40-5 through 6A has amended the definition of proceeds in ASC 860 to include beneficial interests.

Control Criteria—Conditions That Constrain a Transferee

Question 22: Assuming that all of the other requirements of ASC 860-10-40-4 through 40-5 are met, has a transferor surrendered effective control over transferred financial assets if the transferee, which is not an entity whose sole purpose is to engage in securitization or asset-backed financing activities is precluded from exchanging the transferred assets but obtains the unconstrained right to pledge them?

Answer: It depends. If the transferee is able to obtain most of the cash flows associated with the transferred financial assets either by transferring or pledging those assets, the transferee would have effective control over the transferred assets.

Question 22A: Entity A transfers a financial asset to Entity B which has a significantly limited ability to pledge or exchange the transferred assets and is not an entity whose sole purpose is to engage in securitization or asset-backed financing activities. The transferor receives cash for the transferred financial assets and has *no* continuing involvement with those assets. Does this transfer qualify under the requirements in ASC 860-10-40-5?

Answer: Yes. The requirements in ASC 860-10-40-5 would *not* be met if Entity B were *not* permitted to pledge or exchange the transferred financial asset and the transferor received a benefit from that limitation that is more than insignificant. However, if a transferor has any continuing involvement after a transfer to an entity that is not a securitization entity, the transferor should evaluate whether the requirements in ASC 860-10-40-5 have been met, in accordance with the guidance in ASC 860-10-40-15-6 through 15-18.

Question 23: In certain loan participation agreements that involve transfers of participating interests, the transferor is required to approve any subsequent transfers or pledges of the interests in the loans held by the transferee. Would that requirement be a constraint that would prevent the transferee from taking advantage of its right to pledge or to exchange the transferred financial asset and, therefore, preclude accounting for the transfer as a sale?

Answer: It depends, and judgment clearly is necessary. A requirement that constrains the transferee from selling or pledging the transferred assets and that provides more than a trivial benefit to the transferor would preclude sale accounting. In that case, the transferor has not given up effective control and should account for such transfers as secured borrowings. However, ASC 860 also indicates that a requirement to obtain the transferor's permission before selling or pledging the transferred assets—if such permission is not unreasonably withheld—typically does not constrain the transferee from selling or pledging the related assets.

Question 24: If a securitization entity issues beneficial interests in the form of Rule 144A securities and the holder of those beneficial interests may not transfer them unless an exemption from the 1933 U.S. Securities Act registration is available, do the limits on the transferability of the beneficial interests result in a constraint on the transferee's right to pledge or exchange those beneficial interests and, therefore, preclude sale accounting by the transferor?

Answer: It depends. The primary limitation on the sale of Rule 144A securities is that the buyer must be a sophisticated investor. If a large number of such investors exist, there would be no effective constraint on the transferee's right to pledge or exchange the asset.

Questions 24a through 30: These questions have been deleted because the concept of a qualifying special-purpose entity has been removed from ASC 860.

Question 31: Credit card securitizations often include a "removal-of-accounts provision" (ROAP) that permits the seller, under certain conditions and with trustee approval, to withdraw receivables from the pool of securitized receivables. Does a transferor's right to remove receivables from a credit card securitization preclude accounting for a transfer as a sale?

Answer: It depends on the rights that the transferor has under the ROAP. A ROAP that does not allow the transferor to unilaterally reclaim specific financial assets from the transferee does not preclude sale accounting.

Question 32: If a transferor is permitted to dissolve a securitization entity (e.g., through the beneficial interests that it holds) and reassume control of the transferred financial assets, is the transferor precluded from accounting for the transfer as a sale?

Answer: Yes. In this case, the transferor effectively maintains control over the assets through its ability to dissolve the securitization entity and reclaim the assets.

Questions 33 through 41: These questions have been deleted because the concept of a securitization entity has been removed from ASC 860.

Control Criteria—Effective Control

Question 42: Dollar-roll repurchase agreements (also called dollar rolls) are agreements to sell and repurchase similar but not identical securities. Dollar rolls differ from regular repurchase agreements in that the securities sold and repurchased, which are usually of the same issuer, are represented by different certificates, are collateralized by different but similar mortgage pools (e.g., conforming single-family residential mortgages), and generally have different principal amounts. Is a transfer of financial assets that are under a dollar-roll repurchase agreement within the scope of ASC 860?

Answer: Yes, if the dollar-roll repurchase agreement pertains to the transfer of securities that already exist.

Question 43: Does ASC 860-10-40-5 preclude sale accounting for a dollar-roll transaction that is subject to the provisions of ASC 860?

Answer: It depends. In order for sale accounting to be precluded, the transferred financial assets to be repurchased must be the same or substantially the same as the assets transferred. All six of the characteristics discussed in ASC 860-40-24(a); ASC 860-10-55-35 must exist in order to meet the substantially-the-same requirement (see ASC 860-10-40-24 and ASC 860-10-55-35, as revised by ASU 2011-3 for further details).

Question 44: In a transfer of existing securities under a dollar-roll repurchase agreement, if the transferee is committed to return substantially the same securities to the transferor but that transferee's securities were to be announced at the time of transfer, would the transferor be precluded from accounting for the transfer as a secured borrowing?

Answer: No. The transferor is only required to obtain a commitment from the transferee to return substantially the same securities. The transferor is not required to determine that the transferee holds the securities that it is committed to return.

Questions 45 through 47: Superseded by the guidance in ASU 2011-3.

Answer: No. If a mechanism does not exist to ensure that adequate collateral is maintained—even for a transaction that is substantially overcollateralized—sale accounting would not be precluded.

Question 48: The example of effective control in ASC 860-10-40-5 states that the transferor maintains effective control over the financial transferred assets through "an agreement that both entitles and obligates the transferor to repurchase or redeem them before their maturity." What does the term *before maturity* mean in the context of the transferor that maintains effective control under the provisions of ASC 860?

Answer: ASC 860 does not define the term *before maturity*. However, in order for the agreement to be viewed as requiring repurchase or redemption before maturity, the remaining term in the life of the financial asset must be sufficient for the asset could be sold again. That is, the remaining term must not be so short that a net cash payment would be made.

Question 49: How do different types of rights of a transferor to reacquire (call) transferred financial assets affect sale accounting under ASC 860?

Answer: Sale accounting is precluded if a transferor's right to reacquire (call) a transferred financial asset constrains the ability of a transferee to (or, if the transferee is an entity whose sole purpose is to engage in securitization or asset-backed financing activities and that entity is constrained from pledging or exchanging the assets it receives, each third-party holder of its beneficial interests) pledge or exchange the transferred financial assets (or beneficial interests) it received and provides more than a trivial benefit to the transferor.

In addition, ASC 860-10-40-5 precludes sale accounting if a transferor, its consolidated affiliates included in the financial statements being presented, or its agents, maintain effective control over transferred financial assets. For example, sale accounting is precluded if a right to reacquire a transferred financial asset results in either of the following:

1. The transferor, its consolidated affiliates included in the financial statements presented, or its agents, maintain effective control through an agreement that both entitles and obligates the transferor to repurchase or redeem the transferred financial asset before its maturity; or
2. The transferor, its consolidated affiliates included in the financial statements, or its agents, maintains effective control through an agreement that provides the transferor with both the unilateral ability to have the holder return the specific transferred financial assets and a more-than-trivial benefit attributable to that ability, other than through a cleanup call.

A unilateral right to reclaim specific transferred financial assets permits a transferor to maintain effective control and precludes sale accounting if the transferor has the unilateral right to reacquire the transferred financial assets and if that right provides the transferor with more than a trivial benefit. ASC 860-10-40-9 through 40-10, 40-33 through 40-34 states that "a call or other right conveys more than trivial benefit if the price to be paid is fixed, determinable or other otherwise potentially advantageous, unless because that price is so far out of the money or for other reasons it is probable when the option is written that the transferor will not exercise it.

Question 50: In certain transactions, the transferor is entitled to repurchase a transferred, amortizing, individual financial asset that is not readily obtainable elsewhere when its remaining principal balance reaches some specified amount, for example, 30% of the original balance. Does ASC 860 permit such a transfer to be accounted for partially as a sale and partially as a secured borrowing?

Answer: If a call enables a transferor to unilaterally force the holder of a transferred financial asset to return the remaining portion of the entire financial asset to the transferor and gives the transferor more than a trivial benefit, the transferor should not account for a transfer of the total financial asset as a sale. Under the guidance in ASC 860, the provisions related to derecognition should be applied to a transfer of a total financial asset, a group of total financial assets, or a participating interest in a total financial asset. Further, accounting for a transfer of a total financial asset or a participating interest in a total financial asset partially as a sale and partially as a secured borrowing is prohibited. (See Question 49.)

Question 51: Would a transferor's contractual right to repurchase a loan participation that is not a readily obtainable financial asset preclude sale accounting?

Answer: Yes, based on the guidance in ASC 860-10-40-5, each transferee should have the right to pledge or exchange the assets it received and that a transferor cannot (*a*) restrict a transferee from using its right to pledge or exchange its assets and (*b*) receive more than a trivial benefit. A transferor's contractual right to repurchase a loan is a call option written by a transferee to the transferor. According to ASC 860-10-40-18, a freestanding call option may benefit the transferor and may restrict a transferee if the transferred financial assets are not readily in the marketplace. If a transferor's right to repurchase a financial asset is not freestanding but is attached to a loan and may be transferred with it, ASC 860-10-40-5 states that a transferor maintains effective control over the transferred financial asset.

Question 52: Deleted.

Question 53: Under the guidance in ASC 860, does a transfer of a debt security classified as held-to-maturity that occurs for a reason other than those specified in ASC 320-10-25-6, 25-9 taint the entity's held-to-maturity portfolio?

Answer: It depends on how the transfer is handled. If the transfer of the debt security is treated as a sale, the entity's held-to-maturity portfolio would be tainted unless the transfer occurred for one of the reasons specified in ASC 320-10-25-6, 25-9. If the transfer is accounted for as a secured borrowing, the held-to-maturity portfolio would not be tainted.

Question 54: Deleted the concept of a securitization entity is removed from ASC 860.

Question 55: Assuming that all of the other criteria of ASC 860-10-40-4 through 40-5 are met, is sale accounting appropriate if a cleanup call on a pool of assets in a qualifying SPE is held by a party other than the servicer? For example, sometimes the fair value of beneficial interests retained by a transferor of financial assets who is not the servicer or an affiliate is adversely affected by the amount of transferred financial assets declining to a "low level." If such a transferor has a call exercisable when assets decline to a specified low level, could that be a cleanup call?

Answer: No. Because the transferor is not the servicer or an affiliate of the servicer, the transferor's call on the assets in the qualifying SPE is not a cleanup call for accounting purposes. However, because the call option can only be exercised when the assets reach a certain pre-specified level, the transfer would be recorded as a partial sale (assuming the other provisions of ASC 860-10-40-4 through 40-5 are met.

Question 56: In a securitization transaction involving not-readily-obtainable assets, may a transferor that is also the servicer hold a cleanup call if it "contracts out the servicing" to a third party (i.e., enters into a subservicing arrangement with a third party) without precluding sale accounting?

Answer: Yes. This is due to the fact that from the SPE's perspective, the transferor remains the servicer. If the subservicer fails to perform under the contract, the transferor remains liable for servicing the assets. However, if the transferor sells the servicing rights to a third party, the transferor could not hold a cleanup call.

Measurement of Assets and Liabilities upon Completion of a Transfer

Question 57: Could a transferor's exchange of one form of beneficial interests in financial assets that have been transferred into a trust for an equivalent, but different, form of beneficial interests in the same transferred financial assets be accounted for as a sale under the guidance in ASC 860?

Answer: No. This type of arrangement definitely does not qualify for sale accounting, and it may not even meet the definition of a transfer in ASC 860. If the exchange is with a trust that originally issued the beneficial interests, a transfer has not occurred.

Question 58: Deleted because ASC 860 requires that derecognition provisions be applied to a transfer of the whole financial asset, a group of whole financial assets, or a participating interest in a whole financial asset. See the guidance in ASC 860-20-40-1; ASC 860-20-25-1 through 25-3; ASC 860-20-30-1 through 30-2.

Question 59: Deleted because a beneficial interest obtained in a transfer of a whole financial asset or a group of whole financial assets accounted for as a sale are considered to be proceeds of the sale and are recognized initially and measured at fair value under the guidance in ASC 860.

Question 60: Deleted because a beneficial interest obtained in a transfer of a whole financial asset or a group of whole financial assets accounted for as a sale are considered to be proceeds of the sale and are recognized initially and measured at fair value under the guidance in ASC 860.

Question 61: An entity transfers debt securities to a qualifying SPE that has a predetermined life, in exchange for cash and the right to receive proceeds from the eventual sale of the securities. For example, a third party holds a beneficial interest that is initially worth 25% of the fair value of the assets of the qualifying SPE at the date of transfer. The qualifying SPE must sell the transferred securities at a predetermined date and liquidate the qualifying SPE at that time. In addition, the beneficial interests are issued in the form of debt securities, and prior to the transfer those securities are accounted for as available-for-sale in accordance with the guidance in ASC 320. Does the transferor have the option to classify the debt securities as trading at the time of the transfer?

Answer: Generally, no. Debt and equity securities under the guidance in ASC 320 that are held by the transferor after a transfer convey rights to the same cash flows as those securities held before the transfer. ASC 320 provides that transfers into and from the trading category should be rare. If, however, the transferred securities were not accounted for under the guidance in ASC 320 prior to the transfer, then the transferor would have the opportunity to decide the appropriate classification of the transferred assets at the date of the transfer.

Question 62: In certain transfers, the transferor retains an interest that should be subsequently accounted for under the guidance in ASC 325-40-05-1 through 05-2, 15-2 through 15-9, 25-1 through 25-3, 30-1 through 30-3, 35-1 through 35-13, 35-15 through 35-16, 45-1, 55-1 through 55-25, 60-7; ASC 310-20-60-1 through 60-2; ASC 310-30-15-5; ASC 320-10-35-38, 55-2 (Recognition of Interest Income and Impairment on Purchased Beneficial Interests and Transferor's Beneficial Interests in Securitized Financial Assets Obtained in a Transfer Accounted for as a Sale). If the transferred asset was accounted for as available-for-sale under the guidance in ASC 320 prior to the transfer, how should the transferor account for amounts in other comprehensive income at the date of transfer?

Answer: The application of that guidance should not result in recognition of earnings of an unrealized gain or loss that had been recognized in accumulated other comprehensive income before it is realized.

Question 63: Deleted because the concept of a securitization entity is deleted. Guidance is provided in Question 62 above.

Question 64: Assume an entity transfers a bond to a qualifying SPE for cash and beneficial interests. When the transferor purchased the bond, it paid a premium (or discount) for it and that premium (or discount) was not fully amortized (or accreted) at the date of the transfer. Would that existing premium or discount continue to be amortized (or accreted)?

Answer: Yes, but only to the extent a sale has not occurred because the transferor retained beneficial interests in the bond.

Question 65: Deleted because under the guidance in ASC 860, derecognition provisions must be applied to a transfer of the whole financial asset, a group of whole financial assets, or a participating interest in a whole financial asset. See the guidance in ASC 860-20-40-1; ASC 860-20-25-1 through 25-3; ASC 860-20-30-1, 30-2.

Question 66: Deleted because ASC 820, *Fair Value Measurement* defines fair value and establishes a framework for measuring fair value.

Question 67: Can the method used by the transferor for providing "recourse" affect the accounting for the transfer?

Answer: Yes. However, before evaluating the accounting treatment for the recourse provision, the transferor must first determine whether a sale has occurred. In some jurisdictions, the recourse provision may suggest that the transferred assets have not been appropriately isolated (i.e., the transferor and its creditors still have access to the assets). If a sale has occurred, the accounting depends on the manner in which the recourse provision is effected. The transferor may agree to reimburse the transferee for amounts not paid by debtors. The transferor would separately recognize a liability for this obligation. Alternatively, the transferor may retain a beneficial interest in the assets that is only receivable after other investors are paid. In such a manner, the transferor in essence retains credit risk. However, in this situation, no recourse liability is needed.

Question 68: What should the transferor consider when determining whether retained credit risk is a separate liability or a part of a retained beneficial interest in the asset?

Answer: If the transferor's liability is limited to a claim on its retained interest in the transferred assets, no separate liability is recognized. The transferor would recognize an asset valuation account for this recourse obligation on the date of transfer. However, if the transferor's obligation under the recourse provision could exceed its retained interest in the transferred assets, a separate liability is recognized.

Question 69: Deleted because the fair value practicability exception has been removed from ASC 860.

Question 70: Deleted because ASC 820 defines fair value and establishes a framework for measuring fair value.

Question 71: Deleted because the fair value practicability exception has been removed from ASC 860.

Question 72: Must a transferor recognize in earnings the gain or loss that results from a transfer of financial assets that is accounted for as a sale, or may the transferor elect to defer recognizing the resulting gain or loss in certain circumstances?

Answer: Sale accounting and the corresponding recognition of gain or loss is not optional if a transfer of financial assets meets the requirements in ASC 860 for sale accounting.

Question 73: Does ASC 860 require disclosures about the assumptions used to estimate fair values of the transferor's retained interests in securitized financial assets or of other assets obtained and liabilities incurred as proceeds in a transfer?

Answer: Yes, see the guidance in ASC 860-20-50-1 through 50-4.

Question 74: Deleted because a beneficial interest obtained in a transfer of a whole financial asset or a group of whole financial assets accounted for as a sale are considered to be proceeds of the sale and are recognized initially and measured at fair value under the guidance in ASC 860.

Question 75: How should a transferor initially and subsequently measure credit enhancements provided in a transfer if the balance that is not needed to make up for credit losses is ultimately to be paid by the transferor?

Answer: Credit enhancements are measured at the date of transfer by allocating previous carrying amounts between assets sold and retained interests, based on relative fair values. Credit enhancements provided by other parties are initially measured at the fair value of the enhancement that is expected to benefit the transferor. The guidance in ASC 860 does not address the subsequent measurement of credit enhancements—other existing authoritative literature should be consulted (e.g., ASC 310-10, Receivables—Overall).

Questions 76 and 77: Deleted because ASC 820 defines fair value and establishes a framework for measuring fair value.

Servicing Assets and Servicing Liabilities

Question 78: ASC 860-50-30-2 states that "typically, the benefits of servicing are expected to be more than *adequate compensation* to the servicer for performing the servicing . . ." (Emphasis added). What is meant by the term *adequate compensation*?

Answer: *Adequate compensation* means the amount of compensation necessary to attract an alternate servicing entity, if one becomes necessary. This amount is determined by the marketplace and includes a provision for normal profit.

Questions 79 through 86: Deleted because the fair value practicability exception has been removed from ASC 860.

Question 87: For sales of mortgage loans, is adequate compensation the same as normal servicing fees previously used in applying the guidance in ASC 948-10 and 948-360?

Answer: No. ASC 860 defines *adequate compensation* as the amount of compensation necessary to attract an alternate servicing entity, should one become necessary. That amount is determined by the marketplace, and includes a provision for normal profit. ASC 948 defines *normal servicing* fees as the amount that was typically charged for servicing a particular type of loan. Often, a normal servicing rate as formerly determined under the guidance in ASC 948 would exceed the definition of *adequate compensation* in ASC 860.

Question 88: Do the types of assets being serviced affect the amount required to adequately compensate the servicer?

Answer: Yes, since different asset classes require different levels of effort to service. The nature of the assets being serviced should be considered a factor in determining the fair value of a servicing asset or servicing liability.

Question 89: Does a contractual provision that specifies the amount of servicing fees that would be paid to a replacement servicer affect the determination of adequate compensation?

Answer: No. A contractually specified amount that would be paid to a replacement servicer could be more or less than adequate compensation.

Question 90: If market rates for servicing a specific type of financial asset change subsequent to the initial recognition of a servicing asset or servicing liability, does ASC 860 include any requirement to adjust the recorded asset or liability?

Answer: Yes. In terms of a servicing asset, a change in market rates may indicate that the asset is impaired. In terms of a servicing liability, a change in market values may increase the liability. Such an increase in the liability would be recorded as a loss in the income statement.

Question 91: Do additional transfers under revolving-period securitizations (e.g., home equity loans or credit card receivables) result in the recognition of additional servicing assets or servicing liabilities?

Answer: Yes. Servicing assets and liabilities arise from the sale of new receivables.

Question 92: The question and answer have been nullified by ASC 860, *Transfers and Servicing*, which provides specific guidance in its amendment to ASC 860-50-45-1 through 45-2, 25-1, 25-4, 30-1, 30-8, -35-1 through 35-5, 35-15.

Question 93: How should an entity account for rights to future income from serviced assets that exceed contractually specified servicing fees?

Answer: If the benefits to servicing are expected to exceed adequate compensation, the servicer should record a servicing asset, an interest-only strip, or both. For example, the servicer may be entitled to receive interest income from serviced assets that exceeds contractually specified servicing fees. This would represent a financial asset, not a servicing asset, and would effectively be an interest-only strip.

Question 94: Should a loss be recognized if a servicing fee that is equal to or greater than adequate compensation is to be received but the servicer's anticipated cost of servicing would exceed the fee?

Answer: No. Recognition of a servicing asset or a servicing liability depends on the marketplace, not on a servicer's cost of servicing.

Servicing—Other

Question 95: Should an entity recognize a servicing liability if it transfers all or some of a financial asset that meets the definition of a participating interest that is accounted for as a sale and retains an obligation to service the asset but is not entitled to receive a contractually specified servicing fee? Is the answer to this question affected by circumstances in which it is not customary for the transferor/servicer to receive a contractually specified servicing fee?

Answer: Yes. A servicer/transferor would be required to recognize a servicing at fair value if the benefits of servicing are less than adequate compensation.

Question 96: A selling entity (*a*) transfers a portion of a loan under a participation agreement that meets the definition of a participating interest and qualifies for sale accounting under FAS-140, (*b*) obtains the right to receive benefits of servicing that more than adequately compensate it for servicing the loan, and (*c*) and continues to service the loan, regardless of the transfer because it (the selling entity) retains part of the participated loan. In these circumstances, is the selling entity required to record a servicing asset?

Answer: Yes, the selling entity is required to record a servicing asset for the portion of the loans it sold. If the benefits of servicing are significantly greater than an amount that would be fair compensation for a substitute service provider, if one were to be required, the transferred portion does not meet the definition of a participating interest. Consequently, the transfer would not qualify for sale accounting.

Question 97: A transferor that sells mortgage loans that it originated in a transfer that is accounted for as a sale takes on the obligation to service them. Immediately thereafter the transferor enters into an arrangement to subcontract that obligation to another servicer. How should the transferor account for the obligation to service the loans in this situation?

Answer: The transferor should account separately for the two transactions. The sale of the mortgage loans and the obligation to service those loans should be accounted for in accordance with the guidance in ASC 860. The obligation to service the loans should be initially recognized and measured at fair value in accordance with the guidance in ASC 860-20-25-1 through 25-2, 40-1B. (A transferor's accounting for the subcontract with another servicer is not under the scope of the guidance in ASC 860, but should be accounted for under existing guidance).

Question 98: When servicing assets are assumed without cash payment, what is the appropriate offsetting entry to be made by the transferee?

Answer: If an exchange has occurred, the transaction should be recorded based on the facts and circumstances. On the other hand, if the investor is in substance making a capital contribution to the investee, the investee should recognize an increase in equity from a contribution by owner.

Question 99: ASC 860 requires that an entity separately evaluate and measure impairment of designated strata of servicing assets. If more than one characteristic exists for stratifying servicing assets, must more than one predominant risk characteristic be used?

Answer: No. Under the guidance in ASC 860-50-35-9, servicers are required to stratify servicing assets based on one or more predominant risk characteristics of the underlying financial assets.

Question 100: Under the guidance in ASC 860-50-35-9, a servicer is required to stratify servicing assets based on one or more of the predominant risk characteristics of financial assets. Should the strata selected by the servicer be used consistently from period to period?

Answer: Yes, generally the strata selected should be used consistently from period to period. If a significant change is made, it should be accounted for prospectively as a change in accounting estimate in accordance with the guidance in ASC 255 (Accounting Changes and Error Corrections).

Question 101: Under the guidance in ASC 860, the impairment of servicing assets must be recognized by a valuation allowance for an individual stratum. The valuation allowance should reflect changes in the measurement of impairment subsequent to initial measurement of impairment. Fair value in excess of the carrying amount of servicing assets for that stratum should not be recorded. How should an entity recognize subsequent increases in a previously recognized servicing liability?

Answer: The revised estimate of the liability should be recorded and a loss should be recognized in earnings. Similar to accounting for changes in the valuation allowance of an impaired asset, increases in the servicing obligation may be recovered, but the obligation should not be reduced below the amortized measurement of the initially recognized servicing liability.

Question 102: Deleted because the fair value practicability exception has been removed from ASC 860.

Question 103: Deleted because ASC 820 defines fair value and establishes a framework for measuring fair value.

Financial Assets Subject to Repayment

Question 104: If an entity recognizes both a servicing asset and the right to receive future interest income from serviced assets in excess of contractually specified servicing fees (an interest-only strip) in a transfer of a whole financial asset to an unconsolidated entity that meets the requirements for sale accounting, should the value of the right to receive future cash flows from ancillary sources (e.g., late fees) be included in measuring the servicing asset or in measuring the interest-only strip?

Answer: Yes, generally in the servicing asset. The value of the right to receive future cash flows from ancillary sources is included in the measurement of the servicing asset if the right to such future cash flow depends, as is customary, on servicing being performed satisfactorily. The value of the right to future cash flows from ancillary sources is generally not included in measuring the interest-only strip.

Question 105: Under the guidance in ASC 860-20-35-2, financial assets, except for instruments accounted for under the scope of ASC 815, that contractually can be prepaid or otherwise settled in such a way that the holder will not recover substantially all of its recorded investment must subsequently be measured like available-for-sale or trading debt securities in accordance with the guidance in ASC 320. Does this mean that those financial assets are included under the scope of ASC 320?

Answer: This depends on the form of the assets, but in either case, the measurement principles of ASC 320, including provisions for recognizing and measuring impairment, should be applied.

Question 106: Can a financial asset that can be contractually prepaid or otherwise settled in such a way that the holder would not recover substantially all of its recorded investment be classified as held-to-maturity if the investor concludes that prepayment or other forms of settlement are remote?

Answer: No. This is not a relevant factor in determining whether the provisions of ASC 860-20-35-2 apply to those financial assets.

Question 107: A transferor transfers mortgage loans in their entirety to a third party in a transfer that is accounted for as a sale but retains servicing. Afterward, the transferor enters into a subservicing arrangement with a third party. If the transferor's benefit of servicing exceeds its obligation under the subservicing agreement, should the difference be accounted for as an interest-only strip?

Answer: No. The transferor should account for the two transactions separately. The transfer of mortgage loans and the obligation to service the loans should be accounted for by the transferor in accordance with the guidance in ASC 860 and the contract with the subscriber should be separately accounted for under other guidance because it is not included in the scope of ASC 860.

Question 108: Can a debt security that is purchased late enough in its life that, even if prepaid, the holder would recover substantially all of its recorded investment, be initially classified as held-to-maturity?

Answer: Yes. A debt security can be classified as held-to-maturity if the conditions of ASC 320-10-25-1, 25-5; ASC 320-10-35-1 are met.

Question 109: May a loan (that is not a debt security), which when initially obtained could be contractually prepaid or otherwise settled in such a way that the holder would not recover substantially all of its recorded investment, be classified as held for investment later in its life?

Answer: Yes, if the following conditions are met: (1) it would no longer be possible for the holder not to recover substantially all of its recorded investment upon contractual prepayment or settlement and (2) the conditions for amortized cost accounting are met.

Question 110: Under the guidance in ASC 860-20-35-2 certain financial assets that are not in the form of debt securities are required to be measured at fair value like investments classified as available-for-sale or classified as trading under the guidance in ASC 320. How should instruments subject to provisions ASC 860-20-35-2 be evaluated for impairment?

Answer: All of the measurement principles of ASC 320 apply, including the recognition and measurement of impairment.

Question 111: Is a financial asset that is not a debt security under the guidance in ASC 320 subject to the requirements of ASC 860-20-35-2 because it is denominated in a foreign currency?

Answer: No. An entity is not required to measure such an investment like a debt security unless it has provisions that allow it to be contractually prepaid or otherwise settled in a way that the holder would not recover substantially all of its recorded investment, as denominated in the foreign currency.

Question 112: Is a note for which the repayment amount is indexed to the creditworthiness of a party other than the issuer subject to the provisions of ASC 860-20-35-2?

Answer: Yes, because the event that might cause the holder to receive less than substantially all of its recorded investment is based on a contractual provision, not on a default by the borrower.

Question 113: Can a residual tranche debt security in a securitization of financial assets using a securitization entity be classified as held-to-maturity?

Answer: The answer depends on the specific facts and circumstances. If the contractual provisions of the residual tranche debt security provide that the residual tranche can contractually be prepaid or otherwise settled so that the holder would not recover substantially all of its recorded investment, the residual tranche debt security should not be accounted for as held-to-maturity. On the other hand, if the only way the holder of the residual tranche would not substantially recover all of its recorded investment is via default of the borrower, then a held-to-maturity classification is acceptable if the conditions specified for that classification in ASC 320-10-25-1(c) and ASC 320-10-25-5(a) are met.

Secured Borrowings and Collateral

Question 114: Are the collateral recognition requirements of ASC 860-30-25-5 limited to transfers by or to broker-dealer entities, or do they apply to other types of borrowings?

Answer: The collateral recognition provisions of ASC 860-30-25-5 apply to the accounting for all transfers of financial assets pledged as collateral that are accounted for as secured borrowings.

Question 115: What is the proper classification by the transferor of securities loaned or transferred under a repurchase agreement that is accounted for as a secured borrowing if the transferee is permitted to sell or repledge those securities, and rights of substitution or termination are not granted to the transferor?

Answer: Pledged assets should be reported in the statement of financial position separately from other assets not so encumbered, but otherwise ASC 860 does not specify the classification or terminology to be used. ASC 860-50-55-22 illustrates possible classifications and terminology.

Question 116: What is the appropriate classification of liabilities incurred in connection with securities borrowing and resale agreement transactions?

Answer: ASC 860 does not specify classification or terminology to be used to describe liabilities by either the secured party or debtor in securities borrowing or resale transactions. Such liabilities should be separately classified.

Question 117: How should a transferor measure transferred collateral that must be reclassified?

Answer: The guidance in ASC 860-30-25-5, requires that transferred collateral that can be sold or repledged by a secured party be reclassified and reported separately by the transferor. However, it does not change the transferor's measurement of that collateral.

Question 118: Does ASC 860 provide guidance for the subsequent measurement of a secured party's obligation to return transferred collateral that the secured party recognized in accordance with the guidance in ASC 860-30-25-5?

Answer: No. ASC 860 generally does not address subsequent measurement of transferred financial assets or the obligation to return transferred collateral. The liability to return the collateral should be measured in accordance with other relevant authoritative literature.

Extinguishment of Liabilities

Question 119: Are liabilities extinguished by legal defeasances?

Answer: Yes, if the condition of ASC 405-20-40-1(b), which requires that the debtor has been legally released, is satisfied.

Question 120: How should a debtor account for the exchange of an outstanding debt instrument with a lender for a new debt instrument with the same lender but with substantially different terms? How should the debtor account for a substantial modification of a debt instrument?

Answer: ASC 405-20-40-1, permits derecognition of a liability only if it is extinguished by the debtor paying the creditor or the debtor being legally released as the primary obligor, either judicially or by the creditor.

Question 121: If an entity is released from being the primary obligor and it becomes a secondary obligor, should the entity recognize the resulting guarantee from being the secondary obligor in the same manner as a third-party guarantor?

Answer: Yes. The entity should recognize the guarantee in the same way it would have as a guarantor that had never been primarily liable.

Question 122: Does the guidance in ASC 860 address impairment of financial assets?

Answer: The guidance in ASC 860 does not address the subsequent measurement of assets and liabilities, except for servicing assets and servicing liabilities and interest strips, other beneficial interests, loans, other receivables, or other financial assets that contractually may be prepaid or settled otherwise so that the holder would not recover all of its recognized investment. Generally, impairment should be measured by reference to other applicable authoritative guidance.

Question 123: Many securitization structures provide for a disproportionate distribution of cash flows to various classes of investors during the amortization period (referred to as a turbo provision). What effect do such provisions have on the accounting for transfers of financial assets under the guidance in ASC 860?

Answer: Distribution provisions that diverge from the stated ownership percentages of different parties do not affect whether (1) sale accounting is appropriate or (2) the transferred assets should be derecognized. Differential distribution provisions should be taken into consideration in determining the relative fair values of the portion of transferred assets sold and portions retained by the transferee.

ASC 860-10-05-11; ASC 860-20-35-10, 55-16 Securitization of Credit Card and Other Receivable Portfolios

BACKGROUND

Banks or other financial institutions form pools of receivables consisting of balances owed by credit card customers and transfer an interest in the receivables to a trust. A bank then sells undivided participation interests in the trust to investors. The trust is commonly referred to as a credit card securitization. It has a limited life that can be divided into two phases:

1. A reinvestment phase, during which all receivables generated by customers in the pool are kept by the trust while investors receive interest payments only
2. A liquidation phase, during which investors receive principal payments as well as interest

During the reinvestment phase, usually 18 to 36 months, the trust purchases additional credit card receivables as balances in the selected accounts increase. Although the percentage of the bank's and investors' participation in the trust's assets may fluctuate up or down during this phase, as a result of charge and payment activities in the selected accounts, the investors' dollar investment in the trust remains constant, because proceeds from repayments (principal payments) allocated to the investors are reinvested in additional credit card receivables.

For example, the following illustrates such activity for a month.

	Credit Card Balances	*Investors' Interest*	*Percentage*
Total receivables in trust, 1/1	$1,000,000	$750,000	75.0
Repayments	(100,000)	(75,000)	75.0
Charges	80,000	75,000	93.8
Total receivables in trust, 1/31	$ 980,000	$750,000	76.5

In this example, a larger percentage of charges (93.8% instead of 75%) was allocated to the investors in order to maintain their $750,000 investment in the trust.

During the liquidation period, principal payments on receivables in the trust are allocated to investors, based on the terms of the agreement. The following methods are used:

- The *participation method,* which consists of:
  - *Fixed participation* Based on investors' interests in the receivables at the end of the reinvestment period.
  - *Preset participation* Based on a preset percentage that is higher than investors' participation interests at the end of the reinvestment period. (Results in a faster payout than the fixed participation method.)
  - *Floating participation* Based on investors' actual participation interests in the trust each month. (Interests will decline each month because of repayments.)
- The *controlled amortization method,* which is based on a predetermined monthly payment schedule; investors' interests are liquidated over a specified period. One of the three participation methods is used to allocate principal payments to investors. If principal payments are greater than the predetermined monthly payment, they are allocated to the bank and used to increase the investors' ownership interests. If allocated principal payments are less than the predetermined monthly payment, payments to investors are reduced by the deficiency. The deficiency is recovered in subsequent months if the amount allocated to investors exceeds the predetermined payments.

Credit losses on receivables in the trust generally are allocated to investors based on their actual floating participation interest (participation interests may fluctuate monthly because of an imbalance between charges and payments on accounts), regardless of the liquidation method. However, some form of credit enhancement, such as a third-party letter of credit that exceeds expected credit losses, may be used to mitigate losses allocated to investors.

ACCOUNTING ISSUES

1. Issues 1 and 2 have been nullified.
2. How should a gain or loss on transfer that is recognized as a sale be calculated?

ACCOUNTING GUIDANCE

1. This guidance has been nullified by the guidance in ASC 860, which has been amended by the guidance in ASC 860-10-35-4, 35-6, 05-8; ASC 860-20-25-5; ASC 460-10-60-35; ASC 860-20-55-46 through 55-48; ASC 860-50-05-2 through 05-4, 30-1 through 30-2, 35-1A, 35-3, 35-9 through 35-11, 25-2 through 25-3, 25-6, 50-5.
2. The guidance on the effect of the liquidation method was nullified by the guidance in ASC 860.
3. A gain, if any, on the sale of receivables should not exceed amounts related to existing receivables at the date of the sale. Amounts related to future receivables expected to be sold during the reinvestment period should *not* be included in the gain. (This guidance has been affirmed in ASC 860-50-25-9.) Based on information about certain transactions, some Task Force members noted that a gain on such transactions generally would not be significant, because the receivables sold have a relatively short life, the high cost of servicing credit card loans, and the yields required by the current interest rate environment. In addition, they noted that a transaction's terms should be reviewed to determine whether a loss should be recognized for costs expected to be incurred for all future servicing obligations, including costs for receivables not yet sold. Under the guidance in ASC 860, a servicer is required to recognize a servicing liability if the servicer expects that the costs of performing the service will exceed the benefits and the work is expected to be performed at a loss. Some members also observed that transaction costs related to sales of receivables may be recognized over the initial and reinvestment periods in a rational and systematic

manner, unless a transaction results in a loss. (The consensus was affirmed in ASC 860 and was not reconsidered in ASC 860-10-35-4, 35-6, 05-8; ASC 860-20-25-5; ASC 460-10-60-35; ASC 860-20-55-46 through 55-48; ASC 860-50-05-2 through 05-4, 30-1 through 30-2, 35-1A, 35-3, 35-9 through 35-11, 25-2 through 25-3, 25-6; 50-5, which amended the guidance in ASC 860.)

In addition, in accordance with the guidance in ASC 860, transaction costs for a past sale are not an asset and consequently should be included in a gain or loss. However, some of the transaction costs incurred at the beginning of a credit card securitization can qualify for asset recognition because they are related to future sales that will occur during the revolving period.

SUBSEQUENT DEVELOPMENT

The SEC Observer stated in July 1995 that the staff believes that above guidance also applies to securitizations of other types of receivables with similar arrangements.

PRACTICE POINTER: ASC 810-10 (Consolidation of Variable Interest Entities) requires the consolidation of variable interest entities by an entity that absorbs a majority of a variable interest entity's expected losses or has the right to receive a greater part of a variable interest entity's expected residual returns or both.

PRACTICE NOTE: Although the guidance in ASC 860-50-35-3, 35-6 through 35-7; 50-5, which amends the accounting guidance in ASC 860 for separately recognized servicing assets and servicing liabilities, it does not affect the guidance in this Issue. The FASB's decision in ASC 860-50-35-3, 35-6 through 35-7, 50-50-5 to replace the term *retained interests* with the term *interests that continue to be held by a transferor* is reflected in this Issue.

ASC 860-10-15-5, 40-40; ASC 815-10-40-2 through 40-3 Accounting for Transfers of Assets That Are Derivative Instruments but That Are Not Financial Assets

BACKGROUND

This Issue was raised because it was unclear how to account for transfers of *nonfinancial* assets that are accounted for as derivatives under the guidance in ASC 815. Transfers of such derivatives are excluded from the scope of ASC 860, which applies only to transfers of *financial* assets and financial liabilities, as defined in ASC *Glossary*.

ACCOUNTING ISSUE

How should transfers of nonfinancial assets that are accounted for as derivatives under the guidance in ASC 815 be accounted for?

ACCOUNTING GUIDANCE

1. Transfers of nonfinancial assets (e.g., a forward contract to purchase gold requiring physical settlement) that are considered to be derivatives under the definition in ASC 815 should be accounted for by analogy to ASC 860. However, this guidance does not apply to contracts that may meet the definition of a derivative in ASC 815, for example, contracts issued by an entity in connection with stock-based compensation arrangements addressed in ASC 718 that are excluded from the scope of ASC 815-10-15-74.
2. If a derivative instrument could potentially be both a nonfinancial asset and a nonfinancial liability—for example, a commodity forward contract that is a nonfinancial derivative instrument—the instrument must meet the criteria in ASC 860 to qualify for derecognition.

A special purpose entity that receives nonfinancial assets in a transfer should not be accounted for as a securitization entity under the guidance in ASC 860.

ASC 860-10-05-21A, 21-2B, 40-42 through 40-46, 55-17A through 55-17C, 55-54 Accounting for Transfers of Financial Assets and Repurchase Financing Transactions

BACKGROUND

The FASB staff addresses the accounting for a transaction that has the following fact pattern: Party A (transferor) transfers a financial asset to Party B (transferee) who pays cash for the asset to Party A. Subsequently or at the same time, Party B enters into a repurchase agreement, as defined in ASC 860-10-05-20 through 05-21 with Party A. Under that agreement, Party A lends cash to Party B, which transfers the financial asset or substantially the same asset, as defined in ASC 86-10-40-24, 55-35 to Party A as collateral for the loan. Under the terms of the arrangement, Party B must repurchase the financial asset, or substantially the same financial asset, from Party A at a fixed or determinable price within a prescribed time period. Party A returns the financial asset, or substantially the same financial asset, to Party B when Party B has made the required payment to Party A under the agreement. The repurchase agreement may occur at the same time as the original transfer of the financial asset by Party A to Party B or at a later date.

Under the guidance in ASC 860, any involvement a transferor has with a transferred asset (even one that occurs some time after the initial transfer) must be considered in an analysis of whether the transferor has relinquished control over the transferred financial asset. ASC 860 does not, however, provide guidance for the repurchase transaction discussed here. Further, there is a presumption in ASC 860 that the counterparties to a transfer of a financial asset will account for the transaction symmetrically.

The question addressed here is whether there are circumstances in which the transfer of a previously transferred financial asset and a repurchase financing agreement related to the same asset between the same counterparties may be accounted for as two separate transactions. Although this question was first asked by entities in the mortgage real estate investment trust industry, the following guidance also will affect entities in other industries.

ACCOUNTING GUIDANCE

The presumption in the following guidance is that an initial transfer and a repurchase agreement between the same counterparties should be linked and accounted for as one transaction under the guidance in ASC 860, unless certain criteria are met. In that case, the two agreements should be evaluated separately under the guidance in ASC 860.

The following three transactions occur in a transfer of a financial asset and a repurchase agreement between the same counterparties:

1. The initial transfer when a transferor transfers a financial asset to a transferee.
2. The execution of a repurchase agreement under which an initial transferee (borrower) transfers a previously transferred financial asset back to the initial transferor (lender) as collateral for a loan.
3. The settlement of the repurchase agreement under which a borrower repays a lender who then returns the collateral to the borrower.

Derecognition and recognition. The counterparties to a transfer of a financial asset and a related repurchase agreement are permitted to account for those transactions separately if: (1) there is a compelling and separate business or economic purpose for entering into separate transactions; and (2) the repurchase agreement is *not* a means for the initial transferor to regain control over the transferred asset. A transaction that lacks a specific business or economic purpose and is entered into only to achieve a specific accounting result by circumventing an accounting standard does *not* qualify for separate accounting.

An initial transfer and a related repurchase agreement entered into between the same counterparties simultaneously or at a later date should be considered to be *linked* and accounted for as one transaction, unless *all* of the following criteria are met:

- The initial transfer and the repurchase agreement do *not* contractually depend on each other and the counterparties have entered into *no* implied commitments, such as the pricing or performance of the initial transfer or the repurchase agreement, which depend on or affect the terms of the transactions and the execution of the other agreement.
- The initial transferor has full recourse to the transferee on default. That is, the initial transferor must be exposed to the initial transferee's, or its affiliates' credit risk, not only to the market risk of the transferred financial asset. In addition, the transferee's repurchase agreement for the previously transferred financial asset, or substantially the same asset, must be for a fixed price, not fair value.
- There is a quoted price in an active market for the previously transferred financial asset and the repurchase agreement (i.e., Level 1 inputs as defined in ASC 820. In addition, the financial asset's initial transfer and the repurchase agreement are executed at market rates. This provision should *not* be circumvented by embedding off-market terms in a separate transaction at the time of the initial transfer or the repurchase financing.
- The repurchase agreement must be settled *before* the financial asset's maturity.

If *all* of the above criteria are met, the initial transfer and the repurchase agreement should be accounted for separately. In that case, (1) the initial transfer should be analyzed to determine whether the transaction meets the requirements for sale accounting in ASC 860 without considering the repurchase agreement, and (2) the initial transferor and the initial transferee should analyze the repurchase financing as a repurchase agreement in accordance with the guidance in ASC 860-10-05-19 through 21, 35-3, 40-4 through 40-5, 40-24, 55-1 through 55-3, 55-35, 55-51 through 53, 55-55 through 55-58, 55-68 through 68A; ASC 860-20-40-1, 40-1A, 40-2, 25-1 through 25-3, 30-1 through 30-2, 55-25; ASC 860–30-25-7. The guidance in ASC 860 requires that both parties to a repurchase agreement use the same criteria to determine how to account for the repurchase agreement.

The initial transfer and repurchase agreement in a transaction that does *not* meet all of the criteria for separate accounting should be accounted for as a *linked* transaction and evaluated to determine whether the requirements for sale accounting in ASC 860 have been met. If the requirements for sale accounting have *not* been met, the linked transaction should be accounted for based on the economics of the combined transactions, generally, as a forward contract. In addition, it is necessary to determine whether a linked transaction should be accounted for as a derivative in accordance with the guidance in ASC 815 and to consider whether other accounting literature applies to the linked transaction, such as how other aspects of a securitization transaction are affected if an initial transferor retains a financial asset that is subject to a repurchase agreement.

ASC 860-10-S40-1, S99-1, 50-40-7 through 40-9; ASC 460-10-60-37 Balance Sheet Treatment of a Sale of Mortgage Servicing Rights with a Subservicing Agreement

BACKGROUND

Mortgage servicers perform administrative services for mortgage investors for which they receive a fee. Among the services they perform are collection of mortgage payments, remittance of escrow taxes and insurance payments to the proper entities, and remittance of the net collections to the investor. The right to receive those fees is recognized in the mortgage servicer's financial statements as an asset referred to as "mortgage servicing rights." A mortgage servicer may sell the right to receive those fees, but may retain the obligation to service the mortgage through a subservicing agreement.

ACCOUNTING ISSUE

Should a transfer of mortgage servicing rights with a subservicing agreement be accounted for (*a*) always as a sale with a gain deferred, (*b*) always as a financing, or (*c*) based on the particular facts and circumstances of the transaction?

ACCOUNTING GUIDANCE

1. A sale of mortgage servicing rights with a subservicing agreement should be accounted for as a sale with gain deferred, if substantially all of the risks and rewards inherent in owning the rights have been effectively transferred to the buyer.
2. The transaction should be treated as a financing if substantially all risks and rewards have *not* been transferred. Risks and rewards associated with a seller performing purely administrative functions under a subservicing agreement would not necessarily preclude sales treatment.
3. Certain factors, if present, provide *conclusive evidence* that substantially all risks and rewards have *not* been transferred and thus preclude sales treatment. Certain other factors, if present, are *presumed to indicate* that substantially all risks and rewards have *not* been transferred. The presumption can be overcome only if there is sufficient evidence to the contrary. Those factors are in the following table:

Conclusive Evidence—No Sales Recognition	*Must Be Overcome for Sales Recognition*
• The seller/subservicer directly or indirectly guarantees a yield to the buyer.	• The seller/subservicer directly or indirectly provides financing or guarantees the buyer's financing. Nonrecourse financing would indicate that risks have not been transferred.
• The seller/subservicer is obligated to make payments of all or a portion of the subservicing fees to the buyer on a nonrecourse basis prior to receipt from the mortgagor.	• The terms of the subservicing agreement unduly limit the purchaser's ability to exercise the rights associated with ownership. An example is a subservicing agreement that is not cancelable by either party (although a reasonable noncancellation period is allowed).
• The seller/subservicer indemnifies the buyer for damages due to causes other than failure to perform its contractual duties.	• The buyer is a special-purpose entity without sufficient capital at risk.

Conclusive Evidence—No Sales Recognition	*Must Be Overcome for Sales Recognition*
• The seller/subservicer agrees to absorb losses on mortgage loan foreclosures not covered by government agencies or other guarantors, including absorption of foreclosure costs of managing foreclosed property.	
• Title to the servicing rights is retained by the seller/subservicer.	

There may be other factors that also indicate that the seller has not transferred substantially all risks and rewards associated with ownership to the buyer.

PRACTICE POINTER: Under the provisions of ASC 460, a guarantor is required to recognize a liability for the obligation assumed at the inception of a guarantee.

PRACTICE POINTER: Although the guidance in ASC 860-50-35-3, 35-6 through 35-7, 50-5 does not affect the guidance in this Issue, changes in the fair value of separately recognized servicing assets or servicing liabilities that are measured at fair value subsequent to adoption of that guidance should be included in earnings in the period in which the fair value changes occur. An additional change in the fair value of servicing assets or servicing liabilities, if any, from the last measurement date to a date of sale should be included in earnings at the date of sale.

SEC OBSERVER COMMENT

The SEC Observer noted that the SEC staff believes that if, in substance, a transaction transfers only a portion of the servicing revenue, substantially all the risks and rewards of ownership have not been transferred. Such a transaction should be accounted for under the guidance in ASC 470-10-25-1 through 25-2, 35-3.

DISCUSSION

The primary concerns were related to the transferor's continuing involvement with the loans and whether the risks and rewards have been transferred.

Those who believed that the determination of whether to account for the transaction as a sale or financing should be based on specific circumstances analogized to sale-leasebacks and to the specific criteria used to determine whether a transaction discussed in ASC 470-10-25-1 through 25-2, 35-3 is a sale or a financing. They also looked to SEC SAB-30 (Accounting for Divestiture of a Subsidiary or Other Business Operation) and SAB-82 (Certain Transfers of Nonperforming Assets) for guidance on factors that would help determine whether the transaction is a sale or a financing.

Each of the factors that provide conclusive evidence that the transaction is *not* a sale is related to aspects of the transferor's retention of risks and rewards of ownership that cannot be overcome. Although the list of presumptive evidence includes factors that also indicate retention of the risks and rewards of ownership, those factors, such as the buyer's ability to cancel the subservicing agreement, may be overcome.

ASC 860-10-55-35, 40-24 Definition of the Term *Substantially the Same for Holders of Debt Instruments*, as Used in Certain Audit Guides and a Statement of Position

BACKGROUND

The following discussion addresses whether two debt instruments are substantially the same. This guidance is designed to help classify various types of repurchase agreements as a sale or as a financing. For example, an entity may sell a debt instrument with an agreement to repurchase another debt instrument. If the debt instrument to be repurchased is substantially the same as the debt instrument that was sold, the transaction would be treated as a financing. Otherwise, the transaction would be treated as a sale.

ACCOUNTING GUIDANCE

Scope

The following guidance pertains to the sale and purchase, or the exchange, of debt instruments between two entities that both hold the debt instrument as an asset. The term *debt instrument* is defined broadly, including those instruments traditionally viewed as securities and those not classified as such. The debt instruments encompassed in this discussion include notes, bonds, debentures, money market instruments, certificates of deposit, mortgage loans, commercial loans, commercial paper, and mortgage-backed certificates. The following guidance does not apply in circumstances in which an entity originates or acquires a whole loan mortgage and then exchanges the loan for a participation certificate issued by a government-sponsored enterprise or agency (e.g., FHLMC, FNMA, or GNMA). However, exchanges of participation certificates are included within the scope of this guidance.

ACCOUNTING GUIDANCE

For debt instruments to be classified as substantially the same, all of the following six criteria must be met. This has the practical effect of making it quite difficult for two debt instruments to be viewed as substantially the same. The six criteria that must be met in order for two debt instruments to be classified as substantially the same are as follows:

1. The debt instruments must have the same primary obligor. However, if the debt instrument is guaranteed by a sovereign government, a central bank, or a government-sponsored enterprise or agency thereof, the debt must be guaranteed by the same party. Also, the terms of the guarantee must be identical.
2. Each debt instrument must be identical in form and type so that all provide the same risks and rights to their holders. For example, the following types of exchanges would not meet this criterion: (*a*) GNMA I securities for GNMA II securities, (*b*) loans to foreign debtors that are otherwise the same except for different U.S. foreign tax credits, and (*c*) commercial paper for redeemable preferred stock.
3. Each debt instrument must carry the same contractual interest rate.
4. In general, the debt instruments must have the same maturity. In the case of mortgage-backed pass-through and pay-through securities, the mortgages underlying the securities must have similar remaining weighted average maturities that result in approximately the same market yield. For example, an exchange of GNMA securities that have a high prepayment record for GNMA securities with a low prepayment record would not meet this criterion.
5. Mortgage-backed pass-through or pay-through securities must be collateralized by a similar pool of mortgages, such as single-family residential mortgages.
6. In general, each debt instrument must have the same unpaid principal amount. In the case of mortgage-backed pass-through or pay-through securities, the aggregate principal amounts of the mortgage-backed securities given up and the mortgage-backed securities reacquired must be within the accepted "good delivery" standard for the type of mortgage-backed security involved. These specific standards are promulgated by the Public Securities Association and are discussed in *Uniform Practices for the Clearance and Settlement of Mortgage-Backed Securities and Other Related Securities.*

Illustration of Applying Criteria

First Interstate Bank of Texas transfers its portfolio of mortgage-backed pass-through securities for a similar portfolio held by First Virginia Bank. At issue is whether this transfer of debt instruments would represent the transfer of instruments that are substantially the same.

Assume that criteria 2-4 and 6 are met. Criterion 5 also is met—both sets of mortgage-backed securities are collateralized by a similar pool of mortgages: single-family residential mortgages. However, criterion 1, which requires the debt instruments to have the same primary obligor, is not met; there is a different set of primary obligors on First Interstate's loans than on First Virginia's loans. Therefore, this transfer does not represent the transfer of debt instruments that are substantially the same.

ASC 860-10-55-3; ASC 310-20-25-20 Accounting for Fees and Costs Associated with Loan Syndications and Loan Participations

---

IMPORTANT NOTICE: Under the guidance in ASU 2014-09, *Revenue from Contracts with Customers*, which becomes effective for public business entities in annual reporting periods that begin after December 15, 2017, and interim periods within those annual periods and in annual reporting periods that begin after December 15, 2018, for nonpublic entities, the guidance in ASC 860-10-55-3(b) will be amended by replacing "investment that is in substance a sale of real estate, as defined in Subtopic 320-20" with "in substance nonfinancial asset (see Subtopic 610-20)."

BACKGROUND

This Issue was discussed because some questioned the FASB staff's interpretation that the guidance in ASC 860 nullifies the previous conclusion that certain participations should be accounted for as "in-substance syndications."

ACCOUNTING ISSUES

1. Does the guidance in ASC 860 apply to loan participations even if they are considered to be in-substance syndications?

ACCOUNTING GUIDANCE

1. All loan participations should be accounted for under the provisions of ASC 860, which applies to all loan participations, even those having the characteristics of loan syndications.
2. All transactions structured legally as loan syndications, including those described as in-substance loan participations should be accounted under the provisions of ASC 310, Receivables.

DISCUSSION

The FASB staff explained that lenders sometimes structure transactions as loan participations rather than syndications because of the administrative difficulties of structuring a syndication. In a participation, the lender originates and funds the total loan but very shortly thereafter sells interests in the loan to other lenders, whereas in a syndication, several lenders initially fund the loan. The fees are the same in both transactions, but the lender in a participation has the credit and interest rate risk until other participants are found. Those who supported accounting for loan participations and loan syndications based on their legal form argued that ASC 860 applies to all transfers of financial assets and that it would be counterproductive to make exceptions to that requirement.

ASC 860-10-55-13 Sale of Bad-Debt Recovery Rights

BACKGROUND

A financial institution and another party enter into an agreement in which the financial institution sells the other party the right to receive the first $5 million collected on loans that had been previously written off by the financial institution. The other party (the buyer) pays the financial institution $5 million for that right and will receive a specified market rate of interest annually on $5 million reduced by loans recovered. The agreement continues until the buyer has recovered the $5 million. The buyer has no recourse to the financial institution and can use its own efforts to recover on the loans if dissatisfied with the financial institution's collection results.

ACCOUNTING ISSUES

Should the transaction be accounted for as:

- A sale of recovery rights and recognize a gain at the date of the transaction?
- A recovery of loans previously written off and recognized as a credit to the loan loss allowance?
- A borrowing secured by the potential recovery rights and recognized as a liability?
- A secured borrowing with the amount of proceeds received from the buyer considered in computing the current year's loan-loss provision?

ACCOUNTING GUIDANCE

The transaction is a secured borrowing. No conclusion was reached on whether proceeds received from a buyer should be considered in the current year's loan loss provision.

DISCUSSION

The following arguments supported the conclusion that the transaction is a secured borrowing:

- The transaction is similar to a nonrecourse financing or a funded guarantee.
- The buyer's stated annual return is more like a return on a financing transaction than a return on an equity transaction, because the buyer has no reward beyond recovery of the principal and interest.
- The buyer has no risk because, based on the institution's experience, the buyer will cover the principal and interest.
- The financial institution does not sell the buyer a right to recoveries on specific loans.
- Loans written off continue to be controlled by the financial institution, which has the incentive to make recoveries and limit the amount of interest paid.

ASC 860-10-55-71 through 55-72 Sale of a Short-Term Loan Made under a Long-Term Credit Commitment

BACKGROUND

A financial institution has made a 90-day short-term loan to a borrower under a five-year long-term credit commitment and subsequently transfers the short-term loan without recourse to a third party. Under the transfer agreement, the risk of loss on the short-term loan is legally transferred to the purchaser, while the transferor retains no obligation to repurchase the short-term loan. The financial institution may relend to the borrower under the long-term credit commitment when the short-term obligation matures, but may refuse to do so based on an evaluation of the borrower's credit or because the borrower does not satisfy a covenant under the long-term credit commitment.

ACCOUNTING ISSUE

Should a transfer of a short-term loan under a long-term credit commitment be accounted for as a sale or as a financing transaction?

ACCOUNTING GUIDANCE

1. A transfer of a short-term loan under the long-term credit commitment described above should be accounted for as a sale.
2. Loan covenants affect the accounting for a transfer as follows:
   a. A transfer of a short-term loan under a long-term credit commitment that includes a substantive *subjective* covenant should be accounted for as a sale.
   b. A transfer of a short-term loan under a long-term credit commitment that includes only *objective* covenants should be accounted for as a sale only if such objective covenants are substantive—that is, they specifically apply to the borrower and are expected to be meaningful and relevant in determining whether the long-term credit commitment obligates the financial institution to relend to the borrower.
3. Commitment fees received for long-term commitments should be recognized based on the guidance in ASC 310, Receivables.

EFFECT OF ASC 815

The guidance in ASC 815 applies if an analysis of the terms of a contract indicate that a put option qualifies as a derivative under the Statement.

EFFECT OF ASC 860

- The guidance in ASC 860 affirms the conclusion that a short-term loan under a long-term credit commitment to a third-party purchaser without recourse should be accounted for as a sale under the circumstances described. Such a transaction could meet the conditions for the surrender of control under the guidance in ASC 860-10-40-4 and 40-5. Specific transactions should be evaluated based on that guidance.
- If a transaction discussed is accounted for as a transfer of a receivable with a put option, recognition of a sale is required if the transaction meets the conditions in ASC 860-10-40-4 through 40-5.
- The guidance in ASC 860-10-40-4 through 40-5 is amended to require that a transferor that effectively retains control over transferred financial assets be precluded from recognizing a sale on the transaction. Examples of when a transferor effectively retains control over transferred financial assets are included in ASC 860-10-40-4 and 40-5.
- The SEC Observer's concerns (see comment below) are partially resolved by the requirement in ASC 860-20-25-1, that a liability be recognized for a put obligation incurred or proceeds in such transactions if the put obligation does not prohibit sales accounting.
- The guidance in ASC 860 does not address a lender's refusal to relend to a borrower based on subjective or objective covenants. (See SEC Observer's Comment.) However, the put option's terms should be analyzed to determine whether the put meets the definition of a derivative in ASC 815. If a loan cannot be readily converted to cash and there is no market mechanism to enable the holder to settle the option in net cash, the put option may not meet the condition in ASC 815-10-15-83, which is further discussed in ASC 860-10-40-4 through 40-5.
- The recognition of commitment fees is not addressed in ASC 860.

SEC OBSERVER COMMENT

The SEC Observer stated that he is uncomfortable with sales accounting and concerned about uncertainties related to the transaction, such as the accounting for commitment fees for long-term commitments under the guidance in ASC 310, the classification of the loan by the borrower as short-term or long-term, and the probability of whether a financial institution will relend to the borrower.

DISCUSSION

Although the risk of loss has been transferred in this transaction, and the transferor has no contractual obligation to repurchase the short term loan receivable, the Issue is complicated by the fact that it deals with a short-term loan under a revolving long-term credit commitment. That is, if the transaction is viewed as a single loan that reprices periodically, the substance of the transaction is that the lender (transferor) either repays the transferee when the loan rolls over or the transferee agrees to purchase the additional portion of the loan.

To address concerns about the probability that the financial institution will relend to the borrower, the effect of loan covenants on the relending decision were discussed. The conclusion was based on a discussion of the following two types of financial-related covenants:

1. *Subjective covenants* Compliance is determined subjectively. For example, a provision that refers to a "material adverse change" may be evaluated differently by the parties to the agreement.
2. *Objective covenants* Compliance is determined objectively based on data such as financial ratios.

ASC 860-20: SALES OF FINANCIAL ASSETS

ASC 860-20-25-08, 25-10 through 25-13, 30-4, 35-9, 55-41 through 55-42, 55-62 through 55-92; ASC 860-40-25-2, 50-25-10 Accounting for Changes That Result in a Transferor Regaining Control of Financial Assets Sold

---

PRACTICE NOTE: The guidance below has been updated based on the guidance in ASU 2020-03, *Codification Improvements to Financial Instruments*.

BACKGROUND

According to ASC 860-20-25-8, a transferor may regain control of financial assets previously accounted for as sold if a transferee no longer meets one of the conditions in ASC 860-10-40-4 through 40-5 that are required for sale accounting. Failure to meet the conditions in ASC 860-10-40-4 through 40-5 is usually a result of a change in law, or other circumstances. If such circumstances occur, a portion of the transferred financial assets may no longer meet the conditions of a participating interest or the transferor may regain control of a transferred financial asset that had been accounted for as a sale, because one or more of the conditions in ASC 860-10-40-4 through 40-5 are no longer met. Under those circumstances, the transferor must account for the transferred financial assets as if they have been repurchased from the transferee in exchange for the liabilities assumed by the transferor. The transferor recognizes the transferred financial assets and liabilities at their fair value on the date the change occurs and thereafter reports the assets and the liabilities in its financial statements to the former transferee or other beneficial interest holders in those assets. The transferee derecognizes the transferred financial assets on that date and accounts for them as if they were sold in exchange for a receivable from the transferor. It is assumed in this Issue that the transferor does not consolidate the transferee. However, a transferor that subsequently consolidates an entity that had been involved in a transfer that was accounted for as a sale should apply current guidance.

ACCOUNTING ISSUES

1. How should a transferor account for retained beneficial interests if portions of the underlying assets that had been sold are rerecognized because the transferor's contingent call option on the transferred assets, such as a removal of accounts provision (ROAP), becomes exercisable? How much of a gain or loss should be recognized under those circumstances?
2. Are there any circumstances under which an allowance should be recorded for assets that are rerecognized at fair value?

3. How does the rerecognition of assets (or a portion thereof) sold as the result of circumstances discussed in ASC 860-20-25-8 affect the accounting for a related servicing asset?
4. How should a transferor subsequently account for its interests, except for servicing assets, after the occurrence of an event discussed in ASC 860-20-25-8?

ACCOUNTING GUIDANCE

1. Under the guidance in ASC 860-20-25-12, a transferor applying the guidance in ASC 860-20-25-10 should not recognize a gain or loss in earnings related to its beneficial interests. However, a transferor may recognize a gain or loss when exercising a removal of accounts provision (ROAP) or a similar contingent right related to a repurchased transferred financial asset that was sold if the ROAP is not a derivative accounted for under the guidance in ASC 815-10 and is not at-the-money. That is, the fair value of repurchased assets should not exceed or be less than the transferor's related obligation to the transferee.
2. Under the guidance in ASC 860-20-25-13, as amended by ASU 2020-03, rerecognized financial assets under the guidance in ASC 860-20-25-10 should be initially recognized at fair value and accounted for under the applicable guidance in ASC 860 on transfers and servicing, ASC 310 on receivables, ASC 320 on investments—debt securities, ASC 321 on investments—equity securities, ASC 323 on investments—equity method and joint ventures, and ASC 325 on investments—other. An allowance for credit losses should be measured in accordance with the guidance in ASC 326, if applicable, as follows:
   a. For financial assets that are not **purchased financial assets with credit deterioration** under the scope of ASC 326, an allowance for credit losses should be recognized with a corresponding charge to credit loss expense as of the reporting date.
   b. For purchased financial assets with credit deterioration (including a beneficial interest that meets the criteria in ASC 325-40-30-1A) under the scope of ASC 326, an allowance should be recognized for credit losses in accordance with the guidance in ASC 326 with a corresponding increase to the asset(s)' amortized cost basis as of the date of recognition.
3. Under the guidance in ASC 860-20-25-10(b), the accounting for a servicing asset related to a previously sold financial asset does not change if an event discussed in ASC 860-20-25-8 occurs. The contractually required cash flows from the rerecognized assets will continue to be paid to the special-purpose entity, which will distribute the proceeds to satisfy its contractual obligations, including to beneficial interest holders. A transferor, as servicer, continues to be contractually required to collect the asset's cash flows for the benefit of the special-purpose entity and to service the asset in other ways. Therefore, a transferor should continue to recognize the servicing asset separately, even if a transferor regains control over the underlying asset, and should evaluate it for impairment as required in ASC 860-50-35-9.
4. In accordance with the guidance in ASC 860-20-25-10(c), a transferor should not combine its interest in the underlying financial assets with rerecognized financial assets after an event discussed in ASC 860-20-25-8 occurs. A transferor's interest should be recombined, however, with the underlying assets, if as a result of a subsequent event, the transferor reclaims the financial assets from a transferee—for example, by exercising a removal of accounts provision or by consolidating a special purpose entity under U.S. GAAP, including the Variable Interest Entities Subsections of ASC 810-10.

ASC 860-20-35-6, 55-17 through 55-19 Accounting for Accrued Interest Receivable under ASC 860 Securitizations

Question: How should the accrued interest receivable related to securitized and sold receivables be accounted for and reported under the guidance in ASC 860?

Answer: When credit card receivables are securitized, a pool of receivables is transferred to a trust and the trust receives the right to future collections of principal, finance charges, and fees. Assuming that the transfer of receivables meets the ASC 860 criteria for treatment as a sale, the transferor will carry on its balance sheet only its retained interests in the transferred receivables.

Some companies that securitize credit card receivables continue to recognize accrued interest receivable as an asset on their balance sheet, even though the right to receive this accrued interest receivable has been transferred to the trust. The accrued interest receivable represents the investors' portion of the accrued fees and finance charges on the transferred credit card receivables. According to the final FSP that was recently issued, this accounting treatment is generally no longer acceptable.

Assuming that the securitization meets the requirements to be treated as a sale and the accrued interest receivable is subordinated, the accrued interest receivable should be considered one of the components of the sales transaction. The accrued interest receivable should be treated as retained beneficial interest. It is not acceptable to refer to the accrued interest receivable as "loans receivable," or as any other title that fails to communicate that the accrued interest receivable has been subordinated to the senior interests in the securitization.

The accrued interest receivable cannot be prepaid or settled in a manner in which the owner would suffer a significant loss of its investment. Therefore, the accrued interest receivable is not subsequently measured like an investment in debt securities that is treated as available-for-sale or trading under the guidance in ASC 320. The subsequent measurement of retained interests that cannot be prepaid or settled in a manner in which the owner would suffer a significant loss on its investment, including accrued interest receivable, is accounted for in accordance with ASC 450 (FAS-5, Accounting for Contingencies). ASC 450 provides guidance in providing for the uncollectibility of receivables including, as in this case, accrued interest receivable.

ASC 860-50: SERVICING ASSETS AND LIABILITIES

ASC 860-50-40-3 through 40-5 Determination of What Risks and Rewards, If Any, Can Be Retained and Whether Any Unresolved Contingencies May Exist in a Sale of Mortgage Loan Servicing Rights

BACKGROUND

A seller/transferor may provide a buyer/transferee with protection provisions in an agreement to sell or transfer servicing rights. Such provisions may include adjustment of the sales price for loan prepayments, defaults, or foreclosures occurring within a specific time period. In addition, most agreements include representations and warranty provisions that apply to eligibility defects discovered within a specific time period.

ACCOUNTING ISSUE

Is sales recognition precluded at the date title passes if the agreement includes any provision under which the seller retains specific risks, or could a sale be recognized at that date if:

- A seller can reasonably estimate and recognizes a liability for the costs related to protection provisions, or
- A sales agreement provides for substantially all risks and rewards to irrevocably pass to the buyer, and the seller can reasonably estimate the minor protection provisions and recognizes a liability for that amount?

ACCOUNTING GUIDANCE

- A transfer of a right to service mortgage loans should be recognized as a sale if the following conditions have been met:
  - — Title has passed.
  - — Substantially all risks and rewards of ownership have irrevocably passed to the buyer.
  - — The seller has retained only minor protection provisions that are reasonably estimable.
- A liability should be accrued for the estimated obligation associated with the minor protection provisions.
- A seller retains only minor protection provisions if:
  - — The obligation related to those provisions does not exceed 10% of the sales price, and
  - — Prepayment risk is retained for a maximum of 120 days.

DISCUSSION

Proponents of the view adopted by Task Force noted that authoritative pronouncements such as ASC 605 and ASC 360, permit sales recognition when some risk has been retained by the seller. It also was argued that sufficient historical and projected information exists about the types of risks retained to enable a seller to estimate the effects of such uncertainties. In addition, provisions related to prepayment protection, early payment defaults, and investor approval are resolved within a short period of time, such as three months or less. The buyer's remedies usually are limited to a reduction of the sales proceeds for the disqualified portion, but the buyer cannot void the sale unless there is fraud. As a result, the seller can estimate the effect of the provisions.

The term *minor* was defined as 10% of the sales price to attain consistent application of the consensus. Ten percent was chosen as the maximum limit, because it is a common definition of minor found in the accounting literature, such as in lease accounting and pooling of interests. Ten percent also is considered a reasonable percentage of risk to be retained by the seller while recognizing a sale.

ASC 860-50-40-10, 50-11 Sale of Mortgage Service Rights on Mortgages Owned by Others

BACKGROUND

A company sells its portfolio of first-mortgage loans and retains the right to service the loans. Because there is a lag between the time the mortgage payments are collected and the time such payments are passed to the mortgage owners, the company invests that "float." As a result, the company can sell the mortgage servicing rights for cash or for participation in the future interest stream produced by the loans.

ACCOUNTING ISSUES

- Should a gain be recognized on the sale of mortgage servicing rights for a participation in the income stream of future interest?
- If so, how should the gain be measured?

ACCOUNTING GUIDANCE

- A gain should be recognized at the date of the sale.
- It is difficult to measure a gain if the sales price is based on the seller's participation in future payments; the accounting literature does not provide guidance on the upper limit of a computed sales price. All available information should be considered, including the gain that would be recognized if the servicing rights were sold for a fixed cash price.

Appendices

APPENDIX A

ASC 912—CONTRACTORS—FEDERAL GOVERNMENT

CONTENTS

GENERAL GUIDANCE

ASC 912-10: OVERALL

OVERVIEW

Government contracts often include certain unique features, such as being based on the costs incurred by the contractor (i.e., cost-plus-fixed-fee). These contracts may also provide that the government may terminate the contract at its convenience. ASC 912 deals with both fixed-price and cost-plus-fixed-fee (CPFF) contracts. It addresses the problems involved in the termination of a government contract by the government; it does not cover terminations resulting from default of the contractor (ASC 912-10-15-3).

TERMINATED WAR AND DEFENSE CONTRACTS

ASC 912 deals with both fixed-price and CPFF contracts. It addresses the problems involved in the termination of a government contract by the government.

The determination of profit or loss on a terminated government contract is made as of the effective date of termination. This is the date that the contractor accrues the right to receive payment on that portion of the contract that has been terminated (ASC 912-275-50-4).

GOVERNMENT CONTRACT RECEIVABLES

A distinction should be made in the balance sheet between unbilled costs and fees and billed amounts. Unbilled costs and fees under cost-plus-fixed-fee contracts are receivables or contract assets rather than advances or inventory (ASC 912-310-25-1).

In the case of terminated contracts, if a reasonable estimate of the termination claim for reporting purposes cannot be made, full disclosure of this fact must be made by note to the financial statements, which should describe the uncertainties involved. For those parts of the termination claim that are included in financial statements after termination, full disclosure of the essential facts must be made (ASC 912-310-50-1).

Termination claims are classified as current assets if the criteria in the ASC Glossary are met (ASC 912-310-45-3). Prior to the termination notice, advances received are deducted from termination claims receivable for reporting purposes. Loans received on the security of the contract or termination claim are shown separately as current liabilities. Advance payments received before the termination may be shown in the financial statements after termination as deduction from the claim receivable (ASC 912-310-45-4). Material amounts of termination claims are classified separately from other receivables in the financial statements (ASC 912-310-50-2).

The cost of items included in the termination claim that are subsequently reacquired by the contractor is recorded as a new purchase, and the amount is applied as a reduction of the termination claim. These types of reductions from the termination claim generally are referred to as *disposal credits* (ASC 912-310-35-1; ASC 912-330-25-1).

DISCLOSURES

When a significant portion of a company's business is derived from government contracts, incremental disclosure must be made in the financial statements or notes thereto, indicating the uncertainties involved with contracts terminated for the convenience of the government (ASC 912-275-05-1). Disclosure is required if 10 percent or more of an enterprise's revenue is derived from sales to the federal government, a state government, a local government, or a foreign government (ASC 280-10-50-42).

Termination claims are stated at the amount estimated as collectible, and adequate provision or disclosure is required for items of a controversial nature even if estimates of ultimate amounts to be realized are not determinable (ASC 912-275-50-3, 5).

APPENDIX B

ASC 92X—ENTERTAINMENT

CONTENTS

PART I: GENERAL GUIDANCE

ASC 92X—ENTERTAINMENT

OVERVIEW

Authoritative accounting literature for companies in the entertainment industry are presented in five categories: broadcasters, cable television, casinos, films, and music. While all of these lines of business have certain things in common, they have unique aspects that are covered in the respective authoritative pronouncements. The FASB standards related to entertainment enterprises draw heavily on former Statements of Position and other work of the AICPA's Accounting Standards Executive Committee.

PRACTICE NOTE: The standards applicable to all entities generally apply to entertainment entities. The standards included in ASC 92X deal with the unique application of those standards to entertainment entities and are described in the ASC as "incremental industry-specific guidance."

ASC 920: BROADCASTERS

BACKGROUND

The term *broadcaster* refers to an entity or an affiliated group of entities that transmits radio or television program material (ASC Glossary). A broadcasting station may be completely independent or may be affiliated with a network. Independent broadcasters purchase or otherwise provide for all of their programming. A network affiliated broadcaster obtains much of its programming from its affiliated network and usually receives an affiliation fee and has lower programming costs than an independent.

Programming costs usually are the largest expense of television broadcasters. Programming costs generally are higher for independent broadcasters, who must obtain all of their programming themselves, than they are for network-affiliated broadcasters. Program material for television broadcasters is purchased under television licenses from producers and distributors. These producers and distributors generally package several films and license the material for one or more exhibitions or for a specified period, at which time the license expires. The license agreement usually provides for installment payments over a period, which is almost always less than the license period. The producer or distributor receives all of its money for the license prior to the expiration of the license.

Many television broadcasters produce some of their programming material either live or on videotape. Local news broadcasts and local interview shows are popular programs produced by television broadcasters.

Television and radio broadcasters are regulated by the Federal Communications Commission (FCC). Broadcasters are licensed periodically to use frequencies in specific areas, which are assigned by the FCC. In licensing a broadcaster, the FCC may consider the (a) financial position of the broadcaster, (b) advertising policies, (c) quality of the programming, and (d) contribution made to the community in which the broadcaster operates. Advertising rates are not regulated by the FCC, but guidelines have been established for advertising rates by the National Association of Broadcasters.

The major assets of a broadcaster are its FCC license and its network affiliation agreement. Thus, network-affiliated broadcasters usually are more valuable than independent broadcasters.

PROGRAM MATERIAL LICENSE AGREEMENTS

A broadcaster (licensee) accounts for a license agreement for program material and any exhibition rights acquired under a license agreement for program material as a purchase of a right or group of rights. The license agreement is reported in the financial statements of the licensee when the license period begins and all of the following conditions are met (ASC 920-350-25-2):

- The cost of each license fee for each program is known or is reasonably determinable.
- The broadcaster has accepted the program material in accordance with the terms of the license agreement.
- The program is available for its first showing or telecast under the license agreement.

The asset and liability that arise from the purchase of program material rights are reported by the licensee or licensor at either (a) the fair value of the liability or (b) the gross amount of the liability. If a present value technique is used to measure fair value, accounting shall be in accordance with applied ASC 835 (ASC 920-405-30-1).

PRACTICE POINTER: One purpose of ASC 835 is to require that interest be imputed on liabilities that bear an unreasonable rate of interest or no interest at all. If a reasonable rate of interest is charged on a liability, the provisions of ASC 835 would not apply and the liability would be recorded at its gross amount. ASC 835 is based on the pervasive principle of **substance over form**. Allowing the licensee or licensor to report the liability or receivable either **gross** or at **present value** is equivalent to permitting the licensee or licensor to report either the **substance** or the **form** of the transaction.

The cost of rights to a package of programs is allocated to each program right in the package, based on the relative value of each program right to the broadcaster. Amortization of program material rights is computed on the estimated number of times that the program will be aired by the broadcaster. Program rights purchased for unlimited broadcast may be amortized over the term of the license agreement if the estimated number of future showings is not determinable (ASC 920-350-30-2, 35-1).

Feature programs are amortized on an individual basis. Series programs, however, are amortized on a series basis. An accelerated method of amortization must be used when the first broadcast of a program is more valuable than its reruns, which usually is the case. The straight-line method of amortization is appropriate only when each broadcast is expected to produce approximately the same amount of revenue (ASC 920-350-35-2).

Unamortized program rights shall not exceed their net realizable value or a write-down is required. Program rights are reported in the balance sheet at the lower of their unamortized cost or their estimated net realizable value (ASC 920-350-30-3).

INTANGIBLE ASSETS

ASC 920 requires that intangible assets in the broadcasting industry are only amortized if they are deemed to have a finite life.

If a network affiliation is terminated, any unamortized network affiliation costs are charged to expense unless a replacement agreement exists. In this event, if the fair value of the replacement agreement exceeds the unamortized network affiliation cost of the terminated agreement, no gain is recognized. If the fair value of the replacement agreement is less than the unamortized network affiliation cost of the terminated agreement, however, a loss is recognized to the extent of the difference (ASC 920-350-40-1).

DISCLOSURE

Unrecorded program material license agreements that have been executed and do not meet the criteria of ASC 920 must be disclosed in notes to the financial statements (ASC 920-440-50-1).

PRACTICE POINTER: ASC 920 is silent on the extent of note disclosure that is necessary for unrecorded license agreements that have been executed but do not meet the criteria of ASC 920. Based other similar situations, the following disclosures seem reasonable in this circumstance.

- A description of the nature and term of the obligation.
- The total determinable amount of unrecorded unconditional purchase obligations as of the latest balance sheet date, and for each of the five years after the latest balance sheet date.
- A description of the nature of any variable component of the unrecorded unconditional purchase obligations.
- For each income statement presented, the amounts actually purchased under the unconditional purchase obligations.

ASC 922: CABLE TELEVISION COMPANIES

BACKGROUND

ASC 922 contains the specialized accounting and reporting principles and practices that were originally published in the AICPA SOP 79-2 (Accounting by Cable Television Companies).

Cable television (CATV) systems are organized and built to provide uninterrupted program entertainment. The distribution of the television programs by a CATV system usually is made over coaxial or fiber optic cables or satellites to a defined area.

Ordinarily, a cable TV company, which is regulated by the Federal Communications Commission, obtains a franchise from a local governmental authority, which permits the distribution of CATV programs in a specified area. The franchise agreement usually provides for payment of fees to the granting authority and contains, among other provisions, the maximum fees that the company can charge a subscriber. In addition, franchise agreements may include many provisions pertaining to the type and quality of service that must be provided, number of TV channels, type of construction, and duration of the franchise. If all of the terms of the franchise agreement are not met, the governmental authority may retain the right to terminate the contract with the cable TV company.

The operation of the CATV system begins with the purchase of program entertainment. Program entertainment from major suppliers and motion picture studios usually is acquired on a long-term contract. The transmission signals of a cable programming company are picked up by the CATV system by microwave relay, antennas, or satellite, then amplified and distributed to subscribers via coaxial cables. The subscriber usually pays an initial hookup charge and thereafter, a monthly subscription fee.

Key provisions of 1992 federal cable law include use of reasonable subscriber rates, better customer service standards, and sale of program entertainment on a nondiscriminatory basis. A cable operator with more than 12 usable channels must set aside four to carry local commercial TV stations upon demand.

The size of the franchise area and the density of the population usually determine the construction period required to install a CATV system. The type of system being built, however, may also affect the period of construction. For example, if the coaxial cables must be installed underground rather than on utility poles, the period of construction will likely take longer. The construction period is completed when all of the equipment used to receive transmissions (head-end equipment) is installed, all main (head-end) and distribution cables are in place, and most subscriber drops (installation hardware) are installed. The CATV system is *energized* when the first transmission is made to subscribers. It is not unusual to energize part of the CATV system before the entire system is built, because large CATV systems generally are built in sections over several years. When this occurs, a *prematurity period* is established. A prematurity period begins when revenue from the first subscriber is recognized in accordance with ASC 606 and ends when construction of the system is completed or when the first major stage of construction of the system is completed. The prematurity period will vary in direct relation to the size of the franchise area and the density of the population.

The capital investment necessary for even a small CATV system is quite substantial. The acquisition of a franchise and the cost of the physical facilities are expensive, and the operating overhead during the construction period requires a great deal of working capital. Space on utility poles or in an underground ducts usually is leased from utility companies.

INITIAL RECORDING OF ASSETS

In the construction of a cable TV company, the *prematurity period* begins on the date that revenue from the first subscriber is recognized in accordance with ASC 606 and ends on the date that the construction of the CATV system is completed or when the first major stage of construction is completed. Some cable TV companies, however, have determined that the prematurity period begins on the date that revenue from the first subscriber is recognized and ends on the date that a predetermined number of subscribers is reached (ASC Glossary).

A portion of a CATV system that meets most of the following conditions is in a prematurity period and is accounted for separately from the rest of the system (ASC 922-360-25-3):

- Geographical differences, such as coverage of a noncontiguous or separately awarded franchise area.
- Mechanical differences, such as a separate head-end.
- Timing differences, such as starting construction or marketing at a significantly different date.
- Separate investment decision differences, such as separate break-even and return-on-investment analyses or separate approval of start of construction.
- Separate accounting records, separate budgets and forecasts, or other accountability differences.

ASC 922 distinguishes between capitalized costs attributable to the main cable television plant and other related capitalized costs of a fully operational system, such as the cost of leases on utility poles or underground ducts, leases on satellite or microwave installations, property taxes, and capitalized interest costs. ASC 922 requires that these other related capitalized costs of a fully operational system be amortized over the same period used to depreciate the main cable television plant (ASC 922-350-35-2).

All costs of constructing the physical facilities of a CATV system, including materials, direct labor, and construction overhead are capitalized (ASC 922-360-25-5). During the prematurity period, however, some subscribers are receiving service while construction continues on the system. Thus, during the prematurity period a distinction must be made between costs related to (*a*) the current period, (*b*) future periods, and (*c*) both current and future periods (ASC 922-350-25-1).

Costs Related to Current Period

Selling, marketing, administrative expenses, and all costs related to current subscribers are accounted for as period costs.

Cost Related to Future Periods

During the prematurity period, all costs of constructing the physical facilities of the CATV system, including materials, direct labor, and construction overhead, continue to be capitalized.

Costs Related to Both Current and Future Periods

Programming costs and other system costs (such as the costs of leases on utility poles or underground ducts, leases on satellite or microwave installations, and property taxes) that are incurred in anticipation of servicing a fully operating system and that will not vary significantly regardless of the number of subscribers should be allocated to both current and future periods.

ASC 922 requires that during the prematurity period, charges for capitalized costs other than those of the main cable television plant are allocated to both current and future periods based on a fraction. The denominator of the fraction is the total expected subscribers at the end of the prematurity period; the numerator of the fraction is the greatest of (1) the average number of actual subscribers, (2) the average number of subscribers expected in a particular month, estimated at the beginning of the prematurity period, and (3) the average number of subscribers that would exist during the month if the expected number of subscribers at the end of the prematurity period were added on a straight-line basis over the prematurity period were added on a straight-line basis over the prematurity period. The fraction results in the amount of amortization, which is charged to expense in the current period (ASC 922-350-35-1).

During the prematurity period, depreciation of the cost of the main cable television plant of the CATV system is allocated by the same fraction. Instead of computing depreciation on the costs incurred to date, however, the total depreciable base of the main cable television plant is estimated, and the total amount of depreciation is determined by applying the depreciation method normally used by the company. After the total amount of depreciation is computed, the fraction described in the previous paragraph is applied to arrive at the amount of depreciation expense that should be charged to the current period (ASC 922-360-35-3).

Under the provisions of ASC 922 (originally issued as FAS 34), certain interest costs, if material, are capitalized and added to the acquisition cost of assets that require a period of time to get ready for their intended use. The cost of assets to which capitalized interest is allocated includes the cost of both those assets acquired for a company's own use and those acquired for sale in the ordinary course of business (ASC 922-835-25-1).

Interest cost is capitalized during the prematurity period on that portion of the CATV system which is undergoing development activities to get it ready for its intended use and is not being used in the earning activities of the system.

PRACTICE POINTER: Capitalization of interest cost may pose particularly difficult problems for CATV systems. For example, capitalization of interest ceases when the asset being constructed is ready for its intended purpose. This requirement is particularly important in the construction of large CATV systems that are completed and placed into service in phases. Take care to ensure that interest is not capitalized on phases of the project that are complete and ready for service.

GAAP for the capitalization of interest also specifies that if the enterprise suspends substantially all activities related to acquisition of the asset, interest capitalization shall cease until activities are resumed. Brief interruptions in actions, interruptions that are externally imposed, and delays that are inherent in the asset acquisition process do not require cessation of interest capitalization. Judge carefully to determine whether delays in CATV system construction require an interruption in the capitalization of interest.

FRANCHISE COSTS

Initial hookup costs for subscribers are capitalized. The depreciation period for initial hookup costs for subscribers should not exceed the depreciation period of the main cable television plant (ASC 922-360-35-5).

Usually, a CATV company makes a formal franchise application to a local governmental unit to provide cable television service in its geographical area. The costs associated with any successful application may be significant and are accounted for in accordance with ASC 922 (ASC 922-350-35-4).

The costs associated with unsuccessful franchise applications and abandoned franchises are charged to expense in the period in which it is determined that they cannot benefit any future period (ASC 922-350-40-1).

PERIODIC REVIEW OF RECOVERABILITY

Plant costs capitalized and certain intangible assets of cable television companies are subject to the impairment guidance in ASC 360.

ASC 926: FILMS

BACKGROUND

The following definitions are particularly important in applying industry-specific GAAP for films (ASC Glossary).

Films. Feature films, television specials, television series, or similar products that are sold, licensed, or exhibited, whether produced on film, video tape, digital, or other video recording format.

Film costs. All direct negative costs incurred in the physical production of a film, as well as allocations of production overhead and capitalized interest in accordance with ASC Topic 835. Examples of direct negative costs include:

- Story and scenario.
- Compensation of cast, directors, producers, extras, and miscellaneous staff.
- Set construction and operations, wardrobe, and accessories.
- Sound synchronization.
- Rental facilities on location.
- Postproduction costs, such as music, special effects, and editing.

Market. A distribution channel within a certain territory. Examples of market include theatrical exhibition, home video, pay television, and the licensing of film-related products.

Participation Costs. Parties involved in the production of a film may be compensated in part by contingent payment based on the financial results of a film pursuant to contractual formulas (participants) and by contingent amounts due under provisions of collective bargaining agreements (residuals). Such parties are collectively referred to as "participants," and such costs are collectively referred to as "participation costs." Participations may be given to creative talent, such as actors or writers, or to entities from whom distributions rights are licensed.

Revenue. Revenue earned by an entity from its direct distribution, exploitation, or licensing of a film before deduction of any of the entity's direct costs of distribution. For markets and territories in which an entity's fully or jointly-owned films are distributed by third parties, revenue is the net amounts payable to the entity by third party distributors. Revenue is reduced by allowances, estimated returns, price concessions and other similar adjustments.

Overall Deal. An arrangement in which an entity compensates a producer or other creative individual for the exclusive or preferential use of that party's creative services.

FILM COST CAPITALIZATION

- An entity shall report film costs as a separate asset on its balance sheet (ASC 926-20-25-1).
- Production overhead is a component of film cost. It includes allocable costs of individuals or departments with exclusive or significant responsibility for the production of film. It does not include administrative or general expenses, the costs of certain deals, or charges for losses on properties sold or abandoned (ASC 926-20-25-2).
- An entity may enter into an arrangement known as an *overall deal*. The entity shall record a reasonable proportion of the costs of overall deals with specific project film costs to the extent those costs are directly related to the acquisition, adaptation, or development of the specific projects (ASC 926-20-25-3, 4).

- Film costs ordinarily include expenditures for properties, such as film rights to books, stage plays, or original screenplays, that generally must be adapted to serve as the basis for the production of a particular film. Costs of adaption or development are added to the costs of the particular property (ASC 926-20-25-5).

FILM COST AMORTIZATION

- For a film that is predominantly monetized on its own, an entity must amortize film costs using the individual-film-forecast computation method, which amortizes such costs in the same ratio that current period actual revenue bears to the estimated remaining unrecognized ultimate revenue as of the beginning of the current fiscal year. In the absence of changes in estimates, this results in film costs being amortized in a manner that yields a constant rate of profit over the ultimate period for each film before exploitation costs, manufacturing costs, and other period expenses (ASC 926-20-35-1).
- Unamortized capitalized film costs as of the beginning of the current fiscal year are multiplied by the individual-film-forecast-computation method fraction. The entity shall begin amortization of capitalized film costs when a film is released and it begins to recognize revenue from that film (ASC 926-20-35-1).
- For a film that is predominantly monetized on its own but also monetized with other films and/or license agreements, an entity must make a reasonable estimate of the value attributable to the film's exploitation while monetized with other films and or license agreements for inclusion in its individual-film-forecast computation (ASC 926-20-35-1).
- For a film that is in a film group, the entity shall make a reasonably reliable estimate of the portion of unamortized film costs that is representative of the use of the film. Amounts are then expensed as it exhibits or exploits the film (ASC 926-20-35-2).
- As a result of uncertainties in the estimating process, actual results may vary from estimates. The entity shall review and revise estimates of ultimate revenue as of each reporting date to reflect currently-available information. If estimates are revised, a new denominator is determined that includes only the ultimate revenue from the beginning of the fiscal year of change. The numerator is unaffected by the change. The entity then applies the revised fraction to the net carrying amount of unamortized film costs as of the beginning of the fiscal year, and the difference between expenses determined using the new estimates and amounts previously expensed are charged or credited to income in the period during the period in which the estimates are revised (ASC 926-20-35-3).

ULTIMATE REVENUE

- Ultimate revenue to be included in the denominator of the individual film-forecast computation method fraction includes estimates of revenue that is expected to be recognized by an entity from the exploitation, exhibition, and sale of a film in all markets and territories with certain limitations (ASC 926-20-35-4, 5):
  - — For films other than episodic television series, ultimate revenue includes estimates for a period not to exceed 10 years following the date of the film's initial release.
  - — For episodic television series, ultimate revenue includes estimates for a period not to exceed 10 years form the date of delivery of the first episode or, if still in production, 5 years from the date of the delivery of the most recent episode.
  - — For previously released films acquired as part of a film library, ultimate revenue includes estimates over a period not to exceed 20 years from the date of acquisition.
  - — Ultimate revenue includes estimates of revenue from a market or territory only if persuasive evidence exists that such revenue will occur or the entity can demonstrate a history of recognizing such revenue in that market or territory.
  - — Ultimate revenue includes estimates of revenue from licensing arrangements with third parties to market film-related products only if persuasive evidence exists that such revenue from that arrangement will occur for that particular film or if the entity can demonstrate a history of recognizing such revenue from that form of arrangement.
  - — Ultimate revenue includes estimates of the portion of the wholesale or retail revenue from an entity's sale of peripheral items (e.g., toys, apparel) that is attributable to the exploitation of themes, characters, or other contents

related to a particular film only if the entity can demonstrate a history of recognizing such revenue from that form of exploitation in similar kinds of films.

— Ultimate revenue does not include estimates of revenue from unproven or undeveloped technologies.

— Ultimate revenue does not include estimates of wholesale promotion or advertising reimbursements to be received from third parties. Such amounts shall be offset against exploitation costs.

— Ultimate revenue does not include estimates of amounts related to the sale of film rights for periods after those identified.

FILM VALUATION, IMPAIRMENT, AND DEROCOGNITION

- Following are examples of events or changes in circumstances that indicate that an entity shall assess whether the fair value of a film is less than its unamortized costs (ASC 926-20-35-12A):
  - — An adverse change in the expected performance of a film prior to release.
  - — Actual costs substantially in excess of budgeted costs.
  - — Substantial delays in completion or release schedules.
  - — Changes in release plans, such as a reduction in the initial release pattern.
  - — Insufficient funding or resources to complete the film and to market it effectively.
  - — Actual performance subsequent to release failing to meet expectations prior to release.
- Following are examples of events or changes in circumstances that indicate that an entity shall assess whether the fair value of a film group is less than its unamortized costs (ASC 926-20-35-12B):
  - — A significant adverse change in technological, regulatory, legal, economic, or social factors that could affect the fair value of the film group.
  - — A significant decrease in the number of subscribers or forecasted subscribers, or the loss of a major distributor.
  - — A current-period operating or cash flow loss combined with a history of operating or cash flow losses or a projection of continuing losses associated with the use or exploitation of a film group.
- If a change in events or circumstances indicate that an entity should assess whether the fair value of a film (or film group) is less than its unamortized cost, the entity shall determine the fair value and write off the amount by which the unamortized capitalization costs exceed the film's (or film group's) fair value (ASC 926-20-35-13).
- The following factors, as well as others, are considered in estimating future cash flows for a film (ASC 926-20-35-15):
  - — If previously released, the film's performance in prior markets.
  - — The public's perception of the film's story, cast, director, or producer.
  - — Historical results of similar films.
  - — Historical results of the cast, director, or producer on prior films.
  - — Running time of the film.
- In determining a film's (or film group's) fair value, when using a traditional discounted cash flow approach, the relevant future cash inflows and outflows are the entity's estimate of the most likely cash flows. When using the expected cash flow approach, all possible relevant future cash inflows and outflows shall be probability-weighted by period and the estimated mean or average by period used. When using a traditional discounted cash flow approach, the discount rate shall not be the entity's incremental borrowing rate, liability settlement rate, or weighted average cost of capital. Rather the discount rate shall consider the time value of money and the expectations about possible variations in the amount or timing of the most likely cash flows and include an element to reflect the price market participants would seek for bearing the uncertainty inherent in such an asset (ASC 926-20-35-16, 17).
- An entity shall periodically review properties to determine whether they will ultimately be used in the production of a film. If it determines that a film property will not be used, it shall recognize a loss by a charge to income. The amount written off shall not subsequently be reestablished as an asset. The losses shall be measured as the amount by which the carrying amount of the asset exceeds its fair value. If the presumption is that the entity will abandon the property, its fair value shall be zero (ASC 926-20-40-1 through 40-3).

ASC 928: MUSIC

BACKGROUND

ASC 928 contains the specialized accounting and reporting principles and practices that were originally published in the AICPA SOP 76-1 (Accounting Practices in the Record and Music Industry).

Music publishers control the copyrights of their music, which may be owned by an artist-composer. On the other hand, record companies usually depend on an artist who is employed under a personal service contract to produce the record master that is used in manufacturing the ultimate product. The caliber and reputation of the recording artist have a direct effect on the success of any album or individual record.

A record master is produced by an expert sound engineer. Each instrument and voice is first recorded separately on magnetic tape. The sound engineer then combines each instrument and voice, emphasizing and de-emphasizing as he or she deems appropriate. This process is called mixing and is an important phase of manufacturing a record. The mixing process produces a record master, which is used to make acetate discs that are coated with metal. The metal coated disc is used to produce the mold that is eventually used to make the final product. Record masters also are utilized to produce tapes for the manufacturer of tape cartridges, cassettes, compact discs, and digital formats. The following costs usually are incurred in the production of a record master:

- Costs for the recording studio
- Costs for engineers, mixing experts, directors, and other technical talent
- Costs for musicians, arrangers, vocal background, and other similar talent
- Costs for manufacturing the record master itself

The more successful recording artists are paid a nonrefundable advance against future royalties and bear no cost of producing the record master.

Music publishers license others, on a royalty basis, to use their music. Additional sources of income for music publishers include royalties from public performance, revenue from the music used in motion picture films, and revenue from the sale of sheet music.

Music publishers usually are members of the ASCAP (American Society of Composers, Authors, and Publishers), BMI (Broadcast Music Incorporated), or some other society or association. Copyright laws provide that each time music is played publicly, the publisher and/or composer are entitled to a minimum royalty for public performance and mechanical rights, (i.e., rights to reproduce musical composition by any mechanical means—records, tapes, and diskettes). By monitoring radio and TV stations and live performances, ASCAP or BMI collects the royalties due to various publishers and/or composers. After collecting the royalties, ASCAP or BMI make periodic remittances to the publisher and/or composer.

ARTIST COMPENSATION COST

Royalties earned by artists, adjusted for anticipated returns, are charged to expense in the period in which the related record sale takes place. Royalty advances are recorded as prepaid royalties (an asset) if the past performance and current popularity of the artist to whom the advance is made indicate that the advance will be recoverable from future royalties to be earned by the artist. Advances made to new or previously unsuccessful artists, as well as those not having current popularity, are expensed in the current period. Capitalized advances are charged to expense as subsequent royalties are earned by the artist. If any capitalized advances subsequently appear not to be fully recoverable from future royalties to be earned by the artist, such advances should be charged to expense during the period in which the loss becomes evident. Advance royalties should be classified as current and noncurrent assets, as appropriate (ASC 928-340-35-1).

PRACTICE NOTE: The general standards concerning impairment losses are not applicable for record and music assets, and accounting for asset impairment is based on ASC 928 standards.

Future royalty guarantees, artist advances payable in the future, and other commitments, if material, should be disclosed in the financial statements (ASC 928-440-50-1).

The cost of a record master is recorded as an asset if it is reasonably assured that such cost will be recovered from expected future revenue. This cost should be disclosed separately in the balance sheet. The cost of a record master is amortized to income in proportion to the net revenue that is expected to be recognized (ASC 928-340-35-2; 928-720-25-2).

Any portion of the cost of a record master that is recoverable from the artist's royalties is accounted for as a royalty advance and disclosed separately in the financial statements (ASC 928-340-25-3).

LICENSEE ACCOUNTING

License agreements usually are based on a minimum guarantee that generally is paid in advance to the licensor by the licensee. The licensee records this minimum payment as a deferred charge (an asset). The deferred charge is then amortized to expense in accordance with the terms of the license agreement (ASC-928-340-35-3). Any other fees required by the licensing agreement that are not fixed in amount by the terms of the license agreement before the agreement expires must be estimated and accrued on a license-by-license basis by the licensee.

PART II: INTERPRETIVE GUIDANCE

ASC 924: ENTERTAINMENT—CASINOS

ASC 924-605: REVENUE RECOGNITION

ASC 924-605-25-2, 55-1 through 55-2, 65-1 (ASU 2010-16) Accruals for Casino Jackpot Liabilities

---

IMPORTANT NOTICE: In accordance with the guidance in ASU 2014-09, *Accounting for Revenue from Contracts with Customers*, which will reside in ASC 606, Revenue from Contracts with Customers, industry specific guidance will be superseded. Therefore, the guidance for accounting for jackpot liabilities in this Issue will be amended and moved to ASC 924-405-25-2 and ASC 924-405-25-1 through 55-2 when the guidance in ASU 2014-09 becomes effective for public business entities in annual reporting periods that begin after December 15, 2017, and interim periods within those annual periods and in annual reporting periods that begin after December 15, 2018, for nonpublic entities. Earlier application would be permitted only for nonpublic entities as of annual reporting periods, including interim reporting periods within that annual reporting period that begin after December 15, 2017, as amended by the FASB in ASU 2015-14.

BACKGROUND

Entities that earn their revenue from gaming activities classify slot machine jackpots as follows:

- "Nonprogressive" jackpots are *fixed* payouts that have been programmed into a slot machine based on certain combinations that are identified on the machine's payout table. Because in most jurisdictions a gaming entity is permitted to remove a machine paying such jackpots from the floor at any time, even if no fixed jackpots have been paid on that machine, a gaming entity is not required to make any payouts on such machines as long as a machine's payouts are within a preapproved percentage, which has been programmed into the machine.
- "Progressive" jackpots are payouts based on a percentage that is programmed into a slot machine and conforms to a machine's payout table, which increases as more customers play the machine. The amount that would be paid out the first time a slot machine is played or immediately after a jackpot has been paid out is referred to as the "base" amount of a progressive jackpot. Any amount paid above the base amount and until a customer wins a jackpot is referred to as the "incremental" amount of a progressive jackpot. The base amount of a jackpot is funded by the gaming entity while the incremental amount is funded by customers who play the machine. Therefore, in most jurisdictions, a gaming entity that removes a machine paying progressive jackpots from the floor is usually required to: (1) transfer the incremental amount to a different machine on the floor; or (2) award that amount in some sort of prize drawing. In some jurisdictions, a gaming entity that removes a progressive slot machine from the floor also has to retain and award the base amount of a progressive jackpot. In those circumstances, the gaming entity usually accrues a liability for the base amount before the jackpot has been won. However, some gaming entities also are accruing the incremental amount as a liability based a specific amount (e.g., five cents) per coin played by customers.

This Issue, which addresses how gaming entities should account for base jackpot liabilities if payment of a jackpot can be avoided, was discussed because some gaming entities are accruing a liability for progressive and nonprogressive base jackpots before a jackpot has been won. Those who support this approach base their view on the guidance in ASC 924-605-25-2, which states that "[b]ase jackpots shall be charged to revenue ratably over the period of play expected to precede payout." However, those who believe that a liability should not be accrued for a base jackpot's amount if the gaming entity is not required to make an award, as in a nonprogressive jackpot, cite the guidance in ASC 924-605-25-1, which states that "[r]evenue recognized and reported by a casino is generally defined as the win from gaming activities, that is, the difference between gaming wins and losses, not the total amount wagered."

SCOPE

The guidance applies to base jackpots and incremental amounts in progressive jackpots paid by entities that earn revenue from gaming activities.

ACCOUNTING GUIDANCE

A liability should *not* be accrued until an entity incurs an obligation to pay a base jackpot. An obligation to pay incremental amounts in progressive jackpots should be accounted for in the same manner as the obligation to pay a base jackpot because the same principle applies.

ASC 926-20: ENTERTAINMENT—FILMS

ASC 926-20-35-12 through 35-12A, 65-1 Accounting for Fair Value Information That Arises after the Measurement Date and Its Inclusion in the Impairment Analysis of Unamortized Film Costs

BACKGROUND

Guidance for the capitalization of film costs for producers and distributors of films is provided in ASC 926-20 (Entertainment—Films). Guidance for the impairment test for unamortized film costs is provided in ASC 926-20-35-12 through 35-13. Under that guidance, an entity is required to evaluate whether events or changes in circumstances indicate that a film's fair value is less than its amortized costs. Indicators include: (1) an adverse change in a film's expected performance before its release; and (2) a film's actual performance after its release does not meet the expectations before the film's release. If an entity determines that events or circumstances indicate that there is a potential impairment in a film's fair value, it is required to determine whether it is less than its recorded unamortized film costs. If so, an impairment loss should be recognized for the amount by which the film's unamortized costs exceed the film's fair value.

Before the issuance of Accounting Standards Update 2012-07, ASC 926-20-35-18 provided guidance on how to include subsequent information about the measurement of a film's fair value in an analysis of impairment as of the balance sheet date. It provided that if evidence that becomes available after the balance sheet date, but before the financial statements are issued, indicates that the unamortized costs of a film released before or after the balance sheet date may need a write-down, there is a rebuttable presumption that the conditions leading to the write-off existed at the balance sheet date. In that case, the financial statements would have been adjusted for the effect of a change in estimate, if any, as a result of the subsequent evidence. The rebuttable presumption could have been overcome if an entity could demonstrate that the conditions leading to the write-down did *not* exist at the balance sheet date. For films released after the balance sheet date, entities in the film industry considered events that occurred after the balance sheet date, but before the financial statements were issued, in their assessment of impairment as of the balance sheet date.

Under the definition of fair value in ASC 820 (Fair Value Measurement), fair value should be estimated using assumptions that market participants would use when they consider a transaction for an asset or a liability as of the measurement date. Generally, information that happens after the measurement date is not considered in the measurement because it represents a form of resolving an uncertainty that would already be priced into the fair value of an item at the measurement date.

The FASB issued the guidance in ASC 926-20-35-12 and 65-1 because there has been a conflict between the guidance in ASC 926, which attempts to provide all known information in the financial statements by including the effect of events that occur after the balance sheet date, while the guidance in ASC 820 requires that an exit price be calculated under current conditions at the measurement date, which may include uncertainty because the amount used for expected cash flows is based on estimates rather than known amounts. The objective of the guidance in ASU 926-30-35-12 is to conform the use of fair value measurements in the impairment test of unamortized film costs to the use of fair value measurements in other situations, including impairment tests of similar nonfinancial assets, such as long-lived assets accounted for under the guidance in ASC 360 (Property, Plant, and Equipment), as well as goodwill and indefinite-lived intangibles accounted for under the guidance in ASC 350 (Intangibles—Goodwill and Other).

SCOPE

The guidance in ASC 926-20-35-12 applies to all entities that assess the impairment of unamortized film costs under the guidance of ASC 926.

SUBSEQUENT EVENTS—OVERALL

The guidance in ASC 855 (Subsequent Events) (ASC 855-10-60-3, under the heading, Entertainment—Films), is superseded at transition by the guidance in ASC 926-855-35-1, because the relevant guidance related to the impairment of unamortized film costs has been moved to ASC 926.

ENTERTAINMENT—FILMS—OTHER ASSETS—FILM COSTS

The guidance in ASC 926-20-35 is amended as follows:

- The guidance in ASC 926-20-35-12, which is related to the valuation of film costs, is amended to include a statement that film costs should be tested for impairment if events or changes in circumstances indicate that a film's value may be less than its unamortized costs; and
- The guidance in ASC 926-20-35-18, which discussed subsequent events and included the rebuttable presumption that conditions leading to a write-down existed at the balance sheet date, is superseded by the guidance in ASC 926-20-35-12.

The guidance in ASC 926-855 also is superseded.

ASC 926-20-35-12 has been amended by ASU 2019-02, *Entertainment—Films—Other Assets—Film Costs (Subtopic 926-20) and Entertainment—Broadcasters—Intangibles—Goodwill and Other (Subtopic 920-350): Improvements to Accounting for Costs of Films and License Agreements for Program Materials*, and some of its guidance was moved to become ASC 926-20-35-12A, which provides the following guidance.

The following are examples of events or changes in circumstances indicating that an entity should assess whether a completed or uncompleted film's fair value is less than its amortized film costs:

1. An adverse change in a film's expected performance before its release.
2. Actual costs are substantially greater than budgeted costs.
3. Substantial delays in completion or release schedules.
4. Changes in release plans, such as a reduction in the initial release pattern.
5. Insufficient funding or resources to complete a film and to market it effectively.
6. Actual performance subsequent to release fails to meet expectations set before release as a result of factors such as the following:
   a. A significant adverse change in technological, regulatory, legal, economic, or social factors that could affect the public's perception of a film or the availability of a film for future showings
   b. A significant decrease in the amount of ultimate revenue expected to be recognized.
7. A change in a film's predominant revenue earning strategy that results in revenue being earned on the film with other films and/or license agreements.

Master Glossary, ASC 926-20-25-1, 25-8 through 25-9, 35-1 through 35-5, 35-12 through 35-17, 35-19, 40-5, 45-2, 50-1A through 50-2, 50-4A through 50-4C, 55-12 through 55-15, 65-2; ASC 920-230-05-1, 15-1, Glossary, 45-1; ASC 920-350-30-3, 35-1 through 35-3, 45-1, 50-1 through 50-4 Entertainment—Films—Other Assets—Film Costs (Subtopic 926-20) and Entertainment—Broadcasters—Intangibles—Goodwill and Other (Subtopic 920-350): Improvements to Accounting for Costs of Films and License Agreements for Program Materials (Consensus of the FASB Emerging Task Force)

BACKGROUND

In the past, the guidance in ASC 926-20 for the film industry provided different capitalization requirements for film production costs based on the type of content being produced. For example, all the production costs for films were capitalized, whereas the production costs of episodes of television series were capitalized up to the amount of contracted revenue for each episode in the initial market in which it was shown until there was persuasive evidence that revenue would be earned from secondary markets or an entity could demonstrate that it had earned such revenue in that market. As a result of significant changes in the entertainment industry's production and distribution models, some in the industry have questioned whether the information about the production costs of television series episodes under the existing capitalization guidance for films in ASC 926-20 represents the economics of those transactions and whether it is relevant for investors and other users. It was also suggested that the guidance in ASC 920-350 for broadcasters, which provides accounting guidance for license agreements for program materials, should be conformed with the guidance in ASC 926-20 for films. The following guidance for broadcasters and entities that produce and distribute films and television series episodes has been developed to resolve those issues.

ACCOUNTING GUIDANCE

Master Glossary

The Master Glossary has been amended by deleting the definitions of "Initial Market," "Secondary Market," amending the term "Significant Changes" by adding "to a Film," and adding the term "Film Group," which is defined as follows:

> The unit of account used for impairment testing for a **film** or a **license agreement** is expected to be predominantly monetized with other films and/or license agreements instead of being predominantly monetized on its own. A film group represents the lowest level for which identifiable cash flows are largely independent of the cash flows of other films and/or license agreements.

ENTERTAINMENT—FILMS—OTHER ASSETS—FILM COSTS

Recognition

ASC 960-20-25-6 and 25-7 related to Episodic Television Series have been superseded.

Subsequent Measurement

Film Costs Amortization

The amended guidance in ASC 926-20 distinguishes between the accounting for revenue earned predominantly on a film on its own and revenue earned on a film predominantly in combination with other films and/or license agreements. The existing guidance in ASC 926-20-35-1 has been amended to provide the following additional guidance. If revenue is mostly earned from a film on its own, but revenue on the film is also earned in transactions in which the film is combined with other films or license agreements, an entity should make a reasonably accurate estimate of the film's value when revenue on the film is earned in those circumstances to be included in the film's individual-film-forecast-computation, which is discussed earlier. When that computation is applied to a television series of episodes, the series' multiple seasons are considered to be a single product.

ASC 926-20-35-2 is amended to include the new concept of a film group, which is defined above. It provides that a reasonably reliable estimate of the portion of unamortized film costs representing a film's use should be made for a film that is in a film group. Such amounts should be expensed as the film is exhibited or exploited. For example, if an entity that has a direct-to-consumer streaming platform without advertising on its platform produces a film that is only presented on its platform, and the entity receives subscription fees from third parties that are not directly related to a specific film. Estimates of ultimate revenue should be reviewed and revised as of each reporting date in order to present the most current available information. In addition, estimates of the remaining use of a film for film costs amortized in accordance with the guidance in ASC 926-20-35-2 should be reviewed and revised as of each reporting date to represent the current information. Changes to estimates of a film's remaining use should be accounted for prospectively.

Predominant Monetization Strategy

When an entity begins to capitalize a film's costs, it should determine whether a film is part of a film group by assessing whether it expects mostly to earn revenue on the film on its own or mostly with other films and/or license agreements.

If an entity significantly changes its revenue earning strategy for a film compared to its revenue earning strategy determined when capitalization of a film's costs began, the entity should reassess the predominant revenue earning strategy for that film. A reassessment of the predominant revenue earning strategy should include an assessment of that strategy over the film's entire life rather than an assessment from the time of the significant change in strategy. Two examples of a significant change in that strategy are (*a*) adding a previously unplanned significant distribution channel, and (*b*) abandoning a previously planned significant distribution channel. Results of the revenue earning strategy for a film that differ from the expected results, should not be considered a significant change to that strategy for the purpose of determining whether a significant change to the strategy has occurred.

The guidance on Episodic Film Series in ASC 926-20-35-9 through 35-11 has been superseded.

Impairment

Unamortized film costs should be tested for impairment whenever events or changes in circumstances indicate that the fair value of a film on which revenue is predominately earned alone or in a film group may be less than its unamortized costs. The following are examples of events or changes in circumstances indicating that an entity should assess whether a completed or uncompleted film's fair value is less than its amortized film costs:

1. An adverse change in a film's expected performance before its release.
2. Actual costs are substantially greater than budgeted costs.
3. Substantial delays in completion or release schedules.
4. Changes in release plans, such as a reduction in the initial release pattern.
5. Insufficient funding or resources to complete a film and to market it effectively.
6. Actual performance subsequent to release fails to meet expectations set before release as a result of factors such as the following:
   a. A significant adverse change in technological, regulatory, legal, economic, or social factors that could affect the public's perception of a film or the availability of a film for future showings
   b. A significant decrease in the amount of ultimate revenue expected to be recognized.
7. A change in a film's predominant revenue earning strategy that results in revenue being earned on the film with other films and/or license agreements.

The following are events or changes in circumstances for a film group that indicate that an entity should assess whether a film group's fair value is less than its unamortized film costs:

1. A significant adverse change in technological, regulatory, legal, economic, or social factors that could affect a film group's fair value.
2. A significant decrease in the number of subscribers or forecasted subscribers, or the loss of a major distributor.
3. An operating or cash flow loss in the current period combined with a history of operating or cash flow losses or a projection of continuing losses associated with the use or exploitation of a film group.

ASC 926-20-35-13 through 35-17 are amended by inserting (film group) after the word "film" throughout those paragraphs.

Allocating Impairment Losses to a Film Group

ASC 926-20-35-19 has been added to provide that only the carrying amounts of a film or a license agreement included in a film group should be reduced for an impairment loss attributed to that film group. The loss should be allocated to the films and license agreements within the film group on a prorated basis using the relative carrying amounts of those assets. However, if an entity can estimate the fair values of a film group's individual films and license agreements without excessive cost and effort, the carrying amounts of those films should not be reduced below their fair value.

Derecognition

ASC 926-20-40-4 has been superseded and ASC 926-20-40-5 has been added.

The remaining balances of unamortized film costs should be written off if a film is substantively abandoned.

Other Presentation Matters

ASC 926-20-45-1 has been superseded and ASC 926-20-45-2 has been added.

Film costs should be presented separately from rights acquired under a license agreement for program materials under the scope of ASC 920-350 on entertainment-broadcasters either on the balance sheet or in the notes to the financial statements.

Disclosure

ASC 926-20-50-1 and 50-3 through 50-4 have been superseded. ASC 926-20-50-1A and ASC 926-20-50-4A through 50-4C are added, and ASC 926-20-50-2 is amended

An entity's accounting methods for film cost should be disclosed, including, but not limited to the following:

1. Methods used to compute amortization.
2. A description of the unit(s) of account used to test impairment and the methods used to determine fair value.

The components of film costs (including released, completed and not released, in production or in development or reproduction) should be disclosed separately for films on which revenue is predominantly earned on their own and films on which revenue is predominantly earned in combination with other films and/or license agreements. The following information should be disclosed in the financial statements or in the notes to financial statements for each period for which an income statement is presented:

1. The total amortization expense for each period, separately for films that predominantly earn revenue on their own and films from which revenue is earned predominantly combined with other films and/or license agreements.
2. The income statement caption where amortization is reported.

The following information should be disclosed separately in the notes to the financial statements of the most recent annual period for which a balance sheet has been presented for films from which revenue is earned predominantly on their own and for films from which revenue is earned predominantly in combination with other films and/or license agreements:

1. The portion of completed and not released films that an entity expects to amortize during the upcoming operating cycle, which is presumed to be 12 months. If not 12 months, an entity's operating cycle should be disclosed.
2. The portion of the costs of released films recognized at the date of the most recent balance sheet that an entity expects to amortize within each of the next three operating cycles.

The following information about the impairment recognized for films or film groups should be disclosed in the notes to the financial statements that include the period in which the impairment is recognized:

1. A general description of the facts and circumstances leading to the impairment.
2. The total amount of impairment losses.
3. The caption in the income statement where the impairment losses are reported.
4. If applicable, the segment(s) under ASC 280 where the impairment losses are reported.

Implementation Guidance and Illustration

ASC 926-20-55-9 through 55-11 and their related headings are superseded, and ASC 926-20-55-12 through 55-15 are amended.

Example 4: *Episodic Television Series—Individual-Film-Forecast-Computation Method*

This example illustrates the individual-film-forecast method of amortization for a series of television episodes with multiple seasons in accordance with the guidance in ASC 926-20-35-1. The example is based on the following assumptions:

1. The entity produces and distributes a series of television episodes. Two seasons of the series are ultimately produced.
2. The entity's fiscal year end corresponds directly with the completion of each production season.
3. The production costs are as follows: (*a*) Season 1: $24,000, (*b*) Season 2: $27,000.
4. Ultimate recognized and remaining revenues are as follows:

As of Season 1	
Recognized and reported in Season 1	$12,000
Recognized and reported in Season 2	N/A
Remaining ultimate revenue Season 1	$60,000
Remaining ultimate revenue Season 2	N/A
	$72,000
As of Season 2	
Recognized and reported in Season 1	N/A
Recognized and reported in Season 2	$16,500
Remaining ultimate revenue Season 1	$60,000
Remaining ultimate revenue Season 2	$15,000
	$91,500

5. Ultimate participation cost are as follows:

As of Season 1	$3,000
As of Season 2	$4,500

Amortization of film costs in accordance with the guidance in ASC 926-20-35-1 is determined as follows for Seasons 1 and 2:

Season 1 $\frac{\$12{,}000^{(a)}}{\$72{,}000^{(b)}} \times \$24{,}000^{(c)} = \$4{,}000$

(a) Recognized and reported revenue during the current season.
(b) Remaining ultimate revenue at the beginning of the current season.
(c) Remaining unamortized film costs at the beginning of Season 1.

Season 2 $\frac{\$16{,}500^{(a)}}{\$91{,}500^{(b)}} \times \$47{,}000^{(c)} = \$8{,}475$

(a) Recognized and reported revenue during the current season.
(b) Remaining ultimate revenue at the beginning of the current season.
(c) Remaining unamortized film costs at the beginning of Season 2 ($20,000 unamortized as of the end of Season 1 plus the $27,000 cost of production in Season 2).

Accrual of participation costs is determined as follows:

Season 1 $\frac{\$12{,}000^{(a)}}{\$72{,}000^{(b)}} \times \$3{,}000 = \$500^{(c)}$

(a) Recognized and reported revenue during the current season.
(b) Remaining ultimate revenue at the beginning of the current season.
(c) Remaining unaccrued participation costs at the beginning of Season 1.

Accrual of participation costs is determined as follows:

Season 2 $\frac{\$16{,}500^{(a)}}{\$91{,}500^{(b)}} \times \$4{,}000 = \$721^{(c)}$

(a) Recognized and reported revenue during the current season.
(b) Remaining ultimate revenue at the beginning of the current season.
(c) Remaining unaccrued participation costs at the beginning of Season 2 (ultimate cost of $4,500 less prior cumulative accrual of $500).

Transition and Effective Date

ASC 926-20-65-2 provides the following guidance:

1. The guidance is effective for public business entities for fiscal years and interim periods within those fiscal beginning after December 15, 2019.

2. The guidance is effective for all other entities for fiscal years and interim periods within those fiscal years beginning after December 15, 2020.

3. Early application of the guidance is permitted, including early adoption in any interim period for:

   a. Public business entities for periods for which financial statements have not yet been issued.

   b. All other entities for periods for which financial statements have not yet been made available for issuance.

4. The guidance should be applied prospectively at the beginning of the interim period that includes the adoption date.

5. For the purpose of the transition guidance in 4., an entity should determine its predominant strategy for earning revenue on all of its existing films based on the predominant revenue earning strategy for a film's remaining life.
6. An entity applying the above guidance should disclose the following information in interim and annual periods of the year of adoption:
   a. The nature of and reason for the change in accounting principle.
   b. Transition method.
   c. A qualitative description of the financial statement line items affected by the change.

ENTERTAINMENT—BROADCASTERS—STATEMENT OF CASH FLOWS

Background

ASC 920-230 has been added to provide guidance to a broadcaster licensee regarding the cash flow statement classification of certain costs incurred for the rights acquired under a license agreement for program material. Guidance is also provided for the presentation of the amortization of license agreements' capitalized costs.

Scope and Scope Exceptions

The scope and scope exceptions in this Subtopic are the same as those discussed in ASC 920-10-15-2 and 15-3, which provide that the guidance applies to entities considered to be broadcasters, except for those who own the film or program material and should follow the guidance in ASC 926. The guidance in ASC 920 applies to all broadcaster transactions and activities, including network affiliation agreements.

Glossary

The following two definitions have been added:

Broadcaster

An entity or an affiliated group of entities that transmits radio or television program material.

License Agreement

A typical license agreement for program material (for example, features, specials, series, or cartoons) covers several programs (a package) and grants a television station, group of stations, network, pay television, or cable television system (licensee) the right to broadcast either a specified number or an unlimited number of showings over a maximum period of time (license period) for a specified fee.

Other Presentation Matters

Reporting Cash Flows

Broadcaster licensees are required to (*a*) report cash outflows for costs incurred to obtain the rights acquired under a license agreement for program material as operating activities in the statement of cash flows and (*b*) include the amortization of capitalized costs of license agreements for program material in a reconciliation of net income to net cash flows from operating activities.

ASC 920-350 Entertainment—Broadcasters—Intangibles—Goodwill and Other

Initial Measurement

ASC 920-35-3 has been amended to require that capitalized costs of rights to program materials be reported in the balance sheet at amortized cost or fair value, whichever is lower, based on an individual program, series, package, or daypart, which is defined as "an aggregation of programs broadcast at a particular time of day (for example, daytime, evening, or late night) or programs of a similar type (for example, sports, news, children's shows)." Broadcasters generally sell advertising on a daypart basis.

License Agreements for Program Material-Valuation

ASC 920-350-35-2A provides that if a license agreement accounted for under the scope of ASC 920-350 is part of a film group, as discussed in ASC 926-20-35-3B through 35-3C, it should be reviewed for impairment in accordance with the guidance in ASC 926-20-35-12 and 35-12B. A license agreement that is not part of a film group should be reviewed for impairment in accordance with the guidance in ASC 920-350-35-3. A write-off to the income statement may be necessary for the amount by which the unamortized capitalized costs of a program, series, package, or daypart exceeds its fair value if the programming's usefulness has been revised downward because it does not meet management's expectations.

Other Presentation Matters

License Agreements for Program Material

ASC 920-350-45-1 has been amended to require that an asset recognized for rights acquired under a license agreement for program materials be presented separately from films accounted for under ASC 926-20 either on the balance sheet or in the notes to financial statements.

Disclosure

License Agreements for Program Material

The following additional disclosures are required:

1. The methods of accounting for rights acquired under a license agreement, including, but not limit to, the following methods:
   a. The method or methods used to compute amortization
   b. For impairment, a description of the unit(s) of account used for impairment testing and the method(s) used to determine fair value.
2. The following information should be disclosed in the financial statements or in the notes to financial statements for each period for which an income statement is presented:
   a. The total amortization expense for the period
   b. The income statement caption in which amortization is reported.
3. For the most recent annual period for which an income statement is presented, disclosure in the notes to financial statements is required about the portion of the costs of license agreements recognized at the date of the most recent income statement that an entity expects to amortize within each of the next three operating cycles. It is presumed that an operating cycle is 12 months. If it is not, an entity should disclose its operating cycle.
4. The following information about impairment amounts recognized for a license agreement that is not included in a film group should be disclosed in the notes to financial statements that include the period in which impairment losses are recognized:
   a. A description of the facts and circumstances leading to the impairment
   b. The amount of impairment losses
   c. The income statement caption in which impairment losses are reported
   d. If applicable, the segment(s) under ASC 280 in which impairment losses are reported.

APPENDIX C

ASC 93X—EXTRACTIVE ACTIVITIES

CONTENTS

INTERPRETIVE GUIDANCE
ASC 93X—EXTRACTIVE ACTIVITIES
ASC 930: EXTRACTIVE ACTIVITIES—MINING
ASC 930-330: INVENTORY

ASC 930-330-05-1, 25-1; ASC 930-10-15-2 Accounting for Stripping Costs Incurred During Production in the Mining Industry

BACKGROUND

Mining entities remove waste materials from a mine in order to extract ore from the ground. The costs of removing waste materials from a mine are referred to in the mining industry as stripping costs. Those costs may be incurred while a mine is under development, as preproduction stripping costs, and after production has begun, as post-production stripping costs. Mining entities generally capitalize stripping costs during the development stage as a component of a mine's depreciable cost, which includes costs related to building, developing, and constructing the mine. Amortization of costs related to preproduction begins when production begins and continues over the mine's productive life. A mine's production phase is defined in this Issue as the period when production begins and revenue is earned from the sale of minerals, regardless of the level of production. Because of a lack of authoritative literature on the accounting for stripping costs after production has begun, there has been diversity in practice in accounting for those costs. Some entities have been expensing those costs, others have been deferring them, and still others have been capitalizing and amortizing stripping costs during production.

ACCOUNTING ISSUE

How should entities in the mining industry account for stripping costs?

ACCOUNTING GUIDANCE

Stripping costs incurred by mining entities involved in finding and removing wasting natural resources, other than oil-and gas-producing entities accounted for under the guidance in ASC 932, are variable production costs. Those costs should be included in the costs of inventory produced during the period in which the stripping costs were incurred. The term "inventory produced" as used here means "inventory extracted."

A mine's *production phase* as referred to in ASC 930-330-25-1 is defined in the ASC Glossary as follows:

> The production phase of a mine is deemed to have begun when saleable minerals are extracted (produced) *from an ore body*, regardless of the level of production (or revenues). However, the production phase does not commence with the removal of de minimis saleable mineral material that occurs in conjunction with the removal of overburden or waste material for the purpose of obtaining access to an ore body.

The guidance discussed above does *not* apply to the accounting for stripping costs incurred during a mine's *pre-production phase.*

ASC 930-360: PROPERTY, PLANT, AND EQUIPMENT

ASC 930-360-35-1 through 35-2; ASC 930-805-30-1 through 35-2 Mining Assets: Impairment and Business Combinations

BACKGROUND

Some mining entities have been excluding estimated cash flows associated with a mining asset's economic value beyond its proven probable (VBPP) reserves and the effects of anticipated fluctuations in the minerals' future market prices over the period of cash flows when testing such assets for impairment in accordance with the guidance in ASC 360-10 and in making the purchase price allocation of business combinations. Both VBPP and an estimate of the future market price of the minerals are generally included in a mining asset's fair value.

VBPP is defined in the SEC's Industry Guide 7 (Using Cash Flow Information and Present Value in Accounting Measurements) as (1) *proven reserves*, for which quantity is computed from certain dimensions, such as workings or drill holes; for which quality is determined from detailed samplings; and the geologic character of which is well defined because of the close proximity of the sites for inspection, sampling, and measurement and (2) *probable reserves*, the quantity, grade, and quality of which is computed based on information similar to that used for proven reserves, but the sites for inspection, sampling, and measurement are farther apart. The degree of assurance is lower than that of proven reserves, but is high enough that continuity can be assumed between the points observed. Proven and probable reserves are distinguished based on the level of geological evidence and the subsequent confidence in the estimated reserves. In addition to information about VBPP, the SEC also requires registrants to complete a feasibility study before accepting a registrant's statement that mining assets are proven and probable reserves.

The guidance below applies to mining entities—which include entities that find and remove wasting natural resources—other than oil- and gas-producing entities under the scope of ASC 932-10.

ACCOUNTING ISSUES

1. Should VBPP be considered when an entity allocates the purchase price of a business combination to mining assets?
2. Should the effects of anticipated fluctuation in the future market price of minerals be considered when an entity allocates the purchase price of a business combination to mining assets?

ACCOUNTING GUIDANCE

The following guidance applies:

1. VBPP should be included in the value allocated to mining assets in the purchase price allocation of a business combination in the same manner that a market participant would include VBPP in determining the asset's fair value.
2. The effects of anticipated fluctuations in the future market price of minerals should be included when the fair value of the mining assets is determined in a purchase price allocation. Estimates of those effects should be consistent with the expectations of marketplace participants—that is, available information, such as current prices, historical

averages, and forward pricing curves should be considered. The assumptions should be consistent with the acquirer's operating plans for developing and producing minerals and should be based on more than one factor.

The cash flows associated with VBPP estimates of future discounted and undiscounted cash flows should be included in the evaluation of mining assets for impairment under ASC 360-10. In addition, estimated cash flows used to determine impairment should include estimated cash outflows necessary to develop and extract the VBPP.

The effects of anticipated fluctuations in the future market price of minerals should be included when estimating discounted and undiscounted cash flows used to determine impairment under ASC 360-10. Estimates of those effects should be consistent with the expectations of marketplace participants—that is, available information, such as current prices, historical averages, and forward pricing curves should be considered. The assumptions should be consistent with the acquirer's operating plans for developing and producing minerals and should be based on more than one factor.

ASC 930-715: COMPENSATION—RETIREMENT BENEFITS

ASC 930-715-05-2, 25-1, 45-1, 50-1; ASC 450-20-60-18; ASC 715-60-60-4 Accounting for Estimated Payments in Connection with the Coal Industry Retiree Health Benefit Act of 1992

BACKGROUND

The United Mine Workers of America (UMWA) and the Bituminous Coal Operators' Association, Inc. (BCOA) established four trusts (1950 and 1974 Pension and Benefit Trusts) to provide pension and health benefits for coal industry retirees and their eligible dependents.

In response to the financial crisis confronting the 1950 and 1974 Benefit Trusts, a commission was appointed to study the funding problem. Based on the results of that study, Congress approved the Coal Industry Retiree Health and Benefit Act of 1992 (the Act).

The Act created a new private plan called the United Mine Workers of America Combined Benefit Fund (Combined Fund), which would provide medical benefits beginning in 1993 to all beneficiaries in the 1950 and 1974 benefit plans who were receiving benefits as of July 20, 1992. The Combined Fund is described by the Act as a multiemployer fund under the Employee Retirement Income Security Act of 1974 (ERISA).

All companies that were party to a coal wage agreement will be responsible for payments to the Combined Fund. Those payments will be based on a formula determined by the Act, which will include assignment of beneficiaries, a per-beneficiary premium, and a percentage of the cost of unassigned beneficiaries (who are referred to as orphans). The premium to be charged will be determined by using the July 1, 1991, cost per individual based on payments required by the 1950 and 1974 Benefits Trusts.

ACCOUNTING ISSUE

How should an entity account for payments required by the Act?

ACCOUNTING GUIDANCE

The following guidance applies:

- Entities currently involved in operations in the coal industry should account for their obligation under the Act as (1) a participation in a multiemployer plan (on a pay-as-you-go basis) or (2) a liability. Entities that choose to account for the obligation as a liability should recognize the entire obligation as a loss under the provisions of ASC 450.
- Entities *not* currently involved in operations in the coal industry should account for the obligation as a liability and recognize the entire obligation as a loss under the provisions of SC 450.
- Entities accounting for the obligation as a loss under the provisions of ASC 450 should report the estimated loss as an unusual or infrequently occurring item.
- Disclosure about the effect of the Act should include information about the estimated amount of the total obligation and the entity's method of accounting for it.

FASB STAFF COMMENT

A member of the FASB staff stated that companies should not include the obligation imposed by the Act in the cumulative effect of a change in accounting principle when adopting the guidance in ASC 715, because this obligation is the result of legislation rather than the result of changing to an accrual method to account for the costs of postretirement benefits.

ASC 932: EXTRACTIVE ACTIVITIES—OIL AND GAS

ASC 932-10: OVERALL

ASC 932-10-S25-1, S50-2, S99-5; ASC 932-815-55-1 through 55-2 Accounting for Gas-Balancing Arrangements

IMPORTANT NOTICE: In May 2016, the FASB issued ASU 2016-11, *Revenue Recognition (Topic 605) and Derivatives and Hedging (Topic 815): Rescission of SEC Guidance Because of Accounting Standards Updates 2014-09 and 2014-16 Pursuant to Staff Announcements at the March 3, 2016 EITF Meeting (SEC Update)*. ASU 2016-11 includes two announcements. In the announcement related to Topic 605, the Staff Observer of the Securities and Exchange Commission (SEC) reported that as a result of the FASB's issuance of the guidance in ASU 2014-09, *Revenue from Contracts with Customers*, the SEC Staff Observer comments on matters, which were codified in Topic 605, *Revenue Recognition*, and in Topic 932, Extractive Activities-Oil and Gas (see ASC 932-10-S25-1, S50-2, and S99-5 below for the SEC Observer comment related to the use of the "entitlement method," which was codified in ASC 932-10-S99-5) will be rescinded as of the effective date of the guidance in ASU 2014-09 (for public business entities in annual reporting periods that begin after December 15, 2017, and interim periods within those annual periods and in annual reporting periods that begin after December 15, 2018, for nonpublic entities).

BACKGROUND

Partners in a gas well may arrange to share in the gas well's production. One partner, Entity A, may decide not to sell its share of the gas production because it does not have a customer or market conditions are unfavorable. In that situation, the other partner, Entity B, may agree to take Entity A's gas production and sell it. At a future date, Entity A will have the right to take more than its share of the gas production to make up for the extra amount taken ("the overtake") by Entity B. Alternatively, Entity B pays for the overtake, either in cash or with gas from another well. Such transactions are known as *gas-balancing arrangements.*

The two predominant methods used to account for those arrangements are the *entitlements method* and the *sales method*. The entitlements method assumes that each unit of gas is jointly owned by the well's partners. In the above scenario, Entity B would recognize revenue from sales only to the extent of its proportionate share of the gas sold, recording a payable to Entity A. Conversely, Entity A would recognize a receivable and a sale for the overtake. Under the sales method, Entity B would recognize sales revenue for the entire amount, recognizing no payable to Entity A, which would record no receivable or revenue currently. Under the sales method, the partners track the imbalance by making memorandum entries. The partners may not use the same accounting method, because each partner makes that choice independently.

To illustrate the difference between the two methods, consider a situation in which Entity A has a 40% interest and Entity B has a 60% interest in a gas well. Production of the entire well during November is 6,000 MCF (thousand cubic feet) and the price is $1.50 per MCF. The allocation of gas production and revenue according to the terms of the partnership agreement would be as follows:

	Percentage Interest	*Gas Production*	*Revenue at $1.50/MCF*
Entity A	40%	2,400MCF	$3,600
Entity B	60%	3,600MCF	5,400
Total	100%	6,000MCF	$9,000

Entity A gives up its share of the November production to Entity B. The accounting under the entitlements method and the sales method would be as follows:

	Entitlements Method			*Sales Method*		
	Entity A	*Entity B*	*Total*	*Entity A*	*Entity B*	*Total*
Cash received	$0	$9,000	$9,000	$0	$9,000	$9,000
Receivable	3,600	0	$3,600	0	0	0
Payable	0	($3,600)	($3,600)	0	0	0
Revenue	$3,600	$5,400	$9,000	$0	$9,000	$9,000

ACCOUNTING ISSUE

How should participants in a gas-balancing arrangement account for the transactions?

ACCOUNTING GUIDANCE

Although practice for accounting for gas-balancing arrangements is not uniform, the question was referred to the AICPA's Committee on Regulated Industries because it is industry-specific and established practice exists.

EFFECT OF ASC 815

The terms of the arrangements discussed should be analyzed to determine whether an arrangement meets the definition of a derivative under the guidance in ASC 815. Even though the derivative may always have a zero value, the disclosures in ASC 815-30-50-1, would be required. Further, the option feature may not qualify for the exception for normal purchases and normal sales in ASC 815-10-15-13.

SEC OBSERVER COMMENT

Notice: As stated in ASU 2016-11, which is discussed above, the SEC will rescind the following comments when the guidance in ASU 2014-09, Revenue from Contracts with Customers, becomes effective.

The SEC Observer made the following comments:

- The SEC staff has not taken a position on which of the two methods is preferable.
- Under the entitlements method, the recorded receivable or liability should be valued at the lower of (*a*) the price at the time of production, (*b*) current market value, or (*c*) the contract price if there is a contract.
- Receivables should be recognized net of selling expenses.
- Registrants are required to disclose their accounting method and the amount of an imbalance in units and value, if significant.
- Management's Discussion and Analysis should include information about the effect of gas imbalances on operations, liquidity, and capital resources.

In addition, the SEC Observer noted that the same method should be used to account for gas imbalances consistently. An overtaker (Entity B) using the sales method that has insufficient reserves to offset the imbalance should recognize a liability for the shortfall at the current market prices; if a different price is specified in the contract, it should be used instead.

ASC 932-350: INTANGIBLES—GOODWILL AND OTHER

ASC 932-350-50-12 Application of ASC 350, *Intangibles—Goodwill and Other*, to Oil- and Gas-Producing Entities

QUESTION

Does the scope exception, related to ASC 932 in ASC 350-10-15-4 apply to the balance sheet classification of and disclosures about drilling and mineral rights of oil- and gas-producing entities?

ACCOUNTING GUIDANCE

The scope exception in ASC 350-10-15-4 applies to the balance sheet classification of and disclosures about drilling and mineral rights of oil- and gas-producing entities that account for their operations under the provisions of ASC 932.

Because the accounting framework of ASC 932 is based on the level of an oil- or gas-producing entity's established reserves, rather than on whether its assets are accounted for as tangible or intangible assets, the scope exception in ASC 350-10-15-4 also applies to the disclosure provisions for drilling and mineral rights of oil- and gas-producing entities. However, if they choose, entities are permitted to provide information about their drilling and mineral rights in addition to the information required to be disclosed under the provisions of ASC 932-235).

The above guidance should *not* be applied analogously to other items included in ASC 350-10-15-4.

ASC 932-360: PROPERTY, PLANT, AND EQUIPMENT

ASC 932-360-25-18 Accounting for Suspended Well Costs

BACKGROUND

The guidance below addresses the accounting for costs of exploratory wells by entities that use the successful efforts method of accounting discussed in the FASB Accounting Standards Codification® (ASC 932) and amends that guidance.

The question is whether there are circumstances in which an entity can continue to capitalize costs related to exploratory wells beyond one year, even if *no* additional exploratory wells are necessary to justify major capital expenditures and the wells are under way or firmly planned for the near future. The guidance in ASC 932-360-35-17 states that the costs of drilling exploratory wells can be capitalized while determining whether proved reserves have been found. If such reserves are found, costs that have been capitalized are recognized as part of the entity's wells, equipment, and facilities. Otherwise, those costs should be expensed, net of salvage value.

Sometimes reserves are found but cannot be classified as proved reserves when drilling is completed, because additional geologic and engineering information is required. In addition, other matters, such as government approvals, sales contracts, and financing must be resolved to verify with "reasonable certainty" that the reserves can be recovered under "existing economic and operating conditions"—that is, based on prices and costs at the date of the estimate. In the past, the accounting guidance in ASC 932-360-35-6, 35-13, and 35-16 through 35-20 has been followed under such circumstances. Under that guidance, at least one of the following conditions had to be met in order to capitalize costs of major capital expenditures in an area in which reserves could not be classified as proved reserves:

- A discovery that a well has sufficient reserves to justify making additional capital expenditures towards its completion as a producing well
- Drilling of additional exploratory wells is in process or firmly planned for the near future

Otherwise, exploratory well costs had to be expensed. Capitalized costs related to exploratory wells *not* under the scope of ASC 932-360-35-13 and 35-20 had to be expensed if reserves could not be classified as proved reserves within one year from the date drilling was completed.

The issue of accounting for the costs of exploratory wells was raised because the manner in which oil and gas companies are performing their exploration activities has changed from that originally contemplated in the guidance in ASC 932-360-35-13 and 35-20. Exploration activities now frequently occur in more remote areas, go to greater depths, and are undertaken in more complex geological formations than previously. As a result, some believe that there is a need to extend the one-year capitalization period in which an entity can determine whether found reserves qualify for classification as proved reserves.

ACCOUNTING GUIDANCE

An entity should continue capitalizing exploratory well costs if (1) a well has sufficient reserves to justify its completion as a producing well and (2) the entity is making satisfactory progress in evaluating the reserves and the project's economic and operating viability.

Amendment of ASC 932 The guidance in ASC 932-360-35-16 through 35-18 is amended based on the above guidance, which is provided in ASC 932-360-25-18 for reserves that cannot be classified as proved reserves when drilling is completed. The guidance in ASC 932-360-35-13, 35-16 through 35-20 also applies to exploratory-type stratigraphic wells.

ASC 932-360-35-13 provides that the value of wells should be assumed to be impaired if the criteria in ASC 932-360-25-18 that have been incorporated in ASC 932-360-35-16 through 35-20 are *not* met or an entity has information that raises doubts about a project's economic or operational viability. In that case, capitalized exploration costs incurred, less salvage value, should be expensed. Further, it is required that exploratory well costs *not* continue to be capitalized based on an expectation that economic conditions will change or that technology will be developed to make a project economically or operationally viable.

The following guidance in ASC 932-360-35-19 provides indicators that should be considered along with other relevant facts and circumstances in determining whether an entity is making enough progress in its evaluation of reserves and a project's economic and operational viability:

- Commitment of appropriate personnel with appropriate skills is being made
- Costs are incurred to assess the reserves and their potential development
- The economic, legal, political, and environmental features of a potential development are being assessed
- Sales contracts (or active negotiations) with customers for oil and gas exist
- Agreements (or active negotiations) with governments, lenders and venture partners exist
- Outstanding requests for proposals for the development of the required facilities exist
- Firm plans, established timetables, or contractual commitments exist
- There is progress on contractual arrangements to permit future development
- Existing transportation and other infrastructure that is or will be available for the project has been identified.

The guidance in ASC 932-360-35-19 provides that long delays in assessing progress or in a development plan may raise questions about whether an entity should continue to capitalize exploratory well costs after the completion of drilling. Justification for the deferral of well exploration costs becomes more difficult the longer that process continues.

Under the guidance in ASC 932-360-35-20, capitalized exploratory costs associated with a well, net of salvage value, if any, should be expensed if activities have been suspended or the entity has *not* participated in substantial activities to assess the reserves or a project's development within a "reasonable" time period after drilling has been completed. Planning to undertake activities in the near future is *not* sufficient to continue capitalization. Brief interruptions of activities, however, should *not* affect continued capitalization.

DISCLOSURES

Under the amendment of ASC 932 in ASC 932-360-25-18 management is required to apply more judgment than previously was required in evaluating whether capitalized costs of exploratory wells meet the criteria for continued capitalization. Consequently, the following required disclosures in the notes to the financial statements are intended to provide financial statement users with information about how management is applying that judgment. The disclosures are not required in interim financial statements unless previous information has changed significantly, for example, if exploratory well costs capitalized for more than one year after the completion of drilling are found to be impaired at the most recent balance sheet date. These disclosures are:

- The amount of capitalized exploratory well costs awaiting the determination of proved reserves
- For each annual period that an income statement is presented, changes in capitalized exploratory well costs as a result of
  - — Additions to wells awaiting determination of proved reserves
  - — Transfer of costs to wells, equipment, and facilities because proved reserves were determined
  - — Expensing of capitalized costs
- For exploratory well costs capitalized for a period longer than one year after the completion of drilling at the most recent balance sheet date
  - — The amount of such costs and the number of projects to which they are related
  - — An aging of the amount by year or by a range of years and the number of projects to which they are related
- For exploratory well costs that continue to be capitalized for a period longer than one year after the completion of drilling at the most recent balance sheet date
  - — A description of the projects and activities *undertaken* to date to evaluate the reserves and the projects
  - — Remaining activities required to classify the related reserves as proved reserves

ASC 932-835: INTEREST

ASC 932-835-25-2 Interest on Receivables and Payables: Accounting Interpretations of APB Opinion No. 21

> *IMPORTANT NOTICE:* The guidance in this Issue will be amended by the guidance in ASU 2014-09, *Revenue from Contracts with Customers*, which becomes effective for public business entities in annual reporting periods that begin after December 15, 2017, and interim periods within those annual periods and in annual reporting periods that begin after December 15, 2018, for nonpublic entities. ASU 932-835-25-2 will be amended to state that the guidance in ASU 606, Revenue from Contracts with Customers, will apply if an advance is in a contract with a customer.

BACKGROUND

ASC 932-835-25-2 provides implementation guidance for ASC 835-30.

ACCOUNTING GUIDANCE

Question: Under the guidance in ASC 835-30, interest must be imputed for some rights to receive or to pay money on fixed or determinable dates. For example, a pipeline entity may make an advance payment to encourage exploration. The intent is for this advance payment to be satisfied by the delivery of future production. However, if future production is not sufficient to discharge the amount of the advance payment, there is an obligation to pay cash to settle the obligation. Does the guidance in ASC 835-30 apply to such advances?

Answer: No. The guidance in ASC 835-30 does *not* apply to amounts that will not be repaid in the future, but rather to amounts that will be applied to the purchase price of property, goods, or services. The advance described above fits this exclusion even though there is an obligation to pay cash if future production is not sufficient to settle the liability.

APPENDIX D

ASC 94X—FINANCIAL SERVICES

CONTENTS

INTERPRETIVE GUIDANCE

ASC 942: FINANCIAL SERVICES—DEPOSITORY AND LENDING
ASC 942-310: RECEIVABLES

ASC 942-310-05-2, 35-1 through 35-4 Income Recognition on Loans to Financially Troubled Countries

BACKGROUND

Many bank loans to financially troubled countries meet the criteria for accrual of losses in accordance with the guidance in ASC 450. In those situations, banks should establish loan loss allowances by charges to income.

If a financially troubled country suspends interest payments, banks with outstanding loans from such a country should suspend the accrual recognition of interest income. Such financially troubled countries may later resume interest payments. Guidance on accounting by a creditor for the receipt of interest payments from a debtor that had previously suspended interest payments is included in the industry audit guide titled *Audits of Banks*.

ACCOUNTING GUIDANCE

When a country becomes current as to principal and interest payments and has normalized relations with the international financial markets, assuming the allowance for loan losses is adequate, the creditor may recognize interest on an accrual basis. Even if these conditions are met, the bank should not automatically return the loan to accrual accounting status. Some period of payment performance generally is necessary to make an assessment of collectibility before returning the loan to accrual status.

ASC 942-310-05-3, 25-2, 30-1 through 30-3, 35-5 through 35-7, 55-1 Accounting for Foreign Debt/Equity Swaps

BACKGROUND

Certain foreign countries, particularly those with rapidly developing economies, may experience periodic financial difficulties. These financial difficulties may call into question the ability of these countries to service debt that they have issued. As a method of dealing with these financial difficulties, foreign countries experiencing financial difficulties may permit U.S. lending institutions to convert dollar-denominated debt, issued by these same countries, into approved local equity investments.

Those foreign debt/equity swaps are generally structured as follows. First, holders of the U.S. dollar-denominated debt are credited with an amount of the local currency approximately equal to the amount of the outstanding debt. This conversion is performed at the official exchange rate, with a discount from the exchange rate imposed as a transaction fee. Second, the local currency credited to the lender must be used to make an approved equity investment—the currency can be used for no other purpose. Third, capital usually cannot be repatriated for several years. In some cases, it may be permissible to sell the investment. However, the proceeds from such a sale are generally subject to the same repatriation restrictions.

ACCOUNTING GUIDANCE

These types of foreign debt/equity swaps represent an exchange of a monetary asset for a nonmonetary asset. The transaction should be measured at its fair value on the date it is agreed to by both parties. Determining fair value for those types of transactions can be challenging. In some cases, the fair value of the equity investment received is unclear, and the fair value of the debt surrendered may be equally difficult to determine. It is not unusual for debt of foreign countries experiencing financial difficulty to be thinly traded.

Regarding the fair value of the exchange, both the secondary market value of the loan surrendered and the fair value of the equity investment/net assets received should be considered. The following factors should be considered in determining the fair value of the equity investment/net assets received:

- Similar transactions for cash
- Estimated cash flows from the equity investment or net assets received
- Market value (if available) of similar equity investments
- Currency restrictions, if any, that affect (*a*) dividends, (*b*) the sale of the investment, or (*c*) the repatriation of capital

If the fair value of the equity investment/net assets received is less than the recorded amount of the loan, the resulting difference should be reflected in income as a loss at the time the transaction is consummated. The amount of any resulting loss recognized should be charged against the allowance for loan losses and should include discounts, if any, from the official exchange rate that are taken as a transaction fee. This treatment is not affected even if some portion of the loan loss may have been due to changes in the interest rate environment (i.e., the fair value of the loan had declined due to an increase in interest rates). It is assumed that the causal factor leading to the debt/equity swap, which precipitates the loss, is the adverse financial condition of the foreign debtor.

Illustration of Loss on Debt/Equity Swap

Countries Bank, Inc., has a long-term $10 million dollar-denominated loan outstanding to the Mexican government. As a result of adverse financial conditions, the Mexican government is having difficulty making payments on the above loan. The Mexican government and Countries Bank have agreed to enter into a debt/equity swap. At the current exchange rate, 1 peso equals $.125; however, as a transaction fee, the exchange rate used for the swap is $.126. Therefore, Countries Bank receives 79,365,000 pesos in exchange for the $10 million of dollar-denominated debt (Countries Bank would have received 80 million pesos if the official exchange rate had been used; the difference is a transaction fee). Countries Bank will use those proceeds to purchase 50,000 shares of MexPower, a state-owned utility. MexPower is not publicly traded; however, a third party recently paid 140 million pesos for a 10% stake in MexPower (100,000 shares). The secondary market for the dollar-denominated debt issued by the Mexican government is thinly traded. Therefore, the fair value of this swap transaction will be measured by the fair value of the shares of MexPower received. Based on the recent cash transaction, the fair value of the MexPower shares received by Countries Bank is estimated to be 70 million pesos. In U.S. dollars, the fair value of Countries Bank's MexPower stake is $8.75 million (70 million pesos × .125). Therefore, Countries Bank will recognize a $1.25 million loss on this debt/equity swap ($10 million - $8.75 million).

OTHER ISSUES

With the exception of a discount from the official exchange rate imposed as a transaction fee, all other costs and expenses associated with the swap should be charged to income as incurred. Any discount from the official exchange rate has the effect of reducing the fair value of the equity investment received by the lender; therefore, such a discount is considered in determining the amount of any loss recognized by the lender as a result of the swap.

Because of the subjective nature of the valuation process, the fair value of the equity investment/net assets received might exceed the carrying amount of the loan. This apparent gain (or recovery of previous losses recognized on the loan) should not be recognized until the equity investment/net assets received are converted into unrestricted cash or cash equivalents.

A particular lender may have loans outstanding to a number of financially troubled countries. A loss recognized in a foreign debt/equity swap would be one piece of evidence suggesting that the allowance for loan losses, relating to loans outstanding to other financially distressed countries, should be increased.

ASC 942-320: DEBT AND EQUITY SECURITIES

ASC 942-320-55-1 through 55-2 Financial Institutions' Ability to Hold Mortgage Securities to Maturity

A policy statement issued by a federal regulator of financial institutions identified criteria for determining regulated financial institutions should consider mortgage derivative products to be *high-risk mortgage securities* that should be disposed of. That statement was later clarified to state that the existence of a bank examiners' authority to ask institutions to dispose of high-risk securities should not preclude institutions from classifying as held-to-maturity securities that are non-high-risk when acquired and when the institution has the ability and intent to hold such securities to maturity.

ASC 944: FINANCIAL SERVICES—INSURANCE

IMPORTANT NOTICE: At the request of stakeholders, the FASB has issued ASU 2019-09, *Financial Services—Insurance (Topic 944): Effective Date,* to extend the effective date of ASU 2018-12, *Financial Services—Insurance (Topic 944): Targeted Improvements to the Accounting for Long-Duration Contracts,* which will delay the effective date of the ASU's guidance for public business entities to fiscal years, and interim periods within those fiscal years that begin after December 15, 2021, except for entities that qualify for consideration as smaller reporting companies (SRCs) in accordance with SEC regulations. For all other entities, the ASU's guidance is effective for fiscal years that begin after December 15, 2023, and interim periods within those fiscal years that begin after December 15, 2024. Earlier application of the guidance is permitted for all entities.

ASC 944-30: ACQUISITION COSTS

ASC 944-30-25-1A through 25-2, 50-1, 55-1 through 55-1G Accounting for Costs Associated with Acquiring or Renewing Insurance Contracts

IMPORTANT NOTICE: As a result of the issuance of ASU 2014-09, *Accounting for Revenue from Contracts with Customers*, which becomes effective for public entities in annual reporting periods that begin after December 15, 2017, and interim periods within those annual periods and in annual reporting periods that begin after December 15, 2018, for nonpublic entities, the guidance in this Issue will be amended as follows: (1) ASC 944-30-25-1A(d) will be superseded; (2) ASC 340-20-25-4 will be amended and moved to become ASC 944-30-25-1AA; (3) ASC 340-20-25-5 through 25-18 will be moved to become ASC 944-30-25-1C through 25-1P, respectively; and (4) the reference to ASC 944-30-25-1A(d) in ASC 944-30-55-1F, will be replaced with ASC 944-30-25-1AA.

BACKGROUND

When insurance entities, which are discussed in Financial Accounting Standards Board (FASB) Accounting Standards Codification™ (ASC) 944, *Financial Services—Insurance*, acquire or renew insurance contracts, they incur certain costs (e.g., agent and broker commissions, salaries of employees who are involved in functions related to underwriting and policy issues, medical and inspection fees, and other costs) that are referred to as "acquisition costs" and defined in the Glossary of ASC 944 as costs "related directly to the successful acquisition of new or renewal insurance contracts." Insurance entities recognize as assets costs meeting that definition and refer to them as "incremental direct costs of contract acquisition," which are amortized over time in proportion to revenues based on a contract's estimated gross profit or on its estimated gross margin. Costs that are not related to the acquisition or renewal of insurance contracts and that do not vary with those contracts (e.g., for administration or costs related to investments) are charged to expense as incurred.

PRACTICE NOTE: The transition guidance in ASU 2010-26, *Financial Services—Insurance (Topic 944): Accounting for Costs Associated with Acquiring or Renewing Insurance Contracts*, included a one-time election to be made if an insurance entity's initial adoption of the guidance in ASC 944-30-25-1A of that ASU would result in the capitalization of acquisition costs that the entity had not previously capitalized. In that case, those entities were permitted to elect not to capitalize those types of acquisition costs. Entities had to make the election before fiscal years beginning after December 15, 2011. After the ASU's effective date would have been met by all the affected entities, the guidance related to the one-time election in ASC 944-30-25-1A was automatically deleted with the transition guidance. Subsequently, constituents asked the FASB to reinstate the guidance related to the election in ASC 944-30-25-1A so that entities that had made the election would be able to justify the accounting in case its appropriateness is questioned at a future date. That guidance was reinstated in ASU 2018-09, *Codification Improvements*.

SCOPE

The following guidance applies to insurance entities accounted for under the guidance in ASC 944 that incur costs in the acquisition of new and renewal insurance contracts.

ACCOUNTING GUIDANCE

The following is guidance related to the accounting for DAC:

- The entire amount of incremental direct contract acquisition costs incurred in transactions with employees or independent third parties should be deferred if the criteria for capitalization are met.
- Variable compensation paid to an employee should be considered part of the employee's overall compensation but only a prorated portion of compensation that is related to successful contract acquisitions should be deferred as DAC.

- DAC should include the following:
  - — Costs related to underwriting, policy issuance and processing, and medical inspection;
  - — For activities performed by a contract sales force, only the portion of an employee's total compensation and fringe benefits that are directly related to the time the employee has spent performing activities related to contracts that were actually acquired and other costs related to those activities that would not have been incurred had the contract not been acquired; and
  - — Medical and inspection fees paid to third parties that are related to successful contract acquisitions.
- Advertising costs should be capitalized only if they meet the requirements in ASC 340, *Other Assets and Deferred Costs*, for the capitalization of direct response advertising. If so, costs related to direct-response advertising should be included in DAC for the purpose of classification, subsequent measurement, and premium deficiency calculation in accordance with the guidance in ASC 944.

RECURRING DISCLOSURES

Insurance entities should disclose the following information:

- The nature and type of **acquisition costs** capitalized;
- The method of amortizing capitalized acquisition costs; and
- The amount of acquisition costs amortized for the period.

PRACTICE NOTE: ASC 944-30, *Financial Services—Insurance—Acquisition Costs*, has been amended in paragraph 59 of ASU 2018-09, *Codification Improvements*, by restoring to ASC 944-30-25-1A guidance about a policy election that was included in the transition guidance of ASU 2010-26, *Accounting for Costs Associated with Acquiring or Renewing Insurance Contracts*, and automatically removed when the ASU became effective. It was a one-time election that could be made when the ASU's guidance was adopted. If the initial application of the guidance would result in the capitalization of acquisition costs that were not previously capitalized, an entity could elect not to capitalize those types of costs. Stakeholders wanted the election to be included in the Codification in case the appropriateness of that accounting is questioned in the future.

ASC 944-80: SEPARATE ACCOUNTS

ASC 944-80-25-2 through 25-3, 25-12; ASC 944-80-65-1 How Investments Held through Separate Accounts Affect an Insurer's Consolidation Analysis of Those Investments

BACKGROUND

Some life insurance products (e.g., variable annuity contracts) provide an investment return and sometimes also insure mortality risk. Separate accounts, which are not separate legal entities and are similar to mutual funds, are established by insurance companies to: (1) help pass through investment return risk; and (2) protect the assets that back the separate account component of a variable interest annuity contract from the insurance company's general creditors if the insurance company were to become insolvent. Separate accounts are accounting entities controlled by an insurance company that holds 100 percent of the separate account's assets. The insurance company cannot make investment allocation decisions for contract holders, but it has certain rights (e.g., voting on behalf of the contract holders).

Some separate accounts are required to file standalone financial statements and are considered to be investment companies. Although separate accounts that hold a majority interest in a mutual fund generally do not consolidate the mutual fund in their standalone financial statements, it is unclear whether that treatment is appropriate. In addition, in view of the issuance of FASB Accounting Standards Codification™ (ASC) 810, *Consolidation* (FAS-160, *Noncontrolling Interests in Consolidated Financial Statements*), questions have been raised about the presentation of a noncontrolling interest if an investment was consolidated. Further, there are questions as to whether an insurer should combine its general account interest with its separate account interest in an investment in determining whether it has a controlling interest in the investment.

ACCOUNTING ISSUES

1. How should an insurer account for a majority owned investment in a mutual fund if the insurer's separate account holds a majority ownership interest?
2. If the conclusion is that an insurer should consolidate the mutual fund in issue 1, how should the consolidated mutual fund be presented in the insurer's financial statements?
3. How should an insurer account for a majority-owned investment in a mutual fund if its majority ownership is a result of a combination of interests held by its separate and general accounts, neither of which has a majority interest in the separate account on an individual basis?

SCOPE

The following guidance applies to an insurance company that holds a majority-owned investment in a voting-interest mutual fund through a separate account that meets all of the conditions in ASC 944-80-25-2 or through the combined interests of a separate account and a general account. However, the following guidance does *not* apply to an insurance company that has a majority interest in a mutual fund held through its general account.

The following guidance applies to investment funds that are considered to be variable interest entities (VIEs) under the guidance in Accounting Standards Update (ASU) 2009-17, *Consolidation (Topic 810): Improvements to Financial Reporting by Enterprises Involved with Variable Interest Entities*, which was issued in December 2009.

ACCOUNTING GUIDANCE

The following accounting guidance applies:

- An insurer that holds a majority interest in a mutual fund through its separate account or through a combination of its general and separate accounts is *not* required to consolidate the mutual fund if the general account does *not* hold a controlling interest in the fund on its own;
- An insurance entity that holds investments for the benefit of policyholders through its separate accounts should *not* be required to consider those investments as its own when applying the guidance in ASC 810-10, except if the holder of the separate account is a related party. In that case, the insurance entity should consolidate the separate account (ASC 944-80-25-3);
- If consolidation is required, an insurance entity should include: (1) the portion of a fund's assets that represent the contract holder's interests as separate account assets and liabilities in accordance with the guidance in ASC 944-80-25-3; and (2) the remaining fund assets, including those owned by other investors, in the entity's general account on a line-by-line basis (ASC 944-80-25-12);
- Noncontrolling assets should be classified as a liability or equity based on other guidance (ASC 944-80-25-12); and
- Entities with arrangements that are not separate accounts are prohibited from applying this guidance to other investments by analogy.

ASC 944-605: REVENUE RECOGNITION

ASC 944-605-25-9 through 25-11 Situations in Which ASC 944-40-30-16 and ASC 944-605-35-2 and 25-6 through 25-7 Permit or Require Accrual of an Unearned Revenue Liability

BACKGROUND

Under the guidance in FASB Accounting Standards Codification (ASC) 944-605-25-5, insurers are required to recognize revenue from universal life contracts in the period in which the contracts are assessed unless there is evidence that the amount assessed is for services that will be performed over more than one period. The guidance in ASC 944-605-25-6 through 25-7 states further that amounts assessed for services that will be performed in the future should be recognized as unearned revenue and recognized in income in the periods in which those services will be performed.

In the Basis of Conclusions section, the FASB argued against commentators' suggestions that revenue be recognized ratably over the life of a contract to show a "level pattern of service." The FASB's view was that revenue should be recognized according to a contract's terms and conditions, unless the substance of the agreement differs from the contract's terms. Here, the FASB stated again that amounts related to services that will be provided in the future should be deferred and recognized over the period during which the insurer will provide the service.

An assessed amount that is unearned would be assessed only in certain contract periods or in such a manner that the insurer would have current profits and incur future losses from a specific function of the contract. The FASB concluded that under those circumstances, specific assessments might result in the recognition of unearned revenue, but that it is necessary to consider the facts and circumstances of the particular situation to reach that conclusion. The issue of when insurers should recognize unearned revenue has been raised again because of diversity in the interpretation of ASC 944-605-25-8, which states:

> For a contract determined to meet the definition of an insurance contract . . . if the amounts assessed against the contract holder each period for the insurance benefit feature are assessed in a manner that is expected to result in profits in earlier years and losses in subsequent years from the insurance benefit function, a liability should be established in addition to the account balance to recognize the portion of such assessments that compensates the insurance enterprise for benefits to be provided in future periods.

The guidance in ASC 944-605-25-8 also can be interpreted as limiting the circumstances in which insurers are required to recognize unearned revenue to those in which current profits will be followed by future losses.

PRACTICE NOTE: In accordance with the guidance in ASU 2018-12, the guidance in ASC 944-605-25-11 has been moved to ASC 944-40-30-22A.

ACCOUNTING GUIDANCE

The FASB staff believes that insurers should accrue an unearned revenue liability for amounts assessed to contract holders that represent compensation for services to be provided in future periods and that the situation discussed in ASC 944-25-8 does *not* restrict the recognition of unearned revenue for insurance benefit features of universal life contracts to situations in which profits are expected to be followed by losses. The requirement in ASC 944-605-30-16; ASC 944-605-35-2; ASC 944-605-25-6 through 25-7 is that an unearned revenue liability be accrued for "any amounts that have been assessed to compensate the insurer for services to be performed over future periods."

The FASB staff also stressed the need to consider the facts and circumstances of each situation. Further, the staff noted that if the amount of an insurance benefit liability is determined according to the guidance in ASC 944-605-25-8, unearned revenue liabilities accrued in accordance with the guidance in ASC 944-605-30-16; 944-605-35-2; 944-605-25-6 through 25-7 should be considered. For that purpose, an increase in the unearned revenue liability during a period should be excluded from amounts assessed against a contract holder's account balance for the period, and a decrease in the unearned revenue liability during a period should be included in that period's assessment.

ASC 946: FINANCIAL SERVICES—INVESTMENT COMPANIES

ASC 946-10: OVERALL

ASC 946-10-05-3, 15-4 through 15-5, 55-22 through 55-23, 55-25 through 55-71, 65-1; ASC 323-55-2 through 55-5, 55-7 through 55-9; ASC 810-15-2, 55-6, 55-8 through 55-12 Clarification of the Scope of the Audit and Accounting Guide Investment Companies and Accounting by Parent Companies and Equity Method Investors for Investments in Investment Companies

NOTE: The FASB has decided to delay the effective date of the guidance discussed below for an indefinite period of time. Entities that opted to adopt that guidance before its effective date was delayed were permitted, but not required, to continue applying that guidance. However, entities that had *not* yet adopted the guidance are prohibited from adopting it, except that a consolidated entity must apply the guidance in its standalone financial statements if that entity was formed or acquired after its parent company had early adopted the guidance and it had decided to continue following it.

ASC 946-10-65-1 has been amended as follows:

> The effective date of the pending content that links to this paragraph is delayed indefinitely. An entity that early adopted that pending content before December 15, 2007, is permitted but not required to continue to apply the provisions of the SOP. No other entity may adopt the provisions of that pending content that links to this paragraph, with the following exception. If a parent entity that early adopted the pending content that links to this paragraph chooses not to rescind its early adoption, an entity consolidated by that parent entity that is formed or acquired after that parent entity's adoption of that pending content must apply the provisions of that pending content in its standalone financial statements. If an entity that early adopted the pending contact that links to this paragraph voluntarily rescinds its early adoption as permitted by this paragraph, that entity shall account for that change according to the provisions of Subtopic 250-10.

The guidance in ASC 810-10-25-15 continues to be effective for entities that did *not* adopt that guidance.

DEFINITION OF AN INVESTMENT COMPANY

An investment company is defined as follows:

- An entity whose business purpose and activity is to invest in various investments, such as the securities of other entities, commodities, securities based on indices, derivatives, real estate, and other forms of investments, for current income, capital appreciation, or both, and has exit strategies for its investments. An investment company does *not* acquire or hold investments for strategic operating purposes and does *not* get benefits from its investees that are *not* available to noninvestors that are *not* related parties to the investees. An investment company: (1) sells its capital shares to investors; (2) invests the proceeds to achieve its investment objectives; and (3) makes distributions to its investors in the form of cash or ownership interests in its investees, income earned on investments, and proceeds realized on investments that have been disposed of, less expenses incurred by the investment company; or
- An entity, including one in a foreign jurisdiction, that is registered or regulated so that it is subject to the requirements of the 1940 Act, the Small Business Investment Company Act of 1958, or similar requirements, and is required to report its investments at fair value for regulatory or similar reporting purposes. Such entities include: (1) management investment companies; (2) unit investment trusts (UITs); (3) small business investment companies (SBICs); (4) business development companies (BDCs); (5) certain offshore funds; (6) separate accounts of insurance companies; and (7) common (collective) trust funds. To determine whether an entity is subject to reporting requirements sufficiently similar to those of the 1940 Act or the Small Business Investment Company Act of 1958, regulations related to the following should be considered: (1) registration requirements; (2) reporting and disclosure to investors; (3) the investment manager's and related entities' fiduciary duties; (4) investment diversification; (5) recordkeeping and internal controls; and (6) purchases and redemptions of shares at fair value.

The determination of whether an entity meets the definition of an investment company should be made when the entity is formed and should be reconsidered in each reporting period.

Activities Inconsistent with the Definition of an Investment Company

The following factors should be considered in determining whether an entity meets the definition of an investment company:

Business purpose. Under the definition, an investment company's business purpose is to invest for current income, capital appreciation, or both. How an entity presents itself to other parties may provide evidence about its business purpose. The business purpose of an entity that presents itself as a private equity investor whose objective is to invest for capital appreciation is consistent with the definition of an investment company. However, the business objective of an entity presenting itself as an investor for strategic operating purposes is *not* consistent with the definition. An entity's prior history of purchasing and selling investments, its offering memorandum, and other corporate partnership documents may provide information about an entity's business purpose.

An entity's activities, assets, and liabilities. To meet the definition of an investment company's business purpose, it should have *no* substantive activities other than its investment activities and *no* significant assets or liabilities other than those related to its investment activities.

Multiple substantive investments. An investment company should invest in and hold multiple substantive investments directly or through another investment company. An entity that has equity investments in other entities should organize those investees as separate legal entities, except for temporary investments as a result of foreclosure or liquidation of the original investment. However, an investment company is *not* required to hold multiple substantive investments at all times (e.g., while completing the entity's initial offering period, while identifying suitable investments, or during an entity's liquidation stage) as long as the entity plans to hold various substantive investments simultaneously.

Exit strategies. The following should exist for each investment:

- A potential exit strategy has been identified, even though a specific method has not yet been identified, such as whether an exit will occur through: (1) a sale of securities in a public market; (2) an initial public offering of equity securities; (3) a private placement of equity securities; (4) distributions to investors of ownership interests in investees; (5) sales of assets; or (6) holding a debt security to maturity.
- The expected time for exiting an investment has been determined in terms of an expected date or a range of dates. It is based on a milestone, the entity's limited life, or an entity's investment objective.

Not for strategic operating purposes. Since investment companies are prohibited from holding investments for strategic purposes, the following relationships and activities are *not* permitted:

- Acquiring, using, exchanging, or exploiting an investee's or its affiliate's technology, intangible assets, or processes;
- Significant sales or purchases of assets between the entity or its affiliates and an investee or its affiliates;
- Joint ventures between the entity or its affiliates and an investee or its affiliates;
- Other arrangements between the entity or its affiliates and an investee or its affiliates for joint development, production, marketing, or provision of products or services;
- Other transactions between the entity or its affiliates and an investee or its affiliates: (1) on terms unavailable to parties unrelated to the investee; (2) at a price not available to other market participants at that date; or (3) that correspond to a significant portion of an investee's or the entity's business activity or that of their affiliates; and
- The entity or its affiliates have disproportionate rights, exclusive rights, or rights of first refusal to purchase or acquire in other ways an investee's or its affiliate's assets, technology, products, or services, held temporarily as a result of a default related to an investment in a collateralized security. However, a right of first refusal to purchase or acquire a direct ownership interest in collateral as a result of a default related to an investment in a collateralized security is *not* inconsistent with the definition of an investment company.

Factors to Consider

When considering whether an entity meets the definition of an investment company, all of the following relevant facts and circumstances should be considered.

Number of substantive investors in an entity (pooling of funds). The fact that an entity has many investors who pool their funds in order to benefit from the entity's professional investment management provides significant evidence that the entity's business purpose is to invest for current income, capital appreciation, or both.

Level of ownership interests in investees. The entity's level of ownership interests in its investees and the significance of the investees to the total investment portfolio should be considered. It is more likely that an entity with minor levels of ownership in its investees is investing for current income, capital appreciation, or both, rather than for strategic operating purposes.

Substantial ownership by passive investors. If a substantial amount of an entity whose purpose is to invest for current income and capital appreciation is owned by passive investors rather than by principal investors who determine the entity's strategic direction or run its day-to-day operations, it is a significant indicator that the entity is investing for current income, capital appreciation, or both, rather than for strategic operating purposes.

Substantial ownership by employee benefit plans. Ownership of a substantial amount of an entity by employee benefit plans is a significant indicator that the entity is investing for current income, capital appreciation, or both, rather than for strategic operating purposes.

Involvement in the day-to-day management of investees, their affiliates, or other investment assets. An entity's involvement in investees' day-to-day management activities is an indicator that the entity is investing for strategic operating purposes and consequently would *not* meet the definition of an investment company. However, an investment company may occasionally become involved temporarily in an investee's day-to-day operations if the investee is having difficulties and the investment company steps in to maximize the value of its investment. If that involvement continues over an extended period of time, it may be an indicator that the entity made the investment for strategic operating purposes.

Provision of loans by noninvestment company affiliates of the entity to investees or their affiliates. If an affiliate of an investment company that is *not* an investment company provides a loan to an investee or its affiliate, depending on the arrangement's terms and conditions, it may be an indicator that the investment was made for strategic operating purposes. However, if *all* of the following conditions exist, such a loan may *not* be inconsistent with the definition of an investment company:

- The loan's terms are at fair value.
- The loan is not required as a condition of the investment.
- The loans are not made to most of the entity's investees or their affiliates.
- Making loans is part of the usual business activity of an affiliate that is *not* an investment company.

Compensation of investee's or its affiliate's management or employees depends on the entity's or its affiliate's financial results. If the compensation of an investee's or its affiliate's management or employees depends on the entity's or its affiliate's financial results, it is an indicator that the entity has made the investment for a strategic operating purpose. Options granted to acquire stock are an example of such compensation.

Directing the integration of operations of investees or their affiliates or the establishment of business relationships between investees or their affiliates. An entity's involvement with an investee's or its affiliate's integration of operations or the establishment of business relationships between investees or their affiliates, such as the creation of joint ventures or significant purchases or sales of assets or other transactions between an investee and its affiliate, is an indicator that the investment was made for strategic operating purposes.

Although none of the factors discussed are individually determinative as to whether an entity meets the definition of an investment company, some should be given more weight than others when the definition of an investment company is applied. Specifically, the indicators related to the number of an entity's investees and an entity's level of ownership interest in its investees provide more significant evidence about an entity's business purpose than the other factors discussed.

ACCOUNTING BY PARENT COMPANIES AND EQUITY METHOD INVESTORS FOR INVESTMENTS IN INVESTMENT COMPANIES

An investment company under the scope of this guidance may be: (1) a subsidiary of another entity; or (2) an investor in an investment company that has the ability to exercise significant influence over it and accounts for its investment under the equity method of accounting.

Overview. A parent company or an equity method investor that chooses to retain investment company accounting in its financial statements may do so only if *all* of the following conditions exist:

- A subsidiary or equity method investee under the scope of the Guide meets the definition of an investment company.
- The established policies of a consolidated group of a parent company that chooses to retain investment company accounting in consolidation follows established policies that distinguish the nature and type of the investment company's investments from the nature and type of the investments made by other entities in the consolidated group that are *not* investment companies. At a minimum, those policies should address the following:
  - — The degree of the investment company's and its related entities' influence over the investment company's investees.
  - — The extent to which the investment company's investees or their affiliates are in the same line of business as the parent company or its related parties.
  - — The consolidated group's level of ownership interest in the investment company. The intent of this requirement is to prevent the consolidated group from selectively making investments in the investment company subsidiary that are similar to investments held by members of the consolidated group that are *not* investment companies and that would account for those investments by the equity method, consolidation, or the cost method.
- The purpose of the parent company's or equity method investor's investments are to earn current income, capital appreciation, or both rather than for strategic operating purposes.

The parent company or equity method investor (through the investment company) is investing for current income, capital appreciation, or both, rather than for strategic operating purposes. One of the requirements to retain investment company accounting in the financial statements of a parent company or an equity investor is that a parent company or an equity method investor should hold its investments for current income, capital appreciation, or both, rather than for strategic operating purposes. That requirement is *not* met if a parent company, an equity method investor, or their related parties have benefited or intend to benefit from relationships with their investees or the investees' affiliates that are not available to entities that are *not* investors and are *not* related parties to an investee. The following relationships or conditions violate that requirement:

- Acquiring, using, exchanging, or exploiting an investee's or its affiliate's technology, intangible assets, or processes.
- Significant sales or purchases of assets between the entity or its related parties and an investee or its affiliates.
- Joint ventures between the entity or its related parties and an investee or its affiliates.

- Other arrangements between the entity or its related parties and an investee or its affiliates for joint development, production, marketing, or provision of products or services.
- Other transactions between the entity or its related parties and an investee or its affiliates: (1) on terms unavailable to parties unrelated to the investee; (2) at a price not available to other market participants at that date; or (3) that correspond to a significant portion of the business activities of an investee or its affiliates, the parent company or equity method investor, or that of their related parties.
- An equity method investor or its related parties (not including insurance companies' separate accounts, trust funds, and other investments held by trust departments of financial institutions, and pension and profit-sharing trusts) have a *direct* investment in an investee or its affiliate enabling the investor to exercise significant influence over the investee or its affiliate.
- The parent company, equity method investor, or their related parties have disproportionate rights, exclusive rights, or rights of first refusal to purchase or acquire an investee's or its affiliate's assets, technology, products, or services in other ways.
- The parent company, equity method investor, or their related parties obtain tax benefits due to their ownership interest in the investment company and obtaining those benefits was a significant reason for making the investment.

Except for certain exceptions to be discussed below, a parent company or equity investor is considered to be holding an interest in an investee for strategic operating purposes, which results in a change in accounting, if transfers of investments, including, but not limited to, transfers made in exchange for cash or other consideration are made:

- From an investment company to its parent company, equity method investor, or to their related parties that are *not* investment companies; or
- From the parent company, equity investor, or their related parties that are *not* investment companies to the investment company.

The following transfers are the exceptions that would *not* lead to a conclusion that a parent company or equity method investor is investing for strategic operating purposes:

- Transfers in circumstances in which the investments and the effects of holding them would be reported in the same manner in the financial statements regardless of which party holds them.
- A transfer that is a pro-rata distribution of an investee's shares to an equity method investor in the investment company if: (1) the equity method investor is not able to initiate the distribution; and (2) the distribution of shares is a final liquidation of the investment company or the shares are publicly traded securities.
- Transfers that occur in rare situations between an investment company and its parent company, equity method investor, or their related parties if there have been: (1) significant changes in the facts and circumstances of the nature of the parent company's, equity method investor's, or their related parties' business activities that are unrelated to the investee or its affiliates; or (2) significant changes in the business activities of an investee or its affiliates that were *not* initiated or directed by the parent company, equity method investor, or their related parties so that retaining the investment in the investment company, parent company, equity method investor, or their related parties would lead to a conclusion that the investment company should *no* longer be accounted for under the Guide's scope.
- Immaterial and insignificant transfers in all respects, for example, in relation to: (1) a parent company's or equity investor's financial statements; (2) a parent company's or equity investor's interest in the investment company; and (3) the total investment portfolio of investment company subsidiaries and investees reported on the equity method.

Factors to Consider

The following factors should be considered in determining whether a parent company or equity method investor is investing in an investment company for strategic operating purposes:

- Involvement in the day-to-day management of investees, their affiliates, or other investment assets;
- Significant administrative or support services provided by the parent company, equity method investor, or their related parties;
- Financial guarantees or assets to serve as collateral provided by investees or their affiliates for borrowing arrangements entered into by the parent company, equity method investor, or their related parties;

- Compensation of an investee's or affiliate's management or employees depends on the parent company's, equity method investor's, or their related parties' financial results;
- Directing the integration of investees' or their affiliates' operations or the establishment of business relationships between investees or their affiliates;
- Active participation in an investee's or its affiliate's organization and formation; and
- Acquiring equity interests in an investment company in exchange for interests in investees.

GUIDANCE FOR EQUITY METHOD INVESTORS (THROUGH THE INVESTMENT COMPANY) THAT INVEST FOR CURRENT INCOME, CAPITAL APPRECIATION, OR BOTH, RATHER THAN FOR STRATEGIC OPERATING PURPOSES

Because an investment company may have a number of equity method investors, those investors should apply the guidance regarding the retention of investment company accounting in a parent company's or equity method investor's financial statements, based on their *own* facts and circumstances without regard to the relationships and activities of other investors in the investment company that are *not* related to the equity method investor. That is, some equity method investors in an investment may apply investment company accounting when applying the equity method in their financial statements while others may not. This guidance does *not* apply to investors that do not exercise significant influence over an investee, even though the guidance in ASC 323-30-S55-1, S99-1, and ASC 272-10-05-3 through 05-4; ASC 323-30-15-4, 35-3 provides that the equity method may be applied in certain situations in which an investor does not exercise significant control. Those investors should retain the specialized accounting for investment companies when applying the equity method to their investment in an investment company.

Changes in Status

An investment company's status as an entity that accounts for its transactions under the guidance in ASC 946 should be determined when the entity is formed. That determination should be reconsidered at each reporting period based on the guidance regarding the scope of ASC 946. If an entity's status changes (i.e., an entity previously not under the scope of the guidance in ASC 946 meets the requirements for investment company accounting or an entity that was under the scope of the guidance in ASC 946 no longer meets those requirements), the entity should adopt the appropriate accounting as of the date on which its status changed, rather than as of the reporting date. A change in status should be accounted for as follows:

- *Change from investment company accounting.* An entity that no longer meets the scope requirements under this guidance should stop accounting for its transactions in accordance with investment company accounting under the guidance in ASC 946 and report its changed status *prospectively* by accounting for its investments in accordance with other generally accepted accounting principles (GAAP) as of the date of the change in status using *fair value* as the carrying amount of the investments in conformity with investment company accounting *at the date of the change.*
- *Change to investment company accounting.* If there is a change in the status of an entity that previously had not met the scope requirements in this guidance to be accounted for in accordance with the guidance in ASC 946, the effect of the change in status, which is the difference between the carrying amounts of the investments in conformity with the provisions of ASC 946 and their carrying amounts in accordance with other GAAP should be reported as of the date of the change as an adjustment to retained earnings in the period in which the change occurred.
- *Disclosure of change in status.* All entities that experience a change in status should disclose that fact in their financial statements. However, entities that change to investment company accounting from other GAAP should disclose the effect of the change in status on the financial statements in the period in which it occurred, including the effect of the change on the reported amounts of investments as of the date of the change in status and how that change has affected net income, change in net assets from operations (for investment companies) or change in net assets (for not-for-profit organizations), and related per share amounts. When making their initial investment in an investment company, a parent company or an equity method investor should make their initial determination whether to retain investment company accounting for that investment in their financial statements. The provisions in this guidance regarding the retention of investment company accounting in a parent company's or an equity method investor's financial statements should be reconsidered at each reporting period and may result in a change in status. A change in status should be accounted for as follows:
- *Parent company no longer meets the requirements for retention of investment company accounting.* If after the initial determination that a parent company should retain investment company accounting for a subsidiary in its financial statements, the parent company no longer meets the requirements in this guidance for retention of investment

company accounting for *any* investment company subsidiary (or if an investment company subsidiary that previously had met the scope requirements under this guidance and had been consolidated in the parent company's financial statements no longer meets the scope requirements for investment company accounting under this guidance), the parent company should discontinue its retention of investment company accounting in its financial statements for *all* of its subsidiaries.

- *Equity method investor no longer meets the requirements for retention of investment company accounting.* If an equity method investor discontinues retention of investment company accounting in its financial statements for its investment in an investment company in accordance with this guidance after it had been determined that investment company accounting should be retained for that investee in the equity method investor's financial statements (or if an equity method investee that previously had met the scope requirements under this guidance and investment company accounting had been retained in the investor's financial statements for that investee no longer meets the scope requirements under this guidance for investment company accounting), the equity method investor should stop using investment company accounting to report its investment in *that* investment company and its equity method investments in *other* investment companies that meet both of the following conditions: (1) the equity method investor has the ability to exercise significant influence over the entity; and (2) the entity is managed by the same general partner, investment advisor, a party with an equivalent role, or a related party of that general partner, investment adviser, or party with an equivalent role for which investment company accounting is *not* permitted.

REPORTING A DISCONTINUANCE OF RETENTION OF INVESTMENT COMPANY ACCOUNTING

A parent company or an equity method investor that no longer retains investment company accounting for a subsidiary or investee in its financial statements in accordance with this guidance should report a change in status *prospectively* by accounting for its investment in accordance with *other* GAAP as of the date of the change in status, rather than as of the reporting date, and should report the carrying amount of the investment at *fair value* in accordance with investment company accounting at the date of the change.

- *Adopting retention of investment company accounting.* If after an initial determination that a parent company does *not* meet the conditions in this guidance for retention of investment company accounting in its financial statements for a subsidiary or an equity method investor for its investee, a change in a parent company's or equity method investor's circumstances may result in the conclusion that investment company accounting should be retained in a parent company's or equity method investor's financial statements in accordance with this guidance. In that case, a parent company or equity method investor should change to the appropriate accounting as of the date of the change in status and should report the effect of that change as an adjustment to retained earnings in the period in which it occurred. The effect of that change equals the difference between the carrying amounts of the investments in accordance with the provisions of the Guide and the carrying amounts of the investments (or assets minus liabilities or consolidated investments) in accordance with GAAP other than that in ASC 946.
- *Disclosure of a change in status.* All entities that have a change in status should report that fact in their financial statements. Parent companies or equity method investors that had initially determined not to retain investment company accounting for their subsidiary or investee in their financial statements and that due to a change in circumstances have started to retain investment company accounting in their financial statements should disclose: (1) the effect of the change in status on the financial statements in the period in which the change occurred; (2) the effect of the change on the reported amounts of investments as of the date of the change in status; and (3) the related effects on net income, change in net assets from operations (for investment companies) or change in net assets (for not-for-profit organizations), and related share amounts.

DISCLOSURE REQUIREMENT

Disclosures about a Parent Company's Retention of Investment Company Accounting

Parent companies should disclose the following information if investment company accounting is retained for investment company subsidiaries in the parent company's consolidated financial statements:

- Retention of investment company accounting in the consolidated financial statements.
- As of each balance sheet date, the carrying amount (fair value) and cost of the portfolio of investment company subsidiaries for which investment company accounting has been retained.

- Disclosures about significant transactions between the parent company or its related parties and investees of the investment company or their affiliates, including:
  - — The nature of the relationships.
  - — A description of transactions for each of the periods for which income statements are presented and other information considered necessary to understand the effects of the transactions on the financial statements, such as the amount of gross profit (or similar measure) from the transactions.
  - — The dollar amounts of transactions, such as sales and similar revenues, for each of the periods for which income statements are presented and the effects of a change, if any, in the method of establishing the terms of the transactions from that used in the preceding period.
  - — Amounts due from or to investees or their affiliates as of the date of each balance sheet presented and, if not otherwise clear, the terms and manner of settlement.
- Gross unrealized total appreciation and total depreciation of investments in the investment company's investment portfolio for each balance sheet date.
- Net realized gains and losses from investments in the investment portfolio of investment company subsidiaries for which investment company accounting has been retained for each year an income statement is presented.
- Net increase (decrease) in unrealized appreciation (or depreciation) of the investment portfolio (change in unrealized amounts during the year) for each year an income statement is presented.
- The policy for distinguishing the nature and type of investments made by the investment company from the nature and type of investments made by other entities within the consolidated group that are *not* investment companies.

Disclosures about an Equity Method Investor's Retention of Investment Company Accounting

Equity method investors should disclose the following information if investment company accounting is retained in the financial statements:

- Retention of investment company accounting for an investment company in the equity method investor's financial statements.
- As of each balance sheet date, the carrying amount (fair value) and cost of the portfolio of equity method investees for which investment company accounting has been retained. Amounts disclosed should correspond to the equity method investor's proportionate interests in the portfolios of its equity method investees.
- Disclosures about significant transactions between the equity method investor or its related parties and investees of the investment company or their affiliates, including:
  - — The nature of the relationships.
  - — A description of transactions for each of the periods for which income statements are presented and other information considered necessary to understand the effects of the transactions on the financial statements, such as the amount of gross profit (or similar measure) from the transactions.
  - — The dollar amounts of transactions, such as sales and similar revenues, for each of the periods for which income statements are presented and the effects of any change in the method of establishing the terms from that used in the preceding period.
  - — Amounts due from or to investees or their affiliates as of the date of each balance sheet presented and, if not otherwise clear, the terms and manner of settlement.

Disclosures Related to Changes in Status Related to the Scope of ASC 946

The following information should be disclosed if in accordance with this guidance there is a change in the status of an investment company's qualification to be accounted for under the scope of ASC 946:

- The nature of and justification for the change in status.
- The disclosures required under this guidance related to the scope of ASC 946.

Disclosures Related to Changes in Status Regarding the Retention of Investment Company Accounting in the Financial Statements of a Parent Company and of an Equity Method Investor

The following information should be disclosed in accordance with this guidance:

- The nature of and justification for the change in status.
- The disclosures required under this guidance related to the retention of investment company accounting in the financial statements of a parent company and of an equity method investor.

EFFECTIVE DATE AND TRANSITION

See the Note above.

ASC 946-605: REVENUE RECOGNITION

ASC 946-605-05-5 through 05-11, 25-4 through 25-7, 50-1 Application of "Distribution Fees by Distributors of Mutual Funds That Do Not Have a Front-End Sales Charge," When Cash for the Right to Future Distribution Fees for Shares Previously Sold Is Received from Third Parties

BACKGROUND

Mutual fund shares referred to as "B shares" are usually sold by a fund's distributor without a sales commission (front-end load) on purchase. Rather, the distributor usually receives an asset-based fee on such shares, known as a 12b-1 fee, which is charged to investors over a period of six to eight years (12b-1 period). In addition, investors that redeem B-shares before the expiration of the 12b-1 plan period usually are charged an asset-based fee, known as a contingent deferred sales charge (CDSC), which also may be referred to as a back-end load or a sales charge. The amount of that fee declines over time until the 12b-1 plan period has expired. Fees related to shares previously sold by a distributor are referred to here as "Rights."

The 12b-1 fees are calculated periodically as a percentage of net asset value. The CDSC is calculated as a percentage of the current net assets or the original cost of shares being redeemed, whichever is less. Both fees are intended to compensate a fund's distributor for costs incurred in the form of sales commissions to broker-dealers, and for other costs related to the distribution of mutual fund shares, such as advertising, marketing, and financing costs. A distributor is usually a subsidiary of a fund's sponsor, but is a separate entity so that the distribution function is separate from the fund's investment advisory function and its record keeping and transaction services functions. However, if a fund replaces its distributor, the original distributor continues to receive 12b-1 fees and CDSC for shares it has sold.

Distributors sometimes sell their Rights to third parties and receive lump sum cash payments. The agreements may include provisions to protect buyers on default as well as indemnities in case a fund's independent board decides to terminate its 12b-1 plan. Under the guidance in "Distribution Fees by Distributors of Mutual Funds That Do Not Have a Front-End Sales Charge" which is discussed below, distributors are *not* permitted to recognize revenues on fees until cash is received. However, that guidance does *not* discuss the accounting for the receipt of cash from parties *other* than investors or the mutual fund. Consequently, some distributors have accounted for sales of Rights to third parties as sales of unrecognized financial assets. Others have recognized revenue on the receipt of cash from a third party for sales of Rights. Still others have accounted for such transactions as loans.

ACCOUNTING GUIDANCE

Question: How should a distributor account for cash received from a third party for a sale of Rights?

Answer: A distributor should recognize revenue on a sale of Rights when cash is received from a third party if the distributor has *no* recourse to those Rights or any continuing involvement with them. That is, neither the distributor nor any member of the consolidated group to which the distributor belongs: (1) retains an excessive interest in the risks and rewards related to the Rights sold; (2) guarantees or provides assurances related to a purchaser's rate of return on the Rights sold; or (3) can restrict the ability of a consolidated group or a mutual fund's independent board to remove, replace, or subcontract any of the entities or individuals that provide services to the fund. Deferred costs, if any, related to shares sold by a distributor to which the Rights pertain should be written off to earnings in the period in which revenue on the sale of those Rights is recognized.

This discussion is *not* intended to provide guidance to mutual funds, investors in mutual funds, or third party investors that obtain the Rights regarding how to account for those Rights. Mutual Funds should follow the accounting guidance provided in ASC 946-20-05-4, 05-7, 25-3, 30-2 through 30-5, 35-2 through 35-4, 45-2, 50-3. No analogies should be made to this guidance when accounting for other transactions.

Basis for Conclusions

This guidance is based on the following concepts:

- *Revenue recognition* If a distributor has *no* recourse or continuing involvement with Rights that have been sold, revenue recognition is appropriate when the distributor receives cash for the sale of those Rights because there is no uncertainty about the amount the distributor will receive on the sale. A sale of Rights is *not* analogous to sales of software as some have suggested because a distributor's right to receive 12b-1 fees or CDSC does *not* require the distributor to perform additional services to receive those Rights, which result from past services.
- *Continuing involvement* Services to investors performed by other members of a mutual fund's consolidated group are distinct and separable from a distributor's services and are *not* affected by the distributor's sale of Rights. However, a distributor maintains a continuing involvement if an arrangement includes the following provisions: (*a*) the distributor or any member of its consolidated group is required to perform future services in connection with the sale of the Rights, including actual or expected performance of a separate service with separate pricing that is a direct result of the transaction between the distributor and the buyer of the Rights, and (*b*) the distributor or any member of its consolidated group is permitted to participate in future risks or rewards in the Rights that are not proportionate to the portion of the Rights sold, for example, retention of risks or rewards of 60% when only 50% of the Rights have been sold.
- *Recourse* A distributor or its consolidated group would have recourse to a buyer that would preclude revenue recognition if an arrangement includes the following provisions:
  - — The consolidated group must make a payment to the buyer if its independent board decides to change the nature of the Rights, for example, provisions related to the computation of fees and the timing of payments
  - — The consolidated group must make a payment to the buyer if its independent board decides to change service providers such as the distributor, advisor, or transfer agent
  - — The arrangement includes provisions that protect the buyer from risks related to fluctuations in a mutual fund's net asset value or to legal or regulatory risks that might result in termination of the 12b-1 plan
  - — The arrangement restricts changes in a fund's investment objectives in accordance with the fund's prospectus or similar restrictions

Separate-Company Financial Statements

Revenue recognition in a distributor's separate-company financial statements is not affected if any member of the consolidated group that includes the distributor has a continuing involvement with a buyer as a result of the retention of a proportionate or pro rata interest. The provisions of this guidance apply to the determination of revenue recognition in a distributor's separate-company financial statements. For example, a distributor should recognize revenue in its separate-company financial statements when receiving cash from an arrangement in which a distributor transfers all or a pro rata interest in Rights to a member of its consolidated group that is *not* the distributor's subsidiary.

ASC 946-605-25-8 Distribution Fees by Distributors of Mutual Funds That Do Not Have a Front-End Sales Charge

> ***IMPORTANT NOTICE:*** As a result of the issuance of ASU 2014-09, *Accounting for Revenue from Contracts with Customers*, which becomes effective for public entities in annual reporting periods that begin after December 15, 2017, and interim periods within those annual periods and in annual reporting periods that begin after December 15, 2018, for nonpublic entities, the guidance ASC 946-605-25-8 will be moved to ASC 946-720-25-4 and will be amended to state that distributors of mutual funds that do not have a front-end load should expense the indirect costs when incurred.

BACKGROUND

Under Rule 12b-1 of the Investment Company Act of 1940, an investment company that sponsors a mutual fund can adopt a plan, known as a 12b-1 plan, which permits it to finance the cost of distributing its mutual fund's shares with the fund's assets, rather than charging a fee (front-end load) to investors when they purchase shares. Funds that have adopted such plans are known as no-load funds.

The fund usually enters into an agreement with a distributor, under which the distributor is paid a fee based on either an annual percentage of the fund's average net assets or an annual percentage of the fund's average net assets limited to actual costs incurred. Although distribution agreements usually continue from year to year, under the rules of a 12b-1 plan the agreement must be approved annually by the investment company's directors and may be terminated at any time with no penalty to the fund.

Because investors do not pay a front-end load, they are required to pay a contingent-deferred sales load (back-end load), which is a sales charge based on a percentage of the redemption proceeds or original cost, whichever is less, if the shares are held for less than a specified period. The percentage decreases (usually by 1% a year) until it is eliminated. The fee is deducted from the shareholder's proceeds on redemption and is paid to the distributor, even if the distribution agreement has been terminated.

When this Issue was discussed in 1985, distributors of mutual fund shares were recognizing distribution fees in income when they were received. Incremental direct costs related to distribution activities, such as sales commissions, were deferred and amortized over six years (the period shareholders would have to hold shares without incurring a fee on redemption). All other distribution costs were expensed as incurred. Because this method resulted in the deferral of a large amount of costs to future accounting periods (so they could be matched with future revenues), some in the industry suggested recognizing the discounted amount of the distribution fee in the period in which shares are sold.

ACCOUNTING ISSUE

Should fees that are expected to be received over a specified future period be recognized at a discounted amount when shares are sold, together with all related distribution costs, or on receipt with deferral of incremental direct costs?

ACCOUNTING GUIDANCE

Distributors should continue to recognize fees on receipt, defer incremental direct costs, and expense indirect costs when they are incurred.

DISCUSSION

The guidance is based on the conservative approach of recognizing revenue when a fee is realized and earned, which is consistent with the guidance in Statement of Financial Concepts No. 5, *Recognition and Measurement in Financial Statements of Business Enterprises*, (not included in the ASC).

ASC 946-830: FOREIGN CURRENCY MATTERS

ASC 946-830-05-1 through 05-2, 50-1 through 50-4, 55-1 through 55-8, 55-10 through 55-16, 45-1 through 45-5, 45-7 through 45-12, 45-14, 45-22 through 45-23, 45-25 through 45-29, 45-31, 45-34 through 45-39 Foreign Currency Accounting and Financial Statement Presentation for Investment Companies

BACKGROUND

A number of U.S. investment companies offer closed-end single-country funds (e.g., the Germany Fund). Those funds typically adopt the U.S. dollar as their functional currency, even though many of the transactions of the fund are denominated in a different currency (e.g., the mark for the Germany Fund). The U.S. dollar is typically adopted as the functional currency because sales, redemptions, and dividends are paid to shareholders in U.S. dollars.

This pronouncement is designed to provide guidance to investment companies in computing and reporting foreign currency gains and losses in two types of investment transactions: (1) transactions involving securities denominated in or expected to be settled in a currency other than the U.S. dollar, and (2) investments in a currency other than the U.S. dollar. This Statement also provides guidance in handling other transactions (e.g., receivables and payables) denominated in a currency other than the U.S. dollar.

ACCOUNTING GUIDANCE

Scope

The provisions of this pronouncement apply to all investment companies subject to the provisions of ASC 946-830, Financial Services-Investment Companies. If a single-country fund invests in a country that is classified as "highly inflationary" in accordance with the guidance in ASC 830-10-45-11, the measurement and disclosure guidelines in this pronouncement may not apply.

PRACTICE POINTER: This pronouncement does not specify the measurement and disclosure guidelines to follow if a single-country fund invests in a country classified as "highly inflationary." However, it seems reasonable to adapt the guidance on "highly inflationary" economies discussed in ASC 830 to the accounting for the single-country fund.

General Conclusions

The following conditions can give rise to a foreign currency gain or loss:

- The value of securities held, based on current exchange rates, differs from the securities cost.
- The amount of a receivable or payable at the transaction date differs from the amount ultimately received or paid upon settlement, or differs from the amount receivable or payable at the reporting date based on current exchange rates.
- The amount of interest, dividends, and withholding taxes at the transaction date differs from the amount ultimately received or paid, or differs from the amount receivable or payable at the reporting date based on current exchange rates.
- Expenses accrued at the transaction date(s) differ from the amount ultimately paid, or differ from the amount payable at the reporting date based on current exchange rates.
- Forward exchange contracts or foreign exchange futures contracts need to be marked to market.

All of those conditions result from changes in the exchange rate between the U.S. dollar and the foreign currency applicable to the fund. Before the settlement date of the transaction, a revaluation of securities, receivables, payables, etc., is classified as an unrealized gain or loss. When the transaction is settled (the cash flow occurs), the gain or loss is realized.

Differences between the amounts that were originally recorded and the amounts at which transactions are settled, or the amounts at which unsettled transactions are measured on the reporting date (based on the current exchange rate), are a function of changes in the exchange rate and changes in market prices. In recording the original transaction, the transaction at settlement, and the unsettled transaction at a reporting date, the reporting currency is used (i.e., typically the U.S. dollar).

The two components of gain/loss identified in the previous paragraph (changes in exchange rates and changes in market prices) must be separately identified, computed, and reported for all transactions other than for investments. Entities can choose to separately disclose the two components of gain/loss for investment transactions, or to combine these two elements.

Investments—Purchased Interest

Interest-bearing securities are often purchased between coupon dates. Accrued interest since the last coupon date is included in the purchase price of the security. The purchaser should recognize this accrued interest as interest receivable, measured on the basis of the spot exchange rate on the transaction date. If a reporting date intervenes before the purchased interest is received, the interest receivable is measured at the reporting date on the basis of the spot exchange rate on that date. After the settlement date, interest should be accrued on a daily basis using each day's spot exchange rate. If the exchange rate is relatively stable, however, interest can be accrued either weekly or monthly.

Illustration of the Accrual of Interest—Stable Exchange Rate

New Millennium Foreign Fund, a single-country closed-end fund, purchases an investment grade corporate bond for 1,000,000FC on December 1, 20X4. The interest rate is 8%, and the investment is purchased at face value. The semiannual interest payment dates are September 1 and March 1. The exchange rate at December 1, 20X4, is $.58 per FC. This transaction would be recorded at December 1, 20X4 (in the fund's functional currency, the U.S. dollar), as follows:

Investment in Corporate Debt (1,000,000 × $.58)	$580,000	
Interest Receivable (1,000,000 × .08 × 3/12 × $.58)	11,600	
Cash		$591,600

The exchange rate is relatively stable during December. New Millennium will accrue interest at December 31, 20X4, using the average exchange rate for December ($.57 per FC). The appropriate journal entry is as follows:

Interest Receivable (1,000,000 × .08 × 1/12 × $.57)	$3,800	
Interest Income		$3,800

Investments—Marking to Market

As discussed previously, due to changes in both exchange rates and market values, the market value of a security at a valuation date (a reporting date) may differ from the amount at which the security was originally recorded on the transaction date. The two components of any unrealized gain or loss on securities *do not* have to be separately reported. However, the guidance in this pronouncement indicates that in many cases such separate reporting would provide valuable information to users of the fund's financial statements.

The two components—changes in exchange rates and changes in market prices—of any unrealized gains or losses can be computed as follows:

Unrealized foreign currency gain or loss

(Cost in foreign currency × Valuation date spot rate) - Cost in functional currency

Unrealized market value appreciation or depreciation

(Market value in foreign currency -Original cost in foreign currency) × Valuation date spot rate

In the above computations, weekly or monthly average exchange rates can be used if daily fluctuations in exchange rates are not significant. Also, if an entity holds a short-term security that is being carried at amortized cost, amortized cost should be substituted for market value in the above formulas.

Illustration of the Computation of Unrealized Gain

The New Millennium Foreign Fund purchases 1,000 shares of WMB Motors on December 1, 20X4, at a price of 40FC per share. The exchange rate on December 1, 20X4, is $.58 per FC. On December 31, 20X4, the market price of WMB Motors is 41FC per share, and the average exchange rate during December was $.57 (the exchange rate was relatively stable during the month). The two components of the unrealized gain recognized by New Millennium would be computed as follows:

Unrealized foreign currency gain or loss

(1,000 shares × 40FC per share × $.57) - (1,000 shares × 40FC per share × $.58) = ($400)

Unrealized market value appreciation or depreciation

[(1,000 shares × 41FC per share) - (1,000 shares × 40FC per share)] × $.57 = $570

PROOF:

(1,000 shares × 41FC per share × $.57) - (1,000 shares × 40FC per share × $.58) = $170

This proof is based on the following formula: (Market value in foreign currency × Valuation date spot rate) - (Cost in foreign currency × Transaction date spot rate)

Investments—Sale

A realized gain or loss on a security sale has two components: a realized exchange gain or loss and a realized market gain or loss. However, separately computing and displaying these two components is *optional*. If the entity chooses to report both pieces of the realized gain or loss, these amounts would be computed as follows:

Realized foreign currency gain or loss

(Cost in foreign currency × Sale date spot rate) - Cost in functional currency

Realized market gain or loss

(Sale proceeds in foreign currency -Original cost in foreign currency) × Sale date spot rate

Upon the sale of securities, a receivable is recorded based on the exchange rate on the trade date. Any change in the exchange rate between the trade date and the settlement date will be recognized as a gain or loss when the trade is settled.

Investments—Sale of Interest

An entity may sell an interest-bearing security between coupon dates. The difference between the recorded interest receivable and the foreign currency received, translated into the functional currency at the current exchange rate, represents a realized gain or loss.

Income—Interest

Interest on a security denominated in a foreign currency is to be accrued daily. First the interest is measured in the foreign currency, and then it is converted into the functional currency using the daily spot exchange rate. If the exchange rate is relatively stable, this calculation can be based on the average weekly or monthly exchange rate.

Interest receivable, which includes both accrued interest and purchased interest, is initially measured in the foreign currency. At the valuation date (which may be daily), the receivable is converted into the functional currency using the current exchange rate. The difference between the interest receivable, converted at the spot exchange date on the valuation date, and interest accrued in the foreign currency is the unrealized foreign currency gain or loss.

Income—Accretion and Amortization

Bonds are often purchased at a premium or a discount. Any such premium or discount should initially be amortized daily on a foreign currency basis. At maturity, the carrying value of the bond in the foreign currency will equal the foreign currency proceeds received. However, in most cases there will be a realized foreign currency gain or loss.

The purchase price of the bond, at the trade date, is converted into the entity's functional currency using that day's exchange rate. Daily amortization of discount or premium, in the entity's foreign currency, is converted into functional currency using the daily exchange rate (again, if exchange rates are relatively constant, a weekly or monthly average rate can be used). The sum of the purchase price of the bond (converted into functional currency on the trade date) plus (minus) amortization of the discount (premium) over the life of the bond (converted into functional currency at periodic spot rates) will produce the carrying value of the bond in the entity's functional currency. The proceeds received upon the expiration of the bond (its face value in foreign currency) is to be converted into the entity's functional currency using the exchange rate in effect on the maturity date. In most cases, the proceeds in functional currency will differ from the carrying value of the bond in functional currency. This is what gives rise to a foreign currency gain or loss.

Illustration of the Computation of a Foreign Currency Gain—Bond Expiration

The New Millennium Germany Fund purchased a 25,000,000 mark bond on October 1, 20X4, at 97%. The exchange rate on this date was $.56 per mark. The carrying value of this bond in U.S. dollars, the functional currency, on October 1, 20X4, is $13,580,000 (25,000,000 marks × 97% × $.56). Over the remaining life of this bond, New Millennium must amortize the discount of 750,000 marks. Based on the spot rates in effect when this discount was amortized, the functional currency amount of the discount amortization was $412,500. The spot exchange rate is $.59 on the bond's due date. Therefore, on the bond's due date the New Millennium Germany Fund will receive 25,000,000 marks, which is convertible into $14,750,000 (25,000,000 marks × $.59). The carrying value of the bond in U.S. dollars is $13,992,500 ($13,580,000 + $412,500). Therefore, New Millennium would have a realized foreign currency gain of $757,500.

Dividends

Dividend income on securities denominated in a foreign currency is to be recognized on the ex-dividend date. The amount of the dividend in foreign currency is to be converted into functional currency using the exchange rate on that date (DR, Dividend Receivable; CR, Dividend Income). The related Dividend Receivable account is to be translated daily at the spot exchange rate; differences that arise as a result of this process are unrealized gains or losses. When the dividend is received, the unrealized gain or loss account is reclassified as realized gain or loss.

Withholding Tax

In some cases, taxes are withheld from investment and dividend income at the source. These withheld amounts may or may not be reclaimable by the fund. If the tax withheld is not reclaimable, it should be accrued on each income recognition date if the tax rate is fixed and known. If the tax withheld is reclaimable, it should be recorded as a receivable and not as an expense. If the tax rate is not known or estimable, the expense (when the tax is not reclaimable) or the receivable (when the tax is reclaimable) is recorded on the date the (net) investment income is received. When the net investment income is received, the realized foreign currency gain or loss is computed on the gross income receivable and the accrued tax expense.

Expenses

Expenses should be accrued as incurred and translated into the functional currency using the exchange rate on the day the expense is incurred. The difference between the expense accrued in the functional currency and the related foreign currency accrued expense balance (a liability) translated into the functional currency using the exchange rate on the valuation date is the unrealized foreign currency gain or loss. When the expense is paid, the unrealized foreign currency gain or loss is reclassified as a realized gain or loss.

Receivables and Payables

Receivables and payables typically arise to record items of income and expense and to record the purchase or sale of securities. At each valuation date, all receivables and payables should be translated into the functional currency using the exchange rate on the valuation date. In most cases, there will be a difference between the amount of the receivable or payable translated at the valuation date and the functional currency amount that was recorded at various spot rates for income or expense items (or for purchases and sales of securities on different dates). This difference is an unrealized gain or loss. When a receivable or payable is settled, the difference between the amount received or paid (in functional currency) and the functional currency amount that was recorded at various spot rates for income or expense items (or for purchases and sales of securities on different dates) is a realized gain or loss.

Illustration of the Computation of a Foreign Currency Loss—Payables

The New Millennium Foreign Fund incurs the following expenses during December 20X4: 10,000FC on 12/7; 11,000FC marks on 12/14; 12,000FC on 12/21; and 13,000FC on 12/28. The spot exchange rates on these dates are $.55, $.59, $.57, and $.58, respectively. Therefore, the functional currency value of these expenses is $26,370 [(10,000FC × $.55) + (11,000FC × $.59) + (12,000FC × $.57) + (13,000FC × $.58)]. The exchange rate on December 31, 20X4, is $.58. Also, these expenses represent the December 31, 20X4, accrued expense balance. New Millennium's accrued expense balance, in its functional currency, is $26,680 at year-end. Therefore, New Millennium would have an unrealized (the liability is not yet settled) foreign currency loss of $310 ($26,680-$26,370).

Cash

Receipts of foreign currency (cash) are to be treated as if a foreign currency denominated security had been purchased. The foreign currency received is to be converted into the functional currency using the exchange rate on the day the cash is received. Every disbursement of foreign currency is to be treated as if a security had been sold. The functional equivalent of the foreign currency disbursed is to be credited (using specific identification, FIFO, or average cost to determine the amount of the functional currency to be released).

The acquisition of foreign currency does not result in a gain or loss. However, the disposition of foreign currency typically does result in a gain or loss. The gain or loss is measured as the difference between the functional currency equivalent on the date the foreign currency was acquired and the functional currency equivalent on the date the foreign currency is disbursed.

The functional currency equivalent of foreign currency held is to be computed on each valuation date. Any difference between this amount and the functional currency equivalent of the foreign currency on the date it was acquired is an unrealized gain or loss.

Forward Exchange Contracts

A *forward exchange contract* is an agreement between two parties to exchange two currencies at a specified rate on a specified date in the future. If a fund enters into a forward exchange contract, the contract is to be initially recorded at the forward rate and marked to market on a daily basis.

Unrealized gain or loss on these contracts is computed as follows: the foreign currency amount valued at the valuation date forward rate minus the amount to be received or paid at the settlement date. On the settlement date, the unrealized gain or loss is reclassified as realized gain or loss.

Financial Statement Presentation

A section of the Statement of Operations is titled "Realized and Unrealized Gain (Loss) from Investments and Foreign Currency." This section follows the presentation of investment income and investment expenses. All foreign currency gains and losses should be reported in this section. Gains or losses from non-investment transactions would have their own line item in the Statement: "Foreign currency transactions" (with separate line items for realized and unrealized gains and losses). If foreign currency gains and losses from investment transactions are computed separately, these amounts would be included in the line item "Foreign currency transactions" as well. If foreign currency gains and losses from investment transactions are not computed separately, they would be aggregated with market gains or losses from investment transactions and reported in the line item "Investments."

The Statement of Assets and Liabilities and the Statement of Changes in Net Assets should reflect the same unrealized and realized gain and loss components. It is permissible to combine (*a*) net realized gains and losses from investments with net realized gains and losses from foreign currency transactions and (*b*) net unrealized appreciation (depreciation) on investments with the net unrealized appreciation (depreciation) on the translation of assets and liabilities in foreign currencies.

The notes to the financial statements should disclose the entity's policy regarding the treatment of unrealized and realized gains or losses from investments. Otherwise these amounts do not have to be separately disclosed; however, such disclosure may provide useful information to financial statement users.

Certain taxes on foreign source income are not reclaimable. To the extent such taxes exist, the relevant amount should be deducted from the related amount of income. Either this reduction in the income amount is shown parenthetically on the face of the income statement or else a contra-account (to the income item) should be presented on the face of the income statement. Taxes that are based on the aggregate income or capital gains of the investment company are to be treated in a manner similar to income taxes.

Other Issues

Investing in foreign securities poses a number of risks. In addition to the foreign currency risks already discussed, risks related to liquidity, size, and valuation need to be monitored by management and considered for disclosure. Some foreign markets are illiquid. Therefore, quoted market prices may not necessarily be indicative of net realizable value. Some foreign markets are relatively small, and a fund may hold an investment that represents a sizable stake in the overall market. In these cases, quoted market prices may not be indicative of net realizable value. For the reasons previously discussed, determining the proper valuation of securities is sometimes subjective. The fund's board of directors has the ultimate responsibility for determining the fair values of securities.

APPENDIX E

ASC 954—HEALTH CARE ENTITIES

CONTENTS

PART I: GENERAL GUIDANCE

ASC 954-10: OVERALL

OVERVIEW

ASC 958 (Not-For-Profit Entities) is the primary source of U.S. GAAP for not-for-profit (NFP) entities. The Health Care Entities Topic (ASC 954) provides incremental industry-specific guidance for most health care entities.

BACKGROUND

ASC 954 is applicable for health care entities that can be classified into one of the following categories:

- Investor-owned health care entities
- Not-for-profit, business-oriented entities

Investor-owned entities are characterized by having ownership by investors or others with a private equity interest, and they provide goods and services with an objective of making a profit. NFP entities are characterized by their lack of any ownership interests, and they rely on fees received for goods and services to remain self-sustaining (ASC 954-10-05-2).

PRACTICE NOTE: Not-for-profit, non-business oriented entities such as voluntary health and welfare entities are not subject to the additional guidance provided by ASC 954 (ASC 954-10-15-3).

TERMINOLOGY

The authoritative literature includes many terms that are important for an understanding of accounting for health care entities. Several of these terms are explained below.

Capitation Fee

A capitation fee is a fixed amount per individual that is paid periodically to a provider as compensation for providing health care services for the period (ASC Glossary).

Charity Care

Charity care represents health care services that are provided to patients with a demonstrated inability to pay, thus these services are not expected to generate any cash flows (ASC Glossary).

Contribution

A contribution is an unconditional transfer of cash or other assets to an entity or a settlement or cancellation of its liabilities in a voluntary nonreciprocal transfer by another entity acting other than as an owner (ASC Glossary).

Inherent Contribution

An inherent contribution is a contribution that results when an entity voluntarily transfers assets or performs services for another entity and receives either no assets or assets of substantially lower value in exchange (ASC Glossary).

Prepaid Health Care Plan

A prepaid health care plan is a plan in which the provider is compensated in advance by the sponsoring entity. The amount of the payment(s) is based on either a fixed sum or a per-enrollee amount. In such a plan, the financial risk of providing the health care services is assumed by the provider (ASC Glossary).

Prepaid Health Care Services

Prepaid health care services are any health care services that are provided in exchange for a scheduled payment and where the amount of that payment is determined before the services are provided and are not dependent on the level of service that is subsequently provided (ASC Glossary).

Prospective Rate Setting

Prospective rate setting is a method of establishing payment rates at the beginning of a period (usually one year). The amount of the payment(s) determines how much third parties will pay for health care services provided during that rate period, and those rates are not intended to change during the period (ASC Glossary).

Retrospective Rate Setting

Retrospective rate setting is a method of establishing payment rates that involves the determination of an interim payment rate that third parties will pay for health care services provided during the rate period (usually one year). After the rate period has ended, a final settlement will be made based on federal or state regulations or contractual agreements, and the provider may be entitled to receive additional payments or may be required to refund a portion of the interim payments received (ASC Glossary).

ASC 954-205: PRESENTATION OF FINANCIAL STATEMENTS

The financial reporting for the two categories of health care entities covered by ASC 954 is consistent except for certain types of transactions that are only applicable to one of the two types of entities. For example, investor-owned entities would not typically have anything to report for contributions, while not-for-profit, business-oriented entities would not have anything to report for stockholders' equity (ASC 954-205-05-1). The basic financial statements for both types of entities would include a balance sheet, a statement of operations, a statement of changes in equity (or net assets), a statement of cash flows, and notes to the financial statements.

ASC 954-210: BALANCE SHEET

Although health care entities must classify their assets and liabilities as current or noncurrent, rather than presenting a classified balance sheet, a continuing care retirement community may instead order their assets based on how close they are to being converted to cash and order their liabilities based on how soon they will mature or be paid (ASC 954-210-45-1).

ASC 954-225: INCOME STATEMENT

Functional Allocations

Not-for-profit, business-oriented health care entities group their expenses according to the purpose for which the costs are incurred. The primary functional expense classifications are program services (e.g., health services) and supporting activities (e.g., general and administrative). More complex entities may use additional classifications (ASC 954-225-45-3).

Performance Indicator and Intermediate Operating Measures

Not-for-profit, business-oriented health care entities must include a performance indicator in their statement of operations. This performance indicator must be clearly labeled with a descriptive term such as revenues over expenses, revenues and gains over expenses and losses, recognized income, or performance earnings. The performance indicator must also be reported in a statement that presents the total changes in net assets without donor restrictions (ASC 954-225-45-4).

PRACTICE NOTE: Performance indicators in a not-for-profit, business-oriented health care entity are analogous to income from continuing operations of a for-profit entity.

The following items must be reported separately from the performance indicator (ASC 954-225-45-7):

- Transactions with owners
- Equity transfers involving other related entities
- Receipt of donor-restricted contributions
- Contributions of long-lived assets
- Items that are required to be reported in or reclassified from other comprehensive income
- Items that are required to be reported separately under specialized NFP standards
- Unrealized gains and losses on investments on other than trading securities
- Investment returns restricted by donors or by law
- An inherent contribution that increases net assets with donor restrictions
- The portion of the total change in the fair value of the liability resulting from a change in the instrument-specific credit risk

Unless restricted by donors or by law, investment returns must be classified as changes in net assets without donor restrictions as follows (ASC 954-225-45-8):

- Included in the performance indicator are:
  - — Dividend, interest, and other similar investment income
  - — Realized gains and losses
  - — Unrealized gains and losses on trading debt securities
  - — Credit loss expense
  - — Unrealized gains and losses and impairments on equity investments accounted for under ASC 321
- Excluded from the performance indicator are:
  - — Unrealized gains and losses on debt securities, unless the debt security is a trading debt security

ASC 954-305: CASH AND CASH EQUIVALENTS

Health care entities should separately report and exclude from current assets any cash or claims to cash that meet any of the following conditions (ASC 954-305-45-1):

- They are restricted as to withdrawal or use for other than current operations.
- They are designated for expenditure in the acquisition of construction of noncurrent assets.
- They are required to be segregated for the liquidation of long-term debts.
- They are limited to use for long-term purposes by a donor-imposed restriction.

ASC 954-310: RECEIVABLES

Health care entities often have arrangements with third-party payors that result in an amount due from third-party payors that is less than the providers' full established rates for the services provided. Thus, the receivable amounts may be determined based on any of the following (ASC 954-310-05-2):

- A contractual agreement with others (e.g., Blue Cross plans, Medicare, Medicaid, HMOs)
- Legislation or regulation (e.g., workers' compensation, no-fault insurance)
- Provider policy or practice (e.g., discounts to medical staff and employees)

Recognition and Measurement

Contractual adjustments and discounts are variable consideration and shall be measured in accordance with ASC 606-10-32-5 through 32-14. An allowance for credit losses must be recorded in accordance with ASC 326 on measurement of credit losses (ASC 954-310-30-1).

Disclosure

ASC 825-10-50 provides guidance on the required disclosures about significant concentrations of credit risk, including risk arising from accounts receivable. Since health care entities generally provide their services to patients from the local or surrounding communities, these entities are particularly susceptible to issues regarding the concentration of credit risk. Thus, these entities must disclose the primary geographic sources of their patients (ASC 954-310-50-2).

ASC 954-340: OTHER ASSETS AND DEFERRED COSTS

Subsequent Measurement

Any prepaid costs, including amounts paid to physicians for future services, must be amortized over the period benefited (ASC 954-340-35-2).

ASC 954-440: COMMITMENTS

A continuing care retirement community enters into contracts that require them to provide services and the use of facilities to individuals over their remaining lives. The nature and extent of such services will vary based on individual circumstances. Although some contracts will permit fee increases in future years as costs increase, other contracts will not permit such fee increases. Thus, the facility must assume the risk of having to provide services in the future that are not fully covered by the periodic fees received. If the advance fees plus periodic fees charged are not sufficient to cover the costs of providing future services and the use of facilities, then a liability must be recorded for the amount of the expected costs in excess of the related expected revenues. When establishing this liability, the facility should consider actuarial assumptions, estimates of future costs and revenues, the facility's own historical experience, and statistical data. A determination of whether a liability is needed must be made annually (ASC 954-440-35-2).

ASC 954-450: CONTINGENCIES

Medical Malpractice Claims

An entity must accrue the costs of malpractice claims when the incident that gives rise to the claim occurs. These costs include the costs associated with litigating or settling the claims. Any liability that is recognized due to exposure to losses arising from claims must not be presented net of anticipated insurance recoveries. Rather, the entity must recognize a separate insurance receivable at the same time the liability is recognized (ASC 954-450-25-2). The amount of the liability recognized must include an estimate of any losses that will result from incidents that have not yet been reported but that are likely to have occurred before the end of the reporting period. An entity must reevaluate their estimated losses at each reporting period and any changes in those amounts are recognized currently as additional expense or as a reduction of expense (ASC 954-450-35-1).

ASC 954-805: BUSINESS COMBINATIONS

If a merger of NFP entities results in a new entity that is both a not-for-profit, business-oriented health care entity and a public entity, the new entity must disclose the performance indicator for the current reporting period as though the merger date had been the beginning of the annual reporting period (ASC 954-805-50-1). For an acquisition by a NFP entity, a not-for-profit, business-oriented health care entity that is a public entity must disclose all of the following (ASC 954-805-50-2):

- The performance indicator attributable to the acquire since the acquisition date that is included in the statement of activities for the reporting period
- The performance indicator as though the acquisition date for all acquisitions that occurred during the current year had occurred the beginning of the annual reporting period
- If the acquirer presents comparative financial statements, the performance indicator as though the acquisition date for all acquisitions that occurred during the current year had occurred as of the beginning of the comparable prior annual reporting period
- The nature and amount of any material, nonrecurring pro forma adjustments directly attributable to the acquisition(s) included in the reported pro forma performance indicator

ASC 954-815: DERIVATIVES AND HEDGING

A NFP health care entity must generally account for derivatives and hedges in the same manner as ASC 815 requires for a for-profit entity. Thus, any gains or losses from derivatives that would be reported in current earnings for a for-profit entity must be included in the performance indicator of a NFP health care entity. Similarly, any gains or losses that would be excluded from current earnings for a for-profit entity (e.g., items reported in other comprehensive income) must be excluded from the performance indicator by a NFP health care entity (ASC 954-815-25-2).

Although a not-for-profit, business-oriented health care entity is not required to report a separate component of equity in the balance sheet, the entity may nonetheless use comprehensive income reporting for qualifying gains and losses from cash flow hedges. These entities must separately disclose the beginning and ending accumulated derivative gain or loss that has been excluded from the performance indicator, the related net change associated with current period hedging transactions, and the net amount of any reclassifications into the performance indicator. In addition, a NFP health care entity must disclose any anticipated reclassifications into the performance indicator of gains and losses that have been excluded from that measure and reported.

PART II: INTERPRETIVE GUIDANCE

ASC 954-280: SEGMENT REPORTING

ASC 954-280-45-1 Meaning of the Term "Customer" as It Applies to Health Care Facilities under ASC 280

BACKGROUND

Under the guidance in ASC 280, disclosure is required if 10% or more of an entity's revenue is derived from sales to a single customer. The disclosures should state that fact and should give the amount of revenue derived from each customer. A group of customers under common control is considered a single customer.

ACCOUNTING GUIDANCE

Question: Is an insuring entity (e.g., Blue Cross) considered a "customer" of a health care facility?

Answer: An insuring entity should *not* be considered a customer of a health care facility as the term *customer* is used in ASC 280. The fact that an insuring entity is a paying agent for a patient does not make the insuring entity the customer of the health care facility. The paying entity does not decide which services to purchase and from whom those services will be purchased.

ASC 954-405: LIABILITIES

ASC 954-405-25-4 through 25-5; ASC 958-405-60-1 Accounting for Costs of Future Medicare Compliance Audits

Health care providers that have settled allegations of Medicare fraud with the U.S. government must commit under their settlement agreements to engage an independent organization annually for the following five years to test and report on their compliance with Medicare requirements. The issue is whether those entities may accrue a liability on settlement for costs related to that commitment.

A promise made in the settlement agreement to have future compliance audits creates a current duty and responsibility only if an obligating event has occurred, in accordance with the definition of a *liability* in paragraph 36 of Statement of Financial Concepts No. 6 (not in ASC), which would allow a provider little or no discretion to avoid incurring that cost. Entering into an agreement is not the obligating event for costs of a future compliance audit and therefore providers should *not* recognize a liability on the date of settlement.

ASC 954-450: CONTINGENCIES

ASC 954-450-25-2; ASC 954-720-25-1 Health Care Entities: Presentation of Insurance Claims and Related Insurance Recoveries

BACKGROUND

Issues related to an insured entity's claims incurred under claims-made insurance and retroactive insurance contracts are codified in FASB Accounting Standards Codification™ (ASC) 720, *Other Expenses* (ASC 720-20). According to that guidance, it is inappropriate to offset prepaid insurance and receivables for expected recoveries from insurers against a recognized incurred but *not* reported liability or a liability incurred due to a past insurable event, unless the transaction meets the conditions in ASC 210-20-45. As a result of that guidance, liability claims and related anticipated insurance recoveries are usually recognized on a gross-basis.

Some constituents have asked whether the guidance in ASC 720-20 applies to health care entities because the language in ASC 954, *Health Care Entities,* has been interpreted by some to permit or require that insurance recoveries be netted against an organization's estimated accrual for medical malpractice claims.

ACCOUNTING ISSUE

How should health care entities record liabilities for medical malpractice and other similar claims and related insurance recoveries?

SCOPE

The following guidance clarifies that the requirements in ASC 210-20-45 apply to health care entities accounted for under the scope of ASC 954, which report medical malpractice claims and similar contingent liabilities, as well as related anticipated insurance recoveries on their balance sheets. In accordance with the guidance in ASC 210-20-45, entities are *not* permitted to offset anticipated insurance recoveries from third parties against conditional or unconditional liabilities.

ACCOUNTING GUIDANCE

Health care entities, similar to entities in other industries, should determine whether to present claims and insurance recoveries in the balance sheet on a gross or net basis based on the guidance in ASC 210-20-45, because a gross presentation shows that the entity is obligated on a claim even though an insurance company may be paying to defend the claim and may eventually pay for a portion of the claim or the total claim. In addition, a gross presentation of an insurance receivable required in ASC 210-20-45 is a better presentation of the retained credit risk if an insurer is unable to pay a claim.

If a health care entity will be indemnified by its insurer, a receivable should be recognized at the same time as the liability and should be measured on the same basis as the liability, conditional on a need for a valuation allowance for uncollectible amounts.

ASC 954-605: REVENUE RECOGNITION

ASC 954-605-25-4, 45-4 through 45-5, 50-4, 55-1 through 55-4; ASC 954-310-50-3, 55-1 through 55-3 Health Care Entities: Presentation and Disclosure of Patient Service Revenue, Provision for Bad Debts, and the Allowance for Doubtful Accounts for Certain Health Care Entities

IMPORTANT NOTICE: The guidance in this Issue will be superseded by the guidance in ASU 2014-09, *Accounting for Revenue from Contracts with Customers*, when it becomes effective for public business entities in annual reporting periods that begin after December 15, 2017, and interim periods within those annual periods and in annual reporting periods that begin after December 15, 2018, for nonpublic entities.

BACKGROUND

In some cases in which a health care entity performs its services, it may be doubtful or not determinable whether the entity will be able to collect all or a portion of the amounts billed or billable. Sometimes, as in the case of charity care, a health care entity may recognize no revenue on such transactions.

It has been practice in the health care industry to adopt a revenue recognition policy for billings to self-pay patients under which revenue is recognized at the gross amount charged with a relatively high provision for bad debt in accordance with the guidance in ASC 954-605-25-3. Under that revenue recognition policy, revenue for insured patients is recognized when the services are provided with adjustments for contractual discounts based on agreements with third-party payors or based on other arrangements. A provision for bad debt is usually recognized for deductibles and co-pays *not* expected to be collectible. The bad debt provision in those circumstances is usually classified as an expense, not as a reduction of revenue. The issue discussed is whether revenue should be recognized only if collectibility is reasonably assured.

SCOPE

The following guidance applies only to health care entities that recognize significant amounts of revenue from fees for patient services at the time the services are rendered without evaluating the collectibility of those fees. Entities that evaluate collectibity *before* recognizing revenue from fees for patient services are not affected by the following guidance.

ACCOUNTING GUIDANCE

Health care entities that recognize significant amounts of revenue from fees for patient services at the time the services are rendered without evaluating collectibility should present the provision for bad debts related to revenue recognized on fees for patient services as a deduction from revenue (net of contractual allowances and discounts) in the income statement, in a manner similar to the following:

Patient service revenue (net of contractual allowances and discounts)	$2,500,000
Provision for bad debts	(250,000)
Net patient service revenue less provision for bad debts	2,250,000
Premium revenue	50,000
Other operating revenue	500,000
Total revenue	$2,800,000

The following kinds of bad debts should be presented as operating expenses in a health care entity's income statement:

- Bad debts related to receivables from revenue other than from patient services; and
- Bad debts related to receivables from patient service revenue if an entity recognizes revenue only for amounts that are expected to be collectible.

DISCLOSURES

A health care entity that recognizes significant amounts of revenue from patient services when the services are provided without evaluating a patient's ability to pay should disclose the following information by major payor revenue source for interim periods:

- The policy for evaluating collectibility in determining the timing and amount of revenue to be recognized for fees from patient services (net of contractual allowances and discounts); and
- The amount of revenue from fees for patient services (net of contractual allowances and discounts) before the provision for bad debts.

An entity's major payor sources of revenue should be identified in a manner that is consistent with the entity's management of its business (e.g., how the entity evaluates credit risk).

In addition, a health care entity should disclose qualitative and quantitative information about significant changes in its allowance for doubtful accounts related to accounts receivable from patients. The information may include significant changes in estimates and underlying assumptions, the amount of self-pay write-offs, the amount of third-party payer write-offs, and other unusual transactions that affect the allowance for doubtful accounts.

The required disclosures should be presented in interim and annual financial statements.

ASC 954-605-50-3 Health Care Entities: Measuring Charity Care for Disclosure

BACKGROUND

Health care entities provide charity care, which is any service provided without the expectation of payment to patients that meet certain guidelines established by the health care entity. Under the guidance in ASC 954-605-25-10 through 25-11, no revenue should be recognized for charity care in the financial statements and judgment should be used to distinguish between bad debts and charity care, which should be based on established criteria. Under the guidance in ASC 954-605-50-3, an entity is required to disclose in the notes to the financial statements management's policy for charity care and the level of such care. Because there has been diversity in practice, some have suggested that the measurement of charity care disclosed in the financial statements should be standardized for improved comparability among health care entities.

ACCOUNTING ISSUE

How should a health care entities measure charity care?

SCOPE

The following guidance applies to entities that provide health care services.

ACCOUNTING GUIDANCE

Information about charity care disclosed in the financial statements of health care entities should be based on the entity's measurement of the direct and indirect costs of providing such services, which should be determined in a manner that is consistent with that used to report charity care to the IRS for regulatory purposes. Such information may be determined by various means, such as by using: (1) information from a cost accounting system; (2) reasonable techniques to estimate the cost of providing charity care, such as a calculation of a ratio of the cost of charity care to gross charges that would be multiplied by the amount of gross uncompensated charges related to charity care; or (3) other reasonable methods. Subsidies related to charity care, such as those from an uncompensated care fund or from gifts and grants, should be separately disclosed.

In addition to disclosing the costs of providing charity care, health care entities also should separately disclose the following information: (1) amounts received from various sources to compensate the entity for providing charity care; and (2) the method used to determine the costs of providing charity care.

APPENDIX F

ASC 958—NOT-FOR-PROFIT ENTITIES

CONTENTS

PART I: GENERAL GUIDANCE

ASC 958-10: OVERALL

OVERVIEW

Historically, accounting principles for not-for-profit (NFP) organizations were fragmented among industry-specific pronouncements prepared by the AICPA and other groups. The result of this fragmentation was that the practices followed by the various types of organizations were inconsistent. The FASB engaged in a broad project to address many of these inconsistencies and to attempt to improve the accounting and reporting of not-for-profit entities.

BACKGROUND

The primary source of U.S. GAAP for not-for-profit entities is ASC 958. Guidance is provided for the accounting for contributions received and made by all entities, as well as for the format and content of financial statements of all NFP organizations. ASC 958 also establishes standards for accounting for business combinations involving NFP entities. Finally, ASC 958 requires NFP entities to disclose information about depreciable assets and depreciation (ASC 958-360-05-1).

FINANCIAL STATEMENTS OF NOT-FOR-PROFIT ORGANIZATIONS

ASC 958 establishes standards for external financial statements of NFP organizations. It requires them to present a statement of financial position at the end of the period, a statement of activities, and a statement of cash flows. ASC 958 amends ASC 230 (Statement of Cash Flows), extending its provisions to NFP entities. All NFP organizations are required to disclose information about all expenses by nature and function in one location, which can be either on the face of the statement of activities, as a schedule in the notes to the financial statements, or in a separate financial statement (ASC 958-205-45-6).

Financial Statements Required

ASC 958 (*a*) specifies three financial statements that must be present in external financial reports and (*b*) standardizes the approach to the disclosure of operating cash flows from net assets without donor restrictions and net assets with donor restrictions. ASC 958 reviews and discusses the fundamental concepts governing financial reporting; it emphasizes that general-purpose financial statements can be prepared to serve a wide range of user needs, including an assessment of management's stewardship responsibilities to safeguard entity assets and use them for authorized activities. ASC 958 further specifies that the user's primary informational needs include (ASC 958-205-05-4):

- Information about assets, liabilities, and net assets
- The effect of transactions and other events that change the amounts of net assets
- Cash flows
- The amount and kinds of inflows and outflows of economic resources
- Service efforts of the organization

Three financial statements are necessary to provide this information (ASC 958-205-45-4):

- Statement of financial position
- Statement of activities
- Statement of cash flows

ASC 958 also requires specific notes to the financial statements which complete the disclosures relevant to the information needs listed above.

ASC 958 also emphasizes that the disclosure requirements contained in all authoritative literature that do not specifically exempt NFP entities remain in effect (ASC 958-205-45-5). Another noteworthy aspect of ASC 958 is that the degree of disaggregated fund information is not limited. Preparers have flexibility regarding the amount of detail provided, the order of line items, and the grouping of assets, liabilities, revenues, expenses, and gains. However, it is expected that the exercise of this flexibility will be similar to that used by business enterprises (ASC 958-205-45-1).

ASC 958 also deals with accounting for a *donor-restricted* endowment fund, which is an endowment fund created by a donor stipulating that the gift be invested in perpetuity or for a specified term (ASC 958-205-45-13).

As a general rule (i.e., unless otherwise restricted by donor stipulation or law), investment returns on a donor-restricted endowment are free of donor restrictions. If a donor or law imposes a restriction on the investment returns, those returns must be reported within net assets with donor restrictions until appropriated for expenditure. Conversely, investment returns that are not subject to any restrictions imposed by a donor or by law must be reported in net assets without donor restrictions (ASC 958-205-45-13B).

ASC 958 does not address issues related to measurement focus, basis of accounting, or measurement methods (ASC 958-205-15-1).

STATEMENT OF FINANCIAL POSITION

The objective of the statement of financial position is to present information about assets, liabilities, and net assets to facilitate analysis of credit, liquidity, ability to meet obligations, and the need to obtain external financing (ASC 958-210-05-2). In particular, ASC 958 emphasizes the need to distinguish between assets with donor restrictions and assets without donor restrictions. However, the focus of ASC 958 is on the organization as a whole, and therefore, the total amounts for assets, liabilities, net assets, net assets with donor restrictions, and net assets without donor restrictions must be reported (ASC 958-210-45-1).

An important objective of the statement of financial position is to provide additional information about the entity's liquidity. This is accomplished by (*a*) sequencing assets in the order of diminishing liquidity or by current/noncurrent classification, and (*b*) sequencing liabilities according to their nearness to maturity (ASC 958-210-45-8).

Particular attention should be paid to disclosing which elements of the statement of financial position have donor-imposed restrictions on their use. Restrictions exist because assets cannot be used until a future period, because they may be used only for certain types of expenditures, or because only the investment income from the assets may be used. Internally imposed restrictions made by the governing board of an entity must also be disclosed. Preparers are given flexibility about where to show disclosures about restrictions: on the face of the statements or in notes to the statements (ASC 958-210-45-10, 11).

ASC 958 requires a NFP entity to prepare a single, combined balance sheet with a net assets section distinguishing between classes of asset restrictions (ASC 958-205-45-13A):

Net assets:	
Without donor restrictions	$ xxx
With donor restrictions	xxx
Total net assets	$ xxx
Total liabilities and net assets	$ xxx

While accounts may be maintained on a fund basis, the above example emphasizes that the reporting focuses on the nature of the restrictions and not on the particular fund in which an asset is carried.

PRACTICE POINTER: ASC 958 makes no specific recommendation about whether the statement of financial position should show assets and liabilities by fund. In discussing the statement of activities, ASC 958 explicitly states that reporting by fund groups is not precluded, but is not a necessary part of external reporting. Accordingly, it seems clear that entities may prepare a statement of financial position that includes disaggregated fund groups, as long as those groups aggregate with net asset classes. It is also important to note that the statement of activities change in net asset class must articulate with the net assets shown on the statement of financial position. ASC 958 emphasizes that information should be simplified, condensed, and aggregated into meaningful totals, and that the statements should not be obscured by unnecessary fund or line item details.

ASC 958 requires that either the statements or the notes thereto give information describing the amount and nature of the various types of donor-imposed restrictions, such as the following examples (ASC 958-210-45-9):

- Assets that may be part of a collection (of art objects, historical treasures, etc.) that were donated with stipulations that they be preserved and not be sold
- Assets that result from gifts and bequests that create a donor-restricted endowment that is perpetual in nature
- Support of particular operating activities
- Investment for a specified term
- Use in a specified future period
- Acquisition of long-lived assets

Entities may disclose board designations on assets without donor restrictions either on the face of the statements or in notes (ASC 958-210-45-11).

STATEMENT OF ACTIVITIES

The statement of activities is the operating statement for a NFP entity, analogous to an income statement for a business. This statement combines the revenues, expenses, gains, and losses with the changes in equities. The statement should use the term *changes in net assets* or *changes in equities* to describe equity (ASC 958-205-45-1). ASC 958 sees net assets or equities as encompassing the whole of the net assets of the entity. The statement of activities must report the changes in total net assets and the change in each net asset class (ASC 958-225-45-1). An important dimension of reporting operations for NFP entities by ASC 958 is the use of net asset classes. The requirement is to report changes in net assets with donor restrictions and net assets without donor restrictions in the statement of activities. Therefore, the statement will contain sections for changes in net assets without donor restrictions (which includes revenues and gains), changes in net assets with donor restrictions (both inflows and outflows), and a line for total changes in net assets.

Illustration of Format of Statement of Financial Position

NFP Organization #1 Statement of Financial Position December 31, 20X5
(in thousands)

Assets:	
Cash and cash equivalents	$ 15
Accounts and interest receivable	425
Inventories and prepaid expenses	120
Contributions receivable	600
Short-term investments	300
Assets restricted to investment in land, buildings, and equipment	1,050
Land, buildings, and equipment	12,300
Long-term investments	43,600
Total assets	$58,410
Liabilities and net assets:	
Accounts payable	$ 500
Refundable advance	75
Grants payable	100
Notes payable	200
Annuity obligations	330
Long-term debt	900
Total liabilities	$ 2,105

Net assets:	
Without donor restrictions	$23,010
With donor restrictions	33,295
Total net assets	56,305
Total liabilities and net assets	$58,410

Illustration of Format of the Statement of Activities

NFP Organization #2 Statement of Activities for Year Ending June 30, 20X8 (in thousands)

Changes in net assets without donor restrictions:	
Revenues and gains:	
Contributions	$ 900
Fees	450
Investment income	25
Other	10
Total income without donor restrictions	$ 1,385
Net assets released from restrictions:	
Program restrictions satisfied	$ 250
Equipment acquisition restrictions satisfied	200
Time restrictions expired	100
Total assets released from restrictions	550
Total support	1,935
Less: Expenses and losses:	
Program A	600
Program B	750
Management and administrative	400
Fund-raising expenses	100
Total expenses and losses	1,850
Increase in net assets without donor restrictions	85
Changes in net assets with donor restrictions:	
Contributions	650
Investment income	250
Net assets released from restrictions	(110)
Increase in net assets with donor restrictions	790
Increase in net assets	715
Net assets, beginning of the year	2,600
Net assets, end of the year	$ 3,315

ASC 958 specifies that the term *changes in net assets* or *change in equity* should be used in the statement (ASC 958-225-45-2).

The reporting of restricted resources is straightforward under ASC 958. When donor-restricted assets are received, they normally are reported as restricted revenues or gains. In cases in which the restrictions are met in the same period the resources are received, it is permissible to classify the receipts as support in net assets without donor restrictions, provided the policy is disclosed and applied consistently (ASC 958-225-45-6). In addition, ASC 958 allows reporting of subtotals for operating and nonoperating items, expendable and nonexpendable items, or other terms as desired to provide additional detail within the two classes of net assets. This additional detail is not required, but preparers can make such distinctions as they deem necessary (ASC 958-225-45-9, 10).

ASC 958 allows the reporting of gains and losses as net amounts if they result from peripheral transactions, such as disposal of assets. In its basis for conclusion, the FASB clearly states that this approach should not be used for special events that are ongoing major activities (ASC 958-225-45-15).

STATEMENT OF CASH FLOWS

ASC 958 amends several sections of ASC 230 to require that NFP organizations include a statement of cash flows in their financial statement package (ASC 230-10-15-2, 15-3, Glossary, 45-14, 45-25, 45-28, 45-29, 45-30, 50-4, 55-6). All these changes involve minor wording changes or additions to ASC 230 to clarify that ASC 230 is applicable to NFP entities. As is the case for business entities, either the direct or indirect method may be used to present the cash flow information. The cash flow statement is best presented on an aggregated basis for the two classes of net assets; to do otherwise would result in a very detailed statement.

PRACTICE POINTER: The statement of cash flows as required by ASC 958 is essentially the same as that required by ASC 230 for business enterprises. The only substantive difference is the substitution of "change in net assets" of the NFP organization for "net income" of the business organization. For that reason, an illustration of the statement of cash flows is not presented here; see Chapter 7, *ASC 230—Statement of Cash Flows*.

PRACTICE POINTER: Receipts from sales of equity instruments of other entities are generally classified as cash inflows from investing activities. Certain donated equity instruments received by NFP organizations are an exception. Cash receipts resulting from the sale of donated financial assets by NFPs that upon receipt were directed without any NFP-imposed limitations for sale and were converted nearly immediately into cash are classified as operating cash flows. If, however, the donor restricted the use of the contributed resource to a long-term purpose, those cash receipts meeting stated criteria are classified as financing activities.

CONTRIBUTIONS MADE

ASC 958 emphasizes full accrual and fair market value in providing guidance for contributions made. The fair market value emphasis is particularly evident in the directions given for accounting for contributions of nonmonetary assets. Contributions of nonmonetary assets are recognized as expenses and decreases in assets (or increases in liabilities) in the period made. Donors should find the most objective way possible to determine the fair market value of nonmonetary assets (ASC 720-25-30-1).

PRACTICE NOTE: Absence of a definite valuation does not justify use of historical cost as a basis for recording the transaction.

Appraisals, present value of estimated cash flows, net realizable value, and quoted market prices are all acceptable ways of determining the fair market value of donated nonmonetary assets. If a present value technique is used to measure fair value of unconditional promises to give cash, subsequent accruals of the interest element are accounted for as contribution income by donees and contribution expense by donors. NFP organizations shall report the contribution increase as an increase in net assets with donor restrictions if the underlying promise to give is donor restricted (ASC 958-310-35-6; 958-310-45-2).

ACCOUNTING FOR INVESTMENTS

Definitions and Applicability

The Codification establishes standards for certain investments in debt and equity securities. The term *securities* is defined as a share, participation, or other interest in property or in an enterprise of the issuer or an obligation of the issuer that has the following characteristics (ASC 958-320-55-1; ASC Glossary):

- It is represented by an instrument issued in bearer or registered form, or it is registered in books maintained to record transfers by or on behalf of the issuer.
- It is of a type that is commonly dealt in on securities exchanges or markets or, when it is represented by an instrument, commonly recognized as a medium for investment in any area in which it is issued or dealt in.
- It is one of a class or series, or by its terms is divisible into a class or series of shares, participations, interests, or obligations.

Equity securities represent an ownership interest in an enterprise (e.g., common and preferred stock) or the right to acquire (e.g., warrants, rights, call options) or dispose of (e.g., put options) an ownership interest at fixed or determinable prices. Convertible debt and preferred stock that by their terms either must be redeemed by the issuing enterprise or are redeemable at the option of the investor are not considered equity securities (ASC 958-321-55-1; ASC Glossary).

Debt securities represent a creditor relationship with an enterprise. Debt securities include U.S. Treasury securities, U.S. government agency securities, municipal securities, corporate bonds, convertible debt, commercial paper, securitized debt instruments and interest only and principal-only strips. Preferred stock that must be redeemed by the issuing enterprise or that is redeemable at the option of the investor, as well as collateralized mortgage obligations that are issued in equity form but are required to be accounted for as nonequity instruments regardless of how the instruments are classified, are considered debt securities. The term excludes option contracts, financial futures contracts, forward contracts, lease contracts, and swap contracts (ASC 958-320-55-1, 2).

An equity security is deemed to have a readily determinable fair value if at least one of the following criteria is met:

1. Sales prices or bid-and-asked quotations for the security are available on a securities exchange registered with the Securities and Exchange Commission (SEC) or in the over-the-counter market. For over-the-counter market prices to qualify, they must be publicly reported by the National Association of Securities Dealers Automated Quotation (NASDAQ) system or by the National Quotation Bureau.

PRACTICE NOTE: Restricted stock does not meet this criterion. The term *restricted stock* refers to equity securities for which sale is restricted at acquisition by governmental or contractual requirement, other than in connection with being pledged as collateral, except if that requirement terminates within one year or if the holder has the power by contract or otherwise to cause the requirement to be met within one year. Any portion of the security that can be reasonably expected to qualify for sale within one year is not considered restricted.

---

2. For an equity security traded only in a foreign market, that market is of a breadth and scope comparable to a U.S. market referred to in 1 above.
3. For an investment in a mutual fund, the fair value per share or unit is determined and published and is the basis for current transactions.

Measurement and Recognition Standards

The most important measurement and recognition requirement is that all investments in debt securities are accounted for at fair value in the statement of financial position (ASC 958-320-35-1). An equity security must be initially measured at its acquisition cost if it is purchased, or at its fair value if it is received as a contribution or through an agency transaction (ASC 958-321-30-1).

ASC 958 provides the following guidance for the income effects of measuring investments at fair value (ASC 958-225-45-18, 20):

- Gains and losses on investments resulting from their measurement at fair value and dividend, interest, and other investment income are reported in the statement of activities as increases or decreases in net assets without donor restrictions, unless their use is limited by donor-imposed restrictions or by law, in which case those amounts are reported as increases or decreases in net assets with donor restrictions.
- Gains and investment income that are limited to specific uses by donor restriction may be reported as increases in net assets without donor restrictions if the restrictions are met in the same reporting period as the gains and income are recognized (provided the organization has a similar policy for reporting contributions received, applies that policy consistently, and discloses that policy).

PRACTICE POINTER: Investment returns must be reported net of external and direct internal investment expenses (ASC 958-225-45-14). This requirement provides a more comparable measure of investment returns across all NFP entities. In addition, NFPs are no longer required to disclose those netted expenses, which eliminates the difficulties and related costs in identifying embedded fees and the resultant inconsistencies in the reported amounts of investment expenses.

Disclosure Standards

The following information related to the statement of financial position is required (ASC 958-320-50-2; ASC 958-325-50-2):

- Basis for determining the carrying amount for investments other than equity securities with readily determinable fair values and all debt securities
- The method(s) and significant assumptions used to determine fair values

For the most recent period for which a statement of financial position is presented, the nature of and carrying amount for each individual investment or group of investments that represents a significant concentration of market risk are required (ASC 958-320-50-3).

DEPRECIATION

NFP entities are required to recognize the cost of using up the future economic benefits or service potential of long-lived tangible assets by reporting depreciation on those assets. In addition, disclosure of the following items is required for those assets (ASC 958-360-35-1). However, depreciation is not required to be taken on works of art or historical treasures considered to have an indefinite service potential or an extraordinarily long useful life. Verifiable evidence should exist which indicates that (*a*) the historical treasures or works of art are of such value that they are worth preserving perpetually and (*b*) the entity has the capacity to preserve the undiminished service potential of the asset for an indefinite period, and is doing so (ASC 958-360-35-3).

COLLECTIONS

To be part of a *collection*, assets must be (ASC Glossary):

- Held for public exhibition, education, or research rather than held for financial gain
- Protected, preserved, and not used as collateral or otherwise encumbered
- Subject to a policy that requires the proceeds of collection items sold to be reinvested in collections

Entities are encouraged by ASC 958 to either (1) capitalize all collection items, (2) capitalize all collection items on a prospective basis (that is all items acquired after a stated date), or (3) do not capitalize any items. Capitalization of selected items is not permitted (ASC 958-360-25-3). An entity that does not capitalize collections is required to disclose additional information.

Additional Disclosures for Collections

A not-for-profit entity that does not recognize and capitalize its collections must report, separately from revenues, expenses, gains, and losses, all of the following (ASC 958-360-45-5):

- Costs of collection items purchased as a decrease in the appropriate class of net assets
- Proceeds from sale of collection items as an increase in the appropriate class of net assets
- Proceeds from insurance recoveries of lost or destroyed collection items as an increase in the appropriate class of net assets

Similarly, an entity that capitalizes its collections prospectively must report proceeds from sales and insurance recoveries of items not previously capitalized separately from revenues, expenses, gains, and losses.

If collections are *not* capitalized, the cash consequences of collection activities appear in the statement of activities within a separate category called "changes in net assets with donor restrictions." This category follows the revenue and expense categories. Substantial descriptive notes regarding the collections are required when collections are not capitalized. These disclosures must include the relative significance of the collection, along with the accounting and stewardship policies followed. In addition, the notes must indicate the values of items sold, lost, or destroyed (ASC 958-360-50-6). A line in the financial statements must refer to the collections note. An NFP must disclose its organizational policy for the use of proceeds from deaccessioned collection items, including whether those proceeds could be used for acquisition of new collection items, the direct care of existing collections, or both. If the collection-holding entity allows proceeds to be used for direct care, the entity must disclose its definition of direct care (ASC 958-360-50-7).

PRACTICE NOTE: The note disclosures required for uncapitalized collections or collections that are capitalized prospectively (after a certain date) are extensive. They emphasize that readers of the financial statements must be made aware of the details of all significant changes in the collection. In particular, statement users must be advised regarding casualty losses, insurance recoveries, accounting policies, and managerial controls in place. The concept of *full disclosure* is very much in evidence in this standard.

CONTRIBUTIONS

ASC 958 provides guidance in accounting for contributions received and contributions given, promises to give cash or other assets, contributed services, collections of works of art, and gifts with donor-stipulated conditions. ASC 958 also specifies when to recognize the expirations of donor-imposed restrictions. ASC 958 standardizes the terminology used to describe the contributions and in the timing of recognition of income for the contributions received and expense for contributions given.

ASC 958 applies to contributions of cash, nonmonetary assets, and services, and to promises to give the same (ASC 958-605-15-1). It applies to exchange transactions in which the value received is substantially different from the value given. It does *not* apply to (*a*) bargained arm's-length transactions without a gift element or (*b*) transactions in which the entity is an intermediary or is acting in some form of agency capacity (ASC 958-605-15-6).

Also expressly excluded from the scope of ASC 958 are transactions that convey only contingent or indirect benefits, such as tax abatements. Transfers of assets from governments to businesses also are not covered by ASC 958, nor are transfers of assets (typically from a government entity) that are part of an existing exchange transaction between a recipient and an identified customer (e.g., payments under Medicare and Medicaid programs, or Pell Grants or similar state or local government tuition assistance programs) (ASC 958-605-15-6).

Contributions in ASC 958 include cash, assets, or services—or unconditional promises to give these in the future. The Statement emphasizes the word *promise* and requires verifiable documentary evidence that a promise has been made (ASC 958-605-25-8). It also distinguishes between donor-imposed *conditions* and donor-imposed *restrictions* to provide a basis for differentiating the way these items are reported. Imposing restrictions on how a gift is to be used does not delay recognition of income or expense. However, recognition of conditional gifts is delayed until the conditions are substantially met.

Contributions Received

ASC 958 generally requires that all unconditional contributions—whether assets, services, or reductions of liabilities—be recognized currently as revenue or gains (ASC 958-605-25-2). ASC 958 takes the current recognition, fair value approach, which embraces the characteristics of relevance and reliability and the qualities of comparability and consistency that are discussed in FASB Concepts Statement No. 2 (Qualitative Characteristics of Accounting Information).

PRACTICE NOTE: The FASB's conceptual framework consists of Statements of Financial Accounting Concepts that are intended to provide conceptual guidance in selecting the economic events recognized and reported in financial statements. This includes the characteristics of accounting information and is useful as a reference to understanding the importance attached to various concepts that are emphasized in the FASB Standards.

ASC 958 also provides guidance in accounting for donated services. In particular, it holds that donated services must create or enhance nonfinancial assets, or must be of a specialized nature, must be provided by individuals possessing those skills, and typically need to be purchased before they can be included as revenue or gains in the operating statement. Routine volunteer services requiring no particular expertise must not be reported as contribution revenue (ASC 958-605-25-16). Finally, ASC 958 requires explanatory footnotes that disclose a disaggregation of the amount of contributed nonfinancial assets recognized within the statement of activities by category that depicts the type of contributed nonfinancial assets. For each category of contributed nonfinancial assets, an NFP must also disclose the following (ASC 958-605-50-1A):

1. Qualitative information about whether the assets were either monetized or utilized during the reporting period.
2. The NFP's policy about monetizing rather than utilizing the assets.

3. A description of any donor-imposed restrictions associated with the assets.
4. A description of the valuation techniques and inputs used to determine the fair value of the assets.
5. The principal or most advantageous market used to determine fair value if it is a market in which the NFP is prohibited by a donor-imposed restriction from selling or using the assets.

Assets to be included in a collection are recognized as revenue or gains if they are capitalized, but may not be included in revenue or gains if they are not capitalized (ASC 958-605-25-19).

Contribution Standards Applicable Only to NFP Entities

ASC 958 requires that NFP organizations distinguish the use of assets and support as donor-restricted support that increases net assets with donor restrictions, and support that increases net assets without donor restrictions (ASC 958-605-45-3, 4). This separation could be accomplished through fund accounting by having a different fund for each of the two classes of net assets. Support that is restricted by donors as being available only in future accounting periods is reported as donor-restricted support (ASC 958-605-45-5).

Gifts of long-lived assets that are received without any donor-imposed stipulations as to how long the donated asset must be used are reported as revenue without donor restrictions. Gifts of cash or other assets that are restricted to acquire long-lived assets are initially reported as donor-restricted support and then reclassified from net assets with donor restrictions to net assets without donor restrictions when the long-lived asset is acquired and placed in service, unless the donor has also placed a time restriction on the use of the long-lived asset (ASC 958-605-45-6).

When restrictions lapse, recognition is required in the statement of activities. In general, a restriction expires when the period of the restriction has lapsed or when an expenditure for an authorized purpose is made. If an expense is incurred for a purpose for which both net assets without donor restrictions and net assets with donor restrictions are available, the donor-imposed restriction is met (ASC 958-205-45-9).

Conditional Promises

Material gifts or promises subject to conditions present accounting issues regarding the appropriate time to recognize the gift revenue or expense. Donor-imposed conditions represent a barrier that must be overcome before the recipient is entitled to the assets promised. They may also create the need for additional note disclosures describing the nature of the conditions. ASC 958 requires that a promise to give be recognized when the donor-imposed conditions of the promise are substantially met (ASC 958-605-25-11). Conditional promises are essentially contingent events. If the contingent event (condition) is remote, the promise is accounted for as an unconditional promise. Otherwise, the gift is not recognized until the conditions have been substantially met. Although ASC 958 requires note disclosure by recipients of conditional promises, there is no similar requirement for the promisor.

Recognition problems also occur for donees when ambiguous wording makes it difficult to determine if conditions for recognition exist. Contributions with donor-imposed conditions are essentially contingent revenue for the donee. ASC 450 (Contingencies) prohibits recognition of contingent gains, and ASC 958 is consistent with ASC 450 in that regard (ASC 958-605-25-5E). The donee need only prepare a note to the financial statements describing the nature and conditions of the promise and the amounts promised (ASC 958-310-50-4). Accrual of conditional promises is not permitted unless the probability that the condition will not lapse is remote. For unconditional promises, the notes to the financial statements must indicate the timing of the cash flows as well as amounts, and disclose the balances in any allowances for uncollectibles (ASC 958-310-50-1).

Donor-Imposed Conditions

For a donor-imposed condition to exist, it must be clear from the agreement that a recipient is only entitled to the transferred assets or a future transfer of assets if it has overcome the barrier related to the condition (ASC 958-605-25-5B). A donor-imposed condition must have both of the following (ASC 958-605-25-5A):

1. One or more barriers that must be overcome before a recipient is entitled to the assets transferred or promised.
2. A right of return to the contributor for assets transferred

An entity must consider the facts and circumstances to determine whether a stipulation represents a barrier that must be overcome before the recipient is entitled to the assets transferred or promised. The likelihood that the recipient will meet the stipulation is not relevant when determining whether an agreement contains a barrier (ASC 958-605-25-5C).

ACCOUNTING FOR DEFINED BENEFIT POSTRETIREMENT PLANS

A NFP entity may sponsor a defined benefit postretirement plan for its employees. The accounting requirements for these plans generally parallel those for business entities. The NFP entity shall recognize in its statement of financial position the funded status of the benefit plan as the difference between the fair value of the plan assets and its benefit obligation. The aggregate status of all *overfunded* plans is recognized as an asset in the statement of financial position. The aggregate status of all *underfunded* plans is recognized as a liability in the statement of financial position. The asset is presented as a noncurrent asset. The liability is presented as a current liability, noncurrent liability, or a combination. The current portion is the amount by which the actuarial present value of benefits included in the benefit obligation payable in the next 12 months, or operating cycle if longer, exceeds the fair value of plan assets.

A NFP entity shall recognize the net gain or loss, the transition asset or obligation, and the prior service costs or credits that arise during the period but are not recognized as components of net periodic benefit cost in accordance with ASC 715 (Compensation—Retirement Benefits). This disclosure shall be a separate line item or items in the changes in net assets without donor restrictions, apart from expenses. There is no requirement as to whether the separate line items are to be included within or outside the intermediate measure of operations or performance indicator, if one is presented (ASC 958-715-45-1).

PRACTICE POINTER: AICPA guidance for certain types of health care organizations requires that certain items of other comprehensive income are reported outside the performance indicator.

The entity is required to reclassify to net periodic benefit cost a portion of the net gain or loss, the transition asset or obligation, and prior service costs and credits previously recognized. The contra adjustments to the initially recognized net gain or loss, the transition asset or obligation, and the prior service costs or credits are reported in the same line item or items within changes in net assets without donor restrictions, apart from expenses, as the initially recognized amounts. Net periodic benefit cost is reported by functional expense classification (ASC 958-715-45-2).

References throughout ASC 715 to accumulated other comprehensive income relate to net assets without donor restrictions for a NFP entity (ASC 958-715-25-1). Any income tax effects are to be determined in accordance with the guidance in ASC 740 (Income Taxes).

NFP entities shall measure plan assets and benefit obligations as of the date of the fiscal year-end statement of financial position unless the exceptions described in the chapters on pension and other postretirement benefit plans apply (i.e., a consolidated subsidiary or an equity method investee).

Disclosures

NFP entities that sponsor defined benefit pension or other postretirement benefit plans need to disclose the following:

- For each annual statement of activities presented, the net gain or loss and the net prior service cost or credit recognized in the statement of activities apart from expenses
- Separate disclosure is required for amounts arising during the period and amounts reclassified as components of net periodic benefit cost during the period
- For each annual statement of activities presented, the net transition asset or obligation recognized as components of net periodic benefit cost for the period
- For each annual statement of financial position presented, the amounts that have not yet been recognized as components of net periodic benefit cost, with separate disclosure of the net gain or loss, net prior service cost or credit, and net transition asset or obligation
- The amounts of net gain or loss, net prior service cost or credit, and net transition asset or obligation that arose previously and are expected to be recognized as components of net periodic benefit cost over the fiscal year that follows the most recent annual statement of financial position presented
- The amount and timing of any plan assets expected to be returned to the plan sponsor during the 12-month period, or operating cycle if longer, that follows the most recent annual statement of financial position presented

The above-mentioned disclosures are to be made separately for pension plans and other postretirement benefit plans.

SERVICE EFFORTS

An important disclosure for NFP organizations is information about service efforts. This disclosure is accomplished by arranging the statement of activities along functional lines. All NFPs must present information about the relationship between functional classification and natural classification for all expenses in an analysis that disaggregates functional expense classifications, such as major classes of program services and supporting activities, by their natural expense classifications, such as salaries, rent, electricity, interest expense, supplies, depreciation, awards and grants to others, and professional fees (ASC 958-720-45-15).

Proper classification of expenditures between program and support is a fundamental disclosure principle. ASC 958 provides detailed guidance about the appropriate classification of items of a support nature. *Supporting activities* are divided into three categories: (1) management and general, (2) fund-raising, and (3) membership development (ASC Glossary).

PRACTICE NOTE: ASC 958 specifies that membership development is an element of support activity and should be so reported.

Also, it is important to emphasize that much information about service efforts may not be presentable in the body of the financial statements. Accordingly, preparers must ensure that notes provide full disclosure of information describing service accomplishments, including program descriptions, statistical data relevant to program inputs and outputs, and narratives about accomplishments.

BUSINESS COMBINATIONS

ASC 958 also establishes standards for accounting for mergers and acquisitions involving NFP entities. ASC 958 provides guidance on (1) determining whether a combination is a merger or an acquisition, (2) applying the carryover method in accounting for a merger, (3) applying the acquisition method in accounting for an acquisition, including determining the entity that is the acquirer, and (4) determining the appropriate disclosures. ASC 958 extends the requirements of ASC 350 to NFP entities, thereby improving the information provided by NFP entities about goodwill and other intangible assets (ASC 958-805-10-1; 958-805-05-1, 2, 4, 5).

Scope

ASC 958 provides guidance on accounting for a combination of NFP entities, which is a transaction or other event that results in a NFP entity initially recognizing another NFP entity, a business, or a nonprofit activity in its financial statements. ASC 958 applies to a combination that meets the definition of either a "merger" of NFP entities or an "acquisition" of a NFP entity (ASC 958-805-15-3; 958-805-05-1).

A "merger" of NFP organizations is a combination in which the governing bodies of two or more NFP entities cede control of those entities to create a new NFP entity. In contrast, an "acquisition" is a combination in which a NFP acquirer obtains control of one or more nonprofit activities or businesses. This is a particularly important consideration in applying ASC 958 because subsequent accounting for a merger is significantly different from that for an acquisition (ASC Glossary).

If the participating entities retain shared control of the new entity, they have not ceded their control. To qualify as a new entity (i.e., an acquisition), the combined entity must have a newly formed governing body. The new entity is often a new legal entity, although this is not a requirement. Control of a NFP entity is the direct or indirect ability to determine the direction of management and policies through ownership, contract, or otherwise (ASC Glossary).

PRACTICE POINTER: Ceding control to a new entity is the sole definitive criterion for identifying a merger. One entity obtaining control over the other is the sole definitive criterion for an acquisition. Other characteristics, however, can be used to help identify a merger. Participating entities must consider all of the characteristics and other pertinent factors and make a professional judgment about whether (1) the governing bodies have ceded control of those entities to create a new entity, (2) one entity has acquired the other, or (3) another form of combination (e.g., the formation of a joint venture) has occurred (ASC 958-805-55-1, 2).

ASC 958 does not apply to the following (ASC 958-805-15-4):

- The formation of a joint venture;
- The acquisition of an asset or a group of assets that does not constitute either a business or a nonprofit activity;

- A combination between NFP entities, businesses, or nonprofit activities under common control; or
- A transaction or other event in which a NFP entity obtains control of another entity but does not consolidate that entity.

Unique Features of NFP Combinations

Combinations by NFP and business entities are similar in many ways, so much so that the same basic accounting method (i.e., the acquisition method) is appropriate for both (see Chapter 47, *ASC 805—Business Combinations*, for a detailed discussion of the acquisition method of accounting). However, there are important differences between for profit and NFP entities and those differences are reflected in the accounting for business combinations.

A fundamental difference between combinations for NFP and business entities is that a NFP entity lacks the type of ownership interests that business entities have and, as a result, negotiations in NFP mergers and acquisitions generally focus on the furtherance of the benefit for the public rather than on maximizing returns for equity holders. Many mergers and acquisitions by NFP entities do not involve a transfer of consideration. They are not fair value exchanges but rather are nonreciprocal transfers. This fundamental difference contributes significantly to ASC 958's requirement that different accounting methods apply to a merger of a NFP entity and an acquisition by a NFP entity. For an acquisition, those combinations result in a contribution of the acquiree's net assets to the acquirer, referred to in ASC 958 as "inherent contribution received," to distinguish it from other contributions received by a NFP entity.

MERGERS

The carryover method is required by ASC 958 for NFP mergers. Under the carryover method, the combined entity's initial set of financial statements carry forward the assets and liabilities of the combining entities, measured at their carrying amounts in the books of the combining entities at the merger date (ASC 958-805-25-6; ASC 958-805-30-1). In applying the carryover method, an entity recognizes neither additional assets nor additional liabilities that are not already recognized in the combining entities' financial statements before the merger (ASC 958-805-25-7). Exceptions are made to reflect a consistent method of accounting for the new entity if the merging entities used different methods and to eliminate the effects of intra-entity transactions (ASC 958-805-30-2, 4).

The measurement date of a merger in ASC 958 is the actual merger date, defined as the date the combination becomes effective. The NFP entity that results from a merger is a new reporting entity. The history of the new entity begins at its inception and has no previous operations. Guidance on the measurement date and related presentation issues in ASC 958 is consistent with the merged entity's status as a new entity (ASC 958-805-30-1).

ASC 958 also provides additional guidance for applying the carryover method. For example, ASC 958 states how to make the classifications and designations that are required to apply other generally accepted accounting principles (GAAP), such as hedge accounting requirements. The new entity is to carry forward into the opening balances in its financial statements the merging entities' classifications and designations unless either of the following applies (ASC 958-805-25-9):

- The merger results in a modification of a contract in a manner that would change the previous classifications or designations; or
- Reclassifications are required to conform the accounting policies of the merging entities.

Disclosures: Mergers

ASC 958 outlines the following disclosure requirements for the new reporting entity that results from a NFP merger (ASC 958-805-50-2, 3, 4, 5):

- The name and a description of each merging entity;
- The merger date;
- The primary reasons for the merger;
- For each merging entity:
  - — The amounts recognized as of the merger date for each major class of assets and liabilities and each class of net assets;
  - — The nature and amounts of any significant assets or liabilities that U.S. GAAP does not require to be recognized;

- The nature and amount of any significant adjustments made to conform the individual accounting policies of the merging entities or to eliminate intraentity balances; and
- If the new entity is a public entity, the following supplemental pro-forma information:
  - — If the merger occurs at other than the beginning of an annual period and the entity's initial financial statements cover less than an annual reporting period, the following information for the current reporting period as if the merger had been at the beginning of the annual reporting period: (1) revenue; (2) for an entity subject to the *Health Organizations Care* Guide, the performance indicator; and (3) changes in net assets without donor restrictions and changes in net assets with donor restrictions.
  - — If the new entity is a public entity the entity should present comparative financial information in the annual reporting period following the year in which the merger occurs, the entity shall disclose the supplemental pro-forma information above for the comparable prior reporting period as though the merger date had been the beginning of that prior annual reporting period.

If disclosure of any of the above information is impracticable, the entity shall disclose that fact and explain why the information is not disclosed. The term "impracticable" as used in ASC 958 has the same meaning as in ASC 250 (Accounting Changes and Error Corrections) (ASC 250-10-45-9).

ACQUISITIONS

The acquisition method in ASC 958 is the same as the acquisition method described in ASC 805 for business entities. It contains additional guidance on items that are unique or especially significant to a NFP entity and eliminates any ASC 805 guidance that does not apply to NFP entities. ASC 958 guidance on identifying both the acquirer and the acquisition date is in substance the same as the guidance in ASC 805, but ASC 958 uses different terminology and adds some details unique to NFP entities (ASC 958-805-25-13).

Applying the acquisition method requires (ASC 958-805-25-13) the following:

- Identifying the acquirer;
- Determining the acquisition date and what is part of the acquisition transaction;
- Recognizing and measuring the identifiable assets acquired, liabilities assumed, and any noncontrolling interest of the acquiree; and
- Recognizing and measuring goodwill or the contribution received.

Identifying the Acquirer

One of the combining entities must be designated as the acquirer in an acquisition (ASC 805-10-25-4). The former guidance in SOP 94-3, *Reporting of Related Entities by Not-for-Profit Organizations*, or the AICPA Audit and Accounting Guide *Health Care Organizations* apply to identify the acquirer (ASC 958-805-25-15, 16).

Determining the Acquisition Date

The acquisition date is the date on which the acquirer obtains control of the acquiree (ASC 805-10-25-6). The acquisition date is generally the date that consideration is transferred, assets acquired, and liabilities assumed. This date is typically the closing date, although the acquisition date can precede the closing date if a contract or other written agreement indicates that control is obtained before the closing date. All relevant facts and circumstances are to be considered in determining the acquisition date (ASC 805-10-25-7).

Recognizing and Measuring Identifiable Assets, Liabilities, and Noncontrolling Interest

In ASC 958, the basic principles of recognizing and measuring identifiable assets, liabilities, and noncontrolling interest are as follows:

- As of the acquisition date, the acquirer recognizes separately from goodwill the identifiable assets acquired, liabilities assumed, and any noncontrolling interest in the acquiree. As a result, the acquirer may recognize certain assets and liabilities that the acquiree had not previously recognized (e.g., internally developed brand names, patents, and customer relationships).
- At the acquisition date, the acquirer classifies or designates the identifiable assets acquired and liabilities assumed as required to subsequently apply other GAAP. The acquirer makes those classifications or designations based on the

contractual terms, economic conditions, operating or accounting policies, and other pertinent conditions that exist at the acquisition date. An exception to this general rule is that lease contracts and insurance contracts are classified by the terms that existed at the inception of the contract.

- The acquirer measures the identifiable assets acquired, liabilities assumed, and any noncontrolling interest at their fair value at the acquisition date.

Exceptions to the General Recognition and Measurement Guidance

The acquirer shall not recognize an acquired donor relationship as an identifiable intangible asset separately from goodwill (ASC 958-805-25-22). In addition, an acquirer that follows an accounting policy of not capitalizing "collections" (e.g., works of art and historical treasures) should not capitalize as an asset acquired works of art, historical treasures, etc. that it adds to its collection. If the work of art, historical treasure, etc. is purchased, the acquirer decreases net assets in the statement of activities and presents a cash outflow for investing activities. And if the work of art, historical treasure, etc. is contributed, the acquirer does not recognize the item as an asset or as contribution revenue (ASC 958-805-25-23). Finally, a conditional promise to give is only recognized if the underlying conditions have been substantially satisfied at the acquisition date, and assets that have already been transferred under a conditional promise are recognized as a liability (i.e., a refundable advance) unless the underlying conditions have been substantially satisfied (ASC 958-805-25-26).

Contingencies

In general, the acquirer recognizes as of the acquisition date assets acquired and liabilities assumed that would be within the scope of ASC 450 (Contingencies), had they not been acquired or assumed in a business combination. If the fair value of an asset or a liability arising from a contingency can be determined during the measurement period, the acquirer recognizes the fair value of the asset or liability at the acquisition date (e.g., a warranty obligation). If the fair value of an asset or liability arising from a contingency is not determinable during the measurement period, an asset or liability is recognized only if the ASC 450 criteria are met during the measurement period (i.e., probable that an asset existed or a liability has been incurred and the amount can be reasonably estimated).

Income Taxes, Employee Benefits, and Indemnification Agreements

The acquirer recognizes and measures a deferred tax asset or liability arising from the assets acquired and liabilities assumed in an acquisition according to ASC 740.

The acquirer recognizes and measures a liability or an asset, if any, related to the acquiree's employee benefit arrangements in according with other GAAP. Refer to Chapter 42, *ASC 715—Compensation—Retirement Benefits*, for additional guidance on postemployment and postretirement benefits.

The seller in an acquisition by a NFP entity may contractually indemnify the acquirer for the outcome of a contingency or uncertainty related to all or part of a specific asset or liability. When the acquirer receives such an indemnity, the acquirer recognizes an indemnification asset at the same time that it recognizes the indemnified item, measured on the same basis as the indemnified item, subject to the need for a valuation allowance for uncollectible amounts.

PRACTICE POINTER: If an indemnification asset is measured at fair value, no valuation allowance is needed because the risk related to uncollectibility is already included in determining the asset's fair value.

Reacquired Rights and Assets Held for Sale

In an acquisition an acquirer may reacquire a right that it had previously granted to the acquiree (e.g., the acquirer could have granted the acquiree a right to use technology under a technology licensing agreement). Such a reacquired right is recognized as an intangible asset at fair value. Fair value is based on the remaining contractual term of the transferred right, regardless of whether market participants would consider potential renewals in determining fair value.

At the acquisition date, the acquirer measures an acquired long-lived asset or disposal group that is classified as held for sale at fair value less cost to sell in accordance with ASC 360.

Recognizing Goodwill or a Contribution Received

ASC 958 differs most significantly from ASC 805 in the area of recognizing goodwill. Unlike business entities, some NFP entities are solely or predominantly supported by contributions and returns on investments (e.g., a soup kitchen). Other NFP entities are more like business entities and receive most, if not all, of their support from fees and services (e.g., a hospital that charges fees to help cover its costs). In general, the more a NFP entity is like a business, the more relevant information about goodwill is to the users of its financial statements.

ASC 958 recognizes that information about goodwill may be of limited use to the donors of a NFP entity in making decisions to provide resources to the entity. Accordingly, the standard requires an acquirer that expects the operations of the acquiree as part of the combined entity to be predominantly supported by contributions and returns on investments to recognize as a separate charge in its statement of activities the amount that would otherwise be recognized as goodwill at the acquisition date. The phrase "predominantly supported by" means that contributions and returns on investments are expected to be significantly more than the total of all other sources of revenues for the NFP entity (ASC 958-805-25-29).

Many acquisitions by NFP entities constitute an inherent contribution received because the acquirer receives net assets without transferring consideration. ASC 958 requires the acquirer to recognize such a contribution as a separate credit in its statement of activities on the acquisition date (ASC 958-805-25-31; 958-805-30-8, 9).

However, if the acquiree is not primarily supported by contributions and returns on investment, goodwill may be recognized as part of the acquisition. The goodwill amount to be recognized is computed as the excess of the purchase price over the fair value of the acquiree's net assets at the acquisition date. The acquisition price includes (1) consideration transferred (measured at fair value), (2) the fair value of any noncontrolling interest in the acquiree, and, (3) if the acquisition is achieved in stages, the fair value of the interest in the acquiree held by the acquirer on the acquisition date (ASC 958-805-25-28; 958-805-30-6). In some cases, an acquirer receives assistance from an unrelated third party in consummating an acquisition. Such assistance is included in the fair value of the consideration transferred by the acquirer (ASC 958-805-25-32). In addition, the acquirer may transfer contingent consideration. The fair value of such contingent consideration is included in determining the acquisition price (ASC 958-805-25-36). Finally, assets transferred where the acquirer retains control over the assets' future economic benefits are *not* to be considered as being transferred (ASC 958-805-25-33).

Noncontrolling Interests

ASC 958 requires that a recognized noncontrolling interest in another entity be measured at its fair value at the acquisition date. This is true whether the other entity is a business entity or another NFP entity. ASC 958 also provides guidance on and illustrates the presentation of a noncontrolling interest in a NFP entity's financial statements.

Other Provisions of the Acquisition Method

ASC 958 provides other guidance on applying the acquisition method in areas that are unique or especially significant for NFP entities, including the following:

- An acquisition achieved in stages;
- What constitutes the "measurement period";
- Determining what is part of the acquisition transaction;
- Acquisition-related costs;
- How to present in the statement of activities and the statement of cash flows various items that are unique to NFP entities, including an immediate charge to the statement of activities for amounts that otherwise would be recognized as goodwill, and an immediate credit to the statement of activities for an inherent contribution received; and
- Subsequent measurement.

Acquisition Achieved in Stages

An acquisition is achieved in stages when two or more transactions result in the acquirer obtaining control of the acquiree. For example, ABC Inc. might hold a 30% noncontrolling equity interest in XYZ Inc. and then acquire another 40% equity interest. Because ABC Inc. now holds a 70% equity interest in XYZ Inc., ABC now has control and that control was achieved in stages.

In an acquisition achieved in stages, the acquirer remeasures its equity stake in the acquiree at fair value at the acquisition date. In the preceding example, at the time of the second acquisition, ABC Inc. would revalue its 30% stake in XYZ Inc. to fair value. Any resulting gain or loss on the remeasurement would appear in ABC Inc.'s statement of activities.

In addition, an entity subject to the AICPA Audit and Accounting Guide *Health Care Organizations* would include the gain or loss on remeasurement in the performance indicator (ASC 954-805-45-3).

Determination of the Measurement Period

If the accounting for an acquisition is incomplete by the end of the reporting period in which the acquisition occurred, the acquirer accounts for the acquisition using provisional amounts. These provisional amounts are to be adjusted during the measurement period using additional information as to conditions that existed on the acquisition date. In addition, if additional information indicates that other assets and liabilities existed at the acquisition date they are to be recorded even if provisional amounts were not established. The measurement period ends when the acquirer obtains all the information it needs to account for the acquisition, but in no case shall the measurement period exceed one year from the acquisition date.

In determining whether information subsequently acquired provides information about the value of assets and liabilities as of the acquisition date or reflects transactions that occurred after the acquisition date, the acquirer recognizes that information received shortly after the acquisition date is more reliable than information received later. Changes to the provisional amounts recorded for assets and liabilities affect goodwill or, for those acquisitions where goodwill is not recognized, are recorded via a direct charge to the statement of activities. And, if the provisional amounts recorded for assets and liabilities are adjusted, amounts reported in prior-period statements are to be adjusted, including recomputing prior-period amounts for depreciation, amortization, etc. Finally, once the measurement period is over, adjustments related to the acquisition can only be recorded to correct errors.

Scope of the Acquisition Transaction and Acquisition-Related Costs

The acquirer and acquiree may have a relationship that precedes the acquisition transaction, or they may enter into a separate transaction during the acquisition negotiations. Any amounts exchanged that are not part of the consideration for the acquisition are to be accounted for separately. In particular, a transaction entered into primarily for the benefit of the acquirer is likely to be a separate transaction. Examples of separate transactions that are not part of the acquisition include the following (ASC 805-10-25-21; 958-805-25-7):

- A transaction to settle a preexisting relationship between the acquirer and acquiree;
- A transaction that compensates employees or former owners of the acquiree for future services;
- A reimbursement of the acquiree or its former owners for paying the acquirer's acquisition-related costs;
- A payment by a former owner of an acquired business that is unrelated to the acquiree.

Acquisition-related costs are costs incurred by the acquirer to consummate the acquisition. With one exception, acquisition-related costs are expensed as incurred. However, the costs to issue debt to fund an acquisition are accounted for in accordance with other applicable GAAP.

Financial Statement Presentation Issues

If the acquiree's operations are primarily supported by contributions and returns from investments, any excess of the acquisition price over the fair value of the net assets acquired is charged to the statement of operations in the period of the acquisition. A suitable line item description might be, "excess of consideration paid over net assets acquired in acquisition of Entity ABC" (ASC 958-805-45-4).

If the fair value of the net assets acquired exceeds the acquisition price, the acquirer has received an inherent contribution. Such an inherent contribution is to be recognized in the statement of activities. A suitable line item description might be "excess of assets acquired over liabilities assumed in donation of Entity ABC." For those entities where the AICPA Audit and Accounting Guide *Health Care Organizations* applies, whether the donation is included within the performance indicator depends upon whether the contribution is restricted or unrestricted. Unrestricted contributions are included within the performance indicator; donor-restricted contributions are not (ASC 958-805-45-5).

The classification of the net assets associated with the inherent contribution depends on any restrictions imposed. Restrictions imposed on the net assets of the acquiree by a donor before the acquisition, or those imposed when the acquiree is donated to the acquirer are to be disclosed. Also, contributions restricted by donors are to be reported as donor-restricted support even if the restrictions are satisfied in the period of the acquisition (ASC 958-805-45-6).

The use of assets by the acquirer to fund an acquisition may result in a change in net asset classifications. If assets restricted for the purchase of works of art are used to purchase an acquiree that has works of art, the acquirer must report the expiration of the restrictions either separately or in aggregate with other restrictions that have expired. The transfer of assets with no associated donor restrictions to acquire assets that have associated donor restrictions results in a reclassification of net assets in the statement of activities (ASC 958-805-45-8, 9, 10).

In addition to the statement of activities, there are presentation issues that affect the statement of cash flows. The acquirer will report as a cash outflow in the investing activity portion of the statement the cash consideration transferred less the acquiree's cash balance, except for cash payments made to settle a contingent consideration liability arising from the acquisition that are not paid soon after the business combination, which are classified as cash outflows for financing activities. Noncash amounts and contributions received or transferred are to be disclosed as noncash transactions in accordance with the guidance in ASC 230 (ASC 958-805-45-11, -12; 958-805-50-15).

Subsequent Measurement

Assets acquired or liabilities assumed in an acquisition are generally accounted for in accordance with other applicable GAAP. ASC 958 provides specific guidance in subsequently accounting for (1) reacquired rights, (2) indemnification assets, (3) contingent consideration, and (4) goodwill.

A reacquired right recognized as an intangible asset is amortized over the remaining contractual term. The gain or loss on any future sale of the reacquired right would consider the carrying value of the reacquired right.

The indemnification asset is measured at each future reporting date using the same (measurement) basis as the indemnified asset or liability, subject to any contractual limitation on the amount of the asset. The indemnification asset should only be derecognized when the acquirer collects the asset, sells the asset, or otherwise loses its right to the asset.

The amount of contingent consideration due may change because of subsequent business developments, say, meeting or failing to meet an earnings, share price, or other performance target. The acquirer is to remeasure the related asset or liability to fair value at the end of each reporting period until the contingency is resolved. Changes in the fair value of contingent assets and liabilities are included in the statement of activities (ASC 958-805-35-3).

The acquirer is to apply ASC 350 in accounting for goodwill and other intangible assets in future periods (ASC 958-805-35-5).

Disclosures: Acquisitions

ASC 958 requires extensive disclosures by the acquirer if an acquisition occurs either during the current period or after the current period but before the financial statements are issued or are available to be issued. However, if the accounting is incomplete for an acquisition occurring after the current period but before the financial statements are issued or are available to be issued, the acquirer must state the disclosures that could not be made and the reasons why (ASC 958-805-50-14).

The disclosures required by an acquirer as a result of an acquisition are as follows (ASC 958-805-50-7, 8, 9, 11, 12):

- The name and description of the acquiree;
- The acquisition date;
- If applicable, the percentage of voting equity ownership obtained;
- The primary reasons for the acquisition and how control was obtained;
- A description of the factors that make up the goodwill recognized or the separate charge recognized in the statement of activities for those acquirees where goodwill is not recognized (i.e., acquirees whose support is primarily from contributions and returns on investment);
- The fair value of the consideration transferred (including by major class of consideration) at the acquisition date;
- For contingent consideration and indemnification assets, the amount recognized, a description of the arrangement and how any future payment is to be determined, and (if practicable) an undiscounted range of possible payment outcomes;
- The amounts recognized as of the acquisition date for each major class of assets acquired and liabilities assumed;
- Assets and liabilities recognized as a result of contingencies, including the measurement basis (i.e., fair value or measured in accordance with ASC 450), and a description of the contingencies;

- If assets and liabilities related to contingencies are not recognized, any required disclosures from ASC 450 (e.g., the contingency is reasonably possible, or the contingency is probable but a reasonable estimate of the amount cannot be developed);
- Goodwill expected to be deductible for tax purposes;
- The dollar amount of "collectible" items (works of art, historical items, etc.) not recognized as an asset but rather recorded in the statement of activities as a decrease in the acquirer's net assets;
- The undiscounted amount of conditional promises to give acquired or assumed, with individual descriptions and amounts for each group of similar promises;
- For transactions with the acquiree that are not part of the acquisition: (1) a description of the transaction, (2) how the acquirer accounted for the transaction, (3) the amounts recognized for each transaction and the financial statement lines where these amounts appear, and (4) how the settlement amount was determined if the transaction settles a preexisting relationship;
- For transactions with the acquiree that are not part of the acquisition: (1) acquisition-related costs, (2) amounts recognized as an expense, and (3) the financial statement lines where these amounts appear;
- For those acquisitions involving an inherent contribution received, a description of why the transaction resulted in a contribution received;
- For those acquisitions achieved in steps: (1) the fair value of the acquirer's equity interest in the acquiree immediately before the acquisition date and (2) any gain or loss in revaluing the acquirer's equity interest and the line item in the statement of activities where this gain or loss appears;
- If the acquirer is a public entity, required additional disclosures are:
  - The amounts included in the statement of activities attributable to the acquiree since the acquisition date for revenues, changes in net assets without donor restrictions and changes in net assets with donor restrictions, and for entities subject to the AICPA Audit and Accounting Guide *Health Care Organizations* the performance indicator;
  - Selected pro-forma information as if all acquisitions during the period had occurred as of the beginning of the period, including revenues, changes in net assets without donor restrictions and changes in net assets with donor restrictions, and for entities subject to the AICPA Audit and Accounting Guide *Health Care Organizations* the performance indicator;
  - If the acquirer presents comparative financial statements, selected pro forma information as if all acquisitions during the period had occurred as of the beginning of the earliest period presented for comparative purposes, including revenues, changes in net assets without donor restrictions and changes in net assets with donor restrictions, and for entities subject to the AICPA Audit and Accounting Guide *Health Care Organizations* the performance indicator.

If disclosure of any of the above information is impracticable, the entity must disclose that fact and explain why the information is not disclosed. The term "impracticable" as used in ASC 958 has the same meaning as in ASC 250 (Accounting Changes and Error Corrections) (ASC 958-805-50-10).

In addition to the above disclosures, the acquirer is to disclose adjustments in the current period that relate to acquisitions in either the current or prior periods. The following items are to be disclosed for all material acquisitions and in the aggregate for immaterial acquisitions that are material when considered together (ASC 958-805-50-16):

- If the accounting for the acquisition is incomplete and provisional amounts are included in the financial statements, the following are to be disclosed:
  - The reasons that the accounting is incomplete;
  - The specific assets, liabilities, equity interests, or consideration amounts where the accounting is incomplete;
  - The nature and amount of any measurement-period adjustments recognized during the period;
- For each reporting period after the acquisition where a contingent consideration asset or liability continues to exist, the following are to be disclosed:
  - Any changes in the amounts recognized, including gains and losses on settlement;

— Any changes in possible undiscounted outcomes and the reasons for these changes;
— A reconciliation of the beginning and ending goodwill balance.

ASC 958-20: FINANCIALLY INTERRELATED ENTITIES

ASC 958 requires a recipient organization to recognize at fair value an asset and liability instead of contribution revenue if the recipient organization accepts cash or other financial assets from a donor and agrees to use those assets, or disburse them and the return from investing the assets, or both, to a specified beneficiary (ASC 958-605-25-24). The specified beneficiary reports its interest in the assets held by the recipient organization as an asset and as contribution revenue (ASC 958-605-25-28). Exceptions to the above are situations in which the recipient organization is granted variance power (i.e., can redirect the use of funds) and in which the recipient and beneficiary organizations are interrelated (ASC 958-605-25-25, 27).

The Codification also specifies criteria for determining when the recipient organization and the specified beneficiary are considered interrelated organizations. These criteria are typically met by a NFP organization and a related foundation (ASC Glossary).

PART II: INTERPRETIVE GUIDANCE

ASC 958-205: PRESENTATION OF FINANCIAL STATEMENTS

ASC 958-205-05-9 through 05-10, 45-13 through 45-13F, 50-1A through 50-1B, 55-1, 55-31 through 55-53 Endowments of Not-for-Profit Organizations: Net Asset Classification of Funds Subject to an Enacted Version of the Uniform Prudent Management of Institutional Funds Act, and Enhanced Disclosures

BACKGROUND

The Uniform Prudent Management Institutional Funds Act of 2006 (UPMIFA) is a model act that was adopted by the National Conference of Commissioners on Uniform State Laws (NCCUSL) to be used as a guideline by states enacting related legislation. It is a modernized version of the Uniform Management of Institutional Funds Act of 1972 (UMIFA) on which 46 states and the District of Columbia have based their primary laws that legislate the manner in which not-for-profit organizations (NFPOs) are required to invest and manage donor-restricted endowment funds.

The UPMIFA provides new guidance for the designation of expenditures of a donor-restricted endowment fund, unless it is superseded by explicit donor conditions. While the UMIFA dealt with the prudent spending of a fund's net appreciation, the UPMIFA addresses the treatment of both the *original* gift and the *net appreciation* of a donor-restricted endowment fund. The UPMIFA also replaces the UMIFA's historic-dollar-threshold with guidance on what represents prudent spending while considering a fund's duration and preservation.

Under subsection 4(a) of the UPMIFA, an endowment fund's assets are considered to be donor-restricted assets until the NFPO has designated them for disbursement, unless the gift instrument states otherwise. Some have raised questions about how that requirement and the UPMIFA's changed focus from the UMFIA's requirement of prudent spending (i.e., historical-dollar-threshold) to the detailed guidelines on what represents prudent spending, which requires consideration of an endowment fund's duration and preservation (see ASC 958-205-45-13 through 45-13F).

ACCOUNTING GUIDANCE

- FASB Accounting Standards Codification® (ASC) 958-205-45-13 through 45-13F provides the following guidance to NFPOs for reporting endowment funds: Endowments, which may be established by a donor or by an NFP's governing board, may be made either with (donor-restricted endowment funds) or without donor restrictions. Endowments with donor restrictions are the result of a gift stipulating that the money be invested either for a long or specified period of time or in perpetuity. Endowments without donor restrictions (board-designated endowment funds) are created when a governing board designates or earmarks a portion of its net assets to be invested without donor restrictions, usually for a long or maybe an unspecified time period.
- ASC 958-205-45-13A provides that an endowment fund's net assets should be presented as follows in the balance sheet separated into the following two classes of net assets: (*a*) net assets with donor restrictions, and (*b*) net assets without donor restrictions, such as a board-designated fund. The latter class of net assets may in rare circumstances also include a portion of net assets with donor restrictions.

- ASC 958-205-45-13B provides that an NFPO should consider a donor's explicit stipulations and applicable laws in the classification of donor-restricted funds. An investment return is generally considered free of donor restrictions unless it is restricted by the donor or by law. Most donor-restricted funds in the United States are governed by an enacted version of the Uniform Prudent Management of Institutional Funds Act of 2006 (UPMIFA), under which a donor's restriction on the use of the donated funds also applies to the investment return until the governing board appropriates for expenditure. Therefore, if the returns are restricted, they should be reported in net assets with donor restrictions until the funds are appropriated for expenditure. However, the original fund plus the returns of an endowment fund created by a governing board should be reported in net assets without donor restrictions, unless the use of those funds are subject to other purpose-type restrictions.
- ASC 958-205-45-13C states that ASC 958-205-45-13D through 45-13F below provide guidance to NFPs that follow an enacted version of UPMIFA for the classification of the net assets of donor-restricted endowment funds.
- Under the guidance in ASC 958-205-45-13D, the original gifted amount of a donor-restricted fund, additional gifts to that fund, if any, and investment returns, should initially be classified as net assets with donor restrictions. Unless a gift instrument states otherwise, an endowment fund's assets are donor-restricted until an NFP's governing board appropriates the funds for expenditure. Donors may provide specific instructions on spending from a donor-restricted endowment fund or from the fund's investment returns.
- ASC 958-205-45-13E provides that a governing board's appropriation of funds from a donor-restricted endowment fund reduces the amount of its net assets. When an appropriation for expenditure is made, the restriction expires for the appropriated amount as long as all of the restrictions related to the period of time that an endowment fund must be held have lapsed and all of the purpose restrictions have been met. At that time, the appropriated amount is reclassified from net assets with donor restrictions to net assets without donor restrictions in accordance with the guidance in ASC 958-205-45-9. But if the purpose restrictions have not been met, the appropriated funds will remain in donor-restricted net assets until those restrictions have been satisfied.
- ASC 958-205-45-13F provides that without an interpretation by legal or regulatory authorities of the phrase "appropriated for expenditure" in subsection 4(a) of the UPMIFA, for the purpose of this guidance, an appropriation for expenditure occurs when it is approved, unless it is approved for a future period. In that case, the appropriation would be considered to have occurred at that future date. Approval for expenditure may occur in different ways, such as part of a formal annual budget or when an unexpected need occurs during the year.

  To help NFPOs understand the requirements of the applicable law in their particular states, the following sources of information may be consulted: (1) discussions of a state's legislative committee that have resulted in the law's adoption; (2) announcements from a state's Attorney General; (3) a consensus of scholarly lawyers in that state; or (4) similar information. The governing board of an NFP in a state that has *not* enacted new legislation based on the UPMIFA should interpret the requirements of the UPMIFA consistently from year to year based on clarifying court decisions, additional guidance issued by their state's Attorney General, or similar developments.
- Regardless of whether it is subject to an enacted version of UPMIFA, a NFP is required to disclose information about the organization's *donor-restricted* and *board-designated* endowment funds to help users of its financial statements to understand: (1) the classification of net assets (e.g., net assets with donor restrictions or net assets without donor restrictions); (2) the composition of net assets (e.g., board-designated endowment funds or donor-restricted endowment funds); (3) changes in the composition of net assets; (4) the organization's spending policies; and (5) related investment policies. At a minimum, the following information should be disclosed for each period for which a NFP presents financial statements:
  - — The governing board's interpretation of the laws based on which net assets of donor-restricted endowment funds are classified, including its interpretation of the ability to spend from underwater endowment funds.
  - — The NFP's spending policies (i.e., its policies for the designation of funds from endowment assets for disbursement), including its policy, and any actions taken during the period, related to appropriation from underwater endowment funds.
  - — The NFP's investment policies for its endowments, including: (1) the organization's goals for returns and risk limits; (2) the relationship of those goals to its spending policies; and (3) the strategies used to achieve those goals.

— The composition of the NFP's endowment by net asset class at the end of the period, in total and by type of endowment fund, with donor-restricted endowment funds presented separately from board-designated endowment funds.

— A reconciliation of the beginning and ending balance of the NFP's endowment, in total and by net asset class, including, at a minimum, all of the following line items, if applicable: (1) investment return, net; (2) contributions; (3) amounts designated for disbursement; and (4) other changes.

ASC 958-720: NOT-FOR-PROFIT ENTITIES—OTHER EXPENSES

ASC 958-720-05-1, 05-7, 15-6 through 15-8, 25-9, 30-2 through 30-3, 45-56, 50-3; ASC 958-10-65-1; ASC 958-605-25-27; ASC 954-10-05-3; ASC 954-220-45-2 Services Received from Personnel of an Affiliate

BACKGROUND

Not-for-profit (NFP) entities in an affiliated group frequently operate under an arrangement in which personnel is hired and used for common purposes and projects. The personnel may be assigned to work for affiliated NFP entities without repayment of those costs to the contributing entity.

Under the existing guidance in FASB Accounting Standards Codification® (ASC) 958, *Not-for-Profit Entities* (ASC 958-605-25-17), a NFP entity is required to recognize "contributed" services and the related assets and expenses if employees of a separately managed affiliate: (1) regularly perform services for the recipient NFP entity under its direction; and (2) meet the criteria for the recognition of contributed services.

Under the existing guidance in ASC 958-605-25-16, contributed services from nonaffiliated entities should be recognized if they:

- Create or augment nonfinancial assets; or
- Require specialized skills, which are provided by individuals with those skills that would otherwise have to be purchased (e.g., skills such as those provided by accountants, carpenters, doctors, lawyers, electricians, plumbers, teachers, nurses, etc.).

According to the guidance in ASC 958-605-30-2, contributions should be measured at their fair value.

The Financial Accounting Standards Board (FASB) has issued Accounting Standards Update 2013-06 because some stakeholders have questioned whether a recipient NFP entity should recognize personnel costs regularly incurred on its behalf by an affiliated entity as contributed services in accordance with the guidance in ASC 958-605-25-17. Some believe that transactions in which a recipient NFP entity has control over services contributed by an affiliate and has access to information about the actual cost of the services provided differ from services contributed by unaffiliated donors and justify different recognition and measurement criteria. However, there is diversity in practice. Some NFP entity recipients have been recognizing in their standalone financial statements only personnel services received from an affiliated entity that meet the criteria provided in ASC 958-605-25-17 and those related to skilled services or the creation or improvement of nonfinancial assets discussed in ASC 958-605-25-16. Other recipients have been recognizing the cost of all personnel services paid for by an affiliated entity.

ACCOUNTING GUIDANCE

The guidance in ASU 2013-06 applies to the financial statements of a NFP entity that receives personnel services from an affiliated entity. The guidance is as follows:

- *Master Glossary*. The term "affiliate" will be added. It is defined as, "[A] party that, directly or indirectly through one or more intermediaries, controls, is controlled by, or is under common control with an entity."
- *ASC 954-10-05-3*. This paragraph in ASC 954, *Health Care Entities*, includes a list of subtopics that provide guidance applicable to business-oriented NFP health care entities. The list is amended to include "services received from personnel of an affiliate (see Subtopic 958-720)."
- *ASC 954-220-45-2*. Equity transfers that are recorded separately as changes in net assets are not included in a NFP's results from operations and do no result in a step-up in the basis of the transferred underlying assets. As discussed in ASC 958-720-30-3, a NFP entity that receives services at no charge from an affiliate's personnel that directly benefit the NFP, business-oriented health care entity should record the fair value of the service received or at the amount that the affiliate recognized for providing the service.

- *ASC 958-605-25-17*. The guidance in the existing paragraph will be superseded effective June 15, 2014, by new guidance that refers readers to ASC 958-720, for guidance related to the accounting for personnel services received from an affiliate that does not seek compensation. The new guidance clarifies that an affiliate that charges for services provided to a NFP entity requires the recipient to pay at least for the approximate amount of the direct personnel costs (e.g., compensation and fringe benefits) that the affiliate incurred or the approximate fair value of providing the service.

- *ASC 958-720*. The following is new guidance in the new subsection, *Services Received from Personnel of an Affiliate*, which has been added to existing section, *Not-for-Profit Entities—Other Expenses:*

  — *ASC 958-720-05-7* in the Overview and Background section of ASC 958-720 repeats the guidance in ASC 958-605-25-17 above.

  — *ASC 958-720-15-6* is the introductory paragraph to the Scope and Scope Exceptions section, which applies to entities and transactions.

  — *ASC 958-720-15-7* provides that the guidance in the subsections related to Services Received from Personnel of an Affiliate applies to all NFP entities that receive services that directly benefit the NFP entity from an affiliate's personnel without being charged for those services.

  — *ASC 958-720-15-8* defines the transaction (i.e., a service received that is provided by an affiliate's personnel) as one in which an affiliate is not seeking compensation, meaning that the affiliate does not request to recover at least an estimated amount of the direct personnel costs that the affiliate incurs to provide the service to the NFP entity (e.g., compensation and fringe benefits related to payroll) or an estimated fair value of the service. This guidance does not apply to other transactions between affiliates if the affiliate charges the NFP entity for at least the estimated amount of direct costs or the estimated fair value of the services.

  — *ASC 958-720-25-9* provides that a NFP entity should recognize the cost of all services received from an affiliate's personnel if they directly benefit the NFP entity (e.g., if the services are performed under the recipient's direction, and shared services, which are provided by individuals in the affiliate's group in a centralized function that the NFP entity would otherwise have to purchase or receive as a donation).

  — *ASC 958-720-30-2* provides guidance for the *initial measurement* of services, which are provided by an affiliate that does not request compensation and that directly benefit the NFP entity. A NFP entity should measure the cost of those services at the affiliate's cost to provide them, except as provided in ASC 958-720-30-3 below. The components of those costs might vary depending on the situation, but should include all direct personnel costs that the affiliate incurred to provide the services.

  — *ASC 958-720-30-3* provides that if recognition in accordance with the guidance in ASC 958-720-30-2 would overstate or understate the value of the services received, a NFP entity may choose to recognize the cost of the service either at: (1) the affiliate's cost for providing the service; or (b) the fair value of the service.

  — *ASC 958-720-45-56* provides that an increase in net assets related to services that directly benefit a NFP entity, which were received gratis from an affiliate, should not be presented as a contra-expense or a contra-asset. If a NFP entity's net assets decrease or if an asset has been created or enhanced as a result of the use of the gratis services received from an affiliate, that amount should be reported in a similar manner to the way other such expenses or assets are presented. (See ASC 958-220-45-21 for guidance on the presentation of services received from an affiliate's personnel.)

  — *ASC 958-720-50-3* provides that a NFP entity should disclose the information required in ASC 850, *Related Party Disclosures*, for services it has received from an affiliate's personnel.

APPENDIX G

ASC 96X—PLAN ACCOUNTING

CONTENTS

INTERPRETIVE GUIDANCE

ASC 960: PLAN ACCOUNTING—DEFINED BENEFIT PENSION PLANS

ASC 960-325: INVESTMENTS—OTHER

ASC 960-325-35-4, 50-4 through 50-5 Measurement Date Practical Expedient

BACKGROUND

In April 2015, the FASB issued ASU No. 2015-04, *Compensation—Retirement Benefits (ASC 715): Practical Expedient for the Measurement Date of an Employer's Defined Benefit Obligation and Plan Assets*, which provides employers with a practical expedient under which a defined benefit plan's assets are measured on an alternative measurement date, which is a month-end date that is nearest to an employer's fiscal year-end, when the end of the fiscal period does not coincide with the month-end. Employers that elect to use the practical expedient are required to apply it consistently each year thereafter by adjusting the measurement of a defined benefit plan's assets and obligations to include contributions and significant events that occur between the alternative measurement date and the employer's fiscal year-end. An employer also is required to disclose using the practical expedient and the alterative measurement date. Some stakeholders believe that employee benefit plans also should be allowed to apply that practical expedient.

SCOPE

The following guidance applies only to entities that follow the requirements in ASC 960, ASC 962, and ASC 965. The specific amendments to the guidance in ASC 962 and ASC 965 are discussed under the applicable Topics in this Chapter.

ACCOUNTING GUIDANCE

The guidance in ASC 960 is amended as follows:

- ASC 960-325-35-4 has been added to state that a plan is permitted to measure investments and accounts related to investments (e.g., a liability for a pending trade with a broker) by using a month-end that is closest to a plan's year-end when the plan's fiscal year-end does not coincide with a month-end. That election would have to be applied consistently in reporting periods thereafter.
- ASC 960-325-50-4 has been added to require a plan to disclose the election to measure investments and accounts related to investments at the month-end that is closest to the plan's fiscal year-end in accordance with the guidance in ASC 960-325-35-4 and the month-end measurement date.
- ASC 960-325-50-5 has been added to require a plan that measures its investments and accounts related to investments in accordance with the guidance in ASC 960-325-35-4 to disclose the amounts of contributions, distributions, and/or significant events (e.g., a plan amendment, a merger, or a termination) that have occurred between the month-end date used to measure investments and accounts related to those investments and the plan's fiscal year-end.

ASC 960-325-45-1 through 45-2, 50-1 through 50-2, 50-6; ASC 960-30-45-2, 50-2; ASC 960-205-55-1 Plan Investment Disclosures

BACKGROUND

The accounting guidance discussed below has been issued under the FASB's Simplification Initiative that is intended to "identify, evaluate, and improve areas of generally accepted accounting principles" in order to reduce the cost and complexity of providing useful information to financial statement users.

Before the issuance of Accounting Standards Update (ASU) No. 2015-12, *Part II: Plan Investment Disclosures*, plans accounted for under the guidance in ASC 960, *Defined Benefit Plans*, ASC 962, *Defined Contribution Plans*, and ASC 965, *Health and Welfare Plans*, were required to disclose information about individual investments that constitute 5% or more of net assets available for benefits and about the net appreciation or depreciation of investments by general type. Stakeholders held that those disclosures, which are less expensive to provide, did not provide users with information that is useful for decision-making. In addition, under the disclosure requirements in ASC 820, *Fair Value Measurement*, entities are required to group and disclose classes of assets based on their nature, characteristics, and risks, while entities accounting for their investments under the guidance in ASC 960, ASC 962, and ASC 965 also were required to group assets based on their general type. Stakeholders argued that disclosure of similar investment information in accordance with the requirements in ASC 820 is costly for preparers and more difficult to use.

SCOPE

The following guidance applies only to entities that follow the requirements in ASC 960, ASC 962, and ASC 965. The amendments to the guidance in ASC 962 and ASC 965 are discussed under the applicable Topics below.

ACCOUNTING GUIDANCE

The guidance in ASC 960 is amended as follows:

- ASC 960-30-45-2 and 45-2(a) has been amended to state that the purpose of information about changes in net assets available for benefits is "to present the effects of significant changes in net assets during the year" and that the presentation of "net appreciation or depreciation in fair value that includes realized gains and losses on investments that were both purchased and sold during the period as well as unrealized appreciation or depreciation of the investments held at year-end" are required "at a minimum." The previous guidance in that paragraph has been deleted.

- ASC 960-30-50-1 has been amended to refer to the investments of a master trust as "measured at fair value."
- ASC 960-30-50-2 has been amended to substitute "investments" for "each significant type of investment."
- Note E of the financial statements included in ASC 960-205-55-1 has been amended: (1) to refer to a detailed example of plan investment disclosures in ASC 962-325-55-17, and (2) to delete a table in Note E of fair value disclosures about investments that represent 5% or more of a plan's net assets—a disclosure that is no longer required.
- ASC 960-325-45-1 has been amended to delete a requirement to present information "in enough detail to identify the types of investments," which is substituted by "that are measured using fair value."
- ASC 960-325-45-2 has been added to require the presentation of "[i]nvestments measured using fair value in the statement of net assets available for benefits or in the notes" by general type. It includes a list of types of nine investments, such as government securities, corporate bonds, and real estate, among others.
- ASC 960-325-50-1 has been amended to state that "defined benefit pension plans are exempt from the disclosure requirements in ASC 820-10-50-2B(a)," which require the disaggregation of assets by nature, characteristics, and risks, but it provides that the information disclosed by classes of assets under the requirements in ASC 820-10-50 should be disclosed by general type of plan assets as required in ASC 960-325-45-2.
- ASC 960-325-50-2 has been superseded.
- ASC 960-325-50-6 has been added to provide that an investment's significant investment strategy, which is discussed in ASC 820-10-50-6A(a), need not be disclosed for an investment (a) measured by using the net asset value per share (or its equivalent) practical expedient discussed in ASC 820-10-35-59, and (b) held in a fund that files U.S. Department of Labor Form 5500 as a direct filing entity.

ASC 962: PLAN ACCOUNTING—DEFINED CONTRIBUTION PENSION PLANS

ASC 962-310: RECEIVABLES

ASC 962-310-35-2, 45-2, 50-1; ASC 962-325-55-16; ASC 310-10-50-5B, 50-7B Reporting Loans to Participants by Defined Contribution Pension Plans

BACKGROUND

Loans to participants against assets in their plan accounts may be permitted under the provisions of some defined contribution pension plans. If so, some of the assets in a participant's account are liquidated to provide cash for the loan. The only collateral against the loan is the remaining balance in the participant's account, which would be offset if the participant defaults on the loan. In addition, because a plan has no recourse against a participant's personal assets, no assets would be returned to the plan if the participant defaults on the loan. The only consequence of default on a loan from a participant's account in a defined contribution plan is that the participant will be taxed on the unpaid balance of the loan.

Pension and welfare benefit plans are required to file an annual report, referred to as a Form 5500 filing, with the Department of Labor. Under that filing, defined contribution pension plans are required to report the plan's assets at "current value," which is defined as "fair market where available." Otherwise, the term "current value" means that fair value is "determined in good faith under the terms of the plan by a trustee or a named fiduciary, assuming an orderly liquidation at the time of determination." If a plan does not meet certain conditions, audited financial statements must be submitted with the filing. A difference, if any, between the valuation of the plan's assets in the Form 5500 filing and the audited financial statements must be reconciled in a note to the financial statements.

PRACTICE NOTE: ASU 2010-25, *Plan Accounting—Defined Contribution Pension Plans* (Topic 962), *Reporting Loans to Participants by Defined Contribution Pension Plans*, changed the requirements for the reporting of loans to participants. Prior to the issuance of ASU 2010-25, participant loans were considered Plan investments for which guidance was provided in ASC 962-325 (Investments). ASU 2010-25 amended the guidance related to participant loans and relocated it to ASC 962-310 (Receivables).

In accordance with the guidance in ASC 962, *Plan Accounting—Defined Contribution Pension Plans* (ASC 962-325-45-10), loans to participants were reported as investments even though the nature of a loan was that of a receivable.

In addition, under the guidance in ASC 962-325-35, most of a plan's investments, including loans made to participants, must be reported at fair value in accordance with the guidance in ASC 820, *Fair Value Measurements and Disclosures*. The fair value of a plan's investments is "the price that would be received to sell an asset or paid to transfer a liability in an orderly transaction between market participants at the measurement date." However, in practice, most defined contribution pension plans carry loans to participants at amortized cost, which is considered to be a good faith estimate of the fair value based on that definition.

Some believe that loans to participants should be valued based on the guidance in ASC 820 because it cannot be assumed that the outstanding principal balance of those loans is an estimate of their fair value. Others hold that doing so would require highly subjective assumptions about market interest rates and credit risk, which would result in information that is unreliable, not comparable, and not useful. Still others argue that the valuation of loans to participants based on the guidance in ASC 820, which might result in a value other than the unpaid balances of participants' loans, would be misleading to the participants and others (e.g., regulators) and would not be relevant because repayments of the unpaid balances of loans to participants are based on the original amounts of the loans, plus interest, less previous payments.

SCOPE

The following guidance applies to all loans to participants in defined contribution pension plans.

ACCOUNTING GUIDANCE

Participants' loans should be classified as notes receivable from participants in a defined contribution plan's financial statements and should be measured at the balance of the unpaid principal, plus accrued but unpaid interest, if any.

Recurring Disclosures

Additional recurring disclosures are not required for participant loans. In addition, the disclosure requirements about fair value in ASC 825, *Financial Instruments* (ASC 825-10-50-10 through 50-16), do not apply to loans to participants.

Loans to participants are exempt from making the disclosures about credit quality required in ASU 2010-20, *Receivables (Topic 310): Disclosures about the Credit Quality of Financing Receivables and the Allowance for Credit Losses.*

ASC 962-325: INVESTMENTS—OTHER

ASC 962-325-35-1B, 50-2A through 50-2B Measurement Date Practical Expedient

BACKGROUND

In April 2015, the FASB issued ASU No. 2015-04, *Compensation—Retirement Benefits (ASC 715): Practical Expedient for the Measurement Date of an Employer's Defined Benefit Obligation and Plan Assets*, which provides employers with a practical expedient under which a defined benefit plan's assets are measured on an alternative measurement date, which is a month-end date that is nearest to an employer's fiscal year-end, when the end of the fiscal period does not coincide with the month-end. Employers that elect to use the practical expedient are required to apply it consistently each year thereafter by adjusting the measurement of a defined benefit plan's assets and obligations to include contributions and significant events that occur between the alternative measurement date and the employer's fiscal year-end. An employer also is required to disclose using the practical expedient and the alterative measurement date. Some stakeholders believe that employee benefit plans also should be allowed to apply that practical expedient.

SCOPE

The following guidance applies only to entities that follow the requirements in ASC 960, ASC 962, and ASC 965. The amendments to the guidance for ASC 960 and ASC 965 are discussed under the applicable Topics in this Chapter.

ACCOUNTING GUIDANCE

The guidance in ASC 962 is amended as follows:

- ASC 962-325-35-1B has been added to state that a plan is permitted to measure investments and accounts related to investments (e.g., a liability for a pending trade with a broker) by using a month-end that is closest to a plan's year-end when the plan's fiscal year-end does not coincide with a month-end. That election has to be applied consistently in reporting periods thereafter.

- ASC 962-325-50-2A has been added to require a plan to disclose the election to measure investments and accounts related to investments at the month-end that is closest to the plan's fiscal year-end in accordance with the guidance in ASC 962-325-35-1B and the month-end measurement date.
- ASC 962-325-50-2B has been added to require a plan that measures its investments and accounts related to the investments in accordance with the guidance in ASC 962-325-35-1B to disclose the amounts of contributions, distributions, and/or significant events (e.g., a plan amendment, a merger, or a termination) that have occurred between the month-end date used to measure investments and related accounts and the plan's fiscal year-end.

ASC 962-325-35-5 through 35-6, 35-9, 35-11 through 35-12, 45-5, 50-3, 50-8A; ASC 962-205-45-2 through 45-3; ASC 815-10-15-68; ASC 825-10-50-8 Fully Benefit-Responsive Investment Contracts

BACKGROUND

The accounting guidance discussed below has been issued under the FASB's Simplification Initiative, which is intended to "identify, evaluate, and improve areas of generally accepted accounting principles" in order to reduce the cost and complexity of providing useful information to financial statement users. Until the issuance of the guidance in Accounting Standards Update (ASU) No. 2015-12, *Part I: Fully Benefit Responsive Investment Contracts,* such contracts, which were accounted for under the guidance in ASC 962, *Plan Accounting—Defined Contribution Plan*, and ASC 965, *Plan Accounting—Health and Welfare Benefit Plans*, had to be measured at contract value. However, under that guidance, if the contract value of such investment contracts differed from their fair value, as measured under the requirements of ASC 820, *Fair Value Measurement*, an adjustment had to be presented on the face of a plan's financial statements to reconcile the difference.

Some stakeholders suggested that the requirement to measure the fair value of those investment contracts and to disclose the difference between their contract value and fair value did not provide the users of a plan's financial statements with useful information. Further, because the contract value is the amount that participants would receive if they were to make permitted transactions under a plan's terms, such as withdrawals, contract value is used for regulatory reporting purposes and was said to be the relevant measurement attribute for those contracts in Statement of Position (SOP) 94-4, *Reporting of Investment Contracts Held by Health and Welfare Benefit Plans and Defined Contribution Plans,* issued by the American Institute of Certified Public Accountants (AICPA). That guidance has been codified in ASC 962.

Under the amended guidance discussed below, fully benefit responsive investment contracts are measured, presented, and disclosed at contract value.

SCOPE

The following guidance applies to reporting entities under the scope of ASC 962 that classify investments as fully benefit-responsive investment contracts, as defined in the Master Glossary's new definition of a fully benefit-responsive contract.

ACCOUNTING GUIDANCE

The following amendments apply to the guidance in ASC 962, except for the amendment of the Master Glossary, which also applies to the guidance in ASC 965.

Master Glossary

The definition of a "fully benefit-responsive investment contract" has been superseded by the following definition:

> An investment contract is considered fully benefit-responsive if all of the following criteria are met for that contract, analyzed on an individual basis:
>
> a. The investment contract is effected directly between the plan and the issuer and prohibits the plan from assigning or selling the contract or its proceeds to another party without the consent of the issuer.
>
> b. Either of the following conditions exists:
>
> 1. The repayment of principal and interest credited to participants in the plan is a financial obligation of the issuer of the investment contract.
> 2. Prospective interest crediting rate adjustments are provided to participants in the plan on a designated pool of investments held by the plan or the contract issuer, whereby a financially responsible third party, through a contract generally referred to as a wrapper, must provide assurance that the adjustments to the interest crediting rate will not result in a future interest crediting rate that is less than zero.
>
> If an event has occurred such that realization of full contract value for a particular investment contract is no longer probable (for example, a significant decline in creditworthiness of the contract issuer or wrapper provider), the investment contract shall no longer be considered fully benefit-responsive.

c. The terms of the investment contract require all permitted participant-initiated transactions with the plan to occur at contract value with no conditions, limits, or restrictions. Permitted participant-initiated transactions are those transactions allowed by the plan, such as any of the following:
   1. Withdrawals for benefits
   2. Loans
   3. Transfers to other funds within the plan.

d. An event that limits the ability of the plan to transact at contract value with the issuer and that also limits the ability of the plan to transact at contract value with the participants in the plan, such as any of the following, must be probable of not occurring:
   1. Premature termination of the contracts by the plan
   2. Plant closings
   3. Layoffs
   4. Plan termination
   5. Bankruptcy
   6. Mergers
   7. Early retirement incentives.

e. The plan itself must allow participants reasonable access to their funds.

If access to funds is substantially restricted by plan provisions, investment contracts held by those plans may not be considered to be fully benefit-responsive. For example, if plan participants are allowed access at contract value to all or a portion of their account balances only upon termination of their participation in the plan, it would not be considered reasonable access and, therefore, investment contracts held by that plan would generally not be deemed to be fully benefit-responsive. However, in plans with a single investment fund that allow reasonable access to assets by inactive participants, restrictions on access to assets by active participants consistent with the objective of the plan (for example, retirement or health and welfare benefits) will not affect the benefit responsiveness of the investment contracts held by those single-fund plans. Also, if a plan limits participants' access to their account balances to certain specified times during the plan year (for example, semiannually or quarterly) to control administrative cost of the plan, that limitation generally would not affect the benefit responsiveness of the investment contracts held by that plan. In addition, administrative provisions that place short-term restrictions (for example, three or six months) on transfers to competing fixed-rate investment options to limit arbitrage among those investment options (equity wash provisions) would not affect a contract's benefit responsiveness.

- The guidance in ASC 962-205-45-2(c) and 45-3 has been superseded.
- The guidance in the first sentence of ASC 962-325-35-5 has been amended to delete "all" and to add "(excluding insurance contracts and fully benefit-responsive investment contracts, [see ASC 962-325-35-6 for special provisions on the valuation of insurance contracts and ASC 962-325-35-5A for special provisions on the valuation of fully benefit-responsive investment contracts])," at the end of the sentence. The second sentence of the existing paragraph has been deleted.
- ASC 962-325-35-5A has been added to state that "[c]ontract value is the relevant measure for the portion of the net assets available for benefits of a defined contribution plan attributable to fully benefit-responsive investment contracts."
- ASC 962-325-35-6 has been amended to delete "[d]efined . . . insurance" at the beginning of the paragraph and to state that a plan should present insurance contracts, as defined in ASC 944-20, in a manner similar to the plan's presentation in its annual report filed with certain governmental agencies in accordance with the Employee Retirement Income Security Act (the Act), "that is, either at fair value or at amounts determined by the insurance entity (contract value)." It provides further that plans that are not required to report under the Act should "present insurance contracts as if the plans were subject to the reporting requirements of the Act."
- The second and third sentences of ASC 962-325-35-9 are deleted.
- The guidance in ASC 962-325-35-12 has been superseded.
- The subheading "Nonparticipant Directed Investments" preceding ASC 962-325-45-5 has been deleted. The paragraph is amended by substituting "[i]nvesments measured using fair value" at the beginning of the sentence for "[t]the presentation of non-participant directed investments" at the beginning of the paragraph. Item (k), "[s]elf-directed brokerage accounts (that is, an investment option that allows participants to select investments outside the plan's core options)" has been added to the list in that paragraph. A sentence has been added after the list, referring a reader to ASC 962-325-35-5A and ASC 962-325-50-3 for the presentation of fully benefit-responsive investment contracts that are measured at contract value.
- The required disclosure in ASC 962-325-50-3(a) has been amended after "investment contracts" by the addition of "(including how they operate) by the type of investment contract (for example, synthetic investment contracts or

traditional investment contracts)." The guidance in subparagraphs ASC 962-325-50-3(a)(1) and 50-3(a)(2) through 50-3(c) has been superseded. Item 50-3(f) has been added to require disclosure of "[t]he total contract value of each type of investment contract (for example, synthetic investment contracts or traditional investment contracts)."

- ASC 962-325-50-4 has been superseded.
- ASC 962-325-50-6 has been amended by the addition of "measured using fair value" after "master trust" and "detailed" has been replaced by "presented". Item (g) has been added for note disclosure of "[s]elf directed brokerage accounts (that is, an investment option that allows participants to select investments outside the plan's core options.)" A sentence has been added after the list, referring a reader to ASC 962-325-35-5A and 50-3 for the presentation of fully benefit-responsive investment contracts that are measured at contract value.

Amendment of ASC 815-10

ASC 815-10-15-68A has been added to state that the scope of the guidance in ASC 815 excludes a wrapper of a synthetic guaranteed investment contract that meets the definition of a fully benefit-responsive investment contract held by an employee benefit plan.

Amendment of ASC 825-10

ASC 825-10-50-8, which provides a list of financial instruments that are excluded from making the disclosures of fair value required in ASC 825-10-50-10 through 50-16, is amended by the addition of item (k) for "[f]ully benefit-responsive investment contracts held by an employee benefit plan."

ASC 962-325-45-1 through 45-5, 45-7, 50-1 through 50-1A, 50-6 through 50-7, 50-9, 55-17 Plan Investment Disclosures

BACKGROUND

The accounting guidance discussed below has been issued under the FASB's Simplification Initiative that is intended to "identify, evaluate, and improve areas of generally accepted accounting principles" in order to reduce the cost and complexity of providing useful information to financial statement users.

Before the issuance of Accounting Standards Update (ASU) No. 2015-12, *Part II: Plan Investment Disclosures*, plans accounted for under the guidance in ASC 960, *Defined Benefit Plans*, ASC 962, *Defined Contribution Plans*, and ASC 965, *Health and Welfare Plans*, entities were required to disclose information about individual investments that constitute 5% or more of net assets available for benefits and about the net appreciation or depreciation of investments by general type. Stakeholders held that those disclosures, which are less expensive to provide, did not provide users with information that is useful for decision-making. In addition, under the disclosure requirements in ASC 820, *Fair Value Measurement*, entities are required to group and disclose classes of assets based on their nature, characteristics, and risks, while entities accounting for their investments under the guidance in ASC 960, ASC 962, and ASC 965 also are required to group assets based on their general type. Stakeholders argued that disclosure of similar investment information in accordance with the requirements in ASC 820 is costly for preparers and more difficult for users.

SCOPE

The following guidance applies only to entities that follow the requirements in ASC 960, ASC 962, and ASC 965. The amendments to the guidance for ASC 960 and ASC 965 are discussed under the applicable Topics in this Chapter.

ACCOUNTING GUIDANCE

The following amendments apply to ASC 962:

- ASC 962-205-45-7, which provides that the purpose of information about changes in net assets available for benefits is "to present the effects of significant changes in net assets during the year." It has been amended in ASC 962-205-45-7(a) to provide that "net appreciation or depreciation" in fair value "includes realized gains and losses on investments that were both purchased and sold during the period as well as unrealized appreciation or depreciation of the investments held at year-end." The existing guidance in that paragraph has been deleted.

- ASC 962-325-45-1 through 45-4 have been superseded.
- ASC 962-325-45-5 has been amended to:
  - — Delete the heading "Nonparticipant-Direct Investments" before the paragraph
  - — Substitute "[t]he presentation of nonparticipant directed investments" at the beginning of the paragraph with "[i]nvestments measured using fair value"
  - — Substitute "presented" for "detailed"
  - — Add item (k) "Self-directed brokerage accounts (that is, an investment option that allows participants to select investments outside the plan's core options"
  - — Add a statement that ASC 962-325-35-5A and ASC 962-325-50-3 should be consulted for information about the presentation of fully benefit-responsive investment contracts that are measured at contract value.
- ASC 962-325-45-7 has been superseded.
- ASC 962-325-50-1 has been amended to state that defined benefit pension plans are exempt from the disclosure requirements in ASC 820-10-50-2B(a) requiring the disaggregation of assets by nature, characteristics, and risks, and the requirements in ASC 820-10-50 regarding the disclosure of information by classes of assets should be required to be provided by general type of plan assets as required in ASC 962-325-45-5.
- ASC 962-325-50-1A has been superseded.
- ASC 962-325-50-6 under the heading "Master Investment Trusts," has been amended in the same manner as ASC 962-325-45-5 (discussed above).
- ASC 962-325-50-7 has been amended by the addition of "total" as the second word, and the substitution of "investments" for "each significant type of "investment."
- ASC 962-325-50-9, which has been added under a new heading, "Investments Measured Using the Net Asset Value per Share Practical Expedient" provides that the investment strategy of an investment measured using the net asset value per share (or its equivalent) practical expedient in ASC 820-10-35-59 need not be disclosed, as discussed in ASC 820-10-50-6(a), if the investment is in a fund that files U.S. Department of Labor Form 5500 as a direct filing entity.
- The guidance in ASC 962-325-55-16 and its related headings have been superseded.
- ASC 962-325-55-17 has been added to provide illustrative financial statements and note disclosures of a defined contribution plan.

PRACTICE NOTE: ASC 962-325-55-17 has been amended under the guidance in ASU 2018-09, *Codification Improvements,* as follows:

1. Key assumptions a. and b. for Example 2. have been deleted.
2. Subparagraph 5 under the Level 3 valuation methodologies is superseded and the Table of Assets at Fair Value has been amended.
3. The Table of Investments Measured Using the Net Asset Value per Share Practical Expedient has been superseded.

For SEC filers, the amendments are effective for annual periods beginning after December 15, 2018, including interim periods within those annual periods. For all other entities, the amendments are effective for annual periods beginning after December 15, 2019, and interim periods within those annual periods beginning after December 15, 2020. Early adoption is permitted for any fiscal year or interim period for which a public business entity's financial statements have not yet been issued, and for all other entities for which financial statements are available to be issued.

ASC 965: PLAN ACCOUNTING—HEALTH AND WELFARE BENEFIT PLANS

ASC 965-325: INVESTMENTS—OTHER

ASC 965-325-35-1, 35-3, 35-6 through 35-9, 45-2, 50-2 through 50-3, 55-3; ASC 965-205-45-2 through 45-3 Fully Benefit Responsive Investment Contracts

BACKGROUND

The accounting guidance discussed below has been issued under the FASB's Simplification Initiative, which is intended to "identify, evaluate, and improve areas of generally accepted accounting principles" in order to reduce the cost and complexity of providing useful information to financial statement users. Until the issuance of the guidance in Accounting Standards Update (ASU) No. 2015-12, *Part I: Fully Benefit Responsive Investment Contracts*, such contracts, which were accounted for under the guidance in ASC 962, *Plan Accounting—Defined Contribution Plan*, and ASC 965, *Plan Accounting—Health and Welfare Benefit Plans*, had to be measured at contract value. However, under that guidance, if the contract value of such investment contracts differed from their fair value, as measured under the requirements of ASC 820, *Fair Value Measurement*, an adjustment had to be presented on the face of a plan's financial statements to reconcile the difference.

Some stakeholders suggested that the requirement to measure the fair value of those investment contracts and to disclose the difference between their contract value and fair value did not provide the users of a plan's financial statements with useful information. Further, because the contract value is the amount that participants would receive if they were to make permitted transactions under the terms of plan, such as withdrawals, contract value is used for regulatory reporting purposes and was said to be the relevant measurement attribute for those contracts in Statement of Position (SOP) 94-4, *Reporting of Investment Contracts Held by Health and Welfare Benefit Plans and Defined Contribution Plans*, issued by the American Institute of Certified Public Accountants (AICPA). That guidance has been codified in ASC 962.

Under the guidance discussed below, fully benefit responsive investment contracts will be measured, presented, and disclosed at contract value.

SCOPE

The guidance that follows applies to reporting entities under the scope of ASC 965 that classify investments as fully benefit-responsive investment contracts, as defined in the Master Glossary's revised definition of a fully benefit-responsive contract. (The revised definition is included in the discussion of fully benefit-responsive investment contracts in ASC 962 above.)

ACCOUNTING GUIDANCE

Except for the amendment of the Master Glossary (see ASC 962-325), which applies to ASC 962 and ASC 965, the following amendments apply to ASC 965.

- ASC 965-20-45-1(c) and ASC 965-20-45-2 have been superseded.
- The guidance in ASC 965-325-35-1 has been amended after "other investments" in the first sentence to add "(excluding insurance contracts and fully benefit-responsive investment contracts, [see ASC 965-325-35-3 for special provisions on the valuation of insurance contracts and ASC 965-325-35-8 for special provisions on the valuation of fully benefit-responsive investment contracts])," and to delete "(excluding insurance contracts)."
- ASC 965-325-35-6 has been amended by deleting the second and third sentences.
- ASC 965-325-35-8 has been amended by deleting the first sentence and adding that contract value is the relevant "measure" for fully benefit-responsive investment contracts.
- ASC 965-325-35-9 has been superseded.
- The subheading "Nonparticipant Directed Investments" preceding ASC 965-325-45-2 has been deleted. The paragraph is amended by substituting "[i]nvesments measured using fair value" at for "[t]the presentation of non-participant directed investments" at the beginning of the paragraph. A sentence has been added after the list, referring a reader to ASC 962-325-35-8 and 50-2 for the presentation of fully benefit-responsive investment contracts that are measured at contract value.
- The disclosure guidance in ASC 965-325-50-2(a) has been amended to require a description of "the nature of those investment contracts (including how they operate) by the type of investment contract (for example, synthetic investment contracts or traditional investment contracts). Subparagraphs 50-2(a)(1) through 50-2(c) have been

superseded. Paragraph 50-2(f) has been added to require disclosure of "[t]he total contract value of each type of investment contract (for example, synthetic investment contracts or traditional investment contracts)."

- ASC 965-325-50-3 has been superseded.
- ASC 965-325-55-3 has been amended by substituting "fully benefit-responsive investment contract" for "benefit-responsive investment."

ASC 965-325-2A, 50-1B through 50-1C Measurement Date Practical Expedient

BACKGROUND

In April 2015, the FASB issued ASU No. 2015-04, *Compensation—Retirement Benefits (ASC 715): Practical Expedient for the Measurement Date of an Employer's Defined Benefit Obligation and Plan Assets*, which provides employers with a practical expedient under which a defined benefit plan's assets are measured on an alternative measurement date, which is a month-end date that is nearest to an employer's fiscal year-end, when the end of the fiscal period does not coincide with the month-end. Employers that elect to use the practical expedient are required to apply it consistently each year thereafter by adjusting the measurement of a defined benefit plan's assets and obligations to include contributions and significant events that occur between the alternative measurement date and the employer's fiscal year-end. An employer also is required to disclose using the practical expedient and the alterative measurement date. Some stakeholders believe that employee benefit plans also should be allowed to apply that practical expedient.

SCOPE

The following guidance applies only to entities that follow the requirements in ASC 960, ASC 962, and ASC 965. The amendments to the guidance in ASC 960 and ASC 962 is discussed under the applicable Topics in this Chapter.

ACCOUNTING GUIDANCE

- ASC 965-325-35-2A has been added to state that a plan is permitted to measure investments and accounts related to investments (e.g., a liability for a pending trade with a broker) by using a month-end that is closest to a plan's year-end when the plan's fiscal year-end does not coincide with a month-end. That election would have to be applied consistently in fiscal year-end reporting periods thereafter.
- ASC 965-325-50-1B has been added to require a plan to disclose the election to measure investments and accounts related to investments at the month-end that is closest to the plan's fiscal year-end in accordance with the guidance in ASC 965-325-35-2A and the month-end measurement date.
- ASC 965-325-50-1C has been added to require a plan that measures its investments and accounts related to investments in accordance with the guidance in ASC 965-325-35-2A to disclose the amounts of contributions, distributions, and/or significant events (e.g., a plan amendment, a merger, or a termination) that have occurred between the month-end date used to measure investments and related accounts and the plan's fiscal year-end.

ASC 965-325-45-2, 50-1 through 50-1A, 50-4, 55-8; ASC 965-20-45-3; ASC 965-205-55-4, 55-6, 55-8 Plan Investment Disclosures

BACKGROUND

The accounting guidance discussed below has been issued under the FASB's Simplification Initiative that is intended to "identify, evaluate, and improve areas of generally accepted accounting principles" in order to reduce the cost and complexity of providing useful information to financial statement users.

Before the issuance of Accounting Standards Update (ASU) No. 2015-12, *Part II: Plan Investment Disclosures*, plans accounted for under the guidance in ASC 960, *Defined Benefit Plans*, ASC 962, *Defined Contribution Plans*, and ASC 965, *Health and Welfare Plans*, were required to disclose information about individual investments that constitute 5% or more of net assets available for benefits and about the net appreciation or depreciation of investments by general type. Stakeholders held that those disclosures, which are less expensive to provide, did not provide users with information that is useful for decision-making. In addition, under the disclosure requirements in ASC 820, *Fair Value Measurement*, entities have been required to group and disclose classes of assets based on their nature, characteristics, and risks, while entities accounting for their investments under the guidance in ASC 960, ASC 962, and ASC 965 also have been required to group assets based on their general type. Stakeholders argued that disclosure of similar investment information in accordance with the requirements in ASC 820 is costly for preparers and more difficult to use.

SCOPE

The following guidance applies only to entities that follow the requirements in ASC 960, ASC 962, and ASC 965. The amendments to the guidance for ASC 960 and ASC 962 are discussed under the applicable Topics in this Chapter.

ACCOUNTING GUIDANCE

The following amendments apply to ASC 965:

- ASC 965-20-45-3(e), which applies to the net appreciation or depreciation in fair value in the statement of changes in net assets available for benefits, has been amended by the deletion of the first sentence and the addition of the requirement that net appreciation or depreciation also should include unrealized appreciation or depreciation of investments held at year-end.
- Except for the first sentence of Note 3 under Example 1 (ASC 965-205-55-2 through 55-4) and Note 3 under Example 2 (ASC 965-205-55-6), the text and the tables that follow have been deleted in each of those notes. A reference to ASC 962-325-55-17, which includes a detailed example of fair value disclosures, has been added to both notes.
- In Example 4 (ASC 965-205-55-8), the schedule for the net increase in net assets available included in Note E has been amended by (1) changing the first line item to read "Net appreciation in fair value of investments" for the amount of $10,800, (2) deleting the line item "U.S. government securities" and adding the revised first line item to the existing line item "Interest" for the amount of $80,200." The total is unchanged.
- ASC 965-325-45-2 has been amended by (1) deleting the heading "Non-Participant Directed Investments," (2) deleting "The presentation of non-participant directed investments" at the beginning of the sentence and inserting "Investments measured using fair value" instead. A sentence is added to the paragraph referring readers to ASC 965-325-35-8 and ASC 965-325-50-2 for the presentation of fully benefit-responsive contracts that are measured at contract value.
- ASC 965-325-50-1 has been amended to state that: (1) health and welfare benefit plans are exempt from the disclosure requirements in ASC 820-10-50-2B(a), which requires the disaggregation of assets by nature, characteristics, and risks, and (2) the requirements in ASC 820-10-50 for the disclosure of information by classes of assets should be presented by general type of plan assets in accordance with the guidance in ASC 965-325-45-2.
- ASC 965-325-50-1A has been superseded.
- ASC 965-325-50-4 as well as a heading "Investments Measured Using the Net Asset Value per Share Practical Expedient" have been added to provide that information about an investment's significant investment strategy, as discussed in ASC 820-10-50-6A(a), need not be disclosed if an investment is measured using the net asset value per share (or its equivalent) practical expedient discussed in ASC 820-10-35-59 and the investment is in a fund that files U.S. Department of Labor Form 5500 as a direct filing entity.
- ASC 965-325-55-8 has been amended to refer to Example 2 in ASC 962-325-55-17, and the phrase "with participant directed and nonparticipant directed investments" at the end of the paragraph has been deleted.

ASC 960: Plan Accounting—Defined Benefit Pension Plans

ASC 962: Plan Accounting—Defined Contribution Plans

ASC 965: Health and Welfare Benefit Plans

ASC 960-325, ASC 962-325, ASC 965-325: Investments—Other

ASC 960-205-45-7, ASC 960-325-50-7 through 50-11; ASC 962-205-45-10, ASC 962-325-50-8 through 50-8C, 50-55-18, ASC 962-10-65-4; ASC 965-205-45-11, ASC 965-325-50-05 through 50-9 Plan Accounting: Defined Benefit Pension Plans (Topic 960), Defined Contribution Pension Plans (Topic 962), Health and Welfare Plans (Topic 965): Employee Benefit Plan Master Trust Reporting

BACKGROUND

The FASB took on this project to improve the usefulness and the extent of information reported in the financial statements of employee benefit plans about those plans' interests in master trusts, which are trusts for which regulated financial institutions (e.g., banks, trust companies or similar financial institutions) serve as trustees or custodians. A master trust may hold the assets of more than one plan sponsored by a single employer or by a group of employers under common control.

ACCOUNTING GUIDANCE

Under the amended guidance in ASC 960, 962, and 965, for each master trust in which an employee benefit plan holds an interest, presentation of the amount of a plan's interest and the amount of a change in that interest, if any, is required in separate line items in a plan's statement of net assets available for benefits and its statement of changes in net assets available for benefits.

Although Health and Welfare Plans, which are accounted for under the guidance in ASC 965, are not required to disclose information (i.e., disclosures required by ASC 815 and ASC 820) for investments in 401(h) assets, those plans are required to disclose the name of a defined benefit pension plan that allocated the funds to the Health and Welfare Benefit Plan and that discloses information about the related investments.

All employee benefit plans under the amended guidance in ASC 960, 962, and 965 are required to include the following information in the notes to the plan's financial statements in each period in which a statement of changes in net assets available for benefits is presented:

a. The net appreciation or depreciation in the fair value of a master trust's investments, including realized gains and losses on investments purchased and sold during the period, and unrealized appreciation or depreciation of investment held at year-end; and
b. Investment income not included in (a).

Disclosure of the following information should be included in the notes to the financial statements of all employee benefit plans under the amended guidance in ASC 960, 962, and 965:

a. A description of the basis used to allocate the following:
   1. Net assets
   2. Total investment income.
b. For a plan with a proportionate, rather than a specific interest in a master trust, the percentage interest as of each statement of net assets available for benefits presented.
c. A master trust's investments measured at fair value and presented by general type of investment, such as the following, as of the date on which a statement of net assets available for benefits is presented:
   1. Registered investment companies (e.g., mutual funds)
   2. Government securities
   3. Common collective trusts
   4. Pooled separate accounts
   5. Short-term securities
   6. Corporate bonds
   7. Common stocks
   8. Mortgages
   9. Real estate
   10. Self-directed brokerage accounts (this investment is only included in plans under ASC 962).

Plans accounted for under the guidance in ASC 962-325-50-8A and ASC 965-325-50-7 are required to present information about the contract value of *fully benefit-responsive investment contracts*, as defined in the ASC's Glossary (see the guidance related to that term in this Chapter's section on ASC 962-325: Investments—Other).

The financial statements of plans accounted for under the guidance in ASC 960, 962, and 965, also are required to disclose the following information:

a. The general types of investments held by a master trust and the dollar amount of a plan's interest in each of those general types of investments; and
b. A master trust's other assets and liabilities and the dollar amounts of a plan's interest in each (e.g., amounts due from brokers for securities sold, amounts due to brokers for securities purchased, receivables relating to derivatives, accrued interest and dividends, and other accrued expenses).

Transition and Effective Date

ASC 962-10-65-4 provides the following transition and effective date guidance for ASC 960, 962, and 965:

- The guidance will be effective for fiscal years that begin after December 15, 2018, but early adoption is permitted.
- The guidance should be applied retrospectively to all periods for which financial statements are presented.
- The disclosures in ASC 250-10-50-1(a) are required in the first annual period in which an entity adopts the guidance.

APPENDIX H

ASC 970—REAL ESTATE—GENERAL

CONTENTS

PART I: GENERAL GUIDANCE

OVERVIEW

The authoritative literature establishes standards for the acquisition, development, construction, and selling and rental costs related to real estate projects. In addition, they cover accounting for initial rental operations and include rules for ascertaining when a real estate project is substantially completed and available for occupancy.

BACKGROUND

Real estate acquisition costs may be classified as (*a*) preacquisition costs and the actual cost of acquiring the property from the seller, and (*b*) post-acquisition costs. Preacquisition costs are those that are incurred prior to the acquisition of the property, such as appraisals, surveys, legal fees, travel expenses, and costs to acquire options to purchase the property. Post-acquisition costs are those that are incurred after the property has been acquired, such as development and construction costs. Post-acquisition costs may be classified further as (*a*) direct costs, (*b*) indirect costs, (*c*) costs of amenities, and (*d*) incidental operational costs.

Direct costs are those that can be directly identified with the real estate project. Indirect costs may or may not be related to a specific real estate project. Indirect costs of several real estate projects may be allocated to each project on a reasonable allocation basis. Incidental operations of a real estate project occur during the development stage of the project and are intended to reduce the cost of the real estate project. Incidental operations do not include activities that result in a profit or return on the use of the real property.

Capitalized costs of a real estate project are allocated to the individual components within the project. The allocation usually is accomplished by the specific identification method, if the individual components within the project can be identified specifically. If specific identification is not possible, capitalized land cost and all other common costs, including common costs of amenities, are allocated based on the relative fair value of each land parcel benefited prior to any construction. Capitalized construction costs are allocated based on the relative sales value of each individual component within the real estate project. Individual components of a real estate project may consist of lots, acres, or some other identifiable unit.

Costs to rent real estate projects under operating leases or direct financing leases are either chargeable to future periods or chargeable to the current period, according to whether their recovery is reasonably expected from future rental revenue.

REAL ESTATE COSTS AND INITIAL RENTAL OPERATIONS

Preacquisition Costs

Certain costs related to the property are frequently incurred before the actual date on which a parcel of real property is acquired. These costs are referred to as *preacquisition costs*. Practically any type of cost may be classified as a preacquisition cost if it is incurred prior to the date of acquisition of a parcel of real property. For example, the cost of an option to purchase real property at a future date is a preacquisition cost and usually is capitalized. If the option is not exercised on or before its expiration date, however, the option becomes worthless and should be expensed.

All other types of preacquisition costs are expensed when incurred, unless they can be identified specifically to the real property being acquired and (ASC 970-340-25-3):

- The preacquisition costs would be capitalized if the property were acquired.
- The costs are directly identifiable with the specific property.
- The acquisition of the property or an option to acquire the property is probable (e.g., the prospective purchaser is actively seeking to acquire the property and can obtain financing).

PRACTICE NOTE: Probable implies that the property is available for sale, the purchaser is currently trying to acquire the property, and the necessary financing is reasonably expected to be available.

Thus, preacquisition costs of a real estate project consist of (*a*) unexpired options to purchase real property and (*b*) other costs that meet all of the above conditions. Preacquisition costs that do not qualify for capitalization should be expensed when incurred (ASC 970-340-25-4).

After a parcel of real property is acquired, preacquisition costs are reclassified as project costs. In the event that the property is not acquired, capitalized preacquisition costs shall not exceed the amount recoverable, if any, from the sale of options, developmental plans, and other proceeds. Capitalized preacquisition costs in excess of recoverable amounts are charged to expense (ASC 970-340-25-4).

Illustration of Preacquisition Costs

Omega Company incurred the following preacquisition costs related to a piece of property:

1. Option to purchase land parcel: $10,000
2. Architectural consultation concerning feasibility of constructing warehouse facility on land parcel: $14,000

Situation 1: At the end of the year in which the above costs were incurred, Omega was actively seeking financing for the land and warehouse facility. Management believes it is probable that financing will be found and the land will be purchased, after which time the warehouse facility will be constructed.

In this situation, the $10,000 option and the $14,000 feasibility study should be capitalized as preacquisition costs, to be reclassified as project costs when the land purchase and warehouse construction commence.

Situation 2: At the end of the year in which the above costs were incurred, preliminary results of the feasibility study were not optimistic. Omega has suspended its search for financing, pending the final outcome of the feasibility study. The company considers the probability of purchasing the land and constructing the facility as no more than reasonably possible, but is optimistic that it can sell the option for at least its $10,000 cost.

In this situation, the $10,000 option cost should be carried as an asset, but the $14,000 for the feasibility study should be expensed in the current period.

Project Costs

Taxes and Insurance

Property taxes and insurance are capitalized as project costs only during periods in which activities necessary to get the property ready for its intended use are in progress (ASC 970-340-25-8).

After real property is substantially completed and ready for its intended use, ASC 970 also requires that property taxes and insurance costs be expensed as incurred (ASC 970-340-25-8).

Amenity Costs of Real Property

Golf courses, swimming pools, tennis courts, clubhouses, and other types of amenities frequently are included in the overall plans of a real estate project. The ultimate disposition of an amenity, however, may vary from one real estate project to another. Thus, accounting for the costs of amenities is based on the developer's (management) ultimate plans for the disposition of the amenity. In this respect, a developer may decide to retain ownership of the amenity and to either (*a*) operate the amenity or (*b*) eventually sell the amenity. On the other hand, the developer may be required under the terms of the individual sales agreements to sell or otherwise transfer ownership of the amenity to the purchasers of the individual components within the project. In this event, the purchasers of the individual components within the project usually form an association for the purposes of taking title to the amenity and operating the amenity for the common benefit of all owners of individual components within the project.

Accounting for the costs of amenities under the provisions of ASC 970 is as follows:

Ownership Not Retained by Developer. When the ownership of an amenity is to be transferred to the individual components within the real estate project, the net cost of the amenity is accounted for by the developer as a capitalized common cost of the project. The capitalized common cost of an amenity is allocated to the individual components within the project that are expected to benefit from the use of the amenity. Thus, the total cost of each individual component in the project that benefits from the amenity will include a proportionate share of the costs of the amenity (ASC 970-340-25-9).

The developer's net cost or gain that is accounted for as a common cost (reduction) of the real estate project may include the sales price, if any, and all other proceeds, if any, from the transfer of the amenity, less the following items:

- Direct costs that clearly are identifiable to the amenity
- Indirect costs that clearly are related to the amenity

- The developer's cost of operating the amenity until the amenity is transferred to the individual components in the project in accordance with the sales contract or other contractual agreement
- Common costs of the project that are allocated appropriately to the amenity

If an amenity clearly benefits specific individual components within a real estate project, the common cost (reduction) of the amenity is allocated only to those specific individual components.

Ownership Retained by Developer. When a developer retains ownership of an amenity, the total cost of the amenity is capitalized as a separate asset. The total cost of an amenity includes direct costs, indirect costs, and the allocation of common costs, including operating results of the amenity prior to its date of substantial completion and availability for its intended use. Under ASC 970, however, the amount capitalized cannot exceed the estimated fair value of the amenity at its expected date of substantial completion. Any costs in excess of the estimated fair value of the amenity at the expected date of its substantial completion are accounted for as common costs of the real estate project (ASC 970-340-25-9). Before an amenity is substantially completed and available for use, operating income (loss) of the amenity shall be included as a reduction of (or additions to) common costs (ASC 970-340-25-11).

After it is substantially completed and ready for its intended use, further revision of the final capitalized cost of an amenity is not permitted. This cost becomes the basis of the amenity for any future sale. The subsequent basis for determining gain or loss on the sale of the amenity is the capitalized cost of the amenity not in excess of its estimated fair value at its date of substantial completion, less any allowable depreciation to the date of the sale.

After its date of substantial completion and availability for its intended use, the operational results of an amenity that is owned by the developer shall be included in the developer's current net income (ASC 970-340-25-11).

Incidental Operations of Real Property

Incidental operations of a real estate project usually occur during the holding or development stage of the project and are intended to reduce the cost of the project. Incidental operations do not include activities that result in a profit or return from the proposed development of the real property. For example, revenue received from billboard advertisements placed on the property or miscellaneous concession income would be classified as incidental operations.

If the incremental revenue received from incidental operations exceeds the related incremental costs, the difference is accounted for as a reduction of the capitalized costs of the real estate project. Thus, when incidental operations of a real estate project result in a profit, the capitalized costs of the project are reduced by the amount of profit. Under ASC 970, however, the same does *not* hold true if the incidental operations result in a loss: if the incremental costs of incidental operations exceed the related incremental revenue, the difference is charged to expense when incurred (ASC 970-340-25-12). The guidance in ASC 970 on accounting for incidental operations does not apply to real estate time-sharing transactions.

Revisions of Estimates

Estimates are used extensively in the acquisition, development, and construction of a real estate project. As a result, revisions of estimated costs occur frequently, and past, present, and future accounting periods may be affected by the revisions.

Revisions of estimates that occur in the acquisition, development, and construction stages of a real estate project are accounted for as changes in accounting estimates (ASC 250). The effects of a change in accounting estimate are accounted for (*a*) in the period of change, if the change affects only that period or (*b*) in the period of change and future periods, if the change affects both. A change in an accounting estimate caused in part or entirely by a change in accounting principle should be reported as a change in accounting estimate. ASC 250 requires that disclosure be made in current period financial statements of the effects of a change in an accounting estimate on (*a*) income from continuing operations, (*b*) net income, and (*c*) related per share data (ASC 250-10-50-4). However, ordinary accounting estimates for uncollectible accounts or inventory adjustments, made each period, do not have to be disclosed, unless they are material (ASC 970-340-35-1).

Selling Costs

Costs incurred to sell real estate projects are accounted for as project costs.

Project Costs

Costs incurred to sell real estate projects must be evaluated for capitalization in accordance with guidance in ASC 340-40-25-1 through 25-8 (ASC 970-340-25-13).

Costs to sell real estate projects that qualify as project costs become part of the capitalized cost of the project and are allocated to the individual components of the project as common costs.

Rental Costs of Real Estate Projects

Initial Rental Operations

Initial rental operations commence when a real estate project is substantially completed and available for occupancy. A real estate project is considered *substantially completed and available for occupancy* when tenant improvements have been completed by the developer, but in no event later than one year after major construction activity has been completed, excluding routine maintenance and cleanup (ASC 970-340-25-19).

The actual rental operation of a real estate project shall commence when the project is substantially completed and available for occupancy. At this time, rental operating costs are charged to expense when incurred. Operating costs include amortization of deferred rental costs, if any, and depreciation expense (ASC 970-340-25-18).

Some portions of a real estate rental project may still require major construction for completion, and other portions of the same project may be substantially completed and available for occupancy. In this event, each portion should be accounted for as a separate project (ASC 970-340-25-17).

Operating Leases

Costs incurred to rent real estate projects under operating leases or direct financing leases are either chargeable to future periods or chargeable to the current period. If the costs can be identified to, and reasonably expected to be recovered from, specific revenue, such costs are capitalized and amortized to the periods in which the specific revenue is earned. If the costs are for goods not used or services not received, such costs are charged to the future periods in which the goods are used or services are received.

If deferred rental costs can be associated with the revenue from a specific operating lease or direct financing lease, other than initial direct costs, such costs are amortized over the lease term. The amortization period commences when the rental project is substantially completed and available for occupancy. If deferred rental costs, other than initial direct costs, cannot be identified with the revenue from a specific lease, such costs are amortized over the periods benefited. The amortization period commences when the rental project is substantially completed and available for occupancy (ASC 970-340-35-2).

PRACTICE POINTER: Expense unamortized rental costs that subsequently become unrecoverable from future operations when they are determined to be unrecoverable. For example, unamortized rental costs related to specific leases that have been, or will be, terminated should be charged to expense.

If the costs to rent real estate projects under operating leases or direct financing leases do not qualify as chargeable to future periods, they are accounted for as period costs and expensed as incurred (ASC 970-340-25-16).

PROJECT COSTS RELATED TO PROPERTY, PLANT, AND EQUIPMENT

Project Costs

Project costs, which are clearly associated with the acquisition, development, and construction of a real estate project, must be capitalized as a cost of that project (ASC 970-360-25-2).

Indirect costs of real estate projects that can be identified clearly with specific projects under development or construction are capitalized as project costs. Indirect costs that are accumulated in one account, but clearly relate to several real estate projects under development or construction, are allocated on a reasonable basis to each of the projects (ASC 970-360-25-3).

Indirect costs on real estate projects not under development or construction are expensed as incurred. In addition, indirect costs that cannot be identified clearly with specific projects such as general and administrative expenses are charged to expense when incurred (ASC 970-720-25-3).

Illustration of Direct and Indirect Project Costs

Zeta Co. incurs the following direct and indirect project costs for two major real estate construction projects, identified as L and M:

Direct project costs:	
Project L	$150,000
Project M	740,000
Indirect project costs:	
Identified with Projects L and M	270,000
Identified with projects not currently under development	145,000
General and administrative	250,000
Total	$1,555,000

The indirect costs associated with Projects L and M are allocable one-third to Project L and two-thirds to Project M.

Treatment of the $1,555,000 of project costs for the year is as follows (in thousands of dollars):

	Project L	*Project M*	*Current Expense*
Direct costs	$150	$740	
Indirect costs:			
Project L ($270 × 1/3)	90		
Project M ($270 × 2/3)		180	
Not allocable ($145 + $250)			$395
	$240	$920	$395

Allocation of Capitalized Costs

All capitalized costs of a real estate project are allocated to the individual components within the project. If practicable, ASC 970 requires that capitalized costs be allocated by the specific identification method. Under this method, capitalized costs are identified specifically with the individual components within the real estate project. However, if it is impractical to use the specific identification method to allocate capitalized costs, ASC 970 requires that allocations be made as follows (ASC 970-360-30-1).

Land Costs

Only capitalized costs associated with the land prior to any construction are allocated as land costs. Land costs prior to any construction include capitalized land costs and other preconstruction common costs related to the land, including preconstruction common costs of amenities.

Total capitalized land costs are allocated based on the relative fair value of each land parcel prior to any construction. A land parcel may be identified as a lot, an acre, acreage, a unit, or a tract.

Construction Costs

Capitalized construction costs are allocated based on the relative sales value of each individual structure or unit located on a parcel of land. In the event capitalized costs of a real estate project cannot be allocated by the specific identification method or the relative sales value method, the capitalized cost shall be allocated on area methods or other methods appropriate under the circumstances (ASC 970-36-25-1).

Abandonments and Changes in Use

Occasionally a real estate project is partially or completely abandoned, or there is a significant change in the use of the property in the project. Under the provisions of ASC 970, if part or all of a real estate project is abandoned, the related capitalized costs must be expensed immediately. The capitalized costs of an abandoned real estate project should not be allocated to other real estate projects (ASC 970-360-40-1).

The cost of land donated to a governmental authority for uses that will benefit the project is not accounted for as abandoned. Under this circumstance, the cost of the donated land is accounted for as a common cost of acquiring the project. Thus, the cost of the donated land is allocated to the other land in the project, based on the relative fair value of each parcel of land prior to construction of any buildings or structures (ASC 970-360-35-1).

After significant development and construction costs have been capitalized in a real estate project, there may be a change in the use of part or all of the land within the project. Under the provisions of ASC 970, capitalized costs incurred prior to a change in use of all or part of the land within a real estate project are charged to expense, except in the following circumstance:

> The enterprise has developed a formal plan that indicates that the change in use of the land will result in a higher economic yield than was originally anticipated. In this event, the maximum costs that can be capitalized must not exceed the estimated value of the revised project at the date of substantial completion and availability for its intended use. Capitalized costs in excess of the estimated value of the revised project when substantially completed, if any, are charged to expense (ASC 970-360-35-2).

Recoverability

Real estate projects that are substantially complete and ready for their intended use are to be carried at the lower of carrying amount or fair market value less cost to sell (ASC 360-10-35-43).

Each individual project is analyzed separately to determine whether a write-down is necessary. An individual project is considered to consist of similar components within the real estate project, such as (*a*) individual residences, (*b*) individual apartments or condominiums, or (*c*) individual lots, acres, or tracts. Thus, a real estate project that includes 50 individual residences, 10 condominium buildings, 20 multifamily buildings, and 100 residential lots would be accounted for as four separate projects for the purposes of determining net realizable values. The net carrying amount of the 100 residential lots may exceed their net realizable value, while the individual net carrying values of the 50 individual residences, 10 condominium buildings, and 20 multifamily buildings may not exceed their individual estimated net realizable values (ASC 970-360-35-3).

PART II: INTERPRETIVE GUIDANCE

ASC 970: GENERAL

ASC 970-340-25-1 through 25-2, 25-5 through 25-7, 35-3 through 35-4; ASC 970-720-25-1 through 25-2 Accounting for Internal Costs Relating to Real Estate Property Acquisitions

BACKGROUND

ASC 970-10-15-8 through 15-11; ASC 970-340-25-2 through 25-4, 25-8 through 25-17, 35-1; ASC 970-360-25-2 through 25-3, 30-1, 35-1 through 35-4, 40-1 through 40-2; ASC 970-605-21-1; ASC 970-720-25-3 provides guidance for the treatment of costs related to the acquisition, development, construction, sale, and rental of real estate projects. The costs addressed under that guidance include preacquisition costs and project costs. Under that guidance, preacquisition costs (e.g., for surveying, zoning studies, or obtaining an option on the property, which are incurred before its acquisition) (*a*) should be capitalized if they are related directly to the property, (*b*) would be incurred if the property were owned, and (*c*) should be capitalized only if it is probable that the property will be acquired or the purchaser will obtain an option to acquire the property.

Under the guidance in ASC 970-360-25-2 through 25-3, project costs are those that are "clearly associated with the acquisition, development and construction of a real estate project" and should be capitalized. Indirect project costs associated with more than one project also should be capitalized and allocated to the related projects.

This Issue has been raised because many real estate companies have full-time property acquisition departments that are involved in finding and acquiring properties and that perform services, such as appraisals and feasibility studies, which otherwise may be provided by outsiders. Because that existing guidance did not distinguish between the accounting for internal and external costs, the treatment of the costs of internal acquisition departments had been diverse—some companies capitalized those costs while others expensed them. Opinions also differed as to whether the existing guidance would apply to all real estate acquisitions or only to properties requiring further development and construction.

ACCOUNTING ISSUE

Should any costs incurred by an internal acquisitions department of a real estate entity to identify and acquire real estate properties be capitalized as part of the acquired property?

ACCOUNTING GUIDANCE

- Costs related to preacquisition activities that are incurred by a real estate entity's internal department to identify and acquire a property that will be classified as *nonoperating* when it is acquired should be *capitalized* as part of the cost of acquiring the property if the costs can be directly identified with the acquired property and were incurred *after* the acquisition was considered probable. If the entity later decides to classify the property as operating when it is acquired, capitalized costs should be expensed and additional costs should be expensed as incurred.

- Preacquisition costs incurred *internally* in connection with the acquisition of a property that will be classified as *operating* on acquisition should be *expensed* as incurred. However, if the entity later decides that the property should be classified as nonoperating when it is acquired, amounts that had already been expensed should *not* be capitalized as part of the cost of acquiring the property. An operating property is (*a*) a property on which major construction activities, not routine maintenance or cleanup activities have been substantially *completed* by the acquisition date; (*b*) a property that will be available for occupancy when tenant improvements are completed; or (*c*) a property that is already income producing. In addition, preacquisition costs related to properties that are partially operating and partially nonoperating should be accounted for based on the guidance in ASC 970-360-25-17, which requires that the two components be accounted for as separate projects and that preacquisition costs incurred be allocated between the respective portions.

The FASB staff noted that guidance on distinguishing between external and internal costs is available in ASC 310-20-55-9 through 55-10. In addition, related guidance on accounting for a service corporation established by a real estate investment trust (REIT) is provided in ASC 974-323-25-1; ASC 840-25-1, "Accounting by a Real Estate Investment Trust for an Investment in a Service Corporation," which is discussed below

DISCUSSION

- Although the original charge was to determine whether the accounting for preacquisition costs incurred by a real estate entity's internal property acquisitions department should differ from that for costs incurred for the same services provided by a third party, the final guidance is based on the guidance in ASC 970-360-25-3, which requires that (*a*) only costs that can be directly identified with a specific property be capitalized, that is, not all costs incurred to identify acquisitions are capitalizable, (*b*) the costs would be capitalizable if a property had already been acquired, and (*c*) it is probable that a property will be acquired. In addition, those who supported this guidance argued that there is no conceptual reason that the accounting for preacquisition costs incurred by an internal department should differ from costs incurred if the same services are provided by an unrelated third party.

  The decision that capitalization of preacquisition costs is appropriate only for properties that will be *acquired* was based on the view that those costs will be recovered over the life of the property through its revenue stream. The benefit of costs related to properties *not* acquired expires in the period in which the costs were incurred, because they will not be recovered from revenues earned in future periods.

- Internal costs related to the identification and acquisition of real estate properties that need further development (*nonoperating* properties) were distinguished from those incurred to identify and acquire *operating* real estate properties. Some argued that the acquisition of an operating property is similar to a business combination and should be accounted for based on the principles in ASC 815.

  The FASB staff, who supported the guidance, analogized to (*a*) the guidance on the capitalization of interest costs in ASC 835-20-25-5 through 25-6 under which capitalization ceases when the status of a property changes from nonoperating to operating and (*b*) the guidance in ASC 310 and ASC 840, both of which distinguish between the treatment of costs related to *originating* loans and leases and those related to *acquiring* existing loans or leases.

ASC 970-360-25-1, 55-1 through 55-3 Recognition of Receipts from Made-Up Rental Shortfalls

BACKGROUND

A public real estate syndication (buyer) purchases a newly constructed office building from a developer (seller). At the date of the sale, the buyer's general partner negotiates a master leaseback agreement with the seller for the building, which is only partially occupied. The agreement provides that the seller will lease vacant space for two years at a market rate and the buyer will pay the seller a reasonable fee, which is described as a fee in exchange for signing a master lease or as an escrowed portion of the purchase price. If a sublease meets certain conditions, the seller will not be required to make future lease payments on space the seller leases to others. The seller's rental payments would exceed the buyer's fee if the seller is unable to lease the vacant space during the two-year lease period.

ACCOUNTING ISSUE

How should a buyer account for (*a*) a fee paid to the seller and (*b*) rental payments received from the seller?

ACCOUNTING GUIDANCE

A buyer should account for the fee paid to a seller and rental payments received from the seller as adjustments to the basis of the acquired property that will affect future depreciation.

The buyer's fee paid to the seller was considered by some, including the SEC Observer, to be an escrowed portion of the purchase price that is conditional on the seller's ability to rent the space.

EFFECT OF ASC 815

The guidance in ASC 815 applies if the agreement meets the definition of a derivative in ASC 815. However, usually the agreement would meet the scope exception in ASC 815-10-15-13 related to sales or service revenue of one of the parties to the agreement because the underlying is the syndicate's leasing rental revenue and consequently the accounting guidance above would not be affected.

ASC 970-360-55-4 through 55-5 Recognition by Homebuilders of Profit from Sales of Land and Related Construction Contracts

---

> *IMPORTANT NOTICE:* The guidance in this Issue will be superseded by the guidance in ASU 2014-09, *Accounting for Revenue from Contracts with Customers*, which becomes effective for public business entities in annual reporting periods that begin after December 15, 2017, and interim periods within those annual periods and in annual reporting periods that begin after December 15, 2018, for nonpublic entities.

BACKGROUND

A homebuilder enters into a contract with a buyer to construct a single-family house on a lot owned by the homebuilder. The sales price stated in the contract does not distinguish between the sale of the lot and construction of the house. Title on the lot is not transferred to the buyer until completion of construction and closing.

If, instead, the house was built on a lot owned by the buyer, the homebuilder would be able to recognize profit on the construction of the house based on the percentage-of-completion method discussed in ASC 605-35-05-1 through 05-13, 15-6, 25-1 through 25-50, 25-54 through 25-88, 25-90 through 25-98, 45-1 through 45-2, 50-1 through 50-10, 55-1; ASC 210-10-60-2; ASC 460-1-60-10; ASC 910-20-25-5; ASC 912-20-25-1, "Accounting for Performance of Construction-Type and Certain Production-Type Contracts."

ACCOUNTING ISSUE

Should a builder recognize profit on the construction of a house on the builder's lot (*a*) separately for the construction of the house using the percentage-of-completion method regardless of the transfer of title on the lot or (*b*) for the construction of the house and sale of the lot when title passes at closing, based on the guidance in ASC 360-20; ASC 976-605?

ACCOUNTING GUIDANCE

Profit recognition on the transaction should be recognized when the conditions for full accrual profit recognition in ASC 360-20-40-5 have been met. Until then, proceeds received for the land and construction of the house should be accounted for based on the deposit method discussed in ASC 360-20-55-17, 55-19.

DISCUSSION

This guidance is based on a strict application of the guidance in ASC 360-20-40-5. Under that guidance, profit should not be recognized under the full accrual method until a sale has closed; the buyer's initial and continuing investments meet the conditions in ASC 360-20-40; the seller's receivable cannot be subordinated to the buyer's other obligations, except for a first mortgage on the property or a loan, the proceeds of which will be used to pay the seller; and the seller has transferred the risks and rewards of ownership to the buyer and will have no continuing involvement with the property.

ASC 970-470-05-2 through 05-3, 25-1, 25-3, 55-2 through 55-14; ASC 460-10-60-40
Accounting for Special Assessments and Tax Increment Financing Entities

BACKGROUND

The construction of infrastructure or improvements may be financed by a municipality through special assessments or by a Tax Increment Financing Entity (TIFE), which is an independent taxing jurisdiction organized under various state statutes to issue bonds used to finance the construction, operation, and maintenance of roads and other capital infrastructure related to a specific project. For example, Company A owns land it wants to develop into an industrial park that requires roads, water, power, and all other infrastructure associated with such a development. Because the only entity receiving direct benefits is Company A, it might be considered unfair to levy an assessment payable by all members of the community. Instead, a TIFE is created to issue bonds to finance the construction and to levy assessments on users (in this case, Company A) to repay the debt and operate and maintain the infrastructure.

A TIFE established for a real estate development may repay a pro rata portion of the bonds as portions of the project are sold or if assessments surpass current tax rates. The entity (developer) provides the funds to repay the bonds or reduce future assessments. The bonds are generally nonrecourse to the sponsoring entity. If there is a default on a TIFE's bonds, however, the entity may be affected because the property would be subject to liens. In some states, such as California, the obligation for repayment of the debt remains with the property as it is sold to new owners. Some states set a minimum amount that must be repaid by the developer.

ACCOUNTING ISSUE

Should an entity that uses a TIFE to finance infrastructure construction recognize an obligation for special assessments or the TIFE's debt?

ACCOUNTING GUIDANCE

- There is a presumption that an entity (the property owner) should recognize an obligation if a special assessment or an assessment to be levied by a TIFE on each individual property owner is a fixed or determinable amount for a fixed or determinable period.
- The following factors indicate that an entity may be contingently liable for a TIFE's debt; recognition of a liability should therefore be evaluated under the provisions of ASC 450:
  - — A shortfall, if any, in annual debt service obligations must be made up by the entity.
  - — The entity has pledged assets.
  - — A letter of credit or other means of supporting the TIFE's debt has been provided by the entity.
- There is a presumption that the TIFE's debt should be recognized as the entity's obligation if the entity is constructing facilities for its own use or operation and any of the criteria stated above is met.

PRACTICE POINTER: An entity that has an interest in a variable interest entity and is required to absorb the majority of that entity's expected losses or is entitled to receive most of the entity's expected residual returns, or both, is required to consolidate that entity in accordance with the guidance in ASC 810-10. ASC 810-10-05-10, 25-38 through 25-38G provides guidance for determining whether an entity has a controlling interest in a variable interest entity and on the consolidation of many special-purpose entities of the type used as TIFEs.

Illustration of Accounting for Special Assessments and TIFEs

A real estate developer organizes a TIFE to issue bonds for the construction of the infrastructure for a subdivision of homes. The infrastructure's assets become the property of the municipality when construction is completed. The company does not guarantee the TIFE's debt.

Case 1

Annual assessments are based on anticipated debt service requirements. Properties are taxed based on their stage of development. (That is, developed property is taxed at the maximum rate, undeveloped property is not taxed or taxed only to supplement shortfalls in the annual debt service requirement. If taxes collected on developed and undeveloped property are not sufficient to meet the obligation, an additional tax may be levied.)

Accounting. Because individual properties are assessed based on their rate of development, assessments are not fixed or determinable and no obligation need be recognized. The entity should, however, evaluate the recognition of an obligation under the guidance in ASC 450 if it is obligated to make up any shortfall in debt service requirements.

Case 2

The total assessment, which is based on the TIFE's annual debt service, is allocated equally to all lots in the development. In addition to their regular property taxes, property owners are assessed over the period that the debt is outstanding. When a portion of the property is sold, the developer must repay a pro rata portion of the TIFE debt or the purchaser must assume the obligation.

Accounting. The developer should recognize a liability because the amount of the assessment is fixed and determinable for a fixed or determinable period of time.

DISCUSSION

In the discussion of the treatment of TIFE debt by entities sponsoring infrastructure construction, it was determined that practice among such entities included recognition of a TIFE's debt and assets and treatment of a TIFE as a tax assessor (i.e., recording the annual tax assessments, user fees, or both as incurred in the assessment period).

The guidance in ASC 450-20-25-2, which requires recognition of a liability if it is probable that a loss will be confirmed by one or more events that will occur in the future and the amount is estimable is applied. Under the guidance in ASC 450, a property owner sponsoring an infrastructure project should account for a TIFE's debt as follows:

- *Debt recognized as a liability.* If assessments are fixed or determinable amounts for a fixed or determinable period, required payments can be estimated. In addition, payments are probable because the company is the primary obligor; the only way the company can avoid payment of the obligation is by selling the property. However, even when the property is sold, the entity must satisfy the debt or reduce the selling price by the amount of debt assumed by the buyer.
- *Debt not recognized as a liability.* A TIFE's debt need not be recognized as an obligation if debt service requirements are met by other than fixed or determinable assessments, because the amount cannot be estimated. The following are examples:
  - — Annual assessments whose rates depend on the land use category (developed or undeveloped)
  - — Assessments computed based on the assessed value of the property
  - — Normal property tax assessments
- *Debt may be a contingent liability.* A developer may remain contingently liable on a TIFE's debt. For example, in certain states, such as California, where the obligation remains with the property, the entity has to make up shortfalls in the annual debt service obligation. In other states, such as Colorado, an entity is required to guarantee a TIFE's debt. In those cases or if an entity guarantees a TIFE's debt by pledging assets, the entity has a contingent liability on the debt and therefore must continue to evaluate its obligation to report the debt based on the guidance in ASC 450.

ASC 970-810-25-1 through 25-3 General and Limited Real Estate Partnerships

BACKGROUND

For many years, preparers of financial statements and auditors have been asking for guidance on how to determine whether a limited partnership should be consolidated in a general partner's financial statements. Until recently, the practice has been to analogize to the guidance in the ASC 970-323-05-2 through 05-3, 15-2, 35-3 through 25-4, 25-6 through 25-12, 30-3 through 30-7, 35-2 through 35-10, 35-12 through 35-17, 35-20, 35-22, 40-1, 55-7; ASC 970-810-45-1; ASC 970-835-35-1; ASC 970-605-25-3 through 25-4; ASC 323-30-60-3 (SOP 78-9), which provides specific guidance on investments in real estate ventures that may include investments in corporate joint ventures, general partnerships, limited partnerships, and undivided interests.

In ASC 810-20-15-1 through 15-3, 25-1 through 25-20; 45-1; 55-1 through 55-16 (Issue 04-5, Determining Whether a General Partner, or the General Partners as a Group, Controls a Limited Partnership or Similar Entity When the Limited Partners Have Certain Rights), the EITF provided guidance for determining whether a limited partnership's general partner, or the general partners as a group, control a limited partnership. Because the EITF believes that such guidance should be consistent for limited partnerships in all industries, the EITF asked the FASB to amend SOP 78-9 so that its guidance would conform to the guidance in Issue 04-5.

AMENDMENT OF SOP 78-9

The guidance in SOP 78-9 is amended as follows:

- In ASC 970-810-25-2 (paragraph 7 of SOP 78-9), the fourth sentence, which addresses the concept that the majority owners may not control a partnership if *major* decisions must be approved by one or more of the partners, is deleted. It is replaced with the concept that a majority interest holder may *not* control an entity if one or more of the other partners have *substantive participating* rights allowing them to participate in certain *significant* financial and operating decisions made in the ordinary course of an entity's business. Whether those rights are substantive and whether the presumption that a majority owner has control has been overcome should be evaluated based on the guidance in ASC 810-10-25-2 through 25-14.
- ASC 970-810-25-3 states that limited partners in a limited partnership that does meet the conditions in ASC 810-10-15-14, and, consequently, is not a variable interest entity, should evaluate whether they have a controlling financial interest in the limited partnership in accordance with the guidance in ASC 810-10-15-8A. Further, the guidance in ASC 810-10 should be applied as follows to determine whether any of the limited partners control the limited partnership:
  - The general partner and limited partners should account for their interests in the limited partnership by the equity method if no single partner controls the limited partnership, except if a limited partner has virtually no influence over the partnership's operations and financial policies because the limited partner has only a very minor interest in the entity (see ASC 323-30-S99-1).
  - A single limited partner that controls a limited partnership should consolidate a limited partnership in its financial statements and account for that interest in accordance with the guidance for investments in subsidiaries in ASC 810.

ASC 974: REAL ESTATE INVESTMENT TRUSTS

ASC 974-323-25-1; ASC 974-840-25-1 Accounting by a Real Estate Investment Trust for an Investment in a Service Corporation

---

PRACTICE POINTER: Under the guidance in ASC 810-10, the consolidation of variable interest entities by an entity that absorbs most of a variable entity's expected losses or has the right to receive a greater part of the variable entity's expected residual returns or both is required. The following guidance does not apply to service corporations considered to be variable interest entities under the provisions of ASC 810-10, but it continues to apply to service corporations that are *not* variable interest entities.

BACKGROUND

To retain their favorable tax status (i.e., the ability to deduct dividends in arriving at taxable income), real estate investment trusts (REITs) may be established in the form of trusts, associations, or corporations, and may distribute a substantial amount of their taxable income to their shareholders annually. Because the Internal Revenue Code restricts the types of operating activities performed by a REIT to retain its qualification, some REITs have established service corporations (SCs) to perform certain services for the REIT or for third parties, such as property management, leasing services, and services involving the acquisition, development, construction, financing, or sale of real estate projects.

REITs are not permitted to own more than 10% of an SC's voting stock for federal income tax purposes. Consequently, a REIT may own a minimal interest in an SC's voting stock while holding a substantial interest in the SC's nonvoting preferred stock or nonvoting common stock, so that the REIT enjoys substantially all of the SC's economic benefits. Most of an SC's voting stock is owned by the REIT's sponsors, officers, or affiliates. Generally, transfers of voting stock are not restricted. Owners of the majority of an SC's voting common stock generally contribute minimal amounts of equity to the SC.

ACCOUNTING ISSUES

1. Should an SC be considered an independent third party, as the term is used in ASC 310, when determining the costs a REIT should capitalize for leasing services?
2. Should a REIT account for its investment in an SC on the equity method or by consolidation, if the REIT receives substantially all of the economic benefits generated by the SC?

ACCOUNTING GUIDANCE

1. A REIT should not consider an SC to be an independent third party, regardless of how it accounts for its investment in the SC. A REIT should not capitalize costs for leasing services provided by the SC the amount of those costs that would have been capitalized under the provisions of ASC 840 if the REIT had incurred those costs directly.

PRACTICE NOTE: The guidance in (1) above will be superseded by the guidance in ASU 2016-02, *Leases*, when that guidance becomes effective for public business entities in fiscal reporting periods beginning after December 15, 2018, and one year later for all other entities. Early application is permitted.

---

2. A REIT should *not* account for its investment on the cost method if some or all of the following factors—which indicate the REIT's ability to exercise at least significant influence over an SC—exist:
   a. The SC's activities are performed primarily for the REIT.
   b. The REIT receives substantially all of the SC's economic benefits.
   c. The REIT can designate a seat on the SC's board of directors.
   d. Individuals serving on the REIT's board of directors also serve on the SC's board of directors.
   e. The REIT and SC share officers and/or employees.
   f. Owners of a majority of an SC's voting common stock contributed a minimal amount to the SC's equity.
   g. The SC's operations are influenced by the views of the REIT's management.
   h. The REIT can obtain the necessary financial information to account for its investment in the SC on the equity basis.

The decision whether to consolidate the SC or account for it on the equity basis depends on facts and circumstances.

If the application of the guidance on Issue 2 results in a change in the method of accounting for a REIT's investment in an SC, the change should be accounted for based on the guidance in ASC 250 for reporting a change in an entity's accounting.

DISCUSSION

A REIT's voting interest in an SC is usually less than 10%. Under a strict interpretation of the guidance in ASC 323, a 20% or greater voting interest in an investee connotes significant influence. Because of a belief that a REIT often has significant influence over an SC's operations, even if it has less than a 20% voting interest in the SC, the list of factors was developed to indicate whether a REIT has significant influence and could overcome the 20% ownership presumption in ASC 323.

ASC 978: REAL ESTATE—TIME SHARING ACTIVITIES

ASC 978-10-05-3 through 05-6, 15-3 through 15-6; ASC 978-230-45-1; ASC 978-250-35-1; ASC 978-310-05-2 through 05-3, 30-1 through 30-2, 35-1 through 35-6, 40-1 through 40-2; ASC 978-340-25-1 through 25-5, 40-1 through 40-2, 60-1; ASC 978-605-10-1, 15-1, 25-1 through 25-17, 25-19, 30-1 through 30-10, 55-1 through 55-25, 55-27 through 55-62, 55-64 through 55-95; ASC 978-720-05-2 through 05-4, 25-1 through 25-3; ASC 978-810-25-1; ASC 978-840-25-1 through 25-2 Accounting for Real Estate Time-Sharing Transactions

---

IMPORTANT NOTICE: Any specific-industry guidance and revenue recognition guidance in this Issue will be deleted, and other guidance will be amended by the guidance in ASU 2014-09, *Accounting for Revenue from Contracts with Customers*, which becomes effective for public business entities in annual reporting periods that begin after December 15, 2017, and interim periods within those annual periods and in annual reporting periods that begin after December 15, 2018, for nonpublic entities.

BACKGROUND

The volume of sales of interests in real estate time-sharing intervals has grown enormously. In addition, the variety of ways in which interests in time-sharing intervals are structured has increased. For example, interests in time-sharing intervals may be purchased for a fixed time, such as a specific week; for a floating time, such as a specific season; or in the form of points, vacation clubs, or fractional interests. Also, buyers may have the right to exchange their time-sharing intervals for other time periods and venues, as well as for other products, such as cruises, through a third-party exchange company. Some sellers of time-sharing intervals establish time-sharing special-purpose entities to which they transfer title in the real estate.

ACCOUNTING GUIDANCE

Scope

The following guidance applies to the accounting for *real estate* time-sharing transactions in which a seller:

- Passes title and ownership of the real estate to a buyer or special purpose entity (SPE) in a fee simple transaction without recourse
- Retains title and ownership of all or a portion of the real estate
- Passes to a buyer title and ownership of all or a portion of the real estate, which subsequently revert to the seller or are transferred to a third party

The following guidance also applies to transactions involving a time-share reseller.

Profit Recognition under ASC 360

Sellers should recognize revenue on sales of real estate time-sharing intervals in accordance with the guidance in ASC 360 for sales of real estate other than retail land sales. The guidance in ASC 360-20-40-37 through 40-38, 40-40 through 40-50, 40-56 through 40-64; ASC 460-10-60-3; ASC 840-10-25-60 regarding continuing involvement should be followed. Revenue may be recognized in accordance with the percentage-of-completion method if the criteria in ASC 360-20-40-50 have been met, but related selling and marketing costs should not be included in computing costs. Contract-for-deed arrangements qualify for profit recognition. Transactions in which title can revert to a seller, however, should be accounted for as operating leases.

Seller Identification of Projects and Phases

Time-share interval projects may be constructed in a single phase or in multiple phases. Under this guidance, sellers of time-sharing intervals are required to (*a*) define a project at its inception in terms of the number of phases to be developed and (*b*) to account separately for each phase of a project.

If the definition of a project or its phases changes because of significant changes in facts and circumstances related to the development of a project, that is, a change in the nature of a project, the change should be accounted for as a change in an accounting estimate by making an adjustment in the current period. Significant changes may include changes in sales prices or discount programs, changes in construction contract prices or inflation, temporary construction delays, design changes, or a seller's decision to significantly increase the proportion of a project's luxury units as compared to the number of standard units in the project. If a change in the definition of a project is *not* the result of a significant change in facts or circumstances in the project's development, such as a change in the number of phases into which a project is divided, which is a change in the way the project is accounted for but is *not* a change in the facts and circumstances of the project, the change should be accounted for as a cumulative effect of a change in the application of an accounting principle in accordance with the guidance in ASC 250-120-45-5 through 45-10.

Determination of Sales Value

Under the guidance in ASC 360, the *sales value* of a sale of real estate must be calculated in order to determine whether a buyer's initial and continuing investment is adequate for full accrual revenue recognition. To determine the sales value of a real estate sale, the stated sales price should be adjusted as follows:

- Reduce the stated sales price of a time-sharing interval by the difference between the amount paid by a buyer to a seller and the fair value of products or services a seller provides or is legally or otherwise committed to provide to a buyer as part of consummating a sale. Such products or services often are used as sales incentives and should be accounted for in accordance with the guidance in ASC 605-50-05-1, 15-2 through 15-3, 25-1 through 25-9, 45-1 through 45-11, S45-1, 55-1, 55-3, 55-5, 55-8 through 55-12, 55-14 through 55-15, 55-17 through 55-22, 55-24 through 55-25, 55-27 through 55-28, 55-30 through 55-31, 55-33 through 55-37, 55-40 through 55-44, 55-46 through 55-47, 55-49 through, 55-50, 55-52, through 55-53, 55-55 through 55-70, 55-71 through 55-72, 55-74 through 55-77, 55-79 through 55-95, 55-97 through 55-107, S99-1 ASC 330-10-35-13; ASC 908-360-55-1, Vendor's Income Statement Characterization of Consideration Given to a Customer Including a Reseller (discussed in Chapter 38, *ASC 606/605—Revenue Recognition*), which differentiates between cash and noncash incentives. Noncash incentives should be accounted for as separate deliverables that have an associated cost of sales. Cash incentives should be accounted for as discounts of the stated sales prices.

- A seller may give a buyer a *cash* incentive in cash or by waiving a payment that the buyer would otherwise have to make, for example, payment for closing costs or for the first year of the owners association's maintenance fees. A *noncash* incentive is one that a buyer could purchase, such as a first-year membership in a time-share exchange program or a voucher for airline tickets. If a *noncash* incentive such as a voucher for airline tickets is provided free as an incentive to consummate a sale, the stated sales price of the time-sharing interval should be *reduced* by the fair value of the voucher, which should be recognized as a separate item in revenue.

  If a time-sharing interval is sold together with a membership in a time-share exchange program, however, and the first year of membership in the program is provided for free, the fair value of the fee for the exchange program should be accounted for as a *cash* incentive, because the buyer would otherwise have to pay the fee. In that case, the fair value of the fee for the exchange program should be deducted from the sales price and accounted for as a reduction of the seller's cost for fees instead of as a separate revenue item. Incentives do *not* include products or services that are included in future maintenance charges or other fees that a buyer pays for at market rates.

  Inducements provided by a seller to prospective buyers regardless of whether they make a purchase are considered to be selling costs, which should be accounted for in accordance with the guidance in the section on costs to sell time-sharing intervals.

- Increase the stated sales price for the purpose of determining sales value by fees charged to a buyer that are unrelated to financing, such as fees for document preparation. Fees that a seller collects for third parties, such as municipalities or taxing authorities, however, should *not* be added to the stated sales price and should *not* be included in a buyer's initial and continuing investment. Fees that are related to financing of time-share purchases, such as loan origination fees, should be accounted for as adjustments to the stated interest rate on financings, in accordance with the guidance in ASC 310. Sellers that offer buyers at the time of sale programs under which buyers can reduce their payments by prepaying their notes, or sellers that consistently make such offers during the term of buyers' notes should include estimated payment reductions in their calculations of sales value.

- Sellers that partially or fully finance buyers' time-sharing transactions at stated interest rates that are less than prevailing market rates for buyers with similar credit ratings in similar transactions should reduce the sales value and the amount of the note in accordance with the guidance in ASC 835.

Application of Test of Buyer's Commitment

When testing for the adequacy of a buyer's commitment under the guidance in ASC 360-20-40-5, sellers should reduce the amount of buyers' initial and continuing investments by the amount that the fair value of products or services offered to buyers as incentives exceeds the amount a buyer would pay for such goods or services. That requirement does not apply if a buyer does *not* receive the incentive until the buyer has met certain contractual obligations related to the purchase of a time-sharing interval. For example, a seller requires a buyer to make timely payments on a note for six months for the seller to pay the buyer's owners association fees in the second year. In that situation, a seller must determine whether future performance meets the initial and continuing investment criterion for a buyer's commitment. To meet that criterion, a buyer's future payments required for eligibility to receive an incentive should at least equal the incentive's fair value. The required payments should equal the value of an incentive and interest on the amount *not* paid for the incentive.

When applying the criterion in ASC 360-20-40-5, a seller should reduce the measurement of a buyer's commitment by the amount that the fair value of an incentive exceeds the amount the buyer paid for the incentive if future performance is deemed *not* to be sufficient. If a portion of a buyer's down payment is considered to apply as a payment for an incentive because the buyer's future payment does *not* at least equal the fair value of the incentive, that amount should *not* be included in the buyer's initial and continuing investment.

Upgrade and Reload Transactions

In a *reload* transaction, an existing owner of a time-sharing interval purchases a new interval, which is accounted for as a separate transaction. The buyer must meet the commitment criterion in ASC 360-20-40-5 by making an additional cash payment or providing other consideration that qualifies. The buyer's initial and continuing investments from the initial transaction should *not* be included in measuring the buyer's commitment for the additional purchase.

In an *upgrade* transaction, a buyer modifies an existing time-share interval. In that case, the buyer's initial and continuing investments in the original transaction are included in determining whether the buyer meets the commitment criterion. The guidance in ASC 360 for profit recognition is applied to the sales value of the new interval.

Accounting for Uncollectibility

Receivables of interest and principal on sales of time-sharing intervals become uncollectible when a seller determines that less than the total amount of the note will be collected. Uncollectibility should be based on a seller's actual collection experience, regardless of who services the receivables, not based on amounts a seller receives as proceeds. In accounting for uncollectible receivables, sellers should:

- Recognize estimates of uncollectible receivables as a reduction of sales revenue when recognizing profit on sales of time-sharing intervals under the full accrual or the percentage-of-completion methods. To recognize the reduction in revenue on estimated uncollectible amounts accounted for under the relative sales value method, a corresponding adjustment is made to cost of sales and inventory by applying the cost-of-sales percentage.
- Charge uncollectible accrued interest income receivable to interest income when it is determined that a receivable is uncollectible.
- Consider modifications, deferments, or downgrades of receivables, which involve only modifications of the terms of notes receivable, as troubled debt restructurings, and account for them under the guidance in ASC 310. The allowance for uncollectible accounts should be charged when a recorded investment in a note receivable is reduced under the provisions of ASC 310. That treatment is necessary, because estimated losses were charged against revenue when a sale was recognized or was subsequently charged against revenue as a change in estimate. Direct costs associated with uncollectible receivables, such as collection costs, should be expensed as incurred.
- Account for assumptions of notes receivable as two separate activities with two different parties as follows:
  - — Charge the allowance for uncollectible receivables with the remaining investment in the original note receivable, which becomes uncollectible when an arrangement with the original buyer is terminated.
  - — Account for a time-sharing transaction with a new buyer in accordance with the profit recognition guidance in ASC 360.

- Account for the allowance for uncollectibles the same as for any receivables after the initial recognition of a sale when revenue is reduced for estimated uncollectibles, except that *no* bad debt expense is recognized.
- Evaluate receivables in each reporting period, and, at least quarterly, estimate the amount of ultimate collections and evaluate the adequacy of the allowance under the guidance in ASC 450. Adjust the allowance and current-period revenue through the account for uncollectibles, which is a contra-revenue account. Adjust cost of sales and inventory for a corresponding amount.
- Determine the amount of the allowance for uncollectibles by considering uncollectibles by year of sale and the aging of notes receivable and other factors such as the location of timeshare units, contract terms, collection experience, economic conditions, and other qualitative factors.
- Adjust interest income if a gain or loss on a sale of a portfolio of receivables without recourse is attributable to a change in market interest rates between the date receivables were generated and the date they were sold. Adjust revenue for a gain or loss on the transaction attributable to other factors, such as a change in the perceived credit quality of the portfolio between the date receivables were generated and the date they were sold.

Accounting for Cost of Sales and Inventory

The following guidance applies only to transactions accounted for under the full accrual, percentage-of-completion, cost recovery, installment, or reduced profit revenue recognition methods discussed in ASC 360. It does *not* apply to transactions accounted for under the deposit method, which is also discussed in ASC 360.

Sellers should account for the cost of sales and time-sharing inventory by the *relative sales value method*, which is similar to a gross profit method. It is used to allocate inventory cost and to determine the cost of sales in conjunction with a sale. Under this method, cost of sales is calculated as a percentage of net sales using a cost-of-sales percentage, which is a ratio of total costs to the total remaining estimated time-sharing revenue. Different phases should be accounted for separately under this method. Common costs, including costs of amenities, should be allocated to inventory by the phase they will benefit.

Estimated total revenue, which is the actual amount to date, and expected future revenue, should include factors such as incurred or estimated uncollectibles, changes in sales prices or sales mix, repossession of intervals the seller may or may not be able to sell, effects of upgrade programs, and past or expected sales incentives to sell slow-moving inventory. Those estimates should be recalculated at least quarterly. The cost-of-sales percentage should be recalculated whenever estimated revenue or cost is adjusted based on newly estimated total revenue and total cost, including costs to complete, if any. The *effects* of changes should be accounted for prospectively in the period in which a change occurred so that the revised estimates will be reported in the balance sheet and in subsequent periods as if those estimates had been made at inception. The effects of changes should be disclosed in accordance with the guidance in ASC 250-10-50-4. The inventory balance in the balance sheet, estimated costs to complete the inventory, if any, is the pool of costs that will be charged against future revenue.

If the relative sales value method is used, inventory is *not* affected if a time-sharing interval is repossessed or reacquired, unless there is a change in expected uncollectibles. Sellers should test inventory for impairment based on the guidance in ASC 360-10.

Costs to Sell Time-Sharing Intervals

Costs incurred to sell time-sharing intervals should be expensed as incurred unless the costs qualify for capitalization under this guidance. Deferral of recognition until a sale transaction occurs, however, is permitted for costs that (*a*) are reasonably expected to be recovered from the sale of time-sharing intervals or from incidental operations and (*b*) are incurred for (1) tangible assets used directly during the selling period for the purpose of making sales (for example, model units and furnishings, sales property and equipment, and semi-permanent signs), and (2) services required to obtain regulatory approval of sales, for example, legal fees and costs of preparing, printing, and filing prospectuses. Such costs should be allocated proportionately to sale transactions based on the number of intervals available for sale in a project or phase to which those selling costs apply.

Other costs may be deferred until a sale occurs if they are (*a*) reasonably expected to be recovered from a sale of time-sharing intervals; (*b*) directly associated with sales transactions accounted for under the percentage of completion, installment, reduced profit, or deposit methods of accounting, such as commissions; and (*c*) incremental costs that a seller would *not* have incurred if a sales transaction had not occurred. Deferred selling costs should be expensed in the period in which the related revenue is recognized. Deferred selling costs related to sales contracts that are canceled before profit has been recognized on the transaction should be expensed in the period in which the cancellation occurred.

Costs of call centers and direct and incremental costs related to bringing potential buyers to tour a property should be expensed as incurred. Other costs that should be expensed as incurred are costs incurred for unsuccessful sales transactions and sales overhead, such as rent for on-site and off-site sales offices, utilities, maintenance, and telephone expenses. The cost of nonrefundable airline tickets purchased for potential buyers who will be touring a property should be expensed on the date of the visit.

Operations During Holding Periods

The holding period for time-sharing operations begins when intervals are available for sale, that is, when they are legally registered for sale as time-sharing intervals, which should be accounted for as inventory during holding periods and should *not* be depreciated. Operating costs during holding periods include (*a*) seller subsidies to an owners association and (*b*) maintenance and other costs related to time-sharing intervals held for sale.

Units rented in periods other than the holding period should be depreciated with rental activities accounted for under the guidance in ASC 840. In each reporting period, sellers should evaluate whether to continue classifying time-sharing intervals as held and available for sale.

During a holding period, revenue and costs of rental and other operations should be accounted for as incidental operations. If incremental revenue from incidental operations exceeds related incremental costs, the pool of inventory costs under the relative sales value method should be reduced by that excess amount. Estimates of future excess amounts should *not* be considered in calculations under the relative value method. Incremental costs that exceed incremental revenue should be expensed as incurred.

Costs related to rentals and other operations (for example, sampler programs and mini-vacations) during a holding period should be deferred if they are (*a*) directly related to rental activities during a holding period and are reasonably expected to be recovered from those activities and (*b*) incremental costs that a seller would not have incurred if a particular rental transaction had not occurred. Such deferred costs should be expensed or netted against inventory costs in the period in which a rental occurs.

Sampler Programs and Mini-Vacations

If a seller applies a portion of a buyer's payment for a sampler program or mini-vacation that has *not* been used in its entirety against the sales price of a time-sharing interval, the payment should be considered a part of the buyer's initial and continuing investment when evaluating the buyer's commitment. A seller should *not* include such a payment in a buyer's initial and continuing investments, however, if the buyer has fully used the sampler program or mini-vacation, even if legal documents state that the payment would be applied to the sales price.

Special Entities, Point Systems, Vacation Clubs, and Similar Structures

Interests in time-sharing intervals structured as special entities established to facilitate sales, point systems, vacation clubs, and variations of those structures, should be accounted for based on the guidance for profit recognition in ASC 360. The transactions should be evaluated primarily based on whether a seller has transferred title to an interest in a time-sharing interval without recourse and whether the seller has a continuing involvement with the buyer, and other requirements necessary to meet the profit recognition criteria in ASC 360. Profit should only be recognized if a time-sharing interval has been sold to an end user. No profit should be recognized on a transfer of time-sharing intervals to a special purpose entity (SPE), which should be considered to have no economic substance for balance sheet reporting purposes if it (*a*) was structured for legal purposes and (*b*) has no debt, and its only assets are the time-sharing intervals. Interests in an SPE not yet sold to end users should be presented in the balance sheet as time-sharing inventory. SPEs that do not meet the conditions in (*a*) and (*b*) above should be accounted for in the same manner as investments in other SPE's structures.

A seller, its affiliate, or a related party that operates a points program, vacation, or exchange program should be considered to have a continuing involvement with the buyer. A seller's accounting should be determined based on whether compensation for those services is set at prevailing market rates. If there is no compensation for the services, or if the fee is at below prevailing market rates, compensation should be imputed when a sale is recognized and charged against the sales value of the interval. Profit should be recognized under the guidance on continuing involvement in ASC 360. Revenue on those services should be recognized as it is earned.

Owners Associations

Until all time-sharing intervals have been sold, a seller is the owner of all unsold units and is required to pay the owners association dues or maintenance fees for those units. Also, sellers will frequently subsidize the operations of an owners association for a limited time rather than pay dues or maintenance fees on unsold units. Sellers' payments for maintenance fees should be expensed as incurred. Subsidies to an owners association also should be expensed. A seller that is contractually entitled to recover all or a portion of its subsidy to an owners association should recognize a receivable only if recovery is probable and the measurement of the receivable is reasonably reliable. A seller that is hired to manage an owners association for a fee should recognize that fee as revenue only if it is earned and realized or realizable. A seller that subsidizes an owners association's operations while acting as its manager should offset its revenue from fees on seller-owned intervals against its subsidy expense.

OBSERVATION: The guidance in the previous paragraph applies if a timeshare development's Owners Association (OA) is not consolidated in the seller's financial statements, but no guidance is provided regarding issues related to consolidation of an OA. Such guidance is provided in ASC 810.

Presentation and Disclosures

In its balance sheet, a seller should present gross notes receivable from time-sharing sales, a deduction from notes receivable for the allowance for uncollectibles, and a deduction from notes receivable for deferred profit under the guidance in ASC 360, if any.

Sellers of time-sharing intervals should make the following disclosures in their financial statements:

- The effects of changes in estimate in the relative sales value method, in accordance with the guidance in ASC 250-10-50-4.
- Maturities of notes receivable for each of the five years following the date of the financial statements and the total for all following years. The total of notes receivable balances displayed with various maturity dates should be reconciled to the amount of notes receivable on the balance sheet.
- The weighted average and range of stated interest rates of notes receivable.
- Estimated cost to complete improvements and promised amenities. Activity in the allowance for uncollectible accounts, including the balance at the beginning and end of the period, additions related to sales in the current period, direct write-offs charged against the allowance, and changes in estimates related to sales in prior periods. The same disclosures should be made for receivables with recourse, if applicable.
- Policies related to meeting the criteria for a buyer's commitment and collectibility of the sales price in ASC 360.

Changes in the amount of time-sharing notes receivable, including sales of those notes, should be reported as cash flows from operations in the statement of cash flows.

APPENDIX I

ASC 980—REGULATED OPERATIONS

CONTENTS

INTERPRETIVE GUIDANCE

ASC 980-605: REVENUE RECOGNITION

ASC 980-605-25-1 through 25-4 Accounting by Rate-Regulated Utilities for the Effects of Certain Alternative Revenue Programs

BACKGROUND

Utility customers generally are billed for their usage based on predetermined rates, which are regulated and approved by the utility's regulatory commission. The rates are set based on costs of service and are designed to recover the utility's allowable costs, which include a return on shareholders' investments.

Certain utility regulators have authorized the use of alternative revenue programs that reduce the volatility in the utility's earnings and have the following objectives:

- To protect the utilities, their investors, and their customers from unexpected fluctuations in sales and earnings caused by changes in weather patterns or by reduced demand because of conservation efforts
- To reward utilities for meeting certain goals

The following two major alternative revenue programs permit utilities to adjust future billings to consider certain past events:

Type A

Type A programs are intended to reduce the effects on a utility's revenue of differences between actual sales volume and estimated sales used to set base rates. Such differences may be caused by abnormal weather patterns, conservation efforts, and other external factors. For example, 50% more kilowatt hours of electricity may be used during a very hot summer, or user conservation efforts may result in decreased usage. Variations between forecasted revenue and actual usage may be adjusted by billing surcharges that are added to or deducted from base rates in future billings. For example, in a period following a hot summer, customers' billings would be increased by a surcharge. Surcharges are most commonly used to recover fuel costs that differ from estimated costs included in base rates. Under Type A programs, the utility recognizes revenue in the future when customers are provided with service at the base rate plus or minus a surcharge.

Type B

Type B programs involve incentive awards that are related to a utility's performance. Such programs commonly set goals that may be achieved by measurable improvement in a utility's effectiveness or efficiency of operations. Examples of such goals are controlling growth in demand, reducing costs, and reducing the number of customer complaints. Achievement of those goals may be measured subjectively and objectively and usually involves an audit by the regulatory authority. If the goals are achieved, Type B programs provide utilities with additional revenue. If they are not achieved, there may be penalties for the utility and refunds for its customers.

ACCOUNTING ISSUES

- What is the appropriate accounting for alternative revenue programs (Type A and Type B) of regulated utilities?
- Should the accounting for Type A and Type B programs be the same?

ACCOUNTING GUIDANCE

If the specific events that would allow a utility to bill additional revenues under Type A or Type B programs have occurred, a utility should recognize those additional revenues if all of the following conditions are met:

- The utility's regulatory commission has approved the additional revenue program, which allows the utility to adjust future rates automatically. Such adjustments are considered automatic even before the regulator has verified the adjustment to future rates.
- The utility can determine the amount of additional revenue for the period objectively, and recovery is probable.
- Additional revenues will be collected no later than 24 months from the end of the annual period in which they were recognized.

DISCUSSION

When this issue was discussed, industry practice was to recognize revenue and the related asset when the condition resulting in future billings occurred, the amount was known, and it was probable that it would be recovered.

The EITF was asked to consider when the economic benefit of alternative rate programs should be recognized in a utility's financial statements. Several alternatives were discussed. The following alternatives were considered:

Proponents of the view that additional revenue should be recognized when the amount is known and realization is probable noted that the guidance in ASC 980-10-15-5 provides that regulated enterprises should follow U.S. GAAP, except if U.S. GAAP conflicts with the guidance in ASC 980. They argued that because ASC 980 does not specifically address that issue, U.S. GAAP for all entities should be followed in recognizing amounts to be received under those programs. Statement of Financial Accounting Concepts No. 5 states that revenue may be recognized when it is realized and has been earned. Assets are defined in Statement of Financial Accounting Concepts No. 6 as "probable future economic benefits obtained or controlled by a particular entity as a result of past transactions." Thus, this view supports recording the revenue and related asset in the year the earnings process and performance were completed, even though the surcharge billing occurs in the future.

ASC 980-605-25-5 through 25-15; ASC 440-10-60-20 Revenue Recognition on Long-Term Power Sales Contracts

IMPORTANT NOTICE: Based on the guidance in ASU 2014-09 Part B, Accounting for Revenue from Contracts with Customers, the guidance in ASC 980-605-25-5 through 25-15 will be treated as follows: (1) A new Subtopic ASC 980-815, Regulated Operations-Derivatives and Hedging has been established. ASC 980-605-25-5 through 25-7 will be moved to ASC 980-815-25-1 through 25-3, respectively, ASC 980-605-25-10 will be moved to ASC 980-605-15-3, and ASC 980-605-25-14 through 25-15 will be moved to ASC 980-815-25-4 through 25-5, respectively; (2) ASC 980-605-25-8 through 25-9 and 25-11 through 25-13 will be superseded. The effective date of the guidance in the ASU, which will reside in ASC 606, Revenue from Contracts with Customers, has been deferred by ASU 2015-14, *Revenue from Contracts with Customers (Topic 606) Deferral of the Effective Date*. Consequently it becomes effective for public business entities in annual reporting periods that begin after December 15, 2017, and interim periods within those annual periods, and for nonpublic entities in annual reporting periods that begin after December 15, 2018.

BACKGROUND

Nonutility generators (NUGs) are entities that supply power to other entities (often rate-regulated utilities), usually under long-term sales contracts (20-30 years), or to builder/users for their own needs. Those entities are not regulated and generally would not be accounted under the guidance in ASC 980. However, accounting guidance for NUGs is included in ASC 980-605 because many of the services provided by those entities are the same as those provided by regulated entities.

Long-term power sales contracts include pricing and terms that create practical issues in accounting, particularly in revenue recognition. Pricing arrangements may include the following:

- Specified prices per unit (e.g., per kilowatt hour or kwh) that increase, decrease, or remain fixed over the term of the contract
- Formula-based prices per kwh (e.g., a price determined annually based on the current cost of power from other sources or based on published rates)

A combination of those pricing arrangements is used in the following billing methods:

- Billings are based on a specified price schedule over the term of the contract, but at the end of the contract term, the NUG either makes or receives a payment so that total revenue recognized and payments made over the contract's term will equal the amount computed under an arrangement in which the pricing is based on a formula. The difference between the payments made and the amount calculated based on a formula pricing arrangement is (1) recorded in an interest-bearing tracker account, or (2) at a defined point in the life of the contract, the cumulative balance in the tracker account may be amortized to zero by adjusting subsequent billings.
- Billings are based on a specified price schedule but the NUG is required to make a payment if at the end of the contract term, the total revenue recognized and total payments received by the NUG under the specified rate schedule exceed the amount computed under a pricing arrangement based on a formula.

The discussion was based on the following three examples of long-term contracts:

Type 1 Contract

The customer (utility) is obligated to take or pay for all power made available by the NUG for the term of the contract (20 years). The price per kwh is specified and increases in years 11 to 20.

Type 2 Contract

The customer is obligated to take or pay for all power made available by the NUG for the term of the contract. Billings are based on specified prices per kwh that increase during the term. However, total payments over the term of the contract will be based on a formula used by the customer annually to compute its *avoided cost,* which is the cost that would have been incurred if power had been purchased from another source or had been self-generated (the source is specified in the contract). Over the term of the contract, the customer uses what is referred to as a "tracker account" to record its avoided cost and to offset actual billings against that amount. At the end of the contract, the tracker account is adjusted, if necessary, and may result in an additional payment to the NUG, if avoided cost is greater than actual billings, or in a refund to the customer, if billings exceed avoided cost.

Type 3 Contract

The contract is the same as a Type 2 contract, except the formula is used to limit the NUG's total revenue to the lesser of total avoided cost or total actual billings (i.e., an adjustment is made only if the customer's cost decreases).

SCOPE

Contracts that are considered to be leases are outside the scope of the following guidance and should be accounted for in accordance with the provisions of ASC 840, *Leases*.

ACCOUNTING ISSUES

1. Should revenue on a power sales contract that provides for scheduled price changes (Type 1 contract) be recognized based on the price schedule or ratably over the term of the contract?
2. Should the accounting required for contracts described in Issue 1 change if the power sales contract provides that total revenues for the term of the contract be determined based on a separate, formula-based pricing arrangement (Type 2 contract)?

3. Should the accounting required for contracts described in Issue 1 change if the power sales contract provides that total revenues for the term of the contract be limited by a separate formula-based pricing arrangement (Type 3 contract)?

ACCOUNTING GUIDANCE

Contracts That Include Scheduled Price Changes

NUGs should account for Type 1 contracts as follows:

a. Recognize revenue at the lesser of
    i. The amount billable under the contract
    ii. An amount determined by the kwhs available to the customer during the period multiplied by the estimated average revenue per kwh over the term of the contract.
b. Determine the lesser amount annually based on the cumulative amount that would have been recognized under either method had it been applied consistently from the beginning of the contract.

Contracts That Determine or Limit Revenue Under Formula-Based Pricing

a. Recognize revenue for Type 2 and 3 contracts in each period based on a contract's separate formula-based pricing arrangement if *total* revenues billed under the contract are determined or limited by that arrangement, but not if the separate formula-based pricing arrangement is used only to establish liquidating damages.
b. Recognize a receivable only if (*a*) the contract requires the customer to pay the NUG for the difference between the amount billed and the amount calculated according to the formula-based pricing arrangement at the end of the contract, and (*b*) it is probable that the receivable will be recovered. A receivable occurs if the amount calculated based on a formula exceeds the amounts billed.

Contracts That Meet the Definition of a Derivative

Long-term power sales contracts that meet the definition of a derivative in ASC 815 should be marked to fair value through earnings, unless a contract has been designated as a hedging instrument. Contracts that do not meet the definition of a derivative should be analyzed to determine whether they contain embedded derivatives that should be accounted for separately under the guidance in ASC 815. Otherwise, the guidance discussed above applies. Some contracts that meet the definition of a derivative may qualify for the normal purchases and normal sales scope exception in ASC 815-10-15-17(b). In that case, those contracts would be accounted for under the guidance discussed above.

DISCUSSION

1. The guidance on Issue 1 was based on two views. Under one view, revenue on a long-term power sales contract should be recognized as an amount that is billable under the contract. Under the second view, periodic revenue should be recognized based on estimated average revenue per kwh over the life of the contract.

    Proponents of the first view believed that the contracts are executory contracts under which customers have no obligation to pay unless the NUG makes power available to them.

    Under the second view, long-term power sales contracts are similar to operating leases and kwhs made available to customers annually are similar to property used by a lessee.

    The guidance on Issue 1 represents a compromise between those two views; it results in recognition of the most conservative amount of revenue, regardless of the method used. In addition, it attempts to associate revenue with the periods in which it was earned while allocating revenue more evenly over the term of the contract. That approach also addresses concerns about possible abuses or manipulation under the first approach; for example, structuring a contract to front-end revenue by charging higher rates in the early years, thereby recognizing revenue before it has been earned and distorting revenue recognized over the term of the contract.

2. Those who supported recognizing revenue on Type 2 and Type 3 contracts based on the avoided-cost formula believed that the tracker account used to monitor the cumulative difference between amounts billed and amounts calculated with the avoided-cost formula shifts the customer's substantial risk of changes in the utility's avoided cost to the NUG over the term of the contract. They further believed that the contract is in substance an arrangement under which a customer provides financing to the NUG in the early years and the NUG sells power to

the customer at the avoided cost over the term of the contract. Although proponents of this view agreed that a power sales contract is not a lease, they argued that if a lease with escalating rents had an alternative calculation based on rents adjusted to, for example, the consumer price index, under the guidance in ASC 840, a lessor would be permitted to recognize revenue based on the CPI only in the early years of the lease.

A working group met with industry representatives to discuss the characteristics of contracts similar to those referred to above as Type 2 and Type 3 contracts, except that they also may have some of the characteristics of Type 1 contracts. All those contracts use a tracking account. They were described as Category A and Category B contracts in the working group's discussions. Some contracts under Category A use a tracking account only to measure liquidated damages if the NUG does not perform under the contract. Revenue is not limited to avoided cost, and the NUG can retain all amounts billed if it performs under the contract. Another type of contract in this category has specified rates in the early years of the contract and fluctuating rates based on avoided cost in the later years. A balance of billings over avoided cost in the tracker account in the early years of the contract is forgiven over the years when rates are based on avoided cost. If the NUG performs over the contract term, the tracker account is amortized to zero. Industry representatives believed that the economic substance of Category A contracts is the same as for Type 1 contracts in Issue 1. That is, the NUG keeps all amounts billed, but here the customer has the additional security that the NUG will perform. They argued that because the NUG's total revenue is not determined by or limited to revenues based on the avoided-cost formula and the tracker account is used only to determine liquidation damages, if necessary, revenue on this category should not be based on the avoided-cost formula. Rather, revenue on those contracts should be recognized the same as for contracts in Issue 1.

In Category B contracts, which measure total revenue on a contract based on the avoided-cost formula, the tracker account is used to accumulate the difference between billings and actual annual avoided cost. The balance of the tracker account must be settled at the end of such contracts with the customer paying no more than total actual avoided cost. The economic substance of such contracts is that the NUG takes on the risk that there will be unexpected changes in avoided-cost projections over the term of the contract or that the projections of avoided cost on which the contract's rates were based were inaccurate. Although they have adequate cash flows, NUGs that recognize revenue based on avoided cost in this category of contracts incur losses in the early years of a contract, because avoided cost is too low to cover the NUG's financing and construction costs. In contrast, actual amounts billed on the contract are based on avoided costs over the long term and always exceed annual avoided cost in the early years and reverse in later years.

Under the guidance, revenue on Type 2 and 3 contracts must be recognized based on avoided cost, because that amount represents revenue earned in each period. Because the NUG's *total* revenue on Type 3 contracts is determined by or limited to total revenue based on the avoided-cost formula over the *term* of the contract, revenue recognition based on the avoided-cost formula also best represents revenue earned over the term of the contract.

ASC 980-605-25-17 through 25-18; ASC 980-350-35-3 through 35-5 Revenue Recognition under Long-Term Power Sales Contracts That Contain Both Fixed and Variable Pricing Terms

---

IMPORTANT NOTICE: Based on the guidance in ASU 2014-09 Part B, Accounting for Revenue from Contracts with Customers, the guidance in ASC 980-605-25-17 through 25-18 will be superseded. The guidance in the ASU, which will reside in ASC 606, Revenue from Contracts with Customers, has been deferred by ASU 2015-14, *Revenue from Contracts with Customers (Topic 606) Deferral of the Effective Date*. Consequently, it becomes effective for public business entities in annual reporting periods that begin after December 15, 2017, and interim periods within those annual periods, and for nonpublic entities in annual reporting periods that begin after December 15, 2018.

BACKGROUND

The following guidance addresses contracts that consist of fixed and variable pricing arrangements, which were not considered under the guidance in ASC 980-605-25-5 through 25-15; ASC 440-10-60-20 discussed above. For example, billings under such contracts are based on a stated price schedule for a certain period of time, such as the first ten years of a 30-year contract, with billings at a variable rate for the remainder of the contract. Unlike the contracts discussed above, total revenues billed under the contracts addressed under the following guidance are not limited by a tracker account that the NUG maintains to record the difference between a utility's avoided costs and amounts that can be billed under the contract, with the difference, if any, repaid at the end of the contract. *Avoided energy cost* is the cost that a utility would have incurred had it purchased the power from another source or had the power been self-generated.

Power sales contracts negotiated on a competitive basis by NUGs prior to developing and constructing a power generation facility usually are long-term contracts (20 to 30 years) that are intended to minimize the NUG's financial risk. Although the contracts usually provide for payments based on both an energy and a capacity component, the following discussion applies only to the energy component, which is arrived at through a complex formula that represents the utility's avoided energy cost.

NUGs generally price long-term powers sales contracts to recover expected fixed and variable costs and to earn a reasonable rate of return. Rates must be sufficiently firm to assure financing for construction of the facility. Utilities are motivated by cost so they usually seek rates that agree with their estimated long-range avoided costs. Most of the contracts addressed here were negotiated in California in the early to mid-1980s. The initial terms of the contracts were at fixed or scheduled prices based on avoided cost to guarantee a revenue stream. It was expected at that time that avoided costs would increase significantly over the term of the contracts (30 years). In reality, avoided costs have decreased.

ACCOUNTING ISSUE

How should NUGs recognize revenue on long-term power sales contracts that consist of separate, specified terms for (*a*) a fixed or scheduled price per kwh for one period of the contract and (*b*) a variable price per kwh (which is based on market prices, actual avoided costs, or formula-based pricing arrangements), for a different portion of the contract, if total revenues billable under the contract over its entire term are not determined or limited by a tracker account or other form of adjustment?

ACCOUNTING GUIDANCE

The contracts addressed here should be divided and accounted for as follows:

- Revenue earned during the contract period in which prices are fixed or scheduled should be recognized in accordance with the guidance discussed above for contracts that include scheduled pricing changes, that is, at the lesser of (*a*) the amount billable under the contract or (*b*) an amount based on the kwh made available during the period multiplied by the estimated average revenue per kwh over the term of the contract. The lesser amount should be determined annually based on the cumulative amounts that would have been recognized had each method been applied consistently from the beginning of the term of the contract.
- During the contract period in which variable prices are used, revenue should be recognized as billed, in accordance with the contract's provisions for that period.

Revenue for the entire contract should be recognized based on the guidance for Issue 1 of ASC 980-605-25-5 through 25-15; ASC 440-10-60-20 discussed above if the contractual terms during the separate fixed and variable portions of the contract do not approximate the expected market rates at the inception of the contract.

Such contracts should be reviewed periodically to determine whether they are profitable or whether immediate loss recognition is required. Premiums related to a contractual rate in excess of current market rates should be amortized over the remaining portions of the respective periods of long-term power sales contracts acquired in purchase business combinations. For example, a premium resulting from an above-market rate related to the fixed or scheduled portion of a contract would be amortized over the remaining portion of that period of the acquired contract.

DISCUSSION

The approach adopted accounts for each phase of the contract separately. Proponents believed that revenues earned during each contract period are not affected by revenues in another contract period. They argued further that total revenues under the contracts discussed here are not the sum of revenues earned in each period of the contract. They noted that the guidance for Issue 1 of ASC 980-605-25-5 through 25-15; ASC 440-10-60-20 discussed above specifically states that it applies only to contracts with scheduled price changes that are determined by the contract and do not require estimating a utility's future avoided cost. They argued that if they had wanted NUGs to recognize level revenues over the contract term, such estimates would have been required for formula-based contracts discussed in ASC 980-605-25-5 through 25-15; ASC 440-10-60-20 discussed above, which usually are based on avoided cost.

Market rates are used in the variable-rate period of the contracts. Proponents analogized to the revenue recognition practices of oil or natural gas producers who enter into long-term contracts and recognize revenue as billed at current market prices on delivery. Similar accounting is followed by the mineral extractive industries and for agricultural commodities.

Illustration of Revenue Recognition on Long-Term Power Sales Contracts with Fixed and Variable Pricing Terms

Highpower Resources Co. has entered into a ten-year contract to provide energy. There is no tracker account. During the first five years of the contract, the rates are fixed at amounts stated in the contract; for the following five years, rates are at the utility's actual avoided energy cost. It is expected that actual avoided costs in the second half of the contract will be higher than those at the time the contract is entered into. Actual avoided costs decrease over the contract term. Annual demand is 1 million kwh per year.

The following energy rates are used in years 1-5 (the fixed portion of the contract):

Year 1	$.06
Year 2	.07
Year 3	.08
Year 4	.09
Year 5	.10

Actual avoided energy costs in years 6-10 are as follows:

Year 6	$.041
Year 7	.038
Year 8	.035
Year 9	.031
Year 10	.027

Revenue recognition during the fixed portion of the contract

1. Calculate the estimated average rate per kwh:

$$\frac{\text{Total revenue per kwh based on contract}}{\text{Number of years}} = \frac{\$.4}{5} = \$.08$$

2. Calculate the cumulative amounts using estimated revenue that is based on the average rate and that is the billable amount. Recognize the amount that results in a lower cumulative amount had each method been applied consistently from the beginning of the contract term. (For example, in year 4, recognizing $90,000 at the billable rate results in the lower cumulative amount of $300,000; had $90,000 been recognized at the average rate, the resulting cumulative amount would be $320,000.)

		Cumulative Amounts		
Estimated	*Avg. Rate*	*Avg. Rate*	*Billable Rate*	*Revenue Recognition*
Year 1	$.08	$ 80,000	$ 60,000	$ 60,000
Year 2	.08	160,000	130,000	70,000
Year 3	.08	240,000	210,000	80,000
Year 4	.08	320,000	300,000	90,000
Year 5	.08	400,000	400,000	100,000

Revenue recognition during the variable portion of the contract

Recognize revenue based on actual avoided energy costs.

Actual Avoided	*Energy Cost*	*Revenue Recognition*
Year 6	$.041	$41,000
Year 7	.038	38,000
Year 8	.035	35,000
Year 9	.031	31,000
Year 10	.027	27,000

ASC 980-715: COMPENSATION-RETIREMENT BENEFITS

ASC 980-715-25-4 through 25-7, 50-1; ASC 715-60-60-6 Accounting for OPEB Costs by Rate-Regulated Enterprises

BACKGROUND

Like other entities, rate-regulated entities were required to apply the provisions of ASC 715-60 for fiscal years beginning after December 15, 1992. Under that guidance postretirement benefits are considered to be deferred compensation arrangements, which involve an exchange of a promise of future benefits for current services performed by employees. The guidance in ASC 715-60 requires recognition of an obligation over the employees' related service period associated with providing future postretirement benefits to retired employees.

Before the guidance in ASC 715-60 became effective, most companies, including regulated entities, were accounting for costs of other postretirement benefits (OPEB costs) on a pay-as-you-go or cash basis. OPEB costs were paid and recognized in the period in which they were incurred. Rate regulators generally permitted including such costs in rates when they were paid. On adoption of the guidance in ASC 715-60, regulated entities not only had to accrue postretirement benefit obligations in their financial statements in the current period, but also had to either recognize a transition obligation relating to prior service costs immediately or amortize that obligation over the employees' average remaining service period, or 20 years, whichever is longer. Therefore, costs recognized under the guidance in ASC 715-60 would be significantly higher than those recognized on a cash basis.

As rate-regulated entities were getting ready to adopt the guidance in ASC 715-60 for financial reporting, the question arose as to how costs recognized under the requirements of that guidance would affect OPEB costs included in rates. If regulators were to permit entities to include in rates all of the costs under the guidance in ASC 715-60 (including amortization of the transition obligation), the costs reported in the entity's financial statements and the costs included in rates would not differ. In this case, no deferral of costs or recognition of a regulatory asset would be necessary. However, if regulated entities were not allowed by the applicable regulator to include in rates, the entire amount of the costs charged to customers under the guidance in ASC 715-60, some questioned whether regulated entities would have sufficient evidence to meet the criteria in ASC 980-340-251 and 40-1 for deferral of the difference between the amount charged in rates and the total cost recognized in the financial statements under the guidance in ASC 715-60. Under the guidance in ASC 980-340-251 and 40-1, all or part of an incurred cost that would otherwise be charged to expense may be capitalized as a regulatory asset if two conditions are met: (*a*) it is probable that by including the cost in rates charged to customers the capitalized cost will be recovered from future revenues and (*b*) future revenue will result in recovery of a previously incurred cost instead of providing for similar levels of future costs.

ACCOUNTING ISSUES

1. What additional criteria or evidence does a rate-regulated entity need in order to meet the requirements in ASC 980-340-25-1, 40-1 for recognition of a regulatory asset related to costs under the guidance in ASC 715-60 for which rate recovery has been deferred?
2. Should the conclusions reached apply to discontinued plans under the guidance in ASC 715-60?
3. If a rate-regulated entity initially fails to meet the regulatory asset recognition criteria, should a regulatory asset be recognized in a subsequent period when the criteria are met?

ACCOUNTING GUIDANCE

The following guidance is limited to accounting for regulatory assets related to costs accounted for under the guidance in ASC 715-60 by regulated entities that apply the guidance in ASC 980).

1. Recognition of a regulatory asset should be based on the following guidelines:
   a. *No* regulatory asset should be recognized for costs under the guidance in ASC 715-60 if a regulator continues to include OPEB costs of a continuing plan in rates on a pay-as-you-go basis.

      [It was noted that OPEB costs should be included in current rates, because they represent current costs of providing the regulated service or product that must be recovered through rates under the provisions of ASC 980.]
   b. A regulatory asset related to a continuing plan should be recognized for the difference between costs under the guidance in ASC 715-60 and OPEB costs included in rates if:

(1) It is probable that at least the amount of the regulatory asset will be recovered from future revenues that include the cost in rates, *and*

(2) All of the following criteria are met:

(a) Deferral of costs under the guidance in ASC 715-60 and subsequent inclusion of those deferred costs in the entity's rates is allowed by the entity's regulator under a rate order, which includes a policy statement or generic order that applies to entities in the regulator's jurisdiction.

(b) Annual costs under the guidance in ASC 715-60, including amortization of the transition obligation, will be included in rates within approximately five years of adopting the guidance in ASC 715-60. Conversion to full accrual accounting may occur in steps, but additional amounts should not be deferred longer than approximately five years.

(c) The regulator's authorized period for combined deferral and recovery of the regulatory asset should not be longer than approximately 20 years from adoption of the guidance in ASC 715-60. If a regulator requires a deferral period that exceeds 20 years, only the proportionate amount of costs that will be recovered within 20 years should be recognized as a regulatory asset.

(d) For each year, the percentage by which rates increase under the regulatory recovery plan should not exceed the percentage by which rates increased in the immediately preceding year. That criterion is similar to that for phase-in plans discussed in ASC 980-340-25-3. This criterion would be met by recovering the regulatory asset in rates on a straight-line basis.

c. *Transition requirement* The guidance discussed above applies to rate-regulated entities that elect to immediately recognize the transition obligation in accordance with the guidance in ASC 715-60 and to entities that elect to delay recognition of the transition obligation and amortize it in accordance with the guidance in ASC 715-60.

d. *Disclosure* Rate-regulated entities should disclose the following information about costs recognized under the guidance in ASC 715-60 in their financial statements:

(1) A description of the regulatory treatment of OPEB costs

(2) The status of any pending regulatory action

(3) The amount of any costs recognized under the guidance in ASC 715-60 that have been deferred as a regulatory asset at the balance sheet date

(4) The expected period of recovery of deferred amounts through rates.

2. A regulatory asset of a discontinued plan related to costs recognized under the guidance in ASC 715-60 should be recognized if it is probable that an amount at least equal to the deferred asset will be included in rates and recovered in future revenues within approximately 20 years after adopting the guidance in ASC 715-60. During that period, rate recovery may continue on a pay-as-you-go basis. For the purpose of this guidance, a discontinued plan is one in which employees do not earn additional benefits for future service (it has no current service costs).

3. A rate-regulated entity that initially does not meet the criteria for recognizing a regulatory asset but that meets the criteria in a subsequent period should recognize a regulatory asset for the cumulative difference between costs under the guidance in ASC 715-60 and OPEB costs included in rates since the date the guidance in ASC 715-60 was adopted.

DISCUSSION

1. This Issue was discussed because of concerns about the recoverability of a regulatory asset for costs recognized under the guidance in ASC 715-60 through rates in future periods. The underlying premise of ASC 980-340 is that rates charged to current customers include current costs of providing the regulated service. However, ASC 980-340-25-1, 40-1 provides for situations in which some costs may be deferred because they are not recovered in rates in the same period in which they are recognized in the financial statements. Some believed that the judgmental criteria in ASC 980-340-25-1, 40-1 are adequate and analogized to accounting for pensions, compensated absences, and taxes by rate-regulated entities.

However, others were concerned about the changing regulatory environment and questioned the probability that capitalized costs would be recovered. They were concerned whether regulators would permit including costs recognized under the guidance in ASC 715-60 in rates because such costs are noncash expenses that represent estimates of costs that will be incurred in the future. Generally, rates charged by regulated entities include costs incurred to provide services in the current period. A further concern was related to the extended time period for recovery of the liability recognized under the guidance in ASC 715-60 including the transition obligation, which is related to prior service and could be amortized over more than 20 years.

The concerns about recoverability were resolved by adding criteria that would tighten the requirements in ASC 980-340-25-1, 40-1 and by requiring that costs recognized under the guidance in ASC 715-60 be fully included in rates within approximately 20 years from adoption of the guidance in ASC 715-60. Those who supported a 20-year recovery period for the regulatory asset argued that the period should not be shorter for rate-regulated entities than for other entities and that at the end of that period, regulated entities would present costs recognized under the guidance in ASC 715-60 in their financial statements in the same manner as other entities.

Another concern was that regulated entities may *backload* the recovery of the regulatory asset for costs under the provision of ASC 715-60. For example, if a portion of costs recognized under the guidance in ASC 715-60 is deferred during the first five years, but the asset will not be recovered through rates until years 16 to 20, there was a concern about the probability of recovery.

That concern was dealt with by adopting the requirement for phase-in plans under the guidance in ASC 980-340, which requires a decreasing or steady percentage increase in rates over the recovery period. It was decided not to differentiate between entities that elect immediate recognition of the transition obligation and those electing to amortize it in accordance with the requirements of ASC 715-60, because the transition method elected would not affect the entity's revenues, net income, or equity during the recovery period if the entity meets the criteria for recognizing a regulatory asset. Although the regulatory asset of an entity that elects immediate recognition of the transition obligation would be larger than that of an entity that elects to recognize it over approximately 20 years, both entities would be recovering the cost through rates based on this guidance.

2. It was considered whether a regulated entity with a discontinued OPEB plan—a plan having a transition obligation related to employees' prior service but no current service costs—should be prohibited from recording a regulatory asset like an entity with a continuing plan, if OPEB costs are included in rates on a pay-as-you-go basis. The question was raised because of concerns that significant amounts of current period operating costs would continue to be deferred over long periods if OPEB costs were to be recovered through rates on a pay-as-you-go basis. Those who supported permitting recognition of a regulatory asset in this situation argued that unlike a continuing plan, which may have increasing deferrals over 30 to 40 years, no current costs would be deferred. Therefore, they did not object to pay-as-you-go recovery if deferred costs will be recovered through rates within approximately 20 years after adoption of the guidance in ASC 715-60.
3. Those who supported recognizing a regulatory asset for an incurred cost when it meets the criteria in ASC 980-340-25-1, 40-1—even though the criteria were not met when the cost was incurred—believed that the asset is created by the regulator's rate action rather than by incurring the cost. They referred to paragraph 180 in Statement of Financial Accounting Concepts No. 6 (not in ASC), which states that "[t]he ultimate evidence of the existence of assets is the future economic benefit, not the cost incurred." They argued that a regulatory asset should be recognized when it becomes probable that it will be recovered in future rates, even if recovery occurs in a period other than the one in which the cost was incurred. Another argument was that recognition of a regulatory asset when its recovery becomes probable is consistent with a balance sheet approach to financial reporting.

APPENDIX J

ASC 985—SOFTWARE

CONTENTS

PART I: GENERAL GUIDANCE

ASC 985-20: COSTS OF SOFTWARE TO BE SOLD, LEASED, OR MARKETED

OVERVIEW

Accounting for computer software has resulted in significant accounting issues, particularly when that software is developed internally. Similar to research and development costs and start-up costs of a new entity, computer software costs are elusive and often difficult to identify and measure. The major issue for internally developed software is the distinction between costs that should be expensed immediately and those that should be capitalized and amortized over some period in the future.

BACKGROUND

The role of computer software in our economy has increased rapidly over the past 20 years and its role is likely to continue to grow in the future. Some entities develop computer software for sale to other parties. These entities need guidance on accounting for the costs of developing such software.

Other entities do not sell computer software, but they use software internally in the operation of their businesses. Such software may be purchased externally or developed internally. These entities need guidance on accounting for the costs of computer software used in the operation of their businesses, particularly the software that is developed internally.

ASC 985 provides guidance on accounting for the costs of developing computer software for those entities that plan to sell that software. Generally, accounting for such software parallels accounting for research and development costs. To the point of establishing technological feasibility, costs are expensed as incurred. Once technological feasibility is established, it is evident that the particular software can be produced in accordance with design specifications. After that point, all costs incurred in developing the computer software product should be capitalized. The development costs of a computer system that improves an enterprise's administrative and selling procedures are not considered R&D costs. Costs incurred for internally developed computer software products that are used in the enterprise's own R&D activities, however, are considered R&D and should be accounted for accordingly.

COMPUTER SOFTWARE TO BE SOLD, LEASED, OR OTHERWISE MARKETED

ASC 985 applies to those costs incurred in purchasing or internally developing and producing computer software products that are sold, leased, or otherwise marketed by an enterprise. The costs covered by ASC 985 may be incurred (*a*) for separate computer software products or (*b*) for integral parts of computer software products or processes. ASC 985 does *not* cover those costs incurred for computer software that are (*a*) research and development assets acquired in a business combination or an acquisition by a not-for-profit entity, (*b*) created for the internal use of an enterprise, or (*c*) related to service contracts requiring significant production, modification, or customization (ASC 985-20-15-3).

Under ASC 985, the terms *computer software product, software product*, and *product* are used interchangeably to mean either (*a*) a computer software program, (*b*) a group of programs, or (*c*) a product enhancement. A product enhancement represents improvement to an existing product that significantly improves the marketability or extends the estimated useful life of the original product. A product enhancement almost always involves a new design or redesign of the original computer software product (ASC 985-20-15-4).

ASC 985 does not apply to research and development assets acquired in a business combination, or in a combination of not-for-profit entities. Those assets are recognized and measured at fair value in accordance with ASC 805 and ASC 958. However, ASC 985 does apply to any costs incurred after the date of a business combination for computer software to be sold, leased, or otherwise marketed, whether internally developed and produced or purchased (ASC 985-20-15-2).

The primary activities that are involved in the creation of a computer software product are the (*a*) planning function, (*b*) design function, and (*c*) production function. The planning function of a computer software product generally includes preliminary product specifications and design and the development of production and financial plans for the product. In addition, the planning function should include a marketing analysis and a marketing plan for the product. The planning function should generate sufficient documentation and detail information for an enterprise to make a determination of the overall feasibility of the proposed computer software product.

The design function of a computer software product includes the product design and the detail program design. The production of a product master generally involves coding, testing, and the development of training materials. Coding is the process in which the requirements of the detail program design are converted into a computer language. Testing includes the steps necessary to determine whether the computer software product works in accordance with its design specifications and documentation.

Computer Software Costs

ASC 985 specifies that all costs incurred in establishing the technological feasibility of a computer software product that is to be sold, leased, or otherwise marketed by an enterprise are research and development costs, which must be accounted for as required by ASC 730 (Research and Development). Thus, until technological feasibility is established in accordance with ASC 985, all costs incurred through the purchase or internal development and production of a computer software product that is to be sold, leased, or otherwise marketed are accounted for as R&D costs and expensed in the period incurred (ASC 985-20-25-1).

The development costs of a computer system that improves an enterprise's administrative or selling procedures are not considered R&D costs. All costs incurred for internally developed computer software products used in an enterprise's own R&D activities, however, are charged to expense when incurred, because the alternative future use test does not apply to such costs (ASC 730-10-25-4).

Production costs incurred for integral parts of a computer software product or process are expensed, unless (*a*) technological feasibility has been established for the computer software product or process and (*b*) all research and development activities have been completed for the other components of the computer software product or process (ASC 985-20-25-4).

Technological Feasibility

Technological feasibility is established upon completion of all of the activities that are necessary to substantiate that the computer software product can be produced in accordance with its design specifications, including functions, features, and technical performance requirements. Thus, all planning, designing, coding, and testing activities that are required to substantiate that the computer software product can be produced to meet its design specifications must have been completed before technological feasibility is established (ASC 985-20-25-2).

Under ASC 985, the method of establishing the technological feasibility of a computer software product depends on whether the process of creating the computer software product includes a detail program design or not. The minimum requirements for establishing the technological feasibility of a computer software product are discussed below (ASC 985-20-25-2).

Including Detail Program Design

If the process of creating the computer software product includes a detail program design, the following criteria establish the technological feasibility of a computer software product (ASC 985-20-25-2):

- An enterprise must complete the product design and detail program design for the computer software product and establish that it has available the necessary skills, hardware, and software technology to produce the product.
- An enterprise must substantiate the completeness of the program design and its consistency with the product design by documenting and tracing the detail program design to the product specifications.
- An enterprise must identify the high-risk development issues in the computer software product through review of the detail program design; if any uncertainties relating to the high-risk development issues are discovered, they must be resolved through coding and testing. High-risk development issues that may be encountered in the production of a computer software product may include novel, unique, or unproven functions and features, and/or technological innovations.

Not Including Detail Program Design

If the process of creating the computer software product *does not* include a detail program design, the following criteria establish the technological feasibility of a computer software product (ASC 985-20-25-2):

- An enterprise must complete a product design and a working model of the computer software product.
- An enterprise must substantiate the completeness of the working model and its consistency with the product design by testing the model.

Computer Software Costs That Must Be Capitalized

After technological feasibility has been established, ASC 985 specifies that all costs incurred for a computer software product that is sold, leased, or otherwise marketed by an enterprise shall be capitalized. Thus, the costs of producing product masters for a computer software product, including costs for coding and testing, are capitalized, but only after technological feasibility has been established (ASC 985-20-25-3).

Production costs for computer software that is to be used as an integral part of a product or process are capitalized, but only after (*a*) technological feasibility has been established for the software and (*b*) all R&D activities for the other components of the product or process have been completed.

Capitalization of computer software costs is discontinued when the computer software product is available to be sold, leased, or otherwise marketed. Costs for maintenance and customer support are charged to expense when incurred or when the related revenue is recognized, whichever occurs first (ASC 985-20-25-6).

PRACTICE NOTE: Under ASC 985, the amount of costs that an enterprise is required to capitalize depends primarily on its choice of production methods. Thus, an enterprise may control the amount of computer software costs that it capitalizes by establishing technological feasibility at a designated time during the production process.

Amortization of Capitalized Computer Software Costs

Amortization of capitalized computer software costs, on a product-by-product basis, begins when the product is available to be sold, leased, or otherwise marketed. Periodic amortization, on a product-by-product basis, is equal to the greater of (*a*) the amount computed by the straight-line method over the estimated useful life of the product or (*b*) the amount computed by using the ratio that current gross revenues bear to total estimated gross revenues (including current gross revenues) (ASC 985-20-35-1).

Inventory Costs

Inventory costs are capitalized on a unit-specific basis and charged to cost of sales when the related revenue from the sale of those units is recognized. Inventory costs include duplicate copies of the computer software product made from the product master, documentation, training materials, and the costs incurred for packaging the product for distribution (ASC 985-330-25-1).

Periodic Evaluation of Capitalized Computer Software Costs

Unamortized computer software costs that have been capitalized previously in accordance with ASC 985 are reported at net realizable value on an enterprise's balance sheet. Net realizable value is determined on a product-by-product basis and is equal to the estimated future gross revenues of a specific product, less estimated future costs of completing and disposing of that specific product, including the costs of performing maintenance and customer support on a product-by-product basis as required by the terms of the sale.

The excess of any unamortized computer software costs over its related net realizable value at a balance sheet date shall be written down. The amount of write-down is charged to periodic income. Capitalized costs that have been written down as a charge to income shall not be capitalized again or restored in any future period (ASC 985-20-35-4).

FINANCIAL STATEMENT DISCLOSURE

The total amount of unamortized computer software costs that is included in each balance sheet presented shall be disclosed in the financial statements. The total amount of computer software costs charged to expense shall be disclosed for each period for which an income statement is presented. The total amount of computer software costs charged to expense shall include amortization expense and amounts written down to net realizable value (ASC 985-20-50-1).

All computer software costs that are classified as R&D costs shall be accounted for in accordance with ASC 730. These costs may include the costs of planning, product design, detail program design, and the costs incurred in establishing technological feasibility of a computer software product (ASC 730-10-50-1).

PART II: INTERPRETIVE GUIDANCE

ASC 985-605: REVENUE RECOGNITION

ASC 985-605-05-1, 05-3, 15- 2 through 15-4, 25-1 through 25-19, 25-21 through 25-31, 25-33 through 25-41, 25-44 through 25-89, 25-91 through 25-107, 55-2, 55-28, 55-127 through 55-129, 55-131 through 55-133, 55-136 through 55-144, 55-146 through 55-148, 55-150 through 55-151, 55-154 through 55-160, 55-162 through 55-168, 55-170 through 55-179, 55-181 through 55-184, 55-205 through 55-210; ASC 985-20-60-3; ASC 450-10-60-12; ASC 605-35-15-3; ASC 730-10-60-5 Software Revenue Recognition

---

IMPORTANT NOTICE: Based on the guidance in ASU 2014-09 Part B, Accounting for Revenue from Contracts with Customers, the guidance in Subtopic ASC 985-605 will be renamed Software-Revenue Recognition-Provision for Losses when the guidance in the ASU, which will reside in ASC 606, Revenue from Contracts with Customers, becomes effective for public business entities in annual reporting periods that begin after December 15, 2017, and interim periods within those annual periods, and for nonpublic entities in annual reporting periods that begin after December

15, 2018. The guidance in this Issue will be affected as follows: ASC 985-605-05-1 will be amended and retained. All of Section 985-605-25 will be superseded, except for 25-2 and 25-7, which will be retained and amended, ASC 985-605-25-86 will be amended and moved to ASC 730-20-15-1A, and ASC 985-605-25-87 will be amended and moved to ASC 985-20-25-12. ASC 985-605-05-3, 15-3 through 15-4 will be superseded. All of Section 985-605-55 will be superseded, except for ASC 985-605-55-121 through 55-122, which will be amended and moved to ASC 985-20-15-5 through 15-6, respectively.

BACKGROUND

This pronouncement provides guidance on when and the amount of revenue that should be recognized from a sale, lease, or licensing of computer software. Software arrangements may be limited to providing a license for a single software product or, at the other end of the spectrum, they may consist of the delivery of software or a software system that requires significant production, modification or customization. The following guidance does *not* apply to sales of products that contain software that is incidental to the product being sold.

SCOPE

The scope of the following guidance applies to all entities and to the following transactions and activities, unless there is a scope exception that is discussed below:

1. Licensing, selling, leasing, or marketing software in other ways.
2. Software and elements, such as software products, upgrades, enhancements, services, or postcontract customer support (PCS), related to software under an arrangement that includes software that is more-than-incidental to the products or services of the total arrangement. The following are some, but not all, indicators that software is more-than-incidental to an arrangement's products or service as a whole:
   a. The marketing effort focuses on the software or it is sold separate.
   b. The vendor provides PCS.
   c. The vendor incurs significant costs discussed under the scope of ASC 985-20.

   A service is included under the scope of the following guidance if the service would not function without the software under the arrangement.
3. Offers of more-than-insignificant discounts with the following characteristics on future purchases:
   a. The discounts are in addition to a range of discounts included in the pricing of an arrangement's other elements.
   b. The discounts are in addition to a range of discounts usually given on comparable transactions.
   c. The discounts are significant.

   Determining whether an additional discount is significant requires judgment. There is a presumption that the existence of more-than-insignificant discounts or other concessions in an arrangement constitutes an offer of an additional element or elements.
4. Arrangements to deliver software or a software system, alone or together with other products that require significant production, modification, or software customization. Software arrangements that include services that are not essential to any of the arrangement's elements or that would be additional to the price of the arrangement (see ASC 985-605-25-78) should be accounted for separately.

The guidance does not apply the following transactions and activities:

1. Arrangements for products or services including software that is incidental to the total arrangement.
2. Leases of software that include property, plant, or equipment (tangible products) if the software is incidental to the tangible product as a whole, or if the tangible product's software and nonsoftware components work together to enable the tangible product to perform its essential function.
3. Marketing and promotional activities that are not unique to software transactions, such as:
   a. Insignificant discounts on future purchases offered in a software arrangement.
   b. Discounts that are not given in addition to discounts usually given in comparable transactions.

4. Nonsoftware components of tangible products.
5. Software components of tangible products that are sold, licensed, or leased with tangible products whose software and nonsoftware components work together to enable the tangible product to perform its essential function.
6. Undelivered elements related to software essential to the ability of the tangible product discussed in (5) (above) to function.

ACCOUNTING GUIDANCE

If the sale of computer software involves significant customization, modification, or production, the transaction should be accounted for as a long-term contract. In all other cases, revenue should be recognized when the following four conditions are met:

1. Persuasive evidence of an arrangement exists.
2. Delivery has occurred.
3. The vendor's price is fixed or determinable.
4. Collectibility of the selling price is probable.

Evidence an Arrangement Exists

Some entities require a written contract to support the sale of computer software. If the entity customarily uses written contracts to support the sale of software, such a written contract—signed by both parties to the contract—must exist to confirm that a sale arrangement exists. If written contracts are not typically used to support the sale of computer software, other evidence that a sale arrangement exists must be present. Other evidence might include a purchase order from the customer or an electronic order. Even if all the other criteria for software revenue recognition specified in this pronouncement are met, a sale should not be recorded unless there is persuasive evidence that a sales arrangement exists.

Delivery Has Occurred

In most cases, delivery is deemed to have occurred at the transfer of the product master or, in cases where the product master is not transferred, at the transfer of the product master, or a first copy. The one exception to this general rule is when the amount of revenue is a function of the number of copies shipped. In this case, revenue is recognized as copies are delivered to the user or reseller. Sometimes the delivery mode for software is electronic dissemination. In those cases, delivery is deemed to have occurred when the buyer: (1) takes possession of the software by downloading it, or (2) has been provided with the access codes necessary to download the software. In addition, if there is uncertainty as to whether the customer has accepted the software, license revenue should be deferred until such acceptance occurs.

Delivery has not occurred until the software is delivered to the customer's place of business or to an intermediate site designated by the customer. In some cases in which a customer specifies an intermediate site as the delivery point, a substantial portion of the revenue is not due until the vendor moves the software from the intermediate site to another location designated by the customer. In those cases, revenue is not recognized until the software is delivered to that other site.

A delivery agent, acting for a vendor, may distribute software to customers. Revenue is not recognized when the vendor delivers the software to the delivery agent. Rather, revenue is recognized when the delivery agent has delivered the software to the customer.

Software may contain authorization keys, which prohibit unauthorized access to the software. The possession of those keys is what allows a customer to access the software. Typically, delivery of a software key is not a prerequisite to a vendor's recognition of revenue.

Price Is Fixed or Determinable and Collectibility Is Probable

A number of situations indicate that the selling price is not fixed or determinable. In those cases, revenue is recognized as payments from customers become due. Situations where the selling price is not fixed or determinable are as follows:

- The selling price is a function of the number of copies distributed or the number of users of the product.
- In general, the presence of extended payment terms exists.

- A significant portion of the license fee is not due until after the expiration of the license period or not due until more than 12 months from the sale date. However, such payment terms are not a problem if the vendor has a history of successfully collecting the sales price using such payment terms, without making concessions.
- The sale includes a cancellation period. The selling price is not fixed or determinable until the cancellation period lapses.

Before revenue can be recognized, collectibility also must be reasonably assured. If a right of return exists, the requirements for revenue recognition in ASC 605-15 must be met.

Additional criteria must be met when the sale is to a reseller. For example, the following four situations suggest that the sale price may not be fixed or determinable, or that collectibility is not reasonably assured:

1. The vendor's payment is substantially contingent on the reseller's success in distributing the software to end users.
2. The reseller's financial situation may be such that it is unable to make fixed or determinable payments to the vendor until it collects cash from its customers.
3. Uncertainties about the number of copies to be sold by the reseller may preclude reasonable estimates of future returns.
4. The vendor provides the reseller protection against future price changes, and there are significant uncertainties about the vendor's ability to maintain its selling price.

Computer Software—Multiple Elements

Note: See ASC 605-25-15-3A, 25-2, 30-2, 30-5, 30-6A through 30-6B, 30-7, 50-1 through 50-2, 55-1, 55-3, 55-7, 55-12, 55-25, 55-29, 55-32, 55-34, 55-36 through 55-47, 55-52, 55-54, 55-6A through 55-57, 55-61, 55-69, 55-75 through 55-6B, 55-93, 65-1, "Revenue Arrangements with Multiple Deliverables" for updated guidance on (1) how a vendor should determine whether an arrangement that involves multiple deliverables should be accounted for as more than one unit of accounting, (2) how to measure consideration on such an arrangement and (3) how to allocate that consideration the arrangement's separate units of accounting.

The sale of computer software often includes other elements in addition to the software itself. Other elements might include a service that cannot function without the software element of an arrangement, the delivery of enhancements/upgrades, services of various types, and post-contract support (PCS). If a sales contract includes multiple elements, revenue should be allocated to the multiple elements based on vendor-specific objective evidence (VSOE) of the relative fair values of each element. Separate prices stated within the contract that apply to each element are often not indicative of relative fair values.

PRACTICE POINTER: This pronouncement originally limited VSOE to two criteria:

1. The price charged when the same element was sold separately
2. For an element not yet being sold separately, the price set for the separate element by an appropriate level of management and where it is probable that the price would not change before the separate element is introduced into the marketplace.

Those two criteria were viewed by many as too restrictive as to what constitutes VSOE. The effective date of this provision was deferred by SOP 98-4 (not in ASC) and it was subsequently permanently eliminated Although the two original limitations on what constitutes VSOE have been eliminated from this pronouncement, entities must still allocate fees received in a multiple element arrangement based on the relative fair values of each element. Those fair values must be supported by VSOE. If VSOE is insufficient to support unbundling of the total fee, the entire fee must be deferred.

In general, if VSOE of relative fair values does not exist, revenue recognition should be deferred until the earlier of (1) the date on which VSOE of relative fair values exists, or (2) the date when all elements under a contract have been delivered. There are four exceptions to this general guidance:

1. If the only undelivered element is PCS, the entire fee is to be recognized ratably.
2. If the only undelivered element are services that do not involve significant production, modification, or customization, the entire fee is to be recognized over the period that the service is performed.

3. If the software sale is essentially a subscription, the entire fee is to be recognized over the subscription period.
4. If the fee is based on the number of copies sold of more than one product, it is often not clear how many of each product will be sold. In most cases, revenue cannot be recognized because total revenue allocable to each software product is not known.

Collectibility may be a problem when software is delivered in installments. The collectibility criterion is not met if the portion of the fee allocated to units already delivered is subject to forfeiture if other elements of the software package are not delivered. In evaluating whether revenue allocated to units already delivered is subject to forfeiture, the focus is on management's intent and not just on the terms of the legal contract. That is, if management typically refunds fees already paid if other elements of the software sale are not delivered, the collectibility criterion is not met even if management is not legally required to provide such refunds.

Multiple Software Elements—Rights to Upgrades and Enhancements

A vendor may deliver a software package and promise to provide upgrades or enhancements to that software as those upgrades/enhancements subsequently become available. The purchase price is allocated between the current software product and the right to future upgrades/enhancements based on VSOE. Some customers may choose not to exercise their right to the upgrade/enhancement. If sufficient evidence exists to estimate the number of customers who will not exercise the upgrade/enhancement right, revenue allocated to this right should be reduced.

Vendors may deliver software and a promise to provide additional software in the future. Again, the fee should be allocated between the current software product and the right to additional software based on VSOE. Unlike the situation of upgrades/enhancements, the fee allocated to the additional software is not reduced for any customers not expected to take delivery of the additional software.

Often the promise to provide customers with future versions of software is, in essence, a subscription agreement. For example, the vendor may promise to deliver all new products that comprise a certain "family" of software that are developed over some number of future years. In the case of subscription agreements, no revenue is allocated to individual software products. Rather, all of the revenue is recognized over the life of the subscription agreement, beginning on the date of delivery of the first product.

Multiple Software Elements—Postcontract Customer Support

Software is often sold with a promise, either contractual or implied by the vendor's normal business practices, to provide postcontract customer support (PCS). An example of postcontract customer support is telephone support (e.g., a help desk maintained by the vendor). Revenue is to be allocated between the software product and the PCS based on the fee to be received if the PCS was sold separately. This fee is best estimated by referring to the rate charged for such service at renewal (i.e., the renewal rate). Revenue allocated to PCS is to be recognized ratably over the PCS period.

In cases where the sale of software includes multiple elements (including PCS), there may not be the VSOE needed to allocate the fee across the multiple elements. In those cases, if the PCS represents the only undelivered element, the entire software fee should be recognized ratably over:

- The PCS contract period if the vendor is contractually obligated to provide these services.
- The estimated period over which the vendor will provide PCS if the vendor's obligation to provide these services is implied based on its past actions.

In some cases, PCS revenue can be recognized along with the initial licensing fee at delivery of the software product if all of the following conditions are met:

- The PCS fee is included with the initial licensing fee.
- The term of the PCS included with the initial license is for one year or less. This criterion is not violated if the vendor provides telephone support for more than one year, if the vendor's past history indicates that the majority of the telephone support will be provided in the first year after the sale.
- The estimated cost of providing the PCS during this period is insignificant.
- Unspecified upgrades/enhancements offered during the PCS period have historically been, and are expected to continue to be, minimal and infrequent.

If PCS revenue is recognized on delivery of the software product, the estimated costs of providing PCS are to be accrued on this date. The estimated costs of providing PCS include the costs of providing software upgrades/ enhancements.

Multiple Software Elements—Services

The sale of software may include the provision of future services (non-PCS related) in addition to the software product itself. These services might include installation, consulting, and training. The vendor must determine whether the service elements qualify for separate accounting treatment as the services are performed. If not, the entire purchase price (for both the software and services) is to be accounted for using contract accounting. To conclude that the service element of the contract can be accounted for separately, the following criteria must be met:

- The fair value of the service element of the contract must be supported by sufficient VSOE.
- The ability to use the software (i.e., functionality) must not depend on the service.
- The price of the contract would be expected to vary based on the inclusion or exclusion of the service.

If the service qualifies for separate accounting, revenue allocated should be recognized as the service is performed. If no pattern of performance is obvious, revenue is recognized over the period during which the service is to be performed.

There may be instances in which there is not sufficient VSOE to allocate the sale price between the software product and the services included. If the only undelivered element of the sale is the service and if the service does not involve significant production, modification, or customization, the entire purchase price is recognized as services are performed.

Software is more likely to be functional without any additional services being rendered if the software is viewed as off-the-shelf software. If the software is not off-the-shelf, or if significant modifications to off-the-shelf software are necessary to meet the customer's functionality, no element of the arrangement would qualify as accounting for a service. Rather the entire purchase price, both for the software and for any services, would be accounted for using contract accounting.

Factors that indicate that the service element of the arrangement is essential to the functionality of the software are as follows:

- The software is not off-the-shelf.
- The services to be rendered include significant modifications to off-the-shelf software.
- It is necessary to build complex interfaces for the customer to use the vendor's software in its own environment.
- The customer's obligation to pay for the software is tied to the completion of the services.
- Customer acceptance criteria (i.e., milestones) affect the realizability of the software-license fee.

Multiple Software Elements—Contract Accounting

Software or software systems that require significant production, modification, or customization do not meet the criteria for separate accounting for the service element. In those cases, contract accounting must be applied. Contract accounting is implemented using either the percentage-of-completion method or the completed-contract method. Guidance on applying those methods is provided in Chapter 38, *ASC 606/605—Revenue Recognition*, of this Guide.

In applying the percentage-of-completion method, both input and output measures of the degree to which the software project is complete can be used. A typical input measure is labor hours incurred. Labor hours incurred provides a good measure of progress toward completion for software projects that are labor intensive (e.g., customization of core software). Milestones toward completion of the software project are examples of output measures. A good example of useful output measures of progress to date is the completion of tasks that trigger independent review.

ASC 985-605-05-4, 55-121 through 55-125 Application of ASC 985-605, Software Revenue Recognition, to Arrangements That Include the Right to Use Software Stored on Another Entity's Hardware

IMPORTANT NOTICE: Based on the guidance in ASU 2014-09 Part B, Accounting for Revenue from Contracts with Customers, the guidance in Subtopic ASC 985-605 will be renamed Software-Revenue Recognition-Provision for Losses when the guidance in the ASU, which will reside in ASC 606, Revenue from Contracts with Customers, becomes effective for public business entities in annual reporting periods that begin after December 15, 2017, and interim periods within those annual periods, and for nonpublic entities in annual reporting periods that begin after December

15, 2018. The guidance in this Issue will be affected as follows: ASC 985-605-05-4 will be superseded as well as the guidance ASC 985-605-55-123 through 55-125. The guidance in ASC 985-605-55-121 through 55-122 will be amended and moved to ASC 985-20-15-5 through 15-6, respectively.

BACKGROUND

Instead of licensing software that is installed on a customer's hardware, some software companies and entities referred to as application software providers (ASPs) are offering customers access to software applications without taking possession of the software. Under such arrangements, the customer can access software—which is installed on a vendor's or a third party's hardware—over the Internet or over a dedicated line. This type of storage or access service is known as hosting.

The form of such arrangements consists of a right to (1) use software and (2) store software on hardware owned by a vendor or a third party. Customers in those arrangements may not have a license to the software and may not be able to access the software through a different host. ASPs consider themselves to be service providers that deploy, host, and manage application solutions for rent.

Although the terms of hosting arrangements may differ significantly, the following guidance applies to arrangements in which a customer purchases a software license as well as a right to store and access the software. It is assumed that payment occurs at the inception of the arrangement.

ACCOUNTING ISSUES

1. Should the guidance in ASC 985-605 apply to arrangements that require a vendor to host the software?
2. Does the guidance in ASC 985-605 apply to arrangements in which a customer can choose to take delivery of the software?
3. If the answer to Issue 2 is affirmative, when does delivery occur and how does a vendor's obligation to host the software affect revenue recognition?

ACCOUNTING GUIDANCE

1. The guidance in ASC 985-605 applies to the software element of a hosting arrangement if
   a. The customer has a contractual right to take physical possession of the software at any time during the hosting period without significant penalty, and
   b. It is feasible for the customer to run the software on its own hardware or to contract for a hosting arrangement with a third party that is unrelated to the vendor or the host.

   Arrangements that do not give those options to a customer are accounted for as *service arrangements*, which are not included under the scope of ASC 985-605.
2. If a customer in a hosting arrangement can choose whether to take physical possession of the software as discussed above, delivery occurs when the customer is able to takes possession of the software. Service arrangements could include multiple elements that would affect the allocation of revenue.
3. The Task Force noted that if the guidance in ASC 985-605 applies to software in a hosting arrangement, revenue for the portion of the fee allocated to the software portion of the arrangement should be recognized on delivery only if *all* of the revenue recognition requirements under that guidance are met. This would include the requirement for vendor-specific objective evidence of fair value and that the portion of the fee allocated to the software cannot be forfeited, refunded, or be subject to any other concession. The portion of the fee allocated to the hosting arrangement would be recognized as the service is provided. In addition to the software and the hosting service, arrangements under this guidance that are accounted for under the guidance in ASC 985-605 also may include other elements, such as specified or unspecified upgrade rights.

The following guidance applies to the accounting for costs of developing software for hosting arrangements:

a. The provisions of ASC 985-20 apply to software development costs incurred by vendors that sell, lease, license, or market to others software that is accounted for under the guidance in ASC 985-605.
b. The provisions of ASC 350-40 apply to the development costs of software accounted for under the scope of ASC 985-605 if it is used only to provide services and is not sold, leased, licensed, or marketed to others.
c. The provisions of ASC 985-20 also apply to software development costs if in the process of developing or modifying the software, a vendor develops a substantive plan to sell, lease, license, or market the software to others.

ASC 985-605-15-3 Applicability of ASC 985-605, Software Revenue Recognition, to Non-Software Deliverables in an Arrangement Containing More-Than-Incidental Software

---

> *IMPORTANT NOTICE:* Based on the guidance in ASU 2014-09 Part B, Accounting for Revenue from Contracts with Customers, the guidance in Subtopic ASC 985-605 will be renamed Software-Revenue Recognition-Provision for Losses when the guidance in the ASU, which will reside in ASC 606, Revenue from Contracts with Customers, becomes effective for public entities in annual reporting periods that begin after December 15, 2016, and interim periods within those annual periods, and for nonpublic entities in annual reporting periods that begin after December 15, 2017. The guidance in this Issue will be superseded.

BACKGROUND

This question has been raised because there is diversity in practice in the application of the provisions of ASC 985-605, Software Revenue Recognition, in arrangements that include non-software deliverables, such as hardware, in addition to software that is more than incidental to the products or services as a whole. The guidance in ASC 985-605-15-3 includes the following indicators that software is more than incidental: (*a*) the company's marketing focuses on the software and or it is sold separately, (*b*) the vendor provides postcontract customer support, and (*c*) the vendor incurs significant costs that are accounted for under the scope of ASC 985-20 (Accounting for the Costs of Computer Software to Be Sold, Leased, or Otherwise Marketed). There has been some confusion, because the guidance in ASC 985-605-15-3 through 15-4 states that revenue related to property, plant, or equipment included in a lease of software should be accounted for under the guidance in ASC 840-10, Leases, but the guidance in ASC 985-605-25-5 discusses accounting for revenue from software arrangements with *multiple elements* and states that "all additional products and services specified in the arrangements" should be accounted for under the guidance in ASC 985-605.

ACCOUNTING ISSUE

Should non-software deliverables included in an arrangement that contains software that is more than incidental to the products or services as a whole be included under the scope of ASC 985-605?

ACCOUNTING GUIDANCE

Software and software-related elements are included under the scope of ASC 985-605 in arrangements that include software that is *more than incidental* to the products or services as a whole. Software-related elements include software products and services, such as upgrades and enhancements and postcontract customer support (PCS), as well as non-software deliverables that require a software deliverable for their functionality. Unrelated equipment that does not require a software deliverable for its functionality is not considered to be software-related and should be *excluded* from the scope of ASC 985-605.

ASC 985-605-15-3 through 15-4A, 25-10, 50-1, 55-211 through 55-236, 65-1 Applicability of ASC 985-605 to Certain Revenue Arrangements That Include Software

---

> *IMPORTANT NOTICE:* Based on the guidance in ASU 2014-09 Part B, Accounting for Revenue from Contracts with Customers, the guidance in Subtopic ASC 985-605 will be renamed Software-Revenue Recognition-Provision for Losses when the guidance in the ASU, which will reside in ASC 606, Revenue from Contracts with Customers, becomes effective for public entities in annual reporting periods that begin after December 15, 2016, and interim periods within those annual periods, and for nonpublic entities in annual reporting periods that begin after December 15, 2017. The guidance in this Issue will be superseded.

BACKGROUND

The guidance in ASC 985-605, Software Revenue Recognition, applies to products or services that contain software that is "more than incidental" to the products or services as a whole and requires that the selling price of separate deliverables in an arrangement that includes multiple elements be based on vendor-specific objective evidence (VSOE). Certain transactions under the scope of ASC 985-605 include software-enabled devices, which are sold only with other deliverables and result in a revenue pattern that is *not* based on the economics of the transaction because VSOE cannot be determined for those devices.

Some constituents have suggested that the model in ASC 985-605 should be amended to exclude some transactions that include software-enabled devices that may *not* have been considered when that guidance was written.

ACCOUNTING ISSUES

1. Should the measurement criteria or the scope of ASC 985-605 be modified?
2. If so, how should the scope of ASC 985-605 be modified?

SCOPE

The following guidance applies to arrangements with multiple elements that include both hardware and software elements. However, hardware elements of a tangible product are never accounted for under the scope of software revenue recognition guidance

ACCOUNTING GUIDANCE

1. The scope of the guidance in ASC 985-605-15-3 should be amended by deleting the existing subparagraph 3b and amending ASC 985-605-15-3c to include a service that cannot function without the software element of an arrangement.
2. This guidance amends the guidance in ASC-985-605-15-4 to *exclude* application of the guidance in ASC 985-605 to the following transactions and activities in addition to those already listed:
   a. Leases of software that include property, plant, or equipment (tangible products) if the software is incidental to the tangible product as a whole, or if the tangible product's software and nonsoftware components work together to enable the tangible product to perform its essential function. (ASC 985-605-15-4b)
   b. Nonsoftware components of tangible products. (ASC 985-605-15-4d)
   c. Software components of tangible products that are sold, licensed, or leased with tangible products whose software and nonsoftware components work together to enable the tangible product to perform its essential function. (ASC 985-605-15-4e)
   d. Undelivered elements related to software essential to the ability of the tangible product discussed in the previous bullet to function. (ASC 985-605-15-4f)
3. A vendor should consider all of the following factors to determine whether software components that function together and are delivered with a tangible product are necessary for the tangible product to perform its basic function:
   a. There is a rebuttable presumption that a software product is essential to a tangible product's ability to perform its function if the tangible product is rarely sold without the software element.
   b. If a vendor sells products that perform similar functions, such as different models of similar products, the products should be considered to be the same products for the evaluation of factor (a) if the only difference between similar products is that one includes software that the other does not.
   c. If a vendor sells software separately as well as tangible products containing the same software, it should not be presumed that the software is not essential to the tangible product's functionality because the vendor also sells the software separately.
   d. The fact that a software element may not be embedded in a tangible product does not mean that it is not considered to be essential to that product's functionality.
   e. Nonsoftware elements of a tangible asset must contribute significantly to a product's essential function. That is, a tangible product should not only be a means of delivering software to a customer. (ASC 985-605-15-4A)

A vendor that has entered into an arrangement that includes software deliverables, which are under the scope of ASC 605-25, and nonsoftware deliverables, which are not under the scope of ASC 605-25, should allocate consideration under that arrangement to the nonsoftware and software deliverables as a group based on the guidance in ASC 605-25-15-3A. If a nonsoftware deliverable includes software deliverables that are considered to be essential to a tangible product's ability to perform its function and the arrangement includes more than one software deliverable, a portion of the consideration on the arrangement should be allocated to the software deliverables as a group based on the guidance in ASC 605-25-15-3A and should be separated and allocated further based on this guidance. In addition, software contained in a tangible product that is *not* essential to that product's ability to perform its function as well as nonessential software and other deliverables under an arrangement (other than the nonsoftware components of a tangible product) related to the nonessential software also are included in the scope of this guidance. An undelivered element related to a deliverable under the scope of this guidance and to a deliverable excluded from the scope of this guidance should be separated into (a) a software deliverable, which is under the scope of this guidance, and (b) a nonsoftware deliverable, which is not under the scope of this guidance. (ASC 985-605-25-10(f))

DISCLOSURE

A vendor should disclose the information required under the guidance in ASC 605-25 for arrangements that apply to multiple elements that may or may not be under the scope of ASC 985-605.

ASC 985-705: COST OF SALES AND SERVICES

ASC 985-705-S25-1, S99-1 Accounting for the Film and Software Costs Associated with Developing Entertainment and Educational Software Products

BACKGROUND

Games incorporating audio, film, graphics, and interactive software technology on CD-ROM are entertainment and educational software (EE) products, which may include film content taken from an existing film or film developed specifically for the software product. The development of such products by both motion picture companies and software companies differs from the development of software for business applications or operating systems; production costs are a significant component of multimedia entertainment product costs.

Motion picture companies had been capitalizing costs related to EE products as inventory and amortizing them over the product's expected revenue stream under the provisions of FAS-53 (not in ASC). In addition, motion picture companies were not applying the guidance in ASC 720-35 on reporting for advertising costs. Motion picture companies considered EE products to be entertainment products similar to films for the following reasons: (*a*) the products usually use previously developed or simple software, so technological feasibility is reached at the beginning of the project, and (*b*) the software content often is minimal. In contrast, software companies have been expensing film production and software costs under the provisions of ASC 605-25. Some software companies were accounting separately for costs related to the film content under the provisions of FAS-53 (not in ASC) and costs related to the software content under the provisions of ASC 605-25.

ACCOUNTING ISSUE

How should companies developing EE products account for related film and software costs?

SEC OBSERVER COMMENT

At the May 1996 meeting, the SEC Observer announced that based on the educational session presented by a working group from the motion picture and software industries the SEC staff believes that EE products that are sold, licensed, or otherwise marketed should be accounted for based on the requirements of ASC 605-25. Therefore, subsequent to May 23, 1996, SEC registrants should account for film costs related to those products under the provisions of ASC 605-25, not under the provisions of FAS-53. In addition, registrants should expense exploitation costs incurred subsequent to May 23, 1996, unless they qualify for capitalization under the provisions in ASC 720-35. Registrants that previously capitalized all costs incurred in the development of EE products should restate prior-period financial statements to account for software development costs, in accordance with the provisions of ASC 605-25, if the related amounts are material. The SEC staff's views are not intended to apply to costs incurred to produce computer generated special effects and images used in products exhibited in theaters or licensed to television stations.

Accounting Resources on the Web

The following World Wide Web addresses are just a few of the resources on the Internet that are available to practitioners. Because of the evolving nature of the Internet, some addresses may change. In such a case, refer to one of the many Internet search engines, such as Google (http://www.google.com) or Yahoo (http://www.yahoo.com).

Accounting Research Manager http://www.accountingresearchmanager.com

AICPA http://www.aicpa.org

American Accounting Association http://aaahq.org

CCH Publications www.cchcpelink.com/books

CPE www.cchcpelink.com

Congress.gov (formerly Thomas Legislative Research http://www.congress.gov

FASAB http://www.fasab.gov

FASB http://www.fasb.org

FedWorld https://www.ntis.gov

GASB http://www.gasb.org

Government Accountability Office http://www.gao.gov

House of Representatives http://www.house.gov

International Accounting Standards Board http://www.ifrs.org

IRS http://www.irs.gov/

Library of Congress http://www.loc.gov

National Association of State Boards of Accountancy http://www.nasba.org

Office of Management and Budget http://www.whitehouse.gov/omb/

CCH® ProSystem *fx*® Engagement https://taxna.wolterskluwer.com/professional-tax-software/prosystem-fx/engagement

Public Company Accounting Oversight Board http://www.pcaobus.org

Securities and Exchange Commission http://www.sec.gov

Wolters Kluwer www.taxna.wolterskluwer.com

Index

A

G

Q

R

T

U

V